W9-CIB-481
Norwegian Sea
NORWAY
SWEDEN
Finland
Lapland
Gulf of Bothnia
Gulf of Finland
Siberia
RUSSIAN EMPIRE
Bergen
Christiania (Oslo)
Stockholm
St. Petersburg
Baltic Sea
Riga
SCOTLAND
North Sea
Iona
Glasgow
Edinburgh
Belfast
Dublin
IRELAND
ENGLAND
London
DEN.
Copenhagen
Kaliningrad (Konigsberg)
Moscow
Perm
Tobolsk
Omsk
Tomsk
Barnaul
Poland
Warsaw
Berlin
Hamburg
Amsterdam
NETH.
GERMANY
Halle
Leipzig
Prague
Kiev
Volga R.
Volgograd
Rostov
Astrakhan
Odessa
BELG.
LUX.
Paris
FRANCE
Basel
Munich
Vienna
Budapest
SWITZ.
Geneva
Lyons
Venice
AUSTRIA-HUNGARY
ROMANIA
Bucharest
Marseille
ITALY
Adriatic Sea
Bosnia
SERBIA
MONT.
ALB.
Danube R.
BULGARIA
Black Sea
Constantinople (Istanbul)
Rome
Naples
Tyrrhenian Sea
Sicily
Ionian Sea
GREECE
Athens
Aegean Sea
Asia Minor
TURKEY
Smyrna
Armenia
Madrid
SPAIN
PORTUGAL
Lisbon
Barcelona
Mediterranean Sea
Algiers
Tunis
Malta
Crete
Cyprus
Aleppo
Beirut
Syria
Damascus
Jerusalem
Amman
Palestine
Euphrates R.
Tigris R.
Bagdad
Caspian Sea
Aral Sea
Russian Turkistan
KHIVA
BOKHARA
Bokhara
Tashkent
TURKMENISTAN
Pamirs
Tabriz
Teheran
Meshed
PERSIA
Isfahan
Shiraz
Persian Gulf
Herat
AFGHANISTAN
Kabul
Peshawar
Jammu and Kashmir
Srinagar
Lahore
Baluchistan
Indus R.
Sind
Karachi
Gwadar
Muscat
Gulf of Oman
Alma-Ata
Irkutsk
Nerchinsk
TANNU TUVA
MONGOLIA
Gobi Desert
Sinkiang
Chinese Turkistan
Yarkand
Kiuchuan (Suchow)
Changyeh
CHINESE EMPIRE
Tsinghai
Tibet
Lhasa
NEPAL
Khatmandu
BHUTAN
Delhi
Agra
Lucknow
Ganges R.
Allahabad
Benares
Calcutta
INDIA (Br.)
Nagpur
Bombay
Poona
Ahmadnagar
Hyderabad
Goa (Port.)
Bangalore
Madras
Mangalore
Mysore
Pondicherry (Fr.)
Madura
Tranquebar
Cochin
Jaffna
Tinnevelly
Kandy
CEYLON (Br.)
Colombo
Arabian Sea
Bay of Bengal
Andaman Is.
Andaman Sea
Maldives (Br.)
Chittagong
Mandalay
BURMA (Br.)
Rangoon
Moulmein
Chiang Mai
SIAM
Bangkok
Tavoy
Gulf of Siam
FRENCH INDOCHINA
Hue
Phnompenh
Saigon
Cochin China
Tong king
Hanoi
Gulf of Tong king
Annam
Lanchow
Sian
Huang He R.
Kaifeng
Peking
Tientsin
Chefoo
Chengtu
Chungking
Wuhan
Yangtze R.
Nanking
Soochow
Hangchow
Shanghai
Foochow
Amoy
Swatow
Canton
Macao (Port.)
Hong Kong (Br.)
Formosa (Jap.)
East China Sea
South China Sea
Manchuria
Amur R.
Vladivostock
CHOSEN (KOREA)
Seoul
Yellow Sea
Sea of Japan
Nagasaki
Hondo
Kyoto
Tokyo
Yokohama
JAPAN
Hakodate
Sapporo
Sakhalin Island (Jap.)
Sea of Okhotsk
Pacific Ocean
Philippine Sea
Luzon
Manila
Philippine Islands (U.S.)
Iloilo
Mindanao
Marianas Is.
Guam (U.S.)
Micronesia
Caroline Islands (Ger., Jap. 1914)
Palau (Pelew) (Jap.)
Melanesia
Celebes Sea
BRUNEI
Sarawak
Borneo (Kalimantan)
Celebes
Moluccas
Ambon Is.
BRITISH MALAYA
Kuala Lumpur
Malacca
Singapore
Penang Is.
Sumatra
Indonesian Islands
DUTCH EAST INDIES
Batavia (Djakarta)
Java
Java Sea
Timor (D & Port.)
Timor Sea
Arafura Sea
Dutch New Guinea
German New Guinea
New Guinea
British New Guinea
Bismarck Archipelago (Ger.)
New Pommern (New Britain) (Ger.)
Port Moresby
Port Darwin
Gulf of Carpentaria
Coral Sea
Northern Territory
Western Australia
Queensland
AUSTRALIA
South Australia
New South Wales
Victoria
Camarvon
Perth
Brisbane
Sydney
Adelaide
Melbourne
Darling R.
Murray R.
Great Australian Bight
Tasmania
Hobart
Indian Ocean
Seychelles (Br.)
Comoros (Fr.)
Mauritius (Br.)
Réunion (Fr.)
MADAGASCAR (Fr.)
Antananarivo
Mozambique Channel
MOROCCO (Fr. & Sp.)
Casablanca
ALGERIA (Fr.)
TUNISIA
Tripoli
TRIPOLI (LIBYA) (It.)
Alexandria
Cairo
Suez
EGYPT (Br.)
Canary Islands (Sp.)
RIO DE ORO (SPANISH SAHARA)
Sahara Desert
LIBYA (It.)
Nile R.
Red Sea
ARABIA
Riyadh
Mecca
Aden
Gulf of Aden
FRENCH WEST AFRICA
Timbuktu
Sudan
SENEGAL (Fr.)
PORTUGUESE GUINEA
FRENCH GUINEA
Freetown
SIERRA LEONE (Br.)
Monrovia
LIBERIA
Harper
Cape Palmas
IVORY COAST (Fr.)
GOLD COAST (Br.)
TOGO (Ger.)
DAHOMEY (Fr.)
Niger R.
Lagos
Kano
NIGERIA (Br.)
FRENCH SUDAN
Khartoum
ANGLO-EGYPTIAN SUDAN
ERITREA (It.)
ABYSSINIA (ETHIOPIA)
Addis Ababa
BRITISH SOMALILAND
FRENCH SOMALILAND
ITALIAN SOMALILAND
KAMERUN (Ger.)
Gulf of Guinea
RIO MUNI (Sp.)
Congo R.
UGANDA (Br.)
BRITISH EAST AFRICA
L. Victoria
Nairobi
Mombasa
FRENCH CONGO
BELGIAN CONGO
Cabinda
GERMAN EAST AFRICA
Dar es Salaam
ZANZIBAR (Br.)
L. Nyasa
Luanda
ANGOLA (Port.)
RHODESIA (Br.)
Blantyre
PORTUGUESE E. AFRICA
Salisbury
Bulawayo
GERMAN SOUTH-WEST AFRICA
BECHUANALAND (BOTSWANA) (Br.)
TRANSVAAL
Johannesburg
UNION OF SOUTH AFRICA (Br.)
Orange R.
NATAL
ZULULAND
Durban
CAPE COLONY
Cape Town
Port Elizabeth
South Atlantic Ocean
Cartography by Meridian Mapping, Minneapolis

Biographical Dictionary of Christian Missions

BIOGRAPHICAL DICTIONARY OF CHRISTIAN MISSIONS

Edited by
Gerald H. Anderson

MACMILLAN REFERENCE USA

NEW YORK

Macmillan Reference USA
1633 Broadway
New York, NY 10019

PRINTED IN THE UNITED STATES OF AMERICA

Printing Number
2 3 4 5 6 7 8 9 10

LIBRARY OF CONGRESS CATALOGING-IN-PUBLICATION DATA

Biographical dictionary of Christian missions / edited by Gerald H. Anderson.
p. cm.
Includes bibliographical references and index.
ISBN 0-02-864604-5 (alk. paper)
1. Missionaries—Biography—Dictionaries. I. Anderson, Gerald H.
BV3700.B56 1997
266'.0092'2—dc21
[B] 96-49922
CIP

This paper meets the requirements of ANSI/NISO Z39.48-1992 (Permanence of Paper).

Contents

Dedicated to

All those through the ages who have worked, witnessed, prayed and given to advance the worldwide mission of Jesus Christ—"so that the world may believe" (John 17:21)

Acknowledgments

A pioneering project of this magnitude and complexity owes much to many. In addition to the distinguished board of editorial advisers who gave generously of their counsel and their contributions, more than fifty other colleagues around the world were consulted in the initial planning of the project, especially in drawing up the list of persons to be included. Most of all we are indebted to the 349 authors in 45 countries who wrote the nearly 2,400 articles included here.

In the actual production of the volume, Robert T. Coote brought his strong editing skills and journalistic experience to the role of assistant editor. Craig Noll, Nancy G. Wright, and Joan Zseleczky shared the task of copyediting, William A. Smalley had primary responsibility for proofreading, Cynthia Crippen prepared the index, and Niki Gekas managed the office and controlled the database. Assisting in manuscript development were Joanne Pemberton Anderson, John N. Jones, Nancy Gratton, and Marian K. Ohara.

Paul Bernabeo, Editor-in-Chief, and his staff at Macmillan Reference were a constant source of counsel and encouragement. The Overseas Ministries Study Center in New Haven, Connecticut, graciously housed the project for five years, where Eugenia N. Dilg, Business Manager, provided financial administration.

Working in proximity to the Day Missions Collection in the library of Yale Divinity School, where Martha Lund Smalley and Joan Duffy were always ready to be helpful, was an enormous advantage.

Finally, the editor wishes to express his deep appreciation for the support given by the Pew Charitable Trusts, without which this project would not have been possible.

Gerald H. Anderson

PREFACE

The history of Christian missions is indebted to the persons who have served in various ways to facilitate the extension of the church and the faith that it proclaims. Since the time of Jesus, it is estimated that ten million persons have served as foreign missionaries or cross-cultural home missionaries.[1] Many millions more at the home base have worked and prayed and given to support the missions.

The *Biographical Dictionary of Christian Missions* includes articles on 2,400 of these persons in the post-New Testament history of Christianity down to the present, representing Roman Catholic, Orthodox, Anglican, Protestant, Pentecostal, independent, and indigenous churches. In consultation with more than fifty scholars around the world from diverse church traditions, persons included in this work were chosen because they made a significant contribution—often a pioneering role—to the advancement of Christian missions. Nearly one hundred were martyrs. Not all those included were missionaries. Some were involved at the home base in promotion, recruitment, administration, missiology, teaching, writing, prayer, funding, "the diffusion of intelligence," and other forms of missions advocacy.

Despite our best efforts, women are not adequately represented because, until the late nineteenth century, women were often "invisible" participants in missions. Their significant role and contribution (often even their names) are not well documented in the records. Similarly, non-Western workers, while represented here, will be more fully recognized in years to come, as scholars discover accounts of their work. Therefore, the persons included here serve only as representatives of a vastly larger number of outstanding persons in the history of Christian missions.

The importance of this project is twofold. First, today there are approximately two billion Christians—or 33 percent of the total world population in 1997—and this global community of believers has come about in considerable measure as a result of the missionary enterprise. Second, the place of biography in Christianity is biblical and pivotal to the faith, yet there has never been a major biographical reference tool for Christian missions. An important reason for producing this work is that it has never been done before and its availability now will facilitate an understanding of the worldwide extension of the church. The names included here comprise a virtual Who's Who in the history of the expansion of Christianity.

Like most works of scholarship, we have built on the work of those who have gone before us. Nearly all of the articles have a bibliography for further study. Some of the most important standard works are not included in the bibliographies since doing so would involve much unnecessary repetition. Instead, they are listed after this Preface and recommended as valuable sources for further information.

For the convenience of the reader, the articles are arranged in alphabetical order. Cross-references, indicated with an asterisk placed before the name of a related subject, enhance the ease and usefulness of finding further information in the *Biographical Dictionary*. In the interests of ease of reading, the use of accented characters and diacritical marks has for the most part been limited to European languages. Where old geographical names are historically accurate but no longer current, present-day names have been added on first mention in an article. Efforts have been taken to reflect the latest changes in geographical names. Chinese place names are given in this dictionary as frequently found in primary sources in European languages. The Wade-Giles spelling generally has been preferred, followed in parentheses by the name in Pinyin, thereafter using only the traditional name. For example: Peking (Beijing), thereafter Peking; Nanking (Nanjing), thereafter Nanking. Romanization of Chinese personal names and terms is complicated. At the beginning of each article dealing with a Chinese per-

1. David B. Barrett, "Annual Statistical Table on Global Mission: 1996," *International Bulletin of Missionary Research* 20 (1996): 24.

son, we have used the romanization system of the name that the person used and was known by. In most cases this is the Wade-Giles system. The first form of the name is followed in parentheses with the same name in the Pinyin system, if available.

The elaborate appendix and index will be of special interest and will greatly facilitate the efforts of readers who wish to explore particular regions of work, types of work, and periods of missionary service. In addition, the appendix lists martyrs, women, non-Western personnel, and the largest groups represented in this work. The endpaper maps are another useful tool to facilitate the study of where these persons worked; the front map shows the world around 1914 and the back one is current.

To read the articles gathered in this dictionary is not only informative and inspiring, but humbling. They are profiles of faith, courage, and sacrifice—testimonies to the work of the Holy Spirit in earthen vessels.

Today there is a misconception that the era of Christian missions is over. Actually, there are far more missionaries working today than ever before in history (403,000 in 1997).[2] The difference is that a great many of these missionaries are now sent out from churches in the non-Western world. This great new fact is itself a result, in part, of the missionary enterprise up to the present.

In his 1991 encyclical *Redemptoris Missio* (The Mission of the Redeemer), Pope John Paul II envisioned—on the eve of the third millennium—"the dawning of a new missionary age," with God "preparing a great springtime for Christianity." Anticipating the twenty-first century as another century of missionary expansion, we recall the injunction of Adoniram Judson, the pioneer Protestant missionary to Burma, "The future is as bright as the promises of God." That is the missionary spirit.

Gerald H. Anderson

2. David B. Barrett, "Annual Statistical Table on Global Mission: 1997," *International Bulletin of Missionary Research* 21 (1997): 25.

Standard Reference Works

Bibliotheca Missionum (1928, 1951)

Biographical Dictionary of Methodist Missionaries to Japan: 1873–1993 (1995)

Blackwell Dictionary of Evangelical Biography, 1730–1860 (1995)

Catholic Encyclopedia (1907)

Concise Dictionary of the Christian World Mission (1971)

Dictionary of American Biography (1928–1958, with supplements)

Dictionary of American Catholic Biography (1984)

Dictionary of Canadian Biography (1987)

Dictionary of Catholic Biography (1961)

Dictionary of Christianity in America (1990)

Dictionary of National Biography (Great Britain) (1885–;1917–)

Dictionary of Scottish Church History and Theology (1993)

Dictionary of the Ecumenical Movement (1991)

Dictionary of Pentecostal and Charismatic Movements (1988)

Dictionnaire d'histoire et de géographie eccélesiastiques (1912–)

Dictionnaire de spiritualité (1937–1995)

Dictionnaire du monde religieux dans la France contemporaine (1985)

Encyclopedia of Missions (1891; 2d ed., 1904)

Evangelisches Kirchenlexikon (3d ed., 1986–1996)

Historical Dictionary of Ecumenical Christianity (1994)

International Who's Who (60th ed., 1996/1997)

Jesuiten-Lexikon (1934)

Lexikon der Mission (1992)

Lexikon für Theologie und Kirche (2d ed., 1957–1965; 3d ed., 1993–)

Lexikon zur Weltmission (1975)

Missionary Biography: An Initial Bibliography (1965)

New Catholic Encyclopedia (1967–1979)

Norsk Biografisk Leksikon (1923–)

Norsk Misjonsleksikon (1965–1967)

Oxford Dictionary of the Christian Church (3d ed., 1997)

Religion in Geschichte und Gegenwart (3d ed., 1957–1965; 4th ed., 1996–)

Theologische Realenzyklopädie (1976–)

Webster's Biographical Dictionary (1988, rev. 1995)

Who's Who of World Religions (1991)

World Christian Encyclopedia (1982)

Abbreviations and Symbols

Abbreviations refer to the names or titles indicated by authors in their articles and not necessarily to the present-day names or titles.

- * An asterisk indicates a cross-reference to the subject following it.
- AACC All Africa Conference of Churches
- ABCFM American Board of Commissioners for Foreign Missions
- ABFMS American Baptist Foreign Mission Society
- ABS American Bible Society
- AEF Africa Evangelical Fellowship (formerly South Africa General Mission)
- *AFER* *Africa Ecclesiastical/Ecclesial Review* (Masaka/Eldoret, 1959–)
- AG Assemblies of God
- AIM Africa Inland Mission
- *AJT* *Asia Journal of Theology* (Singapore, 1987–)
- AME African Methodist Episcopal Church
- *AMZ* *Allgemeine Missions-Zeitschrift* (Gütersloh, 1874–1923)
- BCMS Bible Churchmen's Missionary Society
- BFBS British and Foreign Bible Society
- BM Basel Mission
- BMS Baptist Missionary Society
- c. circa, about
- CBMS Conference of British Missionary Societies
- *CC* *Christian Century* (Chicago, 1900–)
- CCA Christian Conference of Asia
- CCIA Commission of the Churches on International Affairs
- CEZMS Church of England Zenana Missionary Society
- *ChH* *Church History* (New York/Chicago, 1932–)
- CICM Congregation of the Immaculate Heart of Mary (Missionaries of Scheut/ Missionhurst)
- CIM China Inland Mission (now Overseas Missionary Fellowship)
- CLS Christian Literature Society
- C&MA Christian and Missionary Alliance
- CMJ Church's Ministry among Jewish People (formerly London Society for Promoting Christianity amongst the Jews)
- CMML Christian Missions in Many Lands
- CMS Church Missionary Society (now Church Mission Society)
- CSC Congregation of the Holy Cross
- CSI Church of South India
- CSM Church of Scotland Mission
- CSP Congregation of Saint Paul (Paulists)
- CSSp Holy Ghost Fathers
- CSSR Redemptorists
- *CT* *Christianity Today* (Washington/Carol Stream, 1956–)
- CWM Council for World Mission (formerly London Missionary Society)
- CWME Commission on World Mission and Evangelism of the World Council of Churches
- D.D. Doctor of Divinity degree
- diss. dissertation
- DRC Dutch Reformed Church
- EACC East Asia Christian Conference
- *EAJT* *East Asia Journal of Theology* (Singapore, 1983–1986). Successor to SEAJT and NEAJT
- ed(s). edited by; editor(s)
- EFMA Evangelical Foreign Missions Association (now Evangelical Fellowship of Mission Agencies)
- e.g. for example
- *EMM* *Evangelisches Missionsmagazin,* Neue Folge (Basel, 1857–1974)
- EMMS Edinburgh Medical Missionary Society
- *EMQ* *Evangelical Missions Quarterly* (Washington and Wheaton, 1964–)
- *EMZ* *Evangelische Missions-Zeitschrift* (Stuttgart, 1940–1974)
- Eng. tr. English translation
- *ER* *Ecumenical Review* (Geneva, 1948–)
- et al. and others
- f., ff. following
- FCSM Free Church of Scotland Mission

fl. flourished
FMB Foreign Mission Board (now International Mission Board), Southern Baptist Convention
FMM Franciscan Missionaries of Mary
Fr. Father
GMU Gospel Missionary Union
HM *Het Missiewerk* (Nijmegen, 1919–1971)
IAMS International Association for Mission Studies
IBMR *International Bulletin of Missionary Research* (Ventnor/New Haven, 1981–). Successor to OBMR
ICHR *Indian Church History Review* (Mysore, 1967–)
IFMA Interdenominational Foreign Mission Association of North America
IHM Immaculate Heart of Mary Missionary Sisters
IMC International Missionary Council
IMR *Indian Missiological Review* (Bombay/Indore, 1979–)
IRM *International Review of Mission(s)* (London/ Geneva, 1912–)
IVCF InterVarsity Christian Fellowship
JRA *Journal of Religion in Africa* (Leiden, 1967–)
LAM Latin America Mission
LMS London Missionary Society
LSPCJ London Society for Promoting Christianity amongst the Jews
LWF Lutheran World Federation
M Afr Missionaries of Africa, also known as Society of African Missions (SMA) and White Fathers (WF)
MCCJ Comboni Missionaries
Med. *Mededeelingen (van wege het Nederlandsche Zendelinggenootschap)* (Rotterdam, 1857–1943)
MHM Mill Hill Missionaries
MM Maryknoll Missioners (Catholic Foreign Mission Society of America)
MMS Medical Mission Sisters
MMS Methodist Missionary Society
MR *Missionswissenschaft und Religionswissenschaft* (Münster in Westfalen, 1938–1941, 1947–1949.)
MRL Missionary Research Library, New York City
MRW *Missionary Review of the World.* New Series (1888–1939). Successor to *Missionary Review* (Princeton, 1878–1887)
MSC Missionaries of the Sacred Heart
MS(S) manuscript(s)
MW *Moslem World* (Hartford, 1911–1960; *Muslim World,* 1961–)
NAE National Association of Evangelicals
NAM North Africa Mission (now Arab World Ministries)
NAMZ *Neue Allgemeine Missionszeitschrift* (Gütersloh, 1924–1939)
NCC National Council of Churches
NEAJT *North East Asia Journal of Theology* (Tokyo, 1968–1982)
NECC Near East Council of Churches
NMS Norwegian Mission Society
NZG Netherlands Mission Society
NZM *Neue Zeitschrift für Missionswissenschaft* (Schöneck-Beckenried, 1945–)
OBMR *Occasional Bulletin of Missionary Research* (Ventnor, 1977–1980)
O Carm Carmelites
OFM Order of Friars Minor (Franciscans)
OFM Cap Franciscan Capuchins
OFM Conv Franciscan Conventuals
OMF Overseas Missionary Fellowship (formerly China Inland Mission)
OMI Oblates of Mary Immaculate
OMS Oriental Missionary Society (now OMS International)
OP Order of Preachers (Dominicans)
OSA Order of Saint Augustine (Augustinians)
OSB Order of Saint Benedict (Benedictines)
OSU Order of Saint Ursula (Ursuline Sisters)
PA *Practical Anthropology* (Tarrytown, 1954–1972)
PCUS Presbyterian Church in the US (Southern)
PCUSA Presbyterian Church (USA)
PECUSA Protestant Episcopal Church in the USA
PEMS Paris Evangelical Missionary Society *(Société des Mission Evangéliques de Paris)*
PFM Paris Foreign Missions *(Missions Etrangéres de Paris)*
PIME Pontifical Institute for Foreign Missions
PSS Priest of San Sulpice
r. reigned
RBMU Regions Beyond Missionary Union
RC Roman Catholic
RCA Reformed Church in America
Rev. Reverend
rev. revised edition
SA Salvation Army
SAGM South Africa General Mission (see AEF)
SAMS South American Missionary Society
SBCFMB Southern Baptist Convention Foreign Mission Board (now International Mission Board of the Southern Baptist Convention)
SCM Student Christian Movement
SDA Seventh-day Adventist
SDB Salesians of Saint Don Bosco
SDS Salvatorians
SEAJT *South East Asia Journal of Theology* (Singapore, 1959–1982)
SIL Summer Institute of Linguistics; see WBT/SIL
SIM Sudan Interior Mission (now Society for International Ministries)
SJ Society of Jesus (Jesuits)
SJA Sisters of St. Joseph of the Apparition
SJT *Scottish Journal of Theology* (Edinburgh, 1948)
SM Society of Mary (Marists)

SMA Society of African Missions, also known as Missionaries of Africa (M Afr) and White Fathers (WF)
SMSM Missionary Sisters of the Society of Mary
SND Sisters of Notre Dame de Namur
SOAS School of Oriental and African Studies, University of London
SPCK Society for Promoting Christian Knowledge
SPF Society for the Propagation of the Faith
SPG Society for the Propagation of the Gospel
SS Sulpicians
SSC Columbans
SSND School Sisters of Notre Dame
St. Saint
SUM Sudan United Mission
SVD Society of the Divine Word
SVM Student Volunteer Movement for Foreign Missions
tr(s). translated by; translator(s)
UBS United Bible Societies
UCBWM United Church Board for World Ministries (successor to ABCFM)
UCCF Universities and Colleges Christian Fellowship
UK United Kingdom of Great Britain and Northern Ireland
UMCA Universities' Mission to Central Africa
univ. university
U.S. United States
USCL United Society for Christian Literature
USPG United Society for the Propagation of the Gospel
vol(s). volume(s)
WBT/SIL Wycliffe Bible Translators/Summer Institute of Linguistics
WCC World Council of Churches
WEC Worldwide Evangelization Crusade
WMMS Wesleyan Methodist Missionary Society
WF White Fathers (see M Afr)
WSCF World (formerly World's) Student Christian Federation
WZ *Wereld en Zending* (Amsterdam, 1972–)
YMCA Young Men's Christian Association
YWAM Youth With A Mission
YWCA Young Women's Christian Association
ZM *Zeitschrift für Missionswissenschaft* (Münster in Westfalen, 1911–1927)
ZMiss *Zeitschrift für Mission* (Basel & Stuttgart, 1975–)
ZMkR *Zeitschrift für Missionskunde und Religionswissenschaft* (Berlin, 1886–1939)
ZMR *Zeitschrift für Missionswissenschaft und Religionswissenschaft* (Münster in Westfalen, 1928–1935; 1950–). Successor to *ZM* and *MR*

Directory of Contributors

Theodor Ahrens
Professor of Missiology and Ecumenics
Faculty of Theology
University of Hamburg
Hamburg, Germany

Michael Amaladoss, SJ
Professor of Theology
Vidyajyoti College of Theology
Delhi, India

Gerald H. Anderson
Director, Overseas Ministries Study Center
New Haven, Connecticut
Editor, *International Bulletin of Missionary Research*

José S. Arcilla, SJ
Professor of History
Ateneo de Manila University
Quezon City, The Philippines

Thomas A. Askew
Professor and Chair of the Department of History
Gordon College
Wenham, Massachusetts

Willem J. van Asselt
Senior Lecturer
History of Reformed Theology
Utrecht University
Utrecht, The Netherlands

Abraham P. Athyal
Dean of Postgraduate Studies
Professor of New Testament
Gurukul Lutheran Theological College and Research Institute
Madras, India

Alvyn Austin
Research Associate
Joint Center for Asia Pacific Studies
York University, Toronto, Canada

Dirk Bakker
Formerly Director
Hendrik Kraemer Institute
Oegstgeest, The Netherlands

Daryl M. Balia
Associate Professor and Dean of Theology
University of Durban-Westville
Durban, South Africa

David B. Barrett
Research Professor of Missiometrics
Regent University
Virginia Beach, Virginia

Daniel H. Bays
Professor of Modern Chinese History
University of Kansas
Lawrence, Kansas

Kwame Bediako
Director, Akrofi-Christaller Memorial Centre for Mission Research and Applied Theology
Akropong-Akuapem, Ghana

H. D. Beeby
Formerly Old Testament Lecturer
Selly Oak Colleges
Birmingham, England

Anthony Bellagamba, IMC
Regional Superior, North American Region
Consolata Missionaries
Somerset, New Jersey

Robert Benedetto
Associate Librarian
Associate Professor of Bibliography
Union Theological Seminary
Richmond, Virginia

Clinton Bennett
Lecturer in Islamic Studies and Anthropological Theology
Westminster College
Oxford, England

John C. Bennett
President
Overseas Council for Theological Education and Missions
Greenwood, Indiana

Ans Joachim van der Bent (died 1995)
Formerly Director of the Library
World Council of Churches
Geneva, Switzerland

Stephen B. Bevans, SVD
Professor of Doctrinal Theology
Catholic Theological Union
Chicago, Illinois

Robert Bireley, SJ
Professor of History
Loyola University
Chicago, Illinois

Otto Bischofberger, SMB
Professor for History of Religions
University of Luzern
Luzern, Switzerland

Nansie Blackie
Formerly on the staff of the Church of Scotland missionary training college
St. Colm's
Edinburgh, Scotland

Nils Egede Bloch-Hoell
Formerly Professor of Missiology and Ecumenics
Oslo University
Oslo, Norway

Edith Blumhofer
Associate Director
Public Religion Project
University of Chicago
Divinity School
Chicago, Illinois

P. Richard Bohr
Associate Professor of History and
Director of Asian Studies
College of Saint Benedict
Saint John's University
Saint Joseph, Minnesota

Edward E. Bollinger
Retired American Baptist
Missionary in Japan and
Okinawa

Jonathan J. Bonk
Associate Director
Overseas Ministries Study Center
New Haven, Connecticut

Henry Warner Bowden
Professor of Religion
Rutgers University
New Brunswick, New Jersey

William H. Brackney
Principal and Professor of
Historical Theology
McMaster Divinity College,
McMaster University
Hamilton, Ontario, Canada

G. Thompson Brown
Emeritus Professor of Missions
and World Christianity
Columbia Theological Seminary
Decatur, Georgia

Mark J. Brummel, CMF
Editor
Claretian Publications
Chicago, Illinois

Paul Brunner, SJ
President
Catechists' Foundation
of the Philippines, Inc.
Quezon City, The Philippines

David Bundy
Librarian and Associate Professor
of Church History
Christian Theological Seminary
Indianapolis, Indiana

Horst W. Bürkle
Emeritus Professor for
Comparative Religious Studies
Ludwig-Maximilians-University
Munich, Germany

Kenelm Burridge
Emeritus Professor of
Anthropology
University of British Columbia
Vancouver, British Columbia,
Canada

Arnulf Camps, OFM
Emeritus Professor of Missiology
Catholic University of Nijmegen
Nijmegen, The Netherlands

Joel A. Carpenter
Provost, Calvin College
Grand Rapids, Michigan

Emilio Castro
Formerly General Secretary
World Council of Churches
Geneva, Switzerland

A. J. V. Chandrakanthan
Professor of Systematic Theology
Concordia University
Montreal, Québec, Canada

Cindy Swanson Choo
Intercultural Specialist
InterVarsity Christian Fellowship
New Haven, Connecticut

Chun Chae Ok
Professor of Missiology and
Religion
Department of Christian Studies
College of Liberal Arts
Ewha Woman's University
Seoul, Korea

Paul Clasper
Formerly Dean of St. John's
Cathedral
Hong Kong

Edward L. Cleary, OP
Professor of Latin American
Studies
Providence College
Providence, Rhode Island

Keith W. Clements
Co-ordinating Secretary for
International Affairs
Council of Churches for Britain
and Ireland
Bristol, England

Norman H. Cliff
Retired Minister
United Reformed Church
Essex, England

Paul Rowntree Clifford
Formerly President of Selly Oak
Colleges
Birmingham, England

Robert G. Clouse
Professor of History
Indiana State University
Terre Haute, Indiana

Thomas Cohen
Assistant Professor of History
Curator of the Oliveira Lima
Library
Catholic University of America
Washington, D.C.

Mary Frances Coleman, OP
Researcher, Project Opus:
A History of the Order of
Preachers in the United States
Chicago, Illinois

Harvie M. Conn
Professor of Missions
Westminster Theological
Seminary
Philadelphia, Pennsylvania
Editor, *Urban Mission*

Demetrios J. Constantelos
Charles Cooper Townsend Senior
Distinguished Professor
of History and Religious
Studies
Richard Stockton College of
New Jersey
Pomona, New Jersey

Robert T. Coote
Assistant to the Director for
Planning and Development
Overseas Ministries Study Center
New Haven, Connecticut

Gary R. Corwin
Editor
Evangelical Missions Quarterly
Charlotte, North Carolina

Dimitrios Couchell
Executive Director
Orthodox Christian Mission
Center
St. Augustine, Florida

Ralph Covell
Formerly Professor of World
Christianity and Academic
Dean
Denver Seminary
Denver, Colorado

James L. Cox
Lecturer
Centre for the Study of
Christianity in the
Non-Western World
University of Edinburgh
Edinburgh, Scotland

Kenneth Cracknell
Research Professor in Mission and Theology
Brite Divinity School
Texas Christian University
Fort Worth, Texas

Kenneth Cragg
Honorary Assistant Bishop
Oxford, England

Terrence Craig
Associate Professor of English Literature
Mount Allison University
New Brunswick, Canada

Clyde F. Crews
Professor of Theology
Bellarmine College
Louisville, Kentucky

J. S. Cummins
Emeritus Professor of Hispanic and Latin American Studies
London University
London, England

R. Emmett Curran, SJ
Associate Professor of History
Georgetown University
Washington, D.C.

Marthinus L. Daneel
Emeritus Professor of Missiology
University of South Africa
Pretoria, South Africa

Dick L. Darr
President Emeritus
Gospel Missionary Union
Kansas City, Missouri

Mohan D. David
Formerly Professor and Head Department of History
University of Bombay
Bombay, India

Allan K. Davidson
Lecturer in Church History
St. John's College
Auckland, New Zealand

Ronald E. Davies
Director, Postgraduate Center for Mission Studies
All Nations Christian College
Easneye, Ware, England

John W. de Gruchy
Robert Selby Taylor Professor of Christian Studies
University of Cape Town
Cape Town, South Africa

Christiaan G. F. de Jong
Research Fellow
Kampen Theological University
Kampen, The Netherlands

Pablo A. Deiros
Professor of Church History
International Baptist Theological Seminary
Buenos Aires, Argentina
and Fuller Theological Seminary, School of World Mission
Pasadena, California

Paul R. Dekar
Professor of Evangelism and Missions
Memphis Theological Seminary
Memphis, Tennessee

Wayne Detzler
Dean and Professor of Mission
Southern Evangelical Seminary
Charlotte, North Carolina

Peter Deyneka, Jr.
Founder and President of Russian Ministries
Wheaton, Illinois

J. A. DiNoia, OP
Professor of Theology
Dominican House of Studies
Washington, D.C.
Editor, *The Thomist*

J. G. Donders, M Afr
Chair of Mission and Cross-cultural Studies
Washington Theological Union
Washington, D.C.

Ian T. Douglas
Associate Professor of World Mission and Global Christianity
Episcopal Divinity School
Cambridge, Massachusetts

Frederick S. Downs
Professor of the History of Christianity
United Theological College
Bangalore, India

Otto Dreydoppel, Jr.
Director of Moravian Studies and Instructor of Church History
Moravian Theological Seminary
Bethlehem, Pennsylvania

Angelyn Dries, OSF
Associate Professor of Religious Studies
Cardinal Stritch College
Milwaukee, Wisconsin

Richard H. Drummond
Emeritus Professor of Ecumenical Mission and History of Religions
University of Dubuque Theological Seminary
Dubuque, Iowa

Joan R. Duffy
Archives Assistant
Yale Divinity School Library
New Haven, Connecticut

Avery Dulles, SJ
Laurence J. McGinley Professor of Religion and Society
Fordham University
Bronx, New York

Jacques Dupuis, SJ
Professor of Dogmatic Theology
Pontifical Gregorian University
Rome, Italy

Donald F. Durnbaugh
Emeritus Professor of Church History
Bethany Theological Seminary
and Archivist at Juniata College
Huntingdon, Pennsylvania

Cornelius J. Dyck
Emeritus Professor of Anabaptist and Sixteenth Century Studies
Associated Mennonite Biblical Seminaries
Elkhart, Indiana

William W. Emilsen
Lecturer in Church History
United Theological College
North Parramatta
Sydney, Australia

Thomas van den End
Mission Historian
Gereformmerde Zendingsbond (Reformed Mission League)
Apeldoorn, The Netherlands

Ido H. Enklaar (died 1994)
Formerly Principal
Hendrik Kraemer Institute
Oegstgeest, The Netherlands

Samuel Escobar
Professor of Missions
Eastern Baptist Theological Seminary
Philadelphia, Pennsylvania

James T. Fisher
Danforth Professor in the Humanities
Saint Louis University
St. Louis, Missouri

Gerald P. Fogarty, SJ
Professor of Religious Studies and History
University of Virginia
Charlottesville, Virginia

Charles W. Forman
Emeritus Professor of Missions
Yale University Divinity School
New Haven, Connecticut

Duncan B. Forrester
Head of the Department of Christian Ethics and Practical Theology
University of Edinburgh
Edinburgh, Scotland

M. Joy Fox
Archivist, Methodist Church Overseas Division (Methodist Missionary Society)
London, England

Albert H. Frank
Pastor
First Moravian Church
Dover, Ohio

Ruth Franzén
Professor of Church History
Uppsala University
Uppsala, Sweden

Angus Fraser
President
George Borrow Society
Kew, Richmond, England

Robert Eric Frykenberg
Professor of History
University of Wisconsin
Madison, Wisconsin

Gernot Fugmann
Area Secretary for Papua New Guinea, Pacific, and East Asia
Department of World Mission
Evangelical Lutheran Church in Bavaria
Neuendettelsau, Germany

Robert Mikio Fukada
Professor of Practical Theology
Doshisha University
Kyoto, Japan

John Garrett
Fellow of the Institute of Pacific Studies
University of the South Pacific
and Research Associate
Pacific Theological College
Suva, Fiji

Paul D. Garrett
Independent Scholar
Latrobe, Pennsylvania

Hans-Werner Gensichen
Emeritus Professor of History of Religions and Missiology
University of Heidelberg
Heidelberg, Germany

Anthony J. Gittins, CSSp
Professor of Theological Anthropology
Catholic Theological Union
Chicago, Illinois

Arthur F. Glasser
Emeritus Dean
Fuller Theological Seminary, School of World Mission
Pasadena, California

H. McKennie Goodpasture
Emeritus Professor of Christian Missions
Union Theological Seminary
Richmond, Virginia

Karen L. Gordon
Independent Scholar
Moscow, Russia

Jan Górski
Professor of Missiology
Pontifical Academy of Theology
Cracow, Poland

Jerald D. Gort
Associate Professor of Missiology
Theological Faculty of the Free University
Amsterdam, The Netherlands

John A. Gration
Emeritus Professor of Missions
Wheaton College Graduate School
Wheaton, Illinois

Richard Gray
Emeritus Professor of African History
University of London
London, England

James Grayson
Director of the Centre for Korean Studies
University of Sheffield
Sheffield, England

Leslie Griffiths
Minister
Wesley's Chapel
London, England

Christoffer H. Grundmann
Lecturer
Department of Missions, Oecumenics and Religion
University of Hamburg
Hamburg, Germany

Lucio Gutiérrez, OP
Professor of Church History and Patrology
Dean of the Faculty of Sacred Theology
University of Santo Tomas
Manila, The Philippines

Waltraud Ch. Haas
Formerly Assistant Archivist
Basel Mission
Basel, Switzerland

Getatchew Haile
Cataloger of Oriental Manuscripts
Regents Professor of Medieval History
Saint John's University
Collegeville, Minnesota

P. E. H. Hair
Emeritus Professor of Modern History
University of Liverpool
Liverpool, England

Gordon M. Haliburton
Formerly Professor of History
University of Botswana, Lesotho, and Swaziland
Roma, Lesotho

Jehu J. Hanciles
Lecturer in Church History and Missiology
Faculty of Theology
Africa University
Mutare, Zimbabwe

Stanley Samuel Harakas
Archbishop Iakovos Emeritus Professor of Orthodox Theology
Holy Cross Greek Orthodox School of Theology
Brookline, Massachusetts

C. David Harley
Dean
Discipleship Training Center
Singapore

Susan Billington Harper
Formerly Lecturer in History and Literature and in Expository Writing
Harvard University
Cambridge, Massachusetts

John W. Harris
Director of the Translation and Text Division
Bible Society in Australia
Canberra, Australia

Adrian Hastings
Emeritus Professor
Department of Theology and Religious Studies
University of Leeds
Leeds, England

Roger E. Hedlund
Professor of Mission Studies (Research)
Serampore College
Serampore, India
Managing Editor, *Dharma Deepika: A South Asian Journal of Missiological Research*

Eugene Heideman
Formerly Secretary for World Mission
Reformed Church in America
New York, New York

Mary J. Heideman
Formerly Missionary in the Church of South India
Reformed Church in America
New York, New York

John R. Hendrick
John William and Helen Lancaster Emeritus Professor of Missions
Austin Presbyterian Theological Seminary
Austin, Texas

Barbara Hendricks, MM
Formerly President
Maryknoll Sisters Congregation
Maryknoll, New York

Willi Henkel, OMI
Director
Pontifical Missionary Library
Rome, Italy
Editor, *Bibliografia Missionaria*

Irving Hexham
Professor of Religious Studies
Department of Religious Studies
University of Calgary
Calgary, Alberta, Canada

Ulrich van der Heyden
Research Fellow
Center for Modern Oriental Studies
Berlin, Germany

Francis X. Hezel, SJ
Director of the Jesuit-run Research Pastoral Institute
Pohnpei, Federated States of Micronesia

Janet Hodgson
Advisor in Local Mission
Diocese of Durham
Church of England
Durham, England

Libertus A. Hoedemaker
Professor of Missions and Ecumenics
Theological Faculty
State University of Groningen
Groningen, The Netherlands

Alle G. Hoekema
Lecturer in Missiology and Practical Theology
Faculty of Theology
University of Amsterdam
and Dean, Mennonite Seminary
Amsterdam, The Netherlands

J. W. Hofmeyr
Professor and Head
Department of Church History
Faculty of Theology
University of Pretoria
Pretoria, South Africa

Edmund M. Hogan, SMA
Provincial Archivist
Society of African Missions
Cork, Ireland

Marjo A. Hogendorp
Doctoral Candidate
Utrecht University
Utrecht, The Netherlands

George A. Hood
Formerly East Asia Secretary
Council for World Mission
London, England

Thomas Hopko
Dean and Professor of Dogmatic Theology and Spirituality
St. Vladimir's Orthodox Theological Seminary
Crestwood, New York

Norman A. Horner
Emeritus Professor of Mission and Evangelism
Louisville Presbyterian Theological Seminary
Louisville, Kentucky

John Hosie, SM
Professor of Church History
Catholic Theological Union
Sydney, Australia

David M. Howard
President
Latin America Mission
Miami, Florida

Lydia Huffman Hoyle
Assistant Professor of Religion
Georgetown College
Georgetown, Kentucky

Everett N. Hunt, Jr. (died 1996)
Formerly Professor of the History of Missions
E. Stanley Jones School of World Mission and Evangelism
Asbury Theological Seminary
Wilmore, Kentucky

Keith L. Hunt
Formerly Special Assistant to the President
InterVarsity Christian Fellowship
Ann Arbor, Michigan

Robert A. Hunt
Lecturer in Practical Theology and Religions
Trinity Theological College
Singapore

George G. Hunter III
Dean and Beeson Professor of Evangelism and Church Growth
E. Stanley Jones School of World Mission and Evangelism
Asbury Theological Seminary
Wilmore, Kentucky

A. Hamish Ion
Professor of History
Royal Military College of Canada
Kingston, Ontario, Canada

E. M. Jackson
Senior Lecturer in Religious Studies
University of Derby
Derby, England

Sylvia M. Jacobs
Professor of African History
North Carolina Central University
Durham, North Carolina

Paul Jenkins
Archivist
Basel Mission
Basel, Switzerland

P. J. G. Jeroense
Minister
Netherlands Reformed Church
Gorssel, The Netherlands

R. Park Johnson
Retired Mission Executive
Presbyterian Church (USA)
Penny Farms, Florida

Geoffrey Johnston
Director of Pastoral Studies
Presbyterian College
Montreal, Quebec, Canada

Richard J. Jones
Associate Professor of Mission and World Religions
Virginia Theological Seminary
Alexandria, Virginia

Jan A. B. Jongeneel
Professor of Mission
Utrecht University
Utrecht, The Netherlands

Leendert J. Joosse
President, Institute for Reformed Theological Training
Editor, *International Review of Reformed Missiology*
Zwolle, The Netherlands

Ogbu U. Kalu
Professor of Church History
University of Nigeria
Nsukka, Enugu State, Nigeria

Wi Jo Kang
Wilhelm Loehe Emeritus Professor of Mission
Wartburg Theological Seminary
Dubuque, Iowa

Hans Kasdorf
Emeritus Professor
Free Theological Academy
Giessen, Germany

Christopher J. Kauffman
Professor of Church History
Catholic University of America
Washington, D.C.
Editor, *U.S. Catholic Historian*

David A. Kerr
Professor and Director
Centre for the Study of Christianity in the Non-Western World
University of Edinburgh
Edinburgh, Scotland

Karen Kidd
Doctoral Candidate in History
Claremont Graduate School
Claremont, California

Gail King
Curator of the Asian Collection
Harold B. Lee Library
Brigham Young University
Provo, Utah

Graham Kings
Henry Martyn Lecturer in Missiology
Cambridge Theological Federation
Cambridge, England

Rita Smith Kipp
Professor of Anthropology
Kenyon College
Gambier, Ohio

Gerishon M. Kirika
Lecturer, Religion Department
Kenyatta University
Nairobi, Kenya

Jeffrey Klaiber, SJ
Professor of Peruvian and Latin American Church History
Catholic University of Peru
Lima, Peru

Fritz Kollbrunner, SMB
Editor *Neue Zeitschrift für Missionswissenschaft*
Luzerne, Switzerland

Anne-Marie Kool
Director
Protestant Institute for Mission Studies
Budapest, Hungary

David Nii Anum Kpobi
Secretary for Inter-Church and Ecumenical Relations
Presbyterian Church of Ghana
Accra, Ghana

John W. Krummel
Formerly Professor of English
Aoyama Gakuin University
Tokyo, Japan

Kwok Pui-lan
Associate Professor of Theology
Episcopal Divinity School
Cambridge, Massachusetts

Creighton Lacy
Emeritus Professor of World Christianity
Duke University Divinity School
Durham, North Carolina

Leny Lagerwerf
Interuniversity Institute for Missiological and Ecumenical Research
Utrecht, The Netherlands

Bartholomew P. Lahiff, SJ
Professor of History
Ateneo de Manila University
Quezon City, The Philippines

Erick D. Langer
Associate Professor of Latin American History
Carnegie Mellon University
Pittsburgh, Pennsylvania

Joseph Lévesque, PPS (died 1995)
Formerly Director
Centre de Recherche Théologique Missionaire
Paris, France

Walter L. Liefeld
Emeritus Professor of New Testament
Trinity Evangelical Divinity School
Deerfield, Illinois

Li Li
Ph.D. Candidate
Department of History
University of North Carolina
Chapel Hill, North Carolina

Eeuwout van der Linden
Minister
Netherlands Reformed Church
Goes, The Netherlands

Peter Lineham
Senior Lecturer
Department of History
Massey University
Palmerston North
New Zealand

Kathleen L. Lodwick
Professor of History
Pennsylvania State University
Allentown, Pennsylvania

Margaret F. Loftus, SND
Formerly Executive Director
United States Catholic Mission Association
Washington, D.C.

Charles Henry Long
Formerly Editor
Forward Movement Publications
Cincinnati, Ohio

Jesús López-Gay, SJ
Dean of the Faculty of Missiology
Pontifical Gregorian University
Rome, Italy

Louis J. Luzbetak, SVD
Formerly Editor, *Anthropos*
Formerly Staff Member of the Vatican's Pontifical Council for Culture
Techny, Illinois

Cyprian Lynch, OFM
Emeritus Professor
Franciscan Institute
St. Bonaventure University
St. Bonaventure, New York

Donald MacInnis
Formerly Director of the China Program
National Council of Churches in the USA and
Coordinator for China Research of the Maryknoll Fathers and Brothers
Maryknoll, New York

James Patrick Mackey
Thomas Chalmers Professor of Theology
University of Edinburgh
Edinburgh, Scotland

H. T. Maclin
Formerly President
Mission Society for United Methodists
Norcross, Georgia

Flemming Markussen
Formerly Instructor in Missiology
Free Faculty of Theology
Aarhus, Denmark

James K. Mathews
Bishop (Retired)
United Methodist Church
Washington, D.C.

L. Grant McClung, Jr.
Coordinator for Research and Strategic Planning
Church of God World Missions
Cleveland, Tennessee

William E. McConville, OFM
Formerly President
Siena College
Loudonville, New York

Gary B. McGee
Professor of Church History
Assemblies of God Theological Seminary
Springfield, Missouri

Mary Nona McGreal, OP
Director of Research for Project Opus: A History of the Order of Preachers in the United States
Chicago, Illinois

G. Stewart McIntosh
Director of MAC RESEARCH
Tayport, Scotland, and
Missiologist in the Facultad Evangélica Orlando E. Costas
Lima, Peru

Edward H. McKinley
Chair of the History Department
Asbury College
Wilmore, Kentucky

Josef Metzler, OMI
Formerly Prefect
Vatican Secret Archives
Vatican City

David J. Michell
Director
Overseas Missionary Fellowship
Toronto, Ontario, Canada

Kenneth P. Minkema
Executive Editor
The Works of Jonathan Edwards
Yale University
New Haven, Connecticut

Min Ma
Professor of History
Dean of the History and Culture College
Central China Normal University
Huazhong, Hubei, China

William Mitchell
Translation Consultant
United Bible Societies
Quito, Ecuador

Eileen Moffett
Formerly Presbyterian Church (USA) Missionary to Korea
Princeton, New Jersey

Samuel Hugh Moffett
Henry Winters Luce Emeritus Professor of Ecumenics and Mission
Princeton Theological Seminary
Princeton, New Jersey

Jacques Monet, SJ
President
University of Sudbury
Director, Canadian Institute of Jesuit Studies
Sudbury, Ontario, Canada

Mary Motte, FMM
Director
Mission Resource Center
Franciscan Missionaries of Mary
North Providence, Rhode Island

Kenneth B. Mulholland
Dean
Columbia Biblical Seminary and Graduate School of Missions
Columbia International University
Columbia, South Carolina

Karl Müller, SVD
Formerly Director
Society of the Divine Word Missiological Institute
Sankt Augustine, Germany

Klaus W. Müller
Lecturer in Missions
Freie Hochschule für Mission
Korntal, Germany

Graeme A. Murray
Formerly Chairman
New Zealand Baptist Missionary Society
Wellington, New Zealand

Jocelyn Margaret Murray
Secretary
British and Irish Association for Mission Studies
London, England

Paul O. Myhre
Doctoral Student of Historical Theology
St. Louis University
St. Louis, Missouri

Alan Neely
Henry Winters Luce Emeritus Professor of Ecumenics and Mission
Princeton Theological Seminary
Princeton, New Jersey

Lesslie Newbigin
Formerly Bishop of Madras
Church of South India
Madras, India

Marc Nikkel
Advisor for Theological Education
Diocese of Bor, Rumbek, and Wau
Sudan

Nyambura J. Njoroge
Executive Secretary of Women and Men in Partnership
World Alliance of Reformed Churches
Geneva, Switzerland

Gerrit Noort
Home Secretary
Board of Mission
Netherlands Reformed Church
Oegstgeest, The Netherlands

Mark Douglas Norbeck
Doctoral Student
General Theological Seminary
New York, New York

Frederick W. Norris
Dean E. Walker Professor of Church History, and Professor of World Mission and Evangelism
Emmanuel School of Religion
Johnson City, Tennessee

Daniel O'Connor
Formerly Canon of Wakefield Cathedral
Wakefield, West Yorkshire, England

Takehiko Oda
Director
Japan Catholic Research Institute for Evangelization
Tokyo, Japan

Matthews Akintunde Ojo
Lecturer
Obafemi Awolowo University
Ile-Ife, Nigeria

J. Steven O'Malley
John T. Seamands Professor of Wesleyan Holiness History
Asbury Theological Seminary
Wilmore, Kentucky

Johannes van Oort
Associate Professor of Ecclesiastical History
University of Utrecht
Utrecht, The Netherlands

G. C. Oosthuizen
Director of NERMIC, a research unit for New Religious Movements and Indigenous/Independent Churches
Durban, South Africa

Rodney H. Orr
Ph.D. Candidate
University of Edinburgh
Edinburgh, Scotland

Charles Partee
Professor of Church History
Pittsburgh Theological Seminary
Pittsburgh, Pennsylvania

James A. Patterson
Professor and Chair
Department of Church History
Mid-America Baptist Theological Seminary
Germantown, Tennessee

Achiel Peelman, OMI
Professor of Theology and Academic Vice-Rector
Saint Paul University
Ottawa, Canada

Jaroslav Pelikan
Sterling Emeritus Professor of History
Yale University
New Haven, Connecticut

Peter Penner
Emeritus Professor of History
Mount Allison University
Calgary, Alberta, Canada

Cindy L. Perry
Coordinator
Nepal Church History Project
Kathmandu, Nepal

James M. Phillips
Formerly Associate Director
Overseas Ministries Study Center
New Haven, Connecticut

Richard V. Pierard
Professor of History
Indiana State University
Terre Haute, Indiana

Paul E. Pierson
Emeritus Dean and Professor of the History of Mission
Fuller Theological Seminary, School of World Mission
Pasadena, California

Stuart Piggin
Master, Robert Menzies College
Fellow, School of History
Macquarie University
Sydney, Australia

Louise Pirouet
Formerly Lecturer in Church History
Makerere University
Kampala, Uganda, and Nairobi University
Nairobi, Kenya

John S. Pobee
Coordinator
Ecumenical Theological Education
World Council of Churches
Geneva, Switzerland

Edward W. Poitras
Professor of World Christianity
Perkins School of Theology
Southern Methodist University
Dallas, Texas

Margaret Prang
Emerita Professor of History
University of British Columbia
Vancouver, British Columbia
Canada

Gregory Rabassa
Distinguished Professor of Romance Languages
Queens College and Graduate School
City University of New York
New York, New York

Lyell M. Rader, Jr.
Major, Director of Curriculum
Salvation Army School for Officer Training
Suffern, New York

Paul A. Rader
General
The Salvation Army
London, England

Yvette Ranjeva Rabetafika
Senior Lecturer
Institute de Civilisations
Musée de l'Université
University of Antananarivo
Madagascar

Werner Raupp
Lecturer in Church History
College for Social Affairs
Reutlingen, Germany

James W. Reapsome
Formerly Executive Director
Evangelical Missions Information Service
Wheaton, Illinois

Ralph Reavis, Sr.
Professor of Historical Studies and Missions
School of Theology
Virginia Union University
Richmond, Virginia

Daniel G. Reid
Reference and Academic Book Editor
InterVarsity Press
Downers Grove, Illinois

Walter Riggans
General Director
Church's Ministry among Jewish People
St. Albans, Hertfordshire
England

Dana L. Robert
Professor of International Mission
Boston University School of Theology
Boston, Massachusetts

W. Dayton Roberts
Latin America Mission
San José, Costa Rica

Peter Rodgers
Pastor
St. John's Episcopal Church
New Haven, Connecticut

Arij A. Roest Crollius, SJ
Director
Center for Cultures and Religions
Gregorian Pontifical University
Rome, Italy

Hans Rollmann
Professor
Department of Religious Studies
Memorial University of Newfoundland
St. John's, Newfoundland, Canada

Sidney H. Rooy
Emeritus Professor of Church History and Missions
Evangelical Higher Institute of Theological Studies (ISEDET)
Buenos Aires, Argentina

Andrew C. Ross
Senior Lecturer
History of Missions
Deputy Director, Centre for the Study of Christianity in the Non-Western World
University of Edinburgh
Edinburgh, Scotland

H. Miriam Ross
Formerly Hannah Maria Norris Associate Professor of Christian Missions and Social Issues
Acadia Divinity School
Wolfville, Nova Scotia, Canada

Leroy S. Rouner
Professor of Philosophy, Religion and Philosophical Theology
Director of the Institute for Philosophy and Religion
Boston University
Boston, Massachusetts

Harold H. Rowdon
Formerly Lecturer in Church History
London Bible College
London, England

John Roxborogh
Head
Department of Mission Studies
Bible College of New Zealand
Henderson, Auckland
New Zealand

Eugene F. Rubingh
Vice President for Translations
International Bible Society
Colorado Springs, Colorado

Beryl J. Russell
Assistant Librarian
Eastern Baptist Theological Seminary
Wynnewood, Pennsylvania

Willem A. Saayman
Professor and Head
Department of Missiology
University of South Africa
Pretoria, South Africa

Stanley J. Samartha
Formerly Director
Dialogue Sub-Unit
World Council of Churches
Geneva, Switzerland

Lamin Sanneh
Professor of History, and D. Willis James Professor of Missions and World Christianity
Yale University
New Haven, Connecticut

Annalet van Schalkwyk
Junior Lecturer
Department of Missiology
University of South Africa
Pretoria, South Africa

David A. Schattschneider
Dean and Professor of Historical Theology
Moravian Theological Seminary
Bethlehem, Pennsylvania

James A. Scherer
Emeritus Professor of Christian Missions and Church History
Lutheran School of Theology
Chicago, Illinois

Lothar Schreiner
Emeritus Professor of Missiology and Comparative Religion
Kirchliche Hochschule Wuppertal
Wuppertal, Germany

Robert J. Schreiter, CPPS
Professor of Doctrinal Theology
Catholic Theological Union
Chicago, Illinois

John N. Schumacher, SJ
Professor of Church History
Loyola School of Theology
Ateneo de Manila University
Quezon City, The Philippines

Robert H. Scott
Director of the Hiram Reynolds Institute
Church of the Nazarene
Kansas City, Missouri

John T. Seamands
Emeritus Professor of Missions
Asbury Theological Seminary
Wilmore, Kentucky

David A. Shank
Formerly Mennonite Missionary
Abidjan, Ivory Coast

Eric J. Sharpe
Emeritus Professor of Religious Studies
University of Sydney
Sydney, Australia

Richard Shaull
Henry Winters Luce Emeritus Professor of Ecumenics
Princeton Theological Seminary
Princeton, New Jersey

Wilbert R. Shenk
Professor of Mission History and Contemporary Culture
Fuller Theological Seminary, School of World Mission
Pasadena, California

E. Morris Sider
Professor of History and English Literature
Messiah College
Archivist for the Brethren in Christ Church and Messiah College
Grantham, Pennsylvania

John H. Sinclair
Formerly Secretary for Latin America
Commission on Ecumenical Mission and Relations
Presbyterian Church (USA)
New York, New York

Adelbert Agustin Sitompul
Professor of Old Testament and Culture
Nommensen University School of Theology
Pematang Siantar
Sumatra, Indonesia

Oskar Skarsaune
Professor of Church History
Norwegian Lutheran School of Theology
Oslo, Norway

C. Philip Slate
Professor and Chair
Department of Missions
Abilene Christian University
Abilene, Texas

Martha Lund Smalley
Curator
Day Missions Collection
Yale Divinity School Library
New Haven, Connecticut

William A. Smalley
Formerly Translations Consultant
United Bible Societies in Southeast Asia
Hamden, Connecticut

A. Christopher Smith
Academic Dean and Professor of Intercultural Studies
Providence College
Otterburne, Manitoba, Canada

David W. Smith
Principal
Northumbria Bible College
Berwick-upon-Tweed, England

Teotonio R. de Souza
Professor of Social and Economic History
Instituto Superior de Matemática Aplicada e Gestâo
Lisbon, Portugal

Jonathan Spence
Sterling Professor of History
Yale University
New Haven, Connecticut

Marc R. Spindler
Emeritus Professor of Missiology and Ecumenics
University of Leiden
Leiden, The Netherlands

Brian Stanley
Director of the North Atlantic Missiology Project
University of Cambridge
Fellow of St. Edmund's College
Cambridge, England

Russell L. Staples
Emeritus Professor of World Mission
Andrews University
Berrien Springs, Michigan

Carl F. Starkloff, SJ
Professor of Missiology
Regis College
Toronto School of Theology
Toronto, Ontario, Canada

Evgeny Steiner
Associated Researcher
Meiji Gakuin University
Yokohama, Japan

Nancy Stevenson
Research Student
Department of Religious Studies
Open University
United Kingdom

Philip C. Stine
Director for Translation, Production and Distribution Services
United Bible Societies
Reading, England

Harry S. Stout
Jonathan Edwards Professor of American Christianity and John B. Madden Master of Berkeley College
Yale University
New Haven, Connecticut

David M. Stowe
Emeritus Executive Vice President
United Church Board for World Ministries
Tenafly, New Jersey

Theo Sundermeier
Professor of History of Religion and Missiology
University of Heidelberg
Heidelberg, Germany

Scott W. Sunquist
Professor of World Missions and Evangelism
Pittsburgh Theological Seminary
Pittsburgh, Pennsylvania

William L. Svelmoe
Doctoral Candidate in American Religious History
University of Notre Dame
South Bend, Indiana

Lalashowi Swai
Executive Secretary for Africa
World Council of Churches
Geneva, Switzerland

John V. Taylor
Anglican Bishop (Retired)
Winchester, England

M. Thomas Thangaraj
D. W. & Ruth Brooks Associate Professor of World Christianity
Candler School of Theology
Emory University
Atlanta, Georgia

Notto R. Thelle
Professor of Missiology and Ecumenics
Theological Faculty
Oslo University
Oslo, Norway

Norman E. Thomas
Vera B. Blinn Professor of World Christianity
United Theological Seminary
Dayton, Ohio

T. Jack Thompson
Lecturer in Mission Studies
Centre for the Study of Christianity in the Non-Western World
University of Edinburgh
Edinburgh, Scotland

John K. Thornton
Associate Professor of History
Millersville University
Millersville, Pennsylvania

Tite Tiénou
President and Dean
Evangelical Seminary of the Christian Alliance
Abidjan, Ivory Coast

Paul E. Toews
Professor of History
Fresno Pacific University
Fresno, California

Edvard Torjesen
Chairman
Evergreen Family Friendship Service
Palm Springs, California

Thomas Forsyth Torrance
Emeritus Professor of Christian Dogmatics
University of Edinburgh
Edinburgh, Scotland

Garry Trompf
Professor in the History of Ideas
School of Studies in Religion
University of Sydney
Sydney, Australia

Ruth A. Tucker
Author and Lecturer
Grand Rapids, Michigan

A. Leonard Tuggy
Formerly Asia Ministries Director
CBInternational
Wheaton, Illinois

Harold W. Turner
Founding Director of the Centre for New Religious Movements
Selly Oak Colleges
Birmingham, England

Horace G. Underwood
Retired Presbyterian missionary
Board of Yonsei University
Seoul, Korea

Werner Ustorf
Professor of Mission
Birmingham University and Selly Oak Colleges
Birmingham, England

Mark Valeri
E. T. Thompson Professor of Church History
Union Theological Seminary
Richmond, Virginia

Charles Van Engen
Arthur F. Glasser Professor of Biblical Theology of Mission
Fuller Theological Seminary, School of World Mission
Pasadena, California

Winifred K. Vass
Formerly Missionary of the Presbyterian Church (U.S.) in Zaire
Dallas, Texas

John A. Vickers
Formerly Principal Lecturer and Head of the Religious and Social Studies Department
Bognor Regis College of Education
West Sussex, England

Winona Wall
Doctoral Student
University of Edinburgh
Edinburgh, Scotland

Andrew F. Walls
Founding Director
Centre for the Study of Christianity in the Non-Western World
University of Edinburgh
Edinburgh, Scotland

Kevin Ward
Lecturer
African Religious Studies
Department of Theology and Religious Studies
Leeds University
Leeds, England

Susan E. Warrick
Independent scholar in United Methodist Missions History
Madison, New Jersey

Charles W. Weber
Professor of History
Wheaton College
Wheaton, Illinois

John C. B. Webster
Historian and Former Missionary in India
Presbyterian Church (U.S.A.)
Waterford, Connecticut

Charles C. West
Emeritus Professor of Christian Ethics
Princeton Theological Seminary
Princeton, New Jersey

Frank Whaling
Reader in Religious Studies
Edinburgh University
Edinburgh, Scotland

Gavin White
Formerly Lecturer in Church History
University of Glasgow
Glasgow, Scotland

Darrell Whiteman
Professor of Cultural Anthropology
E. Stanley Jones School of World Mission and Evangelism
Asbury Theological Seminary
Wilmore, Kentucky
Editor, *Missiology: An International Review*

Jean-Paul Wiest
Research Director
Center for Mission Research
Maryknoll, New York

Bernward H. Willeke, OFM (died 1997)
Emeritus Professor of Missiology
University of Würzburg
Würzburg, Germany

Peter Williams
Vicar
Ecclesall Parish Church
Ecclesall, Sheffield, England

Dorothy Clarke Wilson
Author
Orono, Maine

Everett A. Wilson
Director
Latin America Language and Research Center
Division of Foreign Missions
Assemblies of God
San José, Costa Rica

John W. Witek, SJ
Associate Professor of East Asian History
Georgetown University
Washington, DC

Klaas M. Witteveen
Formerly Lecturer in Church History
University of Utrecht
Utrecht, The Netherlands

Timothy Man-kong Wong
Doctoral Candidate
Department of History
Chinese University of Hong Kong

Timothy Yates
Honorary Canon
Derby Cathedral
Derby, England

Betty Young
Archivist
United Mission to Nepal
Centre for the Study of Christianity in the Non-Western World
University of Edinburgh
Edinburgh, Scotland

Cassian Yuhaus
Executive Director
Ministry for Religious Research and Consultancy
Clarks Summit, Pennsylvania

Hwa Yung
Principal of Seminari Theoloji Malaysia (Malaysia Theological Seminary)
Petaling Jaya, Malaysia

Hesdie S. Zamuel
Chairman
Mission Board of the Moravian Church
Dean
Moravian Theological Seminary
Paramaribo, Surinam

Barbara Brown Zikmund
President and Professor of American Religious History
Hartford Seminary
Hartford, Connecticut

Jean-François Zorn
Professor of Practical Theology
Institut Protestant de Théologie
Faculté Libre de Théologie
Montpellier, France

Biographical Dictionary of Christian Missions

Abdul Masih, Salih (1765–1827), early Indian Muslim convert to Christianity. Abdul Masih was the most influential indigenous Christian to shape Christian mission to Islam in early nineteenth-century India. Born to a socially respected and devout Muslim family in Delhi, he spent his early life as a scholar and teacher in Lucknow, where he earned recognition as a religious *shaykh*. In this capacity he befriended Henry *Martyn, one of the first chaplains of the British East India Company to direct his energies almost wholly to the evangelization of Muslims. Attracted by Martyn's faith and preaching, he studied Martyn's Urdu translation of the New Testament and took catechetical instruction from two other company chaplains, David *Brown and Daniel *Corrie. His conversion and baptism in 1811 caused social unrest in Lucknow, so he moved to Agra, where he worked as an itinerant preacher and healer, assisting the early development of the Church Missionary Society (CMS) in the city. His success in winning both Muslim and Hindu converts led the CMS to hope that he would be the vanguard of indigenous evangelists. This did not materialize due to the failure of the first Anglican bishop of Calcutta (Thomas *Middleton, 1769–1822) to ordain him into Anglican orders, which was the result of poor relationships between the company chaplains, the CMS, and the new diocese. Although Abdul Masih became a Lutheran, in 1825 he reentered the Anglican Church as the first Indian-ordained minister under Bishop *Heber of Calcutta. As a consequence, he was able to exercise considerable influence over both Anglican and Lutheran approaches to mission among Muslims in the first half of the nineteenth century. His application of the rationalistic methods of Islamic religious scholarship to interpretation of the Bible is illustrated in his extensive journals. An abridged translation is available in the CMS *Missionary Register* (1814–1826). His work prepared the way for the German CMS evangelist Karl Gottlieb *Pfander (1803–1865), who followed Abdul Masih in Agra and dominated later nineteenth-century methods of Muslim evangelism.

BIBLIOGRAPHY Daniel Corrie, "Memoir and Obituary of Rev. Abdool Messeeh," *Missionary Register* 15 (1827): 449–453; Avril Powell, *Muslims and Missionaries in Pre-Mutiny India* (1993); "Sheikh Salih Abdul Masih," *Bulletin of the Henry Martyn Institute of Islamic Studies* 53 (1964): 3–4; Lyle Vander Werff, *Christian Mission to Muslims: The Record—Anglican and Reformed Approaches in India and the Near East, 1800–1938* (1977).

David A. Kerr

Abeel, David (1804–1846), pioneer American missionary to China. Born in New Brunswick, New Jersey, Abeel had begun medical studies when a religious conversion turned him toward the Christian ministry. He graduated from New Brunswick Seminary and was ordained in 1826, serving at Athens, New York, until ill health forced him to spend the winter of 1828–1829 in the West Indies. Feeling a call to foreign missionary service, he was appointed a chaplain of the Seamen's Friend Society and sailed for Canton in October 1829 with Elijah C. *Bridgman, first missionary to China of the American Board of Commissioners for Foreign Missions (ABCFM). After performing his chaplaincy duties in Canton for a year while studying Fukienese, Malay, and Siamese, his appointment by the ABCFM as a missionary to China was confirmed.

Abeel went to Java to visit the Dutch Reformed Churches there in 1831, then traveled to Singapore and to Bangkok, where he undertook exploratory work for the ABCFM. Returning home for health reasons in 1833, he traveled via England, Switzerland, France, Germany, and Holland, speaking on behalf of missions and attending conferences. In England he helped found the Society for Promoting Female Education in the East. From 1835 to 1838 he actively promoted interest in missions within the

Dutch Reformed Church. He arrived again in Canton in 1839, but with the first of the "Opium Wars" then in progress, he elected to visit Dutch Reformed Churches in Borneo. Returning to China in 1841, he established a mission at Kolongsu, a small island at Amoy, one of the five ports opened to missionaries. In 1844 he was joined at Amoy, destined to become a major mission of his church, by Elihu Doty and William John Pohlman from Borneo. Ill health compelled him to return to America in 1845, and he died the following year at Albany of the pulmonary tuberculosis which had long hampered him. His influence in the early missionary movement was greatly increased by his writings.

BIBLIOGRAPHY David Abeel, *To the Bachelors of India, by a Bachelor* (1833), *A Narrative of a Residence in China* (1834), and *The Claims of the World to the Gospel* (1838). Abeel wrote a number of tracts and pamphlets, and articles in the *Chinese Repository*. J. L. Good, *Famous Missionaries of the Reformed Church* (1903); G. R. Williamson, *Memoir of the Rev. David Abeel* (1848). For obituary see *Missionary Herald* 42 (1846): 354.

David M. Stowe

Abel, Charles William (1863–1930), English missionary to Papua New Guinea. Born in London, Abel was converted to evangelical faith through the preaching of Dwight L. *Moody. At age 18 he went to New Zealand for several years and worked among the Maori. In 1884 he returned to England and studied at Chestnut College and took medical training at London Hospital. He was sent to Papua in 1890 by the London Missionary Society (LMS) and was located on the small island of Kwato near the eastern tip of Papua. He and his wife, Beatrice, who was from a wealthy Anglican family, endeavored to develop their mission according to their middle-class English standards. They emphasized industriousness, cleanliness, punctuality, good sportsmanship, group singing, and knowledge of the English language, along with strong personal faith. Abel's wife taught women domestic skills and English virtues. The Abels took a strong stand against racial prejudice, and people of all races on Kwato worked together. The mission also emphasized sports, and the Kwato cricket teams were well-known.

Abel developed technical and vocational education along with local industries, including logging, boat building, furniture making, and plantation establishment. He needed capital and sought large contributions and investments from wealthy evangelical business people in Britain and Australia, and later, America. His work was quite different from other LMS operations, and his need for funds put him in competition with other LMS work. To end the tensions the LMS agreed in 1918 that he establish a separate mission, the Kwato Extension Association. He continued to guide it successfully until his death during a visit to England. Thereafter his sons continued along the same lines. In 1964 the Kwato church rejoined the Papuan LMS church.

BIBLIOGRAPHY Russell W. Abel, *Charles W. Abel of Kwato: Forty Years in Dark Papua* (1934); John Garrett, *Footsteps in the Sea: Christianity in Oceania to World War II* (1992); David Wetherell, "Monument to a Missionary: C. W. Abel and the Keveri of Papua," *Journal of Pacific History* 8 (1973): 30–48 (tells of outreach from Kwato to mainland Papua).

Charles W. Forman

Abhishiktananda (Swami). *See* Le Saux, Henri.

Abraham, Samuel (1860–1918), Methodist leader in Malaya. Born in Jaffna, Ceylon (Sri Lanka), to Hindu parents, Abraham converted to Christianity at age 14. He worked first for the Church Missionary Society and then the American Methodist Mission. In 1898 he was sent to Malaya to pastor the Tamil Methodist Church of Kuala Lumpur. There he founded the Anglo-Tamil school in 1899. He traveled extensively visiting Tamil workers on rubber estates and founded numerous churches. In 1913 he became the first Asian district superintendent of the Methodist Church in Malaya. He died in Malacca.

BIBLIOGRAPHY "Samuel Abraham, Minister of God," *Malaysia Message* 28, no. 2 (November 1918): 10; *Minutes of the Malaysia Annual Conference* (1919), p. 360 (Methodist Church of Singapore archives).

Robert A. Hunt

Abraham Malpan (1796–1845), leader of a reformation in the Syrian church of Kerala, South India. Born in the ancient family of Palakunnathu, Abraham studied Syriac, and was ordained a priest in 1815. Subsequently he was appointed a professor at the "Old Seminary," Kottayam, where he taught Syriac and came to be known as "Malpan," a term used for a Syriac teacher.

In close contact with Church Missionary Society (CMS) missionaries who were sent as a "mission of help" to the Syrian Christians, Abraham was drawn to an evangelical understanding of the gospel and was inspired to work for the removal of superstitious beliefs and practices prevalent in the church. Meanwhile, tension was developing between the missionaries who were proposing various changes and the Metropolitan, who refused to accept them. At its Mavelikara Synod in 1836, the church severed all connections with the missionaries. Nevertheless, Abraham determined to take steps in his own parish at Maramon, where the people were in sympathy with his ideas. He revised the eucharistic liturgy and translated it into Malayalam, the local language. The revision included the deletion of prayers for the dead, and of the invocation of saints and the Virgin Mary. Using the revised liturgy, he celebrated the eucharist in Malayalam, instead of Syriac, a language little understood by the worshipers. He also destroyed the image of a saint believed to have miraculous powers and in whose honor an annual festival was held. In 1840 Abraham resigned from the seminary and began to concentrate on reformation at a wider level. This led to his excommunication, though it did not sway him from his commitment. Wanting the support of a bishop, he sent his nephew, Deacon Mathew, to the patriarch at Mardin in Mesopotamia and had him consecrated a bishop. This new bishop, Mathew Mar Athanasius, returned in 1843. Then followed a long tussle between the reformed party and the established church, leading finally to their separation. Meanwhile, Abraham died, having played a pioneering role in the evangelical awakening of his people.

BIBLIOGRAPHY Alexander Mar Thoma Metropolitan, *The Mar Thoma Church: Heritage and Mission* (1986); Juhanon Mar Thoma, *Christianity in India and a Brief History of the Mar Thoma Syrian Church* (1968); M. M. Thomas, *Toward an Evangelical Social Gospel: A New Look at the Reformation of Abraham Malpan* (1977).

Abraham Athyal

Abraham Mar Thoma (1880–1947), metropolitan of the Mar Thoma Syrian Church in India. Born at Kalloppara, Travancore, Abraham Mar Thoma received his basic education at Tiruvella, Kerala, and the Madras Christian College. He studied theology at Wycliffe College, Toronto, Canada, was ordained as a deacon in the Mar Thoma Syrian Church in 1911, and was consecrated bishop in 1917. Even though he was the metropolitan of the Mar Thoma Church for only a short period (1944–1947), he was very influential in church and society, noted for the simplicity of his lifestyle and for his spiritual leadership. He was deeply concerned with the contemplative, ashram way of life, although this did not prevent him from being actively involved with the life of the church in society. His enthusiasm for evangelism led to the formation of the Mar Thoma voluntary evangelistic association, of which he was president for many years. He gave much of his energy to efforts to indigenize the rituals and practices of the church. He was strong and outspoken in his protests against the autocratic and repressive measures of state authorities who tried to keep the state of Travancore separate and outside the union of India. He was held in great respect by the people as shepherd, prophet, and spiritual guru.

BIBLIOGRAPHY Short writings about Abraham Mar Thoma exist in Malayalam, but little is written by or about him in English.

Stanley J. Samartha

Abrams, Minnie F. (1859–1912), missionary to India. Born in Lawrenceville, Wisconsin, Abrams attended the Methodist-related Chicago Training School for Home and Foreign Missions. She arrived in Bombay, India, in 1887 as a missionary with the Woman's Foreign Missionary Society of the Methodist Episcopal Church. In 1898, she left the Methodist post to work with Pandita *Ramabai at the (undenominational) Mukti mission in Kedgaon.

When word of the Welsh Revival reached India, spiritual awakenings soon occurred in many Protestant mission stations beginning in early 1905. Subsequent events at Mukti became well known through reports of extended times of prayer, public confession of sins, visions, dreams, and a burning sensation felt by those seeking the sanctification and baptism of the Holy Spirit.

Abrams, an advocate of Wesleyan holiness theology, viewed baptism in the Holy Spirit as a separate work of grace occurring after conversion and designed to sanctify and empower believers for evangelism. She traveled widely in India promoting revival, and her holiness views were popularized through a series of articles published in 1906 entitled "The Baptism of the Holy Ghost and Fire," which appeared in two major Christian newspapers in India: *The Bombay Guardian* (independent) and *The Indian Witness* (Methodist).

When word of the Azusa Street revival (Los Angeles, California) reached India later that year with news of the restoration of the gifts of the Holy Spirit (e.g. speaking in tongues, prophecy), Abrams and others at the mission prayed that they, too, might receive the fullness of the Spirit. When this new impetus gave fresh life to the revival there, Abrams revised her newspaper articles and published them in book form with the title *The Baptism of the Holy Ghost and Fire* (1906). Unlike many other Pentecostals, however, she did not insist on the evidential nature of tongues for baptism in the Spirit.

A year later, Abrams sent a copy of her book to former Chicago Training School classmate May Hoover and her husband Willis *Hoover, M.D., Methodist missionaries in Chile. The revival in Chile that followed led to the founding of the Methodist Pentecostal Church and the larger Pentecostal movement in that country.

Abrams died from a fever in 1912 while evangelizing unreached people in India in the company of several other single women missionaries.

BIBLIOGRAPHY Minnie F. Abrams, *The Baptism of the Holy Ghost and Fire,* Memorial Edition (c. 1913). See also "Minnie F. Abrams of India," *MRW* 26 (February 1913): 156; Helen S. Dyer, *Pandita Ramabai: Her Vision, Her Mission and Triumph of Faith,* 2d ed. (n.d.); Effie G. Lindsay, *Missionaries of the Minneapolis Branch of the Woman's Foreign Missionary Society of the Methodist Episcopal Church* (1904); Gary B. McGee, "Early Pentecostal Hermeneutics: Tongues as Evidence in the Book of Acts," in *Initial Evidence: Historical and Biblical Perspectives on the Pentecostal Doctrine of Spirit Baptism,* Gary B. McGee, ed. (1991).

Gary B. McGee

Acosta, José de (1540–1600), Jesuit missionary to Peru. Born in Medina del Campo, Spain, Acosta had completed most of his studies as a Jesuit when he arrived in Lima in 1572. He taught theology in the Jesuit major seminary in Lima and between 1573 and 1574 conducted a study tour of southern Peru and Bolivia. In 1576 he was named provincial superior of his order. He served as a theologian-adviser to the Third Lima Council, convoked by Archbishop Toribio de *Mogrovejo in 1582. This, the most important of all the Lima councils, influenced pastoral practices in the Andes into the nineteenth century. Acosta was instrumental in preparing the catechism approved for use among priests in Indian parishes. It was written in Spanish, Quechua, and Aymara. Acosta also founded the Jesuit mission in Juli, by Lake Titicaca, which served as a model for the more famous Paraguay missions.

Acosta returned to Spain in 1587 after spending a year in Mexico while completing his two major works, *De Procuranda Indorum Salute* (1588, On how to bring about the salvation of the Indians) and *Historia Natural y Moral de las Indias* (1590, A natural and moral history of the Indies). *De Procuranda,* published in Spain, soon became one of the most influential guides for missionaries in the new world. In it Acosta blamed the slow progress in evangelizing on missionaries who gave bad examples, treated the Indians harshly, or failed to understand their language and culture. He expressed his belief that the Indians were basically good and docile and could be converted to Christianity by a combination of firmness and gentleness.

In *Historia Natural y Moral,* Acosta saw the hand of God in the great Indian civilizations of the Incas and the Aztecs, which for him represented a providential preparation for the coming of the gospel. However, he did not esteem the contemporary Indian religions, but rather saw them as the work of the devil and their Indian rituals as a parody of Christian sacraments. Acosta stood out most of all for his combination of humanism, zeal, and common sense. He was the prime spokesman among second generation missionaries to the Andean regions who found fault with the superficial means used by the first generation. After returning to Spain in 1587 he held several important positions in his order. He died in Salamanca.

BIBLIOGRAPHY León Lopétegui, *El Padre José de Acosta y las misiones* (1942); Sabine MacCormack, *Religion in the Andes* (1991), pp. 261–280; Luis Martín, *The Intellectual Conquest of Peru: The Jesuit College of San Pablo, 1568–1767* (1968); Francisco Mateos, *Obras del P. José de Acosta, SJ* (1954).

Jeffrey Klaiber, SJ

Acquaviva, Rudolf (1550–1583), Italian Jesuit martyr in Goa. Acquaviva came from a family of Neapolitan nobility, and an uncle, Claude Aquaviva, was a general superior of the Jesuits. He entered the Society of Jesus in 1568 despite delicate health and opposition from his parents. He volunteered for India, was ordained in Portugal in 1578, and arrived in Goa in 1579. That same year an embassy from the Mogul emperor Akbar also arrived in Goa, inviting Jesuit priests to the court at Fathpur-Sikri, near Agra. The Jesuits selected Acquaviva to head a three-man mission (Antonio Monserrate and Francis Henriquez were the others), the beginning of nearly one and a half centuries of Jesuit presence and influence at the Mogul court, although the Jesuit dream of converting Akbar and his successors was never realized. Acquaviva and the other Jesuits were greatly respected and were treated affectionately by Akbar. When the mission was recalled to Goa, Akbar reluctantly agreed to let Acquaviva leave his court. On his return to Goa, Acquaviva was appointed superior of the Salcete region in South Goa, which was assigned to the Jesuits for evangelistic work. The region had been under repeated assults by the Bijapur ruler from whom the Portuguese had acquired it by force. The local Hindu leaders also took advantage of these situations to express their disaffection by revolting against the Portuguese authority. The Jesuit priests joined the Portuguese punitive military expeditions and were at times directly involved in destroying temples and idols. Against this background, Acquaviva and four other Jesuits were mobbed and killed in the village of Cuncolim, where they had gone to choose a site for a new church; today they are known as the Blessed Martyrs of Cuncolim. Their beatification was announced in 1893.

BIBLIOGRAPHY John Correia-Afonso, *Letters from the Mughal Court* (1980); F. Goldie, *The First Christian Mission to the Great Mogul, or the Story of Blessed Rudolf Acquaviva and his Four Companions in Martyrdom* (1897); E. Maclagan, *The Jesuits and the Great Mogul* (1932); Teotonio R. de Souza, "Why Cuncolim Martyrs? An Historical Re-Assessment," in Teotonio R. de Souza and Charles J. Borges, eds., *Jesuits in India: In Historical Perspective* (1992); Josef Wicki, ed., *Documenta Indica,* vol. 12 (1972).

Teotonio R. de Souza

Adalbert (d. 705), English missionary in Germany and the Netherlands. Perhaps a son of Oswald, king of Northumbria, Adalbert became a disciple of Egbert of Iona at the monastery of Rath Melsigi in Connacht, Ireland. With ten others he accompanied *Willibrord on a mission to Germany. The two were eventually sent by Pépin II to Friesland. Adalbert's ministry was marked by patience and kindness. He became archdeacon of Utrecht but is most noted for his work at Egmond, Netherlands, where he preached and built a church. His tomb there became a pilgrimage site. In the tenth century Theodoric II rebuilt the church and founded a monastery to honor Adalbert.

BIBLIOGRAPHY Charles H. Talbot, *The Anglo-Saxon Missions in Germany* (1954); Herbert Thurston and Donald Attwater, ed., rev., suppl., *Butler's Lives of the Saints* (1963), vol. 2, pp. 641–642.

Frederick W. Norris

Adalbert of Bremen (c. 1000–1072), missionary bishop in northern Europe. A descendant of a Saxon noble family, Adalbert served as canon at Bremen and then became archbishop of Hamburg-Bremen in 1043 with jurisdiction over the Scandinavian churches. Advocate of church reform and promoter of mission in northern Europe, he succeeded in extending his archdiocese by founding the dioceses of Ratzeburg and Mecklenburg in largely pagan territory. He was blamed for exercising undue political influence on the young emperor Henry IV and for his ambition to enhance his metropolitan authority throughout the north. While his missionary zeal cannot be doubted, he frequently disregarded the borderline between ecclesiastical organization and political design.

BIBLIOGRAPHY Edgar N. Johnson, "Adalbert of Hamburg-Bremen," *Speculum* 9 (1934): 147–179; Friedrich Knöpp, "Adalbert, Erzbischof von Hamburg-Bremen," in Friedrich Knöpp, ed., *Die Reichsabtei Lorsch* (1973), pp. 335–346.

Hans-Werner Gensichen

Adalbert of Prague (c. 956–997), missionary to the Slavs. Prince Vojtěch, as Adalbert was first known on account of his birth of Czech nobility, was educated at

Magdeburg. Inspired by the church reform movement of Cluny, he became the second bishop of Prague in 983. Tensions in his diocese led to his resignation. Having joined the Benedictine order, he eventually labored as a missionary in Bohemia, Hungary, and Poland. During a mission campaign in Prussia, initiated by the Christian duke Boleslav Chrobry of Poland, he was slain by a pagan priest. Pope Sylvester II canonized him in 999. Adalbert is also considered one of the protagonists of western Slavonic culture.

BIBLIOGRAPHY Rudolf Holinka, *Svatý Vojtěch* (1947); Heinrich G. Voigt, *Adalbert von Prag* (1898).

Hans-Werner Gensichen

Adam, William (c. 1799–1861?), missionary to India. Born in Dunfermline, in the Fife region of Scotland, Adam was educated at St. Andrews University and the University of Glasgow, and at the Baptist college at Bristol. In 1818 he married Phoebe, elder daughter of Charles *Grant, the renowned champion of mission for India within the directorate of the East India Company. The same year he was appointed to Calcutta by the Baptist Missionary Society (BMS). During the trinitarian controversy (1820) between Indian reformers, led by Ram Mohun Roy (1771–1833), and Serampore missionaries, Adam expressed doubts about the doctrine of the Trinity. He was tried for heresy in 1821, was expelled from the BMS, and joined the Unitarians. William Bentinck, Governor General of Bengal, appointed Adam (1835) to survey vernacular education in Bengal during the education controversy which pitted Thomas B. Macaulay and his elitist anglicizing policy against orientalists such as Henry Prinsep. Though "Macaulayism" was adopted in Calcutta, Adam's recommendation to employ the vernacular in Western-type education in order to benefit the majority was widely adopted elsewhere and helped to lay foundations for modern education in India.

From 1838 to 1849 Adam served as a Unitarian minister in Toronto and Chicago; he then returned to England. Near the end of his life he confessed to Charles Dall that he had renounced Unitarianism.

BIBLIOGRAPHY William Adam's principal writings were *The Principles and Objectives of the Calcutta Unitarian Committee* (1827), *Reports on the State of Education in Bengal, 1835 and 1838*, A. Basu, ed. (1941), *A Lecture on the Life and Labours of Rajah Rammohun Roy* (1838), and *The Law and Custom of Slavery in India* (1840). M. A. Laird, *Missionaries and Education in Bengal, 1793–1837* (1972); Spencer Lavan, "The Unusual Career of William Adam," in *Unitarians and India* (1977), pp. 41–55; Peter Penner, *The Patronage Bureaucracy in North India: The Robert M. Bird and James Thomason School, 1820–1870* (1986); E. Daniel Potts, *British Baptist Missionaries in India, 1793–1837* (1967).

Peter Penner

Addai (2d century?), considered the Apostle to Edessa. Little is known about Addai, also known as Thaddaeus, other than that he is acclaimed as the first missionary to cross the Roman border into the principality of Edessa (today northeast Turkey). He is said to have converted its first-century king (ostensibly Abgar V) and established a church in the Jewish-Christian community (which rapidly outgrew its Jewish roots). Addai appointed a successor, Aggai. From these beginnings came the ancient church of the East (later called the Nestorian church). Although the tradition includes obviously fictitious embellishments, if the story is transposed to second-century Edessa under Abgar VIII (177–212), it gains arguable plausibility. By the late third century, Edessa was already being called the first Christian kingdom.

BIBLIOGRAPHY For early sources see Eusebius, *Ecclesiastical History* 1:3 and W. Cureton, "The Doctrine of Addaeus the Apostle," in *Ancient Syriac Documents* (1864, repr. 1967). For critical and historical analysis, see J. B. Segal, *Edessa: The Blessed City* (1970), chap. 3, notes, and bibliography.

Samuel Hugh Moffett

Adejobi, Emmanuel Owoade Adeleke (1919–1991), second primate of the Church of the Lord (Aladura). As a Nigerian schoolteacher with an Anglican background, Adejobi joined Joshua O. *Oshitelu's Church of the Lord (Aladura) in 1940. He pioneered branches first in Lagos, then in Sierra Leone from 1947 and in Ghana in 1953, but government refusal prevented expansion in Gambia. A long-held desire for study abroad led him to the Glasgow Bible Institute (1961–1963).

After assessing the situation and visiting the archbishop of Canterbury and W. *Visser 't Hooft in Geneva, he opened a branch of the church in London in 1964. Returning to Nigeria, he founded a secondary school, printing press, and seminary near Lagos, headed by an American Mennonite missionary. Upon Oshitelu's death in 1966, Adejobi became primate. In 1976 this church became one of the first independent African churches to join the World Council of Churches (WCC), and in 1983 Adejobi was elected to the WCC Central Committee. His numerous travels and statesmanlike vision made him the chief agent of the church's international expansion and ecumenical acceptance.

BIBLIOGRAPHY H. W. Turner, *African Independent Church,* 2 vols. (1967), vol. 1, chap. 9 and throughout. Adejobi's numerous publications and obituary materials are held in the library of the Selly Oak Colleges, Birmingham, England.

Harold W. Turner

Adeney, David H(oward) (1911–1994), missionary and university evangelist in China and East Asia. Adeney was born into a British missionary family. His parents worked in Romania with the London Jews' Society (later known as the Church's Ministry among the Jews) and an aunt and uncle worked in Egypt. During his youth, family life was limited, with his father in Bucharest and his mother and three brothers in England. Years in boarding school aggravated the separation. He studied theology at Cambridge, attended the China Inland Mission (CIM) training school in London for a year, and sailed for China in 1934.

There he was involved in church planting in central China until Pearl Harbor (1941). This was followed by joint service with the CIM and InterVarsity Christian Fellowship (IVCF) in the United States and England until the end of World War II made return to China possible. He led student work with the China IVCF until the Maoist triumph, then worked again with the U.S. IVCF. After that his career turned to training Christians: eight years as Dean of the Discipleship Training Center in Singapore, two years in the China Graduate School of Theology in Hong Kong, and more than a decade as professor of Christian missions, New College, Berkeley, California. Greatly beloved, especially by Asian students, he embodied all the best characteristics of the twentieth century Western missionary.

BIBLIOGRAPHY David H. Adeney, *The Unchanging Commission* (1955) and *China, the Church's Long March* (1985). Carolyn Armitage, *Reaching for the Goal: The Life Story of David Adeney* (1993).

Arthur F. Glasser

Adriani, Nicolaus (1865–1926), Dutch missionary linguist in Central Celebes (Sulawesi), Indonesia. Adriani was born in Oud Loosdrecht, Netherlands. In 1887 he was chosen by the Netherlands Bible Society to receive linguistic training in order to support the missionary effort in Indonesia. After finishing his doctoral dissertation in 1893 at Leiden University on the grammar of the Sangirese language (East Indonesia), he was sent to Poso, Central Celebes, to analyze and describe the Bare'e language and to translate the Bible. He also assisted missionaries in other parts of Indonesia.

Adriani did not simply wish to complete a Bible translation as soon as possible; he also understood linguistic study primarily as a tool to grasp the essence of tribal culture and religion. He found a strong ally in A. C. *Kruyt's ethnological approach to mission. The description of priestly litanies and folktales was an integral part of his work. According to Adriani, Bible translation was not to be commenced before Christianization had regenerated the soul and language of the people. His method became exemplary in Indonesia, but it also met with opposition from less patient missionaries. Adriani died at the age of 61 and was buried in Poso. At the time of his death the translation of a major part of the New Testament into Bare'e was finished.

BIBLIOGRAPHY Adriani's main work on the growing church in Central Sulawesi is *Posso (Midden Celebes)* (1919). See also his "Work of a Linguistic Missionary in the Dutch East Indies," *IRM* 12 (1923): 580–590. His Bare'e grammar *"Spraakkunst der Bare'e-taal"* (1931) and a dictionary, *"Bare'e—Nederlands Woordenboek"* (1928), were posthumously published. His collected writings, *Verzamelde geschriften,* were published in 3 vols. (1932). Hendrik Kraemer, *Dr. N. Adriani, schets van leven en arbeid* (1930).

Gerrit Noort

Aea, Hezekiah (c. 1835–1872) *and*
Debora (c. 1835–1871), Hawaiian pioneer missionaries to the Marshall Islands. Debora and her first husband, Berita Kaaikaula, were in the first group of missionaries sent by the Hawaiian Auxiliary Missionary Society to the Caroline Islands in 1852, in cooperation with the American Board of Commissioners for Foreign Missions. They served on Ponape until 1859, when Berita died. Back in Hawaii Debora married Hezekiah Aea and in 1860 they sailed on the *Morning Star* to Ebon in the Marshalls. Designated a "helper" to missionary Edward T. *Doane, Hezekiah became principal leader of the Ebon station, using methods of the Hawaiian churches to train deacons for pastoral service, preparing hymns with local words and music, and adapting local social forms and festivities. Contributions for missionary work on other islands were collected at monthly meetings, principally in coconut oil. There was an annual cycle of itineration among the atolls, with couples stationed at the larger ones: David Kapali and his wife Tamara on Namorik and Jaluit, S. P. K. Nawaa and his wife Mary on Mille, and others. Hezekiah was ordained and started a new station at Majuro in 1869, in spite of the hostility of the king and others. Debora died there in 1871, and Hezekiah in Hawaii in 1872.

BIBLIOGRAPHY Sketches are found in Albertine Loomis, *To All People* (1970), pp. 98ff.; John Garrett, *To Live among the Stars* (1982), pp. 140ff., 146ff. Hezekiah and Debora Aea are mentioned briefly in the ABCFM annual reports and in *Missionary Herald* for these years, and in the records of the Hawaiian Evangelical Association.

David M. Stowe

Aedesius. *For* Aedesius, *see* Frumentius.

Affonso (Alphonse) (1455?–1543), king of Kongo. His father having been baptized by Portuguese missionaries in 1491, Affonso committed himself to the Christianization of his kingdom. Nicknamed Mbema a Nzinga, "the son and heir of the old King," he struggled with and later expelled his unbaptized brother Mpanzu. Inadequately supported by Portuguese authorities, Affonso himself became coercive, adopting a "clean sweep" policy and destroying local ritual objects (*minkisi*). He alienated many people; some of them followed Mpanzu while others abandoned Christianity.

Affonso sent his son to Portugal to study for the priesthood and tried to train an indigenous elite. By catechizing 400 sons of local chiefs and baptizing huge numbers of people, Affonso attempted to create a Christian society. The lack of adequate missionary support led him to establish his own seminary, and though this was opposed by Portugal, he continued to extend Christian education in his kingdom, even creating girls' schools. His son Henrique returned as the first African bishop (1521) but died prematurely, and the budding church withered for lack of sustenance. The Portuguese were more concerned with commerce than with Christianity, and Affonso died disillusioned.

BIBLIOGRAPHY Marie-Louise Martin, *Kimbangu: An African Prophet and His Church* (1975).

Anthony J. Gittins, CSSp

Agbebi, Mojola (David Brown Vincent) (1860–1917), early leader of the independent church movement in Africa. The son of a Nigerian (Yoruba) Anglican catechist, Agbebi was given the name David Brown Vincent at baptism. Educated by the Church Missionary Society (CMS) and appointed a teacher in 1878, he left the CMS in 1880 following a disciplinary measure. Converted about 1883 at a Baptist revival service, he and his wife, Adeline Adeotan, then became Baptists. Agbebi played a prominent role in the March 1888 establishment of the Native Baptist Church in Lagos, the first indigenous church in West Africa. Understanding the importance of indigenous African leadership for an African church, he affirmed the richness of African culture and in 1894 discontinued using David Brown Vincent as his name. An exemplary preacher and pastor, he initiated evangelistic work in Yorubaland and in the Niger Delta.

While maintaining his Baptist convictions, Agbebi was an apostle of ecumenism and an ambassador for Africa at large. His contact in 1895 with a Welsh Baptist, William Hughes, resulted in training for some Africans at the African Training Institute in Wales. In 1903 he visited the United States and Britain to raise money to support his evangelistic work in West Africa. In 1898 he founded the African Baptist Union of West Africa. He was the first president of the Yoruba Baptist Association, formed in 1914, and he supported his wife's efforts in establishing the nationwide Baptist Women's League in 1919. A visionary, he dedicated his life to evangelism, education, and the advancement of African leadership.

BIBLIOGRAPHY Mojola Agbebi, "The West African Problem," in G. Spiller, ed., *Papers on Interracial Problems Contributed to the First International Races Congress...* (1911), reprinted in H. S. Wilson, *Origins of West African Nationalism* (1969); Akinsola Akiwowo, "The Place of Mojola Agbebi in the African Nationalists Movements, 1890–1917," *Phylon* 26 (1965): 122–139; E. A. Ayandele, *A Visionary of the African Church: Mojola Agbebi, 1860–1917* (1971); Hazel King, "Cooperation in Contextualization: Two Visionaries of the African Church—Mojola Agbebi and William Hughes of the African Institute, Colwyn Bay," *JRA* 16 (1986): 2–21; J. B. Webster, *The African Churches among the Yoruba, 1888–1922* (1964).

Matthews A. Ojo

Aggai. *For* Aggai, *see* Addai.

Aggrey, James Emman Kwegyir (1875–1927), African minister and educator. Aggrey was born in Anamabu, Gold Coast Colony (now Ghana), seventeenth son of an important chiefdom counselor and of chiefly lineage on his mother's side. The family converted during his childhood. Taken into the house of a Wesleyan missionary, he became teacher and preacher, and by 1898 he was headmaster of a Wesleyan school at Cape Coast. That year the African Methodist Episcopal Zion Church gave him the opportunity to study at Livingstone College, North Carolina, and at the associated Hood Theological Seminary. He excelled there (B.A. with honors, 1902; M.A. and D.D., 1912), became professor at Livingstone (1902–1920), was ordained an elder of the AME Zion Church, and married an African American, Rosebud Douglass. From 1914 he was also pastor of two rural black churches, combining evangelism with community development. The latter led him into schemes for credit unions and African American land ownership. He was appointed to the influential commission on African education initiated by the Phelps-Stokes Foundation and supported by combined missionary societies, visiting West, Central, and South Africa (1920–1921) and East and South Africa (1923–1924).

As the only black commissioner, he met racial discrimination in several colonies, but his personal and intellectual qualities, powerful utterance, and conciliatory tone made an overwhelming impression, especially in his native Gold Coast and in South Africa (where he was offered a professorship at Fort Hare College). Despite his increasing celebrity, he resumed doctoral studies in sociology at Columbia University, until he agreed in 1924 to be assistant vice-principal to A. G. *Fraser at Achimota College, Gold Coast. His mediation with African society was vital to the success of the visionary college. He died in New York while on leave, seeking to complete the book intended as his doctoral dissertation.

Aggrey's goal was an Africa characterized by Christianity, education (classical, social, and practical, all to the highest standards), agricultural development, and civilization (but not Westernization). His famous unscripted speeches, studded with memorable aphorisms, stressed interracial cooperation, African self-help, and the distinctive contribution of African culture to world civilization.

BIBLIOGRAPHY T. J. Jones, *Education in Africa* (1922) and *Education in East Africa* (n.d.); E. W. Smith, *Aggrey of Africa* (1929); C. K. Williams, *Achimota: The Early Years* (1962).

Andrew F. Walls

Agnew, Eliza (1807–1883), first unmarried American woman missionary to Ceylon (Sri Lanka). Known in later life as the Mother of a Thousand Daughters, Agnew at age ten decided to become a missionary after hearing missionary-physician John *Scudder speak. A Presbyterian, she sailed to Ceylon under the American Board of Commissioners for Foreign Missions (ABCFM) in 1839 and never returned to the United States. She went to Ceylon to relieve the overworked missionary wives by taking charge of the Uduvil Girls' Boarding School, the oldest girls' boarding school of the ABCFM. Under her principalship, over 600 of the 1,300 girls she educated became Christians. The Uduvil graduates returned to their villages as the wives of Christian men and as teachers. Uduvil converts provided the anchor for the small Christian community in an unresponsive mission field. During her vacations, Agnew itinerated among former students, giving advice and strengthening their Christian commitment. She also supervised forty Bible women.

In 1855 an ABCFM deputation led by Rufus *Anderson reduced the size of Uduvil and eliminated English instruction in efforts to promote "three-self" principles. Agnew, however, outlived the reverses caused by the deputation. Upon her retirement from Uduvil in 1879, female education was more advanced in Ceylon than in other mission fields of the ABCFM. She died and was buried in Ceylon.

BIBLIOGRAPHY Short treatments of Agnew's life include the pamphlet "Eliza Agnew" by Ethel Hubbard (1917) and an entry in Annie Ryder Gracey, *Eminent Missionary Women* (1898). The Congregational journal *Life and Light for Women* contains articles by and on Agnew, including an obituary. Minnie Hastings Harrison's history of Uduvil Seminary (1824–1924) was printed in Ceylon in 1925. A file on Eliza Agnew is located in the ABCFM archives at Harvard Univ., Cambridge, Mass.

Dana L. Robert

Ahui, John (*or* Jonas) (c. 1888–1992), Ivorian leader of the Harrist Church of West Africa. Born Nanghui Togba, son of Ebrié chief Akadja Nanghui of the Côte d'Ivoire village of Abia-Gnambo (Petit Bassam), Ahui was renamed Boghui Ahui by his tutor. He became warrior chief of his age-group and married Jeanette Tohi in 1910. In 1914, during William Wadé *Harris's mission at Bingerville, he and his father were baptized. Having been drafted into the colonial army, he was discharged after an accident and became lead chorister in his village. Uncertainty amid resurgence of traditional practices as well as British Methodist activity led him to undertake a trip in December 1928 to visit Prophet Harris near Cape Palmas, Liberia. Harris gave Ahui his blessing, his cross-staff, and his Bible, along with a letter addressed to Ahui's father, charging Ahui with responsibility as Harris's successor. Ahui hesitated to obey, but after a nearly fatal sickness in 1936, he activated Harris's mission in the face of colonial opposition. He rallied an Ivorian multiethnic grassroots movement, and despite illiteracy, was for 57 years acknowledged as Supreme Preacher of the Harrist Church of West Africa, an African-initiated Christian community that extended from Côte d'Ivoire into Liberia, Burkina-Faso, Ghana, Togo, and Bénin.

BIBLIOGRAPHY Ahui's story with biographical details is given by his son: Paul William Ahui, *Le Prophète William Wade Harris: son message d'humilité et de progrès* (1988). See also Lobo Kouassi, "John Ahui, légataire universel s'est éteint," *Fraternité Matin*, December 11, 1992, p. 4; Sheila S. Walker, *The Religious Revolution in the Ivory Coast: The Prophet Harris and the Harrist Church* (1983).

David A. Shank

Aidan (d. 651), Irish missionary monk from Iona. At the request of Oswald, the Christian king of Northumbria, England, Aidan came from the monastery established by *Columba on the Scottish island of Iona to strengthen Christian missions in Northumbria that had begun with the work of *Paulinus. The king represented Aidan to the nobility and the king's county seats became centers for his preaching. Aidan established his base of operations on the peninsula of Lindisfarne off the northeast coast of England and was consecrated bishop in 635. Much of the time he traveled in the British mainland to undergird existent churches and set up new congregations. He followed Celtic ascetic and liturgical traditions and picked twelve young men to educate for future leadership. He was known as peaceable, generous, and concerned for the poor.

BIBLIOGRAPHY Bede, *Ecclesiastical History*, 3.3, 5, 14–17, 25; E. W. Frierson, *The Story of Northumbrian Saints: S. Oswald, S. Aidan, S. Cuthbert* (1913); Henry Mayr-Harting, *The Coming of Christianity to Anglo-Saxon England* (1972, 1977, 1991).

Frederick W. Norris

Aina, J. Ade (1903–1960s?), Ijebu leader in the Nigerian Aladura movement. After dismissal as a Church Missionary Society schoolmaster, Aina participated in the early developments of the Faith Tabernacle movement and in 1924 founded a small congregation in Ibadan. He was caught up in the Aladura revival of Joseph *Babalola in 1930, along with J. O. *Oshitelu, whose Church of the Lord he joined in 1931. He seceded in 1935 with a group which called itself the Aladura Church, which had a subsequent history of divisions and name changes, such as Aladura Apostolic Church (1942) and Living Faith Apostolic Church (1952), all in Ibadan. In 1949 he published a pamphlet in Yoruba, *The Silver Jubilee of the Establishment of the Aladura Church in Ibadan*, but his hopes of using it to set up a union of Aladura churches were unrealized. Some fourteen other printed publications included hymnbooks, church constitutions, a catechism, a service book and ordinal, and treatises on the Second Coming, polygamy, and Islam. His *Present Day Prophets and the Principles upon Which They Work* (c. 1932) defended the Aladura movement and included an ingenious theology of its sacramental use of water. He was biblical and theological, sophisticated and original as an independent African church leader.

BIBLIOGRAPHY Harold W. Turner, *African Independent Church*, vol. 1 (1967) and introduction to 1964 reprint of Aina's *Present Day Prophets*.

Harold W. Turner

Akinyele, Isaac Babalola (1882–1964), Christian and traditional Yoruba leader in Nigeria. Born in Ibadan, a large and predominantly Muslim city, Akinyele was educated in a Church Missionary Society school and had three distinguished careers. In the civil service he rose to be chief judge of the native court and in 1961 minister of state without portfolio in the Western Region Government, after having been knighted by Queen Elizabeth. As a traditional leader, he became an Ibadan chief in 1935 and in 1955 was elected to the supreme office of *olubadan* (i.e. king) of Ibadan, but only on his conditions that there be no traditional ceremonies and sacrifices. As a Christian leader, he first served the Anglican Church as synodsman and from the mid-1920s moved into the new Aladura movement with its faith healing and rejection of traditional medicines; he rejected all medicines for the rest of his life. His section of the Aladura movement became allied with the British Apostolic Church from 1931, but he resented missionary domination and by 1941 had separated as the ascetic and noncharismatic leader of the

Christ Apostolic Church. This became the largest and best organized of the Aladura churches. Among his many publications, secular and religious, is a tract entitled "How to Confess Sins Wholeheartedly."

BIBLIOGRAPHY J. D. Y. Peel, *Aladura: A Religous Movement among the Yoruba* (1968); Harold W. Turner, "The Late Sir Isaac Akinyele, Olubadan of Ibadan," *West African Religion* 4 (1965): 1-4.

Harold W. Turner

Akrofi, Clement Anderson (1901-1967), Ghanaian linguist and Bible translator. Akrofi was born in Apirede, in the Akuapem kingdom of southeastern Ghana, of parents who were among the first to join the Basel Mission church established there in 1873. He came early under the influence of the piety of the Basel Mission. Later, in the middle school and the teacher-training program at the mission headquarters in Akropong, he was influenced by the educational ideals of Scottish missionaries who succeeded the Basel missionaries between the two world wars. Convinced that language was essential to the effective communication of the gospel, Akrofi intensively studied his own Twi language and produced an impressive range of reference tools. His *Twi Kasa Mmara: A Twi Grammar in Twi* (1937) was the first instance of "an African language being interpreted by an African scholar writing in his own language" (Dietrich *Westermann, in the foreword). Akrofi was once introduced to Queen Elizabeth II of England by President Kwame Nkrumah of Ghana as "the Chaucer of our language." His crowning work was the revision of the Twi Bible of his missionary predecessor, Johannes *Christaller. Upon its completion in 1960, Akrofi was awarded a Th.D. from the Johannes Gutenberg University of Mainz, Germany. In his acceptance address, he stated: "I do not forget that I am receiving this honour primarily as a servant of the gospel.... In view of the general tendency to regard Christianity as a foreign religion, I will remind my fellow Africans that although Christianity is Europe's greatest gift to Africa, it is not exclusively the white man's religion; it is not the religion of the imperialist. Christianity is a world religion because Jesus Christ is the Lord and King of the universe."

BIBLIOGRAPHY In addition to his Twi grammar, Akrofi's other significant works are *A Twi Spelling Book* (produced jointly with E. L. Rapp; 1938), *Twi Mmebusem* (n.d.), an annotated collection of 1018 Twi proverbs, and *English-Twi-Ga Dictionary* (produced jointly with G. L. Botchey; 1968). For Akrofi's place in Ghanaian Christian scholarship, see Kwame Bediako, *Christianity in Africa: The Recovery of a Non-Western Religion* (1995), chap. 3.

Kwame Bediako

Alcina (*or* Alzina), Francisco Ignacio (1610-1674), Jesuit missionary in the Philippines. Born in Gandia, Spain, Alcina entered the Society of Jesus in 1624 and went to the Philippines in 1632. There he served as parish priest, principally in the Visayan islands of Leyte and Samar, for over 30 years. In his later years Alcina wrote a number of Visayan linguistic and practical books for missionaries and some devotional ones for lay Christians, of which two were published. His major work was *Historia natural del sitio, fertilidad y calidad de las Islas, e Indios de Bisayas,* the first half of which was prepared for publication in 1668, but for unknown reasons, never saw print. It is the most informative existing account of a particular region of the Philippines, its flora and fauna, the customs of the people, their social organization, their pre-Christian beliefs, and other historical, linguistic, and ethnological information, accompanied by drawings in color. Although the manuscript has been partially exploited by a few scholars, all attempts to publish it, from the seventeenth to the twentieth centuries, have failed. However, a critical edition, in translation, is now in progress.

BIBLIOGRAPHY H. de la Costa, *The Jesuits in the Philippines, 1581-1768* (1961); Evett A. Hester, "Alzina's Historia de Visayas: A Bibliographical Note," *Philippine Studies* 10 (1962): 331-365; Paul S. Lietz, "More about Alzina's Historia de Visayas," *Philippine Studies* 10 (1962): 366-375. Maria Luisa Martin-Meras and Maria Dolores Higueras, eds., *La Historia de Las Islas e Indios Visayas del Padre Alcina, 1668* (1975) is a facsimile edition of an inferior manuscript of Alcina's major work, with reproductions of the drawings from the two principal manuscripts.

John N. Schumacher, SJ

Aldersey, Mary Ann (1797-1868), independent pioneer woman missionary in China. A Londoner from a well-to-do nonconformist family, Aldersey attended classes in Chinese taught by Robert *Morrison when he was on home leave from 1824 to 1826. Not then free from family ties, she made gifts to the London Missionary Society (LMS) that enabled Maria *Newell to go to Malacca (1827). In 1837 she herself was able to go to Batavia (present-day Jakarta), where she started a school for Chinese girls. When the treaty ports in China were opened (1843) she moved the school to Ningpo, where she continued to work until 1861. Never an agent of any society, she maintained close links with the LMS. Several of her teaching staff were Chinese-speaking daughters of missionaries; at least four became missionary wives, including Maria Dyer (see Maria Dyer *Taylor), who married James Hudson *Taylor (against Aldersey's wishes). Another protégée, Mary Ann Leisk, became the wife of William *Russell, later bishop in north China. In 1861 Aldersey handed her school over to the Church Missionary Society and retired to Adelaide, Australia, where she lived until her death. She appears to have been the first single woman missionary to have worked in China.

BIBLIOGRAPHY E. Aldersey White, *A Woman Pioneer in China: The Life of Mary Ann Aldersey* (1932). See also John Pollock, *Hudson Taylor and Maria: Pioneers in China* (1962); Donald MacGallivray, ed., *A Century of Protestant Missions in China (1807-1907)* (1907).

Jocelyn Murray

Aleni, Giulio (1582-1649), Jesuit missionary in China. A native of Brescia, Italy, Aleni entered the Jesuit order in

1600 and studied astronomy under Christopher Clavius at the (Jesuit) Roman College. He reached Peking (Beijing) in 1613 and then accompanied *Hsü Kuang-ch'i, the Christian convert who later became grand minister of the Ming dynasty, on his way to Shanghai. In 1619 Aleni was at Hangchow (Hangzhou) where he baptized 250 adults. At the invitation of Christians who had been baptized away from home but had returned to their native places, he opened new missions in Shansi (Shanxi) and Chekiang (Zhejiang) provinces. He is best known for founding the Jesuit mission in Fukien (Fujian) Province in 1625. For four months he personally visited all the scholar officials of the capital city, Foochow (Fuzhou), and spent another eight months visiting all the other officials in the province. More than fifty scholars wrote testimonials praising Christianity. Forced to go to Macao because of persecution in 1638, he secretly returned to Fukien a year later. From 1641 to 1646 he was the Jesuit vice-provincial for southern China. He died at Yenping (Nanping) during the Manchu consolidation of Fukien province.

BIBLIOGRAPHY Among Aleni's principal works, many of them reprinted over the centuries, are *Sanshan lunxue ji* (Discussions at Sanshan) (1627), *Wanwu zhenyuan* (True origin of all things) (1628), *Zhifang waiji* (Geography of nontributary countries) (1623), and *Misa jiyi* (Sacrifice of the Mass) (1629). L. Carrington Goodrich, "Aleni, Giulio," in L. Carrington and Chaoying Fang, eds., *Dictionary of Ming Biography*, vol. 2 (1976), pp. 2–6; Bernard Hung-kay Luk, "A Serious Matter of Life and Death: Learned Conversations at Foochow in 1627," in Charles E. Ronan and Bonnie Oh, eds., *East Meets West: The Jesuits in China, 1582–1773* (1988), pp. 173–206; Eugenio Menegon, *Un Solo Cielo: Giulio Aleni, S.J. (1582–1649). Geografia, arte, scienza, religione, dall'Europa alla Cina* (1994).

John W. Witek, SJ

Alexander VI (1431–1503), pope during early years of discovery and Christianization of new lands by Spain and Portugal. Born in Játiva, near Valencia, in Spain, Rodrigo Borja (in Italian, Borgia) was advanced quickly by his uncle, Pope Callistus III. Borja became vice-chancellor of the Holy See in 1457, a position from which he amassed great wealth. He lived an openly licentious life, fathering several children, including the infamous Cesare and Lucrezia. He was elected to the papacy in 1492, partially through bribery and simony. As Pope Alexander VI (r. 1492–1503), he devoted his considerable political talent to European affairs, first in the Italian peninsula, and after 1498, in France; he also exercised his powers to enrich his family. He died either from malaria or from poisoning.

Although mission was not the principal interest of Alexander VI, his actions had significant influence on mission history. He called for the re-Christianization of Greenland in 1492 and regulated relations between Portugal and Spain in newly discovered lands by establishing the Line of Demarcation in 1493. He also created the *patronato real* (royal patronage) of Spain, whereby the monarchs were given responsibility for the evangelization of the new territories and were also given authority to nominate bishops. This system shaped church-state relations into the nineteenth century.

BIBLIOGRAPHY O. Raynaldus, "Alexander VI," in *Annales ecclesiastici*, J. D. Mansi, ed. (1747–1756), 11: 208–416; Johann Burchard, *At the Court of the Borgia*, G. Parker, ed. (1963); P. de Roo, *Materials for a History of Pope Alexander VI: His Relations and His Times* (1924).

Robert J. Schreiter, CPPS

Alexander, Michael Solomon (1799–1845), first Protestant bishop in the Ottoman Empire. Born of a Jewish family in Posen, Prussia, Alexander's introduction to Christianity came in 1820 at a meeting of the London Jews' Society, which he attended out of curiosity while seeking a teaching post in England. It made a deep and lasting influence on him, so that when he received a rabbinical post in Plymouth he was happy to teach Hebrew to Christian clergy there. One Anglican priest so impressed Alexander that he began to attend services secretly, until in 1825 he confessed his faith in Jesus and was baptized. Following theological training he was ordained in Ireland as an Anglican priest and joined the London Jews' Society, serving as a missionary in Poland and England. He played a significant part in translating the Anglican liturgy into Hebrew and in revising the Hebrew New Testament. In 1841 this former rabbi became the first Protestant missionary bishop in Jerusalem (and the Ottoman Empire). He founded the Christ Church congregation in Jerusalem one year later. He died while traveling to Egypt on a pastoral missionary visit.

BIBLIOGRAPHY A. Bernstein, *Some Jewish Witnesses for Christ* (1909); Muriel W. Corey, *From Rabbi to Bishop* (n.d.); Kelvin Crombie, *For the Love of Zion* (1991); W. T. Gidney, *The History of the London Society for Promoting the Gospel amongst the Jews* (1908); J. F. A. de le Roi, *Michael Solomon Alexander: Der erste evangelische Bischof in Jerusalem* (1897).

Walter Riggans

Alexander, William Patterson (1805–1884), American missionary to Hawaii. Trained at Centre College, Danville, Kentucky, and Princeton Theological Seminary, Alexander was ordained in 1831, married Mary Ann McKinney, and was sent by the American Board of Commissioners for Foreign Missions (ABCFM) to Hawaii. After an exploratory visit to the Marquesas Islands, the young couple in 1833 joined an effort to establish a mission on Nukuhiwa. Alexander prepared a vocabulary of the Marquesan language, but the people were unreceptive and hostile to his ministry. When responsibility for the Marquesas was divided with the London Missionary Society in 1834, the Alexanders returned to Hawaii, where he founded the station at Waioli, Kauai, serving there for nine years and participating in the great Hawaiian revival of 1836 to 1838. From 1843 to 1856 he was in charge of the Lahainaluna Seminary. In 1856 he became pastor at Wailuku and in 1863 launched a theological school to which he gave virtually all his time after 1869. Alexander's numerous translations into Hawaiian include *Bowditch on Navigation, Evidences of Christianity, A System of Theology, A Pastor's Manual, A Nat-*

ural Philosophy, Form of Church Government, and *A Confession of Faith.* His force and decisiveness, together with his humor and congeniality, made him widely liked and influential.

BIBLIOGRAPHY Rufus Anderson, *The Hawaiian Islands...* (1865), pp. 76–77, 217; *Missionary Album* (1969), pp. 18–23; *Missionary Herald* 81 (1885): 102–103.

David M. Stowe

Ali, Wallayat (?–1857), Indian evangelist, pastor, and martyr. Born in Agra, son of a wealthy haji, Ali's Muslim family persecuted him bitterly when he found Christ through the influence of a British colonel by the name of Wheeler. Baptized in 1838, he worked for seven years as an evangelist in Chitoor, during which time his wife, Fatima, learned to read and was baptized. In 1845 he went to Delhi to nurture and lead the Baptist church there. On the first day of the Sepoy Mutiny of 1857 he was martyred, having attempted to save John Mackay, his new missionary colleague. His wife escaped to record that he refused to recant and died crying, "Father, lay not this sin to their charge" (*Oriental Baptist,* October 1857).

BIBLIOGRAPHY Rajaiah Paul, *They Kept the Faith* (1968); M. A. Sherring, *The Indian Church during the Great Rebellion* (1859).

E. M. Jackson

Allamano, Joseph (1851–1926), founder of the Consolata Missionary Fathers and Consolata Missionary Sisters. Born in Castelnuovo d'Asti, Italy, Allamano wanted to become a missionary from early life. Unable to do so because of poor health, he became a diocesan priest of Turin. He received the D.D. degree from Turin seminary in 1877. For 46 years (1880–1926), he was the counselor of priests at the Convitto Ecclesiastico. Some of them became the first Consolata missionaries in Kenya. He was also rector of the Consolata shrine in Turin. He founded the Consolata Missionary Fathers in 1901 and the Consolata Missionary Sisters in 1910 and was superior general of both institutes until he died. The missionary formation given to Consolata missionaries broke new ground. Evangelization and development were equally important; he also emphasized proper use of local cultural values and customs, and preparation of local leaders and their immediate incorporation in the missionary work. He promoted the involvement of religious women and brothers as full partners in evangelization and development. As a consequence, Consolata missionaries established the first college for catechists in Kenya, the first seminary, and the first local religious institute for women. Allamano was also responsible for persuading the pope to establish a day of prayer and support for all the Catholic missions. He inspired James Alberione, the founder of St. Paul's Society, and James A. *Walsh, cofounder of the Catholic Foreign Missionary Society of America (Maryknoll Missioners). He supported mass media as a means of evangelization and began publishing missionary news in the Consolata bulletin.

BIBLIOGRAPHY Joseph Allamano, *Le conferenze spirituali del servo di Dio Giuseppe Allamano* (1981), *The Spiritual Life* (1982), and *Lettere,* 3 vols. (1990). Domenico Agasso, *Joseph Allamano: Founder of the Consolata Missionaries* (1991); Candido Bona, *La fede e le opere: Spigolature e richerche su Giuseppe Allamano* (1989); Igino Tubaldo, *Giuseppe Allamano: il suo tempo, La sua vita, La sua opera* (1986; vol. 4 includes extensive bibliography). The Allamano museum is located on the grounds of the Consolata mother house in Turin.

Anthony Bellagamba, IMC

Allan, George (1871–1941) *and*
Mary (Sterling) (1871–1939), founders of the Bolivian Indian Mission (BIM). Following their studies and their marriage at Angus Missionary Training College in Australia, New Zealanders George and Mary Allan set out in 1899 for Argentina under the Canadian branch of the South American Evangelical Mission, for which they also helped establish an Australasian council. After serving initially in Argentina, they felt a growing burden for the Quechua Indians of Bolivia. They relocated to Cochabamba, Bolivia, in 1903 but soon focused their ministry on the rural indigenous Indian population. In 1907 they incorporated the BIM and in 1909 established their base in San Pedro, about 350 miles north of Cochabamba. In addition to his ministry and leadership responsibilities, George Allan wrote extensively in the mission periodical *The Bolivian Indian.* Much of his writing focused on the history and culture of the Quechuas, as well as on the progress of the gospel among them. Together with a native Bolivian, Crisologo Barron, he translated the New Testament and the Psalms into the Quechua language. By 1990 some 45,000 members of the Union of Evangelical Churches were worshiping in over 600 churches in Bolivia, a direct outgrowth of the Allans' labors. The Allans lived in Bolivia until their deaths, and both are buried there. BIM later became the Andes Evangelical Mission, and finally merged with SIM International in 1982.

BIBLIOGRAPHY George Allan, *Reminiscences: Being Incidents from Missionary Experience* (1936). W. Harold Fuller, *Tie Down the Sun* (1990); Margarita Allan Hudspith, *Ripening Fruit: A History of the Bolivian Indian Mission* (1958). Papers related to the Allans' work and that of the BIM may be found in the SIM archives in Charlotte, North Carolina.

Gary R. Corwin

Allen, David Oliver (1799–1863), Congregational missionary to Western India. Born in Barre, Massachusetts, Allen attended Amherst College, graduating in 1823. In 1827 he graduated from Andover Theological Seminary and was ordained and commissioned by the American Board of Commissioners for Foreign Missions. The same year he married Myra Wood, and they sailed for Bombay. While mastering the Marathi language Allen became secretary of the Bombay Tract and Book Society. From 1832 on he was active in the British and Foreign Bible Society, serving for 12 years as its local secretary; as principal editor, he worked to bring out a Marathi Bible. He was also involved with the Seamen's Friend Society, the Bombay District Benevolent Society, the Royal Society, and the American Oriental Society. For his last ten years in India he superintended the mission press. He left India for health reasons in 1853. After his first wife's death in 1831 he married Orpah Graves (1838–1842), then Azuba Condit (1843–1844), and finally Mary S. Barnes (1848), who survived him. In addition to Marathi tracts, Allen published the 650-page *India, Ancient and Modern* (1856).

BIBLIOGRAPHY *Missionary Herald* (1832–1842) contains material from Allen's voluminous journal, and vol. 59 (1863): 285 has an obituary notice. Allen figures in ABCFM annual reports between 1828 and 1854, in Rufus Anderson's *History of the Missions of the ABCFM in India* (1875), and in "The Literary Work of the American Marathi Mission," *Memorial Papers of the American Marathi Mission, 1813–1881* (1882), pp. 73–121.

David M. Stowe

Allen, Horace Newton (1858–1932), American Presbyterian and first resident Protestant missionary in Korea. Allen was born in Delaware, Ohio. He graduated from Ohio Wesleyan College in 1881 and from Miami Medical College in Oxford, Ohio, in 1883. In that same year he married Frances Messenger and was appointed a medical missionary to China by the Board of Foreign Missions of the Presbyterian Church in the U.S.A. The Allens were assigned to Nanking (Nanjing), but did not like China; Horace Allen was therefore reappointed to Korea. He arrived in Korea in September 1884, and soon after, his family joined him in Seoul. As a medical missionary, he established a hospital, introduced Western medicine and medical education, and paved the way for successful evangelistic missionary work in Korea. In 1887 the king of Korea appointed him foreign secretary of the first Korean legation in the United States, and in 1890 he became the minister and consul general of the United States in Seoul. In his position in the diplomatic service, he tried to encourage American business interests in Korea. Allen disagreed with the U.S. policy toward Korea and Japan and warned the U.S. government of the dangers Japan posed. In 1905 he was recalled to the United States and settled in Toledo, Ohio, where he practiced medicine.

BIBLIOGRAPHY Horace Newton Allen, *A Chronological Index: Some of the Chief Events in the Foreign Intercourse of Korea from the Beginning of the Christian Era to the Twentieth Century* (1901) and *Things Korean* (1908). Fred Harrington, *God, Mammon, and the Japanese* (1961); Wi Jo Kang, "The Legacy of Horace Newton Allen," *IBMR* 20, no. 3 (1996): 125–128. The unpublished Allen diaries are in the New York City Library.

Wi Jo Kang

Allen, Roland (1868–1947), missiologist and radical critic of the church. Allen was born in Bristol, England, the youngest of five children of an Anglican priest. He was orphaned early in life but obtained an education on scholarship at St. John's College, Oxford, and at the (Anglo-Catholic) Leeds Clergy Training School. In 1892 he was ordained a deacon, and the following year he became a priest in the Church of England. In 1895 he was sent by the Society for the Propagation of the Gospel (SPG) to its North China Mission. While preparing to head a new seminary for Chinese catechists in Peking (Beijing), he was trapped with other foreigners in the Boxer Rebellion of 1900. After rescue by foreign troops, Allen wrote about his experience in *The Siege of the Peking Legations* (1901). While on furlough in England he married Mary B. Tarlton. In 1902 they returned to north China, where their first child was born, but Allen soon became ill and the family had to be sent home. There he took charge of a parish until 1907, when he resigned in protest against the rule of the established church that he must baptize any child presented for the sacrament whether or not the parents had any Christian commitment. Thereafter he held no official post but continued as a voluntary priest, supporting himself by writing and lecturing until his death in Kenya, nearly 40 years later.

The crises of his early experience led him to a radical reassessment of his own vocation and the theology and missionary methods of Western churches. He was an early advocate of the *Nevius plan to establish churches that from the beginning would be self-supporting, self-propagating, and self-governing. He wanted the forms of the church to be adapted to local cultural conditions and not be mere imitations of Western Christianity. To accomplish this, missionaries would have to hand over responsibility to the local leaders in the community, who would not be professional clergy either in their training or in their compensation. Allen criticized missionaries for their paternalistic and protective attitudes and their failure to trust in the Holy Spirit to guide the new church in its development. He continued to be an Anglican, however, and to insist on the importance of sacraments and creeds and the supervision of bishops in order to maintain discipline and provide links with the church universal.

Allen's views were confirmed by a trip to India in 1910 and by later research in Canada and East Africa. In 1912 he published what became his most famous and enduring book, *Missionary Methods: St. Paul's or Ours?* After World War I, he began a long association with the Survey Application Trust and World Dominion Press, an independent missionary research group founded by the Congregationalist layman Sidney J. W. Clark. With the help of the trust he published other books and pamphlets elaborating his reconception of Christian mission, notably *Pentecost and the World* (1917), *The Spontaneous Expansion of the Church and the Causes Which Hinder It* (1927), and *The Case for Voluntary Clergy* (1930).

Allen's ideas had little effect on the churches and missionary societies of his day but as he himself predicted, his work was rediscovered (in the 1960s) and has exercised a growing influence on missiology and ecclesiology in many places, not least in China.

BIBLIOGRAPHY Other works by Roland Allen include *Educational Principles and Missionary Methods* (1919), *Voluntary Clergy* (1923), and *Voluntary Clergy Overseas* (1928). David M. Paton, ed., *Reform of the Ministry: A Study of the Work of Roland Allen* (1968) contains a history of the Survey Application Trust, a list of publications of the World Dominion Press, an account of Allen's last years in East Africa, and selected correspondence. David M. Paton and Charles H. Long, eds., *The Compulsion of the Spirit* (1983) contains selected writings of Roland Allen with brief introductions by the editors. Hubert J. B. Allen, *Roland Allen: Pioneer, Priest, and Prophet* (1995), is a biography by his grandson. See also Charles Henry Long and Anne Rowthorn, "Roland Allen," in Gerald H. Anderson et al., eds., *Mission Legacies* (1994), pp. 383–390.

Charles Henry Long

Allen, Young John (1836–1907), American missionary, educator, and translator in China. A graduate of Emory University, Georgia, Young was appointed as a missionary by the Methodist Episcopal Church, South. With his family, he arrived in China in July 1860. His initial missionary activity was to preach in Shanghai and nearby villages. But the financial straits of his mission during the American Civil War forced him to combine his Christian ministry with secular employment in a government school in Shanghai, where he taught English and science. This educational experience helped him see that preaching alone would not meet China's needs. In May 1868 he became editor of the Chinese-language periodical *Shanghai xinbao* (Shanghai Daily News). He also founded the *Jiaohui xinbao* (Church news), which was designed to bring general news to Chinese Christians, to help Chinese know more about the West, and to print religious news. These experiences in journalism led him in 1871 to help the government-run Kiangnan Arsenal translate into Chinese material on history, current events, geography, and other subjects. In 1874 Allen changed the name of *Jiaohui xinbao* to *Wanguo Gongbao* (Globe Magazine) to reflect the fact that it now included more local and world news than church news. The magazine became increasingly secular as it expanded its readership to include officials, gentry, merchants, and foreigners living in China. During his later years, Allen continued to edit *Globe Magazine* and to work with his mission board, serving until 1895 as superintendent of its China mission and as director of a system of schools in Shanghai that he called the Anglo-Chinese School. Throughout his long period in China, Allen creatively combined both religious and secular activity to bring the Christian faith to the Chinese. Shortly before his death, he attended the China Centenary Missionary Conference in Shanghai (1907).

BIBLIOGRAPHY Adrian A. Bennett, *Missionary Journalist in China: Young J. Allen and His Magazines, 1860–1883* (1983); Warren A. Chandler, *Young J. Allen: "The Man Who Seeded China"* (1931).

Ralph R. Covell

Alli, Janni (1838–1894), Indian cleric and Church Missionary Society (CMS) missionary. Born of a Persian family, Alli was raised in a devout Shi'i Muslim environment. At age 15 he entered the CMS Anglo-Vernacular School (later, Robert Noble College) in his native town of Masulipatam (Hyderabad). Under the influence of headmaster Robert *Noble, he was baptized in 1855. Dedicating his life to Christian education, he taught for several years in Noble's school, then went to England to study theology and philosophy at Cambridge (1873–1876). Ordained at St. Paul's Cathedral, London, in 1877, he became the first Indian engaged as a missionary by the CMS and was appointed to Bombay, where he pioneered a student hostel for young men studying in the CMS school. On a second visit to Britain he made an influential contribution to the Decennial Missionary Conference (1882), which raised the priority of Anglican mission work in Bengal. In 1884 he was appointed the first full-time CMS missionary in Calcutta, where he pioneered Anglican educational work among Bengali Muslims. His missionary career challenged the CMS to explore issues of equality of status between national and expatriate missionaries. He also challenged his missionary colleagues to engage more deeply with Islam as the religious context of their Christian educational and preaching work. Struck by paralysis, he died and was buried in Calcutta.

BIBLIOGRAPHY P. Ireland Jones, "From Islam to Christ: Some Memories of the Late Rev. Janni Alli," *Church Missionary Intelligencer* 46 (n.s. 20, 1895): 6–16; Rajaiah Paul, *Lights in the World: Life Sketches of Maulvi Safdar Ali and the Rev. Janni Alli* (1969).

David A. Kerr

Allier, Raoul (1862–1939), French Protestant mission advocate. Born in Vauvert, Gard, France, of Huguenot stock, Allier received an excellent classical education. He was an evangelical Free Church layman committed to the Social Gospel represented in France by Tommy Fallot. He was a research fellow in Germany (1885–1888) and a lecturer in religious philosophy in the theological faculty, first in Montauban (1886–1889) and then in Paris (1889–1933); from 1920 he served as dean. He earned a doctorate in 1902. Allier was instrumental in the creation of the French Federation of Student Christian Associations in 1898 and became its first president, remaining in that post until 1920. He was a powerful journalist who fought many campaigns for democracy and religious freedom. He defended Alfred Dreyfus and fought for Protestant rights in France and in Madagascar. In 1897 he became a member of the Paris Evangelical Missionary Society governing board and was later its vice-president. His love for missions was inspired by their contribution to social progress, but he was increasingly fascinated by the problem of authentic religious conversion. Against the anthropological teaching of his time, which despised the "noncivilized," he affirmed the common humanity of all those united to the living Christ. Missions, he believed, also falsified J. M. Guyau's predictions about "the non-religion of the future."

BIBLIOGRAPHY Raoul Allier, *La philosophie d'Ernest Renan* (1895), *Le protestantisme au Japon* (1908), *Psychologie de la conversion chez les peuples non-civilisés* (1925), and *Le non-civilisé et nous* (1927; English translation, *The Mind of the Savage*, 1929). Gaston Richard, *La vie et l'oeuvre de Raoul Allier* (1948; includes autobiographical material).

Marc R. Spindler

Allouez, Claude Jean (1622–1689), French Jesuit missionary and explorer. Allouez was born at Saint-Didier-en-Forez in the Haute-Loire, France. He entered the Society of Jesus at Toulouse in 1639. A solidly built man of medium height, he possessed an enterprising and outgoing character. After his studies and teaching assignments in Billom, Rodez, and Toulouse, he left for Canada in 1658, arriving in Quebec in July of that year. He spent two years in the city of Quebec studying native languages, and five more years in Three Rivers, where he held office as superior of the residence and devoted himself to pastoral ministry among the Algonquins. In 1663 Bishop Laval of Quebec appointed him vicar general for all the territories that today constitute northwestern Ontario and the central regions of the United States: some 3,000 miles of land belonging to twenty-three nations of different races, languages, and customs. He set out in August 1665 and in October reached Pointe-du-Saint-Esprit on the southwestern shore of what is now Chequamegon Bay, on Lake Superior (Wisconsin). La Pointe, on Madeline Island, was to be the base of his ministry for the next 24 years. In the beginning, the small birchbark chapel he built at La Pointe was the only church west of Montreal. He began with Christian Hurons and eventually worked among some dozen or so nations, journeying as far north as Lake Nipigon (north of Lake Superior) to reach the Christian Nipissings in 1667. In 1671 he traveled to Sault Sainte Marie when Daumont de Saint-Lusson held a great assembly there to ratify an alliance with fourteen nations. This inaugurated the French strategy of alliance and planned exploration that was to lead to James Bay, the Gulf of Mexico, and the Rocky Mountains. Allouez was chosen to deliver the principal address, as much because of the respect in which he was held by the native people as because of the way his eloquence and fluency delighted them.

Allouez's writings are many and significant. He wrote important parts of the *Jesuit Relations* between 1667 and 1676, with remarkable accounts of the First Nations, particularly the Illinois. Calm, courageous, and stubbornly persevering, he was said to have personally baptized some 10,000 persons. Certainly he designed and established the first organization of the church in mid-America. In the opinion of many of his Canadian contemporaries, he was the greatest Jesuit missionary of his time. He died near Niles, Michigan.

BIBLIOGRAPHY Gilbert J. Garraghan, *The Jesuits of the Middle United States,* vol. 1 (1938), pp. 3ff; Camille de Rochemonteix, *Les Jésuites et la Nouvelle-France,* vol. 2 (1895–1896), pp. 357ff; Reuben Gold Thwaites, ed., *The Jesuit Relations and Allied Documents, 1610–1791,* vol. 73 (1959), p. 43.

Jacques Monet, SJ

Allshorn, Florence (1887–1950), Anglican missionary and trainer of missionaries. Born in Sheffield, England, Allshorn was orphaned by the age of three and was brought up by her mother's governess. She studied art and domestic science and came into active Christian faith through contact with the cathedral in Sheffield, where she later worked. In 1920 she went under the Church Missionary Society (CMS) to Uganda, where she taught in the girls' school at Iganga, Busoga. The relationship with a senior missionary was very difficult, and this highlighted for her the need for love between missionary colleagues. On leave in 1925, she was found to have tuberculosis and spent two years in treatment. The CMS then invited her to run their training college for women missionaries, which she did until 1940. Her emphasis was very much on spiritual life and on relationships. With a vision of founding a community where such emphases could be continued, she founded St. Julian's Community, now at Coolham, West Sussex, which continues to the present day. A guest house and retreat center, it draws mostly unmarried women, many of them connected with CMS. In the training of CMS missionaries, Florence Allshorn's concerns have remained important.

BIBLIOGRAPHY Florence Allshorn, "Corporate Life on a Mission Station," *IRM* 23 (1934): 497–511. Eleanor Brown, "Florence Allshorn," in Gerald H. Anderson et al., eds., *Mission Legacies* (1994), pp. 110–116; J. H. Oldham, *Florence Allshorn and the Story of St. Julian's* (1951); Margaret Potts, ed., *The Notebooks of Florence Allshorn* (1951). See also Max Warren, *Crowded Canvas: Some Experiences of a Life-time* (1974).

Jocelyn Murray

Alopen (7th century), Persian Nestorian missionary to China. Alopen was the first recorded Christian missionary to enter the Chinese empire, reaching the T'ang dynasty capital, Changan (Xian), in 635. Known to history only by his Chinese name as inscribed on the Nestorian Monument (erected in 781), Alopen was a Syriac-speaking Persian. He undoubtedly traveled across Asia by the Old Silk Road and was welcomed by the second T'ang emperor, the great T'ai-Tsung (626–649), who providentially had reversed his father's anti-foreign, anti-Buddhist policy, adopting a policy of religious toleration. Attracted by the fact that the foreigner's faith was the religion of a book, the emperor, a zealous patron of learning, brought Alopen into the imperial library and ordered him to begin translation of his sacred books. Of the earliest Chinese documents identified as Christian or Christian-influenced which were discovered along the Old Silk Road in Central Asia's Takla Makan desert, four have been described very tentatively by the Japanese scholar P. Y. Saeki as dating to the period of Alopen, that is, mid-seventh century.

In 628, three years after Alopen's arrival, the policy of religious toleration was reinforced by an official edict; the first Christian church in China was built in the capital at the emperor's expense; and the presence of twenty-one Nestorian monks in the empire was recognized. The monks were probably all Persian.

This was the beginning of the first opening of China to the Christian faith. The Nestorians were sometimes persecuted and sometimes granted unusual favor by T'ang rulers, and they prospered for at least two and half centuries, but they disappeared about A.D. 907 along with the great dynasty that had protected them. For at least the next 300 years there is no record of Christians in China. Not until the Mongol dynasty (1260–1368) do Nestorians reappear in the empire.

BIBLIOGRAPHY The only early source on Alopen is that of the Nestorian Monument itself. Complete English translations of the text are in John Foster, *The Church of the T'ang Dynasty* (1939) and P. Y. Saeki, *The Nestorian Documents and Relics in China* (1951). In addition to Foster's and Saeki's works on the T'ang Dynasty church, see Samuel Hugh Moffett, *A History of Christianity in Asia,* vol. 1 (1992), chap. 15, and A. C. Moule, *Christians in China before the Year 1550* (1930), chap. 2, both with bibliographical references.

Samuel Hugh Moffett

Altham, John (1589–1640), pioneer English Jesuit missionary in colonial Maryland. Altham emerged from obscure origins. He is thought to have been born in Warwickshire, England, possibly of Roman Catholic parents, but even his name is uncertain, many referring to him as Gravenor throughout his life. He entered the Society of Jesus around 1623 and was educated on the Continent, probably at Douay, since his order was under parliamentary ban in England. He returned to England, though, and filled pastoral offices in London and Devonshire. In 1633 he and fellow Jesuit Andrew *White joined Leonard Calvert, brother to Lord Baltimore, as the aristocrat led Maryland's first 200 colonists to the New World for settlement in Maryland. Landing in March of the following year, Altham helped explore Chesapeake Bay and the Potomac River, also celebrating mass at the fort and the first township which was named St. Mary's. He became particularly interested in spreading the gospel among neighboring Native Americans. Such work prospered especially on Kent Island, where he spent most of his time after baptizing the local chieftain and his wife. Despite physical hardships and a frail constitution, Altham labored to understand native cultural patterns in order to bring Christian principles effectively to bear on them. Growing numbers of Indian converts exacerbated a rivalry that had already sprung up between resident Catholics and Virginia Protestants who also claimed the land. More serious than the hostilities, however, was yellow fever, which claimed Altham's life after a short illness.

BIBLIOGRAPHY E. W. Beitzell, *The Jesuit Missions of St. Mary's County, Maryland* (1976); John T. Ellis, *Catholics in Colonial America* (1965); W. P. Treacy, *Old Catholic Maryland and Its Early Jesuit Missionaries* (1898).

Henry Warner Bowden

Amadeus, Mary (1846–1919), missionary to Native Americans. Born of Irish immigrants in Akron, Ohio, and determined from youth to be a missionary, Sarah Theresa Dunne was professed in 1864 as an Ursuline Sister, and took the religious name Mary Amadeus. She taught, handled her congregation's finances, and in 1874 became the first elected superior of the American Province. In 1884 she established a boarding school in Miles City, Montana, as a step to founding several missions among the Cheyennes and other tribes. Allied initially with the Jesuits in education at St. Labré Mission, Montana, her sisters continued to work there after the men found the territory too difficult.

Called the Great White Woman and Chief Lady Black Robe by the Native Americans, Amadeus's approach to mission emphasized presence to and companionship with native women and attention to their spiritual formation, education, and physical development. She noted and appreciated the keen intuitive sense of Indians, a perspective she contrasted with the scientific approach of American and European education. She brought a young Native American woman with her as a companion when she visited Pope Leo XIII in November 1900. Though in ill health most of her life from an accidental poisoning, Amadeus made six trips to Alaska from 1907 to 1918, founding missions among the Innuits and Aleuts. She died in Alaska.

BIBLIOGRAPHY Sister Saint Angela Louise Abair, "Mustard Seed in Montana," *Montana: The Magazine of Western History* 34 (Spring 1984): 17–31; Florence Gilmore, "Sarah Dunne: An American Missionary in Alaska," *The Sign,* July 1923, pp. 489–492; Mother Angela Lincoln, *Life of the Reverend Mother Amadeus of the Heart of Jesus: Foundress of the Ursuline Missions of Montana and Alaska* (1923); Mother Clotilde Angela McBride, OSU, *Ursulines of the West* (1935).

Angelyn Dries, OSF

Amalorpavadass, Duraiswami Simon (1932–1990), Roman Catholic priest and leader of church renewal in India. Born in Kallery, near Pondicherry, Tamilnadu, Amalorpavadass studied at St. Peter's Major Seminary in Bangalore and was ordained in 1959. The agenda for his life and work was set by his doctoral dissertation at the Institute Catholique of Paris, *Destinée de l'église dans l'Inde d'aujourdhui* (Destiny of the church in India today), published in 1967. He was the founder-director of the National Biblical, Catechetical, and Liturgical Centre (NBCLC), at Bangalore, India (1966–1985), and editor of its journal *Word and Worship.* He was also secretary to the Catholic Bishop's Conference of India for their Biblical, Catechetical, and Liturgical Commissions. He promoted renewal and research through courses and seminars at the NBCLC and also in the dioceses. In 1981 he founded the department of Christianity in the (state) University of Mysore.

Amalorpavadass was active in many international organizations, including the Ecumenical Association of Third World Theologians, the International Commission for English in the Liturgy, the World Catholic Federation for the Biblical Apostolate, and the International Association for Mission Studies. He was one of the two special secretaries for the Roman Episcopal Synod on Evangelization in 1974. In the last years of his life he founded the Anjali Ashram in Mysore and promoted Indian Christian spirituality. He died in an automobile accident on his way to a meeting in Bangalore.

BIBLIOGRAPHY D. S. Amalorpavadass, *Approach, Meaning, and Horizon of Evangelization* (1973), *Gospel and Culture* (1978), *NBCLC Campus, Milieu of God-Experience* (1982), *Poverty of the Religious and the Religious as Poor* (1984), and *Integration and Interiorization* (1990). Gerwin van Leeuwen, gives a complete bibliography both of Amalorpavadass and of the renewal movement in India in *Fully Indian, Authentically Christian* (1990). There have been two memorial volumes: J. Russell Chandran, ed., *Third World Theologies in Dialogue* (1991), and Paul Puthanangady, ed., *Church in India: Institution or Movement?* (1991).

Michael Amaladoss, SJ

Amandus of Elnon (c. 584–c. 676), Apostle of Flanders. Born in Poitou, France, Amandus was an itinerant evangelist in Flanders (today part of Belgium). In 629 he was consecrated a missionary bishop without see. He evangelized the region of Ghent and went on missions to Slavs along the Danube and to Basques in Navarre. His permanent field was the region of Antwerp. Protected by the Frankish kings, he baptized Dagobert's son Sigebert in 630. In 646 and 647 he was temporarily bishop of Tongeren (Tongres) at Maastricht. His method included establishing permanent monastic centers, the most famous of which was the monastery of Elnon on the Scarpe, in northwest France, where he died.

BIBLIOGRAPHY Bruno Krusch, ed., critical edition and commentary of "Vita Amandi," in *Monumenta Germaniae, Scriptores rerum Merovingicarum* 5: 395–485 (1910); E. de Moreau, *Saint Amand, apôtre de la Belgique et du nord de la France* (1927).

Marc R. Spindler

Ambrazis, Nicholas (c. 1854–1926), Greek Orthodox theologian, author, and ecumenist. Ambrazis studied at the Patriarchal Theological School of Chalke, in Constantinople (Istanbul). He then served as a preacher in Smyrna (Izmir), Turkey, and as a teacher, including service at the Barbakeion Lykeion in Athens. He was an author of significant theological works, most of which dealt with interchurch and interreligious topics. His first work, *Protestantism,* was published at age 22 in 1876. He is especially remembered for a missionary novel, *The Greek Orthodox Missionary Philotheos,* published in 1892. The story describes the adventures of a missionary to a tribe of cannibals and evidences an ecumenical approach to mission. It embodies the main principles of Orthodox missiology, such as translation of Scripture, worship in the language of the people, incarnational theology, and rapid indigenization of the clergy. It also contains some typical nineteenth-century racial prejudice and Western cultural attitudes. Filled with adventures and implausibly humorous deus ex machina resolutions to problems, *Philotheos* was republished several times, ultimately as a children's story, and was translated into English (1948).

BIBLIOGRAPHY Elias Boulgarakis, "Nicholaos Ambrazis," *Porefthendes* 10 (1968): 2–4, 41–46, 55–56, 59–62; Stanley S. Harakas, "Philotheos Revisited: The Reawakening of Mission Outlook," *Greek Orthodox Theological Review* 32 (1987): 252–269.

Stanley Samuel Harakas

Ambrose (c. 339–397), bishop of Milan and one of the four great Latin fathers of the church. Born in Trier, Ambrose received a rhetorical and juridical education in Rome. About 370 he became governor of Aemilia-Liguria, with his headquarters in Milan. After the death of the Arian bishop Auxentius, the laity of Milan insisted that Ambrose should succeed him, and eight days after his baptism he was ordained (probably December 7, 374). Brought up on the Nicene Creed since his boyhood, Ambrose defended this orthodoxy against paganism, Judaism, and Christian heresies such as Manichaeism, Marcionism, Sabellianism, and, above all, Arianism. In his diocese he persuaded many pagans by his arguments, particularly those of social and intellectual prominence; he also encouraged missionaries in the Tyrolean regions by his letters. Although in his lifetime Catholics had the support of the state and, moreover, although Ambrose as their friend and adviser exerted a profound influence on the Christian emperors Gratian, Valentinian II, and Theodosius, still a significant percentage of the population (particularly of the aristocracy) seems to have remained attached to the traditional cults. Nevertheless Ambrose's biographer Paulinus records that even pagans and Jews from all ranks attended the bishop's funeral. In any case, it is through Ambrose that northern Italy was decisively won for the Catholic faith.

BIBLIOGRAPHY H. Bloch, "The Pagan Revival in the West at the End of the Fourth Century," in A. Momigliano, ed., *The Conflict between Paganism and Christianity in the Fourth Century* (1963), pp. 193–218; H. von Campenhausen, *Ambrosius von Mailand als Kirchenpolitiker* (1929), pp. 186–188; L. Cracco Ruggini, "Ambrosio e le oppozioni anticattoliche fra il 383 e il 390," *Augustinianum* 14 (1974): 409–449; J. Mesot, *Die Heidenbekehrung bei Ambrosius von Mailand* (1958); W. Wilbrand, "Heidentum und Heidenmission bei Ambrosius von Mailand," *MR* 1 (1938): 193–202, and "Ambrosius von Mailand als Missionsbischof," *MR* 4 (1941): 97–104.

Johannes van Oort

Amiot, Jean Joseph Marie (1718–1793), Jesuit missionary and author at the court of the Chinese emperor. Born in Toulon, France, Amiot entered the Jesuit order in 1737 and was ordained in 1746. He reached Peking (Beijing) in August 1751 and was granted an audience with the Qianlong emperor. His research on the peoples and spoken languages of China led to lifelong study of many aspects of Chinese and Manchu culture. He engaged in considerable correspondence with learned people in Europe, including Henri Bertin, minister to Louis XV, who raised many questions about China. Amiot published voluminous accounts of the history, chronology, physics, literature, mathematics, and music of China, as well as an extensive life of Confucius. When he learned in 1775 that the pope had suppressed the Jesuit order, he suggested to the French government that the Paris Foreign Mission Society take charge of the Peking mission, but the pope sent the Congrégation de la Mission (Lazarists, also known as Vincentians), which Amiot welcomed. His last letters to his sister reflect his concern about the French Revolution and its impact on the mission in China. Overwhelmed by news of the regicide of Louis XIV, which he received on the evening of October 8, he died during the night.

BIBLIOGRAPHY Most of Amiot's essays are in *Mémoires concernant l'histoire, les sciences, les arts, les moeurs, les usages, etc., des Chinois par les missionnaires de Pékin*, 17 vols. (1777–1814). Joseph Dehergne, "Une Grande collection: Mémoires concernant les chinois (1776–1814)," *Bulletin de l'École française de l'Extreme-Orient* 70 (1983): 267–298; "Jean-Joseph-Marie Amiot," in Louis Pfister, *Notices biographiques et bibliographiques sur les Jésuites de l'ancienne mission de Chine* (1932–1934; repr. 1971 and 1975), pp. 837–860; Camille de Rochemonteix, *Joseph Amiot et les derniers survivants de la mission française à Pékin* (1915).

John W. Witek, SJ

Amu, Ephraim Kwaku (1899–1995), Ghanaian composer and musicologist. Amu, whose life spanned almost the entire twentieth century, embodied most of the transitions of Christianity in Ghana in the period. He was born in the town of Peki-Avetile, in the Ewe-speaking Volta region of present-day Ghana, where his early upbringing was influenced by the Bremen Mission. Having responded personally to the Christian faith at 15, Amu desired to be a teacher in church schools. With the outbreak of World War I, the repatriation of German missionaries, and the closing of the Bremen Mission seminaries, Amu was trained as a teacher-catechist under Scottish Presbyterian missionaries at the Abetifi Seminary founded by the Basel Mission. Amu the Ewe thus began his intellectual association with Twi language and culture.

As a teacher at Peki, Amu's early interest in music was intensified through association with local Methodist minister and music tutor Allotey-Pappoe. Moving to Akropong, Amu taught music, nature, agriculture, and Ewe from 1925 to 1933 at Akropong Training College. This was a momentous period for him as he researched the rhythms and meter of African music. He emphasized the critical significance of the drum and maintained that indigenous musical forms need not be at variance with the Christian religion. In 1932 he published his *Twenty-five African Songs.* Reaffirming "the excellence of African culture," he discarded European dress, took to African food, and drank water from a gourd. His most startling innovation was to preach from the pulpit dressed in African cloth, which, combined with his musical innovations, angered the Presbyterian leadership. Faced with the choice of abandoning his African attire and his research into African musical idiom or being dismissed from the Presbyterian Training College, Amu chose the latter.

The church soon recognized that Amu was not wrong; he was simply ahead of his time. But Amu now set aside earlier thoughts of ordination. His career subsequently took him to Achimota College, where he taught from 1934 to 1936 and from 1941 to 1950, to the Royal College of Music, London, where he engaged in research from 1937 to 1940, to the new Kumasi College of Science and Technology (1951–1960), and finally, to the new music department of the Institute of African Studies of the University of Ghana, Legon (1961–1971). In 1965, the University of Ghana awarded him its first Doctor of Music degree; this was followed, in 1976, by another doctorate from the University of Science and Technology, Kumasi.

For Amu, the most important single influence was the life and career of James Emmanuel Kwegyir *Aggrey of Anomabu, who believed that no first-rate educated African would want to be a carbon copy of a white man. No cultural jingoist, Amu never broke away from the church, and his Christian self-consciousness remained consistent. Half of his 200 or so musical compositions derive from and express his Christian convictions.

BIBLIOGRAPHY Fred Agyemang, *Amu the African: A Study in Vision and Courage* (1988).

Kwame Bediako

Anastasios. *See* Yannoulatos, Anastasios.

Anastasius (d. 1036/39), archbishop of Esztergom, in north central Hungary. Anastasius was a priest under *Adalbert of Prague. Successively, he became abbot of the monastery in Brevnov, near Prague, the abbot of a monastery in Miedzyrzecz, Poland, and the abbot of a monastery founded by *Stephen in Pannonhalma, Hungary. An eloquent preacher, he strengthened each institution he led. A story about his traveling to Rome for the crown Stephen of Hungary was to wear is probably false, but his assistance of Stephen earned him the title "Apostle of Hungary."

BIBLIOGRAPHY Francis Dvornik, *The Making of Central and Eastern Europe* (1949); Bálint Hóman, *König Stephan I der Heilige* (1941); Konrad Schünemann, *Die Deutschen in Ungarn bis zum 12. Jahrhundert* (1923).

Frederick W. Norris

Anawati, Georges Chehata (1905–1994), Dominican scholar of Islam. Anawati (the Arabic form was Qanawati) personified the Dominican commitment to religious scholarship as a form of Christian witness. Born in Alexandria, Egypt, of Syrian and Orthodox parentage, he found the intellectual foundations of his faith in Thomism. He entered the Dominican order, taking the name Marie-Marcel, and was ordained a Catholic priest in 1939. His initial missionary service in Algeria (1940–1953) forged a lifelong relationship with the French Dominican Islamicist Louis Gardet (1937–1977). Returning to Egypt, he devoted himself to developing the Dominican Institute for Oriental Studies in Cairo. Under his 50-year leadership, it became the leading center in the Middle East for Christian study of Islam and for dialogue between Muslim and Christian scholars. His goal was to recreate the intellectual discourse between Arabic-speaking Muslims and Christians that had been a feature of medieval learning. In addition to his talents as teacher, international lecturer, and renowned host, he is remembered for his vast literary output. He played a leading editorial role in the Institute's journal, *Mélanges: Institut Dominicain d'Études Orientales du Caire* (founded in 1953), which publishes theological research of international Christian and Muslim scholars. He influenced the Second Vatican Council's rethinking of Christian relations with other religions (*Nostra Aetate*) and subsequent Catholic initiatives in Christian-Muslim dialogue.

BIBLIOGRAPHY "Georges Chehata Anawati, OP (1905–1994)," *Mélanges: Institut Dominicain D'Études Orientales du Caire (MIDEO)* 22 (1995; includes the full bibliogrpahy of Anawati's works); G. Scattolin, "Fr. George Anawati (1905–1994): Pioneer and Witness of Muslim-Christian Dialogue," *Encounter: Documents for Muslim-Christian Understanding* 203 (March 1994), repr. in *Pro Dialogo Bulletin* 88, no. 1 (1995): 69–78.

David A. Kerr

Anchieta, José de (1534–1597), Jesuit missionary in Brazil. A Portuguese Jesuit, Anchieta, along with Manoel da *Nóbrega and Antonio *Vieira, is considered one of the principal founders of the Jesuit missions in Brazil. Known popularly as the Apostle of Brazil, Anchieta was born in the Canary Islands. He studied at the Jesuit college of Coimbra and entered the Society of Jesus in 1551. After two years of novitiate training, he was sent to Brazil to recover from a spinal injury and stayed 44 years. He became proficient in the Tupí-Guaraní language and served other missionaries as interpreter and guide. In this capacity, in 1554, he accompanied his superior, Father Manoel da Nóbrega, to found a mission in the Indian village of Piratininga. This mission, named in honor of St. Paul, evolved into present-day São Paulo. For the next two decades Anchieta worked in the mission, teaching Latin to candidates for the priesthood and catechism to Tupí and Portuguese children. He also wrote the first grammar and dictionary of the Tupí language. In addition, he composed numerous canticles, dialogues, and religious plays in Latin, Spanish, Portuguese, and Tupí. Given his prolific writings, and the fact that he strove to communicate to both the Indians and the Portuguese in Brazil, he is considered the father of Brazilian national literature. A man of action, he accompanied Nóbrega on a trip in 1563 to negotiate a peace settlement between the Tupí, the Portuguese, and the warlike Tamayos Indians. Held as a hostage by the Tamayos for five months, he composed a poem in honor of the Virgin Mary that is considered one of his finest literary productions. On another expedition, in 1566, he and Nóbrega cofounded Rio de Janeiro. In the same year he was ordained a priest. Appointed the superior of the São Paulo–Rio de Janeiro mission, he converted many Indians. He served as the fifth provincial of all the Jesuits in Brazil between 1577 and 1587, and spent his last years preaching to the Indians and writing.

BIBLIOGRAPHY Anchieta's complete writings can be found in Afranio Peixoto, ed., *Cartas Jesuíticas,* vol. 3, *Cartas Informacoñes, Fragmentos Históricos e Sermoñes do Padre Joseph de Anchieta, SJ (1554–1594)* (1933). Norwood Andrews, Jr., "Anchieta, Father José de," in Irwin Stern, ed., *Dictionary of Brazilian Literature* (1988), pp. 17–18; Helen G. Dominian, *Apostle of Brazil: The Biography of Padre José de Anchieta* (1958); Jerome V. Jacobsen, "Jesuit Founders in Portugal and Brazil," *Mid-America* 24 (January 1942): 3–26; Richard A. Preto-Rodas, "Anchieta and Vieira: Drama as Sermon, Sermon as Drama," in *Luso-Brazilian Review* 7, no. 2 (December 1970): 96–103.

Jeffrey Klaiber, SJ

Andel, H(uibert) A(ntonie) van (1875–1945), Dutch pioneer missionary in central Java and one of the founders of the Javanese Christian Church (GKJ). After pastoring Dutch Reformed churches at Zuidland (1900–1908) and Baarn (1908–1911), van Andel served as a missionary from 1912 to 1942 at Surakarta (Solo), central Java. In his doctoral dissertation, "De zendingsleer van Gisbertus Voetius" (1912), he advocated that in the mission field the sacraments of baptism and the Holy Supper should not be separated, and rejected mission conducted by private societies, since he believed that all missionary work was the church's responsibility; its goals were converting sinners and planting churches. In *Een grootsche poging om de wereldzending in de macht van het modernisme te brengen* (1935), he warned against the rising tide of modernism, which, according to him, was prepared to have the "gospel of salvation" replaced by the "gospel of social justice." Pointing at the close relationship between religion and culture, he stated in *Cultuur en Christendom onder de Javanen* (1921) that the duty of both the colonial state and Christian mission is to raise the indigenous people to a higher cultural and moral level by establishing a Christian church and conducting politics according to Christian principles. In this view he was in line with his government's political ethics. His main importance lies in his having been one of the most outspoken representatives of orthodox Reformed theology in the Dutch East Indies in his time. He died in a Japanese internment camp.

BIBLIOGRAPHY D. Pol, *Midden-Java ten Zuiden* (2d ed., 1939); Ph. Quarles van Ufford, *Grenzen van internationale hulpverlening* (1980).

Christiaan G. F. de Jong

Anderson, Christopher (1782–1852), promoter of the Serampore Mission and a founder of home mission societies in Scotland. A native of Edinburgh and a Baptist minister, Anderson met Andrew *Fuller during Baptist Missionary Society (BMS) promotional tours in Scotland at the turn of the century. He resolved to go to India as a missionary and trained under BMS leaders in England for service with the BMS Serampore Mission in Bengal. When health problems prevented him from leaving Britain, he became minister of Charlotte Baptist Chapel in Edinburgh and one of the BMS's chief Scottish supporters. Fuller wished him to become his assistant secretary and successor, but the English BMS committee would not agree to it. Even before the BMS and the Serampore Mission parted company in 1827, he became the chief fund-raiser and advocate in Britain for William *Carey and his partners. As their trusted counselor, Anderson partly filled the void left by William *Ward's death. In the midst of great difficulties, he supported Serampore's Baptists during their extended periods of furlough from Bengal and through correspondence. Anderson also spearheaded vernacular mission work and Bible translation in the Gaelic-speaking Scottish Highlands and in Ireland (from 1805 to the 1830s). This led him to write *Historical Sketches of the Native Irish* (1828) and *The Annals of the English Bible* (1845).

BIBLIOGRAPHY Hugh Anderson, *The Life and Letters of Christopher Anderson* (1854); Donald E. Meek, ed., *A Mind for Mission: Essays in Appreciation of the Rev. Christopher Anderson, 1782-1852* (1992); A. Christopher Smith, "The Edinburgh Connection: Between the Serampore Mission and Western Missiology," *Missiology: An International Review* 18 (1990): 185-209.

A. Christopher Smith

Anderson, David (1814-1881), first bishop of the Church of England in western Canada. Born in London, and educated at Edinburgh Academy and the University of Oxford, Anderson became a priest in Liverpool in 1838. He accepted the position of vice-principal at St. Bees College in 1841 and took curateship in Lichfield in 1847. In 1849 he was named bishop of Rupertsland, a vast area in western Canada covering the lands draining into Hudson Bay. He arrived in the fledgling community of Red River Settlement (area of present-day Winnipeg) in 1849, and remained there until 1864, making only a few trips into the extremities of his see and one brief fund-raising voyage to England (1856). His term was marked by unpleasant sectarian dispute with Scottish Presbyterians who acquired their own minister in 1851 and severed their relations with the local Anglican church, which had been serving them. Furthermore, he was swept up in political wrangling between Hudson's Bay Company officials (the company largely financed the see) and those settlers who desired some form of representative government. Despite these controversies, he succeeded in attracting numbers of new missionary priests to Rupertsland and in establishing St. John's Collegiate School.

Retired in England, Anderson assumed the position of Chancellor of St. Paul's Cathedral in London in 1866, and he continued to speak and write, raising funds for Rupertsland. A scholar and educator, it was Anderson's misfortune to have moved to Red River at a very volatile time. Nevertheless, he was successful in laying the foundation on which the see still stands today.

BIBLIOGRAPHY *The Net in the Bay; or, Journal of a Visit to Moose and Albany* (1854; repr. 1967) is Anderson's only book, although nine sermons and charges delivered in Red River were published in pamphlet form in London between 1851 and 1861. O. R. Rowley, *The Anglican Episcopate of Canada and Newfoundland* (1928); M. P. Wilkinson, "The Episcopate of the Right Reverend David Anderson, D.D., First Lord Bishop of Rupert's Land, 1849-1864" (M.A. thesis, Univ. of Manitoba, 1950).

Terrence Craig

Anderson, James Norman Dalrymple (1908-1994), British scholar of Islamic law and mission theologian. Born in Aldeburgh, England, Anderson experienced a call to missionary service as a law student at Cambridge University. With his wife, Pat (Givan), he devoted seven years to cross-cultural work with the interdenominational Egypt General Mission (EGM) (1933-1940), where he learned to admire the scholarly approach to Muslim evangelism of W. H. T. *Gairdner (1873-1928). Though World War II ended his overseas missionary service, he remained closely involved with the EGM as it evolved into the Middle East General Mission (1956), and he facilitated its union with the Lebanon Evangelical Mission and the Arab Literature Mission to form Middle East Christian Outreach (1976). After a postwar appointment as first warden of the Inter-Varsity Fellowship's residential library for theological research at Tyndale House, Cambridge (1946-1949), he chose a career as an academic specialist in Islamic law. Appointed to a lectureship at London University, he was soon appointed to the Chair of Oriental Laws (1954), which he held concurrently with the directorship of the university's prestigious Institute of Advanced Legal Studies (1958). He acted as consultant in matters of Islamic legal reform to several governments of Muslim countries in Africa and Asia. He encouraged evangelical involvement in social issues and exercised his love of preaching the gospel at universities, churches, and cathedrals in many parts of the world. His literary output reflects his parallel concerns for comparative legal studies and religious studies. In the latter, he established himself as a leading evangelical thinker about Christian-Muslim relations. Elected a lay member of the General Synod of the Church of England in 1970, he served as chair of the House of Laity from 1970 to 1979. He was knighted in 1975.

BIBLIOGRAPHY Anderson's major works include *Islamic Law in Africa* (1954), *Islamic Law in the Modern World* (1959), *Into the World: The Need and Limits of Christian Involvement* (1968), *Christianity and Comparative Religion* (1971), *A Lawyer among Theologians* (1974), *Law Reform in the Muslim World* (1976), *The Teaching of Jesus* (1983), *Christianity and World Religions: The Challenge of Pluralism* (1984), and *An Adopted Son: The History of My Life* (1985). G. Janzon, "Kristen tro och religionerna: en kommenterande litteraturversikt," *Svensk Missionstidskrift* 76, no. 1 (1988): 50-58; M. J. McVeigh, "The Fate of Those Who've Never Heard? It Depends," *Evangelical Missions Quarterly* 21, no 4: (1985): 370-379.

David A. Kerr

Anderson, John (1805-1855), pioneer Scottish missionary in India. Born in Scotland and educated at Edinburgh University, Anderson was the first Church of Scotland missionary to South India, arriving in Madras early in 1837. He was convinced, like Alexander *Duff, his Scottish colleague in Calcutta, that education was the best means of imparting Christian truth. The demand for education was so strong, especially among the Brahman gentry, that the school he established outgrew its premises three times within its first decade. After the founding of Madras University in 1862, his school became one of its earliest affiliated colleges. Renamed in 1877 as Madras Christian College and later relocated in Tambaram, the school remains an elite institution of higher learning to this day. Anderson was brought into special prominence by public controversies surrounding the admission of Untouchable students in 1838; the conversion and baptism of some of his high-caste students in 1841; and the giving of asylum and baptism to a newly converted high-caste, teenage girl named Muniatha in 1845. The Muniatha episode climaxed in a notorious court scene in which European doctors testified to examining the girl to determine whether she had reached puberty; the near riot that ensued could hardly be controlled by mounted police. This incident provoked the first concerted effort by the Madras Hindu Community to petition the British Parliament, with more than 7,000 Indian "loyal subjects" signing a document in protest against missionary interference in their sacred traditions.

BIBLIOGRAPHY J. Braidwood, *True Yoke-Fellows in the Mission Field* (1862); R. E. Frykenberg, "Conversion and Crises of Conscience under Company Raj in South India," in Marc Gaboreieau and Alice Thorner, eds., *Asie du sud, traditions et changements: VIth European Conference on South Asian Studies, Sèvres, 8–13 juillet 1978* (1979), pp. 311–321; G. Pittendrigh and W. Meston, *Mission of the United Free Church of Scotland: The Story of Our Madras Mission* (1907).

Robert Eric Frykenberg

Anderson, Louisa (Peterswald) (?–1882), Presbyterian missionary in Jamaica and Nigeria. Probably born a free woman of color in Jamaica, Louisa Peterswald was teaching at the mission school at Carron Hall when she met William *Anderson, a newly arrived Scottish missionary in January 1840. They were married in 1841, and Louisa continued to teach until they left Jamaica to join the United Presbyterian mission at Calabar, Nigeria. There she worked extensively among the free women. She also ran a home for orphans and other children given into her charge. In 1866 she had sixteen children in her care. Beside regular schooling, the girls learned household arts, including knitting, sewing, and crochet work. Because of her extraordinary energy and competence, Anderson was known in Calabar as "de best man for de mission." She died in Calabar.

BIBLIOGRAPHY W. Marwick, *William and Louisa Anderson: A Record of their Life and Work in Old Calabar* (1897). See also Geoffrey Johnston, *Of God and Maxim Guns: Presbyterianism in Nigeria, 1846–1966* (1988).

Geoffrey Johnston

Anderson, Rufus (1796–1880), American Congregational administrator and theorist of foreign missions. Anderson was the son of a pastor in Yarmouth, Maine, and his boyhood call to foreign missions was cultivated during his years at Bowdoin College (graduated 1818) and Andover Seminary (graduated 1822). He offered for overseas service, but in 1826 he was appointed assistant secretary of the American Board of Commissioners for Foreign Missions. Primarily responsible for overseas correspondence, he soon became senior secretary, the Board's principal policymaker and administrator. He traveled in Latin America (1819, 1823–1824), the Mediterranean and Near East (1828–1829, 1843–1844), India, Ceylon, Syria, and Turkey (1854–1855), and Hawaii (1863). His writings include biographies of notable converts and other promotional pieces, numerous articles and papers on missionary theory and strategy, and four major historical works. He was involved in the founding and governance of a number of educational, cultural, and philanthropic institutions. He and his wife were renowned for hospitality to missionaries and their personal concern. He resigned as secretary in 1866 but continued on the Prudential Committee until 1875.

Anderson contended that mission should aim at nothing more or less than the establishment of self-supporting, self-governing, and self-propagating churches; its mandate does not require the "civilizing" of heathen peoples. Conversion and the establishment of truly indigenous and missionary churches is best accomplished by proclamation of the gospel through preaching. Although the spread of "civilization" is desirable, the gospel itself is the most effectual means to that end. In 1854 and 1855 Anderson led a deputation to the missions in India, Ceylon, and the Near East urging that educational work for the preparation of native pastors and their wives be conducted only in the vernacular. Investment in schools, presses, and other institutions should be minimal. Missionaries should move out of central stations into the villages and tour the countryside. Native pastors should be ordained speedily, and congregations should form their own ecclesiastical organization, with the mission serving only as helper and for a limited time. The "Outline of Missionary Policy" in the ABCFM *Annual Report* for 1856, pp. 53–58, summarizes many of these principles. In 1863 Anderson went to Hawaii to press these concerns and to close the mission.

Anderson's efforts alienated some missionaries and precipitated major debate. Although the three-self goal was widely accepted, Protestant missions became heavily invested in education, health, and social welfare. But by the mid-twentieth century Anderson's emphasis on the indigenous church and the separation of the gospel from "civilization" again became prominent in missionary thinking.

BIBLIOGRAPHY Anderson's writings include *Memorial Volume of the First Fifty Years of the American Board of Commissioners for Foreign Missions* (1861); *History of the Sandwich Islands Mission* (1870), *History of the Missions of the American Board of Commissioners for Foreign Missions to the Oriental Churches* (1872), and *History of the Missions of the American Board of Commissioners for Foreign Missions to India* (1875). R. Pierce Beaver, ed., *To Advance the Gospel: Selections from the Writings of Rufus Anderson* (1967) includes an excellent introduction and bibliography, and "Rufus Anderson," in Gerald H. Anderson et al., *Mission Legacies* (1994), pp. 548–553. Robert A. Schneider, "The Senior Secretary: Rufus Anderson and the ABCFM, 1810–1860" (Ph.D. diss., Harvard Univ., 1980) is the most extensive study of his life and thought. Robert E. Speer, *Studies of Missionary Leadership* (1914) contains an appreciative assessment. A bound volume of the "Reports and Letters of the India, Ceylon, Syrian, and Constantinople Missions, with Report of the Deputation to India" (1856) details Anderson's aggressive and controversial initiative. His personal papers are in the ABCFM collection at Harvard Univ., Cambridge, Mass.; many secretarial letters are available in microfilms.

David M. Stowe

Anderson, William (1769–1852), pioneer missionary among the Griquas of South Africa. Born in London of

Scottish parents, Anderson was one of the second party of London Missionary Society (LMS) volunteers to go to South Africa, arriving in 1800. In 1801 he went north of the Orange River, joining Johannes *Kircherer who was working among the Khoisan. However, he soon began to work with the people of many tribes who were gathering around the settlements established by two Cape Coloured clans, the Koks and the Waterboers, who came to call themselves Griquas. In 1806 he married Johanna Schonke, from Stellenbosch, who joined him in the work. The Griquas built their own churches and schools with Anderson's help. People who sought to join the community were expected to join the church. In 20 years the Griquas became a self-governing Christian ministate beyond the Cape Colony frontier. In 1820 Anderson was transferred by the LMS to Pacaltsdorp, back in the colony, to begin a more traditional but still successful and effective mission station. In 1848 his wife died, and he retired from the service of the LMS. He spent his final years at Pacaltsdorp.

BIBLIOGRAPHY Peter S. Anderson, *Weapons of Peace: The Story of William and Johanna Anderson* (1994); Robert Ross, *Adam Kok's Griquas* (1976). Many letters to and from Anderson are in the LMS archives housed in the SOAS library, Univ. of London.

Andrew C. Ross

Anderson, William (1812–1895), Scottish Presbyterian missionary in Jamaica and Nigeria. Anderson was born in Galashiels, Scotland. His formal education was limited, but he had a keen mind and a taste for reading. In 1839 the Scottish Missionary Society sent him as a catechist to Jamaica, where he met and married a local woman, Louisa Peterswald (see Louisa [Peterswald] *Anderson). After four sessions in theology with William *Jameson, Anderson was ordained in 1845. He went to Calabar, Nigeria, in 1849, and served as "head of station" in Duke Town until his resignation in 1891. With Hope *Waddell he initiated a number of social reforms, most notably the abolition of human sacrifices at aristocratic funerals. However, he argued repeatedly and violently both with his colleagues and the Calabar aristocracy. Indeed, his quarrels were a major reason for the formation of the Presbytery of Biafra, now the Presbyterian Church of Nigeria. Nevertheless, Calabar people not only put up with him but came to love him. Duke Town was never a successful station; Anderson worked hard and faithfully, but the church in Duke Town did not really begin to grow until after 1890, about the time Anderson retired. He returned to Calabar in 1895 and died there.

BIBLIOGRAPHY W. Marwick, *William and Louisa Anderson: A Record of their Life and Work in Old Calabar* (1897). See also Geoffrey Johnston, *Of God and Maxim Guns: Presbyterianism in Nigeria, 1846–1966* (1988). Anderson's journals for 1851 and 1852 are in the offices of the Church of Scotland, Edinburgh.

Geoffrey Johnston

Anderson, William H(arrison) (1870–1950), pioneering Seventh-day Adventist (SDA) missionary in Africa. A native of Indiana and a graduate of Battle Creek College in Michigan (1895), Anderson organized a Student Volunteer Movement-style foreign mission band at the college in the the early 1890s and remained a lifelong popularizer of missions. After the SDA Church opened its first mission station (Solusi) among non-Christian people near Bulawayo in what is now Zimbabwe in 1894, Anderson and his bride, Nora Haysmer, were called to join the first group of American SDA missionaries going there. After several years at Solusi, the Andersons traveled north, crossing the Zambezi River, and in 1905, established an agricultural mission near Pemba, in present-day Zambia. This became the center of a satellite system of self-supporting schools. As the educational system in the country developed, many graduates of these schools became fulltime farmers and formed the core of a significant cohort of Adventist entrepreneurial farmers. Anderson subsequently worked in Botswana, where he was instrumental in opening a hospital and several mission stations, and in Angola, where he spent almost ten years evangelizing and establishing stations. The final decade of his service in Africa was spent as a field secretary—traveling, advising, inspiring, raising money, and opening new work. He did much to maintain the interest of the U.S. SDA Church in African missions by his letters, periodical articles, and public activities. He returned to the United States in 1945 after 50 years of service in Africa. He wrote *On the Trail of Livingstone* (1919) and many articles that appeared in denominational periodicals.

BIBLIOGRAPHY Harold E. Peters, "The Contributions of Education to the Development of Elites among the Plateau Tonga of Zambia: A Comparative Study of School-leavers from Two Mission Schools, 1930–1965" (Ph.D. diss., Univ. of Illinois at Urbana-Champaign, 1976); R. W. Schwarz, *Light Bearers to the Remnant* (1979); Arthur W. Spalding, *Origin and History of Seventh-day Adventists,* vol. 4 (1962); "Anderson, William Harrison," "Solusi College," and "Zambia," in *Seventh-day Adventist Encyclopedia* (2d rev. ed., 1996).

Russell L. Staples

Andrade, Antonio de (1580–1634), Jesuit missionary in India and Tibet. A native of Vila de Oleiros, Portugal, Andrade entered the Society of Jesus in 1596 at Coimbra. His desire to serve the missions in the east was fulfilled when he left Portugal in 1600 to continue his studies toward the priesthood at St. Paul's College in Goa, India. After several years as a missionary on Salsette Island, north of Bombay, he returned to Goa to become rector of the college. In 1621 he was appointed superior of the mission at Agra, capital of the Mogul empire. Upon learning of reports that Christian communities existed to the northeast, he embarked on his first trip into Tibet in 1624, thereby becoming the first European missionary to cross the Himalayan mountains into Tibet. During his audience with Tibetan authorities at Tsaparang, he emphasized that he had come to preach the gospel and would not become involved in any way with Portuguese trade.

After receiving permission to establish a mission, he returned to Agra. The following year, with four confreres, he opened the mission at Tsaparang. The reports of his two trips were sent to Europe and were quickly translated into several languages. In late 1629 or early 1630 he left Tibet to become provincial of India from 1631 to 1634. In 1631, lamas opposed to the Tibetan Christian community (nearly 400 members) destroyed the mission station at Tsaparang. In early January of 1634, Andrade was named visitor of the vice-province of China and the province of Japan, but he did not live to fill that position. In Goa he was a deputy of the Holy Office which was investigating an accusation of heresy against a Portuguese native, João Rodrigues. The latter's son was a hired servant in the Jesuit college and apparently poisoned the water that Andrade drank. The case could not be proved, but the young man, tainted by the accusation of murder, fled to Manila.

BIBLIOGRAPHY Antonio de Andrade, *O Descobrimento do Tibet... em 1624, narrado em duas cartas do mesmo religioso,* Francisco Maria Esteves Pereira, ed. (1921). Giuseppe Toscano, *La Prima Missione Cattolica nel Tibet* (1951); Cornelis Wessels, *Early Jesuit Travellers in Central Asia, 1603–1721* (1924), pp. 43–93.

John W. Witek, SJ

André, Louis (1631–1714), French Jesuit missionary in North America. André was born in Saint-Rémy, Bouches-du-Rhône and joined the Society of Jesus in 1650. After several years of teaching, in 1669 he was sent to the missions in New France (North America), where he was assigned to Sault Sainte-Marie, with Gabriel *Druillettes. When a group of Ottawa Indians stopped on their way toward Manitoulin Island, fleeing from an expected attack by the Sioux, Druillettes directed André to join them. André subsequently served one year on Manitoulin, and then at other Algonquian missions around the western Great Lakes. In 1671 he made his headquarters at the Saint-François Xavier mission on Green Bay. Despite difficult conditions, including having his residences there and at Menominee set on fire, he remained at Saint-François Xavier until 1682. He practicali, lived in his canoe, visiting his missions along the bay. In 1684 he took a teaching position in Quebec. He later served missions in Chicoutimi and Sept-îles (present-day Seven Isles), Quebec. He is also notable for his linguistic and scientific research: he compiled Ottawa and Algonquian dictionaries, prepared an Algonquian catechism, and wrote a journal of the Green Bay tides. He died at Quebec.

BIBLIOGRAPHY Charles Douniol, ed., *Mission du Canada: Relations inédites,* vols. 1 and 2 (1861): 103–104, 118–122; Camille de Rochemonteix, *Les Jésuites et Nouvelle-France au XVIIe siècle* (1896); Carlos Sommervogel, *Bibliothèque de la Compagnie de Jésus,* vol. 1 (1890), col. 333–334; R. G. Thwaites, ed., *The Jesuit Relations,* vol. 54, *Iroquois, Ottawas, Lower Canada 1669–1671* (1899), pp. 240–241; vol. 57, *Hurons, Iroquois, Ottawas 1672–1673* (1899), p. 318; vol. 58, *Ottawas, Lower Canada, Iroquois 1672–1674* (1899), pp. 272–289; vol. 60, *Lower Canada, Illinois, Iroquois, Ottawas: 1675–1677* (1900), pp. 200–207.

Achiel Peelman, OMI

Andrew of Perugia (c. 1270–c. 1329), Franciscan missionary and bishop in China. Andrew and six other Franciscans were elected by Pope Clement V to be consecrated as bishops and sent to China. They left Italy in 1307 and arrived between 1309 and 1313 at Khanbalik (Beijing). As directed by Clement, Andrew and his companions consecrated *John of Montecorvino, OFM, archbishop and patriarch of the entire Orient, and they served in China as assistant bishops. Andrew served first in Khanbalik and later moved to Zaitun (present-day Quanzhou) on the southeast coast of Fukien (Fujian) Province, where he built a monastery and became full bishop shortly after 1322. A gravestone containing his name was found during World War II. One of his letters, written in 1226 to the Franciscan guardian of Perugia, has been preserved.

BIBLIOGRAPHY *Sinica Franciscana,* vol. 1, Anastasius van den Wyngaert, ed. (1929), pp. 369–377; Folker E. Reichert, *Begegnungen mit China: Die Entdeckung Ostasiens im Mittelalter* (1992), pp. 77–79.

Arnulf Camps, OFM

Andrews, Charles Freer (1871–1940), Anglican educational missionary and freelance Christian worker in India. Born in Newcastle-upon-Tyne, in northeast England, Andrews was educated in Birmingham and at Cambridge University. He was ordained an Anglican deacon in 1896 and priest in 1897. In 1904, after three years of urban mission work in London and four years of teaching in Cambridge, he began a decade of teaching at St. Stephen's College, Delhi, as a missionary with the Society for the Propagation of the Gospel. In these years he was moderately high church in theology and passionately anticapitalist in economic politics. For a short time he joined S. E. Stokes and Sundar *Singh in a quasi-Franciscan missionary fellowship, but the experiment did not last. In 1912 Andrews met the Bengali poet Rabindranath Tagore in London, and two years later he resigned his teaching post and joined Tagore in his ashram. In 1914 he also began an association with Mohandas K. Gandhi which was to last for the remainder of his life. He was now at the service of India, especially India's poor, traveling, lecturing, writing, and lobbying on their behalf wherever they happened to be as a result of indentured labor policies, most notably in Fiji and in South Africa. He was always a ready and lucid writer, and his books include an autobiography, *What I Owe to Christ* (1932), several volumes on Indian social and religious topics, and studies of Gandhi and Sundar Singh. In a period when Europeans and Indians often found personal relationships difficult, Andrews made many Indian friends. Early in his career he had been one of those who succeeded in having S. K. Rudra appointed principal of St. Stephen's College, and throughout his career he was a warm supporter of the Indian national movement. His friendships with Gandhi and Tagore were close and mutual. Gandhi, in particular, often cited Andrews as a model Christian missionary who never proselytized but was always prepared to serve the people of India. Andrews's theology began in the style of "high church pietism" with a strong social component, though in later years he moved more in a Quaker direction and his writing became more devotional in tone. He was also influenced in the 1930s by

Frank Buchman's Oxford Group Movement. In 1936 he resumed his Anglican ministry. He died in Calcutta.

BIBLIOGRAPHY Benarsidas Chaturvedi and Marjorie Sykes, *Charles Freer Andrews: A Narrative* (1949); Daniel O'Connor, *The Testimony of C. F. Andrews* (1974) and *Gospel, Raj, and Swaraj: The Missionary Years of C. F. Andrews 1910–1914* (1990); Eric J. Sharpe, "C. F. Andrews," in Gerald H. Anderson et al., eds., *Mission Legacies* (1994), pp. 316–323; Hugh Tinker, *The Ordeal of Love: C. F. Andrews and India* (1980).

Eric J. Sharpe

Andrews, Lorrin (1795–1868), American missionary and civic leader in Hawaii. Educated at Jefferson College, Canonsburg, Pennsylvania, and at Princeton Theological Seminary (graduated 1825), in 1827 Andrews married Mary Ann Wilson, was ordained, and sailed for Hawaii under the American Board of Commissioners for Foreign Missions (ABCFM). He was instrumental in founding Lahainaluna Seminary in 1831 and then served as its principal and teacher, training Hawaiians for leadership in church, missionary, and civic affairs. In 1834 he published the first periodical in Hawaiian.

In 1842 Andrews resigned from the ABCFM to protest its refusal to take a strong public stand against slavery. He then managed the printing office and bindery at Lahainaluna and opened a school for his own and other children. In 1845 he was appointed a judge of the Court of Oahu, which dealt with cases involving foreigners, and in 1846 he was made secretary of the Privy Council, keeping records in both English and Hawaiian. In 1851 he became the first associate justice of the Hawaiian Supreme Court and in 1855 a judge of probate and divorce cases. Andrews compiled a Hawaiian vocabulary, a grammar, and a Hawaiian dictionary defining some 17,000 words. He translated twelve textbooks, mostly in practical fields, a catechism, Bible studies, and, with William *Richards, six books of the Bible, as well as two ancient Hawaiian *meles* in meter. He died in Honolulu.

BIBLIOGRAPHY Rufus Anderson, *The Hawaiian Islands...* (1865), pp. 262–268. The Rev. and Mrs. O. H. Gulick, *The Pilgrims of Hawaii* (1918); *Missionary Album* (1969), pp. 24–27; *Missionary Herald* 65: 42–43.

David M. Stowe

Andrianaivoravelona, Josefa (1835–1897), one of the first Malagasy ministers of the Reformed Church of Madagascar. Andrianaivoravelona was born into a non-Christian noble family of the central part of Madagascar. After his baptism in 1857, he dropped his original name Andriantseheno and adopted Andrianaivoravelona as more in keeping with his Christian faith. Thereafter he applied all his energy to the conversion of his people, hiding in various places because of religious persecution by the queen, Ranavalona I, who was hostile to Christianity and foreign influence. While in southern Madagascar he founded the first church of Fianarantsoa. On his return to Antananarivo, the capital, he was able to work as a self-educated preacher until the persecution ended in 1861, thanks to the secret protection of the queen's son and the prime minister. He was elected as pastor in 1866 by the congregation of Ampamarinana, thus becoming the first native minister of the church and its dependent communities. When the new queen, Ranavalona II, converted to Christianity, he also became one of the pastors of the palace church in 1869, remaining pastor of the two churches until 1897. In spite of his age and heavy pastoral and family responsibilities, Andrianaivoravelona pursued his studies brilliantly in the London Missionary Society College at Antananarivo from 1869 to 1873. He was a prolific hymn writer, an indefatigable and immensely popular preacher, and a member of the committee for the revision of the Bible from 1873 to 1887. He drew praise from fellow countrymen and foreign missionaries alike, although some of the latter were distrustful of his independent spirit. Such a formidable character attracted the suspicion of the French government, so that he was sent into exile to the island of Réunion with the last queen, Ranavalona III. There he died.

BIBLIOGRAPHY Josefa Andrianaivoravelona's hymns appear in Malagasy hymnbooks. Joseph Andrianaivoravelona, "Andrianaivoravelona," in *Mpanolotsaina* 34, nos. 139–142 (1937). Ratovonarivo, *Tantaran'ny Fiangonana Ambonin'Ampamarinana* (History of the Ampamarinana church) (1974). See also Françoise Raison-Jourde, *Bible et pouvoir à Madagascar au XIXe siècle* (1991). The most extended biographical note is in Ravelojaona, ed., *Firaketana* (Malagasy encyclopedic dictionary) (1937).

Yvette Ranjeva Rabetafika

Anselm (c. 1033–1109), archbishop of Canterbury and outstanding theologian. Born into an Italian family of means in Aosta, Lombard, Anselm left for France in 1056 and entered the monastic school of Bec in Normandy during 1059. By 1060 he had declared his monastic vows; in 1063 he followed Lanfranc as prior; by 1078 he was abbot. Anselm exemplified "faith seeking understanding" through a deep spirituality and a keen intellect. His works have been read as both supporting and denying apologetics. While his *Proslogium* develops the ontological argument for God's existence as well as it has ever been presented, the entire treatise is written from within a community of prayerful contemplation. The *Cur Deus Homo?* is a contextualization masterpiece. It uses the Frankish legal system of wergild, which calculated how much one should pay for different deeds that wounded the honor of people at various status levels in society, to explain how the anger of a righteous and just God might be appeased. Humanity must pay, but only God possesses enough to make the payment.

Anselm's battles with the English kings, William and Henry I, over the homage an archbishop should give a ruler, the investiture of bishops, and the control of church lands and income, kept the English church from becoming an appendage of the state. This was no small victory for mission.

BIBLIOGRAPHY Pierre Crapillet, *Le "Cur Deus Homo" d'Anselme* (1984); Eadmer, *The Life of St. Anselm: Archbishop of Canterbury,*

Richard W. Southern, ed. and tr. (1962); K. M. Staley, *"Exemplum Meditandi*: Anselm's Model of Christian Learning," in *Faith Seeking Understanding: Learning and the Catholic Tradition,* George Berthold, ed. (1991).

Frederick W. Norris

Ansgar (*or* Anskar) (c. 801-865), Apostle of Scandinavia. Ansgar was born in Amiens (Picardy, France) and entered the Benedictine monastery of Corbie as a child, taking his vows at the age of 14. In 826 Harald Klak, King of Denmark, was baptized, and Ansgar was sent by papal authority to Denmark as royal chaplain and missionary. Between 829 and 831 Ansgar worked in Sweden, on the island of Björkö, an important trading center close to present-day Stockholm, and was well received by King Björn. This mission, however, did not long survive his departure. Returning to Rome, he was appointed bishop of Hamburg, with responsibility for missionary work in Scandinavia, in which connection he visited Denmark frequently. At this time the politics of northern Europe were in turmoil. In 847 the bishopric of Hamburg was temporarily shut down due to war, but it was reestablished the following year, this time combined with Bremen. Ansgar, now archbishop, was able to establish churches in Denmark (Schlesvig, Ribe), and in 852 he again visited Sweden (Björkö), recruiting priests and reestablishing the mission. In terms of numbers of conversions, Ansgar's mission was never greatly successful, but he laid foundations on which others were able to build. A chapel dedicated to his memory was consecrated on the island of Björkö by archbishop Nathan *Söderblom in 1930. Ansgar died in Bremen and was buried in his cathedral.

BIBLIOGRAPHY There are no substantial Ansgar studies in English. The traditional Latin hagiography, Rimbert's *Vita Ansgarii* (Life of Ansgar), was published in Germany in 1884, in a Danish translation (5th ed.) in 1926, and in Swedish (2d ed.) in 1930. See also Hal Koch, in *Nordisk Teologisk Uppslagsbok,* vol. 1 (1952), cols. 110-113, and most recently, C. F. Hallencreutz, *Ansgar: visionär och politiker* (Ansgar: visionary and politician) (1980).

Eric J. Sharpe

Anthing, F(rederik) L(odewijk) (1818-1883), Dutch evangelist and advocate of indigenous leadership in Indonesia. Born in Batavia (Jakarta) of a Dutch Lutheran father and a mother of German descent, and educated in the Netherlands, Anthing was a member and later vice-president of the supreme court of the Dutch East Indies in Batavia. About 1855 he began evangelizing among the indigenous population of Batavia and its surroundings. He believed that the nations of the Indies could "only be won for Christ by workers from those nations." Consequently he trained and sent Christian workers who traveled the whole of Java, teaching them to use Javanese cultural and religious elements as a means for spreading the gospel. In this way he succeeded in establishing a number of small congregations and inspiring a "Javanese Christianity." Initially he cooperated with the missionary societies, which employed Europeans almost exclusively, persuading them to establish the Depok Seminary, the first mission-run training school for Indonesian evangelists (1878-1926). But he found their methods still too Western and broke off relations. When he had spent his whole fortune in the mission and had not received any help from Holland, he turned to the Hersteld Apostolische Zendingskerk (Restored Apostolic Mission Church), which ordained him Apostle for the East Indies (1879). After his death, some of his followers continued to constitute the Apostolic Church, which in the twentieth century split into several groups. For the most part, they were gradually absorbed by Dutch mission bodies working in Java.

BIBLIOGRAPHY A. J. Bliek, *Mr. L. F.* [sic] *Anthing* (1938); S. Coolsma, *De Zendingseeuw voor Nederlandsch Oost-Indie* (1901); Th. van den End, *De Nederlandsche Zendingsvereeniging in West-Java, 1858-1963: Een bronnenpublicatie* (1991); Sutarman S. Partonadi, *Sadrach's Community and Its Contextual Roots: A Nineteenth-Century Javanese Expression of Christianity* (1990).

Th. van den End

Anzer, Johann Baptist (von) (1851-1903), Catholic missionary and bishop in China. Born in Weinrieth, near Regensburg, Germany, Anzer was the fourth student to join a new mission house at Steyl, Holland, which was later to become the Society of the Divine Word (SVD). He was ordained in 1876 and, together with Joseph *Freinademetz, left for China in 1879; they were the first SVD missionaries. In 1882 Anzer became pro-vicar of South Shantung (Shandong), and in 1886 vicar apostolic of the new vicariate. In 1882 he began with 158 Catholics; when he died, after 21 years of tireless activity, the extensive territory had 26,000 baptized Catholics and 40,000 catechumens, numerous institutions (seminaries, schools, orphanages, homes for the elderly, hospitals), an impressive number of beautiful churches, and many small chapels. Anzer made his residence in the historically important city of Yenchowfu (Yanzhou), capital of South Shantung and stronghold of opposition to Christianity. In 1884 he opened a school for catechists and a seminary. In 1889 he ordained the first two Chinese priests. He played an important part in the question of the German protectorate, for which he was both praised and criticized. While his position in connection with the "reparation churches" after the murder of missionaries Franz Nies and Richard Henle and later the occupation of Kiaochow by Germany is questionable, it is quite clear that he was not motivated by political interests. He always had the good of the mission and the safety of the missionaries at heart.

Anzer was one of the most brilliant missionary organizers and strategists of the time. He placed great emphasis on the Holy Spirit, to whom he dedicated the two large churches in Yenchowfu and Tsining (Jining) and in 1892 his whole mission. Rather unusual for that time, he obtained permission from Pope Leo XIII to portray the Holy Spirit in human form. As a result of his many journeys, his correspondence, and his widely disseminated New Year's greetings, he made a substantial contribution to the spread of mission awareness in Germany and the United States. He died of a heart attack while on a visit to Rome.

BIBLIOGRAPHY "Bischof Johann Bapt. von Anzer," *Steyler Missions-Bote* 31 (1903/1904): 60–62, 76–78, 88–91, 105–108; H. Gründer, *Christliche Mission und deutscher Imperialismus. Eine politische Geschichte ihrer Beziehungen während der Kolonialzeit (1884–1914) unter besonderer Berücksichtigung Afrikas und Chinas* (1832); R. Hartwich, *Steyler Missionare in China,* vol. 1, *Missionarische Erschliessung Südshantungs, 1879–1903* (1983); P. Horbach, *Bischof v. Anzers China-Mission in ihren Beziehungen zur Politik* (1901); K. J. Rivinius, *Weltlicher Schutz und Mission*(1987); "Die im Jahre 1903 verstorbenen Missionsbischöfe," *Die katholischen Missionen* (1903/1904): 265–267.

Karl Müller, SVD

Ao, Longri (Longritangchetba) (1906–1981), indigenous Nagaland missionary, prophet, and peacemaker. Longri Ao was born and buried in Changki village, Mokokchung district, Nagaland, India. He was educated through the level of the Serampore Licentiate in theology. He married Subokyimia in 1932, taught at the Bible school in Jorat, Assam, from 1934 to 1950, and in 1950 was appointed by the Council of Baptist Churches in Northeast India as missionary to the Konyak Naga people. During his 17 years in that position (1950–1967) the Konyak church grew from 1,100 members to more than 12,000. From 1967 to 1980 he served as executive secretary of the Nagaland Baptist Church Council. During those years he sought to make the private and public life of the largely Christian Nagaland state a testimony to the power of Christ. He is best remembered for his contributions to the peace movement in Nagaland. He sought to convince those rebelling against the government of India to be reconciled to a position within that nation, and to persuade the government to act justly in its relationships with the Naga people. He was responsible for establishing the controversial Peace Mission, and later, of the Nagaland Peace Council (NPC), of which he was president from 1974 until his death. Under his leadership, the NPC was largely responsible for bringing an end to the major hostilities through the Shillong Accord of 1975.

BIBLIOGRAPHY The most comprehensive account of Longri Ao's life and work is found in O. M. Rao, *Longri Ao: A Biography* (1986). His life and ministry prior to 1970 is described in Richard G. Beers, *Walk the Distant Hills: The Story of Longri Ao* (1969). Reports of Longri Ao's activities can be found in the annual reports of the Council of Baptist Churches in Northeast India after 1950, and in the annual reports of the Nagaland Baptist Church Council from 1967 to 1981.

Frederick S. Downs

Appasamy, Aiyadurai Jesudasen (1891–1976), Indian Christian theologian. Appasamy was born in a Christian family in Palayamkottai, in the district of Tirunelveli (formerly Tinnevelly), one of the first and greatest centers of Protestant Christianity in the extreme south of India. His intellectual gifts were early recognized and in 1915 he went abroad for his theological studies, first to Hartford, Connecticut, then to Oxford, and finally for a time to Marburg. On his return in 1923 he was employed by the Christian Literature Society in Madras to conduct research and writing. There he produced his most influential works, *Christianity as Bhakti Marga* (1927) and *What Is Moksha?* (1931). In 1932 he moved to Calcutta to teach at Bishop's College, but in 1936 he returned to his birthplace to serve the church there as an archdeacon, working for the theological education of schoolteachers and organizing evangelistic campaigns, prayer meetings, and revivals. For 18 years he was a member of the Joint Committee for Church Union in South India. His advocacy of union was shown in his book *Church Union: An Indian View* (1930). In 1950, three years after the formation of the Church of South India, he was consecrated as bishop of Coimbatore, where he stayed until his retirement in 1959.

Continuing his writing throughout his life, Appasamy's great concern was always to express Christian faith in a way that would be congenial to India. He believed that to do this he needed to link Christianity to the *bhakti,* or devotional tradition, of which the chief exponent was Ramanuja. He presented the Christian life as one of loving devotion to God in Christ. The goal is faith-union with Christ, which is not absorption into the divine, as Hindu *advaita* philosophy would teach, but a loving personal union. He rejected ideas of metaphysical unity between God and Christ, as Chalcedon had taught, in favor of an eternal conformity of wills and union of love.

BIBLIOGRAPHY A. J. Appasamy, *A Bishop's Story* (1969); Robin H. S. Boyd, *An Introduction to Indian Christian Theology* (1969), ch. 7.

Charles W. Forman

Appenzeller, Henry Gerhard (1858–1902), pioneer Methodist missionary to Korea. Born in Souderton, Pennsylvania, Appenzeller graduated from Franklin and Marshall College, Lancaster, Pennsylvania, in 1882 and from Drew Theological Seminary, Madison, New Jersey, in 1885. After ordination he sailed to Korea with his wife, Ella, landing with Presbyterian pioneer missionary Horace G. *Underwood at Inchon on Easter day, April 5, 1885. Overt evangelistic missionary activity was forbidden by the Korean government at that time, so Appenzeller pursued educational work, winning royal approval in 1887 for Paichai Hakdang, a school for young men. Later that year public worship became possible, and he founded Chong Dong First Methodist Church (begun as Bethel Chapel), with Korean leadership and with Appenzeller as pastor until his death.

Appenzeller explored mission opportunities in other regions of Korea but concentrated upon a variety of projects in Seoul, beginning with the translation of the Bible into Korean, which he pursued as an ecumenical effort with other Protestant groups. He opened a bookstore in 1894, wrote many religious tracts, edited the *Korean Repository* and *Korea Review* to introduce Korea internationally, and was active in the Korea branch of the Royal Asiatic Society. At Paichai school he began the Trilingual Press, which published the first Korean-language Christian newspaper, the *Korean Christian Advocate,* and an organ of the Korean independence movement, the *Independent.* Especially concerned about training Korean church leaders, he fostered the development of theological education based upon a liberal arts tradition. While his main contributions were made through establishing institutions and training leaders, his character and views also helped shape Korean Methodism, with its evangelical spirit, fidelity to the Bible, and concern for social justice and Korean independence. Although he began with a firm confidence in the virtues of American culture and the hope of building a Westernized Christian Korea, Appenzeller later acknowledged values in Korean culture and religion. He died at age 44 when the vessel taking him to a Bible translation meeting in Mokpo sank off the western coast of Korea.

BIBLIOGRAPHY Articles by Appenzeller are in such publications as *Independent* (1885–1902), *Korean Mission Field* (vols. 2–37), *Korean Repository* (vols. 1–5), and *Methodist Review* (1885–1902). An early biography with useful information is William T. Griffis, *Henry G. Appenzeller: A Modern Pioneer in Korea* (1912). Everett N. Hunt, Jr., *Protestant Pioneers in Korea* (1980); Edward W. Poitras, "The Legacy of Henry G. Appenzeller," *IBMR* 18 (1994): 177–180. Appenzeller's personal papers are in the library of Union Theological Seminary, New York. The best bibliography is in Daniel M. Davies, *The Life and Thought of Henry Gerhard Appenzeller (1858–1902), Missionary to Korea* (1988).

Edward Poitras

Aquinas, Thomas. *See* Thomas Aquinas.

Arbousset, (Jean) Thomas (1810–1877), French Protestant pioneer missionary in Lesotho and church leader in Tahiti. Born in Pignan, France, of Huguenot stock, Arbousset decided to become a missionary at the age of 15. Educated at Mazéres by the Rev. André Gachon, an admirer of Moravian missions, he entered the Paris Evangelical Missionary Society (PEMS) School of Missions in 1829. He was ordained to the ministry in 1832 and sailed for southern Africa with Eugène *Casalis and Constant Gosselin. Looking for a mission field, the missionaries found King *Moshoeshoe of Lesotho prepared to receive them. They hoped he would become a Christian and bring his people with him to the gospel and to civilization. Arbousset furthered the so-called native agency: he set up a home missionary society in Lesotho in 1848, consisting of companies of Christian men who were responsible for the itinerant evangelization of the districts, and who reported to the mission center at Morija. Arbousset preceded Livingstone in combining mission with exploration; his reports received an award from the Geographical Society of Paris. In 1837 he married Katherine Rogers, of Cape Town. They had nine children. The family returned to France in 1860, but Katherine Arbousset drowned during the journey. Arbousset was sent in 1863 to Tahiti, a new field assigned to the PEMS in the wake of the French occupation. The task was to save the national Protestant church in Tahiti from harassment by the French administration and aggressive proselytism by Catholic missionaries. Arbousset stayed at Papeete, Tahiti, as head of the main congregation, with Queen Pomare as his parishioner. He succeeded in restoring trust among Protestants in Tahiti and returned to France in 1865. He accepted the call of the Reformed congregation at Saint Sauvant, near Poitiers, where he served as pastor until his death. His evangelical ministry was a blessing for the parish but a thorn in the flesh of the liberal Reformed consistory at Lusignan.

BIBLIOGRAPHY Thomas Arbousset and François Daumas, *Narrative of an Exploratory Tour to the North-East of the Colony of the Cape of Good Hope* (1846, 1852, 1968); Thomas Arbousset, *Missionary Excursion into the Blue Mountains: Being an account of King Moshoeshoe's Expedition from Thaba-Bosiu to the Sources of the Malibamatso River in the Year 1840,* David Ambrose and Albert Brutsch, trs. and eds. (1991); Henri Clavier, *Thomas Arbousset: Recherche historique sur son milieu, sa personnalité, son oeuvre, parallèle avec Livingstone* (1965; abridged version, *Thomas Arbousset pionnier,* 1963).

Marc R. Spindler

Archbell, James (1798–1866), English Methodist missionary and politician in southern Africa. Born in Tadcaster, Yorkshire, England, Archbell arrived in 1819 at the Cape Colony with his new wife, Elizabeth (Haigh), and began work north of the Orange River among the Nama people. In 1824 he went to the Rolong, a Tswana people and in 1833 he negotiated with the Sotho king, *Moshoeshoe, for land for the then dispossessed Rolong. He published a full grammar of Tswana based on the model of grammatical structure used by W. B. *Boyce for Xhosa; earlier he had published a hymnbook and prayer book in Tswana. In 1836 he persuaded the Rolong to help the Boers of the Great Trek and was pastor to the Trekkers while they remained in the area. After a furlough he worked for three years among the Xhosa before moving to Natal in 1841. There he again ministered to the Trekkers while opening the first Methodist churches in Natal.

In 1848 Archbell resigned from the ministry. In his subsequent career as a journalist and politician in Natal, he was a leader in the cause of white supremacy, repeatedly expressing distaste for African people and bitter opposition to all so-called negrophile missionaries like John *Philip.

BIBLIOGRAPHY J. du Plessis, *A History of Christian Missions in South Africa* (1911, 1965); L. A. Hewson, *An Introduction to South African Methodists* (1951); A. E. Walker, *The Great Trek* (1931, 1965).

Andrew C. Ross

Arias, Mortimer (1924–), Uruguayan Methodist bishop in Bolivia. Arias graduated from Union Theological Seminary, Buenos Aires (1956); received a doctor of ministry degree at Perkins School of Theology, Southern Methodist University, Dallas (1977); and was awarded an honorary doctorate from DePauw University, Greencastle, Indiana (1985). As Methodist bishop of Bolivia, he developed a public ministry articulated in his "Manifesto to the Nation" (1970) and in "Bolivian Theses on Evangelization in Latin America Today" (1974). He described evangelism as biblical, holistic, liberating, and conscientizing. His prophetic ministry in Bolivia led to repression, jail, and exile, but also to renewal in the life of the church, including the transfer of responsibility for leadership to the Indian constituency. As a member of the Commission on World Mission and Evangelism of the World Council of Churches (WCC), Arias was fully involved in the world missiological debate. He attended the Lausanne Congress on World Evangelization in 1974, and he was a speaker at the Nairobi (1975) assembly of WCC on the theme "That the World May Believe." He served as professor of evangelism at Claremont (California) School of Theology (1981–1987) and at Iliff School of Theology in Denver (1989–1991), while also serving as president of the Latin America Biblical Seminary in San José, Costa Rica (1986–1989). Now retired, he is pastor emeritus in Uruguay.

BIBLIOGRAPHY Mortimer Arias, *Jesús y nosotros* (1960), *Evangelización y revolución en América Latina* (1967), *Salvación es liberación* (1973), *The Cry of My People* (1980), *Announcing the Reign of God* (1984), *Evangelización hoy en Mesoamérica* (1987), *The Great Commission* (1992), and *La Gran Comisión* (1994). An autobiographical article, "My Pilgrimage in Mission," was published in *IBMR* 16 (1992): 28–32.

Emilio Castro

Armstrong, Annie Walker (1850–1938), Southern Baptist women's missionary leader. Born in Baltimore, Maryland, Armstrong grew up in the city's Seventh Baptist Church. Unlike many women of her day, Armstrong was independent, opinionated, and outspoken, and she had extraordinary organizational skills. An interdenominational women's missionary prayer group that began in Baltimore in 1867 inspired the formation of the Maryland Baptist Woman's Mission to Women three years later. Armstrong was particularly involved in the latter. The appointment of the first single women missionaries by the Southern Baptist Foreign Mission Board in 1872 inspired Baptist women throughout the South to organize local societies for the support of missions. When Lottie *Moon in 1887 wrote from China proposing that Southern Baptist women unite in a week of prayer and giving for foreign missions, Armstrong became the principal promoter. The following year, at Richmond, Virginia, she led in founding the Woman's Missionary Union (WMU) as an auxiliary to the Southern Baptist Churches and was chosen to be the organization's first executive. She outlined the role of WMU as threefold: missionary education of women and children, praying, and raising money. She was influential in initiating the now well-known Lottie Moon Christmas Offering for missions among Southern Baptists. Armstrong resigned her position in 1906, having served for 16 years (and without salary). She remained unmarried throughout her life.

BIBLIOGRAPHY Elizabeth Marshall Evans, *Annie Armstrong* (1963); Bobbie Sorrill, *Annie Armstrong: Dreamer in Action* (1984); Ruth Tucker, *Guardians of the Great Commission* (1988).

Alan Neely

Armstrong, Hannah Maria (Norris) (1842–1919), Canadian Maritime Baptist missionary in Burma and India. Born in Nova Scotia and educated as a teacher, Hannah Norris (known within her family circle as Maria), was a talented language learner who worked with Micmac Indians before applying to Maritime Baptists to serve in Siam. Lacking funds, officers of the mission board urged her to appeal directly to her "sisters" in the churches for support. Within ten weeks in the summer of 1870, she organized thirty-three Woman's Mission Aid Societies, the first such Baptist groups, and three weeks later she sailed for Burma to work in conjunction with American Baptists. Rapidly acquiring several Karen languages, she taught in schools and made evangelistic tours.

Marrying William F. *Armstrong shortly after his arrival in 1874, she served with him in Burma and later among the Telugus in India until forced by ill health to return home in 1880. Appointed again to Burma in 1884, this time by American Baptists, she combined major responsibilities in schools, orphanages, and church ministry with care for her own three children. As the only woman to speak at plenary sessions of the 1888 Centenary Conference on Protestant Missions in London, she described Christian witness among the Karens. Though in poor health, she supervised her children's education in England and Canada while translating tracts, searching out "redemptive analogies" in Karen and Telugu folklore, and writing or translating poetry and hymns in these languages. After attending some classes at Wilbert W. White's Bible Teachers Training School in Montclair, New Jersey (later moved to New York City), she determined to set up a similar school in Rangoon where educated Hindus, Buddhists, and Muslims could study the Bible in English. Distrusting the degree of control over the school planned by White, her Baptist missionary colleagues withdrew their support, so she turned for help to friends in other denominations on three continents. Determined to make the school self-supporting, she tried to develop first a teak, then a cotton, plantation to supplement donations. Meanwhile she carried on her work in children's schools, orphanages, and evangelistic efforts and established a reading room and adult Bible classes in Rangoon (intended as forerunners for her school). But after hopes for assistance from her two sons dwindled and her husband sickened and died, she returned to Canada in 1918. She keenly anticipated a part in jubilee celebrations of the United Baptist Woman's Missionary Union (UBWMU), whose fledgling societies she had founded in 1870, but death intervened. Armstrong is fondly remembered as "Our Pioneer," whose independent spirit still serves as a rallying point for Baptist women of the Atlantic Provinces. In 1985 the UBWMU established at Acadia Divinity College the Hannah Maria Norris Chair of Christian Missions and Social Issues.

BIBLIOGRAPHY Armstrong edited *Tamil Hymns... Telugu and Hindustani... Churches in Burma* (1899) and translated "Karen Folk-Lore, an Unwritten Bible" (1913). Reports and articles by Armstrong appear in issues of *Tidings* (1870–1918), *Canadian Missionary Link* (1878–1881), and *Missionary Review of the World* 13, no. 4 (1890): 248–254 and 17, no. 2 (1894): 99–102. Obituaries in *The News* (American Baptist Mission Press, Rangoon) 32, no. 10 (1918): 1–2 and *Canadian Missionary Link* 35, no. 3 (1919): 33–35.

H. Miriam Ross

Armstrong, Philip E. (1919–1981), executive secretary, Far Eastern Gospel Crusade (FEGC). Born in Bronson, Michigan, Armstrong was ordained to the Baptist ministry in 1943 after graduating from Moody Bible Institute, Chicago. As a freshman at Saint Olaf College, Minnesota, he was drafted for military service and sent to the Philippines, where he joined others in organizing "G.I. Gospel Hour" evangelistic meetings. In Manila in 1945, he and his companions prayed for the establishment of the Far Eastern Bible Institute and Seminary (launched in 1947). As Christian servicemen moved on to occupied Japan, they envisioned a G.I. Gospel Crusade for the evangelization of Japan. In 1947, the two visions merged in the founding of FEGC (known as SEND International since 1982), with Armstrong appointed U.S. home secretary in 1948 and then executive secretary in 1950. Under his leadership, the mission focused on the Philippines, Japan, and Taiwan, in subsequent years adding Alaska, Europe, and the Commonwealth of Independent States. Armstrong served as president of the Interdenominational Foreign Mission Association and played a formative role in the early years of *Evangelical Missions Quarterly* (founded in 1964). He resigned his FEGC post in 1980 but continued to serve the mission in an advisory capacity. He died in a plane crash on mission business in Alaska.

BIBLIOGRAPHY Edwin L. Frizen, Jr., "A Study of Candidate Procedures as Followed by the Far Eastern Gospel Crusade" (M.A. thesis, Columbia Graduate School of Bible and Missions, 1954). Biographical material and a selection of Armstrong's writings may be found in a SEND International memorial publication, *With My Heart There* (1984). Personal papers are housed at the Billy Graham Center, Wheaton, Ill.

Robert T. Coote

Armstrong, Richard (1805–1860), American missionary and civic leader in Hawaii. Armstrong graduated from Dickinson College, Carlisle, Pennsylvania, in 1827 and from Princeton Theological Seminary in 1831. In 1831 he also married Clarissa Chapman, was ordained, and sailed to Hawaii under the American Board of Commissioners for Foreign Missions. In 1833 the Armstrongs shared in an effort to found a mission on Nukuhiwa in the Marquesas Islands, but native hostility and unresponsiveness led to withdrawal in 1834. After pastorates at Haiku and Wailuku, Maui, in 1840 Armstrong was called to Kawaiahao Church, Honolulu, where he also shared responsibility for the mission dispensary. Always deeply interested in education and other public issues, he resigned from the mission in 1848 to accept the position of Minister of Public Instruction offered by King Kamehameha III. He served in that capacity for 12 years, presiding over the creation of a national system of education. A system of English schools was developed at the urging of parents. He died at age 55 after falling from his horse while touring island schools. His work in translation included Wayland's *Moral Philosophy*, and he wrote a tract on popery. In 1852 he received an honorary D.D. from Washington College (later Washington and Lee University). One of his ten sons was General Samuel Chapman Armstrong, founder of Hampton Institute.

BIBLIOGRAPHY *Missionary Album* (1969), pp. 30–33; *Missionary Herald* 57 (1861): 12–15. A manuscript memoir by Gen. S. C. Armstrong is in the Congregational History archives at the Pacific School of Religion, Berkeley, Calif.

David M. Stowe

Armstrong, William Frederick (1849–1918), Canadian Maritime Baptist missionary in Burma and India. Born in Nova Scotia, Armstrong studied at Acadia College and Newton Theological Institute before leaving for Burma (now Myanmar) in 1873 as an ordained missionary of the Maritime Baptist Convention. After marrying Hannah Maria Norris (see Hannah Maria *Armstrong) in Rangoon, he served with her in Burma, then among the Telugus in India, where Maritime Baptists established an independent mission in 1875. Returning to Canada for health reasons in 1880, the Armstrongs severed relations with the Maritime Board, and in 1884 they joined the American Baptist Missionary Union to work among the Tamil and Telugu immigrants in Moulmein and Rangoon. After reporting on this work in 1888 at the Centenary Conference on Protestant Missions in London, they assisted A. J. *Gordon and A. T. *Pierson at mission conferences in Scotland. As evangelist, educator, and sometime interim pastor of Immanuel Church and of the English Baptist Church in Rangoon, Armstrong was noted for his diplomacy and tact; his advocacy for Tamils, Telugus, and Anglo-Indians; and his skills in reasoned presentation of the Christian faith during formal public debates with learned Muslims and Hindus. He was often named as representative to denominational, interdenominational, and interfaith commissions. Acadia University awarded him an honorary D.D. in 1910. Though partially paralyzed and totally blind by 1916, he dictated for publication a long treatise entitled *Thoughts for Thoughtful Men* and shorter tracts directed toward educated Muslims. He died in Burma.

BIBLIOGRAPHY Reports and articles by Armstrong appear in issues of *The Messenger and Visitor* (1872–1881), *Canadian Missionary Link* (1879–1880), *The Christian* (1888): 725 and 2168 and (1911): 13, *Missions* 1, no. 3 (1910): 152–158, *The Baptist Missionary Magazine* (1885–1903), and in reports of the Foreign Mission Board (Maritime) of the American Baptist Missionary Union. See also James Johnston, ed., *Report of the Centenary Conference on the Protestant Missions of the World* (1888) and *The News* (American Baptist Mission Press, Rangoon) 31, no. 6 (1918): 29–31 (obit.).

H. Miriam Ross

Arnot, Frederick Stanley (1858–1914), pioneer Plymouth Brethren missionary in central Africa. Arnot was born in Glasgow and brought up in a devout Scottish family, friends of David *Livingstone's wife and children. In 1874 he attended Livingstone's funeral in Westminster Abbey. Determined to continue Livingstone's work, he arrived in Africa in 1881 as an independent missionary connected with the Plymouth Brethren and proceeded north from Durban, eventually reaching Lealui, the capital of the area ruled by Lewanika, the paramount chief of the Lozi, in what is now Zambia. After two fruitless years he moved on to Angola and then to Garenganze, in the Katanga (now Shaba) district of Zaire, then unannexed by any European power. Ill health dogged him, and after seven years mostly on his own, he handed this work over to Dan *Crawford and others. He made several other major central African journeys, planning and helping to open new mission stations and bringing the South Africa General Mission into Northern Rhodesia (now Zambia), but he was forced by recurrent malaria to base himself in Johannesburg. Arnot had little education but nevertheless became a prolific though unexciting writer in the cause of missions. His great gift was to lead and inspire others; he was utterly dedicated to his understanding of the missionary calling. He was awarded a fellowship of the Royal Geographical Society for his journeys on the Zambezi-Congo watershed. He died in Johannesburg.

BIBLIOGRAPHY Frederick Stanley Arnot, *From Natal to the Upper Zambezi* (1883), *Garenganze, or Seven Years Pioneer Mission Work in Central Africa* (1889), and *Bihé and Garenganze, or Four Years Further Work and Travel in Central Africa* (1893). Arnot also edited an edition of David Livingstone's *Missionary Travels and Researches in South Africa* (1899). A popular biography dealing with Arnot's early years is Tony Lawman, *From the Hands of the Wicked* (1960), and a full biography is Ernest Baker, *The Life and Explorations of Frederick Stanley Arnot, F.R.G.S.* (1920) which largely reprints sections of Arnot's own writings. The only scholarly evaluation is by Robert Rotberg in his introduction to the 1969 reprint of *Garenganze.*

M. Louise Pirouet

Arriaga, Pablo José de (1564–1622), Jesuit missionary in Peru. Arriaga is famous for his work *Extirpación de la idolatría en el Perú* (On the extirpation of idolatry in Peru), written in 1621. Born in Spain, Arriaga arrived in Peru in 1585. After teaching rhetoric for three years, he was appointed rector of the Jesuit college of San Martín in Lima and later of the Jesuit college in Arequipa. He returned to Spain in 1601 for a brief period to conduct business of his order.

Arriaga is remembered principally as one of the official visitors assigned to investigate lapses into idolatry among the Indians. His work on that subject was the fruit of many trips throughout the Andes. In 1618 he oversaw the building of the House of Reclusion of Santa Cruz (a kind of detention home) in Lima for recalcitrant Indians who clung to the old ways. He was also instrumental in founding a school for the sons of Indian *caciques* (chiefs) in Lima in 1621. His minute description of Indian customs, rites, and idols is a valuable primary source. Charged with uprooting idolatry, Arriaga displayed little sympathy toward Indian beliefs. He died in a shipwreck near Cuba on his way back to Spain.

BIBLIOGRAPHY Pablo José de Arriaga, *Extirpación de la idolatría en el Perú,* in *Crónicas peruanas de interés indígena,* Francisco Esteve Barba, ed., vol. 209, *Biblioteca de Autores Españoles* (1968); Pierre Duviols, *La lutte contre les religions autochtones dans le Pérou colonial* (1971); Sabine MacCormick, *Religion in the Andes* (1991).

Jeffrey Klaiber, SJ

Arrupe, Pedro (1907-1991), general of the Society of Jesus through the critical post–Vatican II years. Arrupe's charismatic personality and strong emphasis on the synthesis of faith, justice, and inculturation greatly influenced the Jesuits and many other religious orders and congregations of the Catholic Church. Born in Bilbao, in Spain's Basque country, he first studied medicine and then in 1927 entered the Jesuit order. Because of anticlerical persecution in Spain, he did most of his priestly studies in other countries: Belgium, Holland, and the United States. Going to Japan as a missionary in 1938, he worked as a parish priest in Yamaguchi and later as master of novices near Hiroshima. He witnessed the atomic explosion in August 1945 and used his medical training to aid victims. In 1954 he was named superior of the Jesuits in Japan, with the title of provincial in 1958. In that capacity he made many trips to appeal for funds and became widely known.

In 1965 Arrupe was elected general of the Society of Jesus, the first general to be elected from outside Europe. His first task as general was to preside over the thirty-first general congregation of the Jesuits (1965–1966), which incorporated the ideals of Vatican II into the order. His worldwide perspective and concern for the Third World led him to create the Jesuit refugee service in 1980. His strong belief in the unity of faith and justice became the cornerstone of the thirty-second general congregation (1974–1975), which set the pace for many other religious orders.

In 1967 Arrupe was elected president of the union of superior generals of major orders, a post he held until 1981. His influence was felt in many important church assemblies, especially in Medellin (1968) and in the bishop's synod in Rome (1971). His most important contribution to missionary thought is his letter on inculturation (1978). In 1981 he suffered a cerebral hemorrhage and spent the last years of his life in the infirmary of the curia of the Society of Jesus in Rome.

BIBLIOGRAPHY Most of Arrupe's major addresses and letters have been published by the Institute of Jesuit Sources at Saint Louis University, Saint Louis, Missouri. Of special interest are *Challenge To Religious Life Today* (1979), *Justice and Faith Today* (1980), and *One Jesuit's Spiritual Journey: Autobiographical Conversations with Jean-Claude Dietsch, SJ* (1986). See also *Recollections and Reflections of Pedro Arrupe, SJ,* with an introduction by Vincent O'Keefe, SJ (1986).

Jeffrey Klaiber, SJ

Arseny of Konev (d. 1444 or 1447), Orthodox monk and missionary to northwest Russia. Arseny was born in Novgorod (northern Russia) and made his living as a coppersmith. In middle age he made a pilgrimage to Mount Athos in Greece, took monastic vows, and was sent back to found a monastery in northern Russia. While sailing on Lake Ladoga during a storm, he ran aground on Konev ("horses") Island, notorious for the pagan worship of its aboriginal people, the Korels. Each autumn they sacrificed a horse near a rock that looked like a horse's head. Arseny built a chapel, converted many of the local people, and put an end to pagan worship. He was canonized shortly after his death. His commemoration day is June 12 in the Julian calendar.

BIBLIOGRAPHY Taisia (Solopova), *Zhitiya Svyatykh* (The lives of Russian saints) (1983, 1991).

Evgeny S. Steiner

Arthington, Robert (1823–1900), missionary philanthropist. Arthington, the only son of Robert and Maria Arthington of Leeds, England, was brought up in the evangelical Quaker faith of his parents. His father, a prosperous brewer, abandoned his business after being persuaded of temperance principles in 1846. In 1838 the Leeds monthly meeting of the Society of Friends (who do not observe the sacraments) disowned his mother after she had been baptized, and a decade later, Robert, having also been baptized, left the Friends. For a time he maintained close links with the Christian (Plymouth) Brethren. Later he became associated with South Parade Baptist chapel. On his father's death in 1864, he inherited a fortune of £200,000.

Arthington's wealth was not used for local philanthropic causes or for his own comfort (he lived as a bachelor in austerity and became known as the Miser of Headingley). Rather, it was dedicated to the consuming passion for overseas missions that characterized his life from the 1850s to his death. The most frequent recipients of his largesse were the Baptist Missionary Society (BMS) and the London Missionary Society (LMS). As a premillennialist, Arthington believed in the urgent priority of pioneer evangelism, and much of his giving was conditional upon the willingness of missionary societies to embark on new projects in virgin territory. The BMS Congo mission and the Central Africa mission of the LMS, both begun in 1877, were the result of his initiative and money. The Arthington Aborigines Mission, established in 1889, pioneered work among the hill tribes of Mizoram, which laid the foundations for the extraordinary success of the Welsh Calvinistic Methodist Mission and the BMS in this part of northeast India.

Arthington left half of his residuary estate of approximately £1 million to the BMS and 40 percent to the LMS. He was perhaps the most remarkable British missionary philanthropist of the nineteenth century.

BIBLIOGRAPHY A. M. Chirgwin, *Arthington's Million* (n.d.); S. Southall, "An Uncommon Life," *Friend's Quarterly Examiner* 35 (1901): 277–286; Brian Stanley, "The Miser of Headingley," *Studies in Church History* 24 (1987): 371–382.

Brian Stanley

Arthur, John William (1881–1952), Church of Scotland missionary in Kenya. Arthur was born in Glasgow and studied medicine at the University of Glasgow (M.D., 1906) with a view to missionary service. He was appointed to a mission in Kenya that the Church of Scotland had taken over in 1901 from a group of Glasgow businessmen. The mission, centered in Kikuyu country, combined evangelistic, educational, medical, and commercial activities. Arthur arrived in 1907 to open the first hospital but entered with equal vigor into the evangelistic and educational fields. In 1912, at not much over 30, he replaced a senior missionary as head of the mission and led it through a period of notable growth that began with a movement of younger men toward church and school during World War I. Arthur was ordained in 1916 and moved his focus from medical to ministerial practice. He remained mission leader until 1937, when he retired from Kenya.

As leader, Arthur encouraged the development of local structures of church government. Often the dominant presence among Western missionaries in Kenya, and with unimpeachable evangelistic credentials, he also worked enthusiastically for inter-mission cooperation. The intermission Kikuyu Conference of 1913 seemed to promise something more, a union of the churches that were arising from the Protestant missions. But any such development was hindered by the furor caused when news was published of the interdenominational Communion service held at the conference. Cooperation in institutions was easier to achieve; Alliance High School, formed by an "alliance" of missions to be a beacon of light in the educational system, is an example.

Arthur worked happily with the colonial government, discreetly applying pressure from the inside for reform or redress of abuses. His characteristic response to a clumsy and heavy-handed government attempt to draft carriers for war service was to raise a volunteer force himself, with better conditions and higher efficiency. The government responded in 1922 by appointing him an adviser to the governor, and he attended the conference in London that declared the paramouncy of African interests for Kenya's colonial policy. In 1924 he joined the colony's Legislative Council as a representative of African interests.

Arthur's most traumatic experience came over a crisis concerning the practice of cliteridectomy for female initiation. Traditionally, the mission had used a variety of strategies to discourage, mitigate, or circumvent the practice. By 1929, however, a ferment was brewing. Arthur sought to stiffen the church's resistance to cliteridectomy and called for church sanctions against any Christian involved in the practice. This caused a Kikuyu reaction against the church; membership was halved and took a decade to recover. No longer recognized as voicing African interests, Arthur resigned from the Legislative Council. On his eventual return to Scotland, Arthur served as minister of Dunbog, Fife, from 1938 to 1948. He received his D.D. from St. Andrews University in 1944.

BIBLIOGRAPHY R. Macpherson, *The Presbyterian Church in Kenya* (1970); Jocelyn Murray, "The Kikuyu Female Circumcision Controversy" (Ph.D. diss., Univ. of California, Los Angeles, 1974).

Andrew F. Walls

Asbury, Francis (1745–1816), pioneer American Methodist bishop. Asbury was born near Birmingham, England, the son of an Anglican tenant farmer. At age 16, after limited formal schooling, and while apprenticed as a blacksmith, he experienced conversion and became a Methodist local preacher in Salisbury. In 1771 he responded to John *Wesley's plea for preachers to go to the American colonies to aid the fledgling work there. Upon arriving in New York he rejected for himself the life of a stationed pastor, choosing instead to travel widely as a lay preacher and evangelist. Of the original missionaries sent by Wesley before the Revolutionary War, only Asbury remained after the colonies won independence, thereby becoming Methodism's acknowledged leader in America.

To provide a ministry qualified to administer sacraments in the new nation, Wesley commissioned Thomas *Coke to ordain Asbury in 1784; he was named "general superintendent," along with Coke. Sensitive to local sentiment, Asbury sought and received election to that post by the organizing conference of Methodist preachers held in Baltimore, Maryland, in 1784. Later, against Wesley's advice, he called himself "bishop." He used his office to spur rapid mission outreach and church growth in the new United States and never returned to England. He modeled what became the normative pattern of Methodist ministry—the "circuit rider" on horseback who sought out converts even in the most remote settlements. Never married, he traveled almost incessantly for 45 years, covering an estimated 300,000 miles on horseback and preaching over 16,000 sermons. Crossing the Appalachian Mountains more than 60 times, he presided over 224 annual conferences. He was an early advocate of camp meetings as a means of evangelism. In 1780 he raised the first gifts for Methodist education in the United States and in 1784 laid foundations for the first Methodist college by establishing Ebenezer Academy (renamed Cokesbury College in 1787). In 1789 he started both the Methodist Publishing House and the *Arminian Magazine.*

Asbury's vision was for all Methodism to be missionary in purpose, with no distinction between mission and evangelism. His was an urgency to present the gospel to all persons, including Native Americans and African Americans. From a church of 13,740 members and 82 preachers in 1784, American Methodism grew under his leadership to include 214,235 members and 695 traveling preachers by 1816. He died during his travels in ministry at Spotsylvania, Virginia, and is buried in Baltimore, Maryland.

BIBLIOGRAPHY *The Journal and Letters of Francis Asbury* was compiled and published in three volumes by an editorial team led by Elmer T. Clark (1958). Narrative biographies include George G. Smith, *Life and Labors of Francis Asbury* (1898), Ezra S. Tipple, *Francis Asbury: The Prophet of the Long Road* (1916), Herbert Asbury, *A Methodist Saint: The Life of Bishop Asbury* (1927), William L. Duren, *Francis Asbury: Founder of American Methodism* (1928), and L. C. Randolph, *Francis Asbury* (1966). For details of the growth and mission of Methodism under Asbury's leadership, see Wade Crawford Barclay, *History of Methodist Missions,* vol. 1 (1949), and Emory Stevens Bucke, ed., *The History of American Methodism,* vol. 1 (1964).

Norman E. Thomas

Ashmore, William (1824–1909), American Baptist missionary in China. Ashmore was born in Putnam, Ohio, the son of Samuel and Nancy Ashmore. He graduated from Granville Literary and Theological Institute (became Denison University, Granville, Ohio), and the Western Baptist Theological Institute in Covington, Kentucky. He served briefly as pastor of First Baptist Church, Hamilton, Ohio. In 1850 he and his wife, Martha (Sanderson), were appointed by the American Baptist Missionary Union (ABMU) for work among the Chinese in Siam. They arrived in Bangkok the following year to join William *Dean and Josiah *Goddard at the American Baptist mission. Ashmore mastered the Tie-chiu dialect and concentrated on street preaching. After seven years, the Ashmores moved to Hong Kong. In 1858, following the death of his wife, Ashmore relocated to Swatow (Shantou), on the mainland, where he established a new field that replaced Hong Kong as the center of American Baptist Chinese missions. He focused on training Chinese workers and had one of the most extensive indigenous staffs among American Baptists. In 1863, during a furlough in the United States, he married Eliza Dunlevy of Lebanon, Ohio. In the 1870s he served as home secretary for the ABMU. During this period Eliza was seriously ill and eventually died. In 1890 he married Charlotte Brown (widow of Nathan *Brown, missionary to Japan) and the couple began their final missionary assignment. In Swatow, Ashmore built a strong theological school, championing "a trained native leadership." In retirement, when he again served as home secretary (1885–1889), he wrote extensively on a variety of subjects, including the authority of the Bible and the history of Baptist missions in the Far East. Primarily an evangelist and church planter, Ashmore organized at Swatow a training school for women and the theological seminary which later bore his name.

BIBLIOGRAPHY William Ashmore, *A Plea for China* (1895), *Outline History of the South China Baptist Mission, 1838–1850* (1902), *The Different Christianities of China* (1903), and *I Don't Believe in Foreign Missions* (1897). George H. Waters, "Missionary Statesmen: The Ashmores—Father and Son," *The Chronicle,* 1951, pp. 40–45; Walter S. Stewart, *Early Baptist Missionaries and Pioneers* (1925), vol. 2, pp. 105–126.

William H. Brackney

Atiman, Adrian (1860s–1956), African Roman Catholic lay catechist and medical doctor in Tanganyika (modern Tanzania). Born at Toundourma, west of Timbuktu, of a Taureg mother and West African father, Atiman was abducted as a youth and sold into slavery. In 1876, as part of a caravan crossing the Sahara, he was ransomed by missionaries of the Society of African Missions (White Fathers), who took him to Algeria and enrolled him in school. He later attended the Lavigerie Institute and a university in Malta where he was trained as a *médecin-catéchiste.* In 1888 he embarked for Tanganyika with a party of Roman Catholic missionaries and began work at the Karema Mission dispensary, where he served for 68 years. His marriage to the daughter of a Bemba chief opened liaisons for advancing the mission. During World War I his medical services to Belgian soldiers won wide acclaim. A skilled surgeon, Atiman had an inquisitive mind and explored the use of indigenous African medicines while gleaning new findings from European doctors. In tandem with his medical practice was his fervent Catholic faith. As a respected catechist he challenged such practices as infanticide and trial by poisoning. For his wide-ranging achievements he was decorated ten times, receiving medals from the Vatican and from governments in Europe and Africa.

BIBLIOGRAPHY For an edited version of Atiman's autobiography in English, see *Tanganyika Notes and Records* 21 (1946): 46–76. Walter Breedveld, *Atiman, de Negerdokter Bij Het Tanganyikameer* (1965); Roger Fouquer, *Le docteur Adrien Atiman, médecen-catéchiste au Tanganyika* (1964). Atiman's letters, 1888–1919, in French, are held in the Lavigerie Archive, Institut des jeunes Negres in Malta (D11/199–207). These include typed manuscripts of Atiman's full-length autobiography and his *Histoire d'un Soudanais.*

Marc R. Nikkel

Atkinson, Maria W. (Rivera) (1879–1963), pioneer missionary in Mexico of the Church of God (Cleveland, Tennessee). Born in Alamos, Sonora, Mexico, in 1905 Maria went with her husband, Dionisio Jesus Chomina, to Douglas, Arizona, where he died. While still a Roman Catholic, she had a deep spiritual experience in 1907, and between 1915 and 1920 founded several prayer groups in Sonora, Mexico. In 1910 she married an American, Mark Wheeler Atkinson, and returned to the United States. In 1924 she was healed of cancer and baptized in the Holy Spirit. She was then appointed as a preacher of the Assemblies of God, ministering in Arizona and Mexico. From 1926 on, she resided permanently in Mexico. She met J. H. *Ingram, joined the Church of God, and after appointment in 1932 as missionary, laid the foundations of that denomination in Obregón and Hermosillo, Mexico. In 1934 the work of the church was prohibited; private meetings were allowed only under police control. Persecutions ended in 1936 when the police chief himself was healed by faith. Atkinson was known as *La Madre de Mexico* (The Mother of Mexico) because of her ministry. She died in Douglas, Arizona.

BIBLIOGRAPHY C. W. Conn, *Where the Saints Have Trod* (1959); Pablo A. Deiros, *Historia del cristianismo en América Latina* (1992); Roberto Domínguez, *Pioneros de Pentecostés en el mundo de habla hispana,* vol. 2, *México y Centroamérica* (1975); Walter Hollenweger, *El pentecostalismo: Historia y doctrinas* (1976); Peggy Humphrey, *María Atkinson: La Madre de Mexico* (1967).

Pablo A. Deiros

Auca Five (Ecuador Martyrs), five young American missionaries who lost their lives along the Curaray River in the jungles of Ecuador, on January 8, 1956. Jim *Elliot, Peter *Fleming, Ed McCully, Nate *Saint, and Roger Youderian were speared by Waorani (Auca) Indians they were trying to reach with the gospel.

BIBLIOGRAPHY Elisabeth Elliot, *Through Gates of Splendor* (1957).

The Editors

Auer, John Gottlieb (1832–1874), missionary bishop of the Protestant Episcopal Church in Cape Palmas, West Africa. Born in Neubulach, Wurtemberg, Germany, Auer was converted while teaching at Geysburg, and attended the mission seminary at Basel, Switzerland. After receiving distinction as a student, especially in preaching, in 1854 he joined the Basel mission station at Akropong in the interior of the Gold Coast to the south and east of Cape Palmas. Here he became a teacher at the mission's seminary. In 1862 he severed his connection with the Basel Mission and was ordained to the Episcopal ministry by Bishop Payne at Cavalla, Cape Palmas, Liberia. After the death of his wife in 1863, Auer sailed to the United States, staying three years and promoting the interests of the mission in Africa. Returning in 1867 to Liberia, he engaged in translation and education. He translated the Psalms into Grebo and other books into the Kru and Grebo languages; in Grebo he printed both a dictionary and translation of the prayer book. At Payne's request he became head of the school at Cavalla. In 1872, while visiting in Germany, the Episcopal Church elected him to the missionary episcopate of Cape Palmas and adjacent areas. Despite serious illness, he entered upon his short-lived episcopate with vigor.

BIBLIOGRAPHY J. G. Auer, *Elements of the Grebo Language for the Use of Schools in the Protestant Episcopal Mission at and near Cape Palmas, W.A.* (1870); K. W. Cameron, *An Index for the Spirit of Missions (1836–1900)* (1977), p. 61; *Proceedings of the Board of Missions of the Protestant Episcopal Church* (1870), p. 21, (1872) p.41, and (1874), p.43.

Peter R. Rodgers

Aufhauser, Johannes Baptist (1891–1963), German Catholic missiologist. Aufhauser was born in Moosham near Regensburg, and was ordained in 1906. In Munich he acquired doctoral degrees in theology (1908) and philosophy (1910). Having qualified as a university lecturer in 1911, he was appointed lecturer of mission history and late modern church history. In 1918 he became assistant professor of missiology and remained in that position until the faculty of theology at Munich University was abolished by the Nazi regime in 1939. He managed to continue his teaching in the field of missiology in Würzburg until his early retirement in 1947. In 1951, as professor emeritus, he returned to Munich to lecture on the history of religions.

For Aufhauser the purpose of university-level missiology courses was not training missionaries destined for work in the field—the religious orders did that—but to promote mission awareness among future theologians, teachers, doctors, engineers, and others (see his brochure *Die Pflege der Missionswissenschaft an der Universität,* [1920; 2d ed., 1925]). From the very start, he emphasized the close link between the history of religions and missiology. This can be seen from the courses he offered in the universities, his frequent trips abroad, and his publications. For a man of his time, he was amazingly open and full of respect for foreign cultures and non-Christian religions. His publications include *Christentum und Buddhismus im Ringen im Fernosten* (1922), *Ethik des Buddhismus* (1929), and *Asien am Scheidewege: Christentum, Buddhismus, Bolschewismus* (1933). He made a critical study of religious art in the mission countries in his *Umweltbeeinflussung der christlichen Mission* (1932). The whole of his scholarly career was overshadowed and hampered by the two world wars, National Socialism, and the cold war. He died in Ölberg, Bavaria.

BIBLIOGRAPHY K. J. Rivinius, "Errichtung des Lehrstuhls für Missionswissenschaft an der Ludwig-Maximilians-Universität München," *NZM* 41 (1985): 18–40, 102–117, 188–208; B. Willeke, "Prof. Dr. Johann Baptist Aufhauser," *ZMR* 48 (1964): 53 (obit.).

Karl Müller, SVD

Augouard, Prosper Philippe (1852–1921), Holy Ghost Fathers (CSSp) missionary to central Africa. Born in Poitiers, France, Augouard joined the Holy Ghost Fathers as a missionary, becoming an intrepid explorer. In 1879 he made a 27-day march to the interior of central Africa, arriving five days after Henry *Stanley at Stanley Pool, springboard for subsequent missionary expansion. He charted the Congo and Ubangi rivers, earning a Paris Geographical Society prize, and established mission stations along 1,300 miles of the Congo River. In 1890 he became bishop and vicar apostolic of Ubangi-Chari (the Republic of Central Africa), and in 1915, archbishop.

Augouard explored and claimed territory three times the size of France, "with crucifix and national flag," persuading local rulers to accept French patronage. His nationalism antagonized Stanley and his patron, the king of Belgium, and when the Conference of Berlin (1885) established the Belgian Congo, French Catholic missionaries were replaced by Belgians. His empire-building was sometimes undisguised, and his nationalism was judged inexcusable, although he did denounce excessive French oppression. Described as impulsive and intransigent by his spiritual director, and considered abrupt, blunt, and patronizing, he was a flawed though tireless missionary. He was nicknamed Cannibal Bishop (a crude reference to his flock) and Diata-Diata (quick-quick) for his rapid expansion. In his final years he returned to Paris and died at the Mother House.

BIBLIOGRAPHY Louis Augouard, ed., *Mgr. Augouard: Lettres* (1905, 1914, 1934); G. Goyau, *Mgr. Augouard* (1926); J. de Witte, *Mgr. Augouard* (1924). See also H. Koren, *The Spiritans* (1958), and *Bulletin Général de Congrégation du St. Esprit,* Paris (1857 ff.).

Anthony J. Gittins, CSSp

Augustine of Canterbury (d. 604), apostle to the English; saint. Augustine, together with thirty or more Italian monks, was sent by Pope *Gregory I to southern England in 596. The party grew faint-hearted en route, and Augustine returned to Rome to seek permission to abandon the enterprise. Instead, he was made abbot of the missionary band, recommissioned, and given commendatory letters to the Frankish rulers and bishops through whose territory the monks would travel. When they arrived on the southeast English coast in the spring of 597, the Anglo-Saxon ruler of Kent, Ethelbert, who had earlier married a French Christian princess, Bertha, was wary. Nonetheless, he not only allowed Augustine and his company to reside in Canterbury but also gave them permission to preach and win whomever they could to the Christian faith. Augustine quickly returned to the Continent—probably to Arles, in southern France—where he was consecrated archbishop of Canterbury. Shortly thereafter he baptized Ethelbert, which opened the way for the conversion of the king's subjects en masse. The ensuing theological, ethical, and practical difficulties Augustine faced were communicated to Rome in a series of nine questions. Gregory's judicious responses, guided by what has come to be called the principle of accommodation, allowed the missionaries a remarkable degree of latitude. Though successful in evangelization, Augustine was unable during his brief apostolate to unite the Celtic and Roman churches, which did not occur until the Synod of Whitby in 664. He was buried at Canterbury.

BIBLIOGRAPHY Bertram Colgrave and R. A. B. Mynors, eds., *Bede's Ecclesiastical History of the English People* (1969); Edward L. Cutts, *Augustine of Canterbury* (1895); Margaret Deanesly, *Augustine of Canterbury* (1964); Henry H. Howorth, *Saint Augustine of Canterbury* (1913); Arthur James Mason, *The Mission of St. Augustine to England* (1897).

Alan Neely

Augustine of Hippo (354–430), Latin patristic theologian and scriptural exegete; saint. Born in North Africa and educated there and at Rome, Augustine was bishop of Hippo from about 396 until his death. The theology he shaped dominated the West until the thirteenth century and greatly influenced the Reformation. His predestinarian views formed the foundation for various mission theologies and practices during those periods.

Augustine's debate about free will with Pelagius empowered some missionaries with the conviction that without God's gift of Jesus Christ and faith itself all non-believers were lost. Others took Augustine's emphasis on God's ordaining of some for salvation and others for damnation as devastating for missions because destiny was already decided. The important monastery of Lérins in southern France, beginning with John Cassian, represented an Eastern tradition in the West which rejected Pelagian extremes but saw Augustine's predestinarian views as a dangerous innovation.

Augustine's controversy with the Donatists was also thorny. He rejected their insistence on full purity for any sacramental act to be valid. He abhorred their violence but did not mind the thought of suppressing them through the use of Roman troops. At the very moment when a Punic-Berber contextualization of the gospel needed strong pastoral guidance, Augustine's own Latin culture left him unable to see the possibilities.

BIBLIOGRAPHY Peter Brown, *Augustine of Hippo* (1967); Henry Chadwick, *Augustine* (1986); William H. C. Frend, *The Donatist Church: A Movement of Protest in Roman North Africa* (1952); Robert C. Sproule, *The Donatist Controversy* (1984); Agostino Trapé, *St. Augustine: Man, Pastor, Mystic* (1986).

Frederick W. Norris

Auna (c. 1790–1835), missionary from Huahine to Hawaii. A Tahitian chief of Raiatea, Auna became a deacon of the church on neighboring Huahine, in the Leeward Islands. He was among early converts of the London Missionary Society (LMS) in the Society Islands and was one of seven Tahitian Christians to go as missionaries to Hawaii in April 1822. The group was led by William *Ellis, an LMS missionary on Huahine, in response to an invitation from the American Board of Commissioners for Foreign Missions (ABCFM) to help its first company of missionaries to Hawaii in their struggle to cope with the new language and culture. The group sailed from Huahine with a two-person deputation from the LMS in London and gained favor, through Auna, with Kaahumanu, the Queen Mother and widow of Kamehameha I ("the Great"). The Tahitians traveled for two months on the islands of Oahu, Maui, and Hawaii. By oral contact and elementary lessons in literacy using two closely related Polynesian languages, they commended the gospel by telling how it was accepted in Tahiti. Ellis assisted the ABCFM group with Bible translation; he eventually transferred to the ABCFM in Hawaii as an associate missionary. Auna returned to the Society Islands in March 1824.

BIBLIOGRAPHY William Ellis, *Narrative of a Tour through Hawaii* (1826); John Garrett, *To Live among the Stars: Christian Origins in Oceania* (1982, 1985); H. E. Maude, "The Raiatean Chief Auna and the Conversion of Hawaii," *Journal of Pacific History*, no. 8 (1973): 188–191; James Montgomery, ed., *Journal of Voyages and Travels by the Rev. Daniel Tyerman and George Bennet, Esq. Deputed from the London Missionary Society*, 2 vols (1904). The Hawaiian journal of Auna (William Ellis, trans.) is preserved in facsimile in the Hawaiian Mission Children's Society Library, Honolulu.

John Garrett

Avison, Oliver R. (1860–1956), Presbyterian medical missionary in Korea. Avison was born in England and immigrated with his family to Canada in 1866, where he trained as a teacher, pharmacist, and medical doctor. As a medical student and in private practice in Toronto, he was active in the YMCA and its missionary work and met Horace G. *Underwood, who recruited him for Korea. Arriving in 1893, he took over the small hospital started by Horace N. *Allen, and also itinerated widely with Underwood to treat rural patients. He saw a need to combine the clinics of individual medical missionaries into a general hospital and medical school, which he accomplished despite opposition of the Presbyterian Korea mission to "institutional work." In 1900 M. L. Severance of Cleveland, Ohio, donated $10,000 for the first modern building, which was named Severance Union Medical College and Hospital. Avison served both Severance and Chosen Christian College (united in 1957 as Yonsei University) as president until his retirement in 1934. Under his leadership Severance established a pharmaceutical company and pioneered in introducing modern medicine, making it one of the leading hospitals in East Asia. In 1885 he married Jennie Barnes. They had eight children, two of whom, Gordon and Douglas, later became missionaries in Korea. Retiring in 1934, he settled in Forida, where he died.

BIBLIOGRAPHY Allen D. Clark, *Avison of Korea* (1955); L. George Paik, *History of Protestant Missions in Korea, 1832–1910* (1934, 1968); Harry Rhodes, *History of the Korea Mission of the Presbyterian Church, U.S.A., 1884–1934* (1934).

Horace G. Underwood

Axenfeld, Karl (1869–1924), Berlin Mission director. Axenfeld, the son of a Lutheran pastor, was born in Smyrna, Turkey, and studied theology at Halle, Germany. As a parish pastor in Erdeborn bei Eisleben, Saxony, he became so involved in promoting mission work that the Berlin Mission in 1904 appointed him executive secretary (*Missionsinspektor*). Although in frail health, he was a diligent worker. He improved the quality of missionary training, took part in the 1910 Edinburgh World Missionary Conference and other ecumenical ventures, and in 1912–1913 visited the East African field. After his return, he was named director of the mission and in 1914, the Halle theological faculty awarded him an honorary doctorate. His fundraising efforts put the mission on a more sound footing, but the outbreak of World War I crippled operations. Seminary enrollment dwindled as young men joined the army and workers abroad were interned or expelled from their places of service. Axenfeld's vehement criticism of Allied policies, especially the treatment of German missionaries, helped raise consciousness for missions at home, but his hard-line stance contributed both to a rupture in the ecumenical movement and to difficulties in reconciliation after the war. In 1919 he was an adviser on colonial and mission questions to the German peace delegation at Paris. In 1921 he resigned to become general superintendent of the Protestant church's Kurmark Province. He died three years later.

BIBLIOGRAPHY Karl Axenfeld, *Küste und Inland* (1912). Hellmut Lehmann, *150 Jahre Berliner Mission* (1974); Julius Richter, *Geschichte der Berliner Missionsgesellschaft, 1824–1924* (1924).

Richard V. Pierard

Axling, William (1873–1963), American Baptist missionary in Japan, and colleague and biographer of Toyohiko *Kagawa. Born in Oakland, Nebraska, of devout Swedish Baptist church planters, Axling graduated from the University of Nebraska and Rochester Theological Seminary. In 1901 he married Lucinda Burrows; they had no children. Initially slated by the American Baptist Missionary Union (later the American Baptist Foreign Mission Society) to go to Burma, the Axlings instead were reassigned to Japan. Axling's missionary service (1901–1943; 1946–1955) began in Morioka, northern Japan, but he soon moved to Tokyo, where he worked at the Baptists' newly built Misaki Tabernacle. Strengthening the programs of the Tabernacle in both social service and evangelistic outreach, he also oversaw its rebuilding after it was destroyed in the 1923 earthquake. In several programs he worked closely with Toyohiko Kagawa, and wrote the biography that introduced Kagawa to a worldwide audience. The growing antagonisms between Japan and the

United States that led to World War II deeply distressed Axling, who sought to interpret the two countries to each other through Christian perspectives. Already beyond retirement by the time Pearl Harbor was attacked, the Axlings stayed on in Japan after the outbreak of hostilities and were interned until their repatriation to the United States in 1943. They returned to postwar Japan for a final term before retiring in Alhambra, California, where he died.

BIBLIOGRAPHY William Axling, *On the Trail of Truth about Japan* (1921), *Kagawa* (1932; rev. ed., 1946), *This is Japan* (1957), and *Japan at the Midcentury: Leaves from Life* (1959). Leland D. Hine, *Axling: A Christian Presence in Japan* (1969).

James M. Phillips

Aylward, Gladys (1902–1970), British missionary in China. A housemaid born in Edmonton, north of London, Aylward went to China as an independent missionary. With little educational background, no specific abilities to commend her for missionary work, and unable to do well in some introductory mission studies, Gladys was turned down by the China Inland Mission. Despite this disappointment and no support, in 1930 she headed for China on the Trans-Siberian railway. Nearly detained in Russia, she managed to get to Tientsin (Tianjin) and from there traveled to the province of Shansi (Shanxi) in northwest China. Learning the rough Mandarin language of the area, she identified herself with China and its people and became a Chinese citizen in 1936. She gained the favor of the mandarin of the city of Yangcheng (Jincheng), who appointed her an inspector to help enforce the local government's edict against binding the feet of young girls.

The late 1930s were days of strife, as government forces fought against the Japanese and Communists. In this chaotic context Aylward gathered many orphans into a home and in 1940 led them on a perilous journey to safety in Sian (Xi'an), capital of the neighboring province of Shensi (Shaanxi), 240 miles west-southwest of Yangcheng. She returned to England during World War II, went back to China in the late 1940s, and then continued work with needy children in Taiwan through the Gladys Aylward Children's Home until nearly the time of her death.

BIBLIOGRAPHY R. O. Latham, *Gladys Aylward, One of the Undefeated: The Story of Gladys Aylward as Told by Her to R. O. Latham* (1950); Catherine Swift, *Gladys Aylward: The Courageous English Missionary* (1989); Phyllis Thompson, *London Sparrow* (1971). The work of Gladys Aylward was memorialized in a 1959 film, *The Inn of the Sixth Happiness,* starring Ingrid Bergman. Most of the material for the film was derived from Alan Burgess, *The Small Woman* (1957). Aylward's letters are in the archives at the SOAS, University of London.

Ralph R. Covell

Azariah, Vedanayagam Samuel (1874–1945), first Indian bishop of the Anglican Church. Born in the village of Vellalanvilai in the southernmost Indian district of Tirunelveli, Azariah was educated in Anglican missionary schools and at Madras Christian College. As a YMCA secretary from 1895–1909, he became a leader of the emerging pan-Asian student missionary movement by establishing the Indian Missionary Society (IMS) in 1903 and the National Missionary Society in 1905. He forged friendships with Western student leaders Sherwood *Eddy and John *Mott and pleaded for better relations between foreign missionaries and "native" Christians at the 1910 World Missionary Conference in Edinburgh.

In 1909 Azariah left the YMCA to become an ordained Anglican missionary of the IMS to Dornakal in the Telugu-speaking dominions of the Nizam of Hyderabad. In 1912 he was promoted to an unprecedented indigenous bishopric in the new diocese of Dornakal. He remained the only Indian diocesan bishop in the Anglican Church until his death.

Known in Dornakal Diocese by the affectionate honorific *Thandrigaru* ("father"), Azariah was the chief inspirational force behind mass movements that brought roughly 200,000 outcaste Malas and Madigas, tribals and low-caste non-Brahmins into his fledgling church during his lifetime. For over two decades, Azariah also played a leading role in church unity negotiations, which resulted in the historic creation of the Church of South India in 1947, the first unification of an episcopal church (Anglican) with non-episcopal churches (Congregational, Presbyterian, Methodist) since the Reformation. He led many other prominent South Asian Protestant enterprises of his age, including the National Christian Council (the central cooperative body for non-Roman churches and missions in India, Burma, and Ceylon [Sri Lanka]), the Bible Society of India and Ceylon, and the General Council of the Anglican Church of India, Burma, and Ceylon. He spoke with authority on major political issues and became, somewhat reluctantly, both an ally and a foe of M. K. Gandhi in battles over communal representation and religious freedom. He also served as an important bridge between India and Britain during the last phases of their imperial association. He was awarded an honorary degree in 1920 from Cambridge University.

BIBLIOGRAPHY Azariah authored over 180 books, articles, addresses, and translations, some of which are no longer extant. Works prepared mainly for educational and pastoral purposes in English or in Indian vernaculars include studies on several books of the Bible, *Holy Baptism* (1919, 1942), *The Pastor and Pastorate* (1936), *Lessons on Miracles* (1937), *Christian Giving* (1939, 1955), *Confirmation* (1942), and *Sabbath or Sunday* (1942). Azariah translated writings of Charles G. Finney and Andrew Murray into Indian vernaculars; he described the progress of Christianity in South Asia in *India and the Christian Movement* (1935, 1936). For a comprehensive bibliography, see Susan Billington Harper, "Azariah and Indian Christianity in the Late Years of the Raj" (D.Phil. thesis, Oxford Univ., 1991). See also Carol Graham, "V. S. Azariah," in Gerald H. Anderson et al., eds., *Mission Legacies* (1994), pp. 324–329. Many of Azariah's papers were lost or destroyed after his death, but substantial correspondence and records still exist: the CMS archives at the Univ. of Birmingham, the USPG archives at Rhodes House, Oxford, the archives at Lambeth Palace Library, London, the Metropolitan Archives of the

Church of India, Pakistan, Burma, and Ceylon at Bishop's College, Calcutta, and the IMS archives in Palayamkottai.

Susan Billington Harper

Azevedo, Ignacio de (1527–1570), Portuguese Jesuit missionary to Brazil. Azevedo was born in Oporto to one of the most distinguished families of Portugal and was a brother of a viceroy of the Indies. In 1548 he joined the Society of Jesus, and in 1565 was named a visitor general of their mission in Brazil. After a prolonged tour of inspection, where he observed a shortage of missionaries, Azevedo returned to Europe to seek more volunteers for the mission. His idea was to recruit young people in Europe and train them in Brazil, especially in the languages of the Indians and in strategies for evangelization. He recruited reinforcements, mostly teenagers between 14 and 16 years of age. A company of 69 missionaries, both Portuguese and Spanish, embarked from Lisbon in three ships with Azevedo in July 1570. He and 40 others in the leading ship were attacked, captured at sea, and put to death by the French Huguenot privateer Jacobo Soria de la Rochela. The rest of the company escaped this attack, but in the following months were chased, caught, and killed. Pius IX beatified Azevedo and his companions on May 11, 1854. Azevedo was considered a Roman Catholic martyr at the hands of Protestant Huguenots sent by the queen of Navarre.

BIBLIOGRAPHY J. Broderick, *The Progess of the Jesuits, 1546–1579* (1946); Ludovico Pastor, *Historia de los papas,* vol. 18. (1931); Simão de Vasconcellos, *Chronica da Companhia de Jesu do Estado do Brasil,* vol. 2 (1865).

Pablo A. Deiros

B

Babalola, Joseph Ayo (1904–1959), leader of the Nigerian Aladura (the praying people) revival of the mid-twentieth century. Babalola was born of Yoruba parents at Ilofa, Nigeria, and was brought up as an Anglican. Having left elementary school, he was employed in the Public Works Department as a steam roller operator. In October 1928, while trying to repair his machine, he claimed that Jesus Christ called him to abandon the job and start preaching. He then joined Faith Tabernacle in Lagos, which was related to an American Pentecostal organization. In September 1930 Babalola was credited with raising a dead man to life. From then on, with bell and Yoruba Bible in hand, he toured Yorubaland and eastern Nigeria, preaching about repentance, the renunciation of idolatry, the importance of prayer and fasting, and the power of God to heal sickness. In 1930 Faith Tabernacle affiliated with the British Apostolic Church. Then following a schism in the Apostolic Church about 1940, Babalola went with a new independent church, Christ Apostolic Church (CAC), where he continued his healing and revivalistic activities until his death. The CAC regards Babalola as an apostle and his revival ministry as the beginning of the church. A CAC retreat center was built where Babalola was first called in 1928.

BIBLIOGRAPHY David Odubanjo, *The History and Works of the Prophet Joseph Babalola,* pt. 1 (c. 1930); E. H. L. Olusheye, *Saint Joseph Ayo Babalola: The African Foremost Religious Revolutionary Leader Ever Lived* (1983); S. G. Adegboyega, *A Short History of the Apostolic Church of Nigeria* (1978); Adeware Alokan, *The Christ Apostolic Church, 1928–1988* (1991); J. D. Y. Peel, *Aladura: A Religious Movement among the Yoruba* (1968); Idris Vaughan, *Nigeria: The Origins of Apostolic Church Pentecostalism, 1931–1952* (1991).

Matthews A. Ojo

Bach, T(homas) J(ohn) (1881–1963), pioneer missionary in western Venezuela. Born in Denmark, Bach immigrated to the United States in 1899 and studied at the Swedish Institute of Chicago Theological Seminary. In April 1906 he sailed from New York to Maracaibo, Venezuela, with his wife, Anna (Anderson), and Anna O. G. and John Christiansen, sent by the Scandinavian Alliance Mission of North America (later the Evangelical Alliance Mission, or TEAM). In spite of opposition from Roman Catholic clergy, they held their first public worship service on May 19, 1907. Bach was also the founder of *La estrella de la mañana* (the first evangelical magazine in Venezuela), a printing shop, a bookstore, and several local congregations. His labors are considered the foundation of the Venezuelan Organization of Evangelical Christian Churches. In 1928 he became general director of TEAM, serving until 1946, when he retired and became chair of its board of directors. He died in Yucaipa, California.

BIBLIOGRAPHY T. J. Bach, *Pioneer Missionaries for Christ and His Church* (1955, later published under the title *Vision and Valor*); Tom Watson, Jr., *T. J. Bach: A Voice for Missions* (1965).

Pablo A. Deiros

Bachmann, (Johann) Traugott (1865–1948), Moravian missionary to East Africa. Bachmann was born in Niesky in Saxony, Germany. After working as a farm laborer, he attended the missionary school of the Moravian Church. In 1892 he was sent on a mission to southwestern Tanzania (then German East Africa). At first, he was stationed in Rungwe, where he baptized the first convert in 1897. Two years later he founded the Mbozi station in the area of the animistic Nyika. Eager to learn from them, he tried to understand their customs and habits in order to adapt the newly developing Christian life as far as possible to the native culture. His preaching, which was influenced by Count Nikolaus Ludwig von *Zinzendorf and Johann Christoph *Blumhardt, found a positive response.

Flourishing parishes were established, leading eventually to Christianization of the people. His translation of the New Testament into the Nyika language (1913) was instrumental in this. Bachmann's work ended in 1916 during World War I, when he was interned by the British. He returned to Germany and became active as an itinerant Moravian preacher in Hesse and as an agent of missions.

BIBLIOGRAPHY Traugott Bachmann, *Praktische Lösung missionarischer Probleme auf einem jungen Arbeitsfeld (Nyassagebiet, Deutsch-Ostafrika)* (1912). J. Taylor Hamilton, *Twenty Years of Pioneer Missions in Nyasaland* (1912); Hans-Windekilde Jannasch, ed., *Traugott Bachmann: Ich gab manchen Anstoss* (1956; abr. ed., 1964) and *Herrnhuter Miniaturen* (enl. ed., 1976), pp. 160–169; Werner Kessler, "Traugott Bachmann (1865–1948): Ein Schüler und Zeuge Jesu," *Der Brüderbote,* no. 329 (1976): 28–32.

Werner Raupp

Bacon, Sumner (1790–1844), missionary evangelist and founder of the Cumberland Presbyterian Church (CPS) in Texas. Born in Massachusetts, Bacon left home around 1810, spent 15 years wandering in the eastern United States, then traveled by river to Little Rock, Arkansas. After two years in the army in Arkansas, he attended a CPS revival, was converted, and decided to become an evangelist. Finding him barely literate in 1826, the CPS denied him ordination. Undeterred, by 1829 he had worked his way into northern Louisiana and into eastern Texas (then a part of Mexico). His preaching among the settlers aroused a positive response. In 1833 the American Bible Society commissioned him its first agent in the region. His primary purpose was to gain conversions, so he cooperated with people of other denominations, including Roman Catholics. In 1835 the CPS ordained him, and that year, during the war for the independence of Texas, he traveled in Louisiana, Mississippi, and Tennessee raising money to distribute Bibles in Texas. While in Nashville, Tennessee, he married Elizabeth McKerall. Later back in Texas, he helped to organize the first presbytery of the CPS in the region (1837) and the first CPS synod (1842). He is remembered as the Apostle of Texas.

BIBLIOGRAPHY R. Douglas Brackenridge, "Sumner Bacon: 'The Apostle of Texas,'" *Journal of Presbyterian History* 45 (1967): 163–179, 247–255.

H. McKennie Goodpasture

Baedeker, Friederich Wilhelm (1823–1906), itinerant evangelist in Russia and eastern Europe. Born in Witten, Westphalia, Germany, Baedeker held a Ph.D. from the University of Freiburg and was fluent in German, French, and English. Having spent his first 43 years as "a proud German infidel," in England in 1866 he came into contact with the evangelical Anglican Bible teacher Lord Radstock and was converted. In 1875 Radstock introduced Baedeker to a growing circle of evangelicals within the Russian nobility of Saint Petersburg. For three years beginning in 1877, Baedeker, with his English wife and adopted daughter, made Saint Petersburg his base for evangelistic tours throughout central and eastern Europe, Russia, and the Caucasus. His travels continued unabated after he returned to his home in Weston-super-Mare, England. Introduced to prison ministry, he requested through his highly placed friends in Saint Petersburg a permit from the director of prisons to distribute Scriptures and to minister the gospel in the prisons of the Russian empire. Soon he enlarged his itinerary to include the penal colonies of Siberia, making the trip of several thousand miles by river steamer and tarantass (a type of horse-drawn buggy) three times within a decade. He continued visiting and preaching to prisoners, nobility, students, and peasants through eastern Europe and Russia well into his eighth decade.

BIBLIOGRAPHY Robert Sloan Latimer, *Dr. Baedeker and His Apostolic Work in Russia* (1907). See also E. Heier, *Religious Schism in the Russian Aristocracy, 1860–1900: Radstockism and Pashkovism* (1970).

Robert T. Coote

Baëta, Christian G(oncalves) K(wami) (1908–1994), Presbyterian church leader from the Gold Coast (Ghana). Born at Keta, Ghana, Baëta studied at the Scottish Mission Teacher Training College, Akropong, Ghana, Evangelisches Missionsseminar, Basel, Switzerland, and King's College, London, where he wrote a doctoral dissertation entitled "Prophetism in Ghana." He was ordained in 1936. In 1938 he participated in the meeting of the International Missionary Council (IMC) at Tambaram, India. He was Synod Clerk (chief executive) of the Evangelical Presbyterian Church (1945–1949) and chair of both the Ghana Christian Council and the Ghana church union negotiations committee. In 1958 he became vice-chair of the IMC and superintended the merger of the IMC with the World Council of Churches (WCC). He was the Henry W. Luce Visiting Professor at Union Theological Seminary, New York (1958–1959), and the Edward Cadbury Visiting Professor at Selly Oak Colleges, Birmingham, England (1965–1970). He also served on the Commission of the Churches on International Affairs, the Central and Executive Committees of the WCC, and the Anglican-Reformed Commission on Church Unity. He was involved in Bible translation, particularly into Ewe.

Between 1949 and 1971 Baëta served on the staff of the divinity department in the University of Ghana. He helped shift this department from emphasizing Christian theology to emphasizing religions and theology in a pluralistic world. Baëta voiced the concerns of younger churches engaged in mission, and pioneered on the African continent in shifting from mission understood as an expression of worldwide Christendom to mission viewed as encounter and peaceful coexistence of persons of different faiths. In his thinking ecumenism and mission were inextricable. His conviction that God was sovereign over all of life led him to accept political responsibility: as a member of the Legislative Council of the Gold Coast (1946–1950); member of the Coussey Committee on Constitutional Reform for the Gold Coast; and member of the Constitutional Assembly, which, after the overthrow of Kwame Nkrumah, prepared the way for return to civilian rule. Thus, for

Baëta evangelism and engagement with issues of peace and justice were already in the 1940s and 1950s inextricably linked.

BIBLIOGRAPHY Baëta's publications include *Prophetism in Ghana* (1963) and *The Relationships of Christians with Men of Other Living Faiths* (1971). He edited *Christianity in Tropical Africa* (1968). See his autobiographical article "My Pilgrimage in Mission," *IBMR* 12, no. 4 (1984): 165–168. John S. Pobee, ed., *Religion in a Pluralistic Society: Essays in Honour of Prof. C. G. Baëta* (1976); Walter Ringwald, "Christian Baëta Führender Christ seiner Afrikanischen Kirche," in *Oekumenische Profile Brückenbauer der Einen Kirche II,* Günter Gloede, ed. (1963); Theo Sundermeier, "Auf dem Weg zu einer Afrikanischen Kirche, Christian G. Baëta, Ghana," in *Theologen der Dritten Welt* (1982).

John S. Pobee

Báez-Camargo, Gonzalo (1899–1983), third-generation Mexican Methodist and ecumenical leader. Born in Oaxaca, Báez-Camargo was educated in the Methodist Mexican Institute in Puebla, Union Evangelical Seminary, and the Universidad Nacional Autónomo de México. During the Mexican Revolution, at the age of 15, he joined the forces of Venustiano Carranza. Following graduation from seminary, he served as an associate Methodist pastor, then as professor and vice-president of the Methodist Mexican Institute. From 1929 to 1941 he was general secretary of Christian education and executive secretary of the Mexican Council of Churches; from 1931 to 1946 he was also manager of the Union Publishing House. He was professor of Christian literature and journalism, Old Testament, and Hebrew at Union Evangelical Seminary (1941–1971), and he taught as an adjunct at a number of other theological and secular institutions. From 1946 to 1960 he was a member of the Latin American Committee on Cooperation, was on the provisional committee for organizing the World Council of Churches (WCC), and served on a number of committees of the International Missionary Council (IMC) and the WCC. Opposed to the merger of the IMC and WCC in 1961 and disillusioned with the direction of the WCC after the Uppsala Assembly in 1968, he became a strident critic of the "leftist takeover" of the ecumenical movement. Besides authoring more than twenty books, he was a member of the editorial committee and exegetical adviser for *La Versión Popular,* the New Spanish Version of the Bible.

BIBLIOGRAPHY John Maust, "Gonzalo Báez-Camargo: God's Man in Mexico" and "An Interview with Gonzalo Báez-Camargo," *CT* 26 (March 5, 1982): 28–31; Gustavo A. Velasco, "Báez-Camargo, Gonzalo," in Nolan B. Harmon, ed., *Encyclopedia of World Methodism,* vol. 1 (1974), p. 195.

Alan Neely

Bagby, William Buck (1855–1939), Southern Baptist pioneer missionary to Brazil. Bagby was born in Coryell County, Texas. He graduated from Waco University (later merged with Baylor) in 1875, was ordained in 1879, and in 1880 married Anne Ellen Luther. Commissioned by the Southern Baptist Foreign Mission Board, the Bagbys arrived in Brazil in March 1881, settling in the American colony of Santa Barbara, São Paulo state. In Santa Barbara they met Antonio Teixeira de Albuquerque, a Brazilian ex-priest who had been converted to Protestantism by Methodist missionaries and was later baptized by a Baptist minister in the American colony. (Teixeira, it is believed, was the first Brazilian Baptist, and he soon became the cornerstone of the Baptist work, serving as both teacher and preacher.) After 15 months of language study in Campinas, the Bagbys were joined by a second missionary couple, Zachary and Kate (Crawford) Taylor, and together with Teixeira, they moved to Salvador, Bahía. There in October 1882 they formed the first Portuguese-speaking Baptist congregation in Brazil. Two years later the Bagbys moved to Río de Janeiro. When the Brazilian Baptist Convention was organized in 1907, it had 83 congregations, 26 ordained pastors, and as many or more lay preachers; the number of baptized members exceeded 5,000. From 1900 to 1929 the Bagbys lived and worked in São Paulo, and after a year's furlough they moved to Porto Alegre in 1930, where nine years later Bagby died. He left behind 694 churches and more than 53,000 Baptists. Anne Bagby lived three more years, dying in Recife on her way to the United States. Five of the Bagbys' nine children became missionaries to South America.

BIBLIOGRAPHY Robert G. Bratcher, *Land of Many Worlds* (1954); Délcio Costa, *Colunas batistas no Brasil* (1964); A. R. Crabtree, *História dos baptistas do Brasil,* 2 vols. (1937); Pablo A. Deiros, *Historia del cristianismo en América Latina* (1992); Helen Bagby Harrison, *The Bagbys of Brazil* (1954); D. B. Lancaster, "In the Land of the Southern Cross: The Life and Ministry of William Buck and Ann Luther Bagby" (Ph.D. diss., Southwestern Baptist Theological Seminary, 1995); R. F. Matthews, *O Apóstolo do sertão* (1967); Walter Wedemann, "A History of Protestant Missions to Brazil, 1850–1914" (Ph.D. diss., Southern Baptist Theological Seminary, 1977).

Pablo A. Deiros

Bailey, Wellesley C(osby) (1846–1937), Irish lay missionary, founder and first secretary of the Mission to Lepers (later, the Leprosy Mission). Bailey went to India on his own in 1869, where he joined the American Mission (Presbyterian) at Ambala, Punjab, a station served by J. H. Morrison. While visiting the leper asylum attached to the mission, he discovered his special calling to serve these people and to share the gospel with them. This vocation was fully shared by Alice Grahame, also from Ireland, whom he married in 1871.

While on furlough in Dublin in 1874, Bailey wrote and spoke about his experiences to the Misses Pims (friends of his wife), who immediately began to collect funds in support for this yet-unorganized work. In 1878 the Mission to Lepers in India was formed in order to receive and properly administer the increasing flow of funds. Bailey built up the mission in India until 1882, when the work expanded beyond India and he returned to Ireland. From 1886 to 1917 he was its full-time secretary. He was a gifted administrator and traveled extensively, expanding the work to twelve countries. His policy was not to engage mission staff but to give small grants-in-aid wherever and to whomever needed them for the welfare of those suffering from leprosy, which could not then be treated medically. The mission's magazine, *Without the Camp,* began publication in 1897.

BIBLIOGRAPHY W. C. Bailey, *A Glimpse of the Indian Mission-Field and Leper Asylums in 1886–87* (1888) and *The Lepers of Our Indian Empire: A Visit to Them in 1890–91* (1891). H. S. Carson *The Story of the Mission to Lepers in India* (1891) and *Fifty Years' Work for Lepers* (1924); A. D. Miller, *An Inn Called Welcome: The Story of the Mission to Lepers, 1874–1912* (1965).

Christoffer H. Grundmann

Baird, William M. (1862–1931), American Presbyterian missionary educator in Korea. Baird was born in Indiana, attended Hanover College (Hanover, Indiana) and McCormick Seminary (Chicago) and was appointed with his wife, Nancy (Adams), to Korea. Arriving in 1891, he was assigned to open new work in Pusan and then Taegu. In 1897 he was assigned to work in Pyongyang, where he spent the rest of his life, itinerating widely in the northwestern districts of Korea. He was one of the leaders in adopting the Nevius method of mission work (see John L. *Nevius), stressing local church self-development and minimizing institutional work. Appointed education officer of the Presbyterian mission, his education policy based on Nevius principles adopted by the Presbyterian mission in 1898 specified that all mission participation in education should be in direct support of the church. Under this policy he established Soongsil Academy and then College, serving as its first president and preparing many of the needed texts in addition to his regular itineration responsibilities. He earned a Ph.D. from Hanover College in 1903. In 1913 he resigned as education officer, partly as a result of the home Board overruling his education policy and specifying support for a more general policy of education. Thereafter he devoted himself to Christian literature work and Bible translation in addition to his normal itineration duties in the Pyongyang district. After the death of his wife in 1916, he married Rose Fetterolf in 1918. His two sons by his first marriage—William M., Jr., and Richard H.—followed him in missionary service in Korea. He died of typhoid fever in November 1931, shortly after widespread celebrations of the fortieth anniversary of his arrival in Korea.

BIBLIOGRAPHY Richard H. Baird, *William M. Baird of Korea: A Profile* (1968); L. George Paik, *The History of Protestant Missions in Korea, 1832–1910* (1934, 1968); Harry Rhodes, *History of the Korea Mission of the Presbyterian Church, U.S.A., 1884–1934* (1934).

Horace G. Underwood

Baker, Amelia Dorothea (Kohlhoff) (1802–1888), missionary in India. Born at Tanjore, South India, Baker was the granddaughter of John Baltasar Kohlhoff (1711–1790), a German Lutheran missionary who arrived in India in 1737. In 1818 she married a young English missionary, Henry Baker, who had been sent to Travancore in 1817 by the Church Missionary Society (CMS). She ran a girls' school at Cottayam and in 1864 was sponsored by CMS. She continued at the school after her husband's death in 1866 and until her own death. One of nine widows sponsored by CMS to continue their missionary work, Baker was particularly distinguished by her long life and her seventy years of service. Henry Baker, Jr., one of her sons, also worked in Travancore, and three of her five daughters, including her eldest daughter, Amelia *Johnson, married missionaries. Five granddaughters and one grandson worked for the Anglican Church in South India, making special contributions with their knowledge of local languages. Amelia Baker's female descendants continued working in girls' education until well into the twentieth century.

BIBLIOGRAPHY CMS, *Register of Missionaries and Native Clergy* (1904); E. Dalton, *The Baker Family in India* (1963); M. E. Gibbs, *The Anglican Church in India, 1600–1970* (1972); E. A. Kohlhoff, comp., *Pastoral Symphony: The Family and Descendants of Johann Baltasar Kohlhoff* (1989).

Jocelyn Murray

Bakker, D(irk) (1865–1932), Dutch missionary and founder of Gereja Kristen Jawa (GKJ; Church of Central Java). Bakker was born in the Netherlands and studied theology at the Free University of Amsterdam. He served as a minister in three Reformed churches before going to Central Java as a missionary. Upon his arrival in Kebumen in 1900, he built up what was left of the young congregations after a conflict between the mission and the indigenous church leader *Sadrach. In 1906, in Yogyakarta, he set up a theological training program for Javanese ministry assistants. For 18 years he was solely responsible for teaching all theological subjects. He wrote, in Javanese, a textbook of dogmatics, a summary of Christian doctrine, a guide for the ministry, and commentaries; he also published many articles in periodicals such as *Muslim World.* His theology was based on the Reformed confession and founded on the authority of the Scriptures. Soon after his return to the Netherlands in 1929, he was awarded an honorary doctorate by the Free University in recognition of his contribution to theological education, advancement of the mission in Java, and revision of the Javanese translation of the Bible.

BIBLIOGRAPHY D. Pol, *Midden-Java ten Zuiden* (2d ed., 1939); Sutarman Soediman Partonadi, *Sadrach's Community and Its Contextual Roots: Nineteenth Century Javanese Expression of Christianity* (1988); Th. Sumartana, *Mission at the Crossroads: Indigenous Churches, European Missionaries, Islamic Associations and Socio-Religious Change in Java, 1812–1936* (1993). Bakker's papers are in the archives of the Zending der Gereformeerde kerken in Nederland, Utrecht, Rijksarchief.

Dirk Bakker

Baldaeus, Philippus (1632–1671), pioneer Protestant missionary in Ceylon (Sri Lanka). Baldaeus was born in

Delft, Netherlands. After his education by Robertus *Junius and examination by the Amsterdam church authorities in September 1654, he offered to serve in the East Indies and was assigned to Formosa (Taiwan). When he arrived in Batavia (present-day Djakarta) on his way, however, the local church council sent him instead to Ceylon. He arrived there in February 1657, via Malacca, to serve as chaplain in the naval forces, care for East India Company personnel, and evangelize indigenous peoples. He was located in the kingdom of Jaffnapatnam, which included some islands; he also reached out to India.

When the Reformed Church and the East India Company debated over whether to use Dutch or Portuguese, Baldaeus argued instead for research into the Tamil language and Hindu religion. He published Malabar (Tamil) grammar introductions and also translated the Heidelberg Catechism and parts of the Bible. On his return to The Hague in 1667, he proposed that the church should make its missions independent from the commercial authorities. He ministered in Geervliet and edited his studies *Naauwkeurige Beschryvinge van Malabar en Choromandel* (1672) and *Afgoderije der Oost Indische Heydenen* (1672).

BIBLIOGRAPHY R. G. Anthonisz, *The Dutch in Ceylon: Early Visits and Settlement in the Island* (1929); R. L. Brohier, *Links between Sri Lanka and the Netherlands: A Book of Dutch Ceylon* (1978); S. D. Franciscus, *Faith of Our Fathers: History of the Dutch Reformed Church in Sri Lanka (Ceylon)* (1983); L. J. Joosse, *Scoone dingen sijn swaere dingen: Een onderzoek naar de motieven en de activiteiten in De Nederlanden tot verbreiding van de gereformeerde religie* (1992); K. Koschorke, *Holländische Kolonial- und Katholische Untergrundkirche im Ceylon des 17. und 18. Jahrhunderts* (1991).

Leendert J. Joosse

Baldwin, Elizabeth (1859–1939) *and* **Jane** (1863–1949), American missionaries in the South Pacific. Sisters from Orange, New Jersey, the Baldwins were single middle-aged schoolteachers who were considered to be too old by their own Presbyterian mission board when they offered themselves as missionaries after their parents died. They consequently volunteered to the American Board of Commissioners for Foreign Missions (ABCFM) for service "where nobody else wants to go" and were appointed in 1897 to teach in Chuuk (formerly Truk), in Micronesia, using both the German language of the colony and the local language. When the German Liebenzell Mission took over ABCFM work in Chuuk, the Baldwins transferred in 1909 to the ABCFM's mission seminary at Mwot on Kosrae (formerly Kusaie), where they trained teachers and pastors for Kosrae, the Marshall Islands, Kiribati (the Gilbert Islands), and Pohnpei (formerly Ponape). Elizabeth translated the entire Bible into the language of Kosrae with help from Kefwas, a local assistant. Jane supervised the printing press. Each acquired two of the four island languages of their pupils, and they were revered, respectively, as Mother Baldwin and Mother Dubois (Jane's middle name). They helped to implant Congregational church government and discipline in Kosrae's monarchical and chiefly society when its survival had been threatened by the injurious influence of sailors and traders. After 1914 they used Japanese, as required by the new Japanese administration. Elizabeth was buried on Kosrae. In 1941 Jane returned, by way of Japan, to Orange, New Jersey, where she died, infirm, at the age of 86.

BIBLIOGRAPHY John Garrett, *To Live among the Stars: Christian Origins in Oceania* (1982, 1985); Paul D. Schaefer, "Confess Therefore Your Sins: Status and Sin on Kusaie" (Ph.D. diss., Univ. of Minnesota, 1976). Harvey Gordon Segal, *Kosrae: The Sleeping Lady Awakens* (1989); Eleanor Wilson, *"Too Old?" A Saga of the South Pacific* (1972); see also Wilson's preface to Maribelle Cormack, *The Lady was a Skipper...* (1956). The papers of the ABCFM and its women's board and files of the *Missionary Herald* contain reports and other writings by the Baldwins.

John Garrett

Ball, Dyer (1796–1866), American Board of Commissioners for Foreign Missions medical missionary to China. Ball was born in West Boylston, Massachusetts, studied at Phillips Academy and at Yale College for two years, then moved to South Carolina, where he tutored until entering Union College, New York, from which he graduated in 1826. The next year he married Lucy Mills, then studied theology for some years at Yale and Andover Theological Seminary. Ordained in 1831, in 1833 he became an agent of the American Home Missionary Society, working in Florida among the Negro population. In 1835 he established a successful school in Charleston, South Carolina, and also studied medicine, receiving an M.D. in 1837. While his sailing was delayed by a financial panic, he studied Chinese.

Ball arrived in Singapore in 1838 and began a lifelong pattern of teaching, preaching, publishing Chinese literature, distributing tracts, and doing medical work, with evangelism always his first concern. In 1841 he moved to Macao for the sake of his wife's health, and in 1844 to Hong Kong, where she died. Ball then moved to Canton and in 1846 married Isabella Robertson, a missionary from Scotland. While running a boys' school and supervising the publication of books and tracts, including a popular *Almanac,* he devoted much of his energy to touring with his medicines and tracts. After furlough from 1854 to 1857, with his health impaired, he spent most of his final years doing tract distribution from his street chapel in Canton, where he died.

BIBLIOGRAPHY *Missionary Herald* 62 (1866): 259–262, has an informative obituary; other issues, e.g., 48 (1852): 86–87, carry his reports. Ball is mentioned several times in Edward V. Gulick, *Peter Parker and the Opening of China* (1973), which describes the context of his medical work.

David M. Stowe

Ball, Henry Cleophas (1896–1989), pioneer of Assemblies of God (AG) Hispanic churches in the United States and of AG missions in Latin America. Sickly and spiritually sensitive as a child, Ball was reared by his widowed mother in the border town of Ricardo, Texas. He joined the Methodist Church and began pastoring while still in his teens, using Spanish to evangelize the local Mexican community. He was ordained by the AG in 1915 and the following year began publication of *La luz apostólica,* later made the organ of the Latin American District of the AG. After his marriage in 1919 to Sunshine Marshall, a musician, he published a hymnal, *Himnos de Gloria,* that included both translated songs and new pieces composed by Latin Pentecostals. From 1925 to 1934 he was the first superintendent of the Latin American District of the AG and in 1926 founded the Latin American Bible Institute in San Antonio, Texas. He served from 1946 to 1953 as the first field secretary for AG missions in Latin America. His approaches were influenced by his colleague, Alice *Luce, a proponent of indigenous church principles. The publishing house he founded in 1946 became Life Publishers International, a leading U.S. producer of Spanish literature.

BIBLIOGRAPHY Víctor De León, *The Silent Pentecostals* (1979); Roberto Domínguez, *Pioneros de Pentecostés,* vol. 1 (1971); Gary B. McGee, "Pioneers of Pentecost: Alice E. Luce and Henry C. Ball," *Assemblies of God Heritage* 5 (Summer 1985): 4–6, 12–15; Inez Spence, *Henry C. Ball: Man of Action* (n.d.).

Everett A. Wilson

Ballantine, Henry (1813–1865), American missionary in Ahmednagar, India. Born at Schodack, near Albany, New York, Ballantine graduated from Ohio University at Athens (1829) and Andover Seminary (1834). He was ordained on April 6, 1835, and married Elizabeth Darling on May 5. They sailed for India on May 16 and arrived at Bombay on October 11 as missionaries of the American Board of Commissioners for Foreign Missions. With only one home furlough (1850–1852), Ballantine labored at Ahmednagar for nearly 30 years. He was noted for his fluency in Marathi and was widely respected as pastor, preacher, Bible translator, and editor of a semi-monthly mission paper in English and Marathi. Described as the Isaac Watts of Marathi hymnology, he prepared two hymnbooks, one for church use and one for children. He translated some of the hymns from English and composed some himself. He was secretary and treasurer of the Marathi mission for several years, and during his last five years he also taught two theological classes of young men who were preparing for the ministry. On a doctor's advice he and his family sailed for home in September 1865, but he died en route and was buried at sea off the coast of Portugal.

BIBLIOGRAPHY A memorial tribute to Ballantine appeared in *Missionary Herald* 62 (1866): 37–41.

Gerald H. Anderson

Baller, Frederick William (1852–1922), British missionary, educator, and translator in China. Following his conversion at age 17, Baller studied at the missionary institute established at Stepney Green, England. He sailed for China in 1873 as a member of the China Inland Mission (CIM) and studied the Chinese language in Nanking (Nanjing), then just recently liberated from the ravages of the Taiping rebels. During his first years of service in China, he was responsible for much of the mission work in Anhwei (Anhui) and Kiangsu (Jiangsu) Provinces and traveled widely as a pioneer in Shansi (Shanxi), Shensi (Shaanxi), Hunan, Hupeh (Hubei), and Kweichow (Guizhou) Provinces. In 1896 he was appointed principal of the new training home for CIM male missionaries at Anching (Anqing), Szechuan (Sichuan). There he not only helped train missionaries in the Chinese language but also published his lectures in *Letters from an Old Missionary to His Nephew* (1907). From 1900 to 1918 he served on the committee to revise the Mandarin New and Old Testaments. Among his many books, the best known are *An Anglo-Chinese Dictionary, The Mandarin Primer* (thirteen editions), *An Idiom a Lesson, An Analytical Vocabulary of the New Testament, Lessons in Wenli, An English Translation of the Sacred Edict,* and *The Life of Hudson Taylor.* He died and was buried in Shanghai shortly after completing his book on Taylor.

BIBLIOGRAPHY Marshall Broomhall, *F. W. Baller: A Master of the Pencil* (1923). Obituaries by James Stark, *Chinese Recorder,* November 1922, pp. 715–716, and J. W. Wilson, *Chinese Recorder,* December 1922, pp. 778–779.

Ralph R. Covell

Banerjea, Krishna Mohan (1813–1885), Indian Christian philosopher and theologian. Banerjea was born into a Brahman Hindu family in Calcutta. He became proficient in both Sanskrit and English while developing more and more into first an agnostic and then an outright atheist. In his late teens he took up the cause of radical Hindu reform, editing a paper called the *Enquirer.* His extreme views soon brought about a break with his family, creating much excitement in the Hindu community. At about this time he met Alexander *Duff. Listening to Duff's lectures, he gradually became convinced of the rational truth of the Christian message and was baptized by Duff in 1832. Soon thereafter he joined the Church of England and was ordained by bishop Daniel *Wilson in 1836. After serving for some years as pastor to a Calcutta congregation, he became in 1852 a professor at Bishop's College, where he remained until his retirement. Here he was able to teach and to engage in a wide range of literary work both in English and Bengali, and he has been called the father of Bengali Christian literature. Much of his writing was in the apologetical mode, and was framed in direct opposition not only to orthodox Hinduism but also to the Brahmo Samaj (a reformist Hindu association). His best-known book, *Dialogues on the Hindu Philosophy,* first appeared in 1861. At the time of his death he was honorary chaplain to the bishop of Calcutta, a member of the Asiatic Society, and a much-respected Calcutta citizen.

BIBLIOGRAPHY K. M. Banerjea, *The Proper Place of Oriental Literature in Indian Collegiate Education* (1868), *The Relation between Christianity and Hinduism* (reprinted in 1897 with a biographical memoir by B. C. Ghose), and *Dialogues on the Hindu Philosophy* (2d ed., 1903). M. A. Laird, *Missionaries and Education in Bengal 1793–1837* (1972); T. V. Philip, *Krishna Mohan Banerjea: Christian Apologist* (1982).

Eric J. Sharpe

Bang Ji Il (1911–), Presbyterian Korean missionary, pastor, lecturer and author. Born in Sun Chon, North Korea, to a Christian family, Bang graduated from Soongsil College and Presbyterian Theological Seminary (Pyongyang). He planted and served the Chungdori church near the border of China (1929–1933) and the Chundachun church (1933–1937). He was a also a missionary to China (1939–1958). On his return to Korea, he served Yongdungpo Presbyterian Church in Seoul as pastor from 1958 to 1979. He also served as chairperson of the Presbyterian church assembly in South Korea in 1972. He continues his zeal for mission by educating Korean missionary candidates, and preaches to Korean congregations in many parts of the world. He is the author of seventy-four books. In 1982 he received an honorary doctorate from Soongsil University, Seoul.

BIBLIOGRAPHY Bang has written (in English) *Principle of Permission* (1962), *The Gospel of the Blood* (1963), *Believer's Life* (1970), *Pastor's Life* (1971), *Half Century in the Gospel Work* (1986), and *Immanuel (Reflection on China Missionary Work)* (1996).

Chun Chae Ok

Baradaeus (*or* Bar'adai; Barada'i), Jacob (c. 500–578), Syrian missionary bishop and Monophysite "apostle to Asia." Jacob Baradaeus was the architect of the survival of the Syrian Monophysites (hence their name as Jacobites) during the mid sixth-century persecutions by orthodox Constantinople. Baradaeus was born in Tella, eastern Syria, and educated as an ascetic in a monastery near Nisibis. During a lessening of persecution under Justinian, whose wife, the Empress Theodora, favored the Monophysite cause, a Christian Arab prince of the Ghassanids asked the empress to arrange the consecration of two missionary bishops and rescue the Monophysite episcopacy from near extinction. Thus in 542 Baradaeus was made bishop of Edessa. For the next 35 years Baradaeus dodged his persecutors, often by disguising himself in beggar's rags; from this came his nickname, al-Barada'i, "the ragged one." His extraordinary activities revived the Monophysites of Syria and Persia with the ordination (according to a doubtful estimate) of 100,000 priests, 27 bishops, and 2 patriarchs.

BIBLIOGRAPHY The classic biography is *Vita Baradeus,* attributed to the early Jacobite historian John of Ephesus (in *Patrologia Orientalis,* 18, with Eng. tr.). See also Aziz S. Atiya, *A History of Eastern Christianity* (1968), pp. 180 ff; W. H. C. Frend, *Martyrdom and Persecution in the Early Church* (1963), pp. 234–254, and *The Rise of the Monophysite Movement* (1972), pp. 285–287; E. Honigmann, "La Hiérarchie monophysite au temps de Jacques Baradée," in *Corpus Scriptorum Christianorum Orientalis,* Subsidia 2 (1951), pp. 542–578.

Samuel Hugh Moffett

Baraga, (Irenaeus) Frederic (1797–1868), Redemptorist missionary and first bishop of the Roman Catholic diocese of Marquette, Michigan. Baraga was born at Mala Vas castle, parish of Dobrnic, Slovenia. As a law student in Vienna, he became interested in Native American missions. After ordination (1823) he volunteered for the diocese of Cincinnati through the Leopoldinen-Stiftung, a foundation to aid the American missions. In May 1831 he arrived among the Ottawa of Arbre Croche (Harbor Springs, Michigan) and completely transformed the deteriorating mission. He founded missions at Grand River (Grand Rapids) in 1833, and among the Chippewas at La Pointe, Madeline Island, in 1835. He wrote *Theoretical and Practical Grammar of the Otchipwe Language* (1850), *Dictionary of the Ojibway Language* (1853), devotional books in Ottawa and Chippewa, and *The History, Character, Life and Manners of the Indians,* published in Slovene, French, and German (1837). He also ministered to white pioneers when copper mines opened on the Keweenaw Peninsula. He was named first vicar apostolic of the Upper Michigan Peninsula in 1853 and bishop in 1857. He was the first bishop to issue pastoral letters in aboriginal languages as well as English. Preliminary steps have been taken toward his beatification.

BIBLIOGRAPHY M. Dezernik, *Frederick Baraga, a Portrait of the First Bishop of Marquette Based on the Archives of the Congregatio de Propaganda Fide* (1968); J. Gregorich, *The Apostle of the Chippewas: The Life Story of the Most Reverend Frederick Baraga D.D.* (1932); A. I. Rezek, *History of the Diocese of Sault Ste. Marie and Marquette,* 2 vols. (1906–1907); C. Verwyst, *Life and Labors of Rt. Rev. Frederic Baraga: First Bishop of Marquette, Mich.* (1900). The Marquette diocesan library contains a holograph of Baraga's journal and many letters. Other materials are in the Newberry Library (Ayer Collection), Chicago, and Notre Dame University archives.

Achiel Peelman, OMI

Barber, Margaret (1865–1930), British missionary educator in China. Barber, who went to China as an Anglican and later became an independent missionary with informal ties to the Plymouth Brethren, is best known for her influence on Nee Tuo-sheng (Watchman *Nee). Stationed in Foochow (Fuzhou) along the south China coast, she and others regularly taught a Bible class at White Teeth Rock. Here she had contact with Nee at a very formative time of his life, when he studied for a time at Anglican Trinity College. As a result of her own spiritual struggles, she was able to refer him to books by J. N. Darby, Jeanne Guyon, T. Austin Sparks, and others that had been of help to her. She also had impact on many other Chinese men and women, the most noted of whom was Leland Wang (Wang Cai), who later became a Chinese leader.

BIBLIOGRAPHY Little information can be found on the life of Margaret Barber. Her impact on the life of Watchman Nee is discussed in Angus I. Kinnear, *Against the Tide* (1973).

Ralph R. Covell

Barclay, Thomas (1849–1935), Scottish missionary scholar in Taiwan. Barclay was born in Glasgow and died in Tainan following 60 years of service. He studied at the University of Glasgow, took ministerial training at the Free Church Divinity School and Leipzig, and in 1874 was ordained to missionary service under the Presbyterian Church of England. He reached Taiwan in 1875. He founded the Tainan Theological College and continued as its principal for most of his life. In 1895 his successful mediation between the invading Japanese army and Tainan saved the city from assault. Apart from his work as a theological educator, through which he influenced generations of Taiwanese ministers, his major contribution was the promotion of the romanized Taiwanese Bible to achieve a Bible-reading church. In 1916 he completed a thorough revision of the Amoy/Taiwanese New Testament, and in 1932 the Old Testament was finally published; both are renowned for their accuracy and style. In 1923 he also published a valuable *Supplement to Carstairs Douglas' Dictionary of the Amoy Vernacular.* In 1918 the British and Foreign Bible Society made Barclay an honorary life governor; in 1919 he received an honorary D.D. from the University of Glasgow, and in 1921 he was elected moderator of the first General Assembly of the Presbyterian Church of England.

BIBLIOGRAPHY Edward Band, *Barclay of Formosa* (1936) and *Working His Purpose Out* (1947).

George A. Hood

Barlow, Arthur Ruffelle (1888–1965), Scottish teacher, linguist, and church superintendent in Kenya. Born in Edinburgh, Barlow arrived in Kenya at the Kikuyu (Thogoto) mission station in 1903 to visit his uncle, D. C. Ruffelle *Scott, who was a Church of Scotland missionary there. He was only 17 years old at the time, just out of high school, and became informally associated with the work of the young mission by serving as Scott's personal secretary until 1909, when he officially became a missionary teacher of the Church of Scotland mission at Tumutumu near Nyeri. He gained the nickname Bwana Barlow, and his station became known as Kwa Bwana Barlow (Barlow's place or village). He studied the Kikuyu language as well as nine Kikuyu-related dialects of the area northeast of Mt. Kenya, including Chuka and Mwimbi. As a result, he played a leading role in writing the standard Kikuyu grammar and other books. With Leonard Beecher (later archbishop of East Africa) and Canon Harry Leakey, both of the Church Missionary Society, he translated the Scriptures into Kikuyu. The trio's language work was also the basis of a Kikuyu-English dictionary of 1964. Barlow served as superintendent of the Tumutumu mission as well as secretary of the mission council in Kenya. He was one of the influential voices in the missionary debate toward church union in Kenya, always insisting that the African opinion must not be ignored if meaningful unity was to be achieved. He was often consulted on African matters by government officials and other missionaries in Kenya. He retired in 1941 but returned to Kenya in 1952 to assist in translating documents during the Mau Mau troubles. He left finally in 1959.

BIBLIOGRAPHY R. Macpherson, *The Presbyterian Church in Kenya* (1970); E. N. Wanyoike, *An African Pastor* (1974).

Gerishon M. Kirika

Barratt, Thomas Ball (1865–1940), founder of Pentecostalism in Europe and the Norges Frie Evangeliske Hedningemission (NFEH). Barratt was born in Alabaston, Cornwall, England, the son of Mary Ball and Alexander Barratt, an expatriate Wesleyan Methodist mining engineer from Norway. From 1886 to 1902 Barratt served as a Norwegian-speaking Methodist Episcopal pastor in Christiania (Oslo), Norway. He created an inner city mission (Bymission) program that used drama and classical music productions as well as charity programs to minister to the unchurched.

In 1907 he became the founder of Pentecostalism in Norway and Europe, and, in 1908, published an appeal for a "spirit alliance" to unite people who had come to Pentecostalism from diverse ecclesiastical backgrounds. This resulted in the first Pentecostal mission organization, the Pentecostal Missionary Union, London, and his church in Christiania sent missionaries to India (1913). He also organized and administered the NFEH (1914–1929), an ecumenical mission reflecting the theories of William *Taylor. Seeking to expand local support for mission, Barratt then withdrew from the NFEH in 1929 and helped organize the Pinsevennenes Ytre Misjon (Pentecostal Foreign Mission). His mission praxis and theory had formative influences on the development of Pentecostalism in Europe, Asia, Africa, and Latin America.

BIBLIOGRAPHY Barratt edited *Byposten* (1904–1909) which continued as *Korsets Seier* (1909–), and published more than 300 books and pamphlets. Thomas Ball Barratt, *When the Fire Fell and an Outline of My Life* (1927; repr. in D. Dayton, ed., *The Works of T. B. Barratt,* 1985) and *Erindringer* (his memoirs), Solveig Barratt Lange, ed. (1941). Studies include N. Bloch-Hoell, *The Pentecostal Movement: Its Origin, Development, and Distinctive Character* (1964); David Bundy, "T. B. Barratt: The Methodist Years," in *Pentecostalism in the Context of the Holiness Revival* (1988), pp. 62–75, "T. B. Barratt's Christiania (Oslo) City Mission: A Study in the Intercultural Adaptation of American and British Voluntary Association Structures," *Crossing Borders* (1991), pp. 1–15, "Thomas B. Barratt and *Byposten:* An Early European Pentecostal Leader and His Periodical," in *Pentecost, Mission and Ecumenism: Essays on Intercultural Theology* (1992), pp. 115–121, and "Spiritual Advice to a Seeker: Letters to T. B. Barratt from Azusa Street," *Pneuma* 14 (1992): 159–171. The Barratt papers are preserved at the University of Oslo, Norway.

David Bundy

Barreira, Balthazar (*or* Baltesar) (1531?–1612), Portuguese Jesuit missionary in Angola and Sierra Leone. Barreira was the first missionary in Angola, arriving there in 1579. In a decade of mission work, he claimed 20,000 converts.

In 1605 he began work in Sierra Leone, where he staunchly opposed the slave trade. But he was also a sympathetic pastor for Portuguese settlers and members of the suppressed (military) Order of Christ who were engaged in commerce and building a local Christian community. Typically, he baptized a local potentate, "King" Philip of Sierra Leone, and family members, who then became evangelizers of the local people. He trekked north, contacting the Susu people, and always, in true Jesuit spirit, attempted to recruit and train local leadership. In 1606 he urged his superiors to support Sierra Leone as the most suitable place for Christianity in West Africa, although his effort to establish a seminary there was opposed by the king of Portugal, who wanted it in his own land.

Barreira's approach shows mature signs of what today is called contextualization or inculturation: he established real local communities and treated peoples, languages, and cultures with respect; he was a man of deep spirituality and empathy; and his was much more than a proselytizing zeal. Barreria remained in West Africa until old age, returning in 1609 to Lisbon.

BIBLIOGRAPHY M. Bane, *Catholic Pioneers in West Africa* (1956); A. Gittins, "Mende and Missionary" (Ph.D. thesis, Univ. of Edinburgh, 1977); M. Harney, *The Jesuits in History* (1941); A. P. Kup, "Jesuit and Capuchin Missions of the Seventeenth Century," *Sierra Leone Bulletin of Religion* 5 (1963); W. Rodney, *A History of the Upper Guinea Coast* (1970).

Anthony J. Gittins, CSSp

Barreto. *See* Nunes Barreto, João.

Barsauma (*or* Barsumas) (405?–491/95), bishop of the East Syrian Church (Nestorian). Barsauma was educated in Edessa. Because of Monophysite oppression, he moved to Nisibis in the Persian Empire, where he helped to establish and then administer the great theological school of Nisibis. This school became the main Persian theological training center for monks, priests, and bishops, who led in the spread of Christianity across Asia. Barsauma is known for his democratic ecclesiastical leadership, non-ascetic approach (he married a former nun and regularized clerical marriages), and unwavering support of the Dyophysite theological tradition. His ability to work with the Sasanian shah Peroz enabled him to gain responsibilities as ambassador to the West (Constantinople), but it also meant that he was misunderstood by his own followers. Most of the information about Barsauma comes from Nestorian synods, personal letters, and polemic writings from Monophysites.

BIBLIOGRAPHY Stephen Gero, *Barsauma of Nisibis and Persian Christianity in the Fifth Century* (1981); Arthur Vööbus, *History of the School of Nisibis* (1965).

Scott W. Sunquist

Bartel, Henry Cornelius (1873–1965), founder of two Mennonite missions in China and facilitator for the development of other Mennonite mission programs. Born in Poland, Bartel came to the United States with other Mennonite immigrants as a small child. In 1900 he married Nellie Schmidt, and in 1901 they went to China with Horace Houlding and his "China Band." In 1905, after working with Houlding for four years, Bartel established what subsquently came to be known as the China Mennonite Mission Society. It drew missionaries from various Mennonite denominational groups and was located in Shantung (Shandong) and Honan (Henan) Provinces. In addition to doing evangelistic work, the mission opened numerous schools and orphanages and the Truth Publishing House. In 1941 Bartel and his wife began a work in West China near the Szechwan-Kansu-Shansi (Sichuan-Gansu-Shaanxi) border; in 1945 it was accepted as a Mennonite Brethren mission project. Through his assistance the General Conference Mennonites opened a mission adjacent to that of the China Mennonite Mission, and the Krimmer Mennonite Brethren established a mission work in Inner Mongolia. In 1951 the Bartels were requested by the government to leave China.

Four of the Bartels' children—Loyal, Paul, Agnes (Wieneke), and Elsie (Eisenbraun)—also worked as missionaries in China. Loyal, who gained Chinese citizenship, remained in China until his death in 1971.

BIBLIOGRAPHY H. C. Bartel, *Mennonite Mission in China* (1913) and *M. B. Missions in West China* (1949). Robert and Alice Pannabecker Ramseyer, *Mennonites in China* (1988).

Paul Toews

Barth, Christian Gottlob (1799–1862), leading figure in the neopietist movement of Württemberg, Germany. Having served as a parish pastor, Barth became a free-lance promoter of the missionary cause while remaining in contact with the Basel Mission. His first achievement was in the field of mission journalism. While several German mission journals were already in existence, Barth founded not only two of his own but also an independent publishing house (Calwer Verlagsverein) which is still in operation. A collection of Bible stories which he compiled sold 2.5 million copies. In addition Barth gained a reputation for composing mission hymns that became popular far and wide, though some of them struck a somewhat military note. As a bachelor he transformed his house at Calw into a missionary museum; after his death this became the nucleus of the collections of the Basel Mission. He met with criticism for supporting Karl *Gützlaff's one-man mission operation in China but did not hesitate to recant when his enthusiasm proved to be premature. He shared with contemporary apocalyptic theologians an ardent expectation of the coming kingdom of Christ but never allowed it to cripple his determination to prove his faith by action.

BIBLIOGRAPHY Werner Raupp, *Christian Gottlob Barth: Studien zur Biographie und Bibliographie einer führenden Gestalt der württembergischen Erweckungsbewegung* (1997); Gottlieb Weitbrecht, *Dr. Barth nach seinem Leben und Wirken* (1875); Karl Werner, *Christian Gottlob Barth,* 3 vols. (1865–1869).

Hans-Werner Gensichen

Barth, Karl (1886–1968), Swiss theologian. Barth would have been the last to claim special missiological competence for himself. Nevertheless his influence on contemporary theologies of mission can hardly be exaggerated. Although only five pages of specific reference to foreign missions are found within the total of 8,000 pages of his *Church Dogmatics* (4.3a, pp. 874–878), Barth's influence must be interpreted in the wider context of his basic theology. Most of the critical potential of Barth's theology had been appropriated by European missiology even before World War II, in connection with his Berlin lecture on "Mission and Theology" (1932). Its influence continued to be felt during the struggle of the German confessing church under Hitler. Barth's lasting contributions may be summarized in three parameters. First, the foundation of mission cannot be found in anthropological, societal, cultural, or religious circumstances or need, but exclusively in God's total revelation through Jesus Christ, the true witness. Second, mission is meant to announce God's salvation to all people and thus is a venture of obedience which transcends the church and accepts solidarity with the world in proclamation and service. Third, the ultimate test of Christian mission is whether it transforms the church into a missionary community, witnessing in order to make others, too, God's witnesses and to equip them as such.

BIBLIOGRAPHY Karl Barth, "An Exegetical Study of Matthew 28:16–20" in Gerald H. Anderson, ed., *The Theology of the Christian Mission* (1961), pp. 55–71. Karl Hartenstein, *Was hat die Theologie Karl Barths der Mission zu sagen?* (1928); Dieter Manecke, *Mission als Zeugendienst* (1972); Jacques Rossel, "Von einer Theologie der Krisis zu einer Theologie der Revolution? Karl Barth, Mission und Missionen," *EMM* 113 (1969): 151–162; Waldron Scott, *Karl Barth's Theology of Mission* (1978).

Hans-Werner Gensichen

Barton, James Levi (1855–1936), missionary and executive of the American Board of Commissioners for Foreign Missions (ABCFM). Barton was born into a Quaker family in Charlotte, Vermont. He graduated from Middlebury College (1881) and, having developed a keen interest in questions of theology and modern thought, he entered Hartford Theological Seminary. Convinced that foreign missions could make a great contribution to human well-being, at his graduation in 1885 he applied for overseas service, married Flora Holmes, and sailed for Turkey. For seven years he supervised a large system of schools at Harpoot. He was elected president of Euphrates College, Harpoot, in 1892, but when his wife's ill health prevented continuing residence in Turkey, Barton became foreign secretary of the ABCFM. First among equals on the board staff, Barton believed that the primary need of indigenous Christian communities was well-trained leadership. Before his retirement in 1927, he helped secure permanent funds for the support of twenty-one international, interdenominational institutions of higher learning, including two medical schools. Barton had wide-ranging interests and significant contacts with secular leaders. He was a principal architect of Near East Relief after World War I, represented the Foreign Missions Conference of North America at the London Conference in 1921, and attended the Lausanne Conference (1922–1923), where an American treaty to end the war with Turkey was framed. Barton held five honorary degrees from four colleges.

BIBLIOGRAPHY James L. Barton, *The Missionary and His Critics* (1906), *The Unfinished Task of the Christian Church* (1908), *Daybreak in Turkey* (1908), *Human Progress through Missions* (1912), *The Christian Approach to Islam,* (1918), and *The Story of Near East Relief* (1930). A manuscript memoir of 339 pages is in the library of the United Church Board for World Ministries and in the Congregational Library, Boston. Fred Field Goodsell, his successor, wrote a summary tribute, *James Levi Barton: Dynamic World Christian Statesman* (1964).

David M. Stowe

Barton, John (1836–1908), Anglican missionary in India and a leader in the Church Missionary Society (CMS). Barton was born in Eastleigh, Hampshire, England, and graduated from Christ's College, Cambridge, in 1859. After ordination he sailed for Calcutta in 1860. He served in Agra and Amritsar before becoming principal of the new cathedral missionary college in Calcutta in 1865. He acted as secretary of the CMS Madras mission (1871–1875) and as a CMS secretary in London (1876–1877). Appointed vicar of Holy Trinity, Cambridge, in 1877, he continued to act for CMS on its committee and in two overseas visits to South India and Ceylon (1884 and 1889), when he did much to resolve strained relationships between R. S. *Copleston and the CMS. He initiated new structures for the church in Tinnevelly (Tirunelveli), where caste had caused difficulty. From his student days, when he organized the Cambridge University Missionary Union in 1858, to his building of the Henry Martyn Memorial Hall in 1880 and beyond, he remained a leading advocate of the missionary cause in Cambridge. He refused bishoprics of Travancore, Tinnevelly, and in Japan.

BIBLIOGRAPHY C. E. Barton, *Life of John Barton* (1911); M. E. Gibbs, *The Anglican Church in India* (1972); E. Stock, *History of the Church Missionary Society* (1899); *Times* obituary of December 1, 1908.

Timothy Yates

Barzaeus (*or* Barzäus; Berze), Gaspar (1515–1553), Jesuit missionary in the kingdom of Hormuz and in Goa, India. Barzaeus was a native of Goes, Netherlands. He received a master of arts degree from the University of Louvain and joined the army of Charles V in 1536. He later became a hermit in the mountains of Montserrat, Spain, and then worked in the royal treasury in Lisbon. In 1546 he entered the Society of Jesus in Coimbra and two years later sailed for Goa. Francis *Xavier ordered him to go to Hormuz, at the mouth of the Persian Gulf, where he was told to spend three years (1549–1551) teaching in the Jesuit college and working among the local population. Xavier's April 1549 letter of instruction to Barzaeus offers insights into the missionary methods Barzaeus was to follow there. Writing from Kagoshima, Japan, in November that year, Xavier ordered Barzaeus to proceed to Japan, but he apparently did not receive these orders. In 1552 he was summoned to Goa and Xavier later appointed him rector of the college there and vice-provincial of India. In April of 1552 Xavier wrote several detailed letters to

Barzaeus on methods a religious superior in India should follow. Barzaeus died in Goa.

BIBLIOGRAPHY M. Joseph Costelloe, ed., *The Letters and Instructions of Francis Xavier* (1992), pp. 230, 313–314, 391–419, 425–434, 445–447; Nicholas Trigault, *Vita Gasparis Barzae* (1610) and *Vie du P. Gaspard Barzée* (1615).

John W. Witek, SJ

Barzana, Alonso de (1528–1598), Spanish Jesuit missionary and linguist in Peru. Born in Córdoba, Spain, Barzana studied arts and theology in Baeza and then entered the Jesuit order in Córdoba in 1565, a disciple of Juan de Ávila, taking his main vows in 1567. Arriving in Peru in 1569, he was sent to work in Cuzco, and in 1576 he took the "fourth vow" under provincial José de *Acosta. He began studying Indian languages, including Quechua, Aymara, Guaraní, Puquina, Tenocotica, and Catamarcana. Some of his works were among the earliest publications of Peru's first printer, Antonio Ricardo: *Un libro de oraciones* (1586), *Arte y vocabulario en lengua Quichua* (1585) (one of Barzana's more famous works), and *Confesionario.* This latter, published in Quechua and Aymara for priests working among Indians, included a longer and shorter catechism. He was also a *visitador* and preacher in other areas of Peru.

Barzana's greatest contribution to missionary work was his help in formulating and translating into Quechua and Aymara the catechism produced by the Third Council of Lima (1582–1583), *Doctrina cristiana para instrucción de los indios,* which remained in use until 1900. Barzana died in Cuzco, Peru, of apoplexy.

BIBLIOGRAPHY Luis Resines Llorente, *Catecismos Americanos del Siglo XVI,* Tomo 1 (1992); Luis Martin, *The Intellectual Conquest of Peru: The Jesuit College of San Pablo, 1568–1767* (1968); Carlos Sommervoegel, *Bibliothèque de la Compagnie de Jésus* (1890).

G. Stewart McIntosh

Bashford, James Whitford (1848–1919), Methodist bishop in China. Born in Fayette, Wisconsin, Bashford studied at the University of Wisconsin and Boston University School of Theology. After serving first as a pastor, then for 15 years as president of Ohio Wesleyan University, he was elected a bishop of the Methodist Episcopal Church in Los Angeles and in 1904 was assigned at his own request to China at age 55, the first resident bishop of the Methodist Episcopal Church in China. (Three branches of American Methodism operated in separate regions of China until they merged in 1939 to form the Methodist Church. The Chinese Methodist churches did not elect their own bishops until 1930.)

An able administrator and a man of vision, Bashford brought great progress to his church and its institutions in his 15 years as episcopal leader in China. Always a loyal Methodist, he led the way toward union and cooperation among Protestant forces in China, especially in educational and medical work, Bible translation, and production of a common hymnal; he was instrumental in introducing a spirit of interchurch cooperation among his fellow Methodists. In 1904 he served as first president of the board of Hwa Nan Women's College, Foochow (Fuzhou), and encouraged the union of colleges for men and for women in four major cities as early as 1905. He helped bring about union theological seminaries in Foochow and Nanking (Nanjing).

Bashford favored the union of the northern and southern branches of Methodism in China as early as 1906, as well as Methodist participation in forming the National Christian Council in 1922. However, he opposed a Chinese Methodist Church independent from the American church, believing that a "world church" like Methodism should maintain its integrity "organically as well as in spirit."

BIBLIOGRAPHY Bashford wrote *China and Methodism* (1906) and (his major work) *China: An Interpretation* (1916; rev. and enlarged, 1919). G. R. Grose, *James W. Bashford: Pastor, Educator, Bishop* (1922); Jerry Israel, "The Missionary Catalyst: Bishop James W. Bashford and the Social Gospel in China," *Methodist History* 14 (1975); Walter Lacy, *A Hundred Years of Methodism* (1948). Bashford's journals are in the Missionary Research Library, New York.

Donald E. MacInnis

Bataillon, Pierre Marie (1810–1877), pioneer Marist missionary bishop in the southwest Pacific. Born at Saint-Cyr-les-Vignes, Loire, France, Bataillon studied in Lyons and after his 1835 ordination joined the Society of Mary to be a missionary. He sailed with Jean-Baptiste François *Pompallier in 1836 and the next year was placed on Wallis (Uvea), between Fiji and Samoa, with Joseph Luzy to found the first Marist Pacific mission. Despite great hardship and organized opposition, he learned the language quickly and within four years converted every inhabitant, in contrast to compatriot Peter *Chanel on nearby Futuna, whose missionary work seemed almost fruitless. Bataillon was then placed in charge of a newly created Vicariate of Central Oceania and ordained a bishop in 1843. Anxious to establish missions on all the major island groups entrusted to him, Pompallier placed too great demands on his missioners, locating them separately and with few provisions in Samoa, Tonga, and Fiji; he disregarded Marist founder Jean-Claude Marie *Colin's request to place them in pairs for mutual support. Nevertheless, the missionaries survived strong opposition from established denominations, and maintained footholds on each of these island groups. Bataillon wanted an indigenous priesthood and brought three candidates with him on what became a triumphant visit to Europe in 1856. (One of them, the Tongan Soakimi Gatafahefa, received ordination in Rome in 1864.) In 1859 Bataillon established a missionary college for islanders at Clydesdale near Sydney, Australia, which closed after ten fruitless years, but he immediately began again in Wallis, and this effort was successful; islander priests were ordained beginning in 1888.

Bataillon manifested an essential greatness. Known as Enossi (the title of his episcopal see), he was tough, autocratic, and a man of vision who became legendary among island peoples.

BIBLIOGRAPHY Pierre-Marie Bataillon, *Language d'Uvea (Wallis)* (1932). A. Mangeret, *Mgr. Bataillon et les missions de L'Océanie Centrale* (1884), rev. anonymously (by Guy de Bigault) as *La Croix dans les iles du Pacifique: Vie de Mons. Bataillon de la Société de Marie, évêque d'Enos. Premier vicaire apostolique de l'Océanie centrale, 1810–1877* (1922). A chapter on Bataillon is included in John Hosie, *Challenge: Marists in Colonial Australia* (1987). Bataillon's letters and his manuscript history of the mission of Central Oceania are in the archives of the Marist Fathers, Rome.

John Hosie, SM

Bates, M(iner) Searle (1897–1978), American missionary in China and missiologist. Bates was born in Newark, Ohio, the son of a Disciples of Christ minister and college president. He graduated from Hiram College, Ohio, and received both A.B. and M.A. degrees as a Rhodes Scholar at University of Oxford; in 1935 he received the Ph.D. in Chinese history from Yale University. He served in India and Mesopotamia with the YMCA in 1917–1918. For a span of 30 years (1920–1950), he taught history as a missionary of the United Christian Missionary Society (Disciples of Christ) at the University of Nanking (Nanjing), China, an institution formed in 1910 by the merger of three colleges sponsored by American Protestant missions.

In addition to teaching, Bates was active in numerous ecumenical enterprises. He was a member of the China delegation to the Madras meeting of the International Missionary Council (IMC) in 1938, and subsequently served as Far Eastern consultant and, from 1941 to 1945, as coordinator of wartime emergency services in China for the IMC. He served with the Fellowship of Reconciliation in wartime contacts with Japan. He served on the Council of Higher Education of China, the Nanking International Relief Committee, and the executive committee of the National Christian Council in China. He served as investigator of opium trade in Japanese-occupied China. His *Religious Liberty: An Inquiry* (1945) was published in seven languages.

From 1950 to 1965, Bates was professor of missions at Union Theological Seminary, New York; he was a trustee of the United Board for Christian Higher Education in Asia, and a member of the China Program Committee of the National Council of Churches in the U.S.A. After his retirement from teaching until his death, he worked tirelessly on a massive research project focused on the history of the Protestant effort in twentieth-century China.

BIBLIOGRAPHY A content guide to the notes and manuscripts of Bates was prepared and published after his death, along with an introductory essay and outline of the register of his papers: Cynthia McLean, "The Protestant Endeavor in Chinese Society, 1890–1950: Gleanings from the Manuscripts of M. Searle Bates," *IBMR* 8 (1984): 108–112. Bates's China research papers are in the China Records Collection, Yale Divinity School; other papers are in the Disciples Historical Society, Nashville, Tennessee.

Donald E. MacInnis

Baughman, Burr (1910–), Methodist missionary in Malaya and Sarawak. Baughman was born in Java to Methodist missionary parents. After attending Duke University and Garrett Biblical Institute in the United States, he joined the Malaysia Mission in 1932 and worked as pastor, teacher, and missionary to the Senoi (Orang Asli) of peninsular Malaysia. After being interned by the Japanese during World War II, he was assigned in 1947 to oversee, with Lucius *Mamora, work among the Iban people of Sarawak. Through the efforts of Baughman and Mamora, the first Iban converts to Methodism were baptized in 1949. Baughman was subsequently involved in translating the Scriptures and numerous hymns into the Iban language, as well as establishing the Methodist Theological School in Sibu, Sarawak. He retired in 1970 to Florida.

BIBLIOGRAPHY J. Andrew Fowler, "Communicating the Gospel among the Iban" (D. Min. diss., Southern Methodist Univ., 1976); Joseph Terrance, "The Longhouse Church in Sarawak" (S.T.M. thesis, Southern Methodist Univ., 1964).

Robert A. Hunt

Bavinck, Johan Herman (1895–1964), Dutch missiologist. Born in Rotterdam, Bavinck studied theology at the Free University of Amsterdam and received a Ph.D. from Erlangen University in 1919. He served as minister of Dutch-speaking Dutch Reformed churches in Indonesia (1919–1926) and in Heemstede, Holland (1926–1929). In 1930 he returned to Indonesia as a missionary in Solo (1930–1933) and Jogjakarta (1935–1939). In 1939 he was appointed the first professor of missions at both the Theological University of Kampen and the Free University of Amsterdam (1939–1964); beginning in 1954 he also taught pastoral theology.

Bavinck had a special interest in religious psychology. His dissertation (1919) dealt with the medieval mystic Henry Suso, and in Java he paid special attention to Javanese mysticism. His study *Christus en de Mystiek van het Oosten* (Christ and eastern mysticism) (1934) was one of the fruits of his encounter with Javanese mysticism.

In 1940 he published a summary in Dutch of Hendrik *Kraemer's *Christian Message in a Non-Christian World* entitled *De Boodschap van Christus en de Niet-Christelijke Religies,* in which Kraemer's influence on his own missionary thinking was evident. In 1949 he published his main work: *Religieus Besef en Christelijk Geloof* (Religious consciousness and Christian faith) in which he combined his interest in religious psychology with a strong biblical orientation. Another major work is his missiological handbook, *Inleiding in de zendingswetenschap* (1954; in English translation, *An Introduction to the Science of Missions,* 1960).

Bavinck was widely influential both inside and outside the Reformed tradition through his writings and his visits to the United States and South Africa, and through his supervision of many dissertations written by Dutch, South-African, American, and Korean doctoral students.

BIBLIOGRAPHY Bavinck's main works in English are *The Impact of Christianity on the Non-Christian World* (1949); *An Introduction to the Science of Missions* (1960), and *The Church between Temple and Mosque: A Study of the Relationship between the Christian Faith and Other Religions* (1966; 2d ed., 1981). J. van den Berg, "Johan Herman Bavinck," in Gerald H. Anderson et al., eds., *Mission Legacies* (1994), pp. 428–434; "Dr. J. H. Bavinck (1895–1964)," in J. Verkuyl, *Contemporary Missiology: An Introduction* (1978), pp. 35–41; P. J. Visser, *Bemoeienis en Getuigenis: Het leven en de missionaire theologie van Johan H. Bavinck (1895–1964)* (Solicitude and Witness: The Life and the missionary theology of Johan H. Bavinck, with summary in English) (1997); R. Van Woudenberg, *J. H. Bavinck: Een keuze uit zijn werk* (1991). A. Wessels, "Bibliografie van Professor Dr. J. H. Bavinck," in J. van den Berg, ed., *Christusprediking in de Wereld* (1965), pp. 223–246.

Jan A. B. Jongeneel

Bax, Jacques (1825–1895), pioneer Catholic missionary in Mongolia. Born in Weelde/Mechelen (Malines), Belgium, Bax was ordained a priest in 1853 and in 1863 became a member of the Congregation of the Immaculate Heart of Mary (CICM), also known as Scheutveld Missionaries (in the U.S., Missionhurst). In 1871 he was appointed pro-vicar of Mongolia, and in 1874 became the first apostolic vicar of the Ordos borderlands between China and Inner Mongolia. In order to stabilize the situation of the Mongolian peoples, who suffered constantly from famine, natural disasters, and political unrest, he opted for developing a type of reduction (settlement) approach to missionary work similar to that used by the Jesuits in sixteenth- and seventeenth-century Latin America. This was the approach generally used by CICM missionaries in Mongolia from 1879 until the mid-1940s. Bax died at Si-Yintze (or Nanhaochan) in Mongolia.

BIBLIOGRAPHY J. Beckmann, *Die katholische Missionsmethode in China in neuster Zeit, 1842–1912* (1931); J. van Hecken, "Les réductions catholiques du pays des Ordos. Une méthode d'apostolat des missionaires de Scheut," *NZM* 11 (1955): 105–121, 191–203, 266–282; 12 (1956): 35–45, 119–137, 199–218.

Stephen B. Bevans, SVD

Baxter, Richard (1615–1691), Puritan missions advocate. Born of Puritan parents in Shropshire, England, Baxter was ordained in the Anglican Church in 1638. His ministry spanned fifty-three years but he was silenced by ecclesiastical authorities from 1662 to 1689, along with nearly 2,000 colleagues, and became known as the leader of the British Nonconformists. His passionate concern was for the unconverted in all lands. He won numerous supporters and great renown by writing hundreds of essays, books, and sermons, and by his broad evangelical commitment to the unity of the church. At many points his life and works touched the great missionary movements of the seventeenth and eighteenth centuries. He was a personal friend and constant supporter of John *Eliot, the Apostle to the Indians; he faithfully promoted the "Corporation for the Promotion of the Gospel in New England" (1649) and collaborated with its president, Robert Boyle; and he was instrumental in facilitating the translation of Christian literature into Middle Eastern, Indian, and other languages for mission work. He was an inspiration to some of the great missionaries to come, including the father of John *Wesley and Charles *Wesley, and later, through his books, the two sons themselves; Daniel *Wilson of Calcutta; Philip Doddridge, through whom Samuel *Wilberforce was converted; Isaac Watts; George *Whitefield, and others. He believed that each person would be judged according to the law under which he providentially lived: Jews under the law of Moses, pagans under the law of nature, and Christians under the law of Christ. Nevertheless, he asserted that all who are saved are so because of the greatness of the love of God and the grace of Christ.

BIBLIOGRAPHY Richard Baxter, *A Christian Directory* (1673), *Reliquiae Baxterianae* (1696; much of this work is republished in *The Autobiography of Richard Baxter,* introduction and notes by J. M. Lloyd Thomas, 1925), and *The Practical Works of Richard Baxter,* 4 vols. (1888). Hugh Martin, *Puritanism and Richard Baxter* (1954); Frederick J. Powicke, *A Life of the Reverend Richard Baxter,* 2 vols. (1924) and "Some Unpublished Correspondence of the Rev. Richard Baxter and the Rev. John Eliot... 1656–1682," *Bulletin of the John Rylands Library* 15 (1931): 138–176 and 442–466; Sidney H. Rooy, *The Theology of Missions in the Puritan Tradition* (1965), pp. 66–155. *Letters* 1–6 and *Treatises* 1–7 are located in the Dr. Williams Library in London.

Sidney H. Rooy

Baynes, Alfred Henry (1838–1914), secretary of the Baptist Missionary Society (BMS). Born at Wellington, Somerset, England, and educated at Devonshire College, Bath, Baynes at age 20 became private secretary to Sir Samuel Morton Peto, the Baptist civil engineering contractor and honorary treasurer of the BMS, who in 1861 seconded Baynes to the society to attend to its accounts. From this humble beginning as accountant Baynes rose to become finance and minute secretary (1870), co-secretary (1876), and, from December 1878 to 1906, general secretary. He presided over a considerable increase in the size and range of operations of the BMS and thus holds an important place in the story of nineteenth-century Protestant missionary expansion. Between 1876 and 1906, the BMS missionary force grew from 109 to 170. Baynes encouraged the growth of the China mission from a minor enterprise into one of the more significant Protestant mission bodies in China. He was the moving spirit behind the BMS Congo mission (1879), which remained his chief enthusiasm. In association with William Holman *Bentley and George *Grenfell, he directed Baptist expansion on the Congo River. Until 1905, Baynes, following Grenfell's advice, was a firm supporter of Leopold II's Congo Free State as a guarantee against Portuguese ambitions in central Africa and sought to defend Leopold against the mounting volume of criticism directed at the "rubber atrocities."

BIBLIOGRAPHY E. A. Payne, *The Great Succession: Leaders of the Baptist Missionary Society during the Nineteenth Century* (n.d.), pp. 43–53; Brian Stanley, *The History of the Baptist Missionary Society, 1792–1992* (1992); *Missionary Herald* 36 (1914): 345–370.

Brian Stanley

Beach, Harlan Page (1854–1933), American missiologist. Beach was born in Orange, New Jersey, and graduated from Yale University (B.A., 1878) and Andover Theological Seminary (B.D., 1883). He served from 1883 to 1889 as American Board of Commissioners for Foreign Missions missionary in North China, where he taught in a high school and seminary in Tung-chau and founded one of China's first YMCAs. He returned to the United States because of his wife's ill health. Working under the direction of John R. *Mott he became educational secretary of the Student Volunteer Movement in 1895, with responsibility for a program of missionary education for students in colleges and seminaries. He served on the executive committee and was chairman of the exhibit committee of the Ecumenical Missionary Conference at Carnegie Hall in New York City in 1900. His work as a statistician and compiler of atlases of foreign missions, his major contribution to scholarship, began during this period with the publication of *A Geography and Atlas of Protestant Missions* (vol. 1, 1901; vol. 2, 1903). In 1906 he became the first professor of missions at Yale Divinity School, and from 1911 he was also librarian of the Day Missions Library at Yale. At the 1910 World Missionary Conference in Edinburgh, Scotland, Beach reported to the commission on "The Preparation of Missionaries" that Yale had the largest collection of missionary literature in America. His greatest achievement at Yale was the expansion and development of the Day Missions Library, which greatly facilitated the work of his successor, Kenneth Scott *Latourette. Beach traveled frequently to visit overseas mission fields in connection with his teaching and research. His other major scholarly works were *World Atlas of Christian Missions* (1911), with James S. Dennis and Charles H. Fahs, *World Statistics of Christian Missions* (1916), with Burton St. John, and *World Missionary Atlas* (1925), with Charles H. Fahs. After retirement from Yale in 1921, he was lecturer in missions at Drew University Theological School until ill health caused his permanent retirement in 1928.

BIBLIOGRAPHY Beach also published *The Cross in the Land of the Trident* (1895), a mission study on India, *Renaissant Latin America,* a report on the conference in Panama in 1916 of Protestant missionaries to South America, and *Missions as a Cultural Factor in the Pacific,* prepared for the 1927 conference of the Institute of Pacific Relations. His letters and diaries are in the special collections of Yale Divinity Library.

Gerald H. Anderson

Beaver, R(obert) Pierce (1906–1987), American missiologist. Born in Hamilton, Ohio, Beaver graduated from Oberlin College and Cornell University (Ph.D., 1933, history). He went to China in 1938 as a missionary of the Evangelical and Reformed Church. After language study in Peking, he taught at Central China Union Theological Seminary in Ling-ling, Hunan Province, from 1940 to 1942. He was interned in Hong Kong by the Japanese for seven months until repatriated in 1943. Beaver taught missions at Lancaster (Pennsylvania) Theological Seminary from 1944 to 1948, then was director of the Missionary Research Library (MRL) at Union Theological Seminary, New York City, from 1948 to 1955. In 1955 he was appointed professor of missions at the University of Chicago Divinity School, where he taught until his retirement in 1971. After retirement he was director from 1973 to 1976 of the Overseas Ministries Study Center, then located in Ventnor, New Jersey. He was a founding member of the Association of Professors of Missions in North America in 1952, serving as its president from 1956 to 1958, and for many years he was a trustee of the Foundation for Theological Education in South East Asia.

Beaver's greatest contributions to missiology were through research and writing, as well as his encouragement of other scholars through his teaching and professional associations. During his tenure at MRL he began publication of the *Occasional Bulletin from the MRL* (later the *International Bulletin of Missionary Research,* published by the Overseas Ministries Study Center), which provided documentation and encouraged scholarship in studies of Christian missions.

Among his numerous publications were several pioneering studies that became standard references, especially *Ecumenical Beginnings in Protestant World Mission: A History of Comity* (1962) and *All Loves Excelling: American Protestant Women in World Mission* (1968; rev. 1980). He edited *The Gospel and Frontier Peoples* (1973) and a large symposium for the American Society of Missiology in 1976, *American Missions in Bicentennial Perspective,* which one reviewer described as "a landmark in the development of missiology in America." On the occasion of his retirement from the University of Chicago, a Festschrift was presented to him, *The Future of the Christian World Mission: Studies in Honor of R. Pierce Beaver.* In 1972 he received an honorary D.D. from Concordia Seminary, Saint Louis, Missouri. He died in Tucson, Arizona.

BIBLIOGRAPHY Beaver's personal library, papers, and unclassified documents are in the library at Memphis Theological Seminary, Memphis, Tenn. A biographical tribute by Wi Jo Kang and a bibliography of Beaver's published work (up to 1969) are in *The Future of the Christian World Mission: Studies in Honor of R. Pierce Beaver,* edited by William J. Danker and Wi Jo Kang (1971). The best survey and assessment of Beaver's work is by F. Dean Lueking, "R. Pierce Beaver," in Gerald H. Anderson et al., eds., *Mission Legacies* (1994), pp. 452–458. Works by Beaver include *Pioneers in Mission: The Early Missionary Ordination Sermons, Charges, and Instructions* (1966), *Church, State, and the American Indians* (1966), and "Missionary Motivation through Three Centuries," in *Reinterpretation in American Church History,* edited by Jerald C. Brauer (1969).

Gerald H. Anderson

Becker, Carl (1894–1990), American pioneer missionary medical doctor in the Belgian Congo (Zaire). Born in Manheim, Pennsylvania, Becker studied medicine at Hahnemann Medical College in Philadelphia and spent seven years in private practice before he and his wife, Marie, began missionary service with the Africa Inland Mission in 1929. In 1934 he founded a medical center at Oicha to serve the needs of pygmies living deep in the Ituri Forest and remained there for the rest of his active ministry. He specialized in leprosy, treating some 4,000 patients in a 1,100-acre leprosy village. Leprosy specialists and medical missionaries from all over the world came to observe his work and borrow from his research at Oicha. In addition, he served as the only resident medical doctor at the hospital and performed more than 3,000 operations and delivered hundreds of babies each year. Also interested in psychiatry, he was the first doctor in equatorial Africa to successfully use electric shock treatment on African patients. In addition to medical work, he also served as an evangelist, going to villages on weekends with crudely drawn illustrations that depicted biblical stories. During the Simba Revolution in 1964, when he was 70, Becker was evacuated but returned the following year and remained at the medical center until 1976, when he returned to the United States.

BIBLIOGRAPHY William J. Peterson, *Another Hand on Mine: The Story of Dr. Carl K. Becker of the Africa Inland Mission* (1967); Ruth A. Tucker, *From Jerusalem to Irian Jaya: A Biographical History of Christian Missions* (1983).

Ruth A. Tucker

Becker, Christoph Edmund (1875–1937), Catholic missionary in Assam, India, and mission educator. Born in Elsoff in the archdiocese of Frankfurt am Main, Germany, Becker entered the Society of the Divine Savior (SDS, also known as Salvatorians) in 1889. Before ordination in 1898, he received doctorates in both philosophy and theology. After ordination he served as professor and eventually rector at the Salvatorian seminary in Merano, Italy, and in 1905 was appointed prefect apostolic of Assam, India. Expelled from India during World War I, he resigned his position and returned to his native Germany. In 1922 he founded the Medical Mission Institute in Würzburg, the first of its kind to train physicians and nurses for missionary work and to provide medical courses for missionary priests. He also served as professor of missiology in Würzburg.

BIBLIOGRAPHY C. E. Becker, *Indisches Kastenwesen und christliche Mission* (1921), *Im Stromtal des Brahmaputra* (1927), and *Missionsärzliche Kulturarbeit* (1928). T. Ohm, *Die ärtzliche Fürsorge der katholischen Missionen* (1935); G. Schreiber, *Deutsches Reich und deutsche Medizin* (1926); G. Wunderle, "Professor C. E. Becker: Gründer des Missionsärzlichen Instituts," *Katholische Missionsärzlich Fürsorge,* Jahresbericht 14 (1937): 3–14.

Stephen B. Bevans, SVD

Beckmann, Johannes (1901–1971), Catholic missiologist. Born in Essen, Germany, Beckmann studied in Switzerland at Immensee and Wolhusen, then at the seminary of the Missionary Society of Bethlehem, at Schöneck-Beckenried, which he joined as a member. After ordination, he studied missiology at the University of Münster, where J. *Schmidlin was his teacher (D.Th., 1930). Until 1960 he taught church history and missiology at the seminary at Schöneck-Beckenried, and lectured at the University of Fribourg and at the Tropeninstitut (tropical institute) in Basel. In 1936 he traveled to China, and in 1938 and 1939 to Southern Rhodesia. In 1945 he founded the *Neue Zeitschrift für Missionswissenschaft (NZM),* which he edited until he died. The last decade of his life he lived at Fribourg.

Beckmann was a prodigious writer. Besides his dissertation *Die katholische Missionsmethode in China in neuester Zeit, 1842–1912* (1931), he published *Altes und neues China* (1944, with G. Frei), *Die katholische Kirche im neuen Afrika* (1947), and *Weltkirche und Weltreligionen* (1960). He was coauthor of *Lexikon für Theologie und Kirche* (1957-1967) and *Handbuch der Kirchengeschichte* (1962–1979). He was also editor of two volumes in the supplemental series of *NZM,* and published articles in various journals. In 1993 the diary of his visit in South Africa was also published.

Beckmann was especially interested in mission history, particularly the church in Latin America in the sixteenth and seventeenth centuries. But he was also so well informed about the current situation in the church that he was invited to write on Catholic missions for several years in the *International Review of Mission.* One of his sidelines was to explore the lives of Swiss missionaries.

BIBLIOGRAPHY Jakob Baumgartner, "Prof. Dr. Johannes Beckmann, 1901–1971. Zum Gedächtnis," *NZM* 28 (1972): 1–19, and "Beginn der Missionstätigkeit der SMB in Simbabwe. Johannes Beckmanns Erkundungsreise ins südliche Afrika, 1938–1939," *NZM* 48 (1992): 81–114; Johann Specker, "Bibliographie Johannes Beckmann, 1961–1971," *NZM* 27 (1971): 143–152; Johann Specker and Walbert Bühlmann, eds., *Das Laienapostolat in den Missionen. Festschrift Johannes Beckmann* (1961).

Fritz Kollbrunner, SMB

Bede (c. 673–735), English biblical scholar and church historian. Educated at Wearmouth, Bede became a monk at Jarrow, in northeast England, and there was ordained a deacon and a priest. A skilled educator and creative writer, he produced an introductory volume on poetry in which he versified the life of St. *Cuthbert, an early mission figure. He recognized that linguistic skills were crucial for mission work. He was most noted in his own time and in the medieval period for his scriptural commentaries; he also wrote a history of abbots, a prose life and miracles of St. Cuthbert, and a history of the English church. This last work is often considered his most significant; it is sometimes the only source on the history of early Christian mission in England. Bede shows careful use of his sources, which he diligently gathered. While separating out what he considers to be unsupported by the evidence, at the same time he affirms God's activity in the conversion of peoples and the preservation of the faith. He emphasizes the unity and order of the church, which he illustrates by the moral examples of its leaders. Although he does not write in such a way as to highlight the development of character, he does describe situations well and paints wonderful images. He often recounts miraculous events that turned the tide.

BIBLIOGRAPHY Gerald Bonner, *Wearmouth, Bede, and Christian Culture* (1974); George H. Brown, *Bede the Venerable* (1987) and *St. Bede: A Tribute (735–1985)* (1985); John M. Wallace-Hadrill,

Bede's Ecclesiastical History of the English People: A Historical Commentary (1988).

Frederick W. Norris

Belavin, Tikhon. *See* Tikhon.

Belcourt, Georges Antoine (1803–1874), Catholic missionary to Indians of western Canada. Belcourt was born in Quebec and ordained in 1827. In 1831 he volunteered for the Red River area in Saint Boniface Diocese (near present-day Winnipeg). He served in a number of missions among the Ojibwa Indians and devoted himself to studying their language. He was the author of *Principes de la Langue des Sauvages appelés Sauteux* (1839) and of *Dictionnaire Sauteux* published after his death by Albert *Lacombe. He was the first Catholic missionary in the Canadian west to preach without aid of an interpreter. He often accompanied the Ojibwa Indians and Métis (mixed blood) on the buffalo hunt, of which he wrote detailed descriptions. He attempted to teach agriculture to the Indians, who were nomadic hunters. This brought him into conflict with his bishop, Joseph-Norbert Provencher. In 1848, after Belcourt assisted the Métis trappers in a dispute with the Hudson's Bay Company, the company governor instigated his recall to Montreal. The following year Belcourt volunteered for the Dubuque Diocese and went to Pembina (North Dakota). He established the settlement of Saint Joseph (Walhalla, now Leroy), where he started schools for Native Americans and again encouraged agriculture. Conflicts with other clergy continued, and in 1859 he was forced to leave the diocese. He spent the rest of his career working in parishes on Prince Edward Island and the Magdalen Islands, where he died.

BIBLIOGRAPHY Mary Aquinas Norton, *Catholic Missionary Activity in the Northwest, 1818–1864* (1980); J. M. Reardon, *George Anthony Belcourt: Catholic Missionary of the Northwest* (1955) and *The Catholic Church in the Diocese of St. Paul, from Earliest Origins to Centennial Achievement: A Factual Narrative* (1952); Alexander Ross, *The Red River Settlement, Its Rise, Progress and Present State* (1856). See also *Georges Antoine Belcourt* (1984), pamphlet published by the Manitoba Department of Heritage, Culture, and Recreation. Correspondence in the Archives Archiépiscopales de St. Boniface and the Belleau Collection of the Assumption Abbey Archives, Richardson, N. Dak.

Achiel Peelman, OMI

Belksma, J(ohannes) (1884–1942), Dutch missionary to Toraja, Indonesia. Born in Tzummarum, Netherlands, the son of a farm laborer, Belksma became a schoolteacher, and in 1916 was sent by the newly founded (1901) Gereformeerde Zendingsbond (Reformed Mission League) to Tana Toraja, Celebes (Sulawesi, Indonesia) to establish and lead a teacher training school. After the murder of his colleague A. A. van de *Loosdrecht (1917), he became the senior missionary of the Toraja mission until his death. He taught nearly all Toraja teachers and evangelists, wrote the hymnbook (1927) and the catechism (1932) of the incipient Toraja church, and drew up its church order, which followed the classical Calvinist pattern (1937; officially accepted by the church in 1947). One of the problems faced by the Toraja mission was determining the attitude to be assumed towards the feudal order of society.

Among his colleagues, Belksma was the most democratic; he accepted children of former slaves into the teacher training school, thereby bringing them into the new emerging elite. Moreover, he quietly gave moral support to Christians who refused to give traditional homage to the local chiefs at funeral ceremonies, a tradition which had religious as well as social significance. However, as a staunch adherent of Abraham Kuyper's antirevolutionary party, he rejected the idea of social or political revolution and therefore opposed the Indonesian nationalist movement. He wanted the Toraja church to participate in a denominational (Calvinist) ecumene rather than in a national one. After national and church independence, the influence of his ideas waned. In 1995 the Toraja church numbered 300,000 members.

BIBLIOGRAPHY Terance W. Bigalke, "A Social History of 'Tana Toraja' 1870–1965" (Ph.D. diss., Univ. of Wisconsin, 1981); Th. van den End, *De Gereformeerde Zendingsbond 1901–1961. Nederland-Tanah Toraja: Een bronnenpublicatie* (1985); Theodorus Kobong, "Evangelium und Tongkonan" (Th.D. diss., Hamburg, 1989); B. Plaisier, "Bruggen en Grenzen: De communicatie van het Evangelie in het Torajagebied (1913–1942)" (Th.D. diss., Utrecht Univ., 1993).

Th. van den End

Bell, L(emuel) Nelson (1894–1973), Presbyterian medical missionary in China. Born in Longsdale, Virginia, Bell initially intended to pursue a career in law but switched to medicine in response to a call to overseas mission. Graduating from the Medical College of Virginia at 21, in December 1916 he arrived at Tsingkiangpu (now Huaiyin), almost 300 miles north of Shanghai, to serve at Love and Mercy Hospital. The hospital expanded under Bell's leadership and became the largest of the Southern Presbyterian overseas medical missions. After three years under Japanese occupation, the family returned to the United States in May 1941, where Bell took up a medical practice in Asheville, North Carolina. His concern for the theological integrity of his church prompted him to launch the *Southern Presbyterian Journal* (renamed *The Presbyterian Journal* in 1959). In 1955 and 1956 he and his son-in-law, Billy *Graham, founded *Christianity Today;* Bell became executive editor and contributed the column "A Layman and His Faith" until his death. In 1972 he was elected moderator of the General Assembly of the Presbyterian Church in the U.S.

BIBLIOGRAPHY John Pollock, *A Foreign Devil in China* (rev., 1988); *Christianity Today* (memorial), Aug. 31, 1973.

Robert T. Coote

Benavente, Toribio de. *See* Motolinía.

Benavides, Miguel de (1552–1605), Dominican missionary and bishop in the Philippines. Benavides was born in Carrión de los Condes, Palencia, Spain. He joined the Dominican order in 1567 in the convent of San Pablo, Valladolid, and sailed for the Philippines in 1586. He arrived in Manila the following year with fourteen Dominicans, founders of the Dominican order in Asia. His first mission was to the *sangleyes,* the Chinese people in the Philippines. Benavides wrote *Doctrina Christiana en letra y lengua china;* published in 1593 in Manila, it is the oldest book in the Philippines. In 1590, with Juan de Castro, he left for China. Quickly imprisoned, they were expelled in 1591. Benavides later accompanied Domingo de *Salazar, first bishop of the Philippines, to Spain. At audiences with Philip II in Madrid (1593–1597), he denounced the conquest of the Philippines, advocated the preaching of the gospel without coercion, and demanded that the Filipinos be given the freedom to submit voluntarily to Spanish authority. In 1595 he was appointed bishop of the Diocese of Nueva Segovia (northern Luzon). Benavides returned to Manila in 1598 and became its second archbishop in 1602. There he passionately defended the Filipinos against the abuses of the conquistadors.

The University of Santo Tomas, Manila, founded in 1611, and a center of missionary expansion and culture in Asia, considers Benavides its founder.

BIBLIOGRAPHY Emma H. Blair and James A. Robertson, *The Philippine Islands: 1493–1898,* vols. 10 and 11 (1905–1909); Jesús Gayo Aragón, *Ideas jurídico-teológicas de los religiosos de Filipinas en el siglo XVI sobre la conquista de las Islas* (1950). Benavides's correspondence and treatises are mainly found in the Archivo General de Indias in Seville, Spain, Audiencia de Filipinas, Legajo 76.

Lucio Gutiérrez, OP

Bender, Carl Jacob (1869–1935), German Baptist missionary in Cameroon. Bender was born in Eschelbach, Baden, but he immigrated to the United States at age 12 and worked as a store clerk in Buffalo, New York. He became a Baptist, decided to enter the ministry, and enrolled in Rochester Seminary's German department. Deeply influenced by Walter Rauschenbusch's social vision, he wanted to work abroad, and upon graduation in 1899 went to Cameroon under the German Baptist Mission. He pioneered work near Duala; in 1909, he relocated at Soppo, in the interior, where he engaged in evangelism, educational work, and scientific research and became an advocate for Africans. After the Allies conquered the German colony in 1916, Bender was allowed to stay because he was a U.S. citizen. He left in 1919; the mission, located in western Cameroon, the area under British mandate, passed to African leadership. He spent the next years in the United States, serving churches and publishing ethnological books, but when the missionaries were permitted to return, he was recalled to his old station at Soppo in 1929. He revived the dormant work and built a new church building before dying from blackwater fever in 1935. Although he lacked formal anthropological training, Bender had a great appreciation for African culture. He contextualized the Christian message and developed an effective indigenous ministry through the schools he founded.

BIBLIOGRAPHY Carl F. H. Henry, *Bender in the Cameroons* (1943); Charles W. Weber, *International Influences and Baptist Mission in West Cameroon* (1993).

Richard V. Pierard

Benedict (c. 480–c. 550), founder of Western monasticism. Born at Nursia in central Italy, Benedict was sent to Rome for his education, but when he found the hedonism and intemperance of Roman student society a threat to his own Christian life, he secretly withdrew from the city and eventually lived in a cavern in Subiaco. Under the guidance of a local monk named Romanus, Benedict spent three years there as a hermit in solitude, prayer, and penance. His reputation for holiness and miracles soon began to attract disciples whom Benedict eventually organized into twelve communities under his authority, each with twelve monks and a prior. Local hostility finally impelled Benedict to move with a small group of monks to Monte Cassino, where he founded an abbey around 530 and composed his Rule to provide for the administration and spiritual life of the monastery. The monks lived together under Benedict as father abbot, held their possessions in common, celebrated daily the full Liturgy of the Hours (the Divine Office), and spent the day in prayer, sacred reading *(lectio divina),* and work. Through the Rule, and through the example of the life of Monte Cassino, Benedict exerted immense influence not only on all subsequent monasticism in the West but also on the civilization and evangelization of Europe in the aftermath of the Roman empire. Monks following the Rule of St. Benedict were the church's principal missionaries for the next five centuries.

BIBLIOGRAPHY Cuthbert Butler, *Benedictine Monachism* (1924); Christopher Derrick, *The Rule of Peace* (1980); Timothy Fry, ed., *The Rule of St. Benedict* (1981); Terrence Kardong, *The Benedictines* (1988); Odo J. Zimmermann and Benedict R. Avery, eds., *The Life and Miracles of St. Benedict* (Gregory the Great, *Dialogues,* Book II) (1949).

Joseph DiNoia, OP

Benedict XIV (Prospero Lorenzo Lambertini) (1675–1758), pope who dealt with Chinese Rites Controversy and other mission-related issues. Prospero Lorenzo Lambertini, a native of Bologna, Italy, completed a degree in civil and canon law in 1694. At almost 50 years of age, after serving as a canon lawyer in Rome for more than two decades, he was ordained a priest and was consecrated a bishop two weeks later. Appointed archbishop of Ancona in 1727, he became a cardinal the following year and was appointed archbishop of Bologna in 1731. After a very prolonged papal conclave in 1740, he was elected pope on the 255th ballot and took the name Benedict XIV. A promoter of economic improvement for the lower classes in the Papal States, he also founded four academies for scholarly discussions about church and Roman history and established a Museum of Christian Antiquities in the Vatican Palace. As a canon lawyer, Benedict sought to decide longstanding disputes in the Christian missions. He issued a bull that parishes in missionary lands, even those administered by religious orders, were to be subject to the local bishops in everything that pertained to the care of souls and the administration of the sacraments. His brief to the bishops in South America forbade anyone to participate in seizing or selling Indians into slavery. By issuing two papal bulls, he settled the long-continuing issues about the Chinese Rites and the Malabar Rites in India. The first bull, *Ex quo singulari* (1742), banned Chinese Christians from using ancestral rites, and Chinese Christian scholars from participating in ceremonies honoring Confucius. The second, *Omnium sollicitudinum* (1744), ordered, for example, that only names of saints listed in the Roman Martyrology could be used for baptismal names, and that missionaries were expected to enter the houses of pariahs, thereby ignoring caste restrictions. His works and extensive extant correspondence portray a scholar committed to guarding purity of doctrine.

BIBLIOGRAPHY Benedict XIV, *Opera omnia,* 17 vols. (1829–1847) and *Heroic Virtue: A Portion of the Treatise of Benedict XIV on the Beatification and Canonization of the Servants of God,* 3 vols. (1850–1852). Tarcisio Bertone, *Il governo della Chiesa nel pensiero di Benedetto XIV* (1977); Marco Cecchelli, ed., *Benedetto XIV (Prospero Lambertini),* 2 vols. (1981–1982); Renée Haynes, *Philosopher King: The Humanist Pope Benedict XIV* (1970).

John W. Witek, SJ

Benedict XV (1854–1922), pope and author of the mission encyclical *Maximum illud.* Benedict was born Giacomo Della Chiesa at Genoa in 1854. He was ordained priest in 1878 and in 1882 became private secretary to the nuncio in Madrid. In 1901 he entered the papal curia as a close collaborator of the cardinal secretary of state and confidant to the pope. He became archbishop of Bologna in 1907; in May 1914 he became cardinal and was elected pope on September 3 of the same year.

Benedict's pontificate (1914–1922) was characterized by repeated, substantial efforts for peace and attempts at mediation during World War I. In 1917 he submitted a plan for peace negotiations. He had the Curia organize aid and care for prisoners of war. Without ceding the inherited papal stance regarding territorial sovereignty, he sought to reduce the tension that had arisen between the Curia and the Italian government because of Italy's annexation of territory previously controlled by the church. Among his achievements internal to the church were the reform and codification of canon law; curial, pastoral, and liturgical reforms; pastoral care for emigrants; and guidelines for preaching God's Word, addressed to bishops and priests.

Benedict's greatest contribution was the far-seeing impetus that he gave to Catholic missionary activity. World War I had brought great harm to the missions. The period of colonialism was ending, and the peoples under colonial rule were vigorously struggling for political independence. From it all, Benedict drew the following conclusions: Base the Christian mission on its purest spiritual foundations and separate it from politics and colonialism; promote the formation of indigenous clergy and entrust the church's leadership into their hands; establish indigenous hierarchies and churches; promote and centralize aid to the Catholic missions and transfer its direction from colonialism-tainted France to the Vatican (a move that almost provoked a breach in diplomatic relations with France); and establish a chair of mission studies in the Propaganda Fide Congregation's Athenaeum (later, Urbanianum University). All these major provisions he outlined in his landmark mission encyclical *Maximum illud* (1919).

BIBLIOGRAPHY Pablo Gúrpide, "Benedicto XV el pontífice de las misiones," *El Siglo de las Misiones* 9 (1922): 66–68, 97–100, 129–132, 161–163; F. Hayward, *Un pape méconnu. Benoît XV* (1955); Cyril C. Martindale, *The Call of the Missions and the Answer of the Popes* (1939); M. di Pietro, *Benedict XV, the Pope of Peace* (1941); "S. S. Benoît XV, pape des missions," *Bulletin des Missions Bénédictines Belges* 6 (1920–1923): 241–245; Josef Schmidlin, *Papstgeschichte der neuesten Zeit,* vol. 3, *Pius X. und Benedikt XV. (1903–1922)* (1936).

Josef Metzler, OMI

Benignus, Pierre (1912-1963), missionary and facilitator of Christian-Muslim relationships in Africa. Born of missionary parents in the French colony of New Caledonia and educated in theology and missiology in his native France, Benignus was ordained into the ministry of the Reformed Church (1937). With his wife, Marianne (Hoepffner), he spent two years prior to the outbreak of World War II as a missionary in New Caledonia. After the war and a brief pastorate in Strasbourg, a second missionary posting took him to Africa, first to Madagascar (1948–1950) and then to Senegal, where he was appointed general secretary of missions of the Protestant churches of West Africa (1951). During the political turmoil of French decolonization, he helped pioneer a new relationship of friendship between Christians and Muslims in the common task of nation building. He was recalled to Paris as secretary for missionary and ecumenical relationships in the Paris Evangelical Missionary Society, and his experience in Christian-Muslim relations inspired the foundation of the Islam in Africa Project (1960), of which he became the first general secretary. He traveled extensively in Africa, consulting with Christian leaders to assist churches in building new relationships with Muslim neighbors based on mutual understanding, trust, and social cooperation. As delegate to the 1961 New Delhi general assembly of the World Council of Churches, he contributed to the emergence of interfaith dialogue as an integral part of the mission of the world church. Though he died prematurely in a tragic plane accident in Cameroon, his leadership of the Islam in Africa Project laid the foundations of what continues as the Project for Christian-Muslim Relations in Africa.

BIBLIOGRAPHY *Pierre Benignus (1912–1963)* (undated pamphlet, c. 1964; preface by Pastor Marc Boegner).

David A. Kerr

Benlloch y Vivó, Juan (1864–1926), cardinal of Burgos. Benlloch was born in Valencia, Spain, where he did his ecclesiastical studies, becoming a doctor of theology and canon law. He was ordained a priest in 1888 and became a bishop in 1901. In 1906 he was named bishop of Urgel and sovereign prince of Andorra; in 1919 he was assigned to Burgos as bishop, and in 1921 he was made a cardinal. He received a letter from Pope *Benedict XV in 1921 encouraging him to establish a seminary for training foreign missionaries. In that same year, with some priests and seminarians from Burgos, he founded the Seminario Español Misiones Extrajeras, which became an institute in 1947. He also worked with José *Zameza to develop the Spanish school of missiology. With his interest in missions, he visited many countries of Latin America. Thanks to him and to the seminary he established, many Spanish diocesan clergy have been trained and sent as missionaries to Latin America, Asia, and Africa.

BIBLIOGRAPHY Benlloch y Vivó's greatest pastoral letters urging the church of Burgos and of Spain to support missionary activity are from 1919 and 1920. On his visit to South America, see A. Villanueva Gutiérrez, *Crónica oficial de la embajada del Card. Benlloch y Vivó a la América española,* vols. 1 and 2 (1916).

Jesús López-Gay, SJ

Bennett, Belle Harris (1852–1922), president of Woman's Missionary Council, Methodist Episcopal Church, South, and founder of Scarritt Bible and Training School. Born near Richmond, Kentucky, Bennett began outreach among the Kentucky poor while in her twenties. Concerned that southern Methodist women were going to the mission field without adequate training, in 1889 she proposed founding a missionary training school and then raised the money to open it in 1892 at Kansas City, Missouri. In 1892 she also joined the central committee of what became the Woman's Home Missionary Society, serving as president from 1896 to 1910. Under her leadership, southern Methodist women founded settlement houses, conducted industrial work among African-Americans, opposed racism, and organized a deaconess movement. In 1910 the women's home and foreign missionary boards of the Methodist Episcopal Church, South, were combined into one organization at the insistence of the men. Bennett took on the leadership of the resulting Woman's Missionary Council even as she led a fight for women's laity rights in southern Methodism. Of ecumenical spirit, she attended the World Missionary Conference in Edinburgh, 1910; chaired the Commission on Woman's Work for the Panama Congress on Christian Work in Latin America, 1916; and was elected to the first International Missionary Council in 1921 at Lake Mohonk, New York.

BIBLIOGRAPHY R. W. Macdonnell, *Belle Harris Bennett: Her Life Work* (1928, 1987); Carolyn Stapleton, "Belle Harris Bennett: Model of Holistic Christianity," *Methodist History,* April 1983, pp. 130–142. See also Alice Cobb, *"Yes, Lord, I'll Do It": Scarritt's Century of Service* (1987); Sara Estelle Haskin, *Women and Missions in the Methodist Episcopal Church, South* (1920); John Patrick McDowell, *The Social Gospel in the South: The Woman's Home Mission Movement in the Methodist Episcopal Church, South, 1886–1939* (1982).

Dana L. Robert

Bennett, Cephas (1804–1885), American Baptist missionary in Burma (Myanmar). Bennett was born in Homer, New York, the son of Baptist minister Alfred Bennett. At 13, Cephas was apprenticed to a printer, and this became his lifelong trade. In 1824 he became the printer of the *New York Baptist Register.* He had a wide interest in publishing religious materials, and while Sunday School superintendent at Broad Street Baptist Church, Utica, New York, he produced a Bible dictionary. In 1827 he offered to print the Burmese Bible, a project of Adoniram *Judson that the Baptist Board of Foreign Missions felt should be accomplished in Burma. Lucius Bolles, secretary to the board, invited Bennett to become a missionary printer. In response, he and his wife, Stella (Kneeland), accepted an appointment as American Baptist missionaries to Burma in 1829. At Moulmein, and later at Rangoon, he superintended the printing of the Bible and countless tracts and served as pastor of a Baptist congregation. In 1862 he organized the Burma Bible and Tract Society; Stella Bennett was an active leader in Burmese women's work.

A longtime resident of Rangoon, Bennett lectured widely on its history and published a historical study of the changes during his residence there. He died in Burma after 56 years of missionary service.

BIBLIOGRAPHY Cephas Bennett, *A Dictionary of the New Testament for the Use of Sabbath Schools* (1857), *Vocabulary and Phrasebook: In English and Burmese* (1857), and *Rangoon Fifty Years Ago: Topographical, Social and Commercial* (1884). A. P. Brigham, *In Memory of Rev. Cephas Bennett: A Sermon, Feb. 26, 1886* (1886); Ruth W. Ranney, *A Sketch of the Lives and Missionary Work of Rev. Cephas Bennett and His Wife Stella Kneeland Bennett* (1892).

William H. Brackney

Bentley, William Holman (1855–1905), Baptist Missionary Society (BMS) missionary in the Congo. Bentley was born at Sudbury, Suffolk, England, where his father was a Baptist minister. He worked as a bank clerk before being accepted by the BMS for its new Congo mission. He sailed for the Congo (Zaire) in April 1879 in the company of Thomas and Minnie *Comber, H. E. Crudgington, and J. S. Hartland. In January 1881, Bentley and Crudgington became the first Europeans to establish a route inland from the mouth of the Congo to Stanley Pool, where modern Kinshasa is situated. In 1884, Bentley returned to England on furlough. He took with him a Congolese assistant, Nlemvo, who worked with him on the compilation of the *Dictionary and Grammar of the Kongo Language* (1887), a work still used today. During this furlough he married Hendrina Margo Kloekers. Bentley returned to the Congo in 1886 to assume responsibility for a station on the upper river, but the death of Thomas Comber in 1887 diverted him to Ngombe Lutete among the Bakongo people. There Bentley remained, nurturing the growth of the Kongo church and devoting his linguistic expertise to the translation of the New Testament into Kikongo, which was completed in 1893. He also translated Genesis, Proverbs, and part of the Psalms. For these achievements he was awarded an honorary doctorate of divinity by the University of Glasgow. He died in Bristol.

BIBLIOGRAPHY In addition to his linguistic work, Bentley published *Pioneering on the Congo*, 2 vols. (1900). H. M. Bentley, *W. Holman Bentley: The Life and Labours of a Congo Pioneer* (1907); Brian Stanley, *The History of the Baptist Missionary Society, 1792–1992* (1992).

Brian Stanley

Berg, Daniel (1884–1963), cofounder of the Assemblies of God Church in Brazil. Berg was born of Baptist parents in Vargon, Sweden, and was baptized at 15. Early in 1902, due to a severe economic depression, he immigrated to New England and worked there and in Pennsylvania for eight years. When he returned to Sweden for a visit in 1909, a boyhood friend awakened in him a fervent desire for the baptism of the Spirit. At a Chicago conference he met Gunmar *Vingren, with whom he was to share the call to missions until the latter died in 1933. Vingren had finished studies in a Baptist Bible institute and had become a Baptist pastor in South Bend, Indiana. There, first Vingren and later Berg received a prophecy by Adolf Uldine that they were to be missionaries to "Para." At a local library they discovered that Para was a state in northern Brazil. After a service of confirmation led by William H. Durham of the North Avenue Mission of Chicago, in 1910 the two men began their work in Belem, the capital city of Para, in cooperation with the local Baptist congregation. However, they were soon cut off from that congregation because of their Pentecostal teachings. With seventeen adult members and their children, they founded the first Assemblies of God church on June 18, 1911. After seven more years of work, the new congregation was officially registered as the Assembleia de Deus.

On a return visit to Sweden in 1920, Berg married, and his wife, Sara, became his co-worker upon their return to Brazil. He was honored with a gold medallion at the fiftieth anniversary celebration of the organization of the first Assemblies of God church. His humble demeanor and evangelistic zeal made him a hero of faith for the church he founded, the largest Protestant church in Latin America. He retired and died in Sweden.

BIBLIOGRAPHY Berg's autobiography is *Enviado por Deus: Memorias de Daniel Berg* (3d ed., 1973). Emilio Conde, *Historia des Assembleias de Deus no Brasil: Belem 1911–1961* (1960); Abroao De Almeida, ed., *Historia des Assembleias de Deus no Brasil* (1982); Walter Hollenweger, *The Pentecostals* (1972).

Sidney H. Rooy

Bergmann, Wilhelm (H. F.) (1899–1987), German missionary in New Guinea. Born in a Westphalian farming community, from early childhood Bergmann had wanted to become a missionary. At the outbreak of World War I he found himself managing his mother's and his married sisters' farmsteads. To better prepare himself for missionary service, he studied Greek, Latin, and music. After the Leipzig Mission rejected him, the Neuendettelsau Mission Seminary accepted him for training in 1921. Graduating with honors, he briefly pursued linguistic studies at Hamburg University. In 1928 he arrived in New Guinea, which was then administered by Australia under a League of Nations mandate. From 1919, Lutheran missions had encouraged indigenous missionaries sent by coastal congregations to contact the peoples of the central highlands. Then when Australian authorities realized it was impossible to keep the central highlanders isolated from outside fortune hunters and traders, they decided to allow Western missionaries to work there, and Bergmann guided a rapidly expanding missionary endeavor. His qualifications for this task were a rare combination of sober-minded missionary determination, organizational competence, a low-key conciliatory approach to the highland people, and a keen anthropological and linguistic interest. He traveled to practically every corner of the highlands placing local evangelists, recording data, and guiding younger staff. Though initially an overall strategist, he later concentrated on pastoral work among the people of the Chimbu Valley. He retired to Australia in 1968. In 1986 the University of Erlangen-Nürnberg granted him an honorary doctorate in theology in recognition not only of his pioneering mission work but also in gratitude for his vast collection of manuscripts and papers containing an enormous wealth of anthropological, social, linguistic, and historical information.

BIBLIOGRAPHY Works written or translated by Wilhelm Bergmann include *Das Neue Testament in der Kuman Sprache* (1953), *Grammatick der Kuman Sprache* (1964–1966), *Mareko: Yesu Singgie Kamo Wakai* (The gospel according to St. Mark in Kuman) (1968), *Yohane: Yesu Singgie Kamo Wakai* (The Gospel according to St. John in Kuman) (1969), *Die Kamanuku (Die Kultur der Chimbu Stämme)*, 4 vols. (1970), and *Vierzig Jahre in Neuguines*, 11 vols. (n.d.) See also T. Ahrens, *Der Neue Mensch im kolonialen Zwielicht* (1993), pp. 49 ff. Bergmann materials, including most of the above, are available in the Neuendettelsau Mission archives and in the archives of the Evangelical Lutheran Church of Papua New Guinea, at Lae.

Theodor Ahrens

Berkeley, Xavier (1861–1944), Catholic missionary in China. Born in Gloucestershire, England, to a noble family, Agnes Mary Berkeley was inspired from youth to "save Chinese babies." In 1882 she entered the Sisters of Charity of St. *Vincent de Paul and received the religious name Xavier. She spent 54 years in China, first in Kiangsi (Jiangxi) Province, and then at Ningpo (Ningbo), Chekiang (Zhejiang) Province, drawn especially to the sick and poor. She rescued countless abandoned babies and organized young Chinese to design and weave silk and satin, thereby making them financially independent. In 1911, on Chou-shan (Zhoushan) Island, she developed House of Mercy, a model mission of charity, and she became known throughout the area as the Mother of the Orphans and the Poor. This mission, adjacent to the island where Chinese pilgrims visited the shrine of Kwan Yin, the Buddhist goddess of mercy, contained an orphanage, homes for old and infirm, and hospitals for the sick poor. With difficulty, she kept the mission open when the Japanese overran the area in World War II. She was buried in the mission garden.

James A. *Walsh referred to her as Maryknoll's cofounder, as she urged him to send women to China. Her manner of living and working with the poor was the pattern he desired the Maryknoll Sisters to assume.

BIBLIOGRAPHY Mary Louise Hinton, *Sister Xavier Berkeley, Sister of Charity of St. Vincent de Paul* (1949); Mark Leo Kent and Mary Just, *The Glory of Christ: A Pageant of Two Hundred Missionary Lives from Apostolic Times to the Present Age* (1955). James A. Walsh narrates her story in *Field Afar* 2, no. 5 (1908), and 5, no. 5 (1911).

Angelyn Dries, OSF

Bermyn (*or* Bermijn), Alphonse (1853-1915), Catholic missionary in Mongolia. Born in St. Paul-Waes in the archdiocese of Ghent, Belgium, Bermyn was ordained a priest in 1876 and became a member of the Congregation of the Immaculate Heart of Mary (CICM; also known as Scheutveld Missionaries, or, in the U.S., Missionhurst) in 1878. That same year he was assigned to the CICM mission in Mongolia, and in 1901 became apostolic vicar of southwest Mongolia (the region known as Ordos), a successor to Jacques *Bax. Due to the nomadic life of the Mongolians, the frequent famines and natural disasters in the region, and the general political unrest in this remote part of China, Bermyn encouraged the development of Christian villages around the mission compound. Such communities, which were similar to the Jesuit reductions of sixteenth- and seventeenth-century Latin America, were a particular contribution of the CICM missionaries to missionary methods in China. Bermyn died at Kangfangyintze in Mongolia.

BIBLIOGRAPHY J. Beckmann, *Die katholische Missionsmethode in China in neuster Zeit, 1842-1912* (1931); J. van Hecken, *Mgr. Alfons Bermijn: Dokumenten over het missieleven van een voortrekker in Monglie, 1878-1915,* 2 vols. (1947), "Les réductions catholiques du pays des Ordos. Une méthode d'apostolat des missionaries de Scheut," *NZM* 11 (1955): 105-121, 191-203, 266-282, 12 (1956): 34-45, 119-137, 199-218.

Stephen B. Bevans, SVD

Bernardino, Ignazio da Asti (c. 1702-1757), Italian author of an early Catholic missionary manual. Bernardino arrived in Luanda, in present-day Angola, as a Capuchin missionary in 1741. Two years later he was sent north to the principal mission, Soyo, which had been without a missionary for six months following a dispute with the ruler. He was instructed to abandon the Soyo mission should the situation prove impossible, but with the help of a strong, loyal corps of Kongolese interpreters, teachers, and servants of the mission, he successfully continued the work. He acted as vice-prefect in Luanda from August 1746 to June 1748. While at Soyo he was cured from an eye illness through a miraculous intervention by his former novitiate master, Ignazio da Santhià. In 1749 he returned to Italy, where he presented two memoranda to Propaganda Fide and composed *Missione in pratica,* a missionary manual. In March 1750 he was assigned to Bahia, Brazil, where he died.

Bernardino's manual was finally published in 1931 with a French translation but with its authorship wrongly attributed. Written as pious advice for those intending to be missionaries, it nevertheless provides fascinating, intimate insights into the daily life of the Soyo mission in the mid-eighteenth century.

BIBLIOGRAPHY T. Filesi and Isidoro de Villapadierna, *La "Missio Antiqua" dei Cappuccini nel Congo* (1978); J. Nothomb, ed., *La pratique missionnaire des PP. Capucins Italiens dans les royaumes de Congo, Angola et contrées adjacentes* (1931).

Richard Gray

Bernardino de Sahagún. *See* Sahagún, Bernardino de.

Bernard-Maitre, Henri (1889-1975), missionary and historian of Jesuit missions in China. Born at Châlons-sur-Marne, France, Bernard (-Maitre added in 1948) became a Jesuit in 1908 and received a degree in mathematics. Having taught in Rheims, then in Amiens, in 1924 he was sent to become professor of mathematics at the École des Hautes Études in Tientsin (Tianjin), China. He worked actively as a missionary among the Chinese, but several articles he published from 1925 onward led to his assignment as a researcher and writer at Zikawei (Xujiahui), near Shanghai, in 1937 and then in Tientsin two years later. From 1940 to 1947 he taught Chinese philosophy at Sienhsien (Xianxian), then at Tientsin. He established the Cathasia printing house to reprint the works of past missionaries such as Léon *Wieger and Seraphim *Couvreur. Returning to France in 1947, he spent 18 years in Paris and 10 at Chantilly. At the Institut Catholique in Paris he established the Institute of Religious Ethnology and Sociology. Besides several books, he wrote many articles about China in more than forty periodicals. Along with Joseph *Dehergne, in 1974 he founded the Colloque International de Sinologie, which meets every three years at Chantilly.

BIBLIOGRAPHY Henri Bernard-Maitre, *Aux portes de la Chine, les missionnaires du XVe siècle, 1514-1588* (1933), *Matteo Ricci's Scientific Contribution to China* (1935), and *Le Père Matthieu Ricci et la Société chinoise de son temps (1552-1610),* 2 vols. (1937). Hugues Beylard, "Bernard, Henri. Bernard-Maitre," in Paul Duclos, ed., *Dictionnaire du Monde Religieux dans la France Contemporaine* (1985), p. 38; Joseph Dehergne, "Henri Bernard-Maitre, Choix d'articles et de livres sur l'Extreme-Orient," *Bulletin de l'École française de l'Extreme-Orient* 63 (1976): 467-479.

John W. Witek, SJ

Berron, Paul (Émile) (1887-1970), founder and first director of Action Chrétienne en Orient. Born in La Petite-Pierre, Alsace (then part of Germany), Berron studied philosophy and theology in Strasbourg and missiology in Halle. He was ordained a Lutheran minister in 1914. Assigned by the Frankfurter Mission to a ministry among Muslims in Syria, he was called up instead to serve with the German army. As a military chaplain, he went to Syria in 1915 to inspect soldier's clubs and was from 1916 stationed at Aleppo with his wife, Madeleine (Hey). They discovered the plight of the martyred and deceived Armenian nation. In 1919 he returned to Alsace, now part of France again, with the same missionary vocation; he studied Islam and learned Turkish. But as a French citizen he was not welcome in Turkey. From 1920 to 1922 he served with the Frankfurter Mission, exploring opportunities in French-controlled Syria. Realizing that a French agency could work there, in 1922 Berron founded a new nondenominational missionary society, Action Chrétienne en Orient, based in Strasbourg. Its aims were relief of displaced Armenians, spiritual support of the old Near-Eastern churches, and mission to Muslims. Branches were established in Switzerland and the Netherlands that were eventually stronger than the French base. Missionaries were French, Swiss, Dutch, Armenians, and Arabs of evangelical persuasion. The first to be appointed were Hedwige Bull from Estonia, Alice Humbert-Droz from Switzerland, and the Armenians Jean Ghazarossian and Krikor Khayiguian; all four transferred from the Frankfurter Mission. The bulk of the work was the planting of evangelical Armenian churches in the Near East and in France, and since the 1950s, social work and Christian witness among North-African Muslim immigrants in France. In 1961 Berron yielded his leadership to Robert Brecheisen. He never left his connection with the Lutheran state church in Alsace but was spiritually at home in the evangelical Free Church movement of Southern Germany (Gemeinschaftsbewegung). He died in Auvernier, Switzerland.

BIBLIOGRAPHY Paul Berron, *Jean-Marie Guyaus Kritik der Religion* (Ph.D. diss., Univ. of Strasbourg, 1914), *Missionsdienst im Orient und Okzident: Entstehung und Werdegang der Strassburger Morgenlandmission "Action Chrétienne en Orient"* (1957), and *Une oeuvre missionnaire en Orient et en Occident: Origine et développement de l'Action Chrétienne en Orient* (1962; partly autobiographical).

Marc R. Spindler

Berthoud, Paul (1847–1930), pioneer missionary of the Swiss Mission Church in South Africa and Mozambique. Berthoud received his theological education at the faculty of the Free Church of the canton Vaud in Lausanne, Switzerland. In 1872 he and Ernest *Creux left for Basutoland (present-day Lesotho) where he served under the auspices of the Paris Evangelical Missionary Society (PEMS). Together with Adolphe *Mabille, he left in 1872 for the northeastern Transvaal in neighboring South Africa. There in 1875 Berthoud and Creux established a mission station named Valdezia after their home canton, Vaud, and began to study the Tsonga (Gwamba) language. In 1877 Berthoud left for Portuguese East Africa (present-day Mozambique) and established a mission station and a training institution at Rikatla and in 1889 another station at Lourenço Marques. Though he retired in 1903, he returned in 1906 to Mozambique where he eventually died.

Besides his pioneering mission work, Berthoud made a major contribution in the field of linguistics. His knowledge of the Tsonga and Ronga languages not only led to Bible translations but also to his writing various hymns and grammars.

BIBLIOGRAPHY Paul Berthoud, *Les Nègres Gouamba* (1896), *Lettres missionaires de M. et Mme. P. Berthoud de la Mission romande, 1873–1879* (1900), *Abuku da Mapsalme* (1905), and *Eléments de grammaire Ronga* (1920). J. du Plessis, *A History of Christian Missions in South Africa* (1911); M. I. Mathebula, "The Relationship between Some Ecumenical Bodies and the Evangelical Presbyterian Church in South Africa (Swiss Mission) (1904–1975): A Historical Study" (M.Th. thesis, Univ. of South Africa, Pretoria, 1989).

J. W. Hofmeyr

Berze, Kaspar. *See* Barzaeus, Gaspar.

Beschi, Constanzo Giuseppe (1680–1747), Italian Jesuit missionary in India. Beschi was born in Castiglione, near Mantua, in northern Italy. After joining the Jesuits, he went to the Madurai mission in South India in 1710. The following year he donned the ocher robe of the Indian sannyasi (holy man). For 36 years he had an active ministry, traveling widely in the mission, ministering to the scattered Catholic communities, and making new converts. In a period of political unrest with competing armies of Hindu and Muslim chieftains, Beschi needed courage and diplomatic skill to protect the mission and seemed to have had the support of some Muslim chieftains. The Tamil version of his name (Constanzo) was *Viramamunivar*—"the brave sannyasi."

With the help of another missionary, Beschi set up a school for catechists, writing textbooks in Tamil and also offering spiritual formation through the *Spiritual Exercises* of St. *Ignatius. What set Beschi apart from other missionaries was his mastery of the Tamil language and literature. Despite his many other labors, his literary production (which often profited by his enforced immobility due to war) was marked by abundance and variety. *Thembavani* (The unfading garland), his greatest work, is an epic of 36 cantos, with over 14,000 lines. Though it is the story of Joseph, the husband of Mary, the poet evokes the whole history of salvation, as narrated by St. Michael to the Holy Family as they are fleeing to Egypt. Literary historians rank it among the best epics in Tamil literature. *Thirukavalur Kalambagam* in praise of Mary and *Kittheriammal Ammanai* in praise of St. Quiteria of Portugal are his other poetic works. He wrote two books of grammar: *Thonnul Vilakkam* in Tamil, and *Clavis* in Latin and Tamil. He compiled two dictionaries. The *Caturagarathi* (Fourfold dictionary), in Tamil, gives meanings, synonyms, technical terms, and rhymes. The *Tamil-Latin Dictionary* contains 9,000 words. The *Tale of the Guru Paramartha,* a humorous story, was translated into Latin (by himself), English, French, German, Telugu, and Kannada. *Vethiyar Olukkam* is a manual for catechists. *Veda vilakkam* (An explanation of religion) and *Pethaga Marutthal* (Refutation of schism) were written against the Lutherans who were enticing the Catholics into their fold.

Beschi is the most outstanding of the followers of Robert de *Nobili in the tradition of creative inculturation. He died at Manapparai. A statue of him in the marina of Madras honors his contribution to Tamil culture.

BIBLIOGRAPHY Beschi's poetic works and commentaries on them in Tamil were published in the 1980s by the Tamil Literature Society, Tiruchirapalli. L. Besse, *Father Beschi of the Society of Jesus: His Times and His Writings* (1918) gives archival and publication information about Beschi's manuscripts and also a bibliography of writings about Beschi, pp. 4–10. A recent biography is Antonio Sorrentino, *L'altra perla dell'India* (1980).

Michael Amaladoss, SJ

Bessieux, Jean Rémi (1803–1876), French missionary bishop in West Africa. Born into a farming family in the south of France, Bessieux was ordained in 1829 and served in his home diocese for 13 years before entering the novitiate of François *Libermann's new missionary society, the Congregation of the Immaculate Heart (soon to become the Holy Ghost Fathers) in 1842. The very next year he was sent out as superior of a group of seven priests to begin work in a new vicariate in West Africa based in Liberia and assigned to Msgr. Edward Barron of Philadelphia. Bessieux was the sole priest survivor from this disastrous expedition; six of his companions died of fever within eight months. He himself escaped on a ship to Gabon, which became henceforth the center of his work. In 1848 he was named vicar apostolic (Barron having resigned), with jurisdiction over virtually the whole west coast of Africa. He was soon able to assign Senegal and the northern half to Aloÿs *Kobès, a coadjutor. A keen linguist, Bessieux published several books in Pongwe, including a grammar and a dictionary in 1847; he was also an enthusiastic agriculturalist. He remained in Gabon until his death. One of the longest missionary survivors on the nineteenth-century African west coast, he may well be hailed as the father of Catholicism throughout French-speaking West Africa.

BIBLIOGRAPHY Paul Coulon and Paule Brasseur, *Libermann 1803–1852* (1988), pp. 637–641.

Adrian Hastings

Besson, Pablo Enrique (1848–1932), pioneer Baptist missionary in Argentina. Born in Nod, near Neuchatel, Switzerland, Besson became an ardent Protestant militant for religious liberty in Argentina. After solid theological preparation and a brief pastorate in the Swiss Free Reformed Church, he worked as an evangelist in France, was baptized by immersion, and became a Baptist pastor. In 1881 he responded to an urgent plea from Swiss-French Baptist colonists in Esperanza, Santa Fe, Argentina, for pastoral help. In 1883 he moved to Buenos Aires to better advance the struggle for Protestant rights in a Catholic land. There he remained for 50 years, working directly with the members of the Argentine congress and ministers of the presidential staff for the legal rights of minorities, acting cooperatively with other churches, publishing tracts, writing articles for most of the leading Argentine newspapers and some foreign ones, establishing the first Baptist congregations in Argentina and personally advancing causes of social reform. During his ministry, the secularization of cemeteries and marriage and the public registry of births and deaths was achieved.

BIBLIOGRAPHY Pablo Besson, *Escritos de Pablo Besson*, 2 vols. (1947). Santiago Canclini, *Pablo Besson, Un Heraldo de la Libertad Cristiania* (1933); Junta Bautista de Publicaciones in Buenos Aires, *Los Que Abrieron el Camino* (1961), pp. 47–58; W. T. T. Millham, *Heroes of the Cross in South America* (1947), pp. 52–56. Besson contributed many articles and his work is frequently mentioned in the contemporary magazines *El Evangelista, El Estandarte,* and *La Reforma,* the first Protestant religious periodicals published in the River Plate area.

Sidney H. Rooy

Betanzos, Domingo de (c. 1480–1549), Spanish Dominican missionary in Española and Mexico. Born in León, Spain, to a noble family, Betanzos studied law at the University of Salamanca and then lived as a hermit for five years. In May 1511 he became a Dominican friar in Salamanca and was ordained in Seville on his way to America. He arrived at Española (island of present-day Haiti and Dominican Republic) early in 1514. Two years later he wrote a letter to Bartolomé de *Las Casas protesting the abuses inflicted on the Indians and the danger of their extinction in the Antilles. He then became a pioneer missionary of his order in Mexico, where he arrived in 1526 with eleven other Dominicans, five of whom died within the first year, and four of whom returned to Spain. Betanzos established convents in Tlascala, Puebla, and Oaxaca. In 1528 twenty-four more Dominicans arrived, and in 1529 Betanzos went with them to Santiago, Guatemala, where they founded a church and a convent.

In 1530 Betanzos returned to Spain, and in 1532 he obtained from Pope Clement VII the bull *Pastoralis officii,* through which the province of Santiago de Mexico was recognized as independent of the province of Española. On returning to Mexico in 1534, he was elected as vicar general of the new Dominican province, and in 1535 he was elected provincial, in which position he served to 1538. Betanzos died in Valladolid, Spain.

Betanzos had never learned an Indian language, and with the passing years he developed a negative attitude toward Indians. He believed that they were not rational beings, were beasts totally incapable of receiving the Christian faith, and were under sin before God, who had condemned them to ruin. He retracted these views at the time of his death, but they influenced the way the Indians were treated by the Spanish colonists, particularly in Mexico. His most vigorous opponent was Las Casas.

BIBLIOGRAPHY Benno Biermann, *Zur Auseinandersetzung um die Menschenrechte der Indianer: Fray Bernardino de Minaya OP und sein Werk* (1968); A. M. Carreño, *Fray Domingo de Betanzos* (1924); Manuel Jiménez Fernández, *Fr. Bartolomé de Las Casas: Tratado de Indias y el doctor Sepúlveda* (1962).

Pablo A. Deiros

Bettelheim, Bernard Jean (1811–1870), missionary to the Ryukyu Islands. Born in Pressburg (present-day Pozsony, Hungary), Bettelheim received a degree in medicine from the University of Padua, Italy. After serving in the Egyptian Navy and the Turkish Army as head physician, he was converted and baptized by the British chaplain of Smyrna. He went to England to seek missionary appointment to work among Jews in the Mediterranean area. This failing, he was sent to the Ryukyu Islands by the British Seaman's Mission, arriving there May 1, 1846. His eight-year residence in Naha was beset by constant opposition despite a policy of official tolerance. He did some outdoor preaching, was beaten on occasion for his importunity, but was credited during his stay with five converts and about fifty inquirers. He developed cow-pox vaccine and secretly trained Okinawan doctors in Western medicine. He produced the first grammar and dictionary of the Ryukyuan language and translated the Gospels of John and Luke and the books of Acts and Romans into Ryukyu. These were republished in a special edition by the Japan Bible Society in 1977. He passed much Western learning to Okinawa's royal court and through that channel to the Satsuma clan of Japan. He served as an interpreter for Commodore Perry's fleet in Okinawa in 1853. Exhausted and ill, he departed Okinawa with his family in 1854, bound for England. Stopping en route in the United States, he chose to remain there and received ordination by the Presbytery of Chicago. He served as a surgeon during the Civil War and died of pneumonia in Brookfield, Missouri.

BIBLIOGRAPHY Teruya Yoshihiko, "Bettelheim: A Study of the First Protestant Missionary to the Island Kingdom" (Ph.D. diss., Univ. of Colorado, 1969), is the most complete study. Some further details are included in Edward E. Bollinger, *On the Threshold of the Closed Empire: Mid-19th Century Missions in Okinawa* (1991).

Edward E. Bollinger

Bettendorf, Johann Philipp (1625–1698), Roman Catholic missionary in Brazil. A German-speaking Jesuit, Bettendorf was born in Luxembourg and studied humanities at the University of Trier and civil law in Italy. He entered the French Belgium province of the Society of Jesus in 1647, and, inspired by Antonio *Vieira, volunteered for the missions in Brazil. He arrived in the state of Maranhão in northeast Brazil in 1660. During his missionary career he served as rector of the Colleges of Maranhão and Pará, and as superior of the entire Brazil mission. During a stay at the court in Lisbon in 1648 he befriended King Pedro II and wrote a compendium of the Christian faith in Portuguese and in the "Brazilian language" (Tupí-Guaraní). Back in Brazil, he used his court connections to defend the rights of the Indians against the Portuguese colonists. A well-rounded humanist, he spoke several languages and was an accomplished painter. His most important work was his chronicle on the missions in the state of Maranhão, which touches upon the geography, fauna and flora, and mineral resources of the region, as well as the story of the Jesuit missionaries. He died in Pará.

BIBLIOGRAPHY Carl Borromäus Ebner, "Johann Philipp Bettendorf, SJ (1625–1698) Missionar und Entwicklungspionier in Nordbrasilien," *NZM* 31 (1975): 81–99; Serafim Leite, *História da Companhia de Jesús no Brasil*, vol. 4 (1943), pp. 317–319; vol. 8 (1949), pp. 98–106.

Jeffrey Klaiber, SJ

Beyzym, Jan (1850–1912), Polish Jesuit missionary in Madagascar. Born in eastern Poland, Beyzym studied in Kiev and Kraków, was ordained a priest, and worked in several parishes as pastor and teacher. In 1899 he began his missionary work in Madagascar among persons with leprosy at Ambahiwuraka. He first created a shelter for them, and then in 1902, with financial help from Poland, he began building a hospital with 200 beds for leprosy patients at Ambatuwuri. The hospital was completed in 1911. He wrote numerous articles for mission magazines about his work and requesting assistance. Eventually he himself contracted leprosy and died at Ambatuwuri, where he is remembered as "servant and protector of lepers."

BIBLIOGRAPHY Czeslaw Drazek, *Vie, activité et sainteté du Serviteur de Dieu Jean Beyzym, prêtre de la Compagnie de Jésus (1850–1912)*, 2 vols. (1989). Beyzym's papers are located in the archive of the Jesuit Superior's House in Kraków, Poland.

Jan Górski

Biard, Pierre (1567–1622), pioneer Jesuit missionary in North America. Biard was born in Grenoble, France. He was teaching theology and Hebrew at Lyons in 1608 when he was appointed by Pierre Coton, confessor to Henry IV, to take charge of the first Jesuit mission in New France. In May 1611 he and Ennémond Massé landed at Port Royal in Acadia (present-day Nova Scotia) where they soon faced the hostility of Sieur de Poutrincourt, founder of the colony. In the spring of 1613, together with Massé and two additional Jesuits, Biard established a mission among the Etchemins on Mt. Desert Island (off the coast of present-day Maine). A short while later, the mission was attacked by an English raiding party from Jamestown, Virginia, under Samuel Argall. One missionary was killed, Massé was sent back to France, and Biard and Jacques Quentin were taken to Jamestown, where the governor threatened to hang them. Protected by Argall, Biard was ultimately sent first to England and then to France, where he returned to teaching at Lyons and published his accounts of the mission. He died at Avignon. His capture marked the end of the first Jesuit mission in New France.

BIBLIOGRAPHY Biard's accounts are in Reuben Gold Thwaites, ed., *The Jesuit Relations and Allied Documents* (1897), vol. 3, pp. 21–289, and vol. 4, pp. 1–167. Other accounts are also found in *The Jesuit Relations*. On the Jesuits in Canada, see J. H. Kennedy, *Jesuit and Savage in New France* (1950).

Gerald P. Fogarty, SJ

Bibliander, Theodor (1504 or 1509–1564), Swiss Reformed theologian and orientalist. Bibliander, whose family name was Buchmann (as an accomplished scholar he went by the Hellenized form of his name), refuted the Calvinist view of predestination, taught a moderate universalism, and emphasized the responsibility of the church for world mission. He had intended to go to Egypt as a missionary, but instead he became one of the most learned philologists of his time, famous for his *Hebrew Grammar* (1535) and for publishing in 1543 the Latin translation of the Qur'an made originally in 1143, which never before (as far as is known) had been available to the scholarly world. For apologetic purposes his edition also contained a refutation of the teachings of the Qur'an. Bibliander, a professor of Old Testament in Zurich (1531–1560), was the first scholar in Switzerland to use methods of comparative religion for the exegesis of the Bible. Seeking to promote the unity of humankind, he followed *Zwingli and stressed the common dimension in all religions. Among his most important writings are *De ratione communi omnium linguarum et litterarum commentarius* (1548; a comparison of more than thirty languages and their histories) and *Relatio fidelis* (1545), which is still of value for the study of the history of religions. He left twenty-four published works and numerous manuscripts.

BIBLIOGRAPHY Emil Egli, *Biblianders Leben und Schriften* (1901) and "Biblianders Missionsgedanken," *Zwingliana* 3 (1913–1920): 46–50; Walter Köhler, "Zu Biblianders Koranausgabe," *Zwingliana* 3 (1913–1920): 349–350; Joachim Staedtke, "Der Zürcher Prädestinationsstreit von 1560," *Zwingliana* 9 (1949–1953): 536–546; Ernst Staehelin, "Die biblischen Vorlesungen Theodor Biblianders," *Zwingliana* 7 (1939–1943): 522–526. Bibliander's published and unpublished writings are in the Zentralbibliothek and his letters in the Staatsarchiv, both in Zurich, Switzerland.

Lothar Schreiner

Bichurin, Iakinf. *See* Iakinf (Bichurin).

Bickel, Luke Washington (1866–1917), mariner and Baptist missionary to Japan. Bickel was born in Cincinnati, Ohio, the son of Philipp Bickel and Katherine Clarke, Baptist missionaries in the United States and later, Germany. After serving as an apprenticed seaman, he fulfilled a childhood dream by receiving certification as a captain by the English Board of Trade. He studied at Spurgeon's College in London for a year and is said to have mastered six languages while at sea. For a time he served with the English Baptist Publication Society. In 1897 the American Baptist Missionary Union (ABMU) received a gift from Robert Allen, a prosperous merchant of Glasgow, Scotland, to build a gospel ship for use in the Japanese Inland Sea. The ABMU appointed Bickel and his wife, Annie (Burgess), as mariner missionaries at Kobe, Japan, where they arrived in 1898. In September 1899 the *Fukuin Maru* was launched and the Bickels set about creating Sunday schools and preaching on the remote islands. From 1911, when Bickel received a new, larger ship, he continued his evangelizing and church planting voyages among the islands of the Inland Sea. In 1916 Bickel reported sixty Sunday Schools and three hundred converts on sixty islands. His work extended cooperatively to various denominations and Bible societies. He died at Kobe, Japan.

BIBLIOGRAPHY Luke Washington Bickel, *The Log of the Gospel Ship* (n.d.), *Put Your Helm Up* (1902), *Eight Bells* (1903), and "First Ten Years on the Inland Sea," *Missions Magazine,* 1910, p. 439. Charles K. Harrington, *Captain Bickel of the Inland Sea* (1919); see also Floyd L. Carr, *Captain Luke Bickel: Master Mariner of the Inland Sea* (1926). A biography in Japanese is in *Gleanings* 23, no. 5 (1917): 107–115.

William H. Brackney

Bickersteth, Edward (1850–1897), Anglican missionary in India and bishop in Japan. Bickersteth was the grandson of the Church Missionary Society (CMS) secretary of the same name. His father, who became bishop of Exeter, was a leading advocate of missions and of the CMS. After education at Highgate School and Pembroke College, Cambridge, he was ordained in the Church of England in 1873. He returned to Cambridge in 1875 as fellow of Pembroke and helped to mount the Cambridge Mission to Delhi, of which he became leader in 1877.

In 1883 Bickersteth returned to England because of ill health. He intended to return to India in 1886 but was invited to become an Anglican bishop in Japan. A highly creative bishop, he is generally recognized as the founder of Nippon Sei Ko Kwai, the Anglican Church in Japan. With Bishop Channing *Williams of the Protestant Episcopal Church U.S.A. and indigenous Japanese leaders, he drafted a church constitution that included the American Episcopal, CMS, and Society for the Propagation of the Gospel (SPG) missions and was accepted synodically in 1887. He encouraged Canadian Anglicans to take part in the church's outreach and introduced religious communities in Tokyo, namely, the St. Andrew's Brotherhood and the St. Hilda's Mission for women, of whose work in mission he was a strong advocate. Recurrent illness caused his final return to England in 1896. He attended the Lambeth Conference of 1897 before his untimely death.

BIBLIOGRAPHY Edward Bickersteth, *Our Heritage in the Church* (1898). M. Bickersteth, *Japan As We Saw It* (1893); S. Bickersteth, *The Life and Letters of Edward Bickersteth* (1899); J. M. Campbell, *Christian History in the Making* (1946); M. Dewey, *The Messengers* (1975); J. Murray, *Proclaim the Good News* (1985); S. C. Neill, *Anglicanism* (1958); SPG, *The Story of the Delhi Mission* (1909); E. Stock, *History of the Church Missionary Society* (1899, 1916); H. P. Thompson, *Into All Lands* (1951).

Timothy Yates

Bickersteth, Edward (1786–1850), missionary administrator. Born in Kirkby Lonsdale, England, the fourth son of a surgeon, Bickersteth left the local grammar school at 14 to work in the post office. He later trained as a solicitor and in 1812 went into practice in Norwich with his brother-in-law. In 1815 Josiah *Pratt, the overworked clerical secretary of the Church Missionary Society (CMS), invited him to become his assistant, commencing with a pastoral visit to West Africa. After ordination in the Church of England he sailed for Africa in January 1816. During three months in Sierra Leone he traveled widely, advised the missionaries, and made good contacts with the British governor. As CMS administrator he was responsible especially for pastoral matters and for training, and he succeeded Pratt as clerical secretary in 1824, continuing until 1829. He then became the rector of Watton, Hertfordshire, where he lived to the end of his life, continuing to support CMS in many ways.

His only son, Edward Henry Bickersteth (1825–1906), the hymnwriter, became bishop of Exeter, and his grandson (also Edward), bishop in Japan. Several others in his family were also missionaries.

BIBLIOGRAPHY T. R. Birks, *A Memoir of the Rev. Edward Bickersteth, Late Rector of Watton, Herts.*, 2 vols. (1851); Francis Keyes Aglionby, *Life of Edward Henry Bickersteth, D.D., Bishop and Poet* (1907).

Jocelyn Murray

Bicknell, Henry (1766–1820), English missionary to Tahiti. Originally a house carpenter and wheelwright, Bicknell was one of the artisan missionaries of the London Missionary Society (LMS) who sailed as pioneers to Tahiti on the ship *Duff* in 1797. Bicknell and his colleagues John Eyre, Henry *Nott, and John *Jefferson survived local wars in Tahiti and isolation from London during the Napoleonic wars. Their preaching and their cooperation with high chiefs—especially King *Pomare II, who was baptized by Bicknell in 1819—established foundations for what became the Evangelical Church of the Society Islands. Between 1808 and 1811, Bicknell went to Sydney, New South Wales, and to England, where he married Mary Ann Bradley. In Sydney he helped negotiate support for the Tahitian mission through Samuel *Marsden, the Anglican colonial chaplain and agent of the LMS, who sympathized with the Calvinistic Methodism of Bicknell and of the LMS's early mentor Thomas *Haweis. Bicknell died of dysentery at Papara, Tahiti.

BIBLIOGRAPHY Niel Gunson, *Messengers of Grace: Evangelical Missionaries in the South Seas, 1797–1860* (1978); Richard Lovett, *The History of the London Missionary Society, 1795–1895*, 2 vols. (1899); [James Wilson], *A Missionary Voyage to the Southern Pacific... in the Ship Duff...* (1799). Archival materials are held in the LMS South Sea collection at the SOAS, Univ. of London (available on microfilm).

John Garrett

Bieder, Werner (1911–), Swiss missiologist and theologian. Bieder was born in Basel, studied theology in his home town, and from 1941 to 1955 was pastor of the Protestant congregation in the capital of the canton of Glarus. He became director of missionary education for the Basel Mission (BM) in 1955, the same year that BM terminated its five-year mission seminary course for men in order to offer missionary education for people of both sexes who had already completed their professional training. He held this post until 1971. He became professor of New Testament and mission studies in the theological faculty of the University of Basel in 1957 and held this post concurrently with his BM responsibilities. He published widely on biblical and missiological themes, especially in *Evangelisches Missions Magazin/Zeitschrift für Mission*, on whose editorial board he served from 1964 to 1979. Under BM auspices he also made a number of important extended visits as lecturer to Reformed and ecumenical theological seminaries in Africa and Asia.

BIBLIOGRAPHY Werner Bieder, *Grund und Kraft der Mission nach dem 1. Petrusbrief* (1950), *Das Mysterium Christi und die Mission: Ein Beitrag zur missionarischen Sakramentalgestalt der Kirche* (1964), *Segnen und Bekennen: Der Basler Mission zum Anlass des 150 jährigen Bestehens von ihrem Studienleiter gewidmet* (1965), *Gottes Sendung und der missionarische Auftrag der Kirche nach Matthäus, Lukas, Paulus und Johannes* (1965), *Die Verheissung der Taufe im Neuen Testament* (1966), "History of the Basel Mission in Relation to the Christian Hope," in *Wholeness in Christ: The Legacy of the Basel Mission in India*, Godwin Shiri, ed. (1985), and *Erfahrungen mit der Basler Mission und ihrer Geschichte* (1991).

Paul Jenkins

Bigandet, Paul Ambroise (1813–1894), Catholic missionary bishop in Burma (Myanmar). Born in Malans, Doubs, France, Bigandet entered the Paris Foreign Missionary Society (MEP) in 1836 and was sent to Siam (Thailand) in 1837. Mission work in neighboring Burma was entrusted to the MEP in 1856, and in 1865 Bigandet was made a bishop and apostolic vicar of Burma. The Burmese church flourished under his leadership. With the help of missionary sisters and brothers, he developed a number of Catholic schools, encouraged the development of a Burmese clergy, and published a series of pastoral and catechetical books in the Burmese language. An expert as well in Burmese Buddhism, he wrote *The Life or Legend of Gaudama, the Buddha of the Burmese*; first published in 1858, this classic work went through five editions. He died in Rangoon.

BIBLIOGRAPHY Paul Ambroise Bigandet, *The Life or Legend of Gaudama, the Buddha of the Burmese* (1858; 5th ed., 1914) and *An Outline of the History of the Burmese Catholic Mission from the Year 1720 to 1887* (1887).

Stephen B. Bevans, SVD

Bigard, Stephanie (1834–1903) *and*
Jeanne (1859–1934), founders of the Society of St. Peter the Apostle for the training of indigenous clergy. Stephanie Bigard was born in France at Mortagne, Séez. After the death of her husband, Charles, in 1878 and of her son, Renato, in 1887, she and her daughter, Jeanne, corresponded with Father Aimé Villion, a missionary in Japan, and with Bishop Julien Cousin of Nagasaki and learned about the financial needs of their Japan mission. In light of the persecution the Japanese church had endured, Cousin considered the establishment of an indigenous clergy to be essential for the Christian mission. On June 1, 1889, he wrote to Stephanie and Jeanne Bigard a letter which is generally considered the foundation of the Society of St. Peter the Apostle. In this letter he said that, for financial reasons, he was not able to receive new students into the seminary in Japan, although he was convinced that they would become good priests. He appealed to the Bigards to find generous benefactors in France who would support the training of local clergy. The Bigards pa-

tiently and persistently asked for help and found it from many sources. On April 4, 1894, Stephanie wrote: "The work has become the whole scope of our lives." In 1902, having received legal recognition, the society was transferred to Fribourg, Switzerland, and in 1920 it was placed under Propaganda Fide in Rome.

BIBLIOGRAPHY P. Lesourd, *Guda delle missioni cattoliche* (1934), pp. 506–511, and *L'holocauset de Jeanne Bigard, 1859–1934, fondatrice de l'Oeuvre Pontidsicle de Saint-Pierre Apôtre* (1938); Joseph F. Lynch, "The Work of the Native Clergy and the Bigards," *Ecclesiastical Review* 102 (1940): 53–61; Celestina A. Obi, "The Bigard Ladies and the Foundation of the Society of St. Peter the Apostle," *Bigard Theological Studies* 10, no. 2 (1990): 12–28; O. Olichon, *Les origines françaises de l'Oeuvre pontificale de Saint-Pierre-Apôtre pour la formation des clergés indigènes en pays de missions* (1929); Ernst Stürmer, "The Bigard Ladies and Their Countless Sons: Stephanie and Jeanne, Mother and Daughter, founded the Society of St. Peter 100 Years Ago," *Omnis Terra* 23 (1989): 334–341.

Willi Henkel, OMI

Bill, Samuel Alexander (1864–1942), British missionary in Nigeria. Born in Belfast, Northern Ireland, and influenced by the preaching of D. L. *Moody, Bill trained for missionary service at Harley College in London. In 1887 the principal, Henry Grattan *Guinness, announced that he had received a letter from Scottish missionaries working in Calabar conveying an appeal for help from peoples farther to the east in the Niger Delta. Bill responded by offering himself for service. He sailed for Africa without organizational support and commenced work among the Efik-speaking people at the mouth of the Qua Iboe River. He devoted the rest of his life to service among the Efik and Annang peoples of what is now southeastern Nigeria. The Qua Iboe Mission was founded to support the work; interdenominational by nature, it drew considerable support from Ulster Presbyterians. Bill lived to see remarkable growth in the Qua Iboe Church, especially following a revival movement which commenced in 1927. His sympathetic response to this "Spirit movement" helped retain converts within the church and led to further expansion of the work northward to the kingdom of Igala. He was awarded the Member of the British Empire in 1938 at a ceremony at Eket. He is buried at Ibuno on the bank of the Qua Iboe River beside his wife, Gracie, and his first convert, David Ekong.

BIBLIOGRAPHY Jean Corbett, *According to Plan: The Story of Samuel Alexander Bill* (1977). On the Spirit movement, see David Smith, "A Survey of New Religious Movements among the Annang of Nigeria," *NZM* 42, no. 4 (1986): 264–275. Archival material is held by the Qua Iboe Fellowship in Belfast, Northern Ireland.

David W. Smith

Billiart, (Marie Rose) Julie (1751–1816), founder of the Sisters of Notre Dame de Namur. Born in Cuvilly, France, of devout Roman Catholic parents, Billiart received an education above the average for girls at that time, and then became involved in the Christian education of the people in Cuvilly. For most of her life she was crippled by a nervous disorder but held classes in her home. In 1790, in the wake of the French Revolution, she was hounded from Cuvilly by those seeking to enforce the antireligious Act of the Civil Constitution of the Clergy. In defiance of the act, she had taught religion, harbored priests, and organized meetings. In 1794 she again had to flee, this time to Amiens, where she was befriended by Françoise Blin de Bourdon, a Catholic noblewoman who became her co-worker.

The French Concordat of 1801 legalized the celebration of Catholic worship, and Billiart and Blin openly began what was to be their life's work: "the service of the poor in the most abandoned places." On February 2, 1804, they vowed themselves publicly to the Christian education of girls and to the training of teachers. Many young women joined them, and schools were opened in rapid succession in France and Belgium. In 1809, Billiart transferred the center of her religious institute from Amiens to Namur, Belgium, because the bishop of Amiens had demanded that each foundation be independent and come under the jurisdiction of the diocesan bishop. Since then, the congregation has been known as the Sisters of Notre Dame de Namur, with one central governing body.

Billiart's outstanding gift was in providing an education designed to include "everything young women need to know to become useful members of society." She wanted her sisters to establish learning centers wherever the underprivileged were found. Sisters of Notre Dame are active on the continents of Europe, America (North, Central, and South), Asia, and Africa.

BIBLIOGRAPHY Several biographies are extant, the most definitive being *The Life of the Blessed Julie Billiart,* by Mary Xavier Partridge, James Clare, ed. (1909). *Memoires,* written by Françoise Blin under her religious name of Mother St. Joseph, outlines the life of Billiart and the history of the founding of the congregation (privately published in English in 1990). The original in French is held in the archives in Namur, Belgium. Billiart's personal letters and exhortations have been privately printed and circulated. They are housed in the archives of the Sisters of Notre Dame in Namur, Belgium.

Margaret Loftus, SND

Bingham, Hiram (1789–1869) *and*
Sybil (Moseley) (1792–1848), pioneer missionaries of the American Board of Commissioners for Foreign Missions (ABCFM) in Hawaii. Born in Bennington, Vermont, Hiram Bingham graduated from Middlebury College (1816) and Andover Theological Seminary (1819). In 1820 he married Sybil Moseley, was ordained and appointed a missionary by the ABCFM, and sailed with the first company of Protestant missionaries to the Sandwich Islands. With abundant courage and an inflexible will, yet cheerful, good-natured, and highly capable, he was from the beginning the natural leader of the mission (caricatured as Abner Hale in James Michener's novel *Hawaii*).

At Honolulu, the principal port and seat of government, Bingham was chief representative of the mission with the Hawaiian king and nobility and with foreign residents and visitors. The phenomenal success of the mission was due in considerable part to the role he and his wife, Sybil, played in winning the strong allegiance of the principal chiefs. Sybil, born in Westfield, Massachusetts, did much to bring the powerful regent *Kaahumanu and others to Christian faith. Hiram, too, won the allegiance of Hawaiians, but his forcefulness not only brought him into conflict with foreigners who resented missionary interference with their commercial, political, and sexual interests, but also irritated colleagues. Bingham was the first pastor of Kawaiahao Church and designed a magnificent stone landmark in the center of Honolulu. He helped create a writing system for the Hawaiian language, translated several books of the Bible, and produced *Elementary Lessons, First Book for Children, Scripture Catechism, First Teacher,* and a hymn and tune book. Sybil's ill health forced the Binghams into a long home leave in 1841. She died in Easthampton, Massachusetts, predeceasing her husband by 20 years. Hiram was never sent back to Hawaii. For a few years he pastored a Negro church in New Haven, Connecticut, and later he was supported by an annuity given by friends. He died in New Haven just before a planned return to the Islands for the semicentenary celebration in 1870.

BIBLIOGRAPHY Hiram Bingham, *A Residence of Twenty-one Years in the Sandwich Islands* (1845); Rufus Anderson, *History of the Sandwich Islands Mission* (1870); Albertine Loomis, *Grapes of Canaan: Hawaii, 1820* (1951); Char Miller, *Fathers and Sons: The Bingham Family and the American Mission* (1982). A sketch and pictures can be found in *Missionary Album* (1969). Sybil Bingham figures prominently in Mary Zwiep, *Pilgrim Path: The First Company of Women Missionaries to Hawaii* (1991).

David M. Stowe

Bingham, Hiram, Jr. (1831-1908), American Congregational missionary to Micronesia. Born in Honolulu of missionary parents, a graduate of Yale College (1853; D.D., 1895) with distinction in academics and sports, Hiram Bingham, Jr., was ordained in 1856 after two years at Andover Theological Seminary. The same year he married Minerva Clarissa Brewster, received appointment as a missionary by the American Board of Commissioners for Foreign Missions (ABCFM), and sailed on the first *Morning Star* to Micronesia. With a Hawaiian couple, the Kanoas, the Binghams began a mission on Abiaiang in the Gilbert Islands. Bingham planned and supervised the work of the mission, devised a writing system for the language, and worked at translation, while Hawaiian colleagues did much of the itineration and evangelizing. After a health furlough in 1865, he returned as skipper of the second *Morning Star,* visiting stations in the Marquesas and Micronesia. By 1875 health problems required the Binghams to live in Honolulu, where they produced a Gilbertese hymn and tune book (1880), a Bible (1890), a Bible dictionary (1895), and a commentary on the Gospels and Acts. Bingham was for a time corresponding secretary of the Hawaiian Board of Missions, which sponsored the Micronesia mission in cooperation with the ABCFM, and he also served as the government-appointed protector of Gilbert Islanders employed as imported laborers by sugar planters.

BIBLIOGRAPHY Hiram Bingham, Jr., *Story of the Morning Stars* (1866, with successive editions to 1907). John Garrett, *To Live among the Stars* (1982), pp. 148-155; Albertine Loomis, *To All People* (1970), pp. 105-131; Char Miller, *Fathers and Sons: The Bingham Family and the American Mission,* chaps. 3 and 4 (1982; highly critical). See also ABCFM *Annual Reports* and *Missionary Herald.* Bingham's papers are at the Houghton Library, Harvard Univ.

David M. Stowe

Bingham, Rowland Victor (1872-1942), cofounder and longtime director of the Sudan Interior Mission (SIM). Born in East Grinstead, Sussex, England, Bingham immigrated to Canada at age 16 and sailed for Africa in 1893 under the nascent SIM to open a way to the unreached people of the interior. Within a year, both of his colleagues, Walter *Gowans and Thomas Kent, were dead from fever and he himself had returned to Canada in broken health. In 1898 SIM was reconstituted as the Africa Industrial Mission, with Bingham serving as its director. After a second failed attempt in 1900, a third attempt in 1902 succeeded in establishing the mission's first station at Patigi, Nigeria. In 1906 the mission returned to "Sudan Interior Mission" as its official name.

By the time of Bingham's death, SIM had grown into what was arguably the largest Protestant presence in Africa—400 missionaries, with hundreds of churches established. Under Bingham, SIM became a somewhat unique representative of the faith missions movement, more open about the need for missionary support and more thoroughly internationalized than the British model of Hudson *Taylor and the China Inland Mission, and more broadly evangelical and more socially involved than many American faith missions. Perhaps most outstanding among the missiological legacies Bingham left through SIM were his emphasis on teaching and promoting missions among the newly established churches of Africa, his utilization of thoroughly integrated international teams, and his holistic model of missions outreach, which addressed social concerns as part of the process of discipling believers into churches equipped to carry on Christ's commission.

As editor of *Evangelical Christian* (Canada's only transdenominational evangelical magazine) from 1904 until his death, Bingham not only was an articulate spokesman regarding the pressing theological issues of his day but carried on a tireless campaign to promote mission and outreach organizations, both foreign and domestic. To the same ends he also established Evangelical Publishers (1912) and the Canadian Keswick Conference Center (1924). He received an honorary D.D. from Wheaton College in 1932. He died in Toronto.

BIBLIOGRAPHY Bingham's *Seven Sevens of Years* (1943) is a largely autobiographical record of the Sudan Interior Mission during his ministry years. Other works by Bingham, in addition to his multitudinous writings in *Evangelical Christian,* include *Matthew the Publican* (n.d.) and *The Bible and the Body* (1921, 1952). James Hunter, *A Flame of Fire* (1961); Brian McKenzie, "Fundamentalism, Christian Unity, and Premillennialism in the Thought of Rowland Victor Bingham (1872-1942): A Study of Anti-Modernism in Canada" (Ph.D. diss., Toronto School of Theology, 1985). A Ph.D. dissertation in process by Gary R. Corwin for Trinity Evangelical Divinity School examines the missiological contributions of Bingham and the work of the Sudan Interior Mission under his leadership, in the context of the larger faith missions movement. Bingham's papers, along with a full set of *Evangelical Christian* magazines, are part of the SIM archives in Charlotte, N.C.

Gary R. Corwin

Bird, Mark Baker (1807-1880), Methodist missionary in Jamaica and Haiti. Born in England, Bird served with the Wesleyan Methodist Missionary Society of London. After four years in Jamaica (1834-1838) and a few months as the first Methodist missionary in the Cayman Islands, he was moved to Haiti in 1840. There he endured the 1842 catastrophic earthquake in Cap Haitien (in which two of his children died) and survived revolutions and several natural disasters. But he always believed in the country and its people. His two books, *The Black Man or Haitian Independence Deduced from Historical Notes* (1869) and *Un paradis terrestre* (published posthumously in 1881), analyze events in Haitian history and culture in a critical but supportive way. He and his mission colleagues decided to concentrate resources on the towns and cities rather than on rural areas. They focused particularly on education. Throughout Bird's time in Haiti, emblazoned over the portal of his Port-au-Prince schools were words penned in 1816 by President Alexandre Pétion when he invited Methodist missionaries to come to Haiti: "L'Education lève un homme à la dignité de son être." Bird's educational work survives to this day. The present Methodist Church's prestigious high school is named "Nouveau Collège Bird." In July 1879 Bird left Haiti after 39 years and died a little over a year later on the island of Jersey, England.

BIBLIOGRAPHY Material on Bird can be found in Catts Pressoir, *Le Protestantisme haitien,* 2 vols. (1945) and in Leslie J. Griffiths, *History of Methodism in Haiti* (1991). See also Joseph A. Boromé, "Mark Baker Bird and His Early Defense of Haiti," *Bulletin of the New York Public Library* (1970): 496-513.

Leslie J. Griffiths

Bird, Mary Rebecca Stewart (1859-1914), missionary in Persia (Iran). Bird was born at Castle Eden, County Durham, England, the daughter of the town's Anglican minister. Educated at home, she was inspired at age five by stories of Africa told by a missionary friend of her father. Thoroughly committed to her call to the mission field, she refused an offer of marriage in preference to working in a foreign land. In 1891 she was accepted by the Church Missionary Society to go to Persia as a pioneer of women's work. She prepared by attending The Willows, a training college for women workers in Stoke Newington, England, for a few months.

Bird lived and worked in Julfa and Isfahan from 1891 to 1897. Because she had some medical training, she opened a small dispensary at Isfahan. On furlough in 1897 and 1898, she spoke of her work to various groups in England and Canada and inspired many. Returning to Persia in 1899, she spent five years in Yezd and Kirman. Her younger sister's marriage necessitated her return to England in 1904 to care for their mother. During the next eight years, in Liverpool, she was an effective advocate of missions. After her mother's death in 1911, she returned to Persia, where she continued her work until her death from typhoid fever.

BIBLIOGRAPHY Mary Bird, *Persian Women and Their Creed* (1899). Clara C. Rice, *Mary Bird in Persia* (1916).

Joan R. Duffy

Birinus (d. 649-650), apostle to the West Saxons of England. Birinus was an Italian monk in Rome who was ordained a bishop by Asterius at Genoa. Pope Honorarius sent him to Wessex, England, where he arrived in 634. By 635 he had baptized King Cynegils. The king set aside Dorchester as Birinus's see. His Italian supporters apparently had intended for him to travel throughout other sections of Great Britain as a missionary, but he remained in Wessex.

BIBLIOGRAPHY John Field, *Saint Berin, the Apostle of Wessex* (1902); Henry Mayr-Harting, *The Coming of Christianity to Anglo-Saxon England* (1972, 1977, 1991); T. Varley, *St. Birinus and Wessex: From Odin to Christ* (1934).

Frederick W. Norris

Birkeli, (Otto) Emil (1877-1952), Norwegian Lutheran missionary and scholar. Birkeli was born at Hurum outside Oslo, graduated from the Stavanger School of Mission in 1902, and was ordained in 1903. He was sent to Madagascar by the Norwegian Missionary Society in 1903 and served there until 1919. Returning to Norway, Birkeli taught at the Stavanger School of Mission from 1923 to 1944, and was its principal from 1937 to 1944. He was also editor of *Norsk Misjonstidende* (1923-1936). He wrote some ethnographic studies published by l'Académie Malgache, of which he was a member. The most important of his more than twenty books include a biography of the first Norwegian missionary to Africa, H. C. Knudson (1925), a two-volume history of Christian missions (1935, 1937), and a doctoral dissertation on ancestor worship in Norway in the Middle Ages (1938). He also wrote a textbook on the history of religion (1946) and a book on Norwegian religious folklore through the ages, with special reference to ancestor worship (1943).

Nils E. Bloch-Hoell

Birkeli, Fridtjov (Søiland) (1906-1983), Norwegian missionary, scholar, and Lutheran bishop. Birkeli, son of missionary parents, was born in Tulear, Madagascar. He graduated from the Norwegian Lutheran School of Theology and from the University of Oslo (D.Th.), and was ordained in 1930. After language study in France Birkeli went to Madagascar in 1933 in the service of the Norwegian Missionary Society (NMS). For several years he taught at Ivory Theological Seminary, Fianarantsoa, Madagascar, but became seriously ill in 1944 and had to return home. He published studies on the local history of Madagascar in *Bulletin de l'Académie Malgache* and a commentary on Galatians in Malagasy. He wrote the missionary history of Madagascar in the hundredth-anniversary publication of NMS. In his doctoral dissertation, "Politikk og misjon" (1952), he investigated the political and interconfessional circumstances in Madagascar and their consequences for the establishment of the Norwegian mission from 1861 to 1875. His second field of research focused on the earliest missionary activities from England to Norway and the transition from paganism to Christianity in Norway.

Birkeli was a man of vision and initiative. He encouraged the development of an independent Lutheran church of Madagascar, arranged the first All-Africa Lutheran conference in Marangu, Tanganyika (now Tanzania) in 1955, and proposed the founding of the Radio Voice of the Gospel in Addis Ababa. He was editor of *Norsk Misjonstidende* (1948–1954), director of the Lutheran World Federation department of World Mission in Geneva (1954–1957), secretary general of the NMS (1957–1960), bishop of Stavanger (1960–1968), and bishop of Oslo (1968–1972). He was awarded Norwegian and British orders and three honorary doctorates.

BIBLIOGRAPHY Nils E. Bloch-Hoell, "Fridtjov Birkeli: Minnetale over biskop Fridtjov Birkeli," *Det Norske Videnskaps-Akademi Årbok 1984* (1985), pp. 145–153.

Nils E. Bloch-Hoell

Birraux, Joseph Marie (1883–1947), superior general of the Society of Missionaries of Africa (popularly known as the White Fathers [WF]). Born in Bernex, Haute Savoie, France, Birraux entered the WF in 1907. Ordained a priest in 1908, he obtained his doctorate in canon law at the Gregorian University in Rome (1911). Arriving in Karema, Tanganyika (Tanzania), the same year, he became the canonical counselor of the vicar apostolic, Adolphe Lechaptois, whom he succeeded in 1920. He improved the education of the local catechists, ordained the first two local priests in 1923, tried to introduce Kiswahili as the pastoral lingua franca, and organized a church tax levy (hoping to make the local church less dependent).

Elected superior general in 1936, he reorganized the WF into national provinces. During his superiorate, the society expanded from 1,800 to 2,272 members. He was present in Rome at the consecration of the first African bishop, Joseph *Kiwanuka, a member of his society (1939). The WF accepted new mission responsibilities in Oyo, Nigeria (1943), and in Beira, Mozambique (1946), and ceded Mbulu and Turu in Tanganyika to the Pallotine Fathers (1939), while the apostolic vicariate of Masaka was entrusted to Kiwanuka (1939).

BIBLIOGRAPHY J. M. Birraux, *Lettres et Circulaires de Monseigneur Birraux, 1936–1947* (1947); G. D. Kittler, *The White Fathers* (1957); A. Wyckaert, *Son Exc. Msgr. J.M. Birraux* (n.d.).

J. G. Donders, M Afr

Bishop, Artemas (1795–1872), American missionary to Hawaii. After graduation from Union College, New York (1819), Bishop attended Princeton Theological Seminary, where he graduated in 1822. The same year he was ordained, married Elizabeth Edwards, and sailed with the second company of American Board of Commissioners for Foreign Missions missionaries to Hawaii. Serving at Waimea, Kauai (1823–1824), Kailua (1824–1836), and Ewa (1836–1846), he then assisted in the pastorate at Kawaiahao Church, Honolulu, also preaching at Ewa until 1860 and conducting classes for ministerial candidates. With others or alone he translated a dozen books of the Bible. He also translated *Pilgrim's Progress* and a number of mathematics textbooks and compiled a Hawaiian-English phrase book.

BIBLIOGRAPHY *Missionary Album* (1969), pp. 46–47; *Missionary Herald* 69:148–149.

David M. Stowe

Bishop, Isabella Lucy (Bird) (1831–1904), traveler, author, and advocate of medical missions. Isabella Bird was the daughter of Edward Bird, curate of Boroughbridge, Yorkshire, England. Encouraged by her father to travel and to write, she visited Canada and the United States in 1854 and wrote *The Englishwoman in America* (1856). She revisited the United States in 1858 to study the revival movement; her *Aspects of Religion in America* appeared in 1859. From 1860 she lived mostly in Scotland, writing on Edinburgh slum conditions and assisting Highland welfare and emigration schemes. By 1872 she faced physical and psychological breakdown, and foreign travel was recommended. A period in Australia and New Zealand availed little, but a dangerous sea passage to Hawaii, six months' residence there, and a subsequent sojourn in the American Rockies rejuvenated her. Two popular books, *The Hawaiian Archipelago* (1875) and *A Lady's Life in the Rocky Mountains* (1879), followed. Thereafter, though a chronic invalid in a spinal brace when at home, she became a celebrated traveler abroad, an outstanding travel writer, and a recognized commentator on overseas affairs—occupations normally then a male province. *Unbeaten Tracks in Japan* (1880) opened aspects of Japanese life (notably the rural areas and the Ainu) that were new to Western readers. A tour of Malaya produced *The Golden Chersonese* (1883).

In 1881 Bird married John Bishop, an Edinburgh doctor, and for a few years her only travels were in fruitless search for a European location suiting his failing health. On his death in 1886, she undertook nursing training, but returned to traveling in 1889 with a two-year journey through India, the Tibetan borderlands, Mesopotamia, Persia, Kurdistan, Azerbaijan, and Turkey. On her return she briefed Gladstone on the Armenian question and gave evidence to a parliamentary committee on the subject. *Journeys in Persia and Kurdestan* appeared in 1889. In 1894 she began a three-year journey in the Far East, writing perceptively on the developing situations in Korea (*Korea and Her Neighbors,* 1898) and China (*The Yangstze Valley and Beyond,* 1899). Her last journey, undertaken at age 70, was to Morocco.

Her faith seems to have matured slowly. Often receiving mission hospitality, she witnessed missionary endeavors at close quarters. Her husband assisted the Edinburgh Medical Missionary Society and through him she became increasingly interested in medical missions. On his death she wished to open a hospital in Nazareth and to work there. When that proved impossible, she established mission hospitals in India, China, and Japan. She also supported Dugald *Christie's medical college in Manchuria. Well known for her respect for indigenous cultures, she became in her later years an eloquent advocate for missions; her speech "Heathen Claims on Christian Duty" (1894) had a profound influence upon the public. She supported a variety of mission agencies, not least the China Inland Mission, which she particularly admired. She died in Edinburgh.

BIBLIOGRAPHY Up to 1880 her works appear under the name of Isabella L. Bird; thereafter under that of Mrs. Bishop. Her principal books have received modern editions. Pat Barr, *A Curious Life for a Lady: The Story of Isabella Bird* (1970); Olive Checkland, *Isabella Bird and "a woman's right to do what she can do well"* (1996); Eugene Stock, *History of the Church Missionary Society,* vol. 3 (1899) and vol. 4 (1916); Anna M. Stoddart, *The Life of Isabella Bird (Mrs. Bishop)* (1906). Obituary, *Blackwoods Edinburgh Magazine,* November 1904, pp. 698–704.

Andrew F. Walls

Bishop, William Howard (1885–1953), founder and superior general of the Glenmary Home Missioners. Bishop, a native of Washington, D.C., was educated at Harvard (1906–1908) and St. Mary's Seminary, Baltimore (1908–1915), and ordained a Catholic priest in 1915. From 1917 to 1937 he was pastor of St. Louis parish, Clarksville, Maryland. With the help of the Catholic Daughters of America he founded and headed the League of St. Louis (1922) to support a parochial school; it became the League of the Little Flower (1924), an archdiocesan organization to supervise funding of catechetical programs and parochial education in rural parishes. He was founder and editor of its quarterly publication, *The Little Flower* (1927–1937).

Bishop was also a founding member of the National Catholic Rural Life Conference (NCRLC) in 1923 and served as president from 1928 to 1934. He founded and edited the NCRLC journal *Landward* (1930), a quarterly dedicated to a back-to-the-land movement. In 1935, drawing upon the rural mission experiences of Thomas F. *Price, the missionary bands promoted by the Paulists, and the foreign mission impulses of Maryknoll, Bishop conceived a plan for a religious community of Catholic rural missionaries. It involved direct-action evangelization to convert the unchurched in rural areas through "camp meetings" led by a team of missioners who would articulate Catholicism and establish mission parishes in the hundreds of counties in rural America that he referred to as "no-priest land." With the support of the founder-superior of Maryknoll, James A. *Walsh, and Archbishop John T. McNicholas, of Cincinnati, the Home Missioners of America was founded in 1937. Later called the Glenmary Home Missioners, the society was composed of priests, brothers, and sisters (1939; the sisters later formed a separate community). In 1938 Bishop founded *The Challenge,* the society's publication. When he died, there were seven rural missions, twenty-one priests, eleven brothers, and twenty-nine sisters.

BIBLIOGRAPHY Christopher Kauffman, *Mission to Rural America: The Story of W. Howard Bishop, Founder of Glenmary* (1991); Herman W. Santen, *Howard Bishop, Founder of the Glenmary Home Missions* (1961). Bishop's personal papers, diaries, and correspondence are located at the Glenmary archives in Cincinnati.

Christopher J. Kauffman

Bisseux, Isaac (1807–1896), pioneer French Protestant missionary in South Africa. Recommended to Paris Evangelical Missionary Society (PEMS) by Reformed pastor Antoine Colani of Lemé, Aisne, France, in 1829 Bisseux sailed for southern Africa with two other PEMS missionaries, Prosper *Lemue and Samuel *Rolland. Afrikaners of French descent inhabiting the Wagenmaker Valley invited Bisseux to evangelize their Khoi (Hottentot) slaves. Though it was originally unplanned, the PEMS allowed this venture to proceed, and the first conversion took place in 1831. When slavery was abolished three years later, the black Christian community numbered fifteen baptized members. It moved to Wellington in 1842, where Bisseux established a school. When he retired in 1881 in Montagu, Cape Province, his congregation joined the Dutch Reformed Church.

BIBLIOGRAPHY Robert Cornevin, "Isaac Bisseux (1807–1896)," in *Hommes et Destins,* vol. 2 (1977), pp. 92–93; C. J. Kriel, "Bisseux, Isaac," in *Dictionary of South African Biography* (1968), pp. 79–80; "Quelques souvenirs du missionnaire Bisseux," *Journal des missions évangéliques* 72 (1897): 131–136; Jean-François Zorn, *Le grand siècle d'une mission protestante: La Mission de Paris de 1822 à 1914* (1993), pp. 363–369, 518.

Jean-François Zorn

Black, William (1760–1834), pioneer of Methodism in Nova Scotia. Black was born in England at Huddersfield, Yorkshire, into a Methodist home. His family immigrated to Nova Scotia in 1775, where he worked for the rest of his life. In 1779 he experienced a spiritual awakening and began to preach, contributing to a revival that began in 1781 and led to the start of Methodism in Canada. Classes, love feasts, and quarterly meetings were set up, and a circuit was formed. He began a circuit ministry in 1781 and in 1782 appealed to John *Wesley for missionaries for Nova Scotia. In 1784 he met Richard Whatcoat and Thomas *Coke at the historic Christmas Methodist Conference in Baltimore, Maryland, where Freeborn Garrettson and James Oliver Cromwell were set aside for Nova Scotia and thus became the first foreign missionaries of American Methodism in the New World. Black spent February to May 1785 in the Boston area on his way back to Nova Scotia, and his skills as a preacher and evangelist were further displayed. In May 1789 he was ordained a deacon, then elder, by Thomas Coke and Francis *Asbury at the Philadelphia Methodist Conference, and he was designated presiding elder for Nova Scotia by Coke. In 1799 he went to England to recruit four more volunteers for the expanding work. In 1816 he was delegated to represent the British Methodist Conference at the American Methodist General Conference to discuss disagreements between American and British missionaries in Nova Scotia about political matters and continuing British Methodist participation in the Church of England. Black wrote an account of his life in Thomas Jackson's *Lives of the Early Methodist Preachers.* He died of cholera in Halifax, Nova Scotia, after spearheading the rise and growth of Methodism in that part of Canada.

BIBLIOGRAPHY *Centennial of Canadian Methodism* (1891); G. S. French, *Parsons and Politics* (1962); M. Richey, *William Black* (1839).

Frank Whaling

Blackmore, Sophia (1857–1945), missionary in Singapore and Malaya. Born in Goulburn, Australia, Blackmore was the first single woman Methodist missionary appointed to the Malay Peninsula, where she worked from 1887 to 1928. Because the Australian church did not send out single women, she was appointed by the Woman's Foreign Missionary Society of the American Methodist Episcopal Church. Within two years of her arrival, she founded two Methodist girls' schools in Singapore, followed by five others in Malaya by 1900. She also founded Nind Home, a boarding school for orphans and for girls seeking refuge or from poor families. Before the turn of the century, she and her colleagues were ahead of their mission in sending local women overseas for further training. Her efforts to train women for evangelistic work led in 1901 to her being appointed the first head of a training institute for "Bible women" in Singapore, later named Eveland Seminary. Her evangelistic zeal and saintliness of character left a lasting legacy in the lives of numerous women who came under her influence. Today a school building atop Mt. Sophia in Singapore is named in her memory.

BIBLIOGRAPHY Theodore R. Doraisamy, ed., *Sophia Blackmore in Singapore—Educational and Missionary Pioneer, 1887–1927* (1987) and "Women Pioneers and Methodism in Singapore and Malaysia: Messengers of Love," *AJT* 4, no. 2 (1990): 344–355. Sophia Blackmore, "A Record of 40 Years of Women's Work in Malaya, 1887–1927," an unpublished and undated manuscript in the United Methodist archives, Madison, N.J.

Hwa Yung

Blackstone, William Eugene (1841–1935), American missions activist and philanthropist, and "Father of Zionism." A devout Methodist, lay evangelist, and successful Chicago businessman, Blackstone devoted his life and fortune to propagating the premillennial view of the Second Coming of Jesus Christ, to missions, and to the welfare and evangelization of the Jews. An avid tract distributor, in 1878 he wrote *Jesus Is Coming,* the most popular statement of premillennial hope in its day. In 1890 he held the first Jewish-Christian conference. The next year he made a presentation to President Benjamin Harrison in which he proposed the establishment of a Jewish state in Palestine. In 1887 he founded the Chicago Hebrew Mission, which advocated that Jews should be able to maintain their cultural identity even as Christians.

Blackstone gave anonymously to hundreds of mission causes. He helped to found the Christian and Missionary Alliance, the Moody Bible Institute, the Bible Institute of Los Angeles, and the Chicago Training School. After the death of his wife in 1909, he went to China and published and distributed Bibles for five years. Returning to America, for years he administered the Milton Stewart fund for the distribution of Christian literature around the world.

BIBLIOGRAPHY Sandy Keck, "W. E. Blackstone, Champion of Zion," *American Messianic Fellowship Monthly* 78–79 (1973–1974); Beth M. Lindberg, *A God-Filled Life: The Story of William E. Blackstone* (n.d.); Cutler B. Whitwell, "The Life Story of W. E. B.—and of 'Jesus Is Coming,'" *Sunday School Times,* January 11, 1936, pp. 19–20. See also Yaakov Ariel, *On Behalf of Israel: American Fundamentalist Attitudes Toward Jews, Judaism, and Zionism, 1865–1945* (1991). Blackstone wrote many pamphlets and articles and edited *The Jewish Era: A Christian Magazine on Behalf of Israel.* His papers are held by the American Messianic Fellowship in Chicago.

Dana L. Robert

Blanchet, Francis Norbert (1795–1883), first Catholic bishop in Oregon. Blanchet was born in Quebec City and ordained in 1819. He ministered among the Acadians and Micmac Indians in New Brunswick from 1820 to 1827, then served the St. Joseph de Soulages church in Montreal from 1827 to 1837. In 1838 he set out with Modeste Demers for the Pacific Northwest. They established missions among the American and French-Canadian settlers and took special interest in setting up missions among the aboriginal population. Blanchet was ordained bishop in 1845. The following year he convinced the Vatican to establish an ecclesiastical province, with himself as archbishop of Oregon City, his brother Augustin Magloire Blanchet as bishop of Walla Walla, Washington (and later of Nesqually, Washington), and Demers as bishop of Vancouver Island. The Whitman Massacre in 1847 and the Cayuses War (1847–1848) were major setbacks for his new diocese; many settlers blamed the Catholic clergy for the massacre. Conflict with the government over Protestant control of Catholic reservations led to the organization of the Bureau of Catholic Missions in 1874. Blanchet's "Catholic ladder," a pictorial device for teaching Catholic doctrine, was copyrighted in 1859. He wrote *Historical Sketches of the Catholic Church in Oregon* (1878) and *Historical Notes and Reminiscences* (1883). He moved his residence to Portland in 1862, where he retired in 1880.

BIBLIOGRAPHY C. P. Bagley, *Early Catholic Missions in Old Oregon,* 2 vols. (1923); L. M. Lyons, *Francis Norbert Blanchet and the Founding of the Oregon Missions, 1838–1848* (1940); Wilfred P. Schoenberg, *A History of the Catholic Church in the Pacific Northwest* (1987).

Achiel Peelman, OMI

Bliss, Anna Elvira. *See* Ferguson, Abbie Park.

Bliss, Daniel (1823–1916), American missionary educator in Lebanon. Bliss entered Amherst College at age 25, supporting himself and graduating in 1852 (D.D., 1863). Three years later he graduated from Andover Theological Seminary, was ordained into the Congregational ministry, married Abby Maria Wood, was appointed by the American Board of Commissioners for Foreign Missions (ABCFM), and sailed for the Near East. After he had served five years at Abeih and Suq al-Gharb, Lebanon, managing schools, itinerating, and preaching, the Syria Mission of the ABCFM voted in 1862 to establish a Syrian Protestant College and Bliss was chosen to organize it and serve as its president. The aim was to "enable native youth to obtain, *in the country,* [a] literary, scientific, and professional education" in a self-governing, self-sustaining indigenous institution not supported or controlled by the mission but nevertheless "conducted on strictly Christian and evangelical principles." Bliss spent two years in America and Britain winning prominent and generous supporters, including W. E. Dodge, his son, D. S. Dodge, the Earl of Shaftesbury, and John Bright. He secured a New York State charter for an institution governed by a self-perpetuating board of trustees, elected in the first instance by the Syria Mission. The college opened in 1866 with two tutors and Bliss as professor and soon began to draw students from all over the region, representing all Christian communities as well as Druze, Jews, and Muslims. Bliss was intensely active in all aspects of the college, cultivating support, developing the campus, and participating in the school's academic and religious life. He described himself as born a Baptist, brought up a Methodist, ordained a Congregationalist, and laboring (in 1881) among Presbyterians. His liberal evangelical perspective is reflected in an *Atlantic Monthly* article (May 1920), "The Modern Missionary," written by his son, Howard Bliss, who succeeded him as president in 1903. The college became the American University of Beirut in 1920. A major thoroughfare in Beirut was named Rue Bliss.

BIBLIOGRAPHY *Reminiscences of Daniel Bliss,* F. J. Bliss, ed. (1920); *The Voice of Daniel Bliss* (1956; sermons and addresses); *Missionary Herald* 59 (1863): 36–38; 112 (1916): 393.

David M. Stowe

Bliss, Edwin Munsell (1848–1919), American missionary, author, and editor. Bliss was born in Erzurum, Turkey, the son of American Board of Commissioners for Foreign Missions (ABCFM) missionaries Isaac Grout and Eunice B. (Day) *Bliss. His father was a representative of the American Bible Society in the Middle East for over 30 years. Edwin studied at Robert College, Constantinople, under Cyrus *Hamlin and graduated from Amherst College (B.A., 1871; D.D., 1896) and Yale Divinity School (B.D., 1877). He assisted his father and succeeded him as a Bible Society agent in the Middle East until 1888, when he resigned and returned to the United States following the death of his first wife, Marie Louise (Henderson). His great contribution to mission studies was the *Encyclopedia of Missions,* which he edited. Published in 1891 in two volumes, it was a remarkable achievement and remains a valuable source of information, primarily on the progress of Protestant missions in the nineteenth century. (A second edition of the *Encyclopedia,* co-edited by Bliss, Henry Otis Dwight, and Henry Allen Tupper, Jr., was published in 1904.) During the academic year 1898–1899 Bliss lectured on foreign missions at Yale Divinity School. He assisted the Ecumenical Conference on Foreign Missions of 1900 with publicity and publications while working as a newspaper editor in New York City. In 1900 he married former ABCFM missionary Ella Theodora Crosby, who wrote *Micronesia: Fifty Years in the Island World: A History of the Mission of the American Board* (1906). From 1902 to 1904 Bliss was a field representative in New England for the American Tract Society. In 1905 he became general secretary of the Foreign Missions Industrial Association, remaining in that post until 1907. He was then called to the U.S. Bureau of the Census in Washington, D.C., as a specialist on religious organizations, where he served until he died.

BIBLIOGRAPHY Bliss was the author of *Turkey and the Armenian Atrocities* (1896), *Concise History of Missions* (1897), and *The Missionary Enterprise* (1908). For the U.S. Bureau of the Census he helped to prepare *Religious Bodies,* 2 vols. (1916).

Gerald H. Anderson

Bliss, Isaac Grout (1822–1889), missionary and agent of the American Bible Society (ABS) in the Near East. Born in Springfield, Massachusetts, Bliss was educated at Amherst College (graduated 1844) and at Andover Theological Seminary. After graduating in 1847, he was ordained a missionary of the American Board of Commissioners for Foreign Missions (ABCFM), married Eunice B. Day, and sailed for Turkey. They were stationed at Erzurum, a new field, where Bliss worked so strenuously that his health failed and they returned home in 1851. He did pastoral work in Massachusetts until his appointment by the American Bible Society in 1856 as agent for the Levant, stationed in Constantinople. The Bible had been translated and published before his arrival, but Bliss energetically undertook the systematization and extension of its distribution and further publication. He toured in Turkey, Syria, Egypt, and Persia, studied the needs and opportunities of many nationalities and tribes, consulted with missionaries, and employed large numbers of colporteurs. One of his major projects was the development of a large Bible House in Constantinople to be the headquarters for the ABCFM and the American and British Bible societies. In 1866 he secured in America most of a $60,000 development fund, and the first of several buildings was completed in 1872. There were rented shops on the ground floor, storerooms for Bible and mission publications, printing facilities, offices, workrooms, and a chapel where evangelistic services were held. In his 1883 report "Twenty-five Years in the Levant," Bliss noted an aggregate distribution of 1,883,157 Bibles and portions, in some thirty languages. He was the brother of ABCFM missionary Edwin Elisha Bliss, and father of the mission encyclopedist Edwin Munsell *Bliss. He died in Assiout, Egypt, and was buried beside fellow missionary John *Hogg.

BIBLIOGRAPHY *Missionary Herald* 85 (1889): 141–142 (obit.). Bliss's work is described in Joseph K. Greene, *Leavening the Levant* (1916), pp. 128–131.

David M. Stowe

Bliss, Kathleen Mary Amelia (Moore) (1908–1989), ecumenical pioneer. Born in Fulham, London, a graduate from Girton College, Cambridge, with a first-class degree in theology as well as a good history degree, Kathleen Moore was a Student Volunteer and much involved in the Cambridge Student Christian Movement. Her red hair attracted an admirer, and her challenging theological arguments a devoted life partner in Rupert Bliss, a former naval engineer who had become an Anglican ordinand through the influence of William *Temple. Together they went to Tamil Nadu, South India, in 1932 under the London Missionary Society. On furlough in 1939, Rupert introduced his wife to Eleanora Iredale, J. H. *Oldham's assistant. Kathleen succeeded Iredale as assistant editor and then editor of the influential *Christian Newsletter* (1942–1949). From 1945 to 1959 she worked for the British Council of Churches and then for the BBC (1950–1955). She was a moving spirit at the Amsterdam Assembly of the World Council of Churches (WCC) in 1948 and is credited with the famous phrase, "We intend to stay together." She was elected to the Central Committee and Executive Committee of the WCC in 1954, and she played an important part in the evolving ecumenical movement. She had a formidable intellect, concerned particularly with laypeople and women, hence her outstanding work as secretary of the WCC commission on the status and role of women in the churches. From 1958 to 1966 as secretary of the Board of Education of the Church of England, she was responsible for policy in the rapidly expanding colleges and universities of the 1960s. Finally, she was senior lecturer in the Department of Religious Studies at the new University of Sussex (1968–1972). Even retirement did not lessen her concern for ecumenism. Increasingly crippled by arthritis, she was unfortunately unable to finish her biography of J. H. Oldham, her mentor and friend. Her crowded memorial service was testimony to how wide her influence was and how precious her friendship. She was a "foremother" of today's women theologians and church leaders. In 1949 she was honored with a D.D. by the University of Aberdeen.

BIBLIOGRAPHY Kathleen Bliss, *The Service and Status of Women in the Churches* (1952), *We, the People* (1963), *The Future of Religion* (1969), and "J. H. Oldham," in Gerald H. Anderson et al., eds., *Mission Legacies* (1994), pp. 570–580. Martin Conway, *ER* 42, no. 1 (January 1990): 68–77 (obit.); Susannah Herzel, *A Voice for Women* (1981).

E. M. Jackson

Bloch-Hoell, Nils Egede (1915–), Norwegian missiologist. Born in Oslo, Bloch-Hoell graduated from the Norwegian Lutheran School of Theology in 1941. In a varied career, his contribution to missions was primarily through his positions as traveling preacher in the Norwegian Mission to the Lapps (1942–1943), general secretary of the Norwegian Mission to the Muslims (1950–1958), and the first professor of missiology and ecumenics at the Theological Faculty of Oslo University (1969–1985). He was also director of Egede Instituttet (Oslo) for missionary study and research, and editor of its missiological journal, *Norsk Tidsskrift for Misjon* (1972–1985). His main academic contribution has been in the field of ecumenics; his 1956 doctoral dissertation about the Pentecostal movement was a pioneering study. He was also involved in various ecumenical dialogue commissions and published textbooks and more general works about ecumenical issues.

BIBLIOGRAPHY Bloch-Hoell's doctoral thesis was published in English as *The Pentecostal Movement: Its Origin, Development, and Distinctive Character* (1964). A special issue of *Norsk Tidsskrift for Misjon* 39 (1985), published in his honor, includes a bibliography. Additional references are found in the same journal 43 (1990): 243–244.

Notto R. Thelle

Blumhardt, Christian Gottlieb (1779–1839), pioneer German mission leader. Blumhardt was born in Württemberg and became pastor of the Württemberg church. From 1803 to 1807 he was assistant secretary of the German Christianity Society in Basel, Switzerland, where he was responsible for communicating much information from the new world of Anglo-Saxon missions to the German-speaking pietist grass roots, thus laying the foundation for the rapid growth of broad public support that characterized the early years of the Basel Mission (BM). Blumhardt was a major figure in the establishment of BM, and from 1816 to his death he was the *Inspektor* (executive head) of the mission. Under his leadership two major periodicals were started: *Magazin für die neueste Geschichte der evangelischen Missions- und Bibelgesellschaften* (quarterly from 1816) and the more popular monthly *Evangelische Heidenbote* (from 1828). He helped create the mission's organizational structure, defined the nature and curriculum of the mission seminary, and set up the first BM fields: Russian Caucasus from the early 1820s, Ghana from 1828, South India from 1834. His ecumenical contacts resulted in many Basel-trained missionaries working for England's Church Missionary Society. He was also involved in the negotiations that led to the founding of the Barmen (Rhineland) Mission and the Paris Evangelical Missionary Society.

BIBLIOGRAPHY Christian Gottlieb Blumhardt, *Versuch einer allgemeinen Missionsgeschichte der Kirche Christi* (1828ff.). See also Karl Rennstich, *Handwerkertheologen und Industriebruder als Botschafter des Friedens: Entwicklungshilfe der Basler Mission im 19. Jahrhundert* (1985); William Schlatter, *Geschichte der Basler Mission* (1915).

Paul Jenkins

Blyden, Edward Wilmot (1832–1912), African American clergyman, educator, politician, and diplomat. Blyden was born in St. Thomas, Virgin Islands, of pious parents associated with the integrated Dutch Reformed Church of

St. Thomas. John P. Knox, American missionary pastor of the church, noted Blyden's abilities and encouraged him. With his parents' approval and encouragement from Knox, he decided to become a Christian minister. In 1850 he visited the United States with Knox's wife and sought matriculation in Rutgers Theological College but was denied admission. Likewise his efforts to enroll at two other theological colleges failed. But while in the United States he came into contact with Presbyterians associated with the colonization movement, under whose auspices he immigrated to Liberia in 1850. In 1851 he enrolled in Alexander High School in Monrovia. He was ordained a Presbyterian minister with the Presbyterian Board of Foreign Missions in 1858. In 1886, having become somewhat sympathetic to Islam and distressed at the arrogance of Christian missionaries, he resigned from the Presbyterian Church. During his lifetime he held a variety of positions in Liberia and Sierra Leone—Secretary of State, ambassador to the court of St. James, Envoy Extraordinary to London and Paris. In 1887 his major work—*Christianity, Islam, and the Negro Race*—was published. He also wrote many other books, pamphlets, and articles in which he sought to vindicate the Negro race. The roots of the philosophy of *négritude*, Pan-Africanism, African nationalism, and African Christian theology can be traced to Blyden's idea of African personality.

BIBLIOGRAPHY Edward W. Blyden, *Vindication of the Negro Race* (1857), *Liberia's Offering* (1862), *People of Africa* (1871), *Origin and Purpose of African Colonization* (1883), *West Africa before Europe, and Other Addresses* (1905), and *African Life and Customs* (1908, repr. 1969). Edith Holden, *Blyden of Liberia: An Account of the Life and Labors of Edward Wilmot Blyden, LL.D., As Recorded in Letters and in Print* (1967); Thomas W. Livingston, *Education and Race: A Biography of Edward Wilmot Blyden* (1975); Hollis R. Lynch, *Edward Wilmot Blyden, Pan-Negro Patriot* (1967), and ed., *Black Spokesman: Selected Published Writings of Edward Wilmot Blyden* (1971).

Tite Tiénou

Boardman, George Dana (1801-1831), pioneer missionary to Burma (Myanmar). Born in Maine and educated at what is now Colby College, Boardman offered himself to the Baptist Foreign Mission Board in 1823. After two years of study at Andover Theological Seminary and marriage to Sarah Hall (*see* Sarah Hall Boardman *Judson), he was commissioned for service to Burma. He arrived there with Sarah and their infant daughter in 1827, shortly after the death of Adoniram Judson's wife, Ann Hasseltine *Judson, and scarcely a week prior to the death of Judson's two-year-old daughter. Boardman's first task was to build a coffin for the child. Located for a brief period in Moulmein, where he opened a school for boys, Boardman was urged by the mission board to extend the work to new areas. He agreed and in 1828 relocated in Tavoy, a largely Buddhist city 125 miles south. Accompanying Boardman and his family was *Ko Tha Byu, a Karen who had become a Christian through Judson's influence but had not been baptized because of his criminal past. Two months after their arrival in Tavoy, Boardman baptized Ko Tha Byu. Three Karens witnessed the rite and asked Ko Tha Byu to come to their villages and tell his story. In the meantime, Boardman organized a church of three members and started a teachers' training school for young men. He spent his time in daily discussions and witnessing to the Burmese, directing the school, and leading the church. By 1830 the Tavoy Church had grown to ten members. When repeated delegations of Karens came to his home, one bearing *The Book of Common Prayer* (which the Karens could not read) and asking if it was a good or evil book, Boardman sensed the evangelistic potential among the animistic, non-Buddhist Karen tribal people. Thus, on February 5, 1829, with Ko Tha Byu and two young men from the school, he went on the first preaching mission to the Karens. Boardman died of tuberculosis only two years later, but his pioneering efforts among the Karens eventually resulted in an ingathering of Christian converts rarely equaled in mission history. After Boardman's death, Sarah Boardman married Adoniram *Judson.

BIBLIOGRAPHY Alonzo King, *A Good Fight: George Boardman and the Burman Mission* (1874); Joseph C. Robbins, *Boardman of Burma* (1940); Robert G. Torbet, *Venture of Faith* (1955); Walter N. Wyeth, *A Galaxy in the Burman Sky* (1892).

Alan Neely

Boardman, Sarah (Hall). *See* Judson, Sarah (Hall) Boardman.

Boaz, Thomas (1806-1861), social reformer and missionary pastor in Calcutta. Born in Scarborough, England, Boaz remained a blunt nautical Yorkshireman, even after his conversion (which occurred during a time of rebellion against his Quaker background). After ordination, he was led to the London Missionary Society (LMS) in 1834 and missionary service in Bengal. In particular, he influenced educated Bengali converts and European youth as pastor of Union Chapel, Calcutta. He united a divided congregation and made it financially self-sufficient, a base for mission and social action. On furlough in England (1849-1850), he raised funds to rebuild and endow the LMS college at Bhowanipore (still a premier educational institution). He created the Bethel Mission to sailors in Calcutta, encouraged ecumenical charities, and edited the *Calcutta Christian Observer*. But it is as a social reformer he should be remembered. He almost single-handedly stopped the trade in indentured laborers in Bengal in 1842, although his efforts were not supported in Europe following the fatiguing, long-running anti-slavery campaigns. In 1849 he married Elizabeth Smith (1823-1884) a woman of equal strength of character, an indefatigable missionary who ran the Union Chapel when he was ill in 1858 and who wrote an excellent memoir of him. They returned to England in 1859.

BIBLIOGRAPHY Mrs. [Elizabeth] Boaz, *The Mission Pastor: Memorials of the Revd Thomas Boaz, by his widow* (1862); Hugh Tinker, *A New System of Slavery* (1974).

E. M. Jackson

Boberg, Folke Anders Adrian (1896–1987), missionary in Mongolia. Born in Kisa, Ostergotland, Sweden, Boberg prepared for mission work at the Swedish Alliance Mission Bible Institute in Jonkoping (1919–1920) and at Moody Bible Institute in Chicago, Illinois (1920–1922). From 1922 until 1951, he served as a missionary of the Swedish Pentecostal churches to Inner Mongolia (in present-day China). While there, he engaged in evangelism and lexicographical work. The fruit of his labors appeared in the highly acclaimed *Mongolian-English Dictionary,* 3 vols. (1954). Several Swedish foundations (e.g., The Langmans Cultural Fund) underwrote his publications.

BIBLIOGRAPHY Boberg's books also include *Med fridsbudskapet till Mongoliet* (With the peace mission to Mongolia, 1931), *Bland pilgrimer i Djungis Khans land* (With the pioneers in Genghis Kahn land, 1945), *Mongolia as a Mission Field* (1946), and *Lessons in the Mongolian Language* (1946).

Gary B. McGee

Bodding, Paul Olaf (1865–1938), Norwegian Lutheran missionary and scholar. Bodding was born in Gjøvik and graduated from the University of Oslo (Christiania) in 1889. He was ordained in 1889 and was sent to Santal Parganas in India. He was a missionary in India from 1890 to 1934, first as a local pastor in Mohulpahari for two long periods, and later as a superintendent of the Santal Mission (1911–1923). But most of his 44 years of service in India was given to research. Bodding was an outstanding Bible translator, and author and editor of a notable Santal-English dictionary. Though not a great preacher, he was a good administrator and spiritual guide. He was a member of the Asiatic Society of Bengal, and the Norwegian Academy of Science and Letters, and an honorary member of the British and Foreign Bible Society. He was awarded King Oscar's Gold Merit medal and was Commander of the Order of St. Olav, and he received the Delhi Durbar medal. Bodding's most important writings include a translation of most of the Santal Bible (1929, done partly in cooperation with L. O. *Skrefsrud); a Santal dogmatics text, and, in addition to his Santal-English dictionary, works on Santal grammar, folk tales, traditions, and institutions (1929–1936).

BIBLIOGRAPHY Sten Konow, "Minnetale over misjonsprest Paul Olaf Bodding," *Det Norske Videnskaps-Akademi in Oslo, Årbok 1938* (1939), pp. 76–86.

Nils E. Bloch-Hoell

Bodelschwingh, Friedrich von (1831–1910), founder of Bethel center and promoter of mission. Born in Westphalia, the son of a nobleman and high official of the Prussian government, Bodelschwingh felt called as a youth to overseas mission service, but he was trained for home ministry and never saw overseas service. In 1872, after several years of pastoral work, he was appointed head of a home for epileptics and an adjoining institution for deaconesses located outside Bielefeld. Under his leadership, these institutions became the nucleus of the world-famous Bethel center of charities and home mission. Because of its outstanding work with the poor and suffering, the reputation of Bethel spread throughout the German emigrant and missionary communities around the world.

Bodelschwingh was so closely connected with Bethel's home mission work that some accounts of his life do not mention his overseas interests. Yet he viewed home and overseas mission as two sides of the same coin. When he was asked in 1890 to join the board of the Protestant Mission Society for German East Africa (EMDOA), founded in 1886 and headquartered in Berlin, he agreed at once and promised to recruit nursing staff for the mission's hospital at Dar es Salaam. In 1906 the EMDOA moved from Berlin to Bielefeld, and in 1920, ten years after Bodelschwingh's death, the mission officially adopted the name Bethel Mission, thereby fulfilling his aim to let the Bethel community of the suffering and dying become a symbol of life eternal to Africa. Bodelschwingh was succeeded by his youngest son, Friedrich (1877–1946).

BIBLIOGRAPHY The only reliable and comprehensive account of Bodelschwingh as a mission leader is found in Gustav Menzel *Die Bethel-Mission: Aus 100 Jahren Missionsgeschichte* (1986).

Hans-Werner Gensichen

Bogue, David (1750–1825), British mission promoter and missionary educator. Bogue was the sixth son of a small landowner and magistrate in Coldingham, Berwickshire, Scotland, and was educated at the University of Edinburgh for the Church of Scotland ministry. As an opponent of the prevailing system of church patronage, he found no ready opening as a minister, and so went to England, where he eventually became pastor at Gosport, Hampshire. His background was Presbyterian, but the congregation was Independent (i.e., Congregational). From 1789 he combined the pastorate with a small seminary for training ministers.

Bogue was a major promoter of missions, at home and abroad. In the former sphere he was a founder of the Hampshire Association, an evangelistic agency in his locality, and a prominent supporter of evangelism in the Scottish Highlands. In the latter, he was perhaps the most important pioneer of the London Missionary Society (LMS). His published sermon in 1792, a gathering with like-minded friends, and his influential article in the *Evangelical Magazine* for May 1794 marked stages toward the formation of the LMS in 1795. He was an early and long-serving director of the society. He assisted the efforts of his friend Robert *Haldane (in whose conversion he had been instrumental) for a mission in Bengal and prepared to serve in it himself. When it became clear that the East India Company would not permit it, he turned his attention to missionary education and preparation. He had steadily opposed the LMS policy (urged by Thomas *Haweis and other directors) of accepting untrained and uneducated missionaries; he believed that India, in particular, needed better. From 1800 his seminary undertook the training of missionaries, giving the often homespun candidates of the LMS an intellectual preparation as rigorous as that for the home ministry. He trained at least 115 missionaries for the LMS, including many for India. His lectures, published years after his death, were long used on the mission field for training indigenous ministers. The Gosport seminary, however, led for a while after his death by Ebenezer *Henderson, did not long survive him.

In 1802 Bogue was part of an LMS-associated mission to France to promote circulation of the Scriptures there during the short-lived Peace of Amiens. A French translation of his book *The Divine Authority of the New Testament* (1801) was intended to help those influenced by atheistic and rationalistic thinking. He was also active in establishing the Religious Tract Society and the British and Foreign Bible Society, and was a proponent of Jewish missions. With his student James Bennett, he wrote a four-volume *History of the Dissenters from . . . 1688 to . . . 1808* (1808–1812), which had a long currency. Yale awarded him a D.D. in 1815.

BIBLIOGRAPHY David Bogue, *Discourses on the Millennium* (1818), *On Universal Peace* (1819), and *Theological Lectures* (1849). James Bennett, *Memoirs of the Life of the Rev. David Bogue* (1827); R. Lovett, *History of the London Missionary Society*, vol. 1 (1899); John Morrison, *The Fathers and Founders of the London Missionary Society* (2d ed., 1844), pp. 156–217; S. Piggin, *Making Evangelical Missionaries* (1984); C. Terpstra, "David Bogue, D.D., 1750–1825" (Ph.D. diss., Univ. of Edinburgh, 1959).

Andrew F. Walls

Böhler, Peter (1712–1774), bishop of the Moravian Church. Böhler was born in Frankfurt and educated at Jena, where he came under the influence of Augustus Gottlieb *Spangenberg. He joined the Moravian Church and was the first minister ordained by Count *Zinzendorf. He was a gifted linguist in Latin, German, French, and English, and one of the best educated clergymen of his day. On a mission journey to South Carolina in 1737, he encountered John *Wesley and aided Wesley's spiritual development with his advice: "Preach faith until you have it, and then because you have it, you will preach faith." Wesley later testified that this counsel from Böhler had a profound impact on his spiritual development. Böhler led a colony of Moravians to Pennsylvania and spent the last 25 years of his life alternating duties between Europe and America. He died in London.

BIBLIOGRAPHY J. T. and K. G. Hamilton, *History of the Moravian Church* (1967); J. E. Hutton, *History of the Moravian Church* (1909); Edwin A. Sawyer, *These Fifteen* (1963).

Albert H. Frank

Bohner, Heinrich (1842–1905), long-serving German missionary in West Africa. Born in the Bavarian Palatinate, Bohner worked for the Basel Mission (BM) in the Ga-Adangme region of Ghana from 1863 to 1889. He was a main influence in the conversion of Paulo Mohenu, a traditional priest who played a major role in the expansion of the BM church in the Ga-Adangme language group, and whose biography Bohner wrote. From 1890 to 1898 he was *Präses* (local head) of BM in Cameroon, playing a key role in building up BM work in this new field. He died in Germany. One of his children, Theodor, published a description of the trials of growing up as the son of a missionary.

BIBLIOGRAPHY Heinrich Bohner, *Die Erziehung des Kamerun-Negers zur Kultur* (1902). Theodor Bohner, *Auf allen Strassen: Geschichte einer Jugend in zwei Romanen* (5th ed., 1921, autobiography of his youth) and *Der Schuhmacher Gottes* (1934; biography of his father).

Paul Jenkins

Böhnisch, Frederick (1710–1763), Moravian missionary to Greenland. Born in Kunewald, Moravia, Böhnisch immigrated in 1724 to Herrnhut, Saxony. His family had old Moravian connections, and he was one of a significant number whose influence and service provided a link between the earlier and later periods of Moravian experience. In 1727 Böhnisch was part of a group that met regularly for Bible study and mutual edification, a discipline he continued throughout his mission career. In 1734 he traveled to Greenland with John Beck as part of the second mission team and served there for the last 30 years of his life, leading Bible study meetings and writing hymns for Greenlanders. This ministry in Greenland was interrupted only by brief trips to Europe and North America. In 1740 he married Anna Stach. He was ordained in 1745, and in 1749 visited the Indian mission station at Gnadenhütten on the Mahoning River in Pennsylvania. He died at New Herrnhut, Greenland, the first Moravian missionary to be buried in that land.

BIBLIOGRAPHY *Die Anfänger der Brüdermission in Grönland* (1841); J. T. Hamilton and K. G. Hamilton, *History of the Moravian Church* (1967); A. C. Thompson, *Moravian Missions* (1882).

Albert H. Frank

Boismenu, Alain de (1870–1953), French missionary of the Sacred Heart and consolidator of Catholic mission work in Papua New Guinea. Arriving at Yule Island in 1898, de Boismenu labored for 47 years along the coast among the Roro people and inland among the Mekeo, Kuni, and Fuyughe. In 1900 he was appointed bishop, and then vicar apostolic in 1908. His explorations in those early years led to opening the Oba Oba station in Kuni country and the Popole station among the Western Fuyughe. Under his oversight small stations staffed by single individuals were replaced by district stations, with supporting sisters, schools and catechetical centers, and technical training facilities. From 1898 to 1945 the districts increased from five to eleven, the people under care from 8,000 to 65,000, the baptized Catholics from 2,400 to 23,500, and school pupils from 800 to 7,000. At Kubuna, in Kuni country, de Boismenu founded an indigenous sisterhood, the Handmaids of Our Lord (1918), and established the first contemplative monastery in Papua New Guinea by recruiting Carmelite nuns for Papua in 1935. As organizer, peacemaker among warring Fuyughe tribesmen, defender of religious liberty against government intrusion, and inspirer of faith during the Japanese assaults on Papua, de Boismenu left an indelible mark. He died in Papua.

BIBLIOGRAPHY George Delbos, *Cent ans chez les Papous: Mission accomplie?* (1984; tr. by Theo Aerts as *The Mustard Seed: From a French Mission to a Papuan Church,* 1985); André Dupeyrat, *Papouasie: Histoire de le mission, 1885–1935* (1935); André Dupeyrat and F. de le Noé, *Sainteté au naturel: Alain de Boismenu évêque des Papous, vu à travers ses lettres* (1958); Garry W. Trompf, *Melanesian Religion* (1991), ch. 7, "The Catholic Mission" (with Theo Aerts).

Gary Trompf

Bojaxhiu, Agnes Gonxha. *See* Teresa, Mother.

Bolaños, Luis (1549–1629), Spanish Franciscan missionary friar in Paraguay. Born in Marchena, Andalusia, Spain, Bolaños arrived in Asunción, Paraguay, in 1575, with eleven other Franciscan friars, under the leadership of Alonso de San Buenaventura, his friend and patron. For ten years as a deacon Bolaños was an itinerant missionary, preaching the gospel to the Indians. He opposed the persecution of the Indians by the Spanish army and the settlers. Beginning in 1580, the converted Indians were gathered into *reducciones* (resettlement towns), for protection, indoctrination, and organized labor. Bolaños was ordained in 1585 and soon became the chief organizer of the Franciscan resettlements, ten of which were founded in Paraguay and Río de la Plata. He mastered the Indian languages and was the author of the first Guaraní grammar and dictionary. He also translated the Lima Catechism, a manual for confessions, and a book of sermons. In 1607 he founded the city of San José de Caazapá and another series of resettlements to the south of Asunción. The governor of Paraguay, Hernando Arias de Saavedra (known as Hernandarias), supported the work because the conversion of the Indians and their pacification improved the security of colonial interests. The last resettlement founded by Bolaños was in Baradero, near Buenos Aires, in 1616. His evangelizing work and his resettlements were important antecedents to the later work of the Jesuits. Old and nearly blind, he retired to the friary of San Francisco at Buenos Aires around 1623, where he died. In 1979 some of his relics were transferred to the church of San Francisco at Asunción.

BIBLIOGRAPHY Mariano Erasti, *América Franciscana,* vol. 1, *Evangelizadores e Indigenistas en el Siglo XVI* (1986), pp. 337–356; Margarita Durán Estrago, *Presencia Franciscana en el Paraguay, 1538–1824* (1987), pp. 225–232; M. A. Habig, "The Franciscans in Paraguay," *Franciscan Studies* 22 (1941): 33–57; Buenaventura Oro, *Fray Luis Bolaños, Apóstol del Paraguay y Río de la Plata* (1934); Elman R. Service, *Spanish-Guaraní Relations in Early Colonial Paraguay* (1954).

Pablo A. Deiros

Bolotov, Ioasaf (c. 1761–1799), pioneer Russian Orthodox missionary and first bishop of Alaska. Born to a clerical family in Strashkov, Russia, Bolotov graduated from the diocesan seminary in Rostov. Tonsured a monk in 1786, he became abbot at the strict Valamo monastery in Finland and gained a reputation for erudition and conscientiousness. In 1792 he was approached to head a mission to Kodiak Island, Alaska. Arriving in September of 1794, he hoped for an active role on the Alaskan mainland, but administrative duties kept him in Kodiak. Much of his time was given over to mediating among the competing companies of Russian fur traders, and between them and the Aleut and Koniag natives they employed and often abused. In 1796 the Holy Ruling Synod of the Russian Orthodox Church elected Bolotov bishop of Kodiak, auxiliary in the diocese of Irkutsk (Russia). He set off for Siberia following the opening of sea routes in the summer of 1798. After reporting in full on the state of the mission and receiving "unqualified praise" following months of scrutiny by Bishop Benjamin of Irkutsk, he was consecrated a bishop on April 10, 1799, by Benjamin alone; as such, he was one of the few exceptions to Apostolic Canon 1, which requires at least two consecrators (no other bishops were able to reach Irkurtsk, before Bolotov had to return to Alaska aboard the last ship for several years).

Taking along three workers to bolster the mission, the first Orthodox bishop for America set sail in the autumn; he was last seen alive on Unalaska on October 28, 1799, where he stopped to visit the flock. The wreckage of his ship, *Phoenix,* drifted ashore in May and June of 1800. Strong winds off Kodiak or an ailing crew were cited as reasons for the tragedy.

BIBLIOGRAPHY Richard Pierce, ed., *The Russian Orthodox Religious Mission in America, 1794–1837* (1978); P. A. Tikhmenev, *A History of the Russian American Company* (1978).

Paul D. Garrett

Bolshakoff, Serge N. (*or* Sergey Nikolaevich Bolshakov) (1901–1991), Russian Orthodox lay theologian, spiritual writer, and ecumenist. Born in St. Petersburg, Bolshakoff emigrated from Russia as a youth in 1918 and settled in Estonia. He studied theology at Pskovo-Petchersky monastery, and subsequently at Chevtogne, eventually committing himself as an Orthodox to the rule of St. Benedict. During World War II, he enrolled at the University of Oxford, from which he earned the D.Phil. degree in 1943. Subsequently he served as editor of the periodical *Church and World.* He had wide-ranging theological interests, which he explored in numerous articles and in several volumes. His main themes were spiritual life (*Russian Mystics,* 1977; *In Search of True Wisdom: Visits to Eastern Spiritual Fathers,* with M. Basil Pennington, 1979), church-state relations (*The Christian Church and the Soviet State,* 1942; *Russian Nonconformity: The Story of Unofficial Religion in Russia,* 1950), and ecclesiology (*The Doctrine of the Unity of the Church in the Works of Khomyakov and Moehler,* 1946). He was one of the first of the expatriate Russian intelligentsia to express theological and historical interest in Orthodox missions.

BIBLIOGRAPHY Serge Bolshakoff, *The Foreign Missions of the Russian Orthodox Church* (1943) and "Orthodox Missions Today," *IRM* 42 (1953): 275–284. James J. Stamoolis, *Eastern Orthodox Mission Theology Today* (1986); Nicolas Zernov, *The Russian Religious Renaissance of the Twentieth Century* (1963).

Stanley Samuel Harakas

Bompas, William Carpenter (1834–1906), pioneer Anglican missionary and bishop in Canada. Born in London, England, to a Baptist family, in 1858 Bompas resigned from the law firm in which he worked and was confirmed and soon ordained a deacon in the Church of England. An appeal by David *Anderson in 1865 inspired Bompas to relieve ailing Church Missionary Society missionary Robert *McDonald in the Yukon. With McDonald's recovery, Bompas was appointed itinerant preacher and quickly established a reputation for evangelistic zeal, indefatigable energy, and linguistic aptitude. The peripatetic Bompas grudgingly accepted his nomination as first bishop of Athabasca, one of four new jurisdictions that had been carved out of the huge Rupert's Land diocese. He was consecrated in England in May 1874 and married Charlotte Selina Cox, his cousin.

Bishop Bompas continued to function as an active missionary, preaching, baptizing, and translating hymns, prayers, and Scripture into the Slavey, Beaver, and Tukudh languages. Diocesan restructuring resulted in Bompas's becoming bishop of the northernmost diocese, Mackenzie River, in 1884. With further subdivision of his diocese in 1891, Bompas became bishop of Selkirk (Yukon). He died at Carcross in the Yukon Territory soon after retiring. One of the best-known Anglican missionaries of his day, the subject of popular juvenile and adult hagiography, and lauded for his bravery, self-sacrifice, and physical endurance, Bompas was described in one obituary as worthy to be "ranked with St. Paul, St. Peter, and St. Augustine."

BIBLIOGRAPHY William Bompas, *History of the Diocese of Mackenzie River* (1888), *Northern Lights on the Bible: Drawn from a Bishop's Experiences during Twenty-five Years in the Great Northwest* (1893), and *The Symmetry of Scripture* (1896). Bompas's numerous translations of religious works into native languages are listed in *Canadiana, 1867–1900.* K. M. Abel, "Bishop Bompas and the Canadian Church," in Barry Ferguson, ed., *The Anglican Church in Western Canada, 1820–1970* (1991); C. S. [Cox] Bompas, *A Heroine of the North: Memoirs of Charlotte Selina Bompas (1830–1917), Wife of the First Bishop of Selkirk (Yukon), with Extracts from Her Journals and Letters,* S. A. Archer, comp. (1929); Kenneth Coates, "Send Only Those Who Rise a Peg: Anglican Clergy in the Yukon, 1858–1932," *Journal of the Canadian Church Historical Society* 28 (1986); Hiram Alfred Cody, *An Apostle of the North: Memoirs of the Right Reverend William Carpenter Bompas* (1908); Eugene Stock, *The History of the Church Missionary Society, Its Environment, Its Men, and Its Work,* 4 vols. (1899–1916).

Jonathan J. Bonk

Bonaventura da Sardegna (c. 1600–1649), Capuchin missionary to Congo and coauthor of early Kikongo dictionary. Having completed classical studies in his native Sardinia, Bonaventura enrolled in the University of Salamanca. Taking the Capuchin habit in Madrid in 1629, he was ordained priest in 1637. Guardian of the convent of Valladolid, in 1643 he was nominated for the first Capuchin mission to Kongo (southern region of present-day Congo and northern Angola), arriving there in May 1645. He worked closely with Manuel Roboredo, the son of a Portuguese father and a mother of royal Kongolese blood. Ordained in the same year as Bonaventura, Roboredo had been sent by King Garcia II to conduct the Capuchins to the royal capital, Mbanza Kongo (about 150 miles southwest of Brazzaville). Bonaventura rapidly organized schools in Mbanza Kongo, training students in the arts and theology. He collaborated with Roboredo in compiling a trilingual dictionary of Kikongo, Spanish, and Latin. This was used by the students and missionaries, and a copy made by the martyr George de Geel was brought back to Rome in 1657. The Kikongo section, with translations into French and Flemish, was eventually published in 1928 by the Jesuits J. van Wing and C. Penders.

Bonaventura was entrusted by Garcia II with important diplomatic negotiations in Luanda, first with the Dutch in 1646, and then, after the Portuguese reconquest, with Salvador Correa da Sa in 1648. After Bonaventura died, Roboredo fittingly preached the sermon at his funeral. In 1652 Roboredo was received into the Capuchin Order. In 1665 he was killed at the battle of Mbwila, accompanying Garcia's successor as military chaplain.

BIBLIOGRAPHY Buenaventura de Carrocera, "Los capuchinos españoles en el Congo y el primer diccionario congolés," *Missionalia Hispanica* 2 (1945): 209–230; Carlo Toso, *Il Congo, cimitero dei Cappuccini, nell'inedito di P. Cavazzi,* sec. xvii (1992); J. van Wing and C. Penders, *Le plus ancien dictionnaire bantu* (1928).

Richard Gray

Bondolfi, Pietro (1872–1943), founder of the Societas Missionaria de Bethlehem (SMB). Born in Rome of Swiss parents, Bondolfi studied in Switzerland, Italy, Austria, and Belgium (licentiate in political and social sciences, Louvain, 1898). After his ordination as a Catholic priest in 1895, he served as archivist of the Diocese of Chur (Switzerland). In 1903 he got a doctorate in canon law. In 1904, when the Bethlehem Institute at Immensee (a society of priests founded in 1896 by the French priest J.-M. Barral) ran into financial difficulty, the bishop of Chur sent Bondolfi to study the situation. In 1906 he became the administrator of the institute, and after the quasicongregation of the Bethlehem Fathers was dissolved in 1908, Bondolfi took responsibility for the house and the school.

In 1921 the SMB was founded under the guidance of Propaganda Fide, and in 1923 Bondolfi became its first superior general. In 1924 he was able to send missionaries to Heilungkiang (Heilongjiang) Province, Manchuria, which he visited in 1929. The mission seminary, which had been opened at Wolhusen in 1922 was transferred in 1932 to Schöneck-Beckenried, where it remained until 1973. In 1936 the constitutions of the SMB were confirmed by Propaganda Fide, and in 1938 SMB missionaries were sent to Southern Rhodesia (Zimbabwe), where they later took over the Vicariate of Fort Victoria.

BIBLIOGRAPHY Josef Friemel, *Dr. Pietro Bondolfi: Leben und Wirken bis 1920* (1993); Walter Heim, *Geschichte des Institutes Bethlehem,* vols. 1–4 (1981–1990).

Fritz Kollbrunner, SMB

Boniface (*or* Bonifatius) (c. 675–754), English Benedictine monk and "Apostle of the Germans." Born at Crediton, in Devon, Boniface was originally known as Winfirth (Winfried). In 716 he went to Utrecht, where he was unable to get permission to preach to the Frisians from their king, Radbod, and he returned home. In 718 he went to Rome, where he got permission from Pope Gregory II (r. 715–731) "to preach the gospel to non-believers." He returned to Utrecht and worked under bishop (later archbishop) *Willibrord. Willibrord wanted Boniface as his successor but Boniface declined. Instead he went to Hesse, where he successfully extended the Christian faith into pagan territory and improved the development of the existing congregations. In 722 Pope Gregory II consecrated him missionary bishop of Germany. While he was in Rome, however, some of the nominal Christians in Hesse reverted to paganism. On his return to Hesse, Boniface decided that the time had come for a confrontation between paganism and Christianity, so he felled the sacred oak of Thor, at Geismar. Thousands of heathen converted to Christianity.

In 724 or 725 Boniface went to Thuringia, where he also did intensive missionary work. In 732 he was consecrated archbishop by Pope Gregory III (r. 731–741) and given the task of establishing papal authority over the church in Central Europe. After a third visit to Rome (737–738), he went to Bavaria, where he reorganized the church. Following the death of Charles Martel (741), he undertook to reform the Frankish church, on which he imposed a measure of discipline. He recruited many helpers, including women; he ordained priests, appointed bishops, and established the famous abbey at Fulda (744). In 747 he became archbishop of Mainz.

In his later years Boniface resigned his see because he wanted to complete the evangelization of the Frisians in the northern part of the Netherlands. He traveled among them, baptized thousands, destroyed temples, and built churches. In June 754 he and fifty companions were waiting for the arrival of some new converts near Dokkum. Suddenly they were attacked by angry pagans who murdered them all.

Boniface left his stamp upon the church in the Netherlands and Germany. Shortly after his death, the Mainz presbyter *Willibald wrote a biography, *Vita Sancti Bonifatii.*

BIBLIOGRAPHY G. F. Browne, *Boniface of Crediton and His Companions* (1910); F. Flaskamp, *Die Missionsmethode des heiligen Bonifatius,* (1929); E. Kylie, *The English Correspondence of Saint Boniface* (1911); G. Kurth, *Saint Boniface, 680–755* (1902); J. Lortz, *Bonifatius und die Grundlegung des Abendlandes* (1954); G. W. Robinson, *The Life of Saint Boniface by Willibald* (1916); Th. Schieffer, *Winfried-Bonifatius und die christliche Grundlegung Europas* (1954, repr. 1972); C. H. Talbot, "St. Boniface and the German Mission," in G. J. Cuming, ed., *The Mission of the Church and the Propagation of the Faith* (1970), pp. 45–57.

Jan A. B. Jongeneel

Bonjean, Ernest Christophe (1823–1892), French Oblate missionary and bishop in Ceylon (Sri Lanka). Born in France at Riom, Puy-de-Dôme, Bonjean entered the Paris Foreign Mission Society in 1846 and went to Coimbatore, South India. In 1857 he joined the Missionary Oblates of Mary Immaculate and worked as a missionary in Jaffna, Ceylon. In 1868 he was appointed vicar apostolic and bishop of Jaffna. He organized the vicariate into five districts and twenty-three mission stations. Through his dedication and missionary visitations, he strengthened the Christian spirit and stimulated the religious life of the people, preaching to Christians and administering the sacrament even in small villages, inspiring the missionaries in their work. An able writer, he defended Christian schools and dealt with marriage questions as well as with the schism in Goa. He participated in the First Vatican Council. In 1883 he was appointed vicar apostolic and in 1886 first archbishop of Colombo. In 1885 he was called back to Rome to participate in planning the establishment of the hierarchy in India. He died in Colombo.

BIBLIOGRAPHY E. C. Bonjean, *A Few Words on Catholic Education* (1860), *Denominational versus Common Mixed Schools* (1861), *The Catholic Church and Civilization* (1862), *Marriage Legislation in Ceylon* (1864), *Answers to the Questions Proposed by the Sub-Committee of Education* (1867), *The Latest about the Goa Question* (1873), *De infidelibus evangelizandis* (1878), *Missions des Oblate de Marie Immaculée à Colombo dans l'Ile de Ceylan* (1885), and *Acta Synodi Provincialis Columbensis primae* (1887). E. Jonquet, *Mgr. Bonjean: Oblat de Marie Immaculée, premier archevêque de Colombo* (1910); Johannes Rommerskirchen, *Die Oblatenmissionen auf der Insel Ceylon im 19. Jahrhundert, 1847–1893* (1931), pp. 97–111.

Willi Henkel, OMI

Bonnand, Clément (1796–1861), Catholic missionary bishop in India. Born in Saint-Maurice-sur-Dargoire, France, Bonnand entered the Paris Foreign Mission Society in 1823, and in 1824 was sent to India. In 1833 he was ordained bishop as coadjutor of the Vicariate of the Coromandel Coast (now Kerala), and became vicar apostolic three years later. One of the most eminent figures of Roman Catholic mission work in nineteenth-century India, Bonnand promoted the foundation of schools and printing presses and was especially concerned with the development of an Indian clergy. As vicar apostolic of Pondicherry, a position to which he was named in 1845, he held two important synods, and in 1858 was named papal visitor to India to create greater unity and cooperation among the various orders and nationalities that were working in India and to encourage the development of Indian clergy. However, he died at Benares, a victim of cholera, before the visitation was completed. Concluded under the bishop of Mysore, Étienne Louis Charbonneaux, the visitation laid the foundation for mission work in modern-day India: questions about caste differences were discussed, provincial councils were introduced, and an Indian hierarchy was eventually established.

BIBLIOGRAPHY F. Coutinho, *Le régime paroissial des diocéses de rite latin de l'Inde* (1958); C. Marces de Melo, *The Recruitment and Formation of the Native Clergy in India* (1955); J. Waigand, *Missiones Indiarum Orientalium SCPF concreditae, juxta visitationem apostolicam 1859–62* (1940); E. Zeitler, "Die Genesis der heutigen Priesterbildung in Indien," in *Verbo Tuo: Festschrift des Missionspriester-seminars St. Augustin* (1963), pp. 312-353.

Stephen B. Bevans, SVD

Boone, William Jones, Sr. (1811-1864), first American Episcopal missionary bishop in China. A native of South Carolina, Boone was admitted to the bar in 1833 but then graduated from seminary and medical school as well. In 1837 he was ordained and commissioned as a Protestant Episcopal Church USA (PEC) missionary to the Dutch East Indies and China. Initially, he served among the Chinese in Batavia, where he established a school for boys. In 1840 he moved his boys' school to Macao, and in 1842 pioneered mission work in Amoy (Xiamen), a newly opened treaty port in Fukien (Fujian) Province. His wife died in 1842 and in 1843 he returned to the United States, where he vigorously championed the cause of the China mission of the church when some leaders were wavering in their support. In 1844 Boone was consecrated missionary bishop to China, was given five new missionaries as reinforcements, remarried, and returned to China. After pausing in Hong Kong to consider strategy, he settled in Shanghai, which would become the most important of the port cities, and served there from 1845 until his death.

In Shanghai, Boone was involved in the early development of almost all PEC mission endeavors in China, including the expansion of the church to other cities. He ordained the first Chinese Episcopal priests and pursued his own literary and translation interests, including a translation of the Book of Common Prayer. He was an important participant in the committee of delegates who gathered in the late 1840s to make a new Chinese translation of the Bible. Controversies arose over the proper Chinese term to use for "God," and Boone, with a few others, commenced their own translation in 1851. One son, William Jones Boone, Jr. (1846-1891), was later missionary bishop of Shanghai; another son, H. W. Boone, M.D., did PEC medical work in Shanghai.

BIBLIOGRAPHY Muriel Boone, *The Seed of the Church in China* (1973); PEC, *The Bishops of the American Church Mission in China* (1906). Boone's official correspondence and reports are in the PEC historical archives at the Episcopal Seminary, Austin, Tex.

Daniel H. Bays

Booth, Ballington (1857-1940) *and*
Maud (Charlesworth) Ballington Booth (1865-1948), leaders of the Salvation Army (SA) in the United States and co-founders of Volunteers of America. Ballington Booth was born in Brighouse, England, son of William *Booth, founder and first general of the SA. Maud Charlesworth was born in Limpsfield, daughter of a clergyman. They were married in 1886 and she adopted Maud Ballington Booth as her full name. Almost as newlyweds, the Booths were placed in charge of the SA in the United States, becoming American citizens in 1895. They resigned from the SA in 1896 after a dispute with William Booth, and soon established the Volunteers of America.

During the years when the Booths administered the SA, the organization greatly expanded its ministry in the United States, including urban and world missions. Programs were started for temporary family crisis care (the "Slum Sisters," 1889), day-care centers (1889), and residential care and rehabilitation of homeless alcoholic men (1891). In addition, special ethnic ministries were started among the immigrant urban poor, and evangelistic activity among and by persons of African descent was attempted. The American branch of the SA began to finance the Army's rapidly expanding world missionary program (first "Self Denial Campaign," 1888).

The Volunteers of America was similar to the Army in form, although more democratic, and had similar programs, with two major differences. The new organization was entirely American, without a foreign missions component. In addition, it emphasized social welfare activity among prisoners, a particular interest of Maud, who became recognized as a national leader in this area. Ballington served as first general of the Volunteers of America until his death; he was succeeded in command by Maud, who remained as second general until shortly before her own death.

BIBLIOGRAPHY Ballington Booth, *From Ocean to Ocean* (1891); with Maud, *Beneath Two Flags* (1889); Maud Ballington Booth, *After Prison—What?* (1903). Both wrote often for the official publications of the SA (*War Cry*, 1887-1896) and of the Volunteers of America (*Volunteers' Gazette*, 1896-1948). Susan F. Welty, *Look Up and Live!* (1961) is a full biography of Maud. See also E. H. McKinley, *Marching to Glory: The History of the Salvation Army in the USA, 1880-1992* (2d rev. ed., 1994).

Edward H. McKinley

Booth, Catherine (Mumford) (1829-1890), "Mother" of the Salvation Army. Born in Derbyshire, England, Catherine Mumford was brought up in a pious Wesleyan family that worshiped in a Reformed Methodist chapel. Although delicate, she received a good education at home. As early as 1850 she was publicly proclaiming the equality of women. In 1852 she met the young Methodist evangelist William *Booth, and they married in 1855. By 1865, when they moved to Hammersmith, London, they had six children under ten years of age. Catherine Booth gave her husband complete support as his call to evangelism led first to his resignation from the Methodist New Connexion, and then to the formation of the Christian Mission, which became a "volunteer army" and ultimately, in 1878, the Salvation Army (SA). Her search for holiness influenced her husband and the movement he began.

In 1859, when the Booths were living at Gateshead, the American holiness preacher Phoebe Palmer, who was preaching locally with her husband, was denounced by an Anglican clergyman. Catherine Booth responded by writing a paper defending female ministry. Shortly afterward she spoke publicly for the first time. Later, as the wife of General William Booth, she became a well-known and effective speaker; she also contributed to SA magazines and wrote other papers and books. Her ministry—for example holding drawing room meetings for women—was of the greatest importance. She died of cancer.

Booth bore eight children, all of whom survived. Never a missionary herself, she was the mother and grandmother of many, and the mother of a missionary church. Her daughter Marian was a lifelong invalid; the other seven children all attained high office in the SA and served outside the United Kingdom. Evangeline (1865–1950), who did not marry, was the SA commander in the United States before becoming the fourth SA general.

BIBLIOGRAPHY Writings by Catherine Booth include *Female Ministry, or Women's Right to Preach the Gospel* (1859; repr. 1975), *Aggressive Christianity* (1880), *Papers on Godliness* (1881), *Practical Religion* (1884; contains "The Training of Children"), and *Holiness* (1887). Frederick Booth-Tucker, *The Life of Catherine Booth, the Mother of the Salvation Army,* 3 vols. (1893); Catherine Bramwell-Booth, *Catherine Booth: The Story of Her Loves* (1970); Clifford W. Kew, ed., *Catherine Booth: Her Continuing Relevance. A Collection of Essays* (1990).

Jocelyn Murray

Booth, Evangeline Cory (1865–1950), the daughter of William and Catherine *Booth and first woman general of the Salvation Army. Born in London, Evangeline Booth began street ministry as a child. She worked her way up through the ranks and became the director of the Salvation Army in Canada in 1896. In 1904 she was appointed commander of the Army in the United States, where she served for the next 30 years. She became the fourth general of the Army in 1934, a post in London she held for five years until her retirement at age 73, when she returned to the United States. She was an internationally known evangelist, noted for her personal magnetism and her colorful and dramatic sermons that drew crowds numbering tens of thousands. During her tenure as general of the Army, she launched the "World for God" campaigns, which took her around the world establishing new centers for gospel ministry and outreach. Her most lasting legacy was the growth and popularity she brought to the Army in the United States, which continues today. When she died, she was one of the best-known women of the twentieth century.

BIBLIOGRAPHY Sally Chesham, *Born to Battle: The Salvation Army in America* (1965); Edward H. McKinley, *Marching to Glory: The History of the Salvation Army in the United States, 1880–1980* (2d rev. ed., 1994); Margaret Troutt, *The General Was a Lady: The Story of Evangeline Booth* (1980); Ruth A. Tucker and Walter Liefeld, *Daughters of the Church: Women and Ministry from New Testament Times to the Present* (1987).

Ruth A. Tucker

Booth, Joseph (1851–1932), English missionary in Africa. Booth was born in Britain, immigrated to Australia, and first went to Africa in 1892 to begin the Zambezi Industrial Mission at Mitsidi in Malawi. For the rest of his life he was almost constantly on the move—both geographically and denominationally. He spent time in Malawi, South Africa, Lesotho, Britain, and the United States; he was affiliated variously with Baptists, Seventh Day Baptists, and Seventh-day Adventists. He aroused the hostility of both mainline missionaries and colonial authorities by advocating higher wages and more political power for Africans, and by what they regarded as fomenting African political discontent. He influenced several important African Christian figures, including John *Chilembwe, Elliot Kamwana Chirwa, Charles Domingo, and John L. Dube (one of the founders of the African National Congress in South Africa). He pursued many pro-African petitions and schemes, summed up in the title of his book *Africa for the Africans* (1897). In 1915 he was wrongly blamed for Chilembwe's uprising in Malawi and was deported from Lesotho to Britain, where he died in poverty and virtual obscurity. An enigmatic figure, Booth stands out as one of the few radically anticolonial missionary figures in south-central Africa.

BIBLIOGRAPHY Brighton G. M. Kavaloh, "Joseph Booth: An Evaluation of His Life, Thought, and Influence" (Ph.D. diss., Univ. of Edinburgh, 1991); Emily Booth Langworthy, *This Africa Was Mine* (1952); Harry W. Langworthy, *Joseph Booth: A Radical Missionary* (1996); George Shepperson and Thomas Price, *Independent African: John Chilembwe and the Nyasaland Rising of 1915* (1958).

T. Jack Thompson

Booth, William (1829–1912), English evangelist and founder of the Salvation Army. Booth was born in Nottingham, in poor circumstances, lost his father in 1843, and was apprenticed to a pawn-broker. Converted at the age of 15, he immediately began preaching in local slums, and with help from a wealthy Methodist, became a full-time preacher, sponsored and trained by the Methodist New Connexion. After his marriage to Catherine Mumford (1855), he worked as a traveling evangelist and served in northern Methodist circuits. When his request to be released for full-time evangelism was refused, he left the Methodists. In 1865 the Booths moved to East London and started the Christian Mission, which became in 1878 the Salvation Army (SA), with Booth as its general. During its early outreach the new organization was much persecuted, but growth continued. By 1880 officers had been sent to Australia and the United States; in 1882 a group went to India. By the end of the century the SA was established throughout the English-speaking world and in several European countries as well.

Booth's wife, his oldest son, Bramwell (1856–1929), and George Scott *Railton were his aides. The abject poverty of the British slums turned the SA toward meeting social and physical needs, and Booth and his wife knew and cooperated with leading British philanthropists. The publication of his *In Darkest England and the Way Out* in 1890, the year of his wife's death, set the SA firmly in its dual role of evangelism and social work. Booth was succeeded as general (1912–1929) by his son and by his daughter Evangeline *Booth (1934–1939).

BIBLIOGRAPHY Harold Begbie, *The Life of William Booth: The Founder of the Salvation Army,* 2 vols. (1919); Richard Collier, *The*

General Next to God: The Story of Willian Booth and the Salvation Army (1965); St. John Ervine, *God's Soldier: General William Booth,* 2 vols. (1934). See also R. G. Moyles, *A Bibliography of Salvation Army Literature in English (1865–1987)* (1988).

Jocelyn Murray

Booth-Tucker, Frederick St. George de Lautour (1853–1929) *and* **Emma Moss (Booth)** (1860–1903), Salvation Army (SA) leaders. Frederick Tucker was born in India into a family with long connections to the East India Company. Educated at Cheltenham College, England, he passed the Indian Civil Service examinations there. While studying law in London in 1875 he was converted at the D. L. *Moody and Ira Sankey mission. He married Louisa Bode, 18 years his senior, in Amritsar, India, in 1877. In 1881 while on leave, he resigned from the Indian Civil Service and joined the Salvation Army. He returned to India in 1882 as leader of a pioneer band of SA missionaries. From Bombay he traveled widely, while Louisa worked in the city. She died of cholera in 1887, and Tucker was recalled to London. There he met and in 1888 married Emma Booth, the second daughter of William and Catherine *Booth, who had been in charge of training women cadets. The Booth-Tuckers (the hyphenated name was at the insistence of her father) returned to India together, but Emma's time there was brief, due to her mother's illness. Back in England in 1891, the Booth-Tuckers were appointed SA commissioners for foreign affairs, and Frederick twice organized tours for General Booth in India. In 1896 they were sent to the United States because of the crisis caused there by the defection of Emma's brother Ballington *Booth. They adapted well and were successful in reestablishing the SA, but in 1903 Emma died in a railway accident. In 1904 Booth-Tucker and the children returned to London, where he became foreign secretary at the SA headquarters; in 1906 he married Minnie Reid, who had an Indian Civil Service background much like his own, and who survived him. He was active in the SA until he retired in 1924. He returned to India for a short while and was involved in writing and editing. His youngest daughter Muriel, born in 1903, also served in India.

BIBLIOGRAPHY Frederick Booth-Tucker, *The Life of Catherine Booth: The Mother of the Salvation Army,* 3 vols. (1893) and *The Consul: A Sketch of Emma Booth-Tucker* (1903). F. A. Mackenzie, *Booth-Tucker, Sadhu and Saint* (1930); Harry Williams, *Booth-Tucker: William Booth's First Gentleman* (1980).

Jocelyn Murray

Borden, William Whiting (1887–1913), intended missionary to Muslims in China. Borden grew up in wealth in Chicago, heir to the Borden Dairy fortune, and came to faith in Christ as a youth at Moody Church through the ministry of Reuben Torrey. In 1909 he enrolled at Yale University, and during his freshman year he met Samuel *Zwemer, a Reformed Church missionary who challenged him to reach out to Muslims, not only in Persia and Arabia, but also in China. Borden was so moved by Zwemer's message that he committed his life to missions that night, and three years later sailed for Egypt to study Arabic before going to China. Prior to going abroad he relinquished his inheritance of nearly one million dollars, specifying that it be given to home and foreign mission agencies. On arriving in Cairo, he immediately became involved in language study and ministry. However, he soon contracted spinal meningitis and within weeks he was dead. Friends found a message scratched on a piece of paper stuffed under his pillow: "No Reserve! No Retreat! No Regrets!"

BIBLIOGRAPHY Mrs. Howard [Mary Geraldine Guiness] Taylor, *Borden of Yale* (1926; rev., 1952).

Ruth A. Tucker

Borghero, Francesco Saverio (1830–1892), pioneer Catholic missionary in Dahomey. Borghero was born in Ronco Scrivia, Italy, and studied at Voghera, Piedmont, and the seminary of Genoa. He was ordained a priest in December 1854. In 1857 he met *Marion Brésillac, founder of the Society of African Missions, and joined the enterprise. In June 1859 Brésillac and four other members died of yellow fever in Freetown, Sierra Leone. Borghero, appointed by Propaganda Fide as interim superior of the Vicariate of Dahomey, was selected to lead the second expedition. He spent four years, from 1861 to 1865, in Africa. During that period he established stations at Whydah and Porto Novo and explored the Guinea Coast, traveling as far as Cape Palmas, Liberia, to locate sites for future missions. He also visited King Gle Gle of Dahomey at Abomey, where he was denied permission to evangelize. Borghero departed for Europe in January 1865. Poor health, the deaths of four confreres, and differences with his superior, Augustin *Planque, over the exercise of authority caused him to be discouraged. Borghero's doubts about the future of the mission alarmed Planque and Cardinal Barnabo, Prefect of Propaganda Fide, and eventually Borghero was forced to resign. He spent the remainder of his life in Italy and died in Ronco Scrivia.

Despite his fears, the church planted by Borghero in Dahomey prospered. From there Christianity spread east to Lagos and the Niger, and west to Togoland and the Gold Coast (Ghana), Ivory Coast, and Liberia. The expansion was based largely on Borghero's study of the coast during his voyages of exploration.

BIBLIOGRAPHY *Dictionnaire Bio-Bibliographique du Dahomey* (1957); Noël Douau, "Le Sacrifice du Pére Borghero," a manuscript in the SMA general archives, Rome; Patrick Gantly, *Mission to West Africa,* vol. 1 (1991); Patrick Gantly and Ellen Thorp, *For This Cause* (1992); Renzo Mandirola, "Padre Francesco Borghero, Primo Missionario S.M.A. Italiano," a manuscript in the SMA general archives, Rome.

Edmund M. Hogan, SMA

Boris I (c. 830–907), first Christian ruler and national saint of Bulgaria. Boris, known also as Boris-Michael, succeeded Presian, his father, and ruled Bulgaria from 852 to 889. During his long and turbulent reign, the official conversion of Bulgaria to Christianity took place. Whether for political reasons or religious considerations, in 864 Boris was baptized by Patriarch *Photios of Constantinople and named Michael, receiving the name of his sponsor, the Byzantine emperor. One account of Boris's conversion attributes it to religious influence and instruction he received from his sister, who had converted to Christianity while in Constantinople. A second story attributes it to the influence of Capharas, a Greek slave in his court. A medieval Greek chronicle records an apocryphal legend according to which Boris saw an icon of the Last Judgment that frightened and conduced him into becoming a Christian.

In any case, the Bulgarian people, imitating their ruler, converted to Christianity. Opposition came from several Bulgarian boyars (privileged aristocrats) who revolted in opposition to the new faith and to influences from Slavic language and literature. But the revolt was suppressed and the Christianization of Bulgaria continued. With the elimination of opposition, a national church was established, many houses of worship and monasteries were founded, and missionary activity was intensified. In 886 Boris received several disciples of *Constantine-Cyril and *Methodius, the great missionaries to the Slavs, who had been expelled from Moravia. With Boris's full support they continued their missionary work in Bulgaria most successfully. In 889 Boris became a monk, retiring to the Saint Panteleemon Monastery, where he died. He received local canonization soon after. His feast day is celebrated May 2.

BIBLIOGRAPHY Ivan Duichev, ed., *Kiril and Methodius: Founders of Slavonic Writing,* Spass Nikolov, trans. (1985), includes accounts of the period by Theophylaktos and Clement of Ochrid, pp. 93–130; Francis Dvornik, *Byzantine Missions among the Slavs* (1970); John V. Fine, Jr., *The Early Medieval Balkans* (1983), pp. 112–131; B. K. Stephanides, *Ekklesiastike Historia* (1948); A. P. Vlasto, *The Entry of the Slavs into Christendom* (1970).

Demetrios J. Constantelos

Borrow, George (1803–1881), author, traveler, and Bible society agent. Borrow was born in East Dereham in Norfolk, England, the son of a militia officer. His schooling was erratic because of constant movement of his father's regiment. In 1816 the family settled in Norwich, where he attended school for a few years before being apprenticed to a firm of solicitors. He did not apply himself to the law, preferring to frequent Gypsy tents and study a variety of languages. In 1824 he went to London to live by his pen but found only ill-paid hack work. Then came several obscure years until, in 1833, he was employed by the British and Foreign Bible Society (BFBS), which sent him to Saint Petersburg to oversee printing of a Manchu New Testament, and then to Portugal and Spain (1835–1840) to distribute the Scriptures. In Spain, civil war made his expeditions risky, while the hostile attitude of the authorities led twice to imprisonment. The BFBS financed the printing of his translation of Luke into Spanish Romani (1838). In 1840 he left the BFBS after marrying a widow, Mary Clarke. On her estate on the shores of Oulton Broad in Suffolk, he began turning his experiences to literary account. His main publications were *The Zincali,* about Spanish Gypsies, *The Bible in Spain* (1843), a stirring account of his adventures in the Iberian Peninsula, *Lavengro* (1851) and *The Romany Rye* (1857), fictionalized autobiographies of his early years, and *Wild Wales* (1862), a classic of Welsh travel literature.

BIBLIOGRAPHY Michael Collie and Angus Fraser, *George Borrow, a Bibliographical Study* (1984); T. H. Darlow, ed., *Letters of George Borrow to the British and Foreign Bible Society* (1911); Herbert Jenkins, *The Life of George Borrow* (1912, 1970); William I. Knapp, *Life, Writings, and Correspondence of George Borrow* (1899, 1967).

Angus Fraser

Bosch, David J(acobus) (1929–1992), South African missiologist. Born near Kuruman, South Africa, Bosch graduated from the Universities of Pretoria, South Africa, and Basel, Switzerland (D.Th. in New Testament, 1957) and then went to the Transkei as a missionary of the Dutch Reformed Church. Nine years later he was appointed to teach at the Theological School of Decoligny, near Umtata, Transkei. In 1971 he was appointed professor of missiology at UNISA (University of South Africa), Pretoria, where he served until his death in a car accident on April 15, 1992. He was the founder of the Southern African Missiological Society (SAMS) in 1968 and served as its general secretary until his death. He was also the first editor of its journal, *Missionalia.*

Bosch influenced missiology worldwide through his numerous articles and books. Within southern Africa he had lasting influence on Christian mission itself, as well as the study of missiology. He was always open to the world around him, listening carefully and with empathy, an incisive theologian with a strong pastoral inclination. His missiology was never a closed dogmatic system but was always open to new insights. He was equally welcome in ecumenical and evangelical circles, well loved in South Africa among both black and white. In 1979 he served as chairperson of the executive committee of the South African Christian Leadership Assembly, the first interracial representative gathering of South African Christians.

Among his most influential publications are *A Spirituality of the Road* (1979), *Witness to the World* (1980), and especially *Transforming Mission: Paradigm Shifts in Theology of Mission* (1991). To celebrate his sixtieth birthday, SAMS devoted its 1990 congress to a dialogue with him. The papers were published in a Festschrift, *Mission in Creative Tension: A Dialogue with David Bosch,* Willem Saayman and Klippies Kritzinger, eds. (1990).

BIBLIOGRAPHY Kevin Livingston, "A Missiology of the Road: The Theology of Mission and Evangelism in the Writings of David J. Bosch" (Ph.D. diss., Univ. of Aberdeen, 1989) and "The Legacy of David J. Bosch," *IBMR* (forthcoming); Willem Saayman and Klippies Kritzinger, eds., *Mission in Bold Humility: David Bosch's Work Considered* (1996). A collection of Bosch's unpublished articles is kept by the Department of Missiology, UNISA, Pretoria.

Willem Saayman

Bosco, Giovanni (John) (1815–1888), founder of the Society of St. Francis de Sales and of the Salesian Sisters.

Born near Turin, Bosco was ordained a Catholic priest in 1841 and felt called to work with youth. In Turin he opened a hospice for boys that became the Oratory of St. Francis de Sales. As part of the training, he offered vocational workshops in shoemaking, sewing, and printing. In 1859, with the encouragement of Pius IX, he founded the Society of St. Francis de Sales, a religious congregation commonly known as the Salesians, which received approval in 1868. The first ten Salesian missionaries were sent to Argentina. Bosco's concept of mission included *diakonia* (service), but his main interest was the salvation of souls and the winning of new church members. He viewed the missionary vocation as a life of sacrifice and danger for the sake of the uncivilized and unconverted. The Salesians opened a novitiate in Argentina in 1876. In 1879 they had a hundred missionaries in Argentina, Uruguay, and Paraguay. Bosco was canonized in 1934.

BIBLIOGRAPHY Karl Bopp, *Kirchenbild und pastorale Praxis bei Don Bosco* (1992); J. Borrego, "Originalità delle missioni Patagoniche di Don Bosco," in M. Midali, ed., *Don Bosco nella storia* (1990), pp. 453–468.

Fritz Kollbrunner, SMB

Bosshardt, R(udolf) Alfred (1897–1993), missionary in China. Brought up in Manchester, England, by Swiss parents, Bosshardt completed an apprenticeship as an engineer. He was accepted for training by the China Inland Mission (CIM) and in 1922 was appointed to western China. He worked in Kweichow (Guizhou) Province, which in 1924 was overtaken by famine and disease; he became engaged in relief work, and nearly died from typhus. In 1931 he married Rose Piaget, a Swiss CIM missionary. In September 1934 the Bosshardts were among a missionary party abducted by a section of the Communist armies and held hostage for a huge ransom (described as a fine for spying). The women were soon released, but Bosshardt and a New Zealander, Arnolis Hayman, were taken by the Second Army on the epic Long March. Beatings and threats of execution heightened their sufferings. Their fate attracted attention in the West and, following the execution of John and Betty *Stam, led to appeals for concerted prayer by the world Christian community. Hayman was released, but Bosshardt was held until Easter 1936, when he had covered more than 6,000 miles. His ability to translate French maps made him useful to his captors as a guide. When released, he was desperately ill and needed long convalescence. He returned to Kweichow in 1940, and when the Communist army reached Panhsien (Panxian) in 1950, he remained with the city's small church until the withdrawal of missionaries in 1951. The Bosshardts then shared in the expansion of CIM (renamed Overseas Missionary Fellowship) activity to Southeast Asia, working in Pakse, Laos, until Rose died in 1965. Alfred returned to Manchester, working with the Chinese church there until paralysis overtook him in 1990.

Bosshardt's book describing his captivity, *The Restraining Hand* (the title indicating the divine restraint on his captors), was reprinted several times. Three decades later, with the help of ghost writers, he retold the story as *The Guiding Hand,* in the wider context of his life. A Chinese version bears a commendatory foreword by the Communist commander, Xiao Ke, the last surviving leader of the Long March, whom Bosshardt met again, in friendship, in the 1980s.

BIBLIOGRAPHY R. A. Bosshardt, *The Restraining Hand: Captivity for Christ in China* (1936) and, with Gwen and Edward England, *The Guiding Hand: Captivity and Answered Prayer in China* (1973). Leslie T. Lyall, *A Passion for the Impossible: The Continuing Story of the Mission Hudson Taylor Began* (2d ed., 1976), chap. 3; Harrison Salisbury, *The Long March: The Untold Story* (1985); Jean Watson, *Bosshardt: A Biography* (1995); *The Guardian,* November 8, 1993 (obit.).

Andrew F. Walls

Boudinot, Elias (Galagina) (c. 1803–1839), Cherokee tribal leader and associate of American Board of Commissioners for Foreign Missions (ABCFM) mission to the Cherokees. Born near Rome, Georgia, Galagina (his original name) was sent in 1818 to the ABCFM's Foreign Mission School at Cornwall, Connecticut, where he was converted and took the name of a prominent statesman and patron of the school. After a year at Andover Theological Seminary (1822–1823) Boudinot returned to Georgia, where he worked with ABCFM missionary Samuel A. *Worcester in translating biblical and educational literature. In 1828 the Cherokee National Council directed him to establish a newspaper, the *Cherokee Phoenix,* using both English and the Cherokee syllabary. This major medium of information and opinion opposed efforts to remove the tribe beyond the Mississippi, and as a result it was suppressed by the Georgia legislature in 1835. However, Boudinot became convinced that removal was the only viable option and joined a few others in signing a removal treaty. This action and the suffering of the tribe along the notorious "Trail of Tears" led to bitter dissension, and Boudinot was assassinated in 1839.

Boudinot's marriage in 1826 to Harriet Gold, a Cornwall girl, had provoked outrage in the Cornwall community but was supported by the ABCFM. After her death in 1836, Boudinot married Delight Sargent, a missionary teacher among the Cherokees.

BIBLIOGRAPHY Boudinot wrote one book in Cherokee, *Poor Sarah, or The Indian Woman* (1833). Other writings can be found in Theda Perdue, ed., *Cherokee Editor: The Writings of Elias Boudinot* (1983). See also R. H. Gabriel, *Elias Boudinot, Cherokee, and His America* (1941); Thomas Wilkins, *Cherokee Tragedy* (1970); Grace Steele Woodward, *The Cherokees* (1963); *Missionary Herald* 89 (1839): 131.

David M. Stowe

Bouey, Elizabeth Coles (1890–1957), African American missionary in Liberia. Born in Monrovia, Liberia, where her parents, John J. and Lucy A. Coles, were missionaries, Elizabeth Coles was brought back to Richmond, Virginia, as an infant. She graduated from Virginia Union University in Richmond (later earning a master's degree from Columbia University in New York) and taught in the Richmond Public Schools. In 1920 she married Edward H. Bouey. Shortly thereafter, they went to Liberia as independent missionaries and worked at the Bendoo Industrial Mission for five years. Two of their three children were born in Liberia, and they adopted a boy of the Gola tribe. In their second term, Elizabeth Bouey served as supervisor of mission schools under the Foreign Mission Board of the National Baptist Convention and built the Carrie Dyer Hospital in Monrovia, Liberia. After returning to the United States in 1931, she resumed her teaching career. In 1940–1941 she founded and for 17 years served as the president of the National Association of Ministers' Wives, now the International Association of Ministers' Wives and Ministers' Widows, Incorporated, which has chapters in forty-one states and twenty-two countries. She became ill at the national conference of the association in 1956 and died a few months later.

BIBLIOGRAPHY Priscilla Rasin Evans, *From a Dream to Reality: The Story of the International Association of Ministers' Wives and Ministers' Widows, International (Interdenominational),* vol. 1, 1941–1980 (n.d.). Bouey's papers and unclassified documents are in the library at the association's international headquarters, Richmond, Virginia.

Ralph Reavis, Sr.

Bourgeoys, Marguerite (1620–1700), founder of the Congregation of Notre Dame de Villemarie. Bourgeoys was the daughter of a small trader in Troyes, France. Twice rejected for the religious life, she was attached without vows to the local convent when Maisonneuve, governor of Montreal, visited Troyes in 1653. She joined his returning party to Canada. In bleak and dangerous conditions, she built up schools for colonists and the Iroquois (the first Iroquois baptized in the colony was her pupil) and established the first Canadian order for women. The sisters (French, Canada-born, and Iroquois) had no cloister or veil, which freed them for service to the poor. Bourgeoy's work was appreciated perhaps more by the state than by church authorities. She retired from leadership, ill, in 1693, and the congregation was ecclesiastically recognized only in 1698. She was beatified in 1950.

BIBLIOGRAPHY *Les écrits de Mère Bourgeoys. Autobiographie et testament spirituel* (1964). Helène Bernier, *Marguerite Bourgeois* (sic) (1958; includes letters); K. Burton, *Valiant Voyager: Blessed Marguerite Bourgeoys...* (1964); Y. Charon, *Mère Bourgeoys (1620–1700)* (1950); (E. M. Faillon), *Mémoires particulières pour servir à l'histoire de l'Eglise d L'Amérique du North,* vols. 1–2, *Vie de la Soeur Bourgeoys...* (1853); A. Jamet, *Marguerite Bourgeoys, 1620–1700* (1942).

Andrew F. Walls

Bouvet, Joachim (1656–1730), Jesuit mathematician and missionary in China. A native of Le Mans, France, Bouvet entered the Society of Jesus in 1673 with the express desire to go to the China mission. This was fulfilled when Louis XIV included him among the five royal mathematicians sent to Peking (Beijing) in 1685. The emperor chose Bouvet and Jean-François *Gerbillon (1654–1707) to work at the court and allowed the other three to live and preach in China wherever they wished. Engaged in teaching mathematics and philosophy to the emperor, in 1693 Bouvet was sent as an imperial envoy to Louis XIV to thank the latter for the astronomical instruments he had presented as gifts to the Chinese court. During his sojourn in France, he corresponded with *Leibniz and published two works about China. Upon his return to Peking, Bouvet deepened his study of the *I-ching* (Book of Changes) and the mythological and historical origins of China. His subsequent system, called figurism, sought to find figures of the Old Testament in the Chinese classics. He attracted a following among some of his confreres, especially Jean-François *Foucquet. This was their attempt to solve the Chinese Rites Controversy. At first the emperor was interested in Bouvet's views, but by 1716 he expressed anxiety about further Western contacts with China. A new emperor ascended the throne in 1723 and subsequently exiled the missionaries in the provinces to Canton. However, Bouvet was allowed to continue his research and apostolic work among the Christian community in Peking.

BIBLIOGRAPHY Joachim Bouvet, *Portrait historique de l'empereur de la Chine* (1697) and *L'Estat présent de la Chine en figures* (1697). Claudia von Collani, *P. Joachim Bouvet, S.J.: Sein Leben und sein Werk* (1985); John Witek, *Controversial Ideas in China and in Europe: A Biography of Jean-François Foucquet, S.J., 1665–1741* (1982).

John W. Witek, SJ

Bowen, George (1816–1888), American missionary editor, linguist, and translator in India. Bowen was born in Middlebury, Vermont, but spent his youth in New York and traveled for more than three years in Europe and the Middle East. At age 17 he rejected his family's Protestant Episcopal faith and his father's business connections in favor of a literary life and agnosticism. Converted at the age of 27 to Christ and to biblical revelation by William Paley's *Evidences of Christianity,* he volunteered as a foreign missionary and sailed for India in 1847 under the American Board of Commissioners for Foreign Missions (ABCFM). Believing his views on infant baptism to be unacceptable to his colleagues and that missionaries should live more simply, he surrendered his salary and subsequently resigned from the ABCFM (but was reinstated ten years later). Under the influence of William *Taylor's evangelistic crusade and emphasis on self-supporting missions, he joined the Methodist Church in India and was appointed a "presiding elder." He later declared, "My passion is for winning souls, but it does not please the Lord to use me that way." Instead he was used to establish the *Bombay Guardian* as a Christian weekly, to direct the Bombay Tract and Book Society, and to write extensively on theological apologetics addressed to Muslims, Roman Catholics, and "educated natives," and devotional works that reached and impressed Queen Victoria, as well as countless readers in India. He died in Bombay, preaching and writing for the *Guardian* to the end.

BIBLIOGRAPHY Robert E. Speer, *George Bowen of Bombay: A Memoir* (1938); John N. Hollister, *The Centenary of the Methodist Church in Southern Asia* (1956), intro. et passim.

Creighton Lacy

Bowen, Thomas Jefferson (1814–1875), Southern Baptist missionary in Nigeria. Bowen was born in Jackson County, Georgia, and arrived in Nigeria in 1850, the pioneer Southern Baptist missionary in the area. In 1853 he settled at Ijaye, in Yorubaland, and with the assistance of American colleagues established other stations in Ogbomosho and Abeokuta. He became a Yoruba scholar of considerable standing, publishing a dictionary and grammar of the language after his early retirement due to poor health. On his return to the United States in 1856 he promoted a colonization scheme, whereby African Americans would settle in Nigeria. The scheme gained some support, but eventually died in the U.S. House of Representatives.

BIBLIOGRAPHY T. J. Bowen, *Central Africa: Adventures and Missionary Labours* (1857) and *Grammar and Dictionary of the Yoruba Language* (1858). F. J. A. Ajayi, *Christian Missions in Nigeria, 1841–1891: The Making of a New Elite* (1965).

Geoffrey Johnston

Bowley, William (c. 1780–1843), pioneer evangelist and church builder in India. The son of a British soldier and an Indian mother, Bowley was proud of his Indian heritage and language skills and would not tolerate racism in any shape or form. Originally a fifer in the East India Company's army, he was a successful businessman when converted through the influence of Daniel *Corrie. From 1814 to 1843, supported by the Church Missionary Society (CMS), he was a tireless street evangelist. He itinerated along the Ganges from Buxar, some 20 miles south-southwest of Benares (Varanasi) to Chunar, about 50 miles east-northeast of Benares, and gave pastoral oversight of converts. Bishop Reginald *Heber of Calcutta ordained him deacon and priest in 1825, five years after he had also received Lutheran orders. Bowley built his own church and mission station at Chunar, which he left to the CMS on condition they support his widow. More important were the congregations he built, consisting mainly of orphans, drummer boys, army invalids, and Indian partners of European soldiers. He was a tireless champion of the rights of Indian women to respect and education. His 130 surviving letters in the CMS archives, as well as his copious journals, are a vital source for understanding church growth along the Ganges.

BIBLIOGRAPHY M. A. Laird, ed., *Journal of a North Indian Journey: The Travels of Bishop Reginald Heber, 1823–5* (1979); Eugene Stock, *The History of the Church Missionary Society, 1795–1895,* vol. 1 (1899).

E. M. Jackson

Bowman, Robert H. (1915–), co-founder of Far East Broadcasting Company (FEBC). Born in California, Bowman attended Southern California Bible School in Pasadena (1933–1936). He joined the Haven of Rest gospel radio program in 1934 as a member of its quartet and back-up radio evangelist for what was one of the first nationwide religious broadcasts in the United States. In December 1945 he and John *Broger founded FEBC. While Broger laid the groundwork for establishing the first station in the Philippines, Bowman left the Haven of Rest program, spoke at churches on the West Coast to generate interest, and raised funds. FEBC began broadcasting as Christian Radio City Manila in June 1948 and was beaming shortwave programs into China by 1949. After 1954, when Broger left for government service, Bowman became president and oversaw the continued growth of FEBC. By the early 1960s gospel radio could be heard on AM mediumwave broadcasting bands in mainland China and the Soviet Union. Today two-thirds of the world's population is within range of FEBC as it broadcasts in more than 150 languages from 32 transmitters in four countries. Bowman retired in California in 1992.

BIBLIOGRAPHY Eleanor G. Bowman and Susan F. Titus, *Eyes beyond the Horizon* (1991); Gleason H. Ledyard, *Sky Waves* (1968); Ruth A. Tucker, *From Jerusalem to Irian Jaya* (1983).

Robert T. Coote

Boyce, William Binnington (1803–1889), English Methodist missionary, administrator, and pioneer linguist. Boyce was ordained in 1829 for service in South Africa where he worked among the Xhosa of the eastern Cape Colony. He was brilliant and aggressive, but his lifelong friendship with William *Shaw was a steadying influence upon him. His great achievement was discovering the "euphonic concord," which provided the essential clue to the syntax of all Bantu languages. In 1834 with Shaw, he published the text of Luke in Xhosa. Between 1834 and 1843 he played a vigorous role in frontier affairs, supporting the English settlers in their attacks on John *Philip and other London Missionary Society pro-African missionaries. After returning to England in 1843, he was sent to Australia in 1845 as head of Methodist missions there. He planned and oversaw the creation of the Australasian Conference of the Methodist Church and later served as president (1885 and 1886). In 1858 he was called back to England to be secretary of the Wesleyan Missionary Society. In this post he encouraged the setting up of autonomous conferences for Methodist mission areas abroad. He retired in 1876 to Australia.

BIBLIOGRAPHY William Binnington Boyce, *Memoir of the Rev. William Shaw* (1874). G. G. Finlay and W. W. Holdsworth, *History of the Wesleyan Methodist Missionary Society,* vol. 3 (1922); L. A. Hewson, "William B. Boyce and the Euphonic Concord," *Journal of the Methodist Historical Society, S.A.,* March 1955.

Andrew C. Ross

Braden, Charles Samuel (1887–1970), Methodist missionary educator, editor, and author in Latin America. Born in Chanute, Kansas, Braden received a B.A. from

Baker University, Baldwin City, Kansas (1909), a B.D. from Union Theological Seminary, New York (1912), and a Ph.D. from the University of Chicago (1926). He was ordained in the Methodist Episcopal Church in 1914. He was a missionary in Bolivia (1912–1915) and Chile (1916–1922). In Chile he was a professor and president of the Union Theological Seminary at Santiago, edited *El Heraldo Christiano,* managed the Union Book Store, and served intermittently as pastor of First Church Santiago. He was assistant secretary of the Methodist Episcopal Board of Foreign Missions from 1923 to 1925. From 1926 until retirement in 1954 he taught religious history and literature at Northwestern University, Evanston, Illinois. He continued adjunct teaching elsewhere: Scripps College, Claremont, California (1954–1955), Facultad Evangélica de Teológica, Buenos Aires (1957), and Perkins School of Theology, Dallas, Texas (1954, 1959). He founded and edited *World Christianity* (1936–1939) and served on the editorial board of the *Journal of Bible and Religion* (1943–1949). He authored *The World's Religions* (1939, 1954) and other books in religious studies, while contributing many articles to journals and encyclopedias.

BIBLIOGRAPHY Braden wrote or contributed to some thirty books, among them *Religious Aspects of the Conquest of Mexico* (1930, 1966) and *These Also Believe* (1949, 1966); he also authored several hundred academic and popular articles. He prepared an annotated bibliography of his writings with autobiographical comments, *The Literary Harvest of a Half-Century* (1967), located at Bridwell Library, Southern Methodist Univ., Dallas, Texas.

Edward W. Poitras

Bradley, Dan Beach (1804–1873), American pioneer medical missionary to Thailand. Bradley is considered one of the most outstanding missionaries to have served in Thailand, although he had no more success in gaining converts and seeing the church established than did others. Born in Marcellus, New York, he graduated from New York Medical College in 1833. Together with his wife, Emilie (Royce), he began work in 1835 under the American Board of Commissioners for Foreign Missions (ABCFM) until forced to resign for theological reasons, after which the ABCFM closed its Thailand mission. On his only return to the United States (1847–1849), Bradley joined the American Missionary Association, which purchased the ABCFM property but did not afford much additional financial help. Through commercial printing he supported not only his family but also an extensive medical program, voluminous publication of Christian material, and widespread evangelistic ministry. As a personal friend of King Mongkut, Bradley taught him English briefly, and often discussed with him the Christian faith, science, and Western culture. At the same time, he repeatedly attacked polygamy and other royal practices in his publications. Bradley became dean among the Protestant missionaries in the country so that interdenominational missionary prayer meetings and social gatherings were held in his home and on his lawn. He is remembered by Thai people for his "firsts." He imported the first press and Thai type font ever used in the country, published the first government decree ever printed in Thai, and produced the first newspapers in English and Thai. He performed the first Western-style surgical operation and introduced the first smallpox vaccinations. After Emilie Bradley died in 1845, he married Sarah Blatchly, who outlived him by 20 years. Both wives contributed greatly to the work. He died in Bangkok. Two daughters, three grandchildren, and one great-grandchild also served as missionaries to Thailand.

BIBLIOGRAPHY William L. Bradley's *Siam Then: The Foreign Colony in Bangkok Before and After Anna* (1981) consists largely of excerpts from Dan Bradley's journals and other publications. Donald Charles Lord, *Mo Bradley and Thailand* (1969); George Bradley McFarland, ed., *Historical Sketch of Protestant Missions in Siam, 1828–1928* (1928); Kenneth E. Wells, *History of Protestant Work in Thailand, 1828–1958* (1958). The Bradley papers are in the Oberlin College archives.

William A. Smalley

Brahmabandhav Upadhyaya. *See* Upadhyaya, Brahmabandhav.

Braide, Garrick Sokari (c. 1880–1918), first major Nigerian independent Christian prophet. Braide was baptized at Bakana in the Niger Delta Pastorate founded by Samuel A. *Crowther. Late in 1915 he led a revival that featured mass baptisms, healing, Sunday observance, and active opposition to traditional religion and to imported articles, especially trade gin. Traditionalist complaints and fear of unrest as being seditious led twice to Braide's being imprisoned. Initial Anglican welcome changed to opposition, but loss of members from the Anglican church to the movement led to Anglican indigenizing reforms. A variety of "Christ Army" independent churches honoring Braide arose from the movement and continue in southeast Nigeria.

BIBLIOGRAPHY H. W. Turner, "Prophets and Politics: A Nigerian Test Case," *Bulletin of the Society for African Church History* 2 (1965): 97–118. See also two articles on Braide as "Elijah II" in *Church Missionary Review,* one by James Johnson, August 1916, pp. 455–462, the other by M. T. Pilter, March 1917, pp. 142–145.

Harold W. Turner

Brainerd, David (1718–1747), New England missionary to Indian tribes of the middle colonies. Born to a farming family in Haddam, Connecticut, Brainerd soon turned his aspirations to the clergy and a life of study. The early death of his parents, combined with a naturally melancholy personality, caused him to be morose and to fixate on the brevity of life, so that his religious life was characterized by prolonged depressions punctuated by ecstatic experiences of God. He began to study for the ministry at Yale College in 1739. During his first year he showed signs of the tuberculosis that was to end his life prematurely. During the following year, the New Light preaching of George *Whitefield and other itinerants such as Gilbert Tennent and James Davenport gained many adherents at the college, including Brainerd, and he became involved in a separate church founded by students. In November 1741 he was reported as saying that one of the local ministers who was a college tutor had "no more grace than a chair." Determined to snuff out the New Light among the students, the Yale Corporation, led by its rector, Thomas Clap, expelled Brainerd for refusing to make a public confession.

Officially barred from the ministry, Brainerd nonetheless became an itinerant preacher, filling pulpits of New Light sympathizers throughout New England and New York. In the process he gained the admiration of many clergymen, including Jonathan Dickinson, a Presbyterian minister of New Jersey and commissioner for the Society in Scotland for Propagating Christian Knowledge. Dickinson in 1742 first proposed that Brainerd become a missionary. To prepare himself, in 1743 Brainerd went to work with John *Sargeant, missionary to the Stockbridge Indians. He was ordained by the Presbytery of New York in 1744. From 1743 to 1747 he ministered to the Indians in western Massachusetts, eastern New York, the Lehigh region of Pennsylvania, and central New Jersey. At the New Jersey Bethel mission (near Cranbury), he achieved his most notable successes. Out of his experiences here came the publication of two installments of his journals that described both the revivals among the Delaware Indians and his own spiritual turmoil and exultation.

For all of his zeal, however, Brainerd's constitution could not stand up to the hardships of wilderness living. In April 1747, seriously weakened by tuberculosis, he left New Jersey for the home of his friend Jonathan *Edwards in Northampton, Massachusetts, where he died in October.

In 1749 Edwards published *An Account of the Life of the Late Reverend Mr. David Brainerd,* drawn from Brainerd's extensive diaries and supplemented by Edwards's own commentary. Edwards sought to portray Brainerd as a model of Christian saintliness who manifested his faith in good works and self-sacrifice, expurgating many passages that recorded Brainerd's depressions and enthusiasms. Over the centuries, this work has achieved international fame, has gone through countless printings, and has inspired many missionaries in pursuing their call.

BIBLIOGRAPHY David Brainerd, *Mirabilia Dei inter Indicos; or, the Rise and Progress of a Remarkable Work of Grace Amongst a Number of the Indians in the Province of New Jersey* (1746) and *Divine Grace Displayed; or, The Continuance and Progress of a Remarkable Work of Grace...* (1748). *The Works of Jonathan Edwards,* vol. 7, Norman Pettit, ed., *The Life of David Brainerd* (1985). Joseph A. Conforti, "Jonathan Edwards's Most Popular Work: 'The Life of David Brainerd' and Nineteenth-Century Evangelical Culture," *Church History* 54 (June 1985): 188–201; David Wynbeek, *David Brainerd, Beloved Yankee* (1961).

Kenneth P. Minkema

Brainerd, John (1720–1781), missionary to Delaware Indians in New Jersey and Presbyterian minister. Born in Haddam, Connecticut, Brainerd was ordained in February 1748 a missionary to the Delaware Indians, following the death of his brother, David *Brainerd, several months earlier. He was released from his appointment in 1755 because of the parceling of the Indian lands but was reinstated in June 1756 to serve the Delaware congregation then gathered near New Brunswick, New Jersey. He was again released in September 1757 because of the failure of authorities to procure permanent lands for the Indians. He preached in the Presbyterian Church of Newark until February 1758, when the government finally provided territory for the Delawares in Burlington County. Here Brainerd served until 1777 as both minister and schoolmaster.

BIBLIOGRAPHY Thomas Brainerd, *The Life of John Brainerd* (1865); Franklin B. Dexter, *Biographical Sketches of the Graduates of Yale College,* vol. 2 (1896), pp. 76–79.

Kenneth P. Minkema

Brancati de Laurea, Lorenzo (Giovanni Francesco) (1612–1693), pioneer of Catholic mission theory. Giovanni Francesco Brancati was born in Lauria, Calabria, Italy, and entered the Conventual Franciscans in 1630, taking the name Lorenzo. After completing his studies he was ordained in 1636 and received his doctorate in 1637. He held various academic posts and became a professor at Sapienza University in Rome. He became prefect of the Vatican Library and in 1665 prefect of studies at the Propaganda Fide college, which brought him into close relationship with the growing Catholic mission. He was adviser to the Roman Curia and various congregations. In 1681 Pope Innocent XI appointed Brancati cardinal and also librarian of the Catholic Church. Brancati's eight-volume commentary (1673) on the theology of Duns Scotus includes the tract "De Fide," a treatise on missions, in which he surveys Christian missionary activity up to the sixteenth century. Brancati made the study of mission integral to his theology. He dealt with when, where, how, and by whom the faith is to be propagated, and how it is to be extended in the future. This is perhaps the earliest attempt to develop a systematic approach to mission and thus is a foundational contribution to the science of mission.

BIBLIOGRAPHY Ronan Hoffman, *Pioneer Theories of Missiology: A Comparative Study of the Mission Theories of Cardinal Brancati de Laurea, O.F.M. Conv.* (1960); Nicola Kowalsky, "Fra Lorenzo Brancati di Lauria: Missionologo quasi sconosciuto di Propaganda Fide," *Euntes Docete* 10 (1957): 383–393.

Wilbert R. Shenk

Brand, Evelyn (Harris) (1879–1974), missionary in India. Evelyn Constance Harris, daughter of a wealthy, devout Londoner, determined at age 30 to become a missionary. Assigned by her Strict Baptist Mission to Madras, India, she met and married Jesse Brand, sharing his urge to serve on the Kolli Malli (mountains of death), so called because of their deadly malarial fevers. For six years they labored without seeing a single convert, then slowly established a Christian community, with schools, orphanage, dispensary, industrial and agricultural services, and a chapel built with Jesse's own hands. It was their dream to take the gospel to four other mountain ranges, but in 1929 Jesse died of blackwater fever.

Stricken but undaunted, for years "Granny Brand," as she was known, marked time in stations on the plains. Then, retiring at age 69, and no longer inhibited by board restrictions, she moved to the second mountain range, repeating the long process, making friends and converts, camping in makeshift shelters in all kinds of weather, riding stony trails on horseback, preaching, teaching, healing, and scorning deprivations, falls, broken bones, and physical debilities that would have put one less intrepid into a wheelchair. Before dying at Karigiri, near Vellore, she saw seven stations with thriving mission work, her son Paul (see below), a world-famous leprosy specialist, and her daughter Connie a missionary to Africa.

BIBLIOGRAPHY Evelyn Brand, *Trust and Triumph* (1970). Dorothy Clarke Wilson, *Granny Brand, Her Story* (1976, 1990) and *Life for the Mountains of Death* (1966).

Dorothy Clarke Wilson

Brand, Paul Wilson (1914–), medical missionary in India and leprosy specialist. Brand was born in India of missionary parents, graduated from University Medical School in London, and qualified as Fellow of the Royal College of Surgeons. In 1946 he went to the Christian Medical College and Hospital in Vellore, India, as an orthopedic surgeon. Visiting a leprosy sanatorium, he was appalled by the victims' stiffened and useless claw hands, many of the fingers gone or reduced to stumps. He devised operations for the claw hand, transferring good muscles from the forearm into the palm of the hand, which, after long rehabilitation, became usable again. He revolutionized the concept of deformity in leprosy by proving that lack of sensation, not the disease, was responsible for destruction of hands and feet. He founded a rehabilitation center at Vellore where patients were taught to avoid mutilation and were trained in new skills to become self-sufficient. He designed shoes to protect the insensitive feet from unnecessary injury.

Trainees came to Vellore from all over the world to learn the new techniques, and Brand himself traveled to centers in Africa and South America to train and perform surgery. His wife, Margaret, also a surgeon, became adept in treating leprous eyes prone to lid paralysis and complications leading to blindness. In recognition of his work, Brand was decorated by the Crown with the award of Commander of the British Empire. In 1960 he received the Albert Lasker Award for service in rehabilitation.

In 1966 he became chief of rehabilitation at the U.S. Public Hospital in Carville, Louisiana, and clinical professor of surgery at Louisiana Medical School, while still traveling widely for surgery and training. His experience with paralysis insensitivity led to application of the same methods to other diseases involving lack of sensation. In his retirement he became a well-known author, expounding in his works one of the basic tenets of his philosophy, that pain is not a curse but a blessing to the human race.

BIBLIOGRAPHY Paul Brand, *The Forever Feast* (1993); with Philip Yancey, *Fearfully and Wonderfully Made* (1980), *In His Image* (1984), and *The Gift Nobody Wants: Memoirs of a Career in Pain* (1993). Dorothy Clarke Wilson, *Ten Fingers for God* (1965, 1989; Swedish tr., 1967; French tr., 1970; German tr., 1957, 1991; Dutch tr., 1969).

Dorothy Clarke Wilson

Braun, Peter (1726–1800), pioneer Moravian missionary in Antigua. Braun was born at Creuznach, Palatinate, and immigrated to Herrnhut, Saxony in 1743. He joined the Moravian Church in 1746 and served in educational work in Maryland and Pennsylvania until 1769. He was united in marriage with Maria Barbara Meyer in 1755 and ordained deacon in 1769 before leaving for Antigua, where he was to revive the earlier work done by Samuel Isles. Upon reaching Antigua, he found 14 converts remaining from Isles's work. Widowed in 1771, he traveled to Saint Thomas in 1772, where he married Bibiana Frederica Göttlich, who with her first husband had traveled with the Brauns to the West Indies.

From 1772 the work in Antigua flourished, and Braun was joined by other workers as well as native helpers whom he appointed. In 1772 he visited neighboring Saint Kitts and held the first Moravian services at Basseterre. In 1791 his health failed, and he retired to Bethlehem, Pennsylvania, where he eventually died. The work in Antigua had grown from the original 14 souls to 7,400 during his ministry. Massa Brown, as he was called by the slaves, oversaw a field that today has grown to 14 congregations.

BIBLIOGRAPHY *Bethlehem Diary,* vol. 39; G. Oliver Maynard, *History of the Eastern West Indies Province of the Moravian Church* (1969); Karl Müller, *200 Jahre Brüdermission,* vol. 1, *Das Erste Missionsjahrhundert* (1931); A. C. Thompson, *Moravian Missions* (1882).

Albert H. Frank

Bray, Thomas (1658–1730), English churchman, missionary educator, philanthropist, and founder of the Society for Promoting Christian Knowledge (SPCK) and the Society for the Propagation of the Gospel in Foreign Parts (SPG). Bray was born in Shropshire, England, the son of a farmer. He attended Oswestry Grammar School and the University of Oxford and was ordained in the Church of England in 1681. For almost 20 years thereafter he served in parishes in the English Midlands. In 1696 he published *A Course of Lectures upon the Church Catechism* (4 vols.), which was well received in high places and earned him royal, political, and episcopal support. Also in 1696 he was appointed "Commissary of the Church of England for Maryland" by the bishop of London, Henry Compton. Although he spent only a few months in the colony in 1700, the effects of his visit were lasting. In March 1699 he had been instrumental in founding a society to provide Christian libraries at home and abroad—the SPCK. Two years later, at his initiative, a royal charter was granted for the SPG. Both initially had their sights set mainly on the Americas, and together they formed a comprehensive support organization for Anglicanism throughout the world. Bray was also concerned with the evangelization of African American slaves, and in 1723, on the basis of funds left to him by a private secretary to the king of Holland, created a foundation, Associates of Dr. Bray, devoted to this end. Bray was no lover of power; having shaped his organizations, he was content to leave the running of them to others. In 1706 he was appointed to a London parish, St. Botolph Without, Aldgate, where he served for the rest of his life as an exemplary parish priest.

BIBLIOGRAPHY John W. Lydekker, *Thomas Bray, 1658–1730, Founder of Missionary Enterprise* (1943); Edgar L. Pennington, *The Reverend Thomas Bray* (1934); Bernard C. Steiner, ed., *Rev. Thomas Bray: His Life and Selected Works Relating to Maryland* (1901); Henry P. Thompson, *Into All Lands: The History of the Society for the Propagation of the Gospel in Foreign Parts, 1701–1950* (1951), pp. 9–43, and *Thomas Bray* (1954).

Eric J. Sharpe

Brébeuf, Jean de (1593–1649), French Jesuit missionary in Canada. Brébeuf was born into French rural nobility and grew up working the family farm. Entering the Society of Jesus in 1617 and receiving ordination in 1622 or 1623, he was sent to the Canadian mission in 1625. Skilled at languages, he first learned one of the Algonquian languages, then sought and obtained the assignment to go to the Hurons to the northwest. He learned the Huron language fluently and served from 1626 to 1629, until taken captive by the English and returned to France. After several assignments in France, he returned to Canada in 1633 and helped establish missions at Ihonatiria and Ossossane, near the southern shore of Georgian Bay. He and the other Jesuits were followed enthusiastically by a number of converts (who had invited him back in 1633), but other Indians suspected and hated them as sorcerers in the service of the Europeans. Tensions with the Iroquois Confederation, based on very complex political alliances, were also constant. In 1639 Brébeuf founded the mission St. Marie Among the Hurons and served there until attacked by Iroquois warriors in March 1649. Brébeuf, several Huron parishioners, and Father Gabriel *Lalemant died under torture after the fashion of the military practice of the area. The mission was destroyed, though a model of it now exists on the spot near Midland, Ontario.

Brébeuf was known as a gentle giant (he was called "Echon" in Huron, "The Strong One"), being of great height but having a refined and patient disposition. He was also renowned for his diplomatic ability. His mission practices followed the basic Jesuit model of adaptation. Like others of his time, he was hardly ecumenical, and his ethnic biases show in his reports; but he nonetheless merited the epithet "Huron among the Hurons." Brébeuf wrote *A Catechism of Father Ledesma for the Montaignais,* later translated into Huron, and *The Travels and Sufferings of Father Jean de Brébeuf among the Hurons of Canada as Described by Himself.* He was canonized by *Pius XI in 1930.

BIBLIOGRAPHY T. J. Campbell, *Pioneer Priests of North America,* vol. 2 (1913), pp. 65–172; Joseph P. Donnelly, *Jean de Brébeuf* (1975); Francis Xavier Talbot, *Saint among the Hurons: The Life of Jean de Brébeuf* (1949); Reuben Gold Thwaites, ed., *Jesuit Relations and Allied Documents,* vols. 6–39 (1898; accounts by Brébeuf and others covering a quarter century of service). Given the controversies surrounding this period, also to be recommended are three recent critical sources of varying degrees of sympathy: Olive Patricia Dickason, *Canada's First Nations* (1992); John Webster Grant, *Moon of Wintertime* (1984); and Bruce Trigger, *Native and Newcomers* (1985).

Carl F. Starkloff, SJ

Brechter, Heinrich Suso (1910–1975), German Benedictine missiologist. Born in Dorndorf, near Ulm, Germany, Brechter became a Benedictine monk of the archabbacy of St. Ottilien, Bavaria. From 1930 to 1937 he studied philosophy and theology and from 1937 to 1941 medieval philology, history, and paleography at the University of Munich. In 1941 the Nazis dissolved the monastery, but in 1945 Brechter became prior and in 1957 archabbot of the reestablished post-war archabbacy. He was also appointed to the chair of mission theology at the University of Munich. As president of the congregation of Bendictine missions he founded abbacies in Caracas, Venezuela, and Waegwan, South Korea, priories in Inkamana, Zululand, and Hanga, Tanzania, and laid foundations for new Benedictine missions in Colombia, Kenya, and Japan. In 1960 he became a member of the Vatican commission on mission. He participated as a "council-father" in all four sessions of Vatican II and became a papal consultant in the Vatican secretariat for the non-Christians after the Council. Highly honored by church and state authorities, he died after contracting an incurable tropical infection.

BIBLIOGRAPHY In addition to his doctoral dissertation, *Die Quellen zur Angelsachsenmission Gregors des Grossen 596–604* (1941), Brechter wrote *Das Apostolat des hl. Bonifatius und Gregors des Grossen Missionsinstruktionen für England* (1954), *Die Regula Benedicti im Decretum Gratiani* (1954), "Einleitung u. Kommentar zum Dekret über die Missionstätigkeit der Kirche, Das Zweite Vatikanische Konzil," in *Lexikon für theologie u. Kirche,* vol. 14 (1968), pp. 9–125, and "De Principiis fundamentalibus dialogi cum religionibus non christianis," in *Acta Congressus internationalis de Theologia Concilii Vatican II* (1968). For a full bibliography see F. Renner, "In Memoriam Erzabt Suso Brechter von St. Ottilien," in *Studïen in Mitteilungen des Benediktinerordens* 86 (1975): 831–833.

Horst W. Bürkle

Breck, James Lloyd (1818–1876), Episcopal missionary in the American midwest. Born in Philadelphia, Pennsylvania, Breck was educated in New York under William Augustus Mühlenberg and at the General Theological Seminary (1838–1841). Responding to Jackson Kemper's appeal for help in Wisconsin, he settled in Nashotah, where with two seminary classmates he founded a monastic style community, which became Nashotah House Seminary. From this center Breck and his fellows evangelized the surrounding countryside, sometimes walking 50 miles to preach. As mission opportunities opened up farther west, Breck resigned from Nashotah and moved to Saint Paul, Minnesota, in 1850. By 1852 he had learned the

Chippewa language and obtained Chippewa prayer books. His mission at Gull Lake provided both educational and medical services. He established a school for Indian children in Faribault, Minnesota, championed the rights of native Americans, and in 1855 founded the Seabury Divinity School. Again he resigned his position and moved west to California in 1867. For the last nine years of his life he worked in northern California, based at Bernica, establishing missions and schools. He is buried at Nashotah. Breck pioneered an Anglo-Catholic style of mission work on the American frontier with special concern for the training of indigenous clergy. He is commemorated in the Episcopal calendar on April 13.

BIBLIOGRAPHY Charles Breck, *The Life of the Reverend James Lloyd Breck* (1883); Robert G. Carroon, "Frontier Churchman," *The Living Church,* March 28, 1976, pp.10–11; Theodore Isaac Holcombe, *An Apostle to the Wilderness: James Lloyd Breck, D.D., His Missions and His Schools* (1903).

Peter R. Rodgers

Breda, Gregorius van (1901–1985), Dutch Capuchin missiologist. Born in Breda, Netherlands, as Lambert J. M. van den Boom, Breda received a doctorate in missiology from the University of Münster, Germany (1933), then continued his studies in ethnology at the University of Vienna, Austria, 1934–1935. He was lecturer in missiology from 1935 to 1960 at the theological seminary of the Dutch Capuchin Friars in Tilburg, and lectured in missiology, cultural anthropology, and non-Western sociology at various institutions in the Netherlands. His research in Tanzania in 1959 was published in *Anthropos.* He wrote two volumes on the sociology of non-Western peoples (1965, 1966) and published more than eighty articles and numerous book reviews in many Dutch and foreign journals. From 1946 to 1971 he was a member of the editorial board of the Dutch missiological review *Het Missiewerk.* From 1939 to 1965 he served as secretary or president of the Dutch Missiological Week, held at Nijmegen. Through the Mission Interacademiale and the Academic Lay Missionary Action, he sought to interest university students in mission and missiology. The Catholic pioneer of missiology and cultural anthropology in the Netherlands, Breda was the first Catholic scholar trained in both fields at the university level.

BIBLIOGRAPHY Arnulf Camps, "In Memory of Father Dr. Gregorius van Breda (van den Boom), OFM Cap (1901–1985)," *ZMR* 70 (1986): 306–307.

Arnulf Camps, OFM

Brennecke, Gerhard (1916–1973), mission leader in the German Democratic Republic. Early in his career Brennecke joined the German student Christian movement, became chairman of the students' league for mission, and took an active part in the struggle of the German confessing church under Hitler. He also was a member of the German delegation to the International Missionary Council world conference at Tambaram in 1938. Even during the war, having taken his examination for the ministry illegally in the confessing church, he volunteered for mission service in China. As this turned out to be impracticable, the Berlin Mission used him in home mission work and appointed him inspector, and, in 1949, director. The political outlook for him, as he continued in the old mission headquarters in East Berlin, implied, as it were, jumping from the frying-pan of the Third Reich into the fire of a Communist state. Brennecke accepted the challenge: renewal of the mission abroad in ecumenical fellowship and restructuring of the home base in full solidarity with the church under pressure. He did not live to see the outcome. But until his untimely invalidism and death he exercised considerable influence, not least as an author, as editor of the only theological magazine in the German Democratic Republic, and as academic teacher.

BIBLIOGRAPHY Martin Fischer, "Gerhard Brennecke zum Gedenken," *EMZ* 30 (1973): 205–209.

Hans-Werner Gensichen

Brent, Charles Henry (1862–1929), missionary bishop in the Philippines and ecumenical pioneer. Brent was born in Newcastle, Ontario, and was educated at Trinity College, University of Toronto. Ordained to the priesthood in 1887 in the Protestant Episcopal Church, he began his career in Buffalo, moving in 1889 to Boston, where he joined the monastic Society of St. John the Evangelist. He left the monastic order in 1891 and was appointed to St. Stephen's City Mission in Boston's South End. In 1901 he was elected the first missionary bishop of the Protestant Episcopal Church in the Philippine Islands. For 16 years, he and his staff provided spiritual and physical help to the American, Chinese, and (to a lesser degree) Roman Catholic Filipino residents of Manila, to the Ilocano and Igorot peoples of northern Luzon, and to the Muslims in Mindanao. When the United States entered World War I, he left the Philippines and became senior chaplain of the American Expeditionary Forces, and then in 1918 he was elected bishop of Western New York.

Brent made several contributions to his country and the international community. Perhaps the most significant was an international crusade against the use of opium and other narcotics in Asia. Indeed, Brent persuaded President Theodore Roosevelt to convene the first and second International Opium Conferences in 1909 (Shanghai) and 1911 (the Hague), and he presided at both. He also represented the United States on the League of Nations Narcotics Committee. Although wracked by ill health after the war, Brent continued to represent the United States at international narcotics conferences. He served for the last time as a delegate to the Second Geneva Opium Conference (1924).

Brent's greatest contribution to the church was in the field of ecumenics. Although inspired by the 1910 Edinburgh World Missionary Conference which he attended, he believed that true Christian unity could arise only from straightforward discussion of the issues that still divided Christendom. Thus he persuaded his denomination to plan a world conference on Faith and Order, which met at Lausanne, Switzerland, in 1927, with Brent presiding.

BIBLIOGRAPHY The best scholarly treatment of missionary work in the Philippines, including important material on Brent, is Kenton J. Clymer, *Protestant Missionaries in the Philippines, 1898–1916: An Inquiry into the American Colonial Mentality* (1986). Mark D. Norbeck, "The Protestant Episcopal Church in the City of Manila, Philippine Islands, from 1898 to 1918: An Institutional History" (M.A. thesis, Univ. of Texas at El Paso, 1992); Emma J. Portuondo, "The Impact of Bishop Charles Henry Brent upon American Colonial and Foreign Policy, 1901–1917" (Ph.D. diss., Catholic Univ. of America, 1969); Leon G. Rosenthal, "Christian Statesmanship in the First Missionary-Ecumenical Generation" (Ph.D. diss., Univ. of Chicago, 1989). The best biography is by Alexander C. Zabriskie, *Bishop Brent: Crusader for Christian Unity* (1948). Brent's personal papers are in the manuscript division of the Library of Congress, Washington, D.C.; his official correspondence is in the archives of the Episcopal Church, U.S.A., Austin, Texas.

Mark D. Norbeck

Brésillac, Melchior de Marion. *See* Marion Brésillac, Melchior Joseph de.

Breton, Raymond (Guillaume) (1609–1679), French Dominican missionary in the French West Indies. Born in Beaume, France, Guillaume Breton entered the Order of Preachers as an adolescent, received the name Raymond and was professed in January 1627. He studied philosophy and theology at the school of Saint Jacques in Paris, where he graduated with honors. In May 1635 he and three Dominican companions left from Dieppe for the French West Indies. They arrived in Guadeloupe, where they began evangelizing the natives. Breton left Guadeloupe in 1641 and went to the island of Dominica, where he ministered until 1651. He then returned to Poitier, France, where for five years he was spiritual director to the Dominican nuns. Later he returned to Beaume, where he composed a catechism, or summary of the first three parts of the Christian catechism, from French into Carib (1664). In 1665–1666 he wrote *Dictionaire François-Caraibe* and *Dictionaire Caraibe-François,* both published at Auxerre. These dictionaries contain valuable historical information which the author included to help elucidate the difficult Carib language. In 1667 his *Grammaire Caraibe* appeared. Breton also left a manuscript giving an account of the works of the Dominican missionaries in the French West Indies, which is considered of great historical importance: "Relatio gestorum a primis ordinis Praedicatorum missionariis in insulis Americanis ditionis Gallica praesertim apud Indos indigenas, quos Caraibes vulgo dicunt, ab anno MDCXXXV ad MDCXLIII" (An account of the labors of the First Order Dominicans among native Indians, the Caribs, in the French West Indies from 1635–1643). Breton died at Caen.

BIBLIOGRAPHY L. Fournier, *Le B. P. Raymond Breton, de l'ordre du fr. precheurs, profes du convent de Beaume, missionnaire aux Antilles, 1609–1679* (1895); Jacques Quetif and Jacques Echard, *Scriptores Ordinis Praedicatorum,* vol. 2 (1721), col. 688a.

Mary Frances Coleman

Brett, William Henry (1818–1886), Anglican missionary in British Guiana (present-day Guyana). While teaching Sunday school in Dover, England, Brett felt a call to missions. In 1840 the Society for the Propagation of the Gospel (SPG) sent him to open a station on the Pomeroon River in British Guiana. There he was enabled to survive physically and to understand the people through the help of an emancipated African slave, Jeanette, and of Sacibarra (Cornelius), the son of an Arawak chief. Brett's work included analysis of the local languages and social and religious practices; he also held worship services, gave instructions to adult inquirers, and set up a school for children. Brett, his wife, and local helpers developed writing systems for four native languages. Much of his work consisted of preparing dictionaries and grammars and translating prayers and portions of Scripture. In 1848 he was ordained and posted as rector of Holy Trinity parish at Essequibo on the coast and given oversight of the Pomeroon and Moruca missions, a responsibility he carried for the next 25 years. He returned to England in 1875. In his major publication, *The Indian Tribes of Guiana* (1852, 1868), he described his travels, the geography of Guiana, and the characteristics of the languages, social life, and religion of the peoples among whom he worked.

BIBLIOGRAPHY F. P. L. Josa, *"The Apostle of the Indians of Guiana": A Memoir of the Life and Labours of the Rev. W. H. Brett, B.D.* (1888); C. F. Pascoe, *Two Hundred Years of the SPG: An Historical Account of the SPG in Foreign Parts, 1701–1900* (rev. ed., 1901), vol. 1, pp. 243–249, 801; Henry P. Thompson, *Into All Lands: The History of the SPG in Foreign Parts, 1701–1950* (1951), pp. 282–284.

H. McKennie Goodpasture

Bridgman, Elijah Coleman (1801–1861), first American missionary to China. Bridgman was born in Belchertown, Massachusetts, and graduated from Amherst College (1826) and Andover Theological Seminary (1829). In response to the urging of Robert *Morrison of the London Missionary Society and of pious American merchants who offered free passage, Bridgman was ordained and was appointed for service in China by the American Board of Commissioners for Foreign Missions in 1829. He arrived in Canton in 1830, where he was welcomed by Morrison. He studied Chinese and soon began the literary labors to which he devoted much of his life. In 1834 he became the first joint secretary of the Society for the Diffusion of Useful Knowledge; he was a founder of the Morrison Education Society and its president for many years, and active in organizing the Medical Missionary Society in China (1838). Later he edited the journal of the North China branch of the Royal Asiatic Society. In 1832 Bridgman started a mission press and began publication of the *Chinese Repository,* which he edited until 1847. From 1839 to 1841 he worked at Macao, preparing a Chinese chrestomathy to aid in language learning. During negotiations to secure American access to China, Bridgman assisted as translator and adviser from 1842 to 1844. Shortly after baptizing his first convert he moved to Shanghai in 1847, where he was primarily occupied in working on Bible translation, his version appearing shortly after his death.

In 1845 Bridgman had married Eliza Jane Gillett (see below), an American Episcopalian missionary. She had founded and managed for 15 years the first girls' school in Shanghai. After her husband's death she moved to Peking, secured substantial property, and started Bridgman Academy, noted for educating a large number of Chinese women leaders.

BIBLIOGRAPHY Eliza Jane Bridgman, *The Life and Labors of Elijah Coleman Bridgman* (1864). *Missionary Herald* 58 (1862): 75–78 and 68 (1872): 110–112, provides informative obituaries of Elijah and Eliza Bridgman, respectively. Eliza's *Daughters of China, or Sketches of Domestic Life in the Celestial Empire* (1853) has an introduction by Elijah.

David M. Stowe

Bridgman, Eliza Jane (Gillett) (1805–1871), pioneer educational missionary in China. A school principal, Gillett had wanted to be a missionary since childhood. After the death of her widowed mother, she was free to apply to the Board of Missions of the Protestant Episcopal Church. Appointed a missionary teacher, she sailed to China in 1844. She immediately met Elijah Coleman *Bridgman of the American Board of Commissioners for Foreign Missions, who believed her to be God's answer to his prayers for a wife. They married, she transferred to the Congregational Church, and the Bridgmans began work in Canton. They adopted two small girls, and after the Bridgmans had transferred to Shanghai, Eliza began a girls' school that became the first Protestant school for girls there. Her successful school work continued until 1862, when her health broke following the death of her husband. After a furlough in America during which she was run over by a sled, she resumed work in Peking in 1864. There she opened Bridgman Academy, the predecessor to the Woman's College of Yenching University. Bridgman was widely acknowledged to be an exceptional teacher, and she gave money liberally to Congregational missions in China. After returning to Shanghai to help open a new school, she died and was buried beside her husband.

BIBLIOGRAPHY Eliza Bridgman, *Daughters of China; or Sketches of Domestic Life in the Celestial Empire* (1853) and *The Life and Labors of Elijah Coleman Bridgman* (1864). See obituary by Henry Blodget, "The Late Mrs. E. C. Bridgman," *The Chinese Recorder* 4 (March 1872): 261–263; (April 1872): 298–302. Eliza Bridgman's handwritten autobiography and journals for 1856 and 1865 are held in the archives at Yale Divinity School, New Haven, Conn. The ABCFM archives at Harvard Univ., Cambridge, Mass., hold her response to the Episcopal Church's unsupportive stance regarding her marriage.

Dana L. Robert

Bright, William ("Bill") Rohl (1921–), founder of Campus Crusade for Christ. Born in Coweta, Oklahoma, Bright graduated from Northeastern State University, Tahlequah, Oklahoma, and moved to California in 1944 to pursue a business career. In 1945, under the influence of Henrietta Mears at First Presbyterian Church, Hollywood, he dedicated his life to Christ and entered seminary. In 1951, leaving seminary without graduating, he began evangelizing students at the University of California at Los Angeles and teaching others how to do it, thereby launching Campus Crusade for Christ. His approach was direct, aggressive, and focused on student leaders. Staff followed rigid formulas for evangelism, according to Bright's *Have You Heard of the Four Spiritual Laws?* (1965). After its rapid growth on American campuses, Campus Crusade expanded overseas to South Korea in 1958. Bright also added specialized evangelism among athletes, business executives, political leaders, and diplomats. In 1979 "the Jesus film," a movie about the life of Christ, became Campus Crusade's most far-reaching evangelistic tool. In *The Secret: How to Live with Power and Purpose* (1989), Bright codified his teaching about the Holy Spirit. By the 1990s Campus Crusade included 40,000 paid and volunteer staff in 152 countries. Bright received the 1996 Templeton Prize for Progress in Religion.

BIBLIOGRAPHY Richard Quebedeaux, *I Found It! The Story of Bill Bright and Campus Crusade* (1979).

James W. Reapsome

Britto, João de (1647–1693), Jesuit martyr of the Madura mission in India. Born in Lisbon, Portugal, Britto entered the Society of Jesus at the age of 16 after serving as a page at the royal court. He arrived in India in 1673 and completed his theological studies in Goa and his final training at Ambalakat before proceeding to Madura, where he assumed the role of the *pandaraswamy* (one who works with the lower castes). In addition to the normal problems of adapting to a new place and people, he had to face constant political instability in the region and the ravages of internecine wars, and his missionary zeal was seriously misinterpreted by one of his provincial superiors. However, his sincerity of purpose enabled him to persevere and his devotion was recognized by most of his Jesuit colleagues. Contrary to the Portuguese nationalist feelings of most of the *padroado* missionaries of the time, Britto's loyalties were with the Indian people. He was keen to bring the Oratorian priests of Goa to the Madura mission, hoping that their knowledge of Marathi could help the mission win favor with the Maratha rulers in the region. His plan, however, was not acceptable to his provincial superior. Britto was nearly martyred in 1683, but he survived to return to Portugal in 1687 as procurator of the Malabar Province of the Jesuits and to fire the imagination of many other Jesuits who offered to serve in the mission. He returned to India in 1689 despite strong objections by the king of Portugal, who with all his court liked and admired Britto. In 1693 he was beheaded at Oriyur in the Ramnad District of Tamilnadu by a Marava chieftain at the instigation of a Brahmin leader, because the ruling caste was unhappy about the values of the gospel that threatened the continued exploitation of the lower castes by the elite. "Arulanandaswamy," as Britto was called, was to be beatified in 1741, but suppression of the Society of Jesus delayed the process until 1852, when the Jesuits went back to Madura. He was canonized by Pope *Pius XII in 1947.

BIBLIOGRAPHY A. M. Nevett, *John de Britto and his Times* (1980); A. Saulière, *Red Sand: A Life of St. John de Britto, S.J.* (1947); Lotika Varadarajan, *India in the 17th Century (Memoirs of François Martin)*, 4 vols. (1981-1985).

Teotonio R. de Souza

Brockman, Fletcher Sims (1867-1944), missionary and YMCA executive in China and the United States. Born in Amherst County, Virginia, and a graduate of Vanderbilt University, Brockman began his career with the YMCA as the first student secretary for the thirteen southern states, 1891-1897. In 1897 and 1898 he was traveling secretary of the Student Volunteer Movement. A member of the Methodist Episcopal Church, South, he served the YMCA in China from 1898 to 1915, first as foreign secretary in Nanking (Nanjing) and from 1901 as the first general secretary of the Chinese YMCA, based in Shanghai. He also helped to organize the National Christian Council of China. In 1915 he handed responsibility for the Chinese YMCA over to C. T. Wang and, at the request of John R. *Mott, returned to the United States to serve as associate general secretary both of the YMCA National War Work Council and of the International Committee. After the National Council of the YMCAs of the United States was formed in 1924, he became its administrative secretary for the Far East. Following his retirement from the YMCA in 1929, he lectured at Vanderbilt University and served as secretary of the Committee on the Promotion of Friendship between America and the Far East. He received an honorary LL.D. from Colgate University in 1929.

BIBLIOGRAPHY Fletcher Sims Brockman, *I Discover the Orient* (1935). Eugene R. Barnett, "Builders of the YMCA-3," *Old Guard News* 25, no. 8 (November 1954); Sherwood Eddy, *Pathfinders of the World Missionary Crusade* (1945), pp. 200-212. Additional biographical information available in a memorial booklet, *Fletcher Sims Brockman, 1867-1944: In Remembrance*, Mott papers, Yale Univ. Divinity School (1944).

Martha Lund Smalley

Broger, John C(hristian) (1913-), American pioneer in missionary broadcasting. After studying at Texas A & M, Broger graduated from Southern California Bible College (1939). During World War II he served as a U.S. Navy officer in the Pacific. With Robert *Bowman he cofounded the Far Eastern Broadcasting Company (FEBC) in 1945, and provided leadership as it established its first broadcasting facilities in the Philippines. In 1954 he became a consultant to the U.S. Joint Chiefs of Staff, and in 1960 he was appointed director of information for the Armed Forces, which involved overseeing 1,100 radio and television stations and 1,900 newspapers worldwide. In this capacity he also lectured at the U.S. Military Academy, the National War College, and Harvard Business School, among others. He developed counseling materials for the Chiefs of Chaplains. In 1977 he retired from government service to found the Biblical Counseling Foundation. Broger received the LL.D. from Wheaton College (1965), as well as numerous governmental awards and citations.

BIBLIOGRAPHY Eleanor G. Bowman and Susan F. Titus, *Eyes beyond the Horizon* (1991); Gleason H. Ledyard, *Sky Waves* (1968); Ruth A. Tucker, *From Jerusalem to Irian Jaya* (1983). Archival material on Broger is available at the Biblical Counseling Foundation, Rancho Mirage, Cal.

Wayne A. Detzler

Bromilow, William E. (1857-1929), Australian Methodist missionary. Born in Geelong, Victoria, Bromilow served in Fiji, New Guinea, and Papua. His father came to Australia from England; his mother dedicated him to mission work before he was born. Educated at Grenville College, Ballarat, at 14 he passed the matriculation examination at the University of Melbourne and became a teacher. A "deepened, more personal religious experience" led to service as a lay circuit preacher. He answered a call for volunteer missionaries in 1879, but Methodist policy required that he be married. He promptly asked Lily Thompson to marry him. The Bromilows immediately went to Sydney for William's ordination. Four days later, aboard the mission ship *John Wesley*, they sailed for Fiji, where they served until 1889. From 1891 to 1907 Bromilow was chair of the Dobu mission station in New Guinea. Known for his linguistic work, in 1910 he was awarded an honorary doctorate by Aberdeen University for his translation of the Bible into Dobu. The next year he was appointed chair of the New South Wales Conference. In 1920 he and his wife returned to Papua for five more years, before retiring in Australia.

BIBLIOGRAPHY William E. Bromilow, *Twenty Years among Primitive Papuans* (1929). Diane Langmore, *Missionary Lives: Papua, 1874-1914* (1989).

Darrell Whiteman

Brønnum, Niels Høegh (1882-1966), Danish pioneer missionary in Nigeria. Brønnum was born in Nørholm, near Aalborg, Denmark. Drafted into military service in 1904, he became a medical orderly at the garrison hospital in Aalborg. There he felt the call to mission through the influence of Anton Pedersen, vicar of Vor Frelser Kirke (Our Saviour's Church). While studying medicine at the University of Edinburgh, 1906-1911, in a meeting of the Edinburgh Medical Missionary Society, Brønnum heard H. K. W. *Kumm speak about the Sudan. Brønnum wanted to serve as a medical missionary in the Sudan but none of the existing Danish missionary societies were willing to send him there, so a new society was established in cooperation with the Sudan United Mission (founded by Kumm in 1904). The Danish branch of the Sudan United Mission was established on November 22, 1911, with Anton Pedersen as chairman.

In 1913 Brønnum was sent to Nigeria, where the Danish society had been assigned the northeastern province of Yola as its field of activity. After visiting several English mission stations, Brønnum arrived at Numan in September 1913. There he studied the language and religion of the Bachama people, built a mission station, and translated the Gospel of Mark, which was published in 1915. Concurrently he worked as a doctor.

During a furlough in Denmark from 1915 to 1916, Brønnum was ordained. His first wife, Margaret Chapel (Young), died in Nigeria in 1913 following the birth of a son, and in 1916 Brønnum married Albertha Tholle. As a visible fruit of his missionary efforts, the first national believer was baptized in 1917, and in 1920 the first church in Numan was dedicated outside the mission station. In 1917 the Brønnums left Nigeria for England due to his wife's health problems, and he was out of missionary service until he returned to Nigeria alone from 1919 to 1921. From then until 1953 he served as secretary of the Sudan United Mission. He visited Nigeria several more times, the last being in 1963, when the church celebrated the fiftieth anniversary of his arrival there. He died in Roskile, Denmark.

Brønnum was one of the most prominent missionaries of the Danish Lutheran Church, and certainly the person whose work yielded the most visible results. As an outcome of the missionary work which was done by him and his successors, an independent church was established—the Lutheran Church of Christ in Nigeria, which today counts several hundred thousand members.

BIBLIOGRAPHY Mogens Jensen, *To mænd og deres mission* [Two men and their mission] (Th.D. diss., Univ. of Aarhus, 1992; includes English summary and extensive bibliography). Margaret Nissen, *An African Church Is Born: The Story of the Adamawa and Central Sardauna Provinces in Nigeria* (1968).

Flemming Markussen

Bronson, Miles (1812–1883), pioneer American Baptist missionary to Assam, India. Born in Norway, New York, and educated at Hamilton Literary and Theological Institute, Bronson reached Assam together with his first wife, Ruth (Lucas), in July 1837. After her death in 1869, he married Frances Danforth, who died two years later; he married Mary Rankin in 1874. Bronson's contributions to the church in Northeast India were the most important of any nineteenth-century missionary. He was the first to live among the hill tribes (Namsang Nagas, 1839–1841); he organized the Garo congregation at Rajasimla (1867), the first Baptist church among the hill tribes, and ordained the first pastor indigenous to Northeast India. He established the Nowgong Orphan Institution (1843), the first coeducational institution in Northeast India, and produced the first English-Assamese dictionary (1867). He is best known and still honored by the Assamese people, Christian and Hindu, for his leadership of the Assamese language agitation, which was successful in preventing the British government from replacing the Assamese language with Bengali in the schools and courts of Assam.

BIBLIOGRAPHY "The Bronson Papers," a collection of letters and other matter received and written by Bronson and his wives from 1834 until his death, are housed in the Andover Newton Theological School library, Newton Center, Massachusetts. A comprehensive biography of her father's life was written by Harriette Bronson Gunn, *In a Far Country: A Story of Christian Heroism and Achievement* (1911). An analysis of his participation in the Assamese language agitation is found in Frederick S. Downs, "Missionaries and the Language Controversy in Assam," *Indian Church History Review* 13, no. 1 (June 1979): 29–69.

Frederick S. Downs

Brooke, Graham Wilmot (1865–1892), Anglican lay missionary in West Africa. Brooke was born at Aldershot, England, into a military family. After study at Haileybury College, a period of medical study at St. Thomas's Hospital, and then travel in Africa, he went to West Africa in 1889, initially as an independent missionary but then joining the Church Missionary Society (CMS) in 1890. He took with him an intense and intolerant spiritual enthusiasm nurtured by the Keswick Convention and tending toward the perfectionism of Charles Finney. Influenced by Brooke's magnetic personal qualities, the CMS entrusted him with the leadership of a missionary party to the Niger while he was still only 25 years old. The party was composed of young, headstrong, very middle-class missionaries, mainly from Cambridge, who looked to the radical missionary methods of Hudson *Taylor as their inspiration and guide. They were stern critics of traditional missionary methods. Niger had been evangelized under the leadership of Samuel *Crowther, the first black African bishop of the nineteenth century. Almost immediately, confrontation developed as Crowther's policy, methods, and agents were critically scrutinized. Brooke's missionaries sought to purge the local church of "sin," with a total insensitivity to differences of culture and age. This produced a full-scale confrontation at Onitsha with the aged, distinguished, saintly, but undeniably over-gentle Crowther, which was inevitably perceived in racialist terms (though arguably Brooke would have acted in much the same way had Crowther been white). Brooke and his fellow missionaries were enraged when they felt that the CMS did not support them sufficiently. They threatened to make public some damaging information about the church on the Niger. The CMS therefore retreated to a position where it, in effect, substantially modified its traditional, *Venn-like support for African missionaries and leadership. Shortly afterward Brooke died of blackwater fever. If his missionary career was a failure, much of the blame must lie with the CMS for giving him responsibilites that were far beyond his experience and wisdom.

BIBLIOGRAPHY Frieder Ludwig, "The Making of a Late Victorian Missionary," *NZM* 47 (1991): 269–290; Andrew Porter, "Evangelical Enthusiasm, Missionary Motivation, and West Africa in the Late Nineteenth Century: The Career of G. W. Brooke," *Journal of Imperial and Commonwealth History* 6 (1977): 23–46.

Peter Williams

Broomhall, Anthony James (1911–1994), physician, pioneer missionary, and historian. Broomhall was born in Chefoo (Yantai), China, the son of Benjamin Charles Broomhall and Marion Broomhall of the Baptist Missionary Society and grandson of Benjamin *Broomhall. He was educated at the Chefoo School and in England at Monkton Combe, Bath, and at the London Hospital, where he received his medical training. He joined the China Inland Mission (CIM) and sailed for China in 1938. In 1942 he married Theodora Janet Churchill. They began pioneer work among the Nosu tribe in southwest China, but soon the Sino-Japanese War forced them to flee to India. After the war they spent four more years among the Nosu doing medical and evangelistic work. In 1951 they and their four daughters were expelled from China by the Communists after several months of house arrest.

Broomhall then explored the possibility of the CIM doing medical work in Thailand, which led to the founding of three hospitals. He also pioneered for 11 years among the Mangyan people on the island of Mindoro in the Philippines, mastering the Tagalog language and laying the foundation for a strong church. In 1988 he paid a return visit to Nosuland and met the grandchildren of early converts.

BIBLIOGRAPHY Anthony James Broomhall, *Strong Tower* (1947), *Strong Man's Prey* (1953), *Fields for Reaping* (1953), *Time for Action* (1956), and his seven volume magnum opus, *Hudson Taylor and China's Open Century* (1989). Obituaries in *East Asia Millions,* October–December 1994, pp. 87, 88, and in Overseas Missionary Fellowship's *Pray for China Fellowship,* September 1994, pp. 1, 2.

Norman H. Cliff

Broomhall, Benjamin (1829–1911), British mission advocate, administrator, and author. Born in Bradley, Staffordshire, Broomhall was the eldest child of Charles and Jane Broomhall. He married Amelia Taylor, sister of J. Hudson *Taylor, in 1859. They had ten children, five of whom went as missionaries to China. After serving as secretary of the Anti-Slavery Association, Broomhall became the general secretary of the China Inland Mission, 1878–1895, and editor of the mission magazine, *China's Millions.* He addressed breakfast gatherings in the homes of titled people and spoke for the mission at meetings throughout Britain. When the *Cambridge Seven had been accepted as missionary candidates, Broomhall organized large farewell gatherings in many centers and produced a book about the men, *A Missionary Band* (1886). A copy was accepted by Queen Victoria and some 20,000 copies were sold.

In 1888 Broomhall formed and became secretary of the Christian Union for the Severance of the British Empire with the Opium Traffic and editor of its periodical, *National Righteousness.* He lobbied the British Parliament on the opium trade. He and James Maxwell appealed to the London Missionary Conference of 1888 and the Edinburgh Missionary Conference of 1910 to condemn the continuation of the trade. When Broomhall was dying, his son Marshall (see below) read to him from the *Times* the welcome news that an agreement had been signed ensuring the end of the opium trade within two years.

BIBLIOGRAPHY A. J. Broomhall, *Hudson Taylor and China's Open Century,* vol. 7 (1989); M. Broomhall, *Heirs Together of the Grace of Life* (1918). Obituaries in *China's Millions,* July 1911, pp. 99, 100, and *National Righteousness,* June 1911, pp. 2–6.

Norman H. Cliff

Broomhall, Marshall (1866–1937), English missionary writer and editor. Broomhall, a nephew of Hudson *Taylor, was one of ten children born to Benjamin *Broomhall and his wife, Amelia Hudson (Taylor). From the age of nine he lived at the London headquarters of the China Inland Mission (CIM). In 1890, after completing a degree at Cambridge, he followed an older brother and sister to China under the auspices of the CIM. He spent the next four years studying Chinese and was married to Flora Corderoy in 1894. In 1899 his wife's health necessitated a permanent return to England, and in 1900 he became the editorial secretary of the CIM, a post he was to hold until 1927. He edited the CIM magazine, *China's Millions,* and wrote numerous books and the CIM annual reports. He made return visits to China and kept in close touch with current writings on China and on political developments. After his retirement he continued to write, and in 1936, despite poor health (he had early lost the sight of one eye), he returned to edit *China's Millions.* He served well the mission with which so many of his family had been associated, both by his writings and by his personal life and witness.

BIBLIOGRAPHY Marshall Broomhall, *The Chinese Empire: A General and Missionary Survey* (1907), *The Jubilee Story of the China Inland Mission* (1915), *Heirs Together of the Grace of Life: Benjamin Broomhall, Amelia Hudson Broomhall, by Their Son* (1918), *Hudson Taylor: The Man Who Believed God* (1929), *Archibald Orr Ewing, "That Faithful and Wise Steward"* (1930), *Our Seal: Being the Witness of the China Inland Mission to the Faithfulness of God* (1933), and *By Love Compelled: The Call of the China Inland Mission* (1936). Broomhall's obituary is in *China's Millions,* December 1937. See also A. J. Broomhall, *Hudson Taylor and China's Open Century,* vol. 7 (1989).

Jocelyn Murray

Broughton, William Grant (1788–1853), first Anglican bishop of Australia. Broughton was born in London and educated at the University of Cambridge. An old-fashioned high churchman, he was conscious of the church's responsibility to educate and evangelize the entire population of settlers, convicts, and Aborigines in Australia. He was appointed archdeacon of New South Wales in 1829 and bishop of Australia in 1836. In 1832 he withdrew from the Church Missionary Society Australian corresponding committee and instead enlisted the support of the Society for the Propagation of the Gospel in procuring clergy and money for the colony. The demands of his own diocese meant he could do little to translate his dream of a converted Pacific into reality. "My mission is not to convert heathens to Christianity," he told Bishop *Selwyn of New Zealand, "but by God's grace to prevent Christians from lapsing into heathenism." In 1850 he presided over the conference of Australasian bishops, which established the Australian Board of Missions committed to training Aboriginal and islander missionaries for work among their own people.

BIBLIOGRAPHY Stephen Judd and Kenneth Cable, *Sydney Anglicans* (1987); G. P. Shaw, *Patriarch and Prophet, William Grant*

Broughton, 1788–1853: Colonial Statesman and Ecclesiastic (1978); F. T. Whitington, *William Grant Broughton* (1942).

Stuart Piggin

Brown, Alfred (Nesbit) (1803–1884), English missionary to the Maori. Born in Colchester, Essex, England, Brown trained at the Church Missionary Society (CMS) college, Islington, and went to New Zealand in 1829. The station he established among the Maori at Matamata in 1835 was closed the following year due to opposition. (However, a leading chief there, Wiremu Tamihana Tarapipipi, was influenced by Brown's ministry and was baptized in 1839.) In 1838 Brown and his wife, Charlotte, developed a new base at Te Papa, Tauranga. Made archdeacon of Tauranga in 1844, he traveled extensively, promoting peace and education, preaching, baptizing, and supervising Maori teachers. His initial success was undermined by social and economic changes in the 1850s and by conflicts in the 1860s pitting the Maori against European settlers and the government. Although Brown strove to be an evangelist, mediator, and protector of the Maori people, he found himself discredited by some Maori, and his efforts to rebuild the mission had limited success. He died in New Zealand.

BIBLIOGRAPHY N. V. Hall, *I Have Planted: A Biography of Alfred Nesbit Brown* (1981). Brown's papers are held by the CMS and at The Elms, Tauranga, and are available on microfilm.

Allan K. Davidson

Brown, Arthur Judson (1856–1963), Presbyterian mission administrator. Born in Holliston, Massachusetts, Brown graduated from Wabash College in 1880 and Lane Seminary in Cincinnati in 1883. He married Jennie S. Thomas in 1883. He held three Presbyterian pastorates and served for 34 years (1895–1929) as administrative secretary of the Presbyterian Board of Foreign Missions in New York City; he never had any other title. He spent the remaining 34 years of his life in retirement, with gradually lessening literary and ecumenical activity. His wife died in 1945.

Brown's portfolio was the Far East. He made two long tours of that region (1901–1902; 1909). From these experiences there came reports and a series of popular books on Christian missions and countries of the Far East. He also wrote a widely used textbook, *The Foreign Missionary* (1907), and a history, *One Hundred Years*, celebrating the anniversary of the Presbyterian Board in 1937.

In his books and in the counsels and correspondence of the mission board, Brown insisted on the importance of mission being centered in national churches. He clearly adumbrated what became standard mission policy many years later. Brown was also a leader in the growth of the ecumenical movement, serving on committees leading to the missionary conferences in New York (1900) and Edinburgh (1910), the formation of the IMC in 1921, and the Life and Work conference in Stockholm in 1925, which underlay the development of the World Council of Churches. He also served as a member of the Hoover Relief Committee (1915) and the American Committee on Religious Rights and Minorities (1920) and for many years was a member of the Church Peace Union. He died in New York City at the age of 106.

BIBLIOGRAPHY In addition to many pamphlets and reports, Brown wrote sixteen books, including *The New Era in the Philippines* (1903), *New Forces in Old China* (1904), *The Why and How of Foreign Missions* (1909), *Unity and Missions* (1915), and *Memoirs of a Centenarian*, W. N. Wysham, ed. (1957). A substantial collection of Brown's papers are in the Yale Divinity School Library. The sole biographical treatment is R. Park Johnson, "Arthur Judson Brown," in Gerald H. Anderson et al., eds., *Mission Legacies* (1994), pp. 554–562.

R. Park Johnson

Brown, David (1763–1812), British Anglican chaplain in Calcutta and advocate of missions. Brown attended school in Hull, in northeast England, run by the noted Anglican evangelical Joseph Milner, and then the University of Cambridge. After being ordained an Anglican priest, he went to Calcutta in 1786 to head an orphanage. Soon after his arrival he was also appointed a military chaplain and became senior chaplain of Bengal in 1797. From 1794 he was in charge of St. John's Church, Calcutta. He was provost of the East India Company's civil service college of Fort William from 1800 to 1807. Although not a missionary, in 1787 he drew up a proposal supported by Charles *Grant and others to inaugurate Protestant missionary work in Bengal. He was a trustee and led services at the Mission Church in Calcutta for 23 years. His plan to set up public schools throughout India to spread British and Christian influence came to nothing. He was a friend of the *Serampore Trio, a member of the Calcutta Church Missionary Society corresponding committee, and founding member and secretary of the Calcutta British and Foreign Bible Society auxiliary. Brown was the first evangelical appointee and leader among the notable group of chaplains who served in Bengal. They included Claudius *Buchanan, Henry *Martyn, Daniel *Corrie, and Thomas Thomason. Brown died in India.

BIBLIOGRAPHY A. K. Davidson, *Evangelicals and Attitudes to India, 1786–1813* (1990); Charles Simeon, ed., *Memorial Sketches of the Rev. David Brown: With a Selection of His Sermons, Preached at Calcutta* (1816).

Allan K. Davidson

Brown, Edith Mary (1864–1956), pioneer English woman doctor in India. Born into a devout Christian family, and with an older sister a missionary by 1873, Brown took a degree in science at Cambridge and then taught until she could afford to study medicine. This she did in London from 1887 to 1891, but as a woman she had to retake the examination in Scotland to receive her certification. In 1891 she left for India as the first medical doctor of the Baptist Zenana mission. She went to a small Zenana mission hospital in the Punjab, at Ludhiana, an interdenominational institution, originally for language study. Her studies were interrupted by requests for her help with surgery and midwifery. She then spent a year establishing new work at Palwal, near Delhi, and the difficulties with which she met led her to conceive of a Christian medical training school for Indian women, who could give skilled help to the missionary staff. A conference to discuss the scheme was held at Ludhiana at the end of 1893. Ludhiana was finally chosen as the place for the experiment. With permission from her society, she returned to Ludhiana, and in October 1894, the North India School of Medicine for Christian Women opened there, with seven societies cooperating.

The school prospered under her leadership and rapidly expanded. It initially trained women only, but male students were accepted from 1951, and from 1953 medical degrees were awarded. Brown was a woman of firm theological views who required assent to a strict basis of faith, even from the missionaries seconded to work at Ludhiana. Her work was recognized by several awards (she was made Dame Commander of the British Empire in 1931). As one who found it difficult to hand over direction to others, she retired reluctantly to Kashmir in 1941 but returned in 1947 to assist during the partition riots. She died in Srinagar 65 years after her first arrival in India.

BIBLIOGRAPHY Francesca French, *Miss Brown's Hospital: The Story of the Ludhiana Medical College and Dame Edith Brown, OBE, Its Founder* (1954); J. C. Pollock, *Shadows Fall Apart: The Story of the Zenana Bible and Medical Mission* (1958); Charles Reynolds, *Punjab Pioneer* (1968).

Jocelyn Murray

Brown, George (1835–1917), English writer, translator, ethnographer, and pioneer missionary of the Wesleyan Missionary Society of Australasia. Brown was born in Barnard Castle, Durham, England, and had only a secondary school education. After spending several years in New Zealand, he went to Samoa in 1860 to help with the resumption of Methodist missions. In 1875 he sailed from Samoa aboard the mission ship *John Wesley* for New Britain, the only European among a team of devoted South Sea island missionaries. Fanning out, the group established a network of centers. In 1878, at the instigation of a chief named Talili, who was fearful of losing his trading monopoloy with the inland tribes, four of Brown's Fijian co-workers were killed and eaten. Brown helped rescue their families. Then, in a controversial move, he and 60 armed men put Talili to flight and demanded from his followers compensation and the bones of the murdered Fijians. In 1887 Brown became general secretary of the mission board of the New South Wales and Queensland Wesleyan conferences. It was he, more than anyone, who formulated the strategy for Wesleyan (later Methodist) missions in Melanesia. In 1902 Brown accompanied John F. *Goldie to the Roviana Lagoon, where Goldie later became leader of the new mission at Munda.

Brown was a botanist, an ornithologist, a philologist, and an ethnologist. He was able to speak the Samoan, Tongan, Fijian, and New Britain languages. While in New Britain, Brown interviewed tribesmen from the Duke of York island group. His *Anthropological Notes and Queries* contains the results of those discussions as well as information on Samoan customs that he obtained while living there. His major ethnological work was *Melanesians and Polynesians* (1910).

BIBLIOGRAPHY George Brown, *George Brown, D.D., Pioneer Missionary and Explorer: An Autobiography* (1908). Charles Brunsdon Fletcher, *The Black Knight of the Pacific* (1944); John Garrett, *To Live among the Stars* (1982).

Darrell Whiteman

Brown, Nathan (1807–1886), American Baptist missionary in Burma, Assam, and Japan. Born in Ipswich, New Hampshire, Brown graduated from Williams College, the valedictorian of his class, and was for a time a student at Newton Theological Institution. For two years he taught school in Bennington, Vermont, and edited the *Vermont Telegraph*, a weekly religious newspaper. In December 1832 Brown and his wife, Eliza, sailed for Burma (Myanmar) under appointment of the Baptist General Convention. In Burma he worked with Adoniram *Judson on translation projects until Judson recommended him for a new work in Assam. In 1834 he became head of the Assam field, organizing the mission among four language groups. In 1845 the Browns moved to Sibsagar, but owing to ill health, Eliza Brown returned to the United States where she was enthusiastically received by the churches. Back in Assam, Nathan translated the first Assamese New Testament (1848) and, by 1851, organized an association of churches. He returned to the United States in 1855 and withdrew from the mission in protest over the bureaucracy and policies of the board. He joined the newly formed American Baptist Free Mission Society, an abolitionist group, and became heavily involved in the abolitionist movement. In 1862 he personally presented President Abraham Lincoln with a memorial respecting emancipation. Eliza Brown died in 1871. With the merger of his original mission with the Free Mission Society in 1872, Brown was recommissioned and sent the next year with his second wife, Charlotte Amelia Worth Marlit (d.1923), to Japan to join Jonathan *Goble. At 65 years of age, he actively engaged in church planting at Yokohama, finished the translation of the Bible into Japanese, and published a Japanese hymnbook. He died in Japan.

BIBLIOGRAPHY Nathan Brown, *Catechism in Tai Lik An thim Au lau* (1838), *History of Assam* (1844), *Two Sermons on the Gospel Message and Christian Ordinances, Preached at Gowhati and Nowgong, Assam* (1847), and *Introduction to the Scholar's Edition of the New Testament in Vernacular Japanese* (1885). Albert A. Bennett, *A Biographical Sketch of Rev. Nathan Brown, D.D.* (1895); Fred H. Wight, "Nathan Brown, Baptist Missionary to Burma, Assam, and Japan," *Watchman-Examiner*, September 9, 1937, p. 1006; Walter S. Stewart, *Early Baptist Missionaries and Pioneers*, vol. 2 (1925), pp. 53–78.

William H. Brackney

Brown, Samuel Robbins (1810–1879), Reformed Church in America missionary in Japan. Brown was the oldest of the six pioneer Protestant missionaries who arrived in Japan with their families in 1859. He combined rich talent with breadth of education and years of ministerial experience in the United States and China before arriving in Japan. His earliest training was in the Congregational Church in his Massachusetts hometown and at Yale College, from which he was graduated in 1832. He received theological education at the Presbyterian seminary in Columbia, South Carolina, and later in the first full class of Union Theological Seminary, New York City. Ordained by the Presbyterian Church, sent first to China by the Reformed Church in America, he was described by a contemporary as a man "preeminently catholic, liberal and tolerant."

Compelled by his wife's health to return to the United States after seven years of primarily educational mission work in Canton, China (1839–1847), Brown served as pastor of the Reformed Dutch Church of Sand Beach, New York, near Auburn. He was one of the founders of Elmira College, the first women's college chartered as such in the United States. Accepting a call to go to Japan as a Reformed Church missionary, he served there from 1859 to 1879, notably in educational and pastoral work and translating portions of the New Testament into Japanese. He was a cooperating missionary in the establishment of the first Japanese Protestant congregation, in Yokohama (1872), and of the first Protestant theological seminary, Meiji Gakuin, in Tokyo (1878), from beginnings in his own home.

BIBLIOGRAPHY Edward R. Beauchamp, "Brown, Samuel Robbins," *Encyclopedia of Japan* (1983); Richard H. Drummond, *A History of Christianity in Japan* (1977); William Elliot Griffis, *A Maker of the New Orient, Samuel Robbins Brown* (1902).

Richard H. Drummond

Browne, Alice. *See* Frame, Alice Seymour (Browne).

Browne, Laurence Edward (1887–1986), Islamic scholar, educator, and author. After studying at Cambridge and being ordained by the Church of England, Browne served in India under the Society for the Propagation of the Gospel. His first 12 years (1912–1924) were spent at Bishop's College, Calcutta, where, in addition to his duties as general editor of the Indian Church Commentaries, he developed an interest in Islam. Three years of furlough (1926–1929) permitted him to concentrate on Islamic studies in Cairo, Istanbul, and Cambridge, preparing him for a new appointment in India as librarian of the Henry Martyn Institute of Islamic Studies, Lahore (prior to its relocation in Aligarh). Here he wrote the work for which he is best known, *The Eclipse of Christianity in Asia* (1933), which analyzes eastern Christian relationships with Islam from the seventh to the fourteenth centuries—at that time, a subject seriously overlooked in Western missionary scholarship. His four years in Lahore were cut short by personal circumstances that necessitated his return to England. After a period of parish ministry and the award of a Cambridge D.D., he became the first Islamicist to hold the chair of comparative religion at Manchester University (1941–1946) and subsequently at Leeds University (1946–1952). In these academic positions he produced significant works dedicated to the challenge of making Christianity intelligible to Muslims.

BIBLIOGRAPHY Laurence Edward Browne, *Early Judaism* (1920), *The Acts of the Apostles: with Introduction and Notes* (1925), *The Eclipse of Christianity in Asia from the Time of Muhammad till the Fourteenth Century* (1933), *Christianity and the Malays* (1936), *The Prospects of Islam* (1944), *Where Science and Religion Meet* (1950), *The Messianic Hope in Its Historical Setting* (1951), *Ezekiel and Alexander* (1952), *The Quickening Word: A Theological Answer to the Challenge of Islam* (1955).

David A. Kerr

Browne, Stanley G(eorge) (1907–1986), missionary doctor and leprologist in the Congo. Browne was born in southeast London, the second son of devout Baptist parents. Despite limited early education, he won a scholarship to King's College, London, where he studied medicine and theology. After graduating as a surgeon in 1936, he went with the Baptist Missionary Society (BMS) to the Belgian Congo (Zaire). He was posted to Yakusu hospital (near modern Kisangani). There he inherited Clement *Chesterman's emphasis on a community health program of preventive medicine, conducted in close cooperation with the colonial government. When a leprosy census revealed that up to half the population was infected with leprosy, Browne opened a leprosarium across the Congo river at Yalisombo. Progress was slow until the late 1940s, when a new drug, dapsone, became available for systematic use in the community health program. By the early 1950s, Browne's work at Yakusu had attracted international acclaim. However, disagreements with missionary colleagues over medical policy led eventually to his resignation from the BMS in 1959. He then succeeded Dr. Frank Davey as senior leprologist at Uzuakoli in Nigeria, working for the Nigerian government. From 1966 to 1978 he served as director of the Leprosy Study Center in London and as medical consultant to the Leprosy Mission.

BIBLIOGRAPHY As well as publishing numerous medical papers, Browne was joint editor of *Heralds of Truth: The Saga of Christian Medical Initiatives* (1985). Sylvia and Peter Duncan, *Bonganga: Experiences of a Missionary Doctor* (1958); Brian Stanley, *The History of the Baptist Missionary Society, 1792–1992* (1992); Phyllis Thompson, *Mister Leprosy* (1980).

Brian Stanley

Brownlee, John (1791–1871), pioneer Scottish missionary among the Xhosa of South Africa. Brownlee went to South Africa with the London Missionary Society (LMS) in 1817. After a year in Cape Colony, he went beyond the colonial frontier to work among the Xhosa. His subsequent acceptance of the colonial authorities' request to be their agent led to his resignation from the LMS. But in 1825 John *Philip proposed that Brownlee resign from government service and serve the LMS again. He agreed and began a new station among the Xhosa (now King William's Town), where he was ordained as a Congregationalist. With the exception of two interruptions, first in the war of 1835 and then again in the war of 1846, he spent the rest of his life among the Xhosa and Mfengu there.

BIBLIOGRAPHY B. F. Holt, *Greatheart of the Border: A Life of John Brownlee* (1976); Richard Lovett, *The History of the London Missionary Society, 1795–1895* (1899).

Andrew C. Ross

Brubaker, Henry Heisey (1900–1972), Brethren in Christ (BC) missionary in Rhodesia. Brubaker was born near Mechanicsburg, Pennsylvania, and attended Messiah College in Grantham, Pennsylvania. Following ordination to the ministry in 1922, he began 29 years of missionary work in Southern and Northern Rhodesia (now Zimbabwe and Zambia, respectively). In 1929 he became superintendent of BC missions in Africa; while on furlough in 1932 he was ordained a bishop. In addition to denominational duties, he served on the executive committee of the Southern Rhodesia Missionary Conference, six years as the conference's president. He wrote and edited tracts in the Sindebele language and served on an inter-mission language committee dealing with matters concerning Sindebele. For many years he also wrote Sunday school lesson helps for *UBaq,* a South African paper published in Zulu. Following his retirement from mission work, he served as president of Niagara Christian College in Ontario, Canada, as superintendent of Messiah Home in Harrisburg, Pennsylvania, and as secretary of the BC Church in North America. He spent his last years in Upland, California, where he was minister of visitation in the local congregation until his death.

BIBLIOGRAPHY Anna Engle et al., *There Is No Difference* (1950); E. Morris Sider, ed., "Henry H. Brubaker: Memoirs of a Missionary," *Brethren in Christ History and Life* 12 (August 1989): 101–104 and 14 (April 1991): 48–74.

E. Morris Sider

Brückner, Gottlob (1783–1857), missionary in Java with the London Missionary Society (LMS) and Baptist Missionary Society (BMS). Brückner was born in Upper Lusatia and studied in Berlin and Rotterdam with a view to service with the Netherlands Missionary Society. When war in Europe thwarted this objective, he went to England and applied to the LMS. After further studies at David *Bogue's Gosport seminary, Brückner (with J.C. *Kam and Joseph Supper) was sent in 1813 to initiate an LMS mission in Java. Brückner settled at Semarang, on the north coast. Through contact with a BMS missionary, Thomas Trowt, he became convinced of Baptist principles, and in 1817 he was accepted by the BMS. Although his evangelistic work saw little success, Brückner completed a translation of the New Testament into Javanese, which he took to Serampore where it was printed by the mission press between 1828 and 1831. Brückner then returned to Semarang, where he spent the rest of his life. The BMS, short of funds and unimpressed by the meager results of Brückner's church planting efforts, withdrew its support in 1847. Nevertheless, Brückner's work prompted the Netherlands Missionary Society to expand its work in Java, and Dutch missionaries used his translation as a basis for a revised Javanese New Testament.

BIBLIOGRAPHY Ernest A. Payne, *South-East from Serampore: More Chapters in the Story of the Baptist Missionary Society* (1945).

Brian Stanley

Bruillard, Philippe de (1763–1860), founder of the Missionaries of Our Lady of La Salette. Born in Dijon, France, De Bruillard went to the Saint Sulpice seminary in Paris and was ordained to the priesthood in 1789. He was priest of the Saint Étienne-du-Mont parish in Paris in 1821. Consecrated bishop of Grenoble, France, in 1826, he paid special attention to religious education and published several diocesan catechisms in 1836 and 1837. Then two young shepherds, Maximin Giraud (10 years old) and Mélanie Calvat (15), said they had seen an apparition of the Virgin Mary on September 9, 1846, on the mountain of La Salette, county of Corps, France, in his diocese. In 1851 he finally authenticated the vision and set about to implement its message: submission to the authority of God and the church, with the promise of Mary's intercession for sinful humankind. In 1852 he founded a society of priests caring for the pilgrims on the apparition site in summer and preaching in the parishes in winter. The society became a religious institute in 1858 and was approved by the pope in 1890. Its foreign missionary outreach began in 1879 in Norway. It promotes a spirituality of reconciliation and provides for pastoral, social, and educational needs.

BIBLIOGRAPHY J. Jaouen, *La grâce de La Salette au regard de l'Église* (1964); J. S. Kennedy, *Light on the Mountain* (1953); J. P. O'Reilly, *The Story of La Salette* (1953).

Marc R. Spindler

Brun(o) of Querfurt (c. 974/978–1009), Benedictine missionary bishop and martyr in Poland. A descendant of Saxon nobility, Brun opted for monasticism instead of a career as court chaplain to Emperor Otto III. He decided to continue the work of *Adalbert of Prague in northern Poland and was appointed missionary archbishop by the pope. After several abortive beginnings, mainly because of political tensions in the area, he reached his destination but was martyred instantly by pagan Prussians, just as his friend and model, Adalbert, had been before him. Unlike other contemporary missionaries, Brun insisted on peaceful mission efforts among pagans while tolerating violent means, if necessary, in order to regain apostates.

BIBLIOGRAPHY Hans-Dietrich Kahl, *Compellere intrare* (1955); Gisbert Voigt, *Brun von Querfurt* (1907); Reinhard Wenskus, *Studien zur historisch-politischen Gedankenwelt Bruns von Querfurt* (1956).

Hans-Werner Gensichen

Brunton, Henry (c. 1770–1813), Scottish missionary in Guinea, West Africa, and Caucasus. Brunton worked with the Edinburgh Missionary Society among the Susu on the Rio Pongas (in modern Guinea) in 1798 and 1799. Returning to Edinburgh because of ill-health, he produced for the Church Missionary Society (CMS) a series of booklets on the Susu language, one of which included a discussion of mission strategy in relation to semi-Islamized peoples. Although never in fact used in the mission field, these were pioneering works in both Susu and African linguistics; and as such they had later intellectual influence. In 1802 he and his family traveled to Russia and established a mission station at Karass among the Nogay Tatar, where his colleagues were several Scotsmen and a Susu youth. Concentrating on linguistic work, he printed material in Tatar. Despite its being located in a region of Russian imperial advance and desultory warfare, the mission operated until the 1820s, at a site still known as Shotlandka (Little Scotland). Shortly before his death Brunton fell into disgrace, apparently because of drunkenness.

BIBLIOGRAPHY W. Brown, *History of the Propagation of Christianity* (1823); P. E. H. Hair, "Susu Studies...1799–1900," *Sierra Leone Language Review* 4 (1965): 38–53, and "A Scottish Missionary in the Caucasus," *Scottish Institute of Missionary Studies Bulletin* 13 (1973): 28–30; Charles Hole, *Early History of the CMS* (1896); M. V. Jones, "The Sad Story... of Karass," *Oxford Slavonic Papers* 8 (1975): 53–81.

P. E. H. Hair

Bucer, Martin (1491–1555), pioneer of the Lutheran cause in Alsace. While still a Dominican monk, Bucer was won for the Reformation when attending Luther's Heidelberg disputation in 1518. With other reformers he shared a theocentric concept of mission: God's will to save all people breaks forth in the intrinsic power of the gospel. The mission is God's and not ours. But as faith is "a living, restless thing" (Luther), all Christian people are called to be witnesses to God's saving grace. Consequently Bucer first reflected on the progress of God's kingdom in history as it dawned in the era of Old Testament patriarchs, reached a first climax in Christ, and continued by means of the church and its universal witness toward ultimate fulfillment in Christ's parousia. Bucer did not attempt to reconcile his view of God's universal saving will with the doctrine of double predestination which he shared with Calvin. He located the call to mission in the context of pastoral care. Not only the individual Christian and the Christian community, but Christian rulers as well are committed to make sure that even their non-Christian subjects find opportunities to save their souls.

BIBLIOGRAPHY Hastings Eells, *Martin Bucer* (1931); Wilhelm Pauck, *Das Reich Gottes auf Erden* (1928); Thomas Forsyth Torrance, *Kingdom and Church* (1956), pp. 73 ff.

Hans-Werner Gensichen

Buchan, Jane (1837–1904), teacher, publisher, and mission society administrator. Born in Paris, Upper Canada (modern Ontario), Jane Buchan committed herself to Christian service during an early period of residence in Toronto (1850–1851), where she was baptized into the membership of Bond Street Baptist Church. Settling permanently in Toronto in 1866, she taught Sunday school and, in 1876, helped create the Women's Baptist Foreign Missionary Society (WBFMS) of Ontario West. Two years later, she and her sister, Margaret, launched a periodical, the *Canadian Missionary Link*. Under Jane Buchan's able administration, it soon had 5,000 subscribers. In 1886 the WBFMS named her corresponding secretary, a position she held until her death. By then, Baptist women of Ontario supported fourteen women missionaries in India and Bolivia. Buchan provided services essential to their ministry. They valued her support and named a unit after her at the Vuyyuru hospital in present-day Andhra Pradesh. In addition to her Sunday school and mission work, Jane Buchan was secretary of the Toronto branch of the YWCA for 20 years.

BIBLIOGRAPHY Jane Buchan's reports as corresponding secretary of the WBFMS appear in *Canadian Missionary Link*. See also Alfreda Hall, *Wheels Begin to Turn: The Baptist Women's Missionary Society of Ontario and Quebec* (1976); Mary Quayle Innis, *Unfold the Years: A History of the Young Women's Christian Association in Canada* (1949).

Paul R. Dekar

Buchanan, Claudius (1766–1815), pioneer Anglican in India. Born in Cambuslang, Scotland, Buchanan was converted in London under John *Newton and became an Anglican. He went to Cambridge and upon graduation was appointed a chaplain to the East India Company. He arrived at Calcutta in 1797 as junior chaplain to David *Brown and set about learning Indian languages. Under Lord Wellesley, Buchanan played a key role in the founding of Fort William College, serving as vice-provost from 1800 to 1806. In addition to providing training for East India Company civil servants, Buchanan and Brown wanted the college to sponsor translations of the Bible into many languages. They soon enlisted William *Carey, from nearby Serampore, as a collaborator. Buchanan's great concern was to see India opened to missionary work. As part of his strategy, he drafted a plan for setting up a full-scale ecclesiastical establishment in India. At the same time he recognized the importance of mobilizing public opinion in support of changing the East India Company charter to allow missionaries to enter India. He instituted in British universities prize essays on Christian missions (1803–1805), which resulted in some notable publications. He believed credible publicity required careful attention to facts, and despite poor health, he undertook an arduous journey (1806–1808) to investigate conditions in South India and Sri Lanka. His findings were published as *Christian Researches in Asia* (1811), a work often reprinted. In 1808 he returned to Great Britain to recuperate and to help in the campaign to open India to Christian missions by speaking and writing. He received honorary D.D. degrees from Glasgow, Aberdeen, St. Andrews, Dublin, and Cambridge universities in recognition of his distinguished service in promoting Bible translation and as a publicist. He died at age 49 in Yorkshire.

BIBLIOGRAPHY Claudius Buchanan, *The Works of the Rev. Claudius Buchanan, L.L.D....* (1812). Allan K. Davidson, *Evangel-*

icals and Attitudes to India, 1786–1813 (1990); Hugh N. Pearson, *Memoirs of the Life and Writings of the Rev. Claudius Buchanan, D.D.*, 2 vols. (1817); Wilbert R. Shenk, "Claudius Buchanan," in Gerald H. Anderson et al., eds., *Mission Legacies* (1994), pp. 255–263.

Wilbert R. Shenk

Buchmann, Theodor. *See* Bibliander, Theodor.

Buchner, Charles (1847–1907), Moravian mission administrator. Buchner was born at Irwinhill, Jamaica, where his parents served the Moravian mission. He was educated in Moravian schools at Kleinwelka and Gnadenfeld, Germany, and served the former as an instructor before ordination and pastoral service at Gnadenfrei, Silesia, from 1870. In 1874 he was called as pastor at Hausfeld, Silesia, and married Anne Elizabeth Rhein at Königsfeld. In 1879 he was appointed director of the Normal School at Niesky and in 1889 was first elected to the mission board of the Moravian Unity. In 1892 he was consecrated bishop before an official visit to the missions in South Africa and from 1896 served as president of the mission board. Official visitations included North America in 1895 and Surinam in 1898 and 1902.

An acknowledged mission authority in Europe, Buchner was elected chairman of the German Evangelical Missionary Union in 1905. The next year he was forced into retirement because of failing health and died at Herrnhut.

BIBLIOGRAPHY Benjamin LaTrobe, "Memoir of Charles Buchner," *Moravian* (1907); *Zum Gedächtnis am 2 Januar 1907 in Herrnhut entschafen Bruders Charles Buchner* (1907).

Albert H. Frank

Buck, Pearl S(ydenstricker) (1892–1973), missionary in China and Nobel Prize winner in literature. Born in Hillsboro, West Virginia, Pearl Sydenstricker was raised in China by her parents, who were missionaries with the (Southern) Presbyterian Church in the U.S. She graduated from Randolph-Macon Woman's College in Virginia and returned to China as an educational missionary, mainly in Nanking. In 1917 she married John Lossing Buck, an agricultural missionary from the Presbyterian Church, U.S.A., whom she later divorced. In 1932 she received the Pulitzer Prize for *The Good Earth* (1931), a novel that described the difficult life of a Chinese peasant couple. In that same year she published a controversial pamphlet, *Is There a Case for Foreign Missions?* and an article in *Christian Century* that praised the report of the Laymen's Foreign Missions Inquiry. Her emphasis on social service instead of evangelism and her criticism of missionary personnel in China sparked conservatives to demand her dismissal from the Presbyterian Board of Foreign Missions, leading to her resignation in 1933. *Fighting Angel* and *The Exile*, both published in 1936, recount the lives of her missionary parents, Absalom and Carrie Sydenstricker. The biographies contributed significantly to the Nobel Prize in literature that Buck was awarded in 1938. Many of her novels about life in China include missionary characters.

BIBLIOGRAPHY Buck's autobiographies are *My Several Worlds* (1954) and *A Bridge for Passing* (1962). The authorized biography is Theodore F. Harris, *Pearl S. Buck* (1969). See also Peter J. Conn, *Pearl S. Buck: A Cultural Biography* (1996) and Nora Stirling, *Pearl Buck: A Woman in Conflict* (1983). On the role of missionaries in her writings, see Charles Silver, "Pearl Buck, Evangelism and Works of Love: Images of the Missionary in Fiction," *Journal of Presbyterian History* 51 (1973): 216–234.

James A. Patterson

Buglio, Lodovico (1606–1682), Jesuit missionary in China. A native of Mineo, Sicily, Buglio entered the Society of Jesus in Palermo in 1622. After completing studies at the Roman College (the Jesuit college in Rome), he was granted permission in 1634 to leave for Macao, which he reached in 1636. By 1639 he was in Kiangnan (area of present-day Anhui and Jiangsu Provinces), where he baptized nearly 700 adults. The following year he became the first European to enter Chengtu (Chengdu), Szechwan (Sichuan) Province, where he established a thriving mission. With the assistance of Gabriel de Magalhães (1610–1677), who joined him in 1642, he expanded the mission to other cities in Szechwan. Buglio and Magalhães reluctantly became astronomers at the court of a Chinese rebel, Zhang Xianzhong, who declared himself prince of the area in late 1644. But Haoge, a Manchu prince, seized the province in 1647 and brought them to Peking (Beijing), where four years later both were freed. There, with imperial permission, they built the Dongtang (East Church). During the persecution of 1665 to 1670, which involved the Chinese rejection of Western methods of astronomy at court, Buglio wrote a reply to charges leveled against Christianity. He composed nearly two dozen works in Chinese and also translated a large part of the Roman Breviary and the *Summa Theologiae* of Thomas Aquinas. His tombstone in Beijing was restored in 1987.

BIBLIOGRAPHY Giuliano Bertuccioli, "Ludovico Buglio," in *Scienziati siciliani gesuiti in Cina nel secolo XVII* (1985), pp. 121–146; "Lodovico Buglio," in Louis Pfister, *Notices biographiques et bibliographiques sur les Jésuites de l'ancienne mission de Chine* (1932–1934; repr. 1971 and 1975), pp. 230–243 (with an annotated list of Buglio's Chinese works).

John W. Witek, SJ

Bühlmann, Walbert (1916–), Swiss Capuchin missionary, missiologist, and theologian. Bühlmann earned his doctorate at the University of Fribourg, Switzerland, writing a thesis on "Christian Terminology as a Missionary Problem in the Bantu Languages." He worked as a missionary in Tanzania (1950–1953), taught missiology at Fribourg, and served for many years in Rome as the secretary general of the Capuchin missions. Since 1983 he has resided in the Capuchin friary in Arth, Switzerland. His influence has come mainly from his writings. His most important book is *The Coming of the Third Church* (1976), in which he predicted that by the year 2000, some 70 percent of all Catholics would be living in the Southern Hemisphere. Drawing on the teachings of Vatican Council II, the theology of Karl Rahner, and the vitality of local churches in Latin America, Africa, and Asia, Bühlmann argued that the missionary dynamism of the church must be rooted in a greater respect for cultural pluralism within the church, a commitment to dialogue with the great non-Christian religious traditions, and an effective advocacy for "integral liberation." His subsequent works have continued to draw upon these themes. Thus he has emerged as a strong critic of Eurocentrism and administrative centralization within the church, as well as a vigorous advocate of the inclusiveness of salvation offered by Christ.

Bühlmann has also contributed to the renewal of the Franciscan missionary tradition through his careful study of the missionary experience of St. Francis of Assisi and Chapter 16 of the Franciscan Rule of 1221. In this tradition he discerns the enduring importance of fraternal life as a form of Christian witness, the challenge of solidarity with the poor, and the attractiveness of Francis of Assisi as focus of interreligious dialogue.

BIBLIOGRAPHY Walbert Bühlmann, *Courage, Church* (1978), *The Missions on Trial* (1979), *All Have the Same God* (1980; 1988), *The Chosen Peoples* (1982), *Build Up My Church: Franciscan Inspirations for and from the Third World* (1984), *The Church of the Future* (1986), "My Pilgrimage in Mission," *IBMR* 10 (1986): 104-105, *Dreaming about the Church: Acts of the Apostles of the Twentieth Century* (1987), and *With Eyes to See: Church and World in the Third Millennium* (1990). James Joseph Ferguson, "Salvation and the Mission of the Church: A Comparative Study of the Writings of André Seumois and Walbert Buehlmann" (Ph.D. diss., Catholic Univ. of America, 1983).

William E. McConville, OFM

Builes, Miguel Angel (1888-1971), founder of the Yarumal Missionary Seminary in Colombia. Builes was born at Donmatías, Colombia. He attended seminary, was ordained in 1914, and in 1924 was ordained bishop of Santa Rosa de Osas. In his pastoral letters he endorsed the Mission Aid Society. In 1927, after careful planning, he founded the first missionary society in Latin America, the Xaverian Missionaries of Yarumal, in charge of the missions of Arauca, Buenaventura, Istmina, and Mitú; it received papal approval in 1939. In 1929 he next founded the Missionary Sisters of Saint Theresa of the Child Jesus for the education of youth and care of the sick. The congregation, which received papal approval in 1964, numbered 453 members in 1977 in Colombia, Ecuador, and Venezuela. The Contemplative Missionary Sisters, founded by Builes in 1939, however, ceased to exist in 1968. Then in 1951 he founded a third congregation of sisters, the Daughters of our Lady of Mercy, which counted eighty professed sisters and twenty novices in 1975. They give catechetical instruction in schools and do social work in Colombia and Ecuador.

BIBLIOGRAPHY Miguel Angel Builes, "Conferencia misional," *Revista Seminario de Misiones,* no. 61 (1956): 12-19, "IMEY: Instituto de Misiones Extranjeras de Yarumal," *Semisiones,* no. 98 (1962): 7-14, and "Mi testamento espiritual: Dedicado a todos los hijos y hijas religiosos que Díos me dió (1959)," *Vinculum,* no. 100 (1971): 40-42. María Dolly Olano García, *Monseñor Builes, el hombre, el apostól el místico* (1978); Jaime Sanin Echeverri, *El Obispo Builes* (1988); Gustavo Vélez Vásquez, *Miguel Angel Obispo* (1988).

Willi Henkel, OMI

Buker, Raymond Bates, Sr. (1899-1992), Baptist missionary in Burma (Myanmar) and mission administrator. Born in Foster, Rhode Island, Buker graduated from Bates College in Maine. Two years after competing in the 1924 Olympics in Paris (where he met Eric *Liddell), Buker and his family joined his twin brother and medical missionary, Richard, as missionaries to tribal people along the Burma/China border, serving with the Northern Baptist Foreign Mission Society. Escaping just ahead of the advancing Japanese army, the Bukers returned to the United States in 1942. In 1944 they were appointed by the newly formed Conservative Baptist Foreign Mission Society (now CBInternational) and Buker was asked to become the mission's first foreign secretary. In this role he profoundly influenced the shaping of the society's field policies, operational principles, and philosophy of ministry, drawing heavily on his own experiences as a pioneer missionary in Burma. In 1956 he resigned from CBFMS to become the first professor of missions at the Conservative Baptist Theological Seminary (now Denver Seminary) in Denver, Colorado, serving in this role until retirement in 1967. He was then asked to serve as coordinator for the Committee to Assist Ministry Education Overseas (CAMEO), a joint project of the Evangelical Foreign Missions Association (now Evangelical Fellowship of Mission Agencies) and the Interdenominational Foreign Mission Association, a post he held until 1974.

BIBLIOGRAPHY Eric S. Fife, *Against the Clock: The Story of Ray Buker, Sr., Olympic Runner and Missionary Statesman* (1981).

A. Leonard Tuggy

Bulck, Gaaston (*or* Vaast) van (1903-1966), Belgian Jesuit ethnographer, linguist, historian, and missiologist. After joining the Society of Jesus upon completion of secondary school, Van Bulck pursued philosophy, linguistics, ethnography, and phonetics at the Sorbonne and in Brussels, followed by ethnology and African linguistics in Vienna, where he received his doctorate. After two years traveling in western and central Africa, he returned to Belgium to study theology prior to his ordination. He was subsequently appointed to the Gregorian Pontifical University, occupying the multi-discipline chair of history of religions, anthropology, ethnography, and ethnology. The outbreak of World War II found him studying Bantu linguistic problems in Africa, and he was sent to Kwango in present-day Zaire to conduct research, particularly among the Yaka, and to teach until he could return to Rome. He returned to Africa in 1950 as part of an international team studying the languages and dialects on the border between the Sudanic and Bantu groups. His area was the region from northwestern Belgian Congo to Juba in the Sudan. In 1951 he became chairman of the Institut

Africain of the University of Louvain, where he taught until 1965, all the while continuing his teaching duties in Rome.

BIBLIOGRAPHY Gaaston Van Bulck, "Cinq nouvelles classifications des langues bantoues," *Zaire, revue congolaise* (1948), *Manuel de linguistique Bantoue* (1949), *Les deux cartes linguistiques du Congo belge* (1952), *Autour du probleme missionnaire: études de missiologie de 1932 a 1957* (1960). Wilma Meier, ed., *Bibliographie afrikanischer Sprachen* (1984; contains a language-related bibliography). Obituary, *Africa* 37 (1967).

Philip C. Stine

Bulmer, John (1833–1913), missionary among Australian Aborigines. Arriving in Victoria State from England in 1852, Bulmer was appalled at the unjust treatment of the Aborigines. Despite concern about his Methodist background, in 1855 the Church of England appointed him to its new Yelta mission in northwestern Victoria, near the junction of the Murray and Darling Rivers. He married Caroline Blay in 1862, and relocating to the eastern coast of Victoria, they founded the Church of England's Lake Tyers mission. By 1863 several important Aboriginal leaders had become Christians. Stressing efficiency and self-sufficiency, Bulmer created a typical nineteenth-century mission compound: neat rows of huts, schoolhouse, mission house, farm, and church of St. John. The Bulmers ran Lake Tyers paternalistically through good and bad times. Bulmer was finally ordained in the Church of England in 1903. The government sent Aborigines to Lake Tyers from elsewhere, creating tensions in the mission. Bulmer became an outspoken critic of government policy, particularly the forced removal of people under the so-called Aborigines' Protection Act. The government, however, took over Lake Tyers in 1907, reluctantly permitting Bulmer to exercise religious duties. At his death, he had spent 51 years there.

BIBLIOGRAPHY John Harris, *One Blood* (1990). The John Bulmer papers are held in the state museum of Victoria.

John W. Harris

Bulu, Joeli (c. 1810–1877), Tongan missionary in Fiji. Bulu was converted to Christianity during the Tongan revival of 1834. Four years later he joined a party of Christian teachers sent by the future king of Tonga to help the new Methodist mission in Fiji. His first work was on Ono-i-lau Island, where he was ordained and stayed eight years. Other postings followed, including three years (1863–1866) as principal of the catechist training college. After his Tongan wife's death, he married a Fijian and became a fully integrated and widely influential member of the Fijian church. He received a high appointment in that church when he was made the chaplain to the high chief Thakombau. He encouraged Fijians to continue the work he had begun by engaging in foreign missions. He spent his later years on the royal island of Bau and died there, universally loved and honored. He was one of the most widely known of Pacific island missionaries.

BIBLIOGRAPHY Joeli Bulu, *The Autobiography of a Native Minister in the South Seas, translated by a Missionary* (1871); John Garrett, *To Live among the Stars: Christian Origins in Oceania* (1982).

Charles W. Forman

Buntain, D(aniel) Mark (1923–1989), missionary in India. Born in Winnipeg, Manitoba, Canada, Buntain was the son of Daniel N. Buntain, a prominent Pentecostal leader. After beginning evangelistic and pastoral work, he married Huldah Munroe (1926–) in 1944. In the same year, he authored a biography of his father entitled *Why He Is a Pentecostal Preacher* (1944). Later, after moving to the United States, the Buntains received appointment as Assemblies of God missionaries to India in 1954.

Buntain's early ministry in Calcutta focused on evangelism and pastoring. Touched by the pain of the starving people, he committed himself to gospel proclamation and social concern. Through the Assembly of God Church in Calcutta, which he pastored, and fund-raising in the United States (under the auspices of Calcutta Mission of Mercy), a variety of ministries emerged: church planting; West Bengal Bible College; private schools; Teachers' Training Junior College; Assembly of God Hospital and Research Centre; Assembly of God School of Nursing; a feeding program, and many others. These projects and activities are highlighted in the publication *The Cry of Calcutta.*

In recognition of his contributions to the people of Calcutta, the University of Missouri-Columbia conferred an honorary Doctor of Humane Letters on Buntain in 1984. After his death, his wife, Huldah Buntain, became senior pastor of the church and director of the work.

BIBLIOGRAPHY Huldah Buntain, *Treasures in Heaven* (1989); Ron Hembree, *Mark* (1979); Amitabh Singh, "Calcutta Assemblies of God Mission: Its Origin and Development, with Special Reference to the Contribution of Rev. (Dr.) D. Mark Buntain" (B.D. thesis, Southern Asia Bible College, Kothanur, Bangalore, India, 1992).

Gary B. McGee

Burgess, Paul (1886–1958), American Presbyterian missionary in Guatemala. Born in Lisle, New York, Burgess and his wife Dora (McLaughlin) served in Quetzaltenango, Guatemala, from 1913 to 1958. A tireless evangelist and organizer, he started sixteen churches and multiple preaching points among Indian and Ladino populations. Speaking six languages besides English, he challenged the conventional wisdom of his day by advocating that tribal people should be reached in their own language rather than Spanish. In 1935, together with L. L. Legters, Cameron *Townsend, and others, he founded the Latin America Indian Mission, predecessor to the Wycliffe Bible Translators. He prepared an elementary grammar of the Quiché language and collaborated in translating the New Testament into that language; he also founded the Quiché Bible Institute, and established an evangelical publishing house and Christian bookstore. His visionary leadership, innovative strategy, identification with the Quiché Indians, and unwearying witness among all social classes created an openness to Protestant Christianity that quite probably laid the foundation for the exceptionally rapid Protestant expansion in Guatemala. A prolific writer, he initiated and edited numerous periodicals and authored over 400 articles and 17 books. His biography of Justo Rufino Barrios, considered Guatemala's greatest president, was widely acclaimed.

BIBLIOGRAPHY Paul Burgess, *Los veinte siglos del cristianismo* (1918), *Justo Rufino Barrios: A Biography* (1926), and *Historia de la obra evangélica presbiteriana en Guatemala* (1957). Anna Marie Dahlquist, *Burgess of Guatemala* (1985; contains an extensive bibliography) and *Trailblazers for Translators: The Chichicastenango Twelve* (1995).

Kenneth B. Mulholland

Burns, William Chalmers (1815–1868), Scottish Presbyterian missionary in China. Born at Duns, Scotland, a son of the manse, Burns studied at Aberdeen and Glasgow and was a leading figure in a revival movement that swept across Scotland and beyond in the decade before the 1843 Disruption of the Church of Scotland. He joined the newly established Free Church of Scotland, which had close ties with the reconstituted Presbyterian Church in England (PCE). In 1847, at Sunderland, England, he was appointed to work in China as the first missionary of the PCE. Such was his reputation as an evangelist that the PCE foreign missions committee allowed him full freedom to develop its work there. He always stressed his calling as an evangelist, but in contrast to the great success he had known at home, he labored for many years in the areas of Canton (Guangzhou), Amoy (Xiamen), Shanghai, Swatow (Shantou), and Foochow (Fuzhou) before any results became apparent. When they did, first at Pehchuia (Baichuan) in south Fukien (Fujian), he was content to leave the work of nurturing to others while he moved on, never daunted by the need to learn another Chinese language. His desire to protect the religious freedom of Chinese Christians, in accordance with the 1860 treaty, took him to Peking (Beijing), and from there he moved on to Newchang (Yingkou), where he died.

The Presbyterian Church in Ireland began its mission in Manchuria in response to his appeal for others to continue his work there. Known as "The man of the Book," he also translated Bunyan's *Pilgrim's Progress,* wrote and translated hymns, and published a Chinese metrical version of the Psalms. He was an inspiration to his colleagues within the English Presbyterian mission, and his spiritual gifts, to which Hudson *Taylor among many others bore personal testimony, were recognized throughout the missionary community in China.

BIBLIOGRAPHY Islay Burns, *Memoir of the Rev. Wm. C. Burns* (1869; rev. 1885); Austin Fulton, *Through Earthquake, Wind and Fire: Church and Mission in Manchuria, 1867–1950* (1967); George A. Hood, *Mission Accomplished? The English Presbyterian Mission in Lingtung, South China* (1986); R. Strang Miller et al., *Five Pioneer Missionaries* (1965, 1993).

George A. Hood

Burton, John Wear (1875–1970), missionary and social reformer in Fiji, champion of Pacific island missions. Born in England and educated in New Zealand, Burton was sent to Fiji in 1902 by the Australasian Methodist mission. He worked among the indentured laborers from India and became critical of the system of indenture. He expressed his views in his book *The Fiji of Today* (1910), which caught the attention of the leaders of India, including Gandhi. This led to investigation and eventual abolition of the indenture system. Burton was attacked by mill owners who imported Indian labor. The Colonial Sugar Refining Company, the principal economic power in the land, demanded that he withdraw his charges; but the head of the mission replied that they would be withdrawn only if disproved.

In 1912 Burton left Fiji because of his wife's health. Later, from 1925 to 1945, he was general secretary of the Australian Methodist overseas missions. In this post he represented a social and humanitarian type of Christianity, but he also pressed for more evangelism among Fiji's Indians. Through his writings he became the world's chief spokesperson for Pacific island missions. From 1945 to 1948 he was president general of the Methodist Church of Australasia, a position to which he would have been elected earlier had it not been for his uncompromising pacifism.

BIBLIOGRAPHY John Wear Burton, *A Missionary Survey of the Pacific Islands* (1930) and *Modern Missions in the South Pacific* (1949). A. Harold Wood, *Overseas Missions of the Australian Methodist Church,* vol. 3 (1978). Also see *Australian Dictionary of Biography,* vol. 7 (1979).

Charles W. Forman

Burton, William Frederick Padwick (1886–1971), missionary to Africa. Born in Liverpool and trained as an engineer, Burton was converted in 1905 and later attended the Bible school of the Pentecostal Missionary Union at Preston, England. Leaving Britain in 1914 for Johannesburg, he was joined there by James Salter, Joseph Blakeney, and George Armstrong; they traveled north to the Belgian Congo to begin mission work among the Baluba people at Mwanza, arriving in 1915.

Disagreement with leaders of the Pentecostal Missionary Union in England led Burton and the others to affiliate with the Pentecostal Mission in South and Central Africa, which was incorporated in the Transvaal (with American headquarters in Newark, New Jersey). By 1919, however, their activities had expanded to such an extent that Burton and Salter founded the Congo (now Zaire) Evangelistic Mission. Support and personnel came largely from Elim Pentecostal congregations in England, the British Assemblies of God, and various independent churches.

During World War I, Burton returned to South Africa in 1918 to recruit new workers, one of whom, Hettie Trollip, he married. Serving as field director in the Congo until 1954, he superintended the growing number of missionaries, evangelism and church planting, and the training of pastors and church leaders. Today, the legacy of these labors is found in the Pentecostal Church of Zaire.

A courageous traveler and evangelist, Burton successfully challenged the dreaded Bambudye Secret Society, breaking its hold on the people to whom he ministered, and evangelized the cannibal villages in the Luvidyo Valley, which subsequently became law abiding and safe for travelers. His talents and accomplishments were many. He was a skilled artist, whose works gained recognition from the South African Academy in Johannesburg; his sketches of landscapes and village life are found in his *Congo Sketches* (1950). He collected Congo fables and proverbs and wrote extensively on tribal culture; he also published a study of the Luba religion, *L'ame Luba* (Éditions de la Revue Juridique du Congo Belge, 1939). He wrote twenty-eight books during his lifetime, including *God Working with Them* (1933), *When God Makes a Pastor* (1934), and *How They Live in Congoland* (1938). He left the Congo in 1960 and died in South Africa.

BIBLIOGRAPHY Max Wood Moorhead, *Missionary Pioneering in the Congo Forests* (1922); Colin C. Whittaker, *Seven Pentecostal Pioneers* (1983); Harold Womersley, *W. F. P. Burton: Congo Pioneer* (1973).

Gary B. McGee

Buss, Ernst (1843–1928), missiologist of theological liberalism. Buss was a Swiss Reformed pastor who, with no missionary experience of his own, made a reputation for himself by producing what amounted to the first comprehensive draft plan of an up-to-date missionary enterprise, conceived on the basis of contemporary liberal Christian thought. First came his book *Die christliche Mission* (1876), with its severely critical review of the missionary enterprise. While Buss was able to draw on the notorious catalogue of the failures of pietist missions produced by his Swiss contemporary E. F. Langhans in 1865, he took care to offer a workable alternative. This he developed by basing mission on the "religion of Jesus," not as a means to convert heathen to what Buss condemned as "dogmatic" Christianity but as an effort to upgrade non-Christian religions and their adherents to a "Christian humane culture" in which the true values of other religions would be preserved. Next came the Evangelical Protestant Missionary Association, founded in 1884, which developed a remarkable style of Christian presence in China and Japan and enjoyed the support of renowned scholars of religion and liberal Christianity. In 1929 it became the East Asia Mission, Swiss and German respectively, and changed its character in order to overcome what critics described as its "theological homelessness." Buss's programmatic book had meanwhile fallen into oblivion, probably not least because—as Gustav *Warneck remarked even in the year of its appearance—Buss's new proposals were "either new but impracticable or practicable but not new" (*AMZ* 3 [1876]: 434).

BIBLIOGRAPHY Ferdinand Hahn, "Das theologische Programm von Ernst Buss," in Ferdinand Hahn et al., eds., *Spuren..., Festschrift zum hundertjährigen Bestehen der Ostasien-Mission* (1984), pp. 10–18.

Hans-Werner Gensichen

Butler, Elizur (1794–1857), medical missionary to the Cherokee Indians. Born in Connecticut, Butler received a commission from the American Board of Commissioners for Foreign Missions to provide medical service at Brainerd Mission, a site in northen Georgia where he began work in 1821. He served there until 1824 and was then stationed at Haweis Mission until 1831. His emphasis on hygiene as part of civilized habits was particularly welcome among the Cherokee people, who were as interested in aspects of Anglo culture as they were in religious ideas and practices. By 1831, however, the missionaries were confronted with a law requiring whites to take an oath of loyalty to the state of Georgia before receiving permission to live among the Indians. Congregationalist, Moravian, and Methodist evangelists refused to comply, and they were arrested in July of that year. Along with others, Butler was chained and imprisoned, mistreated physically and psychologically. Two months later, he was sentenced to four years of hard labor. After he and co-worker Samuel A. *Worcester spent more than 16 months in prison, they were released early in 1833. Butler resumed his practical ministrations the following year. He had proved his dedication to missionary endeavors and loyalty to this one tribe of Native Americans. He became an ordained minister in 1838 and continued to labor effectively among people who trusted him. When the Cherokees were forcibly relocated to reservations in Indian Territory (now Oklahoma), he accompanied his charges during their time of uprooting and great tribulations. Once accommodated to new surroundings, the Cherokees established Fairfield Mission and Park Hill Mission under Butler's guidance. There he labored for the rest of his life, serving notably as steward of the Cherokee Female Seminary at Park Hill.

BIBLIOGRAPHY Bibliographic sources for Butler's life are focused on his years in Georgia: W. J. McLoughlin, "Civil Disobedience and Evangelism among the Missionaries to the Cherokees, 1829–1839," *Journal of Presbyterian History* 51 (1973): 116–139; R. S. Walker, *Torchlights to the Cherokees: The Brainerd Mission* (1931).

Henry Warner Bowden

Butler, Fanny Jane (1850–1889), first English missionary woman doctor. Born and brought up in London the eighth of ten children, Butler had most of her education at home. When in 1872 she felt a vocation toward medical mission work, she had to embark on intensive study to gain entrance to medical training. This she did and in 1874 became the first woman to enroll in the London-based School of Medicine for Women. She qualified in 1880, and later in the same year, at 30 years of age, sailed for India under the Church of England Zenana Missionary Society. She worked for several years in the Bengal area, notably in Bihar, and in her vacations traveled in the Punjab, surveying the work of other mission hospitals. After a furlough in 1887, she asked to be transferred to Kashmir, where Arthur and Ernest Neve were carrying on the medical work started by William *Elmslie in Srinagar. The evangelistic and hospital outreach in Kashmir was shared by several societies, and she worked happily there with the Church Missionary Society. Her medical experience with

Hindu women was invaluable, but she soon died at her post. It was to be many years before another female doctor worked in Srinagar.

BIBLIOGRAPHY E. M. Tonge, *Fanny Jane Butler, Pioneer Medical Missionary* (n.d.).

Jocelyn Murray

Butler, William (1818–1899) *and* **Clementina (Rowe)** (1820–1913), founders of American Methodist missions in India and Mexico. The Butlers were probably the best-known Methodist missionary couple in the late nineteenth century. Born in Ireland, William Butler underwent a conversion experience, joined the Wesleyan church, and became a minister. He immigrated to the U.S. in 1850. After being twice widowed, he wrote to Clementina Rowe in Ireland, who had been influenced by his preaching some years before. Clementina crossed the ocean and they married in 1854.

In 1856 the Butlers sailed to India as founders of American Methodist work. After their arrival, the Sepoy Mutiny broke out and they fled to the mountains, where they remained under siege for eight months. After the uprising was crushed, they opened orphanages for children left homeless by the rebellion. In 1865, after putting the church on a firm footing, the Butlers returned to the United States, where they vigorously promoted foreign missions. Clementina spoke to groups of Congregational and Methodist women about the needs of women in India. In response, women in both denominations founded women's missionary societies to support single women missionaries. Clementina was a founder of the Woman's Foreign Missionary Society of the Methodist Episcopal Church and served over the years as an officer and recruiter.

As secretary of the American and Foreign Christian Union, an organization devoted to missions in "papal lands," William was deemed the best person to found Methodist work in Mexico in 1873. As they had done in India, the Butlers established a printing press, schools, a girls' orphanage, and church buildings. William wrote *The Land of the Veda* (1871), *From Boston to Bareilly and Back* (1886), and *Mexico in Transition* (1892). Clementina established the Zenana Paper Fund that published Christian women's literature in five vernaculars.

Two children continued the work of their parents. John W. Butler spent 44 years in Mexico as a Methodist missionary. Their daughter, Clementina Butler, wrote mission books for women, was secretary of the American Ramabai Association, and founded in 1912 the Committee on Christian Literature for Women and Children in Mission Fields.

BIBLIOGRAPHY Clementina Butler, *William Butler: The Founder of Two Missions* (1902) and *Mrs. William Butler: Two Empires and the Kingdom* (1929). On William Butler, see Charles C. Creegan and Josephine Goodnow, *Great Missionaries of the Church* (1895); D. V. Singh, "Social Activities of the Methodist Episcopal Church in India in the Nineteenth Century," *Indian Church History Review* 5 (1971): 133–152. John Butler wrote *The History of the Methodist Episcopal Church in Mexico* (1918), *Mexico Coming into Light* (1907), and *Sketches of Mexico* (1894).

Dana L. Robert

Buxton, Alfred (1891–1940), missionary in Belgian Congo (Zaire) and Ethiopia. Buxton was born in Japan, the second son of Barclay Fowell *Buxton. In 1913, before completing his medical course at Cambridge, he volunteered to go with his father's old friend, C. T. *Studd, to a new work in the Congo, which became the Heart of Africa Mission, later the Worldwide Evangelization Crusade. He married Studd's daughter, Edith, in the Congo in December 1917. The Buxtons lived at Ibambi in the Ituri Forest, two days' journey from Studd's center at Nala. In 1924, a rare tropical illness caused a partial physical collapse, and Buxton continued to be troubled by attacks for the rest of his life. When differences arose between the strongly individualistic Studd and his colleagues in the 1920s, Buxton felt obliged to differ with his father-in-law. He traveled to the United States in 1927 to try to repair relationships with their American supporters. He was then dismissed by Studd as "disloyal," although Buxton's and Studd's personal links were never broken. Buxton and some other former Congo missionaries linked with T. A. *Lambie and the Sudan Interior Mission to open new work in Ethiopia and Somalia. Buxton also encouraged the Bible Churchmen's Missionary Society to evangelize in northern Kenya. The Italian invasion of Ethiopia necessitated returning to England, and the Buxtons were living in Devon when World War II broke out.

Still involved in church and mission enterprises, Buxton also spent time in London. He arranged for the publication of a revised translation of the Amharic Bible. In October 1940 he and his brother Murray were in a committee meeting at Church House, Westminster, when it was struck in an air raid, and they died together.

BIBLIOGRAPHY B. Godfrey Buxton, *The Reward of Faith in the Life of Barclay F. Buxton, 1860–1946* (1949); Edith Buxton, *Reluctant Missionary* (1968); Norman Grubb, *Alfred Buxton of Abyssinia and Congo* (1942).

Jocelyn Murray

Buxton, Barclay Fowell (1860–1946), missionary in Japan and evangelist with the Japan Evangelistic Band. Born in Essex County, England, of devout Anglican parents, Buxton graduated from Harrow and Trinity College, Cambridge, and was ordained a Church of England priest (1885). He married Margaret Railton (1886), and they had four sons and one daughter. Volunteering to serve with the Church Missionary Society, the Buxtons went to Japan (1890), where they lived in Matsue. Here they carried out extensive evangelistic work centered on biblical studies, with a Holiness orientation. Buxton's speaking and writing stimulated the devotional life of many Christian groups throughout Japan. Returning to England in 1902 for his family's sake, he became the first chairman of the Japan Evangelistic Band, formed by his colleague

Paget *Wilkes. He was invited to carry out evangelistic and spiritual training programs in Australia, Egypt, Switzerland, Korea, and the United States, as well as back in Japan. He served as vicar at Tunbridge Wells (1921–1935) before his retirement to Wimbledon, England, where he died.

BIBLIOGRAPHY Buxton wrote several biblical studies for the Japan Evangelistic Band. B. Godfrey Buxton, *The Reward of Faith in the Life of Barclay Fowell Buxton, 1860–1946* (1949).

James M. Phillips

Buxton, B(arclay) Godfrey (1895–1986), British evangelical missions leader. A great-grandson of Sir Thomas Fowell *Buxton, son of Barclay Fowell *Buxton, and the younger brother of Alfred *Buxton, Godfrey Buxton served in the British Army during World War I and was awarded the Military Cross. In 1920 he became president of the Cambridge Inter-Collegiate Christian Union. Unable to serve overseas due to injuries sustained during the war, he founded the Missionary Training Colony. Between 1921 and 1939 under spartan conditions this institution trained nearly 300 young men, including many university graduates for pioneer missionary work. Buxton was active in the Officers' Christian Union and in InterVarsity Fellowship. From 1946 to 1976 he was chairman of the Japan Evangelistic Band. He frequently lectured at All Nations Bible (later, Missionary, then Christian) College, founded in 1923. With his help, All Nations was relocated in 1964 from Taplow, west of London, to his old family home in Hertfordshire.

BIBLIOGRAPHY B. Godfrey Buxton, *The Reward of Faith in the Life of Barclay Fowell Buxton* (1949). Ian Dobbie, *Captain B. Godfrey Buxton* (1986); J. Pollock, *A Cambridge Movement* (1953). Buxton's private papers and records relating to the Missionary Training Colony and the Japan Evangelistic Band are in the archives of All Nations Christian College, Easneye, Ware, U.K.

C. David Harley

Buxton, Thomas Fowell (1786–1845), British philanthropist and mission theorist. Buxton was born in Castle Hedinghan, Essex, England, and educated at Trinity College, Dublin. The Anglican and Quaker traditions within his family both affected him, and following an evangelical conversion in 1813 he was much influenced by Josiah *Pratt of the Church Missionary Society. From 1818 to 1837 he served as a member of Parliament, nominally as a Whig, in practice as an independent. He specialized in penal and prison reform, working to reduce the incidence of capital punishment, until in 1821 William *Wilberforce asked him to take over leadership of the parliamentary campaign against slavery. Thereafter his immediate concern was for the emancipation of all slaves in the British dominions, eventually achieved by legislation in 1833. He was created baronet in 1840.

Buxton's concerns extended over the whole field of "aborigines' rights"—that is, colonial issues and the effect of white settlement on indigenous peoples. He was president of the Aborigines Protection Society, set up for "protecting the defenseless and promoting the advancement of uncivilized tribes"; and he chaired and largely drafted the report of a parliamentary committee that highlighted colonial abuses and the unjust seizure of land and demoralization inflicted by British settlers. Witnesses called by the committee included the secretaries of the Church, London, and Wesleyan Methodist Missionary Societies. Buxton also supported John *Philip in his stand against settler interests in South Africa over the status of the Cape Xhoi and the Xhosa frontier War of 1835.

After emancipation Buxton's main preoccupation became the continuing resilience of the Atlantic slave trade and its desolation and depopulation of Africa. After losing his parliamentary seat, he concentrated on research, issuing a book *The African Slave Trade and Its Remedy.* This argued that Britain and other "Christian" nations were responsible for the systematic pillage of Africa by the slave trade, producing dependence and barbarism for Africa; that Africa's redemption lay in calling forth its own potentially rich resources, both natural and human (the latter exemplified in the Christian communities in the Caribbean and Sierra Leone); and that Africa's development as an equal trading partner could stifle the slave trade at its source. The interests of genuine commerce, he argued, thus intersected with those of Christianity and the human development usually called "civilization"; in his view, each made conditions favorable for the other. In 1841 Buxton persuaded the British government to underwrite an expedition up the Niger as a pilot project. J. F. *Schön and Samuel Adjai *Crowther participated on behalf of the missions. The project failed disastrously, with the loss of forty lives, and Buxton died distressed and discredited. His principles, however, deeply influenced British mission thinking. Henry *Venn's ideas of indigenous leadership and evangelization by native agency, and his skillful use of cotton production as an adjunct to the Yoruba mission, owe much to Buxton. The Scottish Calabar mission (1846) arose directly from the impact on churches in the Caribbean of Buxton's books, and the whole career of David *Livingstone exemplified Buxton's vision and convictions.

From the same family came Barclay *Buxton and Alfred *Buxton and other distinguished missionaries, as well as several representatives of his humanitarian concerns in public life.

BIBLIOGRAPHY T. F. Buxton, *The African Slave Trade and Its Remedy* (1839, 1840, repr. 1967) and *Report of the Parliamentary Select Committee on Aboriginal Tribes* (repr. with additions by the Aborigines Protection Society, 1837). Charles Buxton, *Memoirs of Sir Thomas Fowell Buxton* (1848); Seymour Drescher, *Econocide: British Slavery and the Slave Trade in the Era of Abolition* (1977); A. F. Walls, "Thomas Fowell Buxton," in Gerald H. Anderson et al., eds., *Mission Legacies* (1994), pp. 11–18.

Andrew F. Walls

Buyl (*or* Boyl; Boil), Bernal (1445–1520?), first vicar apostolic of the New World. Buyl was born near Tarragona, Spain. He entered the Benedictine monastery of Montserrat in 1481 and remained there until 1492. After getting to know the founder of the Minims, Francis of Paula, he joined the order and was appointed vicar general of the Minims in Spain. In 1493 a papal bull named him vicar apostolic in the Indies and in the same year, he accompanied Columbus on his second expedition to America. However, his missionary activity was brief because of conflict with Columbus, so in 1494 he returned to Spain, and from 1495 to 1497 he worked for his order in Rome. From 1498 to 1504 he was abbot of Cuxá.

BIBLIOGRAPHY Fidel Fita, "Fray Bernal Buil y Pedro Magarit," *Congreso Internacional de Americanistas,* vol. 2 (1883), pp. 173–179; a series of articles in *Boletin Histórico de la Real Academia de Historia* 19 (1891): 173–233, 267–348, 354–356, 557–560; 20 (1892): 160–178, 179–205, 573–615, and *Fray Bernal Buyl, ó el primer apóstol del Nuevo Mundo, De Documentos Raros y Inéditos relativos a este varon ilustre* (1884); E. Ward Loughran, "The First Vicar Apostolic of the New World," *American Ecclesiastical Review* 82 (1930): 1–14; Herbert Thurston, "The First Evangelist of America," *The Month* 122 (1913): 1–12, 152–169.

Willi Henkel, OMI

Buzacott, Aaron (1800–1864), London Missionary Society (LMS) missionary in the Cook Islands. Born in South Moulton, Devonshire, England, Buzacott arrived in Rarotonga in 1828, just seven years after the introduction of Christianity. He and Charles *Pitman became the chief architects of the Cook Islands Christian Church. He was noted for his skills in shipbuilding, house building, and furniture making, and he taught these to future ministers, along with a strong Calvinistic theology. In 1838 and 1839 he erected the first theological college building in the Pacific islands, Takamoa College, which has continued as the training place for Cook Islands pastors. He inspired his pupils to missionary service in distant parts of the Pacific, and he traveled to Samoa and Niue to place teachers there. The style and standard of living which his pupils adopted spread widely in the island world. He retired in 1857.

BIBLIOGRAPHY Aaron Buzacott, *Mission Life in the Islands of the Pacific* (1866, 1985); John Garrett, *To Live among the Stars: Christian Origins in Oceania* (1982).

Charles W. Forman

Byington, Cyrus (1793–1868), missionary to the Choctaw Indians. Byington was born in modest circumstances in Massachusetts. After graduating from Andover Theological Seminary in 1819, he was licensed to preach by the local presbytery, and he volunteered for missionary service at the same time. In 1821 he accompanied others appointed by the American Board of Commissioners for Foreign Missions to Mississippi for work among the Choctaws. When many of the party died of disease, Byington stayed on as a replacement. He labored to bring both salvation and civilization to his charges, and to that end he prepared a grammar and dictionary to help the Choctaws become literate. He also translated several books and most of the Bible into Choctaw. After removal of the Choctaws to the west, Byington settled in 1834 at Eagletown (Oklahoma) and organized seven new churches and constructed Iyannubbee Seminary to enhance native clerical leadership. Declining health and constant penury forced him to retire from the field in 1866.

BIBLIOGRAPHY The best edition of Byington's grammar, edited by Daniel G. Brinton, is published in the *Proceedings of the American Philosophical Society* (1871); his most complete dictionary, edited by J. R. Swanton and H. S. Halbert, is published in bulletin 46 of the *Bureau of American Ethnology* (1915).

Henry Warner Bowden

C

Cable, (Alice) Mildred (1877–1952), missionary pioneer in Central Asia, and author. Born and brought up in Guildford, England, Cable became a Christian early in her life and trained as a pharmacist. Joining the China Inland Mission in 1901, she met Evangeline (Eva) *French, who was returning to China following her first home leave; they were to be together for the rest of their lives. Stationed in Hwochow (Huoxian), in Shansi (Shanxi) Province, a center of violence during the Boxer uprising, they traveled constantly in the surrounding area. Eva's younger sister, Francesca *French, joined them in 1910, and they became a well-known trio. In June 1913 Cable and the two sisters set out for central Asia. After eight months, having traveled 1,500 miles, they reached Kanchow (Zhangye), and then went on to Suchow (Jiuquan), in Kansu (Gansu) Province. Chinese Christians from Kanchow joined them, and a new church was begun before the trio went on to England via Russian Siberia. After their return to Suchow they took a year-long journey west into Chinese Turkestan, where for several months they were kept virtual prisoners by a Mongol brigand leader, to tend his wounds. In 1932 they took their first journey into the Gobi Desert, and Cable was severely hurt by the kick of a donkey. On all their treks they met local people and "gossiped the gospel," selling Gospels and Bibles. They returned to Suchow via Russia for the last time in 1933. Mildred was often ill, and instability in the country was increasing. Finally, in August 1936, all foreigners were ordered to leave Suchow.

During retirement in Dorset, England, Cable was much in demand as a speaker. She also worked for the British and Foreign Bible Society. She and Francesca French continued writing and made several international tours. Their books opened wide contacts for them everywhere. Cable died in Dorset, the first of the trio to go.

BIBLIOGRAPHY Mildred Cable and Francesca French, *Dispatches from North-West Kansu* (1925), *Through Jade Gate and Central Asia* (1927), *Something Happened* (1933), *A Desert Journal: Letters from Central Asia* (1934), *Ambassadors for Christ* (1935), *Toward Spiritual Maturity: A Handbook for Those Who Seek It* (1939), *A Parable of Jade* (1940), *The Gobi Desert* (1942), *The Book which Demands a Verdict* (1946), and *George Hunter, Apostle of Turkestan* (1948). W. J. Platt, *Three Women: Mildred Cable, Francesca French, Evangeline French: The Authorised Biography* (1964); Phyllis Thompson, *Desert Pilgrim: The Story of Mildred Cable's Venture for God in Central Asia* (1957).

Jocelyn Murray

Cabral, Francisco (1528–1609), member of the sixteenth-century Jesuit mission to Asia. Cabral, a Portuguese aristocrat who went to Asia originally as a military officer, joined the Society of Jesus while in Asia in 1554. In 1568 he was appointed regional superior for Malacca, Macao, and Japan, with Japan as his base; he arrived there in June 1570. A deeply pious and dynamic man, Cabral brought a new sense of order and purpose to the mission. He oversaw a vast expansion of the church, first in Kyushu, and then on Honshu, particularly in the counties around the capital, Kyoto. However, he was unable to escape from the racial prejudice of the conquistador and did not adapt to living in Japan outside the area of Portuguese cultural domination. Because of this he clashed with Alessandro *Valignano, Jesuit Visitor to the East, over Japanese membership in the Society of Jesus and over the training of Japanese seminarians. As a result, in September 1583 Valignano made him superior in Macao. In 1587 Cabral went to India, where he served as superior of the Jesuit House, first in Cochin, then in Goa. In 1592 he was made provincial of the Jesuit missions in India, which post he retained until his death.

BIBLIOGRAPHY There is no life of Cabral in English, but see C. R. Boxer, *The Christian Century in Japan* (1951); J. F. Moran, *The*

Japanese and the Jesuits (1993); J. F. Schutte, *Valignano's Missionary Principles for Japan* (1980).

Andrew C. Ross

Cabrini, Frances Xavier (1850–1917), missionary to immigrants and orphans. Born at Sant'Angelo, near Milan, Maria Francesca Cabrini graduated from a teachers college in Arluno in 1868, taught, and became principal of an ophanage. In 1880, taking the religious name Frances Xavier, she founded the Institute of Missionary Sisters of the Sacred Heart of Jesus and had to defend inclusion of the word "missionary" in the title because clergy insisted it was a masculine concept. After founding schools and orphanages in Milan, Grumello, Borghetto, and Rome, Cabrini intended to begin missions in China. She was dissuaded from this by Bishop John Scalabrini and Pope Leo XIII, who urged her to aid Italian emigrants. She arrived in New York in 1889 and founded orphanages, schools, and hospitals in the United States, Latin America, and Europe. In 1909, Mother Cabrini, as she was known, became a naturalized citizen of the United States.

Though in frail health, Cabrini crossed the ocean thirty times, often becoming a liaison between family members separated from each other. She possessed keen business sense and adroitness in dealing with American churchmen. When she died of malaria in Chicago, she had founded nearly seventy institutions and was superior general of 4,000 women. In 1946, Pope *Pius XII declared her a saint, the first American citizen to be canonized by the Catholic Church.

Cabrini's *Travels of Mother Frances Xavier Cabrini: Foundress of the Missionary Sisters of the Sacred Heart of Jesus* (1944) encapsulates her mission perspective. She adopted the spiritual teachings of Francis de Sales, encouraged an expression of mission that sprang from contemplating the love of Christ, and presented the value of the dignity of work.

BIBLIOGRAPHY The best recent biography is Mary Louise Sullivan, *Mother Cabrini, Italian Immigrant of the Century* (1992). Other popular biographies are *Frances Xavier Cabrini* (1944), by a Benedictine of Stanbrook Abbey, Lucille Papin Borden, *Francesca Cabrini: Without Staff or Scrip* (1945); Pietro DiDonato, *Immigrant Saint: The Life of Mother Cabrini* (1960); and Theodore Maynard, *Too Small a World: The Life of Francesca Cabrini* (1945).

Angelyn Dries, OSF

Caffray, D(aisy) Willia (1880–1975), Methodist missionary evangelist. Caffray was born in Baton Rouge, Louisiana. Although raised an Episcopalian, she experienced conversion and sanctification in the Methodist Episcopal Church. At the age of 22, she completed deaconess training at the Chicago Training School and began work as a traveling Methodist evangelist in the Wisconsin conference. In 1920 she became one of the first women in the Methodist Episcopal Church to receive a local preaching license. Five years later, after serving as an associate pastor and an evangelist at large, Caffray extended her ministry beyond the United States. For the next 30 years she toured the world, preaching the need for both conversion and holiness. She labored extensively in South America, Africa, India, and China. According to the reports of Caffray and others, tens of thousands responded to her message. When she was in the United States, Caffray regularly taught a course in missions at Chicago Evangelistic Institute (later Vennard College) and lectured and preached widely at Methodist colleges and camp meetings.

BIBLIOGRAPHY Caffray's sermon and lecture notes, as well as her travel diaries and prayer letters, are included in the microfilm collection at Asbury Theological Seminary, Wilmore, Ky. A biography that quotes extensively from these materials is Kenneth L. Robinson, *From Brass to Gold: The Life and Ministry of Dr. D. Willia Caffray* (1971).

Lydia Huffman Hoyle

Cairns, David Smith (1862–1946), Scottish theologian and ecumenical leader. Born in the south of Scotland, Cairns entered Edinburgh University in 1880, but his course was interrupted by illness. A voyage of recuperation to Egypt brought him into contact with the missionary John *Hogg, whose son Alfred (A. G. *Hogg) later became a close friend. Cairns studied for a time at Marburg, familiarizing himself with developments in German theology. From 1895 to 1907 he served a tiny congregation, Ayton, on the southeast coast of Scotland, and he published his first book, *Christianity in the Modern World,* in 1906. On the strength of this he was appointed, in 1907, professor of dogmatics and apologetics at the United Free Church College in Aberdeen, a post which he held until his retirement 30 years later. He was a fine all-around theologian, best remembered for his brilliant chairmanship of Commission IV on "The Missionary Message in Relation to Non-Christian Religions" at the Edinburgh World Missionary Conference of 1910, for his involvement with the Student Christian Movement, and for his sensitive book *The Faith that Rebels* (1928).

BIBLIOGRAPHY *David Cairns: An Autobiography,* edited by his son and daughter, with a memoir by D. M. Baillie (1950).

Eric J. Sharpe

Cakobau, Ratu Seru (1817–1883), Fijian chief and champion of missionaries. Cakobau was a chief of Bau Island, off Viti Levu, Fiji, who prevailed against neighboring chieftainships by monopolizing firearms. He dominated most of Fiji between 1830 and 1850, when settlers and missionaries first arrived there. Pressed by revolts, Cakobau eventually became a Christian in 1854, supporting the Wesleyans. King George *Tupou of Tonga, instrumental in his conversion, helped him through his military difficulties. His conversion meant Christianization went on apace, Christianity being called "Cakobau's religion." He became king of Fiji in 1871, and three years later ceded power to Britain.

BIBLIOGRAPHY Stanley Brown, *Men from under the Sky: The Arrival of Westerners in Fiji* (1973); John Garrett, *To Live among the*

Stars: Christian Origins in Oceania (1982), chap. 4; Deryk Scarr, *Fragments of Empire* (1967) and "Cakobau and Ma'afu: Contenders for Preeminence in Fiji," in James W. Davidson and Deryk Scarr, eds., *Pacific Island Portraits* (1976), pp. 95–126; Joseph Waterhouse, *The King and People of Fiji* (1884).

Gary Trompf

Calder, Helen (1877–1970), missions advocate and administrator. Born in Hartford, Connecticut, Calder graduated from Mount Holyoke College in 1898 and Hartford Theological Seminary in 1900. She taught Latin and algebra at Western College in Oxford, Ohio, from 1898 to 1899. She served as YWCA secretary, first at Hartford from 1899 to 1902 and then at Mount Holyoke from 1902 to 1905. Then for 27 years, until 1932, she held the position of home secretary for the Woman's Board of Missions of the Congregational Church in Boston. From 1927 to 1932, assuming an additional role as secretary of the American Board of Commissioners for Foreign Missions (ABCFM), she traveled to China and Japan to visit mission stations. She attended the World Missionary Conference (Edinburgh, 1910), the International Missionary Council (IMC) (Oxford, 1923), and the IMC committee (Herrnhut, Germany, 1932). In 1929 she became the first woman to be elected chair of the Foreign Missions Conference of North America. She retired officially in 1932 but continued to serve on ABCFM committees.

BIBLIOGRAPHY Calder's published work includes *The Preparation of Women for Foreign Missionary Service* (1916) and numerous articles in the *Missionary Herald* and *Light and Life for Women*. Her personal papers are available at the Mount Holyoke College library/archives, South Hadley, Massachusetts.

Joan R. Duffy

Calder, Matilda S. *See* Thurston, Matilda S. (Calder).

Caldwell, Robert (1814–1891), missionary bishop and scholar in South India. Caldwell was born near Belfast, Ireland, in utter poverty. He began working in Glasgow at nine years of age and educated himself by reading voraciously. In 1834, after joining the Congregational Church and being accepted as a missionary candidate by the London Missionary Society (LMS), he entered the University of Glasgow, where he was tutored by Daniel Sanford, a pioneer of comparative philology. Caldwell studied Latin and Greek as well as theology. He was ordained just before he sailed to Madras in 1838, but after three years of service there he became an Anglican and joined the Society for the Propagation of the Gospel, then at a very low ebb with only two India-born European missionaries in Tamil Nadu. Caldwell increased the growing comity and ecumenical atmosphere by marrying the daughter of the senior LMS missionary. In December 1841 they settled at Idaiyangudi, where in less than three years he was superintending twenty-one congregations and nine schools, with 2,000 inquirers organized into a proper catechumenate, the fruits of a mass movement among the Nadar subcaste. Caldwell's wife started a girls' boarding school in 1844 and launched a lace-making program for widows, enabling them to achieve financial independence. Caldwell organized the construction of a vast, cathedral-like church, where he and his wife (d. 1899) lie buried, and built St. Peter's Church, Kodaikanal, which served as a private chapel for his retirement home.

In 1877, Caldwell was consecrated assistant bishop of Tinnevelly together with his friend Edward *Sargent of the Church Missionary Society. It seemed necessary to appoint two bishops, as no single Indian candidate was acceptable (including even W. T. *Satthianadhan). But Caldwell was now too old to travel as much as was necessary to hold the diocese together, and Sargent was too conservative. Caldwell moved from his beloved Idaiyangudi to Tuticorin to found a theological school in 1881. After the death of Sargent in 1887, he was persuaded to retire so that a unified church structure (as opposed to mission structure) could be created.

Caldwell is still a legend among the Tamil people. He is principally remembered for his great works of scholarship, particularly *A Comparative Grammar of the Dravidian or South Indian Family of Languages* (first printed in 1856 and frequently reprinted), *A Political and General History of the Districts of Tinnevelly* (1881), and *A Record of the Early History of the Tinnevelly Mission* (1881). His work proved invaluable in the revival of Tamil literature and culture after 1940.

BIBLIOGRAPHY Mildred E. Gibbs, *The Anglican Church in India, 1600–1970* (1972); Eugene Stock, *A Centenary History of the CMS* (1899); J. E. Wyatt, *Reminiscences of Bishop Caldwell* (1894).

E. M. Jackson

Calhoun, Simeon Howard (1804–1876), educational and evangelistic missionary in Turkey, Greece, and Syria. Calhoun was born in Boston and graduated from Williams College in 1829. Although at first indifferent to religion, he was converted in 1831 while tutoring at Williams. He became an effective Christian witness and a competent expounder of the Scriptures. He studied theology under Drs. Griffin and Mark Hopkins and was ordained in 1836. Sent as an agent of the American Bible Society to Turkey and Greece, he became fluent in modern Greek. In 1844 he was appointed a missionary in Syria by the American Board of Commissioners for Foreign Missions, and in less than two years he was teaching and preaching in Arabic. During a furlough in 1846 he married Emily Reynolds.

Calhoun's assignment placed him in charge of the mission school and seminary in Abeih in the Lebanon mountains. This area of the Turkish empire frequently suffered from conflicts among Druze, Muslims, and Christians. At one point the Christians were driven from the mountain area by the Druze, and many Christian men fled, leaving their wives, children, and possessions with Calhoun. When the French army came to Lebanon, the Druze fled, and left their wives, children, and material treasures with Calhoun. Trusted by all groups, he was known as the Saint of Mount Lebanon. In 1864 he received a doctor of divinity degree from his alma mater. He died in Buffalo, New York.

BIBLIOGRAPHY Henry H. Jessup, *Fifty-three Years in Syria*, vol. 1 (1910), pp. 97–105; H. C. Trumbull, "A Cedar of Lebanon: Simeon H. Calhoun," in *Old Time Student Volunteers* (1902), pp. 150–155.

R. Park Johnson

Callaway, Henry (1817–1890), Anglican missionary bishop in South Africa. The eleventh child of a Lymington, England, bootmaker, Callaway qualified as a surgeon at St. Bartholomew's Hospital, London. In 1854 he was ordained a priest, and he and his wife joined Bishop J. W. *Colenso to pioneer the Natal mission of the Society for the Propagation of the Gospel (SPG). As a missionary, Callaway deemed it essential to be proficient in African languages and sensitive to the local culture. His publications include Zulu translations of the Bible and the prayer book, a revised Xhosa prayer book, a compendium of Zulu folklore and history, and *The Religious System of the Amazulu* (1870). Callaway founded two Zulu missions, Springvale and Highflats in Natal, and Clydesdale among the Griqua in northern Kaffraria. Averse to the mission compound ethos, he pioneered the model of an indigenous priesthood evangelizing people in their own environment. He was consecrated first bishop of Kaffraria (later, St. John's, Transkei) in Edinburgh in 1873, with the Scottish Episcopal Church maintaining a commitment to the diocese together with the SPG. Having developed Umtata, the new Transkeian capital, into a hub of pedagogical and church activity, Callaway retired in 1886 to England.

BIBLIOGRAPHY Marian S. Benham, *Henry Callaway, M.D., D.D. First Bishop for Kaffraria: His Life-history and Work* (1896); Stanier Green, *The First Hundred Years, 1873–1973: The Story of the Diocese of St. John's* (1974), pp. 56–72; Cecil Lewis and G. E. Edwards, *Historical Records of the Church of the Province of South Africa* (1934), pp. 357–365, 534–541.

Janet Hodgson

Callenberg, Johann Heinrich (1694–1760), missionary to Jews. A German Lutheran, Callenberg taught theology and oriental languages at the University of Halle from 1727. The university itself was founded as an expression of the revival of pietism in Germany, and a major aspect of that revival was a new concern for mission to Jewish people, a concern shared by Callenberg. As well as writing important commentaries on the prophetic books of the Old Testament, he published *Introduction and Dictionary of Yiddish* for training missionaries to Jews. At his own expense he ran a Hebrew and Arabic printing press to publish materials for evangelizing among Jews of Europe and North Africa. In 1728 he founded the Institutum Judaicum at Halle expressly to train Christians for holistic missionary work within the Jewish community. No institution has ever been more influential in Jewish evangelism. It led to the founding of similar institutes in Europe, and by 1884 there were 168 students registered in these schools. It also became the model for the London Society for Promoting Christianity amongst the Jews (now the Church's Ministry among Jewish People).

BIBLIOGRAPHY A. E. Thompson, *A Century of Jewish Missions* (1902); A. Lukyn Williams, *Missions to the Jews: An Historical Retrospect* (1897).

Walter Riggans

Calverley, Edwin Elliot (1882–1971), Protestant missionary scholar of Islam. Born in Philadelphia and educated at Princeton University, Calverley served with the Arabia Mission of the Reformed Church of America (RCA) from 1909 to 1930. Most of these years were spent in Kuwait, where he and his wife, Eleanor, a physician, established an enduring reputation for scholarship and medical care. With an excellent command of Arabic, he was the first missionary scholar to graduate (1923) through the innovative field-based Ph.D. program of the Kennedy School of Missions in the Hartford Seminary Foundation. His doctoral translation of al-Ghazali's treatise on prayer was published as *Worship in Islam* (1925, 1957). Forced by illness to leave Kuwait, he succeeded his teacher Duncan Black *Macdonald as professor of Arabic and Islamic studies in the Kennedy School of Missions (1930) and trained a generation of missionaries for service in Muslim countries. In 1938 he joined his RCA missionary colleague Samuel *Zwemer as associate editor of *The Moslem World,* which Zwemer had founded in Princeton (1911) as a quality journal for missionary debate and instruction. On Zwemer's retirement, the journal moved to the Hartford Seminary Foundation, where Calverley succeeded to the full editorship in 1948, a position he held until 1952. His concept of mission owed more to the influence of Macdonald than to that of Zwemer, and it evidences the missiological breadth of the Arabia Mission.

BIBLIOGRAPHY Edwin Calverley, *Worship in Islam* (1925, 1957) and *Islam: An Introduction* (1958). Elmer Douglas, "Edwin Elliott Calverley, October 26, 1882–April 21, 1971," *The Muslim World* 61 (1971): 155–158.

David A. Kerr

Calvert, James (1813–1892), British Wesleyan Methodist missionary in Fiji. Born in Torquay, Yorkshire, England, Calvert was a printer, bookbinder, and bookseller. During an illness in 1831, he was persuaded by a mystical experience that God was calling him to the mission field. In 1837 he completed studies at Hoxton (Wesleyan) Theological Institution. The next year he married Mary Fowler, and they set sail for Fiji in response to an appeal by James Watkin of Tonga in the British Wesleyan Methodist press. Calvert was accompanied on the voyage by his friend John *Hunt and by Thomas Jagger, a printer. The trio provided much-needed assistance to David *Cargill and William *Cross, Wesleyan missionaries already in Fiji. The Hunts followed Cross to Rewa, and the Calverts remained in Lakeba for the next ten years. In 1856 Calvert returned to England to oversee the publication of the Fijian Bible. The following year he returned to Fiji. He lived to see Fiji almost entirely Christianized. Around 1871 Calvert went to South Africa, where he served as a missionary until 1881. In 1885 he went to Fiji for the mission jubilee, then toured Australia and America on behalf of the mission before retiring to England.

BIBLIOGRAPHY James Calvert, *Fiji and the Fijians,* vol. 2, *Mission History,* G. Stringer Rowe, ed. (1884; new ed. with an introduction by Fergus Clunie, 1985). G. Stringer Rowe, *James Calvert of Fiji* (1893); R. Vernon, *James Calvert; or, From Dark to Dawn in Fiji* (1890?); A. H. Wood, *Overseas Missions of the Australian Methodist Church,* vol. 2 (1978).

Darrell Whiteman

Calvin, John (1509–1564), leader in the Protestant Reformation. Calvin was born in Noyon, France, and was educated at the University of Paris in law, letters, and theology. He was converted to the Protestant faith about 1533 and soon thereafter became a lifelong exile from his homeland. Except for a three-year expulsion (1538–1541) he spent the rest of his life in ministry and teaching in Geneva, Switzerland. From this center radiated the profound influence that Calvin exercised as reformer over half a continent for about 25 years. Artisans, students, and pastors went to Geneva from numerous countries for pastoral and theological training directly related to their return, each to his own country, in order to extend the church and the kingdom of God. Through hundreds of letters to his former students and to rulers and church leaders of many lands, Calvin vigorously promoted the mission of the church. His theology of mission was the *missio Dei;* God himself so governs the whole world, especially through his church, apostles, ministers, and believers, that his will comes to pass. To proclaim the glory of the Lord, to advance the history of redemption, to bring about the conversion of the peoples of the earth, and to establish the kingdom of God with the restoration of all creation, the Gospel must reach beyond "the isles of the sea" and to "the most remote nations" of the earth. The means God uses include the preaching of the Word, sending workers to the harvest, communicating the Spirit's gifts to others, personal testimony and prayer, seeking the general welfare of one's neighbors, unity of the faith that overcomes racism, gentle persuasion rather than force, martyrdom, and especially the example of a just life. In 1556 Calvin and the pastors of Geneva sent pastors and theological students to Brazil with reinforcements for the new colony of Huguenots there (see Jean de *Lery). Calvin's concept of general revelation and "seeds of religion" in every person (also "rays of light," "sparks of divinity," "natural conscience of God," and the "gifts of the Spirit") provides a basis for dialogue with people of other faiths.

BIBLIOGRAPHY Calvin's missionary ideals are presented in his *Commentaries, Institutes,* and *Letters* in many editions. A complete classified bibliography of books and articles in many languages, prepared by Peter De Klerk, appears annually in the *Calvin Theological Journal.* David B. Calhoun, "John Calvin: Missionary Hero or Missionary Failure?" *Presbyterian Covenant Seminary Review,* Spring 1979, pp. 16–33; Philip E. Hughes, "John Calvin: Director for Missions," in John H. Bratt, ed., *Heritage of John Calvin* (1973), pp. 40–73; Sidney H. Rooy, "Los Reformadores y la misión," *Boletín Teológico* 25, no. 52 (1993): 239–270; Pete Wilcox, "Evangelisation in the Thought and Practice of John Calvin," *Anvil* 12 (1995): 201–217.

Sidney H. Rooy

Camara, (Dom) Helder Pessoa (1909–), Roman Catholic archbishop of Olinda and Recife, Brazil. Born in Fortaleza, Ceará, Brazil, Camara graduated from the diocesan seminary in that city and was ordained in 1931. As a priest he worked primarily in education and social service for the dioceses of Fortaleza (1931–1936) and Rio de Janeiro (1936–1964); he served as archbishop of Olinda and Recife from 1964 until his retirement in 1985. His work, locally and nationally, reflected his vision of the church in Latin America responding to the historical situation in which it is living. He played a major role in the creation of the National Conference of Brazilian Bishops in 1952, serving as its first general secretary for 12 years, and in the formation and early development of the Latin American Conference of Bishops.

During the years of military rule in Brazil, Camara was one of the first bishops to take a strong position in defense of human rights and contributed significantly to the church's courageous stand on that issue. He worked vigorously for economic development that would serve the interests of the poor and for nonviolent action to bring about structural changes in society. He also traveled widely in Europe and North America as a prophetic voice for the people of the Third World.

Camara received honorary degrees from leading universities in North America and Western Europe and his writings have been widely read not only in Portuguese but also in German, French, Spanish, and English translations. What stands out most about Camara is his saintliness, demonstrated by his openness to and concern for people, especially the very poor, his willingness to bear their suffering and his espousal of poverty and simplicity of life.

BIBLIOGRAPHY In *The Conversions of a Bishop* (1979), Camara reflected on his life and work in interviews with José de Broucker, who also wrote *Dom Helder Camara: The Violence of a Peacemaker* (1970). An assessment of Camara's work is found in a St. Louis Univ. doctoral dissertation, "Dom Helder Camara: A Study in Polarity," by Patrick Joseph Leonard (1974). An abridged version of his extensive bibliography is in the *Latin American Research Review* 10, no. 2 (summer 1975): 147–166. Most of this material is also available on microfilm in the Pius XII Library at St. Louis Univ.

Richard Shaull

Cambridge Seven. Seven Cambridge students of distinction who gave up everything to go to China to join J. Hudson *Taylor and the China Inland Mission in 1885. They were Montagu Beauchamp, W. W. *Cassels, D. E. *Hoste, A. T. Polhill-Turner, C. H. Polhill-Turner, S. P. *Smith, and C. T. *Studd.

BIBLIOGRAPHY John Pollock, *The Cambridge Seven* (1955, 1996).

The Editors

Campbell, John (1766–1840), Scottish Congregationalist pastor, director of the London Missionary Society (LMS), and missionary pioneer. Campbell attended the Royal High School of Edinburgh before being apprenticed to a goldsmith. In 1793 he helped found the Religious Tract Society of Scotland, and in 1796 he founded the *Missionary Magazine* in Edinburgh. He entered the Congregational ministry as a result of the Haldane revival and went on to found a church, known as "Kingsland," and a school in London. In 1812 he was sent to South Africa by the LMS to investigate the situation of its missions there, the first person ever to visit all the missions inside and outside the colony. He helped John Anderson establish a permanent Christian presence among the Griqua and returned to London with the most comprehensive report on the missions hitherto and the first good maps of the colony and its hinterland. In November 1818, he accompanied John *Philip to South Africa to plan together the future of the LMS there. Again he made long and arduous journeys far beyond the colonial frontier, examining and encouraging all the missionaries. In 1820 he reassumed the pastorate of Kingsland and became a prolific writer on African missions, specializing in children's books, a genre which he pioneered.

BIBLIOGRAPHY Campbell published journals in two volumes titled *Travels in South Africa* (1822). Robert Philips, *The Life, Times, and Missionary Enterprises of the Rev. John Campbell* (1841).

Andrew C. Ross

Camphor, Alexander Priestly (1865–1919), African American missionary of the Methodist Episcopal Church. Camphor was born to slave parents in Jefferson Parish, Louisiana. They died while he was a small child, and he was adopted and raised by Stephen Priestly, a white Methodist minister. Camphor was educated in Methodist Freedmen's Aid schools, established in the South after the American Civil War. In 1887 he was graduated from New Orleans University. He taught mathematics there for four years and organized the Friends of Africa Society. He was graduated from Gammon Theological Seminary in 1895, after which he did postgraduate work at Columbia University and Union Theological Seminary, New York. Camphor and his wife, Mamie (Weathers), whom he married in 1893, were commissioned by the Methodist Episcopal Church in 1896 as missionaries to Liberia. He served as superintendent of Methodist schools in Liberia from 1896 to 1907. He also served as president of the College of West Africa (formerly Monrovia Seminary) until 1907, when he and his wife returned to America, where they remained for nine years. In 1916 he was elected the last missionary bishop for Liberia of the Methodist Episcopal Church and he returned there for three years. He died in South Orange, New Jersey.

BIBLIOGRAPHY Alexander Camphor, *Missionary Story Sketches: Folklore from Africa* (1909, 1981). See also Wade Crawford Barclay, *History of Methodist Missions*, 4 vols. (1949–1973); Frederick Leete, *Methodist Bishops: Personal Notes and Bibliography* (1948); Walter Williams, *Black Americans and the Evangelization of Africa 1877–1900* (1982).

Sylvia M. Jacobs

Camps, Arnulf (1925–), Dutch Catholic missiologist. Born in Eindhoven, Netherlands, Camps entered the Franciscan order in 1943 and was ordained a priest in 1950. After receiving his doctorate in missiology from the University of Fribourg, Switzerland, in 1957, he went to Pakistan to teach at the Catholic regional seminary in Karachi. In 1961 he returned to the Netherlands in ill health, then served as mission secretary of the Dutch Franciscan province. In 1963 he succeeded Alphons *Mulders as professor of missiology at the Catholic University of Nijmegen, Netherlands, where he served until he retired in 1990.

Camps's special interest is in relations with people of other faiths, especially interreligious dialogue. Three of his books in Dutch on this subject were published in one volume in English, *Partners in Dialogue: Christianity and Other World Religions* (1983). From 1964 to 1980 he was a consultant to the Vatican Secretariat for Interreligious Dialogue. In ecumenical involvements he was one of the founders of the International Association for Mission Studies and was its president from 1974 to 1978. For ten years (1981–1991) he was president of the board of the Interuniversity Institute for Missiological and Ecumenical Research in the Netherlands. He was also active in the World Conference on Religion and Peace. In 1967 Camps discovered in the National Library in Rome the long-lost Sanskrit grammar and manuscripts of Heinrich Roth, the seventeenth-century Jesuit missionary at Agra in the Mogul Empire, which Camps co-edited for publication in 1988. He once described his vocation as being a pilgrim on the road, with people of other faiths, professing his Christian faith in the spirit of St. *Francis of Assisi.

BIBLIOGRAPHY Arnulf Camps, "My Pilgrimage in Mission," *IBMR* 20 (1996), 33–36, *Jerome Xavier S.J. and the Muslims of the Mogul Empire* (1957), and with Patrick McClosky, *The Friars Minor in China (1294–1955), Especially the Years 1925–1955* (1996). For a bibliography of works by Camps, see J. Van Nieuwenhoven and B. Klein Goldewijk, eds., *Popular Religion and Contextual Theology: Essays Dedicated to A. Camps* (1991), pp. 235–249.

Gerald H. Anderson

Cáncer de Barbastro, Luis (1510?–1549), martyred Catholic missionary in Florida. Cáncer was born in Saragossa, Spain, and entered the Dominicans. In 1543 he arrived in Guatemala, where he used peaceful means to evangelize the Indians and gained the title "Standard-Bearer of the Faith." Convinced that he could use similar means for missionary success in Florida, in December 1547 he obtained a royal cedula ordering the viceroy of Mexico, Don Antonio de Mendoza, to provide him with passage and necessary supplies for an expedition to Florida. Early in 1549, together with three other priests, a lay brother, and an Indian woman interpreter, he set out from Veracruz. Contrary to the viceroy's instructions to convey the missionaries to a place where no Spaniards had been, the ship's pilot landed them near Tampa Bay, where the armed expeditions of Narváez and De Soto had been a few years before. On May 29 Cáncer waded ashore with two missionaries and their interpreter. Encouraged by their reception from the natives, Cáncer returned to the ship for more presents for them. When he returned to shore, his companions had disappeared. Landing at another spot, he discovered that the two Dominicans had been slain and the interpreter had rejoined the Indians. On June 26, against the advice of one of his companions, he again went ashore, and was clubbed to death.

BIBLIOGRAPHY Victor Francis O'Daniel, *Dominicans in Early Florida* (1930); "Relacíon de la Florida para el Ilmo. Señor Visorrei de la Nueva España la qual trajo Fr. Gregorio de Beteta," in Buckingham Smith, ed., *Collecíon de varios documentos para la historia de la Florida y tierras adyacentes (1516–1794)* (1857). See also Michael V. Gannon, *The Cross in the Sand* (1983).

Gerald P. Fogarty, SJ

Candidius, Georgius (1597–1647), pioneer Protestant missionary in Formosa (Taiwan). Born at Küchardt, the Palatinate, Germany, Candidius went to Leiden, Netherlands, in 1621 and finished his studies there in 1623. Sebastiaen Danckaerts, who had organized a school to evangelize children in Ambon, East Indies, persuaded him to minister overseas. The Amsterdam classis assigned him to the East Indies in 1623. After he worked in Ternate in the Maluccas, the church council at Batavia (present-day Jakarta) sent him as the first Reformed missionary to Formosa (Taiwan) where he arrived in 1627. Instead of living in the Dutch castle in Zeelandia, he lived among villagers in Sinckan. He suggested that Formosan students should take their theological education in the Netherlands, but was opposed by Justus *Heurnius, who wanted to establish theological education in the East Indies. Candidius described the indigenous language and religion in his *Discours ende cort verhael van't eylant Formosa.* In 1639 he returned to the Netherlands, at Alkmaar, and advised the church on mission matters. In 1643 he returned to Batavia, where he served as rector of the Latin school until his death.

BIBLIOGRAPHY C. R. Boxer, *The Dutch Seaborne Empire, 1600–1800* (repr. 1988); L. J. Joosse, *Scoone dingen sijn swaere dingen: Een onderzoek naar de motieven en de activiteiten in De Nederlanden tot verbreiding van de gereformeerde religie* (1992); J. J. A. M. Kuepers, *The Dutch Reformed Church in Formosa, 1627–1662: Mission in a Colonial Context* (1978).

Leendert J. Joosse

Canut, Juan Bautista (1846–1896), early Protestant leader in Chile. Born in Valencia, Spain, Canut entered the Jesuit order in 1865 and five years later was sent to Chile. In 1871, however, he left the order and later married. His first acquaintance with the gospel, he maintained, occurred in 1876, when he found a New Testament in a rubbish heap outside the Santiago railroad station. The Presbyterian mission became aware of Canut, and in 1879 he was employed as a "native licentiate." Eventually, conflict resulted in his termination. Confused and disillusioned, he returned in 1884, albeit briefly, to the Catholic Church. By the end of the decade, however, he was working with the Methodists, who ordained him. He was moderately effective as a Methodist pastor, but in his work as an evangelist and utilizer of nationals as lay preachers, Canut was unequaled. He was especially effective among the European immigrant settlers in the frontier areas of southern Chile. Ill health forced him to resign his pastorate in Temuco in 1896, as well as to discontinue his work as an itinerant evangelist. He went to Santiago to seek medical help but died there at the age of 50. So widely known was Canut among Chileans that Protestants in that country, even as late as the 1960s, were frequently referred to as "Canutos."

BIBLIOGRAPHY J. B. A. Kessler, Jr., *A Study of the Older Protestant Missions and Churches in Peru and Chile* (1967); Arturo Oyarzún, *Reminiscencias históricas de la obra evangélica en Chile* (1921); Ignacio Vergara, *El Protestantismô en Chile* (1962).

Alan Neely

Capadose, Abraham (1795–1874), promoter of missions to Jews. A Portuguese Jew living in the Netherlands, Capadose studied medicine at Leiden University. His conversion to Christian faith was influenced by the poet Willem Bilderdijk (1756–1831). Together with his uncle, Isaac da *Costa, he was baptized in Leiden in 1822. He lived most of his life in the Hague (1833–1874). His account of his conversion, *Conversion de Dr. A. Capadose* (1837), was widely read and was translated into many languages. He also published the conversion story of his brother, Joseph. A vigorous advocate of mission and evangelism among the Jews, Capadose started a Sunday school in his own house. He founded the Friends of Israel (1846) and encouraged the members to pray and work for the conversion of Israel. The Jewish community in the Netherlands reacted strongly to his missionary activities. Nevertheless, Capadose supported various missions, while strongly criticizing the syncretism and confessional indifference of the Netherlands Mission Society.

BIBLIOGRAPHY Works by Capadose translated in English include *Conversion of Dr. Capadose, a Jewish Physician of Amsterdam... Written by Himself* (1839), *Speech of Dr. Abraham Capadose, of Holland, in the General Assembly of the Free Church of Scotland* (2d. ed., 1846), and *Meditations on the Vocation and Future of Israel* (1847). F. Hausig, *Dr. Capadose, ein christlicher Israelit* (1890); D. Kalmijn, *Abraham Capadose* (1955); L. Engelfriet, *Bilderdijk en het Jodendom* (1995), pp. 179–185.

Jan A. B. Jongeneel

Capillas, Francisco de (1607–1648), protomartyr of China. Born in Palencia, Spain, Capillas joined the Dominican order in Valladolid in 1623 and then, as a deacon, left for the East in fulfillment of his missionary vocation. After his ordination in Manila in 1632, he was sent to the Cagayan Valley (northern Luzon) and worked there from 1632 to 1641. The poor and the sick were the main beneficiaries of his ministry. After his martyrdom, people bore witness to his ardent zeal during these years in the Philippines.

In 1641 he volunteered to go to China, where a mission in Fookien (Fujian) Province had been established by the Italian Dominican Angel Cocchi in 1631. From 1642 to 1646 Capillas worked tirelessly as an itinerant preacher, especially among farmers, fishermen, and the sick. In 1644 the Manchus invaded China, and by 1646 they were in Fookien. Capillas was imprisoned, and on January 15, 1648, he was condemned to death. He was beheaded the next day. *Benedict XIV proclaimed him protomartyr of China in 1748, and Pius X beatified him in 1909.

BIBLIOGRAPHY F. Calva, *Vida del Venerable Padre Fr. Francisco Fernández de Capillas* (1787); Juan García, *Relación del martirio del V. P. Francisco de Capillas en el Reino de China,* in *Monumenta Sinica* (1684); *Positio super martyrio, causa martyrii signis seu miraculis* or *Summarium* (1906). Original letters of Capillas are held in the Archivo de la Provincia del Santísimo Rosario in Avila, Spain, Sección China, vol. 21.

Lucio Gutiérrez, OP

Capitein, Jacobus Elisa Joannes (1717–1747), first African ordained by the Netherlands Reformed Church. Born on the west coast of Africa, Capitein was enslaved at the age of eight and taken to the Netherlands where, after his basic education, he entered the University of Leiden to study theology. He graduated in 1742 with a controversial dissertation defending slavery as compatible with Christian freedom. The Netherlands Reformed Church ordained him the same year and appointed him chaplain and missionary to Elmina in the Gold Coast (present-day Ghana). His ministry in Elmina achieved an initial success but soon faced problems in interpersonal relationships. The African community in Elmina could not accept him fully, nor were the European traders ready to accept an African as their pastor. The support he was expecting from the church in the Netherlands also never came. He died in Elmina after barely five years of service.

BIBLIOGRAPHY A. Eekhof, *De Negerpredikant* (1917); David N. A. Kpobi, *Mission in Chains* (1993); K. K. Prah, *Jacobus Elisa Johannes Capitein* (1989).

David Nii Anum Kpobi

Cardoso, Mattheus (1584–1625), Portuguese Jesuit missionary in the Kongo kingdom. The diocese of São Salvador, capital of the Kongo (large area including present-day People's Republic of the Congo and northern Angola), had been established in 1596. Some years later the Jesuits, already based in the Portuguese colonial town of Loanda, agreed to open a college in São Salvador. Cardoso was named first rector, arriving in August 1625. While previously working in the Kongo, he had learned Kikongo and had translated the Portuguese catechism into it. He also wrote an interesting history of the country, which was not published until the twentieth century. He arranged to have the catechism printed in Lisbon with both Kikongo and Portuguese texts, and he brought it with him to São Salvador in 1625. Unfortunately he died shortly afterward. His catechism remains the only printed work in Kikongo before the late nineteenth century and is of great linguistic interest for Bantu studies. Both as linguist and as historian and recorder of culture, Cardoso is the only early seventeenth-century missionary in central Africa who might be compared with his Jesuit contemporaries Matteo *Ricci and Robert de *Nobili.

BIBLIOGRAPHY F. Bontinck and D. Ndembe Nsasi, *Le catéchisme kikongo de 1624: Réédition critique* (1978); F. Bontinck and J. Castro Segovia, eds., "Histoire du royaume du Congo," *Études d'histoire africaine* 4 (1972).

Adrian Hastings

Carey, Charlotte Emilia (von Rumohr) (1761–1821), second wife of William *Carey. A lifelong invalid, this petite lady of means from German/Danish Schleswig traveled to Danish Tranquebar in South India for health reasons. In 1800 she moved to Danish Serampore, near Calcutta, where she met William Carey, who taught her English, led her to Christ, and baptized her in 1802. In spite of open opposition from Carey's doughty mission colleagues, they married in May 1808, six months after the death of his first wife, Dorothy (Plackett). Charlotte Carey committed herself wholeheartedly to supporting the Serampore Mission's Bible translation work and evangelistic activities. Her husband, a studious linguist and part-time pastor, prized her knowledge of European languages and her refreshing attitude toward life in India. After the distressing circumstances of his years as a pioneer missionary (1793–1807), she brought great domestic comfort to his harried life, even though she was frail. To benefit from her company, the "father of the Serampore Mission" limited his travel to commuting along the 13-mile stretch of river that connected colonial Serampore and cosmopolitan Calcutta. Their 13 years of marriage were productive in the scholarly realm and contrasted significantly with the spartan, peripatetic existence that characterized the first half of Carey's life both in England and in interior Bengal.

BIBLIOGRAPHY The only information on Charlotte Carey is to be found in William Carey's correspondence and in detailed biographical studies of his life. See, for example, S. P. Carey, *William Carey, D.D.* (1923, 1934, 1993) and George Smith, *The Life of William Carey, D.D.: Shoemaker and Missionary* (1885).

A. Christopher Smith

Carey, Felix (1786–1822), oldest son of William *Carey and the first Christian missionary to Burma (Myanmar). Born in England, Carey spent six years in rural Bengal before he put down roots in Serampore in 1799. Fluent in various North Indian languages, he was trained by William *Ward to work for the Serampore Mission press and to engage in evangelistic work. In 1807 he undertook missionary reconnaissance in Burma and provided translation services to its government. After three years as a widower, he remarried but tragically lost his second family at sea. In 1814 he was appointed as Burmese ambassador to the British government in Bengal. This political arrangement backfired and he had to flee Burma for his life. For three years he wandered in the wilds of Burma and India in a pitiful state. After William Ward discovered him near Chittagong in 1818, he returned to Serampore and resumed Bible translation. His volatile life and early death (in Serampore) caused his father much concern and grief.

BIBLIOGRAPHY Sunil Kumar Chatterjee, *Felix Carey: A Tiger Tamed* (1991).

A. Christopher Smith

Carey, Lott (c. 1780–1828), leader of the first African American mission to Africa. Carey was born to slave parents in Virginia. Though his father and grandmother were devout Baptists, he was not converted until 1807. He obtained a Bible and taught himself to read, later enrolling in a night school for blacks established by William Crane, a white Baptist leader. Meanwhile, he had married, fathering two children. He had also gained a reputation as an effective evangelist, preacher, and leader. In 1815 he and Crane led in organizing the Richmond African Missionary Society (RAMS). Carey (who remarried after the death of his first wife) and his friend Colin *Teague were appointed as missionaries to Africa by the RAMS and the Baptist Triennial Convention as a part of a plan of the American Colonization Society to settle freed blacks in newly established African colonies. The two missionaries, their wives, Teague's 16-year old son, and another couple organized themselves into a church before sailing in January 1821. Arriving first in the British protectorate and newly established colony of Sierra Leone in March, the American colonists were delayed in settling in Liberia until August of the following year.

Carey was named health officer by the colony's white governor, a task that absorbed much of his time and energy. He also acted as director of the schools and pastor of the newly established Providence Baptist Church. Repeated attacks by indigenous tribes, a lack of adequate supplies, fevers and other maladies, and internal dissension complicated life for the colonists. When the governor was forced by illness to return to America, Carey was named the colony's first (albeit provisional) governor of African heritage. Responsible for the defense of the threatened settlement, he along with several others were killed by an accidental explosion of gunpowder in November 1828.

BIBLIOGRAPHY Miles Mark Fisher, "Lott Carey: The Colonizing Missionary," *Journal of Negro History* 7 (1922): 380–418, 427–448; Leroy Fitts, *Lott Carey: First Black Missionary to Africa* (1978) and *The Lott Carey Legacy of African American Missions* (1994); Sandy D. Martin, *Black Baptists and African Missions* (1989).

Alan Neely

Carey, William (1761–1834), English Baptist Bible translator, pastor, and father of the Serampore Mission. Born into an Anglican home in rural Northamptonshire, England, Carey was largely self-taught in geography and European languages. Drawing from the thinking of Baptist and Dissenting pastor-theologians in the Edwardsian tradition, such as Philip Doddridge, Andrew *Fuller, and John Sutcliff, he challenged the hyper-Calvinist view, prevalent among British Baptists, that God would bring the nations to Christ without human assistance. In 1792, as a young Baptist pastor in Leicester, he published *An Enquiry into the Obligations of Christians, to Use Means for the Conversion of the Heathens* (1792). This missiological pamphlet argued that Christians should undertake evangelistic missions overseas. Expecting "great things" from God, he urged the leaders of the Northampton Baptist Association to found a "society for propagating the gospel among the heathen." Thus was a Particular Baptist voluntary society born in 1792 that became known as the Baptist Missionary Society (BMS).

Carey, the first Baptist missionary of the modern era, arrived in colonial Calcutta in November 1793 without any travel permits. His family managed to survive because he accepted employment as manager of an indigo plantation in the interior of Bengal. After missionary colleagues arrived from England in 1799, he moved to the Danish colonial enclave of Serampore, 13 miles up the River Hooghly from Calcutta. There he spent the rest of his life with Joshua *Marshman and William *Ward in a unique partnership dubbed by mission promoters "the *Serampore Trio." A strange combination of stiff political opposition and unusual emoluments from the East India Company significantly shaped the nature and work of the mission Carey established at Serampore. He spent well over half his time working as a professor of Bengali and Sanskrit at Fort William College, Calcutta. In partnership with several veteran colleagues and scores of Indian pundits, he accomplished much in the areas of philology, Bible translation (into dozens of languages), Orientalism, literacy, education (founding Serampore College in 1818), publishing, technology, relief work, social reform, botany, evangelization, and mission promotion. During his last 20 years, he was stymied by rampant dissension between younger and veteran Baptist missionaries that led to a costly split between Serampore and the London-based BMS in 1827. He died like a humble patriarch and has been highly revered by generations of Bengalis for his contributions to the renaissance of their culture.

BIBLIOGRAPHY The most comprehensive studies of Carey's life and work are John C. Marshman, *The Life and Times of Carey, Marshman, and Ward, Embracing the History of the Serampore Mission* (1859); S. P. Carey, *William Carey, D.D., Fellow of Linnaean Society* (1923, 1934, 1993); and E. Daniel Potts, *Baptist Missionaries in India, 1793–1837: The History of Serampore and Its Missions* (1967). An evaluation of some of the older biographies is Ernest A. Payne: "Carey and His Biographers," *Baptist Quarterly* 19 (1961): 4–12. For a survey of Carey's major writings and a missiological analysis of his significance, see A. Christopher Smith, "William Carey," in Gerald H. Anderson et al., eds., *Mission Legacies* (1994), pp. 245–254. An extensive collection of Carey's letters, writings, and publications is housed in the BMS archives, Regent's Park College, Oxford. Much of this is available in microfilm at the Historical Commission of the Southern Baptist Convention, Nashville, Tennessee.

A. Christopher Smith

Cargill, David (1809–1843), Scottish Methodist missionary in Tonga and Fiji. Cargill was born in Brechin, Scotland, the son of a banker, and graduated from King's College, Aberdeen (M.A., 1830). He became a Methodist as a student and was accepted as probationer preacher in 1831. The next year he was appointed a missionary, and, having married Margaret Smith of Aberdeen, sailed for Tonga, which the Wesleyan mission had recently taken over from the London Missionary Society. He was stationed on Vavau during an important period of Christian development that included a revival and mass movement in 1834. In 1835, with William *Cross and several Tongan missionaries, he was transferred to Fiji, where Christian influence was minimal. From October 1835 to July 1839 he was on Lakeba, in the east, and from then until July 1840 he was at Rewa, Viti Levu, in the west. In 1838, he became the first chairman of the Fiji district. When Margaret Cargill, who had been his anchor, died in 1840, he returned to Britain with their four children and some manuscript translations. In 1841 he married Augusta Bicknell of London, and was reassigned to Vavau, but grief, depression, and dengue fever had broken, and perhaps unhinged, him. He died of a laudanum overdose three months after landing.

Cargill's superior education and Scottish background made him singular among his missionary colleagues; most thought him gifted but difficult. He was probably the best missionary linguist of his day in the Pacific, and his studies in Tongan, and especially in Fijian, languages, though now largely forgotten, were foundational for the work of others.

BIBLIOGRAPHY David Cargill, *Memoirs of Mrs. Margaret Cargill* (1841), and "A Brief Essay on the Feejeean Language," appendix to *Report of the Wesleyan Methodist Missionary Society* (1840). Mora Dickson, *The Inseparable Grief: Margaret Cargill of Fiji* (1976); J. Garrett, *To Live among the Stars: Christian Origins in Oceania* (1982), chap. 4; Niel Gunson, *Messengers of Grace: Evangelical Missionaries in the South Seas, 1797–1860* (1978); A. J. Schütz, *The Diaries and Correspondence of David Cargill, 1832–1843* (1977).

Andrew F. Walls

Carlson, Paul (1928–1964), American missionary medical doctor in the Belgian Congo. Born in Culver City, California, Carlson did his medical studies at Stanford University. After a time in private practice he volunteered with his wife, Lois, for short-term medical ministry, which led to a career commitment beginning in 1963. He was assigned by the Evangelical Covenant Church to a mission station in Wasolo, a remote area of the Ubangi Province, where he worked in a primitive hospital serving some 200 patients a day. In 1964 this "forgotten corner of the Congo" was infiltrated by Simba rebel soldiers. He was taken captive and was shot to death while trying to escape. Soon after his death the Paul Carlson Medical Foundation was established.

BIBLIOGRAPHY Lois Carlson, *Monganga Paul: The Congo Ministry and Martyrdom of Paul Carlson, M.D.* (1966); James and Marti Hefley, *By Their Blood: Christian Martyrs of the 20th Century* (1979).

Ruth A. Tucker

Carmichael, Amy Beatrice (1867–1951), founder of the Dohnavur Fellowship. Born in Belfast, Ireland, to a devout family of Scottish ancestry, Carmichael was educated at home and in England, where she lived with the family of Robert Wilson after her father's death. While never officially adopted, she used the hyphenated name Wilson-Carmichael as late as 1912. Her missionary call came through contacts with the Keswick movement. In 1892 she volunteered to the China Inland Mission but was refused on health grounds. However, in 1893 she sailed for Japan as the first Keswick missionary to join the Church Missionary Society (CMS) work led by Barclay *Buxton. After less than two years in Japan and Ceylon, she was back in England before the end of 1894. The next year she volunteered to the Church of England Zenana Missionary Society, and in November 1895 she arrived in South India, never to leave. While still learning the difficult Tamil language, she commenced itinerant evangelism with a band of Indian Christian women, guided by the CMS missionary Thomas *Walker. She soon found herself responsible for Indian women converts, and in 1901, she, the Walkers, and their Indian colleagues settled at Dohnavur. During her village itinerations, she had become increasingly aware of the fact that many Indian children were dedicated to the gods by their parents or guardians, became temple children, and lived in moral and spiritual danger. It became her mission to rescue and raise these children, and so the Dohnavur Fellowship came into being (registered 1927). Known at Dohnavur as Amma (Mother), Carmichael was the leader, and the work became well known through her writing. Workers volunteered and financial support was received, though money was never solicited. In 1931 she had a serious fall, and this, with arthritis, kept her an invalid for the rest of her life. She continued to write, and identified leaders, missionary and Indian, to take her place. The Dohnavur Fellowship still continues today.

BIBLIOGRAPHY Amy Carmichael, *From Sunrise Land* (1895), *Things as They Are* (1901), *Walker of Tinnevelly* (1916), and *Ragland, Spiritual Pioneer* (1951). Carmichael's books on Dohnavur include *Lotus Buds* (1909), *Gold Cord: The Story of a Fellowship* (1932), and *Windows* (1937). Elisabeth Elliott, *A Chance to Die: The Life and Legacy of Amy Carmichael* (1987); Frank Houghton, *Amy Carmichael of Dohnavur: The Story of a Lover and Her Beloved* (1953); Eric J. Sharpe, "The Legacy of Amy Carmichael," *IBMR* 20, no. 3 (1996): 121–125.

Jocelyn Murray

Carneiro Leitão, Melchior Miguel (1519–1583), Portuguese Jesuit missionary and bishop of China and Japan. Born in Coimbra, Portugal, Carneiro entered the Society of Jesus in 1543. *Ignatius of Loyola, the founder of the order, did not want Jesuits to become bishops, but he acceded to the 1554 request of King John III of Portugal to promote Carneiro, João *Nunes Barreto, and Andres *Oviedo to the episcopate, since no benefices or honors but rather hardships were attached. Carneiro was appointed bishop of Nicaea and one of two auxiliary bishops to Nunes Barreto, patriarch of Ethiopia. The king of Ethiopia had asked the Portuguese monarch for military assistance against the Muslims. King John, under the impression that the Ethiopian church would unite with Rome, sent the Jesuit bishops, along with a dozen confreres, to Goa, India, the gateway to Ethiopia. Carneiro arrived in Goa in 1555 and was consecrated a bishop in 1560. Named bishop of China and Japan by Pius V, he proceeded to Macao in 1568, where the next year he founded a hospital. He wanted to resign the title of bishop in 1573, but three years later the diocese of Macao was established.

Only Oviedo ever reached Ethiopia, whose ruler rejected the Portuguese overtures. With the death of Oviedo in 1577, Carneiro became patriarch of Ethiopia but actively assisted in the new diocese of Macao until Leonardo de Sá, newly appointed as the first bishop there, was able to come in 1581. The following year Carneiro resigned as bishop (having received papal permission to do so in 1578); he died in Macao.

BIBLIOGRAPHY Philip Caraman, *The Lost Empire: The Story of the Jesuits in Ethiopia, 1555–1634* (1985); Joseph Dehergne, *Répertoire des Jésuites de Chine de 1552 à 1800* (1973), p. 45; John O'Malley, *The First Jesuits* (1993), pp. 327–328; Manuel Teixeira, *Macau e a sua Diocese* (1940) 2:73–83; 3:149–156; Josef Wicki, ed., *Documenta Indica* (1954) 3: 5–6.

John W. Witek, SJ

Carpenter, Chapin Howard (1835–1887), American Baptist missionary in Burma and Japan. Born in Milford, New Hampshire, the son of a Baptist minister, Carpenter was a graduate of Harvard College (1859) and Newton Theological Institution (1861). With his wife, Harriet (Rice), he was appointed to Burma (Myanmar) by the American Baptist Missionary Union (ABMU). After teaching for five years in the Karen Theological Seminary, he was placed in charge of the Bassein Sgau-Karen mission of about seventy churches. Briefly serving as president of the Rangoon Theological Seminary in 1874, he returned to Bassein in 1875. There he established a highly regarded school, building the facilities from Karen contributions. He convinced the Karens to accept responsibility for their own work; they raised several thousand dollars to establish the Elisha L. Abbott Fund of the ABMU. Carpenter developed strong views on the matter of self-support and he published them widely. Unable to convince his superiors of this strategy, he resigned from the ABMU in 1886. Subsequently, he and Harriet established a mission among the Ainus of Japan, independent of any board. He died at Nemuro, a remote Japanese village.

BIBLIOGRAPHY Chapin Howard Carpenter, *The Great Commission and Its Fulfillment by the Church* (1873), *Self-Support, Illustrated in the History of the Bassein Karen Mission from 1840 to 1880* (1883), and *The American Baptist Missionary Union: Its Present Standing As an Economical Agency for Propagating the Gospel* (1885). A biographical sketch is in the 1887 annual of the American Baptist Foreign Mission Society, pp. 12–13.

William H. Brackney

Carpini, John of Plano. *See* John of Pian di Carpine.

Carroll, John (1736–1815), first American Catholic bishop in the United States. Born to Daniel Carroll and his wife, Eleanor (Darnall), in Upper Marlboro, Prince Georges County, Maryland, Carroll, with his cousin, Charles Carroll of Carrollton, traveled to Europe in 1748 to do classical studies at the English Catholic school at Saint-Omer, Flanders. Five years later he entered the Jesuit novitiate at Watten. Ordained in 1761, he subsequently taught in the English colleges at Liège and Bruges. In 1774, a few months after the Society of Jesus was suppressed by Pope Clement XIV, the embittered Carroll returned to his native land, where from his mother's estate he functioned for a dozen years as pastor to Catholic congregations in the Maryland and Virginia countryside bordering the Upper Potomac. He supported the American Revolution and in 1776 became a member of an unsuccessful mission to persuade the French Canadians to join the colonists' cause. He welcomed the religious liberty and separation of church and state that came in the wake of the country's declaration of independence, as he made clear in his 1784 *Address to the Roman Catholics of the United States,* a rebuttal of a pamphlet by a former Jesuit-turned-Anglican attacking the repressive and un-American character of Roman Catholicism.

The revolution, together with the suppression of the Jesuits, in effect dissolved the traditional ties of Catholic America to Rome through England. In 1783 Carroll organized the ex-Jesuit priests into a representative body to administer the former property of the Jesuits in Maryland and Pennsylvania for the good of the Catholic community and to plan for the needs of a rapidly expanding Catholic population. A year later the Holy See named him superior of the church in the United States. In 1789 the American clergy elected him the first Roman Catholic bishop in the new republic, with his see in Baltimore. To provide the institutional means for a properly trained clergy, he founded Georgetown College (later University) in the newly created District of Columbia and St. Mary's Seminary in Baltimore. In 1791 he called the first national synod to establish rules and guidelines for church administration. By 1803 his diocese stretched from Maine to Louisiana, and in 1808 his see was raised to an archepiscopal one and suffragan sees were created in Boston, New York, Philadelphia, and Bardstown, Kentucky. He brought the first community of religious women, the Carmelites, to the United States in 1790, and under his auspices other indigenous female religious communities began at Georgetown in 1799 under Alice Lalor and in Emitsburg in 1809 under Elizabeth Ann Seton.

BIBLIOGRAPHY John Carroll, *The John Carroll Papers,* 3 vols. (1976). Peter Guilday, *The Life and Times of John Carroll: Archbishop of Baltimore (1735–1815),* 2 vols. (1922) and Annabelle M. Melville, *John Carroll of Baltimore: Founder of the American Catholic Hierarchy* (1955) are the principal biographies. See also Thomas W. Spalding, *The Premier See: A History of the Archdiocese of Baltimore, 1789–1989* (1989) and "'A Revolution More Extraordinary': Bishop John Carroll and the Birth of American Catholicism," *Maryland Historical Magazine* 84 (Fall 1989): 195–222.

R. Emmett Curran, SJ

Carver, William Owen (1868–1954), Southern Baptist missiologist. Born and reared in a pious Southern Baptist home in Tennessee, Carver graduated with an M.A. from Richmond College (now Richmond University) in 1891. Five years later, after serving briefly as a pastor and a college professor, he received a Th.M. and a Th.D. from Southern Baptist Theological Seminary, Louisville, Kentucky. He began teaching the New Testament there while a student and was elected to the faculty in 1896. Substituting for an ill colleague, Carver concluded a class in mission in 1897, and two years later he initiated a course in comparative religions and missions. He became head of the newly founded missions department in 1900, a post held until his retirement in 1943. He was thus one of the first in the United States to teach missions exclusively. Though his firsthand experience in other lands was limited to extended visits, he became a recognized authority in his field. Ecumenical and theologically progressive, Carver was one of the first named to the American theological committee of the World Conference on Faith and Order. A prolific writer, he published twenty-one books, including *Missions and the Plan of the Ages* (1909), *Missions and Modern Thought* (1910), *The Course of Christian Missions* (1932), and *The Glory of God in the Christian Calling* (1949).

BIBLIOGRAPHY W. O. Carver, *Out of His Treasure: Unfinished Memoirs* (1956). Hugo H. Culpepper, "William Owen Carver," in Gerald H. Anderson et al., eds., *Mission Legacies* (1994), pp. 85–92; John N. Johnson, "W. O. Carver," in *Baptist Theologians,* Timothy George and David Dockery, eds. (1990), pp. 284–399.

Alan Neely

Cary, Lott. *See* Carey, Lott.

Cary, Maude (1878–1967), missionary to Muslims in Morocco. Cary was raised on a Kansas farm and became interested in missions through missionaries who were entertained in her home when she was growing up. In 1901 she sailed for North Africa, where she served for more than 50 years with the Gospel Missionary Union. Her initial adjustment to missionary work was difficult. The fact that she outscored a male counterpart in language study, combined with her tendency toward "gaiety, friendliness, and laughter" and "pride of dress," led to an internal mission board decision that she should return home. Her pleas to be retained and her promise to mend her ways kept her on the field, but her struggles continued. She desperately desired to be married but finally accepted her fate of being "an old maid missionary." Her ministry among the Muslims was difficult and slow. During World War II all the missionaries were evacuated except for herself and three other single women. She was placed in charge of the work, and following the war she served as the mission's elder stateswoman. In that capacity she founded a Bible institute and trained new missionaries. At the age of 74 she returned to Morocco for the last time; after three more years of ministry, she retired.

BIBLIOGRAPHY Evelyn Stenbock, *"Miss Terri": The Story of Maude Cary, Pioneer GMU Missionary in Morocco* (1970); Ruth A. Tucker, *From Jerusalem to Irian Jaya: A Biographical History of Christian Missions* (1983).

Ruth A. Tucker

Casalis, Eugène (1812–1891), French Protestant pioneer missionary in Lesotho and mission administrator. Casalis was born in Orthez, France, of Huguenot stock. He was educated by Henry Pyt at Bayonne and converted in the Swiss revival. At the age of 15 he decided to become a missionary. He entered the Paris Evangelical Missionary Society (PEMS) School of Missions in 1830, taking courses in Islam and Arabic, preparing for Algeria. Instead, the PEMS elected to send him to Cape Town. He was ordained to the ministry in 1832, learned Dutch, the lingua franca in South Africa at that time, and eventually preached his first missionary sermon in Dutch. On his arrival, he made the strategic decision not to serve with either the colonists of Huguenot stock or with the Hottentots, but with the Africans of the interior. He set out on an exploratory trip without knowing exactly where he was going. Arriving at Philippolis, on the Orange River, in 1833, he heard of the desire of *Moshoeshoe, king of the Basothos, to receive missionaries. Casalis established the mission at a place he called Morija, later at the foot of the royal mountain, Thaba Bossiu, where he served for 20 years. He translated the Gospel of Mark into Sotho and published linguistic and anthropological studies. He is revered particularly for his role as political adviser of King Moshoeshoe in foreign affairs and in the process of nation building. In 1849 and 1850 he was on furlough in Europe, bringing the first eyewitness reports of the planting of the church in Lesotho. The Lesotho mission became the PEMS emblem and paradigm. From 1856 to 1882 he was PEMS director and principal of the School of Missions. He greatly expanded the activity of the society, opening a new field in Senegal and accepting the responsibility of Tahiti from the London Missionary Society in 1862.

BIBLIOGRAPHY Eugène Casalis, *Études sur la langue séchuana, précédées d'une introduction sur l'origine et les progrès de la mission chez les Bassoutos* (1841), *Les Bassoutos, ou vingt-trois années d'études et d'observations au sud de l'Afrique* (1859, 1933; English trans., *The Basutos,* 1861, 1965), and *Mes souvenirs* (1884; English trans., *My Life in Basuto Land,* 1889). Jean-François Zorn, *Le grand siècle d'une mission protestante: La Mission de Paris de 1822 à 1914* (1993).

Marc R. Spindler

Casas, Bartolomé de las. *See* Las Casas, Bartolomé de.

Case, Isaac (1761–1852), pioneer Baptist missionary in New England. Born in Rehoboth, Massachusetts, Case received no formal education. He was ordained in 1783 as an evangelist. Under the influence of Baptist ministers Isaac Backus and Job Macomber, he preached in central Massachusetts and Vermont, ultimately moving to the district of Maine. He itinerated along the south coast and among the islands, starting a church at Thomaston in

1784. In his eight-year pastorate there, he married a convert, Joanna Snow, and began several other congregations, notably at Bowdoinham, East Brunswick, and Readfield. In 1800 he began full-time missionary work for the Bowdoinham Baptist Association (which he had organized) in eastern Maine. As the first appointed American Baptist missionary in British North America, he helped to organize Baptist work in the Canadian Maritime provinces. In 1802 he became one of the first missionaries of the Massachusetts Baptist Missionary Society, the first general domestic mission society of the Baptists in the United States. In order to focus attention on the vast unchurched areas of northern and eastern Maine, plus the Maritime provinces, Case organized the Maine Baptist Missionary Society in 1804.

BIBLIOGRAPHY Henry S. Burrage, *Rev. Isaac Case: A Memorial* (1887) and *History of the Baptists in Maine* (1904); William B. Sprague, *Annals of the American Baptist Pulpit* (1860), pp. 205–206. Case did not publish, but there are some letters and certificates in the collections of the American Baptist Historical Society in Rochester, N.Y.

William H. Brackney

Case, William (1780–1855), pioneer Methodist missionary to Canadian Indians. Case was born in Swansea, Massachusetts. In 1805 the New York Methodist Annual Conference sent him to the Bay of Quinte circuit in Upper Canada (the southern part of present-day Ontario) where in one year he traveled some 2,500 miles and preached more than 360 times. Over the next several years he was assigned to circuits in Canada, Michigan, and New York. In 1810 he was named a presiding elder of the newly formed Genesee (New York) Conference. He returned to Canada in 1815 as presiding elder of the Upper Canada District. In 1821 he was named to a new Genesee Conference committee on Indian missions. From this date, although he continued as presiding elder, he became increasingly involved in Indian affairs. In 1824 he requested transfer to the New Canada Conference, and when that conference became independent in 1828, he was elected conference president and named superintendent of Indian missions and schools. In 1833 he resigned from the presidency and was named "General Missionary to the Indian Tribes." From 1837 to 1851 he served as superintendent of the Alderville Mission and the Manual Labor School he founded there.

BIBLIOGRAPHY John Carroll, *Case and His Contemporaries: or, The Canadian Itinerant's Memorial: Constituting a Biographical History of Methodism in Canada, from Its Introduction into the Province, till the Death of the Rev. Wm. Case in 1855*, 5 vols. (1867–1877); William R. Phinney, "William Case: Apostle to the Canadian Indians," in *Canadian Methodist Historical Society Papers* (1978).

Susan E. Warrick

Cash, William Wilson (1880–1955), missionary, mission administrator, and Anglican bishop. Born near Manchester, England, Cash served as a missionary in Egypt under the Egypt General Mission from 1901 to 1909. In 1909 he was accepted by the Church Missionary Society (CMS) and was ordained a deacon in 1910 and a priest in 1911. He continued to serve in Egypt until 1915 but then spent four years in the British army. He became the CMS Middle East secretary in 1920 and was named home secretary in 1924. In 1926 he was appointed CMS general secretary. This followed a time of theological controversy that had led to a division within CMS and the founding of the more conservative Bible Churchmen's Missionary Society in 1922. Having inherited this legacy of controversy, Cash, in the years that followed, restored the confidence of many conservative evangelicals while maintaining the role of CMS as a church society and not a parachurch agency. In 1928 he participated in the meeting of the International Missionary Conference in Jerusalem. When he became bishop of Worcester in 1941, he left the society in good heart and financially solvent. He wrote several books on relations with Islam; he also introduced the *CMS Newsletter*, carried on to such effect by his successor, Max *Warren. He was the first CMS general secretary to have served as an overseas missionary.

BIBLIOGRAPHY W. Wilson Cash, *The Muslim World in Revolution* (1925) and *The Missionary Church* (1939). Gordon Hewitt, *The Problems of Success: A History of the Church Missionary Society, 1910–1942*, vol. 1 (1971); Max Warren, *Crowded Canvas: Some Experiences of a Life-time* (1974).

Jocelyn Murray

Caspari, Carl Paul (1814–1892), Jewish-Christian theologian and chairman of the Norwegian Committee for the Mission to the Jews. Born of Jewish parents in Dessau, Germany, Caspari studied oriental languages at the University of Leipzig and was converted to Lutheran pietism and baptized at age 24. A promising scholar in the Old Testament and in Oriental linguistics, he accepted a position as lecturer and later professor of Old Testament at the University of Christiania (now Oslo), Norway, in 1847. He soon became a leading authority on the history of the Apostolic and Nicene Creeds and also took an active part in Norwegian church life. From 1861 to 1892 he was chairman of the Norwegian Mission to the Jews. Shortly after his conversion he said that only as a Christian did he "feel like a Jew." As a youth he had been educated in the ideas of the Jewish enlightenment and had lost faith in the Old Testament as a book of divine revelation. Through faith in Christ, he regained belief in the divine authority of the Bible and became a major apologist for the Old Testament against the higher criticism of German scholarship. As the leader of the Norwegian Mission to the Jews, he emphasized the need to preach the Old Testament Law to the Jews, to awaken in them the need of a savior and of the forgiveness of sins. He was always a staunch Lutheran, but under his leadership the Norwegian Mission to the Jews supported not only the work of the German Lutheran Mission to the Jews but also of several interdenominational missions and the London Society for the Propagation of Christianity among the Jews. He died in Christiania, still active at the university.

BIBLIOGRAPHY An autobiographical letter recounting the story of Caspari's conversion is in G. Nathanael Bonwetsch, *Aus vierzig Jahren Deutscher Kirchengeschichte. Briefe an E. W. Hengstenberg, Erste Folge* (1917), pp. 33–42. J. Belsheim, "Caspari, Carl Paul," *Real-Encyklopädie für Theologie und Kirche,* vol. 3 (1897), pp. 737–742; Jacob Gartenhaus, *Famous Hebrew Christians* (1979), pp. 53–56; O. Skarsaune, "From Jewish Enlightenment to Lutheran Pietism: The Spiritual Odyssey of Carl Paul Caspari (2 Feb. 1814–11 April 1892)," in T. Elgvin, ed., *Israel and Yeshua: Festschrift Celebrating the Tenth Anniversary of Caspari Center for Biblical and Jewish Studies* (1993), pp. 57–64.

Oskar Skarsaune

Cassels, William Wharton (1858–1925), Anglican missionary bishop in China. Born to British parents in Portugal, Cassels moved in 1868 to England, where he received most of his education, culminating in a degree at Cambridge. He then served as curate at All Saints, Lambeth. Going to China with the China Inland Mission (CIM) in 1885 as one of the famed *Cambridge Seven, he studied language for two years in Shansi (Shanxi), north China, and then began his missionary work in Paoning (Langzhong) in northern Szechuan (Sichuan), western China, where the CIM assigned all its Church of England missionaries. In 1894 the Church Missionary Society also began work in Szechuan. By 1895 Cassels was consecrated bishop of western China, with ecclesiastical jurisdiction over the missionary work of both societies. His mission authority, however, extended only to the CIM. This unusual pattern worked well, but only because Cassels was able to blunt the criticism that came from supporters of both groups over ecclesiastical and doctrinal matters. In his 30 years as bishop, he labored tirelessly in administrative, pastoral, educational, and evangelistic activities. He was married in 1887 to Mary Louisa Legg, and the couple had six children.

BIBLIOGRAPHY Marshall Broomhall, *W. W. Cassels: First Bishop in Western China* (1926).

Ralph R. Covell

Castiglione, Giuseppe (1683–1766), Jesuit missionary and painter at the imperial court of China. A native of Milan, Castiglione entered the Society of Jesus in 1707 to become a coadjutor brother, not a priest. Trained as a portrait artist and desiring to go to China, he left Italy in 1709 but was delayed in Coimbra, Portugal, for five years. In December 1715 he arrived in Peking (Beijing), where for the rest of his life he served K'ang-hsi (Kangxi), Yung-cheng (Yongzheng), and Ch'ien-lung (Qianlong) emperors of the Ch'ing (Qing) dynasty. Since Chinese painting styles infrequently incorporated portraits, Castiglione concentrated on nature and became famous in the history of Chinese art for his remarkable style in depicting horses. He was the principal designer and builder of the gardens in the Yuan Ming Yuan summer palace, then located on the outskirts of Peking. The Qianlong emperor took a personal interest in Castiglione's work. On two occasions, in 1737 and 1746, when the emperor visited the artist's workshop, Castiglione went on his knees to ask that the persecution of Christians be lifted. For Castiglione's seventieth birthday, the emperor ordered that gifts and an inscription he had personally written, be sent to the Jesuit residence in a public ceremony. After Castiglione's death, by a special decree the emperor conferred honors on him.

BIBLIOGRAPHY C. and M. Beurdeley, *Giuseppe Castiglione: A Jesuit Painter at the Court of the Chinese Emperors* (1971); Joseph Dehergne, *Répertoire des Jésuites de Chine de 1552 à 1800* (1973), pp. 48–49; Mikinosuke Ishida, "A Biographical Study of Giuseppe Castiglione," *Memoirs of the Research Department of the Toyo Bunko,* no. 19 (1960): 79–122; George R. Loehr, *Guiseppe Castiglione, pittore de Corte de Ch'ien-Lung* (1940); Victoria Siu, "Castiglione and the Yuanming Yuan Collections," *Orientations* 19, no. 11 (November 1988): 72–79.

John W. Witek, SJ

Castro, Emilio (1927–), ecumenical mission leader from Uruguay. Born in Montevideo, Castro graduated from Union Theological Seminary (ISEDET) in Buenos Aires, Argentina, in 1950, did postgraduate study from 1953 to 1954 with Karl Barth in Basel, Switzerland, and pastored Methodist congregations in La Paz, Bolivia, and Montevideo from 1954 to 1965. From 1965 to 1972 he was coordinator of UNELAM, the Commission for Evangelical Unity in Latin America; from 1966 to 1969 he was executive secretary of the South American Association of Theological Schools; and from 1970 to 1972 he was president of the Evangelical Methodist Church of Uruguay. He was director of the Commission on World Mission and Evangelism of the World Council of Churches (WCC) and editor of the *International Review of Mission* from 1973 to 1983. He received a doctorate from the University of Lausanne in 1984, and from 1985 to 1992 he was general secretary of the WCC and editor of the *Ecumenical Review.* In 1993 he returned to Uruguay, where he continues to be active as a Methodist minister. His publications include *Amidst Revolution* (1975), *Freedom in Mission: The Perspective of the Kingdom of God—An Ecumenical Inquiry* (1985), and *When We Pray Together* (1989).

BIBLIOGRAPHY Many of Castro's articles and reports to the WCC appeared in *IRM* and *ER* during his years in Geneva. See also his article "Mission in the 1990s," *IBMR* 14, no. 4 (1990): 146–149.

Gerald H. Anderson

Castro, Matheus de (c. 1594–1677), first Indian bishop of the Catholic Church. Castro belonged to the Mahale Brahmin family of Navelim on the island of Divar across from the old city of Goa. He did his early studies with the Franciscans at their Reis-Magos college at Bardes in Goa. In keeping with the policy of the Portuguese church authorities and particularly of the religious orders in India at that time not to admit Indians into their ranks, his request for ordination to the priesthood was not entertained. Castro then succeeded in reaching Rome in the company of some friendly Carmelite fathers in 1625. The dynamic secretary of the newly established Propaganda Fide, Francesco *Ingoli, took notice of the young man and promoted his studies for priesthood at the Collegio Urbano. After being ordained a priest in 1630, he pursued studies for a doctorate in theology, impressing people with his abilities. In 1633 he was appointed apostolic pronotary to accompany Bishop Myra to Japan but could not proceed beyond Goa because of hostile developments in Japan. Returning to Rome, he was consecrated Bishop of Chrysopolis *in partibus infidelium* in 1635 and was sent as vicar apostolic to the territories of Adilkhan in Bijapur, near Goa. The *padroado* authorities in Goa refused to accept his appointment or prerogatives as bishop. Castro sent strong reports to Rome against them and against the Jesuits in particular, whom he blamed for the discriminatory policies employed against the Indians. He also conspired with the Dutch and the Muslim Adilshah to expel the Portuguese from Goa. His 1653 pastoral letter *Speculum Brachmanorum* (Mirror of the Brahmins) incited the Indians to rise against the Portuguese rule and their church control. He also ordained several Goan boys, including relatives, without consulting the archbishop of Goa. He convinced the Mogul emperor Shah Jahan that the Jesuits at his court were political agents of the Goa government, so that the priests there suffered for a while until a friendly Armenian general of the Moguls came to their rescue. The Portuguese authorities in Goa tried to catch him and deport him to Portugal. Finally, the church authorities recalled Castro to Rome, where he died. His nephew, Thomas de Castro, became a vicar apostolic of Propaganda Fide in the vicariate of Canara in 1674.

BIBLIOGRAPHY Th. Gasquière, *Mathieu de Castro* (1936); Carlos Mercês de Melo, *The Recruitment and Formation of the Native Clergy in India* (1955); Teotonio R. de Souza, "An Unsung Hero: Matheus de Castro Mahale," *Goa Today*, January 1975.

Teotonio R. de Souza

Catalani, Jordan (c. 13th–14th cent.), French Dominican missionary bishop and martyr in India. Catalani (sometimes referred to as Jordanus) came from Sévérac, near Toulouse, in France. He worked for some years at the Dominican monastery at Tabriz in Persia (Iran). In 1320 he joined a group of four Franciscans on their way to China. He himself intended to go to India to fill the vacancy left by his Dominican confrere Nicolas de Pistoia, who had accompanied *John of Monte Corvino and had died at Mylapore. When the four Franciscans were killed at Thana, near Bombay, Catalani took care of their burial and labored single-handedly there for about two and a half years before returning to Europe in 1328. He was appointed bishop of Quilon in 1330, and returned to India with more missionaries to work in different parts of the country. He himself was martyred at Thana.

Catalani is known for his *Memorabilia Descripta*, in which he left a record of his field experience in India, particularly in the regions of Thana, Broach, and Sopara, where he succeeded in converting some non-Christians as well as some Nestorians. The Franciscan John de Marignolli, who visited Quilon in 1346–1347, reported the continued existence of a Latin Church there. Catalani's activities remain associated with the first presence of Latin Christianity in India prior to the arrival of the Portuguese. The Great Schism in the Western church and the black death did not permit continued missionary effort.

BIBLIOGRAPHY G. M. Moraes, *A History of Christianity in India* (1964); A. C. Moule, "Brother Jordan of Severac," *Journal of the Royal Asiatic Society* (1928); L. M. Zaleski, *The Martyrs of India* (1913).

Teotonio R. de Souza

Cattaneo, Lazzaro (1560–1640), Jesuit missionary in China. A member of a noble family in Sarzana near Genoa, Italy, Cattaneo entered the Society of Jesus at Rome in 1581. After completing his training in Portugal, he went to Goa, India, and in 1589 became superior of the mission on the Fishery Coast. In 1593 he arrived in Macao to study Chinese and the following year was with Matteo *Ricci in Shao-chou (Shaoguan). As interim superior of that mission, Cattaneo was the first to discuss Christianity with *Hsü Kuang-ch'i, one of the pillars of the early church in China. Cattaneo accompanied Ricci on his first trip to Peking (Beijing), but no imperial audience was possible because of Chinese participation in the war against Japanese invaders in Korea. During this journey Cattaneo added the five tones and aspiration marks for all the words in the Mandarin official language dictionary that Ricci composed. This system remains today a standard feature of Sino-Western dictionaries. Cattaneo later worked at Nanking (Nanjing), spent some years at Macao, and then returned to Nanking and Nan-ch'ang (Nanchang) in 1606. At the urging of Hsü, he opened the mission in Shanghai, where the entire Hsü family became converts. He later went to Hangchow (Hangzhou), where he continued his apostolic labors until his death there.

BIBLIOGRAPHY Lazzaro Cattaneo, "Ling-hsing i-chu" (Introduction of the soul to God) and "Hui-tsui yao-chi" (On contrition and sorrow for sin), described in Pasquale M. d'Elia, ed., *Fonti Ricciane*, 3 vols. (1942–1949), 1:332–334, 2:31–33. George Dunne, *Generation of Giants: The Story of the Jesuits in China during the Last Decades of the Ming Dynasty* (1962), pp. 49–50, 55–56, 68–70, 118–126; Louis Gallagher, *China in the Sixteenth Century: The Journals of Matthew Ricci* (1953), pp. 257–258, 287–291; D. E. Mungello, *The Forgotten Christians of Hangzhou* (1994), pp. 15–18, 54, 72.

John W. Witek, SJ

Cavazzi da Montecuccolo (1621–1678), Capuchin missionary in Angola. Born in Montecuccolo, Modena, Italy, Cavazzi was known in his early life for his piety, but his teachers and the Capuchin order, which he joined in 1632, found his intelligence lacking. Nevertheless, he was dispatched to the Capuchin mission to Congo and Angola in 1654, where he traveled widely, visiting the most powerful kingdoms in the area—Mpungu a Ndongo, Matamba, Kongo, Kasanje, and the Portuguese colony of Angola. He spent many years at the court of Queen Ana de Sousa Njinga Mbande of Matamba, who although baptized in

1622 lived in a state of apostasy from 1631 until her reconciliation with the church in 1655. Cavazzi became her confidant and presided over her funeral. In 1665 he wrote an extensive manuscript history of the Capuchin mission in central Africa, the life of Queen Njinga, and a general description of the societies of central Africa illustrated with watercolor paintings. In 1669 Vatican officials commissioned him to write a general history of the mission, which he completed in 1671 using his earlier manuscript and accounts of other Capuchin missionaries to supplement it. The publication of the manuscript was delayed for many years because of his attachment to miracle stories. It finally appeared after his death as *Istorica Descrizione de' tre regni Congo, Matamba, ed Angola* (Bologna, 1687). His account remains one of the most important sources for the history and customs of seventeenth-century central Africa.

Cavazzi had a hostile attitude towards African society and customs and was skeptical about the conversion to Christianity of all but the Kongo, which he visited in 1666. He was never inclined to accept the sincerity of Queen Njinga, although he maintained good relations with her.

BIBLIOGRAPHY A good biography of Cavazzi by Francisco Leite da Faria and full bibliographic references are found in the Portuguese translation of Cavazzi's *Istorica Descrizione,* Graziano Maria da Leguzzano, ed. (1965). Jean Cuvelier, "Notes sur Cavazzi," *Zaire* 3 (1949): 175–184; a full history of the Angola mission is found in Graziano Saccardo, *Congo e Angola con la storia de la missione dei Cappuccini* (1983–1984). Cavazzi's unpublished manuscript of his travels is found in the private library of the Araldi family in Modena, Italy.

John K. Thornton

Cecile, Mother Isherwood. *See* Isherwood, Annie Cecile.

Céspedes, Gregorio (1551–1611), Jesuit missionary to Japan and Korea. Céspedes was born in Madrid, Spain, studied literature and canon law at the University of Salamanca, and became a Jesuit in 1569. In March 1574, he left Lisbon for India. Ordained to the priesthood in Goa at the end of 1575, he sailed for Macao and then reached Japan in 1577. Chosen by the vice-provincial of the Jesuits to give pastoral care to Christians involved in the war in Korea, he spent more than a year in Komunkai, Korea, from 1594 to 1595, accompanied by a Japanese Jesuit brother, León Hankan. Céspedes was not a military chaplain in the usual sense, but rather a pastor to thousands of Korean and Japanese Christians who had been uprooted from their homes. He worked for an armistice, but peace was not forthcoming. He died in Kokura, Japan.

BIBLIOGRAPHY J. Ruiz de Medina, *The Catholic Church in Korea: Its Origins, 1566–1784* (John Bridges, Eng. tr., 1991), pp. 47, 205. Many reports about the life and work of Céspedes are in J. F. Schütte, ed., *Monumenta Historica Japoniae I. Textus Catalogorum Japoniae... 1549–1654,* Monumenta Historica Societatis Iesu (1975).

Jesús López-Gay, SJ

Chabanel, Noël (1613–1649), French Jesuit missionary martyr. Born at Saugues, France, Chabanel entered the Society of Jesus in Toulouse in 1630. After his ordination in 1641, he taught rhetoric at Rodez—contemporaries claimed he was a brilliant orator. In 1643 his requests to be assigned to Canada's "dangerous missions" were granted; he left for Quebec in the late spring and worked among the Wendat and Tobacco nations along the eastern shores of Georgian Bay and Lake Huron. It seems that of all the seventeenth-century Jesuit missionaries in North America, Chabanel alone lacked a flair for languages; furthermore, he disdained the ways and customs of the native peoples. Still, in June 1647, he vowed to remain on the mission. In December 1649 he was asked by Paul Ragueneau, superior of the mission, to join his Jesuit companions at Sainte-Marie II (now Christian Island, Georgian Bay, Ontario). Enroute, he was killed by Louis Honarreennha, a Wendat apostate. Chabanel was canonized by Pope *Pius XI on June 29, 1930.

BIBLIOGRAPHY Angus Macdougall, ed., *Martyrs of New France* (1962); François Roustang, *An Autobiography of Martyrdom* (1964); Reuben Gold Thwaites, ed., *The Jesuit Relations and Allied Documents, 1610–1791* (1959).

Jacques Monet, SJ

Chakkarai, V(engal) (1880–1958), pioneer of an Indian Christian theology. A member of the Chetty caste, Chakkarai was born into a well-to-do Hindu family in Madras. After going through a period of doubt and agnostic inclinations, he accepted Jesus as his Lord under the influence of his teachers in school and college and was baptized in 1903. He left the practice of law and ended his association with the Danish Lutheran mission in Madras, then joined Gandhi's freedom campaigns, and later the labor movement as well. As mayor of Madras and trade union leader he became a public figure in the 1940s and 1950s. His lasting contribution was in the field of a reconsideration and restatement of the theological task in India as developed in his main works *Jesus the Avatar* (1927) and *The Cross and Indian Thought* (1932). He and his brother-in-law, *Chenchiah, were among the founders of the Christo Samaj at Madras, which worked for the Indianization of the church. Chakkarai felt that Indian theology ought to satisfy the two great urges of Indian Christians—"for a direct contact with Jesus and an aspiration of rebirth, to be born a son of God in the image of Jesus." He sought to write merely the prolegomena for such a theology, leaving the main task to others whom he expected to abandon Greek and Latin theology and to work out a new expression of the faith on the basis of Scripture and experience with critical use of Hindu terminology.

BIBLIOGRAPHY P. T. Thomas, Introduction to vol. 1 of Chakkarai's writings, *Vengal Chakkarai* (1981), pp. 1–41; Herwig Wagner, *Erstgestalten einer einheimischen Theologie in Südindien* (1963), pp. 198–259.

Hans-Werner Gensichen

Chakko, Sarah (1905–1954), Indian Christian leader. Chakko was born in Trichur, Kerala, South India, the fourth of ten children born to the much-respected commissioner of police. She was nurtured in the ancient Syrian Orthodox community there and was educated at government institutions so that she would understand the Hindu society surrounding her. Graduating from Queen Mary's College, Madras, she refused to marry and dedicated her life to education. In 1930, after postgraduate study and some teaching experience in Madras, she was appointed to a post at Isabella Thoburn College, a Methodist school in Lucknow. She became principal there in 1945 after studying at the University of Chicago and the University of Michigan (1937). Invited to attend the inaugural assembly of the World Council of Churches (WCC) in Amsterdam in 1948, she was already well known in ecumenical circles from her contribution to World's Student Christian Federation student conferences in Java (1933), and San Francisco (1936), her work for the World Alliance of YWCAs, and her participation in a delegation from the Indian Student Christian Movement that visited university students in China in 1947. From 1948 to 1949 she was chair of the WCC Commission for the Life and Work of Women in the Church. She took a sabbatical from her post from January 1951 to August 1952 to work full time for the commission, and by her tact and diplomacy on her travels not only built up its work but also enhanced the reputation of the WCC in both East and West. In particular, she stimulated between thirty and forty major churches to examine the situation of women in their organizations, and she even caused Karl Barth to reassess his theology. Elected a president of the WCC in 1951 when T. C. *Chao resigned, she persuaded the Central Committee of the WCC to meet in her college in Lucknow in January 1953, a meeting so successful that little further persuasion was necessary to bring the WCC World Assembly to New Delhi in 1961. She died of a heart attack while playing basketball in January 1954.

BIBLIOGRAPHY Susanne Hertzel, *A Voice for Women* (1981); M. L. Slater, *Future Maker of India: The Story of Sarah Chakko* (1968); Hedwig Thöma, *Sarah Chakko–eine grosse Inderin* (1955); H. R. Weber, *Asia and the Ecumenical Movement* (1966).

E. M. Jackson

Chalmers, John (1825–1899), London Missionary Society (LMS) missionary in China. Chalmers was born in northeastern Scotland and graduated from the University of Aberdeen. After theological training at Cheshunt College, he was ordained in 1852 and appointed by the LMS to join his fellow countryman James *Legge, in Hong Kong. When Legge went on leave, Chalmers had sole responsibility for the mission's work, including school and printing press. On Legge's return, Chalmers moved to Canton to reopen the society's work there. He combined that task and the extension of work in the surrounding districts with increasing his already considerable knowledge of Chinese language, literature, and culture. In 1878 he received the degree of LL.D. from his old university, and in 1879 he moved back to Hong Kong to take sole charge of the work there. His published works include *Origin of the Chinese* (1868), *Lau-tsze* (1868), *The Concise Kang-Hi Chinese Dictionary,* (1877) and *The Structure of the Chinese Characters* (1882). He also played a leading part in the committee for revision of the Wen-li (classical Chinese) version of the Bible. His missionary career exemplified the conviction that in China a task of centuries rather than years lay before the church; he devoted his whole life to laying a sound foundation. He died in Korea on his way back to China and was buried in Hong Kong.

BIBLIOGRAPHY George Cousins, *A Life for China: A Sketch of the Late Rev. John Chalmers, LL.D.* (1900).

George A. Hood

Chalmers, Thomas (1780–1847), Scottish church leader and mission advocate. Chalmers had a conversion experience after eight years of ministry in Kilmany, Fife. Interest in Bible societies, Moravian and Baptist missions, and the London Missionary Society shaped his theological identity, together with both the moderate and evangelical traditions within the Church of Scotland. He believed strongly in education and in community schemes for the relief of the poor. From 1819 to 1823 his "St. John's Experiment" sought to encourage gospel progress in industrial Glasgow through news of missionary success overseas. From 1823 to 1828 he taught moral philosophy and political economy in St. Andrews University. His students, including Alexander *Duff, founded one of the early student missionary societies and provided the first generation of Church of Scotland missionaries to India. The 1830s saw Chalmers in Edinburgh involved in church extension and disputes over the boundaries of church and state, which led to the Disruption of 1843 and the formation of the Free Church of Scotland, of which he became the first moderator. By then, widespread acceptance of missions was assured.

Although there were flaws in his schemes, his place in the affections of Scotland was undisputed. His publications included missionary and other sermons plus works on political economy, social ministries, theology, and biblical reflections.

BIBLIOGRAPHY Stewart J. Brown, *Thomas Chalmers and the Godly Commonwealth* (1982); A. C. Cheyne, ed., *The Practical and the Pious* (1985); Stuart Piggin and John Roxborogh, *The St. Andrews Seven* (1985); John Roxborogh, *Thomas Chalmers, Enthusiast for Mission* (1997). An extensive collection of Chalmers's papers is in New College Library, Univ. of Edinburgh.

John Roxborogh

Chamberlain, Jacob (1835–1908), Reformed Church in America medical missionary in India. Born in Sharon, Connecticut, and educated at Western Reserve College, Ohio, Chamberlain arrived in India in April 1860 and was based in Madanapalle throughout most of his career. A firm advocate of evangelistic touring throughout the Telugu-language area, he reported in 1871, for example, that he had been on six preaching tours of five weeks each.

He and his Indian associates had preached 739 times to 538 audiences in 351 towns and villages to 18,730 people, selling 2,403 Scriptures. Through such tours, Chamberlain gained an intimate knowledge of the Telugu language and customs. He served from 1873 to 1896 on the American Bible Society committee for revision of the Telugu Bible. He also compiled and composed hymns for the *Telugu Hymnal,* which went through five editions. In his last years before his death in India, he wrote the first volume of a Bible dictionary in Telugu.

Chamberlain was a physician who claimed to have ministered to 30,000 patients in his first decade in India and who advocated the intimate relationship between the healing and preaching ministries. A strong champion of unity in mission, he was a leading supporter of the South India United Church in the years 1902–1905. He hailed the National Missionary Society of India for its insistence upon management by Indian leaders, supported by Indian money, and for the principle of beginning no new denomination but working in strongest loyalty to existing churches.

BIBLIOGRAPHY Jacob Chamberlain, *In the Tiger Jungle* (1896), *The Cobra's Den* (1900), *A Telugu Bible Dictionary* (1906), and *The Kingdom in India: Its Progress and Promise* (1908). Personal papers of Chamberlain are located in Reformed Church in America archives, New Brunswick Theological Seminary, New Brunswick, N.J.

Eugene Heideman

Chamberlain, John (1777–1821), Baptist Missionary Society (BMS) missionary in north India. Chamberlain was the eldest son of John and Ann Chamberlain of Welton, Northamptonshire, England. He studied under John Sutcliff at Olney and John *Ryland at Bristol. Appointed to India in 1802, he pioneered BMS expansion in north India, working principally at Katwa and Agra. An ardent and independent spirit, he was expelled from Agra in 1812 by the East India Company for preaching to the soldiers there. He spent his final years at Monghyr in Bihar. Chamberlain died at sea off Ceylon (Sri Lanka) while sailing home to recover his health.

BIBLIOGRAPHY C. B. Lewis, *John Chamberlain* (1976); Ernest A. Payne, *The First Generation: Early Leaders of the Baptist Missionary Society in England and India* (1936); William Yates, *Memoirs of Mr. John Chamberlain, Late Missionary in India* (1824).

Brian Stanley

Chaminade, Guillaume Joseph (1761–1850), founder of the Marianist Sisters and of the Marianists (Society of Mary). Chaminade was born in Périgueux, France, and ordained in 1784. After obtaining his doctorate in theology, he taught at the seminary in Mussidan. Since he refused to take the government oath in support of the Civil Constitution of the Clergy, his life was continuously in danger, and in 1797 he was expelled from France. At the shrine of Our Lady of the Pillar in Saragossa, Spain, he discovered his calling as apostle of Our Lady for the renewal of Christian life. Having returned to France in 1801, he began to found various Marian sodalities and religious societies, which developed into the Marianist congregations. The Marianist Sisters or Daughters of Mary (1816) spread from France to Corsica and Spain, the Marianists (male branch) (1817) across Europe, Africa, and the Americas. The sisters concern themselves chiefly with the education of girls, the priests and brothers with education in institutions of all kinds, promoting an elite among youth for the development of lay Catholic Action and fostering religious and priestly vocations. The Marianist sisters, priests, and brothers take a fourth vow of "stability," that is, daily consecration to the Blessed Virgin Mary.

BIBLIOGRAPHY A. Aigner and V. Vasey, "Chaminade," in R. Bäumer and L. Scheffczyk, eds., *Marienlexikon,* vol. 2 (1989), p. 16; K. Burton, *Chaminade: Apostle of Mary* (1949); M. Heimbucher, *Die Orden und Kongregationen der katholischen Kirche,* vol. 2 (2d ed., 1965), pp. 445–447; J. G. Roten, "Chaminade," in R. Bäumer and L. Scheffczyk, eds., *Marienlexikon,* vol. 4 (1992), pp. 303–305; H. Rousseau, *William Joseph Chaminade* (1914); J. Simler, *Guillaume Joseph Chaminade* (1902).

Karl Müller, SVD

Champagnat, Marcellin (Joseph Benôit) (1798–1840), founder of the Marist Brothers of the Schools. Born in Le Rozey, parish of Marlhes, Loire, France, Champagnat studied theology in Lyons, joining Jean-Claude Courveille, Jean-Claude *Colin, and others in planning a multibranched religious order of Marists (to include priests, brothers, sisters, and laity). After ordination Champagnat, as curate at Lavalla, urged inclusion of teaching brothers—originally Petits Frères de Marie—and was made responsible for them. He began the brothers when he brought together his first two candidates in January 1817, in a house that Courveille later helped him buy. Despite continuing financial and other difficulties, the order grew and spread. Champagnat's Lavalla headquarters also became a major center for the Marist Fathers. However, Courveille, who had originated the Marist concept, saw himself as the rightful superior and made a bid to replace Champagnat. After he failed, Courveille finally departed in 1826. When Rome made an offer in 1836 to give separate approval for the priests' branch if Marists undertook Pacific missions, Champagnat accepted but hoped—vainly as it proved—for recognition at the same time for other Marist branches. Although Champagnat himself volunteered for the Pacific, Colin, by now the overall head of the Marist project, asked him to stay in France. Champagnat sent three brothers with the first group of Marist missionaries, twelve more before he died; the brother-catechists became an integral part of the pioneer Marist missions. Rome's recognition of the brothers as an independent order finally came in 1863, and they spread rapidly throughout the world.

BIBLIOGRAPHY *Letters of Marcellin J. B. Champagnat, 1789–1840, Founder of the Institute of the Marist Brothers,* vol. 1, *Texts,* Paul Sester, ed. (1991), vol. 2, *References,* Raymond Borne and Paul Sester, eds. (1992); both vols. tr. by Leonard Voegtle. Stephen Farrell,

Achievement from the Depths: A Critical Historical Survey of the Life of Marcellin Champagnat (1984); Jean-Baptiste [Furet], *Vie de Joseph-Benôit-Marcellin Champagnat* (1856; repr. with critical notes, 1989; edited English trans., *Life of Father Champagnat,* 1947). Champagnat's notebooks, letters, sermons, conferences, and other papers are preserved in the archives of the Marist Brothers, Rome.

John Hosie, SM

Chandran, J(oshua) Russell (1918–), first Indian principal of United Theological College, Bangalore, India. Chandran was born in Kodamankuly, South India. After university studies and a brief period of pastoral work, he received his theological education at the United Theological College, Bangalore (1941–1945), Mansfield College, Oxford (1947–1949), and Union Theological Seminary, New York (1949–1950). His most enduring contribution was to theological education and ministerial training during three decades at the United Theological College, Bangalore, where he was appointed a faculty member in 1950 and then its first Indian principal in 1954. He was also president of the senate of Serampore College from 1968 to 1971. He was convener of the theological commission of the Church of South India and was secretary of the Joint Council of the Church of North India, the Church of South India, and the Mar Thoma Church, working for the unity of the church in India. He was associated with the World Council of Churches as a member of its Faith and Order Commission and its Central and Executive Committees, of which he served as vice-moderator (1961–1968), enabling him to contribute to the wider ecumenical movement. As president of the Christian Peace Conference (1975), president of the Ecumenical Association of Third World Theologians (1976), and founder-president of the Christian Union of India, he sought to relate the concerns of the church to the political and social realities of the world.

BIBLIOGRAPHY Two collections of Chandran's writings have been published: *The Church in Action* (1992) and *I Believe* (1993). A book of essays in his honor was published under the title *A Vision for Man,* Samuel Amirtham, ed. (1978).

Stanley J. Samartha

Chanel, Pierre Louis (1803–1841), Marist missionary martyr on Futuna. Born in Cuet, France, Chanel was ordained a diocesan priest but in 1831 entered the newly founded Marist Fathers. Recruited to work in the Pacific by Jean-Baptiste *Pompallier, Chanel left France in 1836 with Pompallier and six other Marists to staff the Vicariate of Western Oceania, established the same year. Chanel was appointed superior of the small band of Marist missionaries. Pompallier and the Marists spent several months wandering about the Pacific, looking for a suitable field for their mission, before they chose the islands of Wallis and Futuna, in the central Pacific. In November 1837 Chanel and a Marist brother were put ashore on Futuna to open the first Catholic mission. The serene and gentle Chanel patiently endured the frustrations of isolation, material want, struggle with the language, and the unpredictability of his relations with the island people. Although Chanel had found protection with one of the two warring local chiefs, the chief's attitude changed as his fortunes of war rose and fell. Despite debilitating illnesses that left him bedridden at times, Chanel continued his ministry to the sick and wounded. He made a few converts but was plagued by worries that his mission was a failure. When the son of his chiefly patron was converted, his former protector turned against him. On April 28, 1841, the priest was struck down by a man who had told him he needed medicine. His skull split by an ax, Chanel prayed for his assassins and comforted his converts. His remains were found and sent to Rome; only in the 1970s were they returned to Futuna. Chanel was canonized a saint in 1954 and declared the patron of Oceania. Chanel's martyrdom renewed interest in the missions of Oceania. Two years after his death the entire population of Futuna was received into the church.

BIBLIOGRAPHY C. Rozier, *Écrits du Père Pierre Chanel* (1960); William Stuart and Anthony Ward, *Ever Your Poor Brother Peter Chanel* (1991); W. Symes, *Life of St. Peter Chanel* (1963). The first two titles are collections of Chanel's writings and include the journal he kept on Futuna.

Francis X. Hezel, SJ

Chang, Barnabas (c. 1895–c. 1960), a founder of the True Jesus Church in China. The True Jesus Church grew out of the Apostolic Faith Mission begun by American Pentecostal missionaries in Shansi (Shanxi) Province in 1912. One of those affected was Barnabas Chang, a Presbyterian from Shantung (Shandong) Province, who received "the baptism of the Holy Spirit" in 1912 while listening to Chang Ling-sheng preach. He, Chang Ling-sheng, and Paul Wei, who died in 1919, founded churches in northern, central, and southern China. The True Jesus Church in Taiwan, totaling 145 churches and 28,237 members in 1968, was begun by Barnabas Chang during a month-long visit to Taiwan in 1926. These and other independent churches reflected the rise of Chinese nationalism in the 1920s.

In 1929 Chang left the church and set up his own work in Hong Kong and countries of southeast Asia. He was excommunicated by the True Jesus Church in 1931. According to True Jesus Church members, Chang went mad before his death in the 1960s.

BIBLIOGRAPHY Barnabas Chang, "The True Jesus Church in Taiwan," *Taiwan chuanjiao sanshi zhounian jiniankan* (Thirtieth anniversary issue of evangelism in Taiwan) (1956). Kenneth Scott Latourette, *A History of Christian Missions in China* (1929); Allen J. Swanson, *Taiwan: Mainline versus Independent Church Growth* (1970).

Donald E. MacInnis

Chao T(zu) C(h'en) (Zhao Zichen) (1888–1979), Chinese theologian and Christian educator. A penetrating thinker and an articulate speaker and writer, Chao endeavored to make Christianity relevant to the needs of Chinese culture and society. Chao reconciled himself to the Communist revolution of 1949 and remained in China, but descended into obscurity after the mid-1950s and apparently lost his faith long before his death. Some of his writings were still in use in Protestant seminaries in Hong Kong and Taiwan long after the revolution. In many ways he was a liberal theologian, although Western terms do not do justice to his thought.

Chao was from Chekiang (Zhejian) Province. He had a solid classical education that later enriched his prose and his thought. He attended the preparatory middle school and then Soochow University, a missionary institution, graduating about 1911. Chao went to the United States in 1914 and received M.A. and B.D. degrees at Vanderbilt University. He returned to Soochow University in 1917 as a professor, becoming dean in 1922. In 1926 he moved to the prestigious Yenching University in Peking, where in 1928 he became dean of the school of religion, a post he held until the early 1950s, when he was attacked politically and removed.

From 1917 until the early 1930s, Chao, along with other colleagues such as those affiliated with Yenching's Life Fellowship group (Liu T'ing-fang [Liu Tingfang], Hsu Pao-ch'ien [Xu Baoqian], and Wu Lei-ch'uan [Wu Leichuan]), tried to establish Christianity's relevance to China's national and social needs and tended to strip it of all supernatural elements. Chao's 1925 book, *Christian Philosophy,* and his *Life of Jesus* (1935), exemplify this. In the 1930s and later, he became more conservative in faith, especially after his imprisonment by the Japanese for several months in 1942; he may also have been influenced by Karl Barth. His *Life of Paul* (1947) and *My Prison Experience* (1948) reflect the change. These major works are all in Chinese. He also wrote many articles in English, especially for the *Chinese Recorder* (Shanghai) in the 1920s and 1930s.

Chao was active on the national Protestant scene, participating in major conferences and organizations, including the National Christian Council and the YMCA. He attended the International Missionary Council meetings of 1928, 1938, and 1947, and served as a president of the World Council of Churches from 1948 to 1951.

BIBLIOGRAPHY Samuel H. Chao, "The Chinese Church and Theology: A Discussion," *EAJT* 2 (1984): 82–93; Winfried Glüer, *Christliche Theologie in China, T.C. Chao, 1918–1956* (1979); Lee Ming Ng, "Christianity and Social Change: The Case of China, 1920–1950" (Ph.D. diss., Princeton Univ., 1971); Philip West, *Yenching University and Sino-Western Relations, 1916–1952* (1976), ch. 3; Winfried Glüer, "T. C. Chao," in Gerald H. Anderson et al., eds., *Mission Legacies* (1994), pp. 225–231. Comprehensive listings of Chao's nearly 100 published works, in Chinese and English, are available in Glüer and in Ng, cited above.

Daniel H. Bays

Chapdelaine, Auguste (1814–1856), missionary of the Paris Foreign Mission Society (PFMS) in China. Born near La Rochelle, France, Chapdelaine was ordained priest for the diocese of Coutances in 1843. After seven years as a diocesan priest, he joined the PFMS and was assigned to China in 1852. Two years later, Chapdelaine began to minister in Kwangsi (Guangxi) Province, which at that time was not open to foreigners. Arrested, he did not heed the advice of a friendly Chinese magistrate to go back to Canton (Guangzhou). In February 1856 he was detained again, tortured, and kept overnight in a small cage to be ridiculed by passersby. He died of exhaustion the following morning. His head was then chopped off and remained on display for several days at the execution ground.

The cruel death of Chapdelaine gave France an excuse to mount a joint armed expedition with Great Britain against China. The conflict, often referred to as the Second Opium War, or the Arrow War, ended in a humiliating defeat for China. In the ensuing Sino-French Treaty of Tientsin (1858) and Convention of Peking (1860), France won considerable rights for the establishment of Christianity throughout China and further enhanced its role as protector for all the foreign missionaries and their Chinese followers. Chapdelaine was beatified in May 1900 by Pope Leo XIII.

BIBLIOGRAPHY Adrien Launay, *La salle des martyrs du Séminaire des Missions-Etrangères* (1900), *Mémorial de la Société des Missions-Etrangères,* vol. 2 (1916), and *Les bienheureux martyrs des Missions-Etrangères* (1921). See also Société des Missions-Etrangères de Paris, *Mémorial de la Société des Missions-Etrangères* (1888).

Jean-Paul Wiest

Chappotin de Neuville, Hélène de (Marie de la Passion) (1839–1904), founder of the Franciscan Missionaries of Mary. Chappotin was born in Nantes, France, and was educated privately according to the nineteenth-century French norms for women of nobility. She entered the cloister of the Poor Clares at Nantes in December 1860, but because of ill health she left the cloister and returned to her family. In 1864 she entered the Congregation of Marie Reparatrix, and in 1865 was sent to Madura, India. From 1867 to 1876 she directed the work of the congregation in the Madura mission. Because of complications that arose in the mission and difficulty in communicating with her superiors in Europe, Chappotin, with nineteen other sisters, decided to leave the Society of Marie Reparatrix and established a new religious society of women for mission. She then left for Rome, where Pius IX approved the new missionary congregation, the Missionaries of Mary, on January 6, 1877. In 1882 this new institute became part of the Franciscan family and its name was changed to Franciscan Missionaries of Mary. Chappotin became the first superior general when the institute was founded and remained in this office until her death in San Remo, Italy, in 1904. Her unique contribution to world mission was in establishing a congregation of women dedicated exclusively to universal mission. From the beginning women were accepted into the institute regardless of their national origin. At the time of her death there were nearly 3,000 members. A century after its founding, the Franciscan Missionaries of Mary numbered approximately 9,000 women of 65 nationalities, working in 77 countries. Through her leadership, Chappotin articulated a thorough and strong missionary spirituality for the women who followed her. She developed this spirituality in the daily meditations she wrote for the sisters, in her letters, and in her own spiritual notes. She was concerned about social problems and directed the members of the institute to work among the poorest, with special emphasis on the promotion of women. She emphasized sending the sisters to those places where people had not heard the gospel. At the same time she set up in Europe communities that were instructed not only to recruit members and raise funds but also to reach out to the poorest. Although unforeseen at the time, the orientations of these European communities became a basis for the awareness of "mission on six continents" that emerged after Vatican II.

BIBLIOGRAPHY Georges Goyau, *Valiant Women: Mother Mary of the Passion and the Franciscan Missionaries of Mary* (1947); Institute of the Franciscan Missionaries of Mary, *La Trés Réverende Mère Marie de la Passion: Fondatrice des Franciscaines Missionnaires de Marie* (1914); Marie-Thérèse de Maleissye, *Petite vie de Marie de la Passion* (1996); Mary Motte, "The Ecclesial Vocation in the Writings of Mary of the Passion," in Romano Stephen Almagno and Conrad L. Harkins, eds., *Studies Honoring Ignatius Charles Brady, Friar Minor* (1976); Pilar la Orden, *Una Mujer y un Mensaje* (1976); Agnes Willmann, *Everywhere People Waiting: The Life of Hélène de Chappotin de Neuville* (1972). The personal papers of Chappotin are in the archives of the Franciscan Missionaries of Mary, Rome, Italy.

Mary Motte, FMM

Charles, Pierre (1883–1954), Catholic missiologist. Born in Brussels, Charles became a Jesuit in 1899, was ordained to the priesthood in 1901, and served as professor of theology at Louvain from 1914 to 1954, with special interest in the problems of missiology, but also in ethnology and in the history of religions. He founded the Louvain school of missiology, which maintained that the aim of missionary activity should be the planting or formation of a church (with its own hierarchy, indigenous clergy, and sacraments) in non-Christian countries. It broke away from the German school of missiology founded by Joseph *Schmidlin at Münster in 1919, which viewed the aim of missions as the conversion of individuals. The theological foundation of Charles's thesis is God's desire for the salvation of everyone not individually but in a church.

Charles was also professor of missiology at the Gregorian University in Rome from 1932 to 1938. His influence was definitive in Catholic missiology up to and including Vatican II (cf. *Ad Gentes,* no. 6). A man of much activity and a prolific author, Charles began publishing articles and books in 1913. He published the *Dossiers* on missionary activity beginning in 1916, and started the Xaveriana series in 1923. He was the secretary of Semaines de Missiologie from 1925 to 1953. During World War II, he worked in Latin America. He died in Louvain.

BIBLIOGRAPHY Published works of Pierre Charles include *La prière missionnaire* (1935), *Les Dossiers de l'action missionnaire* (1927–1929; 2d ed., 1938–1939), *Missiologie* (1939), and *Études missiologiques* (1956). P. Van Bulck published a complete list of his writings in *Studia Missionalia* 10 (1960): 3–56. In 1954 many journals dedicated an article to his work; see *Nouvelle Revue Theologique* 76 (1954): 254–273, *Revue Philosophique de Louvain* 52 (1954): 187–194, and *World Mission* 5 (1954): 465–468. Joseph Masson, "Pierre Charles, S.J.," in Gerald H. Anderson et al., eds, *Mission Legacies* (1994), pp. 410–415.

Jesús López-Gay, SJ

Charp (*or* Carp), Stephen *See* Stephen of Perm.

Chartier, Guillaume. *See* Léry, Jean de.

Chatterjee, Kali Charan (1839–1916), Indian church leader. Chatterjee came from a Bengali Brahman family and was converted to Christ while a student in a mission school, prompting his family to disown him. He studied in Alexander *Duff's college and then went to the Punjab to head the Presbyterian school in Jullundur. He taught for a time at the Presbyterian college in Lahore and in 1868 was ordained and was given charge of the newly opened Presbyterian mission district of Hoshiarpur, where he remained for the rest of his life. He was a capable administrator and an indefatigable evangelist both in the city and the countryside. He baptized a number of high-caste families as well as large numbers of outcastes; by the end of his labors there were 3,000 baptized Christians and 1,500 catechumens in his district. He was elected president of the Hoshiarpur municipal committee and also served as president of the Board of Governors of Forman Christian College (1886–1915). He worked for Christian unity, and when a single Presbyterian church for all of India was formed in 1904, he was made its moderator by acclamation. Chatterjee was one of the very few non-Westerners to be a delegate to the World Missionary Conference at Edinburgh in 1910.

In his beliefs he emphasized the atoning death of Christ and salvation by grace through faith, which, he thought, set Christianity apart from other faiths. He strongly opposed the practice of reserving power in the church to Western missionaries and pressed for equal rights for all ordained workers. He also supported movements for greater independence for India.

BIBLIOGRAPHY J. C. R. Ewing, *A Prince of the Church in India, Being a Record of the Life of the Rev. Kali Charan Chatterjee, for 48 Years a Missionary at Hoshyarpur, Punjab, India* (1918); John C. B. Webster, *The Christian Community and Change in Nineteenth Century North India* (1976).

Charles W. Forman

Chatterton, Percy (1898–1984), missionary statesman and prominent figure in Papua New Guinean history. Growing up in London, Chatterton served as an ambulance bearer in World War I before resuming his studies in science. During a short period as schoolteacher in a Quaker school at Penketh, he responded to an advertisement by the London Missionary Society (LMS) and was sent to Papua in 1924. There he worked as an educator with the coastal Motu and Roro peoples, eventually being ordained for missionary work as a Congregationalist minister (1943). He entered colonial politics by 1964 and was a key speaker of the Papua and New Guinea House of Assembly. In 1963 he was instrumental in uniting LMS and Methodist work into the Papua Ekalesia; but he was disappointed with the later, broad amalgam called the United Church in Papua New Guinea and the Solomon Islands (1968) because its bishops offended his Congregationalist sensibilities. He turned back to Quakerism, becoming a member just before his death. He was knighted by the Governor General of Papua on behalf of the Queen of England in 1981. Chatterton's best-known literary publications include the translation of the whole Bible into Motu and an autobiography. In his later years he contributed to the radio and press almost daily. He is also famous for initiating the Boy Scout movement in Papua. He died in Papua.

BIBLIOGRAPHY Percy Chatterton, "The Missionaries: Working Themselves out of a Job?" *New Guinea and Australia, the Pacific and South East Asia* 3, no. 1 (1968): 12–18, and *Day That I Have Loved* (1980). Ian Stuart, "Percy Chatterton: Pastor and Statesman," in James Griffen, ed., *Papua New Guinea Portraits* (1978), pp. 195–223. Personal papers are found in the National Library of Papua New Guinea; archival materials in the National Archives, the Michael Somare Library of Papua New Guinea, and the Univ. of London.

Gary Trompf

Chaumont, Denis (1752–1819), Catholic missionary in China and administrator. Born in Eragny, France, Chaumont entered the Paris Foreign Mission Society (PFMS) in 1775 and went as a missionary to China in 1776. In 1784 he was recalled to Paris as representative of the China mission. Many letters written to him from China are published in *Nouvelles Lettres Édifiantes* (vols. 2–5, 1818–1820). In 1792 he was forced by the French Revolution to immigrate to England. The priests exiled in England, Germany, and Russia continued the work of promoting the missionary cause. Chaumont's appeal *Adresse aux âmes charitables en faveur des missions chez les peuples idolâtres de la Chine, de la Cochinchine et du Tonkin* (1814) became famous. Together with Denis Boiret he published *Nouvelles des missions orientales* (1787 and 1808). In 1814 he returned to Paris.

After Napoleon's abdication and the return of the Bourbons, Chaumont was able to reopen the seminary and buy back the buildings that had been seized. He became superior general and was responsible for reorganizing the PFMS, which he did in an unassuming but effective manner. His friend and confrere M. Langlois said: "He combined sound judgment and an upright spirit with solid piety. He was blessed with unusual wisdom and kindly simplicity" (A. Launay, *Histoire Générale*, vol. 2: p. 430).

BIBLIOGRAPHY Johannes Beckmann, "Die Wiederaufnahme der Missionsarbeit," in *Handbuch der Kirchengeschichte*, H. Jedin, ed., vol. 6 (1971), pp. 231–232, especially note 8; A. Launay, *Histoire Générale de la Société des Missions Étrangères*, vol. 2 (1894) and *Mémorial de la Société des Missions Étrangères*, vol. 2 (1916).

Karl Müller, SVD

Chavara, Kuriackos Elias (1805–1871), founder and first superior general of the Syro-Malabar Carmelites in southern India. Chavara was born in Kainakary, Kerala, India, and ordained a priest in 1829. In 1831 he founded the Carmelites of Mary Immaculate (CMI) in the Syro-Malabar rite, for which he received full approbation in 1855. In 1866 he also founded two congregations for women, one in the Syro-Malabar rite (Sisters of the Congregation of the Mother of Carmel) and one in the Latin (Teresian Carmelites of Verapoly). In 1861 he was appointed vicar general of the Syro-Malabar vicariate apostolic of Verapoly and worked to reconcile a schismatic group of Christians headed by Bishop Thomas Rocco. Indeed, throughout his life he worked both for greater union with the Roman church and greater development and autonomy for his own Syro-Malabar rite. Having decided to reactivate the apostolate of the press in southern India, he designed his own press and used locally made type to publish a number of devotional and catechetical books, as well as Syro-Malabar liturgical books. He was beatified by Pope *John Paul II on February 8, 1986.

BIBLIOGRAPHY K. C. Chacko, *Father Kuriackos Elias Chavara* (1959); W. Herbstrith, *Begegnungen mit Indien und einem seiner grossen Pioniere* (1969); J. Kanjiramattahil, *Pastoral Vision of Kuriakos Elias Chavara* (1986); Fr. William, *The Carmelite Congregation of Malabar, 1831–1931* (1932).

Stephen B. Bevans, SVD

Chavoin, Jeanne-Marie (Mother Saint Joseph) (1786–1858), founder of the Marist Sisters. Born at Coutouvre, Loire, France, Chavoin was invited by Marist founder Jean-Claude *Colin to join him in Cerdon in 1817 to establish the Marist Sisters. She took the name Mother Saint Joseph and in 1825 moved headquarters to Belley, Ain. The sisters mainly worked on educating local poor, but from 1837 they took a keen interest in the new Oceania mission. Soon they received invitations from Marist Pacific missionaries to work among island women. Chavoin sought missionary vocations, and many sisters would have volunteered for the work, but Colin opposed the idea. The difficulties his men had faced convinced him that island conditions would make it impossible for women to live the religious life there, and he vetoed any departures during his lifetime. The Marist Sisters first began working in the Pacific at Levuka, Fiji, in 1892.

BIBLIOGRAPHY Selections from Chavoin's papers are published as *Correspondence* (1966), *Recollections Mother St. Joseph* (1974), and *Index Mother Saint Joseph* (1977). Jessica Leonard, *Triumph of Failure: Jeanne Marie Chavoin, Foundress of the Marist Sisters* (1988). A chapter on Chavoin appears in Antoine Forissier, *For a Marian Church: Marist Founders and Foundresses* (1992). Chavoin's personal papers and correspondence are preserved in the archives of the Marist Sisters, Rome.

John Hosie, SM

Chawner, C(harles) Austin (1903–1964), missionary in South Africa. The son of pioneer Canadian Pentecostal missionaries to South Africa, Chawner graduated from Bethel Bible Training School in Newark, New Jersey, and was ordained in 1925 by the Pentecostal Assemblies in Canada. In the same year, he received missionary appointment and traveled to South Africa. In 1935, he married Ingrid Lökken, a missionary supported by Norwegian Pentecostal Churches.

Chawner began mission work in Natal, but when Portuguese authorities refused him entry into Portuguese East Africa (present-day Mozambique), he settled in the Transvaal. There he ministered to the Tsonga people who had come from Portuguese East Africa to work in the gold mines. After much opposition from the Portuguese authorities, he established a permanent station in the Gijani district, the first Pentecostal endeavor in the country. His activities focused on ministerial training and publications that included tracts, hymnbooks, correspondence courses, and books in both English and Tsonga. Chawner also wrote a grammar for the Tsonga language entitled *Step by Step in Thonga: A Series of Lessons in the Thonga Language* (1938), and he served on the translation committee of the British and Foreign Bible Society.

When the Portuguese curtailed Protestant missionary activities (c. 1950), the membership of the two hundred Pentecostal Assemblies of God Churches that had been established by Chawner were prepared to carry on under the direction of trained national church leaders.

BIBLIOGRAPHY C. Austin Chawner's books include *Have You Heard about Mozambique?* (1936) and *Christ Conquering in Thongaland* (1938). See also Charles and Emma Chawner, *Called to Zululand,* 2d ed. (c. 1923; C. Austin Chawner's parents are the authors of this volume); Ingrid Lökken Chawner, *Nkosazana: The King's Daughter* (1936); Gloria G. Kulbeck, *What God Hath Wrought: A History of the Pentecostal Assemblies of Canada* (1958).

Gary B. McGee

Cheek, Landon N(apoleon) (1871–1964), African American Baptist missionary to Malawi. Born in Canton, Mississippi, Cheek was the son of a former slave and Baptist minister; his mother was a Cherokee Native American. He migrated to Bridgeton, Missouri, where he pastored Bridgeton Baptist Church while working as a letter carrier. At the age of 28 he volunteered to the National Baptist Convention to go to Africa as a missionary and eventually arrived in Malawi in 1901. He assisted John *Chilembwe, founder and head of the Providence Industrial Mission (PIM) in Malawi, who later led an uprising against the colonial government. Shortly after arriving, Cheek married Rachel Chilembwe, niece of John Chilembwe, and they had three children during Cheek's term of service. Cheek and fellow missionary Emma B. *Delaney set up an industrial-based education curriculum for the PIM more than 20 years before it was recommended by the Phelps Stokes Commission as the best educational method for Africa. Colonial pressure, lack of financial support, and health problems led Cheek to return to the United States in 1906. During the next 50 years he served various congregations as pastor, raised funds for foreign missions, and preached a positive message about his missionary experience.

BIBLIOGRAPHY Landon N. Cheek, "Reminiscences of a Missionary," *Mission Herald* 43 (March–April 1939): 15, (May–June 1939): 16–17, and 44 (September–October 1940): 17–18, and "Adventures of a St. Louis Missionary in Darkest Africa," *St. Louis Globe Democrat,* July 12, 1908. George Shepperson and Thomas Price, *Independent Africa* (1958).

Rodney H. Orr

Cheese, John Ethelstan (1877–1959), independent missionary in Somalia. Evidencing a mixture of eccentricity and piety, Cheese was described as "the holiest man in Somalia" by one who knew the affection in which he was held by the Somali peoples. He graduated from Cambridge University, was ordained by the Church of England, and began his missionary career among Druze villagers in pre–World War I Lebanon. In 1925, following a period of itinerant preaching among Palestinian bedouins, he moved to British Somaliland. Here, for 33 years, he lived the life of a simple holy man, emulating what he believed to be "the Presence of Christ" among the Somali peoples. Never employed by a mission agency, Cheese paved the way for the work of the Sudan Interior Mission among Somali Muslims.

BIBLIOGRAPHY Philip Cousins, "Twentieth Century St. Francis," *Theology* 81 (1978): 90–96; Constance Padwick, "Unpredictable: Impressions of the Life and Work of John Ethelstan Cheese," *The Muslim World* 57 (1967): 265–276.

David A. Kerr

Chen, Wen-Yuan (1897–1968), bishop of the Methodist Episcopal Church in China. Chen was educated in Methodist schools in Foochow (Fuzhow), earned B.A. and M.A. degrees at Syracuse University, New York, and returned to serve as pastor of the Church of Heavenly Peace (Tianantang) in Foochow. He received his Ph.D. degree from Duke University in 1929 and returned to Fukien Christian University in Foochow, where he taught psychology and later became dean and acting president. In 1936, while serving in Shanghai as head of the national YMCA's Youth and Religion department, he was elected general secretary of the National Christian Council. He was elected a delegate to the International Missionary Council at Madras in 1938 and served as a vice-chairman. In 1941 he became one of the four Methodist bishops in China, serving the west China area. As late as 1946 he continued in active service to the National Christian Council, as honorary general secretary, attending its first postwar meeting in December of that year.

Once designated by *Time* magazine as "China's No. 1 Protestant," Chen became an early target of the anti-imperialism movement in the Chinese church. At a denunciation meeting in 1951 in Peking (Beijing) attended by 151 Protestants, he was one of four Chinese church leaders attacked. In a speech entitled, "I Denounce That Christian Reprobate W. Y. Chen," his fellow Methodist, Z. T. Kaung, charged him with supporting the Nationalist regime of Chiang Kai-shek, both at home and abroad. He was placed in detention in 1951 and was released in 1959 due to illness. He died of cancer.

BIBLIOGRAPHY Francis P. Jones, *The Church in Communist China* (1962); Walter Lacy, *A Hundred Years of China Methodism* (1948); National Council of Churches of Christ of the U.S.A., *Documents of the Three-Self Movement* (1963); Roderick Scott, *Fukien Christian University* (1954).

Donald E. MacInnis

Chenchiah, Pandipeddi (1886–1959), leading Indian lay theologian. Chenchiah was born in Madras in a Telugu family all of whom became Christians in 1901. He had an excellent record in school, college, and law school and became judge in a small princely state in South India without, however, finding full satisfaction in his profession. Having read widely and attained a remarkable degree of independent scholarship in various fields of learning, Chenchiah became a prominent member of the progressive Rethinking Christianity group, advocating the secular mission of the church "in the spirit of self-forgetting love so much needed for nation building." While deprecating the mission-compound mentality of many Indian Christians, he led the way to an interaction of Hinduism and Christianity that met with criticism in many Christian circles. So did his secret initiation into a Hindu yoga school, as well as his contacts with the Ramakrishna Mission and the Theosophical Society. As a lay theologian he did not produce any systematic formulation of an Indian Christian theology. But he did make a unique contribution to a theological synthesis of Western naturalist philosophy, Indian spirituality, and Christian cosmology—as a "confluence of three streams, East and West, and fertilized by the stream of Christ's teaching of the kingdom of God."

BIBLIOGRAPHY D. A. Thangasamy, *The Theology of Chenchiah* (1966); Herwig Wagner, *Erstgestalten einer einheimischen Theologie in Südindien* (1963), pp. 107–197.

Hans-Werner Gensichen

Ch'eng Ching-Yi (Cheng Jingyi) (1881–1939), Chinese Protestant statesman. From about 1910 to well after 1930 Ch'eng played a key inspirational and administrative role in shaping church trends in the Chinese Protestant community. Deeply committed to shifting the focus from foreign missions to the Chinese church, he did much in this cause, yet without alienating the missionary community. He burned himself out in the process, and by the mid-1930s his health was failing and his activities had to be curtailed.

Ch'eng had a remarkably rapid rise to prominence. He grew up in Peking, where his father was a preacher associated with the London Missionary Society. He had just completed theological school in Tientsin (Tianjin) in 1900 when the Boxer uprising erupted. Ch'eng joined the Allied relief force as an interpreter. In 1903 he began assisting in a new Chinese Bible translation; this resulted in a total of five years in England and Glasgow. He then became pastor of a small church in Peking and pushed for its independence from mission control. At age 29, one of only three Chinese delegates to the 1910 Edinburgh World Missionary Conference, he electrified the assembly with an eloquent declaration in favor of rapid indigenization and elimination of Western-derived denominationalism.

Ch'eng became associated with John *Mott upon the latter's important visit to China in 1913, then served as secretary of the China Continuation Committee, preparatory to the National Christian Conference of 1922, of which he was chairperson. This seminal meeting's equal representation of Chinese and foreign delegates, and its clear theme, "The Chinese Church," owed much to Ch'eng. From 1924 to 1934 he was a secretary of the new ecumenical Sino-foreign National Christian Council; he was also a strong supporter of the union Church of Christ in China, formed in 1927, of which he became secretary in 1934.

BIBLIOGRAPHY Ch'eng wrote several articles in the English-language *Chinese Recorder* (Shanghai), and his reports and opinions run through the publications and bulletins of the National Christian Council after its founding in 1924. Howard L. Boorman and Richard C. Howard, eds., *Biographical Dictionary of Republican China*, vol. 1 (1967), pp. 284–286; Charles Boynton, "Dr. Cheng Ching-Yi," *Chinese Recorder* 70 (1939): 689–698 (obit.).

Daniel H. Bays

Chesterman, Clement C(lapton) (1894–1983), Baptist Missionary Society (BMS) medical missionary in the Belgian Congo (Zaire). In 1920 Chesterman, an Englishman, was sent by the BMS to Yakusu, in the upper Congo, the first resident doctor at that station. He supervised the erection of a new hospital and secured government recognition for Yakusu as a center for training medical auxiliaries. Confronted by evidence that up to 30 percent of the population was infected with sleeping sickness, he developed a network of health centers and dispensaries to implement a comprehensive program of preventive medicine using the new drug tryparsamide. His policy of mass chemotherapy was widely adopted in tropical Africa and succeeded in virtually eliminating the disease. Similar methods were later applied to the containment of yaws and leprosy. In 1936 Chesterman succeeded R. Fletcher *Moorshead as medical secretary of the BMS. He was knighted by the British crown for his work.

BIBLIOGRAPHY Clement C. Chesterman, *In the Service of Suffering: Phases of Medical Missionary Enterprise* (1940). S. G. Browne et al., eds., *Heralds of Health: The Saga of Christian Medical Initiatives* (1985); Brian Stanley, *The History of the Baptist Missionary Society, 1792–1992* (1992).

Brian Stanley

Chestnut, Eleanor (1868–1905), medical missionary in China. Chestnut served 11 years in China under the mission board of the Presbyterian Church, U.S.A., and suffered a martyr's death at the hands of a rioting mob. She was born in Waterloo, Iowa, orphaned in infancy, and raised by relatives. Graduating from Park College, Missouri, and the Women's Medical College of Illinois, she dedicated her life to mission. She sailed for China in 1894 to take responsibility for the recently opened women's hospital at the isolated mission station of Lianzhou (Lienchow), 300 miles up the Bei Jiang River from Guangzhou (Canton). She became well known for her travels on horseback to hold clinics in neighboring villages and for her sacrificial living in cramped and uncomfortable quarters on the second floor of the hospital.

In 1905 a confrontation occurred between Dr. Edward Machle and Buddhist priests at the temple adjacent to the hospital over the erection of a small, temporary Buddhist structure on hospital property. Although the dispute was amicably settled, a gang of ruffians enraged the gathering mob, which burned the mission station to the ground. The missionaries escaped to a nearby Buddhist grotto, where a priest had invited them to take refuge. When the mob arrived, four of the seven missionaries and a child (Rev. and Mrs. John Peale, Ella Machle, her ten-year-old daughter, and Miss Chestnut) were found and killed. The death of the young medical doctor made a deep impression on the populace, and witnesses said that her last act was to treat a Chinese boy who had been hit with a flying stone. Two years later the missionaries returned, the hospital and church were rebuilt, and the work went on.

Bibliography The best account of the Lianzhou affair, the investigation into its causes by the Chinese viceroy and the United States consular officials, and biographical sketches of the martyred missionaries are found in a pamphlet by Arthur J. Brown, *The Lien-Chou Martyrdom* (c. 1906). A shorter account appears in Arthur J. Brown, *One Hundred Years* (1936). See also Robert E. Speer, *Servants of the King* (1909).

G. Thompson Brown

Chevalier, Jules (1824–1907), French founder of two Catholic missionary societies. Born in Richelieu, near Tours, France, and educated at Bourges, France, Chevalier was ordained to the priesthood in 1851 and served in Issoudun, France. He founded the Society of the Missionaries of the Sacred Heart of Jesus in 1854, and, assisted by Marie-Louise Hartzer, the Congregation of the Daughters of Our Lady of the Sacred Heart in 1883. Both religious orders are based on devotion to the heart of Jesus, symbol of God's infinite love for the world. Their motto reads, *"Amatur unique terrarum Cor Jesu Sacratissimum"* (May the Most Sacred Heart of Jesus be loved everywhere). Chevalier also had a special devotion to the Blessed Virgin Mary, connecting the foundation of his new society with the papal definition of the dogma of the Immaculate Conception in the same year, 1854. He created new forms of accession to priesthood and religious life when he opened apostolic schools where poor students were admitted freely. The first was founded in 1867 by Jean Vandel in Chezal-Benoît, France. Others followed abroad. The foreign missionary outreach of the society began in 1881, in obedience to a papal commission, in New Guinea and the South Pacific.

Bibliography J. Chevalier, *Le Sacré-Coeur de Jésus dans ses rapports avec Marie, ou Notre-Dame du Sacré-Coeur* (1884). C. Piperon, *Le Très Révérend Père Jules Chevalier* (1952). See also *Annales de Notre Dame du Sacré Coeur* (1866 ff., also published in English).

Marc R. Spindler

Child, Abbie B. (1840–1902), leader of Protestant women's foreign mission work. Born in Lowell, Massachusetts, Child served as home secretary of the Woman's Board of Missions of the Congregational Church and editor of *Life and Light for Women* from 1870 until her death. During this time, she developed fifteen auxiliaries and many local branches of the board. In London in 1888, at the Centenary Conference on Protestant Missions of the World, she presented an inspiring paper encouraging women's increased participation in missions. At that conference, leaders from women's foreign mission boards in the United States, Canada, and Great Britian initiated the World's Missionary Committee of Christian Women, electing Child as chair. Under her leadership, the Committee held a conference of women's missionary societies during the Woman's Congress of Missions in Chicago in 1893; it planned sessions on women's work for the Ecumenical Missionary Conference in New York in 1900; and it formed the Central Committee on the United Study of Foreign Missions, which produced books and study material for all the American women's boards. Child instituted a weekly hour of prayer, from five to six o'clock each Sunday, for all member societies of the World's Missionary Committee. Other boards followed suit by observing days or weeks of prayer. This practice served as the inspiration for the World Day of Prayer.

Child made two journeys around the world to visit the mission fields in Turkey and Spain (1888) and in China, Japan, and India (1895–1896). She died suddenly at her home in Boston. The World's Missionary Committee existed nominally for a few more years after her death, and then was succeeded by the Interdenominational Conference of Woman's Boards of Foreign Missions.

Bibliography Biographical information on Child is included in R. Pierce Beaver, *American Protestant Women in World Mission: History of the Feminist Movement in North America* (1968); Patricia R. Hill, *The World Their Household: The American Woman's Foreign Mission Movement and Cultural Transformation, 1870–1920* (1985); "Death of Miss Abbie B. Child," *Missionary Herald* 98 (1902); "In Memoriam," *Life and Light for Women* 32, no. 12 (December 1902).

Joan R. Duffy

Chilembwe, John (c. 1871–1915), Malawian independent church leader and protonationalist hero. Born near Chiradzulu, Malawi, in the 1890s Chilembwe fell under the influence of Joseph *Booth, who baptized him in July 1893. Going to the United States with Booth in 1897, he split with his mentor and spent two years studying at Lynchburg (Virginia) Theological Seminary, where he seems to have been ordained by the National Baptist Convention. He returned to Malawi (then a British protectorate) in 1900 and formed the Providence Industrial Mission, near his birthplace. Between 1900 and 1914 he worked quietly, building up a small following and attracting little publicity. As World War I approached, he became increasingly upset by the unjust employment practices of neighboring European-owned estates. The outbreak of war in 1914 and the conscription of large numbers of Africans as soldiers and carriers led him to instigate a military uprising against colonial rule in January 1915. He may have modeled himself on John Brown. Although the uprising was a military fiasco, Chilembwe's death in its aftermath assured for him a martyr's place in the subsequent history of African anticolonial struggle.

BIBLIOGRAPHY George Simeon Mwase, *Strike a Blow and Die* (1967); Bridglal Pachai, *Malawi: The History of the Nation* (1973); George Shepperson and Thomas Price, *Independent African: John Chilembwe and the Nyasaland Rising of 1915* (1958).

T. Jack Thompson

Ching T'ien-Yin (Jing Dianying) (1890–1973?), founding member of the Jesus Family in China. Ching was born into a strong Confucian family in Shantung (Shandong) Province. Educated in a Methodist school in T'ai-an (Tai'an), Shantung (Shandong) Province, he made a commitment to Christ in 1911. A few years after his conversion, he was reconciled to his wife, whom he had abandoned some years earlier. She was converted in 1920, and in 1921 they started a cooperative project on land he owned. This led gradually to the formation of a community that later came to be known as the Jesus Family (Yesu Chiat'ing) and which eventually had several hundred members gathered into a number of Christian communes. In the early 1930s Ching, his wife, and others preached the gospel widely in north China. The communist government closed the Christian communes in 1953 and Ching was imprisoned for 20 years.

BIBLIOGRAPHY D. V. Rees, *The "Jesus Family" in Communist China* (1959).

Ralph R. Covell

Chini, Eusebio Francesco. *See* Kino, Eusebio Francisco.

Chi-Oang (1872–1946), Taiwan tribal evangelist. Chi-Oang was the daughter of a chief of the Tayal tribe in the mountains of northeast Taiwan. Her clan resisted Japanese rule and continued to fight for ten years after Taiwan was ceded to Japan in 1895. Peace finally came through the mediation of Chi-Oang, who was known by both sides as "the reconciler."

Through her marriage to a Taiwanese of Chinese extraction, she learned the dominant language of the island and became accustomed to life on the plains. She also became a Christian and in her early fifties studied in a Bible school. Chinese were not allowed to enter the tribal areas and Christian preaching was very strictly prohibited by the Japanese rulers, but this did not inhibit Chi-Oang. In 1931, already frail, she returned to her own people and began an itinerant evangelistic ministry. By foot, by train, and sometimes on the backs of young men she evangelized her people. When travel became impossible, they came to her. Chi-Oang, the political reconciler, reconciled men and women to God until she died, and the hundreds of mountain churches now in existence honor her as their apostle.

BIBLIOGRAPHY Edward Band, ed., *He Brought Them Out* (1950); George Vicedom, *Faith that Moves Mountains* (1967).

H. Daniel Beeby

Chitambar, Jashwant Rao (1879–1940), leader of the Methodist Church in India. Chitambar was born in Allahabad, India, the son of converts from Hinduism. He secured his B.A. from Lucknow Christian College and did his theological training at the Methodist Theological Seminary in Bareilly. On completing his seminary course, he served effectively as pastor of the Central Methodist Church in Lucknow and then as superintendent of the Eastern Kumaon district in north India. He was one of few non-Western participants at the 1910 World Missionary Conference in Edinburgh. Chitambar's career was marked by a series of extraordinary firsts. For five years he served as the first general secretary of the Epworth League for India and Burma (now Myanmar). He was one of the founders of the National Missionary Society in 1905 and helped to organize the India Methodist Missionary Society, which he served as the first executive secretary. In 1922 he was appointed the first Indian principal of Lucknow Christian College, and from that position he was elected the first Indian bishop of the Methodist Church in India. He served effectively in this capacity from January 1931 until his death in 1940. Chitambar was known widely for his preaching ability. Whether speaking in Urdu, Hindi, or English, he was fluent and forceful, preaching always with passion and power.

BIBLIOGRAPHY B. T. Badley, *The Making of a Bishop* (1943); John N. Hollister, *The Centenary of the Methodist Church in Southern Asia* (1956), pp. 255–256. The September 12, 1940, issue of *The Indian Witness* is devoted entirely to the life and ministry of Bishop Chitambar, with articles of tribute by many colleagues.

John T. Seamands

Choi Chan Young (1927–), Korean missionary in Southeast Asia, Presbyterian pastor, missiologist, and lifelong worker of the United Bible Societies. Choi was born in China to a third-generation Christian family. He graduated from the Presbyterian Seminary in Seoul and for 38 years (1955–1993) served as the first Korean missionary after Korean independence sent by the Presbyterian Church in the Republic of Korea; he was supported by the Yungnak Presbyterian Church in Seoul. He and his wife, Esther (Kim Kwang Myung), a medical doctor, pioneered Korean cross-cultural work in Thailand. This represented a new venture by the Korean church, as he worked among the Thai people, not the Korean diaspora. Beginning in 1962 he was the secretary of the Thailand Bible Society for 14 years, and became regional secretary for the United Bible Societies for 4 years in the Philippines, and for 14 years in Hong Kong. In 1987 he played an important role in the establishment of Amity Press in Nanking, China; it has printed some 600 million Bibles and 400 million hymnbooks in six different Chinese languages. His vision is to evangelize China by distributing the Scriptures. He is fluent in Chinese and Thai. Since 1992 he has been on the faculty of Fuller Seminary School of World Mission in Pasadena, California, as director of extension studies for Korean students.

BIBLIOGRAPHY Choi's autobiography was published in Korean in 1995.

Chun Chae Ok

Chong Yak-Jong, Augustine (1760–1801), early Korean Catholic martyr. Chong came from a noble, educated family residing near Seoul. His worldview was Confucian, but through the study of Taoism and other academic subjects (including philosophy, ethics, literature, and medicine) and an encounter with *I Sung-Hun, Chong discovered Christianity. Against the express wishes of his father and brothers, he was baptized in 1786 and became a leading figure in early Korean Christianity. He survived the persecution of 1791, in which many Christians lapsed from the faith and others died as martyrs, and fearlessly continued his activity. *Chou Wen-mo from China, the first Catholic priest to enter Korea (1793), nominated him president of the Myong Do Hoe (The Bright Way Association). The object of this association, which consisted of groups of five or six persons, was to study and spread the Christian faith. Chong compiled a catechism in Korean so that ordinary people would be able to understand Christian doctrine; it was approved by Chou and used in Korea until 1932. In 1797 Chong was brought before a local court and then before the supreme court in Seoul in 1799. Together with Chou, for whom he interceded to the very end, he was beheaded in the persecution of 1801/1802. One of Chong's last statements was: "I would never regret [having become a Christian] even if I had to die a thousand times."

BIBLIOGRAPHY C. Dalles, *L'Église de Corée,* 2 vols. (1874); H. Diaz, *A Korean Theology, Chu-Gyo Yo-Ji: Essentials of the Lord's Teaching by Chŏng Yak-jong (1760–1801)* (1986); Sung-Hae Kim, "Liberation and Inculturation: Two Streams of Doing Theology with Asian Resources," *Interreligio,* no. 12 (1987): 67–83.

Karl Müller, SVD

Chou Wen-Mo (Zhou Wenmo, *also* Chou Mon-mo) (1753–1801), Chinese diocesan priest and missionary to Korea. Chou Wen-mo, known in Korean as Chou Mun-mo and in Portuguese accounts as Diogo Vellozo, was a native of Suchow (Suzhou), Anhwei (Anhui) Province, China. Orphaned at the age of 8 and raised by an aunt, he was married at 20 and widowed three years later. He was 30 when he entered the seminary at Peking (Beijing). The bishop of Peking chose him as the first priest permanently assigned to the Korea mission, with its 4,000 Christians. In December 1794, with the help of two Korean Christians, he crossed the Yalu River and the following month entered Seoul. For six months he was a very busy pastor, but reports from an informer masquerading as a convert, led to an order for his arrest. Several Christians helped him escape, and he pursued underground pastoral activities in various areas for the next several years. During the 1801 nationwide persecution, when more than 300 Christians died, an apostate told the police about Chou's hideout. Already on his way back to China, since he believed that his presence was the cause of the persecution, Chou was near the border when he decided to return to Seoul in the hope that his surrender would mitigate the harshness of the persecution. Condemned to death, he was executed at Sae-nam-t'o on Trinity Sunday, May 31. Korean officials secretly buried his body so that Christians would never find it.

BIBLIOGRAPHY Andreas Choi, *L'érection du premier vicariat apostolique et les origines du catholicisme en Corée, 1592–1837* (1961), pp. 48, 49, 64, 110, 113, 117; Charles Dallet, *Histoire de l'église de Corée,* 2 vols. (1874), vol. 1, pp. 70–81, 128–148; Joseph Chang-mu Kim and John Jae-sun Chung, eds., *Catholic Korea Yesterday and Today* (1964), pp. 46–50, 55–65.

John W. Witek, SJ

Christaller, Johannes Gottlieb (1827–1895), Basel Mission linguist, Bible translator, and missionary to Ghana. Born in a poor home in Winnenden, southwest Germany, Christaller showed unusual intelligence, great eagerness to learn, and exceptional ability in languages. A product of the pietist fellowships within the Lutheran Church, he early sensed a call to missionary service. After four years of training at the Mission House in Basel, he was sent to the Gold Coast (modern Ghana), arriving in January 1853. In addition to teaching at the recently founded (1848) Basel Mission Seminary at Akropong-Akuapem, his major task was Scripture translation and the production of other Christian literature for the growing indigenous Christian communities.

Christaller rapidly mastered the Twi language and began his translation of the Bible. In 1859 the four Gospels and the Acts of the Apostles were printed. By 1863 all the books of the New Testament were available in separate volumes. Psalms and Proverbs followed in 1866. Of rather weak constitution, Christaller had to return to Europe in 1868, but he took with him the complete text of the Bible in Twi, which was printed in 1871. From Schondorf, where he had settled, he continued to serve the Twi-speaking churches in the Gold Coast. In 1875 he published his scientific grammar of the Twi language, followed in 1881 by his magnum opus, *Dictionary of the Asante and Fante Language—called Twi* (two volumes), a veritable lexicon of Akan cultural, religious, and social ideas. From 1883 until his death Christaller edited *The Christian Messenger,* which continues today as Ghana's oldest Christian periodical. Christaller was twice awarded the Prix Volney of the French Academy. His contribution to the development of indigenous Christianity in Ghana was well assessed by Noel Smith: "Christaller's work achieved three things: it raised the Twi language to a literary level and provided the basis of all later work in the language; it gave the first real insight into Akan religious, social, and moral ideas; and it welded the expression of Akan Christian worship to the native tongue" (*The History of the Presbyterian Church in Ghana, 1835–1960* [1965]).

BIBLIOGRAPHY Johannes G. Christaller, *Missionar J. G. Christaller: Erinnerungen aus seinem Leben* (1929). For two Ghanaian assessments of Christaller's missionary career, see J. B. Danquah, *The Akan Doctrine of God: A Fragment of Gold Coast Ethics and Religion* (1944), pp. 185ff., and Kwame Bediako, *Christianity in Africa: The Renewal of a Non-Western Religion* (1995), chaps. 3 and 5.

Kwame Bediako

Christie, Dugald (1855–1936), Scottish medical missionary in China. Christie was the son of a Glencoe sheep farmer. His parents died during his childhood and he was apprenticed to a Glasgow draper. Following an evangelical conversion during D. L. *Moody's mission of 1874, he studied medicine under the auspices of the Edinburgh Medical Missionary Society and became a resident physician in their inner city mission. In 1882, with his wife, Elizabeth Hastie (Smith), he began work in Manchuria as a medical missionary of the United Presbyterian Church (after 1900, the United Free Church) of Scotland. From Newchang (now Ying-k'ou), he soon moved to the capital, Mukden (Shen-yang). Itinerant medical work gave way to a chain of dispensaries, and after two years he opened Manchuria's first hospital, which played a notable part amid the natural disasters and endemic warfare afflicting the area. Christie's policy of training an indigenous staff culminated in 1912 in Mukden Medical College, which offered a full curriculum for doctors and laid the basis of modern medical education in the region. Elizabeth Christie died in 1888; Christie married Liza Inglis, a United Presbyterian missionary, in 1892. He retired in 1923 and died in Edinburgh.

Christie's address at the Centenary Missionary Conference in Shanghai in 1907 articulated a coherent, christologically grounded philosophy of medical missions as integral, not ancillary, to the gospel. He argued for the highest professional standards (higher than some thought necessary in the West); due regard to local context, with deep respect for language and custom; the concomitance of medical, evangelistic, and pastoral work; the development of a skilled indigenous medical staff; and free treatment (healing should be as free as preaching). The last ran counter to much mission practice, and Christie's own mission avoided financial responsibility for Mukden Medical College and other major developments. Christie, insisting on theological grounds that the Christian church should rise to the financial challenges of the gospel of healing, raised support for the college from Western and especially Chinese sources.

BIBLIOGRAPHY Dugald Christie, *Ten Years in Manchuria* (1893) and *Thirty Years in Moukden* (1914). Liza Inglis Christie, *Dugald Christie of Manchuria* (1932); A. Fulton, *Through Earthquake, Wind, and Fire: Church and Mission in Manchuria, 1867–1950* (1967); J. A. Lamb, *Fasti of the United Free Church of Scotland* (1956), p. 549.

Andrew F. Walls

Christlieb, Theodor (1833–1889), German Protestant missiologist. A native of Württemberg, Germany, Christlieb served seven years as German pastor in London and became professor of practical theology at Bonn University in 1868. As coeditor of Gustav *Warneck's *Allgemeine Missions-Zeitschrift* (1874), he put his knowledge of Britain and of English church life and theology to good use. His affinity to the Anglo-Saxon revival movement led him to advocate evangelistic lay preaching in Germany and to cofound the German Association for Evangelization, and the Johanneum, a college for the training of evangelists at Barmen. He was also one of the first missiologists to deal with the ministry of healing as an integral part of the Christian mission. His book *Ärztlich Missionen* (Medical missions, 1889), though not the first of its kind in German, was a truly pioneering effort. It offered a well-documented survey of the history of medical missions, including a special chapter on the importance of the activities of women. It also appealed to missionary societies and medical personnel to take part in this important branch of the missionary enterprise, which, in Christlieb's opinion, called for a strictly ecumenical approach.

BIBLIOGRAPHY Emily Christlieb, *Theodor Christlieb of Bonn* (1892); Arno Pagel, *Theodor Christlieb: Ein Leben* (1960); Thomas Schirrmacher, *Christlieb* (1985).

Hans-Werner Gensichen

Christoffel, Ernst Jakob (1876–1955), pioneer of mission to the blind in the Near East. Prototype of a solitary charismatic, Christoffel, a German pastor, decided to go to the Near East in order to witness to the love of Christ by charitable work among Muslims. He began by founding two orphanages at Siwas, Turkey, in the years 1904 to 1907, commissioned by a Swiss agency for aid to Armenians. He continued with a Christian asylum for the blind at Malatya in 1908 without any organized backing. Expelled after World War I, he made a new start with institutions for the blind in Persia. After imprisonment by British authorities during World War II, he was able to begin again at Isfahan where he died in 1955 after more than a half century of service, including three periods of imprisonment and two of internment. The work at Isfahan was taken over by the Church Missionary Society. Christoffel did not live to see its expansion into one of the largest organizations of its kind, operating all over the world as Christoffel-Blindenmission International with headquarters at Bensheim, Germany.

BIBLIOGRAPHY Fritz Schmidt-König, *Ernst J. Christoffel: Vater der Blinden im Orient* (1969); Marietta Peitz, *Wurzeln und Zweige: 80 Jahre Christoffel-Blindenmission* (1988).

Hans-Werner Gensichen

Chrysostom, John (c. 347–407), patriarch of Constantinople. Chrysostom was born in Antioch, son of a general in the imperial army, Secundus, and a Christian mother, Anthusa. Best known for his liturgies, homilies, and writings in defense of Christian faith, he was also an ardent missionary advocate.

He was baptized (c. 370), became a hermit (c. 381), and was ordained a priest (387). As the ablest preacher of the fourth-century Greek church, he came to be called Chrysostom, "golden-mouthed." He was consecrated bishop of Constantinople in 398 and sent monks from Constantinople to evangelize pagan peoples, including Goths. Refusing to depend on imperial decrees or the use of force to win converts, he insisted that the example of Christian living is the most effective way to evangelize non-Christians.

Chrysostom's episcopal tenure in Constantinople was cut short because of theological and administrative controversies with the bishops of Alexandria and Rome, and with the Empress Eudoxia, who resented his preaching against the extravagant ways of the rich. Exiled in 403, he continued to encourage missions to Cilicia and Phoenicia. He was recalled to his episcopal office after one year but was again exiled to Cucusus in Armenia. In 407 he was summoned to a more remote exile in Iberia, but he died en route.

BIBLIOGRAPHY Paul Andres, *Der Missionsgedanke in den Schriften des heiligen Johannes Chrysostomus* (1935); Donald Attwater, *St. John Chrysostom* (1959); Chrysostomus Baur, *John Chrysostom and His Times,* M. Gonzaga, tr., 2 vols., 2d ed. (1988); Jaroslav Pelikan, ed., *The Preaching of Chrysostom: Homilies on the Sermon on the Mount* (1967); Aimé Puech, *St. John Chrysostom,* Mildred Partridge, tr., 2d ed. (1917); Jacques Paul Migne, *Patrologiae Graicai,* tomes 47-64 (1965).

Norman A. Horner

Church, John E. ("Joe") (1899-1989), a leader in the East African Revival. Son of an English country clergyman, Joe Church, as he was known, was educated at St. Lawrence's School and at Cambridge, qualifying in medicine at St. Bartholomew's Hospital, London. In 1927 he joined the Church Missionary Society (CMS) Rwanda mission. From Kabale, Uganda, he went to Gahini, Rwanda, at the time of a serious famine. This crisis in part triggered a searching for a victorious spiritual life that resulted in contact with a Ganda Christian, Simeon *Nsibambi, who was engaged in the same search. From 1929, with Nsibambi and other African Christians, and soon with other missionaries, he spearheaded a movement known as the East African Revival. Revival spread rapidly into Kenya and Tanganyika (Tanzania), and Church led teams that took the message near and far. He still worked as a doctor at Gahini, cooperating with the hospital staff in evangelism as well as healing. Conventions were arranged, locally and in other centers, that continued the spread of the revival. In 1934 William Church, a brother and also a doctor, went to Gahini, allowing Joe Church to take on a more active evangelistic role. Revival Christians became the core of many Protestant churches throughout East Africa. Joe remained deeply involved until his retirement in 1975.

Joe and his wife, Decima (Tracey) (1904-1991), also a doctor, had five children. Their son, John, a doctor, also served at Gahini. A brother, Howard, was a CMS missionary in Kenya.

BIBLIOGRAPHY J. E. Church, *Quest for the Highest: An Autobiographical Account of the East African Revival* (1981). George E. Mambo, "The Revival Fellowship (Brethren) in Kenya," in D. B. Barrett et al., eds., *Kenya Churches Handbook* (1973), pp. 110-117; Patricia St. John, *Breath of Life: The Story of the Ruanda Mission* (1971); Max Warren, *Revival: An Enquiry* (1954).

Jocelyn Murray

Claret, Anthony Mary (1807-1870), founder of the Claretians. Born in Sallent, Spain, Claret worked in the textile industry until he discerned a vocation to the priesthood. Ordained at 28, he felt a missionary calling and entered the Jesuits in Rome, but his health broke down and he was advised to return to Spain. There he gained a notable reputation as a preacher of parish missions. In 1849 several priests joined him and together they formed the Congregation of the Sons of the Immaculate Heart of Mary, known today as the Claretians. Soon afterward, Claret was appointed archbishop of Santiago, Cuba. For seven years he served the poor and brought about needed reforms in church life.

In 1857 Queen Isabella asked for him to be her personal chaplain, a position he accepted only on the condition that he could continue his preaching and writing. He wrote or compiled numerous books and pamphlets and founded a major publishing house. A revolution in 1868 forced the queen out of Spain and Claret with her.

Claret was a participant in the First Vatican Council in 1870. He died in the Cistercian Monastery in Fontfrode, France. He was declared a saint by Pope *Pius XII in 1950. His feast day is celebrated on October 24. Claretian missionaries now serve in fifty-three countries around the world.

BIBLIOGRAPHY Saint Anthony Mary Claret, *Autobiography* (Eng. tr., 1976); John M. Lozano, *Mystic and Man of Action: Saint Anthony Mary Claret* (1977) and *Anthony Claret: A Life at the Service of the Gospel* (1985).

Mark J. Brummel, CMF

Clark, Charles Allen (1878-1961), missionary of the Presbyterian Church, U.S.A., in Korea. A graduate of McCormick Seminary (1902), Clark and his first wife, Mabel (d. 1946), were stationed in Seoul through 1923 and then in Pyengyang until 1941. He had a part in founding more than 100 churches, personally pastoring fifty-three congregations. The editor of three periodicals during his lifetime, he served as a faculty member of the Presbyterian Theological Seminary in Pyengyang (1908-1941) and was a prodigious writer of theological textbooks. When he left Korea in 1941, under threat of imprisonment by the Japanese government, he had written six books in the English language and thirty-eight in Korean, including eighteen full-length biblical commentaries, two texts on homiletics, and two on pastoral theology. Unable to return to Korea because of the outbreak of the Korean War (1950-1953), he spent the last years of his life in Oklahoma, pastoring a number of smaller churches and continuing to write Bible commentaries for the Korean church.

BIBLIOGRAPHY Clark's Ph.D. dissertation (Univ. of Chicago, 1929) was published in Korea as *The Nevius Plan for Mission Work: Illustrated in Korea* (rev. 1937). His 1932 *Religions of Old Korea* was a pioneer study of the country's religious history. His biblical commentaries appeared in the Standard Bible Commentary series, authorized in 1934 by the General Assembly of the Korean Presbyterian Church. From Clark came the first volume, *Job and Psalms* (1937). Interrupted by World War II and the Korean War, his titles continued to appear, including *Numbers* (1957), *Leviticus* (1957), *Mark* (1958), and *Luke* (1962). Allen D. Clark, *All Our Family in the House* (1975); Harry Rhodes, ed., *History of the Korea Mission, Presbyterian Church, U.S.A., 1884–1934* (1934); Harry Rhodes and Archibald Campbell, eds., *History of the Korea Mission, Presbyterian Church, U.S.A., vol. II, 1935–1959* (1964).

Harvie M. Conn

Clark, Ephraim W. (1799–1878), American missionary to Hawaii. Born in Haverhill, New Hampshire, a graduate of Dartmouth College (B.A., 1824; M.A., 1827) and of Andover Theological Seminary (1827), Clark was ordained in 1827. He married Mary Kittredge and sailed under the American Board of Commissioners for Foreign Missions (ABCFM) to the Sandwich Islands, arriving in 1828 at Honolulu, where he was first stationed. From 1835 to 1843 Clark taught at the Lahainalunu high school on Maui, then did evangelistic work at Wailuku. From 1848 to 1863 he was pastor of the large First Church of Honolulu. In 1852, as secretary of the newly formed Hawaiian Missionary Society, he went to Micronesia with the first company of American and Hawaiian missionaries. In 1856 he made a trip to New York to supervise the printing of the Hawaiian New Testament, and in 1859 he again returned to the United States to marry Sarah Helen Richards Hall (his first wife having died in 1857). Clark resigned from the mission in 1864 to superintend publication of the Hawaiian Bible by the American Bible Society in New York. He did not return to the islands. He was also in charge of Hawaiian printing at the Tract House in New York. He translated the Tract Society's Bible dictionary and published several other books and tracts, including a hymn and tune book for Sunday schools. While in Hawaii he had translated *Mathematical Texts,* an almanac, tracts on marriage and on astronomy, and Abbott's *Little Philosopher.*

BIBLIOGRAPHY *Missionary Album* (1969) contains a sketch of Clark's life and work; *Missionary Herald* 74 (1878): 281–282 provides an obituary.

David M. Stowe

Clark, Henry Martyn (c. 1857–1916), Church Missionary Society (CMS) doctor in North India. In 1859, when his Afghan mother died outside Peshawar, Clark was taken into the family of Robert *Clark, CMS missionary in the Punjab. He was educated in Scotland from 1869, at George Watson's School and at Edinburgh University. He studied medicine, and in 1882, with a Scottish wife, left to begin the Amritsar Medical Mission. Receiving his M.D. in 1892, he continued to serve in the Punjab until 1905. With a good knowledge of Urdu and Punjabi from his childhood in Peshawar, and as an excellent and caring doctor, he became a skilled controversialist with Muslims. He wrote extensively; for five years he was editor of *Punjab Mission News,* and he wrote papers and pamphlets on Islam, Hinduism, and medical matters. He was the editor in chief of the official *Dictionary of Punjabi* and wrote a life of his adoptive father.

After retiring from the mission in 1905, he lived in Edinburgh, Scotland, where he lectured in tropical medicine at the university.

BIBLIOGRAPHY H. M. Clark, *Robert Clark of the Punjab: Pioneer Missionary and Statesman* (1907); Arthur Neve, "In Memoriam," *C. M. Intelligencer,* November 1916, pp. 559–561.

Jocelyn Murray

Clark, Robert (1825–1900), Church Missionary Society (CMS) missionary in the Punjab. Born in Harmston, Lincolnshire, England, Clark and his colleague Thomas Fitzpatrick were the first CMS missionaries in the Punjab. Clark founded the CMS mission station in Amritsar (1852), the CMS Afghan Mission in Peshawar (1854), and the Kashmir Mission (1864). When the Lahore Diocese was established in 1877, he became the first chairman of its Punjab Native Church Council, as well as the first secretary of both its CMS mission (1878–1898) and the Church of England Zenana Missionary Society (1878–1900). Throughout his lifetime he was recognized by the CMS, other missions, and the government as one of the most respected missionary leaders in the Punjab. He died at Kasauli in the Himalayas.

BIBLIOGRAPHY Robert Clark, *A Brief Account of Thirty Years of Missionary Work of the Church Missionary Society in the Punjab and Sindh* (1883, 1884; revised by Robert Maconachie as *The Mission of the Church Missionary Society and the Church of England Missionary Society in the Punjab and Sindh,* 1904). Henry Martyn Clark, *Robert Clark of the Punjab: Pioneer Missionary and Statesman* (1907).

John C. B. Webster

Clark, William Smith (1826–1886), American educator in Hokkaido, Japan. Clark spent less than a year in Japan but his name is probably better known than that of any other foreigner who contributed to the modernization of Japan. A graduate of Amherst College with a doctorate in chemistry from the University of Göttingen, Germany, he was president of Massachusetts Agricultural College when he went to Japan in June 1878. Employed by the Japanese government, he organized an agricultural school in Sapporo, Hokkaido. In addition to his other duties, he was charged with the moral training of the students. He used the Bible as a textbook and as a result of the influence of this Congregational Church layman, all of the students in the class accepted Christ. They then led many of the members of the next entering class to Christ, forming what became known as the Sapporo Band. Among them were several who made noteworthy contributions to the world of education and to the Christian movement in Japan, including Kanzo *Uchimura, Shosuke Sato, and Inazo Nitobe. After leaving Japan Clark resigned from Massachusetts Agricultural College because of problems with its board of trustees and then entered into an unsuccessful business venture in New York. He died in Massachusetts after several years of ill health.

BIBLIOGRAPHY John M. Maki, "William Smith Clark, *Yatoi,* 1826–1886," in Edward R. Beauchamp and Akira Iriye, eds., *Foreign Employees in Nineteenth-Century Japan* (1990); Shingo Osaka, *Kuraaku Sensei Shoden* (1956; short biography of Clark); Yuzo Ota, *Kuraaku no ichinen* (1979; on Clark's one year in Japan); D. P. Penhallow, *William Smith Clark* (1908). A book-length manuscript by John M. Maki, *William Smith Clark: A Yankee in Hokkaido,* in the Univ. of Massachusetts archives, was shortened and translated by Shinichi Takaku as *Kuraaku: Sono Eiko to Zasetsu* (Clark: His glory and collapse) (1978).

John W. Krummel

Clarke, John (1802–1879), Baptist Missionary Society (BMS) missionary in Jamaica, Fernando Póo, and the Cameroons. Clarke, an Englishman, sailed for Jamaica in 1829, where he worked until 1840. In response to the desire of many newly emancipated slaves to send the gospel to their native continent, he and G. K. Prince were sent by the BMS to West Africa in 1840 to explore the possibilities of a mission to the Niger. They landed on the island of Fernando Póo in January 1841 and began work among the freed slave population. Rather than proceeding to the Niger, Clarke and Prince recommended that the BMS establish a mission on the island and on the neighboring Cameroonian mainland. In the course of 1842 and 1843, Clarke visited Jamaica twice and England once to recruit volunteers for the new mission. In February 1844, he returned to Fernando Póo with a party of forty-two Jamaican teachers and settlers. This experiment was not a success, as it was dogged by problems of ill health and quarreling. In 1847 Clarke led many of the migrants home to Jamaica. Nonetheless, the Cameroons mission survived and later became the springboard for the BMS Congo mission. Clarke spent the rest of his life as a Baptist minister in Jamaica.

BIBLIOGRAPHY John Clarke, *Introduction to the Fernandian Tongue* (1848) and *Memorials of Baptist Missionaries in Jamaica* (1869). D. J. East, "The Late Rev. John Clarke, of Jamaica," *Missionary Herald* (1879): 359–364; Lamin Sanneh, *West African Christianity: The Religious Impact* (1983); Brian Stanley, *The History of the Baptist Missionary Society, 1792–1992* (1992).

Brian Stanley

Classe, Léon (1874–1945), French Catholic missionary in Rwanda. Born in Nancy, Lorraine, France, Classe was ordained a priest in the Society of Missionaries of Africa (also known as the White Fathers) in 1900. The same year he was appointed one of the first two missionaries to Rwanda, where he suffered the hostility of the Batutsi king, Musinga. In 1907 he was appointed pro-vicar of Kivu and in 1912 vicar apostolic. In 1922 he was appointed vicar apostolic of Rwanda. After the king decreed freedom of religion, the mission began to flourish. In 1943 Classe baptized King Mutara III, son of Musinga, in the presence of the fifty-two chiefs of Rwanda (all but two of whom were Christians by then). Many of the church buildings needed for the growing number of faithful were designed by Classe. He died in Bujumbura, Burundi.

BIBLIOGRAPHY "S. E. Léon Classe," *Rapports Annuels, Notices Nécrologiques, 1939–1945, Pères Blancs* (1946), pp. 28–83; G. D. Kittler, *The White Fathers* (1957); Antoine van Overschelde, *Monseigneur Léon Paul Classe: Premier Vicaire Apostolique du Ruanda (1945).*

J. G. Donders, M Afr

Claver, Peter (1580–1654), Jesuit saint famed for his work among the black slaves in Cartagena, Colombia. Born in Verdú, Catalonia, Claver studied at the University of Barcelona and entered the Society of Jesus in 1602. While studying at the Jesuit college of Montesión in Mallorca, he befriended the porter, Brother Alfonso Rodríguez, who was widely esteemed for his holiness. Rodríguez (later canonized) urged Claver to go to the New World as a missionary, and in 1610 Claver was summoned by his provincial to do just that. With three other Jesuits he arrived in Cartagena, a major port and center for the African slave trade on the Caribbean coast of Colombia. He finished his theology studies in Bogotá and in 1615 returned to Cartagena, where he was ordained a priest a year later. Another Jesuit, Alonso de *Sandoval, had already begun working among the slaves. Sandoval, who sharply criticized abuses against the slaves in his writings, took Claver under his guidance. Claver, however, won fame not so much for his denunciation of slavery as for his human charity toward the slaves. He entered newly arriving ships with a band of interpreters, most of them former slaves. He fed the new arrivals and attended to their health needs. Through his interpreters and by means of pictures, he managed to communicate with them. According to his own claims, during his lifetime he baptized around 300,000 slaves. He regularly visited the slave quarters in the city as well as the hospitals, especially the one for lepers. In 1650 he fell victim to a plague and remained bedridden for the last four years of his life. He styled himself the "slave of black slaves for all time." Modern critics note that neither Sandoval or Claver raised a voice, at least in a clear and public way, against the system of slavery. On the other hand, by not making himself a nuisance to the authorities, Claver was allowed to carry out his humanitarian mission. He was canonized in 1888.

BIBLIOGRAPHY Arnold Henry Moore Lunn, *A Saint in the Slave Trade: Peter Claver, 1581–1654* (1935, 1947); Angel Valtierra, *Peter Claver, Saint of the Slaves* (1960).

Jeffrey Klaiber, SJ

Clement VIII (1536–1605), pope who implemented the Council of Trent (1545–1563) and undertook thoroughgoing church reform. An Italian lawyer and diplomat, Ippolito Aldobrandini was ordained in 1580, serving as papal legate in Poland prior to his election as Pope Clement VIII in 1592. He initiated the reform of religious communities, revised liturgical books and the Vulgate translation of Sixtus V, and promoted strict orthodoxy. There were inconsistencies. Piety and abnegation were mixed with nepotism and flamboyance. His reactivated inquisition sent more than thirty "heretics" to the stake, although he defended Huguenot religious freedom and abrogated the excommunication against Henri IV of France.

Though a Roman Catholic restorationist, Clement was a missionary pontiff of some finesse. In Europe he reunited millions of Orthodox with Rome, confirmed Ruthenian and Ukrainian liturgical practices, and supported Maronites, Italo-Greeks, and Serbs. His attempts to restore Sweden and Britain to Roman influence failed, although he claimed greater success in Switzerland. He minimized Spanish influence on the papacy, thus retaining the independence of the Holy See.

Beyond Europe he was an outstanding champion of missions, initially favoring Portuguese Jesuits over Spanish Franciscans in Japan, China, and Korea, but later encouraging the expansion of all the mendicant orders. He established dioceses in the Philippines, and during his pontificate, cordial contact was made with the Great Mogul of India and the Shah of Persia. In Africa, diocesan expansion continued in Kongo (Congo), Angola, Guinea, and Abyssinia (Ethiopia). Mexico, Peru, Chile, and Brazil were supported, and by 1601 there were 32 dioceses, 2 universities, 400 religious houses, and numerous hospitals and mission stations in Spanish America alone.

His Congregation for the Missions, established in 1594 and renamed in 1599 the Congregation for the Propagation of the Faith, was the forerunner of the 1622 congregation Propaganda Fide, the central Roman congregation for all missionary activity.

BIBLIOGRAPHY N. Chirovsky, *The Millennium of Ukrainian Christianity* (1988); H. Jedin, *History of the Church,* vol. 5 (1980); K. S. Latourette, *A History of the Expansion of Christianity,* vol. 3 (1937); W. Miller, *Medieval Rome from Hildebrand to Clement VIII* (1902); L. von Pastor, *The History of the Popes,* vols. 23, 24 (1952).

Anthony J. Gittins, CSSp

Clement XI (1649–1721), pope and promoter of missions. Giovanni Francesco Albani, born of a noble Umbrian family, was educated at the Roman College and later studied philosophy and law. He entered curial service in 1677, serving in governorships in Rieti, the Sabine Province, and Orvieto in central Italy. In 1687 he was appointed secretary of briefs and created cardinal in 1690. He was ordained a priest in September 1700 and two months later, after a 46-day conclave, was elected pope (r. 1700–1721).

Although Clement XI was known both for his upright life and for his administrative skills, papal influence was on the wane in Europe. Two-thirds of his reign coincided with the War of the Spanish Succession, in which he unavoidably antagonized different parties, was ignored in the peace settlements, and lost papal territory. He also tried to mobilize forces against the Turks in Poland and the Peloponnese. Within the church he struggled against Jansenism, ending in the condemnation of the errors of the leader of the Jansenist party, Pasquier Quesnel, in the bull *Unigenitus Dei Filius* in 1713. He was an important benefactor of the Vatican library and did much to ease the plight of the poor.

Clement had a passionate commitment to foreign missions. That included, for him, reuniting the Western church in northern Europe and encouraging Uniate groups in eastern Europe, Persia, Egypt, and Abyssinia. He promoted the foundation of missionary colleges in Rome and in northern Europe. He pressed new missionary initiatives throughout Asia and the Philippines. But he is especially remembered for ending the Chinese Rites Controversy in 1704, by confirming the decision of the Holy Office against the veneration of Confucius and of ancestors by Christians in China. The decision did great damage to the church there and hampered subsequent evangelizing activity. The ban was lifted in 1939.

BIBLIOGRAPHY Much of Clement's writing was collected and published by his nephew, Annibale Cardinal Albani (1729); see also *Magnum Bullarium Romanum* 21: 1–866. The only extensive description of his papacy in English is in Ludwig von Pastor, *History of the Popes,* vol. 31. (1941). The Catholic University of America acquired his library in 1930. See also George Minamiki, *The Chinese Rites Controversy* (1985).

Robert J. Schreiter, CPPS

Clement of Ochrid (9th century), apostle to the Bulgarians. Apparently the first Bulgarian-speaking bishop, Clement became a priest under the supervision of the famous Orthodox missionary *Methodius. Driven from Moravia after Methodius's death, he went into Bulgaria. *Boris, its king, sent him to Macedonia to convert Bulgarian-speaking Slavs who lived there. He set up a renowned school in Macedonia to train priests and to translate important ecclesiastical books into Bulgarian. At the same time he founded primary schools to find able candidates for the priesthood. He educated 3,500 young leaders and divided them about equally to serve in the twelve regions of Bulgaria.

BIBLIOGRAPHY Francis Dvornik, *Byzantine Missions among the Slavs: Sts. Constantine-Cyril and Methodius* (1970) and *Les Slaves: Byzance et Rome au IXe siècle* (1926, 1970); Dimitar Kornakov, *St. Clement in Ochrid* (1967); Dimitri Obolensky, *Six Byzantine Portraits* (1988); Steven Runciman, *A History of the First Bulgarian Empire* (1930, 1981).

Frederick W. Norris

Clifford, James (1872–1936), pioneer Plymouth Brethren missionary in Argentina. Born in Kilbirnie, Scotland, in a working-class home, Clifford was converted to Christ at 18 and became a self-taught preacher among the Plymouth Brethren. A leader of mining workers with lifelong sympathies for socialism, he left a political career in the Labour Party in response to a call to missionary service. Recruited by lay missionary Henry Ewen, he left Liverpool for Buenos Aires in October 1896 with Ewen and three other missionaries, under the Plymouth Brethren–related group Christian Missions in Many Lands. It was a time of successful expansion of Brethren work following routes opened by the British Rail in Argentina, using open-air preaching, gospel meetings in tents, and lay leadership. In 1898 Clifford, William Payne, and James Bathgate traveled by horse across the Andes to preach in Chile, Peru and Bolivia. Established first in Córdoba, in 1900 he moved on to Tucumán. His first wife, Harriet, having died in 1903, Clifford married Jane Thomson in 1906, and their home became a center for missionary work of several denominations. An accomplished poet, he wrote more than 100 hymns in Spanish and was the founder and editor of *El sendero del creyente,* an influential Christian magazine in South America. He died in Argentina.

BIBLIOGRAPHY A.C.T., *Un hombre bueno* (1957); Arno W. Enns, *Man, Milieu, and Mission in Argentina* (1971).

Samuel Escobar

Clough, John Everett (1836–1910) *and* **Emma (Rauschenbusch)** (1859–1940), pioneer American Baptist missionaries in Andhra Pradesh, South India. John Clough was born in Frewsburg, New York. His farming family moved to Iowa, where he worked on the farm, did survey work, and graduated from Upper Iowa University of Fayette in 1862 (M.A., 1865). In 1882 he was awarded an honorary D.D. by Kalamazoo (Michigan) College. Appointed as missionaries to India by the American Baptist Missionary Union, he and his first wife, Harriet (Sunderland), arrived in Andhra Pradesh in 1865. In 1866, they moved to Ongole, where he remained for the rest of his missionary career. After his wife died in 1893, Clough married Emma Rauschenbusch, another missionary, in 1894. They retired in 1906 but remained in India until 1910. John Clough died soon after returning to the United States that year.

Emma Clough, the sister of the famous social gospel theologian, Walter Rauschenbusch, was a scholar in her own right. She attended Wellesley College and Rochester Female Seminary and was granted a Ph.D. by the University of Berne, Switzerland, in 1894. In recognition of her scholarly accomplishments, she was made a member of the Royal Asiatic Society of Great Britain and Ireland.

John Clough is well known for his famine relief work in 1877 and 1878 and his association with the Ongole mass movement. In a six-week period during the summer of 1878, he and his assistants baptized nearly 9,000 members of the Madiga (Dalit) community in and around Ongole. More significant, though not so well known, were his insights into the importance of maintaining converts in their traditional social environments. For this purpose his evangelistic work was centered on villages, where he encouraged inquirers to wait until a family or group was ready to be baptized with them. Churches were organized in the villages in accordance with indigenous social structures, and continuing relationships with neighbors of other faiths were encouraged. He placed emphasis on the work of indigenous preachers, encouraging them to adopt as their model the Hindu guru.

BIBLIOGRAPHY John E. Clough, *Social Christianity in the Orient: The Story of a Man, a Mission, and a Movement* (1914) is the most authoritative primary source for the work and missiological thought of the Cloughs; see also Emma Rauschenbusch Clough, *While Sewing Sandals* (1899). Robert C. Torbet, *Venture of Faith: The Story of the American Baptist Foreign Mission Society and the Woman's American Baptist Foreign Mission Society, 1814–1954* (1955).

Frederick S. Downs

Coan, Titus (1801–1882), American missionary to Hawaii. Born in Connecticut and educated at East Guilford Academy, Coan went to western New York, where he was converted in a Charles G. Finney revival. After graduation from Auburn Theological Seminary and ordination in 1833, he explored the Argentine region of Patagonia on behalf of the American Board of Commissioners for Foreign Missions (ABCFM). In 1834 he married Fidelia Church, sailed for Hawaii, and was stationed at Hilo. He made an extended evangelistic tour of the island in 1836, which produced dramatic results. In 1837 and 1838, thousands flocked to Hilo for days and nights of fervent preaching, prayer, and manifestations of the power of the Spirit. Prior to 1837, prospective church members were rigorously examined and less than 1,200 had been admitted. After that year admissions averaged nearly 2,000 annually. By 1853, in a native population of about 71,000, over 56,000 were Protestants. The ABCFM moved to declare Hawaii Christianized and terminate the mission. Coan advocated a mission by Hawaiians to the Marquesas Islands and made two voyages there as a delegate of the Hawaiian Missionary Society. In 1873 he married Lydia Bingham, daughter of Hiram and Sybil *Bingham, his first wife having died in 1872. He wrote *Adventures in Patagonia* (1880) and *Life in Hawaii* (1882). He died in Hawaii.

BIBLIOGRAPHY Rufus Anderson, *History of the Sandwich Islands Mission* (1870), chap. 21; Lydia Bingham Coan, *Titus Coan* (1884); John Garrett, *To Live among the Stars* (1982), pp. 55–57; F. F. Goodsell, *When Faith Meets Faith* (1961), pp. 281–282; Albertine Loomis, *To All People* (1970), pp. 16–19; *Missionary Album* (1869), pp. 70–71; *Missionary Herald* 81 (1885): 50–52.

David M. Stowe

Coates, Dandeson (d. 1846), secretary of the Church Missionary Society (CMS). Coates joined the home staff of the Church Missionary Society in 1820, becoming assistant secretary in 1824 and lay secretary in 1830. An able administrator, he introduced sound management practices. He guarded the CMS's position as a lay voluntary society, but the CMS moved to secure episcopal patronage in 1839. After Henry *Venn's appointment as clerical secretary in 1841, Coates's influence waned. With colleagues from the Methodist Missionary Society and the London Missionary Society, Coates gave testimony before a parliamentary committee in 1837 in defense of the rights of aboriginal peoples.

BIBLIOGRAPHY Dandeson Coates, *The New Zealanders and Their Lands* (1844). Eugene Stock, *History of the Church Missionary Society*, 3 vols. (1899).

Wilbert R. Shenk

Cobo, Bernabé (1580–1657), Jesuit missionary in Peru. Cobo was the last of the great colonial chroniclers of the Indian past and Spanish beginnings. He first went to America as part of a fortune-hunting expedition, but in 1599 he began studying at the Jesuit college of San Martín in Lima, and in 1601 he joined the order. After his ordination as a priest he worked in Lima, Cuzco, Juli, Arequipa, and Callao. In Juli he learned Quechua and Aymara. In all of these places, as well as in Mexico, where he lived between 1630 and 1652, he took extensive notes on local history, culture, fauna, and flora. He published his four volume *Historia del nuevo mundo* in 1653 in Lima.

Cobo's history covers the Incas as well as the Indians under Spanish rule. His description of Andean religious beliefs and practices is one of the most detailed and systematic. He offers one of the first eyewitness accounts of the practice of coca-chewing, and he was the first European to describe the quinine tree. His chronicle also provides one of the most complete descriptions of colonial Lima, including then current religious practices and organizations. In many ways his account of the past is more than a chronicle. His is a critical synthesis of earlier chronicles, and as such it may be considered the first real history of Peru. He died in Lima.

BIBLIOGRAPHY Bernabé Cobo, *Historia del nuevo mundo* (1653), Francisco Mateos, ed., vols. 91–92, *Biblioteca de Autores Españoles* (1964); Luis Martín, *The Intellectual Conquest of Peru* (1968); Manuel Marzal, *Historia de la antropología indigenista: México y Perú* (1981, 1986), pp. 108–121.

Jeffrey Klaiber, SJ

Cocceius, Johannes (1603–1669), Reformed theologian. Born in Bremen, Germany, Cocceius studied philology and theology at Bremen and at Franeker, Netherlands. In 1636 he was appointed to a position at Franeker first as professor of Hebrew and seven years later as professor of Reformed theology. In 1650 he moved to Leiden University. Drawing upon Old and New Testament prophecies, he developed a "prophetic" theology in which he interpreted church history as history of the kingdom (reign) of God. In his main work, *Summa doctrinae de foedere et testamento Dei* (1648), he distinguished seven periods in the history of God's covenants, starting with a universal prelapsarian covenant of works and a postlapsarian covenant of grace. The seventh and last period preceding the parousia of Christ he saw as the period of great flowering of Protestant missions. The primary goal in this period would not be the expansion of the Christian commonwealth by establishing churches but the proclamation of God's kingdom. In his view mission is a preparation for the parousia of Christ. The urgency of preaching the gospel before the coming of Christ is an important motive of his missionary theology. He contributed to the revitalization of theology in the Dutch Reformed Church and influenced Protestant theologians on both sides of the Atlantic.

BIBLIOGRAPHY W. J. van Asselt, *Amicitia Dei: Een onderzoek naar de structuur van de theologie van Johannes Cocceius* (1988) and "Missionaire motieven en perspectieven in de theologie van Johannes Cocceius," *Kerk en Theologie* 41 (1990): 227–236.

Willem J. van Asselt

Cochran, George (1833–1901), Canadian Methodist missionary in Japan. Born in Cavan County, Ireland, and self-educated, Cochran was one of the pioneers of Canadian Methodist missions in Japan. Arriving there in 1873, he taught in a school in Tokyo operated by Nakamura Keiu, a prominent Japanese liberal. As a teacher, he capitalized on the Japanese desire to learn English. He returned to Canada in 1879 because of his wife's poor health but returned to Japan in 1882 to be principal of Toya Eiwa Gakko, in Tokyo, a Christian school for boys and girls. He also taught in the theological department. Cochran left Japan when religious instruction was banned in 1899 and returned to Canada. He then moved to Los Angeles, California, and began teaching at McLay Theology School. He was also dean of the College of Liberal Arts of the University of Southern California.

BIBLIOGRAPHY A. Hamish Ion, *The Cross and the Rising Sun: The Canadian Protestant Missionary Movement in the Japanese Empire, 1872–1931* (1990).

Geoffrey Johnston

Cochran, Joseph Gallup (1817–1871), American missionary to Persia (Iran). Born at Springville, New York, Cochran graduated from Amherst College (1842) and Union Theological Seminary, New York (1847); within a month he married Deborah W. Plumb, was ordained, and sailed under the American Board of Commissioners for Foreign Missions (ABCFM). He reached Urumia (Rezaiyeh), Persia, in June, 1848. As a member of the Nestorian Mission he worked among adherents of the Syriac-speaking Assyrian Church of the East, serving many years as principal or associate principal of the mission seminary at Seir, effectively equipping preachers and teachers. A prolific author and translator in Syriac, he published books on Bible geography and history, pastoral theology and homiletics, algebra, astronomy, and philosophy. In the year of his death at Urumia the ABCFM mission in Persia was turned over to the Presbyterians.

BIBLIOGRAPHY *Missionary Herald* 68 (1872): 133 has a short obituary. Other information is found in the files and archives of the ABCFM and in Presbyterian missionary publications.

David M. Stowe

Cochran, Joseph Plumb (1855–1905), Presbyterian medical missionary in Persia. The son of American Presbyterian missionary Joseph G. *Cochran, Cochran grew up in Urumia, northwestern Iran. He left at age 15 for schooling in America. After attending high school in Buffalo, New York, he studied medicine at Yale and in 1877 received his M.D. degree from the College of Physicians and Surgeons, New York. He was then appointed a Presbyterian medical missionary to Persia, and married Kathleen Dale. They reached Urumia in 1878.

In addition to medical work, Cochran built the first mission hospital in Iran, trained a dozen helpers to become physicians, went on numerous medical trips throughout the area, took part in church and evangelistic work, and became the friend and counselor to provincial governors, Kurdish chieftains, and members of the royal family. He was a wise conciliator and diplomat as well as a skillful doctor. In becoming a conspicuous, influential citizen of Urumia, Cochran had several advantages: he spoke flawlessly from childhood the two languages of the common people, Turkish and Syriac; he knew the cultural terrain and ways of thought of the people; he was a pioneer of modern medicine in a provincial area where it was unknown; and he lived before the nationalistic, anti-foreign distrust that became endemic in the twentieth century.

Exhausted by his tireless medical work and as an upholder of justice, he died in Persia at the age of 50. The whole area of Urumia joined in mourning.

BIBLIOGRAPHY Robert E. Speer, *"The Hakim Sahib." The Foreign Doctor: A Biography of Joseph Plumb Cochran, M.D., of Persia* (1911).

R. Park Johnson

Cochrane, Thomas (1866–1953), medical missionary in China and promoter of mission surveys. Cochrane was born and brought up in Greenock, Scotland. He left school at an early age to work to support his widowed mother and the younger children of the family. Listening to D. L. *Moody in 1882 brought him to a strong evangelical faith, which determined the rest of his life. In the face of great difficulties, he trained as a doctor in Glasgow and offered himself for service with the London Missionary Society (LMS), requesting appointment "where the work was most abundant and the workers fewest." In 1897 the LMS appointed him and his wife to Chaoyang, Liaoning Province, in northern China to take up the work James *Gilmore had begun. Conditions there, including the desperate shortage of trained personnel, medical equipment, and supplies, made a deep impression. He survived the Boxer Rebellion, and in its aftermath the LMS appointed him to rebuild its hospital in Peking (Beijing). Out of his vision and through his diplomatic skills, the Peking Union Medical College was born, with support from other mission bodies and the empress dowager, and he became the college's first principal. Its high standards were recognized throughout China and beyond, and in 1915 he negotiated the underwriting of its financial needs by the Rockefeller Foundation. From his China experience grew his lifelong concern for the best use of the available resources for mission and the need of cooperation to achieve this. In 1913 the Christian Literature Society of China published his *Survey of the Missionary Occupation of China* with an accompanying *Atlas of China in Provinces Showing Missionary Occupation.*

After his return to England in 1915, Cochrane served at the headquarters of the LMS and also with the National Laymen's Missionary Movement. In 1918 a Survey Trust was formed with Cochrane, Roland *Allen and Sidney J. W. Clark (a wealthy Congregationalist businessman with a lifelong commitment to world mission) as its three trustees. In 1920, in conjunction with Roland Allen, Cochrane published *Missionary Survey as an Aid to Intelligent Co-operation in Foreign Mission,* and in 1924 the Survey Application Trust was formed. Although "Survey" featured prominently in both the name and activities of the trust, the deed specifically charged the trustees to promote and apply, anywhere in the world, the principles asserted by Clark in his pamphlets and Allen in his two principal books, *Mission Methods: St. Paul's or Ours?* and *The Spontaneous Expansion of the Church.* The World Dominion Press was the publishing branch of the trust, and a list of its publications indicates how it sought to fulfill this dual function of survey and the promotion of indigenous principles.

In all of this survey work, Cochrane's managerial skills and ability to reconcile those of different traditions were at work. The compiling of the first edition of the *World Christian Handbook,* issued in 1949, edited by E. J. Bingle and K. G. *Grubb, fulfilled one of Cochrane's long-standing ambitions. In another direction, he purchased the Mildmay Centre in London in 1931 as a base for the Movement for World Evangelization, with the task of mission on its doorstep, which exemplified his combination of vision and broad evangelical concern. He died in Pinner, Middlesex.

BIBLIOGRAPHY Francesca French, *Thomas Cochrane: Pioneer and Missionary Statesman* (1956); Kenneth G. Grubb, *The Story of the Survey Application Trust,* part 3 of *Reform of the Ministry,* David M. Paton, ed. (1968).

George A. Hood

Codrington, Robert Henry (1830–1922), English missionary in Melanesia. Son of a Church of England clergyman, Codrington was born in Wroughton, England. He was educated at Charterhouse School and at the University of Oxford and in 1857 was ordained in the Church of England. Later he immigrated to Nelson, New Zealand, and in 1871 began service with the Melanesian Mission on Norfolk Island under Bishop John Coleridge *Patteson. This was during the era when unscrupulous labor traders forcibly abducted island men. After one such kidnapping episode in 1871, Bishop Patteson, in a misdirected retaliation by Islanders, was murdered on the atoll of Nukapu. Codrington was forced to assume Patteson's leadership role until 1877, although he turned down the opportunity to be bishop. During this period, the mission developed greatly. Under his leadership the work of evangelization progressed, indigenous teachers were trained and given charge of village schools, and several islanders were ordained to the diaconate. In 1888 he returned to England and devoted himself to church work.

Codrington's anthropological writing, which came largely at Lorimer *Fison's encouragement, is of great importance. He extensively and systematically inquired into

Melanesian practices and social regulations. He also researched their languages. He set out to record "what the natives themselves said, not what the Europeans said about them." All this he tells in the preface of *The Melanesians: Studies in Their Anthropology and Folk-lore* (1891, 1957), a companion to *The Melanesian Languages* (1885). Codrington's writing became important in anthropology because of his concept of mana, which has greatly influenced writing on "primitive" religion. He also encouraged Pacific Islanders to write about their conversions and the sociological factors involved, an example being Clement Marau, *Story of a Melanesian Deacon,* Robert Henry Codrington, tr. (1894). Codrington also wrote (with J. Palmer) *Dictionary of the Language of Mota* (1896).

BIBLIOGRAPHY David Hilliard, *God's Gentlemen: A History of the Melanesian Mission, 1849–1942* (1978); Darrell Whiteman, *Melanesians and Missionaries* (1983).

Darrell Whiteman

Coe, Shoki (C. H. Hwang) (1914–1988), Taiwanese leader in ecumencial theological education. Coe, a third-generation minister of the Presbyterian Church of Taiwan, studied in Tainan, Taipei, Tokyo, Birmingham, and Cambridge and taught at London University. In 1947 he returned to Taiwan and served as principal of Tainan Theological College (1949–1965) before joining his family in England and becoming the director of the World Council of Churches (WCC) Theological Education Fund/Program for Theological Education (1965–1979).

Combining intellectual brilliance, vision, charisma, persuasiveness, charm, and energy with a deep Christian faith, he left his mark in many places. Out of a defunct Bible school he created a large, influential theological college and research center in Tainan. He played a large part in establishing both the Southeast Asia and the Northeast Asia associations of theological education before his final work on the world scene within the WCC. For almost 20 years he was the outstanding leader of the Presbyterian Church of Taiwan and for the whole of his working life was an ecumenical statesman of note. A citizen of the world, he was also a passionate fighter for Taiwan's self-determination and eventual independence.

BIBLIOGRAPHY Shoki Coe, *Recollections and Reflections,* introduced and edited by Boris Anderson (1991; 2d ed., 1993) and *Joint Action for Mission in Formosa* (1968).

H. Daniel Beeby

Coerper, Heinrich Wilhelm (1863–1936), founder of the Liebenzeller Mission. Born and brought up in a Protestant parsonage in southwestern Germany, Coerper had a personal awakening while studying for the ministry that brought him into contact with pietist circles. After ten years as a parish pastor he was called in 1899 to Hamburg, where, following Hudson *Taylor's suggestion, he founded a German branch of the China Inland Mission (CIM). A similar attempt had already been made in 1897 at Kiel, after a visit by Taylor, but this effort had been taken over by the Breklum Mission. Thus it was left to Coerper to transplant the CIM heritage to Germany—a difficult undertaking in a country where several notable mission operations for China already had been initiated. Transfer of the headquarters to Liebenzell, in southwestern Germany, the hinterland of the powerful Basel Mission, led Coerper to enlist support of neo-pietist groups like the German branch of Christian Endeavor, which enabled him to set up his Liebenzeller Mission as a more self-contained agency. Overseas work was begun in the Chinese provinces of Hunan (1901) and Guizhou (1906), then in Micronesia, and, after World War I, in Japan. Even after Coerper's retirement in 1936, the mission retained its specific stance of evangelicalism in loyalty to the German regional churches.

BIBLIOGRAPHY Kurt Emil Koch, *Heinrich Coerper und sein Werk* (1964).

Hans-Werner Gensichen

Coillard, François (1834–1904), French Protestant missionary in central Africa. Coillard was born of a Huguenot peasant family in Asnières-lès-Bourges, France. His spirituality was shaped by the Swiss revival brought by Ami Bost. Educated at Glay and Strasbourg, he entered the Paris Evangelical Missionary Society (PEMS) School of Missions under Eugène *Casalis, together with Adolphe *Mabille. Ordained in 1857, he sailed to Lesotho with the second generation of PEMS missionaries. The Orange Free State was busy encroaching upon Basotho territory and the PEMS was forced to move somewhat northward; Coillard was sent to Leribe, a town that had been placed under the authority of Molapo, a son of *Moshoeshoe. It was the home of Coillard, and soon of his wife, for 20 years. In 1861 Christina Mackintosh (1829–1891), a daughter of a Scottish minister, whom he had met in Paris, came over to marry him. Coillard spoke excellent Sesotho and wrote hymns, poems, tales, and translations, which were used in the schools. He organized missionary excursions with Basotho evangelists, planting new churches in the district. In 1865 warfare with the Boers forced Coillard to hide in Natal until Lesotho became a British protectorate in 1868. Upon his return to Leribe in 1869, Coillard found the missionary drive among the Basotho stronger than ever. In 1875 a first joint mission of the Basotho church at Leribe and PEMS missionaries to the Banyaï in Rhodesia failed. A second expedition led by Coillard, with five Basotho missionaries—Asser Sehahoubane, Azael, Andreas, Aaron Mayoro, and Eleazar Marathane—departed in 1877 and reached the Zambesi after two difficult years of exploring but proved abortive, too. But in 1885 Coillard was finally able to found the Zambesi mission, received by Lewanika, king of the Barotsi, first at Sefula and later at Lealui, Zambia. A dedicated network of *Zambezias* in Europe was organized by Coillard and Alfred Bertrand to support the mission. Coillard died at Lealui, having incarnated the heroic, self-sacrificing missionary and explorer.

BIBLIOGRAPHY F. Coillard, *On the Threshold of Central Africa: A Record of Twenty Years' Pioneering among the Barotsi of the Upper*

Zambesi (1897; French, *Sur le Haut-Zambèze,* 1898). Édouard Fabre, *La vie d'un missionnaire français: François Coillard, 1834–1904* (1922); Catherine Winkworth Mackintosh, *Coillard of the Zambesi: The Lives of François and Christina Coillard, of the Paris Missionary Society, in South and Central Africa, 1858–1904* (1907). The best historical assessment of Coillard's career and influence is Jean-François Zorn, *Le grand siècle d'une mission protestante: La Mission de Paris de 1822 à 1914* (1993).

Marc R. Spindler

Coke, Thomas (1741–1814), pioneer Methodist bishop and missionary. Coke was born in Brecon, Wales, of well-to-do parents. Educated at Jesus College, Oxford University, with a B.A., M.A., and a doctorate in civil law, he worked first as a burgess and bailiff in Brecon, and then as an ordained Anglican curate in South Petherton. Dismissed in 1777 for his Wesleyan leanings, Coke joined John *Wesley, who found in him a valued legal mind, a gifted evangelical preacher, a skilled administrator, and in later years, his most trusted companion. After serving as superintendent of Methodism's London circuit (1780) and first chairman of the Irish Conference (1782), Coke was ordained and appointed by Wesley in 1784 as superintendent for the work in the newly independent United States. Coke convened the organizing conference for American Methodism at Baltimore, Maryland, in 1784 and, with authorization from Wesley, ordained Francis *Asbury and consecrated him joint superintendent. Through nine subsequent visits to the growing church in the United States, Coke symbolized the unity of Methodists on both sides of the Atlantic, although he had continual disputes with Asbury over church policies. They agreed, however, to make a stand against slavery, threatened slaveholders with excommunication, and presented an antislavery petition to President George Washington at Mount Vernon in 1785.

Coke was rightly called Father of the Methodist Missions. His pamphlet *An Address to the Pious and Benevolent Proposing an Annual Subscription for the Support of Missionaries* (1786) was the first Methodist missionary tract. He intended to establish missionaries in Nova Scotia in 1786, but a gale forced his landing in Antigua, West Indies, instead. Thrilled with the opportunities there, mission in the British West Indies and other British colonies became his dominant passion for the remainder of his life. At the last conference attended by John Wesley at Bristol in 1790, Coke was named to head the first Methodist missionary committee (he later was made its president, upon the organization's revision in 1804). "I beg from door to door," he told his friends without embarrassment, and he donated his family's wealth to the missionary effort. Beginning in 1792, he led in sending pioneer missionaries to most islands in the West Indies, as well as to new missions in Sierra Leone, Nova Scotia, Ireland, and France. During the Napoleonic Wars he organized work among the 70,000 French prisoners of war held in England. He died in 1814 on board a ship en route to India, leading a missionary band of preachers for India and South Africa. Wesleyan Methodist missions advanced spectacularly following Coke's death, building on the visionary foundations he had laid.

BIBLIOGRAPHY John Vickers, *Thomas Coke: Apostle of Methodism* (1969) is the best documented biography and contains a full list of Coke's writings. Samuel Drew, *Life of the Rev. Thomas Coke, L.L.D.* (1816) was the official biography commissioned upon his death. W. A. Candler, *The Life of Thomas Coke* (1923) and S. Sowton, *Thomas Coke* (1956) are later biographies. For details of Coke's missionary leadership, see Wade Crawford Barclay, *History of Methodist Missions,* vol. 1 (1949), Cyril Davey, *Mad about Mission: The Story of Dr. Thomas Coke* (1985), and George E. Lawrence and Cyril Dorsett, *Caribbean Conquest: The Story of Dr. Coke and Methodism in the West Indies* (1947); John A. Vickers, "One-man Band: Thomas Coke and Origins of Methodist Missions," *Methodist History* 34 (1996): 135–147.

Norman E. Thomas

Coker, Daniel (1780?–1846), first African-American missionary to Sierra Leone, West Africa. Born Isaac Wright, a slave, to a white mother who was an indentured servant and a slave father in Maryland, he was educated with his white half brothers. In New York, where he fled to avoid slave hunters, he took the name Daniel Coker and came in contact with Methodists. Returning to Baltimore, he put himself in danger of being returned to slavery, but his freedom was purchased by four freedmen and he became a leading preacher, writer, and educator. He was ordained a deacon in the Methodist Episcopal Church by Bishop Francis *Asbury in 1802. With Richard Allen and others he was a founder in 1816 of the African Methodist Episcopal (AME) Church. In 1820 he was sent by his church as a missionary to Sierra Leone, West Africa, and sailed with other emigrants under the American Colonization Society. On shipboard he organized a society of believers. Landing on Sherbro Islands, Sierra Leone, in March 1820, he found himself the adminstrator of the colony within three months because of the deaths of the three appointed agents. With disease and death increasing, the survivors moved to the mainland, where Coker's wife and children joined him the following year. He spent the remainder of his life in Sierra Leone, working as a government administrator and church organizer. Later, when a split developed in his church, he became superintendent of an independent group, the West African Methodist Church.

BIBLIOGRAPHY *Journal of Daniel Coker, a Descendant of Africa, from the Time of Leaving New York, on the Ship Elizabeth, Capt. Sebor, on Voyage for Sherbro, in Africa, in Company with Three Agents and about Ninety Persons of Colour* (1820, repr. 1983). Wade C. Barclay, *History of Methodist Missions: Early American Methodism, 1769–1841,* vol. 1 (1949); Josephus R. Coan, "Daniel Coker: 19th Century Black Church Organizer, Educator and Missionary," *Journal of the Interdenominational Theological Center* 3 (1975): 17–31; Larry G. Murphy, J. Gordon Melton, and Gary L. Ward, eds., *Encyclopedia of African American Religions* (1993); Isaiah H. Welch, *The Heroism of the Rev. Richard Allen* (1910).

H. T. Maclin

Colenso, Elizabeth (Fairburn) (1821–1904) *and* **William** (1811–1899). Elizabeth Fairburn was born of British missionary parents in New Zealand. She taught at her father's Church Missionary Society (CMS) station at Otahuhu. William Colenso came from England as a CMS printer in 1834. He produced the New Testament in Maori in 1837 and made several exploratory journeys combining his interests in botany and missionary outreach. They married in 1843 and worked at St. John's College, where William was ordained a deacon in 1844. They moved to a remote mission station at Ahuriri. William's stubborn evangelical zeal alienated him from Bishop G. A. *Selwyn and many Maori. A child he had by a Maori woman resulted in his suspension in 1852.

Elizabeth Colenso separated from her husband and taught at Taupiri from 1854 to 1861. She went to London and acted as a Maori interpreter for the Colonial Office and during the presentation of Maori to Queen Victoria in 1863. While in London she also contributed to the revision of the complete Maori Bible printed in 1868. From 1869 to 1875 she taught Maori at Paihia, New Zealand. She then went with the Melanesian mission to Norfolk Island, where she trained girls and translated the Book of Common Prayer into Mota, retiring in 1898.

William Colenso became a largely unsuccessful colonial politician but continued his significant botanical and scientific contributions and wrote in defense of Maori rights. He was rehabilitated as a deacon in 1894.

BIBLIOGRAPHY A. G. Bagnall and G. D. Peterson, *William Colenso: Printer, Missionary, Botanist, Explorer, Politician: His Life and Journeys* (1948); A. L. Rowse, *The Controversial Colensos* (1989). Elizabeth and William Colenso papers are at the Alexander Turnbull Library, Wellington, New Zealand.

Allan K. Davidson

Colenso, John William (1814–1883), Anglican bishop of Natal, South Africa. Colenso was born at St. Austell, Cornwall, England, and was educated at Cambridge. He became a fellow of St. John's College, a master at Harrow School (producing in 1843 a standard textbook of arithmetic), and rector of Forncett St. Mary, Norfolk. His concern for missions led in 1853 to appointment as first bishop of Natal, then a new colony. South African missions invariably found difficulty in reconciling ministry to a growing white population with African missions. Colenso's instincts were missionary. He threw himself into Zulu studies, producing a major grammar and dictionary and much Bible translation, and developed a model mission at Ekukanyeni. He envisioned the gradual Christianization of Zulu society, with Zulu institutions left as far as possible intact and polygamy tolerated in the meantime, a policy which offended the existing missions. Meanwhile, tensions arose between Colenso and the white laity, the white clergy (mainly Tractarian), and Robert *Gray, bishop of Cape Town, who claimed metropolitan jurisdiction over Natal. A dispute over eucharistic theology overflowed into charges of serious heresy on publication of Colenso's *St. Paul's Epistle to the Romans... Explained from a Missionary Point of View* (1861), which offered an objective and universalist view of atonement. Gray brought his accusations before the English bishops, but the universalist issue was soon overshadowed by Colenso's *The Pentateuch and Book of Joshua Critically Examined* (1862), which applied arithmetical analysis and rationalistic literary criticism to the Old Testament. Most English bishops, and the Convocation of Canterbury, denounced Colenso's opinions. In 1863 Gray summoned him to Cape Town for trial for heresy, and deposed him, allowing appeal to Canterbury. Colenso did not attend, denying Gray's jurisdiction in English law, and appealed, not to Canterbury, but to the Queen in Council. The matter kept him in England for three years, during which he became a national celebrity, excoriated by orthodox churchmen and lauded by scientific and literary figures. In 1865 the Judicial Committee of the Privy Council ruled that Gray had no legal authority to depose Colenso. The judgment did not address the theological issue. Colenso returned as legal bishop but to uproar in his cathedral, war with his clergy, and litigation over diocesan finances. Gray and his confrères eventually secured the consecration of a new bishop, institutionalizing two parallel Anglican churches in Natal. In Colenso's last ten years, his ecclesiastical notoriety faded, but he was marginalized and starved of resources both human and financial. Nevertheless, he became an outstanding spokesman for African rights through a decade of imperial expansion. He defended the Hlubi chief Langalibalele against the colonial authorities, obstructed as far as possible the imperial dismemberment of Zululand, and befriended Zulu king Cetshwayo, viewed as the archenemy of Britain. Such actions cost the popularity with settlers he had gained over his resistance to Gray. After Colenso's death, his daughters, Harriette and Frances, continued his campaign for Zulu rights.

Colenso belonged to no one definable party in Anglicanism. F. D. Maurice influenced him but was shocked by his later rationalism. Colenso's biblical criticism had little permanent influence. Anglican synodical government and the Lambeth conferences of bishops were permanent but unintended outcomes of his career. His early missionary tracts and his linguistic works are monuments of what might have been, had other controversies not distracted him from the issues of the gospel and Zulu culture.

BIBLIOGRAPHY G. W. Cox, *The Life of John William Colenso, D.D., Bishop of Natal,* 2 vols. (1888); Jeff Guy, *The Heretic: A Study of the Life of John William Colenso, 1814–1883* (1983); Peter Hinchliff, *John William Colenso, Bishop of Natal* (1964), "John William Colenso: A Fresh Appraisal," *Journal of Ecclesiastical History* 13 (1962), and *The Anglican Church in South Africa* (1964). Hinchliff is stronger on theological and constitutional issues, Guy on African issues. Some of Colenso's early works are collected in R. Edgecombe, *Bringing Forth Light: Five Tracts on Bishop Colenso's Zulu Mission* (1982).

Andrew F. Walls

Colin, Jean-Claude Marie (1790–1875), priest and founder of the Marist Fathers and Sisters. Born at Saint-Bonnet-le-Troncy, Rhone, France, Colin followed his brother Pierre to seminary, studying theology in Lyons. He joined Marcellin *Champagnat and others there in planning the Society of Mary (Marists) as a four-branched order of laypeople, sisters, brothers, and priests. In 1816, twelve of the planners signed a pledge to achieve this goal. Appointed assistant to his brother, Colin invited Jeanne *Chavoin to join them at Cerdon to begin the Marist Sisters. He became defacto leader of the Marist project, making an 1834 trip to Rome in an unsuccessful effort to gain approval of the organization.

The failure of plans by Henri de *Solages for a Pacific mission caused Rome to seek missionaries in Lyons, which gave opportunity to the Marists. Rome offered approval of the Marist priests' branch if the priests would undertake a mission to western Oceania. This they accepted, and the order was approved in April 1836. Bishop Jean-Baptiste François *Pompallier and seven Marists left in December. Colin sent more missionaries but soon found that he had to raise vast funds, mostly from Pauline *Jaricot's organization, the Society for the Propagation of the Faith, to repay Pompallier's huge borrowings. The bishop neglected his missioners badly; he blamed Colin yet vetoed Colin's proposal for a Marist house in New Zealand to ensure food supplies. In 1842 Colin submitted a plan to Rome's Propaganda Fide to divide responsibility for western Oceania. It was approved, and the Vicariate of Central Oceania was created in 1842 under Bishop Pierre-Marie *Bataillon; the Vicariate of Melanesia in 1844 under Bishop Jean-Baptiste *Epalle; and the Vicariate of New Caledonia under Bishop Guillaume Douarre in 1847. Villa Maria, a supply base in Sydney, Australia, was established in 1845. In 1848 Pompallier met Colin in Rome to discuss continuing problems. They could only agree that the Marists would withdraw from Pompallier's jurisdiction, which was thereby reduced to the Diocese of Auckland. Unsupported by Rome, and facing similar difficulties with Bataillon, a saddened Colin sent fewer Marists to the Pacific after 1845, and none at all between 1849 and 1854, the date of his resignation as superior general. But his successor, Julien Favre, asked Colin to renegotiate in Rome. This time Propaganda Fide was persuaded to draft moderate proposals regarding care for the missionaries, and the Marists resumed sending missionaries in 1855. Bataillon was asked to come to Rome, where he accepted a rule for the missions in 1857, including a Marist visitor general to work from Villa Maria.

Although he never saw the Pacific, Colin played a major role in helping establish missions there, and he vitally influenced Roman Catholic mission policy.

BIBLIOGRAPHY Selections from Colin by Jean Coste appear in *A Founder Speaks: Spiritual Talks of Jean-Claude Colin*, 2 vols. (1975) and *A Founder Acts: Reminiscences of Jean-Claude Colin by Gabriel-Claude Mayet* (1983). His anonymously published biography (by Jean Jeantin) is *Le Très Révérend Père Colin, fondateur et premier superieur general de la Société de Marie*, 6 vols. (1895–1898). Stanley W. Hosie, *Anonymous Apostle: The Life of Jean Claude Colin, Marist* (1967). Colin's papers are preserved in the archives of the Marist Fathers, Rome. They also contain "Mémoires Mayet," which comprises Colin's addresses, conversations, and activities recorded daily in notebooks by Gabriel-Claude Mayet.

John Hosie, SM

Colley, William W. (1847–1909), African American missionary in Liberia. Colley was born in Rice's Depot, a rural community in Prince Edward County, Virginia. His father was a Scottish clergyman and his mother an African American. In 1873 he graduated from Richmond Theological Seminary (later Virginia Union University) and was ordained a Baptist minister. In 1875, after a brief pastorate in Connecticut, he was appointed a missionary to Africa by the Foreign Mission Board of the Southern Baptist Convention and worked in Liberia for nearly five years. In 1879 the Virginia Baptist State Convention secured Colley's services to canvas African American churches throughout the South concerning the need for more black missionaries in Africa. In November 1880, a meeting was called in Montgomery, Alabama, to organize the Foreign Mission Convention of the United States, the beginning of the first national effort among black Baptists toward the support of foreign missions. Colley was elected corresponding secretary. In 1883 the convention sent Colley and five others to establish mission stations in Liberia, giving birth to the Bendoo and Jundoo missions. It is believed that Colley and his wife perished in Liberia from hardship and disease.

BIBLIOGRAPHY Charles H. Corey, *A History of the Richmond Theological Seminary* (1895); Miles Mark Fisher, *A Short History of the Baptist Denomination* (1933); Larry G. Murphy et al., *Encyclopedia of African American Religions* (1993); Carter G. Woodson, *The History of the Negro Church* (1921); Davis Collier Wolley, *Baptist Advance: The Achievements of the Baptists of North America for a Century and a Half* (1964).

Ralph Reavis, Sr.

Collins, Judson Dwight (1823–1852), American Methodist pioneer missionary in China. Collins was one of eight children in a pious Methodist farm family in Michigan. While still a college student, he determined to become a missionary to China, but there was no Methodist mission work there, so after graduation he taught for two years at Albion College. In 1847 he was called to New York, where he was ordained an elder and commissioned with Dr. and Mrs. Moses C. *White, the first Methodist missionaries to China. They sailed on April 15 and arrived in Foochow (Fuzhou), one of the five treaty ports, four months later. To create an opening for the gospel, Collins opened a school for boys in 1847 and another in 1848. He worked with other missionaries on Bible translation and distribution of tracts. In 1850 he was appointed superintendent of the Foochow Mission. Plagued with illness, he returned to the United States in 1851 and died the following year.

BIBLIOGRAPHY F. C. Bald, "First Missionary to China," *Quarterly Review* (Univ. of Michigan, n.d.); Frank T. Cartwright, "Notes on Early Foochow History," unpublished manuscript in archives of the United Methodist Church, Madison, N.J.; Walter Lacy, *A Hundred Years of China Methodism* (1948).

Donald E. MacInnis

Columba (*or* Colum Cille) (c. 521–597), Irish missionary. Columba, along with *Patrick and Brigid, is the patron of all the Scotti, as the Irish were called in early times. His work provides an important example of enculturating

Christianity in non-Greco-Roman cultures. He was born of such high lineage in the Irish Ui Neill dynasty as would have made him a candidate for high kingship in the territories of northern and central Ireland, had he not chosen otherwise. His training was in the monastery of Clonard, 30 miles north-northwest of Dublin, under its abbot, Finnian. Little is known of his life or person in Ireland until at age 42 (an old man in that era), he went into exile as a result of his part in bringing about the bloody battle of Cul Drebne (561). This led him to found a monastic missionary community on the island of Iona off the western coast of Scotland, from which the influence of his monastic *familia* eventually spread over much of Ireland and Britain. Needing to provide institutional support for a spreading religion in a culture unfamiliar with Roman imperial models which had produced episcopacy and diocesan structures, Columba copied the institutions of the secular dynasty to which he belonged. He and his successor abbots from the same royal kin ruled the increasingly far-flung family of monastery-churches, just as his secular kinsman ruled their territories; indeed Columba's *familia* spread right along with the extension of Ui Neill influence, either through conquest or alignments with other dynasties, and included not only monastery-churches in the Ui Neill territories in Ireland but also extended beyond in the kingdoms of Dal Riada, the Picts, and eventually Northumbria and further south into England.

Adomnan's *Vita Columbae,* going back to earlier records containing living memories, is a miracle-laden portrait of one who was the equal of any Christian saint, including biblical figures like Moses, and also the equal of kings. It also shows the old exile particularly as a man of prayer and scholarship, and supervisor of the daily round of work, liturgy, and discipline in an Irish monastery-church. One of the earliest pieces of Irish vernacular literature (itself the oldest vernacular literature in Europe) is a traditional praise poem on Columba's death, in which the man's sanctity and his learning are equally revered. That learning comprised both continental Christian authors and the extensive learning of a hitherto nonliterate culture.

BIBLIOGRAPHY A. O. Anderson and M. O. Anderson, eds., *Adomnan's Life of Columba* (1991); Marie Herbert, *Iona, Kells, and Derry: The History and Hagiography of the Monastic Familia of Columba* (1988), "The Legacy of Colum Cille and His Monastic Community," in James P. Mackey, ed., *The Cultures of Europe: The Irish Contribution* (1994), and "A Poem in Praise of Colum Cille," in Thomas Kinsella, ed., *The New Oxford Book of Irish Verse* (1986); Alfred P. Smith, *Warlords and Holy Men: Scotland, A.D. 80–1000* (1984).

James P. Mackey

Columban (*or* Columbanus) (c. 543–615), Irish missionary in Europe. Trained as a monk by Comgall at Bangor in northern Ireland, Columban left Ireland about 591 on a *perigrinatio* through Europe. (A *perigrinatio* was neither pilgrimage nor evangelizing mission but appears to have served as a final farewell to the securities of life, on the model of Abraham taking leave of his home and kin. Those who undertook an Irish *peregrinatio* saw themselves as journeying by faith alone to their only true home with God.) Columban set up his first monastery-church near Strasbourg, at Annegray in the Vosges mountains west of Strasbourg, where he deliberately built on the ruins of a temple to Diana. He then set up others at Luxeuil, southwest of Strasbourg, and at Fontaine in the southeast of France. He inevitably became involved with Roman imperial politics, secular and ecclesiastical, arousing attempts to deport him to Ireland in 610. But he escaped, continued his travels, and extended his monastery-churches to Bregenz (on the southern border of Lake Constance at the western end of modern Austria), and finally to Bobbio in northern Italy, where he died.

Columban's writings include sermons and letters; rules for monks and a penitential for monks, secular clergy, and laity; and some lyric poetry. Together they provide a compact but comprehensive picture of early Irish Christianity. Columban defended with great passion and conceptual precision the distinctive Christian forms of his own people and, concomitantly, the unity of the whole Christian community under the leadership of the bishop of Rome, so that neither could or should threaten the other; "for," he wrote, "we are all joint members of one body, whether Franks or Britons, or Irish, or whatever our race may be" (Letters 2.9).

BIBLIOGRAPHY G. S. M. Walker, ed., *Sancti Columbani Opera* (1957). T. O'Fiaich, *Columbanus in His Own Words* (1974) and "Irish Monks on the Continent," in James P. Mackey, ed., *An Introduction to Celtic Christianity* (1989); H. Concannon, ed., *Jonas' Life of Columban* (1915).

James P. Mackey

Comber, Thomas James (1852–1887), Baptist Missionary Society (BMS) missionary in the Cameroons and Congo. Comber was born in Camberwell, South London, to a strong Baptist family. He was trained at Regent's Park College, London, and was accepted by the BMS for service in the Cameroons. From 1876 to 1878 he served in the Cameroons alongside George *Grenfell. With Grenfell he made two journeys to the Congo River in 1878 to investigate the possibilities of a Congo mission. After Grenfell resigned from the BMS in difficult circumstances, Comber was left to press the claims of the new missions on the British public. He led the first BMS missionary party to sail for the Congo in 1879. The death in June of his wife, Minnie, was followed by the loss in 1884 of his sister, a missionary in the Cameroons, and in 1885 of his brother, a fellow missionary in the Congo. In 1886, at São Salvador do Congo (now Mbanza Kongo, in Angola), Comber's Congolese servant, William Mantu Parkinson, became the first BMS convert to be baptized. Comber deserves to be remembered as one of the architects of the Baptist church among the Bakongo people. He died of fever on board ship en route for England.

BIBLIOGRAPHY J. B. Myers, *Thomas J. Comber: Missionary Pioneer to the Congo* (1888); Ernest A. Payne, *The Great Succession: Leaders of the Baptist Missionary Society during the Nineteenth Century* (1938).

Brian Stanley

Comboni, (Anthony) Daniel (1831–1881), Roman Catholic missionary bishop and founder of the Verona

(Comboni) Fathers. Comboni was born at Limone, Italy, and attended the missionary Institute of Don Mazza at Verona. Ordained a priest in 1854, he departed for Sudan with the institute's expedition to central Africa in 1857. There Comboni joined a team sent to the Holy Cross mission station among the Dinka on the Upper Nile, but the endeavor was beleaguered by high missionary mortality and the incursions of slave merchants. A dying colleague's plea for apostolic perseverance provided inspiration for Comboni's later motto, "Africa or death." Suffering chronic fever, Comboni withdrew to Italy, but he was soon assisting in efforts to ransom young Africans from slavery and to transfer them to Europe for education. For three years he served as vice-rector of the African colleges at Verona, overseeing the education of African men. In 1864, while praying at the tomb of St. Peter, he first conceived his "Plan for the Regeneration of Africa by Africa," which envisioned the creation of seminaries, trade schools, and Christian communities on African soil for the formation of a genuinely African apostolate. Centers established on Africa's Mediterranean coast would allow Africans to be trained in a familiar environment while Europeans could be acclimatized for forays into the interior. His plan called for the effort to be international in nature, with personnel drawn from clergy, laity, and religious. Once the proposal was embraced by Propaganda Fide and by Pope Pius IX, Comboni traveled extensively seeking international support. In 1867 he founded the African Mission at Verona and established two institutes for training African men and women in Cairo, Egypt. An institute for missionary sisters was opened at Verona in 1872. In the same year Comboni was named pro-vicar apostolic of Central Africa, a territory stretching from Egypt to Zimbabwe and from the Red Sea to Mali. With the mission entrusted to his institute, Comboni traversed Sudan, challenging the institutions of slavery and founding new stations. In 1877 he was named vicar apostolic of Central Africa. Tragically, Comboni's early death coincided with the rise of the Mahdiyah and suppression of the church he had struggled to establish. Nevertheless, his fervent spirituality and farsighted methodology have remained an inspiration for succeeding generations of missionaries committed to the creation of an indigenous apostolate.

BIBLIOGRAPHY The complete writings of Comboni have been published and annotated as *Scritti,* 10 vols. (1983); a condensed one-volume edition, also in Italian, is available as *Daniele Comboni, gli scritti* (1991). Since 1960 the Archivio Comboniano in Rome has published twice annually a guide to archival documents and literature concerning the life of Comboni. The most authoritative biography remains Michelangelo Grancelli, *Mons. Daniele Comboni e la Missione dell' Africa Centrale* (1923); in English, see Pietro Chiocchetta, *Daniel Comboni: Papers for the Evangelisation of Africa* (1982) and Aldo Gilli, *Daniel Comboni: The Man and His Message* (1980).

Marc R. Nikkel

Comenius (*or* Komensky), Jan Amos (1592–1670), Moravian theologian and educational reformer. Born in eastern Moravia, Czechoslovakia, Comenius was the last bishop of the Moravian Brethren. He studied theology at Herborn and Heidelberg (1611–1614), served as teacher, rector, and minister in Prerov and Fulnek (in 1614 and 1618, respectively), was uprooted by the Thirty Years' War (1618–1648), lost his library and writings, and traveled as a refugee through Europe. He stayed several times in Lissa, Poland, and finally settled in Amsterdam (1656–1670), where he induced some colleagues to produce a Turkish Bible translation. (The unpublished MS is at Leiden University.) He also had significant influence on Gottfried Wilhelm *Leibniz and German pietism. Comenius advocated the propagation of *pansophia* (universal wisdom), a true knowledge of God, who, according to Comenius, is already served by the nations, though unconsciously. In *Angelus Pacis* (1667) he appealed to the Dutch and English mercantile companies to care for Asians, Africans, and Native Americans.

Comenius's main work is the seven-volume *De Rerum Humanarum Emendatione Consultatio Catholica* (A general consultation concerning the improvement of human affairs) (published 1960). It treats Christianity, in its ecumenical and missionary dimensions, as a means to improve human relations. This improvement will best be achieved through "universal education," "universal language," and "universal reform." As a theologian, Comenius dreamed of a church in which all religions would be united by Christian love; as an educator, he dreamed of schools that would convey divine wisdom to implant the image of Christ in all students. The Comenius Gesellschaft, in Berlin, and the Comenius Theological Faculty, in Prague, keep the thought of Comenius alive.

BIBLIOGRAPHY H. Geissler, "Johann Amos Comenius als Wegbereiter Evangelischen Missionsdenkens," *EMZ* 14 (1957): 74–82; S. S. Laurie, *John Amos Comenius, Bishop of the Moravians: His Life and Educational Works* (1893); J. M. van der Linde, *Die Welt hat Zukunft: Johann Amos Comenius über die Reform von Schule, Kirche und Staat* (1992), pp. 173–193; W. Rood, *Comenius and the Low Countries: Some Aspects of Life and Work of a Czech Exile in the Seventeenth Century* (1970; includes a complete bibliography of Comenius); C. J. Wright, *Comenius and the Church Universal* (1942); R. F. Young, *Comenius and the Indians of New England* (1927).

Jan A. B. Jongeneel

Condit, Azubah Caroline (c. 1810–1844), Reformed Church in America missionary in southeast Asia. The first single woman to engage in foreign mission work, Condit responded to a plea from David *Abeel and joined Jacob Ennis, Elihu Doty, Elbert Nevius, William Youngblood, and their wives, who sailed from New York for Borneo in June 1836. She was given the title of assistant missionary. A sister of Mrs. Nevius, Condit studied Chinese and taught Chinese girls on Java, as well as starting a boarding school for Chinese girls at Pontianak, Borneo, in 1842. Her early death cut short a promising missionary career.

BIBLIOGRAPHY R. Pierce Beaver, *American Protestant Women in World Mission* (1968); Eugene Heideman, *A People in Mission: The Surprising Harvest* (1980); *Tercentenary Studies: Reformed Church in America* (1928). Also see materials in Reformed Church in America archives, New Brunswick Theological Seminary, New Brunswick, N.J.

Charles E. Van Engen

Conforti, Guido Maria (1865–1931), Italian bishop and promoter of missions. Conforti was born at Casalora di Ravadese di Cortile S. Martino, Parma. After his ordination he was appointed professor and rector of the Parma seminary. He wanted to join the Society of Jesus or the Salesian Fathers of Don Bosco, but poor health impeded him. In 1893 he was appointed diocesan director of the Propagation of the Faith. Between 1889 and 1895 he planned the Society of Emilia for the Missions, whose members would take religious vows. Unable to go to the missions himself, he sent the society's first missionaries, Cajo Rastelli and Odoardo Manini, to China in 1898. They were accompanied by the Franciscan missionary Francesco Fogolla. In 1899 Conforti founded an organization for missionary cooperation, Apostolate of Faith and Civilization (also the title of the organization's Italian bulletin). In 1902 he was appointed archbishop of Ravenna, but resigned in 1904 because of poor health. He was then appointed auxiliary bishop and from 1907 ordinary bishop of Parma. Conforti promoted a missionary spirit among the clergy. He gave great support to Paolo *Manna during the foundation of the Pontifical Missionary Union of the Clergy and served as its first president. In 1921 the society for Emilia for the Missions received papal approval.

BIBLIOGRAPHY L. Ballarin, *L'anima missionaria di Giovanni Maria Conforti* (1962); G. Bonardi, *Giovanni Maria Conforti* (1936); A. Dagnino, *Dottrina spirituale di mons. Giovanni Maria Conforti* (1966).

Willi Henkel, OMI

Congar, Yves (1904–1995), Catholic theologian of mission. Congar was born at Sedan, in the French Ardennes. In 1921 he entered the Paris seminary of the Carmelites; later he nearly joined the Benedictines but in 1925 he chose instead the Dominican novitiate of the Province of France at Amiens. His studies were carried out at the Dominican Study House of Le Saulchoir in Belgium, where teachers and pupils had sought refuge from the anticlerical legislation of the Third French Republic. Congar's master, Marie-Dominique Chenu (1895–1990) communicated to him his own enthusiasm for the infant ecumenical movement, and this marked the beginning of Congar's passion for ecumenical theology and ecclesiology. However, dark years followed with the Roman condemnation of Chenu's academic work which was judged as having dangerous historicist tendencies. Congar was assigned—at his own request—to the École Biblique of Jerusalem, eventually returning to France to resume pastoral and theological ministry in 1955.

Everything changed with the election of Pope *John XXIII (r. 1958–1963) who named him theological consultor to the preparatory commission for Vatican II. At the council itself Congar helped write major documents, among them the Constitutions on Divine Revelation, on the Mystery of the Church, and on the Church in the Modern World, as well as the Decrees on the Church's Missionary Activity and on Ecumenism. Congar approached the theology of religions and mission from the standpoint of Christian unity and witness. He saw the church and the churches as the sign of the appearance of God's grace in Jesus Christ, which encompassed the entire history of humankind. All human beings saved in Jesus Christ were in God's providence ordained to participate in the church's sacrament of salvation, at once unique and diverse.

BIBLIOGRAPHY Yves Congar, *The Wide World My Parish* (1961), *The Mystery of the Temple* (1962), *Power and Poverty in the Church* (1964), *Diversity and Communion* (1984), and *The Word and the Spirit* (1986). W. Henn, *The Hierarchy of Truths according to Yves Congar* (1987); C. MacDonald, *Church and World in the Plan of God: History and Eschatology according to Yves Congar* (1982); A. Nichols, *Yves Congar* (1989).

Jacques Dupuis, SJ

Considine, John Joseph (1897–1982), Maryknoll missiologist. Considine was born in New Bedford, Massachusetts, entered the Catholic Foreign Mission Society (Maryknoll) in 1915, and was ordained in 1923. Sent in 1925 as Maryknoll's "man in Rome," he also founded and directed the Fides International Service (1927–1934), a service of the Propaganda Fide Office. From 1934 to 1946 he served on the general council of Maryknoll and directed Maryknoll Publications. In the 1950s he participated in the Fordham University Missionary Institutes and taught at the Maryknoll Seminary in Ossining, New York, until 1960. He chaired the Latin America Bureau of the National Catholic Welfare Council in Washington, D.C. (1961–1966), directed the Papal Volunteers for Latin America, and was a member of the national Advisory Council of the Peace Corps.

Through his many writings and presentations, which combined statistics and personal narratives gathered from trips to missions around the world, Considine developed a theology of global Christianity (*World Christianity*, 1945), argued for a mission education that emphasized an intelligent acquaintance with people and their cultures, influenced the direction of the U. S. Roman Catholic mission effort to Latin America in the 1950s and 1960s (*Call for Forty Thousand*, 1946), and explored the relationship between mission and contemplation. He died at Maryknoll.

BIBLIOGRAPHY Considine's extensive diaries, writings, and correspondence are well organized in the Maryknoll Mission Archives, Ossining, New York. Works by Considine include "An Outline of Missiography," *The Missionary Academia* 1: 8 (1944); *Across a World* (1942); *Fundamental Teaching on the Human Race* (1960); and as editor, John J. Considine, *The Church in the New Latin America* (1964). See also Angelyn Dries, "Toward a U.S. Theology of Global Christianity: John Considine, M.M.," *Records of the American Catholic Historical Society* 103, no. 4 (1992): 23–32.

Angelyn Dries, OSF

Constantine-Cyril. *See* Cyril-Constantine.

Constantine the Great (c. 280–337), first Christian emperor and ruler of the later Roman or early Byzantine empire. Constantine the Great, also known as Constantine I, was born at Naissus (modern Nis in Serbia). The son of Constantius Chlorus and his wife, Eleni, he was brought up in the eastern part of the Roman empire and received his military training in Emperor Diocletian's court at Nicomedia in Asia Minor. He spoke Greek and Latin and inclined toward religious mysticism. Constantine was raised to serve in various military ranks, and after defeating his adversaries, Maxentius and Licinius, he emerged sole emperor in 324. As emperor he founded Constantinople and introduced several political, military, and economic measures of lasting importance.

Constantine's significance for Christianity lies in several aspects of his life and work. His conversion influenced its future. His example served as a model for his subjects and created a precedent to be followed by other medieval rulers such as *Clovis of the Franks, *Boris of Bulgaria, and *Vladimir of Russia. Constantine's adoption of Christianity has been attributed to both political motives and religious experiences. Ancient sources relate that the turning point in his conversion was his victory against Maxentius in 312, when he officially invoked the help of the Christians' God.

Constantine's commitment to Christianity after 312 is revealed by several measures and reforms that aided its advance, including his proclamation of the Edict of Toleration (Milan, 313), which made Christianity a legal religion; the issuing of several laws granting the church and its clergy legal and economic privileges; his interest in the unity of the church by convoking in 325 the Council of Nicaea, which issued the Nicene Creed as an authoritative synopsis of Christian beliefs; his interest in church building and his encouragement of philanthropic works; and his adoption of humanitarian legislation by which cruel practices, such as punishment by crucifixion, were abolished. In 324 he selected Byzantium to be his new capital and in 330 renamed it Constantinople after himself. Constantine was baptized in 337 and died soon after in Nicomedia. Because of his contributions to the Christian movement, the church proclaimed him *isapostolos* (equal to the Apostles). His feast day is celebrated May 21.

BIBLIOGRAPHY Norman H. Baynes, *Constantine the Great and the Christian Church,* Proceedings of the British Academy, vol. 15 (1929); Hermann Dörries, *Constantine the Great,* Roland H. Bainton, tr. (1972); Eusebius, *Ecclesiastical History* and *On the Life of Constantine,* both in A Select Library of Nicene and Post-Nicene Fathers of the Christian Church, 2d ser., vol. 1 (1961); A. H. M. Jones, *Constantine and the Conversion of Europe* (1948, 1962); Lactantius, *De Mortibus Persecutorum,* J. L. Creed, ed. and tr. (1984).

Demetrios J. Constantelos

Cook, Albert Ruskin (1870–1951), Church Missionary Society (CMS) doctor in Uganda. Cook was born in Hampstead, London, son of a doctor. His father died when he was twelve. His mother, Harriet Cook, was the daughter of Edward *Bickersteth. Cook was a scholar at St. Paul's School, London, and studied medicine in London and Cambridge, being awarded the M.D. (Cambridge) in 1901. In 1895 he volunteered to the CMS and arrived in Uganda in 1897. His first task was to persuade his colleagues that a hospital was viable and would be profitable work for medically trained personnel. Not until the arrival of his brother, John Cook, to become a second doctor (1899) could Mengo Hospital, Kampala, really develop. The following year Albert Cook married Kate Timpson, a well-qualified nurse. The hospital was accepted and grew. Cook was not only a gifted doctor but he also had linguistic gifts and participated in evangelistic outreach. However, the personality clashes between Kate Cook and the other medical personnel marred the work of the hospital while she continued as matron. Finally compelled to resign in 1919, she established the Lady Coryndon Maternity Training School (opened 1921), also in the Kampala area. Both Albert and Kate Cook were decorated for their work, and in 1932 Albert Cook was knighted. The Cooks retired in 1934, remaining in Uganda, where Kate Cook died in 1938. Albert Cook lived to see the golden jubilee of the hospital he had founded.

BIBLIOGRAPHY Albert R. Cook, *Uganda Memories (1897–1940)* (1945) and *Proclaiming Liberty, 1897–1947: Jubilee Book of Mengo Hospital* (1947). W. D. Foster, *The CMS and Modern Medicine in Uganda: The Life of Sir Albert Cook K.C.M.G. 1870–1951* (1978); Joyce Reason, *Safety Last: The Story of Albert Cook of Uganda* (1954); A. Stanley Smith, "Sir Albert Cook's Legacy" (Uganda Medical Association lecture, 1967).

Jocelyn Murray

Cook, J. A. B. (1854–1926), English missionary to Singapore. Born in South Shields in northern England, Cook determined to become a missionary upon reading an account of the death of David *Livingstone. In 1881 he accepted appointment by the English Presbyterian Mission to take charge of the Chinese Presbyterian Church in Singapore, which had languished after the death of its founder, Benjamin *Keasberry. He arrived in Singapore in 1882 after a year in China during which he studied the Swatow dialect. After reforming the existing congregation, he initiated the establishment of new congregations to serve Chinese Christians outside the city and those of dialects other than Swatow. He also obtained land grants from the sultan of Johor through James Meldrum, son-in-law of Keasberry and prominent company manager in Johor. This led to the formation of the first Chinese Presbyterian churches in peninsular Malaysia. In addition to his administrative and pastoral duties, Cook oversaw for many years a monthly missionary meeting which brought together all of the Protestant church workers in Singapore and fostered extensive cooperative ministries. He was an influential leader of the temperance and anti-opium movements in Singapore and was an outspoken critic of the brothel trade in Chinese women. This, and his interest in history, was reflected in his books and numerous articles for the Christian press in Singapore.

BIBLIOGRAPHY J. A. B. Cook, *Sunny Singapore* (1907); Bobby Sng, *In His Good Time* (1993).

Robert A. Hunt

Cooke, Mary Ann. *See* Wilson, Mary Ann (Cooke).

Cooke, Sophia (1814–1895), agent of the Society for Promoting Female Education in India and the East. Cooke worked as a governess in England for 20 years before applying to the Church Missionary Society (CMS). Assigned to Singapore, in 1853 she took over the Chinese Girls' School, which had been founded in 1846. (It continues a century and a half later as the St. Margaret's Girls' School.) Under Cooke, the school served as a home for abandoned or abused Chinese girls and as a base for evangelistic work among Chinese women. Several of its pupils went on to work for the CMS mission in Foochow (Fuzhou), China. Cooke was actively involved in social work on a wide scale. She was a founder of the Sailors' Rest, fed and clothed sailors who were destitute or ill, and led Bible studies and worship for sailors, soldiers, and policemen. Her weekly worship services for Chinese were the direct predecessor to the first Anglican and Presbyterian Chinese churches in Singapore. Cooke was also founder of the Singapore YWCA and helped organize branches of the Ladies' Bible and Tract Society and the British and Foreign Bible Society. Through these agencies she played a leading role in mobilizing the European population of Singapore for Christian mission. In her projects she worked closely with Brethren, Presbyterian, Anglican, Wesleyan, and later Methodist missionaries in Singapore. She instituted and inspired extensive ecumenical social work whose legacy continues until today. She died in Singapore.

BIBLIOGRAPHY Bobby Sng, *In His Good Time* (1993); E. A. Walker, *Sophia Cooke* (1899).

Robert A. Hunt

Cook González, Eulalia (1913–), American Methodist missionary and literacy specialist in Cuba. Trained at Columbia University, New York, and Scarritt College, Nashville, Cook was commissioned to work in Cuba by the Methodist Woman's Division of Christian Service in 1940. She arrived in Báguanos in 1942 and immersed herself in that rural community. In 1943 Frank *Laubach visited Cuba, and Cook learned his methods and applied them contextually. Through literacy work she founded several rural churches. A publishing program for new readers developed in cooperation with educators Justo and Luisa *González. In 1952 and 1953, Cook visited rural mission centers in South America, Puerto Rico, and Haiti, establishing a network that would later serve as a basis for Alfabetizacion y Literatura (ALFALIT). Having systematized her experience as a church-based movement for community renewal and evangelism, from 1957 to 1960 she taught at the Evangelical Seminary in Matanzas and founded its department of rural mission. In November 1960 political tensions forced her to move from Cuba to Costa Rica, where with the Gonzálezes she founded ALFALIT and during 25 years traveled extensively promoting literacy and the improvement of the conditions of poor women. Methodist women from Florida supported Cook's program of simple literature in Spanish. Five years after Luisa González died, Cook married Justo in 1992, and from retirement in Miami they continued to promote ALFALIT.

BIBLIOGRAPHY Justo González, *Story of a Miracle* (1985).

Samuel Escobar

Coolen, C(oenraad) L(aurens) (1775–1873), Indonesian layman, cofounder of the church in East Java. Coolen was born in Java, Indonesia, of a Russian father and a Javanese mother of noble descent. He mastered the *wayang* (Javanese mythical puppet play) and Javanese music and dance. He served in the army and in the government forestry service. About 1816 he became a Christian through contact with Johannes *Emde. In 1827 he started clearing a forest in East Java and established a prosperous village that attracted many Javanese Muslims. Standing in a patriarchal relation to his tenants, who considered him to have supernatural powers and great wisdom, he proclaimed the gospel by means of the *wayang* and Javanese religious concepts and rituals, and formed the first Javanese Christian congregation, but without administering the sacraments. After 1844 his influence waned as a consequence of conflicts with government officials and even more because a number of his followers came into contact with Emde and had themselves baptized. As European pietists, Emde and his missionary colleagues pressed the Javanese Christians to abandon their Javanese cultural identity. After some hesitation, and with the approval of Jelle *Jellesma, the Javanese Christians chose a middle course: they accepted restrictions on the use of *wayang* and other quasi-religious features of Javanese culture, but retained their Javanese names, clothing, and other elements of their culture. Despite this shift in allegiance, Coolen is still honored, and his grave continues to attract Christians and Muslims alike. Together with Emde, he is considered to be the founder of the Christian church in East Java.

BIBLIOGRAPHY Philip van Akkeren, *Sri and Christ: A Study of the Indigenous Church in East Java* (1970; with bibliography); S. Coolsma, *De Zendingseeuw voor Nederlandsch Oost-Indië* (1901).

Th. van den End

Coombs, Lucinda L. (1849?–1919), American Methodist medical missionary in China. Coombs graduated from the Woman's Medical College of Pennsylvania and was sent to China by the Woman's Foreign Missionary Society (WFMS) of the Methodist Episcopal Church. Possibly the first female medical missionary of any denomination in that country, she arrived in Peking (Beijing) in September 1873; two years later she opened the first hospital for women in China. In November 1877 she married fellow Methodist missionary Andrew Stritmatter and moved to his station at Kiukiang (Jinjiang), Kiangsi (Jiangxi) Province. There she continued to work as a medical doctor, although her marriage automatically removed her from the roll of WFMS missionaries. In 1880 her husband, suffering from tuberculosis, was forced to retire from the mission field. The Stritmatters and their two small sons arrived in San Francisco in October and began traveling east to his family home in Ohio. However, he could travel no further than Denver, where he died on November 22. Little is known about "Lucy's" later life. She evidently moved on to Ohio with her children. She did not remarry, and died in Columbus, Ohio.

BIBLIOGRAPHY There is no complete biography of Lucinda Coombs. Some information about her can be gleaned from Wade Crawford Barclay, *History of Methodist Missions,* vol. 3 (1949).

Susan E. Warrick

Cope, Marianne (1838–1918), remembered as Mother Marianne of Molokai. Cope was born Barbara Koob in Germany. The family immigrated to the United States in 1840 and changed their name to Cope. In 1862 Barbara Cope joined the Sisters of St. Francis in Syracuse, New York, and received the religious name Marianne. A woman of remarkable leadership abilities, she eventually became Mother Superior of her congregation. In 1883 Mother Marianne, with six of her Franciscan Sisters, sailed for Hawaii to work among persons with leprosy. Thus Mother Marianne became one of the first sisters of an American foundation to start missionary work in a foreign land (Hawaii was an independent kingdom at the time). After working on other islands, she and some of her sisters went to Molokai in 1888, in response to an urgent request from Father *Damien to work there among the victims of leprosy. She remained in the leprosy settlement until her death twenty years later and is buried on Molokai.

BIBLIOGRAPHY Margaret R. Bunson, *Father Damien: The Man and His Era* (1989); Mary Laurence Hanley and O. A. Bushnell, *Pilgrimage and Exile: Mother Marianne of Molokai* (1980, 1991); Edward Anthony Lenk, "Mother Marianne Cope (1838–1918): The Syracuse Franciscan Community and Molokai Lepers" (Ph.D. diss., Syracuse Univ., 1986).

Gerald H. Anderson

Copleston, Reginald Stephen (1835–1925), Anglican bishop in South Asia. Copleston was born and educated in England. After a few years teaching at Oxford, he was consecrated bishop of Colombo in Ceylon (Sri Lanka), a position he held from 1875 to 1902. Thereafter, he was bishop of Calcutta and metropolitan of the Church of India until retirement in 1913. Two outstanding aspects distinguish his work. First, he seriously sought to understand Buddhism. He both studied the Pali texts and made close observations of current Buddhist practice, producing a series of articles and a major book. Nineteenth-century missionary derogation of Buddhism in Ceylon, that did much to provoke its revival, was moderated in Copleston's case. Second, he promoted the constitutional integrity of the local church. This involved a painful controversy with the Church Missionary Society missionaries in Ceylon, initially over their involvement in the Tamil Coolie Missions, as he asserted episcopal authority and church unity. Less controversially, he steered the Anglican Church in Ceylon through its disendowment, and in India he took a leading part in the development of the church's independence.

BIBLIOGRAPHY Copleston asked that no biography of himself be written. His formal but often revealing correspondence with the SPG is in the SPG archives, Rhodes House, Oxford, but Copleston destroyed almost all his correspondence regarding the Ceylon controversy with the CMS. His main published work is *Buddhism Primitive and Present in Magadha and in Ceylon* (1892); reviews of this work and of his articles on Buddhism are listed in S. Hanayama, *Bibliography on Buddhism* (1961). There is a judicious account of the Ceylon controversy in M. E. Gibbs, *The Anglican Church in India, 1600–1970* (1972); C. J. Grimes, *Towards an Indian Church* (1946) refers to his constitutional work. The *Ceylon Diocesan Gazette* provides glimpses of him.

Daniel O'Connor

Coppin, Fanny Marion (Jackson) (1837–1913), African-American educator and missionary. Jackson was born into slavery in Washington, D.C., but her freedom was purchased by an aunt. Eventually she moved to Newport, Rhode Island, as a domestic servant. After completing a teaching course, she enrolled at Oberlin College, the first college in America open to blacks. Driven by a sense of mission to African Americans, she opened a night class for freedmen. Oberlin then appointed her as the first black student to teach in its preparatory department. After graduating in 1865, she became principal of the Female Department of the Institute for Colored Youth in Philadelphia, a Quaker institution. In less than five years, she became principal of the entire school. Under her leadership, the institute specialized in educating African Americans as teachers and also added industrial training to its curriculum. The first black woman to head an institution of higher learning, she remained until her retirement in 1902.

In 1881 she married Levi Coppin, an African Methodist Episcopal (AME) minister. She joined the AME and became active in mission work, serving for years as president of the AME Women's Home and Foreign Missionary Society. In 1888 she represented the society at the London Centenary Conference and spoke on women's desire for "the Christianization of the colored races of the earth." In 1900 Levi Coppin was elected bishop for South Africa. In 1902 Fanny joined him and began speaking on temperance among Cape Coloured and African women. Because oppressed farm workers were partly paid in wine, temperance had special significance in the South African context (although Coppin claimed to be apolitical). She accompanied her husband to the interior and spoke to women, organizing mission societies and supporting mission education. After leaving South Africa at the end of 1903, she suffered from arteriosclerosis until her death.

BIBLIOGRAPHY Coppin's autobiography was published as *Reminiscences of School Life, and Hints on Teaching* (1913). She also had a column in the *Christian Recorder,* the oldest black periodical in the United States. See also Levi Coppin, *Unwritten History* (1913); Margaret E. Burton, *Comrades in Service* (1919); Linda M. Perkins, *Fanny Jackson Coppin and the Institute for Colored Youth, 1865–1902* (1987).

Dana L. Robert

Corbett, Hunter (1835–1920), pioneer Presbyterian missionary in Shandong (Shantung), China. Born in Clarion County, Pennsylvania, Corbett graduated from Washington and Jefferson College (Washington, Pennsylvania) and from Princeton Theological Seminary. With his wife, Lizzie (Culbertson), he sailed for China in 1863, and after a six-month voyage around the Cape of Good Hope and shipwreck off the China coast, they finally arrived at Yantai (Chefoo) in the middle of winter, 1865. After several years in Dengzhow (P'eng-lai, or Tengchow), they established a permanent residence at Yantai and began evangelistic work. Along with colleagues Calvin *Mateer and John *Nevius, Corbett developed the methodology that would plant the gospel in the soil of northern China and make Shandong the strongest Presbyterian mission in China. Wide itineration throughout the countryside, rather than concentrated efforts in the cities, was the main feature of the Shandong plan. Corbett was described as an "indefatigable itinerator," and he traveled over the whole province by horse, mule cart, and foot. Added to his travel difficulties were incidents in which he was reviled and stoned.

Corbett believed in using unconventional methods. He rented a theater and converted the back rooms into a museum stocked with objects of interest from around the world. After a service, the museum doors would be opened. In 1900, 72,000 people listened to his preaching and visited the museum. A crowning achievement was the organization and development of Shandong Presbytery. By the year of Corbett's death, there were 343 organized churches and chapels throughout the province, with more than 15,000 communicant members. In 1906 he was elected moderator of the General Assembly of the Presbyterian Church, U.S.A. Altogether, Corbett ministered in China for 56 years.

Bibliography Hunter Corbett, ed., *The American Presbyterian Mission in Shantung During Fifty Years: 1861–1911* (c. 1914). James R. E. Craighead, *Hunter Corbett: Fifty-Six Years a Missionary to China* (1921); John J. Heeren, *On the Shantung Front: A History of the Shantung Mission of the PCUSA, 1861–1910* (1921). See also the tribute by his colleagues, "A Memorial of Dr. Hunter Corbett: A Prince in Israel has fallen!" in *1920 Minutes of the Annual Meeting of the Mission Council, Shantung Mission* (archives, Presbyterian Department of History, Philadelphia).

G. Thompson Brown

Corbinian (d. after 725), apostle of Bavaria. Although little is known about his life, Corbinian—like his contemporaries Emmeran and Rupert—is regarded as an apostle of Bavaria. A native of Melun, France, he went to Rome, where he became a bishop and was assigned to work in Bavaria as a missionary, stationed at Freising, where he is to this day venerated as patron of the archdiocese of Freising-Munich. His activities there marked the end of the missionary phase proper and the beginning of an independent Bavarian church province.

Bibliography Romuald Bauerreis, *Kirchengeschichte Bayerns* (1949, 1973), pp. 1, 41ff.

Hans-Werner Gensichen

Córdoba, Pedro de (1482–1521), superior of first Dominican missionaries to Latin America. Born in Córdoba, Spain, Córdoba joined the Dominicans and in 1510 arrived with other Spanish Dominican missionaries in Hispaniola (present-day Haiti and Dominican Republic). He and his comrades, including Antonio de *Montesinos, questioned the social and religious system imposed by the early Spaniards. With his strong theological background, Córdoba raised questions about property rights of the Indians, the obligation to restore property taken from the people, their right to baptism and to peaceful, voluntary acceptance of Christian faith, and limitations to the power of the monarch. He encouraged discussion of these and similar questions in Dominican community meetings (chapters) and fostered community support for the pastoral decisions reached there. Montesinos's illustrious sermons, the "Gritos," resulted from these meetings. Córdoba also had a strong influence on Bartolomé de *Las Casas. Despite a hearing from the Spanish king Fernando in 1513, Córdoba succeeded in obtaining only a little amelioration for the people. He made what may be the first systematic efforts to evangelize in the New World, later elaborated in a publication that appeared after his death, *Doctrina cristiana.* Until recently obscured by the figure of Las Casas, Córdoba was eulogized by Pope *John Paul II and many others during the Fifth Centenary commemorations.

Bibliography Pedro de Córdoba, *Doctrina cristiana para instrucción de los indios,* Miguel Angel Medina, ed. (1987), and *Doctrina cristiana y cartas* (1988). Rubén Boria, *Fray Pedro de Córdoba, O.P.* (1982; includes bibliography); P. Henríquez Ureña, *La cultura y las letras coloniales en Santo Domingo* (1936); María-Graciela Crespo Ponce, *Estudio histórico-teológico de la "Doctrina cristiana"* (1988).

Edward L. Cleary, OP

Corrado, Alejandro María (1830–1890), Italian Franciscan missionary in Bolivia. Corrado, who worked most of his life in southeastern Bolivia, is best known for his history of the missions of the Colegio de Propaganda Fide in Tarija, Bolivia, covering the period from 1810 to 1880. In this work he portrays the vast labors of the nineteenth-century Tarija Franciscans, as they founded eight missions incorporating almost 10,000 Indians. Although most of his work was among the Chiriguano Indians, Corrado also helped initiate the missionary efforts among the Chaco tribes. He was also the founder of San Francisco Solano del Pilcomayo in 1860, a mission established for the Toba Indians. He incorporated a group of Chiriguano into the mission because he felt that the Toba were untrustworthy and might assassinate the resident missionary. In his later years, he became the prefect of the Tarija missionary system and administered the missions in the 1870s, their period of greatest flowering. He died in Bolivia.

Bibliography Alejandro M. Corrado, *El Colegio Franciscano de Tarija y sus misiones* (1884, 1990) and *Reglas elementales de la lengua chiriguana* (1896).

Erick D. Langer

Corrie, Daniel (1777–1837), first bishop of Madras. Corrie was born in Ardchaton, Argyll, Scotland, and was educated at Clare College and Trinity College, Cambridge (1799–1805). There he came under the influence of Charles *Simeon, fellow of King's College and minister of Holy Trinity Church. Through the influence of Simeon and following two brief curacies, Corrie was appointed as a chaplain to Bengal with the British East India Company. From 1807 to 1823 he held chaplaincies at Chunar, Cawnpore, Agra, and Benares and served as senior chaplain at Calcutta. In 1823 he was made archdeacon of Calcutta by his bishop, Reginald *Heber. His final service to the Indian church was as bishop of Madras from 1835 to 1837.

Corrie made numerous contributions to the religious establishment and missionary movement in India. In addition to his reputation as an effective and responsible chaplain, he joined David *Brown in organizing the Calcutta auxiliary of the British and Foreign Bible Society and in cooperating with William *Carey and the Serampore Baptists in various Bible translation projects. Corrie also served as an able secretary of the Calcutta Corresponding Committee of the Church Missionary Society (CMS). Bishop Heber and fellow chaplain Henry *Martyn warmly affirmed Corrie's rapport with Indian nationals.

BIBLIOGRAPHY G. E. Corrie and H. Corrie, eds., *Memoirs of the Right Rev. Daniel Corrie, first Bishop of Madras: Compiled Chiefly from His Letters and Journals* (1847); Angus Macnaghten, *Daniel Corrie: His Family and His Friends* (1969). Collections of Corrie's papers are held in the archives of the CMS (University of Birmingham) and to a lesser extent in the India Office Library and Records (London).

John C. Bennett

Costa, Isaac da (1798–1860), Portuguese Jewish convert and promoter of Christian mission. Da Costa studied law and arts in Leiden, Netherlands, where the Christian poet Willem Bilderdijk (1756–1831) directed his attention to the Old Testament messianic prophecies and promises. In 1822 he, his wife, Hanna (Belmonte), and his nephew, Abraham *Capadose, were baptized in Leiden. He moved to Amsterdam, where he devoted his life to Bible study and poetry. A lay preacher, he became a leader in the nineteenth-century Réveil (revival) movement and wrote courageously for the Christian faith. His most influential work is *Bezwaren tegen de Geest der Eeuw* (Objections against the spirit of the century, 1823), which was an attack on Enlightenment concepts.

Da Costa was cofounder of the Friends of Israel (1846). He welcomed the conversion of Jews but in contrast to Capadose, did not personally engage in missionary work among them. He expected God to bring the Jewish people to the Messiah and to restore Israel as a nation in the Holy Land. Nevertheless, da Costa engaged in general missionary work: he addressed missionary gatherings, wrote missionary hymns, and taught at the Scottish Seminary for Mission at Home and Abroad, located in Amsterdam. He also criticized the Netherlands Mission Society as being theologically syncretistic.

BIBLIOGRAPHY Isaac da Costa, *The Four Witnesses: Being a Harmony of the Gospels on a New Principle* (1855), *Israel and the Gentiles: Contributions to the History of the Jews from the Earliest Time to the Present Day* (1855), and *Noble Families among the Sephardic Jews*, B. Brewster, ed. (1936). J. G. Bomhoff et al., *Isaäc da Costa* (1961); H. Bremmer, *Isaäc da Costa en het Réveil* (1951); L. Engelfriet, *Bilderdijk en het Jodendom* (1995), pp. 165–170; J. Haitsma, *Isaäc da Costa (1798–1860)* (1993); J. Meijer, *Isaac da Costa's Weg naar het Christendom* (1941, 2d ed. 1946).

Jan A. B. Jongeneel

Costantini, Celso (1876–1958), Italian-born promoter of indigenous local churches and first apostolic delegate to China. Given the rank of archbishop, Costantini reached China in late 1922 and immediately began to push for implementation of the directives outlined by Pope *Benedict XV in his missionary encyclical *Maximum illud* (1919). In the so-called First Council of China, held in Shanghai from May 15 to June 13, 1924, he convened all the foreign heads of Catholic missions in China, delegates of various missionary institutes, and representatives of the Chinese clergy to plan a general reform of the Catholic Church in China. Together they addressed pressing problems, such as the tension between native and foreign priests, the promotion of the Chinese clergy and the ordination of Chinese bishops, the creation of new commissions for the work of the apostolate, and the liberation of the church from the political influence of the French protectorate. Despite resistance by some foreign bishops, Costantini's relentless efforts during his 13-year term in China produced good results. Missionary training began to emphasize understanding of and respect for Chinese culture. Chinese priests in increasing number acceded to important positions. When Costantini arrived in China, the Catholic Church was under foreign missionary control; by the time the 1924 council met, three prefectures apostolic were already headed by Chinese prelates. Two years later, in October 1926, Pope *Pius XI ordained six Chinese bishops (the first such ordinations since 1685). By 1933, when Costantini finished his mandate, 19 of the existing 119 ecclesiastical territories were in Chinese hands. The prelate also contributed to the idea that the Chinese had primary responsibility for converting their own people when he founded, in 1926, the Disciples of the Lord, a Chinese religious congregation for the purpose of imparting the missionary spirit to the local clergy. Costantini, who had a deep appreciation for the sacred arts, strongly advocated the development of Chinese forms of expression. Through his influence, Chinese-style buildings, statues, images, and music began to gain acceptance in the Catholic Church. From 1935 to 1953, Costantini was secretary of Propaganda Fide in Rome. In 1953 Pope *Pius XII made him a cardinal. Till his death, Costantini remained a champion of missionary accommodation and of local churches rooted in their own cultures and headed by native bishops. He succeeded in helping the Holy See free itself from the protectorate system and its nationalistic implications.

BIBLIOGRAPHY Costantini's most important books are *La Crisi Cinese e il Cattolicismo* (1931), *Aspetti del problema missionario* (1935), *L'arte Christiana nella missioni. Manuale d'arte per i missionari* (1940), *Con i missionari i Cina* (1954; the three vols. of his memoirs as apostolic delegate), and *Ultime foglie* (1954; his memoirs as secretary of Propaganda Fide). Jean Bruls compiled and translated many of these writings in Celso Costantini, *Réforme des Missions au XXe siècle* (1960).

Jean-Paul Wiest

Costas, Orlando E(nrique) (1942–1987), Latin American evangelical missiologist. Born in Ponce, Puerto Rico, Costas grew up in the Hispanic community in the United States and graduated from Bob Jones University and Garrett Evangelical Seminary. He served as a Baptist minister in Yauco, Puerto Rico, and Milwaukee, Wisconsin, where he became a political activist defending the rights of Hispanic workers. With his wife Rose (Feliciano), Costas moved to Costa Rica in 1970 and worked in evangelism and theological education under the Latin America Mission. His missiological teaching and writing, which blended the best of the evangelical and the ecumenical missionary experience, was propagated through the Latin American Theological Fraternity. In 1973 he created the Latin American Center for Pastoral Studies (CELEP), based in San José, which became formative for a new generation of missionaries and national leaders.

Costas was active in the evangelical congresses of Lausanne (1974) and Pattaya (1980), as well as in the World Council of Churches mission conference of Melbourne (1980); he taught in six continents. After doctoral studies at the Free University of Amsterdam (1974–1976), he returned to Latin America. In 1980 he was appointed professor of missiology at Eastern Baptist Theological Seminary in Philadelphia. With other missiologists from the non-Western world, he was among the founders of the International Fellowship of Evangelical Missiologists from the Two Thirds World. Among his best-known books are *The Church and Its Mission: A Shattering Critique from the Third World* (1974), *Christ outside the Gate* (1982), and his posthumous work *Liberating News* (1989). At the time of his death he was the dean and professor of mission at Andover Newton Theological School near Boston.

BIBLIOGRAPHY Costas's published doctoral dissertation is *Theology of the Crossroads in Contemporary Latin America: Missiology in Mainline Protestantism, 1969–1974* (1976). An extensive evaluation of his work is in Antonio Barro, "Orlando Enrique Costas: Mission Theologian on the Way and at the Crossroads" (Ph.D. diss., Fuller Theological Seminary, 1993). The most complete catalog of his publications is Raul Fernández Calienes, "Bibliography of the Writings of Orlando E. Costas," *Missiology* 17, no. 1 (1989): 87–105. Costas's personal library, books, and unclassified papers are in the library of Andover Newton Theological School.

Samuel Escobar

Cotta, Anthony (1872–1957), Catholic missionary in China. Born into a cultured Egyptian Catholic family, Cotta began his studies for the priesthood in Lebanon, then entered the Vincentian seminary in Paris, where he began a lifelong friendship with Vincent *Lebbe. Ordained in 1898, he was sent to Madagascar and barely escaped death during the bloody Malagasy uprising against French rule. In 1906 he was assigned to China and went to Tientsin (Tianjin), where he was reunited with Lebbe. Like Lebbe, he became a staunch advocate of the Chinese and found himself increasingly opposed to the elitist mentality prevailing in the missionary community. In 1914, at a meeting of missionary bishops and specialists in Peking (Beijing), Cotta spoke boldly in favor of giving greater responsibility to Chinese priests and preparing them for the episcopacy. Two years later, when the French consul in Tientsin, in the name of the French protectorate on Christian missions, attempted to annex a piece of land linking the French concession to the cathedral, Cotta and Lebbe sided openly with the Chinese in the city to oppose the measure. They also informed the Vatican of the collusion between the missionary bishop and the consul. Cotta followed up with a thirty-page memoir to Cardinal Serafini, prefect of Propaganda Fide, in which he argued for the establishment of a Chinese episcopacy and a church truly "acclimatized" to China. The document served as a principal source of inspiration and information for the missionary encyclical *Maximum illud* from Pope *Benedict XV in 1919 and paved the way for Pope *Pius XI to ordain six Chinese bishops in 1926.

Meanwhile, the attitude of Cotta had not only angered the French government but caused much resentment against him among the missionary leadership in China. In December 1920 he was recalled from China by his superiors and never allowed to return. In 1922 he withdrew from the Vincentians and joined the Maryknoll Society in the United States. He left a profound influence as a professor at the major seminary in Maryknoll, New York, and as a spiritual director for the seminarians and for the Maryknoll sisters.

BIBLIOGRAPHY Raymond J. de Jaegher, "The First Chinese Bishops and Father Cotta," *World Mission* 6 (1955): 267–277; "Father Anthony Cotta," in Robert E. Sheridan, ed., *Profiles of Twelve Maryknollers,* (1963), chap. 4; Claude Soetens, ed., *Recueil des Archives Vincent Lebbe. Pour l'Eglise chinoise,* vol. 1, *La Visite apostolique des missions de Chine, 1919–1920* (1982) and vol. 3, *L'Encyclique Maximum illud* (1983). These two volumes contain many letters from and to Cotta, his memoir to Cardinal Serafini, as well as a detailed analysis of his role as a missionary figure.

Jean-Paul Wiest

Cotton, George Edward Lynch (1813–1866), educator and Anglican bishop of Calcutta. A soldier's son, Cotton served his educational apprenticeship under the renowned Matthew Arnold at Rugby, where he served as a master from 1837 to 1852. From 1852 to 1856 he was headmaster of Marlborough. In 1858 he became bishop of Calcutta in succession to Daniel *Wilson. His time in India was short, and although it is said that he was not fond of Indian life, he was a good administrator and made valuable contributions in the area of education. His background was evangelical, and though a liberal educationist, he was never really a Broad Churchman. In October 1866, returning from a trip, he drowned in the Ganges at Kushtia. His body was never found.

BIBLIOGRAPHY Sophia Anne Cotton, *Memoir of George Edward Lynch Cotton* (1871).

Eric J. Sharpe

Coudrin, Pierre Marie Joseph (1768–1837), founder of the Congregation of the Fathers of the Sacred Hearts of Jesus and Mary and of the Perpetual Adoration of the Most Holy Sacrament of the Altar (CSSCC). In 1792 Coudrin, a French priest, founded the CSSCC. The aim of this religious group is to emulate the four ages of Christ: his *infancy,* by the instruction of children and the formation of youths for the priesthood; his *hidden life,* by the adoration of the Eucharist; his *public life,* through missionary works; his *crucifixion,* by exercises of mortification. In 1805 Coudrin opened a seminary in Paris for the young candidates to his new congregation. The buildings were located at the Rue Picpus, hence the name Picpus Fathers, by which CSSCC members are commonly known. Under Coudrin's leadership the congregation expanded rapidly. In 1825 the Picpus missionaries began evangelizing in the New Hebrides (modern Vanuatu) in the South Pacific. By the time of Coudrin's death, Picpus missionaries were at work throughout the archipelagoes of Oceania as well as in Peru and Chile.

BIBLIOGRAPHY W. H. Hünermann, *Les maquisards de Dieu* (1954); A. Lestra, *Le Père Coudrin* (1952); S. Perron, *Vie du Très Révérend Père M.-J. Coudrin* (1950).

Jean-Paul Wiest

Coughlan, Laurence (?–1785), Irish missionary and founder of Methodism in Newfoundland. Nothing is known about Coughlan prior to his conversion through Methodist missionaries in the early 1750s at Drumsna, County Leitrim, Ireland. From 1755 to 1757 he was an itinerant preacher in Ireland and subsequently served Methodist societies in England. In the 1760s he aligned himself with Calvinistic and enthusiastic Methodist circles in London and received unauthorized ordination at the hands of the Greek bishop Erasmus, causing a break between himself and John *Wesley. In 1766, after receiving Anglican ordination, he went as a missionary of the Society for the Propagation of the Gospel in Foreign Parts (SPG) to Harbour Grace, Conception Bay, Newfoundland. Here, alongside his Anglican clerical duties, he preached from door-to-door the Methodist religion of the heart and, in the winter of 1769, effected a revival. Soon, however, he incurred the anger of the ruling merchant class because his preaching involved rigorous ethical demands and resulted in greater independence of the lower classes from merchant controls. He also held a position as a magistrate, but through the intervention of the merchants with the authorities, he was deprived of it. After losing his SPG support as well, through the combined opposition of the merchants and the governor, he had to leave Newfoundland. He continued until his death as a preacher among Calvinistic Methodists, especially in London.

BIBLIOGRAPHY Laurence Coughlan, *An Account of The Work of God, in Newfoundland, North America...* (1776). Hans Rollmann, "Laurence Coughlan and the Origins of Newfoundland Methodism," in John Webster Grant and Charles S. Scobie, eds., *The Contribution of Methodism to Atlantic Canada* (1992), pp. 53–76.

Hans Rollmann

Couplet, Philippe (1623–1693), Jesuit missionary in China. Couplet was the principal editor of the first European translation of Confucian teachings. Born in Malines, Belgium, he entered the Society of Jesus in 1640. His interest in China was sparked by a lecture by Martino *Martini, a Jesuit missionary in China then traveling through Europe on his way to Rome. Couplet went to Lisbon in 1655 and reached Macao three years later. Active in several provinces of China, he was exiled to Canton (Guangzhou) during the persecution of 1665 to 1670. The next year he returned to Sungchiang (Songjiang), 25 miles southwest of Shanghai, and he later worked on the island of Chongming, north of Shanghai. Elected procurator of the mission, he left for Rome in 1681 to seek permission for missionaries to celebrate the liturgy in Chinese. En route he stopped at the court of Louis XIV, where he was instrumental in getting royal support for Jesuit mathematicians to come to Peking. In Rome he presented the pope with a library of Christian books in Chinese. Having taken an oath supporting the authority of the vicars apostolic in the Asian missions, which was opposed by the Portuguese patronado system, Couplet waited for eight years in Europe before the two sides settled their differences. En route to China again, he lost his life aboard ship in a storm off the coast of Goa, India.

BIBLIOGRAPHY In addition to seven catechetical works and books of prayer in Chinese, Couplet wrote *Tabula Chronologica Monarchiae Sinicae* (1686), *Confucius Sinarum Philosophus* (1687), *Breve raguaglio delle cose piu notabili spettanti al grand'imperio della Cina* (1687), and *Histoire d'une dame chrétienne de la Chine* (1688). Jeroom Heyndrickx, ed., *Philippe Couplet, S.J. (1623–1693): The Man Who Brought China to Europe* (1990; essays by ten scholars).

John W. Witek, SJ

Cousins, William E(dward) (1840–1939), English missionary to Madagascar. Born in Abingdon, England, Cousins studied at Bedford and married Abigail Williams. He was one of the first group of missionaries sent by the London Missionary Society (LMS) to Madagascar in 1862 after the end of a long period of persecution. He was put in charge of one of the chief city churches in Antananarivo, which like other city churches, carried responsibility for a cluster of village churches in central Madagascar. In 1872 the five Protestant missions in the country decided to produce a new translation of the Bible, since growing missionary knowledge of the language had revealed many weaknesses in the first translation. Cousins was put in charge of the work, which was his chief occupation for 14 years. He was a strong advocate of missionary control over the admission of church members and over the appointment of all local pastors and preachers. At the same time, he tried to defend the church from control by the government, which assumed that the pre-Christian unity of state and religion would continue after national conversion to Christianity. He resigned from the mission in 1899 and was sent the following year as an LMS delegate to the Ecumenical Missionary Conference in New York. After a long period of retirement in England, he was killed in a street accident shortly before his ninety-ninth birthday.

BIBLIOGRAPHY Norman Goodall, *A History of the London Missionary Society, 1894–1945* (1954); Bonar Gow, *Madagascar and the Protestant Impact: The Work of the British Missions, 1818–95* (1979); J. T. Hardyman, *Madagascar on the Move* (1950).

Charles W. Forman

Couvreur, Séraphin (1835–1919), Jesuit missionary in China, translator of Chinese classics, and compiler of several dictionaries. Couvreur was a native of Varenne, Somme, France. After his studies at the seminary in Amiens, he entered the Society of Jesus in September 1853. Upon completion of his philosophical and theological studies at Vals and Laval respectively, he was ordained a priest in 1867. While teaching grammar at the college in Amiens, he asked to go to the China mission. He arrived in April 1870, and after language training at Hochienfu (Hejian), Hopei (Hebei) Province, he became a parish priest for several years and was then appointed a professor in the seminary at Sien-hsien (Xianxian), about 150 miles south of Peking (Beijing). Aware of the need for missionaries to improve their communication with the Chinese, he published a Latin-Chinese dictionary in 1877. This work launched his long career of publishing a French-Chinese, then a Chinese-French, dictionary, and also dual-language translations (French and Latin) of the Five Classics and the Four Books—the key writings of Chinese civilization. Many of these works had several editions and have been reprinted in Paris and Taipei in recent decades. For his sinological contributions Couvreur twice received the Stanislas Julien Prize from the Académie des Inscriptions et Belles-Lettres in Paris. The greater part of his life he spent at the Jesuit residence in Sien-hsien, where he died.

BIBLIOGRAPHY Séraphin Couvreur, *Dictionarium linguae Sinicae Latinum* (1877), *Choix de documents* (4th ed., 1906), *Dictionarium Sinicum et Latinum* (2d ed., 1907), *Dictionnaire Français-Chinois* (2d ed., 1908), *Seu Cheu: Les Quatre Livres,* (2d ed., 1910), *Dictionnaire classique de la langue Chinoise* (3d ed., 1911), *Li Ki ou mémoire des bienséances,* 2 vols. (2d ed., 1913), *Tch'ouen Ts'iou et Tso Tchouan,* 3 vols. (1913), *Cérémonial* (1916), *Cheu King* (2d ed., 1916), *Chou King,* (2d ed., 1916), *Guide de la conversation Français-Anglais-Chinois. Guide to Conversation in French, English, and Chinese* (10th ed., 1920), and *Géographie ancienne et moderne de la Chine* (2d ed., 1934).

John W. Witek, SJ

Cowman, Charles Elmer (1864–1924) *and*
Lettie (Burd) (1870–1960), missionaries in Japan and founders of the Oriental Missionary Society. Born in Toulon, Illinois, Charles Cowman moved with his family to Thayer, Iowa, birthplace of Lettie Burd, when he was two years old. They became childhood sweethearts and were married in 1889. They moved to Chicago and were converted at Grace Methodist Episcopal Church. After hearing A. B. *Simpson, founder of the Christian and Missionary Alliance, give a missionary challenge, they dedicated themselves to missionary service. After brief training at Martin Wells Knapp's God's Bible School in Cincinnati, they went to Japan as independent missionaries in early 1901. There they teamed up with Juji *Nakada, a Japanese whom they met when Nakada was a student at Moody Bible Institute in the late 1890s.

Leasing a hall in Tokyo, they began by conducting nightly evangelistic rallies and a daytime Bible training school for workers. A distinctive feature of their ministry was the Every Creature Crusade, an effort to reach every home in Japan with the gospel of Jesus Christ, a feat they claimed was accomplished between the years 1912 and 1918. Together with Nakada and E. A. *Kilbourne, they organized their work as the Oriental Missionary Society (today, OMS International). Eventually they also established work in Korea and China as well as Japan.

After Charles's untimely death, Lettie continued to play a significant role in OMS. After Kilbourne's death in 1928 she held the office of president until 1949, longer than anyone else. She traveled the world speaking in behalf of missions, and is best remembered for her compilation of devotional materials in *Streams in the Desert* (1925). OMS International was born in the holiness movement and continues today in the tradition of Wesleyan Arminian theology, with an emphasis on evangelism, church planting, and training.

BIBLIOGRAPHY Lettie B. Cowman, *Charles E. Cowman: Missionary Warrior* (1928, 1939); John J. Merwin, "The Oriental Missionary Society, Holiness Church in Japan, 1901–1983" (D.Miss. diss., Fuller Theological Seminary, 1983); Ben H. Pierson, *The Vision Lives* (1961); Robert D. Wood, *In These Mortal Hands* (1983).

Everett N. Hunt, Jr.

Cox, Melville Beveridge (1799–1833), pioneer Methodist Episcopal missionary in Liberia. Born near Hallowell, Maine, Cox entered the New England Methodist Conference in 1822 as an itinerant preacher. After contracting tuberculosis in 1825, he was unable to preach and moved to Baltimore, where he worked in a bookstore and edited a weekly newspaper. He married Ellen Cromwell, but within two years both she and their young daughter died in a cholera epidemic. Resigning his final pastorate in 1831 in Raleigh, North Carolina, again because of his illness, he volunteered the next year as a missionary to South America. He was appointed instead to Liberia. Chided for even considering the assignment, he replied, "Let a thousand fall before Africa be given up." Arriving in Liberia in March 1833, he quickly organized the first Methodist Episcopal church among the immigrants (freed slaves from the United States), some of whom were already Christians. He established a mission at Grand Bassa and another along the Niger with a school of agriculture and art and a vigorous Sunday school. A month later, ill with malaria, he refused to return to America. He was dead within 4 months of his arrival in Africa. When news of Cox's death reached the United States, many others volunteered their services to carry on his brief but effective ministry.

BIBLIOGRAPHY Wade C. Barclay, *History of Methodist Missions: Early American Methodism,* vol. 1 (1949); G. F. Cox, *Remains of Melville B. Cox* (1835); Roger S. Guptill, *Though Thousands Fall* (1932).

H. T. Maclin

Cragg, Albert Kenneth (1913–), British Christian interpreter of Islam. Educated at Oxford, Cragg was ordained to the Anglican priesthood in 1936. His lifelong association with the Middle East began with service under the British Syria Mission in Lebanon, where he taught during World War II at the American University of Beirut. After the war, he returned to Oxford to write a doctoral thesis, "Islam in the Twentieth Century: The Relevance of Christian Theology and the Relationship of Christian Missions to Its Problems" (1950). Cragg then crossed the Atlantic to become professor of Islamic studies at the Hartford Seminary Foundation, where he taught missionary candidates and edited *The Muslim World* as a forum of intellectual debate about Islam and Christian-Muslim relations. His most influential book, *The Call of the Minaret* (1956), was based on American lectures in which he elaborated an irenic Christian approach to Islam through ministries of understanding, service, social action, interpretation of the gospel, and "retrieval"—a term that expressed his vision of a renewed relationship with Muslims in Christ.

Cragg returned to the Middle East in the late 1950s to begin his long association with St. George's Cathedral, Jerusalem. There, and later as a faculty member (1959) and principal (1961) of St. Augustine's College, Canterbury, he developed two major missionary study programs, Operation Reach and Emmaus Furlongs. Three years on the faculty of Ibadan University, Nigeria (1967–1970), preceded his appointment as assistant bishop of Jerusalem residing in Cairo. When Egypt gained its own diocesan status within the Anglican communion, he relinquished his post in favor of an Egyptian bishop and returned to Britain, briefly to a university lectureship (Sussex) and then to pastoral ministry in Yorkshire, an area settled by large immigrant Muslim communities. Since 1981 he has lived in retirement in Oxfordshire, where he continues to write on Islamic and Christian themes.

BIBLIOGRAPHY Among the most important of Cragg's more than thirty books are *The Call of the Minaret* (1956, 1986), *Sandals at the Mosque* (1959), *The Dome and the Rock: Jerusalem Studies in Islam* (1964), *The Event of the Qur'an* (1971), *The Mind of the Qur'an* (1973), *The Christian and Other Religion* (1977), *Muhammad and the Christian: A Question of Response* (1984), *Jesus and the Muslim: An Exploration* (1985), *The Christ and the Faiths: Theology in Cross-Reference* (1986), *The Arab Christian: A History in the Middle East* (1991), *Troubled by Truth: Life Studies in Inter-Faith Concern* (1992), and *Faith and Life Negotiate: A Christian Story-Study* (1994). Studies on Cragg include "A Bibliography of Kenneth Cragg," *The Muslim World* 83 (1993): 177–191; George Braswell, "The Encounter of Christianity and Islam: The Missionary Theology of Kenneth Cragg," *Perspectives in Religious Studies* 8 (1981): 117–127; Andreas D'Souza, "Christian Approaches to the Study of Islam: An Analysis of the Writings of Watt and Cragg," *Bulletin of the Henry Martyn Institute of Islamic Studies* 11 (January–June 1992): 55–87, and 11 (July–December 1992): 33–80; Sydney Griffith, "Kenneth Cragg on Christians and the Call to Islam," *Religious Studies Review* 20 (1994): 29–35; Richard Jones, "Wilfred Cantwell Smith and Kenneth Cragg on Islam as a Way of Salvation," *IBMR* 17, no. 3 (1993): 105–110; Christopher Lamb, "The Call to Retrieval: Kenneth Cragg's Christian Vocation to Islam" (Ph.D. diss., Birmingham Univ., 1987); Jan Slomp, "Kenneth Cragg and the Qur'an," in L. Hagemann, ed., *Ihr Alle Aber Seid Bruder* (1990), pp. 167–189.

David A. Kerr

Crawford, Daniel (1870–1926), Scottish missionary to Zaire. Born in Gourock, Scotland, Crawford left school at 14 to work as a bookkeeper. His was a devout Church of Scotland family, and he taught in the local Sunday school. Despite this, he was converted at a Brethren meeting in 1887 and received adult baptism. He gave up work and became a freelance preacher, relying on God to provide for his sustenance, which was to be his way for the rest of his life. At that time he influenced many who later became his base of support. Feeling called to Africa, in March 1889 Crawford set off as an independent missionary associated with the Plymouth Brethren of Scotland and England and spent the rest of his life in Katanga (modern Shaba, in southeast Zaire). After some months working with others, he struck out alone and settled among the Nyamwezi. With headquarters on Lake Mweru, he itinerated constantly, preaching and setting up local schools, aiming simply at literacy in the local language. He married Grace Tilsley in 1896. Crawford's only absence from Africa occurred from mid-1911 to mid-1915, two years of which were spent pleading the cause of African missions in Europe and the United States. He was a brilliant linguist and by 1926 had completed the translation of the whole Bible into Luba. This and other languages he learned by living as the sole European among Africans, thus learning to "think black," an attitude that made him something of an exception among missionaries of that era.

BIBLIOGRAPHY Daniel Crawford, *Thinking Black: 22 Years without a Break in the Long Grass of Central Africa* (1913) and *Back to the Long Grass: My Link with Livingstone* (1923). James J. Ellis, *Dan Crawford of Luanza* (1927); A. R. Evans, *Dan Crawford* (1956); George E. Tilsley, *Dan Crawford, Missionary Pioneer in Central Africa* (1929).

Andrew C. Ross

Crawford, Isabelle (Belle) (1865–1961), Baptist missionary to and spokesperson for Native Americans. Born of Canadian parents, Crawford served as her father's assistant in his pastorate in Saint Thomas, North Dakota, from 1884 until she went to Chicago for missionary training in 1892. In 1893 she began work with the Kiowa Indians under the Woman's Baptist Home Missionary Society (WBHMS) in the Oklahoma Territory. She identified with them to such an extent that she became the leader of what was, in effect, an independent Baptist congregation of the Saddle Mountain Kiowa. She traveled far and wide during her vacations, appealing against the injustice endured by Native Americans. This made her unpopular in the white population of the territory, including the leading white churchmen. The pressure led to her resignation in 1906 and a brief breakdown of her health. The WBHMS continued to employ her as a missionary in the West. In 1914 she moved to Buffalo, New York, to campaign against the unjust treatment of the Seneca Indians. Until she retired in 1931, she campaigned constantly on behalf of Native American people and Native American churches, becoming one of the best-known missionaries in the United States. She was buried in the Indian Cemetery at Saddle Mountain, Kiowa County, Oklahoma.

BIBLIOGRAPHY Isabelle Crawford, *Kiowa: The Story of a Blanket Indian Mission* (1915), *A Jolly Journal* (1932), and *A Joyful Journey* (1951). The best assessment of Crawford's life is a series of three articles in *Foundations: A Baptist Journal of History and Theology* 21 (1978): 332–339, 22 (1979): 28–42 and 99–115. A large collection of her papers has been preserved by the American Baptist Historical Society, Rochester, New York.

Andrew C. Ross

Crawford, T(arleton) P(erry) (1821–1902) *and* **Martha (Foster)** (1830–1909), Southern Baptist missionaries in China. Early in 1851, knowing that as a missionary appointee of the Southern Baptist Convention Foreign Mission Board (SBCFMB) he had to be married before leaving the United States, and learning of a single young woman who wanted to be a missionary, T. P. Crawford journeyed to Alabama where he met, proposed to, and married Martha Foster in less than a month. They arrived in Shanghai in 1852 and worked there until 1863, when they moved to northern China.

More competent and compatible than her dogmatic and often irascible husband, Martha Crawford was proficient in the language, greatly respected, and unusually productive—traits that were annoying to her husband. (Early in her career she wrote in her diary that God wanted her to be a missionary wife, but later she crossed out the word "wife.") She evidenced unusual ability as a teacher of Chinese children, and though she was convinced that this was her calling, she was equally effective as an evangelist among Chinese women.

Her husband presented an unfortunate contrast. Repeatedly absorbed in conflicts with missionary colleagues and nationals, T. P. Crawford became an outspoken critic of the SBCFMB, primarily because they refused to agree that evangelism and preaching were the only legitimate missionary methods. He compelled Martha, against her will, to cease doing school and medical work and to engage only in evangelism. When he intensified his attacks upon the mission board, he was dismissed in 1892. Although the board wished to retain Martha, she voluntarily withdrew to join her husband in his newly organized Gospel Mission, an independent society that dissolved the year after her death. Before that time she apparently had advised her Gospel Mission colleagues to return to the SBCFMB, and most of them did. Like other Westerners during the Boxer Rebellion, the Crawfords were forced to leave China in 1900. He died in Alabama shortly thereafter. Martha Crawford returned to China in 1902 to continue her work, and she died in China.

BIBLIOGRAPHY Catherine B. Allen, *The New Lottie Moon Story* (1980); L. S. Foster, *Fifty Years in China: An Eventful Memoir of the Life of Tarleton Perry Crawford* (1909); Irwin T. Hyatt, Jr., *Our Ordered Lives Confess* (1976); Adrian Lamkin, Jr., *The Gospel Mission Movement within the Southern Baptist Convention* (1981).

Alan Neely

Creux, Ernest (1845–1929), pioneer missionary of the Swiss Mission Church in northeastern Transvaal, South Africa. Creux completed theological studies at the faculty of the Free Church of canton Vaud in Lausanne, Switzerland. Together with Paul *Berthoud, he offered his services as a foreign missionary "whether under the tropics or on the northern ice." In 1875 he and Berthoud established in the Transvaal a station named Valdezia after their home canton, Vaud. In 1879 he left Valdezia and established a second mission in this area at Elim where an important mission hospital and a school were developed.

In 1902 Creux was transferred to Pretoria. Here he embarked on a ministry which was to make the Swiss mission famous: caring for lepers, the imprisoned, and the insane. Eventually he was made director of the Swiss mission in the Transvaal. Through his leadership, links were forged between the Swiss mission and other churches in the South African Missionary Conference (1904) and the Transvaal Missionary Association (1905).

BIBLIOGRAPHY J. du Plessis, *A History of Christian Missions in South Africa* (1911); H. A. Junod, *Ernest Creux et Paul Berthoud: les fondateurs de la mission suisse dans L'Afrique du Sud* (1933); M. I. Mathebula, "The Relationship between Some Ecumenical Bodies and the Evangelical Presbyterian Church in South Africa (Swiss Mission) (1904–1975): A Historical Study" (M.Th. thesis, Univ. of South Africa, Pretoria, 1989).

J. W. Hofmeyr

Criminali, Antonio (1520–1549), first Jesuit martyr. Born near Parma, Italy, Criminali was received into the Society of Jesus by *Ignatius of Loyola in 1542 and was assigned by him to serve in Asia. In 1544 he was ordained a priest at Coimbra, Portugal, and in 1545 left for India, arriving in Goa the same year. He was assigned to the missions of Cape Comorin, on the Pescheria coast, where he worked with missionary zeal, learning the Tamil language. Francis *Xavier, who preceded him to India, considered him the Jesuit missionary prototype, writing to Ignatius in 1549, "He is really a holy man, and excellently suited for the cultivation of these fields." Criminali was named superior of the Jesuit mission there by Xavier, who also wanted him to go to Malacca. Before he could undertake this trip, however, he was killed, probably in Vedalai, in an invasion by barbarians along the coast where he worked. Criminali is the protomartyr of the Society of Jesus. Although his apostolate lasted only four years, he deserves a special place in the history of Jesuit missionaries.

BIBLIOGRAPHY J. Castets, *Venerable Anthony Criminale, Successor of St. Francis Xavier on the Indian Mission and First Martyr of the Society of Jesus* (1926); G. Schurhammer, "Leben und Briefe Antonio Criminali's des Erstlingsmartyrer des Gesellschaft Jesu," in *Archivum Historicum Societatis Iesu,* 5 (1936): 131–167; *Documenta*

Indica, vol. 1 (1540–1549), vol. 2 (1550–1553), edited by J. Wicki, Monumenta Historica Societatis Iesu (1948, 1950).

Jesús López-Gay, SJ

Cripps, Arthur Shearly (1869–1952), Anglo-Catholic missionary in Rhodesia. A high Anglo-Catholic Anglican with an Oxford degree, Cripps volunteered his services to the Society for the Propagation of the Gospel and was sent in 1901 to Rhodesia (now Zimbabwe), where he spent most of the next half century. Critical of church policy but still more critical of government and settler attitudes, he fought a lifelong battle for African rights. Acquiring 7,700 acres of farmland, he built a thatched church at Maronda Mashanu (Five Wounds) and a round hut, in which he lived. His tenants paid no rent and farmed as they liked. After 1930 he formally cut his Anglican links, becoming simply a "Christian missionary in Mashonaland." His poetry, novels, and a play entitled *The Black Christ* challenged at a fundamental human and spiritual level the assumptions of colonialism. He battled against government policies like the hut tax and befriended black political leaders, but his greatest significance lay simply in what he was—a sort of Francis of Assisi of the African countryside, enduring the greatest poverty and blind for the last decade of his life, but unconquerable in his hope.

BIBLIOGRAPHY G. Brown, A. Chennells, and L. Rix, eds., *Arthur Shearly Cripps: A Selection of His Prose and Verse* (1976); M. Steele, "'With Hope Unconquered and Unconquerable...': Arthur Shearly Cripps, 1869–1952," in T. Ranger and J. Weller, eds., *Themes in the Christian History of Central Africa* (1975), pp. 152–174; D. V. Steere, *God's Irregular: Arthur Shearly Cripps* (1973).

Adrian Hastings

Crook, William Pascoe (1775–1846), London Missionary Society (LMS) missionary in the Marquesas Islands and Tahiti. Crook was born at Dartmouth, Devonshire, England, and joined a pioneer contingent of LMS missionaries who sailed on the ship *Duff* in 1796. He was inspired by Matthew Wilks, preacher at The Tabernacle, London. He was one of two unmarried missionaries stationed in June 1797 at Tahuata in the Marquesas Islands, remaining in frequent isolation, learning the language and handling difficult situations successfully (sexual initiative by women was often customary there). A year later he was taken to the Marquesan island of Nukuhiva on a passing American ship. In January 1799, he returned to England where he married Hannah Dare, by whom he had one son and eight daughters. He upgraded his skills as teacher and preacher and returned to Sydney, Australia. The LMS posted him a second time to Tahiti in 1816. He served successively on the island of Mooréa and at two stations on the Tahitian mainland. He revisted Tahuata in 1825 and left three Tahitian missionaries in the Marquesas, taking a continuing interest in the mission and the language. In Tahiti he was involved in both evangelism and education; he witnessed the baptism of King *Pomare II in 1819, as well as the king's moral decline by 1823. In 1830 he retired to Sydney, where he helped found Congregational churches. After his wife's death he retired to Melbourne, where he lived with his son until his death.

BIBLIOGRAPHY Greg Dening, *Islands and Beaches: Discourse on a Silent Land* (1980); John Garrett, *To Live among the Stars: Christian Origins in Oceania* (1985); Niel Gunson, *Messengers of Grace: Evangelical Missionaries in the South Seas, 1797–1860* (1978); Richard Lovett, *The History of the London Missionary Society, 1795–1895* (1899). Crook's papers and journals are in the Council for World Mission collections at SOAS, Univ. of London, and the Mitchell Library, Sydney.

John Garrett

Crosby, Aaron (1745–1824), missionary to Native Americans of the Iroquois League in New York. Crosby, about whom little is known, seems to have been chosen for missionary work by Eleazar *Wheelock, who boarded him at Moor's Charity School, Lebanon, Connecticut, to sharpen his evangelical capabilities. Crosby was expelled sometime thereafter, a cryptic notation in the records saying only that he broke "three severall commandments." He nevertheless received a degree from Harvard College in 1770 and settled as a missionary teacher on the eastern branch of the Susquehanna River. His work among the Oneida Indians was financed by the Boston commissioners of the Scottish Society for the Propagation of Christian Knowledge. After surviving the Revolutionary War with his charges, Crosby received support from the Northern Missionary Society and expanded his ministerial attention to the Tuscarora tribe in addition to the Oneidas who remained in the newly formed state of New York.

BIBLIOGRAPHY Eleazar Wheelock, *A Plain and Faithful Narrative... of the Indian Charity-School* (9 vols., 1763–1775). Clifford K. Shipton, *Biographical Sketches of those Who Attended Harvard College in the Classes 1768–1771* (1975), pp. 381–383.

Henry Warner Bowden

Crosby, Thomas (1840–1914), pioneer Methodist missionary in British Columbia. Crosby was born in Pickering, Yorkshire, England, and went to Canada with his parents in 1856. In 1862, volunteering for missionary service, he immigrated to Victoria, British Columbia. Initially employed as a laborer, he won the confidence of local Methodists, who made him head of the mission school in Nanaimo one year later. He mastered the Ankomenum language, taught and preached in the region for nine years, and accepted ordination in 1871 to become the first full-time Methodist missionary among the Indians of British Columbia. Following a furlough and his marriage to Emma Douse, he and his bride returned to British Columbia and almost immediately (1874) transferred to Port Simpson, the site of William *Duncan's early endeavors among the Tsimshians. For the next 25 years, Crosby traveled along the coast of British Columbia and throughout the Queen Charlotte Islands in the launch *Glad Tidings* and into the interior by canoe and on foot, preaching and establishing the first medical missions of the Methodist Episcopal Church of Canada. His election as president of the Methodist Conference in 1897 necessitated his transfer to Victoria, bringing his itinerating to a conclusion. Crosby's most enduring legacy is the effective advocacy which his Indian protégés and their descendants exercised on behalf of their own people.

BIBLIOGRAPHY Thomas Crosby, *Among the An-ko-me-nums or Flathead Tribes of Indians of the Pacific Coast* (1907), *Up and Down the North Pacific Coast by Canoe and Mission Ship* (1914), *David Sallosalton* (n.d.), and "Ancient Warriors of the North Pacific," in *Warriors of the North Pacific: Missionary Accounts of the Northwest Coast, the Skeena and the Stikine Rivers and the Klondike, 1829–1900,* Charles Lillard, ed. (1984). Clarence Bolt, *Thomas Crosby and the Tsimshian: Small Shoes for Feet Too Large* (1982).

Jonathan J. Bonk

Cross, William (1797–1842), English Methodist missionary in Tonga and Fiji. Cross was born at Cirencester, Gloucestershire, England. He had served in Tonga since 1827 when in 1835 he and David *Cargill became the copioneers of the British Wesleyan Methodist mission to the Fiji Islands. With them came a group of Tongan Islander missionaries to Fiji, where marauding Tongan soldiers were involved in warfare. The missionaries landed at Lakeba in 1835 and were aided by Tongan and Fijian Christian chiefs, notably Josua Mateinaniu, who facilitated the missionaries' approach to a belligerent Seru *Cakobau, who eventually became the paramount chief and king of Fiji. Cross began by gaining a foothold for the mission with neighboring chiefs at Rewa and Viwa. In the meantime he witnessed and carefully recorded appalling battles and episodes of cannibalism in wars between rival Fijian confederacies. After John *Hunt and the Tongan missionary Joeli *Bulu reinforced the mission from 1839 onward, the tide slowly turned in favor of the gospel in central and eastern Fiji. Cross died from dysentery six years before his gifted colleague Hunt, who wrote a memoir as his eulogy.

BIBLIOGRAPHY G. G. Findlay and W. W. Holdsworth, *The History of the Wesleyan Methodist Missionary Society,* vol. 3 (1921); John Hunt, *Memoir of the Rev. William Cross* (2d ed., 1858); A. Harold Wood, *Overseas Missions of the Australian Methodist Church,* vols. 1–3 (1975–1980). Diaries and other records of and about Cross are in the Mitchell Library, Sydney, and the national archives of Fiji, Suva.

John Garrett

Crowe, Frederick (1819–1846), Baptist pioneer missionary to Guatemala. Born in Bruges, Belgium, to British parents, Crowe left home a rebel and went as a sailor to Central America in 1836. In Belize he was converted, got married, and in 1837 was baptized. A Baptist church there sent him as a missionary to Guatemala. He arrived in Veracruz in 1840, served as a colporteur, and taught English and French, using the New Testament as a textbook. He also taught music and organized the first orchestra in Guatemala. In 1843 he moved to the capital city. He began to preach and was finally expelled to Belize by the government in 1846. His efforts not only promoted the distribution of the Bible but also fostered liberal reforms, such as lay education and religious freedom. He later went to England, where he died. His book, *The Gospel in Central America,* was published in London in 1850.

BIBLIOGRAPHY Justo C. Anderson, *Historia de los bautistas,* vol. 3 (1990); Horace O. Russell, *The Baptist Witness: A Concise Baptist History* (1983); Juan C. Varetto, *Federico Crowe en Guatemala* (1940).

Pablo A. Deiros

Crowther, Dandeson Coates (1844–1938), West African church leader. Born in Freetown, Sierra Leone, Crowther was the youngest son of Anglican Bishop Samuel Adjai *Crowther. Ordained by his father in 1870, Crowther joined the Niger Mission of the Church Missionary Society (CMS) the following year and became archdeacon of the Niger Delta in 1876. He was an indefatigable organizer and inspirational leader; it was mainly due to his enthusiasm and evangelistic zeal that a mass movement toward Christianity grew in the Niger Delta during the 1870s and 1880s. However, the Niger crisis of the early 1890s (which produced racial conflict, high-handed reform by the CMS missionaries, and rebellion of the national leadership) marked a turning point in his career. Among other things, European agency was introduced into the hitherto all-African Delta Mission, ultimately causing the Niger Delta to secede from the CMS. This revolt was spearheaded by Crowther. Then, in April 1892 he launched the Niger Delta Pastorate. This experience of independence lasted for only six years, but it represented one of the first significant, wholly African attempts to establish a self-supporting, self-governing church in western Africa. As its prime mover, Crowther deserves special recognition in the study of Christian missions.

BIBLIOGRAPHY J. F. A. Ajayi, *Christian Missions in Nigeria, 1841–1891: The Making of a New Elite* (1965); W. O. Ajayi, "A History of the Niger and Northern Nigeria Missions, 1854–1914" (Ph.D. diss., Univ. of Bristol, 1963); E. A. Ayandele, *The Missionary Impact on Modern Nigeria, 1842–1914* (1966); E. M. T. Epelle, *The Church in the Niger Delta* (1955); Jehu J. Hanciles, "Dandeson Coates Crowther and the Niger Delta Pastorate: Blazing Torch or Flickering Flame?" *IBMR* 18, no. 4 (1994): 166–172; G. O. M. Tasie, *Christian Missionary Enterprise in the Niger Delta, 1864–1918* (1978). The CMS archives, Univ. of Birmingham, contain Crowther material.

Jehu J. Hanciles

Crowther, Samuel Adjai (*or* Ajayi) (c. 1807–1891), African missionary and bishop. Crowther was born with the name Ajayi in Osogun, in the Egba section of the Yoruba people, in what is now western Nigeria. When about 13, he was taken as a slave by Fulani and Yoruba Muslim raiders and sold several times before being purchased by Portuguese traders for the transatlantic market. His ship was intercepted by the British navy's anti-slave trade patrol, and the slaves were liberated in Sierra Leone. There he became a Christian, taking at baptism the name of an eminent clergyman in England, Samuel Crowther. Excelling at school, he became a mission teacher and one of the first students of the Fourah Bay Institution, founded by the Church Missionary Society (CMS) in 1827 to train able Sierra Leoneans for Christian service. He assisted John *Raban and (probably) Hannah *Kilham in their studies of African languages, and in 1841 he joined J. F. *Schön as a CMS representative on T. F. *Buxton's Niger Expedition, contributing signally to it. He studied at the CMS college in London preparatory to ordination in 1843—a landmark for the Anglican ministry. With Henry *Townsend and C. A. *Gollmer, he then opened a new mission in Yorubaland, centered in Abeokuta, by now the homeland of Crowther's Egba people. (He discovered some close relatives there and was the means of conversion of his mother and sister.) His role in producing the Yoruba Bible, which set new standards for later African translations, was crucial. Crowther's visit to Britain in 1851 influenced government, church, and public opinion about Africa. The CMS secretary, Henry *Venn, saw Crowther as a potential demonstration of the feasibility of self-governing, self-supporting, and self-propagating African churches and in 1857 sent him to open a new mission on the Niger. The entire staff was African, mainly from Sierra Leone, and Venn moved toward an Anglican version of the "three-self" formula by securing Crowther's appointment in 1864 as "Bishop of the countries of Western Africa beyond the Queen's dominions." In the upper and middle Niger territories Crowther pioneered an early form of Christian-Muslim dialogue for Africa. He oversaw J. C. *Taylor's ground-breaking work in Igboland and directed the evangelization of the Niger Delta, with notable results at such centers as Bonny.

In the 1880s clouds gathered over the Niger Mission. Crowther was old, Venn dead. The morality or efficiency of members of Crowther's staff was increasingly questioned by British missionaries. Mission policy, racial attitudes, and evangelical spirituality had taken new directions, and new sources of European missionaries were now available. By degrees, Crowther's mission was dismantled: by financial controls, by young Europeans taking over, by dismissing, suspending, or transferring the African staff. Crowther, desolated, died of a stroke. A European bishop succeeded him.

Part of the Niger Mission retained its autonomy as the Niger Delta Pastorate Church, under Crowther's son, Archdeacon D. C. *Crowther, and at least one of the European missionaries, H. H. *Dobinson, repented of earlier hasty judgments. Everyone recognized Crowther's personal stature and godliness; his place in the history of translation and evangelization has often been undervalued.

BIBLIOGRAPHY S. A. Crowther, *Journal of an Expedition up the Niger in 1841* (with J. F. Schön, 1843), *Journal of an Expedition up the Niger and Tschadda Rivers* (1855), *The Gospel on the Banks of the Niger* (with J. C. Taylor, 1859, repr. 1968), and *Experiences with Pagans and Mohammedans in West Africa* (1892). J. F. A. Ajayi, *Christian Missions in Nigeria: 1841–1891* (1965); P. E. H. Hair, *The Early Study of Nigerian Languages* (1967); P. R. McKenzie, *Inter-religious Encounters in Nigeria: S. A. Crowther's Attitude to African Traditional Religion and Islam* (1976); G. O. M. Tasie, *Christian Missionary Enterprise in the Niger Delta, 1864–1918* (1978); A. F. Walls, "A Second Narrative of Samuel Ajayi Crowther's Early Life," *Bulletin of the Society of African Church History* 2 (1985): 5–14, and "Samuel Ajayi Crowther," in Gerald H. Anderson et al., eds., *Mission Legacies* (1994), pp. 132–139.

Andrew F. Walls

Crummell, Alexander (1819–1898), African American Episcopal missionary to Liberia. Crummell was born in New York of free black ancestry. He had a good general education, and though racial prejudice denied him entrance to General Theological Seminary, he was ordained in the Episcopal Church (deacon, 1842; priest, 1844). Fund-raising in England for his new black congregation in New York brought him a place at Queens College, Cambridge, where he graduated in 1853. He then went as a Protestant Episcopal missionary to Liberia, taking citizenship and combining pastoral work with the headship of schools in Monrovia and in Maryland County. From 1862 to 1866 he was professor of philosophy and English at Liberia College, a stormy period; and from 1867 to 1873, he lived at the Caldwell settlement, where he built a church and school, established an educational outreach for indigenous people, and served two other mission stations. Crummell influenced Liberian intellectual and religious life as preacher, prophet, social analyst, and educationist, proclaiming a special place for Africa, with its God-given moral and religious potential, in the history of redemption. He wanted Liberia to be marked by democratic institutions, flourishing arts and letters, commerce, and law, and to that end Christian teaching was necessary. His enthusiasms included agricultural development, opening the interior to evangelization and trade, women's education, and public libraries. He helped reconstruct the Protestant Episcopal Mission as a Liberian church. In his vision, African Americans had a particular responsibility for Africa, but as a "pure black" (as he frequently asserted), he sought to identify with the interests of the indigenous population, opposing government attempts to concentrate power and resources in the mulatto community. In 1873, fearing his life was in danger from the mulatto ascendancy, he returned to the United States. He was rector of St. Luke's, Washington, D.C., until 1894 and taught at Howard University from 1895 to 1897. He continued his work for African American Christian scholarship and African redemption and founded the American Negro Academy in 1897.

BIBLIOGRAPHY Alexander Crummell, *Alexander Crummell, 1844–1894: The Shades and Lights of a 50 Years' Ministry* (1894), *The Relations and Duties of Free Colored Men in America to Africa* (1861), *The Future of Africa* (1862, 1969), *The Greatness of Christ and Other Sermons* (1882), and *Africa and America* (1891). M. B. Akpan, "Alexander Crummell and His African 'Race Work': An Assessment of His Contribution to Liberia to Africa's Redemption," in D. W. Wills and R. Newman, eds., *Black Apostles at Home and Abroad: Afro-Americans and the Christian Mission from the Revolution to Reconstruction* (1982), pp. 283–310; W. J. Moses, *Alexander Crummell: A Study of Civilization and Discontent* (1989); J. R. Oldfield, *Alexander Crummell (1819–1898) and the Creation of an African-Amer-*

ican Church in Liberia (1990); G. U. Rigsby, *Alexander Crummell: A Pioneer in Nineteenth-Century Pan-Africa Thought* (1987); O. M. Scruggs, "'We the Children of Africa in this Land': Alexander Crummell," in L. A. Williams, ed., *Africa and the Afro-American Experience* (1977).

Andrew F. Walls

Cusanus, Nicholaus. *See* Nicholas of Cusa.

Cushing, Ellen Winsor (Howard) Fairfield (1840–1915), American Baptist missionary and educator. Born at Kingston, Massachusetts, Ellen Howard began her career as a schoolteacher. In 1862 she joined a volunteer mission group, Gideon's Band, to work with slaves in the Port Royal Experiment in Beaufort, South Carolina. There she married a plantation owner, Josiah Fairfield. After he was lost at sea in 1865, she returned to Boston to be the administrator of the Home for Little Wanderers. In 1866 she married Josiah Nelson Cushing (1840–1905), a missionary candidate at Newton Theological Institution. The couple arrived in Rangoon, Burma (Myanmar), in 1867 and established a station in the Shan State at Toungoo. They worked jointly on a translation of the Gospels into Shan, as well as on the first English-Shan dictionary. In a second term, they separately administered stations at Bhamo and at Toungoo from 1877 to 1880. During a furlough in 1886, Ellen Cushing began work as field secretary to the Philadelphia Baptist Missionary Union; her task was missionary education. To respond to the need for women missionaries, in 1892 she established in Philadelphia a school which became the Baptist Training School for Christian Work. That same year, her husband returned to Rangoon, where translation work continued, and he served as pastor of the church and principal of Rangoon Baptist College. In 1905, while on furlough with his wife, Cushing died, his translation projects still unfinished. After a 20-year absence from Burma, Ellen Cushing returned for three years to complete her husband's work. The Baptist Training School for Christian Work, then located in Bryn Mawr, Pennsylvania, was renamed Ellen Cushing Junior College in 1970 (it closed in 1980).

BIBLIOGRAPHY The American Baptist Historical Society, Rochester, New York, holds in its archives a biographical paper and a publicity brochure that outline the career of Ellen Cushing. An obituary is included in the *Pennsylvania Baptist General Convention Annual* for 1915, pp. 54–55. On Josiah Cushing, see Wallace St. John, *Josiah Nelson Cushing: Missionary and Scholar: Burma* (1912).

William H. Brackney

Cushing, Richard James (1895–1970), cardinal, archbishop of Boston, and founder of the Missionary Society of St. James. Born in Boston, Massachusetts, and ordained a priest of the archdiocese in 1921, Cushing expressed a desire to go abroad as a missionary. Instead, he was appointed assistant director of the Boston office of the Society for the Propagation of the Faith and in 1928 was promoted to director. He garnered a reputation as an effective fund-raiser for missionary causes and as an enthusiastic promoter for the missions, especially among young people. In 1939 he was ordained auxiliary bishop of Boston, and in 1944, archbishop. Pope *John XXIII appointed him cardinal in 1958. After World War II he organized a "lend lease" program by which he sent priests of his archdiocese to serve in other dioceses of the United States that had a shortage of priests. Building on this commitment, Cushing founded the Missionary Society of St. James in 1958 to provide an opportunity for priests of his archdiocese and other dioceses to engage in missionary activity in Latin America. Within five years almost 100 priests were working in Peru, Ecuador, and Bolivia. A vocal anti-Communist and vigorous proponent of evangelization and care for the poor, Cushing was a frequent visitor to Latin America.

BIBLIOGRAPHY John Henry Cutler, *Cardinal Cushing of Boston* (1970); M. C. Devine, *The World's Cardinal* (1964).

William E. McConville, OFM

Cust, Robert Needham (1821–1909), British orientalist, linguist, and missionary strategist. Born in the Manor House at Cockayne, Bedfordshire, where his father was the rector, Cust was educated at Eton and Haileybury (then the College of the East India Company) and had a distinguished career in the Indian Civil Service. He was able to speak eight European and eight Asian languages, was an able administrator, and had a great love for people. A certain brittleness in his character meant that he never quite reached the top, and he retired with a deep sense of failure in 1867 after the death of his second wife in childbirth. Always a fiercely independent thinker with more than a touch of intolerance, he became a passionate orientalist with a particular interest in missionary strategy. He had a tempestuous relationship with the Church Missionary Soceity (CMS), where for a period he was a leading figure on some of its key committees. His uncompromising views were always likely to alienate. He was never entirely at home in an evangelical culture, being, for example, much more accepting of Roman Catholicism (and even other religions) than evangelical orthodoxy thought appropriate. Above all, he and J. B. *Whiting led the fight against what he castigated as "the unsympathetic and cruel line of policy adopted by the majority of the Committee towards our Negro fellow Christians." He was referring to the society's abandonment of Henry *Venn's policy, which had placed the development of indigenous leadership at the top of the agenda. In reaction, key CMS figures openly criticized him. Eugene *Stock, for example, described Cust as "inconsistent, cantankerous and far too liberal." Cust was a prolific writer, publishing more than sixty volumes between 1870 and 1909. Those on missionary subjects mixed learning, passion, perceptiveness, idiosyncrasy, and abuse in such a manner that those who were most in need of his considerable insights were least likely to hear or heed them.

BIBLIOGRAPHY Robert Cust, *Memoirs of Past Years of a Septuagenarian* (1899). Peter Penner, *Robert Needham Cust, 1821–1909: A*

Personal Biography (1987); Eugene Stock, "Dr. Cust on Missions and Missionaries," *CM Intelligencer,* February 1895, pp. 103–110.

Peter Williams

Cuthbert (d. 687), British missionary bishop. Raised within the monastery at Melrose, Scotland, near the English Northumberland border, Cuthbert learned the Irish monastic tradition under Eata. He became a monk there and later followed Eata to Ripon, in Northumberland. By 661 he had returned to Melrose, where he served as prior. At the Synod of Whitby in 662, he adopted Roman practice in place of the Celtic. He made his way by 664 to Lindisfarne where he also served as prior. From 676 to 684, he lived as a hermit on the island of Farne. Bishop of Lindisfarne from 684 or 685 to 686 or 687, he was at the center of great missionary activity. His warm compassion for common folk, his virtuous character, and his miraculous deeds impressed his colleagues.

BIBLIOGRAPHY Gerald Bonner, David Rollason, and Clare Stancliffe, eds., *Saint Cuthbert: His Cult and His Community: To A.D. 1200* (1989); Betram Colgrave, *Two Lives of St. Cuthbert* (1940, 1985); Elizabeth W. Frierson, *The Story of Northumbrian Saints: S. Oswald, S. Aidan, S. Cuthbert* (1913); Henry Mayr-Harting, *The Coming of Christianity to Anglo-Saxon England* (1972, 1977, 1991); Theodore Johnson-South, *The Historia de Sancto Cuthberto: A New Edition and Translation* (1990).

Frederick W. Norris

Cyril-Constantine (826–869), founder of Slavic literature and, with his brother, *Methodius, considered apostle to the Slavs. Born in Thessalonica, Cyril's baptismal name was Constantine. He received an advanced education in both classical and Christian studies, which earned him the sobriquet "the Philosopher." In Constantinople, he was appointed librarian of Hagia Sophia, where he was closely associated with the scholar *Photius and became known as Photius's best friend. When Photius was named patriarch of Constantinople, Constantine succeeded him at the "university." He was active in the theological disputes of the day, defending the use of images against the iconoclasts and the Trinity against the Muslims, and proclaiming the Christian gospel to the Khazars. But his decisive place in history came with a petition presented in 862 to the Byzantine emperor Michael III, that he send missionaries to Greater Moravia, where Irish and German missionaries had been working. The Moravian mission illustrates a basic difference between Eastern and Western missionary methods: the West taught its converts the Latin Mass, while the East translated the liturgy. To prepare for his missionary work, Constantine undertook to translate the Gospels, and eventually (apparently after arriving in Moravia) the Byzantine liturgy, into Old Church Slavonic. He created for that purpose the so-called Glagolitic alphabet—not the Cyrillic, which was mistakenly attributed to him. In Moravia in 863, Constantine and Methodius evoked opposition from those who insisted on the Latin liturgy. In 867 and 868 they journeyed to Rome, where they secured papal approval of their Slavonic liturgy. At Rome Constantine became a monk, taking the name Cyril, by which he is known to history. He died less than two months later and was buried at San Clemente, probably because he and Methodius had borne the relics of Clement of Rome from the Crimea back to Rome.

BIBLIOGRAPHY Francis Dvornik, *The Slavs: Their Early History and Civilization* (1956) and *Byzantine Missions among the Slavs: SS. Constantine-Cyril and Methodius* (1970).

Jaroslav Pelikan

D

Dablon, Claude (1618 or 1619–1697), French Jesuit superior of North American missions. Dablon was largely responsible for recording and publicizing the accounts of the great exploratory journeys of Jacques *Marquette to the Mississippi and Charles Albanel to Hudson Bay. He also took firm stands during the many disputes with those involved in the liquor trade. According to his contemporaries, he proved to be a successful negotiator because of his cordial and tactful manner.

A Norman from Dieppe, France, Dablon became a Jesuit at twenty-one and landed in Quebec during the summer of 1655. Apart from ministry in that city before and during his terms as superior (1671–1680, and 1686–1693), he worked among the native people during three significant periods—one among the Onondagas in the mid-1650s, in what is now upstate New York; another in 1661, during an expedition into what is now northern Quebec, when he reached the watershed into Hudson Bay; and the third from 1669 to 1679, when he was superior at Sault Sainte-Marie at the western end of Lake Huron. During all of these missions he kept precise descriptions of everything he saw, notably details about the natural resources of the country and the customs of the indigenous nations. He also drew detailed maps of these regions, which, with his other documents, have remained invaluable sources. He died in Quebec.

BIBLIOGRAPHY Reuben Gold Thwaites, ed., *The Jesuit Relations and Allied Documents, 1610–1791,* vol. 73 (1959), p. 189.

Jacques Monet, SJ

Dahl, Otto Christian (1903–1995), Norwegian missionary and scholar. Dahl graduated from the Stavanger School of Mission in 1927 and was ordained the same year in the Lutheran church. After language study in France he was sent to Madagascar by the Norwegian Missionary Society (NMS) and served there from 1929 to 1957. Dahl was superintendent for west Madagascar (1952–1957) and president of the Lutheran Church of Madagascar (1955–1957). From 1958 to 1966 he was in the home service of the NMS, for some of the time as acting secretary general. From 1967 to 1974 he had a state research stipend. Dahl studied linguistics in Oslo, Hamburg, Leiden, and London. In addition to his doctoral dissertation (a linguistic comparison of Malagasy and Malay, 1951), he wrote forty-six contributions in books, periodicals, and dictionaries, mostly linguistic studies, often related to problems in mission work. His publications appeared in Norwegian, French, German, English, and Malagasy. His first linguistic study, published in Paris in 1938, was *Le système phonologique du Proto-Malgache.* Dahl was a member of L'Académie Malgache and the Norwegian Academy of Science and Letters, and was Officier de l'Ordre National de Madagascar.

BIBLIOGRAPHY Norwall Hessen, ed., *Prester i Den norske kirke og andre teologiske kandidater* (1990), p. 79.

Nils E. Bloch-Hoell

Dahle, Lars Nilsen (1843–1925), Norwegian Lutheran missionary and mission leader. Born in Hen, Romsdal, Dahle studied at a teachers' college, at the Stavanger School of Mission, and at the University of Oslo (Christiania). In 1870 he was ordained and sent by the Norwegian Missionary Society (NMS) to Madagascar. He taught at the theological seminary in Antananarivo from 1871 to 1887 and was also superintendent of the mission from 1876 to 1887. He then became secretary general of the NMS and also taught at the Stavanger School of Mission until 1920. Dahle was learned and conservative and had a powerful personality. When he finished his 50 years of service, the NMS had become the largest missionary society in Scandinavia. Lord Balfour, speaking at the Edinburgh missionary conference in 1910, referred to Dahle as follows: "It seems to me, in summing up the lessons of this Report, the words of my Norwegian friend stand out as the quintessence of good sense and guidance." At Antananarivo in 1877 Dahle published *Specimens of Malagasy Folk-Lore,* a collection of myths, proverbs, riddles, and ballads. In 1893 he published a comprehensive eschatological study. Together with W. E. *Cousins he completed a new translation of the Malagasy Bible. Dahle was named a Knight of the Order of St. Olav and was a member of the Norwegian Academy of Science and Letters and of the Jena Wissenschaftgesellschaft.

BIBLIOGRAPHY Lars Dahle, *Tilbageblik paa mit liv* (Memories), 3 vols. (1922–1923).

Nils E. Bloch-Hoell

Dake, Vivian Adelbert (1854–1892), holiness pastor, evangelist, and founder of Pentecost Bands. Born in Oregon, Illinois, to parents who were charter members of the Free Methodist Church, Dake attended Chili Seminary (present-day Roberts Wesleyan College) and the University of Rochester (New York), before returning to the Midwest. In 1882 at Mankato, Minnesota, Dake organized the first "Pentecost Band" for short-term evangelistic work. In 1885, while he served as a Free Methodist pastor in Michigan, the enterprise took permanent form. At a time when church-sponsored activities for young people were rare, the notion of groups of holiness youth traveling to evangelize and plant churches at home and abroad soon became popular, and Dake found himself at the head of a movement.

Although Pentecost Bands gained the blessing of B. T. Roberts, founder of the Free Methodist Church, the movement resisted denominational control. Dake traveled widely in the United States and overseas, promoting and encouraging the efforts of the various bands. At the time of his death in Sierra Leone, Pentecost Bands were active in Europe, Africa, India, and the United States. Afterward, the organization drew further away from the Free Methodist Church. In 1925, it changed its name to Missionary Bands of the World. Due to aging personnel and declining funds, it merged with the Wesleyan Methodist Church (the present-day Wesleyan Church) in 1958.

BIBLIOGRAPHY Charles Edwin Jones, *Perfectionist Persuasion: The Holiness Movement and American Methodism, 1867–1936* (1974); Thomas Hiram Nelson, *Life and Labors of Rev. Vivian A. Dake, Organizer and Leader of Pentecost Bands* (1894); Ida Dake Parsons, *Kindling Watch-Fires, Being a Brief Sketch of the Life of Rev. Vivian A. Dake* (1915).

Gary B.McGee

Dalle Périer, Luis (1922–1982), Catholic missionary to Peru and first director of Instituto de Pastoral Andina. Born in France, Dalle's missionary training in Châteaudun was interrupted in 1943 when he volunteered to accompany young Frenchmen conscripted to forced labor by the Nazis. Within the horrors of the Zwieberg camp, he secretly gave spiritual assistance to hundreds of prisoners, and was at the point of death from dysentery and exhaustion when he was liberated in April 1945. Ordained as a priest of the Sacred Heart in July 1946, he was assigned to Peru as a teacher, arriving in Lima in 1948. A restless social activist, in 1954 he was sent to work in an indigenous rural parish north of Lima, where he discovered an unsuspected religious world of syncretic practices among the Quechua Indians. In 1959 as father provincial in Ayaviri in the Peruvian southeast highlands, Dalle implemented pastoral methods newly approved by Vatican II. At age 45 he studied anthropology at a secular university in order to systematize his wealth of pastoral observations. He contributed to the renewal of the Catholic Church in Peru, first as the director of the Instituto de Pastoral Andina in Cuzco from 1968, and then as bishop of Ayaviri from 1971. In one of his frequent bus trips, he died in an accident near Arequipa and was buried in his beloved Ayaviri.

BIBLIOGRAPHY Gabriel Campredon, a companion priest of Dalle, wrote his biography, *Luis Dalle: Un hombre libre* (1985), based on hundreds of letters that Dalle sent to his family in France. Most of Dalle's writings appeared in the periodical *Allpanchis Phutunrina,* which he started in 1968.

Samuel Escobar

Dalman, Gustav Hermann (1855–1941), missionary to Jews. Born into a pious German family that had close contact with leading Jewish Christians in the Netherlands, Dalman studied at a Moravian school and theological seminary and became a professor of Old Testament exegesis for six years. He gained a reputation as a specialist in Aramaic, Targum studies, and Palestinian customs and folklore. In 1871 he met Franz *Delitzsch and began active involvement in Jewish evangelism. Under Delitzsch's influence he left the Moravian Church, became a Lutheran, and was appointed professor of theology at the University of Leipzig in 1887. In 1895 he was appointed professor of the Institutum Judaicum Delitzschianum in Leipzig, a center for training specialists in mission to the Jewish community. He supervised training in Hebrew, Aramaic, and Yiddish, Jewish religious sources, and strategies in Jewish ministry. He was ahead of his time in his commitment to help Jews and Christians better understand one another and to support contextualized worship and evangelism for Jews who accepted Jesus as the Messiah. He was a firm defender of the work of Joseph *Rabinowitz and became a passionate advocate of using Hebrew New Testaments in Jewish mission.

BIBLIOGRAPHY Gustav Hermann Dalman, *Jesus Christ in the Talmud, Midrash, Zohar, and the Liturgy of the Synagogue,* A. W. Streane, tr. (1893) and *Christianity and Judaism,* G. H. Box, tr. (1901). Julia Männchen, "Gustav Dalman and Jewish Missions," *Mishkan* 14 (1991): 64–73.

Walter Riggans

Damien of Molokai (Joseph Damien De Veuster) (1840–1889), Flemish Catholic missionary to the exiled colony of persons with leprosy at Kalawao, on Molokai, one of the Hawaiian Islands. Born at Tremelo, near Louvain, Belgium, Damien joined the Congregation of the Sacred Hearts of Jesus and Mary in 1859, taking the religious name Damien, and arrived in Honolulu in 1864. In 1873 he volunteered to serve the isolated and neglected Hawaiians confined in the leprosy asylum at Kalawao. He arrived there in May 1873 and stayed until his death. Damien built houses, two churches, an orphanage, and a hospital, comforted the afflicted, and buried the dead. In response to his pleas for help and support, other priests and brothers from his congregation eventually joined him, and in 1886 Brother Joseph *Dutton came to Kalawao to carry on the work for nearly half a century. In 1888 the Franciscan Sisters of Syracuse, led by Mother Marianne *Cope, arrived to help. By the early 1880s Damien himself had contracted the disease, and he subsequently became known as Damien the Leper. He continued his ministry with single-minded devotion even as his health deteriorated. In 1881 he was decorated by the Hawaiian monarch with the Cross of Knight Commander of the Royal Order of King Kalakaua. Damien rarely wore the jeweled medal, professing, "The Lord decorated me with his own particular cross—leprosy." In 1936 his remains were removed from Molokai and taken to Louvain.

Damien was beatified by Pope *John Paul II in 1994. Statues of Damien are found in front of the State Capitol in Honolulu and also in Washington, D.C., inside the U.S. Capitol.

BIBLIOGRAPHY Margaret R. Bunson, *Father Damien: The Man and His Era* (1989); Gavan Daws, *Holy Man: Father Damien of Molokai* (1973,1984) (includes extensive bibliography); John Farrow, *Damien the Leper* (1937); Vital Jourdain, *The Heart of Father Damien, 1840–1889* (1955). The Damien Museum is located on the grounds of Saint Augustine Church, 130 Ohua Avenue, Honolulu, Hawaii.

Gerald H. Anderson

Dammann, Ernst (1904–), German academician and specialist in African studies. Dammann pursued theological and oriental studies at the University of Kiel, with emphasis on Africa, and received a doctoral degree in 1929. After ministerial service in northern Germany, he worked in Tanganyika (now Tanzania) from 1933 to 1936, both as a missionary and as pastor of a German parish. In 1940 he became lecturer in African languages at Hamburg University. He continued this career after the war, first in Hamburg, then, from 1957, as professor of African studies at Humboldt University in East Berlin, and from 1962, at Marburg University where he also taught history of religions. For several years he served as president of the Berlin Mission. Heidelberg University recognized his scholarly achievements by conferring on him an honorary doctor's degree in theology in 1968. As a teacher, author, and editor of learned journals, Dammann continued the tradition of his teachers Carl *Meinhof (1857–1944) and Diedrich *Westermann (1875–1956), and acquired an outstanding reputation among Africanists and missiologists. He retired in 1973.

BIBLIOGRAPHY There is yet no critical survey or assessment of Dammann's work. His major books are *Dichtungen in der Lamu-Mundart des Suaheli* (1940), *Die Religionen Afrikas* (1963), *Das Christentum in Afrika* (1968), and *Grundriss der Religionsgeschichte* (1972, 1989). A Festschrift for Dammann, *Wort und Religion: Kalima na dini,* edited by Hans-Jürgen Greschat and Hermann Jungraithmayr, was published in 1969.

Hans-Werner Gensichen

Danbolt, Erling Gauslaa (1904–), Norwegian Lutheran missionary and scholar. Danbolt was born in Bergen and graduated from the Norwegian Lutheran School of Theology, Oslo, in 1930. In 1931 he was ordained, went to France for language study, and in the same year was sent by the Norwegian Missionary Society (NMS) to Madagascar. He first taught at the Protestant Teachers' College at Fianarantsoa, then did parish work and taught at the Ivory Theological Seminary in Fianarantsoa from 1948 to 1954. In his missionary service Danbolt emphasized the proclamation of the gospel and high standards of education for teachers and pastors. He wrote a Malagasy commentary on the First Epistle to the Corinthians and a Norwegian one on the same epistle from the point of view of mission. His doctoral dissertation, *Misjonstankens gjennombrudd i Norge* (1946), was a study of the missionary awakening in Norway during the years 1800 to 1830, leading up to the establishment of the NMS in 1842, and also tracing the missionary concept and activity in Norway in the eighteenth century. In 1948 he published a dictionary of NMS missionaries from 1842 to 1948. After some years of parish service, he concluded his career as a professor and principal of the Norsk Laererakademi in Bergen from 1969 to 1974.

BIBLIOGRAPHY Norwall Hessen, ed., *Prester i Den norske kirke og andre teologiske kandidater* (1990), p. 84.

Nils E. Bloch-Hoell

Dandoy, Georges (1882–1962), Jesuit missionary in India. Born in Hemptinne, Belgium, Dandoy entered the Society of Jesus in 1899 and went to India in 1909; he was ordained there in 1914. He worked in India all his life, first as professor of theology in Kurseong and then, from 1922 onward, in Calcutta. Together with W. Wallace, J. Bayart, and P. Johans he belonged to the so-called Calcutta school, which continued the work of *Upadhyaya Brahmabandhav in close cooperation with Brahmachari Animananda to help India gain a new knowledge and new understanding of Jesus. In 1922 they founded a monthly journal, *Light of the East,* for which Dandoy was the chief editor until it ceased publication in 1946. He worked as chaplain in the Christian Hostel of St. Xavier's College, Calcutta, as spiritual director for many priests and laypeople (Catholics and non-Catholics), and as canon lawyer in the marriage tribunal of the archdiocese. He was strongly influenced by the missionary methods of Robert de *Nobili and by Pierre *Charles's adaptation theory, placing his trust in these words of the Lord: "I have come not to abolish [the Law or the Prophets] but to complete [them]."

In his work for *Light of the East* Dandoy provided ideas, did the day-to-day routine work of publishing, and personally wrote many articles, some of which were published in condensed form as books; for example, *An Essay on the Doctrine of the Unreality of the World in the Adwaita, Catholicism and National Culture, Karma-Evil-Punishment,* and *Religion versus Religions According to Radhakrishnan.* Though not everybody could identify with his ideas, an obituary in the *Examiner* stated: "Of all the minds that have served the church in India in our century, none was greater than Fr. Dandoy's."

BIBLIOGRAPHY J. Bayart, SJ, "In Memoriam: Georges Dandoy, S.J. (1882–1962)," *Clergy Monthly* 26 (1926): 103–115; F. Wilfred and M. M. Thomas, *Theologiegeschichte der Dritten Welt: Indien* (1992).

Karl Müller, SVD

Daniel, Antoine (1601–1648), early Jesuit missionary in Canada. A Norman from Dieppe, France, who came from a family of seafaring merchants, Daniel had studied law before entering the Society of Jesus in October 1621. After his formation in the order, he taught and served in the administration of the Jesuit college in Eu. In 1632 he sailed for Acadia (present-day Nova Scotia), where he spent a year at Fort Sainte Anne, Cape Breton Island (then under the command of his brother, Charles Daniel). A year later he was in Quebec city, and another year later, after a difficult journey up the St. Lawrence River, in Wendake, the land of the Huron Indians, along the eastern shore of Georgian Bay, Ontario. A kindly, gentle man, he was well liked by the native peoples. He learned languages easily and was the first to translate the basic Christian prayers into Huron. He also founded a children's choir to help with church services. Back in Quebec, for two years (1636–1638), he took charge of a new boarding school for native boys at Notre-Dame-des-Anges, but the experiment was a failure. Returning to Wendake, he remained there until the end of his life, first at Ossossane, and then among the people of the Rock Nation at Cahiague (1638–1647) and at Teanaostaiaë (1647–1648), near present-day Orillia, Ontario. On July 4, 1648, as he was finishing Mass, the Iroquois attacked Teanaostaiaë. After urging his congregation to flee, he walked toward the enemy, blocking their way to gain time for those escaping. He was struck by musket shot and pierced by many arrows. He was canonized by Pope *Pius XI on June 29, 1930.

BIBLIOGRAPHY Angus Macdougall, ed., *Martyrs of New France* (1962), pp. 25–32; Reuben Gold Thwaites, ed., *The Jesuit Relations and Allied Documents, 1610–1791* (1959).

Jacques Monet, SJ

Daniélou, Jean (1905–1974), Catholic theologian of mission and religions. Daniélou was born at Neuilly-sur-Seine, France, and enrolled in the Sorbonne, Paris, at an early age, obtaining there the licence-ès-lettres. In 1929 he entered the Jesuit novitiate at Laval. Having obtained the licentiate in philosophy in 1934, he attended the course of theological studies at the Jesuit scholasticate of Fourvière, where he developed a passion for the Fathers of the Church, becoming the cofounder of the French collection *Sources Chrétiennes.* In 1938 he was ordained priest and he defended a doctoral thesis in theology at the Institut Catholique de Paris, which he later presented also at the Sorbonne (1944) under the title "Platonisme et théologie mystique: Essai sur la doctrine spirituelle de Saint Grégoire de Nysse." He succeeded Jules Lebreton in the chair of history of Christian origins at the institute, and was appointed editor of the periodical *Études.*

Daniélou's interest in Christian origins led him to reflect theologically on the mission of the church in relation to other religions and on issues of dialogue with other traditions. These reflections are published in part in *Bulletin du Cercle Saint Jean Baptiste* and in *Axes.* Becoming a *peritus* (expert consultant) at Vatican II, he contributed to the council's documents concerned with the same issues. He thus was one of the first among pre-Vatican II Roman Catholic theologians to devise a theology of religions and of the church's mission in the context of dialogue. In 1969 Pope *Paul VI made him a cardinal.

Daniélou's theological position on religions and Christian mission is characteristic of what has been called the "fulfillment theory." Other religions represent humanity's inborn quest for God based on God's cosmic revelation through nature; Christianity, on the other hand, is the God-given response to the human quest. Other religions are, moreover, doubly anachronistic, in that they are superseded first by Judaism, and definitively by the Christ-event and Christianity. Whatever positive values can be recognized in them can only serve as *praeparatio evangelica,* clearly distinct from God's unique and universal intervention in history in Jesus Christ. Christianity is the God-intended means of salvation for all human beings, even while salvation in Jesus Christ is possible outside the boundaries of the visible church. Although Daniélou's "fulfillment theory" represents an important step in the Roman Catholic reflection on religions and mission, post-Vatican II developments have tended to supersede it.

BIBLIOGRAPHY Jean Daniélou, *The Salvation of the Gentiles* (1955), *Holy Pagans of the Old Testament* (1957), *The Lord of History: Reflections of the Inner Meaning of History* (1958), *The Advent of Salvation: A Comparative Study of non-Christian Religions and Christianity* (1962), *Myth and Mystery* (1968), and *Gospel Message and Hellenistic Culture* (1973). Paul Lebeau, *Jean Daniélou* (1967); *Jean Daniélou, 1905–1974* (1975); Dominic Veliath, *Theological Approach and Understanding of Religions: Jean Daniélou and Raimundo Panikkar. A Study in Contrast* (1987).

Jacques Dupuis, SJ

Darling, David (1790–1867), English missionary in the South Pacific. Sent by the London Missionary Society, Darling arrived in Tahiti in 1817, together with several protégés of David *Bogue of the Gosport Academy (Hampshire, England), whose training gave them some advantages over the "godly mechanicks" among their pioneering forerunners. During a long career, Darling helped his talented fellow missionary John *Davies of Wales to prepare Tahitians to become Islander missionaries. He was present at the baptism of King *Pomare II by Henry *Bicknell in 1819, tried in the 1830s to introduce the gospel to the Marquesas group, and officiated at the first baptisms in the Austral Islands. He translated some Scriptures into Marquesan and supervised printing at Papeete. He left Tahiti in 1859 following the death of his wife, Rebecca (Woolston), in 1858 and died in retirement at Sydney, New South Wales.

BIBLIOGRAPHY John Davies, *The History of the Tahitian Mission, 1799–1830,* C. W. Newbury, ed. (1961); Niel Gunson, *Messengers of Grace: Evangelical Missionaries in the South Seas, 1797–1860* (1978); Richard Lovett, *The History of the London Missionary Society, 1795–1895* (1899). Manuscript materials by and relating to Darling are in LMS South Sea collection at SOAS, Univ. of London (available on microfilm).

John Garrett

Darling, Thomas Young (1829–1909), Church Missionary Society (CMS) missionary in South India. Born in India an Anglo-Indian of partly Scottish descent, Darling was educated at the Church Missionary Institute, Madras. In 1847 he was assigned to Bezwada as a catechist in the Telegu Mission. In 1851 he was enrolled as a regular member of CMS and was later ordained. In 1852 he married Mary Nicholson, sister of a CMS missionary. He continued at Bezwada and in 1858 played a central role in the Telegu mass movement among the Mala, a subcaste people of Bezwada and Raghapur districts. A group of Mala men who had heard of Christ but had never met a missionary came to Darling and asked for instruction. After intensive teaching, a large number of Mala were baptized, and the expansion continued. A fluent speaker of Telegu, Darling took part in Telegu Bible revision. In 1875 he retired to England, where for several years he was a CMS association secretary and later a rector in Dorset. His work with CMS, and that of his sister, Jesse Darling, who also worked briefly for the mission, exemplify the debt of CMS in India to the "country born."

BIBLIOGRAPHY CMS, *Register of Missionaries and Native Clergy* (1904); M. E. Gibbs, *The Anglican Church in India, 1600–1970* (1974); Eugene Stock, *History of the Church Missionary Society,* 3 vols. (1899).

Jocelyn Murray

Datta, S(urendra) K(umar) (1878–1948), Indian Christian leader. Datta was born in Lahore, in present-day Pakistan. After his education in Lahore and Edinburgh, he served as lecturer in Forman Christian College, Lahore, of which he later became president. He served as the national secretary of the YMCAs of India, Burma, and Ceylon (1919–1927) and gave an address at the Jerusalem meeting of the International Missionary Council in 1928. He was a nationalist active in the political life of the country and served as a member of the Central Legislative Assembly from 1924 to 1926. He served as president of the All India Conference of Indian Christians in 1923, 1933, and 1934. In 1931 he attended the Round Table Conference in London as an Indian Christian delegate.

Although Datta believed that Indian religions do indeed search for truth, he argued that they did not provide moral and spiritual support for reform and renewal. He was particularly critical of Hinduism, arguing that some of its doctrines like *karma* and *transmigration* weakened the demand for moral responsibility and social reform. According to him, only the basic teachings of Christianity—the righteousness of God, the moral order of the created universe, the redeeming love of God manifest in Jesus Christ, and the eternal value of the human soul—could give hope to the people of India. He emphasized a twofold contribution of Christianity to India: through the work of educational institutions, and through the visible Indian church, which he believed to be influential far beyond its minority status. He was strongly critical of the Indian church, however, for its lack of spiritual depth, the absence of a distinctive Indian Christian theology, and its dependence on foreign money and leadership. He was also severely critical of the caste system operating within the Indian churches.

BIBLIOGRAPHY S. K. Datta, *The Desire of India* (1909) and *Asiatic Asia* (1932).

Stanley J. Samartha

Daubanton, François Elbertus (1853–1920), Dutch professor of missions. Born in Amsterdam, Daubanton was a minister of the French Reformed Church in Zwolle, Netherlands, and of the Netherlands Reformed Church in Heemstede and Amsterdam (1878–1903). From 1903 to 1920 he was professor of biblical theology, practical theology, and the history of mission at Utrecht University. He also edited *Theologische Studiën* (1883–1917). His major missiological work was *Prolegomena van Protestantsche Zendingswetenschap* (1911). This large volume was the first serious history of mission studies and the first formal study of the science of mission. It deals with the structure, name, and history of the science of mission; the place of mission studies in the encyclopedia of theology; and the methodology of mission studies. Daubanton differed from Gustav *Warneck in his methodology but wrote out of the same theological convictions. He disagreed with the approach of the *Religionsgeschichtliche Schule,* represented by Ernst *Troeltsch and others. Christian mission, he said, is based on revelation, not evolution; the purpose of mission is neither civilization nor social work, but the preaching of the gospel, the planting of churches, and the Christianization of cultures. The missionary enterprise has to avoid two extremes: the rigidity of the early pietists on one hand, and the accommodation of the Jesuits on the other.

BIBLIOGRAPHY J. A. B. Jongeneel, "De Ethische Zendingstheologie van François E. Daubanton (1853–1920)," *Nederlands Theologisch Tijdschrift* 44 (1990): 288–307. See also O. G. Myklebust, *The Study of Missions in Theological Education,* 2 vols. (1955, 1957), passim; J. A. B. Jongeneel, *The Philosophy, Science, and Theology of Mission in the Nineteenth and Twentieth Centuries: A Missiological Encyclopedia,* 2 vols. (1995, 1997), passim.

Jan A. B. Jongeneel

Daüble, Carl Gustav (1832–1893), German missionary with the Church Missionary Society (CMS) in India. Born in Würtemberg, Daüble trained at the Basel Mission Institute and then at the Church Missionary College in Islington, England. He received Anglican orders and in 1857—the year of the Indian Mutiny—proceeded to North India. After several years in Benares and Agra, he served at the Secundra Orphanage, just outside Agra, from 1860 to 1870. The orphanage had been begun by CMS in the 1830s after severe famines in North India and had become well-known for its Orphan Press, operated by former residents. The Christian village at Secundra, and most of the other buildings, were demolished during the mutiny, and the press was transferred to Allahabad. At the time, no one proposed rebuilding the orphanage, but new famines intervened, and Daüble responded by reactivating the orphanage. His 36 years in India exemplify the faithful work of the many German CMS missionaries. After Daüble's death, his second wife, who had been a missionary at Secundra, was enrolled as a CMS member to continue work in North India, and his daughter married a CMS missionary.

BIBLIOGRAPHY CMS, *Register of Missionaries and Native Clergy* (1904); M. E. Gibbs, *The Anglican Church in India, 1600–1970* (1972); Eugene Stock, *History of the Church Missionary Society,* 3 vols. (1899).

Jocelyn Murray

David, Christian (1690–1751), itinerant evangelist and renewal agent of the Moravian Church. Born of Roman Catholic parents in Senftleben, Bohemia, David was early impressed by Protestant neighbors who were willing to suffer for their faith. He became religiously confused as a young man because attacks on Protestants by his family conflicted with the influence of Protestant friends who expressed their disagreements with Catholicism. Trained in carpentry, he continued his religious pursuits and was influenced by a German Protestant pastor who ministered to him during an illness. This led to religious peace of mind.

Meeting the young Count *Zinzendorf at Dresden in 1722, David agreed to lead refugees from Moravia to Saxony, where they might find asylum. He made ten trips back to Moravia and, with the first group, founded the settlement of Herrnhut on Zinzendorf's estate in 1722. As he felled the first tree, he quoted Psalm 84:4 and helped choose the name for the settlement, which means "On Watch for the Lord." In 1727, the formative year of revival at Herrnhut, he worked tirelessly for the renewal of the community and continued his refugee-saving journeys to Moravia.

David was one of the first Moravian missionaries to go to Greenland in 1733, ministering there until 1735, when he returned to Herrnhut. In 1741 he was in the Wetterau area of Germany, in 1742 at Pilgerruh, in 1747 back in Greenland to build a mission house. In 1748 he went to Pennsylvania and in 1749 returned to Greenland for a two-week visit, during which he built a school for the mission. He died at Herrnhut. Zinzendorf, who conducted the funeral, characterized him as a man of great and respectable gifts.

BIBLIOGRAPHY C. J. Fliegel, tr., *Christian David: Servant of the Lord* (1962); *Gräfin von Zinzendorf, Christian David und Leonhard Dober in kurzen Umrissen* (1841).

Albert H. Frank

Davidson, Andrew (1836–1918), pioneer medical missionary to Madagascar. Born in Kincardineshire, Scotland, Davidson studied medicine and graduated from the University of Edinburgh before completing postgraduate studies in Brussels. He was a member of the Free Church of Scotland and joined the London Missionary Society (LMS), which appointed him to Madagascar. He arrived at Antananarivo with his wife in August 1862 and served at the mission dispensary in the center of the city while working toward establishing a mission hospital. The hospital—the first medical facility of its kind in Madagascar—opened in July 1865, and he became its first director. He was also responsible for training the first native physicians, midwives, and nurses. Two of his most famous students were Andrianaly and Rajaonah, the first Malagasy doctors to graduate from a European university (Edinburgh). After a furlough in Britain in 1866, he resumed his work at the hospital but severed his connection with the LMS in 1868. He remained in the country, conducting a medical mission supported by Scottish benefactors. Disagreement with the Malagasy prime minister caused him to leave the country in November 1876, and he stayed in Mauritius for some time.

In 1898, after his final return to Scotland, Davidson was appointed professor on the medical faculty at the University of Edinburgh as a specialist in oriental diseases. He wrote many pamphlets in English and Malagasy, mostly on medical matters but also on native customs.

BIBLIOGRAPHY Short biographies of Davidson appear in Régis Rajemisa Raolison, *Dictionnaire historique et géographique de Madagascar* (1966), and John Owen Whitehouse, *Register of Missionaries Deputations..., 1796–1896* (1896). Passages relating to the medical mission and to the social context appear in Mervyn Brown, *Madagascar Rediscovered* (1978) and James Sibree, *Fifty Years in Madagascar* (1924).

Yvette Ranjeva Rabetafika

Davidson, Benjamin (1860–1948), founder and director of evangelical mission agencies. Born in Scotland, Davidson was serving as a tea company agent in Ceylon (Sri Lanka) when he became concerned for the spiritual welfare of the "soldiers, sailors, railway employees, postmen, police and coolies" of Ceylon and India. Leaving his business career, he became the founder and longtime director of two missions that began with an exclusive focus on the Indian subcontinent. The first, Ceylon and India General Mission (of which he was director from 1893 to 1921) was one of the groups that merged in 1968 to become International Christian Fellowship, which later merged into SIM International (1989). The second, the India Mission (director, 1930–1948), changed its name to International Missions upon its entrance into Pakistan in 1954. A man of dedication, determination, and zeal, Davidson was almost legendary for his frugality and tight control of mission activity, even when he was 12,000 miles away.

BIBLIOGRAPHY Margaret Chamberlain, *Reaching Asians Internationally: A History of International Missions* (1984). Davidson's papers having to do with the founding and his directorship of the CIGM are part of the SIM archives in Charlotte, N.C.

Gary R. Corwin

Davidson, Hannah Frances (1860–1935), Brethren in Christ (BC) missionary in Rhodesia. Davidson was born near Smithville, Ohio, the daughter of Henry Davidson, first editor of the *Evangelical Visitor,* the denominational paper of the BC. She was educated at Ashland College, Ohio, and Kalamazoo College, Michigan, and taught at McPherson College, Kansas (1888–1897). In 1898 she and four other missionaries founded the first BC mission in Africa at Matopo, located about 30 miles southwest of Bulawayo in Southern Rhodesia (now Zimbabwe). In 1906 with Adda Taylor she founded the first BC mission in Northern Rhodesia (now Zambia) at Macha, where she was superintendent until her retirement in 1923. The system of elementary education that she introduced remained largely in effect until the governments of the two countries became responsible for the denomination's schools. Her book *South and South Central Africa* (1915) is still one of the best descriptions of early American missionary work in Africa. On returning to the United States, she taught at Messiah College in Grantham, Pennsylvania, until shortly before her death and served as missions editor for the denomination's paper.

BIBLIOGRAPHY Anna Engle et al., *There Is No Difference* (1950); E. Morris Sider, "Hannah Frances Davidson," in *Nine Portraits* (1978).

E. Morris Sider

Davies, John (1772–1855), London Missionary Society (LMS) missionary in Tahiti. A Calvinistic Methodist teacher-minister with the Missionary Society (later LMS), Davies was born at Pontrobert, Wales, and arrived in Tahiti in July 1801. He survived a testing period of isolation during the Napoleonic and Tahitian wars, and in 1808 he moved to Huahine with the mission's protector, King *Pomare II. In 1809 he went with other missionaries to Sydney, where he married his first wife, Sophia Browning (who died in 1812). Returning to Tahiti in 1810, he instructed converts and joined in forming a church on Moorea. Pomare was victorious in war in 1815 and was baptized in 1819. For a time, Davies joined with a newly arrived group of critically disposed missionaries on Huahine. After 1820 he moved to Papara, Tahiti, where his second wife, Mary Ann (Bradley) Bicknell, the widow of Henry *Bicknell, died in 1826. He trained local Islander missionaries to establish out-stations in the Tuamotu, Austral, and Marquesas groups, and later in Tonga and Fiji. In lonesome years spent at Papara he translated New Testament books and the Psalms, compiled the first dictionary, and wrote his highly regarded manuscript history of the Tahitian mission. He died at age 83 at Papara.

BIBLIOGRAPHY C. W. Newbury, ed., *The History of the Tahitian Mission, 1799–1830* (1961) presents Davies's manuscript history in printed and annotated form. John Garrett, *To Live among the Stars: Christian Origins in Oceania* (1982); Niel Gunson, *Messengers of Grace: Evangelical Missionaries in the South Seas, 1797–1860* (1978); Richard Lovett, *The History of the London Missionary Society* (1899); Jacques Nicole, *Au Pied de l'écriture: Histoire de la traduction de la Bible en Tahitien* (1988). Manuscripts and other items are in LMS South Sea collection at SOAS, Univ. of London.

John Garrett

Davis, J(ohn) Merle (1875–1960), YMCA missionary in Japan, and International Missionary Council (IMC) executive. Davis was born in Japan, son of the pioneer missionary Jerome Davis. He graduated in 1899 from Oberlin College in Oberlin, Ohio, and began work on a doctorate in Germany with the hope of returning to Japan to teach. His abilities were known to John R. *Mott, who invited him to head the new YMCA in Nagasaki. He accepted and began work in 1905, moving later to the Tokyo YMCA. On furlough from 1923 to 1924, he threw himself into a study of race relations in California, hoping to reduce anti-Japanese feeling there. This led to an invitation to help in organizing a pan-Pacific conference in Hawaii and thereafter to become the founding secretary of the Institute of Pacific Relations, devoted to reducing East-West tensions. In 1929 he became the director of the new Department of Social and Economic Research and Counsel of the IMC, in which position he continued until his retirement in 1949.

Davis's task at the IMC was to study the economic and social environment of the younger churches, in order to give the missionary movement a clearer understanding of the conditions facing new churches. He traveled widely and wrote reports on the African Copperbelt, Sumatra, the Caribbean, and South America. His work was often criticized by Europeans as being the quintessence of American social gospel activism, but his influence was widely felt, especially in the Madras meeting of the IMC in 1938.

BIBLIOGRAPHY J. Merle Davis, *New Buildings on Old Foundations: A Handbook on Stabilizing the Younger Churches in Their Environment* (1945) and *John Merle Davis: An Autobiography* (1960). Fred Field Goodsell, "Serenity Amid Labor: Observations Concerning the Life and Work of John Merle Davis, 1875–1960," *IRM* 49 (1960): 443–445.

Charles W. Forman

Day, David A(lexander) (1851–1897), American Lutheran missionary in Liberia. Born in Dillsburg, Pennsylvania, Day fought in the Civil War at the age of 14. He grew up deeply troubled by poverty and injustice. He studied theology and medicine at the Missionary Institute at Susquehanna University and was ordained for service in

Liberia by the Lutheran General Synod Mission Board in 1874. He sailed for Africa with his wife, Emily, arriving in Monrovia in June 1874, which was 14 years after the founding of the original Lutheran mission by Morris *Officer. Of the original seven missionaries, three had died of disease, while the others were forced to abandon their posts in the "white man's graveyard." (The Days later buried three of their own children in Africa.) Finding only dilapidated buildings at Muhlenberg, the former mission site, Day began rebuilding the school, replanting the mission farm, securing more government land, and opening carpenter, blacksmith, and machine shops. He constructed the first side-wheeler steamboat to navigate the Saint Paul River. Emma Day, going on long bush walks, became known as Ma Day, teacher and friend of Liberians.

Never swerving from his purpose of devoting his entire career to the coming of God's kingdom in Liberia, Day declined positions in the mission board home office and with the U.S. government. In failing health, he died aboard ship en route home.

BIBLIOGRAPHY George Drach, ed., *Kingdom Pathfinders: Biographical Sketches of Foreign Missionaries* (1942); L. B. Wolf, ed., *Missionary Heroes of the Lutheran Church* (1911).

James A. Scherer

Day, George Edward (1815–1905), founder of the missions library at Yale University Divinity School. Day graduated from Yale College and Yale Divinity School. After serving as pastor of Congregational churches in Marlboro and Northampton, Massachusetts, and as professor and librarian at Lane Theological Seminary in Cincinnati, Ohio, he returned to Yale in 1866 as professor of Hebrew. From 1888 until his retirement in 1895 he was dean of Yale Divinity School. In 1891, before Yale had a professor of missions, Day established a missions library at Yale with an initial gift of his personal collection of mission books, and he solicited gifts and support for the library from others. Day and his wife, Olivia Hotchkiss Day, also provided in their wills for a building and an endowment for the library.

Day stipulated that the scope of the missions collection would include the history of modern missions, missionary biography, history and annual reports of missionary societies, missionary periodicals, works prepared and issued by missionaries for the use of the natives for whom they labored, and missions to the Jews. After his retirement, Day devoted another seven years to the development of the missions library. On the occasion of the centennial anniversary of the library, the Day Missions Library at Yale was said to rank "as the strongest resource in North America for both Protestant and Roman Catholic missions."

BIBLIOGRAPHY Stephen L. Peterson, "A 'Steady Aim toward Completeness,'" *The Day Missions Library Centennial Volume* (1993).

Gerald H. Anderson

Day, John (1797–1859), African American Baptist missionary, chief justice and lieutenant governor in Liberia. Born in Hicksford, Virginia, probably a free man, Day was licensed to preach by a Baptist church in 1821. Like many others of his era, his only theological training came from a scholarly pastor, in Greensville County, Virginia. Excited by the opportunity that African colonization offered for blacks, he immigrated to Liberia with his wife and four children in 1830. His preaching ability and evangelistic passion led to his appointment as a missionary by the Baptist Triennial Convention in the United States in 1836; he was assigned to preach and teach school. He served as pastor of several Liberian Baptist congregations as well as teacher in various schools. In 1845, when northern and southern Baptist churches split in the United States, he severed his relationship with the Triennial Convention and the following year was appointed a missionary by the Foreign Mission Board of the Southern Baptist Convention. He eventually became the superintendent of Baptist work in Liberia and Sierra Leone. Subsequently he also served as chief justice of the Supreme Court and lieutenant governor of Liberia.

Day firmly believed in evangelism and in the necessity of repentance for salvation and was critical of missionaries who assumed "a little education" and "a little civilization" were substitutes for preaching the gospel. Though aware that white support of African colonization was largely motivated by racism, Day viewed it as God's instrument for liberating American blacks as well as extending the gospel to heathen Africa.

When he died, E. W. *Blyden gave the eulogy in which he praised Day's "excellences as a preacher, a soldier, a physician, a judge, a legislator, a lieutenant-governor, and educator and a theologian."

BIBLIOGRAPHY *African Repository* 30 (November 1854): 341–342; G. Winfred Hervey, *The Story of Baptist Missions in Foreign Lands* (1884); Sandy D. Martin, *Black Baptists and African Missions* (1989); Garnet Ryland, *The Baptists of Virginia, 1699–1926* (1955); Nan F. Weeks and Blanche Sydnor White, *Liberia for Christ* (1959); B. I. Wiley, ed., *Slaves No More* (1980).

Alan Neely

Day, Lal Behari (1824–1894), notable Bengali convert. Enrolled in Alexander *Duff's pioneering school in Calcutta in 1833, Day was deeply influenced by the teaching and the teachers there and was baptized in 1843. Appointed a catechist in the same year, he studied for the ministry and was ordained in 1855 by the Free Church of Scotland Presbytery of Calcutta. In Duff's missionary strategy, Day and the other early converts were to be the leaders in a process of reformation and renaissance in India, led by Indian Luthers and Knoxes. From the beginning, however, the missionaries were reluctant to share power with their Indian fellow ministers and resisted independent thought on the part of the converts. As a consequence, Day left the employ of the Free Church and became professor of English in the government Hooghly College. The Scottish missionaries encouraged their converts to write in mission newsheets such as the *Calcutta Christian Observer* and the *Madras Native Herald.* Some went on to make significant contributions to Indian literature.

Michael Madhasudhan Dutt became well known for his poems; Day's works included a collection of folktales and *Govinda Samanta* (1874), later known as *Bengal Peasant Life.* This last work is still in print and is a sensitive and accurate portrayal of rural life in Bengal; in its own way it is a significant work of Victorian English literature. Day's importance is as a leading member of a band of notable and able converts to Christianity in mid-nineteenth-century Bengal, who was also a fine interpreter between the Bengali tradition and culture and the English-speaking world.

BIBLIOGRAPHY Lal Behari Day, *Recollections of Alexander Duff, D.D., LL.D.* (1879). M. A. Laird, *Missionaries and Education in Bengal, 1793-1837* (1972); G. Macpherson, *Life of Lal Behari Day* (1900).

Duncan B. Forrester

Day, Samuel Stearns (1808-1871), pioneer of the American Baptist Telugu mission. Born in Leeds County in southeastern Ontario, Day was educated at Hamilton Literary and Theological Institution in New York and ordained at Cortland (New York) Baptist Church. In 1835 he and his wife, Roenna (Clark), were appointed by the Baptist Board of Foreign Missions to the Telugus in southern India. The Days worked in Vishakhapatnam, Madras, and Nellore, establishing congregations and translating the Scriptures and important theological works; Day is credited with baptizing the first Telugu convert in 1840. For 26 years the station at Nellore was the only location of missions to the Telugus, earning the name "Lone Star Mission." The Days found that traditional methods of evangelism did not work with the Telugus, owing to their Hindu religious culture; several times the Days' lives were threatened. The results of their mission were so meager that in 1848 the Telugu mission was retained by the Baptist board only after an impassioned plea by Edward Bright, secretary of the board, and Samuel Francis Smith, a prominent New England Baptist pastor. Although Day had successfully used a chain of Christian day schools to conduct the mission work, the board rejected the use of schools as a mission strategy. In 1853, he returned to the United States in failing health. From 1855 to 1859 he traveled in Canada and the United States as an agent of the American Baptist Missionary Union until his health again failed. He died at Homer, New York.

BIBLIOGRAPHY Day's writings include a translation of Adoniram Judson's *A View of the Christian Religion, First Diglott Edition* (1839) and *The History of Christ* (1854). David Downie, *The Lone Star: The History of the Telugu Mission of the American Baptist Missionary Union* (1893); Thomas S. Dunaway, *A Pioneer for Jesus* (1925). A negative assessment of the Telugu mission that proved to be influential is Howard Malcolm, *Travels in South Eastern Asia, Etc.* (1837).

William H. Brackney

Dean, William (1807-1895), American Baptist missionary in Siam (Thailand) and Hong Kong. Dean was born in Eaton, New York, the oldest of eight children of Joshua and Mary Dean. He graduated from Hamilton Academy and Hamilton Literary and Theological Institution; while there he also studied at the Burma School operated by Maung Sway Moung. In 1834 he and his wife, Matilda (Coman), were appointed to Siam (Thailand) to work with the Chinese and begin a new mission for the Baptist Board of Foreign Missions, the first American missionaries appointed to work among the Chinese. The Deans entered Siam via Moulmein, Burma, where they met Adoniram and Sarah B. *Judson, with whom they became close friends. In Bangkok, Dean organized a church, distributed tracts, operated a dispensary, and translated Scripture. Following a lengthy furlough and the death of his wife, Dean married Theodosia Barker and was again appointed, in 1838, to the mission in Bangkok. When China ceded Hong Kong to the British in 1842, the Deans immediately relocated to that island. There he started the first Protestant church composed of Chinese members. During the years in Siam, Dean had become a trusted friend of the Siamese king, Chulalongkorn, and in 1880 he prepared an edition of the Gospel of John in honor of Queen Sunanda. In addition to Bible translation work, his literary achievements include notes on several books of the Bible, a devotional guide, a hymnal, and a catechism. He retired in the United States and died in San Diego.

BIBLIOGRAPHY William Dean, *Genesis, with Explanatory Notes* (1850) and *The China Mission: Embracing a History of the Various Missions of All Denominations among the Chinese* (1859; this volume was the first of its kind). Francis W. Goddard, *Called to Cathay* (1948). William Dean's autobiographical "Reminiscences" is an unpublished typescript held by the American Baptist Historical Society, Rochester, N.Y. Of related interest is Pharcellus Church, *Notices of the Life of Theodosia Ann Barker Dean, Wife of Rev. William Dean, Missionary to China* (1851).

William H. Brackney

Deck, (John) Northcote (1875-1957), pioneering Australian medical missionary. After studying medicine at Sydney University, Deck, the nephew of Florence Young, founder of the South Sea Evangelical Mission (SSEM), visited the work of this mission in the Solomon Islands in 1908. He was immediately captivated and threw himself into the work of the mission, serving until 1928. An adventurous spirit, he toured the Solomon Islands, principally Malaita and Guadalcanal, in the mission vessel *Evangel,* serving as captain and engineer of the vessel, photographer, explorer, doctor, and teacher in his missionary service.

Deck was joined by his brother Norman and three sisters, Kathleen, Joan, and Constance, as members of the SSEM, which was known at the beginning as the Deck Mission. His missionary adventures were described in a quarterly letter that reached a circulation of 2,000 in the 1920s, and he also wrote some devotional books and accounts of the SSEM work in the Solomons, including *South from Guadalcanal: The Romance of Rennel Island* (1945). Upon his retirement, first in England for ten years and later in Canada, he became a popular speaker at mission conventions retelling his exploits as a missionary in the Solomon Islands.

BIBLIOGRAPHY Allison Griffiths, *Fire in the Islands* (1977); Florence Young, *Pearls from the Pacific* (1925).

Darrell Whiteman

Dehergne, Joseph (1903–1990), historian of Jesuit missions in China. Born in La Gaubretière, Vendée, France, Dehergne entered the major diocesan seminary at Luçon, Vendée, in 1921. He became a Jesuit novice in 1925 at Beaumont-sur-Oise and was ordained a priest in Paris in 1934. He departed for China in 1936 and two years later began a career of teaching history and French at Aurora University, Shanghai. During this period he published one book and a number of articles, especially in the *Bulletin de l'Université l'Aurore.*

Expelled from China in 1951, Dehergne went to Chantilly, France, where he became the librarian and later the archivist in the Jesuit house of studies. In 1959 he received a diploma from the École practique des Hautes Études for his study on the French Revolution, for which he received a prize from the Académie Française. In 1965 he received his doctorate from the University of Paris. A cofounder with Henri *Bernard-Maitre of the triennial Colloque Internationale de Sinologie, at Chantilly, he edited the proceedings of the first three meetings. He continued to assist others in their research on the China mission. He died at La Seilleraye, Thouaré, near Nantes.

BIBLIOGRAPHY Joseph Dehergne, *Les Vendéens (1793). La "Grande Armée." La vie regionale* (1939), *Répertoire des Jésuites de Chine de 1552 à 1800* (1973), and *Juifs de Chine: A travers la correspondance inédite des Jésuites du dix-huitième siècle* (1980; 2d ed., 1984; coedited with D. D. Leslie). E. Malatesta, "Necrology," and T. S. Foss, "Bibliography of Works of Joseph Dehergne, S.J.," in [Joseph Dehergne and Theodore N. Foss, eds.,], *Chine et l'Europe: Evolution et particularités des Rapports Est-Ouest du XVIe au XXe siècle* (1991), pp. 306–314.

John W. Witek, SJ

Dehqani-Tafti, H(assan) B(arnaba) (1920–), first Persian Anglican bishop in Iran. Born in Taft, Persia, of a Muslim father and a Christian mother, Dehqani-Tafti's faith came alive when he attended a Christian school in Isfahan. He studied Persian literature at the University of Tehran and theology at Ridley Hall, Cambridge, and was ordained in 1949. In 1961 he was consecrated bishop of Iran. He described his diocese as "the smallest numerically, and perhaps the largest geographically, within the Anglican Communion." He also became presiding bishop of the Episcopal Church in Jerusalem and the Middle East, 1976 to 1986. After the Islamic revolution he survived an assassination attempt by three revolutionary guards on October 26, 1979. Four bullets ringed his head in a semicircle on his pillow, and his wife was wounded. The next month he left Iran for conferences in Cyprus, England, and Kenya and was not permitted to return. On May 6, 1980, his 24-year old son Bahram was murdered in Iran.

In England Dehqani-Tafti lived at Ridley Hall, Cambridge, and then became assistant bishop of Winchester from 1982 to 1990. In retirement he lives in Basingstoke, where he wrote an important missiological trilogy in Persian—*Christ and Christianity amongst the Iranians.*

BIBLIOGRAPHY Dehqani-Tafti's autobiographical works are *Design of My World* (1959) and *The Hard Awakening* (1981), the latter recounting the revolution, assassination attempt on his life, and the murder of his son. An illuminating account of the same period by his chaplain, Paul Hunt, is *Inside Iran* (1981). Dehqani-Tafti's trilogy volumes are entitled *A Short Historical Survey* (1992), *In the Classical Period of Persian Poetry* (1993), and *In Contemporary Poetry, Prose, and Art* (1994).

Graham Kings

Delany, Emma Bertha (1871–1922), African American missionary in Malawi, and Liberia. Delany was born in Fernandina Beach, Florida. She graduated from Spelman Seminary (now College), Atlanta, in 1894 and worked for several years at Florida Institute, Live Oak, Florida, before going to Malawi in 1902. Under appointment of the National Baptist Convention and the National Baptist Convention of the U.S.A., Inc., she was supported in Africa by the Baptist women of Florida. Delany was first stationed at Chiradzulu, Blantyre, where she cofounded the Providence Industrial Mission with Landon N. *Cheek, the first African American missionary to arrive in Malawi. She worked as a teacher at the mission and eventually established a women's society and weekly sewing classes for girls. She left the country in 1906 and returned to the United States.

In 1912 Delany went to Liberia, where she worked for eight years. She supervised the construction of Suehn Industrial Mission and served as the first principal of Suehn Industrial Academy. In 1920 she returned to the United States with the idea of raising funds for continued work and for establishing a chain of schools in Liberia. However, she died at the age of 51 of yellow fever.

BIBLIOGRAPHY C. C. Adams and Marshall A. Talley, *Negro Baptists and Foreign Missions* (1944); Nuper Chaudhuri and Margaret Strobel, *Western Women and Imperialism: Complicity and Resistance* (1992); Edward A. Freeman, *The Epoch of Negro Baptists and the Foreign Mission Board* (1951); Florence Matilda Read, *The Story of Spelman College* (1961).

Sylvia M. Jacobs

d'Elia, Pasquale. *See* Elia, Pasquale d'.

Delitzsch, Franz Julius (1813–1890), biblical exegete, Semitist, and scholar of mission to Jews. Born in Leipzig, Delitzsch's proficiency with Hebrew and Jewish religious sources have led many to presume a Jewish origin for this pious and committed Lutheran scholar. After a conversion experience in his youth he became a passionate believer in missions, especially to the Jewish people. He is remembered as the founder of the Institutum Judaicum at Leipzig in 1886, which was dedicated to training Christians for evangelism among Jewish people. There he taught Mishnah, Talmud, and Jewish hermeneutics to the students whom he sent to Jewish communities all over Europe. He was also at the forefront of those who have promoted a contextualized Jewish church.

During his lifetime Delitzsch served as professor of Old Testament theology at three different German universities and published commentaries of such quality that they are still regarded as classics in the field. A fierce opponent of anti-Semitism, he exposed prejudice in the churches, worked closely with leading Jewish scholars, and advocated a genuine interest in the perspectives of Orthodox Judaism. He is famous for his magisterial translation of the New Testament into Hebrew for use in evangelism among Jewish people. The first edition of this New Testament was published in 1877 by the British and Foreign Bible Society, and the tenth edition, completed by his student and successor Gustav *Dalman, is still in use. At his death, many rabbis and Jewish scholars gave appreciative obituaries. The *Encyclopedia Judaica* numbers him among the most eminent Christian Hebraists.

BIBLIOGRAPHY Arnulf Baumann, "Frans Delitzsch als Missionar," *Friede über Israel* 3 (1990): 101–108; S. I. Curtis, *Franz Delitzsch* (1891); A. E. Thompson, *A Century of Jewish Missions* (1902); Siegfried Wagner, "Franz Delitzsch, Scholar and Missionary," *Mishkan* 14 (1991): 46–55.

Walter Riggans

Del Valle, Juan. *See* Valle, Juan del.

Dengel, Anna (1892–1980), physician and founder of the Catholic Medical Mission Sisters. Born in Steeg, Austria, Dengel attended boarding school in Lyons, France, headquarters for the Society for the Propagation of the Faith. Upon advice from Agnes McLaren, Scottish suffragist and a physician who promoted medical missions, especially for women in India, Anna studied at the medical school of Cork University, Ireland, graduating in 1919. After a nine-month internship in Derbyshire, England, Dengal began her medical mission work in Rawalpindi, India, in 1920. Because the Muslim law of purdah and the Hindu caste system often left women without medical care, her policy at St. Catherine's hospital and dispensary was to aid women and children of all religions.

She spent most of 1924 in the United States, writing and speaking on behalf of medical missions. In Washington, D.C., she met Michael Mathis, CSC, a former missionary in India, who helped her write a constitution for herself and three women who joined her to devote their lives to medical missions. Formed as a Pious Society on September 30, 1925, the Society of Catholic Medical Missionaries became a religious congregation in 1936, after *Pius XI lifted the medieval ban on women religious entering the medical profession. The pontiff's decision was influenced by earlier discussions with the Vatican by McLaren, Dengel, and some American bishops. The society moved its headquarters to Fox Chase, Pennsylvania, a few years later. In 1927, Mother Dengel began editing *The Medical Missionary,* which was published through 1968.

The sisters expanded their services to provide medical supervision in government hospitals and city health centers; they also trained native women as midwives and nurses, and provided home health care and education in public health and nutrition. The Medical Mission Sisters became the first Roman Catholic congregation to provide surgeons and obstetricians for mission work. As superior general from 1925 to 1967, Dengel saw the community grow to over 700 women working in 40 countries. She died in Rome.

Dengel laid the theoretical foundations for medical missions in *Mission for Samaritans* (1945). She noted three reasons for this practical response to the sick and poor of mission countries: the example of Christ the healer; the charity of the Good Samaritan who tended the man injured on his journey; and restitution for the debt which the white race "owed to the peoples subjected and exploited by our forefathers." This latter point also identified the systemic relationship between health problems and oppressive conditions for women in many countries. Justice, therefore, became essential to healing.

BIBLIOGRAPHY Correspondence, talks, and writings of Mother Dengel and correspondence with founding associates are well organized at the Society of Catholic Medical Missionaries archives, Philadelphia, Pennsylvania. For biographical information and Dengel's role in the development of Catholic medical missions, see Katherine Burton, *According to the Pattern: The Story of Dr. Agnes McLaren and the Society of Catholic Medical Missionaries* (1946); M. M. McGinley, "Mother Anna Dengel, M.D.—A Pioneer Medical Missionary," *Worldmission* 31 (1980): 26–31; Floyd Keeler, *Catholic Medical Missions* (1925); and Richard F. Long, *Nowhere a Stranger* (1968). See also Margaret Mary Reher, "Den[n]is J. Dougherty and Anna M. Dengel: The Missionary Alliance," *Records of the American Catholic Historical Society* 101, nos. 1–2 (1990): 21–33; and M. Bonaventure Beck, "The Society of Catholic Medical Missionaries: Origin and Development" (M.S. thesis, Catholic Univ. of America, 1955).

Angelyn Dries, OSF

Denis (*or* Denys; Dionysius) of Paris (?–c. 258), first bishop of Paris, martyr, and a patron saint of France. Knowledge of St. Denis is entirely based on hagiographic tradition. Gregory of Tours, in his *History of the Franks* (A.D. 576), reports that Denis was sent from Rome to establish the church in Paris in 250, a member of a party of seven missionaries who organized the church in Gaul. His companions were Gatian (from Tours), Trophimus (Arles), Paul (Narbonne), Saturninus (Toulouse), Austremonius (Clermont-Ferrand), and Martial (Limoges). Denis was probably beheaded on the hill now called Montmartre ("martyr hill"), during the persecution of 258, directed by Emperor Valerian against bishops in particular. The cult of the martyr is attested in the fifth century; a basilica was erected about 475 on the site of martyrdom; and an abbey was built about 624 next to the basilica upon the initiative of King Dagobert.

BIBLIOGRAPHY Léon Levillain, "Saint Trophime et la mission des Sept en Gaule," *Revue de l'histoire de l'Église de France* 13 (1927):

145-189; Luce Pietri, "Des origines à l'an Mil," in Bernard Plongeron, ed., *Le diocèse de Paris des origines à la Révolution* (1967), pp. 15-19.

Marc R. Spindler

Dennis, James Shepard (1842-1914), American Presbyterian missionary, author, teacher, and statistician of missions. Dennis was born and raised in Newark, New Jersey, and took his formal education at the College of New Jersey (Princeton University) and at Princeton Theological Seminary. After ordination in 1868 by the Presbyterian Church, U.S.A. (PCUSA), the American Board of Commissioners for Foreign Missions sent him to its mission in Sidon, 20 miles south of Beirut; he was there from 1868 to 1871. During a brief return to the United States, he married Mary Elizabeth Pinneo, and together they returned to Syria. Sponsored this time by the PCUSA, Dennis served as principal and professor of theology at the newly established Beirut Theological Seminary. While there, he wrote three textbooks in Arabic for use in seminary classes.

After returning to the United States in 1891, Dennis compiled detailed world missionary statistics and wrote extensively on missiological themes. At Princeton and several other seminaries in 1892 and 1895, he delivered the "Students' Lectureship on Missions." He served on the Board of Foreign Mission of the PCUSA and was their delegate to the Ecumenical Missionary Conference in New York City in 1900 and to the Edinburgh 1910 World Missionary Conference, where he took a leading part. Dennis believed that Christianity, as propagated by foreign missions, was the social hope of the nations. In his lectures and writings, he was an optimistic apologist for missions. He wrote *Social Evils of the Non-Christian World* (1892), *Foreign Missions after a Century* (1893), *Christian Missions and Social Progress,* 3 vols. (1897-1906), *Centennial Survey of Foreign Missions* (1902), *The New Horoscope of Missions* (1908), and *The Modern Call of Missions* (1913). With Harlan P. *Beach and Charles H. Fahs he edited *World Atlas of Christian Missions* (1911).

BIBLIOGRAPHY William H. Berger, "James Shepard Dennis: Syrian Missionary and Apologist," *American Presbyterians: Journal of Presbyterian History* 64, no. 2 (Summer 1986): 97-111. Dennis's papers are in the Speer Library at Princeton Theological Seminary, Princeton, N.J.

H. McKennie Goodpasture

Dennis, Thomas John (1869-1917), British missionary in West Africa. Dennis was born in Sussex, England. He was a gardener before he volunteered with the Church Missionary Society (CMS), which trained him at the Preparatory Institute, Clapham (1889), and at their college in Islington, near London (1890-1893). For 24 years he served in Sierra Leone and Igboland (Nigeria). Assigned to Fourah Bay College, Sierra Leone, he showed commitment to hard work, excellent education, and love for African people. In Igboland, he devoted himself to evangelism, education, rigorous administration, and especially a new vernacular translation of the Bible incorporating elements from various dialects. He advanced the mission into central Igboland from 1906. Dennis earned Durham's B.A. (1897) and Oxford's honorary M.A. (1916) for his *Union Ibo Bible.* He died in a ship mishap. Miraculously, his Bible manuscript washed ashore, a gift from a caring, humble missionary. The first grammar school in Igboland—Dennis Memorial Grammar School, Onitsha (1925)—is a worthy tribute to the "greatest of all who have made a lasting impression on Igbo life and thought."

BIBLIOGRAPHY F. K. Ekechi, "The Missionary Career of the Venerable T. J. Dennis in West Africa, 1893-1917," *Journal of Religion in Africa* 9, no. 1 (1978): 1-26; Frances M. Hensley (née Dennis), *Niger Dawn* (n.d.; 1948?); G. O. M. Tasie, "Igbo Bible Nso and the Evolution of the Union Igbo, 1905-1913," *Journal of the Niger Delta Studies* 1, no. 2 (1977): 61-70.

Ogbu U. Kalu

Depelchin, Henri (1822-1900), Belgian Jesuit missionary in India. Born in Russignies, France, Depelchin entered the Society of Jesus in 1842. He studied theology and was a teacher for five years. He went to India in 1859, where he became the founder and first superior of the mission of the Belgian Jesuits in West Bengal. He first did "work in the bush" and later was a teacher. From 1864 to 1871 he was rector of the University College in Calcutta. During this time the number of students grew from 100 to 500. Afterward he wanted to work in the interior of the mission but instead had to take over the administration of St. Xavier's College in Bombay (1872-1876) and at the same time lecture in philosophy, dogmatics, church history, and exegesis. In 1878 he was called to Europe by the superior general to prepare for entering Africa and to organize the Zambezi mission there. Together with five priests and five brothers he arrived in Zambezi territory in 1879 and remained until 1883, when he returned to Belgium. In 1888 he went back to India as rector of St. Joseph's College in Darjeeling, in the Himalayas. At age 74 he was given responsibility for the initiation of the young Jesuit missionaries who made their third year of probation in Ranchi, the heart of the Khol mission. He died in Calcutta. His letters from India were published in numerous missionary periodicals in Europe. His letters and reports from the Zambezi mission were published in the collection *Trois ans dans l'Afrique australe* (1882 and 1883).

BIBLIOGRAPHY "Le Révérend Père Henri Depelchin," *Missions belges de la Compagnie de Jésus* (1900): 289-294 (obit.); E. Moreau, "Les exploits d'un missionaire belge: Le P. Depelchin et ses compagnons," *Revue du Clergé Africain* 1 (1946): 428-436.

Karl Müller, SVD

Desideri, Hippolytus (1684-1733), Jesuit scholar of Tibetan religion and culture. Born at Pistoja, Italy, Desideri entered the Society of Jesus in 1700 and went to India in 1712. Together with his companion, Manuel Freyre, he left for Tibet in 1714, starting from Delhi in the Mogul Empire, passing through Kashmir and Baltistan to Ladakh, and finally arriving in Lhasa. Desideri traveled all over Tibet visiting the main Buddhist monasteries and schools, studying the religion of the Tibetans and their sacred books, and writing refutations of their errors as well as treatises on Catholic doctrines (all in Tibetan). Desideri was not aware that in 1704 Propaganda Fide had entrusted the mission in Tibet to the Capuchin Fathers, and indeed up to 1716 he did not meet any Capuchins in Lhasa. After they arrived there was discussion between the Jesuits and the Capuchins both in Tibet and in Rome on the question of jurisdiction. Rome decided in 1718 to give exclusive rights to the Capuchins, and when in 1721 this was communicated to Desideri by his superior general in Rome, he left Tibet for India. He returned to Rome in 1727, where he later died. Desideri was an excellent scholar and a keen observer, and his Tibetan works are now being published.

BIBLIOGRAPHY G. Toscano, *Opere Tibetane di Ippolito Desideri S.J.*, 5 vols. (1981ff.); L. Petech, *I missionari italiani nel Tibet e nel Nepal*, pts. 5–7 (1954–1956; critical edition of Desideri's Italian letters and works). See also Augusto Luca, *Nel Tibet Ignoto: Lo straordinario viaggio di Ippolito Desideri S.J. (1684–1733)* (1987).

Arnulf Camps, OFM

De Smet, Pierre-Jean (1801–1873), Jesuit missionary to American Indians. De Smet went to the United States from his native Belgium in 1821 as a Jesuit novice and was sent to Saint Louis to help start the Jesuit center there. In 1837 he went with a group to begin a Jesuit mission to the Potawatomi Indians in Council Bluffs, Iowa, who were in desperate condition after being transplanted by the government from their homelands. But the Indians were not receptive, and in 1839 De Smet returned to Saint Louis. The next year he volunteered to answer the plea for missionaries which had been issued by the Flatheads in western Montana. There his reception was enthusiastic and he dreamed of creating a Christian republic under priestly guidance which would influence all the western tribes. But perhaps because of his efforts to transform these nomadic people into sedentary agriculturists and change their marriage patterns, the enthusiasm vanished and he left in 1842. For two years (1844–1846) he visited and administered five new missions that had come to the Pacific Northwest. His travels there included an arduous and perilous winter journey into the land of the Blackfoot Indians, during which he urged them to make peace with other tribes.

Thereafter his years were spent raising funds for missions, writing about the Indians, and undertaking peace expeditions at the request of the U.S. government. His fund-raising efforts included seven trips to Europe. In his peace expeditions he always tried to travel alone, rejecting government companions and protection, and he refused compensation. He was highly critical of the ways white men were treating Indians, pushing them into war, for he believed that war was suicidal for the Indians. His most famous exploit was in 1868, when he set out alone through hostile territory in time of war and persuaded the leaders of the Sioux to return with him to a peace council. Though he wanted the best for the Indians, ironically, the result of his pacification efforts was to open the country for white settlement.

BIBLIOGRAPHY Pierre-Jean De Smet, *Oregon Missions and Travels over the Rocky Mountains in 1845 and 1846* (1847, 1978) and *Western Missions and Missionaries: A Series of Letters* (1859, 1972). The largest publication of his papers is Hiram M. Chittenden and A. T. Richardson, eds., *Life, Letters, and Travels of Father Pierre-Jean De Smet, S.J., 1801–1873,* 4 vols. (1905, 1969). The standard biography is E. Laveille, *The Life of Father De Smet (1801–1873)* (1915, 1981). Two recent works are John J. Killoren, *"Come, Blackrobe": De Smet and the Indian Tragedy* (1994), and Robert C. Carriker, *Father Peter John De Smet: Jesuit in the West* (1995).

Charles W. Forman

Devanandan, Paul David (1901–1962), Indian theologian and pioneer in interreligious dialogue. Born in Madras, Devanandan studied at Nizam College, Hyderabad, and Presidency College, Madras, and did his theological studies at Pacific School of Religion in Berkeley, California. He later obtained his doctorate in comparative religion from Yale University, with a dissertation on the concept of maya in Hinduism. From 1932 to 1949 he was professor of philosophy and religions at United Theological College, Bangalore, India. From 1949 until 1956 he was with the Indian YMCA, first as secretary at the Delhi YMCA, and later as national literature secretary. In 1954 he was ordained a presbyter of the Church of South India. In 1956 he was appointed director of the Center for the Study of Hinduism, which later became the Christian Institute for the Study of Religion and Society (CISRS), Bangalore, from where he and his work are most known in the world church. With M. M. *Thomas he edited the journal *Religion and Society,* which was published by CISRS. Devanandan's contribution can rightly be described as preparation for dialogue because, at a time when conversations between Christians and people of other faiths were mostly controversies or monologues, he initiated a series of dialogues with Hindu scholars and thinkers. In doing so, he worked toward a deeper understanding of religions based on the actual experience of dialogue. Drawing attention to "the surging new life manifest in other religions," he affirmed, "It would be difficult for the Christian to deny that these deep, inner stirrings of the human spirit are in response to the creative activity of the Holy Spirit." Thus he prepared the way for a credible theology of religions. The new creation in Christ, the work of the Holy Spirit in history, the gathering of all people into the kingdom of God, and the call to witness to the renewing power of God in Christ are the major points in his theology. His address to the Third Assembly of the World Council of Churches at New Delhi in 1961, under the title "Called to Witness," delivered just a few months before his death, is a summing up of his convictions. He died at Dehra Dun, India.

BIBLIOGRAPHY Paul David Devanandan, *The Concept of Maya* (1950), *The Gospel and Renascent Hinduism* (1959), *Christian Concern in Hinduism* (1961), *Christian Issues in Southern Asia* (1963), *I Will Lift Up Mine Eyes,* S. J. Samartha and Nalini Devanandan, eds. (1963, a collection of sermons and Bible studies), *Preparation for Dialogue,* M. M. Thomas and Nalini Devanandan, eds. (1964), and *Selected Writings, with an Introduction,* Joachim Witzke, ed., 2 vols. (1983–1986). A personal tribute and a summary of Devanandan's theological contribution by S. J. Samartha was published in *IRM* 52 (1963): 183-194. Devanandan's papers and manuscripts are in the archives of United Theological College, Bangalore.

Stanley J. Samartha

Devasahayam, John (1786-1864), first South Indian Anglican priest and missionary. A third-generation Christian, Devasahayam was baptized by Christoph *John of the Royal Danish Tranquebar mission (whose name he took) and educated by C. F. *Schwartz. Entering the service of the Church Missionary Society (CMS) in 1815, he took over J. C. *Schnarre's work after the latter's death, then worked with G. T. Bärenbruck in Mayaveram. He was close to Carl *Rhenius but declined to follow him into schism. Ordained deacon in 1830 when Daniel *Corrie came to investigate the schism, he was ordained priest in 1836, the first South Indian to be ordained in the Anglican church. In 1844 he was transferred to Kadachapuram, Tinnevelly District with the status and responsibilities of a European missionary. Noted for his resolute stand against caste, Devasahayam's leadership qualities, spirituality, and achievements were outstanding. He married twice, both times to a granddaughter of the first Indian Lutheran minister (known only by his Christian name, Aaron).

Two of Devashahayam's sons achieved distinction in mission—Jesudasen John (in CMS service 1847-1889) and Samuel John, minister of Tucker Church, Madras, and an ecumenical pioneer. His daughter, Annal Arokium, a teacher in Kadachapuram, married a notable convert, W. T. *Satthianadhan, and on her husband's appointment to Zion Church, Madras, in 1861, she pioneered education systems for women in their homes.

BIBLIOGRAPHY Samuel John, *A Brief Memoir of the Revd John Devasahayam, First Native Minister of the Church of England in South India* (1895); Rajaiah Paul, *Chosen Vessels* (1961); S. Satthianadhan, *Sketches of Indian Christians: Collected from Different Sources* (1896).

E. M. Jackson

Deyneka, Peter (1898-1987), evangelist and founder of the Slavic Gospel Association. Born in Belorussia, Deyneka immigrated to the United States in 1914. In Chicago he encountered Russian members of the International Workers of the World and embraced atheism, but contacts with the gospel climaxed with his conversion under the ministry of Paul D. *Rader. From the start he exhibited a gift for evangelism, exercised not least in the Russian émigré communities of the Dakotas. Word of the 1918-1922 famine in Russia, which claimed members of his own family, spurred his desire to evangelize his homeland. Trips to Russia and eastern Europe in 1925-1926, 1930, and 1933 led to the founding of the Slavic Gospel Association (1934). Deyneka's extensive survey and preaching trips among Slavic peoples led to hundreds of young people entering Slavic ministries in North America, Argentina, Uruguay, Alaska, and in later years, in eastern Europe and the Union of Soviet Socialist Republics. In 1941 Deyneka pioneered in gospel broadcasts to Russia from radio station HCJB, Quito, Ecuador, an outreach that soon extended to Slavic peoples in eastern Europe and South America.

The Russian Bible Institute, launched by Deyneka and Oswald J. *Smith in Toronto in 1941 and transferred to Argentina in 1950, has trained hundreds of Slavic young people. Deyneka died in Wheaton, Illinois.

BIBLIOGRAPHY Norman B. Rohrer and Peter Deyneka, Jr., *Peter Dynamite: The Story of Peter Deyneka, Missionary to the Russian World* (1975).

Robert T. Coote

Dick, Amos Daniel Maurice (1894-1979), Brethren in Christ (BC) missionary in India. Dick was born in Mechanicsburg, Pennsylvania, and studied at Messiah College in Grantham, Pennsylvania. In 1918 he was ordained to the ministry, and went to India with his wife, Nellie, under the BC. He served there for 45 years, mostly in the province of Bihar, and in 1936 became superintendent and bishop of the denomination's missions in India. He read widely in the literature of India, including sacred Hindu texts. He was fluent in Hindi, Nepali, Bengali, and Urdu, and could read Sanskrit. His language facility and knowledge of Indian literature gave him access to prominent Indian leaders, including Mahatma Gandhi. In 1952 the Dicks moved to Ulubaria, West Bengal, where for ten years he was a superintendent with the Churches of God missions, and also taught at the Calcutta Bible College. On their return to the United States, Dick was pastor from 1962 to 1970 of the Silverdale BC Church in Pennsylvania.

BIBLIOGRAPHY Anna Engle et al., *There Is No Difference* (1950); *Evangelical Visitor,* December 10, 1979, pp. 5-7 (obit.).

E. Morris Sider

Dickson, James (1900-1967) *and*
Lillian (Glazier) (1901-1983), Canadian Presbyterian missionaries in Taiwan. The Dicksons were sent to Taiwan (Formosa) in 1927, where Canadian Presbyterians first opened work in 1865. Their names became known throughout the island for their work both with the native mountain tribespeople and with those of Chinese descent in the plains areas. They served in Taiwan until 1940, and after World War II from 1946 to 1964. During the war (1940-1946) they served in British Guiana. While the Dicksons were instrumental in establishing medical clinics, leprosy care, and other kinds of Christian service, they are best known for training pastors and establishing local churches. They spearheaded the growth of the church among the mountain people; 386 congregations, a theological institute, a monthly magazine, and many agricultural and self-help projects were established during their years of service. James Dickson was principal of the Taiwan Theological College for over 30 years; under him it grew from a small student body and two teachers to a seminary with 160 students and 11 professors. He also served on many agencies of the

General Assembly, synod and presbyteries of the Taiwan church, and on the boards of schools, hospitals, and evangelical organizations. Lillian Dickson developed and promoted through her newsletter world-famous "Mustard Seed" projects throughout the island.

BIBLIOGRAPHY Lillian Dickson, *These My People: Serving Christ Among the Mountain People of Formosa* (1958); Kenneth L. Wilson, *Angel at Her Shoulder: Lillian Dickson and Her Taiwan Mission* (1964). Obituaries and personal records exist in the archives of the Presbyterian Church in Canada, Knox College, Toronto.

Donald E. MacInnis

Dindinger, Johannes (1881–1958), missiologist, bibliographer, and librarian. Born at Heinrichsdorf, Lorraine, (now part of France), Dindinger joined the Missionary Oblates of Mary Immaculate in 1901. He studied in Rome, where he learned other European languages in addition to his mother tongues of German and French, and took a special interest in history. From 1908 to 1926 he taught philosophy at Hünfeld, Germany, where he met Robert *Streit, who invited him to collaborate in preparing the bibliography *Bibliotheca Missionum.* In that project he became acquainted with some of the pioneers of Catholic missiology such as Joseph *Schmidlin, A. Huonder, and Friedrich *Schwager. When Streit moved to Rome, he asked his superiors to assign Dindinger there as well so that he might continue to collaborate on the bibliography and build up the Pontifical Missionary Library, which had been founded in 1925. When Streit died in 1930, Dindinger was appointed director of the library, a position he held until his death. In collaboration with his assistant Johannes *Rommerskirchen, he compiled the first catalogue of the library: authors, subjects, periodicals, and a special catalogue of 530 languages. Dindinger also served as professor of mission history at the Missiological Institute of the Propaganda Fide Athenaeum from 1932 to 1948. He continued the *Bibliotheca Missionum* as editor of volumes 6–11 (Asia), 15–20 (Africa), and 21 (Australia and Oceania). In 1952 he received an honorary doctorate from the University of Münster.

BIBLIOGRAPHY Dindinger's 70th birthday Festschrift was *Missionswissenschaftliche Studien: Festgabe... Johannes Dindinger O.M.I.* (1951). His complete bibliography is in *Bibliografia Missionaria* 22 (1958): 4–6. Johannes Beckmann, "Hochwürden Herrn P. Dr. Johannes Dindinger O.M.I. zum 70. Geburtstag," *NZM* 7 (1951): 305–308; W. Henkel, "Johannes Dindinger," in Gerald H. Anderson et al., eds., *Mission Legacies* (1994), pp. 394–400.

Willi Henkel, OMI

Dirks, Heinrich (1842–1915), Mennonite missionary in Indonesia and missions promoter. Dirks was born in Gnadenfeld, Ukraine. In Germany his father had been influenced by the Moravian Brethren; after immigrating to Russia, the elder Dirks became a promoter of missions and church renewal among the Mennonites. Following secondary school, Heinrich Dirks went to Germany, where he studied at the Barmen Missions School, graduating in 1866. The next year he studied Javanese, Malay, Dutch, and English in Amsterdam. In 1869 he married Agnes Schroeder, was ordained for missionary service, and was sent to Indonesia by the Dutch Mennonite mission board. In 1871 he founded the Mennonite mission at Pakanten, Sumatra. The family returned to Russia in 1881 to educate their children. There Dirks exerted decisive influence among the Mennonites as an evangelist and promoter of missions. He also traveled widely in Germany, the Netherlands, and North America on behalf of the missionary cause. Nine couples and eleven single people from Russia entered missionary service as a result of his efforts. He instituted annual mission festivals and developed financial support for missions. A gifted writer and speaker, he was widely appreciated for his warm evangelical piety and concern to unify the churches.

BIBLIOGRAPHY P. M. Friesen, *Die Alt-Evangelische Mennonitische Bruederschaft in Russland, 1789–1910* (1911), pp. 265–266, 552–559; Waldemar Janzen, "Foreign Mission Interest of the Mennonites in Russia before World War I," *Mennonite Quarterly Review* 42, no. 1 (January 1968): 57–67; Gerhard Lohrenz, "The Mennonites of Russia and the Great Commission," in C. J. Dyck, ed., *A Legacy of Faith* (1962).

Wilbert R. Shenk

Doane, Edward T(oppin) (1820–1890), American Board of Commissioners for Foreign Missions (ABCFM) missionary in Pohnpei. Doane was born in Tomkinsville, Staten Island, New York, and graduated from Illinois College, Jacksonville, Illinois (1848), and Union Theological Seminary, New York (1854). Doane reached Pohnpei (then Ponape) in 1855, but in 1857 the mission there decided to send him with the pioneer mission group to the Marshall Islands, where he settled on Ebon. Following his wife's death, he returned to the United States in 1863, where he remarried, and then went back to Pohnpei in 1865. After a hostile chief burned a church and seized land, Doane asked an American warship to come and arrange restitution, which was done. From 1874 to 1879 he was in Japan and America because of his wife's health and her disaffection with him. Returning to Pohnpei alone, he carried on the work of teaching, supervising, and protecting the church. The arrival of Catholic missions along with the Spanish government in 1886 involved him in struggles to maintain the Protestant position. The Spanish governor had him arrested and taken to Manila for trial, which set off a storm of protest in America and an insurrection in Pohnpei. The governor was killed and the Spanish power fled the island. Doane was cleared of all charges in Manila and returned to Pohnpei in September 1887 in time to help negotiate the return of Spanish rule. All this weakened him and in 1890 sickness forced his departure for Honolulu, where he died.

BIBLIOGRAPHY David Hanlon, *Upon a Stone Altar: A History of the Island of Pohnpei to 1890* (1988); *The Missionary Herald at Home and Abroad,* August 1890, pp. 313–315.

Charles W. Forman

Dober, Johann Leonhard (1706–1766), first Moravian missionary and last chief elder of the Unity. Born in Münchsroth, Swabia, Dober joined his older brother Martin at Herrnhut in 1725 and the following year committed his life to the Savior. A potter by trade, he was assistant to Martin Linner as the leader of the Single Brothers' Choir. In 1731 he heard Count *Zinzendorf speak of the slave Anthony Ulrich, whom the count had met in Copenhagen, and after a sleepless night, Dober offered himself for mission service. His offer was confirmed by lot, and he set out for Saint Thomas on August 21, 1732, the first missionary of the Moravian Church.

Accompanied by David *Nitschmann, a carpenter, Dober found work as a watchman and labored among the slaves with little success until he contracted malaria and was nursed back to health by those to whom he had preached. In 1734 he was joined by another 18 missionaries, including a former companion, Tobias Leupold. In 1735 Dober returned to Herrnhut, where he had been elected chief elder of the Brethren's Unity on the death of Martin Linner. He married Anna Schindler in 1737.

The office of chief elder was that of intercessor for the church, chief arbiter of disputes, and spiritual head of the entire denomination. He filled the office for six years until 1741, when he resigned. The office was never again filled by a human, the lot confirming a decision to commit the office to Christ himself. He was consecrated a bishop on July 4, 1747, and continued to serve various congregations in Europe until the death of Zinzendorf, when he became part of the governing body of the Unity. Twelve of his hymns were published in the Brethren's hymnals. He died at Herrnhut.

BIBLIOGRAPHY *Gräfin von Zinzendorf, Christian David und Leonhard Dober in kurzen Umrissen* (1841); J. T. Hamilton and K. G. Hamilton, *History of the Moravian Church* (1967); L. Schneider, *Dober, der erste Missionar der Brüdergemeinde* (1906; 2d ed., 1932).

Albert H. Frank

Dobinson, Henry Hughes (1863–1897), Anglican archdeacon of the Niger. Dobinson was born in a well-to-do family at Stanwix, near Carlisle, England, and educated at Repton School and Brasenose College, Oxford. He was noted more for sporting than for academic prowess. He was ordained by Bishop Lightfoot after attending the latter's reading parties and served a curacy in Lightfoot's Durham diocese. In 1890 he joined his vicar, F. N. Eden, in offering to serve with the Church Missionary Society in West Africa. Dobinson and several men of similar background were appointed to the hitherto African-staffed Niger Mission of Bishop S. A. *Crowther. They represented a new type of missionary in Africa—upper class, well educated, confident, and possessing an eager spirituality stressing holiness and sacrifice. Dobinson shared in the events that led to Crowther's humiliation and the dismissal of most of the African staff, but he stayed in the mission longer than any of his European colleagues and came to lament publicly his earlier attitudes and actions. Empathetic and irenic, he impressed on successive missionary bishops the importance of "more trust on God and more trust in the Africans." He urged the recruitment of more African workers from Sierra Leone, valued the Niger Delta Pastorate (see D. C. *Crowther), and fought for its continued independence from missionary society control. He worked principally from Onitsha, where he devoted himself to the Igbo language (translating or revising parts of the Bible and prayer book), developed medical and educational work, and expanded the mission among the Igbos west of the Niger. In 1893 he became secretary of the Niger Mission (though he loathed administration) and was later archdeacon of the Niger under Bishop Tugwell. He died of fever in Onitsha at age 33.

BIBLIOGRAPHY Henry Hughes Dobson, *Letters of Henry Hughes Dobinson... with a Prefatory Memoir* (1899). Church Missionary Society, *Register of Missionaries* (1894 and 1904), no. 1137; P. E. H. Hair, *The Early Study of Nigerian Languages* (1967); G. O. M. Tasie, *Christian Missionary Enterprise in the Niger Delta, 1864–1918* (1978), esp. pp. 150ff.

Andrew F. Walls

Dobrizhoffer, Martin (1718–1791), Jesuit missionary in Paraguay. One of the more notable of the non-Spanish Jesuit missionaries in Paraguay, Dobrizhoffer's work on the Abipon Indians in the Argentine Chaco is a classic in ethnology. He was born in Bohemia and joined the Austrian province of the Society of Jesus in 1736. Sent to Paraguay in 1749, he spent 18 years working principally among the Abipon Indians, who were incorporated into the great mission system of the Guaraní Indians. A keen observer of native customs and rituals, he became fluent in their language. Before the expulsion of the Jesuits in 1767, he worked in the reduction (Indian settlement organized by the missionaries) of San Joaquín in the Gran Chaco, north of Asunción. After the expulsion, he spent his remaining years as a preacher at the court of Empress Maria Theresa of Austria. Fascinated by his stories of life in the missions, she urged him to put his experiences into writing. Between 1777 and 1782 Dobrizhoffer composed a three-volume history of the Abipones in Latin. Not long after his death, the work was translated into German and English; it is considered one of the key sources for the history of the Paraguay missions as well as a pioneering work in the field of ethnology.

BIBLIOGRAPHY Martin Dobrizhoffer, *History of the Abipones*, 3 vols., Sara Coleridge, tr. (1822). Philip Caraman, *The Lost Paradise: The Jesuit Republic in South America* (1975); Jerome V. Jacobsen, "Dobrizhoffer: Abipón Missionary," *Mid-America* 29 (1947): 122–131.

Jeffrey Klaiber, SJ

Dodge, Grace Hoadley (1856–1914), philanthropist, humanitarian, and founding president of the YWCA. Born into a mercantile family in New York City, Dodge devoted herself full time to the welfare of working girls and women. In 1881 she founded a club for factory women, the germ of a national association for working girls. She founded the Industrial Education Association and became the first woman appointed to the New York City Board of Education. Through her funds and leadership, the industrial association evolved into the Teachers College of Columbia University, with Dodge as treasurer until 1911. Her most impressive achievement was in unifying two Christian women's movements into the American Young Women's Christian Association and acting as its first president in 1906. An active Presbyterian of broad outlook, Dodge contributed to world mission in her work for the YWCA, promoting indigenous control of foreign YWCA workers. She oversaw the transformation of a small Congregational mission college in Turkey into Constantinople Woman's College. Dodge underwrote the expenses of Ruth *Rouse in establishing work among women for the World's Student Christian Federation. As a member of the Educational Commission she attended the World Missionary Conference at Edinburgh in 1910. She never married.

BIBLIOGRAPHY Margaret E. Burton, *Comrades in Service* (1919); Abbie Graham, *Grace H. Dodge: Merchant of Dreams* (1926); Marion O. Robinson, *Eight Women of the YWCA* (1966).

Dana L. Robert

Dodge, Ralph E(dward) (1907–), Methodist missionary and bishop in Africa. Dodge was born in Terril, Iowa, and educated at Taylor University, Indiana (B.A.), Boston University (M.A.), and Hartford Seminary Foundation (S.T.M., Ph.D.). Ordained in the Methodist Episcopal Church, he served as a missionary in Angola (1936–1950), as executive secretary for Africa, Board of Missions of the Methodist Church (1950–1956), and as a bishop for Rhodesia (now Zimbabwe, 1956–1968); he was reelected bishop for life. Churches under Dodge's leadership moved from being compliant partners with colonial white rule to becoming advocates of radical social change. António Agostinho Neto, Dodge's secretary in Angola, whom he enabled to study medicine in Portugal on a Methodist Crusade scholarship, later became founder and president of the Movimento Popular de Libertação de Angola (MPLA) and of the People's Republic of Angola. Dodge's friend Eduardo Mondlane became first president of Frente de Libertação de Moçambique (FRELIMO). Among the more than 100 Zimbabweans sponsored by Dodge and the Methodist Church for overseas study was Abel Tendekai Muzorewa, his successor as bishop, who became prime minister of Rhodesia.

With passionate commitment to African majority rule in both state and church, Dodge was expelled from Rhodesia in 1964 by the Ian Smith regime, but he was supported as president by the Southern Rhodesia Christian Conference and by his church. From exile in Zambia he authored *The Unpopular Missionary* (1964) and *The Pagan Church* (1968). Dodge retired in the United States in 1968.

BIBLIOGRAPHY Ralph E. Dodge, *The Revolutionary Bishop Who Saw God at Work in Africa* (1986; his autobiography). *Who's Who in the Methodist Church* (1966) and *The Encyclopedia of World Methodism* (1974) contain short biographies. Dickson A. Mungazi, *The Honoured Crusade: Ralph Dodge's Theology of Liberation and Initiative for Social Change in Zimbabwe* (1991) assesses Dodge as social reformer. Dodge's personal papers are in the Syracuse Univ. library.

Norman E. Thomas

Doig, Andrew Beveridge (1914–), Scottish missionary and church statesman. After study at Glasgow University and at Union Theological Seminary (New York), Doig was sent by the Church of Scotland Mission (CSM) to Blantyre, Malawi (then Nyasaland), in 1938. From 1941 to 1945 he served as a chaplain with Nyasaland troops in East Africa and Burma. In 1954 he was appointed to the parliament of the new, and short-lived, Federation of Nyasaland and the Rhodesias to represent African interests until white intransigence forced his resignation in 1958. Meanwhile, he played a large role in the integration of the CSM into the indigenous church, the Church of Central Africa Presbyterian. Back in Scotland in 1962 he served a parish in Dalkeith, then became secretary of the National Bible Society. In 1981 he was moderator of the General Assembly of the Church of Scotland.

Andrew C. Ross

Doke, Clement Martyn (1893–1980), pioneer scholar of Bantu linguistics. Doke was born in Bristol, England, grew up in New Zealand, and later moved to South Africa. In 1914 he was one of the founders of the Baptist Mission in Lambaland in Northern Rhodesia (now Zambia). As a result of his efforts to learn Lamba, he became convinced of the need to develop a framework that described Bantu languages in terms of their own internal structure; thus began a career in Bantu linguistics. Forced by illness to leave the mission field in 1920, he taught at the University of Witwatersrand, Johannesburg, from 1923 to 1953. In addition to more than 150 publications on Bantu linguistics, Doke edited the *South African Baptist* for 26 years, served as president of the Baptist Assembly in 1949, and was translator of the Bible into Lamba.

BIBLIOGRAPHY *African Studies* 30, nos. 3 and 4 (1971) contain a tribute to Doke and a list of his publications. Desmond T. Cole, *African Studies* 39, no. 1 (1980) (obit.); G. Fortune, "Clement Martyn Doke: A Biographical and Bibliographical Sketch," in *Catalogue of the C. M. Doke Collection on African Languages in the Library of the University of Rhodesia* (contains an extensive catalog of Doke's books and MSS). Wilma Meier, ed., *Bibliographie afrikanischer Sprachen* (1984; contains a language-related bibliography).

Philip C. Stine

Doke, Joseph John (1861–1913), English Baptist minister and missionary. Doke was born in Chudleigh, Devon, where his father served 34 years as pastor of a Baptist church. After moving to South Africa for health reasons, he organized Baptist work and was ordained at Graaff-Reinet in 1882. In 1886, after his marriage to Agnes Hannah Biggs, a descendant of William *Carey, Doke returned to England. He ministered as pastor of Chudleigh Baptist Church (1887–1888) and City Road Baptist Church, Bristol (1889–1894). A call to mission service led him to New

Zealand (1894–1901), Grahamstown, South Africa (1903–1907), and Johannesburg (1907–1913). He served as president of the South African Baptist Union (1906–1907). His arrival in Johannesburg coincided with Gandhi's campaigns on behalf of South Africa's Indian population. Aligning himself with Ghandi's cause, he protested against unjust racial laws and published the first biography of Gandhi, *M. K. Gandhi: An Indian Patriot in South Africa* (1909).

In July 1913, in memory of his missionary brother, William Henry Doke, Doke and his son Clement Martyn *Doke set out to explore the possibilities for evangelizing central Africa. (The journey was financed through the publication of Doke's novel, *The Secret City: A Romance of the Karroo* [1913].) Doke died en route, at Umtali, in what was then Southern Rhodesia (Zimbabwe). At the memorial service in Johannesburg, Ghandi praised Doke's Christian vision of love conquering hatred and virtue overcoming vice.

BIBLIOGRAPHY F. W. Boreham, *The Man Who Saved Gandhi: A Short Biography of John Joseph Doke* (1948); William E. Cursons, *Joseph Doke, The Missionary-Hearted* (1929); James D. Hunt, *Gandhi and the Nonconformists: Encounters in South Africa* (1986). The Baptist Theological College of Southern Africa, Johannesburg, houses documents relating to Doke and Gandhi.

Paul R. Dekar

Dole, Charlotte (Close) Knapp (1813–1874), American missionary teacher in Hawaii. Dole was born Charlotte Close in Greenwich, Connecticut. She arrived in Hawaii in 1837 with her first husband, Horton O. Knapp, in the eighth company of missionaries sent by the American Board of Foreign Missions (ABCFM). They served at Waimea, Hawaii, for a year; at Lahainaluna, Maui, until 1839; then at Honolulu, where Horton Knapp died in March 1845. In June 1846 Charlotte married Daniel Dole of the ninth company, a widower who was principal of the mission's Punahou school in Honolulu and was stationed after 1855 as pastor-teacher at Koloa, Kauai. Charlotte Dole's varied accomplishments included proficiency in Hebrew, Greek, Latin, and "all kitchen branches of information into the bargain." She was one of many New England women who introduced special skills—praying, reading, teaching, weaving, and quilting—to the Hawaiian church. She died in Honolulu four years before her husband.

BIBLIOGRAPHY *Missionary Album: Portraits and Biographical Sketches of the American Protestant Missionaries to the Hawaiian Islands* (1969). Papers relating to Charlotte Dole and her two husbands are in the Hawaiian Mission Children's Society Library, Honolulu. Other materials are in the ABCFM collection of Sandwich Islands papers at the Houghton Library, Harvard Univ.

John Garrett

Doll, Ludwig (1846–1883), German missions advocate. Doll was born into the family of a pastor in Kirchen an der Sieg, Germany, and at age 20 had a dramatic conversion experience. He studied theology at various universities and while in Berlin was influenced by the piety of the Berlin Mission. In 1872 he was named the assistant pastor at the Neukirchen, Moers (Rhineland), church of Andreas Bräm (1797–1882), a prominent revival preacher and founder of the Neukirchen Educational Association. After his ordination in 1873, he succeeded Bräm as pastor. A man of deep faith, in 1878 Doll founded an orphanage on the George *Müller model, and then, in 1882, purchased a building to use as a mission house where people could be trained for foreign service. Although Doll died the following year, Engelbert Julius *Stursberg (1857–1909), who had joined the pastoral staff in 1880, brought his dream of a thriving mission society to fruition. The Neukirchener Mission still functions as a faith mission and has close ties with the German Evangelical Alliance.

BIBLIOGRAPHY Ulrich Affeld, *Er mache uns im Glauben kühn: 100 Jahre Neukirchener Mission* (1978); Wilhelm Nitsch, *Unter dem offenen Himmel: Aus der Geschichte der Waisen- und Missionsanstalt Neukirchen, 1878–1928* (1928); Karl Rahn, *Dennoch gestrost: 75 Jahre Waisen und Missionsanstalt Neukirchen* (1953).

Richard V. Pierard

Dominic (1170–1221), founder of the Order of Friars Preachers, or Dominicans. Dominic was born in Calaruega, Spain, of the Guzman family. He became a canon of Osma in 1199 and in 1203 accompanied his bishop, Diego, on a preaching mission directed to the conversion of the Albigensian sect in southern France. This early experience persuaded him of the need for a mendicant band of itinerant preachers who would be free of the monastic obligations theretofore characteristic of all religious communities in the church. Dominic drew his inspiration from the example of the missionary activities of the apostles as recounted in Acts. By 1216 Dominic won the approval of Pope Honorius III for such a new religious community called the Order of Preachers. With a sophisticated governmental structure, this order of friars (as distinct from monks) was to follow the rule of *Augustine and the religious observances of the abbey of Premontré but be free of any monastic commitment to a particular place. Dominic saw prayer, poverty, mobility, and solid theological training as fundamental to the success of missionary preaching in the evangelical model. The first friars were sent to university towns throughout Europe, and soon flourishing Dominican communities developed at Paris, Bologna, Madrid, and Rome. Although he never realized his dream personally to evangelize the Cuman Tartars in eastern Europe, Dominic's friars were already active there by the time of his death at Bologna. He was canonized in 1234.

BIBLIOGRAPHY Guy Bedouelle, *Saint Dominic: The Grace of the Word* (1987); F. C. Lehner, ed., *Saint Dominic: Biographical Documents* (1964); M. H. Vicaire, *Saint Dominic and His Times* (1964).

Joseph DiNoia, OP

Donaldson, Dwight Martin (1884–1976), missionary in Iran and India, and Islamic scholar. An American Presbyterian from Ohio, Donaldson first became acquainted with Islam in India, where he taught for three years at Forman College, Lahore (1907–1910). Following theological education in Pittsburgh and Harvard, he served as a Presbyterian missionary in Meshed, one of the holy cities of Shi'i Islam in the Khorasan province of northeastern Iran. For 26 years (1914–1940) he shared his faith with Shi'i religious leaders, at the same time learning of their faith from them. His wealth of knowledge was invested in a doctoral thesis for the Hartford Seminary Foundation's Kennedy School of Missions on the history and doctrines of the twelve Imams of mainstream Shi'ism. His wife, Elizabeth, added a further dimension to their research through her study of popular Islam in Iran.

In 1940 the Donaldsons were called to India, where Dwight succeeded Lewis Bevan *Jones as principal of the Henry Martyn School of Islamic Studies in Aligarh. Committed to training Christians for missionary service among Muslims, the institute under his leadership maintained a cordial academic relationship with Aligarh (Muslim) University that continued through the political turmoil of Indian partition in 1947. His decision to keep the institute in India, rather than move it to Pakistan, reflected his hope that the liberal trends of Indian Islam would be more hospitable to Christian witness. The Donaldsons retired to the United States in 1951, where they continued to write on aspects of formal and popular Islam.

BIBLIOGRAPHY Dwight Donaldson, *The Shi'ite Religion: A History of Islam in Persia and Irak* (1933) and *Studies in Muslim Ethics* (1953); Elizabeth Donaldson, *The Wild Rose: A Study of Muhammedan Magic and Folklore in Iran* (1938) and *Prairie Girl in Iran and India* (1972). William Miller, "Dwight Martin Donaldson," *Al-Basheer, the Bulletin of the Christian Institutes of Islamic Studies* 5 (1976): 105–108.

David A. Kerr

Donders, Peter (1809–1887), Dutch missionary in Surinam. Born at Tilburg, Netherlands, Donders was ordained priest in 1841 and volunteered for the mission in Surinam in 1842. This mission was entrusted to the secular clergy from the Netherlands, of which Donders was a member. After the mission was handed over to the Redemptorist Fathers in 1865, Donders received admission into that congregation. He engaged in pastoral work in the capital of Paramaribo and in the plantations. For 27 years he was the pastor of the leprosarium of Batavia, Surinam, and also did missionary work among the Indians and African Americans. His spirituality stressed self-sacrifice in the service of God, listening to the will of God in prayer, and striving after unity with God through the Holy Eucharist. He died at Batavia. On March 25, 1945, his virtues were recognized by the Vatican as being heroic. On May 23, 1982, he was beatified by Pope *John Paul II in Rome.

BIBLIOGRAPHY J. L. F. Dankelman, *Peerke Donders, schering en inslag* (1982) and *Twee missionarissen onder de Melaatsen en Indianen van Suriname (P. Donders en J. B. Romme)* (1894); Historical Institute of the Redemptorists, *Studia Dondersiana* (1982). From Donders's correspondence, 53 letters have been preserved in the general archives of the Redemptorists in Rome.

Arnulf Camps, OFM

Dooley, Thomas Anthony (1927–1961), jungle doctor of Laos. Dooley was born in Saint Louis, Missouri, of a wealthy family involved in railcar manufacturing. He attended the University of Notre Dame and, after graduating from the Saint Louis University School of Medicine in 1954, enlisted in the United States Navy Medical Corps. He was assigned to a task force aiding the transplantation of refugees from North Vietnam to South Vietnam following the defeat of the French by the Vietminh at Dienbienphu. Dooley's work among the eight hundred thousand Catholics fleeing communism was chronicled in his best-selling work *Deliver Us from Evil* (1956). After being discharged from the Navy because of his homosexuality in 1956, Dooley returned to southeast Asia as a private citizen to establish village clinics in Laos on behalf of the International Rescue Committee and, later, MEDICO, a private nonsectarian agency he helped found in 1958. Dooley was often assumed to be a Catholic missionary, an impression he struggled to overcome. The great majority of his moral and financial support in the United States came from Catholics who viewed Dooley as a saintly figure serving Laos peasants threatened by communism as well as disease, a view dramatically heightened when Dooley contracted malignant melanoma in 1959. Though critics accused Dooley of egocentricity and unsound medical practices, he continued with his work until his death at the age of thirty-four.

BIBLIOGRAPHY Thomas Anthony Dooley, *The Edge of Tomorrow* (1958) and *The Night They Burned the Mountain* (1960). James Terence Fisher, *"Dr. America": The Lives of Thomas A. Dooley, 1927–1961* (1996) and *The Catholic Counterculture in America, 1933–1962* (1989).

James T. Fisher

Doremus, Sarah Platt (Haines) (1802–1877), founder of the Woman's Union Missionary Society. Doremus was the wife of a New York City merchant and mother of nine children. She became a member of the Dutch Reformed Church when she married, and continued her Presbyterian family's tradition of mission interest and charitable activity. In 1828 she organized a ladies' relief society to alleviate the suffering of Greek women. She helped to found and lead the Women's Prison Association and the New York House and School of Industry. She founded the Nursery and Child's Hospital, the Presbyterian Home for Aged Women, and the Woman's Hospital in New York City. She also distributed tracts, collected medical supplies, and raised funds for worthy causes.

Doremus became interested in foreign missions as a child. In 1834, when David *Abeel, first Dutch Reformed missionary from the United States, returned from five years in China, she arranged for him to speak to women in New York on the necessity of women organizing themselves to send missionaries. However, Rufus *Anderson of the American Board of Commissioners for Foreign Missions opposed the idea of a women's organization and the women deferred to his authority. But in 1861, after hearing a missionary from Burma tell of the needs of women, Doremus became founding president of the Woman's Union Missionary Society (WUMS), the first American non-denominational women's missionary society, whose object was to send single women as teachers and missionaries to Asia. From its headquarters, at her home, she directed its activities until her death. Throughout her life, Doremus assisted missionaries of many denominations by providing hospitality, outfits, money, correspondence, and support. Besides the WUMS, she raised money for schools in Hawaii and in 1835 organized a mission society to support Swiss Baptist work in Canada. An ecumenist at heart, she made the first financial contribution for Methodist women's work in North India.

BIBLIOGRAPHY Mrs. Doremus's life was reviewed in the memorial issue of the March 1877 *Missionary Link.* See also Annie Ryder Gracey, *Eminent Missionary Women* (1898). For her mission influence in the Dutch Reformed Church, see Mrs. W. I. Chamberlain, *Fifty Years in Foreign Fields* (1925). The archives of the Woman's Union Missionary Society are located at the Billy Graham Center in Wheaton, Ill.

Dana L. Robert

Dorville, Albert (1621–1662), Jesuit missionary in China and Tibet. A native of Brussels, Belgium, Dorville entered the Society of Jesus in 1646 at Landsberg, Germany. Eleven years later he left Lisbon, Portugal, bound for Macao, which he reached in July 1658. After two years of language training, he was sent to Kiangchow (present-day Xinjiang), in Shansi (Shanxi) Province. His missionary endeavors there were cut short, since he was ordered to go to Sian (Xi'an), Shensi (Shaanxi) Province to meet Johannes *Grüber. The Jesuit superior general in Rome had instructed Johann Adam *Schall von Bell, then in Peking (Beijing), to assist Grüber to find a land route from China to Europe or to India. This would avoid the many dangers and long delays that occurred on trips taken by way of the Cape of Good Hope, the Indian Ocean, and the South China Sea. Accompanied by a Muslim interpreter, Dorville and Grüber left Sian and in three months they crossed the deserts through Tsinghai (Qinghai) Province and entered Tibet. They spent two months at the capital, Lhasa, and then proceeded to Nepal, Bengal, Benares, and finally Agra, in India. The trip, which lasted 214 days not counting stopovers, weakened Dorville, and he died in Agra on Holy Saturday.

BIBLIOGRAPHY Henri Bosmans, "Documents sur Albert Dorville," *Analectes pour servir à l'histoire ecclésiastique de la Belgique* 37 (1911): 329–384, 470–497; Henry Heras, "The Tomb of Father Albert d'Orville," *Archivum Historicum Societatis Jesu* 2 (1933): 17–24; Cornelis Wessels, *Early Jesuit Travelers in Central Asia, 1603–1721* (1924), pp. 164–204.

John W. Witek, SJ

Douglas, Carstairs (1839–1877), Scottish Presbyterian missionary in China. A son of the manse, Douglas was educated at the University of Glasgow and trained for the ministry at the Free Church Divinity School. During his final year he was recruited by William *Burns, the pioneer missionary of the Presbyterian Church in England, for work in China. Ordained in 1855, he worked throughout his life in south Fukien (Fujian), the first missionary to be supported by the Scottish Auxiliary of the English Presbyterian Mission. He devoted himself, for some periods without any missionary colleagues, to extending and developing a self-supporting, self-propagating Chinese church, training church workers, and producing the standard Chinese-English dictionary of the Amoy language, published in 1873. When he died, the single congregation at Pehchuia (Baichuan) had grown into a church of twenty-five congregations organized as a presbytery that was predominantly Chinese in membership. After visiting Taiwan in 1860 and during his first furlough in 1862, he persuaded the foreign missions committee of the Presbyterian Church in England to undertake work there. In 1863 he again visited Taiwan, accompanied by J. L. Maxwell, who in 1865, following language study in Amoy, became its first resident English Presbyterian missionary.

The University of Glasgow honored Douglas with an LL.D. for his Amoy dictionary, and his British missionary colleagues were unanimous in choosing him as one of the two joint chairmen (British and American) of the 1877 Shanghai Missionary Conference. Soon after that conference he died of cholera at the age of 47, with the reputation of never having wasted a moment of his life.

BIBLIOGRAPHY Edward Band, *Working His Purpose Out* (1947); J. M. Douglas, *Memorials of Rev. Carstairs Douglas, M.A., LL.D.* (1877).

George A. Hood

Draper, Minnie Tingley (1858–1921), faith healer and missions executive. Born in Waquit, Massachusetts, Draper grew up in Ossining, New York, and became a member of the Presbyterian Church. Later, in broken health and with little assistance from the medical profession, she visited A. B. *Simpson's Gospel Tabernacle in New York City and subsequently testified to miraculous healing.

Draper eventually became an associate of Simpson, assisting him in prayer for the sick at various conventions of the Christian and Missionary Alliance (C&MA). Beginning in 1906, she identified increasingly with the Pentecostal movement, and she left the C&MA in 1912 because it rejected the evidential nature of speaking in tongues for baptism in the Holy Spirit.

Draper helped found the Bethel Pentecostal Assembly in Newark, New Jersey. As board chairwoman at the Newark church, she helped establish and directed until her death the Pentecostal Mission in South and Central Africa (1910). The large Full Gospel Church of God in South Africa represents an important legacy of this mission agency. Initial efforts in Central Africa, however, developed under another Pentecostal agency, the Zaire Evangelistic Mission, founded by William F. *Burton and James Salter.

Draper also helped initiate, in 1916, the Bethel Bible Training School in Newark, New Jersey. Many of the graduates joined the Assemblies of God and held important posts of leadership.

BIBLIOGRAPHY C. J. Lucas, "In Memoriam," *Full Gospel Missionary Herald* (April 1921): 3–5; Gary B. McGee, "Three Notable Women in Pentecostal Ministry," *Assemblies of God Heritage* 1 (1986): 3–5, 12, 16; Charles W. Nienkirchen, *A. B. Simpson and the Pentecostal Movement* (1922).

Gary B. McGee

Draskóczy, László (1905–1967), Hungarian missions leader. Draskóczy, a Reformed pastor, was born in Khust (Hungarian: Huszt), a city in the eastern foothills of the Carpathian mountains, in what is present-day Ukraine. He gained a vision for missions during his student days and served in various capacities with the Hungarian Reformed Foreign Mission Society from 1929 to 1949. He wrote over a hundred articles on foreign missions, edited the Reformed mission periodical *Hajnal* (Dawn), and co-edited the missiological journal *Református Külmissiói Szemle* (Reformed foreign mission review) as well as the successful popular series *Missziói Füzetek* (Mission brochures). He emphasized the special missionary calling of Hungarian Christians to work among the Muslims in the Balkans. He wrote a book on the history of Hungarian mission work (1940), and therefore could be considered the first Hungarian mission historian. After World War II he advocated Hungary's participation in mission work in Indonesia. He protested against limiting the scope of mission as imposed by the postwar Hungarian regime. In 1949 Hungarian foreign mission involvement was officially banned, and he was given a minor administrative position in the church. In 1956 he tried in vain to reestablish the Hungarian Foreign Mission Society.

BIBLIOGRAPHY László Draskóczy, *A Magyar keresztyénség külmissziói szolgálata* (The foreign mission ministry of Hungarian Christianity) (1940), *Hősők és vértanuk: Képek a misszió történetéből* (Heroes and martyrs: Pictures from mission history) (1943), and *Mindhalálig* (Till death) (1948). Anne-Marie Kool, *God Moves in a Mysterious Way: The Hungarian Protestant Foreign Mission Movement (1756–1951)* (1993).

Anne-Marie Kool

Drebert, Ferdinand (1890–1981), Moravian missionary and Bible translator in Alaska. Born in Volhynia, Russia, Drebert emigrated with his family to Alberta, Canada, when he was four years old. After graduating from Moravian College and Theological Seminary in Bethlehem, Pennsylvania (1912), he was ordained a deacon of the Moravian Church and entered mission service in Alaska. Drebert's first assignment was to establish a mission station at Kwigillingok, on the west coast of Kuskokwim Bay. In 1917 he married Marie Stecker, daughter of Moravian missionaries and missionary teacher in Alaska. In 1920 they were transferred to Quinhagak, on the eastern coast. From there Drebert traveled extensively by dog team, doing evangelistic and pastoral work. In 1931 he moved to the headquarters at Bethel and in 1939 became superintendent of all Moravian work in Alaska. It was in large part through his efforts that that mission survived during World War II, when southwestern Alaska was threatened with invasion. Drebert was one of the few missionaries to master the Yup'ik Eskimo language. His most significant contribution was a translation of the New Testament completed shortly before his retirement in 1954.

BIBLIOGRAPHY *Alaska Missionary* (1959) is Drebert's autobiography. James W. Henkelman and Kurt Vitt, *Harmonious to Dwell: The History of the Alaska Moravian Church, 1885–1985* (1985); Anna B. Schwalbe, Gertrude Trodahl, and Harry Trodahl, *Dayspring on the Kuskokwim: The Story of Moravian Missions in Alaska* (1985). Drebert's letters and papers are in the Moravian Archives, Bethlehem, Pennsylvania. The Moravian Archives, Bethel, Alaska, holds an extensive collection of photographs that Drebert took between 1912 and 1954.

Otto Dreydoppel, Jr.

Drexel, Katherine (1858–1955), founder of the Sisters of the Blessed Sacrament. Drexel was born in Philadelphia, Pennsylvania. The second daughter of a wealthy banking family, she was educated privately by tutors. With her two sisters, she was taught from her earliest years to share her wealth with the poor. She understood the emerging cultural ethos of the United States during the late nineteenth and early twentieth centuries. She perceived the special importance of education as an instrument of change and used her influence and wealth to develop educational opportunities for Native Americans and African Americans. These efforts eventually led her, in 1891, to establish a religious order of women, the Sisters of the Blessed Sacrament, to carry on this work. Drexel served as superior general of the order until 1937. In spite of strong resistance, she founded educational institutions for African Americans in the racially segregated parts of the United States. Of these, Xavier University, New Orleans, was the first Catholic institution of higher learning for African Americans; it received its charter as a college of liberal arts and sciences in 1925 and became a university in 1932. In 1954, Xavier became integrated to include students without regard to race or creed. Today, the religious community founded by Drexel continues to work for interracial justice.

BIBLIOGRAPHY Katherine Burton, *The Golden Door: The Life of Katherine Drexel* (1957); C. M. Duffy, *Katherine Drexel: A Biography* (1966); Boniface Hanley, "A Philadelphia Story," *The Anthonian* 58, no. 11 (1984); Elizabeth Letterhouse, *The Francis A. Drexel Family* (1939). The personal papers of Katherine Drexel are in the archives of the Sisters of the Blessed Sacrament, Bensalem, Pennsylania.

Mary Motte, FMM

Droese, Ernest (1817–1891), pioneering German missionary in North India. Born in Toruń (Thorn), West Prussia (presently Poland), Droese was a silver- and goldsmith by profession, until he trained at the seminary of the Berlin Mission Society and went to India in 1842. There he first evangelized among Hindus and Muslims in Ghazipur (lower Ganges, Uttar Pradesh) and also briefly for the London Missionary Society, in Benares (presently Varanasi, Uttar Pradesh). When the Berlin Society ended its involvement in India in 1849, Droese joined the Church Missionary Society, which in 1850 commissioned him for pioneering work in Bhagalpur (lower Ganges, Bihar). Supported by the British colonial government, he established a mission center by founding a church, schools, and orphanages. His main focus, however, was evangelizing the Paharis, an animistic hill tribe in the Rajmahal Hills. Within the first ten years he baptized over 500. He translated the Gospels, the Psalms, and the Book of Common Prayer into Malto, their Dravidian language, and wrote grammar books and dictionaries. He was also a pioneer missionary in Santal country and founded schools in several places. After nearly half a century of mission work, Droese retired in 1888 to Mussoorie in the Himalaya region. His daughter, following her father's example, joined the mission and distinguished herself in Urdu and Hindi literature.

BIBLIOGRAPHY A. W. Baumann, "The Late Rev. E. Droese," *Church Missionary Intelligencer* 42 (1891): 758–769; Julius Richter, *Geschichte der Berliner Mission* (1924), pp. 134–138; Eugene Stock, *The History of the Church Missionary Society,* vol. 3 (1899), pp. 187–190.

Werner Raupp

Druillettes, Gabriel (1610 or 1613–1681), French missionary priest, diplomat, and explorer in New France (Canada). Born in Garat, Limoges, France, Druillettes (or Dreuillette and other variations) joined the Society of Jesus in 1629 and left for New France in 1643. He quickly mastered the local Algonquian language and spent two years with the people, accompanying them to their winter hunting grounds, as he also did subsequently many times in his missionary career. In 1646 he opened a mission among the Abenaki Indians and went as far as the Penobscot River near present-day Augusta, Maine, where he met Capuchin missionaries. In 1650 government officials of Quebec sent him to Boston to negotiate an "eternal alliance" between New England and New France. In 1661 he and fellow Jesuit Claude *Dablon undertook a voyage toward Hudson Bay, officially to explore the possibilities for the mission but also in search of a passage to the "Sea of Japan." They got as far as Nékouba (Nikabau), near Lake Mistassini in central Quebec, when news of an Iroquois invasion made them turn back. Druillettes died in Quebec.

BIBLIOGRAPHY Thomas J. Campbell, *Pioneer Priests of North America,* vol. 3 (1911), pp. 70–109; Marie de S.-Jean d'Ars, "A la recherche de la mer du Nord, 1661," *Revue d'histoire de l'Amérique Française* 8 (1954): 220–235; Camille de Rochemonteix, *Les Jésuites et la Nouvelle-France au XVIIe siècle,* vols. 1 and 2 (1896); R. G. Thwaites, ed., *The Jesuit Relations,* vol. 32 (1898), pp. 94–112, vol. 36 (1899), pp. 83–111, and vol. 46 (1899), pp. 247–295.

Achiel Peelman, OMI

Drummond, Henry (1851–1897), Scottish evangelist, biologist, and apologist. Born in Stirling, Scotland, Drummond entered the arts class of the University of Edinburgh in 1866 and proceeded to New College in 1870 to train for the ministry. His interests, however, centered more on science than on theology. He later confessed that he never had any intention of becoming a minister, though he was eventually ordained. In 1873 he was caught up in the Moody-Sankey evangelistic campaigns and proved to have extraordinary gifts as an evangelist, especially, though not exclusively, to young people. His admiration for Dwight L. *Moody was unbounded. In 1877 he was appointed lecturer in natural science (zoology, botany, and geology, together with the relations of science to religion) at New College, Edinburgh, and in 1884 he took up a similar post in Glasgow, at which time he was ordained. His evangelistic work continued, but it was the publication in 1883 of his controversial book *Natural Law in the Spiritual World* that made him famous. It urged that science and religion, natural law and spiritual law, are one and the same, governed by identical laws and it won him many friends and many enemies. In his last years, Drummond traveled the world and made many acute observations on missionary matters. A consummate stylist in all he did, said, and wrote, he had a powerful influence on students in the 1880s and 1890s. He died in 1897 of an unidentified disease perhaps contracted in Africa a decade earlier.

BIBLIOGRAPHY Cuthbert Lennox, *Henry Drummond: A Biographical Sketch* (1901); George Adam Smith, *The Life of Henry Drummond,* 2d ed. (1899). For memorial sketches by W. Robertson Nicoll and Ian Mclaren, see Henry Drummond, *The Ideal Life and Other Unpublished Addresses by Henry Drummond* (4th ed., 1899).

Eric J. Sharpe

Dubois, Jean Antoine (c. 1765–1848), Catholic missionary in India. Born in Saint-Remèze (Ardèche), France, Dubois was ordained a priest in the diocese of Viviers in 1792. He left for India the same year as a member of the Missions Etrangères de Paris (MEP), to work in the Pondicherry mission. He worked for a few years in Tamil Nadu and later moved to Mysore. In Seringapatam, he tried to reconvert Christians who had become Muslims under Tippu Sultan, a local Muslim chieftain. To help the Christians he founded agricultural colonies, the principal one being in Sathalli, near Hassan. He also encouraged vaccination against smallpox on a mass scale. In order to promote knowledge about the people of South India he compiled (in French) *Hindu Manners, Customs, and Ceremonies,* for which he is most widely remembered. He returned to France in 1823 as director of MEP and was superior general from 1836 to 1839.

Dubois maintained that it was impossible to convert high-caste Hindus to Christianity. He himself had made between 200 and 300 converts, two-thirds of whom were outcastes. He translated into French the *Pancha-Tantra* (Five tricks—a book of fables) and *The Exploits of the Guru Paramartha* (humorous stories by the Jesuit missionary C. G. *Beschi).

BIBLIOGRAPHY Dubois's principal work, *Hindu Manners,* was first published in 1806 and revised and enlarged in 1821. The shorter first edition was first published in English, edited by G. U. Pope, in 1816. The enlarged version was translated and edited by Henry K. Beauchamp (3d ed., 1906). Dubois also authored *Letters on the State of Christianity in India,* which was published together with *A Vindication of the Hindoos* in London in 1823. See also J. Hough, *A Reply to the Letters of the Abbé Dubois on the State of Christianity in India* (1824).

Michael Amaladoss, SJ

Dubose, Hampden Coit (1845-1910), Presbyterian missionary in China and founder of the Anti-Opium League. A native of South Carolina and a graduate of Columbia (South Carolina) Theological Seminary, Dubose arrived in China with his wife, Pauline (McAlpine), in 1872 and settled in Suzhou (Soochow), a city of gardens and canals. He served there 38 years until his death. Although an eloquent preacher to non-Christian audiences, he is best remembered as the founder of the Anti-Opium League. The league sought to publish facts about the curse of opium and mobilize public opinion against its trade. To this end Dubose enlisted the support of President Theodore Roosevelt, the U.S. Congress, and the International Opium Commission. Success came in 1906 when the British Parliament declared the trade "morally indefensible." A petition signed by over a thousand China missionaries was presented to the emperor. An imperial edict, following verbatim the petition Dubose had drafted, prohibited its trade and use. He was honored in Suzhou by the erection of a stone tablet and in the United States by being elected moderator of the General Assembly of the Presbyterian Church, U.S. (Southern) in 1891.

BIBLIOGRAPHY Hampden Coit Dubose, *Preaching in Sinim: The Gospel to the Gentiles, with Hints and Helps for Addressing a Heathen Audience* (1873), *The Image, the Dragon, and the Demon: Or the Three Religions of China—Confucianism, Buddhism, and Taoism* (1887), and *Memoirs of Dr. J. Leighton Wilson* (1895). Dubose also published a popular book of sermons and a number of Bible study aids in Chinese. Nettie Dubose Junkin, ed., *For the Glory of God: Memoirs of Dr. and Mrs. H. C. Dubose* (c. 1910); P. Frank Price, *Our China Investment* (1927).

G. Thompson Brown

Duchesne, Rose Philippine (1769-1852), frontier missionary among Native Americans. Duchesne was born in Grenoble, France. After the upheavals of the French Revolution, she became a member of the newly founded Society of the Sacred Heart of Jesus and resolved to offer her life by teaching in a foreign land. To fulfill this vow, she arrived in 1818 with four other members of the Sacred Heart at Saint Charles, Missouri, where she established the first free school west of the Mississippi and was responsible for the congregation's work with Native Americans beginning in 1825 at Florissant, Missouri. Rather than having Indians come to schools in town, Duchesne believed that living among them was a better way to "change their nature." She personally carried out this approach when she was 71 years of age and in diminished health. She went among the Potawatomis at Sugar Creek (Kansas), where the Indians called her the Woman-Who-Prays-Always. Called back by her superior after one year, she died in Saint Louis.

Duchesne struggled throughout her life with the tension between the cloister and the needs of the missions, as well as with the prevailing attitude that missions were the work of men and not of women. She was beatified in 1940 and canonized by Pope *John Paul II in 1988.

BIBLIOGRAPHY Louise Callan, *Philippine Duchesne: Frontier Missionary of the Sacred Heart, 1769-1852* (1957); Marjory Erskine, *Mother Philippine Duchesne* (1926); Mother L. Keppel, *Blessed Rose Philippine Duchesne: Religious of the Sacred Heart and Missioner, 1769-1852* (1940); Catherine Mooney, *Philippine Duchesne: A Woman with the Poor* (1990).

Angelyn Dries, OSF

Duff, Alexander (1806-1878), Scottish missionary in India and missiologist. Duff was born in Moulin, Perthshire, the son of a Gaelic-speaking farm servant. At St. Andrews University he was a distinguished student in arts and divinity and helped to found a student missionary society. As his studies were concluding, the Church of Scotland was preparing to institute its first mission, which would have education at its center, and appointed him superintendent of the General Assembly's institution at Calcutta. He arrived in Calcutta in 1830, after two shipwrecks. Desiring to influence Hindu society as a whole by producing a core of thinking people who would change thought patterns and value systems, Duff's institution offered a complete system of science and letters in English, set in a Christian philosophy with constant use of the Bible. He was crucially assisted by the Hindu reformer Ram Mohun Roy, who gained him acceptability among Hindu parents and, after 1835, by the new status of English as the language of local administration. At the government Hindu College many young Brahmins were rebelling against traditional Hinduism and proclaiming their atheism under the influence of Western secular education. Duff engaged them in debate; four prominent leaders, including K. M. *Banerjea, were converted. To reach a wider intellectual public he produced a magazine, the *Calcutta Christian Observer.*

In 1834, his health broken, Duff returned to Scotland to recuperate. A powerful speech (published as *The Church of Scotland's India Missions* [1835, 1836]) at the General Assembly disarmed critics, gave new prominence to missions in church agendas, and gained support for a new mission to Madras (see John *Anderson). He traveled throughout Scotland, producing enthusiasm in congregations and creating a local infrastructure that transformed mission finances. A lecture series (the basis of his book *India and Indian Missions* [1839]) expounded a systematic theory of mission in the context of "the gigantic system" of Hinduism. The crown of such missions was to be the emergence of a native ministry to evangelize India. Duff went on to develop a theology of the church as missionary in its essence (*Missions the Chief End of the Christian Church* [1839]).

From 1840 to 1851 Duff was back in India. The school, while giving an excellent Western education, was seeing conversions and producing a deeply committed and intellectually grounded Christian leadership. In 1843, at the time of the Church of Scotland Disruption, Duff and the missionaries who had joined him declared for the Free Church, but the old Church claimed the property. Duff and his colleagues began anew, with uncertain finances. The work expanded beyond Calcutta, and the foundations of an indigenous church were laid. In 1850 Duff was recalled to Scotland to restore collapsing mission finances by his advocacy. A busy visit to the United States in 1854 was made the occasion of perhaps the first-ever international conference on missions, held in New York City.

Duff's final period of Indian service lasted from 1855 to 1863. Educational work still prospered, but the remarkable conversions were no longer so obvious; high-caste Hindu reformism now had other outlets. Following the 1857 mutiny he wrote *The Indian Rebellion and Its Results* (1858), a book that was critical of British government policy. By 1863 he was chronically ill and left India, with universal honor, to become convener of the Free Church's foreign mission committee. He visited South African missions on his way back to Scotland.

As convener, he encouraged expansion in Africa and India and campaigned for mission studies as a necessary ingredient of the theological curriculum. In 1866 he proposed a missionary professorship, with a missionary institute that would study Asian and African languages and cultures, a vision partly inspired by Propaganda Fide in Rome. Next year he was appointed to a new chair of Evangelistic Theology at New College, Edinburgh, the first chair of missions anywhere. But he was not attuned, personally or theologically, to a changed Scotland, and the innovation did not have the impact he sought.

Nevertheless, few missionaries ever did so much to raise consciousness about mission or expounded a more coherent philosophy of mission. In India, although the period of dramatic high-caste conversions soon ended, and despite the limitations of his policies (underemphasis on vernacular language, the cultural uprooting of converts), he made an immense impression, above all on students like Lal Behari *Day. In Scotland, the best missionary tradition retained his association of the gospel with learning and scholarship, and a readiness for intellectual engagement with indigenous thought.

BIBLIOGRAPHY Lal Behari Day, *Recollections of Alexander Duff* (1879); W. P. Duff, *Memorials of Alexander Duff* (1890); M. A. Laird, "Alexander Duff," in Gerald H. Anderson et al., eds., *Mission Legacies* (1994), pp. 271–276, and *Missionaries and Education in Bengal, 1793–1837* (1972); O. G. Myklebust, *The Study of Missions in Theological Education,* vol. 1 (1955); S. Piggin and J. Roxborogh, *The St. Andrews Seven: The Finest Flowering of Missionary Zeal in Scottish History* (1985); H. Scott, *Fasti Ecclesiae Scoticaenae* 7 (1928): 691–692; George Smith, *The Life of Alexander Duff* (1879; popular ed., abridged but updated, 1881); Thomas Smith, *Alexander Duff* (1883).

Andrew F. Walls

Dufresse, Jean-Gabriel-Taurin (1750–1815), Catholic missionary bishop and martyr in China. Born in Lezoux, France, Dufresse entered the Paris Foreign Mission Society in 1774 and was sent to China in 1775. In 1785 he was deported by the hostile Chinese government, but returned secretly in 1789. In 1800 he became a bishop and was appointed apostolic vicar of Szechwan, and in 1803, at a time of relative peace, he presided over the first synod in China, a synod which would have great importance for the future development of the Chinese church. A decree in 1811 condemned to death all leaders of European religions, and in 1815 Dufresse's identity was discovered. At the order of the emperor, he was beheaded (along with another bishop and nine priests). In 1900, in the company of a number of Chinese martyrs, Dufresse was beatified by Pius X. Their feast is celebrated on November 27.

BIBLIOGRAPHY J. Beckmann, "Die Lage der katholischen Missionen in China um 1815," *NZM* 2 (1946): 217–223; J. Metzler, *Die Synoden in China, Japan, und Korea 1570–1931* (1980); J. de Moidrey, *Confesseurs de la Foi en Chine* (1935), p. 84; Louis Wei Tsing-Sing, *La Politique Missionaire de la France en Chine, 1842–56* (1960); B. H. Willeke, *Imperial Government and Catholic Missions in China during the Years 1784 to 1785* (1948).

Stephen B. Bevans, SVD

Duncan, John (1796–1870), Scottish orientalist and Hebraist. Duncan was sent to Hungary by the Free Church of Scotland in 1841 in recognition of his vocational call and his extraordinary gifts in language and persuasion. While serving as a missionary to Jews there, his health broke down; as a result, in 1843 he accepted a prestigious post as the first professor of Hebrew in the Free Church of Scotland at New College, Edinburgh. Few non-Jewish missionaries have had such an impact on missions to Jews, especially in the training of others.

BIBLIOGRAPHY David Brown, *Life of the Late John Duncan, LLD* (1872); A. Moody Stuart, *Recollections of the Late John Duncan, LLD* (1872). See also Gavin Carlyle, *"Mighty in the Scriptures": A Memoir of Adolph Saphir, DD,* especially app. B (1893).

Walter Riggans

Duncan, William (1832–1918), Anglican missionary in British Columbia. Born at Bishop's Burton, Yorkshire, England, Duncan enrolled in the Church Missionary Society (CMS) training school at Highbury and was commissioned (though never formally ordained) for educational work among the Tsimshian Indians of British Columbia. Arriving at Fort Simpson, British Columbia, in 1858, he gradually gained a following among the younger people. But in 1862, having become convinced of the need for a stable and self-supporting Christian community, he and about fifty Tsimshians relocated to Metlakatla, across from present-day Prince Rupert. There he established and presided over a model Victorian village complete with streets and sanitation and regulated by means of stringent, rigorously enforced rules. With 1,000 to 2,000 inhabitants and its own church, school, sawmill, salmon cannery, community store, and police force, the settlement was widely lauded as a missiological model. But Duncan's overbearing and stubborn individuality, combined with certain theological eccentricities (forbidding the sacrament of Holy Communion, for example) resulted in his dismissal from CMS in 1882. Five years later, he and a remnant established New Metlakatla on Annette Island, across from Ketchikan, Alaska, on the American side of the border. Duncan worked there until his death. Despite his shortcomings, he was a strong champion of Indian rights and played a significant role in the lives of a number of Indians who became influential advocates on behalf of their people.

BIBLIOGRAPHY Early hagiographical accounts of Duncan abound. Among the better studies are Jean Usher, *William Duncan of Metlakatla: A Victorian Missionary in British Columbia* (1974) and Peter Murray, *The Devil and Mr. Duncan* (1985). John Williams Arctander, *The Apostle of Alaska: The Story of William Duncan of Metlakahtla* (1909); John Webster Grant, *Moon of Wintertime: Missionaries and the Indians of Canada in Encounter since 1534* (1984); H. S. Wellcome, *The Story of Metlakahtla* (1887). The William Duncan Papers, 1853–1916, are located in the Public Archives of Canada in Ottawa.

Jonathan J. Bonk

Dunger, George Albert (1908–), Baptist missionary in Cameroon. Dunger was born in Saxony, Germany, and immigrated to the United States in 1930. After pursuing education at various places, including New York University, he left in 1938 with his wife, Louise, for British Mandated Cameroon under the auspices of the German Baptist Mission. He served in Cameroon until 1948 (and again briefly from 1973 to 1975) and was responsible for significantly reorganizing and expanding the Baptist work there during World War II. He emphasized education work and brought about a legal separation between the German Baptist Mission and Cameroons Baptist Mission (U.S.A.). He devised the first general plan for developing and operating Baptist endeavors in western Cameroon, coordinating and expanding the educational, medical, and evangelistic efforts under Cameroonian leadership and with high regard for African customs. In 1946 he received his master's degree and in 1950 his Ph.D. from the Hartford Seminary Foundation's Kennedy School of Missions. From 1951 to the present he has been variously professor of missions, librarian, and archivist at the North American Baptist Seminary, Sioux Falls, South Dakota.

BIBLIOGRAPHY George A. Dunger, "The Dynamics of Religious Behavior of the North-Western Bantu as Illustrated by the Bakweri" (Ph.D. diss., Hartford Seminary Foundation, 1950). Charles W. Weber, *International Influences and Baptist Mission in West Cameroon* (1993).

Charles W. Weber

Dunne, Sarah Theresa. *See* Amadeus, Mary.

Duparquet, Charles (1830–1888), first modern Roman Catholic missioner to the interior of central Africa. Duparquet was born in L'Aigle, Normandy, and was ordained a priest in the missionary Congregation of the Holy Ghost (Spiritans) in 1855. He devoted his next 33 years to opening up the African heartlands to Roman Catholic missions. Illness marked his strenuous life, forcing his early return from Dakar (Senegal) and Libreville (Gabon). Back in France, he learned Portuguese, researched the Congo River region, and initiated a memorandum to Propaganda Fide in Rome, offering Spiritan personnel for that territory. In 1865 Rome created the Prefecture of the Congo and assigned it to the Spiritans. His health renewed, Duparquet was appointed to the new mission, but, meeting with the bishop of Angola, he was persuaded to work in that country. As the first Spiritan in Angola, Duparquet found that his French citizenship made him unwelcome to Portuguese authorities. Returning to Lisbon, he was instrumental in establishing the Holy Spirit College of Braga and founding a Portuguese (Spiritan) province. But his sights remained on the interior of Africa.

Appointed to the Zanzibar Prefecture, in 1870 Duparquet left Bagamoyo (opposite Zanzibar on the mainland) by donkey caravan for the interior. After a ten-day trek, no suitable site had been found. The destruction of parts of Bagamoyo and Zanzibar in a cyclone forced him to rebuild, while the outbreak of the Franco-Prussian war virtually cut off financial support from France. Weakened by recurrent illness, he left eastern Africa, and, in 1876, attempted a new initiative on the west coast, advancing far up the Congo River and finding traces of the early Portuguese missions.

From France, where illness again drove him in 1877, Duparquet next planned a route to the interior of Africa from the south. Named vice-prefect of the Prefecture of Cimbebasia (a million square miles between Angola and the Cape), he sailed for southern Africa and, in 1878, tried to reach the heart of the continent through Kimberley; however, political unrest halted him. The next year he sailed round to Walvis Bay (in present-day Namibia) and up the Cunene River. In 1881, undaunted by vicissitudes, he was back in Kimberley, heading toward present-day Botswana by way of the Kalahari Desert. Five years later he tried again via Mafeking, withdrawing because of conflict with Methodist missionaries. Through negotiations in Rome in 1885, Duparquet helped establish the Vicariate of French Congo, a territory extending from present-day Zaire through central Africa to Chad. It was assigned to the Spiritans over strenuous opposition from Cardinal *Lavigerie, who wanted to control the whole of the hinterland of sub-Saharan Africa. Finally back in Africa in 1888, Duparquet was stricken by peritonitis and died at Loango, Congo.

BIBLIOGRAPHY Henry J. Koren, *To the Ends of the Earth* (1983) and *The Spiritans* (1958); *Le R. P. Duparquet* (1888; n.a.).

Anthony J. Gittins, CSSp

Du Plessis, David Johannes (1905–1987), international Pentecostal and ecumenical leader. Born near Cape Town, South Africa, and converted in 1916, du Plessis attended Grey University in Bloemfontein. Rising in the ranks of the Apostolic Faith Mission (a Pentecostal denomination in South Africa), he served as general secretary (1932–1947) until his selection as organizing secretary of the newly formed Pentecostal World Conference (1947).

In 1948, du Plessis moved with his wife and family to the United States, where he traveled widely in Pentecostal circles and later joined the Assemblies of God (AG) (1955). In 1951, he visited the offices of the World Council of Churches (WCC) in New York City and found a warm welcome. Through his friendship with John *Mackay, president of Princeton Theological Seminary, he met other ecumenical leaders. Du Plessis subsequently addressed the International Missionary Council (IMC) meeting at Willingen, Germany, in 1952, attended the first six WCC assemblies, and lectured on Pentecostalism at influential theological centers in the United States and Europe.

With his significant involvement in the emergence of the charismatic movement (1960–), du Plessis forged relationships between Pentecostals, charismatics, conciliar Protestants, and Roman Catholics, earning him the title "Mr. Pentecost." An observer at the third session of Vatican II (1963–1965), he was also received by three pontiffs during his lifetime (*John XXIII, *Paul VI, and *John Paul II). With Fr. Kilian McDonnell, OSB, du Plessis inaugurated the International Roman Catholic–Pentecostal Dialogue, serving as first Pentecostal cochair (1972–1982). Numerous honors accorded him included the Pax Christi award in 1976 from St. John's University, Minnesota, and the Benemerenti award in 1983 from John Paul II; he was the first non-Roman Catholic to be so honored.

At a time when Pentecostal denominations were identifying ever more closely with conservative evangelicals, du Plessis inspired Pentecostals to look and minister beyond narrow confessional and organizational confines and recognize that the renewal of the Holy Spirit represented an ecumenical grace in all the churches. Due to perceptions that he officially represented the AG, he was criticized by NAE leaders for his relations with the WCC and NCC leaders and had to surrender his AG ministerial credentials in 1962; his reinstatement came in 1980.

Bibliography David J. du Plessis, *The Spirit Bade Me Go* (rev. 1970), *Simple and Profound* (1986), and, with Bob Slosser, *A Man Called Mr. Pentecost: David du Plessis* (1977). Martin Robinson, "To the Ends of the Earth: The Pilgrimage of an Ecumenical Pentecostal, David J. du Plessis (1905–1987)" (Ph.D. diss., Univ. of Birmingham, England, 1987). For his participation in the Roman Catholic–Pentecostal Dialogue, see Arnold Bittlinger, *Papst und Pfingstler: Der romisch katholisch-pfingstliche Dialog und seine okumenische Relevanz* (1978); Jerry L. Sandidge, *Roman Catholic-Pentecostal Dialog (1977–1982): A Study in Developing Ecumenism* (1987). See also Edith L. Blumhofer, *Restoring the Faith: The Assemblies of God, Pentecostalism, and American Culture* (1993). The papers of David J. du Plessis are held at Fuller Theological Seminary, Pasadena, Calif.

Gary B. McGee

Du Plessis, Johannes (1868–1935), South African missiologist. Du Plessis graduated from the theological seminary at the University of Stellenbosch and from the University of Edinburgh, Scotland, with a doctorate in theology (having studied briefly also in Halle, Germany). He was ordained a minister of the Dutch Reformed Church (DRC) in 1894, and became general secretary for mission of that church in 1903. In this capacity he traveled on foot across sub-Saharan Africa. From 1913 to 1930 he was professor of Christian mission and later also of New Testament at Stellenbosch. In this capacity he had a strong influence on missiological thinking within the DRC.

Bibliography The most important works by du Plessis are *A History of Christian Missions in South Africa* (1911), *Een toer door Afrika* (1917), *The Life of Andrew Murray* (1919), *The Evangelisation of Pagan Africa* (1929), and *Wie sal gaan?* (1932). G. B. A. Gerdener, *Die boodskap van 'n man: Lewenskets van prof. J. du Plessis* (1943; a biography). The March 1986 issue of *Theologia Evangelica* 19, no. 2, contains articles about du Plessis by South African theologians.

Willem Saayman

Dürr, Johannes (1904–1972), Swiss mission theologian. As a member of the Basel Mission, Dürr taught from 1928 to 1932 at the Basel Mission seminary in Bandjermasin, Kalimantan, Indonesia. Back in Switzerland in 1939 he served as home secretary of the mission, lecturer in missiology, and editor of *Evangelisches Missions Magazin* (1949–1963). He obtained a professorship in practical theology and missiology in the theological faculty of Basel University (1951–1972), and in that capacity he made an outstanding contribution to the study of missions in theological education. He initiated a fresh and critical encounter with Gustav *Warneck in his doctoral dissertation "Sendende und werdende Kirche in der Missionstheologie Gustav Warnecks" (1947). In the wake of World War II he also pleaded for a thorough "purification of missionary motives" (*Die Reinigung der Missions-Motive*, 1951). Finally, he paved the way for an improved cross-fertilization of mission and academic theology in Switzerland.

Bibliography "Professor Johannes Dürr zum Gedenken," *EMM* 117, nos. 1–2 (1973).

Hans-Werner Gensichen

Dutton, Ira Barnes (Brother Joseph) (1843–1931). A veteran of the Union Army in the American Civil War, divorced, a recovered alcoholic, and a convert to Roman Catholicism, Dutton read a newspaper article about the work of Father *Damien in the leprosy settlement at Molokai in the Hawaiian Islands and felt attracted to the work as a new beginning for his life. He went on his own initiative to Hawaii in 1886, without prior contact, and offered his services. Damien put him to work and named him unofficially Brother Joseph. Dutton served tirelessly in the leprosarium for the rest of his life and is buried on Molokai.

Bibliography Howard D. Case, ed., *Joseph Dutton: His Memoirs* (1931); Gavan Daws, *Holy Man: Father Damien of Molokai* (1973,

1984); Charles J. Dutton, *The Samaritans of Molokai: The Lives of Father Damien and Brother Dutton among the Lepers* (1932).

Gerald H. Anderson

Dwane, James Matta (1848–1915), a leader of Ethiopianism in South Africa. Born into Xhosa royalty at Debe Nek, in the eastern Cape, Dwane is known for his role in promoting Ethiopianism, a nationalist pan-African church movement in the late nineteenth century. He served as a Methodist minister before heading up the African Methodist Episcopal Church. In 1900 he founded the Order of Ethiopia, which he affiliated with the Anglican Church of the Province of Southern Africa. The order has continued as a quasi-independent indigenous body. Dwane eventually became its provincial, but not its bishop as he had hoped. He is renowned for his commitment to the education, evangelization, and liberation of his people.

BIBLIOGRAPHY Sigqibo Dwane, *Issues in the South African Theological Debate* (1989), pp. 1–6, 83–101; D. M. Balia, *Black Methodists and White Supremacy in South Africa* (1991); Cecil Lewis and G. E. Edwards, *Historical Records of the Church of the Province of South Africa* (1934), pp. 217–226; L. T. Moeti, *Ethiopianism: Separatist Roots of African Nationalism* (1981); T. D. Verryn, *A History of the Order of Ethiopia* (1972).

Janet Hodgson

Dwight, Harrison Gray Otis (1803–1862), American missionary in the Near East. Dwight was born in Conway, Massachusetts, and graduated from Hamilton College (1825) and Andover Theological Seminary (1828). In 1829, after 15 months as agent of the American Board of Commissioners for Foreign Missions (ABCFM) among the home churches, he was ordained a missionary, and in January 1830 he married Elizabeth Barker and sailed for Malta. Dwight then undertook with Eli *Smith an investigation of opportunities for mission in the interior of Asia Minor. Their 16-month journey of 2,400 miles took them as far as the Caucasus and northwestern Persia. Dwight then settled in Constantinople; his work among the Armenians in the city and throughout Turkey led to the development of the Armenian Evangelical Church. In addition to extensive touring, preaching, and lecturing and the organization of schools and churches, he did much literary work, including translations. He wrote a number of tracts in Armenian, a geography, and many articles for the *Avedaper* (Messenger), which he edited after 1854. His first wife and a son died in the plague of 1837. In 1839 he married Mary Lane, who died in 1860; he had five children with her, and four by his first wife. He was killed in a railway accident in Vermont while promoting the cause of missions among the churches.

BIBLIOGRAPHY With Eli Smith, Dwight wrote *Researches of Rev. Eli Smith and Rev. H. G. O. Dwight in Armenia,* 2 vols. (1833). He also wrote *A Memoir of Elizabeth B. Dwight* (1840) and *Christianity Revived in the East* (1850), and prepared a catalogue of Armenian literature for the *Journal of the American Oriental Society* (1853). *Missionary Herald* 58 (1862): 73–75 has his obituary; many of his letters appear in that magazine between 1830 and 1862. Fred Field Goodsell, *They Lived Their Faith* (1961), pp. 170, 222–223, 414–415, reports on Dwight and three generations of the missionary family he founded.

David M. Stowe

Dyer, Alf(red) John (1884–1968), Australian missionary to the Aborigines. Dyer was born in Melbourne and worked as a salesman until accepted as a Church Missionary Society (CMS, Australia) missionary in 1915. Posted to the Roper River Mission in Arnhem Land in the Australian Northern Territory, he married Mary Crome who had been working there as a nurse. In 1921 he assisted Hubert Warren in establishing a CMS mission at Groote Eylandt and in 1925 founded the CMS Oenpelli mission in western Arnhem Land. He was part of the celebrated CMS "peace expedition" that persuaded a number of Aborigines who had killed five Japanese fishermen and a white policeman to give themselves up to the authorities to prevent a punitive police expedition. A farcical trial followed that was a great ordeal for Dyer, but he stood by the accused, who were acquitted on appeal. The trial led to improvements in procedures for Aboriginal justice. After 19 years on CMS mission stations, Dyer resigned and settled in Sydney where his wife died of cancer in 1940. He served as rector of three Sydney parishes, retired in 1949, and died following a car accident.

BIBLIOGRAPHY A. J. Dyer, *Unarmed Combat: An Australian Missionary Adventure* [c. 1954?]. Keith Cole, *Oenpelli Pioneer: A Biography of the Revd Alfred John Dyer* (1972); John Harris, *One Blood* (1992).

Stuart Piggin

Dyer, John (1783–1841), secretary of the Baptist Missionary Society (BMS). Born in Devizes, Wiltshire, England, Dyer entered the Baptist ministry in 1810 and held pastorates in Plymouth and Reading. He became a member of the BMS committee in 1812. In 1817 he was appointed assistant secretary of the BMS, and a year later he relinquished his Reading pastorate to become full-time salaried secretary of the BMS, a position he held until his death. In that role, he was involved in the deteriorating relationships between the BMS committee and the Serampore missionaries, which led eventually to the separation of the Serampore mission from the BMS in 1827. William *Carey once complained that Dyer's letters were "like those of a Secretary of State." In 1832 Dyer, after considerable initial hesitation, threw the BMS behind William *Knibb's campaign for an immediate end to slavery in the British West Indies. In his later years in office, Dyer came under increasing strain through overwork and anxiety over the society's finances. A period of intense depression culminated in his suicide in July 1841.

BIBLIOGRAPHY Ernest A. Payne, "The Diaries of John Dyer," *Baptist Quarterly* 13 (1950): 253–259, and *The First Generation: Leaders of the Baptist Missionary Society in England and India* (1936);

Brian Stanley, *The History of the Baptist Missionary Society, 1792–1992* (1992).

Brian Stanley

Dyer, Samuel (1804–1843), London Missionary Society (LMS) missionary to the Chinese. Dyer, educated in law at Cambridge, was one of the early group of LMS missionaries who worked in Batavia (Indonesia) in the period before China became open to evangelism. He was especially involved in Bible translation and distribution. His invention of moveable metal type for printing the Chinese Scriptures greatly facilitated their publication. He was stationed in Penang, Malaya, then in Malacca, and finally in Macao. In 1827 he married Maria Tarn, the daughter of the director of the British and Foreign Bible Society (BFBS); she was one of a group of women who had studied Chinese in London with Robert *Morrison in 1825. After Dyer died, Maria Dyer remarried, but she died four years later. The three Dyer children were sent to England and brought up by their maternal uncle, William Tarn, an executive of the LMS. All three returned to Indonesia or China in Christian service. Burella Dyer, who married John Burdon of the Church Missionary Society, taught in Ningpo; Maria Dyer (see Maria [Dyer] *Taylor), who accompanied her, married James Hudson *Taylor of the China Inland Mission; Samuel Dyer, Jr., was a BFBS agent in Shanghai from 1877.

BIBLIOGRAPHY W. Canton, *History of the British and Foreign Bible Society,* vol. 2 (1904); R. Lovett, *The History of the London Missionary Society,* 2 vols. (1904); John Pollock, *Hudson Taylor and Maria: Pioneers in China* (1962).

Jocelyn Murray

E

Eastman, Elaine (Goodale) (1863–1953), missionary teacher among American Indians. Born in Mount Washington, Massachusetts, Elaine Goodale and her younger sister, Dora, wrote poems about their lives. In 1877, when they were ages 13 and 10, they produced *Apple Blossoms: Verses of Two Children.* At age 20, Elaine took her first teaching post at a missionary school for Indians and blacks, in Virginia. In 1884, she visited the Great Sioux Reservation in Dakota Territory and wrote detailed reports, which were published in New York and Boston newspapers. She convinced the commissioner of Indian Affairs, John Atkins, of the need for an Indian industrial day school, where cooking, sewing, and gardening would be taught along with academic subjects. She became the first government-appointed teacher at White River camp. Her desire to expand her efforts to other areas resulted in her appointment in 1890 as supervisor of education in Dakota Territory. She traveled several hundred miles to visit fifty Sioux schools and organize teachers' institutes. In 1891 she married Charles A. Eastman, a Sioux physician whom she met while nursing wounded prisoners. She relinquished her career for a role as wife and mother to six but continued to write about her Indian experiences until her death.

BIBLIOGRAPHY Elaine Goodale Eastman, *In Berkshire with the Wild Flowers* (1879), *Wigwam Evenings* (1909), *Yellow Star: A Story of East and West* (1920), *The Voice at Eve* (1930; see autobiographical chapter "All the Days of My Life"), and *Pratt: The Red Man's Moses* (1935). Kay Graber, ed., *Sister to the Sioux: The Memoirs of Elaine Goodale Eastman, 1885–91* (1978).

Joan R. Duffy

Eastman, George Herbert (1881–1974), Congregational minister and London Missionary Society (LMS) missionary to the Cook Islands and Kiribati. Eastman was born in Suffolk, England, in 1881, and went in 1913 to Rarotonga, Cook Islands, where, with his wife, Winifred (Grimwade), he learned the Maori language and ministered to the community, including young Islanders who served in World War I. In 1918 he succeeded William E. *Goward at Rongorongo, Beru, Kiribati (Gilbert Islands). A liberal evangelical and systematic innovator, Eastman developed Rongorongo in new directions. He trained a generation of Gilbertese pastors and deployed and visited them on the mission ship *John Williams.* He and his wife, who trained pastors' wives, stressed basic medical care, carpentry, and appropriate technical skills as part of a rounded ministry. The Rongorongo Press produced vernacular books and periodicals ranging from theology to geography and natural history. During World War II the Japanese occupied and plundered Rongorongo. Eastman had been evacuated to New Zealand, but he returned after the war in chaplain's uniform alongside British colonial administrators, to plan the reconstruction of the mission. He revised the translation of the Gilbertese Bible in Fiji, then retired with his wife to Dorset, England, in 1949.

BIBLIOGRAPHY John Garrett, *Footsteps in the Sea: Christianity in Oceania to World War II* (1992); Norman Goodall, *A History of the London Missionary Society, 1895–1945* (1954). Eastman's papers, together with many imprints of the Rongorongo Press, are in the George Knight Library, Pacific Theological College, Fiji. His correspondence with the LMS is in the society's archives at SOAS, Univ. of London.

John Garrett

Eddy, G(eorge) Sherwood (1871–1963), American student missionary leader and evangelist. Born in Leavenworth, Kansas, Eddy was educated at Yale, Union Theological Seminary, and Princeton Theological Seminary.

Inspired by Dwight L. *Moody's appeal to a Northfield (Massachusetts) student conference and by the Student Volunteer Movement (SVM) watchword "the evangelization of the world in this generation," he promoted the student missionary cause on American and Canadian college campuses as an SVM secretary in 1893 and 1894. He went to India in 1896 as a secretary for the SVM and YMCA under the auspices of the American Board of Commissioners for Foreign Missions, and from 1911 he served as the YMCA's chief evangelist in Asia. With the outbreak of World War I, he returned to Europe as a YMCA secretary with British and American armies.

"The war did something to me," Eddy recalled in 1934; "I could never be quite the same again." Emerging as a pacifist and socialist, he promoted a radical social gospel during the years before his retirement from the YMCA in 1931. From 1921 to 1957 he led the influential Fellowship for a Christian Social Order, a liberal organization that hosted traveling seminars for American leaders to England, Europe, and the Soviet Union in search of Christian solutions to the reformation of industrial capitalism. He also helped to organize the Christian Socialist Delta Cooperative Farms in 1936, a project in Mississippi that provided land for families of evicted tenant farmers. His latter-day explorations of psychic evidence for life after death are described in his book *You Will Survive after Death* (1950).

BIBLIOGRAPHY Eddy published two autobiographies, *A Pilgrimage of Ideas: or The Re-education of Sherwood Eddy* (1934) and *Eighty Adventurous Years* (1955), and over thirty-five other works, including *The Students of Asia* (1915), *Suffering and the War* (1916), *The Abolition of War* (with Kirby Page, 1924), *The Challenge of Russia* (1931), *A Century with Youth* (1944), and *Pathfinders of the World Missionary Crusade* (1945). Eddy's papers are in the Day Missions Library at Yale Divinity School.

Susan Billington Harper

Eddy, Mary Pierson (1864–1923), pioneer medical missionary in Syria. Eddy was born in Sidon of missionary parents and was the first woman doctor to receive the imperial permit of the Turkish empire to practice medicine. She went to the United States in 1880 and enrolled at Elmira College (New York). After she recovered from an illness, she felt a call to relieve the sufferings of Syrian women. She earned a medical degree from Woman's Medical College of Pennsylvania, Philadelphia, and in 1892 she was appointed by the Presbyterian church to the Syria mission.

Eddy spent several years in medical itineration among the villages of southern Lebanon. She believed that medical work should be centered in fields where opposition to evangelical work was greatest. She began a dispensary for women in the area of Junieh, 15 miles north of Beirut, where the Maronite Christians had prevented any Protestants from living. By her service, Eddy soon made friends and opposition faded. In 1903 she established a hospital and a sanatorium for tuberculosis patients, who were moved to the cool 4,000-foot level in the mountains near Hamana for the summer months. During World War I, when patients could not be taken back to the sea coast, they spent the winter in the mountains and were found to be in much better health than expected. Thenceforth the mountains became a year-round location for the sanatorium. Her health failing, Eddy left Syria in 1914 and lived in Washington, D.C., where she died.

BIBLIOGRAPHY Henry H. Jessup, *Fifty-three Years in Syria*, vol. 2, (1910), pp. 545, 597–598, 720–721. The Presbyterian Historical Society, Philadephia, holds some of Eddy's letters and reports.

R. Park Johnson

Edersheim, Alfred (1825–1889), Hebraic scholar and mentor of missions to Jews. Edersheim was born into a Viennese Jewish family who gave him the best possible education. He became the first Jewish student at the gymnasium in Vienna to receive an academic prize. In 1842 he moved to Budapest, where he began to learn English, which at one point involved instruction from John *Duncan, a Scottish missionary. After regular attendance at the mission station in Budapest, Edersheim accepted Jesus as his Messiah. He followed Duncan to Edinburgh to study theology and was ordained by the Free Church of Scotland in 1846. He served as a missionary in Romania, Scotland, and England, especially as a teacher and writer of textbooks on the Jewish milieu of Jesus and Jesus' fulfillment of prophecy. His books are still required reading in many training programs for this ministry.

BIBLIOGRAPHY Edersheim's three most influential works are *The Temple: Its Ministry and Services at the Time of Jesus Christ* (1874), *Sketches of Jewish Social Life in the Days of Christ* (1876), and *Life and Times of Jesus the Messiah*, 2 vols. (1884). Jacob Gartenhaus, *Famous Hebrew Christians* (1979); Louis Meyer, *Eminent Hebrew Christians of the 19th Century* (1904).

Walter Riggans

Edkins, Joseph (1823–1905), British missionary in China. Edkins was appointed as a missionary by the London Missionary Society (LMS) and arrived in China in July 1848. With his colleagues in Shanghai, Walter *Medhurst, William *Lockhart, Alexander *Wylie, and William C. *Milne, he engaged in evangelism, participated in a training school for pastors, and produced scholarly books for the work of missions in China. During his years in Shanghai he made several contacts with the leaders of the Taiping Heavenly Kingdom in an effort to determine the precise beliefs of this movement. In 1863 he became one of the first Protestant missionaries to live in Peking (Beijing), where he stayed for 30 years.

He was a part of the team in the capital that produced a Mandarin version of the New Testament. He was an active member of the China and North China branches of the Royal Asiatic Society. He is most noted for two of his later books, *Religion in China* (1880) and *Chinese Buddhism* (1880). In these he claimed that missionaries should regard Buddhism, particularly in its eschatology, as a preparation for Christianity. Edkins retired from the LMS in 1880 but remained in Peking with the Imperial Maritime Customs until 1893. He lived again in Shanghai from

1893 to 1905 and continued to be active in writing until his death.

BIBLIOGRAPHY Alexander Wylie, *Memorials of Protestant Missionaries to the Chinese* (1867).

Ralph R. Covell

Edmiston, Althea (Brown) (1874–1937), African American missionary among the Bushoong people in the Belgian Congo. Althea Brown was born in Russelville, Alabama. After graduating from Fisk University in 1901, she was appointed by the foreign missions committee of the Presbyterian Church in the United States for service in the Congo Free State. She prepared with one year of graduate study at the Chicago Training School for City and Foreign Missions. Arriving in Ibanche in 1902, she served as a teacher at the Maria Carey Home for Girls and then went to work among the Bushoong people. She compiled a dictionary and grammar of their language, which was published 30 years later. She opened a school to teach people to read and write and translated enough literature to form a small library.

In 1904 Alonzo Edmiston joined the mission, and he and Althea married the following year. They had three sons. On furloughs, Althea Edmiston spoke at the American Missionary Association of the Congregational Board in the East (1906); at Fisk University, where she gave the commencement address in 1921; and at the Missionary Conference of Negro Women (1935). In 1922 the Edmistons worked among the Congo royalty at Mushenge. Later they worked among the Lulua, the Zappo Zaps, and the Luba peoples. Althea Edmiston was in charge of the Mutoto Girls' Home for three years and was principal of the day-school system for four years. She died in Mutoto, Belgian Congo, from sleeping sickness and malaria.

BIBLIOGRAPHY Althea Edmiston, *Grammar and Dictionary of the Bushonga or Bukuba Languages as Spoken by the Bushonga or Bukuba Tribe Who Dwell in the Upper Kasai District, Belgian Congo, Central Africa* (1932?) and *Maria Fearing: A Mother to African Girls* (1938). Julia Lake Kellersberger, *A Life for the Congo: The Story of Althea Brown Edmiston* (1947).

Joan R. Duffy

Edwards, Jonathan (1703–1758), American theologian, minister, and missionary. Edwards was born in East Windsor, Connecticut, the son of Timothy Edwards and grandson of the famed Solomon Stoddard. From birth he was set aside for the ministry, and at an early age he resolved to be great in the cause of Christianity. Following his education at Yale College, Edwards served briefly at pastorates in New York City and Bolton, Connecticut, and then moved to Northampton, Massachusetts, where he served with his grandfather and, upon Stoddard's death in 1729, as senior pastor of the First Congregational Church. In his years at Northampton Edwards began producing the philosophical and theological works that would make him early America's most eminent Christian philosopher. His intellectual leadership during the Great Awakening of the 1740s succeeded in rearticulating historic Calvinist theology within the categories of the "New Learning" championed by John Locke and Isaac Newton.

Following his dismissal from the Northampton congregation in 1750 over the issue of Communion and church membership, Edwards accepted a call to a Native American mission in Stockbridge, Massachusetts, where he remained until 1758. During these years, he completed many of his famous theological treatises including *Freedom of the Will* (1754) and *Original Sin* (1758). Edwards's prodigious scholarship, however, did not come at the expense of his missionary activity with the Mohawk Indians. As evangelist and Native American school reformer, he worked tirelessly to meet the religious and educational needs of Native Americans and, by his example as much as his words, established the foundation for Calvinist ("Edwardsian") missions in the nineteenth and twentieth century.

In 1758 Edwards reluctantly accepted an appointment as president of the College of New Jersey (later Princeton College). He died of a smallpox inoculation, however, before serving his new appointment.

As minister, theologian, and missionary, Edwards has exercised profound influence not only on the thought, culture, and literary life of his own time but on American society to the present. He is a window into a critical period in American history and was a shaper of spiritual life in America. When historians seek a person who represents the Puritan, intellectual strain in the American character, they turn almost universally to Edwards.

BIBLIOGRAPHY C. C. Cherry, *The Theology of Jonathan Edwards* (1966); Ronald E. Davies, "Jonathan Edwards: Missionary Biographer, Theologian, Strategist, Administrator, Advocate—and Missionary," *IBMR* 21 (1997): 60–67; Perry Miller, *Jonathan Edwards* (1949); Iain Murray, *Jonathan Edwards: A New Biography* (1987); and editors' introductions to the Yale Edition of *The Works of Jonathan Edwards* (1957–).

Harry S. Stout

Edwards, Mary (Kelley) (1829–1927), founder of Inanda Seminary, Natal, South Africa. Born a Quaker in Ohio, Kelley became a teacher and in 1856 married William Edwards. After his death in 1867, she volunteered to the American Board of Commissioners for Foreign Missions and was sent to Natal as the first missionary of the newly founded (Congregational) Woman's Board of Missions. In 1869 she founded Inanda Seminary for Zulu girls, where she introduced academic subjects, domestic science, modern methods of agriculture, and, at age 80, nurses' training. She pushed constantly to raise the intellectual standards of the school, despite prejudice against higher education for African girls. Early Inanda graduates became teachers at day schools. Financial support of the school was always difficult, so the pupils did their own housework and gardening. Taking only one furlough, in 1875, Edwards remained in Africa for the rest of her life. After 1892 she no longer supervised the academic side of Inanda but continued to lead the agricultural and industrial work. By 1909 she was practically blind but remained at Inanda as a spiritual support until her death. Inanda became the best secondary school for Zulu girls in South Africa and continued despite severe disabilities forced upon it by the apartheid regime.

BIBLIOGRAPHY Edwards wrote articles for the women's missionary periodical *Life and Light for Heathen Women.* Mabel E. Emerson, *Mary K. Edwards* (pamphlet in Pioneer Series, 1917); Agnes A. Wood, *"Shine Where You Are": A Centenary History of Inanda Seminary, 1869–1969* (1972). Material on Edwards can be found in the archives of the ABCFM at Harvard Univ., Cambridge, Mass.

Dana L. Robert

Edwins, August W(illiam) (1871–1942), American founder of the Augustana Lutheran Church mission in central China. Edwins was the fourth son of Swedish immigrant parents who migrated to Swede Valley, Iowa, in 1868. Due to poverty, at age 16 Edwins left home to seek a trade; at 22 he enrolled in Augustana Academy, Rock Island, Illinois, graduating as valedictorian of both his college and his seminary classes. Gifts as scholar and linguist became important for his missionary career. He was ordained in 1902 and called to a pastorate in Stillwater, Minnesota. When no one responded to a call for volunteers for the newly formed (1901) China Mission Society, Edwins himself volunteered. Commissioned for China, Edwins married Alfreda Anderholm and sailed from Seattle, arriving in Shanghai in October 1905. After language study in Fancheng, Hupeh (Hubei) Province, the Edwinses journeyed north to Honan (Henan) Province in April 1906, in search of a field of service for the Augustana mission. In consultation with missionaries of the China Inland Mission and others, Edwins was directed to an unoccupied field in central Honan. Moving to Hsu-ch'ang (Xuchang) in 1906, Edwins obtained a foothold in Loyang (Luoyang), Jiaxian, and other strategic centers, where land and property were purchased and groundwork was laid for future expansion. In 1910 the first nine converts were baptized in Hsu-ch'ang.

Among other accomplishments, Edwins started a union language school for new missionaries, initiated a Chinese Lutheran church paper, promoted indigenous literature, and taught dogmatics in the Union Lutheran Theological Seminary near Wuhan, Hupeh, for 20 years. Interned by the Japanese after Pearl Harbor, he contracted typhus, died, and was buried at sea while being repatriated.

BIBLIOGRAPHY S. Hjalmar Swanson, *Three Missionary Pioneers and Some Who Have Followed Them* (1945).

James A. Scherer

Egede, Hans (Povelsen) (1686–1758), Norwegian Lutheran missionary known as the Apostle of Greenland. Born in Harstad and graduated from the University of Copenhagen in 1705, at 19 years of age, Egede was ordained in 1706 and served as a chaplain in Vaagan, Norway, from 1707 to 1718. In 1708 Egede began to wonder what had become of the descendants of the Norwegian settlers in Greenland in the Middle Ages, when a bishop had been in charge of the church in Greenland. After research he concluded that it was the duty of the churches of Norway and Denmark to proclaim the gospel to the Eskimos and possible Norwegian descendants in Greenland. In 1710 he wrote the first of many impressive proposals for a mission to Greenland and sent it to the bishops of Bergen and Trondheim and to King Frederik IV.

Egede, representative of Lutheran orthodoxy, insisted that the Great Commission (Mt. 28:19) is always urgent for the church and for every Christian. He proposed regular church collections and voluntary gifts as the financial foundation of the mission, but the king decided to combine mission with colonization. After intense missionary work in Greenland from 1721 to 1736, Egede went to Copenhagen, where he established the Seminarium Groenlandicum for the training of missionary personnel. His sons Poul and Niels, his son-in-law, and his nephews Niels Bloch and Peder Egede were missionaries to Greenland. German Moravian missionaries also worked there, but Egede was the pioneer. He was appointed honorary bishop of Greenland in 1740. He wrote an Eskimo grammar, a small dictionary, and a catechism; he translated parts of the Bible, and he wrote a 228-page description of the mission in Greenland and a 136-page description of Greenland's geography and ethnography. His most important writings were *Kort Beretning om den Grønlandske Missions Beskaffenhed* (Brief report on the nature of the mission to Greenland, 1738); and *Det gamle Grønlands ny Perlustration eller Naturel Historie* (A description of Greenland, showing the natural history, 1741; English trans., 1745).

BIBLIOGRAPHY Louis Bobé, *Hans Egede: Colonizer and Missionary of Greenland* (in Danish, 1944; in English, 1952); O. G. Myklebust, ed., *Hans Egede: Studier til 200-årsdagen for hans død* (1958); Nils E. Bloch-Hoell, "Hans Egede: Grønlands apostel. Norges og Danmarks første Misjonaer," *Norsk Tidsskrift for Misjon* 40 (1986): 13–37.

Nils E. Bloch-Hoell

Ehrenfeuchter, Friedrich (1814–1878), pioneer of missions as a theological discipline. Born and educated in southwest Germany, Ehrenfeuchter was serving there as teacher and parish pastor when in 1854 he received a call to Göttingen University as professor of practical theology. Later he also occupied leading positions in the regional church of Hanover. In both capacities Ehrenfeuchter was foremost among the prominent theologians of his time to make the cause of mission an integral part of theological teaching. O. G. *Myklebust observed, "Through Schleiermacher the subject of missions had achieved theological citizenship; through Ehrenfeuchter it became a theological science." In his published lectures on practical theology (1859), Ehrenfeuchter devoted the greater part to a discussion of the expansion of the church through mission, in obedience to Christ's Great Commission "to go, to teach, to baptize." He was highly respected by Karl *Graul, C. H. C. *Plath, Gustav *Warneck and others as one of the pioneers of missionswissenschaft.

BIBLIOGRAPHY Friedrich Ehrenfeuchter, *Die praktische Theologie* (1859). Olav Guttorm Myklebust, *The Study of Missions in Theological Education,* vol. 1 (1955), pp. 89-93.

Hans-Werner Gensichen

Elia, Pasquale d' (1890-1963), Jesuit missionary in China, and missiologist. A native of Pietracatella, Italy, d'Elia entered the Society of Jesus in 1904. He studied philosophy on the Island of Jersey and was in Zikawei (Xujiahui), near Shanghai, China, from 1913 to 1917, after which he completed his theological education at Woodstock, Maryland, and Hastings, England. Returning to China in 1923, he was a professor of English and philosophy at Aurora University in Shanghai until 1930. He later was a researcher and writer at the Jesuit center at Zikawei. He became a professor at the Gregorian University in Rome in 1933, where he instituted a chair of missiology. He is best known for his publications about Matteo Ricci.

BIBLIOGRAPHY Pasquale d'Elia, *The Triple Demism of Sun Yat-sen* (1931), *Il mappamondo cinese del P. Matteo Ricci, S.I.* (1938), *Fonti Ricciane,* 3 vols. (1942-1949), and *Il Lontano confino e la tragica morte del P. João Mourão, S.I., Missionario in Cina (1681-1726)* (1963). The latter includes a list of d'Elia's publications up to 1959 (pp. 554-581). Johannes Beckmann, "Pasquale d'Elia, S.J.," *NZM* 20 (1964): 146-147.

John W. Witek, SJ

Eligius (c. 590-c. 660), missionary in Flanders and bishop of Noyon, France. Born at Chaptelat, near Limoges, Eligius was a goldsmith and coin maker of great skill. He worked at the courts of Clothar II and Dagobert I, Frankish kings. As a trusted counselor of Dagobert, he preached in the regions of Antwerp, Courtrai, and Ghent. Entering the priesthood in 641 after Dagobert's death, he set up monasteries and erected churches in Flanders. His compassion led to his being known for his good deeds, and particularly for his persuasive work in raising funds to redeem captives given sentence of death or sold into slavery.

BIBLIOGRAPHY Pierre Cristus, *The Legend of Sts. Eligius and Godeberta* (1963); P. Morel, "Étude critique de la vie de S. Éligius" (Ph.D. diss., Paris, 1930).

Frederick W. Norris

Eliot, John (1604-1690), Puritan minister and pioneer missionary among Native Americans. Eliot left England, the land of his birth, in 1631 as a young Puritan pastor. He worked in Boston for a year, then established a church five miles away in Roxbury, where he remained for 58 years, until his death. From the beginning he established an excellent relationship with the Narragansett Indians in the area and gradually also with other peoples speaking related languages. From 1660 he was called the Apostle of the American Indian. He carried on his work with the Indians parallel to his pastoral duties at the Roxbury congregation and to his general duties for the New England church as a whole.

Beginning at Natick, where he preached biweekly until he was past 80, Eliot was instrumental in organizing fourteen Indian villages. No whites were resident, and a form of self-government was instituted according to the pattern given in Exodus 18. Interested neighboring pastors were encouraged to participate in regular instruction. Although most of the evangelization was carried out by personally trained Indian evangelists, Eliot himself traveled on foot and on horseback, taxing his strength to the utmost, sometimes drenched by rain, in order to bring the gospel to the people. He brought cases to court to fight for Indian property rights, pleaded for clemency for convicted Indian prisoners, fought the selling of Indians into slavery, sought to secure lands and streams for Indian use, established schools for Indian children and adults, translated the Bible (1663) and twenty other books into Indian languages, and attempted to train Indians to adopt a settled way of life.

Hostilities and mutual suspicion increased between whites and Indians, until in 1675 during King Philip's War, most of the Indian villages were damaged or destroyed, and many of the Indian Christians joined the war or were relocated. Eliot spent the remainder of his life reestablishing some of the villages.

BIBLIOGRAPHY Sidney H. Rooy, *The Theology of Missions in the Puritan Tradition* (1965), pp. 156-241 (includes summary of Eliot's missionary tracts); O. E. Winslow, *John Eliot: "Apostle to the Indians"* (1968).

Sidney H. Rooy

Ellinwood, Frank F(ield) (1826-1908), Presbyterian mission administrator. Ellinwood was born in Clinton, New York, and graduated from Hamilton College, New York, and from Princeton Theological Seminary. He served pastorates at Second Presbyterian Church of Belvidere, New Jersey (1853-1854), and Central Presbyterian Church of Rochester, New York (1854-1865). After holding administrative posts for the Presbyterian Committee of Church Erection (1866-1870) and the Memorial Fund Committee (1870-1871), he was appointed corresponding secretary for the Presbyterian Board of Foreign Missions (1871-1906). In that capacity he worked with such notables as Robert E. *Speer and Arthur Judson *Brown to shape one of the more vibrant Protestant mission agencies in America during the late nineteenth and early twentieth centuries. Ellinwood's board responsibilities included editing the *Foreign Missionary Magazine* and supervising relations with women's auxiliaries, the YMCA, and the Student Volunteer Movement. He also steered the board to establish mission posts in newly opened fields, including China, Korea, and the Philippines. He wrote *The Great Conquest* (1876), *Oriental Religions and Christianity* (1892), *Questions and Phases of Modern Missions* (1899), and numerous pamphlets on missions. In addition, from 1886 to 1903 he lectured on comparative religion at the University of the City of New York (now New York Univ.), which awarded him two honorary doctorates.

BIBLIOGRAPHY Mary G. Ellinwood, *Frank Field Ellinwood: His Life and Work* (1911).

James Patterson

BIBLIOGRAPHY Maurice Caldwell, "Missionary of God," Church of God *Missions* (June 1992).

L. Grant McClung, Jr.

Elliot, Philip James ("Jim") (1927-1956), missionary martyr in Ecuador. Raised in a godly Plymouth Brethren home, in Portland, Oregon, Elliot developed from an early age a deep desire for God and a keen insight into the Scriptures. In 1945 he enrolled at Wheaton College, Illinois, where he graduated *summa cum laude* and was a champion wrestler. He gave rigorous leadership to missions interest among students and attended the 1946 (Toronto) and 1948 (Urbana, Illinois) missionary conventions of InterVarsity Christian Fellowship. In 1952 he went with Peter *Fleming to Ecuador, to work among the Quichua Indians. He was soon joined by his college classmate Ed McCully and his wife, Marilou; in 1953 he married Elisabeth Howard in Quito.

In 1955 Nate *Saint, a pilot with Missionary Aviation Fellowship, discovered from the air a settlement of Auca (now known as Waorani) Indians, an isolated tribe. Elliot had been praying for several years about reaching this tribe. For twelve weeks Saint, Elliot, and McCully made weekly flights over the Auca village, dropping gifts from the air. On January 3, 1956, the three men, along with Peter Fleming and Roger Youderian, established a base on a beach of the Curaray River, near Auca territory. After they made an initial friendly contact with three Auca Indians, on January 8 a group of Aucas killed the five men with wooden spears. They were buried on that site a few days later by a rescue team of several missionaries, Quichua Indians, and U.S. military personnel from Panama.

BIBLIOGRAPHY Elisabeth Elliot, *Through Gates of Splendor* (1957) and *Shadow of the Almighty* (1958); Elisabeth Elliot, ed., *The Journals of Jim Elliot* (1978).

David M. Howard

Elliott, Benjamin Franklin (1858-1926), educator, preacher, and missionary of the Church of God (Anderson, Indiana). Born in Maine, Elliott was converted at the age of 15 in a Methodist class meeting. Called to preach at the age of 16, he entered the East Maine Methodist Conference seminary, where he completed a three-year course before enrolling in Wesleyan University, Middletown, Connecticut, in 1878. In 1882, three years prior to leaving the Methodist Episcopal Church and joining a holiness group, he was a circuit rider serving six Methodist churches in the San Diego, California, area. In 1892, after the death of his first wife, Mary, Elliott, accompanied by his five-year old son, Clark, began missionary work in Mexico. Two years later he married Georgia Cook. The Elliotts then spent 15 years printing and distributing tracts and papers in Spanish. In 1913, after the political revolution of 1910 forced them from Mexico to El Paso, Texas, they relocated to Los Angeles, California, where for 13 years, up to the time of his death, they continued their evangelistic and printing ministries.

Elliott, Walter (1842-1928), American Catholic missionary strategist. Elliott was born in Detroit, Michigan, and graduated from the University of Notre Dame. A Civil War veteran, he was later a partner in a Detroit law firm. In 1868 he joined the newly formed Paulist Fathers and became an effective mission preacher throughout the United States. In 1882, Elliott renewed Isaac *Hecker's plan for mission to non-Catholics, based on the principles of persuasion, noncontroversiality, the presumption of the Spirit in his listeners, and emphasis on topics of similarity between Protestants and Catholics. His inauguration of the "Question Box," a protocol for entering into cordial discussions about Catholicism with Protestants, attempted to focus these principles. In 1896, he became cofounder of the Catholic Missionary Union (CMU), which spiritually and financially supported missionaries to non-Catholics and hosted missionary congresses (1901-1909) where missionaries shared their strategies, successes, and failures. Elliott edited the CMU's magazine, *The Missionary*.

After a cloud of suspicion in Rome enveloped Elliott because of the French translation of his *Life of Fr. Hecker* (1897), Elliott became novice master, rector, and teacher at the Apostolic Mission House, the training center for missionaries he and Alexander Doyle founded at Catholic University, Washington, D.C., in 1904. During this period, Elliott wrote *A Manual of Missions* (1925), a synthesis of his class notes and his preaching experience.

BIBLIOGRAPHY Angelyn Dries, "Walter Elliott's Foundations for Evangelization," *Journal of Paulist Studies* 1 (1992): 1-10; Thomas Joseph Jonas, *The Divided Mind, American Catholic Evangelism in the 1890s* (1988); Joseph McSorley, *Father Hecker and His Friends* (1952); James McVann, *The Paulists, 1858-1970* (1983). The memorial issue of *The Missionary* 42 (June 1928) highlights various aspects of Elliott's life.

Angelyn Dries, OSF

Ellis, William (1794-1872) *and*
Mary Mercy (Moor) (1793-1835), London Missionary Society (LMS) missionaries to Polynesia. Born in England, William and Mary Mercy Ellis went to Tahiti in 1817 as part of a new group of highly educated workers sent out by the LMS. They brought with them the first press and set it up in Moorea. They soon moved to Huahine, where William Ellis helped draft the code of laws. In 1822 a visiting LMS deputation took him with them to Hawaii and in 1823 he and Mary moved there. They were both influential in royal circles and helped in organizing the Hawaiian church. Because of Mary's health they returned to England in 1824, but William continued his service to Polynesia by writing his carefully collected observations, which have continued to be an important source of information. In 1832 he began a decade of service as foreign secretary of the LMS.

When the persecutions in Madagascar were drawing to a close, William Ellis was asked by the LMS to negotiate with the Malagasy court about the return of missionaries and freedom for Christianity. He made three trips to the island in 1853, 1856, and 1862, on the first of which he was rebuffed. On the others he was able to guide the reestablishment of the Malagasy church, and by his writings he stirred the churches of England to a great interest in that island. His wisdom and experience made him one of the most influential missionary statesmen of his time.

BIBLIOGRAPHY William Ellis, *Memoir of Mrs. Mary M. Ellis, Wife of the Rev. William Ellis, Missionary to the South Seas and Foreign Secretary of the London Missionary Society* (1835), *Polynesian Researches* (1829), *History of the London Missionary Society* (1844), and *The Martyr Church of Madagascar* (1870). John Eimeo Ellis, *Life of William Ellis, Missionary to the South Seas and to Madagascar* (1873).

Charles W. Forman

Elmslie, Walter Angus (1856–1935), Scottish missionary of the Livingstonia Mission in Malawi. Born in Aberdeen and educated at the University of Aberdeen, Elmslie began his service in Malawi as a doctor at Njuyu. In 1889 he opened a new station at Ekwendeni among the Ngoni people, where he spent most of the rest of his missionary career. He was ordained by the Free Church of Scotland in 1897. He is chiefly remembered for his patient and pioneering work among Chief M'mbelwa's Ngoni people, building on the foundation already laid by William Mtusane *Koyi, Xhosa evangelist to the Ngoni. Elmslie is also important for his early linguistic and historical studies. In 1886 he published *Izongoma zo 'Mlungu,* a collection of hymns and Scripture selections, which was the first printed book in the Ngoni language. This was followed in 1891 by a translation of Mark's Gospel and two books on ChiNgoni grammar and history. A close ally of Robert *Laws, Elmslie is representative of the more conservative stream in the Livingstonia tradition, which was fairly negative about African culture and cautious about the pace of African leadership. Remembered by local Christians with respect rather than affection, he was important for his steadfastness and courage in the period before the Ngoni began to respond to the gospel. He died in Scotland.

BIBLIOGRAPHY Walter Angus Elmslie, *Introductory Grammar of the Ngoni (Zulu) Language* (1891) and *Among the Wild Ngoni* (1899, 1970). K. J. McCracken, *Politics and Christianity in Malawi, 1875–1940* (1977); T. Jack Thompson, *Christianity in Northern Malawi* (1995).

T. Jack Thompson

Elmslie, William J. (1832–1872) *and*
Margaret (Duncan) (1852–1882), early Church Missionary Society (CMS) missionaries in Kashmir. From the 1850s CMS sought to establish work in the Himalayan foothills and into Kashmir. This was much encouraged by British Christian administrators and army officers, some of whom recruited William Elmslie and paid his expenses. A Scottish Presbyterian doctor from Aberdeen, Elmslie joined CMS in 1864 and began work in Srinagar in 1865. His service was limited to the summers only, as Maharajah Rambhir Singh, the Muslim ruler of Kashmir, would not allow any foreigners to remain through the winter. Early in 1872, while on leave in Scotland, Elmslie married Margaret Duncan and returned to Kashmir with her. Later that year, leaving Srinagar too late in the season, they became trapped in snow. William, who had been ill before leaving, was confined to a litter. Margaret Elmslie struggled on with her husband, but he died at Gujrat. After his death, permission to remain in Kashmir year round was received. Elmslie's medical successors, Theodore Maxwell and the brothers Arthur and Ernest Neve, built up a successful hospital. Margaret Elmslie, who was greatly loved by her colleagues, continued to work in orphanages in Amritsar until 1878. In 1881, after her return to Britain, she married Francis Baring, a former CMS missionary, but she died in Kulu, North India, only a year later.

BIBLIOGRAPHY Margaret Duncan Elmslie and W. Burns Thomson, *Seedtime in Kashmir: A Memoir of William Jackson Elmslie... Late Medical Missionary, CMS, Kashmir* (1875); M. E. Gibbs, *The Anglican Church in India, 1600–1970* (1972); Eugene Stock, *History of the Church Missionary Society,* 3 vols. (1899).

Jocelyn Murray

Elwin, H(arry) Verrier H(olman) (1902–1964), Anglican anti-imperial missionary in India. Born in England, Elwin studied English literature and theology at Oxford and received ordination. He joined John Copley *Winslow's pioneer Christian ashram, the Christa Seva Sangh, at Poona (Pune) in western India in 1927. During five years there, he became involved with Gandhi and the national movement. Then, persuaded to devote his life to the service of India's tribal peoples, and in partnership with Shamrao Hivale, an Indian companion, he established an ashram and welfare organization serving the tribals in central India. They continued this work for 21 years, usually in great poverty, but with irrepressible humor. Elwin, earned the title *Din Sevak* (servant of the poor). Because of his association with Gandhi, his bishop refused to license him for this work; increasingly isolated from the church, he resigned his membership in 1935. His interest in India's tribes led to study as well as welfare work, and he became a respected anthropologist, though he preferred the term "philanthropology." In 1954 Prime Minister Nehru appointed him to an advisory post in northeast India, through which he significantly influenced official policies toward the tribal peoples.

Elwin contributed creatively to the Christa Seva Sangh's policy of inculturation with a series of comparative studies in spirituality, including *Christian Dhyana* (1930; dealing with *The Cloud of Unknowing* and the Indian bhakti tradition), *Richard Rolle: A Christian Sannyasi* (1930), *The Religion of Adoring Love* (serially in the *Christa Seva Sangh Review,* August 1931–May 1932), and *St. Francis* (1933). He also wrote books and articles on Gandhi and Indian nationalism. His later substantial anthropological work, including over a dozen major monographs (from the early *Songs of the Forest,* 1935, through to the magisterial *Religion of an Indian Tribe,* 1955) and his work for tribal advancement, were eventually valued by the church. He died at Shillong in northeast India.

BIBLIOGRAPHY Elwin's autobiography is *The Tribal World of Verrier Elwin* (1964). Two volumes of selections from Elwin, with introductory essays, are Nari Rustomji, ed., *Verrier Elwin, Philanthropologist* (1989), and Daniel O'Connor, ed., *Din-Sevak: Verrier Elwin's Life of Service in Tribal India* (1993). A part-biography is Shamrao Hivale, *Scholar Gipsy: A Study of Verrier Elwin* (1946); a missiological study is William W. Emilsen, *Violence and Atonement: The Missionary Experiences of Mohandas Gandhi, Samuel Stokes and Verrier Elwin in India before 1935* (1994). Studies of his work as an anthropologist include M. C. Pradhan et al., *Anthropology and Archaeology: Essays in Commemoration of Verrier Elwin, 1902–1964* (1969), and Babagrahi Misra, *Verrier Elwin: A Pioneer Indian Anthropologist* (1973). Large collections of Elwin's papers are in the India Office Library and Records, London, and the Nehru Memorial Library, New Delhi.

Daniel O'Connor

Ely, Charlotte Elizabeth (1839–1915) *and* **Mary Ann Caroline** (1841–1913), American missionaries in Turkey. Daughters of a Presbyterian minister, Charlotte and Mary Ely (born in Philadelphia, Pennsylvania, and in Wilmington, Delaware, respectively) studied at Elmira Female College and at Mount Holyoke Seminary. Returning to the United States after travel and study in Europe, the sisters met American Board of Commissioners for Foreign Missions (ABCFM) missionaries the Rev. and Mrs. George C. Knapp aboard ship and were persuaded to seek appointment under the ABCFM. They returned with the Knapps to Bitlis, Turkey, in 1868. The sisters opened a boarding school for girls that came to be known as the Mount Holyoke of Kurdistan. Approximately fifty girls were trained in academic subjects, music, art, dressmaking, and needlework. As native teachers became available, Charlotte and Mary devoted more time to evangelistic touring throughout eastern Turkey. During one year, 1909, the sisters had sole charge of the Bitlis mission, as they were the only foreigners in the city and the only English-speaking missionaries within three days' journey. The population of Bitlis, approximately one-third Armenian and two-thirds Muslim Kurds, suffered greatly during the Turkish massacres. Throughout difficult times the sisters were renowned for bravery and dedication to their work. Charlotte died in Bitlis; Mary died in Beirut.

BIBLIOGRAPHY Memorial tributes, *The Missionary Herald,* July 1913 and October 1915; brief biographical sketches are in Joseph K. Greene, *Leavening the Levant* (1916).

Martha Lund Smalley

Emde, J(ohannes) (1774–1859), cofounder of the church in East Java. Born in Arolsen, Germany, Emde joined the Dutch East India Company and settled in Surabaya, East Java, where he married a Javanese woman and worked as a watchmaker. He was part of a small group of devout Christians who were stimulated by Joseph *Kam to evangelize the indigenous population, which had remained practically unreached during two centuries of Dutch presence in Java. Nicknamed the Saints of Surabaya, Emde and his friends formed a Bible tract and missionary society and started distributing tracts and Bible portions. Their activities were opposed by ministers of the established church, who even sent Emde to prison in 1820. In 1837 a group of Javanese Muslims living on the estate of C. L. *Coolen responded positively to the Gospel of Mark. Coolen explained it to them and remained their spiritual leader for several years until he sent them to Emde, whose ideas about the inculturation of the gospel were different from Coolen's. Emde not only had the Javanese Christians baptized but also told them to cut their hair, wear European clothes, and shun *wayang* (Javanese mythical puppet play), gamelan (Javanese orchestra/music), and other traditional elements of Javanese culture that he considered pagan. Eventually, under the leadership of Paulus *Tosari from Java and the Dutch missionary Jelle *Jellesma, the Javanese Christians adopted a middle course by keeping some elements of their traditional culture and rejecting others. Together with Coolen, Emde is considered the founder of the church in East Java.

BIBLIOGRAPHY Philip van Akkeren, *Sri and Christ: A Study of the Indigenous Church in East Java* (1970).

Th. van den End

Emmerich, Heinrich (1901–1984), German Catholic missiologist and cartographer. Emmerich was born in Dössel, near Paderborn. He entered the Society of the Divine Word (SVD) in 1922 and was ordained in 1929. From 1929 to 1941 he taught in the schools of the SVD in Tirschenreuth, near Regensburg, and in Marienburg, Switzerland. While treasurer of the Anthropos Institute in Posieux (from 1941), he studied statistics in Fribourg. From 1952 to 1983 he was cartographer and statistician at the SVD Generalate in Rome. Apart from numerous reports and maps in SVD journals and the booklet *Tatsachen, Zahlen, Leistungen* (1965) published for publicity purposes, he produced *SVD Atlas* (1952, 1972) and *Atlas of the Catholic Missions* (1958); constructed a missionary globe for Pope John XXIII; and prepared the map sections for Anton *Freitag's *Die Wege des Heils* (1960) and the third edition of Karl *Streit's *Atlas Hierarchicus* (1968), which includes a geographic and statistical description of the whole Catholic Church of the Roman Rite and the Oriental Uniate churches. He also prepared a separate fascicle with a historical section and explanatory notes for the maps in German, English, French, Italian, and Spanish, which is inserted in the atlas (the 2d ed. of *Atlas Hierarchicus* was published in English in 1930). Whereas the textual supplement received criticism, the geographic part was praised as "a magnificent achievement" (*ZMR* 53 [1969]: 89). At the urging of Pope Paul VI, Emmerich published another edition of the atlas in 1976, for which the pope himself wrote the foreword. A fifth edition with an updated map section, a revised statistical and geographic section, and an additional historical section was published in 1993, edited by Zenon Stezycki.

BIBLIOGRAPHY *Steyler Missionschronik* (1985/1986): 191 (obit.). Regarding the *Atlas Hierarchicus,* see *Internationaler Fidesdienst* no. 2822 (March 6, 1976): 139–141.

Karl Müller, SVD

Enbaqom (Abu l-Fath) (?–1561), eleventh abbot of the monastery of Debre Libanos in Shewa, Ethiopia. According to oral tradition, Enbaqom was originally a Muslim merchant from Yemen. Sometime early in the sixteenth century, he settled in Ethiopia and undertook a careful study of Islam and its literature, and this resulted in his conversion to Christianity. He was christened with the name Enbaqom (Habakkuk) in the Debre Libanos monastery, where he later served as abbot.

Enbaqom's conversion occurred only a few years before the revolt (1526–1543) of Ahmad ibn Ibrahim al-Ghazi ("Ahmad Gran"), who sought to establish Islamic rule in place of the Christian rule of Ethiopia. Strengthened by the Ottoman Turks with soldiery and modern weaponry previously unknown in Ethiopia, Ahmad crushed almost every contingent of the royal army sent against him. Emperor Lebna Dengal (1508–1540) died while fleeing before one of Ahmad's attacks. Ahmad's assaults were characterized by systematic destruction of churches and monasteries—the repositories of the kingdom's literary wealth—in every part of the country. Their faith shaken to the roots, Christians were forced to choose between conversion to Islam or death. Their teachers were not prepared to challenge the Islamic faith because their knowledge did not go beyond the polemics recorded in hagiographic sources. Enbaqom, however, with his Muslim background and careful study, was in an admirable position to meet their needs, and his presence was seen as providential. While Ahmad did all he could to capture and execute him, Enbaqom moved from place to place comforting the faithful. For close to 40 years he was abbot of the monastery of Debre Libanos and held the rank of *echege,* the highest ecclesiastical rank after the metropolitanate. In addition to composing the *Gate of Faith* (in Ethiopic, or Ge'ez), Enbaqom is remembered as having translated Chrysostom's commentary on the Epistle to the Hebrews and the Indian story *Barlaam and Josaphat.* He is commemorated each spring in the Ethiopian calendar.

BIBLIOGRAPHY Enrico Cerulli, "Gli Abbati di Dabra Libanos, capi del monachismo etiopico, secondo la 'lista rimata' (sec. XIV–XVIII)," *Orientalia* 13 (1944): 137–182 (see especially pp. 150–152); Lanfranco Ricci, "Le *Vite* di Enbaqom e di Yohannes, Abbati di Dabra Libanos di Scioa," *Rassegna di Studi Etiopici* 13 (1954): 91–120, and 14 (1959): 69–107; E. J. Van Donzel, *Enbaqom Anqasa Amin (La Porte de la Foi)* (1969).

Getatchew Haile

England, John (1786–1842), Catholic missionary bishop in America. England was born in Cork, Ireland, and ordained a priest in 1808. After extensive pastoral experience in Ireland, he immigrated to the United States and became the first bishop of Charleston, South Carolina (1820–1840), which then included only three congregations in a vast mission area: all of South Carolina, North Carolina, and Georgia. His mission strategy entailed forming congregations led by laypersons who would conduct Sunday prayer. He published a catechism (1822), *A Missal for the Laity* (1822), a *Laity's Directory* (1822), and the first Catholic newspaper in the nation, *The United States Catholic Miscellany* (1822). He was also appointed apostolic delegate to Haiti (1833–1837) to restore Vatican-Haitian diplomatic relations. Committed to the inherent compatibility of Catholicism and the republican ethos, he established a constitution for his diocese that provided a strong voice for the laity. He also promoted regular meetings of the bishops at the provincial councils of Baltimore, Maryland. A noted orator, he frequently addressed gatherings of Protestants and addressed a joint session of Congress in 1826. He founded the Sisters of Charity of Our Lady of Mercy and a diocesan seminary; when he died his diocese had eighteen priests, while the Catholic population had increased from about 1,100 to 7,000.

BIBLIOGRAPHY *The Works of the Right Reverend John England, First Bishop of Charleston,* Ignatius Reynolds, ed., 5 vols. (1849); Peter Guilday, *The Life and Times of John England, First Bishop of Charleston, 1786–1842,* 2 vols. (1927); Patrick W. Carey, *An Immigrant Bishop: John England's Adaptation of Irish Catholicism to American Republicanism* (1982); Peter Clarke, *A Free Church in a Free Society* (1982).

Christopher J. Kauffman

Epalle, Jean-Baptiste (1808–1845), Marist bishop and first vicar apostolic of Melanesia and Micronesia. Epalle was born at Marlhes, Loire, France, and was ordained a priest in Lyons in 1837. He joined the Society of Mary (Marists) to be a missionary, sailing to New Zealand in 1839 to work under Jean-Baptiste François *Pompallier, who seriously neglected the Marist missioners. Epalle's colleagues sent him back to Europe in 1842 seeking help. After Marist founder Jean-Claude *Colin persuaded Rome to reduce Pompallier's jurisdiction, Epalle was named vicar apostolic of Melanesia and Micronesia and was ordained bishop in 1844. Reaching Sydney in 1845 with twelve priests and brothers, he chartered a ship for the Solomons. At Isabel, people from the town came aboard to trade, but Epalle naively disregarded their warnings about an enemy tribe nearby. He landed among those warriors and made the sailors leave their weapons in the boat as a sign of peace. Fatally wounded within minutes, he died three days later on board ship. The shattered missionaries regrouped at Makira, later moving nearer New Guinea to Murua (Woodlark) and briefly to Umboi (Rook). Further lives lost from violence and malaria caused Colin to withdraw the Marists gradually from 1852. They handed Murua over to Milan missionaries, who closed the mission in 1855.

BIBLIOGRAPHY John Hosie, *Challenge: Marists in Colonial Australia* (1987); Hugh Laracy, *Marists and Melanesians: A History of Catholic Missions in the Solomon Islands* (1969); Ralph Wiltgen, *The Founding of the Roman Catholic Church in Oceania 1825 to 1850* (1979).

John Hosie, SM

Erasmus, Desiderius (c. 1467–1536), Dutch Christian humanist who heralded a new era in European history but opposed the Reformation. Born in Rotterdam, Erasmus became a Catholic priest and influential scholar. On several occasions he dealt with missionary issues, such as salvation outside the visible church, the role of non-Christian religions in the providence of God, and practical issues such as Turkish expansion in Europe. Near the end of his life Erasmus appealed to the clergy of the Roman Catholic Church, especially the Franciscans and the Dominicans, to take up missionary work in the whole world. There is no excuse, he said, for staying at home. In his treatise *Ecclesiastes sive concionator evangelicus* (1535) he called attention to Asia and Africa, to unknown religions and Islam, and to the necessity of sending missionaries. Missionaries, he said, cannot convert the heathen abroad unless they offer themselves totally to God. Missionary work is difficult, but it is the most noble work. His *Ecclesiastes* was reprinted and translated several times. In 1730 Thomas *Bray reprinted it again and recommended it for the preparation of missionaries.

BIBLIOGRAPHY J. R. Coates, "Scholarship and Missions: Erasmus," *East and West Review: An Anglican Missionary Quarterly Review* 2, no. 3 (1936): 244–249; J. Schmidlin, "Erasmus von Rotterdam über die Heidenmission," *ZM* 4 (1914): 1–12; George Hunston Williams, "Erasmus and the Reformers on Non-Christian Religions and Salus Extra Ecclesiam," in Theodore K. Rabb and Jerrold E. Seigel, eds., *Action and Conviction in Early Modern Europe: Essays in Memory of E. H. Harbison* (1969), pp. 319–370; Eike Wolgast, "Erasmus von Rotterdam über die Weltmission," *ZMR* (1995): 111–119.

The Editors

Errico, Gaetano Cosma Damiano (1791–1860), founder of the Missionaries of the Sacred Hearts of Jesus and Mary. Errico was born in Secondigliano, near Naples, Italy. After receiving his training in the diocesan seminary in Naples, he was ordained in 1815 and began a fruitful period of pastoral ministry in Secondigliano, particularly with youth. After Our Lady of Sorrows church in Secondigliano was completed (1835), he devoted himself completely to the religious society he planned and founded, the Missionari dei Sacri Cuori di Gesù e di Maria. Its purpose was to spread devotion to the Sacred Hearts of Jesus and Mary, general apostolic activities, home and foreign missions, retreats, and youth apostolate. The motherhouse is still in Secondigliano, but the superior general now resides in Rome. The congregation works mostly in Italy and South America. Shortly after Errico's death the process for his beatification was initiated.

BIBLIOGRAPHY N. Angelini, *Vita del venerabile Gaetano Errico* (several eds.); G. Coniglio, "Errico, Gaetano Cosma Damiano," *Enciclopedia Cattolica* (1949ff), id., in *Bibliotheca Sanctorum*, vol. 5, pp. 76–78; L. M. Grande, "Missionari dei Sacri Cuori di Gesù e di Maria," in *Dizionario degli Istituti di perfezione*, vol. 5, pp. 1472–1474; *Memorie storiche sulla Pia Unione dei S. S. Cuori* (1893).

Karl Müller, SVD

Eto, Silas (1905–1984), prophet-leader of a Melanesian independent church. From the Roviana culture of New Georgia, Solomon Islands, Eto trained to be a pastor-teacher under the Methodist missionary J. F. *Goldie. Visionary experiences convinced Eto that he was Goldie's successor, and in 1960 he organized the Christian Fellowship Church, which was marked by ecstatic and glossolalic phenomena. Eto dressed for worship in white robes and was considered by many of his flock to be a manifestation of God. His congregations ritually assented to his pronouncements, and the name "Holy Mama" was often added to the Trinitarian formula. Eto has thus provided the closest parallel to African black messiahs like Simon *Kimbangu or Isaiah *Shembe to be found in Melanesia. Rejection by leading Methodist missionaries carrying on Goldie's work made it difficult for Eto to accept reunification in the 1980s, but many of his followers eventually drifted back during the 1990s. Eto's church is marked by a rich hymnology, idiosyncratic prayer techniques, and a mixture of indigenous and Wesleyan-influenced iconography. Following Eto's death, Sam Kuku continued the church's organization, which includes schools, a theological college (initially funded by the World Council of Churches), and businesses. Eto's son, Job Dudley, became premier of the Western Province of the Solomons and eventually national environment minister.

BIBLIOGRAPHY Frances Harwood, "The Christian Fellowship Church: A Revitalization Movement" (Ph.D. diss., Univ. of Chicago, 1971) and "Intercultural Communication in the Western Solomons: The Methodist Mission and the Emergence of the Christian Fellowship Church," in James Boutilier, Daniel T. Hughes, and Sharon W. Tiffany, eds., *Mission, Church, and Sect in Oceania* (1978), pp. 231–250; Garry Trompf, "Independent Churches in Melanesia," *Oceania* 54, no. 1 (1983): 51–72, no. 2 (1983): 122–132; Esau Tuza, "The Emergence of the Christian Fellowship Church" (M.A. thesis, Univ. of Papua New Guinea, 1975) and "Silas Eto on New Georgia," in Garry W. Trompf, ed., *Prophets of Melanesia* (1977, rev. 1981), pp. 65–88.

Gary Trompf

Eulogius (d. 859), proponent of confrontational Christian witness in Muslim societies. Born in a Christian aristocratic family in Cordoba, capital of Muslim Spain, Eulogius was educated in Latin and Arabic. He devoted his priesthood to propounding a Christian missiology of martyrdom with which to confront Islam. He was appointed bishop of Toledo (c. 851) but was unable to take up office due to his conflict with the Muslim political authorities. Opposed to the affinity with Islamic culture which then characterized the Christian population, he developed a theology of confrontation that drew heavily upon biblical apocalypse (e.g., Daniel 7). In two books, *Memoriale Sanctorum* and *Liber Apologeticus Martyrum*, he provided a spiritual hagiography and theological vindication of a group of contemporary Cordoban Christians who witnessed to their faith by publicly defaming the prophet Muhammad, bringing upon themselves capital punishment through the Muslim courts. Known as the Cordoban martyrs' movement, it involved perhaps as many as thirty martyrs during the middle decade of the ninth century (851–859). Eulogius's work perpetuated the movement's influence as a theological motif in the Christian reconquest of Spain. He was executed in 859 and his remains were reinterred on the pilgrim route to Santiago de Compostela, where they were visited by later generations of Christian crusaders. His legacy helped shape the medieval concept of militant Christian mission against Islam, especially under the crusading Pope Innocent III.

BIBLIOGRAPHY Allan Culter, "The Ninth-Century Spanish Martyrs' Movement and the Origins of Western Christian Missions to the Muslims," *The Muslim World* 55 (1965): 321–339; Norman Daniel, *The Arabs and Medieval Europe* (1979); Jean Marie Gaudeul, *Encounters and Clashes: Islam and Christianity in History* (1984); Benjamin Kedar, *Crusade and Mission: European Attitudes Towards the Muslims* (1984); Richard Southern, *Western Views of Islam in the Middle Ages* (1962); Justo Pérez de Urbel, *San Eulogio de Cordoba* (1927) and *A Saint under Muslim Rule* (1937); James Waltz, "The Significance of the Voluntary Martyrs' Movement of Ninth-Century Cordoba," *The Muslim World* 60 (1970): 143–159; 226–236; Kenneth Wolf, *Christian Martyrs in Muslim Spain* (1988).

David A. Kerr

Eusebius of Caesarea (260–339), bishop of Caesarea in Palestine and author of the first important ecclesiastical history. From many documents obtained at the Caesarean library founded by *Origen and from insights from his own travels in Palestine and Egypt, Eusebius constructed the story of early Christianity. Histories of early Christian missionary expansion depend heavily upon this work. Eusebius reports legends about the apostles' travels eastward and speaks of events from Gaul and Germania to Ethiopia and India. He also wrote five apologies for the Christian faith. Although his own Christology only approximated Nicene orthodoxy, he quoted the pagan Porphyry as supporting Christ's divinity and ridiculed attempts to depict Jesus as a deceptive magician.

BIBLIOGRAPHY Harold Attridge and Gohei Hata, eds., *Early Christianity, Judaism, and Eusebius* (1992, 1993); Timothy D. Barnes, *Constantine and Eusebius* (1981); Robert M. Grant, *Eusebius as a Church Historian* (1980).

Frederick W. Norris

Evald, Emmy C(hristina) (Carlsson) (1857–1946), Lutheran church woman and missions advocate. Born in Geneva, Illinois, to Rev. and Mrs. Erland Carlsson, Emmy Carlsson was educated in Chicago public schools. At age 13 she went to Sweden to spend four years in a girls' school in Kalmar and was confirmed in that city's cathedral. She later attended Rockford (Illinois) College for three years and became a lifelong friend of Jane Addams. In 1880 she organized the first young people's society in her father's Augustana Lutheran congregation, which in 1907 became the impetus for the synod's Luther League of America. Married to Carl A. Evald, pastor of Immanuel Lutheran Church in Chicago, the mother church of Augustana Lutheranism in Chicago, Emmy taught a Bible class of 300, formed mission study groups, and in 1888 organized a local Women's Missionary Society at Immanuel. She took a leading role in Immanuel's parish school, confirmation and Sunday school classes, and choirs. In 1892 at the Augustana Synod national assembly in Lindsborg, Kansas, she founded the synod's Women's Home and Foreign Missionary Society (WMS), which she headed until 1935. The WMS paid the salaries of women missionaries, built a Bible school and hospital in India, underwrote costs of a hospital and the Emmy Evald School for Girls in China, and provided for a hospital, school for missionaries' children, and thirty-five primary schools in Tanzania. At her retirement in 1935, she moved to New York City to head the Lutheran Home for Young Women. She was awarded a gold medal for her work by King Gustav V of Sweden.

BIBLIOGRAPHY G. Everett Arden, *Augustana Heritage: A History of the Augustana Lutheran Church* (1963); George F. Hall, *The Missionary Spirit in the Augustana Lutheran Church* (1985).

James A. Scherer

Evans, James (1801–1846), Methodist minister, ethnographer, linguist, and missionary to Canadian Indians. Born in Kingston-upon-Hull, England, Evans received a basic education and entered the grocery business. In 1822, he married Mary Blithe Smith. They had two daughters, one of whom died in infancy. In 1822 the family immigrated to Lower Canada (modern-day Quebec) and he taught near L'Orignal. About three years later, he moved to Augusta, Upper Canada (modern-day Ontario) on the Saint Lawrence River, where he was converted at a Methodist camp meeting. In 1828 he accepted an appointment at the Rice Lake school for Indian children. An aptitude for language enabled him to devise an Ojibwa syllabary and to begin publishing hymns, Scripture, and other texts in Ojibwa—a major linguistic achievement. Between 1831 and 1833, he served on the Credit, Ancaster, and Saint Catharines circuits. Ordained in 1833, he took an appointment at the Saint Clair mission near Sarnia, where he was responsible for leading a number of Ojibwas to Christianity.

In 1839 Evans undertook a tour of the north shore of Lake Superior with Thomas Hulburt. This led to the opening of work at Norway House, Manitoba, where he prepared a syllabary for another Algonquin language, Cree, and began to publish hymns and Scripture. He became embroiled in controversy regarding policies of the Hudson's Bay Company. In 1844 he was involved in the accidental death of Thomas Hassall, a trusted teacher and interpreter. He never recovered from the shock and returned to England, where he died of a heart attack after a missionary rally.

BIBLIOGRAPHY Among translations into Ojibwa and Cree, Evans produced *The Speller and Interpreter, in Indian and English, for the Use of the Mission Schools, and Such as May Desire to Obtain a Knowledge of the Ojibwa Tongue* (1837) and *Cree Syllabic Hymn Book* (1841; repr. 1954). Vera Fast, "Holy Men of Different Orders," *Journal of the Canadian Church Historical Society* 33 (1991): 95–106; John Webster Grant, *Moon of Wintertime* (1984); Gerald M.

Hutchinson, "James Evans' Last Year," *Bulletin* (Archives of the United Church of Canada) 26 (1977): 42–56; John McLean, *James Evans, Inventor of the Syllabic System of the Cree Language* (1890); Nan Shipley, *The James Evans Story* (1966); Egerton R. Young, *The Apostle of the North: Rev. James Evans* (1900). Victoria University Library, Toronto, and the University of Western Ontario house important Evans collections.

Paul R. Dekar

Evans, R(obert) M(ilton) (c. 1847–1924), missionary to Nassau, from the Church of God (Cleveland, Tennessee). Born in rural Mississippi and reared in Live Oak, Florida, Evans served as a Methodist pastor for 34 years. In 1907, after he retired from the ministry, he and his wife, Ida, had a Pentecostal experience. They joined the Church of God in 1909, sold their home and livestock in order to support their missionary venture, and set sail for Nassau (1910). In the Bahamas they were joined by friends Edmond and Rebecca Barr, native Bahamians. Many home cells were established and calls for revival meetings came from numerous surrounding islands. These activities not only laid the foundation for new Church of God congregations but also became the basis for racial integration between blacks and whites. W. V. Eneas, an early convert, became the first black bishop of the Church of God in the Bahamas. Late in 1912, with personal funds depleted and health failing, Evans retired to Florida.

BIBLIOGRAPHY C. W. Conn, *Where the Saints Have Trod* (1959); James E. Cossey, *R. M. Evans: The First of His Kind* (1985).

L. Grant McClung, Jr.

Evans, Robert Philip (1918–), American evangelical mission administrator. Evans was born in Baltimore, Maryland, to Rowland and Bertha Evans, who were Presbyterian (U.S.A.) missionaries to Cameroon. Evans graduated from Wheaton College (1939) and Eastern Baptist Seminary (1943) and in 1974 earned a Ph.D. from Manchester University, England. During World War II he was a U.S. Navy chaplain in France, where he was wounded in action. Evans was a founder of Youth for Christ International, which he served as executive director and vice president from 1945 to 1948. In 1949 he formed Greater Europe Mission (GEM) and served as European director until 1986. During his tenure GEM established the European Bible Institute in Lamorlaye, France (1952), and nine more Bible institutes and three seminaries in Europe. For 46 years Evans assisted Billy Graham in his European operations. Evans received an honorary LL.D. from Wheaton College (1962) and an honorary L.H.D. from Eastern College (1969). He wrote *Transformed Europeans* (1963) and *Let Europe Hear* (1963), published numerous articles, and served as visiting professor at seminaries in Europe and the United States.

BIBLIOGRAPHY Evans's doctoral dissertation was "The Contribution of Foreigners to the French Protestant *Réveil*, 1815–1850" (Manchester Univ., England, 1971).

Wayne A. Detzler

Evarts, Jeremiah (1781–1831), early leader of the American Board of Commissioners for Foreign Missions (ABCFM). Evarts was an influential editor and a prominent advocate of Indian rights and civic and religious causes. Educated at Yale College (B.A., 1802; M.A., 1805), he married Mehitabel Barnes in 1804 and was admitted to the Connecticut bar in 1806. In 1810 he moved to Boston to edit the *Panoplist,* an organ of orthodox Congregationalism. The next year he was elected treasurer of the newly formed ABCFM, and in 1812 he became a member of the board and of its prudential committee. At the same time the *Panoplist* became an official ABCFM organ (renamed *Missionary Herald* in 1820).

When Samuel *Worcester, corresponding secretary of the ABCFM, died in 1821, Evarts succeeded him, continuing also as editor. In spite of persistent ill health, he traveled extensively on behalf of the ABCFM and among its missions to the Cherokees, Chickasaws, and Choctaws. Evarts became deeply involved in the issue of Indian rights, combating the frontier mentality reflected in Andrew Jackson's policy of displacing the tribes. His articles in major periodicals, later published in book form, together with his lobbying in Washington and elsewhere, were central in the struggle; his strenuous efforts contributed to his early death. He was prominent in many other causes—the American Bible Society, training for the ministry, and temperance and Sabbatarian movements.

BIBLIOGRAPHY The most comprehensive treatment is John Andrew III, *From Revivals to Removals: Jeremiah Evarts, the Cherokee Nation, and the Search for the Soul of America* (1992). E. C. Tracy, *Memoir of the Life of Jeremiah Evarts* (1845) lists all Evarts's papers relating to the Indian question. *Missionary Herald* 27:305–313 and 337–347 has an extensive tribute.

David M. Stowe

Ewing, Greville (1767–1841), early supporter of missions and of Congregationalism in Scotland. Born in Edinburgh and graduated from the University of Edinburgh, Ewing was a founding member and the first secretary of the Edinburgh (later Scottish) Missionary Society, formed in March 1796. In July 1796 he helped found the *Missionary Magazine.* From 1800 to 1839 he was minister of the mother church of Scottish Congregationalism in Glasgow. His leadership was important for rebuilding the denomination after the Haldane Brothers left in 1808 to start Baptist churches. Ewing was instrumental in starting the Glasgow Theological Academy with Ralph Wardlaw in 1811 and the Congregational Union the following year. He was awarded an honorary D.D. by Princeton Theological Seminary in 1821.

BIBLIOGRAPHY Harry Escott, *A History of Scottish Congregationalism* (1960); J. J. Matheson, *Memoir of Greville Ewing* (1843).

John Roxborogh

Ewing, James C(aruthers) R(hea) (1854–1925), Presbyterian missionary in India. Born in Armstrong County, Pennsylvania, Ewing was assigned to Mainpuri, Allahabad, in 1879 and then in 1883 to the newly created North India Theological College in Saharanpur. However, beginning in 1888 he found his major work in Lahore as principal of the Presbyterian school that became Forman Christian College. He began two years after the college was founded, when it had just over 100 students and a single building; by 1917, it had over 800 students, a large campus, and an outstanding faculty and reputation. Ewing enjoyed widespread respect as both educator and administrator. He was dean of the Faculty of Arts of Punjab University (1890–1907) and its vice-chancellor (1910–1917), one of only three missionaries to have held that position in an Indian university. He was awarded three honorary degrees by colleges in the U.S. The British government gave him the Kaiser-i-Hind Gold Medal (for Kangra Valley Earthquake Relief Fund work), and named him Honorary Companion of the Indian Empire and then Honorary Knight Commander of the Indian Empire. He ended his India career as secretary of the India council of the Presbyterian Church in the U.S.A. (1918–1922). Later he was president of the PCUSA Board of Foreign Missions from 1924 until his death.

BIBLIOGRAPHY J. C. R. Ewing, *A Prince of the Church in India, Being a Record of the Life of the Rev. Kali Charan Chatterjee, D.D., for Forty-eight Years a Missionary at Hoshiarpur* (1918). Robert E. Speer, *Sir James Ewing: A Biography of Sir James C. R. Ewing* (1928).

John C. B. Webster

Ezana (4th century), first Christian King of Aksum. In the fourth century Aksum (later Ethiopia) was a prosperous kingdom on the Red Sea coast, trading with Egypt and other areas. From inscriptions and coins Ezana appears to have been the most important of the Aksumite rulers. Early inscriptions show him as polytheist, worshiping a wide range of deities, but another of later date refers only to the "Lord of Heaven." Still another proclaims his faith in the Trinity. Evangelized by *Frumentius, who was ordained a bishop for Ezana's kingdom by Athanasius of Alexander, Aksum appears to have been converted from the king down, the Christianization of the people in general only beginning in Ezana's time. Ezana stands with *Constantine and Tiridates of Armenia as one of a group of fourth-century royals who established a new political Christendom.

BIBLIOGRAPHY Steven Kaplan, "Ezana's Conversion Reconsidered," *JRA* 13 (1982): 101–109.

Adrian Hastings

Fabri, Friedrich (1824–1891), leader of the Rhenish Mission (RM). After serving as a Lutheran pastor in his native Bavaria, Fabri moved to Barmen to take the position of inspector in the RM from 1857 to 1884. He succeeded in coordinating the Lutheran, Reformed, and United elements in the society and in improving the standards of training in its seminary. In his theology of mission he developed a peculiar vision of the coming kingdom that combined the traditional view of individual salvation with a contemporary philosophy of history as the field of God's redeeming action in the world of nations, including the spread of Western civilization by means of the colonial movement. This highly ambivalent ideology allowed him both to agitate freely for German participation in the international quest for overseas colonies and to continue as a leader of one of the most prominent German Protestant mission agencies. In 1884 he was appointed to a professorship at Bonn University. Fabri's mission legacy is marked by the memory of a pioneer of German colonial imperialism.

BIBLIOGRAPHY Klaus J. Bade, *Friedrich Fabri und der Kolonialismus in der Bismarckzeit* (1975).

Hans-Werner Gensichen

Fabricius, Johann Philipp (1711–1791), linguist and Bible translator of the Danish-Halle Mission in South India. Born near Frankfurt am Main, Germany, Fabricius, after finishing a full course of studies in both law and theology, arrived in South India in 1740 and soon took charge of the small Tamil Lutheran congregation at Madras. In spite of many setbacks, it grew from 300 to 2,200 members during the 30 years of his ministry. Fabricius's forte was linguistic and translation work. In 1774 Fabricius brought out a collection of 335 Tamil hymns, most of them translated from the German. It soon replaced earlier Tamil hymnals, and many of Fabricius's hymns have been included in more recent hymnals. In 1777 he published the first Tamil-English dictionary, containing 9,000 words, which became the basis of all later efforts in the field. His Tamil-English grammar appeared in 1778. His outstanding contribution to the progress of Christianity in Tamil proved to be his Bible translation, the first comprehensive effort of its kind in any Indian language. A famous Tamil poet called it the "golden version." It passed the highest tests of Hindu pandits and retained its peculiar quality even in many later revised versions. Fabricius did not live to see the complete work in print (1796). Also, his last years were clouded by mismanagement of the mission, unsuccessful financial transactions, and other failures. But even today his memory as one of the greatest missionary translators in India lives on. He died in Madras.

BIBLIOGRAPHY Wilhelm Germann, *Johann Philipp Fabricius* (1865); E. Arno Lehmann, *It Began at Tranquebar* (1956).

Hans-Werner Gensichen

Falkner, Thomas (1707–1784), English Jesuit missionary in Argentina. Falkner was born in Manchester, England, of Calvinistic, perhaps Scottish parentage. His early career is obscure, but he studied medicine (he wrote a treatise on the human body), knew Isaac Newton, and had a scientific reputation that produced a commission from the Royal Society to report on the medicinal properties of plants in the Americas while acting as surgeon on a slave ship from Africa. Nursed from sickness by Jesuits in Buenos Aires, he became a Catholic in 1731, a Jesuit in 1732, and after study at Córdoba (Argentina) University, a priest in 1738 or 1739. Between 1743 and 1756 he worked as priest and doctor in Jesuit colonies for Indians on the pampas and in the Buenos Aires highlands, maintaining his studies of flora and fauna. From 1756 he taught mathematics at Córdoba, until the expulsion of the Jesuits in 1767 forced him out, first to Spain and eventually to England. There he wrote a remarkable account of Patagonia and its peoples, described the curative powers of American drugs, and developed a new map of South America.

BIBLIOGRAPHY Thomas Falkner, *A Description of Patagonia and the Adjoining Part of South America, with an Account of the Soil, Produce, etc. of Those Countries* (1774; facs. ed. by A. E. S. Neumann, 1935). G. Furlong Cardiff, *Tómas Falkner y su Acerca de los Patagones* (1954) and *La personalidad y la Obra de Tómas Faulkner* (1929); V. O. Cutolo, *Nuevo Diccionario Biografico Argentino (1750–1930)*, vol. 3 (1971), pp. 19–21.

Andrew F. Walls

Farquhar, John Nicol (1861–1929), Scottish educational missionary and orientalist. Farquhar was born in Aberdeen, Scotland, and served an apprenticeship as a draper. He returned to school at 21, and completed studies at Oxford. In 1891 he arrived in India as a lay educational missionary for the London Missionary Society, teaching at Bhowanipur, Calcutta, for 11 years. He was never ordained. In 1902 he joined the staff of the Indian YMCA, first as national student secretary and later as literary secretary, a post he held until 1923. During these years he wrote several important books, notably *The Crown of Hinduism* (1913) and *Modern Religious Movements in India* (1915), and edited many more. The key word in Farquhar's missionary theology was "fulfilment." He did not invent but did much to popularize the idea that Christ came to fulfill and bring to completion not only the law and the prophets (Matt. 5:17) but all the world's higher religions. It is in this sense that Christ is the "crown" of Hinduism. Farquhar was an excellent linguist in Bengali and Sanskrit and had an encyclopedic grasp of the Hindu source material, as his *Outline of the Religious Literature of India* (1920) demonstrates. As an editor, he was able to inspire a whole missionary generation to write to the highest standards of accuracy, sympathy, and Christian centrality. He was less successful in finding Indian Christian co-workers, never coming fully to terms with the changed climate of opinion in India after 1919. Having left India because of ill health in 1923, he spent the last six years of his life as professor of comparative religion in the University of Manchester. He died in Manchester.

BIBLIOGRAPHY Eric J. Sharpe, *J. N. Farquhar: A Memoir* (1963), *Not to Destroy but to Fulfil* (1965), *Faith Meets Faith* (1977), pp. 19–32, and "J. N. Farquhar," in Gerald H. Anderson et al., eds., *Mission Legacies* (1994), pp. 290–296.

Eric J. Sharpe

Farrington, Sophronia (1801–1880), first woman missionary of the Methodist Episcopal Church. Farrington grew up in Herkimer, New York, one of ten children. She graduated from Cazenovia (New York) Seminary and taught school for several years. In November 1833 she sailed with Rufus Spaulding and Samuel O. Wright and their wives for the mission in Liberia, begun by Melville *Cox that March. The missionaries landed in Monrovia on New Year's Day 1834 and immediately fell ill. Phebe Wright died February 4, her husband March 29. When the Spauldings decided to return to the United States, Farrington refused to go with them, fearing that the church would abandon the mission if she left. She wrote, "I laid my life on the altar on leaving America, and I am willing that it should remain there." She remained alone and ill with fever in Liberia from May 17, 1834, until reinforcements arrived that fall. Her health did not improve, and she returned to the United States the following spring, arriving in New York on April 29, 1835. She settled in Utica, New York. In 1851 she married George Cone, a grocer.

BIBLIOGRAPHY There is no complete biography of Farrington, but information about her missionary experiences appears in Wade Crawford Barclay, *History of Methodist Missions*, vol. 1 (1949), and John M. Reid, *Missions and Missionary Society of the Methodist Episcopal Church* (1879).

Susan E. Warrick

Faulding, Jennie. *See* Taylor, Jennie (Faulding).

Favier, Pierre-Marie Alphonse (1837–1905), missionary pastor and vicar apostolic of Peking. Born at Marsanny-la-Côte (Côte d'Or), France, Favier entered the Congrégation de la Mission (Lazarists, also known as Vincentians) in 1858. Ordained a priest in 1861, he arrived in Peking (Beijing) in July 1862, where he had an active pastoral ministry. In 1897 he became coadjutor to the vicar apostolic, whom he succeeded two years later. He obtained an imperial decree placing Catholic bishops on a par with the Chinese governors and governors general, an unpopular move with a number of Catholics, Protestants, and the Chinese. Living through the month-long siege of the Beitang (North Church) during the Boxer Rebellion of 1900, he condemned the international relief expedition's excessive use of force against the Chinese rebels. He wrote many articles in mission journals, an account of the Boxer Rebellion, and a general history of Peking. He died in Peking.

BIBLIOGRAPHY Pierre-Marie Favier, *Peking: Histoire et Description* (1897; repr. 1900) and *The Heart of Peking: Bishop A. Favier's Diary of the Siege* (1901). See also Robert Streit, ed., *Annales de la Congrégation de la Mission* 70 (1905): 339–350.

John W. Witek, SJ

Feild, Edward (1801–1876), first Anglican bishop of Newfoundland. Feild was born near Worcester, England, the third son of a local gentleman farmer. He was educated at Rugby and at Queen's College, Oxford (1823). Ordained a priest in the diocese of Oxford in 1827, he served as curate of Killington and later as rector of English Bicknor, in Gloucestershire. In 1840, during a time of controversy over the Anglican monopoly of state-supported education, he was made a special inspector of church schools on behalf of the National Society, the educational arm of the Church of England. In 1844 he was appointed colonial bishop for Newfoundland, Bermuda, and the Labrador Coast, a new jurisdiction separated from the diocese of Nova Scotia. He proved to be a faithful pastor and vigorous organizer of widely scattered congregations of settlers and native peoples, most of whom could be reached only by boat. To visit the congregations in Labrador alone required a dangerous voyage of 1,600 miles, lasting three months or more. He attracted clergy and financial support from the Society for the Propagation of the Gospel (SPG), founded Bishop Feild College in St. John's, Newfoundland, and built up local stewardship and self-support through the establishment of a central fund. Annual reports of his missionary journeys published by the SPG made him something of a celebrity in England. In 1875 ill health forced his return to England where he died the following year.

BIBLIOGRAPHY Edgar House, *Edward Feild, the Man and His Legacy* (n.d.) contains extended reference to Bishop Feild College, illustrations, and a bibliography; Frederick Jones, *Edward Feild, Bishop of Newfoundland, 1844–1876* (n.d.; pamphlet published by the Newfoundland Historical Society); H. W. Tucker, *Memoir of the Life and Episcopate of Edward Feild, D.D.* (1877). Several of Feild's journals and annual reports are in the SPG archives in London.

Charles Henry Long

Feller, Henriette (Odin) (1800–1868), founder of the French Canadian Protestant mission at Grande-Ligne, Lower Canada (Quebec). Born in Montagny, Switzerland, Henriette Odin acquired medical knowledge from her father, who in 1803 moved to Lausanne as director of the city hospital. In 1822 she married Louis Feller, a 41-year old widower, father of three children, and director of the Lausanne police. Sympathetic to converts of Scottish revivalist Robert Haldane, the Fellers protected those oppressed for activities outside official Protestantism.

Between 1822 and 1827, Henriette Feller suffered the deaths of her daughter, husband, sister, and mother, and was afflicted by typhoid fever. During her convalescence, her sympathies with dissident Protestants deepened and she began working with the Société des Missions Evangéliques de Lausanne (founded 1828), which had a mission in French Canada. In 1835 she left for Canada and, despite intense Catholic opposition, took up residence in Grande-Ligne, near Montreal. The absence of public services provided openings for witness. She taught, dispensed rudimentary medical services, distributed Bibles, and provided children's care. By the time of the 1837 rebellion, a Protestant community numbering sixteen converts and a few sympathizers had formed.

Persecution prompted Feller and the congregation to flee to Vermont. This provided an opportunity to strengthen the work at Grande-Ligne through fund-raising and affiliation with the Foreign Evangelical Society of New York. Feller founded the Evangelical Society of Grande-Ligne. She was the instrument of the conversion of a number of educated French Canadians and the inspiration of Baptists who formally organized a French Canadian missionary society.

BIBLIOGRAPHY J. M. Cramp, *A Memoir of Madame Feller* (1876); Harry A. Renfree, *Heritage and Horizon: The Baptist Story in Canada*, chap. 14 (1988); Paul Villard, *Up to the Light: The Story of French Protestantism in Canada* (1928); W. N. Wyeth, *Henrietta Feller and the Grande-Ligne Mission, A Memorial* (1898). The Canadian Baptist archives, Hamilton, Ontario, house papers of the Grande-Ligne Mission.

Paul R. Dekar

Fenn, Christopher Cyprian (1823–1913), Anglican mission administrator. Fenn was born in South India, where his father, Joseph, was a pioneer missionary of the Church Missionary Society (CMS). After graduating with a first class degree in classics from the University of Cambridge (Trinity College) and ordination in the Anglican Church, he commenced a lifetime of missionary service in 1851 when he went to Ceylon (Sri Lanka) under the CMS as principal of the Cotta Institute. He returned to England in 1863 and became a secretary of the CMS, bearing much of Henry *Venn's burden as Venn came to the end of his secretariat. After Venn's death, Fenn was the guardian of the Venn tradition. His areas of special responsibility included Ceylon, and he became a key figure in an acrimonious "Ceylon controversy" with Bishop R. S. *Copleston in the late 1870s. This was partly a boundary dispute between the CMS and Copleston, partly a theological dispute concerning the extent and nature of a bishop's authority, and partly a conflict about how quickly a local church could move to self-governing status. After his retirement in 1894, Fenn continued to be involved in CMS affairs, and, for example, served on the Centenary Committee on "Communities of Native Christians." Its report was a reiteration of Venn's views, but it was later heavily altered by the secretariat, which effectively abandoned the traditional commitment to self-governing churches.

BIBLIOGRAPHY Eugene Stock, *History of the Church Missionary Society: Its Environment, Its Men, and Its Work*, 4 vols. (1899–1916). Obituary in *Church Missionary Review*, November 1913.

Peter Williams

Ferguson, Abbie Park (1837–1919) *and*
Bliss, Anna Elvira (1843–1925), founders of Huguenot College, and leaders of the early South African Dutch Reformed women's missionary movement. New Englanders and daughters of Congregationalist ministers, Ferguson and Bliss graduated from Mount Holyoke Female Seminary in 1856 and 1862 respectively. Having absorbed the missionary legacy of Mount Holyoke's founder, Mary *Lyon, Ferguson and Bliss became teachers. In 1873 they answered the appeal of Andrew *Murray for teachers from Mount Holyoke to open a female seminary in South Africa. With financial support from the Dutch Reformed Church (DRC) in South Africa, Ferguson and Bliss founded Huguenot Seminary (later Huguenot College) in Wellington as the first woman's college in South Africa. Ferguson became the first president, and in 1910 Bliss became the second. Graduates from Huguenot fanned out across southern Africa, establishing schools and trans-

forming the education of girls. Ferguson especially inculcated missionary fervor in her students, and in 1875 Johanna *Meeuwsen left Huguenot for missionary service in the Transvaal. In 1878, upon reading the ten-year report of the Woman's Board of the American Board of Commissioners for Foreign Missions, Ferguson and her students founded the Huguenot Missionary Society, which supported alumnae as missionary teachers and also supported pioneer male missionaries in southern Africa, such as A. A. *Louw. Virtually the entire first generation of women missionaries from the DRC, both single and married, were Huguenot graduates. Approximately fifty Huguenot students had become missionaries by 1904.

Ferguson herself wished to become a missionary in the South African gold fields but was persuaded to remain at Huguenot. In 1889, with Mrs. Andrew Murray and Huguenot graduates as officers and leaders, the Vrouesendingbond (Woman's Missionary Union) emerged from the Huguenot Society as the first national organization for Afrikaner women. The Vrouesendingbond appointed and paid all salaries of single women missionaries in the DRC. In 1890 Ferguson used her own money to begin a mission study class at Huguenot that became the nucleus of the Student Volunteer Movement in the Cape Colony. In 1904 the class became a separate missionary training school for women, Friedenheim, under the DRC. Ferguson's brother, George, joined her in 1877 until his death in 1896 as head of a missionary training institute for men. Abbie Ferguson and Andrew Murray participated together in movements to promote higher spiritual life. After her retirement from the presidency of Huguenot, Ferguson helped to establish a Women's Interdenominational Missionary Committee in South Africa.

BIBLIOGRAPHY See Ferguson, Bliss, and Andrew Murray's accounts of their work in the 1898 *Huguenot Seminary Annual.* Other sources on Ferguson and Bliss include George P. Ferguson, *The Builders of Huguenot* (1927); Dana L. Robert, "Mount Holyoke Women and the Dutch Reformed Missionary Movement, 1874–1904," *Missionalia* 21 (1993):103–123. The archives of Mount Holyoke College, South Hadley, Mass., contain files on Ferguson and Bliss. The major collection of their papers, journals, and correspondence is held in the NGK archives in the Cape Archives, Cape Town, Republic of South Africa.

Dana L. Robert

Ferguson, Samuel David (1842–1916), American Episcopal missionary bishop in Liberia. Ferguson was born in Charleston, South Carolina, to a former slave mother and Baptist deacon father. In 1848 his family immigrated to the newly independent Republic of Liberia. Ferguson was educated at Mount Vaughan High School in Cape Palmas, where he later served as teacher and principal (1862–1865). Trained for the ministry under Bishop John Payne, Ferguson was ordained a priest in 1868 and placed in charge of St. Mark's (Episcopal) Church, Cape Palmas (1868–1885). Elevated to the episcopate in 1885, he became the first bishop of African descent consecrated for a jurisdiction of the American Episcopal Church (PECUSA). Ferguson's episcopacy was marked by institutional growth, advances in education, and increased Liberian identity. During his tenure many churches became self-supporting, indigenous teachers and clergy assumed leadership, and the number of communicants in the district increased fivefold. A strong nationalist, Ferguson believed that divisions between the indigenous population and Americo-Liberians could be healed through education. At his initiative, Cuttington College was founded in 1889 and the Bromley School for Girls reorganized. Supporting fifty-six schools, the Episcopal mission led all churches in education and enrolled more "native" students than the Liberian government schools.

BIBLIOGRAPHY D. Elwood Dunn, *A History of the Episcopal Church in Liberia, 1821–1980* (1992); Dean Arthur Holt, "Change Strategies Initiated by the Protestant Episcopal Church in Liberia from 1836 to 1950 and Their Effects" (Ed.D. diss., Boston Univ., 1970); National Council of the Protestant Episcopal Church, *Handbooks on The Missions of the Episcopal Church: Liberia* (1924).

Ian T. Douglas

Fernbaugh, Hettie Luzena (1870–1904), first missionary of the Brethren in Christ. Fernbaugh was born in Indiana of pioneer stock; her mother's ancestors were Baptist missionaries to the Kansas territory. In 1892 she joined the Brethren in Christ Church of Abilene, Kansas. Although some Brethren in Christ people supported her, she was almost excommunicated for joining the Gospel Missionary Union (GMU), a premillennial nondenominational faith mission founded to evangelize the interior of Africa. In 1894 she sailed with the first GMU party bound for Morocco. An uneducated person, she kept house for the missionaries and watched their children to release them for evangelistic work among the Muslims and Jews. After studying Arabic, she was able to engage in house-to-house visitation with other missionary women. Remaining loyal to the Brethren in Christ, she continued to dress plainly, which included keeping her head covered. Fernbaugh lived by the "faith-mission" method, existing without salary. She believed in the imminence of Christ's second coming and in divine healing. Returning to the United States in 1900, she died a few years later of jaundice, after refusing medical treatment. Her example inspired the Brethren in Christ to establish its own denominational mission work.

BIBLIOGRAPHY Wilma Wenger Musser, "Hettie L. Fernbaugh, Missionary Pioneer," *Notes and Queries in Brethren in Christ History,* July 1865, pp. 16–22. There is a collection of Fernbaugh's letters in the archives of the Brethren in Christ Church, Grantham, Pa.

Dana L. Robert

Fielde, Adele M. (1839–1916), Baptist missionary to China known for her work with Bible women. Fielde was born in New Hampshire and grew up in the Universalist church tradition. In her late 20's she became engaged to a Baptist missionary candidate to Siam (Thailand), agreeing to become a Baptist and to join him on the field to be married. When she arrived in Siam in 1865 after a long ocean voyage, she learned that he had died months earlier. She took over his ministry amid her grief but did not fit in with the Baptist missionary community. Her dancing, card-playing, and associations with the diplomatic community resulted in her dismissal from the mission. She returned home to the United States but later was reinstated and reassigned to China. Settling at the port city of Swatow (Shantou), Kwangtung (Guangdong) Province, she initiated Bible women's work, training native women to go out as evangelists and Bible teachers. During her 20-year tenure in China she established schools, wrote curriculum, and trained some 500 Bible women. After her retirement she returned to the United States and became involved in scientific research. Ten years following her death she was eulogized by her Baptist mission agency as the "mother of our Bible women and also the mother of our Bible schools."

BIBLIOGRAPHY Helen N. Stevens, *Memorial Biography of Adele M. Fielde: Humanitarian* (1918); Ruth A. Tucker, *Guardians of the Great Commission: The Story of Women in Modern Missions* (1988).

Ruth A. Tucker

Figurovskii, Innokentii (1864–1931), Russian Orthodox missionary to China. Dispatched from Russia to Peking (Beijing) in 1897, Figurovskii found that the Russian Orthodox mission there was virtually dormant. Six formal missions had been mounted since 1728, but after ministering to expatriate Russian merchants until such time as the latter assimilated to Chinese culture and drifted away from the church, they limited themselves to studying Chinese and translating; the archimandrite in charge of the mission often doubled as the de facto Russian ambassador. Figurovskii refocused the work on missionary outreach and Christian witness. He instituted daily services for Chinese converts and potential catechumens, established charitable agencies for destitute émigrés, and ordered his fellow preachers, sent out into the villages, to double as social workers. Following the violently anti-Christian Boxer Rebellion (1901), which saw the Russian missionaries suffer more than the numerically larger Roman Catholics and Protestants, Figurovskii reported on the status and needs of the Chinese mission to the Holy Synod in Saint Petersburg. He was elevated to the episcopacy and returned to China, along with several priests. Utilizing reparation payments from the Chinese government, he opened thirty-two mission centers that provided elementary education to some 500 children. His clergy baptized over 5,000 people and a seminary was opened to train native clergy. It is known that in 1904 he was working in Manchuria, but after that the record is silent.

BIBLIOGRAPHY Serge Bolshakoff, *The Foreign Missions of the Russian Orthodox Church* (1943), pp. 63–68; James J. Stamoolis, *Eastern Orthodox Mission Theology Today* (1986), pp. 41–42.

Paul D. Garrett

Filofei (Leshchinsky) (1650–1727), Russian Orthodox missionary in Siberia. Filofei was of Malorossian extraction and had the surname Leshchinsky. He graduated from the Theological Academy in Kiev and ministered there as a priest. In the last decade of the seventeenth century, after the death of his wife, he joined the famous Kiev-Pechery Lavra (Monastery of grottoes), taking the monastic name Filofei. In 1701 he was appointed abbot of the Svensk Dormition Monastery in the province of Orel, and less than a year later was consecrated metropolitan of Siberia and Tobolsk. On April 4, 1702, with a group of young monks, he set off for Tobolsk to evangelize the aboriginal people. Gravely ill in 1709, he delegated all his public duties and secluded himself in the Troitsky monastery in Tyumen, which he had founded in 1708. But the following year, upon recovery of his health, Filofei returned to his work as an ordinary missionary under the name Fyodor, which he adopted with the highest degree of monastic vows in 1709. In 1715 he sent an Orthodox mission to Peking, headed by Archimandrite Hilarion. In 1716, Czar Peter the Great ordered him to return to the metropolitan see in Tobolsk and to govern the Siberian diocese again. Filofei obeyed, but in 1720, at the age of 70, he requested that the Czar relieve him of his official responsibilities. From then until his death Filofei traveled tirelessly across the Tyumen region, teaching and baptizing. It is claimed that he and his fellow missionaries converted about 40,000 persons throughout Siberia. The number of churches in Filofei's diocese increased from 160 to 448 in the years of his service. He established several schools and seminaries. A contemporary wrote that Filofei "doomed to fire their pagan shrines, but toward the people he acted with a spirit of meekness and convinced them by arguments, without any force or violence."

BIBLIOGRAPHY N. A. Abramov, *Filofei Leshchinsky: Mitropolit Sibirsky i Tobolsky* (Metropolitan of Siberia and Tobolsk) (1861) and *Svyatitel Filofei, V Skhime Fyodor: Prosvetitel Sibirskikh Inorodtsev* (The Very Reverend Filofei, Feodor in schema: illuminator of Siberian natives) (1882). Also see *Missioner* (Missionary), 1875, nos. 34 and 37.

Evgeny S. Steiner

Fisch, Rudolf (1856–1946), pioneer Swiss missionary doctor in Ghana. Fisch was born in the Swiss canton of Aargau, was trained as a doctor by the Basel Mission (BM), and served in southern Ghana, based at Aburi, from 1885 to 1911. As the first BM missionary in Ghana with scientific training, he pioneered the application of new discoveries (like the nature of malaria and the available forms of prophylaxis and prevention) to the actual living situation of Europeans and Africans there. He was a frequent contributor to the *Archiv für Schiffs- und Tropenhygiene* and published a widely read guide to health in the tropics (*Tropische Krankheiten,* 1891; 4th ed., 1912). As a scientific pioneer, however, he faced skepticism on the part of many missionary colleagues who had experienced the benefits of traditional African knowledge of medicinal herbs or who were more interested in homeopathy. He also founded the Blue Cross, a temperance movement in Ghana. For several decades after his return to Switzerland, he was a father in the faith to pietist and mission groups in his home region. Occasionally, it seems, he also helped out a local district nurse with inoculation programs. However, lacking full academic qualifications as a medical doctor, he was not able to practice medicine in his homeland.

BIBLIOGRAPHY Friedrich Hermann Fischer, *Der Missionsarzt Rudolf Fisch und die Anfänge medizinischer Arbeit der Basler Mission an der Goldküste (Ghana)* (1991).

Paul Jenkins

Fisher, George S. (1856–1920), founder of Gospel Missionary Union (GMU). Fisher, who was born of missionary parents near Cass Lake, Minnesota, became secretary of the Kansas YMCA in 1890. It soon became the fastest growing YMCA in the country, proving him a gifted leader of people, an able administrator, an effective evangelist, and a much-sought-after pulpit speaker. As a result of a challenge by H. Gratton *Guinness, many YMCA members volunteered for missionary work in the vast unreached interior of sub-Saharan Africa. In 1890 nine American young men and women went out in what became known as the Sudan Party, five of whom died of fever within three months of reaching Sierra Leone. Fisher's involvement with the Sudan Party made him the center of a major controversy in the national YMCA, leading to his resignation in 1892. The same year, he became instrumental in founding the World's Gospel Mission (later, Gospel Missionary Union). His stated purpose was to "promote Bible study, consecrated Christian living, sound doctrine, and the preaching of the Gospel where Christ is not named." He led GMU into four frontier fields: Morocco in 1894, Ecuador in 1896, Colombia in 1908, and French Sudan (Mali) in 1919. Fisher died on a field trip in Guayaquil, Ecuador, and is buried there.

BIBLIOGRAPHY Fisher's writings appeared from 1891 to 1920 in the *Kansas Pilgrim* and the *Gospel Message*, both magazines of GMU. Details on the Sudan Party and Fisher's 1913 survey trip of the French Sudan are found in Dick L. Darr, "George C. Reed and the French Sudan" (unpublished manuscript held by GMU). C. Howard Hopkins, in "The Kansas-Sudan Missionary Movement in the YMCA, 1889–1891," *Church History* 21 (1954): 314–322 gives an overview of the controversy that led to Fisher's resignation from the YMCA. See also D. P. Shidler, *Exploits of Faith* (1982), pp. 113–114.

Dick L. Darr

Fisher, Welthy (Honsinger) (1879–1980), American Methodist educational missionary in China, and literacy pioneer in India. Welthy Honsinger was born in Rome, New York, and grew up hoping to be an opera singer. But upon hearing a missionary speaker, Honsinger discarded her plan, completed her education as a teacher, and sailed to China in 1906. As headmistress of the Bao Lin school in Nanchang until 1917, she promoted higher academic standards and Chinese leadership. Upon choosing a Chinese to succeed her and then leaving, she was terminated by the (Methodist) Woman's Foreign Missionary Society. Back in the United States, she became a YWCA war worker and then edited *World Neighbors*, a Methodist mission magazine. In 1924, she married Frederick Bohn Fisher, American Methodist bishop of India and Burma and friend of Gandhi and Tagore.

The Fishers' commitment to indigenization caused Frederick to resign his bishopric in 1930 in favor of an Indian successor. After her husband died in 1938, Welthy Fisher wrote his biography and studied educational systems throughout the world. Stylish and articulate, she became a popular lecturer on missions, women's topics, and international friendship. She supported Chinese industrial cooperatives and was accused of being a communist. In 1948 she was chairman of the World Day of Prayer. Six weeks before his death in 1947, Gandhi asked her to work for India's villages. In 1952 she returned to India to work with Frank *Laubach, Christian literacy pioneer. In 1953 she founded Literacy House at Allahabad. Breaking with Laubach, she developed secular methods to encourage functional literacy, linking it with agricultural and industrial development. Literacy House moved to Lucknow and became famous for its effectiveness and its House of Prayer for All People. Fisher was much-honored by the Indian government, which based its village literacy programs on her ideas. She returned to the United States in 1973 and died in Connecticut.

BIBLIOGRAPHY Autobiographies by Welthy Fisher are *Beyond the Moongate* (1924) and *To Light a Candle* (1962). She also authored *Twins Travelogues* (1922–1923), *A String of Chinese Pearls* (1924), *Top of the World* (1926), *Freedom: A Story of Young India* (1930), *Frederick Bohn Fisher: World Citizen* (1944), and *Handbook for Ministers' Wives* (1950). Sally Swenson, *Welthy Honsinger Fisher: Signals of a Century* (1988); Colleen Kelly, "The Educational Philosophy and Work of Welthy Honsinger Fisher in China and India, 1906–1980" (Ph.D. diss., Univ. of Connecticut, 1983).

Dana L. Robert

Fisk, Pliny (1792–1825), pioneer of the Near East mission of the American Board of Commissioners for Foreign Missions (ABCFM). Born in Shelburne, Massachusetts, Fisk graduated from Middlebury College and Andover Theological Seminary (1818). After ordination as a missionary, he served briefly as agent of the ABCFM in Georgia. With Levi *Parsons he embarked on November 3, 1819, on the first American mission to the Near East, with the primary aim of converting the Jews of Palestine, widely believed to be a necessary preliminary to the millennial age of Christ's reign on earth. First based at Smyrna, they soon moved to Scio, where they studied modern Greek and published and distributed a tract made up of evangelical passages from *Chrysostom. After returning to Smyrna they toured Asia Minor. When Parsons went on to Jerusalem in December 1820, Fisk remained in Smyrna and for a year was acting British chaplain there, preaching and distributing literature. After Parson's death at Alexandria in February 1822, Fisk went to Malta and was joined by Jonas *King. They toured Upper Egypt, crossed the Sinai Desert, and reached Jerusalem in April 1823. They went on to Beirut, but Fisk was back in Jerusalem before the end of the year. There were troubles with the authorities, instigated by Latin Catholics and Maronite and Syrian patriarchs who disliked these "Bible-men." In the summer of 1824, Fisk and King toured the major centers of Syria, then returned to Beirut and Jerusalem. In the spring of 1825 Fisk returned to Beirut where he died in October, having nearly completed an Arab and English dictionary.

BIBLIOGRAPHY The obituary of Fisk in *Missionary Herald* 22 (1826): 128–132 is largely an edifying account of his death. His journeys and activities are reported in some detail in Joseph Tracey, *History of the ABCFM* (1842), a summary compilation of material from annual reports and the *Missionary Herald* for the years 1819 to 1825.

David M. Stowe

Fiske, Fidelia (1816–1864), first single woman missionary in Persia and founder of the Nestorian Female Seminary. As a precocious and devout child in rural Massachusetts, Fiske read Timothy Dwight's *Theology* at age eight. A Congregationalist, she pursued the best education available to girls and was one of the first pupils at Mount Holyoke Seminary, the first woman's college in America. Upon graduation, she became a teacher at Mount Holyoke and was known for bringing her pupils to Christ. Fiske secretly longed to be a missionary, as her uncle Pliny *Fisk had been one of the first American Board of Commissioners for Foreign Missions (ABCFM) missionaries to the Holy Land. In 1843 ABCFM missionary Justin *Perkins visited the seminary and requested two single women to pursue educational work among Nestorian girls. Fiske was chosen from the volunteers and she embarked that year, the first of many unmarried women missionaries educated at Mount Holyoke.

Fiske opened a boarding school for girls at Urmia that she sought to manage along "Mount Holyoke principles." The purpose of the seminary was to make Nestorian girls better wives and mothers and to revive their Christian faith. During her 15 years at Urmia, Fiske led numerous revivals that converted approximately two-thirds of her students. Rufus *Anderson, whose vernacular policies she supported, compared her to Jesus Christ in spirituality. During school vacations, she visited former pupils in their homes and held women's meetings, encouraging former pupils to evangelize other women. In 1858 she returned to Massachusetts in hopes of regaining her health. She spoke about missions to women's groups and prepared the memorial volume for the twenty-fifth anniversary of Mount Holyoke, after turning down an offer to be its principal. She edited *Recollections of Mary Lyon,* which was published posthumously. Fiske was probably the best-known female ABCFM missionary of her generation.

BIBLIOGRAPHY D. T. Fiske, *The Cross and the Crown; or, Faith Working by Love: As Exemplified in the Life of Fidelia Fiske* (1868); [Thomas Laurie], *Woman and Her Saviour in Persia* (1863); Annie Ryder Gracey, *Eminent Missionary Women* (1898).

Dana L. Robert

Fison, Lorimer (1832–1907), English anthropologist and Wesleyan missionary to Fiji. While studying law at the University of Cambridge, Fison committed some infraction and was suspended. He then set sail for Australia and the goldfields of Victoria. After learning of his father's death, he committed his life to Christ at a Wesleyan open-air service. Soon afterward, he volunteered for Fiji as a missionary. Serving two terms, a total of 16 years (1863–1871 and 1875–1884), he became known as a brilliant missionary anthropologist and historian of colonial Fiji. When Fiji became a British colony, he wrote a series of 35 articles for the *Sydney Morning Herald,* which are a major historical and ethnological contribution. He is best remembered for *Kamilaroi and Kurnai* (1880, coauthored with Alfred L. Howitt), on the Aborigines of Australia's southwest. He is also recognized for his work with the American anthropologist Lewis Henry Morgan. He provided Morgan with much valuable kinship data on Pacific tribal groups. Fison encouraged Fijians to tell their own stories, and he recorded and published them. His *Tales of Old Fiji* (1904) and other writings reflect an astonishing grasp of the island mind. His linguistic work anticipated what is now called ethnolinguistics. His study of Fijian land tenure (*Land Tenure in Fiji,* 1881) was republished as an official Australian government reference work. For 17 years he was editor of the weekly Methodist journal *The Spectator.* In addition, he was a frequent lecturer before scientific bodies in Australia and elsewhere.

BIBLIOGRAPHY Arthur Gordon, *Fiji: Records of Private and of Public Life, 1875–1880,* vol. 1 (1897–1912); A. Harold Wood, *Overseas Missions of the Australian Methodist Church,* vol. 2 (1975–1980).

Darrell Whiteman

Fitch, George A(shmore) (1883–1979), YMCA worker in China. Fitch was born in Soochow, China, the son of Presbyterian missionaries George F. and Mary (McLellan) Fitch. He graduated from the College of Wooster, Ohio (1906), and Union Theological Seminary, New York (B.D., 1909). He was ordained in the Presbyterian Church in 1909 and went to China to work with the YMCA in Shanghai. When the Nanking (Nanjing) Massacre by the Japanese army occurred in 1937–1938, Fitch, who was head of the YMCA there, served as director of the International Committee for the Nanking Safety Zone. His diary report on atrocities committed by the Japanese army in Nanking was carried to Shanghai by the first person able to leave Nanking after its occupation by the Japanese in December 1937. Writing later in his autobiography, Fitch said, "My story created a sensation in Shanghai, for it was the first news of what had happened in the capital since its evacuation, and it was copied and mimeographed and widely distributed there." In 1938 Fitch traveled throughout the United States giving talks about the Nanking Massacre and showing films to document it. He returned to China in 1939 to serve with the YMCA and later with the United Nations Relief and Rehabilitation Agency until 1947. He then served the YMCA in Korea and Taiwan until 1961, when he retired in the United States. He died in Claremont, California.

Bibliography George A. Fitch, *My Eighty Years in China* (1967).

Martha Lund Smalley

Fjellstedt, Peter (1802–1881), pioneer of the missionary movement in Sweden. Fjellstedt was born in the province of Värmland in western Sweden and studied for the ministry at the University of Lund. After his ordination in 1828, he went immediately to the Basel Mission's school for a short period of missionary training. He was sent first to Palamcottah in South India, but after only a short time there (1832–1835) he was forced home by ill health. Fjellstedt's second mission assignment, to Turkey and Malta, also proved debilitating, both physically and spiritually. In 1840 he was compelled to return to Europe; and by 1843 he was again in Sweden. The second half of Fjellstedt's life was spent as a missionary motivator and organizer in his homeland. There he was instrumental in founding in 1845 the Lund Missionary Society, one of the forerunners of the present-day Church of Sweden Mission, and the missionary training institute which in 1862 became the Fjellstedtska School in Uppsala. In his last years he was much appreciated as a preacher and especially as a devotional writer and Bible commentator. In 1853 he was awarded an honorary doctorate of theology at the University of Halle. His ability to learn languages was legendary, as was his memory. He died in Uppsala.

Bibliography Carl Anselm, *Peter Fjellstedt,* 2 vols. (1930, 1935); Emmet E. Eklund, *Peter Fjellstedt: Missionary Mentor to Three Continents* (1983); Bengt Sundkler, *Svenska Missionssällskapet, 1835–1876* (1937); Herman Schluyter, *Nordisk Teologisk Uppslagsbok,* vol. 1 (1952), cols. 897–900.

Eric J. Sharpe

Flad, Johann Martin (1831–1915), German missionary to Ethiopia. A native of Württemberg and trainee of the famous St. Chrischona Mission seminary near Basel, Switzerland, Flad was one of four young missionaries who in 1855 were sent to Ethiopia by Samuel *Gobat, Anglican bishop of Jerusalem. After a short period of work as a craftsman in the service of the emperor Theodoros, Flad discovered his personal opportunity for mission among the Falashas, an indigenous Jewish minority in and around Addis Ababa. The mission was supported mainly by the London Society for Promoting Christianity amongst the Jews, of which Flad became a member. During a persecution initiated by the emperor, Flad was arrested in 1863, together with other Europeans. They were eventually freed by a British military expedition in 1868, but Flad had to leave the country. He managed to continue his work from outside Ethiopia, chiefly by sending Bibles for distribution among the Falashas, and later by dispatching evangelists. In 1885 he joined the British and Foreign Bible Society and is said to have delivered altogether eighty-four camel loads of Amharic Bibles and New Testaments. When the country again became accessible for missionaries in 1922, Martin Flad's son Friedrich and others were able to continue the work until the occupation by Italy in 1936.

Bibliography Julius Flad, *J. M. Flad, Ein Leben für Äthiopien* (1968).

Hans-Werner Gensichen

Fleming, Archibald Lang (1883–1953), Anglican missionary and bishop among the Inuit (Eskimo). A Glasgow naval architect who immigrated to Canada and studied at Toronto, in 1909 Fleming accompanied the experienced missionary J. W. Bilby to Lake Harbour, Baffin Island, Canada, under the auspices of the Church Missionary Society. Ordained in 1912, he was chaplain of Wycliffe College, Toronto, from 1918 to 1921 and served a church in New Brunswick (1921–1927). He then served as archdeacon of the Arctic (1927–1933) and first bishop of the Arctic (1933–1949). His diocese, which gave him the nickname "Archibald the Arctic," was amalgamated from many previous jurisdictions and covered all Inuit and much Indian work spread over 2,250,000 square miles of northern Canada. He was able to draw continuing support from England, but despite his long residence in Canada he never succeeded in adequately tapping Canadian sources. The Arctic he knew was one of fur-trapping under the Hudson's Bay Company, and he saw no reason to suppose that this life-style would not last forever. The church as Fleming found it depended on a network of local leaders, with a scattering of missionaries at certain trading posts. This proved durable among Inuit, but was less successful among Indians.

Bibliography A. L. Fleming, *Dwellers in Arctic Night* (2d ed., 1929), *Perils of the Polar Pack: or, The Adventures of the Reverend E. W. T. Greenshield, KT. O. N., of Blacklead Island, Baffin Land* (1932), and *Archibald the Arctic* (1956). T. C. B. Boon, *The Anglican Church from the Bay to the Rockies* (1962).

Gavin White

Fleming, Daniel Johnson (1877–1969), American missiologist. Fleming was born in Xenia, Ohio, and graduated from the College of Wooster. After completing a short-term mission assignment in India, he earned advanced degrees at Columbia University (M.A., physics) and at the University of Chicago (M.S., chemistry). He also studied theology at Union Theological Seminary in New York. In 1904, the Presbyterian Board of Foreign Missions appointed him and his wife, Elizabeth (Cole), missionaries to Lahore, India, where they served for eight years. While on furlough, Fleming completed a Ph.D. at the University of Chicago Divinity School. When family health problems made a return to India impossible, he accepted a position at Union Theological Seminary, New York, serving first as director of the newly established Department of Foreign Service and later as professor of missions (1918–1944). In addition to his work at Union, he lectured widely at other academic institutions and missionary conferences. He also served on the staff of the Laymen's Foreign Missions Inquiry in India.

Although Fleming had an impact on many through his teaching, his greatest contribution to the Christian mission was through his writing. He wrote or edited twenty-three books and published seventy-five articles. Through his writing he sought to rethink the missionary enterprise in response to the questions raised by biblical higher criticism, the social sciences, and increasing global consciousness. He hoped to build a theory and practice of mission that would be viewed as ethical by thinking people both in the United States and in countries where American missionaries were sent. *Whither Bound in Missions* (1925) provides the most comprehensive statement of his thinking. His later books, which were more widely recognized, and which were devoted to the cause of world unity, include *Each with His Own Brush* (1938), *The World at One in Prayer* (1942), and *Bringing Our World Together* (1945).

BIBLIOGRAPHY Lydia Huffman Hoyle, "Making Missions Ethical: Daniel Johnson Fleming and the Rethinking of the Missionary Enterprise" (M.A. thesis, Univ. of North Carolina, 1987) and "Daniel Johnson Fleming," in Gerald H. Anderson et al., eds., *Mission Legacies* (1994), pp. 486–493. Fleming's published works and some unpublished papers are available at Union Theological Seminary in New York.

Lydia Huffman Hoyle

Fleming, John (1807–1894), Presbyterian missionary to Native Americans. Born in Pennsylvania, Fleming graduated from Jefferson College in 1829 and, after studying at Princeton Seminary, was ordained in 1832 as a Presbyterian minister. The following year he was appointed by the American Board of Commissioners for Foreign Missions to work among the Creek Indians, one of the Five Civilized Tribes who had been removed by treaty from their homeland in the southeastern United States to Indian Territory (later Oklahoma). At first he preached through an interpreter, but diligent study of the Muskhogean language allowed him eventually to communicate directly with the people. Fleming was also able to prepare a writing system for that language. Thereafter he published hymns, sermons, and portions of the Bible for local use. He traveled widely to stay in touch with the scattered Creeks, but, through no fault of his own, results were meager and government authorities closed the mission station permanently. Fleming tried in 1838 and 1839 to make a place for himself in the Great Lakes region by working with the Weas, the Ojibwas, and the Ottawas, all to no avail. Shortly after his wife died, he became pastor to a conventional church of white parishioners in Fairfield, Pennsylvania. After eight years of such work he moved to LaSalle County, Illinois, where he again took up missionary activities from 1849 to 1875 among scattered settlements of white farmers. Among other things, he served during these years as supervisor of the Presbyterian boards of missions and publication.

BIBLIOGRAPHY John Fleming, *The Muskokee Semahayeta, or Muskokee Teacher* (1836). Also see annual reports of the Presbyterian Church from the mid-1830s to 1875.

Henry Warner Bowden

Fleming, Louise ("Lulu") Cecilia (1862–1899), African American missionary of the Woman's Baptist Foreign Missionary Society. Fleming was born a slave in Hibernia, Clay County, Florida. In 1885 she graduated from Shaw University, Raleigh, North Carolina, and in 1886 became the first black woman to be appointed and commissioned for career missionary service by the Woman's Baptist Foreign Missionary Society in the West (WBFMSW) and one of the first three single women sent out by that society. She reached the Congo in 1887 and was stationed at Palabala. During her first term of service, she supervised girls at the station and taught the primary classes and the upper English classes in the day and Sunday schools. She returned to the United States to regain her health in 1891, and while on furlough completed the full course in 1895 at the Woman's Medical College of Pennsylvania in Philadelphia. The same year she sailed to the Congo representing the Woman's Baptist Foreign Missionary Society, with headquarters in the East. Fleming was stationed at Irebu, where she worked as a medical missionary. In 1898, when the Irebu station was closed, she was reassigned to the Bolenge station. She was stricken with African sleeping sickness before the end of her second term and returned to the United States for medical treatment. She died at the Samaritan Hospital in Philadelphia.

BIBLIOGRAPHY Lulu C. Fleming, "A Letter from the Congo Valley," *Missionary Review of the World,* n.s. 1 (1888): 207–209; Rosalyn Terborg-Penn, Sharon Harley, and Andrea Benton Rushing, *Women in Africa and the African Diaspora* (1987).

Sylvia M. Jacobs

Fleming, Paul William (1910–1950), founder of New Tribes Mission (NTM). Born of Swedish immigrant parents in California, Fleming had little formal education but was deeply influenced by evangelist Paul D. *Rader in Los Angeles and in Fort Wayne, Indiana. In 1937 he sailed as an independent missionary for Singapore. Receiving the blessing of Robert *Jaffray, he soon focused his efforts on the largely unreached Sakai people in British Malaya. Returning to the United States in 1940 after his ministry was cut short by cerebral malaria, and convinced that many tribal groups in otherwise evangelized areas of the world had yet to hear of Christ, Fleming traveled across the country, showing films of his work in Malaya to quicken interest. With Cecil Dye, a pastor from Saginaw, Michigan, Lance Latham (an associate of Rader), and others, Fleming founded NTM in 1942.

The work suffered an inordinate number of tragedies in its early years: five men of the first party of recruits disappeared into the Bolivan jungle in 1943; in 1946 fire destroyed two dormitories at the mission's training camp in California, claiming the life of an infant; two NTM planes crashed in 1950, taking many lives, including that of Fleming himself; another pioneer missionary lost his life along the Bolivian-Brazil border in 1951; and in 1953, fourteen recruits lost their lives fighting a forest fire. Defying the odds, the mission continued to grow, and as of the mid-1990s, it was the third-largest North American Protestant agency, with 2,000 missionaries in 21 countries, among 200 tribal groups.

BIBLIOGRAPHY Kenneth J. Johnston, *The Story of New Tribes Mission* (1985); New Tribes Mission brochure "Great Is Thy Faithfulness" (1993).

Robert T. Coote

Fleming, Peter Sillence (1928–1956), missionary martyr in Ecuador. Fleming was born in Seattle, Washington, and earned B.A. and M.A. degrees in American literature at the University of Washington. A longtime friend of James *Elliot of Portland, Oregon, he and Elliot had discussed remaining single in order to be pioneer jungle missionaries. In 1952 they sailed for Ecuador, hoping to find an elusive tribe of jungle Indians known as Aucas (a Quichua term for "wild men"; now known by their tribal name, Waorani). Pending an opportunity to locate and reach the Aucas, they initially worked among the Quichua. After Elliot married Elisabeth Howard, in 1954 Fleming married his college sweetheart, Olive Ainslie. They worked in Quito and then in the jungle village of Puyupungu.

After the Aucas were located, Fleming, along with Elliot, Ed McCully, Roger Youderian, and the missionary pilot, Nate *Saint, began making friendly contacts with the Aucas from the air, followed by a meeting on a sand bar along the Curaray River. Two days later, on Sunday, January 8, 1956, what was expected to be another friendly conversation turned out to be hostile. Fleming and his companions were speared to death. Eventually about one half of the Waorani, including all five of the killers, became Christians. Three of the killers became pastors and evangelists, and the believers endeavored to contact other villages still hostile.

BIBLIOGRAPHY Elisabeth Elliot, *Through Gates of Splendor* (1957); Olive Fleming Liefeld, *Unfolding Destinies: The Untold Story of Peter Fleming and the Auca Mission* (1990).

Walter L. Liefeld

Fliedner, Federico (1845–1901), Protestant missionary in Spain. Born in Kaiserwerth, Germany, where his father, Theodore, was a pastor and a famous philanthropist, Fliedner went as a missionary to Spain in 1870 and established himself in Madrid where he remained the rest of his life. The mandate he received from the independent missionary committee that sent him from Berlin was to work for the unity of the Protestant churches, and he dedicated his talents and energy to that end. He founded schools, an orphanage, and a publishing enterprise to serve all churches. Fliedner established contact with liberal intellectuals and writers, some of whom published in the magazine *Revista cristiana* that he founded in 1880. His pedagogical experiments and the textbooks he published inspired several reforms to modernize the educational system of Spain. As a result of his constant traveling and unifying efforts, several Protestant denominations joined in the Iglesia Evangélica Española, in which his own family has continued his work to the present. Through teaching and the publication of classic books of Spanish Protestants, he also tried to connect the so-called Second Reformation of Spain in the nineteenth century with the aborted Protestant Reformation of the sixteenth century, which was decimated by the Inquisition. In 1873 Fliedner attended the sixth conference of the Evangelical Alliance in New York and presented the case of Spanish Protestants.

BIBLIOGRAPHY Fliedner's memoirs were gathered in *Aus meinen Leben*, 2 vols. (1901–1903) edited by his son Jorge. There is a brief account of his work in Carmen de Zulueta, *Misioneras, feministas, educadoras. Historia del Instituto Internacional* (1984).

Samuel Escobar

Flierl, Johann (1858–1947), Lutheran pioneer missionary in New Guinea. Flierl grew up in a Lutheran farmer's household in northern Bavaria. The village pastor encouraged him to volunteer for training in the seminary of the Neuendettelsau Mission. In 1878 he was sent out for service among Australian Aborigines. Having applied for transfer to the newly established German colony in northeastern New Guinea in 1886, he became the pioneer of Lutheran missions among the Papua. He served there as field director of the mission until 1930, even though Australia began occupation of the territory in 1914. He played an important part in the exploration of the eastern highlands and paved the way for the mission to the hill tribes. Learning by doing rather than relying on preconceived strategies, he became largely responsible for introducing a system of church mission "from below," compensating for the shortage of foreign missionaries by involving local elders and teachers in evangelistic service and introducing a Christian life-style by means of cautious inculturation of the faith. As Flierl considered indigenous religion a strictly public affair, he also tended to postpone individual baptism of converts until larger numbers of people came forward. It was left to his successors to develop this approach in terms of the more closely knit German Volk-church pattern. Flierl also worked for wider Lutheran fellowship through his close connection with Australia, which allowed the mission churches to survive the hardship of two world wars.

BIBLIOGRAPHY Johann Flierl, *Forty Years in New Guinea* (1927), and *Christ in New Guinea* (1932). Charles W. Forman, *The Island Churches of the South Pacific* (1982); Herwig Wagner and Hermann Reimer, *The Lutheran Church in Papua New Guinea: The First Hundred Years* (1987).

Hans-Werner Gensichen

Florovsky, Georges V(asilievich) (1893–1979), premier Orthodox historical theologian. Florovsky was born in Odessa, Russia (in what is now Ukraine), and educated at the Theological Academy, where his father was rector. In 1920 the family immigrated to Sofia, Bulgaria. The following year he was invited to teach philosophy of law in Prague. In 1922 he married and moved to Paris. With others, he founded St. Sergius Theological Institute there, teaching patristics from 1926 to 1948. He was ordained a priest of the Ecumenical Patriarchate of Constantinople in 1932. In 1948 he moved to the United States, where he taught at St. Vladimir's Orthodox Theological Seminary, Crestwood, New York, until 1955, serving also as dean from 1950 to 1955. Beginning in 1954 he taught at Harvard Divinity School, and, concurrently, at Harvard's Slavic Department and at Holy Cross Greek Orthodox School of Theology, Brookline, Massachusetts. He was active in ecumenical affairs throughout his life. Upon retirement from Harvard he taught from 1965 to 1979 at Princeton Seminary and Princeton University. His theological legacy is enormous; he published in almost all areas of Orthodox theology, provoking a neopatristic synthesis that has influenced every phase of Orthodox theology, including the theology of mission, where his major contribution was on the issues of culture and faith.

BIBLIOGRAPHY Georges Florovsky, "Empire and Desert: Antinomies of Christian History," *Greek Orthodox Theological Review* 3 (1957): 133–159, *Christianity and Culture: The Collected Works of Georges Florovsky,* vol. 2 (1974), and "Russian Missions: An Historical Sketch," in *Aspects of Church History: The Collected Works of Georges Florovsky,* vol. 4 (1975), pp. 139–155. Andrew Blane, ed., *Georges Florovsky: Russian Intellectual and Orthodox Churchman* (1993); "Orthodoxy and the Ecumenical Movement: Esssays in Honor of Fr. Georges Florovsky," *Greek Orthodox Theological Review* 41, no. 2 (1996); George Hunston Williams, "Georges Vasilie Florovsky: His American Career (1948–1965)," *Greek Orthodox Theological Review* 11 (1965): 7–107.

Stanley Samuel Harakas

Flynn, John (1880–1951), Presbyterian minister and founder of the Australian Inland Mission of the Presbyterian Church of Australia. Flynn was born in Moliagul, Victoria, Australia. In 1902, after four years with the Education Department of Victoria, he joined the home mission staff of the Presbyterian Church, working among remote and working-class communities. Ordained in 1911, he was assigned for two years to what was known as the Smith of Dunesk Mission based at Beltana, South Australia. In 1912 he reported on the needs of remote aboriginal and white communities in the Northern Territory, presenting a vision of the church's mission to the sparsely populated areas of inland Australia. For the next 39 years, as superintendent of the mission, he was guided by the motto "For Christ and the Continent" and put need before creed. In 1928 he founded the mission's Aerial Medical Service at Cloncurry, Queensland, later known as the Royal Flying Doctor Service, which fulfilled his dream of a "mantle of safety" for outback Australians. From 1939 until 1942 he was moderator general of the Presbyterian Church of Australia. The John Flynn Memorial Church at Alice Springs is his official memorial.

BIBLIOGRAPHY Max Griffiths, *The Silent Heart: Flynn of the Inland* (1993); W. Scott McPheat, *John Flynn: Apostle to the Inland* (1963); Michael Page, *The Flying Doctor Story, 1928–1978* (1977).

William W. Emilsen

Focher, Juan (d. 1573), Franciscan missionary theoretician in Latin America. Born in France, Focher (also known as Foucher, Fucer, Fuchens, Fucher, Francher, and Frucher) received a doctor of law degree before entering the Franciscans. Going to New Spain in 1540, he became an eminent consultant for other missionaries and for episcopal commissions concerning the increasingly complex problems of church organization, marriage law, and pastoral practice in the New World. His written responses to queries were passed from hand to hand, as were his more systematic treatises, which addressed the major problems of colonization and evangelization. Besides its importance for religious history, Focher's work also figured in the development of Mexican civil law. He developed a theory of evangelization and showed painstakingly its application to the Americas. His works thus became manuals for Franciscan missionaries in Mexico and other countries. Many of his productions have been lost through time, but a major work of missiology survives—*Itinerarium catholicum proficiscentium ad infedeles convertendos* (1574) albeit with additions and corrections by Pedro Valadés. Among many other themes, this pioneering work in mission theory puts forward the theory of royal vicarship to explain the relations between Spain and the church in the Indies. Focher died in Mexico.

BIBLIOGRAPHY Juan Focher, *Itinerario del misionero en América,* Antonio Eguiluz, tr., with introduction and biographical source notes (1960). J. de Mendieta, *Historia eclesiástica indiana* (1870); R. Streit, "Focher: Ein unbekannter Missionstheoretiker des 16. Jahrhunderts," *ZM* 3 (1913): 275–283.

Edward L. Cleary, OP

Forbin-Janson, Charles de (1785–1844), founder of the Association of the Holy Childhood. Born in Paris of noble parents who fled from the city with him during the French Revolution, de Forbin-Janson went to the Saint Sulpice seminary in 1808, where he shared missionary dreams with Henri de *Solages and Eugène de *Mazenod. He was ordained to the Catholic priesthood in 1811 and wanted to go to China. Instead, the pope commissioned him to re-Christianize France. He founded the Missionaries of France in association with Abbé de Rauzan, leading home missions during the French Restoration. Appointed bishop of Nancy and Toul in 1824, he emigrated anew after the 1830 revolution in France. From 1839 he carried out preaching missions in New York, Philadelphia, Saint Louis, New Orleans, Baltimore, Quebec, Montreal, and Ottawa. Back in France in 1842, he met Pauline *Jaricot. Involving children in mission was a new idea that led to the foundation of the Holy Childhood in 1843. Funds were raised after the pattern of Pauline Jaricot, including the monthly donation of coins offered by children for the salvation of children. The first campaigns were for Chinese orphans. Helping these children implied the hope that they would eventually become "priests" to their own nation.

BIBLIOGRAPHY Philpin de Rivière, *Vie de Mgr Forbin Janson, missionnaire, évêque de Nancy et Toul, primat de Lorraine, fondateur de la Sainte Enfance* (1892); Paul Lesourd, *Mgr de Forbin Janson* (1944);

N.E. Dionne, *Mgr de Forbin Janson: sa vie, son oeuvre en Canada* (1895, 1910). See also *Annales de la Sainte Enfance* (1846–1966).

Marc R. Spindler

Ford, Francis X(avier) (1892–1952), Maryknoll missionary and bishop in China. Born in Brooklyn, New York, in 1912 Ford became the first student to apply to the seminary of the recently established Catholic Foreign Mission Society, also known as Maryknoll. Ordained in 1918, he was one of the first four Maryknoll missioners to leave for China. In 1925 he was appointed head of the newly created mission territory of Kaying, or Meihsien (Meizhou), in the northeastern corner of Kwangtung (Guangdong) Province. Ten years later, when the area became a vicariate apostolic, Ford was made bishop. For his episcopal motto he chose the word *condolere,* meaning "to have compassion," from Hebrews 5. In December 1950 he was arrested by the Communists for alleged spying activities. Four months later, he was pronounced guilty and sentenced to the provincial prison in Canton. He died in jail of exhaustion and illness in February 1952.

Ford used the encyclical *Maximum illud* of Pope *Benedict XV (1919) as the cornerstone of his efforts to implement a native church. His goal was a self-governing Chinese church financially self-reliant and not burdened by Western institutions. His plans called not only for a well-trained local clergy and sisterhoods but also for a well-educated lay leadership to take responsibility in building modern China. Ford was one of the first Roman Catholic prelates to emphasize direct evangelization by religious women. The small experiment he and a few Maryknoll sisters started in 1934 helped to enhance the role of women in mission and their place in the church.

BIBLIOGRAPHY Francis X. Ford, *Come, Holy Ghost* (1953; rev. 1976). John F. Donovan, *The Pagoda and the Cross: The Life of Bishop Ford of Maryknoll* (1967); Raymond A. Lane, *Stone in the King's Highway: The Life and the Writings of Bishop Francis Xavier Ford* (1953); Robert E. Sheridan, *Compassion: The Spirit of Francis X. Ford, M.M.* (1982); Mark Tsai, "Bishop Ford, Apostle of South China," *American Ecclesiastical Review* 127 (October 1952): 241–247; Jean-Paul Wiest, "Francis X. Ford, M.M.," in Gerald H. Anderson et al., eds., *Mission Legacies* (1994), pp. 232–241.

Jean-Paul Wiest

Forgács, Gyula (1878–1941), founder of the Hungarian Christian Student Movement. A Reformed minister, Forgács was assistant pastor of the Scottish Mission among the Jews in Budapest from 1904 to 1910 and subsequently served congregations in Pécel and Sárospatak. In different capacities he pioneered and served the Hungarian (Reformed) Foreign Mission Society from 1903 to 1936. In 1925 he published a comprehensive handbook on the home mission work of the Hungarian Reformed Church; it remains a standard text. In preparing the mission article of the church constitution of 1933, he worked out his vision for a missionary congregation. He served the revival of the whole Reformed church by theologically linking the numerous home mission societies to the church by broadening the concept of mission to all regular church activities. But he emphasized the teaching component of the Great Commission almost to the exclusion of evangelism. This emphasis, further pursued by Sándor *Makkai, limited mission activity to what occurred within the church. Forgács nevertheless contributed in a theological and practical way to the growth of mission awareness in the Hungarian Reformed Church, which effort saw significant fruits in the revival following World War II.

BIBLIOGRAPHY Gyula Forgács, "Az evangéliomi keresztyén diákmozgalom" (The Evangelical Christian Student Movement), *Protestáns Szemle* 17 (1906), "Mott János és a diákok evangelizációja" (John Mott and the evangelization of students), *Protestáns Szemle* 21 (1909): 164–175, *A belmisszió és cira pastorális kézikönyve* (Handbook for home mission and pastoral care) (1925), "A Zsidómissió hazánkban" (Mission to the Jews in our home country), in László Draskóczy and Sándor Virágh, eds., *Jubileumi Emlékkönyv (Jubilee album), Református Külmissziói Szemle* 2 (1934): 56–64, and "A száz éves skót misszió" (The hundred year old Scottish Mission), in *És lõn világosság* (The light dawns) (1941), pp. 414–425. Anne-Marie Kool, *God Moves in a Mysterious Way: The Hungarian Protestant Foreign Mission Movement (1756–1951)* (1993), pp. 297–305.

Anne-Marie Kool

Forman, Charles W(illiam) (1916–), American missiologist. Forman was born in Gwalior, India, the son, grandson, and great-grandson of American Presbyterian missionaries to India (Forman Christian College, in Lahore, is named for his grandfather). After receiving a Ph.D. in history from the University of Wisconsin and a B.D. from Union Theological Seminary, New York City, he married Helen Janice Mitchell and they went as Presbyterian missionaries to India, where he taught at North India United Theological College in Saharanpur, Uttar Pradesh, 1945–1950. In 1953 he became successor to Kenneth Scott *Latourette as professor of missions at the Divinity School of Yale University until he retired in 1987. He was also chairman of the Theological Education Fund of the World Council of Churches from 1965 to 1971, chairman of the Commission on Ecumenical Mission and Relations of the United Presbyterian Church in the U.S.A. from 1965 to 1971, chairman of the Foundation for Theological Education in Southeast Asia from 1970 to 1989, and president of the American Society of Missiology from 1980 to 1981. An authority on Christianity in the South Pacific, he authored *The Island Churches of the South Pacific* (1982) and *The Voice of Many Waters: The Story of the Life and Ministry of the Pacific Conference of Churches* (1986). In retirement he served as visiting professor at seminaries in Egypt and on Fiji, American Samoa, and Western Samoa.

BIBLIOGRAPHY Forman's other publications include *A Faith for the Nations* (1958), *The Nation and the Kingdom* (1964), *Christianity in the Non-Western World* (1967), "A History of Foreign Mission Theory in America," in *American Missions in Bicentennial Perspective,* edited by R. P. Beaver (1977), "Evangelization and Civilization: Protestant Missionary Motivation in the Imperialist Era—The Americans," *IBMR* 6 (1982): 54–56, and autobiographical reflections in "My Pilgrimage in Mission," *IBMR* 18 (1994): 26-28.

Gerald H. Anderson

Forman, Charles William (1821-1894), American Presbyterian missionary to India. After growing up without religion in a landed family in Kentucky, Forman was converted at the age of 20 and, after training at Princeton Seminary, volunteered for mission service. He arrived in India in 1847 and two years later settled in Lahore, where he remained for the rest of his life. He founded the Rang Mahal School in the center of the old city. In 1865 a college department under his leadership was added to the school. He built up a fine corps of Indian teachers and the college produced leaders of Punjab society in business, government, and the professions. He was a member of virtually every committee on education appointed by the Punjab government during his lifetime. Theologically conservative, he nevertheless favored adaptation of Christianity to Indian custom on matters such as polygamy and he wrote appreciatively of the Sikhs and their founder. He was a friend of all, walking the streets to and from school and talking with the people daily for 40 years. At the time of his death the college department was named Forman Christian College.

BIBLIOGRAPHY Stanley E. Brush, "Protestants in the Punjab: Religion and Social Change in an Indian Province in the Nineteenth Century" (Ph.D. diss., Univ. of California, Berkeley, 1971); S. K. Datta, *The History of the Forman Christian College: Selections from the Records of the College, 1869-1936* (1936); John C. B. Webster, *The Christian Community and Change in Nineteenth Century North India* (1976).

Charles W. Forman

Formosus (c. 816-896), Latin missionary to the Bulgarians and, later, pope who worked for the expansion of the church. As reward for success in heading the Latin mission to the Bulgarians (866-867), Formosus was offered the archbishopric of the Bulgarian church by a grateful King *Boris. However, he declined on demand of Pope *Nicholas I. Despite disagreements over the legitimacy of the use of the Slavic vernacular and the Byzantine Rite in worship, in 868 he obediently ordained his ideological rival, *Methodius, to the priesthood during the latter's visit to Rome. Political intrigues forced him into exile in France for more than five years before he was restored to the See of Porto, and in 891 he was elevated to the papacy. As pope, he promoted missions in England and across northern Germany.

BIBLIOGRAPHY Francis Dvornik, *Byzantine Missions among the Slavs* (1970), pp. 132-138.

Paul D. Garrett

Forsyth, Christina Moir (1844-1919), missionary of the United Presbyterian (later United Free) Church of Scotland to the Mfengu people of South Africa. Born in Glasgow, Christina Moir early decided on a missionary career but because of various family demands was not free to serve until 1878 when she went to Paterson in the eastern Cape Colony as an unpaid missionary.

In 1881 she returned to Scotland where, in 1884, she married a Mr. Forsyth who was drowned a year later. Christina Forsyth then again became an unpaid missionary in South Africa. She lived in a traditional house among the Mfengu of the Xolobe Valley, who had long resisted any advance by missionaries. She got to know every family well through constant visits, which she continued for 30 years despite many rebuffs and even threats of violence. Slowly but surely she won the community over to Christianity simply by her presence among them. She took no furloughs and rarely left the valley until ill health and advanced age forced her retirement in 1916. The Mfengu sent a delegation to beg her to die among them, since "you are not white but one of us." This she wanted to do, but the mission authorities and European friends would not allow it, and she returned to Scotland.

BIBLIOGRAPHY The only biography of Christina Forsyth is an unsatisfactory one by W. P. Livingstone with whom she refused to cooperate, *Christina Forsyth of Fingoland: The Story of the Loneliest Woman in Africa* (1919). The book contains ample evidence to counter the negative title. Archives of the Foreign Mission Committee of the United Free Church of Scotland, in the National Library of Scotland, contain material on Forsyth.

Andrew C. Ross

Foucauld, Charles Eugène de (1858-1916), Christian hermit among the Muslim Tuareg tribes of North Africa. Born in Strasbourg, de Foucauld discovered his missionary calling after living the dissolute life of a French aristocrat and soldier. His spiritual quest began during a scientific visit to Morocco, where he was moved by the simplicities of sincere Muslim piety. The French Abbé Huvelin, spiritual director of several French intellectuals, brought him to Christian faith and guided his choice of an ascetic life following a pilgrimage to Jerusalem in 1889. For seven years, de Foucauld lived as a Trappist in a remote Syrian village (1890-1897); then he left the order for the more arduous life of giving unpaid service to the convent of the Poor Clares in Nazareth and Jerusalem. Ordained in 1901, he devoted himself to what he called "Nazarene spirituality," which found most austere expression in French Algeria. There he felt himself drawn by irresistible urge, first to the oasis of Beni-Abbes and finally to Tamanrasset in the Ahaggar Mountains, which was to be his spiritual home for the remaining 11 years of his life (1905-1916). He lived an uncompromising asceticism among the Tuareg tribes, who related to him as *marabout* (holy man), drawn less by his Christian creed and daily Eucharist than by his unspoken imitation of Christ, in which they recognized the Qur'anic portrayal of *Isa* (Jesus). In the estimation of the Tuareg chieftain who knew him best, his spirituality transcended the culture of French colonialism, which the tribesmen detested. His modern Muslim biographer, Ali Merad, asks whether, "though belonging to Christianity spiritually, the great hermit of the Sahara belongs in some way to Islam?" In answer to his question, he opines: "This fragile light was like a joyful sign of a fraternal presence." In 1916 de Foucauld died at the hand of a young Tuareg tribesman in what was probably a tragic accident. He lies buried in Tamanrasset. The rule he devised was taken up in 1933 by the Little Brothers and in 1936 by the Little Sisters of Jesus. They maintain their spiritual center in Tamanrasset but also work in the poorest conditions of African and Asian cities. De Foucauld also had a profound spiritual influence on the French Catholic scholar of Islam, Louis *Massignon (1883–1962), who in turn influenced the Second Vatican Council's teaching on Christian-Muslim reconciliation.

BIBLIOGRAPHY R. Bazin, *Charles de Foucauld: Explorateur du Maroc, Ermite au Sahara* (1921; Eng. tr., 1923); M. Gibbard, "Charles de Foucauld," in C. Jones and G. Wainwright, eds., *The Study of Spirituality* (1986); E. Hamilton, *The Desert My Dwelling Place: A Study of Charles de Foucauld* (1968); A. Merad, *Charles de Foucauld au Regard de l'Islam* (1975); N. Robinson, "Massignon, Vatican II, and Islam as an Abrahamic Religion," *Islam and Christian Muslim Relations* 2 (1991): 182–205; R. Voillaume, *Seeds of the Desert: The Legacy of Charles de Foucauld* (1955).

David A. Kerr

Foucquet, Jean-François (1665–1741), Jesuit missionary in China. Foucquet was born in Vézelay, Yonne, France, and entered the Society of Jesus in Paris in 1681. There he completed his studies for the priesthood and was ordained in 1693. The following year he volunteered for the missions in the East. Assigned to China, he arrived in Amoy (Xiamen) in 1699. Successful in developing mission stations in Fukien (Fujian) and Kiangsi (Jiangxi) Provinces, he was called to Peking (Beijing) in 1711 by the emperor, who wanted him to assist Joachim *Bouvet in studying the I-ching (Book of changes). He was soon asked to explain principles of astronomy and mathematics.

Over the next seven years Foucquet wrote several essays on figurism, which aimed at finding the figures of the Old Testament in the Chinese classics. As part of this enterprise, he was perhaps the first Jesuit to cite Taoist literature. While in Canton, Foucquet had denied the common Jesuit position on the Chinese rites. He saw figurism as a way between that position and its opposing view, which understood the Chinese philosophers as atheists. Foucquet's refusal to accept a confrere as his superior led to his recall to France in 1720. Seeking to present his figurist ideas to the Holy See, he went to Rome, where he was consecrated a bishop in St. Peter's Basilica in 1725. In Paris he had become acquainted with Voltaire and the Duc de Saint-Simon, and in Rome Montesquieu had several discussions with him. Moreover, his correspondence helped several French scholars to develop sinology in France.

Having received Foucquet's letter containing some of his figurist views, a prelate in Canton wrote Propaganda Fide that these were contrary to sacred Scripture. In 1736 its investigation commission concurred, and the cause of figurism ended. A year after Foucquet's death the papacy condemned the Jesuit interpretation of the rites.

BIBLIOGRAPHY Catherine Jami, "The French Mission and Ferdinand Verbiest's Scientific Legacy," in J. Witek. ed., *Ferdinand Verbiest (1623–1688): Jesuit Missionary, Scientist, Engineer, and Diplomat* (1994), pp. 531–542; Jean Claude Martzloff, "Espace et temps dans les textes chinois d'astronomie et de technique mathématique astronomique aux XVIIe et XVIIIe siècles," in C. Jami and Hubert Delahaye, eds. *L'Europe en Chine: Interactions scientifiques, religiquese, et culturelles aux XVIIe et XVIIIe siècles* (1993), pp. 217–230; John W. Witek, *Controversial Ideas in China and in Europe: A Biography of Jean-François Foucquet* (1982).

John W. Witek, SJ

Fox, Charles Elliot (1878–1977), Anglican missionary in Melanesia. Fox was born in England, the son of a clergyman who was appointed vicar of Gisborne (diocese of Waiapu, New Zealand); he received all his education in New Zealand. Joining the Melanesia Mission, a high-church Anglican society, in 1902 he went to Norfolk Island, where he was ordained. He taught there, and later on Mota, before going to the Solomon Islands in 1908. Quick to learn local languages, he lived as much as possible as a Melanesian, going through an adoption ceremony with a Christian teacher from San Christóbal. Small in stature, he was named Kakamora by the locals, the name of a type of bush spirit. He was the only missionary ever to be a member (from 1932 to 1943) of the Melanesia Brotherhood, a largely lay indigenous order founded in 1926. He was offered the diocese of Melanesia in 1932 but declined it. After meeting the anthropologist W. H. R. Rivers, he embarked on a scientific investigation of Melanesian culture, which resulted in a D.Litt (1922) and a number of publications; he also made Bible translations in Arosi. Never married, he died in Waipukurau, New Zealand, at the age of 99, never really having retired. His ashes were buried in the cathedral in Honiara, in Melanesia.

BIBLIOGRAPHY Charles E. Fox, *The Threshold of the Pacific: An Account of the Social Organization, Magic, and Religion of the People of San Cristoval in the Solomon Islands* (1924), *Lord of the Southern Isles: Being the Story of the Anglican Mission in Melanesia, 1849–1949* (1958), and *Kakamora* (autobiography, 1962). John Garrett, *Footsteps in the Sea: Christianity in Oceania to World War II* (1992); David Hilliard, *God's Gentlemen: A History of the Melanesian Mission, 1849–1942* (1978).

Jocelyn Murray

Fox, Henry Watson (1817–1848), Church Missionary Society (CMS) missionary in India. Fox was educated at Durham Grammar School, Rugby, and Oxford University's Wadham College, from which he received a degree in 1837. Appointed by the CMS for work in India, he and his wife reached Madras in July 1841. He worked with Robert T. *Noble at Masulipatam (Machlipatnam). Developing remarkable eloquence in Telugu, he concentrated on village evangelism and saw many conversions. But his health began to fail, and by late 1845 he had to abandon the work. His wife and one of his three children died before he could book passage home to England. In Britain, his forceful appeals, published in *Chapters on Missions in South*

India (1848), persuaded many to go into missionary service. Returning to India late in 1846, his health again declined. Forced to return to England in early 1848, he was appointed to work under Henry *Venn, as assistant secretary of the CMS. But his health did not stand up, and he died in October of that year. The force of his personality and spirituality had a strong influence, both in England and in India.

BIBLIOGRAPHY Henry W. Fox, *The Claims of India, on Members of Our Universities, Being Extracts from Unpublished Letters* (1861) and *Missionary Letters Addressed to Oxford Undergraduates' Church "Missionary Collectors" Association by the Late Rev. Henry W. Fox* (1861, listing twelve individuals inspired by Fox to enter missionary service). See also George Townshend Fox, *A Memoir of Henry Watson Fox, B.A.* (1850 and later editions); J. S. Reynolds, *Evangelicals at Oxford* (1953).

Robert Eric Frykenberg

Frame, Alice Seymour (Browne) (1878–1941), American Congregationalist missionary and dean of Women's College, Yenching University. Browne was born in Turkey where her parents were missionaries with the American Board of Commissioners for Foreign Missions (ABCFM). Graduating from Mount Holyoke College in 1900, she was inspired by the Boxer Rebellion to set her sights for China. Students and alumnae of the school sponsored her missionary service. In 1903 she graduated from Hartford Theological Seminary in religious pedagogy and in 1905 sailed to China to take charge of a Congregationalist girls' school. In 1913 she married ABCFM missionary evangelist Murray Scott Frame, but within five years she lost two children and had become widowed.

In 1918 she began to teach at the North China Union Women's College in Peking and became dean in 1922 after it affiliated with Yenching University. In 1928 the college was merged with the university. In 1931, after resigning under pressure to make way for a Chinese dean, Frame became secretary of religious education of the North China Congregational Church and undertook itinerant evangelism and rural education. In 1938 she attended the Madras Conference of the International Missionary Council as a delegate of the China Christian Council. Her service in China was cut short by cancer.

BIBLIOGRAPHY Frame's papers and letters are held in the archives of the UCBWM, Boston, and in the ABCFM archives at Harvard Univ., Cambridge, Mass. She corresponded from 1905 to 1940 with her supporters at Mount Holyoke College. Some letters are also held in the China Collection at Yale Divinity School, New Haven, Conn. Her obituary is in *Missionary Herald,* October 1941, pp. 47–48.

Dana L. Robert

Francesca, Maria. *See* Cabrini, Frances.

Francescon, Luigi (1866–1964), Pentecostal evangelist and founder of the Congregacioni Christi in Brazil. From his birthplace in Cavasso Nuova, province of Udine, Italy, Francescon immigrated to Chicago in 1890, where he pursued his vocation as a mosaic artisan. After a conversion experience in a Waldensian church, he participated in establishing the Italian Presbyterian Church of Chicago (1892). He married Rosina Balzano in 1895. His submission to adult baptism in 1903, with twenty-five fellow Presbyterians, became the occasion for separation from the Presbyterian Church. In 1907 he attended a meeting led by William H. Durham where, together with his wife, he experienced the baptism of the Spirit and speaking in tongues. With others he established the first Italian Pentecostal church in Chicago, the Assemblea Cristiana (1907). As an evangelist he helped found churches among Italian communities in Los Angeles, Philadelphia, Saint Louis, New York, and elsewhere. In 1910, leaving his wife and six children in the United States, he traveled to Argentina and Brazil, where he established Italian congregations in San Antonio de la Platina and Sao Paulo. Through eleven such trips from the United States to Brazil, he saw the Congregacioni Christi grow to 305 congregations by 1940, 815 by 1951, and nearly 2,500 before his death. Today the denomination is one of the largest in Brazil.

Francescon's broader Waldensian heritage is evidenced in his church's advocacy of social responsibility, rejection of legalistic ethics, ventures into industry to resolve unemployment woes, and use of elders and deacons, rather than clergy, for the work of the church.

BIBLIOGRAPHY Louis Francescon, *Resumo de una ramificacao da obra de Deus, pelo Espiritu Santo, no seculo actual* (1942, 1953, 1958). Francescon's untitled autobiography was published in G. Bongiovanni, *Pioneers of the Faith* (1971). See also Walter Hollenweger, *The Pentecostals* (1972).

Sidney H. Rooy

Francis, Mabel (1880–1975), missionary to Japan with the Christian and Missionary Alliance (C&MA). Francis grew up in New Hampshire, began teaching school at age 15, and soon after became involved in itinerant evangelism. At 19 she sensed a call to foreign missionary service and enrolled at Gordon Bible Institute (founded by A. J. *Gordon), and later transferred to the C&MA Nyack Missionary Training Institute. She began her ministry in Japan in 1909, where she served for 56 years, working alongside her sister Anne and her brother Tom much of the time. She served as an evangelist and church planter, helping to found 20 C&MA churches. She became known to the Japanese as the American woman who rode a bicycle and was always smiling. During World War II she refused to be evacuated with other missionaries, insisting that her home was Japan. She was placed under house arrest in a Roman Catholic monastery, where she continued her ministry. After the war, her ministry expanded and many Japanese viewed her as a true friend. She was invited to speak at official functions and was awarded Japan's highest civilian honor, membership in the Fifth Order of the Sacred Treasure. She retired to the United States in 1966 at the age of 86.

BIBLIOGRAPHY Mabel Francis with Gerald B. Smith, *One Shall Chase a Thousand* (1968); Ruth A. Tucker, *Guardians of the Great Commission: The Story of Women in Modern Missions* (1988).

Ruth A. Tucker

Francis of Assisi (1181–1226), founder of the Franciscan order. Francis was born in the small Umbrian city of Assisi; his father, Pietro Bernardone, was a wealthy textile merchant; his mother, Pica, was from a distinguished French family. Francis's wealth and love of life made him the leader of Assisi's youth. He took part in the intercity feuding between Assisi and Perugia and at one point was captured by the Perugians. After his release, Francis turned his back on a military career and decided on a profession in the business world. A meeting with a leper, however, and hearing a voice from the cross at the chapel of San Damiano resulted in his conversion and total renunciation of all possessions. On February 24, 1208, he heard the missionary discourse of Matthew 10:7–19 at the church of Santa Maria degli Angeli, the Portiuncula, outside the walls of Assisi. After that experience, he became an itinerant preacher of penance and peace and formed a brotherhood, approved by Innocent III, dedicated to living according to the gospel. He attempted to go to Syria in 1212, to Morocco in 1213–1214, and to Damietta, Egypt, in 1219. The last journey was successful. Though he was not able to stop the Fifth Crusade, he had a friendly meeting with the sultan of Egypt, Malik-al-Kamil, and obtained some privileges for his brothers, enabling them to settle in the Holy Land. Thus he and his brothers became a strong force for religious renewal not only in Europe but also in the lands of the church's missionary activity.

In his rule of 1221, chapter 16, Francis and his brothers laid down their missionary views, which are to be found in abbreviated form in the rule of 1223. This chapter is entitled "Those Who Are Going among the Saracens and Other Nonbelievers." This rejects the mentality of the Crusades, which was directed *against* (not *among*) the Muslims. Francis considered the vocation of a missionary to be a divine inspiration. He taught his brothers not to engage in arguments or disputes but to be subject to every human creature for God's sake, to acknowledge that they are Christians, and to proclaim the Word of God when they see that it pleases the Lord. Moreover, they should remember that they gave themselves and abandoned their bodies to the Lord. Francis was the first founder of a religious order who explicitly mentioned missionary activity in his rule and who reformed the traditional missionary approach in a radical and evangelical way.

BIBLIOGRAPHY Regis J. Armstrong and Ignatius C. Brady, eds., *Francis and Clare: The Complete Works* (1982), pp. 3–4, 121–122; David Flood, *Francis of Assisi and the Franciscan Movement* (1989); Marion A. Habig, ed., *St. Francis of Assisi: Writings and Early Biographies* (1983); J. Hoeberichts, *Franciscus en de Islam* (1994). See also Leonardo Boff and Walbert Bühlmann, eds., *Build Up My Church: Franciscan Inspirations for and from the Third World* (1984).

Arnulf Camps, OFM

Francke, August Hermann (1663–1727), German pietist educator. It is not easy in retrospect to obtain an accurate impression of Francke's importance to the earliest Protestant missionary efforts. He holds an undisputed place as Philipp Jakob *Spener's successor in the leadership of Lutheran Pietism and in the development of Halle as a center of pietist theology and of a faith active in love in a large variety of works of charity. At the same time, the Danish-Halle mission in South India, initiated by King Frederick IV of Denmark in 1705 and led by two of Francke's former students, Bartholomäus *Ziegenbalg and Heinrich *Plütschau, was launched without Francke's cooperation. It was only after reviewing the first reports of the missionaries that he joined his colleagues at Berlin and F. J. *Lütkens, German court chaplain at Copenhagen, in lending support to the new venture of faith. Even then he expressed doubts whether Ziegenbalg had been the best choice for the job. Later Francke clearly discouraged Ziegenbalg's effort to reach a deeper understanding of the Hindu way of life by refusing to have Ziegenbalg's relevant writings published. As late as 1715 Francke made an effort to put down in writing a lengthy admonition addressed to the missionaries at Tranquebar concerning a truly pietist missionary life-style as he saw it—with surprisingly little reference to the hard facts of mission work under Indian circumstances. The missionaries themselves never failed to regard Francke as their spiritual mentor. In fact, they seem to have contributed to the learning process he underwent, combining the specific pietist emphasis on the narrow path to personal salvation with the invitation to all and sundry to enter the open door of the kingdom. Eventually Halle became the heart of the mission, while Copenhagen remained the administrative center, with Francke and his co-workers readily assuming responsibility for steady material support of the mission, recruitment and training of missionaries, and ecumenical publicity for the growing Indian church.

BIBLIOGRAPHY Most of the existing biographies of Francke are outdated, and there is none in English. F. E. Stoeffler's excellent study *The Rise of Evangelical Pietism* (1965) does not include the era of Francke. Among historical works on the Danish-Halle mission that take Francke into account, E. Arno Lehmann's *It Began at Tranquebar* (1956) can still be recommended. The most recent authentic analysis is by a Danish scholar, Anders Nørgaard, *Mission und Obrigkeit: Die Dänisch-hallische Mission in Tranquebar, 1706–1845* (1988).

Hans-Werner Gensichen

Francke, August Hermann (1870–1930), Moravian missionary to Indian Tibet. Francke, a descendant of the eighteenth-century Halle theologian of the same name, was born in Gnadenfrei, Silesia. He served from 1896 to 1908 in Ladakh, a major region of Jammu and Kashmir Province in the Himalayan mountains at the western end of the Tibetan culture sphere. After returning home to Germany because of the health of his wife, Anna Theodora (Weiz), he made research trips in 1909 and 1914 to Ladakh, on the second of which he was interned by the British because he was German. He was not allowed to return to Ladakh after the war. During his missionary career Francke engaged primarily in evangelism, education, translation, and publication. He started the first Ladakh newspaper, which also included Christian teaching. He made translations of Mark in Ladakhi and in three dialects of Lahuli. He also contributed to the translation of parts of the Tibetan Old Testament. Response to the gospel was limited, but Francke was the first major Western student of the area, and no one has written more about it. His scholarly publications in German and English covered such diverse topics as folklore, art, customs, language, rock carvings, and archeology. After the war he became professor of Tibetan at Berlin University.

BIBLIOGRAPHY Two of Francke's major works are *The Antiquities of Indian Tibet* (vol. 1, 1914; vol. 2, 1926) and *A History of Western Tibet* (1907, repr. as *A History of Ladakh*, 1977). The major source of information on Francke, including essays and annotated bibliography of works by and about him, is Harmut Walravens and Manfred Taube, *August Hermann Francke und die Westhimalaya-Mission der Herrnhuter Brüdergemeine: Eine Bibliographie mit Standortnachweisen der Tibetischen Drucke* (1992); also see Hilde Deskyid Klingner-Francke, "Life of August Hermann Francke, Missionary and Linguist...," in *The Himalayan Mission: Moravian Church Centenary, Leh, Ladakh, India 1885–1985* (1985).

William A. Smalley

Franson, Fredrik (1852–1908), evangelist, church planter, and pioneering mission developer. Born in Sweden, Franson arrived in the United States as an immigrant at age 17. Converted at 20, he got his basic training in the Swedish Baptist church in his Nebraska frontier settlement. He was motivated toward interchurch cooperation, particularly on the local level. In 1878 he transferred his membership to the Moody Church in Chicago. He ministered in Colorado and Nebraska in 1880 and brought five new local churches into being, incorporating a distinctive sense of mission and expectation of the imminent return of Christ. He organized these churches as simply "free" and "evangelical." Later this ecclesiology was a foundation on which developed the Evangelical Free Church of America.

In Europe from 1881 to 1890, Franson developed productive evangelistic strategies for his native Sweden, and for Norway, Denmark, Germany, Switzerland, France, and Finland. These ministries, together with his probes along the Mediterranean and in eastern Europe, convinced him that only through specialized mission-oriented evangelization could the goal of the Great Commission be met. He inspired the founding of several organizations: Mission Covenant Church of Norway, Holiness Union (Sweden), Evangelical Orient Mission (Norway), Danish Mission Covenant, Finnish Free Church, Alliance Mission (Germany), and Swiss Alliance Mission.

Franson then committed himself to mobilizing the church for special-purpose missions in all the world. From 1890 to 1901 he was influential in founding or in the early history of the following mission organizations: The Scandinavian Alliance Mission of North America (today the Evangelical Alliance Mission [TEAM], 1890); North China Mission of the Christian and Missionary Alliance (1893); Mongolia Field of the Evangelical East Asia Mission, Sweden (1897); Himalaya Mission of the Finnish Free Church (1898); Fellowship Deaconess Home of the Marburg Mission, Germany (1899); Swedish Alliance Mission (1900); Women's Missionary Association of Finland (1900); and Norwegian Missionary Alliance (1901). In 1901 he left on an unhurried round-the-world mission and study tour, which lasted until 1908. He worked and consulted with missionaries and national church leaders and engaged in evangelistic campaigns. He also sorted out and evaluated the applied missiologies he observed. He died soon after arriving back in the United States.

BIBLIOGRAPHY O. C. Grauer, *Fredrik Franson: An Evangelist and Missionary in Worldwide Service* (1938–1940); Edvard Torjesen, "Fredrik Franson," in Gerald H. Anderson et al., eds., *Mission Legacies* (1994), pp. 48–54.

Edvard Torjesen

Fraser, Alexander Garden (1873–1962), Church Missionary Society (CMS) missionary educator in Africa and Sri Lanka. Fraser was born in Tillicoultry, Clackmannanshire, Scotland, son of an Indian government officer and grandson of a missionary. He was educated at Edinburgh University and Trinity College, Oxford. After an evangelical conversion, he served as a staff worker for the Student Volunteer Missionary Union (with J. H. *Oldham, who became his brother-in-law). In 1900, despite his Presbyterian upbringing, he joined the CMS as an honorary lay missionary in Uganda. There he initiated a plan for improved education that eventually issued in the prestigious King's College, Budo. In 1903 his wife's health forced withdrawal and reassignment to Ceylon (Sri Lanka), where he was appointed principal of Trinity College, Kandy, which was then in a perilous state. Fraser rescued it, raised standards and discipline, deepened the links with Sri Lankan culture by introducing Sinhala and Tamil, and increased involvement with the local community. His service there lasted effectively until 1922, interrupted by two years spent as a wartime army chaplain (during which he was gassed in France). With Trinity recognized as a model Christian school, Fraser was appointed to lead a missionary commission to inquire into Indian educational policy. The published report (*Village Education in India*, 1920) anticipated many of the recommendations of the Phelps-Stokes commissions on West Africa, which soon followed, and which coincided with the vision of Sir Gordon Guggisberg, governor of the Gold Coast (Ghana). Through Oldham, Fraser was offered the principalship of Guggisberg's proposed new college at Achimota. Fraser accepted on the condition that J. E. K. *Aggrey receive a senior post. Guggisberg (whom Fraser had led to Christian commitment), Aggrey, and Fraser made Achimota an institution unique in West Africa; it was publicly funded but independent of government, with a council involving the African community; it was marked by high academic standards, broad curriculum, public service, cultural relevance, and Christian ethos, and aimed toward ultimate university standards and status. Fraser, increasingly ill, left in 1935 and spent his later active life in adult education and school chaplaincy in Scotland and Jamaica. Inspirational, uncompromising, sometimes difficult, with intense if unconventional spirituality, and impatient of missionary and colonial orthodoxies, he was one of the outstanding educators of his time.

BIBLIOGRAPHY G. Guggisberg and A. G. Fraser, *The Future of the Negro* (1929); W. E. F. Ward, *Fraser of Trinity and Achimota* (1965); C. K. Williams, *Achimota: The Early Years* (1962); R. E. Wraith, *Guggisberg* (1967).

Andrew F. Walls

Fraser, Donald (1870–1933), missionary to Africa and international mission statesman and strategist. Fraser was born in Scotland at Lochgilphead, Argyllshire, the son of a Free Church minister. As a young man, he helped found the Student Volunteer Movement (SVM) in Britain and became its traveling secretary in 1892. He was also involved with John R. *Mott in discussions leading to the formation of the World's Student Christian Federation in 1896. Before beginning missionary service in Malawi with the Free Church of Scotland, Fraser toured both Europe and South Africa in 1896 to encourage the SVM. In Malawi Fraser was assigned to the Ngoni people, with whom he became closely identified. He encouraged huge sacramental conventions which soon attracted thousands. These were modeled after nineteenth-century Scottish Highland gatherings, but in Africa included both baptism and Communion. He was much more open to African culture than were most of his Scottish colleagues. He encouraged indigenous church music by organizing annual hymn-writing competitions and encouraged local leadership in the church, including the leadership of women through an unofficial order of women elders, long before such initiatives were officially recognized in either Scotland or Malawi. He also spent a very high proportion of his time itinerating around the huge area for which he was responsible. At such times his wife Agnes (Robson), herself a medical doctor, carried on the administration of the mission station at Loudon (Embangweni). In 1925, somewhat unwillingly, Fraser was recalled to Scotland to become a United Free Church mission secretary. In 1926 his considerable international reputation was recognized when he was asked to chair the international conference at Le Zoute on the topic "The Christian Mission in Africa." After his death, Fraser's ashes were returned to Malawi and buried at Embangweni, among the people he had served so well.

BIBLIOGRAPHY Donald Fraser, *Winning a Primitive People* (1914), *African Idylls* (1923), *The Autobiography of an African* (1925), and *The New Africa* (1927). Agnes R. Fraser, *Donald Fraser of Livingstonia* (1934); T. Jack Thompson, *Christianity in Northern Malawi: Donald Fraser's Missionary Methods and Ngomi Culture* (1995) and "Donald Fraser," in Gerald H. Anderson et al., eds., *Mission Legacies* (1994), pp. 166–172.

T. Jack Thompson

Fraser, James Outram (1886–1938), English missionary in southwest China. A graduate engineer born near Saint Albans, England, with an unusual gift in music, Fraser went to China in 1908 with the China Inland Mission. After a period of studying Chinese, he arrived in 1910 in the southwest China province of Yunnan. He was forced by the chaos accompanying the Chinese revolution of 1911 to divide his time between western Yunnan and Burma. He learned the language of and commenced his work among the Lisu, a Tibeto-Burmese minority people who lived in the high mountains along the borders of the two countries. By 1918, sparked by family evangelism carried on by the people themselves, 60,000 believers had been baptized. Fraser was known for his ability to organize the people into strong indigenous churches that became models for church-planting ventures not only for other minority peoples in China's southwest but in other countries as well. He wrote many articles in English for *The Chinese Recorder.* He also developed a script for the Lisu language and used it to prepare a catechism, portions of Scripture, and eventually, with much help from his colleagues, a complete New Testament. He died in Paoshan (Baoshan), in western Yunnan, of malignant malaria.

BIBLIOGRAPHY Mrs. Howard Taylor, *Behind the Ranges: Fraser of Lisuland, Southwest China* (1944); Eileen Crossman, *Mountain Rain* (1982).

Ralph R. Covell

Fraser, John (Andrew) Mary (1877–1962), Canadian Catholic missionary and founder of the Scarboro Foreign Mission Society. Born in Toronto, Fraser studied with the Vincentian order in Italy, where he became interested in the missions. After ordination he volunteered for China, becoming the first English-speaking Canadian Catholic missionary in that country. From 1902 to 1918 he served in Ninghsien (Ningpo) and other cities in the province of Chekiang (Zhejiang). In 1918 he succeeded in opening a seminary to train missionary priests in Almonte, Ontario. One year later he founded a missionary journal, *China* (later *Scarboro Missions*). In 1921 the seminary was moved to Scarborough, near Toronto. The Vatican assigned the new missionary society to the Chuchow (Lishui) area of Chekiang, to where Fraser set out in 1926 with five new members of his society. He was recalled by his board of directors in 1929 but returned to China in 1932. He worked in Kinhwa (Jiuhua) until 1949, engaged in individual ministry, which was more suited to his temperament. After the Communist victory, he went to Japan, where he supervised the reconstruction of churches in Nagasaki, Fukuoka, and Osaka, where he died. By then, his society had approximately one hundred members, serving in Canada, Asia, Latin America, and the West Indies.

BIBLIOGRAPHY Grant Maxwell, *Assignment in Chekiang: 71 Canadians in China, 1902–1954* (1982). Fraser's autobiography and selected early letters are printed in consecutive issues of *Scarboro Missions* from January 1959 to January 1961.

Achiel Peelman, OMI

Fraser, Kenneth (1877–1935), Church Missionary Society (CMS) medical missionary pioneer in Sudan. Born at Crock Ban on the Isles of Lewis, Scotland, Fraser qualified as a doctor in the Royal Army Medical Corps with a view toward overseas missions. In 1920, under the CMS's Gordon Memorial Sudan Mission, he and his wife, Eileen, arrived at Lui (formerly Yilu) among the Moru of southern Sudan. There, drawing upon his military background, he established a well regimented hospital, the centerpiece of a system designed to extend services to every sector of Moruland's 15,000 square miles. Young Christian converts were trained as evangelists with specialized skills as teachers or medical workers. Equipped with standardized medical kits, they were sent out in pairs, following identical routines and sending back periodic reports to Lui Hospital. Centers that harmonized the services of a dispensary, school, and church were constructed at intervals of 15 miles along the main roads of the district, thus penetrating every Moru chieftaincy. Fraser's industrious and generous Christian character, his organization of leper communities, his well-informed efforts to reform harmful indigenous practices, and his numerous successes in surgery won him legendary status. Under his methodology, the Moru became one of the best educated and most pervasively Christian peoples in Sudan. He died at Lui.

BIBLIOGRAPHY Brian de Saram, *Nile Harvest: The Anglican Church in Egypt and the Sudan,* privately published (1992). Eileen Fraser, *The Doctor Comes to Lui* (1943).

Marc R. Nikkel

Freed, Paul E. (1918–1996), founder of Trans World Radio (TWR). Growing up in Palestine as the son of missionaries, Freed graduated from Wheaton (Illinois) and Nyack (New York) Colleges and earned a Ph.D. in mass communications from New York University. As a Youth for Christ staff worker, he noted that Spain was neglected by evangelical missions and became convinced that radio was the ideal entrée. He established the first small studio in Tangier, Morocco, and began broadcasting in 1954, with his father serving as on-site director. After they had gained more powerful facilities in Monaco in 1960, Freed began developing regional offices in Europe to provide national leadership and programming, with the result that by 1965 more than half of the support was coming from Europe. Freed continued to press for increased coverage, ultimately making TWR programs available to 80 percent of the world's population, with broadcasts in 120 languages from nine primary locations: Monte Carlo, Netherlands Antilles, Sri Lanka, Swaziland, Cyprus, Guam, Uruguay, Albania, and Siberia. In 1993 Freed retired from the presidency but continued as chairman of the board of TWR. He was honored that year by the National Religious Broadcasters as the broadcaster who "has done the most to promote and extend the reach of international Christian broadcasting."

BIBLIOGRAPHY Paul E. Freed, *Towers to Eternity* (rev, 1994). E. Brandt Gustavson, "Paul E. Freed," in John D. Woodbridge, ed., *Ambassadors for Christ* (1994). The fortieth anniversary issue of *TWRadio* magazine features a historical summary of TWR.

Robert T. Coote

Freeman, John Joseph (1774–1851), mid-nineteenth-century leader of the London Missionary Society (LMS). Freeman, born in London, was educated at Hoxton Academy and became a Congregational pastor in Kidderminster. In March 1827 he was sent to Madagascar as a missionary on a limited-time appointment by the LMS. In September 1829 he was expelled from Madagascar. His wife and family sailed to England, but Freeman stopped in Cape Town, where he assisted John *Philip. In 1831 he was able to return to Madagascar, where his wife and children joined him in 1834. Political difficulties again forced the Freemans to leave Madagascar, and they returned to Cape Town, where Freeman finished the period of his contract. Back in Britain by the beginning of 1837, he became a pastor in Walthamstow. In May 1841 he was made joint foreign secretary of the LMS with A. Tidman. He spent 1842 and 1843 inspecting and revitalizing the LMS missions in the Caribbean. In 1846 he became full-time home secretary of the LMS. From February 1849, he spent 18 months inspecting the work in South Africa, and then tried to reenter Madagascar but was turned back. Before Freeman died, he managed to see through to publication his very important *Tour in South Africa.*

BIBLIOGRAPHY A very large number of letters to and from Freeman can be found in the LMS archives, which are housed in the library of the School of Oriental and African Studies, Univ. of London. See also Richard Lovett, *The History of the London Missionary Society, 1795–1895* (1899).

Andrew C. Ross

Freeman, Thomas Birch (1809–1890), British Methodist missionary to West Africa. Freeman was born in Twyford, Hampshire, England. Little is known of his early life. His mother was English, his father an African freed slave. When he was accepted as a Wesleyan Methodist missionary in 1837, he had been head gardener on a Suffolk estate but had lost his post because of his Methodist activism. In 1838 he arrived in Cape Coast, Gold Coast (Ghana), where a Methodist church of indigenous origin was being tenuously supported by a succession of short-lived English missionaries. Freeman was unusual in surviving, despite a strenuous program. In his early months he built a church in Cape Coast, extending preaching and schools along the coastal plain, and identified a young Fanti preacher, William de Graft, as a suitable minister. He then made his way to Kumasi, capital of Ashanti, forming a promising relationship with the Asantehene and other important chiefs. In 1841, taking de Graft with him, he visited Britain to appeal for funds and recruits for the expanding work. The publication of his Kumasi journals made him a celebrity, and the then-current popularity of the African vision of T. F. *Buxton favored his success. He returned with more missionaries, revisited Kumasi, and finding still greater promise, left a missionary there. Meanwhile some Yorubas who had become Christians in Sierra Leone and had made their way back to their homeland, had asked the Wesleyan mission for help. Freeman, again with de Graft, went to investigate. He had a cordial meeting with the Egba paramount Sodeke at Abeokuta, and on his own initiative he established a mission in Yorubaland, first at Badagri, with de Graft, later at Lagos, and eventually at Abeokuta. He never, however, obtained the resources for the large-scale mission he envisioned. He several times met Ghezo, the powerful king of Dahomey, and placed a preacher at Ouidah, but he could neither persuade Dahomey to abandon a slaving economy nor persuade his mission to underwrite evangelistic efforts there. Missionary mortality in the Gold Coast continued, deteriorating relations between Britain and Ashanti clouded the Kumasi mission, and tensions arose with his home committee over finance. In 1857 charges of overspending forced his resignation as general superintendent. To repay what had exceeded the budget, he took the thankless government post of civil commandant of Accra but was dismissed by a new governor in 1860. He remained in the Gold Coast, farming, writing, and preaching; he had married a local woman in 1854 (two previous wives had died soon after their respective arrivals in Africa). In 1873, at age 63, he reentered the Wesleyan ministry and became an active and innovative pastor, prominent in revival movements and skilled in conciliation.

Freeman was limited linguistically, and as he fully recognized, financially incompetent. But in forging relationships with African rulers, he was preeminent, and he also worked well with the more farsighted of British officials. His vision, tact, humanity, energy, and durability underlie the now substantial Methodist presence in Ghana, Western Nigeria, and Benin.

BIBLIOGRAPHY Thomas Freeman, *Journal of Various Visits to the Kingdom of Ashanti, Aku, and Dahomi in Western Africa* (2d ed., 1843, with a new introduction by H. M. Wright, 1968), and *Missionary Enterprise No Fiction* (a semi-autobiographical novel; 1871). J. F. Ade Ajayi, *Christian Missions in Nigeria, 1841–1891: The Making of a New Elite* (1965); F. L. Bartels, *The Roots of Ghana Methodism* (1965); Allen Birtwistle, *Thomas Birch Freeman, West African Pioneer* (1950); P. Ellingworth, "Christianity and Politics in Dahomey, 1843–1867," *Journal of African History* 5 (1964): 209–220; G. E. Metcalfe, *Maclean of the Gold Coast* (1962); John Milum, *Thomas Birch Freeman* (n.d.).

Andrew F. Walls

Freinademetz, Joseph (1852–1908), Catholic missionary in China. Freinademetz was born in Abtei, near Badia, South Tyrol, Austria (area ceded to Italy in 1919). He was ordained in 1875 and entered the Steyl mission house of the Society of the Divine Word (SVD) in 1878. Zeal for souls moved him to abandon his beloved Tyrol, his family, and his position as assistant priest and go off to China in 1879. He and J. B. von *Anzer were the first SVD missionaries. After working in Hong Kong for some time in 1881 he moved to South Shantung (Shandong), which had been assigned to the SVD. At that time there were only 158 Catholics among a population of 12 million.

Freinademetz devoted himself wholeheartedly to his people and mission. His tenderness counterbalanced the rather hotheaded personality of Anzer. From 1886 to 1900 and again from 1903 to 1908 Freinademetz was the provicar of the mission. Good catechesis and the training of catechists was a top priority, and for this purpose he prepared catechetical material in Chinese. He also availed himself of every opportunity to promote the cause of a Chinese clergy. Another of his great concerns was the spiritual care of missionaries; as provincial from 1900 to 1908, he established a central house in Taikia near Tsining (Jining) to foster renewal. He was also convinced of the crucial importance of prayer for the success of the Chinese mission and was himself a man of prayer. When the missionaries left the danger zones during the Boxer Rebellion, he remained with his people. He reacted calmly to ill-treatment, even death threats. Chinese Christians said of him: "He is like Kungdse [Confucius], everything about him is good, everything perfect: he is always friendly, modest, humble." In 1907 he was made administrator of the mission for the sixth time. While caring for typhoid victims during this period, he contracted the illness that led to his death. When he died, the South Shantung SVD mission reported 45,000 Catholics and almost as many aspirants for baptism. In 1975 he was beatified by Pope *Paul VI.

BIBLIOGRAPHY J. Baur, *P. Joseph Freinademetz,* 4th ed. (1956); Fritz Bornemann, *Der selige P. J. Freinademetz, 1852–1908: Ein Steyler China-Missionar* (1977; English trans., *As Wine Poured Out: Blessed Joseph Freinademetz, SVD, Missionary in China, 1879–1908* [1984]); A. Henninghaus, *P. Joseph Freinademetz,* 2d ed. (1926); J. Reuter, *Das Schrifttum über Arnold Janssen und Josef Freinademetz* (1990).

Karl Müller, SVD

Freitag, Anton (1882–1968), German Catholic missiologist. Born in Altenbeken, Freitag became a member of the Society of the Divine Word (SVD) in 1903. After ordination in 1908 he studied missiology under Joseph *Schmidlin at Münster; seven years later, he was the first to receive a doctorate in Catholic missiology. Henceforth missiology and the promotion of mission awareness became the goal of his life. He published in numerous journals (especially in *ZM, HM, Theologie und Glaube,* and *Akademische Missionsblätter*), spoke at many missionary congresses and other such events, and was the initiator and first editor of *Jesusknabe* (today *Weite Welt*), a mission magazine for children, the first issue of which appeared in January 1921. His most important scholarly publications are *Katholische Missionskunde im Grundriss* (1926), *Paulus baut die Weltkirche* (1951), *Die neue Missionsära—das Zeitalter des einheimischen Klerus* (1952), *Die Wege des Heils* (1960; British ed., *The Universal Atlas of the Christian World* [1963] and American ed., *The Twentieth Century Atlas of the Christian World* [1963]), and *Mission und Missionswissenschaft* (1962). His main interest was missionography; from 1920 to 1953 he regularly published "Missionsrundschauen" (Mission panorama) in *ZM* (later *MR, ZMR*); he wrote the articles on most of the key words about mission in the *Lexikon für Theologie und Kirche.*

Freitag's health problems prevented him from accepting a regular teaching position in missiology, but he lectured in Steyl (1915–1921), Paderborn (1922–1926), and Roermond (1938–1952). Apart from academic pursuits, all his life he was engaged in the pastoral ministry. He was a popular preacher, retreat master, and spiritual director, and published numerous devotional works.

BIBLIOGRAPHY Johannes Beckmann, "Würdigung der wissenschaftlichen Verdienste des Jubilars," *ZMR* 49 (1965): 222–224 and "Drei verdiente Pioniere des Missionswissenschaft," *NZM* 24 (1968): 202–206; J. Brunner, "Das Verständnis von Mission bei Anton Freitag" (M.A. thesis, St. Gabriel's Major Seminary, Vienna-Mödling, 1982); SVD, *Missie nu: Aktuele Missieproblemen* (1958).

Karl Müller, SVD

French, Evangeline ("Eva") (1869–1961) *and* **Francesca** (1871–1961), missionary pioneers in central Asia. The sisters Evangeline and Francesca French were born to an Anglo-French family and were educated mainly in Geneva. Francesca came early to Christian faith; Eva experienced years of rebellion that ended in the 1890s. Going to China under the China Inland Mission (CIM) in 1895, Eva found herself in the center of the Boxer uprising in Shansi (Shanxi) Province and the leader of a group of women who escaped with their lives. In 1901 she met the younger CIM recruit, Mildred *Cable, and the two were never to be separated. They returned to Hwochow (present-day Xinjiang) in Shansi to help rebuild the shattered church. Francesca had remained in England with their widowed mother, but at the mother's death she became the third member of the trio, and coauthor, with Mildred Cable, of many books. From this point until Cable's death in 1952, the three lived and worked together. From 1913 they turned their attention to Kansu (Gansu) Province, Chinese Turkestan (Xinjiang Uygur), and the Gobi Desert. In the 1920s they took into their home a Tartar girl, known as Topsy, who proved to be a deaf mute. She lived with them for the rest of their lives and was especially close to Eva. In the 1930s political unrest increased and they were compelled to leave Suchow (Jinquan), their base in Kansu. In August 1936 they made their last journey home by the Trans-Siberian railway and retired together in Hampstead, Dorset, England. Francesca continued to write and travel with Mildred. Eva, the leader of the trio in China, stayed at home with Topsy. They were able to use their reputation as pioneering women travelers to gain publicity and support for the CIM, for the British and Foreign Bible Society, and above all for the gospel. Eva died in Dorset, Francesca at their Hampstead home three weeks later.

BIBLIOGRAPHY Mildred Cable and Francesca French, *Dispatches from North-West Kansu* (1925), *Through Jade Gate and Central Asia* (1927), *Something Happened* (1933), *A Desert Journal: Letters from Central Asia* (1934), *Ambassadors for Christ* (1935), *Toward Spiritual Maturity: A Handbook for Those Who Seek It* (1939), *A Parable of Jade* (1940), *The Gobi Desert* (1942), *The Book which Demands a Verdict* (1946), and *George Hunter, Apostle of Turkestan* (1948). W. J. Platt, *Three Women: Mildred Cable, Francesca French, Evangeline French: The Authorised Biography* (1964).

Jocelyn Murray

French, Thomas Valpy (1825–1891), missionary evangelist, educator, and Islamicist in India. Born in England, French served with the Church Missionary Society (CMS) in India during the second half of the nineteenth century. His early years in the Northwest Provinces (1850–1863) saw the emergence of the two motifs which marked his missiology. The first was education as a means of evangelism. In Agra he founded and developed St. John's College, a secondary school that offered quality education to Hindu and Muslim children. His second passion was for direct evangelism. Cofounder of the Derajat Mission in the frontier regions of Baluchistan, he was reputed as the "seven-tongued evangelist." His skill in languages and appreciation of poetry combined to make him an effective if controversial preacher in village markets.

The second phase of French's life was committed to nurturing the growth of an indigenous Indian convert church. In 1869 he founded St. John's Divinity School in Lahore for the training of Indian Christian pastors. After several years of teaching, he was appointed Anglican bishop of Lahore in 1877. To encourage the Indian church to acquire the best of theological education, he founded the Cambridge-Delhi Mission. To help root the Indian church in Indian culture, independent of foreign cultural norms, he pioneered the preparation of theological literature that respected Indian literary traditions, and he experimented with indigenous patterns of worship reflecting the cultural backgrounds of Muslim and Hindu converts. The catholicity of an indigenous church required ecumenical openness, for which he articulated the vision of "one common church for all India." In these ways he foresaw the indigenous Indian church being able to take over the task of evangelism from the Western missionary.

French retired to Britain in 1887, but four years later he responded to a CMS call for evangelists to Arabia. The last months of his life were spent as an itinerant preacher in Muscat, where he hoped to find ways of bringing the gospel to the historical heartland of Islam. His death in 1891 shortly predated the formation of the (American) Arabia Mission, which was inspired by his example.

BIBLIOGRAPHY For French's personal account of Christian mission, see "Missionary Efforts Among Muhammadans," *Church Missionary Intelligencer* (1877): 577–588. Herbert Birks, *The Life and Correspondence of Thomas Valpy French, First Bishop of Lahore*, 2 vols. (1895); Arvil Powell, *Muslims and Missionaries in Pre-Mutiny India* (1993); Vivienne Stacey, "Thomas Valpy French, First Bishop of Lahore," *Al-Mushir (the Counselor): Theological Journal of the Christian Study Centre, Rawalpindi, Pakistan* 23 (1981): 135–144, and 24 (1982): 1–22, and "Thomas Valpy French," in Gerald H. Anderson et al., eds., *Mission Legacies* (1994), pp. 277–282; Eugene Stock, *An Heroic Bishop: The Life Story of French of Lahore* (1913); Lyle Vander Werff, *Christian Mission to Muslims: The Record* (1977).

David A. Kerr

Frey, Joseph Samuel C(ristian) F(rederick) (1771–1850), father of modern Jewish missions. Frey was born in German Franconia into a rabbinical family. Through a perfunctory "conversion," an uncle had identified with Christianity, and in reaction his family indoctrinated Frey against the gospel from the beginning. Nonetheless, a chance meeting with a Christian in a nearby city led to his becoming a believer in Jesus in 1798. Feeling a call to mission, he left for London to train with the London Missionary Society (LMS) for work in Africa. However, he discovered the plight of the Jews in London's East End and began a mission to them in 1805. A pioneer of the concept of holistic mission, he proposed the establishment of a center for training Jewish believers for wage-earning employment, but the LMS declined to be involved. Therefore, in 1809, he founded the first modern mission to Jews, commonly known as the London Jews' Society, now the Church's Ministry among Jewish People. It served as a model for most of those that followed. In 1816 Frey also visited America, where he was instrumental in establishing a society known as the Society for Ameliorating the Conditions of the Jews in New York.

BIBLIOGRAPHY Frey wrote two autobiographical works and a major piece of apologetic polemic concerning the Jewish people: *The Converted Jew, or, Memoirs of the Life of Joseph Samuel C. F. Frey, Who Was Born a Jew* (1815), *Narrative of the Rev. Joseph Samuel C. F. Frey* (1817), and *Joseph and Benjamin: A Series of Letters on the Controversy between Jews and Christians* (1837). See also A. Bernstein, *Some Jewish Witnesses for Christ* (1909); W. T. Gidney, *The History of the London Society for Promoting Christianity amongst the Jews* (1908).

Walter Riggans

Freytag, Walter (1899–1959), German Protestant missiologist. Born in a merchant's family of Moravian tradition in Thuringia, Germany, Freytag studied theology and philosophy at Tübingen, Marburg, and Halle, completing a doctorate in 1925. In 1928 he started his long career in missions as director of Deutsche Evangelische Missionshilfe, the central Protestant German agency for promoting mission work. When political complications prevented him from becoming a missionary in China, he concentrated on teaching missiology and history of religions both at Hamburg and Kiel universities, at the same time serving in leading positions in German and international mission agencies as well as in the ecumenical movement. Due to pressure from National-Socialist authorities he lost his missiological lectureship at Hamburg University and was reinstated only after the war. A man of many talents, he was repeatedly called to high office in the German church and in international Christian bodies, but he decided to devote his gifts and strength to the cause of mission, with special emphasis on Christianity and non-Christian religions, the psychology of conversion, and what he called "the miracle of the church among the nations." Although he was equally unforgettable as speaker, teacher, and writer, he left behind only one major book, an analysis of the importance of the so-called younger churches for the church universal, which he wrote after a study tour in Asia in 1938. His lasting contribution to missiology has been preserved, first, in two volumes of collected essays and speeches, published after his untimely death at the age of 60, and, second, in a postwar generation of missiologists. Under his guidance, the latter acquired a new understanding of "mission as God's reality in this world," a vision of the "missionary dimension of the whole church and of all churches," "witnessing by word and deed in real brotherhood and sacrificial service for the sake of mankind," and so proclaiming the Lord's death until he comes.

BIBLIOGRAPHY Walter Freytag, *Reden und Aufsätze,* 2 vols. (1961). Tributes by colleagues and a bibliography of Freytag's published work to 1956 will be found in Jan Hermelink and Hans Jochen Margull, eds., *Basileia: Walter Freytag zum 60. Gerburtstag* (1959). Also see, Hans-Werner Gensichen, "Walter Freytag," in Gerald H. Anderson et al., eds., *Mission Legacies* (1994), pp. 435–444.

Hans-Werner Gensichen

Fridelli, Xaver-Ehrenbert (*or* Ernbert) (1673–1743), Jesuit missionary in China. A native of Linz, Austria, Fridelli entered the Society of Jesus in 1688. During his studies he volunteered to go to the China mission and embarked from Lisbon in 1704. Arriving in Macao in August 1705, he was assigned to Chen-chiang (Zhenjiang) in Jiangnan Province (area of present-day Anhui and Jiangsu Provinces), where he began language study and started to propagate devotion to the Sacred Heart of Jesus, which he continued to do for the rest of his life. Called to Peking (Beijing) because of his knowledge of mathematics, he assisted two confreres, Jean-Baptiste *Régis (1663–1738) and Pierre *Jartoux (1669–1720), in making maps of China at the request of the imperial court. From Peking he traveled through Manchuria to the Russian border (1710–1711); then accompanied by Guillaume Fabre Bonjour (1669–1714), he traveled to Szechwan (Sichuan) and Yunnan (1713–1714). Fridelli used the occasion to preach in these areas, where mission stations had not yet been established. He was appointed superior of the residence of St. Joseph in Peking and built a church of St. Joseph nearby in 1721. Later he had a six-year term as rector of the parish of the Portuguese college in Peking and then returned to the parish of St. Joseph, where he served until his death.

BIBLIOGRAPHY Fridelli's letters are in Joseph Stöcklein, ed., *Der Neue Welt Bott* (1726–1758), no. 103, 5: 47–49, no. 194, 8:18, no. 589, 30:97–98, no. 674, 34:37–38. Alfred Zerlik, *P. Xaver Ernbert Fridelli, China-Missionar und Kartograph* (1962).

John W. Witek, SJ

Fridolin (*or* Fridold) (6th century), Irish missionary abbot in France and the Upper Rhine. From an Irish noble family, Fridolin traveled to France, became a monk, and was then made abbot of Hilary's monastery in Poitiers. He rediscovered Hilary's relics, rebuilt Hilary's church, and built a church in the Vosges Mountains which became St. Nabor's monastery. Fired by missionary zeal, he ministered in Strasbourg and Coire, but finally settled on the small island of Säckingen in the Rhine River, north of Basel. Although not originally well received by the people there, he eventually gained permission from the ruler—sources differ as to his identity—to build a church, a monastery, and a nunnery. He died at Säckingen and a series of churches in the region are dedicated to him or to Hilary.

BIBLIOGRAPHY Louis Gaugaud, *Christianity in Celtic Lands* (1932); Gottfried Heer, *St. Fridolin, der Apostel Alamanniens* (1889).

Frederick W. Norris

Fries, Karl (1861–1943), leader of the Swedish and international student movements. Fries was born in Stockholm into an upper middle-class family with maritime connections. In school and at Uppsala University he developed a warm evangelical faith. He initially intended to become a missionary to Ethiopia, but his health did not permit it. In the 1880s he became deeply involved in the work of the YMCA, organizing a world conference in Stockholm in 1888, with appointment as a full-time paid YMCA secretary. In the following year, Fries visited the United States and met John R. *Mott for the first time. Unable to attend Moody's Northfield Conference in 1890, he sent Nathan *Söderblom in his place, thus launching Söderblom's ecumenical career. In 1895, Fries was one of the founders of the World's Student Christian Federation, at a conference in Vadstena, Sweden, which he organized almost single-handedly. Thereafter, the record of Fries's career was one of tireless traveling, organizing, and conference-going. In 1912 he was elected the first chair of the newly created Swedish Missionary Council, a position he held for eight years. In 1920 he became general secretary of the YMCA, based in Geneva, holding the post during the difficult postwar years. Fries's personal faith was warmly evangelical, with strong Keswick-style "holiness" leanings; he was an accomplished linguist, and his social connections with Swedish royalty and aristocracy made him uniquely influential at home and opened many doors internationally.

BIBLIOGRAPHY Karl Fries, *Mina minnen* (My reminiscences) (1939).

Eric J. Sharpe

Friesen, Abraham J. (1859–1920), missionary in southern India. Friesen was born in the Mennonite colony of Chortitz (near present-day Zaporozhye), Ukraine. He trained for missionary service at the German Baptist missionary school at Hamburg-Horn. His father, Johann, a well-known industrialist, supported his son's dedication to founding a Mennonite Brethren (MB) mission among the Telugus in southern India, and Friesen found support among the Russian MB for his proposal to work in India under the aegis of the American Baptist Missionary Union (ABMU) of the American Baptist Foreign Mission Society, headquartered in Boston. His career in India was momentous for the MB church of Russia and America. Beginning in 1889 he laid the foundation for a spiritually dynamic church as well as a large station at Nalgonda, east of Hyderabad city. He also managed, with strong financial support from Rueckenau (the MB headquarters), to place another six couples and four single women from Russia in the Nalgonda district before 1914. Together they built up two other equally pivotal stations: Suryapet and Jangaon. Most importantly, in 1900 he launched and edited a widely read missionary periodical entitled *Das Erntefeld* (The Harvest Field). From 1899 to 1904 he played a key role in assisting the American MB (principally churches in Kansas and Minnesota) in their pioneering work in adjacent Mahbubnagar district, south of Hyderabad city. In 1904–1905, with his mediation, a plan of cooperation and shared expenses matured between Rueckenau and the ABMU. When World War I disrupted Rueckenau's financial participation in 1914, the AMBU took responsibility for Nalgonda, Suryapet, and Jangaon. Friesen continued to promote missions until he died in Rueckenau of typhoid fever in the aftermath of revolution, famine, and civil war in Russia.

BIBLIOGRAPHY P. M. Friesen, *The Mennonite Brotherhood in Russia (1789–1910)* (1911, 1978); Peter Penner, "Baptist in All But Name: Molotschna MB in India," *Mennonite Life* (March 1991): 17–23, "The Holy Spirit and Church Renewal: Coimbatore, India, 1906," *Direction* (Fall, 1991): 135–142, "The Russian Mennonite Brethren and the American Baptist Tandem in India (1890–1940)," in Paul Toews, ed., *Mennonites and Baptists: A Continuing Conversation* (1993), pp. 133–146, 243–247. The Abraham Friesen Collection, American Baptist archives, Valley Forge, Pennsylvania.

Peter Penner

Fritz, Samuel (1651–1728?), Jesuit missionary in Peru. Fritz worked in the Peruvian Amazon basin and made the first scientific map of the region. Born in Bohemia, he entered the Society of Jesus in 1673 and was sent to Ecuador in 1684 along with Enrique *Richter, a fellow German Bohemian Jesuit. Fritz set out to evangelize the Omaguas (near present-day Iquitos) by the Marañón-Amazon River. In three years he founded thirty-eight mission towns along the riverbanks or on river islands. He then directed his efforts to preaching among the Yurimaguas, along the Huallaga River. In 1689 he fell sick and sought aid from an expedition of Portuguese adventurers who had advanced up the Negro River in present-day Brazil. The Portuguese sent him to the city of Gran Pará (Belém) where he remained for 19 months. He later reported to the viceroy in Lima on the activities of the Portuguese in what he believed to be Spanish territory. He also supported his belief with a detailed map of the entire Amazon region of Ecuador, Colombia, Peru, and part of Brazil. His map was finally perfected in 1707 and is considered a basic instrument for studying the history of the Amazon. Fritz's interest was not merely scientific. He aimed to keep the Portuguese out of the Spanish Amazon because they raided native communities and carried off the Indians for the slave trade. He served as superior of the Mainas missions between 1704 and 1712. He died in Peru.

BIBLIOGRAPHY Samuel Fritz, *Journals of the Travels and Labours of Father Samuel Fritz in the River of the Amazons between 1686 and 1723*, George Edmundson, tr. (1922). José Chantre y Herrera, *Historia de la misiones de la Compañía de Jesús en el Marañón español* (1901); José Jouanen, *Historia de la Compañía de Jesús en la antigua provincia de Quito (1570–1774),* vol. 1 (1941); Rubén Vargas Ugarte, *Historia de la Iglesia en el Perú,* vol. 3 (1960).

Jeffrey Klaiber, SJ

Fróis, Luis (1532–1597), Jesuit missionary in Japan. Portuguese by birth, Fróis became a Jesuit in 1548 and in the same year left for India, where he met the Jesuit pioneer Francis *Xavier. He was ordained a priest in 1561 and became the provincial secretary of the Jesuits. He worked in Malacca from 1554 to 1557, returned to India, and then from July 1563 worked in Japan except from 1592 to 1595 in Macao. He died in Japan. He traveled widely, gathering news of every type. He left extremely important written material on the history, culture, and religions of Japan. Especially valuable is his *História de Japão,* through which we know of the first steps of the church in that country, and the cultural and religious meeting of East and West. With some of this historical material, he also wrote a treatise on the differences between Europe and Japan, and one on the first ambassador of Japan to Rome. He left behind many letters as well. Fróis showed himself to be a careful observer of the religious folklore and customs of the Japanese.

BIBLIOGRAPHY Luís Fróis, *História de Japâo,* 5 vols., J. Wicki, ed. (1980–1984) and *Tratado em que se contem muita susinta e abreviadamente algumas contradicões e diferencas de costumes antre a gente de Europa a esta provincia de Japâo,* J. F. Schütte, ed. (1955). H. Feldmann, "As disputas de S. Francisco Xavier com bonzos da doutrina Zen relatadas por Luís Fróis, SJ y J. Rodrigues, SJ," in *O Sécolo Cristâo do Japâo: Actas do Coloquio internacional commemorativo dos 450 anos de amizade Portogal-Japâo* (1994), pp. 70–78; A. Maria Costa-Lopes, "Imagens do Japâo. 'Do que toca as mulheres, e de suas pessoas e costumes' no Tratado de Luís Fróis," ibid., pp. 591–602; Rui Manuel Loureiro, "A visão de outro nos escritos de Luís Fróis, SJ," ibid, pp. 645–663.

Jesús López-Gay, SJ

Frost, Henry W(eston) (1858–1945), North American director of the China Inland Mission (CIM). Frost, who was born in Detroit, lived in several cities as a child. He graduated from Princeton University, was ordained in the Presbyterian Church, and was much influenced by the premillennialist Niagara conferences of the late 1880s. After Hudson *Taylor's important 1888 visits to the Northfield and Niagara prophetic conferences at the invitation of D. L. *Moody, Frost was designated in 1889 by Taylor as secretary-general (later home director) of the CIM for North America. He set up a formal CIM branch (council) in Toronto on an equal footing with the London council and built a sophisticated support network all through Canada and the United States. In 1901 he moved the North American headquarters to the Philadelphia area.

Frost was an effective manager and presided over the internationalization of the CIM. By the 1930s North America contributed one-third of the international CIM missionary force and half the total budget. Frost maintained strong doctrinal views and eschewed ecumenical fellowship and cooperation with more liberal groups. Thus he cofounded in 1917 and served as first president of the Interdenominational Foreign Mission Association of North America. He also contributed to *The Fundamentals* (1910–1915).

BIBLIOGRAPHY Alvyn J. Austin, "Blessed Adversity: Henry W. Frost and the China Inland Mission," in Joel A. Carpenter and Wilbert R. Shenk, eds., *Earthen Vessels: American Evangelicals and Foreign Missions, 1880–1980* (1990); Dr. and Mrs. Howard Taylor, *By Faith: Henry W. Frost and the China Inland Mission* (1938, 1988). Most of the North American CIM records are in the Billy Graham Center archives, Wheaton College, Ill.; Frost left an autobiography of over 900 pages in manuscript preserved in the OMF archives in Toronto.

Daniel H. Bays

Frumentius (4th century), Apostle of Ethiopia. Born in a Christian family in Tyre, Frumentius and his brother Aedesius were taken as children on an expedition up the Red Sea that ended in their being brought into the service of a king of Aksum (later Ethiopia). After some years during which, apparently, Frumentius was given much administrative responsibility, the brothers were allowed to leave for home about the year 340. While Aedesius returned to Tyre, Frumentius went first to Alexandria to explain to its bishop, Athanasius, the religious position in Aksum and its need for a bishop to advance its evangelization. Athanasius chose Frumentius himself to fulfill this role and consecrated him a bishop. Rufinus (345–410) in his *Historia Ecclesiastica* is our authority for this account and he obtained it directly from Aedesius, who had become a priest in Tyre. Back in Aksum Frumentius was probably instrumental in bringing about the conversion of its king, *Ezana, and in establishing the ecclesiastical tradition of Ethiopian Orthodoxy, which until the twentieth century received its bishops from the patriarch of Alexandria. For the Ethiopian church, Frumentius has always been its revered founder, "Abba Salama, Revealer of the Light."

BIBLIOGRAPHY G. Haile, "Ethiopian Church," *The Encyclopedia of Religion,* Mircea Eliade, ed. (1987), vol. 5, pp. 173–177; Carlo Conti Rossini, *Storia d'Etiopia: Dalle origini all'avvento della dinastia Salomonide* (1928).

Adrian Hastings

Fuller, Andrew (1754–1815), Baptist theologian and first secretary of the Baptist Missionary Society (BMS). Fuller was born in Soham, Cambridgeshire, England, where in 1775 he was ordained pastor of the Baptist church. Originally schooled in the hyper-Calvinist theology then prevalent in parts of the Particular Baptist denomination, he became convinced in 1775 that the hyper-Calvinist position was not scriptural. In 1785 he published *The Gospel Worthy of All Acceptation,* which did much to prepare his denomination for accepting the missionary obligation. As pastor in Kettering, Northamptonshire, from 1783, Fuller became firm friends with John Sutcliff of Olney, John *Ryland of Northampton, and later the young William *Carey. The strengthening missionary vision of this group bore fruit on October 2, 1792, when the Particular Baptist Society for Propagating the Gospel among the Heathen (later known as the Baptist Missionary Society) was formed in the home of one of Fuller's deacons in Kettering. Fuller was appointed secretary. Until his death he combined the demands of a busy pastorate with managing the affairs of the BMS. He traveled extensively to raise funds for the society, especially in Scotland, which he visited five times.

BIBLIOGRAPHY A. G. Fuller, *The Complete Works of the Revd Andrew Fuller, with a Memoir of his Life* (1841); J. W. Morris, *Memoirs of the Life and Writings of the Rev. Andrew Fuller* (1816); John Ryland, *The Work of Faith, the Labour of Love, and the Patience of Hope Illustrated in the Life and Death of the Reverend Andrew Fuller...* (1816); Brian Stanley, *The History of the Baptist Missionary Society, 1792–1992* (1992).

Brian Stanley

Fuller, Jennie (Frow) (1851–1900), missionary with the Christian and Missionary Alliance (C&MA) in India. Born in Winchester, Ohio, Jennie Frow left Oberlin College to join Albert and Mary Norton's faith mission work in Ellichpur, Berar Province (present-day Maharashtra), India, engaging in evangelism and orphan ministry from 1877 to 1880. Returning from the United States in 1882 with her new husband, Marcus B. Fuller, she worked with him in establishing a mission center in Akola. While on furlough from 1890 to 1892 they joined the newly formed C&MA and returned to India as superintendents of the Alliance mission headquartered in Bombay. In the late 1890s Jennie Fuller wrote articles for the *Bombay Guardian,* a Christian weekly newspaper, including a well-researched series concerning the social conditions of women in India. She died in India from cholera.

BIBLIOGRAPHY Mrs. Marcus B. Fuller, *Texts Illuminated, or God's Care* (1898) and *The Wrongs of Indian Womanhood* (1900; first printed in the *Bombay Guardian*). Helen S. Dyer, *A Life for God in India* (n.d.).

Martha Lund Smalley

Fulton, Thomas Cosby (1855–1942), Irish Presbyterian missionary in Manchuria. Fulton was born near Carnmoney, County Antrim, Northern Ireland, and was educated at Queen's College, Belfast. Appointed to Manchuria in 1884 and stationed at Newchwang (Yingkou), he spent much time in pioneer evangelism over a wide area. He may have opened more stations and churches than any other missionary of his time in Manchuria. In 1899 he joined the staff of Union Theological College, Mukden (Shenyang), and spent most of the rest of his missionary career in theological education. He retired in 1941.

BIBLIOGRAPHY T. C. Fulton, *Reminiscences* (1937). R. H. Boyd, *Thomas Cosby Fulton* (n.d.) and *Waymakers in Manchuria* (1940); Austin Fulton, *Through Earthquake, Wind, and Fire: Church and Mission in Manchuria, 1867–1950* (1967).

T. Jack Thompson

Fumasoni-Biondi, Pietro (1872–1960), cardinal and head of the Congregation of Propaganda Fide. Born in Rome, Fumasoni-Biondi was ordained a priest and taught rhetoric in Propaganda Fide College, becoming an official of Propaganda Fide in 1904. In 1916 *Benedict XV appointed him apostolic delegate to India; in 1919, first apostolic delegate to Japan, and from 1921 to 1922, secretary of Propaganda Fide. *Pius XI then appointed him apostolic delegate to the United States. In 1933 Pius XI made him a cardinal and put him in charge of Propaganda Fide. Fumasoni-Biondi continued his predecessor's emphasis on indigenous clergy, and the second conference of African bishops (1936) in Leopoldville, Congo, studied the practical implications of such appointments. In 1947 Fumasoni-Biondi founded St. Peter's College in Rome for indigenous priests and attached it to Urban College. By 1950, eighty-nine seminaries had been established in Africa with 4,291 students, and the number of African priests reached 1,096. Fumasoni-Biondi recommended nineteen Africans to the pope for the episcopacy, the first one being ordained by *Pius XII in 1939. During his time as prefect, the Asian bishops increased from 18 to 125. In many countries the ordinary hierarchy was established, and China and India received their first cardinals. Under Fumasoni-Biondi's leadership, Propaganda Fide adopted a new attitude toward indigenous rites. In 1935, in a letter to the apostolic vicar of Kirn (Manchuria), it permitted the honoring of pictures of Confucius. In 1936 Japanese Christians were allowed to take part in ceremonies of the Shinto cult and in marriages and funerals. In 1939 the congregation issued the instruction that finally ended the Chinese rites controversy. After World War II Fumasoni-Biondi took new initiatives for renewing missionary activity. During the Holy Year of 1950 an International Congress of missions was organized in Rome. An exposition of Christian art in missions attracted wide attention. Fumasoni-Biondi died in Rome.

BIBLIOGRAPHY *Sylloge Praecipuorum documentorum recentium Summorum Pontificum et Sacrae Congregationis de Propaganda Fide necnon aliarum SS. Congregationum Romanarum. Ad usum missionariorum* (1939). Many documents concerning the indigenous clergy and indigenous rites appear in "L'enciclica del Sommo Pontefice Pio XII sulle missioni" (Evangelii Praecones), *Euntes Docete* 5 (1952): 1–10.

Willi Henkel, OMI

Furman, Charles Truman (1876–1947), Church of God (Cleveland, Tenn.) missionary in Guatemala. Furman, along with fellow Pentecostal T. A. Pullin, was trained in the Missionary Training Institute, Nyack, New York. He arrived in Guatemala in 1916 under the auspices of the Pennsylvania United Free Missionary Society. Initially they collaborated with C. Albert Hines, an independent Pentecostal, and Charles F. Secord, a Plymouth Brethren missionary, who had previously gathered several congregations in the department of Tontonicapán. In 1919 Furman married Nyack alumna Carrie Smith, an evangelist in her own right. Released by their mission in 1922, the couple did not resume their work in Guatemala until 1929, when they returned with the Primitive Methodists. Shortly thereafter, their church experienced a spontaneous revival in San Cristóbal, El Quiché. Leaving the Primitive Methodists in 1934, the Furmans affiliated with the Church of God (CG), accompanied by fourteen of the Primitive Methodist churches. For the next 14 years Furman served as the general overseer of the CG mission, which became one of the denomination's largest overseas efforts. When Furman died in Guatemala, he was mourned as the patriarch of a movement with eighty churches and 3,000 members.

BIBLIOGRAPHY Charles W. Conn, *Where the Saints Have Trod* (1959); Richard E. Waldrop, "A Historical and Critical Review of the Full Gospel Church of God of Guatemala" (D.Miss. diss., Fuller Theological Seminary, 1993); Everett A. Wilson, "The Central American Evangelicals: From Protest to Pragmatism," *IRM* 77 (January 1988): 94–106.

Everett A. Wilson

G

Gabet, Joseph (1808–1853), pioneer Catholic missionary in Mongolia. Born in Névy, France, Gabet was ordained in 1833 and entered the Vincentians in 1834. He went to Macao in 1835 and Mongolia in 1837, took part in a scientific expedition to Tibet from 1844 to 1846, and then returned to Europe. He is regarded as the founder of the modern Catholic mission to the Mongols. He became more widely known through the two-volume report published by his confrere E. R. *Huc, *Souvenir d'un voyage dans la Tartarie et le Tibet* (1851). His memorandum presented to the Holy See and Propaganda Fide, entitled "Reseignements sur l'état des missions en Chine," which he soon afterward published in *Coup d'oeil sur l'état des missions de Chine présenté au Saint Pére, le Pape Pie IX* (1848), got a mixed reception. Apart from the very realistic description of the missionary situation in China, his unambiguous demand for a Chinese clergy caused offense. In 1850 E. J. F. Verrolles, the vicar apostolic of Manchuria, succeeded in getting the memorandum formally condemned by Propaganda Fide. After submitting a report in Rome, Gabet went to Brazil (1849), where he left the order. He died in Rio de Janeiro.

BIBLIOGRAPHY N. Kowalsky, "Das 'verlorene' Manuskript zu Gabets Denkschrift über den einheimischen Klerus," *NZM* 14 (1958): 150–151; G. B. Tragella, "Le vicende d'un opuscolo sul clero indigeno e dul suo autore," in *Der einheimische Klerus in Geschichte und Gegenwart,* Johannes Beckmann, ed. (1950), pp. 189–202.

Karl Müller, SVD

Gabra Michael. *See* Gebhre Michael.

Gaebelein, A(rno) C(lemens) (1861–1945), missionary to Jews and fundamentalist Bible teacher. Born in Thuringia, Germany, Gaebelein immigrated to the United States in 1879, found work in a woolen mill, and joined a German Methodist Episcopal church. After studying privately for the Methodist ministry, he was ordained in 1885, pastored various congregations, and in 1891 was assigned to work among Jews in New York under the Methodist church's City Mission Society. He quickly mastered Hebrew and Yiddish and two years later founded the Hope of Israel Movement, a mission that engaged in social work among poor Jews and preached a gospel message that stressed the Second Coming of Christ. In 1894 he started *Our Hope,* a Bible study magazine that was a strong voice for premillennialism, foreign missions, and Zionism. In 1899 Gaebelein severed his Methodist ties, left the mission, and spent the rest of his life writing and speaking on the Bible conference circuit. He wrote dozens of books and tracts on prophetic themes and was a harsh critic of modernism, communism, and anti-Semitism.

BIBLIOGRAPHY A. C. Gaebelein, *Half a Century: The Autobiography of a Servant* (1930) and, as editor, *Our Hope* (1894–1957). Yaakov Ariel, *On Behalf of Israel* (1991); David A. Rausch, *Arno C. Gaebelein, 1861–1945: Irenic Fundamentalist and Scholar* (1983).

Richard V. Pierard

Gairdner, W(illiam) H(enry) Temple (1873–1928), Church Missionary Society missionary in Egypt. Gairdner, a seminal figure in Christian-Muslim relations, was equipped with singular gifts of imagination and pastoral energy. The son of a distinguished professor of medicine at the University of Glasgow, Gairdner came to evangelical faith and missionary vocation at Oxford. Cairo was his sphere of service from 1899 to 1928, except for brief periods of study leave at the Edinburgh World Missionary Conference of 1910 (on which he wrote a telling report) and at Hartford Seminary, where his mentor was Duncan Black *Macdonald.

Despite administrative duties and the loss of Douglas *Thornton, his early colleague, Gairdner "fulfilled the gospel" in sustained ventures of mind and pen. Tireless in conversation, he grew steadily more perceptive about communication with the Muslim community. The journal *Orient and Occident* was his lively forum. Against much opposition, he pioneered the use of drama and he wrote plays on biblical themes and Arabic commentaries in the style of the Muslim exegete Al-Baidawi (1226–1260). Applying his musical skills, he combined Egyptian lyrics and Christian hymnology. After his death at the height of his powers, the Church of Jesus, Light of the World was built and dedicated to his memory in Old Cairo.

BIBLIOGRAPHY W. H. Temple Gairdner, *The Reproach of Islam* (1909), had several editions prior to the fifth (1920), when "Reproach" became "Rebuke," to move the onus more squarely onto Christians. Also by Gairdner: *W. H. T. G. to His Friends* (1930; letters) and *The Value of Christianity and Islam* (with W. A. Eddy, 1927). Constance E. Padwick, *Temple Gairdner of Cairo* (1929; appendix lists his plays and pamphlets and works in Arabic); Lyle L. Vander Werff, *Christian Mission to Muslims: The Record* (1977), pp. 184–224 and 279–282.

Kenneth Cragg

Gale, James Scarth (1863–1937), Canadian missionary in Korea. Gale was born in Pilkington, Ontario, and graduated from University College, Toronto, in 1888. He was sent to Korea that same year as a lay missionary of the University College YMCA but joined the mission of the Presbyterian Church (U.S.A.) in 1891, when support from the YMCA became uncertain. He traveled widely in Korea, established a mission in Wonsan, opened work in remote areas, participated in translating the Bible and Christian literature into Korean, wrote a Korean grammar and dictionary, and translated Korean literature into English. After ordination in 1897, he served as a pastor, devoted years to education, and wrote widely, including articles on Korean politics, educational materials in Korean, a novel, and accounts of his experiences. A major interpreter of Korea to the West and of things Western to Korea, Gale devoted much of his time to Korean studies. His *Folk Tales* (1913) and *Cloud Dream of the Nine* (1922) (a translation of an old Korean novel) were both well received, and his *History of the Korean People* (1927) reveals an appreciation of the culture and religious background of Korea. Retiring to England in 1927, he revised some earlier writings and expressed regret at Korea's modernization and the loss of the spirit of old Korea. As a missionary pioneer in Korea, he explored the nation geographically, historically, and culturally and became an important early Korean studies scholar.

BIBLIOGRAPHY Gale's writings in English include *The Unabridged Korean-English Dictionary*, 3d ed. (1931), *Korean Sketches* (1898), *The Vanguard* (1904), *Korea in Transition* (1909), and numerous articles in such periodicals as *Transactions of the Royal Asiatic Society*, *Korean Repository*, and *Korea Magazine*. Richard Rutt, *James Scarth Gale and His History of the Korean People* (1972) contains extensive annotated bibliographies. References to Gale appear in A. Hamish Ion, *The Cross and the Rising Sun* (1990).

Edward W. Poitras

Gall (Gallus) (c. 550–c. 640), Irish missionary to France and Switzerland. Firm evidence about Gall's career is extremely sketchy—only a brief mention in Jonas of Bobbio's seventh-century biography of *Columban, a fragmentary eighth-century "Life" of Gall, and ninth-century biographies by the monks Walafrid of Strabo and Wettinus. These accounts suggests that Gall was from a good Irish family and as a child was offered to the service of God at Bangor Abbey. There he was placed under the guidance of Columban and accompanied the famous missionary on his journey to the Continent (c. 590). Gall quickly mastered the Alemanni language and worked with Columban in spreading Christianity among this Germanic people. Around 610 Columban left for Italy, but Gall remained behind because of illness, lived in a hermitage at the east end of Lake Constance, and engaged in meditation and missionary work. By the time of his death the Alemanni had largely been Christianized. In the Middle Ages he was renowned for his preaching, personal holiness, and miracle-working power; contrary to tradition, however, he did not found the famous Benedictine Abbey of St. Gall. Although located on the site of his Swiss hermitage, it was actually established in the early ninth century. The feast day of St. Gall is October 16.

BIBLIOGRAPHY *Monumenta Germaniae Historica, Scriptores Rerum Merovingicarum*, vol. 4 (1902) provides the text and a discussion of the biographies of Gall. An English translation of the Walafrid biography is contained in Maud Joynt, *The Life of St. Gall* (1927). James F. Kenney, *The Sources for the Early History of Ireland: Ecclesiastical* (1966) gives a comprehensive bibliography.

Richard V. Pierard

Galland, Emmanuel Arnold (1888–1944), YMCA worker among students in South America. Born in Lausanne, Switzerland, to a distinguished Swiss family, Galland was a member and later central treasurer and editor for the Student Christian Movement of French-speaking Switzerland. He graduated from preparatory school for theology in 1909, and in 1913 studied in the School of Theology of the Free Church of Vaud. For a brief period he also worked as an assistant to his father, Alfred Galland, a banker and also the British counsel in Lausanne. Galland married Yvonne M. B. van Berchern in 1916 and later that year was sent by the International Committee of the YMCA to Uruguay and Argentina as student and religious secretary. He and his wife became active members of the Methodist Episcopal Church in Uruguay and Argentina but worked with many Protestant groups, especially with the Waldensian churches of the River Plate area. Galland's principal task was to teach Bible classes and to organize evangelical high school and university students in local and national bodies of the World's Student Christian Federation. Returning from furlough in Europe to Buenos Aires in 1922, he became traveling student secretary for the South American Federation of the YMCA, a position he held until 1934.

BIBLIOGRAPHY Kenneth S. Latourette, *World Service: A History of the Foreign Work and World Service of the Young Men's Christian As-*

sociations of the United States and Canada (1957); Hans Jürgen Prien, *La historia del Christianismo en América Latina* (1985).

Alan Neely

Galvin, Edward J. (1882–1956), founder of the Columban Fathers. Galvin was born in County Cork, Ireland, studied for the priesthood at St. Patrick's College, Maynooth, and was ordained in 1909. He served a parish in Brooklyn, New York, until 1912, when he was drawn to missionary service in China. There he first served in the mission territory of the French Vincentians. In 1915 two Irish priests joined him in his work. Back in Ireland in 1916, together with a fellow Irish priest John Blowick, he founded the St. Columban's Foreign Mission Society. Formal approval from Rome came in 1918.

The new society opened houses in Galway and the United States that year and rapidly gained recruits who trained to serve in their new mission territory centered in Hanyang, Hupei (Hubei) Province, China. By 1920 they numbered forty priests and sixty seminarians. In that year Galvin and seventeen other priests formed the pioneer group that opened the Columbans' work in central China.

Galvin was appointed prefect apostolic in 1924, vicar apostolic in 1927, and first bishop of the new Hanyang Diocese in 1946. After the Communist victory in 1949, all 146 Columbans were expelled from China. Galvin was placed under house arrest, tried, and expelled in 1952. Already ill with leukemia, he returned to Ireland via the United States and died four years later, having witnessed the expansion of Columban missions into other regions, eventually reaching eleven nations in East Asia and Latin America.

BIBLIOGRAPHY William E. Barrett, *The Red Lacquered Gate: Life of Edward J. Galvin* (1967); P. Crosbie, *March Till They Die* (1956); R. T. Reilly, *Christ's Exile: Life of Bishop Edward J. Galvin* (1958).

Donald E. MacInnis

Gamewell, Frank (Francis) Dunlap (1857–1950), American Methodist educational missionary in China. Gamewell received world acclaim for organizing the defense of the Methodist Mission and the British Legation in Peking (Beijing) during the Boxer Rebellion of 1900. Born in South Carolina, he earned three degrees from Dickinson College, Carlisle, Pennsylvania, but was also trained in engineering at Rensselaer Polytechnic Institute and at Cornell University, New York. He received honorary degrees from Syracuse and Columbia Universities. He began his missionary service under the Methodist Episcopal Church in 1881 as principal of a boys' school in Peking. In 1884 he was appointed superintendent of the West China mission. Three years later he was forced out of Chungking (Chongqing), Szechwan (Sichuan) Province, by antiforeign riots, and returned to Peking to teach physics and chemistry as acting president at the future Yenching University. During the 56 days of the Boxer siege, he was "chief of staff" in charge of fortifications and the administration of vital services for some 3,500 people. Subsequently he served for 12 years as executive secretary of the Educational Association of China and then as an associate general secretary of the Methodist Episcopal Board of Foreign Missions in New York City.

His first wife, Mary (Porter) (1848–1906), was the fourth appointee of the Methodist Woman's Foreign Missionary Society and the first to go to China. In 1872 she opened one of the pioneer schools for girls (insisting on unbound feet). After her marriage to Frank Gamewell she showed remarkable courage in resisting mob attacks on the West China mission, as well as later, in Peking, where she ministered to refugees and wounded Legation defenders. Gamewell's second wife, Mary (Ninde) (1858–1947), was a daughter of Bishop William X. Ninde, a former president of Garrett Biblical Institute. She served with her husband for 21 years and wrote a number of books on mission work in China.

BIBLIOGRAPHY Frank D. Gamewell, *The Siege in Peking* (1900) and *China Old and New* (1906). Mary P. Gamewell, *Mary Porter Gamewell and Her Story of the Siege in Peking* (1907); Mary N. Gamewell, *Ming-Kwong, "City of the Morning Light"* (1924), *The Gateway to China* (1916), and *New Life Currents in China* (1919); Ethel Daniels Hubbard, *Under Marching Orders: A Story of Mary Porter Gamewell* (1909).

Creighton Lacy

Gante, Pedro de. *See* Peter of Ghent.

Garcés, Julián (1451?–1542), cofounder of the church in Mexico. Born in Aragón, Spain, of a noble family, Garcés studied at the Sorbonne and then entered the Dominicans. He served for a while as a court chaplain and in 1527 Charles V named him first bishop of Tlaxcala, Mexico. En route to his new diocese Garcés conferred with fellow Dominicans Antonio de *Montesinos and Bartolomé de *Las Casas in Santo Domingo. In Mexico he supported the work of Juan de *Zumárraga, the first bishop of Mexico City and cofounder (with Garcés) of the church in Mexico. Like Zumárraga, Garcés also defended the Indians against the abuses of fellow Spaniards. He wrote a letter in 1533 to Pope Paul III in which he took up the cause of the Indians and praised their human qualities. This letter influenced the Pope's bull, *Sublimis Deus* (1537), in which the pontiff solemnly defended the humanity of the Indians and rejected all arguments in favor of enslaving them. Shortly after Garcés's death the seat of his diocese was moved to modern-day Puebla.

BIBLIOGRAPHY Mariano Cuevas, *Historia de la Iglesia de México,* vol. 1 (1921–1928); Enrique Dussel, *El Episcopado latinoamericano y la liberación de los pobres, 1504–1620* (1979); Antoine Touron, *Sketches of Illustrious Dominicans: St. Louis Bertrand, Julián Garcés, Jerome de Loaysa,* tr. from the French (1884).

Jeffrey Klaiber, SJ

Gardiner, Allen Francis (1794–1851), pioneer of South American Protestant missions. Gardiner was born into a country gentleman's family in Berkshire, England. He joined the navy at 16 and saw service in the Napoleonic

Wars and in South America, but he was not employed again after reaching the rank of commander in 1826. Before this, he had experienced evangelical conversion. Following his wife's death in 1834, he devoted his life to missions. In South Africa, he tried to persuade the Zulu king Dingane to receive missionaries and to help reform the nearby down-at-the-heels European settlement of Port Natal. He returned to England in 1836 to urge the government to bring Natal into Cape Colony and to persuade the Church Missionary Society to establish a Zulu mission. The government compromised by appointing him magistrate in Port Natal (a post in which he was largely impotent); the missionary society sent Francis *Owen. The Piet Relief massacre and the subsequent war between Dingane and the Dutch led to Gardiner's withdrawal and the end of the mission.

Gardiner spent most of the years 1838 to 1843 in extraordinary voyages of missionary reconnaissance, often with his family (he had remarried in 1836). He visited Brazil, Buenos Aires, Chile, Australia, and the Dutch East Indies, then came back via Cape Town and Rio de Janeiro to Chile. Everywhere government opposition or Catholic presence blocked any chance of a mission. In 1841 he turned to Patagonia and desolate Tierra del Fuego, which contained independent unreached peoples who would be accessible from the British Falkland Islands. Encouraged by his visit, he returned to England to plead with the established missionary societies to follow it up, but in vain. Returning to South America, he distributed Bibles and tracts in a cross-continental land journey. In Britain again in 1844, he established the Patagonia Mission, which evoked only a modest response, and he accompanied its first missionary to the Straits of Magellan. Settlement proved impossible and they withdrew the next year. Gardiner now traveled to Bolivia to help establish Federico Gonzales, a Spanish Protestant, in a short-lived mission there. This was followed by another campaign around Britain on behalf of Patagonia and then another reconnoitering party to Tierra del Fuego. Having concluded that a Fuegian mission could work from its own boat, in 1850 he returned to Tierra del Fuego with two lay missionaries in two launches crewed by three Cornish fishermen and a carpenter. Supply arrangements for the underfunded expedition broke down, and the whole party died of starvation and scurvy. Gardiner's tragic death had a powerful public impact; his Patagonia Mission (in which his only son served) eventually blossomed into the South American Missionary Society.

BIBLIOGRAPHY A. F. Gardiner, *Narrative of a Journey to the Zoolu Country, in South Africa...* (1836), *A Visit to the Indians on the Frontiers of Chili* (1840), and *A Voice from South America* (1847). G. P. Despard, *Hope Deferred, not Lost: A Narrative of Missionary Effort* (1852); J. W. Marsh, *A Memoir of Allen F. Gardiner* (1857); J. W. Marsh and W. H. Stirling, *The Story of Commander Allen Gardiner... with Sketches of Missionary Work in South America* (1867); Monica Wilson and Leonard Thompson, *Oxford History of South Africa*, vol. 1 (1982).

Andrew F. Walls

Garnier, Charles (1606–1649), French Jesuit missionary in New France. Garnier was born in Paris into a family of the lesser nobility. After studies at the Jesuit Collège de Clermont, he entered the Society of Jesus in 1624 and was ordained a priest in 1635. He volunteered for the Canadian missions, landed in Quebec in June 1636, and arrived in Wendake—the land of the Huron Indians, east of Georgian Bay, Ontario—two months later. He enjoyed consistent good health and had easy fluency in the native languages. This made him very popular among the native peoples, who called him, appreciatively, *Ouracha*, "Rainmaker." For the next 13 years he labored at the Saint-Joseph (Teanaostaiaë) mission, near present-day Orillia, Ontario, and on two occasions in the land of the Tobacco Nation (southern Ontario below Georgian Bay). There, at the mission of Saint-Jean, he was killed by the Iroquois at the time of the destruction of the Huron missions. He refused to flee, and when his body was found a few feet from the chapel, it had two bullet wounds and two blows from a tomahawk. He was canonized by Pope *Pius XI on June 29, 1930.

BIBLIOGRAPHY François Roustang, *An Autobiography of Martyrdom* (1964); Reuben Gold Thwaites, ed., *The Jesuit Relations and Allied Documents* (1959); Camille de Rochemonteix, *Les Jésuites et la Nouvelle-France*, vol. 2 (1895–1896).

Jacques Monet, SJ

Garr, A(lfred) G(oodrich), Sr. (1874–1944), early Pentecostal missionary to India and China. In China between 1907 and 1911, Garr played an important role in establishing a Pentecostal mission base in Hong Kong. After he returned to the United States, he became a well-known Pentecostal evangelist and pastor.

Garr was from Kentucky, where he started preaching at an early age. After attending Asbury College, he and his wife, Lillian (Anderson), moved to Los Angeles, where he was pastor of the Burning Bush Mission. Garr was an early participant in the multiracial Azusa Street Mission revival in 1906, and he was allegedly the first Caucasian pastor to receive baptism in the Holy Spirit with speaking in tongues.

Convinced that some of the tongues were real languages, given for the purpose of missions, the Garrs participated in the strong thrust of the early Pentecostal movement into foreign missions. Garr believed that he had been given an Indian language and his wife Tibetan and Chinese. They went to India in 1907 where, disappointed in not having the hoped-for supernatural linguistic skills, they persisted briefly, having a considerable and controversial impact on the missionary community. They went on to Hong Kong in October 1907, where they preached the new Pentecostal doctrines at an American Board of Commissioners for Foreign Missions church, until they were evicted. A deacon of the church who acted as interpreter, Mok Lai Chi (Mo Lizhi), became an early convert, and meetings continued in a building he owned. Mok was the driving force behind the small but dynamic Sino-foreign Pentecostal community in Hong Kong.

Beginning in 1908, the foreign contingent suffered from sickness and death, accounting for the Garrs' frequent absences and their final departure in 1911. But Mok and the Chinese Pentecostal community nurtured by the Garrs continued in active witness.

BIBLIOGRAPHY Daniel H. Bays, "The Impact of Pentecostalism on Established American Missions in China," in Edith Blumhofer, ed., *Pentecostal Currents in the American Church* (1996); E. May Law, *Pentecostal Mission Work in South China* (c. 1915); William A. Ward, ed., *The Trailblazer: Dr. A. G. Garr* (n.d.)

Daniel H. Bays

Gaspais, Auguste Ernest (1884–1952), Catholic missionary and bishop in Manchuria. Born in Brittany, France, Gaspais, a member of the Paris Foreign Mission Society, was ordained in 1907 in Penang, Malaysia. That same year, he sailed to China for the vicariate apostolic of northern Manchuria, later known as the Kirin (Jilin) vicariate. In 1923 he became bishop of that mission territory. After Japan created the puppet state of Manchukuo in 1932, direct contacts between Catholic missions in Manchuria and Celso *Costantini, the apostolic delegate to China, were interrupted. The Holy See therefore appointed Gaspais as its temporary representative to look after the interests of the Catholic Church in Manchukuo. Gaspais is best remembered for his role in bringing about a reversal in the Holy See's intransigent attitude toward Chinese Confucian and ancestral ceremonies. When the government of Manchukuo made the cult of Confucius obligatory on all citizens, Gaspais inquired whether the prescribed ceremonies were conceived of as religious in character or deemed a "purely civil homage to a distinguished man and philosopher." The answer received from the Ministry of Education stated that the ceremonies had no religious significance and were only manifestations of the country's affection for Confucius and his teaching. After discussing the matter with the other bishops of the region, Gaspais submitted his findings to the Holy See, which in May 1935 officially authorized Catholics in Manchukuo to render homage to Confucius and all the great people of the past as well as to their ancestors. In December 1939 the permission was extended to the whole of China. In similar moves, in May 1936 the Holy See permitted the use of Shinto rites and other Japanese customs and, in April 1940, approved the Malabar rites of India. During the civil war that followed the return of Manchuria to China in 1945, Gaspais stayed at his post. In June 1951 he was put under house arrest by the Communist authorities. In December he was jailed for a few weeks and sentenced to extradition. He died less than a year after his return to France.

BIBLIOGRAPHY *Annuaire des Missions Catholiques du Manchoukuo* (1938, 1939); *Bulletin de la Société des Missions Etrangères de Paris* (1953): 69–70; Georges Minamiki, *The Chinese Rites Controversy from Its Beginning to Modern Times* (1985); *Le Siège apostolique et les missions,* vol. 1 (1959); *Missionnaires d'Asie,* vol. 69 (1953): 154–159.

Jean-Paul Wiest

Gebauer, Paul (1900–1977), Baptist missionary in Cameroon. Gebauer was born in Silesia, Germany, and immigrated to the United States in 1925. From 1928 to 1931 he studied at Southern Baptist Theological Seminary, Louisville, receiving a master of arts in theology. In 1931 he went to British Mandated Cameroon as a missionary under the German Baptists and served there for 30 years. He and his wife, Clara Katherine, located in the grasslands of western Cameroon, where they helped establish churches as well as educational and medical programs. They became experts in the people, history, culture, and arts of the region. They promoted the preservation and appreciation of Cameroon culture through such publications as *Spider Divination in the Cameroons* (1964; based on Gebauer's 1958 master's thesis at Northwestern University), *A Guide to Cameroon Art from the Collection of Paul and Clara Gebauer* (1968), and *Art of Cameroon* (1979), based on the Gebauers' own photographs and collection. Paul obtained a B.A. degree in 1943 and an honorary D.D. in 1952 from Linfield College, McMinnville, Oregon, where he taught after retiring from the mission in 1962. He also helped train early Peace Corps volunteers to Cameroon. The Gebauers contributed artifacts and photographs of the grasslands to the Metropolitan Museum of Art in New York City, Field Museum of Chicago, Milwaukee Public Museum, and Portland Art Museum.

BIBLIOGRAPHY Charles W. Weber, *International Influences and Baptist Mission in West Cameroon* (1993); Frank H. Woyke, *Heritage and Ministry of the North American Baptist Conference* (1979).

Charles W. Weber

Gebhre Michael (*or* Ghebre Michael; Gabra Micha'el) (1791–1855), indigenous pioneer of Ethiopian Catholicism. Gebhre Michael was born in Mertoulé Mariam, Gojjam, Ethiopia. A dissident Coptic monk of deep piety, he was impressed by the theological profundity and personal integrity of Justin (Guistino) de *Jacobis, a Vincentian missionary from Naples. Dissatisfied with his church's endemic corruption and poorly articulated theology, he became a Catholic in 1844 and embarked upon the work that was to be his major contribution to Ethiopian Catholicism—producing a catechism and translating a textbook of moral theology into Amharic. He was admitted to the Vincentians after being secretly ordained in 1851. Arrested by Coptic authorities for heresy in 1855, he died in August of that year after several months of torture. He was beatified on October 31, 1926.

BIBLIOGRAPHY Donald Attwater, *The Golden Book of Eastern Saints* (1938); Donald Crummey, *Priests and Politicians: Protestant and Catholic Missions in Orthodox Ethiopia, 1830–1868* (1972); M. M. Vaussard, ed., *The Golden Legend Overseas* (1931).

Jonathan J. Bonk

Geddie, John (1815–1872), Presbyterian missionary to New Hebrides. Geddie was born in Banff, Scotland, and was raised in Nova Scotia. His father was a clockmaker. His family closely followed the progress of Congregational missions in the South Seas Islands. Geddie was educated at Pictou Academy (Presbyterian Church of Nova Scotia) and Dalhousie University. He was then ordained and married Charlotte McDonald. He became pastor of the Succession Church on Prince Edward Island and was the prime mover in the formation of a mission society among the Presbyterians of Nova Scotia, becoming their first appointee. After a brief time in Tutuila, Samoa (1847–1848), he and his wife boarded the ship that served the various stations of the London Missionary Society. They and two other couples were to be stationed at Aneityum, New Hebrides. Within a short time, however, the others withdrew, one couple for health reasons, the other because of the husband's adultery. Progress was slow and discouraging. In 1852 John *Inglis and his wife, Presbyterians from Scotland, came to assist. Geddie and Inglis worked well together and were of one mind on how to win the island. By 1854 more than half the island's population had become Christians. Within a few more years, the New Testament had been translated and published, and as many as half the population had been taught to read. As more workers arrived from Nova Scotia and Scotland, the mission fanned out to other islands. The traditional, orderly Presbyterian pattern set by Geddie and Inglis was followed. On Erromanga in 1861, two missionaries died in a measles epidemic. But Christianity continued its spread through the southern New Hebrides islands through the Presbyterian work. In 1866 Queen's University in Kingston, Ontario, conferred an honorary doctorate on Geddie. By the time of his death, all the population of Aneityum were said to be Christians.

BIBLIOGRAPHY R. S. Miller, *Misi Gete, John Geddie, Pioneer Missionary to the New Hebrides* (1975); George Patterson, *Missionary Life among the Cannibals: Being the Life of the Rev. John Geddie, D.D., First Missionary to the New Hebrides: with the History of the Nova Scotia Presbyterian Mission on That Group* (1882).

Darrell Whiteman

Gensichen, Hans-Werner (1915–), German Protestant missiologist. Born in Lintorf, Germany, Gensichen came from a family of ministers and missionaries. He obtained his doctorate and qualified as a university lecturer (1950) in church history at Göttingen. In the missiological field he regarded Walter *Freytag as his mentor, but more important for his missiological thinking was his activity in India (1952–1957), where he taught in theological colleges at Tranquebar and Madras. From 1957 until his retirement in 1983, he held the newly established chair of history of religions and missiology in the faculty of theology at the University of Heidelberg, interrupted by three years' work for the Theological Education Fund of the World Council of Churches (1961–1964). Here, as secretary for a special Africa program, he fostered theological training on the African continent and contributed to developing the concept of contextual theology. Gensichen was not only a successful teacher with whom students from all over the world came to study, but he also served on many missiological and ecumenical boards. Among other things he was from 1965 to 1991 president of the Deutsche Gesellschaft für Missionswissenschaft (German Society for Missiology) and founding member and first president (1972–1974) of the International Association for Mission Studies. He published numerous works in comparative religion and particularly in mission history. His missiological legacy is reflected in his main work, *Glaube für die Welt: Theologische Aspekte der Mission* (1971). Gensichen always presents missiology in its historical context, believing that only in continuity and dialogue with history can the church accomplish its task in the world. For him, mission is the decisive dimension of the life of the worldwide church. To highlight all facets of mission with a view to practical application has been the lifelong goal of his scholarly work.

BIBLIOGRAPHY Other works by Gensichen include *Missionsgeschichte der neuren Zeit* (1961, 1976), *Living Mission: The Test of Faith* (1966), *Mission und Kulture: Gesammelte Aufsätze* (1985), *Weltreligion und Weltfriede* (1985). His autobiographical reflections are found in "My Pilgrimage in Mission," *IBMR* 13 (1989): 167–169. Theo Sundermeier et al., eds., *Fides pro mundi vita: Missionstheologie heute. Festschrift Hans-Werner Gensichen zum 65. Geburtstag* (1980); Henning Wrogemann, "Bibliographie der Werke Hans-Werner Gensichens (1980–1994)," *ZMR* 79 (1995): 183–188.

Theo Sundermeier

George, David (c. 1742–1810), early African American promoter of mission. With energy and dedication, George urged the importance of mission at a time when Protestant Christianity was far from committed to it and when the organizational basis for mission was virtually nonexistent. With indomitable will and a preparedness to take risk that was born of faith, he became leader of the outreach to Africa that opened a new chapter in the modern history of the continent.

George was born to slave parents on a plantation in Essex County, Virginia. At an early age he ran away but soon after passed into the hands of a new master in South Carolina. He converted to evangelical Christianity and became a colleague of the black preacher George *Liele, a veteran missionary to Jamaica and the Bahamas. When the American Revolutionary War broke out in 1776, George joined the British side and in 1782 was demobilized with other black loyalists to Nova Scotia, Canada, where he continued his preaching activity. He impressed the British authorities with his leadership qualities, and he was appointed a leader of an expedition to repatriate the black loyalists to West Africa. They made landfall in Freetown, Sierra Leone, in March 1792, the commencement of what the English evangelical cause, led by William *Wilberforce, termed "a Christian experiment." It established in tropical Africa a bridgehead from where the trade in slaves could be attacked and the rest of the continent reached for the gospel.

In Freetown George combined the roles of preacher, community leader, official representative with the British authorities, humanitarian campaigner against the slave trade, and lightning rod for missionary awakening among Baptists in England, where he visited in 1793. He and William *Carey were thus active at about the same time, though George by then had accumulated an abundance of field experience. By the time of George's death in Freetown the cause was virtually assured—this was four years after the

Williamstown (Massachusetts) Haystack Prayer Meeting, an event that lit the American missionary impulse. The success of the Sierra Leone "Christian experiment," in which George's hand was so prominent, led to the abolition of the slave trade and the peaceful, economic mobilization of Africa for commerce, civilization, and Christianity.

BIBLIOGRAPHY I. E. Bill, *Fifty Years with the Baptist Ministers and Churches* (1880); W. H. Brooks, "The Priority of the Silver Bluff Church and Its Promoters," *Journal of Negro History* 2 (1922): 172–196; Christopher Fyfe, "The Baptist Churches in Sierra Leone," *Sierra Leone Bulletin of Religion* 2 (December 1963): 55–60 and *A History of Sierra Leone* (1962); Grant Gordon, *From Slavery to Freedom: The Life of David George, Pioneer Black Baptist Minister* (1992); Anthony Kirk-Green, "David George: The Nova Scotian Experience," *Sierra Leone Studies*, n.s., 14 (1960): 93–120; Lamin Sanneh, "Prelude to African Christian Independency: The Afro-American Factor in African Christianity," *HTR* 77, no. 1 (1984): 1–32; Mechal Sobel, *Trabelin' On: The Slave Journey to an Afro-Baptist Faith* (1979); Andrew F. Walls, "The Nova Scotians and Their Religion," *Sierra Leone Bulletin of Religion* 1 (1959): 19–31.

Lamin Sanneh

George, Eliza (Davis) (1879–1980), African American missionary to Liberia and founder of the Elizabeth Native Interior Mission. Eliza Davis grew up in Texas and studied at Central Texas College, where she became involved in the Student Volunteer Movement and made plans to serve in Africa. Her plans were nearly thwarted when she learned from Texas Baptist leaders that they had no intention of sending a black woman to Africa. They told her that if she wanted to reach black people with the gospel, she could do so at home. She refused to give up, and in 1914, supported by the National Baptist Convention, arrived in Liberia to begin her ministry, which continued for more than a half century. She served as an evangelist, church planter, and founder of the Bible Industrial Academy. Despite her success, however, she faced problems with financial support. In 1919, when a British businessman proposed marriage, she refused at first, but then accepted, having concluded that his promised support was the only means by which she could remain in Africa. Although they worked together for 20 years, the marriage was filled with conflict. After her husband died in 1939, she was forced to become independent and rely on small contributions given through Eliza Davis George Clubs. By the 1960s the Eliza George Baptist Association had 27 churches. George remained active in the ministry until she reached her 90s, when the work was taken over by Liberians. She retired in Austin, Texas.

BIBLIOGRAPHY Lorry Lutz, *Born to Lose, Bound to Win: The Amazing Journey of Mother Eliza George* (1980); Ruth A. Tucker, *Guardians of the Great Commission: The Story of Women in Modern Missions* (1988).

Ruth A. Tucker

Gérard, Joseph (1831–1914), Oblate missionary in South Africa. Born in the French village of Bouxiérès-aux-Chênes, near Nancy, Gérard joined the Missionary Oblates of Mary Immaculate in 1851. In 1853 he was appointed deacon and was sent to the new Oblate mission in Natal, South Africa, arriving in January 1854 at Durban, where he was ordained a priest. He first worked among the white population, learning English and especially the Zulu languages. In 1862 he went to Basutoland (Lesotho), where the king, *Moshoeshoe, welcomed him and gave land for a mission station. The place was called Village of the Mother of Jesus and, later on, Roma. In 1865 he baptized the first Basotho; at his death the Catholic population numbered 15,000, plus 44,000 catechumens. His method consisted of simply talking to the Basotho, who called him "One who talks to the people." He presented Christian doctrine in a lively way, paying special attention to solemn occasions such as baptisms, confirmations, and marriages. Gérard emphasized solid formation for the catechumens. From the catechists he expected vocations of future priests and religious sisters. The Basotho consider him to be their apostle. He died in Africa.

BIBLIOGRAPHY Gerard O'Hara, *Father Joseph Gérard, Oblate of Mary Immaculate* (1988); A. Roche, *Clartés australes, Joseph Gérard, O.M.I. le "prêtre bien-aimés des Basotho"* (1951) and *Le Cavalier de Malouti, Joseph Gérard O.M.I., 1831–1914* (1955); Francis Santucci, "Father Joseph Gérard, O.M.I.: An Over-View of His Life and the Background of His Times," *Vie Oblate Life* 51 (1992): 259–278.

Willi Henkel, OMI

Gerbillon, Jean-François (1654–1707), Jesuit missionary in China. Gerbillon was born in Verdun, France, and entered the Society of Jesus in 1670. During his fourth year of theological studies in Paris, he volunteered to join five confreres designated to go to China as mathematicians of King Louis XIV. Arriving in Peking (Beijing) in 1688, Gerbillon and Joachim *Bouvet were chosen to work at court. After teaching geometry to the emperor for a number of months, Gerbillon accompanied another Jesuit, Tomas Pereira, to Nerchinsk, Russia. As interpreters and negotiators, they were instrumental in concluding the 1689 Sino-Russian treaty, the first agreement in Asia based on the law of nations.

Gerbillon's eight trips to Mongolia and Manchuria are recorded in his travel accounts published in Europe. He completed Manchu and Chinese translations of French works on philosophy and geometry. As superior of the French Jesuits in China, he discussed the Chinese Rites issue with Charles Thomas Maillard de *Tournon, the first papal legate sent to Peking. A rupture of relations between legate and the emperor ensued. Apparently, because Gerbillon, in the eyes of the emperor, had taken the side of Tournon, no imperial funds were allocated to defray Gerbillon's funeral expenses when he died.

BIBLIOGRAPHY "Lettre du P. Gerbillon," in M. L. Aimé-Martin, ed., *Lettres édifiantes et curieuses*, 4 vols. (1843), 3:157–160. Henri Cordier, "Cinq lettres inédites du Père Gerbillon," *T'oung Pao* 7 (1906): 437–468; "Observations historiques sur la Grande Tartarie" and "Relations de huit voyages dans la Grande Tartarie de

1688 à 1699," in Jean-Baptiste du Halde, *Description géographique, historique, chronologique, politique, et physique de l'Empire de la Chine et de la Tartarie chinoise,* 4 vols. (1735; 1736), 4:33–59, 87–422; "Lettre du 30 decembre 1706," in Gonzalez de St. Pierre, *Relation abregée de la nouvelle persécution à la Chine* (1712), pp. 88–94; Joseph S. Sebes, *The Jesuits and the Sino-Russian Treaty of Nerchinsk (1689): The Diary of Thomas Pereira, S.J.* (1961); Yves de Thomaz de Bossierre, *Jean-François Gerbillon, S.J. (1654–1707)* (1994).

John W. Witek, SJ

Gericke, Christian Wilhelm (1742–1803), German Lutheran missionary in South India. A native of Kolberg (Pomerania), Gericke was one of the German missionaries who, after training at Halle, joined the Danish-Halle mission under the sponsorship of the (English) Society for Promoting Christian Knowledge. After a period of apprenticeship in the rather neglected congregation at Cuddalore, south of Madras, he was stationed farther south at Negapattam and later transferred to the Lutheran mission at Vepery, Madras, where he succeded J. P. *Fabricius. During the British-French war Gericke saved the town of Cuddalore and the mission from capture by Haidar Ali through successful negotiation with the French. Probably no other member of the Danish-Halle mission labored as incessantly as Gericke by traveling all over South India, even under pressure of colonial warfare, famine, and epidemics, in order to gather and encourage the scattered members of the Lutheran church. In the last years of his life he took part in paving the way for the great Christian awakening in Tirunelveli, in the far south. A monument was erected to Gericke's memory in the Fort Church at Madras.

BIBLIOGRAPHY Reinhold Vormbaum, *C. W. Gericke, evangelisch-lutherischer Missionar in Trankebar* (1852).

Hans-Werner Gensichen

Geyer, Francis Xavier (1858–1943), Catholic missionary bishop, educator, and mission strategist in the Sudan. Born in Regen, Germany, Geyer studied at Munich University and in 1881 entered the Institute for African Mission founded by Daniel *Comboni at Verona, Italy. Ordained two years later, he promptly departed for Sudan under an expedition of the institute. With Christian missionaries forced into exile during the Mahdiyah, Geyer retreated to Suakin, on the Red Sea, where he supervised the care of African children and became vicar general of the mission. In 1897 he returned to Europe as superior of a community in Bressanone and began a seminary to train future missionaries. In 1903 he returned to Sudan as vicar apostolic of Central Africa, undertook a series of expeditions by land and river, and founded eight stations across a vast territory. The academic and trade schools he established won the esteem of British authorities and opened a new era of Catholic mission in Sudan. From 1913 he served as vicar apostolic of Khartoum until his resignation from the mission in 1922. Returning to Europe, he began a seminary for immigrants where he invested his remaining years.

BIBLIOGRAPHY F. X. Geyer, *Durch Sand, Sumpf und Wald: Missionreisen in Zentral-Afrika* (1914) and *Ein Zentrum der Kultur in Inner-Afrika*(1907). Lilian M. Passmore Sanderson and Neville Sanderson, *Education, Religion, and Politics in Southern Sudan, 1899–1964* (1981); and articles in *Nigrizia,* 1895, pp. 170–176, 184–187, in *Bericht Negerkinder,* 1898, pp. 23–75, and in *Stern der Neger,* 1904–1914.

Marc R. Nikkel

Giannecchini, Doroteo (1837–1900), Italian Franciscan missionary in Bolivia. Giannecchini was a leader in expanding the Franciscan missions among the Chaco tribes of Bolivia, and the most forceful spokesperson for the missionary enterprise among government officials and frontier settlers. He came to the Franciscan convent in Tarija in the mid-nineteenth century, when the mission system established by the Franciscans was at its height among the Chiriguano, Toba, and Mataco in southeastern Bolivia. Because of his linguistic talents and his forceful personality, he became the primary missionary of the Tarija convent. He was mission prefect at Tarija various times in the 1870s and 1880s. Under his leadership, the Tarija convent tried to establish missions in Cuevo and Ivo, only to fail because missionaries were lacking. He was chaplain to two expeditions into the Gran Chaco: one in 1882, and the other in 1886–1887 led by Daniel Campos, which reached Asunción (Paraguay). He vigorously defended the mission enterprise against the anticlerical opposition of Campos, publishing his memoirs of the expedition a decade later. He was an accomplished speaker of Guaraní and compiled a dictionary, published posthumously in 1916. In addition, some of his annual reports on the state of the missions have been published, providing a vital source of information about the Tarija missionary system in the 1880s.

BIBLIOGRAPHY Doroteo Giannecchini, *Diario del viaje del padre Doroteo Giannecchini, capellán castrense de la expedición del Chaco central en 1882* (1882), *Relación de lo obrado por los PP del Colegio de Tarija en la expedición fluvial y terrestre del Pilcomayo* (1883), *Diario de la expedición exploradora boliviana al Alto Paraguay de 1886–1887* (1896), and *Diccionario chiriguano-español y español-chiriguano* (1916). Many of Giannecchini's writings appear in Erick D. Langer and Zulema Bass Werner de Ruiz, eds., *Historia de Tarija: Corpus documental,* vol. 5 (1988).

Erick D. Langer

Giannelli, José (1823–1891), Italian founder of nineteenth-century Franciscan missions in southeastern Bolivia and explorer of the Gran Chaco. Giannelli arrived in Bolivia in 1845 and was assigned in 1848 to the frontier outpost of Villa Rodrigo on the western side of the Gran Chaco. Here he founded two of the most important missions among the Chiriguano: Aguairenda (1851) and Taiairí (1854). These missions prepared the way for the religious and military conquest of this ethnic group in the following decades. An expedition into the Gran Chaco headed by Giannelli in 1863 resulted in the establishment of San Antonio de Padua del Pilcomayo, a mission for the Mataco people. After the Toba threatened to destroy that mission in 1866, he transferred it to the east, on the other side of Mission San Francisco Solano del Pilcomayo. In 1870 he became prefect of the Tarija mission system for a six-year term. Afterward, he went to Santa Cruz de la Sierra and became the head of all Franciscan missions in Bolivia. He died in Santa Cruz.

BIBLIOGRAPHY Giannelli's work is mentioned in Alejandro M. Corrado, *El Colegio Franciscano de Tarija y sus misiones* (1884, 1990). The diary of his expedition is published in the 1990 edition above and in Erick D. Langer and Zulema Bass Werner de Ruiz, eds., *Historia de Tarija: Corpus documental,* vol. 5 (1988).

Erick D. Langer

Gibson, John Campbell (1849–1919), Scottish Presbyterian missionary in China. The son of a Free Church of Scotland theological professor, Gibson had a distinguished academic record at the University of Glasgow before training for the ministry in the Free Church Divinity School. With his lifelong friend and future brother-in-law Thomas *Barclay, he was accepted by the English Presbyterian Mission for service in China, and they sailed together in 1874—Gibson to work in the Swatow (Shantou) field, and Barclay in Taiwan. Gibson shared with Barclay a profound belief in the virtues of the romanized script to achieve a Bible-reading church and became its chief protagonist throughout China. But he also played a major role at the national level in the Easy Wen-li translation of the New Testament. His Duff lectures of 1898, published as *Mission Problems and Mission Methods in South China* (1901), detail his experience of evangelism and the building up of a Chinese church. Both as a joint chairman of the 1907 Shanghai Centenary Missionary Conference and as chairman of the Commission on The Church in the Mission Field, reporting to the 1910 Edinburgh World Missionary Conference, he stressed the right of the Chinese church to unity and independence from foreign control. The Presbyterian Church of England elected him its moderator in 1910, and in 1919 he was called to preside over the first General Assembly of the Presbyterian Church in China.

BIBLIOGRAPHY George A. Hood, *Mission Accomplished? The English Presbyterian Mission in Lingtung, South China* (1986), chap. 3 (contains a full bibliography); P. J. Maclagan, *J. Campbell Gibson, D.D., A Biographical Sketch* (1920).

George A. Hood

Giffen, J(ohn) Kelly (1853–1932), Presbyterian missionary in Egypt and Sudan. Born in Saint Clairsville, Ohio, Giffen was educated at Franklin College and Pittsburgh Theological Seminary. From the time of their arrival in Egypt in 1854 American Presbyterians had dreamed of helping Egyptian Christians evangelize Africa, beginning in Sudan and then Ethiopia. During the Mahdi's reign (1881–1885) it was impossible to plant a Christian outpost in Sudan, but one year after Kitchener's victory at Omdurman (1898), Giffen was sent to Khartoum to reconnoiter. When the British government initially refused permission to evangelize among the Muslim population, Giffen and his wife, Grace, established a mission station 600 miles up the Nile at Doleib Hill (1900). A few years later the Giffens returned to Khartoum and then traveled with fellow missionary Thomas A. *Lambie into Ethiopia. In 1922 Giffen was elected moderator of the United Presbyterian Church of North America before returning to Sudan. He died in Khartoum.

BIBLIOGRAPHY J. Kelly Giffen, *The Egyptian Sudan* (1905).

Charles Partee

Gih, Andrew (Ji Zhiwen) (1901–1985), independent Chinese evangelist. Born in Shanghai, Gih became a Christian while a student at Bethel School, Shanghai. Moved by the preaching of Paget *Wilkes, he became an evangelist at age 25. In 1928 he joined the Worldwide Evangelistic Band, led by George Rideout of Asbury College, Wilmore, Kentucky. While on a preaching tour in south China, Gih met the famed evangelist John *Sung. They formed the Bethel Worldwide Evangelistic Band in 1931. After Sung left this work in 1933, Gih continued it under the name of Bethel Mission until 1947, when he founded the Evangelize China Fellowship (ECF) and opened the Mandarin Church in Shanghai. When Shanghai fell to the Communists, he moved his work to Hong Kong. In 1947 Gih appointed Paul Shen to open ECF work in Taiwan, resulting eleven years later in seven churches and an orphanage.

Throughout his life Gih traveled the world, preaching in many countries. During wartime he organized refugee centers and orphanages for war victims. Under his leadership the ECF established 375 churches and chapels, seven schools, and two seminaries in seven countries of Southeast Asia. The work of ECF continues in those countries, in Hong Kong, and in the United States.

BIBLIOGRAPHY Andrew Gih, *Twice Born—and Then? The Life Story and Message of Andrew Gih,* J. Edwin Orr, ed. (n.d.; autobiography); Leslie Lyall, *Three of China's Mighty Men* (1973).

Donald E. MacInnis

Gilbert, Nathaniel (c. 1721–1774), Antiguan planter and Methodist preacher. Gilbert was sent to London in 1741 to train for the legal profession at Gray's Inn and was called to the bar in 1747. Returning to Antigua, he succeeded his father as a member of the island's Assembly. A chance encounter with John Wesley's *Earnest Appeal to Men of Reason and Religion* led him to return to England in 1757, where on January 17, 1758, *Wesley preached at Gilbert's home in London. On his father's death in 1761 Gilbert inherited the family estate. Returning again to Antigua, he was reelected to the Assembly and in 1763 became speaker of the house, but then he resigned from public life in 1769. Influenced by Wesley and the antislavery writings of the American Quaker Anthony Benezet, Gilbert evangelized his slaves, although legal and social factors deterred him from emancipating them. The religious society he formed for the slaves was the beginning of British Methodist overseas work. After his death, leadership of this group passed to two women—Mary Alley, of mixed parentage, and a black woman, Sophia Campbell—and then to his sister-in-law Mary Gilbert.

BIBLIOGRAPHY Frank Baker, "The Origins of Methodism in the West Indies: The Story of the Gilbert Family," in *London Quarterly and Holborn Review,* January 1960, pp. 9–17; G. G. Findlay and W. W. Holdsworth, *The History of the Wesleyan Methodist Missionary Society,* vol. 2 (1921), pp. 29–32; Edgar W. Thompson, *Nathaniel Gilbert, Lawyer and Evangelist* (1960).

John A. Vickers

Gill, William Wyatt (1828–1896), London Missionary Society (LMS) missionary in the Cook Islands. Gill was born in Bristol, England, and was educated in London. He married Mary Harrison in Sydney, Australia, in 1851; they had ten children. Between 1852 and 1872 Gill worked on Mangaia, Cook Islands, recording mission activity and Polynesian customs and cultures. In 1872 he accompanied Archibald W. *Murray of Samoa to the Torres Strait Islands, where they settled pioneer Islander missionaries, including six from the Cook group. Gill reported on the voyage before the Royal Geographical Society in 1873. He worked at Rarotonga between 1877 and 1883, when his wife died. In 1884 and 1885 he settled Islander missionaries in Papua, and in 1887–1888 he visited London to see the Rarotongan Bible through to publication. The University of St. Andrews honored him with a doctorate in 1889 in recognition of his contributions to Oceanian studies. He died in retirement in Sydney.

BIBLIOGRAPHY Gill's published works include *Work and Adventure in New Guinea* (with James Chalmers) and *Jottings from the Pacific* (both 1885), *Life in the Southern Isles: or, Scenes and Incidents in the South Pacific and New Guinea* (1876), *Historical Sketches of Savage Life in Polynesia, with Illustrative Clan Songs* (1880), and *From Darkness to Light in Polynesia* (1894). MSS and references are in LMS South Sea collection at the SOAS, Univ. of London.

John Garrett

Gilman, Frank Patrick (1853–1918), pioneer Presbyterian missionary to Hainan, China. Gilman was born in Sparta, New York, and graduated from Princeton College in 1879. He taught at the Territorial University in Seattle, Washington (1880–1882), then graduated from Princeton Theological Seminary in 1885. He accepted an appointment from the Presbyterian Church to open their new station on Hainan Island, Kwangtung (Guangdong), China. En route he traveled via India, there marrying Marion MacNair of Sparta, at the Woodstock School, where she had taught for a year. The Gilmans and Henry M. *McCandliss were the first Americans to reside on Hainan. Marion Gilman died in New York in 1899. Their surviving children were a son Charles and a daughter Janet (who also served as a missionary in China). In 1903 Gilman married Mrs. Wellington J. White, widow of a Canton missionary. They had no children, and she died in 1917. Gilman frequently journeyed to the interior stations of Nodoa, or Nada (Danxian), established 1888, and Kachek, or Jiaji (Qionghai), established 1900, and to the Liuchow (Liuchou) peninsula on the mainland. He had a special interest in converting the aboriginal Miao people of the interior of Hainan. Gilman died in Hainan.

BIBLIOGRAPHY Frank P. Gilman, "Hainan and Its Missionary Work," *Chinese Recorder* 21 (1890): 271–280. "Frank P. Gilman," *Chinese Recorder* 50 (1919): 480 (obit.); Margaret Moninger, ed., *The Isle of Palms: Sketches of Hainan* (1919, 1980), pp. 108–110.

Kathleen L. Lodwick

Gilmour, James (1843–1891), missionary to the Mongolians. A Scottish Congregationalist, born near Glasgow, Gilmour trained at Glasgow Theological Hall, and then at Cheshunt College and Highgate. In 1870 the London Missionary Society appointed him to reopen the work in Mongolia, pioneered by Edward *Stallybrass and William *Swan from 1817 to 1841. In contrast to his predecessors, Gilmour worked from the southeast with a base in Peking (Beijing), making contact with Mongolians there during the winter, and in the summer itinerating across Mongolia. In 1874, in Peking, he married Emily Prankard, with whom he had corresponded in England. Four strenuous and lonely years, sharing the life of the nomadic Mongolians, brought no converts; eleven more passed before the first baptism. Throughout his service he lacked a medical colleague, which he considered essential for the task. His colleagues in Peking were not wholly sympathetic to his single-minded commitment to work among the nomadic Mongolians. From 1885 onward he agreed to work among the more-settled agricultural Mongolians in the eastern areas, and he labored there in three main centers: Ta Cheng Tzu (Dazhengzi), Ta Ssu Kou (Dasigou), and Chao-yang (Zhaoyang).

Gilmour's books, *Among the Mongols* (1883; rev. 1888) and *More about the Mongols* (1893), with their vivid account of his experiences of life in the Gobi Desert, opened Western eyes to a hitherto largely unknown country. His ascetic life and patient, whole-hearted commitment in the face of such little response challenged both his own and later generations to missionary service. Gilmour died of typhus in Tientsin.

BIBLIOGRAPHY H. P. Beach, *Princely Men in the Heavenly Kingdom* (1903), pp. 77–106; Richard Lovett, *James Gilmour of Mongolia: His Diaries, Letters, and Reports* (1892) and *James Gilmour and His Boys* (1894).

George A. Hood

Gilmour, John (1792–1869), Baptist minister and missionary advocate in Canada. Born in Ayr, Scotland, John Gilmour was raised a Presbyterian and apprenticed as a merchant mariner. He was captured and imprisoned in France from 1809 to 1814. After returning to Scotland, Gilmour adopted Baptist convictions and was baptized in 1814. Trained at Horton College, Bradford, Gilmour served as pastor in Greenock from 1820 to 1821 and in Aberdeen from 1821 to 1830. In 1822, he married Jannet Walker. They had one son.

In 1830 the Gilmours sailed to Montreal, where John served as pastor of St. Helen Street Baptist Church (later First Baptist Church). In 1835 the family moved to Clarence, near Ottawa, where Gilmour participated in a revival in the Ottawa river valley. Modeled upon the work of James and Robert Haldane in Scotland, the 1836 revival resulted in many conversions. Gilmour helped form a home missionary society and the Ottawa Valley Baptist Association. He then returned to the United Kingdom, where he founded the Baptist Canadian Missionary Society and raised funds for missionaries to serve in Canada and for a Baptist theological college in Canada. Once again back in Canada, he helped establish Canada Baptist College in Montreal, the Grande-Ligne Mission, the Regular Baptist Missionary Convention of Canada West, and the *Canada Baptist Magazine and Missionary Register.*

A man of deep faith, a powerful preacher, and an advocate of open communion, Gilmour was the dominant Baptist evangelist of the period. From 1837 to 1868, he served as agent of the nondenominational New England Company, which pioneered work among Indians. He also collaborated with Presbyterians through the Canada Education and Home Missionary Society.

BIBLIOGRAPHY Articles by Gilmour may be found in *Canada Baptist Magazine and Missionary Register, Canadian Baptist, Montreal Register, Union Baptist,* and *Christian Freeman.* See also Paul R. Dekar, "The Gilmours: Four Generations of Baptist Service," in P. R. Dekar and M. J. S. Ford, eds., *Celebrating the Canadian Baptist Heritage* (1984) and an obituary in *McMaster University Monthly* 4 (1894): 49–59. The Canadian Baptist archives, Hamilton, Ontario, house Gilmour's papers.

Paul R. Dekar

Glass, Frederick C. (c. 1870–1960), British evangelist and Bible colporteur in Brazil. Born in Walthamstow, England, Glass worked briefly for the *Daily Chronicle* in London before leaving for Brazil in 1892 to work in a railway company. In 1897 he had a conversion experience while working in a gold mine in Minas Gerais and became an enthusiastic evangelist. In 1900 he associated with the British and Foreign Bible Society, specializing in Bible distribution in the Brazilian interior, especially in the towns and villages without evangelical churches. In 1911 he joined the staff of the Evangelical Union of South America. From his residence in Garanhuns he crossed Brazil numerous times in several directions by horse, muleback, boat, and automobile, sometimes accompanied by New Zealander Rod Gillanders. Glass published articles about his trips in the *Daily Chronicle* and later collected them in two books that circulated widely in British missionary circles and attracted others to missionary work in Latin America. He became a permanent resident of Brazil and was buried in the British Cemetery of Rio de Janeiro.

BIBLIOGRAPHY Frederick C. Glass, *Adventures with the Bible in Brazil* (n.d.) and *Through Brazilian Junglelands with the Book* (n.d.).

Samuel Escobar

Glasser, Arthur Frederick (1914–), American missiologist. Born in Paterson, New Jersey, Glasser was educated at Cornell University as a civil engineer, graduated from Faith Seminary in 1942, married Alice Oliver, served as a marine chaplain in World War II, and worked in China under the China Inland Mission from 1947 to 1951. Returning to the U.S.A., he taught at Columbia Bible College and later at Westminster Seminary. He was North American director of the Overseas Missionary Fellowship from 1954 to 1969. He studied at Union Theological Seminary, New York, under Hans *Hoekendijk in 1969 to 1970 (STM degree), and also at the Jewish Theological Seminary.

In 1970 he began to teach theology of mission in the School of World Mission at Fuller Theological Seminary, Pasadena, California, serving as dean from 1971 to 1980. Then he became senior professor and dean emeritus. His theology of mission focused on the kingdom of God as its central motif. He was president of the American Society of Missiology (1982–1983) and edited its journal, *Missiology,* from 1976 to 1982. While maintaining a high view of biblical authority and a strong focus on world evangelization, he embraced a broader view of the church than the separatist movement from which he came. Thus he encouraged other evangelicals to join him in participating in ecumenical dialogue and associations. His lifelong concern for the communication of the gospel to the Jews led him to establish a program of Judaic Studies and Jewish Evangelism at Fuller Seminary.

Among his publications are *Missions in Crisis* with Eric Fife (1961), and *Contemporary Theologies of Mission* with Donald *McGavran (1983). In 1996 the School of World Mission at Fuller Seminary established the Arthur F. Glasser Chair of Biblical Theology of Mission.

BIBLIOGRAPHY A bibliography of Glasser's writings was published in the Festschrift, *The Good News of the Kingdom: Mission Theology for the Third Millennium,* Charles Van Engen, Dean S. Gilliland, and Paul Pierson, eds. (1993). See also his "My Pilgrimage in Mission," *IBMR* 14 (1990): 112–115. Most of Glasser's writing consists of articles, many published in *Missiology.*

Paul Pierson

Glazik, Josef (1913–), German Catholic missiologist. Born in Hagen, North Rhine-Westphalia, Glazik entered the Sacred Heart Missionaries in 1934 and was ordained in 1939. Several years in Russia with the German army and as a prisoner of war were instrumental in shaping his future as a specialist in Russian Orthodox missions. He obtained his doctoral degree with the thesis "Die russisch-orthodoxe Heidenmission seit Peter dem Grossen" (Münster, 1953) and qualified as university lecturer in missiology with a dissertation on "Die Islammission der russisch-orthodoxen Kirche" (Münster, 1958). At first he lectured in the institute of his own mission order in Oeventrup (Kreis Arnsberg, Westphalia); then from 1959 to 1961 he was associate professor of missiology in Würzburg. In 1961 he was appointed professor of missiology as successor of Thomas *Ohm in Münster. He took part in the preparatory meetings and was *peritus* (adviser) at the Second Vatican Council and played a decisive part in the drafting of the mission decree *Ad Gentes.* After the council he became consultor of the Secretariat (later Pontifical Council) for Non-Christians and adviser of the General Synod of the Dioceses of Germany.

For many years Glazik was director of the Internationales Institut für missionswissenschaftliche Forschungen and from 1962 to 1974 was editor-in-chief of *Zeitschrift für Missionswissenschaft und Religionswissenschaft.* He edited the Festschrift *50 Jahre katholische Missionswissenschaft in Münster* (1961). His publications were mostly focused on Russian Orthodox missions, the missionary activity of his own congregation, and missionary issues arising from the Second Vatican Council. In 1990 he published *Vor 25 Jahren Missionsdekret "Ad Gentes." Erinnerungen eines Augenzeugen des Konzils.* Because of poor health resulting from his war experience, he retired in 1970.

BIBLIOGRAPHY "Josef Glazik MSC, Selbstdarstellung," in *50 Jahre katholische Missionswissenschaft in Münster, 1911–1961,* Josef Glazik, ed. (1961), pp. 57–58; H. Waldenfels, ed., *"...denn ich bin bei Euch" (Mt 28:20): Festschrift für J. Glazik und B. Willeke* (1978).

Karl Müller, SVD

Glen, William (1779–1849), Scottish missionary in Russia and translator of the Persian Old Testament. After ten years as a secession minister at Annan, Scotland, Glen entered missionary service with the Scottish Missionary Society at Astrakhan, Russia, on the delta of the Volga River. His initial role was pastoral, and he first saw the mission task as itineration to the Tatars. He formed a mission academy, and a distinguished convert was A. Kazem-Bek, the future Russian Orientalist. Glen's priorities changed, however, as a result of contact with Persians in Astrakhan. The Russian Bible Society had printed Henry *Martyn's Persian New Testament in 1815. After discussion with A. H. Dittrich of the Basel Mission, Glen embarked on a translation of the Old Testament, as well as revisions of Martyn's New Testament. When the British and Foreign Bible Society (BFBS) withdrew funding in 1833 and the mission closed in 1834, the United Associate Synod in Scotland took on Glen's support, funding a return to confer with Persian scholars in 1837. St. Andrews University awarded him a D.D. in 1845. The complete Glen/Martyn Persian Bible was printed in 1846, with two later editions, superseded only in 1895. Glen returned to Persia in 1847 and presented the first copy to the shah. He died there in early 1849, engaged in distribution.

BIBLIOGRAPHY William Glen, *Journal of a Tour from Astrachan* (1823). His Bible MSS are at the BFBS. See also M. V. Jones, "The Sad and Curious Story of Karass, 1802–35," *Oxford Slavonic Papers,* n.s., 8 (1975): 52–81.

Nancy Stevenson

Glover, Archibald Edward (1850–1954), English missionary in China. The son of Richard Glover, Glover graduated from Worcester College, Oxford, and was ordained a deacon in the Church of England in 1887 and a priest in 1890. From 1887 to 1895 he had a number of curacies, finally serving under the evangelical clergyman H. W. Webb-Peploe at St. Paul's, Onslow Square, London. In 1896 he went to China with the China Inland Mission and joined Stanley P. *Smith, one of the *Cambridge Seven, in Lu'an (present-day Changzhi), Shansi (Shanxi) Province. A year later his wife, Flora, joined him with baby son and daughter, Hedley and Hope. When Smith went on furlough in 1899, Glover was put in charge of the station. Soon after this the Boxer Rebellion spread to Shansi Province, with an outbreak of hostilities in Lu'an. Glover, with his pregnant wife, two children, and fellow missionary Caroline Gates, fled by mule litter, traveling half naked and with little food, and constantly facing insults from the mobs and threats of death from officialdom. At Hankow (Wuhan), Hupeh (Hubei) Province, the Glovers' child, Faith Edythe, was born, only to die eleven days later. When they reached Shanghai, Glover's wife died of peritonitis, and he returned to England. His *Thousand Miles of Miracle in China,* describing the group's 67 days of hardship and suffering, became a classic. It went through twenty-two editions, and was translated into German, Swedish, Danish, and Arabic.

BIBLIOGRAPHY Archibald E. Glover, *A Thousand Miles of Miracle in China* (1904, 1957). Pat Barr, *To China with Love: The Lives and Times of Protestant Missionaries in China, 1860–1900* (1972); A. J. Broomhall, *Hudson Taylor and China's Open Century,* vol. 7 (1989); M. Broomhall, *Martyred Missionaries of the China Inland Mission* (1901). See also the CIM periodical *China's Millions* for the years 1900–1904.

Norman H. Cliff

Glover, Robert Hall (1871–1947), missionary and missions administrator. Canadian by birth, Glover spent most of his life in China and the United States. A graduate of the University of Toronto, New York Missionary Training College, and New York University Medical College (M.D.), he was appointed a medical missionary to China in 1894 by the Christian and Missionary Alliance (C&MA). He lived through the Boxer rebellion, when many missionaries were killed and others were forced to flee the country. In response to the crescendo of calls to quit China, Glover wrote a stirring defense of missionary efforts there entitled "Shall Suffering and Danger Halt Our Missionary Work?" His service with the C&MA in China continued until 1913. During his years in China he was ordained, married Caroline Robbins Prentice, and founded two educational institutions. In 1913 he was appointed C&MA foreign missions secretary. In 1921 Moody Bible Institute recruited him to serve as director of missionary studies, a position he occupied until 1926, during which time he wrote *The Progress of World-Wide Missions* (1924), one of the most widely used mission histories ever written; it was translated into multiple languages. In 1926 he became a missionary administrator for the China Inland Mission (CIM), serving as assistant home director (1926–1929) and as home director (1930–1943). He retired in Germantown, Pennsylvania, in 1943.

BIBLIOGRAPHY Obit., *New York Times,* March 25, 1947, 25:5.

Alan Neely

Glukharev, Makarii (Mikhail Yakovlevich) (1792–1847), Russian Orthodox missionary in southwestern Siberia. Glukharev was born to a clerical family in Vyazma, 125 miles southwest of Moscow. Following basic theological education at the Smolensk diocesan seminary and advanced training at the Saint Petersburg Theological Academy, he was tonsured a monk in 1819 with the name Makarii and served as rector of the Kostroma Seminary in north central Russia. In 1821 he was elevated to the rank of archimandrite. Two years later he retired from academic life to pursue a life of contemplation in the Glynsk hermitage. Recalled from seclusion in 1830, he was assigned to the expanding Siberian missions and took up residency in Oirot Tura (formerly Ulala; now Gorno-Altaisk), a small town on the Katun River in the rugged Altai Mountains. He found the Kalmyks distrustful of Russian intentions and began to work quietly by acquiring a systematic knowledge of their language. He compiled a bilingual dictionary and translated the Gospels, selections from the Old and New Testaments, the Nicene Creed, selected prayers, and devotional treatises into the Mongolian Telengut dialect. Opposed to the politically motivated mass conversions that predominated in some areas of Siberia, he insisted on thorough catechetical preparation of each individual prior to baptism. He supplemented this instruction by the example of his own humble life and a clear, practical concern for the physical well-being of the indigenous people. He considered such concern to be the clearest explanation of the spirit of Christianity. In 13 years at the head of the Altai mission, he baptized 675 Altaic people.

Fearful that the Kalmyks might backslide into the dominant Tibetan Buddhism, which was strongly intermixed with indigenous beliefs and shamanism, Glukharev sought to remove them from their nomadic way of life by organizing Christian villages governed by his fellow missionaries. In these villages—five were completed by the time he retired from the mission—the Kalmyks were taught to read and write and learned arithmetic, basic construction, farming techniques, and various crafts. Two churches, three schools, and an orphanage were also constructed. Glukharev left Altai seriously ill in 1843. He ended his career as abbot of the monastery at Bolkhov.

BIBLIOGRAPHY Nikita Struve, "Macaire Glukharev: A Prophet of Orthodox Mission," *IRM* 54 (1965): 308–314; Paul R. Valliere, "Russian Orthodoxy and the Challenge of Modernity: The Case of Archimandrite Makary," *St. Vladimir's Theological Quarterly* 22 (1978): 3–15.

Paul D. Garrett

Gnecci-Soldi, Organtino (1535–1609), Italian Jesuit missionary in Japan. An Italian from Brescia, Organtino, as he is usually known, became a Jesuit in 1555 and arrived in Japan in 1567 to serve the Society of Jesus there. He differed deeply with his provincial, Francisco *Cabral, over the latter's attitude to Japanese people and culture, but was vindicated when Alessandro *Valignano adopted Organtino's views and built them into his missionary strategy of acculturation. Organtino tried to be Japanese in order to win Japan. He was a close friend of Oda Nobunaga, the de facto ruler of Japan, and opened the first seminary for secular priests in Japan under Oda's patronage at Azuchi in 1582.

BIBLIOGRAPHY There is no biography in English of Organtino, but he figures significantly in J. F. Schutte, *Valignano's Missionary Strategy for Japan* (1983). See also C. R. Boxer, *The Christian Century in Japan* (1951).

Andrew C. Ross

Gobat, Samuel (1799–1879), Church Missionary Society (CMS) missionary to Abyssinia. Born to a Lutheran family in Crémine, Berne, Switzerland, Gobat studied at the Basel Mission Institute, the Missionary Institute in Paris, and the CMS training institution in Islington (London), England. Ordained in the Lutheran church, he nevertheless volunteered for service with the CMS. During six years of service in Abyssinia (Ethiopia), broken by a short stint in Europe from 1833 to 1834, during which he married Maria Zellerin, Gobat worked energetically and to some degree successfully at building rapport with the Orthodox Coptic Church. In 1836 he was forced by poor health to return to Europe. He was subsequently sent to Malta, where, between 1839 and 1845, he supervised the translation of the Bible into Arabic and served as vice-president of the Malta Protestant College. In 1846 he was nominated by King Friedrich Wilhelm IV of Prussia to succeed the recently deceased bishop in Jerusalem, Michael Solomon *Alexander. Within the space of a few days, Gobat was ordained an Anglican priest and consecrated (at Lambeth, on July 5, 1846) as bishop of Jerusalem. Until his death (in Jerusalem), Gobat was notable for the energetic practicality and consummate Christian diplomacy that marked his fulfillment of this difficult and frequently exasperating role. In addition to his several publications cited below, and the Arabic translation of the Bible mentioned above, Gobat left behind thirty-seven Palestinian schools with a combined enrollment of 1,400 students, and twelve indigenous churches.

BIBLIOGRAPHY Samuel Gobat, *Journal of Three Years' Residence in Abyssinia, in Furtherance of the Objects of the Church Missionary Society...* (1834) and *Samuel Gobat: His Life and His Work* (1884). John S. Conway, "The Jerusalem Bishopric: A 'Union of Foolscap and Blotting-paper,'" *Studies in Religion* 7, no. 3 (1978); Eugene Stock, *The History of the Church Missionary Society: Its Environment, Its Men, and Its Work* (1899).

Jonathan J. Bonk

Goble, Jonathan (1827–1896), maverick missionary in Japan. Goble, a native of Wayne, New York, and imprisoned as a felon, prayed that God would make him a missionary. Released from prison in 1851, he enlisted in the U.S. Marine Corps hoping that as a member of Commodore Perry's 1852–1853 expedition to Japan he could enhance his knowledge and determine his possibilities for being a missionary. Discharged in 1855, he enrolled in Madison (later Colgate) University, Hamilton, New York, married in violation of a school rule, and was suspended before completing his studies. In 1859 the vehemently abolitionist American Free Mission Society nonetheless appointed Goble and his wife missionaries to Japan, where he survived largely by his own resourcefulness. Effective as a colporteur, storyteller, and inventor, he translated a hymn and the Gospel of Matthew, which became the first Protestant hymn and New Testament book published in the Japanese language. The Gobles returned to the United States on furlough in 1870 and were commissioned to return to Japan under the American Baptist Missionary Union in 1872. Less than a year later, however, the mission terminated him. He continued as an independent Baptist missionary despite many difficulties, spending his final years in Japan as a colporteur for the American Bible Society. Independent, cantankerous, and sometimes violent, Goble was singularly tenacious; critics considered him to be of dubious reputation. He left Japan in 1883 and returned to the United States.

BIBLIOGRAPHY Jonathan Goble, "Jonathan Goble's Book," Keith Seat, ed., *Transactions of the Asiatic Society of Japan,* 3rd ser., 16 (1981): 109–152; F. Calvin Parker, *Jonathan Goble of Japan: Marine, Missionary, Maverick* (1990) and "Jonathan Goble, Missionary Extraordinary," *Transactions of the Asiatic Society of Japan,* 3rd ser., 16 (1981): 77–107.

Alan Neely

Gockel, Mary (1874–1925), founder of the American branch of the International Missionary Association of Catholic Women (MACW). Gockel saw the MACW to be important for its eucharistic emphasis in mission and its stress on women's (laity) membership and funds management. A business secretary in Milwaukee, Wisconsin, Gockel engaged thousands of Catholic women in mission activity through annual retreats, mission conferences, the spread of an apostolic spirit in Catholic homes, and financial commitment to meet specific missionary needs. Gockel died from complications of a fall after her return from the 1925 Vatican Missionary Exposition, where she had devised a display for the MACW. The association disbanded in 1982.

BIBLIOGRAPHY Angelyn Dries, "Mary Gockel: Early Twentieth Century Evangelization and Mission," *Catholic Evangelization* 2 (March/April 1989): 75–76; C. M. Thuente, *A Sketch of the Life and Work of Mary Gockel* (1926). Papers of the MACW are at the World Mission Office, Archdiocese of Milwaukee, Wisconsin.

Angelyn Dries, OSF

Goddard, Josiah (1813–1854), American Baptist missionary in Siam and China. Born in Wendell, Massachusetts, Goddard was the son of the Reverend David and Hannah B. Goddard. He graduated from Brown University in 1835 and from Newton Theological Institute three years later. Ordained to the Baptist ministry, Goddard and his wife, Eliza (Abbot), were appointed by the Baptist Board for Foreign Missions to work with the Chinese in Siam (Thailand) and they sailed in 1839. At Bangkok in 1842 Josiah Goddard succeeded William *Dean as pastor of the first Chinese Baptist church, and labored there for six years until his health failed. In 1848 the Goddards moved to Ningpo (Ningbo), northeast Chekiang (Zhejiang) Province, China. Though suffering from a lung disease, Josiah mastered the Tie-Chu dialect and preached to a new congregation. He was best known for the quality of his translation work, some of which was among the first English to Chinese. From 1842 to 1854 he completed five tracts, a catechism, a vocabulary, and the entire New Testament. The Goddard children, some of whom married members of the William Dean family, produced several generations of Baptist missionaries in China, including Josiah Ripley Goddard, Augusta Fanny Dean, Anna Kate Goddard, Francis Wayland Goddard, and Anna M. Corlies.

BIBLIOGRAPHY Goddard published a number of tracts, including *A Temperance Tract: An Inquirer's Guide* and *A History of Elijah.* His New Testament in Chinese was first published in 1853 for the American and Foreign Bible Society. A nineteenth-century biographical sketch of Goddard is included in William B. Sprague, *Annals of the American Baptist Pulpit* (1860); a more recent biography is Francis W. Goddard, *Called to Cathay* (1946).

William H. Brackney

Goes, Bento de (1562–1607), first Jesuit missionary to cross Asia en route to China. Goes was a native of Villa Franca do Campo in the Azores. As a young solider in India, he visited a chapel along the Travancore coast and decided to enter the Society of Jesus as a coadjutor brother. He studied Persian and accompanied Jerome *Xavier to visit Akbar (r. 1556–1606), the Mogul ruler in Agra, in northern India. There the Jesuits, interested in a land route from India to China via central Asia, learned that a Muslim merchant had recently traveled overland to Khanbaliq (Peking), the capital of Cathay. With letters of introduction from Akbar, Goes and several companions joined a caravan that left Agra in October 1602, crossed the Pamirs (the high altitude region in the northwest corner of India), and reached Yarkand (now Shache), in western Sinkiang, which was then the capital of the kingdom of Kashgar. With a new caravan, he went on to Aksu and Kucha (Kuqa) in November 1604. At Yen-ch'i (Yanqi) he met a Muslim merchant who had lived with Matteo *Ricci in a hostel for foreigners in Khanbaliq. Convinced that Cathay and China were identical, Goes and a few companions went on their own via Turfan (Turpan) and Hami and entered Suchow (now Jinquan), Kansu (Gansu) Province, in late 1605. In reply to a letter from Goes, Ricci sent a Jesuit brother, Chung Ming-li, who arrived less than two weeks before Goes died.

BIBLIOGRAPHY Goes's letters are listed in Carlos Sommervogel, *Bibliothèque de la Compagnie de Jésus,* 12 vols. (1890–1932), 3:1529–1531. The original account of the trip, in Italian, is in Pasquale M. d'Elia, ed., *Fonti Ricciane,* 3 vols. (1942–1949), 2:391–445. Henri Bernard, *Le Frère Bento de Goes chez les Musulmans de la Haute Asie, 1603–1607* (1934); Vincent Cronin, *The Wise Man from the West* (1955), pp. 236–256 (repr. 1984, pp. 226–245); L. Carrington Goodrich, "Goes, Bento de," in L. Carrington Goodrich and Chaoying Fang, eds., *Dictionary of Ming Biography,*

2 vols. (1976), 1:472–474; Cornelis Wessels, *Early Jesuit Travellers in Central Asia, 1603–1721* (1924), pp. 1–41.

John W. Witek, SJ

Goforth, Jonathan (1859–1936) *and* **Rosalind (Bell-Smith)** (1864–1942), first Canadian Presbyterian missionaries to mainland China. Jonathan Goforth became the foremost missionary revivalist in early twentieth-century China and helped to establish revivalism as a major element in Protestant China missions. He grew up on an Ontario farm, the seventh of eleven children. Hearing G. L. *Mackay, Presbyterian missionary to Formosa (Taiwan), speak, he sensed God's call to go to China. Attending Knox College for training, Goforth met Rosalind Bell-Smith at the Toronto Union Mission. She had been born in London, England, and had grown up in Montreal. They married in 1887 and eventually had eleven children, six of whom survived childhood. They pioneered the North Honan (Henan) mission in 1888.

In 1900 the Goforths barely escaped the Boxers and returned to Canada. After their return to Honan in 1901, Jonathan Goforth felt increasingly restless. In 1904 and 1905 he was inspired by news of the great Welsh revival and read Finney's *Lectures on Revivals.* In 1907, circumstances brought him to witness firsthand the stirring Korean revival (*When the Spirit's Fire Swept Korea* [1943] represents his response). As he returned to China through Manchuria, congregations were so fascinated by his accounts that they invited him back in early 1908. During this extended visit there occurred the unprecedented "Manchurian revival," which transformed Goforth's life and ministry; from then on he was basically an evangelist and revivalist, not a settled missionary. He also became one of the best known of all China missionaries, admired by many, but disliked by some for his "emotionalism."

Goforth remained active well into the 1930s, especially in Manchuria; in 1931 the Goforths coauthored *Miracle Lives of China.* After his death in Toronto, Rosalind, a capable writer who had first published in 1920, wrote the popular *Goforth of China* (1937, with many reprints), and her own autobiography, *Climbing: Memories of a Missionary's Wife* (1940).

Bibliography Writings by Jonathan Goforth include *By My Spirit* (1929, 1942, 1964, 1983); and by Rosalind Goforth, *Chinese Diamonds for the King of Kings* (1920, 1945) and *How I Know God Answers Prayer* (1921). Alvyn Austin, *Saving China: Canadian Missionaries in the Middle Kingdom, 1888–1959* (1986), chaps. 2, 6; Daniel H. Bays, "Christian Revival in China, 1900–1937," in Edith L. Blumhofer and Randall Balmer, eds., *Modern Christian Revivals* (1993); James Webster, *"Times of Blessing" in Manchuria* (1908). The Goforth's papers are in the Billy Graham Center archives, Wheaton College, Wheaton, Ill., collection 188.

Daniel H. Bays

Gogerly, Daniel John (1792–1862), Methodist missionary in Ceylon (Sri Lanka). Gogerly was born in London, the child of American Loyalists, and had an evangelical conversion at 14. A printer by trade, he was recruited by Richard Watson, an architect of the Wesleyan Methodist Missionary Society, for the mission press in Colombo. He spent the rest of his life, apart from two brief furloughs, in Ceylon. He entered the ministry there in 1823 and was ordained two years later. In 1839 he became an energetic general superintendent of the mission, developing mission education, raising teaching standards, and in the face of Anglican opposition, obtaining government recognition of the Methodist Church and public endowment of a number of indigenous ministers.

From the first, Gogerly studied Pali, the language of the Buddhist scriptures, as well as modern Sinhala. With no linguistic training, he built up a competence never before attained by any European. Working with the Lankan David de Silva, he translated Buddhist texts and provided some of the earliest Western scholarly analysis and commentary. He was, however, diffident about publication; unlike his colleague R. S. *Hardy, he never produced a major work, and his surviving papers were mostly undertaken for the Ceylon branch of the Royal Asiatic Society (of which he was president). Gogerly was also a translator of the Sinhala scriptures. During his lifetime his best-known work was a substantial controversial tract, *Kristiyani Prajñapti* (1848), republished in an English version as *Evidences and Doctrines of Christianity* (1862), which drew fierce polemics from the Buddhist community. His other writings, collected posthumously, are calm and investigative; the eminent Buddhologist T. W. Rhys Davids saluted Gogerly as the "greatest Pali scholar of his age."

Bibliography A. S. Bishop, ed., *Ceylon Buddhism: Being the Collected Writings of Daniel John Gogerly* (1908); Elizabeth J. Harris, "A Case of Distortion: The Evangelical Missionary Interpretation of Buddhism in Nineteenth Century Sri Lanka," *Dialogue,* n.s., 2, no. 1 (1994): 19–42; *Minutes of the Methodist Conference* (1862); K. M. de Silva, *Social Policy and Missionary Organizations in Ceylon, 1840–1855* (1965); J. Telford, *Makers of Our Missions* (1895).

Andrew F. Walls

Goh Hood Keng (1886–1961), Methodist lay evangelist in Malaya and Java. Goh came from a Malay-speaking, Singapore Straits Chinese family. He was converted at age 12 while attending the Methodist Anglo-Chinese School in Singapore. There, upon graduation, he became first a teacher and then a supervisor of a branch campus until 1924. From 1912 to 1951 he also served as pastor of the Middle Road Methodist Church in Singapore, which had over 1,000 members at the time of his retirement. In 1924, he was struck with Hansen's disease (leprosy), but after being treated in India, he returned to Singapore in 1926 as a full-time pastor. He was well known as an evangelist and made preaching tours of Malaya and Java. A prolific lecturer and writer in the local press, he had a ministry that played a key role in establishing the influence of Christianity among the Straits-born Chinese.

Bibliography Wong Hoon Hee, ed., *Memoirs of the Late Rev. Goh Hood Keng* (n.d.); Bobby Sng, *In His Good Time* (1993).

Robert A. Hunt

Goldie, Hugh (1815–1895), Presbyterian missionary in Jamaica and Nigeria. Goldie was born in Kilwinning, Scotland, and was appointed as a lay missionary to Jamaica in 1840. In Jamaica he first worked as schoolmaster at Stirling, Westmoreland, with Rev. William Niven. In 1844 he moved to Negril, where he was more or less on his own. While in Jamaica he studied under William *Jameson, subsequently a missionary in Calabar.

The Jamaica Missionary Presbytery ordained Goldie for service in Africa in 1846. He arrived in Calabar, in what is now southeastern Nigeria, in 1847. His first posting was in Duke Town, the largest of the Calabar communities. In 1856 he went to open a new work among the Efik, at Ikunetu, a settlement some distance up the Cross River, but in 1858 he returned to Calabar itself, succeeding Hope Masterton *Waddell at Creek Town. In 1862 he brought out the first translation of the New Testament in Efik. His Efik-English dictionary was published two years later. He remained as "head of station" at Creek Town until his death. In 1890 he published an account of the Calabar mission up to that time. Goldie's work on the Efik New Testament, with his long and successful ministry in Creek Town, makes him one of the founding fathers of the Presbyterian Church of Nigeria.

BIBLIOGRAPHY Hugh Goldie, *Calabar and Its Mission* (1890, reissued in 1901) and *Dictionary of the Efik Language* (1862). Geoffrey Johnston, *Of God and Maxim Guns: Presbyterianism in Nigeria, 1846–1966* (1988).

Geoffrey Johnston

Goldie, John Francis (1870–1954), founder of Methodism in the Solomon Islands. Goldie was a forceful personality who dominated the Methodist mission in the western Solomons from 1902 to 1951. Born in Tasmania to Scottish parents and converted at the age of 17, he soon became a powerful evangelist, attracting large crowds. After serving as a Methodist minister in home mission work in Queensland, he offered his services to the Australasian Methodist Board of Missions.

Invited by Solomon Islanders who had been converted in Fiji under the Wesleyans, the mission led by Goldie began work in 1902. His wife Helena joined him in 1903. This frontier setting among people engrossed in warfare and headhunting appealed to Goldie's strong personality. He quickly learned the local language and was preaching within four months, although it took him six years to receive his first converts. A champion of industrial missions, he believed that investing in plantations would help the church to be self-supporting and enable Solomon Islanders to learn Western working skills appropriate for an emerging cash economy. Unfortunately he was also very slow to train Solomon Islanders for leadership in the church, but he was nevertheless a champion of islanders' rights and interests before the British colonial government. He retired in Sydney, Australia, in 1951. In 1952 he returned to the Solomon Islands for the Jubilee celebration. He died in Sydney.

BIBLIOGRAPHY David Hilliard, "Protestant Missions in the Solomon Islands, 1849–1942" (Ph.D. diss., Australian National Univ., 1966); C. T. J. Luxton, *Isles of Solomon: A Tale of Missionary Adventure* (1955); Alan R. Tippett, *Solomon Islands Christianity* (1967); Ronald G. Williams, *The United Church in Papua, New Guinea, and the Solomon Islands: The Story of the Development of an Indigenous Church* (1972).

Darrell Whiteman

Goldsack, William (1871–1957), Australian Baptist missionary in India. Goldsack began service with the Australasian Baptist Missionary Society in 1899. After language study, at which he excelled, he was stationed at Pabna, East Bengal (present day Bangladesh). Influenced by George Henry *Rouse, head of the Baptist Mission Press at Calcutta, Goldsack turned to Islamic studies and literary work, writing many apologetic tracts and pamphlets. In 1911 he attended the Lucknow Conference of Missionaries to Muslims and was elected to the continuation committee. In 1912 he spent six months studying Arabic in Syria, supplemented later by six months in Cairo (1917). Frustration with district duties led him to transfer to the British Baptist Missionary Society in 1912 (as first suggested by Rouse in 1905), and in 1914 he was designated exclusively for Muslim work. While Secretary of the Bengal Branch of the Christian Literature Society, he produced a Bengali rendering of the Qur'an (1918) and a collection of Muslim traditions (1923). Although dismissive of Islam and largely self-taught, he was meticulous in his use of original sources. He retired in 1923, suffering from malaria and recurrent boils. With his wife, Charlotte (Somerville, 1874–1969) and their two children, he became a successful South Australian fruit farmer.

BIBLIOGRAPHY Works by Goldsack include *Christ in Islam* (1905), *Muhammad in Islam* (1916), and *The Bible in Islam* (1922). Goldsack's personal papers are in the BMS archives, Regents' Park College, Oxford.

Clinton Bennett

Gollmer, Charles Andrew (Carl Anders) (1812–1886), missionary of the Church Missionary Society (CMS) in Yorubaland. Gollmer was born in Kircheim-unter-Teck, Germany, a Württemberg pietist stronghold that produced a succession of missionaries. In 1835 he entered the Basel Mission seminary and in 1840 the CMS college in Islington, London. The following year, after Anglican ordination, he went with CMS to Sierra Leone. In 1845 he was appointed with Henry *Townsend and Samuel Ajayi *Crowther to open the Yoruba mission in what is now Nigeria. The intended focus was the Egba state of Abeokuta (present-day Ogun State), but war confined them at first to the port of Badagri. When Townsend and Crowther were able to move inland in 1846, Gollmer stayed on. Badagri was a discouraging post: impoverished, unresponsive, politically volatile, and embroiled in the succession disputes of its more powerful neighbor, Lagos. Like other CMS missionaries, and in spite of frequent physical danger, Gollmer supported the cause of Akitoye against Kosoko in the Lagos succession, believing that with Akitoye in ascendancy Lagos would be kept out of the slave trade. On leave in

1849, he addressed (through the agency of Henry *Venn) a House of Commons committee in favor of retaining a British naval presence in the area and on his return he was instrumental in securing the British intervention that restored Akitoye to his throne in 1851. In 1852 he himself moved to Lagos, building up evangelistic and educational work there. His acquisition of property for these operations and his support of Abeokuta as the best means of promoting Christianity and of undermining the slave trade created hostility with European merchants, who had other interests, and complicated relations with the local representatives of the British government. In 1857 he was transferred to Abeokuta, where he extended the work westward into Ketu. In 1862, shattered in health, he retired to Margate, England, and engaged in translation and deputation work. Among African houseguests was a son of Kosoko, who grew up to work for the mission.

Gollmer's Yoruba name, Alapako ("owner of the board [house]"), indicates his reputation as a builder. He was also a prolific translator of tracts and schoolbooks and a reviser of the Yoruba Scriptures. As an educationist, he was remembered for his readiness (as against, e.g., Townsend) to open the whole range of Western learning to Africans. Grammar school scholarships were endowed in his memory.

Gollmer married three times. His first wife, Catherine Schmidt, died in Sierra Leone in 1842; the second, Eliza Phillips, died soon after arriving in Badagri in 1845; Sarah Hoar died in Margate in 1883. One of their sons, Charles Henry Vidal, became a CMS missionary in Lagos and Palestine.

BIBLIOGRAPHY [C. H. V. Gollmer], *Charles Andrew Gollmer: His Life and Missionary Labours in West Africa* (1889; by his eldest son, includes essay by Gollmer on Yoruba symbolic messages); J. F. A. Ajayi, *Christian Missions in Nigeria, 1841–1891: The Making of a New Elite* (1965); Church Missionary Society, *Register of Missionaries and Native Clergy*, no. 320 (cf. no. 875).

Andrew F. Walls

Gomer, Joseph (1834–1892), African American missionary of the United Brethren in Christ (UBC). Gomer was born in Michigan and served in the Union Army during the Civil War. After the war he moved to Dayton, Ohio, where he became active in the United Brethren Church and married Mary Green (see Mary *Gomer). In 1870 the Gomers' application for missionary work was approved. They arrived in Sierra Leone in 1871 and were stationed at Shenge. Earlier, in 1855, the UBC had begun work on Sherbro Island, settling at Shenge. The Shenge mission station grew coffee and rubber trees. Gomer taught improved farming methods and opened an industrial school with funds raised from a tour in the United States. He befriended the local chief at Sherbro and converted him. In ensuing years he was able to build up the mission, multiplying preaching places and increasing converts. He devoted the remainder of his life to mission work in Africa, and died at his post of apoplexy.

BIBLIOGRAPHY Emmett D. Cox, *The Church of the United Brethren in Christ in Sierra Leone* (1970); Christopher Fyfe, *A History of Sierra Leone* (1962); Walter L. Williams, *Black Americans and the Evangelization of Africa, 1877–1900* (1982).

Sylvia M. Jacobs

Gomer, Mary (Green) (?–1896), African American missionary of the United Brethren in Christ (UBC). Born in Dayton, Ohio, Mary Green married Joseph *Gomer, and in 1870 they applied for mission work in Africa. They reached Sierra Leone in 1871 and were stationed at the Shenge station. The UBC had begun mission work in Africa in 1855. It had acquired the American Missionary Association station in Sierra Leone, and the Gomers were the first black American missionaries sent there. At Shenge Gomer worked with the women and children. As a teacher, she taught many useful and practical lessons. In her religious and domestic training classes she encouraged her female students to become model wives and housekeepers. After her husband died at his post in 1892, Mary Gomer remained at the Sierra Leone mission for two years. She returned to the United States in 1894 and died in Dayton, Ohio.

BIBLIOGRAPHY Daniel Berger, *History of the Church of the United Brethren in Christ* (1897); Christopher Fyfe, *A History of Sierra Leone* (1962); Walter L. Williams, *Black Americans and the Evangelization of Africa, 1877–1900* (1982).

Sylvia M. Jacobs

González Carrasco, Justo (1902–1994), Cuban educator and founder of ALFALIT. González was a Methodist and graduated from Candler College in Havana. He was involved in a revolution against dictator Gerardo Machado and later became director of publications in the Ministry of Agriculture. The success of his short novel *Cubaqua* made him a specialist in literature for new readers, and he participated in a campaign applying the literacy methods of Frank *Laubach. From 1944 to 1961 he and his wife, Luisa (García), cooperated with missionary Eulalia *Cook in teaching members of rural churches to read and motivating them to teach others. In 1959 the Branscomb Fund was created by the Methodist Church in Florida to support these efforts, but in 1961 pressures from the revolutionary government of Fidel Castro forced González to leave for Alajuela, Costa Rica.

In 1962 González helped start ALFALIT—Alfabetizacion y Literatura—a movement for popular education and literacy in Costa Rica. Literacy, books for new readers, and mobilization of volunteers constitute the core of the ALFALIT program that the Gonzálezes and Cook propagated all over Latin America. By 1971 ALFALIT was established in twelve countries and in Peru it received the 1983 UNESCO prize for outstanding service in literacy. From 1971 until his death González lived in Miami. In 1992, five years after the death of Luisa, he married Cook.

BIBLIOGRAPHY Justo González, *Story of a Miracle* (1985).

Samuel Escobar

González de Santa Cruz, Roque (1576–1628), Paraguayan Jesuit and missionary martyr in his own land.

Born to Spanish parents, González was raised in Asunción and learned Guaraní as a child. He became a diocesan priest and went to work among the Indians in Jejui, in the northern Chaco region. In 1609 he entered the Society of Jesus and was soon sent to help build San Ignacio Guazú, the first Jesuit reduction (Indian settlement organized by the missionaries) in Paraguay. From there he founded the reduction of Encarnación, by the Paraná River, and was the first Jesuit to found missions along the Uruguay River. Shortly after founding a new reduction, All Saints, in southern Brazil, he and two other Jesuit companions were martyred by Indians at the instigation of a local shaman. He thus became the first native-born martyr in the New World.

González was considered a holy man in his own time, even by non-Christian Indians who admired his courage and zeal. He also criticized the encomienda labor system by which the Spanish colonists exploited the Indians. In 1614, in a lengthy letter to his brother, the lieutenant governor of Asunción, he defended the newly founded missions against charges made by the encomenderos, and in turn accused them of mistreating the Indians. Not an intellectual, he was most of all a practical man. He was a mason, carpenter, architect, preacher, and organizer. He built the mission towns that he founded and offered leadership and protection to the Indians. He also translated the catechism of the Third Lima Council (1582–1583) into Guaraní. He was canonized in 1988.

BIBLIOGRAPHY Philip Caraman, *The Lost Paradise* (1975, 1990); Clement J. McNaspy, *Conquistador without Sword, The Life of Roque González, SJ* (1984).

Jeffrey Klaiber, SJ

Good, Adolphus Clemens (1856–1894), Presbyterian missionary to Cameroun. Good, born in West Mahoning, Pennsylvania, graduated from Washington and Jefferson College (1879) and Western Theological Seminary, Pittsburgh (1882). The Presbyterian Board of Foreign Missions appointed him to Gabon in West Africa on September 28, 1882. He married Lydia B. Walker of the Gabon mission in 1883. Assigned to Baraka station, he did wide evangelistic itineration along the Ogowe River and on Corisco Island during the next decade. An able linguist, he revised the Mpongwe New Testament.

French colonial insistence on the use of French rather than vernacular languages in mission schools prompted Good and his colleagues, in 1892, to recommend transfer of the Presbyterian work in Gabon and the Ogowe region to the Paris Evangelical Mission Society. On Good's recommendation, the American Presbyterians moved into German Kamerun, using Batanga station (established 1889) as base. From here Good pioneered in the interior of southern Cameroun. Between 1892 and 1894 his exploratory trips inland from Batanga led to a decision to work among the Bulu. He compiled the first Bulu-English dictionary and made the earliest Bulu translation of the four Gospels. He located and established the first two inland stations, Efulan (1893) and Elat (1894). He died at Efulan of blackwater fever at age 38, after only 12 years in Africa.

BIBLIOGRAPHY Charles W. McCleary, *The Beloved* (1904), passim; Ellen C. Parsons, *A Life for Africa: Rev. Adolphus Clemens Good, Ph.D.* (1900); W. Reginald Wheeler, *The Words of God in an African Forest: The Story of an American Mission in West Africa (1931),* pp. 80–101 and passim.

Norman A. Horner

Goodall, Norman (1896–1985), British missionary statesman and architect of the integration of the International Missionary Council (IMC) with the World Council of Churches (WCC). Born in Birmingham, Goodall early displayed his administrative gifts as a member of the British civil service during World War I. After the armistice, he graduated from Mansfield College at Oxford, was ordained to the Congregational ministry and in 1936 was appointed member of the staff of the London Missionary Society with secretarial responsibility for India and the South Pacific. On the basis of the wide experience this gave him, Goodall was chosen to succeed William *Paton in 1944 as London secretary of the IMC and editor of the *International Review of Missions.* This placed him at the center of the developing ecumenical movement.

A changed world at the end of World War II demanded fresh thinking about missionary strategy, and Goodall played a leading role. He was instrumental in planning the IMC conferences at Whitby, Ontario (1947), and Willingen, Germany (1952), leading to the integration of the IMC and WCC at New Delhi (1961). He remained on the staff of the WCC for a further two years as assistant secretary, and in a period of semi-retirement was actively involved in the International Congregational Council and the UK Free Church Federal Council. Final retirement in 1968 did not lessen his ecumenical influence, particularly in lectures to Roman Catholics, culminating with visits to the Pontifical Gregorian University in Rome. He was an outstanding expositor and a master of the English language, but above all, someone with remarkable pastoral gifts. He is chiefly remembered for his gracious Christian character.

BIBLIOGRAPHY Norman Goodall, *One Man's Testimony* (1949; repr. with a memoir by Kenneth Slack, 1985), *Missions under the Cross* (1953), *History of the London Missionary Society* (1954), *The Ecumenical Movement: What It Is and What It Does* (1961; 2d ed., 1964), *Ecumenical Progress: A Decade of Change in the Ecumenical Movement, 1961–1971* (1972), and *Second Fiddle: Recollections and Reflections* (1979). A comprehensive collection of Goodall's numerous articles and pamphlets is included in the archives of the LMS held at the School of Oriental and African Studies, London. See also Paul Rowntree Clifford, "Norman Goodall," in Gerald H. Anderson et al., eds., *Mission Legacies* (1994), pp. 602–607.

Paul R. Clifford

Goodell, William (1792–1867), American missionary to the Near East. Born at Templeton, Massachusetts, in a two-room house, Goodell was one of twelve children of parents "full of the millennium and of the missionary spirit." At age 15 he walked 60 miles to Phillips Academy in Andover with his trunk on his back; there his evident promise won support in the form of scholarship funds. In

February 1812 he walked from Andover to Salem to witness the ordination of the first American foreign missionaries, an experience to which he often alluded. Goodell graduated from Dartmouth College in 1817 and from Andover Theological Seminary in 1820. After attending medical lectures he traveled as an agent of the American Board of Commissioners for Foreign Missions (ABCFM) and visited its Cherokee and Choctaw missions. In 1822 he was ordained, married Abigail Perkins Davis, and sailed under appointment by the ABCFM to Syria and the Holy Land. Prevented from proceeding to Jerusalem after language study at Malta, he and Isaac *Bird, with their families, inaugurated the mission at Beirut. Goodell began a special study of Armenian and when driven back to Malta in 1828 by wars and plunder, superintended the mission press and in 1831 published his first version of the Armeno-Turkish New Testament. He then moved to Constantinople to inaugurate a mission to the Armenians. Until his retirement in 1865 he played a major role in the Turkey Mission, exercising his unusual gifts of scholarship combined with an affable and winning personal presence and strong religious sense. His translation of the Old Testament first appeared in 1842, and his final revision of the Bible was published in 1863. During his only furlough in America he published *The Old and the New; Or, The Changes of Thirty Years in the East, with Some Allusions to Oriental Customs as Elucidating Scripture* (1853); in 1870 a volume of his sermons in Armenian appeared. He returned home in 1865 and died in Philadelphia.

BIBLIOGRAPHY *Missionary Herald* 63 (1867): 129–133 has an extensive obituary; see also 66 (1870): 46–47. J. K. Greene, *Leavening the Levant* (1916); E. D. G. Prime, *Forty Years in the Turkish Empire; Or, Memoirs of Rev. William Goodell, D.D.* (1876).

David M. Stowe

Gordon, A(doniram) J(udson) (1836–1895), pastor, author, poet, hymn writer, educator, social reformer, and missions leader. Born in New Hampton, New Hampshire, Gordon graduated from Brown University (1860) and Newton Theological Institution (1863). From 1869 to 1895 he was pastor of the Clarendon Street Baptist Church of Boston, Massachusetts, where he promoted the cause of foreign missions. On the executive committee of the American Baptist Missionary Union (ABMU) from 1871, and chair after 1888, Gordon stimulated Baptist missions expansion. One of the most influential evangelical leaders of his era, he made an impact on missions well beyond Baptist circles through his writing and speaking. In 1884 he negotiated the ABMU takeover of the Congo River Livingstone Inland Mission, founded in 1878 by H. Grattan *Guinness. In 1886 he addressed Dwight L. *Moody's Northfield Conference when the initial 100 student volunteers launched what became the Student Volunteer Movement. At the 1888 London Centenary Conference on the Protestant Missions of the World, Gordon emerged as an international apologist for missions and toured Scotland to advance the cause. In 1889 he founded the Boston Missionary Training Institute, one of America's first Bible schools, which graduated fifty missionaries in its initial decade and later evolved into Gordon College and Gordon-Conwell Theological Seminary.

Gordon's mission theory, largely premillennial in emphasis, was expounded in his books, including *The Ship Jesus* (c. 1884) and *The Holy Spirit in Missions* (c. 1893), and in articles in his journal *The Watchword*, and in *Missionary Review of the World*, of which he was associate editor after 1890. Rejecting optimistic, civilizing colonialist theories popular in the imperial era of missions, Gordon separated Christianity and culture and questioned the efficacy of Western colonialism. To hasten the Second Coming of Christ, he advocated worldwide evangelization and indigenous church planting over against incremental institutional approaches. Though a loyal denominationalist, he viewed the decentralization of missions and the rise of "faith mission" as efficient ways to enlist the human and financial resources of local congregations. An outspoken advocate of women in ministry, he welcomed females and minorities to his training school and to the larger mission enterprise.

BIBLIOGRAPHY A. J. Gordon, *The Ministry of the Spirit* (1894), *How Christ Came to Church* (c. 1895), and *In Christ* (1872). Ernest B. Gordon, *Adoniram Judson Gordon: A Biography with Letters and Illustrative Extracts* (1896, 1986) remains the fullest treatment of Gordon's life. *The Vision Continues: Centennial Papers of Gordon-Conwell Theological Seminary*, Garth M. Rosell, ed. (1992), contains essays analyzing Gordon's legacy. *Journal of Our Journey*, John Beauregard, ed. (1989), relates Gordon's experiences promoting missions in Britain in 1888. See also Dana L. Roberts, "Adoniram Judson Gordon," in Gerald H. Anderson et al., eds., *Mission Legacies* (1994), pp. 18–27. Gordon's personal papers are in the Gordon College archives and the Gordon-Conwell Theological Seminary archives.

Thomas A. Askew

Gordon, Andrew (1828–1887), Presbyterian missionary in India. Born in Putnam, New York, Gordon arrived in Calcutta in February 1855 under appointment by the Associate Presbyterian Church of North America (soon to enter into a union forming the United Presbyterian Church of North America). In August of that year, he established the first mission station at Sialkot, Punjab. In 1865 he returned to the U.S. for reasons of health but went back to India in 1875. From 1875 to 1885 he was stationed at Gurdaspur, one of the earliest centers of the Chuhra mass movement in the Punjab. There, in addition to the work associated with the mass movement, he was involved in the early stages of putting the Psalms into Punjabi meter so that they might be sung to Punjabi tunes in Punjabi style. Returning to the United States in 1885 because of his daughter's health, Gordon wrote *Our India Mission* (1886). What sets this work apart from other contemporary mission histories is that it reveals so much, not just about missionaries and their work, but about converts, mass conversion movements, and the Christian communities that emerged during the mission's first 30 years. Gordon died soon after completing the book. In 1895 the Sialkot mission named its new college in Rawalpindi the Gordon Mission College.

BIBLIOGRAPHY W. W. B., "Sketch of the Rev. Andrew Gordon, D.D.," *The Women's Missionary Magazine of the United Presbyterian Church* 1 (September 1887).

John C. B. Webster

Goreh, Nilakantha (Nehemiah) (1825–1895), Indian Christian philosopher and theologian. "God's doubting Thomas for his church in India," Goreh was born into a high Brahmin caste in Maharashtra and grew up in Varanasi (Benares). In his early twenties, reading John Muir's *Mataparikśha* (an apologetical work in Sanskrit) and later the Bible convinced him of the reality of eternal punishment, and in March 1848 he was baptized, taking the name "Nehemiah." At this stage he was an evangelical with Church Missionary Society affiliations. In the early 1850s he paid his first visit to England as tutor to Maharaja Dhuleep Singh, meeting among others Queen Victoria and the orientalist professor Max Müller. Returning to India, he wrote the work for which he is chiefly remembered, *Saddarshan Darpan* (Rational refutation of Hindu philosophical systems, 1861), but, troubled by the question of authority in the church, he moved from evangelical to high-church Puseyite Anglicanism. He was ordained deacon in 1868 and priest in 1870. In his later years he was associated with (though never a full member of) the Anglican Society of St. John the Evangelist (Cowley Fathers), and his counsel was a decisive factor in the conversion of Pandita *Ramabai (1883).

BIBLIOGRAPHY C. E. Gardner, *The Life of Father Goreh* (1900); Balwant A. M. Paradkar, *The Theology of Goreh* (1970); Richard Fox Young, *Resistant Hinduism: Sanskrit Sources on Anti-Christian Apologetics in Early Nineteenth-Century India* (1981), pp. 101ff., 169ff.

Eric J. Sharpe

Gorham, Sarah E. (1832–1894), African American missionary of the African Methodist Episcopal (AME) Church. Gorham was born either in Fredericktown, Maryland, or Fredericksburg, Virginia. Little is known of her life before 1880, when she visited relatives who had immigrated to Liberia. She spent a year traveling throughout the country preaching and comforting the needy. It was on this trip that she became interested in mission work. She returned to the United States, but in 1888 she offered her services to the AME Church as a missionary. At the age of 56 she became the first single woman AME missionary appointed to a foreign field. She was supported by the Ohio Conference. After her arrival in Sierra Leone, she was stationed at Magbele, one of the leading AME missions in the country, where she worked among the Temne women and girls. At Magbele she established the Sarah Gorham Mission School, which gave both religious and industrial training. In July 1894 she was bedridden with malaria and died the next month. She was buried in Kissy Road (now Street) Cemetery in Freetown.

BIBLIOGRAPHY Lewellyn L. Berry, *A Century of Missions of the African Methodist Episcopal Church, 1840–1940* (1942); Rosemary Skinner Keller, Louise L. Queen, and Hilah F. Thomas, eds., *Women in New Worlds* (1982).

Sylvia M. Jacobs

Gossner, Johannes Evangelista (1773–1858), founder of the Gossner Mission. Gossner was born and brought up in a Roman Catholic farmer's family in Bavaria and was ordained priest in 1796. After joining a group of young clerics who worked for spiritual revival in the Catholic Church, he went through a period of doubt and frustration. He officiated in various congregations but was repeatedly involved in disputes and conflicts with representatives of the official church. While serving as priest of a German church in St. Petersburg, Russia, he was forced to resign. After years of unsettled life, the alleged heretic at last found a haven in the Lutheran church and in 1829 was appointed pastor of the (Moravian) Bohemian Bethlehem church in Berlin, where he was successor to Johann *Jänicke, founder of the first mission seminary in Germany and brother of a former missionary in South India. Jänicke's example probably encouraged Gossner to combine the concern for foreign mission work with his spiritual leanings, which were expressed mainly in a translation of the Greek New Testament into German (1815), and in exegetical and devotional literature.

Characteristically, however, Gossner hesitated to start a mission of his own. Instead, he joined the board of the Berlin Missionary Society, which had been founded in 1824, and cooperated loyally until 1836, when a group of young men urged him to give them what they did not find in the Berlin society: "preparation in the power of the Spirit" as the Lord's own disciples and as the Moravian brethren had received it. Having already started a mission magazine of his own, Gossner in 1836 embarked on a loosely knit one-man missionary enterprise, with Jesus as "president" and every believer willing to pray for the mission as a potential member. In 1842 the Gossner Mission was organized as a chartered society. Of the 141 missionaries who were sent out during Gossner's lifetime, mainly to North India, only sixteen had a theological education. After his death a board of trustees reformed the association as a conventional missionary society.

BIBLIOGRAPHY The only fully reliable account of Gossner and his mission is Walter Holsten, *Johannes Evangelista Gossner: Glaube und Gemeinde* (1949). The author was the last one to use the Gossner Mission archives in Berlin before they were almost completely destroyed in the last days of World War II.

Hans-Werner Gensichen

Goupil, René (1608–1642), French Jesuit missionary in Canada. Goupil was already a surgeon when he entered the Jesuit novitiate in Paris at the age of 31. But because he suffered from deafness, he left the order and volunteered instead to accompany the Jesuits to Canada. He arrived at the city of Quebec in 1640 and worked as a surgeon at nearby Sillery until he was asked to accompany Isaac *Jogues to Wendake (the land of the Huron Indians in eastern Ontario) in the summer of 1642. Their party, comprising twelve canoes with forty people, was captured by the Iroquois, who took many of them, including Jogues and Goupil, to their own territory. There, at Ossernenon (now Auriesville, New York), he was killed with a hatchet by an Iroquois angry that he had made the sign of the cross over a child. A few days before, he had asked to return to the Jesuit order and had taken first vows. He is venerated as the first of the Jesuit Canadian martyrs; he and seven of his companions were canonized by Pope *Pius XI on June 29, 1930. He is invoked as the patron saint of surgeons and of those who are hearing impaired.

BIBLIOGRAPHY Reuben Gold Thwaites, ed., *The Jesuit Relations and Allied Documents* (1959); J. Wynne, *The Jesuit Martyrs of North America* (1925).

Jacques Monet, SJ

Govan, William (1804–1875), Scottish missionary and educational administrator in South Africa. A graduate of the University of Glasgow, an experienced schoolmaster, and an ordained minister, Govan was appointed to be the first principal of Lovedale Institution, which the Glasgow Missionary Society founded in 1841 on the troubled Xhosa frontier of Cape Colony, South Africa. Lovedale, a high school, was shaped by Govan as a nonracial institution giving the best possible education up to university entrance. The first incoming class consisted of nine white and eleven black students. All shared the same classes and did manual labor to help support the school. In the 1850s Govan added courses in carpentry, wagon making, smithing, printing, and bookbinding, but his primary aim was to produce a Christian academic elite (black and white) to lead the nation.

In 1867, James *Stewart joined the staff and soon challenged Govan's emphasis. The church, Stewart believed, should provide the widest possible spread of primary education for Africans rather than concentrating on the few. When the church authorities in Scotland backed Stewart in 1870, Govan resigned. In Scotland he wrote a classic missionary history, *Memorials of the Reverend James Laing of Kaffraria* (1875).

BIBLIOGRAPHY R. H. W. Shepherd, Lovedale's fourth principal, writes very fully about Govan in *Lovedale, South Africa: The Story of a Century* (1940). There are also revealing passages in J. W. McQuarrie, *Reminiscences of Sir Walter Stanford* (1958) (McQuarrie was one of Govan's pupils).

Andrew C. Ross

Gowans, Walter (1868–1894), Canadian cofounder of Sudan Interior Mission. It was the vision and burden of Gowans's mother, Margaret, passed on to her son, that inspired Gowans, Rowland *Bingham, and Thomas Kent in 1893 to set out for the interior of West Africa, known then as the Soudan. Of the three founders, Gowans seems to have been the leader. In spite of his early death at Ghirku in present-day Nigeria in November 1894, Gowans has remained an important inspiration to many, particularly through quotations like these from an 1893 letter to friends: "Our success in this enterprise means nothing less than the opening of the country for the gospel: our failure, at the most nothing more than the death of two or three deluded fanatics"; and again, "Sixty millions are at stake! Is it not worth even risking our lives for so many?"

BIBLIOGRAPHY An unpublished biography of Gowans by Kerry Lovering is available from SIM, Scarborough, Ontario. Papers related to Gowans's life and work may be found in the SIM archives in Charlotte, N.C.

Gary R. Corwin

Goward, William E(dward) (1860–1931), London Missionary Society (LMS) missionary in Samoa. An Englishman educated at Hackney College, London, Goward began work for the LMS in Samoa in 1887. In 1900 he was dispatched to the Gilbert Islands (now Kiribati) to try to stem the advance of the Roman Catholic mission, which was fast replacing the long-established Protestant church there. Protestants were under the leadership of Samoan LMS pastors in the south and Hawaiian American Board of Commissioners for Foreign Missions (ABCFM) pastors in the north. Goward exercised strict control over the Samoans, driving them to harder work. He also began a pastoral school on the dry and barren island of Beru to train local Gilbertese ministers to replace the Samoans. Graduates of the school provided effective leadership, and the Catholic advance was stopped. Goward then tried working with the ABCFM in the north, but because of his domineering character, that proved difficult, and in 1917 the ABCFM decided to turn over its work to Goward and the LMS. He retired in 1919 as one of the most powerful men in the country, and spent his remaining years in England.

BIBLIOGRAPHY Barrie Macdonald, *Cinderellas of the Empire: Towards a History of Kiribati and Tuvalu* (1982); Charles W. Forman, *The Island Churches of the South Pacific: Emergence in the Twentieth Century* (1982).

Charles W. Forman

Goyau, Georges (1869–1939), French Catholic missions scholar and author. Born in Orléans, Goyau studied in France and Rome, obtaining a doctorate in history. From 1927 to 1938 he was professor of mission history in the Institut Catholique in Paris. His first wife was Lucie Félix-Faure; his second wife, Juliette Heuzey, was also his biographer. In 1922 he became a member of the Académie Française, in 1930 consultor of the Congregation of Rites. He was one of the cofounders of Amis des Missions and was also closely allied with the journal *Revue d'histoire des missions.* He was member of the Order of Leopold, commander in the Order of St. Gregory, and chevalier of the Legion of Honor. A fervent Catholic, he was praised at his death by *Pius XII for his Christian charity.

Goyau became world famous through his literary activity, which included nearly 100 books, together with innumerable articles (170 articles alone for the *Catholic Encyclopedia*). His best-known publications are *Le pape, les catholiques et la question sociale* (1890–1900), *L'Allemagne religieuse* (1896–1913), *Histoire religieuse de la nation française* (1922), and *L'Église en marche* (1928). The idea of mission found its way into all his books. The obituary written by L. Deyrieux lists twenty books about mission in the strict sense: missionary biographies (Jean Colin, Cardinal Lavigerie, Mons. Augouard, Mother Javouhey, H. de Solages, Mother Marie de la Passion), histories of orders (Dames de la Charité, Picpus Missionaries, the Paris Foreign Mission Society, Spiritans, Sisters of Our Lady of the Apostles, Vincentians), as well as systematic studies on mission such as *Missions et missionnaires* (1931), *La femme dans les missions* (1933), and *A la conquêt du monde païen* (1934).

BIBLIOGRAPHY L. Deyrieux, "Hommage à Georges Goyau (1869–1939)," *Les Missions Catholiques* 71 (1939):482–484; "Un grand écrivain catholique français Georges Goyau (1869–1939)," in *La Documentation Catholique* 41 (1940): 399–412; J.-P. Heuzey-Goyau, *Dieu premier servi: Georges Goyau. Sa vie et son oeuvre* (n.d.) (see *NZM* 4 [1948]: 304–305); G. B. Tragella, "Giorgio Goyau, academico missionario," *Studium* 45 (1949): 235–243; F. Veuillot, *G. Goyau* (1942).

Karl Müller, SVD

Graham, James Robert III (1898–1982), American Presbyterian missionary in China and Taiwan. Born in Rock Hill, South Carolina, the son of Presbyterian missionaries, Graham grew up in China. After graduating from Hampden-Sydney (Virginia) College (B.A., 1918) and serving one year in the U.S. Marine Corps, he married Louise Garrett and went as a Southern Presbyterian missionary to China. He served in Yencheng (Yangcheng) (1921–1927) and Chinchiang (Zhenjiang), Kiangsu (1929–1936), from where he carried out an itinerant ministry throughout north China. In 1936 he and his family returned to the United States, and in 1938 he left the Presbyterian Church over issues of liberalism.

From 1936 to 1950 Graham ministered in various capacities, including lecturing at Wheaton College, Illinois (1939–1940), which awarded him a D.D. in 1939. After a thwarted attempt to return to China in December 1941, he spent the period 1942–1950 ministering in Los Angeles. His first wife died in 1948. In 1950 he married Sarah Chapel and at the suggestion of Billy *Graham (no relation), he went to Taiwan as an independent missionary, and in 1955 founded the Chung Yuan College of Science and Engineering in Chung Li. In 1958 he established Christ's College in Tanshui, near Taipei, serving as president until he retired in 1980 and remaining actively involved until his death. His wife, Sarah, having died, in 1979 he married Louise Hunter, a longtime friend and missionary widow from Japan. Graham was well known to thousands of Chinese and was highly respected for his exceptional command of Mandarin.

BIBLIOGRAPHY J. R. Graham, "Old China Hand," *Decision*, July, 1974. Some anecdotal material appears in J. C. Pollock, *A Foreign Devil in China* (1971).

Daniel G. Reid

Graham, John Anderson (1860–1942), Church of Scotland missionary in the eastern Himalayas and founder of the Kalimpong Homes. Graham was born in London, son of a Scottish customs officer who returned to farm in his native Dunbartonshire a year later. His schooling was patchy and interrupted. He was a clerk and a minor civil servant before entering the University of Edinburgh to study for the ministry (M.A., 1885). While a divinity student, he became secretary to the committee producing the church periodical *Life and Work*, in which capacity he initiated the *Church of Scotland Yearbook* in 1886. He became national secretary for the Young Men's Guild, and in 1888 he was ordained as the first missionary supported by the guild. He married Katherine McConachie soon afterward, and they arrived next year in Kalimpong in the Himalayan region then called British Sikkim. The church had begun to grow in the district, mainly among Lepcha people, with some Nepali. Graham helped more churches emerge and grow, developed a strong local organization (based on heads of Christian households) and leadership (based on *panchayats*, or councils, of catechists), and raised finances from Scotland for an imposing church building, a hospital, and economic development activities. He gained publicity for the mission in *Life and Work*, which he had once served. A long furlough (1895–1898) enabled him to promote Kalimpong throughout Scotland, especially through the guild network and through his book on the mission, *On the Threshold of Three Closed Lands* (1897; 2d ed., 1905). A further book, *The Missionary Expansion of the Reformed Churches*, followed in 1898. Graham also persuaded the church to undertake the pastoral care of the (mostly Scottish) tea planters of the area and to begin missionary work among their laborers.

Returning to India, Graham turned his attention to the children of the planters, offspring of unofficial unions with local women. In 1900 he initiated St. Andrews Colonial and Industrial Settlement project to provide these children with Christian homes, education, and the opportunity to immigrate to rewarding work. Neither the guild nor the missionary committee would fund the project, so he turned to the British government of India, to commerce, and to the wider Scottish public.

He maintained his work as a district missionary and representative of the guild, though some tensions and conflicts of interest arose between the mission concerns and the homes. His regional impact among people of all faiths was considerable. He sought to develop local industries, agriculture, and technical skills. He maintained a lively interest in the neighboring "closed lands" of Tibet and Nepal, and especially Bhutan, where he formed close relations with the rulers. Graham's wife, an innovative presence in all the work, was awarded the Kaisar-i-Hind Medal. She died in 1919. Graham received several honors, British and Bhutanese, and several honorary degrees. He was moderator of the Church of Scotland in 1931. The fiftieth anniversary of his missionary service was marked in 1939 by the presentation of a house in Kalimpong, where he lived in semiretirement until his death.

Graham's theology, always based on the love of God and the humanity of Christ, broadened with the years as he was influenced by Hindu thought and notably by Sri Ramakrishna. He wrote *Stray Thoughts on the Possibility of a Universal Religion and the Feasibility of Teaching It in Our Schools* (1937) for a Bengal teachers' conference and in response to a Hindu friend who was devoted to Christ.

BIBLIOGRAPHY John A. Graham, *The Education of the Anglo-Indian Child* (1934). J. R. Minto, *Graham of Kalimpong* (1974).

Andrew F. Walls

Graham, William ("Billy") Franklin (1918–), foremost Protestant evangelist of the twentieth century. Graham was born on a farm near Charlotte, North Carolina, and was converted at age 16. He attended Wheaton College, Illinois, where he received a B.A. in anthropology in 1943 and met his wife, Ruth, the daughter of Dr. and Mrs. L. Nelson *Bell, Presbyterian missionaries to China. After a brief pastorate, he began working for Youth for Christ as an itinerant evangelist and made several trips to England and Europe. He gained national prominence during a successful evangelistic crusade in Los Angeles in 1949. In 1950 he founded the Billy Graham Evangelistic Association (BGEA) and his crusades around the world, his radio, film, and television ministries, *Decision* magazine, and his best-selling books enhanced his reputation. Graham's warm personality and irenic spirit enabled him to be the confidant of presidents and other world leaders and a respected figure both in ecumenical and evangelical circles.

Graham had a keen interest in foreign missions. He met with missionaries and local Christians during his visits to Korea (1952), other countries in Asia (1956), and Africa (1960), a practice that he continuously followed on his later crusades in non-Western countries. Graham's moderation of his early anticommunism, and his consistent opposition to racism (he refused to speak at segregated meetings), were widely noted abroad. Desirous of renewing evangelicalism and enhancing its global vision, the BGEA organized the Berlin Congress on Evangelism (1966), regional conferences in Asia, Latin America, Africa, the United States, and Europe, and above all, the International Congress on World Evangelization at Lausanne, Switzerland (1974). In the next two decades the Lausanne Committee promoted cross-cultural evangelism and the development of indigenous churches throughout the world. This vision was reiterated particularly at the Consultation on World Evangelization at Pattaya, Thailand, in 1980, and in a second international congress at Manila in 1989. The BGEA also organized two international conferences for itinerant evangelists in Amsterdam (1983 and 1986), most of whose delegates were from the non-Western world. The ministry's earnings were invested in the Billy Graham Center at Wheaton College, which emphasized missionary education and preservation of documents on missions, and in the Billy Graham Training Center at Porter's Cove, North Carolina.

BIBLIOGRAPHY Graham's autobiography is *Just As I Am* (1997). By far the finest biography is William Martin, *A Prophet with Honor: The Billy Graham Story* (1991). John Pollock, *Billy Graham: The Authorized Biography* (1966), *Billy Graham: Evangelist to the World* (1979), and *To All the Nations: The Billy Graham Story* (1985) are useful as inside accounts. Jerry B. Hopkins, "Billy Graham and the Race Problem" (Ph.D diss., Univ. of Kentucky, 1986) is the definitive work on its subject. For Graham's ecumenical development, see Richard V. Pierard, "From Evangelical Exclusivism to Ecumenical Openness: Billy Graham and Sociopolitical Issues," *Journal of Ecumenical Studies* 20 (1983): 425–446. Some BGEA correspondence and papers and materials pertaining to Graham and his associates are available at the Billy Graham Center Archives, Wheaton, Ill. The BGEA published the papers and proceedings of the major congresses.

Richard V. Pierard

Grandin, Vital Justin (1829-1902), French Catholic missionary and bishop in western Canada. Grandin was born in Saint Pierre-la-Cour, France. Following a brief stint with the Foreign Missions of Paris, he entered the Oblates of Mary Immaculate in 1851 and was ordained in 1854 to become one of only five Catholic missionaries to serve all of western Canada and the north. In December of 1857, at the age of 28, Grandin was appointed auxiliary bishop of the diocese of Saint Boniface (part of modern Winnipeg, Manitoba), although he did not hear of his assignment until 1859. In 1871 he became the first bishop of the vast, newly created diocese of Saint Albert (today the archdiocese of Edmonton). In the face of tremendous obstacles, including his own chronic poor health, Grandin worked tirelessly to bring Christianity to the Indians and those of mixed race, logging more than 25,000 miles on snowshoe in addition to countless additional miles on dogsled and horseback, and leaving behind sixty-five missions, fifty schools, three hospitals, and two seminaries. A vocal and effective critic of the treatment of aboriginal peoples by the Canadian government and Hudson's Bay Company, Grandin became known as the Indian Bishop. In 1937, the Vatican issued a decree for the introduction of Grandin's cause for sainthood and declared him venerable in 1966.

BIBLIOGRAPHY Vital Justin Grandin, *The Diaries of Bishop Vital Grandin*, Alan D. Ridge, tr. (1989). Claude Champagne, *Les débuts de la mission dans le nort-ouest canadien: mission et église chez Msgr. Vital Grandin, O.M.I.* (1983); Frank J. Dolphin, *Indian Bishop of the West: The Story of Vital Justin Grandin, 1829–1902* (1986).

Jonathan J. Bonk

Grant, Anthony (1806–1883), Anglo-Catholic advocate for missions. Grant was born on Portsea Island, England, and was educated at Winchester and at New College, Oxford, of which he was a fellow. He married Julia Carey in 1838. Ordained an Anglican priest in 1834, he became curate of Chelmsford and vicar of Romford, Essex (1838–1862), and of Aylesford, Kent (1862–1877). In 1846 he was appointed archdeacon of St. Albans.

Grant was Bampton lecturer at Oxford for 1843 and delivered a course on *The Past and Prospective Extension of the Gospel by Missions to the Heathen* (1844). This was the first attempt by an Anglo-Catholic to develop a comprehensive theory of mission. His main premise was that the apostolic tradition requires that missions be led by a bishop. This placed him in opposition to the Church Missionary Society, sponsored by evangelical Anglicans, and other voluntary and lay mission societies that had gained ascendancy in the nineteenth century.

BIBLIOGRAPHY Wilbert R. Shenk, *Henry Venn, Missionary Statesman* (1983).

Wilbert R. Shenk

Grant, Asahel (1809–1844), American physician and explorer among the Nestorians in Persia (Iran). After the death of his first wife, Grant moved to Utica, New York, where he was elected a Presbyterian elder. In 1835 he married Judith Campbell (see Judith *Grant) and sailed for Urmia, Persia, becoming the second physician to go out under the American Board of Commissioners for Foreign Missions (ABCFM). In 1837 he wrote an "Appeal to Pious Physicians," arguing that medical missionaries could gain access to people and so should be sent on exploratory missions to new areas.

In 1839 Grant's wife and twin daughters died. Over the next five years, he undertook five exploratory tours of the mountain Nestorian villages in Kurdistan. Seeking places to open missions, he established schools and dispensaries. Oblivious to political dynamics, he entered a religious dispute with Anglican missionaries. The resulting ethnic feud culminated in a combined Turkish-Kurdish assault on the Nestorians in which 10,000 died by 1846. Grant died in an epidemic among the refugees, and the American Board gave up attempts to work in the mountains. Grant had believed the Nestorians were a remnant of the ten lost tribes of Israel and that their redemption would signal the end of Islam.

BIBLIOGRAPHY Asahel Grant, *The Nestorians; or the Lost Tribes* (1841). Grant wrote for the *Missionary Herald* on the Nestorians, and he left an unpublished manuscript, "Life in Kurdistan." A. C. Lathrop, comp., *Memoir of Asahel Grant, M.D., Missionary to the Nestorians* (1947); Thomas Laurie, *Dr. Grant and the Mountain Nestorians* (1853); Joseph L. Grabill, *Protestant Diplomacy and the Near East: Missionary Influence on American Policy, 1810–1927* (1971).

Dana L. Robert

Grant, Charles (1746–1823), noted British evangelical layman, politician, businessman, philanthropist, and missionary advocate. Grant was born in Scotland and went to India in 1767, where, after some setbacks, he prospered financially, becoming a director of the East India Company. In 1787 he supported David *Brown's "A Proposal for Establishing a Protestant Mission in Bengal and Bahar." The same year he purchased the Mission Church (or Old Church) in Calcutta, which had belonged to John *Kiernander, a missionary of the Society for the Propagation of Christian Knowledge (SPCK). He also supported a mission at Gaumalti, staffed by John *Thomas (1787–1789).

In 1790 Grant returned to England and attempted unsuccessfully to encourage the SPCK to take a greater interest in India. He wrote *Observations on the State of Society among Asiatic Subjects of Great Britain* in 1792 (published by the House of Commons in 1813). This was a significant missiological apologia for integrating education and Christianity. He supported William *Wilberforce's unsuccessful campaign in 1793 to make provision for missionary work in India. While he was often cautious, Grant used his influential position as a director of the East India Company to advance the evangelical and missionary cause. He appointed evangelical chaplains and defended the Baptist missionaries in India. A member of parliament from 1802 to 1818, Grant identified with the Clapham Sect's campaigns to abolish the slave trade and to provide for missionary work in India in the 1813 East India Company charter. He was a founding director of the Sierra Leone Company, a vice-president of the Church Missionary Society and of the British and Foreign Bible Society, and a pioneer of Sunday schools in Scotland.

BIBLIOGRAPHY A. K. Davidson, *Evangelicals and Attitudes to India, 1786–1813* (1990); A. T. Embree, *Charles Grant and British Rule in India* (1962); Henry Morris, *The Life of Charles Grant* (1904).

Allan K. Davidson

Grant, G(eorge) C(opeland) ("Jack") (1907–1978) *and* **Ida Madeline (Russell)** (1905–1994), Congregationalist educators and ecumenical leaders in South Africa and Zimbabwe. Born in Trinidad, West Indies, Grant was educated in Trinidad and at Cambridge University, earning a B.A. and an M.A. in history and a diploma in education. From 1931 to 1949 he served in British colonial education in Southern Rhodesia (1931–1932), Trinidad (1932–1935), Grenada (1935–1944), and in Zanzibar (1944–1949) as high school headmaster and acting director of education. As principal of Adams College, South Africa (1949–1956), he led in the struggle against apartheid in education, which led to the college's closing.

Ida M. Russell, born in Capetown, South Africa, was the daughter of a former chief justice of the supreme court and acting governor of Rhodesia. Educated at the University of Capetown and at Cambridge University, she taught at Hope Foundation (a London Missionary Society school in Rhodesia) and at Adams College and was a member of the Natal Regional Commission of the South African Institute of Race Relations.

Married in 1932, the Grants served as the International Missionary Council's (IMC) organizing secretaries for the All-Africa Church Conference in Ibadan, Nigeria, and assisted in the formation of the All-Africa Conference of Churches in 1958. From 1959 to 1972 Jack Grant was field secretary of the American Board of Commissioners for Foreign Missions and superintendent of the United Church of Christ in Rhodesia (now Zimbabwe). An ecumenical leader, he served as secretary of the Southern Rhodesia Christian Conference and as a founder and treasurer of the Christian Council of Rhodesia. Strong advocates of African advancement and majority rule in Zimbabwe, the Grants led in establishing scholarship programs for political detainees and restrictees, the multiracial Cold Comfort Farm Society, and Christian Care in

Zimbabwe, which was the joint Roman Catholic-Protestant social welfare arm of the churches.

BIBLIOGRAPHY G. C. Grant, *Jack Grant's Story* (1980).

Norman E. Thomas

Grant, Judith (Campbell) (1814–1839), American missionary to Nestorians and founder of female education in Persia (Iran). Campbell was reared by her aunt, Sabrina Campbell, a well-known medical worker among the poor in Connecticut. Proficient in French, Latin, and Greek, Judith Campbell was probably the best educated of the early American missionary women, having received a thorough classical and mathematical education. After being accepted by the American Board of Commissioners for Foreign Missions (ABCFM), she met and married Asahel *Grant who had been appointed physician to the Nestorian mission. They married and sailed for Persia in 1835.

Grant did medical work alongside her husband. She also introduced female education to the Nestorians by teaching her domestics to read and thereby interesting women in educating their daughters. She attained such ability to speak Turkish, and to read ancient and modern Syrian, that the Nestorian bishops were glad to receive from her instruction in geography and the Greek Scriptures. She lost an eye to ophthalmia, but in 1838 she was able to open a female seminary, the first school for girls among the people. Her untimely death, leaving three babies, provoked a revival. The bishops whom she had tutored had her buried within their church walls. Grant's educational work for girls was continued by Fidelia *Fiske.

BIBLIOGRAPHY H. G. O. Dwight, *Memoir of Mrs. Elizabeth B. Dwight, with a Sketch of the Life of Mrs. Judith S. Grant, Missionary to Persia* (1840); A. C. Lathrop, comp., *Memoir of Asahel Grant, M.D., Missionary to the Nestorians* (1847); Thomas Laurie, *Dr. Grant and the Mountain Nestorians* (1853).

Dana L. Robert

Grassman, Andrew (1704–1783), Moravian missionary in Europe and Greenland and member of the governing board of the Unity. Grassman was born at Senftleben, Moravia, and came under the influence of Christian *David in 1725. In 1728 he immigrated to Herrnhut, Germany. Following brief military service, he was called to mission service in Europe, and in 1734 he went to the Lapps in Sweden, accompanied by David Schneider and John Nitschmann, Jr. The group withdrew when they found that the people were under the nominal care of the state church.

In 1737, accompanied by Schneider and Michael Miksch, Grassman went to Russia to work among the Samoyeds along the shores of the Arctic Ocean. The party was arrested and taken to Saint Petersburg, where they were released. In 1740 he went to Greenland and in 1741 to Holland. In 1743 he was a member of the synod that gave Count *Zinzendorf total powers of management and oversight of the Moravian Church, a decision which proved to be fiscally ruinous. Consecrated a bishop in 1756, Grassman served as a member of the interim board of management after the count's death, charged with solving the community's financial problems. In 1761 he developed plans for an expansion of Moravian work in Bohemia. He died at Herrnhut.

BIBLIOGRAPHY J. T. Hamilton and K. G. Hamilton, *History of the Moravian Church* (1967); *Nachrichten aus der Brüder-Gemeine* (1845).

Albert H. Frank

Graul, Karl (1814–1864), leader of Leipzig Mission and Tamil scholar. Born in a poor weaver's family in central Germany, Graul had a first-rate education, especially in classical and modern languages and in theology. He was, however, entirely self-taught in mission and missiology. In 1844 he was appointed director of the Lutheran Leipzig Mission that had succeeded the Danish-Halle mission in South India. His truly formative experience was a four-year stay in India. Intensive language study gave him a mastery of both high and colloquial Tamil as reflected in his *Bibliotheca Tamulica* (1854–1865) and *Tamil Grammar* (1855). Having himself set an impressive example, Graul insisted on thorough academic training of missionaries, enabling them to work on a firm theological basis and with a contextual approach toward an indigenous church. For the sake of truth as he saw it, he did not mind involving himself and his mission in controversies, especially by proposing what appeared to many as too lenient an approach to the Indian caste system. He also took a somewhat exaggerated view of the primacy of the Lutheran church and the leadership of the Leipzig Mission. After he had resigned from the directorate in 1860, he succeeded in obtaining qualification as a university lecturer in missiology at Erlangen (1864), but he died before he was able to begin teaching.

BIBLIOGRAPHY There is as yet no satisfactory biography of Graul. A list of his published works (139 titles) can be found in Siegfried Krügel, *Hundert Jahre Graul-Interpretation* (1965).

Hans-Werner Gensichen

Gray, Robert (1809–1872), first Anglican bishop of Cape Town, South Africa. Son of the bishop of Bristol, England, Gray was appointed bishop of Cape Town in 1848. His high churchmanship significantly shaped the Anglo-Catholic ethos of early Anglicanism in South Africa. Sponsored by the Society for the Propagation of the Gospel and the Society for Promoting Christian Knowledge, Gray envisioned a mission strategy that facilitated the twin goals of imperial expansion and the religious conversion of indigenous peoples of southern Africa. Missionary dioceses were established spanning the existing colonial territories, and mission stations were founded with the substantial backing of Governor Sir George Grey. These two leaders of church and state, respectively, were true to the spirit of the times in equating Christianity with Western civilization and loyalty to the Crown. Gray's commitment to education led to the establishment of numerous church schools in newly emerging urban centers. As a pastor he was untiring in his countrywide visitations, often made under appalling conditions. His missionary zeal took him on extensive fund-raising tours to England. In consequence of doctrinal controversies with Bishop J. W. *Colenso of Natal, who challenged Gray's metropolitan authority in the English courts, the Anglican Church in South Africa was made an autonomous province, with Gray presiding over its first synod in 1870. He can be regarded as the father of Anglicanism in southern Africa.

BIBLIOGRAPHY A. E. M. Anderson-Morshead, *Pioneer and Founder* (1905); C. N. Gray, *Life of Robert Gray,* 2 vols. (1876); Peter Hinchliff, *The Anglican Church in South Africa* (1963), pp. 27–53, 69–75, 82–117; Janet Hodgson, "Mission and Empire: A Case Study of Convergent Ideologies in 19th-Century Southern Africa," *Journal of Theology for Southern Africa* 38 (1982): 34–48; Cecil Lewis and G. E. Edwards, *Historical Records of the Church of the Province of South Africa* (1934), pp. 31–112.

Janet Hodgson

Graybill, Anthony Thomas (1841–1905), American Presbyterian missionary in Mexico. Born in Virginia, Graybill served in the Confederate Army, then studied at Roanoke College and Union Theological Seminary in Virginia. The Presbyterian Church, U.S. (PCUS) ordained Graybill in 1873, and the following year, just as Protestants were finding some acceptance in Mexico, the PCUS sent him and his wife, Frances Douglas (Taylor), to be the denomination's first missionaries to that country. They began their mission in Matamoros, across the Rio Grande from Brownsville, Texas. Graybill preached and taught in Matamoros and at ranches and villages within a radius of 60 miles. By 1884 enough people had come into the Presbyterian congregations and enough ministers had been trained that the first Mexican presbytery could be formed. By 1887 Graybill and his wife could move to Linares, 200 miles southwest of Matamoros. By 1898, with the help of Mexican Presbyterian leaders and other missionaries who had arrived, Graybill reported that ten congregations had been organized in the region, with nineteen Sunday schools and six elementary day-schools. The first synod, called the National Presbyterian Church of Mexico, was formed in 1901; Graybill was elected moderator for 1903–1904. He died at his home in Linares.

BIBLIOGRAPHY Alice J. McClelland, *Mission to Mexico* (1960); William A. Ross, *Sunrise in Aztec Land* (1922).

H. McKennie Goodpasture

Green, Samuel Fiske (1822–1884), American Congregational medical missionary in Ceylon (Sri Lanka). Born in Worcester, Massachusetts, Green was sent by the American Board of Commissioners for Foreign Missions (ABCFM) to Ceylon in 1847 "first to be physician to the missionaries and then to be of use to the heathen" (i.e., the Tamils). At Manepay, where the Green Memorial Hospital still stands, he began an intensive program of training native physicians. He developed a medical nomenclature in Tamil, translated textbooks, and altogether published some 4,000 pages in the fields of anatomy, physiology and hygiene, obstetrics, surgery, chemistry, and the Indian pharmacopoeia. His medical vocabularies were used in India as well as Ceylon, and he published medical tracts that were distributed by the thousands, particularly in connection with the cholera epidemics of 1855 and 1866. He trained some sixty Ceylonese physicians, many employed by the government in various parts of the island, others working in the Jaffna field of the mission. Friend-in-Need Hospital in Jaffna served 8,000 patients a year. Green believed that patients should pay something for treatment. An ardent evangelist, he systematically commended Christ to every patient and student. After suffering from cholera, Green returned to the United States in 1858; in 1862 he married Margaret Phelps Williams and returned to Ceylon. After the ABCFM reduced support for medical work, Green returned to the United States in 1873, but continued his Tamil publishing for several years. Released by the ABCFM in 1877, he died in Worcester.

BIBLIOGRAPHY Helen I. Root, *A Century in Ceylon* (1916), pp. 43–45. The *Missionary Herald* has a brief obituary in vol. 82 (1884): 284, and excerpts from his letters in issues from 1849 to 1855 and 1862 to 1873 (vols. 45 to 51 and 58 to 60). ABCFM *Annual Reports* for those years refer to his work, as does Fred Field Goodsell in *You Shall Be My Witnesses* (1859), pp. 67, 72.

David M. Stowe

Greene, Elizabeth "Betty" Everts (1920–1997), cofounder with J. Grady *Parrott and James Truxton, of Mission Aviation Fellowship (MAF). Born in Seattle, Washington, Greene served with the Women's Air Service Pilots (WASP) during World War II. She presented the need for missionary aviation in a Christian magazine article, which sparked an interest in other pilots, who joined her in 1945 to form a missionary aviation support service. She served as the first full-time staff worker and the first pilot, assigned to southern Mexico to fly for the jungle training camp program of the Wycliffe Bible Translators. Other overseas assignments took her to Peru, Nigeria, Sudan, Ethiopia, Uganda, Kenya, the Congo, and Irian Jaya. These assignments involved flying missionaries, national church workers, and medical patients as well as making overland, sometimes harrowing, treks through the jungle to check out new landing strips to qualify them for service. She was the first woman to fly over the Andes in a single-engine airplane. Between assignments she worked at MAF headquarters in the United States in public relations and recruitment. She retired in 1982.

BIBLIOGRAPHY Dietrich G. Buss and Arthur F. Glasser, *Giving Wings to the Gospel: The Remarkable Story of Mission Aviation Fellowship* (1995); Ruth A. Tucker, *From Jerusalem to Irian Jaya* (1983), "Female Mission Strategists: A Historical and Contemporary Perspective," *Missiology* 15 (January 1987): 86–97, and *Guardians of the Great Commission* (1988).

Charles E. Van Engen

Gregory I (the Great) (c. 540–604), pope, saint, doctor of the church, and mission advocate. Born in Rome into a devout patrician family, Gregory received what was for his troubled times an excellent education. He entered the civil service and about 570 became prefect of Rome; but about 575 he resigned and became a Benedictine monk, establishing his monastery at his own family home on the Coelian Hill. In 579 he was sent as a deacon to act as papal representative at the Byzantine Court in Constantinople, and although he returned to his monastery about 585, he was often asked by Pelagius II to serve the church of Rome. In 590, when Pelagius died in an epidemic, Gregory was elected pope by popular acclamation but assumed the papacy with great reluctance (legend has it that he attempted to have himself smuggled out of Rome in a basket). He was, however, a dedicated and brilliant churchman and statesman, and served as a bridge in an era of transition from classical to medieval times. Gregory is spoken of both as the last of the church fathers and the first scholastic; as liturgical reformer, defender of Rome from the Lombard invaders, and promoter of the Roman primacy, he is recognized as the architect of the medieval papacy. His extensive writings include homilies, letters, the *Moralia, Pastoral Care,* and the *Dialogues.* This last work had vast influence in medieval devotion to the saints and in the development of the doctrines of heaven, hell, and purgatory.

Gregory is best remembered in mission history for his determination to reevangelize Britain. In sending Augustine (later referred to as *Augustine of Canterbury) and forty companions (all from his monastery on the Coelian) in 596 to evangelize the Anglo-Saxon invaders, Gregory was the first pope to authorize a mission to non-Christians. With the help of Bertha, the Christian wife of King Ethelbert, Ethelbert and 10,000 others were converted in 597. Bede's *Ecclesiastical History* (1: 27–30) contains a number of letters to Augustine in Britain in which Gregory offers very practical and sometimes quite culturally sensitive pastoral advice to the missionaries.

BIBLIOGRAPHY Gregory's works are found in Migne's *Patrologia Latina,* vols. 75–79. For more modern editions and English translation, see the bibliography in C. J. Peifer, "Gregory I the Great," in *Dictionary of the Middle Ages,* vol. 5 (1985), p. 669. Works on Gregory that have appeared in the last quarter century are found in *Bibliographia Patristica: Internationale Patristiche Bibliographie* under "Gregorius I Magnus." See also P. Batiffol, *St. Gregory the Great,* J. Stoddard, tr. (1929); C. Dagens, *Saint Grégoire le Grand: Culture et expérience Crétienne* (1977); F. H. Duden, *Gregory the Great,* 2 vols. (1905, 1967); K. S. Latourette, *A History of the Expansion of Christianity,* vol. 2, *The Thousand Years of Uncertainty A.D. 500–A.D. 1500* (1938), pp. 116–174; and J. Richards, *Consul of God: The Life and Times of Gregory the Great* (1980).

Stephen B. Bevans, SVD

Gregory VII (Hildebrand) (c. 1020–1085), ecclesiastical statesman, reformer, and pope. Gregory was born of poor parents in Tuscany and is believed to have been a monk at Cluny. Ordained by Gregory VI in 1049, he served as prior of a monastery for some 20 years, and was elected pope in 1073 by popular acclaim in a process which has been called a "somewhat tumultuous affair." He was a man of great intellectual power, vision, and determination who at once set to work to reestablish the reign of law in the church, and to demand the submission of every Catholic to the papacy, no matter what that person's status in society. In 1059 he decreed that henceforth, popes should be elected only by the cardinals, without political interference. Another of his passions was the reform of the clergy, particularly with regard to celibacy, nepotism, and simony (trading in ecclesiastical preferment). This involved him in fierce controversy, especially with the Salian (German) emperor Henry IV. In 1075 and 1076 the pope and the emperor excommunicated and dismissed each other, with civil war the result. At the same time, Pope Gregory genuinely wished to unite his church under one authority, and to this end he involved himself in the politics of the whole of Europe, even as far afield as Scandinavia. His interests also extended to North Africa, Spain, Poland, and Hungary. He wished to see more bishops and smaller dioceses, the better to provide pastoral care for, and exercise control over, the people. The world was, in a manner of speaking, his pastorate, but his strict notion of authority did little to ensure his popularity. In the end he died in exile in Salerno, saying on his deathbed, "I have loved righteousness and hated unrighteousness; that is why I am in exile." He was canonized in 1606.

BIBLIOGRAPHY J. N. D. Kelly, *The Oxford Dictionary of Popes* (1986), pp. 154b–156a.

Eric J. Sharpe

Gregory XV (1554–1623), pope (r. 1621–1623), established the mission coordination agency Propaganda Fide (PF). Born into a noble family in Bologna, Alessandro Ludovisi studied at the Roman College and then pursued law in Bologna, receiving his doctorate in 1575. He was ordained a priest shortly thereafter. Gregory XIII appointed him chairman of judges of the Campidoglio in Rome. Under Clement VII he was appointed to the Segnatura, where he mediated a number of difficult cases with great tact and often to the satisfaction of both sides. He also took on increasingly important diplomatic missions. He became archbishop of Bologna in 1612 but shortly afterward was asked to mediate the dispute between Charles Emmanuel I of Savoy and Philip III of Spain. He was created cardinal in 1616. In 1621 he was elected pope by acclaim, taking the name Gregory XV.

In frail health at the time of his election, Gregory reigned only two and a half years. The first Jesuit-trained pope, he pressed forward the renewal of the church and the recovery of some of its lost influence. Two of his efforts were to be lasting achievements. The first changed the procedure for electing a pope, which had been subject to undue influence from secular rulers and powerful cardinals. In two bulls (November 1621 and March 1622), Gregory decreed that voting would begin only after the conclave had been closed to outsiders, and specified the procedure in meticulous detail. With some modifications made by Pius X and *Pius XII in the twentieth century, the procedure has continued to the present time. The second was the establishment of PF in 1622, which coordinated the church's missionary activity for the first time. It gathered information, assigned mission fields, supervised colleges in Rome, restricted the *patronato real* of Spain and Portugal, and supervised those parts of the church in northern Europe whose episcopal hierarchies had been dissolved.

BIBLIOGRAPHY The most thorough account available is Ludwig von Pastor, *History of the Popes,* vol 27 (1938). For Gregory's decrees, see *Magnum Bullarium Romanum* 12: 483–824.

Robert J. Schreiter, CPPS

Gregory XVI (1765–1846), pope responsible for renewal of the church's world mission in the nineteenth century. Born into a noble family, Bartolomeo Alberto Cappellari entered the Camaldolese order in 1783. He was ordained a priest in 1787. From 1790 he taught science and philosophy. He went to Rome in 1795 to work in the general curia of his order. He fiercely resisted Napoleonic encroachments on papal sovereignty and was expelled from Rome in 1807, during the Napoleonic occupation. He returned in 1814, resuming his duties as abbot of San Gregorio (he had been elected in 1805) and as professor of theology. He declined two episcopal sees but was created cardinal in 1826. He was named prefect of the Propaganda Fide in 1826 (having served as a consultor since 1821). In 1831 he was elected pope (r. 1831–1846) and took the name Gregory XVI.

An austere and learned monk, Gregory was deeply suspicious of liberalism and republicanism, resisting any claims of natural rights and democracy, especially in the papal states. His encyclical *Mirari vos* foreshadowed Pius IX's *Syllabus of Errors* (1864). Yet he was an adroit diplomat and was able to secure autonomy for the church in many difficult situations throughout Europe. More important, he was responsible for the great revival in Catholic missionary activity in the nineteenth century. He brought new order and energy to a missionary effort that had declined in the eighteenth century. He also brought to an end the power of the *patronato real* of Portugal and Spain over the missions in their colonies. He encouraged the founding of new missionary orders and encouraged existing orders to staff more missions. He established residential bishops in parts of Latin America, created more than seventy new dioceses and vicariates apostolic, and promoted indigenous clergy and bishops as a policy. In 1843 he instituted the Society for the Propagation of the Faith and the Pontifical Association of the Holy Childhood as papal aid societies to help the financial support of the missions.

BIBLIOGRAPHY *Acta Gregorii papae XVI,* A. M. Bernasconi, ed. (1901–1904) is defective, and no other compilation exists to cover Gregory's entire pontificate. *Bullarii Romani Continuatio,* vols. 19–20, covers the first four years of his pontificate. For his contribution to mission, see Joseph Schmidlin, "Gregor XVI als Missionspapst," *Zeitschrift für Missionswissenschaft und Religionswissenschaft* 21 (1931): 209–228. See also Nicholas Wiseman, *Recollections of the Last Four Popes and of Rome of Their Times* (1858), pp. 415–532.

Robert J. Schreiter, CPPS

Gregory Thaumaturgus (c. 213–270), missionary bishop and church father. Born to a distinguished pagan family in Neocaesarea, Pontus (Asia Minor), Gregory prepared for a career in law, studying in Alexandria, Athens, and Berytus (present-day Beirut). About 233, he and his brother, Athenadorous, traveled to Caesarea, Palestine, where they came under the influence of *Origen and enrolled at his school. Gregory converted to Christianity and was baptized. Soon after his return to Neocaesarea (c. 238) he received a letter from Origen urging him to dedicate himself to work in the church. About 240, he was elected bishop of Neocaesarea. He was an eloquent preacher, and his missionary efforts led to the conversion of nearly the entire town. The great number of miracles attributed to his prayers led the faithful to name him Thaumaturgus (Wonder Worker). During the persecution of Christians by Decius (c. 250), he advised his flock to go into hiding and he himself fled to the desert, returning when a plague struck Neocaesarea. In his *Canonical Epistle,* he describes the devastation of Pontus by the Goths in the years 252–254. He participated in the Synod of Antioch (264–265), which dealt with the heretic Samosata, and fought the heresies of Sabellianism and Tritheism. His feast day is November 17.

BIBLIOGRAPHY Gregory's writings include *Panegyric to Origen* (c. 238), *On The Holy Trinity,* and *The Metaphrase of Ecclesiastes.* These and other works can be found in *Ante-Nicene Fathers,* vol. 6, Alexander Roberts and James Donaldson, eds. (1986), pp. 7–79. See also Berthold Altaner, *Patrology* (1960), pp. 238–239; J. T. Migne, *Patrologia Graeca,* vol. 46, cols. 893–958 (contains a brief biography of Gregory Thaumaturgus by Gregory of Nyssa).

Dimitrios G. Couchell

Gregory the Illuminator (c. 240–332), Apostle of the Armenians. Born to an aristocratic family in the Caucasus Mountains, at an early age Gregory joined many of his compatriots in fleeing Persian-occupied Armenia. While in exile in Cappadocian Caesarea, he was converted to Christianity. Following the expulsion of the Persians, he returned home and began to preach among his pagan countrymen, many of whom had been forcibly converted to Mazdaism (related to Zoroastrianism). King Trdat II quickly had him arrested as an enemy of the gods and as the son of the man who had assassinated his father, King Trdat I. Gregory spent 15 miserable years in the dungeon of the Artashat Fortress in Ararat while the persecution of Christians became widespread and ferocious. His release was achieved when Trdat's sister saw Gregory in a dream, his face illumined, calling for an end to the persecution. He was summoned to court, and his prayers restored the king's health and sanity and effected his conversion. Gregory himself subsequently saw an apocalyptic vision that inspired him to build the Church of Echmiadzin ("the Only-Begotten has descended") near Vagarshapat, at the foot of Mount Alagot.

The converted King Trdat II nominated Gregory to become catholicus of the Armenian Church, and he was consecrated in Caesarea in 301. Under royal auspices and with frequent personal participation of the monarch, Christianity spread rapidly among the Armenian people by way of mass conversions, the transformation of pagan temples into churches, and the ordination of converted pagan priests. The church was established as the state religion of Armenia a dozen years before Christianity gained toleration in the Roman Empire. While legends of Gregory's missionary feats—four million baptisms and four hundred episcopal consecrations—are overstatements, he did succeed remarkably in organizing the church and Christianizing the population.

BIBLIOGRAPHY Agathanelos, *Patmowt'ian Hayots: The History of the Armenians* (1980); Adrian Fortescue, *The Lesser Eastern Churches* (1931), p. 399.

Paul D. Garrett

Grenfell, George (1849–1906), Baptist Missionary Society (BMS) missionary and explorer of the Congo River. As a young man Grenfell was interested in the exploits of David *Livingstone and Alfred *Saker. In November 1874, after study at Bristol Baptist College, he was accepted for service in the Cameroons. He sailed the following month for West Africa in the company of Saker. Initially Grenfell worked alongside Saker at Cameroons Town (now Douala), teaching practical skills to the young men of the mission community. In 1877 he lost his first wife, Mary (Hawkes), whom he had married only 11 months previously. Shortly after her death, he was joined by another young recruit, Thomas *Comber. The two missionaries began a series of exploratory journeys inland from Cameroons Town that foreshadowed the role that Grenfell was subsequently to play in the Congo.

In October 1877 the BMS invited Comber and Grenfell to investigate the prospects for a mission to the Congo River. Two exploratory journeys in 1878 led to the commencement of the Congo mission in the following year. Grenfell, however, resigned from the BMS in August 1878 following the discovery that his Jamaican housekeeper in the Cameroons, Rose Edgerley, was pregnant by him. He returned to the Cameroons to marry her. After working for a commercial concern in the Cameroons from 1878 to 1880, Grenfell was reengaged by the BMS. He was soon recalled to England to supervise the construction of a mission steamer, the *Peace*, to facilitate advance on the upper Congo River. By December 1886 the *Peace* had made six journeys of exploration of the upper Congo and its tributaries. By 1896 Grenfell's work had borne fruit in a chain of mission stations stretching from Stanley Pool (modern Kinshasa) to Yakusu (just downriver from modern Kisangani).

In 1884 and 1885 the European powers had recognized the sovereign rights over the Congo of Leopold II, king of Belgium. Grenfell held to a belief in the essentially humanitarian character of Leopold's Congo Free State until long after most informed observers had revised their estimate of Leopold's alleged benevolence. By the mid-1890s evidence was accumulating of widespread atrocities perpetrated by state agents in the conduct of the rubber trade. Leopold responded in 1896 by appointing a Commission for the Protection of the Natives, comprising six missionaries, one of whom was Grenfell. Grenfell by now admitted the existence of abuses, but he remained persuaded of Leopold's personal good intentions until 1904.

Grenfell's abiding significance is as a mission strategist for central Africa. He was influenced by Robert *Arthington's vision of a chain of mission stations stretching across Africa to meet the westward advance of the Church Missionary Society from Uganda. Grenfell's determination in his later years to press further along the upper Congo and its tributaries, though thwarted by the Congo Free State authorities, was founded on an astute perception that in the twentieth century the sub-Saharan belt would become the principal area of conflict between Islam and evangelical Christianity.

BIBLIOGRAPHY G. Hawker, *The Life of George Grenfell* (1909); H. H. Johnston, *George Grenfell and the Congo* (1908); D. Lagergren, *Mission and State in the Congo* (1970); R. M. Slade, *English-Speaking Missions in the Congo Independent State (1878–1908)* (1959); Brian Stanley, *The History of the Baptist Missionary Society, 1792–1992* (1992). Grenfell's papers are preserved in the BMS archives at Regent's Park College, Oxford.

Brian Stanley

Grenfell, Wilfred Thomason (1865–1940), British medical missionary and social reformer in Labrador and northern Newfoundland. Born in Parkgate, Cheshire, England, the son of an Anglican clergyman, Grenfell graduated from the University of London as a surgeon, and was decisively influenced by his medical mentor, Frederick Treves, and by Dwight L. *Moody, whom he heard in London. He joined the interdenominational Royal National Mission to Deep Sea Fishermen, and in 1892, after service in the North Sea, he joined the crew of the hospital ship *Albert* on its journey to Labrador, becoming keenly aware of the adverse living conditions and great physical and spiritual needs of the Labrador settlers and fishermen. In 1893 he returned to Newfoundland and Labrador with a small medical team, thus initiating a lifelong medical mission as well as efforts to improve living conditions through agricultural and industrial development. He was aided by private philanthropists, governmental support, his lecture tours in England and North America, as well as numerous publications. Among his many writings were the best-selling *Adrift on an Ice Pan* (1909) and his autobiography, *A Labrador Doctor* (1919). In 1912 he established the International Grenfell Association with headquarters in Saint Anthony, Newfoundland, which raised funds for his medical and social work. Ill health forced Grenfell's retirement in 1935 to Vermont, where he died five years later. He left behind an impressive medical and social edifice, which not only included several hospitals and nursing stations but also orphanages, industrial self-help centers, agricultural stations, community centers, and cooperative stores. Recognition for his achievements came through countless honors, among them a knighthood in 1927.

BIBLIOGRAPHY Wilfred Thomason Grenfell, *Vikings of Today, or, Life and Medical Work among the Fishermen of Labrador* (1895), *Labrador Looks at the Orient: Notes of Travel in the Near and Far East* (1928), *On Immortality* (1912), and *Forty Years for Labrador* (1932). Ronald Rompkey, *Grenfell of Labrador: A Biography* (1991). See also the periodicals *Toilers of the Deep: A Monthly Record of Work amongst Them* (1895–1939) and *Among the Deep Sea Fishers: Organ of the International Grenfell Association* (1903–present).

Hans Rollmann

Grentrup, Theodor (1878–1967), Catholic missiologist. Born in Ahlen, Germany, Grentrup entered the Society of the Divine Word (SVD) in 1898 and was ordained a priest in 1902. Obtaining a doctorate in Rome, he taught canon law at St. Gabriel's Mission House, an SVD seminary near Vienna, and spent several years on the SVD General Council (1920–1924). From 1929 until 1933 he taught at the University of Berlin, but lost his position with the ascendancy of the Nazi government. After World War II he distinguished himself with studies in linguistics and on German migrants in Europe and other countries. Grentrup allied himself with the school of thought in missiology that linked mission closely to Roman Catholic canon law, a notion he developed in his 1925 work, *Jus Missionum*. In a way similar to that of the Louvain school, he argued in this work that mission is that aspect of the church's ministry that works for the implantation and consolidation of the Catholic faith among non-Catholics. Unlike the Münster school, therefore, mission for Grentrup was not so much geared toward preaching the gospel exclusively among non-Christians as it was the building up of the church and its hierarchical structure (*plantatio ecclesiae*) wherever it is weak.

BIBLIOGRAPHY Theodor Grentrup, "Die Definition des Missionsbegriffes," *ZM* 3 (1913): 265–274, *Jus Missionarium* (1925), and *Religion und Muttersprache* (1932). *Analecta SVD* 48: 62–87; J. Beckmann, "P. Theodor Grentrup, S.V.D. (1878–1967)," *NZM* 24 (1968): 202–203; U. Crentz, "P. Dr. Theodor Grentrup. Ein Leben im Dienste von Glauben und Volkstum," *Christ unterwegs*, 12 (1958): 1–3.

Stephen B. Bevans, SVD

Gribble, Ernest Richard (1868–1957), missionary among Australian Aborigines. Gribble was born in Geelong, Victoria, the son of missionaries John and Mary *Gribble. He studied for the Anglican ministry. In 1892, while catechist at Tumbarumba in southern New South Wales, Gribble was called by his ill father to take over Yarrabah mission in the far north of Queensland. Stern, hardworking, and physically strong, Gribble put immense effort into the material, educational, and spiritual development of the people of Yarrabah, and many were converted and baptized. He was ordained in 1898. His protégé, James Noble, became the first ordained Aborigine.

Gribble broke down from overwork in 1908. In 1913, following his recovery, he was asked to resurrect the failing Forrest River mission in northwest West Australia. Dismantling its stockade, he established friendly contact with Aborigines. James and Angelina Noble joined him, initiating Sunday services and a day school. For 14 years he administered the mission with autocratic paternalism. When he publicized police brutality of the Aborigines, the white community shunned him. His deep anger at the mistreatment of Aborigines drove him to an obsession with protecting them. Desperate to "save the remnant," Gribble became more despotic and was dismissed in 1928. Hurt and bitter, he nevertheless volunteered as chaplain to the Aboriginal penal settlement, Palm Island, off the northeast coast of Queensland, where, with the Nobles, he spent his happiest years.

BIBLIOGRAPHY Ernest Gribble, *Forty Years with the Aborigines* (1930), *The Problem of the Australian Aboriginal* (1932), and *A Despised Race* (1933). John Harris, *One Blood* (1990).

John W. Harris

Gribble, John Brown (1847–1893), missionary among Australian Aborigines. Leaving England with his parents in 1848, Gribble grew up in Geelong, Victoria, and was converted at age 14. Marrying Mary Bulmer in 1867, he entered the Methodist ministry and later the Congregational Union, becoming the first minister in Jerilderie, southern New South Wales. Angered at injustices the Aborigines suffered, he published *Plea for the Aborigines of Australia* (1879). He opened Warangesda mission on the Murrumbidgee River in New South Wales, initially funding it himself but later accepting Anglican and government subsidies. Displaced Aborigines fled there, many becoming converted. Reordained by the Anglican bishop, and invited to Carnarvon, Western Australia, in 1885, Gribble was appalled at the oppressive system of forced Aboriginal labor. He protected fugitives at his Galilee mission, which antagonized local residents. Ostracized in Carnarvon, condemned in the *West Australian* newspaper, Gribble wrote *Dark Deeds in a Sunny Land* (1886). Called a liar, he sued the newspaper, lost his case, and left Western Australia sick and penniless. He cashed in his life insurance, chose a remote site in the far north of Queensland, and began in 1892 what became the Yarrabah mission. Seriously ill within months, he wrote "I have given my life and substance to defend the blackman of Australia . . . would that I had fifty lives that I might spend in such service."

BIBLIOGRAPHY John Gribble, *Black but Comely* (1884) and *Dark Deeds in a Sunny Land* (1886). Ernest Gribble, *The Problem of the Australian Aboriginal* (1932); John Harris, *One Blood* (1990).

John W. Harris

Griffiths, Bede (Alan Richard) (1906–1993), contemplative Benedictine missionary monk in India. Born in Walton-on-Thames, England, in an Anglican family, and educated at the University of Oxford, Griffiths became a Benedictine monk from 1936 and pursued a contemplative vocation in India from 1955 onward. After an initial year attempting to establish a Benedictine ashram near Bangalore and studying with Raimundo *Panikkar, Griffiths, with Alapatt (an Indian Benedictine) and Mahieu (a Belgian Cistercian), founded the Kurisumala Ashram in Kerala. With this firmly established, he became leader of the Saccidananda Ashram (Hermitage of the Holy Trinity) at Shantivanam in Tamil Nadu in 1968, in succession to Jules *Monchanin and Henri *Le Saux (Abhishiktananda). Here, apart from journeys in India and lecture tours in the West, he spent the rest of his life. His conviction was that Hindus and Christians meet in the mystical realization of God; a continuing concern was with what he regarded as the spiritual disinheritance of the modern West. His writings, lectures, and striking appearance in saffron robes made him something of a Christian guru to many.

BIBLIOGRAPHY Griffiths's autobiographical *The Golden String* (1954) covers his life until his departure to India; autobiographical material in some of his later books such as *Christian Ashram: Essays towards a Hindu-Christian Dialogue* (1966) and *The Marriage of East and West* (1982) continue the story. Other important texts are his *Vedanta and Christian Faith* (1968, with an expanded version in 1973), *Return to the Centre* (1976), and *A New Vision of Reality* (1990). Kathryn Spink, *A Sense of the Sacred* (1988); Wayne Teasdale, *Toward a Christian Vedanta: The Encounter of Hinduism and Christianity according to Bede Griffiths* (1987).

Daniel O'Connor

Griffiths, David (1792–1863), Welsh missionary in Madagascar. Griffiths was born in Carmarthenshire, Wales, and educated at Nevaddlwyd, Wrexham, and Gosport. He and his wife, Mary (Griffiths [her maiden name]), were sent by the London Missionary Society (LMS) to Madagascar in 1821. They arrived in Antananarivo just six months after the other LMS pioneer, David *Jones. Together they founded the first Protestant mission in Madagascar. Each of these men started a school at the behest of the king, Radama I. They also began to translate the Bible. The first Bible to be printed in an African language, it was published in 1835. In 1824 Radama gave them permission to preach in Malagasy, and church attendance rapidly swelled. In 1831, under a new monarch, Queen Ranavalona I, Griffiths's ten-year residence permit expired, but he managed through negotiations to remain a further three years. He baptized freely and organized the first church, actions that the other missionaries thought premature. His activities may have also stirred fears in the queen, leading her to begin persecuting Christians. The other missionaries threatened to leave the country if he did not depart, which he did in 1834.

Later, when no missionaries were allowed in the country, Griffiths returned as a trader and found ways to help some of the persecuted Christians. In 1840 he went back to Britain and became a pastor in Wales for the remainder of his life. He published a history of Madagascar in Welsh, and a Malagasy grammar in English.

BIBLIOGRAPHY David Griffiths, *Hanes Madagaskar* (1842) and *A Grammar of the Malagasy Language* (1854). Bonar Gow, *Madagascar and the Protestant Impact: The Work of the British Mission, 1818–95* (1979); Richard Lovett, *The History of the London Missionary Society* (1899); James Sibree, *The Madagascar Mission: Its History and Present Position Briefly Sketched* (1907).

Charles W. Forman

Grignion de Montfort, Louis-Marie (1673–1716), founder of the Missionaries of the Company of Mary (Montfort Fathers) and of the Daughters of Wisdom. Born in Montfort-la-Cane, near Rennes, France, Grignion de Montfort started high school at the Jesuit College of Rennes, where he met *Poullart des Places. When he was 20 years old, he went to Paris to enter Saint-Sulpice Seminary. In 1700 he was ordained a priest. He was well known for his devotion to Mary and for his educational method of catechetical songs. In 1702 he founded the Daughters of Wisdom, a congregation for teaching and nursing, and in 1705 the Montfort Fathers, a missionary congregation of men. A traveling missionary in France for much of his career, Grignion de Montfort also wrote many devotional works of Marian piety. He was canonized in 1947.

BIBLIOGRAPHY Louis-Marie Grignion de Montfort, *Complete Works of Saint Louis-Marie Grignion de Montfort* (1966). Bernard Guitteny, *Grignion de Montfort: Missionnaire des pauvres* (1993); Louis Perouas, *Grignion de Montfort: Les pauvres et les missions* (1966).

Joseph Lévesque, PSS

Grimké, Charlotte (Forten) (1837–1914), educator, antislavery poet, and civil rights and home missions advocate. As an African American, born in Philadelphia, Pennsylvania, who experienced racial discrimination, Charlotte Forten was motivated to support the abolitionist movement. In 1855 she joined the Salem (Massachusetts) Female Anti-Slavery Society. One year later she began teaching at the Epes Grammar School in Salem, and in 1862 went to South Carolina to teach African Americans under the auspices of the Port Royal Relief Association. In 1878 she married Francis Grimké, a prominent African American minister and civil rights advocate. She organized a women's missionary group at her husband's Laura Street Presbyterian Church in Jacksonville, Florida, in 1885. She became a founding member of the Colored Women's League in 1892 and the National Association of Colored Women in 1896. Grimké kept a detailed journal of her life and published numerous poems and essays. She died in Washington, D.C.

BIBLIOGRAPHY Charlotte Forten Grimké, "A Visit to the Birthplace of Whittier," in *Scribner's Magazine,* September 1872 and "Personal Recollections of Whittier," in *New England Magazine,* June 1893. Ray Allen Billington, ed., *Journal of Charlotte L. Forten* (1953); Anna Julia (Haywood) Cooper, ed., *Life and Writings of the Grimké Family* (1951); Brenda Stevenson, ed., *Journals of Charlotte Forten Grimké* (1988). See also Darlene Clark Hine, ed., *Black Women in America: An Historical Encyclopedia,* vol. 1 (1993) and *Black Women in American History: The Twentieth Century,* vol. 2 (1990).

Joan R. Duffy

Griswold, Hervey DeWitt (1860–1945), Presbyterian missionary in India. Born in Dryden, New York, Griswold went to India in 1890 as a missionary of the Presbyterian Church in the U.S.A. After four years in Jhansi, Uttar

Pradesh, he became professor of philosophy at Forman Christian College in Lahore from 1894 to 1913. From 1913 to 1918 and from 1922 to 1925 he was secretary of the India Council, which coordinated the work of his church's three India missions. A leading student of both classical and modern Hinduism, he produced several scholarly works including "Brahman: A Study in the History of Indian Philosophy" (Ph.D. diss., Cornell Univ., 1900), *The God Varuna in the Rig-Veda* (1910), and *The Religion of the Rigveda* (1923). In addition, he wrote a large number of articles on popular religion and religious movements in the Punjab, which formed the basis of the northern India portions of J. N. *Farquhar's *Modern Religious Movements in India* (1915). Some of these were presented in revised form in Griswold's *Insights into Modern Hinduism* (1934). Griswold was a theological liberal, current with the latest developments in Vedic exegesis and comparative religions. He applied evolutionary theory to the development of religion and considered Christianity, not post-Vedic Hinduism, to be the fulfillment of Rigvedic faith.

BIBLIOGRAPHY John C. B. Webster, *The Christian Community and Change in Nineteenth-Century North India* (1976), pp. 98-102.

John C. B. Webster

Grossman, Guido (1871-1945), Moravian missionary leader and bishop in Nicaragua. Grossman was born at Neustadt, Saxony, and educated in Moravian schools. After serving as pastoral assistant at Königsfeld and Niesky, he was ordained in 1899 and entered mission service in Bluefields, Nicaragua, in 1900. He served in Nicaragua from 1900 until poor health forced his retirement in 1937; he served as superintendent of the mission after 1914. He was consecrated a bishop at Bethlehem, Pennsylvania, in 1925 by six bishops of the Moravian Unity. Failing health led to his retirement in Kleinwelka, Germany, in 1937. He died at Dresden.

BIBLIOGRAPHY "The Bishop's Book" (MS in Moravian archives, Bethlehem, Pa.); see also correspondence with S. H. Gapp; J. T. Hamilton and K. G. Hamilton, *History of the Moravian Church* (1967); *The Moravian*, December 15, 1945.

Albert H. Frank

Grotius, Hugo (*or* Huigh de Groot) (1583-1645), Dutch jurist, Arminian theologian, and missions apologist. In 1618 Grotius was sent to prison for his Arminian theological sympathies, by order of the Calvinist Prince Maurice of Nassau, but he escaped and settled in Paris. He wrote juridical, political, and theological works. His most famous book, intended as a handbook for the use of Dutch sailors traveling to the Far East, is *De Veritate Religionis Christianae* (On the truth of the Christian religion, 1627). In this book Grotius gives evidence of the truth of the Christian religion and refutes paganism, Judaism, and Islam. He concludes his defense of Christianity with an admonition for all Christians to live simple, devout lives in peace and harmony. During his lifetime *De Veritate* was translated into English, French, and German; after his death 144 editions and translations were published, including an Arabic edition in 1660 and an Urdu edition in 1839. Richard *Baxter recommended the Arab translation to the East India Company. Grotius influenced his student and friend Peter *Heyling, a jurist, who in 1632 went to Egypt and Ethiopia, hoping to contribute to the renewal of the oriental Orthodox churches.

BIBLIOGRAPHY J. P. Heering, *Hugo de Groot als Apologeet van de Christelijke Godsdienst* (1992; includes a summary in English); *The World of Hugo Grotius (1583-1645)*, Proceedings of the International Colloquium Organized by the Grotius Committee of the Royal Netherlands Academy of Arts and Sciences, Rotterdam 6-9 April 1983 (1984).

Jan A. B. Jongeneel

Groves, A(nthony) N(orris) (1795-1853), founder of the so-called Plymouth Brethren. A dentist in Exeter, England, Groves volunteered to the Church Missionary Society but developed doubts about ordination and the state church. Instead, he moved among those who began to form less structured fellowships of believers. His active career as an independent missionary was somewhat unproductive. Four traumatic years in Baghdad, working in extremely adverse conditions (1829-1833), were followed by 20 years in India (1833-1853), where his attempts to work with existing missionaries were largely negated by his idealistic approach.

Groves's influence on an understanding of Christian mission, however, has been immense. A fundamental concept was literal obedience to the precepts of Jesus, as expounded in Groves's influential book *Christian Devotedness* (1825). He repudiated social and racial distinctions and all contrived methods of obtaining financial support, relying instead solely on prayer. His largely unsuccessful efforts to make his work self-supporting by growing cotton and sugar and by manufacturing silk have been seen by some as conflicting with this ideal; others see it as complementary. He clearly influenced his brother-in-law, George *Müller of orphanage fame, and James Hudson *Taylor.

Groves's suspicion of institutionalism became somewhat tempered by experience (e.g., he saw the value of providing basic education), but he always viewed evangelistic preaching as the core activity of Christian mission. His cultural sensitivity, allied to his humble spirit, enabled him to identify to an unusual degree with those he was endeavoring to evangelize.

In his lifetime, few adopted his methods, apart from an Indian disciple, Aroolappen, and a handful of English missionaries. Later, however, Brethren missionaries became a sizable proportion of the total Protestant missionary force, establishing churches—sometimes in large numbers—in well over a hundred countries, and his faith principle was adopted by many interdenominational faith missions. Groves died in the home of George Müller, while visiting England.

BIBLIOGRAPHY Groves published *Journals* (1832) describing his journey to Baghdad (1831) and his work there in 1830 and 1831.

His widow published *Memoir of A. N. Groves* (1856), and G. H. Lang has written two biographies: *Anthony Norris Groves* (1939) and *The History and Diaries of an Indian Christian (J. C. Aroolappen)* (1939). See also W. T. Stunt et al., *Turning the World Upside Down: A Century of Missionary Endeavor* (1972), pp. 15–31.

Harold H. Rowdon

Groves, Charles Pelham (1887–1973), church historian of Africa. Groves was born in Cambellport, Wisconsin, the son of a Methodist minister who moved to England in 1897 and thereafter became superintendent of the Countess of Huntingdon's Connexion in Sierra Leone. Charles studied at University College, Reading, and at the University of Manchester before entering the Primitive Methodist ministry. He was appointed to Eastern Nigeria in 1911 and from then until 1923 trained teachers and evangelists at the Oron Training Institute. Following a brief circuit ministry, he spent the years 1926 to 1954 (with the exception of a visiting professorship, from 1937 to 1939, at the Kennedy School of Mission at Hartford Seminary, Connecticut) in the Selly Oak Colleges, Birmingham, during the colleges' most influential period in ecumenical and mission studies. He was tutor at Kingsmead, the Methodist missionary college, both before and after the 1932 union of the Methodist churches, and professor of missions in the colleges from 1945. His first major book, *Jesus Christ and Primitive Need* (1934), explores the relation of Christianity ("The Christian message is not the submission of an idea; it is an announcement about a Person") to the worldviews current in primal, and especially African, societies. His magnum opus, *The Planting of Christianity in Africa* (4 vols., 1949–1958), was the first serious attempt at a full-scale African church history. Though it is inevitably missions centered, its scope is immense; it treats the entire continent and presents a continuous Christian history from New Testament times to the 1950s, making exhaustive use of the limited sources then available. It earned Grove the title "the Eusebius of Africa."

BIBLIOGRAPHY *Minutes and Yearbook of the Methodist Conference* (1973), pp. 143 ff.

Andrew F. Walls

Grubb, Kenneth George (1900–1980), Anglican layman, missionary explorer, and public servant. Grubb, born in Oxton, England, spent the years prior to World War II traveling and researching throughout Latin America, first on behalf of the Worldwide Evangelization Crusade, and then for the World Dominion Press. This unique experience led to his appointment as director of the Latin American section of the Ministry of Information, set up by the British government at the outbreak of World War II, and later to his promotion to Overseas Controller of the Ministry of Information, a position he held with growing influence and distinction until 1946. Two years earlier he had accepted the invitation of Canon Max *Warren to become president of the Church Missionary Society, supervising its development for the next quarter of a century. In 1946 Grubb was invited to become the first chairman of the Commission of the Churches on International Affairs, and in partnership with Federick Nolde he played a decisive role in the World Council of Churches throughout the period up to the fourth assembly in Uppsala in 1968. Later he added to his responsibilities by thrice accepting election as chairman of the House of Laity in the Assembly of the Church of England. He also continued to accept government assignments, as secretary general of the Hispanic and Luso-Brazilian Councils, and as chairman of the high level Committee on Strategic Studies in Britain. In recognition of his public service as well as his service to the church he was awarded a knighthood by the queen.

Grubb did not find personal relations easy. By temperament he was a loner, an authoritarian who found it difficult to suffer fools gladly. With his deep Christian convictions he battled successfully to overcome this throughout his public life. It may be said of him that he was probably the most influential Protestant layman in the world mission of the church in the postwar years.

BIBLIOGRAPHY Most of Grubb's voluminous publications are to be found in the archives of the CMS and WCC. Notable among these are the *World Christian Handbook*, successive issues of which he edited with E. J. Bingle and H. Wakelin Coxill from 1949 to 1968, *Amazon and Andes* (1930), *Parables from South America* (1932), *Advancing Church in Latin America* (1936), *A Layman Looks at the Church* (1964), and *Crypts of Power* (1971; an autobiography).

Paul R. Clifford

Grubb, Norman P(ercy) (1895–1993), leader of Worldwide Evangelization Crusade (WEC). Born in Bournemouth, England, the older brother of Kenneth *Grubb, Norman Grubb was active in Christian witness in his regiment during World War I, when he also received the Military Cross for meritorious action. He enrolled at Cambridge University and helped to establish InterVarsity Christian Fellowship in Britain. Marrying Pauline Studd, the daughter of C. T. *Studd, founder of WEC, Grubb served from 1920 to 1927 in the northern Belgian Congo (Zaire), where he helped translate the New Testament into Bangala. In 1928 he accepted responsibility for representing WEC in Britain, and after C. T. Studd's death in 1931, was appointed general secretary. Inheriting a faltering force of thirty missionaries and insufficient support, Grubb implemented a consensus style of leadership, introduced the "faith mission" basis of support for home-based personnel, and pressed for expansion. When he retired in 1965, WEC numbered 800 missionaries in twenty countries. With his personal encouragement, the Christian Literature Crusade, a sister mission, was founded in 1947.

Continuing his ministry as author and speaker in his later years, Grubb emphasized "union life" in Christ and is credited with helping many around the world find a richer spiritual life. From 1957 the Grubbs made their home on WEC property at Fort Washington, Pennsylvania, where his wife Pauline predeceased him in 1981.

BIBLIOGRAPHY Norman Grubb, *C. T. Studd: Cricketeer and Pioneer* (1946), *Jack Harrison, Successor to C. T. Studd* (1949), *Once*

Caught, No Escape (1969; his autobiography), and several works on "deeper life" themes.

Robert T. Coote

Grubb, W(ilfrid) Barbrooke (1865–1930), Anglican missionary and explorer in Paraguay. Born in Scotland in Liberton, Midlothian, Grubb was appointed by the South American Missionary Society (SAMS) as a lay catechist to a chaplaincy position in Keppel Island in the West Falkland Islands, where he arrived in 1886. Engaged to May Bridges, he could marry her only 12 years later, because in 1889 he was asked to move to Paraguay, then a little-known country with vast areas of unexplored territory. He first worked with the Lengua Indians, endeavoring to inculturate the gospel among them and to establish an indigenous church. His explorations lasted for more than 20 years, during which he traveled by horse an average of 25 kilometers (15 miles) per day. His interest in serving the Indians took him also to remote areas of Bolivia and Argentina where many Paraguayan Indians migrated in search of work. An expert in the cultures of the Lengua, Sanapana, Mataco, and Toba peoples, Grubb was called the Pacifier of the Indians. His writings made known in Europe the vast Chaco region of the American continent. His *Unknown People in an Unknown Land* (1910) became a classic description of the land and the people and a valuable source of geographic description and anthropological observation. In 1914 he returned to England in poor health but did deputation for SAMS until his death.

BIBLIOGRAPHY W. B. Grubb, *Church in the Wilds* (1914). N. J. Davidson, *Barbrooke Grubb Pathfinder* (1924); R. J. Hunt, *The Livingstone of South America: The Life of Barbrooke Grubb* (1933).

Samuel Escobar

Grüber, Johannes (1623–1680), Jesuit explorer of land routes to China. A native of St. Florian, Austria, Grüber entered the Society of Jesus in Vienna in 1641 and was ordained a priest in Graz in May 1655. In response to his request to be sent to the China mission, the superior general called him to Rome and instructed him to travel via the Middle East and the Silk Route to China. Not finding this possible, he followed the southern sea route via Surat, India, and Macao. In July 1658, ten months after his arrival in Macao, he received orders to go to Peking (Beijing) and proceed along a northern route to Europe. Again finding this impossible, Grüber left Peking in 1661 and went to Sian (Xi'an) to meet Albert *Dorville, and together they traveled via the western region of Sinkiang (Xinjiang), Tibet, and Nepal to Agra, India, where Dorville died. Grüber reached Hormuz by sea, went overland through the Middle East, and proceeded to Rome. Still intent on entering China via a northern land route, he traveled to Riga, Latvia, where he learned that the Russians would not issue him a transit visa. Traveling to Constantinople, he fell ill and returned to Italy. He became a military chaplain for two years and was a pastor at Tyrnau (or Trnava, in present day Slovenia) and at Trenčn until his death at Sárospatak, Hungary.

BIBLIOGRAPHY Johannes Grüber, *Notizie varie dell'imperio della Cina* (1687). Franz Braumann, ed., *Johannes Grueber als Kundschafter des Papstes nach China, 1656–1664: Die Erste Durchquerung Tibets* (1985); Athanasius Kircher, *China monumentis qua sacris qua profanis...* (1667), pp. 64–66; Cornelis Wessels, *Early Jesuit Travellers in Central Asia* (1924), pp. 164–204, and "New Documents Relating to the Journey of Fr. John Grueber," *Archivum Historicum Societatis Iesu* 9 (1940): 281–302; Bruno Zimmel, "Johann Grueber in China," *Biblos* 13 (1964): 161–188.

John W. Witek, SJ

Grundemann, Peter Reinhold (1836–1924), German mission scholar and publicist. A Protestant parish pastor from 1869 until his death, Grundemann was Gustav *Warneck's right hand in all aspects of mission studies and publications. This applied, first, to his coeditorship of *Allgemeine Missions-Zeitschrift* from 1874 until Warneck's death in 1910. Second, Grundemann became a self-taught but highly competent expert in mission statistics and a pioneer in mission geography and cartography. His *Allgemeiner Missionsatlas* (1866–1871) and a smaller edition published in 1886 remained unequaled for decades. Third, he gradually discovered his talent for writing popular mission literature and made extensive and successful use of it. As a scholar he gained a reputation for unrelenting criticism of unfounded propagandist claims in mission literature. Though not always welcome, it was effective because he applied it also in his own publications, especially in his revised edition of G. C. Burckhardt's popular *Kleine Missionsbibliothek* (4 vols., 1881), which was widely used but never replaced, and in a large number of contributions to *Allgemeine Missions-Zeitschrift.*

BIBLIOGRAPHY Julius Richter, "In piam memoriam," *NAMZ* 1 (1924): 210–216; Olav G. Myklebust, *The Study of Missions in Theological Education,* vol. 1 (1955), pp. 297–300. There is no biography of Grundemann.

Hans-Werner Gensichen

Gründler, Johann Ernst (1677–1720), German missionary of the Danish-Halle Mission at Tranquebar, South India. A senior colleague of Bartholomäus *Ziegenbalg, Gründler arrived in India in 1709 after working as a teacher in one of *Francke's schools at Halle. He devoted himself to the study of both Tamil and Portuguese. He became the first missionary ever to study indigenous Indian methods of healing, which he found described in a Tamil book and parts of which he translated into German (though it remained unpublished). He also had a way with children and put it to good use in the mission schools. Gründler shared the discontentment of his colleagues with the local Danish garrison commander. Yet in 1714 to 1716, when he was put in charge of the mission during Ziegenbalg's home leave, Gründler managed to improve relations with the authorities and also with the Dutch and British representatives in South India. In order to mitigate the social misery of converts, he experimented with a papermill as a means for providing jobs. But as it failed to pay its way, it had to be closed. Mission friends in Europe were concerned about Gründler's marriage to the wealthy widow of a Danish official, because it was interpreted as an offense against the pietist integrity of the mission. All this contributed to Gründler's early death. As Gründler had preached the sermon at Ziegenbalg's funeral in 1719, fellow-missionary Benjamin *Schultze preached the sermon at Gründler's funeral in 1720.

BIBLIOGRAPHY There is no biography of Gründler. However, see E. Arno Lehmann, *It Began at Tranquebar* (1956) and Anders Nørgaard, *Mission und Obrigkeit: Die Danisch-hallische Mission in Tranquebar 1706–1845* (1988).

Hans-Werner Gensichen

Gsell, Francis Xavier (1872–1960), Roman Catholic missionary bishop of northern Australia. Born in Alsace-Lorraine, Gsell became a Missionary of the Sacred Heart, studying at Rome's St. Apollinaire University before ordination in 1896. He arrived in Australia in 1897, at first teaching in Sydney. In 1900 he took up missionary work in Papua. Assigned in 1906 to Darwin as apostolic administrator of Australia's Northern Territory, he made the conversion of the Aboriginal people his lifelong goal. Obtaining a 10,000 acre grant, he established the Bathurst Island mission in 1912, living there until 1938. He studied Aboriginal language and culture and gained a deep understanding of the Tiwi people. He had a strategy of "buying" girls for his convent school to save them from polygamous marriages. He educated them and arranged their marriages to schooled young men who accepted monogamy. Nevertheless, Gsell held no illusions. He baptized hundreds of children but after 30 years claimed no adult convert. He was appointed bishop of Darwin in 1938 and established missions at Arltunga and Garden Point. Awarded both the Order of the British Empire and the Legion of Honor, he is best remembered for the title of his perceptive autobiography, *The Bishop with 150 Wives* (1954).

BIBLIOGRAPHY C. W. M. Hart and A. R. Pilling, *The Tiwi of North Australia* (1960).

John W. Harris

Gual, Pedro (1813–1890), Franciscan missionary who played a key role in restoring the church in Peru after independence. Born in Canet del Mar, Barcelona, Gual entered the novitiate in 1831. Expelled from Spain in 1835 with other Catholic clergy during anticlerical disturbances, he finished his studies in the Papal States. He left for Peru in 1845 and served as guardian of the newly reopened monastery of Santa Rosa of Ocopa in the central Andes. In 1852 he founded a hospice in Lima for incoming missionaries, which a year later became the missionary college of the discalced (members of barefooted religious orders) in Lima. Gual continued the work of Andrés *Herrero, the Franciscan who restored his order's missions in Peru and Bolivia after independence. He served as the delegated leader of the Franciscans in Peru, and later as superior of the Franciscan missionary colleges in Peru, Chile, Ecuador, Colombia, and Venezuela. In 1870 he represented archbishop Goyeneche of Lima at the first Vatican Council. A vigorous polemicist, he wrote tracts against Freemasonry and liberalism. He especially attacked the ideas of Francisco de Paula González Vigil, a Peruvian priest who was excommunicated for proposing the creation of a national Catholic church.

BIBLIOGRAPHY Jeffrey Klaiber, *The Catholic Church in Peru, 1821–1985* (1992); Odorico Sáiz, *Restauración de la Orden Franciscana en el Perú en el siglo XIX* (1993).

Jeffrey Klaiber, SJ

Gubernatis, Dominicus de (c. 1620–1690), Franciscan mission historian. Gubernatis was born in Sospitello in the diocese of Turin, Italy. He joined the order of the Strict Observants of the Franciscan family, and served as a lecturer of sacred theology and as a chronicler of the whole order. He planned to write thirty-five volumes, entitled *Orbis Seraficus*, on the history of the three branches of the Franciscan Order. He completed five of them, the fifth being on the missions. The sixth and final volume (the remainder were never undertaken) was published in 1886 on the basis of his notes; it continued the mission history up to 1622. Gubernatis was not only a historian of missions; he also provided an exposition on mission theory, in which he systematically followed his contemporary Cardinal *Brancati de Laurea (1612–1693). Both belonged to a group of pioneer missiologists of the seventeenth century. Gubernatis's history of the Franciscan missions is especially valuable because he could make use of the then still-existing archives of the Franciscan Order at the Ara Coeli monastery in Rome.

BIBLIOGRAPHY Dominicus de Gubernatis, *Orbis Seraficus*, vol. 5 (1689), vol. 6 (1886). See also Ronan Hoffman, *Pioneer Theories of Missiology: A Comparative Study of the Mission Theories of Cardinal Brancati de Laurea, OFM Conv., with Those of Three of His Contemporaries: José de Acosta SJ, Thomas a Jesu O.Carm., and Dominicus de Gubernatis OFM* (1960).

Arnulf Camps, OFM

Gudwal (*or* Gurwal; Gurvalus) (d. c. 640), English missionary in Brittany. The sources for Gudwal's life credit him with the founding of a monastery at Plec, on the isle of Locoal-Mendon, Brittany. He also seems to be responsible for church settlements as far west as Guer. Some sources say he was the regional bishop at Alet, but claims that he was the earliest bishop of Saint-Malo appear to be incorrect.

BIBLIOGRAPHY F. Duine, *S. Gudwal, évêque et confesseur* (1934).

Frederick W. Norris

Guébriant, Jean-Baptiste Budes de (1860–1935), missionary bishop and promoter of the indigenous Catholic Church in China. Born in Paris, de Guébriant joined the Paris Foreign Mission Society (PFMS) in 1883 and two years later was ordained and sent to China. In 1910 he became the first vicar apostolic of Kientchang (Xichang), Szechwan (Sichuan) Province, and then was moved to the seat of Canton (Guangzhou) in 1916. In 1918 he was one of six missionary bishops selected by Cardinal Van *Rossum, prefect of the Propaganda Fide, to answer a questionnaire on the situation of the church in China. In the November 1919 encyclical *Maximum illud* from Pope *Benedict XV, several directives echo points made by de Guébriant: for instance, choosing heads of mission with good leadership skills, improving the language proficiency of missionaries, forming a native clergy on a par with foreign missionaries, and freeing the Catholic Church in China of its foreign character. Van Rossum also followed up on two other recommendations made by de Guébriant: sending an apostolic visitor to tour all the China missions, and naming a permanent representative of the Holy See in Peking (Beijing). In July 1919 de Guébriant found himself appointed apostolic visitor *in missiones sinensis,* and in August 1922 Archbishop Celso *Costantini was appointed the Vatican's first apostolic delegate to China.

Following a reorganization of the PFMS in accordance with the Code of Canon Law promulgated by the Holy See in 1917, in 1921 de Guébriant became the first to assume the responsibility of superior general of his society. During his 14-year term, he ended his society's monopoly over large mission fields by partitioning them and inviting other missionary groups to assume the evangelization of some of these smaller territories. He also began implementing the policy that missioners who were pioneers should move on once a local church had been established in a particular place. Two high points of his life were viewing the ordination of the first six Chinese bishops in Rome by Pope *Pius XI (1926) and joining Archbishop Costantini at the Temple of Heaven in Peking in reciting the *Pater Noster* (1932).

BIBLIOGRAPHY Celso Costantini, "Monseigneur J. Budes de Guébriant," *Collectanea Commissionis Synodalis* 8 (April 1935): 329–331; Antoine Flachère, *Monseigneur de Guébriant. Le Missionnaire* (1946); Société des Missions-Etrangères de Paris, *Compte-rendu annuel des travaux de 1935* (1935), pp. 244–262. For an analysis of the important roles played by de Guébriant, see introductions in Claude Soetens, ed., *Recueil des Archives Vincent Lebbe. Pour l'Eglise chinoise,* vol. 1, *La Visite apostolique des missions de Chine, 1919–1920* (1982), vol. 2, *Un Nonciature à Pékin en 1918?* (1983), and vol. 3, *L'Encyclique Maximum illud* (1983). Numerous articles on and by de Guébriant can be found in issues of *Field Afar* between 1918 and 1935.

Jean-Paul Wiest

Guerrant, Edward Owings (1838–1916), Presbyterian minister, medical doctor, and missionary to Appalachia. Born in Sharpsburg, Kentucky, Guerrant attended Centre College, 1859–1860, and Danville Seminary, 1860–1861. During the Civil War, Guerrant left the seminary to join General Humphrey Marshall's Kentucky forces. Following the war, he studied medicine at Jefferson Medical College in Philadelphia and Bellevue Hospital Medical College in New York. He then returned to Kentucky, where he established a medical practice and in 1868 married Mary Jane DeVault. In 1873 Guerrant became ill with typhoid fever. Recovering, he vowed to devote the rest of his life to the gospel ministry. He enrolled at Union Theological Seminary in Virginia and was licensed in 1875. He served three small churches in Kentucky before he was called to First Presbyterian Church of Louisville, where he ministered from 1879 to 1882. From his position as chair of the Synod of Kentucky's Committee of Home Missions, Guerrant aroused the church to the spiritual and social plight of the people of Appalachia. In 1882 he resigned his pastorate to become an evangelist in the southern highlands, where he built several churches. In 1897 he organized the Society of Soul Winners: American Inland Mission, which issued a monthly publication, *The Soul Winner,* beginning in 1902. By 1913, his organization operated seventeen schools and mission stations and an orphanage, and employed fifty missionaries.

BIBLIOGRAPHY Edward O. Guerrant, *The Soul Winner* (1896), *The Galax Gatherers* (1910), *The Gospel of the Lilies* (1912), and, as editor, *The Soul Winner* (1902–1913). Martha B. Crowe, "'A Mission in the Mountains': E. O. Guerrant and Southern Appalachia, 1839–1916," *Journal of Presbyterian History* 68 (1990): 46–54; J. Gray McAllister and Grace Owings Guerrant, *Edward O. Guerrant: Apostle of the Southern Highlands* (1950); Louis B. Weeks, *Kentucky Presbyterians* (1983).

Robert Benedetto

Guinness, Henry Grattan (1835–1910), British evangelist, author, and missionary trainer. Born in Dublin of a nonconformist family related to the wealthy brewers of the same name, Guinness briefly studied theology and then, in 1857, became an independent evangelist of the second Evangelical Awakening. He spent 15 years traveling and preaching in Britain, Europe, and North America. In 1860 he married Fanny Fitzgerald, which strengthened his Plymouth Brethren ties. She traveled with him and also became a well-known speaker. As friends and supporters of James Hudson *Taylor, they offered to go with him to China but were refused on account of their age. In 1872 the Guinnesses settled in East London and founded Harley College, a training institute for missionaries; later a northern branch was established at Cliff House, Derbyshire. Their interest in the Congo led to the founding of the Livingstone Inland Mission (1878) and later the Congo and Balolo Mission (1889), which became the Regions Beyond Missionary Union. In 1878 Guinness published *The Approaching End of the Age,* the first of several books by him on prophecy, eschatology, world history, and Zionism that led to new demands for him to speak on biblical prophecy. His wife died in 1898. In 1903 he married Grace Hurditch (b. 1878), who bore him two more sons. They traveled widely for five years and on their return settled in Bath. He became involved with the affairs of the Congo Reform Association, visiting the Congo in 1910, shortly before his death. All four surviving children of his first marriage worked as missionaries overseas: his daughter Geraldine, a prolific writer, married Hudson Taylor's son Howard; Lucy married Karl *Kumm, founder of the

Sudan United Mission; G(ershom) Whitfield Guinness also served with the CIM; and Harry Guinness worked with the Congo and Balolo Mission.

BIBLIOGRAPHY Henry Grattan Guinness, *Light for the Last Days* (1886), *The Divine Programme of World History* (1888), *Key to the Apocalypse* (1899), and *On This Rock* (1909). Michelle Guinness, *The Guinness Legend* (1990); J. Edwin Orr, *The Second Evangelical Awakening in Britain* (1949). See also Joy Guinness, *Mrs. Howard Taylor: Her Web of Time* (1949; biography of Mary Geraldine [Guinness] Taylor).

Jocelyn Murray

Gulick, Alice (Gordon) (1847–1903), American missionary in Spain and founder of the Instituto Internacional. Born in Boston, Alice Gordon graduated from Mount Holyoke College in 1867 and married William Hooker Gulick in 1871. Commissioned to work in Spain by the American Board of Commissioners for Foreign Missions (ABCFM) and the Congregational Woman's Board of Missions, the couple served in Santander beginning in 1872 and gained great acceptance among the poor and among upper-class liberals, but experienced intense opposition from Roman Catholic clergy. Alice started a boarding school in 1877. Relocated to San Sebastián in 1881, it was incorporated in 1892 as the International Institute for Girls in Spain. Modeled after Mount Holyoke, the school became highly respected when its graduates performed with distinction at the University of Madrid. During the Spanish-American War (1898), the Gulicks moved to Biarritz, France, and in 1899 they returned to the United States, where Alice became dean of women for Cuban teachers at Harvard College. In 1901 they returned to Biarritz, and she founded the International Institute in Madrid. Sponsored by a special corporation and league in the United States, it became an intellectual center that influenced the modernization of Spanish education during the twentieth century. Alice died in London and was buried in Madrid.

BIBLIOGRAPHY Elizabeth Putnam Gordon, *Alice Gordon Gulick: Her Life and Work in Spain* (1917); Carmen de Zulueta, *Misioneras, feministas, educadoras. Historia del Instituto Internacional* (1984).

Samuel Escobar

Gulick, Luther Halsey (1828–1891) *and* **Louisa Mitchell (Lewis)** (1830–1894), Congregational missionaries in many fields. One of seven missionary sons of American Board of Commissioners for Foreign Missions (ABCFM) missionaries Peter and Fanny *Gulick, Luther Gulick was born in Honolulu and educated in the United States; he received an M.D. from the New York College of Physicians and Surgeons in 1850. He attended lectures at Union Theological Seminary, engaged in city missionary work, and was also ordained in that year. In 1851 he married Louisa Lewis, who had taught in North Carolina and done city missionary work in New York. Within a month they sailed for Micronesia as missionaries of the ABCFM. En route Luther organized in Honolulu the Hawaiian Mission Children's Society, which became a major factor in Hawaiian development and support of the Micronesia Mission. With Albert and Susan Surges and a Hawaiian couple, the Kaaikaulas, the Gulicks were stationed on Ponape in the Caroline Islands, where they established churches and schools and did medical work. In 1854 Luther countered a smallpox epidemic with a vaccine he cultured in himself from an active case. Louisa translated a language primer into Ponapean. In 1859 they were transferred to Ebon, in the Marshall Islands, but for health reasons returned to the United States, where Luther proved a popular and effective missionary speaker. In 1863 he became secretary of the newly organized Hawaiian Evangelical Association, successor to the ABCFM Sandwich Islands Mission. In 1871 he founded an ABCFM mission in Spain in which two of his brothers served; after investigation it was concluded that a similar venture in Italy would be inadvisable. In 1875 he became Far East agent for the American Bible Society, located first in Yokohama and then in Shanghai. He edited the *Chinese Recorder and Missionary Journal* (1885–1889) and founded the *Medical Missionary Journal*. Luther Gulick died at Springfield, Massachusetts, Louisa Gulick at Kobe, Japan.

BIBLIOGRAPHY John Garrett, *To Live among the Stars* (1982), pp. 139–142; Albertine Loomis, *To All People* (1970), pp. 53–77; *Missionary Album* (1969), pp. 106–107; *Missionary Herald* 87 (1891): 237–239. Gulick wrote "Notes on the Grammar of the Ponape Dialect" in *Journal of the American Oriental Society* 10 (1872).

David M. Stowe

Gulick, Orramel Hinckley (1830–1923) *and* **Ann Eliza (Clark)** (1833–1938), American missionaries in Hawaii and Japan. Son of pioneer Sandwich Islands missionaries, Peter and Fanny *Gulick, Orramel was educated at Punahou School and began missionary service under the American Board of Commissioners for Foreign Missions (ABCFM) on the *Morning Star*, which provided transportation for the Micronesia mission. He was ordained in 1862 and stationed first at Waiohinu on Hawaii, then on Oahu, where he founded the Kaumakapili Church and he and his wife established a female boarding school. Ann Clark had also been born in Hawaii, daughter of missionaries Ephraim and Mary *Clark. She was educated at Punahou School, spent two years at Mount Holyoke College, and married Gulick in 1855.

In 1870 the Gulicks were sent to Japan, the second couple of the ABCFM mission to arrive there. They worked in Kobe from 1871 to 1883, then transferred to Nugata in the North Japan mission. In 1893 they visited the United States, then settled in Hawaii for ministry to the Japanese, who were pouring into the islands to work on the plantations. Orramel was continued on the Japan Mission roster until 1896. Both died in Honolulu, Ann at the age of 105.

Gulick was by coincidence associated with the revocation of Japan's proscription of Christianity. Ishikawa, his language tutor, was arrested with his wife in 1871 for aiding in Scripture translation and died in prison of neglect a year later, the first Japanese Protestant martyr. During that time a high-level commission from Japan visited the

West, seeking abolition of the extraterritorial privileges granted when Japan was forced open. The American secretary of state indicated that American citizens could not be subject to Japanese law as long as laws against Christianity were in force. To rebut the claim that there was no religious persecution, the Ishikawa case was cited, and in 1873 the proscription was ended. Gulick founded the first Christian newspaper in Japan in 1875, the weekly *Shichi-Ichi Zappo*. In 1918 the Gulicks published a history, *The Pilgrims of Hawaii.*

BIBLIOGRAPHY ABCFM annual reports; Fred Field Goodsell, *They Lived Their Faith* (1961), pp. 24–25; 367–368; *Missionary Herald* 119 (1922): 149.

David M. Stowe

Gulick, Peter Johnson (1797–1877) *and* **Fanny Hinckley (Thomas)** (1798–1883), American missionaries to Hawaii, progenitors of five generations of missionaries. Born in New Jersey, Peter Gulick graduated from Princeton College (1825) and Princeton Theological Seminary (1827). A few months later he married Fanny Thomas, was ordained and sailed with the third company of the Sandwich Islands Mission of the American Board of Commissioners for Foreign Missions (ABCFM). They were stationed at Waimea, Kauai (1828–1835), Koloa (1835–1843), and Kaluaaha (1843–1846), where he was superintendent of Molokai schools. After a final decade at Waialua, Oahu, they undertook self-support by ranching near Honolulu in 1857. In 1874 they went to live with their son, Orramel, a missionary at Kobe, Japan.

At age 27 Fanny was converted under the preaching of Charles G. Finney and worked in the early Sabbath Schools in New York City. In Hawaii she taught women sewing and began a home industry in the plaiting of straw from sugar cane blossoms into hats and bonnets. Her primary efforts were focused on rearing a family of seven sons and a daughter, six of whom became missionaries of the ABCFM, and one a tent-making missionary in Japan (another died at age 20). Luther served in Micronesia, Hawaii, Spain, Italy, and China; Orramel in Hawaii and Japan; William and Thomas in Spain; Julia and Theodore in Japan; along with their brother John Thomas, who combined educational work with active study and publication in the field of conchology, making significant contributions to the development of evolutionary theory and its ultimate acceptance in religious circles. A grandson, Sydney L. Gulick, served as a missionary in Japan and later became the first race relations secretary of the Federal Council of Churches. In 1993 a great-great-granddaughter was serving in Thailand as a fifth-generation missionary under the United Church Board for World Ministries, successor of the ABCFM.

BIBLIOGRAPHY Fred Field Goodsell, *They Lived Their Faith* (1961), pp. 173ff.; Addison Gulick, *John Thomas Gulick: Evolutionist and Missionary* (1932); Sydney L. Gulick, *The White Peril in the Far East* (1905); *Missionary Album* (1969), pp. 110–111; *Missionary Herald* 74 (1878): 203; 75 (1879): 103; 79 (1883): 296–297.

David M. Stowe

Gulliford, Henry (1852–1937), Wesleyan missionary in India. Born in Dunster, England, Gulliford entered the Wesleyan Methodist ministry in 1876 from Didsbury College, Manchester. Stationed in Mysore from 1877 to 1937, he raised standards in high schools (1878–1903) and saw the beginning of effective training of indigenous ministers. From 1892 he was editor of *Harvest Field, Orithanta Patrike,* and *Bodhaha Bodhini* (Kanarese periodicals) and sometime editor of *Vrittanta Patrike.* He was appointed secretary of the Christian Literature Society, Madras (1903–1908), and was awarded the Kaiser-i-Hind medal in 1916 for these services. He integrated the former Basel Mission work in the Nilgiri Hills into the Methodist District (1919) and was secretary of the committee seeking South India church union. Esteem for his ministry is reflected in his having been twice named chairman of the Provincial Synod (in 1907 and in 1927). His publications include *Handbook of Wesleyan Methodism* (1910) and *Methodist Law and Discipline* (1925).

BIBLIOGRAPHY G. G. Findlay and W. W. Holdsworth, *The History of the Wesleyan Methodist Missionary Society,* vol. 5 (1924); a popular appreciation of Gulliford's work giving a broad overview of his achievements in India appeared after his death in the periodical *The Kingdom Overseas* (July 1937); and *List of Missionaries (Methodist Mission, Mysore District), 1821–1933.* Official correspondence, a set of *Harvest Field,* and *Mysore District Reports,* 1930 and 1933–1947, are held in the Methodist Missionary Society archives at the library, SOAS, Univ. of London.

M. Joy Fox

Gundert, Hermann (1814–1893), German mission publisher and linguist in South India. Gundert was born in Stuttgart. His father was a leader of the Württemberg Bible Society and a key early supporter of the Basel Mission (BM). After receiving his doctorate in Tübingen, Gundert went to Tamil Nadu, India, in 1836 as tutor to the children of A. N. *Groves, an independent English missionary. In 1838 he joined the BM in India, without any training in the mission seminary in Switzerland (an occurence unique in BM's nineteenth-century history). Relocating to Kerala, he became an internationally respected authority on the Malayalam language. He typically insisted that missionaries concern themselves with the whole language and culture, not merely with a sanitized or Christianized segment.

After a short interlude in Indian government service as inspector of schools, Gundert returned to Europe in 1859. He was appointed head of the Calwer Verlag, a publishing house in the northern Black Forest area of Germany that specialized in missionary and pietist literature. On his retirement, he was succeeded in this office by his son-in-law, Johannes Hesse, the father of the poet and novelist Hermann Hesse.

In Kerala, Gundert's reputation as scholar of, and writer in, the Malayalam language is still strong in all religious communities. His German and Malayalam works have been reprinted in recent years. The centenary of his death was celebrated in Kerala and in Stuttgart by notable international and multireligious conferences on his life and work.

BIBLIOGRAPHY Albrecht Frenz and Scaria Zacharia, *Dr. Hermann Gundert and Malayalam Language* (1993).

Paul Jenkins

Gunning, Jan Willem (1862–1923), Dutch missions educator and administrator. Gunning was a minister of the Netherlands Reformed Church at Eerbeek (1886–1896), director of the Mission House at Rotterdam (1897–1913), and secretary of the Netherlands Mission Society (1897–1923). An influential missionary statesman, he helped establish the Mission Consulate at Batavia (now Djakarta) in 1906, the Mission Study Council in the Netherlands in 1909, and the Mission House at Oegstgeest in 1917. He also trained many missionaries, including Hendrik *Kraemer. Placing the Dutch missionary enterprise in a worldwide perspective, he pleaded for national and international cooperation in missions and established collaboration among the main mission societies in the Netherlands. He improved the training of missionaries at the Mission House. He also emphasized the need for education in the indigenous churches of the Dutch East Indies in preparation for their independence. Western patterns of theological thinking, he urged, should not be transplanted by missionaries to native churches in the non-Western world.

BIBLIOGRAPHY Gunning published much in Dutch but only one article in English: "Government, Islam, and Missions in the Dutch East Indies," *IRM* 7 (1917): 209–220. A. den Besten, "God Werkt . . . daarom Moeten Wij ook Werken: een Onderzoek naar het Missiologisch Denken van Dr. Jan Willem Gunning (1862–1923)" (M.Th. thesis, Utrecht Univ. 1990, with bibliography and a summary in English); H. M. van Nes, *Vijftig Jaren Zending "Oegstgeest" (1897–1947)* (1948), pp. 15–131; S. C. Graaf van Randwijck, *Handelen en Denken in Dienst der Zending: Oegstgeest, 1897–1942,* vol. 1 (1981), pp. 47–62.

Jan A. B. Jongeneel

Gurney, Samuel (1860–1924), pioneer Methodist medical missionary in Zimbabwe. Gurney was born at Long Branch, New Jersey. After receiving his education for ministry at the New York Missionary Training School and Drew Theological Seminary, he was ordained in 1891 in the New York East Conference of the Methodist Episcopal Church. While serving pastorates in New York and Connecticut, he earned an M.D. at Yale University (1901). From 1903 until his death, except for two furloughs, he served as a Methodist church superintendent and medical missionary in Southern Rhodesia (Zimbabwe). As a result of his medical ministry, chiefs Mutasa and Mangwende became supporters of mission work in their areas. Initially, "Everyone was against him," one white settler related; a government official once told him, "We have been spared two evils—cattle sickness and missionaries." But Gurney persevered and led in establishing new centers of the church's work at Nyakatsapa (1907), Mrewa (1909), Mtoko (1915), and Nyadiri (1923).

He was a catalyst in a partnership of government and church in health services that began in the colonial era of Southern Rhodesia and continues in Zimbabwe today. His openness in working cooperatively with all was recognized as he chaired the Southern Rhodesia Missionary Conference (1922–1924). He died in Salisbury.

BIBLIOGRAPHY Henry I. James, *Missions in Rhodesia under the Methodist Episcopal Church, 1898–1934* (1935).

Norman E. Thomas

Gusinde, Martin (1886–1969), German Catholic anthropologist and missionary in Chile. Born in Breslau, Silesia (present-day Wroclaw, Poland), Gusinde studied at the Divine Word mission seminary in Mödling, near Vienna. Ordained in 1911, he was sent by the Society of the Divine Word to Chile, where he taught physiology and biology at the Liceo Alemán in Santiago. His primary interest, however, was the study of the cultures, languages, and racial traits of South American Indians. He became a curator at the national museum in Santiago and soon became known as a capable field researcher. He is best known for his fieldwork among the remnants of the almost extinct Ona Indians in Tierra del Fuego. His four field trips to Tierra del Fuego (1918–1924) included his initiation into the tribe and an important discovery of the Indians' belief in a supreme being. On his return to Austria, he completed his doctoral studies in anthropology at the University of Vienna (1926), basing his thesis on his Tierra del Fuego field notes. The subsequent publication (in 1937, 1938, and 1939) of three large volumes reporting on his expeditions won him world recognition. He worked as an associate of Wilhelm *Schmidt on the editoral staff of Schmidt's ethnological and linguistic journal *Anthropos,* and later as his assistant at the ethnological mission museum in Rome. Except for a professorship at the Catholic University of America (1948–1957), he devoted the rest of his professional life to worldwide ethnographic, linguistic, and anthropometric field research, writing, and lecturing.

BIBLIOGRAPHY Of Gusinde's more than 200 publications, the most important are his three *Die Feuerland-Indianer* volumes: *Die Selk'nam* (1931), *Die Yamana* (1937), and *Anthropologie der Feuerland-Indianer* (1939). Of special missionary interest is *Die völkerkundliche Ausrüstung des Missions* ("Ethnological Preparation for Missionaries," 1958). For biographical information and an evaluation see Fritz Bornemann, *P. Martin Gusinde 1886–1969* (1971). For a listing of Gusinde's publications, see Wilhelm Saake, *Verzeichnis von Beiträgen zur Anthropologie, 1916–1966* (1966). Archival materials are preserved at the SVD Mödling mission seminary, at Anthropos Institute, Sankt Augustin, Germany, and at the SVD Generalate in Rome.

Louis J. Luzbetak, SVD

Gutmann, Bruno (1876–1966), missionary ethnographer in East Africa. A native of Dresden, Saxony, Gutmann had a difficult childhood before he applied for admission to the Leipzig Mission seminary. At Leipzig he came under the influence of diverse social science theories that helped him to form a social philosophy of his own and later supplied the motivation for ethnographic research.

Gutmann served as a missionary from 1902 to 1938 among the Chagga people in the Kilimanjaro area of what is now Tanzania and became justly famous for his studies on Chagga religion, society, and customs, which remained unsurpassed in spite of their methodological shortcomings. Gutmann attempted to identify ethnic "life power" among the Chagga as determinative for the incorporation of tribal "primeval links" into the community of Christ. As a corollary, he expressed violent opposition to the power of modern civilization, fearing that it would destroy the tribal order of creation which, in his view, had not been affected by human sin. While his ideas proved successful in the congregations at Old Moshi and its surroundings, they could not but lead to misgivings regarding the encounter of Chagga Christians with the postwar world. As he was unable to return to Africa during 28 years of retirement, much as he wished to do so, he had no opportunity to adjust his views to changed conditions.

BIBLIOGRAPHY Among Gutmann's major works are *Dichten und Denken der Dschagganeger* (1909), *Das Dschaggaland und seine Christen* (1925), *Christusleib und Nächstenschaft* (1931), and *Die Stammeslehren der Dschagga,* 3 vols. (1932, 1935, 1938). The preferred modern account of Gutmann and his work is J. C. Winter, *Bruno Gutmann, 1876–1966: A German Approach to Social Anthropology* (1979). See also Ernst Jäschke, *Bruno Gutmann: His Life, His Thoughts, and His Work* (1985), and Jäschke's essay in Gerald H. Anderson et al., eds., *Mission Legacies* (1994), pp. 173–180.

Hans-Werner Gensichen

Gützlaff, Karl Friedrich August (1803–1851), pioneer Protestant missionary in China. Born in a pietist family in Pomerania, Gützlaff received missionary training in Johann *Jänicke's mission institute in Berlin and under the auspices of the Dutch Mission Society. Having met Robert *Morrison in London, he decided to learn Chinese and began to work among expatriate Chinese in Java and Siam, where he also acquired some medical skill. As an interpreter and medical practitioner Gützlaff made three journeys along the China coast between 1831 and 1833, which were decisive for the following years. In 1833 he succeeded in entering mainland China as a free-lance missionary, and he remained through 1839. He saw to it that accounts of his activities were published far and wide in the West, where they received an enthusiastic reception. After conflicts with Chinese authorities he found a new opening as a Chinese-language secretary in British diplomatic services. He also began a translation of the Bible into Chinese and devoted himself to recruiting and training Chinese assistants and tract distributors. He supported the formation of a Chinese evangelization society that was mainly Chinese led and that, in his opinion, represented a significant step toward the evangelization of all of China. Due to lack of supervision and material support, the enterprise collapsed before Gützlaff's death (in China), but it was eventually taken over by other mission associations. Gützlaff has rightly been called the grandfather of the China Inland Mission later established by J. Hudson *Taylor.

BIBLIOGRAPHY The Swedish scholar Herman Schlyter has written two definitive studies of Gützlaff's life and achievements: *Karl Gützlaff als Missionar in China* (1946) and *Der China-Missionar Karl Gützlaff und seine Heimatbasis* (1956). A careful assessment of his importance for medical missions will be found in Christoffer H. Grundmann, *Gesandt zu heilen* (1992), pp. 130–143.

Hans-Werner Gensichen

Gwynne, Llewellyn Henry (1863–1957), Church Missionary Society (CMS) missionary and bishop in Sudan. A native of Wales, Gwynne was ordained in 1886 after studies at London College of Divinity. In 1899, amid continuing British indignation surrounding the death in Sudan of General Charles "Khartoum" Gordon, Gwynne was sent as a missionary to Sudan under the CMS's Gordon Memorial Sudan Mission. British officials, however, were unwilling to allow direct evangelization among Sudanese Muslims. Made chaplain to British forces in Sudan, Gwynne displayed an unpretentious style that won favor, and he succeeded in establishing girls' schools open to Muslims and Christians alike. Named archdeacon of the Sudan in 1905, he oversaw the founding of the first CMS mission in southern Sudan, and in 1908 he became suffragan bishop of Khartoum. He served in France during World War I and became deputy chaplain-general to the British forces. In 1920 he was named the first "Bishop in Egypt and the Sudan," his diocese stretching from the Mediterranean to Uganda and from Darfur to Aden. Under his initiative, cathedrals were constructed in Khartoum and Cairo. Inspired as much by Gordon's writings as by the Bible, Gwynne became a venerable symbol of British Christianity in North Africa. He retired in 1946 and returned to England.

BIBLIOGRAPHY Numerous articles and sermons by Gwynne are contained in *The Sudan Diocesan Review.* H. C. Jackson, *Pastor on the Nile, Being Some Account of the Life and Letters of Llewellyn H. Gwynne* (1960); Brian de Saram, *Nile Harvest: The Anglican Church in Egypt and the Sudan,* privately published (1992). Most of Gwynne's papers are held at the CMS archives (Acc. 18), Birmingham Univ. Library, Birmingham, England. A smaller collection is located at the Sudan archive, Univ. of Durham, England.

Marc R. Nikkel

H

Hadfield, Octavius (1814–1904), British missionary and bishop in New Zealand. Hadfield was born at Bonchurch, Isle of Wight, England. He was ordained a deacon in Sydney in 1838 and a priest at Paihia, New Zealand, in 1839. Despite chronic ill health, he pioneered Church Missionary Society work along the Kapiti coast, acting as teacher and peacemaker, and becoming archdeacon of Kapiti in 1849. He defended Maori land rights against aggressive colonial settlement, writing three strongly worded pamphlets in 1860 and 1861 appealing for justice. In 1870 he became second bishop of Wellington and was increasingly absorbed in colonial church affairs. From 1890 until his retirement in 1893, he was Anglican primate of New Zealand.

BIBLIOGRAPHY Christopher Lethbridge, *The Wounded Lion: Octavius Hadfield, 1814–1904: Pioneer Missionary, Friend of the Maori, and Primate of New Zealand* (1993); Barbara MacMorran, *Octavius Hadfield* (1971).

Allan K. Davidson

Hagenauer, Friedrich August (1829–1909), German Moravian missionary among Australian Aborigines. Born in Saxony and trained at Herrnhut, the Moravian missionary center, Hagenauer was ordained in 1858. He accompanied F. W. Spiesecke when Spiesecke returned to Australia for a second attempt to found a Moravian mission, and in 1859 they began the Ebenezer mission on the Wimmera River in northwest Victoria. They learned the Wotjabaluk language and opened a school. Several Aborigines were converted, the first, Nathanael Pepper, becoming Hagenauer's protégé and lifelong associate. In 1861, Christiana Knobloch arrived from Germany to marry Hagenauer. Invited by the Presbyterians, the couple opened the Ramahyuck mission at Lake Wellington, Gippsland (eastern Victoria), in 1863, striving to develop a model Christian village and replacing traditional customs with European practices. Many Aborigines accepted Hagenauer's autocratic paternalism, relinquishing their freedom in order to survive in a hostile colonial world. A church was opened and two converts were baptized in 1866; fifty-one had been baptized by 1875.

Hagenauer's apparent success led to his appointment as secretary of the Aborigines' Protection Board, overseeing implementation of its oppressive rules. Some Ramahyuck residents respected him, but others resented his interference in their lives. Ruling Ramahyuck for a half century, Hagenauer was among the first of Australia's many loyal Moravian missionaries, but his attempt to serve two masters marred his achievement.

BIBLIOGRAPHY John Harris, *One Blood* (1990); A. Massola, *Aboriginal Mission Stations in Victoria* (1970).

John W. Harris

Hahn, Carl Hugo (1818–1895), pioneer German missionary in Namibia. Born in Riga, Latvia, Hahn was converted as a young man and in 1842 was sent to South-West Africa (Namibia) by the Rhenish Mission. As a pioneer missionary, strongly supported by his English wife, Emma (Hone), he studied the language and compiled the first Herero grammar. After almost 20 years of fruitless missionary effort, he developed a small missionary community of laypeople and African Christians, a so-called mission colony at Otjimbingue, where he also opened a theological seminary in 1868. He invited the Finnish Missionary Society to take up mission work among the Ambo tribes in northern Namibia. During his missionary career Hahn developed a more decidedly Lutheran orientation and laid the foundations for the establishment of a Lutheran church in Namibia. In 1873 he left the mission and became the pastor of a German Lutheran Congregation in Cape Town, where he died.

BIBLIOGRAPHY C. H. Hahn, *Tagebücher, 1837–1860* (1895). Theo Sundermeier, *Mission, Bekenntnis und Kirche. Missionstheologische Probleme des 19. Jh. bei C. H. Hahn* (1962).

Theo Sundermeier

Hahn, Heinrich (1800–1882), Catholic missions advocate. Born in Aachen, Germany, Hahn became a physician and devoted his life to public service and charitable work. He remained a layperson all his life and distinguished himself by zealously promoting mission awareness among the German people. His efforts found particular support from Cardinal Johannes von Geissel of Cologne, whose annual Lenten pastoral letters spoke of the missionary obligation of all Christians. In 1842 Hahn founded the Francis Xavier Mission Society (*Franziskus-Xaverius-Verein*) in Germany, known after 1922 as the Pontifical Work of the Propagation of the Faith (*Päpstliches Werk der Glaubensverbreitung*) and today as Missio. Between 1857 and 1863 he published a five-volume history of the church's missionary activity, the first work of its kind in scope. Narrative in style and not particularly accurate as history, the work nevertheless reflects the missionary spirit prevalent in the nineteenth century. He also published a short exposition of the history of missions in China.

BIBLIOGRAPHY Heinrich Hahn, *Geschichte der katholischen Missionen seit Jesus Christus bis auf die neueste Zeit für Mitglieder der katholischen Missions-Vereine und alle Freunde der Missionen* (1857–1863). F. Bäumker, *Dr. med. Heinrich Hahn, ein Apostel im Leienkleide, 1800–1882* (1930); R. Streit, *Die katholische deutsche Missionsliteratur: Die geschichtliche Entwicklung der katholischen Missionsliteratur in deutschen Landen von Beginn des 19. Jahrhunderts bis zur Gegenwart* (1925).

Stephen B. Bevans, SVD

Haines, Byron Lee (1928–1990), Presbyterian missionary in Pakistan. Trained at McCormick Seminary, Chicago, Haines received ordination in the Presbyterian Church, U.S.A., and went to Pakistan (1956–1960) as chaplain and chemistry teacher in Forman Christian College, Lahore. After doctoral studies at Harvard, he returned to Pakistan in 1967 to work with the Christian Study Center in Rawalpindi. His task of promoting mutual understanding between Christians and Muslims exposed him to the pioneering thought of South Asian Christian theologians in interfaith dialogue. On returning to the United States in 1977, he deployed his Pakistan experience in the service of the National Council of the Churches of Christ, U.S.A. (NCCC), which, through a special task force Haines directed, was just beginning to explore the significance of Christian-Muslim dialogue within the United States. During the 1979 Iranian revolution, he emerged as an able interpreter of events in the Muslim world. From his base at Hartford Seminary, where he served as academic dean, he initiated several national meetings of American Christians and Muslims and became nationally known and admired through his editorship of the NCCC *Newsletter on Christian-Muslim Relations.* Two years before his death, he undertook administrative responsibility for the Presbyterian Church's work throughout the Middle East and South Asia.

BIBLIOGRAPHY Works edited by Byron Haines: Yvonne Haddad, Byron Haines, Ellison Findly, eds., *The Islamic Impact,* (1984); Byron Haines, Frank Cooley, eds., *Christians and Muslims Together: An Exploration by Presbyterians* (1987), and Byron Haines, R. Marston Speight, eds., *Newsletter of the Task Force on Christian-Muslim Relations* (1977–1985; renamed *Newsletter of the Office on Christian-Muslim Relations,* 1985–1990). R. Marston Speight, ed., *Concerning Means and Ends: Writings of Byron Lee Haines on Interfaith Relations* (1992).

David A. Kerr

Hale, Mathew Blagden (1811–1895), Anglican missionary and bishop in Australia. An English clergyman, Hale keenly supported overseas missions. In 1847, Augustus Short, first Anglican bishop of Adelaide, invited him to Australia as his archdeacon responsible for Aborigines. Hale rapidly became an outspoken critic of colonial society, demanding justice for Aborigines. "We profess to admitting them [as] British subjects," he declared, "but in reality the only [privilege] they enjoy is that of being hanged." In 1850 he opened his Aboriginal Institution at Poonindie, near Port Lincoln, South Australia, envisaging young people growing up in a healthy Christian environment. Despite deaths from European diseases, the Poonindie Aboriginal people became a confident Christian community, widely admired as a successful Christian mission. Reluctantly becoming bishop of Perth (1857) and Brisbane (1875), Hale used his position to influence public opinion about the plight of the Aboriginal people.

BIBLIOGRAPHY Mathew Hale, *The Aborigines of Australia* (1892). Peggy Brock and D. Kartinyeri, *Poonindie: The Rise and Destruction of an Aboriginal Agricultural Community* (1989); John Harris, *One Blood* (1990).

John W. Harris

Hale, Sarah Josepha (Buell) (1788–1879), editor and champion of women's education. Born in Newport, New Hampshire, educated at home, and married in 1813, Hale was widowed nine years later with five children to raise. In 1828 she moved to Boston to edit the *Ladies' Magazine,* the first substantial magazine in the United States for women. It was merged ten years later with Louis Godey's *Lady's Book,* and she relocated to Philadelphia in 1841, since Godey's offices were there. With a circulation that reached 150,000 in the 1860s, the journal she edited set the standards of progressive feminism. A supporter of the Female Medical School of Pennsylvania (1850), she was also a supporter and served as secretary of the Ladies' Medical Missionary Society (1851), which merged with the Woman's Union Missionary Society in 1860. During the 1860s Hale headed the Philadelphia branch of the latter. A constant advocate of women's education, she urged that women be trained as medical doctors to deal with feminine needs at home and in the work of overseas missions.

BIBLIOGRAPHY Isabelle Webb Entrikin, *Sarah Josepha Hale and "Godey's Lady's Book"* (1946); Ralph Nading Hill, "Mr. Godey's Lady," *American Heritage* 9, no. 6 (October 1958); Edward T. James, ed., *Notable American Women* (1971); Sherbrooke Rogers, *Sarah Josepha Hale, A New England Pioneer* (1985).

Robert T. Coote

Hall, Elizabeth (Garland) (1867–1933), African American missionary in Congo and Jamaica. Born in Augusta, Maine, orphaned early, and adopted by a Christian woman in Boston, Elizabeth Garland decided from childhood to be a missionary. She graduated in 1891 from the Baptist Missionary Training School in Chicago, where, for the first time, she was designated "colored." In 1893 she married William Hall, a Jamaican Baptist missionary, and returned with him to the Congo, serving at several stations before spending 13 years at Palabala, where the work of "Mama Hall" with children and the sick was long remembered. Although she recovered several times from blackwater fever (which usually proves fatal), it eventually necessitated her withdrawal from Africa. Later she worked in Jamaica (1918–1932), where for 18 months she operated a private isolation hospital for victims of alastrim, a disease like smallpox, all the while refusing remuneration. A founder and first organizing secretary of the Jamaica Baptist Women's Federation, for seven years she had an orphanage for twelve children in her own home, raising most of the money for their support herself, by lectures and assistance from friends abroad. The Garland Hall Children's Home in Anchovy, Jamaica, was built in her memory. Her last 14 months were spent as a very sick patient in Graduate Hospital, New York City, where her witness and influence reached every level of the hospital community. She was buried in Westchester County, New York.

BIBLIOGRAPHY Beryl J. Russell, "A Biographical Study of the Life and Work of Elizabeth Garland Hall" (M.A. thesis, Eastern Baptist Theological Seminary, 1996).

Beryl J. Russell

Hall, Gordon (1784–1826), pioneer missionary in India. Born in Tolland, Massachusetts, Hall graduated with highest honors from Williams College in 1808. Entering Andover Theological Seminary in 1810, he joined the group of students whose enthusiasm for missionary service led to the formation of the American Board of Commissioners for Foreign Missions (ABCFM) later that year. Appointed a missionary in September 1811, Hall studied medicine at Boston and Philadelphia. In February 1812 he was ordained by the ABCFM at Salem, Massachusetts, along with Adoniram *Judson, Samuel *Newell, Samuel *Nott, and Luther *Rice. Hall, Rice and the Notts sailed from Philadelphia on February 18, reaching Calcutta on August 8. Refused residence by the British East India Company, Hall and the Notts evaded authorities, sailed for Bombay and persuaded the governor, a vice president of the British and Foreign Bible Society, to allow them to stay, constituting the first American missionary station overseas.

Hall first studied the local languages, gave medical treatments to English and Indians, preached in the English church, and prepared literature in Marathi. In 1814 the first of thirty-five schools was opened. Hall married Margaret Lewis, a young English woman resident in Bombay who was proficient in the local language, in 1816. For the following ten years he evangelized and provided medical services, usually in Hindu temples and in bazaars, translated much of the New Testament, opened and supervised schools, and distributed literature. He was instrumental in forming the Bombay Missionary Union. After two children died, Mrs. Hall and two sons returned to America in 1825. In March of the following year Hall died of cholera at Doorlee Dhapur.

BIBLIOGRAPHY Hall's sermon "The Duty of American Churches in Respect to Foreign Missions" was published in 1815. With Samuel Newell he wrote *The Conversion of the World, or the Claims of the Six Hundred Millions* (1818). Horatio Bardwell, *Memoir of Rev. Gordon Hall* (1834); A. M. Colton, *Gordon Hall, A Memorial* (1882); John Crozier, *I Cannot Turn Back: The Adventures of Gordon Hall* (1977); Daniel M. Hall, *Gordon Hall: A Family Portrait of a Committed Man* (1973). Histories of the ABCFM by Tracy (1842) and Strong (1910), and histories of missions in India, particularly in the Bombay area, refer extensively to Hall. His correspondence with the ABCFM is included in the ABCFM papers in Houghton Library, Harvard, and extensively excerpted in the *Panoplist* and *Missionary Herald* 1813–1826. His letter condemning American slavery appeared in the *Boston Recorder* 17 (1832): 1.

David M. Stowe

Hall, Marian (Bottomley) (1896–1991), medical missionary of the American Methodist Church in Korea and India. Born in Epworth, England, Marian Bottomley immigrated with her widowed mother to Athens, Ontario, Canada. A graduate of Mount Union College, Alliance, Ohio, she completed medical training at the Woman's Medical College of Pennsylvania in Philadelphia in 1924. In 1922 she married Dr. Sherwood *Hall, a medical missionary, and went with him to Haeju, Korea, in 1926. She organized a baby welfare clinic and mothers' clubs to teach hygiene. After expulsion from Korea in 1940 by the Japanese, the Halls were reassigned to Madar in Rajasthan, India. There Marian Hall did extensive medical work in the villages, using a mobile clinic van and working especially for the eradication of trachoma. She was instrumental in founding a branch of the Association of Planned Parenthood. She died in Richmond, British Columbia, a few months after her husband's death. Her ashes were interred with her husband's in the Foreigner's Cemetery in Yanghwa-jin, Seoul, Korea.

BIBLIOGRAPHY Sherwood Hall, *With Stethoscope in Asia: Korea* (1978, 1981; the *Tonga ilbo* newspaper published a Korean translation of this work in 1984).

James H. Grayson

Hall, R(onald) O(wen) (1895–1975), Anglican bishop of Hong Kong. Hall was born in Newcastle, England, the eldest son of the vicar of a working-class parish. At the outbreak of World War I he enlisted in the infantry and spent nearly the whole war in France (1914–1919), rising to the rank of major and receiving the Military Cross. He returned to Brasenose College, Oxford, for an abbreviated university education and one term at Cuddesdon Theological College. He soon emerged as an energetic and articulate leader of the British Student Christian Movement and was appointed to the national staff in 1920. As missionary secretary he was a delegate to the World's Student Christian Federation conference in Peking in 1922. He formed deep friendships with a group of young Chinese Christian leaders, including the student evangelist T. Z. *Koo and the YMCA leader, Y. T. *Wu. From then on he attempted to understand and interpret Chinese politics from the Chinese point of view. His experience in the war and in the industrial north of England also led him to give priority to the needs of ordinary people, especially the victims of social upheaval. Later, as bishop of Hong Kong (1932–1966), he was criticized for his advocacy of the poor and his support for the Chinese revolution.

Ordination (1921), marriage (1922), a return visit to China on a peacemaking mission (1925–1926), and some experience as a parish priest in Newcastle (1926–1932) preceded his appointment to Hong Kong. The diocese then included most of south China and was about to be engulfed by the Sino-Japanese War and the civil war that followed. "R. O." brought to these turbulent years vigorous and creative leadership and an extraordinary ability to recruit able people, both Chinese and foreign, to assist him. Something of his spirit was captured in *The Art of the Missionary,* a book he wrote in 1940 that became a classic. (It was reprinted in the United States as *A Missionary Artist Looks at His Task.*) The capture of Hong Kong and Canton by the Japanese left the diocese divided by battle lines. Hall moved to Kunming and assigned responsibility for continuing the church's work on both sides of the lines to Chinese assistant bishops. In 1944, in order to provide pastoral care for an isolated congregation, he ordained the first woman priest in the Anglican Communion, Li Tim-oi, an action at first repudiated, but years later confirmed by both Chinese and Church of England authorities. The reconstruction of the church in Hong Kong after World War II included establishment of thirty new churches, sixty-five schools, what became the Chinese University of Hong Kong, and a host of welfare agencies to deal with the needs of refugees and a rapidly growing industrial population. In 1966 he and his wife retired to Lewknor, their home near Oxford, where they lived until his death.

BIBLIOGRAPHY Books by Hall include *The Nature of the Missionary Enterprise* (1924), *A Family in the Making* (1925), *China and Britain* (1927), and *T. Z. Koo* (1950). Numerous articles by Hall appear in *The Student World* (WSCF), *The Student Movement* (British SCM, 1920–1927), and *The Outpost* (magazine of the Hong Kong Diocesan Assocation in England). David M. Paton, *"R. O.": The Life and Times of Bishop Hall of Hong Kong* (1985).

Charles Henry Long

Hall, Sherwood (1893–1991), Canadian medical missionary to Korea and India. Born in Seoul of Methodist medical missionary parents, William James Hall and Rosetta Sherwood Hall, Sherwood Hall graduated from Mount Union College, Alliance, Ohio, served with the U.S. Army Reserve Medical Corps in World War I, and completed medical training at the University of Toronto in 1923. Hall married Marian Bottomley (see Marian Bottomley *Hall), also a medical doctor, in 1922. They received specialized medical training at the School of Tropical Medicine, University of London, before assignment to Norton Memorial Hospital in Haeju, Korea, in 1926. In 1928 Hall founded the Haeju School for the Tuberculous, the first tuberculosis sanatorium in Korea, and for his work was granted a certificate of merit by Japanese Emperor Hirohito in 1929. To support tuberculosis work, Hall started a program of selling Christmas seals in 1932. Expelled from Korea by the Japanese in 1940 on charges of being British spies, the Halls were reassigned to the Madar Union Tuberculosis Sanatorium near Ajmer, in Rajasthan, India. Hall introduced the Christmas seals program to India in 1941. He built up the sanatorium from 24 beds in 1941 to a complex center of nearly 500 beds with specialized treatment and retraining facilities before his retirement in 1963. The Halls visited Korea in 1960, and again in 1984 when he received the Order of Civil Merit, Moran Medal. He died in Richmond, British Columbia; his ashes were interred in the Foreigner's Cemetery in Yanghwa-jin, Seoul, Korea.

BIBLIOGRAPHY Sherwood Hall, *With Stethoscope in Asia: Korea* (1978, 1981; the *Tonga ilbo* newspaper published a Korean translation of this work in 1984).

James H. Grayson

Hallbeck, Hans Peter (1784–1840), Swedish-born Moravian missionary bishop in South Africa. Hallbeck was educated in Lund and taught for a few years in Gothenburg, where he came into contact with the Moravians. He was received into their fellowship in 1804. After working as a teacher in Germany and Ireland, in 1815 he became minister of the Moravian congregation in Manchester, England, and in 1817 he was sent to Gennadendaal (Gnadenthal), Cape Province, South Africa. There he became an effective, energetic, and much respected organizer, administrator, and educator. He was appointed bishop in 1836.

BIBLIOGRAPHY Carl Anshelm, *Biskop Hans Peter Hallbeck* (1927).

Eric J. Sharpe

Halliwell, Leo B(lair) (1891–1967) *and* **Jessie (Rowley)** (1894–1962), American Seventh-day Adventist (SDA) missionaries in Brazil. During an early period of missionary service in eastern Brazil, Leo Halliwell, a native of Nebraska with a degree in electrical engineering from the University of Nebraska (1916) and Jessie, his wife and a graduate nurse, came to realize the possibility of using the Amazon and its tributaries to gain access to the peoples of the interior. Commencing in 1931, the couple made twenty-five annual expeditions from Belem, of six to seven months' duration and covering 10,000 to 12,000 miles, up the Amazon and its tributaries in shallowdraft boats designed by Halliwell and named *Luzeiro* ("morning star" in Portuguese). The *Luzeiro* served as both residence and floating clinic on these long trips, as they treated the ill, gave lectures on health, and taught the gospel. As the work developed, Leo supervised the construction of chapels and a fleet of vessels for the use of colporteurs, evangelists, and medical workers and built a clinic at Belem that developed into a hospital. In 1956 the Halliwells relinquished their long riverboat expeditions and moved to Rio de Janeiro, where Leo served as supervisor of the Adventist missionary fleet of some twenty-five vessels on the rivers of South America. In 1958 the Halliwells retired to the United States and the following year were presented with the National Order of Cruzeiro do Sul by the government of Brazil for their "outstanding medical and religious work."

BIBLIOGRAPHY Leo Halliwell, *Light Bearer to the Amazon* (1945) and *Light in the Jungle* (1959). Floyd Greenleaf, *The Seventh-day Adventist Church in Latin America and the Caribbean,* vol. 1 (1992); "Halliwell, Leon Blair" and "Missionary Vessels," in *Seventh-day Adventist Encyclopedia,* 2d rev. ed. (1996); R. W. Schwarz, *Light Bearers to the Remnant* (1979).

Russell L. Staples

Hambroeck (Hambroek), Antonius (1605–1661), Dutch Reformed missionary in Formosa (Taiwan). Born in Rotterdam, Hambroeck studied in Leiden. After ministering in Schipluiden, near Delft, from 1622 to 1647, he was sent by the church to the East Indies. The church in Batavia (Jakarta) asked him to serve on Formosa, so in 1648 he settled in the village of Mattau. Assisted by indigenous teachers, he followed up on the work of Georgius *Candidius and Robertus *Junius and organized a teachers college in 1657. He also translated the Gospels of Matthew and John into the local language. These were revised by Daniël Gravius before being published in 1661. Hambroeck promoted school education designed to bring about conversion and the advancement of church life rather than the development of society. Many children and adults were therefore educated in Latin.

During Hambroeck's time, war broke out frequently between villages. He warned the governors in Batavia that political turmoil was coming, but his pleas for military help were not heeded. In addition, the ongoing war with the Chinese worsened. When he tried to mediate between the Dutch and "Coxinga" (Tcheng Tch'eng-Koung), the Chinese military leader, he as well as his entire family was taken captive and decapitated. Hambroeck thus became a martyr for the Reformed faith. The Dutch lost the island to the Chinese in 1662.

BIBLIOGRAPHY W. A. Ginsel, *De Gereformeerde Kerk op Formosa of de lotgevallen eener handelskerk onder de Oost Indische Compagnie, 1626–1662* (1931); L. J. Joosse, *Scoone dingen sijn swaere dingen: Een onderzoek naar de motieven en de activiteiten in De Nederlanden tot verbreiding van de gereformeerde religie* (1992); J. J. A. M. Kuepers, *The Dutch Reformed Church in Formosa, 1627–1662: Mission in a Colonial Context* (1978).

Leendert J. Joosse

Hamlin, Cyrus (1811–1900), founder and first president of Robert College in Constantinople. Hamlin was born in Waterford, Maine, son of Hannibal and Susanna Faulkner Hamlin. He graduated from Bridgeton Academy (1830), Bowdoin College (1834), and Bangor Theological Seminary (1837). He was appointed in 1837 by the American Board of Commissioners for Foreign Missions (ABCFM) to serve in the Near East. In September 1838 he married Henrietta Jackson, and the couple sailed for Constantinople in December of that year.

Hamlin directed Bebek Seminary, a mission school in Constantinople, from 1840 to 1860. He resigned from the mission in 1860 over disputes with fellow missionaries and the leadership of the ABCFM concerning his philosophy of education and highly successful "secular labors" to raise money for student support. With financial backing from American philanthropist Christopher Robert, he founded the college on the Bosphorus that bore Robert's name. Hamlin served as its president from 1863 to 1873. He then returned to the United States, where he attempted for two years with limited success to secure endowment funds for Robert College.

Prevented by colleagues from returning to his work in Constantinople, Hamlin taught for three years at Bangor Seminary. In 1880 he became president of Middlebury College in Vermont, a position he held with distinction until he retired to Lexington, Massachusetts, in 1885.

BIBLIOGRAPHY Cyrus Hamlin, *Among the Turks* (1878) and *My Life and Times,* 2d ed. (1893). Marcia and Malcolm Stevens, *Against the Devil's Current: The Life and Times of Cyrus Hamlin* (1988); George Washburn, *Fifty Years in Constantinople* (1909).

Norman A. Horner

Hamlin, James (1803–1865), pioneer Church Missionary Society (CMS) missionary in New Zealand. Born in Somerset, England, Hamlin was the first student at the Church Missionary College at Islington, near London. Appointed by the CMS to New Zealand as a catechist in 1825, with skills as a flax dresser and spinner, Hamlin had little success using his trade. With Alfred *Brown he investigated missionary opportunities in the Waikato area in 1834. He was involved in developing mission stations at Waimate (1830), Mangapouri in the Waikato (1835), Moeatoa and Orua Bay in the Manukau area (1836–1839), and Wairoa, Hawke's Bay (1844). A fluent Maori speaker, he contributed to the Old Testament translation and was a member of Bishop G. A. *Selwyn's translation committee that revised the Prayer Book in 1844. He was ordained a deacon by Selwyn in 1844, but because he lacked knowledge of Greek he was denied priest's orders. Selwyn moved him in 1844 from the growing European settlement at Orua, where he had acquired land for his family, to a Maori area in Wairoa. Many Maori were baptized during his time at Wairoa, where he had responsibility for a large district in which he developed fifteen outposts. A conscientious and dedicated missionary, Hamlin and his wife, Elizabeth, who had twelve children, struggled with ill health over a long period. Elizabeth died in 1858, and James died two years after he had been ordained a priest by William *Williams.

BIBLIOGRAPHY H. J. Ryburn, *Te Hemara: James Hamlin, 1803–1865, Friend of the Maoris* (1979). Hamlin's papers are held by the CMS (available on microfilm) and the Hocken Library, Univ. of Otago, Dunedin, New Zealand.

Allan K. Davidson

Han Kyung Jik (1902–), Presbyterian pastor, prominent preacher in Korea, theologian, and author. Han was born in Kanri Pyongannamdo, North Korea. He was educated at Osan School, where he was introduced to the Christian faith, and at Soongsil College, where he received his call to ministry in 1924. He graduated from Princeton Theological Seminary in 1929 and was ordained in 1934. He founded Yungnak Church in Seoul and served as its pastor from 1944 to 1994; Yungnak is the largest Presbyterian church in Korea. He served as president of Soongsil College (now a university in Seoul), as chair of the fortieth Presbyterian church assembly in South Korea, and as chair of the Korean National Council of Churches in 1956. His emphasis on evangelism, education, and service led to establishing numerous centers for social welfare, vocational schools, a seminary for women, and over 200 churches. He initiated Korean cross-cultural missions by sending *Choi Chan Young to Thailand after Korean independence. Han has a high view of Scripture, emphasizes a pietistic lifestyle, and promotes ecumenical work among churches and in society. He received honorary doctorates from Yonsei University (1956) and Soongjun University (1977), the alumni award from Princeton Seminary (1985), and the Templeton Award (1992).

BIBLIOGRAPHY All available material by and about Han is written in Korean.

Chun Chae Ok

Hanlon, Henry (1866–1937), English Mill Hill bishop in Uganda. Hanlon joined the Mill Hill Missionaries and after ordination was sent to India (1890–1894). In Buganda, meanwhile, after the establishment of British rule, tensions and civil war between the Catholics (evangelized by the French White Fathers) and Protestants (evangelized by the British Church Missionary Society) had led to recognition of the need to make the difference between church and nationality completely clear. Léon *Livinhac, general of the White Fathers, suggested to Cardinal *Vaughan that the Mill Hill Fathers, as British Catholics, should take over part of the Nyanza Vicariate. Consequently in 1894 its eastern section was detached to form the Vicariate Apostolic of the Upper Nile and assigned to Mill Hill. Hanlon was recalled from India and placed in charge of it. His task was to ensure harmonious relations between the Catholic Church and the British authorities while developing the evangelization of eastern Uganda. In both tasks he succeeded well. He founded a new missionary headquarters at Nsambya, near Kampala, on land granted him by King Mwanga, while his missionaries began to work in Buganda and Busoga before advancing into Bukedi, Bugisu, Teso, and Kavirondo. He introduced the Franciscan Sisters in 1902. When he retired on account of ill health in 1911, there were some 25,000 Catholics in his vicariate and 12,000 children in his schools.

BIBLIOGRAPHY H. P. Gale, *Uganda and the Mill Hill Fathers* (1959).

Adrian Hastings

Hannington, James (1847–1885), first Anglican bishop of East Africa. Hannington was educated at St. Mary Hall, Oxford, and ordained a priest in 1876. He was first sent by the Church Missionary Society (CMS) to Zanzibar in 1882, but illness forced him to return to England the following year. He recovered and returned to East Africa as bishop in January 1885. His diocese included missions of the CMS at the coast and inland in Buganda. At Freretown, a freed slave settlement near Mombasa, Hannington ordained two African deacons. He determined to pioneer a shorter and healthier highland road to Buganda, using Christian porters and undercutting the Arab slave route to the south. He was oblivious to the political consequences of traversing Busoga, a strategically sensitive area for the Buganda state. The sudden intrusion of German imperialism at the coast made the Bugandan ruler, Kabaka Mwanga, even more suspicious of Hannington's motives. He was arrested in Busoga, just before crossing the Nile. The bishop and forty-six Freretown porters were executed. Suspicion of collaboration then focused on the Christian converts in Buganda, young men at the court. Some 100 Anglican and Catholic Christians were killed. The fears of the authorities had a large measure of justification, in that within ten years Buganda lost its independence. Hannington has been criticized for naïveté and tactlessness. His last journals, nevertheless, reveal a person who faced death with brave resignation and faith. He is commemorated as a martyr on October 29.

BIBLIOGRAPHY E. C. Dawson, *James Hannington* (1887), gives an account of the bishop's last days based on Hannington's journals. M. S. Kiwanuka, *A History of Buganda* (1971), provides the cultural and political background. J. F. Faupel, *African Holocaust* (1962), gives a vivid account of the Uganda martyrs who died in the aftermath of Hannington's execution.

Kevin Ward

Hanxleden, Johann Ernst (1681–1732), Jesuit missionary in India and pioneer Sanskrit scholar. Born in Osterkappeln/Osnabrück, Germany, Hanxleden entered the Society of Jesus in 1699. He volunteered for the East Indian mission and completed his novitiate en route. An eminent linguist with knowledge of East Syrian, Malayalam, and Sanskrit, he was one of the first Europeans to write a

Sanskrit grammar. He also wrote lexicons for Sanskrit-Portuguese and Malayalam-Portuguese and composed numerous religious poems and songs in Malayalam. He is known among the people of Kerala as *Arnos Pathiri* (Malayalam for Father Arnold).

BIBLIOGRAPHY L. Koch, "Hanxleden, Ernst," *Jesuiten-Lexikon* (1934); M. Mundadan, "John Ernest Hanxleden (*Arnos Pathiri*): His Contribution to the Sanskrit and Malayalam Languages and Literatures," in A. Amaldass, ed., *Jesuit Presence in Indian History: Commemorative Volume on the Occasion of the 150th Anniversary of the New Madurai Mission, 1838–1988* (1988), pp. 171–181, and "An 'Unknown' Oriental Scholar: Ernest Hanxleden (*Arnos Pathiri*)," *Indian Church History Review* 23 (1989): 39–63; S. Rajamanickam, *The First Oriental Scholar* (1972).

Stephen B. Bevans, SVD

Happer, A(ndrew) P. (1818–1894), Presbyterian minister, medical doctor, educator, and missionary in China. Born near Monongahela, Pennsylvania, Happer graduated from Jefferson College, Canonsburg, in 1835 and taught school for five years. Prior to going overseas, he studied theology at Western Theological Seminary, Pittsburgh (1840–1843), and medicine at the University of Pennsylvania (1843–1844). In 1844 he sailed for China and settled near Canton. In 1847 he married Elizabeth Ball (d. 1864), with whom he had five children. He subsequently married A. L. Elliott (d. 1873) in 1869 and Hannah J. Shaw in 1875. Happer's evangelistic work grew slowly, but his medical and educational work flourished. Within ten years he established two dispensaries which annually treated 10,000 patients. In 1854 he turned over the medical work to Dr. John G. *Kerr, who developed the practice into a major medical center. Happer then devoted himself to education. During the 1850s he founded several day schools and a training school for pastors and teachers. He served on the China-wide committee to revise the Chinese Bible, chaired the editorial committee of the Presbyterian Press at Shanghai, and served as editor of the *Chinese Recorder* (1880–1884). In 1862 he also organized the First Presbyterian Church in Canton, where he served as pastor. Happer's educational work culminated in 1886, when he founded Canton Christian College, now Lingnan University. He left China in 1891 and returned to the United States where he died in Wooster, Ohio.

BIBLIOGRAPHY A. P. Happer, *The State of Religion in China* (1881) and *Influence of the College in the Civilization of the World* (1895). Loren W. Crabtree, "Andrew P. Happer and Presbyterian Missions in China, 1844–1891," *Journal of Presbyterian History* 62 (1984): 19–34; Henry V. Noyes, "In Memoriam: Rev. A. P. Happer, M.D., D.D., LL.D.," *Chinese Recorder* 26 (January 1895): 31.

Robert Benedetto

Harada Tasuku (1863–1940), Japanese pastor and educator. Harada was born into the samurai class in Kumamoto and received his earliest education in the clan school for foreign studies under the Christian influence of Captain Leroy Lansing *Janes. In 1880 he entered Doshisha, a Congregational school in Kyoto, and was baptized a year later. Ordained in 1885, he studied in America at the University of Chicago Divinity School and at Yale University (1888–1891) and then in England and Germany before returning to Japan in 1896. Pastor of major Congregational churches and active in Christian journalism, the YMCA movement, and interdenominational cooperation, he was one of four official Japanese representatives at the Edinburgh World Missionary Conference in 1910. He was called to the presidency of Doshisha in 1907 and served as such for 13 years, during which time the school received official university accreditation from the government. In 1920, Harada was invited to the University of Hawaii to set up a department of Asian studies and served as its dean until 1932. During these years and until his death he was active in movements to promote international understanding and peace. He was the author of numerous works, including *The Faith of Japan* (1914), and received honorary degrees from Edinburgh University, the University of Hawaii, and Amherst College.

BIBLIOGRAPHY Ken Harada, *Harada Tasuku Ishu* (1971; posthumously collected works).

John W. Krummel

Haraldsson, Olav (995–1030), Norwegian viking chief, king, mission leader, and national saint of Norway. Haraldsson was the great-great-grandson of Harald Haarfagre, the first king of all Norway. Also known as Olav II and St. Olav, he was born in the southeastern part of Norway and took part in the first of many viking raids when he was 12 years old. He was baptized in Rouen, France, in 1013 or 1014 and arrived back in Norway in 1015 to claim the throne and to force people to accept Christianity. He brought with him British priests, including four bishops. Norway was then ruled by the Danish king and partly by local chiefs. Olav conquered Norway, uniting the country under one administration. He followed a severe mission strategy, destroying pagan idols and forcing people to accept Christianity and be baptized. In 1024 he started the organization of one national church of Norway. He is the single most important person in the Christianization of Norway, although the way had been prepared through two centuries, partly by influence from the south, but mostly by Norwegians who had been converted in England. In 1028 Olav was forced to leave Norway, but after two years of exile in Sweden and Russia he returned to regain the throne and complete the Christianization of the country. He was killed in the battle of Stiklestad on July 29, 1030. In 1031 Olav was declared a martyr and a saint by his principal bishop, Grimkell. Churches were dedicated to St. Olav all over Europe and pilgrims visited his tomb in the cathedral at Trondheim.

BIBLIOGRAPHY Fredrik Paasche, *Olav den hellige* (1921); Sigrid Undset, *Norske helgener* (1937); Andr. Seierstad, *Olavsdyrking i Nidaros og Nord-Europa* (1930); Olav Bö, *Heilag-Olav i norsk folketradisjon* (1955); Vera Henriksen, *Saint Olav of Norway, King, Saint, and Enigma* (1985).

Nils E. Bloch-Hoell

Hardy, Robert Spence (1803–1868), British Methodist missionary in Sri Lanka. Hardy was born in Preston, Lancashire, England, and worked for his grandfather, a Methodist printer and bookseller, in York. Entering the Wesleyan ministry in 1825, he was appointed to Ceylon (Sri Lanka), where he spent 23 years over three periods of service, the last as chairman of the South Ceylon District (1862–1864). With Daniel *Gogerly he was one of the first serious Western students of Buddhism, though by the time he left Sri Lanka, missionary dialogue with Buddhists there had largely broken down. He translated and abstracted Sinhala Buddhist manuscripts and also worked with the Lankan minister David de Silva on Pali texts. His *Manual of Buddhism* (1853; 2d ed., 1880), despite evident limitations, is the earliest work of its kind. Other writings include an influential pamphlet on British government support for Buddhism (1841), *Eastern Monachism* (1850), *The Legends and Theories of the Buddhists* (which critiques Buddhist sources from a contemporary Western historical and scientific standpoint; 1866); and works in Sinhala. He was elected an honorary member of the Royal Asiatic Society. He left Ceylon for the last time in 1864 and died as a minister in the Leeds District.

BIBLIOGRAPHY *Wesleyan Conference Minutes,* 1868, pp. 253–254. K. M. de Silva, *Social Policy and Missionary Organization in Ceylon, 1840–1855* (1965); E. J. Harris, "A Case of Distortion: The Evangelical Missionary Interpretation of Buddhism in Nineteenth-Century Sri Lanka," *Dialogue* (n.s.) 21 (1994): 19–42.

Andrew F. Walls

Haringke Bai (c. 1888–1938), pioneer Lutheran evangelist and hymn writer in Papua New Guinea. Born near Finschhafen, Papua New Guinea, Haringke was one of the first four local evangelists to volunteer for a lifelong missionary career among hostile people in the neighboring Hube area. Trained by Christian *Keysser, Haringke and his fellow evangelists were commissioned in 1908; this marked the beginning of the mission program that the incipient congregations had accepted as their responsibility. While working among the Kuat people in Tobou, Haringke also influenced the spiritual growth of the Kotte-speaking congregations with the hymns he composed. In 1931 he retired to his home village, there assisting the translation of the Bible into his language until his death.

BIBLIOGRAPHY Christian Keysser, *Der Prophet von Tobou* (1931).

Gernot Fugmann

Harms, Ludwig (1808–1865), founder of the Hermannsburg Mission. The son of a Lutheran pastor, Harms grew up, was educated, and worked as a pastor in the Lüneburg Heath, in north Germany, mainly in the village of Hermannsburg, where he founded his own "peasants' mission" in 1849. Rooted in the traditional Lutheran piety of his age, he became the revivalist of his parish and the surrounding countryside by means of preaching, teaching, pastoral care, and prayer. As the regional church authorities hesitated to support his activities, Harms began dispatching his own missionaries, trained in his local seminary. They went first to the Oromo people in Ethiopia (1853), and then, after the collapse of that mission, to South Africa (Natal, 1854; Transvaal, 1857) and to the Telugu-speaking part of South India (1864). Because of his critical attitude toward the institutional church, Harms's brother and successor, Theodor, initiated the formation of a Lutheran free church in the Hermannsburg area. But the separation did not seriously affect the growth of the Hermannsburg Mission. To the present day it has preserved much of the peculiar spirituality of its founding father, whose watchword was, "the mission can never be a sign of the glory of the Christian church but merely a sign of the kingdom to come."

BIBLIOGRAPHY Hans Otto Harms, *Ludwig Harms, Theodor Harms und die Hermannsburger Mission* (1980). Harms's own writings consist almost exclusively of sermons and meditations.

Hans-Werner Gensichen

Harnack, Adolf von (1851–1930), German patristic scholar and historian of early Christian mission. Harnack's major contribution to missiology came out of his research into the history and expansion of Christianity in the first three centuries *(Die Mission und Ausbreitung des Christentums in den ersten drei Jahrhunderten,* 1902, 4th enlarged edition, 1924; English translation of the first edition by James Moffatt, 1904–1905). As a native of the Baltic part of the Russian empire, he had grown up in an atmosphere of conventional Lutheran piety, including familiarity with the work of Lutheran missions. His criticism of traditional Christian dogma could not but affect his attitude to missions as well. In his opinion, the Great Commission in Matthew 28 could not possibly be ascribed to Jesus but had to be regarded as a compilation by the early church, which at that time had already started its fateful journey under the auspices of Hellenic thought. Harnack thought that he had thus cleared the way for a fair treatment of the early spread of the Christian faith. It was left for later scholarship to show, contrary to Harnack, that the proclamation of the gospel for the whole world was grounded in the ministry of Jesus and not just in the literary productions of later generations.

BIBLIOGRAPHY From the large number of biographies and other studies on Harnack, an outstanding account in English is by G. Wayne Glick, *The Reality of Christianity: A Study of Adolf von Harnack as Historian and Theologian* (1967).

Hans-Werner Gensichen

Harris, George Kaufelt (1887–1962), American missionary to Muslims in China. Harris was born in Winona, Minnesota. After studying at Moody Bible Institute, Chicago, he joined the China Inland Mission in 1916 and was stationed in the northwestern and largely Muslim province of Xining. In 1917 Samuel *Zwemer visited China, encouraging mission work among Chinese Muslims. As a result of Zwemer's visit, Harris became one of the few China missionaries to develop interest in Islam and in the evangelization of Muslims. Between 1925 and 1946 he contributed several articles to the *Moslem World.* In 1927 he cofounded the Society of Friends of Moslems in China. In 1946, he wrote *How to Lead Moslems to Christ,* with a foreword by Zwemer. Intended as a manual for China missionaries, this book drew on the conciliatory approach of Lewis Bevan *Jones. One of Harris's major concerns was the production of literature appropriate for China. Rejecting controversy, he aimed to communicate the gospel so that it could take root in the cultural milieu of Chinese Islam. In one *Moslem World* article, he wrote about secret Christians in Tibet who were "outwardly still Mohammedans." He also translated works by Lilias *Trotter into Chinese.

BIBLIOGRAPHY Articles by Harris in *Moslem World* include: "On the Borders of Tibet," 15, no. 2 (April 1925), "Literature for Chinese Moslems," 17, no. 2 (April 1927), "The Rebellion in Kansu," 19, no. 3 (July 1929), "The Moslem Mind and the Gospel in China," 19, no. 4 (October 1929), "El Azhar Through Chinese Spectacles," 24, no. 2 (April 1934), "The Moslems of China Today," 25, no. 4 (October 1935), and "Northwest China: A Challenge for Today," 36, no. 3 (July 1946).

Clinton Bennett

Harris, Merriman Colbert (1846–1921), American Methodist missionary to Japan. Harris was born in Ohio, served in the Union Army in the War between the States, and was a graduate of Allegheny College, Meadville, Pennsylvania. He arrived in Japan in 1873, the first Protestant missionary in Hokkaido, where he baptized the members of the famous Sapporo Band of students who had been converted by William Clark *Smith. He also played a significant role in establishing Methodist work in Tokyo from 1878. He was superintendent of the Methodist Episcopal mission to the Japanese on the West Coast of the United States from 1886 and took a strong public stance against the periodic anti-Asian outbreaks in California, leading the movement for Japanese to be granted the right to attend public schools in that state. He returned to Japan as a Methodist missionary bishop in 1904. An enthusiastic but uncritical Japanophile, he gave unqualified support to the expansionist policies of the Japanese government, believing that the Japanese were the best equipped by nature and culture to lead the Far East into the modern world. Bishop Harris was thrice decorated by the emperor, his highest decoration being the Second Order of the Sacred Treasure, which was conferred at the time of his retirement in 1916. He was the author of *Christianity in Japan* (1908). He died in Tokyo and is buried there.

BIBLIOGRAPHY Edwin T. Iglehart, "Bishop Merriman C. Harris," *The Japan Evangelist* 28, no. 5 (May 1921): 143; "Merriman Colbert Harris," in Samuel John Umbreit, ed., *The Christian Movement in Japan, Korea, and Formosa: A Year Book of Christian Work* (1922), p. 295; "Missionary Society of the Methodist Episcopal Church: Foreign Missionaries Past and Present," *The Gospel in All Lands,* January 1900, pp. 41–44.

John W. Krummel

Harris, William Wadé (c. 1860–1929), prophet and leader of a West African mass movement. Wadé (his original family name) was born in the village of Half-Graway, near Cape Palmas, Liberia, a quarter century after the arrival of missionaries and black American colonists. The son of a heathen father, he nevertheless claimed to have been "born Methodist," presumably in reference to his mother's faith. He was schooled, converted, baptized as "William Harris," and became a lay preacher under Methodist influences. In 1888, after marrying Rose Farr, daughter of a teacher at the U.S. Episcopal Church's Half-Graway boarding school, he accepted employment with the Episcopal mission. From 1892 to 1908 he rose on the mission staff, teaching and evangelizing among his people. All the while the Liberian bishop, Samuel Ferguson, shifted from a pro-Glebo stance to identification with the immigrant black authorities. In 1899 Harris became the official interpreter for the Glebo population and his loyalties were severely tested. His deep differences with Ferguson, his embracing of the apocalypticism of Jehovah's Witnesses, and the influence of Dr. Edward *Blyden led to collaboration in a pro-British plot. Condemned as a traitor and dismissed by the Episcopal mission, Harris was imprisoned during the disastrous Liberian-Glebo war of 1910, which he had abetted. There an anointing of the Spirit during a trance visitation of the Angel Gabriel provoked obedience to Christ's Great Commission and transformed him into "the prophet of the last times."

Accompanied by women singers, Harris saw himself as a black Elijah "in the last days" before Christ's return, on a mission of power confrontation, charged to bring in a reign of peace. White-robed, turbaned, barefoot, and bearing a cross-staff, Bible, calabash rattle, and baptismal bowl, he proclaimed the power of God and the cross of Christ, calling for repentance and the destruction of all fetishes. Refusing money for his ministry, he baptized, cast out spirits, and healed. He taught the Lord's Prayer, the Ten Commandments, and strict observance of Sunday as a day of prayer and rest. He sent thousands of baptized persons to Catholic and Protestant missionaries for teaching. Where missionaries were not available, he named "Twelve Apostles" from the local population, promising that "whites with the Bible" would come as teachers.

Beginning in 1924, in Ivory Coast, the Methodist Mission Society's William J. *Platt established the Methodist Church on some 160 such congregations with over 32,000 adherents. Harris's power confrontation and symbolism found its greatest continuity in Ghana's Church of the Twelve Apostles and Ivory Coast's Harrist Church under Ebrié John *Ahui.

BIBLIOGRAPHY Gordon Mackay Haliburton, *The Prophet Harris: The Study of an African Prophet and His Mass Movement in the Ivory Coast and the Gold Coast* (1971); John Hargreaves, ed. and tr., "The Prophet Harris," in *France and West Africa* (1969), pp. 257–262; David A. Shank, *The "Black Elijah" of West Africa* (with abridgment by Jocelyn Murray; 1994) and "William Wadé Harris," in Gerald H. Anderson et al., eds., *Mission Legacies* (1994), pp. 155–165; Frank Deaville Walker, *The Day of Harvest in the White Fields of Africa* (1925); Sheila S. Walker, *Religious Revolution in the Ivory Coast: The*

Prophet Harris and the Harrist Church (1983). Harris left no writings and only a couple of signed letters.

David A. Shank

Harrison, Paul Wilberforce (1883–1962), Reformed Church in America medical missionary in the Middle East. Born in Scribner, Nebraska, Harrison graduated from Johns Hopkins University, Baltimore, Maryland, in 1909. He saw his medical skills as a tool that he could use to present Christianity to the Arabs, whom he came to love and respect. For more than four decades (1910–1954) he served throughout the Arabian Gulf area, including Oman, Bahrain, Kuwait, and Iraq, and made many exploratory visits into Saudi Arabia. He made pioneering contributions to medical science in the fields of spinal anesthesia and hernia surgery. Respecting the fact that Arabs feared that Christianity would make them Westerners, he maintained that they could become Christians and remain Arabs. An evangelist as much as a physician, while on his evening hospital rounds he gathered patients and read Bible stories to them. He wrote commentaries on the Gospel of John and the book of Hebrews. Although he had few converts, he believed that he was preparing the way for the time when Christianity would be accepted by the people with whom he worked.

BIBLIOGRAPHY Paul W. Harrison, *The Arab at Home* (1924), *Doctor in Arabia* (1940), *The Light That Lighteth Every Man* (1958), and *Meditations on Hebrews* (1962). Ann M. Harrison, *A Tool in His Hand* (1958).

Mary J. Heideman

Hartenstein, Karl (1894–1952), German mission theologian and administrator. One of the pivotal figures in modern German missions and missiology, Hartenstein went from church service in his native Württemberg to a prominent career as director of the Basel Mission (1926–1939). Thereafter until his untimely death he occupied leading positions in his home church. Before, during, and after World War II, in a period of rigorous testing of church and mission alike, his contribution to missiology appeared as an existential witness to the redemptive work of God in the vicissitudes of history rather than a unified theological system. Rooted in the soil of Swabian pietism, Hartenstein's thought underwent a circular process of theological formation. In his encounter with Karl *Barth he became the first missiologist to develop the concept of "missio Dei" as "an inalienable indication of God's revelation." However, in Hartenstein's opinion, Barth's radically transhistorical eschatology appeared to lack a proper "focusing on the end" which places mission and church under God's judgment. Thus Hartenstein's study of New Testament eschatology and his reinterpretation of the pietist heritage led him to attribute to the mission the "central salvation-historical meaning of the interim period between the ascension and the return of the Lord," as envisaged even by eighteenth-century Swabian theologians and reaffirmed by Hartenstein's friend Walter *Freytag. From this view it also follows that the mission cannot become church centered, inasmuch as the church's commission itself is structured as *missio-unio-passio*. On the basis of this eschatological perspective Hartenstein was able both to take a determined stand against Nazi ideology and to align himself with the "Confessing Church" and the ecumenical movement.

BIBLIOGRAPHY Gerold Schwarz, *Mission, Gemeinde und Ökumene in der Theologie Karl Hartensteins* (1980). Also see Schwarz's essay on Hartenstein in Gerald H. Anderson et al., eds., *Mission Legacies* (1994), pp. 591–601.

Hans-Werner Gensichen

Hartmann, (Joseph Alois) Anastasius (1803–1866), Swiss Capuchin missionary bishop in India. Hartmann was born at Altwis, Switzerland, joined the Capuchin Order in 1821, and was ordained priest in 1825. In 1844 he reached Agra, India, and was appointed chaplain at Gwalior. In 1846 he was consecrated bishop and appointed vicar apostolic of Patna, in northeast India. In 1850 he was transferred to Bombay, where the church was divided between a padroado and a Propaganda Fide party. As the chief representative of the Catholic community to the government of India, he managed to improve the status of Catholics in government policy. He upgraded theological education for the priesthood by inviting the Jesuits to Bombay, where they started a boys' college. However, tensions were created between the Capuchins and the Jesuits because the Jesuits wanted to be in charge of the vicariate apostolic of Poona and also of Bombay. In 1856 Hartmann returned to Europe and was put in charge of all the missions of the Capuchins. In 1860 he was able to return to his beloved Patna, where he later died.

Hartmann translated the New Testament into Hindi. He was an outstanding prelate, a linguist of distinction, gentle in his dealings with all kinds of people, a man of devotion and humility, and a person with the capacity for getting things done in very difficult circumstances.

BIBLIOGRAPHY Adelhelm Jann published Hartmann's *Autobiography* (1917), his letters (1943), and the *Monumenta Anastasiana,* 5 vols. (1939–1948). Walbert Bühlmann, *Pionier der Einheit: Bischof Anastasius Hartmann* (1966); Fulgentius [da Camugnano], *Bishop Hartmann* (1946); Stephen Neill, *A History of Christianity in India, 1707–1858* (1985), pp. 289–294.

Arnulf Camps, OFM

Hartmann, Maria (d. 1853), Moravian missionary widow who worked among free Negroes in Surinam. Hartmann accompanied her husband, John Gottlieb Hartmann, to Surinam in 1826 and served with him at Paramaribo and Charlottenburg. The couple had five children, of whom one son served the church in Surinam and one daughter in Tibet. When her husband died in 1844, Hartmann worked among the Bush Negroes at Berg-en-Dal and New Bombay, from where she made trips into the bush country teaching the free blacks. Her work included instructing younger missionaries in methodology of service. She continued to labor until her death, despite suffering from elephantiasis.

Following her death a number of articles appeared in the *Periodical Accounts of Moravian Missions* applauding her singular service as one of the outstanding aspects of the work in Surinam.

BIBLIOGRAPHY J. T. Hamilton and K. G. Hamilton, *History of the Moravian Church* (1967); *Periodical Accounts Relating to the Missions of the Church of the United Brethren,* 21 (1853); A. C. Thompson, *Moravian Missions* (1882).

Albert H. Frank

Hastings, Eurotas Parmelee (1821-1890), American missionary and educator in Ceylon (Sri Lanka). Born in Clinton, New York, Hastings graduated from Hamilton College (1842) and Union Theological Seminary, New York (1846), and sailed for Ceylon as missionary of the American Board of Commissioners for Foreign Missions (ABCFM). He served as an instructor in the Batticotta Seminary from 1847 to 1850, then was stationed at Manepy until he returned in 1852 to the United States, where he married Anne Cleveland in 1853. Returning to Ceylon in 1853, he was stationed in Batticotta before moving to Chavagacherry (1855) and Manepy (1858). While on furlough in the United States in 1870 he solicited funds for the establishment of a new college in Jaffna. Jaffna College, an English-language school, was started on the initiative of Tamil Christian leaders and was a full-fledged college, affiliated with the University of Madras. This affiliation ended in 1907 due to changes of educational policy at Madras, and Jaffna had high-school status until 1920. Hastings was appointed president of the new Jaffna College at Batticotta in 1872 and served in that position until forced by health problems to retire in 1889. He then had charge of the Manepy station until his death there the following year. Though involved primarily in educational work, Hastings also had oversight of several churches. He was awarded a D.D. from Hamilton College while on a brief visit to the United States in 1882.

BIBLIOGRAPHY ABCFM, *Historical Sketch of the American Ceylon Missions: Jaffna, 1858-1879* (1879) and *Ceylon* (1927). Memorial tribute, *The Missionary Herald,* November 1890.

Martha Lund Smalley

Hastings, Harry (?-1951), medical missionary in Nigeria with the United Free Church of Scotland. After military service in Germany during World War I, Hastings studied medicine at the University of Edinburgh. He served his entire missionary career in Nigeria from 1924 to 1949, at Uburu Hospital. He is remembered for his skill as a surgeon, his development of Nigerian staff to the point where they could run the hospital by themselves, and his leprosy work. He developed a network of clinics in the settlements that the Uburu people had already established for leprosy patients, and these led to the founding of the Southern Ogoja Leprosy Service in 1946. Hastings was awarded the Order of the British Empire in 1945. He returned to Scotland for medical reasons in 1949.

BIBLIOGRAPHY Geoffrey Johnston, *Of God and Maxim Guns: Presbyterianism in Nigeria, 1846-1966* (1988); M. Ross and N. Obini, *Presbyterian Joint Hospital, Uburu, 1913-1988* (1988).

Geoffrey Johnston

Haven, Jens (1724-1796), Danish Moravian missionary to Greenland and Labrador. Haven was born in Vust, Jutland, into a Lutheran family of farmers. In his youth he came under the influence of Andreas Langgaard, a Lutheran pastor whose congregation had close ties with the Moravians. He was also apprenticed to a Moravian carpenter and joiner in Copenhagen. In 1748, upon completing his training, Haven went to the Moravian center of Herrnhut, Saxony, where he was employed in the printing shop. From 1758 to 1763 he served as a missionary in Lichtenfels, Greenland, where he learned the Inuit language. He felt a strong call to serve in Labrador, where the first missionary journey in 1752 had ended in the murder of Johann Christian Erhardt and several of his crew. On three exploratory trips to Labrador (1764, 1765, 1770), Haven established successful contact with the Eskimos, using the Inuit language. After protracted negotiations with the British colonial authorities and their agreement to a Moravian settlement in Labrador, Haven and his wife, Mary (Butterworth), participated in establishing the Nain mission in 1771. Exploratory voyages to northern and southern Labrador followed, along with new mission stations at Okak (1776) and Hopedale (1782). Haven and his wife retired to Hernnhut in 1784, where he died.

BIBLIOGRAPHY "Account of the Life of Brother Jens Haven, The First Missionary Sent by the Brethren to the Esquimaux Indians on the Coast of Labrador," *Periodical Accounts Relating to the Missions of the Church of the United Brethren, Established among the Heathen,* vol. 2 (1798), pp. 99-115; Mercella Rollmann, "The Role of Language in the Moravian Missions to Eighteenth-Century Labrador," *Unitas Fratrum* 34 (1993): 49-64; H. G. Schneider, "Jens Haven in Labrador," *Beiblatt zur Allgemeinen Missions-Zeitschrift* 1 (January 1901): 1-16; W. H. Whiteley, "The Establishment of the Moravian Mission in Labrador and British Policy, 1763-83," *Canadian Historical Review* 45 (1968): 29-50.

Hans Rollmann

Hawaweeny, Raphael (1860-1915), first Orthodox bishop consecrated in North America. Born in Beirut, Lebanon, and educated in Damascus, Halki (Turkey), and Kiev, Hawaweeny was serving on the faculty of the School for Missionaries to Muslims in Kazan, Russia, when he received a call from the Syrian Orthodox Benevolent Committee in New York City to serve the church in North America. Immigrating in 1895 and serving under the aegis of the Russian Orthodox mission, he had pastoral responsibility that extended to isolated communities spread thinly across North America. He traveled repeatedly across the continent for nine years before being consecrated bishop of Brooklyn. While continuing his travels, he established a journal, *al-Kalimat*. His translations of Greek liturgical books into Arabic, distributed at his own expense to communities throughout the Middle East and to émigrés in the Americas, Africa, and Australasia, greatly helped preserve Orthodox Christianity in those regions.

BIBLIOGRAPHY André G. Issa, *The Life of Raphael Hawaweeny, Bishop of Brooklyn, 1860–1915* (M.Th. thesis, St. Vladimir's Theological Seminary, 1991).

Paul D. Garrett

Haweis, Thomas (1734–1820), Anglican cofounder of the London Missionary Society. Haweis was born in Redruth, Cornwall, England, served apprenticeship as a surgeon, and after an evangelical conversion, studied at Oxford and was ordained in 1757. From 1764 he was rector of Aldwincle, Northamptonshire, ministering there until his retirement to Bath in 1809. He combined regular, if controversial, Anglican churchmanship with service to Lady Huntingdon and her Connexion and with unusual openness to Dissenters. He campaigned for Protestant missions, popularizing Melville *Horne's *Letters*. He himself planned several early missions. Dispatch of two of Lady Huntingdon's preachers to Tahiti in 1791 was frustrated by their unrealistic demand for Anglican ordination; a mission to Bulama (now in Guinea Bissao) in 1794 was also aborted. In 1795 Haweis, David *Bogue, and John *Eyre were principal founders of the Missionary Society (later, the London Missionary Society), of which he remained a prominent director. He was responsible for choosing the Pacific as the first main field, securing assistance from Sir Joseph Banks, Captain Bligh, and other notables, and arguing consistently for a ship to give logistical support.

BIBLIOGRAPHY Thomas Haweis, *Sermons . . . at the Formation of the Missionary Society* (1795), *A Word in Season Designed to Encourage My Brethren of the Missionary Society* (1796), *A Plea for Peace and Union . . . to the Missionary Society* (1796), *Missionary Instructions . . .* (1796), *Memoir Respecting an African Mission* (1796), *Thanksgiving Sermons . . . before the Missionary Society* (1798), *A Missionary Voyage to the Southern Pacific Ocean* (1799), and *A View of the Present State of Evangelical Religion throughout the World* (1812). R. Lovett, *History of the London Missionary Society*, vol. 1 (1899); R. H. Martin, *Evangelicals United: Ecumenical Stirrings in pre-Victorian Britain* (1983); A. Skevington Wood, *Thomas Haweis, 1734–1820* (1957) and "Sierra Leone and Bulama: A Fragment of Missionary History," *Sierra Leone Bulletin of Religion* 3, no. 1 (1961): 16–22.

Andrew F. Walls

Hawkins, Ernest (1802–1868), mission secretary of the Society for the Propagation of the Gospel (SPG). Hawkins was the son of a military officer who served in India in the forces of the East India Company. After graduating from Balliol College, Oxford, in 1824, he was ordained in the Church of England and worked in the parish of Burwash in Sussex as a curate before returning in 1831 to Oxford as fellow of Exeter College and curate of St. Aldate's church. He was appointed an undersecretary of the SPG in 1838 and became secretary in 1843. His period of office (until 1864) largely coincided with the secretaryship of Henry *Venn of the Church Missionary Society. The two men established a good relationship, prayed regularly together, and consulted frequently on issues that affected their two societies in relation to the developing colonial church. From 1841 Hawkins acted as secretary to the newly created Colonial Bishoprics Fund during a period when Anglican dioceses overseas grew from eight to fifty-seven. In 1856 he launched the chief monthly periodical of SPG, *The Mission Field*. By the time of his retirement, the number of missionaries of the society had increased from 180 to 493, and the number of supporting parishes from 290 to 7,270. Like Henry Venn, Hawkins was created a prebendary of St. Paul's Cathedral (1844–1864). On retirement from SPG, he became a canon of Westminster Abbey.

BIBLIOGRAPHY Ernest Hawkins, *Documents Relative to the Erection and Endowment of Additional Bishoprics in the Colonies* (1855). J. McCleod Campbell, *Christian History in the Making* (1946); M. Dewey, *The Messengers* (1975); C. F. Pascoe, *Two Hundred Years of the SPG* (1900); H. P. Thompson, *Into All Lands* (1951); T. E. Yates, *Venn and Victorian Bishops Abroad* (1978). Contemporary obituaries appeared in the *Guardian* of October 14, 1868, and the *Illustrated London News* of October 10, 1868.

Timothy Yates

Hawley, Gideon (1727–1807), American Congregational missionary. Born at Stratfield (now Bridgeport), Connecticut, Hawley graduated from Yale in 1749 and was licensed to preach a year later. Feeling called to be a missionary to the Indians, in 1752 he was appointed by the Society for Propagating the Gospel to the Indians as a schoolteacher in the Iroquois boarding school attached to the mission at Stockbridge, Massachusetts, where Jonathan *Edwards was missionary to the Indians and pastor of the white congregation. Hawley had been appointed to replace Martin Kellogg, who was considered incompetent, but the whites at Stockbridge, who were already opposed to Edwards, supported Kellogg and used the situation to cause more trouble. Hawley left Stockbridge in May 1753 to establish a new mission at Onohoghgwage, on the Susquehanna River, returning to Stockbridge in 1754. He was ordained as a minister and missionary, and in 1755 returned to Onohoghgwage, taking Jonathan Edwards, Jr., with him. They returned to Stockbridge in February 1756 due to the French and Indian War. Hawley made two unsuccessful attempts to return to Onohoghgwage in 1756 and 1757, spent a short time as army chaplain, and eventually became missionary pastor to the Mashpee Indians on Cape Cod, where he remained until his death.

BIBLIOGRAPHY W. B. Sprague, *Annals of the American Pulpit*, vol. 1 (1857), pp. 497–500, includes a biographical sketch. Letters describing Hawley's missionary work and adventures appear in *Massachusetts Historical Society Collections*, ser. 1, vol. 4, pp. 50–67 and ser. 6, vol. 4, pp. 617–619, 627–630. Hawley's manuscript journal is held in the Congregational Library in Boston.

Ronald E. Davies

Haymaker, Edward M. (1859–1948), pioneer Presbyterian missionary in Guatemala. Born in Murraysville, Pennsylvania, Haymaker graduated from Lafayette College, Pennsylvania, and Princeton Theological Seminary and worked as a home missionary in Pennsylvania. He then served as a Presbyterian missionary in Mexico for three years prior to his long and fruitful career in Guatemala (1887–1947), which included his retirement years beginning in 1933. He established the Colegio La Patria in Guatemala City and later the Colegio La Cooperacion in El Rancho, El Progreso, for those who were among the poorest and who were more receptive to the gospel message but had no access to education. He opposed the common mission policy of not paying national workers, whose work he considered more effective than that of foreign missionaries. He summarized his mission theory in a report to the Presbyterian mission board in 1937, stressing the importance of itinerant ministries, especially to the indigenous peoples; the organization of the national church; the use of schools for Christian orientation; the urgency for pastoral training; the need for medical work in the interior; the importance of biblical and theological publications; and the relevance of the missionary mandate for the United States as well as for foreign lands. His unpublished "Footnotes" are an invaluable commentary on the beginnings of Protestant work in a Central American country. He received the honorary doctor of divinity degree from Lafayette College in 1926.

BIBLIOGRAPHY Edward M. Haymaker, "Footnotes on the Beginnings of the Evangelical Work in Guatemala," United Mission Library, the Interchurch Center, New York, 1946, 137 pp., mimeographed. *El Mensajero*, Guatemala, founded by Haymaker in 1888 and edited for many years by him, carried a large number of his articles. The Iglesia Evangélica Nacional Presbiteriana de Guatemala published a historical study, *Apuntes para la Historia,* for its centennial celebration with a section on Haymaker, pp. 76–86 (1982). David G. Scotchmer, "Called for Life: The Literary Contributions of Edward M. Haymaker to an Ethnohistory of Protestant Missionary Ideology, Guatemala, 1887–1947," in Darrell Whiteman, ed., *Missions, Anthropology, and Cultural Change* (1985), pp. 323–368.

Sidney H. Rooy

Hayward, Victor E. W. (1908–1988), missionary in China, foreign secretary of the Baptist Missionary Society (BMS), and ecumenical statesman. Born in London, Hayward studied at Mansfield and Regent's Park Colleges, Oxford, and then went to China with the BMS in 1934. After five years in Shansi Province, the Japanese occupation compelled him and his wife, Eva, to move to Guizhou Province in southwest China, where they ministered mainly to students and officials. After a year working with refugees in Guangxi Province, Hayward moved to Shanghai to become the British secretary of the National Christian Council of China during the closing years of the missionary era. As general foreign secretary of the BMS from 1951 to 1959, he sought to adjust the missionary thinking of British Baptists to the implications of the age of nationalism and mounting anti-Western feeling. Always more enthusiastic about the ecumenical movement than many in his denomination, he moved to Geneva in 1959 to become the executive secretary of the department of missionary studies of the World Council of Churches (WCC). In 1969 he was appointed as associate general secretary of the WCC, with special responsibility for relationships with national and regional Christian councils. In 1972 he became research secretary of the China Study Project of the British Council of Churches.

BIBLIOGRAPHY Victor E. W. Hayward, *The Church as Christian Community: Three Studies of North Indian Churches* (1966) and *Christians and China (1974).* Brian Stanley, *The History of the Baptist Missionary Society, 1792–1992* (1992); H. R. Williamson, *British Baptists in China, 1845–1952* (1957).

Brian Stanley

Heath, George Reinke (1879–1956), pioneer Moravian missionary in Honduras. Heath was born at Fairfield, Jamaica, where his English parents served the Moravian mission. Educated at the Moravian school at Fulneck, England, he studied at the University of Manchester until 1901, when he was called to serve as an English-speaking missionary in Nicaragua. In 1902 he was married in Jamaica to Marguerite Mellowes. They served in Nicaragua until 1923. From 1923 until 1926, they resided at Winston-Salem, North Carolina, where Heath taught at Salem College and began work on translation of the Scriptures into Miskito. In 1926 the couple returned to Jamaica and served there for four years. In 1930 they went to Honduras as the first Moravian missionaries among the Miskito people there. At first an extension of the work in Nicaragua, the mission became independent in 1938, and Heath became the first superintendent, serving until retirement in 1945.

Following retirement, the Heaths lived in Winston-Salem, where he continued his translation work of hymns, liturgies, and further portions of the Bible.

BIBLIOGRAPHY J. T. Hamilton and K. G. Hamilton, *History of the Moravian Church* (1967); *The Wachovia Moravian,* September 1956.

Albert H. Frank

Heber, Reginald (1783–1826), second Anglican bishop of Calcutta. Heber came from a family of Yorkshire gentry. After attending Oxford University, he traveled extensively in northern Europe and Russia. He was ordained in 1807 and was a conscientious vicar at Hodnet in Shropshire, England. He supported the Church Missionary Society (CMS), the Society for the Propagation of Christian Knowledge (SPCK), and the British and Foreign Bible Society. His broad-minded outlook was reflected in his suggestion in 1818 that the CMS and the Society for the Propagation of the Gospel (SPG) should unite. He was a poet of some note, and his popular hymns include "Holy, Holy, Holy" and "From Greenland's Icy Mountains." His scholarship was seen in his Bampton lectures in 1815, in his edition of Jeremy Taylor's works, and in his contributions to the *Quarterly Review.* He was consecrated bishop of Calcutta in 1823 and gained support from the SPCK, SPG, and CMS. He ordained the first Indian Anglican clergy. In contrast to his predecessor, T. F. *Middleton, Heber resolved the issue of episcopal jurisdiction over the CMS missionaries and established good relationships with them and with other Protestant missionaries. He supported Bishop's College, Calcutta, and the use of education and translations to spread Christian influence. His extensive travels are recorded in his *Narrative of a Journey* (1828), where he shows a positive appreciation of India and Indians and expresses support for missionary work undertaken in a spirit of moderation.

BIBLIOGRAPHY Reginald Heber, *Sermons Preached in England* (1829) and *Sermons Preached in India* (1829). Amelia Heber, ed., *The Life of Reginald Heber,* 2 vols. (1830) and *Narrative of a Journey,* 2 vols. (1828); M. A. Laird, ed., *Bishop Heber in Northern India: Selections from Heber's Journal* (1971)

Allan K. Davidson

Hebich, Samuel (1803–1868), Basel Mission leader in southwest India. Hebich was born of a country pastor's family near Ulm, Württemberg, Germany. In 1834 he was one of the first three missionaries commissioned by the Basel Mission for service in southwest India. He established mission stations at Mangalore and Cannanore; the latter became the base for a unique Christian community composed of British and Indian soldiers. Hebich was exceptionally successful in the conversion of young British officers, although his autocratic inclinations made him a difficult person to work with. His rather oversimplified revivalist preaching and his uncompromising fight against Hindu "paganism" aroused considerable criticism in India and Europe so that Hebich became the favorite target of radical opponents of pietism like the Swiss theologian E. F. Langhans. Still, when Hebich retired after 25 years of service, a solid foundation had been laid on which an Indian church could be built.

BIBLIOGRAPHY G. S. Thomssen: *Samuel Hebich of India* (1905).

Hans-Werner Gensichen

Hecker, Isaac Thomas (1819–1888), founder of the Missionary Society of St. Paul the Apostle (CSP; known as Paulist Fathers). Born in New York City of German-American parents and baptized a Lutheran, Hecker left public school to help support his family during the early 1830s. A voracious reader and an activist in reform politics, he was influenced by Romanticism, Transcendentalism, and the thought of Orestes Brownson. His conversion to Catholicism in 1844 was a gradual process rather than a single identifiable experience. After theological training in Europe, he returned to the United States as a Redemptorist priest in 1851 and immersed himself in missionary life with an emphasis upon evangelizing non-Catholics. During this period he wrote *Questions of a Soul* (1855) and *Aspirations of Nature* (1857), works that reveal his self-understanding as a missionary to America: the intellectual and spiritual stirrings of contemporary culture could be satisfied only by Catholic life and thought based upon the natural law truths, since these were fundamental to the American republican ethos. Frustrated with the confinements of the Redemptorist old world spirit, Hecker and others successfully appealed to Rome for recognition of their missionary vision, an appeal that led to the founding of the CSP in 1858. Under his leadership, the Paulists founded a monthly magazine, *The Catholic World* (1865–), took charge of St. Paul's Church in New York City, and engaged in parish missions. A theologian at the First Vatican Council, Hecker believed that the proclamation of papal infallibility ended post-Reformation defensiveness and began an era of the Holy Spirit most evident in American Catholic life. The French edition of Walter *Elliot's 1891 biography of Isaac Hecker ignited a controversy in 1898; right-wing polemicists coined the term "Heckerism," equated with a heterodox capitulation to modernity. Putative Heckerism was influential in Pope Leo XIII's condemnation of Americanism (1899).

BIBLIOGRAPHY Hecker's personal papers are held in the Paulist Fathers archives, Washington, D.C. Also see John Farina, *An American Experience of God: The Spirituality of Isaac Hecker* (1981) and ed., *Hecker Studies: Essays on the Thought of Isaac Hecker* (1983); David J. O'Brien, *Isaac Hecker, An American Catholic* (1992).

Christopher J. Kauffman

Heckewelder, John Gottlieb Ernestus (1743–1823), pioneer in the North American Moravian Indian missions. Born at Bedford, England, of a Moravian family, Heckewelder was educated in Moravian schools there and went to America with his family in 1754. He lived in the Bethlehem, Pennsylvania, Moravian community until 1762, when he accompanied Christian Frederick Post to Ohio on the first Moravian mission venture in the Northwest Territory. Though unsuccessful in establishing a settlement, he continued his work with the Indian missions and was the first schoolmaster at Schönbrunn, Tuscarawas County, Ohio, in 1772. He became fluent in the Delaware tongue and produced works on the history, customs, and manners of the Delaware Indians among whom he lived.

From 1777 to 1810 he served as agent for the Moravian Society for Propagating the Gospel. For many years, Heckewelder was chief assistant to David *Zeisberger and was ordained at Lititz, Pennsylvania, in 1778. In 1780 he founded and became resident missionary at Salem, Ohio, where he married Sarah Ohneburg. The couple had three daughters.

In 1781 Heckewelder and Zeisberger were tried in Detroit for treason but were exonerated. For the next 32 years Heckewelder traveled continuously in the work of the Indian missions and his denomination, journeying over 30,000 miles betwen 1754 and 1813. In 1798 he refounded the settlement at Gnadenhütten, Ohio, as a white congregation. He was employed as assistant peace commissioner at Vincennes (oldest town in what is now Indiana) in 1792 and at Detroit in 1793. Heckewelder retired to Bethlehem, where he died.

BIBLIOGRAPHY J. T. Hamilton and K. G. Hamilton, *History of the Moravian Church* (1967); J. E. Hutton, *History of the Moravian Church* (1909); Paul A. W. Wallace, *Thirty Thousand Miles with John Heckewelder* (1958).

Albert H. Frank

Heim, Karl (1894–1958), German theologian and mission spokesman. One of the most influential German systematic theologians of the early twentieth century, Heim is remembered by generations of students for his concern for the Christian mission. A native of Württemberg, he taught at Tübingen University beginning in 1920, attended a World's Student Christian Federation conference in East Asia in 1922, and took an active part in the world missionary conference at Jerusalem in 1928, both as a member of the German delegation and as one of the key speakers. Another important stage in his missiological development was marked by three essays he contributed to the first three issues of the newly founded *Evangelische Missions-Zeitschrift* in 1940; they dealt with the trinitarian foundation, the unity, and the purpose of mission. Appearing in the early stages of World War II, Heims's missiological appeal made a remarkable impact on a wide Christian audience at a time when the cause of mission seemed to be more at risk than ever before.

BIBLIOGRAPHY A popular introduction to Heim's thought in English is E. L. Allen, *Jesus Our Leader* (1950).

Hans-Werner Gensichen

Heine, Carl (1869–1944), Australian-born missionary in the Marshall Islands, Micronesia. Heine left his New South Wales home as a young man to become a trading agent for a New Zealand firm. During his first visit to the Marshalls in 1892, he decided to remain there. Settling on the island of Namorik, he married a Marshallese woman whose influence led to his religious conversion. When his wife died, Heine married again. He had nine children by his two marriages. He entered the service of the American Board of Commissioners for Foreign Missions and in 1906 was ordained to the ministry. Traveling throughout the island group, he helped coordinate Protestant church work. When Japanese rule forced the American missionaries to withdraw, Heine remained and assumed leadership of the church in the Marshalls. His quiet courage and unremitting effort strengthened the Protestant church during the troubled period of World War II. In 1944 he and his eldest son, Claude, were executed by the Japanese military.

BIBLIOGRAPHY John Garrett, *Footsteps in the Sea* (1992). Biographical information is also scattered throughout the DeBrum Papers, copies of which are contained at Alele Museum, Majuro, and the Micronesian Area Research Center, Guam. Additional information can be found in Heine's correspondence in the ABCFM Micronesia letters and papers, Houghton Library, Harvard Univ., Cambridge, Mass.

Francis X. Hezel, SJ

Heinrichs, Maurus (1904–1996), Franciscan missionary in China and Japan. Heinrichs was born at Gladbeck, Germany, joined the Franciscan Order in 1923, and was ordained a priest in 1929. He received a doctorate in theology at Innsbruck and another in sinology at Berlin before his departure for China in 1931. For more than 20 years he taught dogmatics in China and then served in the same capacity in Japan beginning in 1954 at St. Anthony Seminary, Tokyo. He wrote three volumes on Catholic dogmatics and one on fundamental theology (all in Latin), in dialogue with the main religions of Asia. These works were translated into Japanese in 1984 and following years. He also published three books on Christian theology and the Asian way of thinking about dialogue. The key themes of his theology are Christian revelation and religious experience.

BIBLIOGRAPHY Maurus Heinrichs, *Die Bedeutung der Missionstheologie, aufgewiesen am Vergleich zwischen den abendländischen und chinesischen Kardinaltugenden* (1954), *Theses dogmaticae*, 3 vols. (1954), *Theologia fundamentalis* (1958), *Katholische Theologie und asiatisches Denken* (1963), and *Christliche Offenbarung und religiöse Erfahrung im Dialog* (1984).

Arnulf Camps, OFM

Hemans, James Henry Emmanuel (1856–1908), Jamaican missionary to Central Africa. Hemans was born in Manchester County, Jamaica, and was the first black missionary sent by the London Missionary Society to Central Africa, arriving at Fwambo in 1888. A trained teacher and agriculturalist, he enjoyed relative success and popularity with Africans around Lake Tanganyika, which generated envy on the part of his white colleagues. They made life difficult for him and his wife (Maria Cecilia Clementina Gale), repeatedly accusing them of insubordination and complaining of Hemans's English pronunciation. He was finally demoted to menial work and was forbidden to hold a schoolbook in his hand each day between 7 A.M. and 4:30 P.M. Although his white colleagues insisted that they be the first to offer spiritual counsel to Africans, Hemans had come to be regarded as a friend who listened and understood the local inhabitants, and the Africans persisted in seeking him out. In the end, the social ostracism, constant criticism, blatant discrimination, and damaging gossip of his white colleagues led to Hemans's retirement and return to Jamaica in 1906. Hemans concluded that "dark-skinned missionaries could never be accepted on equal terms by their colleagues, and that their presence was therefore harmful to good relations between missionaries." A biographical study of this significant black missionary remains to be undertaken.

BIBLIOGRAPHY Jonathan J. Bonk, *The Theory and Practice of Missionary Identification, 1860–1920* (1989); Robert I. Rotberg, *Christian Missionaries and the Creation of Northern Rhodesia, 1880–1924* (1965).

Jonathan J. Bonk

Henderson, Ebenezer (1784–1858), pioneering contributor to the Bible Societies of Iceland, Scandinavia and Russia. A Scot, Henderson's only higher education was two years at Robert Haldane's congregational seminary. He became a noted biblical scholar and linguist, with honorary doctorates from Kiel (1816), Copenhagen, and Amherst (1840). His major achievement was the organization of Bible printing for Iceland. In Denmark from 1805 with John *Paterson, he was soon extending links with the British and Foreign Bible Society and with the Religious Tract Society to Sweden, Lapland, and Finland. Called to Russia to assist Paterson in 1816, he supervised Oriental and Hebrew translations for the Russian Bible Society, for which both men worked exclusively from 1822 to 1825. Returning to England in 1825, Henderson became David *Bogue's successor in the London Missionary Society training school, and was theological tutor at the amalgamated Highbury College until 1850. He published extensively. In 1842 he helped found the British Society for the Propagation of the Gospel among the Jews.

BIBLIOGRAPHY Henderson's works include *Iceland; or, A Journal of a Residence in That Island during the Years 1814–1815,* 2 vols. (1818) and *Biblical Researches and Travels in Russia* (1826). Elizabeth Bini, "British Evangelical Missionaries to Sweden in the First Half of the Nineteenth Century" (Ph.D. diss., St. Andrews Univ., 1983); James H. Glassman, "Ebenezer Henderson, Missionary, Traveller, Teacher, Bible Scholar" (Ph.D. diss., Edinburgh Univ., 1958); Thulia S. Henderson, *Memoir of Rev. Ebenezer Henderson* (1859).

Nancy Stevenson

Henderson, James (1867–1930), Scottish educational missionary in South Africa. Henderson was educated at Edinburgh University and New College before going to Malawi, in 1895, to serve the Livingstonia Mission. Initially he did pioneer work in what is now Zambia, but then he became head of the Training School at Khondowe, in Malawi. In 1906 he was called to become the third principal of the Lovedale Institution in the Cape Colony, the most important center of African education in the southern hemisphere. Almost as soon as he arrived, he was involved in the foundation of Fort Hare University College. He continued to keep Lovedale at the forefront of African education and a center of ecumenical cooperation. He edited the *South African Outlook,* in which Africans could express their opinions on any subject to do with Christianity or society in South Africa. At the time of his death he was still actively seeking to give South Africa an educated Christian African leadership whether the state wanted it or not.

BIBLIOGRAPHY Henderson's letters home from Malawi have been published as *Forerunners of Modern Malawi* (1968). A very good study of his life is contained in R. W. H. Shepherd, *Lovedale, South Africa: The Story of a Century* (1941).

Andrew C. Ross

Henriques, Henrique (1520–1600), Jesuit missionary in India. Henriques was born in Vila Viçosa, Portugal. Entering the Society of Jesus in 1545, he departed for India a year later. From 1547 to 1549 he worked as a missionary on the Fishery Coast. In 1549 he was elected superior of the mission and retained this post until 1576. His regular reports, mostly to the superior general, give a good picture of the external and internal development and concrete problems of the mission. All his life he was concerned about the transmission of the faith by means of the local languages. He himself arranged for printing a book on Christian doctrine in Tamil (1578), another book on Christian doctrine by Marcos Jorge, translated by himself into Tamil (1579), and *Flos Sanctorum* in Tamil (by various authors, 1586). Some of his works in the "Malabar" language (Tamil) are no longer extant, including a grammar, a dictionary, a booklet for confession, and a religious history from Creation to the Ascension. A total of sixty-five letters and other documents from his pen exist, mostly published in the *Monumenta Historica SJ* edited by J. *Wicki. One of his concerns from 1570 was to found and gain approval for the Brotherhood of Charity, a fraternity for which he had written the statutes and for which the Society of Jesus was to take responsibility. He hoped this organization would contribute to the consolidation of the faith. Among the more striking features of his character were a zealous striving for perfection, concern about the spirit of the Society of Jesus, love for prayer, loyalty to his vocation, willingness to endure long periods in difficult assignments, great understanding and affection for the local Christians; on the less positive side, he manifested an inclination to anxiety and overscrupulousness.

BIBLIOGRAPHY A. L. Farinha, *Vultos missionários da India quinhentista* (1955), pp. 71–132; J. Wicki, "P. Henrique Henriques S.J. (1520–1600): Ein vorbildlicher Missionar Indiens," *Studia Missionalia* 13 (1963): 113–168, reprinted in *Indian Ecclesiastical Studies* 4 (1965): 142–150; 5 (1966): 36–72, 175–189.

Karl Müller, SVD

Henry, Antonin-Marcel (1911–1987), French Dominican missiologist and theologian. Henry was a prolific writer and editor whose works appeared in thirty-seven languages. His interest in missions led to his founding *Parole et Mission* in 1958, which he edited for many years, and to teaching theology of missions at the Institut Catholique de Paris. His best-known mission publication before Vatican II, *A Mission Theology* (1962), emphasized hearing the Word of truth and apostolic preaching. While he had his eye on non-Christian areas of the world as especially the domain for missionary activity, he also saw the need in Europe of reaching out to social environments, such as that of the working class in France, where the Word of God was virtually unknown. Trained in systematic theology, he had special interest in Christology and the sacraments, the Holy Spirit, and, above all, spirituality. For many years he edited *La vie spirituelle* and its *Supplement.* He emphasized spiritual growth for laypersons, especially in married life. Within a missionary framework he emphasized Asia, cooperation with other Christians, and the relation of Christianity to other religions.

BIBLIOGRAPHY Antonin-Marcel Henry, ed., *Relation of Christianity with non-Christian Religions* (1966), *La force de l'Evangile*

(1968), *L'Asie nous interpelle* (1973), *La long marche de L'Eglise* (with Jean Chilini, 1981), and *Vivre et combattre la pauvrete* (1986).

Edward L. Cleary, OP

Henry (*or* Henrik) of Uppsala (d. 1156), the Apostle of Finland. Henry of Uppsala is in many ways a shadowy figure. Apparently born in England, though it is not known when or where, he was the fourth bishop of Uppsala, having arrived in Sweden with Cardinal Breakspear in 1153. He left for Finland in 1155 together with King Erik Jedvardson on what was more a political crusade than a missionary tour. There was already a small Christian presence in the Swedish-speaking west of Finland, and when Erik returned to Sweden, Henry remained to organize and care for the local Christians. His apostolic period was short but energetic. It has been said of him that he worked with apostolic zeal, though occasionally hardly with apostolic wisdom. Clearly he made enemies, and in 1156 he was assassinated. He was buried in Nousi Church, and his remains were later removed to Åbo Cathedral in Turku, Finland, of which diocese he was acknowledged as the apostle.

BIBLIOGRAPHY C. J. A. Oppermann, *The English Missionaries to Sweden and Finland* (1937), pp. 197–205.

Eric J. Sharpe

Hepburn, James Davidson (1840–1893), London Missionary Society (LMS) missionary to the Ngwato people of Botswana. Born in Newcastle upon Tyne into a poor home, Hepburn educated himself while working in a flour mill and later as a salesman. He was converted in his mid-twenties and volunteered to serve the LMS, which trained him and sent him to South Africa in 1870, immediately after his marriage and ordination. Initially he worked at the Ngwato capital, Shoshong, assisting John *Mackenzie until the latter went to Kuruman, Griqualand, in 1876. Hepburn stayed on with his growing family, becoming a close friend of the brilliant Christian king of the Ngwato, *Khama III, who had come to power in 1875. Hepburn moved with Khama to the new capital of Palapye in 1889, but by this time relations between them were breaking down. Khama saw his role as that of leader of his people and of the church among his people. Angry at having his authority as church leader challenged, Hepburn left for London in 1891. Repenting of his haste he returned the next year, but Khama would not receive him, so he retired to Britain in 1892.

BIBLIOGRAPHY *Twenty Years in Khama's Country, As Told in the Letters of Rev. J. D. Hepburn,* C. H. Lyall, ed. (1895); Elizabeth Hepburn, *Jottings, by Khama's Friend, Mrs J. D. Hepburn* (1928).

Andrew C. Ross

Heras, Enrique (*or* Henry) (1888–1955), Spanish Jesuit missionary and historian in India. Born in Barcelona, Heras went to Bombay, India, in 1922 as a Jesuit to work at St. Xavier's College, where he was appointed a lecturer in history. He became better known as Henry Heras and made a significant contribution as a historian and archaeologist. He founded the Indian Historical Research Institute in Bombay (1926), a center for research and teaching, where he trained some of the outstanding scholars of the country in his field. After his death, the institute was renamed the Heras Institute of Indian History and Culture. He worked on deciphering the Indus script of the early civilization of Mohenjodaro, which he classified as Proto-Dravidian. His *Aravidu Dynasty* (1927) remains a classic contribution to south Indian history. His involvement in Indian history and culture led him to promote Christian themes through Indian symbols and styles of art in painting, sculpture, iconography, and architecture. He also wrote *The Conversion Policy of the Jesuits in India* (1933) to defend his order against accusations of forced conversions, although he did not deny the misguided zeal of some individuals.

BIBLIOGRAPHY Bernard Anderson and John Correia-Alfonso, eds., *H. Heras: Indological Studies* (1990; contains a bibliography of Heras's writings). Melchior Balaguer, "Three Jesuits in Modern India Who Left a Mark," in Teotonio R. de Souza and Charles J. Borges, eds., *Jesuits in India: In Historical Perspective* (1992); John Correia-Afonso, George M. Moraes, and H. D. Sankalia, "Henry Heras: The Scholar and His Work," *Indica* 13 (1976).

Teotonio R. de Souza

Herman of Alaska (c. 1756–1837), Russian Orthodox missionary to Alaska. A monk of unknown birth and background prior to his entry into the Holy Trinity/St. Sergius Monastery in Zagorsk (formerly Sergiev), Russia, Herman (also known as "German" in Russian) became renowned for his simplicity and for zealously following the traditional ascetic life. After transferring in 1778 to the more stringent Valamo Monastery on an island in Lake Ladoga, Finland, he was recruited in 1794 to participate in a mission to the inhabitants of the newly discovered Aleutian Islands. Repeatedly declining ordination to the priesthood on the grounds of his unworthiness, Herman arrived on Kodiak Island in 1794 as the least of the ten monks. His lay status severely limited his ability to participate in the most active work, which presupposed the right to administer the sacraments to converts, but by his patience and irenic disposition he served a vital role as intermediary between the naive and idealistic brothers and the Russian colonial authorities, who resented any infringement of their unlimited license to enslave and exploit the people. When the head of the mission, the archimandrite Ioasaf *Bolotov, returned to Siberia in 1798, it was Herman rather than the surviving clerics who was named interim head; when news arrived that Bolotov had perished at sea, Herman was confirmed in the office permanently.

One by one the remaining missionaries retired from the rigors of life on Kodiak, leaving Herman alone. He dedicated the last three decades of his life to instructing the native Koniag Eskimos and the transplanted Aleuts in the rudiments of Christianity and in ways of improving their lives through agriculture and simple crafts. Most of them by then had been baptized and had learned to speak

Russian as employees of the Russian-American Company. Twice his courageous defense of the indigenous people's rights and his opposition to the calloused ways of the Russian fur hunters led to his exile on tiny Spruce Island, northeast of Kodiak. A coterie of indigenous people followed their *apa* (Father) there, drawn by his radiant personality. Following his death, they preserved his memory for over 60 years before his name was considered for canonization by the Russian Orthodox Church in 1900. Following the Bolshevik Revolution in 1917, his cause was pursued by Russian émigrés in 1936, 1953, and 1957. Finally in 1970, he was proclaimed the New World's first Orthodox saint.

BIBLIOGRAPHY Michael Oleksa, ed., *Alaskan Missionary Spirituality* (1987); Richard Pierce, ed., *The Russian Orthodox Religious Mission in America, 1794–1837* (1978); Vsevolod Rochcau, "Saint Herman of Alaska and the Defense of Alaskan Native Peoples," *St. Vladimir's Theological Quarterly* 16 (1972): 17–39.

Paul D. Garrett

Hermosilla, Jerónimo (1800–1861), Dominican missionary and bishop in Vietnam. Hermosilla was born in Santo Domingo de la Calzada, La Rioja, Spain, and joined the Order of Preachers (Dominicans) in Valencia in 1823. As a student, he left for the missions in the Far East, arriving in Manila in 1825, where he completed his studies at the University of Santo Tomas. After ordination he left for Tonkin (northern Vietnam) in 1829, where he worked for 32 years. Emperors Minh Mang (1820–1840) and Tu Duc (1847–1883), the Nero and Diocletian of Vietnam, persecuted Christianity violently, martyring some 150,000 Christians. More than half a million Christians also perished in the mountains, forests, and sea.

Appointed bishop in 1841, Hermosilla preached the gospel unceasingly, ordained Vietnamese clergy (both secular and Dominican), and trained catechists and laypersons. He was forced to live in hiding. To some contemporaries, Hermosilla was for Vietnam what the apostle Paul had been for the churches of Asia Minor. Taken captive by his persecutors, he and some of his companions were beheaded in Haiphong. Pius X beatified him in 1906, and in June of 1988 *John Paul II canonized him, along with a group of 116 other martyrs from Vietnam.

BIBLIOGRAPHY Telesforo Galarreta, *Vida y Martirio del Beato P. F. Jerónimo Hermosilla, Dominico, Obispo de Mileto y Vicario Apostólico del Tonquin Oriental* (1906); Pelayo S. Ripa, *Jerónimo Hermosilla, misionero y mártir riojano* (1988). Hermosilla's papers are in the Archivo de la Provincia del Santísimo Rosario in Avila, Spain, Sección Tonquin, 8.

Lucio Gutiérrez, OP

Hernández, Venancio (1914–), Mexican evangelist and missionary. A Mexican Otomí Indian born in San Nicolás, municipality of Ixmiquilpan, Hernández was converted in the 1930s through reading the Bible and comparing it with books of magic he had been reading and following. After his conversion, he decided to evangelize his own people in the Mezquital Valley in the state of Hidalgo, north of Mexico City. He worked as a foreman on a ranch near his own village for a year, responding to the people's needs and gaining their confidence, then began to witness and to preach. "Serve first and preach Christ afterward" became his motto and determined his mode of evangelism. In subsequent years, many churches were established in the valley and in the hills around it, with a total Christian community of about 8,000 Indians. Pastors who range in age from 25 to 65 are chosen for the respect they command in the various communities. Services are generally held in the Otomí language. The congregations are not dependent upon outside groups for funding or on missionaries for church work. More recently, their evangelistic efforts have spread to other indigenous and mestizo groups in four Mexican states. Hernández has collaborated with Bible translators of the Summer Institute of Linguistics (Wycliffe Bible Translators) in the Otomí Mezquital language.

BIBLIOGRAPHY Donald McGavran, *Church Growth in Mexico* (1963); Justo Gonzalez, *Historia de las Misiones* (1970), pp. 409–410; Hugh Steven and James C. Heffley, *Miracles in Mexico* (1972).

Sidney H. Rooy

Herrero, Andrés (1782–1838), Franciscan priest who restored his order's missions in Peru and Bolivia after the wars of independence. Born in Arnedo, Spain, Herrero entered the Franciscan province of Burgos and left for the New World in 1810. He worked in the mission college of San Francisco of Moquegua in southern Peru, spent a few years in the Bolivian jungle, and in 1820 was elected superior of all the Franciscan mission colleges in Peru and Bolivia. During the wars of independence (1810–1824), most Spanish missionaries were forced to return to Spain and their mission centers were closed. Herrero undertook the task of restoring them and sought aid from General Andrés de Santa Cruz, the Bolivian dictator, who supported his plans. In 1833 Herrero went to Spain and Italy, where he was received by the pope, and returned with a small band of new missionaries. After a second trip to Italy, in 1836, he was far more successful and returned with eighty-three Spanish and Italian Franciscans for Bolivia and Peru. The most famous of the mission colleges was Saint Rose of Ocopa, in the central Peruvian Andes. Herrero died while visiting the missions in Bolivia.

BIBLIOGRAPHY Fernando Domínguez, *El Colegio Franciscano de Propaganda Fide de Moquegua* (1955); Ordorico Sáiz, *Restauración de la Orden Franciscana en el Perú en el siglo XIX* (1993).

Jeffrey Klaiber, SJ

Herron, Walter (1910–1964), Australian-born pioneer of missionary aviation. Following the death in childbirth of his first wife, Violet, Herron—then a missionary in the remote lowlands of Bolivia—became convinced that air service could not only have saved her life but could also play a crucial role in bringing the gospel and improving the lives of people in Bolivia's El Beni Department. In 1941 he established the first permanent missionary air service, and the rest of his life was committeed to the development of missionary aviation. In 1961 he was awarded Bolivia's highest distinction, The Condor of the Andes, for his "untiring humanitarian services, cooperation with national and civil authorities, and above all, his leadership in the establishment of Tane Leprosarium with his own resources, and his valiant contribution to the progress of the country through the evangelization of tribes and the inauguration of air taxi service." It was signed by President Victor Paz Estenssoro.

BIBLIOGRAPHY C. Peter Wagner and Joseph S. McCullough, *The Condor of the Jungle* (1966). Papers related to Herron's work may be found in the SIM archives in Charlotte, N.C.

Gary R. Corwin

Herschell, Ridley Haim (1807–1864), missionary to Jews. Born in Strzelno, Poland, to Orthodox Jewish parents, Herschell was intensely religious and determined to become a rabbi. Intellectually gifted and spiritually sensitive, he felt a sense of sin covering his people. After encountering Reform Judaism and assimilated Jews in Germany, he traveled throughout Europe searching for answers to his questions about life. He came across a copy of the Beatitudes, later received and read a New Testament, and after a struggle, came to faith in Jesus as the Messiah in 1826. He was transformed and set out on a life of mission to Jewish people. In 1828 he went to study in London, eventually becoming an ordained Baptist minister. Herschell then helped to found the British Society for the Propagation of the Gospel among the Jews, in 1842, which became an effective agency for witness. He had a successful ministry in England and saw several other societies grow out of his own. A characteristic emphasis of his work was the distribution of New Testaments.

BIBLIOGRAPHY Ridley Haim Herschell, *Jewish Witnesses that Jesus Is the Christ* (1848). Jacob Gartenhaus, *Famous Hebrew Christians* (1979); Louis Meyer, *Eminent Hebrew Christians of the 19th Century* (1904).

Walter Riggans

Hetherwick, Alexander (1860–1939), Church of Scotland missionary in Malawi. Hetherwick graduated from Aberdeen University, the best mathematician of his class. He turned away from an academic career and trained for the Church of Scotland ministry. In 1885 he was ordained for missionary service with the Blantyre mission in Malawi, where D. C. *Scott sent him to open up new work among hitherto hostile groups beneath the Zomba plateau. Although very different temperamentally from Scott, Hetherwick soon became Scott's principal assistant and succeeded him as head of the mission in 1898. Hetherwick was an able linguist and chaired the committee that produced the complete Nyanja Bible, which was used until the late 1970s in Malawi, Zambia, and parts of Mozambique. Following in Scott's footsteps, he never flinched from challenging the colonial authorities over African rights and served as representative of those interests in the legislative council of the Protectorate from 1908 to 1913 and again from 1922 to 1925. His speeches before the government commission of enquiry into the John *Chilembwe rebellion of 1915 were, for the time, a startling insistence on the oneness of humanity transcending racial difference. Along with Robert *Laws, he was one of the main architects of the autonomous Church of Central Africa Presbyterian, which was inaugurated in 1924.

BIBLIOGRAPHY Hetherwick, as well as producing a new edition of D. C. Scott's *Cyclopediac Dictionary of the Cimang'anja Language,* wrote *Robert Hellier Napier* (1926) and *The Gospel and the African* (1932). In 1931, W. P. Livingstone produced Hetherwick's biography, *A Prince of Missionaries.*

Andrew C. Ross

Heurnius, Justus (1587–1652), Dutch pioneer missionary in the East Indies. Born in Leiden, Heurnius took a medical degree, traveled throughout Europe, became a theological student in Groningen, and subsequently served as pastor in Kalslagen beginning in 1620. He wrote *De legatione evangelica ad Indos capessenda admonitio* (1618) and asked the East India Company and the Amsterdam church to send him overseas. Through the efforts of Sebastiaen Danckaerts, one of the first pioneers of Dutch missions in the East Indies, Heurnius was sent to Batavia (present-day Jakarta) in 1624. There he organized the Dutch East Indies church and its order. Approaching the Chinese population, he prepared a Dutch-Latin-Chinese dictionary and translated the Heidelberg Catechism into Chinese. Temporarily barred from his work by fierce opposition from the colonial government, he was restored to office in 1632 and extended his work to several remote islands, starting from the island of Ambon. He proposed that a theological college should be established for indigenous students in the East Indies. After he returned to the Netherlands in 1639, he became a minister at Wijk bij Duurstede, where he and others translated the Bible into Malay.

BIBLIOGRAPHY J. van den Berg, *Constrained by Jesus' Love: An Inquiry into the Motives of the Missionary Awakening in Great Britain in the Period between 1698 and 1815* (1956); L. J. Joosse, *Scoone dingen sijn swaere dingen: Een onderzoek naar de motieven en de activiteiten in De Nederlanden tot verbreiding van de gereformeerde religie* (1992); G. M. J. M. Koolen, *Een seer bequaem middel: Onderwijs en Kerk onder de 17e eeuwse VOC* (1993).

Leendert J. Joosse

Heyer, John Christian Frederick (1793–1873), Lutheran missionary to India. A native of Helmstedt, in central Germany, Heyer received his early education in Philadelphia, Pennsylvania, where he stayed with his uncle. He studied for the Lutheran ministry at Göttingen University, Germany, and then returned to the United States where he served as a Lutheran home missionary. At the same time, he held himself in readiness to be sent out as a foreign missionary. After the death of the German

Lutheran missionary Carl *Rhenius of Tinnevelly, Heyer offered his services and after several delays was appointed to India by the missionary society of the Pennsylvania Lutheran ministerium. In 1842 he took up work among Telugu-speaking people north of Madras, with headquarters at Guntur. Reports on his successful start led to cooperation by the mission society of the (U.S.) Lutheran General Synod. In addition, the North German Missionary Society, assisted by Heyer, began work at Rajahmundry. In 1846 Heyer returned to the United States, became pastor of a German congregation, and obtained private medical training at Washington, D.C. Returning to Guntur in 1849, he began his most fruitful period of mission work, including medical service. In 1853 the missions of Guntur and Rajahmundry joined hands and organized the first Lutheran synod in India, with Father Heyer, as he was affectionately called, as president. After another sojourn in the States, Heyer returned to India for the third time, at age 76, in order to reorganize the work at Rajahmundry. His task fulfilled, he returned to the United States and died in Philadelphia.

BIBLIOGRAPHY E. Theodore Bachmann, *They Called Him Father* (1942); C. H. Swavely, "The India Mission of the United Lutheran Church in America," in C. H. Swavely, ed., *The Lutheran Enterprise in India* (1952), pp. 32–48.

Hans-Werner Gensichen

Heyling, Peter (1607/1608–c. 1652), missionary in Egypt and Ethiopia. A native of the Hanseatic city of Lübeck, Germany, Heyling studied law and theology in Paris (1628–1632), where he was influenced by Hugo de *Groot. Together with some fellow students he set out to "reawaken the derelict churches of the Orient to genuine evangelical life." After a period in Egypt, he traveled to Ethiopia in 1634, where he became an influential minister, teacher, and doctor at the court of King Fasilides (1632–1667) and attempted to bring about reform and renewal in Coptic Christianity. This resulted not only in Christological disputes but also in an Amharic translation of the New Testament. He was expelled from the country and died, probably in Sudan as a martyr. There are traces of his work in the Ethiopian Evangelical Church Mekane Yesus (founded in 1959).

BIBLIOGRAPHY Gustav Arén, *Evangelical Pioneers in Ethiopia: Origins of the Evangelical Church Mekane Yesus* (1978), pp. 34–38, 409 f.; P. A. Bredvey, "Peter Heyling: Etiopias første evangeliske misjonær," *Norsk Tidsskrift for Misjon* 11 (1957): 39–46; Otto F. A. Meinardus, "Peter Heyling, History and Legend," *Ostkirchliche Studien* 14 (1965): 305–326, and "De Petro Helingo Germano Lubecensi," *Zeitschrift des Vereins für Lübeckische Geschichte und Altertumskunde* 68 (1988): 139–157; Johann Heinrich Michaelis, *Sonderbarer Lebens-Lauff Herrn Peter Heylings* (1724) (extracted in Werner Raupp, ed., *Mission in Quellentexten,* 1990, pp. 97 ff.).

Werner Raupp

Hiebert, N(ikolas) N(ikolai) (1874–1957), Mennonite Brethren missionary and mission administrator. Born in the village of Lichtfelde, Molotschna, Ukraine, Hiebert came to the United States with his Mennonite Brethren parents when he was an infant. The family settled near Mountain Lake, Minnesota, where he grew up in a church with a missionary emphasis; he pursued studies at McPherson College in Kansas.

Following several years of teaching, Hiebert was ordained a minister of the gospel in January 1899 and married Susanna Wiebe in May. That same year he stood at the Mennonite Brethren annual conference to recite Luke 4:18–19 as his call to missions. He and his wife were commissioned as the first American Mennonite Brethren missionaries to India, traveling to their destination via the churches in Russia, which had sent their first missionaries to India in 1889. Illness forced the Hieberts to return to the United States within two years. Despite ongoing health problems, Hiebert made major contributions to Mennonite Brethren mission work as secretary of the mission board (1901–1936), Bible teacher, itinerant preacher, writer (1901–1947), and pastor in Mountain Lake (1918–1930), at the church that had shaped his missions perspective.

BIBLIOGRAPHY Hiebert's correspondence, papers, and notes are in the archives of the Center for Mennonite Brethren Studies in Fresno, California. They include his unpublished manuscript "A Brief Survey of My Life" (1874–1945); a tribute by his children, "N. N. Hiebert," *Zionsbote,* October 1947, p. 15; *Missions-Album aus der Mission der Mennoniten Brüdergemeinde von Nord Amerika* (1914?); and *Der Mitarbeiter: Ein Organ im Interesse der Reichsgottesarbeit* (n.d.).

Hans Kasdorf

Higginbottom, Sam (1874–1958), agricultural missionary in India. Born in England, Higginbottom went to the United States in 1894. After graduating from Princeton University, he went to India on a two-year appointment, which he spent teaching in a college in Allahabad. Concerned about the isolation of college students from the poverty of India's peasants, he planned an agricultural school that would train people to work with the farmers, unlike government agricultural schools, which trained people for desk jobs in agricultural departments. Back in the United States from 1909 to 1911, Higginbottom secured an agricultural degree and raised funds, which his Presbyterian mission board would not provide. He raised enough to make a gradual start and finally, in 1919, the Allahabad Agricultural Institute was founded.

His project attracted wide attention. Gandhi became an eager supporter, as did several maharajahs, and the Indian government decorated him repeatedly. He was a world pioneer in soil reclamation, starting with the barren land on which his institute stood. The institute expanded greatly over time, though Higginbottom lost some of his best faculty recruits because of his domineering ways. He had no interest in the evangelistic work of the mission, believing that Christianity should be commended only by good works. He retired in Florida in 1945.

BIBLIOGRAPHY Sam Higginbottom, *Sam Higginbottom, Farmer: An Autobiography* (1949) and *The Gospel and the Plow: Or, The Old*

Gospel and Modern Farming in Ancient India (1921, 1938). Gary R. Hess, *Sam Higginbottom of Allahabad: Pioneer of Point Four to India* (1967).

Charles W. Forman

Hill, David (1840–1896), British Wesleyan Methodist missionary to China. Hill, who was from York, received theological training at Richmond. After ordination, he was posted to the English Wesleyan Methodist Central China field, based in Wuchang, Hupeh (Hubei) Province. Unmarried, he was more mobile than most Protestant missionaries. In 1878 a famine ravaged Shansi (Shanxi) Province, prompting Hill and a few others (including the British Baptist Timothy *Richard) to devote nearly two years to famine relief work. This experience transformed Hill's ministry into one with an expanded social vision and considerable ecumenicity. While in Shansi in 1879, through an essay contest, he was instrumental in the conversion of *Hsi Sheng-mo (Xi Shengmo), a talented and dynamic leader who as an independent pastor had a considerable regional impact until his death in 1896.

In his later years Hill established a hospital and homes for the aged, the blind, and orphans; he also helped to begin the Central China Religious Tract Society. In 1890 he had a major role in the nationwide Shanghai missionary conference. He seems to have been respected and beloved in all quarters, and his early demise was counted a great loss.

BIBLIOGRAPHY *Days of Blessing in Inland China, Being an Account of Meetings Held in the Province of Shan-si, etc.,* intro. by J. Hudson Taylor (1887); William T. A. Barber, *David Hill, Missionary and Saint* (1898); Harold B. Battenbury, *David Hill, Friend of China: A Modern Portrait* (1949); Jane Elizabeth Hellier, *How David Hill Followed Christ: A Biography* (n.d.); Mrs. Howard Taylor, *One of China's Scholars: The Culture and Conversion of a Confucianist* (1900, 1907). Hill's official correspondence is in the Central China field section of the Wesleyan Methodist Missionary Society archive, now at the School of Oriental and African Studies, Univ. of London.

Daniel H. Bays

Hill, John Henry (1791–1882), American Episcopal missionary in Greece. Hill was born in New York City and educated at Columbia University. After commercial pursuits, he studied at Virginia Theological Seminary, was ordained in 1830, and sailed for Greece with his wife, Frances M. (Mulligan). In Athens, which was recovering from the war of independence, the Hills established in their home a school that nurtured three generations of Greek women in Christian faith and learning. Other schools were established for girls and boys, which afterward became the models and source of teachers for state schools. In their 50 years of service in Greece they took pains not to proselytize or to speak against the Greek Orthodox Church. Their sensitivity won wide respect from the authorities. In addition to educational work, Hill translated many sacred and secular works into modern Greek and published editions of Greek classics. For many years he served as chaplain to the British Legation. He was awarded an honorary D.D. from Harvard University in 1856 and an LL.D. from Columbia University in 1868. His modesty led him to refuse decoration from the Greek government, but when he died in Athens, the government gave him a state funeral.

BIBLIOGRAPHY W. A. R. Goodwin, *History of the Theological Seminary in Virginia and Its Historical Background,* vol. 2 (1923), pp. 252–272; *Proceedings of the Board of Missions of the Protestant Episcopal Church* (1872), p.36.

Peter R. Rodgers

Hill, Mary (Beardsmore) (1791–1847), pioneer missionary in Berhampore, Bengal, and writer. Born in Newcastle-under-Lyme, England, Mary Beardsmore was 20 when she married Micaiah Hill, a Congregational minister, and sailed to Calcutta with him for work there under the London Missionary Society (LMS). She quickly became fluent in Bengali and started girls' schools. In 1824, the Hills were sent to Berhampore, a very conservative town and a military station, where they persevered in the face of European and Indian opposition. Mary Hill came to concentrate on orphans (especially following the 1837–1838 floods) and Indian Christian women, complementing her husband's work and sharing his courage. He was the first in India to develop a model farm, rural industries, and handicrafts as a vehicle of evangelism and social uplift, as well as a printing press and orphanage. Despite repeated pregnancies, Mary was the first woman missionary to itinerate regularly with her husband. When she returned from furlough in 1839, she discovered her talent for writing. The LMS could not get enough of her vivid articles on religious and social issues. She also wrote fiery letters to the LMS about the injustices suffered by her husband who was overworked and in debt. Eventually their sons William (served 1847–1863) and Samuel (served 1852–1891) were accepted by the LMS, the latter reaping the fruits of his parents' work at Berhampore when he took over the schools and orphanage in 1864 and reformed them. Her children's piety comforted Mary after a fall and injuries in Calcutta that eventually led to her death. Her husband was already in poor health, and his grief broke him. He died on the Ganges below Varanasi (Benares) while traveling to their daughter's home in Jullender and is buried in Varanasi.

BIBLIOGRAPHY LMS Berhampore Mission papers, CWM archives, SOAS, London.

E. M. Jackson

Hinderer, David (1820–1890) *and*
Anna (Martin) (1827–1870), missionaries in Yorubaland (now in Nigeria). David Hinderer came from rural Württemberg, near Schorndorf, Germany, and trained at the Basel Mission seminary. Accepted by the Church Missionary Society, he entered their training college in London in 1846 and received Anglican ordination (deacon 1847, priest 1848). He joined the Yoruba mission in 1849, with a view to expanding the work up the Niger to Hausaland. Since Henry *Townsend was absent in England, Hinderer was first stationed at Abeokuta, where, like

Townsend, he concluded that Ibadan City, rather than Hausaland, was the proper target of expansion. In 1851 he was the first Western visitor to Ibadan. On sick leave in England next year, he married Anna Martin. Born in Hempnall, Norfolk, and early left motherless, Anna was living in the family of Francis Cunningham, vicar of Lowestoft, a connection by marriage of T. F. *Buxton.

The Hinderers went to Yorubaland in 1856, opening work in Ibadan. Though their reception was cordial, the Christian response was not spectacular. The small church that emerged, however, was later to blossom under Daniel Olubi, who himself grew up in the Hinderer household. The striking characteristic of the Hinderers was human warmth; they made friends readily—among them Olubi, J. C. Akielle, Henry and Samuel *Johnson, and others who became leading lights in the West African churches. Longstanding mutual affection bound Anna and the many children who lived in or visited their compound. David became an effective translator and as the mission's Hebraist, its chief Old Testament reviser.

The Ijaye War long clouded their work. Abeokuta and Ibadan were on opposing sides, and Hinderer lamented the missionary tendency, illustrated in Townsend, to take Abeokuta's part. The war circumscribed missionary activity, and the Hinderers were cut off for several years from colleagues, mission headquarters, money, and supplies, with David at times in real danger. They finally left Ibadan in 1869, the city having resisted pressure from Abeokuta to expel them in the *Ifole*—the movement for expulsion of all whites. Both were broken in health, and they retired in England to take pastoral charge of the village of Martham, Norfolk. Here Anna died. David returned to Yorubaland in 1874, laying the foundation of the church in Ondo and other areas east of Lagos. He finally retired in 1877, while continuing to work on Yoruba translation. A memoir based on Anna's journal and letters became a popular and much-quoted classic of women's missionary work.

BIBLIOGRAPHY J. F. A. Ajayi, *Christian Missions in Nigeria, 1841–1891* (1965); S. O. Biobaku, *The Egba and Their Neighbours, 1842–1872* (1957); *CMS Register of Missionaries*, no. 391; [Anna Hinderer], *Seventeen Years in the Yoruba Country*, R. B. Hone, ed., (1872); Ellen Thorp, *Swelling of Jordan* (1950; a novel based on Anna Hinderer's life).

Andrew F. Walls

Hinsley, Arthur (1865–1943), visitor apostolic to Catholic missions in British Africa and Cardinal Archbishop of Westminster. Hinsley, a Yorkshireman, was ordained a priest in 1893. With many years of pastoral service at home behind him, he was serving as rector of the English College in Rome when in 1927 he was selected for the special appointment of visitor apostolic to Catholic missions throughout British Africa. The Phelps-Stokes Reports (1920 and 1924) had pointed the way toward a new concentration by colonial governments on African education, especially secondary education, following a trail blazed by some Protestant missions. It was clear that the future of Africa would be decided educationally, but most Catholic missions lagged badly behind. Hinsley's task was to convince Catholic missionaries that education through the medium of English and full cooperation with the British authorities was the top priority. "Collaborate with all your power," he told a conference of bishops and leading missionaries at Dar es Salaam in August of 1928, "and where it is impossible for you to carry on both the immediate task of evangelization and your educational work, neglect your churches in order to perfect your schools." Hinsley's mission was decisively important for a shift in Catholic policy, though his advice has also been criticized. His African success led to his appointment in 1935 as Archbishop of Westminster (London). He was made a cardinal by *Pius XI in 1937.

BIBLIOGRAPHY John Heenan, *Cardinal Hinsley* (1944); R. Oliver, *The Missionary Factor in East Africa* (1952).

Adrian Hastings

Hislop, Stephen (1817–1863), Scottish missionary and scientist in India. Hislop was a son of a small builder in Duns, Berwickshire. He showed early talents as a naturalist. Paying his way through university by teaching and tutoring, he studied arts at Edinburgh (where scientific training was good) and divinity at Glasgow and Edinburgh. His evangelical conversion came through W. C. *Burns, his missionary vocation through John *Wilson. In 1844 the Free Church of Scotland appointed him to western India, from where Wilson had called for a scientist. Soon, however, he was sent to open a mission recently endowed by an army officer at Nagpur, in central India. He spent the rest of his life there, except for a period in 1850–1851 when he relieved the invalided John *Anderson in Madras, and a sick leave in 1858–1860, when he assisted the revival in eastern Scotland, attended the Liverpool Conference on Missions, and continued Alexander *Duff's rehabilitation of mission organization and finance in the Free Church of Scotland.

Hislop followed Duff's model of mission, based on Christian education with a view to creating a new intellectual environment. His school, for long the only one in Nagpur, developed into the university-level Hislop College. He differed from Duff in constantly preaching in the vernacular (he excelled in Marathi) and in having a clearer view of the complexities of Indian religion. Furthermore, the Free Church being then the only Protestant mission in Nagpur, Hislop addressed all strands of the population: majority and minority communities, migrants, European and Indian troops, and administrators. The small Christian church drew upon all these sectors. Hislop spent a month of each year with the neglected aboriginal Gondh people. His posthumous *Papers Related to the Aboriginal Tribes of the Central Provinces* (R. Temple, ed., 1866) includes an ethnographic survey, a vocabulary distinguishing dialects and offering parallels with Telugu and Tamil, and a translation of the Gondh myth, which Hislop used as a starting point for Christian teaching. His scientific work gradually attained major significance. A pioneer of Indian geology, he was also a botanist, zoologist, and archaeologist, declaring such activities "glorifying to the God of truth." Nagpur's status changed during his time: the princely state became a "non-regulation" British administered territory, and then the core of the Central Provinces of British India. The uncompromising Hislop often had uncomfortable relations with officialdom, both Indian and British. The former he thought corrupt, the latter (until the arrival of Sir Richard Temple), inept. In the 1857 mutiny, a warning from a Muslim friend saved Hislop and the Europeans resident in Nagpur. Six years later he drowned crossing a swollen river while on an archaeological expedition. He left few writings apart from his scientific papers.

BIBLIOGRAPHY W. Ewing, *Annals of the Free Church of Scotland* 1 (1914), p. 186; S. Neill, *History of Christianity in India, 1707–1858* (1985), pp. 316–319; George Smith, *Stephen Hislop, Pioneer Missionary and Naturalist in Central India from 1844 to 1863* (2d ed., 1889); John Wilson, *Memorial Discourse on the Death of the Rev. Stephen Hislop of Nagpur* (1866).

Andrew F. Walls

Hitchcock, John William (1882–1919), medical missionary in Nigeria with the Free Church of Scotland. Born in England at Bures, St. Mary, Suffolk, Hitchcock studied at Edinburgh Royal Infirmary and went to Nigeria in 1911. He first did a tour of relief duty at Itu hospital, then went north on an exploratory journey into Igbo land to locate a site for a mission hospital. He recommended Uburu, the site of a significant regional market; a hospital was built there, and Hitchcock became the first doctor. After serving there from 1912 to 1917, he contracted influenza during the epidemic of 1918 and died at Itu in January 1919.

BIBLIOGRAPHY Geoffrey Johnston, *Of God and Maxim Guns: Presbyterianism in Nigeria, 1846–1966* (1988); W. P. Livingstone, *Dr. Hitchcock of Uburu* (1920); M. Ross and N. Obini, *Presbyterian Joint Hospital, Uburu, 1913–1988* (1988).

Geoffrey Johnston

Hitotsuyanagi, William Merrell Vories. *See* Vories, William Merrell.

Hobson, Benjamin (1816–1873), pioneer medical missionary in China. Born in Welford, Northamptonshire, England, Hobson studied medicine in University College, London, married Jane Abbey, and was sent to China by the London Missionary Society (LMS). Arriving at Macao in 1839, shortly after his colleague William *Lockhart, Hobson began his career by working in close cooperation with Peter *Parker. He worked at Macao until 1843, when he took charge of a new mission hospital in Hong Kong. It drew a much greater number of patients than anticipated, compelling him to rely heavily on help from Chinese nationals. This development made him think about systematic medical training for Chinese, a need felt also by other medical missionaries. In 1845 he left for England because of the ill health of his wife, who died on the voyage.

In England, Hobson married Rebecca Morrison, daughter of Robert *Morrison, then returned to the hospital in Hong Kong in 1847. But his idea of medical training for Chinese—which he conceived as early as 1844—remained unfulfilled, since he was requested by the LMS to move to Canton (1848), then to Shanghai (1858), before he finally left China for good because of health problems. Nevertheless, he laid the foundation, and his vision came to realization in 1881 at Tientsin (Tianjin) under John Kenneth *MacKenzie, another LMS medical missionary, who compiled and translated medical textbooks into Chinese. Hobson died at Forest Hill, near London.

BIBLIOGRAPHY William Lockhart, *The Medical Missionary in China* (1861); K. Chimin Wong, *Lancet and Cross* (1950); K. Chimin Wong and Wu Lieh-Teh, *History of Chinese Medicine* (1932).

Christoffer H. Grundmann

Hocking, William Ernest (1873–1966), philosopher of religion. Born in Cleveland, Ohio, Hocking received his M.A. and Ph.D. from Harvard. From 1914 until his retirement in 1943, he was professor of philosophy at Harvard. His work focused on analyzing human experience, especially the experience of God. In *The Meaning of God in Human Experience* (1912), he advocated "widened empiricism" that located the ideal forms of transcendent reality within the bounds of pragmatic experience. His concern for Christian missions began in his teenage years with his conversion during a Methodist "experience meeting." His mature philosophy of missions was summarized in *The Coming World Civilization* (1958), in which he foresees Christian faith as the "binding ingredient" of a world culture. Prior to that he published three books dealing with mission themes: *Human Nature and Its Remaking* (1918), *Re-thinking Missions* (1932), and *Living Religions and a World Faith* (1940). The fame and controversy of *Re-thinking Missions,* in which he summarized a group report of the Laymen's Foreign Missions Inquiry, overshadowed and somewhat distorted his other work. He later commented that there was much he personally believed that could not be included. *Human Nature and Its Remaking,* a study of the ethical need to reshape the human will-to-power in a creative direction, proposes the Christian world mission as the ultimate instrument of that creativity since it confers power on others rather than seeking to gain power over them. *Living Religions and a World Faith* argues that there is a fundamentally human "nuclear experience" of God that is best interpreted in Christian terms, an argument that has much in common with St. Augustine's view that Christianity is the natural religion of humankind.

Hocking's famous debate with Hendrik *Kraemer began when Kraemer's *The Christian Message in a Non-Christian World* (1938) stated that there was no word of authentic Christianity in *Re-thinking Missions.* Twenty-five years later, however, in the Hocking festschrift, Kraemer called Hocking a "shining example of truly Christian urbanity," and Hocking had moved much closer to Kraemer's modified neo-orthodox position.

BIBLIOGRAPHY Among Hocking's twenty-two published books are *Thoughts on Death and Life* (1937), *Science and the Idea of God* (1944), and *The Meaning of Immortality in Human Experience*

(1957). The Hocking Festschrift, *Philosophy, Religion, and the Coming World Civilization* (1966), Leroy S. Rouner, ed., contains a bibliography of Hocking's work by Richard Gilman. Hocking's philosophy is the subject of Leroy S. Rouner's *Within Human Experience: The Philosophy of William Ernest Hocking* (1969). Hocking's personal library is located on the grounds of the family home in Madison, New Hampshire. Most of his professional papers are in the Houghton Library at Harvard.

Leroy S. Rouner

Hodges, Melvin Lyle (1909–1988), missionary to Latin America and Pentecostal missiologist. Hodges was born in Lynden, Washington, to parents who had left the Methodist Church to join the Pentecostal movement. Although he lacked a formal theological education (with the exception of courses in New Testament Greek at Colorado College), he became an evangelist in 1928, the same year in which he married Lois M. Crews. Ordination with the Assemblies of God (AG) came a year later.

During the process for gaining missionary appointment in 1935, Hodges was urged by Noel *Perkin, AG missionary secretary, to read the books of Roland *Allen, which shaped his missiology before he reached El Salvador in 1936. Under the initial tutelage of Ralph D. *Williams, Hodges helped redirect the AG in Nicaragua from a paternalistic structure dependent upon American financial assistance to one based on indigenous church principles.

Beginning in 1945, Hodges assumed editorial and added administrative responsibilities in Central America and at the mission headquarters in Springfield, Missouri. Through his lectures, the publication of *The Indigenous Church* (1953), and his work editing the *Missionary Forum*, he began retraining the existing missionary personnel and preparing candidate missionaries to work toward the growth of strong evangelistic "New Testament" churches overseas led by national church leaders. Hodges also served as field director of AG missionaries in Latin America and the Caribbean from 1954 to 1973. Upon his retirement, he became professor of missions at the Assemblies of God Theological Seminary, Springfield, Missouri; he left that post due to ill health in 1985.

Hodges's formative influence in AG missions stemmed from his Pentecostal adaptation of the missiology of Roland Allen and his belief that the role of the Holy Spirit in evangelism and church growth as portrayed by the Book of Acts is indispensable for successful mission work today. His many books include *A Theology of the Church and Its Mission* (1977) and *The Indigenous Church and the Missionary* (1978).

BIBLIOGRAPHY Luisa Jeter de Walker, *Siembra y Cosecha Reseña histórica de las Asambleas de Dios de México y Centroamérica*, vol. 1 (1990); Gary B. McGee, *This Gospel Shall Be Preached: A History and Theology of Assemblies of God Foreign Missions*, 2 vols. (1986, 1989), and "Assemblies of God Missiology by the 1990's: A Pilgrimage of Change and Continuity Since 1914," paper presented at the twenty-first annual meeting of the Society for Pentecostal Studies, Lakeland, Fla., November 7–9, 1991. A comprehensive bibliography of Hodge's publications is available through the AG archives, Springfield, Mo.

Gary B. McGee

Hodgkin, Henry Theodore (1877–1933), Quaker missionary and administrator in China. Born in England, Hodgkin received his education at King's College, Cambridge. He was chairman of the English Student Missionary Union from 1902 to 1905. He went to China with the Friends' Foreign Missionary Association in 1905 and remained until 1909. For the next ten years (1910–1920) he was secretary of the Friends' Foreign Missionary Association. He lectured in China in 1921 and then assumed duties (1922–1929) as one of the secretaries of the National Christian Council of China. During the last four years of his life he directed a graduate school in England for the Society of Friends. A prolific author, he wrote *The Christian Revolution* (1923), *Friends beyond the Seas* (1916), and *Living Issues in China* (1932).

BIBLIOGRAPHY George Herbert Wood, *Henry T. Hodgkin: A Memoir* (1937). See also various issues of *The Chinese Recorder.*

Ralph R. Covell

Hodgson, Thomas Laidman (1787–1850), English Methodist missionary in southern Africa. Ordained in 1815, Hodgson sailed with his wife, Anne, to South Africa in 1821. He and his colleague, Samuel Broadbent, sought to work beyond the area already influenced by other missionaries. Making the very arduous journey to beyond the Vaal River, they contacted the Rolong division of the Tswana people. There, near present-day Wolmeransstad, they were pioneers in adding agricultural innovation to evangelism and education as part of the missionary task. After a brief stay in Cape Town in 1824, Hodgson returned to the Rolong in 1825, accompanied by James *Archbell. In 1828 he went to work among unevangelized Griqua at Boetsap. His wife's death while on leave in England in 1831 led to a decision not to return. However, after a few years he changed his mind and in 1838 arrived in Cape Town with his new wife, Elizabeth, to succeed Barnabas *Shaw as chairman of the district. In these last years he made the so-called Cape Coloured people his main pastoral concern.

BIBLIOGRAPHY T. Smith, *Memoirs of the Rev. Thomas Laidman Hodgson* (1854).

Andrew C. Ross

Hoecken, Christian (1808–1851), Jesuit missionary to Native Americans. Hoecken was born in the Netherlands and educated at St. Joseph's College, Tournout, Belgium, where he was influenced by Pierre-Jean De Nef, a Catholic layman who served as director of the school. De Nef encouraged him, as he had Pierre *DeSmet and John *Schoenmakers, to consider mission work among Native Americans. He also studied at the Minor Seminary of St. Michael, Gestel, Belgium. In 1832 he joined the Society of Jesus in Belgium, was ordained a priest, and departed for America. Going to Missouri and later to Kansas, he served the Kickapoo Indians from 1836 to 1838. Not only did he learn their language and write a dictionary, but they called him Father Kickapoo because of his facility with the Kickapoo language and his established relationships with them. In 1838 he founded a Catholic mission among the Osage River Potawatomi and served them there until they were relocated in 1841. From 1841 until 1847 he worked among the Potawatomi at Sugar Creek, Kansas, and wrote a Potawatomi grammar and dictionary. He also accompanied them during their relocation in 1847 to the Kaw Valley in Kansas and established a mission station among them there. Under his guidance the mission was headquartered at Mission Creek, which was near St. Mary's, the home of many of the other Jesuit missionaries among the Potawatomi. During the 1840s he also visited the Sauk, Piankashaw, Miami, and Peoria in Kansas. He established two churches in 1849—Our Lady of Sorrows Church, at Mission Creek, and St. Joseph's Church, at Mechgamiinak, Kansas. These churches were constructed to serve the Potawatomi and the Kansa Native Americans respectively. During this same year, he sought to enroll children from the Kansa Indians for the mission school. In 1850 and 1851 he accompanied Pierre DeSmet on a mission to the Sioux. He contracted cholera and died on a journey accompanying DeSmet to a Great Council of all Native Americans east of the Rocky Mountains.

BIBLIOGRAPHY Gilbert J. Garraghan, *The Jesuits of the Middle United States,* 3 vols. (1938); John Francis Xavier O'Connor, *The Jesuits in the Kaw Valley: An Account of the Missionary and Educational Work of the Jesuits of St. Mary's, Kansas* (1925); Francis Xavier Kuppens, "History of St. Mary's Mission among the Potawatomies," unpublished manuscript in the Jesuit Missouri Province archives, Saint Louis, Mo., the location also of Hoecken's letters and papers.

Paul O. Myhre

Hoekendijk, J(ohannes) C(hristiaan) ("Hans") (1912–1975), Dutch missiologist. Hoekendijk was born and raised in western Java (Indonesia), where his parents were missionaries until 1925, when the family returned to the Netherlands. He prepared himself for a missionary career in Indonesia and studied theology at the State University of Utrecht. World War II both delayed his plans and had a lasting influence on his later thinking about mission as the confrontation of the kingdom of God and the secular world. Hoekendijk served as missionary consul in Indonesia for one year (1945–1946) and then had to return to the Netherlands because of health problems. He became secretary of the Netherlands Missionary Council (1947–1949) and of the Department of Evangelism of the World Council of Churches (WCC) (1949–1953). He taught at the State University of Utrecht as church professor in practical theology (1953–1959) and as state professor in church history of the twentieth century (1959–1965). In 1965 he was appointed to the chair of World Christianity at Union Theological Seminary in New York, where he remained until his death. His contributions to the International Missionary Council and the WCC include especially his work on the world mission conference of Willingen (1952) and on the WCC study project "The Missionary Structures of the Congregation" (1961–1966).

Hoekendijk participated in the ecumenical discussions on mission with emphases that have often been labeled radical. Insisting that the church can be no more than a function of God's work for worldly *shalom,* he criticized all tendencies toward ecclesiocentrism and toward the elevation of the categories of church and mission over categories of "people" and "nation." There is a strong eschatological element in this position, and also an effort to take the secular world seriously as the arena where *kerygma, koinonia,* and *diakonia* appear as references to the coming kingdom. Although himself critical of emerging forms of liberation theology, Hoekendijk is rightly considered to have been a major influential figure behind post-1970 paradigm changes in missionary thinking.

BIBLIOGRAPHY Hoekendijk's major academic work is his dissertation *Kerk en Volk in de Duitse Zendingswetenschap* (1948), edited in German with an added appendix as *Kirche und Volk in der Deutschen Missionswissenschaft* (1967). Some of his important earlier essays are collected in *The Church Inside Out* (1966); some of his contributions to the WCC study project on the missionary structures can be found in *Planning for Mission,* edited by Thomas Wieser (1966). G. Coffele, *Johannes Christiaan Hoekendijk: Da una teologia della missione ad una teologia missionaria* (1976); P. van Gurp, *Kerk en zending in de theologie van Johannes Christiaan Hoekendijk* (1989); L. A. Hoedemaker, "The Legacy of J. C. Hoekendijk," *IBMR* 19, no. 4 (1995): 166–170. A collection of documents related to Hoekendijk's work is kept at the library of the State Univ. of Utrecht, Netherlands.

Libertus A. Hoedemaker

Hoëvell, Wolter Robert van (1812–1879), Dutch Reformed minister in the Dutch East Indies. Born in Deventer, Netherlands, a descendant of an old patrician family, van Hoëvell enrolled as a theological student in Groningen in 1829. In addition to his theological studies, he trained himself in literature and rhetoric. After finishing a thesis entitled "The Unity of the Church According to Irenaeus" (1836), he was ordained and embarked with his wife to the Dutch East Indies. He demonstrated his linguistic talent both in preaching and in writing. He edited the first Christian journal in the East Indies: *Tijdschrift ter Bevordering van den Christelijken zin in Neêrland's Indiê* (1846–1847); his essays reflected his critical views of Dutch colonial policy about education, poverty, and slavery in the indigenous population. Conflict with the colonial authorities was inevitable, and he finally resigned and returned home in 1848, where he campaigned as a member of the Dutch parliament for an enlightened policy toward the people in the colonies.

BIBLIOGRAPHY Van Hoëvell published impressions of his travels in *Reis over Java, Madura en Bali in het miden van 1847,* 2 vols. (1849, 1854) and *Uit het Indisch leven* (1860). Two friends wrote biographical tributes on the occasion of van Hoëvell's death: G. J. von Soest, in *Tijdschrift voor Nederlandsch-Indië,* 1879, pp. 1–72, and P. J. Veth, in *De Nederlandsche Spectator,* no. 12 (March 22, 1879): 90–93.

Marjo A. Hogendorp

Hoffman, C(adwallader) Colden (1819–1865), American Episcopal missionary in West Africa. A native of New

York City, Hoffman studied at Virginia Episcopal Seminary, and went as a missionary to Cape Palmas, Liberia, in 1849. He learned the Glebo language and established missions and schools. In 1854 ill health forced his return to the United States. On his return to Africa in 1855, his wife died of consumption, but Hoffman continued his work with ever greater determination and self-sacrifice. He preached not only in the area of Cape Palmas but for 60 miles into the interior, where people thronged to hear the gospel. In order to reach remote villages, he slept on bare floors in small smoky huts and often missed meals. These long journeys on foot to the interior broke his health. In 1858 he married Caroline Hogan, a veteran missionary of the Cape Palmas station. After his death she directed the orphan asylum in Cape Palmas, then returned to Philadelphia, Pennsylvania, to found a home for missionary children.

BIBLIOGRAPHY K. W. Cameron, *An Index for the Spirit of Missions, 1836–1900* (1977), p. 24; George Townshend Fox, *A Memoir of The Rev. C. Colden Hoffman* (1868); W. A. R. Goodwin, *History of the Theological Seminary in Virginia and Its Historical Background,* vol. 2 (1923), pp. 312–318.

Peter R. Rodgers

Hoffmann, Johannes Baptist (1857–1928), Jesuit missionary linguist in India. Born in Wallendorf, Eifel, Germany, Hoffmann entered the Belgian province of the Society of Jesus in 1877 and a year later, still a novice, was sent to Chota Nagpur, India. As an ordained missionary, he labored zealously among the people of the forested highlands and converted many aboriginals, especially Mundas, until his expulsion from India in 1915. He reported and evaluated his work in a booklet *37 Jahre Missionär in Indien. Tröstliche Erfahrungen beim Naturvolk der Mundas: der Misserfolg in der Missionierung höherer Kasten und seine Ursachen* (1923). His memory lives on because of three undertakings in particular. First, through the founding of a Catholic cooperative—the first in India—he helped to save the peasants from the exploitation of Hindu usurers, his system serving as a model for later legislation on cooperative societies in India. Second, he helped the aboriginals to secure their land against expropriation by Hindus; the Chota Nagpur Tenancy Act of 1908 is due to his efforts. The people gratefully called him King of Chota Nagpur. Finally, all his life he dedicated himself to the study of Mundari. His earliest publications go back to the nineteenth century. In 1903 he published *Mundari Grammar,* followed by *A Mundari Grammar with Exercises,* part 1 (1905), *Specimens and Dictionary of Mundari Language* (1906), and *Mundari Poetry, Music, and Dances* (1907). After his expulsion from India, despite poor health, he worked until his death on *Encyclopaedia Mundarica,* posthumously published in 1930 in 4 volumes.

BIBLIOGRAPHY A. V., "P. Johann B. Hoffmann SJ," *Die katholischen Missionen* 57 (1929): 53–54 (obit.); C. Blesses, "Father J. B. Hoffmann SJ: The Man and His Work," *Our Field* 21 (1946): 1–5; P. Ponette, ed., *The Munda World: Hoffmann Commemoration Volume* (1978); P. v. Wynsberghe, *Le champion d'une race opprimée, le Père J.-B. Hoffmann SJ* (1935).

Karl Müller, SVD

Hoffmann, L(udwig) F(riedrich) Wilhelm (1806–1873), German mission and church leader. Hoffmann was born in Württemberg. His father was the leading initiator of the pietist settlement of Korntal. Founded by royal charter in 1819, Korntal was a reference point for nineteenth-century pietist social ideals, including the "Christian village" policy of the Basel Mission (BM) in Ghana. His younger brother Christoph (1815–1885), a proponent of the separation of Christian believers from general society, founded the German Templar movement and led an emigration to settle in Palestine in 1868. Wilhelm Hoffmann himself was elected *Inspektor* (executive head) of BM in 1839. In 1850 he moved to Berlin, where he served until his death as a senior ecclesiastical official in both the court and state of Brandenburg-Prussia, with close links to Friedrich Wilhelm IV. He was thus involved in the restoration of conservative royal authority after the revolutionary disturbances of 1848–1849.

As *Inspektor* of BM, Hoffmann was interested in the Anglo-Saxon missionary experience. For example, he was keen to get BM women's work started in India along the lines of the British Society for the Education of the Female Sex in India and China. He was also an important publicist for mission and for a pietist view of the world, authoring more than a dozen works on Protestant and Catholic mission history (including in-depth German studies of mission in Tahiti and Abeokuta based on the existing English literature).

No proper modern study of his work or the broader family history exists. The continuities that led him from Korntal to Berlin via Basel are unknown, although they indicate the existence of strong links between some strands of southern German agrarian pietism in the middle of the nineteenth century and the emerging Prussian/German nationalism soon to be focused in the Protestant figure of Bismarck.

BIBLIOGRAPHY Waltraud Haas, *Erlitten und Erstritten: Der Befreiungsweg von Frauen in der Basler Mission, 1816–1966* (1994; an English summary of part of this book, including material relevant to Hoffmann, was published under the title *Mission History from the Woman's Point of View* [1989]); Hartmut Lehmann, *Pietismus und weltliche Ordnung in Württemberg* (1967); Wilhelm Schlatter, *Geschichte der Basler Mission* (1915).

Paul Jenkins

Hofinger, Johannes (1905–1984), Austrian Jesuit missionary in the Philippines, and leader in catechetical renewal. Born in Austria, missionary in China (1937), Hofinger was exiled to Manila, where he founded the East Asian Pastoral Institute, which became the headquarters of his worldwide apostolate. From there he profoundly influenced the liturgical and catechetical renewal of the Catholic Church worldwide. His main activities were lecturing, writing, and organizing international study weeks during which experts in liturgy and religious education gathered to share their experiences and to prepare plans for action. In religious education he advocated the "kerygmatic" approach he had learned from his teacher in Innsbruck, the great Joseph Andreas Jungmann. Sixteen times from 1953 to 1970, Hofinger went around the world lecturing. Through his numerous writings he also reached audiences vastly wider than those who listened to his voice. He organized six international study weeks: Nijmegen, Holland (1959), Eichstätt, Germany (1960), Bangkok, Thailand (1962), Katigondo, Uganda (1964), Manila, Philippines (1967), Medellin, Colombia (1968). Eventually he settled down in New Orleans, Louisiana, where he died after a short illness.

BIBLIOGRAPHY The book which sums up Hofinger's approach to religious education is his *The Good News and Its Proclamation* (1968). Also see his *Geschichte des Katechismus in Österreich von Canisius bis zur Gegenwart* (1937). The papers of the international study weeks were published in several languages, including *Liturgy and the Missions* (1960), *Teaching All Nations* (1961), *Katigondo: Presenting the Christian Message to Africa* (1965), and *International Study Week on Catechesis, Medellin* (1969). For a short biography and a complete list of Hofinger's writings, see *East Asian Pastoral Review* 2 (1984): 103–127.

Paul G. Brunner, SJ

Hofmeyr, Stefanus (1839–1905), pioneer South African missionary. Born in Cape Town, Hofmeyr went to school there and later became a farmer in the Cape Province. In 1863 he qualified as teacher of religion in Stellenbosch and in 1864 became a missionary in the Soutpansberg in the far northern Transvaal. He was the first South African-born "foreign" missionary of the Dutch Reformed Church (DRC). In 1866 he was ordained as missionary (not minister) in Cape Town before returning to Soutpansberg, where a church revival from 1875 to 1877 led to rapid growth in the congregation. Because of ill health Hofmeyr returned to the Cape Province between 1887 and 1889. During this time he wrote *Twintig jaren in Zoutpansberg* (1890). He established several mission stations and outstations, and his work laid the foundation for what later became the Northern Transvaal region of the DRC in Africa. He also had an abiding interest in the black people north of the Limpopo (in present-day Zimbabwe) and sent some of his own black evangelists there. Out of these efforts was born the Mashona mission of the DRC.

BIBLIOGRAPHY D. Crafford, *Aan God die dank*, vol. 1 (1982); J. du Plessis, *A History of Christian Missions in South Africa* (1911); W. L. Maree, *Lig in Soutpansberg: Die sendingwerk van die Ned. Geref. Kerk in Noord-Transvaal, 1863–1963* (1962).

Willem Saayman

Hogan, J(ames) Philip (1915–), Pentecostal missionary and missions executive. Born on a ranch near Olathe, Colorado, Hogan graduated from Central Bible Institute in 1936. After graduation, he and his wife Virginia (Lewis) engaged in evangelistic and pastoral work before sailing to Ningpo, China, as Assemblies of God (AG) missionaries in 1947. Their stay lasted eighteen months due to the Communist takeover. Moving to Taiwan to evangelize, the family was eventually evacuated; Virginia and their two children returned to the United States and Hogan remained for another six months to train a national minister to carry on the work.

In 1952 the family moved to Springfield, Missouri, and Hogan began work in the foreign missions department at AG headquarters. With the retirement of Noel *Perkin as executive director of foreign missions in 1959, the AG general council elected Hogan as his successor.

During Hogan's long tenure as director, the AG witnessed spectacular growth overseas. Hogan's concern to follow the leading of the Holy Spirit in planning, his openness to creative new ventures, as well as his successful efforts to maintain the unique status of the mission enterprise within the denominational structure offered a stable environment for expansion. His strong commitment to indigenous church principles, respect for the work of Melvin L. *Hodges, and concern for the missionary family led to improved training for missionary candidates, enhanced continuing education for those who were home on furlough, and establishment of a personnel and family life department. Hogan also played a key role in the founding of the Assemblies of God Theological Seminary and its program in missiology.

His stature as a leader in Christian missions led to his election three times as president of the Evangelical Foreign Missions Association and membership on the board of directors of World Relief Corporation. Following retirement in 1989, Hogan was a guiding force in the development of the World Assemblies of God Fellowship, serving as its first president (1988–1992).

BIBLIOGRAPHY J. Philip Hogan, "The Holy Spirit and the Great Commission," *World Pentecost* 1 (1972): 4–5; Virginia Hogan, "Fleeing Shanghai," *Assemblies of God Heritage* 9 (Spring 1989): 8, 15; Gary B. McGee, *This Gospel Shall Be Preached: A History and Theology of Assemblies of God Foreign Missions since 1959*, vol. 2 (1989).

Gary B. McGee

Hogg, Alfred George (1875–1954), Scottish educational missionary. Born in Egypt of missionary parents, Hogg was educated in Scotland at George Watson's College and at Edinburgh University (1893–1897), where he acquired a lifelong taste for philosophy. In 1897 a crisis of faith caused him to suspend his studies for the ministry, and therefore he first went to India in 1903 as a lay educational missionary of the United Free Church to teach in Madras Christian College. Finally ordained in 1912, he was an atypical missionary, sure by now of his faith but always prepared to revise his theology. He seems often to have left his Indian students in a state of admiring bewilderment, but he impressed his missionary contemporaries as an unusually acute thinker. He did not believe in easy accommodation between Christian and Hindu forms of religious expression but sought always for what he called "cardinal issues" and fundamental disagreements. For this reason he was suspicious of the fulfillment theory of J. N. *Farquhar and others. Consistent with his own ethical interests, Hogg found the most important of these cardinal issues in the contrast between the Hindu notion of karma and the Christian view of redemption (*Karma and Redemption,* 1909). His most widely read book, *Christ's Message of the Kingdom,* appeared in 1911, *Redemption from this World* in 1922, and *The Christian Message to the Hindu* in 1947. After 25 years teaching mainly philosophy, in 1928 he became principal of the college and was at the helm during the college's move from downtown Madras to its new Tambaram campus (1937). He was also much involved in the early 1930s in the work of the Lindsay Commission of inquiry into Christian higher education in India. He personally favored the setting up of a Christian university, but in a period of intense communal and factional fighting, he realized its impracticability. In 1938 the International Missionary Council held a major conference on the Tambaran campus. Hogg, who had never been a conference-goer and disagreed profoundly with dialectical theology, crossed swords with Hendrik *Kraemer on that occasion. Shortly thereafter he retired to Scotland, spending the war years as a parish minister in various parts of southern Scotland. He died at his home in the village of Elie, Fife.

BIBLIOGRAPHY James L. Cox, "Faith and Faiths: The Significance of A. G. Hogg's Missionary Thought for a Theology of Dialogue," *SJT* 32 (1979): 241–256; Eric J. Sharpe, *Not to Destroy but to Fulfil* (1965), pp. 272–297, *The Theology of A. G. Hogg* (1971), and "A. G. Hogg," in Gerald H. Anderson et al., eds., *Mission Legacies* (1994), pp. 330–338.

Eric J. Sharpe

Hogg, John (1833–1886), Protestant missionary in Egypt. Hogg was born in the mining village of Penston, Scotland. From the age of nine, he worked in a coal mine as a pit boy, but an accident set him free to study. An evangelical conversion, followed by the death of an elder brother, convinced him of a missionary vocation, and in 1856 he accepted a call to Alexandria, Egypt, in connection with the Scottish Society for the Conversion of the Jews. In 1860 the work passed to the American (United Presbyterian) Mission. Thereafter Hogg worked mostly as an educational and literary missionary out of Asyūt. He was a firm believer in the establishment of independent, self-sustaining, and self-propagating churches. He was a fine Arabic scholar, a notable personality, and a tireless preacher, teacher, translator, and administrator. Of his twelve children, the eldest, Hope Waddell Hogg (1863–1912), carried on his father's work in Egypt; Alfred George *Hogg and Laurence Alexander Hogg became missionaries in India. John Hogg died in Asyūt.

BIBLIOGRAPHY Rena L. Hogg, *A Master Builder on the Nile: Being a Record of the Life and Aims of John Hogg, D.D.* (1914).

Eric J. Sharpe

Hohenheim, Theophrastus Bombastus von. *See* Paracelsus.

Holland, Henry Tristram (1875–1965), English missionary surgeon in India. Born in Durham, England, Holland was sent by the Church Missionary Society in 1900 to Quetta Hospital on the frontier between Baluchistan and Afghanistan. He won legendary fame as a surgeon, performing over 60,000 operations for cataract alone in the next half-century. In 1910 he married a colleague, Effie Tunbridge, daughter of missionaries in India. The hospital grew from 20 to 120 beds but was demolished by an earthquake in 1935. Rescued from the debris by one of his missionary sons, Holland rebuilt the facility more solidly. Having traveled throughout India, advising on medical policy for both churches and government, he received the Kaiser-i-Hind silver and gold medals, and a knighthood in 1936. His combined roles of surgeon, administrator, evangelist, and man of God influenced generations of British soldiers and officials and so impressed the fervently Muslim Pathans that numbers of them were converted, some paying with their lives for their change of religious allegiance. In 1909 a banker of the (then) exclusively Hindu city of Shikarpur in Sind invited Holland to his own home to operate on hundreds of poor patients; thereafter the banker built a hospital where Holland could bring a team of surgeons for six weeks every winter. The hospital ministry continued for many years after Holland's retirement to England in 1948.

BIBLIOGRAPHY *Frontier Doctor* (1959), the autobiography Holland wrote at age 83, conveys the true flavor of his personality. For further insight into his motivation, see his article, "Surgery," in *Medical Practice in Africa and the East,* Hugh Martin and H. W. Weir, eds. (1923), pp.1–12. For his professional authority, see his "Notes on 221 Intracapsular Cataract Extractions Performed in Three Weeks in Khaipur in 1947," *British Journal of Ophthalmology,* February 1949, pp. 101–106.

John V. Taylor

Holly, James Theodore (1829–1911), missionary in Haiti and first African American to be ordained a bishop in the Protestant Episcopal church. Holly was born in Washington, D.C., of freeborn Roman Catholic parents. From early youth he felt called to participate in the struggle for liberation from oppression and the evils of racism. Though baptized and confirmed in the Roman Catholic Church, he was ordained a deacon in the Protestant Episcopal Church in 1855 and a priest in 1856 with the express commitment to work in Haiti. He went to Haiti as pastor in 1861 with 112 African Americans, but tragedy struck. Within seven months, forty-seven died from illnesses, including his mother, wife, daughter, and one of three sons. Yet he persevered and ministered there as pastor, teacher, evangelist, and counselor for 50 years, often supporting himself and his new family by shoemaking, teaching, tutoring, and secretarial work. He was consecrated as Episcopal bishop of Haiti in 1874. When he died, the Episcopal Church in Haiti had fifteen parishes, seven missions, fifteen national clergy, and a church community of over 2,000 persons. Since he believed that the incarnation of Christ required concern for the bodies as well as the souls of his people, he established schools, medical clinics, and a mutual fund society. Two of his sons became clergymen; four were medical doctors; one was a music teacher. His seven books and eighteen published articles showed erudition in many fields, though much of his education was self-acquired, including his knowledge of Latin, Greek, Hebrew, French, and Creole. He believed that through centuries of oppression the black race had gained a sense of righteousness, justice, forbearance, and love of peace that prepared them to be specially qualified agents in the coming kingdom of Christ.

BIBLIOGRAPHY James Theodore Holly, "A Vindication of the Capacity of the Negro Race for Self-Government and Civilized Progress as Demonstrated by Historical Events of the Haytian Revolution; and Subsequent Acts of that People since their National Independence," in Howard H. Bell, ed., *Black Separatism and the Caribbean, 1860* (1970), pp. 16–66. David Dean, "James Theodore Holly, 1829–1911, Black Nationalist and Bishop" (Ph.D. diss., Univ. of Texas, 1972); J. Carleton Hayden, "James Theodore Holly (1829–1911), First Afro-American Episcopal Bishop: His Legacy to Us Today," in Randall K. Burkett and Richard Newman, eds., *Black Apostles: Afro-American Clergy Confront the Twentieth Century* (1978), pp. 129–140; William Louis Wifler, "The Establishment and Development of L'Eglise Orthodoxe Apostolique Haïtienne" (S.T.M. thesis, General Theological Seminary, 1955). See also *Handbooks, The Missions of the Episcopal Church,* vol. 5, *The West Indies* (1926), pp. 13–49.

Sidney H. Rooy

Holmes, Elkanah (1744–1832), American Baptist missionary among Native Americans. Born in Canterbury, New Hampshire, the son of farmers, Holmes received no formal education. He entered the colonial militia in New York in the French and Indian War and served during the American Revolution as a chaplain. After the war, he pastored several congregations in the Hudson Valley, notably on Staten Island. As moderator of the New York Baptist Association, he became interested in missionary work among the Indians. In 1797 he visited the Tuscaroras and Senecas in the Niagara region; the following year he established himself on the Niagara River near Lewiston. Serving under the authority of the New York Missionary Society (a coalition of Baptists, Presbyterians, and Reformed in New York City), he became the first Baptist missionary to the Indians of the northeast and the first American Baptist missionary to work in what became Upper Canada (Ontario). His station at the border became a regular point of departure for Baptist work in Canada. In 1807 he withdrew from the ecumenical society owing to Baptist principles. For a number of years before the War of 1812 he actively established and strengthened congregations in the Canadian Niagara Peninsula, notably at Beamsville. He authored a polity manual for the Baptists that had a wide influence on the missionary frontier.

BIBLIOGRAPHY Elkanah Holmes, *A Church Covenant, Including a Summary of the Fundamental Doctrines of the Gospel* (1797). Biographical details are sketchy and based upon William Parkinson, *The Funeral Sermon of Elder Elkanah Holmes, Preached in the Meetinghouse of the First Baptist Church in the City of New York, Lord's Day, Feb. 26, 1832* (1832).

William H. Brackney

Holsten, Walter (1908–1982), German missiologist and academician. Holsten was the first German missiologist after World War II to be appointed to a newly established university chair at Mainz University. He had been trained as a pastor and had served in the Lutheran church of Hanover until 1947. But during these years he had become a missiologist by inclination, though he never actually worked abroad. His chair at Mainz was originally sponsored by the Gossner Mission of Berlin, but it was funded by the university in 1953. His major scholarly book was an analysis of Johannes E. *Gossner's personality and the Gossner mission and church in India (which Holsten had never been able to visit), based on documentary material later destroyed in the final days of World War II. Probably no other contemporary missiologist in Germany has so comprehensively covered his field in creative research, in teaching, and in writing, including work on the history and theory of missions, the phenomenology and theology of religions, Christian anthropology, and not least, the Christian approach to the Jews. Holsten received an honorary doctorate from Göttingen University in 1952. After his retirement in 1973 he gained a reputation as an expert in general university and student affairs. As a missiologist Holsten was unique in what he described as the founding of the Christian mission on the Pauline kerygma ("the kerygma is the mission"), a proposition which evoked more criticism than agreement.

BIBLIOGRAPHY Walter Holsten, *Johannes Evangelista Gossner: Glaube und Gemeinde* (1949) and *Das Kerygma und der Mensch* (1953). See also "Deutsche Missionsaufgabe Heute," *Evangelische Theologie,* September/December 1947, pp. 155–170.

Hans-Werner Gensichen

Höltker, Georg (1895–1976), German Catholic mission anthropologist in New Guinea. Born in Ahaus in Münsterland, Germany, Höltker was educated at St. Gabriel Mission Seminary, Mödling, Austria, and ordained for the Society of the Divine Word (SVD) in 1925. He studied anthropology at the Universities of Vienna (1926) and Berlin (1927–1929), served on the staff of Wilhelm *Schmidt's journal *Anthropos,* and was its editor from 1932 to 1935. He was also Schmidt's assistant at the papal ethnological mission museum in Rome. He was known for his great interest and skill in training missionaries—as teacher, their guide in fieldwork, and advisor in preparing manuscripts for publication. In 1936 he left for New Guinea, where he did ethnographic, linguistic, and somatological fieldwork that brought him recognition as one of the outstanding New Guinea mission anthropologists of his time. Shortly before the outbreak of World War II, he had to leave New Guinea because of illness. On his return to Europe, he joined Schmidt's collaborators at the Anthropos Institute (then in Switzerland), where he assumed teaching posts at the Tropeninstitut in Basel and later at the University of Fribourg (1954–1962) as Schmidt's successor. Some years later, when the Anthropos Institute moved to Germany, he taught at the SVD mission seminary at Sankt Augustin, near Bonn. He continued his work on his New Guinea field notes and guided missionaries in their anthropological research by mail. This missionary interest is also reflected in his close collaboration with the journal *Neue Zeitschrift für Missionswissenschaft* and its founder, Johannes *Beckmann.

BIBLIOGRAPHY A Festschrift honoring Hőltker was published as no. 29 of *Studia Instituti Anthropos* (1975). It contains an account of his life, lists his publications, and reprints his eleven more significant articles on his New Guinea fieldwork. Materials of archival interest from his fieldwork are preserved at the Univ. of Fribourg, Switzerland, and at the mission museum at Sankt Augustin, Germany.

Louis J. Luzbetak, SVD

Honda Yoichi (Honda Yoitsu) (1848–1912), Japanese Methodist bishop and educator. Born in Hirosaki into a samurai family of the highest rank, Honda went to Yokohama in 1870 to study the new Western learning. He was baptized by Reformed Church missionary James H. Ballagh in 1872. He returned to Hirosaki that year to become principal of the old clan school and in 1874 brought Methodist missionary John Ing to the school. Many students became Christians and were organized into a church which sent more than 200 people into full-time Christian service during the ensuing 100 years. Honda went to America in 1888 to study at Drew Theological Seminary, New Jersey, and returned to Japan to become the first Japanese chancellor of the Methodist boys' school in Tokyo, Aoyama Gakuin, in 1890. It was largely through his leadership that the three major Methodist bodies in Japan united in 1907 to form the autonomous Japan Methodist Church, of which he was elected the first bishop. He was chairman of the Japan YMCA (1903–1909) and was elected the first president of the Japan Federation of Christian Churches (1911). A vice-chairman of the World's Student Christian Federation (WSCF) (1900–1909), he was also a delegate to the 1910 Edinburgh World Missionary Conference and one of three Asians on its continuation committee.

BIBLIOGRAPHY Shigemi Kega, "Bishop Yoichi Honda, Founder of the Japan Methodist Church," in Norimichi Ebizawa, ed., *Japanese Witnesses for Christ* (1957); Takeo Kega, *Honda Yoitsu* (1968); F. D. Leete, *Methodist Bishops* (1948); Tetsuzo Okada, *Honda Yoitsu Den* (1936); Mizutaro Takagi, ed., *Honda Yoitsu Sensei Iko* (1918; posthumous collection of Honda's writings).

John W. Krummel

Honoratus (c. 350–429), archbishop of Arles, France, and founder of the monastery at Lérins. From a well-positioned family in Gaul, perhaps at Trier, Honoratus and his brother, Venantius, traveled in Syria and the Holy Land to visit pilgrim sites and monastic centers. Venantius died on the journey. After his return through Rome, Honoratus settled first at the grotto of Estéval, in Provence, and about 410 went to the island of Lérins, off the coast of southern France. From that island base, Christianity spread throughout France both through the foundation of other monasteries and through continued contact with a number of missionary monks, including Patrick of Ireland and Augustine of Canterbury.

BIBLIOGRAPHY Hilary of Arles, *Sermon on the Life of St. Honoratus*, Roy Deferrari, ed., tr., *Fathers of the Church*, vol. 15 (1952); S. Cavallin, *Vitae SS. Honorati et Hilarii* (1952); B. Munke, ed., *Die Vita S. Honorati: Zeitschrift für Romanische Philologie*, Beiheft 33 (1911).

Frederick W. Norris

Honsinger, Welthy. *See* Fisher, Welthy (Honsinger).

Hooper, Handley Douglas (1891–1966), Church Missionary Society (CMS) missionary and mission administrator. The son of a pioneer missionary in East Africa, Hooper was born at Jilore, north of Mombasa, Kenya. His mother died in 1893, and he was brought up in England by family friends. After graduation from Cambridge (Queen's College, B.A., 1912), he received theological training in Durham, and was ordained. In 1915 he married Cicely Winterbotham, and they were sent by CMS to Kahuhia, Kenya, to a station among the Kikuyu people that his father had developed. He spent ten years in Africa, two with the Mission Volunteer Carrier Corps in German East Africa. He and his wife became particularly close to the Kikuyu men and women they served. Cicely Hooper started a girls' boarding school, and he began teacher training; he gave encouragement to young educated Africans whose political concerns were developing. In 1926 he became Africa secretary of CMS, a post he held until 1950. He was especially interested in agriculture and initiated the Rural Life Conferences for members of the British Conference of Missionary Societies.

In 1961 he retired to Cheltenham; his older son Cyril (b. 1916) also served as a CMS missionary at Kahuhia.

BIBLIOGRAPHY H. D. Hooper, *Leading Strings* (1921). M. C. Hooper, *New Patches: Women's Customs and Changes in East Africa* (1935), *If I Lived in Africa* (1937), *Beyond the Night* (1938), and *The Way of Partnership* (1939). Also see Jocelyn Margaret Murray, "The Kikuyu Female Circumcision Controversy, with Special Reference to the Church Missionary Society's 'Sphere of Influence'" (Ph.D. diss., Univ. of California Los Angeles, 1974); Harry Thuku, *Harry Thuku: An Autobiography* (1970). The Hooper Papers, including personal letters to and from Kikuyu friends, and reports on African ecclesiastical and political development, are held in the CMS archives, Univ. of Birmingham.

Jocelyn Murray

Hoornbeeck (*or* Hoornbeek), Johannes (1617–1666), Reformed theologian. Born in Haarlem, Netherlands, Hoornbeeck studied at the Universities of Leiden and Utrecht. At Leiden he was a pupil of Gisbertus *Voetius and Antonius *Walaeus. He moved to Germany to serve as pastor of a refugee Reformed church in Mülheim (1639–1643). Forced to leave Germany, he returned to the Netherlands and in 1644 was appointed professor of theology at Utrecht and ten years later at Leiden. In his important missionary treatise *De conversione Indorum ac gentilium* (published posthumously in 1669), he pointed to the great perspectives opened up for Christian missions by the new possibilities of travel and to the religious responsibility of the Dutch government for its colonies. Economic concerns should not prevail, only things that promote Christ's kingdom. Theological disputes should be replaced by missionary activity as a completion of the missionary task of the apostles. Hoornbeeck regarded especially the Old Testament as filled with God's promises for the Gentiles. In his *Summa controversiarum religionis* (1653) and *De convincendis et convertendis Judaeis et Gentilibus* (1655), he also gave attention to mission to Jews and Muslims. His works are important not only for the study of the beginnings of a Protestant missionary theology in the Dutch Reformed Church, but also for the history of religions.

BIBLIOGRAPHY M. Galm, *Das Erwachen des Missionsgedankens im Protestantismus der Niederlande* (1915); J. W. Hofmeyer, *Johannes Hoornbeeck as polemicus* (1975); B. Oosterom, "Johannes Hoornbeeck als Zendingstheoloog," *Theologia Reformata* 13 (1970): 81–98; P. J. Ypma, "Johannes Hoornbeek als Missionstheoretiker" (Ph.D. diss., Gregorian Univ., Rome, 1958).

Willem J. van Asselt

Hoover, James Matthews (1872–1935), Methodist missionary in Borneo. A layman from Pennsylvania, Hoover was widely known as "Tuan Hoover of Borneo," *tuan* meaning something like "sir" or "lord." His biographer calls him "one of the last great missionary pioneers." After graduation from Shippensburg (Pennsylvania) Normal School, Hoover served as teacher and principal in an African American school and organized a local YMCA to provide more wholesome social life for the youth of Chambersburg, Pennsylvania. In 1899 he answered a call from Bishop J. M. *Thoburn for India but was sent instead to Penang, Malaya. There he taught school and was fascinated by the variety of races, religions, languages, cultures, and customs.

Meanwhile, the second "White Rajah of Sarawak," Sir Charles J. Brooke, had invited (or "imported") nearly 1,000 Chinese from the southern Chinese province of Fukien (Fujian), in the hope that they would develop agricultural enclaves in the jungles of Borneo. Since many of them were Christians (Methodists), they presented an opportunity and a challenge to the Methodists of Malaya. After his apprenticeship on the peninsula, Hoover requested this appointment and sailed in 1903 to Sibu, Sarawak, near the mouth of the Rejang River. Here, for more than 30 years, he provided not only spiritual guidance but economic and technological stimulus for the new settlers, introducing to this primitive frontier bicycles, motor launches, a rice-hulling mill, rubber plantations, electricity, and even an ice plant. He once confessed, "Next to the churches and schools I have helped to build, and next to the lives I have helped God to make over, I am proudest of my boats."

Except for his wife, Ethel Mary (Young), whom he married in 1904, Hoover labored almost alone; his few missionary colleagues did not remain long in that difficult climate. He learned the language of the region and managed to win cooperation and devotion not only from the Chinese immigrants but also from the Malays and Sea Dyaks (Iban) of Sarawak. He died of malaria and was buried where he served.

BIBLIOGRAPHY Frank T. Cartwright, *Tuan Hoover of Borneo* (1938).

Creighton Lacy

Hoover, Willis Collins (1856–1936), founder of indigenous Pentecostal movements in Chile. A native of Freeport, Illinois, who had been influenced by the Methodist bishop William *Taylor, Hoover studied medicine in preparation for a missionary career in Chile. He married Mary Anne Hilton. Beginning as a teacher and Methodist lay pastor in 1889, he was named superintendent of the Methodist Iquique district in 1897 and in 1902 pastor of the large Valparaíso church. Versatile in his methods, he was undoubtedly influenced by the work of Juan Bautista *Canut, who had previously made use of street preaching and lay leadership. Hoover was also aware of recent revivals, including the healing emphasis of A. B. *Simpson, the Welsh revival led by Evan Roberts in 1904, the Azusa Street Pentecostal mission in Los Angeles, and the work of William H. Durham in Chicago. He was especially impressed by an account of a 1905 revival in India, written by his wife's training school classmate Minnie F. *Abrams. Moreover, he had employed decentralized home meetings and lay leadership for more than a year after his church was destroyed in the 1906 earthquake. Both spiritually sensitive and pragmatic, he directed his efforts to the common people. When Pentecostal phenomena appeared in his meetings in 1909, he permitted displays that were considered by his critics to be unseemly and unbiblical. Pressured to conform, he resigned from the Methodist Church and, with a sizable Chilean following, formed the Iglesia Metodista Pentecostal in 1909. Against a backdrop of urban migration and social deterioration, the group grew steadily for a quarter century under his leadership. Following a major split in 1932, he founded the Iglesia Evangélica Pentecostal (now the second largest Chilean Pentecostal group), which he led until his death. Chilean Pentecostals now make up scores of organizations with an aggregate adherence of as much as one-fifth of the national population.

BIBLIOGRAPHY Willis C. Hoover, *Historia del avivamiento pentecostal en Chile* (1948). John B. A. Kessler, *A Study of the Older Protestant Missions and Churches in Peru and Chile* (1967); Christian Lalive d'Epinay, *Haven of the Masses* (1969).

Everett A. Wilson

Hopkins, Samuel (1721–1803), American Congregational minister, theologian, and early advocate for African missions. Born in Waterbury, Connecticut, Hopkins graduated from Yale and trained as a Calvinist minister under Jonathan *Edwards. As a pastor in the Massachusetts frontier town of Housatonic, he began largely unsuccessful efforts to educate and evangelize local Native American tribes. In 1769 Hopkins moved to Newport, Rhode Island, where he encountered the slave trade and began to agitate for abolition. Joining other antislavery reformers in Britain, Scotland, and Africa, he was one of the first Americans to propose sending freed African American Christians to Africa as missionaries. From 1771 to 1775 he developed a network of financial support for an African mission, soliciting funds from New England Calvinist churches and the Scottish Society for the Propagation of the Gospel. During the American Revolution, he continued to write against the slave trade. From 1783 to 1799 he renewed his campaign for an African mission, shifting his emphasis to the colonizing of free blacks in Africa rather than simply sending missionaries. Failing to garner adequate support, he proposed as an alternative that American blacks join an English colony in Sierra Leone. Although he died without success in these efforts, his missionary efforts, and their foundation in his millennial views, fostered in New England Calvinism the missionary spirit that became more successful in the nineteenth century.

BIBLIOGRAPHY William K. Breitenbach, "Unregenerate Doings: Selflessness and Selfishness in the New Divinity Theology," *American Quarterly* 34 (1982): 479–502; Joseph A. Conforti, *Samuel Hopkins and the New Divinity Movement: Calvinism, the Congregational Ministry, and Reform in New England between the Great Awakenings* (1981); Joseph Haroutunian, *Piety versus Moralism: The Passing of the New England Theology* (1932); Edwards A. Park, *Memoir of the Life and Character of Samuel Hopkins, D.D.* (1854).

Mark Valeri

Hore, Edward Coode (1848–1912), London Missionary Society (LMS) missionary in Central Africa. Hore was part of that band of missionaries whose public protests resulted in the collapse of the slave trade in Central Africa and in the creation of Northern Rhodesia (Zambia). He was born at Frizinghall, near Bradford, Australia, and became a member of the Mariner's Church in Sydney. He was appointed to the Lake Tanganyika mission of the LMS, arriving in Zanzibar on August 1, 1877. Credentialed as a master mariner, he captained first the *Morning Star,* a 32-foot lifeboat, and later the *Good News,* a 54-foot, two-masted screw steam yacht financed by Robert *Arthington of Leeds and dragged overland piece by piece for reassembly on Lake Tanganyika. In 1888, ill health dictated his taking a medical leave in England. Hore resumed his association with the LMS in 1892, serving as first officer on the Polynesian-based barque *John Williams* until his resignation in 1900. He settled in Tasmania, where he died at the age of 64.

BIBLIOGRAPHY Edward Coode Hore, *Tanganyika: Eleven Years in Central Africa* (1892) and *Missionary to Tanganyika, 1877–1888: The Writings of E. C. Hore, Master Mariner,* selected, edited, and with an introduction by J. B. Wolf (1971). Jonathan J. Bonk, *The Theory and Practice of Missionary Identification, 1860–1920* (1989); Annie B. Hore, *To Lake Tanganyika in a Bath Chair* (1886); Richard Lovett, *The History of the London Missionary Society, 1797–1895* (1899); James Sibree, *London Missionary Society: A Register of Missionaries, Deputations, Etc., from 1797–1923,* 4th ed. (1923).

Jonathan J. Bonk

Horne, Melville (c. 1761–1841), Anglican clergyman and British missionary advocate. Horne began his ministry in Madeley, Shropshire, England, where he was deeply involved in the Methodist movement. In January 1792 he and his brother-in-law, Nathaniel *Gilbert, went to Sierra Leone as chaplains to the Sierra Leone Company. Although Horne saw his role as a missionary one, he never learned an African language, and the adverse climate forced him to return home in 1793. In 1794 he published *Letters on Missions: Addressed to the Protestant Ministers of the British Churches,* which called on all British Protestants to unite in a common missionary enterprise. His appeal was taken up by Thomas *Haweis and led to the formation of the London Missionary Society in 1795; but after the Church Mission Society (CMS) was founded in 1799, Horne transferred his support there. In 1811 he was one of the first to urge the CMS to send a mission to revive the Syrian church of Malabar.

BIBLIOGRAPHY Charles Hole, *The Early History of the Church Missionary Society for Africa and the East* (1896); Stiv Jakobsson, *Am I Not a Man and a Brother? British Missions and the Abolition of the Slave Trade and Slavery in West Africa and the West Indies, 1786–1838* (1972); Roger H. Martin, *Evangelicals United: Ecumenical Stirrings in Pre-Victorian Britain, 1795–1830* (1983).

Brian Stanley

Horton, Azariah (1715–1777), pioneering missionary among Native Americans on Long Island. Born in New York, Horton graduated from Yale in 1735 and was ordained by the Presbytery of New York in 1740. In 1742, he was sent as minister to Indians near Montauk Point near Southampton, thus becoming the first officially commissioned Presbyterian missionary in colonial times. Financial support came from the Scottish Society for the Propagation of Christian Knowledge, and this enabled Horton to lead the way for all subsequent Presbyterian work among Native Americans. With one station at Pooseputrick, he resided at a larger site, Shinnecock. Sometime between 1748 and 1752, Horton moved to a church of white parishioners in what is now part of Madison, New Jersey. He served there until 1776, when he resigned. He died the following year of smallpox.

BIBLIOGRAPHY Annual reports of the Presbyterian Church.

Henry Warner Bowden

Hoste, Dixon Edward (1861–1946), British missionary, administrator, and evangelist in China. Born in Brighton, England, and raised in a Christian family, Hoste was converted when he attended the evangelistic meetings of D. L. *Moody near his home in 1883. Accepted by the China Inland Mission (CIM) in 1884, he resigned his commission as a lieutenant in the Royal Artillery and sailed for China in 1885 as one of the famed *Cambridge Seven, although he was not himself a Cambridge graduate. He was sent to Shansi (Shanxi) Province for language study, and there he developed a close relationship with the respected pastor *Hsi Shengmo, a converted Confucian scholar who directed much of the CIM work in Shansi and founded many opium refuges. Hoste worked until 1896 in Shansi, spending several months each year living in villages with an evangelist and preaching at country fairs. He exhibited wise leadership in the sensitivity that he showed in being a peacemaker among both his missionary associates and his Chinese colleagues. Following a sick leave in Australia in 1896, he was made superintendent of the CIM work in Honan (Henan) Province, and he was then appointed acting general director of the CIM in 1901 and general director in 1902. Although some had predicted the demise of the mission following the death of Hudson *Taylor in 1905, Hoste gained the ongoing confidence of both missionaries and Chinese. He was married to Amelia Gertrude Broomhall in 1894, and they had three sons. He retired from the CIM in 1935, was imprisoned by the Japanese (1941–1945), and died in London.

BIBLIOGRAPHY Phyllis Thompson, *D. E. Hoste* (1947). See also A. J. Broomhall, *Hudson Taylor and China's Open Century*, vols. 6 and 7 (1988, 1989).

Ralph R. Covell

Hotuntsevsky. *See* Ioasaf (Hotuntsevsky).

Hough, George H. (1788–1859), American Baptist missionary in Burma. Little is known of Hough's early life, except that he was born in Concord, New Hampshire, and was trained as a printer. Without formal education, he became a Baptist minister and from 1813 to 1815 was pastor of the Baptist church in New Bedford, Massachusetts. In April 1815 he became the first recruit of the Baptist Board of Foreign Missions, which appointed him its first missionary printer. With his wife, Phebe (Mann), and their children, he joined the Adoniram *Judsons in Burma (Myanmar) in 1816 and remained for 12 years. With equipment supplied by the English Baptists at Serampore, he established the American Baptist Mission Press in Rangoon. Under his direction, the press produced the first tracts, Scripture portions, and other Christian literature in Burmese. Twice Hough was imprisoned by the Burmese government (in 1818 and 1824); both times he and his family subsequently fled to Calcutta with the press. In the 1818 removal, Hough was reprimanded by the board for leaving his station without its permission, and this led to stricter regulations over missionary appointments. In 1827 Hough became the first American Baptist missionary to remain in an overseas context following missionary service. Upon his retirement, he became superintendent of government schools in Tenasserim Province and served as a government interpreter.

BIBLIOGRAPHY Hough's publications include *An Anglo-Burmese Dictionary*, pt. 1 (1845). A few biographical details are found in *The Missionary Jubilee* (1865) and in published correspondence in the *Latter Day Luminary* and the *American Baptist Magazine*. Robert G. Torbet, *Venture of Faith: The Story of the American Baptist Foreign Mission Society and the Woman's American Baptist Foreign Mission Society, 1814–1954* (1955), pp. 37–45, 92, relates a significant part of Hough's work. His correspondence is in the American Baptist Historical Society in Rochester, New York.

William H. Brackney

Howard, Leonora (1851-1925), Methodist medical missionary in China. A native of Ontario, Canada, Howard graduated in 1876 from the University of Michigan, Ann Arbor, her medical education having been paid for by the Woman's Foreign Missionary Society (WFMS) of the Methodist Episcopal Church. In 1877 she went to Peking (Beijing) under WFMS auspices and took charge of the Peking hospital. In March 1879 she was called to Tientsin (Tianjin) to care for Lady Li Hung Chang, wife of the viceroy. Lady Li, having recovered, wanted Howard to remain in Tientsin. The viceroy had turned a temple into a medical dispensary under the auspices of the London Missionary Society (LMS), and as an inducement to stay, the viceroy proposed that Howard open a women's ward. In 1881 the Methodists opened the Isabella Fisher Hospital (named after the mother of the principal donor, in Baltimore, Maryland) in Tientsin. Howard managed the hospital until her 1884 marriage to Alexander M. King of the LMS, which ended her connection with WFMS. The Kings remained in China; she maintained her contacts with the vice-regal families and then with the Nationalist government until her death, although she never became an official LMS missionary.

BIBLIOGRAPHY Margaret Negodaeff-Tomsik, *The Good Fight* is a full-length biography (1994). Information about Howard can also be found in Frances J. Baker, *The Story of the Woman's Foreign Missionary Society* (1896) and in Mary Isham, *Valorous Ventures* (1936).

Susan E. Warrick

Howe, Gertrude (1847–1928), Methodist missionary in China. Howe attended the University of Michigan and in 1872 went to Kiukang, China, as the pioneer missionary of the Woman's Foreign Missionary Society (WFMS) of the Methodist Episcopal Church. For a few years she was joined by her sister, Dr. Delia Howe. In 1873 she founded what became the Rulison Girls' High School, which insisted on unbound feet for admittance. To the shock of fellow missionaries, she adopted four Chinese girls and began to teach them English. After a dispute between the WFMS and the Methodist mission board over her mission policies, in 1883 she transferred to Chungking to open a girls' school that was destroyed by riots two years later. Returning to Kiukang, she continued her educational work, preached throughout the countryside, and trained "Bible women."

With confidence in Chinese ability, she tutored Chinese students in higher branches of Western learning. In 1892 she took five Chinese pupils to the University of Michigan and supported them. Two were among the first Chinese women to become medical doctors, Mary *Stone and Ida *Kahn. Kahn, who was one of Howe's adopted daughters, founded a hospital in Nanchang. Howe's other daughters married prominent Chinese educators and government ministers, and one became an itinerant evangelist. Howe mothered and educated many other Chinese children, refusing to leave them for vacations in "Westerners only" resorts, and living as a Chinese so as to have money for the children. She did a lot of translation work, including the *Methodist Hymn Book,* and compiled *The History of the Reformation* in Chinese. In 1926 she moved to Nanchang to live with Ida Kahn and to superintend the work of Bible women. After surviving the 1927 civil war, she died as one of Methodism's most well-known missionaries.

BIBLIOGRAPHY The most valuable source on Howe's life are the clippings in her file at the archives of the United Methodist Church in Madison, N.J., and the correspondence about her in the files of other missionaries. See pamphlets "Gertrude Howe" by Frances J. Baker, and "Miss Gertrude Howe" by Mary Stone. She wrote articles for *Heathen Woman's Friend* and other religious publications.

Dana L. Robert

Howells, George (1871–1955), Baptist Missionary Society (BMS) missionary in India. Howells was born in Monmouthshire, south Wales. After theological study at Regent's Park College, London, and Mansfield College, Oxford, he was accepted by the BMS in 1895 for service in Orissa. Involved in educational and translation work in Cuttack from 1896 to 1906, he was appointed principal of Serampore College in Bengal in 1906. Howells played a large part in ensuring the survival of the college as an institution of higher education when influential figures within the BMS wished it to revert to a narrower role in training leaders for the Baptist churches. He reactivated the college's historic right to award degrees in theology. Howells was probably the most learned British Baptist missionary of his day. He believed, like J. N. *Farquhar, that the relationship of Christianity to Hinduism should be seen as one of fulfillment rather than confrontation. His book advocating this position, *The Soul of India* (1913), was attacked by conservative elements in the Baptist denomination in the 1920s as evidence of the inroads of theological liberalism. He retired to Wales in 1929 but continued to serve Serampore College as chairman of its council in Britain until 1941.

BIBLIOGRAPHY E. W. Price Evans, *Dr. George Howells: Missionary Statesman and Scholar* (1966); Brian Stanley, *The History of the Baptist Missionary Society, 1792–1992* (1992).

Brian Stanley

Hoy, William Edwin (1858–1927), pioneer American missionary to Japan and China. After graduating from Franklin and Marshall College (1882) and Lancaster Theological Seminary (1885), Hoy was ordained and appointed by the Reformed (German) Church in the United States and sailed for Japan in 1885. He quickly identified Sendai in northern Japan as strategic, and upon arrival there in January 1886 launched a small school for training Japanese pastors, while also carrying on active evangelistic work. He helped start a girls' school, now Miyagi Gakuin, and the following year married Mary Ault, one of its teachers. In 1891 Hoy's school became Tohoku Gakuin (North Japan University).

Burdened with a wide variety of responsibilities, including publication of a bimonthly English journal, the *Japan Evangelist,* and suffering from asthma, he went to Shanghai in 1898 for a three-month health furlough. After traveling up the Yangtze to Hankow, he determined to launch a mission in Hunan Province, resigned from the Japan Mission, and in 1900 settled at Yochow. For 25 years Hoy was at the center of a rapidly developing program of schools for boys and girls, evangelistic outstations, and medical work. He was granted the D.D. by Franklin and Marshall (1903) and the LL.D. by Heidelberg College (1925). In the turmoil of revolutionary civil war, the Hoys were evacuated in 1927, and William Hoy died on shipboard. His daughters Gertrude and Mabel also served as missionaries in China.

BIBLIOGRAPHY Arthur Vale Casselman, *It Happened in Hunan* (1953); William H. Daniels, "The Life and Labors of William Edwin Hoy" (B.D. thesis, Lancaster Theological Seminary, 1945); *Fifty Years of Foreign Missions of the Reformed Church in the United States, 1877–1927* (1927), chaps. 2 and 3; C. William Mensendiek, *Not Without Struggle: The Story of William E. Hoy and the Beginnings of Tohoku Gakuin* (1986). Hoy wrote extensively for the *Messenger,* magazine of the Reformed Church in the United States, throughout his years of service. His voluminous correspondence is in the archives at Lancaster Theological Seminary.

David M. Stowe

Hsi Shengmo (Pastor Hsi) (c. 1835–1896), Chinese missionary evangelist. Born in Shansi (Shanxi) Province, China, Hsi came from a literary class family of above-average means. A Confucian scholar, he nevertheless became addicted to opium in his thirties. He adopted the name Shengmo, meaning "Demon overcomer," at his conversion in 1879, which took place after contact with the British Methodist missionary David *Hill. Subsequently, he worked with missionaries of the China Inland Mission in pioneer evangelism in Shansi and surrounding areas, at that time almost untouched by the gospel. His education, forceful personality, and natural gifts, together with a fervent faith and deep prayer life, quickly led to his emergence as a spiritual leader. Despite character weaknesses of impatience, dogmatism, and authoritarianism, which mellowed with years, he eventually came to exercise a ministry rightfully described as apostolic. His pastoral gifts and leadership were recognized in 1886 when Hudson *Taylor ordained him as superintending pastor over a wide area. His most notable achievement was to establish some forty-five refuges for curing opium addicts in four provinces; these also functioned as centers for church planting. His regular exercise of the spiritual gifts within a traditional Chinese context has continuing relevance to the Asian church as it deals with charismatic renewal.

BIBLIOGRAPHY Mrs. Howard Taylor [Geraldine Taylor], *Pastor Hsi: Confucian Scholar and Christian* (1900; rev. 1949, 1989).

Hwa Yung

Hsu Kuang-ch'i (Xu Guangqi) (1562–1633), grand minister of the Ming dynasty. Hsu, sometimes described as one of the Three Pillars of Christianity in China, was a native of Shanghai. He was the first Chinese to translate European books. After passing the lowest official examinations in 1581 but failing the next level, he taught in Kwangtung (Guangdong) Province, where he met the Jesuit Lazzaro *Cattaneo in 1596. En route to Peking (Beijing) to take the metropolitan examinations in 1600, he met Matteo *Ricci in Nanking (Nanjing). He was baptized by João *da Rocha (1565–1623) and received the name Paul. In 1604 he passed the highest level examinations and was appointed to the Hanlin Academy in Peking where he helped Ricci translate books on astronomy, geography, hydraulics, and mathematics, including the first half of Euclid's *Elements.* During this period, his father and a son were also baptized. After his father's death in 1607, Hsu twice went to visit the churches in Macao. He returned to Peking after Ricci's death but resigned his official position because of poor health. He moved to Tientsin (Tianjin), where he wrote extensively on agronomy. From 1616 to 1628 he held various positions at court with interludes of retirement from service. In 1628, with the help of the Jesuit missionaries, he accurately predicted a solar eclipse in contradiction to the calculations of the Chinese and Muslims. During the next two years he secured the assistance of Johann Adam *Schall von Bell and was also involved in getting Portuguese troops with cannon to enter China to help defend it against the Manchus. From 1630 onward, peace was established and Hsu was elevated to various government positions. Because of unrest in the Shanghai area, his remains were not buried in his native Zikawei (Xujiahui, Hsu's family village) until 1644.

BIBLIOGRAPHY Hsu Kuang-ch'i, *Zengding Xu wending gongji* (1933, collected writings); Hsu's letters are in *Xu wending gong moji* (1933). George H. Dunne, *Generations of Giants* (1962), pp. 98–100, 115–116, 121–123, 208–215, 220–225; Liang Jiamian, *Xu Guangqi nianpu* (1981); Nicholas Standaert, *Yang Tingyun: Confucian and Christian in Late Ming China* (1988), pp. 35–37, 92–94; J. C. Yang, "Hsu Kuang-ch'i," in Arthur Hummel, ed., *Eminent Chinese of the Ch'ing Period,* 2 vols. (1943–1944; repr. 1967), pp. 316–319; Xi Zezong, *Xu Guangqi yanjiu lunwen ji* (1986; collected essays on Hsu).

John W. Witek, SJ

Huc, Évariste-Régis (1813–1860), Vincentian missionary in Mongolia and Tibet. Huc was born in Caylus, Tarn-et-Garonne, France. After theological studies at Toulouse, he entered the Congrégation de la Mission (Lazarists or Vincentians) in 1836 and three years later reached Peking (Beijing) via Macao. The vicar apostolic of North Chihli (the region of Chihli comprised what is largely today's Hebei and Liaoning Provinces), Martial *Mouly, wanted Huc and his confrere, Joseph *Gabet, to travel to Mongolia and Tibet to learn customs and culture of these regions. After studying Mongolian dialects for several years, Huc and Gabet left for Mongolia in 1844. They preached there and then proceeded to the Buddhist monastery at Kumbun in Kansu (Gansu) Province, where they learned Tibetan. Later they published a translation of the forty-two essential points of the teaching of the Buddha as recorded in Mongolian. In January 1846, Tibetans welcomed them in Lhasa, the capital of Tibet, but a Chinese commissioner forced them to leave by late February. They reached Canton (Guangzhou) in September. Because of frail health, Huc returned to Paris in 1852. After leaving the Vincentians the following year, he published an extensive travelogue on China, Mongolia, and Tibet (translated into eight languages), a two-volume sequel on the Chinese empire, and a history of Christianity in these lands. He died in Paris.

BIBLIOGRAPHY Évariste-Régis Huc, *Souvenirs d'un voyage dans la Tartarie et le Thibet,* 5th ed., 2 vols. (1868; repr. 1925), *Recollections of a Journey through Tartary, Tibet, and China,* 2 vols. (1852), *L'empire chinois,* 3d ed. (1857), *The Chinese Empire,* 2d ed., 2 vols. (1855; repr. 1970), and *Les quarante-deux points d'enseignement professés par Boudha* (1850). See also *Mémoires de la Congrégation de la Mission,* vol. 3 (1911–1912), pp. 407–410.

John W. Witek, SJ

Huddleston, Trevor Ernest Urban (1913–), Anglican leader in the struggle against apartheid. Educated at Oxford and a member of the Anglican Community of the Resurrection, Huddleston was greatly influenced by the Christian Socialist movement. In 1943 he was posted to take charge of the Anglican mission based at the Church of Christ the King, Sophiatown, Johannesburg, and six years later he was made provincial superior of his order, with responsibility for St. Peter's School and Theological College. However, his gift for friendship and passion for justice were what marked him. He returned to Britain in 1956, the year in which he published *Naught for Your Comfort,* a best-selling classic of the anti-apartheid struggle. In 1960 he was consecrated bishop of Masasi, Tanzania, where he became a personal friend of Julius Nyerere. He left Masasi in 1968 to make way for an African successor and was appointed suffragan bishop of Stepney in East London where he once more met problems of racism and poverty. In 1978 he was appointed bishop of Mauritius and archbishop of the Indian Ocean, finally retiring in 1983.

Although he left South Africa in 1956, Huddleston retained strong ties with the country throughout his life, and his name was synonymous with the struggle against apartheid. He became president of the Anti-Apartheid Movement in 1981. He was a close friend of Nelson Mandela, Oliver Tambo, and Desmond Tutu. In his retirement he worked tirelessly on behalf of the church in Africa and against apartheid in South Africa. He was able to return to South Africa for the 1994 elections. He is now living in retirement at Mirfield in Yorkshire, the Mother House of the Community of the Resurrection.

BIBLIOGRAPHY Huddleston's writings include *The True and Living God* (1964), *I Believe: Reflections on the Apostles' Creed* (1986), and *God's World* (1988). Biography and comment include Eric James, *On Safari: In the Steps of Bishop Huddleston* (1991) and Deborah D. Honoré, *Trevor Huddleston: Essays on His Life and Work* (1988).

M. Louise Pirouet

Hudson Taylor, James. *See* Taylor, James Hudson.

Huegel, Frederick J(ulio) (1889–1971), American missionary, theological educator, and pastor in Mexico. Born in Madison, Wisconsin, in a family of German Lutheran immigrants, Huegel graduated from the University of Wisconsin in English literature and philosophy. Frederick Farrar's *Life of Christ* deeply influenced his commitment to Christ and call to ministry. He joined the Disciples of Christ, taught four years at Culver-Stockton College, Canton, Missouri, and served during 1918–1919 as a chaplain in the United States Army. In 1920 he and his wife, Alleen (de Garis), were commissioned by the Disciples for missionary service in Mexico, first in Aguas Calientes, and then in San Luis, Potosí. Suffering brought by the death of their first daughter prompted his book *The Cross of Christ* (1932). In 1931 he moved to Mexico City and began a long teaching career at the Centro Evangélico Unido. He was a frequent speaker in interchurch activities. After retirement in 1957, he traveled extensively preaching throughout Latin America and Japan. He was appreciated particularly as a teacher of spirituality. He published hundreds of articles in English and Spanish. Among his best-known books translated from Spanish are *Bone of His Bone* (1932), *High Peaks of Redemption* (1937), and *Prayer's Deepest Secrets* (1959). The Huegels had two daughters. Their son John is a missionary in Mexico.

BIBLIOGRAPHY Juan Huegel, *Apóstol de la cruz* (1995).

Samuel Escobar

Hueting, André (1868–1961), Dutch missionary in eastern Indonesia. Born in a village near Leiden, Netherlands, and educated at the training institute of the Netherlands Mission Society at Utrecht (1891–1896), Hueting was part of a movement in Dutch missions that stressed the importance of approaching individuals as part of their cultural group. In Halmahera, Indonesia, where Hueting served from 1897 to 1915, earlier missionaries had used an individualistic approach that was critical of traditional culture. Mass movements towards Christianity, which were less critical of indigenous culture, met with no positive response from missionaries and thus were allowed to taper off. However, when a new mass movement arose in 1898, Hueting did not allow it to ebb away. He gave the people involved an interim status by issuing "learner's certificates," and requirements for baptism were lowered, since he viewed baptism as initiation into the Christian religion. On the other hand, the newly baptized were not allowed to participate in Holy Communion until they had received further catechetical instruction. Hueting took a selective approach toward traditional culture. Traditional marriage was considered legal, the dowry was lowered but not abolished, and the taking of Western or biblical names was not encouraged. Between 1901 and 1908, Christian custom was codified by mass assemblies attended by Christian and pagan tribal people. From 1915 to 1930 Hueting worked in Buru (also in eastern Indonesia), following the same principles.

BIBLIOGRAPHY Hueting's many publications include a Tobelo-Dutch dictionary and an elementary Tobelo grammar, a Tobelo hymnbook, and a history of Christian missions in Halmahera. J. Haire, *The Character and Theological Struggle of the Church in Halmahera, Indonesia, 1941–1979* (1981). Hueting's papers are in the archives of the Raad voor de Zending der Nederlandse Hervormde Kerk, Oegstgeest, Netherlands.

Th. van den End

Hughes, Thomas Patrick (1838–1911), Anglican missionary and Islamic scholar. Hughes was educated at the Church Missionary Institute, Islington, near London, and ordained at Calcutta, India, in 1865. He spent his entire missionary career (1864–1884) at Peshawar, capital of the Northwest Frontier Province, 18 miles from the Khyber pass. He blended with the populace through adopting Afghan dress and mastering Pushtu. He wrote the official government textbook for learning that language. His careful and extensive scholarship of Islam, its sources, history, and popular beliefs and practices, resulted in his *Notes on Mohammedanism* (1878) and *Dictionary of Islam* (1885). For these he received the B.D. (1876) and the D.D. (1886) from the Archbishop of Canterbury and membership in the Royal Asiatic Society (1877); he was made a fellow of Punjab University (1882). His ultimate aim was to refute Islam, but copies of his dictionary, edited and revised by Muslim scholars, are still easily obtainable anywhere in the Indian subcontinent. Hughes moved to the United States, where he gained the LL.D. (1897) from St. John's, Annapolis, Maryland, and was rector of churches in Lebanon Springs, New York (1885–1888), and on Long Island, New York (1889–1902). After retirement in 1902, he devoted himself to literary work, writing the introduction on church law in *Lloyd's Clerical Directory*.

BIBLIOGRAPHY Thomas Patrick Hughes, *Translation of the Ganj-Pakkhto* (1882) and *The Kalid-i-Afghani* (1885). Hughes's personal papers are in the CMS archives, Birmingham Univ.

Clinton Bennett

Hulbert, Homer Bezaleel (1863–1949), missionary and educator in Korea. Born in New Haven, Vermont, Hulbert graduated from Dartmouth College in 1884. After two years of study at Union Theological Seminary in New York, he arrived in Korea in 1886 and served for five years as a teacher at the Royal English School in Seoul. A

Congregationalist, his only missionary service was with the Methodist Episcopal Church in Korea from 1893 to 1897. In this period he directed the Trilingual Press, supported the progressive and independence movements, preached, and wrote of his research on Korea. A confidant of the Korean king, he served from 1897 to 1905 as principal of the Imperial Normal and Middle Schools and published a series of texts for modern education in Korean. He published his *History of Korea* in 1905 and *The Passing of Korea* in 1906, which reflect his growing disillusionment with Japan's aggression in Asia. An indefatigable advocate of Korean progress and independence, he played an active, though unsuccessful, role in Korea's behalf during the diplomatic negotiations that led to Japanese control and annexation of Korea between 1905 and 1910.

Returning to the United States, Hulbert was ordained in the Congregational Church in 1911 and spent over a decade championing the Korean cause on the lecture circuit. He was invited to Korea by President Syngman Rhee when the Republic of Korea was established in 1948, but his wife's death delayed his travel until 1949. He died soon after his arrival and was buried with full national honors in Seoul.

BIBLIOGRAPHY Most of Hulbert's important articles can be found in *Korea Review* and *Korean Repository.* A short biography is in vol. 1 of Hulbert's *History of Korea,* Clarence Norwood Weems, ed. (1962), while vol. 2 provides an annotated bibliography of his writings.

Edward W. Poitras

Hulstaert, Gustaf (1900–1990), Catholic missionary in the former Belgian Congo. Born in Melsele, Belgium, Hulstaert studied at the University of Louvain and became a member of the Missionaries of the Sacred Heart (MSC). Ordained in 1924, he was assigned to the Vicariate Coquilhatville (now Mbandaka, Zaire) in 1925 and was superior at the mission stations Flandria (now Boteka) and Bokuma. From 1936 to 1946 he was superior of the MSC missionaries in that district. Freed in 1950 from missionary duties, Hulstaert was allowed to concentrate on his research at Bamanya, where a group of missionaries and colonial administrators interested in the authentic traditions of the people regularly gathered around him in the institute Centre Aequatoria. In 1934 he started to work on a translation of the Bible into the language of the Mongo. This highly regarded work was completed in 1977. His numerous scientific studies cover a wide range of topics in the fields of ethnography and linguistics. Most smaller studies were published in the periodical *Aequatoria* (since 1980, *Annales Aequatoria*), which he cofounded in 1937. He received honorary doctorates from the University of Mainz (1972) and the National University of Zaire (1973).

BIBLIOGRAPHY Among Hulstaert's major studies are *Dictionnaire Français-Lomongo (Lonkundo)* (1952), *Dictionnaire Lomongo-Français* (1957), *Proverbes Mongo* (1958), *Contes Mongo* (1965), and *Fables Mongo* (1970). Short biographies were published in *Africa-Tervuren* 16 (1970): 107–112, in *ZMR* 57 (1973): 33–38, and on the occasion of his eightieth birthday, with the bibliography of his publications up to 1980, in *Annales Aequatoria* 1, no. 1 (1980): 3–57. This was updated and expanded in *Annales Aequatoria* 12 (1991): 1–75.

Otto Bischofberger, SMB

Hume, Edward H(icks) (1876–1957), founder and organizer of the Yale Mission hospital and medical college in Changsha, China. Hume was born in Ahmednagar, India, where his father and grandfather had worked as teachers and missionaries. He received his B.A. from Yale (1897) and his M.D. from Johns Hopkins Medical School (1901). Married to Lotta Carswell, he was at work on plague prevention projects in India (1903–1905) when the newly formed Yale-in-China Mission invited him to launch a university medical school in China. This project became his most important lifework. From humble beginnings in 1906 in a Changsha, Hunan, inn that served as the first hospital, Hume gathered Chinese medical co-workers, raised funds, negotiated agreements, and laid the groundwork for the Yale-China hospital which opened in 1917. He served as senior physician, dean of Hunan Medical College, professor of medicine, and liaison with Chinese medical boards and professional journals. His aim was to develop educational and medical work "under the strongest Christian influence and under the highest intellectual and scientific standards of teaching and research." Despite mission opposition, and facing intense nationalistic pressures during the 1920s, Hume advocated giving greater authority to the Chinese. In 1926 he offered his resignation to the Yale-China board in a dispute over policy. He later lectured on Chinese medical history, published books on Eastern and Western approaches to medicine, and served as medical consultant in various church-related situations.

BIBLIOGRAPHY Edward H. Hume, *The Chinese Way of Medicine* (1940), *Doctors East, Doctors West* (1946), and *Doctors Courageous* (1950). A biography of Hume was written by his wife, Lotta Carswell Hume, *Drama at the Doctor's Gate: The Story of Doctor Edward Hume of Yale-in-China* (1961), and a biographical sketch appears in Jonathan Spence, *To Change China: Western Advisers in China, 1620–1960* (1969).

James A. Scherer

Hume, Robert Allen (1847–1929), American Congregational missionary in India. Hume was born in Bombay, India, of missionary parents serving with the American Board of Commissioners for Foreign Missions (ABCFM). He graduated from Yale University and Andover Seminary and was sent by the ABCFM to India, where he was assigned to the Marathi Mission, based in the city of Ahmednagar. He remained there his entire missionary career (1874–1926) and thus became known as Hume of Ahmednagar. In 1878 he founded and headed the Ahmednagar Divinity College, his main responsibility for 43 years. One of his most notable students at the seminary was the Marathi Christian poet Narayan Vaman *Tilak. During that time he was superintendent of the Parner mission district near Ahmednagar. He also served as English editor of *Dnyanodaya,* the mission's Anglo-Marathi newspaper, as president of the Bombay Christian Council, and as the first moderator of the United Church of North India when it was formed in 1925. In 1893 he addressed the World Parliament of Religions in Chicago on "Christian and Hindu Thought." Hume received an honorary D.D. from Yale University in 1895, and Queen Victoria conferred upon him in 1901 the Kaiser-i-Hind gold medal for his public service in India. He was the author of *Missions from the Modern View* (1905), *An Interpretation of India's Religious History* (1911), and nearly 200 pamphlets in English and Marathi. Hume returned to the United States in 1926 where he retired and died in Brookline, Massachusetts.

BIBLIOGRAPHY A series of autobiographical articles, "Hume of Ahmednagar," was published in *The Congregationalist* during 1921 (vol. 106). Additional material on Hume can be found in issues of *The Missionary Herald* (1874–1929), especially those of February 1925 and September 1929. See also Alden H. Clark, "Hume of Ahmednagar," *MRW* 52(1929): 821–827.

Gerald H. Anderson

Hume, Robert Wilson (1809–1854), American missionary to western India. Born in Stamford, New York, Hume graduated from Union College, New York (1834), and Princeton Theological Seminary (1837). He was ordained a missionary by the American Board of Commissioners for Foreign Missions (ABCFM) in 1839, married Hannah D. Sackett, and sailed for Bombay. They stopped en route at Zanzibar, where the sultan was intrigued by Hannah's musical ability and offered to trade six young women for her. Apart from some touring, Hume served his entire career in Bombay, doing literary work, preaching, and managing schools. He was for a time secretary of the Bombay Temperance Union and editor of its journal. For ten years he was secretary of the Bombay Tract and Book Society and instrumental in instituting a system of colportage and payment for literature. He also edited for ten years the semimonthly magazine *Dnyanodaya,* the only Christian journal in a native language in western India. Forced by ill health to return home, he died and was buried at sea. Three of his seven children became missionaries; through three generations, nineteen Hume missionaries worked in India. His son Robert Allen *Hume was at the center of the ABCFM's 1886 "Andover controversy" over a liberalized theology.

BIBLIOGRAPHY Fred Field Goodsell, *They Lived Their Faith* (1961), pp. 11–12, 112–113; *Missionary Herald* 51 (1855): 175–178.

David M. Stowe

Hung Hsiu-ch'uan (Hong Xiuquan) (1814–1864), founder of the Taiping Heavenly Kingdom and leader of the Taiping Rebellion. Hung was the fourth of five children in a Kwangtung (Guangdong) peasant family. Depressed after twice failing examinations for the *shengyuan* degree, he traveled to Canton, where he met *Liang Fa, a Chinese evangelist working with an American missionary. The Bible tract *Good Words for Exhorting the Age,* given to him by Liang Fa about 1836, changed his life. He had dreams and visions in which he conversed with two bearded men. After six years as a village schoolteacher, and twice again failing the government exams, he came to believe that the two men were God and Jesus and that he, Hung, was the younger brother of Jesus Christ. He began to preach, baptize converts, and destroy ancestral shrines and idols. In 1847 he returned to Canton, where he studied the Bible with Issachar *Roberts, an American Baptist missionary. He then joined a group known as the Society of God Worshipers in eastern Kwangsi (Guangxi) Province, where his movement spread among the remote mountain people.

Hung advocated the creation of a new theocratic, egalitarian communal society of believers and the destruction of the Manchu government, which he considered to be in demonic opposition to the true God. By 1850 he had attracted over 20,000 followers who were organized into military units under rigorous discipline. In 1850, after the first Qing government army sent against him was defeated, Hung named himself the Heavenly King of the Heavenly Kingdom of Great Peace. Hung's Taiping armies moved north, capturing arms and booty as city after city fell. The Taipings ruled from Nanking (Nanjing) for 11 years (1853–1864) under Hung as Heavenly King. Their strict code of conduct banned opium smoking, prostitution, alcohol, and sexual immorality. Yet in the end they failed, due largely to Hung's eccentricities and erratic leadership. His religious ideology was finally regarded by missionaries to be a heretical Chinese sect, with himself as a false messiah. It is estimated that upward of 20 million people died in the course of the rebellion.

BIBLIOGRAPHY P. Richard Bohr, "The Politics of Eschatology: Hung Hsiu-chüan and the Rise of the Taipings, 1837–1853" (Ph.D. diss., Univ. of California, Davis, 1978); Chien Yu-wen, *The Taiping Revolutionary Movement* (1973); William R. Doezema, "Western Seeds of Eastern Heterodoxy: The Impact of Protestant Revivalism on the Christianity of Taiping Rebel Leader Hung Hsiu-ch'uan, 1836–1864," *Fides et Historia* 25 (1993): 73–98; Kenneth Scott Latourette, *A History of Christian Missions in China* (1929); Franz Michael and Chang Chung-li, *The Taiping Rebellion: History and Documents,* 3 vols. (1966–1971); Jonathan D. Spence, *God's Chinese Son: The Taiping Heavenly Kingdom of Hong Xiuquan* (1996).

Donald E. MacInnis

Hunnicutt, Benjamin Harris (1886–1962), American Presbyterian agricultural missionary and college president in Brazil. Hunnicutt graduated from Mississippi Agricultural and Mechanical College (Mississippi State University) in 1905, and in 1907 the Board of Foreign Missions of the Presbyterian Church, U.S. sent him to Gammon Institute in Lavras, near Belo Horizonte in eastern Brazil, where he was appointed director of the new Agricultural Department. Within 15 years the department had grown into a college-level, four-year program; by 1923 the school had graduated 50 students and had an enrollment of 326. Hunnicutt published several books in Portuguese on agriculture and farm animals. He was married to

Gladys Allyn (died in 1914) and later to Nannie Hall Kolb (died 1955).

Hunnicutt was executive secretary for the Eleventh World Sunday School Convention, São Paulo, 1932. In 1934 he became president of Mackenzie College in São Paulo. With William W. Reid, Hunnicutt wrote *The Story of Agricultural Missions* (1931), a carefully researched description of the work of the churches to improve agriculture and upgrade livestock in seven major countries of Asia, the Middle East, and Latin America. He also wrote two books introducing Brazil to general, international readers—*Brazil Looks Forward* (1945) and *Brazil, a World Frontier* (1949, 1969). Hunnicutt remained as president of Mackenzie until his retirement in 1951.

BIBLIOGRAPHY James E. Bear, *Mission to Brazil* (1961) and "The Mission Work of the Presbyterian Church in the United States in Southern Brazil, 1869-1958" (microform of a 1960 manuscript at Union Theological Seminary in Virginia). Many materials relating to Mackenzie College are in the Presbyterian Historical Society, Philadelphia.

H. McKennie Goodpasture

Hunt, Bruce Finley (1903-1992), American Presbyterian missionary in Korea, associated with the "repentance movement" in Korean Presbyterianism. Born in Pyengyang of missionary parents serving with the Presbyterian Church, U.S.A., Hunt labored under the same board from 1928 to 1935, then joined the Orthodox Presbyterian Church in 1936 and gave leadership to its Korean mission. In 1941 he was imprisoned in Manchuria for his opposition to Shinto worship. Repatriated with his wife and five children in 1942, he returned to Korea in 1946 and associated with those concerned over compromises with Shinto worship and the growth of theological liberalism. He joined the staff of Koryu Seminary in Pusan, created by Korean leadership to promote renewal. When the supporting presbytery was ousted by the denomination in 1951, a new denomination, nicknamed the Koryu Group, was formed. Hunt was associated with it until his retirement in 1976. Following his return to the United States, he carried on an active preaching ministry in Korean-American churches.

BIBLIOGRAPHY Bruce Finley Hunt, a foreword to *The Planting and Development of Missionary Churches* by John Nevius (1958), *For a Testimony* (autobiography, 1966), and *Korean Pentecost and the Sufferings which Followed,* coauthored with William Blair (1977). Harvie M. Conn, "Studies in the Theology of the Korean Presbyterian Church: An Historical Outline," *Westminster Theological Journal* 30 (1967): 24-49, and 31 (1968): 135-184; Ung-kyu Pak, "The Significance of Bruce F. Hunt's Ministry in Korea and Manchuria (1928-1952): With Particular Attention to Shinto Shrine Worship" (Th.M. thesis, Westminster Theological Seminary, 1992).

Harvie M. Conn

Hunt, John (1811-1848), English Methodist missionary in Fiji. Hunt arrived in Fiji with his wife in 1839 and worked successively in Rewa, Somosomo, and Viwa. His main task was Bible translation; he completed the New Testament and had begun work on translating the Old Testament before his untimely death from dysentery. He was a person of deep religious feeling whose beauty of character and total devotion made a strong impact on the Fijians, even when they did not accept his faith. He respected the Fijian culture and learned to know it well, recognizing both its bad and its good qualities. He worked to develop forms of worship that made use of Fijian cultural styles.

The last island where he worked, Viwa, was the place with which he was most closely associated and where his grave still attracts Fijians. It was his Bible reading and prayer which moved the warrior Varani, nephew of Viwa's chief, to give himself to Christ. Varani's conversion in 1845 changed the scene in the Bau-Rewa-Viwa center of power in Fiji and was one of the factors leading to the conversion in 1854 of Varani's friend and Fiji's greatest chief Thakombau. Varani's conversion was also followed by an outbreak of Pentecostal-style revival in the Viwa church, which Hunt welcomed, trusting that even its emotional excesses would lead to transformed lives.

BIBLIOGRAPHY Allen Birtwhistle, *In His Armour: The Life of John Hunt of Fiji* (1954). See also John Garrett, *To Live among the Stars: Christian Origins in Oceania* (1982), pp. 105-111.

Charles W. Forman

Hunt, Phineas Rice (1816-1878), printer for the American Board of Commissioners for Foreign Missions (ABCFM) in India and China. Born in Arlington, Vermont, in 1839 Hunt went to India, where for 27 years he supervised the sizable ABCFM press in Madras, producing an improved Tamil Bible as well as a Tamil dictionary compiled by Miron *Winslow. He also served as treasurer of the mission until it closed in 1866. After a sojourn in the United States, he and his wife took up similar work in China in 1868, establishing the first metallic movable type operation in Peking (Beijing) and overseeing production of a new Mandarin translation of the Bible and of the Prayer Book. Though trained only as a printer and apparently without having learned any local languages, Hunt worked closely with English-speaking residents and congregations in both India and China, often voicing his hope that "God will let me win some souls for him before I die." He died in China of typhus fever, a year after his wife died.

BIBLIOGRAPHY H. Blodget, "Phineas R. Hunt," *Missionary Herald,* September 1878.

Creighton Lacy

Hunter, George W. (1861-1946), China Inland Mission (CIM) missionary in Turkestan. A Scotsman who never married, Hunter went to China in 1889. After several years working among Muslims in Kansu (Gansu), Tsinghai (Qinghai), and Ningsia (Ningxia) in northwest China, he began a ministry among the several Islamic minority peoples of Central Asia in what is now Sinkiang (Xinjiang) Province. Although he considered Tihwa (Urumqi) to be his base, he itinerated widely through the province, distributing literature that he had translated and doing personal evangelism. As he traveled, he helped the Swedish mission work in Kashgar and a very conservative community of 200 families of Russian Baptists living in Kuldja (Gulja), Chuguchak, and other nearby cities in northwest Sinkiang. In Tihwa, Hunter prepared translations of scripture portions into Kazak and a dialect of Kalmuk or Western Mongolian. When the Russians took control of the province in the mid-1930s, he was held prisoner for 13 months and tortured by the Soviet secret police. Upon his release, he was deported by plane to Lanchow (Lanzhou), Kansu (Gansu) Province, where he received medical treatment, recuperated, and helped the missionaries in their work. He tried once again to return to Sinkiang at the end of World War II. He got no farther than Kanchow (Zhangye), where he died.

BIBLIOGRAPHY Mildred Cable and Francesca French, *George Hunter: Apostle of Turkestan* (1948).

Ralph R. Covell

Hunter, Leslie Stannard (1890–1983), founder of the Sheffield, England, Industrial Mission. Hunter, the son of a Congregational minister in Glasgow, was educated at Kelvinside Academy and New College, Oxford, and became an Anglican in 1913. He was a study secretary of the Student Christian Movement (1913–1920). He developed ideas about relating the church to industry while first a canon of the cathedral and then an archdeacon in the diocese of Newcastle-on-Tyne. In 1944 he founded the Sheffield Industrial Mission as bishop of Sheffield (1939–1962) and appointed E. R. ("Ted") Wickham, another pioneer in the field, to lead it.

BIBLIOGRAPHY Leslie S. Hunter, *A Mission of the People of God* (1961). P. Bradshaw, *The Church beyond the Church* (1994); G. H. G. Hewitt, ed., *Strategist for the Spirit* (1985); E. R. Wickham, *Church and People in an Industrial City* (1957). Obituary in *The Times*, July 19, 1983.

Timothy Yates

Hurlburt, Charles E. (1860–1936), a founder and general director of the Africa Inland Mission (AIM). Born in Iowa and raised in Oberlin, Ohio, Hurlburt left a successful plumbing business to work with the YMCA, becoming state secretary of the Pennsylvania YMCA in 1889. With Peter Cameron *Scott and others, Hurlburt helped to found AIM in May 1895. Named AIM general director in 1897, and confronted with the near collapse of the mission after the death of Scott in December 1896, he led his family and new workers to Kenya in 1901. Beginning in 1909, Hurlburt extended the work of the mission to include areas in Tanzania and the Belgian Congo (Zaire), gaining permission to enter the latter through the intervention of President Theodore Roosevelt (who had consulted Hurlburt in 1908 regarding East African affairs). Hurlburt pioneered in the concept of educating missionary children on the field, founding the Rift Valley Academy boarding school in Kenya. He represented AIM at the World Missionary Conference, Edinburgh (1910), and at the Foreign Missions Convention at Washington (1925), there giving an address, "The Gospel among Primitive Peoples." He had a major influence on the formation of the Interdenominational Foreign Mission Association in 1917. In 1925 differences of interpretation over the "faith" principle of missionary support figured in his forced resignation from AIM. From his home in California, Hurlburt founded the Unevangelized Africa Mission and continued for 11 more years to recruit missionaries for the Congo and French Equatorial Africa.

BIBLIOGRAPHY Dick Anderson, *We Felt Like Grasshoppers* (1994); Kenneth Richardson, *Garden of Miracles: A History of the Africa Inland Mission* (1968). A brief biographical sketch appears in Edwin L. Frizen, Jr., *Seventy-Five Years of IFMA, 1917–1992: The Nondenominational Missions Movement* (1992).

Robert T. Coote

Hut, Hans (1490?–1527), missionary of early south-German and Austrian Anabaptism. A bookdealer by trade, Hut was an early Anabaptist convert and evangelist in southern Germany. Whereas the converts of other Anabaptist missionaries often went to Moravia for security, Hut's converts did not emigrate but formed countless small cells of believers wherever he went. This was due in part to his emphasis on the unity of personal and social salvation, to his rootedness in late medieval mysticism, and to his apocalyptic emphasis that the end of the age was at hand. His own baptism at the hands of Hans Denck in 1526 was less a complete turning away from the violence of Thomas Müntzer after the abortive 1525 Peasants' War, as earlier historiography described it, than an expedient muting of his earlier vision. His date for the endtime was postponed from 1525 to 1528. During this period, absolute pacifism, suffering, and community of goods became the norm, but believers expected that in the endtime they would be armed by the returning Christ to help destroy the wicked. His baptisms were made with the sign of the Greek letter tau on the forehead, to indicate that the baptized were among the elect 144,000; the rite was covenantal, sealing the believer both to God and to the congregation through the Spirit, water, and blood. Hut's trademark emphasis upon the "gospel of all creatures" (Rom. 1:20) suggested that the gospel has been, and is, preached in and through all creation; it was meant to stress that the suffering of Christ must be fulfilled in all his members; justification requires inner and outer suffering. Hut was captured and put on trial in Augsburg. Following torture, he was returned unconscious to his cell. A candle ignited the straw where he lay. The guard found him dead when he returned.

BIBLIOGRAPHY Hans Hut, "Of the Mystery of Baptism," in Gordon Rupp, ed., *Patterns of Reformation* (1969); Ray C. Gingerich, *The Mission Impulse of Early Swiss and South German-Austrian Anabaptism* (1980); Werner O. Packull, "Gottfried Seebass on

Hans Hut: A Discussion," *Mennonite Quarterly Review* 49 (1975), and *Mysticism and the Early South German-Austrian Anabaptist Movement, 1525–1531* (1977); Gottfried Seebass, *Müntzers Erbe: Werk, Leben und Theologie Hans Hut* (1972).

Cornelius J. Dyck

Hwang, C. H. *See* Coe, Shoki.

Hyde, John (1865–1912), Presbyterian missionary to India. The son of a Presbyterian minister in Carrollton, Illinois, Hyde graduated from Carthage College, Illinois, and McCormick Seminary (1892). During the ocean voyage to the United Presbyterian Mission in the Punjab, India, he wrestled with issues of holiness and sought the infilling of the Spirit. Initially slow at learning language—attributed to his being hard of hearing and to his preoccupation with Bible study—he nevertheless became fluent in Urdu, Punjabi, and Hindustani. Gifted in personal evangelism and devoted to itinerant village evangelism, he came to the fore beginning in 1904, when the Sialkot annual convention was organized to revive missionaries and Indian pastors, evangelists, and other Christian workers.

During the annual conventions, Hyde typically spent most days and nights in the convention prayer room, indifferent to meals and sleep. His eccentric intensity was a source of contention and embarrassment in the missionary community, but friends credited his prayers as the source of the revival that swept through the Punjabi mission in the first decade of the twentieth century. Broken in health, he sailed for England in 1911 and then on to the United States, where he died of a brain tumor in his forty-seventh year. He never married.

Bibliography Francis A. McGaw, *Praying Hyde* (rep., 1970); Basil Miller, *Praying Hyde* (1943).

Robert T. Coote

Hynd, David (1895–1991), Nazarene minister and medical missionary in Swaziland. Hynd was born in Perth, Scotland. A graduate of the University of Glasgow and London School of Tropical Medicine, he prepared for both ministry and medicine and was ordained in 1924. He began missionary work in 1925 in Swaziland, establishing the first Church of the Nazarene and the nation's first hospital, Raleigh Fitkin Memorial Hospital. Through remarkable energy and leadership, he established rural outpatient clinics, the country's first nurses training college, the first branch of the Red Cross, and the first colony for person's with leprosy. He developed primary and secondary schools and the first teachers training college.

In 1947 Hynd was made Commander of the British Empire, one of a number of honors he received over the years from the British and Swaziland monarchs. After his retirement in 1961, the Swazi government issued a postage stamp that bore his image. He received the LL.D. from the University of Swaziland in 1987. He died at Manzini, Swaziland.

Bibliography J. Fred Parker, *Mission to the World* (1988); Mendell Taylor, *Fifty Years of Nazarene Missions* (1956). Numerous documents and personal papers are held in the Nazarene archives, Kansas City, Mo.

Robert H. Scott

I

Iakinf (Bichurin) (1777-1853), outstanding Russian sinologist and corresponding member of the Russian Academy of Sciences. A monk from 1800, Iakinf was appointed in 1807 as the superior of the Orthodox mission in Peking (Beijing) and spent 14 years there. He translated the Orthodox liturgy and compiled a catechism in Chinese. More scholar than monk by nature, Iakinf immersed himself in Chinese studies. He devoted most of his time to compiling dictionaries, translating Chinese classics, and writing original works on Chinese history, geography, and religion. Upon his return to Russia, he lived in the Valaam monastery and in the St. Petersburg Alexander Nevsky Lavra (from 1826), where he wrote books on sinology that were translated into many languages.

BIBLIOGRAPHY Iakinf (Bichurin), *Avtobiograficheskaya Zapiska* (Autobiographical note) (1855) and *Opisaniye Religii Uchenykh* (The description of religion of scholars) (1840). P. Ye. Skachkov, *Iakinf Bichurin: Materialy k Biografii* (Materials for biography) (1933).

Evgeny S. Steiner

Ibiam, (Francis) Akanu (1906-1995), Nigerian medical missionary and statesman. Ibiam was born in Unwana, southeast Nigeria, and educated at Hope Waddell Training Institute, Calabar, and King's College, Lagos, before becoming the first African medical graduate of the University of St. Andrews in 1934. Rejecting well-paid government service, he was (after some hesitation) accepted as a medical missionary of the Church of Scotland. He pioneered Abiriba hospital (1936-1945) and then superintended mission hospitals at Itu and Uburu. In the period preceding Nigerian independence he was increasingly recognized as a popular leader and representative; he served in local government, in the Eastern Regional House of Assembly, and in the Legislative and Executive Councils. He was a vigorous advocate of universal primary education and one of the early voices calling for a Nigerian university. In 1957 he became principal of Hope Waddell Institution. With independence in 1960 he was appointed governor of Eastern Nigeria. When the events of 1966—two military coups, the secession of Biafra, and the civil war—overturned all constitutional arrangements, Ibiam became adviser to the Biafran military government, often representing Biafra abroad, where his church contacts were useful in obtaining relief supplies. He renounced his two knighthoods (awarded in 1951 and 1960 by the British monarch) in protest against British support for the Nigerian federal government. When war ended in 1970, he remained in Nigeria, working for reconstruction and relief and returning to honorary hospital service.

In Nigeria Ibiam was a key Christian figure, responsible for new initiatives such as the Bible Society of Nigeria and the Christian Medical Fellowship, and serving as president of the Christian Council of Nigeria (1955-1958) and in many other representative capacities. He was also an outstanding African ecumenical figure of the decolonization period, serving as chairman of the conference that led to the All Africa Conference of Churches (AACC), a president of the AACC and of the World Council of Churches, chairman of the council of the United Bible Societies, and leader of the AACC peace mission to Sudan. In his home area he was a respected traditional ruler, Eze Ogo Isiala I of Unwana and Osuji of Uburu.

BIBLIOGRAPHY Geoffrey Johnston, *Of God and Maxim Guns: Presbyterianism in Nigeria, 1844-1946* (1988); D. C. Nwafo, *Born to Serve: The Biography of Dr. Akanu Ibiam* (1988); *The Scotsman,* July 24, 1995.

Andrew F. Walls

Ibuka Kajinosuke (1854-1940), pioneer pastor and educator in the Presbyterian-Reformed Church in Japan. Ibuka was born in Wakamatsu, north of Tokyo, in a family of high rank in the Tokugawa regime. His family suffered total confiscation of their property upon the overthrow of that regime by the southwestern clan of Choshū and Satsuma in 1867. In Tokyo and later in Yokohama he realized that the best education was now to be Western learning and that through English. He made the acquaintance of Samuel R. *Brown and was ultimately able to enter Brown's newly formed school in Yokohama.

From this background Ibuka studied further under Brown, his daughter, and his niece, then, from 1877, at the new Union Theological School in Tokyo. After ordination in November 1878, Ibuka served in the pastorate for a year and then was appointed instructor in the same school. When that school joined Meiji Gakuin in 1886, Ibuka was first vice-president and then, in 1891, president, following a year's study under Philip Schaff at Union Theological Seminary in New York City. Ibuka served as moderator of the Nihon Kirisuto Kyōkai (Church of Christ in Japan) and as a member of many of its committees. He became internationally known as an outstanding representative of Japanese Protestant Christianity, and gave an address at the World Missionary Conference in Edinburgh, 1910, which he attended as a delegate of the Board of Foreign Missions of the Presbyterian Church, U.S.A.

BIBLIOGRAPHY William Imbrie, "Biographical Sketch of Kajinosuke Ibuka," in Mutoh Tomio, ed., *Ibuka Kajinosuke to Sono Jidai,* vol. 1 (1969).

Richard H. Drummond

Iglehart, Charles W(heeler) (1882–1969), American Methodist missionary and leader of Protestant Christianity in Japan. Iglehart was born in Evansville, Indiana, and spent much of his youth in New York City, where his father was a prominent Methodist pastor. Educated at Columbia University (B.A., 1902) and Drew University (M.Div., 1906; Ph.D., 1934), he received honorary degrees from Syracuse University and Tokyo Union Theological Seminary. After brief pastorates near New York City, Iglehart went to Japan as a Methodist missionary in 1909, married Congregational missionary Florence Allchin in 1911, and did evangelistic, educational, and publishing work in Sendai. During World War I, he served the YMCA's army department in Siberia, returning to Tokyo as a missionary in 1919. There he served as professor at Aoyama Gakuin, district superintendent of the Methodist Church (Kanto district), educational secretary for the National Christian Council of Japan, and editor of the Japan Christian Yearbook. He was a delegate to the Jerusalem (1928) and Madras (1938) conferences of the International Missionary Council (IMC), and served as IMC Far East consultant. During World War II, he assisted the Methodist Board of Missions in New York as East Asia secretary, and also taught missions at Union Theological Seminary. In 1946 he returned to Japan as adviser on educational and religious matters to Allied occupation authorities. He later served as visiting professor at Tokyo International Christian University and wrote that institution's history. Iglehart prepared the centennial history of Japanese Protestantism (1959). He was awarded an imperial decoration by Emperor Hirohito in 1953. He died in Florida.

BIBLIOGRAPHY Charles W. Iglehart, *Cross and Crisis in Japan* (1957), *A Century of Protestant Cooperation in Japan* (1959), and *International Christian University: An Adventure in Christian Higher Education in Japan* (1964).

James A. Scherer

Ignatius of Loyola (*or* Iñigo López de Loyola) (1491–1556), founder of the Society of Jesus, popularly known as the Jesuits. Iñigo was born at the castle of Loyola in the Basque province of Guipúzcoa in northeastern Spain. At about age 15, he was sent to join the household of the chief treasurer of Castile at Arévalo and to be educated as a courtier. Subsequently, he passed into the service of the viceroy of Navarre. In 1521 a French cannon ball wounded him seriously in both legs as he was leading the defense of the city of Pamplona. While recuperating back at Loyola, Iñigo experienced a conversion that changed the course of his life.

Departing Loyola in early 1522—his goal Jerusalem and a life of penance there—Iñigo stopped at Manresa, a town north of Barcelona, where in the course of nine months he underwent a series of religious experiences and mystical illuminations that provided the basis for his *Spiritual Exercises.* His goal became apostolic, "the help of souls." Unable to remain in Jerusalem as he had hoped, Iñigo returned to Spain, where he began to study for the priesthood at Barcelona, Alcalá, and Salamanca. In 1528, when church authorities restricted his evangelizing activities, he moved to the University of Paris, where he later took the name Ignatius. Here the first companions of the nascent Society of Jesus gathered about him, including the young Frances *Xavier. On August 15, 1534, in a small chapel on Montmartre, six of them took vows of poverty and promised to go to Jerusalem to labor for the salvation of souls. The trip to Jerusalem ultimately proved impossible, so in late 1538, now joined by a handful of others, they put themselves at the service of the pope. Faced with the spread of apostolic missions in Europe and overseas, they determined to found a new religious order. And so on September 27, 1540, Pope Paul III issued the bull *Regimini militantis ecclesiae* formally creating the Society of Jesus, of which Ignatius was elected the first superior general.

Ignatius spent most of his final years in Rome composing the *Constitutions* of the society and overseeing its growth. Nearly 7,000 of his letters survive from this period. During this time the efforts of the society turned to education, so that at Ignatius's death there were thirty-one colleges. Altogether, in 1556 roughly 1,000 Jesuits were divided into twelve provinces, including India, Brazil, and the short-lived Ethiopian Province.

Ignatius's two principal works are the *Spiritual Exercises,* which have had an enormous impact in the Catholic world and beyond up to the present day, and the *Constitutions,* which included many innovations in religious life. Both incorporate a spirituality that is open to the world, and so to inculturation, and that seeks to combine in a new way an intense prayer life with apostolic activity.

BIBLIOGRAPHY Most available documentation regarding Ignatius is in the multivolume *Monumenta Historica Societatis Jesu* (1894–). English editions of the *Spiritual Exercises* and the so-called *Autobiography,* along with selections from the *Spiritual Diary,* the *Constitutions,* and correspondence appear in George E. Ganss, ed., *Ignatius of Loyola: The Spiritual Exercises and Selected Works* (1991); *The Constitutions of the Society of Jesus* (1970), also edited by Ganss, is much more fully annotated. Cándido de Dalmases, *Ignatius of Loyola, Founder of the Jesuits: His Life and Work* (1985) is a factually accurate and concise biography. A major study of the early years of the Jesuits is John W. O'Malley, *The First Jesuits* (1993). For current scholarship, see the annual bibliography in the *Archivum Historicum Societatis Jesu.*

Robert Bireley, SJ

Ihmels, Carl (1888–1967), director of the Leipzig Mission. Son of a Lutheran bishop, a native of northwest Germany, Ihmels studied theology and philosophy and worked as a parish pastor before he was appointed director of the Lutheran Leipzig Mission in 1923 at the age of 35. No other German mission leader in modern times held office for so long and in so turbulent and critical a period. Ihmel's administration was marked by two simultaneous processes of change—from Western missions to younger churches, and from a Christian establishment in fairly intact surroundings to a secularized and fragmented society for which first the Nazi ideology and later the radical socialism of the German Democratic Republic regime paved the way. Although Ihmels served as part-time lecturer in missiology at Leipzig University, he never claimed to be a scholar and never produced a major book. However, he did become the prototype of a mission administrator who, without overseas missionary experience of his own, derived his strength from imperturbable loyalty to the Lutheran confession and the Lutheran church at home and abroad, demanding strict discipline and self-restraint from himself and his missionaries.

BIBLIOGRAPHY Niels-Peter Moritzen, *Werkzeug Gottes in der Welt: Leipziger Mission 1836–1936–1986* (1986).

Hans-Werner Gensichen

Ilminskii, Nikolai Ivanovich (1822–1891), Russian Orthodox missionary linguist to Muslim Tatars. Born to a clerical family in Penza, Russia, Ilminskii graduated from the Kazan Theological Academy and was assigned to study the Tatar language spoken in the southern provinces of the Russian empire. In 1847 he was named to the Bible translation committee, and over the course of 11 years translated most of the liturgical books of the Orthodox Church into Tatar; he also wrote numerous books and articles on missiology. Dispatched by the Russian Orthodox mission in 1850 to the Middle East to master Arabic, Turkish, and Persian, he returned home a recognized orientalist, fluent also in Hebrew, Greek, Latin, Tatar, Mordvin, Chuvash, Cheremish, Kirghiz, Altai, and Yakut. Never ordained for active missionary service, he remained a lay professor. By 1858 he began advocating the abandonment of Arabic as the language for evangelizing among Muslim Tatars, substituting instead the readily understood spoken vernacular as transcribed in Russian characters. This he saw as the only means of severing the resilient cultural bonds to Islam, which Muslim polemicists used successfully among the politically (rather than religiously) motivated convert masses. The tide of apostasy was stemmed. In 1872, under the patronage of Metropolitan *Innocent of Moscow, he was named director of the Kazan Native Training College, which began training an indigenous clergy.

BIBLIOGRAPHY Serge Bolshakoff, *The Foreign Missions of the Russian Orthodox Church* (1943), pp. 38–40; James J. Stamoolis, *Eastern Orthodox Mission Theology Today* (1986), pp. 31–33.

Paul D. Garrett

Imad ud-Din (c. 1830–1900), Muslim scholar, Christian convert, and apologist. Imad ud-Din (Pillar of the Faith) was a descendant of a family of Muslim notables and religious scholars in the Punjab. Trained in traditional Islamic sciences, he was appointed as a young man to a preaching position in the central mosque of Agra. His anti-Christian polemic contributed to the controversy between Muslim *ulema* and Christian missionaries that preceded the Indian mutiny of 1857; it may also have deepened his youthful doubts about the formalist character of the Indian *ulema* of his day. Abandoning his position, he took to the life of an itinerant ascetic, until, stricken by inner restlessness, he temporarily rejected all religions. As a language teacher in Lahore, in contact with Christian missionaries and government servants, he began intense study of the Bible. Following his conversion he was baptized in Amritsar by Robert *Clark, the senior Church Missionary Society representative in the Punjab. Ordained an Anglican deacon (1868) and priest (1872), he became chaplain to Bishop Thomas Valpy *French of Lahore, the two men sharing a common approach to Muslim evangelism. In 1884 he became the first Punjabi Christian to receive the Canterbury D.D. on French's recommendation. His voluminous writings laid the foundations of Urdu Christian literature and pioneered the exposition of an Islamically inculturated evangelical faith. His work was hailed by his friend and fellow convert *Safdar Ali as "the best of teaching for non-Christians and especially for Mohammedans." His polemic against the modernist rethinking of Islam by his contemporary Sayyid Ahmad Khan of Aligarh influenced missionary criticism of the so-called "new Islam." He declined an invitation to participate in the 1893 Parliament of World Religions in Chicago but sent a paper which assessed the history of Christian missions in India.

BIBLIOGRAPHY Imad ud-Din's Urdu writings include *How I Accepted Christianity* (1866), *Commentary on the Book of Revelation* (1870), *The Commentaries on St. Matthew, St. John, and the Acts of the Apostles* (in conjunction with Robert Clark, 1875, 1879, 1884), *History of Rev. Imad-ud-Din's Generation* (1886), and *New Translation of the Qur'an* (1894). Robert Clark, *The Missions of the Church Missionary Society and the Church of England Zenana Mission in the Punjab and Sindh* (1904); Ernest Hahn, *The Life of the Reverend Mawlawi Dr. Imad ud-Din Lahiz* (1978); Avril Powell, *Muslims and Mission-*

aries in Pre-Mutiny India (1993); Christian Troll, *Sayyid Ahmed Khan: A Reinterpretation of Muslim Theology* (1978); E. M. Wherry, *The Muslim Controversy* (1905).

David A. Kerr

Ingalls, Marilla Baker (1828–1902), American Baptist missionary in Burma. Marilla Baker was born in Greenville, New York, the daughter of Selah and Sally Baker. In 1850 she met Lovell Ingalls, a furloughed missionary from Burma (Myanmar) and guest in her parents' home. The couple married and sailed for Burma the following year. Marilla joined the Arakan field of the Burma mission and taught school. Her effectiveness as a teacher attracted many inquirers, and the mission compound facilities had to be expanded. Upon the death of her husband, the American Baptist Missionary Union in 1858 appointed her for "independent work." She centered her efforts at Thongze, a village deep in the jungle, and concentrated on teaching and tract distribution. When the railroad reached her isolated region in 1867, she designed a plan to distribute tracts at the stations. Having acquired a copy of the Bible autographed by Queen Victoria, Ingalls used this gift to gain an audience with the queen of Burma, to whom she preached. Once, when she was under intense pressure from gangs and local Buddhists, a reward of 10,000 rupees was placed on her head, but her Christian friends prevented her capture. It is said she won one hundred Buddhist priests to the Christian faith. She died in Thongze, after a ministry of more than 40 years in Burma.

BIBLIOGRAPHY Marilla Ingalls's works include *Ocean Sketches of Life in Burma* (1857) and *A Golden Sheaf from the Judsons' Work at Ava* (1881). Ingalls refused to allow memoirs to be published, so autobiographical data is nonexistent. Two items written posthumously provide some insight: Grace M. Everts, *By the Banyan Tree: In Memory of Marilla Baker Ingalls* (1907), and Dietrich Brandis, "Mrs. Marilla B. Ingalls," *The Standard,* June 6, 1903, p. 1292. Sarah F. Whiting, *The Story of the Queen's Bible as Related by Marilla Baker Ingalls* (1909) provides an interesting chapter of Ingalls's ministry.

William H. Brackney

Inglis, John (1808–1891), Scottish Presbyterian missionary in New Hebrides (Vanuatu). Born at Moniaive, Dumfriesshire, Inglis wanted to work with New Zealand's Maori and was disappointed when assigned instead to minister to European settlers in Otago and Southland. But in July of 1852, he and his wife, Jessie, joined John and Charlotte *Geddie on Aneityum in the New Hebrides. He had previously visited the island with Captain John Erskine of the HMS *Havana,* and Geddie had welcomed him. The two liked each other and, though from two somewhat diverging streams of Presbyterianism, were of one mind on strategy. Inglis located in the north of Aname. Both traveled round the coast in open boats and trekked unarmed to inland villages. They supervised the Polynesian teachers who were assisting in the work, mastered the language, began translating the Scriptures (Mark, then Jonah), and started schools. Friendly tribal chiefs, like Noahat and Womra, were of immense help. Inglis, a stronger linguist than Geddie, went to England to oversee the publication of the New Testament (1863). He received an honorary doctorate from the University of Glasgow for his work. Traditional Presbyterian polity and simple white churches and houses were part of their legacy. Their approach became the model for Presbyterian work in the New Hebrides.

BIBLIOGRAPHY John Garrett, *To Live among the Stars: Christian Origins in Oceania* (1982); R. S. Miller, *Misi Gete, John Geddie, Pioneer Missionary to the New Hebrides* (1975).

Darrell Whiteman

Ingoli, Francesco (1578–1649), pioneer missionary strategist of the papal curia. Born in Ravenna, Italy, to a well-established family, Ingoli graduated in 1601 in civil and canon law at the University of Padua. Ordained priest, he was auditor for Cardinal Boniface Caetani, papal governor of the Romagna, and accompanied him back to Rome in 1611. On Caetani's death in 1617, he entered the service of Cardinal Orazio Lancellotti. Ingoli became known in the curia for his scientific and pastoral interests and was called as an expert in two legal cases against Galileo. An able linguist, with Greek and Arabic among his languages, he became tutor of Cardinal Ludovico Ludovisi, whose uncle became Pope *Gregory XV in 1621.

On January 6, 1622, Ingoli was appointed secretary of the newly created Sacred Congregation of Propaganda Fide, charged with the control of Catholic missions in Europe and overseas. Gregory XV provided Propaganda Fide with extensive powers and unprecedented financial autonomy, but it was Ingoli who ensured its effective operation and survival. He rapidly made Propaganda Fide the center of an unrivaled network of information with reports from papal nuncios and the heads of religious orders, supplemented by personal correspondence and contacts with missionaries. Capable of great intellectual industry, he noted critically the contents of practically every letter received by the Propaganda Fide until his death. Armed with this information, he produced numerous notes, instructions, and memoranda, which firmly established Propaganda Fide's concerns and strategy.

Convinced that the printed word was an essential means of evangelism, Ingoli supported a polyglot press with compositors expert in Slavic, Middle Eastern, Indian, and Ethiopian languages, vigorously defending this work despite the considerable costs involved. He also guided the early progress of the Collegio Urbano, set up to train priests from the mission territories.

One of the greatest problems facing the Propaganda Fide was the vested interests and abuses arising from patronage rights in Latin America, Asia, and Africa granted to the crowns of Portugal and Spain in the fifteenth century. Confronted with this colonialist challenge, Ingoli quickly recognized the need to create and ordain an indigenous clergy, to appoint indigenous bishops, and to create vicariates apostolic directly responsible to Propaganda Fide. Although during his lifetime success was limited, these aims and activities shaped the policy of Propaganda Fide in the following centuries.

BIBLIOGRAPHY The sources on Ingoli's work are scattered throughout the archives of Propaganda Fide up to 1649. By far the most useful assessment is in J. Metzler's chapters in *Sacrae Congregationis de Propaganda Fide Memoria Rerum,* J. Metzler, ed. (1971). Ingoli's firm attachment to the principles of Catholic reform is clearly portrayed in the memorandum published by J. Grisar, "Francesco Ingoli über die Aufgaben des kommenden Papstes nach dem Tode Urbans VIII (1644)," *Archivum Historiae Pontificiae,* vol. 5 (1967), pp. 289–324. See also N. Kowalsky, "Il testamento di Mons. Ingoli, primo segretario della Sacra Congregatione 'de Propaganda Fide,'" *NZM* 19 (1963): 272–283.

Richard Gray

Ingram, James Henry (1893–1981), foreign missions field representative for the Church of God (CG) (Cleveland, Tenn.). As overseer of the CG for California and Arizona, Ingram was long interested in Latin America and was appointed in 1921 to serve the CG as foreign missions field representative. In 1931 he recruited Maria W. *Atkinson, the Mexican-born wife of an American businessman, to the CG; along with her came several congregations that she had formed in the state of Sonora, Mexico. In Guatemala in 1934, he annexed the work of Charles T. *Furman when the latter was released by his mission. In 1940 he negotiated the incorporation of eighty congregations of the National Christian Church of the Assemblies of God (AG) (a group that had broken away from the AG of Mexico in 1934) as well as the independent Pentecostal groups associated with Fredrick *Mebius in El Salvador. The same year he annexed groups in Costa Rica and Panama. In June 1940, on a trip through South America, he met Marcos Mazzucco, whose Isla Maciel church had recently seceded from the Swedish AG. Mazzucco affiliated his work with the CG and became the CG overseer for Argentina. Ingram also established relations with Pentecostal groups in Europe, Asia, and the Middle East. He died in California.

BIBLIOGRAPHY J. H. Ingram, *Around the World With the Gospel Light* (1937). Charles W. Conn, *Where the Saints Have Trod* (1959); Roberto Domínguez, *Pioneros de Pentecostés,* vol. 2 (1973), pp. 181–189; P. Humphrey, *J. H. Ingram: Missionary Dean* (1966); Richard E. Waldrop, "An Historical and Critical Review of The Full Gospel Church of God of Guatemala" (D.Miss. diss., Fuller Theological Seminary, 1993).

Everett A. Wilson

Inman, Samuel Guy (1877–1965), advocate of Protestant missions in Latin America. Originally from Trinity, Texas, Inman was profoundly influenced by his ministry in Hell's Kitchen, New York City, and the broad emphasis of the social gospel. His entire ministry was marked by a concern for the whole person and his or her social context. Ten years of intensive and creative mission work for the Disciples of Christ in Monterrey and Rio Piedras, Mexico, during its revolutionary period fired his enthusiasm for Latin America. When the Edinburgh World Missionary Conference (1910) decided not to consider missions in Roman Catholic lands, the North American mission societies took action and organized the Committee on Cooperation in Latin America (CCLA). As secretary for 25 years (1913–1938) and with Robert E. *Speer as chairman, Inman guided the ambitious program of CCLA from its base in New York City. He spearheaded plans for the Panama Mission Conference (1916) and cooperated in the subsequent conferences in Montevideo (1925) and La Habana (Havana) (1929). His philosophy of missions aimed at the conversion of Latin American leaders; sought the elevation of moral character, especially through education; proclaimed Jesus Christ as the savior both of individuals and of society; and, despite concerns about Latin American Roman Catholicism, believed dialogue to be the right approach for interchurch relations. He rejected military intervention of the United States in Latin American lands, helped form President Theodore Roosevelt's "good neighbor" policy, and participated in the movement for Pan-Americanism. His later years, spent in Brooklyn, New York, were dedicated to teaching and to civil and ecumenical affairs.

BIBLIOGRAPHY Samuel Guy Inman, *Christian Cooperation in Latin America* (1917), *Problems in Pan Americanism* (1921), and *Latin America: Its Place in the World* (1937). Karla Koll, "Samuel Guy Inman: Venturer in Inter-American Friendship," *Union Seminary Quarterly Review* 42, no. 3 (1988): pp. 45–66; K. F. Woods, *Samuel Guy Inman: His Role in the Evolution of Inter-American Cooperation* (Ph.D. diss., American Univ., 1962).

Sidney H. Rooy

Innis, Etta. *See* Schmelzenbach, Harmon Faldean.

Innocent IV (d. 1254), pope of the Inquisition and interreligious coexistence. Born Sinibaldo Fieschi in Genoa, Innocent combined apparent opposites. Assertive enough to declare himself supreme authority on earth, he pioneered what would later be called interreligious dialogue; judged a notorious nepotist, he steadfastly argued for personal integrity and religious freedom in an era of Christian self-righteousness. His legacy rests on three pillars: his legal skills, his attitude to unbaptized potential Christians, and his defense of the rights of Muslims and Jews.

"The greatest lawyer that ever sat upon the chair of Peter" (Maitland), Innocent overturned the uncritical assumption that Europe was rightfully and forever "Christian"; and when new lands outside Europe proved to be populated by adherents of indigenous religious systems, he developed legal protocols for relations between the papacy and "infidels." He championed interreligious coexistence, endorsed the rights (*dominium*) of other people, and declared coercion indefensible. All this represented a monumental change.

This complex person, who sent missionaries to the Great Khan, thereby undertaking the Mongol Mission (1245), who worked tirelessly though unsuccessfully for reunion with the Emperor John III of Nicea, and who convoked the First (General) Council of Lyons, also established a permanent Inquisition (1252), endorsed a crusade to regain the Holy Places, and deposed Emperor Frederick II.

BIBLIOGRAPHY F. W. Maitland, "Moral Personality and Legal Personality," in *The Collected Papers of F. W. Maitland,* H. A. L. Fisher, ed., vol. 3 (1911); James Muldoon, *Popes, Lawyers, and Infidels* (1979).

Anthony J. Gittins, CSSp

Innocent Veniaminov (Ivan Popov-Veniaminov) (1797–1879), Russian Orthodox apostle to America. Born to a clerical family and educated at the provincial theological seminary in Irkutsk, Russia, Veniaminov quickly showed himself to be a bright prospect for the Russian Orthodox Church in Siberia. After initially declining his bishop's request that he take up missionary work on Unalaska Island in the north Pacific, he felt himself divinely called to aid the island people there. Taking his growing family overland to the Pacific, he arrived on Unalaska in 1822 and quickly accepted pastoral responsibility for the inhabitants of the neighboring islands, the Alaskan peninsula, and the remote Pribilof Islands.

He assiduously studied the Fox Aleutian dialect to the point of being able to translate into it the Gospel of Matthew and to write a short devotional pamphlet, *An Indication of the Pathway into the Kingdom of Heaven.* (In Russian translation it became a classic in his homeland.) Feeling the physical toll of ten years of rowing kayaks and hiking through the island mountains, he sought a disability retirement in 1832. Instead, he was transferred to the relative comfort of Sitka, where he set to work among the less receptive Tlingit Indians. Summoned home in 1839 to report on the status of the American mission to the Holy Synod, Veniaminov sailed to Saint Petersburg. While there he learned that his wife had died, and, no longer married, he became canonically eligible to head a newly created diocese stretching from California to Yakutsk. He accepted reluctantly and returned to Alaska as a bishop in 1840. He insisted that the missionaries under his jurisdiction follow his own example of mastering the local dialects, studying the local cultures sympathetically in order to incarnate the gospel, and establishing schools advancing all phases of education. In order to prepare an indigenous clergy, which he saw as the logical next step in evangelization, he established a seminary in Sitka.

In 1868, blind and physically worn out, he sought retirement but was instead advanced to the rank of metropolitan of Moscow. There Metropolitan Innocent used his influence to found the Russian Missionary Society, whose local chapters throughout the empire raised funds to support home and foreign missions. The society flourished until the Bolshevik revolution ended its activities. In 1977 he was honored by the Orthodox Church in America as "Evangelizer of the Aleuts and Apostle to America." The synod of the Russian Orthodox Church, on the 200th anniversary of his birth, designated 1997 as the "Year of St. Innocent."

BIBLIOGRAPHY Innocent Veniaminov, *Notes on the Unalaska District* (1984), *Indication* (included in Michael Oleksa, *Alaskan Native Spirituality,* 1987), and *Journals of the Priest Ioann Veniaminov in Alaska, 1823–1836* (1994). The most extensive study is Paul D. Garrett, *St. Innocent, Apostle to America* (1979). Veniaminov's collected writings, in six volumes, are in Russian. His Russian-language diary covering his early years in America is held by the Library of Congress.

Paul D. Garrett

Intorcetta, Prospero (1625–1696), Jesuit missionary in China. Born in Sicily, Intorcetta entered the Jesuit order in 1642 and accompanied Martino *Martini to China in 1657. He spent his first five years of active ministry in Chiench'ang (present-day Nanfeng) in the province of Kiangsi (Jiangxi). There he demonstrated the qualities of leadership and judicious temperament that characterized his 37-year apostolate in China. In 1665, following a nationwide anti-Christian resurgence, he was arrested and exiled to Canton with twenty-five other missionaries. Four years later, he was recalled to Rome as procurator and did not return to China until 1676. He was then assigned to Hangchow (Hangzhou) in the province of Chekiang (Zhejiang), where he remained stationed until his death. From 1676 to 1684 he also served as Jesuit visitor of China and Japan, and from 1686 to 1689 as vice-provincial of the Jesuits in China.

Intorcetta was a pioneer in developing a technique for producing Sino-European xylographic works (woodblock printing) in which both Chinese and Latin characters appeared on the same page. A prolific writer and editor, he published Latin translations of the Chinese classics, Chinese translations of the *Rules of the Society of Jesus* and the *Exercises of Saint Ignatius,* and countless other Christian works. He also authored a long treatise in Latin defending the Jesuit position on the Chinese Rites honoring ancestors and Confucius.

While in Hangchow, Intorcetta revived the Jesuit attempt to develop an indigenous Chinese clergy by establishing a seminary. He also had the interior of the Church of the Savior decorated with seventy-two paintings that were used to teach Christian doctrine. Illiterate Chinese could relate to the religious images, while the literati were drawn to the classical Chinese texts and the skillful calligraphy that accompanied them.

BIBLIOGRAPHY Joseph Dehergne, *Répertoire des Jésuites de Chine* (1973), pp. 129–130; David E. Mungello, *The Forgotten Christians of Hangzhou* (1994), pp. 42–66; Louis Pfister, *Notices biographiques et bibliographiques sur les Jésuites de l'ancienne mission de Chine, 1552 à 1773,* vol. 1, (1923), pp. 321–328; Abel Rémusat, *Nouveaux mélanges asiatiques,* vol. 2 (1829), p. 229. See also "T'ai-hsi Yin Chüeh-szu hsien-sheng hsing-lüeh" (Biography of Intorcetta) (c. 1696) in Bibliothèque Nationale, Paris, Chinese manuscript 1096.

Jean-Paul Wiest

Ioasaf (Hotuntsevsky) (d. 1759), Russian Orthodox missionary to the Kamchatka peninsula in the Russian Far East. Ioasaf was born in Small Russia (present-day Ukraine) with the surname of Hotuntsevsky (or Hotuntsevich). His secular first name as well as his birthdate are unknown; Ioasaf was his monastic name. He graduated from the Kievan Theological Academy and in 1739 was sent to the Slavo-Graeco-Latin Academy in Moscow as chaplain. At the end of 1742, he was appointed superior of the mission for Kamchatka with the rank of archimandrite. During the six years of his missionary career he opened three schools (in Bolsheretsk, Verkhne-Kamchatsk, and Nizhne-Kamchatsk) where about two hundred pupils were enrolled at a time. He built several churches (there were only three on the whole peninsula when he arrived), and he personally baptized 1,719 people of different tribes. In 1748 he was called to Saint Petersburg for consecration as bishop of Irkutsk, but while traveling through Siberia he fell severely ill, and thus was not consecrated. In 1754 he became the rector of the Slavo-Graeco-Latin Academy in Moscow, the highest educational institution of those days in the Russian Empire. Less than a year before his death he was finally consecrated a bishop of Keksholm and Ladoga (in the north of Russia).

BIBLIOGRAPHY References to Ioasaf are found in Philaret, *Istoriya Russkoi Tserkvi* (History of the Russian Church), vol. 5; Piotr Slovtsov, *Istoricheskoye Obozreniye Sibiri* (Historical account of Siberia), vol. 2 (n.d.); and in an article by A. Popov in *Letopis Russkoi Literatury* (Annals of Russian literature), vol. 2 (1859). Documents related to Ioasaf are stored in the archive of the Synod in Saint Petersburg, years 1752 (case no. 79); 1754 (no. 355); 1757 (no. 176).

Evgeny S. Steiner

Ioasaph. *See* Bolotov, Ioasaf.

Irenaeus of Lyons (c. 126–202?), theologian and bishop of Lyons, France. Likely from Smyrna (present-day Izmir) in Asia Minor, Irenaeus is known chiefly for his work in Lugdunum (now Lyons), a Celtic religious stronghold. Although he has been traditionally studied primarily as theologian and churchman, he would likely regard himself more as a missionary and pastor. Deductions about his missiology come from his polemical and catechetical writings and what others, like *Eusebius, wrote about him.

His chief work, *Against Heresies,* was designed to equip others to answer local Gnostics, reclaim weak Christians, and "confirm the mind" of the new believers. His *Proof of the Apostolic Preaching* sought, by using a form of biblical theology, to instruct former pagans about the Christian way of life. No reclusive theological writer, he worked so familiarly among the Celtic people that he learned and used their "barbarous dialect" rather than the Latin and Greek of the local Roman administration. He knew and addressed pointedly the pressing concerns of daily life.

Later writers exaggerated the immediate effects of Irenaeus's evangelistic work, all of which, from 177 onward, was done under the oppression of persecution and martyrdom. But he clearly provided a style of ministry and type of literature that served future Christian purposes. He possessed a lively sense of evangelizing Gentiles and elaborated a Christology appropriate to the pagan context. Indeed, some of his urgency, excitement, and biblical perspective on evangelizing Gentiles reminds one of Acts of the Apostles. His adjustments to specific situations, emphasis on stabilizing the newly converted, creation of a useful literature, and constructive blending of the roles of missionary, theologian, and churchman serve as useful models for subsequent missionaries.

BIBLIOGRAPHY Everett Ferguson, "Irenaeus' *Proof of Apostolic Preaching* and Early Catechetical Instruction," *Studia Patristica* 18, no. 3 (1989): 119–140; R. M. Grant, "Irenaeus and Hellenistic Culture," *Harvard Theological Review* 42 (1949): 41–51; F. R. Montgomery Hitchcock, *Irenaeus of Lugdunum* (1914); J. Lawson, *The Biblical Theology of St. Irenaeus* (1948); C. Philip Slate, "Two Features of the Missiology of Irenaeus," *Missiology* 23, no. 4 (1995): 431–442; Terrence L. Tiessen, *Irenaeus on the Salvation of the Unevangelized* (1993).

C. Philip Slate

Isaiah of Rostov (d. 1089), missionary bishop in the Rostov-Suzdal area of Russia. Born in the Kiev oblast and tonsured in the Kiev Caves Monastery by Saint Theodosii, Isaiah became abbot of Saint Dmitrii's monastery. In 1077 he was raised to bishop of Rostov, succeeding Saint Leontii, first bishop of Rostov. Leontii had brought Christianity to the area and laid the foundations for successful work against paganism. When Isaiah arrived, he found new Christians who needed instruction and pagans who had not yet heard the gospel. He tried to cut the roots of paganism by destroying pagan idols. He traveled in both the Rostov and Suzdal areas, preaching to pagans and encouraging new Christians. He combined his preaching with acts of mercy, helping the sick and poor. Many were converted before his death on May 15, now his feast day. He was canonized in 1164 or 1474.

BIBLIOGRAPHY Mitropolit Evgenii, *Slovar' istoricheskii o svyatykh proslavlennykh v russkoi tserkvi* (2d ed., 1862), p. 108; V. O. Klyuchevskii, *Drevnerusskie zhitiya svyatykh kak istoricheskii istochnik* (1871), chap. 1.

Karen L. Gordon

Isakovich, Nikolai Fedorovich (1798–1874), Russian Orthodox missionary to the Buryat people. Born in Mogilev, Russia, Isakovich attended seminary in Orsha. Graduating the top of his class, he was sent to Saint Petersburg Spiritual Academy in 1821. He graduated in 1825 and was tonsured as a monk with the name Nil. He was sent to Chernigov, where he became master of theology in 1827, and in 1828 was made inspector and professor at Kiev Spiritual Academy. In 1830 he became rector of the seminary at Yaroslavl and archimandrite. In 1835 he was appointed bishop of Vyatsk and was involved in mission among the Udmurty and Mariitsy. Transferred to Irkutsk in 1838 and made archbishop in 1840, he gave himself to missionary work among the Buddhist Buryat people, becoming the leading specialist at that time in Buddhism and learning the Mongolo-Buryat language. He translated the service books (published 1852 and 1853) of the Orthodox Church as well as other literature into Buryat and oversaw the selection and sending of educated priests, supporting and encouraging them in their work among the Buryat. Between 1838 and 1850, 20,810 baptisms were held, and

42 churches were built. In 1854 he was moved to Yaroslavl, where he was archbishop until his death. During this time he continued to translate.

BIBLIOGRAPHY K. D. Golovshchikov, *Yaroslavskii arkhiepiskop Nil* (1894).

Karen L. Gordon

Isenberg, Karl Wilhelm (1806–1864), missionary and linguist in Ethiopia and India. A German Lutheran, Isenberg trained at the Basel Mission seminary in Switzerland and received Anglican orders in 1832 when accepted by the Church Missionary Society (CMS). He joined Samuel *Gobat in Cairo and studied Amharic and Arabic before the two men left for Ethiopia in 1834. After Gobat left Ethiopia in 1836, Isenberg was joined by his fiancée, Henrietta Geerling and J. L. *Krapf. His unwillingness to accept Gobat's advice over the siting of the mission and his inability to reach any accommodation with the Ethiopian Orthodox clergy, led first to the mission's removal to Shoa and then contributed to its expulsion from Ethiopia in 1843. When it became clear that there was no possibility of returning to Ethiopia, Isenberg transferred to the CMS mission in Bombay where, amidst many activities, he worked briefly in a settlement for freed African slaves, some of whom returned to Africa as evangelists. Diagnosed in India in 1864 as terminally ill, he returned to Germany, died in Stuttgart, and was buried in Korntal.

Isenberg's *Dictionary of Amharic* was published in 1841, and a competent grammar the following year, as well as several other books intended for use in the school the mission tried to establish in Ethiopia. This pioneering language work was to be his most significant contribution to mission.

BIBLIOGRAPHY The main sources for Isenberg's life are H. Gundert, *Biography of the Rev. Charles [Karl] Isenberg, Missionary of the Church Missionary Society to Abyssinia and Western India from 1832 to 1864* (1885); J. L. Krapf and C. W. Isenberg, *The Journals of the Rev. Messers Isenberg and Krapf, Missionaries of the Church Missionary Society, Detailing Their Proceedings in the Kingdom of Shoa, and Journeys in other Parts of Abyssinia in the Years 1839–1842* (1843; repr. as *The Journals of Isenberg and Krapf*, 1968), and Eugene Stock, *The History of the Church Missionary Society*, vol. 1 (1899), pp. 351–353. Donald Crummey, *Priests and Politicians: Protestant and Catholic Missions in Orthodox Ethiopia, 1830–1968* (1972), pp. 29–59.

M. Louise Pirouet

Isherwood, Annie Cecile (1862–1906), English missionary in South Africa. Isherwood came from a comfortable home in England. Orphaned in her early teens, she volunteered for mission work in South Africa. Ordained a deaconess, she became, at 21, the first member and head of the Anglican community of the Resurrection of Our Lord, founded by Bishop Allan Becher Webb in Grahamstown. She worked among the poor and destitute of all races in the eastern Cape and was far ahead of her time in seeking to heal a divided society. Despite the enduring poverty of her community at St. Peter's Home, she established schools, hostels, missions, and orphanages throughout the region. She also founded the Grahamstown Teacher Training College, the first in South Africa for women. Though she died young, she had laid the foundation of a community strong enough to expand her work.

BIBLIOGRAPHY *Mother Cecile in South Africa, 1883–1906,* compiled by a sister of the community (1930); Margaret Cropper, *Shining Lights: Six Anglican Saints of the 19th Century* (1963), pp. 135–165; Horton Davies, *Great South African Christians* (1951), pp. 160–168.

Janet Hodgson

I Sung-Hun, Peter (1756–1801) (also spelled Seng-hun-i, Lee [Ly, Yi] Seung Hun, Ri Seung-hon-i), first Korean Christian. An intellectual of noble origin, I Sung-Hun accompanied a Korean delegation to Peking in 1783 to continue his study of mathematics and to get acquainted with the Catholic faith. Before returning to Korea in 1784, he enthusiastically received baptism and took the name Peter. He returned to Korea with many religious books, crosses, and holy pictures. It was hoped that as the first Korean Christian, he would be the cornerstone of a new Korean church. Because of his witness and inspired by the books he distributed, many Koreans embraced the Christian faith. Since foreign priests were not allowed to enter Korea, the Christians themselves chose priests, among them I Sung-Hun. However, when the bishop of Peking declared these elections invalid in 1790, the Christians complied. At the same time the bishop of Peking also forbade ancestor worship; this decree led to serious conflicts and bloody persecution by the political authorities. On several occasions, I Sung-Hun succeeded in saving his life by denying his faith. But in the more politically motivated persecution of 1801 he was condemned to death. Together with others—Christians and witnesses of the Christian faith—he was beheaded. He died without professing his faith.

BIBLIOGRAPHY A. Choi, *L'érection du premier vicariat apostolique et les origines du Catholicisme en Corée,* 1592–1837 (1961); C. Dallet, *Histoire de l'Église de Corée,* 2 vols. (1874); E. Fourer, *Koreas Märtyrer und Missionare* (1895); Jai-Man Park, *La spiritualità dell'apostolato dei laici della primitiva comunità cristiana in Corea, 1784–1838* (1985).

Karl Müller, SVD

Itzem, Julio (1902–1993), Kekchi Presbyterian evangelist in Guatemala. Born in Guatemala and converted in the Nazarene Church, Itzem witnessed and gave leadership as a plantation worker in the areas of Palestrina Chineval and Los Angeles Pencala. He was named a lay evangelist and later ordained a pastor by the national Presbyterian Church, which was responsible for evangelizing the more than a quarter million Kekchi people in the northeastern part of Guatemala.

The Kekchis were 95 percent illiterate and were exploited by the white population. Under Itzem's leadership,

Kekchi Christians witnessed first to their peers in their own community. To evangelize other communities, scouts first evaluated the situation; then evangelists representing half of the church families took living necessities with them and spent twenty days in the new community, carrying on family-to-family evangelism. Meanwhile, the other half of the congregation cared for the families of the evangelists. Every night worship was conducted, and the newly converted families became the nucleus of the new church.

Among the Kekchis, only older, experienced Indians are ordained pastors; there are no educational requirements. Native musical instruments and dress are used, and all activities are conducted in the Kekchi language. In Itzem's lifetime, nearly all of the Kekchi people became Christians through this self-evangelization process.

BIBLIOGRAPHY Moises Colop, "Julio Itzem, El Pionero Kekchi," unpublished study written for the Institute Misionologico de Las Americas, San Jose, Costa Rica; Mardoqueo Munez, "Un Estudio del Ministerio Pastoral y del Inglecrecimiento entre los Presbiterianos en Guatemala" (D.Miss. thesis, Fuller Theological Seminary, 1984).

Sidney H. Rooy

Iuvenalii (Iakov Fedorovich Govorukhin) (c. 1761–1796), pioneer Russian Orthodox missionary to Alaska. Born the son of a mine foreman in Sverdlovsk (formerly Ekaterinburg), in the Ural Mountains, Govorukhin was trained as a mining engineer. Widowed in 1791, he entered the monastic life at Valamo, Finland, where he gained a reputation for obedience. In 1793 he was ordained to the priesthood (taking the name Iuvenalii) and then was recruited for the American mission.

Although known for his sensibility, he and Makarii *Glukharev became "almost like madmen" in their eagerness to preach on mainland Alaska. In 1795 he was assigned to Yakutat Bay, on the southern shore of the Gulf of Alaska, but apparently proceeded independently to Kenai and on north to Iliamna Lake, west of Cook Inlet. The next year Russian-American Company officials reported that he was almost certainly killed among the Aglemiuts but no reliable details are available. Forced baptisms and adamant demands that the natives conform to a little-understood Christian life-style were later suggested as reasons for his being killed. In 1977 the Diocese of Alaska, Orthodox Church in America, canonized Iuvenalii as the first Orthodox martyr in America.

BIBLIOGRAPHY Gregory Afonsky, *A History of the Orthodox Church in Alaska* (1977), p. 21; Michael Oleksa, "The Death of Hieromonk Juvenaly," *St. Vladimir's Theological Quarterly* 30 (1986): 231–268; Fern A. Wallace, *The Tides of Change* (1977), pp. 22–33.

Paul D. Garrett

Ivanovskii, Nikolai Ivanovich (1875–1919), Russian Orthodox missionary in Korea. Ivanovskii graduated from Tula Seminary in 1894, became a monk in 1896, and went as a missionary to Zabaikal (present-day Buryat Republic, east of Lake Baikal). In 1900 he was sent to Vladivostok, where he studied Korean in the Oriental Institute, and in 1904 he joined the Korean mission in Seoul as archimandrite. During his time there he made a special study of the other Christian missions. In 1912 he was made suffragan bishop in the Vladivostok diocese of Nikolsk-Ussuriisk and head of the Korean mission, covering Korea and Korean emigrants in the far east of Russia. The mission flourished under his leadership. He concentrated on providing translations of Scriptures, service books, and other literature and also on training catechists and lay workers, including women. He set up groups for study and prayer in villages where there was no church or priest. The degree of Korean participation in the mission rose greatly during this time, providing a foundation for a Korean Orthodox Church. Ivanovskii was attacked by Korean nationalists for Russifying native Koreans in Russia, although he in fact opposed Russification as an end in itself. Both sides, however, identified Orthodoxy with Russianness. He died in the Russian Far East.

BIBLIOGRAPHY Ivanovskii's diaries and letters from Seoul appear in *Pravoslavnyi Blagovestnik* (signed A.P.). His articles on mission are printed in *Vladivostokskie Eparkhial'nie Vedemosti (VLEV)*, as are the instructions produced for missionaries and catechists in the Korean mission. A short biographical note appears in *VLEV* 1912 on the occasion of his ordination as bishop. Ivanovskii's work in the Korean mission within Russia is discussed in Karen L. Gordon, "A Study of Russian Orthodox Missions in the Russian Far East, 1700–1917" (M.Phil. thesis, Univ. of Leeds, England, 1994).

Karen L. Gordon

J

Jabavu, Davidson Don T(engo) (1885–1959), Bantu educator, author, and social activist of the Eastern Cape, South Africa. The eldest son of Mary and John Tengo *Jabavu, Jabavu was born at King Williamstown and was educated there by Wesleyan Methodists and at the Lovedale High School. On being refused admission to white colleges, he entered the University of London and graduated there in 1912, the first black South African to gain a British degree. He trained further in journalism and religious and social work in England and wrote a report on the United States education system for the Union of South African government. Returning to South Africa in 1914, he edited and published *Imvo Zabantsundu* (The people's opinion), a weekly newspaper, and in 1915 was appointed the first professor at the South African Native College, Fort Hare, concentrating on Bantu languages and social anthropology. He taught there for 29 years. As a writer, he continually promoted the black cause, also founding and organizing the South African Farmers' Association. He served as president of the Cape Teachers' Association, worked in other educational bodies, and chaired numerous conventions and conferences. He attended the meeting of the International Missionary Council at Jerusalem in 1928. In 1954 he was awarded an honorary doctorate by Rhodes University and the Bronze Medal of the Royal African Society. He was also known for directing student and church choirs and other Methodist church activities.

BIBLIOGRAPHY Davidson Don T. Jabavu, *The Life of John Tengo Jabavu* (1922), "Native Unrest in South Africa," *IRM* 11 (1922): 249–259, *The Influence of English on Bantu Literature* (1942), *The Black Problem* (1953), and with others, *Criticisms of the Native Bills* (1935). Robert H. W. Shepherd, *African Affairs* (1958), *Bantu Literature and Life* (1955), and *Lovedale and Literature for the Bantu: A Brief History and a Forecast* (1945).

Gerhardus C. Oosthuizen

Jabavu, John Tengo (1859–1921), Bantu newspaper editor, teacher, preacher, and champion of education and justice in the Eastern Cape, South Africa. Son of Mtwanambi (from forebears Citywa), Jabavu was born in a village near the Methodist mission school of Healdtown. Staunch Methodists, the family also attended Quaker meetings. One brother, Jonathan James, became a minister. Jabavu became a teacher, working in Somerset East (1877–1881), there apprenticing himself to the Wesleyan Methodists as a local preacher, as well as to the local newspaper office. He became editor of *Isigidimi sama-Xhosa* (The Xhosa Express) at the Lovedale Institution, where he developed as a brilliant debater. Then he became editor of *Imvo Zabantsundu* (The people's opinion, 1884–1921), which was oriented toward Christian justice. He was an ardent, nonviolent advocate of an impartial administration of justice, without regard to race, and was continually alert to the African cause. His editorial power frequently drew the attention of the Cape Parliament. He traveled to London in 1909 to fight the Colour Bar clause in the Union Constitution, and was elected to attend the Universal Races Congress (1911). From 1906 he worked at what became the South African Native College (ultimately, the University of Fort Hare), also championing the cause of women's education.

BIBLIOGRAPHY Davidson D. T. Jabavu, *The Life of John Tengo Jabavu: A Great Bantu Patriot* (1922); M. Stauffer, *Thinking with Africa* (1927).

Gerhardus C. Oosthuizen

Jaca, Francisco José de (c. 1645–1688), Spanish Capuchin missionary in the Caribbean. Having ministered to black slaves brought to Cartagena (Colombia), the principal port of entry and market of the slave traders, Jaca wrote from Cuba in 1681 a stinging abolitionist document:

"Resolución sobre la libertad de los negros y sus originarios en el estado pagano y después ya cristianos" (Resolution on the freedom of the blacks and their pagan ancestry, but who are now Christians). He challenged the conventional defense of slavery and condemned the enslavement not only of Africans but of Native Americans as well. Likely influenced by Bartolomé de *Las Casas, he and his fellow Capuchin, Epifanio de *Moirans, were among the earliest abolitionists in American history.

BIBLIOGRAPHY Gustavo Gutiérrez, *Las Casas: In Search of the Poor of Jesus Christ* (1993); José Tomás López Garcia, *Dos defensores de los esclavos negros en el siglo XVII* (1982); Angel Valtierra, *Pedro Claver: El santo redentor de los negros* (1980).

Alan Neely

Jackson, Sheldon (1834–1909), architect of Protestant missions in Alaska. Born in upstate New York of devout Presbyterian parents, Jackson studied theology at Princeton Seminary where he became interested in foreign missions. After graduation and ordination in 1858, he worked briefly as a missionary teacher among the Choctaw Indians in Oklahoma, but due to illness was reassigned as a home missionary for new church development in Minnesota. In 1869 the Missouri River Presbytery appointed him district missionary in charge of a vast area extending from western Iowa to Idaho. For the next ten years, he traveled extensively, organizing Presbyterian mission work throughout the Rocky Mountain region.

After visiting Alaska in 1877 and 1879, Jackson encouraged Protestant churches to begin work in the territory, culminating in a historic meeting held in New York in 1880 where a comity agreement for Alaska was endorsed. Jackson spent most of 1883 in Washington, D.C., lobbying Congress to establish both a civil government and a school system for Alaska. These contacts resulted in his appointment in 1885 as U.S. general agent for education in Alaska, for which he had prepared by arranging to be assigned as minister in charge of the Presbyterian Church in Sitka. Jackson used his dual roles as missionary and government education officer to establish English-speaking mission schools whose aim was to replace indigenous forms of housing, clothing, marriage, religion, and economy with those he considered typical of Protestant Christians in the United States. By 1894, twenty-four schools run by Protestant missionary teachers had been established across Alaska. Jackson's last major endeavor was to persuade the U.S. government to import 1,200 reindeer into Alaska in order to change the nomadic subsistence patterns of Alaskan natives. In 1908, Jackson resigned as general educational agent, suffering from poor health and amid disputed charges of fiscal mismanagement surrounding his reindeer domestication scheme.

BIBLIOGRAPHY Sheldon Jackson, *Alaska and Missions on the North Pacific Coast* (1880) and annual reports on education in Alaska in *Reports of the Commissioner for Education for the Years 1878 through 1906.* James L. Cox, *The Impact of Christian Missions on Indigenous Cultures* (1991); Theodore Charles Hinckley, Jr., "The Alaska Labors of Sheldon Jackson, 1877–1890" (Ph.D. diss., Univ. of Indiana, 1961); Arthur J. Lazel, *Alaskan Apostle: The Life Story of Sheldon Jackson* (1960); Robert Laird Stewart, *Sheldon Jackson* (1908). The largest collection of Sheldon Jackson manuscript material is found in the Presbyterian Historical Society, Philadelphia.

James L. Cox

Jacob Baradaeus. *See* Baradaeus, Jacob.

Jacobis, Justin de (1800–1860), Italian Vincentian missionary to Ethiopia. A Neapolitan, de Jacobis entered the Congregation of the Vincentians (also known as Lazarists) and was ordained in 1824. In 1839 he was appointed prefect apostolic in charge of a new mission in Ethiopia and after ten years in the country was made vicar apostolic; he was consecrated bishop by Guglielmo *Massaja at Massowa. De Jacobis's mission was to use the Ethiopian rite. This he did with conviction, showing outstanding sympathy for the Ethiopian Christian tradition in all its aspects. He gained some remarkable converts, most notably the future martyr *Gebhre Michael. In consequence he established a well-rooted and lasting Catholic Church in northern Ethiopia. However, the favorable relations he achieved with Ethiopian authorities in the early years changed after the arrival of the new Egyptian patriarch, Salama, in 1855. Salama naturally saw in him a rival and a threat. De Jacobis was arrested and thus prevented from further activity during his final years in Ethiopia. If his church survived and grew, it was largely because of his ordination of numerous priests, some of them married men, who remained as a group profoundly loyal to the memory of "Abuna Jacob." No Western missionary has ever demonstrated greater love and understanding for an Eastern Christian tradition.

BIBLIOGRAPHY M. E. Herbert, *Abyssinia and Its Apostle* (1867) is the only biography of de Jacobis in English. S. Pane, *Il Beato Giustino de Jacobis della Congregazione della Missione* (1949) is the most exhaustive study. Donald Crummey, *Priests and Politicians: Protestant and Catholic Missions in Orthodox Ethiopia, 1830–1868* (1972) places de Jacobis best in his political and ecclesiastical context.

Adrian Hastings

Jaeschke, Heinrich August (1817–1883), Moravian missionary among Tibetan refugees and Bible translator. Jaeschke, a direct lineal descendant of early Moravian families who had emigrated under the influence of Christian *David, was born at Herrnhut, Germany, and was educated at the pedagogium at Niesky where he showed a strong gift for languages. Following training at the theological seminary of the Brethren's Unity at Gnadenfrei, he served as a teacher at Christiansfeld, Denmark, and then returned to the pedagogium at Niesky, where he taught from 1842 to 1856. In 1856 he went to India, where he worked for 11 years as a missionary among Tibetan refugees in Ladakh; he settled at Kyelang, where he began his work with the Tibetan language. This included the beginnings of translations of the Gospels into Tibetan along with typical preaching, teaching, and medical ministries. In 1868, due to ill health, he returned to Herrnhut and continued translation into Tibetan, including the New Testament. He also wrote a small dictionary and grammar, and numerous other church-related works. He died at Herrnhut.

BIBLIOGRAPHY J. T. Hamilton and K. G. Hamilton, *A History of the Moravian Church* (1967); *The Moravian*, January 18, 1884 (obit.).

Albert H. Frank

Jaffray, Robert Alexander (1873–1945), Christian and Missionary Alliance (C&MA) missionary in China and southeast Asia. Son of the owner and publisher of the Toronto *Globe*, Jaffray converted under the preaching of C&MA founder A. B. *Simpson. He was trained in Simpson's New York Missionary Training Institute and was sent to Wuzhou, Guangxi, China, in 1897. This became his headquarters for 35 years, and from there he soon began to serve as leader of all C&MA work in south China. In addition to extensive mission administration, preaching, and evangelistic itineration, he helped found the Wuzhou Bible School (later the Alliance seminary in Hong Kong) and served as its principal. The Chinese-language *Bible Magazine*, which he edited and for which he wrote many of the articles, was read in Chinese communities all over the world. In 1916 Jaffray opened for the C&MA the first Protestant mission field in the French colony of Annam (now Vietnam), directly to the south of Guangxi. He served as its superintendent, visiting frequently from Wuzhou. In 1928 Jaffray surveyed the need for C&MA missionaries in the East Indies (Indonesia) and sent Chinese missionaries to serve in Borneo. In 1931 he moved with his family to Makassar, Celebes, Indonesia. From there he led a rapidly growing mission until 1942, when he was arrested by the Japanese, who had captured Indonesia. He was kept in a series of internment camps until he finally died of illness and malnutrition just before the Japanese surrender. Jaffray married Minne Donner in 1890, and had a daughter, Margaret; both were effective participants in the programs he led. The enormous energy Jaffray manifested in his work was expended even though he had been weakened from childhood by both a heart condition and diabetes.

BIBLIOGRAPHY A. W. Tozer, *Let My People Go: The Life of Robert A. Jaffray* (1947, 1990).

William A. Smalley

Jameson, William (1807–1847), Scottish Presbyterian missionary in Jamaica and Nigeria. Jameson was born in Methven, Perthshire, to a family of ministers. He studied at the University of Edinburgh and the Divinity Hall of the United Associate Synod. In 1833 he was licensed to preach by the United Associate Presbytery of Perth and spent some three years in missionary appointment before being ordained as a missionary to Jamaica in September 1836. The next day he married Nicolis Mackersy, also of Perthshire. The couple arrived in Jamaica in January 1837 and took up residence at Goshen, in the north-central part of the island. Jameson's task was to establish a congregation among the newly emancipated slaves, or apprentices, as they were then called. Despite the usual difficulties, the work went well, and he was able to form a congregation in 1839. His wife died in July of the same year. In July 1840 the Jamaica Missionary Presbytery asked Jameson to take on the training of Scottish catechists working in the mission there who wished to become ministers. Among his students were William *Anderson and Hugh *Goldie, both of whom were soon to go to the Calabar mission. In 1846 the Presbytery appointed Jameson to their new mission in what is now Calabar, Nigeria. He arrived there in January 1847, taking up work in Creek Town. His genuine affection for people and acute sense of justice immediately won a place in the town's affections. He died of fever a few months later.

BIBLIOGRAPHY Alexander Robb, *The Gospel to the Africans: A Narrative of the Life and Labours of The Rev. William Jameson in Jamaica and Old Calabar* (2d. ed., 1861); Geoffrey Johnston, *Of God and Maxim Guns: Presbyterianism in Nigeria, 1846–1966* (1988).

Geoffrey Johnston

Janes, Leroy Lansing (1837–1909), Reformed Church of America educational missionary to Japan. Janes, a graduate of West Point, served for some years as an artillery officer (captain) in the United States Army. In 1871 or 1872 he was invited by the daimyo (feudal lord) of Higo in Kyūshū, Japan, to open a school in the castle town of Kumamoto. This school was intended by its Japanese sponsors to introduce new Western learning but not to teach the Christian faith. Janes, however, had been recruited through the offices of the Reformed Church in America, and as soon as it was prudent, he began to include systematic teaching of the New Testament as a part of the academic program of the school.

Thinking that such knowledge would help the students better to reject Christian faith, the school authorities approved of the program. However, as a result of Janes's teaching and his personal character, about forty of the young men went to the top of Mount Hanaoka, near the city, on January 30, 1876, and solemnly pledged their loyalty to Jesus Christ as Lord. Thus was formed the Kumamoto Band, one of the three Christian bands (the others were the Yokohama and the Sapporo Bands) that became seedbeds of the leadership of nascent Protestant Christianity in Japan. Persecution arose from conservative elements in Kumamoto. As a result the school was forced to close in August 1876. Following the behest of Janes, the members of the Kumamoto Band moved to the Dōshisha school in Kyoto. In later life Janes turned from evangelical Protestant faith and accepted liberal theological views.

BIBLIOGRAPHY Otis Cary, *A History of Christianity in Japan* (1909); Richard H. Drummond, *A History of Christianity in Japan* (1972); *Kodansha Encyclopedia of Japan* (1983).

Richard H. Drummond

Jänicke, Johann (1748–1827), revivalist and mission educator. Jänicke (or Jenjk) was born and grew up in a settlement of Bohemian weavers in Berlin. After serving an apprenticeship in weaving, he became a schoolteacher and underwent training for the ministry. After ordination in 1779 he was called as a Lutheran pastor to the Bohemian Bethlehem Church in Berlin. His peculiar gift for revivalist preaching and his service for the poor made him popular and contributed to the Berlin awakening. In 1800 Jänicke and Baron von Schirding, another leader of the Berlin awakening, founded a mission seminary that became a model for the Berlin Mission seminary (established in 1824). The Jänicke seminary is said to have trained about eighty mission candidates for service in several mission organizations. A brother, Joseph Daniel Jänicke, worked in the Danish-Halle mission of Tranquebar, in South India, from 1788 to 1800.

BIBLIOGRAPHY K. F. Ledderhose, *Johann Jänicke* (1863).

Hans-Werner Gensichen

Janssen, Arnold (1837–1909), founder of the Society of the Divine Word (SVD). Born in Goch, Rhineland, Janssen was ordained in 1861, taught for 12 years in a secondary school in Bocholt, and in 1869 became director of the Apostleship of Prayer of the Diocese of Münster. In 1873 he founded the magazine *Kleiner Herz-Jesu-Bote* for the reunification of Christians and the promotion of mission. In 1875 he moved to the Netherlands, where he founded St. Michael's Mission House in Steyl as a house of formation for future missionaries; this soon developed into a missionary order of priests and brothers, the SVD. He also founded two missionary congregations of sisters, the Servants of the Holy Spirit in 1889 and a contemplative order, the Servants of the Holy Spirit of Perpetual Adoration in 1896. The society spread rapidly. When he died, there were 293 priests, 137 brothers, and 329 sisters working in Asia, New Guinea, Africa, Latin America, and the United States.

Undoubtedly one reason for this extraordinary development was the personality of the founder: he was totally committed, single-minded, and hard-working, a man of faith, vision, and deep spirituality. Janssen was a pioneer of the modern German missionary movement, head of a missionary society that incorporated the social sciences in the curriculum for future missionaries, zealous advocate of the reunification of divided Christians, promoter of the retreat movement, bold pioneer of the Catholic press apostolate, and untiring champion of the lay apostolate.

Since he himself had no missionary experience, he refrained from giving too many concrete instructions, but he stressed certain features that were to have a lasting effect on missionary strategy. He always emphasized the theological and spiritual basis of mission. He kept the society as a whole in mind and, considering the missionary goals, established a strong central administration. He laid the foundations for the international nature of the society. He supported the efforts of the superiors in the missions to develop a native clergy and saw the possibility of religious services without priests. He placed great emphasis on health care for his missionaries. The society administered local seminaries and founded teachers' training colleges, secondary schools, and technical schools in the Third World. He trained the young sisters in Steyl mostly as teachers, but some also as midwives (despite the fact that Propaganda Fide did not permit religious sisters to work as midwives until 1936). He allowed Wilhelm *Schmidt a large degree of freedom in the development of the journal *Anthropos*. Janssen's beatification in 1975 was a recognition not only of his heroic virtue but also of his extraordinary importance for the whole missionary movement.

BIBLIOGRAPHY For a complete bibliography, see J. Reuter, *Das Schrifttum über Arnold Janssen und Josef Freinademetz* (1990), which lists 132 monographs for Janssen. Fritz Bornemann, *Arnold Janssen, der Gründer des Steyler Missionswerkes* (1969; in English, 1975); H. Fischer, *Arnold Janssen* (1919).

Karl Müller, SVD

Jansz, Pieter (1820–1904), pioneer Dutch Mennonite missionary in Indonesia. Jansz was born in Amsterdam and became a teacher. The Dutch Mennonite mission appointed him their first missionary, and he and his wife arrived in Java in 1851. They settled in north Central Java, where Jansz started working as a teacher and lay missionary. Encountering a strong constraining influence from Islam throughout the area, he concluded that people were not free to become Christians, and began searching for new mission methods. His contribution to missionary theory is his book (in Dutch), *Land Reclamation and Evangelism* (1874), in which he proposed the formation of Christian colonies as a solution.

He brought to his ministry a bias favoring the weak and disenfranchised members of society, which brought him into conflict with the colonial government. He promoted formation of an association of missionaries in the Dutch Indies (organized in 1880) and served many years as its secretary.

In addition to his role in founding the church in north Central Java, Jansz's most lasting contribution was his work as Bible translator and lexicographer under sponsorship of the British and Foreign Bible Society. He found the existing Gericke translation of the New Testament (1848) too literal in its approach, and he soon began translating Scripture passages with his fledgling congregation. He secured appointment with the British and Foreign Bible Society in 1881 and finished the Javanese New Testament in 1888 and the Old Testament in 1892. A second edition of the entire Bible appeared in 1895. In addition, he produced several Javanese readers and a two-volume Javanese-Dutch dictionary. For his literary labors he was knighted by the Dutch government in 1902. Jansz never returned to the Netherlands but died near Kudus, Java.

BIBLIOGRAPHY *Mennonite Encyclopedia,* vol. 3, p. 94; Alle Hoekema, "Pieter Jansz (1820–1904), First Mennonite Missionary to Java," *Mennonite Quarterly Review* 52, no. 1 (January 1978): 58–76; J. L. Swellengrebel, *In Leijdeckers Voetspoor,* part 1 (1974).

Wilbert R. Shenk

Janzen, Aaron A. (1882–1957), Mennonite Brethren pioneer missionary in Belgian Congo (Zaire). Born in Mountain Lake, Minnesota, into a Mennonite family that had recently emigrated from Russia, Janzen studied at Moody Bible Institute in Chicago and the German Baptist Seminary in Rochester, New York. In 1911 he married Ernestina Strauss, who had studied nursing in preparation for a missionary career. Going to the Belgian Congo, between 1912 and 1919 the Janzens developed a Christian presence in the Kasai region under the auspices of the Congo Inland Mission. In 1922 they began an independent work (taken over by the Mennonite Brethren Board of Missions in 1943). Janzen traveled some 300 miles investigating possible locations before establishing this new work at Kikandji on the Kwilu River, not far from the commercial center of Kikwit. Two years later he shifted to Kafumba, six miles away, and there on a 120-acre tract of land established the first center of what became the Mennonite Brethren Church of Zaire. He founded a training center, linked with many outlying village schools, which provided religious training as well as literacy development. By 1940, some 450 students were studying annually in the station school, and 1,500 in the village schools; the church he established numbered more than 1,600. Janzen's contribution to the Congo was officially recognized by the Belgian colonial government in 1954 when he was knighted and received the honorary title "Chevalier of the Crown." He left Africa in 1956 and retired to Mountain Lake, Minnesota. He died the next year in Winnipeg, Manitoba.

BIBLIOGRAPHY Abraham E. Janzen, *Pioneering for God in the Congo Jungle* (1962); J. B. Toews, *The Mennonite Brethren Church in Zaire* (1978).

Paul Toews

Jaricot, Pauline-Marie (1799–1862), founder of the Society for the Propagation of the Faith. Jaricot was born in Lyons, France. At the age of 17, she began to lead a life of unusual sacrifice and self-denial. On Christmas Day, 1816, she made a vow of perpetual virginity. From her youth she had a talent for organizing people in order to accomplish a goal. One of her first such efforts was to gather a group of pious servant girls in a society for prayer. They were known as les *Reparatrices du Sacre-Coeur.* She also succeeded in helping a number of servant girls, who worked for her brother-in-law, to transform their lives. When Jaricot began focusing on foreign missions, the first contributions came from among these girls. In 1820 she formed an association to assist the work of the Foreign Mission Society of Paris. She also worked intently to promote apostolic works for women of all classes. Among her other initiatives she founded the Loretta, a home for working girls in Lyons. In 1826 she formed the Association of the Living Rosary, whose members committed themselves to daily prayer and the distribution of books. In the midst of many activities, she concentrated mainly on helping the foreign missions through collecting alms and through the prayers of the faithful. By setting up a group of ten promoters among her friends and collaborators, each of whom collected contributions from a group of ten on a regular basis, Jaricot was able to raise a considerable sum of money. Angelo Inglesi, vicar general of New Orleans, visited Lyons in 1822. He formed a group of twelve men for the purpose of raising funds for mission work. Because of her successful fundraising, Jaricot was invited to join the group. This led to the establishment of the Society for the Propagation of the Faith on May 3, 1822. At the time it was also called the Missionary Society of Lyons and the St. Francis Xavier Society. Jaricot is recognized as the founder. She also promoted the Association of the Holy Childhood, which specifically sought to help children understand the importance of sharing in the work of mission through their prayers and contributions. Many future missionaries received their first introduction to missionary work through this association. A laywoman known for her virtue and holiness, Jaricot made a significant and lasting contribution by organizing and educating people for missionary awareness. Her means were simple and effective, and they enabled people of all walks of life to participate in the work of missionaries through their interest, prayers, and contributions.

BIBLIOGRAPHY K. Burton, *Difficult Star: The Life of Pauline Jaricot* (1947); G. Gorce, *Pauline Jaricot: Une Laique engagée* (1962); J. Jolinon, *Pauline Jaricot: Patronne des Chrétiens Sociaux* (1957); D. Lathoud, *Marie-Pauline Jaricot,* 2 vols. (1937); J. Maurin, *Pauline Marie Jaricot,* E. Sheppard, tr. (1906); Georges Naidenoff, *Pauline Jaricot* (1986; Eng. ed., 1988); J. Servel, ed., *Un Autre visage: Textes inédits de Pauline Jaricot* (1961).

Mary Motte, FMM

Jarlin, Stanislas François (1856–1933), Vincentian missionary in China. Jarlin left his native France for China in 1888 and was ordained priest in Peking (Beijing) the following year. In 1899 he became bishop coadjutor of the vicariate apostolic of Peking and gained fame almost immediately for his role in organizing the defense of the foreign legations besieged by the Boxers. At the death of Pierre-Marie *Favier in 1905, Jarlin took over the direction of the vicariate. From then on until the arrival, in November 1922, of Archbishop Celso *Costantini, first papal delegate apostolic to China, Jarlin was the de facto intermediary between the Holy See and the Chinese government. For many years, he distrusted the methods and pro-Chinese attitude of one of his fellow Vincentians, Vincent *Lebbe. He also remained a decided partisan of continuing the French protectorate over Catholic missions. In 1926, however, following the ordination of six Chinese bishops by Pope *Pius XI, he began to favor change. Jarlin was an outstanding administrator. At the beginning of his 33 years as a missionary bishop, Peking was just a large vicariate with 40,000 Chinese Catholics; by the time of his death, the territory had been split into five vicariates and contained more than 400,000 Catholics.

BIBLIOGRAPHY *Annales de la Congrégation de la Mission et de la Compagnie des Filles de la Charité* 98 (1933): 544–558, and 124 (1959): 121–122; J. Van den Brandt, *Les Lazaristes en Chine,*

1697–1935 (1936); Paul Goffard and Albert Sohier, eds., *Lettres du Père Lebbe* (1960).

Jean-Paul Wiest

Jartoux, Pierre (1669–1720), Jesuit mathematician and cartographer in China. Jartoux was a native of Embrun, France. In 1687 he entered the Society of Jesus at Avignon and was ordained 11 years later. In 1701 he was in China and was soon called to Peking (Beijing) to work in the calendar bureau. The emperor took notice of his skills in theoretical mathematics as well as with clocks and other mechanical devices. When not occupied at court, Jartoux ministered to Christians in the capital. In 1708 he assisted two Jesuit confreres, Joachim *Bouvet and Jean-Baptiste *Régis, in the first stages of making a map of the Chinese empire. His travels took him to the Great Wall north of the capital and throughout Manchuria, where he also ministered to the Christians. Illness forced him to return to Peking, where he began to collate the maps of the provinces in preparation for a general atlas. The final version was presented to the emperor one year after Jartoux died in Manchuria.

Bibliography Jartoux's letter on ginseng is in M. L. Aimé-Martin, ed., *Lettres édifiantes et curieuses* (1843), 3:183–187; other works are listed in Louis Pfister, *Notices biographiques et bibliographiques sur les Jésuites de l'ancienne mission de Chine* (1932–1934), pp. 584–586. Theodore N. Foss, "A Western Interpretation of China: Jesuit Cartography," in C. Ronan and B. Oh, eds., *East Meets West: The Jesuits in China, 1582–1773* (1988), pp. 209–251; Walter Fuchs, *Der Jesuiten Atlas der K'ang-hsi Zeit* (1943); John W. Witek, *Controversial Ideas in China and in Europe: A Biography of Jean-François Foucquet, 1665–1741* (1982), pp. 110, 175, 196–198, 235, 243, 247.

John W. Witek, SJ

Javouhey, Anne-Marie (1779–1851), founder of the Sisters of St. Joseph of Cluny. Javouhey was born in Jallanges, in the Burgundy region of France, to hardworking and deeply religious farmers. Javouhey was ten years old at the time of the French Revolution. About half of the clergy refused to take an oath of allegiance to the revolutionary government and were forced to go into hiding. Although still young, Javouhey demonstrated the initiative and force of character that would mark her throughout life in the assistance she gave to priests who refused to sign the oath. At the same time she was actively engaged in the religious education of young children. In 1807, desiring to continue her commitment to religious education, she and a small group of women who taught with her founded the Sisters of St. Joseph of Cluny; Javouhey, then 27 years of age, was approved by her colleagues to be the superior of the new congregation. As with many founders, she suffered much misunderstanding and was continually confronted with obstacles in her efforts to provide a stable foundation. The most serious opposition came from within the church, and especially from the bishop of Autun. But in the aftermath of the revolution, there was a dire need for education, with many young people able neither to read nor write. The Sisters of St. Joseph were well prepared to respond. While in Paris in 1815, Javouhey discovered the Lancaster System, which gave accelerated education to older and brighter students so that they, in turn, could assist other students. A number of Catholic bishops, among others, opposed this system and Javouhey as well. However, the government recognized her educational leadership, and she was ultimately invited to send sisters to Bourbon Island (present-day Reunion Island). Soon thereafter the government also requested sisters for the French West Indies, French Guiana, and the West Coast of Africa. When she visited the colonies and witnessed the effects of slavery, she recognized that slavery had created subhuman conditions that had become a way of life, and that it would take much effort to prepare people for emancipation. Here again her vision and initiative contributed to the development of a unique system of agricultural and family education. In French Guiana, under her direction, there developed a nearly independent colony of freed slaves, "Mana." Her legacy continues today through the Sisters of St. Joseph of Cluny, who are engaged in teaching, pastoral ministry, religious education, nursing, and rural ministry throughout the world.

Bibliography Jean Hébert de Segonzac and Marie-Cécile de Segonzac, eds., *Anne-Marie Javouhey: Correspondence, 1798–1851*, 4 vols. (1994); P. Keiffer, *Blessed Mother Anne-Marie Javouhey* (1979); Glenn D. Kittler, *The Woman God Loved: The Life of Blessed Anne-Marie Javouhey* (1959); C. C. Martindale, *The Life of Mère Anne-Marie Javouhey* (1953); Brian Moore, *A Little Good* (1982); Joanne Turpin, *Women in Church History: 20 Stories for 20 Centuries* (1990). Five volumes, containing more than 1,000 letters written by Javouhey, were translated into English and published privately in 1974. The original French letters are in the archives of the Motherhouse of the Sisters of St. Joseph of Cluny in Paris, France.

Mary Motte, FMM

Jefferson, John Clark (1760–1807), London Missionary Society (LMS) missionary in Tahiti. Formerly an actor and teacher, Jefferson was the acknowledged leader and secretary of twenty-nine pioneer missionaries sent to Tahiti in 1796 by the Missionary Society (later the LMS). He was one of four ordained ministers in the group, the rest of whom were artisans expected to combine evangelism with the teaching of useful crafts and trades, but these aims were frustrated by their exposure to local warfare, sexual temptation, and difficulties of communication with England during the Napoleonic wars. Jefferson toured Tahiti extensively. His letters to his London directors described his progress in learning Tahitian, in which he could preach by 1801, and his instruction of King *Pomare II of Tahiti in literacy and Christian faith. He and his longer-lived but less well-educated colleague Henry *Nott took the first steps toward Pomare's eventual conversion and the adoption of Christianity by a majority of Tahiti's chiefs and people. Jefferson's deteriorating health led to his death at Matavai, Tahiti, where the mission had begun.

Bibliography John Davies, *The History of the Tahitian Mission, 1799–1830*, C. W. Newbury, ed. (1961); Niel Gunson, *Messengers of Grace: Evangelical Missionaries in the South Seas, 1797–1860* (1978); Richard Lovett, *The History of the London Missionary Society, 1795–1895* (1899). Letters and other papers are in the LMS archives at SOAS, Univ. of London (available on microfilm).

John Garrett

Jellesma, J(elle) E(eltjes) (1817–1858), one of the founding fathers of the Javanese church. Jellesma was born in Hitzum, Netherlands, the son of a primary school teacher. After working as a farmhand and a peddler, and attending the missionary training institute in Rotterdam (1841–1843), he was sent by the Netherlands Mission Society (NZG) to Ceram in eastern Indonesia. There he founded a Christian colony, Damej ("peace"). From 1846 to 1848 he served as secretary to a visiting NZG executive. Thereafter he preferred the more populous mission field of East Java. Initially he lived in Surabaya; from 1851, having obtained permission from the government to establish himself in the interior, he lived in Mojowarno, a village founded in 1846 by Javanese Christians. The day-to-day tasks in the congregation were performed by the Javanese pastor Paulus *Tosari, freeing Jellesma to found an institute for the training of Javanese teachers, preachers, and evangelists. The New Testament in Javanese served as the textbook for general and religious instruction. Jellesma's importance lies mainly in the fact that he resolved the deadlock between C. L. *Coolen's syncretism and the pietistic legalism of Johannes *Emde. By accepting the desire of Coolen's followers to keep their Javanese names and clothing, Jellesma opened the way for the further development of the Javanese church.

Bibliography Philip van Akkeren, *Sri and Christ: A Study of the Indigenous Church in East Java* (1970). Jellesma's papers are in the archives of the Raad voor de Zending der Nederlandse Hervormde Kerk, Oegstgeest, Netherlands.

Th. van den End

Jensen, Christian (1839–1900), founder of the Breklum Mission. A Lutheran country pastor in Schleswig-Holstein, the northernmost part of Germany, Jensen belonged to a group of churchmen who in the wake of the neopietist revival of the early nineteenth century were led to establish regional centers of mission in which the concern for foreign and home missions went hand in hand with Christian charity in the neighborhood. Thus the remote village of Breklum became a rallying point not only for evangelistic activities at home and abroad (India, China) but also for related efforts in public education and communication. Criticism came from those who feared for the evangelistic and confessional integrity of the foreign mission enterprise and therefore advocated an institutional segregation of home and foreign mission. Jensen reacted by conceding a juxtaposition rather than full integration, or, in his own words, a "keeping apart" (*Auseinanderhaltung*), a policy of differentiation between two allied pursuits, each of which remained an essential element of the church.

Bibliography H. Dunker, *Christian Jensen* (1970); K. Sensche, *Christian Jensen und die Breklumer Mission* (1976).

Hans-Werner Gensichen

Jessup, Henry Harris (1823–1910), Presbyterian missionary in Syria and Lebanon. Jessup was born in Montrose, Pennsylvania. Ordained in 1855, he sailed the same year from Boston to Beirut, under appointment by the American Board of Commissioners for Foreign Missions. The Syria/Lebanon field was subsequently transferred to the Board of Foreign Missions of the Presbyterian Church, U.S.A. Exercising his gifts as evangelist, teacher, and writer, he served there for 53 years, residing successively at Tripoli, Abeih, and Beirut. In 1882 he declined an offer by President Chester A. Arthur to appoint him ambassador to Persia.

Jessup was a persuasive advocate of the Protestant mission to Muslims, one of the most prominent figures of his day in directing the attention of American churches to the Middle East. He regarded the traditional churches in the area, and especially their hierarchies, as merely "nominal Christians," unsuited for the missionary task. In a speech to the Presbyterian General Assembly in 1879, he argued for a British protectorate over Turkey, insisting that Great Britain and the United States in particular had the necessary religious and educational means to convert Muslims to Christianity and should have political powers to assure the legal right of such converts to declare their conversions openly.

Bibliography Henry H. Jessup, *The Mohammedan Missionary Problem* (1879), *The Greek Church and Protestant Missions* (1891), *Kamil Abdul Messiah: The Setting of the Crescent and the Rising of the Cross* (1899), and *Fifty-three Years in Syria,* 2 vols. (1910). Jean-Michel Hornus, "Le Protestantisme au Proche-Orient," *Proche Orient Chrétien,* vol. 8 (1958), pp. 243–262, vol. 9 (1959), pp. 42–5, 350–357, and vol. 10 (1960), pp. 26–41.

Norman A. Horner

Jesu, Thomas á. *See* Thomas of Jesus.

Jeune, Paul le (1591–1664), French Jesuit missionary in Canada. Born in Vitry-le-François, France, of Calvinist parents, Le Jeune became a Catholic and joined the Jesuits in Paris in 1613. An eminent teacher and philosopher-theologian, in 1631, while Jesuit superior at Dieppe, he was named superior to the Canadian mission. Leaving for Quebec in 1632, he held office until 1639. He rebuilt church properties (in ruins after the English war and occupation), instituted the first parish of Quebec, and reorganized the downriver missions. He spent some months with Algonquin Indians on their winter hunt, learning their language and customs, and established a Jesuit college, a hospital, two schools, and a reservation for the Indians at nearby Sillery. He founded and wrote the first eleven issues of *Jesuit Relations,* a serial newsletter (now an invaluable historical document) recording and commenting on the activities of settlers, Indians, missionaries, and on the administration of the colony. He made several visits home to raise funds and assistance for the colony and mission and was finally recalled to France in 1649 to act as agent for the Jesuit mission in Canada. His sermons and letters on the spiritual life (*Épistres spirituelles*) were published in Paris by friends in 1665.

BIBLIOGRAPHY T. J. Campbell, *Pioneer Priests of North America* (1908); Edna Kenton, *The Jesuit Relations and Allied Documents* (1954); Edmund Bailey O'Callaghan, *Jesuit Relations* (1847); Francis Parkman, *Pioneers of New France in the New World* (1915) and *The Jesuits in North America in the Seventeenth Century* (1915).

Kenelm Burridge

Jing Jing (8th century), Persian priest and scholar who settled in China during the eighth century. Jing Jing, a scholar and priest also known as Adam, is credited as the author of the inscription on the famous Nestorian monument near Si-an (Xi'an), Shensi (Shaanxi) Province. Discovered in 1625 by a Jesuit priest, the monument—a single block of fine-grained limestone about 10′ × 3′ × 1′—was erected in 781 to commemorate the propagation in China of the Luminous Religion, the Chinese term for the (Nestorian) Church of the East. The inscription provides the first known record of a Christian presence in China, tracing it to the arrival in 635 of the Nestorian monk *Alopen. Jing Jing is also credited with translating thirty or so Nestorian books into Chinese.

BIBLIOGRAPHY Mar Aprem, *Nestorian Missions* (1976); C. E. Couling, *The Luminous Religion* (1925); John Foster, *The Church of the T'ang Dynasty* (1950); Dennis Hickley, *The First Christians of China* (1980); John Kaserow, "Christian Evaluations of Buddhism from Clement of Alexandria to the Renaissance" (Ph.D. diss., Univ. of St. Michael's College, Univ. of Toronto, Canada, 1976); A. C. Moule, *Christians in China before the Year 1550* (1930); P. Y. Saeki, *The Nestorian Documents and Relics of China* (1951); John M. L. Young, *By Foot to China* (1984).

Jean-Paul Wiest

Jocz, Jakób (1906–1983), missionary, theologian, and advocate of missions to Jews. Jocz was born in Vilnius, Lithuania, of Hebrew Christian parents whose instruction brought him to faith. In 1920 his father joined the Church's Ministry among the Jews (CMJ) as an evangelist. During World War I the family encountered severe anti-Semitism despite their Christian identity. As a teenager, Jakób was drafted for army service in postwar Poland. Following demobilization he offered himself for evangelistic service with the CMJ. He began three years of study under CMJ direction coupled with missionary service in Poland followed by two years in Frankfurt-am-Main at the German Methodist Seminary. Because he showed unusual promise, the CMJ then sent him to St. Aidan's College in England to complete training for Anglican ordination.

Marriage to Joan Gapp followed, and in 1935 Jakób and his wife were assigned to Jewish evangelism in the Polish countryside and to a Yiddish-speaking congregation in Warsaw. They met with much opposition but also with unprecedented response to the gospel. An unexpected call to England just prior to the Nazi assault in 1939 spared their lives. During the war and afterward Jocz directed CMJ's London mission. This made possible doctoral studies at the University of Edinburgh (D.Phil., 1945) and later service in an Anglican congregation. In 1956 Jocz was called to direct the CMJ Nathaniel Institute in Toronto. By 1960 he knew that his future lay in theological education. From 1960 until 1976 he occupied the chair of systematic theology at Wycliffe College (Univ. of Toronto). His writings and his long association with the International Hebrew Christian Alliance greatly enlarged his influence and resulted in many lectureships and conference engagements. In many ways he was a prophet to both Jews and Gentiles. He challenged the churches because they tolerated anti-Semitism and were indifferent to Jewish evangelism, and he reminded Jewish people that salvation is not by convenant or race but through personal encounter with the living God. He was probably the outstanding Jewish Christian theologian of the twentieth century.

BIBLIOGRAPHY Jakób Jocz, *The Jewish People and Jesus Christ* (1949), *A Theology of Election: Israel and the Church* (1958), *The Spiritual History of Israel* (1961), *Christian and Jews: Encounter and Mission* (1966), *The Covenant: A Theology of Human Destiny* (1968), and *The Jewish People and Jesus Christ after Auschwitz* (1981). The only comprehensive survey and assessment of Jocz's life, ministry, and publications is Elizabeth Louise Myers, "The Literary Legacy of Jakób Jocz" (M.A. thesis, Fuller Theological Seminary, 1989). See also Arthur F. Glasser, "Jacób Jocz," in Gerald H. Anderson et al., eds., *Mission Legacies* (1994), pp. 523–531.

Arthur F. Glasser

Jogues, Isaac (1607–1646), French Jesuit missionary among the Huron and the Iroquois Indians. Born in Orléans, France, into a prosperous family, Jogues entered the Society of Jesus in 1624. After his studies and ordination in 1636, he volunteered to go to New France and arrived in Quebec in July. From there he traveled to Wendake (territory of the Huron Indians in eastern Ontario) in 19 days, reaching Ihonateria, the principal Huron village, in September.

Between 1636 and 1642 he worked among the Hurons, the Tobacco Indians, and the Chippewas during critical and difficult times. Disease and famine ravaged the country, and the Indian wars were intensifying. In 1639 Jogues was entrusted with building Sainte-Marie Among the Hurons, on the southeastern shore of Georgian Bay. In 1642, during a trip to Quebec for supplies, he was taken prisoner, tortured, and enslaved by the Mohawks. He escaped in August 1643 with the assistance of the Dutch from Rensselaerswyck (now Albany, New York), who arranged to ship him back to France. After a convalescence and a memorable reception at the court of the regent, Anne of Austria, he came back to Canada in 1644 and spent two years ministering to the French colonists at Montreal, although he kept insisting that he wished to be sent to Mohawk country. In May 1646 he was at last asked to go there on a peace embassy, which he did, making two trips—one in the spring and a second in September. Negotiations went well on the first, but during his absence, Mohawk attitudes changed. The Mohawks became alarmed and frightened by the sacred vessels and liturgical vestments Jogues had left behind. He was killed by a hatchet blow at Ossernenon (now Auriesville, New York).

A devout man with a mystical prayer life and deep sensitivity, and also a writer of classical elegance and remarkable taste, Jogues was especially a person of great courage and hope. He was canonized by Pope *Pius XI on June 29, 1930.

BIBLIOGRAPHY Guy Laflèche, *Les Saints Martyrs Canadiens,* 2 vols. (1988, 1989); François Roustaing, *An Autobiography of Martyrdom* (1964); F. X. Talbot, *Saint among Savages* (1935); Reuben Gold Thwaites, ed., *The Jesuit Relations and Allied Documents, 1610–1791* (1959).

Jacques Monet, SJ

Johanns, Pierre (1882-1955), Jesuit missionary to India and Vedanta scholar. Johanns was born in Luxembourg. After training and ordination to the priesthood in the Society of Jesus, he studied Sanskrit in Brussels and Oxford, specializing in the philosophic system of Sankara. He went to India in 1921 and taught philosophy at Saint Xavier's College, Calcutta. In 1922, together with G. *Dandoy and in collaboration with Animananda, a disciple of Brahmabandhab *Upadhayaya, Johanns started a journal, *The Light of the East.* Its policy was spelled out in its first issue: "We shall try to show that the best thought of the East is a bud that fully expanded blossoms into Christian thought." Though Johanns wrote many articles introducing Indian philosophy and theology, his major work was a series of 137 articles under the general title "To Christ through the Vedanta," showing how Sankara, Ramanuja, Vallabha, and Chaitanya lead to Christ as understood by the Scholastic theology of *Thomas Aquinas. He saw in Hinduism a natural *praeparatio evangelica.* Even Hindus acknowledged his mastery of Hindu thought. He returned to Belgium in 1939 because of ill health.

BIBLIOGRAPHY P. Johanns, *A Synopsis of "To Christ through the Vedanta"* (1930–1933), *Introduction to the Vedanta* (1938), and *Hinduism* (1948). See also Joseph Mattam, *Land of the Trinity* (1975).

Michael Amaladoss, SJ

Johanssen, Ernst (1864-1934), missionary among the Bantu peoples of East Africa. Born and educated in north Germany, Johanssen was inspired by the great Nordic theologians J. G. Hamann and Søren Kierkegaard. He was recruited for mission work in what used to be German East Africa by Friedrich von *Bodelschwingh, founding father of the Bethel Mission. In nearly 40 years of pioneering service Johanssen carried the idea of a comprehensive Christian witness by word and deed under specific African conditions to Usambara, and later, with the participation of Usambara Christians, to Rwanda and finally to Bukoba, west of Lake Victoria. He was responsible for the promotion of African languages, both tribal idioms and Swahili, as well as the training of African church leadership in English. In his retirement he taught missiology at Marburg University. He had a special gift for understanding Africans and their religion in depth and became one of the first renowned Africanists among German Protestant missionaries.

BIBLIOGRAPHY Johannsen's pioneering study is *Mysterien eines Bantu-Volkes* (1925). For a reliable assessment of his achievements see G. Jasper, *Ein Herold Gottes* (1952).

Hans-Werner Gensichen

John XXIII (1881-1963), pope and convener of Second Vatican Council. John XXIII (r. 1958-1963) was born Angelo Giuseppe Roncalli in Sotto il Monte, near Bergamo, to a family of sharecroppers. A scholarship permitted him to attend the Roman Seminary, where he gained a doctorate in theology in 1904. Ordained a priest, he became secretary to the bishop of Bergamo and a seminary professor. In 1921 he became national director of the Society for the Propagation of the Faith. Pius XI made him titular archbishop of Areopolis and posted him to Bulgaria as apostolic visitator in 1925. He held subsequent diplomatic positions in Turkey, Greece, and France. He was created a cardinal in 1953 and became patriarch of Venice.

Already 77 years old when elected pope in 1958, John was regarded as a transition figure. Instead, he ushered in a new era for the Roman Catholic Church and for ecumenical relations. His greatest achievement was convening the Second Vatican Council, which began in 1962 and continued after his death until 1965. He intended the council to update the church in all areas, in a pastoral manner, with an attitude of openness to the modern world. In 1959 he initiated a revision of canon law that was completed in 1983. And he convoked the first synod in history for the diocese of Rome in order to renew the church there.

Of his seven encyclicals, *Pacem in Terris* (1963) is best remembered. Addressed to all people of goodwill, it promoted peace based on justice and liberty. His ecumenical efforts led to the first Vatican contact with the World Council of Churches in 1959. He established the Secretariat for Promoting Christian Unity in 1960 and invited thirty-nine non-Catholic observers and guests to the Vatican Council. He fostered growth in the missions in many ways. In 1959 he published the encyclical *Princeps pastorum,* on the fortieth anniversary of *Benedict XIV's *Maximum Illud.* In it he sought to promote indigenous clergy and greater involvement of the laity. He also consecrated twenty-eight bishops for Africa, Asia, and Oceania.

BIBLIOGRAPHY Angelo Giuseppe Roncalli published several works on Bergamo church history, and *Gli Atti della Visita Apostolica di S. Carlo Borromeo a Bergamo,* 5 vols. (1936–1958); *Acta Apostolicae Sedis,* vols. 50–55, gives the *acta* of his pontificate. His *Journal of a Soul* (1965) gives a posthumous window into his interior life. Peter Hebblethwaite, *John XXIII: Shepherd of the Modern World* (1985); Paul Johnson, *Pope John XXIII* (1975).

Robert J. Schreiter, CPPS

John, Christoph Samuel (1747–1813), pioneer missionary educator in India. Born at Fröbersgrün near Greiz, Germany, the son of a clergyman, John studied at Halle while teaching in the famous orphanage there. Following a discussion with Professor Knappsen and much family prayer, he was ordained as a missionary in Copenhagen in 1769 and arrived in India with Wilhelm Jacobus Müller, landing at Tranquebar in June 1771. He died in Tranquebar after more than 42 years' labor and was buried in the New Jerusalem churchyard there.

An intellectual, John was distinguished by his great love of and skill in teaching. He also raised the morale of his discouraged colleagues, as his letters show. He and his wife suffered terrible poverty for the first six years of their work in India, until John arrived at a solution later emulated in Serampore, which was to establish reputable European schools in addition to Tamil schools. These were financed by fees and by the pupils making and selling stockings. His faith was sorely tested by the deaths of three of his children within one year and by his failure to find European colleagues for his schools. The mission was under continual attack from Danish traders and colonial administrators, yet Danish academics with whom he corresponded appreciated his scientific contributions. Outside Tranquebar his work was appreciated partly because of C. F. *Schwarz's support. He died, exhausted and blind, as a result of a stroke.

BIBLIOGRAPHY J. Ferd Fenger, *History of the Tranquebar Mission* (1906); James Hough, *The History of Christianity in India from the Commencement of the Christian Era,* vols. 3–4 (1845); Daniel Jeyaraj, *Inkulturation in Tranquebar* (1996); E. Arno Lehmann, *It Began at Tranquebar* (1956).

E. M. Jackson

John, Griffith (1831–1912), London Missionary Society (LMS) missionary in China. Born at Swansea, Wales, John trained for the Congregational ministry at Brecon College, Wales, and Bedford Academy, England. After ordination he offered himself for service in Madagascar. But he was persuaded by LMS to accept appointment to China and arrived at Shanghai in September 1855. An inveterate itinerator, he became well known for his extensive missionary journeys into the Chinese interior—journeys that sometimes stretched to 3,000 miles or more. In July of 1861 he moved to Hankow (Hankou), which remained his base until his final departure from China in 1912. There, John, fluent in both spoken and written Chinese, made his major contribution to the Chinese church as author, translator, and preacher. A powerful and eloquent speaker, he was immensely popular with the Chinese, who would gather in great numbers to hear him preach. He was notably successful in training and mentoring numerous Chinese evangelists. He was also a prolific pamphleteer, authoring numerous popular tracts and serving for many years as chairman of the Central China Tract Society. He is credited with a Mandarin translation of the New Testament, Psalms, and Proverbs, as well as a Wen-li New Testament, published in 1885. Elected chairman of the Congregational Union of England and Wales for 1889, he declined the honor, remaining instead in Hankow among his beloved Chinese. The University of Edinburgh conferred on him the degree of D.D. (1889) in recognition of his service to the Chinese. During a career spanning 60 years, John left China only three times, returning finally to England in January of 1912.

BIBLIOGRAPHY Griffith John, *A Voice from China* (1907). Jonathan J. Bonk, *The Theory and Practice of Missionary Identification, 1860–1920* (1989); Richard Lovett, *The History of the London Missionary Society, 1795–1895* (1899); James Sibree, *London Missionary Society: A Register of Missionaries, Deputations, Etc., from 1796–1923,* 4th ed. (1923); Ralph Wardlaw Thompson, *Griffith John: The Story of Fifty Years in China* (1906).

Jonathan J. Bonk

John Chrysostom. *See* Chrysostom, John.

John of Montecorvino (1247–c. 1328), first Roman Catholic missionary to reach China proper and first bishop of Khanbaliq (Beijing). After civil, military, and perhaps medical service, Montecorvino, an Italian, entered the Franciscan order and in 1280 was sent as a missionary to Armenia and Persia. In 1289 he was the leader of an embassy from Haiton II of Armenia to Pope Nicolas IV, who sent John as his legate to the Great Khan, Kublai, in Khanbaliq.

Traveling by way of Armenia and Persia and spending some months in India, he reached Beijing in 1294, just after Kublai Khan's death. Befriended by the new Khan, Timur, John built the first Catholic church in China in 1299. In 1303 Arnold of Cologne, a Franciscan colleague, arrived to assist him. By 1305 they had won a thousand converts and built a second church. John's most notable convert was the Nestorian prince George of Tenduc (Inner Mongolia). The conversion of this prince and thousands of his people aroused bitter opposition from the larger Christian community of Nestorians in China. Pope Clement V appointed John archbishop of Beijing and primate of all the East in 1307, sending seven Franciscan suffragan bishops to support him, only three of whom survived to reach China around 1310. Another bishop, the Franciscan Pietro da Firenze, arrived in 1312. Under John's direction, the new bishops expanded Franciscan missions south into Fujien Province, three months' journey from Beijing, building a cathedral at Zaitun (modern Quanzhou). John baptized some 6,000 Mongols in Beijing, according to two of his letters that have survived (dating from 1305 and 1306).

John learned the Mongolian language and translated the New Testament and the Psalms in that language. None of these missions survived the fall of the Mongol dynasty in 1368.

BIBLIOGRAPHY J. Charbonnier, *Histoire des Chrétiens de Chine* (1992), pp. 61–67; J. de Ghellinck, *Les Franciscains en Chine aux XIIIe–XIVe siècles, ambassadeurs et missionaires,* vol. 1, *Xaveriana* no. 42 (1927); *International Study Workshop on John of Montecorvino, OFM, 1294–1994* (1994); T. Lapolla, *Giovanni da Montecorvino,*

Raccolta documentaria, scoperte archeologiche, testimonianze (1993); A. C. Moule, *Christians in China before the Year 1550* (1930), chap. 7; F. E. Reichert, *Begegnungen mit China: Die Entdeckung Ostasiens in Mittelalter* (1992), pp. 76–79; Anastasius van den Wyngaert, *Sinica Franciscana*, vol. 1 (1929), pp. 333–355 (3 letters).

Samuel Hugh Moffett

John of Pian di Carpine (*or* Plano de Carpine) (c. 1190–1252), Franciscan envoy to central Asia. Born in an Umbrian town in Italy, John joined *Francis of Assisi around 1215. In 1221 he was sent to Germany where until 1230 he played a decisive role in founding the Franciscan order. He was transferred to Spain, then back to Germany from 1232 to 1239. In 1245 Pope *Innocent IV appointed him papal envoy to the court at Karakorum in Mongolia. John carried a papal letter seeking favorable treatment for Christians. He left Lyons on April 16, 1245, arriving in Karakorum on July 22, 1246. He attended the enthronement of the Great Khan, Güyüg. After receiving a written answer to the papal letter, he returned to Lyons on November 18, 1247, where the pope was anxiously waiting for him. During the return journey from Karakorum John and his companions prepared *Historia Mongalorum quos nos tartaros appellamus,* a long report on the Mongols and how to deal with them. It contains extensive details on many aspects of the life of the peoples encountered, especially on the Mongols. It also makes clear that the Mongols believed they had a divine mission to conquer all countries. The report, therefore, called on the kingdoms in Europe to unite in order to prepare a strong defense.

John undertook another papal mission to King Louis of France, then was appointed archbishop of Antivari in Dalmatia in 1248. He probably died in Antivari.

BIBLIOGRAPHY Giovanni di Pian di Carpine, *Storia dei Mongoli,* Enrico Menestò et al., eds. (1989). I. de Rachewiltz, *Papal Envoys to the Great Khans* (1971), pp. 89–111; *Sinica Franciscana,* vol. 1, Anastasius van den Wyngaert, ed. (1929), pp. 1–130.

Arnulf Camps, OFM

John of Segovia (c. 1400–1458), Spanish theologian. At the divisive Council of Basel (1433–1437) John of Segovia championed reform through conciliarity against papal authority. Briefly a cardinal under the ill-fated Felix V (1440–1449), he retired to an academic life in which he set his mind on global issues facing the medieval church. Significant among these was Islam. He argued against crusades on the grounds that it was unprincipled and ineffective for Christianity to use what he regarded as the essentially Islamic means of war to propagate religion. He also had little confidence in the practicability of missionary preaching, given the fact that Muslim law denied Christians the freedom to make this possible. His alternative was *contraferentia,* a word that appears nowhere else in the contemporary Latin literature. It suggests the idea of intellectual disputation, and in the last years of his life, John advocated the convening of an international Christian-Muslim conference. As preparation, he labored to produce a new Latin translation of the Qur'an which has not survived. Though the conference was not convened, his vision of intellectual confrontation between the two faiths was embraced by his friend and contemporary *Nicholas of Cusa (1401–1464).

BIBLIOGRAPHY James Beichler, "A New Face toward Islam: Nicholas of Cusa and John of Segovia," in Gerald Christianson and Thomas Izbicki, eds., *Nicolas of Cusa in Search of God and Wisdom* (1991); Jean Marie Gaudeul, *Encounters and Clashes: Islam and Christianity in History* (1984); Thomas Izbicki, "The Possibility of Dialogue with Islam in the Fifteenth Century," in Gerald Christianson and Thomas Izbicki, eds., *Nicolas of Cusa in Search of God and Wisdom* (1991); Jessie Mann, "The Historian and the Truths: Juan de Segovia's *Explanatio De Tribus Veritatibus Fidei*" (Ph.D. diss., Univ. of Chicago, 1993); D. Cabanelas Rodrigues, *Juan de Segovia y el Problema Islamico* (1952).

David A. Kerr

John Paul II (Karol Jozef Wojtyla) (1920–), pope known for his global apostolate. Karol Josef Wojtyla was born in Wadowice, Poland, studied poetry and drama at the Jagiellonian University, Krakow, and then, under the Nazi occupation, did seminary studies secretly while working in a chemical plant and in a quarry. Ordained to the priesthood in 1946, he obtained doctorates in theology at the Angelicum in Rome and at the Jagiellonian University. After presenting a thesis on the ethical system of Max Scheler, he taught at the seminary in Krakow (from 1953) and the Catholic University of Lublin (from 1954). As auxiliary bishop of Krakow (beginning in 1958), he attended Vatican Council II (1962–1965), contributing especially to the *Pastoral Constitution on the Church in the Modern World.* *Paul VI named him archbishop of Krakow in 1964 and cardinal in 1967. While teaching and writing about moral theology and philosophy, he governed his diocese, traveled extensively, and participated, between 1969 and 1977, in four meetings of the synod of bishops at Rome. At the 1974 synod, dealing with evangelization, he composed the second half of the final report.

Elected pope in 1978, he transformed the papal ministry into a global apostolate. In Mexico in 1990 he declared that the Lord "has wished my pontificate to be that of a pilgrim pope of evangelization, walking down the roads of the world, bringing to all peoples the message of salvation." From 1979 through 1993 he made sixty-one foreign trips and saw every continent; he made ten visits to Africa. Since 1983 he has repeatedly called for the Catholic Church to commit its full energies to a "new evangelization"—new, he says, in its ardor, its methods, and its expression. His views on missionary activity are synthesized in the encyclical *The Mission of the Redeemer* (1990), in which he declares: "I sense that the moment has come to commit all of the Church's energies to a new evangelization and to the mission *ad gentes.*"

BIBLIOGRAPHY Works by Wojtyla include *The Acting Person* (1979), *Sources of Renewal: The Implementation of Vatican II* (1980), and *Crossing the Threshold of Hope* (1994). His encyclicals and other important documents are published in English by the United

States Catholic Conference, Washington, D.C. Tad Szulc, *John Paul II: The Biography* (1995); George H. Williams, *The Mind of John Paul II* (1981) and "John Paul II," in *New Catholic Encyclopedia,* supplementary volume 18 (1989), pp. 221–233.

Avery Dulles, SJ

Johns, David (1796–1843), missionary to Madagascar with the London Missionary Society. Born in Cardiganshire, Wales, Johns (whose original surname was Jones) studied at Newton Academy and at Gosport. He reached Madagascar in 1826 and in 1831 was put in charge of the second church organized in the country. He changed his surname to Johns because there was already a David *Jones in the mission. In 1835 the government began persecuting Christians, causing the missionaries to leave, but Johns and the printer, Edward Baker, stayed on for another year to complete Johns's Malagasy dictionary and his translation of *Pilgrim's Progress* and to bind copies of the Bible to leave with the Christians. This was a time of great distress. The missionaries' servants were forced by the government to undergo an ordeal by poison, from which two of them died. When he finally left, Johns went to Mauritius and tried to keep in touch with and encourage the Malagasy Christians. He ventured back to Madagascar briefly four times, making fruitless efforts to establish a haven for Christians on the part of the coast that was under French influence. The coastal island of Nosy Be was his headquarters for some of these operations. Once, between these trips, he and his wife took six refugees to Britain and he published, with J. J. *Freeman, *A Narrative of the Persecutions of Christians in Madagascar* (1840). On his last trip to Madagascar, Johns died of fever, having declared, "If I had a thousand lives, I would willingly lay down every one for Madagascar."

BIBLIOGRAPHY William Ellis, *The Martyr Church of Madagascar* (1852); Richard Lovett, *The History of the London Missionary Society* (1899).

Charles W. Forman

Johnson, Amelia Dorothea (Baker) (1820–1904), missionary of the Church Missionary Society (CMS) in India. The daughter and granddaughter of missionaries in South India, in 1840 Amelia Baker married John Johnson, a CMS missionary to South India. Their son William was born in 1843. John Johnson died in 1846, and his widow, already involved in teaching, remained at Cottayam in charge of the girls' schools until 1855, when she took her son to England. Her two sisters also married missionaries in South India; three daughters of her brother, Henry Baker, Jr., became missionary teachers, and the Baker Memorial School in Kottayam stands as a tribute to three generations of women who served female education in South India for well over a century.

BIBLIOGRAPHY CMS, *Register of Missionaries and Native Clergy* (1904); E. Dalton, *The Baker Family in India* (1963); Eugene Stock, *History of the Church Missionary Society,* 3 vols. (1899).

Jocelyn Murray

Johnson, James (c. 1836–1917), West African Anglican church leader. Johnson was born in the former Sierra Leone colony. Educated at the Fourah Bay Institution (later College), he joined the Church Missionary Society (CMS) in 1858 and was ordained an Anglican minister in 1863. He labored for 11 years as missionary and pastor in the prestigious Christ Church, Pademba Road, Freetown, where his piety and aggressive evangelism earned him the accolade "Wonderful Johnson"; later his reputation for being a highly genuine West African Christian earned him the sobriquet "Holy Johnson." Uncompromising, forceful, and in many ways an enigma, he became a champion of the native pastorate ideal advocated by Henry *Venn. He was also an advocate of African nationalism, though his calls for an independent African church—underlined with vigorous denunciations of ethnocentric European missionary control and enterprise—sat uneasily with his lifelong and deep-seated loyalty to the CMS.

Johnson was transferred to Nigeria in 1874, where he gained a reputation as an outspoken defender of his race, a capable administrator, and an indefatigable missionary. He played a leading role in forming and developing the Lagos Native Pastorate Church. During his brief elevation as superintendent of the CMS Yoruba Mission (1877–1879), he endeavored to expand that mission with characteristic zest, but his demand for ecclesiastical independence was a significant factor in the short-lived secession of the Niger Delta from CMS control in the 1890s. He was considered for the episcopate as early as 1876 and was eventually consecrated assistant bishop of Western Equatorial Africa in 1900, with oversight of the Niger Delta and Benin.

Johnson's life reflected the conflicts and ambiguities of his age. Thus, he failed, for instance, to realize his dream of an independent, nondenominational, African church, even when the opportunity seemed to present itself. Yet he stands like a colossus among nineteenth-century West African clergy. His vision and militancy challenged both mission and church.

BIBLIOGRAPHY E. A. Ayandele, *The Missionary Impact on Modern Nigeria, 1842–1914: A Political and Social Analysis* (1966) and *Holy Johnson: Pioneer of African Nationalism, 1836–1917* (1970); C. Fyfe, *A History of Sierra Leone* (1962); Jehu J. Hanciles, "The Sierra Leone Native Pastorate (1850–1890): An Experiment in Ecclesiastical Independence" (Ph.D. diss., Univ. of Edinburgh, 1995); Lamin Sanneh, *West African Christianity: The Religious Impact* (1983) and *Translating the Message: The Missionary Impact on Culture* (1989).

Jehu J. Hanciles

Johnson, Mammie (early 1820s–1888), Jamaican Baptist teacher and evangelist in Cameroon. Born a slave, Johnson was one of several pioneer freed Jamaicans who in 1843 traveled to Clarence on the island of Fernando Po and in 1845 settled at Douala, along the Cameroon river estuary. In 1853 Baptist Missionary Society missionary Alfred *Saker (1814–1880) baptized her and encouraged her and her husband, Sam Johnson, to open a mission station in Douala. As a colleague of another Jamaican missionary, Joseph Jackson Fuller (1825–1908), Mammie Johnson helped lay the foundations of Protestant work in Cameroon. They studied the native languages, undertook translation work, formed churches, and provided services in the areas of medicine, education, agriculture, and industrial training. As part of the Jamaican pastoral team, Johnson pioneered women's work and encouraged formation of indigenous church leadership in Cameroon.

British Baptist missionary colleagues gratefully acknowledged her care of the sick and of missionary children. At her death, they remembered Johnson as an inspiring Christian lay worker.

BIBLIOGRAPHY Horace Orlando Russell, "The Missionary Outreach of the West Indian Church to West Africa in the Nineteenth Century, with Particular Reference to the Baptists" (Ph.D. diss., Oxford Univ., 1972); Brian Stanley, *The History of the Baptist Missionary Society, 1792–1992* (1992). BMS sources such as Thomas Lewis, *These Seventy Years, An Autobiography* (1930) and Joseph Jackson Fuller, manuscript autobiography housed at Regent's Park College, Oxford, refer frequently to Johnson.

Paul R. Dekar

Johnson, Samuel (1846–1901), Yoruba minister, diplomat, and historian. Johnson was born in Hastings, Sierra Leone. His father was Henry Johnson, a liberated African descended from the former king of Oyo in Yorubaland; his eldest brother was Henry Johnson. When Samuel was ten years old, David *Hinderer recruited his father for Yorubaland as his assistant in Ibadan. Samuel attended the Hinderers' school, and then the Abokuta Training Institution. In 1865 he became schoolmaster at Aremo, Ibadan, and catechist there in 1876, taking increasing responsibility in the frequent prolonged absence of missionary staff. He also traveled to keep contact with the scattered Christians beyond Ibadan.

During the Yoruba Wars (1877–1893), he became an emissary, trusted on all sides, between the Ibadan chiefs, the king of Oyo, and the British. During a visit from the bishop of Sierra Leone in 1886, he was ordained deacon and priest and, after a brief period at Ondo, in 1887 became pastor at Oyo. There he remained until his untimely death.

In Oyo, Johnson had access to rich sources of Yoruba tradition. By 1897 he had completed the remarkable *History of the Yorubas,* an account of Yoruba culture and tradition down to his own day. The work made excellent use of oral sources and of his own experiences. The Church Missionary Society would not publish the manuscript but passed it to another publisher, who lost it. Johnson thus died without seeing the work in print. His younger brother Obadiah, a Lagos medical doctor, rewrote the book from his papers, and after many vicissitudes (the second manuscript was sent to England on a ship that was captured during the World War I) it was published, with a dedication to Hinderer's memory, in 1921. It has often been reprinted.

Johnson says that he wrote from patriotic motives; educated Yoruba knew the history of Britain, Greece, and Rome, but not of their own country. He envisaged an originally unitary Yoruba state, of which Oyo and Ife were respectively the political and cultural pillars, and saw Christianity as crowning, not as overturning, Yoruba history. His book is a monument to the scholarship and cultural sensitivity to be found among Christian West Africans of his generation.

BIBLIOGRAPHY Samuel Johnson, *The History of the Yorubas from the Earliest Times to the Beginning of the British Protectorate,* O. Johnson, ed. (1921). J. F. Ade Ajayi, *Christian Missions in Nigeria, 1841–1891* (1965) and "Samuel Johnson, Historian of the Yoruba," *Nigeria Magazine* 81 (1964): 141–146; *CMS Register of Missionaries and Native Clergy,* no. 348; *Lagos Weekly Record,* May 4, 1901 (obit.).

Andrew F. Walls

Johnson, Thomas Sylvester (Claudius) (1873–1955), Sierra Leonean Anglican bishop. Johnson was born in Sierra Leone to a farming and trading family of mixed Igbo and Yoruba stock. Making the best of a village education, he taught in his village and then in Freetown, where he gained a scholarship to Fourah Bay College and became headmaster of the Church Missionary Society (CMS) "Mohammedan School." The difficulties of Muslim evangelism fueled his desire to improve his education; he took arts and theology degrees at Fourah Bay College. Rejected for the ministry, he returned to teaching but was eventually ordained as bishop's chaplain in 1909. In 1911 he joined the staff of Fourah Bay College, assisting in its financial rescue and increasing its impact (as a Christian institution with high academic standards) on local education. In 1933, after service as diocesan inspector of schools and as a pastor, he became principal of the prestigious Church Missionary Society grammar school, which had once refused him as a pupil. Thereafter, he was successively canon, archdeacon, and, in 1937, first assistant bishop of Sierra Leone. He attended the Tambaram Missionary Conference of 1938. In 1947, he retired to his village, Benguema, remaining active in community affairs.

Johnson, while zealous for both education and evangelism (his interest in Muslim evangelism remained), was innovative in giving Christian direction and interpretation to cultural practices. His book *The Fear Fetish: Its Cause and Cure* (1949) insists on taking African worldviews seriously. He also wrote a history of the Sierra Leone church, *The Story of a Mission* (1953). His influence on Harry *Sawyerr and others merits a place in the history of African theology.

BIBLIOGRAPHY *Crockford's Clerical Directory,* 1951–1952, p. 688; M. Markwei, "Harry Sawyerr's Patron (Bishop T. S. Johnson)," in M. E. Glasswell and E. W. Fasholé-Luke, eds., *New Testament Christianity for Africa and the World* (1974), pp. 179–197; A. F. Walls, "The Theological Significance of Harry Sawyerr," in *The Practice of Presence: Selected Papers of Harry Sawyerr,* J. Parratt, ed. (1995).

Andrew F. Walls

Johnson, William Augustine Bernard (1787–1823), German-born missionary of the Church Missionary Society (CMS) in Sierra Leone. Born in Hanover, Germany, Wilhelm Augustin Bernhard Janzen moved with his wife to England in 1812. Working as a laborer in London, he Anglicized his name to "Johnson." He offered his services to the CMS and in 1816 was sent to Sierra Leone as a schoolmaster. In 1817 he was ordained "according to the rites of the Lutheran church" by other German missionaries of the CMS. Large numbers of African captives rescued from slave ships were being landed, reclothed, and formed into village communities in the hills above Freetown. Johnson worked for seven years at the village of Regent as evangelist, social organizer, and eventually official superintendant. While the governor of Sierra Leone provided facilities, Johnson made striking progress in turning the flood of uprooted individuals—men, women, and children of diverse cultural traditions—into an orderly body, English speaking and church attending, with many individuals eager to acquire Western education and "civilized" forms of social bonding. He also encouraged initial work on the local African languages. Sent home because of ill health, he died at sea. Publication of his journals made Regent a Victorian byword for the success of Protestant missions. Several of the pupils, converts, and assistants of the Apostle of Regent, as Johnson was known, later became influential figures in Sierra Leone.

BIBLIOGRAPHY *A Memoir of the Rev. W. A. B. Johnson, Missionary of the Church Missionary Society, in Regent's Town, Sierra Leone* (1852). *Church Missionary Society African Missions (No. 1, Sierra Leone)* (1865); Christopher Fyfe, *History of Sierra Leone* (1962, 1994); John Peterson, *Province of Freedom: A History of Sierra Leone, 1787–1870* (1969); Arthur T. Pierson, *Seven Years in Sierra Leone* (1897); E. Stock, *History of the CMS* (1899).

P. E. H. Hair

Johnson, William Percival (1854–1928), Anglican missionary to central Africa. Educated at University College, Oxford, Johnson intended to follow a career in the Indian civil service. However, he was attracted by a notice asking for volunteers for the Universities' Mission to Central Africa and volunteered. He reached Zanzibar in 1876, a few months after his close friend Chauncy Maples. By 1878 he was priest in charge at Mbweni in Malawi. In 1880, during one of what were to be many attacks of illness, he was treated at Cape Maclear by the Scottish Presbyterian missionary Robert *Laws. In spite of considerable theological differences between them, an intimate friendship developed and lasted until Johnson's death. Laws referred to Johnson as the Apostle of the Lake (i.e., Nyasa), indicating both his pioneering missionary work and his tireless traveling. Johnson, who remained single throughout his life, had an ascetic life-style and a burning concern not to impose European culture unnecessarily on the African church. He was awarded an honorary D.D. by Oxford in 1911. He was most at home in the African bush, where he died, at Liuli, on the eastern side of Lake Nyasa.

BIBLIOGRAPHY W. P. Johnson, *Nyasa the Great Water* (1922) and *My African Reminiscences, 1875–95* (1924). Bertram Herbert Barnes, *Johnson of Nyasaland: A Study of the Life and Work of William Percival Johnson D.D.* (1933); G. H. Wilson, *The History of the Universities' Mission to Central Africa* (1936).

T. Jack Thompson

Jones, Charles Colcock, Sr. (1804–1863), Presbyterian minister, educator, and missionary to American slaves. At one time professor of church history at Columbia Theological Seminary, and secretary of the Presbyterian Board of Domestic Missions (Old School), Jones was born into a slaveholding family in Liberty County, Georgia. Educated by William McWhir at Sunbury Academy, Jones worked as a clerk for six years in a "counting house" in Savannah, Georgia. At 17 years of age he experienced a critical illness, and his subsequent conversion prompted him to study for the ministry. He enrolled at Phillips Academy in Andover, Massachusetts, and later at Andover Theological Seminary and Princeton Theological Seminary. While at seminary Jones became troubled by the evils of the plantation system and was determined to improve the physical and spiritual welfare of plantation slaves. Following graduation in 1830, he returned to Liberty County, where he organized the Liberty County Association for the Religious Instruction, Orally, of the Colored Population, a nondenominational association that organized Sunday schools and worship services. Though a slaveholder himself, who never came to repudiate the system, Jones was nevertheless a reformer and missionary who worked to improve both the living conditions and the spiritual lives of southern slaves. His publications include *A Catechism . . . for the Oral Instruction of Colored Persons* (1837) and *The Religious Instruction of the Negroes in the United States* (1842).

BIBLIOGRAPHY Eduard Nuessner Loring, "Charles C. Jones: Missionary to Plantation Slaves, 1831–1847" (Ph.D. diss., Vanderbilt Univ., 1976); Robert Mason Myers, *A Georgian at Princeton* (1976); Robert Mason Myers, ed., *The Children of Pride* (1972); Donald G. Mathews, "Charles Colcock Jones and the Southern Evangelical Crusade to Form a Biracial Community," *Journal of Southern History* 41 (1975): 299–320; Wayne C. Tyner, "Charles Colcock Jones: Mission to Slaves," *Journal of Presbyterian History* 55 (1977): 363–380.

Robert Benedetto

Jones, Clarence W(esley) (1900–1986), missionary radio pioneer. Born in Sherrard, Illinois, and a graduate of Moody Bible Institute, Jones was mentored by evangelist Paul D. *Rader in the 1920s and had his first taste of radio ministry in Rader's pioneering programs on Chicago's first commercial station. Concerned for the evangelism of South America, he seized upon radio as the key. After a fruitless survey trip in 1928 through Venezuela, Colombia, Panama, and Cuba, which seemed to confirm his critics' appellation "Jones's folly," Jones was affirmed by Reuben *Larson, missionary to Ecuador, who set out to negotiate permission to broadcast from Quito. Jones played his trombone and Larson preached in Spanish for the inaugural broadcast on Christmas Day, 1931—this at a time when there were less than a score of receiving sets in all of Ecuador. Despite financial crises during the Great

Depression, by 1940 radio station HCJB (Heralding Christ Jesus' Blessings) boasted a 10,000-watt transmitter capable of delivering signals to India, New Zealand, and Russia. In 1944 Jones helped to found the National Religious Broadcasters (NRB). He retired as president of HCJB in 1970 but continued to represent the mission in North America and Europe. In 1975 he was the first recipient of the NRB's Hall of Fame Award. He died in retirement in Largo, Florida.

BIBLIOGRAPHY C. Jones, *Radio: The New Missionary* (1946), repr. in Joel Carpenter, ed., *Missionary Innovation and Expansion* (1988); Lois Neely, *Come up to This Mountain: The Miracle of Clarence W. Jones and HCJB* (1980).

Robert T. Coote

Jones, David (1797–1841), the first in a long line of Welsh missionaries to Madagascar. Ordained in 1817, Jones was sent to Madagascar by the London Missionary Society in 1818, accompanied by his wife and his colleague Thomas Bevan and his wife. On arrival in Madagascar, the whole party, including two infant children born en route, was stricken with fever and all but Jones died; he himself was left with a permanent weakness. Retiring briefly to Mauritius, he returned to Madagascar and made his way to the capital, Antananarivo. He told the king, Radama, that if he was permitted to stay he would preach the word of God, establish schools, and bring artisans to teach European skills. Radama was not interested in the preaching but nevertheless gave permission in order to secure the other benefits. More missionaries soon joined Jones. Together they began industries, started a network of schools, and translated the Bible. In 1822, Jones and David *Griffiths settled the orthography of the Malagasy language on a fully phonetic basis. Public worship was inaugurated and attendance increased. By the late 1820s converts were being baptized.

Radama's death in 1828 was followed by the assassination of his friends and the ascent to the throne of Queen Ranavalona, who bitterly persecuted the Christians and forced the missionaries to leave the country. Jones departed in 1830, but then tried to return. In June 1840 he sought redress from the queen and was held prisoner. Managing to escape, he fled to Mauritius, where he died.

BIBLIOGRAPHY William Ellis, *The Martyr Church: A Narrative of the Introduction, Progress, and Triumph of Christianity in Madagascar* (1869); Ernest Hayes, *David Jones, Dauntless Pioneer* (1923); R. Lovett, *History of the London Missionary Society*, vol. 1 (1899), pp. 673–710.

Charles W. Forman

Jones, David Picton (1860–1936), London Missionary Society (LMS) missionary to central Africa. Jones was born in New Quay, Cardiganshire, Wales. His training for the Congregational ministry at Carmarthen was followed by a course in tropical medicine and first aid at Bristol General Hospital in preparation for his appointment to the Central Africa Mission of the LMS, in an area now part of Zambia. When Jones arrived in Uguha in March 1883, slave raiding had reduced the region to a state of virtual anarchy, forcing him to move frequently. He eventually settled at Kambole on the Ulungu plain. Between 1887 and 1889 he played a key role in the short-lived experiment of establishing missionary-governed stockaded villages for the protection of the local Mambwe and Lungu populations, long the prey of Bemba and Arab slave raiders. The experiment rapidly degenerated into draconian comprehensive control over political, judicial, and social aspects of African life. Early on, LMS directors expressed strong disapproval of the system, but missionaries continued to exercise temporal authority as late as 1905.

Jones's flair for languages resulted in the translation of *Aesop's Fables*, the New Testament, and various hymnbooks into Kimambwe. Upon completion of his translation work, Jones was appointed to Matabeleland, settling at Inyati until ill health induced his retirement from missionary service in 1903. Back in Great Britain, Jones pastored churches at Llansamlet (near Swansea), Glamorganshire (1903–1923), and Clydach (1916–1918). He died at Warmley, Bristol.

BIBLIOGRAPHY David Picton Jones, *After Livingstone* (1968). Jonathan J. Bonk, *The Theory and Practice of Missionary Identification, 1860–1920* (1989); Richard Lovett, *The History of the London Missionary Society, 1795–1895* (1899); Robert I. Rotberg, *Christian Missionaries and the Creation of Northern Rhodesia, 1880–1924* (1965); James Sibree, *London Missionary Society: A Register of Missionaries, Deputations, Etc., from 1796–1923* (1923).

Jonathan J. Bonk

Jones, E(li) Stanley (1884–1973), American Methodist missionary to India, global evangelist, and author. Born in Clarksville, Maryland, Jones was converted at age 17, studied law, and graduated from Asbury College (1906). In 1907, under the Board of Missions of the Methodist Episcopal Church, he went to Lucknow, India, where he had a fruitful pastorate. Ordained both a deacon and an elder in 1908, he worked as district missionary superintendent and revival preacher.

Responding to a call to serve India's intelligentsia, he delivered carefully prepared addresses (later published as widely influential books), followed by grueling question periods, in public halls throughout India. His early narrow and individualistic approach became more liberal and social. His roundtable conferences predated the interfaith dialogue emphasis of the World Council of Churches. He attended meetings of the International Missionary Council at Jerusalem (1928) and at Madras (1938). He founded a Christian ashram at Sat Tal in the Himalayas (1930) and later an international ashram movement. He was a friend of Mahatma Gandhi and other national leaders of all religions; his sympathies with the nationalist movement antagonized the British authorities and kept him out of India during World War II. In a valiant effort to avoid war between Japan and the United States, Jones worked with his Christian contacts in the Japanese embassy in Washington to stimulate last-minute communication between President Roosevelt and Emperor Hirohito. His interest in mental health led to the founding of Nur Manzil Psychiatric Center, Lucknow (1948).

From the 1930s, Jones's evangelistic work extended to six continents, including ten visits he made to postwar Japan. His interest in church union led to 500 addresses to Christian gatherings across the United States. He wrote twenty-eight books, giving all royalties back to the church for scholarships and evangelism. His labors brought missions and evangelism to the forefront again and furthered peace and social witness. He declined episcopal election (1928). He received honorary degrees from Syracuse University, Duke University, and many other schools. He received the Gandhi Peace Prize in 1961 and was twice nominated for the Nobel Peace Prize.

BIBLIOGRAPHY E. Stanley Jones, *The Christ of the Indian Road* (1925), *The Christ of the Round Table* (1928), *The Christ of Every Road* (1930), *The Way* (1946), *A Song of Ascents* (1968; his autobiography), and *The Divine Yes* (1974). Martin Ross Johnson, "The Christian Vision of E. Stanley Jones: Missionary, Evangelist, Prophet, and Statesman" (Ph.D. diss., Florida State Univ., 1978); Richard W. Taylor, "E. Stanley Jones," in Gerald H. Anderson et al., eds., *Mission Legacies* (1994), pp. 339-347; C. Chacko Thomas, "The Work and Thought of Eli Stanley Jones with Special Reference to India" (Ph.D. diss., Univ. of Iowa, 1955). Jones's papers are to be placed in the archives of Asbury Seminary, Wilmore, Ky.

James K. Mathews

Jones, Edward (1807-1865), Afro-American missionary to Sierra Leone. Born in Charleston, South Carolina, Jones became the first black American to graduate from Amherst (Massachusetts) College. Ordained by the Episcopal Church in 1830, he arrived in the Sierra Leone colony the following year and joined the Church Missionary Society (CMS) there in 1840. He became the first black principal of Fourah Bay College (1841-1859) and also served as secretary of the Sierra Leone Mission (1855-1858 and 1861-1864). He was an outstanding scholar, and Henry *Venn attested that his "powers and knowledge of Africa" were "superior to all his brethren." As principal, Jones was singularly committed to the educational development of the native African; he had a major influence on the men who later became the first pastors of the Sierra Leone Native Pastorate. Inexorably propelled into the vanguard of the perennial racial tension in the mission, he became an intrepid champion of native advancement and frequently challenged European missionary prejudice. He was the mainstay of the mission during the notoriously unsettled period between 1850 and 1862, when three bishops died in quick succession. Although his last few years in the colony were clouded by failing health and beleaguered relations with the CMS, to the native clergy and congregations he remained an immensely popular missionary and a highly esteemed role model. He died in England.

BIBLIOGRAPHY Michael Crowther, "From Amherst to Fourah Bay: Principal Edward Jones" (paper presented at the Bicentenary of Sierra Leone Symposium, Fourah Bay College, Univ. of Sierra Leone, May 1987) includes a comprehensive bibliography on Jones. Christopher Fyfe, *A History of Sierra Leone* (1962). Reference materials in the CMS archives are numerous, but see especially C A1/0 129 (Jones's personal correspondence and reports), C A1/0 3 (official correspondence as mission secretary), and C A1/L4-L7 (letters from CMS secretaries to, and about, Jones).

Jehu J. Hanciles

Jones, Evan (1788-1873) *and*
John Buttrick (1823-1876), Baptist missionaries to the Cherokees. Born to an Anglican family at Brecknockshire, Wales, Evan Jones married Elizabeth Lanigan in 1808 and moved to London. In 1821 they immigrated to the United States, settled in the Welsh community at Berwyn, Pennsylvania, and became Baptists. Jones and his wife soon answered the Baptist Foreign Mission Board appeal for missionaries to serve among the Cherokees in North Carolina. There John Buttrick Jones was born three years after his parents began their missionary service. After graduating from Rochester Seminary in 1855, he married Jennie Smith (d. 1867) and began missionary service with his father.

The Joneses had outstanding evangelistic success. Together father and son won more Indians to the Christian faith than any other Protestant missionaries. Their effectiveness rested on several considerations. They identified with Cherokee culture and became fluent Cherokee speakers and Bible translators. They preached a gospel that embraced all people and resisted the prevailing trend to "Americanize" the Indians. They championed Cherokee rights and autonomy and repeatedly sided against the U.S. government and the white majority when policies or laws disadvantaged the Cherokees. The Joneses opposed all government attempts to detribalize the Cherokees. Perhaps the most contentious issue they faced was black slavery, in which some Cherokees were implicated as slaveholders. During their long missionary service, between them they were expelled from the Cherokee Nation four times, including twice for their antislavery stand. The Joneses' evangelical faith led them to oppose Indian practices that Scripture expressly forbade, but they refused to condemn Indian culture or treat it in a condescending manner. They emphasized training Cherokees for Christian ministry in their own context and ordained many for the pastorate. The Joneses were frequently embroiled in controversy. White settlers were continually extending their occupation of Indian territory. This was further complicated by the North-South tensions among the States. President Ulysses S. Grant appointed John Jones a federal agent to the Cherokees, a position he held from 1870 to 1874.

BIBLIOGRAPHY William G. McLoughlin, *Champions of the Cherokees: Evan and John B. Jones* (1990).

Wilbert R. Shenk

Jones, George Heber (1867-1919), American Methodist missionary to Korea. Educated in public schools in Utica, New York, Jones went to Korea at the age of 20 under the auspices of the Methodist Episcopal Church only three years after the beginning of Protestant missionary work in that country. His first five years were spent mainly in Seoul, teaching at the Pai Chai high school and college, while continuing his own education by correspondence with the American University at Harriman, Tennessee, from which he received his B.A. in 1892. In the same year he went to Chemulco, where he spent the next decade establishing churches in an area where there had been none. He had the rare distinction of having established every one of the forty-four churches in the district and having baptized each one of the 2,800 Christians. He served for two periods as the superintendent of the Methodist Episcopal mission throughout Korea, was a member of the board of translators of the Bible into Korean, and established and edited two theological journals. He was involved with other missionaries in helping the Korean royal family after the murder of the queen in 1895, and later organized the Korean immigration movement to the newly acquired American territory of Hawaii, for which he secured the support of the Korean government. He returned to the United States permanently in 1909 and for the next ten years until his death lectured, wrote, and served as editorial secretary and associate secretary of the Board of Foreign Missions of the Methodist Episcopal Church.

BIBLIOGRAPHY L. G. Paik, *The History of Protestant Missions in Korea* (1929).

Ronald E. Davies

Jones, John (1737–1800), soldier and Congregationalist minister, founder of Newfoundland Congregationalism. Born in Wales, Jones was enlisted in the Royal Artillery and experienced a conversion at Saint John's, Newfoundland, when he observed a soldier curse God after being mortally wounded in a fight. When his company returned to England he joined a Calvinistic Methodist congregation in Kent, but within a couple of years he was again stationed in Saint John's, where he organized an evangelical society. The congregation suffered persecution through the governor and the local magistrate (who was an Anglican priest). In 1778 Jones returned to Plymouth, England, where he resigned his military positions and took up theological studies with the dissenting minister Christopher Mends. Following his ordination as a Congregational minister, he returned in 1779 to Saint John's, where despite initial difficulties with the colonial authorities he succeeded in establishing a thriving independent congregation, which in 1794 had grown to four hundred members. He exhibited a spirit of civility and tolerance not only among his fellow Protestants but also toward Roman Catholics, as the correspondence with the first Roman Catholic bishop James Louis *O'Donel shows. With the financial help of English dissenters, he and his congregation carried out evangelistic and charitable activities. Most notably they built and maintained a charity school open to all denominations. When Jones died in Saint John's, he had laid the foundation for the island's subsequent Congregational presence.

BIBLIOGRAPHY The major source for Jones's life and work is his handwritten "Journal," kept by the Kirk Session of St. David's Presbyterian Church, Saint John's, Newfoundland. *The Dissenting Church of Christ at St. John's, 1775–1975* (1976; a memorial volume published at St. John's); Samuel Greatheed, "The Life of John Jones," *Evangelical Magazine* 8 (1800): 441–449; Hans Rollmann, "John Jones, James O'Donel, and the Question of Religious Tolerance in Eighteenth-Century Newfoundland: A Correspondence," *Newfoundland Quarterly* 80, no. 1 (1984): 23–27; Edmund Violet, *Remarks upon the Life and Manners of the Rev. John Jones...* (1810).

Hans Rollmann

Jones, John B. *See* Jones, Evan, and John Buttrick.

Jones, John Peter (1847–1916), American Congregational missionary to India. Of Welsh birth and extraction, Jones graduated from Western Reserve University, Ohio (which awarded him its D.D. in 1895), and Andover Theological Seminary, Massachusetts. He joined the Madura Mission of the American Board of Commissioners for Foreign Missions in 1878. He was among the founders of Union Theological Seminary in Pasumalai (forerunner of Tamil Nadu Theological Seminary in Madurai) and was founding editor of the *Year Book of Missions in India.* His books and articles, which include *India's Problem: Krishna or Christ* (1903), *India: Its Life and Thought* (1908), and *The Modern Missionary Challenge* (1911), contributed to early twentieth-century reflection on the theology of religion. These writings influenced the reformulation of missionary policy in the period of the 1910 World Missionary Conference at Edinburgh, in which he took an active part. In 1914 he became a professor at the Kennedy School of Missions in Hartford, Connecticut, where he served until his death.

BIBLIOGRAPHY Kenneth R. Cracknell, *Justice, Courtesy, and Love: Missionaries and Theologians Encountering the World Religious Traditions, 1846–1914* (1995).

Kenneth R. Cracknell

Jones, John Taylor (1802–1851), American Baptist missionary to Siam (Thailand). Taylor and his first wife, Eliza Grew, were the first American Baptist missionaries to Siam; his wife was the first American woman missionary in that country. The Joneses went to Thailand in 1833 from Burma, where they had joined Adoniram *Judson in 1831. Jones's major ministry was to Thai people, unlike other Baptists in Thailand, who worked primarily with Chinese. He saw few converts but made a significant contribution in what he translated and wrote in Thai. Most notably, he was principal translator of the first published Thai New Testament, the first edition of which was finished in 1844, having been published in several separate portions as each was completed. A revision of the full New Testament followed in 1850. This work helped to standardize for a time some Christian theological vocabulary in Thai. Eliza Jones died in Thailand in 1838 after extensive work on the first English-Thai dictionary, which incorporated earlier work done by Carl *Gutzlaff. Jones married twice more. He died in Thailand as he was beginning to translate the Old Testament. Baptist work among the Thai virtually ceased after his death.

BIBLIOGRAPHY William Gammell, *A History of American Baptist Missions* (1851); Howard Malcolm, *Travels in South-Eastern Asia* (1839, rev. 1853); George B. McFarland, ed., *Historical Sketch of Protestant Missions in Siam, 1828–1928* (1928).

William A. Smalley

Jones, Lewis Bevan (1880–1960), British Baptist missionary to Muslims in India. Bevan Jones, as he was generally known, was born in Agra, India, where his father was a Baptist Missionary Society (BMS) missionary. Jones was educated at Eltham College, University College, Cardiff, and at Regent's Park College, London (B.A., B.D.). Later, he received an M.A. from Cardiff for a thesis on the status of women in Islam. Ordained in 1907, he proceeded to Agra with the BMS. In 1909 he was transferred to Dhakka, in East Bengal; there, after the 1911 Lucknow Conference of Missionaries to Muslims, he began to specialize in Muslim evangelization. In 1914 he was officially designated for this work. In 1916 he married Violet Rhoda Stanford, a BMS nurse, who soon began to share his interest in Islam. In 1917, accompanied by his wife, Jones spent six months learning Arabic at Temple *Gairdner's study center in Cairo, and in 1924 they attended the Jerusalem Conference of Missionaries to Muslims.

Jones combined his work as secretary of the Missionaries to Muslims League in India and the Far East and as a member of the National Missionary Council's Committee for Muslim Work with part-time lecturing on Islam at Serampore College and at Bishop's College, Calcutta. In 1930, in Lahore, an ecumenical school of Islamic studies was founded, which he served as principal until 1941 and which he named the Henry Martyn School. During his years at the school, he wrote *The People of the Mosque* (1932), *Christianity Explained to Muslims* (1938), and *Women in Islam* (coauthored with his wife, 1941). He stressed the need for personal friendship, and he valued spiritual experience more than doctrinal confession. After pastoring churches in Delhi, and then in Surrey, England, Jones retired in 1947 but still served on the Council for the Muslim World (Church of England) and as chairman of the Fellowship of Faith for Muslims, for which he wrote several booklets.

BIBLIOGRAPHY Other works by Jones include *The Best Friend: A Life of Our Lord* (1925), *The Five Pillars of Islam* (1952), *The Ahmadiyya Movement* (1952), *From Islam to Christ: How a Sufi Found His Lord* (1952), and *Christ's Ambassador to the Muslim* (1952). Clinton Bennett, "Lewis Bevan Jones," in Gerald H. Anderson et al., eds., *Mission Legacies* (1994), pp. 283–289, and "A Theological Approach of Lewis Bevan Jones, Baptist Pioneer in Christian Muslim Relations," *The Baptist Quarterly* 32 (January 1988): 237–252.

Clinton Bennett

Jones, Mabel Lossing (1878–1978), Methodist missionary educator in India. Mabel Lossing was born in Clayton, Iowa, and graduated from Upper Iowa University in 1903. She was a public school teacher and principal. In 1904 she was commissioned as a missionary to India by the Woman's Foreign Missionary Society of the Methodist Episcopal Church. Married to E. Stanley *Jones in Bombay, India, in 1911, she served in Khandwa, Jabalpur (Madya Pradesh), and at Isabella Thoburn College, Lucknow. She founded two teachers' training schools and for 30 years was a master educator at Sitapur, Uttar Pradesh. She wrote many missionary articles, raised scholarships for thousands of boys, and by her long residence in one place made for an influential witness among all classes. With her husband, she left everything to India, endowing an extensive scholarship program. She received a D.H.L. degree from Upper Iowa University and was named Iowa Woman of the Year in 1990, 12 years after her death.

BIBLIOGRAPHY Mabel Jones's papers are to be consigned to the United Methodist Archives, Madison, N.J.

James K. Mathews

Jones, Nancy (1860–?), African American missionary of the American Board of Commissioners for Foreign Missions (ABCFM). Jones was born in Hopkinsville, Christian County, Kentucky; during her childhood her family moved to Memphis, Tennessee. She graduated from Fisk University, Nashville, in 1886. Although a Baptist, she applied to the Congregational ABCFM for a missionary appointment. The first unmarried black woman commissioned by the ABCFM, Jones served in Mozambique from 1888 to 1893 and later in Southern Rhodesia (Zimbabwe) from 1893 to 1897. In Mozambique she was stationed at Kambini and worked with two other black missionaries, Benjamin and Henrietta Bailey Ousley. She taught in, and soon took charge of, the mission school's primary department. She also visited nearby areas, working with women in the villages and eventually opening a school for area children. In 1893 Jones was transferred to the Gaza mission in Southern Rhodesia, where she initially worked as a teacher in the day school. However, having been relieved of that duty, in 1897 she resigned, stating that as the only black person at the Gaza Mission, she had faced prejudice from some of her co-workers. She returned to her home in Memphis. There is no extant record of the date and place of her death.

BIBLIOGRAPHY Fred Field Goodsell, *You Shall Be My Witnesses* (1959); William E. Strong, *The Story of the American Board: An Account of the First Hundred Years of the American Board of Commissioners for Foreign Missions* (1910); Walter L. Williams, *Black Americans and the Evangelization of Africa, 1877–1900* (1982).

Sylvia M. Jacobs

Jones, Thomas Jesse (1873–1950), U.S. educator and sociologist. Jones was born in Llanfaethraeth, Wales, came to the United States in 1884, where he studied at Washington and Lee University, Virginia, Marietta College, Ohio (A.B.), Union Theological Seminary, New York (B.D.), and Columbia University, New York (Ph.D.). He developed a lifelong interest in research on education; he served as acting head of the University Social Settlement in New York City (1901–1902), as director of the research department at Hampton Institute in Virginia (1902–1909), as statistician for the U.S. Bureau of the Census (1909–1912), and as a specialist in education for the U.S. Bureau of Education (1912–1919). His major contribution to mission education resulted from his work with the Phelps-Stokes Fund from 1913 to 1946. He chaired the fund's education commission to West, South, and Equatorial Africa (1920–1921) and the subsequent commission to East Africa (1924). The commission's reports he edited, *Education in Africa* (1922) and *Education in East Africa* (1925), provided mandates and guidelines for that partnership of missions and colonial governments that was to characterize African education for the next generation. Widely implemented in English-speaking Africa were the commission's recommendations that the missions give priority to the establishment of teacher training institutions and that governments give grants-in-aid to mission schools maintained at approved standards.

BIBLIOGRAPHY Thomas Jesse Jones, *The Sociology of a New York City Block* (1904), *Negro Education in the United States* (1917), *Four Essentials of Education* (1926), and *Essentials of Civilization* (1929).

Norman E. Thomas

Jones, William Henry (c. 1840–1904), Anglican clergyman in East Africa. A Yao from the Malawi area, Jones was one of many slaves rescued by the British navy and landed in Bombay, India, where they were put under the care of the Church Missionary Society (CMS) at Sharanpur, near Nasik (hence their nickname, "Nasik boys"). In 1864 he was one of several sent by the CMS to Mombasa to help Johannes *Rebmann. Jones and Ishmael Semler (from Mozambique) were ordained deacons by Bishop James *Hannington in May 1885, and Jones led the party that accompanied the bishop on his expedition to Buganda. After the murder of Hannington in Buganda in October 1885, Jones and his party returned to the coast, where they arrived in February 1886. It is recorded that from their trade goods they made a blue banner with the word, in white, "Ichabod" (Alas! The glory!) which they carried as they entered Rabai. In 1895 Jones and Semler were ordained priests by Bishop Alfred *Tucker. They were among the first African co-workers with the missionaries in Eastern Equatorial Africa.

BIBLIOGRAPHY W. G. Blaikie, *Personal Life of David Livingstone* (1880); Church Missionary Society, *Register of Missionaries and Native Clergy* (1904); Jocelyn Murray, *Proclaim the Good News: A Short History of the Church Missionary Society* (1985); Donald Simpson, *Dark Companions: The African Contribution to the European Exploration of East Africa* (1975); Eugene Stock, *The History of the Church Missionary Society: Its Environment, Its Men, and Its Work* (1899).

Jocelyn Murray

Jordan, Johann Baptist (Francis Mary of the Cross) (1848–1918), German founder of two Catholic mission societies. Born in Gurtweil, Baden, Jordan was ordained in 1878. The recipient of a scholarship, he studied in Rome, where he founded the Salvatorians in 1881 and the Sisters of the Divine Savior in 1888. He assigned no special field of work to his foundations. He wished, rather, "with every means inspired by the love of God," to work for the kingdom of God everywhere on earth in the homeland and in foreign lands. In 1889 the prefecture apostolic of Assam was entrusted to the Salvatorians. In 1893 the society went to the United States, and in 1896 to Brazil. Simultaneously it expanded in several countries of Europe. The male branch is mainly engaged in pastoral ministry, education of boys, and foreign missions. The female branch works in numerous charitable institutions at home and overseas. Jordan was notable for his prayerfulness and extraordinary trust in God.

BIBLIOGRAPHY M. Heimbucher, *Die Orden und Kongregationen der katholischen Kirche*, vol. 2 (3d ed., 1965), pp. 411–416; P. Pfeiffer, *Jordan und seine Gründungen* (1930); Anton Kiebele, ed., *Die Salvatorianer in Geschichte und Gegenwart, 1881–1981* (1981).

Karl Müller, SVD

Jordan, Lewis G(arnett) (1854?–1939), corresponding secretary of the National Baptist Convention Foreign Mission Board (NBCFMB). Born a slave in Lauderdale County, Mississippi, Jordan took the name Lewis from a Union soldier who gave him his first pair of trousers and Jordan from another Union soldier. He received the rudiments of education from a missionary in a Union army camp. He responded to the gospel and was baptized in the Mississippi River on the Warren County plantation of Jefferson Davis. He graduated from Roger Williams University in Nashville, Tennessee, in 1883. While pastoring a Baptist church in Waco, Texas, a group of his parishioners sent him to Liberia to investigate emigration opportunities. In Liberia he met a number of missionaries and began a lifelong interest in missions. While he was corresponding secretary of the NBCFMB (1896–1921), he inaugurated the *Mission Herald* magazine and helped recruit African American missionaries like Emma B. *Delany and Landon N. *Cheek. He also helped over 200 Africans like John *Chilembwe from Malawi to get training in Baptist schools in the United States. He made four mission trips to Africa, two to the West Indies, and six to Europe. Upon retiring, he was given a pension of $1,200 per year, half of which he annually gave to the NBCFMB as a contribution for support of missions.

BIBLIOGRAPHY Lewis G. Jordan, *Up the Ladder in Foreign Missions* (1901), *Pebbles from an African Beach* (1917), *Negro Baptist History, U.S.A., 1750–1930* (1930), and *On Two Hemispheres: Bits from the Life Story of Lewis G. Jordan* (1930; 2d ed., 1939). Additional articles by Jordan are in the *Mission Herald* magazine. Edward A. Freeman, *The Epoch of Negro Baptists and the Foreign Mission Board* (1953); Owen D. Pelt and Ralph Lee Smith, *The Story of the National Baptists* (1960). Most of Jordan's books and magazines are available in the Schomburg Collection of the New York City Public Library.

Rodney H. Orr

Josenhans, F(riedrich) Joseph (1812–1884), German mission leader. Josenhans was *Inspektor* (executive head) of the Basel Mission (BM) from 1850 to 1879. Born of pietist parents, he was a pastor of the established Protestant church in the German state of Württemburg. In the BM's oral history Josenhans is known as the great organizer, regulator, and codifier. During his regime were issued printed regulations concerning such matters as BM congregations, the personal life of the missionaries, their correspondence, and the life of the mission seminary in Basel. These regulations amount to a major text on pietist organizational principles and social ethics. They were partly based on experiences Josenhans had while inspecting BM work in India in 1851, the only field visit made by a member of the BM home leadership before the 1880s.

Josenhans was a complex character of considerable intelligence, and with a remarkable ambition to provide dynamic pastoral guidance in the many complex conflicts that troubled the BM in the third quarter of the nineteenth century. But his view of his own authority and that of the BM leadership ("The voice of the [BM] Committee is the voice of God") raises a smile nowadays. The way this authority was built up and exercised to provide long-distance control over missionaries in the field stands as a cautionary lesson on the destructive effects of eurocentric authoritarianism.

BIBLIOGRAPHY Waltraud Haas, *Erlitten und Erstritten: Der Befreiungsweg von Frauen in der Basler Mission, 1816–1966* (1994; an English summary of part of this book, including the material relevant to Josenhans, was published under the title *Mission History from the Woman's Point of View* [1989]). Johannes Hesse, *Joseph Josenhans, ein Lebensbild* (1895); Jon Miller, *The Social Control of Religious Zeal: A Study of Organizational Contradictions* (1994); Wilhelm Schlatter, *Geschichte der Basler Mission* (1915).

Paul Jenkins

Jowett, William (1787–1855), English missionary and mission administrator. German volunteers were the first missionaries sent out by the Church Missionary Society (CMS) because ordained Anglican clergymen were not responsive. Thus Jowett, brother-in-law to Josiah *Pratt, the CMS clerical secretary, became the first English missionary of CMS. Well-qualified in Oriental languages, in 1815 he went to Malta, which was seen as a stepping-stone to work in the Mediterranean and Middle East. Direct evangelism was not permitted, but over the next 15 years Jowett traveled widely, making contact with Orthodox churches and establishing a printing facility in Malta that became a center for Bible translation and distribution. Jowett was reponsible for procuring for printing an Amharic version of the Bible; other portions produced by the press in Malta were in Maltese, Italian, Arabic, and modern Greek. He married Martha Whiting in 1815. She died in 1829, and in 1832 he became clerical secretary at the CMS headquarters in London, working alongside Dandeson *Coates. From 1840 to his death he was priest of St. John's Clapham, in south London.

BIBLIOGRAPHY William Jowett, *Christian Researches in the Mediterranean, Syria, and the Holy Land* (1820). Jocelyn Murray, *Proclaim the Good News: A Short History of the Church Missionary Society* (1985); Eugene Stock, *The History of the Church Missionary Society: Its Environment, Its Men, and Its Work,* 3 vols. (1899). Also see [Miss Childe], "Mrs. Jowett," in *The Finished Course: Brief Notices of Departed Church Missionaries* (1865), pp. 157–183.

Jocelyn Murray

Juanmartí y Espot, Jacinto (1833–1897), Roman Catholic missionary in Mindanao, the Philippines. Born in Llarvent, Lerida, Spain, Juanmartí entered the Society of Jesus after ordination to the priesthood in 1857. Having arrived in the Philippines in 1867, after four years in various apostolates he was sent to the Rio Grande mission in Tamontaka, Cotabato, where he spent the rest of his life, the last 22 years of it as its superior. From this Christian community of slaves ransomed from the Magindanao, intended as a Christian agricultural colony among the Muslims, he also exercised an apostolate among the animistic Tiruray of the mountains as well as making friendly contacts with the Muslim Magindanao. Though sharing many of the prejudices of his contemporaries against Islam, he mastered the Magindanao language, of which he published the first grammar and dictionary. Having been gradually accepted and trusted by the Magindanao, he was able to serve successfully as intermediary in various hostilities between them and the Spanish military. The mission with its school and hospital became a center of attraction for the Muslims. He died a year before the mission was dispersed with the withdrawal of the Spanish Jesuits during the Philippine Revolution.

BIBLIOGRAPHY Jose S. Arcilla, ed. and tr., *Jesuit Missionary Letters from Mindanao,* vol. 1, *The Rio Grande Mission* (1990), contains a considerable number of Juanmartí's letters from Mindanao in translation. See also Francis C. Madigan and Nicholas P. Cushner, "Tamontaka Reduction: A Community Approach to Mission Work," *NZM* 17 (1961): 81–94; Pablo Pastells, *Misión de la Compañía de Jesús de Filipinas en el siglo XIX,* 3 vols. (1917). Juanmartí's Maguindanao works are the *Diccionario moro-maguindanao-español* (1892) and *Gramática de la lengua de maguindanao según se habla en el centro y en la costa sur de la isla de Mindanao* (1892), together with the anonymously published religious work *Compendio de historia universal desde la creación del mundo hasta la venida de Jesucristo* (1888).

John N. Schumacher, SJ

Judd, Gerrit Parmele (1803–1873), American missionary and Hawaiian statesman. Judd was born at Paris, New York, and graduated from medical school at Fairfield, New York, in 1825. Converted in 1826, the following year he was appointed by the American Board of Commissioners for Foreign Missions (ABCFM) to serve as physician to the Sandwich Islands Mission. The same year he married

Laura Fish and sailed for the islands. Having developed great facility in the Hawaiian language and many professional contacts with the king and chiefs, he resigned from the mission in 1842 in order to become the king's translator, recorder, and adviser on finance. In 1843 King Kamehameha III was forced under the guns of a British warship to cede the kingdom to Great Britain. Judd as foreign minister drafted protests to be smuggled abroad; Britain and France then jointly guaranteed the independence of the kingdom. In 1845 Judd became interior minister, in 1846 finance minister, and in 1849 his diplomatic journey to Britain, France, and the United States achieved some progress in securing better treaty status. He represented the king in the drafting of the liberal constitution of 1852 but in 1853 was forced out of the government. In the constitutional convention of 1864 he opposed the effort of Kamehameha V to increase the royal prerogatives. In 1863 he became a member of the Board of the Hawaiian Evangelical Association, indigenous successor to the Sandwich Islands Missions. His book *Anatomia* was published at Lahainaluna (date not available). He died in Honolulu.

BIBLIOGRAPHY Laura Fish Judd, *Honolulu . . . from 1828 to 1861* (1880, 1928); *Missionary Album* (1969), pp. 28-129; *Missionary Herald* 69 (1873): 330-331, and many issues between 1828 and 1842. Standard histories of Hawaii, such as Ralph S. Kuykendall, *The Hawaiian Kingdom, 1778-1854* (1957), describe Judd's public activities.

David M. Stowe

Judd, Walter H(enry) (1898-1994), medical missionary to China. Judd, a Nebraskan, served in the U.S. Armed Forces in World War I. After medical school at the University of Nebraska, he went to China in 1925 under the American Board of Commissioners for Foreign Missions. He served in a mission hospital in Fukien (Fujian) Province (1926-1931). Frequent bouts of malaria forced him to return for a time to the United States, but he was back in China in 1934 to direct a mission hospital in Fenchow (Fenzhou), Shansi (Shanxi) Province. He lived under Japanese occupation for several months in late 1937 and 1938 before returning again to the United States, where between 1938 and 1940 he made over 1,400 speeches warning of Japanese aggression.

After World War II, as a U.S. congressman from Minnesota (1943-1962), Judd was an eloquent and vigorous defender of Nationalist China, playing an important role in U.S. Far Eastern policy. No U.S. former China missionary ever served in so high an elected office. He promoted overseas recovery programs. At the 1960 Republican National Convention he gave a rousing keynote address and nearly received the vice-presidential nomination. He was defeated in his Congressional reelection bid in 1962.

BIBLIOGRAPHY Ena Chao, "The China Bloc: Congress and the Making of Foreign Policy, 1947-1952" (Ph.D. diss., Univ. of North Carolina, 1990); Lee Edwards, *Missionary for Freedom: The Life and Times of Walter Judd* (1990); Floyd R. Goodno, "Walter H. Judd: Spokesman for China in the United States House of Representatives" (Ed.D. diss., Oklahoma State Univ., 1970); Edward J. Rozek, ed., *Walter H. Judd: Chronicles of a Statesman* (1980). Obituaries appeared on February 15, 1994, in the *New York Times* and the *Washington Post*. Judd's papers on national and international affairs are at the Hoover Institution, Stanford Univ.; several items are also in record groups 9 and 42 in the Yale Divinity School Library archives, New Haven, Conn.

Daniel H. Bays

Judson, Adoniram (1788-1850), pioneer American Baptist missionary in Burma. Born in Malden, Massachusetts, the son of Adoniram Judson, Sr., a Congregational clergyman, and Abigail (Brown), Judson graduated from Brown University (B.A., M.A.) and in the first class of Andover Theological Seminary (1810). His interest in missions began in 1809 when he read Claudius *Buchanan's sermon "The Star in the East." With ministerial friends he started the Society of Inquiry, a seminary study group on missions. In 1810 he was licensed to preach by the Orange, Vermont, Congregational Association preparatory to the pastoral ministry; however, he had strong inclinations toward overseas missions. In June of that year, Judson, Samuel *Newell, Samuel *Nott, Jr., and Gordon *Hall presented themselves to the Massachusetts General Association for missionary service, and the American Board of Commissioners for Foreign Missions (ABCFM) was formed as a result. Following an unsuccessful attempt to secure an appointment from the London Missionary Society in England, Judson persuaded the ABCFM to support three couples and two single men on a mission to the East. Judson was the lead candidate of the first commissioning service for American overseas missionaries held at Salem (Massachusetts) Tabernacle on February 6, 1812.

Following a sendoff with great fanfare, Judson and his bride, Ann (Hasseltine), sailed with the Newells for India in 1812. During the four-month voyage, the couple carefully studied the baptismal positions of the English Baptists in order to controvert the Baptist position; however, when they arrived at Calcutta, they adopted Baptist principles and were baptized by William *Carey. Upon their change of sentiments, the Judsons resigned from the ABCFM and plans were laid for the creation of a Baptist mission society in the United States.

By order of the British East India Company, the Judsons were forced to leave India. Surreptitiously escaping to Rangoon, Burma (Myanmar), in 1813, they established a station that became the first mission of American Baptists. Their work included evangelism and Bible translation. In 1824, following completion of Judson's first dictionary, the couple relocated to Ava, to establish greater influence with the government. However, Adoniram Judson was charged with being an English spy and was imprisoned in June 1824. In a 21-month period of incarceration during the Anglo-Burmese War, he suffered from fever and malnutrition and underwent a forced march. As a result of the courage and resourcefulness of his wife, he was released in February 1826 to serve as a translator for the Burmese government during negotiations for the Treaty of Yandabo. Ann Judson died of complications of smallpox later the same year.

To enlarge his efforts, Judson moved his mission to Moulmein in 1828. There, with the assistance of Jonathan *Wade, he built a church and school and continued work on the Burmese Bible, which he completed in 1834. Later that year, he married Sarah Hall *Boardman, widow of George Dana *Boardman and a gifted linguist and teacher. In 1845, following the birth of their tenth child, Sarah's health declined and the Judsons embarked for the United States. Sarah died en route; Judson completed the trip and remained in the United States for nine months' furlough. While his strength had been greatly reduced and he suffered chronic laryngitis, he was hailed as a hero throughout the Christian community.

While at Madison University in upstate New York, he met and married Emily Chubbock, a writer and educator. They returned to Burma in 1846 for continued work on an enlarged Burmese dictionary, which was finished in 1849. Shortly afterward, Judson contracted a respiratory fever and, attempting to travel to a better climate, died at sea.

BIBLIOGRAPHY Judson published several sermons and tracts, plus *A Dictionary of the Burmese Language* (1826) and a Burmese Bible (1840). Early works about him include John Dowling, *The Judson Offering, Intended as a Token of Christian Sympathy with the Living and a Momento of Christian Affection for the Dead* (1846); Rufus Babcock, *A Discourse Commemorative of the Life and Labors of the Rev. Adoniram Judson* (1851); and Francis Wayland, *A Memoir of the Life and Labors of the Rev. Adoniram Judson* (1853). Two important modern interpretations are Courtney Anderson, *To the Golden Shore: A Life of Adoniram Judson* (1956) and Joan J. Brumberg, *Mission for Life: The Story of the Family of Adoniram Judson; The Dramatic Events of the First American Foreign Mission, and the Course of Evangelical Religion in the Nineteenth Century* (1980). Judson's personal papers are in the American Baptist Historical Society in Rochester, New York, and Valley Forge, Pennsylvania.

William H. Brackney

Judson, Ann ("Nancy") (Hasseltine) (1789–1826), pioneer Baptist missionary to Burma (Myanmar). A school teacher from Bradford, Massachusetts, Ann Hasseltine met Adoniram *Judson when he stayed at her father's house during the organizational meeting of the American Board of Commissioners for Foreign Missions (ABCFM). Her decision to marry Judson made her the wife of one of America's first foreign missionaries, appointed in 1812 by the ABCFM. On their way to India, the Judsons were convinced of the biblical basis for believer's baptism, and accordingly they were baptized after their arrival in India. As a teacher committed to the evangelization of her pupils, Ann Judson observed with interest the mission schools of Hannah *Marshman. The Judsons waited with William *Carey while American Baptists organized themselves for missions until, in 1814, they were adopted by the American Baptists as their first foreign missionaries.

Prevented from working in India, the Judsons sailed to Burma (Myanmar). Ann did evangelistic work, adopted orphan girls, and educated children. In 1824, war broke out between the British and the Burmese, and Adoniram Judson was arrested with other foreigners. Ann saved his life by lobbying government officials, bringing him food in prison, and pressing for his freedom relentlessly over the next two years. After British victory and Adoniram's release, she died, exhausted by persecution and family responsibilities. Her last words were in Burmese. Her surviving child died shortly afterward.

With her translation of the Gospel of Matthew in 1819, Ann was the first person to translate any part of the Bible into Siamese (Thai). She also translated the Books of Daniel and Jonah into Burmese and wrote a Burmese catechism. While home on furlough in 1822 and 1823 to recover her health, she wrote *A Particular Relation of the American Baptist Mission to the Burman Empire* (1823), one of the earliest histories of an American mission. Her letters and example kept missions alive for American Baptists. Because of her numerous biographies, she remains the most influential missionary woman in American history.

BIBLIOGRAPHY Joan Jacobs Brumberg, *Mission for Life: The Story of the Family of Adoniram Judson* (1980); Ethel Daniels Hubbard, *Ann of Ava* (1913); James B. Knowles, *Memoir of Mrs. Ann H. Judson, Late Missionary to Burmah. Including a History of the American Baptist Mission in the Burman Empire* (1829); Arabella Stuart Willson, *The Lives of Mrs. Ann H. Judson and Sarah B. Judson, with a biographical sketch of Mrs. Emily C. Judson* (1851). A few of Judson's letters are in the American Baptist Historical Society archives in Rochester, New York.

Dana L. Robert

Judson, Emily Chubbock (1817–1854), third wife of Adoniram *Judson. Emily Chubbock grew up amid poverty in central New York. With great courage she acquired an education and became a teacher in the Utica Female Seminary and eventually a well-known literary figure, writing novels and magazine feature articles under the pen name "Fanny Forester." When Adoniram Judson returned to the United States in 1845, he was eager to find an able writer to do a biography of his second wife, Sarah. Recognizing Chubbock's outstanding writing ability, he met her. Very quickly she became his wife and in 1846 they sailed together for Burma (Myanmar). She had a great zest for life, a rich sense of humor, a vivid writing style, and a total love for Judson and the mission in Burma. She brought a lightness of touch and great gaiety to his life after many years of hardship and struggle. After the death of both Adoniram and a newborn son in 1850, she returned to the United States in 1851, where she assembled materials for Francis Wayland's famous biography of her husband, wrote three more books of her own, and cared for her daughter and five stepchildren. She died of tuberculosis.

BIBLIOGRAPHY Courtney Anderson, *To the Golden Shore: The Life of Adoniram Judson* (1956); Daniel Eddy, *The Three Mrs. Judsons* (1860); A. C. Kendrick, *The Life and Letters of Mrs. Emily C. Judson* (1860).

Paul Clasper

Judson, Sarah (Hall) Boardman (1803–1845), pioneer missionary to Burma (Myanmar). Born in New Hampshire, Sarah Hall grew up in Salem, Massachusetts, the oldest of thirteen children. Unusually precocious, she gained an early knowledge of composition, geometry, logic, Latin, and theology. When George D. *Boardman read her published poem memorializing a Baptist missionary to Burma who had died soon after arriving, he set out to meet her. He was delighted to find that this young woman of 18 shared his desire to be a missionary. They were married in July 1825 and soon departed for Burma. Forced to wait in Calcutta until the end of the Anglo-Burmese War, they began to study Burmese and thus had a basic knowledge of the language by the time they arrived in Burma in early 1827. They began their work in Moulmein and later moved to Tavoy, where she established a school for girls and worked on translating the Karen New Testament. Her husband opened a school for adolescent boys, and then began evangelistic itineration of Karen villages. Their baby daughter died in 1829, and George himself fell victim to tuberculosis two years later. Sarah, however, refused to give up and continued their work, journeying from Karen village to village, preaching and teaching, while caring for their son. In 1834 she married Adoniram *Judson, and though this required her to leave Tavoy and the Karen work, new missionaries had come to assume this responsibility and the Karen churches continued to multiply. She lived 11 more years and her companionship and encouragement enabled Judson to finish his translation of the Burmese Bible and begin the massive project of compiling a Burmese dictionary. Together they had eight children. Sarah translated some twenty hymns into Burmese, as well as Bunyan's *Pilgrim's Progress.* Because of her declining health, it was decided that she should return to the United States for medical treatment and rest. The Judsons sailed in 1845, but she died en route and was buried on the island of Saint Helena.

BIBLIOGRAPHY Courtney Anderson, *To the Golden Shore: The Life of Adoniram Judson* (1961); Fanny Forrester, *Memoir of Sarah B. Judson* (1848); Stacy R. Warburton, *Eastward: The Story of Adoniram Judson* (1937); Walter N. Wyeth, *Sarah B. Judson* (1889).

Alan Neely

Julian (6th century), first known missionary to Nubia. Julian was a Monophysite priest from Constantinople who evangelized Nubia (542–544) with the support of the Empress Theodora and was accompanied by an Egyptian bishop named Theodore. The king of the Nobades, a Nubian group, was converted. Julian returned to Constantinople after two years, though Theodore remained until 551. There seems to have been a rival, or subsequent, Orthodox mission backed by the Emperor Justinian that had more lasting effect. There were certainly Christians in Nubia before Julian, while the conversion of the Alwa and the south dates from after his time (c. 580). Nevertheless, though we know little about him, Julian remains as the principal apostle of Nubia.

BIBLIOGRAPHY U. Monneret de Villard, *Storia della Nubia Cristiana* (1938); P. L. Shinnie, "Christian Nubia," in *Cambridge History of Africa,* vol. 2, J. D. Fage, ed. (1978), pp. 556–588.

Adrian Hastings

Junípero Serra. *See* Serra, Junípero.

Junius (de Jonghe), Robertus (1606–1655), Dutch missionary in Formosa (Taiwan). Born in Rotterdam, Junius studied in Leiden at the seminary of Antonius *Walaeus, graduating in 1628. He was first sent to Batavia (present-day Jakarta) in 1629, and then to Formosa, where he arrived later that year. He worked for two years in the area around the Dutch castle Zeelandia in Formosa, and then, from 1631 to 1643, reached out to the indigenous population of Sinckan (present-day Hsinying). Considered in Dutch church history as the reformer of Formosa, he baptized about 5,500 adults and educated 50 primary school teachers. He proposed to send pupils to the Netherlands for theological training; he translated sermons and the Heidelberg Catechism, and emphasized the importance of teaching in the vernacular.

Upon his return to Middelburg, Netherlands, in 1644, Junius reported on missionary progress. He was involved in a controversy over his missionary methods because his successors in Formosa did not adapt their teaching to the Formosans as much as Junius did. Having ministered in Delft until 1653, he moved to a church in Amsterdam, where he educated students, including Philippus *Baldaeus, who were sent to the Indies. He thereby in effect reestablished the seminary of Antonius Walaeus.

BIBLIOGRAPHY Inez de Beauclair, *Neglected Formosa: A Translation from the Dutch of Frederic Coyett's 't Verwaerloosde Formosa* (1975); L. J. Joosse, *Scoone dingen sijn swaere dingen: Een onderzoek naar de motieven en de activiteiten in De Nederlanden tot verbreiding van de gereformeerde religie* (1992); J. J. A. M. Kuepers, *The Dutch Reformed Church in Formosa, 1627–1662: Mission in a Colonial Context* (1978).

Leendert J. Joosse

Junod, Henri Alexandre (1863–1934), missionary ethnographer in South Africa. Junod was born at Saint Martin, Neuchâtel, Switzerland, the son of the founder and pastor of the Independent Protestant Church. Educated at Neuchâtel, Basel, and Berlin, he was ordained in 1885 and served for two years as a pastor. Experiencing a call to mission service, he set sail for Mozambique in 1889 after training in Scotland and marriage to Emilie Biolley of Couvet.

His initial appointments in the Swiss Romande Mission were as a teacher at Ricatla and principal of the Bible school at Shiluwane, Transvaal. A gifted linguist, he published grammars in Ronga (1896) and Tsonga (or Shangane, 1909). His two-volume classic study of the Tsonga people, *The Life of a South African Tribe* (1912–1913), was judged in its day to be "the finest monograph written on an African tribe." His sympathetic analysis of traditional African beliefs and ritual behavior, including divination, set a high standard. Other interests included traditional African music and the taxonomy of African butterflies. Retiring to Geneva in 1921, he served as president of the International Bureau for the Defence of Native Interests and as consultant to the mandates commission of the League of Nations. He received an honorary doctorate from the University of Lausanne.

BIBLIOGRAPHY Works by Junod include *Manuel de conversation et dictionnaire ronga, portugais, français, anglais* (1896), *Les Chants et les Contes des Ba-Ronga* (1897), and *Mission Suisse dans l'Afrique du sud* (1933). Henri-Philippe Junod, *Henri A. Junod: Missionnaire et Savant, 1863–1934* (1934).

Norman E. Thomas

Justin Martyr (c. 100–165), early Christian apologist and martyr. Born to pagan parents in Palestine, Justin traveled throughout the eastern Mediterranean. His conversion evidently took place in Ephesus, after he made considerable study of philosophies and religions. He founded a Christian school in Rome.

What we know of him rests primarily on his extant works: a carefully constructed dialogue with a Jew he named Trypho, and a two-volume apology. Perhaps his most important insight was his insistence that the logos doctrine found in Greek philosophers could be used to claim that Christ the Logos was present wherever truth was known. For him Greek philosophy instructed Greeks in the way that the Old Testament instructed Jews.

Not so well read as Tatian, and lacking eloquence, Justin still holds first place among the second-century apologists. He honored and claimed the best from the prevailing Greek learning and culture while insisting that Christian revelation was both older and better. In Rome, after a lifetime of effective witness, he was denounced as a Christian, scourged, and beheaded.

BIBLIOGRAPHY Leslie W. Bernard, *Justin Martyr: His Life and Thought* (1967); Eric F. Osborn, *Justin Martyr* (1973); Kwame Bediako, *Theology and Identity: The Impact of Culture upon Christian Thought in the Second Century and Modern Africa* (1992).

Frederick W. Norris

Juvenaly. *See* Iuvenalii.

Kaahumanu (1772–1832), regent of Hawaii. Kaahumanu, who came to power after the death of her husband, King Kamehameha the Great, in 1819, was the leader in overthrowing the traditional religious taboos, while her son Liholiho, the official king, followed timorously in her wake. She received the first missionaries (New England Congregationalists) from the United States in 1820 and was immediately interested in Christianity. In 1822 she made the first of a number of tours of her kingdom in which she took the missionaries with her, encouraged literacy, and burned idols, many of which she ferreted out from their hiding places. With encouragement from missionaries, she enacted laws barring Hawaiian women from visiting foreign ships, and in consequence, was menaced by rioting sailors. She expelled the first French Catholic missionaries, an order which was circumvented for a time, and she later arrested twelve Hawaiians who had Catholic loyalties. With her strong character she also had deep affections and a warm piety. On her deathbed she said, "Lo, here am I, O Jesus. Grant me thy gracious smile."

Bibliography John Garrett, *To Live among the Stars: Christian Origins in Oceania* (1982); Ralph Kuykendall, *The Hawaiian Kingdom 1778–1854* (1938).

Charles W. Forman

Kafarov, Petr Ivanovich (1817–1878), Russian Orthodox sinologist and missionary. In 1840, after study at the Kazan seminary, Kafarov was ordained and sent as a missionary to Peking (Beijing). On a second mission to China in 1849, he was made archimandrite. In 1864, at the time of the launching of his third mission, he was made head of the mission. His major contribution to missionary work was through his philological and cultural studies, for he spent more time on academic pursuits than on the preaching and teaching work of the mission. He made an expedition with the (Russian) Imperial Geographic Society to Ussurisk, and frequently visited Buddhist temples. He mastered Chinese and translated several Chinese and Mongolian texts into Russian, as well as various Christian texts into Chinese. These included Scriptures, service books, teaching materials, and missionary literature. His translations proved of value not only for the China mission but also for those in Korea, Japan, and the Russian Far East. Not only were the translations used as such, but they helped greatly the work of translating such materials into Korean and Japanese. Kafarov died enroute back to Russia. He is best known for his Chinese-Russian dictionary, which was completed after his death by the consul general in Peking and published in 1889.

Bibliography Kafarov's translations include *Starinoe mongol'skoe skazanie o Chingis-khane, Puteshestvie daosskogo monakha Chuan-chunya na Zapad,* in *Rossiiskaya dukhovnaya missiya. Pekin. Trudy,* vol. 4 (1853), and *Kitaiskaya literatury magometan* (1887). Some biographical information is in S. A. Arkhangelov, *Nashi zagranichnye missii* (1899). Further information on his publications appears in A. Vinogradov, *Kitaiskaya biblioteka i uchenye trudy Imperatorskoi dukhovnoi i diplomaticheskoi missii v g. Pekine ili Bei-Tszine (v Kitae)* (1889).

Karen L. Gordon

Kafiar, Petrus (c. 1873–1926), indigenous evangelist in western New Guinea (Irian Jaya, Indonesia). Kafiar was born on Supiori Island (Biak) in western New Guinea, the son of a headman. At the age of seven he was kidnapped and subsequently ransomed by an Indonesian missionary couple at Mansinam. Baptized in 1887, he attended the mission seminary in Depok, Java (1892–1896), and became a teacher-preacher. After working in several places, he returned to his native village in 1908 and pioneered mission work in Biak.

BIBLIOGRAPHY F. J. F. van Hasselt, *Petrus Kafiar, de Biaksche evangelist* (n.d.); F. C. Kamma, *Dit wonderlijke werk: Het probleem van de communicatie tussen Oost en West op Nieuw-Guinea (Irian Jaya) 1855–1972. Een socio-missiologische benadering,* vol. 2 (1977), pp. 491, 531, 661ff.

Th. van den End

Kagame, Alexis (1912–1981), African Catholic linguist and author. Born in Kiyanja, Rwanda, Kagame was ordained a Catholic priest in 1941. Even as a student in Nyakibanda Regional Seminary (1936–1940), he spent all his free time studying and collecting the poetic literature of the Tutsi; he also did some composing himself, and wrote for various African journals. In 1950 he was the first African to become a corresponding member of the Institut Royal Colonial Belge (later Académie Royale des Sciences Coloniales; since 1959 Académie Royale des Sciences d'Outre-Mer). In 1952 his bishop sent him to the Gregorian University in Rome for doctoral studies in philosophy. His thesis, published in 1956, was *La philosophie bantu-rwandaise de l'Etre.* To a volume entitled *Des prêtres noirs s'interrogent* he contributed "La littérature orale au Rwanda," a comparison of Tutsi dynastic poetry with its equivalent in the Hebrew psalter. An expert in his mother tongue, he translated the Bible, the missal, and various liturgical texts into Kinyarwanda. Drawing mainly from oral sources, he wrote numerous historical works. Of these the most important are *Un abrégé des l'ethno-histoire du Rwanda* (1972) and *Un abrégé de l'histoire du Rwanda, de 1855–1972* (1975). He also wrote for his own people in the local language. Because of his political, social, and family background, he naturally became prominent in the independence movement of his country and so made enemies. He was professor at the National University of Rwanda, contributor to the "Histoire Générale de l'Afrique," and visiting professor at the University of Lubumbashi. He was also a member of the Institut International des Civilisations Différentes, the Commission de Linguistique Africaine, and the American Academy of Political and Social Sciences. He died in Nairobi.

BIBLIOGRAPHY F. Bontinck, "In memoriam Alexis Kagame," in *Revue Africaine de Théologie* 6 (1982): 113–115; M. Walraet, *Les sciences au Rwanda. Bibliographie (1894–1965)* (1966). See also obituaries in *Mondes et cultures* 42, no. 2 (1982): 228–230, and *Académie Royale des Sciences d'Outre-Mer* 28, no. 1 (1981), 67–68 (by J. P. Harroy).

Karl Müller, SVD

Kagawa, Toyohiko (1888–1960), Japanese evangelist and social movement leader. Kagawa was born in Kobe to Kame and Junichi Kagawa. In lonely years following the death of his parents at age four, he met Harry W. Myers and Charles A. Logan, missionaries of the (Southern) Presbyterian Church, U.S., and was baptized by Myers on February 14, 1904, at the Tokushima church. He pursued theological study at Meiji Gakuin in Tokyo and Kobe Theological Seminary. During his student days in Kobe he moved into the Shinkawa slum to serve the physical and spiritual needs of some 7,500 people. Between August 1914 and May 1917 Kagawa studied in the United States at Princeton Theological Seminary and then became involved in labor and peasants' movements in Japan and in organizing religious programs, with the Jesus Band of Kobe as the base of his work.

In 1921 Kagawa organized the Friends of Jesus. This Franciscan-like band of young people strove for spiritual discipline, compassion for the poor, and an evangelical life of witness. When Tokyo suffered a massive earthquake in 1923, he shifted the main emphasis of his work to that city. He promoted economic cooperatives in Japan and peace and social reform programs before and after World War II.

Kagawa was a prolific writer. Most of his writings are collected in the twenty-four volume *Kagawa Toyohiko Zenshu* (The work of Kagawa Toyohiko) (1964). His theological focus was on the redemptive love of God, manifest in the life of Jesus Christ, to whom people can commit themselves through a mystical experience of faith and intellectual creativity. Kagawa was known more as a Christian social reformer than as a religious leader both in and out of Japan, but he was fundamentally an evangelist throughout his life.

BIBLIOGRAPHY Toyohiko Kagawa, *Before the Dawn* (1925), *Love the Law of Life* (1929), *Meditation on the Cross* (1935), and *Songs from the Slums* (1935). The most helpful bibliography appears in Robert Schildgen, *Toyohiko Kagawa: Apostle of Love and Social Justice* (1988). See also George B. Bikle, Jr., *The New Jerusalem: Aspects of Utopianism in the Thought of Kagawa Toyohiko* (1976).

Robert M. Fukada

Kähler, Christiane (Mues) (1800–1871), German missionary deaconess in South Africa. Christiane Mues was born in Osnabrück, Germany, and was raised by an uncaring grandmother after her father's debilitating stroke and her mother's death. Against this background of an unhappy childhood, she had a crisis conversion experience as a teenager, and unwavering piety marked her subsequent life. She worked as a store clerk and for a while taught a girls' sewing class. In July 1832 she married Heinrich Kähler, a Rhenish Mission appointee. They left immediately to work at the Stellenbosch station in the Cape Colony. Shortly after arriving in January 1833, Heinrich drowned in a river, and three months later, Christiane gave birth to a son, who died in 1840. At first she taught newly freed slave women and girls at the Cape and ministered to sick and dying Africans; later she moved into the mission house, where she cared for a widowed missionary's children, oriented new arrivals, and received guests. Her deep devotion and spiritual power energized the mission. Kähler carried on such an extensive correspondence with the home base that she truly was the chronicler of the South African work. She remained in Africa until her death.

BIBLIOGRAPHY Gustav Menzel, *Die Rheinische Mission* (1978); J. C. Wallmann, *Leiden und Freuden rheinischer Missionare* (1856); Gustav Warneck, *Christiane Kähler, eine Diakonissin auf dem Missionsfelde* (1873, 1898); Johannes Warneck, *Christiane Kähler* (1939).

Richard V. Pierard

Kähler, Martin (1835–1912), German theologian and champion of mission. Kähler, a famous representative of "biblical realism" in nineteenth-century German systematic theology, has not always been recognized as a missiologist. Yet as a contemporary, colleague, and close friend of Gustav *Warneck at Halle University, he made a significant contribution to scholarly theological reinforcement of the Christian mission. In 1971 H. Frohnes collected and published Kähler's writings on Christology and mission, which demonstrate that for Kähler the Christian world mission, both as a privilege and an obligation of the church, has its roots in the atoning work of Christ and is therefore to be regarded as an integral element of the Christian faith. Kähler expressed and promoted this conviction not only in several exegetical and theological essays but also in a number of sermons, meditations, and book reviews, all of them accessible in the 1971 volume. There exists also a draft of an unpublished memorandum by Kähler, solicited by John R. *Mott, on the question "In what respects does the state of the Home Church affect the expansion of Christianity?" Kähler's distinctly critical reply was not used by Mott during the World Missionary Conference at Edinburgh in 1910, but it remains a significant statement of Kähler's convictions.

BIBLIOGRAPHY H. Frohnes, ed., *Schriften zu Christologie und Mission* (1971). For an analysis of some of Kähler's christological and missiological writings see C. E. Braaten and R. A. Harrisville, eds., and trans. *The Historical Jesus and the Kerygmatic Christ* (1964), pp. 79–105.

Hans-Werner Gensichen

Kahn, Ida. *See* K'ang Ch'eng.

Kalbermatter, Pedro (1884–1968), Argentinean evangelist, educator, and health worker. With his wife, Guillermina, Kalbermatter was a Seventh-day Adventist missionary among Aymara and Quechua Indians in southern Peru from 1919 to 1939. Born in Pilar, Argentina, he grew up on his father's farm and was educated as an Adventist. After a successful period as a businessman and farmer, he volunteered for missionary service and was invited to Peru by Ferdinand *Stahl, who was working among the Aymaras. Kalbermatter and his wife had been trained in nursing, and there was great need for their services. Adventist work began in Peru in 1898 and became heavily involved in health and education. Kalbermatter founded the first school for Quechua Indians in Lallahua (1920), and in the following years he organized twenty-five more Quechua schools. He was also an untiring promoter of the rights of the Indians. A big, tall man, in many instances he became quite literally a defender of the Indians against physical attacks from fanatics. Despite Roman Catholic opposition, the government of Cusco asked him to be head nurse of the state hospital. After retirement, he returned to Argentina and went back to farming in Crespo, until his death.

BIBLIOGRAPHY Barbara Westphal, *A Man Called Pedro* (1975) is a biography based on Pedro Kalbermatter's memoirs in Spanish, *Veinte años como misionero entre los indios del Perú* (1950).

Samuel Escobar

Kalkar, Christian (1802–1886), mission leader in the Danish Lutheran church. Kalkar was one of the most prominent clergymen, theologians, and mission leaders in the nineteenth-century Danish state church. Born in Stockholm, the son of a Jewish rabbi, he lived with his sister in Copenhagen after his father's death in 1812. He was baptized in 1823 into the Danish Evangelical Lutheran Church. He received a degree in theology from the University of Copenhagen in 1826. His post-graduate studies concentrated on church history and Old Testament. He received doctorates from the University of Kiel, Germany (1833), and Copenhagen (1836). From 1843 to 1868 he served as a minister, and he was chairman of the Danish Foreign Mission Society from 1861 to 1872. He was a pioneer in writing Danish mission history; his principal work, *Den christelige Mission blandt Hedningerne* (The Christian mission among the Gentiles), 2 vols. (1879), was translated into German as *Geschichte der christlichen Mission unter den Heiden* (1879). He was also a leader in the Danish translation of the Old Testament, authorized by the king in 1871. As a young man he had wanted to write about the true relationship between Christianity and Judaism, but not until late in his life was he able to devote himself to this study. Kalkar saw evidence of divine providence in the fact that Israel had succeeded in keeping herself separate from other peoples. In the end times, he believed, Israel would be at the head of the church as the Jewish people converted to Christ. He was skeptical of the effort to gather Jews into the Holy Land and into specifically Jewish-Christian congregations. At the same time, Kalkar was a strong advocate of mission to the Jews and he criticized the Danish church for its neglect in this endeavor. Before his death he had an opportunity to address the small group of people who founded the Danish Israel Mission in 1885.

BIBLIOGRAPHY Christian Kalkar, *De Cantico Deboræ* (1833), *Lamentationes critice et exegetice illustratæ cum præmisis disputationibus historico-criticis tribis* (1836), *Missionen blandt jøderne* (Mission among the Jews, 1868), and *Israel og Kirken* (Israel and the Church, 1881). Niels Bundgaard, *Dr. Christian Kalkars Betydning for dansk Kirkeliv og Missionsvirksomhed* (Dr. Christian Kalkar's significance for Danish church life and mission, 1951).

Flemming Markussen

Kalley, Robert Reid (1809–1888), independent Scottish medical missionary in Madeira and Brazil. Kalley was born of wealthy parents in Glasgow, Scotland. After medical studies he was a ship's doctor from 1829 to 1831 on routes between Glasgow and the Far East. Converted in 1834, he applied to the London Missionary Society (LMS) to serve in China as a medical missionary. Upon acceptance, he returned to medical studies at Glasgow, graduating with an M.D. in 1838. His marriage to Margaret Crawford broke LMS rules, however, and Kalley resigned from the society. Nevertheless in October 1838 the couple left for Madeira, hoping to go to China later. The success of his medical, educational, and evangelistic work in Madeira provoked fierce opposition by the Roman Catholic hierarchy and led to expulsion from the island in 1848. Some 2,000 of his converts also left at that time and migrated to the West Indies and to Illinois. In the following years Kalley visited these exiles and also worked in southern Ireland, Malta, and Lebanon. His wife died in Lebanon in 1851, but he continued his medical and evangelistic work in Palestine, beginning a small congregation in Safed. In 1852 he married Sarah Poulton Wilson, daughter of a Nottingham industrialist and niece of the politician Samuel Morley. There followed pastoral and evangelistic visits to the Madeiran "diaspora." In 1855 the Kalleys went to Brazil, where Jansenist influences in the Roman Catholic Church and the policies of Pedro II had created favorable conditions for their activities. They were helped from an early date by co-workers from the Madeiran "diaspora." In 1858 in Rio de Janeiro they established a church on Congregational principles—Igreja Evangélica Fluminense—today regarded as the oldest Brazilian Protestant church. In addition to their pioneering role, they are also remembered for their part in the struggle for religious liberty and their contribution to the hymnody of the Brazilian church. In 1876 they retired to Edinburgh, where they continued to support a number of evangelical causes. Hudson *Taylor, a friend of many years, led Kalley's funeral service.

BIBLIOGRAPHY William B. Forsyth, *The Wolf from Scotland* (1988); Michael P. Testa, *O Apóstolo da Madeira* (1963).

William Mitchell

Kals, Jan Willem (1700–1781), Dutch promoter of missions. Born in Düren, Germany, Kals attended a Jesuit grammar school, studied theology at Utrecht University (1722–1728), and was appointed a minister of the Netherlands Reformed Church in Surinam (1731). Wanting to see the conversion of the local peoples, he urged his church to engage in mission and protested to the colonial authorities against the slave trade and the expulsion of Indians. He argued that Indians and blacks were entitled to civilization and Christianization, and that therefore they should be permitted to attend the church services of the European colonists and to enroll in the schools that had been established for the colonists' children. Within two years the authorities sent him back to the Netherlands.

At home and in England, Germany, and North America, Kals continued his fight on behalf of Indians and blacks. In 1756 he published *Neerlands Hooft—en Wortel—sonde, het Versuym van de Bekeeringe der Heydenen* (The Netherlands' main and root sin, the neglect of the conversion of the heathen), and (as the second part of the same volume) *Nuttige en Noodige Bekeeringe der Heidenen in Suriname en Berbices enz., enz., waar zulk nogh Versuymt Word* (Useful and needful conversion of the heathen in Surinam and Berbice, etc., etc., where it is still neglected).

Kals spent from 1745 to 1756 in London, Oxford, and Bremen, studying languages and publishing books. From 1758 to 1774 he was in the United States, serving as minister of German Reformed immigrants in Pennsylvania. In 1774 he returned to the Netherlands to spend his final years. He died and is buried at Maastricht.

BIBLIOGRAPHY J. M. van der Linde, *Jan Willem Kals (1700–1781), Leraar der Hervormden, Advocaat van Indiaan en Neger* (1987; includes a bibliography and summaries in German and English).

Jan A. B. Jongeneel

Kam, Joseph (1769–1833), apostle of the Moluccas. Kam was born at 's Hertogenbosch, Netherlands, and died at Ambon, Netherlands Indies (now Indonesia). Born and brought up in the Dutch Reformed Church, Kam nonetheless was strongly influenced by the Moravian Brethren center at Zeist. In 1808 he first offered his services to the recently founded Netherlands Mission Society (NZG). In 1813 he was sent out by the London Missionary Society to Java as one of the first missionaries to the Netherlands Indies in the nineteenth century.

At Batavia (now Djakarta) Kam accepted an appointment by the colonial government as pastor of the large indigenous church in the Moluccas, the result of two centuries of Dutch East India Company missionary work. During the last 18 years of his life he was preoccupied on the one hand with church order and discipline, preaching, administration of the sacraments, and education (both religious and secular). But on the other hand, he devoted much attention to training preacher-teachers, printing and distributing Bibles, hymnbooks and Christian literature, erecting church buildings, promoting church music, and most of all to unceasing evangelistic endeavor. He defended the Calvinistic character of the church against Baptist influences introduced by William *Carey's youngest son, Jabez.

Kam's main field of work was among the scores of congregations at Ambon and adjacent islands, but he also traveled extensively, covering thousands of miles by sea, partly in his self-built schooner, to the remotest islands of eastern Indonesia. At his urgent request the NZG sent out a large number of new missionaries, whom he placed and supervised. Though his methods were not especially imaginative, he earned fame as the great promoter of modern mission in the Moluccas.

BIBLIOGRAPHY I. H. Enklaar, *Joseph Kam, "Apostel der Molukken"* (1963).

I. H. Enklaar

Kamma, F(reerk) (Christiaan) (1906–1987), Dutch linguist and missionary in western New Guinea. Kamma was born in the Netherlands, the son of a bargeman. He worked as a sailor and a baker, and through the local YMCA he was led to mission work. He studied at the Netherlands Mission Society training institute in Oegstgeest from 1925 to 1931. From 1931 to 1942 Kamma worked in western New Guinea (Irian Jaya). During an eight-year convalescence after internment in the Japanese camps, he took a Ph.D. in anthropology at Leiden University. Returning to New Guinea in 1955, he guided the Evangelical Christian Church of Irian to independence (1956) and became its first general secretary. His publications on cargo cults and mission history display a thorough knowledge of the oral traditions and the indigenous perception of the Christian faith. He also supervised the translation of the New Testament into the Biak language.

BIBLIOGRAPHY Kamma's publications include *Koreri: Messianic Movements in the Biak-Numfor Culture Area* (1972), *Dit wonderlijke werk: Het probleem van de communicatie tussen Oost en West op Nieuw-Guinea (Irian Jaya), 1955–1972. Een socio-missiologische benadering* (2d ed., 1977), and *The Origin and Sources of Life: The Threat to Life and its Defense against "Natural" and "Supernatural" Phenomena, Collected and Translated by Freerk Kamma,* vols. 3 and 8 of the Nisaba Religious Texts Translation Series (1975, 1978). Kamma's papers are in the archives of the Raad voor de Zending der Nederlandse Hervormde Kerk, Oegstgeest, Netherlands.

Th. van den End

Kamwana, Elliot Kenan (c. 1870–1956), African independent preacher and initiator of the Wacitawala (Watch Tower) churches in central Africa. Kamwana was a Lake Malawi Tonga. Though not yet baptized, he was a leader in a mass conversion movement in northern Malawi in the 1890s. Frustrated by the Livingstonia missionaries' suspicion of this revival, in 1900 he went to Blantyre, where he was baptized by Joseph *Booth as a Seventh-day Baptist in 1902. Going to South Africa to work, in 1907 he spent six months in Cape Town with Booth, being trained as a preacher for Charles Taze Russell's Watch Tower Bible and Tract Society. In September 1908 he was back in Malawi and began preaching a fiery millennial message of the expected return of Jesus in 1914. Within a year he had baptized nearly 10,000 people and alarmed the British authorities. The British exiled him but allowed him to return in 1914. The next year he was exiled again, this time to the Seychelles, although he had deliberately distanced himself from the *Chilembwe uprising. He returned in 1937 to find not only that many small Wacitawala congregations were flourishing in Malawi but also that the movement had spread across central Africa. Under Kamwana Wacitawala became a widely dispersed African indigenous church (separate from the Russellite Watch Tower Society), whose congregations have a large degree of autonomy. From 1937 until his death Kamwana lived quietly as a Wacitawala pastor.

BIBLIOGRAPHY David Barrett, *Schism and Renewal in Africa* (1968); George Shepperson and Thomas Price, *The Independent African* (1958).

Andrew C. Ross

Kanamori, Tsurin ("Paul") (1857–1945), Japanese evangelist. Kanamori was born in Kumamoto, Japan, and attended the school founded by L. L. *Janes, where he was converted to Christianity in 1875 and took the name Paul. Kanamori and several former classmates entered the first theological class of Doshisha University and graduated in 1879. This Kumamoto Band founded the Kimiai or Congregational Churches in Japan.

Kanamori served briefly in Okayama, sponsored by American Board of Commissioners for Foreign Missions missionaries. He became pastor of one of the largest congregations in Tokyo, then was called by Joseph Hardy *Neeshima to teach theology at Doshisha University.

In the early 1890s, higher biblical criticism undermined Kanamori's evangelical theological position. He demitted the ministry and for twenty years worked with a politico-social reform movement. He published his new theological beliefs under the title *The Present and Future of Christianity in Japan.*

The death of his wife prompted his return to the earlier evangelical conservatism. In 1915 he became a traveling evangelist, preaching a renowned three-hour sermon more than eight hundred times to over 300,000 people in all parts of Japan and among Japanese populations in Formosa, China, Korea, Hawaii, and Manchuria, and along the Pacific coast of the United States. His evangelistic campaigns are said to have produced some 50,000 conversions to Christianity. A total of 150,000 copies of his booklet in Japanese, *The Christian Belief,* were circulated. He was called by some "the Dwight L. Moody of Japan."

BIBLIOGRAPHY Paul Kanamori, *Paul Kanamori's Life Story Told by Himself* (1921) and *The Three-hour Sermon on God, Sin and Salvation* (1920).

Norman A. Horner

Kane, J(ames) Herbert (1910–1988), North American evangelical missiologist. Kane was born in Montreal, Quebec, graduated from Moody Bible Institute, Chicago, in 1935, and under the China Inland Mission with his wife, Winnifried Mary (Shepherd), went to China, where they worked in Anhwei Province (except for a furlough during World War II) until 1950, when they returned to Canada. Coming from the very conservative background of the Plymouth Brethren, Kane discovered the writings of E. Stanley *Jones soon after his arrival in China, and said they "opened up a whole new world of ideas and convinced [him] for the first time of the social and political implications of the Gospel." When he heard Jones speak in 1937, he said "[his] 'conversion' was complete." He taught missions at Providence (Rhode Island) Bible Institute (later named Barrington College) (1951–1963), Lancaster (Pennsylvania) Bible College (1963–1967), and Trinity Evangelical Divinity School (Deerfield, Illinois) (1967–1980). During his tenure at Trinity he served as president of the Association of Evangelical Professors of Mission, and he was the first evangelical to be elected president of the American Society of Missiology (1976–1977). Kane was one of the most productive and influential American evangelical missiologists of his time. After revising and enlarging Robert Hall *Glover's *Progress of Worldwide Missions* in 1960, Kane published *A Global View of Christian Missions* (1971), *Understanding Christian Missions* (1974), *Christian Missions in Biblical Perspective* (1976), *A Concise History of the Christian World Mission* (1978), *Life and Work on the Mission Field* (1980), and other books that were used extensively as texts in evangelical schools.

BIBLIOGRAPHY Kane's autobiographical reflections are in "My Pilgrimage in Mission," *IBMR* 11 (1987): 129–132. His letters and papers are in the archives of the Billy Graham Center, Wheaton, Ill.

Gerald H. Anderson

K'ang Ch'eng (Kang Cheng; *or* Ida Kahn) (1873–1930), prominent medical doctor and leader of the Chinese church. Born in Kiukiang (Jiujiang), Kiangsi (Jiangxi), to a poor family, K'ang Ch'eng was adopted by an American Methodist missionary, Gertrude *Howe, and was also known as Ida Kahn. During K'ang's childhood they lived in San Francisco, Japan, and China. In 1892, upon graduation from the Kiukiang girls' school, she and her friend *Shih Mei-yü studied in the medical school of the University of Michigan. Graduating in 1896, she was sent by the Woman's Foreign Missionary Society of the Methodist Episcopal Church as a medical missionary to Kiukiang. In 1901, she and Shih Mei-yü established the Elizabeth Skelton Danforth Hospital. Invited by officials in Nanchang, K'ang established a medical program in that city in 1903, supported by contributions of local people. Later, she studied literature at Northwestern University in the United States, receiving a bachelor's degree in 1911. She was given an honorary master's degree from the University of Michigan in 1920.

K'ang was frequently involved in welfare and relief work. Her hospital at Nanchang treated many wounded refugees during the revolution of 1911 and again during the Northern Expedition of 1926. When a flood struck Tientsin (Tianjin), she served as a member of the Tientsin Christian Union Flood Relief Committee to help the needy. In addition to taking care of patients, she was concerned about medical education, evangelistic work, social welfare, and women's issues. She was a delegate from China to a number of ecumenical and church conferences. She spoke at the Edinburgh World Missionary Conference of 1910 and attended the world conference of the YWCA in Berlin the same year. She also served as a committee member of the National Christian Council of China, formed in 1922. She was the author of *An Amazon in Cathay* (1912) and numerous articles.

BIBLIOGRAPHY K'ang's articles include "The Doctor's Opportunity in Visiting Homes," *Woman's Work in the Far East* 35, no. 4 (December 1914): 170–174 and "The Place of Chinese Christian Women in the Development of China," *Chinese Recorder* 50 (1919): 659–662. Her biography is found in Margaret Burton, *Notable Women of China* (1912). Her personal papers are in the archives of the United Methodist Church in Madison, New Jersey.

Kwok Pui-lan

Karrer, Otto (1888–1976), Catholic theologian and pioneer of the ecumenical movement. Karrer was born in Ballrechten, Germany, and became a member of the Jesuit order. In 1923 he joined the Lutheran Seminary in Nuremberg, but rejoined the Catholic Church in 1924 and thereafter lived in Lucerne, Switzerland, where he devoted himself to writing. Karrer went back to the sources of the Christian faith and translated many of them into German, including the New Testament and the *Imitatio Christi*. Of special missionary relevance was his book *Das Religiöse in der Menschheit und das Christentum* (1934). In it he presented non-Christian religions in a positive light and viewed them as signs of the permanent guiding presence of God among humanity. While he refused to see religions as merely natural phenomena, neither did he consider them ordinary ways to salvation. He pioneered a more open perspective in understanding other religions, a position that would be expressed in Vatican II.

BIBLIOGRAPHY Liselotte Höfer, *Otto Karrer, 1888–1976: Kämpfen und Leiden für eine weltoffene Kirche* (1985; 2d ed. 1986).

Fritz Kollbrunner, SMB

Kasatkin, Nikolai (Ivan Dmitriyevich) (1836–1912), first Russian Orthodox missionary to Japan and founder of the Orthodox Church there. In 1860, while a student at the Saint Petersburg Theological Academy, Kasatkin volunteered to serve as chaplain of the newly opened Russian consulate in Hakodate, Japan. Tonsured a monk with the name Nikolai and ordained a priest, he crossed Siberia and arrived in Japan in June 1861. He quickly tired of his limited post but was reinvigorated by a chance meeting with the missionary bishop *Innocent Veniaminov (later metropolitan of Moscow), who convinced him to master the Japanese language and culture. Nikolai threw himself into the task, engaging a samurai warrior and Shinto priest, Takuma *Sawabe, as his tutor. Initially belligerent toward Christianity, Sawabe was drawn into the faith, and in 1868 he became one of Nikolai's first converts. Meanwhile, the now fluent missionary translated the liturgical books of the Russian Orthodox Church into a highly literate form of Japanese and began celebrating services in the vernacular. Rather than adopting earlier Roman Catholic or Protestant translations of Scripture, he pioneered a fresh version utilizing vocabulary he assumed to be purged of non-Christian connotations.

Kasatkin's strict policy was to transform newly baptized catechumens immediately into lay catechists responsible for gathering seekers and organizing twice-weekly meetings to explain the meaning of the Creed, the Lord's Prayer, and the Ten Commandments. Lingering Japanese xenophobia made such an indigenous approach especially appropriate. By 1871 the number of converts reached the point that a formal mission was established by the Holy Synod of the Russian Orthodox Church. In response, a persecution was ordered by alarmed Hakodate officials. Soon afterward, the mission transferred to more strategically located Tokyo, purchased land for the future Holy Resurrection Cathedral (better known as *Nikolai-Do* [House of Nikolai]), and opened two schools. Funds flowed in from Metropolitan Innocent's Russian Missionary Society, and Nikolai's first two converts were ordained to the priesthood in 1875. By 1880 the mission required a resident bishop, and Nikolai was duly elected. Within ten years he supervised 215 mission stations, 24 clergy, 125 catechists, and 17,614 faithful. Though a dedicated Russian patriot, Nikolai neither fled nor was expelled from Japan when hostilities broke out between Russia and Japan in 1905, but he quietly cared for the 70,000 Russian prisoners of war. Following peace in 1906, Nikolai was elevated to archbishop of Japan, and when he died six years later, he left behind an organized, disciplined church prepared for continued growth. In 1970 he was canonized by the Russian Orthodox Church and is known as Nikolai of Japan.

BIBLIOGRAPHY John Bartholomew, *Missionary Activity of St. Nicholas of Japan* (M.Div. thesis, St. Vladimir's Seminary, 1987); Serge Bulgakoff, *The Foreign Missions of the Russian Orthodox Church* (1943), pp. 76–78; James J. Stamoolis, *Eastern Orthodox Mission Theology Today* (1986), pp. 35–40; Evgeny Steiner, "Nikolai of Japan," *Monumenta Nipponica* 50 (1995): 433–446; Proclus Yasuo Ushimaru, "Japanese Orthodoxy and the Culture of the Meiji Period," *St. Vladimir's Theological Quarterly* 24 (1980): 115–127.

Paul D. Garrett

Kats, Wilma (1920–1980), Reformed Church in America (RCA) missionary to the Sudan. Born in Holland, Nebraska, and educated at Central College in Pella, Iowa, Kats was the first RCA missionary to be sent to the Sudan, arriving there in 1948. She was joined by Robert and Morrell Swart to work among the Anuak in Akobo, in the Upper Nile region. In 1956 the congregations established there were organized as the Church of Christ in the Upper Nile. In 1964, when missionaries were expelled from the Sudan, Kats went to Ethiopia to continue work there. She contracted malaria with complications and returned to the United States in poor health, where she remained until her death.

BIBLIOGRAPHY Arie R. Brouwer, *Reformed Church Roots* (1977); Eugene Heideman, *A People in Mission: The Surprising Harvest* (1980).

Charles E. Van Engen

Kaundinya, Hermann Anandaraja (1825–1893), the first Indian to be trained as a missionary by the Basel Mission (BM). The son of a Brahmin lawyer, Kaundinya was born in Mangalore where he attended the traditional Kannada school. He was orphaned at the age of nine and was brought up by one of his uncles. At age 15 he was sent to an English-language school founded by missionaries of the BM. In 1843 he was baptized by one of his missionary teachers, Hermann *Moegling, who became one of his closest friends. His wife remained a Brahmin and refused to live with him after his baptism. Kaundinya was accepted as a missionary student, trained at the Basel seminary (1846–1851), and ordained at the Stadtkirche Leonberg in Württemberg before returning to India. His wife then agreed to join him but died soon afterward (1853). He was coeditor of a Kannada hymn book and editor of a Kannada Christian weekly; he translated school books into Kannada and worked with Moegling on translating the *Calwer Bible Dictionary,* a popular reference work among pietists in Germany. When called by the BM to work at the Mangalore catechist training center as a teacher and housefather, he applied to the BM home board for a wife from Germany. Marie Reinhardt (1837–1919), the daughter of the mayor of Schoemberg, near Stuttgart, was then asked by Moegling's mother if she was willing to become Kaundinya's wife. After being accepted by the BM home board she agreed to travel to India and marry him (1860). The couple had eleven children, five of whom died early. Two daughters became missionaries' wives, and one son worked in Ghana as a BM missionary trader.

BIBLIOGRAPHY *Lebensgeschichte des in Mangalur bekehrten Brahminen Hermann Anandaraja Kaundinya,* an autobiography Kaundinya read at his ordination (1853). Some reports from India are printed in BM publications. Kaundinya's handwritten letters and reports in German, as well as the couple's extensive private correspondence and his second wife's diary, are in the BM India archive, Basel, Switzerland.

Waltraud Ch. Haas

Keasberry, Benjamin Peach (1811–1875), missionary in Singapore. Keasberry was born in Hyderabad, India, to British parents who moved to Java in 1814. While working in Batavia he was converted and employed by the London Missionary Society (LMS) missionary Walter *Medhurst. In 1834 he attended Andover Seminary in Massachusetts. He returned to Singapore in 1837 as a missionary for the American Board of Commissioners for Foreign Missions but became a missionary for the LMS in 1839. When the LMS closed its mission in 1847, he stayed in Singapore as an independent missionary.

Aided by Abdullah bin Abdul Kadir, Keasberry translated into Malay the New Testament, *Pilgrim's Progress,* storybooks, and textbooks. In 1843 he built the Malay Chapel in Singapore, now known as the Prinsep Street Presbyterian Church, and opened a mission among the Chinese. In 1847 or 1848 he established a boarding school in Singapore with Malay as the medium of instruction. Alongside orphaned boys, a number of Malay princes attended the school. One of them became the sultan of Johore and another the raja of Kedah. After Keasberry's death, the school continued under government sponsorship. His congregations subsequently came under the supervision of Presbyterian missionaries.

BIBLIOGRAPHY J. A. B. Cook, "A Short Sketch of the late Rev. B. P. Keasberry," *The Chinese Recorder and Missionary Journal* 40 (1909): 413–416; J. H. Haines, "A History of Protestant Missions in Malaya During the Nineteenth Century, 1815–1881" (Th.D. diss., Princeton Theological Seminary, 1962).

Robert A. Hunt

Keith-Falconer, Ion G(rant) N(eville) (1856–1887), pioneer Scottish missionary to the Arabian peninsula. Keith-Falconer succumbed to malarial fever within six months of his arrival in Shaikh Uthman, a place just north of the harbor of Aden where caravan routes converged in the Arabian peninsula. Here he intended to set up a Christian ministry envisioned against a background of long reflection on the nature of Islam and the Christian obligation. Born in Edinburgh, Scotland, a gifted mathematician and linguist at Cambridge University, Falconer first fulfilled his Christian calling in a city mission in East London. His academic Arabic studies and contact with General Charles Gordon inspired him to think of an active location in an Arab context where his ideals of medicine and education as urgent components of the gospel could be pursued.

On his personal initiative, he went to Aden Territory (now part of Yemen). Having first visited Arabia, he then committed the cause to the Free Church of Scotland in a series of public addresses in which he expounded his perception of Islam as pointing beyond itself to Christ via the reality of its faith in divine unity. He saw his task also as a correction to the negative effect on the Arab mind of the British imperial presence in the Aden Territory. Although he died of malaria at an early age, his vision and talents inspired Samuel *Zwemer and Zwemer's brother, Peter, and Scottish and Danish recruits who took up his labors.

BIBLIOGRAPHY Robert Sinker, *Memorials of Ion Keith-Falconer* (1888).

Kenneth Cragg

Kekela, James (1824–1904), Hawaiian missionary to the Marquesas Islands. Kekela was ordained in 1849 and initially served a congregation at Kahuku, Oahu. In 1852 he went as cosupervisor on an expedition to place the first Protestant missionaries in Micronesia. The next year he was in Hawaii when a sailor returned from the Marquesas with a message from a prominent chief asking for missionaries. The chief was hoping for wider trade contacts. The Hawaiian church responded and Kekela volunteered for service along with eight others. He stayed in the Marquesas for 46 years. With his colaborers he established a Protestant community, but the Marquesans experienced disease, disruption, and despair to a far greater extent than other Pacific peoples, and the church never flourished. Eventually French Catholics won the allegiance of the majority of the people and Kekela was left to tend his small flock, watching his children intermarry and his family merge into Marquesan life. His most famous exploit was when he persuaded an enraged chief not to kill an American sailor. For this achievement he received an inscribed gold watch from President Abraham Lincoln. In his final years he returned to his homeland for retirement.

BIBLIOGRAPHY John Garrett, *To Live among the Stars: Christian Origins in Oceania* (1982), pp. 47, 140–141, 268–269; Nancy Jane Morris, "Hawaiian Missionaries Abroad, 1852–1909" (Ph.D. diss., Univ. of Hawaii, 1987), pp. 346–358.

Charles W. Forman

Keller, Otto C. (1888–1942), *and*
Marian (Weller) (1889–1953), missionaries to Tanzania and Kenya. Born at Parry Sound, Ontario, Canada, to devout Anglican parents, Marian Weller graduated from the Normal Training School and began her career as a schoolteacher. In 1909 she came into contact with the Pentecostal movement and soon after enrolled at the Rochester (New York) Bible Training School, directed by Elizabeth V. Baker and her sisters, and felt called to Africa as a missionary.

While at the Rochester school, Marian Weller met and married Karl Wittich, a Baptist minister and fellow student. The Wittichs left for Tanganyika (present-day Tanzania) in 1913 as independent Pentecostal missionaries. After three months, they became ill from drinking the water; Karl died, but Marian recovered and remained in the country to continue as a missionary. Five years later, she married Otto C. Keller, an American Pentecostal missionary who had come to Africa about 1914. They moved north to British East Africa (present-day Kenya), and, in 1924, affiliated with the Pentecostal Assemblies of God of Canada. Additional Canadian missionaries joined the work and a strong evangelistic and educational ministry resulted. The legacy of the Kellers can be found in the (Kenyan) Pentecostal Assemblies of God, a strong national church with indigenous leadership. After Otto's death, Marian carried on the ministry in Kenya until 1946, when she retired to Victoria, British Columbia.

BIBLIOGRAPHY Gordon C. Atter, *The Third Force,* 2d ed. (1965). Marian Keller, *Twenty Years in Africa* (c. 1933); Gloria G. Kulbeck, *What God Hath Wrought: A History of the Pentecostal Assemblies of Canada* (1958).

Gary B. McGee

Kellersberger, Eugene R(oland) (1888–1966) *and*
Julia Lake (Skinner) (1897–1986), Presbyterian medical missionaries in the Congo. Born in Cyprus Mills, Texas, Eugene Kellersberger was a graduate of the University of Texas (1911) and Washington University Medical School in St. Louis (1915). He also held a certificate from the London School of Tropical Medicine (1921) and a diploma in Tropical Medicine and Hygiene from the Royal College of Physicians and Surgeons in London (1922). At the Edna Kellersberger Memorial Hospital at Bibanga, named for his first wife, Edna (Bosché; 1888–1923), he treated over 10,000 cases of *trypanosomiasis* (African sleeping sickness) and wrote the chapter on this disease in the standard medical textbook, Strong's *Diagnosis and Treatment of Tropical Diseases.* He founded the Bibanga Agricultural Leprosy Colony and was decorated three times by the Belgian government for his outstanding medical contributions. Ordained in 1928 by the Upper Missouri Presbytery, Presbyterian Church U.S. (Southern), he preached every Sunday and was active in the governing bodies of the denomination. In 1938 he attended the First International Leprosy Congress in Cairo, Egypt, as an official representative of the United States. From 1940 to 1953, he served as general secretary of the American Leprosy Missions. The first Protestant member of the Père Damien Leprosy Foundation, he was also a member of the American and New York Societies of Tropical Medicine, the International Leprosy Association, the New York Academy of Sciences, and the Advisory Committee on Leprosy of the U.S. Public Health Service.

Julia Lake (Skinner) Kellersberger, his second wife (they were married in 1930) and constant travel companion, was an outstanding public speaker for missionary and leprosy causes. She was the author of nine books, including *Congo Crosses: A Study of Congo Womanhood,* the 1936 interdenominational mission book published by the Central Committee on the United Study of Foreign Mission.

BIBLIOGRAPHY Julia Lake and Eugene R. Kellersberger, *Doctor of the Happy Landings* (1949); Winifred K. Vass, *Dr. Not Afraid: E. R. Kellersberger, M.D.* (1986).

John R. Hendrick and Winifred K. Vass

Kelley, Francis Clement (1870–1948), promoter of Catholic rural missions in the United States. Kelley was born in Vernon River, Prince Edward Island, Canada. Ordained a priest in Nicolet, Quebec, he did pastoral work at Lapeer, Michigan, and served as a chaplain in the U.S. National Guard during the Spanish-American War. In 1905 he founded the Catholic Church Extension Society for rural white congregations, to complement the work of the Catholic committee of Indian and Colored Missions. In 1910 he obtained a pontifical charter for the society and remained its president until 1924. With headquarters in Chicago, the organization raised money to build and support rural churches, to provide railroad "chapel cars" and "motor chapels" for missionary priests, and to support priests in rural areas. He also founded the American Catholic Board for Missions, which, contrary to his desires, collected funds only for home missions. His outspoken condemnation of Mexican persecution of the Catholic Church won from the Mexican bishops his appointment as a monsignor. In 1924 he was named bishop of Oklahoma. His success among the state's African American community was overshadowed by his failure to reach the Native American and Mexican populations. He died in Oklahoma City.

BIBLIOGRAPHY Francis Clement Kelley, *The Book of Red and Yellow* (1915), *Blood-Drenched Altars* (1935), and *The Bishop Jots It Down* (1939). James P. Gaffey, *Francis Clement Kelley and the American Catholic Dream,* 2 vols. (1980).

Gerald P. Fogarty, SJ

Kemp, Johannes Theodorus van der (1747–1811), pioneer Dutch missionary in South Africa. Van der Kemp was born at Rotterdam, Netherlands, the son of a professor of theology. After service as an officer in the army, he went to Scotland where he received his medical degree in 1782 from the University of Edinburgh. He practiced medicine in Holland from 1782 to 1795. The drowning death of his wife and only child in a boating accident in 1791 led to his conversion.

He came into contact with the Moravian Brethren at Zeist, where he learned about the newly founded London Missionary Society (LMS). He applied to LMS and in 1797 was ordained for service in South Africa. Before leaving he also helped to found the Netherlands Missionary Society in Holland. Arriving in Cape Town in 1799, he left for Kaffraria and ministered among the Xhosa for two years, but saw no Christian conversions despite his contacts with King Ngqika.

In 1801 Van der Kemp shifted his concern to the distressed Khoikhoi (Hottentot) people in the Graaff-Reinet area. There he experienced tensions and conflicts, first with the colonists and later also with the government. In 1803 he founded Bethelsdorp, a mission station near Algoa Bay through which he hoped to evangelize and civilize, and build character and society among the Khoikhoi. From the beginning, however, Bethelsdorp was bitterly resented by the Dutch colonists, as well as by the Xhosa and Khoikhoi. Van der Kemp's identification with his "colored" flock, and especially his marriage in 1807, at age 60, to a teenage Malagasy slave girl, shocked both his foes and friends. New conflicts arose due to his struggle against slavery and his fight for social and economic equality for the Khoikhoi. Still, he remained the natural leader of the missionaries and was appreciated by the Xhosa. Some of the converted Khoikhoi gradually took the initiative as evangelists among their own people.

The missionaries at Bethelsdorp, in the face of much hostility from white settlers, rejoiced at the abolition of the slave trade in 1807. Van der Kemp composed a hymn for the day of public thanksgiving at Bethelsdorp to mark this event. He also wrote a commentary on Romans 13–16 and a textbook on midwifery for use at Bethelsdorp. When he died at Cape Town his funeral was attended by vast numbers of Cape inhabitants, including leaders of church and state. It was a testimony to his life and work as well as inspiration for many who faced discrimination and oppression.

BIBLIOGRAPHY In 1804 Van der Kemp published a catechism, *Principles of the Word of God for the Hottentot Mission.* I. H. Enklaar, *Life and Work of Dr. J. Th. Van der Kemp, 1747–1811: Missionary Pioneer and Protagonist of Racial Equality in South Africa* (1988); A. D. Martin, *Dr. Vanderkemp* (1931).

I. H. Enklaar

Kempers, John R. (1900–1995) *and*
Mabel (van Dyke) (1902–), missionaries of the Reformed Church in America (RCA) to Chiapas, Mexico. A graduate of Princeton Seminary, John Kempers was invited by the National Presbyterian Church of Mexico to pioneer work in Chiapas, the southernmost state of Mexico. Supported by the RCA, the Kempers traveled by boat and oxcart to Chiapas in 1925. Working first in Tapachula and later in the capital city of Tuxtla Gutiérrez, they began an evangelistic work that developed into strong churches and a Bible school, all officially related to the National Presbyterian Church of Mexico. The Kempers' policy of identifying with the national church, giving to local consistories and presbyteries final approval of projects, and relying on the national church for support of the work led to rapid church growth in Spanish-speaking churches as well as in five Mayan language groups. In 1943 they were joined by Garold and Ruth Van Engen; and in the 1950s the DeVoogds, the Meyerinks, the Stegengas, and the Hofmans came to work among the Mayan groups. By 1990 the Presbyterians in Chiapas numbered more than 200,000. The Kemperses taught at the National Presbyterian Seminary in Mexico City from 1965 to 1968, followed by retirement in the United States.

BIBLIOGRAPHY Arie R. Brouwer, *Reformed Church Roots* (1977); Eugene Heideman, *A People in Mission: The Surprising Harvest* (1980) and *A People in Mission: Their Expanding Dream* (1984). See also *Charm and Challenge of Chiapas* (RCA annual publication) during the years of the Kemperses' service.

Charles E. Van Engen

Kendall, Thomas (1788–1832), pioneer Church Missionary Society (CMS) missionary to New Zealand. Kendall was born in North Thoresby, Lincolnshire, England, and was among the first CMS missionaries in New Zealand in 1814. He started a school in 1816, but it closed two years later. He made important progress in understanding the Maori language, shaping its orthography and writing. He described its grammar with the help of Samuel Lee at Cambridge University and with assistance from Maori chiefs Hongi Hika and Waikato. He published the first Maori grammar later that year. While he was in England in 1820 he was ordained a deacon and a priest. Kendall's relations with his colleagues, including Samuel *Marsden, were strained by isolation and jealousy and exacerbated by his fiery temper. His involvement in the musket trade with Maori and his adulterous relationship with a Maori woman led to his dismissal in 1823. He made important (although limited) pioneering attempts to understand Maori religion and cosmology. Together with his wife, Jane, the mother of their nine children, he left New Zealand in 1825 and served as minister and schoolteacher in the British community in Valparaiso, Chile, for two years. From 1827 he farmed land in New South Wales, Australia. He drowned in 1832. Kendall was a tortured and tragic evangelical figure in a pioneering missionary context.

BIBLIOGRAPHY Judith Binney, *The Legacy of Guilt: A Life of Thomas Kendall* (1968); J. R. Elder, *Marsden's Lieutenants* (1934). Kendall's papers are in the Hocken Library, Univ. of Otago, Dunedin, New Zealand.

Allan K. Davidson

Kentigern (St. Mungo) (c. 525–612), missionary to Britons and Picts and patron saint of Glasgow. Hagiographic sources about Kentigern, none contemporary, radiate miracles from his conception to death. Royally if illegitimately born, allegedly brought up by St. Serf, and divinely directed to Cathures (Glasgow), Kentigern established a large Christian community there around 580. Ordained bishop of Glasgow by an Irish bishop, Kentigern evangelized continuously and extensively throughout a huge diocese, so that Glasgow became the religious center for the Britons. His enduring influence is confirmed by dedications that range from Invernessshire to Berwickshire and Cumbria, and he is even credited with founding great monasteries in Wales, at Llanelwe and Llancarfen.

BIBLIOGRAPHY Bishop Forbes of Brechin, *Kalendars of the Scottish Saints* (1871); E. Towill, *Saints of Scotland* (1978).

Winona Wall

Keough, George D(orkin) (1882–1971), Irish Seventh-day Adventist (SDA) missionary to the Middle East. Born of Irish parents in Crieff, Scotland, Keough was educated at the SDA British Training College in London, and entered the ministry in the south of England in 1905. He and his wife, Mary (Alderson), accepted a call to mission service in Egypt in 1909. Aware that an earlier intellectual approach to city dwellers had yielded slender results, he took up residence among the fellahin in a village in upper Egypt and sought to enter into the life of the community. He was more successful in influencing Copts, some of whom were converting to Islam, than in winning Muslims; nevertheless, his work sparked renewed interest in mission to Muslims among Adventists. After spending about 15 years in this work, he was transferred to Cairo as superintendent of SDA missions in Egypt and Syria. He and his German colleague, W. K. Ising, alternated in this position from 1923 to 1942. During this time they sent several prospective European missionaries to the School of Oriental Studies in Cairo, where they studied under Samuel *Zwemer. In 1942 Keough was temporarily assigned to the SDA theological seminary in Washington, D.C., to prepare missionaries for work among Muslims. He returned to Beirut in 1946 as head of the Voice of Prophecy, a Bible correspondence school, to develop Bible lessons in Arabic. Retired in 1955, he continued to teach Bible and promote missions at Newbold College (near London) for another decade. His final home was in Bangor, Northern Ireland.

BIBLIOGRAPHY Erich W. Bethmann, *Bridge to Islam,* (1950); Baldur E. Pfeiffer, *The European Seventh-day Adventist Mission in the Middle East, 1879–1939* (1981); "Egypt, Arab Republic of," and "Keough, George D.," in *Seventh-day Adventist Encyclopedia,* 2d rev. ed. (1996); Nabil G. Mansour, "Seventh-day Adventist Mission in Egypt" (unpublished paper, 1975), Adventist Heritage Center, Andrews Univ., Berrien Springs, Mich.

Russell L. Staples

Kepler, Asher Raymond (1879–1942), first general secretary of the Church of Christ in China. A missionary of the Presbyterian Church, U.S.A, Kepler and his wife, Jeannette (Fitch), served in evangelistic work in Chekiang (Zhejiang) Province (1901–1909), and in institutional work in Hunan Province (1910–1921). He was general secretary of the Nantao Institute, Shanghai (1921–1924) and organizing secretary for the National Convention of Young People's Societies of Christian Endeavor. Deeply committed to interchurch cooperation and church union, he was asked at the close of the 1922 National Christian Conference to take charge of organizing a general assembly to formally establish the Church of Christ in China (CCC). At the constituting general assembly of the CCC in 1927, Kepler was elected both stated clerk and general secretary of the CCC, the latter position continuing until his colleague *Ch'eng Ching-yi (Cheng Jing-yi) assumed responsibility in 1934. Thereafter, until his death, he served as associate general secretary, and served concurrently as executive secretary of the Missions Cooperating Council (1940–1942).

Kepler traveled widely in China and abroad, preaching the cause of church unity in China. In the early years of the war with Japan (1931–1945) he was asked by the Chinese Red Cross and other service agencies to organize help for wounded soldiers. He became the director of the National Christian Service Council for Wounded Soldiers, which by 1939 had nine regions and 973 full-time staff, plus thousands of volunteers. A colleague in a memorial tribute said, "From the beginning of his service, Dr. Kepler had a peculiar singleness of purpose—the upbuilding and strengthening of the church."

BIBLIOGRAPHY Articles by A. R. Kepler appear in the *Chinese Recorder.* Arthur Judson Brown, *One Hundred Years: A History of the Foreign Missionary Work of the Presbyterian Church in the U.S.A.* (1950); Wallace Merwin, *Adventure in Unity: The Church of Christ in China* (1974); Reginald W. Wheeler, ed., *The Crisis Decade: A History of the Foreign Missionary Work of the Presbyterian Church in the U.S.A., 1937–1947* (1950).

Donald E. MacInnis

Kerr, George McGlashan (1874–1950) *and* **Isabel (Gunn)** (1875–1932), Scottish missionary pioneers of leprosy treatment in India. George Kerr was born in Aberdeen and joined the Methodist society there. Through meeting Robert *Laws, he volunteered for missionary service in Africa. He took arts, divinity, and medical courses (though without graduating) at Aberdeen University and trained for the Wesleyan ministry at Didsbury College, Manchester. In 1901 he was appointed to Southern Rhodesia but was restricted to working among European settlers and soon returned home. In 1903 he married Isabel Gunn, who had just qualified in medicine at Aberdeen.

After a brief ministry in England, in 1907 the Kerrs entered missionary service in the Indian princely state of Hyderabad with the Wesleyan Methodist Missionary Society, George superintending an industrial school, Isabel working in hospitals. Both became stirred by the conditions of lepers in the area and attempted measures of relief. What began as an adjunct to their work became a principal concern with a substantial gift (from a Hindu) to set up a home for lepers, for which the nizam of Hyderabad provided a site at Dichpali. Meanwhile, a local mass movement of some 6,000 people into the church laid heavy pastoral responsibilities upon them. The leprosy home at first concentrated on relief and care, rather than treatment, until hydnocarpus treatment was developed in 1920. Isabel worked with its pioneer, Ernest Muir, and introduced it at Dichpali. The treatment (the most advanced until sulfone drugs came into use), with the imaginative development of the hospital and its rehabilitation services provided by George, made Dichpali one of the world's leading centers in the campaign against leprosy. George Kerr saw it as "very largely an Indian Institution and . . . an indication of the response of Indian people to the Spirit of Christ." The Kerrs each received the Kaiser-i-Hind medal in 1923. After Isabel's sudden death in 1932, George continued to superintend Dichpali until his retirement in 1938 to Cove in the West of Scotland where he assisted the local church of Scotland.

BIBLIOGRAPHY A. D. Miller, "A Memorial to Dr. Isabel Kerr of Dichpali," *Kingdom Overseas,* June 1936, pp. 137–138; *Minutes of the Methodist Conference,* 1950; Dermot Monahan, *The Lepers of Dichpali* (1938; rev. ed., *The Story of Dichpali,* 1948); A. F. Walls, *Some Personalities of Aberdeen Methodism* (1973). The Kerr papers are in the Centre for the Study of Christianity in the Non-Western World, Univ. of Edinburgh.

Andrew F. Walls

Kerr, John Glasgow (1824–1901), American Presbyterian medical missionary in China. Born in Duncansville, Ohio, Kerr graduated from Jefferson Medical College in Philadelphia, arrived in Hong Kong in 1854, and as successor to Peter *Parker, was in charge of the Ophthalmic Hospital in Canton for 44 years. He also founded in 1898 the first Refuge for the Insane in China at Canton, where he served until his death. It is estimated that during his career in China he treated 780,000 patients and performed 48,000 surgical operations. Kerr also translated 34 volumes of medical works into Chinese, was the author of many articles and treatises, and taught 150 Chinese medical students. One of his students in 1886 was Sun Yat-sen, who later became the first president of the Chinese republic. Robert E. *Speer, in the *Monthly Missionary Survey,* wrote of him, "Vast as was his distinctly medical work, Dr. Kerr was above all things a missionary. He never lost an opportunity to preach Christ. Kindly, just, dignified in his manner, he was always at work doing good and commending Christ to the Chinese.... He was a missionary first, and all his medical knowledge was used to commend the Gospel." He was buried in the Protestant cemetery outside Canton, near three of his missionary colleagues, Dr. Dyer *Ball, Dr. Henry V. Noyes, and Dr. Joseph C. Thomson.

BIBLIOGRAPHY C. C. Seldon, "Life of John G. Kerr," *Chinese Medical Journal* (April 1935); William Warder Cadbury and Mary Hoxie Jones, *At the Point of a Lancet: One Hundred Years of the Canton Hospital, 1835–1935* (1935), pp. 101–143.

Gerald H. Anderson

Kersten, Christoph (1733–1796), Moravian tailor and missionary to Surinam. Kersten was born at Dorse Staats in der Altmark, Germany. He settled in the Moravian community of Herrnhut in July 1758. In 1759 he was admitted to the Herrnhut Holy Communion and worked in the Schreiber-Collegium and as house manager in the seminary.

In 1765 he was ordained a deacon and was sent as a missionary to Surinam, where he spent the first year in language study and worked as a tailor. He was married to Anna Maria Paulson, a widow, in 1768. The next year he began service in Paramaribo, where he continued his trade and established a cottage industry that grew into a prosperous business in the interests of the church. He returned to Europe in 1784 and retired in Gnadau, where he died.

The small tailor shop in Paramaribo became the center for a large mercantile enterprise of Moravian missions that supported the work in Surinam and beyond for many years, at one time forming the largest holding of the worldwide Moravian Church Foundation. In recent years this work has been placed under a national board of governors and continues to support diverse mission efforts in Surinam.

BIBLIOGRAPHY A. Helman, *Merchant, Mission, and Meditation* (1968); *Nachrichten aus der Brüder-Gemeine* (1876).

Albert H. Frank

Kevin, Mother (Kearney, Teresa) (1875–1957), founder of the Franciscan Missionary Sisters for Africa. Born in County Wicklow, Ireland, Teresa Kearney entered the Franciscan convent at Saint Mary's Abbey, London, in 1892, taking the name "Sister Kevin." Five years later, she volunteered to go to Uganda at the request of Bishop Henry *Hanlon of the Mill Hill Missionaries. She was soon struck by the inadequacy of the church's response to sickness and disease there. She was especially concerned with the problem of leprosy and the inadequacy of maternity and child care services. Encouraged by her bishop, she set up several dispensaries, clinics, and a hospital. During World War I she was made a Member of the Order of the British Empire by the king of England for her treatment of soldiers during the East Africa campaign. In 1923 in Nsambya, Sister Kevin founded the Congregation of the Little Sisters of Saint Francis, a community of African nuns for teaching and nursing; she was appointed superior, with the title "Mother." In 1928 she founded an exclusively missionary novitiate in England to serve her growing number of convents in Uganda. Both Mother Kevin and her bishop had long since concluded that the major obstacle to a meaningful Catholic medical apostolate was the church's refusal to allow priests and nuns to practice maternity nursing, medicine, and surgery. She was one of a group of bishops and others who made representations in Rome in the late 1920s and early 1930s to have the prohibition modified or withdrawn. (Repeal eventually came in 1936.) In 1935 she opened an Irish novitiate at Mount Oliver, near Dundalk. This was to become the headquarters of the Franciscan Missionary Sisters for Africa, which was established as a separate missionary order in 1952. Today sisters of the order work in hospitals, clinics, schools, and social centers in Uganda, Kenya, Zambia, and South Africa.

BIBLIOGRAPHY Edmund M. Hogan, *The Irish Missionary Movement* (1990); Marian Keaney, *They Brought the Good News: Modern Irish Missionaries* (1980).

Edmund M. Hogan, SMA

Keysser, Christian (J. E.) (1877–1961), German Lutheran missionary in New Guinea. Keysser was born in Bavaria, was trained at the seminary of the Neuendettelsau Mission (1895–1899), and was sent to northeastern New Guinea (Papua) in 1899, where he lived and later headed the mission station at Sattelberg. He analyzed the local Kate language; collected ethnographic, geographic, and botanical data; soon became aware of the different quality of the language-associated cognitive behavior of Papuan and Melanesian peoples; and acquired a high reputation among them. His insights decisively changed his approach to frontier missions. He advocated using evangelists from the established indigenous church under the guidance of missionaries; culturally appropriate proclamation of the gospel, starting with the concept of God; content before form; and an emphasis on an integral approach, considering religious and secular interests as equally important. He compiled hymns, translated parts of the New Testament, wrote teaching materials, and trained evangelists. On reconnaissance trips he explored the region of the Adler River north of Lae and the Finisterre Mountains; he was appointed corresponding member of the German Geographical Society for his first ascent of Mount Saruwaged.

In 1920 Keysser went to Germany with his family and was not permitted to return to New Guinea because of the political situation during and after World War I. He worked on his ethnographic and linguistic data and published a dictionary of the Kate language in 1925. In 1929 the University of Erlangen awarded him an honorary doctorate for his scientific achievements. A member of the Deutsche Evangelische Missionsrat, he was a leading figure in German missions. At the mission seminary in Neuendettelsau he trained a new generation of missionaries, sensitive to the mentality and culture of the people among whom they worked. As mission inspector, he advised and encouraged missionaries and other missions, especially during the oppressive Nazi period. His strong sense of national and cultural identification was criticized during the denazification process, and he lost all his offices, most of which his former student Georg F. *Vicedom took over.

BIBLIOGRAPHY Christian Keysser, *Anutu im Papualande* (1926), *Eine Papuagemeinde* (1929, Eng. tr., *A People Reborn,* 1980), *Gottes Weg ins Hubelan* (1936), *Lehret alle Völker* (1960), and *Das bin bloss ich* (1966). Wilhelm Fugmann, *Christian Keysser: Bürger zweier Welten* (1985); G. F. Vicedom, *Church and People in New Guinea* (1961). Keysser wrote several hundred essays, reports, treatises, and books that were published in church journals or preserved in manuscript in the archives of the Missionswerk der Evang.-Luth. Kirche in Bayern at Neuendettelsau.

Klaus Müller

Khama III (c. 1835–1923), eldest son of Chief Sekgoma I of the Ngwato people of Bechuanaland (now Botswana). In about 1858 Khama (correctly Kgama) and his father met missionaries of the (Lutheran) Hermannsburg Mission while in exile as guests of Sechele of the BaKwena. One of the missionaries, Heinrich C. Schulenburg, went home with them, and Khama joined the church. Khama's father objected to the practices of the new faith and was exiled in 1875; Khama then ruled at Shoshong. He worked hand in hand with missionaries of the London Missionary Society (LMS; the Lutherans withdrew), and together they labored to build up a strong church. In this partnership Khama—who was known as Khama the Great and Khama the Good—was the senior partner. The LMS church he helped create was very much a state church for the BaNgwato, and indeed no rival was allowed. Missionaries who offended Khama were soon ordered out of his kingdom.

Khama was publicly praised by the LMS for his prohibition of the liquor trade and the drinking of spirits, his observance of the Sabbath, and his curtailing of traditional ceremonies such as rainmaking and the initiation rites for youth. He welcomed the offer of British protection in 1885. In 1895 he journeyed to Britain with fellow chiefs to oppose Cecil Rhodes, who was demanding administrative rights over the protectorate. He continued to rule his people strictly until his death.

BIBLIOGRAPHY J. Mutero Chirenje, *Chief Kgama and His Times c. 1835–1923* (1978) and *A History of Northern Botswana 1850–1910* (1977); Anthony Dachs, *Khama of Botswana* (1971).

Gordon M. Haliburton

Khrisanf (Shchetkovsky) (1871–1906), pioneer Russian Orthodox missionary to Korea. Upon graduating in 1895 from the Theological Academy in the city of Kazan (West Siberia), which was at that time the principal educational center for missionaries, Khrisanf was ordained and sent to evangelize the Kalmycks, who lived between the Don and Volga rivers in Southeast Russia. He spent five years there and then was appointed the superior of the mission in Korea. He arrived in Seoul in 1900, apparently the first Orthodox missionary in the area. After initial pastoral work among Russian settlers in Korea and Korean language study, he consecrated an Orthodox church in Seoul and began work among Koreans. The first fruit of his labors were Koreans who had long before converted to Christianity when they had lived at the Russian Border but who had forgotten almost all they knew about the faith (including sometimes their own Christian names). Khrisanf conducted a recatechization of these people who had lived for years without church and clergy. He translated liturgical books into Korean, established a school for Korean children, and constructed a mission compound near Seoul. He made several missionary trips throughout Korea on horseback. He visited "the Korean Mount Athos," a cluster of 40 Buddhist monasteries in the Diamond mountains, and conducted theological dialogues with the monks. He wrote in his travel diary, "Monks of all nations are usually very good people." During the Russo-Japanese war, Korea was occupied by the Japanese and all Russians had to leave. In 1904 the mission property was closed and Khrisanf returned to Russia, where he was consecrated bishop of Yelizavetgrad. He died of tuberculosis.

BIBLIOGRAPHY Khrisanf Shchetkovsky, *Iz Pisem Koreiskogo Missionera* (From letters of a Korean missionary) (1904) and *Ot Seoula Do Vladivostoka* (From Seoul to Vladivostok) (1905). See also S. Bolshakoff, *The Foreign Missions of Russian Orthodox Church* (1943); L. Anisimov, "The Orthodox Mission in Korea," *Journal of the Moscow Patriarchate* (1991), no. 3.

Evgeny S. Steiner

Kidder, Daniel Parish (1815–1891), pioneer American Methodist missionary in Brazil. As a result of an 1835 investigative tour by Fountain E. Pitts of the Methodist Episcopal Church, reporting on spiritual conditions in Brazil, Kidder was sent to begin Methodist work in Rio de Janeiro, arriving in January 1838. The American Bible Society made consignments of Scriptures to Kidder for distribution, and he opened a mission home, preached, and visited with people. His work aroused opposition from Catholic priests, one of whom wrote *O cathólico, o methodista,* which strongly attacked Kidder. In 1840, his wife, Cynthia Harriet (Russell), died, leaving two small children, so Kidder returned to a Methodist pastorate in New Jersey. In 1844 he became editor of Sunday school publications for the denomination. From 1856 to 1871 he taught practical theology at Garrett Biblical Institute, then joined the faculty at Drew Seminary. From 1880 to 1887 he was secretary of the Methodist Episcopal Board of Education. He died in Evanston, Illinois.

BIBLIOGRAPHY Harlan P. Beach et al., *Protestant Missions in South America* (1900); G. E. Strobridge, *Biography of the Rev. Daniel Parish Kidder, D.D., LL.D.* (1894).

Pablo A. Deiros

Kidder, Mary Eddy (c. 1845–1910), Reformed Church in America missionary to Japan. Kidder arrived in Yokohama, Japan, in 1869 and began teaching four Japanese girls in 1870. Very soon she opened a girls' day school under the patronage of the governor of the port. This led later in the 1870s to the establishment of the Ferris Seminary, a school for women in Yokohama, which has had a long-standing reputation for quality education. She married E. Rothesay Miller in July 1873. Her missionary service in Japan continued until her death.

BIBLIOGRAPHY Arie R. Brouwer, *Reformed Church Roots* (1977); *Tercentenary Studies: Reformed Church in America* (1928). See also material in RCA archives, New Brunswick Theological Seminary, New Brunswick, N.J.

Charles E. Van Engen

Kiernander, John Zacharias (1710 or 1711–1799), first Protestant missionary to Bengal. Kiernander was born in Akstad, Sweden, and educated both at Uppsala University and at Halle, Germany. In 1739 he responded to a request by the Society for the Propagation of Christian Knowledge for a worker at Cuddalore in Bengal, and after ordination he went to India via London, arriving there in 1740. He rapidly built up a congregation and gained some financial security by marrying an English woman of modest means. When the French captured the city in 1758, he was expelled and relocated in Calcutta, where he opened a school and mission and occasionally preached in nearby Serampore. When his wife died three years later, he married a wealthy English widow, thereby acquiring social status and money to expand the work. Because the Protestant church in Calcutta had been destroyed in the 1756 uprising, he built a new structure, along with a school and mission house, all at his own expense. Completed in 1770, it was later known as the Old

Church, or Mission Church. However, his entrance into high society hurt the effectiveness of his ministry, and his second wife's death in 1773, as well as some bad business dealings, ruined him financially. After losing the property in a bankruptcy proceeding in 1787, he became chaplain at the Dutch settlement of Chinsurah. When war broke out in 1795, he returned to Calcutta and died destitute and forgotten.

BIBLIOGRAPHY John Carne, *Lives of Eminent Missionaries* (1832); James Hough, *The History of Christianity in India* (vol. 4, 1845); Herman Sandegren, *Sveriges Första Missionär i Indien: J. Z. Kiernander och Hans Tid* (1924); G. F. Westcott, *175 Years at the Old or Mission Church, Calcutta* (1946).

Richard V. Pierard

Kigozi, Blasio (c. 1909–1936), East Nigerian revival pioneer. Born of Mugandan parents, Kigozi was educated in Uganda. In 1928 he was ordained deacon by the Anglican Church of Uganda and posted to Gahini, in eastern Rwanda. During 1929 and 1930, a severe famine struck, killing thousands. With his elder brother, Simeoni Nsimbambi, Kigozi then entered into a new charismatic experience of the Holy Spirit, joining a group of churchmen called Abaka (Men on fire). They then began eight years of ceaseless village-to-village itineration and preaching as the Rwanda Revival, begun in Gahini in 1927, gathered momentum. In late 1935 Kigozi took the lead in a great ten-day Anglican Revival convention in Kabale, accompanied by outbreaks of pentecostal enthusiasm. Shortly after, in January 1936, Kigozi was called back to Uganda to attend the church's synod in Kampala, but on the way he contracted tick fever. At the synod he delivered a fervent appeal to Ugandan clergy on the need for repentance and revival but then died suddenly in a hospital in Mengo before the synod's close, crying "Awake! Awake!" Waves of revival swept through the Church of Uganda throughout 1937 and then across the entire country. Kigozi may be regarded as the major founder and developer of the East African Revival in its first decade as it began its rapid spread across East and Central Africa.

BIBLIOGRAPHY Joe E. Church, *Awake Uganda* (c. 1940), provides a biography of Blasio Kigozi. Church's later work, *Forgive Them: The Story of an African Martyr* (1967), is a biography of Kigozi's Rwandese protégé, Tutsi pastor Yona Kanamuzeyi, who was murdered in 1964. See also Church's *Quest for the Highest: The East African Revival* (1982); A. C. Stanley Smith, *Road to Revival: The Story of the Rwanda Mission* (1946).

David B. Barrett

Kijne, I(zaak) (Samuel) (1899–1970), Dutch missionary, remembered as the father of the Evangelical Christian Church of New Guinea (Irian Jaya). Born at Vlaardingen, Netherlands, Kijne completed teacher training and received missionary and linguistic training in the Netherlands and Germany (1918–1923). In 1923 he went to New Guinea. There he founded a training school for teacher-preachers (from 1925 onward, located in Miei, on the north coast), which he led until 1941. After internment by the Japanese (1942–1945), he became the leader of Dutch mission work in New Guinea (1948–1953) and rector of the theological school in Serui (1955–1958). He belonged to a generation of Dutch missionaries who had freed themselves of the limitations of pietism, and he took a different attitude toward indigenous religion and culture from most missionaries before him. He collected the regional mythologies and made them the object of ethnological and theological study. He was a gifted musician and composed five books of hymns, one of which was used by many Indonesian churches for half a century. He educated the first generation of church leaders and wrote the church order, liturgy, and catechism of the incipient church of Irian.

BIBLIOGRAPHY F. C. Kamma, *Dit wonderlijke werk: Het probleem van de communicatie tussen Oost en West op Nieuw-Guinea (Irian Jaya), 1855–1972. Een socio-missiologische benadering,* vol. 2 (1977), pp. 721ff., 752ff., bibliography. Kijne's papers are in the archives of the Raad voor de Zending der Nederlandse Hervormde Kerk, Oegstgeest, Netherlands.

Th. van den End

Kilbourne, Ernest Albert (1865–1928), cofounder of the Oriental Missionary Society (OMS). Born in Niagara Falls, Ontario, Canada, Kilbourne was attracted to telegraphy and was assigned to the Chicago office of Western Union, where he met Charles *Cowman and later became Cowman's first convert. Together they organized the Telegraphers Mission Band, destined to be the foundation of the OMS. In August 1902, some 18 months after the Cowman's arrived in Japan, Kilbourne and his wife joined them in Toyko. Some of the mission's most effective programs grew out of Kilbourne's prayer life and vision. He began the mission magazine *Electric Messages,* which he edited until his death. He played a leading role in expansion of OMS into Korea after 1906 and into China in the 1920s. With Cowman he organized and supervised the Great Village Campaign (1917–1918), an attempt by dozens of single men to reach all 10,300,000 homes in Japan, distributing gospel tracts and sharing the gospel. At Cowman's death in 1924, Kilbourne became president of OMS.

The Kilbournes had three children. Their son, Edwin Lawson (Bud) Kilbourne, made his own 65-year contribution to OMS beginning in 1915. Three of his sons have been missionaries of OMS as well.

BIBLIOGRAPHY Lettie B. Cowman, *Charles E. Cowman: Missionary Warrior* (1928); Robert D. Wood, *In These Mortal Hands* (1983).

Everett N. Hunt, Jr.

Kilbuck, John Henry (1861–1922), pioneering Moravian missionary and educator in Alaska. Kilbuck was born in Kansas, a descendant of the Delaware Indian chief Gelelemend, who was baptized by the Moravian missionary David *Zeisberger in 1789. He was the first Native American graduate of Moravian College and Theological

Seminary in Bethlehem, Pennsylvania. After his ordination in 1885, Kilbuck and his wife, Edith (Romig), the daughter of the superintendent of the Moravian Indian mission in Kansas, volunteered to begin a mission field in the Kuskokwim region of Alaska, along with William and Caroline *Weinland. When ill health forced the Weinlands to withdraw in 1887, the Kilbucks took sole charge of the new work. For 37 years they were active as mediators between Yup'ik and Western cultures, preaching to the Eskimos not only the Christian gospel but also the virtues of Western civilization and education, while at the same time explaining the complexities and value of the Yup'ik way of life to the missionary authorities in Pennsylvania. In 1900 they left mission service and Alaska but returned in 1905 when Kilbuck accepted an appointment with the U.S. Bureau of Education. He taught at Barrow and Wainwright in the north and at Douglas in the southeast before returning to the Kuskokwim as teacher (1911), assistant superintendent (1916), and district superintendent (1919) at Akiak. In July 1921, seven months before his death, Kilbuck reentered the service of the Moravian Church.

BIBLIOGRAPHY Ann Fienup-Riordan, *The Real People and the Children of Thunder: The Yup'ik Eskimo Encounter with Moravian Missionaries John and Edith Kilbuck* (1991) and *The Yup'ik Eskimos as Described in the Travel Journals and Ethnographic Accounts of John and Edith Kilbuck* (1988); James W. Henkelman and Kurt Vitt, *Harmonious to Dwell: The History of the Alaska Moravian Church, 1885–1985* (1985); Anna B. Schwalbe, Gertrude Trodahl, and Harry Trodahl, *Dayspring on the Kuskokwim: The Story of Moravian Missions in Alaska* (1985). Kilbuck's papers, including extensive diaries and travel accounts and a large correspondence between him and his wife, are in the Moravian archives, Bethlehem, Pennsylvania.

Otto Dreydoppel, Jr.

Kilger, Laurenz (1890–1964), Catholic missiologist. Born in Munich, Germany, Kilger became a Benedictine monk of Saint Ottilien, at Saint Ottilien, Germany. In 1910 and 1911 he was one of the first students of Joseph *Schmidlin at the University of Münster. From 1920 to 1925 he lectured in Rome at Urbaniana University and St. Anselmo, then worked in Saint Ottilien, mainly as an editor. In 1936 he moved to Uznach, Switzerland (probably to escape the Nazis), and edited the Benedictine missionary magazine. In 1958 he moved to Fribourg, where he had already been lecturing part-time in missiology since 1944.

Although he worked behind the scenes, Kilger had great influence on the establishment of the Institut für missionswissenschaftliche Forschungen at Münster (1911) and of the Missiological Faculty of the Urbaniana University in Rome (1932). In 1921 he became co-editor of the *Zeitschrift für Missionswissenschaft,* and in 1935 and 1936 the editor in chief. He was also one of the initiators of the *Neue Zeitschrift für Missionswissenschaft* in 1945. In 1951 he was named a corresponding member of the Academy of American Franciscan History. His main interest was in the history of missions, especially in Africa (16th–18th centuries), and in the early Christianization of the Germans.

BIBLIOGRAPHY Johannes Beckmann, "P. Dr. Laurenz Kilger, OSB (1890–1964) zum Gedächtnis," *NZM* 20 (1964): 161–167; Aegidius Kolb, *Bibliographie der deutschsprachigen Benediktiner 1880–1980,* vol. 2 (1987); Ivo Auf der Maur, "Der Missionswissenschaftler P. Dr. Laurenz Kilger, OSB," in Basilius Doppelfeld, ed., *Mönche und Missionare,* (1988), pp. 189–202; Frumentius Renner, *Der fünfarmige Leuchter,* vol. 3 (1990).

Fritz Kollbrunner, SMB

Kilham, Hannah (Spurr) (1774–1832), English Quaker missionary educator and linguist in West Africa. Hannah Spurr was born in Sheffield in a working-class family and brought up as a devout Anglican. Well educated for her time and gender, she showed independence of mind and in 1794 became a Methodist. In 1798 she married a widower, Alexander Kilham, leader of the breakaway Methodist New Connexion. He died eight months later, leaving Hannah with a stepdaughter and expecting a child of her own. She settled in Nottingham, where her daughter was born and died in infancy. She supported herself and her stepdaughter by teaching. Returning to Sheffield, she joined a Quaker Meeting in 1803 and became involved in charitable work and in the antislavery movement. Her interests in West Africa and in education came together as she heard of early missionary work in Sierra Leone. Pondering the problems of teaching freed slave children, she advocated the use of vernacular languages. With help from her Quaker community, she sailed for the Gambia in 1823 with six companions, two of them Gambians, former slaves. In six months there and in Freetown, Sierra Leone, schools and agricultural projects were set up and she developed her knowledge of the vernaculars. Although her Quaker supporters felt she should have stayed longer, she left Africa and spent the next three years in London, still convinced of the value of her linguistic theories in educating "liberated Africans." She returned privately to Sierra Leone at the end of 1827 in the company of some Church Missionary Society missionaries. She started a school for girls (continued by a gifted West Indian woman) but because of illness again left for England in February 1828. In October 1830 she was able to return to Sierra Leone and to establish, in Charlotte, a boarding school for recently liberated African girls. Despite difficulties the venture prospered, and early in 1832 she visited Monrovia, Liberia. She spent a profitable month there but died on the return journey to Freetown and was buried at sea. She spent less than two years in West Africa, but her legacy has endured.

BIBLIOGRAPHY Reports and pamphlets by Hannah Kilham include *Scripture Selections on the Principles of the Christian Religion* (1819), *Lessons on Language* (1818), *First Principles of the Christian Religion for Schools of Early Instruction* (1827), *Report on a Recent Visit to the Colony of Sierra Leone* (1828), *The Claims of West Africa to Christian Instruction through the Native Languages* (1828); all are in the Friends' Library, Euston Square, London. Sarah (Kilham) Biller, *Memoir of the Late Hannah Kilham* (1837); Mora Dickson, *The Powerful Bond: Hannah Kilham, 1774–1832* (1980). See also Andrew Walls, "Alexander Kilham," in *Some Personalities of Aberdeen Methodism, 1760–1970* (1973).

Jocelyn Murray

Kilian (Kyllena) (c. 640–689), apostle of Franconia, in south central Germany. Kilian, who was Irish, was perhaps already a bishop when he went to work among Frankish tribes around Aubigny. He made a pilgrimage to Rome. On his return he located in Würzburg, apparently won Duke Gozbert to Christianity, and had much success among people in East Franconia and Thuringia. Early records describe him as a miracle worker.

BIBLIOGRAPHY Ferninand Emmerich, *Die heilige Kilian* (1896); Aubrey Gwynn, "New Light on St. Kilian," *Irish Ecclesiastical Record,* 6th ser. 88 (1957): 1–16.

Frederick W. Norris

Kim, Andrew Tae-kon (1821–1846), first Korean Catholic priest. Kim was born in Nol-mae, Ch'ung-ch'ong Province (south central Korea); his father, Ignatius Kim, was martyred in 1839. Kim entered seminary in Macao in 1836 and six years later proceeded to Manchuria in order to reenter Korea; he was successful in 1845, on his third attempt. Later that year he and several Korean Christians sailed in their own craft to Shanghai, where in August he was ordained a priest. Upon returning to Korea in October, Kim undertook pastoral activities. In June 1846, while surveying the southwest coast for a possible point of entry for missionaries, he was arrested and eventually sent to Seoul for interrogation. He was beheaded at the Han River on September 16, his body exposed for three days and then buried near the execution site. Later, Christians retrieved his body and buried it on Mount Mi-ri-nai, about 35 miles from Seoul. Beatified in 1925 along with seventy-eight other martyrs, including his father, Kim was designated in 1949 the principal patron of the Korean clergy. Along with the other martyrs, he was canonized by Pope *John Paul II on May 6, 1984.

BIBLIOGRAPHY "Epistolae Beati Andreae Kim, Primi Sacerdotis Coreani Martyris," *Pro Corea. Documenta* (1938), pp. 19–125; Clarence A. Herbst, "Korea's Martyr-Patron," *American Ecclesiastical Review* 137 (1957): 330–341; Joseph Chang-mun Kim and John Jae-son Chung, *Catholic Korea: Yesterday and Today* (1964), pp. 197–200, 206–222; Adrien Launay, *Martyrs français et coréens, 1838–1846: Beatifiés en 1925* (1925), pp. 209–250.

John W. Witek, SJ

Kim, Helen (1899–1970), Korean educator, stateswoman, evangelist, and author. Kim served the Ewha Womans University as teacher, professor, dean, president, president emeritus, and chair of its board of trustees (1918–1970). Under her leadership, Ewha became the largest women's university in Asia. A Christian school, it seeks to advance women through higher education.

Kim was born in Chemulpo (Inchon) and graduated from Ewha, Ohio Wesleyan University, Boston University, and Columbia University Teachers College. Her Ph.D. (Columbia, 1931) was the first earned by a Korean woman. She also received five honorary doctorates. A Methodist, she was strongly devoted to Christ, establishing the Korean YMCA (1922) and the Upper Room Evangelistic Association (1961). She led a Sunday Bible class in the Ewha university church from 1935 until her death. She attended over fifty international conferences as a speaker and served over thirty institutions and organizations in various capacities, including the International Missionary Council and the World Council of Churches. She was ambassador-at-large for Korea. Her short haircut and Korean traditional costume became a model for many Korean women who found their vocation in society. Slight in stature, she was a giant in achievement. She received the Order of Cultural Merit of the Republic of Korea, the Ramon Magsaysay award (Philippines), and the Upper Room citation for World Christian Leadership, all in 1963. She died in Seoul.

BIBLIOGRAPHY Helen Kim, *Grace Sufficient* (1964).

Chun Chae Ok

Kimbangu, Simon (1889?–1951), founder of the Church of Jesus Christ through the Prophet Simon Kimbangu. Born in Nkamba, Lower Zaire, Kimbangu had charismatic gifts, but apart from catechistic instruction by the British Baptist Missionary Society (BMS), leading to his baptism in 1915, he had no formal education. In the midst of a colonialism of nearly genocidal dimension, he experienced the leading of God into a ministry of healing and preaching. BMS missionaries, regarding Kimbangu as uneducated, rejected his application to become a catechist and thus refused to provide his ministry a legitimate place within the mission church. Kimbangu's decisive spiritual experience, pushing him into public ministry outside the mission (1921), was explicitly linked to his rejection by the missionaries.

Kimbangu's religious activity, which was characterized by strong charismatic phenomena (cases of resuscitation are reported), lasted from March to September 1921, mainly in Nkamba, the "New Jerusalem." His preaching emphasized the uselessness of traditional African means of protection (resulting in the burning of "fetishes"), the direct intervention of God on behalf of the Africans (questioning the mediation and authority of the missionaries, at the same time rejecting African violence), and the prediction of the end of colonial and white rule (resulting in black self-awareness). As early as May 1921 Kimbangu was on the "wanted" list of the colonial police.

In September 1921 Kimbangu gave himself up to the Belgian authorities. Sentenced to death for allegedly having endangered public security, his punishment was commuted into life imprisonment, and he was treated as a dangerous convict in Elisabethville (Lubumbashi) for the rest of his life. His twelve "apostles" and thousands of followers were banned. Kimbanguism became a deeply rooted Christian movement in the then Belgian Congo. Sociologically, the prophet and his church offered a new model of social authority; religiously, Kimbangu expressed God's love through the mediation of African symbols; and psycho-culturally he set in motion a grand narrative of the black people's special place in God's world.

On his death bed Kimbangu received baptism in the Catholic church. Like Jesus, he left no writings and became a figure of legend, myth, and theology. For missionaries, for Western scholars of Kimbanguism, and for the theologians of the Kimbanguist church itself, it has always been theologically difficult to define who Kimbangu was.

BIBLIOGRAPHY Apart from archival sources (Archives Africains, Brussels; BMS archives, Oxford) the principal documentation on Kimbangu's life and ministry is Paul Raymaekers, ed., "L'Histoire de Simon Kimbangu prophète d'après les écrivains Nfinangani et Nzungu," *Archives de sociologie des religions* 31 (1971): 7-49 and Paul Raymaekers and Henri Desroche, eds., *L'Administration et le sacré. Discours religieux et parcours politiques en Afrique Centrale (1921-1957)* (1983). Oral history has been collected in W. MacGaffey, "The Beloved City: Commentary on a Kimbanguist Text," *JRA* 2 (1969): 129-147, and in Kuntima Diangienda, *L'Histoire du Kimbanguisme* (1984), written by the youngest son of Kimbangu, the late head of the Kimbangu Church. M.-L. Martin, *Kimbangu: An African Prophet and His Church* (1975); Werner Ustorf, *Afrikanische Initiative* (1975).

Werner Ustorf

Kincaid, Eugenio (1797-1883), pioneer American Baptist missionary in Burma. Kincaid was born in Wethersfield, Connecticut, the oldest of eight children of Noah Kincaid and Lydia (Hough). He was educated at Hamilton Literary and Theological Institution, New York, and graduated in the first class with Jonathan *Wade. From 1822 to 1827 he served Baptist churches at Galway, New York, and Milton, Pennsylvania, and in 1827 also edited a monthly newspaper, *The Literary and Evangelical Register.* The Baptist General Association of Pennsylvania having appointed him a domestic missionary, he itinerated in 1828 and 1829 in central and northern parts of the state. In 1829 the Baptist Board of Foreign Missions appointed Kincaid and his wife, Almy, as missionaries to Burma (Myanmar). They arrived at Moulmein in 1830 to join his friend, Jonathan Wade. Almy having died in 1831, Kincaid married Barbara McBain, and together they made a seven-hundred-mile journey up the Irrawaddy River in 1833 to explore a mission at Ava. Under much opposition from the government, the Kincaids focused their attention on the Karen peoples in the state of Arakan (now Rakhine, area along northeast border of Bay of Bengal). At the city of Sittwe they worked in intense tropical heat and won hundreds to the faith. In 1837 Kincaid began evangelistic work among the Kachins, a people of the northern Burmese hills. Owing to difficulties with the government, Kincaid returned to the United States in 1842 and traveled widely on behalf of the mission board. His articulate stories of mission work increased support dramatically and earned for him the title "Hero missionary." He was reappointed in 1849 and returned to Rangoon, Prome, and Ava; in 1857 Kincaid was appointed an official emissary to the United States for the royal court at Ava. From 1857 to 1865 he again served in Burma at Prome, primarily among the Karen and Shan peoples. In failing health, Kincaid returned to the United States in 1866, retiring first as a supply preacher in Philadelphia and later in Girard, Kansas, where he died.

BIBLIOGRAPHY Kincaid was a popular speaker and contributed much to the genre of missionary hagiography. Among his best literary efforts were an essay on Burma in *The Missionary Offering* (1853) and an article in *Free Mission Record* (1854) in which he defended the work of Justus Vinton and Durlin L. Brayton. His own story is told in Alfred S. Patton, *The Hero Missionary, or A History of the Labors of Rev. Eugenio Kincaid* (1858) and in Willis S. Webb, *Incidents and Trials in the Life of Rev. Eugenio Kincaid, the "Hero" Missionary to Burma, 1830-1865* (1890).

William H. Brackney

King, Clifford J. (1888-1969) founder of the Catholic Students Mission Crusade. Born in Mineville, New York, King entered the Divine Word Seminary at Techny, Illinois, in 1909. He was professed in the first class of the American Province of the Society of the Divine Word (SVD) in 1916 and was sent as a seminarian in 1919 to replace expelled German missionaries in Yenchowfu, China. He and Robert Clark were the first American SVD priests ordained there in 1921. When the Japanese invaded China in 1941, King escaped to the Philippines. After three years of hiding while the Japanese occupied the Philippines, King returned to Techny. From 1944 to 1960, he was secretary to the exiled archbishop of Peking, Thomas Cardinal Tien. At 72, King volunteered for work at a leprosarium in Papua New Guinea. He returned to the United States six years later and died at Techny.

King is best remembered for his part in founding the Catholic Students Mission Crusade (CSMC), begun while he was a seminarian in 1918 at Techny. Influenced by the Protestant example of the Student Volunteer Movement and by reading stories from Maryknoll's *Field Afar,* the CSMC leadership organized thousands of seminarians and college and high school students nationally for study, prayer, and participation in missions.

BIBLIOGRAPHY Clifford J. King, *I Remember* (1968); the CSMC *Golden Jubilee Booklet of the Catholic Students Mission Crusade* (1968) features King's work, along with the extended program for a pageant chronicling U.S. Catholic mission work. One section of the pageant highlights King's life.

Angelyn Dries, OSF

King, Copland (1863-1918), cofounder with Albert *Maclaren, of the New Guinea Anglican Mission. Born at Parramatta, Australia, King was the son of a clergyman and a graduate of the University of Sydney. After ordination in 1887 he served in Sydney's evangelical Anglican diocese before responding to the appeal of Maclaren, a high churchman, to begin the mission in northeastern New Guinea at the future cathedral site of Dogura. Following Maclaren's early death and his own illness and temporary withdrawal in 1892, he returned as head of the mission and persevered in isolated and malarial areas until 1918, when he died of heart disease. He was buried at Camden, New South Wales. A self-effacing and often lonely unmarried priest, King declined nomination as the first Anglican bishop of New Guinea. He worked in the remote Mambare River region and devoted himself to evangelism, exploration, and mastery of the Wedau and Binandere languages. His scientific botanical and linguistic studies and his observations of New Guinea cultures developed from his missionary vocation.

BIBLIOGRAPHY David Wetherell, *Reluctant Mission: The Anglican Church in Papua New Guinea 1891–1942* (1977); Gilbert White, *A Pioneer of Papua: Being the Life of the Rev. Copland King* (1929). The Dogura papers are in the New Guinea Collection, Univ. of Papua New Guinea, Port Moresby; detail about King is in the Australian Board of Missions' library collections, Sydney.

John Garrett

King, Johannes (c. 1830–1898), Surinam prophet and evangelist. Born in the coastal area of Surinam, King moved as an adolescent with members of his family to Maripaston on the Saramacca River. In 1855 he had an illness which he attributed to witchcraft, and at a point when all hope of recovery seemed lost, his spirit was carried away by an angel of God—as he later wrote—to have a look into heaven and hell. As a result, he was converted and called to preach the gospel to his own people. Further visions—which he resisted for two years—led him to contact the Moravian missionaries. Thus, in 1857 he went to Paramaribo and requested baptism. After training, in 1861 the missionaries appointed him leader of the church in Maripaston. Guided by visions, in 1865 he also began taking missionary journeys to the tribal area of the interior of Surinam. A powerful preacher, especially when relating his visions, he saw hundreds converted to Christ. In 1867, however, the Moravian missionaries instructed him to preach Christ alone and not speak about his visions. King obeyed but lost his charisma. Between 1870 and 1890 he made no missionary journeys. In 1895 he was elected chief of his tribe, which again roused conflict with the missionaries, and he ended his career in isolation.

BIBLIOGRAPHY Hesdie S. Zamuel, *Johannes King: Profeet en apostel van het Surinaamse Bosland* (1994); H. F. de Ziel, *Johannes King: Life at Maripaston* (1973). King's diaries about his visions, the customs of Surinam blacks, his journeys, and the history of Maripaston are held in the Moravian archives in Paramaribo, Surinam, and Herrnhut, Germany, and also in the Moravian archive in the State archive (Rijksarchief) in Utrecht, Netherlands.

Hesdie S. Zamuel

King, Jonas (1792–1869), American missionary to Greece and the Near East. Born in Hawley, Massachusetts, King prepared for higher education by his own efforts and graduated from Williams College (1816), Andover Theological Seminary (1819), and the College of New Jersey (Princeton; D.D., 1831). He was ordained in the South Carolina Congregational Association, did evangelistic work among Negroes and seamen, and returned to Andover for graduate study in 1820. When Amherst College was founded in 1821, King was named professor of Oriental languages and literature and went to Paris to study under noted Orientalist De Sacy. Asked to help establish the Palestine Mission of the American Board of Commissioners for Foreign Missions (ABCFM), King secured support from friends, a group which developed into the Paris Evangelical Missionary Society. King joined Pliny *Fisk, toured Egypt, worked in Jerusalem, studied Arabic in Lebanon, and toured in Syria. Leaving Jerusalem in 1825, he returned to America via Beirut and Smyrna. In 1828, after a period of missions promotion, King accompanied a shipment of relief supplies to Greece for victims of the Turkish-Greek war. In 1829 he married Annetta Aspasia Mengous, a Greek woman, and was reappointed a missionary. Settling in Athens in 1831, he developed a school and church. King's efforts to effect a reformation of the Orthodox Church led to protracted controversy and the formation of the Greek Evangelical Church. For several periods between 1851 and 1868 King served as United States consular agent in Athens.

BIBLIOGRAPHY King in 1825 published *Farewell Letter,* which was widely circulated in Greek and Turkish, and he published many translations and original works in Greek, including *Defence* (1845), *Speech before the Areopagus* (1847), *Hermeneutics of the Sacred Scriptures* (1857), and two volumes of *Sermons* (1859). F. E. H. Haines, *Jonas King: Missionary to Syria and Greece* (1979). *Missionary Herald* 65 (1869): 245–256 has his obituary; his letters and journals are quoted throughout vols. 19–65. Joseph Tracy, *History of the ABCFM* (1842) refers extensively to King in the annual summaries.

David M. Stowe

Kingsbury, Cyrus (1786–1870), missionary to American Indians. Born in Alstead, New Hampshire, Kingsbury graduated from Brown University (1812) and Andover Theological Seminary (1815). He was ordained and worked in Virginia and East Tennessee under the Connecticut Missionary Society. Assigned to the Cherokees by the American Board of Commissioners for Foreign Missions (ABCFM) in 1816, he met with President James Madison and the secretary of war and secured a significant subsidy for educational work. He was encouraged by the Cherokees' Great Council and in January 1817 established a station near Chattanooga, later named Brainerd. He married Sarah Bowdoin Varnum in 1818. After she died in 1822 he married Electa May in 1823.

In the summer of 1818, Kingsbury, with Loring and Matilda Williams, journeyed by wagon through the wilderness to open a mission among the Choctaws 400 miles to the southwest in Mississippi. Fifteen months after the first building was erected at Elliott, he responded to Choctaw urging and opened a second station at Mayhew, 100 miles to the east. When the Choctaws were forced to sell their lands to the United States in 1830 and move beyond the Mississippi, Kingsbury continued with them and settled at Pine Ridge (now Oklahoma) in 1836. When the ABCFM pressed the missionaries to expel slaveholding Choctaws from the church, Kingsbury pointed to white slaveholders all around them and argued that more, not less, of the gospel was the only hope for improvement. After closure of the mission in 1859, Kingsbury worked under the Presbyterian and Southern Presbyterian boards until his death.

BIBLIOGRAPHY R. Pierce Beaver, *Church, State, and the American Indians* (1966), pp. 67–73; Fred Field Goodsell, *They Lived Their Faith* (1961), pp. 13–14; William E. Strong, *The Story of the American Board* (1910), pp. 36–46, 186–187. See also annual reports of the ABCFM dealing with the Cherokee and Choctaw missions, 1816–1859, and especially 1864, pp. 54–63.

David M. Stowe

Kino, Eusebio Francisco (1644–1711), Jesuit missionary in Mexico and the American Southwest. An Italian born with the family surname Chino in Segno, Tyrol, Kino attended German schools, became a Jesuit in 1665, was ordained to the priesthood in 1677, and then asked to be sent on a mission. In 1678, he sailed to Cadiz, but was delayed for two years in Seville, during which time he learned agricultural techniques he would later teach to the Indians and also studied mathematics and astronomy. He observed the appearance of a comet using instruments he made himself and published his findings. During this time he also began contact with the Duchess of Aveiro, Arcos, and Maquedá, who resided in Madrid and was a noted benefactress of Jesuit missions. The seven-year correspondence between Kino and the duchess (beginning 1680) demonstrated a profound spiritual friendship.

After he arrived in Mexico in 1681, Chino changed the spelling of his surname to Kino, to avoid a bad pronunciation in Spanish. He crossed Mexico and sailed in 1683 to Baja California, to the city of La Paz, where he took ecclesiastical responsibility for the government of the city. He returned to Sinaloa, crossing deserts and heading toward northern Baja California, but instead, stayed to work in Pimeria Alta, which includes Sonora and the northwest deserts, where he became the Apostle to the Pimas. Achievements of his first decade in the new world include founding many missions, at least fourteen expeditions as far as the Colorado River, thirty-one maps from his explorations, and defense of the rights of the Indians even though his confrere, Francisco Javier Saeta, was killed in 1695 by Indians. He wrote about the life and death of Saeta, along with other news of great ethnological, geographical, and missionary value.

Kino's second decade in Mexico, roughly from 1698 to 1711, was a time of colonial and religious consolidation. He founded nine mission stations and in 1702 determined that Baja California was not an island but a peninsula. He wrote "Favors from Heaven," explaining the evangelization of California. He was loved by everyone, from the Indians to the king of Spain, who helped him. Kino was a man of the desert and of the inner life, a multifaceted person—missionary, writer, cosmographer, explorer, colonizer, and defender of the liberty and rights of Indians. Today his statue is found in the National Hall of Statuary in Washington, D.C., representing the state of Arizona. He died in Magdalena, in Baja California.

BIBLIOGRAPHY Works by Kino include H. E. Bolton, ed. and tr., *Kino's Historical Memoir of Pimeria Alta* (original text in Spanish: *Favores Celestiales...*) (1919); *Kino's Biography of Francisco Javier Saeta, S.J.* (original text in Spanish), C. W. Polzer and E. J. Burrus, ed. and tr. (1971). From Kino's correspondence, E. J. Burrus, ed., and tr., *Kino Reports to Headquarters: Correspondence of E. F. Kino, SJ, from New Spain with Rome* (1954) and *Kino Writes to the Duchess* (1965). H. E. Bolton, *Rim of Christendom: A Biography of E. F. Kino* (1936); C. W. Polzer, *The Evolution of the Jesuit Mission System in Northwestern New Spain, 1600–1767* (1972); F. J. Smith et al., *Father Kino in Arizona* (1966).

Jesús López-Gay, SJ

Kinsolving, Lucien Lee (1862–1929), pioneer Episcopal Church missionary to Brazil. Kinsolving was born in Middleburg, Virginia, in the midst of the American civil war, to a distinguished family. His father was an Episcopal priest. His mother died soon after his birth. After graduation from the Episcopal High School, Alexandria, he spent three years as a lay missionary in charge of mountain missions in West Virginia, followed by two years at the University of Virginia, where he determined to be a priest and an overseas missionary. At Virginia Theological Seminary (1886–1889) he decided to apply for Brazil, but the official position of the Episcopal Church was to refrain from establishing missions in Roman Catholic countries. Instead, the American Church Missionary Society agreed to sponsor him and a companion, James W. Morris.

Kinsolving was ordained in 1889 and the two men left immediately for Cruziero and São Paulo to study Portuguese. The times were propitious for starting new work in Brazil. Shortly after their arrival, the emperor Dom Pedro II was deposed, and a republic was established with a new constitution guaranteeing freedom of worship to all. Kinsolving and Morris then moved to Rio Grande do Sul, a progressive city full of foreign businessmen. Both English-speaking and Brazilian congregations were established; Kinsolving also started a small theological school. In 1891 he returned to the United States to marry Alice Brown of Mt. Holly, New Jersey. Four more recruits for the mission were also enlisted. Bishop George Peterkin of West Virginia was sent to make an official visit to the new mission in 1893. He was much impressed with its rapid growth, arranged for Portuguese translations of the Bible and the Prayer Book, and continued to supervise the mission from his home diocese until 1899. In that year Kinsolving was elected bishop of Brazil both by the missionaries in the field and by the House of Bishops of the Episcopal Church. Five years later, the American Church Missionary Society decided to turn over its Brazilian work to the Episcopal Church, thus making southern Brazil an official missionary district (diocese) of the Episcopal Church. Kinsolving had to resign in order to be reelected bishop of the new district.

There followed a period of rapid economic development and growth of the urban population (and Protestantism) in Brazil. In 1912 Kinsolving founded the Southern Cross school for boys in Porto Alegre. By the time he retired in 1928, five self-supporting parishes had been established, with twenty-three Brazilian clergy in addition to missionary clergy from United States, England, and Japan. Kinsolving died in retirement in the United States.

BIBLIOGRAPHY Arthur B. Kinsolving, *A Portrait Sketch of the Rt. Rev. Lucien Lee Kinsolving* (1947) is a brief pamphlet by the bishop's brother. Anson Phelps Stokes, *Lucien Lee Kinsolving of Brazil* (1955) is a pamphlet in the Episcopal Church series "Pioneer Builders for Christ." A collection of Kinsolving's correspondence and reports is preserved in the library of the General Theological Seminary, New York. See also chapter 25 of James Thayer Addison, *The Episcopal Church in the United States, 1789–1831* (1951).

Charles Henry Long

Kircher, Athanasius (1601–1680), Jesuit sinologist and scholar of hieroglyphics. Kircher was born in Germany at Geisa, Fulda. In 1618 he entered the Society of Jesus. After studying in Brunswick, Cologne, and Koblenz, he was ordained a priest in 1628. In 1629 he was appointed professor of philosophy and mathematics in Würzburg. After the invasion of the Swedes in 1632, he fled to Lyons and Avignon, France, where he began to decipher the Egyptian hieroglyphics on Roman obelisks. In 1634 he was appointed professor of mathematics, physics, and Oriental languages at the Jesuit college in Rome, where he taught for the rest of his life. In 1636 he defended his hieroglyphics research with the book *Prodromus Coptus sive Aegyptiacus.* In 1643 followed his publication *Lingua Aegyptiaca restituta.* His principal work on hieroglyphics is the three-volume *Oedipus Aegyptiacus h.e. universalis hieroglyphicae veterum doctrinae temporum iniuria abolitae instauratio* (1652–1655). With this he tried to promote the return of the Oriental Christians to the Catholic Church. He was the founder of a famous museum in Rome named after him. Kircher corresponded with many missionaries. He is considered one of the founders of sinology, and his book on China provides a comprehensive historical investigation of European and missionary contacts with China and a history of the various Oriental peoples, including their literature, customs, and cultures.

BIBLIOGRAPHY Athanasius Kircher, *China monumentis qua sacris qua profanis, necnon variis naturae et artis spectaculis, aliarumque rerum memorabilium argumentis illustrata* (1667) and *Romani Collegii Societatis Jesu Musaeum Celeberrimum cujus magnum antiquariae rei, statuarum, imaginum, picturarumque partem ex Legatu Alphonsi Domini S.P.Q.R. a Secretis munifica liberalitate relictum* (1678). See also "Die Miscellanea Epistolarum des P. Athanasius Kircher S. J. in missionarischer Sicht," *Euntes Docete* 21 (1968): 221–254. A bibliography of Kircher's works appears in C. Sommervogel, *Bibliothèque de la Companie e Jésus,* vol. 4 (1893), pp. 1046–1077. The most recent bibliography is Lázló Polgár, *Bibliographie sur l'histoire dela Compagnie de Jésus, 1901–1980,* vol. 3 (1990), pp. 300–305.

Willi Henkel, OMI

Kircherer, Johannes Jacobus (c. 1775–1825), missionary in South Africa. A Dutchman, Kircherer was one of the first two London Missionary Society missionaries at Cape Colony, South Africa. He landed there in March 1799 in the company of J. T. van der *Kemp and was warmly welcomed by ministers of the Dutch Reformed Church. He was commissioned as missionary to the Bushmen (San) in an area north of Cape Town (the Zak River). He moved frequently, journeying into unknown country to the north as far as the Orange River. In this way he was instrumental in opening the way for the first three missionaries of the Rotterdam Missionary Society to be settled among the Nama people on both sides of the Orange River (including what is today Namibia). His San mission on the Zak River was a failure, but he exerted lasting influence in opening the way to the north. In 1806 he accepted the pastorate of the DRC at Graaff-Reinet, from where he moved to the DRC at Tulbagh in 1815. He died in Tulbagh.

BIBLIOGRAPHY Kircherer's story is told in vol. 1 of R. Lovett, *The History of the London Missionary Society* (1899) and in J. du Plessis, *A History of Christian Missions in South Africa* (1911).

Willem Saayman

Kirkland, Samuel (1741–1808), missionary to Native Americans of the Iroquois League. Kirkland was born in Connecticut. In preparation for college he attended Eleazar *Wheelock's boarding school and formed lasting friendships with several Indian youths, notably Joseph Brant. He studied for a while at the College of New Jersey (later Princeton) and in 1765 received a degree in absentia because he had been serving as a missionary with the Seneca Indians for almost a year. He adapted to an Indian life-style without complaint, was readily accepted by his hosts, and was adopted into one of their major clans. In 1766 he was ordained as a Congregationalist minister and entered upon 40 years of labor among another Iroquois tribe, the Oneidas. Based at Canowaroghare, he made slow progress teaching his charges elementary grammar and mathematics, songs and Bible verses. Interested in inculcating habits of temperance and industry as well as saving souls, Kirkland convinced the people to build churches and a gristmill and to expand their economy by raising livestock. The Revolutionary War scattered his flock, but he was successful in keeping the Oneidas neutral during the conflict. Afterward he eased negotiations between the U.S. government and Iroquois tribes, persuading the latter to accept treaty terms. Thereafter he continued to advise the Indians in ways that safeguarded their interests. Finally, in 1793, he realized a long-cherished goal by establishing the Hamilton Oneida Academy for Indians. Though he donated land and funds for training natives to cope with modern culture, the school slowly evolved into an institution for whites, receiving the name Hamilton College in 1812.

BIBLIOGRAPHY Samuel K. Lothrop, *Life of Samuel Kirkland* (1848); Walter Pilkington, ed., *Journals of Samuel Kirkland* (1980); Herbert J. Lennox, "Samuel Kirkland's Mission to the Iroquois" (Ph.D. diss., Univ. of Chicago, 1935); Christine S. Patrick, "The Life and Times of Samuel Kirkland, 1741–1808: Missionary to the Oneida Indians, American Patriot, and Founder of Hamilton College" (Ph.D. diss., State Univ. of New York at Buffalo, 1993).

Henry Warner Bowden

Kitagana, Yohana (1860–1939), apostle of Bunyaruguru and of Kigezi, western Uganda. Born in Buganda, Kitanga was a subchief with five wives, baptized by Catholic missionaries in 1896. He had already set aside all his wives, declaring, "God must suffice for me." In 1901, announcing his intention to work as a missionary to peoples other than his own, he resigned his chiefdom, distributed his property to the poor, and left for Bunyoro, west of Buganda. After some time he was brought back by the White Fathers for a year of catechist training at Lubaga. He was then sent to the kingdom of Bunyaruguru, and in 1911 was moved to the district of Kigezi to begin its evangelization. For 12 years, until the arrival of the first White Father in 1923, he led the entire Catholic missionary work in Kigezi, supervising other resident catechists while ceaselessly itinerating across its valleys and mountains. Apart from the white gown he wore on Sundays, he was dressed only in an animal skin. He remained permanently celibate, became the subject of many miracle stories, and continued as an evangelist until his death.

BIBLIOGRAPHY Y. Ssebalijja, "Memories of Rukiga and Other Places," and J. Nicolet, "The Religious Impact of Yohana Kitagana," both in D. Denoon, ed., *A History of Kigezi* (1972), pp. 177–199 and 231–240.

Adrian Hastings

Kittel, Ferdinand (1832–1903), German missionary linguist in South India. Kittel was born in the remote northern German coastal province of Friesland, where there were nevertheless strong traditional links with the Basel Mission (BM). He showed missionary interest even during his time as a student in gymnasium (high school). He was accepted for missionary training by the BM, and worked for the mission in what is now the Karnataka State of India from 1853 to 1891. After some difficult years conducting normal missionary tasks, he was given responsibility for editing publications in the Kannada language put out by the Basel Mission Press in Mangalore. His qualities as linguist attracted the attention of colonial officials, and his extensive work was partly financed by Indian government funds. In 1891 Kittel returned to Germany where he remained for the rest of his life. The peak of his career was the publication of his *Kannada-English Dictionary* (1894; rev. ed., 1968), which has become a classic. Like his older colleague Hermann *Gundert, Kittel enjoys a high reputation to this day among all communities speaking the language he studied. A notable conference was held in the University of Dharwad in 1994 to celebrate the centenary of the publication of his dictionary.

BIBLIOGRAPHY Srinivasa Havanur, "Contribution of the Basel Mission to Kannada Literature," in *Wholeness in Christ: The Legacy of the Basel Mission in India,* Godwin Shiri, ed. (1985).

Paul Jenkins

Kitto, John (1804–1854), missionary researcher and writer. Although coming from a deprived English background, and totally deaf because of a fall, Kitto possessed remarkable intellectual curiosity and literary skill. At the suggestion of a patron, A. N. *Groves, he was trained as a printer by the Church Missionary Society and spent 18 months in Malta, where he worked as a compositor and also indulged his literary interests, to the displeasure of the society. He subsequently tutored A. N. *Groves's two sons in Baghdad, where he researched the Middle East for the benefit of missionaries (1829–1832). After his return to England, he earned a precarious living as a writer. His publications include three parts of a projected account of all existing missionary organizations and a series of volumes illustrative of the Bible and Palestinian culture.

BIBLIOGRAPHY J. E. Ryland, *Memoirs of John Kitto* (1856).

Harold H. Rowdon

Kivebulaya (Waswa), Apolo (c. 1864–1933), Uganda's apostle to the Pygmies. Waswa (Kivebulaya's original name) was baptized by a Church Missionary Society missionary when he was 30; Apolo (Apollos) was his baptismal name. For the previous ten years of political upheaval he had served different factions as a mercenary, and it was probably a British officer who gave him the scarlet tunic that earned him the nickname Kivebulaya, "the thing from England." Within months of his conversion he offered himself as an evangelist to the kingdom of Toro, and later, even farther west to Mboga in Belgian Congo (Zaire). In the first four years of his Christian life he endured extraordinary suffering, being falsely accused, chain-ganged, and flogged, yet he was upheld by a vivid vision of Christ. He was ordained an Anglican priest in 1903; he never married. From 1899 to 1915 he was a pastor in various districts of Toro. Then, instead of taking the year's leave he had been granted, he asked permission to spend it renewing the church at Mboga, which remained his headquarters until his death. In 1921 a vision of Jesus, "as if I saw a man who was my brother," directed Apolo to seek out the Bambuti, or Pygmies, and other little-known peoples, deep in the Congo forest. His respect and affection won their devotion to himself and to Christ.

BIBLIOGRAPHY The one well-researched biography is Anne Luck's *African Saint* (1963) which makes good use of Apolo's diaries. A. B. Lloyd, *Apolo of the Pygmy Forest,* especially the enlarged ed. of 1936, gives a fair portrait of Apolo's character (pp. 44–46) but presents a highly fabricated version of events. Alfred R. Tucker, *Eighteen Years in Uganda and East Africa* (1908), pp. 139–142, provides a contemporary's evidence for Anne Luck's account.

John V. Taylor

Kivengere, Festo (c. 1919–1988), Anglican Bishop of the Church of the Province of Uganda, Rwanda, Burundi, and Boga-Zaire. Kivengere was a leading figure in the East African Revival (Balokole [saved ones]) movement. Born in Uganda and trained as a teacher, he was originally rejected for ordination in Uganda; but he was ordained a deacon in the United States and a priest in 1967 in Uganda. He won a reputation as a preacher and evangelist and launched the work of African Evangelistic Enterprise (a pan-African movement) in East Africa. He was consecrated bishop of Kigezi in 1972 during President Idi

Amin's reign of terror and fled the country in 1977 when Amin attacked the churches and Bishop Janani Luwum was murdered. He returned to Uganda when Amin was overthrown but continued to travel widely, attracting large audiences in America, Australia, and Britain. He became an international spokesman for the Church of Uganda and courageously denounced the human rights violations that continued unabated during Milton Obote's second presidency. In 1982, when thousands of Banyarwanda refugees were expelled from their homes, Kivengere organized assistance for them although it was unpopular and dangerous to do so. He warned against the dangers posed to the Church of Uganda by the way in which Obote drove a wedge between Catholics and Protestants through favoring the Church of Uganda. In 1983 he ordained three women as priests in his diocese in spite of official opposition but with the support of his own diocese. He died of leukemia at the height of his powers and influence.

BIBLIOGRAPHY With Dorothy Smoker, Kivengere wrote *Revolutionary Love* (1983). J. E. Church, *Quest for the Highest: An Autobiographical Account of the East African Revival* (1981); Anne Commes, *Festo Kivengere, a Biography* (1990); Margaret Ford, *Janani: The Making of a Martyr* (1978); Louise Pirouet, "Religion in Uganda under Amin," *JRA* 9, no. 1 (1980): 12–29.

M. Louise Pirouet

Kiwanuka, Joseph (1892–1966), first African Catholic bishop in modern times. Kiwanuka was born in Buganda just as its religious wars were ending and British rule became established. Raised a Catholic, he was educated in Bukalasa and Katigondo seminaries and was ordained in 1929. Selected for further study in Rome, where he became the first African Doctor of Canon Law, he then joined the White Fathers missionary society. In 1939 he was chosen as first vicar apostolic of Masaka and consecrated bishop by *Pius XII in Rome. Twenty years later he became archbishop of Kampala, attended Vatican II and died just after it ended.

Kiwanuka was the first black diocesan bishop in any mainline church since Samuel *Crowther's death in 1891. For 12 years he remained the only African bishop in the Catholic Church, apart from those in Madagascar and Ethiopia. Masaka, wholly staffed by local priests, was seen as an experiment, one often criticized by missionaries. In fact, however, Kiwanuka's achievement was outstanding. His development of elected lay parish councils and parents' associations for church schools went far ahead of current Catholic practice as did his regular dispatch of priests abroad for further studies. His political influence was extensive. In such ways Kiwanuka pioneered the African church of the next generation.

BIBLIOGRAPHY A. Hastings, *The Church in Africa, 1450–1950* (1994); John Waliggo, *A History of African Priests* (1988).

Adrian Hastings

Klein, Frederick Augustus (1827–1903), Church Missionary Society (CMS) missionary in the Middle East. Born in Strasbourg, France, Klein studied at the Basel Mission Institute before going to the Church Missionary College, Islington (London), and receiving Anglican ordination. In 1851 he left for Palestine under the CMS. He worked in Nazareth until 1855 and then in Jerusalem for 22 years. In 1877 he went to Germany and devoted himself to Arabic translation. From 1882 to 1893 he worked in Cairo, where the CMS had reopened work, wishing to evangelize among Muslims. He established public worship in Arabic. On his final return to Europe, he continued his translation work, revising the Arabic version of the Book of Common Prayer, and translating Ryle's commentary on Luke.

Klein will be ever remembered for his discovery, in 1868, at Diban, east of the Dead Sea, of the Moabite Stone, dating from about 840 B.C.; it gives independent confirmation of events mentioned in the Book of Kings. But he ought to be remembered also as one of a number of long-lived German missionaries who acquired great fluency in Arabic and gave their lives in quiet proclamation of Christ among Muslims.

BIBLIOGRAPHY Jocelyn Murray, *Proclaim the Good News: A Short History of the Church Missionary Society* (1985); Eugene Stock, *History of the Church Missionary Society* (1899).

Jocelyn Murray

Kleinschmidt, Johann Conrad (1768–1832), Moravian missionary to Greenland and Bible translator. Born in Thuringia, Germany, Kleinschmidt determined while still a youth to live at the Moravian community at Neudietendorf. He was confirmed at Easter in 1781 and admitted to the Herrnhut Holy Communion in 1782. He was an active member of the Single Brethren's Choir at Neudietendorf from 1786. In 1793 he was called to service in Greenland, leaving Herrnhut on February 25 and arriving at New Herrnhut, Greenland, on August 2. In 1800 he married Anna Maria Hameless and was ordained a deacon by J. F. Reichel in the same week. Their children were placed in Moravian schools in Germany, as was the normal pattern for mission families well into the twentieth century.

Kleinschmidt's major contributions were in the philological field. His translation of the New Testament into the language of Greenland was published by the British and Foreign Bible Society in 1823. His other works include some Old Testament portions, a revised grammar that improved on earlier work done by Matthew *Stach, and a few minor pieces. He died at Friedensthal, Greenland.

BIBLIOGRAPHY J. T. Hamilton and K. G. Hamilton, *History of the Moravian Church* (1967); *Nachrichten aus der Brüder-Gemeine* (1834).

Albert H. Frank

Klinkert, Hillebrandus Cornelius (1829–1913), Mennonite missionary in the Dutch East Indies (Indonesia). Klinkert was a land surveyor and engineer in a Rotterdam factory before becoming a missionary. In 1856 he became a co-worker of Pieter *Jansz in Jepara, Central Java. Three years later he moved to Semarang. There he translated parts of the Bible into a local Malay dialect; he was the first editor of the Malay newspaper *Slompret Melaijoe* (The Malay trumpet), and published other Christian material. In 1863 the Dutch Bible Society appointed him to prepare a new translation of the Bible into Malay. From 1864 to 1867 he lived under miserable conditions on the island of Riau, where a high literary form of Malay was used as the vernacular. Here he collected numerous valuable literary manuscripts and ultimately produced a translation in Arabic characters. Back in the Netherlands, he finished his translation into Latin characters in 1878. He struggled with differences in the Malay dialects of western and eastern Indonesia and uncertainties about the intended readers (Christians or Muslims). His New Testament translation served until 1938, the Old Testament until 1974 as the predominant translation in the whole country.

From 1878 to 1904 Klinkert was a lecturer for Malay studies in Leiden. He published several Malay dictionaries and translated and annotated a number of Malay manuscripts.

BIBLIOGRAPHY A list of lexicographic and linguistic studies by Klinkert appears in *Encyclopedie van Nederlandsch Indië,* vol. 2 (1918), pp. 350–351. Alle Hoekema, "H. C. Klinkert: Missionary, Journalist, Bible translator, Linguist," *Mennonite Quarterly Review* 67 (1993): 225–240; J. L. Swellengrebel, *In Leijdeckers voetspoor,* vol. 1 (1974), pp. 173–208. Klinkert's letters and research notes are in the archives of the Netherlands Bible Society and the Dutch Mennonite Missionary Society.

Alle G. Hoekema

Knak, Siegfried (1875–1955), director of the Berlin Mission. Knak was born into a family of Lutheran ministers associated with the north-German neopietist awakening. He did his theological studies at Halle, mainly under Martin *Kähler, and for a few years served as a parish pastor. In 1910 he was named inspector of the influential Berlin Mission, and in 1921 he began a twenty-seven-year tenure as director. In 1950 he became lecturer in missiology at the Berlin and Halle universities. Both as a mission administrator and as a mission theologian, Knak conceived the task of missions primarily in terms of inculturation of the gospel, the planting of folk churches, and respect for the God-given orders of society, largely along the lines of Bruno *Gutmann in East Africa and Christian *Keysser in New Guinea. Knak's first questioning of this approach came when the Nazi-controlled German Christians tried to dominate both churches and missions in Germany. Knak, after some hesitation, found himself on the side of the "Confessing Church" movement. A more thorough revision of his missiological stance was initiated after World War II under the influence of the ecumenical movement and J. C. *Hoekendijk's criticism of the "organological" ideology in German missions. Meanwhile, the devastating loss of most of the East German constituency of the Berlin Mission after 1945 required a painful renewal of the mission's leadership.

BIBLIOGRAPHY Knak's only major publication is *Zwischen Nil und Tafelbai: Eine Studie über Evangelium, Volkstum, und Zivilisation* (1931). There is as yet no critical biographical study of Knak.

Hans-Werner Gensichen

Knibb, William (1803–1845), Baptist Missionary Society (BMS) missionary and antislavery campaigner. Knibb was born in Kettering, Northamptonshire, England, but from the age of 13 lived in Bristol. In 1824 he offered himself to the BMS for service in Jamaica, to replace his brother, Thomas, who had died after just four months on the island. Once in Jamaica, Knibb adhered to the BMS committee's instruction not to preach against slavery, but he found the slave owners increasingly hostile to evangelical religion. Following a slave insurrection in December 1831, Knibb was arrested and wrongly charged with inciting the slaves to rebellion. Released, he returned to England to persuade the Baptist denomination that religious liberty now demanded that slavery in the British West Indies be brought to an immediate end. Knibb was the chief actor in a public campaign in the later months of 1832 that swung British Christian opinion in favor of emancipation and led to the Emancipation Act of August 1833. In 1834 he returned to Jamaica, where he spent the rest of his life. He was instrumental in bringing about an early end to the apprenticeship of the former slaves in 1838, and in his final years he earned the contempt of the plantation owners by his consistent defense of the interests of their workers.

BIBLIOGRAPHY J. H. Hinton, *Memoir of William Knibb, Missionary in Jamaica* (1847); Brian Stanley, *The History of the Baptist Missionary Society, 1792–1992* (1992); Mary Turner, *Slaves and Missionaries: The Disintegration of Jamaican Slave Society, 1787–1834* (1982); Philip Wright, *Knibb "the Notorious": Slaves' Missionary, 1803–1845* (1973).

Brian Stanley

Knight-Bruce, George Wyndham Hamilton (1852–1896), Anglican bishop and pioneer missionary in southern Africa. Educated at Oxford (Merton College, B.A., 1876), Knight-Bruce was ordained a priest in 1877 and married Lillian (d. 1937) in 1878. Until 1886 he worked in parishes in England. At the time that Cecil Rhodes and his associates were pushing British sovereignty in southern Africa northward, and boundaries were not yet fixed, Knight-Bruce was consecrated as third bishop of Bloemfontein (Orange Free State). In 1888 he made a notable journey to the Zambezi and back and visited the Ndebele paramount chief, Lobengula. After the setting up of the British South African Company (1889) and the establishment of Salisbury (1890), the Anglican diocese of Mashonaland was formed in 1891. Knight-Bruce became its first bishop, and stations were begun at Salisbury and Penhalonga, near Umtali, with assistance from the Society for the Propagation of the Gospel. During the years of his activities in southern Africa, Knight-Bruce's wife remained in England gathering support. In 1894 he was invalided to Britain. The first Shona converts were baptized in 1896; the Anglican work was later extended into Matebeleland.

BIBLIOGRAPHY G. W. H. Knight-Bruce, *Journals of the Mashonaland Mission, 1888–1892* (1892) and *Memories of Mashonaland* (1895). C. E. Fripp and V. W. Hiller, eds., *Gold and the Gospel in Mashonaland* (1949); C. F. Pascoe, *Two Hundred Years of the SPG: An Historical Account of the Society for the Propagation of the Gospel in Foreign Parts, 1701–1900,* vol. 1 (1901); Titus Presler, "Missionary Anglicanism Meets an African Religion: A Retrospect of the Centenary of Bishop Knight-Bruce's Entry into Zimbabwe," *Missionalia* 17, no. 3 (1989): 162–175.

Jocelyn Murray

Knoblecher, Ignaz (1819–1858), Catholic missionary to central Africa. The vicariate apostolic of the Sudan was established by Propaganda Fide in 1846 to be staffed by a nationally mixed group deriving from the Austrian Empire. Knoblecher, a Slovene, had studied in Propaganda Fide's own college in Rome and was ordained there in 1845. He then became a member of the first party to the Sudan led by Maximilian Ryllo, a Polish Jesuit, in 1847. After Ryllo died Knoblecher was appointed pro-vicar apostolic in 1851.

The mission established its base at Khartoum. Its boat, the *Stella Matutina,* was used to reach the mission's chosen field farther south, perhaps the earliest example of missionary ownership of a boat for inland water travel in Africa. In 1852 a station was opened at Gondokoro, among the Bari, and in 1854 another was opened among the Dinka. At the time no other mission had penetrated nearly so far into the interior of Africa. However, it was grimly unsuccessful. The peoples targeted were unresponsive while the mortality rate among the missionaries was extremely high. The work was brought to a close eight years after Knoblecher's death.

Knoblecher was outstanding in his missionary approach. An excellent linguist, he was the author of interesting works on the language and customs of the Bari and the Dinka, writings far in advance of those of most of his missionary contemporaries. He was also someone able to adapt his appearance and life-style to the society he had entered. Dressed in a white turban and flowing purple robe, he was known up and down the Nile as Abuna Suleiman. Predating the White Fathers by 20 years, he well represented the best in the nineteenth-century Catholic approach as it contrasted with the Protestant—adaptationist rather than civilizing.

BIBLIOGRAPHY D. McEan, *A Catholic Sudan: Dream, Mission, Reality* (1987); E. Schmid, *Alle origini della missione dell'Africa centrale* (1987).

Adrian Hastings

Kobès, Aloÿs (1820–1872), vicar apostolic to Guinea and Senegambia. Born in the Rhineland, Kobès studied in Strasbourg and was ordained in 1844. Two years later he joined the Holy Ghost Fathers (founded by François *Libermann) and, in 1848, was named coadjutor-bishop for Mgr. Jean Rémi *Bessieux. For the rest of his life he was responsible for the young church in the northern half of the vast West African mission, with Bessieux directing the southern half. In 1863 he became vicar apostolic, based in Senegambia. Handing over Sierra Leone to the newly founded SMA of de *Marion-Bresillac, Kobès concentrated on Dakar, Bathurst, and the surrounding area; but his apostolate in this largely Muslimized area, with exceptionally heavy mortality among his missionaries, was extremely hard. Kobès was outstanding as a pioneer in the formation of an African clergy and was able in 1864 to ordain his first African priest, Guillaume Jouga, to be followed by several others. He was also concerned with the foundation of a local sisterhood, the Daughters of the Holy Heart of Mary, which by his death had twenty-eight professed members. These were unique achievements for his time. He was also an excellent linguist: *Principes de la langue wolof* was published in 1865.

BIBLIOGRAPHY Paul Coulon and Paule Brasseur, *Libermann, 1802–1852* (1988), pp. 649–657.

Adrian Hastings

Koechlin, Alphons (1885–1965), Swiss mission and ecumenical church leader. Born into an elite Protestant family in Basel, Koechlin was an early enthusiast for the ecumenical movement. By late 1939 he was president of the cantonal Protestant church of Basel-Stadt, president of Basel Mission (BM), and president of the Federation of Swiss Protestant churches. He was able to maintain contact with the Confessing Church in Germany during the Third Reich, in part via his BM colleague Karl *Hartenstein in Stuttgart. In 1945 Koechlin helped organize the rapid restoration of ecumenical contact with German church leaders, in which the signing of the Declaration of Stuttgart in October 1945 played a key role; and he was an energetic supporter of the founding of the World Council of Churches.

Koechlin successfully stressed the neutral Swiss (and therefore non-German) nature of the Basel mission when World War II broke out; he was the force behind the reorientation of the mission's seminary in 1955 from a five-year theological school for men to a missionary training institution for men and women who had completed their academic or professional education; and he led the BM away from its pietist past toward an ecumenical future. The church struggle in Germany, World War II, the coming of national independence to India and Indonesia, and the Communist revolution in China all represented major crises for the BM during his term of office. That the mission entered the 1950s in good heart and then grew stronger is a tribute to Koechlin's vision and leadership. He retired as president of the BM in 1959.

BIBLIOGRAPHY George Bell, *Alphonse Koechlin: Briefwechsel, 1933–54* (1969); Henri d'Espine, *Alphonse Koechlin: Pasteur et chef d'Eglise, 1885–1965* (1971).

Paul Jenkins

Koelle, Sigismund Wilhelm (1823–1902), German missionary of the Church Missionary Society (CMS) in Sierra Leone and the Middle East. Koelle's West African period (1847–1853) was one of outstanding linguistic distinction. While teaching various subjects including Hebrew and Arabic at the CMS Institute at Fourah Bay in Sierra Leone, he investigated many African languages, mainly using liberated African slaves as informants. Returning to England, in 1853–1854 he oversaw publication of his studies on the Vai language of Liberia and on the Kanuri language of northern Nigeria, as well as an extensive and renowned collection of vocabularies, the *Polyglotta Africana.* He transferred to the Middle East in 1859 partly for health reasons and after 1868 was alone at the Constantinople station. Because of official hostility to the mission the CMS withdrew in 1877, but Koelle stayed on as an independent missionary until 1879, when he was forced to leave after a clash with the authorities that caused a minor international crisis. During this later career he studied Turkish and prepared material, but little appeared in print. Though retired in England, in 1889 he published *Mohammed and Mohammedanism,* a scholarly work but uncompromisingly hostile to its subjects.

One of the dozen native Germans who served the CMS well in the early decades of the society, Koelle became a British citizen, and his son an Anglican clergyman. For his African linguistic work he received honors, including an honorary doctorate from the University of Tübingen; all his African language works have recently been reprinted. His name is irrevocably linked with the progress of African linguistics, as he was one of its most skillful and successful early pioneers. While his devotion to mission was lifelong, the contrast between the intellectual productivity of his few years in Africa and the relative obscurity of the later decades in the Middle East is striking.

BIBLIOGRAPHY P. E. H. Hair, intro. to repr. of S. W. Koelle, *Polyglotta Africana* (1963) and *The Early Study of Nigerian Languages* (1967); Eugene Stock, *The History of the Church Missionary Society* (1899). The CMS archives on West Africa, Univ. of Birmingham, contain material on Koelle, including some translations into Turkish.

P. E. H. Hair

Koo, T. Z. (Koo Ts-Zung; [Ku Zi-Zong]) (1887–1971), preeminent Chinese Christian leader. Koo, a graduate of St. John's University, Shanghai, entered service with the Chinese YMCA after nine years as an administrator with the Chinese national railways. From 1919 to 1930 he was associate general secretary and student executive secretary of the Chinese YMCA National Committee. Under his leadership the number of Student Christian Associations rose to more than 100. From 1929 to 1934 he was vice-chairman of the World's Student Christian Federation and from 1934 to 1947 its general secretary. During those years he visited forty-five countries, speaking to student audiences. Always an advocate of Christian principles in international relations, he was a member of the Second World Opium Conference in 1924, adviser to the Chinese delegation to the United Nations Conference at San Francisco in 1945, and a speaker at numerous world Christian gatherings, including the Oxford Conference on Life and Work in 1937, the Madras meeting of the International Missionary Council in 1938, and the Amsterdam Conference of Christian Youth in 1939. Beginning in 1945, he taught courses at the University of Iowa, the University of Florida, and Bucknell University, Pennsylvania, where he was visiting professor in the field of Oriental studies. He retired in 1959.

BIBLIOGRAPHY R. O. Hall, *T. Z. Koo: Chinese Christianity Speaks to the West* (1950); Kenneth Scott Latourette, *World Service: A History of the Foreign Work and World Service of the YMCA of the United States and Canada* (1957). Koo materials are in the archives of the YMCA, University of Minnesota, and of the World's Student Christian Federation, Geneva.

Donald E. MacInnis

Koob (*or* Koop), Marianne. *See* Cope, Marianne.

Kosmas Aitolos (*or* Cosmas of Aitolia) (1714–1779), Greek Orthodox itinerant missionary in Greece, Albania, and Turkey. Born in the Greek province of Aitolia (Aetolia), in the village of Mega Dendron (Great Tree), Konstas (his baptismal name) left home at age 20. Acquiring a basic education, he became a teacher. In 1749, he entered the Athonias Theological Academy on Mount Athos. Ten years later he entered the Philotheou Monastery, and became a monk, at which time he took the name Kosmas (Cosmas), and was ordained to the diaconate and priesthood. In 1760 he received permission to leave Mount Athos and serve as an itinerant preacher. For 19 years he preached throughout Greece, Albania, and European Turkey.

Kosmas considered education an indispensable tool for understanding Christianity. After three centuries of foreign rule, the educational system in Greece had deteriorated. Among the illiterate and poor, defections to Islam were increasing. As a result of Kosmas's preaching, schools were established in more than 200 villages and towns. He also spoke out against social injustice, abuse of the poor and uneducated, and societal inequities between men and women. Having alienated some with his preaching, he was apprehended surreptitiously in Berat, Albania. Charged with various crimes, he was taken to the neighboring village of Kalinkontasi and hanged. He was venerated by the faithful for 200 years as a saint. Sainthood was proclaimed officially on April 20, 1961, by the Patriarchate of Constantinople. His feast day is August 24.

BIBLIOGRAPHY Constantine Cavarnos, *Modern Orthodox Saints, St. Cosmas Aitolos* (1971); Dennis Michelis, *The Champions of the Church* (1986), pp. 110–112; George Poulos, *Orthodox Saints* (1978); Nomikos Vaporis, *Father Kosmas, The Apostle of the Poor* (1977; contains an English translation of his teachings and letters, compiled by his followers).

Dimitrios G. Couchell

Ko Tha Byu (1778–1840), the Karen Apostle. A rebellious adolescent of one of the Karen ethnic groups of Burma (Myanmar), Ko Tha Byu left home at age 15 and entered a life of crime and violence. Facing enslavement because of debt, he was ransomed by a Burmese Christian. Displays of uncontrolled rage, however, proved too much for his master, who turned him over to Adoniram *Judson, who taught him to read the Burmese New Testament. Observing the missionary's exemplary life, Ko Tha Byu was dramatically changed, but his nefarious reputation raised doubts in the minds of the church about the genuineness of his conversion, and his baptism was delayed.

In 1828, when George and Sarah *Boardman moved from Moulmein to Tavoy, the mountainous region and principal home of the Karen tribal people, they took Ko Tha Byu with them. Two months after their arrival, Boardman baptized him in a service witnessed by three other Karens, who began pressing him to come to their village and tell his story. Encouraged by Boardman, he began 12 years as an evangelist to the Karens. Though the Karens were animists, their belief in a single Creator and in the existence of a sacred book lost by their ancestors prepared them for Ko Tha Byu's witness, and they began to respond en masse. He later carried the Christian message to Karens in other areas of the country and was an integral part of the ensuing Christianization of his people. Today, Karens constitute the largest cluster of Christianized tribal groups and comprise nearly half of the professing Christians in Myanmar.

BIBLIOGRAPHY Courtney Anderson, *To the Golden Shore* (1956); Harry I. Marshall, *The Karen People of Burma: A Study in Anthropology and Ethnology* (1917); Francis Mason, *The Karen Apostle: or Memoir of Ko Thah-byu* (1843); Robert G. Torbet, *Venture of Faith* (1955).

Alan Neely

Kowalsky, Nicolas (1911–1966), mission historian, librarian, and archivist of Propaganda Fide. Born at Berlin-Spandau, Kowalsky entered the Missionary Oblates of Mary Immaculate in 1933. He studied missiology at the missiological institute of the Propaganda Fide Athenaeum in Rome, where he obtained a doctorate in 1950 dealing with the establishment of the apostolic vicariates in India. From 1951 to 1958 he served as assistant librarian of the Pontifical Missionary Library, and from 1952 to 1958 he was also professor of mission history in the Athenaeum. In 1958 he was appointed archivist of Propaganda Fide, a position he held until his death. He compiled a useful and valuable research tool, "Inventory of the Historical Archives," first published in *Neue Zeitschrift für Missionswissenschaft* (1961) and later as a monograph in the "Schriftenreihe" of the same publishers. He made valuable contributions to *Bibliotheca Missionum* (vols. 13–14, China) and to *Bibliografia Missionaria* (vols. 17–29). From 1961 to 1965 he published a supplement to *Bibliografia Missionaria* containing missionary documents and problems. He served as consultant in preparing the missionary decree *Ad Gentes* of Vatican II and was a member of the council committee for the missions.

BIBLIOGRAPHY Anthony Debevec, "Rev. Fr. N. Kowalsky," *Catholic Historical Review* 52 (1966): 427–429 (obit.); Joseph Metzler, "P. Nikolaus Kowalsky OMI zum Gedächtnis," *NZM* 22 (1966): 293–296.

Willi Henkel, OMI

Koyi, William Mtusane (1846–1886), Xhosa evangelist to the Ngoni of Malawi. Koyi was born near the Thomas River in South Africa, baptized as a Methodist around 1869, and educated at the Free Church of Scotland Lovedale Institute, Cape Province, South Africa, from 1871 to 1876. In 1876 he volunteered for service with the Livingstonia Mission in Malawi. He served briefly at Cape Maclear and Bandawe but is best remembered for his work among the Ngoni in the north. Because the Ngoni had their origins in South Africa, Koyi was very close to them both culturally and linguistically, which proved to be vitally important in the early years of contact when no other missionary could speak their language. He gained their confidence (and especially the confidence of their chief, M'mbelwa) at a time of great tension and social change. He thus laid the foundation for the later work of W. A. *Elmslie and Donald *Fraser, pioneering the first permanent mission station among the Ngoni at Njuyu, where he died of tuberculosis. This was just at the time when the Ngoni, after several years of opposition, had agreed to the opening of schools in their territory. Koyi was undoubtedly one of the key figures in the evangelization of northern Malawi.

BIBLIOGRAPHY George H. Campbell, *Lonely Warrior* (1975); W. A. Elmslie, *Among the Wild Ngoni* (1899, 1970); T. Jack Thompson, *True Love and Roots* (1986, 1989) and *Touching the Heart: Xhosa Evangelists to Malawi 1876–1888* (1997).

T. Jack Thompson

Kraemer, Hendrik (1888–1965), Dutch Reformed lay theologian, linguist, and missiologist. After studying at the Mission House in Rotterdam from 1905 to 1909, Kraemer studied Indonesian languages at Leiden University from 1911 to 1921 and was awarded a Ph.D. under the supervision of the Islamic scholar Christiaan Snouck Hurgronje (1921). As a linguist Kraemer served the Netherlands Bible Society in Indonesia (1922–1937). Then he was appointed professor of the history and phenomenology of religion at Leiden University (1937–1947). Finally he served as the first director of the World Council of Churches' Ecumenical Institute at Château de Bossey, Céligny near Geneva (1948–1955). During his years at Leiden he supervised only one Ph.D. candidate, Arend Th. van *Leeuwen (1947), who later wrote Kraemer's biography (1959).

In Indonesia, Kraemer was more than just a linguist. He acquired expert knowledge about Indonesian Islam, established the Higher Theological School at Jakarta (1934), and traveled widely to develop Indonesian Christianity "from mission field to independent church" (the title of his 1958 book). In 1936, he was invited to write a book in preparation for the meeting of the International Missionary Council at Tambaram (Madras) in 1938. That book, *The Christian Message in a Non-Christian World* (1938), distinguished sharply between what he called "biblical realism" and non-Christian religious experience. His views, which reflect the work of Karl *Barth and Emil Brunner, evoked strong opposition in liberal circles and among Indian theologians.

After World War II Kraemer modified his views somewhat, as reflected in his books *Religion and the Christian Faith* (1956) and *World Cultures and World Religions: The Coming Dialogue* (1960). In these works he no longer used the term "biblical realism," and new terms such as "dialogue" were introduced. However, in *Why Christianity of All Religions?* (1962) he made it very clear that his prewar and postwar views cannot be played off against each other.

Although Kraemer dealt with all religions, he had a special interest in Islam. After Indonesian independence his study on Islam (2 vols., 1928, 1933) was banned by the Indonesian government. His *Islam as a Religious and Missionary Problem* (in Dutch, 1938) was criticized by scholars of religion. However, Muslims such as Isma'il Ragi A. al Faruqi invited Kraemer to write prefaces to their publications.

After leaving Indonesia, Kraemer involved himself in Dutch church and mission work. He contributed significantly to the revitalization of the Netherlands Reformed Church in the postwar situation. At Bossey he developed a "theology of the laity," publishing a book of that title in 1958. From 1938 to 1961 Kraemer dominated the scene in mission theology.

BIBLIOGRAPHY C. F. Hallencreutz, *Kraemer towards Tambaram* (1966); L. A. Hoedemaker, "Hendrik Kraemer," in Gerald H. Anderson et al., eds., *Mission Legacies* (1994), pp. 508-515; J. A. B. Jongeneel, "Christianity and the -Isms: A Description, Analysis, and Rethinking of Kraemer's Theology of Missions," *Bangalore Theological Forum* 20, nos. 1-2 (1988): 17-41 and "Hendrik Kraemer and Stanley J. Samartha, Two Adverse Brothers," *Bangalore Theological Forum* 21, no. 1 (1989): 3-15; P. D. Latuihamallo, "Church and World: A Critical Study about the Relation of Church and World in the Writings of Hendrik Kraemer" (Th.D. diss., Union Theological Seminary, 1959); I. Wajan Mastra, "The Salvation of Non-Believers: A Missiological Critique of Hendrik Kraemer and the Need for Alternatives" (Ph.D. diss., Aquinas Institute, 1970); Retnowinarti et al., *Hendrik Kraemer: Bibliografie en Archief* (1988); S. J. Samartha, "Contact, Controversy and Communication," *Indian Journal of Theology* 17 (1968): 21-26; A. Th. van Leeuwen, *Hendrik Kraemer: Dienaar der Wereldkerk* (1959; German tr., 1962). A special issue of *The Ecumenical Review* 41, no.1 (1989), was devoted to "The Church and the World of Religions and Cultures: Kraemer in Retrospect."

Jan A. B. Jongeneel

Krapf, Johann Ludwig (1810-1881), German Lutheran pioneer missionary in Kenya. Born in Tübingen, Krapf trained for mission work at the Basel Mission seminary in Switzerland. He was accepted by the Church Missionary Society (CMS) and sent to Ethiopia in 1837 to work with C. W. *Isenberg among the non-Christian Galla (now known as Oromo). They taught a few boys but were expelled at the instigation of the Ethiopian Orthodox clergy.

Krapf settled at Mombasa in 1844, hoping to find a southern route to the Galla, but he failed in this although he made a few Galla contacts. The same year he married Rosina Dietrich, but she died two years later and is buried together with their infant daughter near Mombasa. In 1846 he was joined by Johannes *Rebmann and in 1849 by Johann Erhardt. They established a station a few miles inland at Rabai on a ridge overlooking the coastal plain, hoping the Mijikenda would prove more responsive than the slave-owning Muslim society of Mombasa. Krapf traveled extensively, reaching Usambara and Ukambani and sighting Mount Kenya. When he visited Europe in 1850 he impressed the CMS with his vision of a chain of missions across Africa from Rabai, but the hinterland and its people were hostile and the right missionaries were not forthcoming. An attempt to find an alternative route inland via the Tana River almost ended in disaster.

In 1855 Krapf returned to Europe in poor health and published an account of his travels in 1860. He returned to East Africa briefly in 1862 to help Charles *New found Methodist work in East Africa before returning to Germany where he died at Korntal. He made only a few converts and failed to found a church. His importance lies in his pioneer work in Swahili and other languages, and in his geographical discoveries, which aroused great interest in the region.

BIBLIOGRAPHY Johann Ludwig Krapf, *Travels, Researches and Missionary Labours* (Eng. tr., 1860; 2d ed., 1968), *The Journals of the Rev. Messers Isenberg and Krapf, Missionaries of the Church Missionary Society, Detailing Their Proceedings in the Kingdom of Shoa, and Journeys in other Parts of Abyssinia in the Years 1839-1842* (1843; repr. as *The Journals of Isenberg and Krapf,* 1968), and *Dictionary of the Suahili Language* (1882). Eugene Stock, *History of the Church Missionary Society,* vols. 1 and 2 (1899), pp. 458-462 and 124-139.

M. Louise Pirouet

Kraus, Johannes (1898-1980), German Catholic missiologist. Born in Fischbach, Saar, Kraus became a member of the Society of the Divine Word (SVD) in 1920. After his ordination in 1927 he began studying church history and missiology at the University of Münster and completed his studies with the doctoral thesis "Die Anfänge des Christentums in Nubien" (1931). He lectured on theological subjects until his retirement in 1969—most of the time at St. Gabriel's Major Seminary (Vienna-Mödling), one year in the seminary in Bucharest (1930), the rest of the time in St. Augustin near Bonn (1936-1938; 1960-1969). Apart from teaching, he served the SVD in various capacities—as prefect of theologians (1948-1950), superior of the Austrian province (1950-1956), and prefect of studies at St. Gabriel's Major Seminary (1956-1959). He lectured on church history, history of art, and patrology, his favorite subject being "mission history as history of salvation." His research and publications are mainly concerned with church history, mission history, and the history of the SVD.

During World War II Kraus worked mainly on behalf of the Catholic Chinese Encyclopedia. He wrote many articles for the *Lexikon für Theologie und Kirche.* From 1965 until late in life he contributed regularly to the *NZM.* He was particularly skillful in writing the biographies of members of his own society, including Damian Kreichgauer, Alfred

Fräbel, Wilhelm *Schmidt, and Theodor Gabriel. He also published *P. August Hättig SVD, ein Kämpfer für Gottes Reich im Reiche des Drachen* (1957), *P. Arnold Janssen als Studiendirektor von St. Gabriel* (1968), *Im Auftrag des Papstes in Russland* (1970), *P. Anton Volpert (1863–1949), Missionar in Shantung und Kansu* (1973), and *Steyler Patres im Priesterseminar Bukarest* (1978).

BIBLIOGRAPHY A. Rohner, "P. Johann Kraus (1898–1980)," *Steyler Missionschronik* (1981/1982): 157–160; J. Specker, "P. Dr. Johann Kraus SVD zum Gedenken," *NZM* 37 (1981): 145; "Johann Kraus SVD (1898–1980): In Memoriam," *Verbum SVD* 21 (1980): 410–414 (includes a long list of Kraus's publications).

Karl Müller, SVD

Krawielitzki, Theophil (1866–1942), pastor in Vandsburg, West Prussia, and founder of the Marburg deaconry movement. In 1900 Krawielitzki became the leader of a new deaconess organization, which started from the modern pietistic revival movement and formed the nucleus of the Deutscher Gemeinschafts-Diakonieverband (DGD; German Fellowship of Deaconry). In 1908 he moved to Marburg, Germany, and worked exclusively for the deaconry movement, starting several organizations: a mother house named Hebron for deaconesses (1908) and a brother house named Tabor for deacons (1909) in Marburg, followed by other organizations nationally and abroad. In 1922 these training centers were amalgamated to form the DGD, led and shaped by Krawielitzki until his death. His reputation was marred, however, by his positive attitude towards the Nazi regime during the Third Reich.

In addition to the nursing and teaching aspects of ministry, Krawielitzki tried to establish evangelistic and missionary aspects for the deaconry. From 1909, in conjunction with the Liebenzeller Mission, the DGD sent deaconesses as faith-missionaries to Hunan, China. In 1929 the China Inland Mission (CIM) allocated the province of Yunnan to the DGD for its mission territory, and brothers from Tabor began working there in 1931. Renamed the Marburger Mission in 1952, it expanded its work to Japan, Taiwan, Thailand and eventually to Spain and Africa. A second branch of the DGD mission work was the Marburger Brasilienmission (founded in 1932), which was active among German colonists in southern Brazil and eventually among the Caingang Indians. In 1989 it joined the Marburger Mission.

BIBLIOGRAPHY Andreas Franz, *Mission ohne Grenzen: Hudson Taylor und die deutschsprachigen Glaubenmissionen* (1993), pp. 258–266; Fritz Mund, *Theophil Krawielitzki: Ein Zeuge aus der neueren Erweckungs-und Diakoniegeschichte* (1954, rev. 1955); Arno Pagel, *Wer mir dienen will: 75 Jahre Deutscher Gemeinschafts-Diakonieverband* (1974); Erich Günther Rüppel, *Die Gemeinschaftsbewegung im Dritten Reich* (1969), pp. 206–221; Norbert Schmidt, *Von der Evangelisation zur Kirchengründung: Die Geschichte der Marburger Brasilienmission* (1991).

Werner Raupp

Krishna Pal. *See* Pal, Krishna.

Krishna Pillai (Henry Alfred) (1827–1900), Indian Christian poet. Krishna Pillai was born at Karaiyiruppa, Tirunelveli District, South India, of an orthodox Hindu family in the Vaishnava tradition. He received his early education in Tamil grammar and literature in the village tradition. In May 1853 he was appointed Tamil pandit (teacher) at Sawyerpuram, a small Christian settlement founded by the Society for the Propagation of the Gospel. Through the influence of Christian friends he became a Christian and was baptized on April 1, 1858, at St. Thomas Church, Mylapore, Madras. He was given the Christian name of Henry Alfred but retained his Hindu family name. In 1875 he was appointed Tamil pandit at the Church Missionary Society (CMS) college at Tirunelveli.

Krishna Pillai's ambition was to write a Tamil Christian classic along the lines of Hindu epics. With his poetic gifts and deep Christian experience, he spent 14 years toward the end of his life in writing the book by which he is well known: *Rakshanya Yatrikam* (The journey of salvation, 1894). Modeled after John Bunyan's *Pilgrim's Progress,* it is not a translation but an adaptation of the story in Tamil verse. Later, he was persuaded to write a book on Christian apologetics: *Rakshanya Samaya Nirnaya* (The determination of the religion of salvation, 1898). He was a devoted Christian but did not hesitate to use insights from the Hindu tradition (e.g., *saccidananda*—truth, consciousness, and bliss) to explain Christian faith.

BIBLIOGRAPHY A. J. Appasamy, *Tamil Christian Poet* (1966); D. Dennis Hudson, *The Life and Times of H. A. Krishna Pillai, 1827–1900* (1970).

Stanley J. Samartha

Kruyt, Albertus Christiaan (1869–1949), Dutch Reformed missionary among the tribal peoples of Central Sulawesi, Indonesia. Born of missionary parents in Java, Indonesia, Kruyt received his training at the Netherlands Mission Society (NZG) school in Rotterdam. He was sent by the NZG to minister in the isolated and sparsely populated interior of Sulawesi (or Celebes). He worked there from 1892 to 1932, becoming the leader of an ever-growing team of missionaries and Christian schoolteachers from North Sulawesi. In 1909 the first group of Torajan people was baptized, and by the time Kruyt retired in 1932 indigenous Christian leadership was already growing.

Kruyt developed an ethnological approach towards mission, saying that in-depth study of the local culture and religion had to be an integral part of the missionary enterprise. Animism was not to be condemned but to be understood as a temporary stage in religious evolution. The preaching of the gospel was to be linked with the essence of animistic beliefs and practices that point to "faith in God that is breaking through in animism." Missionaries should not preach against or forbid animistic practices but rather foster already existent faith in God. The missionary should monitor the transformational process in such a way that the animists would obtain a deeper understanding of spiritual truth. In principle the converts had to decide for themselves what practices could and could not be maintained, but in some cases the Dutch colonial authorities decided for them (banning of headhunting and certain burial practices). In 1913 Kruyt received an honorary doctorate from the University of Utrecht, Netherlands. After retirement Kruyt moved to the Netherlands and dedicated much of his time to writing and teaching at the NZG school (in 1917 relocated to Oegstgeest).

BIBLIOGRAPHY Albertus Christiaan Kruyt, *Het animisme in den Indischen archipel* (1906), *Van heiden tot christen* (1925), *De Bare'e sprekende Toradja's van Midden Celebes* (3 vols., 1910–1912; vol. 3 was co-authored with N. Adriani), and *De West-Toradja's op Midden-Celebes* (4 vols., 1938). K. J. Brouwer, *Dr. A. C. Kruyt, Dienaar der Toradja's* (1951; includes bibliography). An extensive collection of Kruyt's personal papers are held in the library at the Hendrik Kraemer Institute, Oegstgeest, Netherlands.

Gerrit Noort

Kuder, John (1906–1990), American Lutheran missionary in New Guinea. Born in Niagara Falls, New York, Kuder was educated at Martin Luther College and Seminary in Buffalo, New York. Kuder arrived in New Guinea in 1934, working first on the Rai Coast. He made several difficult expeditions over uncharted mountain ranges to discover unknown peoples of the interior. At the outbreak of World War II, when German missionaries were expelled, he was sent to the highlands to hold the work together, but in 1943 he himself was expelled. After the war he and Theodore Fricke, the Lutheran mission board secretary, surveyed the country and planned the resumption of work. In 1953 Kuder took the lead in uniting the German, American, and Australian Lutheran work into one Lutheran Mission New Guinea. He became its president until the year before its dissolution into the national church in 1970. His chief concern was the creation of an indigenous church, and under his leadership the Evangelical Lutheran Church of New Guinea (now Papua New Guinea) was established in 1956. He became its first bishop and continued to hold that office until 1973, when the first indigenous bishop was elected and he retired.

BIBLIOGRAPHY Herwig Wagner and Hermann Reiner, eds., *The Lutheran Church in Papua New Guinea. The First Hundred Years, 1886–1986* (1986).

Charles W. Forman

Kugler, Anna Sarah (1856–1930), Lutheran missionary doctor and founder of Kugler Hospital at Guntur, Andhra Pradesh, India. Kugler was raised in Ardmore, Pennsylvania, and studied at Friends School in Philadelphia and Miss Markley's School in Bryn Mawr before graduating with honors from the Woman's Medical College of Pennsylvania (1879). After working three years in the State Hospital for the Insane in Norristown, she applied for service as a medical missionary in India in 1882. Her initial application for service as a missionary doctor was rejected by the mission board of the Lutheran General Synod, which assigned her to evangelistic zenana work with Indian women and children. Arriving in Guntur in 1883, she persisted in her dream of serving as a missionary doctor, and in 1884 treated 276 female patients in her own home, plus 185 in private homes. Pleading for suitable buildings for medical work, she itinerated in outlying villages and rented houses in Guntur as dispensaries. In 1885 she was appointed a medical missionary, the only woman physician in Madras Presidency. In 1897 the Kugler Hospital, considered one of the best in India, was erected in Guntur, with maternity and children's wards, chapel, and nurses' home. Kugler was both founder and supervising doctor. Her motto was "Ourselves your servants for Christ's sake," and her principles were to work in accordance with the best scientific teaching, avoid extravagance, encourage fee payments by patients, and regard competent medical practice as effective witness to the love of Christ. Hundreds of Indian nurses and medical assistants received training. In 1904 she received the Kaiser-i-Hind medal from the government of India. She died in the hospital she founded.

BIBLIOGRAPHY George Drach, *Kingdom Pathfinders: Biographical Sketches of Foreign Missionaries* (1942) and ed., *Our Church Abroad: The Foreign Missions of the Lutheran Church in America* (1926).

James A. Scherer

Kuhn, Isobel (Miller) (1901–1957), missionary to southwest China. Born in Canada, Isobel Miller studied at Moody Bible Institute, Chicago. She went to China with the China Inland Mission because of the influence on her life of J. O. *Fraser. Shortly after her arrival, she married her fiancé, John Kuhn, and eventually they were assigned to work in west Yunnan, among the Lisu people, a minority nationality in southwest China. She played a key role in establishing the Rainy Season Bible Schools among minority peoples, in translating the Lisu New Testament, and in ministering to the needs of Lisu women. She and her husband helped the Lisu Christians resist the efforts of the Japanese to advance east of the Salween River into west China as they attacked from Burma. Unsettled conditions in west China in the late 1940s made it necessary for Isobel and her family to leave China. They continued their ministry among the Lisu in northern Thailand from 1951 to 1954. She went to the United States in 1954 to treat the cancer from which she died in 1957. During the course of her missionary career she wrote eight books that enjoyed great popularity among the Christian public. Among these were *Ascent to the Tribes* (1956), *Nests above the Abyss* (1947), *Green Leaf in Drought Time* (1957), and *Stones of Fire* (1960).

BIBLIOGRAPHY Kuhn's *By Searching* (1959) reveals much about her early personal life and commitment. Carolyn Canfield, *One Vision Only* (1959); Lois Headley Dick, *Isobel Kuhn* (1987).

Ralph R. Covell

Kuksha (early 13th century), Russian Orthodox missionary and martyr. Kuksha was tonsured as a monk in the Kiev Cave Monastery, where he lived until about 1215. Under Grand Prince *Vladimir of Kiev, the leading Vyatichi families (a people related to the Polish) had been baptized and settled in towns where the Russian lands and Vyatichi lands met. Kuksha's non-Russian name probably indicates that he was from such a Vyatichi family. He left the monastery and started preaching among the non-Christian Vyatichi living along the river Oka. He attacked paganism by burning idols and shrines, and according to tradition, his preaching was accompanied by various miracles. Although he baptized some pagans, the pagan priests incited people against him until he and a disciple were tortured and beheaded. His feast day is August 27, the date of his martyrdom.

BIBLIOGRAPHY Mitropolit Evgenii, *Slovar' istoricheskii o svyatikh proslavlennykh v russkoi tserkvi* (1836; 2d ed., 1862), p. 142; A. V. Kartashev, *Ocherki po istorii russkoi tserkvi* (1959, 1991), vol. 1, pp. 154–155.

Karen L. Gordon

Kulp, H(arold) Stover (1894–1964), Church of the Brethren missionary in Nigeria. Born in Chester County, Pennsylvania, Kulp graduated from the Chester State Normal School, Juniata College (honorary D.D., 1948), and the University of Pennsylvania (M.A., 1920); he also studied at the Kennedy School of Missions, Hartford Seminary, Connecticut (1930–1931). After spending his early years as a teacher and pastor, he and Albert D. Helser were sent by the Church of the Brethren in 1922 to initiate missionary work in the Northeastern State of Nigeria, locating in Garkida. Neta Ruth (Royer) (b. 1896) joined her husband in 1923 but died the next year in childbirth. In 1926 Kulp married Christine Masterson (1896–1952), a Scottish missionary. Kulp built up a flourishing pioneer mission program with numerous congregations, created a system for writing the Bura and Margi languages, published primers, translated Scriptures, and established schools and a noted leprosarium. Shortly after his retirement and return to the United States in 1964, he died and was buried in Coventry, Pennsylvania.

Kulp was hailed as a church father by hundreds of Nigerians and as a pioneer leader by missionary colleagues. He served as chairman of the Mission Council of Northern Nigeria and president of the Christian Council of Nigeria. The Kulp Bible School at Nkwarhi honors his memory. After initial modest growth, the Nigerian Church of the Brethren has expanded rapidly since the 1950s.

BIBLIOGRAPHY The standard biography is Mary Ann Moyer Kulp, *No Longer Strangers: A Biography of H. Stover Kulp* (1968). See also Chalmer E. Faw, ed., *Lardin Gabas: A Land, a People, a Church* (1973); Church of the Brethren, *Gospel Messenger*, September 12, 1964, pp. 22–23, and December 19, 1964, pp. 14–16; Inez Long, *Faces among the Faithful* (1962, on Ruth and Christine Kulp); and Elgin S. Moyer, *Missions in the Church of the Brethren* (1931). On the growth of the church in Nigeria, see Charles H. Kraft, *Christianity in Culture: A Study of Dynamic Biblical Theologizing in Cross-Cultural Perspective* (1979) and *Communicating the Gospel God's Way* (1980).

Donald F. Durnbaugh

Kumm, (Hermann) Karl Wilhelm (1874–1930) *and* **Lucy Evangeline (Guinness)** (1865–1906), founders of the Sudan United Mission (SUM). Kumm, born in Wiesbaden, Germany, felt called to missionary work among Muslims. He was serving with the North Africa Mission in Egypt when, in 1899, he met Henry Grattan *Guinness, the celebrated evangelist, and his daughter Lucy. Lucy Guinness was known as a writer and editor, and a Christian worker in London's East End. She and Kumm were married in Cairo early in 1900; two sons were born, in 1901 and 1902. In 1901 the Sudan Pioneer Mission was begun; in 1904 Karl Kumm and two others left for Tripoli to study Hausa. In 1904 Lucy, in England with her children, convened a meeting of supporters for the work, renamed the Sudan United Mission. Karl completed a fact-finding expedition to the Upper Benue River area, spent Christmas 1905 with his family in England, and soon afterwards left for the United States, where Lucy and her sons joined him at Northfield, Massachusetts, nearby D. L. *Moody's conference center. In July 1906 he left for the Sudan, and shortly afterward in Northfield, Lucy suffered a miscarriage and died as a consequence. Lucy's sister, Geraldine Taylor, took care of the children until Kumm's remarriage in 1911. The work of the mission continued and expanded, with branches in British Commonwealth countries, Europe, and the United States. Kumm continued as its leader and director until 1924; in 1925 he retired to California. Today the society founded by the Kumms is known as Action Partners—Christians Reaching the World. The largest national churches arising from the work of SUM are the Church of Christ in Nigeria and the Sudanese Church of Christ (Nuba Mountains, Sudan).

BIBLIOGRAPHY Karl Kumm, *The Sudan: A Short Compendium of Facts and Figures about the Land of Darkness* (1907). Irene V. Cleverdon, *Pools in the Glowing Sands* (1936; biography of Karl Kumm); Michele Guinness, *The Guinness Legend* (1990); J. Lowry Maxwell, *Half a Century of Grace: A Jubilee History of the Sudan United Mission* (1954).

Jocelyn Murray

L

Lacombe, Albert (1827–1916), Catholic missionary in western Canada. Lacombe was born at Saint Sulpice, Quebec, and ordained in 1849. After two years at Pembina, North Dakota, with Georges *Belcourt, he accompanied Alexandre Taché, new auxiliary bishop of Saint Boniface, to Red River (present-day Winnipeg, Manitoba). He went on to Lac-Saint-Anne, near Edmonton, Alberta, where he joined the Oblates of Mary Immaculate in 1855. At Edmonton he founded the missions of Saint Joachim in 1858 and Saint Albert in 1861, and the mixed-blood colony of Saint-Paul-des-Cris in 1865. Assigned as a missionary to the Blackfoot and Cree Indians in the Calgary area in 1864, he acted as peacemaker between the two tribes when they went to war. In 1874 Taché named him pastor of Saint Mary's, Winnipeg, with responsibility for Catholic immigrants. In 1882 he returned to the Calgary district, where he acted as intermediary between the Canadian Pacific Railway and the Blackfoot Indians (1883) and founded the Indian residential school at Dunbow (High River) in 1884. During the Northwest Rebellion of 1885, on the request of the Canadian prime minister, he intervened with the Blackfoot Indians, convincing them not to join the uprising. He accompanied the commissioners for Treaties 8 and 11 in the immense Athabasca-Mackenzie district (1899). His name is associated with a widely used adaptation of François *Blanchet's *Catholic Ladder* and a Cree dictionary and grammar. He was loved by the Cree and the Blackfoot as one of their own. The Blackfoot Indians called him the Man of the Good Heart.

BIBLIOGRAPHY Paul-Emile Breton, *The Big Chief of the Prairies* (1955); Gaston Carrière, "Le père Albert Lacombe o.m.i. et le Pacifique Canadien," *Revue de l'Université d'Ottawa* 37 (1967): 287–321, 510–539, 611–638, and 38 (1968): 97–131, 316–350; James G. MacGregor, *Father Lacombe* (1975); J. Phelan, *The Bold Heart: The Story of Father Lacombe* (1956); Une Soeur de la Providence, *Le Père Lacombe d'après ses mémoires et souvenirs* (1916). There are extensive materials in the Oblate archives of Grandin Province, Saint Albert, Alberta.

Achiel Peelman, OMI

Lacroix, Alphonse François (1799–1859), pioneer missionary in Bengal. At age 15, Lacroix ran away from his home near Neuville, Switzerland, but heeding a voice on the road, he returned home and was converted. Commissioned as a missionary of the Netherlands Missionary Society in 1820, he served in the Dutch colony of Chinsurah (22 miles north of Calcutta) from 1821 to 1826. When it became British in 1825, he joined the London Missionary Society (LMS) and worked in the fishing villages of South Calcutta, where there was a small mass movement. He was a tireless street preacher, drawing crowds by his personality and good use of Bengali. In 1837 he moved to Bhowanipore, where he concentrated on evangelism and theological training in Bengali. A truly ecumenical figure, he was a founding member (1829) of the Calcutta Missionary Council. Periodically he served as LMS mission secretary.

Lacroix married Hannah Herklots of Chinsurah, a protégée of Hannah *Marshman. His wife worked tirelessly to educate Bengali women and raised their three daughters to continue the work. Lacroix and his wife took furlough only once, from 1839 to 1842, when on the heels of a revival, he swept French-speaking Switzerland and parts of France into the missionary movement by his oratory. On the return voyage their daughter Hannah became engaged to Joseph *Mullens, later a missiologist. Joseph and Hannah Mullens wrote the only biography of Lacroix just before Hannah Mullens's tragically premature death. Alphonse Lacroix died in Calcutta; Hannah Lacroix died in Brighton, England, in 1880.

BIBLIOGRAPHY Joseph Mullens, *Brief Memorials of the Revd. Alphonse Francois Lacroix* (1862). Lacroix's letters, in the LMS archives at SOAS, London, are practically the only surviving record of his work, since apart from a few tracts and a volume of sermons, he could not bring himself to write anything, even on his great hobby, botany, in which field he made a number of discoveries.

E. M. Jackson

Ladurie, Marie le Roy. *See* Marie de l'Assomption.

Lafitau, Joseph-François (1681–1746), French Catholic missionary in Canada. Born into a wealthy family in Bordeaux, Lafitau became a Jesuit in 1696, studied at the best schools in France, and went to Canada as a missionary in 1711. Living among the Mohawks at Caughnawaga (Sault Saint Louis) near Montreal, he was a good observer, read the reports of previous missionaries, and learned from Julien Garnier (1643–1730). After five years he was sent to France to plead that alcoholic beverages be prohibited to Indians. Detained in France, he wrote *Moeurs des sauvages Amériquains, comparées aux moeurs des premiers temps* (1724), published in two volumes. Two more four-volume editions were published in the same year. Lafitau described the customs of the Iroquois, comparing them with peoples of classical antiquity. He argued for the historic unity of the human race sharing originally a common God-given religion. This comparative method was fashionable at that time, but the reliability of his documentation on the Iroquois placed Lafitau far ahead of his contemporaries. What he wrote about age grades, initiation, and the matriarchy was taken up again more than 150 years later by Arnold van Gennep, W. *Schmidt, and others. Lafitau is regarded by many as a precursor of the modern ethnographer. In the years from 1727 to 1740 he lived again in the Jesuit mission of Canada. He died in Bordeaux.

BIBLIOGRAPHY Early translations of Lafitau's main work were published in Dutch (1731, 1751) and German (1752). William N. Fenton and Elizabeth L. Moore prepared an English edition, *Customs of the American Savages, Compared with the Customs of Primitive Times* (1977). William N. Fenton, "J. F. Lafitau (1681–1746), Precursor of Scientific Anthropology," *Southwestern Journal of Anthropology* 25 (1969): 173–187; K. Kälin, *Indianer und Urvölker nach Jos. Fr. Lafitau (1681–1746)* (1943).

Otto Bischofberger, SMB

Laiser, (Loirera) Lazarus (1892?–1958), Masai teacher, evangelist, pastor, and church administrator. Laiser was a Mwarusha, an offshoot of the Masai people of Tanganyika Territory (now Tanzania). Given the name Lazarus at his baptism (1911), he was educated at a Lutheran school in Arusha, at the Marangu Teacher Training School, and in the Lutheran Pastors' Course at Machame, Moshi. He was ordained in 1943. With the internment of German missionaries of the Leipzig Mission during World War II, Laiser emerged as the local leader for the work, becoming vice-president of the Lutheran Church of Northern Tanganyika (1948–1956), with most of its members in the areas around Meru and Kilimanjaro Mountains. He played a decisive role in getting his church to start mission work among the Sonjo, a Bantu people to the west of Lake Natron in the Great Rift Valley of eastern Africa, near the border with Kenya. He had persistently urged his colleagues to start such work and had made a personal visit in 1928 to familiarize himself with the country and its people; finally the church was able to send missionaries in 1949.

Concern for health and education were basic to Laiser's mission strategy. He also sought to affirm the cultural values of his people in the context of the Christian faith, thus becoming an early pioneer of indigenization/inculturation. The work was supported entirely by local contributions. Laiser never formally retired after leaving his leadership position in the church in 1956, but continued to supervise and consolidate the mission work. He died in a car accident near the Ngorongoro Crater, Monduli district, while on one of his regular visits to the new mission field.

BIBLIOGRAPHY Max Pätzig, *Laiser, Lasaros: Ein Leben für junge Kirchen in Ostafrica* (1959); *UMOJA* (monthly newsletter of the Lutheran Church of Northern Tanganyika), 10 (September 1958): 125 (obit.).

Lalashowi Swai

Lake, John Graham (1870–1935), missionary to South Africa, faith healer, and pastor. Called to preach, and prompted by several healings in his immediate family under the ministry of John Alexander Dowie, Lake left Methodism to join Dowie's Christian Catholic Apostolic Church at Zion City (present-day Zion), Illinois, in 1901. During services held in the city by Charles F. *Parham in 1906, he became a Pentecostal.

In 1908, Lake and Thomas Hezmalhalch and their families sailed as independent missionaries to South Africa, where the Dowie Movement, or the "Zionists," had already gained a foothold. Reports of miraculous healings at Lake's services in Doornfontein and later in Johannesburg attracted widespread attention and contributed to the advancement of the Pentecostal movement. In the same year, he and other missionaries established the Apostolic Faith Mission of South Africa (registered with the government in 1913), currently the largest organized Pentecostal denomination in the country. Though paternalistic in his attitude toward blacks, the Coloured, and Indians, Lake denounced segregated worship. He left South Africa permanently in 1913 and continued in evangelistic, faith healing, and pastoral work, centering his activities in Portland, Oregon.

BIBLIOGRAPHY John G. Lake, *The Astounding Diary of John G. Lake* (1987); C. R. De Wet, "The Apostolic Faith Movement in Africa: 1908–1980. A Case Study in Church Growth in a Segregated Society" (Ph.D. diss., Univ. of Cape Town, 1989); J. Nico Horn, "South African Pentecostals and Apartheid: A Short Case Study of the Apostolic Faith Mission," in *Pentecost, Mission, and Ecumenism: Studies in Intercultural Theology*, Jan A. B. Jongeneel, ed. (1992); Gordon Lindsay, *John G. Lake—Apostle to Africa* (n.d.).

Gary B. McGee

La Lande, Jean de (?–1646), French lay worker martyred in New York. Very little is known about La Lande. He was born in Dieppe, Normandy, and met his death in the Mohawk village of Ossernenon (now Auriesville, New York). Five times official Jesuit documents of the early 1640s refer to him as a "young man" and once as a "young lad." He went to Canada about 1642 as a *donné*, a man who voluntarily bound himself by contract to serve the missionaries in return for lodging and food. He seems to have lived in Three Rivers, Quebec, until September 1646, when he set out with Isaac *Jogues for Mohawk country. Jogues and La Lande met a hostile reception: they were taken prisoner, beaten, robbed, stripped, and eventually tomahawked to death on October 18 and 19. La Lande was canonized by Pope *Pius XI on June 29, 1930.

BIBLIOGRAPHY Reuben Gold Thwaites, ed., *The Jesuit Relations and Allied Documents, 1610–1791,* vol. 31 (1959), p. 122; J. Wynne, *The Jesuit Martyrs of North America* (1925).

Jacques Monet, SJ

Lalemant, Gabriel (1610–1649), French Jesuit missionary martyr. Born in Paris, Lalemant entered the Jesuit novitiate on March 24, 1630, and within two years had volunteered for foreign missions. It would take 14 years for his wishes to be fulfilled, but after various assignments for studies and for teaching (1632–1646), he left for Quebec, arriving in September 1646. He is said to have been the most delicate and frail of all the seventeenth-century Jesuit missionaries in North America. Still, in 1648 he left Quebec for Wendake (the land of the Huron Indians east of Georgian Bay, Ontario), where he worked zealously. He was reported to be unusually fluent in the language within a few months. Along with Jean de *Brébeuf he was captured by the Iroquois at the Wendake mission of Saint-Louis on March 16, 1649, and taken to Saint Ignace (west of present-day Orillia, Ontario), where he was tortured for some 12 hours before he died. Lalemant's reputation for sanctity spread with the years. He was canonized by Pope *Pius XI on June 29, 1930. In 1954 the grave where his remains were buried with those of de Brébeuf was discovered at Sainte-Marie Among the Hurons, Ontario, by Dennis Hegarty, and the site has since become the focus of many pilgrimages.

BIBLIOGRAPHY Camille de Rochemonteix, *Les Jésuites et la Nouvelle-France,* vol. 2 (1895–1896), pp. 81 ff; Reuben Gold Thwaites, ed., *The Jesuit Relations and Allied Documents, 1610–1791* (1959).

Jacques Monet, SJ

Lalemant, Jérôme (1593–1673), French Jesuit missionary to New France, where he was given the Huron name Achiendassé. Born in Paris, Lalemant entered the Jesuit novitiate there in 1610. After his studies, he spent 15 years in teaching, divided between the Collège de Clermont, Rouen, and the Collège de Blois. In 1638 he arrived in Quebec and succeeded Jean de *Brébeuf as superior of the Huron mission at Sainte Marie, on the eastern shore of the Georgian Bay (Ontario), the most important establishment west of Quebec in New France. He introduced key innovations, including employment of lay brothers and the use of a Huron catechism.

In 1645, Lalemant took up a new post as superior of the Jesuits in Canada. During the next five years many Indians and seven Frenchmen, including his nephew, Gabriel *Lalemant, were martyred. This prompted him to return to France to plead the cause of the mission. Returning again to France in 1656, he intended to remain, but in 1659 Bishop Laval requested that he resume his post as superior of the Jesuits, and under his leadership their work was renewed.

Lalemant wrote many letters and reports documenting the Huron mission in the years 1639 to 1644. From 1645 to 1672, he was also spiritual director of *Marie de l'Incarnation, who described him as "father of the poor, French as well as Indian . . . the ardent servant of the Church." The Sainte-Marie-des-Hurons complex has been restored and is a major pilgrim site.

BIBLIOGRAPHY T. J. Campbell, *Pioneer Priests of North America, 1642–1710,* vol. 2 (1914); John Webster Grant, *Moon of Wintertime* (1984); Irene Mahoney, ed., *Marie of the Incarnation: Selected Writings* (1989); Reuben Gold Thwaites, ed., *Jesuit Relations and Allied Documents,* 73 vols. (1896–1901); Bruce G. Trigger, *The Children of Aataentsic* (1976).

Paul R. Dekar

Lambert de la Motte, Pierre (1624–1679), pioneer Catholic missionary to Siam and Indochina, and one of the founders of the Société des Missions Etrangères de Paris (Paris Foreign Mission Society). La Motte was born near Lisieux, France. After practicing law for nine years at the Cour des Aides in Rouen, he entered the Seminary of Coutances and was ordained a priest in 1655. Drawn at first toward mission in Canada, he was asked by his friend François *Pallu to accompany him to Rome to get nominations of apostolic vicars for China. La Motte went and was himself appointed titular bishop of Beirut, with responsibilities as vicar apostolic of Cochin China and apostolic administrator of southern China. He left Paris in 1660 and, traveling mostly on foot, reached Ayuthia, Siam (Thailand), in 1662. He experienced extortion and persecution from the Portuguese and from the Goa Inquisition. Trying to bring order into the missions, he founded a seminary for Siamese young men, and also for those from Tonkin and Cochin China. He also founded the congregation of the Lovers of the Cross for women in Siam and Indochina. He was on especially good terms with the king of Siam, Phra-Narai, and was the main supporter for priests of Missions Etrangères in the Far East. He died in Ayuthia, Siam.

BIBLIOGRAPHY Jean Guennou, *Missions Etrangères de Paris* (1986); Adrien Launay, *Histoire générale de la Société des Missions Etrangères* (1894).

Joseph Lévesque, PSS

Lambie, Thomas A. (1885–1954), American medical missionary in Ethiopia. Born in Pittsburgh and raised in a godly Presbyterian home, Lambie received his medical degree from the University of Pittsburgh in 1907 and the same year sailed for Sudan as a United Presbyterian missionary. Soon after meeting missionary Charlotte Clave in Alexandria, Egypt, he married her, and together they opened a new station in 1911 at Nasir among the Nuer, on the southeastern border of Sudan. They crossed the border into Ethiopia in 1919 to help fight a flu epidemic, and later, after he had successfully treated a provincial governor, Lambie was commended to the future emperor, Haile Selassie, who asked him to open a hospital in Addis Ababa. Lambie also became Selassie's personal physician. In 1927, impatient with the inaction of his U.S. mission headquarters, Lambie launched the Abyssinian Frontiers Mission, which quickly established several new stations in the south and southwest. The same year he merged the new work with the Sudan Interior Mission (SIM). Additional stations were established some 200 miles to the north of Addis Ababa. In 1934 he gave up U.S. citizenship in order to hold property in Ethiopia, but later lost his Ethiopian citizenship after falling out of favor with the emperor, who disagreed with Lambie's decision to treat casualties on both sides in the war with Italy. During the Italian occupation (1935–1941), Lambie served as executive director of the Ethiopian Red Cross. Although heart problems prompted his return to the United States in 1942, in 1945 he was able to sail for Palestine under the Independent Board for Presbyterian Foreign Missions. His wife died enroute and was buried at Port Said, Egypt. His second wife, Irma Schneck, an SIM missionary from Ethiopia, helped him open Berachah Tuberculosis Sanatorium in Bethlehem in 1952. He died in Jerusalem in 1954 as he prepared a message to be given on Easter morning at the Garden Tomb. He is buried in Pittsburgh.

BIBLIOGRAPHY Thomas A. Lambie, *Abayte! or, Ethiopia's Plea* (1935), *A Doctor without a Country* (1939), *A Doctor Carries On* (1942), *Boot and Saddle in Africa* (1943), and *A Doctor's Great Commission* (1954).

Robert T. Coote

Lamburn, Roger George Patrick (1904–1993), Anglican missionary in Tanganyika (Tanzania). Lamburn was known as Robin Lamburn, born in London, and studied pathology at Cambridge. After theological training and a curacy, he went to the Diocese of Masasi in 1930 with the Universities' Mission to Central Africa. He served at Chidya and Luatala, Tanganyika, and then at Lukwika, where he supported circumcision rites for boys in a Christian framework. He was warden of St. Cyprian's Theological College, Namasakata (1936–1949), then archdeacon, and finally education secretary. In 1961 he moved to the Rufiji Delta for an itinerant ministry, and from 1965 until his death lived at Kindwitwi, a leprosy village, founded under German rule. In addition to a modern clinic, he provided it with cultivated land and thousands of cashew trees for self-support. In 1985 he was awarded the Albert Schweitzer Prize. In his acceptance address he declared, "If you go to give, you must also be prepared to receive from those to whom you aspire to give; if you wish to teach, you must be prepared to learn from those whom you teach." And, "My friends, we do not go into the Third World to give or to teach, but to share."

BIBLIOGRAPHY R. Lamburn, "Some Notes on the Yao," *Tanganyika Notes and Records* (1950). A. G. Blood, *The History of the Universities' Mission to Central Africa*, vol. 3 (1962); N. Q. King and Klaus Fiedler, with Gavin White, *Robin Lamburn—from a Missionary's Notebook: The Yao of Tunduru and Other Essays* (1991).

Gavin White

Lambuth, Walter Russell (1854–1921), Methodist missionary physician in China and Japan, and missionary bishop in Brazil and Africa. Lambuth was born in Shanghai, the son of the founding missionaries of Methodist Episcopal Church, South (MECS) missions in China. Having decided to be a medical missionary, he obtained both the M.D. and ordination as elder in 1877. Also in 1877 he married Daisy Kelley, daughter of China missionaries and granddaughter of Mrs. M. L. Kelley, who organized the first Southern Methodist women to support foreign missions. From 1877 until 1885, with the exception of further medical study in the United States, he did medical work in China, including founding an opium treatment center in Shanghai, opening Soochow hospital, and beginning what became Rockefeller Hospital in Peking. In 1887 he and his parents founded the MECS mission in Japan. As superintendent of the Japanese mission, he turned from medical to educational and evangelistic work.

In 1891 the Lambuths returned to the United States and Walter became editor of the *Methodist Review of Missions*. From 1892 until 1910 he served as secretary of the board of missions. He led in ecumenical causes, including the Foreign Missions Conference of North America, the Ecumenical Missionary Conference of 1900, and the Edinburgh World Missionary Conference of 1910, including its Continuation Committee. Under his leadership, Southern Methodists began missions in Cuba and Korea. In 1910 he was elected bishop of the church in Brazil and Africa. With linguist John Wesley Gilbert of the Colored Methodist Episcopal Church, Lambuth in 1911 traveled 4,100 miles through the Belgian Congo and opened Methodist missions in central Africa. In 1919 he initiated missions to Russians and Koreans in Siberia and Manchuria. He died in Japan, as had his father before him; his ashes were buried next to his mother's in Shanghai.

BIBLIOGRAPHY Walter Russell Lambuth, *Side Lights on the Orient* (1908), *Winning the World for Christ: A Study in Dynamics* (1915), and *Medical Missions: The Twofold Task* (1920). An obituary by Bishop James Atkins is in the Nashville *Christian Advocate*, November 18, 1921, pp. 1447–1448. Eugene Clayton Calhoun, *Of Men Who Ventured Much and Far: The Congo Quest of Dr. Gilbert and Bishop Lambuth* (1961); W. W. Pinson, *Walter Russell Lambuth: Prophet and Pioneer* (1924). Lambuth's journals are held at the J. B. Cain Archives, Millsaps-Wilson Library, Millsaps College, Jackson, Miss.

Dana L. Robert

Lanneau, Sophie Stephens (1880–1963), Southern Baptist missionary in China. Born in Lexington, Missouri, Lanneau moved to Wake Forest, North Carolina, at the age of eight. After graduating summa cum laude from Meredith College in 1902, she pursued her missionary dream under strong influence from the Student Volunteer Movement and arrived in China in 1907. In 1911 she founded Wei Ling Girl's Academy in Soochow (Suzhou), Kiangsu (Jiangsu) Province, where she was principal (1911–1927) and teacher (1911–1950). Starting with only seventeen students, between 1911 and 1950 she saw more than 1,000 Chinese women graduated from the institution. In the 1920s and the 1930s, Lanneau also served as a trustee of the College of Shanghai for eight years and was a council member of the East China Christian Educational Association. During World War II, she was interned by the Japanese but was repatriated in 1943. Immediately after the war in 1946, she rushed back to China to her academy, but retired to Wake Forest after the Chinese Communists took over the school in 1950. Lanneau remained a devotee of China affairs, giving many reports about China on behalf of the Southern Baptist Convention Foreign Mission Board.

BIBLIOGRAPHY Li Li, "'Sparing Alas! But Also Lengthening and Strengthening in Soochow': Sophie Lanneau's Response to Chinese Nationalist Revolution," *American Baptist Quarterly* 13 (September 1994): 249–261, and "Mission in Suzhou: Sophie Lanneau and Wei Ling Girl's Academy, 1907–1950" (Ph.D. diss., Univ. of North Carolina, 1997).

Li Li

Lapsley, Samuel Norvell (1866–1892), Presbyterian missionary in the Congo. Born in Selma, Alabama, and a graduate of McCormick Seminary in 1889, Lapsley was an ordained minister and missionary of the Presbyterian Church U.S. (Southern). He served in the Congo Free State from May 1890 to March 1892. Together with his African American co-worker William H. *Sheppard, he founded the American Presbyterian Congo Mission (APCM). Together they explored the Kwango and Kasai river systems, selected the site of Luebo Station, pioneer station of the APCM on the Lulua River, set basic principles for the work, and established relationships with the state administration. Lapsley began the analysis and study of the Tshikete, Bushongo, and Tshiluba languages of the Kasai area of the Congo, recorded native songs and customs, initiated the translation of hymns and portions of the Bible, and launched the organization of a strong indigenous church. His untimely death from blackwater fever occurred at Matadi, Lower Congo, where he is buried at the former Swedish Mission site called "Underhill." From the APCM emerged the Presbyterian Church of Zaire.

BIBLIOGRAPHY James Lapsley, ed., *Life and Letters of Samuel Norvell Lapsley* (1893); William E. Phipps, *The Sheppards and Lapsley: Pioneer Presbyterians in the Congo* (1991); E. C. Scott, *Ministerial Directory of the Presbyterian Church, U.S., 1861–1941* (1942). Additional material can be found at the Department of History, Presbyterian Church (U.S.A.), Montreat, N.C.

John R. Hendrick and Winifred K. Vass

Larsen, Lars Peter (1862–1940), Danish missionary in India. Larsen was born not far from Copenhagen, the son of a country blacksmith. Thanks to the generosity of a local landowner, he received a thorough education, including university. In 1889 he was sent by the Danish Missionary Society (DMS) to work in Madras. In 1899 he left the DMS to work under YMCA auspices among students; and in 1910 he was appointed to the faculty of the newly established United Theological College in Bangalore, becoming principal the following year, a position he held until 1924. Theologically he was a liberal, mistrusted by confessional Lutherans; but in his life of faith he was a model of devotion, with leanings toward a Keswick-style holiness spirituality, and greatly in demand as a convention speaker. In 1924 Larsen was appointed to supervise a revision of the Tamil Bible, which task occupied him for the remainder of his missionary career and was concluded within a day of his seventieth birthday in 1932. He left India for the last time on March 20, 1933, leaving behind a unique reputation for spirituality, scholarship (he was an outstanding linguist), and personal integrity. His written output was extensive in Danish, English, and Tamil, and his Bible studies were especially valuable. What many consider his best book, a study of the relationship of Christianity to Hindu spirituality (*Hindu-Aandsliv og Kristendommen,* 1907), was unfortunately published only in Danish. Larsen's last seven years were spent in retirement in Denmark. He died ten weeks after the German invasion.

BIBLIOGRAPHY Carl Bindslev, *L. P. Larsen: Evangelist and Theologian* (1962); James M. Gibbs, ed., *L. P. Larsen: A Theology for Mission* (1978), which contains a good selection of Larsen's own writings on a range of subjects; Eric J. Sharpe, "Lars Peter Larsen," in Gerald H. Anderson et al., eds., *Mission Legacies* (1994), pp. 297–306.

Eric J. Sharpe

Larson, Reuben E(mmanuel) (1897–1981), missionary in Ecuador and a founder of missionary radio station HCJB. Born in Bancroft, Iowa, Larson graduated from Boone Biblical College, Boone, Iowa and St. Paul Biblical Institute in Saint Paul, Minnesota. Commissioned by the Christian and Missionary Alliance (C&MA), he arrived with his wife, Grace, in Ecuador in 1924 with a sense of call to evangelize the Quichua Indians. The Larsons established a mission station at Dos Ríos, the junction of the Tena and Misauwali Rivers, an eight-day trek from the capital, Quito. Because of their rapport with the Indians and the many services they provided to them, the government asked Larson to supervise schools and road construction in the area. These contacts were helpful when in 1930 Clarence *Jones and Larson asked for a license and contract to start HCJB, the first missionary radio station in Latin America. Seconded by C&MA to this project, the Larsons eventually moved to Quito, where they served until 1972. From retirement in Florida, and until his death, Larson still traveled to Ecuador promoting a program of pastoral and theological literature for national pastors and missionaries. In 1965 Wheaton College granted him an honorary LL.D.

BIBLIOGRAPHY Frank S. Cook, *Seeds in the Wind* (1961); Lois Neely, *Come up to This Mountain* (1980). Biographical material under the care of Larson's daughter, Margaret (Larson) Carlson, is being arranged for deposit in the Billy Graham Center archives, Wheaton, Ill.

Samuel Escobar

La Salle, Jean-Baptiste de (1651-1719), founder of the Brothers of the Christian Schools. Born in Rheims, France, de La Salle was ordained to the priesthood in 1678. He established the Congregation of the Brothers of the Christian Schools in 1680 at Rheims. His aim was to provide Christian educators who took their teaching task as a consecration to God and a service to the church. From 1682 he sent brothers to public schools that requested them. The Institute of the Brothers of Christian Schools, at once a novitiate and a normal school, was founded in 1694 in Paris. De La Salle was elected superior but maintained that the Brothers were laymen. He died at Saint Yon, near Rouen, France, where he had established the headquarters of his congregation. He wrote spiritual treaties which were published after his death. The Brothers of the Christian Schools spread throughout France in their founder's lifetime. Their missionary outreach overseas began after the French Revolution; Brother Philippe, superior general from 1838 to 1874, gave the congregation its international dimension with hundreds of new foundations in the territories under the jurisdiction of the Propaganda Fide in Europe, America, Africa, and Asia. The Generalate of the Christian Brothers was transferred to Rome in 1936.

BIBLIOGRAPHY Educational treatises by de La Salle include *Les règles de la bienséance et de la civilité chrétienne* (1702, 1964) and *Les devoirs d'un chrétien envers Dieu et les moyens de pouvoir bien s'en acquitter* (1703, 1964). Among many biographers, W. J. Battersby has contributed several important studies, including *St. John Baptist de la Salle* (1957), *De La Salle: A Pioneer of Modern Education* (1949), and *History of the Institute of the Brothers of the Christian Schools* (vol.1: 1719-1798; vol.2: 1800-1850; vol.3: 1850-1900) (1960-1963). See also Frère Alban, *Histoire de l'Institut des Frères des Écoles chrétiennes, expansion hors de France, 1700-1966* (1970).

Marc R. Spindler

Las Casas, Bartolomé de (1484-1566), celebrated defender of the Indians in sixteenth-century Spanish America. Raised in Seville, Las Casas went to America in 1502 as an encomendero, with official license to exact tribute from the Indians. He became a priest in 1507, and was influenced by the Dominicans, who denounced their fellow Spaniards for abusing the Indians. In 1514, after experiencing a deep conversion, he set out to champion the cause of the New World natives.

He returned to Spain in 1515 and received the title of Protector of the Indians from Cardinal Cisneros. In a second visit he won the favor of Charles V, emperor of France, who was also king of Spain. From that point on his words and deeds had a powerful influence on imperial policy with respect to the Indians, even though he also won many enemies, especially among the encomenderos. In 1523 he joined the Dominican order. On the practical side Las Casas not only denounced specific abuses, but in 1520 also founded a colony in Venezuela made up of Spanish farmers and free Indians. Although that experiment failed, he tried others. Later, as bishop of Chiapas (1544-1547) he carried his cause to Mexico and Central America.

Las Casas was most successful in influencing opinion through the pen. In his tract "The Only Method of Attracting All Peoples to the True Faith" (1537), he argued in favor of peaceful means to evangelize the Indians. In 1552 he published "A Brief Account of the Destruction of the Indies." This polemical essay became the main source for the "black legend," the widespread belief especially among non-Spanish authors that Spain did nothing but exploit and decimate the Indians in the New World. His major works, *Historia de las Indias* and *Apologética Historia,* were published after his death.

In his own lifetime Las Casas saw evidence of the success of his campaign. In 1542 the Crown decreed laws that significantly limited the power of the encomenderos, and in 1537 Pope Paul III declared in his bull *Sublimis Deus* that the Indians are rational beings with the same rights as European Christians. Returning to Valladolid, Spain, in 1547, Las Casas engaged in a major debate with Juan Ginés de Sepúlveda in 1550 and 1551 over the legitimacy of the Spanish conquest. Modern critics point out that Las Casas inflated numbers and exaggerated abuses, thus diminishing his reliability as a historical witness. But his admirers note that the Spanish Dominican won a major moral battle, in theory if not in practice, by forcing Europeans to recognize the rights of the Indians. Known as the Apostle of the Indies, he is credited with making a major contribution to the modern concept of human rights. He died in Madrid.

BIBLIOGRAPHY Las Casas's major works can be found in *Obras completas* (1989-1990) and *Obras escogidas, Biblioteca de Autores Españoles,* 5 vols, Luis Pérez de Tudela, ed. (1957-1958). Among the few English translations of his works are Stafford Poole, *In Defense of Indians* (1974), and Helen R. Parish, ed., *Bartolomé de las Casas: The Only Way* (1992). For introduction to Las Casas in English, see Lewis Hanke, *The Spanish Struggle for Justice in the Conquest of America* (1949, 1965), *Aristotle and the American Indians* (1959), and *All Mankind Is One* (1994); Helen R. Parish and H. R. Wagner, *The Life and Writings of Bartolomé de Las Casas* (1967); Juan Friede and Benjamin Keen, eds., *Bartolomé de Las Casas in History: Toward an Understanding of the Man and His Work* (1971). The best analysis of Las Casas as a theologian may be found in Gustavo Gutiérrez's *Las Casas: In Search of the Poor of Jesus Christ* (1993).

Jeffrey Klaiber, SJ

Latourette, Kenneth Scott (1884-1968), American Orientalist, missiologist and historian of the expansion of

Christianity. Born in Oregon City, Oregon, Latourette was educated at McMinnville (later Linfield) College (B.S., 1904) and Yale University (B.A., 1906, M.A. 1907, Ph.D. 1909), then spent a year as traveling secretary for the Student Volunteer Movement, before going to China in 1910 on the teaching staff of Yale-in-China at Changsha in Hunan province. He returned home in ill health after two years. Following two years of recovery in Oregon, Latourette taught part time at Reed College in Portland until he joined the faculty of Denison University in Granville, Ohio, in 1916. While at Denison his first major book, *The Development of China,* appeared (1917), he wrote *The Development of Japan* (1918; later reissued as *The History of Japan*), and he began working on *A History of Christian Missions in China* (1929). In 1918 he was ordained to the Baptist ministry. In 1921 he was appointed (as successor to Harlan Page *Beach) the D. Willis James Professor of Missions at Yale University Divinity School; in 1949 he was named Sterling Professor of Missions and Oriental History at Yale, his post until he retired in 1953. In 1945 his presidential address to the American Society of Church History was titled "A Historian Looks Ahead: The Future of Christianity in the Light of Its Past"; his presidential address to the American Historical Association in 1948 was "The Christian Understanding of History." He also served as president of the American Baptist Convention, the Japan International Christian University Foundation, and the Far Eastern Association (later the Association for Asian Studies). Unmarried, Latourette lived on the campus at Yale Divinity School where he was affectionately known as "Uncle Ken" especially by his student secretaries and those who joined his weekly discussion groups for prayer and Bible study. An evangelical, he regularly taught a Sunday morning class for students at a local Baptist church. In 1952 he was serving on thirty boards and committees in New Haven and New York. He received honorary doctorates from seventeen universities in five countries.

Latourette's career at Yale was marked by a steady stream of publications that established his international reputation as historian and apologist of Christian missions. Most notable were two monumental series, *A History of the Expansion of Christianity* (7 vols., 1937–1945) and *Christianity in a Revolutionary Age: A History of Christianity in the Nineteenth and Twentieth Centuries* (5 vols., 1958–1962). His central thesis was that "throughout its history [Christianity] has gone forward by major pulsations. Each advance has carried it further than the one before. Of the alternating recessions, each has been briefer and less marked than the one which preceded it" (*History of the Expansion,* vol. 7 [1945], p. 494). He believed that "in A.D. 1944 Christianity was affecting more deeply more different nations and cultures than ever before." Yet at the time of his death he was unsure whether the period from 1914 to 1960 was a period of advance or retreat. Latourette was killed when an automobile accidentally hit him in front of his family home in Oregon City.

BIBLIOGRAPHY *Beyond the Ranges* (1967) is Latourette's autobiography. A Festschrift, *Frontiers of the Christian World Mission since 1938,* Wilber C. Harr, ed. (1962), includes Latourette's autobiographical reflection "My Guided Life," a biographical essay by E. Theodore Bachmann, and a detailed bibliography of Latourette's publications through 1960. For other assessments see William Richey Hogg, "Kenneth Scott Latourette," Gerald H. Anderson et al., eds., *Mission Legacies* (1994), pp. 416–427, Tracey K. Jones, Jr, "History's Lessons for Tomorrow's Mission," *IBMR* 10 (1986): 50–53, and Norman Kutcher, "The Benign Bachelor: Kenneth Scott Latourette between China and the United States," *Journal of American-East Asian Relations* 2 (1993): 399–424. A memorial tribute by M. Searle Bates, "Christian Historian, Doer of Christian History: In Memory of Kenneth Scott Latourette, 1884–1968," appeared in *IRM* 58 (1969): 317–326. The *New York Times* had an obituary, January 1, 1969. For his historiography, see William Lee Pitts, Jr., "World Christianity: The Church History Writing of Kenneth Scott Latourette" (Ph.D. diss., Vanderbilt University, 1969), and William A. Speck, "Kenneth Scott Latourette's Vocation as Christian Historian," *Christian Scholar's Review* 4 (1975): 285–299. Latourette's manuscripts, letters and papers are in the library of Yale Divinity School.

Gerald H. Anderson

Laubach, Frank Charles (1884–1970), Congregational missionary and apostle of world literacy. Born in Benton, Pennsylvania, Laubach graduated from Princeton University (1909), from Union Theological Seminary, New York (1913), and from Columbia University (Ph.D., 1915). He married Effa Emaline Seely, a nurse, in 1912, and in 1915 they sailed to the Philippines as missionaries of the American Board of Commissioners for Foreign Missions (ABCFM). When local hostilities frustrated his aim of working among the Muslims of southern Mindanao, he did evangelistic work among the Catholic population in northern Mindanao until he was appointed to the faculty of Union Theological Seminary in Manila in 1921. Combining teaching with administration and fund-raising, he also wrote two popular books on the Philippines and did evangelistic work in the city and among students. In 1929 he began work at Dansalan in Mindanao, a Muslim area. As he struggled to reach the highly resistant Moros, he found that the system he had developed for learning Maranao could be adapted to teach people to read their own language. Enthusiastic reception of the program led to rapid expansion, and when American mission support for literacy teachers dried up with the onset of the Depression, a local chief ordered each learner to teach others. The "Each One Teach One" principle, together with graphic charts linking pictures with words and syllables and wide distribution of simple reading materials for new readers, constituted the Laubach method. It proved highly successful throughout the Philippines. In 1935 Laubach began to introduce his method in other countries, and in 1945 he was appointed "missionary at large" of the ABCFM to work with Lit-Lit (the Committee on Literacy and Christian Literature) of the National Council of Churches in the U.S.A., which he had helped establish. After he retired in 1945, Laubach formed Laubach Literacy Inc. to work worldwide, and in 1968 he launched Laubach Literacy Action to work in the United States. His work touched 103 countries, involved 313 languages, and taught 100 million people to read. His fifty-six books promoted both literacy and the intense spirituality which marked his life. In 1984 a U.S. postage stamp in the Great Americans series was issued in his honor.

BIBLIOGRAPHY Laubach's *Letters by a Modern Mystic* (1937) and *Channels of Spiritual Power* (1954) reflect his spiritual quest; *Toward a Literate World* (1938), *Teaching the World to Read* (1947), *How to Teach One and Win One for Christ* (1964), and *Forty Years with the Silent Billion* (1970) deal with his literacy work. See also the essay by Peter Gowing, a younger missionary colleague, in Gerald H. Anderson et al., eds., *Mission Legacies* (1994), pp. 500–507. David E. Mason, *Apostle to the Illiterates* (1966) is a useful short biography with an extensive list of Laubach's writings. Bob Laubach's *The Vision Lives On* (1984) is an intimate family reminiscence with many photos.

David M. Stowe

Laufer, Carl (1904–1969), Catholic missionary and anthropologist. Born at Güsten, Germany, Laufer became a member of the Missionaries of the Sacred Heart (MSC). Inspired by the writings of Wilhelm *Schmidt, during his theological studies he showed a special interest in anthropology, the science of religions, and missiology. In 1929 he was sent to Rabaul, New Britain (today part of Papua New Guinea), where he was responsible for the mission station at Rakunai. In 1955 he had to return to Germany for health reasons. From 1959 to 1969 he was a lecturer at the high school of the MSC at Oeventrop, Germany. He published numerous articles in various journals and became a member of several anthropological societies. Although he had no degree in anthropology, he was a keen observer with an empathetic approach toward Melanesians, mainly the Baining people. He was convinced that God had already been in Melanesia before the missionaries arrived and that Christians should seek the *logoi spermatikoi* (the word of God that is scattered among human cultures). Laufer's work anticipated the inculturation of the church in Melanesia.

BIBLIOGRAPHY Hermann Janssen et al, eds., *Carl Laufer, MSC, Missionar und Ethnologe auf New-Guinea* (1975).

Fritz Kollbrunner, SMB

Launay, Adrien (1853–1927), Catholic mission historian. A member of the Paris Foreign Mission Society, Launay left France in 1877 for Saigon, in what was then known as Western Cochin China. Because of failing health, he returned to Paris within five years. Appointed archivist of his society, he then embarked on a prolific career as a mission historian. Between 1884 and his death, he published forty-five books, sketched maps for the weekly French magazine *Les Missions Catholiques,* and contributed ten chapters to the five-volume work *Les Missions catholiques françaises au XIXe siècle,* directed by Jean-Baptiste Piolet. His many projects were based not only on archival documents he found at the Paris Foreign Mission Society, the Bibliothèque Nationale, Propaganda Fide, and the British Museum but also on research he conducted in India and the Far East. At the same time, he gathered up-to-date information through extensive correspondence with missionaries in the field. His two most significant publications of general mission history are *Histoire générale des Missions-Etrangères* (1894), in three volumes, and *Mémorial de la Société des Missions-Etrangères* (1916), in two volumes. His studies of particular missions include those to Japan, Korea, Manchuria, Tibet, Szechwan (Sichuan), Kweichow (Guizhou), Kwangsi (Guangxi), Kwangtung (Guangdong), Annam, Tonkin, Cochin China, Siam, Burma, and India.

BIBLIOGRAPHY A. Sajot, *Adrien Launay des Missions-Etrangères* (1928); Société des Missions-Etrangères, *Compte-Rendu annuel des travaux de 1927* (1927), pp. 210–218.

Jean-Paul Wiest

Laurea, Brancati de. *See* Brancati de Laurea, Lorenzo.

Laurie, Thomas (1821–1897), American missionary in the Middle East and author-promoter of missions. Born in Craiglieth, Scotland, Laurie graduated from Illinois College (1838) and Andover Seminary, Massachusetts (1841). He arrived in Mosul (present-day Al Mawsil, Iraq) in 1842 to begin work with the American Board of Commissioners for Foreign Missions (ABCFM) mission to the Nestorian communities of southeastern Turkey. After that mission was discontinued, Laurie was transferred to the Syrian mission in 1844. Ill health forced his return to the United States in 1846, and thereafter he served as a pastor in Massachusetts and Rhode Island. He was made a corporate member of the ABCFM in 1875. He wrote extensively on missions, his most prominent publication being *The Ely Volume: Or, The Contributions of Our Foreign Missions to Science and Human Well-Being* (1881).

BIBLIOGRAPHY Thomas Laurie, *Dr. Grant and the Mountain Nestorians* (1853), *Woman and Her Saviour in Persia* (1863), and *Assyrian Echoes of the Word* (1894). Biographical sketch, ABCFM, "Vinton" book, vol. 3, Near East (1869–1910); memorial tribute, *The Missionary Herald,* December 1897.

Martha Lund Smalley

Laval, Jacques Désiré (1803–1864), French Catholic missionary to Mauritius. Laval was born in Croth, near Evreux, France, was educated in Paris, and became a medical doctor in 1830. A serious horse-riding accident prompted his conversion in 1835, and he was ordained to the priesthood in 1838. At Saint-Sulpice Seminary he became a friend of François *Libermann. After three years of parish work in France, he was sent to Mauritius in 1841 for the evangelization of the black slaves. He was the first missionary of the Congregation of the Holy Heart of Mary, founded by Libermann, which merged with the Congregation of the Holy Ghost in 1848. Laval succeeded in organizing the religious life of the former slaves, emancipated in 1835 but neglected by the white clergy. His missionary method consisted in taking progessive steps, employing a catechism in Creole adapted to illiterates, training of catechists and women advisers (*conseilleuses*), providing intensive pastoral care, setting up of a relief fund managed by the Christians themselves, offering rural outreach by means of chapels built by the faithful, and cooperating with other missionary societies. The Roman Catholic Church in Mauritius owes its renewal to Laval; thousands of pilgrims visit his tomb each year on the day of his death, September 9.

BIBLIOGRAPHY Jacques Laval, *Extraits de sa correspondance choisis et présentés par Joseph Lécuyer CSSP* (1978). Joseph Michel, *Le Père Jacques Laval, le "saint" de l'île Maurice (1803-1864)* (1984) and *De l'esclavage à l'apostolat, les auxiliaires laïcs du Bienheureux Jacques Laval, apôtre de l'île Maurice* (1988).

Marc R. Spindler

Lavigerie, Charles Martial Allemande (1825-1892), French cardinal, founder of the White Fathers and White Sisters. Lavigerie, son of a middle-class family in Gascony, studied at the Paris seminary of St. Sulpice and was ordained in 1849. After an academic period, he was made director in 1860 of the Oeuvre des Écoles d'Orient, an organization aimed at helping the Maronites of Lebanon. Henceforth, both Christian-Muslim relations and the needs of Eastern Christian communities were important to him.

Lavigerie was bishop of Nancy from 1863 to 1867. Soon one of the best-known French bishops and a candidate for the primatial see of Lyons, he accepted instead the recently established archbishopric of Algiers at the request of its governor general, Marshal MacMahon. In the government's eyes its ministry was only to French settlers. Lavigerie, however, viewed it as a base for missionary activity, and conflict with MacMahon soon developed. In 1884 he was also appointed archbishop of the revived see of Carthage and in 1882 was named a cardinal.

In 1868 he had founded a missionary society, Missionaries of Our Lady of Africa, soon universally known as White Fathers because of their Arab-style white robes. The White Sisters followed a year later. While the original purpose of these societies was evangelization of North African Muslims, a secondary purpose soon became the real heart of their work—a mission to the central African interior, east and west. Particularly important was the mission to Buganda of 1878. Lavigerie's *Instructions aux missionnaires* is valuable for its emphasis on language learning and also on a lengthy catechumenate before baptism. His increasing concentration upon central Africa led to his 1888 campaign against the slave trade in which he addressed mass meetings in several European capitals including London.

Lavigerie was a man of tremendous energy and large ideas. His founding in 1882 in Jerusalem of a college for the training of eastern-rite priests and his insistence that they must not be "latinized" expresses perhaps better than anything else the key to his missionary approach—a deep respect for cultural pluralism. His autocratic, ambitious, and hot-tempered nature damaged his work at times and undermined relationships even with those most devoted to him, but he remains unquestionably the most influential single figure in the nineteenth-century missionary revival of the Catholic Church.

BIBLIOGRAPHY Lavigerie's *Instructions aux missionnaires* (1950) is a collection of his main letters of guidance to the White Fathers. François Renault, *Le Cardinal Lavigerie 1825-1892: L'église, l'Afrique et la France* (1992; Eng. tr., *Cardinal Lavigerie: Churchman, Prophet, and Missionary*, 1994) is the standard biography. See also Xavier de Montclos, *Lavigerie: Le Saint-Siège et l'église* (1965) and *Le Toast d'Alger* (1966); J. Dean O'Donnell, *Lavigerie in Tunisia: The Interplay of Imperialist and Missionary* (1979); F. Renault, *Lavigerie: l'esclavage africain et l'Europe*, 2 vols. (1971).

Adrian Hastings

Lawes, W(illiam) G(eorge) (1839-1907), London Missionary Society (LMS) missionary to Niue and Papua. Born in Berkshire, England, Lawes arrived in Niue as the first resident European in 1861. He proceeded to train pastors, translate the New Testament, and send Niuean mission volunteers to distant islands. He joined the initial LMS mission to Papua and in 1874 became the first white man to live on the island of New Guinea. From his center at Port Moresby he trained and dispatched Papuans to help the mission along the coast. To protect Papuans from land-hungry Australians, he urged the British government to declare a protectorate. This was done from the steps of his house by a British military officer in 1884. He did not want annexation but it came in 1888. He then worked with the British government to establish laws protecting Papuan rights and in this he was remarkably successful. To bind together the diverse peoples he advocated the common use of the Motu language of Port Moresby. He taught and translated in that language and consequently Motu became the lingua franca of most of Papua until recent times. His *Grammar of the Motu Language* was published in 1885 and his Motu translation of the New Testament in 1891. Lawes above all others laid the foundations and established enduring structures for the Papuan LMS church. He retired to Sydney, Australia, in 1906, where he died.

BIBLIOGRAPHY John Garrett, *To Live among the Stars: Christian Origins in Oceania* (1982); J. King, *W. G. Lawes of Savage Island and New Guinea* (1909).

Charles W. Forman

Lawrence, Edward A(lexander) (1847-1893), pioneer American mission theorist. Lawrence studied at Yale College, Princeton Seminary, and the University of Berlin and then served Congregational pastorates in Syracuse, New York, and Baltimore, Maryland. In 1886 and 1887 he made a 20-month tour of missions in Japan, Korea, China, Sri Lanka, India, Egypt, Palestine, and Turkey. Subsequently, he delivered a lecture series at Andover Newton Theological Seminary, Yale Divinity School, and Beloit College, the substance of which was published posthumously as *Modern Missions in the East: Their Methods, Successes, and Limitations* (1894; repr., 1897). A competent and discerning observer, he argued that missions required a solid missiological foundation based on clearly articulated mission theory. This was especially necessary as the basis for training young people for missionary service. He followed established scientific procedures by gathering relevant historical and empirical data, critically evaluating findings, and proposing basic principles for missionary work. The reviewer of Lawrence's book in *The Missionary Review of the World* (September 1895) commented, "Though so recently issued, this book has already taken its place by general consent in the foremost ranks of the literature of missions... one of the most princely of modern contributions to missions." Lawrence died in Baltimore, Maryland.

Wilbert R. Shenk

Laws, Robert (1851–1934), Scottish Presbyterian leader of the Livingstonia Mission in Malawi. Born near Aberdeen, Laws became an apprentice cabinetmaker and studied in the evenings to achieve university entrance qualifications. He graduated from Aberdeen University, then studied theology at the United Presbyterian College in Edinburgh while taking medical classes in Glasgow, qualifying in both disciplines in 1875. When the Free Church of Scotland and the established Church of Scotland each planned a mission to Malawi in Livingstone's memory, Laws felt compelled to go, despite his own United Presbyterian Church's indifference toward the project. The Free Church was persuaded to take him as medical officer to the Livingstonia Mission whose pioneer party arrived in Malawi in 1875. In 1878 Laws became head of the mission.

The first site of the mission on Cape Maclear at the south end of Lake Malawi proved a mistake, and Laws moved the headquarters to Bandawe, further north, on the east shore of the lake. From there all the peoples of what is now northern Malawi and northeastern Zambia were reached. In 1891 on the Khondowe Plateau, Laws began the Overtoun Institution, modeled on Lovedale in the Cape Colony. From Overtoun there radiated out a network of primary schools that Laws developed so vigorously that by 1901 Livingstonia had more schools than all the other missions in Malawi and Zambia put together. The schools were linked to a network of pastors and evangelists that had an astonishing impact on the whole area. Laws persuaded the Dutch Reformed Church, Cape Synod, to send its first mission party to Malawi, where it was known as the Mkhoma mission. Under W. H. *Murray, the Mkhoma mission occupied the area south of the Livingstonia area and north of the Church of Scotland Blantyre mission area. Thus Malawi was completely covered by Presbyterian missions which produced in 1924 the autonomous Church of Central Africa Presbyterian, of which Laws was one of the guiding forces.

Laws was never able intellectually and spiritually to enter African culture and society as some of his colleagues did, but he had a genius for spotting talented individuals whom he encouraged and supported. Among them was David Kaunda, whom he sent into northeastern Zambia as a missionary and whose son Kenneth was Zambia's first president. In the years after World War I he encouraged educated Christians to form native associations to help deal with the impact of the modern world. In 1938 these associations combined to form the Nyasaland African National Congress.

BIBLIOGRAPHY Robert Laws, *Reminiscences of Livingstonia* (1934). W. P. Livingstone, *Laws of Livingstonia* (1922); J. McCracken, *Politics and Christianity in Malawi: The Impact of Livingstonia Mission* (1977); H. McIntosh, *Robert Laws* (1993).

Andrew C. Ross

Leander of Seville (c. 550–600), missionary bishop of Seville. Leander came from a family of church figures. With a sister, Florentina, and two brothers, Fulgentius of Astigi and the more famous Isidore, he evangelized Arian Visigoths in Spain. Leander converted King Leorigild's son, Hermonegild, about 579. Leorigild sent him into exile to Constantinople about 582, where he met the young man who became Pope Gregory I and later dedicated the *Moralia on Job* and the *Pastoral Rule* to him. Leander returned to win the second royal son, Reccared, to Catholic faith in 587. In 589 he presided over the Synod of Toledo, which further organized the Catholic mission among Arians in Spain.

BIBLIOGRAPHY Ursicino Dominguez del Val, "Algunos temas mon sticos de San Leandro de Sevilla," *Studia Patristica* 16, no. 2: 1–14; Angelus C. Vega, ed., *El "de institutione virginum" de San Leandro de Sevilla* (1948).

Frederick W. Norris

Lebbe, Frédéric-Vincent (1877–1940), Catholic missionary in China. Lebbe was born in Ghent, Belgium. At the age of 12, after reading a book on the life and martyrdom of the Vincentian missionary Jean Gabriel *Perboyre, Lebbe took Vincent as his name and decided to go to China as a Vincentian priest. In 1895 he entered the Vincentian seminary of St. Lazare in Paris and, six years later was assigned to the vicariate apostolic of Peking (Beijing). From the beginning, Lebbe was convinced that missioners should become Chinese in dress, language, attitude, and even loyalty in order to win Chinese people to Christ. Remarkable success in the countryside brought him to the large city of Tientsin (Tianjin), where he attracted throngs of non-Christian Chinese intellectuals to his public lectures and he organized Catholic Action for laymen. In 1912 he and *Ying Lianzhi launched the first Catholic weekly newspaper. Three years later, with the collaboration of a group of talented Chinese Catholics, he published the first Catholic daily, *Yi shih pao* (The social welfare). Appreciated by Chinese people for its accurate reporting and its independent outlook, it rapidly became the most widely circulated publication in northern China.

Lebbe and his friend Anthony *Cotta were outspoken members of a small movement calling for the expatriate church leadership to relinquish the protection of foreign powers and to become truly Chinese. In 1916 they jolted the missionary community when they openly denounced the attempt by the French consul in Tientsin to annex to the French concession, with the collusion of the church authorities, a piece of land the Chinese authorities had refused to grant. Angry, the church authorities transferred Lebbe to a different part of China and eventually sent him back to Europe for several years. His stand, however, began a process of transformation that, in the short run, led *Benedict XV to issue the apostolic letter *Maximum illud* of 1919 and *Pius XI to ordain six Chinese bishops in 1926. In the long run, Lebbe's ideals paved the way for the revocation in 1939 of the condemnation of the Chinese rites and for the establishment in 1946 of a Chinese local church with its own hierarchy.

Between 1920 and 1927, Lebbe crisscrossed Europe helping Chinese students with room, board, and tuition and organizing them into an association. He also helped launch the priests' Society of Auxiliaries of the Missions and the Women Lay Auxiliaries of the Missions. He then returned to China to serve under one of the newly ordained Chinese bishops. In 1928 he adopted Chinese nationality and gave impetus to Chinese monasticism by founding two Chinese religious orders: The Little Brothers of St. John the Baptist, and The Little Sisters of St. Therese of the Child Jesus. After the Sino-Japanese war started in 1931, he organized his brothers into a stretcher-bearer corps. Caught in the power struggle between Chiang Kai-shek and Mao Tse-tung (Mao Zedong), Lebbe was taken captive by the Communists for six weeks in the spring of 1940 and died of exhaustion shortly after his release.

BIBLIOGRAPHY Vincent Lebbe, *En Chine, il y a du nouveau* (1930); Raymond de Jaegher, *Father Lebbe: A Modern Apostle* (1950); Jacques Leclerc, *Thunder in the Distance: The Life of Père Lebbe,* George Lamb, tr. (1958); Léopold Levaux, *Le Père Lebbe: Apôtre de la Chine moderne* (1948); Claude Soetens, *Inventaire des Archives Vincent Lebbe* (1982) and *Recueil des Archives Vincent Lebbe,* 4 vols. (1982–1984); Vincent Thoreau, *Le tonnerre qui chante au loin* (1990).

Jean-Paul Wiest

Leber, Charles Tudor (1898–1959), American Presbyterian mission executive. Leber was born in Baltimore, Maryland, and was educated in Johns Hopkins University (A.B., 1920) and Princeton Theological Seminary (S.T.B., 1923). In 1936, after several years in the pastorate, Leber was brought to the staff of the Board of Foreign Missions of the Presbyterian Church in the U.S.A. as the successor of Robert E. *Speer. He was able to see the new situation then developing in the world and recognized that the churches that had grown out of mission work must now be treated as equal partners in mission. In one after another of the Presbyterian mission fields he persuaded the missions to dissolve themselves and merge into the indigenous churches they were to serve. He worked in close consultation with the heads of other American missions and was chosen as the first chairman of the Division of Foreign Missions of the National Council of Churches in the United States. In 1954 he suggested that the churches of East Asia start working together in mission, and his representative, John Coventry *Smith, then led those churches to form the world's first regional ecumenical body, the East Asia Christian Conference (now the Christian Conference of Asia). In 1956 he brought together the leaders of all churches derived from Presbyterian U.S.A. missions, so that they might plan jointly what they and the Presbyterian board should do. In 1958 he effected a change in the name of that board, making it the Commission on Ecumenical Mission and Relations. More than any other single American, he moved missions into the ecumenical age.

BIBLIOGRAPHY Charles Tudor Leber, ed., *World Faith in Action: The Unified Missionary Enterprise of Protestant Christianity* (1951); John Coventry Smith, *From Colonialism to World Community: The Church's Pilgrimage* (1982).

Charles W. Forman

Lebuin (d. c. 780), Anglo-Saxon Benedictine missionary in Frisia and Westphalia. Lebuin (also known as Lebwin, Levinus, Liafwin, Liebwin and Liefuvyn) was born into a Saxon English family, and became a missionary preacher in Frisia (area of modern Netherlands) and eastern Westphalia, Germany. Having enjoyed some success among the Frisians, he began working among the continental Saxons, among whom he encountered much more resistance. He won some converts in Overijssel on the Wilpa (Wulpel) River near Deventer (eastern Netherlands) and built the first church in Deventer itself. He endured personal attacks, his churches were burned, and converts were killed. Nevertheless, he braved the national Saxon assembly at Marklo (where he was almost lynched) and received the right to preach in the region. However, he made few inroads.

BIBLIOGRAPHY Wilhelm Arndt, *Leben des h. Bonifazius von Wilibald, der h. Leoba von Rudoft von Fuld, des Abtes Sturmi von Eigil, des h. Lebuin von Hucbald* (1888); Charles H. Talbot, *The Anglo-Saxon Missions in Germany* (1954).

Frederick W. Norris

Lechler, Paul (von) (1849–1925), German Protestant businessman, philanthropist, and key figure in the advancement of German medical missions. After apprenticeship as a salesman at Rotterdam, London, and Antwerp, Lechler took over his family's small varnish production plant in Stuttgart, Germany, and soon prospered. He decided to tithe the firm's income for Christian purposes, beginning charitable work among the poor in and around Stuttgart. Still searching for his true vocation, he sold the company to his employees for a nominal price and took to contemplation, only to discover that he ought to remain a businessman. Starting a very successful new business enterprise, he consciously maintained a Christian business ethic and also wrote about it. In 1906 he succeeded in bringing together nearly all Protestant German mission societies to cooperate in establishing the German Institute for Medical Missions at Tübingen, and saw to its adequate support. When the institute was opened in 1909, he was awarded an honorary doctorate from the medical faculty of Tübingen University and given the title "von" by the king of Württemberg.

BIBLIOGRAPHY Paul Lechler, *Geschäftserfolg und Lebenserfolg* (1912; 10th enlarged and rev. ed., 1936; highly regarded for decades by German Protestant businessmen). See also Christoffer Grundmann, "Lechler, Paul (von)," in *Biographisch-Biblio-*

graphisches Kirchenlexikon, ed. Traugott Bautz, vol. 4 (1992), pp. 1183–1188.

Christoffer H. Grundmann

Lechler, Rudolf (1824–1908), leader of the Basel Mission in China. Born in a pastor's family in Württemberg, Lechler served an apprenticeship as a merchant but soon entered the Basel Mission's seminary. In 1846 he was the first Basel missionary to be sent to China, together with his Swedish-born colleague T. Hamberg. Both of them were assigned to a Chinese evangelization society founded by Karl *Gützlaff and became as Chinese as possible. After the dissolution of the association and Hamberg's death, Lechler concentrated on work among the Hakka Chinese, which brought him in contact with the "Taiping revolution" (mainly a Hakka affair). Against considerable odds he pursued an in-depth study of Chinese philosophy and religion and perfected his knowledge of Hakka Chinese. In 1874 he became the head of the Basel mission in China. After his return to Germany in 1899 he finished the Hakka Chinese dictionary begun by Hamberg and compiled a Chinese hymnal.

BIBLIOGRAPHY W. Schlatter, *Rudolf Lechler* (1911).

Hans-Werner Gensichen

Le Comte, Louis (1655–1728), Jesuit missionary in China. Le Comte, one of five Jesuit mathematicians sent to China by Louis XIV in 1685, was born in Bordeaux, France. He entered the Society of Jesus in 1671. En route to China, he recorded many astronomical observations. Although the emperor did not select him for service at court after he arrived in 1688, he and two confreres were allowed to preach anywhere in China. He worked in the provinces of Shansi (Shanxi) and Shensi (Shaanxi). Due to Portuguese pressures against the presence of French Jesuits in China, Le Comte was sent to France to report on the status of the mission. From Paris he proceeded to Rome, where he discussed these matters with Jesuit superiors. Shortly after his return to Paris, he published a book of eight letters addressed to different nobles and clerics. In it he upheld the Jesuit accommodation policy toward the Chinese Rites and customs. The condemnation of this work by the Sorbonne in 1700 was a catalyst in opening the discussion of the Chinese Rites controversy in Europe. Despite his desire to return to China, Le Comte became the confessor of the Duchess of Burgundy and later died in his native city.

BIBLIOGRAPHY Louis Le Comte, *Nouveaux mémoires sur l'état de la Chine* (1696; repr., F. Touboul-Bouyere, ed.), *Un Jésuite à Pékin: Nouveaux mémoires sur l'état présent de la Chine, 1687–1692* (1990). See also Jacques Davy, "La condemnation en Sorbonne des 'Nouveaux mémoires sur la Chine' de P. Le Comte," *Recherches de science religieuse* 37 (1950): 366–397.

John W. Witek, SJ

Ledóchowska, Maria Teresa (1863–1922), Polish Catholic founder of mission support services. Ledóchowska, a Catholic nun, devoted herself to promoting and organizing support in Europe for missions in Africa. In 1889 she founded *Echo from Africa,* a monthly mission magazine, first in German, then in Polish (1893), English (1912), and other languages. She also arranged for printing Bibles, catechisms, and religious brochures in African languages. Visiting many European countries, she raised interest and support among Catholics for missions by her lectures and contacts. She also organized committees and aroused public opinion in Europe to oppose slavery and to support human rights. To provide information, prayer, and support for missions, she established a missionary society, the Sodality of St. Peter Claver for the African Mission, as well as the League of Children for Africa, St. Peter Claver's Penny for Africa, and St. Anthony's Bread for Africa. She was declared blessed in 1975.

BIBLIOGRAPHY Ledóchowska published a series of articles in *Echo from Africa.* Maria Giertych, *A Shared Vision, a Shared Mission* (1994); Marie-Thérèse Walzer, *Auf neuen Wegen* (1972) and *Deux mains ouvertes pour donner* (1976); Maria Winowska, *Allez dans le monde entier...* (1975). The Ledóchowska archive is located in the Istituto San Pietro Claver, Rome.

Jan Górski

Ledochowski, Wladimir (1866–1942), superior general of the Society of Jesus. A native of Loosdorf in Lower Austria, Ledochowski served as a page to the empress of Austria while studying at the academy for nobles in Vienna. He studied law in Cracow for one year and then entered the seminary at Tarnow to become a diocesan priest. In 1899 he earned a doctorate at the Gregorian University in Rome and later that year entered the Society of Jesus. Several years after his ordination to the priesthood in 1894, he became the chief editor of the *Universal Review* in Cracow. On the day he took his final vows as a Jesuit in 1901, he was appointed vice provincial of Galicia and the following year became provincial. Five years later he was elected assistant for Germany, an important advisory position to the superior general. In 1915 Ledochowski was elected the twenty-sixth superior general of the Society of Jesus, for life. His letters reflect a keen interest in the missions. He stressed that all Jesuits sent to the missions were to study the native language for two years before embarking on apostolic work. This was especially true for the study of Chinese. In a letter in 1919 he urged the Jesuits in China to develop an indigenous clergy both for the Jesuit order and for the dioceses. In 1925, in connection with the Vatican Mission Exhibition, he held a congress of Jesuits to discuss measures to promote the development of the missions worldwide. By 1940, 3,902 Jesuits were on the missions, compared with 1,971 when he became superior general. He died in office and was buried in the Jesuit crypt at the Campo Verano in Rome.

BIBLIOGRAPHY Wladimir Ledochowski, *Selected Writings of Father Ledochowski* (1945). Francis Xavier Montalban, "El P. Ledochowski y las misiones," *El Siglo de las misiones* 30 (1943): 42–45;

Laszlo Polgar, *Bibliographie sur l'histoire de la Compagnie de Jesus, 1901–1980,* vol. 3, pt. 2 (1990), pp. 396–397; Joseph Slattery, "In Memoriam. Very Rev. Fr. Wladimir Ledochowski," *Woodstock Letters* 72 (1943): 1–20; "Una grand' anima missionaria. Il defunto generale della Compagnia di Gesù. P. Wlodimiro Ledochowski," *Missioni della Compagnia di Gesù* 29, no. 1 (1943): 3–7; Andreas Villanyi, "Ein Missionsschreiben des Jesuitengenerals Ledochowski," *ZMR* 48 (1964): 27–33.

John W. Witek, SJ

Ledyard, Gleason H. (1919–), mission aviator and evangelist to the Eskimos. Born in Ashland, Ohio, and educated at the Fort Wayne (Indiana) Bible College, Ledyard realized his childhood calling when he established the Eskimo Gospel Crusade in 1946. He and his wife, Kathryn, made their first home at a small trading post on the eastern edge of the Northwest Territories, traveling hundreds of miles through Arctic wilderness by dogsled, and later by air, to share the gospel with nomadic Eskimo communities. Kathryn Ledyard established a school for Eskimo children, and her husband often flew the students in by plane. Turning the work over to the Christian and Missionary Alliance (C&MA) in 1961, the Ledyards made their home in Canby, Oregon, and began work on the *New Life Testament* (1969) and the *New Life Bible* (1986). This New Testament, with a vocabulary of only 850 words, was considered extraordinarily easy to read, and as a result it has been used in missions around the world where English is taught as a second language. More than five million copies of the New Testament had been sold as of 1995, and the Bible was in its seventh edition. As of the mid-1990s, Ledyard continued to be active in preparing Bible study materials to accompany the *New Life* Scriptures.

BIBLIOGRAPHY Gleason H. Ledyard, *Eskimos: Now the World* (1958, 1977).

Robert T. Coote

Lee, Daniel (1807–1896), Methodist missionary to Native Americans in the Pacific Northwest. Born in New England and a member of the New Hampshire Conference of the Methodist Episcopal Church (MEC), Lee was commissioned in 1833 by the MEC Foreign Missionary Society to serve as a missionary to the Indians of the Pacific Northwest. His service entailed a difficult cross-continental passage to the Oregon Territory, over which the U.S. government had not yet established sovereignty. He served from 1833 to 1843 under the superintendency of his uncle, Jason *Lee, working in the Willamette Valley in a self-supporting mission and also opening a highly successful mission at The Dalles of the Columbia River. Ill health forced him and his wife, Marie (Ware), whom he married in 1840, to return to his native New Hampshire in 1843. He coauthored *Ten Years in Oregon* (1844), an important history of the Oregon mission, which contributed significantly to educating his church with regard to the opportunities and challenges of the work. In later years he served Methodist churches in the Midwest.

BIBLIOGRAPHY Cornelius J. Brosnan, *Jason Lee, Prophet of the New Oregon* (1932); Erle Howell, *Methodism in the Northwest* (1966); John Parsons, *Beside the Beautiful Willamette* (1924).

J. Steven O'Malley

Lee, Jason (1803–1845), pioneer Methodist missionary to the Oregon Territory. Born at Stanstead, Lower Canada (present-day Quebec), Lee was converted during a Wesleyan Methodist revival in 1826. Four years later, he accepted the recommendation of Wilbur Fisk, president of Wesleyan University, to lead a missionary journey to the Indians of the Pacific Northwest. The party included his nephew, Daniel *Lee. High points of Lee's expedition included the first Protestant sermon given west of the Rocky Mountains, which he preached near present-day Pocatello, Idaho, in July 1834. His mission in the Willamette Valley included founding the Indian Manual Labor Training School, which was the forerunner of Willamette University, the first college formed west of the Rockies. Two successive wives died amid the rigors of frontier life. As he encouraged Christian families from the East to migrate to the Northwest, he actively advocated that American political sovereignty be extended into the region of present-day Washington and Oregon states. His successful efforts to have the British-American boundary dispute resolved in favor of the American position brought him into controversy with fellow missionaries, who succeeded in persuading the Methodist Episcopal mission board to replace him as superintendent. He returned in declining health to his childhood home in Stanstead, where he died.

BIBLIOGRAPHY James W. Bashford, *The Oregon Missions: The Story of How the Line Was Run between Canada and the United States* (1918); Cornelius J. Brosnan, *Jason Lee, Prophet of the New Oregon* (1932); Erle Howell, *Methodism in the Northwest* (1966); Robert J. Loewenberg, *Equality on the Oregon Frontier: Jason Lee and the Methodist Mission, 1834–43* (1976).

J. Steven O'Malley

Leenhardt, Maurice (1878–1954), French Reformed pioneer missionary in New Caledonia, missiologist, and anthropologist. Born in Montauban, France, Leenhardt is remembered for his keen combination of observation and theology, which he learned from his father, Franz Leenhardt, a professor in the theological faculty at Montauban. Maurice Leenhardt graduated from Montauban in 1902 with a ground-breaking dissertation on the Ethiopian (African indigenous) movement in southern Africa, interpreted as social protest against racial discrimination. "Under the present political circumstances," he concluded, "mission work includes not only evangelization of the heathen, but the duty to urge forward an indigenous legislation based on justice in the different countries." From 1902 to 1926 Leenhardt served with the Paris Evangelical Missionary Society (PEMS) in New Caledonia. The archipelago had already been reached by Melanesian evangelists connected with the London Missionary Society; Leenhardt received their blessing on his arrival. He established a base of operations called Do Neva (The

True Country); pioneered in unreached language groups; founded a pastoral school in order to strengthen and upgrade the already existing native ministry; and defended the rights of Protestants against the combined threats of French anticlericalism, local harassment by the military, and aggressive proselytism by the Marists—all the while observing people, customs, and artifacts carefully. He spent a furlough in 1921 and 1922 visiting all PEMS fields in Africa and Madagascar. In 1922 his Houailou translation of the New Testament was published.

Beginning in 1926 he lived in Paris, combining scholarly work with a pastoral ministry with the Mission Populaire Évangélique in a working-class neighborhood. Occasionally he taught a course in missionary methods at the PEMS School of Missions and published essays and books about the customs and languages of New Caledonia, making his way to a full professorship in primitive religions at the Sorbonne in 1942, as a successor to the leading French anthropologist Marcel Mauss. A special assignment of the French government brought him back to New Caledonia in 1947 and 1948 as the founding director of the French Institute of Scientific Research in Oceania at Nouméa. He made outstanding contributions to cultural anthropology and missiology. He paved the way for a more realistic approach to so-called primitive people, accepting them as human subjects with rights and as creators of complex cultural systems. He persuaded Lucien Lévy-Bruhl to change his mind and to accept the cognitive value of mythical thought. He affirmed the reality of divine adoption experienced in the process of mission: "God is not an import; he reveals himself." Leenhardt followed Raoul *Allier in the field of French Protestant missiology, wary of confessional strings, but warmly believing in evangelical catholicity. He died in Paris from cancer.

Bibliography Maurice Leenhardt, *Alfred Boegner (1851–1912) d'après son journal intime et sa correspondance* (1939) and *Do Kamo: Person and Myth in the Melanesian World,* translated from the French (1979); also see numerous notes and papers in the periodicals he edited, *Les Propos Missionnaires* (1927–1940) and *Le Monde Non Chrétien* (1931–1937; new ser., 1947–1968). James Clifford, *Person and Myth: Maurice Leenhardt in the Melanesian World* (1982); Marc R. Spindler, "Maurice Leenhardt," in Gerald H. Anderson et al., eds., *Mission Legacies* (1994), pp. 494–499.

Marc R. Spindler

Leeuwen, Arend Th. van (1918–1993), Dutch missions theologian. Born in Utrecht, Netherlands, van Leeuwen grew up in an intellectual, liberal environment. At the urging of Hendrik *Kraemer, he opted for a missionary career. In 1947 he received his Ph.D. at the University of Leiden as a student of Kraemer, with a thesis on the Muslim mystic al-Ghazali. From 1950 he worked on behalf of the Dutch Reformed Church as a teacher at the Balé Wyoto in Malang, Indonesia. During leave in the Netherlands he was severely injured in a car accident, which made it impossible for him to return to Indonesia and forced him to end his missionary activities in 1954. From 1960 to 1971 he was director of the institute Kerk en Wereld (Church and World) at Driebergen, Netherlands. From 1971 to 1985 he was professor of social activities at the Catholic University of Nijmegen. Van Leeuwen carried on three missionary dialogues: concerning Islam, Marxism, and secularization. In 1964 he published *Christianity in World History,* which made him famous, especially in Asia and America. His later research on Marx, whom Van Leeuwen chose to look upon as a "substitute" theologian, alienated him ultimately from the church and mission.

Bibliography Th. Salemink wrote a biographical article entitled "De ontwikkeling tot een economische theologie," in *De burger en z'n religie* (1988), pp. 9–22. See also J. C. Hoekendijk, "Discussion: Technology, Theology, and the Christian Faith," *Union Seminary Quarterly Review* 21, no. 4 (1966): 426–433: R. Shaull, "The Christian World Mission in a Technocratical Era," *ER* 17, no. 3 (1965): 205–218. For a comprehensive biography and a description of Van Leeuwen's theology, see P. J. G. Jeroense, *Theologie als zelfkritiek: Een ondersoek naar de missionaire theologie van A. Th. van Leeuwen* (1994).

P. J. G. Jeroense

Lefroy, George Alfred (1854–1919), Anglican missionary bishop in India. Born in County Down, Ireland, educated at Marlborough and at Trinity College, Cambridge (where he came under the influence of B. F. *Westcott), Lefroy was ordained and joined the Cambridge Mission to Delhi in 1879. A good linguist and a capable administrator, he took over the leadership of the mission in 1882, which he held until 1899, when he became bishop of Lahore. Lefroy's years in Lahore were politically tense, due not least to the rise of the Indian national movement. He tried, and failed, to make Sadhu Sundar *Singh an Anglican clergyman and to keep S. K. Rudra from becoming the first Indian principal of St. Stephen's College, Delhi. In 1913 he became bishop of Calcutta, in which position his wise and cautious leadership during the war years was invaluable. Lefroy seems always to have found it easier to relate to Muslims than to Hindus. Crippled by arthritis, he died suddenly on New Year's Day, 1919.

Bibliography Martin Maw, *Visions of India* (1990), pp. 231ff; H. H. Montgomery, *The Life and Letters of G. A. Lefroy* (1920).

Eric J. Sharpe

Legge, James (1815–1897), Scottish missionary and sinologist. Legge was born at Huntly, Aberdeenshire, the youngest in a family of seven. He received an M.A. at King's College, Aberdeen, and, after affiliating with the Congregational Church, did further study at Highbury College, London. He was appointed by the London Missionary Society and joined the Chinese mission to Malacca in January 1840. He became principal of the Anglo-Chinese College in that city later the same year and moved with it to Hong Kong in 1843. Shortly after this move, the mission changed the college into a theological seminary and Legge continued as its principal until 1856. During this period he also pastored the English Union Church in Hong Kong, helped in the development of an independent Chinese congregation, wrote many articles in Chinese as tracts or for various periodicals, and became widely known for his seven-volume translation into English of the Chinese classics. In the long-lasting controversy over the proper term for God in the Chinese language, Legge, along with most English missionaries, advocated the use of the name Shang Di. He was often criticized by fellow missionaries because of his high view of Confucius and his belief that the "natural theology" of the Chinese as found in their ancient classics contained some Christian truth. In 1875 he was appointed a fellow at Corpus Christi College, Oxford, and from 1876 to 1897 he was the first professor of Chinese studies at Oxford University. He was "probably the most important sinologist of the nineteenth century" (A. F. Walls). In 1894 he became the first person, other than a member of the British royal family, to be depicted on a Hong Kong postage stamp—a testimony to his legacy.

BIBLIOGRAPHY Helen Edith Legge, *James Legge: Missionary and Scholar* (1905); Lauren Pfister and Norman Girardot, *The Whole Duty of Man: James Legge and the Victorian Translation of China* (forthcoming). See also Alexander Wylie, *Memorials of Protestant Missionaries to the Chinese* (1867), pp. 117–122.

Ralph R. Covell

Legge, Mary Isabella (Morison) (1816–1852), missionary educator in China. Mary Morison's father, John Morison, was a Congregational theologian and a director of the London Missionary Society (LMS). In 1839 she married James *Legge and they immediately departed for Malacca, which was a major station for those going to the China mission prior to the opening of the treaty ports. In Malacca Mary Legge pioneered in education for Chinese girls while her husband taught and preached at the Anglo-Chinese college. In 1843 the mission moved to Hong Kong, and the LMS resolved to convert the college into a theological school with a preparatory school attached. The latter began in 1844 and in 1846, when it became coeducational, Legge had six Chinese girls enrolled. It reached its zenith in 1851 with sixty boys and thirteen girls. Early in 1850 the LMS had planned to rent a house to found a boarding school in Hong Kong for forty girls under Legge's supervision. This proposal was unrealized, however, because she died in childbirth in 1852, and no other woman missionary in Hong Kong was deemed qualified to carry out the project.

Legge worked closely with her husband, raising her children, handling family affairs such as their children's education, and dealing with other Westerners, mostly missionaries, who stayed in or passed through Hong Kong.

BIBLIOGRAPHY John Morison, "Sketches of the Life and Labours of the Late Mrs. Mary Isabella Legge, of Hong Kong," *Evangelical Magazine, and Missionary Chronicle* 31 (December 1853): 697–707; *Supplement to the Evangelical Magazine, for the year 1853,* pp. 757–764. See also Helen Edith Legge, *James Legge: Missionary and Scholar* (1905); James Legge, "Note on My Life" (1897), typescript at the Bodleian Library, Oxford, and in the LMS archives at the School of Oriental and African Studies, Univ. of London.

Timothy Man-kong Wong

Lehmann, E. Arno (1901–1984), Leipzig missionary in South India, and Halle missiologist. Lehmann was probably the dominating figure in his generation of Leipzig missionaries in South India. After a hard childhood and inadequate schooling, he was trained in the seminary of the Leipzig Mission. During his years of active service in Tamil Nadu (1926–1934) he grew in stature as a Lutheran missionary, an Indologist, and a Dravidologist. An early product of his studies was a translation of hymns by the Tamil poet Tayumanavar, published in 1935. After repatriation during World War II he was put in charge of deputation work for the mission in Saxony while his scholarly work continued. In 1947 he received a doctorate in philosophy at Leipzig University for a translation and analysis of a collection of Tamil Saivite hymns. Lehmann's career reached its climax when he was called to Gustav *Warneck's former chair of missions at Halle University in 1950, with the inclusion of the history of religions and Dravidology. Even under the Communist regime in the German Democratic Republic, Lehmann was able to develop his scholarly capacity to the fullest, concentrating his research on the history of the Danish-Halle Mission of Tranquebar and on Christian art in overseas churches. When missiology proper was outlawed by Marxist authorities, he returned to his scholarly beginnings by opening up new vistas of the encounter of the Christian gospel with Tamil mentality and culture.

BIBLIOGRAPHY Arno Lehmann, *Die Hymnen des Tayumanavar* (1935), *Die sivaitische Frömmigkeit der tamulischen Erbauungsliteratur* (1948), *Es begann in Tranquebar* (1955, 1956), and *It Began at Tranquebar* (1956). No biography is available.

Hans-Werner Gensichen

Leibniz, Gottfried Wilhelm von (1646–1716), German philosopher. Leibniz undoubtedly stands out as one of the most creative philosophers, mathematicians, and diplomats of his age. A native of Leipzig, Leibniz was brought up in the Lutheran faith. His interest in missions was stimulated only toward the end of his life, mainly by contact with Jesuit missionaries working in China. He published a selection of their reports (*Novissima Sinica,* 1697), suggesting in the introduction that Protestant princes and churchmen, too, might attempt to get in touch with the Chinese. Leibniz regarded China as a kind of oriental Europe, with a religion and culture which were at least as highly developed as those of Western Christendom. Hence he called not for unilateral missionary efforts but for a bilateral transfer of messengers able to initiate an exchange of values on the basis of a common knowledge (*scientia generalis*) of God's providence. Propagation of the Christian faith as practiced by the Jesuits would not be excluded. Yet essentially the aim would be *propagatio fidei per scientias,* mission by science rather than by spreading the gospel of universal salvation in Jesus Christ. Leibniz even made sure that mission, as he conceived it, was included in the statutes of the Prussian Academy, founded in 1700. After his death this mandate was disregarded and eventually eliminated. A minor positive effect of what Leibniz intended may be seen in the fact that his efforts were instrumental in stimulating A. H. *Francke to become deeply involved in missions.

BIBLIOGRAPHY Conventional research on Leibniz has paid little or no attention to his missiological interests, with the notable exception of C. D. Zangger, *Welt und Konversation: Die theologische Begründung der Mission bei G. W. Leibniz* (1973). See also F. R. Merkel, *G. W. von Leibniz und die China-Mission* (1920), *Leibniz und China* (1952), and "The Missionary Attitude of the Philosopher G. W. von Leibniz," *IRM* 9 (1920): 399–410.

Hans-Werner Gensichen

Leimena, Johannes (1905–1977), Indonesian layman, medical doctor, and leader in church and state. Leimena was born on the island of Ambon in Indonesia but from his youth lived in Jakarta. He was active in the Student Christian Movement of Java, became one of the organizers of the World's Student Christian Federation conference at Citeureup, West Java (1933), and attended the Tambaram meeting of the International Missionary Council in 1938. From 1930 to 1941 he served as a medical doctor in the missionary hospital at Bandung. He was a member of most national cabinets from 1946 to 1966 and maintained close relations with President Sukarno. He was a leading personality within ecumenical Protestant circles of Indonesia and Asia. He was chairperson of Parkindo, the Christian poltical party; vice-chairperson of the Council of Churches in Indonesia; and a participant in the East Asia Christian Conference and the World Council of Churches.

Both as a cabinet minister and as an influential layperson, Leimena gave much attention to issues of social justice and the well-being of society. He published articles about human rights for laborers, public health, medical ethics, and unity. These concerns cannot be seen apart from his participation within the nationalist movement before 1945 and his efforts in behalf of unity within the young Republic of Indonesia, which faced severe problems from Muslim factions and a separatist movement for a Moluccan republic. Leimena acted as a patient reconciler during these conflicts. Striving after unity also characterized his work for the Council of Churches. Though influenced by Barthian theology, in his later thinking the antithetical relation between church and state seemed to diminish.

BIBLIOGRAPHY Johannes Leimena, "Nationalistische stroomingen in Ned. Indië," *Eltheto* 90, no. 6 (1935): 222–228, "De zending en wij," *CSV Blad* 7, no. 1 (1940): 10–14, *The Ambon Question: Facts and Appeal* (c. 1950), "World Health and World Community," *ER* 8, no. 4 (1956): 407–409, and "The Task of Restoring Fellowship within the Church and the Indonesian Nation," *SEAJT* 9, no. 3 (1968): 57–64. A. G. Hoekema, *Denken in dynamisch evenwicht: De wordingsgeschiedenis van de nationale protestantse theologie in Indonesië* (1994), pp. 114–117, 204–206; J. Verkuyl, "In Memoriam," *Wereld en zending* 6, no. 3 (1977): 329–335 (obit.).

Alle G. Hoekema

Leite, Serafim (1890–1969), Portuguese Jesuit historian. Leite was born in São João da Madeira, Portugal, and spent part of his youth as a trader in the Amazon, where he traveled extensively and began his lifelong interest in the Brazilian Indians. He entered the Society of Jesus in 1914 and was educated in Belgium and in Spain. He returned to Lisbon in 1929 to serve as editor of the Jesuit journal *Brotéria,* and began work in 1932 on the *História da Companhia de Jesus no Brasil,* 10 vols. (1938–1950).

The *História* and his many other writings are informed by Leite's conviction that the Jesuits' most important contribution to Brazilian society was their work as missionaries among the Indians. He provided detailed accounts of all aspects of the Jesuit enterprise, including the Jesuits' catechetical and educational work, their relations with crown officials and settlers, their contributions to arts and letters in the Luso-Brazilian world, and their economic activities. Among his greatest achievements was the collection and interpretation of a vast body of archival materials from repositories in Brazil and throughout Europe. He transcribed and edited many of these documents for publication, including the Jesuit letters in the five-volume *Monumenta Brasiliae* (1956–1968). In addition to the *História* and the collections of documents, Leite's significant publications include biographies of notable missionaries, studies of slavery and other central themes in colonial Brazilian history, and a pioneering study of artisans and laborers who worked for the Jesuits in Brazil.

BIBLIOGRAPHY Miguel Batllori, *Bibliografia de Serafim Leite, S.I.* (1962); works published after 1962 may be found in László Polgar, *Bibliographie sur l'histoire de la Compagnie de Jésus, 1901–1980,* 6 vols. (1981–1990) and in Polgar's annual bibliographies of Jesuit writings in *Archivum Historicum Societatis Iesu,* vols. 32–37 (1963–1968). Biographical material may be found in the obituaries in *Brotéria* 90, no. 2 (February 1970): 164–173, *Archivum Historicum Societatis Iesu* 39 (July–December 1970), and *The Americas* 17 (April 1971): 456–457, as well as in the *História,* particularly in the preface, acknowledgments, and other supplementary materials of volumes 1 and 10.

Thomas M. Cohen

Lemmens, Leonard (1864–1929), German Catholic mission historian. Lemmens was born at Bocket, Rheinland, entered the Franciscan order in 1878, and was ordained a priest in 1888. A zealous historian, he was among the first who applied the modern critical method to the history of the Franciscan order. In 1899 he was called to Rome to work on a history project and soon was made professor of church history at St. Anthony's College. From 1903 until 1907 he was director of the Franciscan Research Institute at Quaracchi, near Florence. Back in Germany in 1907 for further research and writing, in 1909 he was granted an honorary doctorate in theology by the University of Münster. Through the influence of Joseph *Schmidlin, he shifted increasingly to mission subjects. Besides two documentary volumes on missions to the Holy Land, he published numerous studies on missions to the Baltic regions and the Near East. From 1919 he was again in Rome, working mainly in the archives of Propaganda Fide and from 1924 teaching mission history to young missionaries at St. Anthony's College. Shortly before his death, he crowned his rich literary career with a standard work, *Die Geschichte der Franziskanermissionen*.

BIBLIOGRAPHY Livarius Oliger, "De Vita et Operabus P. Leonardi Lemmens, OFM," *Antonianum* 4 (1929): 337-350 (full bibliography).

Bernward H. Willeke, OFM

Lemue, Prosper (1804-1870), pioneer French Protestant missionary in South Africa. The first French recruit of the Paris Evangelical Missionary Society (PEMS), as recommended by the Reformed pastor Antoine Colani, Lemue left in 1829 for southern Africa with Isaac *Bisseux and Samuel *Rolland. John *Philip, the London Missionary Society (LMS) superintendent at the Cape, first directed him to Caffraria, but he finally settled in Botswana, as a colleague of the LMS pioneer Robert *Moffat. He established the Motito station in 1833, working among Arutsi refugees and Korana people. In 1847 PEMS fellow missionaries called him to Lesotho to start a school for teachers and evangelists at the Carmel station. But the Afrikaner Voortrekkers overran the territory and the proposed school did not materialize. Nevertheless, Lemue remained and served the small Carmel congregation until he died.

BIBLIOGRAPHY Eugène Casalis, "Biographical Notice of the Late Reverend Prosper Lemue, French Missionary," tr. from *Journal des missions évangéliques* 45 (1870); Victor Ellenberger, *Un siècle de Mission au Lessouto (1833-1933)* (1933); J. W. Sauer and G. M. Theal, *Basutoland Records,* vol. 1 (1883).

Jean-François Zorn

Lenkeevich, Nikolai (Nikodim) (1673-c. 1740), Russian Orthodox missionary. Born in Poland, Lenkeevich became a monk of the Kiev Cave Monastery and was tonsured as Nikodim in 1715. In 1725 he and five students were sent to the Kalmyks, a nomadic Mongol people living between the Ural mountains and the rivers Volga and Don. Initially the mission was based around a mobile church accompanying a nomadic baptized Kalmyk chief. The missionaries were unique in adopting the same nomadic life-style as the people among whom they worked. Lenkeevich had two aims: to learn the language and to educate the children. The mission did not attempt widespread preaching but concentrated on working with one group at a time and preparing the people well for baptism. The result was about 400 baptisms. In 1731 Lenkeevich settled in Astrakhan, which he made the center of the mission. In 1732 a school was built there for the Kalmyk children. This broke the links between the now settled missionaries and the nomadic Kalmyks, and the mission work suffered. Lenkeevich retired from the mission in 1734, returning in 1738 for an unsuccessful attempt to make Stavropol on the Volga a new center of the mission through settling baptized Kalmyks. Lenkeevich left because of failing health in 1739 and retired to the Kiev Cave Monastery.

BIBLIOGRAPHY Archimandrite Gurii (Stepanov), *Ocherki po istorii rasprostraneniya khristiantsva sredi mongol'skikh plemen* (1915), vol. 1, chap. 2; P. D. Shestakov, *Nekotoryya svedeniya o rasprostranenii khristianstva u kalmykov* (1869), chap. 145, p. 125.

Karen L. Gordon

Lenshina Mulenga, Alice (c. 1925-1978), leader of Lumpa church in Zambia. In 1953 Alice Lenshina—as she was popularly known—claimed to have died and had a vision of Jesus during which he showed her a book of life, taught her a number of hymns, and told her to act against witchcraft. She reported all this to the missionary in charge of the Scottish Presbyterian mission at Lubwa, near her home village of Kasomo. At first the Presbyterian Church treated her with sympathy, and she was baptized in November 1953. She began preaching to large crowds, urging them to destroy their traditional fetishes. But growing disagreement with the Presbyterian Church led to her suspension in 1955, together with that of many of her followers. In the period before Zambian independence, Lenshina—possibly at the behest of the colonial government—urged her followers to tear up their party political cards. This led to clashes with the emerging UNIP party of Kenneth Kaunda, during which several hundred people were killed. As a result, Lenshina and many of her followers were detained, and the movement banned. She was released in 1975. Her movement, already on the decline by the time it was banned, never recovered, though tiny pockets of it remain.

BIBLIOGRAPHY W. M. J. van Binsbergen, "Innovation and Political Conflict in Zambia," *African Perspectives* 2 (1976) and *Religious Change in Zambia* (1981); Arie N. Ipenburg, *The Presbyterian Mission and the Eastern Bemba* (1984); Fergus Macpherson, *Kenneth Kaunda of Zambia* (1974); Robert I. Rotberg, "The Lenshina Movement in Northern Rhodesia," *Rhodes-Livingstone Journal* 29 (1961): 63-68.

T. Jack Thompson

Leontiev, Maxim (d. 1698), Russian Orthodox missionary priest in China. In the last quarter of the seventeenth century, Maxim Leontiev served as chaplain to a group of five hundred Russian frontiersmen who traveled south on the Amur River from Siberia into China in 1683. They established themselves in a fortified bastion, where they were attacked by Chinese forces, overwhelmed, taken prisoner, and transported to Peking (Beijing). Leontiev had with him all the liturgical items needed for conducting Orthodox worship services. The prisoners were treated well; not only was Leontiev permitted to conduct regular services, including the Divine Liturgy, but the Chinese government also gave an old Buddhist temple to the Russians for use as a church. Ten years later, Leontiev came in contact with a caravan going to Tobolsk and asked them to convey a request for some needed liturgical items. The return caravan carried with it the requested articles, two additional Orthodox clergy, and a message from the metropolitan bishop of Siberia with words of encouragement regarding the spread of the light of the gospel among the Chinese people. Peter the Great of Russia welcomed the existence of Leontiev's mission as a political and economic entrance point for Russian imperial policies (a strategy that did not succeed.) Leontiev died in China.

BIBLIOGRAPHY Michael Oleksa, *Orthodox Alaska: A Theology of Mission* (1992); James J. Stamoolis, *Eastern Orthodox Mission Theology Today* (1986).

Stanley Samuel Harakas

Lepsius, Johannes (1858–1926), founder of the Deutscher Hülfsbund Mission (DHM). Son of a famous Egyptologist in Berlin, Lepsius obtained a doctorate in philosophy with honors before he decided to become a pastor. After ordination by court chaplain Rudolf Kögel of Berlin, Lepsius accepted an opportunity to serve as an assistant pastor in the German Protestant congregation in Jerusalem (1884–1886). After his return he remained in close contact with the Near East. In 1895 he and two friends decided after insistent prayer to make arrangement for a new mission to the Near East especially devoted to supporting Christian Armenians. They learned later that on the very day of their decision the Armenians had been caught by the first persecution at Constantinople. Officially launched in 1897, the DHM operated against heavy odds both in Turkey and in Germany. Later the problems of possible or actual interference in politics, and differences about engagement in evangelistic work among Muslims, led to schisms. Lepsius left the mission in 1917 and died in 1926, two years after its temporary dissolution.

BIBLIOGRAPHY Among Lepsius's major works are *Armenien und Europa* (1896), *Ex oriente lux* (1903), *Der Todesgang des armenischen Volkes* (1919), and *Deutschland und Armenien* (1919). The only up-to-date account of Lepsius and the Deutscher Hülfsbund Mission is U. Feigel, *Das evangelische Deutschland und Armenien* (1989).

Hans-Werner Gensichen

Le Roux, Pieter Louis (1865–1943), Afrikaner missionary to the Zulu people of South Africa. Born in the Wellington district of South Africa, Le Roux initially trained and worked as a teacher but later felt called to the Dutch Reformed Church (DRC) mission and was ordained in 1893. That year he married Adriana Josina van Rooyen, a devout and competent missionary who was responsible with him for the impact of their seven-year Zulu ministry in Wakkerstroom, about 175 miles southeast of Johannesburg. Le Roux rejected pedobaptism and emphasized faith healing; he resigned from the DRC in 1903, after contact with the Christian Catholic Church (based in Zion City, Illinois), through its publication *Leaves of Healing*. In 1904 he was ordained an elder and his wife an evangelist in this church. As many as 400 DRC Zulu converts followed them. The hallmark of their work was the education of outstanding African evangelists and leaders such as Daniel Nkonyane, Muneli Ngobese, and Elias Mahlangu. Their influence on the Zion church movement in southern Africa was decisive because of the quality of such African leadership. (Today approximately 80 percent of the African Independent church movement in southern Africa is Zionist.) Le Roux joined the Apostolic Faith Mission at its founding in 1908, serving as its president (1913–1942) and developing it substantially.

BIBLIOGRAPHY I. S. Burger, *History of Faith of the Apostolic Faith Mission* (1987); *Leaves of Healing*, publication of the Christian Catholic Church (1897–1914); G. C. Oosthuizen, *The Birth of Christian Zionism in South Africa* (1987); B. G. M. Sundkler, *Zulu Zion and Some Swazi Zionists* (1976).

Gerhardus C. Oosthuizen

Le Roy, Alexander (1854–1938), Holy Ghost Fathers (CSSp) missionary, linguist, and ethnographer in Africa. Le Roy was born at La Gralemois, France, in 1854 and was ordained to the priesthood in 1876. He went initially to Pondicherry, India. In 1881 he arrived in Africa, and for 15 years he traveled untiringly in Somalia, Mozambique, Kenya, and Tanganyika (Tanzania), before being appointed to Gabon, West Africa, as vicar apostolic (1892). A born student of people and of languages, he committed himself to intensive research of belief and values, explicitly as part of his theological and missionary methodology. Apparently self-taught, Le Roy wrote widely in ethnography, ethnology, and linguistics. He freed slaves as a preamble to evangelization and made contact with Pygmy people as well as the Chaggas and Masais. But his more lasting legacy was that he established a network of local catechists and a seminary for training indigenous priests.

In 1896 he was elected superior general of the Holy Ghost Fathers, which he reorganized and regionalized. In 1921 he founded the Missionary Sisters of the Holy Ghost. He was committed to disseminating an integrated, cross-disciplinary approach to mission and wrote numerous articles and several widely read books. His *Religion of the Primitives* (1922) remains available as a good example of the anthropology of its time. Resigning in ill health in 1926, he died in Paris.

BIBLIOGRAPHY Alexander Le Roy, *Mes Souvenirs* (no date), *A travers le Zanguèbar* (1884) (vol. 5 of *Les Missions Catholiques françaises au XIX siècle*, J. Piolet, ed.), *Religion of the Primitives* (1922), and *Au Kilema-Ndjaro* (4th ed., 1928). There are virtually no resources in English, except a short assessment by G. Collins in *The Interracial Review*, July 1938, pp. 102–104. References can be found in H. Koren, *The Spiritans* (1958) and *Spiritan East Africa Memorial* (1993). In French are E. Baur and A. Le Roy, *Voyage dans l'Oudoé, l'Ouzigoua, et l'Ousogara* (4th ed., 1899); Henri Goré, *Mgr. Alexander Le Roy* (1952).

Anthony J. Gittins, CSSp

Le Roy Ladurie, Marie. *See* Marie de l'Assomption.

Léry, Jean de (1534–1611), member of an ill-fated Protestant mission to Brazil in 1557. Born in Margeil, Burgundy, France, Léry became an early supporter of the Reformation. A cobbler by trade, at 18 years of age he became a student of John *Calvin in Geneva, taking courses in theology and preaching. During this time both the Geneva city council and Calvin received letters from Nicolas Durand de Villegagnon, a distinguished Knight of Malta in the service of the French empire, requesting two pastors and additional settlers for Brazil. Through the influence of Admiral Gaspard de Coligny de Chatillon, Villegagnon had established Fort Coligny, a small French colony on the island of Serigipe in the bay of Rio de Janeiro. Calvin and the council acted favorably on the request and sent the pastors Pierre Richier and Guillaume Chartier with fourteen theological students, including Jean de Léry, along with about 300 colonists, mostly Huguenots. After a six-month voyage, the group arrived in Brazil on March 7, 1557. At the age of 21, Léry was the historian of the ill-fated expedition. When Villegagnon later expelled the Huguenots from the island for religious reasons, he killed three; others lived among the Indians for a time before returning to their homeland; some were hanged as aggressors by the Portuguese; and one was martyred by the Inquisition.

Léry describes his motivation for going to Brazil: ". . . so that the gospel would be preached not only in the whole kingdom, but also in the whole world." His published account had gone through six editions in French by 1600 and was translated into other languages. Noteworthy is his account of living among the Tupinamba Indians. The ethnographic description of the people, their customs, and their religion is remarkably objective, with favorable comparisons to contemporary European culture. His testimonial and dialogical approach in sharing the Christian faith, rather than the then typical practice of imposition, is related naturally in the text. Léry returned safely to France, where he suffered persecution in the sieged city of Sancerre and finally was released. He went to Geneva for writing and publishing, later served as pastor in Switzerland, and died in Berne. His motives and experience, as well as the expressions of gratitude to God by Calvin and the Genevan church for opening this door for the expansion of Christ's kingdom, confirm the interest and concern for missions of the Reformed churches of Geneva.

BIBLIOGRAPHY Jean de Léry, *Indiens de la Renaissance: Histoire d'un voyage fait en la terre de Brésil* (1578, 1975), *Histoire memorable de la ville de Sancerre* (1574), and *Discours du siège tenu devant La Charité* (1574). For a biography of Léry, consult Philibert Papillon, *Biblioteque des auteurs de Bourgogne* (1742; 3d ed. 1970). R. Pierce Beaver, "The Genevan Mission to Brazil," *The Reformed Journal* 17 (July–August 1967): 14–20; Jean Crispin, "Los Mártires de Rio de Janeiro," in G. Baez-Camargo, ed., *Documentos* (1955; facsimile edition of the 1564 French edition); A. G. Gordon, "The First Protestant Missionary Effort: Why Did It Fail?" *IBMR* 8 (1984): 12–18.

Sidney H. Rooy

Le Saux, Henri (Swami Abhishiktananda) (1910–1973), pioneer in Christian-Hindu dialogue. Born in France, Le Saux became a Benedictine monk in 1931 and went to India in 1948. Under the name of Swami Abhishiktananda and guided by Hindu sages, he became an adventurous explorer of the advaitic religious experience enshrined in the Upanishads, and of *sannyasa,* the Hindu monastic tradition. He was convinced that such explorations must precede the emergence of an Indian church. With Jules *Monchanin, he established the Saccidananda Ashram in South India in 1950. After Monchanin's death, he was increasingly drawn to the solitary life, and passed the leadership of the ashram to Bede *Griffiths. For his final years he settled at the hermitage he had built at Gyansu in the Himalayas.

Overcoming initial suspicion, Le Saux had increasing influence within the Roman Catholic Church in India, reinforcing the new dialogic and contextualizing attitudes of Vatican II; he influenced other Christians also, proposing, for example, the Eucharistic preface for the Church of North India, and was respected by many traditional Hindus. Many articles and eighteen books widened his influence. Best known are *Prayer* (1967), *Hindu-Christian Meeting Point* (1976), *Guru and Disciple* (1970) and *The Secret of Arunachala* (1978; both are accounts of his Hindu spiritual teachers); *Saccidananda: A Christian Approach to Advaitic Experience,* (1965) and *The Further Shore* (1975; on *sannyasa* and the Upanishads).

BIBLIOGRAPHY There are full-length studies of Le Saux by M.-M. Davy, E. Vattakuzhy, and Andre Gozier, and a collection of papers (including the important C. Murray Rogers, "Swamiji—the Friend") in Vandana, ed., *Abhishiktananda: The Man and His Message* (1986). James Stuart's *Swami Abhishiktananda: His Life Told through His Letters* (1989) includes a comprehensive bibliography. Many of Le Saux's published and unpublished papers are preserved in the archives of the Abhishiktananda Society, Delhi.

Daniel O'Connor

Leshchinsky, Filofei. *See* Filofei (Leshchinsky).

Leupolt, Charles Benjamin (1805–1884), German missionary in India under the Church Missionary Society (CMS). Born in Reichenall, Saxony, son of a prosperous manufacturer, Leupolt was trained at Basel and the CMS college at Islington, London. He served in Benares (Varanasi), in what he called "the heart of Hinduism," from 1832 to 1873. A frequent correspondent with the CMS committee, Leupolt found a wide readership for his published writings through his enthusiastic, though not uncritical, approach. As his experience grew, his critical stance toward government education policies following the Indian Mutiny of 1857 became evident in succeeding editions of his *Recollections.* The principle of "official neutrality," he said, tended to produce "atheists, skeptics, and materialists." Always optimistic, however, he believed Christianity was gaining ground on Hinduism, a system of which he remained extremely critical.

The *Recollections* clearly show the difficulty in trying to develop a native pastorate as called for by Henry *Venn, when the institution building that seemed essential unavoidably fostered paternalistic relationships with converts and ordinands. Leupolt's various attempts to encourage pastors such as David Mohun and Christian Triloke toward greater independence met with mixed results.

After 1857 Leupolt asked for a sabbatical to tour the North India CMS stations affected by the uprising. He was concerned to recover lost ground, focusing particularly on Oudh, an area of wide disaffection because the British government annexed it in 1856. In these endeavors he received considerable support from such evangelical administrators as Henry Carre *Tucker at Benares and William *Muir at Allahabad. In England during the Liverpool missionary conference of 1860, Leupolt was a leading contributor to the discussions of the native pastorate and church in India.

BIBLIOGRAPHY Leupolt's chief publications were the four editions of his *Recollections of an Indian Missionary* (1844, 1863, 1872, 1884). M. E. Gibbs, *The Anglican Church in India 1600–1970* (1972); Peter Penner, *Robert Needham Cust, 1821–1909: A Personal Biography* (1987); Eugene Stock, *The History of the CMS* (1899); H. C. Tucker, ed., *Conference [at Liverpool] on Missions* (1860). Leupolt's correspondence with the CMS committee is in the CMS archive, the University of Birmingham (CI 1/079, 0177).

Peter Penner

Lewis, Marianne (Gould) (c. 1820–1890), pioneer of the Baptist Zenana Mission in India. Marianne Gould was born in Bristol, England, to a strong Baptist family. She married Charles Bennett Lewis, who had studied at Bristol Baptist College and had been accepted by the Baptist Missionary Society (BMS) for service in Ceylon (Sri Lanka). They sailed for Ceylon in 1845 but were transferred to Calcutta in 1847, following the death of William *Yates. Marianne devoted herself to the work of female education in the Calcutta area. She became closely acquainted with Elizabeth *Sale's work of visiting the Hindu zenanas (the secluded women's sections of high-caste Hindu homes), and on furlough in 1866 she wrote a pamphlet, *A Plea for Zenanas*, advocating the opportunities for women's evangelism presented by zenana visiting. As a direct result of her pamphlet, the "Ladies' Association for the support of Zenanah work and Bible women in India in connection with the Baptist Missionary Society" was established in 1867. This body became known as the Baptist Zenana Mission in 1897, and in 1914 it evolved into the Women's Missionary Association of the BMS. Marianne and Charles Lewis remained in Calcutta with the BMS until 1878, when Charles's ill health forced them to return to England.

BIBLIOGRAPHY Ernest A. Payne, *The Great Succession: Leaders of the Baptist Missionary Society during the Nineteenth Century* (1938); Brian Stanley, *The History of the Baptist Missionary Society, 1792–1992* (1992).

Brian Stanley

Lewis, Thomas (1859–1929), Baptist Missionary Society (BMS) missionary in the Cameroons, Portuguese Congo (Angola), and Belgian Congo (Zaire). Lewis was born in southern Wales and studied for the Baptist ministry at Haverfordwest Baptist College. He was accepted by the BMS for service in the Cameroons, where he arrived in March 1883. His work was soon overshadowed by the scramble of the European powers for Africa, which led to the Cameroons becoming a German territory in 1885 and the BMS handing over its Cameroons mission to the Basel Mission in 1886. Lewis was reassigned to the Portuguese Congo, where from 1887 he was instrumental in planting the church at São Salvador do Congo (Mbanza Kongo). Earlier that year he had married one of his Cameroon colleagues, Gwen Thomas. In 1899 he left São Salvador to establish a new station at Kibokolo (formerly Quibocola) among the Zombo people. In 1913 and 1914, as the senior BMS missionary in the Congo, he expressed caution about some of his colleagues' willingness to risk confrontation with the Portuguese during an anticolonial rising. A strong believer in indigenous and self-supporting evangelistic agency, he was appointed in 1909 as principal of a new ecumenical institute for training evangelists and teachers at Kimpese in the Belgian Congo. After his retirement in 1915, he served the BMS as its first full-time representative in Wales.

BIBLIOGRAPHY Thomas Lewis, *These Seventy Years: An Autobiography* (1930); Brian Stanley, *The History of the Baptist Missionary Society, 1792–1992* (1992).

Brian Stanley

Leydecker, Melchior (1645–1701), Reformed missionary in the East Indies. Born in Amsterdam, Netherlands, Leydecker studied theology and medicine and took both his D.D. and his M.D. at the University of Leiden. He was minister of the Dutch Reformed Church (DRC) in Flanders (1671–1674). In 1675 the DRC of Walcheren sent him to the East Indies (Indonesia), where he first served as a chaplain in the army in East Java. In 1678 he was ordained minister of the Malay church at Batavia (Djakarta). He devoted much of his time to the study of Malay and compiled a Malay dictionary, which became very important for Malay lexicography. In 1691 the church board of Batavia commissioned him to translate the whole Bible into Malay. At his death he had completed it as far as Ephesians 6:6, and it was finished by others. Leydecker's work was ignored for 22 years because the church leaders had a more popular Amboinese version, translated by François Valentijn. Eventually, however, Leydecker's translation into literary Malay was preferred for its wider range. It was printed in 1723 and then reprinted in 1731 (New Testament only), 1733, and 1758 (in Arabic characters). Its importance for the Indonesian Reformed Church can be compared with that of the Authorized Translation for the DRC and the King James Bible for the Church of England. Still in use, it paved the way for other Bible translations in the East Indies.

BIBLIOGRAPHY Hendrik Kraemer, "Eenige aanteekeningen over de Maleische Bijbelvertaling van Leydekker," *Maandblad van het Nederlandsch Bijbelgenootschap*, January 1941; J. L. Swellengrebel, *In Leydekkers voetspoor*, 2 vols. (1974).

Willem J. van Asselt

Liang Fa (1789–1855), Chinese evangelist. Liang, a printer, was won to Christian faith about 1815 through the work of William *Milne, a Scottish missionary. Insofar as is known, he was the first ordained Chinese Protestant evangelist. After Milne's death in 1822, Liang continued as an evangelist and colporteur with the London Missionary Society in Malacca, and later with the American Bible Society, based in Canton and Macao. In 1836, then in the employ of an American missionary, he gave a copy of a Christian pamphlet, "Good Words for Exhorting the Age," to *Hong Xiuquan, a young scholar who had failed in the official examinations. This pamphlet, a summary of Protestant missionary teachings, inspired Hong to study Christian doctrine further and eventually to found the movement called the Heavenly Kingdom of Great Peace, which gave rise to the Taiping Rebellion.

BIBLIOGRAPHY Kenneth Scott Latourette, *A History of Christian Missions in China* (1929); Eliza A. Morrison, *Memoirs of the Life and Labors of Robert Morrison*, vol. 2 (1839); Bob Whyte, *Unfinished Encounter: China and Christianity* (1988).

Donald E. MacInnis

Libermann, François Marie Paul (1802-1852), founder of the Missionaries of the Most Holy Heart of Mary. Born in Saverne, Alsace, of Orthodox Jewish parents, Libermann was educated at the rabbinical school in Metz, France, to become a rabbi like his father. Liberal influences and spectacular conversions of leading Jews to Christianity influenced his own conversion in Paris on November 13, 1826. He entered the Saint-Sulpice Seminary in 1827. Attacks of epilepsy from 1829 to 1831 acted as an impediment to ordination, but Libermann's superiors trusted him and gave him pastoral assignments. In 1837 he was sent to serve with the Eudists in Rennes, Britanny, as master of novices. His calling, however, was the evangelization of Africa. He went to Rome in 1839 with a plan for a new missionary congregation, drawing upon the ideas of Frédéric Le Vavasseur. Libermann introduced his *Little Memorandum on Foreign Missions* at the Propaganda Fide in 1840 and drafted *Provisional Rule of the Missionaries of the Holy Heart of Mary*: "A fellowship of priests, who in the name and as envoys of Our Lord Jesus Christ, dedicate themselves entirely to announce his holy Gospel and to establish his reign among the poorest and most neglected souls in the church of God." Ordained to the priesthood in 1841, Libermann opened his first novitiate at La Neuville near Amiens, France. The first missionary was a former fellow seminarian at Saint-Sulpice, Jacques Désiré *Laval, who went to Mauritius in 1841. The next party went to West Africa. Libermann wrote to them on November 19, 1847: "Put off Europe, its customs, its spirit. . . . Become Negroes to the Negroes, in order to form them as they should be, not in the fashion of Europe, but allow them to keep what is peculiar to them." In 1848, upon request of the Propaganda Fide, he agreed to take over the congregation of the Holy Ghost Fathers, founded in 1703 by Claude-François *Poullart des Places, but devastated by the French Revolution. The Missionaries of the Holy Heart of Mary, though losing their name in favor of the Holy Ghost Fathers, brought their fresh missionary spirituality into the merger. Shocked by the high mortality rate of the first missionaries, Libermann saw indigenous clergy and episcopacy as the key to permanent evangelization. He tried to set up a seminary for future African priests in France or in Rome; the first seminaries were eventually established in Senegal and Gabon (1847-1848). Libermann never visited his missionaries; instead he sent letters of direction, forging a powerful spiritual bond throughout the congregation.

BIBLIOGRAPHY Libermann wrote no books but hundreds of letters and pamphlets. See *Lettres spirituelles* (1874, 1889) and Adolphe Cabon, ed., *Notes et documents relatifs à la vie et à l'oeuvre du Vénérable François-Marie-Paul Libermann* (1929-1956). The fundamental writings are reprinted with scholarly notes in Paule Brasseur and Paul Coulon, eds., *Libermann (1802-1852): Une pensée et une mystique missionnaires* (1988; includes an extensive bibliography on pp. 72-86 and a critical literature survey on pp. 133-160). J. Daly, ed., *Spiritan Wellsprings: The Original Rules, with Commentaries, of the Holy Ghost Congregation* (1986); A. L. Van Kaam, *A Light to the Gentiles: The Life-Story of Fr. Libermann* (1958, 1962, 1985); H. J. Koren, *To the Ends of the Earth: A General History of the Congregation of the Holy Ghost* (1983).

Marc R. Spindler

Li Chih-tsao (Li Zhizao) (1565-1630), one of the so-called Three Pillars of the Catholic Church in seventeenth-century China. A native of Hangchow (Hangzhou), Li received the highest scholarly degree in 1598 and became an assistant department director in the Board of Works in Nanking (Nanjing). Upon meeting Matteo *Ricci soon after Ricci's arrival in Peking (Beijing) in 1601, Li became interested in his world map and in Western science and wrote prefaces to several of Ricci's Chinese works. In 1610 Ricci baptized Li with the Christian name of Leo. When Ricci died later that year, Li obtained imperial permission for his burial in Peking.

In 1611 Li was in Hangchow and invited several Jesuits to preach there. During the 1616 persecution of Christianity, his residence was a place of refuge for the Jesuit missionaries. He wrote a short essay on Nestorian Christianity as found in the text of the Sian (Xi'an) Monument and edited a collection of nineteen works by missionaries (*T'ien-hsüeh*). In 1629 he was appointed to the calendar bureau in Peking, where he assisted *Hsü Kuang-chi and several Jesuits in revising the astronomical methods for the Chinese calendar.

BIBLIOGRAPHY "Li Chih-tsao," in A. Hummel, ed., *Eminent Chinese of the Ch'ing Period* (1943-1944), pp. 452-454; Willard J. Peterson, "Why Did They Become Christians? Yang T'ing-yün, Li Chih-tsao, and Hsü Kuang-ch'i," in C. Ronan and B. Oh, eds., *East Meets West: The Jesuits in China, 1582-1773* (1988), pp. 129-152; N. Standaert, *Yang Tingyun: Confucian and Christian in Late Ming China* (1988), pp. 35-37, 53-58, 79-80, 164-165, 225.

John W. Witek, SJ

Lichtenstein, Isaac (1824-1909), a pioneer of Messianic Judaism. As a district Jewish rabbi in Hungary, Lichtenstein one day confiscated a New Testament from a teacher at a Jewish school and threw it into a corner of his own library. Decades later, during a bout of savage anti-Semitism, he decided to discover for himself what it was about the New Testament that poisoned its readers against Jews. Remembering the confiscated copy, he read it, was fascinated by Jesus, was absorbed by Paul's theology, and became a believer in Jesus as Messiah. Deciding not to declare his faith openly, he exercised a mission to his people from within his prestigious leadership role. He limited himself to quoting from the New Testament in his sermons and counseling and speaking positively about Jesus. This made him a pioneer of the movement to present Jesus as a thoroughly Jewish Messiah. Eventually his secret was uncovered, and he resigned from his rabbinic post under pressure. Nevertheless, he still refused to be baptized, claiming that God wanted Jews to find true Judaism in Jesus, not join churches. This is still a debated issue in the Messianic Jewish world.

BIBLIOGRAPHY Isaac Lichtenstein, *Judaism and Christianity* (1893) and *A Jewish Mirror* (n.d.). Henry Einspruch, *When Jews Face Christ* (1932); Jacob Gartenhaus, *Famous Hebrew Christians* (1979).

Walter Riggans

Liddell, Eric Henry (1902–1945), Olympic gold-medalist and Scottish missionary in China. Liddell was born in Tientsin (Tianjin), China, of missionary parents serving with the London Missionary Society (LMS). His schooling was at the LMS School for Sons of Missionaries at Blackheath and Eltham College in England, and at the University of Edinburgh (B.Sc., 1924). He excelled in rugby and track and in 1924 was chosen to represent Britain in the 100-meter dash at the Olympic games in Paris. The 1981 Academy Award-winning film *Chariots of Fire* powerfully depicts his decision not to enter the 100-meter race because the preliminary heats were scheduled on Sunday. Instead, he competed in the 400-meter race, for which he was not as well prepared. The victory of "The Flying Scotsman" in Olympic-record time has ranked him for all time among the most memorable of Olympic heroes.

In 1925 Liddell returned to China with the LMS and taught at the Anglo-Chinese Christian College in Tientsin. In 1934 he married Florence Mackenzie, daughter of Canadian missionaries. With Japanese hostilities increasing, Liddell arranged for his wife and young family to return to Canada, planning to follow when he could no longer continue missionary work. World War II intervened, and along with about 1,500 others, he was interned in 1943 in Weihsien (Wiefang) Prison Camp, Shantung (Shandong) Province, where he was admired and loved by the scores of imprisoned children from the Chefoo School of the China Inland Mission who were separated from their parents. As teacher, friend, and guide, he modeled a godly life that brought inspiration and spiritual strength. He died from a brain tumor six months before the war ended.

BIBLIOGRAPHY Eric H. Liddell, *The Sermon on the Mount* (1937), *Prayers for Daily Life* (1942), and *Disciplines of the Christian Life* (1985). Sally Magnusson, *The Flying Scotsman* (1981); David J. Michell, *A Boy's War* (1988) and *The Spirit of Eric Liddell* (1992); Russell W. Ramsey, *God's Joyful Runner* (1987); D. P. Thompson, *Eric H. Liddell, Athlete and Missionary* (1971); William J. Weatherby, *Chariots of Fire* (1983).

David J. Michell

Lieberkühn, Samuel (1710–1777), Moravian missionary to the Jews. Born in Berlin, Lieberkühn studied theology and oriental languages at Halle and Jena. He learned Yiddish as a result of his association with Jews in Prussia beginning in 1732. In 1735 he joined the Moravians in Herrnhut. There his concern for the Jewish people and culture found affirmation in Nikolaus *Zinzendorf's plan for evangelism. In 1739 he took over a mission to the Jews in Amsterdam that had been begun by Leonhard *Dober, continuing this work even after his appointment as pastor at Zeist, the Moravian headquarters in the Netherlands. He traveled extensively in Germany, Austria, Bohemia, and England, carrying out the Jewish mission. Lieberkühn baptized no Jews himself, and his method was not to teach through sermons but instead to touch hearts through personal contact and pastoral care. He declined to engage in disputation, and rather than trying to demonstrate that Old Testament prophesies had been fulfilled in Jesus Christ, he presented the resurrection as proof of Christ's messiahship and the experience of the believer's heart as witness to Christ as redeemer. His extensive knowledge of Jewish tradition and his respect for Jewish law and custom led to his being known as Rabbi Shmuel. Lieberkühn also had a deep concern for the Christian instruction of the young. In 1774 he drafted the first catechism of the Renewed Moravian Church.

BIBLIOGRAPHY J. F. A. de le Roi, *Die Evangelische Christenheit und die Juden,* 3 vols. (1884–1892); Adolf Schulze, *Abriss einer Geschichte der Brüdermission* (1901) and *S. Lieberkühns Missionsmethode* (1895).

Otto Dreydoppel, Jr.

Liele, George (c. 1750–1828), first African American to be ordained and first Baptist to go as a missionary to any other land (Jamaica). Born a slave in Virginia, Liele was taken to Georgia, where he was converted in 1773 in the church of his master, Henry Sharp. He soon became concerned about the spiritual condition of his fellow slaves and began preaching to them. In 1775 he was ordained as a missionary to work among the black population in the Savannah area. Like many other black slaves, he sided with the British in the Revolutionary War, as did his master, who set Liele free in 1778.

In order to be evacuated with other royalists and British troops, Liele obtained a loan and accepted the status of indentured servant to pay the passage for himself, his wife, and his four children on a ship bound for Jamaica. Landing there in January 1783, he soon repaid the debt and secured permission to preach to the slaves on the island. Thus by the time William *Carey—often mistakenly perceived to be the first Baptist missionary—sailed for India in 1793, Liele had worked as a missionary for a decade, supporting himself and his family by farming and by transporting goods with a wagon and team. Apparently, he never received or accepted remuneration for his ministry, most of which was directed to the slaves. He preached, baptized hundreds, and organized them into congregations governed by a church covenant he adapted to the Jamaican context. By 1814 his efforts had produced, either directly or indirectly, some 8,000 Baptists in Jamaica. At times he was harassed by the white colonists and by government authorities for "agitating the slaves" and was imprisoned, once for more than three years. While he never openly challenged the system of slavery, he prepared the way for those who did; he well deserves the title "Negro slavery's prophet of deliverance." Liele died in Jamaica.

BIBLIOGRAPHY Clement Gayle, *George Liele: Pioneer Missionary to Jamaica* (1982); E. A. Holmes, "George Liele: Negro Slavery's Prophet of Deliverance," *Baptist Quarterly* 20 (October 1964): 340-351, 361; G. W. Rusling, "A Note on Early Negro Baptist History," *Foundations* 11 (January-March 1968): 362-368.

Alan Neely

Lievens, Constant (1856-1893), Jesuit missionary in northeast India. Lievens was born in Moorslede, Belgium, to a devout peasant family. He entered a Catholic seminary in 1876, but desiring to be a missionary, joined the Society of Jesus in 1878. He left for the Bengal mission the very day that he took his religious vows in 1880, reaching Calcutta later that year. After his theological studies and priestly ordination, he was sent to Chotanagpur in 1885. After acquiring a working knowledge of the Munda and Oraon languages and after surveying the country and the people, he settled down at Torpa, where he developed his first mission station.

Lievens soon became aware that the tribal people were being exploited by landlords and moneylenders. When a group of Protestants promised to become Catholic if they were helped, he took up their case in the law courts and obtained justice from the magistrates. This success brought him an avalanche of requests from all sides, asking not only for justice but also for the faith. Catechists were employed to instruct the people in the elements of the Christian faith, and thousands were baptized. When help arrived, he toured the whole area of Chotanagpur, spreading faith and justice. Some older missionaries did not approve of his meddling with the secular affairs of the tribals and risking the antagonism of the government and police officials as well as the landlords. Others thought that he baptized people without sufficient preparation and built the mission without proper foundations. Lievens himself was aware of the risks, but he saw God's hand in his work. His vision and method gave rise to a flourishing church in Chotanagpur. He had to withdraw from his mission and return to Europe in 1892 because of ill health. He died at Louvain a year later.

BIBLIOGRAPHY F. J. Brown, *The Apostle of Chota Nagpur* (1936); L. Clarysse, *Father Constant Lievens, SJ* (1984); H. Josson, *La mission du Bengale occidental,* 2 vols. (1921); A. Marlier, *Pater Constant Lievens* (1929); L. Monbaliu, *Constant Lievens: De ridder von Chota-Nagpur* (1983); Peter Tete, "The Apostle of Chotanagpur," in J. Lawrence Sundaram, ed., *Jesuit Profiles* (1991).

Michael Amaladoss, SJ

Liggett, Thomas J. (1919-), Disciples of Christ missionary, theological educator, and administrator. Liggett was born in Nashville, Tennessee, and attended college and seminary in Lexington, Kentucky. In 1946 he sailed for Argentina, where he served pastorates in Resistencia and Buenos Aires and became professor of church history at the Evangelical Faculty of Theology (known as ISEDET). In 1951 and 1952 he completed his residence requirements for a doctorate at Columbia University and Union Theological Seminary, New York, after which he continued teaching in Buenos Aires. In 1957 he was named president and professor of the Protestant Seminary in Rio Piedras, Puerto Rico; in 1965, executive secretary for Latin America for the Disciples of Christ; in 1968, president of the Disciples united home and foreign missions board; and in 1974, president of Christian Theological Seminary, Indianapolis, Indiana, where he was also professor of Ecumenism and Expansion of Christianity until his retirement in 1986. He was a delegate to the World Council of Churches Assembly in Uppsala, Sweden, in 1968 and moderator of his church's general assembly from 1985 to 1987.

BIBLIOGRAPHY Thomas J. Liggett, *Where Tomorrow Struggles to Be Born: The Americas in Transition* (1970) and *A Challenge to Protestantism* (1959). Justo Gonzalez, ed., *Por la renovacion del entendimiento: La educacion teologica en America Latina. Ensayos en honor de Thomas J. Liggett* (1965); J. Dexter Montgomery, *Disciples of Christ in Argentina, 1906-1956* (1956); Joseph M. Smith, *A Guide to Materials Related to the United Christian Missionary Society* (1987), pp. 36-38, 117-121; Clark M. Williamson, ed., "The Witness of a Faculty: Essays Presented to Thomas J. Liggett," *Encounter* 48, (1987): 1-161.

Sidney H. Rooy

Liggins, John (1829-1912), first Protestant missionary appointed to Japan. Liggins was born in Warwickshire, England, in 1829, but emigrated with his family to Philadelphia, Pennsylvania, in 1841. He graduated from Virginia Theological Seminary in Alexandria in 1855 and was sent immediately to China as an Episcopal missionary. Two years later he was injured by a mob, developed malaria, and went to Nagasaki, Japan, to recover his health. Since he was on the scene when Japan was opened to missionaries in 1859, the Episcopal Board assigned him to begin missionary work. He was joined a few months later by his classmate Channing Moore *Williams. They began by teaching English to government interpreters, using texts in science and history prepared in Chinese. Liggins published the first Japanese-English phrasebook in 1860 (2d ed., 1867). Continued ill health forced his early return to the United States in 1860. He spent the rest of his life speaking and writing on behalf of foreign missions.

BIBLIOGRAPHY Among Liggins's American publications were *Opium: England's Coercive Policy* (1882) and *The Great Value and Suc-*

cess of Foreign Missions (1888). Otis Cary, *The History of Christianity in Japan*, vol. 2 (1909), p. 47.

Charles Henry Long

Lijadu, Emmanuel Moses (1862–1926), Yoruba catechist, author, and evangelist. Born in Osiele at Ake, Abeokuta, Nigeria, to an early Anglican convert, Lijadu qualified as a teacher in 1885 from the prestigious Teachers' Training Institute at Abeokuta. As an Anglican teacher, catechist, and deacon (1894), he was an outspoken activist, orator, prolific writer, and ardent evangelist. His lecture on Aribilosho, an Egba-Yoruba poet, won acclaim, and in 1897 he wrote a classic study on Yoruba mythology, a pioneering work on the Ifa traditional religion. Believing, as did Mojola *Agbebi, that mission must be built upon a native foundation, he compared Ifa with Christianity. As a delegate to the Pan-Anglican Congress in England in 1898, he worked on the revised version of the Yoruba Bible, initiated by Bishop Samuel *Crowther.

Lijadu exercised charismatic healing gifts, especially during the influenza epidemic of 1895. His Evangelistic Prayer Band (1898) won the approval of Charles Phillip, the bishop of Ondo. Soon, however, Lijadu criticized missionary strategy for lacking roots in indigenous culture and villages. He devised a self-funding (by trading) evangelistic program for rural areas, equipped with a clinic. A crisis came in 1899 when Thomas Harding, an Anglican missionary administrator in the Ondo episcopal area, rebuffed the appeal by African workers for a salary increase, and his rude language was fanned into a racist slur by nationalists. In reaction seventeen independent Yoruba African churches arose between 1888 and 1922. Lijadu, a leading petition-writer, and his Evangelistic Band separated from the Anglican Church on January 1, 1901. He achieved remarkable indigenization in liturgy and spirituality, tramping to village nooks and corners with much ardor. He left an enduring legacy, namely, "to make Christianity . . . our national religion."

BIBLIOGRAPHY E. A. Adegbola, "Ifa and Christianity among the Yoruba" (Ph.D. diss., Univ. of Bristol, 1967); J. B. Webster, *The African Churches among the Yoruba, 1888–1922* (1964).

Ogbu U. Kalu

Limbrock, Eberhard Michael (1859–1931), missionary to China and founder of the Society of the Divine Word (SVD) New Guinea mission. Born in Ahlen, Germany, Limbrock studied at the SVD motherhouse in Steyl, Netherlands (1877–1883), and was sent to China as a deacon. After completing his theological studies in China, he was ordained to the priesthood and assigned to seminary teaching. In 1892 the SVD expanded its activities to Kaiser Wilhelmsland (present-day Papua New Guinea), with Limbrock the religious superior and prefect apostolic (a papal appointee with a quasi-episcopal jurisdiction). This new frontier mission, largely in Stone Age level of technology, lacked basic economic infrastructures and means of communication needed in the modern world. An enterprising and practical man, Limbrock was convinced that to make his spiritual mission possible and to help advance the living standards of the people, the new mission would have to be deeply involved in development. His mission undertook the development of schools and health facilities, large scale food production, cattle raising, new agricultural techniques, road and bridge construction, and plantations and other industries, such as sawmills. Cargo ships were acquired and docking facilities built. Financial independence from the homeland was made an important missionary goal. This many-sided effort became an integral part of the spiritual challenge itself. When Limbrock died in 1931, the New Guinea mission counted some 20,000 Christians and 5,000 catechumens.

BIBLIOGRAPHY For biographical information, see Mary Taylor Huber, *The Bishop's Progress* (1988), pp. 54–74. A listing of Limbrock's publications can be found in *SVD Authors in PNG* (1992). Archival materials are kept at Divine Word Institute, Madang, Papua New Guinea.

Louis J. Luzbetak, SVD

Lindell, Jonathan Luther (1923–1985), Lutheran missionary in Nepal. Born in Honan, China, of missionary parents, Lindell graduated from Augsburg College, Minneapolis, and Colorado State College of Education. As a member of the World Mission Prayer League, he worked among Nepalis in North India (1941–1946), and in Nepal (1956–1979). He made a marked contribution to education in Nepal, first pioneering a community service project in an isolated area, and later directing a prominent boarding school. He was director of the United Mission to Nepal (UMN) for 11 years, unifying and solidifying a very diverse young mission composed of member missions from around the world and carrying out a widely varied program of work in Nepal. He developed practical policies for the operation of the UMN, and set the strategy guidelines for its future. He used every opportunity to contribute to the young Nepali church by fellowship and advice and by his outstanding gift of teaching. His *Nepal and the Gospel of God* (1978), covering the whole story of the country, church, and missions, is an invaluable reference book. After retirement from Nepal in 1979, he continued in mission leadership in the United States.

BIBLIOGRAPHY *Fellow Workers,* magazine of the World Mission Prayer League, Minneapolis, Minn., contains relevant material by and about Lindell, especially the issues of 1979 and 1985. A collection of Lindell's writings, correspondence, diaries, and magazine articles is in the UMN archives in Edinburgh, Scotland.

Betty Young

Lindley, Daniel (1801–1880), American missionary to South Africa. Born in Washington County, Pennsylvania, Lindley graduated from Ohio University (1824), where his father, Jacob Lindley, was the founder and first president, and from Union Theological Seminary, Richmond (1831). In 1834 he married Lucy Allen, was ordained, and under appointment by the American Board of Commissioners for Foreign Missions (ABCFM), embarked with the first company of American missionaries to South Africa. From Cape Town, Lindley, Alexander Wilson, Henry Venable, and their wives set off on a year-long thousand-mile trek by ox wagon to Matabeleland. Arriving at the capital of the Matabele chief Mosilikatse, they were caught in bloody fighting between Dutch voortrekkers and the Matabele and were forced to retire to Natal. Fighting between Boers and Zulus again forced retreat, but in 1839 Lindley reoccupied his station, opened a school for the Boers' children, and in 1842 agreed to be *predikant* (pastor) of their scattered settlements, believing that the aggressive Dutch needed Christianizing as much as the Zulus. One of his confirmands was Paul Kruger, later the first president of the Republic of South Africa. In 1847 Lindley established a station at Inanda, centering his efforts on the Zulus and helping set aside large "native locations" to protect them from land-hungry settlers. At the Lindleys' retirement in 1873, Zulus and Boers expressed deep regard. He retired to the United States in 1874 and died in Morristown, New Jersey. In 1967 a new bridge at Pietermaritzburg was named the Daniel Lindley Bridge.

BIBLIOGRAPHY The principal biography is E. W. Smith, *The Life and Times of Daniel Lindley (1801–1880): Missionary to the Zulus, Pastor of the Voortrekkers, Umbebe Omhlope* (1949). *Missionary Herald* 104 (1906): 26–27 has a sketch and portraits; vol. 76 (1880): 480 has his obituary and many issues contain Lindley letters or reports. Clifton Jackson Phillips, *Protestant America and the Pagan World...* (1969), pp. 212–221, has a good summary account.

David M. Stowe

Lindsay, Gordon (1906–1973), *and*
Freda Theresa (Schimpf) (1916–), leaders in a healing movement, advocates of foreign missions, and founders and directors of Christ for the Nations Institute. Gordon Lindsay's spiritual roots are traced to his parent's membership in John Alexander Dowie's Christian Catholic Apostolic Church in Zion City, Illinois, and his conversion under the ministry of Charles F. *Parham. Influenced by the healing ministry of John G. *Lake, he accompanied him for a time as an evangelist and later pastored in California, Oregon, Washington, and Montana.

Lindsay married Freda Schimpf in 1937 and together they promoted the salvation/healing movement that emerged in the United States after World War II by editing and publishing *Voice of Healing* magazine (renamed *World-Wide Revivial* and now *Christ for the Nations*). Supporters of Pentecostal and charismatic missions, they pioneered several related programs, including Winning the Nations Crusade (1956), Native Church Crusade (1961), and (with W. A. Raiford) the Full Gospel Fellowship of Churches and Ministers International (1962). In 1967 their projects were consolidated and renamed Christ for the Nations, Inc., which sponsors Christ for the Nations Institute (1970) in Dallas, Texas, a ministerial and missionary training school. Gordon Lindsay was a prolific writer, authoring over 250 books and pamphlets in addition to many magazine articles. Freda Lindsay, a capable administrator, succeeded him as president of Christ for the Nations after his death.

BIBLIOGRAPHY Freda Lindsay's books include *My Diary Secrets* (1976), *Freda* (1987), and *The ABC's for Godly Living* (1922). Gordon Lindsay's books include his autobiography *The Gordon Lindsay Story* (n.d.), *William Branham: A Man Sent from God* (1948), *Bible Days Are Here Again* (1949), *John G. Lake—Apostle to Africa* (n.d.), *The Life of John Alexander Dowie* (1951), *Men Who Heard from Heaven* (1953), and *Miracles in the Bible,* 7 vols. (n.d.). See also David Edwin Harrell, Jr., *All Things Are Possible: The Healing and Charismatic Movements in Modern America* (1975).

Gary B. McGee

Lioba (*or* Leobgytha) (c. 710–780), English missionary in south Germany. Descendant of an English noble family and educated in the Benedictine monastery of Wimborne, England, in 738 Lioba followed a call to Germany from her relative and mentor, St. *Boniface. In connection with Boniface's intention to entrust a larger share of the missionary task to women, Lioba became abbess of a convent at Tauberbischofsheim, south Germany, and superintendent of two other nunneries in the vicinity. She was respected by princes and prelates for her erudition as well as for her commitment to evangelism and charity in pagan surroundings. Her remains were laid to rest close to those of Boniface at Fulda. Lioba has rightly been hailed as a prototype of the countless women to whom the Christian missionary movement has opened avenues of service at a time when the church offered few opportunities for them.

BIBLIOGRAPHY *Bibliotheca Sanctorum,* vol. 8 (1967), pp. 60–61; C. H. Talbot, *Anglo-Saxon Missionaries in Germany* (1954).

Hans-Werner Gensichen

Lith, Franciscus van (1863–1926), Dutch Jesuit missionary in Indonesia. Born in Eindhoven, some 50 miles southeast of Rotterdam, Lith was trained as a teacher before entering the Society of Jesus in 1881. Having completed his novitiate and studies of philosophy, he became a teacher in Katwijk College. In 1896 he was sent as a missionary to Central Java, Indonesia. He felt that a good knowledge of the people's language and customs was a prerequisite for evangelistic work. The school system was structured in the Dutch fashion, but he constantly tried to establish contact with the simple people, poor peasants, workers, the sick, and the oppressed. His attempts at adaptation were not welcomed by the conservative local population of the time, so he tried to change this mentality by the formation of an elite class. In 1906 he founded a teachers' college at Moentilan. He also had plans for a school for local chieftains. His basic idea was to conserve the Javanese culture and enrich it with outside influences. The method was a great success. Many of the students were baptized and became active advocates of the faith or even priests. Soon a Jesuit novitiate was established in Moentilan, then a school of philosophy, and in 1936 a diocesan seminary for local clergy. In 1906 Lith published a Javanese prayer book. In *Het Missiewerk* 3 (1921–1922): 96–101 he wrote about the formation of local clergy. At the First International Mission Congress in

Holland (Utrecht, 1922) he spoke about the importance of formation in mission countries. His political ideas, as in his *De politiek van Nederland ten opzichte van Nederlandsch-Indië,* (1922), aroused both approval and opposition. He died in Java.

BIBLIOGRAPHY L. J. M. Feber, "Pastoor Van Lith, S. J.," *St. Claverbond* 38 (1926): 35–39; M. Muskens, *Partner im nationalen Aufbau: Die katholische Kirche in Indonesien* (1979), esp. pp. 131–139, *Indonesië: een strijd om nationale identiteit: nationalisten, islamieten, katholieken* (1969), pp. 375–384; L. van Rijckevorsel, *Pastoor F. van Lith S.J. De Stichter van de missie in Midden-Java, 1863–1926* (1952); A. Soegija, "Aan de nagedachtenis van onzen Vader Franciscus Van Lith," *St. Claverbond* 38 (1926): 97–106; C. Vriens, "De ondergand der Java-Missie in 1898: Uit de herinneringen van Pastoor van Lith SJ," *St. Claverbond* 47 (1935): 182–184, 207–212, 228–235; 48 (1936): 20–24; 32–40.

Karl Müller, SVD

Little, Paul Eagleson (1928–1975), American campus evangelist and professor. Little began his career as a campus worker with InterVarsity Christian Fellowship, U.S., and became a leader in that movement, as well as a popular speaker and writer, and a seminary professor at Trinity Evangelical Divinity School, Deerfield, Illinois. Born in Philadelphia, Pennsylvania, he graduated from the University of Pennsylvania (1950) and joined InterVarsity to work on campuses in Illinois. In succession, he worked with international students in New York City, became regional director in Dallas, Texas, and then national director of evangelism. He spoke on more than 200 campuses in the United States, Canada, Latin America, Europe, and Africa. Although best known as a campus evangelist, he developed a keen interest in world missions as well. He directed InterVarsity's student missions conference at Urbana, Illinois, in 1970 and was program director of the International Congress of World Evangelization, Lausanne, Switzerland, in 1974. He taught evangelism at Trinity from 1964 until his death in an automobile accident in Ontario, Canada. Based on his considerable experience as a campus evangelist, he wrote *How to Give Away Your Faith* (1966), *Know Why You Believe* (1967), and *Know What You Believe* (1970). Still in print, these books have been published in more than twenty languages.

BIBLIOGRAPHY Paul E. Little and Marie H. Little, *Know What and Why You Believe* (1980).

James W. Reapsome

Litwiller, John T(imothy) N(elson) (1928–1971), Mennonite and Presbyterian missionary in Argentina, Uruguay, and Chile. Born of Mennonite missionary parents in Trenque Lauquen, Argentina, Litwiller served under the (Old) Mennonite Board of Missions and the Commission on Ecumenical Mission and Relations of the Presbyterian Church (U.S.A.). He grew up claiming Argentina as home and Spanish as his mother tongue. Educated at Goshen College, Indiana, Hartford Seminary, and Yale Divinity School, he married Mary Ann (Troyer), and they had three children. Litwiller and his wife began missionary service in 1953 among the Toba Indians in the Argentine Chaco and later served in Chile. There he was a founder of the Comunidad Teológica Evangélica, a unique ecumenical model of theological education utilizing both residential and extension programs. He was elected in 1970 the first rector of the Instituto Superior Evangélico de Estudios Teológicos, a merger of El Seminario Evangélico Luterano Rioplatense and La Facultad Evangélica de Teología in Buenos Aires. He served there until his early death. Empowered by a strong evangelical faith, possessed with wisdom, humor, and charisma, and gifted with an inquiring mind on mission strategy, Litwiller identified actively with movements of social change, was passionately ecumenical, and evidenced a keen theological awareness of the needs of the Latin American Protestant community. In his ministry, he displayed a sensitivity to the unique contributions that both North and Latin Americans bring to mission endeavors.

BIBLIOGRAPHY John H. Sinclair, "The Life and Ministry of John T. N. Litwiller" (1993), an unpublished manuscript that includes an interpretive biography, anthology of his sermons, and addresses and memories of friends and colleagues; held at the Presbyterian Historical Society, Philadelphia, Pennsylvania.

John H. Sinclair

Liu, Timothy Ting-Fang (Lew, T. T.) (1891–1947), Chinese Protestant leader and educator. Born in Wenchow (Wenzhou), Chekiang (Zhejiang) Province, Liu received his B.D. from Yale University in 1918 and his Ph.D. from Columbia University in 1920. He was ordained in the Congregational Church, New York City (1920). He joined the faculty of Yenching University in 1921, where he taught theology and psychology. A member of the North China Kung Li Hui (Congregational Church), he was an inveterate ecumenist. A founding member and cooperating secretary of the National Christian Council of China, he gave one of the three major addresses at the first annual meeting of the council in May 1923, where thirty-eight of sixty-four delegates were Chinese.

From 1926 to 1928 he was visiting professor of missions at Boston University School of Theology and at Union and Hartford Theological Seminaries, perhaps the first non-Western professor of missions in the United States. In later years he represented the Chinese church at five of the great world ecumenical conferences: the Life and Work Conference on Church, Community, and State at Oxford, England (1937); the Faith and Order Conferences in Lausanne (1927) and Edinburgh (1937); the International Missionary Council in Madras (1938); and the Conference of Christian Youth in Amsterdam (1939). He was editor of the journal *Truth and Life.* Perhaps his greatest legacy is the body of hymns, both original and translations, credited to his name. In 1932 he became chairman of the Union Hymnal Committee, which produced *Putian Songzang* (Hymns of universal praise). This lists 171 hymns written or translated by Liu. He died in Albuquerque, New Mexico.

BIBLIOGRAPHY *China Christian Yearbook, 1938–1939*; Wallace Merwin, *Adventure in Unity: The Church of Christ in China* (1974); *Yale University Obituary Record, 1947.*

Donald E. MacInnis

Livingstone, David (1813–1873), geographer and missionary in Africa. Born in Blantyre, Scotland, Livingstone began work in the local cotton mill at the age of ten but attended the mill school from eight until ten o'clock each evening and achieved university entrance qualifications. He attended the Andersonian Medical School in Glasgow while working in the mill for part of the year to support himself. He was accepted for service by the London Missionary Society (LMS) and in 1838 went to London for theological training while continuing his medical studies there. He returned to Glasgow only to take his medical final exams.

A speech by Robert *Moffat, his future father-in-law, persuaded him that Africa was where he should serve. After his ordination in London, he sailed for Cape Town and arrived in March 1841. He served for a time under Robert Moffat among the Tswana, in whose language he was soon fluent, and in 1845 married Moffat's daughter Mary (see *Livingstone, Mary). He was determined to bring the gospel to the free peoples beyond the white-dominated south. In 1852, after sending his family back to Scotland, he went north to Zambia and with Kololo companions walked west to Luanda on the coast of Angola. He then turned around and walked across Africa to Mozambique. On his return to Britain he was a national hero, and the sales from his *Missionary Travels and Researches in South Africa* (1857) guaranteed security for his family for some time.

In March 1858 Livingstone embarked upon a government-backed expedition to introduce commerce, civilization, and Christianity to the lands of the Zambezi River and Lake Malawi. The expedition vastly increased geographical knowledge but was otherwise a disaster. His wife Mary's death on the Zambezi in 1862, withdrawal from Malawi of the Universities' Mission to Central Africa, and bad relations with most of his white colleagues left Livingstone's reputation in tatters when he returned to Britain in 1864. But the Royal Geographical Society and a few loyal friends supported him and sent him back to Africa in 1866 to explore the headwaters of the Nile, Congo, and Zambezi Rivers. He did this with his loyal Kololo friends, often disappearing from European view for months and becoming more and more obsessed with the devastation the slave trade was spreading throughout the region. It was under these circumstances that he was "found" and greeted in November 1871 by H. M. *Stanley of the *New York Herald*, "Dr. Livingstone, I presume?" He died at Chitambo's village in Zambia, May 1, 1873. Susi, Chuma, and other African companions buried his heart at Chitambo's village and then carried his mummified body to Dar es Salaam. It was brought back to Britain for a hero's funeral in Westminster Abbey.

For the next 50 years a large number of writers created their own Livingstones, most shaped to justify the "Scramble for Africa." Modern writers have not wholly shaken off these distortions, largely ignoring his bitter attacks on British policy and his defense of the right of Africans to fight for their lands. They also rarely note his constant insistence that without the help of African companions, particularly the Kololo, he could never have completed his astonishing journeys.

BIBLIOGRAPHY G. W. Clendennen and I. C. Cunningham, *David Livingstone: A Catalogue of Documents* (1979) and *Supplement* (1985) are essential resources along with T. Holmes, ed. *David Livingstone Letters and Documents: The Zambian Collection* (1990). Of the many biographies the best are Cecil Northcott, *David Livingstone* (1973), T. Holmes, *Journeys to Livingstone: Exploration of an Imperial Myth* (1993), and the old but good W. G. Blaikie, *The Life of David Livingstone* (1905). See also Andrew F. Walls, "David Livingstone," in Gerald H. Anderson et al., eds., *Mission Legacies*, (1994), pp. 140–147.

Andrew C. Ross

Livingstone, Mary (Moffat) (1821–1862), oldest child of Robert *Moffat and wife of David *Livingstone. Born at Griqua Town, South Africa, Mary Moffat grew up speaking Tswana more fluently than English. She spent five years at Salem School in the eastern Cape Colony followed by some teacher training at Cape Town. From 1839 to 1843 she was in Britain with her parents and disliked the life there intensely. From 1843 she taught happily in the school at Kuruman in Griqualand, and then in 1845 she married David Livingstone. She and their children accompanied him on his two great treks to the north in 1850 and again 1851. Although she loved this life as much as her husband did, her parents were appalled, and when David decided to explore the Zambezi Valley everyone insisted that she not go. There followed four desperately unhappy years in Britain which she still found alien. When David returned to Britain in 1856 she spent two very happy years with him, though still disliking life in Europe intensely. She insisted on joining her husband on the next Zambezi expedition and in 1861 she sailed for her beloved Africa. On April 27, 1862, she died in David's arms at Shupanga on the Zambezi.

BIBLIOGRAPHY Edna Healey, *Wives of Fame* (1986) contains the only serious attempt at a life of Mary Livingstone. Timothy Holmes, *Journey to Livingstone* (1993) contains much information and some sympathetic insights.

Andrew C. Ross

Livinhac, Auguste Simon Léon (1846–1922), superior general of the Missionaries of Africa (or White Fathers [WF]). Born in Ginals, Sévérac, Aveyron, France, Livinhac left the major seminary of the diocese of Rodez to join the WF recently established by Charles Allemand *Lavigerie, archbishop of Algeria. Ordained a priest in 1873, he dedicated himself to the African mission in 1874. In 1878 he was chosen to head the first group of ten missionaries going to Equatorial Africa. They left North Africa on Easter Day, April 21, 1878, and arrived in Uganda on February 17, 1879. Studying Rugunda, he composed a grammar and a dictionary. Ordained a bishop in 1884, he returned as apostolic vicar to Uganda in 1885 at the height of religious persecutions there. Several of the Ugandan Catholic martyrs killed in 1886 had been baptized by him. With a group of Ugandans, he attended the International Antislavery Conference in Paris (1890). The same year he was appointed vicar general of the WF, and after Lavigerie's death in 1892, he was chosen to be superior general. His poor health and his continuous reappointments as superior general (1894–1912) never allowed him to return to Uganda. When he resigned as superior general in 1920, he organized the documentation that would lead to the beatification of the martyrs of Uganda. During his term of office the three equatorial vicariates in Africa grew into nine equatorial vicariates, two Sudanese ones, and two apostolic prefectures. The WF grew from 233 to 930 members. It established itself in Germany (1894), Argentina (1898), Canada (1901), Belgium (1902), Switzerland (1911), Great Britain (1912), and the Netherlands (1917).

BIBLIOGRAPHY G. D. Kittler, *The White Fathers* (1957); Pères Blancs, *Notices Nécrologiques,* supplément no. 17 (1923), pp. 21–36.

J. G. Donders, M Afr

Llinás, Jesús Maria Antonio (1635–1693), Spanish Franciscan founder of missionary colleges in Latin America. Born at Artá, Majorca, Spain, Llinás entered the Franciscan order of strict observance in 1652. In 1664 he went to Mexico, where he taught theology in Valladolid (now Morelia) (1668–1674) and from 1671 to 1674 was also guardian of the convent there. He went to Spain in 1679 and returned to Mexico with 22 Franciscans after he attended the Franciscan general chapter in Toledo, Spain, as a representative in 1683. Realizing that sufficient missionary vocations were no longer coming from Mexican convents, Llinás prepared a plan for missionary colleges in Latin America, for which the Franciscan minister general allowed him to recruit twenty-four missionaries in Spain. He prepared statutes for the colleges, which were approved by Innocent XI in 1682. Shortly afterward, Propaganda Fide issued a decree authorizing the colleges, and for this reason they were called colleges of Propaganda Fide. The first one was opened in 1683 at Querétaro, Mexico, in the Holy Cross monastery, and many more followed. Llinás established the principle that missionary activity should be the fruit of strict religious observance, and missionaries were to devote special time for contemplation. They should also study Indian languages. When a group of Indians were converted, the missionaries were to hand over the parishes to the diocesan clergy. The missionary colleges existed up to the beginning of the twentieth century, when they were taken over by the Franciscan Order. Llinás died in Madrid.

BIBLIOGRAPHY Isidro Felis de Espinosa, *Chronica apostólica y seráphica de todos los colegios de Propaganda Fide de esta Nueva-España de Missioneros Franciscanos Observantes* (1746; 1964 edition with notes and introduction by Lino G. Canedo); Michael B. McCloskey, *The Formative Years of the Missionary College of Santa Cruz de Querétaro, 1683–1733* (1955); Emmanuel R. Pazos, "De Padre Antonio Llinás Collegiorum Missionariorum in Hispania et America Fundatore (1635–1693)," *Archivo Ibero-Americano* 22 (1935): 5–44, 161–188, 321–352; also as off-print (1936).

Willi Henkel, OMI

Lloyd, Arthur (1852–1911), English Anglican missionary and student of Japanese religions. After a distinguished academic career at Cambridge University, where he was fellow and dean of Peterhouse, Lloyd, an ordained minister, responded to a call from the Society for the Propagation of the Gospel to do educational work in Japan. His first period of service in Tokyo began in 1884 and ended in 1890 when he went to Canada with his wife, who was seriously ill. After her death, he returned to Japan in 1894 under the auspices of the Protestant Episcopal Church in the U.S.A. (on account of which he is sometimes wrongly referred to as an American missionary). He began a long period of service as a teacher in the Imperial University, Naval College, and Higher Commercial College in Tokyo. He wrote many books and articles on Japanese religions, and especially on Amitabha Buddhism, notably, *The Praises of Amida* (1907), a translation of Buddhist sermons, and *The Creed of Half Japan* (1911). His theology of mission, expressed in *The Wheat among the Tares* (1908), was influential in the 1908 Pan Anglican Congress in London and at the 1910 World Missionary Conference in Edinburgh. He died in Tokyo.

BIBLIOGRAPHY Kenneth R. Cracknell, *Justice, Courtesy, and Love: Missionaries and Theologians Encountering the World Religious Traditions, 1846–1914* (1995).

Kenneth R. Cracknell

Loayza, Gerónimo de (1498?–1575), evangelizer of Peruvian Indians and first archbishop of Lima. Born in Trujillo in Extremadura, Spain, Loayza entered the Dominican order in Córdoba. After teaching philosophy and theology for a few years, he went to Santa Marta, Colombia, as a missionary, and returned to Spain in 1536. The following year he was ordained bishop of Cartagena, Colombia, where he served until 1543, when he was transferred to Lima. As Lima's first bishop and later its archbishop (1548), Loayza was also the metropolitan over all Spanish dioceses in Central and South America. In that key post he summoned all the bishops to attend the first two general councils of Lima, in 1551 and 1567. The first council, poorly attended, laid down basic norms for evangelizing the Indians. The second, better attended and more important, incorporated the decrees of the Council of Trent and applied them to Latin America. Both councils exhorted pastors to learn the Indian languages and to encourage the Indians to receive the sacraments. In 1549 Loayza published a manual (*Instrucción*) in which he laid down norms for working with the Indians. He began the building of Lima's cathedral, and helped to found San Marcos University (1551), as well as many other cultural and charitable institutions. The most noted of the latter was the Hospital of Santa Ana for Indians, founded in 1549. He also established the Inquisition in 1570. During his 32 years as head of the church in Lima, he had to face many political and social difficulties, ranging from the civil war between the Pizarro brothers and the followers of Diego de Almagro to the forced relocation of the Indians under Viceroy Toledo. Throughout it all he consistently defended the Indians and opposed forcing them to do personal service or work in the mines.

BIBLIOGRAPHY Enrique Dussel, *El Episcopado latinoamericano y la liberación de los pobres, 1504-1620* (1979); Manuel Olmedo Jiménez, "Fray Gerónimo de Loayza, pacificador de españoles y protector de indios" (Ph.D. diss., Univ. of Seville, 1982); Rubén Vargas Ugarte, *Concilios limenses, 1551-1772,* vols. 1-3 (1951-1954), and *Historia de la Iglesia en Perú,* vol. 1 (1953).

Jeffrey Klaiber, SJ

Lock, Annie (1877-1943), Australian missionary to the Aborigines. Born in South Australia, Lock worked with the United Aborigines' Mission from about 1902 in all five Australian states and the Northern Territory. First helping in havens for abandoned Aboriginal children, then deciding she worked best alone, she joined some Aborigines in the desert near a source of water known as Harding soak. She was there in the late 1920s when, following the slaughter of settlers' cattle for food by Aborigines in a drought, and the coincidental killing nearby of a white roustabout caught interfering with Aboriginal women, police and settlers ambushed and shot several Aborigines. Determinedly espousing the cause of the Aborigines during court hearings in Darwin, in an atmosphere of virulent racism, she was mocked and insulted in the streets there and in Alice Springs and reviled in the press. Undaunted, she continued her lonely mission in the Central Desert until her health broke down. When she recovered, about 1933, she and a colleague started a mission for Aborigines congregating at Ooldea, then a watering point in the Nullabor Plain for the transcontinental railway. She retired in 1935, married soon after to a bank manager, James Johansen (d. 1970), and continued her mission work in smaller ways until her death.

BIBLIOGRAPHY The best authority is Violet E. Turner, *The "Good Fella Missus"* (1938) and *"Ooldea"* (1950). See also Kenelm Burridge, *In the Way* (1991); John Cribbin, *The Killing Times* (1984); and John Harris, *One Blood* (1990).

Kenelm Burridge

Lockhart, William (1811-1896), first British medical missionary. Born in Liverpool, Lockhart was trained at the Meath Hospital, Dublin, and at Guy's Hospital, London, and was sent to China by the London Missionary Society (LMS). Arriving in China early in 1839, he married Catherine Parkes (d. 1918) in 1841. Lockhart worked at various places—Macao, Chou-shan (Zhoushan), Tientsin (Tianjin), Hong Kong, Shanghai, and Peking (Beijing)—but his main station was Shanghai, where he worked for 14 years. When he returned to England in 1864, he served the LMS as one of their directors and in 1878 became the president of the newly formed Medical Missionary Association, London. Lockhart advocated a strict separation of the vocations of preacher and physician, a maxim he propounded in his book *The Medical Missionary in China: A Narrative of Twenty Years' Experience* (1861). Thus, he always concentrated on medical work in the hospitals that he directed.

BIBLIOGRAPHY *The Medical Missionary Record* 6 (1891): 198-200; much from Lockhart's pen and about him appears in the pages of *Medical Missions at Home and Abroad,* the monthly publication of the Medical Missionary Association, London, during the years 1879-1888.

Christoffer H. Grundmann

Lo Gregory (*or* Lo Wen-Tsao). *See* Lopez, Gregorio.

Löhe, Johann Konrad Wilhelm (1808-1872), founder of the Neuendettelsau Mission (NM). Löhe was born and brought up in the family of a businessman at Fürth, in northern Bavaria. After studying for the ministry at Erlangen, he made a reputation for himself as one of the most resolutely Lutheran churchmen and theologians in the country. His village parish at Neuendettelsau became a center of Lutheran worship, preaching, and charity on a parochial level, counterbalanced by a vivid concern for German Lutheran immigrants in the United States and the founding of the NM in 1849. It was Löhe's hope that mission among American Indians would be stimulated through the Neuendettelsau parish's interest in the welfare of the German immigrant community. For Löhe, mission was essentially "the one church of God on the move," embracing both evangelistic witness and works of charity, on the basis of unswerving loyalty to the Lutheran confession. A mission seminary and an institution for the training of deaconesses were founded in 1853. Löhe's hope that the American churches themselves would assume responsibility for the mission was not fulfilled because, as Löhe himself became aware, mission to the immigrant population amounted to little more than service for people preoccupied by concern over their uncertain future. Besides, it was difficult to convince the German home base that this was mission in the fullest sense of the term. Löhe did not live to see the wider outreach of the mission to New Guinea after 1886, when the specific missionary heritage of Neuendettelsau came to fruition in a new church overseas.

BIBLIOGRAPHY Wilhelm Löhe, *Gesammelte Werke,* 12 vols., Klaus Ganzert, ed. (1951-1986); J. L. Schaaf, "Wilhelm Löhe's Relation to the American Church" (Th.D. diss., Heidelberg Univ., 1961).

Hans-Werner Gensichen

Lohmann, Ernst (1860-1936), leader in the German Orient Mission (Near East Mission). Lohmann was born in Glowitz, Pomerania, the son of a pastor. He served in Halle as a city missionary and spent a formative period in Frankfurt am Main as pastor of the independent Christ Church Community, which was dedicated to working among those who were destitute. Turkish assaults on the Armenians in 1894 at the instigation of Sultan Abdül

Hamid II led him to start the Deutsche Hilfsbund für Christliches Liebeswerk im Orient in 1896. He retired from the pastorate in order to promote the new venture. This relief agency founded and supported several orphanages, a preachers and a teachers college in Uchtenhagen in Brandenburg, hospitals, and a school for women church workers. Impressed by the example of the Swedes, he suggested starting the Deutsche Frauenmissionsgebetsbund (German Womens' Mission Prayer Federation) in 1899. In connection with this initiative he helped to open a Bible school in Bad Freienwalde in 1898 for mission sisters and women teachers. He taught there from 1910. While in Frankfurt he helped to organize Christian student conferences in 1893 and 1894, which led to the Deutsche Christliche Studentenvereinigung, which joined the World's Student Christian Federation.

Lohmann's writings were influential for evangelism and mission work in the Near East. He started the first Christian weekly, *Für alle,* and the well-known weekly *Licht und Leben.* He published about seventy titles on a wide range of topics, including *Pfingstbewegung und Spiritismus* (1909), *Die jetzige Weltlage in ihrer Bedeutung für die Mission* (1909), *Werden und Wachsen des Deutschen Frauenmissionsbundes* (1914), *Das Geheimnis der Gesetzlosigkeit* (1921), *Die Kirche der Armen* (1928), and *Der Epheserbrief, zur Weltharmonie durch Christus* (1930).

BIBLIOGRAPHY Ernst Lohmann, *Nur ein Leben* (1936; autobiography). Theodor Brandt, *Ernst Lohmann, ein Pionier im Dienst Jesu* (1962); Karl Heinz Voigt, "Lohmann, Ernst," *Biographisch-bibliographisches Kirchenlexikon,* vol. 5 (1993), pp. 182–186 (includes full bibliography).

Lothar Schreiner

Lohr, Oscar T. (1824–1907), German missionary, founder of the Central India Mission. Born in Laehn, Silesia, Germany, Lohr was trained in surgery and pharmacy, and then was commissioned by the Gossner Missionary Society of Berlin and arrived at Ranchi, India, in 1850. Soon thereafter he married a missionary widow, Mrs. Berner. After the Indian Mutiny of 1857 he sailed for the United States, was ordained in the German Reformed Church, and began serving pastorates in New Jersey. Still deeply interested in missions, he was instrumental in organizing the German Evangelical Mission Society (GEMS) in 1865. In 1867 Lohr was commissioned by the GEMS to begin work in India. Arriving in Bombay in 1868 with his wife and three children, he set out for Raipur, in Chhattisgarh, to work among the Satnamis, a tribe unreached by missionaries. He bought some 1800 acres of jungle land at Bisrampur and Ganeshpur on which converts were to settle. In 1870 Lohr baptized three converts, and a church was built in 1874. Conversions continued and new missionaries joined Lohr in what became known as the Central India Mission. Together they developed a wide range of ministries; education of children and evangelists; medical services, including his own work as a pharmacist; the teaching of trades; and better agriculture. Lohr built a lithographic press, utilizing local stone, and printed a catechism, a hymnbook, and other materials for church and school. His son Julius translated the Gospel of Mark into Chhattisgarhi, the first portion to be available in that language. In 1884 GEMS was dissolved and the work in Chhattisgarh was turned over to the (German) Evangelical Synod of North America. Lohr served as president of the mission conference until 1894. He died in India and was buried at Bisrampur.

BIBLIOGRAPHY John W. Flucke, *Evangelical Pioneers* (1931), chap. 12; Emil W. Menzel, ed., *I Will Build My Church* (1943), pp. 1–4; Theodore C. Seybold, *God's Guiding Hand, A History of the Central India Mission, 1868–1967* (1967), chaps. 1–6. Manuscript materials are in the library of Eden Theological Seminary, Saint Louis, Mo.

David M. Stowe

Lohrenz, Henry W. (1878–1945), Mennonite Brethren missionary statesman and educator. Born near Moundridge, Kansas, Lohrenz married Anna M. Friesen, graduated from McPherson College, received an M.A. from Kansas University in 1911, studied theology in four seminaries, and in 1929 was awarded a D.D. by Northern Baptist Theological Seminary in Chicago. He taught post-secondary natural science and biblical studies for over 30 years, was president of Tabor College (1908–1931), and served as chairman of the Board of Foreign Missions of the Mennonite Brethren Church (1919–1936) and as its first executive secretary-treasurer (1936–1945). A gifted speaker, he also promoted the cause of mission in churches and at conferences for more than 40 years. He was the first American Mennonite Brethren leader to shape principles and policies to give unity and direction to the entire mission operation. His letters to missionaries were filled with missiological insights and words of encouragement. The extent of his impact was made evident in papers and other tributes read at a symposium entitled, "H. W. Lohrenz and the Mennonite Brethren: Shaping a Tradition, 1900–1945," held in Fresno, California, April 15–16, 1983.

BIBLIOGRAPHY Board of Foreign Missions, *Foreign Missions Memorial Number: Henry W. Lohrenz* (1946). Lohrenz's classified papers, pamphlets, letters, and missiological writings entitled *Greetings* (1940–1944) are in the archives of the Center for Mennonite Brethren Studies in Fresno, California; a portion of his correspondence is with the family in Kansas City, Kansas.

Hans Kasdorf

Lombard, Eva (1890–1978), first woman missionary doctor of the Basel Mission (BM). Born in Geneva, Switzerland, Lombard was the daughter of a bank manager who left his profession to become an evangelist to prisoners. Her mother worked with women prisoners. Eva Lombard graduated from the University of Geneva as a medical doctor in 1918, after practicing in hospitals in Basel and Geneva. As a member of the Student Christian Movement she attended the world conferences at Constantinople (present-day Istanbul) in 1911 and Mohonk Mountain House, New York, in 1913. In 1920 she went to Mysore, South India, to work with the Kanarese Mission (an organization based in French-speaking Switzerland that took over BM work in South Kanara in 1916). In 1923 she transferred to Udupi and started a small cottage hospital of six beds. The Kanarese Mission was taken over by the BM in 1926. The hospital grew into a well-known 200-bed general hospital with a training school for nurses, serving thousands of people in the area. In 1954 she handed over the work to an Indian woman doctor and returned to Switzerland in 1957. After her death the Indian staff at Udupi dedicated their annual report of 1978 to her memory.

BIBLIOGRAPHY Lombard wrote several articles for *Der Evangelische Heidenbote* and *Unser Dienst in der Frauenmission,* both Basel Mission publications. Obituary in P. A. Kundargi, ed., *Mission Hospital Udupi, South Kanara, Mysore State: Golden Jubilee Souvenir 1979.* Circular letters and correspondence are in the BM archive.

Waltraud Ch. Haas

Long, James (1815-1887), Church Missionary Society (CMS) missionary in eastern India. Long, an Irishman, went to Calcutta in 1840 and worked in eastern India until 1872. He was especially interested in Christian vernacular literature and education, and he built up close personal relationships with Bengali people. In the late 1850s, when the violence of the Indian Mutiny was still vividly remembered, Long became involved in the struggle of Bengali peasants who were being pressured by English planters to grow indigo at the expense of food crops. He acted as sponsor and publisher for a Bengali play, *Nil Darpan,* translated into English as *The Mirror of Indigo.* It was a work of propaganda, with a violent preface contributed by the translator, a Bengali Christian. For his part in this, Long was prosecuted in 1861 at the instigation of the Landholders' Association of British India. He was fined 1000 rupees (paid immediately by a wealthy Bengali) and given a month's imprisonment. The CMS authorities, although sympathetic with his intervention, felt he had exceeded his mandate. He retired in 1872. In 1885 he made a gift to CMS of £2000 to be used to fund the Long Lectures on Eastern religions, which continued into the twentieth century.

BIBLIOGRAPHY CMS, *Register of Missionaries and Native Clergy* (1904); M. E. Gibbs, *The Anglican Church in India, 1600-1970* (1972).

Jocelyn Murray

Long, Retta Jane (Dixon) (1878-1956), Australian founder of the Aborigines Inland Mission (AIM). Retta Dixon was converted as a teenager, joining Sydney's Petersham Baptist Church. Through the Christian Endeavour Union, she accompanied other young Christians visiting Aboriginal people at La Perouse on Sydney's outskirts. At only 20 years of age, she became a resident missionary there, traveling also to Aboriginal camps along the New South Wales coast. In 1905 she left La Perouse to work among Aboriginal people at Singleton, about 100 miles north of Sydney. There, with a group of local Christians, she founded the AIM. In 1906 she married Leonard Long and they became codirectors. The mission expanded, sending missionaries to Aboriginal communities throughout New South Wales, Queensland, and the Northern Territory.

On her husband's death in 1928, Long became sole director of AIM. Among her major projects were a large children's home in Darwin and a Bible Training Institute for Aboriginal Christians. The mission had grown to sixty-two missionaries by 1944. Ill health finally forced her retirement in 1953.

BIBLIOGRAPHY Retta Long, *Providential Channels* (1935) and *In the Way of His Steps* (1937); John Harris, *One Blood* (1990).

John W. Harris

Longinus (6th century), pioneer evangelizer of Nubia. Longinus was a Syrian monophysite long imprisoned in Constantinople for his theological beliefs. With lower Egypt a battleground between partisans of Chalcedonian and non-Chalcedonian theologies, the Byzantine emperor Justinian grew anxious to pacify the boundaries of his empire by Christianizing the natives. About 566 the Coptic patriarch Theodosius I of Alexandria consecrated Longinus as bishop of Napata (capital of the Nubian kingdom) to carry on the work of *Julian two decades earlier. Amid intermittent persecution and exile, he directed the transformation of the pre-Christian temples of Upper Egypt (Nobatia) and Sudan ('Alwa) into churches and the erection of new edifices along the course of the Nile.

BIBLIOGRAPHY William Y. Adams, *Nubia, Corridor to Africa* (1977), pp. 441-443.

Paul D. Garrett

Loosdrecht, A(ntoine) A(ris) van de (1885-1917), pioneer Dutch missionary to Toraja, Indonesia. Van de Loosdrecht was born in Veenendaal, Netherlands, the son of a factory worker. He received his training at the Nederlandse Zendingsschool (the mission school of the Netherlands Mission Society) at Rotterdam and in 1913 left for Celebes (Sulawesi), Indonesia, to become the pioneer missionary of the Sa'dan Toraja mission field. He belonged to the orthodox movement in the Dutch Reformed (Hervormde) Church and was sent by the Gereformeerde Zendingsbond (Reformed Mission League), which was an exponent of that movement. Van de Loosdrecht was influenced by the newly emerging missiology that sought to separate supposedly neutral "culture" from pagan "religion" and to weld Christian faith and traditional culture together into a new way of life for the community and the individual (in that order). He followed the approach used by the famous missionary duo Albert C. *Kruyt and Nicolaus *Adriani in the adjoining area of Poso (Central Celebes). For example, he insisted on using the Toraja language and not Malay in evangelization and education, and he chose the name of a Toraja creator god to translate the word "God." Yet he was critical of feudalism and its excesses in the culture. Fluent in Toraja, and enjoying the confidence of the lower classes, he heard their complaints about abuses by feudal lords and reported these complaints to the colonial officials. When some of the lords rose against the Dutch rulers, Van de Loosdrecht was assassinated.

BIBLIOGRAPHY Terance W. Bigalke, "A Social History of 'Tana Toraja,' 1870–1965" (Ph.D. diss., Univ. of Wisconsin, 1981); Th. van den End, *De Gereformeerde Zendingsbond 1901–1961. Nederland-Tanah Toraja: Een bronnenpublicatie* (1985); Theodorus Kobong, "Evangelium und Tongkonan" (Th.D. diss., Hamburg Univ., 1989); B. Plaisier, "Bruggen en Grenzen: De communicatie van het Evangelie in het Torajagebied (1913–1942)" (Th.D. diss., Utrecht Univ., 1993).

Th. van den End

Lopez, Gregorio (Lo Wen-Tsao) (1611–1691), first Chinese Catholic priest and bishop. Lo Wen-tsao, baptized in 1633 by a Franciscan, Antonio de Santa Maria, was the first Franciscan convert in China. Later to be known as Gregorio Lopez, he studied in Manila, was admitted to the Dominican order, and in 1656 was ordained the first Chinese priest on record. The French vicar apostolic, François *Pallu, a missionary of the newly formed Société des Missions-Étrangeres, proposed that a native secular clergy should be rapidly built up, with a native episcopate under supervision of the foreign vicars apostolic. Rome did not agree but did accede to his proposal that Lopez be appointed successor to the French missionary Cotolendi (who had died on his way out to China) as vicar apostolic of Nanking. Lopez modestly declined, but in 1679 a papal decree ordered him to accept. His own superior, the head of the Dominicans in China, gave his consent on condition that a "wise and learned" Dominican missionary serve as counselor to the new bishop because the Dominicans, who later opposed the Jesuits' leniency on the practice of Chinese ancestral rites, were concerned that Lopez would compromise the strict Dominican position. Because he would not accept missionary supervision, Lopez was refused consecration at Manila. His consecration was finally consummated in Canton in 1685, by the Italian Franciscan, Bernardino della Chiesa, who was vicar apostolic. Lopez was well past 70.

Five years later Lopez was appointed to the newly created see of Nanking, but he did not use the title of bishop and died a year later. Not until 1926 was the next Chinese bishop consecrated, a lapse of 241 years.

BIBLIOGRAPHY Benno M. Biermann, *Die Anfänge der neueren Dominikanermission in China* (1927); Adrien Launay, *Histoire général de la Société des Missions-Étrangeres* (1894); A. C. Moule, "The Life of Gregorio Lopez," *New China Review* 1 (1919): 480–488.

Donald E. MacInnis

López de Mendoza Grajales, Francisco (1525?–1569?), establisher of the first Catholic parish in the present-day United States. López was born in Jerez de la Frontera, Spain. One of four secular priests who sailed with the expedition of Pedro Menéndez de Avilés to Florida, he was the fleet chaplain and wrote an account of the voyage and the first settlement. On September 7, 1565, he landed at St. Augustine, and the next day, which was the Feast of the Nativity of the Blessed Virgin, he celebrated the first Mass there. A few months later, he took part in an expedition that tried to start a colony at Santa Lucia, Florida, but was attacked by Indians. He and a small party next attempted to reach Havana by boat but were blown back to Florida, where they were rescued. In June 1566, as pastor of the Spanish settlement in St. Augustine, he received five more newly arrived secular priests. The final documented mention of his work in Florida dates from 1569, when he intervened on behalf of a group of mutineers. Although Jesuits and, later, Franciscans arrived to work with Native Americans, he was the pioneer missionary and first pastor of a permanent Spanish settlement.

BIBLIOGRAPHY López's memorial is in B. F. French, ed., *Historical Collections of Louisiana and Florida* (1875). See also Michael V. Gannon, *The Cross in the Sand* (1983).

Gerald P. Fogarty, SJ

Lorrain, James Herbert (1870–1944), Baptist missionary in Mizoram, northeast India. Brought up in south London as a Congregationalist, Lorrain came to Baptist principles as a young man. With his co-worker F. W. Savidge, he arrived in the remote Lushai Hills area of northeast India (now Mizoram) in January 1894 under the auspices of Robert *Arthington's Aborigines Mission. Within four years Lorrain and Savidge learned the Lushai (Mizo) language, translated Luke, John, and Acts, and published a Lushai grammar and dictionary. In 1897 Arthington withdrew his workers, prompting Lorrain and Savidge to form their own Assam Frontier Pioneer Mission, and they returned to northeast India in 1899 to work in Arunachal Pradesh. In 1903 they resumed work in the southern Lushai Hills at the invitation of the Baptist Missionary Society. Building on a small Christian community planted by Welsh Calvinistic missionaries from the north, Lorrain (who had married Eleanor Atkinson in 1904) presided over a remarkable process of church growth that placed great stress on indigenous evangelism and self-support. In 1907, and more fully from 1919 to 1924, the church experienced movements of revival. By the time of Lorrain's retirement in 1932, the status of Mizoram as one of the most Christian states of modern India could already be anticipated.

BIBLIOGRAPHY C. L. Hminga, *The Life and Witness of the Churches in Mizoram* (1987); D. Kyles, *Lorrain of the Lushais* (1944); Brian Stanley, *The History of the Baptist Missionary Society, 1792–1992* (1992).

Brian Stanley

Lourdel, Siméon (1853–1890), Catholic missionary pioneer in Uganda. Born in the Pas-de-Calais, France, Lourdel became a White Father, being ordained in 1877. He was chosen for the first caravan to East Africa led by Leon *Livinhac and arrived in Buganda in February 1879. He soon became the mission's principal spokesman, being a good linguist with a manifest faith and an enthusiasm which quickly drew many Baganda to him ; he acquired the personal name of "Mapera" (Mon père), by which he is still remembered. In the tense uncertain atmosphere of the Ganda court of King Mutesa and his son Mwanga, Lourdel's quick spirit was frequently called into action as when, at a moment of crisis in 1881, he offered to walk through fire carrying the Gospels if a Muslim spokesman would do the same with the Koran. The offer was not taken up and an immediate threat to the Christian community was averted. Lourdel baptized at least 15 of the martyrs killed in King Mwanga's persecution of 1885 and 1886, including Joseph Mukasa Balikuddembe and Andrew Kaggwa (all have since been canonized). Expelled from Buganda in 1888 by the usurping Muslim king Kalema, he returned after the Christian victory in 1889 but died shortly afterwards. Buganda Catholicism considers him its true founding father.

BIBLIOGRAPHY A. Nicq, *Vie du Réverend Père Siméon Lourdel* (1895); J. F. Faupel, *African Holocaust: The Story of the Uganda Martyrs* (1962).

Adrian Hastings

Lourenço da Silva de Mendonça (fl. 1681–1686), Afro-Brazilian envoy to Rome whose petitions induced the papacy to condemn the major abuses of the Atlantic slave trade. Claiming descent from "the kings of Congo and Angola," Lourenço was of racially mixed ancestry, probably born in Brazil of slave parents. By 1681 he was recognized as a leader of "all the mulattos" in Portugal, Castile, and Brazil. He presented a petition to Innocent XI that was placed before Propaganda Fide on March 6, 1684. The petition revealed the concern of elite slaves over the perpetual slavery of baptized Christians, but his description of the cruelties inflicted on slaves suddenly awakened the cardinals at Propaganda Fide to the horrors of the slave trade. On January 14, 1686, a further petition from Lourenço was considered, and as a direct result the Holy Office formally approved a set of propositions submitted by Capuchin missionaries that condemned the fraudulent enslavement and sale of innocent "Negroes and other natives" and demanded their emancipation and compensation. The limited concerns of Lourenço's petitions were thus expanded into a solemn papal condemnation of the Atlantic slave trade.

BIBLIOGRAPHY R. Gray, *Black Christians and White Missionaries* (1990), pp. 11–27; G. Saccardo, "La schiavitù e i Cappuccini," *L'Italia Francescana* 53 (1978): 75–113, repr. in G. Saccardo, *Congo e Angola con la storia dell'antica missione dei Cappuccini,* vol. 3 (1983), pp. 263–305.

Richard Gray

Louw, Andries Adriaan (1862–1956), South African missionary. Known as "Andrew," Louw was born at Fauresmith, South Africa, the son of a Dutch Reformed Church (DRC) minister. While studying theology at the University of Stellenbosch, he developed a serious lung affliction and had to give up his studies in order to move to a drier area inland. He worked on a sheep farm near Colesberg for five years before offering his services to the Cape DRC mission committee to accompany S. P. Helm to the new mission field in Mashonaland (present-day Zimbabwe). With the help of black evangelists trained by Stephanus *Hofmeyr, he founded the DRC mission in Mashonaland, with its headquarters at Morgenster. With the help of his wife, Cinie (Malan), he translated the Bible into Karanga. He also started the first theological courses for evangelists, out of which a full-fledged theological seminary later developed. In recognition of his outstanding contribution, he was ordained a minister of the DRC in 1919, without having completed his theological studies. In 1954 the queen of England awarded him the Order of the British Empire in recognition of his service in the development of Southern Rhodesia (Zimbabwe).

BIBLIOGRAPHY Andrew Louw's biography, *Andrew Louw van Morgenster* (1965), was written by his son A. A. Louw. See also W. J. van der Merwe, *From Mission Field to Autonomous Church in Zimbabwe* (1981).

Willem Saayman

Love, John (1757–1825), mission strategist and a founder of the London Missionary Society (LMS). A Church of Scotland minister in London, Love was one of several mission enthusiasts who gathered at the Dissenters' Library in 1794 in support of establishing a Congregational mission. He wrote the 1795 circular convening the LMS. As joint secretary with W. Shrubsole (1795–1798), he worked unstintingly on administration, and with David *Bogue he strove to obtain well-educated missionaries; for this, he exploited his Scottish links.

Returning to Scotland, Love became a distinguished preacher at Anderston from 1800. In 1820, after Robert Balfour's death, he revitalized the long-inactive Glasgow Mission Society (GMS), serving as secretary. He drew his evangelical intensity from David *Brainerd; Samuel Rutherford nourished his mysticism; and his Glasgow enlightenment studies also left a mark. His writings, labeled natural religion, have been justly appreciated posthumously. Love is commemorated in the Lovedale Mission, Cape Colony, founded in 1824 by the GMS.

BIBLIOGRAPHY John Love, *Public Sermons and Otaheite Addresses* (1826; includes a memoir). P. McBride, ed., *Letters of John Love DD, Minister of Anderston Church, Glasgow* (1839); John Morison, *The Fathers and Founders of the London Missionary Society* (1840); Gavin White, "'Highly Preposterous': Origins of Scottish Missions" *Records of the Scottish Church History Society* 19 (1976): 111–124.

Nancy Stevenson

Loveless, Sarah (Farquhar) (1774–1839), first foreign missionary from the United States. Born on Long Island, New York, Farquhar studied with famed female educator and founder of charitable works Isabella Graham, and then became an assistant at Graham's school in New York City. In 1804, she nearly died, and was told to travel to a warm climate to save her life. Setting sail for India, she passed through England, where the ship picked up London Missionary Society missionaries William C. Loveless and John Taylor. They arrived at Madras in 1805, and in 1806 she married Loveless. William Loveless was the first English missionary in Madras. Hostility to missions by the English government meant that the Lovelesses turned their attention to work with Eurasian residents. He supervised an orphan asylum, opened two schools, and founded the Madras Bible and Tract Societies. She did educational work, bore four children, and managed money for the building of a chapel. The Davidson Street Church became the site where the early American missionaries Gordon *Hall and Samuel *Nott held services. Sarah Loveless's greatest accomplishment was founding the Missionary Free School for Girls. She was famous for providing hospitality for visiting missionaries in Madras. In 1824 the Lovelesses retired to England.

BIBLIOGRAPHY Richard Knill, *The Missionary's Wife; or, A Brief Account of Mrs. Loveless, of Madras, the First American Missionary to Foreign Lands* (1839); Richard Lovett, *The History of the London Missionary Society, 1795–1895,* vol. 2 (1899).

Dana L. Robert

Lowe, John (1835–1892), independent Scottish medical missionary. Born in Banchory, Aberdeenshire, Lowe held both an ordination degree and a medical degree. He worked with the London Missionary Society at Neyoor, Travancore, India, from 1861 to 1870. After his wife's ill health forced them to return to Scotland, in 1871 he was appointed superintendent of the Edinburgh Medical Missionary Society's training institution at Edinburgh, and in 1883 he became the society's secretary, serving both offices until his sudden death almost a decade later. Lowe paid much attention to insuring adequate education for aspiring medical missionaries, made the society prosper, and rallied tirelessly for medical missions, especially with his book *Medical Missions: Their Place and Power* (1886), which became the standard reference work on the subject for generations.

BIBLIOGRAPHY John Lowe, *Jubilee Memorial Historical Sketch of the Edinburgh Medical Missionary Society* (1891, 1892). A memorial volume produced by the society was *Rev. John Lowe, F.R.C.S.E., Secretary and Superintendent, Edinburgh Medical Missionary Society* (1892). John Wilkinson, *The Coogate Doctors* (1992).

Christoffer H. Grundmann

Lo Wen-Tsao. *See* Lopez, Gregorio.

Lowrie, John C(ameron) (1808–1900), first American Presbyterian missionary to India. Lowrie was born in Butler, Pennsylvania, and was educated at Jefferson College, Canonsburg, Pennsylvania. In 1833 he and his wife, Louisa Ann, went to Calcutta, where she died six weeks after landing. Within a few months Lowrie himself took sick and was told he could not survive in India. Nevertheless, he explored alone into the far northwest territory among the Sikhs of the Punjab for the benefit of those who would follow and were expected to continue into Afghanistan, Kashmir, and Tibet. Lowrie left India in 1836 and, with health somewhat restored, became an assistant to his father, Walter Lowrie, who had resigned from the U. S. Senate to become secretary of the Western Missionary Society, predecessor of the Presbyterian Board of Foreign Missions. In this capacity, from 1838 to 1891 he wrote a number of books of great sensitivity and strategic vision. His brother, Reuben, served in China for six years before his death. A second brother, Walter M. (1819–1847), also a missionary, was drowned by Chinese pirates. Lowrie was moderator of the Presbyterian General Assembly in 1865.

BIBLIOGRAPHY John C. Lowrie, *Travels in North India* (1842), *Two Years in Upper India* (1850), *A Manual of the Foreign Missions of the Presbyterian Church in the United States of America* (1868), *Missionary Papers* (1881), and *Memoirs of the Hon. Walter Lowrie* (1896). *Memoirs of Mrs. Louisa A. Lowrie, Wife of the Reverend John C. Lowrie, Missionary to Northern India: Who Died at Calcutta, November 21st, 1833, aged 24 years,* compiled by Ashbel G. Fairchild, introduction by Elisha P. Swift, (1836); *Memoirs of the Reverend Walter M. Lowrie, Missionary to China,* ed. by his father (1849); Walter M. Lowrie, *Sermons Preached in China* (1851).

Charles Partee

Loyola, Ignatius. *See* Ignatius of Loyola.

Lozada, Jorgelina (1906–1995), missionary pastor and administrator in the area of the River Plate Republics. Born in Bragado, Argentina, Lozada offered more than 60 years of service for church and mission. After preparatory studies in Christian education and social service, she worked as pastoral assistant for five years before her ordination as missionary pastor in Buenos Aires, thereby becoming the first ordained woman of the Disciples of Christ. She pursued additional studies in the United States and lectured widely on Latin American and women's issues. As executive secretary for the Federation of the Protestant Churches of the River Plate region, she was crucial to the organization of the First Protestant Conference of Latin American Churches in Buenos Aires in 1949. She was a delegate to the World Sunday School Convention in Río de Janeiro (1932) and Toronto (1950); the International Missionary Council in Madras, India (1938), and Willingen, Germany (1952); and the World Council of Churches (WCC) Assembly in Evanston, Illinois (1954). She taught at and was a member of the governing board of the Evangelical Faculty of Theology (known as ISEDET) in Buenos Aires, worked with the YWCA, and served on the WCC committee on the Life and Work of Women in the Church (1950–1958). Her innumerable ecumenical activities included significant functions in the Argentine League of Protestant Women and work with its magazine, *Guía del Hogar;* the World Day of Prayer; and CONDECOORD, an association of nongovernmental social service agencies uniting women volunteers in Argentina.

BIBLIOGRAPHY Jorgelina Lozada, *Breezes in the Wind* (1973). James J. Montgomery, *Disciples of Christ in Argentina, 1906–1956*

(1956); Margaret Richards Owen, *The Reverend Jorgelina Lozada: Ecumenical Witness* (1991).

Sidney H. Rooy

Lubac, Henri de (1896–1991), Catholic theologian of mission and religions. De Lubac was born at Cambrai, France, and joined the novitiate of the Lyon Province of the Society of Jesus in 1913. He served in the French Army for the duration of World War I (1914–1918). His first academic training in philosophy and theology was done in England (1920–1926) and continued in Lyon-Fourvière (1926–1928). He was nominated professor of fundamental and dogmatic theology at the Facultés Catholiques de Lyon (1929) and of history of religions (1939). With Jean *Daniélou he became a cofounder of the French collection *Sources Chrétiennes.* As a theological consultant at Vatican II (1962–1965) he contributed to council documents on religions and the church's mission. Subsequently he also served as a consultor to the pontifical secretariat for non-Christians and nonbelievers.

De Lubac's approach to the theology of mission had a threefold source: deep familiarity with early Christianity and the Fathers of the Church; passion for the catholicity and universality of the Christian message; and a will to enter into a sincere dialogue with other traditions on their own terms. His early studies on Buddhism—even if somewhat dated—witness to this openness to others in their differences.

At the center of de Lubac's theology of mission is the unity of the plan of God for humankind as this has been realized in the person of Jesus Christ and continues to unfold in history through the mission of the church. This seminal theme, brilliantly illustrated in his early work *Catholicism,* was the inspiring axis of his whole theological vision. De Lubac's posture on non-Christian religions came under the category of "fulfillment theory": Jesus Christ alone fulfills human aspirations for union to the divine, as he is personally the God-given answer to humankind's eternal quest for God. To announce him as the one in whom all people of good will may be saved is the church's irreplaceable mission to the world.

BIBLIOGRAPHY Henri de Lubac, *Le fondement théologique des missions* (1946), *La rencontre du Bouddhisme et de l'Occident* (1952), *Aspects of Buddhism* (1953), *The Splendour of the Church* (1956), *The Drama of Atheist Humanism* (1963), *Catholicism* (1964), *The Mystery of the Supernatural* (1967), *The Religion of Teilhard de Chardin* (1968), and *The Church, Paradox and Mystery* (1970). Hans urs von Balthasar, *Henri de Lubac: Sein Organisches Lebenswerk* (1976); Nikola Eterovic, *Cristianesiomo e religioni secondo H. de Lubac* (1981); *L'homme devant Dieu: Mélanges offerts au Père de Lubac,* 3 vols. (1964).

Jacques Dupuis, SJ

Lucas, Bernard (1860–1921), English missionary in India. Lucas went to India in 1886 with the London Missionary Society. He worked first in Bellary and became one of the founders of United Theological College, Bangalore, and a prominent leader in the South India United Church. He was a prolific writer, both of articles and of books. Theologically and missiologically a radical, he defended J. N. *Farquhar's fulfillment theory against attacks from Dugald *Mackichan and others; he went further than Farquhar in a liberal direction. Lucas makes a clear distinction between proselytism and evangelism. The former involves extracting individuals from their culture and their community and Westernizing them; the latter refers to the gradual penetration and transformation of a culture and a society by "the spirit of Christ." The institutional church, Lucas claimed, played little part in the proclamation of Jesus, and he accused fellow missionaries of being obsessed with the institution and incapable of discerning that the Spirit of God was active far beyond the sphere of Judeo-Christian faith, preparing the way for the gospel. The central issue for him was the salvation not of individuals but of nations. Applying his insights to caste, he distinguished the system, which is inherently good, from the "caste spirit," which corrupts the system and should be tackled head-on by Christians. Involved in constant controversy, Lucas effectively challenged narrow and individualistic understandings of evangelism and encouraged Christians to attend more closely to the positive features of Hinduism. But it was by no means clear that the church had a role in his scheme, and he was criticized for having too optimistic a view of political and religious developments in India. He died in England.

BIBLIOGRAPHY Bernard Lucas, *The Empire of Christ* (1907), *Christ for India* (1910), and *Our Task in India* (1914). Of Lucas's many articles, "Not to Destroy but to Fulfil," *Harvest Field* 34 (1914), is particularly important. D. B. Forrester, *Caste and Christianity* (1980), pp. 144–148; Eric Sharpe, *Not to Destroy but to Fulfil* (1965); T. K. Thomas, "The Christian Task in India: An Introduction to the Thought of Bernard Lucas," *Religion and Society* 15, no. 3 (1968): 20–31.

Duncan B. Forrester

Lucas, William Vincent (1883–1945), Anglican missionary and bishop in Tanganyika (Tanzania). After study at Oxford, ordination, and a curacy, Lucas joined the Universities' Mission to Central Africa in 1909, serving in parishes until 1926, when he became the first bishop of the Diocese of Masasi on the death of Bishop Frank *Weston of Zanzibar. Work among the Masasi had begun when Bishop Edward *Steere arrived in 1876 with freed slaves despairing of finding their original homes; the diocese covered southeastern Tanzania and was little developed. Lucas began as bishop with only ten British and nine African clergy, but after 1935 numbers of both rose and pressures eased. In his first ten years schools increased from 89 to 237. But World War II brought such destitution that some people reverted to bark clothing, though the country was not a war zone (as it had been in World War I). Lucas had welcomed colonial indirect rule through chiefs in 1930, but later he felt this was artificial and led to abuse. In 1921 the *jando* (circumcision rites) of the Yao were brought into a Christian framework, Lucas being cautiously in favor. Elsewhere such rites were dying, but Lucas hoped that their real value might endure. He resigned in 1944 and returned to England, where he soon died.

BIBLIOGRAPHY W. V. Lucas, *Christianity and Native Rites* (1948), "The Christian Approach to Non-Christian Customs," in E. R. Morgan, ed., *Essays Catholic and Missionary* (1928) and "The Educational Value of Initiatory Rites," *IRM* 16 (April 1927): 192–198. A. G. Blood, *The History of the Universities' Mission to Central Africa,* vols. 2 (1957) and 3 (1962); Lyndon P. Harries, "Bishop Lucas and the Masasi Experiment," *IRM* 34 (Oct. 1945): 389–396.

Gavin White

Luce, Alice Eveline (1873–1955), missionary to India and to Hispanics in the United States. Born in the home of an Anglican minister in Gloucester, England, Luce was educated at Cheltenham Ladies' College, and then studied nursing and theology. In 1896 she sailed to India as a Church Missionary Society (CMS) missionary and ministered to women at Azimgarh, United Provinces. Beginning in 1905, she served as principal of Queen Victoria High School in Agra. While she was there (1905–1912), two important events changed the direction of her ministry: the publication of Roland *Allen's *Missionary Methods: St. Paul's or Ours?* (1912), and her identification with the Pentecostal movement.

Recovering from illness, Luce returned to England in 1912. A year later, the CMS seconded her to the Zenana Bible and Medical Mission. Sent to work at the branch office in Vancouver, British Columbia, Canada, she resigned from the CMS in 1914. Meanwhile, she felt called by God to go to Mexico as a missionary. When the Mexican Revolution altered her plans, she remained in the United States to evangelize Hispanics in Texas and later in California, gaining ordination from the Assemblies of God (AG) in 1915. In 1926 she founded Berean Bible Institute in San Diego, California (now Latin American Bible Institute in La Puente, California), to train Hispanics for the ministry; she remained there until her death.

Luce was the first missiologist of stature in the AG. By writing a three-part article entitled "Paul's Missionary Methods" in the *Pentecostal Evangel,* she influenced the adoption in 1921 of a more developed strategy of applying indigenous church principles in the AG mission enterprise. Luce's influence continued through her teaching, writing, and mentoring of Ralph D. *Williams and Henry C. *Ball. Her books include *The Messenger and His Message* (1925), *The Little Flock in the Last Days* (1927), *Pictures of Pentecost* (n.d.), and, with Henry C. Ball, *Glimpses of Our Latin-American Work in the United States and Mexico* (1940).

BIBLIOGRAPHY Alice Eveline Luce, "Paul's Missionary Methods," *Pentecostal Evangel,* Jan. 8, 1921, pp. 6–7; Jan. 22, 1921, pp. 6, 11; Feb. 5, 1921, 6–7. See also Victor de Leon, *The Silent Pentecostals: A Biographical History of the Pentecostal Movement among the Hispanics in the Twentieth Century* (1979); Gary B. McGee, "Pioneers of Pentecost: Alice E. Luce and H. C. Ball," *Assemblies of God Heritage* 5 (Summer 1985): 4–6, 12–15. Information on Luce's activities in India can be found in *Proceedings of the Church Missionary Society for Africa and the East,* 1896–1915.

Gary B. McGee

Luce, Henry Winters (1868–1941), missionary educator in China. Born in Scranton, Pennsylvania, Luce was first a supporter and later a recruit of the Student Volunteer Movement (SVM), and a lifelong friend of Sherwood *Eddy, John R. *Mott, and Robert E. *Speer. His commitment to missions came during his time at Yale University, from which he was graduated in 1892. He spent two years at Union Seminary (New York), and completed his seminary training at Princeton in 1896. He devoted two years—the year before graduating from Princeton, and the year following graduation—to the promotion of SVM. In 1897 he was ordained, married, and appointed by the Presbyterian Board of Missions for service in China, where he spent 31 years. Luce was a professor in Shantung Christian (Cheeloo) University founded by Calvin *Mateer, and later vice-president of Yenching University in Peking. Distinguished in appearance, convivial, and persuasive, he raised sizable amounts of money for both Chinese institutions, enabling them to become renowned Christian schools of higher learning. He published five books in Chinese and helped initiate the Yale-in-China Association. He resigned in 1928 to accept a professorship at the Kennedy School of Missions in Hartford, Connecticut, from which he retired in 1935.

Luce devoted the remaining six years of his life principally to two endeavors: the Associated Boards for Christian Colleges in China, and conference-like "institutes" he initiated to help North Americans become aware of what he called the "other five-sixths of the world." He is buried in Utica, New York. One of his four children, Henry R. Luce, was the founder and longtime editor-in-chief at Time-Life.

BIBLIOGRAPHY Sherwood Eddy, *Pathfinders of the World Missionary Crusade* (1945), pp. 54–57; B. A. Garside, *One Increasing Purpose: The Life of Henry Winters Luce* (1948); Irwin T. Hyatt, Jr., *Our Ordered Lives Confess* (1976), pp. 228–230; Patricia Neils, *China Images in the Life and Times of Henry Luce* (1990).

Alan Neely

Ludger (*or* Luidger; Liudger) (c. 744–809), missionary to Frisia and Westphalia. A native of Frisia, Ludger studied with Gregory in Utrecht and with Alcuin in York. By 776 he was preaching in Deventer, and from 777 to 784 he worked in Dokkum, West Frisia, among people converted by English missionaries. He rebuilt the church of Deventer, which had been burned in a rebellion, and established a seminary. During 784 a revolt forced him to flee to Rome and Monte Cassino. Charlemagne, after his 786 victory over the Frisians, brought Ludger back to the region, where he renewed the church; but when he burned the pagan worship centers the Frisians revolted and drove him out again. Sent to Mimigardeford (Münster), he established forty parishes, a convent at Nottuln and abbeys at Helmstedt and Werden.

BIBLIOGRAPHY Hubert Schrade, *Die vita des heiligen Liudger und ihre Bilder* (1960); Klaes Sierksma, ed., *Liudger 742–809. De confrontatie tussen heidendom en christendom in de Lage Landen* (1984).

Frederick W. Norris

Lugo, Juan Leon (1890–1984), early Pentecostal leader in Puerto Rico. A Puerto Rican who was converted in Hawaii in 1913, Lugo took part in Pentecostal work in California and was ordained as an Assemblies of God (AG) minister in 1916. Determined to evangelize his homeland, he left for Puerto Rico with financial help from a local church. Working with other Puerto Rican Pentecostals, he established a congregation in Ponce, his hometown. After several other churches were also organized, the work was affiliated with the AG in 1921, along with legal registration and adoption of a suitable name. In the meantime, Lugo married the recently converted daughter of a devout, socially established Puerto Rican family. In the following years they were reinforced by other missionaries, including Frank Finkenbinder, the father of the Latin American radio evangelist "Hermano Pablo" Finkenbinder. After 15 years, Lugo left thirty-seven Pentecostal churches on the island. He established a large church in New York City in 1931 and returned to Puerto Rico to begin a Bible institute in 1937. After 1940 he lived in New York.

BIBLIOGRAPHY Juan L. Lugo, *Pentecostés en Puerto Rico* (1951). Victor De Leon, *The Silent Pentecostals* (1979); Roberto Domínguez, *Pioneros de Pentecostés,* vol. 1 (1971), pp. 55–122.

Everett A. Wilson

Lull, Raymund (*or* Ramón) (1235–1315), martyred missionary to Muslims. Born into a distinguished family on the island of Majorca, Spain, Lull spent his youth as a page, tutor, poet, and troubadour in the Court of Aragon. Although married and father to two children, he lived a dissolute life until his dramatic conversion in 1257. The facts of his life often are interlaced with legend, but he is reported to have forsaken family and wealth to become a mendicant and scholar. His life goal was to preach the Christian faith and write books to convert unbelievers, persuade princes and popes to establish colleges for the training of missionaries to the Muslims, and give his life as a martyr. For nearly a decade he prepared himself for his work by studying Arabic, engaging Muslim and Jewish scholars in debate, and writing books. He convinced Prince James (later King James II) to establish a monastery, Miramar, in 1276 for would-be missionaries to Muslims. He traveled widely, urging other rulers and church leaders to do the same; and he preached, lectured, debated, and continued to write books in Latin and in Arabic. He is said to have considered becoming a Franciscan but it is uncertain if he ever took Holy Orders.

He made at least four missionary journeys, three to North Africa and one as far as Cyprus, from which he hoped to go on to Syria. The first, in 1291, was to Tunis, where he challenged the Muslim literati and attacked directly the Islamic view of God. Imprisoned, he barely escaped death. In 1301 he made an unsuccessful attempt to enter Syria, but did evidently contact some leaders of the Eastern branches of Christianity and tried to convince them to submit to the authority of Rome. His third mission was to Bugie, a North African town 100 miles east of Algiers. Because of his preaching, he was imprisoned for six months and then deported. At 80 years of age, Lull journeyed again to Tunis and apparently gained his first Muslim converts. Then, in 1314 and 1315, for reasons not entirely clear, he returned to Bugie and, according to tradition, was stoned to death, a martyr.

Lull is significant for his extensive writings designed to persuade believers and non-Christians, especially Muslims, of the truth of the Christian faith; for the college established on Majorca for training missionaries in Arabic language and philosophy; and for his determined missionary efforts in the Muslim world. A mystic, he is often thought of as having opposed the Crusades, but the evidence is mixed. No complete listing of his writings was made, but a partial catalog consists of more than 280 titles.

BIBLIOGRAPHY Raymund Lull, *Obres* (1905–1952). E. Allison Peers, *Ramón Lull: A Biography* (1929) and *Fool of Love: The Life of Ramón Lull* (1946); Samuel M. Zwemer, *Raymund Lull: First Missionary to the Moslems* (1902; informative, but not always reliable in details).

Alan Neely

Luquet, Jean Félix Onésime (1810–1858), French Catholic missionary in India. Luquet was born in Langres, Haute-Marne. As a student at the École des Beaux Arts, he lost his faith. Later, however, he returned to the church and entered the seminary of Saint Sulpice. In 1841 he transferred to the seminary of the Paris Foreign Mission Society. In 1842 he was ordained and sent as a missionary to the Coromandel Coast of India. In 1844 he was a delegate at the Synod of Pondichéry convened by the vicar apostolic of Pondichéry, Clément *Bonnand. As one of the most active participants, he was subsequently sent to Rome to explain the resolutions. He also presented a long memorandum about the establishment of an Indian hierarchy and an Indian clergy: *Eclaircissement sur le Synode de Pondichéry.* Rome was impressed and nominated him coadjutor to Bonnand. He was consecrated by Cardinal Fransoni, prefect of Propaganda Fide, on September 7, 1845, but Bonnand refused to accept him as coadjutor. So he stayed in Rome, resigned as coadjutor in 1851, and spent the few remaining years of his life in the French seminary in Rome. Many of his suggestions could only be realized at a later date.

BIBLIOGRAPHY Jean Félix Onésime Luquet, *Retraite ecclésiastique des missionnaires de Pondichéry* (1847) and *Considérations sur les missions catholiques et voyage d'un missionnaire dans l'Inde* (1853). Bede Barcatta, *A History of the Southern Vicariate of Colombo, Sri Lanka* (1991); C. Constantini, "Ricerche d'archivio sull'istruzione 'De Clero Indigeno,'" *Miscellanea Pietro Fumasoni-Biondi* (1947), pp. 1–78; A. Launay, *Histoire des missions de l'Inde,* vol 2 (1898); F. Pinus, "Quand un 'Champion terrible' entre en lice," *Spiritus* 1 (1959/1960): 455–468. A complete list of Luquet's writings is found in A. Launay, *Memorial,* vol. 2 (1916), pp. 412–413.

Karl Müller, SVD

Luther, Martin (1483–1546), Protestant reformer. As long as the nineteenth-century pattern of foreign missions was the standard by which Christian missions were measured, Luther and the other reformers of the sixteenth century were widely regarded as lacking in both missionary thought and action. With the development of modern Reformation research on the one hand, and the reconsideration of the Christian mission on the other, a more balanced view has emerged, reflecting the essentials of Luther's theology.

(1) The mission is God's, not ours. The living Word moves out into the world, beginning from Jerusalem and proceeding to the ends of the earth. (2) The precedence of God's own initiative, far from paralyzing human action, stimulates the witness of Christians to God's saving grace, which is operative in and through faith. (3) The missionary dimension of the church as a whole must not be narrowed into one special department of Christian action among others. "Nobody should hear the gospel for himself only, but everyone should tell those who do not know it," Luther once said.

If Luther and other reformers did "exceedingly little" (Stephen Neill) to put such insight into practice, this was at least partly due to unfavorable circumstances: a desperate shortage of preachers at home, no Protestant monastic orders, preoccupation with the Protestant struggle for existence in Europe, and lack of contacts with non-Christian lands and peoples. The achievements of sixteenth-century Roman Catholic missions would hardly have invited Protestant competition, even less so since during Luther's lifetime the Jesuits had made it clear that their mission efforts overseas were also meant to compensate for losses in Europe due to the progress of the Reformation. In contrast, Luther's theocentric concept of mission "is not measurable in terms of statistical growth, financial expenditure, or the other tokens of success. Its ultimate vindication is eschatological" (James A. Scherer).

BIBLIOGRAPHY H.-W. Gensichen, "Were the Reformers Indifferent to Missions?" *The Student World* 52 (1960): 119–127; James A. Scherer, *Mission and Unity in Lutheranism* (1969).

Hans-Werner Gensichen

Luthuli, Albert John Mbumbi (1899–1967), Zulu Christian leader. Albert Luthuli was born to a Christian family. Groutville, the mission station of the American Board of Commissioners for Foreign Missions (ABCFM), became the family home, and the Groutville Congregational Church the focal point of their life. Luthuli was educated at the ABCFM Adams College, south of Durban, where he became a member of the staff; in 1921 he became the first African to be appointed a teacher-training instructor in South Africa. In 1934 he was appointed a chief and returned to Groutville to serve his people. Elected a deacon of the Groutville church, he also served for a term as chairman of the Bantu Congregational Church (now part of the United Congregational Church of Southern Africa). He became involved in the political struggles of the time, was elected president of the African National Congress (ANC) in 1952, and was banned by the new Afrikaner Nationalist regime. Nevertheless, he led the ANC Defiance Campaign of the late 1950s. Arrested with many others for treason in 1957, he was found not guilty in 1961 but was banished to Groutville. In 1960 he received the Nobel Peace Prize.

BIBLIOGRAPHY Albert Luthuli, *Let My People Go: An Autobiography* (1962); E. S. Reddy, ed., *Luthuli: Speeches of Chief Albert John Luthuli* (1991).

John W. de Gruchy

Lütkens, Franz Julius (1650–1712), facilitator of the Tranquebar mission. Lütkens's place is not among active foreign missionaries, nor, for that matter, among missiologists. Rather, he represents those who in a decisive hour follow God's call for new and daring ventures in the propagation of the faith. Born a miller's son in a north German village, Lütkens was trained as a Lutheran minister at Wittenberg University and served as an inconspicuous parish pastor until he was transferred to Berlin in 1687. There he was deeply influenced by the pietist reform ideas of his colleague in the ministry, Philipp J. *Spener. When King Frederick IV of Denmark called him to Copenhagen as his court chaplain in 1704, Lütkens made use of his connections to propose two young German Pietists, Bartolomäus *Ziegenbalg and Heinrich *Plütschau, as pioneer missionaries in the newly projected mission in the Danish trade settlement of Tranquebar, South India. He thus helped to initiate a significant historical development which was well under way when, due to disputes with the king, he was removed from office.

BIBLIOGRAPHY G. G. Küster, *Lebensbeschreibung des D. Frantz Julii Lütkens* (1727).

Hans-Werner Gensichen

Luzbetak, Louis J. (1918–), Divine Word missionary and anthropologist. Born in Joliet, Illinois, Luzbetak received his training, from high school to ordination, from the Society of the Divine Word (SVD). After his ordination in 1945, he went to Rome for further theological studies, receiving degrees in theology and in canon law from the Gregorian University. In 1947 he was transferred to the Anthropos Institute in Fribourg, Switzerland, an SVD anthropological center founded and directed by the internationally known scholar Wilhelm *Schmidt, who became Luzbetak's mentor and lifelong inspiration. In 1951 Luzbetak received a doctorate from the University of Fribourg, with which the institute was then associated. His studies at Fribourg, as well as later in Vienna, were in ethnology, linguistics, and the study of religions.

While doing ethnographic and linguistic field research in New Guinea (1952–1956), Luzbetak was increasingly attracted by missiological challenges, especially by the relationship between faith and culture. While uncompromising in matters of faith, he was opposed to all forms of manipulation or pressure in mission action, and his foremost concern was the challenge of what is known today as inculturation and contextualization. His lectures and research took him to many parts of the world. His best-known works are *The Church and Cultures: An Applied*

Anthropology for the Religious Worker (1963) and *The Church and Cultures: New Perspectives in Missiological Anthropology* (1988). His publications include other full-length books and many articles dealing mostly with his favorite theme, the church's need for cultural sensitivity, for which anthropology, he felt, might best provide the necessary light.

From 1963 to 1973 Luzbetak served as director of the Center for Applied Research in the Apostolate in Washington, D.C. He taught anthropology, linguistics, and missiology at various schools and in special cross-cultural training programs, including the Catholic University of America and Georgetown University in Washington, D.C., and at his alma mater at Techny, Illinois. He served as president of the Divine Word Seminary College at Epworth, Iowa (1973–1979). He was acting director of the Anthropos Institute (Sankt Augustin, Germany) and editor of Wilhelm Schmidt's internationally acclaimed journal *Anthropos* (1979–1982). He also served on the Vatican's Pontifical Council for Culture. In 1995 he was semiretired at the SVD Techny headquarters, continuing his research and doing occasional lecturing and consulting.

BIBLIOGRAPHY Louis J. Luzbetak, "My Pilgrimage in Mission," *IBMR* 16 (July 1992): 124–128.

Darrell Whiteman

Lyall, Leslie Theodore (1905–1996), missionary of the China Inland Mission (CIM), and writer on China. Lyall was born in Chester, England, the son of an itinerant evangelist who died when Lyall was five. Educated at Emmanuel College, Cambridge, Lyall was a leader of the Cambridge Inter-Collegiate Christian Union in the period that the Inter-Varsity Fellowship of Evangelical Unions was coming into being. In 1929 he joined the CIM, teaching for a time at the Chefoo (Shantung Province) School for missionaries' children and then working in Shansi (Shanxi) Province. He was one of several CIM missionaries who encouraged the development of Christian student fellowships in Chinese universities, where anti-Christian sentiment was often vocal.

After World War II the Christian movement among students burgeoned. Lyall and his CIM colleague David *Adeney were active in support of the China Inter-Varsity Christian Fellowship, which for a time looked as if it would become the largest affiliate of the International Fellowship of Evangelical Unions. By 1951, however, the political situation required its formal dissolution and the withdrawal of all missionaries from China. Lyall joined the home staff of his mission (now the Overseas Missionary Fellowship), first as men candidate's secretary, then as literature secretary. He wrote prolifically himself and promoted missionary consciousness in the British student world. He was a widely respected "China watcher" and the animator of a study group especially interested in the "unofficial" churches there. He was the main originator of the Evangelical Fellowship for Mission Studies.

Lyall was inspired by Chinese Christian leaders, many of whom he knew from his student contacts. Following Yang Shao T'ang and Watchman *Nee, he stressed the place of suffering in Christian development. He also introduced the work of John *Sung to Western readers.

BIBLIOGRAPHY Leslie Lyall, *John Sung* (1954, rev. 1961), *Come Wind, Come Weather: The Present Experience of the Church in China* (1961), *The Church Local and Universal* (1962), *Urgent Harvest* (1962), *A Passion for the Impossible: The Continuing Story of the Mission Hudson Taylor Began* (1965, rev. 1976), *Red Sky at Night* (1969), *A World to Win* (1972), *Three of China's Mighty Men* (1973), and *New Spring in China? A Christian Appraisal* (1979). Obituaries: *The Independent,* February 24, 1996; *Daily Telegraph,* February 19, 1996; *The Guardian,* February 16, 1996. See also Douglas Johnson, *Contending for the Faith: A History of the Evangelical Movement in the Universities and Colleges* (1979).

Andrew F. Walls

Lyman, David Belden (1803–1884), American missionary in Hawaii. Born in New Hartford, Connecticut, Lyman was converted at an early age and prepared for missionary service at Williams College (graduated 1828) and at Andover Theological Seminary (graduated 1831). Ordained in October 1831, he married Sarah Joiner on November 2 and they sailed as members of the American Board of Commissioners for Foreign Missions fifth company of Sandwich Islands missionaries on November 26. After a voyage of almost six months on the whaler *Averick* they arrived at Honolulu and were assigned to Hilo on the island of Hawaii. There they remained for 52 years without returning to the United States. Lyman worked as an evangelist for four years. As the great awakening of 1836–1838 began, he founded the Hilo Boarding School for Boys, remaining as its head until 1873. The school produced hundreds of graduates, many of them teachers, whose influence was felt throughout the islands. Sarah Lyman was actively associated with the school, particularly in the music program. Instruments for her first school band were made by students out of native materials; later a sea captain donated brass instruments. The band led the singing at the large Hilo church; the famous Haili church choir began with a group of Sarah Lyman's students. The Lymans had eight children, the first of which died in childhood.

BIBLIOGRAPHY *Missionary Herald* 80 (1884): 508–509; *Missionary Album* (1969), pp. 142–143. Sarah Lyman's experience is described in Patricia Grimshaw, *Paths of Duty* (1989). Rufus Anderson tells of the great awakening at Hilo and elsewhere in *History of the Sandwich Islands Mission* (1870), chap. 18.

David M. Stowe

Lyon, D(avid) Willard (1870–1949), pioneer YMCA missionary in China. Born on a houseboat in China, the son of Presbyterian missionaries, Lyon graduated from the College of Wooster, Ohio, and McCormick Theological Seminary and also worked with John R. *Mott. In 1895, his first year back in China, he founded in Tientsin (Tianjin) the first student YMCA. In 1930, after 34 years of continuous service as a YMCA secretary, he was honored by the speaker at a farewell dinner in Shanghai, who commented, "The 'Y' movement in China stands as a perpetual monument of Dr. Lyon's life work." Halfway through his first term, the Boxer troubles forced Lyon and his wife to seek refuge in Korea, where they founded the Korean YMCA movement. In later years he helped start the YMCA in the Philippines. In 1928 he gave an address at the Jerusalem meeting of the International Missionary Council.

During his later years of service in China, Lyon gave major attention to training Chinese YMCA secretaries and to developing literature for students. Various centers were organized where leadership training classes were held. A loan library and a publications department, precursors of the Association Press, were started under his leadership. He began a college student newspaper that became a widely read student magazine, *The Chinese Intercollegian* (later called *China's Young Men*). Always an advocate of indigenous leadership, he enlisted an eminent scholar, Zia Hong-lai, to develop the literature of the student movement. A gifted linguist, Lyon helped organize language schools and worked on the Mandarin Romanization Committee of the China Christian Educational Association. He wrote *The Christian Equivalent of War* (1915) and edited for publication Mott's China addresses. In his final years, he translated Tang dynasty poetry into English. In 1949, on his last visit to China, Mott committed Lyon's "sacred dust . . . to the deep at the mouth of the Yangtze."

BIBLIOGRAPHY Willard D. Lyon, *The First Quarter Century of the Young Men's Christian Association in China* (1920), and twenty-seven signed letters on various topics in the *Chinese Recorder* between 1896 and 1937. C. Howard Hopkins, *History of the YMCA in North America* (1951); Kenneth Scott Latourette, *World Service: A History of the Foreign Work and World Service of the YMCA's of the United States and Canada* (1957). Lyon materials are in the archives of the YMCA, Univ. of Minnesota.

Donald E. MacInnis

Lyon, Mary (1797–1849), founder of Mount Holyoke Female Seminary. Born in Buckland, Massachusetts, Lyon's interest in missions was sparked with the founding of the American Board of Commissioners for Foreign Missions in 1810. Inspired at age 19 by a sermon preached by her great-uncle Enos Smith, and later by her teacher Joseph Emerson at Byfield Female Seminary, she decided to commit her life to furthering the missionary cause through education. For a while, she taught at Ipswich Seminary but then turned her efforts toward establishing a new college for women, with an emphasis on missions. She obtained support by traveling from town to town requesting financial contributions and donations of domestic furnishings. Initially rebuffed by the general assembly of Massachusetts, she ultimately won approval for chartering the Mount Holyoke Female Seminary, at South Hadley, Massachusetts.

On November 8, 1837, Lyon welcomed the first class of eighty students. Serving as principal for the first 12 years, she selected her teachers from among her former pupils from Ipswich Seminary and Mount Holyoke itself. Her ideal was to educate the entire woman, each student having her share of academics, domestic chores, and spiritual enrichment through Bible study, prayer, and worship. Her philosophy was "study and teach nothing that cannot be made to help in the great work of converting the world to Christ." In *A Missionary Offering* (1843), her only published work, she stressed the importance of supporting missions. She frequently invited missionaries to speak at the seminary, and many of her students were inspired to travel overseas or serve at home as missionaries and teachers, some founding schools based on Mount Holyoke's principles.

Lyon's health began to decline during the winter of 1846–1847. She died two years later at age 52, following a bout with erysipelas. In 1888 Mount Holyoke received college status and remains a well-respected institution for the education of women.

BIBLIOGRAPHY Beth B. Gilchrist, *The Life of Mary Lyon* (1910); Elizabeth Alden Green, *Mary Lyon and Mount Holyoke: Opening the Gates* (1979); Edward Hitchcock, *The Power of Christian Benevolence, Illustrated in the Life and Labors of Mary Lyon* (1858); Louise Porter Thomas, *Seminary Militant: An Account of the Missionary Movement at Mount Holyoke Seminary and College* (1937). Personal papers of Lyon are available at the Mount Holyoke College library/archives, South Hadley, Mass.

Joan R. Duffy

Lyons, Lorenzo (1807–1886), American missionary, "the Isaac Watts of Hawaii." Born in Coleraine, Massachusetts, Lyons graduated from Union College, New York (1827), and from Auburn Theological Seminary (1831). He married Betsy Curtis on September 4, 1831, was ordained, and sailed on November 26 with the fifth company of American Board of Commissioners for Foreign Missions (ABCFM) missionaries to the Sandwich Islands. Lyons was stationed at Waimea, on the island of Hawaii, where he worked for 54 years without returning to the United States and for his last 23 years without leaving his station. His wife died in 1837 and the next year he married Lucia G. Smith, a missionary who had been an ABCFM teacher on the Tuscarora Indian reservation in New York and had recently arrived in Hawaii. An ardent evangelist of the Finney school, Lyons toured indefatigably about the rugged terrain of his district which extended 40 miles along the shore and 10 miles in both directions from Waimea on the central ridge. An eloquent preacher in Hawaiian, he won thousands of converts in the revival of 1836–1838 and oversaw the construction of a dozen churches. A prolific writer, he prepared lesson helps for the International Sunday School Lessons. Above all, he was a lyric poet, for years sending a new hymn each week to the newspapers and editing numerous collections. Over half the hymns in the 1983 edition of the Hawaiian hymnbook were written by "Makua Laiana," as he was affectionately known. He was much beloved, both by fellow missionaries and by Hawaiians, and at the time of Lyons's death, King Kalakaua sent a Hawaiian flag for his shroud.

BIBLIOGRAPHY Emma L. Doyle, *Makua Laiana: The Story of Lorenzo Lyons* (1945). Summary sketches of Lyons's life and work are found in *Missionary Album* (1969), pp. 144–145, *Missionary Herald* 83 (1887): 17–19, and *Na Himeni* (1972), the Hawaiian hymnbook, pp. 49–50. John Garrett, *To Live among the Stars* (1982), pp. 55–56, describes Lyons's share in the revival which began in 1836. Lyons himself published *Essay on Hawaii in 1820* (1860), catechisms, hymns, and scriptural writings.

David M. Stowe

M

Maas, Otto (1884–1945), German Catholic missiologist. Maas was born at Neheim, in Westphalia, joined the Franciscans in 1904, and was ordained a priest in 1911. Attending the University of Münster, he studied Sanskrit and Pali and published a book on Buddhism in 1913. Under Joseph *Schmidlin he studied missiology at Münster and in 1914 went to Spain to consult important archives for his doctoral dissertation. War conditions kept him there for five years. He became a specialist on mission archives and published three collections of documents on Mexico and China. Back in Germany, he edited a popular mission magazine and finished his university studies in 1924 with a dissertation, *Die Wiedereröffnung der Franziskanermission in China in der Neuzeit* (published in 1926). For many years he was a member of the circle around Schmidlin and was an influential secretary of the International Institut für missionswissenschaftliche Forschungen at Münster. Concurrently he taught missiology for more than 20 years at the Franciscan House of Theology at Paderborn. He published numerous books and articles, both scholarly and popular, on themes of Christian missions, mostly in German and Spanish, but also in other languages.

BIBLIOGRAPHY Benno Biermann, "P. Dr. Otto Maas OFM," *MR* 32 (1947–1948): 11–14; B. H. Willeke, "P. Dr. Otto Maas OFM," in Joseph Glazik, ed., *50 Jahre Katholische Missionswissenschaft in Münster, 1911–1961* (1961), pp. 82–93 (full bibliography).

Bernward H. Willeke, OFM

Mabie, Catherine Louise Roe (1872–1963), missionary doctor, teacher, and educational advocate in the Belgian Congo. Mabie was born in Rock Island, Illinois. She was inspired at age nine by missionary talks and Methodist revivals and was baptized in a Baptist church. At age ten, she began to teach Sunday school to hoodlum boys in an unchurched area of Chicago. Having become interested in missionary work through the Christian Endeavor Society, she studied medicine at Rush Medical College to prepare for work as a missionary doctor.

In 1898 the Woman's Baptist Foreign Missionary Society (WBFMS) appointed Mabie for service at Banza Manteke, Belgian Congo (Zaire), and at age 26, she sailed for Africa. She served her internship at the Banza Manteke hospital and for many years had charge of the medical work in that district. In 1911 she became a member of the faculty of the Congo Evangelical Training Institution at Kimpese. In 1913 she took part in a meeting in Detroit to unify the home and foreign Woman's Baptist Mission Societies, resulting in the World Wide Guild. Mabie served as the secretary of the WBFMS for 20 years. In 1920 she was appointed to serve in the Belgian Congo with the Phelps-Stokes Commission to study educational, economic, social, and religious conditions in Africa. Following a furlough and tour of schools in the southern United States, she attended the Third Baptist World Alliance Congress, held in 1923 in Stockholm, Sweden. In 1926 she was appointed as a delegate to the conference on Christian Mission in Africa, held at Le Zoute, Belgium. She returned to Kimpese to translate and print school readers and textbooks in the Kikongo language. In 1932 Albert, king of Belgium, bestowed upon her the honor of becoming a Chevalier of the Royal Order of the Lion. In 1941 Mabie retired to the United States at age 70, after 30 years of service in Kimpese. She continued giving talks and papers, doing deputation work, and attending conventions until her death at age 91.

BIBLIOGRAPHY Catherine L. Mabie, *Our Work on the Congo: A Book for Mission Study Classes and for General Information* (1917) and *Congo Cameos* (1952). James Henry Franklin, *Ministers of Mercy* (1919), includes a chapter about Catherine L. Mabie.

Joan R. Duffy

Mabille, Adolphe (1836–1894), Paris Evangelical Missionary Society (PEMS) missionary in Lesotho. Born at Baulmes, Vaud, Switzerland, Mabille received a strong formal education in Yverdon and at the Paedagogium in Basel. He taught French in the Netherlands and in Great Britain, where he received his call to become a missionary. In 1856 he entered the PEMS School of Missions in Paris, where he met his future wife, Adèle Casalis (1840–1923), who was born at Thaba Bosiu, Lesotho, the daughter of PEMS director Eugène *Casalis. They married in 1859, wanting to serve in China, which was a new project of the PEMS inspired by Mabille; instead they were sent to Lesotho. Mabille served with great distinction at Morija from 1860 until his death.

His contribution pertains to four important areas of missionary service. First, in 1856, when he was still a missionary candidate, he suggested the use of "small change" collection cards for fund-raising, which in spite of its modest goals became a major source of income for the PEMS. Second, he worked toward complete translation of the Bible into Sotho, which was achieved in 1879. He launched the first newspaper in Sotho, *Leselinyana* (The little light of Lesotho) in 1863, still published today, and in 1889 started a quarterly for church workers, *Motsualle oa Baboleli le Nalisa ba likolo* (The friend of preachers and shepherds of schools). Third, he encouraged and organized indigenous ministry. He installed the first Sotho minister, Esaia Leeti, at Kolo, near Morija, in 1863. He trained men for the ministry; a theological college was planned very early and finally opened in 1882. Fourth, he encouraged the church of Lesotho to engage in foreign missions. The first Sotho foreign missionary was Isaiah Seële, sent to pioneer among the Pedis of Transvaal in 1863. Other Sotho missionaries were sent in 1875 to the Banyais of Mashonaland (now Zimbabwe) and in 1883 to the Barotsis of Zambesi (now Zambia).

BIBLIOGRAPHY Works by Adolphe Mabille include a Sotho translation of the Bible, the *Sesuto-English Dictionary* (1876, 1894; revised and enlarged by H. Dieterlen in 1904 and 1911), and numerous articles and papers published in Sotho. James E. Siordet, *Adèle Mabille, née Casalis (1840–1923) d'après ses souvenirs et sa correspondance* (1933); Edwin W. Smith, *The Mabilles of Basutoland* (1939).

Marc R. Spindler

MacCallum, (Frank) Lyman (1893–1955), agent for the American and the British and Foreign Bible Societies in the Middle East. MacCallum was born of Canadian missionary parents who served under the American Board of Commissioners for Foreign Missions (ABCFM) in Turkey, where his father trained Armenian Christians for the ministry. He was sent to Ontario at age 14 to attend school and to live with relatives until he entered Queen's University in Kingston, intending to become an engineer. At the outbreak of war in Europe, MacCallum enlisted, fought in the battle of the Somme, and was evacuated in 1918 with a critical lung ailment, from which he never fully recovered. In 1925 he rejoined his parents in Constantinople (Istanbul) and volunteered to serve as "acting sub-agent" of the American Bible Society, engaged in translation (with his father), publication, and circulation of Scriptures. During the 1930s he participated actively in uniting the work of the American Bible Society and the British and Foreign Bible Society, culminating in the establishment of the "Bible Lands Agency, North" in Beirut. His most notable gift was in personal relations. "He loved Turkey and the Turkish people," said Wilfred Smith, and when he visited their mosques he was, his biographer notes, "never an irreverent sightseer there but, rather, a worshipper."

BIBLIOGRAPHY Constance E. Padwick, *Call to Istanbul* (1958).

Creighton Lacy

Macdonald, A(nnie) Caroline (1874–1931), Christian missionary in Japan. Born in Wingham, Ontario, Macdonald graduated from the University of Toronto in mathematics and physics. One of the first professional YWCA secretaries in Canada, she went to Japan in 1904 to help establish the YWCA there and was national secretary until 1915. Drawn into a new vocation when a young Christian friend murdered his wife and two sons, she developed an extensive ministry in Tokyo prisons and promoted penal reform among the bureaucrats in the Ministry of Justice. *A Gentleman in Prison,* her English translation of the autobiography of a notorious murderer converted through her care, later appeared in five additional languages. She established a settlement house in Tokyo named Shinrinkan ("Home of the Friendless Stranger") to serve wives and children of prisoners, ex-prisoners, juvenile delinquents, and factory workers. She also organized labor schools for men and women and became a mentor to the conservative wing of the labor movement.

Over many years she was a part-time teacher of English and the Bible at Tsuda College for Women. Honored by the emperor in 1924 for her social work, a year later she became the first woman to receive an LL.D. from the University of Toronto. Macdonald's intense identification with her adopted country was aided by her membership in Fujimicho Presbyterian church, where she was the only foreigner, and by her friendship with its minister, Masahisa *Uemura. An exceptional fluency in Japanese, a genuine egalitarianism, and a never-failing sense of humor underlay her unusual capacity for friendship and influence among all social classes. She became ill with lung cancer in May 1931, returned to Canada, and died at London, Ontario.

BIBLIOGRAPHY Macdonald translated *A Gentleman in Prison, with the Confessions of Tokichi Ishii Written in Tokyo Prison* (1919, 1950). John McNab, *The White Angel of Tokyo: Miss Caroline Macdonald LL.D.* (n.d.); Margaret Prang, *A Heart at Leisure from Itself: Caroline Macdonald of Japan* (1995); N. W. Rowell, "The Late Caroline Macdonald," *University of Toronto Monthly* 32, no. 1 (1931): 19–30 (supplement).

Margaret Prang

Macdonald, Andrew Buchanan (1892–1970), Scottish medical missionary in Nigeria. Born in Stepps, Glasgow, Macdonald studied medicine at the University of Glasgow, graduating in 1920. He served in Nigeria with the United Free Church and subsequently the Church of Scotland from 1921 to 1954. At first he was the doctor at Itu hospital on the Cross River, but he began treating leprosy in 1926 and within two years had so many patients that he founded Itu Leper Colony, which provided a holistic approach to treating the disease. Because most patients were well enough to work, Macdonald and his colleagues were able to develop a largely self-sustaining agricultural settlement with "an atmosphere of activity and joy and hope." He was awarded the Member of the British Empire in 1934 and Commander of the British Empire in 1957. He retired in 1952 but was called back, retiring again in 1954.

BIBLIOGRAPHY A. B. Macdonald, *Can Ghosts Arise? The Answer of Itu* (1946, 1957) and *In His Name* (1964). Itu Leper Colony, *They Were Cleansed: The Thirtieth Anniversary Report of the Itu Leper Colony* (1958); Geoffrey Johnston, *Of God and Maxim Guns: Presbyterianism in Nigeria, 1846–1966* (1988).

Geoffrey Johnston

MacDonald, Duff (1850–1929), missionary of the Church of Scotland Mission (CSM) in Malawi. Born at Keith, in northeast Scotland, MacDonald was educated at Aberdeen University and was ordained as minister of a parish near Wick in 1877. Almost immediately he was called by the CSM to go to the new mission in Malawi, headquartered at Blantyre. Late in 1878 he became the sole ordained member of the staff there. It appears that the home committee, in spite of defining his duties in terms that were more pastoral than executive, wanted him to save the mission from disaster due to earlier errors in recruiting. Some of the staff had left to become virtual freebooters, the rest were running their growing community of freed slaves as a miniature colony. MacDonald deplored this but did not intervene. In 1881 a CSM commission was sent to investigate. They recommended that all staff be dismissed and the mission begun again from scratch.

MacDonald was scapegoated for what had been errors in planning by the home authorities. Back in Scotland, after trying unsuccessfully to clear his name, MacDonald became a minister in Motherwell, where he was a much-loved pastor until his retirement.

BIBLIOGRAPHY Duff MacDonald, *Africana*, 2 vols. (1885). Basic information about MacDonald can be found in *Fasti Ecclesiae Scoticanae* 3:250, 7:131, 698, 8:257. See also Andrew C. Ross, "The Origins and Development of the Church of Scotland Mission, Blantyre, Nyasaland, 1875–1926" (Ph.D. diss., Univ. of Edinburgh, 1968).

Andrew C. Ross

Macdonald, Duncan Black (1863–1943), pioneer of Arabic and Islamic studies in the United States. Born in Glasgow, Scotland, and educated at Glasgow University, Macdonald studied Semitic languages in Berlin prior to his appointment as professor of Semitic languages in Hartford Theological Seminary (1892). In addition to his initial teaching of Hebrew language and scriptures, he taught Arabic and Islamic studies. Visiting Cairo in 1907 and 1908, he was shocked by the lack of understanding of Muslim life and culture that he encountered among missionaries. He urged the Hartford Seminary Foundation to redress this deficiency. Following the 1910 Edinburgh World Missionary Conference, Hartford inaugurated its Kennedy School of Missions (1911). Macdonald was appointed head of the Islamics department and played a major role in the development of the school, including its unique field-based Ph.D. degree program. With missionaries on furlough he worked on the textual study of Islamic religious classics; through correspondence he guided missionaries in the field in the contextual study of Muslim life and culture. He exemplified his approach in his own writings on Islamic religion and in his lifelong study of the *Arabian Nights,* in which he found a mine of information about traditional Muslim culture. Many of his doctoral students produced distinguished works of scholarship, especially annotated translations of Islamic religious works in Arabic. He aimed to cultivate a love of Islam in the hearts of missionaries, as well as an understanding of elements of Muslim faith and practice to which they could relate the biblical message. Without diminishing doctrinal differences, he urged Christians to cultivate spiritual friendship with Muslims in shared witness against the moral decadence of secular materialism. He retired in 1932 and devoted his remaining years to writing on Hebrew religion.

BIBLIOGRAPHY Macdonald's publications include *Development of Muslim Theology, Jurisprudence and Constitutional Theory* (1903), *Religious Attitude and Life of Islam* (1909), *Aspects of Islam* (1911), *Hebrew Literary Genius: An Interpretation, Being an Introduction to the Old Testament* (1933), and *Hebrew Philosophical Genius: A Vindication* (1936). For a listing of Macdonald's entire published works, see William Shellabear, Edwin Calverley, Elbert Lane, and Ruth Mackensen, eds., *The Macdonald Presentation Volume* (1933), pp. 473–487. Willem Bijlefeld, "A Century of Arabic and Islamic Studies at Hartford Seminary," *The Muslim World* 83 (1993): 103–117; John Bodine, "The Romanticism of Duncan Black Macdonald" (Ph.D. diss., Hartford Seminary, 1973), "Magic Carpet to Islam: Duncan Black Macdonald and the Arabian Nights," *The Muslim World* 67 (1977): 1–11, and "Duncan Black Macdonald" in Gerald H. Anderson et al., eds., *Mission Legacies* (1994), pp. 469–474; Edwin Calverley, "Duncan Black Macdonald," *The Muslim World* 34 (1944): 1–6; Peter Ipema, "The Islam Interpretation of Duncan B. Macdonald, Samuel M. Zwemer, A. Kenneth Cragg, and Wilfred C. Smith: An Analytical Comparison and Evaluation" (Ph.D. diss., Hartford Seminary, 1971); Gordon Pruett, "Duncan Black Macdonald: Christian Islamicist," in Asaf Hussain, Robert Olson, and Jamil Qureshi, eds., *Orientalism, Islam, and Orientalists* (1984), pp. 125–176.

David A. Kerr

MacGillivray, Donald (1862–1931), Canadian Presbyterian missionary in China. MacGillivray's linguistic and literary skills made him prominent as longtime editor and then general secretary of the Christian Literature Society (CLS), Shanghai (1921–1929). Born on a pioneer farm in Ontario, he graduated with honors from the University of

Toronto. In late 1888 he followed Jonathan and Rosalind *Goforth to the new north Honan mission field, where he worked for several years. He learned Chinese rapidly and soon became an authority on the language. He took on the task of revising and updating a standard dictionary, and its publication in 1898 established his scholarly credentials. Upon his return to China, after a furlough in Canada (1897–1898), the eminent Timothy *Richard asked him to join the CLS.

For the next 30 years MacGillivray was a prolific scholar and a popular writer, translator, and editor. At the same time he continued to revise his dictionary, *A Mandarin-Romanized Dictionary of Chinese*, which had seven editions through 1925. He was compiler and editor of the volume *A Century of Protestant Missions in China* (1907) and editor of the first six editions of the *China Mission Year Book*, 1910–1915. He also wrote dozens of articles for the *Chinese Recorder*.

BIBLIOGRAPHY Donald MacGillivray, *Timothy Richard of China: A Prince in Israel; An appreciation* (1920). Margaret H. Brown, *MacGillivray of Shanghai* (1968); *Chinese Recorder* 62 (1931): 444–447 (obit.).

Daniel H. Bays

Macgowan, Edward (1795–1860), medical missionary in Jerusalem. A British physician with a successful practice in Exeter, England, in 1841 Macgowan accepted a call from the London Society for Promoting Christianity amongst the Jews to develop their medical mission in Jerusalem. He accompanied the newly appointed first Anglican bishop of Jerusalem, Michael Solomon *Alexander, and arrived there in January 1842. He immediately set out to expand the existing dispensary into a viable hospital. The society's intention to serve the needs of the poor was evident from the location of this hospital next to the Jewish quarter. Completed in December 1844, it was described by John *Nicolayson, the leader of the mission there, as "the first modern hospital in the Holy Land." Both the medical care and the personal attention were of the highest standard, and the hospital therefore attracted Jewish people in spite of fierce opposition by the rabbis and other Jewish community leaders who warned against the missionaries. However, such was Macgowan's influence that he inspired both Sir Moses Montefiore and Baron Edmund Rothschild, famous Jewish philanthropists from Britain and France, to provide funds for Jewish medical work in the growing city of Jerusalem. Thus he played a substantial role in helping Jewish people take a more favorable view of the work of Christian missions in Palestine. He is buried in the Protestant cemetery on Mt. Zion.

BIBLIOGRAPHY Kelvin Crombie, *For the Love Of Zion: Christian Witness and the Restoration of Israel* (1991); W. T. Gidney, *The History of the London Society for Promoting Christianity amongst the Jews* (1908); Alexander McCaul, *The Old Paths* (1886).

Walter Riggans

Machray, Robert (1831–1904), missionary bishop in western Canada. Machray was born in Aberdeen, Scotland, and educated at the King's College, Aberdeen, and Sidney Sussex College, Cambridge. Raised a Presbyterian, he reacted to the acrimonious divisions in the Church of Scotland by turning to the Episcopalian traditions of his mother's family, and he was ordained in the Church of England in 1856. After earning a master's degree in mathematics at Cambridge, he was appointed in 1859 dean of Sidney Sussex College—a post he held in conjunction with the vicarage of Madingly until his 1865 consecration as successor to David *Anderson as Bishop of Rupert's Land. When Machray arrived in the Red River Settlement (Manitoba) in 1866, the diocese encompassed the vast area now comprising Manitoba, Saskatchewan, Alberta, the Yukon Territory, most of the Northwest Territories, northern Ontario, and northern Quebec. While there were six missions scattered throughout the diocese, most of the settled parishes and the majority of the twenty-two clergy were located within the Red River Settlement. During his lengthy tenure he established schools in every parish, reorganized the native missions, rejuvenated and directed St. John's College (1866–1904), and served as the University of Manitoba's first chancellor (1877–1904). He also orchestrated the division of his unwieldy diocese into the dioceses of Saskatchewan, Moosonee, and Athabasca (each of which was later further subdivided) and oversaw the appointments of John Horden, William Carpenter *Bompas, and John McLean as bishops there. Moreover, he successfully reorganized the church in Rupert's Land in preparation for its independence from the mother church in England in 1893. At that point he became archbishop and the first primate of the Anglican Church for all Canada. From a single diocese and a scattered handful of Anglican clergy in 1865, Machray saw the Anglican Church grow to more than 200 clergy serving in nine episcopal sees by 1904.

BIBLIOGRAPHY Robert Machray, *Life of Robert Machray, D.D., LL.D., D.C.L., Archbishop of Rupert's Land, Primate of All Canada, Prelate of the Order of St. Michael and St. George* (1909). T. C. B. Boon, *The Anglican Church from the Bay to the Rockies: A History of the Ecclesiastical Province of Rupert's Land and Its Diocese from 1820 to 1950* (1962); Berry Ferguson, ed., *The Anglican Church and the World of Western Canada, 1820–1970* (1991), pp. 94–103; W. J. Fraser, *St. John's College, Winnipeg, 1866–1966: A History of the First Hundred Years of the College* (1966); Christopher Hackett, "The Anglo-Protestant Churches of Manitoba and the Manitoba School Question" (M.A. thesis, Univ. of Manitoba, Winnipeg, 1988); R. C. Johnstone, "Robert Machray," *Leaders of the Canadian Church*, W. B. Heeney, ed. (1920), pp. 179–200; Frits Pannekoek, *A Snug Little Flock: The Social Origins of the Riel Resistance of 1869–70* (1991).

Jonathan J. Bonk

Mack, John (1797–1845), Scottish missionary educator at Serampore College, Bengal. Born and educated in Edinburgh, Mack prepared to enter the ministry of the Church of Scotland. While in Gloucester, he became a Baptist and in 1818 entered Bristol Baptist College for training. William *Ward, at home from Serampore for medical reasons, noted Mack's potential. After preparation in Edinburgh University to teach natural philosophy in India, Mack, accompanied by Ward, set sail for missionary service in 1821. He went with the support of Christopher *Anderson's Charlotte Baptist Chapel in Edinburgh. On arrival at Serampore, the young classics scholar began to teach chemistry at the college. Two years later Ward died, and Mack shouldered some of the burden that fell on the surviving mission pioneers. In 1832 he joined William *Carey and Joshua *Marshman as a co-pastor of the Baptist church. Five years later, in partnership with John C. *Marshman, he negotiated a form of reunion between the Baptist Missionary Society and the Serampore Mission. As principal, he elevated Serampore College's scholarly standards and furthered the training of Christian leaders in North India. Like Ward, he died suddenly from cholera in the prime of his life.

BIBLIOGRAPHY Very little has been written specifically on Mack's life and work. The main summaries are to be found in: W. H. Carey, *Oriental Christian Biography* (1852), vol. 1, pp. 282–286; E. A. Payne, *The First Generation: Early Leaders of the Baptist Missionary Society in England and India* (1936), pp. 128–132; and Donald E. Meek, ed., *A Mind for Mission: Essays in Appreciation of the Rev. Christopher Anderson* (1992), pp. 38–42.

A. Christopher Smith

Mack, (Johann) Martin (1715–1784), Moravian missionary to North America and the Caribbean. Born in Laichingen, in the Swabian Mountains of Germany, Mack was sent to North America in 1735 by the Moravian Brethren and in 1741 was involved in founding Bethlehem, Pennsylvania, the first North American Moravian settlement. Appointed a missionary by Nikolaus Ludwig von *Zinzendorf in 1742, Mack evangelized among the Indians in Pennsylvania, Connecticut, and New York for two decades. From 1762 until his death he directed the Moravian missions in Saint Thomas, Saint Croix, and Saint John in the Virgin Islands, where the work included a ministry among the black slaves. In 1770 he was appointed bishop. Mack was the first evangelical missionary to emerge from Württemberg Pietism, which ultimately produced a vast number of missionaries.

BIBLIOGRAPHY Mack's autobiography is in *Nachrichten aus der Brüder-Gemeinde* 39 (1857): 767–781 (extracted in Werner Raupp, ed., *Gelebter Glaube: Erfahrungen und Lebenszeugnisse aus unserem Land* [1993], pp. 162–166). Werner Raupp, "'Ein vergnügter Herrnhuter': Johann Martin Mack, Württembergs erster evangelischer Missionar," *Blätter für Württembergische Kirchengeschichte* 92 (1992): 97–118.

Werner Raupp

Mackay, Alexander M(urdoch) (1849–1890), pioneer missionary in Uganda with the Church Missionary Society (CMS). Mackay was raised in Scotland in the Free Church and was educated at Aberdeen Grammar School and the University of Edinburgh before going to Berlin to gain experience in engineering. He applied to the CMS in 1875 after reading an appeal in the *Edinburgh Review* for missionaries for Uganda. Letters from the explorer, H. M. *Stanley, claimed that King Mutesa of Buganda would welcome Christian missionaries. In 1876 Mackay was a member of the first CMS party that left for Uganda and was the only missionary to remain for any length of time.

Mutesa feared the encroaching power of Egypt, and his first concern was to acquire European arms and engineering skills such as Mackay could offer. But he was also interested in religion. Arab traders from the East African coast had already introduced Islam, and after partially adopting this faith, Mutesa had executed some two hundred Muslim converts for defying him in the name of Allah. Christianity, he thought, might provide a counterweight to Islam.

Mackay quickly set up a printing press and printed reading sheets and portions of Scripture in Swahili, the coastal language introduced by the Arabs, using existing Scripture translations. But Mackay also spent time in repairing guns for Mutesa and in other tasks demanded of him.

In 1879 Roman Catholic White Fathers arrived; Mackay's Calvinistic upbringing led him into controversy with them in public at Mutesa's court. He also debated with Muslims, who feared that his superior debating and technological skills were edging them out of their position of influence. Many young men in training at court for future high office were attracted to Christianity by Mackay's passionate dedication.

From 1885 to 1887 Mutesa's successor, Mwanga, turned against the Christians at court for the same reason that Mutesa had earlier turned against the Muslims for questioning his authority in the name of a higher power. The names of fifty Protestant and Catholic martyrs are known, and others perished too. During this dangerous time Mackay was the only missionary in the country, the White Fathers having temporarily retreated south of Lake Victoria. He thus ensured the continuance of the CMS in Uganda.

In 1888 a Muslim coup forced both missionaries and converts to flee, and Mackay died suddenly from malaria at Nassa, in what is now Tanzania. In 1927 his body was reinterred outside Namirembe Cathedral, Kampala.

BIBLIOGRAPHY The CMS *Church Missionary Intelligencer* carried extensive reports on Uganda, often reprinting missionaries' letters in toto. The most important sources for Mackay's life are J. W. Harrison [Mackay's sister], *A. M. Mackay: Pioneer Missionary of the Church Missionary Society to Uganda* (1890) and *The Story of Mackay of Uganda, Pioneer Missionary* (1989). R. P. Ashe was a contemporary of Mackay, and his *Two Kings of Uganda* (1889) is a useful source. For important aspects of the martyrdoms, see J. F. Faupel, *African Holocaust* (1962) and J. A. Rowe, "The Purge of Christians at Mwanga's Court," *JRA* 5, 1 (1964), pp. 55–72.

M. Louise Pirouet

Mackay, George Leslie (1844–1901), pioneer Canadian Presbyterian missionary in northern Taiwan. Born near Zorra, Oxford County, Ontario, Canada, Mackay was christened by William Chalmers *Burns, an English Presbyterian missionary to China, whose example inspired the younger man to become a missionary also. A graduate of Princeton Theological Seminary, Mackay arrived in Taiwan in 1872 as the first foreign missionary of the western division of the Presbyterian Church in Canada. After consulting English Presbyterian missionaries already working in southern Taiwan, Mackay decided to establish his mission in the north with its headquarters at Tamsui (Danshui). He indefatigably conducted Christian work not only among the Chinese but also among the aboriginal populations. In his evangelistic work, he was greatly assisted by his Chinese wife, Tui Chang Mia (Minnie Mackay), and by A. Hoa, his first convert and lifelong disciple. Mackay was a missionary entrepreneur skilled at raising funds to build churches and to found schools, the most important of which were Oxford College in Tamsui and a theological school that became Taiwan Theological College near Taipei. The Taiwanese referred to him as the Black-Bearded Barbarian of Formosa. He received an honorary D.D. from Queen's University in Kingston, Ontario, and his name is perpetuated by the Mackay Memorial Hospital in Taipei.

BIBLIOGRAPHY George Leslie Mackay, *From Far Formosa: The Island, Its People, and Missions,* J. A. Macdonald, ed. (1896). M. Keith, *The Black Bearded Barbarian* (1912); R. P. MacKay, *Life of George Leslie Mackay, D.D., 1844–1901* (1913); Duncan MacLeod, *The Island Beautiful: The Story of Fifty Years in North Formosa* (1923).

A. Hamish Ion

Mackay, John A(lexander) (1889–1983), influential missiologist, theologian, and leader of the ecumenical movement. Born in Inverness, Scotland, Mackay studied philosophy and theology in Aberdeen and Princeton. When in Spain, he came under the influence of existential philosopher Miguel de Unamuno. This experience gave him a unique understanding of the Iberian soul and permeated his thought with an existential note that explains his unique appeal to Latin Americans. Sent by the Free Church of Scotland with his wife, Jane Logan (Wells), he was a missionary educator in Lima, Peru, from 1916 to 1925, where he was the founder and president of the Anglo-Peruvian school. He then moved to Montevideo, Uruguay, and later to Mexico City, as a traveling lecturer with the YMCA. As a successful evangelist among university students, his influence on well-known Latin American intellectuals was decisive. His forceful plea at the Jerusalem meeting of the International Missionary Council (IMC) in 1928 influenced the ecumenical movement to recognize the legitimacy of a Protestant missionary presence in Latin America.

Mackay's classic *The Other Spanish Christ* (1932) is an unsurpassed missiological interpretation of Latin America. In 1932 he became secretary for Africa and Latin America in the Board of Foreign Missions of the Presbyterian Church in the U.S.A. From 1936 to 1959 he was professor and president of Princeton Theological Seminary. His administration reflected a commitment to the "restoration of theology" after the crisis of the early decades of the century; in 1944 he founded the journal *Theology Today*. From 1947 to 1957 he was chairman of the IMC. At the founding of the World Council of Churches (WCC) in 1948, he became a member of the Central Committee and was chairman of the joint committee of IMC and WCC from 1948 to 1954. He was also president of the World Presbyterian Alliance from 1954 to 1959. Among his best-known books are *A Preface to Christian Theology* (1943), *Christianity on the Frontier* (1950), *God's Order* (1953), and *Ecumenics: The Science of the Church Universal* (1964). Mackay's theology was marked by the Reformed tradition with an existential note, deep roots in Scripture, and a continuous confrontation with questions and challenges that came from the missionary frontier. After retirement from the presidency of Princeton, in 1959, he continued an active writing and teaching ministry.

BIBLIOGRAPHY The most complete list of Mackay's extensive writings is Stanton R. Wilson and William O. Harris, "John Mackay: Bibliographical Resources for the Period 1914–1992," *Studies in Reformed Theology and History* 1, no. 4 (1993): 1–58. Samuel Escobar, "The Legacy of John A. Mackay," *IBMR* 16 (1992): 116–122; E. J. Jurji, ed., *The Ecumenical Era in Church and Society: A Symposium in Honor of John A. Mackay* (1959). Mackay's library, files, and classified documents are in the Speer Library at Princeton Theological Seminary.

Samuel Escobar

Mackenzie, Charles Frederick (1825–1862), Anglican missionary bishop in central Africa. Born in Scotland at Portmore, Perthsire, Mackenzie was educated partly in Scotland, partly in England. He distinguished himself as a mathematician at Cambridge, where he became a fellow of Caius College. Attracted to missionary work, he at first considered joining the Delhi Mission but decided against it. In 1854 he was persuaded by Bishop William *Colenso to join him as his archdeacon in Natal, South Africa. Under the influence of Colenso, Mackenzie took a radical stand on the issue of equal ecclesiastical rights for African and European congregations—an issue on which he was defeated at a church conference at Maritzburg in 1858. Shortly afterward he returned to Britain, partly as a result of ill health, and there he was persuaded to head the newly formed Universities' Mission to Central Africa—established as a result of a speech by David *Livingstone at Cambridge in 1857. In January 1861 Mackenzie was consecrated bishop "of the mission to the tribes dwelling in the neighbourhood of Lake Nyassa and the River Shire." He met Livingstone on the Zambezi, and the explorer helped choose the site for the mission—at Magomero in the Shire highlands of Malawi. It was isolated, unhealthy, and dominated by Yao slave traders. Almost immediately Mackenzie became involved in direct and physical opposition to the slave trade, and this interventionist policy made enemies of the powerful Yao people. In January 1862, while going down the Shire River to meet Livingstone, Mackenzie's canoe capsized, and he lost all his medicines. Both he and his colleague Henry Burrup died soon afterward. These difficulties forced the mission to withdraw temporarily to Zanzibar, but it eventually returned in 1886 to Likoma Island in Lake Malawi. Mackenzie is remembered as a brave and principled—albeit somewhat naive—pioneer.

BIBLIOGRAPHY Owen Chadwick, *Mackenzie's Grave* (1959); G. Harvey Goodwin, *Memoir of Bishop Mackenzie* (1864); David Livingstone and Charles Livingstone, *Narrative of an Expedition to the Zambezi and Its Tributaries* (1865); R. H. Rowley, *The Story of the Universities' Mission to Central Africa* (1866); Landeg White, *Magomero: Portrait of an African Village* (1987).

T. Jack Thompson

Mackenzie, Helen Pearl (1913–), medical missionary and founder of the Ilsin Women's Hospital (IWH), now Christian Hospital, in Pusan, Korea. Mackenzie was born in Pusan of Australian missionary parents. She went to Australia for her education, graduating from Melbourne University Medical School. In 1945 she was appointed by the Australian Presbyterian Church to work in Yunnan Province, southwest China, where with her sister Catherine Margaret, a nurse, she established a thirty-bed hospital. Forced to leave China over the Burma Road in 1950, they were assigned to Korea, where they established the IWH in 1952 in a borrowed kindergarten building, serving impoverished refugees and training doctors and midwife nurses. Begging assistance from many sources, Mackenzie saw the hospital grow under her management from a few makeshift beds and cribs in 1952 to a first-class hospital of 150 beds when she retired in 1976. In recognition of her work she was awarded a citation by the prime minister of Korea (1961), the medal of the British Empire (M.B.E.) by Queen Elizabeth II (1962), and Korean Board Certification in Obstetrics and Gynecology (1965). She retired to Australia in 1976. Catherine, her right hand throughout, also received the M.B.E., the International Red Cross Florence Nightingale Medal, and the Korean Government Medal of Civilian Merit, Magnolia. IWH was designated one of ten maternal and child care centers by the Korean government and was the first hospital in Korea to be designated a "Baby Friendly Hospital" by UNICEF.

BIBLIOGRAPHY *Ilsin Kidok Pyongwon 40 Yon Sa* (40-year history of Ilsin Christian Hospital) (1993).

Horace G. Underwood

Mackenzie, Jean Kenyon (1874–1936), Presbyterian missionary in West Africa. Mackenzie was born in Elgin, Illinois, the first child of Robert and Lydia Ann (McLeon) Mackenzie. Her father was a Presbyterian minister. She attended Van Ness Seminary in San Francisco (1888–1890), the Sorbonne (1891–1892), and the University of California at Berkeley (1895–1896).

Mackenzie served under the Board of Foreign Missions of the Presbyterian Church, U.S.A. in West Africa from 1904 through 1913. She lived in German Kamerun at Lolodorf and Efulan stations, except for a brief interlude (1908–1909) when she was given a special assignment in the French Gabon at Baraka station on the Ogowe River. She worked primarily with the rapidly growing mission schools and with African women, doing extensive itineration throughout the villages of the rainforest.

In 1914 she returned to New York City because of illness. Thereafter she devoted full time to writing and made only one further visit to Kamerun, for 18 months between 1916 and 1918. A gifted writer, she published numerous articles, chiefly in the *Atlantic Monthly* and in *Women's Work*, a journal of the women's missionary societies of the Presbyterian Church. Author of seven books, she had unusual insight into the life and character of Africans, and few people of her generation did more to stir American Protestant interest in the missionary challenge of West Africa.

BIBLIOGRAPHY Jean Kenyon Mackenzie, *Black Sheep* (1916), *African Adventurers* (1917), *An African Trail* (1917), *African Clearings* (1924), *The Venture* (1925), *Friends of Africa* (ed., 1928), and *The Trader's Wife* (1930).

Norman A. Horner

Mackenzie, John (1835–1899), London Missionary Society (LMS) missionary in South Africa. Perhaps after John *Philip, the missionary with the most influence on South African history was John Mackenzie. Brought up in a devout Church of Scotland family in northeastern Scotland, he volunteered for service with the LMS in 1855 and in 1858 was sent to South Africa. He served at Kuruman and at Shoshong among the Tswana peoples. Returning from furlough in 1871, he became tutor in the school for teachers and evangelists, first at Shoshong then at Kuruman. The Tswana peoples were threatened with the loss of their land to Afrikaners of the Transvaal or to speculators from the Cape. Mackenzie became a firm advocate of direct imperial rule of native territories to prevent settler takeover of the land so essential to the integrity of an African people. After a very long and complex struggle against the forces of both the Transvaalers and of Cape politicians like Cecil Rhodes, he achieved success when in 1885 the British government declared the present Botswana a British Protectorate and preserved it from white settler occupation. In 1890 Mackenzie left the Tswana and spent his last years as pastor to the Cape Coloured people of Hankey, the last resting place of John Philip.

BIBLIOGRAPHY A prolific writer, Mackenzie's most important books are *Ten Years North of the Orange River* (1871) and *Austral Africa* (1887). His son W. D. Mackenzie published a full biography, *John Mackenzie: South African Missionary and Statesman* (1902). See also A. Sillery, *Founding a Protectorate* (1965).

Andrew C. Ross

Mackenzie, John Kenneth (1850–1888), British medical missionary in China. Born in Yarmouth, England, Mackenzie made a commitment to Christ in 1868 through a YMCA Bible class and under the influence of the D. L. *Moody evangelistic campaigns. After studying medicine in Bristol and Edinburgh, he was appointed by the London Missionary Society (LMS) and sailed for China in 1875. His first appointment was to Hankow (Hankou), where he studied Chinese, worked in the LMS hospital, and engaged in evangelism, most often as a colleague of Griffith *John. His work was varied and included general medicine, surgery, and working to cure opium addiction. In 1878 he transferred to Tientsin (Tianjin), where, with the patronage of wealthy Chinese and Li Hongzhang, viceroy of the Metropolitan Province, he was able to build a hospital. His effort to establish a medical school in 1881 failed because the Chinese army and navy did not want to use foreign-trained doctors. Mackenzie emphasized evangelism as the principal rationale for medical work. With this emphasis and his widely acclaimed medical skills, he established unusual rapport with the Tientsin community. In 1886 he helped to organize the Medical Missionary Association of China. He died from smallpox contracted from a patient.

BIBLIOGRAPHY Mrs. (Mary Isabella) Bryson, *John Kenneth Mackenzie: Medical Missionary to China* (n.d.)

Ralph R. Covell

Mackichan, Dugald (1851–1932), Scottish educational missionary in India. Born in Glasgow and a graduate of Glasgow University, Mackichan was a missionary of the Free Church of Scotland, and from 1900 of the United Free Church. He served as principal of Wilson College, Bombay (1878–1920), and was for four terms vice-chancellor of Bombay University. He was an educator of great eminence, a prominent public figure, and a missionary statesman. While not a scholar of the first rank, his *Missionary Ideal in the Scottish Churches* (1927, Chalmers Lectures) is still a useful and authoritative survey. He rejected the fulfillment approach espoused by J. N. *Farquhar and others on the ground that it would make Hindus reluctant to convert to Christianity and that it did not adequately distinguish in Hinduism what was denied and displaced by Christianity and what found its completion in Christian faith. Unlike Farquhar, he regarded the emerging nationalist movement as basically hostile to the Christian mission.

BIBLIOGRAPHY D. Mackichan, "A Present-Day Phase of Missionary Theology," *IRM* 3 (1914): 243–254. M. D. David, *John Wilson and His Institution* (1975); Eric Sharpe, *Not to Destroy but to Fulfil* (1965); D. Williamson, ed., *Forty-five Years in India: Memoirs and Reminiscences of Principal Mackichan* (1934).

Duncan B. Forrester

Mackie, Robert Cuthbert (1899–1984), ecumenical leader and missions advocate. Born in Bothwell, Scotland, Mackie studied at the University of Glasgow (M.A., 1922) and the United Free College (1922–1925). He was ordained in the United Free Church of Scotland in 1925 (as of 1929, the Church of Scotland), and from 1925 to 1938 he was Scottish and British general secretary of the Student Christian Movement. From 1938 to 1948 he was based in Geneva and Toronto as general secretary of the World's Student Christian Federation. He was associate general secretary of the World Council of Churches (WCC) from 1948 to 1955 and also director of its largest department—Inter-Church Aid and Refugee Service—and then its chairman until 1961. During much of this time he was also pastor of the Scots congregation in Geneva. In 1955 he returned to Scotland, where he became the inspiration behind the Scottish ecumenical movement. For his generation, he was probably the best-known and most-respected Scottish churchman outside Scotland. A world vision lay behind his early recognition of a missionary vocation and his commitment, persistence, and administrative skills made an essential contribution to the eventual integration of the International Missionary Council and the WCC in 1961. "The ecumenical movement only has meaning in relation to the missionary movement. . . . Mission may be regarded as the way in which the whole Church shares its resources," he wrote in *The Student World* (1946). Already in the 1920s he saw mission as intensive as well as extensive, and it is no coincidence that J. H. *Oldham founded his Christian Frontier Council in Mackie's sitting room. Described as "the heart of the ecumenical movement," Mackie embodied, with modesty and humor, a style of enabling leadership that spanned traditions and continents. He received honorary doctorates from the University of Glasgow (1948) and St. Sergius Orthodox Theological Academy in Paris (1955). He died in Edinburgh.

BIBLIOGRAPHY Nansie Blackie, *In Love and in Laughter: A Portrait of Robert Mackie* (1995).

Nansie Blackie

Maclaren, Albert Alexander (1853–1891), pioneer Anglican missionary to New Guinea. A Scotsman born in southern England, Maclaren was an Anglican priest and became convinced of God's call to be a missionary. After persistently applying for an overseas assignment, he was finally assigned to Australia, where he served several parishes. From there he made two exploratory visits to New Guinea in 1890, which led to the founding of the Anglican mission. The next year Maclaren and three lay colleagues set sail for New Guinea, arriving in August. After bartering for land, they assembled a prefabricated house to serve as headquarters. Four months later, however, Maclaren collapsed and was placed on board a ship, where he died.

BIBLIOGRAPHY Graeme Kent, *Company of Heaven: Early Missionaries in the South Seas* (1972); Edgar Rogers, *Pioneer of New Guinea: The Story of Albert Alexander Maclaren* (1920); Frances M. Synge, *Albert Maclaren: Pioneer Missionary to New Guinea. A Memoir* (1908); David Wetheral, *Reluctant Mission: The Anglican Church in Papua New Guinea, 1891–1942* (1977).

Darrell Whiteman

Maclay, Robert Samuel (1824–1907), American Methodist missionary in China and Japan. Born in Concord, Pennsylvania, Maclay graduated from Dickinson College, Carlisle, Pennsylvania, in 1846. He arrived in China in 1848 and was secretary, superintendent, and treasurer for Methodist missions in China from 1852 to 1872. In 1861 he wrote *Life among the Chinese.* He also helped translate the Bible into Min. In 1872 he was appointed superintendent of Methodist work in Japan. He was also asked to study the possibilities for beginning Methodist work in Korea, and in June 1884, he arrived in Seoul to make a survey. He was subsequently appointed the first superintendent of the work in Korea, working from Japan. Much as he wanted to begin the work in Korea himself, this fell to Henry *Appenzeller and William *Scranton, who arrived in Japan with their wives in March 1885. Within a month—on Easter Sunday, April 5, 1885—Henry and Ella Appenzeller arrived in Juchon, the first Methodist missionaries in Korea. Maclay returned to the United States in 1887; he is buried in Los Angeles, California.

BIBLIOGRAPHY Robert S. Maclay, "A Fortnight in Seoul, Korea, 1884" and "Commencement of the Korea Methodist Episcopal Mission," *Gospel in All Lands* 22 (August 1896): 354–356, 498–502. Everett N. Hunt, Jr., *Protestant Pioneers in Korea* (1980); L. George Paik, *The History of Protestant Missions in Korea, 1832–1910* (1971); Charles D. Stokes, "History of Methodist Missions in Korea, 1885–1930" (Ph.D. diss., Yale Univ., 1947).

Everett N. Hunt, Jr.

MacNicol, Nicol (1870–1952), Scottish missionary in India and scholar of Hinduism. MacNicol studied at Glasgow University and the Glasgow College of the Free Church of Scotland. He was ordained a minister of the Free Church in 1895. From 1895 to 1931 he worked as a missionary in western India, based first in Bombay and then in Poona. India was at that time going through profound social, political, and religious changes, and Poona was a particularly important center of revivalist and reform movements, with which MacNicol maintained close contact. As a district missionary, he developed also a deep understanding of the very different popular Hinduism of the villages. He gained a considerable well-deserved reputation as a sympathetic yet critical student of Hinduism, on which he published several well-regarded books. His best-known work is *Indian Theism* (1915), in which he presented an authoritative account of the varieties of Hindu theistic belief and assessed them in the light of the Christian gospel. His overall approach was very similar to that of J. N. *Farquhar, whose *Crown of Hinduism* was published in 1913. Both men saw Christianity as the fulfillment of the best in Hindu belief. "The faith of which [the Lord Jesus Christ] is the centre," MacNicol wrote, "confirms the institutions and crowns the longings of the long centuries of Indian Theistic aspiration." MacNicol retired in Scotland in 1931.

BIBLIOGRAPHY Notable among MacNicol's other writings are *Psalms of Maratha Saints* (1915), *Pandita Ramabai* (1926, a biography of a convert), his magisterial *The Making of Modern India* (1924), and a popular examination of the role of the church in modern India, *India in the Dark Wood* (1930). The final statement of his position was in his Wilde Lectures, published as *Is Christianity Unique?* (1936).

Duncan B. Forrester

MacVicar, Neil (1871–1949), medical missionary in southern Africa. MacVicar graduated in medicine from Edinburgh University in 1893, winning the medal for the outstanding student of the year. He had been deeply influenced by D. C. R. *Scott and went to join him as medical officer at the Church of Scotland Mission, Blantyre, Malawi. There he was a close ally of Scott and succeeded him as editor of the periodical *Life and Work in British Central Africa* after Scott resigned in 1898. But in 1901 MacVicar also resigned, unable to work any longer with Alexander *Hetherwick, Scott's successor as head of the mission.

James *Stewart of Lovedale persuaded the United Free Church of Scotland to appoint MacVicar as head of the new hospital at Lovedale in Cape Colony. MacVicar threw himself wholeheartedly into the new challenge, as doctor, educator, administrator, and evangelist. For 20 years he trained African women as nurses to the official state registration standards before this was available to them anywhere else in southern Africa. He carried out two brilliant pieces of research on medical problems of great importance to society: tuberculosis among Africans, urban and rural; and scurvy among miners. His reports led to major governmental reforms in public health and to drastic changes in diet and accommodation in the vast mining hostels. He was a brilliant popular writer of evangelistic and public health pamphlets. He died in South Africa.

BIBLIOGRAPHY *Life and Work in British Central Africa* was not only edited by MacVicar but also largely written by him during the years 1899 to 1901. Many articles by him also appear in *The South African Outlook* in issues published between 1922 and 1942. His biography, by R. H. W. Shepherd, is *A South African Medical Pioneer* (1952).

Andrew C. Ross

Magee, John G(illespie) (1884–1953), missionary in China. Born in Pittsburgh, Pennsylvania, Magee finished high school in Connecticut, then graduated from Yale (B.A., 1906) and from Episcopal Theological School (B.D., 1911) in Cambridge, Massachusetts. Ordained in the Episcopal Church, he went to China in 1912, where he worked most of his career in Nanking (Nanjing). In 1921 he married Faith E. Backhouse, an English missionary from the China Inland Mission. They had four sons.

Magee played an important role in saving thousands of Chinese from being murdered by the Japanese army during the occupation of Nanking in 1937–1938. He established a refugee hospital to take care of wounded soldiers and refugees, served as chairman of the Nanking branch of the International Red Cross, and was a member of the International Committee for the Nanking Safety Zone. Films taken by Magee in Nanking and sent to the West were among the first available visual documentation of the Nanking Massacre. After the war, Magee was a witness at the Tokyo War Crimes Trial (1946). Jiro Takidani's *Witness to the Nanking Incident* (1993) documents Magee's work during the Nanking Massacre. When Magee returned to America in the summer of 1938, after 28 years of service in China, he made an extensive tour to speak about the Nanking Massacre. He died in Pittsburgh.

BIBLIOGRAPHY Films of the Nanking Massacre made by Magee are in the Special Collections of Yale Divinity School Library. See the *Historical Register of Yale University, 1937–1951* (1952).

Martha Lund Smalley

Maigrot, Charles (1652–1730), French Roman Catholic mission administrator in China. Born in Paris, Maigrot was ordained a priest in 1676 and received a doctorate from the Sorbonne two years later. In 1680 he entered the Missions Étrangères de Paris (Paris Foreign Mission Society) and early the following year left for China. In 1684 he was named pro-vicar of Fukien (Fujian), Kiangsi (Jiangxi), and Chekiang (Zhejiang) Provinces. Later that year, upon the death of François *Pallu, he became administrator of the missions of China and, in 1687, vicar apostolic of Fukien. In 1692 the emperor of China granted the Edict of Toleration, by which Chinese could freely embrace Catholicism. Maigrot was consecrated a bishop in March 1700.

In 1693 Maigrot reopened the Chinese Rites Controversy by condemning the rites honoring Confucius and one's ancestors as superstitious, and prohibited the practices in Fukien, sending a copy of his edict to Rome. When the papal legate to the imperial court, Charles Thomas Maillard de *Tournon, arrived in China in 1705 to try to settle the controversy, he called Maigrot to assist him in the capital. During an imperial audience, Tournon referred to Maigrot as a noted scholar of Chinese studies. In a later audience in Manchuria, Maigrot contended that Confucian teaching was contrary to Christianity, but he also showed his linguistic weaknesses in Chinese. This led the emperor to question Maigrot's ability to understand the Chinese classics, which were a key element in the Rites Controversy. In 1706 the emperor ordered that all missionaries wishing to remain in China must apply for residence permits and uphold the practices of Matteo *Ricci; Tournon issued an edict against this in February 1707. The next month the emperor ordered Maigrot expelled from China. Two years later he was designated a bishop assisting at the papal throne in the Vatican, a position he held until his death.

BIBLIOGRAPHY Claudia von Collani, "Le Père Joachim Bouvet et le mandement du vicaire apostolique Charles Maigrot," in Edward Malatesta and Yves Raguin, eds., *Succès et échecs de la Rencontre Chine et Occident du XVIe au XXe siècle* (1993), pp. 77–100; A. Launay, *Memorial de la Societé des Missions Étrangères de Paris,* vol. 2 (1916), pp. 417–423; Antonio Sisto Rosso, *Apostolic Legations to China of the Eighteenth Century* (1948), pp. 130–136, 166–171.

John W. Witek, SJ

Mailla, Joseph Marie Anne de Moyriac de (1669–1748), Jesuit missionary, cartographer, and historian in China. Mailla was born in the château of Maillac, which had been in his family for more than 500 years, located in the diocese of Belley, France. He renounced all claims to a patrimony and entered the Society of Jesus in 1686. He embarked for China in 1701 and arrived in Macao in 1703. After Chinese language training, he worked in Kiangsi (Jiangxi) Province. Called to Peking (Beijing) to assist his confreres in making maps of the empire, from 1710 to 1714 he traveled to several provinces and also made a trip to Taiwan. When Mailla returned to the capital, the emperor assigned him to work at court, where he learned Manchu. He wrote several spiritual works in Chinese, including one on devotion to the Sacred Heart of Jesus and another on giving an eight-day retreat according to the *Spiritual Exercises* of *Ignatius of Loyola. In his French publication of a lengthy twelfth-century history of China that had been recently translated into Manchu, Mailla at times added other material, including data on the Ming and Ch'ing (Qing) dynasties. He sent a copy of this work to Lyons, and it was published posthumously. He died in Peking.

BIBLIOGRAPHY Joseph Mailla, *Histoire générale de la Chine,* 12 vols. (1777–1783). M. Milsky, "Les souscripteurs de 'l'Histoire générale de la Chine' du P. de Mailla," in *Les Rapports entre la Chine et l'Europe au temps des lumières* (1980), pp. 101–123; Louis Pfister, *Notices biographiques et bibliographiques sur les Jésuites de l'ancienne mission de Chine* (1932–1934; repr., 1975), pp. 596–605 (with a list of Mailla's Chinese works).

John W. Witek, SJ

Main, D(avid) Duncan (1856–1934), Scottish medical missionary in China. Born and raised in Scotland, Main performed brilliantly at school and studied business at Glasgow, where he had a conversion experience in 1873, and joined the evangelistic revival movement, meeting D. L. *Moody and Ira Sankey in 1874. An encounter with a medical missionary inspired him to become a medical missionary himself. Educated at Edinburgh with the help of the Edinburgh Medical Missionary Society, he sailed with his wife, Florence Nightingale (Smith), for China in 1881 under the Church Missionary Society. They lived at Hangchow (Hangzhou) for their entire service, in spite of frequent revolutionary unrest. When the Mains left China in 1926, at least thirty different medical and welfare institutions had been established through their efforts.

BIBLIOGRAPHY Alexander Gammie, *Duncan Main of Hangchow* (1935); Kingston de Gruchè, *Dr. Apricot of "Heaven Below"* (1910) and *Dr. D. Duncan Main of Hangchow, Who Is Known in China as Dr. Apricot of Heaven Below* (1930). A personal file is in the CMS archive, Univ. of Birmingham.

Christoffer H. Grundmann

Makarii Altaiskii (Mikhail Andreevich Nevskii) (1835–1926), Russian Orthodox missionary and metropolitan. Born in Vladimir Guberniya, Makarii studied in Tobolsk and graduated in 1854. He went to work in the Orthodox mission in the Altai Mountains region, some 800 miles to the southeast, where he taught children and organized discussions with newly baptized adults. He became a monk in 1857 and hieromonk (i.e., also a priest) in 1861. He was made archimandrite in 1883. He spent 37 years in the Altai mission, from 1883 to 1891 as head of the mission, from 1884 as bishop of Bisk. He learned the language of the natives well enough to preach and to translate. He traveled constantly, visiting, preaching, and tending to the needs of the sick. He taught agriculture, construction, and other skills and also encouraged the building of schools and houses for the poor. In 1883 he opened a school for catechists. He encouraged the work of women in the mission. He was always open to visitors and would stop his work to pray with the sick. He produced 1,100 pages of printed sermons in addition to his translation work. He put the liturgy to music in the Altaian and Tatar translations, making it possible for the first time to hold orthodox liturgical services in these languages. He made a practice of inviting priests for tea and during the conversation giving them a theme for a sermon, and a date by which to produce a written sermon (which he would then discuss). In 1912 he was made metropolitan of Moscow. He was relieved of his duties in 1917 and retired to the Nikolo-Ugreshskii monastery, where he died. In 1984 he was canonized as a local saint of Siberia.

BIBLIOGRAPHY David N. Collins, "The Role of the Orthodox Missionary in the Altai: Archimandrite Makarii and V. I. Verbitskii," in Geoffrey A. Hosking, ed., *Church, Nation, and State in Russia and Ukraine* (1991); Tatyana Groyan, ed., *Tsaryu Nebesnomu i zemnomu vernyi. Mitropolit Makarii Moskovskii, Apostol Altaiskii (Parvitskii-Nevskii), 1835–1926* (1966).

Karen L. Gordon

Makarii of Altai. *See* Glukharev, Makarii.

Makemie, Francis (1658–1708), Scotch-Irish Presbyterian minister, theologian, and itinerant missionary preacher in the British colonies of North America and Barbados. Born in County Donegal, Ireland, educated in Glasgow, Scotland, and ordained by his Irish presbytery in 1682, Makemie and other dissenting ministers were urged by immigrants to join them in British North America. Beginning in 1683, Makemie traveled to Maryland, Virginia, the Carolinas, and Barbados. After a brief return to London in 1691, where he made contacts with New England Puritans, he promoted a Reformed alliance against Quakers and Anglicans in America. Making his principal residence in Barbados from 1692 to 1698, he established several Presbyterian congregations in Virginia and Maryland. He also wrote several tracts in support of Presbyterianism in those colonies, most successfully in Virginia. Partly through his efforts, the Virginia legislature enacted the English Act of Toleration, which permitted the activities of dissenting congregations in the colony. Makemie continued to travel widely, including several journeys back to England. He subsequently wrote *A Plain and Loving Persuasion to the Inhabitants of Virginia and Maryland for Promoting Towns and Cohabitation* (1704); it lamented the paucity of civil and religious institutions and encouraged further colonization. In 1706 in Philadelphia, Makemie and several other Presbyterians formed the first presbytery in America, with strong ties to New England Puritan and London dissenting congregations. He thus became known as the founder of American Presbyterianism.

BIBLIOGRAPHY L. P. Bowen, *The Days of Makemie* (1885); B. S. Schlenther, ed., *The Life and Writings of Francis Makemie* (1971); Leonard J. Trinterud, *The Forming of an American Tradition: A Reexamination of Colonial Presbyterianism* (1949).

Mark Valeri

Makkai, Sándor (1890–1951), bishop and professor of mission in the Hungarian Reformed Church. Makkai was born in Nagyenyed, Hungary, the son of Domokos Makkai, professor at the Bethlen Kollegium. He studied at the divinity school of the University of Kolozsvar (Cluj, in present-day Romania), earning a doctorate in systematic and practical theology in 1917. He served as a bishop from 1926 to 1936 in Transylvania and then was appointed to teach practical theology, including mission, at the University of Debrecen (later, Reformed Theological Academy). His threefold mission concept of pastoral, congregational, and foreign mission, although criticized by János *Victor in 1941 for its inadequate biblical and dogmatic foundations, was strongly influenced by the Hungarian church situation. His failure to define the theological content of mission and the true nature of the church, as well as his strong focus on congregational mission, had unexpected consequences with the communist takeover, leading to a concept of mission that was limited to the four walls of the church. The new church leaders, appointed in 1948 and 1949, gave it a new political content: the mission of the church was to serve the purposes of the Socialist state. Makkai's desire had been to awaken congregations to their missionary calling, but he saw with regret that his well organized network of mission committees became an instrument of the state.

BIBLIOGRAPHY Sándor Makkai, *Szolgálatom: Teológiai Önéletrajz 1944* (My ministry: Theological autobiography, 1944) (1990), *Az egyház missziói munkája* (The mission work of the church) (1938), "Mi a 'missziói munka'?" (What is "mission work"?) *Theológiai Szemle* 17 (1941): 31–43, *A gyülekezeti missziói munka mai értelmeze és feladatai* (The present meaning and obligation of congregational mission work) (1947), and *Élőgyülekezet. Tanulmányok, előadások a gyülekezeti misszió közösségi szolgálatról* (Living congregation. Studies and lectures on the community ministry of the congregational mission) (1948). Anne-Marie Kool, *God Moves in a Mysterious Way: The Hungarian Protestant Foreign Mission Movement (1756–1951)* (1993), pp. 319–340.

Anne-Marie Kool

Maldonado de Buendía, Alonso (1510/1520–c. 1596), Spanish Franciscan missionary and reformer. Maldonado labored to correct the abuses of Spain's colonial administration in New Spain (Central America, Mexico, and southwest United States). A fervent idealist, he was especially strident in his condemnation of the injustices inflicted on the native population. After ten years in New Spain, he returned to Europe in 1561 and devoted the next 20 years campaigning for humane colonial policies, reform of the Franciscan Order, and fair treatment of Jewish converts to Catholicism. He submitted petitions urging enactment of such measures to the Council of the Indies, Philip II, and Pope Pius V. In 1582 he was imprisoned by the Inquisition for unknown reasons.

BIBLIOGRAPHY Pedro Borges, "Un reformador de Indias y de la Orden Franciscana bajo Felipe II: Alonso Maldonado de Buendía, OFM," *Archivo Ibero-Americano* 20 (1960): 280–337, 487–535; 21 (1961): 53–97; M. Monica, *La gran controversia del siglo diez y seis acerca del dominio español sobre America* (1952), pp. 137–196.

Cyprian J. Lynch, OFM

Malinki, James M(orrison) (1893–1982), pioneering Seventh-day Adventist (SDA) missionary in Malawi, Zaire, and Zambia. Son of the the first SDA African minister in Malawi, Malinki was one of the first students at Malamulo, the SDA mission station among the Chewa-speaking people. He subsequently taught at the mission and did evangelistic work in the surrounding district. His success led to a transfer to Zaire in 1920. He learned both French and Chiluba and did evangelistic work in the Lubumbashi area for seven years. Returning to Malawi, he established several new SDA communities and two mission stations (at Luwazi and Lunjika). A delegate to the SDA General Conference session in San Francisco in 1930, he inspired delegates with reports of what God was doing in central Africa. After several more years as an evangelist and station director in Malawi, he was transferred to Zambia, where he spent 20 years planting churches and promoting Christian stewardship. On June 2, 1962, the governor of Malawi presented Malinki with a gold medal in the name of Her Majesty Queen Elizabeth II in recognition of 45 years of service to his country and the British empire. Malinki had consistently promoted productive methods of farming, and his retirement farm became a model for which he was awarded a progressive farmer citation by President Banda in 1971. Following his example in evangelistic work and church planting, a number of workers from Malawi became successful cross-cultural missionaries in other parts of Africa.

Bibliography Jaspine D. Bilima, "James Malinki of Malawi: Church Leader in Cross-cultural Ministry" (D.Min. thesis, Andrews Univ., 1993); "Malawi" and "Malinki, J. Morrison," in *Seventh-day Adventist Encyclopedia,* 2d rev. ed. (1996).

Russell L. Staples

Malpan, Abraham. *See* Abraham Malpan.

Mamora (*or* Sinamora), Lucius (c. 1920–), Indonesian missionary to Sarawak. Lucius Mamora was a Batak Christian who received training in Methodist schools in Sumatra and Java before he was sent as one of the first Methodist missionaries to the Iban people of Sarawak in 1940. His evangelistic work was based in Kapit. At the time of the Japanese invasion of 1942, he and his family went into hiding among the Iban and carried out their ministry through the war years. After the war, in 1946, he and Burr *Baughman established a school for Iban boys. His efforts with Baughman led to the baptism of the first Iban Methodist converts in 1949. He subsequently translated many hymns into the Iban language and helped translate the New Testament.

Bibliography Joseph Terrance, "The Longhouse Church in Sarawak" (S.T.M. thesis, Southern Methodist Univ., 1964).

Robert A. Hunt

Manikam, Rajah B(ushanam) (1897–1969), Indian church leader and ecumenical statesman. On his father's side Manikam was Tamil and Lutheran, and on his mother's side Telugu and Anglican. His career led him through a Ph.D. at Columbia University and a B.D. at Lutheran Theological Seminary, Philadelphia, to prominent positions in Indian Christianity. After eight years as a college teacher in Andhra, Manikam joined the staff of the National Christian Council of India in 1937, specializing in church-mission relationships, ecumenical activities, and higher education. In 1950, as a logical continuation of his work on an international level, he was appointed as East Asia secretary of the International Missionary Council and World Council of Churches. Almost simultaneously he was ordained to the ministry of the Tamil Evangelical Lutheran Church whose fourth bishop he became in 1956. His outstanding ecumenical achievement was the creation of the East Asia Christian Conference in 1957. His hopes and expectations for wider church union in India, with Lutheran participation, failed to come to fruition. Manikam is remembered by many as a world Christian whose primary loyalties were nonetheless claimed by India and Asia. As a writer, he made a significant contribution to ecumenical thought in his book *Christianity and the Asian Revolution* (1954).

Bibliography Carl Gustav Diehl and E. Theodore Bachmann, *Rajah Bushanam Manikam* (1975).

Hans-Werner Gensichen

Manna, Paolo (1872–1952), founder of the Pontifical Missionary Union of the Clergy. Born in Avellino, Italy, Manna entered the Missionaries of SS. Peter and Paul (Milan) in 1891. After being a missionary in Burma from 1895 to 1907, he returned to Italy, becoming a pioneer in the contemporary missionary movement. In 1908 he published a book on the need for missionaries and the necessity to organize the clergy in order to promote missionary cooperation. His plan became concrete when he proposed to Guido Maria *Conforti, the archbishop of Parma, a plan for a missionary union of the clergy. On October 31, 1916, the prefect of Propaganda Fide, Cardinal Serafini, communicated full approval. At the end of 1917 the Missionary Union of the Clergy in Italy counted 1,254 members, and by 1934, 38,085 priests, or 84 percent of the Italian clergy. From 1924 to 1934 Manna was also superior general of the Milan Pontifical Institute for Foreign Missions. *Benedict XV and *Pius XI encouraged the Missionary Union of the Clergy, giving it pontifical status. Manna was its first secretary (1936–1941) when it became an international institution under Propaganda Fide.

Bibliography Paolo Manna, *Operarii autem pauci* (1908, 1912, 1923, 1946; Eng. tr., *The Workers Are Few: Reflections upon Vocation to the Foreign Missions,* 1911; 3d ed., 1912; new ed., 1954), *Per una Unione Missionaria del Clero* (1916), *La conversione del mondo infedele* (1920; Eng. tr., *The Conversion of the Pagan World,* 1920, 1923), and *Il problema missionario e i sacerdoti* (1938; Eng. tr., *Priests and the Missionary Problem,* 1938). Ferdinando Germani, *P. Paolo Manna,* vol.

1, *Da Avellino alla Birmania (1872–1907)* (1989), vol. 2, *L'Unione Missionaria del Clero e il. Seminario Meridionale per le Missione Estere (1907–1924)* (1990), vol. 3, *Superiore Generale (1924–1934)* (1992), and *Paolo Manna maestro di spiritualità missionarie* (1993).

Willi Henkel, OMI

Manso, Alonso (c. 1470–1539), first Catholic bishop in the New World. Born at Becerril de Campos near Palencia, Spain, Manso attended the Colegio Major de San Bartolomé in the University of Salamanca, where he earned the degree of licentiate in theology. When he was ordained to the priesthood is not known. He served as *sacristán major* to Don Juan, only son of Ferdinand and Isabella. After the death of that prince in 1497, Manso was appointed a *visitador* of the University of Salamanca and later a canon of the Salamanca cathedral chapter.

The first three dioceses in the New World were created by Julius II in 1511: two on Española (Haiti) and the third on San Juan (Puerto Rico). Appointed bishop of the third, Manso received episcopal ordination in 1512 and took up residence at San Juan the following year. In 1519 Manso was also appointed apostolic inquisitor of the Indies. The apostolic zeal and administrative skill he expended over the next 20 years established the church of Puerto Rico as a vibrant extension of the universal church.

BIBLIOGRAPHY Antonio Cuesta Mendoza, *Historia eclesiástica del Puerto Rico colonial (1508–1700)* (1948), vol. 1, pp. 23–36; Juan Augusto Perea and Salvador Perea, *Early Ecclesiastical History of Puerto Rico, with Some Account of the Social and Political Development of the Island during the Episcopate of Don Alonso Manso, the First Bishop of the New World (1513–1589)* (1929).

Cyprian J. Lynch, OFM

Maranke, John (1912–1963), founder of the African Apostolic Church of John Maranke in Rhodesia (Zimbabwe). A Manyika-Shona born in the Maranke district near Umtali (Mutare), Maranke was raised and educated as a Methodist. Accustomed to receiving visions from an early age, in July 1932 he experienced a divine revelation in which he was called to be Christ's apostle with a distinct missionary mandate, his first task being to convert the members of his extended family in the Mufararikwa chiefdom of Maranke. By appointing numerous relatives to the church's hierarchy, he developed an ecclesiastical nucleus that served as a basis for his remarkable missionary career and the growth of the Apostolic movement, which became the largest African Initiated Church in Rhodesia.

For 30 years Maranke traveled regularly, often on foot, through Rhodesia and the neighboring countries of Botswana, Zambia, Malawi, and South Africa and as far north as Zaire. In response to his prophetic message of salvation for Africa through the Spirit-inspired proclamation of African Apostles, thousands were converted, baptized, and organized into congregations. His message included confrontation of traditional African religion and a contextualized healing/exorcistic ministry. Setting the example of an itinerant missionary, Maranke modeled his church as a missionizing/evangelizing body of African believers without church buildings, involvement in secular education, or the use of medicine.

Maranke's visions figured prominently in Apostolic theology and became a major focus in Apostolic preaching. While his leadership had distinct messianic traits, constant reference to his encounters with Jesus Christ served to preserve and protect the mediating and salvific functions of the biblical Christ. Annual paschal celebrations, popularly referred to as Pendi (from "Pentecost"), last for 17 days, culminating in Holy Communion ceremonies, and at times involve the participation of up to 100,000 Apostles from Zimbabwe and neighboring countries. Pendi celebrations near Maranke's old homestead serve to consolidate church membership and inspire renewed outreach and church growth.

After his death, Maranke's three senior sons—Abero, Makebo, and Judah—succeeded to his leadership. Despite a minor schism, they maintained and further expanded the Apostolic sphere of influence. No firm figures are available, but the Apostolic movement in Zimbabwe and beyond probably had an overall membership in excess of one million in 1996.

BIBLIOGRAPHY Marthinus L. Daneel, *Old and New in Southern Shona Independent Churches,* vol. 1, *Background and Rise of the Major Movements* (1971); Bennetta Jules-Rosette, *African Apostles: Ritual and Conversion in the Church of John Maranke* (1975).

Marthinus L. Daneel

Maretu (c. 1802–1880), preacher and missionary in the Cook Islands. Maretu was one of the first converts to Christianity in the Cook Islands. He worked under the early missionary Charles *Pitman and began conducting services and preaching about 1833, when Pitman became ill for a year. When trouble broke out in the island of Mangaia between the Tahitian missionaries and the local people, Maretu was sent in 1839 to restore peace. His strong, genial nature and his use of the Mangaian language instead of Tahitian brought unity and progress to the church. In 1845, when Pitman became ill again, he insisted that Maretu return to Rarotonga to help him, but in 1854 he was again sent out, this time to Manihiki Atoll, to establish the first church community there. He stayed nearly two years and supervised the building of two churches on Manihiki and one on nearby Rakahanga, a great accomplishment in light of his limited resources.

In 1856 he was appointed as Pitman's successor at Ngatangiia, in Rarotonga, where he continued to serve until his death. He was beloved by all for his saintliness and guilelessness and was the strongest and most effective preacher in the Cook Islands Church of that time. His preaching was described as "soul-stirring," or, as one of his converts put it, "like fire in my stomach." In his later years he wrote his memoirs and the early and more recent history of Rarotonga. He gave vivid descriptions of the wars and cannibalism of the earlier times and of the struggles surrounding the changeover to Christianity. These writings, which now have been translated and published, constitute one of the most important sources for the history of the Cook Islands.

BIBLIOGRAPHY Maretu, *Cannibals and Converts: Radical Change in the Cook Islands* (Marjorie Tuainekore Crocombe, tr. and ed., 1983); see especially ch. 1.

Charles W. Forman

Margil, Antonio (1657-1726), Spanish Franciscan missionary in the New World. Arriving in the New World in June 1683, Margil traveled, largely by foot, from central Mexico to what is now Costa Rica and Guatemala and later to the territory of northern Mexico and Texas. He was largely concerned with the conversion of Indians to Christianity through instruction and preaching. He became a major figure in the design and administration of Propaganda Fide's missionary colleges, an idea developed by Franciscans in Europe and adapted first by Antonio *Llinás and then by Margil and others in Mexico and Guatemala. Margil took over administration of the first college, Santa Cruz de Querétaro, and helped found two other missionary colleges: Cristo Crucificado in Guatemala City, and Nuestra Señora de Guadalupe in Zacatecas. In this era, more than a century after the initial missionaries arrived in Latin America, Margil and other Franciscans promoted the missionary colleges as autonomous communities of friars dedicated to missionary work. For friars from these colleges, Margil modeled the life of a highly mobile missionary who reached out to Indians dispersed from their pueblos. He dedicated a great deal of time to prayer and was revered for personal sanctity. He died at San Francisco convent, Mexico City.

BIBLIOGRAPHY Antonio Margil, *Nothingness Itself*, Marion A. Habig, ed., and Benedict Leutenegger, tr. (1976). Alberto María Carreño, "The Missionary Influence of the College of Zacatecas," and Kieran McCarty, "Apostolic Colleges of the Propagation of the Faith—Old and New World Background," both in Thomas E. Sheridan et al., eds., *The Franciscan Missions of Northern Mexico* (1991); William H. Oberste, *The Restless Friar* (1970); Eduardo Enrique Ríos, *Life of Fray Antonio Margil, O.F.M.* (1959).

Edward L. Cleary, OP

Margull, Hans Jochen (1925-1982), German missiologist. Margull was born near Danzig (present-day Gdansk, Poland) and studied theology in Griefswald, Halle, Mainz, and New York. From 1953 he served the Student Christian Movement in Germany as general secretary until he joined the University of Hamburg in 1955 as assistant to Walter *Freytag. His early scholarly work dealt with the missiological debate within the World Council of Churches (WCC), which at that time reflected a Christocentric approach as well as Freytag's eschatological perspective on mission. Later in Margull's thinking both perspectives faded. From 1961, as secretary of the Department for Evangelism within the WCC, he contributed to the debate on appropriate structures for local churches in mission, a prelude to the recognition of Europe as a context for mission. A lectureship in Japan in 1965 radicalized his views on the meaning of missionary presence in the modern industrial world. From 1967, in the chair for missiology and ecumenics at Hamburg University, he helped prepare the missiological work of the 1968 WCC Uppsala Assembly. Subsequently, he served as chairperson for the WCC's committee on mission and evangelism, and from 1975, as chairperson for the work of the dialogue unit within the WCC. This made him one of the early advocates of interreligious dialogue within the ecumenical movement.

BIBLIOGRAPHY Hans Jochen Margull, *Theologie der missionarischen Verkündigung: Evangelisation als ökumenisches Problem* (1959; Eng. tr., *Hope in Action: The Church's Task in the World* [1962]), *Aufbruch zur Zukunft: Chiliastisch-messianische Bewegungen in Afrika und Südostasien* (1962), *Basileia: Walter Freytag zum 60. Geburtstag*, ed. with Jan Hermelink (1959, 1961), *Mission als Strukturprinzip: Ein Arbeitsbuch zur Frage missionarischer Gemeinden* (1968), and *Zeugnis und Dialog: Ausgewählte Schriften*, T. Ahrens et al., eds. (1992; Margull's collected essays).

Theodor Ahrens

Marianne of Molokai (Mother). *See* Cope, Marianne.

Marie de l'Assomption (Marie Le Roy Ladurie) (1896-1973), French Catholic nun, founder of a lay society for missionary prayer and study. Born in Châlons-sur-Marne, France, Le Roy Ladurie joined the congregation of the Helpers of the Holy Souls in 1919, first at Overyssche, Belgium, later in Paris. She took the religious name Marie de l'Assomption. She edited the mission quarterly of her congregation, *Au-Delà* (1932-1939), and *Cahiers J.C.S.*, a bulletin for girls, many of whom became missionaries. In 1944, encouraged by Jean *Daniélou, she founded the Cercle Saint Jean-Baptiste. Membership was open to women students who had a love for missions but were reluctant to take religious vows. She set up a program of missiological education by extension; leading scholars contributed material that was published in the quarterly *Bulletin du Cercle Saint Jean-Baptiste* (1944-1968), continued as *Axes: Recherches pour un dialogue entre christianisme et religions*. She led seminars and summer courses for lay women and even for nuns in their monasteries. She was involved in founding Aide à l'Implantation Monastique in 1956, for promoting monastic life in Asia and Africa. She combined missionary mysticism with missiological formation. Her interests stretched from biblical missiology to world religions, considered as stepping-stones for the coming of Christ.

BIBLIOGRAPHY Works by Marie Le Roy Ladurie include *Pâques africaines: De la communauté clanique à la communauté chrétienne* (1965; a dissertation in religious anthropology based on field study among African nuns in Ouagadougou, Central African Republic) and *Femmes au désert* (1972). A selection from her columns in the *Bulletin du Cercle Saint Jean-Baptiste* was published in a memorial issue of *Axes: Recherches pour un dialogue entre christianisme et religions* 5, no. 5 (1973): 29-35.

Marc R. Spindler

Marie de l'Incarnation (Marie Guyart) (1599-1672), French mystic and founder of the Ursulines of Quebec. Born in Tours, France, Guyart married a silk merchant, Claude Martin, in 1615, bore a son who eventually became a Benedictine, and was widowed after two years of marriage. She dated her conversion, March 24, 1620: "I saw myself immersed in the blood of the Son of God, shed because of the sins which had been shown to me . . . realizing that it was for my salvation that this Precious Blood had been shed." While progressing in mystical life, she worked successfully in the waterway transport business of her brother-in-law. In 1631 she joined the Ursulines of Tours, taking the religious name Marie de l'Incarnation and leaving her son to the responsibility of her family. In 1635 she had a vision in which she heard a specific missionary calling from God: "It is Canada that I have shown you; you must go there to build a house for Jesus and Mary." In the meantime, a rich laywoman, Madeleine de la Peltrie, had made a vow to build a school for Indian girls in Canada and was prepared to fund the mission. The two women sailed from Dieppe to Quebec in 1639. Within a week after her arrival, Marie had opened a school for Indian girls, the first girls' school in Canada. It was held in the house of the sisters, later the cloister, as the sisters were bound by the rule of closure. The Indian girls shared their life, were instructed in the faith, and learned about piety and virtues, including bodily cleanliness. The Indians, accustomed to smearing bear grease on their bodies as a protection against the elements, were confused by the sisters' perception of dirt. Marie, who became the first Mother Superior of the Ursuline Sisters in Canada, compiled Iroquois and Algonquin dictionaries and a catechism in Huron.

BIBLIOGRAPHY The writings of Marie de l'Incarnation were first edited by her son, Claude Martin, O.S.B., in four volumes (1677–1684). A critical edition was provided by A. Jamet, *Marie de l'Incarnation: Écrits spirituels et historiques* (1929–1939) and by G. M. Oury, *Correspondance de Marie de l'Incarnation* (1971). See also Marie of the Incarnation, *Selected Writings,* Irene Mahoney, ed. (1989; provides an excellent introduction and bibliography); Françoise Deroy-Pineau, *Marie de l'Incarnation: Marie Guyart, femme d'affaires, mystique, mère de la Nouvelle France, 1599–1672* (1989) and *Madeleine de la Peltrie, amazone du Nouveau Monde (Alençon 1603–Québec 1671)* (1992).

Marc R. Spindler

Marion Brésillac, Melchior Joseph de (1813–1859), founder of the Society of African Missions. Brésillac was born at Castelnaudary, France, studied at the seminary of Carcassone, and was ordained a priest in 1838. In 1841 Brésillac joined the Missions Étrangères de Paris and the following year went to Pondicherry, India. In 1846 he was appointed bishop of the Provicariate of Coïmbatore, India. Brésillac favored rapid progress toward the ordination of indigenous clergy. He rejected the existing uncertainty toward the Malabar Rites, many of which, he felt, could be adapted for use by Christianity. He met with much opposition from other missionaries who found his views too progressive. His hopes that Propaganda Fide might provide a firm ruling on the question of Indian customs were misplaced, so that after eight years he felt he had no option but to resign. Brésillac now wanted to go to Africa as a missionary, but Propaganda Fide insisted that he should first found a missionary society. Brésillac's Society of African Missions (SMA), specifically for "the most abandoned souls in Africa," was founded at Lyon on December 8, 1856. Entrusted with the Vicariate of Sierra Leone, Brésillac led his society's first missionary venture, arriving in Freetown in May 1859. Within six weeks he and four of his companions died of yellow fever.

Brésillac gave the church a society that was to play a major role in the modern missionary movement. He also made a significant contribution to thinking on missions. He saw the missionary essentially as an apostle who founds new churches, and the key to founding new churches, in his view, was the formation of an indigenous clergy. What was at issue here was not the education of individual priests but rather the formation of a clergy that would in time be capable of producing its own bishops. Brésillac differed from many of his contemporaries in refusing to accept the view that the formation of such a clergy was impractical or inopportune and that missions could be successfully conducted without indigenous clergy. In 1994 the SMA numbered 1,229 members.

BIBLIOGRAPHY Jean Bonfils, *Mgr. de Marion Brésillac* (1962); Patrick Gantly, *Marion Brésillac in India* (1991) and *Mission to West Africa,* vol. 1 (1991); Patrick Gantly and Ellen Thorp, *For This Cause* (1992); Edmund H. Hogan, "Marion Brésillac's Views on Mission," *SMA Bulletin,* no. 86 (June 1992): 18–26.

Edmund M. Hogan, SMA

Marks, John Ebenezer (1832–1915), Anglican educational missionary in Burma (Myanmar). Marks was born in London and taught in its East End before offering himself to the Society for the Propagation of the Gospel for service in Burma in 1859. After three years of lay service at Moulmein, Burma, he prepared for ordination at Bishop's College, Calcutta, and was ordained in 1863. He worked at Rangoon and then moved to Mandalay in 1868, the capital of Upper Burma, where his school was attended by nine of the sons of the king, Mindon Min. John Lawrence, viceroy of India, had advised against this move, but Marks retained the king's favor between 1868 and 1874. In 1874 it was withdrawn, probably because Marks proved no help in strengthening the king's hand with the British. Marks returned to Rangoon, where he developed St. John's as a school of high reputation, modeled on the methods of Thomas Arnold of Rugby. Marks carried on after the British annexation of Burma in 1885. In 1898, having become one the greatest of all educational missionaries, he returned to England because of failing health.

BIBLIOGRAPHY John E. Marks, *Forty Years in Burma* (1917). J. McCleod Campbell, *Christian History in the Making* (1946); H. P. Thompson, *Into All Lands* (1951).

Timothy Yates

Marmoiton, Blaise (1812–1847), French Marist brother martyred in New Caledonia. A gentle and devoted French lay brother of the Society of Mary from Yssac-la-

Tourette, Puy-de-Dôme, Marmoiton went in 1843 with the Marist bishop Guillaume Douarre, his former parish priest, to found the first New Caledonian Catholic mission station at Balade. He learned the language from attentive neophytes. Covetous and alienated local clans repeatedly threatened the mission house, and in 1847 it was attacked, looted, and burned. Although his confrères escaped, Marmoiton was lamed and speared, lagged behind, and was finally beheaded. Rome has admitted his cause for beatification as a martyr.

BIBLIOGRAPHY V. Courant, *Le Martyr de la Nouvelle-Calédonie, Blaise Marmoiton...* (1931); Georges Delbos, *L'Église Catholique en Nouvelle-Calédonie* (1993); John Garrett, *To Live among the Stars: Christian Origins in Oceania* (1982); Claude Mayet, *Le Premier vicaire apostolique de la Nouvelle-Calédonie...* (1879); Ralph M. Wiltgen, *The Founding of the Roman Catholic Church in Oceania, 1825 to 1850* (1979).

John Garrett

Marquette, Jacques (1637-1675), French Jesuit missionary explorer, linguist, and pastor to the Algonquian Indians. Born of a wealthy family in Lyon, France, Marquette attended the Jesuit College at Reims from age 9 to 17, entered the Society of Jesus in 1654, and volunteered for the Canadian mission, where he was sent following his ordination in 1666. His first assignment was to the mission-related Indian settlement of Sillery, in Quebec, where he grew close to the local Algonquian Indians and learned their language. Linguistically gifted, he became fluent in seven Algonquian languages. In 1668 he traveled up the Ottawa River, then down the French River to Georgian Bay and west to Sault Sainte Marie, where another mission was located. Here he met a Shawnee captive and listened eagerly to him speak about his country to the south. In 1673 Marquette set out with explorer Louis Joliet southward on Lake Michigan and with the help of an Illinois Indian taken slave by the Odawas and their allies, began his famous journey down the Mississippi River. He traversed the Mississippi as far as the mouth of the Arkansas River and came to the conviction that the river flowed all the way into "Florida" and to the gulf to the south. He records his declining health (he probably suffered from amoebic dysentery) beginning in 1674 but continued his ministry as energetically as possible. The party returned to the southeastern shore of Lake Michigan in 1674, where Marquette died. Not content with the conventional burial given to him, his native flock eventually exhumed his body and gave it an appropriate aboriginal-style interment, drying his bones and placing them in a birchbark casket.

Marquette accomplished much in his short life; his writings and reports are of missiological, ethnological, historical, geographical, and horticultural value. His own mission methods would today be described as "adaptation" and perhaps "functional equivalence." He was loved by his flock and left the reputation of being a sensitive and conscientious pastor. He was said to have been a fine teacher when still in France, to have had a joyous and enthusiastic temperament, and to have become a superb preacher who successfully adopted the style of Amerindian oratory.

BIBLIOGRAPHY Joseph P. Donnelly, *Jacques Marquette, SJ, 1637-1675* (1968; contains valuable bibliography); Reuben Gold Thwaites, *Father Marquette* (1898); Reuben Gold Thwaites, ed., *Jesuit Relations and Allied Documents,* vol. 57, pp. 244-263 and vol. 59, pp. 86-211 (1959). Vol. 59 contains Marquette's journal.

Carl F. Starkloff, SJ

Marsden, Samuel (1764-1838), apostle to the Maori. Born at Bagly, Yorkshire, England, Marsden was educated at Hull Grammar School under Joseph Milner and at Cambridge University, where he became a friend of Charles *Simeon. On the recommendation of William *Wilberforce, he was appointed assistant chaplain to the colony of New South Wales (NSW), Australia. He had a vision, acquired from Simeon at Cambridge, of the Christianization of the South Sea Islands. Arriving in the colony in March 1794, he became one of the best-known evangelical missionaries in Australia. Marsden and other evangelicals largely failed in attempts to evangelize convicts and Aboriginal people but their labors among the Polynesian peoples of the South Sea Islands bore significant results.

In 1798 Marsden extended hospitality to eleven London Missionary Society (LMS) missionaries who had fled from Tahiti. In 1804 he was appointed LMS agent in the South Sea Islands. In February 1810 a second group of LMS missionaries arrived in NSW, again dislodged from Tahiti. Marsden encouraged them to persevere with the Tahiti mission until, within a few years, King *Pomare became a Christian and the entire population converted to Christianity.

On a visit to England in 1807, Marsden appealed to the Church Missionary Society for a civilizing mission to the Maori in New Zealand, and in 1814 the mission was finally launched along lines recommended by him. Marsden arrived on December 20 and on Christmas Day, 1814, he preached the first sermon in New Zealand. He made seven voyages to the New Zealand mission, the last when he was over 70 years of age, lame, and almost blind. He was called Flogging Parson from his time as a magistrate issuing punishment to convicts, disqualifying him from admiration in the popular history of Australia. But among evangelicals his counsel was always sought and usually respected. For three decades his name appeared in the minutes of CMS with more frequency than that of any other individual.

BIBLIOGRAPHY Published primary material on Marsden includes J. B. Marsden, ed., *Memoirs of the Life and Labours of the Rev. Samuel Marsden of Paramatta* (1858), John Rawson Elder, ed., *The Letters and Journals of Samuel Marsden, 1765-1838* (1932), and George Mackaness, *Some Private Correspondence of the Rev. Samuel Marsden and Family, 1794-1824* (1942). Biographies include S. M. Johnstone, *Samuel Marsden: A Pioneer of Civilization in the South Seas* (1932) and A. T. Yarwood, *Samuel Marsden: The Great Survivor* (1977). Manuscript material is in the Mitchell and Moore College libraries in Sydney, the Hocken Library in Dunedin, and the CMS archives in the Univ. of Birmingham.

Stuart Piggin

Marshman, Hannah (Shepherd) (1767-1847), mother of the Serampore Mission. Born in Bristol, England, Shepherd became a Baptist, married Joshua *Marshman, and urged him to develop proficiency as a schoolteacher and preacher instead of immigrating to America. Called to missionary service by the Baptist Missionary Society in 1799, they arrived in Bengal and promptly set up a residential school to raise financial support for the Serampore Mission family. Given her strong character and indefatigable commitment to Christian service, Hannah Marshman became a vital pillar of support to her family of six, to William *Carey's turbulent family, to a series of missionary widows, and to many orphans (both native and missionary) over many years. She managed scores of domestic servants from many castes, organized elementary schools for native girls, and ran a girls' boarding school for Anglo-Indians. She served industriously for 47 years in Bengal, outliving the rest of the first generation of Baptist missionaries to India.

BIBLIOGRAPHY Sunil Kumar Chatterjee, *Hannah Marshman: The First Woman Missionary in India* (1987); Rachel Voigt, "Memoir of Mrs. Hannah Marshman's Earlier Years" (BMS archives, Regent's Park, Oxford, n.d.; Voigt was Marshman's daughter).

A. Christopher Smith

Marshman, John C(larke) (1794–1877), scholar of Indian history and supporter of Serampore College. The eldest son of Joshua and Hannah *Marshman, Marshman spent many years working in Serampore's printing and publishing press before becoming editor of the *Calcutta Review*. Later he founded the first vernacular Bengali newspaper, *Samachar Darpan* (News mirror) and the first English newspaper in India, the *Friend of India*. Thoroughly at home in Bengali, Marshman was a leading British scholar of Indian history between the 1820s and 1870s. Official translator to the British government of Bengal between 1834 and 1852, he is best known to missiologists for his large two-volume work *The Life and Times of Carey, Marshman, and Ward: Embracing the History of the Serampore Mission* (1859). Although he never became a Baptist Missionary Society missionary, he voluntarily managed Serampore College after his father's death. He put his literary earnings into the institution to help it survive financially from 1837 until the BMS agreed to take it over in 1855.

BIBLIOGRAPHY J. C. Marshman, *Guide to the Civil Law of the Presidency of Fort William [Bengal]* (1848) and *The History of India* (3 vols., 1867).

A. Christopher Smith

Marshman, Joshua (1768–1837), English missionary pioneer of education and evangelism in Bengal. Born in Wiltshire, England, Marshman's passion for books took him to London, where he worked as a bookseller's porter. He returned home and took up weaving until he was appointed an elementary teacher in a church school in Bristol. After five years of part-time study at the city's Baptist academy, he applied to the Baptist Missionary Society (BMS) and was accepted for service in India. He and his family arrived at the Danish entrepôt of Serampore in October 1799. There he took steps to render the new Bengal mission self-supporting by setting up a private school for Anglo-Indian children. He managed the Serampore Mission during William *Carey's prolonged spells of duty in Calcutta. With an iron constitution and formidable drive, Marshman outlived his peers and challenged young missionary recruits to exert themselves in evangelizing India. He was a good friend of Henry *Martyn and Christopher *Anderson.

Marshman's theology and work style had a particularly Puritan slant. Unlike Carey and William *Ward, he was ever ready to contend in theological, institutional, and political defense of Baptist mission work in Bengal. This resulted in substantial pamphlet skirmishing with Raja Ram Mohun Roy and Abbé J. A. *Dubois in India, as well as with British opponents of the *Serampore Trio. Ever eager to "take all Asia for Christ," he undertook the huge task of translating the Bible into Chinese, even though he never managed to travel beyond Bengal. He was cofounder of Serampore College (1818), was responsible for most of its administration, and lectured in various theological subjects. He was the lightning rod for most of the clashes that occurred between the BMS and the Serampore Mission and participated in their formal separation in 1827. An early missiologist, he died in Calcutta at the end of the pre-Victorian mission era.

BIBLIOGRAPHY Besides polemical pamphlets, Marshman wrote *Hints Relative to Native Schools* (1816), *Thoughts on Propagating Christianity More Effectually among the Heathen* (1827), and a *Brief Memoir Relative to the Operations of the Serampore Missionaries, Bengal* (1827). He also produced an edited version of thirty-two of William Carey's letters, from the turbulent period of 1815 to 1828, under the title *Letters from the Rev. Dr. Carey* (1828). John Fenwick, *Biographical Sketches of Joshua Marshman, D.D.* (1843). A. Christopher Smith, "The Protégé of Erasmus and Luther in Heroic Serampore," *Indian Journal of Theology* 37, no. 1 (1995): 15–44. Some of Marshman's letters, papers, and publications are in the archives of the Baptist Missionary Society, housed in Regent's Park College, Oxford.

A. Christopher Smith

Marston, Sarah Hall (1813–c. 1875), American Baptist missionary in Burma. Born in Boston, Massachusetts, Marston served as a schoolteacher and governess in her early years and was active in the South Boston Baptist Church. In 1861, when Ellen Mason (see Francis *Mason) issued a call for assistance in children's education in Burma, Marston was among the first applicants to the newly formed Woman's Union Missionary Society (WUMS), and was its first commissioned missionary when she sailed from Boston in November 1861. She arrived in Burma, took charge of the school at Toungoo, and collaborated with the Moses H. Bixbys, pioneer American Baptist missionaries to the Shan peoples. With the assistance of a native Bible woman, she traveled widely and organized and taught in schools. Her time in Burma was not without difficulty. She questioned the unorthodox biblical interpretations of Ellen Mason, her supervisor, and lost the support of the Boston and Philadelphia chapters of WUMS. In

1865, she returned to the United States because of failing health. She died at Boston, having reconnected with her home church.

BIBLIOGRAPHY Not much is known directly concerning Marston. She is mentioned in the surviving records of the WUMS and in excerpted letters in its publication, *Missionary Crumbs.* Some biographical data is included in a manuscript history of WUMS in the Margaret Tenney Papers at the Billy Graham Center in Wheaton, Illinois. Her appointment to Burma is mentioned in Robert G. Torbet, *Venture in Faith: The Story of the American Baptist Foreign Mission Society and the Woman's American Baptist Foreign Mission Society, 1814–1954* (1955).

William H. Brackney

Martin, Frederick (1704–1750), pioneer Moravian missionary in the Caribbean. Born of a Silesian family, Martin was described by Count *Zinzendorf as the Apostle to the Negroes of Moravian Missions. He went to Saint Thomas in 1736 and was ordained in 1737 in absentia by Bishop David *Nitschmann. He bought Estate Posaunenberg in Saint Thomas for the church and renamed it New Herrnhut. There he organized the first Moravian congregation in the New World. Later in 1737 he baptized three slaves, which brought a storm of opposition from the local Reformed cleric, Pastor Borm, who succeeded in having Martin and three other Moravian missionaries jailed in 1738. They remained in jail until the providential arrival of Zinzendorf in 1739. The count stormed the jail, as he told the story, and demanded their release. In 1748 Martin was consecrated a bishop of the Brethren's Unity at Herrnhaag, Wetteravia, by Zinzendorf and others.

While Moravian work was started in Saint Croix in 1740 and the first converts baptized in 1744, it remained for Martin to lay a firm foundation, which he undertook on what proved to be his last trip in 1750. He suffered an attack of dysentery soon after he arrived and he lingered until February 1, when he died in his 47th year. His body is buried on the Princess Plantation, where occasional services are still held.

BIBLIOGRAPHY J. T. Hamilton and K. G. Hamilton, *History of the Moravian Church* (1967); G. Oliver Maynard, *History of the Eastern West Indies Province of the Moravian Church* (1968); C. G. A. Oldendorp, *Geschichte der Mission der evangelischen Brüder auf den caraibischen Inseln S. Thomas, S. Croix und S. Jan* (1770, 1987).

Albert H. Frank

Martin, Marie-Louise (1912–1990), missionary and theological educator in Africa. Born in Lucerne, Martin served as a Reformed Church minister in Switzerland from 1938 to 1944. In 1946 she was appointed by the Swiss Mission in South Africa to work as chaplain, minister, and teacher of religion at the Lemana Training Institution in North Transvaal. In 1957 she became a lecturer in theology at the pastoral school of Morija, Lesotho, and lecturer/reader in theology at the University in Roma, Lesotho. She defended her doctoral thesis on African messianism at the University of South Africa in 1962. In 1968 she visited the Church of Jesus Christ on Earth through the Prophet Simon Kimbangu (EJCSK) in Zaire, which had applied for membership in the World Council of Churches. Her acquaintance with the EJCSK changed her critical attitude toward African Independent Churches. After she became persona non grata in South Africa, she agreed to work with the EJCSK, and started a modest theological college in Kinshasa in 1970. It was gradually upgraded to a theological faculty. Fully devoted to the EJCSK, she trained the students theologically and spiritually, meanwhile facing increasingly worsening socioeconomic conditions. She became critically ill in 1990 and was taken to Lucerne, where she died. Her major publications were *The Biblical Concept of Messianism and Messianism in Southern Africa* (1964), and *Kimbangu: An African Prophet and His Church* (1975; German original, 1972).

BIBLIOGRAPHY André Droogers, "Kimbanguism at the Grass Roots," *JRA* 11 (1980): 188–189; Leny Lagerwerf, "Dr. Marie-Louise Martin (1912–1990): Portrait of a Missionary," in *Changing Partnership of Missionary and Ecumenical Movements: Essays in Honour of Marc Spindler* (1995), pp. 144–158 (includes a bibliography of her writings).

Leny Lagerwerf

Martin, William Alexander Parsons (1827–1916), American Presbyterian missionary in China. Martin graduated from the University of Indiana in 1846 and from New Albany (Indiana) Theological Seminary (later relocated to Chicago and renamed McCormick Theological Seminary) in 1849. In 1850 he and his wife, the former Jan VanSant, went to Ningpo (Ningbo), China, one of the five treaty ports opened to foreign residence by the Treaty of Nanking in 1842. During ten years of general missionary service in this south China port city, Martin involved himself in two major events of Chinese history. First, he went on public record to advocate to his government in four newspaper articles that it should support the Taiping Heavenly Kingdom, a large-scale revolt against the reigning Manchu government. Second, he participated actively in the American delegation that produced the Treaty of Tientsin, the second of unequal treaties between China and the Western powers, which opened the entire country to traders, diplomats, and missionaries.

After a short transition period of one year in Shanghai, Martin moved to Peking (Beijing) in 1863, and with an interruption of only three or four years, remained there until his death. During 25 of these years in Peking, although he continued to think of himself as a missionary, he worked primarily as a teacher, administrator, and translator in the government-sponsored Tong Wen Kuan (Interpreters' school), in the new Imperial University in Peking, and in a school in Wuchang, Hupei (Hubei) Province, in central China. He also filled many other roles. He was editor of *Peking Magazine,* an early Chinese reform magazine; special correspondent for the *New York Times;* adviser to the Chinese government on education and international politics; reformer; Bible translator; and author. The last ten years of his life in Peking were spent as an honorary missionary with the American Presbyterian Board.

Martin was widely acclaimed for his writings in both Chinese and English. His major Chinese book, *Tiantao Suyuan* (Evidences of Christianity), was recognized by the 1907 Centennial Missionary Conference as the single best Christian book of the century. He also wrote *Tiantao Hechiao* (Christianity and other creeds) and a seven-volume work, *Kowu jumen* (Natural philosophy). He translated into Chinese the well-known work *Elements of International Law* by Henry Eaton. His best-known works in English are *A Cycle of Cathay* (3d ed., 1900), *Siege in Peking* (1900), and *The Lore of Cathay* (2d ed., 1912).

BIBLIOGRAPHY Ralph Covell, *W. A. P. Martin, Pioneer of Progress in China* (1978); Peter Duus, "Science and Salvation in China: The Life and Mission of William Alexander P. Martin" (A.B. thesis, Harvard Univ., 1955); Norma Farquhar, "W. A. P. Martin and the Westernization of China" (M.A. thesis, Indiana Univ., 1954). See also essays by Ralph Covell in *The Westminster Theological Journal,* 1977, pp. 273–300, *American Presbyterians,* 1993, pp. 233–242, and "W. A. P. Martin," in Gerald H. Anderson et al., eds., *Mission Legacies* (1994), pp. 183–189.

Ralph R. Covell

Martines, Francesco (c. 1568–1606), Chinese Jesuit lay brother and martyr. Martines is the Italian name of Huang Mingsha; in some records he is also known as Francisco Martinez (Spanish) or Martins (Portuguese). Born in Macao, Martines joined Matteo *Ricci in Shaochow (Shaoguan) in 1589 as a brother candidate, and two years later, he and Sebastian Fernandez (Zhong Mingren) became the first two Chinese to enter the Society of Jesus. He served as a language instructor for Western missionaries and as catechist. In 1606 Martines was denounced to the Chinese authorities by an apostate Christian for being part of a supposed Jesuit-led foreign conspiracy to invade and conquer China. He died in a Canton (Guangzhou) jail after several days of brutal torture.

BIBLIOGRAPHY Joseph Dehergne, *Répertoire des Jésuites de Chine* (1973), p. 167; George H. Dunne, *Generation of Giants* (1962), pp. 31, 119; Pasquale M. d'Elia, ed., *Fonti Ricciane: Storia dell'introduzione del Cristianesimo in Cina* (1942–1949), 1: 289–293, 2: 374–379; Jonathan Spence, *The Memory Palace of Matteo Ricci* (1976), pp. 49–51; Nicolas Trigault, *China in the Sixteenth Century: The Journals of Matthew Ricci, 1583–1610,* Louis J. Gallagher, tr. (1953), pp. 467, 485–490.

Jean-Paul Wiest

Martínez, Pedro (1523–1566), Spanish Jesuit missionary in Florida. Martínez was born in Celda, Aragon, Spain. In 1565 he was named superior of a group of Jesuits who were to accompany Menéndez de Aviles on the conquest of Florida. Martínez, however, sailed several months later with another expedition. Near the Florida shore a storm separated his vessel from the fleet. He volunteered to join a landing party to search for a settlement, becoming the first Jesuit to set foot on North American soil. Another storm drove their ship from the coast, leaving the landing party stranded. As they continued along the coast, they were attacked by Native Americans. Martínez was killed; all but one of the others eventually reached safety.

BIBLIOGRAPHY John Gilmary Shea, *Catholic Missions among the Indian Tribes of the United States* (1855), p. 56; Carlos Sommervogel, *Bibliothèque de la Compagnie de Jésus* (1960), vol. 5, col. 634–635.

Achiel Peelman, OMI

Martínez Compañón y Bujanda, Baltasar Jaime (1737–1797), bishop of Trujillo, Peru. Born in Navarre, Spain, Martínez studied law, was ordained a priest in 1761, and served as rector of the University of Oñate. In 1767 Charles III appointed him a canon of the cathedral in Lima, Peru, where he held several posts including that of rector of the seminary, 1770–1779. In 1779 he was ordained bishop of Trujillo, on the northern coast of Peru. Between 1782 and 1785, accompanied by a large retinue of secretaries, sketch artists, and mapmakers, he traveled the length and width of his diocese, which covered most of northern Peru. In 1786 he published the first detailed map of the diocese, along with 1,300 sketches in nine volumes depicting the fauna, flora, and the human conditions in that vast area. A bourbon bishop par excellence, he displayed administrative skills equal or superior to those of any viceroy. During his tenure he founded six seminaries, twenty new towns for Indians, and moved seventeen other Indian towns to new sites. He also founded fifty-four primary schools and four boarding schools for Indians. In addition he established forty-one new parishes and laid out six new roads. In 1791 he was named archbishop of Bogotá and served in that capacity until his death.

BIBLIOGRAPHY José Manuel Pérez Ayala, *Baltasar Jaime Martínez Compañón y Bujanda* (1955); Rubén Vargas Ugarte, *Historia de la Iglesia en el Perú,* vol. 4 (1961).

Jeffrey Klaiber, SJ

Martini, Martino (1614–1661), Jesuit missionary, geographer, and historian of China. Martini was born in Trent, Italy. After studying at the Roman College (the Jesuit college in Rome), he volunteered for missions and entered China in 1643. By using astronomy, he determined the locations of several cities he visited. The Manchus invaded Hangchow (Hangzhou) but showed him respect and gave him a permit to stay. By 1650 a number of Chinese had become converts because of his leadership. That year he was appointed the procurator of the mission to go to Rome for discussions on the Chinese Rites issue with church officials.

En route to Europe, Martini was temporarily held prisoner by the Dutch in Batavia, but he arrived in Rome in 1654. Also that year his *Novus Atlas Sinensis* (New atlas of China) appeared, as did his study of the Manchu conquest, which was soon reprinted and translated. During his return voyage to China, he translated a Chinese historical work, which later was published in Munich. (For decades, this was the only such work translated into a Western language.) In 1659, after obtaining in Rome the 1656 decree favoring the Jesuit views of the rites, Martini returned to Hangchow, where he built a new church in 1660 and died a year later.

BIBLIOGRAPHY Martino Martini, *De bello tartarico in Sinis historia* (1654), *Novus Atlas Sinensis* (1655; the 1981 repr. includes Eng. tr.), and *Sinicae historiae decas prima* (1658). B. Bolognani, *L'Europa scopre il volto della Cina. Prima biografia di Padre Martino Martini, missionario, sinologo, geografo (1614–1661)* (1978); Franco Demarchi and Riccardo Scartezzini, eds., *Martino Martini, umanista e scienziato nella cina del secolo XVII* (1995); G. Melis, ed. *Martino Martini: geografo, cartografo, storico, teologo* (1983).

John W. Witek, SJ

Martin of Tours (c. 316–397), a patron saint of France. Born in Sabaria (now Szombathely, Hungary), Martin of Tours served 25 years with the Roman army, until 356. About this time, he had an epic encounter with a freezing beggar at Amiens, when he cut his cloak in half to share it. This led to a vision of Christ, baptism, and the religious life. He joined Hilary of Poitiers in 360 and founded a monastic community, the first in Gaul, on the site of today's Ligugé, France. Elected bishop of Tours in 371, he was an ardent missionary, reaching out to the Rhine and the Rhone, to Paris and Trier, destroying paganism, winning masses, planting monasteries, and training a clergy with a passion for holiness.

BIBLIOGRAPHY Sulpice-Sévère, *Vie de Saint Martin*, critical edition, French translation, and with commentary by J. Fontaine (1967); *Saint Martin et son temps: Centenaire du monachisme en Gaule, 361–1961* (1961). See also G. K. Van Andel, *The Christian Concept of History in the Chronicle of Sulpicius Severus* (1976).

Marc R. Spindler

Marty, Martin (1834–1896), Benedictine missionary to the Sioux Indians, abbot, and bishop. Born in Schuryz, Switzerland, Marty studied theology at the Benedictine College at Einsiedeln. He became a monk in 1855, was ordained in 1856, and after four years of teaching, came to the United States to serve as prior of the recently established Benedictine community at Saint Meinrad, Indiana.

Named abbot in 1871, he was appointed vicar apostolic of Dakota Territory in 1879. At Standing Rock, the Benedictines and other Catholic religious groups engaged in mission work among the Sioux Indians. Within five years the vicariate had established thirteen parochial schools and eighty-two churches served by forty-five priests. After the division of the territory into two states, Marty was appointed bishop of the diocese of Sioux Falls, South Dakota. His mission work entailed planting the institutional church on the frontier, encouraging immigrants to settle in the area, and especially fostering the faith of the Sioux tribe by establishing annual Indian congresses, urging them to participate in the liturgy and in parish societies. In 1890 he published his revised edition of a Catholic ritual for the Sioux. Even after he was appointed to the diocese of Saint Cloud, Minnesota (1895), he maintained his pastoral responsibility for the Dakota tribes.

BIBLIOGRAPHY M. C. Duratcheck, *Beginnings of Catholicism in South Dakota* (1943); R. Karolevitz, *Bishop Martin Marty* (1890); Joel Rippinger, "Martin Marty: Monk, Abbot, Missionary and Bishop," *American Benedictine Review* 33 (1982): 223–240; 376–393.

Christopher J. Kauffman

Martyn, Henry (1781–1812), Anglican chaplain in India and missionary to Muslims. Martyn was born in Truro, England, where his father worked as head clerk of a merchant house. After attending Truro Grammar School, he proceeded to Cambridge to read mathematics. Influenced by his younger sister, and by Charles *Simeon, he soon professed evangelical faith. He graduated (as Senior Wrangler) in 1801, also earning the Smith's Prize. In 1802 he became a fellow of St. John's. Admiration for David *Brainerd persuaded him to abandon legal ambitions for missionary service.

A curacy with Simeon at Holy Trinity Church, Cambridge, followed. Changed personal circumstances made missionary service impossible for him, so instead, he accepted a chaplain's commission with the East India Company. During the 305-day voyage to Calcutta, he studied Urdu and Bengali. Until he was posted inland, he assisted the Serampore Baptists in Bible translation work. He was chaplain from 1806 to 1809 at Dinapore and from 1809 to 1810 at Cawnpore. In both places, his refusal to regard Indians as inferior and his respect for Indian culture annoyed and alienated many of his peers. Encouraged by fellow evangelicals, he took as his main task Bible translation. With the assistance of *munshis* (translators), he produced Urdu, Arabic, and Persian versions of Scripture, thus focusing on Muslim languages. Confessing that ignorance of Islam handicapped his ability to communicate the gospel, he also "read everything [he] could pick up about Mohammedans."

Late in 1810, suffering from consumption, Martyn took a leave of absence to travel through Iran, to test his Persian translation, and to benefit from a drier climate. He hoped eventually to return to England to persuade a childhood sweetheart, who had refused an earlier request, to marry him. In Iran, he thoroughly revised his Persian translation of the New Testament, which, with the help of Sir Gore Ouseley (1779–1844), was presented to the shah. Reluctantly, Martyn also agreed to exchange tracts with the Muslim *ulema* (religious scholars), later published as his *Controversial Tracts on Christianity and Mohammedanism* (1824). Martyn died at Tocat at age 31, cared for and buried by Armenians, whose ancient church he had long admired. Martyn's ecumencial openness, his desire to implant the gospel in Indian culture, and his concern for spiritual exchange with Muslims have often been obscured by his reluctant use of polemic. Nevertheless, his legacy inspired later missionaries, such as Thomas Valpy *French and Temple *Gairdner toward a more irenic approach to Muslims and to Islam.

BIBLIOGRAPHY Henry Martyn, *Journal and Letters*, S. Wilberforce, ed. (1837). Clinton Bennett, *In Dialogue with Truth: A Critical Biography of Henry Martyn* (1994) and "Henry Martyn," in Gerald H. Anderson et al., eds., *Mission Legacies* (1994), pp.

264–270; John Sargent, *Memoir of the Revd Henry Martyn* (1819); George Smith, *Henry Martyn* (1892).

Clinton Bennett

Mashtots. *See* Mesrob.

Masih, Abdul. *See* Abdul Masih, Salih.

Mason, Francis (1799–1874), American Baptist missionary to Burma. Mason was born in York, England, the son and grandson of Baptist preachers. Apprenticed as a shoemaker, he was self-taught in mathematics, classical literature, and geography. In 1818 he immigrated to the United States and settled in Massachusetts, where, in 1825, he married Lucinda Gill (d. 1828). He studied at Newton Theological Institution (1827–1830), married Helen Maria Griggs (d.1846), applied for missionary service, and was appointed to Burma by the Baptist Board in 1829. Mason settled in Tavoy, replacing George Dana *Boardman. There he spent 22 years as a translator, mission superintendent, and seminary teacher. At Toungoo, with the cooperation of Sau Quala, a Karen, more than 6,000 converts were baptized and 126 churches begun in a ten-year period. Francis's ministry was clouded in the late 1850s when his third wife, Ellen (Ballard) claimed special revelation. Her teachings severely divided the churches and the American Baptist Missionary Union was forced to withdraw their support from 1865 to 1871. Eventually, Mason renounced his wife's declarations and rebuilt the unity of the churches in the region; this led to restoration of his appointment.

A prolific author, Mason translated Scripture into Bghai Karen and Sgau Karen and produced language aids in Pali, Burmese, and Sanskrit. He published an authoritative study on flora and fauna in Burma and was elected a member of the Royal Asiatic Society. In the early 1870s Mason traveled widely in Burma, gathering data for a second edition of his Burmese history and geography as well as writing his memoirs. He died at Rangoon.

BIBLIOGRAPHY Francis Mason, *The Karen Apostle, or Memoir of Ko Thah-byu, the First Karen Convert* (1843), *Burmah, Its People and Natural Productions, or Notes on the Nations Fauna, Flora, and Minerals of Tennasserim, Pegu, and Burmah* (1860), *A Burmese Handbook of Medicine* (1868), and *Story of a Workingman's Life, with Sketches of Travel in Europe, Asia, Africa, and America as Related by Himself* (1870). For biographical data, consult Ellen B. Mason, *Last Days of Rev. Francis Mason* (1874) and "Francis Mason, D.D.," *Baptist Missionary Magazine,* June 1874, pp. 161–164.

William H. Brackney

Massaja, Guglielmo (1809–1889), Italian Capuchin missionary in Ethiopia. Born at Piova, Massaja's baptismal name was Lorenzo. He joined the Capuchin order, receiving the name Guglielmo, and taught philosophy and theology for ten years (1836–1846) near Turin while exercising a wide ministry that included the royal family of Piedmont. In 1846 he was appointed vicar apostolic for a new Latin Rite mission in Ethiopia to be staffed by Capuchins, distinct from the Vincentian mission for the Ethiopian Rite headed by de *Jacobis. Massaja's mission was understood to be one to the "Gallas" (Oromo), the non-Christians of Ethiopia. However the division was not in reality so clear-cut. Orthodox Christian influence had affected many of the Gallas, and very few of Massaja's converts were truly of "pagan" background. Massaja himself was in theory a committed Latinizer, extolling the superior qualities of the Latin Rite, but in practice he was far more pragmatic. He adopted the Ethiopian calendar and fasting practices and did not fight against circumcision. He cooperated well with de Jacobis but was of a grander, more flamboyant character and lacked de Jacobis's deep appreciation for Ethiopian Christianity. The presence of a Latin Rite mission in Ethiopia was always problematic. He was expelled in 1861, though he managed to remain in the country secretly for two years. He returned in 1866 and established friendly relations with Menelik, King of Shoa, but was finally expelled by Emperor Yohannes in 1879 as part of an antiforeign policy. Like de Jacobis, Massaja had wisely ordained a number of young Ethiopians who secured the survival of the church in Kafa, southwest Ethiopia, where his principal work had been done.

Massaja was made a cardinal in 1884 and was encouraged by Leo XIII to write his memoirs, which he did at very great length. Massaja had always been a man at home with princes and comfortable on a public stage as well as an imaginative and determined field missionary. With a public status comparable to that of *Lavigerie, he became something of an Italian national hero, but it is unfair to see him as a conscious precursor of Italian imperialist aspirations in the Horn of Africa.

BIBLIOGRAPHY Massaja's reminiscences were published in the 12 vols. of *I miei trentacinque anni di missione nell'Alta Etiopia* (1885–1895); also see his *Memorie storiche del Vicariato Apostolico dei Galla,* Antonio Rossi, ed., 6 vols. (1984) and *Le Lettere del Cardinale Massaja dal 1846 al 1886,* G. Farina, ed. (1936). No authoritative modern biography exists; the best available is probably E. Cozzani, *Vita di Guglielmo Massaja,* 2 vols. (1943). A comprehensive bibliography may be found in A. Dalbesio, *Guglielmo Massaja, Bibliografia-Iconografia, 1846–1967* (1973).

Adrian Hastings

Massanet, Damian (c. 1660–c. 1710), Catholic founder of Texas missions. Massanet was born on the island of Majorca, Spain. After joining the Franciscan order, Massanet (sometimes known as Manzanet) arrived in Mexico in 1683 and became the head of Caldera Mission in Coahuila. Spanish interest in territory farther north was quickened in the 1680s by French exploration down the Mississippi River and their establishment of a fort on Matagorda Bay. In 1689, Alonso de Leon led an expedition to expel the French from the area, and Massanet, together with a few other priests, accompanied the train as chaplains. A Native American chief of a tribe originally called "Tejas" requested that a missionary be placed among his people. Accordingly, in 1690 Massanet built the first Spanish mission north of the Rio Grande, calling it

San Francisco do los Tejas. The site was abandoned in 1693 and its exact location is unknown, but it flourished briefly somewhere near the Neches River. Massanet returned to Mexico City and repeatedly urged the government to spread civilization and the gospel into the Tejas (Texas) region. His plan of four presidios and eight missions eventually proved feasible, and his success at recruiting thirteen associates for the work enhanced his reputation as an instigating force for missions along the northern border of the Spanish empire.

BIBLIOGRAPHY C. E. Castaneda, *Our Catholic Heritage in Texas, 1519–1936,* 7 vols. (1936–1950); J. A. Marfi, *The History of Texas, 1673–1779,* 2 vols. (1935).

Henry Warner Bowden

Massignon, Louis (1883–1962), Catholic orientalist and author of works on Islamic history and mysticism. Born in Nogent-sur-Narne (Seine), France, Massignon was interested from an early age in Arab and Oriental studies. His contact with the writings of the ninth century Muslim mystic al-Hallaj, on whom he wrote his doctoral thesis at the Sorbonne, was decisive. In 1919 he became a professor at the prestigious Collège de France in Paris. On an archaeological mission in Iraq, he was thrown into prison on suspicion of being a spy. At a moment of utter despondency he was saved from his despair by a mysterious visitor on the night of May 2, 1908. There he formulated his first prayer; that night remained for him the night of his conversion. He also felt a special call to intercessory prayer, which led to his formulation of a spirituality of "substitution" (in Arabic, *Badaliyya*). At Damietta, Egypt, in February 1934, he founded, together with Mary Kahil, an order devoted to prayer and named *Badaliyya.*

In the awareness that through his contacts with Muslims he had found the way back to his own Christian faith, Massignon desired to live this faith in a spiritual sharing and exchange with Muslims. The spirituality of the *Badaliyya* is nourished by this desire of communion in the fullness of truth and grace that has become manifest in Christ. A Catholic priest of the Byzantine rite, Massignon died in Paris where he was a professor at the College of France.

BIBLIOGRAPHY *La Passion de Hallaj, martyr mystique de l'Islam,* 4 vols. (1975) is Massignon's main work. His *L'hospitalité sacrée* contains a biography by J. Keryell, and also a selection of texts on the *Badaliyya.* Y. Moubarac, *L'oeuvre de Louis Massignon* (1972–1973) contains his complete bibliography.

Arij Roest Crollius

Masson, Joseph Armand (1908–), Catholic missiologist. Masson was born in Montegnée, Belgium, entered the Society of Jesus in September 1925, and was ordained a priest in 1938. He obtained a doctorate at the Oriental Institute in Louvain in 1943 and worked as a chaplain and missiologist in Louvain and Namur. He was professor of mission theology, missionography, and Buddhism at the Gregorian University, Rome, from 1958 to 1978. He was involved in pastoral ministry and teaching in Bujumbura, Burundi, from 1978 until his expulsion in 1985. He then continued his literary work in Belgium. His main interests are mission theology and world religions, especially Buddhism. From 1946 onward, as collaborator and successor of Pierre *Charles, he was responsible for the Louvain Missiological Week. During Vatican II he was Bishop Sevrin's theologian and in this position helped to influence the missionary decree *Ad gentes* in accordance with the ideas of the "Louvain school." At his suggestion, the phrase "preaching the Gospel" was supplemented by "and implanting the church," a meaningful compromise about the aim of missionary activity. He was consultor to Propaganda Fide and the Pontifical Council for Interreligious Dialogue. He has published more than 200 articles, some for the collection *Unam Sanctum,* with commentaries on the conciliar decrees *Ad gentes* and *Nostra aetete.*

BIBLIOGRAPHY Among the more important of Masson's books are *Missions Belges sous l'Ancien Régime* (1947), *L'attività missionaria della chiesa* (2d ed., 1967, 1968; text and commentary to *Ad gentes*), *La missione continua: Inizia un'epoca nuova nell'evangelizzazione del mondo* (1975), *Le Bouddhisme, chemin de libération* (2d. ed., 1975, 1992), *Père de nos pères* (1988), and *Mystiques d'Asie* (1992).

Karl Müller, SVD

Mateer, Calvin Wilson (1836–1908), pioneer Presbyterian missionary in Shandong (Shantung) province and founder of the first Christian college in China. A native of Pennsylvania and a graduate of Western Theological Seminary, Pittsburgh, Mateer and his wife, Julia (Brown), arrived in the treaty port of Dengzhow (P'eng-lai, or Tengchow) in 1864. Progress in the boys' school, which he and Julia started, came slowly. By 1872 Mateer had developed a three-point formula for success: all instruction would be in Chinese (not English as in the case of other mission schools); traditional Chinese education would be supplemented by the disciplines of Western science; and standards of admission were raised and Christian character was emphasized. Soon the school was known throughout China. In 1898 classes were extended to include college level, making the school the first Christian college in China. In 1904 it moved inland to the more central location of Weixian (Wei-fang, or Weihsien). A later move took the college to Jinan (Tsinan), the provincial capital. By the time of Mateer's death, graduates of Shantung Christian University (as it was finally known) were spread over sixteen provinces, serving as Christian teachers in more than a hundred schools. Another achievement was Mateer's work on a translation of the Bible into Mandarin (1907), the language spoken by the 300 million people of northern China.

BIBLIOGRAPHY Daniel W. Fisher, *Calvin Wilson Mateer: Forty-Five Years a Missionary in Shantung, China* (1911); Irwin T. Hyatt, Jr., *Our Ordered Lives Confess: Three Nineteenth-Century American Missionaries in East Shantung* (1976), and "The Missionary as Entrepreneur: Calvin Mateer in Shantung," *Journal of Presbyterian History* 49 (1971): 303–327; Robert M. Mateer, *Character Building in China: The Life Story of Julia Brown Mateer* (1912). For a history of the college, see William Purviance Fenn, *Christian Higher Education in Changing China, 1880–1950* (1976) and Jessie G. Lutz, *China and the Christian Colleges, 1850–1950* (1971).

G. Thompson Brown

Mather, Cotton (1663–1728), Puritan minister, theologian, and missions advocate. Mather, the grandson of two famous Puritan divines, John Cotton and Richard Mather, was born in Boston, the son of Increase Mather. His notable capacity for Latin, Greek, and Hebrew at age 12, and receiving his Bachelor's degree from Harvard at 16, presaged his significant contribution to New England's "progress in the gospel." In Cotton Mather's view, the Christian mission sought first to establish the "New England Israel," the extension of the gospel by the planting of the true church in Western lands, and second to convert Native Western Americans to Christian faith. A significant number of his 500 publications dealt with both aspects of the mission. Like John *Eliot, he appealed to the Great Commission of Christ, among other motives, to promote mission. He established and supported a school for the education of African Americans, condemned their ill treatment by whites, promoted their Christianization, and participated in the organization of a black religious society. He entertained blacks in his home and welcomed them by baptism into the membership of the largest New England church, Second Church in Boston, where he preached for 43 years.

His concern for the work among Native Americans was even more significant. His personal approach to them was mainly through writing books and catechisms for them, through letters and appeals to fellow colonists to further the Indian work, by his diligent service for 30 years as one of the commissioners for the Corporation for the Propagation of the Gospel, and by his personal mediation on their behalf.

BIBLIOGRAPHY Cotton Mather, *Magnalia Christi Americana: The Ecclesiastical History of New England,* 2 vols. (1853) and *Diary of Cotton Mather,* Worthington Ford, ed., 2 vols. (1911–1912). Sidney H. Rooy, *The Theology of Missions in the Puritan Tradition* (1965), pp. 242–285.

Sidney H. Rooy

Mather, Percy Cunningham (1884–1933), missionary pioneer in central Asia. Born in Fleetwood, England, the son of an Irish nurse and a railway employee, Mather followed his father into railway service. In 1903 he was converted through the ministry of J. H. Doddrell of the Wesleyan Methodist Church and became a Sunday school teacher and local preacher. When his ordination was delayed, he heard the call of the China Inland Mission (CIM) and vowed to go to China after he had financed his sisters' education. In 1910 he sailed to Shanghai, then moved upriver to Anking (Anqing) language school and afterward to Ningkwo (Ningguo) in Anhwei (Anhui) Province. Greatly influenced by Roland *Allen's book, *Missionary Methods: St. Paul's or Ours?* he volunteered to join George *Hunter in Urumchi (Urumqi), Chinese Turkestan (present-day Xinjiang Uygur Autonomous Region), arriving there in 1914. Until 1926 the two itinerated in Outer Mongolia, developing a ministry among the Mongol tribes as well as the Chinese traders and border settlers. Following intensive medical studies while on furlough in 1927, Mather concentrated on medical work and on translations, grammars, and dictionaries of Mongolian languages, but was increasingly caught up in hostilities in China, being falsely accused of political intrigue. He died of fever during the siege of Urumchi and was buried there.

BIBLIOGRAPHY Mildred Cable and Francesca French, *The Making of a Pioneer: Percy Mather of Central Asia* (1935).

E. M. Jackson

Mather, Robert Cotton (1808–1877), London Missionary Society (LMS) missionary and pioneer of newspaper evangelism in India. Although Mather had been a successful minister in a large Congregational church in York before he arrived in Calcutta in 1833, he failed to collaborate effectively with his LMS missionary colleagues. No more successful in Varanasi (Benares), in 1838 he moved to Mirzapore with Mirza John and John Hussain, two excellent evangelists who were Muslim converts. His knowledge of Hindustani, Urdu, and Hindi, as well as his wife's support, enabled him to create an effective mission, with a press for his Bible translations and popular apologetic works. His vernacular newspaper was an influence in social and religious matters because of the quality of his prose and the comparatively high literacy rate, enhanced by the LMS schools in the area. The schools and two orphanages were run by Mather's wife (a daughter of John *Philips) and his daughter, who together also developed zenana work among secluded Hindu women. Mellowing with age, Mather trained younger colleagues to carry on the work. His ministry showed that Muslims could be won to the Christian faith contrary to the received wisdom of his day. He died near London.

BIBLIOGRAPHY M. A. Sherring, *The History of Protestant Missions in India* (1875). LMS archives, Bengal-Benares Mission, CWM, SOAS, London.

E. M. Jackson

Matthews, Daniel (1837–1902) *and*
Janet (Johnston) (1848–1939), missionaries among Australian Aborigines. Daniel Matthews and Janet Johnston both left England with their families for Australia in 1853. The Matthews family opened a ship chandlery, purchasing land on the Murray River in New South Wales. Encountering the cruelly exploited Aboriginal people, Daniel befriended and championed them through newspaper articles and petitions to government. He also challenged the prevailing dogma of their inevitable extinction.

After Matthews and Janet Johnston married in 1872, they became independent missionaries, setting aside land on the Murray River for their Maloga mission ("Maloga" being the Aborigine's name for an important bend in the river). Aboriginal people sought refuge there, exchanging freedom for survival. Daniel traveled seeking financial support, while Janet served as the mission's leader. Through her gentle influence as much as Daniel's forceful preaching, many became Christians. A man of great physical and moral strength, Matthews became the target of the hostility of the local settlers and the government as a result of his denunciation of the mistreatment of the Aborigines. Persecuted on all sides, the Matthews were finally forced out in 1899. They founded another mission at Mannum, some 300 miles to the west, in South Australia, but Daniel died two years later. His gravestone bears the inscription *Maranooka* (friend). Janet struggled on alone, retiring in 1911. Their Maloga mission, renamed Cumeroogunga, remained a Christian community.

BIBLIOGRAPHY Nancy Cato, *Mister Maloga: Daniel Matthews and His Mission, 1864-1902* (1976); John Harris, *One Blood* (1990).

John W. Harris

Matthews, Thomas Trotter (1842-1928), missionary in Madagascar. Born in Aberdeen, Scotland, Matthews was influenced by the 1859 revival movement and volunteered to the London Missionary Society. He studied theology at the Congregational colleges in Manchester and Highgate and took some medical studies. He was appointed to Madagascar in 1870 as part of the reinforcement and development of the mission there that followed the accession of Rànavàlona II, the first Christian monarch, in 1868. His departure for the field was delayed by typhoid, and his later service was several times interrupted by ill health. He spent the period to 1880 as a district missionary in the Vònizòngo area, which had experienced rapid church growth. He concentrated on developing Christian understanding and quality of church life. After return from leave in 1882, he was appointed to the church at Ambàtonakànga, in the capital, Tananarive, where he went through a turbulent period during the French annexation. In Tananarive his literary work in Malagasy developed; he assisted in the revision of the Malagasy Bible and translated many other works. In addition he composed original works in Malagasy, including sermons, Bible study aids (including a substantial book on biblical archaeology), a biography of a noted Malagasy pastor, and accounts of the Scottish Covenanters and French Camisards, the latter no doubt arising from the French Catholic presence in Madagascar. Ill health forced him to leave Madagascar in 1899. He undertook deputation speaking in Scotland for the next five years, retiring in 1904 to Aberdeen, where he became a well-known figure.

BIBLIOGRAPHY T. T. Matthews, *Notes on Nine Years' Mission Work in the Province of Vonizongo, North West, Madagascar...* (1881), *Thirty Years in Madagascar* (1904), and ed., *Reminiscences of the Revival of 1859, and the Sixties* (1910). *Aberdeen University Review* 15 (1927-1928): 286-287; B. A. Gow, *Madagascar and the Protestant Impact: The Work of the British Missions, 1818-1895* (1979); J. Sibree, *Fifty Years in Madagascar* (1924) and *London Missionary Society, A Register of Missionaries, Deputations, etc....* (4th ed., 1923), no. 676.

Andrew F. Walls

Matthews, Z(achariah) K(eodirelang) (1901-1968), South African educator, politician, and ecumenist. Though his family came from Botswana, Matthews was born in Cape Colony (present-day Cape Province), South Africa. He graduated in humanities at University College of Fort Hare, South Africa, in 1924, then studied anthropology and law at Yale and at the London School of Economics under Bronislaw Malinowski. He taught at Adams High School in Natal and for 24 years was lecturer in social anthropology and native law at Fort Hare. He was active in the Council of Europeans and Africans for Interracial Harmony in Durban and with the Native Bantu Teachers' Union. In 1936, when the Native Representation Bill removed Africans from the common voter's roll, he served on the Native Representative Council and was active in the African National Congress (ANC). In 1952-1953 he was the Henry W. Luce Visiting Professor at Union Theological Seminary, New York. He also served on the royal commission that investigated higher education for Africans in Uganda, Kenya, Tanganyika (Tanzania), and Anglo-Egyptian Sudan.

At the ANC's Cradock Congress in 1953 Matthews broached the idea of "a national convention (of all races)... to draw up a Freedom Charter for the democratic South Africa of the future." His draft of the Freedom Charter was adopted in part by the 1955 congress of people. In these activities he was a collaborator with African political leaders such as Albert *Luthuli and Alphaeus Zulu. For these activities he was charged with high treason in 1956 but acquitted in 1962. From 1966 to 1968 he was Botswana's ambassador to the United States and permanent representative at the United Nations.

After involvement in the Cottesloe Consultation in 1960, Matthews served as Africa Secretary of the Division of Inter-Church Aid, Refugee and World Service of the World Council of Churches. In that capacity his report, *Africa Survey,* addressed the refugee situation created by Christian-Muslim conflict in the Sudan and the Congo crisis of 1962-1963. His efforts sensitized the United Nations to the extent of the refugee situation. In his ecumenical career he served on the planning committee of the WCC Evanston Assembly in 1954. He was also active in the All Africa Conference of Churches. At its first assembly in Kampala in 1963, he chaired the constitutional committee.

BIBLIOGRAPHY Z. K. Matthews, *Freedom for My People: The Autobiography of Z. K. Matthews,* Monica Wilson, ed. (1981) and ed., *Responsible Government in a Revolutionary Age* (1966). Willem Saayman, *A Man with a Shadow: The Life and Times of Professor Z. K. Matthews* (1996).

John S. Pobee

Matthopoulos, Eusebius (1849-1929), foremost home missionary of the Church of Greece in the twentieth century. Born in the village of Trestaina (now Melissopetra), Matthopoulos entered the monastery of Megaspylaeon at age 14. He took monastic vows at 17 and was named Eusebius. Ordained a deacon at 21, he went in 1872 to Athens to complete college. Ordained to the priesthood in 1876, he began the lifelong practice of celebrating divine liturgy daily and receiving Holy Communion. He became chaplain and spiritual director of the School of the Logos, founded in 1876 by Apostolos Makrakes, then the foremost preacher in Greece. But the government closed the school, and the Holy Synod in 1878 condemned Makrakes and his followers for "teachings of error." In 1879, Matthopoulos and other clergy were brought to trial, found guilty, and exiled. Later, the exile of Makrakes and his followers was lifted.

Matthopoulos parted from Makrakes in 1884. In 1895, he was commissioned by the Holy Synod to preach throughout Greece. Living simply and having given away his inheritance, he traveled wherever he was invited, preaching, teaching, hearing confessions, and leading many back to the church. He possessed great knowledge of the Scriptures and the church fathers, knowledge which he applied to his own life and conduct. In 1907, with several friends, he founded the Zoe Brotherhood of Theologians to carry on his work. The periodical *Zoe,* which first appeared in 1911 and continues to be published, was intended to reach those who could not be reached by the spoken word. Such a movement was unknown to the Church of Greece. He was called before the Holy Synod twice and exonerated both times. The brotherhood expanded rapidly in the last years of his life. The Zoe movement has had a profound effect on the spiritual life of the Church of Greece and in reviving the practice of frequent Holy Communion.

BIBLIOGRAPHY Works by Eusebius Matthopoulos include *The Passion of the Lord* (1893), "Commentaries on the First 28 Psalms," *Agape* (1895–1897), "Commentaries on Epistles of St. Paul," *Zoe,* and *The Destiny of Man* (1913). Theophilos Kanavos, *Eixan Potami Ta Trestaina* (A river from Trestaina): *Archimandrite Eusebius Matthopoulos* (1989); Elia Mastrogiannopoulos, *Skapaneis Tou Evangeliou* (Workers of the gospel) (1994), pp. 55–94; Serafim Papakosta, *Eusebius Matthopoulos, Founder of Zoe* (1930), Eng. trans. by A. Massaouti (1939); Panayiotis Trembelas, "Eusebius Matthopoulos," in *Religious and Ethical Encyclopedia,* vol. 8 (1966; in Greek).

Dimitrios G. Couchell

Maturana, Margarita Maria (1884–1934), founder of the Mercedarian Sisters as a missionary order. Born in Spain, Maturana entered the convent of the Mercedarian nuns at Berriz in 1903. She served as principal of the girls' school, forming a missionary association for the students. Even before being elected superior of the Berriz motherhouse in 1927, she had been the driving force of the movement to transform the Mercedarians into a missionary order. Founded in the thirteenth century to ransom captives from Muslims, the Mercedarians had evolved into a cloistered order in which the sisters vowed to spend their entire lives. But with papal approval, the Mercedarians began sending their sisters overseas. In 1926 six sisters were sent to China. Within the next two years other groups of sisters left for Micronesia, and a band later set out for Japan. The Mercedarians of Berriz adopted a new constitution and were formally approved as a missionary institute in May 1930. Mother Margarita was elected the first superior general of the new institute the following year. For the few remaining years of her life she dedicated herself to expanding the missionary work of the Mercedarians. By the mid-1990s, Mercedarian sisters worked on four continents. Mother Margarita died of cancer.

BIBLIOGRAPHY Pedro Lamet, *La Buena Noticia de Margarita* (1977); Manuel Sancho, *La Madre Margarita Maria Maturana: Angel de Caridad* (1945); Jose Zameza, *Una Virgen Apostel* (1959). Mother Margarita's major writings, including the diary she kept during her missionary journeys, can be found in *Viaje Misionero: Alrededor del Mundo* (1960).

Francis X. Hezel, SJ

Maunsell, Robert (1810–1894), pioneer Church Missionary Society (CMS) Bible translator in New Zealand. An Irishman, Maunsell graduated from Trinity College, Dublin, with honors in classics. He attended the Church Missionary College at Islington, near London, and was ordained deacon in 1833 and priest in 1834. He arrived in New Zealand in 1835 and supervised pioneering mission work in the Waikato area, becoming archdeacon in 1859. An advocate for education, he set up boarding schools at Maraetai and Kohanga. Recognized as the preeminent CMS scholar in Maori, he served on Bishop G. A. *Selwyn's translation committee. He was responsible for the translation of the Old Testament completed in 1857 and involved in the revisions of the Bible published in 1868 and 1887. However, his idiomatic classical translation was criticized by some as too far removed from everyday Maori. During the Waikato War in 1863, he moved his family to Auckland, where he served as a military chaplain and as vicar of St. Mary's of Parnell. He was archdeacon of Waitemata from 1868 to 1870 and of Auckland from 1870 to 1883. He and his first wife, Susan (d. 1851), had seven children, and he and his second wife, Beatrice (d. 1864), had three.

BIBLIOGRAPHY Helen Garrett, *Te Manihera: The Life and Times of the Pioneer Missionary Robert Maunsell* (1991). Maunsell's papers are held by the CMS (available on microfilm) and the Hocken Library, Univ. of Otago, Dunedin, New Zealand.

Allan K. Davidson

Ma Xiangbo (1840–1939), Chinese Catholic patriot and educator. Ma was born into a well-to-do Catholic family of Kiangsu (Jiansu) Province that had been Christian since the mid-seventeenth century. At baptism he received the name of Joseph. By age 11 he had mastered the Chinese classics and later received a thorough Western education from French Jesuits in Shanghai. In 1876 he began an impressive career as a consultant in the private and public sectors. He also became a personal advisor to the grand secretary and superintendent of trade on matters of foreign relations and Western technology. He was sent on several economic missions abroad.

In 1896 the drowning of his wife and youngest child in a boating accident and his disillusionment with political life caused him to reassess his values and priorities. He decided to concentrate his efforts in higher education. He wanted to promote institutions where Chinese and Western culture could meet and lay a sound cultural and spiritual foundation for China's modernization. In 1903 he founded Aurora as a Roman Catholic university in Shanghai, which soon fell under the control of the French Jesuits; he then founded Fudan University (1905), a secular institution. Together with *Ying Lien-chih, he was also instrumental in creating Fu Jen Catholic University, which opened in 1927 in Peking (Beijing). He also laid the foundation of the Central Research Academy, which opened in 1928 in Beijing.

Ma was a prolific writer. His religious Chinese translations include the Gospels, Pope *Benedict XV's encyclical *Maximum illud,* and St. *Thérèse of Lisieux's *Story of a Soul.* Following the Japanese invasion of 1931, the elderly Ma relentlessly urged Chinese people to unite and resist. In 1938 he fled to Kueilin (Guilin), Kwangsi Chuang (Guangxi), and then to Vietnam, where he died. The Shanghai municipal government, in 1952, brought his remains from Vietnam to Shanghai, where he is now buried.

BIBLIOGRAPHY Fang Hao, *Ma Xiangbo xiansheng wenji* (Writings of Ma Xiangbo) (1947); Ruth Hayhoe, "A Chinese Catholic Philosophy of Higher Education in Republican China," *Tripod* 48 (December 1988): 16–21, and "Towards the Forging of a Chinese University Ethos: Zhendan and Fudan," *China Quarterly* 94 (June 1983): 323–341; Ruth Hayhoe and Lu Yonglin, eds., *Ma Xiangbo: The Mind of Modern China, 1840–1939* (1996).

Jean-Paul Wiest

Mayhew, Experience (1673–1758), New England Congregational missionary to the Indians of Martha's Vineyard in Massachusetts Bay Colony. The fourth in as many generations of his family to minister to the Massachusett Indians on Martha's Vineyard, Mayhew began preaching in 1694 to five or six congregations of both Indians and English. Having grown up on the Vineyard, he was proficient in the Massachusett language. Consequently, the commissioners of the Society for the Propagation of the Gospel in New England, a missionary organization based in London, assigned him the task of producing new Massachusett translations of the Psalms and the Gospel of John, which were published in 1709. Mayhew also oversaw the translation of major Puritan devotional works and published several books containing the spiritual testimonies of Indian converts. In recognition of his accomplishments, he received an honorary M.A. from Harvard College in 1723. Mayhew was a stringent advocate for the Massachusett to the colony's General Court, presenting petitions for self-government and exposing forged deeds to Indian lands.

Mayhew condemned the preaching of George *Whitefield and other itinerants during the Great Awakening of the 1740s, largely because of fears that antinomian notions of direct revelation would take hold among the Massachusett.

BIBLIOGRAPHY Experience Mayhew, *Massachusee Psalter* (1709), *A Discourse Shewing that God Dealeth with Men as with Reasonable Creatures* (1720), and *Indian Converts; or, Some Account of the Lives and Dying Speeches of a Considerable Number of the Christianized Indians of Martha's Vineyard* (1727). *Sibley's Harvard Graduates,* vol. 7 (1943), pp. 632–39; William B. Sprague, *Annals of the American Pulpit,* vol. 1 (1857), pp. 131–33.

Kenneth Minkema

Mayhew, Thomas, Jr. (1621–1657), New England Puritan settler and Congregational missionary to the Massachusett Indians of Martha's Vineyard. In 1641, with his father, Thomas Mayhew, Sr., Mayhew founded a Puritan settlement at Edgartown on Martha's Vineyard in Massachusetts Bay Colony, and in 1642 was ordained pastor. He quickly became interested in the natives of the island, learned their language, and began ministering to them in 1644. In contrast to the largely failed effort to create settlements of "praying Indians" on the mainland, by 1650, 100 Massachusett Indians had professed the Christian faith and received baptism; within the next decade, the number more than doubled. Mayhew wrote several tracts sponsored by the London-based Society for the Propagation of the Gospel in New England, aimed at publicizing missionary efforts in the New World. In 1649 he contributed a summary of his labors to a collection by Edward Winslow, and a few years later coauthored a work with John *Eliot, the famous "Apostle to the Indians."

Mayhew died when the ship in which he was sailing to England was lost, but he had begun a long family tradition of ministry to the Massachusett Indians on the Vineyard. His son John, grandson Experience (see Experience *Mayhew), and great-grandson Zechariah all followed in his footsteps.

BIBLIOGRAPHY Thomas Mayhew, Jr., and John Eliot, *Tears of Repentance; or, A Further Narrative of the Progess of the Gospel amongst the Indians in New England* (1653). William B. Sprague, *Annals of the American Pulpit,* vol. 1 (1857), pp. 131–133; Henry Whitfield, *The Light Appearing More and More Towards the Perfect Day* (1651) and *Strength Out of Weakness* (1652); Edward Winslow, *The Glorious Progress of the Gospel amongst the Indians in New England* (1649).

Kenneth Minkema

Mazenod, Charles-Joseph-Eugène de (1782–1861), founder of the Missionary Oblates of Mary Immaculate (OMI). Born in Aix-en-Provence of a French noble family, Mazenod immigrated to Italy in 1791, during the French revolution. In 1802 he returned to France, where he studied at Saint-Sulpice Seminary. After his ordination in 1811 he devoted himself to the poor and youth, preaching in the Provence dialect. Realizing the deep religious need caused by the French revolution, in 1816 he gathered some priests with the aim of undertaking preaching missions, thus laying the foundation for the Missionaries of Provence. In 1826 the society received papal approval and also the new name of OMI. Leo XII asked Mazenod first to promote religious renewal in France. In 1832 he was appointed auxiliary bishop of Marseilles, and in 1837 bishop, as he spared no effort in restoring and reorganizing the diocese. He awakened Christian life in Provence through numerous missions to the people and took special care in training new generations of priests. He invited nine religious congregations of men and twenty-four female orders to support his efforts.

Ever since 1818, when Mazenod had written the first rules and constitution of the OMI, he had wanted to send missionaries to foreign missions. Membership of the congregation began to increase after 1841, when Mazenod accepted missions in Canada and later also in Ceylon (1847) and South Africa (1851). Mazenod also wrote "Instruction on Foreign Missions," and his letters to the missionaries reveal his passionate interest in their work of evangelization and concern for their personal well-being. In 1975 *Paul VI celebrated his beatification, proposing him as a model for missionaries. *John Paul II canonized him in 1995.

BIBLIOGRAPHY Yvon Beaudoin, *Bx de Mazenod, lettres aux correspondants d'Amérique, 1841–1860,* 2 vols. (1977; Eng. tr., 1978–1979), *Lettres aux correspondents de Ceylan et de Afrique, 1847–1860* (1979; Eng. tr., 1980), and *Lettres à la S. Congrégation et à l'Oeuvre de la Propagation de la Foi, 1832–1861* (1981; Eng. tr., 1982). *Kerygma* 9 (1975) is a special issue dealing with Mazenod's missionary vocation. Jean Leflon, *Eugène de Mazenod, évêque de Marseille, fondateur des missionnaires Oblats de Marie Immaculée,* 3 vols. (1957–1965, Eng. tr. 4 vols., 1961–1970); Martin Quéré, *Monseigneur de Mazenod, évêque de Marseille, fondateur de la Congrégation des Missionnaires Oblats de Marie Immaculée et les Missions Etrangères* (1960).

Willi Henkel, OMI

Mazzuchelli, Samuel (1806–1864), Italian missionary in the United States. Born in Milan, Mazzuchelli entered the Order of Preachers, or Dominicans, at age 17. After initial studies, in 1828 he was sent to the frontier Diocese of Cincinnati, which embraced what are now Ohio, Michigan, and Wisconsin. Assigned to the northern wilderness, he preached the gospel and pleaded for justice for the Indians as they were being removed from ancestral lands. In 1835 he was sent to the upper Mississippi valley, where he formed Christian communities among the settlers and helped establish their first churches. By 1844 he had founded a college for men at Sinsinawa Mound in southwestern Wisconsin; he also opened a girls' academy, which led to the founding of two colleges for women. In 1847 he formed the Sinsinawa Dominican Sisters, who have numbered more than 3,000 members in the service of the church. Mazzuchelli became a leader among all the people of the region, who called him to civic as well as religious service. He died in Benton, Wisconsin, mourned by Catholics and Protestants. Six generations have kept alive the memory of his faith, courage, and charity. In July 1993 he was given the title "Venerable," a first step toward canonization.

BIBLIOGRAPHY Samuel Mazzuchelli, *Memorie . . . d'un Missionario Apostolico* (1844), which concerns 13 of his 36 years in the United States, was translateed by Maria Michele Armato and Mary Jeremy Finnegan as *The Memoirs of Father Samuel Mazzuchelli* (1967). Mary Nona McGreal, *Samuel Mazzuchelli O.P., A Kaleidoscope of Scenes from His Life* (1973, 1994); Milo Quaife, "Reverend Samuel Charles Mazzuchelli," *Wisconsin: Its History and Its People* (1924). In 1989 the Vatican produced a documentary, *Positio super Vita, Virtutibus et Fama Sanctitatis.*

Mary Nona McGreal, OP

Mbulu, Joeli. *See* Bulu, Joeli.

McBeth, Sue L. (1830–1893), Presbyterian missionary among the American Indians. Born in Scotland, McBeth moved to Wellesville, Ohio, as a young child. After study at Steubenville Female Seminary, she taught school briefly in Fairfield, Iowa. In 1860 she joined the Presbyterian missionaries at work among the Choctaws in Indian Territory (Oklahoma). There she taught the older girls in a boarding school and began work on a history of the mission. When the Civil War forced the closing of the school, she worked as a nurse in a military hospital, an experience she recorded in *Seed Scattered Broadcast: or, Incidents in a Camp Hospital* (1871). She also served for ten years as a city missionary in Saint Louis, Missouri. Her greatest contribution to missions came when she again labored under the auspices of the Presbyterian Board of Foreign Missions. From 1873 until her death, she worked among the Nez Percé Indians, assisted much of the time by her sister, Kate McBeth. Their work was dedicated to the training of young men for the ministry. Sue McBeth also produced the *Dictionary and Grammar of the Nez Percé Language* (1893), which was published by the Smithsonian Institution upon her death.

BIBLIOGRAPHY Michael Coleman, "Christianizing and Americanizing the Nez Percé: Sue L. McBeth and Her Attitudes to the Indians," *Journal of Presbyterian History* 53 (1975): 339–361; Kate C. McBeth, *The Nez Perce since Lewis and Clark* (1908). McBeth's correspondence is included in the American Indian correspondence collection maintained by the Presbyterian Historical Society in Philadelphia, Pa. Portions of her diary are among the Indian Archives of the Oklahoma Historical Society.

Lydia Huffman Hoyle

McCandliss, Henry M. (1859–1931), pioneer medical missionary to Hainan, China. McCandliss was born in Mt. Pleasant, Iowa, and graduated from the Jefferson Medical College in Philadelphia in 1885. Responding to an appeal for medical students to become missionaries to China, he applied to the Presbyterian Board of Foreign Missions and was assigned to Canton. In 1885 the Canton mission sent McCandliss, Frank P. *Gilman, and C. C. Jeremiassen, a Danish seaman, to Hainan Island to open a new station. In 1888 McCandliss married Olivia Kerr, daughter of John G. *Kerr, a Presbyterian missionary doctor in Canton, Kwangtung, (Guangdong). Their three children served as missionaries in China. McCandliss established a hospital at Hoihow (Haikou) on the northern coast of Hainan. He was a member of the China Medical Missionary Association and frequently represented the Hainan mission at meetings of the Presbyterian China Council, which decided policy matters. He retired from the mission in 1925 and died in Pasadena, California.

BIBLIOGRAPHY Kathleen L. Lodwick, "Hainan in Missionary Eyes in the Late 19th Century," *American Asian Review* 9 (Summer 1991): 54–69; Margaret Moninger, ed., *Isle of Palms: Sketches of Hainan* (1919, 1980).

Kathleen L. Lodwick

McCartee, Divie Bethune (1820–1900), medical missionary, educator, and U.S. diplomat in China and Japan. Born in Philadelphia, McCartee entered Columbia University, New York, at the age of 14 and graduated from the University of Pennsylvania Medical School at 20. Arriving in Ningpo in 1844 under the Presbyterian Board, he was probably the first Protestant missionary, and certainly the first physician, to reside on Chinese soil following the First Opium War. (See also Peter *Parker.) In addition to his medical work, he became an adviser and interpreter for American officials and was later vice-consul in Chefoo (present-day Yantai) and Shanghai. In this capacity he helped persuade the "Heavenly King" of the Taipings to promise "non-molestation not only to Americans and Christians, but to all Chinese in their employ."

On a Chinese government assignment to Japan, McCartee remained in Tokyo as professor of law and science at the Imperial University (now Tokyo University), curator of the botanical gardens, and later secretary to the Chinese Legation there. In 1879 he advised General Ulysses S. Grant, the former U.S. president, mediating on the Loochoo (Ryukyu) Islands, although both China and Japan rejected his compromise. From 1885 to 1887 McCartee served as counselor to the Japanese Legation in Washington. After this he was reappointed by the Presbyterian Board as a missionary to Japan. He died in San Francisco.

BIBLIOGRAPHY Carole Ann Duff, *Christianity, Science, and Society: Two Nineteenth-Century American Missionaries in the Far East* (1977); Robert E. Speer, ed. *A Missionary Pioneer to the Far East: A Memorial of Divie Bethune McCartee* (1922).

Creighton Lacy

McCaul, Alexander (c. 1799–1863), missionary to Jews. McCaul was a British scholar of Hebrew and Judaism who became professor of Hebrew and rabbinical literature at King's College, London. The *Encyclopaedia Judaica* lists him as one of the great Christian Hebraists. McCaul desired passionately to see Jewish people come to Christ. In 1821 he was recruited by Lewis *Way to work for the London Jews' Society (LJS), and he established a mission in Poland which was still flourishing on the eve of World War II. He later became the society's principal agent in London and was offered appointment as first Protestant bishop in Jerusalem in 1841. Instead, he convinced the LJS to choose a Jewish believer and then preached at the consecration of Michael Solomon *Alexander.

McCaul supported the Reform movement in Anglo-Jewry because he hoped it would pave the way for a wholesale turning from Judaism to the gospel. He wrote several major missionary books, the most important being *The Old Paths,* in which he presented his views of Judaism, producing an apologetic and polemic almost without rival in its ongoing influence among many missions to Jews. He rejected any notion of continuity between Christianity and Judaism and insisted that "converts" abandon everything Jewish. The tide of thinking was changing, however, and his type of confrontationist attitude and antithetical theology was soon to be challenged. McCaul therefore marked the end of an era in Jewish missions.

BIBLIOGRAPHY Alexander McCaul, *The Old Paths, or, A Comparison of the Principles and Doctrines of Modern Judaism with the Religion of Moses and the Prophets* (1837) and *Lectures on the Prophecies Proving the Divine Origin of Christianity* (1846). David Feldman, "Popery, Rabbinism, and Reform: Evangelicals and Jews in Early Victorian England," in Diana Wood, ed., *Christianity and Judaism* (1992); W. T. Gidney, *The History of the London Society for Promoting Christianity amongst the Jews* (1908).

Walter Riggans

McClure, W(illiam) Don(ald) (1906–1977), American Presbyterian missionary in Africa. Born in Blairsville, Pennsylvania, McClure began teaching in Khartoum, Sudan, in 1928 after graduating from Westminster College, New Wilmington, Pennsylvania. Returning for study at Pittsburgh Theological Seminary, he and his wife, Lyda (Boyd), went back to Sudan in 1934 to evangelize among the Shulla people at Doleib Hill. In 1938 he initiated a new mission to the Anuak people at Akobo on the Sudan-Ethiopia border. The Anuak project was designed to employ a large missionary staff for a limited period. Thus a team of specialists in education, agriculture, medicine, and evangelism expected to work for 15 years to foster a self-sustaining, self-governing, self-propagating Anuak church. Interrupted by World War II, the Akobo mission became so successfully established that in 1950 the McClures were able to open new work among the Anuaks of Ethiopia at Pokwo ("village of life"). After 1960 he directed the Gilo River station while living in Addis Ababa and was serving as general secretary of the American (Presbyterian) Mission when the emperor of Ethiopia, Haile Selassie I, requested a replication of his Anuak project on the Somali border. At Gode, McClure was shot to death by guerrillas. McClure's half-century in Africa spanned dugout canoes to jet boats. Geographically, his relentless missionary pilgrimage covered a 1,250-mile arc through Sudan and Ethiopia.

BIBLIOGRAPHY Charles Partee, *Adventure in Africa: The Story of Don McClure* (1990).

Charles Partee

McCoy, Isaac (1784–1846), American Baptist missionary to Native Americans. Born in Fayette County, Pennsylvania, McCoy was raised on the frontier in Indiana Territory and received no formal education. He was ordained at Silver Creek, Indiana, Baptist Church; for seven years he was pastor at Maria Creek Baptist Church. He took an interest in the Indian tribes of the Old Northwest (later, Northwest Territories; region around the Great Lakes) and in 1817 offered himself to the Baptist Board of Missions. Stationed at Fort Wayne, Indiana, he received a one-year appointment to work with the Miami tribe in Illinois and Indiana. In 1822 he moved to Michigan to become a government teacher with the Potawatomies; he named his station after William *Carey in the hopes of gaining greater attention for his efforts. When the U.S. government determined to remove the Indians to lands beyond the Mississippi River, McCoy supervised the process. He advocated establishing an Indian Territory that would be free from white encroachment. Once in Kansas Territory, he set up schools and model farms among the Delawares and Shawnees, the two tribes assigned to the Baptists. When Baptist Board support for McCoy's work waned in the 1840s, he organized the American Indian Mission Association to unite all Baptists behind his programs. Ultimately, when the Southern Baptist Convention began its domestic mission program in 1846, McCoy transferred his affiliation to that convention.

BIBLIOGRAPHY McCoy wrote a few tracts, of which two are noteworthy: *History of the Baptist Indian Missions* (1840) and *Address to Philanthropists in the United States Generally and to Christians in Particular, on the Conditions and Prospects of the American Indians* (1831). E. J. Lyon, *Isaac McCoy: His Plan of and Work for Indian Colonization* (1945); George Schultz, *An Indian Canaan: Isaac McCoy and the Vision of an Indian State* (1972); Timothy S. Smith, *Missionary Abominations Unmasked* (1833). There is a biographical sketch in William H. Brackney, *The Baptists, with a Biographical Dictionary* (1988).

William H. Brackney

McCully, Edward. *See* Elliot, Philip James ("Jim").

McDonald, Alexander (1837–1911), Canadian Baptist home missionary. McDonald was born at Osgoode, Ontario, the third son of James McDonald and Ann (McLean), Scottish immigrant homesteaders. He graduated from an academy in Brockville, Ontario, and finished secondary school in Morrisburgh, New York. For a time he studied at Madison University, Hamilton, New York; later he graduated from Canadian Literary Institute, Woodstock, Ontario. At the institute, McDonald became close friends with John MacLaurin and Robert A. Fyfe, leading missionary enthusiasts; both deeply influenced his thinking as a missionary. After his first pastoral ministry at Sparta, Ontario, which concluded in 1873, McDonald became a missionary to the Northwest Territories for the Baptist Home Mission Convention of Ontario and Quebec. Known as a pioneer, McDonald started congregations from Winnipeg to Edmonton. In 1880 he organized the Red River Baptist Association and in 1882 the Regular Baptist Missionary Convention of Manitoba and the Northwest; these were the first of their kind among Baptists in the Canadian West. Following his missionary work in Manitoba, McDonald moved to the United States to start Baptist work in Grafton, Dakota Territory. Returning to Canada in 1892, he was the first pastor of the Baptist Church at Fort Edmonton, Alberta, after which he pioneered the church at Leduc. In retirement he began a mission Sunday school near Edmonton, where he died.

BIBLIOGRAPHY Two secondary sources tell the frontier saga of McDonald's life: C. C. McLaurin, *Pioneering in Western Canada: A Story of the Baptists* (1939), and Theo T. Gibson, *Beyond the Granite Curtain: The Story of Alexander McDonald, Pioneer Baptist Missionary to the Canadian North-West* (1975). A scrapbook of his letters and newspaper clippings, plus fragments of his journal and diary, exist at the Canadian Baptist Archives, McMaster Divinity College, Hamilton, Ontario.

William H. Brackney

McDonald, Robert (1829–1913), Canadian Anglican missionary in the Yukon. McDonald's maternal grandmother was an Ojibway from Sault Sainte Marie, and his parents, Neil and Anne (Logan) McDonald, were Port Douglas, Ontario, farmers. He graduated from St. John's College, Manitoba, receiving ordination at the hands of David *Anderson in 1853 and proceeding to White Dog, Yukon Territory, to assume his missionary duties. He relocated to Fort Yukon in 1862 and to Fort McPherson in 1871. Shortly after his appointment as archdeacon of Mackenzie in 1875, McDonald married one of his students, Julia Kutug, a full-blooded Indian 30 years his junior. Fluent in Ojibway, French, and English, he is exemplary among missionaries of his era for his keen interest in and respectful appreciation for indigenous culture. His entire missionary career of over 40 years was spent among the Tukudh people (also known as the Loucheux and the Kutchin), into whose language he translated the whole New Testament, parts of the Old Testament and Prayer Book, some hymns, and other practical religious writings.

BIBLIOGRAPHY A. C. Garrioch and I. O. Stringer, "Robert McDonald," in W. B. Heeney, ed., *Leaders of the Canadian Church* (1920); Frank A. Peake, "Robert McDonald (1829–1913): The Great Unknown Missionary of the Northwest," *Journal of the Canadian Church Historical Society* 17 (September 1975): 54–72; Eugene Stock, *The History of the Church Missionary Society: Its Environment, Its Men, and Its Work,* 4 vols. (1899–1916). The McDonald papers are held in the archives of the Ecclesiastical Province of Rupert's Land, Winnipeg.

Jonathan J. Bonk

McDougall, Francis Thomas (1817–1886), pioneer Anglican missionary and bishop in Sarawak. Born of a military family and growing up in Malta and Corfu, McDougall trained as a surgeon in London (M.R.C.S. 1839, F.R.C.S. 1854). He studied at Oxford (B.A. 1842, M.A. 1845) and married Harriette Bunyon in 1843. The McDougalls agreed to go to Sarawak at the request of Rajah James Brooke and arrived there in June 1848. McDougall was valued for his medical and surgical skills and for some time enjoyed cordial relations with the Brooke regime. He was consecrated bishop in 1855. His wife, Harriette, became well known for her sensitive descriptions of life in Sarawak. However, controversy developed in Britain over McDougall's enthusiastic descriptions of his part in attacks on local "pirates" in 1862 and disagreements with the rajah over the disinheritance of the heir apparent the following year. The McDougalls finally left Sarawak in 1867.

Rough in manner and dress, McDougall at times used language that was more naval than episcopal. In contrast to his crass behavior, McDougall's theology was orthodox and unadventurous. He did not win the Malay converts he hoped for, but he successfully set in place the foundation of the Anglican Church in Borneo.

BIBLIOGRAPHY Max Saint, *A Flourish for the Bishop and Brooke's Friend Grant: Two Studies in Sarawak History, 1848–1868* (1985); Graham Edward Saunders, *Bishops and Brookes: The Anglican Mission and the Brooke Raj in Sarawak, 1848–1941* (1992); Brian Taylor, *The Anglican Church in Borneo, 1848–1962* (1983).

John Roxborogh

McDowell, Henry Curtis (1894–1989), African American pioneer of a black Congregational mission in Angola. McDowell was born in Epes, Alabama, and was educated at Talladega College in Alabama (B.A., 1915; B.D., 1917; D.D., 1937). He was chosen by the Colored Congregational Churches of Raleigh, North Carolina, to establish a station staffed by African Americans, in cooperation with the American Board of Commissioners for Foreign Missions (ABCFM). McDowell and his bride, Bessie Farnsville, were sent to Angola in 1919, and in 1923 they settled in the unevangelized area of Galangue. They were joined by Samuel Coles, an ABCFM agricultural-industrial missionary, and a thriving program of schools, churches, and agricultural work developed. Medical services were expanded in 1931 with the arrival of Dr. Aaron M. McMillan, who attracted many European patients as well as Africans and built a hospital and an outstanding training program for nurses and physician's assistants. In 1937 McDowell became principal of Lincoln Academy at King's Mountain, North Carolina, and in 1944 he became the pastor of the historic Dixwell Avenue Congregational Church in New Haven, Connecticut. In 1947 he returned to Angola with his second wife, Ruth, Betsy having died in 1942. Retiring from the ABCFM in 1959, he briefly occupied the Africa chair at the Kennedy School of Missions in Hartford, Connecticut, then served as founding pastor of the Church of the Open Door in Miami, Florida, until 1967.

BIBLIOGRAPHY Samuel B. Coles, *Preacher with a Plow* (1966); Lawrence W. Henderson, *Galangue* (1986) and *The Church in Angola* (1992), pp. 79–80. ABCFM *Calendar of Prayer, Annual Reports,* and *Missionary Herald* describe his years of service. McDowell's papers are held at the library of the United Church Board of World Ministries.

David M. Stowe

McDowell, Robert James (1767–1841), Reformed Church in America (RCA) missionary to Canada. Educated at Williams College, Massachusetts, McDowell showed interest in church extension and was sent by the Classis of Albany of the RCA as a missionary to Canada to work among Tories who had fled the colonies during the Revolutionary War. He started fourteen churches in Ontario, organizing three in 1798 that numbered more than 400 families of Dutch, German, and English descent. Because the Reformed Church did not send more ministers to help him, he joined the Presbyterian Church in 1819, taking eleven of the new churches with him. Several remain part of the Presbyterian Church in Canada today.

BIBLIOGRAPHY Eugene Heideman, *A People in Mission: Their Expanding Dream* (1984); *Tercentenary Studies: Reformed Church in America* (1928). See also material in RCA archives, New Brunswick Theological Seminary, New Brunswick, N.J.

Charles E. Van Engen

McFarland, Samuel Gamble (1830–1897), American Presbyterian missionary to Siam. McFarland and his wife, Jane (Hays), arrived in Siam (Thailand) in 1860. They helped open the first Protestant mission station outside of Bangkok, located in Phetchaburi, where they developed a church and operated schools for boys and girls. Unusually skilled in Thai, McFarland evangelized widely and wrote and published several books and pamphlets, including translations of parts of the Old Testament and a hymnbook. Education for girls was previously not considered necessary by Thai people, but the McFarlands organized an industrial school for females; when the mission board could supply only half the money needed for a building, King Chulalongkorn and other officials subscribed the rest. Then, in 1878, the king invited McFarland to Bangkok to establish a school for sons of nobility as a step toward instituting modern education in Thailand. McFarland resigned from the mission and became superintendent of the first successful government school in the country and an official in the Department of Education until 1894. In this role he exercised influence on a generation of Thai leaders, continuing a Christian ministry on the side. The McFarlands returned to the United States in 1896.

BIBLIOGRAPHY Bertha Blount McFarland, *Our Garden Was So Fair* (1943) and *McFarland of Siam: The Life of George Bradley McFarland* (1958); George Bradley McFarland, ed., *Historical Sketch of Protestant Missions in Siam, 1828–1928* (1928); Kenneth E. Wells, *History of Protestant Work in Thailand, 1828–1958* (1958); David K. Wyatt, "Samuel McFarland and Early Educational Modernization in Thailand, 1877–1895," in *Felicitation Volumes of Southeast-Asian Studies Presented to His Highness Prince Dhaninivat,* vol. 1 (1965).

William A. Smalley

McFarlane, Samuel (1837–1911), London Missionary Society (LMS) missionary to New Caledonia and New Guinea. Born at Johnstone, Scotland, McFarlane was a railway mechanic before he trained as an LMS missionary at Bedford, England. With his wife, Elizabeth (Joyce), he went in 1859 to the Loyalty Island of Lifou in French New Caledonia and, helped by Samoan missionaries, built on previous work of the pioneering Cook Islander missionary *Pao'o (Fao). He inaugurated the training school for Loyalty Islander pastors at Chépénéhé, where confrontations erupted between rival chiefs, Protestant and Catholic, and with neighboring French Marist missionaries. Charles Guillain, the colony's governor, sent troops to occupy Chépénéhé and counter what he saw as Anglicizing tactics implemented by Samoan turbulence. McFarlane's subsequent "paper war" directed pleas for religious liberty, through Sydney, London, and Paris, to the French emperor Napoleon III. The troops were withdrawn: the Marists and the LMS established an uneasy truce. The French insisted McFarlane should leave Lifou. He wrote *The Story of the Lifu Mission*; then, in 1871, with A. W. *Murray, took eight of his Loyalty Islander students as missionaries to the Torres Strait islands between Queensland and New Guinea. He reconnoitered the Papuan coastline and founded an industrial school on Darnley Island. In 1887 he joined the English home staff of the LMS and wrote an account of his New Guinea experiences. The University of St. Andrews gave him an honorary LL.D. He died at Southport, England, as did his wife in 1913.

BIBLIOGRAPHY Samuel McFarlane, *The Story of the Lifu Mission* (1873) and *Among the Cannibals of New Guinea...* (1888). John Garrett, *To Live among the Stars: Christian Origins in Oceania* (1982); Raymond H. Leenhardt, *Au vent de la grande terre: Histoire des Isles Loyalty de 1840 à 1895* (1957).

John Garrett

McGavran, Donald A(nderson) (1897–1990), American "church growth" missiologist. Born of missionary parents in Damoh, India, McGavran graduated from Butler University, Yale Divinity School, and Columbia University (Ph.D.) and served the Christian Church (Disciples of Christ) as an educator, evangelist, church planter, and mission executive in India. Stimulated by J. Wascom *Pickett's research of India's "mass movements" into Christian faith, McGavran wondered, "Why do some churches grow and others do not?"

This question guided twenty years of field research in varied churches and cultures in which McGavran hoped to discover the "reproducible principles" behind the effective spread of the gospel. His early conclusions were published in *The Bridges of God* (1955). In time, he became recognized within the mission community and beyond as the "Father of the Church Growth Movement." In 1965, he became founding dean of Fuller Theological Seminary's School of World Mission, contributing to a renaissance in mission studies, and particularly to the development of "mission strategy." The publication of *Understanding Church Growth* (in 1970, 1980, and 1990 editions) established MacGavran as a premier mission strategist.

McGavran's distinctive legacy involves several paradigms that are widely influential in world mission. He challenged the "mission station" paradigm that became dominant in the nineteenth century and still prevails today, in which the mission becomes largely confined to the mission compound's services and institutions and thereby arrests the development of the wider mission; he believed that mission stations should be merely a stage in a mission that leads to the indigenization of leadership and the wider expansion of the national church. He challenged the naive individualism of the Western missionary establishment which regarded only one-by-one conversions as valid; he advocated the validity of what he described as "group conversions" and "people movements" within peoples who have a group identity and make important decisions together. He advocated deploying mission personnel to what he termed receptive populations while they are receptive. McGavran perceived that Christianity spreads most naturally and contagiously within homogeneous population units, and specifically within kinship and friendship networks; he counseled churches to cooperate with these insights in reaching undiscipled people, while also nurturing believers into a wider Christian brotherhood.

McGavran believed that mission is essentially apostolic, so that evangelism and church planting are indispensable and perennial expressions of mission, though postcolonial approaches are now required. McGavran believed that "It is God's will that His Church grow, that His lost children be found."

BIBLIOGRAPHY Donald A. McGavran, *How Churches Grow* (1959), *Ethnic Realities and the Church: Lessons from India* (1979), *Momentous Decisions in Missions Today* (1984), and *Understanding Church Growth* (1970, 1980, and 1990 editions). McGavran's correspondence (before 1965) is at the Billy Graham Center, Wheaton College, Illinois; his later correspondence is at Fuller Theological Seminary, Pasadena, California. A Festschrift, edited by A. R. Tippett, *God, Man, and Church Growth,* was published in 1973.

George G. Hunter III

McGilvary, Daniel (1828–1911), American Presbyterian missionary to Siam (Thailand). McGilvary was born in Moore County, North Carolina, and graduated from Princeton Seminary. In 1858 he joined the American Presbyterian mission in Siam and, in 1860, married Sophia Bradley, daughter of Dan *Bradley. In 1861 the McGilvarys helped the Samuel *McFarlands establish a mission station in Phetchaburi, the first Protestant work outside of Bangkok. In 1867 they moved on to start the first Christian work in Chiang Mai, Laos (now northern Thailand), a semi-independent vassal state under the king of Bangkok. Initial response to the McGilvarys' evangelism was encouraging, but the prince of Chiang Mai ordered two of their converts murdered. McGilvary confronted the prince, prompting the regent for the Bangkok king to issue an edict of tolerance. This lessened persecution but did not restore the church's rate of growth. However, acceptance of the gospel in northern Thailand was still greater than around Bangkok. The McGilvarys lived and worked in Chiang Mai the rest of their lives. Until he was 70, McGilvary made repeated tours of several weeks' to several months' duration by elephant through northern Thailand, eastern Burma, northern Laos, and southwestern China, areas where people spoke languages closely related to Thai. Each stop lasted a few days or weeks, so that he could preach, teach people to read, and dispense medicine. Occasionally, small churches or even mission stations resulted from his visits. In 1898, McGilvary also established churches among the Khmu' (not a related language group) in present-day Laos. Even in the final years of his life McGilvary rode horseback to minister in churches ten or more miles away. For her part, Sophia McGilvary informally taught girls, for whom no education was available, an effort that led to establishing a mission school for them. She also contributed to literary work, including scripture translation in the Northern Thai language.

BIBLIOGRAPHY Daniel McGilvary, *A Half Century among the Siamese and the Lao* (1912). George Bradley McFarland, ed., *Historical Sketch of Protestant Missions in Siam, 1828–1928* (1928); Herbert R. Swanson, *Khrischak Muang Nua: A Study in Northern Thai Church History* (1984); Kenneth E. Wells, *History of Protestant Work in Thailand, 1828–1958* (1958). Archives on McGilvary are at Payap University, Chiang Mai, Thailand.

William A. Smalley

McKechnie, Elizabeth (1845–1939), missionary nurse in China. Born in Glasgow, Scotland, McKechnie studied nursing at the Female Medical College of Pennsylvania, in Philadelphia (later Woman's Medical College of Pennsylvania), and went to Shanghai in 1884 with the Woman's Union Missionary Society of America. In Shanghai, McKechnie worked with Elizabeth Reifsnyder at the Margaret Williamson Hospital. The hospital, which opened in 1885, was the third in China established to serve women and children exclusively, and it was financed, staffed, and administered by women. In time, other American nurses joined them, Chinese nurses were trained, and McKechnie became head nurse. In 1896 she left the hospital and the mission to marry E. H. Thomson, a prominent leader in the Shanghai American Episcopal Mission. She continued to assist the hospital with her outside connections. McKechnie retired to the United States in 1917 after the death of her husband.

BIBLIOGRAPHY *Chinese Recorder* 16 (1884): 237; *Margaret Williamson Hospital: 1885–1935* (1935); *The Missionary Link* 92, no. 6 (1961; WUMS centenary issue).

Cindy Swanson Choo

McLaurin, John (1839–1912), Canadian Baptist missionary in India. Born in Osgoode, Ontario, McLaurin graduated from the Canadian Literary Institute, Woodstock, Ontario, in 1868 and was ordained the same year at Stratford, Ontario. With A. V. *Timpany, another Canadian, McLaurin and his wife, Mary (Bates), were appointed by the American Baptist Missionary Union (ABMU) in 1869 for India. The McLaurins served at Ramapatam and later Ongole. In 1872 McLaurin, succeeding John *Clough, took charge of the extensive field at Ongole. During one year, in what became known as the Great Revival at Ongole, he baptized more than 1,500 converts. In 1874 he opened for Canadian Baptists a new field in India at Cocanada, and in 1882 founded a seminary at Samulcotta. In broken health by 1888, he returned to Canada and served as the first secretary of the Board of Missions of the Regular Baptist Foreign Missionary Society of Ontario and Quebec. From 1892 to 1907 he again served under the ABMU at Bangalore, among the Telugus. A translator and writer, McLaurin was editor of the *Telugu Baptist Magazine and Missionary Review* and secretary of the Telugu Baptist Publication Society. In 1905 he represented the Telugus at the Baptist World Alliance inaugural meetings in London. McMaster University awarded McLaurin its first honorary doctor of divinity degree in 1892.

BIBLIOGRAPHY McLaurin's translation work includes a Telugu edition of the New Testament in 1894, and he prepared a *Commentary on the New Testament, in Telugu* (1892–1912). He wrote sixteen major tracts or pamphlets in Telugu and English on subjects ranging from baptism to self-support of missions and total abstinence. For his biography, see "John McLaurin," *McMaster University Monthly,* November 1912, pp. 50–57, and "John McLaurin's Part in the Great Awakening at Ongole, Recalled by Mrs. Clough's Death," *Canadian Baptist,* September 1940, p. 10.

William H. Brackney

McLaurin, John Bates (1884–1952), Canadian Baptist missionary to Telugu-speaking people of India, and mission administrator. McLaurin was born at Samalkot, near Cocanada, in the modern state of Andhra Pradesh, India. His missionary parents served in Andhra Pradesh with the Canadian auxiliary of the American Baptist Missionary Union. He trained in Ontario, Canada, at Woodstock Literary Institute and McMaster University. Ordained in 1908, he married Mary Stillwell the following year, and from 1909 to 1939, they served in India. After Telugu language studies, the McLaurins served at Akividu, Avanigadda, and Ramapatnam, where John taught at a union seminary founded by American Baptists. Amid rapid growth in the work, he recognized the need to organize the national church. To this end, in 1926 he helped establish at Cocanada the School of Eternal Life, Jeevamruta Sala, which evolved into a high school and theological seminary. In 1934, he helped found the Protestant church council of Indian Christians.

In 1934, while on furlough in Canada, he was awarded a D.D. by McMaster University. In 1939, he accepted appointment as general secretary of the Canadian Baptist Foreign Mission Board (renamed in 1970 the Canadian Baptist Overseas Mission Board; since 1995, Canadian Baptist Ministries). Serving in this position until his death, he helped consolidate Baptist work in India and Bolivia; oversaw the transition from mission situations to partnership with national churches; and envisioned possibilities for a new field for Canadian Baptists, in Angola. He supported many voluntary societies, including the Baptist World Alliance, the Bible Society of Canada, the Canadian committee for the Christian Medical College at Vellore, the Canadian Council of Churches, the Canadian Overseas Missions Council, and the World Council of Churches.

BIBLIOGRAPHY Orville E. Daniel, *Moving with the Times* (1973); Earl C. Merrick, *John Bates McLaurin: A Biography* (1955). Personal papers and a number of pamphlets by McLaurin are in the Canadian Baptist archives, Hamilton, Ontario.

Paul R. Dekar

McNairn, A. Stuart (1873–1953), general secretary of the British Evangelical Union of South America. Born in Edinburgh, Scotland, the son of an artist, McNairn studied at Harley House Bible Institute, London. In October 1902 he answered the call to replace William Newell, who had died of typhoid, in the Regions Beyond Missionary Union mission in Cuzco, Peru. Arriving in 1904, he worked there until returning to Britain in 1911 because of his wife's health. Thereafter he served the British Evangelical Union of South America for 40 years as general secretary.

McNairn's talents lay in his graphic descriptions of missionary life and work through articles in the magazine *South America* and in twelve small books, including *Why South America?* (1936), *The Lost Treasure of the Incas* (1947), and *Intercepted Letters* (1953). He created a caring family approach among missionaries and supporters. Earlier in his career, he zealously wished to see the mission involved in holistic mission, typified by its involvement in such issues as the rubber traffic atrocities at Putumayo River (1912–1915), the struggle for constitutional religious liberty in Peru (1913–1915), and the promotion of family planning in Latin America (1920–1924). By 1927, however, he limited the mission's focus to evangelism and church planting, casting doubts on the social aspects of mission.

BIBLIOGRAPHY John Savage, "A. Stuart McNairn," *South America* 23, no. 3 (1953); G. Stewart McIntosh, *The Life and Times of John Ritchie* (1988).

G. Stewart McIntosh

McPherson, Aimee (Kennedy) Semple (1890–1944), American evangelist and founder of the International Church of the Foursquare Gospel. The daughter of James and Minnie Kennedy, McPherson was born on a farm near Salford, Ontario. Her father's evangelical Methodism and her mother's Salvation Army fervor shaped her early religious impressions. In 1908, she embraced Pentecostalism and married Robert Semple, a young Irish evangelist who had converted her. In 1910 the two sailed for Hong Kong, where they joined a small group of Pentecostal missionaries and began language study. They intended to devote their lives to missionary work in mainland China. That dream faded when Robert Semple died of dysentery and malaria barely 11 weeks after their arrival. Aimee sailed for North America with her newborn daughter, Roberta. In 1912, she married a bookkeeper, Harold McPherson. Their son, Rolf, was born in 1913. The couple began evangelistic work in 1915, but from the start, Harold McPherson felt out of place. By the time they divorced in 1921, Aimee's barnstorming evangelism had won her national recognition. With Los Angeles as her headquarters after 1918, McPherson built a religious organization, the International Church of the Foursquare Gospel, that trained and supported missionaries as well as stateside evangelists. Through her publication, the *Bridal Call*, she raised funds and gave visibility to missionary projects. In 1922, she spent several months conducting evangelistic meetings in Australia. Over the years, she made extensive trips to encourage and assist missionary outreach, several times sailing around the world. Under the leadership of her son Rolf McPherson, the organization she left behind cultivated her missionary endeavors and established particularly vigorous national churches in the Philippines, Colombia, and Brazil.

BIBLIOGRAPHY Aimee Semple McPherson, *This Is That* (1919, 1921, 1923); Edith L. Blumhofer, *Aimee Semple McPherson: Everybody's Sister* (1993), which includes a bibliographical essay; Daniel M. Epstein, *Sister Aimee: The Life of Aimee Semple McPherson* (1993).

Edith Blumhofer

Mebius, Frederick (1869–1944), pioneer Pentecostal missionary in El Salvador. A resident of Victoria, British Columbia, Mebius arrived in Latin America perhaps as early as 1906. After a period as a Bible colporteur in Bolivia, he settled in El Salvador, where he eventually gathered several congregations in the western coffee region of Santa Ana. He married locally and never returned to Canada. Anecdotal accounts suggest that his bold, impetuous manner especially endeared him to the country people. After losing some of his churches to the Assemblies of God (AG) in 1930, he affiliated the remainder with the Church of God (Cleveland, Tennessee) in 1940.

BIBLIOGRAPHY Charles W. Conn, *Where the Saints Have Trod* (1959); Roberto Domínguez, *Pioneros de Pentecostés,* vol. 1 (1975); Everett A. Wilson, "Sanguine Saints: Pentecostalism in El Salvador," *ChH* 52 (June 1983): 186–198.

Everett A. Wilson

Medhurst, Walter Henry (1796–1857), London Missionary Society (LMS) pioneer in Malaya, Indonesia, and China. Medhurst was born in London and trained as a printer. After a brief enrollment at Hackney College, London, he joined the LMS with the intention of working among the Chinese. Embarking for Malacca in 1816, he met, courted, and married Elizabeth Braun when his ship put in at Madras, and he disembarked at Malacca in 1817 a married man. Located variously at Malacca, Penang, and Batavia, he early demonstrated enviable facility in both Malay and Chinese, and in addition to his work among orphans, engaged in energetic and effective preaching and publishing ministry. With the opening of five treaty ports following the first Opium War, he settled in Shanghai in 1843, continuing there until ill health forced his return to England in 1856. The author of numerous pamphlets and several substantial reference works, including a *Chinese-English Dictionary,* Medhurst is perhaps best known for his key role in producing the groundbreaking Chinese Delegates Translation Bible, published in 1853.

BIBLIOGRAPHY Walter Henry Medhurst, *China: Its State and Its Prospects...* (1838). Richard Lovett, *The History of the London Missionary Society, 1795–1895* (1899).

Jonathan J. Bonk

Meeuwsen, Johanna (1857–1942), first single woman missionary of the Dutch Reformed Church (DRC) in South Africa. Through the solicitation of Andrew *Murray, two women—Abbie *Ferguson and Anna Bliss—went from Mount Holyoke College in Massachusetts to South Africa to establish the Huguenot Seminary for girls in Wellington, Cape Province. Born in Wellington of Dutch immigrant parents, Meeuwsen was in the first class, starting in 1874. She took an active part in a growing student missionary movement that originated under Ferguson. Before completing her course, Meeuwsen sensed God's call to go to the DRC's mission field in the northwestern Transvaal. At the beginning of 1875, together with Sarie Horak and Rev. and Mrs. Pieter Brink, she departed for the Transvaal. With Horak, she then worked at the pioneer mission station Saulspoort until 1883. They learned Setswana, started a school for children of the Batlhako tribe, and held prayer meetings and singing lessons. Many children were converted. The two teachers worked under arduous conditions and sometimes suffered malaria attacks. Growing interest in missions at the Huguenot Seminary led to the founding of the Huguenot Missionary Society in 1878. Meeuwsen was the first of many single women missionaries who were supported by the society and after 1889 by the Vrouesendingbond (Women's Mission Union) of the DRC.

BIBLIOGRAPHY D. Crafford, *Aan God die dank* (1982; history of the mission of the DRC within the Republic of South Africa and some neighboring states); J. M. Cronje, *Vroue met nardusparfuum* (1984; the contribution of women to the mission work of the DRC); W. L. Maree, *Uit duisternis geroep* (1966; the early mission work of the DRC in the northern and western Transvaal); Dana Robert, "Mount Holyoke Women and the Dutch Reformed Missionary Movement, 1874–1904," *Missionalia* 21 (1993): 103–123.

Annalet Van Schalkwyk

Megapolensis, Johannes (1601–1670), Dutch Reformed pastor in New York. Born in Keodyek, Netherlands, Megapolensis was contracted by Kitian Van Rensselaer to serve as pastor in the Albany, New York, area (1642–1649) and thereafter in New Amsterdam (present-day New York) from 1649 to 1670. In 1643 he arranged the escape of Jesuit missionary Isaac *Jaques from Indians who planned to kill him. Megapolensis had great interest in converting the Indians and often provided hospitality to them. He sought to learn the Mohawk language and customs but also continued to believe it necessary to introduce them to Western civilization. In spite of his years of effort, the cultural and religious gap remained too great; it is questionable whether he gained any converts. He died in New Amsterdam.

BIBLIOGRAPHY *Reply of Rev. Johannes Megapolensis to a Letter of Father Simon Le Moyne, 1658,* on file in Reformed Church archives, New Brunswick Theological Seminary, New Brunswick, N.J. See also Gerold G. De Jong, *The Dutch Reformed Church in American Colonies* (1978), pp. 22–27, 42–54, 149–153.

Eugene Heideman

Meinhof, Carl (Friedrich Michael) (1857–1944), leading German Africanist. Meinhof was born in Barzwitz, near Rügenwalde, Germany. He studied theology and literature in Halle and Erlangen, became a teacher, and was later pastor at Zizow for 17 years. His interest in African languages was aroused by young Africans sent to Germany from the colonies. In 1899 he published the epoch-making *Grundriss einer Lautlehre der Bantusprachen.* Applying the method of comparative linguistics to the study of African languages, he postulated an original parent Bantu language. Several articles in *AMZ* and *EMM* treated linguistic problems and stressed the importance of the knowledge of traditional religions for missionaries. He did fieldwork in Zanzibar (1902–1903), Sudan (1914), and South Africa (1927). From 1903 to 1909 he taught at the Seminar für Orientalische Sprachen in Berlin, and from 1909 he was on the staff of the Kolonialinstitut in Hamburg where he founded the *Zeitschrift für Kolonialsprachen,* later renamed *Zeitschrift für Eingeborenen-Sprachen.* In 1919 he became professor of African languages at the University of Hamburg. His research was not confined to Bantu languages but extended to the Hottentot and Bushman. Having discovered the linguistic unity of the hamitic languages, he wrote *Die Sprachen der Hamiten* (1912). He was awarded honorary doctorates by the universities of Edinburgh (law, 1910), Greifswald (theology, 1919), and Leipzig (philosophy, 1927). He died in Greifswald.

BIBLIOGRAPHY Meinhof's *Grundriss einer Lautlehre der Bantusprachen* (1899, rev. 1910) was translated into English by N. J. van Warmelo as *Introduction to the Phonology of the Bantu Languages* (1932, rev. 1984). An important follow-up study was *Grundzüge einer vergleichen den Grammatik der Bantusprachen* (1906, 2d. ed., 1948). Another important linguistic publication was *Die moderne Sprachforschung in Afrika* (1910; A. Werner, Eng. tr., *Introduction to the Study of African Languages* [1915]). Written for nonspecialists are *Christus, der Heiland auch der Naturvölker* (1907), *Die Dichtung der Afrikaner* (1911), *Afrikanische Religionen* (1912), and *Afrikanische Märchen* (1921). C. M. Doke, "The Growth of Comparative Bantu Philology," *African Studies* 2 (1943): 41–64 (particularly pp. 56–59); C. M. Doke et al., "In Memory of Carl Meinhof," *African Studies* 5 (1946): 73–81; J. Lukas, "Nachruf Carl Meinhof," *Zeitschrift für Eingeborenen-Sprachen* 34 (1943–1944): 81–93. Linguists honored Meinhof's seventieth birthday with *Festschrift Meinhof: Sprachwissenschaftliche und andere Studien* (1927).

Otto Bischofberger, SMB

Mel, Conrad (1666–1733), German Reformed theologian. Born and educated in Hesse and trained in Holland, Mel was influenced by the pietist leaders Philipp J. *Spener and August H. *Francke. In 1697 he became court chaplain of King Frederick I of Prussia and professor of theology at Königsberg, Prussia. After trying his hand at oriental and sinological studies, he followed *Leibniz's lead in conceiving a scheme of foreign missions that largely depended on the political leadership of contemporary European powers and that would be associated with the newly founded Berlin academy of sciences, of which he had become a member. However, his memorandum proposing a Protestant missionary operation, which, in his opinion, should eventually lead to a merger of all religions, remained unpublished. (Both the German and the Latin text were discovered only in the nineteenth century.) A revised printed version entitled "Missionarius Evangelicus" (1711), dedicated to the members of the Berlin academy and the British Society for the Propagation of the Gospel, also failed to attract notice. Meanwhile the Danish-Halle mission at Tranquebar, South India, successfully set an entirely different example.

BIBLIOGRAPHY Franz Rudolf Merkel, *G. W. von Leibniz und die China-Mission* (1920), pp. 174–190.

Hans-Werner Gensichen

Melrose, Margaret (Rae) (1868–1951), Presbyterian missionary to Hainan Island, China. Margaret Rae was born in Iowa. She arrived on Hainan in 1890 with her husband, John Melrose, whom she had married earlier that year; both were graduates of Lenox College, Hopkinton, Iowa. Assigned to the Nodoa, or Nada (Danxian), Melrose assisted her husband until his death in 1897, which followed by thirteen days the death of their only daughter. The new widow traveled to the United States and placed her sons, Andrew and Paul, in her sister's care. (Paul, with his wife, would later serve the Hainan mission.) Mother Melrose, as she became known, then returned to Hainan, where she served as a teacher in the girls' school and as an itinerating missionary in Nodoa for the rest of her career. She carried a Colt .45 revolver and demonstrated its use in target practice before retiring for the night in remote villages, where thieves often preyed on the unprepared. She retired in 1929 and moved to California, where she provided a home for her grandchildren from Hainan while they were attending high school. She died in California.

BIBLIOGRAPHY Margaret Moninger, ed., *The Isle of Palms: Sketches of Hainan* (1919, 1980).

Kathleen L. Lodwick

Men (*or* Menn), Aleksandr Vladimirovich (1935–1990), Russian Orthodox priest, writer, preacher, and catechist. For 20 years Men was the main link between Soviet intelligentsia and the Christian church. Born to a Jewish family in Moscow during the reign of terror under Stalin, he was baptized as an infant by Seraphim Batyukov, a priest in the "Catacomb Church" who lived in seclusion near the Sergiev Trinity Laura (monastery) not far from Moscow. Men became a spiritual child of Batyukov, from whom he acquired the living tradition of Orthodox spirituality and nonconformist courage. In 1953–1958, he studied in the Fur Institute, as he could not enter any other university at that time because of anti-Semitism; but two weeks before graduation he was expelled because of his religious views. In 1958 he was ordained a deacon, and in 1960 he became a priest. He served in several country churches around Moscow until 1970, when he was appointed to a church of Novaya Derevnya near Moscow. Novaya Derevnya became a meeting point of Soviet intellectuals (many of whom were Jewish) and Christianity. Not afraid to talk with educated and irreligious intellectuals, Men brought hundreds of people into the church though personal contacts or secret catechetical seminars. At the same time, he influenced thousands by his books, which circulated clandestinely from the beginning of the 1970s. His first two books—*The Son of Man* and *Heaven on Earth: A Liturgy of the Eastern Orthodox Church*—were published (in Russian) in 1969 in Brussels. Later he published five volumes of his history of pre-Christian religions: *In Search of the Way, Truth, and Life* (1970–1972). During the years of perestroika, he began to preach publicly in large auditoriums and on television. His fame grew, so also did criticism and opposition in antiecumenical and anti-Semitic religious circles. On Sunday morning, September 9, 1990, on his way to church, he was murdered. No one was ever charged for the crime.

BIBLIOGRAPHY Aleksandr Men published thirteen books and numerous articles before his death; additional titles have appeared posthumously. Yves Hamant wrote a biography in French (1993; Eng. tr., *Alexander Menn: A Witness for Contemporary Russia,* 1995); Elizabeth Roberts and Ann Shukman, eds., *Christianity for the Twenty-first Century: The Life and Work of Alexander Men* (1996).

Evgeny S. Steiner

Ménard, René (1604–1661), French Jesuit missionary in North America. Ménard was born in Paris and joined the Society of Jesus in 1624. He arrived in Montreal in 1640 and was sent to work among the Nipissing Indians and other Algonquian tribes. After the destruction of the Huron missions by the Iroquois, he was stationed at Trois-Rivières (present-day Three Rivers, Quebec). Opening a mission among the Iroquois in 1656, the Jesuits sent Ménard to work among the Cayuga and Oneida Indians of central New York. At first the object of ridicule and physical violence, he gradually won their affection and remained with them until the Iroquois mission was suspended in 1660. Although by now in poor health, he was sent to the Ottawa Indians, on the south shore of Lake Superior. He established the mission of Saint-Thérèse on Keweenaw Bay. Abandoned there by the Ottawa, he spent a winter marked by extreme physical hardship. In the summer of 1661 he received an appeal from some fugitive Huron Indians camped near the mouth of the Black River (Wisconsin). Setting out to visit them, he became separated from his companion and perished in an unknown manner. He had traveled farther west than any other member of his order. A county in Illinois is named for him.

BIBLIOGRAPHY Thomas Joseph Campbell, *Pioneer Priests of North America, 1642–1710* (1908–1911), vol. 1, pp. 158–171; R. G. Thwaites, ed., *The Jesuit Relations,* vol. 46, pp. 26–29, 126–145; vol. 48, pp. 115–151; Chryostomus Verwyst, *Missionary Labors of Fathers Marquette, Menard and Allouez in the Lake Superior Region* (1886).

Achiel Peelman, OMI

Menasce, Pierre Jean de (1902–1973), Dominican missiologist. De Menasce was born in Alexandria, Egypt, of a Jewish father, and was educated in law and philosophy in Alexandria and Cairo and at Oxford. He was secretary of the Zionist Bureau in Geneva in 1925 when he converted to Catholicism. He was baptized in 1926 in Paris. Louis *Massignon encouraged him to undertake Syriac studies; this was the beginning of his outstanding contribution to Oriental studies. In 1930 he joined the Dominicans and was ordained to the priesthood in 1935. From 1936 he taught history of religions and missiology at the University of Fribourg, Switzerland. He was instrumental in the creation, in 1945, of the multilingual *Nouvelle Revue de Science Missionnaire/Neue Zeitschrift für Missionswissenschaft,* edited by Johannes *Beckmann. In 1949 he was appointed research professor of the religions of ancient Iran in Paris. Disabled by strokes in 1957 and 1967, he was still very active in writing and correspondence until his death in Paris. He had affinities with the neo-Thomist revival led by Jacques Maritain and Charles Journet, but his closest links were with Massignon, Abd-el Jalil, Louis Gardet, and other Islamists. The relationship of Christianity to Judaism, Islam, and all the great world religions was central to his missiology, and in this he disagreed emphatically with the theology of Hendrik *Kraemer. In all this he contributed to the theological renewal of Roman Catholic missiology after World War II.

BIBLIOGRAPHY A full bibliography of Menasce's writings has been compiled in P. Gignoux and A. Tafazzoli, eds., *Mémorial Jean de Menasce* (1974). In addition to Oriental studies and translations of ancient Iranian texts like *Skand-Gumanik Vicar, Solution décisive des doutes: Une apologétique mazdéenne du 9e siècle* (1945), he published *Permanence et transformation de la mission* (his collected missiological essays, including the famous rebuttal of Hendrik Kraemer; 1967) and "Contemplative Life and Missions," *IRM* 56 (1967): 330–337. See also Adrian Hastings, "The Legacy of Pierre Jean de Menasce," *IBMR* 21 (October 1997), and V. Python, "L'oeuvre du P. de Menasce OP (1902–1973) sur les missions et le mazdéisme," *NZM* 30 (1974): 161–172.

Marc R. Spindler

Mendez, Alphonsus (1579–1639), Portuguese Jesuit and patriarch of Ethiopia. Mendez had been professor of Scripture for some years in the University of Evora, Portugal, when he was chosen by the king of Spain to become the patriarch of Ethiopia. Pedro *Paez, leader of the Jesuit mission in Ethiopia, had converted the emperor Susenyos to Catholicism in 1622; Paez died within a few weeks of Mendez's appointment, after almost 20 years in Ethiopia.

Mendez arrived in 1625, ignorant of the country but totally self-assured. Received with great solemnity by the emperor, he set about a policy of immediate and complete ecclesiastical revolution. Having decided that Ethiopian sacraments were of dubious validity, he decreed that everyone should be rebaptized and all the clergy reordained. The Ethiopian calendar of feasts was to be replaced by the Roman one. Circumcision was prohibited, as was the keeping of Saturday. While Susenyos endeavored to carry out this extraordinary program, rebellions multiplied throughout the country until, in 1632, he sadly rescinded his decrees and handed over power to his son, Fasiladas. Mendez was expelled after appealing to the Portuguese to depose Fasiladas. He died in Goa after writing an account of his mission, *Expeditio Aethiopica,* in which he recognized some of his mistakes. He represents the quintessence of missionary insensitivity to an eastern Christian tradition.

BIBLIOGRAPHY Mendez's own writings are in C. Beccari, *Rerum Aethiopicarum Scriptores Occidentales* (1903–1917); vols. 8 and 9 contain his *Expeditio Aethiopica,* vols. 12 and 13 contain letters. G. Beshah and M. Aregay, *The Question of the Union of the Churches in the Luso-Ethiopian Relations* (1964); P. Caraman, *The Lost Empire* (1985).

Adrian Hastings

Mendieta, Jerónimo (1525–1604), Franciscan missionary in Mexico. Born at Vitoria, Spain, Mendieta joined the Franciscan order at an early age and studied arts and theology. He arrived at Veracruz, Mexico, in June 1554 and became a disciple of Toribio de *Benavente, one of the first twelve Spanish missionaries in Mexico. Mendieta had great facility in Indian languages and became an effective preacher. He tried to improve the socioeconomic situation of the Indians and pleaded for self-sufficient communities. To the king of Spain he proposed a new system of government wherein Spanish and Indian people could live in separate areas. He returned to Spain in 1569 but was sent back in 1573 to write the history of the Franciscan mission to the Indians in Mexico. His *Historia eclesiástica indiana* was completed in 1596 but was not published until the nineteenth century. He died in the monastery of St. Francis in Mexico City.

Mendieta divided Indian church history into three parts: the period before the arrival of the Spaniards (which he called the Egyptian captivity); the "golden age" of the Indian church, from 1524 to 1564; and the period of the "Babylonian captivity," after 1564. His vision never dimmed of a future when the friars and the Indians could create the millennial kingdom of the Apocalypse.

BIBLIOGRAPHY Gerónimo de Mendieta, *Historia eclesiástica indiana,* 4 vols. (1945). Mario Cayota, *Siembra entre brumas, utopía franciscana y humanismo renacentista: Una alternativa a la conquista* (1990), pp. 348–360; Mariano Erasti, *América Franciscana,* vol. 1, *Evangelizadores e Indigenistas en el siglo XVI* (1986), pp. 241–251; John Leddy Phelan, *The Millennial Kingdom of the Franciscans in the New World* (1970).

Arnulf Camps, OFM

Meneses, Aleixo de (1559–1617), Portuguese Augustinian archbishop in Goa, India. Meneses was a descendant of Portuguese and Castilian royal families and was brought up in a courtly environment. He entered an Augustinian convent in Lisbon at the age of 15 and took vows in the order in 1575, taking the religious name Aleixo de Jesus. He completed his studies for priestly training with distinction and was appointed prior at various Augustinian monasteries in Portugal until King Phillip II made him court chaplain and preacher. In 1595 he was sent to Goa as archbishop, where he sought to tighten ecclesiastical discipline. He visited the churches of the Portuguese "Province of the North" in 1596 as well as those in Malabar in 1598. In 1599 he convened the controversial Synod of Diamper, through which he sought to Latinize the Christians of St. Thomas of Malabar. He was responsible for the creation of the diocese *ad honorem* of Angamali, and also of the suffragan diocese of St. Thome of Mylapore. In Goa he promoted the establishment of various convents, such as the Bom Jesus of the Jesuits, the College of Populo of the Augustinians, the Convent of St. Bonaventure of the Franciscans, and the Nunnery of Santa Monica. His concern for the social problems of white women in Portuguese India led him to establish two houses of protection for orphans and widows. On two occasions he acted as governor of the Portuguese *Estado da India* in the absence of the incumbent viceroys. He called the fifth church provincial council in Goa in 1606, and there assumed the title *Primaz do Oriente* (Primate of the Indies), which is still retained by archbishops of Goa. He left Goa after fifteen and a half years to take charge of the archdiocese of Braga, Portugal. He could do little there because he was soon called to Madrid to help as royal adviser in the administration of Portugal. (The crowns of Portugal and Spain were merged at this time and government was seated in Madrid.) He was eventually appointed viceroy of Portugal. He died in Madrid.

BIBLIOGRAPHY M. V. d'Abreu, *Real Mosteiro de Santa Monica de Goa* (1882); A. Bocarro, *Década 13 da História da India* (1876); J. F. Ferreira Martins, *Cronica dos Vice-Reis Governadores da India* (1919); C. C. de Nazareth, *Mitras Lusitanas no Oriente* (1893); Stephen Neill, *A History of Christianity in India: The Beginnings to AD 1707* (1984), pp. 208–219.

Teotonio R. de Souza

Merensky, Alexander (1837–1918), missionary in South Africa. Born in Panten, Silesia, Germany, Merensky studied at the Berlin Mission (BM) seminary and went to the Transvaal in 1859. He first labored among the Sotho Pedi in the north and then in 1864 founded a new station, Bothshabelo near Middelburg. It became the center of the BM work, with workshops, printing press, and training school for evangelists. Merensky mastered several African languages, studied indigenous cultures, and published the results of his scientific research in Europe in many books and articles, beginning with *Beiträge zur Kenntniss Süd-Afrikas* (1875). He returned to Germany in 1882, strongly advocated missions and economic development in Germany's newly acquired colonies, and encouraged the BM to open a work in Tanganyika (Tanzania). In 1891 he led a research expedition to Tanganyika's southeastern region to gather data about the Konde people, which paved the way for BM to occupy this field. In his later years he moderated his excessive emphasis on colonial missions and to some extent became a spokesperson for African rights. Although a highly respected scholar of African geography and ethnology (some even compare him with David *Livingstone), his ambivalent stance toward imperialism remains a matter of contention.

BIBLIOGRAPHY Alexander Merensky, *Erinnerungen aus dem Missionsleben in Südost-Afrika (Transvaal)* (1888), *Deutsche Arbeit am Njassa, Deutsch-Ostafrika* (1894) and *Die Stellung der Mission zum Volkstum der Heidenvölker* (1901). Ulrich van der Heyden, "Alexander Merenskys Beitrag zur ethnographischen und historischen Erforschung der Völkerschaften Südafrikas," *Ethnographisch-Archäologische Zeitschrift* 32 (1991): 263–268; O. Lehmann, *Alexander Merensky, ein deutscher Pionier in Südafrika* (1965).

Ulrich van der Heyden

Merrick, James Lyman (1803–1866), American Congregational missionary to Persia (Iran). Born in Monson, Massachusetts, Merrick graduated from Amherst College (1830) and Columbia (South Carolina) Seminary (1833), was ordained at Charleston the next year, and received detailed instructions from the American Board of Commissioners for Foreign Missions (ABCFM) for testing the possibilities of a mission to Muslims in Persia. He reached Constantinople (present-day Istanbul) in November 1834, studied Turkish as the language of northern Persia, then traveled to Tabreez (Tabriz) in the fall of 1835. In June 1836, accompanied by two workers of the Basel Mission, Merrick went to Teheran, proceeding from there to Shiraz in September 1836, and then to Isfahan, meeting strong resistance in both places. In May of 1837 he returned to Tabreez. He married Emma Taylor, an Englishwoman, in 1839, and the next year secured authorization to start a school. Convinced by the strong opposition not only of Muslims but also of Roman Catholics that the field was unpromising, Merrick went to Oroomiah (Rezaiyeh) and worked there in the Nestorian Mission until 1845, when he returned to the United States. From 1849 to 1864 he was pastor of the Congregational church in South Amherst, Massachusetts.

BIBLIOGRAPHY A series of Merrick's letters in the *Missionary Herald* between 1836 and 1841 provide considerable information, as do the annual reports of the ABCFM. Detailed instructions for his mission of inquiry are found in *Missionary Herald* 30 (1834): 402–405. Joseph Tracy, *History of the American Board of Commissioners for Foreign Missions* (1842) reports Merrick's activities in a year-by-year narrative.

David M. Stowe

Merwe, Willem J(acobus) van der (1906–1990), South African missiologist. Born near Ceres, South Africa, van der Merwe studied theology at the University of Stellenbosch, Princeton Seminary, and the Kennedy School of Missions of the Hartford Seminary Foundation, where his Ph.D. dissertation was "The Development of Missionary Attitudes in the Dutch Reformed Church in South Africa" (1936). From 1934 until 1958 he was a Dutch Reformed Church missionary in Zimbabwe, where he ended up as principal of the theological school at Morgenster. From 1952 to 1954 he served as president of the Southern Rhodesian Missionary Conference and as president of the Southern Rhodesian Christian Conference in 1954. From 1959 to 1974 he was professor of missiology at the University of Stellenbosch, and from 1975 to 1978 he served as principal of the Orumana Theological School in Namibia. In 1985 the University of Stellenbosch conferred on him an honorary doctorate in theology.

As professor of missiology at Stellenbosch and author of the missiological textbook, *Gesante om Christus wil* (1967), van der Merwe exercised great influence on missionary thinking and practice. From 1968 to 1971 he was the first chairperson of the Southern African Missiological Society. His ministry was characterized by strong pastoral and ecumenical concern. He also made a serious study of the religious and cultural life of the African people among whom he lived, as *The Shona Idea of God* (1957) illustrates. His last major work was *From Mission Field to Autonomous Church in Zimbabwe* (1981).

BIBLIOGRAPHY *Sendinggenade* (1986), a Festschrift edited by J. du Preez, C. M. Pauw, and P. J. Robinson, contains a complete bibliography of all van der Merwe's books and articles.

Willem Saayman

Mesrob (*or* Mashtots) (c. 350–439/440), Armenian missionary in Georgia and Albania. In his early years, Mesrob served in the military and then studied classical languages. He became a monk about 395, after which he was ordained a priest and evangelized extensively in the remote parts of Armenia. Accompanied by some of his pupils, he evangelized and established schools in Georgia and Caucasian Albania. Armenian tradition credits him with creating writing systems for both Georgian and Albanian and with contributing to the translation of the Bible into Georgian. Mesrob had already devised the brilliantly conceived Armenian writing system (c. 400), greatly strengthening the place of Christianity in his own country. In addition, he led in translating the New Testament and Proverbs into Armenian. He and his students also gathered from other countries manuscripts of the works of Greek and Syrian church fathers, which they studied and translated. Their work led to the flowering of Armenian Christian literature and liturgy. Mesrob also founded several monasteries, was canonized a saint, and, six months before his death, became patriarch of Armenia. He is recognized by the Armenian Church on two feast days.

BIBLIOGRAPHY The only surviving contemporary source of information concerning Mesrob is a biography by his pupil Koriun, *The Life of Mashtots,* Bedros Norehad, trans. (1964).

William A. Smalley

Methodius (c. 815–885), archbishop of Moravia. Methodius and his brother, *Cyril-Constantine, were considered apostles to the Slavs. A native of Thessalonica, Methodius began a career in the civil service but later became a monk. After the death of Cyril at Rome in 869, Methodius, who was still only a monk, was ordained priest and then consecrated archbishop for Moravia, and the Slavonic liturgy of Cyril and Methodius was approved by the pope. At the instance of the opponents of Slavonic, who claimed that the only proper liturgical languages were the three that had appeared in Pilate's superscription on the cross, Methodius was held captive in Germany. After his release and return to Moravia, he was charged with heresy and summoned back to Rome. In the interest of church unity, Pope John VIII placed limitations on the use of the Slavonic liturgy and withdrew the general approval. However, disciples of Methodius, and their disciples in turn, spread the use of the liturgy among other Slavic peoples. Coming as it did in a century that had begun with the coronation of Charlemagne as Roman emperor and that climaxed in the Photian schism, the mission of Methodius was caught in the crossfire between Rome and Constantinople: those Slavic peoples who followed Cyril and Methodius in their loyalty to Rome (including Poles, Czechs, Slovaks, and Croats) were eventually forced to give up the Slavonic liturgy, while those who followed Cyril and Methodius in the use of the Slavonic liturgy (including Russians, Bulgarians, Serbs, and, until the Union of Brest in 1596, Ukrainians) sided with Constantinople. Nevertheless, as apostles to the Slavs, Cyril and Methodius are revered as saints in both the Eastern and the Western church, and Pope *John Paul II named them patron saints of Europe in 1980.

BIBLIOGRAPHY Francis Dvornik, *The Slavs: Their Early History and Civilization* (1956) and *Byzantine Missions among the Slavs: SS. Constantine-Cyril and Methodius* (1970); Jaroslav Pelikan, *Confessor between East and West* (1990), pp. 23–37 ("The Disputed Legacy of Cyril and Methodius").

Jaroslav Pelikan

Meyendorff, John (1926–1992), Orthodox scholar and promoter of church and mission renewal. Born in France of Russian parents and educated at the Sorbonne and at the Orthodox Theological Institute of St. Sergius in Paris, Meyendorff was a world-renowned authority on Byzantine history, theology, and culture who devoted his life to service in the Orthodox Church. He taught at St. Sergius and was a founder of Syndesmos, the international fellowship of Orthodox youth organizations. He came to the United States in 1959, a year after he was ordained a priest. Working at Harvard's Byzantine Research Center (Dumbarton Oaks) and Fordham University, he was based at St. Vladimir's Orthodox Theological Seminary in New York, where he taught patristics and church history. There he was dean from 1984 to 1992. For many years Meyendorff edited *St. Vladimir's Theological Quarterly* and *The Orthodox Church* (a newspaper). He was heavily involved in ecumenical activities, including serving as moderator of the World Council of Churches Faith and Order Commission (1967–1975). He wrote scholarly and popular books on a variety of subjects and countless articles and editorials.

Meyendorff exemplifies the neopatristic movement in modern Orthodox scholarship and church service. He advocated a "catholic" church life over against ecclesiastical nationalism and provincialism, and promoted a missionary orientation, with full administrative unity, for the ethnically divided Orthodox churches in Europe and America.

BIBLIOGRAPHY John Meyendorff, *A Study of Gregory Palamas* (1959), *Orthodoxy and Catholicity* (1966), *Christ in Eastern Christian Thought* (1969), *Byzantine Theology* (1973), *Marriage: An Orthodox Perspective* (1975), *Living Tradition* (1978), *The Byzantine Legacy in the Orthodox Church* (1981), *Catholicity and the Church* (1983), *Witness to the World* (1987), *Vision of Unity* (1987), and *Imperial Unity and Christian Division: The Church, 450–680* (1989).

Thomas Hopko

Meyer, Louis (1862–1913), archivist, writer, and historian of the Jewish Christian movement. Meyer was born of Orthodox Jewish parents in Crivitz, Germany. Suppressing a desire for an academic career (since university appointments were denied Jews), he turned to medicine and qualified as a surgeon. After contracting blood poisoning and spending four years recovering from the illness, he went to the United States to resume his surgical career. In his thirtieth year a providential conversation with the pastor of a Reformed Presbyterian Church eventuated in Meyer becoming a disciple of Jesus, to the dismay of his father, who formally separated him from the family with a "funeral" service. This deepened his commitment to Christ, and he sought theological education and ordination. During his studies at the Reformed Presbyterian Seminary in Allegheny, Pennsylvania, he was assigned to write a historical essay on Jewish missions in America. He scoured university libraries and became a walking encyclopedia of facts and statistics. Although he served as a pastor for eight years, he rapidly became known as a lecturer and writer on Jewish missions. His knowledge of German, Hebrew, French, and Yiddish gave him unparalleled command of the Jewish missionary scene in Europe and America. He sensed the growing significance of missions to the Jews and compiled records of outstanding Jewish Christians throughout the nineteenth century. Indeed, no writer was more prolific in championing the cause of Jewish missions and no Christian was more widely loved for his Christlike character. He became prominent in the Hebrew Christian Alliance, was an early supporter of premillennial evangelical Zionism, and resigned the pastorate to serve the Chicago Hebrew Mission as its field secretary. He firmly believed that indifference to Jewish evangelism was largely due to ignorance of the Scriptures. He served as an associate editor of *Missionary Review of the World.* His last major project was editing five volumes of *The Fundamentals.* He was the outstanding historian of the Jewish Christian movement in his day.

BIBLIOGRAPHY Meyer's handwritten manuscript *Eminent Hebrew Christians of the Nineteenth Century* was published 80 years after its completion, edited and with an essay on Meyer by David A. Rausch (1983).

Arthur F. Glasser

Meyer, Lucy Jane (Rider) (1849–1922), founder of the Chicago Training School for City, Home, and Foreign Missions and pioneer of the Methodist deaconess movement. Born in New Haven, Vermont, Lucy Rider was converted at age 13 during a Methodist revival. She attended local schools, worked briefly in Canada, and taught at a Quaker freedmen's school in North Carolina before entering Oberlin College. After graduation, she prepared for a missionary career by studying at the Woman's Medical College of Pennsylvania, but the death of her fiancé prompted a change of direction. She studied chemistry at the Massachusetts Institute of Technology, returned to teaching, and eventually accepted a position with the Illinois State Sunday School Association. Convinced that young women entering Christian service needed both theological preparation and practical skills, she launched the Chicago Training School for City, Home, and Foreign Missions in 1885, shortly after her marriage to Josiah Meyer. Together, Lucy and her husband built the training school into a large and diversified organization, where more than 5,000 persons were prepared for missions and social work. In 1887 she completed her M.D. at the Women's Medical College of Chicago and founded America's first deaconess home. Deaconesses were recognized by the Methodist Church in 1888, and Meyer became a key figure in the movement, preparing young women for ministry as social workers and nurses and serving as editor of the *Deaconess Advocate* for nearly 30 years. By the time she retired in 1917, more than forty philanthropic organizations could be traced to her influence.

BIBLIOGRAPHY Lucy Meyer, *Deaconesses: Biblical, Early Church, European, American...* (1887), *Deaconess Stories* (1900), and *The Mother in the Church* (1901). Irva Colley Brown, *In Their Time: Lucy Rider Meyer and Josiah Shelley Meyer: One Hundredth Anniversary, Chicago Training School* (1985), Isabelle Horton, *High Adventure: Life of Lucy Rider Meyer* (1928).

Karen Kidd

Meyer, Theodore J(onas) (1819–1896), scholar, teacher, and missionary to Jews. Meyer was born into an illustrious rabbinical family in Crivitz, Germany, and was destined for the rabbinate himself. However, a deprived childhood and sterile training led him to lose his faith. Later he returned to Judaism, deeply influenced by the prophetic books of the Bible. Distressed by the dispute between Orthodox and Reform Jews, he was persuaded by a friend to read the New Testament's interpretation of the prophets. This led to his conviction that Jesus was the Messiah, and he was baptized in 1847. After studying theology in Scotland, he became assistant professor of Hebrew at Edinburgh University, during which time he translated into English the classic *Christology of the Old Testament* by E. Hengstenberg. He trained many clergy in Jewish mission. From 1858 to 1871 he served the Free Church of Scotland as a pioneer missionary in Romania, Italy, and the Netherlands, mastering all the languages. In 1871 he took charge of the London Jewish mission of the Presbyterian Church of England, which flourished under his leadership for over two decades.

BIBLIOGRAPHY Theodore J. Meyer, *The Autobiography of Theodore J. Meyer,* Max J. Meyer, tr. (1912). Also valuable are A. Bernstein, *Some Jewish Witnesses for Christ* (1909); Gavin Carlyle, *"Mighty In the*

Scriptures": A Memoir of Adolph Saphir, DD (1893); *Church and Synagogue, A Quarterly Magazine* 1 (1896): 85–91.

Walter Riggans

Mezzabarba, Carlo Ambrogio (1685–1741), second papal legate in Peking (Beijing), China. A native of Pavia, Italy, Mezzabarba obtained a doctorate in canon and civil law. He worked in the papal secretariat in Rome and became governor of Todi and later of Sabina. He was ordained a priest in 1718 and was consecrated a bishop the following year. In 1719 *Clement XI appointed him legate to Peking, where he was to settle the Chinese Rites Controversy, which had arisen as a result of the discussions of the emperor with the first papal legate, Charles Thomas Maillard de *Tournon in 1705 and 1706. Mezzabarba went to Lisbon for an audience with the Portuguese king and reached Macao in 1720. From late December of that year until early February 1721, he was cordially received by the emperor in Peking. However, Mezzabarba's defense of the 1715 papal decree that condemned the rites displeased the emperor, who had hoped that Mezzabarba would personally explain the imperial position to the pope and then return to China.

Mezzabarba left Peking in March and reached Macao in May 1721. His pastoral letter, sent to missionaries with instructions not to translate it into Manchu or Chinese, indicated that he had no intention of suspending the 1715 decree on the rites but explained eight agreements on the rites that he had presented to the emperor. The missionaries could discuss these concessions with the Chinese if the need arose. Contrary to claims that Mezzabarba had acted on his own in issuing the eight agreements, archival research has shown that he had received them just before leaving Lisbon. Taking the remains of Cardinal Tournon for burial in Rome, he left Macao in late 1721 and, traveling eastward through Brazil and Portugal, arrived in Rome in May 1723. Two years later he was given the title of Patriarch of Alexandria and was named bishop of Lodi, Italy. He died in office.

Bibliography Giovanni di Fiore, *La legazione Mezzabarba in Cina, 1720–1721* (1989); Ludwig von Pastor, *History of the Popes* (1941), 33:468–484; R. Ritzler and P. Sifrin, *Hierarchea catholica medii et recentioris aevi* (1952), 5:77, 238; Antonio Sisto Rosso, *Apostolic Legations to China of the Eighteenth Century* (1948); Sostegno Maria Viani, *Istoria delle cose operate nella China da Monsignor Gio. Ambrogio Mezzabarba* (1739).

John W. Witek, SJ

Middleton, Thomas Fanshaw (1769–1822), first Anglican bishop of Calcutta. Middleton was born in Kedleston, Derbyshire, England, where his father was rector, and was educated at Christ's Hospital and Pembroke College, Cambridge. He was consecrated bishop of Calcutta in 1814, after the British government in 1813 renewed the charter of the East India Company (and, for the first time, provision was legally made for an ecclesiastical establishment). In 1820 he founded Bishop's College, Calcutta (originally Bishop's Mission College), for the education of missionaries and teachers. He was a supporter of both the Society for Promoting Christian Knowledge and the Society for the Propagation of the Gospel but was uncertain how to view the presence of ordained missionaries in his diocese sent out by the Anglican voluntary society, the Church Missionary Society.

Bibliography C. W. le Bas, *Life of T. F. Middleton* (1831); M. E. Gibbs, *The Anglican Church in India* (1972); J. W. Kaye, *Christianity in India* (1859); S. C. Neill, *A History of Christianity in India, 1707–1858* (1985).

Timothy Yates

Millar, Robert (1672–1752), early Protestant apologist for missions. Millar was minister at Paisley Abbey, Scotland, from 1709. In a period preoccupied with politics and orthodoxy, he rose above the concerns of the restored Presbyterian Church of Scotland to document and promote the global mission of Christianity. His two-volume *History of the Propagation of Christianity and Overthrow of Paganism* (1723) was a pioneering work in English on the history of missions. It had two further editions (1726, 1731) and was translated into Dutch. Millar's interest paralleled the development of the work of the Scottish Society for Promoting Christian Knowledge in North America and the Scottish Highlands. He was one of the few of his time to take practical steps to facilitate world mission. Some connections claimed for Millar's influence are tenuous, but the alacrity and generosity with which the Paisley community as a whole supported the London Missionary Society in 1795 is notable, as is the fact that later obstacles to mission from Scotland had more to do with opportunities and priorities than theology. He advocated shunning a worldly life-style and avoiding worldly means in favor of the examples of John *Eliot and the Danish-Halle Mission. By his own example he also demonstrated a measured approach to other religions and to doing one's historical and theological homework.

Bibliography Ronald E. Davies, "Robert Millar—an Eighteenth Century Scottish Latourette," *Evangelical Quarterly* 62 (1990): 143–156; John Foster, "A Scottish Contributor to the Missionary Awakening: Robert Millar of Paisley," *IRM* 37 (1948): 138–145.

John Roxborogh

Miller, Harry W(illis) (1879–1977), American Seventh-day Adventist (SDA) physician in China. Miller, a native of Ohio, graduated from John Harvey Kellogg's American Medical Missionary College in Battle Creek, Michigan, in 1902. After an internship in Chicago, he and his wife, Maude (Thompson), went to China with medical instruments and a hand-operated printing press. They arrived in Shanghai in late 1903. Maude Miller died less than two years later. Harry married Marie Iverson in 1908, and she shared his missionary life until she died in 1950. The Orient became the Millers' home and apart from interludes in the United States, Miller remained in China until 1956. He was both a specialist in surgery and a missionary generalist to the extent that he served at one time as leader of the SDA Church in China. Endeavoring to treat everybody, regardless of ability to pay, he administered hospitals in Shanghai and Hankow, Hupei (Hubei) Province, at which many of the important leaders of China were treated. Evacuated from Shanghai several months after the Communists occupied the city in 1949, he established the SDA hospital in Taipei. On March 26, 1956, he was awarded the Blue Star of China by Chiang Kai-shek for meritorious service to the peoples of China. He retired to the United States later that year but returned in 1959 to Hong Kong, where he worked on and off for another decade and sponsored the foundation of a hospital there before his final return to the United States. His publications include *The Way to Health* (1920; repeatedly revised, translated, and republished), *Tuberculosis: A Curable Disease* (1954), and dozens of shorter pieces in English and Chinese.

BIBLIOGRAPHY "China, People's Republic of" and "Miller, Harry Willis," in *Seventh-day Adventist Encyclopedia,* 2d rev. ed. (1996). Raymond S. Moore, *China Doctor: The Life Story of Harry Willis Miller* (1961); R. S. Schwarz, *Light Bearers to the Remnant* (1979); A. W. Spalding, *Origin and History of Seventh-day Adventists,* vol 4 (1962); Joy Swift, *The Long Road to China* (1990).

Russell L. Staples

Miller, Walter Richard Samuel (1872–1952), Church Missionary Society (CMS) pioneer among the Hausa peoples. Miller spent nearly 50 years in northern Nigeria as medical doctor, educator, and writer. Born in England and raised among the Plymouth Brethren, he became active in mission as a medical student in London (1890–1896) where he committed himself to overseas mission through the Student Volunteer Missionary Union (SVMU). On graduation he was appointed the SVMU traveling secretary. After a year's medical work in Freetown, Sierra Leone (1897), he joined the 1899 CMS expedition to Hausaland led by Bishop Herbert Tugwell. A short period of Hausa language training in Tripoli, Libya, preceded an arduous journey on foot from Lagos to Zaria in northern Nigeria. For the next 27 years (1902–1929) he remained in Zaria to develop the CMS mission among the Hausa peoples. He established a school for boys. Throughout these years he worked on a Hausa translation of the Bible. The British and Foreign Bible Society published his New Testament translation in 1912 (rev. 1925) and his complete Bible translation in 1932. His estimation of Islam's spiritual values increased through his contact with a small group of *Isawa* (Jesus) Muslims whose interpretation of the quranic portrait of Jesus led them to convert to Christianity and to pioneer an indigenous Christian community in Gimi village, near Zaria. Most of the villagers died in an outbreak of sleeping sickness (1914), but Miller always saw them as a sign of spiritual potential within Hausa Islam. From Zaria he moved to Kano (1929 to 1935) to establish another CMS mission center. The difficulties he faced there prompted him to criticize harshly Muslim social and political traditions. Espousing Christian Socialism also made him critical of the British colonial administration of Nigeria. Failing to remake a home in Britain after retirement in 1935, he returned to Nigeria in 1939 to spend his final years in Jos.

BIBLIOGRAPHY Works and Bible translations by Miller include *Hausa Notes* (1902), *Reflections of a Pioneer* (1936), *The Coiners: A Story of Africa* (1938), *Yesterday and To-Morrow in Northern Nigeria* (1938), *Have We Failed in Nigeria?* (1947), *Success in Nigeria? Assets and Possibilities* (1948), *Walter Miller, 1872–1952: An Autobiography* (1949), and *For Africans Only* (1950). E. A. Ayandele, "The Missionary Factor in Northern Nigeria, 1870–1918," in O. U. Kalu, ed., *The History of Christianity in West Africa* (1980); Edward Hulmes, "Walter Miller and the Isawa: An Experiment in Christian-Muslim Relationships," *Scottish Journal of Theology* 41, no. 2 (1988): 233–246.

David A. Kerr

Miller, William (1838–1923), educational missionary to India. Miller was born in the far north of Scotland and was educated at the universities of Aberdeen and Edinburgh. He arrived in Madras, India, early in 1862 as a missionary of the Free Church of Scotland to teach at the school first opened in 1837 by John *Anderson. At Miller's initiative the school was affiliated with the University of Madras (which had been founded in 1857), while retaining its Christian basis. The first BA class started in 1867. Miller then extended the school's basis by negotiating with the Wesleyan Methodists and the Church Missionary Society to create, in 1877, the Madras Christian College, which he served as principal. New courses were mapped out, new professors were appointed, a library was built up, and in 1883 *Madras Christian College Magazine* was started. Miller was an outstanding educator and trained many Christian and national leaders. He did not, however, believe in the use of education as an inducement to conversion. This, together with his somewhat liberal theology and his concern for problems of social reform, involved him in controversy. Miller was also an early advocate of the theology of fulfillment, believing that India should be allowed to make its own unique contribution to world culture. In 1896, while on furlough, he served as moderator of the General Assembly of the Free Church of Scotland. In 1901 he was appointed vice-chancellor of the University of Madras. He left India for the last time in March 1907 and died in Edinburgh.

BIBLIOGRAPHY O. Kandaswamy Chetty, *William Miller* (1924); George Sherwood Eddy, *Pathfinders of the World Missionary Crusade* (1945), pp. 95–104.

Eric J. Sharpe

Miller, William McElwee (1892–1993), American Presbyterian missionary in Iran. Miller's early childhood was spent in Virginia. He graduated from Washington and Lee University and Princeton Seminary and was ordained in the Presbyterian Church, U.S. (Southern) in 1916. Impacted deeply by the Student Volunteer Movement, he was appointed in 1919 by the Presbyterian Church, U.S.A. (Northern) to its Persia Mission. The beginning of his missionary career coincided with the coming to power of Reza Shah Pahlevi and sweeping reform for the Muslim country. Before his ministry closed in 1962, he had seen service in Meshed in northeast Iran, and in Teheran, Tabriz, and Resht. He witnessed the first General Assembly of the Evangelical Church of Iran, formed in 1934 of Assyrian, Armenian, and Persian-speaking churches. Always the enthusiastic evangelist, he pursued his calling through personal contacts, preaching in the churches (sometimes as pastor), showing lantern slides of the life of Christ, supporting summer schools of evangelism, and so forth. He wrote commentaries in Persian on about half the books of the New Testament. His continuing contacts with Baha'i followers in Iran produced in 1931 the first of his many written studies of that religion. His retirement years in Philadelphia were active in writing and in evangelism.

BIBLIOGRAPHY William McElwee Miller, *Baha'ism: Its History, Origin, and Teachings* (1931), *Ten Muslims Meet Christ* (1969), *The Baha'i Faith: Its History and Teachings* (1974), *Beliefs and Practices of Christians* (1975), *A Christian's Response to Islam* (1976), and *My Persian Pilgrimage* (1989). Much of Miller's correspondence and a complete list and collection of his writings are held by the Presbyterian Historical Society, Philadelphia. His books, documents, and correspondence on the Baha'i religion are in the library at Princeton Theological Seminary.

Harvie M. Conn

Mills, Samuel John, Jr. (1783–1818), prime mover in the founding of the first foreign mission societies in North America. Mills led in the formation of the American Board of Commissioners for Foreign Missions (ABCFM), the American Bible Society, the United Foreign Missionary Society, and a number of other missionary and benevolent organizations. Son of a Congregational pastor in Connecticut, he learned stories of missionary pioneers from his mother. He was one of five participants in the famous 1806 Williams College "haystack prayer meeting" that soon led to the beginning of a secret missionary fraternity called the Society of Brethren, the first Protestant foreign missions organization in America. After he enrolled in Andover Theological Seminary, the society's membership grew to include not only Gordon *Hall and Luther *Rice, companions from Williams College, but also Samuel *Nott, Samuel *Newell, and Adoniram *Judson. In 1810, four of these, including Mills, appeared before the Congregational General Association of Massachusetts and offered themselves to be foreign missionaries. The ABCFM was formed the next day. In February 1812, Judson, Newell, Nott and their wives, together with Hall and Rice, sailed for India, the first foreign missionaries to be sent from North America. Why Mills was not also sent is unclear, but apparently he was needed more in the United States to promote the cause to which he was so committed.

Always involved in multiple projects and activities, Mills engaged for a time in missionary work in the Mississippi valley and later among the poor and destitute in New York City. Returning in 1818 from a journey to West Africa, where he and a colleague had been sent by the American Colonization Society to locate a site for the repatriation of freed African-American slaves, Mills died at sea. He was only 35. Though distinguished neither in appearance nor as an orator, Mills was a natural leader. During his brief lifetime he inspired, as few others, individuals, churches, and denominations to be part of the world mission endeavor.

BIBLIOGRAPHY George Sherwood Eddy, *Pathfinders of the World Missionary Crusade* (1945), pp. 37–40; Thomas C. Richards, *Samuel J. Mills* (1906); Gardiner Spring, *Memoirs of the Rev. Samuel J. Mills* (1820; 2d ed., 1829).

Alan Neely

Mills, W(ilson) Plumer (1883–1959), missionary in China. Born in Winnsboro, South Carolina, Mills graduated from Davidson College (B.A., 1903), Davidson, South Carolina. He taught for three years in Camden, South Carolina, then did a year of graduate study at the University of South Carolina (M.A., 1907). One of the early Rhodes Scholars at Christ Church College, the University of Oxford, Mills graduated with honors in theology (B.A., 1910). He was YMCA secretary at the University of South Carolina from 1910 to 1912. During this time he also studied at Columbia (South Carolina) Theological Seminary (B.D., 1912). In 1932 he received an S.T.M. degree from Union Theological Seminary, New York, and in 1951 an honorary D.D. from Davidson College. He served under the YMCA in China from 1912 to 1932, largely in ministry to students.

In 1932 Mills resigned from the YMCA, was ordained, and began work under the Presbyterian Foreign Mission Board in Nanking (Nanjing), where he coordinated the work of the Presbyterian mission and worked with Chinese pastors. Just before the Japanese occupation of Nanking, Mills played an important role in efforts to bring about a truce that would allow the Chinese army to withdraw from Nanking and the Japanese army to enter the city without fighting. With approval from General Tang Sheng-chih, Mills and fellow missionary M. Searle *Bates went to see the U.S. consul, J. Hall Paxton, on board the USS *Panay*, to transmit the truce-negotiating messages. After the Japanese army occupied Nanking, Mills was appointed vice-chairman of the International Committee for the Nanking Safety Zone when it was founded in November 1937, and chairman in February 1938. The Nanking Safety Zone had a population of about 250,000, of which about 70,000 people were dependent upon the zone committee for food and fuel. Mills received the Order of the Green Jade, the highest honor given to Westerners by the Chinese government in recognition of his work in Nanking during 1937–1938. During World War II he was interned for nine months in Shanghai by the Japanese, was repatriated in 1943, and returned to China in 1944. The next five years were spent in Chungking (Chonqing) and Shanghai. He left China in 1949 and retired formally in 1951 but continued to work in New York City on the staff of the Missionary Research Library at Union Theological Seminary until 1955. He died in New York City.

BIBLIOGRAPHY Martha Lund Smalley, ed., *American Missionary Eyewitnesses to the Nanking Massacre, 1937–1938* (1997) includes excerpts from Mills's letters and reports in Nanking during the Japanese occupation.

Martha Lund Smalley

Milman, Robert (1816–1876), Anglican bishop of Calcutta. Milman was educated at Westminster School and Exeter College, Oxford. In 1840 he was appointed to the parish of Chaddleworth and in 1862 to Great Marlow on the invitation of Samuel *Wilberforce; he also lectured at the bishop's theological college, Cuddlesdon. Appointed the seventh bishop of Calcutta in 1867, he acquired the Bengali, Hindustani, and Hindi languages. A vigorous and highly respected bishop, he supported the work of both the Society for the Propagation of the Gospel and the Church Missionary Society. In 1868 he ordained a notable Muslim convert, *Imad-ud-din. In 1869 he received 7,000 Kol converts of the Lutheran Gossner mission and ordained three German pastors after their dispute with newer Lutheran missionaries in Chota Nagpur. He visited Burma (Myanmar), part of his diocese, and in 1875 received some Karen Baptists as Anglicans. Although he wanted more bishops in India, he disapproved of placing missionary society bishops within the diocese of Madras, a scheme supported by the archbishop of Canterbury in 1873. His death from overwork led to his huge diocese being subdivided, with new sees at Lahore, where T. V. *French was appointed in 1877, and at Rangoon.

BIBLIOGRAPHY E. Chatterton, *Fifty Years Mission Work in Chota Nagpur* (1901); M. E. Gibbs, *The Anglican Church in India, 1600–1970* (1972); F. M. Milman, *Memoir of the Rt. Revd. Robert Milman* (1879); E. Stock, *History of the Church Missionary Society* (1899); H. P. Thompson, *Into All Lands* (1951). Obituaries in *The Times* March 20, 1876, and *The Guardian* March 22, 1876.

Timothy Yates

Milne, Andrew Murray (1838–1907), Bible colporteur in South America. Milne was born in Aberdeenshire, Scotland. Named for Andrew *Murray, the famous South African minister and devotional writer, he was orphaned at age two and raised by pious grandparents. Converted in a London revival at 19, but frustrated in his desire to become a missionary, he immigrated to Argentina in the employ of a fruit trader. He married Harriet Leggat, who had been converted in the same London revival and had also immigrated to Argentina. There he came to the attention of William Goodfellow, a Methodist missionary, who recommended him to the American Bible Society. He was hired in 1864 as the society's first agent in South America, and from his base in the River Plate area, served with unusual dedication and distinction for 43 years, until his death. His travels were wide and constant in all of South America except the Guiyanas. He suffered persecution, hostility, prejudice, and times of cholera and war. Yet he succeeded in establishing bases for the Bible society's work in all the lands he visited. He opened the way for future missionaries in many countries, distributed more than 850,000 Bibles, translated portions into the Quichua language, and preached the gospel in a popular and appealing way wherever he went.

BIBLIOGRAPHY Andrew Murray Milne, *From Cape Horn to Quito,* Arthur Walker, ed. (1942; contains selections from his diaries, reports, and letters). Daniel P. Monti, *Presencia del Protestantismo en el Rio de la Plata durante el siglo XIX* (1969), pp. 205–209.

Sidney H. Rooy

Milne, Rachel (Cowie) (1783–1819), missionary in China. Born and brought up in Aberdeen, Scotland, Rachel Cowie married William *Milne of the London Missionary Society (LMS). After he finished missionary training and was ordained in 1812, they departed for China, where he was the second Protestant missionary to arrive. The Milnes had intended to settle in Macao as an alternative to Canton, where the Ch'ing government prohibited missionary activity. However, after being evicted from Macao, in 1815 they settled in Malacca, where the LMS mission established the Anglo-Chinese College, of which William Milne became the first principal.

Rachel Milne's duties, as outlined by her husband, were to nurture her spiritual life, look after and educate their children, learn the Chinese language, take care of her health, and prepare herself to assist the missionary work. But, unable to tolerate the tropical climate and frequently ill, she died in 1819, leaving three children. She was the first China missionary wife to die in the mission field. She was buried in the Dutch cemetery in Malacca. Her son, William Charles Milne, later became a missionary of the LMS in China.

BIBLIOGRAPHY Robert Morrison, *Memoirs of the Rev. William Milne, D.D., Late Missionary to China, and Principal of the Anglo-Chinese College* (1824); Robert Philip, *The Life and Opinions of the Rev. William Milne, D.D., Missionary to China, Illustrated by Biographical Annals of Asiatic Missions, from Primitive to Protestant Times; Intended as a Guide to Protestant Spirit* (1840); Alexander Wylie, *Memorials of Protestant Missionaries to the Chinese: Giving a List of Their Publications, and Obituary Notices of the Deceased, with Copious Indexes* (1867).

Timothy Man-kong Wong

Milne, William (1785–1822), early Protestant missionary in China and collaborator of Robert *Morrison. Raised in rural Scotland, Milne became a carpenter. In 1809, at age 24, he was accepted by the London Missionary Society and given three years' theological training at their college in Gosport, England, before his ordination in 1812. He and his new wife, Rachel (Cowie) *Milne, arrived on the China coast in 1813, joining Morrison, who had arrived there in 1807. In the next nine years, Milne learned the Chinese language and lived in Canton, Java, Penang, and Malacca. Even more than Morrison (who stayed in Canton), Milne was a cultural pioneer in this network of China-oriented posts ranging from the China coast to Southeast Asia. He translated the books Deuteronomy through Job for Morrison's famous Bible, and in his own right made a signal contribution to the beginnings of the writing, printing, and distribution of Christian literature in Chinese. In 1819 he published a tract *The Two Friends,* which became the most widely used Chinese Christian tract until the early twentieth century. Milne was also principal of the Anglo-Chinese College at Malacca from its founding until his death. His first convert (1815), *Liang Fa, later became renowned as the author of the Christian literature that inspired *Hung Hsiu-ch'üan and the Taiping Rebellion (1850–1864).

Milne was remarkably prolific for one who came to literary work so late in life, and twenty-one Chinese works are attributed to him. Several were of substantial length; one was a monthly magazine that ran from 1815 to 1822 and totaled several hundred pages. In addition, he produced two substantial books and a Malacca periodical in English. Predeceased by his wife in 1819, he was survived by a daughter and three sons, one of whom, William Charles Milne (1815–1863), later became an LMS China missionary (1839–1863).

BIBLIOGRAPHY William Milne, *A Retrospect of the First Ten Years of the Protestant Mission to China* (1820). Daniel H. Bays, "Christian Tracts: *The Two Friends,*" in Suzanne Wilson Barnett and John King Fairbank, eds., *Christianity in China: Early Protestant Missionary Writings* (1985); Brian Harrison, *Waiting for China: The Anglo-Chinese College at Malacca, 1818–1843, and Early Nineteenth-Century Missions* (1979); Robert Morrison, *Memoirs of the Rev. William Milne, D.D.* (1824); Robert Philip, *The Life and Opinions of the Rev. William Milne, D.D., Missionary to China* (1840).

Daniel H. Bays

Miner, Luella (1861–1935), American missionary educator in China. Miner was born at Oberlin, Ohio. Her father was a missionary to the Chippewa Indians and after Civil War service, a teacher in schools for the freedmen. After graduation from Oberlin College (1884), she taught for three years in American Missionary Association schools in the South, then was appointed to serve in China under the American Board of Commissioners for Foreign Missions (ABCFM), with support from the ABCFM-related Woman's Board of Missions of the Interior. She sailed in 1887, and after language study at Paotingfu, taught in North China College at Tungchow, near Peking, and published a geology textbook in Chinese.

During the reconstruction period following the Boxer disturbances of 1900, she turned to education for girls. She moved to Peking in 1903 to reorganize and for ten years head Bridgman Academy; in 1905, she also founded North China Women's College, which later added "Union" to its name by virtue of Presbyterian, Methodist, and London Missionary Society participation. That institution became the Women's College of Yenching University in 1920. Miner resigned as dean in 1922 and joined the faculty of Cheeloo University (Shantung Christian University), Tsinan, serving first as dean of women and then in the school of theology until 1932. She received the D.Litt. from Oberlin in 1914 and in 1928 was a delegate to the International Missionary conference in Jerusalem. She died in Jinan, China.

BIBLIOGRAPHY In 1903 Miner published two books about the Boxer episode which are notable for their focus on the experiences of Chinese Christians rather than on missionary sufferings: *China's Book of Martyrs: A Record of Heroic Martyrdoms and Marvelous Deliverances of Chinese Christians during the Summer of 1900,* and *Two Heroes of Cathay, an Autobiography and a Sketch* (a translation of Fei Chi Hao's *Autobiography,* and a sketch of Kung Hsiang-hsi). Mary H. Porter, *Luella Miner, A Sketch* (1916); *Missionary Herald* 126 (1930): 393–394; 132 (1936): 92–93 (obit.).

David M. Stowe

Mingo de la Concepción, Manuel (1726–1807), Spanish Franciscan missionary and chronicler of the Tarija missions of southeastern Bolivia. Born in Cuença, Spain, Mingo arrived in the New World in 1755, precisely when the Tarija convent was designated a missionary center for the Chiriguano Indians of southeastern Bolivia. His attempts to convert the Indians largely met with failure, though in 1767 he took over the mission of Salinas after the Jesuits were expelled. Mingo gave up evangelism among the unconverted in 1771 and devoted much of his life to preaching among Christians throughout the viceroyalties of Lima and Buenos Aires. He returned twice to Spain to recruit new missionaries. In 1788 he was designated the official historian of the Tarija convent and in 1797 finished a lengthy history. The convent refused to publish his account because of the work's presumed errors and lack of synthesis, but Antonio Comajuncosa based his work *El Colegio Franciscano de Tarija y sus misiones* (1810, 1884, 1990) on Mingo. Almost two centuries later Mingo's work finally appeared in print as *Historia de las misiones franciscanas de Tarija entre los Chiriguanos* (1981). He died in Tarija.

BIBLIOGRAPHY The 1981 publication of Mingo's history contains a brief biography of Mingo by Bernardino del Pace. Thierry Saignes, "L'ethnographie missionnaire en Bolivie: Deux siècles de regards franciscains sur les Chiriguano, 1780–1980," in *The Franciscan Presence in the Americas* (1983), pp. 345–366, gives an analysis of Mingo's work.

Erick D. Langer

Mirbt, Carl (1860–1929), church historian at Marburg and Göttingen universities. A specialist in the history of the papacy, Mirbt also made a name for himself as one of the first modern academic missiologists in Germany. Raised and educated in Silesia in a Moravian Brethren family, as a student he became deeply impressed by Gustav *Warneck, pioneer of the scientific study of mission and professor of missiology at Halle University. As a historiographer, Mirbt combined rigorous standards of research with a sincere commitment to the spread of the faith in evangelical terms. Along with his professorship of church history at Göttingen, he held a lectureship in mission studies, founded a regional conference for missiology in Hanover, and together with like-minded colleagues, laid the foundation for the German Society for the Study of Mission (1918), the first organization of its kind in the world. He was president of the society until his death. At the world missionary conference at Edinburgh (1910) Mirbt also made a notable contribution.

BIBLIOGRAPHY Mirbt's most important missiological publication is *Mission und Kolonialpolitik in den deutschen Schutzgebieten* (1910). Hans-Werner Gensichen, *Invitatio ad Fraternitatem: 75 Jahre Deutsche Gesellschaft für Missionswissenschaft* (1993), pp. 45–55; Ernst Strasser, "Carl Mirbt als Missionswissenschaftler," *Lutherisches Missionsjahrbuch* 44 (1931): 24–46.

Hans-Werner Gensichen

Misley, Róza (Puchlin) (1864–1944), mission advocate among Hungarian Protestant women. Born in Miskolc, Hungary, Róza Puchlin was introduced to the Young Women's Association by her friend Iréne Kunst. The news that Kunst would leave for China as a missionary in 1904 aroused in Puchlin an interest in foreign missions. After reading some issues of the magazine *China's Millions,* she came to feel that Hungarian women ought to support Kunst. In 1907, now the widow of Sándor Misley, she initiated a missions committee within the Lorántffy Zsuzsanna Christian Women's Association. She promoted an interest in Chinese mission, mobilizing women of nobility to pray and donate money for Kunst's mission work. She used a system of pledge forms, appointing contact people in every city to distribute and collect them. Under her zealous leadership, within a few years enough money was collected to support two Chinese indigenous workers and a German missionary of the Liebenzell Mission. She regularly wrote articles on foreign missions—especially on Chinese mission—in the women's association's magazine *Olajág* (Olive-branch) and in that of the Sunday school association, the *Örömhír* (Good news). "Aunt Róza" carried on the work for more than three decades—the last years in affiliation with the Hungarian Reformed Foreign Mission Society—thus affecting whole generations of women and children and securing support for Hungarian foreign mission work.

BIBLIOGRAPHY Mrs. Sándor Misley, "10 év" (10 years), *Olajág* 18, no. 5 (1918): 9–10, "Hogyan gyűjthetünk a misszióra?" (How can we collect for missions?), *Hajnal* 16, no. 11 (1930): 4–7, and "Magyarok munkája Kínában," *Református Külmissziói Szemle,* 1932, pp. 59–62. László Draskóczy, "Misley Sándorné," *Hajnal* 30, no. 6 (1944): 2–4; Anne-Marie Kool, *God Moves in a Mysterious Way: The Hungarian Protestant Foreign Mission Movement (1756–1951)* (1993), pp. 203–206, 363–365.

Anne-Marie Kool

Mitchell, John Murray (1815–1904), Scottish missionary in India. Mitchell was one of four sons of a substantial citizen of Aberdeen, all of whom entered the Church of Scotland ministry. After distinguished studies in arts at Marischal College, Aberdeen, and in divinity at Edinburgh University, and a brief period as a schoolmaster, Mitchell was ordained as a missionary to Bombay in 1838. With all the other missionaries of the Church of Scotland, he joined the Free Church when the Church of Scotland divided in 1843. He worked in western India (often in Pune, where he took charge of the government college for a time) until 1863, when he returned to parish ministry in Scotland. In 1867 Alexander *Duff brought him back to India for six years' service in Duff's old college in Calcutta. In 1873 he became secretary of his church's foreign mission committee; in 1880 he began two more years of lecturing and preaching in India. From 1888 until 1898 he was ministering in France, first in Cannes and then in the Scots Church in Nice. In 1903, at age 88, he undertook the Duff Missionary Lectureship. The resulting lectures were posthumously published in 1905 as *The Great Religions of India.*

Though western India was Mitchell's first concern—he was a fine linguist who loved Marathi poetry and venerated the mystic Tukaram—he was often influential and instrumental elsewhere. He assisted Stephen *Hislop in the establishment of the Central India Mission at Nagpur, surveyed the prospects in Hyderabad (which led to the Jalna mission), negotiated the creation of a united congregation at Simla, and advised both the United Presbyterian Church on the opening of the Rajputana mission and his own church on that of the Santal tribal mission. In outlook he resembled Alexander Duff, devoted to education as the main mode of mission and secure in a Christian worldview which united all the arts and sciences with biblical understanding. He was a trenchant critic of popular Hinduism, yet eager to maintain intellectual rapport with Hindu reformers. He translated vernacular poetry and published extensively both in Britain and in India. His wife, Maria Hay (Flyter), was also a well-known writer on life in India.

BIBLIOGRAPHY J. Murray Mitchell, *In Western India: Records of My Early Missionary Life* (1899); M. H. (Mrs. Murray) Mitchell, *Sixty Years Ago* (1905). W. Ewing, *Annals of the Free Church of Scotland,* vol. 1 (1914), p. 272; J. A. Lamb, *Fasti of the United Free Church of Scotland* (1956), p. 528; H. Scott, *Fasti Ecclesiae Scoticanae* 7 (1928), p. 702.

Andrew F. Walls

Mizeki, Bernard (c. 1861–1896), Mozambican catechist, Bible translator, and martyr. Born in Ihambane, Mozambique, Mizeki trained as a linguist while living as a migrant worker in Cape Town. G. W. H. *Knight-Bruce recruited him in 1891 as a catechist for the new Anglican diocese of Mashonaland in Rhodesia (Zimbabwe). Based near Marondera, he translated into Chishona much of the Bible and Prayer Book. During the war of resistance to colonialism in 1896, Mizeki refused to leave his mission and was stabbed to death. He is remembered as the "Mashonaland martyr," and his shrine in Zimbabwe has become a place of pilgrimage. In South Africa, the Bernard Mizeki Men's Guild and numerous churches commemorate him as a symbol of black Anglicanism.

BIBLIOGRAPHY Jean Farrant, *Mashonaland Martyr: Bernard Mizeki and the Pioneer Church* (1966).

Janet Hodgson

Moe, Malla (1863–1953), missionary to Swaziland with the Scandinavian Alliance Mission. As a young woman, Moe left Norway and immigrated to Chicago, where she came under the influence of Fredrik *Franson, who persuaded her to enroll in his two-week Bible school and then go to Africa as a missionary. Arriving in Swaziland in the mid-1890s, she quickly identified with the people and their culture but was often viewed as difficult and domineering by her missionary colleagues. She established the Bethel mission station near Mhlosheni and Nhlangano, in southern Swaziland, as her base of operations. Conducting her ministry, with no regard to gender limitations, she served as evangelist, church planter, teacher, and preacher. She was not ordained, but she also functioned as a bishop, assigning ministers to churches she planted and overseeing their development. In 1928 she initiated a new ministry of itinerant evangelism, traveling from region to region in her "gospel wagon." She continued for more than a decade and left behind dozens of new churches. The climax of her career came in 1949 when a new brick church was opened at Bethel. She died two months before her 90th birthday, surrounded by African friends.

BIBLIOGRAPHY Maria Nilsen, as told to Paul H. Sheetz, *Malla Moe* (1956); Ruth A. Tucker, *Guardians of the Great Commission: The Story of Women in Modern Missions* (1988).

Ruth A. Tucker

Moegling, Herrmann Friedrich (1811–1881), Basel Mission pioneer in South India. Born in the southern German state of Württemberg, Moegling studied theology in Tübingen, was taught by D. F. Strauss, experienced conversion as a graduate student, and became one of the earliest missionaries of the Basel Mission (BM) to work in India. In 1836 he arrived in what is now the South Indian state of Karnataka. Early on, he was involved in one of the typical BM attempts to live close to the people. Not least for this reason he was also involved in serious strife with colleagues, as when he would travel on foot when others went on horseback. In the long run, however, his creative energies did much to establish the substantive pattern of BM's work in Karnataka, both in education and in the idea of encouraging craft production among Christians, the direct predecessor of the industries. Moegling was also important in the early BM studies of the Kannada language and its literature, including his involvement in the production of the *Bibliotheca Carnataca,* a large-format six-volume collection of traditional Kannada literary texts (including the songs of the early Lingayat poet Basavanna). It was printed lithographically by BM in Mangalore in the 1840s and financed by two wealthy English friends of BM in the area. Moegling left India in 1860.

BIBLIOGRAPHY Hermann Gundert, *Herrmann Mögling: Ein Missionsleben in der Mitte des Jahrhunderts* (1882; English tr., 1997); Srinavasa Havanur, "Contribution of the Basel Mission to Kannada Literature," in *Wholeness in Christ: The Legacy of the Basel Mission in India,* Godwin Shiri, ed. (1985), pp. 216–223.

Paul Jenkins

Moffat, John Smith (1835–1918), London Missionary Society (LMS) missionary in South Africa. Born in Kuruman, South Africa, Moffat was the son of Robert and Mary *Moffat. Educated at Cheshunt College and New College, London, he was ordained in 1858 and returned to Africa in the company of LMS recruits. In Africa he remained with them as an unofficial assistant in their work among the Amandebele people in present-day Zimbabwe. In 1862 he was officially recognized as a missionary by the LMS. In 1865 he moved to Kuruman and began working with his father, but because of his wife's ill health he went to Cape Town in 1867. He returned in 1868 and for four years worked with his father on the revision of the Tswana Bible. His wife's health then forced a further withdrawal until 1874.

In 1878 he resigned from the LMS and became a colonial official, serving the administration of what is now Botswana with distinction until his retirement in 1895.

BIBLIOGRAPHY Moffat published a massive biography of his parents, *The Lives of Robert and Mary Moffat* (1885). Details of his career can be found in Richard Lovett, *The History of the London Missionary Society, 1795–1895* (1899).

Andrew C. Ross

Moffat, Robert (1795–1883), pioneer missionary and linguist in southern Africa. Moffat grew up in central Scotland, but in 1813 he moved to England, where he began to work for James Smith, a pious Scottish merchant in Manchester. Smith's daughter Mary would later join Moffat in South Africa as his wife. The London Missionary Society (LMS) accepted him for missionary service and sent him to South Africa in 1817. There, working on the northern frontier, he gained fame as a result of the conversion of a notorious bandit, Jager Afrikaner, and his followers. In 1819 in Cape Town, Moffat married Mary Smith. Working together as full partners, they began their long stay among the Tswana. While Robert was away on his many long treks, Mary not only ran the home but also the mission. After some moves they settled at Kuruman, which was to be their home until they left Africa. Here they created a large oasis of high fertility in a semiarid area. In 1829, Mzilikazi, chief of the Ndebele (a Zulu offshoot), contacted Moffat, who then visited the chief and began a most extraordinary friendship. Moffat visited Mzilikazi a second time in 1835 and then three more times after the Ndebele moved across the Zambesi. The last visit, in 1859, resulted in the establishment of an LMS mission near Bulawayo.

Almost from the beginning Moffat plunged into the work of translation. In 1840 he published the complete New Testament in Tswana. His translations set a style for Tswana, a language spoken across the breadth of southern Africa, from Namibia to the Free State. In 1857 the whole Bible in Tswana was published at Kuruman. On a visit to Britain he published his *Missionary Labours* (1840), which went through four editions in the next three years and made Moffat the best known missionary in Britain.

After 1860, Moffat took no more long treks but worked on consolidating the work at Kuruman. He preached there for the last time in March 1870; then he and Mary set sail for Britain, where Mary died in 1871. Moffat continued to work hard and did not give up addressing public meetings until 1878. His translation work was a great achievement and his role as a propagandist has rarely been surpassed. However, he never gained a deep understanding of African culture nor any closeness with individual Africans, even with those like Mzilikazi who were fond of him.

BIBLIOGRAPHY R. Moffat, *Missionary Labours* (1840). J. S. Moffat, *The Lives of Robert and Mary Moffat* (1885); C. Northcott, *Robert Moffat: Pioneer in Africa*(1961); J. P. R. Wallis, ed., *The Matabele Journals of Robert Moffat* (1945).

Andrew C. Ross

Moffett, Samuel Austin (1864–1939), pioneer Presbyterian missionary to Korea. Born in Madison, Indiana, and educated at Hanover College (B.S., 1884) and at McCormick Seminary (Th.B., 1888), Moffett was one of the early Presbyterian missionaries to Korea, arriving there in 1890, six months before the decisive visit of John L. *Nevius. The seven Presbyterian missionaries in Korea at the time were fully persuaded by Nevius and adapted to their fledgling work his then controversial plan and methods. The results were dramatic. Moffett stressed two facets of the plan especially: intensive Bible study for all believers, and evangelism by all believers. Beginning in August 1890, Moffett made several excursions to the north, and three years later he moved permanently to Pyongyang, where the response to the gospel and the growth of the church became legendary. Later analyses indicate a number of reasons, apart from missionary methods, that help to account for the remarkable growth of Korean Presbyterian churches during this era, but Moffett's contribution is indisputable.

In 1901 he began the Presbyterian Theological Seminary with two students meeting in his home. He served as the school's president for 17 years and as a member of its faculty until 1935. When the first class graduated in 1907 and the Korean Presbyterian Church was organized, Moffett was elected the first moderator. He was the Korean Presbyterian representative at the Edinburgh missionary conference in 1910, and again at the 1928 Jerusalem Conference of the International Missionary Council. From 1918 to 1928 he was president of Soongsil College in Pyongyang. He retired in 1934 at age 70 but chose to remain in Korea. In January 1936 tension between the Japanese governor and Presbyterian leaders in Pyongyang erupted over whether students in Christian institutions should be required to participate in ceremonies at a newly erected Buddhist shrine. Moffett, then president of the seminary board, and G. S. McCune, president of the college, were issued an ultimatum. The missionaries and the U.S. board voted to close the schools rather than violate their principles. Both McCune and Moffett were forced to leave the country, and Moffett died three years later in Monrovia, California. Of Moffett's five sons, four became ordained Presbyterian ministers and three of these missionaries, including Samuel Hugh *Moffett.

BIBLIOGRAPHY Charles A. Clark, "A Great Church and A Great Evangelist," in Board of Foreign Missions, Presbyterian Church in U.S.A., *One World A-Building* (1946), pp. 87–96; Jong H. Lee, "Samuel A. Moffett's Reform Theology and His Mission in Korea in the Maturing Period: 1920–1936," *The Journal of Modern Korean Studies* 4 (May 1990): 53–77, and "Samuel Austin Moffett" (Ph.D. diss., Union Theological Seminary, Richmond, Va., 1983); Harry A. Rhodes, ed., *History of the Korea Mission, Presbyterian Church U.S.A., 1884–1934* (c. 1935)

Alan Neely

Moffett, Samuel Hugh (1916–), American missiologist. Born in Pyongyang, the son of Samuel A. *Moffett, Moffett received his basic education in Korea, then returned to the United States and graduated from Wheaton College (B.A., 1938), Princeton Theological Seminary (Th.B., 1942), and Yale University (Ph.D., 1945). In 1942 he married Elizabeth B. Tarrant. After ordination and a period as an assistant and interim pastor, he was youth director for the Presbyterian Board of Foreign Missions before he and his wife were appointed missionaries to China in 1947. He was a member of the faculty of Yenching University and Nanking Theological Seminary until 1951, when he was expelled from the People's Republic of China. He served as visiting lecturer in missions and homiletics at Princeton Theological Seminary (1953–1955) and as acting candidate secretary for the Presbyterian Board of Foreign Missions (1954–1955). His wife died January 17, 1955. In October 1955 he returned to Korea, where he was professor, dean of the graduate school, and co-president of the Korean Presbyterian Seminary in Seoul. In 1956 he married Eileen Flower whom he had met in Princeton. He was also director of the Asian Center for Theological Studies and Mission (1974–1981). Following his return to the United States in 1981, he was appointed the Henry Winters Luce Professor of Ecumenics and Mission at Princeton Theological Seminary. He retired from this post in 1986. Moffett served as president of the Royal Asiatic Society and the American Society of Missiology, and as a member of the U.S. Educational Commission on Korea. His published works include *Where'er the Sun* (1953), *The Christians of Korea* (1962), and *A History of Christianity in Asia, vol. 1: Beginnings to 1500* (1992).

BIBLIOGRAPHY *Princeton Seminary Alumni News* 20 (June 1986): 14.

Alan Neely

Mogrovejo, Toribio Alfonso de (1535–1606), second archbishop of Lima. Mogrovejo, who is known by his first name, Toribio, was responsible for reorganizing the Peruvian church and systematizing the evangelization of the Indians. Born in Mayorga, Spain, he studied law at the University of Valladolid and canon law at Salamanca. In 1574 Toribio was named president of the tribunal of the inquisition in Granada, a post he exercised for five years. Prior to his ordination (c. 1579), King Philip II named him archbishop of Lima. He was consecrated in Seville in 1580 and arrived in Lima in 1581. One of his first actions was to call the third Lima council, held between 1582 and 1583. This council, considered the most important of all colonial councils in South America, drew together eight bishops from Colombia to Chile and twenty-two theologians and religious superiors. The principal issue on the agenda of the council was how to evangelize the Indians more effectively. The council produced legislation that influenced all subsequent church councils even into the nineteenth century. The council also produced a catechism in three languages, Spanish, Quechua, and Aymara. In general the council emphasized the importance of preaching in the languages of the Indians and using gentle persuasion.

Toribio is famous for his many visits to his archdiocese, which included nearly all of modern Peru. Indeed, 17 of his 25 years were spent as archbishop traveling. His longest visit (1584–1590) took him through the Callejón de Huaylas in the north central region of Ancash. On these visits he preached to the Indians and baptized, confirmed, and married them. Toribio wrote to the king criticizing the abusive practices of the corregidores, or king's officials, and the reduction system that forced the Indians to live in towns controlled by the Spanish. Toribio himself was criticized by the viceroys who ruled Peru during his administration for his absences and his defense of the church's rights. Toribio founded the seminary of Lima (1584), which to this day bears his name.

BIBLIOGRAPHY Enrique Bartra, *Tercer concilio limense 1582–1583* (1982); Enrique Dussel, *El Episcopado latinoamericano y la liberación de los pobres, 1504–1620* (1979); Mary McGlone, "The King's Surprise: The Mission Methodology of Toribio de Mogrovejo," *The Americas* 50 (July 1993): 65–83; Vicente Rodríguez Valencia, *Santo Toribio de Mogrovejo, organizador y apóstol de Sur América,* 2 vols. (1957).

Jeffrey Klaiber, SJ

Moirans, Epifanio de (1644–1689), French Capuchin missionary in the Caribbean. At the age of 21, Moirans was sent as a missionary to Cuba and Venezuela. Together with another Capuchin, Francisco José de *Jaca, Moirans was one of the first in history to condemn the institution of slavery. After many setbacks, frustrations, and conflicts with Spanish colonial authorities, Moirans settled in Cuba and wrote his *Servi liberi seu naturalis mancipiorum libertatis iusta defensio* (Free servants, or a lawful defense of the natural liberty [of the Slaves], 1682), for which he, along with Jaca, was returned as a prisoner to Spain. The two have been referred to as "prophets of liberty" who condemned the entire slave trade on a doctrinal and moral basis.

BIBLIOGRAPHY José Tomás López García, *Dos defensores de los esclavos negros en el siglo XVII* (1982), contains not only the biographical data on Moirans and Jaca, but also the texts of their writings.

Alan Neely

Mokone, Mangena Maake (1851–c. 1936), South African pioneer of the Ethiopian Church movement. Mokone was born at Bokgaga, Gauteng, South Africa. After ten years of teaching and lay preaching, he entered the Methodist ministry and immediately became involved in the educational life of black people through the Kilnerton school, where he also served as principal. Because of alleged racial discrimination in the Methodist Church, Mokone resigned in 1892 and formed the first Ethiopian Church. His pan-African dream included uniting his church with other discontented black Christians throughout Africa. He was joined by other Methodist preachers, and soon the growth of the new church was a cause of concern for other denominations. Links with the African Methodist Episcopal (AME) Church in the United States were established when Bishop Henry M. *Turner visted South Africa to organize two conferences and ordain a number of new ministers.

Though overlooked as supreme office bearer when the Ethiopian Church formally became a district of the AME Church, Mokone refused to resign because of his determination to prove that black people could work together. Mokone is significant for being the first South African to initiate a church whose motto was "Africa for the Africans" and to challenge openly the racism of European missionaries, and he was one of the first black Christians to articulate a missionary strategy for black solidarity. Indirectly, he sowed the seeds of African nationalism and black theology.

BIBLIOGRAPHY Daryl M. Balia, *Black Methodists and White Supremacy in South Africa* (1991); J. M. Chirenje, *Ethiopianism and Afro-Americans in Southern Africa, 1883–1916* (1978); E. Roux, *Time Longer than Rope* (1948); Donald C. Veysie, *The Wesleyan Methodist Church in the Transvaal, 1823–1903* (1969).

Daryl M. Balia

Molnár, Mária (1886–1943), Hungarian missionary to the Admiralty Islands (Papua New Guinea). Molnár was born in Várpalota, Hungary. In 1902 she joined the Bethania Association, which had recently been established as the Hungarian branch of the pietistic Christian Endeavor (CE) movement. She trained as a nurse and midwife in the Hungarian Philadelphia Deaconess Union from 1904 to 1908. During World War I she worked in a hospital at the Hungarian front in Galicia. Through links with CE she went to Liebenzell, Germany, in 1925, initially for language study. Soon she felt called to work in the Admiralty Islands, a field of the Liebenzell Mission, and was sent there in 1927 by the Hungarian Reformed Mission Society. Known as Missis Doctor, she did pioneering work, especially on the islands of Manus and Pitilu with her co-worker Joseph Lomon.

Difficulties in sending hard currency forced the Hungarian mission contributors to seek alternative ways of supporting their missionaries. Many sent packages of various supplies, which helped to bring foreign mission closer to the heart of the ordinary church members. In a period of nationalistic tendencies, this focus on the worldwide spread of the kingdom of God helped to prepare for the revival of the Hungarian churches in the late 1940s. The martyr death of Molnár and her Liebenzell colleagues in 1943 by the Japanese military deeply shocked Hungarian Christians. Applications to replace her increased, but were in vain, due to the prohibition of foreign mission by the

Communists who ascended to power after World War II. Nevertheless, Molnár's legacy has kept the flame of foreign missions alive at the grass-roots level in Hungary.

BIBLIOGRAPHY Angéla Beliczay, *Engem várnak a szigetek: Molnár Mária tizenöt éve a pápuak között* (The islands await me: Mária Molnár's fifteen years among the Papuans) (1987); László Draskóczy, *Mindhalálig* (Till death) (1948); Lajos Ivanyos, *Hét év a kannibálok földjén; Molnár Mária missziói munkája Mánuszon* (Seven years among the cannibals: Mária Molnár's mission work at Manus) (1935); Friedrich Walter, *Das Kreuz unter Palmen: Ein Bericht über die Missionsarbeit auf den Admiralitätsinseln* (1959) and *Building Christ's Church at Manus: A Chronological Survey* (1981).

Anne-Marie Kool

Monchanin, Jules (Parama-Arubi-Ananda) (1895–1957), Catholic pioneer in Christian-Hindu dialogue. Monchanin was born, educated, and ordained in France. After a fruitful ministry there, he joined the Société des Auxiliares des Missions in 1939 and became the pioneer of that group of Roman Catholic contemplatives who represented the second wave of founders of Christian ashrams in India (the first wave was Anglican, Oriental [Syrian Orthodox, etc.] and Protestant). In Tamil Nadu, doing parish work initially, he was joined in 1948 by Henri *Le Saux; in March 1950 they established Saccidananda Ashram at Shantivanam, and Monchanin adopted the name Parama-Arubi-Ananda. Adapting the Rule of St. Benedict to local conditions, his aim was "nothing less than the assumption into the Church of the age-old Indian *sannyasa* [life of total renunciation] itself." His concern to identify with the poor in frugality and simplicity, and his obvious holiness, were admired by Hindus. Developing the thought of Brahmabandhav *Upadhyaya, but increasingly skeptical about the possibility of harmonizing Vedanta and Christianity, he explored in several works the object of the ashram's adoration and contemplation, the Trinity, or *Saccidananda.* In ill health, he returned to Paris, where he died.

BIBLIOGRAPHY Monchanin's *Indian Benedictine Ashram* (with Henri Le Saux, 1951) describes the principles of their adaptation. His other main works include *Écrits spirituels* (1965; Eng. version, J. G. Weber, ed., *In Quest of the Absolute: The Life and Work of Jules Monchanin,* 1970), *De l'esthétique à la mystique* (1967), *Mystique de l'Inde, mystère chrétien* (1974), and François Jacquin, ed., *Lettres à sa mère, 1913–1957* (1989). An excellent chapter on his ideas and a comprehensive bibliography appear in J. Mattam, *Land of the Trinity: A Study of Modern Christian Approaches to Hinduism* (1975).

Daniel O'Connor

Mondreganes, Pio M. de (1891–1964), Spanish Catholic missiologist. Mondreganes was born in Spain and played an important role in missiology from 1930 to 1960. A Franciscan Capuchin (OFM Cap), he studied missiology at the University of Münster, Germany, and spent his life teaching in this field at the Pontifical Urban University and at the University of the Capuchins in Rome. He was a prolific writer, publishing in Spanish and Italian. His *Manual of Missiology* (three Spanish editions 1933, 1947, 1951; Italian edition 1950) followed the traditional order of subjects introduced by Joseph *Schmidlin. His many articles were collected in *Missionary Problems* (Spanish, 1960) and revealed his broad interests. Mondreganes was inspired by the theological ideas of Theodor *Grentrup (Germany) and Pierre *Charles (Belgium) and not by the Spanish school of missiology, which centers on the notion of the Corpus Mysticum.

BIBLIOGRAPHY Angel Santos Hernández, *Misionologia: Problemas introductorios y ciencias auxiliares* (1961), pp. 163–164.

Arnulf Camps, OFM

Money, Herbert (1899–1996), missionary to Peru. Money was born in Hughenden, Queensland, Australia, and moved to Christchurch, New Zealand, in 1904. Attending evening classes and graduating from New Zealand Technical College, he was the first student in New Zealand to gain first-class honors for a master's degree in education. "As I understood it," he wrote, "the function of primary education involves not only the three R's but the cultivation of habits such as punctuality, truthfulness, honesty, neatness, obedience and courtesy." Throughout his career, he attempted to inculcate these values in school and church practice. He served first as a missionary in the Free Church of Scotland's Colegio San Andrés, Peru (1927–1939); here he married Netta Kemp. He later served as executive secretary of the Peruvian National Evangelical Council of Churches (1940–1967). Like many evangelicals of his time, Money was anti-communist and anti-ecumenical. Through his efforts Lima saw the first citywide evangelistic campaign (1957) under Oswald J. *Smith, a Billy *Graham campaign (1961), and the Latin American Consultation on Evangelism (Huampani, 1962), which led to the Evangelism-in-Depth program in Peru in 1967. Money returned to Christchurch in 1957.

BIBLIOGRAPHY G. Stewart McIntosh, ed., *The Money Memoirs, New Zealand and Peru,* 3 vols. (1988).

G. Stewart McIntosh

Mongiardino (*or* Monguiardino; Monnggiardino), José (?–1877), pioneer Bible colporteur in South America. An Italian by birth, Mongiardino became an agent of the British and Foreign Bible Society (BFBS) and, according to one chronicler, set forth in 1876 on "the greatest colportage journey" ever made in South America. The following year he entered Bolivia via Potosí and Sucre and, according to the society's records, sold more than 1,000 copies of the Scriptures in Spanish. Attempting to return to Argentina by his original route, Mongiardino was attacked and stoned to death near the town of Santiago Cotagaita, Bolivia. The civil authorities discovered his body in a nearby river with a large rock tied to his neck. Because money was found among his possessions, religious fanaticism, not robbery, was considered to be the motive for the homicide. Mongiardino was thus the first victim of anti-Protestant violence in Bolivia. Because he was not Roman

Catholic, the church refused to allow interment of his body in the local cemetery. Reporting Mongiardino's death, the BFBS's director in Buenos Aires wrote that the society "never had a braver or more devoted labourer than José Mongiardino."

BIBLIOGRAPHY Mortimer Arias, "Protestantismo," *Presencia,* August 6, 1976, p. 81; José Roberto Arze, *Figuras eclesiásticas en Bolivia* (1985); R. Kilgour, "Bible Work in Chile, Peru, and Bolivia," in Webster E. Browning et al., eds., *The West Coast Republics of South America* (1930); *The Seventy-Fourth Report of the British and Foreign Bible Society* (1878), pp. 171–172; C. Peter Wagner, *The Protestant Movement in Bolivia* (1970).

Alan Neely

Moninger, (Mary) Margaret (1891–1950), American Presbyterian missionary in China. Born near Marshalltown, Iowa, Moninger graduated Phi Beta Kappa from Grinnell College (B.A., 1913; M.A., 1922), where she was a member of the Student Volunteer Movement. Following two years' teaching in high schools, she was appointed by the Presbyterian Board of Missions to Hainan Island, China. She taught or served as principal at the girls' schools at Kachek, Ndoa, and Kiungchow during most of her career, but also worked as an itinerating missionary. A tireless worker for the cause of female education, she accompanied her students to meetings associated with the May Fourth movement and sought to instill in them a sense of nationalism. As a hobby she collected botanical specimens which now reside at the National Arboretum of the Philippines and Harvard University. Violence forced her to flee to Haiphong, Indochina, for six weeks in 1925, and to the United States in 1927 to 1929. She was prevented from leaving Nodoa for 15 months (1937–1939) because of Japanese military activities, and was working at Kiungchow in July 1941 when she and her colleagues were formally placed under house arrest. Well treated by the Japanese, she was repatriated first to Shanghai and then to the United States on the *Gripsholm* in 1942. She died in Marshalltown.

BIBLIOGRAPHY Kathleen L. Lodwick, "Women at the Hainan Presbyterian Mission: Ministry and Diversion," *American Presbyterians: The Journal of Presbyterian History* 65 (1987): 19–28, "The Presbyterian Mission on Hainan Under the Japanese, 1937–1941," *American Presbyterians: The Journal of Presbyterian History* 70 (1992): 247–258, "Teaching the Chinese Nationalism: Margaret Moninger at the Hainan Presbyterian Mission Schools, 1915–1927," *Journal of Church and State* 36 (1994): 833–846, and *Educating the Women of Hainan: The Career of Margaret Moninger in China, 1915–1942* (1995).

Kathleen L. Lodwick

Monnier, Henri (1896–1944), Swiss Seventh-day Adventist (SDA) missionary in Rwanda. Born in Pieterien, Bern Canton, the fifth of twelve children, Monnier worked in the watchmaking industry after eight years of formal education. He moved to London in the watch trade in 1915 and in 1919 married Winfred Maddams. A few months later, D. E. Delhove, a Belgian missionary who had worked in East Africa, persuaded the couple to accompany him to Rwanda, which had just become a Belgian trust territory. Arriving in 1919, they occupied two of the former Bethel Lutheran mission stations. Winfred died at Kirinda in 1920, shortly after childbirth. Delhove established Gitwe, near Nyanza, and Monnier settled at Rwankeri, in the northwest. In 1924 Monnier returned to Switzerland and married Olga Pavlov, who joined him in his work. Monnier and Delhove employed the traditional threefold Protestant missionary approach of the time, which included direct communication of the gospel, networks of schools, and medical dispensary work. Monnier exerted a powerful influence upon the Banyarwanda and in the early 1930s this work culminated in one of the most notable people movements in SDA mission history. Hutu and Tutsi were united in an outbreak of enthusiasm that brought thousands into the church. Monnier was a natural linguist and an active member of the British and Foreign Bible Society-sponsored team that translated the Bible into Kinyarwanda under the direction of H. E. Guillebaud. The Kinyarwanda New Testament was published in 1931; Monnier worked on revisions and on parts of the Old Testament for the remainder of his life. He died of typhoid fever in Beirut, Lebanon, during a trip. In addition to his translation work, which included a hymnal, Monnier wrote a Kinyarwanda grammar for English-speaking people and a series of Kinyarwanda pamphlets on the gospel and the major doctrines of the Christian church.

BIBLIOGRAPHY A. Long, "Christianity in Rwanda, with Special Emphasis on the Seventh-day Adventist Church" (M.A. thesis, Andrews Univ., 1973); Ian Linden, *Church and Revolution in Rwanda* (1977); "Monnier, Henri" and "Rwanda," in *Seventh-day Adventist Encyclopedia,* 2d rev. ed. (1996); M. Twagirayesu and Jan van Butselaar, eds., *Ce don que nous avons reçu* (1982).

Russell L. Staples

Monsen, Marie (1878–1962), Norwegian missionary in China. Monsen was a catalyst for the Shantung revival of the early 1930s. She had had an apparently disastrous first trip to China soon after 1900; then, in 1911, she came to Nanyangfu, Honan (Henan) Province, with the Norwegian Lutheran Mission. When missionaries fled the interior of China in late 1926 and early 1927, she visited missions in Manchuria, then went to Chefoo (Yantai), Shantung (Shandong) Province. There she met U.S. Southern Baptist missionaries and participated in some dramatic prayer and healing sessions. She returned to Shantung in late 1929 or 1930, and this visit helped to spark a province-wide revival that soon included the U.S. Southern Baptists, Presbyterians, and others. It also influenced a more openly Pentecostal native Chinese "spiritual gifts" revival movement.

Monsen seems to have been a quasi-Pentecostal, stressing the baptism or fullness of the Holy Spirit in addition to an initial conversion experience, and her meetings were emotional if not disorderly. She was by all accounts soft-spoken, and it is not altogether clear why she prompted such strong response. An interesting feature of the Shantung revival was its clearly Pentecostal features occurring in anti-Pentecostal mission bodies.

Well known after the Shantung events, Monsen visited many other missions in the early 1930s. She dropped out of sight after 1933 and presumably returned to Norway. Her book, *The Awakening: Revival in China, A Work of the Holy Spirit,* was published (in Norwegian) in 1959 (English translation by Joy Guinness, 1961).

BIBLIOGRAPHY Marie Monsen, *A Present Help,* Joy Guinness, trans. (1960; later published under the title *Wall of Fire,* 1967). Gustav Carlberg, *China in Revival* (1936), pp. 67–83; Mary K. Crawford, *The Shantung Revival* (1933); C. L. Culpepper, *The Shantung Revival* (1968).

Daniel H. Bays

Montalbán, Francisco Javier (1895–1945), Jesuit seminary professor in Shanghai and mission historian. Born in Gordejuela, Vizcaya, Spain, Montalbán entered the Society of Jesus in 1912 and was ordained in 1926. In 1930 he earned his doctorate in Munich with the dissertation *Das spanische Patronat und die Eroberung der Philippinen.* In China from 1930 to 1936, he taught church history in the Jesuit seminary in Zikawei, near Shanghai. There he published his *Manuale Historiae Missionum* (1935), although it was incomplete because European sources were not available to him. Nevertheless it was a useful handbook because it was based on Joseph *Schmidlin's *Catholic Mission History* and Descamps's compendium *Histoire générale comparée des missions* as well as *Revue d'histoire des missions* and *Zeitschrift für Missionswissenschaft.* In 1938 a Spanish translation was published. In 1936 Montalbán returned to Spain, where he lectured at the theological faculty at Marneffe-Oña and worked at the Secretariado de Misiones in Pamplona. He died in Oña, Spain.

BIBLIOGRAPHY Montalbán published chiefly in the journal *El Siglo de las Misiones.* See especially his articles "Maria en la teologia de las misiones," 25 (1938): 193–198, "El P. Ledóchowski y las misiones," 30 (1943): 42–45, and his book *La Compañía de Jesús Misionera 1540–1940* (1941). For biographical information see *El siglo de las misiones* 33 (1946): 68–69, and *NZM* 2 (1946): 132.

Karl Müller, SVD

Montesinos, Antonio de (*or* Antón Montesino) (c. 1486–c. 1530), Dominican missionary to the West Indies. Details about Montesinos's life are as uncertain as his name. He joined the Dominicans in Salamanca in 1502, and two years later was sent with others of his order to Hispaniola (now Haiti and the Dominican Republic). In his sermons he forcefully condemned Spanish colonists for their mistreatment of indigenous peoples. "You are all living in mortal sin!" he cried. "Know that you can no more be saved than Moors or Turks." Incensed by this unexpected denunciation, the colonists protested vigorously. He was recalled to Spain, where he had opportunity to exert his influence directly in behalf of the Indians. The ensuing Laws of Burgos (1512) and Valladolid (1513) evidence his struggle on their behalf. He was in the Americas at least three additional times, in 1515, from 1522 to 1524, and in 1527. In 1527, he joined an expedition to Jamestown, Virginia, but the attempt to found a colony there failed. Nothing specific is known of his death except the four words written in the margin of the record of his entry into the Dominican Order: "*Obit Martr in Indiis.*" *Las Casas often paid tribute to Montesinos as his mentor, and Montesinos's impact on this renowned Apostle to the Indians is undeniable.

BIBLIOGRAPHY Enrique Dussel, *A History of the Church in Latin America* (1981); Gustavo Gutiérrez, *Las Casas: In Search of the Poor of Jesus Christ* (1993); "The Sermons of Friar A. de Montesinos, 1511," in Lewis Hanke, *The Spanish Struggle for Justice in the Conquest of America* (1965), pp. 17–18.

Alan Neely

Montfort, Louis-Marie Grignion de. *See* Grignion de Montfort, Louis Marie.

Montgomery, Helen (Barrett) (1861–1934), American Baptist missions author and promoter. Helen Barrett was born in Kingsville, Ohio, the eldest of three children of Adoniram Judson Barrett and Emily B. Barrows. She graduated from Wellesley College and Brown University, where she majored in classical literature. For a time she taught school in Philadelphia; in 1887 she married William A. Montgomery and the couple moved to Rochester, New York, where William Montgomery became a successful automobile industrialist. In Rochester Helen Montgomery became active in civic and educational affairs. She advocated a women's college at the University of Rochester and became the first woman elected to the city school board. She also became interested in overseas mission work and was much in demand as a platform speaker and writer. In 1914 she was elected the first president of the national Woman's American Baptist Foreign Mission Society. With her close friend Lucy W. *Peabody, Montgomery joined the Central Committee on the United Study of Foreign Missions and wrote widely for the development of cooperative women's missionary work. In 1910 she wrote *Western Women in Eastern Lands,* which sold over 100,000 copies; that same year she toured the United States on behalf of the International Jubilee of Women's Missions, delivering almost 200 speeches. In 1913, in response to an invitation to attend the Edinburgh Continuation Committee meeting in The Hague, she and Lucy Peabody toured Europe, the Middle East, India, and the Far East, assessing the conditions of women's education. Everywhere she visited she spoke boldly on behalf of Christian schools and the training of women teachers. Seven Christian schools in the Far East were started or strengthened as a result of the tour. At the conclusion of the trip, Montgomery and Peabody advocated the establishing of an annual day of world prayer to unite women of the world and emphasize their issues; the Federation of Women's Boards of Foreign Missions adopted this timely suggestion, which eventually became the World Day of Prayer. In 1920, Montgomery was elected the first woman president of an American denomination, the Northern Baptist Convention. In this role she advocated the Baptist principle of "soul liberty" against a rising tide of fundamentalism and urged that priority be placed on the missionary task of the church rather than on divisive theological issues. Her greatest literary achievement was the *Centenary Translation of the New Testament* (1924), the first New Testament translation by a woman scholar. The sales derived from this translation went directly to mission projects supported by Northern Baptists.

BIBLIOGRAPHY Among Montgomery's most important works are *The King's Highway: A Study of Present Conditions on the Foreign Field* (1915), *From Jerusalem to Jerusalem* (1929), and *The Preaching Value of Missions* (1931). Her autobiography, *Helen Barrett Montgomery: From Campus to World Citizenship* (1940), can be supplemented with R. Pierce Beaver, *American Protestant Women in World Mission: A History of the First Feminist Movement in North America* (1980) and William H. Brackney, "Helen B. Montgomery and Lucy W. Peabody," in Gerald H. Anderson et al., eds., *Mission Legacies* (1994), pp. 62–70.

William H. Brackney

Montgomery, Henry Hutchinson (1847–1932), Anglican bishop of Tasmania and secretary of the Society for the Propagation of the Gospel (SPG). Montgomery was born in Cawnpore, India, the son of Richard Montgomery, lieutenant governor of Punjab and chief commissioner of Oudh. He was educated at Harrow and studied moral sciences at Cambridge. He was ordained in 1871 and served as a curate at Hurstpierpoint. In 1881 he married Maud Farrar, daughter of the well-known Victorian churchman, F. W. Farrar. He became vicar of St. Mark's, Kennington, the same year, and served there until being appointed bishop of Tasmania in 1889. He became secretary of SPG in 1901, in which post he was an active and inspiring missionary leader, visiting Canada, China, Japan, Korea, Malaya, and Borneo during his time of office. He attended the Lambeth Conference of 1897 as a bishop and was active as secretary to the 1908 and 1920 conferences. In his time, annual giving to SPG rose from £88,000 to £151,000. He retired in 1918 to the family home in County Donegal, Ireland.

BIBLIOGRAPHY Montgomery wrote widely between 1896 and 1932, mostly in SPG publications. He also wrote *Foreign Missions* (1902), *Service Abroad* (1910), and *Life's Journey* (1916). M. M. [Maud Montgomery], *Bishop Montgomery: A Memoir* (1933).

Timothy Yates

Moody, Campbell Naismith (1866–1940), English Presbyterian missionary in Taiwan. The most distinguished student of his class in the Glasgow Free Church College, Moody had already spent five years in mission work in Glasgow before he reached Taiwan in 1895, where he became an outstanding missionary evangelist. In his first four years he established eleven churches, and in ten years he had preached in 900 of the 1,100 villages in the central Chiang-hoa region. Usually accompanied by apprentice preachers and other colleagues and with a trumpet to herald his presence, he announced the good news in impeccable Taiwanese. Moody the scholar took great pains to develop the best means of expressing the message and clarifying its content. Concerned that converts should not be too far from an established church, he adopted what came to be known as the planetary system, in which the mission center is the sun and outstations are planets, each with its growing number of satellites. He was well read in early church history and wrote a number of scholarly academic studies.

BIBLIOGRAPHY Campbell Naismith Moody, *The Heathen Heart* (1907), *The Saints of Formosa* (1911), *The Mind of the Early Converts* (1920), *The Purpose of Jesus* (1928), *Christ For Us and In Us* (1935), and *The Childhood of the Church* (1938). Edward Band, *Working His Purpose Out: The History of the English Presbyterian Mission 1847–1949* (1948).

H. Daniel Beeby

Moody, D(wight) L(yman) (1837–1899), American evangelist. Born in Northfield, Massachusetts, Moody left home at age 17 to work in his uncle's shoe store in Boston. Converted under the influence of his Sunday school teacher, he joined a Congregational church. In 1856 he headed for Chicago, where he engaged in a variety of business pursuits and evangelistic work. He started a Sunday school in 1858 and served as an evangelist and relief worker with the U.S. Christian Commission during the Civil War. In 1863 he organized the independent Illinois Street Church in Chicago, and in 1866 he became president of the city's YMCA. Moody made a preaching tour of major British cities during the years 1873 to 1875, during which he and songster Ira Sankey attracted enormous crowds. For the next five years he conducted urban revivals in America's largest cities, then returned to Great Britain for another series of meetings from 1881 to 1884. His urban campaigns in North America continued until 1891, when he began to focus on other endeavors.

Moody's efforts helped to shape a new and ardently evangelical transatlantic network. In 1880 he founded the Northfield Conferences, which were used to promote holiness teachings, premillennial views of the end times, and the use of nondenominational agencies to propagate the gospel. Speakers such as James Hudson *Taylor, founder of the China Inland Mission, were featured at Northfield. A YMCA conference for college students at Northfield in 1886 led to the formation of the Student Volunteer Movement for Foreign Missions, which adopted the watchword "the evangelization of the world in this generation." In 1889 Moody assisted in the founding of a Bible institute in Chicago to train urban evangelistic workers and foreign missionaries. This school, renamed the Moody Bible Institute after Moody's death, proved to be his greatest contribution to the missionary enterprise. It has trained more missionaries than any other single institution in the United States.

BIBLIOGRAPHY The most careful and insightful treatment of Moody's life and times is James F. Findlay, *Dwight L. Moody* (1969); the second edition of William R. Moody, *D. L. Moody* (1930) is helpful as well. On the transatlantic evangelical network and Moody's central role, see Ernest R. Sandeen, *The Roots of Fundamentalism* (1970), chap. 7, "The Millenarian Meridian." See also Stanley M. Gundry, *Love Them In: The Proclamation Theology of Dwight L. Moody* (1982) and Gene A. Getz, *M.B.I.: The Story of Moody Bible Institute* (1969). Of the many collections of Moody's sermons and addresses, one of the best is W. H. Daniels, ed., *Moody, His Words, Work, and Workers* (1877). Significant collections of Moody's papers are held at the library of the Yale University Divinity School, the Library of Congress, the Moody Bible Institute, and the Mount Hermon School in Northfield, Mass.

Joel Carpenter

Moomaw, Ira W. (1894–1990), Church of the Brethren missionary and director of Agricultural Missions (AM). Born in Hartville, Ohio, Moomaw married Mabel Winger in 1920. In 1923 they began 17 years of agricultural mission in India. When Mahatma Gandhi formed the All India Committee for Basic Education, he invited Moomaw to be a member, the only missionary so recognized. This experience proved decisive. As a result of Gandhi's insistence on goals and program methods appropriate to village life and culture, Moomaw understood the intimate relationship between poverty, injustice, and world peace. In 1940 he was awarded a Ph.D. from Ohio State University, and in 1946 he joined the staff of AM as educational secretary, then served as executive secretary from 1954 to 1962. His leadership was characterized by focused purpose and insistence on practical programs. Traveling throughout the world to promote development through agricultural missions, he encouraged the highest standards of professional preparation. During his tenure the number of AM missionaries with advanced training in agriculture, home economics, and rural sociology tripled. At the same time he promoted the training of local people for leadership in their communities. In retirement he taught at his alma mater, Manchester College, Indiana, and at Bethany Theological Seminary. He also wrote prolifically. His best-known works include *Deep Furrows* (1957), *To Hunger No More* (1963), *What Future for Aid* (1966), *Crusade Against Hunger* (1966), and *The Challenge of Hunger* (1966).

BIBLIOGRAPHY J. Benton Rhodes, "Moomaw, Ira Wilbur," *The Brethren Encyclopedia*, vol. 2 (1983), p. 874, and "Agricultural Missions Today and Yesterday," *International Review of Mission* 64, no. 256 (October 1975): 346–353 (reprinted in *Brethren Life and Thought* 21, no. 4 [Autumn 1976]: 209–214).

Wilbert R. Shenk

Moon, Charlotte ("Lottie") Diggs (1840–1912), revered Southern Baptist missionary in China. Born in Albemarle County, Virginia, Moon was educated at the Virginia Female Seminary (now Hollins College), near Roanoke, and at the Albemarle Female Institute in Charlottesville, where she received an M.A. in classics in 1861. She returned home and remained there during the final years of the Civil War; then, for three brief periods, she taught school in Alabama, Kentucky, and Georgia. Moon was appointed a missionary to China in 1872, one of the first unmarried women to be sent by the Southern Baptist Convention Foreign Mission Board. Her entire 40-year career was spent in northern China, first in Tengchow and later in Pingtu. Not satisfied to be only a teacher of Chinese children, she also became an effective evangelist of Chinese women.

Her most conspicuous contributions, however, were her challenge to Southern Baptist women to form their own missionary organization for the support and promotion of foreign missions, and her admonition to young women to heed the call of China. Her constant stream of letters and articles appealing for more recruits and financial support prompted Southern Baptist women to initiate an annual Christmas offering for foreign missions in 1888—an offering later named for Moon—which grew from an initial $3,000 to more than $82 million in 1993. Her impact on board policy was extraordinary and included her advocacy for women to be utilized as missionary evangelists, for newly appointed missionaries to be involved in mission work immediately (rather than waiting to complete language study), and for establishing regular furloughs for all missionaries. Her deep respect and belief in the ability of the Chinese people was in sharp contrast to the attitude of some of her colleagues. "It is comparatively easy to give oneself to mission work," she once said, "but it is not easy to give oneself to an alien people. Yet the latter is much better and truer work than the former."

Moon chided Southern Baptists for their doctrinal disputes, the inconsistency of their sending missionaries to Africa while oppressing or ignoring blacks in the United States, and their meager interest in and support of foreign missions. Forty years of such admonitions and appeals had their effect, and the Southern Baptist Convention became one of the leading missionary sending bodies in the world.

Moon survived numerous hardships, including the Boxer Rebellion of 1900–1901, but loneliness and recurring bouts with illness and emotional depression brought on by malnutrition during a national famine induced her colleagues to insist that she return to the United States. In December 1912 she was carried on board a ship bound for America, but she died on Christmas Eve, while the vessel was anchored in the harbor of Kobe, Japan. Her stature and impact have increased since her death.

BIBLIOGRAPHY Catherine B. Allen, *The New Lottie Moon Story* (1980), and "Charlotte (Lottie) Moon," in Gerald H. Anderson et al., eds., *Mission Legacies* (1994), pp. 205–215; Irwin T. Hyatt, Jr., *Our Ordered Lives Confess* (1976), pp. 63–136; Una Roberts Lawrence, *Lottie Moon* (1927); Helen Albee Monsell, *Her Own Way: The Story of Lottie Moon* (1958).

Alan Neely

Moore, Joanna Patterson (1832–1916), American Baptist home missionary. Moore was born in Clarion County, Pennsylvania, the daughter of Irish immigrants. Reared in an Episcopalian home, she completed secondary school and taught school in Reedsburg, Pennsylvania. In 1852, following revival meetings, she joined the Baptist church at nearby Greenville. While attending

Rockford Seminary in Illinois, she developed an interest in freed slaves, and in 1863, went to live at Island Number 10 in the Mississippi River, in the midst of a large colony of destitute former slaves. With an appointment but no salary from the American Baptist Home Mission Society, Moore taught literacy skills on the island and later followed the community to Helena, Arkansas, where she opened a school for black soldiers. In the 1870s, after she turned down an invitation to become an overseas missionary for American Baptist women, she organized schools among the freedmen in Chicago and New Orleans, obtaining the first appointment of the Woman's Baptist Home Mission Society in 1877. Known as the Swamp Angel of the South in the 1890s, Moore established training institutes for mothers and children, and the Bible Bands and Sunshine Bands for churches and homes to promote Christian education and moral values. In her later years, she traveled in the southern states, visiting the schools and homes to which she had given her life. She died at Selma, Alabama.

BIBLIOGRAPHY Joanna Patterson Moore, "Reminiscences," *Baptist Home Mission Monthly* (1888): pp. 289–293, *For Mother, While She Rocks the Cradle* (1899), *In Christ's Stead* (1902; autobiography), and *The Power and Work of the Holy Spirit* (1912). Grace Eaton, *A Heroine of the Cross: Sketches of the Life and Work of Miss Joanna P. Moore* (1920); Walter S. Stewart, *Later Baptist Missionaries and Pioneers*, vol. I (1928).

William H. Brackney

Moorshead, Robert Fletcher (1874–1934), first medical secretary of the Baptist Missionary Society (BMS). Moorshead grew up in Bristol, England, and from his youth was determined to become a medical missionary. He qualified as a surgeon but was prevented by family responsibilities from going to China as a missionary. Instead, in 1902, he was appointed honorary secretary of the newly formed Medical Mission Auxiliary of the BMS, at a time when medical missions were struggling to establish their credentials within the Protestant missionary movement. He remained as secretary until the auxiliary was absorbed fully into the BMS in 1925, after which he continued as medical officer of the society until his death. From 1927 he also served as medical superintendent of the London Medical Mission. Moorshead visited India in 1906. His vision for the potential of medical work among the animistic Konds of Orissa was fulfilled in the opening of the Moorshead Memorial Christian Hospital at Udayagiri in 1939.

BIBLIOGRAPHY H. V. Larcombe, *First, the Kingdom! The Story of Robert Fletcher Moorshead, Physician* (1936); Brian Stanley, *The History of the Baptist Missionary Society, 1792–1992* (1992).

Brian Stanley

Morales, Juan Bautista de (1597–1664), Dominican missionary in China. Morales was born in Ecija, Sevilla, Spain. He entered the order of St. Dominic in 1614, and six years later left for Manila, where he studied the Amoy dialect to minister to the Chinese community. In 1628 and 1629 he made two trips to Cambodia to open a mission, but ultimately the Cambodian king forced the missionaries to leave. Morales returned to the Philippines but then left in March 1633 for Fu-an (Fu'an), Fukien (Fujian) Province, China. During his early years in China, he became convinced that new converts were involved in superstitious acts when honoring their ancestors and Confucius. After traveling to Foochow (Fuzhou) in late 1635 for discussions with the Jesuits, he sent a report and a list of thirteen questions to the archbishop of Manila. Despite Chinese persecution of the church, Morales continued his pastoral ministry until his expulsion to Macao in 1638. He returned to Manila, where church authorities decided that the questions about the rites could be settled only by the pope. Sent to Rome, Morales arrived there in 1643 and submitted the questions to Pope *Urban VIII. His successor, Innocent X, formally condemned certain Chinese rites as superstitious in his decree of September 1645. Meanwhile Morales went to Madrid to recruit more missionaries for Asia. Arriving back in Manila in 1648, he reached Fu-an the following year and there announced the papal decision. In 1656 he went to Chekiang (Zhejiang) Province; three years later he participated in the Dominican conference at Manila on affairs of China. He returned to Chekiang and in 1661 participated in the meeting of the Dominicans at Lan-ch'i (Lanqi) to discuss pastoral problems, including the favorable view of the rites that the Jesuit Martino *Martini had obtained from Rome in 1656. Because of poor health, Morales returned to Funing (Xiapu), Fukien, in 1662, where he died two years later.

BIBLIOGRAPHY Juan Bautista de Morales, *Sheng-chiao hsiao-ch'in chieh* (Explanation of Catholic filial piety) (n.d.). Benno Biermann, *Die Anfänge der neueren Dominikanermission in China* (1927); Henri Cordier, *Bibliotheca Sinica*, 5 vols. (1904–1924), 5:3910 (on Morales's Chinese-Spanish dictionary in the Vatican Library); José M. González, *Historia de las Misiones Dominicanas de China, 1632–1700* (1964), 1:82–87, 91–96, 114–119, 127–135, 149–161, 266–273, 342–348, 381–393, 684–687 (with a list of Morales's manuscripts).

John W. Witek, SJ

Moreau, Basile Antoine (1799–1873), French priest and founder of three religious congregations. Born in Laigné-en-Belin, France, Moreau was educated at the major seminary at Le Mans, France, and ordained to the priesthood in 1821. He asked permission from his bishop to join the Paris Foreign Missionary Society. Instead, he was sent for further theological studies with the Sulpicians at Issy (1821–1823). He became a seminary professor at Tessé, France (1823–1825), and at Le Mans (1825–1830). In 1834 he founded the Pious and Charitable Association of the Good Shepherd. In 1835 his bishop appointed him superior of the Brothers of St. Joseph, a community founded in 1820 by Jacques-François Dujarié at Ruillé-sur-Loir for the purpose of teaching catechism and other subjects in the villages. In 1837 Moreau created the Association of St. Joseph, meant for promoting devotion to St. Joseph and support of the Brothers. In 1835 he set up a network of what were called auxiliary priests to carry out missions in the country. In 1837, on his suggestion, the Brothers of St. Joseph and the auxiliary priests merged into one body. It was soon called the Congregation of Holy Cross, because its motherhouse was located in the neighborhood of Sainte Croix in Le Mans. In 1841 Moreau founded a female branch of his institute, the Sisters of Holy Cross. His vision was of one religious institute consisting of three autonomous societies. His model was the Holy Family; this is why he called the priests Salvatorists, the brothers Josephites, and the sisters Marianites of Holy Cross. The Congregation of Holy Cross grew rapidly; colleges and schools were opened in France and, beginning in 1842, in the United States and Canada. The North American schools were visited by the founder in 1857. Mission work was started in Algeria in 1841, and in Eastern Bengal (now Bangladesh) in 1852. In 1866 Moreau resigned as superior general and worked as an auxiliary priest in Le Mans until his death.

BIBLIOGRAPHY Étienne and Tony Catta, *Basil Anthony Mary Moreau,* translated from the French by Edward L. Heston (1955); James J. Denn, *The Theology of Preaching in the Writings of Basil Anthony Moreau* (1969). See also E. L. Heston, ed., *Circular Letters of the Very Reverend Basil Anthony Mary Moreau, founder of the Religious of Holy Cross* (1945; French ed., 1835–1866).

Marc R. Spindler

Morris, John Webster (1763–1836), English pastor and writer and an early supporter of the Baptist Missionary Society (BMS). A printer by trade, Morris left Norfolk, England, in 1785 to become pastor of Clipston Baptist Church, only seven miles from William *Carey in Northamptonshire. They entered the Northamptonshire Baptist Association simultaneously and became close friends. Morris joined the BMS committee in March 1793 and for some years assisted Andrew *Fuller in the arduous duties of secretary. He edited and printed the society's *Periodical Accounts* from 1798 to 1809. He wanted to be the first to publish Carey's memoirs but was turned down by Carey in 1831. Editing and printing was his avocation.

BIBLIOGRAPHY John Webster Morris, *Memoirs of the Life and Writings of the Rev. Andrew Fuller* (1816, 1826) and *Biographical Recollections of the Rev. Robert Hall* (1833)

A. Christopher Smith

Morris, William Case (1864–1932), founder of the Philanthropic Schools and Institutes of Argentina. Born in England, Morris went to Argentina as a boy with his widowed father. As a young businessman he developed a passion for educating poor children and went back to England to study for the Anglican priesthood. After ordination in 1898, he was accepted by the South American Missionary Society and returned to Buenos Aires where he opened his first school for children of the poor with eighteen students. His work grew to include twenty-two schools with 7,000 students; by the time of his death, more than 160,000 children had been educated in them. Until he received some support from the national government, he himself raised all the money needed to sustain these schools. He witnessed to his profound Christian faith not only through his educational work but also by regularly conducting religious services, editing a monthly Christian review, and publishing translations of religious books into Spanish. John *Mackay spoke of him as "the best-loved man in Argentina," one of that country's "most Christian and creative citizens."

BIBLIOGRAPHY John A. Mackay, *That Other America* (1935), pp. 136–140.

Richard Shaull

Morrison, Mary (Morton) (1791–1821), missionary in China. Mary Morton was born and brought up in Dublin, Ireland. She accompanied her father, John Morton, a surgeon of the East India Company (EIC), on a business trip to Macao, where they met Robert *Morrison of the London Missionary Society (LMS), the first Protestant missionary in China. Morrison and Mary Morton were married in February 1809 and made their home in Macao because no foreign women were allowed in Canton.

Life as a missionary wife was difficult for Morrison because she suffered from poor health and the tropical climate. Moreover, she was often alone in Macao because her husband was away on business for the EIC and the LMS. Her social life with the Western community, which was composed mostly of Catholic Portuguese, was severely restricted, even though she had learned Portuguese. This was evident in 1811 when her infant son, who lived less than a day, had to be buried under the city wall because permission was denied for him to be buried in the Catholic cemetery. In January 1815 Mary Morrison, with her two children, went to England to restore her health, returning to Macao in 1820. The next year, while pregnant, she died of cholera, and was buried in the newly established Protestant cemetery in Macao. Her son John Robert Morrison returned to Malacca to study at the Anglo-Chinese College and later inherited his father's position in the EIC. He became Chinese secretary to the superintendent of trade for the Hong Kong government. Her daughter Mary Rebecca Morrison became the second wife of Benjamin *Hobson, a medical missionary of the LMS in China.

BIBLIOGRAPHY Marshall Broomhall, *Robert Morrison: A Master Builder* (1924); Eliza Morrison, comp., *Memoirs of the Life and Labours of Robert Morrison, D.C., F.R.S., M.R.A.S., Member of the Society of Asiatique of Paris &c, &c., Compiled by His Widow; with Critical Notices of His Chinese Works by Samuel Kidd; and an Appendix Containing Original Documents,* 2 vols. (1839); Alexander Wylie, *Memorials of Protestant Missionaries to the Chinese: Giving a List of their Publications, and Obituary Notices of the Deceased, with Copious Indexes* (1867). An unpublished MS, "Domestic Memoir of Mrs. Morrison," is held by the Hong Kong Baptist Univ.

Timothy Man-kong Wong

Morrison, Robert (1782–1834), pioneer Protestant missionary to China. Morrison was born in Buller's

Green, Morpeth, Northumberland, England, and grew up at Newcastle-upon-Tyne. Following a rudimentary education, he was apprenticed to his father as a last and boot-tree maker. He joined the Presbyterian Church in 1798. Following the death of his mother in 1802, he decided to prepare for missionary work. He studied at Hoxton Academy, North London (1803), and at the Missionary Academy, Gosport, Hampshire (1804), where David *Bogue, one of the founders of the London Missionary Society (LMS), was principal. The LMS appointed Morrison as a missionary and he then studied medicine, astronomy, and Chinese in London. Following ordination in January 1807, he sailed for China by way of North America. He married Mary Morton (see Mary *Morrison) in Macao on February 20, 1809, and the same day was appointed translator to the East India Company (EIC), which gave him a legal footing for remaining on Chinese soil. His years in China were marked by constant tension with a government that discouraged its people from contact with foreigners. Morrison divided his time between official duties with the EIC, by which he supported himself, and his missionary and literary work. In 1813 he completed a translation of the New Testament into Chinese; it was published the following year. Chinese officials reacted with hostility and this alarmed the EIC, which nevertheless retained Morrison. In 1817 he was Lord Amherst's interpreter on an abortive mission to Peking (Beijing). In recognition of his work as lexicographer and translator, the University of Glasgow conferred its D.D. degree on him in 1817. Soon after arriving in China, Morrison proposed establishing a base on Prince of Wales Island (later known as Penang, off the west coast of Malay Peninsula) for training missionaries in Asia. He envisaged a triennial missionary conference. With his colleague William *Milne, he founded the Anglo-Chinese College at Malacca in 1818. Together they completed the translation of the entire Bible in 1819. Morrison's wife died in 1821, and he returned to Great Britain in 1823 with a collection of several thousand Chinese books, which were eventually deposited with University College, London. In 1824 he became a fellow of the Royal Society (FRS) and helped establish the short-lived Language Institution in London. That year he married Eliza Armstrong. In 1826 the Morrisons returned to Canton, where Robert died eight years later. He regarded his translation of the Bible as only a first step, a work that would be superseded by others in the future. His magnum opus was his three-volume Chinese-English dictionary (1815–1823). In addition, he wrote a Chinese grammar and several treatises on language. He translated hymns and a prayer book into Chinese and wrote various tracts and articles.

BIBLIOGRAPHY Eliza Armstrong Morrison, comp., *Memoirs of the Life and Labours of Robert Morrison, D.D.*, 2 vols. (1839). Marshall Broomhall, *Robert Morrison, A Master Builder* (1924); William Milne, *Retrospect of the First Ten Years of the Protestant Mission to China* (1820); W. J. Townsend, *Robert Morrison, The Pioneer of Chinese Missions* (1888). See also J. Sibree, ed., *Register of Missionaries, Deputations, Etc., London Missionary Society* (1923), p. 7.

Wilbert R. Shenk

Morrison, William McCutchan (1867–1918), Presbyterian missionary linguist and social reformer in the Congo. Morrison was born on a farm near Lexington, Virginia. He graduated from Washington and Lee University (1887) and was then employed for six years as a schoolteacher. He then entered the Presbyterian Theological Seminary at Louisville, from which he graduated in 1895. At seminary he volunteered for the African missions field and was sent to the American Presbyterian Congo Mission, founded at Luebo in 1890 by Samuel N. *Lapsley and William H. *Sheppard. Morrison quickly became the leader of the mission and began to develop a writing system for the widely spoken Tshiluba language. He published the important *Grammar and Dictionary of the Buluba-Lulua Language* (1906) and translated *Malesona* (Lessons from the Bible, 1913), and *Lumu Luimpe* (Gospels and Acts of the Apostles, 1919). Morrison also joined with British reformer E. D. Morel in publicly denouncing the human and economic exploitation perpetrated by the regime of Belgian King Leopold II in the Congo. Morrison's protests made him a marked man, and in 1909 he and Sheppard were sued for libel by the government-controlled Kasai Rubber Company. The trial received international publicity and the acquittal of the missionaries led to important reforms. Both Morrison and his spouse, Bertha Stebbins (d.1910) are buried in the church cemetary at Luebo.

BIBLIOGRAPHY Robert Benedetto, "The Presbyterian Mission Press in Central Africa," *Journal of Presbyterian History* 68 (1990): 55–69; Mary Kirkland, "Sketch of the Heroic Life Work of Rev. W. M. Morrison, D.D., in Africa," *Christian Observer,* August 21, 1918, pp. 825–826; Stanley Shaloff, *Reform in Leopold's Congo* (1970); T. C. Vinson, *William McCutchan Morrison: Twenty Years in Central Africa* (1921).

Robert Benedetto

Morse, Jedediah (1761–1826), American Congregational missions leader. Morse was born in Woodstock, Connecticut, and graduated from Yale (B.A., 1783). He was ordained in 1786 and in 1789 married Elizabeth Ann Breese and settled as pastor of the First Congregational Church of Charlestown, Massachusetts. A staunch Calvinist, in 1805 he founded a monthly magazine, the *Panoplist,* to rally New England orthodoxy against Unitarianism and to promote the cause of missions. Renamed the *Panoplist and Missionary Magazine* in 1808, it soon became an organ of the newly formed American Board of Commissioners for Foreign Missions (ABCFM). From 1820 on, it was the *Missionary Herald,* and until 1950 it was the oldest magazine of continuous circulation in the United States. Morse was elected a member of the ABCFM in 1811 and maintained a lifelong relationship with it. He had been instrumental in organizing the trinitarian General Association of Massachusetts clergy whose meeting at Bradford in 1810 created the ABCFM; he was also a principal founder of Andover Theological Seminary in 1808, which graduated many early missionaries. Morse also helped found the New England Tract Society (1808) and the American Bible Society (1816). He was secretary of the Society for Propagating the Gospel among the Indians, an interest he pursued after leaving his Charlestown parish in 1819. His *Report to the Secretary of War . . . on Indian Affairs* was published in 1822. He promoted missions to educate and Christianize the Indians and proposed intermarriage of whites and educated Indians so that "they would then be literally of one blood with us, be merged in the nation, and saved from extinction." Morse was most widely known as the "Father of American Geography"; a series of his publications on the subject virtually monopolized the field during his lifetime and beyond. He was the father of Samuel F. B. Morse, artist and inventor of the telegraph.

BIBLIOGRAPHY Morse's *Geography Made Easy* (1789) was the first book on the subject published in the United States. He also wrote *A Compendious History of New England* (1824) and *Annals of the American Revolution* (1824). J. K. Morse, *Jedediah Morse: A Champion of New England Orthodoxy* (1939); W. B. Sprague, *The Life of Jedediah Morse* (1874). Also see annual reports of the ABCFM between 1811 and 1827 and issues of the *Panoplist.*

David M. Stowe

Moses, David G. (1902–1974), Indian theologian. Moses was born in Tamil Nadu, South India, and received his education at Madras Christian College, where he studied philosophy under A. G. *Hogg. He devoted his life to Christian education, beginning his career as a lecturer and later serving as principal of Hislop College, Nagpur. He believed that Christian education prepared the Indian mind to receive the gospel. He served as president of the National Christian Council of India and gave an address at the Tambaram conference of the International Missionary Council (IMC) in 1938. He helped to bring about the integration of the IMC with the World Council of Churches in 1961. He took an active part in negotiations leading to the union of five denominations in the Church of North India (1970).

Moses's main contribution was to develop a philosophy of religious truth as a basis for a theology of mission and interreligious relationships. Maintaining that religious truth is different from other forms of truth and that other religions too contain truth values, he argued that the truth of the Christian faith is qualitatively different from others. On this basis he tried to define the content and practice of the church's mission in the world. He affirmed, however, that only through lives that are transformed by the truth in Christ can Asia be truly won for Christ.

BIBLIOGRAPHY Moses wrote *Religious Truth and the Relation between Religions* (1950); his articles include "The Problem of Truth in Religion," in *The Authority of Faith* (IMC, Madras Series, vol. 1, 1939), "Christianity and the Non-Christian Religions," *IRM* 43 (1954): 146–154, "India," in M. S. Bates and W. Pauck, eds., *Prospects of Christianity Throughout the World* (1964), pp. 227–244, and "To the Hindu: The Costliness of Salvation," in Gerald H. Anderson, ed., *Sermons to Men of Other Faiths* (1966), pp. 65–73.

Stanley J. Samartha

Moshoeshoe (also Moshesh, and various other spellings) (1786?–1870), founder of the Kingdom of Lesotho. Moshoeshoe was born at Menkhoaneng, in what is now northern Lesotho, son of a village headman. His original name was Lepoqo. He was early influenced by the religious and political reformer Mohlomi. About 1820, Moshoeshoe migrated to set up his own village. By military and diplomatic skill he incorporated various groups, many of them displaced by Zulu conquest, and in 1824 consolidated the process by migration to Thaba Bosiu, which he made a well-nigh impregnable mountain fortress. Having effectively formed a new nation, he had now to adjust to the encroaching white presence and for this purpose invited missionaries. Eugene *Casalis and Thomas *Arbousset of the Paris Evangelical Missionary Society arrived in 1833, and Moshoeshoe offered them every facility and encouragement, bringing Sotho institutions under Christian influence while avoiding disruption of the community. Education was encouraged, Christian burial introduced, the killing of witch suspects forbidden, and the powers of diviners curtailed; most remarkably, the "circumcision schools" for manhood initiation were discontinued. While he himself held back from full commitment, Moshoeshoe encouraged conversions in his family. Casalis became a trusted counselor, writer of Moshoeshoe's letters, and his intermediary in dealing with whites. Moshoeshoe handled relations with British and Boers with the same sagacity as he had shown with his African neighbors, maintaining the integrity and autonomy of Lesotho as far as he could, eventually accepting British protection as the least undesirable option, and forestalling white land ownership and future absorption into South Africa.

After 1847 Sotho disillusionment with whites slowed Christian progress; leading converts gave up their profession, and the circumcision schools returned. After Casalis left in 1855, no subsequent missionary held Moshoeshoe's confidence to the same degree. But in the 1850s Moshoeshoe was assuring the missionaries that the total victory of Christianity in the country was only a matter of time and patience. He was attracted to French Catholic missionaries who arrived in 1862, and inter-mission rivalries complicated matters. As death approached, however, Moshoeshoe told Adèle *Mabille (Casalis's daughter) that he had been a believer for three months. The date for his public baptism by the Paris missionaries was announced; he died the night before. He had, however, opened his nation to Christian conversion, in Protestant and Catholic forms, as a key to its survival and welfare in the new world. His rule fostered a long dialogue between Christianity and African culture, and it became a paradigm of the modern spread of Christianity in Africa. Today the Kereke ea Moshoeshoe, a large Independent church, claims to perpetuate his legacy by maintaining an African version of Christianity.

BIBLIOGRAPHY E. Casalis, *Les Bassoutos, ou vingt-trois années d'études et d'observations au sud de l'Afrique* (1859) and *My Life in Basutoland* (1889, 1971); D. F. Ellenberger and J. C. MacGregor, *History of the Bassuto, Ancient and Modern* (1912); E. W. Smith, *The Mabilles of Basutoland* (1939); Leonard Thompson, *Survival in Two Worlds: Moshoeshoe of Lesotho, 1786–1870* (1975).

Andrew F. Walls

Motolinía (Toribio de Benavente) (1495?–1565), one of twelve Franciscan "apostles" who first evangelized New Spain. Born in Spain as Toribio de Benavente, Benavente chose to call himself Motolinía, which means "poor" in the Tlaxcalan tongue. He arrived in 1524 and served as the first superior of the Franciscans in Mexico City. In 1529 he aroused the ire of authorities when he offered asylum to Indian leaders who complained of harsh taxation. He also served as guardian of the monastery in Tlaxcala and helped to found the town of Puebla. He made three different trips to Guatemala to aid in Christianizing the Indians.

In 1536 the Franciscan chapter of New Spain commissioned him to write an account of the life and beliefs of the Indians in pre-conquest times, as well as a chronicle of the Franciscans' efforts since their arrival in 1524. His work, finished in 1541, is the first ethnography of the Mexican Indians done by a European. Although influenced by the providentialist theories of his time, Motolinía nonetheless gives an accurate eyewitness account of Spanish mistreatment of the Indians. Although he himself took the Spanish to task, he also criticized *Las Casas for his many exaggerations. Motolinía's work became a basic sourcebook for other religious chroniclers and a guide for contemporary ethnologists.

He served as provincial of his order in Mexico from 1546 to 1551, and spent his last years in the friary of Mexico City.

BIBLIOGRAPHY Manuel Marzal, *Historia de la antropología indigenista: México y Perú* (1981, 1986); Robert Ricard, *The Spiritual Conquest of Mexico* (1933, 1966); Francis Borgia Steck, *Motolinía's History of the Indians of New Spain* (1951).

Jeffrey Klaiber, SJ

Mott, John R(aleigh) (1865–1955), missions and ecumenical statesman. Mott was born in Livingston Manor, New York. Raised in Postville, Iowa, in a pious Methodist home, he graduated from Cornell University in 1888 with a bachelor of philosophy degree and later received honorary degrees from Yale, Edinburgh, Princeton, Brown, Toronto, and other universities. While a Cornell undergraduate, he passed from agnosticism to faith through an evangelical conversion. Shortly thereafter, at Dwight L. *Moody's summer conference at Mount Hermon, Massachusetts, he was among the first hundred to sign the Student Volunteer Movement (SVM) declaration "It is my purpose, if God permit, to become a foreign missionary."

It was as Methodist layman, student leader, and international church statesman that Mott was to fulfill that commitment. While an undergraduate he built the Cornell University Christian Association into the largest and most active YMCA chapter on American campuses and served as its president. A one-year assignment upon graduation as traveling secretary with the intercollegiate YMCA stretched into 44 years of service as its student secretary (1888–1915) and general secretary (1915–1931). His charisma, evangelical fervor, and call for the "evangelization of the world in this generation" at successive SVM conferences resulted in enlistment of over 20,000 missionary volunteers by 1951.

Believing that Christian students could be the lever to move the world toward God, Mott led in the formation of the World's Student Christian Federation in 1895, becoming its general secretary (1895–1920) and its chairman (1920–1928). His world travels on behalf of the YMCA, the SVM, and the WSCF (a total of 1.7 million miles) stimulated the formation of national cooperating bodies, as well as the first ecumenical links between Orthodox and Protestant Christians and reconciliation between Christians of nations that had been at war.

As one of the founders of the Foreign Missions Conference of North America (1893), Mott led the planning for the World Missionary Conference at Edinburgh in 1910, served as its chairman, and headed its continuation committee. In 1912 and 1913 he circled the globe to stimulate the formation of national associations of students, youth, and churches and to conduct mass evangelistic crusades in China and India. He was instrumental in 1914 in establishing the Missionary Research Library in New York City. In 1921 he teamed with J. H. *Oldham to form the International Missionary Council (IMC), with Mott as chairman (1928–1946). Through the IMC he promoted global cooperation in missions and developed a pattern of representative leadership from churches of East and West, North and South, that became normative for the ecumenical movement.

Mott can rightly be called the father of the World Council of Churches (WCC) having been a leader in each of the movements that led to its formation. He played a large part in the first world conferences on Faith and Order (Lausanne, 1927; Edinburgh, 1938), and in those of the Life and Work movement (Stockholm, 1925; Oxford, 1937). Having chaired the provisional committee of the WCC, he was named its honorary president at the inaugural assembly at Amsterdam in 1948.

Mott saw the value of international Christian witness concerning issues of world peace and justice. Under his leadership, both the IMC and the YMCA engaged creatively in many partnerships with goverments. The American YMCA's National War Work Council under his chairmanship enlisted 20,000 men and women for relief work and service to soldiers and prisoners in 1915. He received the American Distinguished Service award for serving on President Woodrow Wilson's peace commissions to Mexico and Russia in 1916 and 1917, honors from more than twenty countries, and the Nobel Peace Prize (1946). He is buried in the (Episcopal) Cathedral Church of St. Peter and St. Paul in Washington, D.C.

BIBLIOGRAPHY Works by Mott include *Evangelization of the World in This Generation* (1900), *The Pastor and Modern Missions* (1904), *The Decisive Hour of Christian Missions* (1910), *The World's Student Christian Federation* (1920), *Cooperation and World Mission* (1935), and *Five Decades and a Forward View* (1939). See also his *Addresses and Papers,* 6 vols. (1946–1947). C. Howard Hopkins, *John R. Mott, 1865–1955* (1979) is the definitive biography; see also Hopkins' "John R. Mott," in Gerald H. Anderson et al., eds., *Mission Legacies* (1994), pp. 79–84; Basil Matthews, *John R. Mott: World Citizen* (1934) covers his early career. The principal sources on Mott's life and work are the John R. Mott and WSCF collections in the Yale Univ. Divinity School Library.

Norman E. Thomas

Motta, Waldomiro (1920–1996), Brazilian Baptist missionary in Bolivia. Motta and his wife, Ligia, were commissioned as missionaries by the Foreign Mission Board of the Baptist Convention of Brazil for work in Bolivia, and arrived at Santa Cruz in July 1946. Motta pioneered evangelistic and social work in a vast region of the eastern part of Bolivia, while Canadian Baptists had developed the Bolivian Baptist Union in the western part since 1898. In spite of strong opposition and even imprisonment because of his evangelistic work, Motta organized the First Baptist Church of Santa Cruz in 1947 and developed a plan for holistic mission including evangelistic, educational, and medical work. By 1957 a total of ten churches had been established, and Motta organized the Bolivian Baptist Convention and started the periodical *El Bautista Boliviano*. He also served for seven years as the chaplain of the prison in Santa Cruz. In 1956 his wife's health forced him to return to Brazil, where for 36 years he pastored the Praça do Carmo Baptist Church in Rio de Janeiro, continuing as an enthusiastic promoter of foreign missions until his retirement in 1992.

BIBLIOGRAPHY Reference material about Motta and Brazilian foreign missions is found in the archives of the Foreign Mission Board of the Brazilian Baptist Convention in Rio de Janeiro, and in the missionary periodical *O Campo é Mundo*.

Samuel Escobar

Moule, Arthur Evans (1836–1918), British Anglican missionary in China. A graduate of the Church Missionary Society (CMS) college, Islington, Moule arrived in Ningpo (Ningbo) with his wife in 1861. He participated in the General Missionary Conference in Shanghai in 1877, delivering a paper, "The Relation of Christian Missions to Foreign Residents." In 1881 he became secretary of the Shanghai district of the CMS. A few years later he was appointed archdeacon and assumed administrative responsibility for the entire work of the CMS in China. In addition to his administrative work, he engaged in local missionary work in Ningpo, Shanghai, and Hangchow (Hangzhou). When he returned to England in 1894, he left a congregation of 180 members with five schools and seven Chinese teachers. As a part of his ministry in Shanghai, he introduced expatriates to the work of Christian missions and showed them how it contributed toward "Christianizing, civilizing, and education in Western knowledge." Three of his major books are *The Glorious Land* (1891), *New China and Old* (3d ed., 1902), and *Half a Century in China* (1911). He also wrote extensively for the church papers *Intelligencer* and *Gleaner*. He and his wife had six sons, several of whom served in education and church-related ministries.

BIBLIOGRAPHY Arthur Evans Moule, *The Story of the Cheh-kiang Mission of the Church Missionary Society* (4th ed., 1891), *Half a Century in China: Reflections and Observations* (1911), *The Chinese People: A Handbook on China* (1914). *Arthur Evans Moule, Missionary to the Chinese: A Memoir by His Six Sons* (1921). See also Eugene Stock, *The History of The Church Missionary Society* (1899).

Ralph R. Covell

Moule, George Evans (1828–1912), Church Missionary Society (CMS) missionary and first Anglican bishop of mid-China. George Moule, his younger brothers Arthur E. *Moule and Handley Moule, were the sons of Henry Moule, Anglican vicar of Fordington in Dorset, England. George Moule was educated at Corpus Christi College, Cambridge, and after ordination in 1851 served as curate to his father. He offered himself to the CMS in 1857 and served at Ningpo, where he was joined by Arthur in 1861. They experienced the Taiping Rebellion at first hand when Ningpo was under siege in 1862. In 1864 George moved to Hangchow (Hangzhou), becoming the first missionary to serve away from a treaty port. In 1880 he became the first Anglican bishop of mid-China. His long and faithful episcopate included translating the Book of Common Prayer into classical Chinese and making a journey of 3,000 miles in 1892; it ended in 1907, when he resigned his see. One son and two daughters joined the Hangchow mission. He died at Auckland Castle on a visit to his brother Handley, then bishop of Durham.

BIBLIOGRAPHY A. E. Moule, tribute to G. E. Moule, *Church Missionary Review*, April 1912. Kenneth Scott Latourette, *A History of Christian Missions in China* (1929); Eugene Stock, *A History of the Church Missionary Society*, vols. 3 and 4 (1899, 1916).

Timothy Yates

Moulton, Ebenezer (1709–1783), American Baptist home missionary. Born in Windham, Connecticut, Moulton was the son of Robert Moulton and Hannah Grove, farmers. With no formal education and with the support of his family, he started a Baptist church at South Brimfield, Massachusetts, in 1736. He was ordained a Regular Baptist in 1741. In 1748 he became an adherent of New Light religious experience and ministered to New Light Congregationalists and Baptists, forming a splinter Baptist congregation in South Brimfield. He helped establish several New Light churches across Massachusetts in the next decade. In order to support his family, he became a shopkeeper, but by the end of the Seven Years' War he was insolvent. Fleeing from his creditors, he settled in Nova Scotia about 1763 and became a surveyor and magistrate in the Township of Yarmouth. In the Annapolis Valley, he again became an itinerant preacher, with regular preaching stations at Yarmouth (Jebogue), Barrington, Cornwallis, and Horton. In 1765 he established the first Baptist congregation in Nova Scotia at the village of Horton, unwittingly becoming the pioneer Baptist missionary to the Maritime Provinces. Opposition to his mission efforts was so strong that he was forced to withdraw to Yarmouth in 1767. In 1772, hearing that his creditors no longer pressed their claims, he returned to South Brimfield, where he died in 1783.

BIBLIOGRAPHY On Moulton's New England Baptist career, see Isaac Backus, *A History of New England with Particular Reference to the Denomination of Christians Called Baptists* (1871), and William G. McLoughlin, *New England Dissent, 1630–1833: Baptists and the Separation of Church and State* (1971), vol. 1, pp. 320–323, 475ff. For the Nova Scotia story, consult M. W. Armstrong, *The Great Awakening in Nova Scotia, 1776–1809* (1948).

William H. Brackney

Mouly, Joseph Martial (1807-1863), Vincentian missionary and bishop in China and Mongolia. Mouly was a member of the Congregation of the Mission founded by St. *Vincent de Paul, better known as Vincentians. At the age of 26, he left his native France for China, where his responsibilities increased steadily. By 1836 he had become superior of the French Vincentians in northern China. In 1842 he was ordained the first bishop of the newly created vicariate apostolic of Mongolia. Five years later the Holy See added to this task that of administrator apostolic of the diocese of Peking (Beijing). Finally, in 1856, when this diocese was abrogated and divided into three vicariates apostolic, Mouly became the first vicar apostolic of North Chihli, with residence in Peking.

Historians of modern China often fault Mouly for excessive displays of Gallic nationalism and heavy reliance on the French protectorate over Catholic missions. On the other hand, he also played a key role in expanding and organizing the Catholic Church in China.

BIBLIOGRAPHY *Annales de la Congrégation de la Mission et de la Compagnie des Filles de la Charité*, vol. 94 (1929), pp. 127-137; Jean Charbonnier, *Histoire des Chrétiens de Chine* (1992), pp. 231–238, and *La Congrégation de la Mission en Chine*, vol. 2, *La Mission française de Pékin* (1912); Antoine Thomas, *Histoire de la Mission de Pékin*, vol. 2, *Depuis l'arrivée des Lazarists jusqu'à la révolte des Boxeurs* (1933).

Jean-Paul Wiest

Moya de Contreras, Pedro (c. 1530-1591), archbishop of Mexico. Moya was born of a noble Castilian family and studied civil and canon law at Salamanca. After his ordination to the priesthood in 1571, Philip II sent him to Mexico to establish the Inquisition. He did so with comparative restraint, but he deferred generally to royal control of the church. He was then appointed archbishop of Mexico in 1571 and received the pallium—indicating full episcopal authority—in 1574. From 1583 to 1586 he was visitador general of Mexico and viceroy of New Spain. He was a bishop of the Council of Trent and of the Catholic Reformation, the views of which he tried to implement in the Third Mexican Council (1585), dedicated to the reform of the clergy and of the religious orders. His approach to the Indians was humanitarian, giving them just treatment. Returning to Spain in 1589, he was appointed president of the Council of the Indies.

BIBLIOGRAPHY Moya's letters appear in *Cartas de Indias* (1877). Stafford Poole, *Pedro Moya de Contreras: Catholic Reform and Royal Power in New Spain, 1571-1591* (1987).

Willi Henkel, OMI

Moye (*or* Moÿe; Moyë), Jean-Martin (1730-1793), French Catholic priest, mystic, founder of the Sisters of Providence, and missionary in China. Born in Cutting, Lorraine, France, Moye studied at the Jesuit college in Pont-à-Mousson, Strasbourg, and in Metz (1745-1754), where he later became apostolic vicar. In 1762, in what was the beginning of the Sisters of Providence, he began sending women to remote villages to teach. This much-disputed initiative and others led to the end of his vicariate in 1767. From 1772 he worked as a missionary of the Paris Foreign Missions in Szechwan (Sichuan) Province, China, where he was briefly imprisoned in 1774 but continued to visit clandestinely the Christian communities. He recruited Chinese Sisters of Providence, sending these Christian celibate women to villages that were barred to men. For health reasons he repatriated in 1782 and worked as apostolic missionary in Lorraine. Exiled to Trier during the French Revolution, he died from typhus in 1793, infected by a soldier he was tending. He wrote *Le dogme de la grace* (1774) and *Directoire des soeurs de la Providence de Portieux* (1858, 1874), as well as numerous works of devotion and prayers written in French and in popular Chinese. He was beatified in 1954.

BIBLIOGRAPHY Anne-Marie Abel, *La pauvreté dans la pensée et l'oeuvre de Jean-Martin Moyë (1730-1793)* (1972; includes complete bibliography); Generosa Callahan, *The Life of Blessed John Martin Moye* (1964); Jean Guennou, *Une spiritualité missionnaire: Le Bienheureux J.-Martin Moyë* (1970); George Tavard, *L'expérience de Jean-Martin Moye: Mystique et Mission, 1730-1793* (1978) and *Lorsque Dieu fait tout: La doctrine spirituelle du bienheureux Jean-Martin Moye* (1984).

Leny Lagerwerf

Muir, William (1819-1905), British colonial administrator in India, Islamic scholar, and advocate of Christian mission. Born in Scotland, Muir and elder brother, John (1810-1882), both served with the Indian Civil Service and were introduced to Oriental languages as part of their training. While John specialized in Sanskrit and Hinduism, William concentrated on Arabic and Islamic studies. Both put their learning to advantage as educators and supporters of Christian mission in India. William Muir's postings included intelligence in Agra (1857), educational development in Allahabad, and the governorship of the Northwestern Provinces (1868-1874). During his years in India he befriended the CMS missionary Karl *Pfander (1803-1865), who encouraged him to undertake his first major piece of academic writing, *The Life of Mahomet* (4 vols., 1858-1861). On retirement from political service, both Muirs returned to Edinburgh, where they continued their commitment to Oriental studies and comparative religion in the university. As Edinburgh University principal, William Muir produced further works on the Qur'an and Islamic history and wrote several studies of Christian-Muslim encounter that reflect his sympathy with the controversialist apologetic of Pfander and others.

BIBLIOGRAPHY Publications by Muir include *The Coran: Its Composition and Teaching* (1877), *The Early Caliphate and the Rise of*

Islam (1881), *Apology of al-Kindi* (tr., 1882), *Annals of the Early Caliphate* (1883), *The Caliphate: Its Rise, Decline, and Fall* (1891), *Mameluke, or Slave Dynasty of Egypt* (1896), *The Mohammedan Controversy* (1897), and *The Old and New Testaments, Tourat, Zabur, and Gospel: Moslems Invited to See and Read Them* (1899). Clinton Bennett, *Victorian Images of Islam* (1992); Avril Powell, *Muslims and Missionaries in Pre-Mutiny India* (1993); Christian Troll, *Sayyid Ahmad Khan: A Reinterpretation of Muslim Theology* (1978).

David A. Kerr

Mukhia, David (1901-1991), first Nepali Christian pastor in Nepal. Mukhia was born into a Gurung family of the Nepali diaspora, near Kurseong, Darjeeling district, India. He began his career as a schoolteacher and local preacher under the Eastern Himalayan mission of the Church of Scotland, then responded in 1931 to a call to work with the Raxaul Medical Mission as one of the first Nepali evangelists along the southern border of Nepal. Over the next 20 years, while Nepal itself remained closed to Christianity, he pioneered an evangelistic and pastoral ministry among dispersed Nepali in North India and Assam. When the Raxaul work was forced to close because of World War II, he and his family joined the Nepali Evangelistic Band (NEB) further along the border at Nautanwa. Urged by the NEB, he accepted ordination in 1943 during a nondenominational ceremony in Calcutta and thus became the first Nepali pastor to serve outside the Darjeeling area. In 1953, two years after Nepal opened to missionary work, he returned to his homeland and founded the first Protestant church in the country, at Ram Ghat, Pokhara. In 1960 he was elected the first president of the Nepal Christian Fellowship (NCF), a body representative of all national Christians in Nepal. After he performed a baptism, a warrant was issued for his arrest, so on the advice of other church leaders, he returned to the NEB border station at Nautanwa, from where he continued to serve as the NCF president until 1964 and performed baptisms on the Indian side of the border. He finally returned to Pokhara in 1969, expecting to retire, but was asked to pastor the church at Ram Ghat once more.

BIBLIOGRAPHY Patricia Hepworth, *Fires at the Foot of Fish-Tail* (1959); NEB Field Literature Committee, ed., *From His Hand to Ours: Being an Account of the Work of the NEB until 1959* (n.d.); L. M. O'Hanlon, *The Church at the Foot of Fish-Tail* (n.d.); Cindy Perry, *A Biographical History of the Church in Nepal* (1990, 1993).

Cindy L. Perry

Mulders, Alfonsus Joannes Maria (1893-1981), Dutch Catholic missiologist. Born at Oudenbosch in the province of Brabant, Netherlands, Mulders entered the minor seminary of the diocese of Breda in 1905 and the major seminary at Hoeven in 1911. Ordained a priest in 1917, he was sent by his bishop to Fribourg in Switzerland, where he obtained a doctorate in theology in 1921 with a dissertation on the vocation of the priesthood. He lectured until 1936 at the major seminary at Hoeven in his diocese, where he taught dogmatic theology and church history. He started teaching missiology at the Catholic University of Nijmegen as a part-time lecturer in 1930. In 1936 he was appointed professor in missiology, fundamental theology, and theology of the Eastern churches. The first professor of missiology in the Netherlands, Mulders established a missiological institute, where missiology, cultural anthropology, history of religions, linguistics, and Islamics were taught. From 1930 to 1970 he edited the missiological journal *Het Missiewerk.* Between 1939 and 1965, he organized a biennial missiology study-week. His most important works were an introduction to missiology (three editions) and a history of missions. He attended the Second Vatican Council as a consultant on missions. On his 60th birthday he received a Festschrift *Scientia missionum ancilla,* and on his departure from the university in 1963 another volume, *Novella ecclesiae Germina.* He died at Nijmegen.

BIBLIOGRAPHY Alphons Mulders, *Levensherinneringen* (Memoirs) (1968). Arnulf Camps, "In Memory of Mgr. Prof. Dr. Alfons J. M. Mulders," *NZM* 37 (1981): 291-293, "Prof. Dr. Alfons Joannes Maria Mulders," *Wereld en Zending* 10 (1981): 130-134, and "Rede ter herdenking, Mgr. Prof. Dr. A. J. M. Mulders," in *Jaarverslag 1981 Katholieke Universiteit Nijmegen* (1982), pp. 69-70.

Arnulf Camps, OFM

Mulenga, Alice Lenshina. *See* Lenshina Mulenga, Alice.

Mulia, Todung Gelar Sutan Gunung (1896-1966), Batak Protestant pioneer of the ecumenical movement in Indonesia. Mulia, born in Padang Sidempuan, Sumatra, was a Protestant layman of Batak heritage. He was a member of the Indonesian delegation at the conference of the International Missionary Council in Jerusalem 1928. He graduated from Leiden University, Netherlands, and earned his Ph.D. from Amsterdam University in 1933 with a dissertation challenging Levy-Bruhl's theories of primitive mentality. From 1922 to 1927 and from 1935 to 1942 he was a member of the Indonesian parliament. Active in Indonesian educational development, following Indonesian independence in 1945 he became a government minister of education and culture and later minister of the Department of Justice. He was a professor from 1947 to 1951 at the Indonesian University in Jakarta, and he also served as president of the Jakarta Theological Seminary. A pioneer of church unity in Indonesia, in 1950 he founded the Indonesian Council of Churches. He helped many churches become members of the East Asia Christian Conference, the World Council of Churches, and the Lutheran World Federation. He served as chairperson of the Indonesian Bible Society and was a member of the standing committee of the United Bible Societies from 1957 to 1960. His greatest contribution to missiology was through Bible translations in modern Indonesian and by his encouragement of younger leaders through teaching and through his activities in professional associations. On his seventieth jubilee, the Indonesian Council of Churches honored him with a Festschrift; he also received an honorary D.D. from the Free University, Amsterdam, in 1966.

BIBLIOGRAPHY Mulia was the author of *India* (1949) and co-editor with K. A. Hidding of *Ensiklopedia Indonesia,* 3 vols. (1950).

His Ph.D. dissertation was published as *Het Primitive Denken in de Moderne Wetenschap* (1933). Simon Rae, "In the Beginning: Five Pioneers of Modern Indonesian Theology," in John McKean, ed., *Proceeding of the Research Group for Asian and Pacific Christianity 1992* (1992), pp. 9–23; T. B. Simatupang, "Dynamics for Creative Maturity," in Gerald H. Anderson, ed., *Asian Voices in Christian Theology* (1975), pp. 87–116; "Todung Gelar Gunung Mulia," in *Ensiklopedia Indonesia,* vol. 4 (1983), p. 2308; Johannes Verkuyl, *Contemporary Missiology* (1978), pp. 267–268.

Adelbert A. Sitompul

Mullens, Joseph (1820–1879) *and* **Hannah (Lacroix)** (1826–1861), London Missionary Society (LMS) missionaries in India. Born in London, Joseph Mullens studied at the universities of London and Edinburgh. He began work in India in 1844, engaging in evangelism and church leadership in Calcutta. There he met his future wife, Hannah, who had been born in that city, the daughter of A. F. *Lacroix. After their marriage she joined her husband in evangelistic work and, at age 19, took charge of a girls' boarding school, which became well known. Raised in India, she was able to depict the Indian scene authentically in several fictionalized publications. She also entered into zenana work, which involved regular visiting and teaching of higher class women in their secluded quarters, a type of mission work growing in emphasis at that time. She died from a sudden illness at age 35.

After the death of his wife, Mullens continued work in Calcutta. His intellectual strength was evident in scholarly writings and in his appointment, in 1857, as fellow of the senate of the new, government-established University of Calcutta. In 1865 he was called to the LMS headquarters in London. He was soon appointed to the office of foreign secretary, the principal office in the society's staff. During his tenure the work by and for women was much expanded and given organized form in a female education department. Also during his time two new missions were begun, New Guinea and Central Africa. Before taking up his work in London, Mullens had traveled among the missions in India and China, and later, in 1873–1874, he made a long visit to Madagascar. In 1879 he proposed going to Africa with reinforcements for the Central Africa mission. The LMS directors were reluctant, but agreed that he go as far as Zanzibar with further travel dependent on the circumstances. He decided in Zanzibar to continue, but was overcome by exposure and fatigue. He died near Mpwapwa, Tanganyika (Tanzania), and was buried in the CMS cemetery there.

BIBLIOGRAPHY Joseph Mullens, *The Religious Aspects of Hindu Philosophy Stated and Discussed* (1860), *Brief Memorial of the Rev. Alphonse François Lacroix: Missionary of the LMS in Calcutta, with Brief Memorials of Mrs. Mullens by her Sister* (1862), *London and Calcutta Compared in their Heathenism, Privileges, and Prospects* (1868), and *Twelve Months in Madagascar* (1875). Hannah Mullens, *Faith and Victory: A Story of the Progress of Christianity in Bengal* (1865). Emma Raymond Pitman, *Heroines of the Mission Field* (1880).

Charles W. Forman

Müller, George (1805–1898), missions promoter and religious philanthropist. Müller, who was of German birth, offered for service with the Church Missionary Society, but became involved in the infant Plymouth Brethren movement and devoted himself to pastoral ministry with the Brethren in Bristol, England. His significance for world mission begins with his philanthropy. His Scriptural Knowledge Institution for Home and Abroad (SKI, 1834) was designed to support the "spread of the gospel" by raising money for schools for children and adults, distributing Scriptures and Christian literature, supporting missionaries "whose proceedings appear to be most according to the Scriptures," and the orphanage he established at Bristol (1835). During his lifetime, almost one and a half million pounds were received for these purposes, of which £260,000 was spent on supporting missionaries. In the early 1870s, Müller was sending abroad £10,000 annually to nearly 200 missionaries. At one critical stage in its early history, the China Inland Mission depended almost entirely on support from the SKI.

A second contribution is Müller's principle of never appealing for funds, except to God in prayer, which derived mediately from A. N. *Groves (his brother-in-law) and ultimately from the words of Jesus (e.g., Matt. 6:30). This was adopted by J. Hudson *Taylor and many other leaders of faith missions.

Müller's third contribution came toward the end of his life in the form of a series of nine tours in different parts of the world (1875–1883). The purpose of these tours was partly evangelistic, but mainly to share his personal convictions with fellow Christians.

BIBLIOGRAPHY The six volumes of Müller's *Narrative of Some of the Lord's Dealings with George Müller* (8th ed., 1881) are the basic source, supplemented by *Preaching Tours and Missionary Work of George Müller* (1883) by his wife Susannah. The most recent biography is R. Steer, *George Müller, Delighted in God* (1975).

Harold H. Rowdon

Müller, Karl (1918–), Catholic missiologist. Müller was born in Blankenberg (now Gologóra) in East Prussia (now Poland) and entered the Society of the Divine Word (SVD) in 1937. After service in the German army from 1940 to 1945 he was ordained a priest in 1948 and completed the doctorate in missiology at the Gregorian University in Rome in 1952. From 1952 to 1960 Müller taught missiology and church history at the SVD seminary (St. Augustin) near Bonn, and in 1962 he received the doctorate in theology from the German state university in Münster. From 1962 to 1967 he served as secretary of studies and formation at the SVD generalate in Rome, and from 1967 to 1977 he was vice superior general of the SVD. After several years as mission secretary for the SVD in Rome and long-distance director of the SVD Missiological Institute at St. Augustin, he returned in 1983 to St. Augustin as professor of missiology (1983–1986), was director of the Anthropos Institute (until 1986), and was on-site director of the Missiological Institute until he retired in 1992.

BIBLIOGRAPHY Of Müller's many works, several are particularly notable: *Geschichte der katholischen Kirche in Togo* (1958), *Mission Theology: An Introduction* (Eng. tr., 1987), and ed. with Theo Sundermeier, *Lexikon missionstheologischer Grundbegriffe* (1987, Eng. tr., 1997). A complete bibliography of Müller's published works until 1993, compiled by Angelika Striegel, along with a short biography by Kurt Piskaty, can be found in Kurt Piskaty and Horst Rzepkowski, eds., *Verbi Praecones. Festschrift für P. Karl Müller SVD zum 75. Geburtstag* (1993).

Stephen B. Bevans, SVD

Mungo. *See* Kentigern.

Murdoch, John (1819–1904), educator and literary evangelist in Ceylon (Sri Lanka) and India. Murdoch was born in Glasgow and attended the University of Glasgow. In 1844 he was appointed to head a government school in Kandy, Ceylon, but after only five years he abandoned teaching for the publication of Christian literature. In 1854 he left Ceylon for India and in 1858 became agent of the Christian Vernacular Education Society, the main object of which was to provide cheap and edifying Christian literature for the newly literate. Out of this initiative later developed the Christian Literature Society (CLS) for India, for which Murdoch wrote a great deal over the years. In his writings he was reasonably well informed on the factual level but fundamentally unsympathetic in his treatment of Hindu beliefs and practices. In two visits to China he was instrumental in establishing the CLS for China and secured the appointment of Timothy *Richard for this work. He received the LL.D. from the University of Glasgow in 1871; the British and Foreign Bible Society made him a life governor of the society in 1889; and in 1904 the Kaiser-i-Hind gold medal was conferred on him for service to India. Never married, Murdoch died in Madras after 60 years in Ceylon and India.

BIBLIOGRAPHY Henry Morris, *The Life of John Murdoch, LL.D.: The Literary Evangelist of India* (1906). Works compiled by Murdoch for publication in India include *Classified Catalogue of Tamil Printed Books* (1865), *Catalogue of the Christian Vernacular Literature of India* (1870), *Indian Missionary Manual: Hints to Young Missionaries to India, with Lists of Books* (2d ed., 1870), and *The History of Civilization in India: A Sketch, with Suggestions for the Improvement of the Country* (1902). Murdoch's views on Hinduism are set forth in his booklet *Swami Vivekananda on Hinduism: An Examination of His Address at the Chicago Parliament of Religions* (1895).

Eric J. Sharpe

Murillo Velarde, Pedro (1696–1753), polymath Jesuit missionary in the Philippines. Born in Laujar, Granada, Spain, Murillo became a Jesuit in 1718 and went to the Philippines in 1723. There he occupied the newly created chair of canon law, at the Jesuit University of San Ignacio, Manila, where he published a treatise on canon law as applied to the Indies that was still being used 150 years later. He became the colony's expert in civil law as well, and published a number of legal works as well as devotional books. His major work of lasting value was his 1749 history of the Philippine Jesuits, wider in coverage of both chronology and island life than its title implies. With it appeared his famous 1734 map, the most accurate one of the Philippines at the time. He also compiled a ten-volume world geography. Though his history is exceptional among religious order chronicles for the attention it gives to Filipinos and their daily life, his evaluation of Filipino character and customs is often negative. He returned to Europe for a meeting in Rome in 1749 as representative of the Philippine Jesuits and died in Spain after having published some of his major works there.

BIBLIOGRAPHY The principal works of Murillo Velarde are *Cursus iuris canonici hispani et indici*, 2 vols. (1943), *Historia de la provincia de Philipinas de la Compañía de Jesús: Segunda parte, que comprehende los progresos de esta provincia desde el año de 1616 hasta el de 1716* (1749), *Catecismo de instrucción christiana en que se explican los mysterios de nuestra santa fe* (1752), and *Geographia histórica*, 10 vols. (1752), of which vol. 8 deals with the Philippines. See also H. de la Costa, *The Jesuits in the Philippines, 1581–1768* (1961).

John N. Schumacher, SJ

Murray, Andrew, Jr. (1828–1917), South African Dutch Reformed Church minister, theologian, evangelist, and mission organizer. Murray was the second son of Andrew *Murray of Graaff-Reinet; four of his brothers also became ministers. He was the prime shaper of the piety that came to characterize the Afrikaner people in the twentieth century. In 1838 he and his brother John were sent to Aberdeen to be educated at the grammar school and university. They then went on to Utrecht, Netherlands, to study theology. Virtually ignoring their professors, their piety and theology were shaped by membership in student societies inspired by the Reveil, a continental revival movement. After ordination at the Hague in 1848, Murray returned home, where he was sent to minister to the Voortrekkers beyond the Orange and the Vaal Rivers. For ten years he served this 100,000-square-mile parish, befriending the extremist leaders Potgeiter and Pretorius and aiding them in negotiating their freedom from the British. In 1856 he married Emma Rutherfoord. The next year saw the first of his 250 publications, some of which were the only books in many Afrikaner homes except for the Bible. He became minister at Worcester in 1860, Cape Town in 1864, and then Wellington in 1871, where he stayed until his retirement in 1906.

Murray's influence on South Africa's Dutch Reformed Church cannot be exaggerated. He was on its initial foreign mission committee and organized and raised funds for its first mission. In 1877 he organized the Mission Training Institute at Wellington. He founded three key organizations: the Ministers Missionary Union, The Bible and Prayer Union, and the Layman's Mission League. He was also an effective evangelist, both in South Africa and abroad. He received honorary degrees from Aberdeen in 1898 and the University of Cape of Good Hope in 1907.

Murray led a movement that transformed his church from an introverted into a missionary institution, but he also helped to confirm it as the church of the Afrikaner

Volk, inadvertently setting it on the path that led to apartheid.

BIBLIOGRAPHY Murray's two most important books are *The Key to the Mission Problem* (1901) and *The State of the Church* (1911). J. du Plessis wrote a massive but now dated biography, *The Life of Andrew Murray of South Africa* (1919).

Andrew C. Ross

Murray, Andrew, Sr. (1794–1866), Scottish pioneer minister and evangelical leader of South Africa. Murray was born into a pious Aberdeenshire family and studied at Aberdeen University, where he felt called to be a missionary to Newfoundland. However, when George Thom went to Scotland (1819–1820) recruiting ministers for the Dutch Reformed Church (DRC) in South Africa, Murray was one of five students who volunteered. In 1822 he was ordained and inducted into the vast frontier parish of Graaff-Reinet. He identified completely with the Afrikaner people, marrying one of them, sixteen-year-old Maria Stegman. She bore him six sons, five of whom became ministers of the DRC, and four daughters, all of whom married ministers. His evangelistic zeal transformed the whole frontier community. He brought so many people to an active Christian faith that out of his original parish eight new self-supporting congregations were created during his lifelong ministry there. He served for many years as clerk of synod and was once synod moderator. Murray was the driving force that began the transformation of the DRC in the Cape from a dry formal state church into a dynamically evangelical church that reached out to all who spoke Afrikaans, Cape Coloureds as well as whites.

BIBLIOGRAPHY The best published source for Murray's life is the biography of his better known son, Andrew Murray, Jr. by J. du Plessis, *The Life of Andrew Murray of South Africa* (1919). A large collection of Murray's papers are in the DRC archives in Cape Town.

Andrew C. Ross

Murray, Archibald Wright (1811–1892), London Missionary Society (LMS) missionary in Oceania. Born at Jedburgh, Scotland, Murray trained at Turvey and Homerton Colleges. He was influenced as a member of the Church of Scotland by Scottish revivals. Married to Ruth Cobden, he began his work in 1836 on Tutuila, Samoa, at Pago Pago and Leone. The Cook Islander missionary *Teava greeted and briefed him on his arrival. He was encouraged, after difficult beginnings, by the outbreak in 1839 of a prolonged ecstatic revival tinged with Samoan cultural elements, which followed news of the murder of his colleague, John *Williams of the LMS, on Eromanga, Vanuatu. Murray emulated Williams's work by helping to recruit and station many Polynesian missionaries in Polynesia and Melanesia. From 1854 he worked at the LMS's Malua seminary and at Apia. He became a "sailing missionary" and located Samoan teacher-pastors in Tuvalu, Vanuatu, New Caledonia, the Torres Strait, and New Guinea, where he and Samuel *McFarlane made the first LMS voyage in 1871. He wrote extensively about the settlement and endeavors of Islander missionaries and their families. He published books filled with colorful detail and recorded the progress of Bible translation. He revised George *Pratt's Samoan translation of the Bible. Contacts in Australia with the LMS colonial agent and Congregationalists led him to write many columns for the *Sydney Morning Herald,* in some of which he castigated French (and Catholic) behavior in the Pacific. He and his wife retired in Sydney, where he died. She died in 1882.

BIBLIOGRAPHY A. W. Murray, *Missions in Western Polynesia...* (1863), *Forty Years' Mission Work in Polynesia and New Guinea...* (1876), *Martyrs of Polynesia...* (1885), and *The Bible in the Pacific* (1888). John Garrett, *To Live among the Stars: Christian Origins in Oceania* (1982).

John Garrett

Murray, William H. (1843–1911), developer of a system for the blind to read Chinese. After losing an arm in a sawmill accident, Murray, a Scot and a devout Christian, became first a letter carrier, then a Bible colporteur. He learned Latin, Greek, and Hebrew on his own. After seven years as an itinerant colporteur for the National Bible Society of Scotland, he was appointed by the society to serve in that capacity in north China. Deeply moved by the fate of the blind in China, he determined to invent a way to make the Scriptures accessible to them. The Braille system, based on the Latin alphabet, was unsuited to the Chinese language. A system based on numerals was revealed to him in a vision, a system that he successfully developed so that blind people could learn to read in a matter of weeks. Over time, the Bible, hymnals, and other books were published in Murray's numerical type, schools were opened, a Mission to the Blind and Illiterate was organized, and thousands learned to read, leading to a flood of Christian conversions among the blind and illiterate. Many former social outcasts found jobs in printing, bookbinding, music, teaching, and preaching.

BIBLIOGRAPHY *Chinese Recorder,* vol. 20 (1889): 128 and 22 (1891): 257; Constance F. Gordon-Cumming, *Inventor of the Numeral Type for China* (1899; repr., 1918?); "Records of the Missionary Conference, Shanghai" (1890).

Donald E. MacInnis

Murray, William Hoppe (1866–1947), South African pioneer missionary in Malawi. Murray, grandson of Andrew *Murray, Sr., became a schoolteacher but felt the call to missionary service and studied for the ministry at Stellenbosch. Graduating in 1892, he went to Edinburgh, Scotland, for a year and took medical classes. In 1894 he was ordained for service with the pioneer Dutch Reformed Church (DRC) mission to Malawi, which had been called to aid the Free Church of Scotland Mission there. Mkhoma became the headquarters of the mission, and William became its head in 1901, remaining in charge until 1937. He was the principal translator in the team that translated the New Testament into Nyanja, a project completed in 1906. The work on the Old Testament took a long time because everyone, including Murray, had so many other tasks to perform, but the whole Bible in Nyanja was published in 1924. This was also the year of the founding of the Church of Central Africa Presbyterian. The churches that had been brought into being by the Mkhoma mission became the Mkhoma Presbytery and, later, the Mkhoma Synod. In 1928 Murray represented the DRC of South Africa at the International Missionary Council Jerusalem meeting. In 1937 Murray retired to Worcester in South Africa where he died.

BIBLIOGRAPHY M. H. Le Roux and M. M. Le Roux, *William Murray of Nyasaland* (1958).

Andrew C. Ross

Mutendi, Samuel (1890–1976), founder of the Zion Christian Church (ZCC) in Rhodesia (Zimbabwe). A muRozvi-Shona born in the Bikita district of Masvingo Province, Mutendi was raised and educated in the Dutch Reformed Church. Even as a young man, Mutendi had dreams and visions reflecting his church leadership ambitions. As a labor migrant in Pretoria, he first obtained membership in the Zion Apostolic Faith Mission, then in 1925 broke away with Enginase Lekganyane and a few other key figures to form the ZCC. Ordained as a ZCC minister, Mutendi founded the Rhodesian branch of the new church, with its headquarters near Nyika Halt in Bikita. Although he retained ideological and historical links with what was to become the largest Christian Church in South Africa, Lekganyane's ZCC, currently based in Pietersburg, he developed the Zimbabwean ZCC into a fully autonomous church, with an estimated 500,000 members in 1996. Zimbabwean-affiliated ZCC congregations also exist in Zambia, Malawi, and Mozambique.

As bishop of the ZCC, and unlike his Apostolic counterpart, John *Maranke, Mutendi focused on building an impressive Zion City, or Moriah, with schools, church, a faith-healing "hospital," and other symbols of the presence of Christ, the Lamb of Mt. Zion (Rev. 14:1). In Zion City, Mutendi's leadership resembled both that of a Rozvi monarch and that of a messianic "man of God," as he is called by his followers. As a black icon, he mirrored the life of Christ in an African setting. His resistance to oppressive colonial rule, which resulted in several detentions, added to his popularity and stature among African chiefs and commoners alike.

In ZCC theology preoccupation with human well-being through exorcistic healing and agro-economic development contributed toward a strong emphasis on this-worldly salvation. Zionist achievement and progress therefore became essential components of the Good News propagated by the ZCC. Nevertheless, Mutendi's church never forfeited its essentially missionary character. The annual paschal celebrations at Zion City serve as a springboard for massive missionary campaigns throughout Zimbabwe and beyond its borders—campaigns of witness, outreach, celebration, and healing that activate entire church communities.

After Mutendi's death, a schism occurred, each faction operating under the leadership of one of his sons, Nehemiah and Ruben. The relationship between the two factions is marked by meaningful interaction rather than alienation.

BIBLIOGRAPHY Marthinus L. Daneel, *Old and New in Southern Shona Independent Churches,* vol. 1, *Background and Rise of the Major Movements* (1971).

Marthinus L. Daneel

Muthiah, Narayana (1872–1959), pioneer Indian Salvation Army leader. Born to a high-caste Hindu family in Palayankottai (Palamcottah), Tirunelveli, Muthiah was drawn to Christ through the witness of Salvation Army officers who entered India in 1882 to "bless and raise" (as William *Booth put it) the offscouring of the earth. Disinherited by his family, Muthiah adopted a fakir life-style to champion a gospel of temporal and eternal salvation for the poor. In the Travancore region of Kerala he belonged to a legendary pioneer band which set the direction for the Salvation Army's evangelistic, educational, medical, relief, and development ministries, notably among Harijans. Through nearly half a century as a Salvation Army officer, he displayed a zeal for intercession and evangelism, an aptitude for servant leadership, and an acute solicitude for the so-called criminal tribes and lepers. Unbowed by imprisonment, deprivation, and multiplied personal sorrows (the graves of six of his children marked the route of his ministry throughout the subcontinent), he attained to the Salvation Army's highest administrative positions, retiring as India's first indigenous commissioner and commander of the Northern Territory in 1938.

BIBLIOGRAPHY Narayana Muthiah, *Triumphs of the Cross in Travancore* (n.d.) and "High-Caste Hindu Becomes Salvationist Territorial Leader: Commissioner Muthiah Tells His Own Remarkable Story for 'All the World,'" *All the World* 5 (October–December 1942): 16–17. Lilly Pennick, *Robes of Renunciation* (n.d.); Solveig Smith, *By Love Compelled: The Salvation Army's One Hundred Years in India and Adjacent Lands* (1981); Rosalie M. Wheaton, *Indian Pilgrim* (1960); Harry Williams, *Booth-Tucker: William Booth's First Gentleman* (1980).

Lyell M. Rader, Jr.

Myers, Estella Catherine (1884–1956), pioneer missionary of the Brethren Church in central Africa. Born in Williamsburg, Iowa, Myers was the daughter of John A. and Anna Stoner Myers; her father was a minister in the Brethren Church. After completing high school in Iowa, Myers spent a year at Jennings Seminary in Aurora, Illinois, but was forced to leave because of mental illness. Upon her recovery she completed the nursing course at Iowa Methodist Hospital in Des Moines (1907), worked for a time, and then enrolled in Ashland (Ohio) College, where she volunteered to join a Brethren mission that was to begin in Africa. While funds were being raised, she served as a nurse at the Lost Creek, Kentucky, mission and spent a term at the School of Religious Pedagogy in Hartford, Connecticut. Finally, she became one of the first four Brethren Church missionaries in Oubangui-Chari (Central African Republic), Africa, serving from 1918 to 1956. "Mama" Myers worked with faith, dedication, and vision as a nurse, teacher, administrator, preacher, and translator. Her Karre language version of the New Testament was published in 1947, and she was at work on a translation of the New Testament into the Pana language at the time of her death.

BIBLIOGRAPHY Florence N. Gribble, *Undaunted Hope* (1932) and *Stranger than Fiction* (1949); Ruth Snyder, *Estella Myers: Pioneer Missionary in Central Africa* (1984).

Robert G. Clouse

Myklebust, Olav Guttorm (1905–), Norwegian Lutheran missiologist. Myklebust was born in Bergen, graduated from the Norwegian Lutheran School of Theology, Oslo, in 1929, and also studied in Berlin with Julius *Richter and in London. He was ordained in 1930 and sent to South Africa by the Norwegian Missionary Society (NMS). After receiving a diploma in education at the University of Natal in 1931, he taught at the Umpumulo teachers' college, and beginning 1934 he was its principal. From 1939 to 1974 he taught missions at the Norwegian Lutheran School of Theology, Oslo, and served as its dean. Active in the ecumenical movement, Myklebust attended conferences of the International Missionary Council at Whitby in 1947, of the Lutheran World Federation at Helsinki in 1963, and of the World Council of Churches (WCC) at Uppsala in 1968. He was a member of the WCC Commission on World Mission and Evangelism from 1961 to 1977. With the publication of his doctoral dissertation, *The Study of Mission in Theological Education* (2 vols., 1955, 1957), Myklebust was recognized as an international authority on the history and place of missiology in theological education. The founder of missiology as an academic discipline in Norway, he founded the Egede Institute for Missiology in Oslo and edited the *Norsk Tidsskrift for Misjon* from 1947 to 1974. He is considered the founding father of the International Association for Mission Studies, and he was instrumental in founding the Nordic Institute for Missiology and Ecumenics. He is a member of the Norwegian Academy of Science and Letters and is a Commander of the Order of Saint Olav. An inspiring teacher, Myklebust demonstrated to his students the inclusive and global aspects of missions and the continuing relevance of the Great Commission. He wrote the history of the NMS in South Africa for the hundredth anniversary of the NMS. His *Misjonskunnskap* (1976) is a comprehensive textbook on missiology. His two volumes on the Norwegian pioneer missionary to South Africa, *H. P. S. Schreuder: Kirke og Misjon* (1980) and *En var den første* (1988), are classics.

BIBLIOGRAPHY Myklebust wrote his autobiographical reflections in "My Pilgrimage in Mission," *IBMR* 11 (1987): 22–23. See also Nils E. Bloch-Hoell, ed., *Misjonskall og forskerglede: Festskrift til professor Olav Guttorm Myklebust* (1975).

Nils E. Bloch-Hoell

N

Nacquart, Charles (1617–1650), French Catholic missionary in Madagascar. Nacquart was born in a village near Soissons and entered the mission congregation known as the Lazarists founded by *Vincent de Paul. He was educated at Saint Lazarus Seminary in Paris and at the Lazarists' residence near Tours before being appointed to Madagascar. The East India Company had asked the mission to send priests to the French colony of Fort-Dauphin (present-day Faradofay, or Tolagnaro, according to the former Malagasy name). Nacquart and fellow Lazarist Nicolas Gondrée arrived in December 1648 together with Etienne de Flacourt, director of the company and commander of the colony, with whom Nacquart's relationship was often irksome, making his task more difficult. The two Lazarists had been preceded by a priest, Bellebarbe, chaplain to the commander, but it was thanks to the help of a colonist, François Grandchamp, that their knowledge of the Malagasy people and language improved. During his eighteen-month stay in Madagascar, Nacquart established good relations with the Malagasy princes and religious leaders, whom he cautiously tried to convert, but concentrated his efforts on teaching and baptizing children. He traveled around the area and made plans for extending the mission work, including building the first large church, whose foundation stone was laid in February 1650. He prepared a handbook for teaching the faith and was probably the principal author of the first catechism in Malagasy, published in 1657, seven years after his death in Fort-Dauphin. He also wrote the first account of that area of Madagascar in his report to his superior (February 5, 1650), which reached Vincent de Paul after Nacquart's death.

BIBLIOGRAPHY Charles Nacquart, *Petit catéchisme avec les prières du matin et du soir* (1657). Jules Chavanon, *Une ancienne relation sur Madagascar (1650)* (1897; contains Nacquart's letter of February 5, 1650); Etienne de Flacourt, ed., *Histoire de la grande isle Madagascar* (1658; 1995); Henri Froideveaux, *Les Lazaristes à Madagascar au XVIIème siècle* (n.d.); Ludwig Munthe et al., *Le catéchisme malgache de 1657* (1987); Modeste Rakotondrabe, *Les premiers catéchismes en langue malgache* (1990).

Yvette Ranjeva Rabetafika

Nagenda, William (1912–1973), Ugandan evangelist and leader in the Balokole revival movement. The son of a prominent Anglican landowner of Buganda (now Uganda), Nagenda was educated at King's College, Budo. He was related to Simeoni *Nsibambi, who with Joe *Church of the Church Missionary Society Ruanda mission initiated the East African revival of the 1930s. Nagenda's own conversion led him to seek ordination, encouraged by Bishop Cyril E. Stuart, who was keen to improve the spiritual and educational quality of a largely peasant clergy. Nagenda's self-assurance and assertion of radical equality between white and black, along with his outspoken criticisms of the "liberal" theology of his missionary teachers, precipitated a crisis at Mukono Theological College. In 1941 he and twenty-eight others were expelled, and he chose to remain a lay evangelist. His commitment to his church, despite its hostility, helped to prevent schism. His uncompromising message of salvation in the blood of Jesus and strict moral discipline profoundly affected Protestant churches throughout East Africa. Nagenda enabled the revival to express itself in vibrant African ways of thinking and living. He was a charismatic leader, intense and single-minded.

BIBLIOGRAPHY J. E. Church, *Quest for the Highest* (1981) is a detailed and illuminating account of the revival and of Church's friendship with Nagenda. For a more distanced assessment, see K. Ward, "Obedient Rebels—The Relationship between the Early Balokole and the Church of Uganda: The Mukono Crisis of 1941," *JRA* 19, no. 3 (1989): 194–227.

Kevin Ward

Nakada Juji (1870–1936), Japanese Holiness leader and cofounder of the Oriental Missionary Society (OMS). Nakada, raised in Japan in a Methodist background, spent most of two years (1897–1898) in Chicago at Moody Bible Institute. There he was befriended by Holiness leaders Charles and Lettie *Cowman and E. A. *Kilbourne, who helped support him. Nakada returned to Japan in 1898 and began the first Japanese Holiness journal in 1899. In 1901, the Cowmans joined him in Tokyo, and together they began vigorous evangelistic activities that led to formation of the OMS. They were joined soon by Tetsusaburo Sasao (1868–1914) and the Kilbournes. Nakada evangelized widely, Sasao taught and ran the Bible school in Tokyo, and the Americans raised funds from abroad.

By 1910, the foreigners' desire to expand OMS work to Korea clashed with the Japanese leaders' wish to develop a Holiness church in Japan. Finally, in 1917, the Japan Holiness Church was established, with Nakada as bishop, and in 1928 it gained full independence from the OMS. After 1930, the church's refusal to sanction Shinto state worship led to increasing persecution. In his last years Nakada came to believe that God would restore Israel through the Japanese people; this split the Holiness Church.

BIBLIOGRAPHY Juji Nakada, *Japan in the Bible* (1933). Florid accounts of the early 1900s activities of Nakada and his OMS colleagues are in the journal *Electric Messages*, available in microfilm from the American Theological Library Association. See also John J. Merwin, "The Oriental Missionary Society Holiness Church in Japan, 1901–1983" (Ph.D. diss., Fuller Theological Seminary, 1983); Robert D. Wood, *In These Mortal Hands: The Story of the Oriental Missionary Society, the First Fifty Years* (1983).

Daniel H. Bays

Nankyama, Theodoros (c. 1924–1997), Orthodox metropolitan of Kampala and all Uganda. Born in Tweyanze, Monde, Uganda, Nankyama was sent at age 21 to study at the Greek Orthodox patriarchate in Alexandria, Egypt, first at the Kaniskerion School (1945–1948) and then at the Photios II College (1948–1954). In 1954 he went to Greece, where he graduated from the School of Theology, University of Athens (1959). In 1959 and 1960, with a World Council of Churches scholarship, he studied at Oxford University.

The Orthodox Church in Uganda was recognized by the patriarchate of Alexandria in 1946. Nankyama was ordained in Alexandria to the priesthood in 1961 and then returned to Uganda. He was elevated to the celibate rank of archimandrite in 1969, elected bishop of Navkratis by the Holy Synod of the Alexandrian patriarchate in 1972, and appointed auxiliary to the metropolitan of Irinoupolis (East Africa). He was one of the first three African Orthodox clergy elected to the episcopacy (all in 1972), and in November 1994 he became the first African elected to the rank of metropolitan.

During his tenure, Uganda suffered greatly through dictatorships and civil war. Nankyama secured numerous scholarships to send young Ugandans to Greece, Romania, and the United States. They were educated in various fields, and some are now back in Uganda, assisting in rebuilding and revitalizing the church. From his headquarters at St. Nicholas Cathedral in Namungoona, a suburb of Kampala, Nankyama continued to head the church during periods of peace and growth.

By 1993 there were 40,000 Orthodox Christians in Uganda, with twenty-two Ugandan priests (nearly all with theological degrees). The church has fifty-one parishes, the Holy Cross Medical Center, eight dispensaries, and several schools.

BIBLIOGRAPHY Theodoros Nankyama wrote numerous articles in Greek mission publications about the Orthodox Church in Uganda. Biographical information is available in the files of the Orthodox Christian Mission Center, Saint Augustine, Fla., and at the Uganda Orthodox Mission Center in Kampala.

Dimitrios G. Couchell

Nanpei, Henry (1880–1928), church leader in Pohnpei, Micronesia. Nanpei was educated at the American Board of Commissioners for Foreign Missions school at Ohwa on Pohnpei and later taught there. He received from his father considerable lands which he used as the basis for profitable ventures and plantations, producing a sizable fortune. He made friends with the successive Spanish, German, and Japanese rulers of Pohnpei, learning something of their languages and selling them goods. When American missionaries were forced out by the Spanish authorities in the 1890s, he became the most respected person in the Pohnpei Christian community and the main pillar of continuing church life. After 1900, when new missionaries came in, he had some quarrels with them about the misdeeds of his relatives, but those missionaries finally had to leave and his influence continued. He traveled to Asia, America, and Europe. He was regarded by some as an opportunist in his business dealings, but his devotion to the advancement of the Pohnpei people and of the Protestant church never flagged. When missionaries of the Liebenzell Mission arrived from Germany (1906), and later others of the Nanyo Dendo Dan from Japan (1920), he cooperated with both, ensuring the harmonious development of the old Protestant church in cooperation with these new endeavors.

BIBLIOGRAPHY Paul Ehrlich, "Henry Nanpei: Preeminently a Ponapean," in Deryck Scarr, ed., *More Pacific Island Portraits* (1978), pp. 131–154; David Hanlon, *Upon a Stone Altar: A History of the Island of Pohnpei to 1890* (1988).

Charles W. Forman

Nassau, Robert Hamill (1835–1921), Presbyterian pioneer in Gabon. Born in Newtown Square, Pennsylvania, Nassau was an ordained minister and a medical doctor. Appointed in 1861 to the Presbyterian mission on Corisco Island off the coast of present-day Equatorial Guinea, he and his first wife, Mary C. (Latta), served there and at Benito on the mainland until her death in 1870.

A mission on the Ogowe River (begun at Baraka in 1842 by the American Board of Commissioners for Foreign Missions) was transferred to the Presbyterian U.S.A. Board of

Foreign Missions in 1871. In 1874 the Presbyterians determined to press into the Ogowe interior, and Nassau established a station at Balimbila, some 200 miles inland. That work was moved to Kangwe two years later. In 1879 the Ogowe church was organized at Kangwe, the beginning of a flourishing work among the Mpongwe people. Nassau's second wife, Mary (Foster) (d.1884), and his sister, Isabel Nassau, were the first white women to live in the Ogowe region.

In 1892 and 1893 France claimed Gabon and the Ogowe as a colony. The Presbyterians transferred their work in those areas to the Paris Evangelical Mission Society. In 1894 Nassau and his sister were assigned to Batanga station in German Kamerun, where they served until their retirement in 1906. After serving churches in Florida for several years, Nassau died in retirement in Ambler, Pennsylvania.

BIBLIOGRAPHY Robert Hamill Nassau, *Corisco Days* (1892), *Fetishism in West Africa* (1904), *The Path She Trod: A Memorial of Mary Foster Nassau* (1909), and *Tales out of School* (1911). See also W. Reginald Wheeler, *The Words of God in an African Forest* (1931), pp. 67–78.

Norman A. Horner

Nau, Semisi (c. 1866–1928), Tongan Methodist missionary in the Solomon Islands. Nau's father, Sioeli, was a missionary in Fiji, and his mother, 'Akosita, was Fijian. He was educated at Tupou College in Tonga. When the Tongan king founded the Free Church of Tonga in 1885, Nau declined to join; instead he identified with the Wesleyan Church, which remained part of the Australasian Methodist Church. This led to a two-year prison sentence. After an inquiry by the high commissioner for the western Pacific, Nau was released and went to Fiji, where he ministered from 1887 to 1890. Returning to Tonga, he worked as a teacher until 1905. Then he went to the Solomon Islands, together with his wife, Matelita. In 1906, he and a Samoan, Polonga, pioneered missionary work at the large coral atoll Ontong Java (also known as the Lord Howe Group). Initially they faced opposition and spent 97 days in a whaleboat in the lagoon, prevented from landing, but eventually they were accepted on shore and had considerable success in establishing the church. Nau served again at Ontong Java (1911–1912, 1914–1918). Although unable to repeat his earlier success, he was highly respected as "an earnest and intelligent Christian." In 1915 he was ordained a Methodist minister at Bilua, in the Solomon Islands. He retired to Tonga in 1919 and is regarded as one of the outstanding Polynesian missionaries who worked in Melanesia.

BIBLIOGRAPHY Semisi Nau, *The Story of My Life,* ed. by Allan K. Davidson (1996). David Hilliard, "Protestant Missions in the Solomon Islands, 1849–1942" (Ph.D. diss., Australian National Univ., 1966). See also *The Australasian Methodist Missionary Review,* 1905–1919. Materials concerning Nau are held in the archives of the Australasian Methodist Overseas Missions, Mitchell Library, Sydney.

Allan K. Davidson

Naudé, C(hristiaan) F(rederick) Beyers (1915–), South African church and mission leader. Born in Roodepoort, Transvaal, in a Dutch Reformed parsonage, Naudé studied theology at the University of Stellenbosch. He served as pastor in various prestigious congregations of the Dutch Reformed Church (DRC), was a prominent member of the secret Afrikaner Broederbond, and was elected moderator of the Transvaal Synod of the DRC. After founding the Christian Institute (CI) at Johannesburg in August 1963, he was forced to resign as moderator, and his clergy status was denied. The CI became very influential in the struggle against apartheid, especially through its Study Project on Christianity in an Apartheid Society. In October 1977 Naudé and the CI were banned by the South African government. The banning order was lifted in 1984, after which he served a term as general secretary of the South African Council of Churches.

BIBLIOGRAPHY An appraisal of Naudé's work with a full bibliography appears in Charles Villa-Vicencio and John W. De Gruchy, eds., *Resistance and Hope: South African Essays in Honor of Beyers Naudé* (1985). An evaluation of the important role played by the CI appears in Peter Walshe, *Church Versus State in South Africa* (1983). See also P. Randall, ed., *Not Without Honor: Tribute to Beyers Naudé* (1982).

Willem Saayman

Navarrete, Domingo Fernandez de (1618–1686), Dominican archbishop, missionary, and controversialist. Navarrete was born in Castrogeriz, Spain, and became a Dominican in 1635. A graduate of and later lecturer in the celebrated San Gregorio College (Valladolid), Navarrete volunteered for the Asian Dominican missions in 1645. After ten years in the Philippines, he moved to China and worked in Fukien (Fujian) and Chekiang (Zhejiang), 1658–1666. He took a prominent part in the Chinese Rites Controversy, opposing the Jesuits, who argued that certain controversial rites should be tolerated in order to facilitate conversions. Imprisoned from 1666 to 1670 in Canton (Guangzhou), he finally managed to return to Europe to present his case and prepare a trilogy on the mission's problems. His first book, *Tratados* (1676), includes a lively account of his travels in America and Asia (including India); his second, the more theological and polemical *Controversias,* was denounced by the Jesuits while still in press and was never published, though five truncated copies exist in libraries. After 1677 his writing plans were frustrated by his promotion to the archbishopric of Santo Domingo (West Indies), where he died after a decade working for the welfare of the colony, particularly of its slave population. His *Tratados,* a monument of missionary and travel literature, was read by Locke, Quesnay, and Voltaire, among others. It made a unique Spanish contribution to eighteenth-century Sinophilism.

BIBLIOGRAPHY J. S. Cummins, ed., *The Travels and Controversies of Friar Domingo Navarrete,* 2 vols. (1962) and *A Question of Rites: Friar Domingo Navarrete and the Jesuits in China* (1993). For background to the Rites Controversy and associated problems, see

J. S. Cummins, *Jesuit and Friar in the Spanish Expansion to the East* (1986).

J. S. Cummins

Nee, (Henry) Watchman (*or* Ni To-sheng; Ni Tuosheng) (1903–1972), founder of the Little Flock movement in China. Born Ni Shu-tsu (Ni Shuzu) in Foochow (Fuzhou), Nee attended Trinity College, Foochow, and was converted at a Dora Yu revival meeting about 1920. In the early 1920s he studied widely in a variety of Christian traditions; his most important mentor at this time was Margaret *Barber, an independent former Church Missionary Society missionary. Close association with women evangelists and teachers was characteristic of his early career. In 1923 he started *Revival,* a small publication in Chinese, which later became an influential journal. In 1928 he published his three-volume *The Spiritual Man* (English trans., 1968), probably the most complete exposition of his basic theology of spirituality. In the late 1920s, his followers began to form separate congregations and acquired the informal name "Little Flock." In 1933 Nee visited England and America. In 1938 he published his major work on ecclesiology, *Concerning Our Missions* (English trans., 1939), which denounced denominations, advocated only one church in each locality, and was somewhat antiforeign in tone.

In 1949, the Little Flock movement had several hundred churches and a membership of perhaps 70,000 nationwide, making it one of the largest Protestant groups in China. Nee himself was savagely denounced in the early 1950s, was arrested in 1952, and died in a work camp.

Nee's thought was strongly premillennialist, shaped by Brethren ideas but also influenced by Holiness and Pentecostal emphasis on the Holy Spirit. Dozens of his lectures, Bible meditations, and sermons were transcribed and published, with most translated into English and some with a worldwide readership. Many Christians in China, especially "house church" Christians, remain followers of the traditions Nee established decades ago.

BIBLIOGRAPHY Transcriptions of Nee's oral presentations, based on the notes of his followers, provided the basis of most publications under his name. Prominent among the many in translation are *The Normal Christian Life* (1957), *Sit, Walk, Stand* (1957), *The Release of the Spirit* (1965), and *Love Not the World* (1968). Angus I. Kinnear, *Against the Tide: The Story of Watchman Nee* (1973); Leslie Lyall, *Three of China's Mighty Men* (1973).

Daniel H. Bays

Neeshima, J. H. *See* Niijima, Jo.

Neill, Stephen Charles (1900–1984), missionary bishop and scholar. Born in Edinburgh, Scotland, Neill—with his sisters Marjorie and Isabel—was the third generation of his family to engage in missionary service in India. Following his conversion while at Dean Close School, Cheltenham, England, and a brilliant career at Trinity College, Cambridge, in 1924 he accompanied his parents, Charles and Daisy (Monro) Neill to Dohnavur. He soon found himself at odds with Dohnavur's Amy *Carmichael and joined G. T. *Selwyn instead, learning Tamil and teaching schoolboys, except when traveling with E. Stanley *Jones. In 1927 Neill was ordained deacon in the cathedral of Tinnevelly. Accepted by the Church Missionary Society (CMS) during furlough in 1928, he was ordained priest and returned to Tinnevelly as a district missionary, later leading Thomas *Ragland's North Tinnevelly Itineracy evangelism program and then teaching in Tamil at the CMS theological college in Palayankottai. He was also involved in negotiations for a united church in South India. Elected bishop in Tinnevelly in 1939, Neill held his diocese together during the war, resisting encroachments by the state and initiating development projects in publishing, banking, and other areas. In 1944 he was forced to resign because of ill health and scandal, which prevented further advancement in the Church of England. He worked for the World Council of Churches from 1947 to 1954, editing with Ruth *Rouse the monumental *History of the Ecumenical Movement 1517–1948* (1954), then edited the World Christian Book series (sixty-four titles in all), and co-edited *Concise Dictionary of the Christian World Mission* (1971). He then went to the University of Hamburg as professor of mission (1962–1967) and to Nairobi as professor of philosophy and religious studies (1969–1973). Retiring to Wycliffe College, Oxford, he regularly visited America on preaching and lecture tours, while writing his magnum opus, the two-volume *History of Christianity in India* and numerous other works. His complete bibliography contains more than 100 titles. This output arose partly because he suffered from chronic insomnia and wrote during the night, and partly because of his indefatigable scholarship. He pioneered vernacular theological education in India and Africa, as well as schemes for producing affordable, readable theological works. Never married, conservative in churchmanship, an inspiring preacher and writer, and a deeply spiritual pastor, he fought all his life against consuming shyness, depression, and ill health.

BIBLIOGRAPHY E. M. Jackson, "The Continuing Legacy of Stephen Neill," *IBMR* 19 (1995): 77–80, and ed., *God's Apprentice: The Autobiography of Bishop Stephen Neill* (1991); Christopher Lamb, "Stephen Neill," in Gerald H. Anderson et al., eds., *Mission Legacies* (1994), pp. 445–51.

E. M. Jackson

Nelson, Daniel (1853–1926), pioneer Norwegian-American Lutheran missionary in central China. Born to a poor Norwegian family near Haugesund, Norway, Nelson went to sea as a young man to earn a living. During 14 years at sea he visited China twice, once as a Norwegian sailor shipwrecked off the China coast, later as a crew member on the U.S.S. *Hartford,* which was stationed in Chinese waters. Back in Norway, Nelson and his wife determined to immigrate to America and take up farming; ultimately they settled in Eagle Grove, Iowa.

In Iowa, while shingling his roof, Nelson heard a voice that said, "Sell your farm, take your family and go to China." By this time an owner of a prospering farm and with a wife and four children, Nelson nevertheless took this word seriously. He was derided by neighbors and local clergy as an impractical visionary, but he was determined to go to China, answering a mystical call shaped by boyhood experiences. Although he had no mission society to support or authorize his work, he proceeded anyway, arriving with his family in Shanghai in 1890. They went first to Wuhan, Hupei (Hubei), which was in the midst of antiforeign rioting, and then briefly to Fanghsien (Fancheng). After the Boxer Rebellion (1900), the Nelsons found a successful field in Hsinyang (Xinyang), in southern Honan (Henan), where they devoted 25 years to church planting and to opening schools and hospitals. Their work was later adopted by a Norwegian-American Lutheran mission society.

Nelson was widely loved for his childlike faith and admired for skills as explorer, groundbreaker, and developer. In February 1926, as missionaries gathered in Hsinyang behind closed doors for protection from marauding troops, Nelson preached his final sermon before being struck in the head by a bullet. He died 40 days later.

BIBLIOGRAPHY Daniel Nelson, *The Apostle to the Chinese Communists* (1935). Mary Lee (Nelson) Latimer, *An Adventure with God: Biography of Daniel Nelson* (1970; previously published as *Daniel Nelson, His Life and Work* [n.d.]).

James A. Scherer

Nerinckx, Charles (1761–1824), Catholic missionary to Kentucky. The Belgian-born Nerinckx was the oldest of fourteen children. He was ordained priest in 1785, served in parish ministry for ten years, and then spent the next decade hiding from anti-Christian forces unleashed by the French Revolution. He offered his ministerial services to the Catholic missions of America and arrived in Baltimore in 1804. After studying English, he joined Stephen Badin on the frontier of Kentucky, where he built fourteen churches and was instrumental in founding the Sisters of Loretto, America's first religious community for native-born women. After a dispute with his bishop, Nerinckx moved to Missouri in 1824, determined to continue his missionary labors, but died there.

The tireless Nerinckx was noted for his concern for children and their evangelization.

BIBLIOGRAPHY W. J. Howlett, *The Life of Rev. Charles Nerinckx* (1915); C. P. Maes, *The Life of Rev. Charles Nerinckx* (1880); H. Magaret, *Giant in the Wilderness* (1956).

Clyde F. Crews

Nesbit, Robert (1803–1855), pioneer Scottish missionary to western India. Nesbit was deeply influenced by the teaching of Thomas *Chalmers while he was a student at St. Andrews University. Along with Alexander *Duff, John Urquhart, and others, he became a leader in the St. Andrews University Missionary Association. After graduation and ordination to the ministry of the Church of Scotland, he volunteered for service to the Scottish Missionary Society. In 1827 he was sent to Bombay, where he worked as a district missionary south of the city. Becoming an expert in the Marathi language and culture, he took a leading part in the revision of the Marathi New Testament. He later served as secretary of the Bombay Book and Tract Society and wrote a number of tracts and short works in Marathi. His *Discourses, Chiefly on Doctrinal Subjects* was published in 1837. He died in Bombay from cholera.

BIBLIOGRAPHY J. M. Mitchell, *Memoir of the Reverend Robert Nisbet* (1858); S. Piggin and J. Roxborogh, *The St. Andrews Seven* (1985).

Duncan B. Forrester

Netsvetov, Iakov Egor (1804–1864), Orthodox missionary to the Eskimos. Born on Atka Island in the Aleutians, the son of a Russian fur trader and a native mother, Netsvetov was chosen to study at the Orthodox diocesan seminary in Irkutsk, Siberia. Before graduating in 1828 he married and was ordained to the priesthood. Returning to Atka as pastor, he found no permanent church building, so he began serving and teaching in Aleut under a tent while overseeing construction of one. After being widowed, he devoted himself to revising the Fox-Aleut translations to accommodate the Atkan dialect, and within five years the Gospels and liturgical hymns were ready for services to be conducted entirely in the vernacular. In 1844, Netsvetov was transferred inland to the Kwikpak mission, and for the next 18 years he traveled the Yukon and Kuskokwim River systems with considerable success in his ministry. Like his mentor, *Innocent Veniaminov, he taught carefully prior to baptizing. In 1994 he was canonized by the Orthodox Church in America.

BIBLIOGRAPHY L. Black, ed., *The Journals of Iakov Netsvetov: The Atkha Years* (1980) and *The Journals of Iakov Netsvetov: The Yukon Years* (1984).

Paul D. Garrett

Nettleton, Asahel (1783–1844), American Congregational evangelist. Nettleton was born in Killingworth, Connecticut, and attended Yale College from 1805 to 1809; he never married. His original intent to go into the foreign mission field never materialized, and he spent his life as an itinerant evangelist. Licensed to preach in 1811 and ordained as an evangelist in 1817, his approach to revivalism was grounded in orthodox Calvinism, rejecting the modified views of Timothy Dwight, Lyman Beecher, and Nathaniel Taylor. Nettleton insisted that conversion was "solely the work of God," and his preaching about the fallen and utterly lost brought many sinners to God. He never used the "anxious seat" or any of the "new measures" encouraged by the followers of Charles Grandison Finney.

Ill health forced Nettleton to curtail his travels in 1820, giving him time to publish *Village Hymns for Social Worship, Selected and Original* (1824) and an accompanying collection of music. After several winters in Virginia and a year in England (1831–1832), he regained a little health, and settled in East Windsor Hill, Connecticut. In 1834 he played a key role in the formation of the Connecticut Pastoral Union, a group of conservative Congregational clergy who founded the Theological Institute of Connecticut (later Hartford Theological Seminary) to counter the liberalizing tendencies of Yale.

BIBLIOGRAPHY George Hugh Birney, Jr., "The Life and Letters of Asahel Nettleton, 1783–1844" (Ph.D. diss., Hartford Seminary Foundation, 1943); Sherry Pierport May, "Asahel Nettleton: Nineteenth Century American Revivalist" (Ph.D. diss., Drew University, 1969); John F. Thornbury, *God Sent Revival: The Story of Asahel Nettleton and the Second Great Awakening* (1977); Bennet Tyler, *Memoir of the Life and Character of Rev. Asahel Nettleton D.D.* (1844). Approximately 900 of Nettleton's letters and diaries are in the Hartford Seminary Library, Hartford, Conn.

Barbara Brown Zikmund

Neumann, J(ohan) H(einrich) (1876–1949), Dutch missionary to the Karo Batak of Sumatra. Born into a poor family in The Hague, Neumann studied in Rotterdam at the missionary school run by the Netherlands Mission Society before going to the Dutch East Indies at age 23. Education, including primary schools and advanced schools for teachers and evangelists, drew much of his energies, but he was a generalist who also delivered babies, engineered an irrigation project, managed a leprosarium, and carried out numerous other projects alongside a spiritual ministry. Above all, his scholarship remains a lasting legacy. A translation of the New Testament and selections from the Old Testament into the Karo language were largely his work and remained the standard for Karo Christians until their revision in the 1980s. Publishing a Karo-language newspaper, *Merga si Lima,* as well as instructional materials for schools and churches, Neumann hoped to preserve the language as well as facilitate literacy. He produced the first systematic grammar of the Karo language and a Karo-Dutch dictionary. In addition, he published over thirty articles, primarily on the traditional religion, and wrote a novel, *Een jaar onder de Karo Bataks* (1949), containing many ethnographic insights. He died in Sumatra.

BIBLIOGRAPHY *Een jaar onder de Karo Bataks* contains a comprehensive bibliography of Neumann's writings. Additional information about him appears in the *Nederland Zendingsblad* of 1939 in an article marking his fortieth year in service to the NZG.

Rita Smith Kipp

Neuner, Joseph (1908–), Jesuit missionary in India. Neuner was born in Feldkirch, Austria. He entered the Society of Jesus in 1926, was ordained a priest in 1936, and was sent to teach theology at the Jesuit seminary in Pune, India. He earned a doctorate in theology from the Gregorian University in Rome, writing a thesis entitled "The Idea of Sacrifice in the Bhagavadgita." He returned to India in 1938 and devoted himself to guiding spiritual retreats and teaching. He served as an expert at Vatican II in the areas of priestly formation, non-Christian religions, and mission. The main areas of his work were the study of Hinduism, the communication of the faith, and teaching theology and spiritual guidance. He contributed scholarly articles to various journals in English and German and was a visiting professor in Germany and Austria. In 1964 he organized an international conference on the theology of other religions in Bombay during the International Eucharistic Congress. He continued to be active in India in his ninth decade.

BIBLIOGRAPHY J. Neuner, *Mission in India* (1979), *Walking with Him* (1985), and ed., *Christian Revelation and World Religions* (1967); J. Neuner and J. Dupuis, eds., *The Christian Faith* (1982); J. Neuner and R. De Smet, eds., *Religious Hinduism* (1964).

Michael Amaladoss, SJ

Nevius, John Livingston (1829–1893), American Presbyterian missionary in China best known for the Nevius method of church planting. Born near Ovid, New York, Nevius attended Union College, Schenectady, New York, and Princeton Seminary (B.D., 1853). Called to missions while at Princeton, Nevius sailed from Boston with his wife, Helen (Coan), in September 1853 and arrived in Ningpo, China, six months later. Both were good students of the Chinese language, and in little more than a year Nevius was preaching and teaching. He and his wife spent most of their time in China in Shantung (Shandong) Province. Itineration formed a key to his missionary method. Most of each year he visited churches on horseback, encouraging, disciplining, and instructing. From June through August each year, however, between thirty and forty men would come to their home for systematic Bible study. He emphasized especially the importance of establishing self-propagating, self-governing, and self-supporting churches, Bible study, strict discipline for believers, cooperation with other Christian groups, and "general helpfulness where possible in the economic life problems of the people." He created a *Manual for Inquirers,* setting forth rules and regulations for believers; these were also mounted on placards in the chapels. The manual included Bible study methods, how to pray, the Apostles' Creed, and passages of Scripture to be memorized.

In 1890 Nevius was invited to explain his method to the new Presbyterian missionaries in Korea. His principles so shaped the Protestant church in Korea that much missionary work as well as local church leadership and organization follow his original design to this day.

In English Nevius wrote *San-Poh* (1869), *China and the Chinese* (1869), *Methods of Mission Work* (1886), and *Demon Possession and Allied Themes,* published in 1894 after his death. He died in Chefoo (Yantai).

BIBLIOGRAPHY Samuel H. Chao, *John Livingstone Nevius 1829–1893: A Historical Study of His Life and Methods* (1996); Charles Allen Clark, *The Korean Church and the Nevius Method* (1937); Everett N. Hunt, Jr., *Protestant Pioneers in Korea* (1980) and "John Livingston Nevius," in Gerald H. Anderson et al, eds., *Mission Legacies* (1994), pp. 190–196; Helen S. C. Nevius, *The Life of John Livingston Nevius* (1895); Roy E. Shearer, *Wildfire: Church Growth in Korea* (1966).

Everett N. Hunt, Jr.

New, Charles (1840–1875), British Methodist missionary and explorer in East Africa. New was born in Fulham, then on the edge of London, the fifth child of a Methodist farm worker and teamster. He was apprenticed as a bootmaker and worked in Northampton until accepted in 1859 into the ministry of the United Methodist Free Churches. Largely self-educated, he had no theological training. After brief ministries in Lancashire and Cornwall, he volunteered for missionary service in 1862. New was at once sent to the East Africa mission, which had begun earlier that year through the inspiration of J. L. *Krapf, joining the only survivor of the mission, Thomas *Wakefield, who was very ill, at Ribe (now in Kenya). The mission strategy was to break through to the supposedly large and developed Galla (i.e., Orma) nation, whose lands, Krapf believed, stretched from behind Mombasa into Ethiopia. Meanwhile the Nyika of Ribe, while friendly, offered little encouragement. New, increasingly dubious about the viability of a Galla mission from Ribe, traveled in 1866 as far as the Tana River. He realized that the Galla were no longer a power in the land and that Maasai raiders disrupted communications there. The mission needed a new direction. New therefore decided to investigate the stories about Mount Kilimanjaro, snow-covered on the equator, which Johann *Rebmann had seen, and which might offer a healthier mission base than the fever-ridden coast. In a remarkable journey in 1871 he climbed Kilimanjaro and established relations with the Chagga people under the formidable chief Mandara. In 1872 he delayed taking leave to join the Royal Geographical Society expedition to find David *Livingstone. When this was abandoned, he returned to Britain, promoting the mission, campaigning against East African slavery, and writing a book about his travels. The Royal Geographical Society made him, like Livingstone, a corresponding member. In 1874 he renewed his search from Ribe for a more promising opening for mission. He returned to the Chagga, but Mandara this time was uncooperative. New became grievously ill and died in a vain attempt to reach missionary colleagues. He was an effective practical linguist and also established the first formal school in East Africa.

BIBLIOGRAPHY Charles New, *Life, Wandering, and Labours in Eastern Africa, with an Account of the First Successful Ascent of the Equatorial Snow Mountain, Kilima Njaro, and Remarks upon East African Slavery* (2d ed., 1873; 3d ed., with introduction by Alison Smith, 1971); S. S. Barton, *The Life of Charles New, Missionary to East Africa* (1889); O. A. Beckerlegge, *United Methodist Ministers and Their Circuits* (1968); R. Elliott Kendall, *Charles New and the East African Mission* (1978); R. Forbes Watson, *Charles New* (1960).

Andrew F. Walls

Newbigin, J(ames) E(dward) Lesslie (1909–), British missionary bishop in India, theologian, and ecumenical statesman. Born in Newcastle-upon-Tyne, England, Newbigin was educated at the University of Cambridge, where he was brought to Christian faith through the ministry of the British Student Christian Movement, which he later served for two years as secretary in Glasgow. In 1936 he was ordained by the Church of Scotland for missionary work in India. He served as a village evangelist (1936–1947), as an architect and interpreter of the Church of South India (CSI), and as bishop of the CSI in Madurai (1947–1959). In 1959 he became general secretary of the International Missionary Council (IMC) and guided it in 1961 to integration with the World Council of Churches (WCC), which he served until 1965 as associate general secretary, with responsibility for the Commission on World Mission and Evangelism. He then returned to India as CSI bishop of Madras until 1974. During his postretirement years in England, he has been professor of ecumenics and theology of mission at Selly Oak Colleges in Birmingham (1974–1979), moderator of the United Reformed Church (1978–1979), and pastor of a small inner city United Reformed congregation in Birmingham (1979–1989). In 1982 he organized the Gospel and Our Culture group to explore the form of Christian mission to pagan Britain, an activity in which he is still engaged.

Newbigin is preeminent as a theologian passionately devoted to the mission and the unity of the church. The influence of his thought and style are found in countless ecumenical conference reports he wrote or edited, in articles, sermons, and biblical studies throughout his career, and in his books, especially *The Household of God* (1953) and *The Open Secret: Sketches for a Missionary Theology* (1978, rev. ed. 1995). At the same time, engagement of Christian faith with the spirits and worldviews of modern society has been his constant theme. His *Honest Religion for Secular Man* (1966) foreshadowed the substantive theology and social analysis of his later works, *Foolishness to the Greeks* (1986) and *The Gospel in a Pluralist Society* (1989).

BIBLIOGRAPHY Lesslie Newbigin, *Unfinished Agenda: An Autobiography* (2d, updated ed., 1993), *The Reunion of the Church* (1948, 1960), *A South India Diary* (1951), *Truth to Tell* (1991), and *A Word in Season* (1994), a collection of his lectures, articles, and sermons. Martin Conway, "Lesslie Newbigin's Faith Pilgrimage," *Mission Studies* 11, no. 2 (1994): 191–202; George L. Hunsberger, "The Missionary Significance of the Biblical Doctrine of Election as a Foundation for a Theology of Cultural Plurality in the Missiology of J. E. Lesslie Newbigin" (Ph.D. diss., Princeton Theological Seminary, 1987; contains extensive bibliography).

Charles C. West

Newcomb, Harvey (1803–1863), Congregational clergyman, journalist, and author of the first American encyclopedia of missions. Born in Thetford, Vermont, Newcomb taught school for several years and then became editor of newspapers in Westfield and Buffalo, New York (1826–1830), and of the Pittsburgh *Christian Herald*, a paper for children (1830–1831). For the following decade he wrote and edited books for the American Sunday School Union. He was licensed to preach in 1840 and served Congregational churches in West Roxbury and West Needham (present-day Wellesley), Massachusetts (1840–1848). He was then editor of the *Boston Traveller* (1849) and assistant editor of the *New York Observer* (1850–1851). He settled in Brooklyn, New York, to head a private girls' school and engage in writing. Having a strong interest in city mission work, he pioneered in the establishment of mission

Sunday schools. In 1859 he became pastor of a church in Hancock, Pennsylvania. Of Newcomb's estimated 178 literary productions (some published anonymously), the most important was his *Cyclopedia of Missions* (1854). He organized this survey of mission work primarily under geographic areas, with additional articles on mission agencies, world religions, and similar topics, but no biographical entries. He also began a series of works on the Indians of North America and missionary work among them, but it was abandoned after two volumes.

BIBLIOGRAPHY Harvey Newcomb, *Manners and Customs of the North American Indians* (1835), *Young Lady's Guide* (1839), *How to Be a Lady* (1846), and *How to Be a Man* (1847). Memorial article, *Congregational Quarterly*, October 1863.

Martha Lund Smalley

Newell, James Edward (1852–1910), London Missionary Society (LMS) missionary in Samoa. Newell was born at Bradford, Yorkshire, and trained at the Lancashire Congregational College. In 1880 he began his Samoan service at Matautu, an important chiefly center on Savai'i. His first wife, Elizabeth (Sidlow), died there in 1882. In 1884, he married Honor Jane Gill, daughter of the missionary W. W. *Gill of the LMS in the Cook Islands. From 1887 he served at the Malua seminary on Upolu, where pastors and teachers were trained for Samoa and for missionary service abroad within Oceania. Newell sailed frequently on the mission ship *John Williams* to place and visit Malua students in Tokelau, Niue, Tuvalu, Kiribati, and Papua. When Western Samoa became a German colony in 1900, Newell's knowledge of Samoans qualified him as adviser and negotiator for the LMS with Wilhelm Solf, the governor. He had already mediated skillfully between Samoans and contending colonial powers in 1898 and 1899. In 1908 he persuaded a powerful Samoan orator-chief, Lauaki Mamoe of Savai'i, a deacon of the church, that a contemplated revolt against Germany would be futile and disastrous.

Newell was an expert on Samoan custom; he edited the church paper *Sulu* (Torch) and guided formation of the *toeaina* (council of elders), the nucleus for the church's future self-government. In 1902 Newell improved his German and visited major missionary societies in Germany to recruit German-speaking staff for Samoa. With August Hanke, a leader in the Rhenish (Barmen) mission, he planned to send Samoan LMS missionaries to serve in the Madang field in German New Guinea between 1912 and the 1930s. In 1910, after attending the World Missionary Conference at Edinburgh, he went to Barmen to arrange for the Samoans to go to Madang, but he died of pneumonia at Gütersloh at the age of 58.

Ralph Wardlaw *Thompson, the general secretary of the LMS, hailed his work for Samoa as "strong and wise." His wife died in England in 1922.

BIBLIOGRAPHY John Garrett, *Footsteps in the Sea: Christianity in Oceania to World War II* (1992). Newell's papers are in the LMS archives, SOAS, Univ. of London (available on microfilm).

John Garrett

Newell, Maria (c. 1800–1831), first single woman missionary of the London Missionary Society (LMS). Born into a comfortable London nonconformist home, Newell studied Chinese under Robert *Morrison during Morrison's home leave in 1824 and 1825. Her friend and fellow student Mary Ann *Aldersey, prevented by home circumstances from becoming a missionary, made a gift to the LMS that enabled Newell to go to Malacca in 1827, the first single woman sent overseas by that society. She worked in Malacca until the end of 1829, then married the German missionary pioneer Karl *Gutzlaff, of the Chinese Evangelization Society. She died in Bangkok two years later.

BIBLIOGRAPHY Robert Lovett, *The History of the London Missionary Society*, 2 vols. (1904).

Jocelyn Murray

Newell, Samuel (1784–1821) *and*
Harriet (Atwood) (1793–1812), pioneers of American foreign missions. Samuel Newell graduated from Harvard College (1807) and from Andover Theological Seminary (1810), where he was active in a society of Christian students seeking to undertake a mission to the heathen. In 1810 he and others proposed to the orthodox Congregational clergy of Massachusetts that they be sent as missionaries. In response, the American Board of Commissioners for Foreign Missions (ABCFM) was formed. Newell studied medicine while awaiting passage to India. Just before embarkation from Salem, Massachusetts, in February 1812, he married Harriet Atwood, who had joined the Congregational church in 1809 and had developed an interest in missions through Samuel's courtship.

When they reached Calcutta in June 1812, they and their fellow missionaries Adoniram and Anne *Judson, Gordon *Hall, and Samuel and Rosanna *Nott, were ordered to leave by the British East India Company. The Newells took ship for Mauritius, but on a long and stormy voyage Harriet gave birth to a child who died and was buried at sea. Harriet died soon after landing, barely 19 years of age and the first American to give her life in foreign missionary service. A memoir prepared by her husband was mailed home and widely read, and it became a powerful missionary tract.

Samuel Newell sailed to Ceylon, where he spent a year preaching and investigating mission opportunities. Learning that Hall and Nott had succeeded in establishing residence in Bombay, he joined them in 1814, inaugurating the first American mission station overseas. With Hall, Newell published an elaborate and widely circulated plan for the evangelization of the world. After several years' activity in the mission's program of schools, evangelism, and publishing, Newell visited cholera victims at Tannah. He succumbed suddenly to the disease in 1821.

BIBLIOGRAPHY Samuel Newell, *A Sermon Preached at Haverhill (Massachusetts) in Remembrance of Mrs. Harriet Newell . . . [and] Memoirs of Her Life* (1814). Samuel Newell and Gordon Hall, *The Conversion of the World, or the Claims of the Six Hundred Millions, and the Ability and Duty of the Churches* (1818). See also Joseph Tracy, *His-*

tory of the American Board of Commissioners for Foreign Missions (1842), pp. 25–104; *Panoplist* 9 (1813): 140.

David M. Stowe

Newton, John (1810–1891), American Presbyterian missionary in the Punjab. Newton was born in Griggstown, New Jersey, and educated at Jefferson College (A.B., 1830) and Western Theological Seminary (B.D., 1834). He was one of the second group of Presbyterians sent to India from the United States in 1834. He reached Ludhiana a few weeks before the only remaining member of the first group left because of illness. Newton proved able to survive and served in the Punjab until his death 56 years later. In 1849 he moved with his son-in-law, C. W. *Forman, to open the mission in Lahore, where he remained for the rest of his days. While Forman worked chiefly in education, Newton devoted himself to evangelistic work and care of the local church. He was a powerful preacher and knew the people well. It was said of him that he was one of the best loved men in the Punjab. He laid the foundations of Punjabi Christian literature, wrote a Punjabi grammar, and was coauthor of the first Punjabi-English dictionary. He had an ecumenical spirit and it was he who invited the Church Missionary Society to come and work in the Punjab. All of his four sons and two daughters became missionaries in India.

At the fiftieth anniversary of the mission he acknowledged that the early hopes for the conversion of India had not been realized, a fact he attributed in part to the spiritual failings of the missionaries, including himself, and in part to external obstacles, some of which could be removed. He remained hopeful that the second 50 years would bring greater success.

BIBLIOGRAPHY Arthur Judson Brown, *One Hundred Years: A History of the Foreign Missionary Work of the Presbyterian Church in the U.S.A.* (1936), pp. 563–567; John Newton et al., *Historical Sketches of the India Missions of the Presbyterian Church in the U.S.A.* (1886); Lodiana Mission, *Fifty-seventh Annual Report of the Lodiana Mission . . . for the Year 1891* (1891).

Charles W. Forman

Ngizaki, Gapenuo (1898–1971), pioneer Lutheran evangelist in Papua New Guinea. Regarded as the apostle of the Gadsup people, Gapenuo (he was generally known by Gapenuo rather than by his family name) led and coordinated the local Lutheran mission expansion into the highlands of Papua New Guinea. Born near Finschhafen and baptized in 1911, by age 15 he was asked to accompany various missionaries in their exploratory trips. Further schooling and short missionary experience in the Markham and Hube areas followed. In 1922 he was appointed to lead a group of evangelists from the town of Sattelberg to the Gadsup area in the highlands. There he settled in Wampar in 1924, although he continued to participate in frequent exploratory trips. Thus he discovered old trade routes, paving the way for Lutheran missionaries to gain easy and friendly access to the highlands as early as 1926. In 1963 he retired after leading many Gadsup people to baptism.

BIBLIOGRAPHY Gapenuo Ngizaki, "Braune Fackelträger" (1985), unpublished autobiography in mission archives, Neuendettelsau, Germany. An abbreviated English translation appears in Gernot Fugmann, ed., *The Birth of an Indigenous Church* (1986).

Gernot Fugmann

Nicholas I (c. 820–867), pope. Born in Rome, Nicholas (r. 858–867) was one of the most significant and energetic popes of the Catholic Church. Convinced of his divine mission, he fought with wisdom and single-mindedness against ambitions of national churches and power-hungry bishops (e.g., John of Ravenna, Hincmar of Reims); he contended for the sanctity of the marital bond in the conflict with Lothair II and struggled with the Eastern church (Emperor Michael III and Patriarch *Photius). This led to a considerable alienation between the two parts of the church but also had strong missionary implications. The pope insisted that the emperor Michael return to the jurisdiction of Rome Illyricum (the vicariate apostolic of Thessalonica), and the ecclesiastical provinces and patrimonies in lower Italy and Sicily. The conversion of Bulgaria, which ecclesiastically belonged to the vicariate of Thessalonica, led to a serious conflict, since Prince *Boris of Bulgaria was baptized in Constantinople (864). But almost simultaneously (866) the prince petitioned Pope Nicholas to send missionaries for his subjects and to answer 106 questions concerning ecclesiastical discipline. The "Respons ad consulta Bulgarorum" of the pope found a favorable reception, in contrast to a previous decree of Patriarch Photius. Nicholas's reply is regarded as a model of wisdom, moderation, and noble consideration for the needs and circumstances of a newly converted but rather unsophisticated people. The pope also attempted to bring under his jurisdiction the missionaries *Cyril and *Methodius sent from Byzantium to Moravia, who had expanded their activities to the neighboring Slavic principality of Pannonia; in this way he would have asserted his claim to Illyricum. The pope invited the two missionaries to Rome, but he died before they arrived.

BIBLIOGRAPHY T. Piffl-Perčević and A. Stirnemann, *Der heilige Method[ius] Salzburg, und die Slawenmission* (1987). I. Dujzev, "Die Responsa Nicolai I Papae ad consulta Bulgarorum," in *Festschrift zur Feier des 200 jährigen Bestandes des Haus-, Hof- und Staatsarchivs,* vol. 1 (1949), pp. 349–362; F. X. Seppelt, *Geschichte der Päpste von den Anfängen bis zur Mitte des zwanzigsten Jahrhunderts,* vol. 2 (1955), pp. 241–288.

Karl Müller, SVD

Nicholas IV (Girolamo Masci) (1227–1292), pope who expanded missions in the East. Born at Lisciano, Italy, Masci joined the Franciscans as a young man. In 1288 he became the first Franciscan to be elected pope, taking the name Nicholas IV. Reflecting the interests of his order, he strove to restore unity with Christians in the East and to expand the missionary work of the church. Shortly after taking office, he met with Rabban Sauma, the envoy of the Nestorian catholicos Yahallaha III, and the two reconciled. The pope allowed Sauma to celebrate mass in St. Peter's

Basilica, gave him Communion and absolution, and sent him back to Persia with letters for the patriarch and the khan of Baghdad. At the same time, he dispatched bands of missionaries to Ethiopia, central Asia, and China. In 1289 he sent a fellow Franciscan, *John of Monte Corvino, as his envoy to the court of Kublai Khan in Khanbalik (Beijing). Four years later, John of Monte Corvino became the first Roman Catholic missionary to set foot on Chinese soil.

BIBLIOGRAPHY E. A. Wallis Budge, tr., *The Monks of Kublai Khan, Emperor of China* (1928); Columba Cary-Elwes, *China and the Cross: A Survey of Missionary History* (1957); Christopher Dawson, *The Mongol Mission* (1955); E. Langlois, ed., *Les registres de Nicholas IV,* 2 vols. (1886–1905); Morris Rossabi, *Voyager from Xanadu* (1992); O. Schiff, *Studien zur Geschichte Papst Nikolaus IV* (1897).

Jean-Paul Wiest

Nicholas of Cusa (1401–1464), German cardinal, philosopher, and bishop of Brixen. As a church politician Nicholas was more conspicuous for his failures than for his successes. But as a religious thinker he is considered one of the deepest, most comprehensive minds of his age. He also was one of the first to develop a Christian theology of religions, based on the principle "one religion in a variety of rites," and he elaborated his ideas in a treatise on peace among the religions (1453) and in a critical analysis of the Qur'an (1459). Just as in God's infinitude all contrasts and differences in the phenomenal world are reconciled, all religions are but "expressions of the one word of God or eternal reason." However, differences of rank do exist among religions, inasmuch as there are degrees of participation in the eternal word of God. Thus the three religions belonging to the tradition of Abraham—Judaism, Christianity, and Islam—are closer to ultimate truth than all the others, with Christianity claiming the highest position. The fact that Nicholas did not hesitate to support a summons for a crusade against the Turks when Rome deemed it opportune is not easily reconciled with his emphatic demand for religious toleration.

BIBLIOGRAPHY W. A. Euler, *Unitas et Pax* (1990); P. M. Watts, *Nicolaus Cusanus: A Fifteenth-Century Vision of Man* (1982).

Hans-Werner Gensichen

Nicolai, Philipp (1556–1608), Lutheran pastor, promoter of mission in its eschatological context. Son of a Lutheran pastor in northwest Germany, Nicolai received his theological education at Wittenberg University. His career in the ministry was beset by encounters with plague, militant Roman Catholicism, and dogmatic strife. Nicolai's existential experience of mortal danger is reflected in his tract "Mirror of the joy of eternal life" (1599), which contains two of the most popular German eschatological hymns. Having eventually settled at Hamburg, he was able to develop a sweeping vision of the missionary task of the church—a task unfinished in spite of the testimony of the apostles, neglected in centuries of unbelief and apostasy, but upheld in view of the coming kingdom. In a truly ecumenical spirit, Nicolai appreciated the successes of Roman Catholic missions and the expansion of the Eastern churches, on which he collected a remarkable wealth of information. On the other hand, he did not hesitate to take to task his own Lutheran Church which had been given great responsibility but had failed to make the most of its talents. Toward the end of his life Nicolai engaged in dubious apocalyptic speculations, which may account for the fact that his call to mission went largely unheeded.

BIBLIOGRAPHY Willy Hess, *Das Missionsdenken bei Philipp Nicolai* (1962).

Hans-Werner Gensichen

Nicolayson, John (*or* Hans Nicolajsen) (1803–1856), pioneer Protestant missionary in Jerusalem. Danish by birth, Nicolayson was brought up in the Lutheran Church but was deeply influenced by evangelical Moravians. In 1821, at the age of 17, he left for Berlin to study at the mission seminary there and was immediately challenged by people involved in Jewish missions. Having studied Arabic at the seminary, he was recruited by the London Jews' Society for service with the Jewish community in Jerusalem, and in 1825 set sail from England. Within a month of his arrival, George Dalton, the man with whom he was to work, became ill and died. Nicolayson was left as the sole evangelical Protestant in Jerusalem and became convinced that he needed more authority to live and serve there. After leaving the region, he met Dalton's widow, married her, went to Basel to be ordained in the Lutheran Church, and in 1833 settled with his family in Jerusalem; they were the first evangelicals to settle permanently there.

By 1836 the London Jews' Society had decided to establish a permanent Church of England mission in Jerusalem. Nicolayson was ordained by the Anglicans in England in 1837 and instructed to buy property in Jerusalem. Political considerations were such as to prompt the Egyptian authorities to allow him to purchase property in the Old City at a site adjacent to the Jewish Quarter and the Jaffa Gate. In 1840 a temporary chapel was built, only to fall to the vagaries of a war between Egypt and Turkey. However, Nicolayson preserved the site and was given permission in 1845 to construct a "consular chapel," the first Protestant church in the Middle East. The consecration service was held in 1849, and Nicolayson preached the sermon. He died in Jerusalem and was buried in the Protestant churchyard on Mount Zion.

BIBLIOGRAPHY Kelvin Crombie, *For the Love of Zion: Christian Witness and the Restoration of Israel* (1991); W. T. Gidney, *The History of the London Society for Promoting Christianity amongst the Jews* (1908); Alexander McCaul, *The Old Paths* (1886).

Walter Riggans

Nida, Eugene Albert (1914–), linguist, teacher, and Bible translation theorist. Born in Oklahoma City, Nida graduated from the University of California at Los Angeles (1936; M.A., 1939) and received a Ph.D. in linguistics and anthropology from the University of Michigan (1943). He was ordained in 1943 by the Southern California Association of the Northern Baptist Convention. Beginning in 1937, he taught linguistics to prospective Bible translators at the Summer Institute of Linguistics. In 1943 he joined the American Bible Society (ABS), soon becoming translations secretary, in which position he roved the world for 40 years, 7 to 8 months a year. He worked in 85 countries and 200 languages, studying the linguistic, cultural, and translation problems that translators faced, giving them guidance, holding seminars, and lecturing. In 1943, he married Althea Lucille Sprague (d. 1993), who accompanied him as his secretary through much of their life together. In 1949 the United Bible Societies (UBS) Subcommittee on Translations became a channel by which Nida's influence spread more widely to translators through other Bible societies. He founded *The Bible Translator*, a UBS journal for translators, and became its editor. An increasing number of UBS consultants worked under his leadership, helping translators around the world. Nida wrote extensively and stimulated his colleagues to write. His lectures and publications covered four primary areas important to Bible translators: analysis of linguistic problems, cross-cultural communication of the gospel, translation theory and practice, and the structure of meaning. In addition to other books, he wrote or coauthored numerous and varied UBS aids for translators. He developed the theory of dynamic or functional equivalence translation, which has deeply influenced the practice of Bible translation all over the world.

Nida was instigator and skillful administrator of some widely used Bible translations and revisions and of such major ecumenical scholarly projects as the UBS Greek New Testament and Hebrew Old Testament texts. He was also a key figure in negotiating guiding principles for cooperative translation between Roman Catholics and Protestants (1968). Since retirement, Nida has continued his writing, has consulted with the ABS on several projects, and has lectured widely, giving several lecture series in China.

BIBLIOGRAPHY Nida's major linguistic publication was *Morphology: The Descriptive Analysis of Words* (2d ed., 1949); his major cross-cultural communication publication was *Message and Mission* (1960); his initial major publication of dynamic/functional equivalence translation was *Toward a Science of Translating* (1964); his major publication on the structure of meaning was Johannes P. Louw and Eugene A. Nida, eds., *Greek-English Lexicon of the New Testament, Based on Semantic Domains* (1988); and there is an autobiographical piece, "My Pilgrimage in Mission," in *IBMR* 12 (1988): 62–65. Matthew Black and William A. Smalley, eds. *On Language, Culture, and Religion: In Honor of Euguene A. Nida* (1974) is a Festschrift, including a biography and bibliography.

William A. Smalley

Nielsen, Alfred Julius (1884–1963), missionary among Muslims in Syria and Palestine. Born in Odense, Denmark, Nielsen went to Copenhagen to study philology. He was involved in the Christian Student Movement, inspired by, among others, John R. *Mott and Robert *Wilder. He approached Osterlandsmissionen (the Near East Mission) with a view to becoming a missionary. After earning a master's degree, he studied theology for two years and was then ordained, married, and sent out in 1911.

The Near East Mission had taken over a mission field north of Damascus, where Nielsen worked as pastor and teacher at a boys' school in Nebk. World War I forced the missionaries to leave the country, and Nielsen did not return to Syria until 1921. He was then encouraged to directly evangelize among Muslims in Damascus. He set up a reading room in "The Street Called Straight," and he walked the streets selling books and booklets. Although the visible results were modest—he only mentions one baptism—the Muslims complained to the authorities, who ordered the reading room closed in 1929. Following this, he taught Arabic at the Newman School of Missions in Jerusalem, where he also served as a missionary and at times as pastor in German and Arab churches. Nielsen acquired a thorough knowledge of Arabic and of Islamic theology, and he wrote several booklets in Arabic. In 1930 he published *Muhammedansk Tankegang i vore Dage paa Grundlag of Damaskusaviser* (Mohammedan thinking in our time, based on Damascus newspapers). He participated as a delegate in the international mission conferences in Jerusalem (1928) and Tambaram, India (1938). In Jerusalem as in Damascus, there were few visible results of mission to Muslims. In his writings Nielsen emphasized that being sent by the Lord and being faithful in his service is the important thing—not whether one can achieve results. He returned to Denmark in 1954 and was an active author, lecturer, and advocate of Palestinians' rights until he died in Askov, Denmark.

BIBLIOGRAPHY Alfred Julius Nielsen, *Vejen vi vandrede* (The road we walked) (1946; autobiography). Chr. Siegumfeldt, *Osterlandsmissionen* (The Near East Mission), vol. 2 (1927).

Flemming Markussen

Niijima, Jo (*or* Joseph Hardy Neesima; Neeshima) (1843–1890), pioneer of Japanese Christianity and education. Born Shimeta Niijima, son of the private secretary of the Annaka clan in Yedo (Tokyo), Niijima received a samurai's education, adding the study of Western languages and sciences. Reading a Japanese translation of *Robinson Crusoe*, books in Chinese on world history and geography, and a part of the Bible telling of a Creator God spurred his resolve to help change his country from an isolated feudalism to a modern society and from Confucian to Christian culture. In 1864 he risked execution by smuggling himself onto an American ship and reached Boston on a vessel owned by the prominent merchant Alpheus Hardy. Already deeply interested in foreign missions, Hardy enabled Niijima to attend Phillips Academy, Amherst College, where he graduated in 1867, and Andover Theological Seminary. In 1866 he was baptized in the Andover Congregational church.

In 1871 and 1872 Niijima traveled as interpreter with a high-level Japanese delegation studying education in America and Europe. In 1874 he finished seminary, was ordained, was appointed a missionary by the American Board of Commissioners for Foreign Missions (ABCFM), and attended the board's annual meeting at Rutland, Vermont, where his impassioned plea that a Christian school be established in Japan raised $5,000 on the spot. In November 1875, with ABCFM missionary Jerome D. Davis, he established Doshisha English School in Kyoto with eight students. The school's purpose was primarily to train pastors. A decisive reinforcement arrived the next year with the enrollment of thirty young men of the "Kumamoto Band," sworn in the samurai spirit to allegiance to Christ and the Christian faith.

In 1876 Niijima established Doshisha Girls' School, and in 1885 and 1886 he successfully sought funds in America and Japan for a comprehensive Christian university. Overburdened with public responsibilities and evangelistic preaching as well as duties to the growing schools, Niijima died at age 46. Doshisha University in Kyoto, Japan's oldest private university, continues today with some 32,000 students in a large complex of schools.

BIBLIOGRAPHY In 1960 Doshisha University published a booklet, *The Founding of the Doshisha and Doshisha University*, written by Niijima himself. Arthur Sherburne Hardy, *Life and Letters of Joseph Hardy Neesima* (1891, 1980) draws heavily on Niijima's own writings. *Missionary Herald* 86 (1890): 91–94 contains an obituary and personal description. The chapter on Niijima in Norimichi Ebizawa, ed., *Japanese Witnesses for Christ* (1957) has an excellent summary. There are extensive references with varying perspectives on Niijima and the Doshisha in Otis Cary, *A History of Christianity in Japan* (1909); Charles W. Iglehart, *A Century of Protestant Christianity in Japan* (1959); and Richard H. Drummond, *A History of Christianity in Japan* (1971).

David M. Stowe

Nikolai (Ziorov) (1851–1915), head of the Russian Orthodox mission in America. Nikolai was born Mikhail Zakharovich Ziorov in the region of Kherson, in southern Russia. After graduation from the Moscow Theological Academy in 1875, he was a lecturer in the Ryazan seminary; from 1883 to 1887 he was an inspector of the Vologda and Mogilev seminaries. In 1887 he was ordained to the priesthood and appointed rector of the Moscow Theological Seminary. In 1891 he was consecrated bishop of Alaska and the Aleutian Islands and made superior of the Russian Mission in North America. A stern, quick-tempered man, he traveled throughout Alaska, visiting the nine parishes and thirty chapels that served the 15,000 Orthodox Christians there. He was the first bishop of the mission to visit Canada (1898). During his administration the *Russian American Messenger*, an English-Russian language weekly, began publication in San Francisco. He admitted twelve parishes to Orthodoxy from the Uniate church. Nikolai had an avid interest in theological studies and maintained a good library, which he left behind for the Orthodox seminary in America. In 1898 he returned to Russia and served as bishop of Tavrida until his death.

BIBLIOGRAPHY Nikolai (Ziorov), *Iz Moyego Dvenika Putevya Zametki i Vpechatieniya vo Vremya Puteshestviya po Alaske i Aleutskim Ostrovam (1893–1894)* (From my diary. Travel notes and impressions made during my itinerary through Alaska and the Aleutian Islands) and *Amerikanskie Propovedi* (American sermons), 3 vols. (1902). Constance J. Tarasar and John H. Erickson, eds., *Orthodox America, 1794–1976: Development of the Orthodox Church in America* (1975).

Evgeny S. Steiner

Nikolai Kasatkin (Archbishop Nikolai). *See* Kasatkin, Nikolai.

Nikon the Metanoeite (c. 930–1000), Greek monk, itinerant preacher, and saint. Nikon is known for his missionary work among non-Christian native Greeks in Lacedaimon, pagan Slavs, and apostates to Islam in Crete. He was born to a wealthy provincial family in the Polemoniake district of Asia Minor. At the age of 20 or 21 he was so disturbed by the conditions under which workers labored in his family's estates that he rejected his family and fled to the monastery of Chryse Petra, by the River Parthenios, near the city of Amastris. After 12 years of monastic life, he left the monastery and traveled extensively, preaching in several towns, cities, and districts of Asia Minor, the island of Crete, and the Greek peninsula. Rather pessimistic about human nature, he made repentance the central theme of his message. Thus the epithet, *ho Metanoeite* (the "you should repent" one). He worked in Crete for seven years, from 961 to 968 or 969, among Christians and former Christians who had apostatized to Islam during the island's occupation by the Arabs (from 827 or 828 to 961). Subsequently he visited several cities in central Greece, including Athens, Chalkis, and Thebes, and others in the Peloponneses, before he settled in Sparta. He worked among Lacedaimon's natives, some of whom adhered to ancient religious practices, and among two small Slavic groups there who practiced Slavic paganism. His method of evangelism was to speak before small groups in an irenic and dialectic manner. He died in the monastery he had established near Sparta. His memory is observed on November 26.

BIBLIOGRAPHY O. Lampsides, *O ek Pontou hosios Nikon ho Metanoeite* (1982), *The Life of Saint Nikon*, Denis F. Sullivan, tr. (1987); D. Tsougarakis, *Byzantine Crete, 5th–12th C.* (1984); E. Voulgarakis, "Nikon Metanoeite und die Rechristianisierung der Kreter von Islam," *ZMR* 47 (1963): 192–204, 258–269.

Demetrios J. Constantelos

Niles, D(aniel) T(hambyrajah) (1908–1970), world leader in ecumenism and evangelism. Niles was born in Jaffna, Ceylon (Sri Lanka), into a family of Congregational and Methodist ministers dating to the first Tamil convert in 1821. He was graduated from what is now United Theological College in Bangalore, India, later earning a doctorate at the University of London. His ecumenical involvement began with the Student Christian Movement for India, Burma, and Ceylon and continued at the International Missionary Council meeting in Madras in 1938. He delivered the keynote address at the founding of the World Council of Churches (WCC) in Amsterdam (1948) and also spoke at Evanston (1954) and Uppsala

(1968). In the WCC he served successively as chairman of the Youth Department, executive secretary of the Department of Evangelism, and one of the six world presidents. Meanwhile, he headed the Methodist Church of Ceylon, the National Christian Council of Ceylon, the World's Student Christian Federation, and the East Asia Christian Conference (which he was instrumental in founding). Though he was an active and faithful Methodist, he was dedicated to worldwide ecumenism rather than national or denominational confessionalism.

Niles considered his primary calling that of an evangelist, a witness to the living Christ as personal savior, a task he once defined as "one beggar telling another beggar where to get food." Influenced by friends as theologically diverse as *Visser t' Hooft, Karl *Barth, Emil Brunner, Reinhold Niebuhr, John R. *Mott, and E. Stanley *Jones, he acknowledged special indebtedness to Hendrik *Kraemer and Paul *Devanandan for complementary approaches to other religions.

His own theology combined the richness of Eastern Orthodoxy and Western Protestantism with the devotion of surrounding Asian traditions. Yet he insisted that "the Christian Faith can be proclaimed; the other faiths can only be taught," because there is "true and essential discontinuity." As both writer and preacher, he consistently drew on the Bible as his principal source, and his published works, numbering at least a score, included several thoughtful and specific studies of Scripture, as well as three major lecture series on preaching. Many of his poems appear in *The East Asian Christian Hymnal,* which he helped to edit. He is remembered most for his commitment to evangelism and ecumenism.

BIBLIOGRAPHY D. T. Niles, *That They May Have Life* (1951), *The Preacher's Task and the Stone of Stumbling* (1958), *Upon the Earth* (1962), and *Who Is This Jesus?* (1968). Creighton Lacy, "D. T. Niles," in Gerald H. Anderson et al., eds., *Mission Legacies* (1994), pp. 362–370; J. Robert Nelson, "D. T. Niles: Evangelist and Ecumenist," *Ecumenical Trends* 9, no. 7, (July–Aug. 1980).

Creighton Lacy

Ninian (*or* Nynias; Niniavus) (c. 360–c. 432), missionary in Scotland. Ninian's father, a chief of Cumbrian Britons who converted to Christianity, sent his son to Rome for a Christian education. Apparently Pope Siricius consecrated Ninian a bishop in 394 and sent him back to evangelize Scotland. At Whithorn in Wigtownshire, in southwest Scotland, he built a church, Candida Casa, apparently dedicated to St. *Martin of Tours, whom he may have met on his travels in France. That church became a monastic mission center from which Ninian worked among Picts and Britons. Many Picts converted but rather quickly relapsed. Yet Candida Casa survived for centuries as an education center for Welsh and Irish missionaries.

BIBLIOGRAPHY Bede, *Ecclesiastical History,* 3.4.1; Mosa Anderson, *St. Ninian* (1964); D. Fahy, "The Historical Reality of Saint Ninian," *Innes Review* 15 (1964): 35–46; John Macqueen, *St. Ninian* (1961).

Frederick W. Norris

Nino (died c. 340), apostle of Georgia in southwestern Asia. A female Christian captive in Georgia, Nino (also Nina, Nunia, Nonna) is said to have performed miraculous healings and converted the Georgian queen. King Mirian followed his queen into Christian faith when, lost in darkness on a hunting trip, he prayed to Christ and found his way.

BIBLIOGRAPHY Rufinus, *Historia Ecclesiastica,* 10.11; V. Nikitin, "St. Nina, Equal to the Apostles, Enlightener of Iberia (Georgia)," *Journal of the Moscow Patriarchate* 2 (1985): 77–82 and "St. Nina, Equal to the Apostles, and the Baptism of Georgia," *Journal of the Moscow Patriarchate* 3 (1986): 49–56; Paul Peeters, "Les débuts du christianisme en Géorgie d'après les sources hagiographiques," *Analecta Bollandiana* 50 (1932): 5–58.

Frederick W. Norris

Nino, Bernardino de (1868–1923), Franciscan missionary and ethnographer among the Chiriguanos in southeastern Bolivia. Born in Prátola, Italy, de Nino arrived in Bolivia in 1891 and became the leader of the Potosí convent's missionary efforts among Bolivia's Chiriguano Indians. He established San Francisco del Parapetí (1901), San Antonio del Parapetí (1903), and Itatiqui (1912) to augment the missions of Potosí, which dated from the late nineteenth century. This was an effort to reinvigorate the missionary enterprise in Bolivia in the face of anticlerical opposition from the Bolivian government. When all three missions were secularized soon after they were founded, he published numerous pamphlets and articles condemning the government's actions. He is best known for his *Etnografía chiriguana* (1912), the best ethnography written on the Chiriguano Indians. After the new Potosí missions failed, de Nino was the prime architect of the Apostolic Vicariate of the Gran Chaco, which in 1919 combined the Potosí and Tarija missions, thereby easing their ultimate transition to secularization by 1949. He died in Buenos Aires.

BIBLIOGRAPHY In addition to *Etnografía chiriguana,* de Nino also published *Guía al Chaco boliviano* (1913) and *Misiones franciscanas del Colegio de Propaganda Fide de Potosí* (1918), a continuation of the mission history begun by Angélico Martarelli (*El Colegio Franciscano de Potosí y sus misiones,* 1893), which de Nino also corrected and augmented. It also includes an earlier work, *Las tres misiones secularizadas de la Provincia Cordillera* (1916). See also Theirry Saignes, "L'ethnographie missionnaire en Bolivie: Deux siècles de regards franciscains sur les Chiriguano, 1780–1980," in *The Franciscan Presence in the Americas* (1983), pp. 345–366.

Erick D. Langer

Nisbet, Henry (1818–1876), London Missionary Society (LMS) missionary in Samoa and Melanesia. Nisbet was born at Laurieston, Glasgow, Scotland. He was ordained a minister of the Presbyterian Relief Church and, after marrying Sarah, daughter of William Pascoe *Crook, went to Tanna, Vanuatu (then the New Hebrides), in 1840, but was forced out by Islander hostility. One of a group of LMS Scottish missionaries based in Samoa, he accompanied the

Canadian-Scots pioneer missionary John *Geddie to found the Presbyterian mission to the New Hebrides on Aneityum in 1848. His subsequent career in Samoa culminated in his work as a Bible translator and teacher of pastors and Islander missionaries at the Malua mission seminary. In 1867 he visited England and Canada. His wife died in 1868; he remarried before returning to Samoa, where he died at Malua. In 1870 his alma mater, the University of Glasgow, honored him with an LL.D.

BIBLIOGRAPHY Niel Gunson, *Messengers of Grace: Evangelical Missionaries in the South Seas, 1797–1860* (1978); Richard Lovett, *The History of the London Missionary Society, 1795–1895* (1899). The Nisbet Papers are in the Mitchell Library, Sydney; also see the LMS collection at SOAS, Univ. of London (available on microfilm).

John Garrett

Nitschmann, David (1696–1772), early Moravian leader in the New World. One of three contemporaries by the same name, Nitschmann became the first bishop of the Renewed Unitas Fratrum, better known as the Moravian Church. He was born at Zauchtenthal, Moravia (in what is now the Czech Republic), and immigrated to Herrnhut in 1724 in one of Christian *David's groups. He learned the carpenter's trade from David. In 1726 he married Rosina Schindler, who, like himself, was from an old Unitas Fratrum family. Earlier that year, Nitschmann was chosen a member of the first elder's conference of the Moravian Church, and he became an eager worker in a home mission team that went throughout Europe. In 1731 he accompanied Count *Zinzendorf to Copenhagen for the coronation of Christian VI and met the slave Anthony from Saint Thomas, who inspired them to begin the mission venture of the Moravians. In August 1732 Nitschmann and Leonard *Dober left Herrnhut for Saint Thomas, where Dober was to become the first missionary. Nitschmann returned to Herrnhut the next year and evangelized in the Netherlands and Denmark in 1734. In 1735 he was consecrated the first bishop of the Moravian Church at Berlin by the Polish Brethren bishop Daniel Ernest Jablonski. In 1737 Nitschmann assisted Jablonski in consecrating Zinzendorf as bishop; also that year he ordained Frederick *Martin for mission service in Saint Thomas. In 1736, as he accompanied the second group of missionaries to Georgia, Nitschmann met Charles and John *Wesley on the voyage. He was one of the members of the party who chose the site for Bethlehem, Pennsylvania, and traveled continuously in the interests of the church during the next 25 years. His wife died at Herrnhaag in 1753, and he returned to America that same year. In 1754 he married the widow of Frederick Martin. From 1756 to 1761 he was at Lititz, Pennsylvania, and then returned to Bethlehem, where he later died.

BIBLIOGRAPHY *Friedrich Martin, David Nitschmann, Friedrich von Watteville, und Petrus Böhler in kurzen Umrissen* (1842); J. T. Hamilton and K. G. Hamilton, *History of the Moravian Church* (1967).

Albert H. Frank

Nobili, Robert de (1577–1656), Jesuit missionary in India. De Nobili was born in a noble family in Rome. He joined the Jesuits in 1597, went to India in 1605, and visited Madurai in South India the following year. Gonzalvo Fernández had been there since 1595, ministering to the Christians from the pearl fishery coast, but was unable to make any local converts. De Nobili soon found the reason: becoming Christian was seen as becoming Portuguese—taking up the Portuguese way of life, eating meat, and so forth. This was anathema to people in Madurai, who were proud of their Indian culture and tradition. De Nobili felt that one need not cease to be Indian to become Christian. To underline this fact he decided to become Indian himself. He mastered Tamil, the local language, and lived like an Indian sannyasi (holy man), dressed in saffron robes and served by Brahmins. He also mastered Telugu and Sanskrit and familiarized himself with the Hindu Vedas and other religious and philosophical works.

In de Nobili's view, allowing Christians to continue to be Indians meant permitting them to keep their ways of dressing and living, like wearing the sacred thread and keeping the tuft of hair, which he considered to be of cultural rather than religious significance. It also meant accepting the social discriminations of the caste system. His policy of cultural accommodation attracted converts not only among the Brahmins but also from the other castes, high and low. Observance of the caste system can be seen in two types of missionaries, starting in 1643: the Brahmin sannyasis for the higher castes and the *Pandaraswamis* (cultic leaders) for the lower ones.

Though de Nobili's approach was approved by the archbishop, Francis Ros of Cranganore, and the Jesuit provincial, Albert Laerzio, it was attacked as syncretistic by others. De Nobili wrote letters and treatises, argued his case in person before the Inquisition in Goa, and appealed to the Jesuit general, Robert Bellarmine (a relative), and to the pope in Rome. This controversy became known as the Malabar Rites controversy. *Gregory XV pronounced himself in favor of de Nobili's methods in the apostolic constitution *Romanae Sedis Antistes,* dated January 31, 1623. The policy bore fruit in rooting the mission firmly in the interior parts of Tamilnadu, among both higher and lower castes, though converts among the Brahmins were not as numerous as expected.

De Nobili has been acclaimed as the first Oriental scholar and the Father of Tamil prose. Excluding his letters and treatises in Italian, Portuguese, and Latin in defense of his missionary method, his writings number 40 Tamil prose works, 3 Tamil poetic works, 8 works in Sanskrit, and 3 works in Telugu, excluding translations into Telugu of some of his works written in Tamil. They are philosophical and theological expositions of the faith, refutations of contrary opinions, and catechisms. He was honored with the title *Tattuva Podagar* (teacher of philosophy). He died in Mylapore, Madras.

BIBLIOGRAPHY S. Rajamanickam, *The First Oriental Scholar* (1972) gives all necessary information about de Nobili and his writings as well as a good bibliography. Rajamanickam has also edited and published most of de Nobili's writings in Tamil at the De Nobili Research Institute, Madras, including *Roberto de Nobili on Adaptation* (1971) and *Roberto de Nobili on Indian Customs* (1972), both of which deal with mission theory. See also S. Arockiasamy, *Dharma, Hindu and Christian, according to Roberto de Nobili* (1986). A popular biography is V. Cronin, *A Pearl to India* (1959).

Michael Amaladoss, SJ

Noble, Robert Turlington (1809–1865), pioneer English missionary and educator in South India. Born in Frisby on the Wreake, Leicestershire, the son of a clergyman, Noble entered Cambridge in 1827 but became ill and withdrew in his third year. After working for several years as a tutor, he finally graduated and was ordained in 1840 before leaving for India in 1841 as a Church Missionary Society (CMS) missionary. He never married and never returned to England. He worked in Masulipatam, in Telugu country, opening the Native English School (later known as Noble College) in November 1843. Over the years, the school became popular and influential. Noble was well-served by local colleagues, including the Eurasian missionaries J. E. *Sharkey and T. Y. *Darling. Two of the school's first converts, baptized in 1852, were ordained in 1864, and other former students made notable contributions to the church and to the community. In 1864 the Masulipatam district was stuck by a disastrous hurricane in which several Indian clergy and their relatives were drowned. Noble's health was affected, and he died a year later. His friends built the Noble Memorial School Hall in Masulipatam to commemorate him.

Bibliography John Noble, *A Memoir of the Rev. Robert Turlington Noble, Missionary to the Telugu People in South India* (1866); Eugene Stock, *The History of the Church Missionary Society: Its Environment, Its Men and Its Work,* 3 vols. (1899).

Jocelyn Murray

Nóbrega, Manoel da (1517–1570), Jesuit missionary to Brazil. As a Portuguese Jesuit Nóbrega played a key role in establishing Portuguese civilization in Brazil and organizing the first missions to evangelize and protect the Indians from the white settlers. He studied at the universities of Coimbra and Salamanca and entered the Society of Jesus in 1544. Although impeded by a speech defect, he became a popular preacher in the countryside of Portugal. In 1549 he was named superior of the small band of Jesuits who accompanied Tomé de Sousa to the New World as first governor general of Brazil. Nóbrega became a close adviser to Sousa and to Mem de Sá, the third governor general, not only in religious matters but also in affairs relating to education, society, and the Indians. He was instrumental in the founding of Salvador of Bahía, the first capital, as well as São Paulo, and Rio de Janeiro. In each of these cities he founded the first schools for boys. He served as first provincial of the Jesuits in Brazil from 1553 to 1559. In August 1553, he and other Jesuits founded São Paulo de Piratininga as a mission for the Indians, and he founded many other *aldeias,* or mission towns, in the interior regions. In his sermons and writings he assumed the defense of the Indians against white exploiters, especially the mestizo raiders who carried Indians off for slavery. In 1562 he interceded between two warring tribes, the Tupis and the Tamóios. The establishment of peace, and the removal of the French who had built a fort in the area, led to the founding of Rio de Janeiro. Nóbrega spent his last years as rector of the college he had founded in Rio de Janeiro. In his own lifetime he was considered the model for all other Jesuits in Brazil, and his policies became a guiding norm for future generations.

Bibliography Jerome V. Jacobsen, "Jesuit Founders in Portugal and Brazil," *Mid-America* 24 (January 1942): 3–26, and "Nóbrega of Brazil," *Mid-America* 24 (July 1942): 151–187; Serafim Leite, *História da Companhia de Jesús no Brasil,* 10 vols. (1938–1950).

Jeffrey Klaiber, SJ

Nommensen, Ingwer Ludwig (1834–1918), pioneer missionary to the Batak in Sumatra. Born in Nordstrand, Schleswig, then a Danish territory, Nommensen graduated from the Rhenish Mission Seminary, Wuppertal, Germany, and went to Sumatra, Indonesia (then the Netherland's East Indies), arriving there in 1862 as a missionary of the Rhenish Mission Society. He settled among the independent Toba Batak in the Silindung Valley and baptized the first converts in 1865. The chief, Pontas Lumbantobing, became his friend and supported the mission. Together with P. H. Johannsen and A. Mohri, Nommensen withstood the opposition of the local *datu* priests. Church rules and a common order of worship were drawn up in 1866. In 1881 he drafted a constitution to organize the growing Christian movement as a "people's church." In 1885 he moved north, pioneering in the Lake Toba region, and some years later he expanded the work to the Simelungun Batak. He consolidated the work by establishing advanced schools, hospitals, and a theological seminary.

Nommensen and his wife lost a child in Indonesia in 1868 and a second one four years later. In 1887 his wife died in Germany, leaving him with four children. He remarried in 1892. In 1901 his son Christian was murdered in Sumatra. In 1909 his second wife died, and another son, Nathaniel, died in World War I.

Often referred to as the Apostle of the Batak, Nommensen was the leading missionary among the Batak from 1864 to 1918 (54 years) and was moderator of the Rhenish Batak Mission from 1881. He was made a knight of the Royal Dutch Order of Orange Nassau in 1893 and an officer of this order in 1911. He received an honorary doctor of theology degree from the University of Bonn in 1904. When he died, the Batak church had 34 pastors, 788 teacher-preachers, and 180,000 members in more than 500 local churches. His published writings include translations into the Batak language of Luther's Small Catechism (1874), the New Testament (1878), Bible Stories (1882), three booklets entitled *Berichte an seine Freunde* (1882, 1883, 1886), and about forty shorter articles and contributions to mission journals.

Bibliography Martin E. Lehmann, *A Biographical Study of Ingwer Ludwig Nommensen* (1996); Gustav Menzel, *Ein Reiskorn auf der*

Strasse: Ludwig Ingwer Nommensen, Apostel der Batak (1984); Lothar Schreiner, "Nommensen in His Context: Aspects of a New Approach," in R. Carle, ed., *Cultures and Societies in North Sumatra* (1987), pp. 179–187, "Nommensen Studies—A Review," *Mission Studies* 9 (1992): 241–251 (includes extensive bibliography), and ed., *Nommensen in Selbstzeugnissen: Unveröffentlichte Aufsätze, Entwürfe und Dokumente* (1996); Johannes Warneck, *Ludwig Ingwer Nommensen, ein Lebensbild* (1919; 4th rev. ed., 1934). Nommensen's personal papers and letters to the mission board are in the archives of the Vereinigte Evangelische Mission, Wuppertal, Germany.

Lothar Schreiner

Norris, Hannah Maria. *See* Armstrong, Hannah Maria (Norris).

North, Frank Mason (1850–1935), Methodist mission executive and ecumenical leader. Born in New York City, North graduated from Wesleyan University, Connecticut. After 20 years in local pastorates, he directed the New York Church Extension and Missionary Society for two decades, edited a pioneer journal called *The Christian City,* and established metropolitan centers for immigrant and minority groups, including New York's Church of All Nations. Between 1912 and 1924 he headed the Board of Foreign Missions of the Methodist Episcopal Church and undertook a world tour of mission fields and relief projects at the outbreak of World War I. He participated in many international and ecumenical conferences and played a major role in the inauguration of the Federal Council of the Churches of Christ in America in 1908, serving as its chairman from 1916 to 1920. He was also the primary author of *The Social Creed of the Churches* (1908), a Christian manifesto for labor and economic justice. Of his many hymns, the most widely known, sung, and translated is "Where Cross the Crowded Ways of Life," published in 1903. Of his three sons, the youngest, Eric McCoy North, served for many years as general secretary of the American Bible Society.

BIBLIOGRAPHY Frank Mason North, *Hymns and Other Verses* (1931), "Christianity and Socialism," *Zion's Herald,* January 14–February 4, 1891, and *The Christian City* (ed., 1892–1912). Samuel M. Cavert, *The American Churches in the Ecumenical Movement, 1900–1968* (1968); *Frank Mason North, December 3, 1850–December 17, 1935,* published by friends (1936); Charles Howard Hopkins, *The Rise of the Social Gospel in American Protestantism, 1865–1915* (1940); Creighton Lacy, *Frank Mason North: His Social and Ecumenical Mission* (1967).

Creighton Lacy

Norton, H(ugo) Wilbert (1915–), American mission educator. Norton was born in Chicago, Illinois, and educated at Wheaton College (B.A., 1936), Columbia Bible College (M.A., 1938; Th.M., 1939), and Northern Baptist Theological Seminary (Th.D., 1955). In 1936 he helped to create the Student Foreign Missions Fellowship, which merged with the Inter-Varsity Christian Fellowship in 1945. In 1940 Norton and his wife, Colleen Woodard, went as missionaries with the Evangelical Free Church of America to Tandala, Belgian Congo (now Zaire), where he became founding director of the Bible Institute of the Ubangi. In 1950 Norton moved to Chicago to serve as missions professor and eventually president of Trinity College. In 1965 he began a 15-year term as missions professor, then dean, at the Wheaton College graduate school. He went back to Africa in 1980 to serve as founding principal of the Jos (Nigeria) Theological Seminary. Then he returned to Wheaton in 1983 to direct the Committee to Assist Ministry Education Overseas. In 1989 he went to the Reformed Theological Seminary in Jackson, Mississippi, to establish a doctoral program in missiology. Norton served on the boards of Inter-Varsity and Evangelical Literature Overseas. He is a charter member of the American Society of Missiology and the founding president of the Association of Evangelical Professors of Missions. He has published five books on missions and church history.

BIBLIOGRAPHY H. Wilbert Norton, *Twenty-five Years in the Ubangi* (1947), *The Diamond Jubilee Story of the Evangelical Free Church of America* (editor; 1959), *European Background and History of Evangelical Free Church Foreign Missions* (1959, rev. ed., 1964), *What's Gone Wrong with the Harvest?* (coauthor with James F. Engel; 1975), and *To Stir the Church: A Brief History of the Student Foreign Missions Fellowships, 1936–1986* (1986).

Joel Carpenter

Nott, Henry (1774–1844), London Missionary Society (LMS) missionary to Tahiti. Nott was born in the village of Bromsgrove, near Birmingham, England. A bricklayer by trade, he was one of the original party of mainly artisan missionaries of the Missionary Society (later LMS) sent in 1896 to Tahiti in the ship *Duff.* A persistent survivor, he endured the trials of the group—defections, deaths, dispersal, and long isolation in a period of wars both in Europe and between chiefs in the Society Islands. He attached himself to the wayward future King *Pomare II of Tahiti, accompanied him in exile to Moorea and the Windward Islands, and after 1816 returned with a few dogged colleagues to share in Pomare's victory, his conversion, his coronation, his dispiriting lapses—and his patronage. Pomare helped him to acquire a stylish "royal" oral Tahitian. Subsequently, as the king became literate, Nott played a major part with Pomare in translating the Bible.

In 1812, on a visit to Port Jackson, Sydney, he married Anne Turner. Between 1825 and 1827 he went to England. By then, though largely self-taught, he had supplemented his ability as a preacher in other ways, helping to frame a code of laws for Christian Tahiti. In 1836 he again visited London, this time in ill health, to see the completed manuscript of the Bible through publication. In September 1840, his return to Tahiti with the Bible helped to consolidate mass conversions and literacy. Both before and during his final retirement at Papeete, his achievements were underestimated by more highly educated incoming missionaries, who viewed the pioneers with a touch of critical disdain. He died and was buried at Papeete, where his modest and long disregarded grave is scant testimony to his exceptional life's work.

BIBLIOGRAPHY John Davies, *The History of the Tahitian Mission, 1799–1830,* C. W. Newbury, ed. (1961); John Garrett, *To Live among the Stars: Christian Origins in Oceania* (1982); Niel Gunson, *Messengers of Grace: Evangelical Missionaries in the South Seas, 1797–1860* (1978); Richard Lovett, *The History of the London Missionary Society, 1795–1895,* 2 vols. (1899); Jacques Nicole, *Au pied de l'écriture: Histoire de la traduction de la Bible en Tahitien* (1988). Nott materials are in the LMS archives, SOAS, Univ. of London (available on microfilm).

John Garrett

Nott, Samuel, Jr. (1788–1869), pioneer American Congregational missionary. Nott was born in Massachusetts, the son of Samuel Nott, a Congregational minister. He graduated from Union College, Schenectady, New York, in 1809 with high honors and from Andover Theological Seminary, Massachusetts, in 1810. He was one of the legendary first group of missionaries appointed to India by the American Board of Commissioners for Foreign Missions in 1812. Immediately following the commissioning of the first five missionaries at Salem, Massachusetts, on February 6, 1812, Samuel married Roxanna Peck and the couple joined Gordon *Hall and Luther *Rice for the second embarkation after the *Judsons and *Newells had left for India. Rice, owing to poor health, soon returned to the United States to organize the Baptist constituency. At Bombay in 1813, Nott and Hall encountered difficulties with the government and the East India Company but were finally permitted to remain. Nott, however, developed liver disease and was advised to return to the United States, which he did in the autumn of 1815. For many years, he served as pastor of the Congregational Church in Wareham, Massachusetts. He and his friend Adoniram Judson met one additional time, in 1845, at Bowdoin Square Baptist Church in Boston. They greeted each other warmly and Nott reaffirmed his friendship and support in spite of Judson's conversion to Baptist principles.

BIBLIOGRAPHY The best sources on Nott's life as a missionary are William E. Strong, *The Story of the American Board: An Account of the First Hundred Years of the American Board of Commissioners for Foreign Missions* (1910) and Courtney Anderson, *To the Golden Shore* (1956). For Nott's own version, see "Recollection of the Rev. Samuel Nott," in *Memorial Volume of the First Fifty Years of the American Board of Commissioners for Foreign Missions* (1861).

William H. Brackney

Noyes, Harriet Newell (1845–1924), American Presbyterian missionary and educator in China. Noyes came from a Presbyterian pastor's family from which one son, two daughters, and two grandsons would serve as missionaries in China. Named after Harriet A. *Newell, a pioneer American missionary, Noyes was accepted as a missionary with the American Presbyterian mission and arrived in Canton in 1868. She ministered there for a period of 50 years, with most of her time devoted to educational work. Within two months of her arrival she established a girls' day school in Wa-lung li, near Canton (Guangzhou), employing Chinese Christian women as teachers. In 1872, after four years of involvement with other girls' day schools, she organized and became the first principal of what became True Light Seminary. One department of this school was the Training School for Women, which was supported largely by the Woman's Work for Foreign Missions in connection with the Presbyterian Board. The purpose of this work was to enable students to become Bible women and teachers and leaders among the neglected women of China. In the period that Noyes was associated with the school it trained 6,000 women. The influence of its graduates led in 1923 to the founding of the Women's Service League, an interdenominational organization that coordinated Bible classes for women.

In 1886 Noyes attended the General Assembly of the Presbyterian Church in the U.S.A. and signed a letter of protest to the U.S. government over its unfair treatment of Chinese in America. The last five years of her life were spent in the United States, where she died.

BIBLIOGRAPHY Harriet Newell Noyes, *A Light in the Land of Sinim* (1919) and *History of the South China Mission of the American Presbyterian Church, 1845–1920* (1927). Obituary in *Chinese Recorder,* March 1924, pp. 185–186.

Ralph R. Covell

Nsibambi, Simeon (1897–1978), Ugandan evangelist and leader in the East African Revival. One of the many sons of a prosperous Ganda subchief, Nsibambi was educated in Anglican schools. During World War I he served in an army medical corps in German East Africa and afterwards became a government health officer. During the 1920s, after a religious conversion, he searched for personal holiness; this was satisfied through a meeting in 1929 with a young missionary doctor from Rwanda, J. E. *Church. Giving up his work, he became an independent evangelist. Through his personal contacts he built up the group that became the foundation of the *Balokole* (Saved Ones) in Buganda. He traveled with Church and others to preach at conventions; his younger half-brother, Blasio *Kigozi, was a worker with the Church Missionary Society Ruanda Mission. His wife, Eva, was sister-in-law to William *Nagenda, the revival's leading evangelist.

After 1943 Nsibambi, although confined almost entirely to his home with heart trouble, continued his influence through personal work. His last years were clouded by Nagenda's serious illness and premature death, and by the formation by some of the Revival Brethren around Kampala of another group known as *Kuzuzuka* (Reawakening).

BIBLIOGRAPHY J. E. Church, *Quest for the Highest: An Autobiographical Account of the East Africa Revival* (1981).

Jocelyn Murray

Ntsikana (c. 1780–1821), early leader of Xhosa indigenous Christianity in South Africa. The son of a hereditary councilor to the chief Ngqika, Ntsikana had a traditional upbringing and was renowned as an orator, singer, and dancer. As a youth, he was probably influenced by the preaching of Johannes *Van der Kemp. In 1815 he experienced a divine call in his cattle kraal and subsequently organized daily Christian worship with a small band of disciples. While attending services at the Kat River mission, he continued to live among his people. He composed the first Xhosa hymns, which were praise songs, with images and symbols rooted in his people's experience, and music drawn from Xhosa singing. His inculturation of the gospel in an African context was the genesis of an authentic indigenous theology.

Following Ntsikana's death, his disciples joined a Western mission yet kept alive his teaching, prophecies, and hymns in oral and written traditions. Africans came to revere him as their own saint, which is reflected in the naming of the St. Ntsikana Memorial Association, founded in 1909 as a cultural and ecumenical Xhosa movement. In recent years he has become a symbol of a much broader African cultural identity.

BIBLIOGRAPHY Janet Hodgson, "Ntsikana: History and Symbol. Studies in the Process of Religious Change among Xhosa-speaking People" (Ph.D. diss., Univ. of Cape Town, 1985), *Ntsikana's Great Hymn: A Xhosa Expression of Christianity in the Early 19th Century Eastern Cape* (1980), and "Fluid Assets and Fixed Investments: 160 Years of the Ntsikana Tradition," in R. Whitaker and E. Sienaert, eds., *Oral Tradition and Literacy: Changing Visions of the World* (1986).

Janet Hodgson

Nunes Barreto, João (1510?-1562), Jesuit missionary in Morocco and India and patriarch of Ethiopia. Born in Porto, Portugal, Nunes Barreto completed his studies at Salamanca and served as a parish priest in the diocese of Braga. In 1545 he entered the Society of Jesus at Coimbra. From 1548 to 1554 he was a missionary in Tetuan, Morocco, where he was deeply involved in offering spiritual consolation to slaves, and he returned to Lisbon to raise funds to ransom them. There, he received news that the founder of the Jesuit order, *Ignatius of Loyola—whose policy was not to allow Jesuits to become bishops—had accepted the request of King John III of Portugal to have Nunes Barreto appointed Patriarch of Ethiopia so that the Catholic mission could be developed further there. Nominated in January 1555 and consecrated in May, Nunes Barreto left Portugal for India in late March 1556 along with Andres *Oviedo, a Jesuit bishop consecrated with him and designated as his successor. Upon arrival in Goa, Nunes Barreto learned from Jesuit confreres recently returned from Ethiopia that the situation there was not favorable. He decided however, to send Oviedo to improve the status of the mission with Ethiopian authorities. Oviedo was somewhat successful with one of the monarchs but not with his successors. Realizing that he was unlikely to enter Ethiopia, Nunes Barreto devoted his talents to an active ministry in Goa. He suggested to Jesuit superiors that they request papal permission to renounce his status as a patriarch and bishop. The negative reply of the superiors reached Goa after his death there.

BIBLIOGRAPHY The patriarch's correspondence was published in Monumenta Historica Societatis Iesu: *Epistolae Mixtae,* vol. 4 (1900), pp. 134-139, 334-336, 422-424 and vol. 5 (1901), pp. 682-691; *Monumenta Ignatiana,* vol. 8 (1901), pp. 707-720, *Litterae Quadrimestres,* vol. 3 (1896), pp. 132-136; Josef Wicki, ed., *Documenta Indica,* vol. 3 (1954), pp. 510-517; vol. 4 (1956), pp. 360-362, 815-819; vol. 5 (1958), pp. 674-677. Philip Caraman, *The Lost Empire: The Story of the Jesuits in Ethiopia, 1555-1634* (1985); John O'Malley, *The First Jesuits* (1993), pp. 327-328; William Van Gulik and Conrad Eubel, eds., *Hierarchia Catholica Medii et Recentioris Aevii,* vol. 3 (1923), p. 97.

John W. Witek, SJ

Nyländer, Gustavus Reinhold (1776-1824), pioneer missionary in Sierra Leone. A German Lutheran from Russian-ruled Livonia (in area of present-day Lithuania), Nyländer trained at the Berlin Mission seminary before being recruited in 1805 by the Church Missionary Society (CMS). He served as chaplain at Freetown, Sierra Leone, from 1806 to 1812 but then opened a mission station on the Bullom Shore of the Sierra Leone estuary, opposite Freetown, where he worked from 1812 to 1818. He finally served as parish minister among liberated slaves at Kissy village, near Freetown, until his death there at the end of 18 continuous years in Sierra Leone. The earliest of the CMS missionaries in West Africa to see his linguistic work in print, he published (1813-1816) a quantity of material in and on the Bullom language, which has been little studied since, and one with a limited printed literature and missionary use to date. He also encouraged a local African, George Caulker, to publish a few pieces on the related Sherbro language. He was thus the founding father of the Freetown school of missionary linguists. He married and buried two wives in Sierra Leone, both Afro-Americans. His two daughters worked in the Sierra Leone mission as teachers and died there. One daughter was the first wife of the missionary linguist, J. F. *Schön, and descendants from this marriage served the CMS during the rest of the century.

BIBLIOGRAPHY P. E. H. Hair, "Freetown and the Study of West African Languages, 1800-1875," *Bulletin de l'Institut Français d'Afrique Noire,* B, 221 (1959): 579-586, "Early Vernacular Printing in Africa," *Sierra Leone Language Review* 3 (1964): 47-52, and *The Early Study of Nigerian Languages* (2d ed., 1995). Nyländer materials are held in the CMS archives, Univ. of Birmingham.

P. E. H. Hair

O

Obookiah (*or* Opukahaia), Henry (1792–1818), intended missionary to his native Hawaii and inspiration for the ABCFM Sandwich Islands Mission. Taken by a Yankee ship captain from Hawaii to New Haven, Connecticut, in 1809, Obookiah was befriended by Samuel *Mills and other mission-minded students. In 1812 he was converted and in 1816 became affiliated with the American Board of Commissioners for Foreign Missions (ABCFM), which enrolled him in its foreign mission school at Cornwall, Connecticut. He was a most effective advocate for the new cause of foreign missions: it was said he "open[ed] the hearts and hands even of enemies." Although he died of typhus at the age of 26, his best-selling *Memoirs* helped inspire a mission which powerfully influenced the history of Hawaii.

BIBLIOGRAPHY Edwin W. Dwight, *Memoirs of Henry Obookiah* (1818, 1968); *Panoplist* 12 (1816): 297–302.

David M. Stowe

Occom, Samson (1723–1792), Native American pastor and missionary. Occom was born at Mohegan, Connecticut, and became a Christian in his youth. He was the first Indian trained by Eleazar *Wheelock at his school in Lebanon, Connecticut, which later became Dartmouth College. In 1749 he moved to eastern Long Island to be teacher and pastor to the Montauk people. His success there led to his ordination by the Long Island Presbytery in 1759, even though he lacked theological education.

Occom made two mission trips to the Oneida Indians in upstate New York, and in 1765, a trip to England with Nathaniel Whitaker to raise funds for Wheelock's school. He made a great impression in England and with Whitaker raised over £12,000. After his return he became an itinerant preacher to the New England Indians and was sometimes in poverty. He was a leader in resisting the encroachments by whites on Indian lands, which made him unpopular in Connecticut. He also took a lead in securing lands for the settlement of New England Indians among the Oneida, who were far from white influence. In 1785, when Brothertown was established in Oneida territory, he became its pastor and remained there the rest of his life.

He was a great orator who gave little attention to doctrine but much to rules of conduct. He composed a number of hymns and published a hymn collection that went through three editions.

BIBLIOGRAPHY A. W. Blodgett, *Samson Occom* (1935); William DeLoss Love, *Samson Occom and the Christian Indians of New England* (1899); L. B. Richardson, *History of Dartmouth College* (1932); L. B. Richardson, ed., *An Indian Preacher in England* (1933).

Charles W. Forman

O'Donel, James Louis (1737–1811), first vicar apostolic of Newfoundland. O'Donel was born near Knocklofty, Ireland, into a prosperous farming family. After private tutoring at home and a classical education in Limerick, he entered the Franciscan order and in 1770 was ordained priest at St. Isidore's College in Rome. He became a seminary teacher in Prague and subsequently held administrative positions within his order in Ireland. When religious liberty was announced to the Roman Catholics of Newfoundland in 1784, the Irish merchants there sought to secure an institutional religious presence for Catholicism, and O'Donel was chosen to be the leader of the mission because of his administrative and pastoral experience. During his stay in St. John's, he succeeded in suppressing unauthorized clergy and establishing parishes, schools, and districts. He also fostered the loyalty of Newfoundland Catholics for Great Britain and cultivated a spirit of religious tolerance for Protestants. In 1796 he was consecrated bishop and placed in charge of the vicariate apostolic of Newfoundland and the French islands of Saint-Pierre and Miquelon. By the time he turned over the island territory to his successor Patrick Lambert in 1807, he had earned the respect of his Irish faithful, the British colonial authorities, and the merchant elite of St. John's. He retired to the Franciscan monastery in Waterford, Ireland, where he died.

BIBLIOGRAPHY Cyril J. Byrne, *Gentlemen-Bishops and Faction Fighters: The Letters of Bishops O'Donel, Lambert, Scallan, and Other Irish Missionaries* (1984); Raymond J. Lahey, *James Louis O'Donel in Newfoundland 1784–1807: The Establishment of the Roman Catholic Church* (1984); Hans Rollmann, "Religious Enfranchisement and Roman Catholics in Eighteenth-Century Newfoundland," in Terrence M. Murphy and Cyril J. Byrne, eds., *Religion and Identity: The Experience of Irish and Scottish Catholics in Atlantic Canada* (1987), pp. 34–52.

Hans Rollmann

Odorico of Pordenone (d. 1331), Franciscan missionary to Asia. Odorico was born between 1265 and 1286 in a small village close to the city of Pordenone in northeastern Italy. He joined the Franciscans and lived the austere life of a hermit. Sometime between 1314 and 1318 he started a 16-year journey to Asia. Traveling by land, he reached Persia, where he lived with his confreres for five or six years. He continued by land to the port of Ormuz; from here he sailed for the northeast coast of India and landed at Thana, where four confreres had been martyred shortly before his arrival. Sailing along the coasts of India, Sri Lanka, Sumatra, Java, Kalimantan, and Vietnam, Odorico arrived at the port of Canton in China. From there he traveled to Khanbalik (Beijing), where he stayed with his confreres for three years. He returned by land via central Asia to Italy, and in 1330 dictated his travel story to William of Solagna. As he intended to return to China accompanied by a large group of Franciscans, he traveled to Avignon to obtain permission of the pope. He fell ill, however, and returned to Udine, where he died.

Odorico was a keen observer. To him we owe a detailed account of the life of the first archbishop and patriarch of the Orient, *John of Montecorvino, and his companions in Beijing and some other cities in China.

BIBLIOGRAPHY Folkert Reichert, *Begegnungen mit China, die Entdeckung Ostasiens im Mittelalter* (1992), pp. 120–123, and *Die Reise des seligen Odorich von Pordenone nach Indien und China (1314/18–1330)* (1987). Anastasius van den Wyngaert, *Sinica Franciscana*, vol. 1 (1929), pp. 379–495.

Arnulf Camps, OFM

Oehler, Theodor Friedrich (1850–1915), German mission leader. Born in Breslau of a Württemberg family, Oehler was *Inspektor* (executive head) of the Basel Mission (BM) from 1885, and then *Direktor* from 1909 until his death. During his years in office, the BM opened two new fields (Cameroon in 1886 and North Togo in 1911) and expanded in all respects, while maintaining the structure left by his predecessor Joseph *Josenhans. Oehler was less than enthusiastic about innovations such as a greater emphasis on the work of unmarried women missionaries. In addition to his leadership of BM, Oehler was important in the national leadership of Protestant missions in Germany, serving as chairman of the German (Protestant) Mission Council from 1890 until his death.

BIBLIOGRAPHY Jonas Dah, *Missionary Motives and Methods: A Critical Examination of the Basel Mission in Cameroon, 1814–1886* (1983); Wilhelm Schlatter, *Geschichte der Basler Mission* (1915).

Paul Jenkins

Officer, Morris (1823–1874), pioneer Lutheran missionary in West Africa and founder of the Lutheran mission in Liberia. Officer was born to poor parents in rural Holmes County, Ohio. Self-reliant and with practical talents, he became the family mainstay at age 15 when his father was disabled. At 20 he underwent a conversion, influenced by revival meetings as well as temperance and anti-slavery causes. In 1846 he entered Wittenberg College, Ohio, and was given responsibility for fund-raising in local congregations, supervising new building construction, and tutoring lower classes. In 1848, through the *Lutheran Observer*, he proposed that Lutherans begin a mission in West Africa. When church authorities demurred, Officer arranged to go to Africa under the auspices of the American Missionary Association but with the intention of eventually establishing a Lutheran mission. In 1852 he sailed for Sierra Leone, spending 18 months prospecting for a field, then returned to Ohio with an appeal to the Lutheran General Synod to sponsor a mission. The synod gave its approval but required Officer to raise all his own funds. In April 1860 Officer and an assistant arrived in Monrovia, where they were received by the Liberian president and given 300 acres for the mission settlement named Muhlenberg. The land was designated for coffee plantation and small farms. Through a remarkable providence, the mission was provided with 40 young African boys and girls, taken from two Congo slave ships intercepted by a U.S. cruiser in African coastal waters. These became the first pupils in the mission schools. In April 1861, one year after landing in Africa, Officer returned to America to report that the African mission had been successfully founded. He dedicated ten more years to superintending home mission development in the American Midwest.

BIBLIOGRAPHY Morris Officer, *A Plea for a Lutheran Mission in Liberia* (1853) and *Western Africa: A Mission Field* (1856). A biographical sketch appears in L. B. Wolf, *Missionary Heroes of the Lutheran Church* (1911).

James A. Scherer

Ofori-Atta, William Eugene Amoako-Atta (1910–1988), Ghanaian Christian patriot. Known affectionately as "Paa Willie," Ofori-Atta made a unique impact as a professional politician during the most turbulent periods of Ghana's modern history. He was one of the so-called Big Six pioneering political leaders—including Kwame

Nkrumah—who in the 1940s initiated the struggle for Ghana's independence from British rule. A graduate in economics from Cambridge University and a trained barrister, Ofori-Atta's admiration for the ideals of British parliamentary procedure led him into the opposition under the First Republic (1960–1966) and into two periods of political detention. During the second, in 1964, he underwent a religious experience that changed his life. He continued to be active in political affairs in government in the Second Republic (1969–1972), and he endured detention in 1972 and 1978 as a leader of the People's Movement for Freedom and Justice that had been founded to resist the new military junta. He also served as chairman of the Council of State in the Third Republic (1979–1981). Despite this consistent political involvement, his ruling passion was to spread the good news of salvation in Jesus Christ. Joint founder of the Maranatha Bible College and of the Christian Outreach Fellowship, an indigenous missionary society, he also advised many other Christian bodies and initiatives. The same revolutionary government that curtailed his political activity in 1981 paid him tribute at his death in July 1988: "He brought to politics a new breath of sincerity, modesty, and honesty.... He did not use his talents or office for the acquisition of personal wealth, and he worked, lived, and died a simple and devoted patriot."

BIBLIOGRAPHY William Ofori-Atta, *Ghana: A Nation in Crisis* (the J. B. Danquah memorial lectures, ser. 18, February 1985) (1988). *Tribute to the Late Mr. William Eugene Amoako-Atta Ofori-Atta (Paa Willie), Member of the Big Six* (1988)

Kwame Bediako

Ohm, Thomas (1892–1962), German Catholic missiologist. Born in Westerholt, Westphalia, Ohm joined the Benedictines of St. Ottilien in 1912. After interruption of his studies by military service in World War I, he became a priest in 1920 and earned his doctorate in theology in Munich in 1923. He taught at the University of Salzburg and then at Würzburg. Dismissed in 1941 by the Nazis, he had time to prepare important works on non-Christian religions. In 1946 he was called to the University of Münster as successor to Joseph *Schmidlin. He founded a new mission institute, reorganized the *Zeitschrift für Missionswissenschaft und Religionswissenschaft,* and revived the International Institute of Missiological Research, which under his guidance held national mission study weeks in Münster (1953), Würzburg (1956), Bonn (1958), and Wien (1961). Field studies led him to India in 1930, to Africa in 1933, to the Far East in 1936, and again to Africa in 1951. At home he was an inspiring teacher, leading many of his students to academic degrees. In 1960 he became a member of the Roman Mission Commission preparing for Vatican II and offered new mission concepts later accepted by the council. He retired in 1961. Several of his publications, including his major work, *"Machet zu Jüngern alle Völker": Theorie der Mission* (1962), were translated into different languages.

BIBLIOGRAPHY Thomas Ohm, *Ex contemplatione loqui: Gesammelte Aufsätze von Thomas Ohm* (1960; full bibliography) and "Meine Tätigkeit im Dienste der Missionswissenschaft in Münster," in Josef Glazik, ed., *50 Jahre Missionswissenschaft in Münster, 1911–1961* (1961), pp. 33–40. Johannes Beckmann, "Prof. Dr. Thomas Ohm OSB zum Gedächtnis," *NZM* 18 (1962): 305–311; H. R. Schlette, "Thomas Ohm zum Gedächtnis," *ZMR* 46 (1962): 242–250.

Bernward H. Willeke, OFM

Olav II. *See* Haraldsson, Olav.

Oldendorp, Christian Georg Andreas (1721–1787), German mission historian. After studies at Jena, Oldendorp joined the Moravian Brethren at Marienborn and for most of the rest of his life worked as an instructor and preacher in Moravian colleges. In 1763 he was entrusted with writing a history of the Moravian mission in the Caribbean, and from 1767 to 1769 he visited the Danish islands of Saint Croix, Saint Thomas, and Saint John (present-day Virgin Islands), where the mission operated, as well as New York and Pennsylvania. An abbreviated version of the material he collected appeared in two volumes in 1777, the first discussing many aspects of the islands, the second detailing the history of the mission from 1732 to 1768. A notable feature of the work was the information on western Africa which he collected from slaves, particularly information on ethnic origins, including pioneering albeit limited vocabularies of some twenty African languages.

BIBLIOGRAPHY Oldendorp's major work was *Geschichte der Mission der evangelischen Brüder auf den caraibischen Inseln S. Thomas, S. Croix und S. Jan* (1777), the African sections of which appeared in Danish and Swedish versions (1784). *Allgemeine Deutsche Biographie,* vol. 24 (1887; includes a bibliography); Soi-Daniel W. Brown, "From the Tongues of Africa: A Partial Translation of Oldendorp's Histories," *Plantation Society* 2 (1983): 37–61 (introduction and a translation of most of the African section); István Fodor, *Pallas und andere afrikanische Vokabularien vor dem 19. Jahrhundert* (1975), pp. 41–43; P. E. H. Hair, "The Languages of Western Africa c. 1770," *Bulletin of the Society for African Church History* 1 (1963): 17–20 and "Collections of Vocabularies of Western Africa before the *Polyglotta,*" *Journal of African Languages* 5 (1966): 208–217.

P. E. H. Hair

Oldham, J(oseph) H(ouldsworth) (1874–1969), English pioneer of ecumenical missionary and social concern. Born of Scottish parents in India, Oldham graduated from Oxford in 1894, then served with the Young Men's Christian Association in India for three years before embarking on theological study in Edinburgh and Germany. In 1908 he was appointed organizing secretary for the epoch-making 1910 Edinburgh World Missionary Conference, and he was subsequently named secretary of the conference's continuation committee. Hopes for rapid advances in ecumemical cooperation among mission boards were set back by World War I, but the *International Review of Missions,* founded by Oldham in 1912, quickly became a most significant organ of research into missionary practice and theology on a world scale. He remained editor until 1927. With the return of peace, in order to consolidate the movement begun at Edinburgh, Oldham successfully proposed the formation of the International Missionary Council and became its secretary in 1921. During the 1920s he traveled widely and became especially concerned with the issues raised by colonial administration in Africa, and with the educational needs of Africans. *Christianity and the Race Problem* (1924), his most substantial book, grew out of this interest.

Meanwhile, Oldham increasingly felt the challenge of the worldwide growth of secular culture. Himself a layperson (Anglican), he was convinced that the future of Christian mission would lie at the interface of faith and secular responsibility in public life. In the 1930s he pioneered the use of the small interdisciplinary study group as the means of research, not least in preparation for the 1937 Life and Work conference, "Church, Community and State," at Oxford, for which he was chairman of the research committee. Thereafter, while closely involved in the negotiations leading to the formation of the World Council of Churches (WCC), Oldham's interests focused more closely on the British scene.

During World War II, along with figures as diverse as Archbishop William *Temple, T. S. Eliot, and John Baillie, he mobilized much new Christian thinking about the nature of modern Western society and Christian responsibility within it, particularly through the medium of his fortnightly *Christian Newsletter.* Out of this movement was born the Christian Frontier Council, one of the leading British postwar inspirations of lay responsibility in society. At the first assembly of the WCC in 1948, Oldham was made an honorary president of the council.

BIBLIOGRAPHY Oldham's letters and papers are in the library of New College, Edinburgh. His works include *The World and the Gospel* (1916), *The New Christian Adventure* (1929), *Real Life Is Meeting* (1941), and *Life Is Commitment* (1953). See also Gerald H. Anderson et al., eds., *Mission Legacies,* pp. 570–580.

Keith Clements

Oldham, William F(itzjames) (1854–1937), Methodist missionary and bishop in India, Southeast Asia, and South America. Oldham was born in Bangalore, India, where his father was an English officer in the Indian Regiment. Although he was baptized a Roman Catholic, his earliest religious contacts came from Protestant military chaplains and the headmaster of the Madras Christian College. He was converted and became a Methodist at Poona while attending evangelistic services held by William *Taylor in 1873. In 1879, married and living in Bangalore, he committed himself to work as a Methodist missionary and traveled to Allegheny College in Meadville, Pennsylvania, for training. In 1884 he was sent to Singapore to initiate a Methodist mission. There he found access to the Chinese merchant population through schools; he established what became the first of a large number of Methodist schools in what was then British Malaya and the Dutch East Indies (Indonesia), as well as the first Methodist Church in Singapore.

Oldham left Singapore in 1889 because of ill health. For the next 15 years he resided in the United States and served as a pastor, lecturer, and secretary for the Methodist Board of Missions. In 1904 he was elected a missionary bishop with responsibility for India and Southeast Asia. In that role he oversaw the rapid expansion of Methodism in the Malay peninsula, the Philippines, and Sumatra. In 1912 he left the missionary episcopacy to serve for four years as one of three corresponding secretaries of the Methodist Board of Missions in New York. In 1916 he was elected a general superintendent (a Methodist bishop who could function throughout Methodism) and took over the supervision of South America until he retired in 1928. He died in Los Angeles.

Oldham participated in the 1910 Edinburgh World Missionary Conference, and his ministry reflected some of the issues that were brought to the fore at Edinburgh. His upbringing in India convinced him of the need for missionaries to understand the religious and cultural context of their work. He was a strong supporter of early efforts at church union in the Philippines and supported the interdenominational Committee on Cooperation in Latin America. In India, Southeast Asia, and the Philippines, he encouraged the development of educational ministries and social ministries as a complement to evangelistic work.

BIBLIOGRAPHY William F. Oldham, *Malaysia: Nature's Wonderland* (1907), *India, Malaysia, and the Philippines: A Practical Study in Missions* (1914), *Thoburn, Called of God* (1918), and "God Keeps: A Personal Testimony of Personal Experiences," *New York Christian Advocate* (1917). Brenton T. Badley, *Oldham: Beloved of Three Continents* (1937); Theodore R. Doraisamy, *Oldham: Called of God* (1979). Biographical tributes to Oldham can be found in *The Malaysia Message,* May 1937, and the *Indian Witness,* April 15, 1937.

Robert A. Hunt

O'Neill, Frederick W. S. (1855–1952), Irish Presbyterian missionary in Manchuria. As a student, O'Neill was active in the Student Volunteer Movement (SVM), serving on its British executive committee and helping to draft the document that led to the adoption of the SVM watchword in 1897. For most of his time in China he served at Fakumen (Faku). His comparatively open attitude to other religions, as expressed for example in his book *The Quest for God in China* (1925), was regarded with great suspicion by many of his more conservative colleagues. The book begins, "Those who are determined to find the beliefs of other people altogether wrong are recommended not to read this book." He left Manchuria in 1945 and retired in Ireland where he died.

BIBLIOGRAPHY F. W. S. O'Neill, *The Call of the East* (1919). Austin Fulton, *Through Earthquake, Wind, and Fire* (1967); Tissington Tatlow, *The Story of the Student Christian Movement* (1933); A. J. Weir, "China," in Jack Thompson, ed., *Into All the World* (1990).

T. Jack Thompson

Oppong, (Kwame) Sam(p)son (c. 1884–1965), Gold Coast prophet-preacher. Oppong (variant spellings: Oppon or Opon) was born in Brong Ahafo (now in Ghana) in a slave family originating in Gurunsi (now in Burkina Faso). He became an itinerant laborer, and, instructed by his uncle, practiced magic enthusiastically. While he was in prison for embezzlement in Ivory Coast (c. 1913), a prophetic dream instructed him to burn his fetishes. He resisted this and other admonitory experiences over several years, during which he prospered through sorcery. He had various contacts with Christians but no sustained church exposure. After a particularly vivid vision about 1917, he began itinerant preaching, calling for destruction of fetishes and abandonment of magic and witchcraft. He seems to have been baptized by an American Methodist Episcopal minister, but he worked independently of the missions, drawing vast crowds in Ashanti where Christianity had made little progress despite a long presence. He confronted powerful chiefs and disturbed the colonial authorities. Illiterate, he was believed to learn Bible texts from a stone he carried (he identified it with the stone of Revelation 2:17). The Basel Mission ignored him, but in 1920, a Wesleyan Methodist missionary, W. G. Waterworth, met and traveled with him, and from then on Oppong worked with the British Methodist mission. Ten thousand baptisms followed in two years, and the Methodist structures could not cope with thousands more seeking Christian instruction. By 1923, 20,000 new converts were in pastoral care. Soon, however, Oppong's uncle got him drinking again, and he became alienated from his church, whose southern Fante ministers he resented. He lost his electrifying preaching powers, could no longer "read" the stone, and in 1929 was convicted of a sexual offense in a traditional court. His later life was spent farming, though he was eventually restored to church membership and preached in his locality.

Oppong's ministry, which transformed Methodist growth in Ashanti, recalls that of his better known contemporary W. W. *Harris, but no direct connection between them has been shown.

BIBLIOGRAPHY H. Debrunner, *The Story of Sampson Oppong* (1967) and *History of Christianity in Ghana* (1965); G. M. Haliburton, "The Calling of a Prophet: Sampson Oppong," *Bulletin of the Society for African Church History* 2, no. 1 (1965): 84–96, and "The Late Sampson Oppong," *West African Religion* 5 (1966): 1–2; A. E. Southon, *Gold Coast Methodism* (1934).

Andrew F. Walls

Opukahaia. *See* Obookiah, Henry.

Orchard, Ronald Kenneth (1911–1989), secretary of the London Missionary Society (LMS). A British Congregationalist, born in Liverpool, Orchard served as secretary of the LMS from 1935 to 1955. Later, as chairman of the board, he played a leading part in the transformation of the LMS into the international Council for World Mission, a multidirectional agency comprising thirty churches on all six continents. He became London secretary of the International Missionary Council (subsequently the new Division and Commission on World Mission and Evangelism of the World Council of Churches) from 1955 to 1965. He was then appointed general secretary of the Conference of British Missionary Societies (CBMS) from 1965 to 1973 and study associate for the next three years.

Orchard was the author of a number of influential books which displayed the sharpness of his mind and his forward looking vision of the mission of the worldwide church. This is encapsulated in an address he gave to the annual meeting of the CBMS when he defined the task as "service to the churches in Asia, Africa, Latin America, the Pacific as the primary bearers of mission within their communities, to help them gain from and contribute to the universal Christian mission; service to the churches in Britain, as the primary bearers of the universal mission here; involvement in the struggle for human meaning and dignity, so that men may know Jesus Christ and come alive."

BIBLIOGRAPHY Ronald Kenneth Orchard, *Tomorrow's Men in Africa* (1948), *Africa Steps Out* (1952), *Out of Every Nation* (1959), *Missions in a Time of Testing* (1964), *Two Minutes from Sloane Square* (1977), and *Servants of Life* (1979). See also Bernard Thorogood, ed., *Gales of Change: Responding to a Shifting Missionary Context. The Story of the London Missionary Society 1945–1977* (1994).

Paul R. Clifford

Organtino. *See* Gnecci-Soldi, Organtino.

Origen (c. 185–253?), early Christian apologist, biblical exegete, and theologian. Origen was born in Alexandria of Christian parents who gave him a good secular and biblical education. Persecution in Alexandria and the martyring of his father, when Origen was not quite 17 made him by default a teacher of Christian inquirers. At 18, he was given charge of all such Christian education. As the school developed, Origen concentrated on its advanced classes, developing there a total approach to knowledge and employing all the learned disciplines of the day. This induced many philosophically educated people to become interested in Christianity and frequently brought them to commitment. Invitations came from students of religion such as Julia Mamaea, mother of future emperor Alexander Severus. The philosopher Porphyry did not believe Origen had been brought up a Christian, so well versed was he in Greek learning. Origen, a layman, taught and preached in the presence of the clergy but tensions developed with his bishop, and in 231 he left Alexandria. Caesarea became his home; he was ordained presbyter there, and his prolific literary output, which had begun about 218, expanded further. In the Decian persecution (250) he was imprisoned and severely tortured; he died not long afterward, in his seventieth year (both 253 and 255 have been proposed).

Origen is arguably the pioneer of mission studies. His *De Principiis* (On first principles) is the first theological treatise written simply as an offering of reverent intellectual exploration. His *Against Celsus* engaged with the fundamental Greek cultural objections to Christianity. His commentaries brought the biblical text (to which he brought a range of scholarly apparatus previously without parallel) into interaction with contemporary intellectual discourse. His industry and devotion to teaching were legendary; both were conducted with the prospect of possible martyrdom. His Christian consciousness was catholic: besides his work in Egypt and Syria he visited Rome, Cappadocia, Nicomedia, and (several times) Greece and Arabia for study, teaching, or dialogue. He was posthumously denounced as heretical by lesser people and never entered the calendar of saints.

BIBLIOGRAPHY H. Crouzel, *Bibliographie critique d'Origène* (1971; supp., 1982) and *Origen* (Eng. tr., 1989); J. Daniélou, *Origen* (Eng. tr., 1955); E. de Faye, *Origène. Sa vie, son oeuvre, sa pensée* (1935); Eusebius, *Ecclesiastical History*, book 6; Gregory Thaumaturgus, *Panegyric of Origen*.

Andrew F. Walls

Orimolade, Moses (1878?–1933), evangelist involved in founding Cherubim and Seraphim independent churches in Nigeria. After his conversion in the 1890s, Orimolade underwent various spiritual experiences associated with his permanent lameness. Although illiterate all his life, he acquired considerable ability to quote the Bible and became a wandering evangelist in his Ondo State and then ranged widely, stressing healing, visions, and the power of prayer. He settled in Lagos about 1924; in 1925 he was called upon to bring Victoria Akinsowon, a young educated Anglican woman, out of a trance. Their continuing association as evangelists led to forming the Seraphim Society, another form of the Aladura movement then developing. Initially supplementary to the churches, it soon became the independent Cherubim and Seraphim Society, which split between the cofounders in 1929, after which Orimolade was rather neglected. However, the many later divisions agree in recognizing him as their spiritual father, and a cult has developed with relics and annual services at his tomb. He remains an example of an unsophisticated but charismatic, ascetic, and meditative response to early Christianity in Nigeria.

BIBLIOGRAPHY J. Akinyele Omoyajowo, *Cherubim and Seraphim: The History of an African Independent Church* (1982); J. D. Y. Peel, *Aladura: A Religious Movement among the Yoruba* (1968).

Harold W. Turner

Orr, J(ames) Edwin (1912–1987), historian of Christian revivals and their impact on missions. Orr was born in Belfast, Northern Ireland, of Christian parents. He tried a business career but was soon drawn to itinerant evangelism and writing when he became associated with Oswald J. *Smith of People's Church, Toronto. For 15 years he traveled widely and wrote books popularizing the dominant themes of evangelicalism. After completing his first doctorate (Th.D., 1942, Northern Baptist Theological Seminary, Chicago), he served as a U.S. Army chaplain, largely in the Pacific (1943–1946). His career came into focus when Kenneth Scott *Latourette endorsed his concern for giving the subject of religious awakenings more careful exploration. This precipitated 30 years of labor, two more doctorates (Oxford, 1948; UCLA, 1971), and further travel to pursue archival research and to interact with academic communities, evangelists, and church leaders worldwide. His concern was to "set the record straight" and challenge the downplaying of religious awakenings by secular historians. This resulted in a score of publications that covered in amazing detail the record of spiritual awakenings in all parts of the world from the eighteenth century onward. He gained international respect for his thoroughness and accuracy. An exciting lecturer, ardent evangelist, and skilled apologist, he devoted his final decade to serving on the faculty of the School of World Mission at Fuller Theological Seminary. He both wrote and made history and has been called a man of "enormous industry" by church historian Martin E. Marty.

BIBLIOGRAPHY Among Orr's popular books are *Full Surrender* (1951; translated into fifteen languages) and *The Faith That Persuades* (1978). His scholarly works on spiritual awakenings are *The Flaming Tongue* (1973; covers the twentieth century), *The Fervent Prayer* (1974; on the worldwide impact of the 1858 awakening), *The Eager Feet* (1975; spans the years from 1790 to 1830), plus the five-volume series *Evangelical Awakenings in Africa* (1975), *Evangelical Awakenings in Eastern Asia* (1975), *Evangelical Awakenings in Southern Asia* (1975), *Evangelical Awakenings in the South Seas* (1977), and *Evangelical Awakenings in Latin America* (1978).

Arthur F. Glasser

Oshitelu, Josiah Olunowo (1902–1966), founder of the Church of the Lord (Aladura, i.e., "praying") independent church in Nigeria. Oshitelu was a charismatic and biblically literate Yoruba who was dismissed as an Anglican catechist after he reported visionary experiences. In 1929 he began a congregation at Ogere. After abortive association with the Aladura revival in Ibadan, he continued independently with church expansion transtribally across Nigeria and internationally to Sierra Leone, Liberia, Ghana, and finally Britain, although membership never totaled more than 15,000. This indigenous church was hierarchically structured and well disciplined; although polygamy was forbidden for the ministry, Oshitelu was allowed seven wives. He developed a catechism, a large hymnbook, a book of rituals, and forms of worship combining Anglican, Pentecostal, and African features. Holy words of power, revealed mainly to Oshitelu, provided a new divine language. A new annual "Mount Taborar" festival at Ogere became an occasion of public pilgrimage for vows, offerings, healings, and blessings and for Oshitelu's "revelations" for the coming year, which passed judgment on the nations but avoided clashing with government. Oshitelu died as a nationally known figure and was succeeded as primate by his nominee, Emmanuel Owoade Adeleke *Adejobi.

BIBLIOGRAPHY H. W. Turner, *African Independent Church*, 2 vols. (1967), vol. 1, chap. 2 and throughout. Oshitelu's papers are in the library of the Univ. of Ibadan, and his publications and church literature are in the library of the Selly Oak Colleges, Birmingham, England.

Harold W. Turner

Otto, Josef Albert (1901–1981), German Catholic missiological author and editor. Born in Celle, Germany, Otto became a Jesuit in 1920 and in 1932 joined the editorial board of *Die katholischen Missionen* (KM) in Bonn. After further studies from 1935 to 1937 at the Gregorian University in Rome, where Pierre *Charles was his most influential teacher, he became the chief editor of *KM* in 1938, but that same year the Nazis banned the magazine. His book *Die Gründung der neuen Jesuitenmission durch General Pater Johann Philipp Roothaan* (1939) could not be accepted by J. *Schmidlin as a doctoral dissertation at Münster because of the political situation. During World War II, he did pastoral work. From 1945 to 1968 he was again chief editor of *KM,* wrote various books and booklets, and often spoke at conferences. His mission theology, expressed in the booklet *Warum Mission?* (1957), was based on the idea of incarnation; through the planting of the church the mystical body of Christ should be incarnated and rooted in various peoples and cultures. He insisted on the importance of the mission *ad extra* (universal) and took part in discussions on mission, development, and dialogue. From 1952 to 1972 he was co-editor of *ZMR.* Through the mediation of a German bishop, he may also have had influence on the decree *Ad Gentes* of Vatican II.

BIBLIOGRAPHY Ludwig Wiedenmann, "Pater Josef Albert Otto, SJ, 1901–1981," *Die katholischen Missionen* 100 (1981): 153–157.

Fritz Kollbrunner, SMB

Otto (*or* Otho) of Bamberg (1062/1063–1139), apostle of Pomerania. Otto was born of a noble family of Swabia, south Germany. He became bishop of Bamberg in 1102 and devoted himself to the reform of his diocese. He was asked by Duke Boleslav III of Poland to undertake a mission in 1122 and 1123 among the people of Pomerania who had promised to accept the Christian faith as a condition of the peace between them and the Poles. Otto gained the confidence of the Pomeranians by his sincerity and liberality, setting an example of evangelization without coercion and violence. This resulted in the conversion of several towns, and during a later journey, of many of the Pomeranian nobility. Even after his return to Bamberg, he continued to supervise the newly established Pomeranian church.

BIBLIOGRAPHY H. Heyden, *Kirchengeschichte von Pommern* (1952).

Hans-Werner Gensichen

Oviedo, André de (1518–1577), Jesuit missionary, Patriarch of Abyssinia. Oviedo was born in Illescas, Spain. He was admitted to the Society of Jesus in 1541 by *Ignatius Loyola himself. He was among five men selected to assist Patriarch João *Nuñez Barreto in the Jesuit mission to Abyssinia (Ethiopia) commissioned by Pope John III, and to that end he was consecrated a bishop in 1554. He and his fellow missionaries (without Nuñez) traveled via Goa, reaching Arquico in 1557. Confounded by regional religious conflicts and local ecclesiastical and political intrigues, Oviedo was eventually granted audience with Emperor Claudius (Galawdewos), at which time he presented the customary letters demanding submission to Rome. This the king and his Coptic priests were understandably loath to do, and Oviedo found the ensuing interminable theological debates so unsatisfactory that he withdrew from the court at the end of 1558. In early 1559 he issued a tactless circular letter describing Abyssinians as "refractory and obstinate against the Church," urging them to disobey their king and forsake their Orthodox religion, and advising Portuguese Catholics to have nothing to do with the "schismatics."

When Nuñez died in Goa in 1561, without ever having seen Abyssinia, the patriarchal office was transferred to Oviedo, who moved to Fremona in Tigré Province. Here, he and his missionary colleagues heroically endured hardship, but their cultural insensitivity combined with increasing impoverishment and isolation ensured ineffectiveness that continued until the arrival years later of his more contextually sensitive countryman, Pedro *Paez.

BIBLIOGRAPHY Tellez Balthazar, *The Travels of the Jesuits in Ethiopia* (1710); Philip Caraman, *The Lost Empire: The Story of the Jesuits in Ethiopia* (1985); C. F. Rey, *The Romance of the Portuguese in Ethiopia* (1929); Taddesse Tamrat, *Church and State in Ethiopia, 1270–1527* (1972).

Jonathan J. Bonk

Owen, Walter Edwin (1878–1945), British Anglican missionary and archdeacon in Kenya and Uganda. Born in Birmingham, England, the son of a British army warrant officer, the family soon settled in Belfast and Owen was educated in Ulster. In 1930 he joined the Church Missionary Society (CMS) and went to their training institution in Islington, London. Ordained deacon in 1904, he sailed for Uganda, where he was ordained priest in 1905. In 1907 Owen married Isobel Barnes, who died in England in 1910. From 1904 to 1918 he worked in several parts of the British East Africa protectorate. In 1911 he married Lucy Olive Walton, a missionary colleague (d. 1953). In 1918 Owen was appointed Anglican archdeacon of Kavirondo (western Kenya), which was then part of the diocese of Uganda, with responsibility for organizing the new, rapidly expanding church among the Luo, Luyia, and Kalenjin peoples. Kenya having been declared a British colony in 1920, Owen founded the Kavirondo Taxpayers' Welfare Assocation (1922) to teach Africans how to run their own affairs. Teaching how economic development actually takes place, he introduced ploughs, watermills, new crops, and bookkeeping as the secret of planned development. Over the years he educated many Luo and Luyia civic and political leaders. From the 1920s onward, he was outspoken in opposition to colonial legislation discriminating against Africans, such as forced labor and the hut tax. He asserted the right of missionaries to take part in local politics; but after 1935 he came to be regarded as politically suspect and was no longer trusted by radical Africans in western Kenya.

Beginning in 1940, he worked on a revision of the Anglican Book of Common Prayer (Luo version) until his death in Limuru, near Nairobi.

BIBLIOGRAPHY Owen's own writings include "The Missionary in Politics," *Church Missionary Review* (1921); "Empire and Church in Uganda and Kenya," *Edinburgh Review* (1927); "The Relationship of Missionary and African in East Africa," *Church Missionary Review* (1927); "Some Thoughts on Native Development in East Africa," *Journal of the African Society* (1931); and a typescript at CMS headquarters (London) written with Alfred Stanway, *The CMS in Kenya,* (book 3) *Nyanza Province.* Charles G. Richards, *Archdeacon Owen of Kavirondo: A Memoir* (1947) covers most of Owen's period.

David B. Barrett

P

Padilla, Juan de (c. 1500–1544), Franciscan missionary and martyr in North America. Padilla's birthplace was probably Andalusia, Spain. He arrived in New Spain (Mexico) in 1528 and was the superior of the convent at Tulancingo until 1540. He worked in Michoacán and Jalisco and also served as head of convents in Zapotlán and Guatitán. For two years he was part of Francisco Vázquez Coronado's expedition that explored Cíbola (New Mexico and Arizona). When the Spaniards returned to New Spain, he and Juan de la Cruz stayed in the territory to evangelize hostile Indians, by whom Padilla was martyred, probably in what is now Kansas. A history of the Franciscan missions in New Spain is wrongly attributed to him; he and others did write a famous letter in 1532 to Charles V commending the work of Juan de *Zumárraga.

BIBLIOGRAPHY Constantino Bayle, *La expansión misional de España* (1936); C. Defouri, *The Martyrs of New Mexico* (1893); M. Engelhardt, *The Franciscans in Arizona* (1899).

Pablo A. Deiros

Padwick, Constance Evelyn (1886–1968), British missionary, author, and literature worker. Padwick grew up near Chichester and in London and was educated mainly at home. She trained as a teacher and worked from 1909 to 1916 on the home staff of the Church Missionary Society (CMS) as editor of its children's magazine, then in Cairo with the Nile Mission Press until 1921. On leave in Britain, she studied Arabic and Arab folklore at the University of London, and in 1923 returned to Egypt under the CMS, with which she served to the end of her career. In the Middle East she developed her knowledge of Arabic and her understanding of Islam. She became secretary of the Central Committee for Muslim Literature, writing as well as editing; she was also one of the editors of *Orient and Occident.* From 1937 she worked in Palestine, and after the war she was asked to go to the Nuba Mountains in Sudan to write appropriate Arabic material for the Nubian peoples. For her friendship and help to Muslim and Christian alike she was much loved and respected. Her time in Sudan ended in 1951 with severe illness, and she officially retired in 1952, but her real retirement in Dorset and then Somerset did not begin until 1957.

Few women, if any, have made as great a contribution to the knowledge and understanding of Islam as Padwick. In the West she is remembered chiefly for her biographical writings—the very influential life of Henry *Martyn, which has been an inspiration to many Christian students, and the life of her colleague Temple *Gairdner of Cairo. She also commemorated Lilias *Trotter, founder of what became the North Africa Mission (later Arab World Ministries) in an anthology of Trotter's writings. But for those whose chief interest is the study of Islam, her most important publication is her definitive study of Muslim prayer manuals, informed by her knowledge of mosques and Muslim devotees all over the Middle East and beyond, published during her retirement.

BIBLIOGRAPHY Constance E. Padwick, *Henry Martyn, Confessor of the Faith* (1923), *Temple Gairdner of Cairo* (1929), *The Master of the Impossible: Sayings, for the Most Part in Parable, from the Letters and Journals of Lilias Trotter of Algiers* (1938), and *Muslim Devotions: A Study of Prayer-Manuals in Common Use* (1961). Kenneth Cragg, *Troubled by Truth: Studies in Interfaith Concern* (1992), pp. 52–73 (chap. on Padwick).

Jocelyn Murray

Paez, (Xaramillo) Pedro (*or* Pero Paez) (1564–1622), Spanish missionary to Ethiopia. Born in Olmedo, Spain, Paez entered the Society of Jesus in 1582 and embarked for Goa (India) in 1588. The following year, enroute to Ethiopia, he was captured by Turkish pirates and enslaved until 1596. Upon his release he returned temporarily to Goa but arrived in Massawa, Ethiopia, in March,

1603, in the guise of an Armenian merchant with the alias "Abedula." He soon mastered Amharic and Ge'ez, translated a catechism, produced a comprehensive report on the theological errors of the Ethiopian Orthodox Church, and wrote a history of the country. Until his death in 1622, Paez, exemplary in his sensitive dealings with suspicious Ethiopian Orthodox clergy, focused his energies on court officials, nobles, and royalty. He achieved the conversion of the formerly Monophysite Emperor Susenyos (Malak Sagad III), who, despite strong resistance from indigenous ecclesiastics, summarily declared Ethiopian allegiance to Rome and abolished the slave trade. When Paez died (probably of malaria), he left behind a Roman Catholic Church that wielded great influence with the nobility. But the appointment to the Ethiopian patriarchate of the tactless and heavy-handed Alfonso *Mendes plunged the country into bloody civil war and resulted not only in the destruction of all that Paez had accomplished but in a two-century ban on Roman Catholic priests.

BIBLIOGRAPHY C. F. Beckingham and G. W. B. Huntingford, *Some Records of Ethiopia 1593–1646* (1954); Philip Caraman, *The Lost Empire: The Story of the Jesuits in Ethiopia 1555–1634* (1985); C. Wessels, "Pedro Paez, 1622–1922," *Studies* 92 (1922): 1–20.

Jonathan J. Bonk

Pal, Krishna (c. 1764–1822), indigenous Baptist pastor, evangelist, and hymn writer; first convert of the Serampore Mission, Bengal, India. Born the son of a carpenter of a Sudra caste, Pal learned and practiced his father's trade. For 16 years he was a follower and activist in a Hindu Vaisnavite reform group, the Khurta Bhojas. He became interested in Christianity and suffered severe persecution when he and his family broke caste by eating with the missionaries. He was baptized in the Hooghly River, near the Serampore mission, on December 28, 1800. Though he had little formal education, he soon learned to read and write and became proficient at writing and speaking publicly in his native Bengali. Ordained in 1806 by Baptist missionaries, who considered him a trusted associate, Pal was made pastor of the Serampore church; he was then transferred to Calcutta, where he had an active ministry for a number of years. There he preached in some fourteen places during a given week, including the British headquarters at Fort William, jails, factories, surrounding villages, and homes scattered throughout the city. In 1813 he was sent to Sylhet, 120 miles northeast of Dacca, specifically to work among Khasi hill peoples. During eight months there he baptized three people, the first Christians in a region that today has one of the highest concentrations of Christians in India. After spending time in different parts of Bengal, he moved back to Calcutta. Shortly thereafter, he died of cholera at 58 years of age. He had served the Serampore Mission for 22 years.

BIBLIOGRAPHY Frequent mention of the activities of Krishna Pal are found in the *Baptist Missionary Society Periodical Accounts* for the years concerned and in various books that have been written about the Serampore Mission since the middle of the nineteenth century, e.g., S. Pearce Carey, *William Carey* (1923) and E. Daniel Potts, *British Baptist Missionaries in India, 1793–1837* (1967). Much of this material has been brought together in Rajaiah D. Paul, *Changed Lives* (1968).

Frederick S. Downs

Palafox y Mendoza, Juan de (1600–1659), bishop of Puebla, Mexico. Born in Navarre (Spain), the illegitimate son of a nobleman, Palafox rose to become a member of the Council of Indies. In 1640, after becoming a priest, he was sent to New Spain to be the bishop of Puebla de los Angeles. He also had the powers of a visitor general, and in 1642, in the absence of both the viceroy and the archbishop, he served for five months as viceroy and administered the archdiocese of Mexico. During that period he attempted to reform the Inquisition. In 1643, back in Puebla, he curtailed many of the privileges of the religious orders, especially those of the Jesuits. As a result of his reforming efforts, he set into motion a bitter and scandalous public battle involving himself, the Inquisition, and the religious orders. In the midst of the storm he returned to Spain in 1649 to become the bishop of Osma, serving in that capacity until his death. As bishop of Puebla he fostered education and culture, leaving as a legacy the Palafox Library. He also wrote prolifically on politics, history, and religion.

BIBLIOGRAPHY Richard E. Greenleaf, "The Great Visitas of the Mexican Holy Office, 1645–1669," *The Americas* 44 (April 1988): 399–420; Jonathan I. Israel, *Race, Class, and Politics in Colonial Mexico 1610–1670* (1975); Charles E. P. Simmons, "Palafox and His Critics: Reappraising a Controversy," *Hispanic American Historical Review* 46 (1966): 394–408.

Jeffrey Klaiber, SJ

Palladius (5th century), missionary in Ireland. No compelling evidence exists about whether Palladius was British or Roman. He fought against English Pelagianism and urged Pope Celestine I to send Germanus to Britain to combat its spread. Although he was ordained by Celestine, it is not clear that Palladius was sent officially to Ireland, though he did go. His headquarters there were in Wicklow (three church sites have been found), but the mission appears to have failed. He left for Scotland and soon after, died there. The story of a long mission in Scotland is false.

BIBLIOGRAPHY Information about Palladius is largely limited to the following biographies of Patrick. Richard P. C. Hanson, *The Life and Writings of the Authentic Saint Patrick* (1983); Thomas O'Rahilly, *The Two Patricks* (1942, 1957, 1971); E. A. Thompson, *Who Was Saint Patrick?* (1986).

Frederick W. Norris

Pallotti, Vincent (1795–1850), founder of the Pallottines. Pallotti was called the saint of Catholic action in reference to his unstinting promotion of the faith both in his native Italy and to unevangelized lands. Of noble stock, he was both austere and academically gifted. Ordained to the priesthood in 1818, Pallotti gained a reputation as a dynamic speaker and retreat preacher. His aim was the universal extension of the church through deepening the faith of Christians and by evangelical outreach to non-Christians.

In 1835 he founded the innovative Society of the Catholic Apostolate (in 1836 renamed the Pious Society of Missions, or the more familiar Pallottines), an organization different from traditional religious orders in that it embraced the laity; it gathered support from all the baptized. Through this society Pallotti sought to involve the laity, clergy, and members of religious orders in some form of the gospel imperative to extend Christ's kingdom. After 1850 the Pallottines extended their ministry into Africa, Australia, Europe, and South America.

Pallotti's influence was enormous. He inspired the revitalization of spiritual life in Italy through seminary teaching and urban preaching. He undertook the training of overseas missionaries, inspiring several subsequent founders of missionary communities. He instituted courses in the English and the Scots College in Rome, and directly influenced Cardinal *Vaughan to establish the missionary Society of Mill Hill, London.

BIBLIOGRAPHY Katherine Burton, *In Heaven We Shall Rest* (1955); Mary E. Herbert, *Venerable Vincent Pallotti* (1942).

Anthony J. Gittins, CSSp

Pallu, François (1626–1684), cofounder of the Missions Étrangères de Paris (Paris Foreign Mission Society [PFMS]) and mission administrator in China and Southeast Asia. A native of Tours, France, Pallu was ordained a priest in 1650. A few years later he met the Jesuit missionary Alexandre de *Rhodes in Paris. Rhodes had left Vietnam and was on his way to Rome to ask that native bishops be appointed for East Asia. Pallu, who supported this move, was named vicar apostolic of Heliopolis in June 1658, consecrated a bishop in November 1658, and given the position of administrator of Laos and southwestern China in September 1659. Before departing for Asia, Pallu and two other bishops founded the PFMS, which was approved by the bishop of Paris in 1663 and by Pope Alexander VII in 1664.

Pallu reached Siam (Thailand) later in 1664, but lacking status among the civil and religious authorities, he returned to Rome for consultation and to obtain additional ecclesial prerogatives. He arrived back in Siam in 1670 and three years later had an audience with the Siamese monarch, who granted permission to preach in the kingdom. Four years later he embarked for China. Caught in a storm off the coast of the Philippines, Pallu was arrested by the Spanish, taken to Manila, and deported to Europe via Mexico. Freed through the intervention of Louis XIV, Pallu went to Rome and obtained the nominations of new vicars apostolic. In 1680 he was named apostolic administrator of all the missions in China. He arrived there in January 1684, but died in Moyang, Fukien (Fujian) Province, later that year.

Pallu and the PFMS worked with Propaganda Fide in Rome as the latter sought to administer control of all the missions of the church. Lisbon opposed such measures, including Pallu's efforts in East Asia, on the grounds that the church had granted the Portuguese crown the rights and duties as sole patron of the Catholic missions in Africa, Asia, and Brazil. With sound judgment and administrative skills, Pallu was a driving force in promoting the development of a native clergy and hierarchy in Asia.

BIBLIOGRAPHY François Pallu, *Lettres*, A. Launay, ed., 2 vols. (1905). L. Baudiment, *François Pallu* (1934); M. Pallu, *Essais biographiques sur François Pallu* (1863).

John W. Witek, SJ

Pamla, Charles (1834–1917), South African Methodist evangelist. Born at Butterworth, Transkei, Pamla had a brief scholastic education at a Dutch school in Nyara and learned the art of public speaking by preaching to trees while herding sheep. He went on to become the first black Methodist superintendent in South Africa and was also appointed as evangelist by the first Methodist conference in 1883. Pamla ministered at Etembeni for 19 years before retiring in 1913. He had printed at his own expense a booklet on African customs and the Christian faith and also contributed to an indigenous hymnbook. His great contribution to Christian missions was his role in securing over 25,000 conversions. This was achieved largely through the inspiration of American Methodist bishop William *Taylor, who visited South Africa in 1866 and conducted evangelistic services; Pamla was his most able translator. Their sermons bore a strong postmillennial mark, polygamy was condemned, and hearers were urged to seek salvation at the altar. The resulting revival of Christianity occurred during economic deprivation, political instability, and religious uncertainty faced by most black South Africans. Use of the "native agency" (black leadership such as Palma provided) during the 1866 revival was instrumental in the development of an indigenous Methodist ministry.

BIBLIOGRAPHY Daryl M. Balia, *Black Methodists and White Supremacy in South Africa* (1991); Leslie Hewson, *Introduction to South African Methodists* (1950); Gordon Mears, *Methodist Missionaries No. 2* (1958); Joseph Whitside, *History of the Wesleyan Methodist Church in South Africa* (1906).

Daryl M. Balia

Pandita Ramabai. *See* Ramabai Dongre Medhavi.

Pandosy, Charles (1824–1891), French Catholic missionary in the Pacific Northwest. Pandosy was born in Marseille, entered the Oblates of Mary Immaculate novitiate in 1844, and left for the Oregon missions in 1847. He spent the next ten years among the Yakima Indians at missions such as Conception, Moxee, and Alachicas. During the Indian War of 1855–1856, he fled the mission at Ahtanum hours before it was burned to the ground by volunteers of the American army. He took refuge with the Jesuits at Colville, Washington. Attempts to reestablish the Yakima mission after the war were unsuccessful, and in 1858 the Oblates left Oregon for British Columbia. Pandosy went to the Okanagan Valley, where he spent most of the rest of his life. He founded the mission at Sand Cove in 1859, moving it a year later to Mission Creek. After serving at Fort Rupert and New Westminster, he was named superior at Okanagan (Kamloops) in 1868. A bay, a lake, and a mountain pass in British Columbia bear his name. He became a legend among the Yakima Indians, who called him Papa Pandosy. He is the author of a Yakima dictionary and grammar.

BIBLIOGRAPHY Letters written during Pandosy's time in Oregon are found in Paul Drouin, ed., *Les Oblats de Marie Immaculée en Orégon, 1847–1860* (1992). Kay Croni, *Cross in the Wilderness* (1961); Achiel Peelman, "Les Missionnaires oblats et les cultures amérindíennes au 19e siècle. Les Oblats en Orégon (1847–1860)," *SCHEC, Études d'histoire religieuse* 62 (1996): 31–47. Archival materials are in the Oblate Deschâtelets archives, Ottawa, and the Archives Départementales de Bouches-du-Rhône, Marseille.

Achiel Peelman, OMI

Panikkar, Raimundo (1918–), ecumencial, interfaith, and global scholar of religion. Born in Barcelona, Spain, the son of a Hindu father and a Roman Catholic mother, Panikkar was brought up in a Hindu-Catholic milieu and spent much of his time, theologically and existentially, in working out how Christians, Hindus, and people of other religious traditions should relate in the developing "one-world" situation. As a Roman Catholic priest, with doctorates in philosophy, science, and theology, he has pursued his academic and spiritual interreligious interests through interfaith dialogue, personal spirituality, and academic appointments at Banares Hindu University, Harvard, and the University of California, Santa Barbara. Panikkar's Christian, interreligious, multidisciplinary, and global scholarship has deeply influenced Roman Catholic, wider Christian, and other religious views through significant writings. These include *The Unknown Christ of Hinduism* (1964), on the universalization of theology; *Christianity and World Religions* (1969), on Christian attitudes to other religions; *The Trinity and World Religions* (1970), on comparative spirituality; *The Intra-Religious Dialogue* (1978); *Myth, Faith, and Hermeneutics* (1978); *The Vedic Experience* (1979), on Hindu studies; and *From Alienation to Atoneness* (n.d.), on the global future. His original and integrative thought also provides clues to a new and more universal Christian theology incorporating elements from other disciplines, cultures, and religions. Now retired, Panikkar divides his time between Spain and India.

BIBLIOGRAPHY Panikkar has written over twenty books in languages other than English, and over five hundred articles in various languages. Miguel Siguan, ed., *Philosophia Pacis: Homenaje a Raimon Panikkar* (1989, Festschrift).

Frank Whaling

Pantaenus (2d century), head of famous catechetical school of Alexandria. A Sicilian Jew trained in Greek philosophy, Pantaenus converted to Christianity and moved to Egypt, winning acclaim as the greatest Christian teacher of his time. *Origen and Clement of Alexandria were his students. Jerome later reported that Indian philosophers, hearing of Pantaenus's fame, sent to ask him to come to India, where he found a Gospel of Matthew in Hebrew and "people who knew Christ." This Pantaenus attributed not to Thomas but to a supposed India mission of the apostle Bartholomew.

BIBLIOGRAPHY Eusebius, *Historia ecclesiasticae,* 5.10; Jerome, *De viris illustribus,* chap. 36; G. M. Moraes, *A History of Christianity in India,* vol. 1 (1964), pp. 43–45; A. Mathias Mundadan, *History of Christianity in India, vol. 1 from the Beginning up to the Middle of the Sixteenth Century (to 1542)* (1982), pp. 118 ff.

Samuel Hugh Moffett

Pao'o (c. 1810–1859), "the apostle of Lifou," Loyalty Islands. Pao'o (called Fao in New Caledonia) was born on Aitutaki in the Cook Islands and served on whaling vessels before his conversion in Rarotonga, where he trained under Aaron *Buzacott of the London Missionary Society (LMS) at the Takamoa Institution. After early posting at Mulifanua, Samoa, where he learned to speak Samoan, he went with Samoans and *Ta'unga, the Rarotongan missionary, to New Caledonia. The Loyalty Island of Maré became the departure point for his mission to Lifou (1842–1858). Landing as a pioneer in a lone canoe, he displayed "perseverance, robust good sense and evident piety," accepting hospitality from Bula, one of several chiefs involved in sporadic interdistrict warfare. He distanced himself from the wars, eventually acquiring neutral land at We between the contestants, sometimes countering overt alignment of less peaceable Samoan colleagues. He taught from the Bible and built a neat and thriving model community of converts at We, preparing the way for LMS missionaries Samuel *McFarlane and William Baker to settle and consolidate in the 1860s. Pao'o's qualities as peacemaker and Christian pastor were applauded by two visiting Catholic Marist missionaries who visited him and his (unnamed) wife. Kanak Protestants in New Caledonia and the Loyalty Islands regard him as the trailblazer of their church. He died on Lifou, after a long illness.

BIBLIOGRAPHY John Garrett, *To Live among the Stars: Christian Origins in Oceania* (1985), Raymond H. Leenhardt, *Au vent de la grande terre* (1947); Samuel McFarlane, *The Story of the Lifu Mission* (1873).

John Garrett

Papadius. *See* Kafarov, Petr Ivanovitch.

Papasarantopoulos, Chrysostom (1903–1972), the first twentieth-century Greek Orthodox missionary to Africa. Born in Vasilitsion, in the department of Messenia in southern Greece, Papasarantopoulos's baptismal name was Christos. At 15, he left home and joined the ascetic religious leader Panagoulakis, giving himself to prayer, fasting, and the study of Scripture. After serving in the Greek armed forces from 1923 to 1925, he entered Marthakion

Monastery and was tonsured a monk in August 1925, taking the name Chrysostom. The following year he was ordained a deacon and a priest, and was appointed abbot of Gardikiou Monastery. In 1935, he moved to the monastery of Chrysokellaris, near his hometown, where he founded catechism schools. Called to Athens by Archbishop Chrysanthos, he was elevated to archimandrite and appointed abbot of Faneromeni Monastery in Salamina. In 1958, at age 55, he graduated from the University of Athens School of Theology. Responding to a call to mission, he spent the next 13 years in Africa, where he learned Swahili, translated liturgical books, preached, built churches and schools, raised money, and prepared candidates for the priesthood. His work in Uganda, Zaire, Tanzania, and Kenya, as well as his voluminous correspondence with individuals and organizations, helped inaugurate within worldwide Orthodoxy a new period of mission endeavor. He died and is buried in Zaire, at the Church of St. Andrew, in Kananga.

BIBLIOGRAPHY *Fos Ethon* (Light of the Nations) 38, no. 1 (1986); 48, no. 3 (1988); 64, no. 1 (1993); *St. Kosmas Aitolos* (1991), nos. 6-8.

Dimitrios G. Couchell

Papeiha (c. 1790–1867), pioneer of Christianity in the Cook Islands. Papeiha was a student of John *Williams at Raiatea, in the Society Islands. In 1821 Williams took him to Aitutaki, the first of the Cook Islands to be entered by a missionary. After a slow start, the whole island became Christian in 15 months. In 1823 Williams took him on to Mangaia, where he was almost killed by the people as he attempted to land. Williams then took him with some others to Rarotonga, but after the first night's horrors, all but Papeiha abandoned the effort. He stayed on under the protection of the chief Makea. Since Makea proved resistant to his teaching, he visited other chiefs and in a few months secured at least the ending of idolatry on the island. After four months an assistant joined him from Raiatea. The first chief he converted was Tinorama, in the village of Arorongi, where polygamy was first abolished on Rarotonga. He married the daughter of this chief and thus became a person of rank and owner of much land in Arorongi. In 1836 he was transferred for missionary work to the island of Atiu, but he soon returned to Arorongi and lived there, helping the mission, for the rest of his days. He has many descendants in Rarotonga, some of whom spell the family name "Papehia."

BIBLIOGRAPHY Taira Rere, *History of the Papehia Family* (1977).

Charles W. Forman

Paracelsus (1493–1541), philosopher and critic of the introverted church. Paracelsus was the name coined for himself by the Swiss-German physician and philosopher Theoprastus Bombastus von Hohenheim. Though he was not personally involved in foreign missions, he deserves to be remembered as an outspoken critic of a static, introverted church, which failed to fulfill its apostolic commission. He regarded non-Christians as potential participants in a salvation as universal as God himself; this salvation was therefore to be shared by all followers of Christ with those who had not yet received it. Paracelsus also condemned crusades against the Turks and pleaded for the use of the vernacular in Christian witness to pagans. While he did not meet with sympathetic response among his contemporaries, except as a naturalist and physician, some of his ideas were later taken up by Justinian von *Welz.

BIBLIOGRAPHY K. Goldammer, "Aus den Anfängen christlichen Missionsdenkens. Kirche, Amt und Mission bei Paracelsus," *EMZ* 8 (1951): 69-81, 104-109.

Hans-Werner Gensichen

Parham, Charles Fox (1873–1929), American Pentecostal pioneer and founder of the Apostolic Faith movement. Born in Muscatine, Iowa, Parham was converted in 1886 and enrolled to prepare for ministry at Southwestern Kansas College, a Methodist institution. After three years of study and bouts of ill health, he left school to serve as a supply pastor for the Methodist Church (1893–1895). His longing for the restoration of New Testament Christianity led him into an independent ministry. Enamored with holiness theology and faith healing, he opened the Beth-el Healing Home in 1898 and the Bethel Bible School two years later in Topeka, Kansas. Parham's theology gained new direction through the radical holiness teaching of Benjamin Hardin Irwin and Frank W. Sandford's belief that God would restore xenolalic tongues (i.e. known languages) in the church for missionary evangelism (Acts 2). Along with his students in January 1901, Parham prayed to receive this baptism in the Holy Spirit (a work of grace separate from conversion). In the ensuing revival, Parham and many of the students reported being baptized in the Spirit, thus forming an elite band of endtime missionaries ("the bride of Christ"), equipped with the "Bible evidence" of speaking in tongues, and empowered to evangelize the world before the imminent premillennial return of Christ. Although this experience sparked the beginning of the Pentecostal movement, discouragement soon followed. Parham's ministry, however, rebounded. As his restorationist "Apostolic Faith" movement grew in the Midwest, he opened a Bible school in Houston, Texas, in 1905. There he influenced William J. *Seymour, future leader of the significant 1906 Azusa Street revival in Los Angeles, California.

Damaged by the scandal of charges of sexual misconduct (later dropped) in San Antonio, Texas, in 1905, Parham's leadership waned by 1907. But his linkage of tongues (later considered by most Pentecostals to be "unknown" tongues rather than foreign languages) with baptism in the Spirit became a hallmark of much Pentecostal theology and a crucial factor in the worldwide growth of the movement. In addition, the revival he led in 1906 at Zion City, Illinois, encouraged the emergence of Pentecostalism in South Africa.

A prolific writer, he edited *The Apostolic Faith* (1889–1929) and authored *Kol Kare Bomidbar: A Voice Crying in the Wilderness* (1902) and *The Everlasting Gospel* (c. 1919).

BIBLIOGRAPHY Robert Mapes Anderson, *Vision of the Disinherited: The Making of American Pentecostalism* (1979); Donald W. Dayton, *Theological Roots of Pentecostalism* (1987); Gordon P. Gardiner, *Out of Zion into All the World* (1990); James R. Goff, Jr., *Fields White unto Harvest: Charles F. Parham and the Missionary Origins of Pentecostalism* (1988).

Gary B. McGee

Parker, Peter (1804–1888), pioneer medical missionary in China. Born in Framingham, Massachusetts, Parker "opened China to the gospel at the point of a lancet." He graduated from both Yale Divinity School (B.D.) and Yale School of Medicine in 1834. After receiving Presbyterian ordination at Philadelphia, in 1834 he sailed for Canton (Guangzhou), China, as a missionary of the American Board of Commissioners for Foreign Missions (ABCFM). He was a skilled surgeon and ophthalmologist, and his hospital in Canton won over the initially suspicious Chinese. As a result, Parker, in cooperation with missionary colleagues from Britain and America and with the support of businessmen (including some Chinese), became instrumental in developing the idea of medical missions. The Medical Missionary Society in China was founded at Canton in 1838, with Parker as a leading figure. Forced out of China during the First Opium War (1840–1842), he promoted medical missions in the United States, England, Scotland, and France, securing financial support and arousing interest in and awareness of the work.

Returning to China in 1842 with his bride, Harriet Webster (who became the first Western woman to be permitted residence in China), in 1844 Parker was appointed part-time secretary and interpreter of the first U.S. legation to China. Thereafter, his relationship with the ABCFM and its secretary, Rufus *Anderson, became strained. Finally in 1847, the ABCFM terminated Parker as a missionary, charging that he was devoting too much time to medical and diplomatic affairs and not giving enough attention to evangelism. He continued his work at the hospital in Canton, at the same time serving as the U.S. chargé d'affaires. It is estimated that during two decades of ministry in China, he treated more than 50,000 patients.

Returning home in 1855, he sailed back to China later the same year, this time as the U.S. commissioner plenipotentiary, in which capacity he served until he was recalled in 1857. Taking up residence in Washington, D.C., he became a regent of the Smithsonian Institution, was active in the newly formed Evangelical Alliance, and finally, as a sign of reconciliation, was made corporate member of the ABCFM. In 1859, in retirement and after 18 childless years of marriage, a son was born—Peter Parker, Jr.

Parker's memorable contribution to missions was undoubtedly his advocacy of medical missions, himself being one of its most outstanding representatives. In making the home bases of missions realize their responsibility for the physical well-being of the people served by other forms of Christian ministry, he not only highlighted the importance of medical services but reclaimed them for the missionary enterprise.

BIBLIOGRAPHY Besides Parker's published reports of the Canton Hospital in the *Chinese Repository* (from 1836 to 1856), see his *Statements Respecting Hospitals in China* (1841). Edward V. Gulick, *Peter Parker and the Opening of China* (1973); Samuel C. Harvey, "Peter Parker: Initiator of Modern Medicine in China," *Yale Journal of Biology and Medicine* 8, no. 3 (1936): pp. 225–241; Kenneth Scott Latourette, "Peter Parker: Missionary and Diplomat," *Yale Journal of Biology and Medicine* 8, no. 3 (1936): 243–248; B. Stevens and W. Fisher Markwick, *The Life, Letters, and Journals of The Rev. and Hon. Peter Parker, M.D.* (repr. 1972). Parker's personal diaries, along with some of his correspondence and sermons, are in the Yale Medical Historical Library, New Haven, Connecticut; his correspondence with the ABCFM is at the Houghton Library, Harvard Univ., Cambridge, Mass.

Christoffer H. Grundmann

Parrinder, (Edward) Geoffrey (Simons) (1910–), British scholar in the study of religion. Parrinder was born in New Barnet, Hertfordshire, England, and was educated for the Methodist ministry at Richmond College. After study at the Faculté de Théologie Protestante in Montpellier, France, he was a missionary in French West Africa (Ivory Coast, Dahomey, and Togo) from 1933 to 1940 and again from 1945 to 1946, much of the time as principal of the Protestant seminary in Porto-Novo, Dahomey. He studied and compared the religious systems of the Akan, Ewe, and Yoruba, the topic of his first book, *West African Religion* (1949; new ed., wider in scope, 1961). Following ministry in the Channel Islands (1946–1949), he was appointed to the department of religious studies at the new University College of Ibadan, Nigeria, where he pioneered the academic teaching of African religions (reflected in his books *West African Psychology*, 1951, and *African Traditional Religion*, 1954) and showed the importance of research into the encounter of Christianity and other religions in Africa (as in his study of Ibadan, *Religion in an African City*, 1953). From 1958 to retirement in 1977 he taught the comparative study of religion at King's College, University of London (reader 1958, professor 1970). Here he moved into the field of Asian religions, with studies of concepts such as avatar, texts such as the Gita, and issues such as Jesus in the Qur'an. He also wrote prolifically on comparative themes across the religions of the world, including mysticism, worship, and sex, and on the issues of religious encounter. He did much to stimulate the serious study of other faiths within the churches and to develop the comparative study of religion as a scholarly discipline (he was secretary and later president of the British Association for the History of Religions, of which he was a founder member). His influence on the scope and the categories used in the study of the primal religions of Africa has been considerable, and not always acknowledged; and he was early in identifying the significance of the African Independent Churches.

BIBLIOGRAPHY Ursula King, ed., *Turning Points in Religious Studies: Essays in Honour of Geoffrey Parrinder* (1990; biography of Parrinder on pp. 309-318); H. W. Turner, "Geoffrey Parrinder's Contributions to Studies of Religion in Africa," *Religion* 10 (1980): 156–164; A. F. Walls, "A Bag of Needments for the Road: Geoffrey Parrinder and the Study of Religion in Britain," *Religion* 10 (1980): 141–150.

Andrew F. Walls

Parrish, Sarah Rebecca (1869–1952), first Protestant woman medical missionary in the Philippines. Parrish was born in Bowers, Indiana, and was orphaned early. After medical training she was sent to the Philippines in 1906 by the Methodist Episcopal Woman's Foreign Missionary Society. Her first Bethany dispensary in Manila was one room with a chair, a desk, an enamel basin, and a pitcher. Soon another room was added with ten bamboo cots. In 1908, with a gift of $12,500 from D. S. B. Johnston of Minneapolis, Minnesota, Parrish founded the Mary Johnston Hospital and School of Nursing in Tondo, a slum district of Manila. Parrish was the central figure and guiding light through the early history of the hospital—which continues today—combining her duties as doctor with evangelistic work and social service. In 1933, after 27 years of service, she returned to the United States. In retirement she lectured widely and wrote her memoirs, *Orient Seas and Lands Afar* (1936). In 1950 Philippine president Elpidio Quirino presented her with a medal of honor from the Civic Assembly of Women, citing "the pioneering effort of this sincere and determined American missionary doctor, who came a long way across the sea, bringing Christian love, healing, and enlightenment, and a better way of life" to the Philippines.

Gerald H. Anderson

Parrott, J(ohn) Grady (1908–), cofounder and president of Mission Aviation Fellowship (MAF). Born in Falls Church, Virginia, Parrott dreamed early of flying after he purchased a ride with a barnstorming aviator. Drafted into the Army Air Corps during World War II, he was eventually seconded to the British Royal Air Force as a flight instructor. He began thinking about the need for airplanes on the mission field after hearing a missionary tell of losing his belongings in a mishap while traveling by canoe. Around the same time, in 1944, three naval aviators, including Jim Truxton, felt the same need and founded the Christian Airmen's Missionary Fellowship. After the war, Parrott, Truxton, and Elizabeth *Greene, a former WASP (Women's Airforce Service Pilots), joined forces to develop what became known as MAF. Parrott served as president of MAF from 1948 to 1970, then as chairman of the board until 1973. MAF was designed to offer air support on a cooperative basis to missions in Third World countries, to "get the missionaries off the trails and out of the dugout canoes." Using primarily former military pilots and airplanes purchased with church donations, MAF first operated in Mexico, then moved into Peru and Ecuador. Today, MAF pilots log almost four million miles per year, serving over 300 Christian organizations in eighteen countries.

Bibliography Dietrich G. Buss and Arthur F. Glasser, *Giving Wings to the Gospel: The Remarkable Story of Mission Aviation Fellowship* (1995); Paul F. Robinson and James Vincent, *A Vision with Wings: The Story of Mission Aviation* (1992); Lee Roddy, *On Wings of Love: Stories from Mission Aviation Fellowship* (1981).

William L. Svelmoe

Parsons, Levi (1792–1822), pioneer American missionary to the Near East. Born into a pastor's family in Goshen, Massachusetts, Parsons manifested unusual piety in his youth and early felt a missionary call. He graduated from Middlebury College (1814) and from Andover Theological Seminary (1817) and was ordained by the American Board of Commissioners for Foreign Missions as a missionary in 1817. For two years he served as an effective missions promoter, soliciting contributions and organizing Palestine Societies, particularly among young people, for the support of a mission to be based in Jerusalem. The millennial hope of Israel's conversion was widespread and sometimes took surprising forms: a group of New York Indians gave Parsons $5.87 and sent a message "to their forefathers in Jerusalem." In a farewell service at Park Street Church, Boston, Parsons and his companion Pliny *Fisk were given a generous mandate: Two great questions were to be ever in their minds, "What good can be done, and by what means?" for Jews, pagans, Mohammedans, and people in Egypt, Syria, Persia, Armenia, or other countries which they might investigate. Fisk and Parsons sailed in November 1819, arrived at Smyrna in January 1820, and went to the island of Scio, where they studied modern Greek. Then they toured Asia Minor, visiting the "seven churches of Asia" noted in the Book of Revelation, and distributing tracts and Testaments. At the end of 1820 Parsons went on to Jerusalem, the first Protestant missionary to enter with the intention of making that city his permanent base. He visited around the city, distributed tracts and Bibles, and talked with people from many places. His reports received much attention in America. In May 1821 Parsons left for Smyrna, suffering a serious illness en route, rejoined Fisk, and with him started again for Jerusalem via Egypt. At Alexandria, Parsons again took sick and died there.

Bibliography Parsons's sermon *The Dereliction and Restoration of the Jews,* preached just before his embarkation, was published in 1819. The annual accounts in Joseph Tracy, *History of the ABCFM* (1842), summarize reports from Parsons and Fisk. See also David Morton, *Memoir of Rev. Levi Parsons* (1824). Parsons's obituary is in *Missionary Herald* 21 (1825): 265–268.

David M. Stowe

Paterson, John (1776–1855), Baltic Bible Society pioneer and executive of the Russian Bible Society (RBS). A Scottish Congregational minister, Paterson, along with Ebenezer *Henderson, fostered Bible printing and Bible societies throughout Scandinavia from 1805 to 1812 and was instrumental in obtaining British and Foreign Bible Society (BFBS) funding for the Swedish and Lapp New Testaments. The BFBS entrée into Russia came through Paterson's work establishing a Bible society for Finland (then subject to Russia). A Bible society was already latent in the minds of pious Russians and of his future collaborator, Robert *Pinkerton, a missionary already in Russia. Paterson was therefore appointed by the BFBS to Saint Petersburg in 1812, which proved to be the catalyst, and the RBS was founded the next year. The Russian Orthodox synod head, A. N. Golitsyn, and Czar Alexander I entered wholeheartedly into the work. Diplomacy and flexibility were essential on the multiconfessional committees. Paterson obtained Henderson's scholarly assistance from 1816 as well. Their standing with the Russian authorities also helped the Scottish (see William *Glen) and London Missionary Society missionaries (see W. *Swan), as well as Saint Petersburg's British-American church. Paterson's dynamism and organizational abilities were required for large-scale printing operations. The RBS was immense, with branches from Poland to Siberia. By 1818 it had produced 91 editions of Bible portions in 26 languages, including the first Russian vernacular New Testament (1821). Paterson toured southern Russia in 1821–1822, peak years for the RBS. The RBS collapsed in 1826; nevertheless, Paterson received an imperial pension. Retiring to Edinburgh, he toured Sweden and northern Scotland for the BFBS in the 1830s.

BIBLIOGRAPHY John Paterson, *The Book for Every Land* (1857, 1858). James M. Alexander, "John Paterson, Bible Society Pioneer, 1776–1855: The Earlier Years—1776–1813," *Records of the Scottish Church History Society* 17 (1971): 131–153; Stephen K. Batalden, "Printing the Bible in the Reign of Alexander I: Toward a Reinterpretation of the Imperial Russian Bible Society," in *Church, Nation, and State in Russia and the Ukraine,* Geoffrey A. Hosking, ed. (1991), pp. 65–78; Elizabeth Bini, "British Evangelical Missionaries to Sweden in the First Half of the Nineteenth Century" (Ph.D. diss., St. Andrews Univ., 1983); Judith Cohen Zacek, "The Russian Bible Society 1812-1826" (Ph.D. diss., Columbia Univ., 1964).

Nancy Stevenson

Paton, David Macdonald (1913–1992), Anglican missionary and friend of China. Named after his maternal grandfather, Ramsay Macdonald, a distinguished English Presbyterian minister and scientist, Paton was born in London, the eldest son of a missionary statesman, William *Paton. He became a Student Christian Movement (SCM) secretary (1936–1939) and established an ecumenical chaplaincy at the University of Birmingham. Ordained a deacon in the Church of England, he then went to China under the influence of his father's friend, R. O. *Hall, first as a YMCA secretary, then as a Church Missionary Society missionary (1939–1945, 1947–1950). The blindness and arrogance of the West, including Western churches and missions, regarding Chinese culture provoked from Paton his prophetic book, *Christian Missions and the Judgement of God* (1953; 2nd ed., with a biographical essay by his son, 1996). Like his first book, *Blind Guides* (1938), it makes for uncomfortable reading and he was an uncomfortable prophet. He also popularized the works of Reinhold Niebuhr and Dietrich Bonhoeffer in Britain and, equally significantly, devoted himself to researching Roland *Allen and Robert Raikes and applying their message today.

Paton became editor of the SCM Press (1964–1969), but although a string of books bears testimony to his abilities, he was unhappy in that role. He was more of a politician than a diplomat, and the Church of England gave him no position higher than that of secretary of the Missionary and Ecumenical Council of the Church Assembly (1964–1969). He had previously been secretary of the Council for Ecumenical Cooperation (1959–1964). Archbishop Michael Ramsey made him a canon of Canterbury in 1966, and he was chaplain to Queen Elizabeth II (1972–1983). He served the World Council of Churches in a variety of capacities, not least through abiding friendships with Chinese church leaders. He was still a valued counselor, a mystic, and an interpreter for the Chinese churches in his last decade, when he was racked with pain and wasting illnesses. Alison, his wife and the daughter of John *Stewart of Manchuria, was also an SCM secretary.

BIBLIOGRAPHY David M. Paton, ed., *Breaking Barriers, Nairobi 1975: The Official Report of the Fifth Assembly of the World Council of Churches, Nairobi, 23 November–10 December, 1975* (1976), *Compulsion of the Spirit: The Collected Writings of Roland Allen* (1983, with Charles Long), and *"R. O.": The Life and Times of Bishop Ronald Hall of Hong Kong* (1985).

E. M. Jackson

Paton, Francis Hume Lyall (1870–1938), missionary in the New Hebrides. Paton was born on the island of Aniwa (Vanuatu, then the New Hebrides), the third son of the celebrated Scottish Presbyterian missionary John G. *Paton. He trained as a minister at Ormond College, Melbourne, and at the universities of Glasgow, St. Andrews, and Bonn. In 1896, after marrying Clara Heyer in Australia, he went, as the first missionary of the John G. Paton Fund, to the island of Tana, in the New Hebrides, where he worked with Lomai, a local leader with previous experience of the labor trade and of Christianity in Queensland, Australia. Paton baptized Lomai and published a book about him. He translated the New Testament and compiled a dictionary. In 1898 a church was formed at Lenakel, but Paton and his wife had to leave in 1902 because of health problems. Appointed foreign missions secretary of the Presbyterian Church of Victoria, he pioneered the Student Volunteer Movement in Australia, working with John R. *Mott in universities and at the parish level. He was moderator of his church in 1922 and 1923. He died at Deepdene, where he had been minister for ten years.

BIBLIOGRAPHY F. H. L. Paton, *Lomai of Lenakel* (1903) and *The Kingdom in the Pacific* (1913). John Garrett, *Footsteps in the Sea: Christianity in Oceania to World War II* (1992); J. Graham Miller, *Live: A History of Church Planting in the New Hebrides (Vanuatu),* 7 vols. (1978–1990).

John Garrett

Paton, John G(ibson) (1824–1907), missionary to the New Hebrides (present-day Vanuatu). Paton was born in Kirkmahoe, Dumfriesshire, Scotland. After serving as a city missionary in Glasgow (1847–1856) and studying theology and medicine at the University of Glasgow, he was sent as a missionary by the Reformed Presbyterian Church of Scotland and began work on the island of Tanna in 1858. He faced disease and danger from the start; both his wife and his infant son died within a year. He fled his isolated post and at the mission conference of 1862 he was sent to Australia to raise funds for the faltering and endangered work. In speaking and fund-raising among the churches he found his greatest usefulness and he devoted himself to that work for most of his remaining years. He soon came to see that the greatest support for Pacific missions could come from Australia, and in 1866 he became a minister and missionary of the Presbyterian Church of Victoria, stationed on the island of Aniwa in the New Hebrides, but spending most of his time on deputations in Australasia, Canada, and Britain. In 1864 he was married to Margaret Whitecross.

In Paton's view, missions were closely tied to the growing British imperialism of the time. He stirred Protestants to resist the French and Catholic influences entering the New Hebrides. He also lent the support of his presence to the shelling by the British navy of a group of Tannese villages. He raised widespread opposition to the labor-trade, which was taking—or forcing—men to leave the islands for plantation labor in Australia and elsewhere. His view of the islanders was paternalistic: he cared for them but did not open doors for them to grow in responsibility or in church leadership. His largest money-raising efforts were devoted to the funding of a succession of mission ships, all named *Dayspring,* the last of which was lost in 1896.

His influence continued long beyond his lifetime: through the enormous popularity of his autobiography, first published in 1889; through the establishment in Britain in 1890 of the John G. Paton Mission Fund, which supported missionaries in up to five stations in the New Hebrides for much of the twentieth century; and through three of his children who served as missionaries in the New Hebrides. Cambridge University conferred on him the D.D. degree in 1891.

BIBLIOGRAPHY John G. Paton, *John G. Paton, Missionary in the New Hebrides, An Autobiography* (James Paton, ed., 1889, 1898), and *Thirty Years Among South Sea Cannibals: The Story of John G. Paton Told for Young Folks* (1964). John Garrett, *To Live among the Stars: Christian Origins in Oceania* (1982), pp. 175–177, 291.

Charles W. Forman

Paton, William (1886–1943), ecumenical pioneer. Born in London, educated at Archbishop Whitgift School, Croydon, Pembroke College, Oxford, and Westminster College, Cambridge, Paton was converted to a living faith in the spring of 1905. He helped rebuild the Student Christian Movement (SCM) when the Cambridge Inter-Collegiate Christian Union went its own way in 1910, then became the men's candidates' secretary of the Student Volunteer Missionary Union. A Presbyterian, he was ordained hastily in 1916 and dispatched to India as a YMCA secretary to prevent his being imprisoned as a pacifist. (Although he was a founding member of the Fellowship of the Reconciliation, he resigned in 1940 because as an indomitable opponent of fascism, racism, and anti-Semitism, he believed Hitler must be opposed by force.)

Paton returned from India in 1919, transformed by the experience, to provide inspiring leadership for the SCM. Recalled to India in 1921, he served from 1922 to 1926 as the first secretary of the National Christian Council of India, making it a church-related Indian concern producing relevant research for evangelism. He then effectively succeeded J. H. *Oldham as secretary of the International Missionary Council, as the latter became more involved with the Life and Work movement. He played a vital role in the creation of the World Council of Churches (WCC) and became secretary alongside W. A. *Visser 't Hooft. He gained enormous influence in the corridors of power in church and state due to sheer knowledge, hard work, and networking. Paton's premature death at the height of his career, as he was planning for the reconstruction of Europe and in dialogue with Bonhoeffer, probably delayed the integration of the WCC and the International Missionary Council. His death was an irreparable loss, for Paton had a broader vision than some of his successors. A writer, preacher, and broadcaster, he always yearned to be a simple evangelist. His 1916 paperback *Jesus Christ and the World's Religions* sold over 50,000 copies.

In 1911 Paton married Grace Mackenzie MacDonald, who radicalized him. She left first the Presbyterian Church and then the Church of England because she considered they did nothing for the poor. In Calcutta she did much for nurses' conditions; then, while making a home for their six children in St. Albans, Herts, she ran a restaurant for striking miners in 1926 and again for workers in World War II. In 1914, she wrote an important paperback, *The Child and the Nation,* on the condition of children, and was still campaigning for nurses when she died in 1967. She became a Roman Catholic in 1936.

BIBLIOGRAPHY E. M. Jackson, *Red Tape and the Gospel: A Study of the Signficance of the Ecumenical Missionary Struggle of Dr. William Paton* (1980) and "William Paton," in Gerald H. Anderson et al., *Mission Legacies* (1994), pp. 581–590; Margaret Sinclair, *William Paton: A Biography* (1949).

E. M. Jackson

Patrick (c. 390–c. 460), missionary credited by legend with the conversion of Ireland to Christianity. Patrick was born somewhere in Britain into a clerical family—his father was a deacon, his grandfather a priest. He was at first a Christian more because of the society into which he was born than as a matter of personal faith and conviction. He relates that the desperate straits of his slavery in Ireland after capture by an Irish raiding party at the age of 16 made him turn to God and supplied the seeds of a personal faith and deep spirituality that directed the future course of his life. When he escaped and returned home, he embarked on a clerical career, was duly ordained deacon and most probably presbyter, and experienced a strong visionary call to return to Ireland as a missionary. This was supported by a decision of his own British church, and so began the work for which history and legend has immortalized him.

Patrick's worthiness for the office of missionary bishop was challenged, possibly at a synod of his British church, while his work was in progress, and to this we owe his *Confession,* a sustained Pauline praise of God's gracious providence through the unworthy Patrick to the people who lived at the end of the known world. To the capture, killing, and enslavement of some of Patrick's converts by a British warlord in a reverse raid on Ireland, we owe his angry, excommunicatory *Letter to Coroticus,* with its implied image of a fifth-century bishop's proprietal lordship over the Christians in his territory. From these two documents we can glean almost all that is historically reliable about Patrick, who also died in Ireland. The rest is legend.

But Patrick did not convert Ireland, as the Christian faith had already taken strong hold, certainly in the southern half of the country. And there is no evidence that he, from his British background, contributed to the inculturation of the faith of his converts. When we get a clear sight of Irish Christianity again, from documents written almost two centuries later, its Christian structures are the indigenized structures of a monastic organization that imitated the organizational patterns of Irish chieftaincies, with some lesser evidence of episcopal/diocesan structure. Thus the inculturation of which modern missionaries speak happened without him. Yet he may well have contributed significantly to two of the most distinctive characteristics of Irish Christianity during its golden age in Europe in subsequent centuries: the powerful ascetic spirituality that accompanied its monastic structures and the ideal of the *peregrinatio pro Christo,* of leaving, and never again returning to the securities of home and kin.

BIBLIOGRAPHY Patrick's authentic writings, with translation and commentary, can best be consulted in Joseph Duffy's *Patrick in His Own Words* (1975) or, with a brief biography attached, in R. P. C. Hanson's *The Life and Writings of the Historical Saint Patrick* (1983). For evaluation of historical problems see J. Carney's *The Problem of Saint Patrick* (1961). For a brief but comprehensive account of Patrick's life, times, and writings, see Hanson's "The Mission of Saint Patrick," in James P. Mackey, ed., *An Introduction to Celtic Christianity* (1995).

James P. Mackey

Patteson, John Coleridge (1827–1871), Anglican missionary bishop and martyr in Melanesia. Born in London, Patteson studied at Eton and Oxford. After a curacy in Devon he joined Bishop G. A. *Selwyn and the Melanesian mission. He arrived in New Zealand in 1855 and went on the annual voyages to Melanesia, recruiting students who were brought back to Auckland for education. Patteson showed a great flair for languages, learning to speak more than twenty and writing a number of grammars. He was admired by the Melanesians for his courage and for the kindness and friendship which he showed irrespective of race or color. He was consecrated missionary bishop for Melanesia in 1861.

In 1867 the mission base was moved from New Zealand to Norfolk Island, which was both warmer and closer to Melanesia. The central school at Norfolk was run on English public school lines and was designed to produce teachers and clergy. Patteson tried to promote "native Churches under native pastors." He emphasized the need to teach "the simple statement of Christian Truth in the Creed, the Lord's Prayer and the Commandments," and proposed to limit translations initially to Luke, John, Acts, some Psalms, the Book of Common Prayer, and hymns. The use of Mota, a Banks Island language, was adopted as the common language for the mission's teaching. Patteson devoted himself to the mission and never returned home for leave. He was influenced by high church views and attempted to spread Christian influence by example as much as by conversion. The activities of labor recruiters in Melanesia undermined the work of the mission. While it is not clear why the local people killed Patteson at Nukapu in the Santa Cruz group on September 20, 1871, it was likely a response to the recent forced removal of islanders by labor traffickers. Two of his companions also died. His death encouraged the regulation of the labor traffic in the Pacific. It gave the mission a martyr and missionary hero who is still venerated in the Church of Melanesia today.

BIBLIOGRAPHY John Gutch, *Martyr of the Islands: The Life and Death of John Coleridge Patteson* (1971); David Hilliard, *God's Gentlemen: A History of the Melanesian Mission, 1849–1942* (1978) and "John Coleridge Patteson: Missionary Bishop of Melanesia," in J. W. Davidson and D. Scarr, eds., *Pacific Island Portraits* (1970); C. M. Yonge, *Life of John Coleridge Patteson: Missionary Bishop of the Melanesian Mission,* 2 vols. (1874).

Allan K. Davidson

Paucke, Florian (1719–1780), Jesuit missionary in Paraguay. Originally named Baucke, Paucke was born in Silesia and joined the Society of Jesus in 1736. He was sent to work in Paraguay along with fellow Jesuit Martin *Dobrizhoffer. After finishing his studies in Córdoba, Argentina, he arrived in 1748 at the reduction (Indian settlement organized by the missionaries) of San Javier, south of Asunción. He spent 20 years in the missions, working among the Mocobie Indians. A practical man, he played the flute, formed a choir of Indian singers, and taught the Indians carpentry, masonry, and tanning. He turned San Javier into a flourishing and prosperous town. After the expulsion of the missions in 1768, he spent the last years of his life in the Bohemian monastery of Zwettl, where he wrote a three-volume work on his experiences among the Mocobies. His work includes a minute description of their customs and religious practices. Equally as valuable as his writings are the 104 drawings, most in color, in which Paucke depicted elements of daily life among the Indians, including their religious processions, military formations, and economic activities.

BIBLIOGRAPHY Angela Blankenburg, "German Missionary Writers in Paraguay," *Mid-America* 29, nos. 1 and 2 (1947); Philip Caraman, *The Lost Paradise* (1975, 1990); Vicente Sierra, *Los Jesuitas germanos en la conquista espiritual de Hispano-América* (1944).

Jeffrey Klaiber, SJ

Paul VI (1897–1978), pope known for his emphasis on evangelization. Giovanni Battista Montini was born in

Brescia, Italy, and lived at home while studying in seminary. After ordination to the priesthood (1920) he was sent to Rome for further studies. From 1924 to 1933 he was a chaplain to Catholic students while working for the Secretariat of State of the Holy See. After the election of *Pius XII, he and Domenico Tardini were the chief officers in the Secretariat of State, while the pope himself remained Secretary of State. Consecrated archbishop of Milan in 1954, he was appointed cardinal in 1958, shortly after the election of *John XXIII. Succeeding John XXIII in 1963, he took the name of Paul in honor of the Apostle to the Gentiles. The first pope since 1809 to travel abroad, he made nine apostolic journeys: to the Holy Land (1964), India (1964), New York City (1965), Portugal (1967), Turkey (1967), Colombia (1968), Geneva (1969), Uganda (1969), and the Far East (Teheran, East Pakistan, Philippines, West Samoa, Australia, Indonesia, Hong Kong, and Sri Lanka, 1970). Sensitive to the unpopularity of the colonial heritage, he spoke of the church as being "at home in all nations," encouraged inculturation, and exhorted Africans to be missionaries to themselves.

In his reorganization of the papal curia in 1967, Paul VI renamed the Congregation for the Propagation of the Faith the Congregation for the Evangelization of Peoples, thus softening the distinction between missionary activity (where the gospel had not yet taken root) and evangelization (which could be done by established local churches). In 1974 he chose as the theme for the synod of bishops "the evangelization of the modern world." On the basis of materials provided by that synod, he issued in 1975 his great apostolic exhortation, *Evangelii nuntiandi.* At his burial an open book of the Gospels was appropriately laid on his coffin, symbolizing the evangelical thrust of his ministry.

BIBLIOGRAPHY Montini's writings as pope, *Insegnamenti di Paolo VI,* were published in various languages for each year of his pontificate by the Libreria Editrice Vaticana. Some of these volumes were reprinted in English by the United States Catholic Conference, Washington, D.C., under the title *Teachings of Pope Paul VI* (1968–1975); *The Church* consists chiefly of pastoral letters and lectures he gave as archbishop of Milan. "Paulus PP. VI," in *Elenchus Bibliographicus* (1981); Peter Hebblethwaite, *Paul VI: The First Modern Pope* (1993).

Avery Dulles, SJ

Paul, K(anakarayan) T(iruselvam) (1876–1931), Christian statesman of India. Paul was born in Salem, southwest of Madras, and was educated under William *Miller at Madras Christian College where he later was history tutor for a short time. In 1905 he was one of the founders of the National Missionary Society (NMS) of India; he was appointed its organizing secretary in 1907 and general secretary in 1909. He and V. S. *Azariah started the monthly journal *National Missionary Intelligencer* (later *National Christian Council Review*). Parallel to his NMS work, Paul was also deeply involved with the YMCA and became national general secretary in 1916. He accompanied J. R. *Mott around India in 1912 and some, recognizing his abilities as organizer and administrator, called him the Mott of India. In the early 1920s he visited Europe and America for the first time. A fervent Indian nationalist who nevertheless remained largely nonpolitical, Paul published in 1927 *The British Connection with India,* a work of outstanding quality and the first of its kind to be written by an Indian Christian. G. Sherwood *Eddy considered Paul the first Christian statesman that India produced. He attended the Jerusalem International Missionary Council conference in 1928 and is credited, along with William *Temple, with having been one of those who prevented theological disagreement from ruining its work. Paul was, however, no real theologian in the technical sense. He was an Indian Christian Gandhian patriot, whose last words are recorded as having been, "I have done my duty to my God and my country. I die in peace."

BIBLIOGRAPHY G. Sherwood Eddy, *Pathfinders of the World Missionary Crusade* (1945), pp. 161–175; H. A. Popley, *K. T. Paul: Christian Leader* (1938).

Eric J. Sharpe

Paulinus of York (584?–644), Roman missionary in England. In 601 Pope Gregory I sent Paulinus, a Roman monk, to Britain as an assistant to *Augustine in Kent. Paulinus worked in that region until 625, when he was ordained a bishop by Justus, archbishop of Canterbury, and was sent to Northumbria. During 627 he baptized Edwin, the Northumbrian king, at York in a wooden church. He soon began work on a stone cathedral there and on another at Lincoln. When Edwin died in battle in 633, Paulinus fled back to Kent with Edwin's family and served as bishop of Rochester. He died there and was buried in the chapter house.

BIBLIOGRAPHY Bede, *Ecclesiastical History,* 1.29; 2.9, pp. 13–14, 16–17, 20; 3.14; Peter Hunter Blair, *The World of Bede* (1970); Henry Mayr-Harting, *The Coming of Christianity to Anglo-Saxon England* (1972, 1991).

Frederick W. Norris

Paul of the Cross (Paolo Francesco Danei) (1694–1775), mystic, founder of the Passionists, and missionary. Born in Ovada, Italy, of poor parents with deep Christian faith, Paul was always attracted to the mystery of the suffering and death of Jesus. In 1720 he experienced a profound mystical moment in which he saw himself destined to establish a community of contemplative missionaries who had vowed to proclaim the gospel of the Passion throughout the world. In a forty-day retreat that followed he wrote the Rule of Life for his disciples and also his spiritual diary. A man of prayer and action, he founded thirteen monasteries, conducted 280 missions and retreats (usually involving all the bishops, priests, and people of an entire district), and wrote some 10,000 letters of spiritual direction. In 1755 he founded the Confraternity of the Passion, a lay movement, to share his vision and mission with the laity. In 1771, together with Faustina Gertrude Constantini, he founded the Passionist Contemplative Nuns.

Paul's mysticism of the Passion is a summons to discover life's fullest meaning in the wounds of Jesus and to reach out courageously to embrace the crucified of our day. Today, Passionist priests and brothers work in fifty-two countries on all continents; Passionist nuns are established in thirty-seven monasteries in fifteen countries. Some thirteen other congregations of men and women share Paul of the Cross's vision of Christian contemplation and action; a secular institute was founded in 1900.

BIBLIOGRAPHY Charles Almeras, *St. Paul of the Cross* (1960); Benet Kelly, *Listen to His Love* (1985); Fabiano Giorgini, *History of the Passionists* (1987); Roger Mercurio, *The Passionists* (1990); Enrico Zoffoli, *San Paolo della Croce, storia critica,* 3 vols. (1968).

Cassian J. Yuhaus, CP

Payeras, Mariano (1769–1823), Spanish-born Franciscan missionary in California. After completing his studies in Mexico, Payeras arrived in San Francisco in 1796. He worked at many missions in California and then in 1804 was assigned to the Mission La Purísima, located north of Santa Barbara. After the mission was destroyed by an earthquake in 1812, he rebuilt it on a safer site. A man of genial character and great organizational skills, he served as president of the missions after 1815 and eventually as commissary prefect. He encouraged the foundation of new missions in the interior and was very concerned about Russian expansion in northern California. Payeras sought to maintain cordial relations between the friars and the Spanish government but protested vigorously against the government's assuming temporal authority over the missions. After Mexico obtained its independence from Spain in 1821, Payeras commanded the friars to pledge their loyalty to the new government. He died at Purísima and was buried in the sanctuary.

BIBLIOGRAPHY John A. Berger, *The Franciscan Missions of California* (1941); Maynard Geiger, *Franciscan Missionaries in Hispanic California* (1969).

William E. McConville, OFM

Payne, Ernest A(lexander) (1902–1980), British Baptist leader, historian, and ecumenical statesman. Payne grew up in east London and studied at Regent's Park College with a view to becoming a Baptist Missionary Society (BMS) missionary in India. Further studies followed at Mansfield College, Oxford, and the University of Marburg (under Rudolf Bultmann). Prevented by family circumstances from going to India, Payne entered the Baptist ministry in England, but in 1932 he became young people's secretary of the BMS. He developed an interest in the history of the Baptist denomination and its missionary society that later issued in a stream of authoritative books. From 1940 to 1951 he taught at Regent's Park College, which had moved to Oxford. From 1951 to 1967 he was general secretary of the Baptist Union of Great Britain and Ireland. A deeply committed ecumenist, Payne served as a member of the central committee of the World Council of Churches (WCC) from 1954 to 1975 and for much of this period was the committee's vice-chairman. He played a part in the integration of the International Missionary Council into the WCC in 1961 and presided over the controversial fourth assembly of the WCC in Uppsala in 1968.

BIBLIOGRAPHY Ernest A. Payne, *Freedom in Jamaica* (1933), *The First Generation* (1936), *The Great Succession* (1938), *The Church Awakes* (1942), and *Southeast from Serampore* (1945). W. M. S. West, *To Be a Pilgrim: A Memoir of Ernest A. Payne* (1983).

Brian Stanley

Payne, William Smith (1870–1924), pioneer of Plymouth Brethren work in Argentina and Bolivia. Payne was born in Dublin, Ireland, and grew up in a devoted Brethren family. He attended Wesley College and married Elizabeth Milne from Scotland in 1890. They were commended to missionary work by the Plymouth Brethren Assembly of Dublin and moved to Spain for language learning. In 1892 they arrived in Argentina and established their base in Córdoba in 1893. From this city Payne traveled intensively, planting new assemblies throughout northern Argentina. He also visited neighboring Chile and Paraguay. In 1895 he and his family traveled 500 miles on muleback to Bolivia and tried to get established in Sucre, but his books and Bibles were confiscated, and they were forced to leave the country. In 1900 Payne made a second attempt to settle with his family in Cochabamba, but his house was burned down by a mob, and he was barely rescued by a military unit. During his third visit to Bolivia, he died of a heart attack in the city of Santa Cruz. His writings influenced many Plymouth Brethren to go as missionaries to Latin America.

BIBLIOGRAPHY Gilberto M. J. Lear, *Un explorador valiente* (1951), a biography of Payne, based mainly on William S. Payne and Charles T. W. Wilson, *Pioneering in Bolivia, with Some Account of Work in Argentina* (1904). See also Peter Wagner, *The Protestant Movement in Bolivia* (1970).

Samuel Escobar

Peabody, Lucy Whitehead (McGill) Waterbury (1861–1949), American Baptist missions promoter. Lucy McGill was born in Belmont, Kansas, the daughter of John and Sarah McGill. She received a secondary education in Rochester, New York, and attended classes at the University of Rochester. In 1881, she married Norman Waterbury, and that year the couple accepted an appointment with the American Baptist Missionary Union to work with the Telugus in Madras, India. After five years in India, Norman died and Lucy returned to the United States to accept a position as home secretary for the Woman's Baptist Foreign Mission Society of the East. She supervised literature production and recruitment of new missionary candidates. In 1906 she left the employ of the society to wed Henry W. Peabody, who died two years later, leaving her with a considerable estate. She returned to mission work and became involved with ecumenical women's organizations, notably the Central Committee on the United Study of Foreign Missions. Peabody made the acquaintance of Helen Barrett *Montgomery in the 1890s and the two collaborated on writing projects and world travel in the promotion of missions. In 1913 and 1914 the two women traveled around the world, also serving as delegates to the 1913 meeting of the Edinburgh Continuation Committee in The Hague. One result of that tour was the establishment of the World Day of Prayer, for the women of the world. Following World War I, Peabody identified with the moderate wing of the Northern Baptist Convention fundamentalists. When a personnel disagreement between the American Baptist Foreign Mission Society and her son-in-law, Raphael C. Thomas, occurred in the 1920s, Peabody led in the formation of an independent Baptist mission agency, the Association of Baptists for Evangelism in the Orient (later, Association of Baptists for World Evangelism—ABWE). Reacting to management policies of the American Baptist board, she protested by walking out of the annual convention sessions in 1927. Her presidency of ABWE ended over differing theological views and opposition by ABWE missionaries to female leadership. In 1923, Peabody became a promoter, with founder Marguerite Doane, of the Houses of Fellowship in Ventnor, New Jersey, later the Overseas Ministries Study Center.

BIBLIOGRAPHY Lucy Peabody's writings include *A Wider World for Women* (1936) and *Just Like You: Stories of Children of Everyland* (1937). The best biographical material is Louise A. Cattan, *Lamps Are for Lighting: The Story of Helen Barrett Montgomery and Lucy W. Peabody* (1972) and William H. Brackney, "Helen B. Montgomery and Lucy W. Peabody," in Gerald H. Anderson et al., eds., *Mission Legacies* (1994), pp. 62–70.

William H. Brackney

Péan, Charles (1901–1991), French Salvation Army (SA) missionary to convicts. Born in Neuilly-sur-Seine, France, Péan entered the SA in 1919. He was an evangelist in Paris and Marseilles with a special concern for liberated convicts. In 1928 he visited the Devil's Island penitentiary settlements in French Guiana. He reported the inhumane conditions of the transported convicts and the plight of the so-called liberated ones. He sailed to French Guiana with six other missionaries in 1933 and created hostels, industrial workshops, and a farm. They organized the first repatriation since 1854 of a number of liberated convicts. The French government decided in 1938 to terminate the Guiana settlement and entrusted the SA with the repatriation of those liberated, which was completed in 1953. Beginning in 1944, Péan held various leadership positions of the SA in France, Switzerland, and Austria. He founded a house for unmarried mothers in Paris and a social center in Lyons. He retired in 1971 and represented the SA before international organizations in Geneva until 1985.

BIBLIOGRAPHY Works by Charles Péan include *Terre de bagne* (1930), *Le salut des parias* (1933), and the partly autobiographical *Conquêtes en terre de bagne* (1947; in English, *The Conquest of Devil's Island,* 1953).

Marc R. Spindler

Pearse, Joseph (1837–1911), English missionary to Madagascar. Born in London and educated at New College, London, Pearse arrived in Madagascar in 1863 as one of a large contingent of missionaries sent by the London Missionary Society (LMS) to triple the LMS staff after Christianity ceased to be persecuted and was officially accepted. His wife, Mary Eyre (Burn), died within a year of their arrival, and he later married Margaret Irvine, the widow of a missionary. Pearse first worked in a time of great prosperity; he was made pastor of a large new church that the people erected, only to find by the time it was completed that it was too small. He then became one of the first missionaries to volunteer for pioneer work among new tribes, starting a mission among the Sihanaka people in 1875. Securing some medical training, he threw himself into medical work along with evangelism. In five years he began fifteen congregations with 2,000 adherents. He was then asked to go to another pioneer district, Betsileo, where his tact and judgment were needed in relating to an advancing Lutheran mission. In the 1890s, however, he endured disasters, empty churches, and the loss of workers forced into exile by anti-LMS policies of the conquering French government. Hoping to resume work with the Sihanaka in 1898, he found everything in ruin because of a rebellion that had swept through that area. He was then called back to his first church, where he enjoyed some stability until ill health forced his retirement in 1904.

BIBLIOGRAPHY Norman Goodall, *A History of the London Missionary Society, 1894–1945* (1954); Richard Lovett, *The History of the London Missionary Society* (1899); C. F. A. Moss, *A Pioneer in Madagascar: Joseph Pearse of the L.M.S.* (1913).

Charles W. Forman

Peck, Edmund James (1850–1924), Anglican missionary to the Inuit (Eskimo). Born in Manchester, England, Peck was converted while serving in the British Navy from 1865 to 1875. After working as a naval seaman, he went in 1876 to Hudson Bay, Canada, for the Church Missionary Society (CMS). While working with Crees, he met Inuit and in 1894 sailed in a Scottish trading vessel to Cumberland Sound in Baffin Island, where Inuit remembered the witness of a Moravian missionary forty years earlier. Peck wished the Inuit themselves to evangelize, which eventually happened, but initially he was "tied hand and feet to ungodly traders," whose tyranny compromised the mission. In 1905 he settled in Winnipeg to raise support. CMS wanted to withdraw, and Canadian Anglicans gave little help, but Peck persevered, and missionaries were ferried between Scotland and Baffin in old sailing vessels. He superintended with visits to Britain and in 1909 to Baffin. He worked also in Nova Scotia and Newfoundland. That almost all Canadian Inuit became Anglican was largely due to Peck, whose hardships were only exceeded by his ingenuity. He translated into Inuit the Bible, the *Book of Common Prayer,* and hymns. His personal life was tragic: his family could not accompany him to the Arctic; his beloved daughter died young, as did one of his two sons. Peck died in Ottawa, and is commemorated on September 10 in the Canadian Anglican Prayer Book.

BIBLIOGRAPHY T. C. B. Boon, *The Anglican Church from the Bay to the Rockies* (1962); A. Lewis, *The Life and Work of the Rev. E. J. Peck among the Eskimos* (1904); Eugene Stock, *The History of the Church Missionary Society,* vol. 4 (1916).

Gavin White

Peck, John Mason (1789–1857), American Baptist home missionary. Peck was born in Litchfield, Connecticut, the son of Asa and Hannah Peck, farmers. In 1813, following extensive voluntary preaching tours, Peck was ordained at Catskill, New York, and married Sallie Paine of Greene County. From 1813 to 1815 Peck was pastor at Amenia, New York. Then, under the influence of a prominent New York State missionary pastor, John Peck (no relation), and Luther *Rice, he took up theological studies in Philadelphia at William Staughton's school. While there, Peck met James E. *Welch, and in 1817 Welch and Peck were appointed by the Baptist Board of Foreign Missions for service in the West among the Indian peoples. After only two years, interest in the western mission waned and the board discontinued support. Peck moved to Illinois, where he received an appointment from the Massachusetts Baptist Missionary Society from 1822 to 1826 to plant churches and itinerate. In 1832 he wrote to an eastern pastor of the plight of the Baptist cause in the western territory, and this led directly to the establishment of the American Baptist Home Mission Society. Later in his career, Peck developed a colportage plan for the field missionaries of the American Baptist Publication Society that was used in conjunction with the home and foreign mission societies. Throughout his career, Peck provided valuable social analysis of the western United States and wrote insightfully of the mission field. He advocated what came to be known as the denominational form of voluntary mission societies and he did much to establish the patterns of Baptist missionary development in the American West. In 1852 Harvard University conferred on Peck an honorary degree in recognition of his work.

BIBLIOGRAPHY Peck edited newspapers and wrote analyses of the Baptist denomination in the periodical *Baptist Memorial and Monthly Chronicle* (1844–1854). His views on Indian missions are found in *The Missionary Offering* (1853). Rufus Babcock, ed., *Forty Years of Pioneer Life: Memoir of John Mason Peck* (1864); Austen K. DeBlois, *John Mason Peck and One Hundred Years of Home Missions, 1817–1917* (1917, 1975).

William H. Brackney

Pedraza, Cristóbal de (1498?–c. 1553), Spanish missionary, Roman Catholic bishop of Honduras. Beginning about 1545, Pedraza was responsible for several isolated colonial towns and villages in Honduras, including the city of Trujillo (composed of some fifty families), and a much larger number of indigenous settlements. Travel was slow and difficult, but Pedraza's greatest problem was making contact with the indigenous peoples. At first, whenever he approached their villages, they fled. He soon learned that the colonists, in an effort to keep him from hearing about their brutal treatment of the Indians, had told the Indians that they would be "strangled, decapitated and thrown to the dogs" if they ever divulged to the bishop what was taking place. When Pedraza learned the truth, he condemned the colonists and protested to the Supreme Council of the Indies. In a letter to the Council, Pedraza noted that the Laws of the Indies commanded the colonists to protect and evangelize the Indians, but contrary to law, they were being enslaved, beaten, tied to posts and trees, and even killed. Though his life and ministry have been overshadowed by the work of the more acclaimed Bartholomew de *Las Casas, Pedraza distinguished himself by his unflagging efforts to "Christianize" the colonists and champion the cause of the Indians.

BIBLIOGRAPHY Enrique Dussel, *A History of the Church in Latin America* (1981), pp. 51–53; José Maria Tojeira, *Panorama histórico de la Iglesia en Honduras* (1987); José Reina Valenzuela, *Historia eclesiástica de Honduras, tomo 1: 1502–1600* (c. 1983).

Alan Neely

Pedro de la Madre de Dios (1565–1608), pioneer Carmelite missionary strategist. Pedro's father was a noted medical doctor in Daroca, Aragon, Spain; his mother was of noble birth. He entered the Discalced Carmelite Order in 1583 and studied at Salamanca. Transferred to Genoa in 1591, he quickly established his reputation as a preacher. Called to Rome in 1596, he was appointed apostolic preacher by *Clement VIII, a post he held also under Leo XI and Paul V. In 1597 Clement VIII placed the Discalced Carmelites in Italy into a separate province and made Pedro the commissary general and prior of Santa Maria della Scala in Trastevere. In 1602 the Carmelites planned a mission to Mount Carmel, in the Holy Land, with financial assistance from Baron Francesco Cimini. When Pedro reported this proposal, Clement VIII suggested that the missionaries should instead go to Persia, where Shah Abbas was in conflict with the Ottomans. Partly financed by Cimini, the mission left Rome on July 6, 1604, the first direct papal mission into territory partly claimed by the Portuguese *padroado* (i.e., the patronage granted by the pope to the Portuguese crown in lands claimed by the papacy).

With the accession of Paul V on May 16, 1605, Pedro became the principal adviser on papal missionary policy. He guided delicate negotiations with the Copts in Egypt, and in April 1606 was responsible for papal instructions for a projected Capuchin mission there. Keenly interested in both Ethiopia and Kongo (present-day southern Congo and northern Angola), in 1607 he actively assisted an ambassador from Kongo to reach Rome, despite Portuguese and Spanish protests. Simultaneously he persuaded *Thomas of Jesus, a Spanish Carmelite, to set aside his fears that missionary work was contrary to a contemplative vocation and to come to Rome to participate in a projected Carmelite mission to Kongo, one of whose aims was to open a route between Kongo and Ethiopia. Pedro died prematurely in the midst of these plans, but his projects later influenced the foundation of Propaganda Fide, for whose work Thomas became a prominent publicist.

BIBLIOGRAPHY V. Buri, *L'unione della chiesa copta con Roma sotto Clemente VIII,* Orientalia Christiana no.72 (1931); Florencio del Niño Jesús, *La Misión del Congo y los Carmelitas y la Propaganda Fide* (1929) and *La Orden de Santa Teresa, la fundación de la Propaganda Fide y las Misiones Carmelitanas* (1923); Johannis a Jesu Maria, "Breve compendium vitae ac virtutum Ven. P. Petri a Matre Dei," in Ildephonsum a S. Aloysio, ed., *Johannes a Jesu Maria Opera Omnia,* vol. 3 (1774). Pluteo 281 in the General Archives of the Discalced Carmelites, Corso d'Italia, Rome, contains copies of Pedro's correspondence and memoranda, several of which are published in the appendix of Buri's volume.

Richard Gray

Peery, R(ufus) B(enton) (1868–1934), early Lutheran missionary in Japan and cofounder of the Japan Evangelical Lutheran Church (1893). Peery was born in Burke's Garden, Virginia, educated at Roanoke College (B.A., 1890) and Gettysburg (Pennsylvania) Seminary (1892), and received the Ph.D. from Pennsylvania College (1895). Called and ordained by the Virginia Synod of the United Lutheran Synod of the South for service in Japan, Peery arrived in Tokyo for language study in 1893 and within a few months joined his friend James A. B. *Scherer, whom he had known at Roanoke, in Saga, Kyushu. Peery's account of the beginnings of Lutheran mission work in Kyushu, *Lutherans in Japan* (1900), describes fierce local resistance to missionary presence, the actual founding of the Japan Evangelical Lutheran Church on Easter Day 1893, and the gradual expansion of the work. Peery married Letitia Rich in 1895, and the couple eventually had six children.

Leaving missionary service in 1903, Peery wrote and lectured on Japanese culture, religion, and philosophy; served pastorates in Denver (1905–1912), Wooster, Ohio (1924–1931), and Raleigh, North Carolina (1931–1934); and was president of Midland College, Atchison, Kansas (1912–1919), and professor of philosophy at Lenoir College, Hickory, North Carolina (1920–1924).

BIBLIOGRAPHY R. B. Peery, *The Gist of Japan: The Islands, Their People, and Missions* (1897) and *Lutherans in Japan* (1900).

James A. Scherer

Peet, Joseph (1798–1865), Church Missionary Society (CMS) missionary in India. Trained at the CMS college at Islington, near London, Peet left for Kottayam, in Travancore, South India, in 1833. Here, in the heartland of Thomas Christianity (Indo-Syrian Orthodox), Peet attempted to establish the Anglican Church and headed a seminary that sought to train young Thomas Christians in Anglican ways. Not surprisingly, ecclesiastical conflict resulted, and neither John *Tucker, secretary of the Madras Corresponding Committee of the CMS, nor Daniel *Wilson, bishop of Calcutta, was able to resolve it. The Mavelikkara Synod of 1836, called by Mar Dionysius IV, repudiated Anglican interference and ended formal relations between the CMS and the Syrian/Thomas Church. As a consequence, Peet was assigned to building a new college for training only the clergy of CMS churches. In 1838 he left Kottayam and settled in Mavelikkara, remaining there for the rest of his life. Apparently a blunt, eccentric, and fiery loner, a former seaman devoid of diplomatic skill or sensitivity, many of his relationships seem to have been marred by trouble.

BIBLIOGRAPHY Leslie Brown, *The Indian Syrian Christians of St Thomas* (1956, 1982); Mildred E. Gibbs, *The Anglican Church in India, 1600–1700* (1972); Stephen Neill, *A History of Christianity in India: 1707–1858* (1985), pp. 236–254; *Register of CMS Missionaries and Native Clergy, from 1804 to 1904,* D. T. B[arry], ed. (1908); Eugene Stock, *History of the Church Missionary Society,* 4 vols. (1899–1916), vol. 1.

Robert Eric Frykenberg

Peña Montenegro, Alonso de (1596–1687), bishop of Quito. Peña was born in Villa de Padrón in Galicia in northwest Spain and studied at the University of Santiago of Compostela. He taught canon law and was ordained a priest in 1639. Appointed bishop of Quito in 1653 and receiving ordination in Bogotá, he reached his diocese in 1654. After extensive visits throughout the diocese, which comprised all of modern Ecuador, he wrote a lengthy manual *Itinerario para párrocos de indios* to guide priests in charge of Indian parishes. Completed in 1666 and published in 1668, the manual directed all priests to learn the languages of the Indians and encouraged them to treat the Indians with kindness, taking into account their customs. Peña's pastoral treatise, divided into five books, became the standard guide for priests in the Ecuadorian and Peruvian Andes in colonial times. For a brief time he served as interim president of the Audiencia (governing board) of Quito.

BIBLIOGRAPHY Rubén Vargas Ugarte, *Historia de la Iglesia en el Perú, vol. 3* (1960); José María Vargas, *Historia de la Iglesia en el Ecuador durante el Patronato español* (1957).

Jeffrey Klaiber, SJ

Pennell, Theodor Leighton (1867–1912), medical missionary in northwest Pakistan. Born in Clifton, Bristol, and losing his father early, Pennell was brought up by his mother, who wanted him to become a missionary. He decided to study medicine at University College, London, where he was an outstanding student. In 1892 the Church Missionary Society sent him to the Punjab Mission to take over the Bannu station, close to the Afghan border. His mother accompanied him and helped him there until her death in 1908.

Pennell's fame was due not only to his medical skills and daring itinerations—mostly on bicycle and always moving unarmed among the heavily armed Muslim peoples of the mountains—but to his irenic missionary existence, of which he gave account in his widely read *Among the Wild Tribes of the Afghan Frontier* (1909). He adopted the Afghan ways of dress, food, and habits; ran a school; and operated a small printing press, from which he issued a newspaper in the vernacular Pushtu. He was honored with the Kaiser-i-Hind Medal for public service in India. He died suddenly of blood poisoning at Bannu, leaving behind his wife, Sorabji, a doctor of a Poona family, whom he had married in 1908 and who wrote his biography.

BIBLIOGRAPHY E. Hume, *Doctors Courageous* (1950); A(rthur) L(ancaster), *Pennell of Bannu* (1913); Alice M. (Sorbaji) Pennell, *Pennell of the Afghan Frontier: The Life of Theodore Leighton Pennell* (1914, 1978); M. Sinker, *Friend of the Frontier: The Story of Dr. Theodore Pennell* (n.d.).

Christoffer H. Grundmann

Pennini, Ricoldo (da Monte Cruce) (1243–1320), Florentine scholar and missionary traveler in the Middle East. In his middle years, Pennini's Dominican superiors sent him by way of Jerusalem (from where he took his pseudonym) to Baghdad. There he studied Arabic and Islamic religion and familiarized himself with indigenous Nestorian Christianity. His public dialogues were forestalled by the repercussions of the Crusaders' defeat at Acre (1291). He retreated to the rural communities of Iraq, where he observed and recorded Muslim customs. His diary, *Itinerarium,* provided medieval Christendom with an unrivaled source of information about Muslim culture. On returning to Italy after ten years, he composed his major work, *Contra Legem Saracenorum* (alternately, *Improbatio Alcorani*)—a comparative account of Christian and Muslim beliefs that represented a summation of medieval Christian knowledge of Islam. In several translations it served as Christendom's primary text on Christian-Muslim theological encounter for the next four centuries, used by Catholics, Orthodox, and Protestants. Though an advocate of a polemical theology, he urged missionaries to learn the languages, scriptures, and beliefs of Islam, value the generosity and sophistication of Muslim peoples, and reciprocate the love of God.

BIBLIOGRAPHY Norman Daniel, *Islam and the West: The Making of an Image* (1960) and *The Arabs and Medieval Europe* (1975); Jean-Marie Gaudeul, *Encounters and Clashes: Islam and Christianity in History* (1984); Monneret de Villard, "La Vita, le Opera, e i Viaggi di Ricoldo da Montecroce," *Orientalia Christiana Periodica* 10 (1944): 227–247.

David A. Kerr

Penzotti, Francisco G. (1851–1925), Bible colporteur in South America. Penzotti left Chiavenna, the city of his birth in northern Italy, for Montevideo, Uruguay, when he was only 13. A carpenter by trade, at age 20 he married Sarah Sagastillense, a Spanish young woman. Profoundly challenged by the preaching of James F. *Thomson, and subsequently converted in 1876 through the ministry of Andrew M. *Milne and Thomas B. *Wood, Penzotti served as pastor to the Waldensians in Colonia, Uruguay, from 1879 to 1886. During this period, in successive years from 1883, he made three missionary journeys as a Bible colporteur, two of them with Milne, to most South American countries and a number of Caribbean islands.

Stoning, death threats, and prison on many occasions did not diminish his efforts. His assignment by the American Bible Society (ABS) to Peru in 1887 increased his difficulties. In 1890 he was imprisoned for eight months on charges that the Peruvian constitution prohibited Protestant preaching and Bible distribution. A national quarrel ensued between liberals and fanatical conservatives until international protest forced his release. For 16 years from 1892 to 1908, his assignment was to Central America, where he became known as the Apostle of the Central American Church. When Milne died in 1908, Penzotti took his place as executive secretary for the ABS in the River Plate region, and continued until the end of his life.

Penzotti personally distributed some 125,000 Bibles, according to one report, and under his direction more than two million New Testaments and smaller portions were placed in the hands of people in Spanish-speaking lands. In recognition of his vast ministry, Bible society Penzotti Institutes in various venues offer training in Scripture distribution and use.

BIBLIOGRAPHY Francisco Penzotti, *Spiritual Victories in Latin America* (1916; autobiography). W. T. T. Millham, *Heroes of the Cross in South America* (1947), pp. 40–46; Daniel P. Monti, *Presencia del Protestantismo en el Rio de la Plata durante el siglo XIX* (1969), pp. 214–223; Luis D. Salem, *Francisco G. Penzotti, Apóstol de la Libertad y de la Verdad* (1964); United Bible Societies, *News and Views,* no. 44 (March 1964).

Sidney H. Rooy

Perbal, Albert (1884–1971), Catholic missiologist. Born in France at Harcourt, Nancy, Perbal entered the Missionary Oblates of Mary Immaculate (OMI) in 1902. In 1919 he was appointed private secretary to Augustin Dontenwill, the superior general of OMI, whom he accompanied to South Africa in 1922. His journal of the trip was published in *Petites Annales des OMI.* He served in Rome as superior of the International Oblate Scholasticate from 1924 to 1930. In 1930 he was named head of the Secretariat of Oblate Missions in Rome and of the Press Office. He was also in charge of the periodical *Missions des Missionares OMI.* In 1932 he served as secretary of the Conference Romaines des Missions Catholiques Africaines and as director of the periodical *Africanae fraternae Ephimerides Romanae.* The same year he was appointed professor at the Missiological Institute of Propaganda Fide. In 1934 he founded the bulletin *Agence Romaine des OMI.* From 1934 to 1939 he was put in charge of courses at the Institut Catholique de Paris. In 1941 he was appointed consultant of Propaganda Fide and made vice-president of the Missiological Institute of Propaganda Fide. At the institute he taught introduction to missiology and Islam; in the years following 1941 he organized the missiological curriculum. He retired in 1954.

BIBLIOGRAPHY Albert Perbal, *Premières leçons de théologie missionnaire* (1935), *What Is Missiology?* (1935), *Les missionnaires français et le nationalisme* (1939), *Prime lezioni di teologia missionaria* (1941), *Ritorno alle fonti* (1942), and *Lo studio delle missioni* (1946). Gaston Carrière, "Albert Perbal, O.M.I., missiologue," *Revue de l'Université d'Ottawa* 42 (1972): 162–166; André Seumois, "Le P. Albert Perbal O.M.I., 1884–1971," *NZM* 28 (1972): 133–135, and

"Albert Perbal O.M.I. et l'Institut Scientifique Missionnaire (1932–1954)," *Euntes Docete* 39 (1986): 221–238 (includes a bibliography of Perbal with some 260 titles).

Willi Henkel, OMI

Perboyre, Jean-Gabriel (1802–1840), Vincentian missionary in China. Perboyre was born at Puech, a hamlet in the diocese of Cahors, France. He became a member of the Congregation of the Mission, better known as Lazarists or Vincentians. Ordained priest in September 1825, he spent the next ten years in his native France, training young candidates in the seminaries of his congregation. He was then sent to China, which at that time was not opened to foreigners. In September 1839 he was betrayed by a new convert and arrested in Hupeh (Hubei) Province. During the nine months he spent in jail, he was tortured; irons were kept at all time around his hands, feet, and neck. Brought several times in front of a tribunal, he always refused to renounce his faith or to reveal the hiding places of Chinese Christians and other missioners. Condemned to death, he was tied to a gibbet and strangled. He was beatified by Leo XIII on November 10, 1899, and canonized by *John Paul II on June 2, 1996.

BIBLIOGRAPHY Vincentian Varig, *Vie du Bienheureux Jean-Gabriel Perboyre* (1899; Eng. tr. by Mary Randolph, *Blessed John Gabriel Perboyre, Priest of the Congregation of the Mission,* 1917); A. Chatelet, *Jean Gabriel Perboyre, Martyr* (1943); J.-B Etienne, *La vie et la mort de M. Jean-Gabriel Perboyre* (1842).

Jean-Paul Wiest

Percival, Peter (1803–1882), Wesleyan Methodist missionary in Ceylon. Percival began his missionary career in 1826, when the English Wesleyan Methodist Missionary Society (WMMS) sent him to Ceylon (Sri Lanka), where he began learning Tamil. In 1829 he opened a new mission field for the WMMS in Calcutta, but after only three years this field was given up and Percival was transferred back to Ceylon. There he put into practice his conviction that educational work must be the basis of missionary activity. In 1834 he opened the Central School (later College) in Jaffna, and later, a girls' boarding school. Believing strongly that worship should take place in the vernacular, he established St. Paul's Chapel in Jaffna as the first center for Tamil worship, composing orders of service that were used in the Jaffna district well into the twentieth century. Called the greatest Tamil scholar Methodism has ever had, he translated the whole Bible into Tamil.

In 1851 a disagreement arose between Percival and WMMS leaders in London, who were reluctant to support his views of the urgency of "native ministry." As a result, he resigned from both the WMMS and the Wesleyan ministry. In 1857 he was appointed professor of Sanskrit and vernacular literature at the newly founded Madras University and was also registrar of the university from 1860; he retired in 1869. In addition to his academic duties, he was a member of the Society for Promoting Christian Knowledge Select Committee in Madras (1857–1859) and published a weekly Tamil newspaper, *Dhinavurtamauni* (1867–1875). In 1870 he was appointed chaplain to the Madras Military Male and Female Orphan Asylums. He retired in 1881 and died at Yercaud, a sanitarium in the Shevaroy Hills, Salem District, Madras. He was buried in Trinity Church cemetery, Yercaud.

BIBLIOGRAPHY Percival's published works include *A Collection of Proverbs in Tamil with Their Translation in English* (1843), *Tamil-English Dictionary* (3d ed., 1877), and *The Land of the Veda: India Briefly Described in Some of...* (1854). Thomas Moscrop and Arthur E. Restarick, *Ceylon and Its Methodism* (n.d.); Walter J. T. Small, ed., *A History of the Methodist Church in Ceylon, 1814–1964* (1964). See also British Library, India Office Records (N/2/63, f.251), Burials at Wellington, Yercaud; *List of European Tombs in the Salem District, with Inscriptions Thereon* (1893).

Kenneth R. Cracknell

Pereira, Eduardo Carlos (1855–1923), Brazilian grammarian and champion of indigenous Protestantism in Latin America. Born in Minas, Brazil, Pereira taught Portuguese grammar and wrote several textbooks. He was converted to the Protestant faith in 1875 and completed theological studies in 1880. His experience in a remote rural church in Lorena was the beginning of awareness about the need to indigenize the Presbyterian Church of Brazil, which had been established by American missionaries. He founded the Brazilian Tract Society in 1884, the Commission of National Missions in 1886, and its periodical *Revista de Missões Nacionais* in 1887. He criticized strongly the foreignness of the educational work supported by the American Presbyterian mission board, and also opposed membership in Masonic lodges, which was practiced by some missionaries and some Brazilian Presbyterians. Confrontation with missionary policies led in 1903 to forming the Independent Presbyterian Church, which severed all links with foreign missionaries and churches and developed rapidly as an indigenous movement under Pereira's leadership. He attended the Panama Congress on Christian Work in Latin America (1916), after which he wrote an interpretation of the religious situation of Latin America. Missiological developments in the United States and Brazil eventually led the Presbyterian Church of Brazil to adopt most of Pereira's ideas.

BIBLIOGRAPHY After the Panama Congress, Pereira wrote *O problema religioso da America Latina* (1920). His biography by Salvador de Moya appears in *Anuário Genealógico Brasileiro* (1943). See also Emile-G. Léonard, *O Protestantismo Brasileiro* (1963).

Samuel Escobar

Perkin, Noel (1893–1979), foreign missions director of the Assemblies of God. Born in England to Wesleyan Methodist parents, Perkin moved to Toronto, Canada, where he identified with the Christian and Missionary Alliance, which influenced his perspectives on missions. Joining the Pentecostal movement, he served for a short time as an independent missionary in Argentina (1918–1921). After pastoring in western New York, he received an invitation in 1926 to work in the Assemblies of

God missionary department in Springfield, Missouri. Appointed director in 1927, Perkin developed policies, promoted missions to the church constituency, and oversaw the growth of the agency from its infancy to remarkable expansion after World War II. Pivotal to the growth of Assemblies of God missions, Perkin encouraged missionaries to read the writings of Roland *Allen. He also influenced Melvin L. *Hodges to further develop theory and strategy for the mission enterprise according to Allen's perspectives. At his retirement in 1959, he was the first Pentecostal to be elected president of the Evangelical Foreign Missions Association.

BIBLIOGRAPHY Edith L. Blumhofer, *"Pentecost in My Soul"* (1989); John Garlock and Noel Perkin, *Our World Witness* (1963); Gary B. McGee, *This Gospel Shall Be Preached,* vol. 1 (1986).

Gary B. McGee

Perkins, Justin (1805–1869), pioneer American missionary to Persia (Iran). Perkins was born at West Springfield, Massachusetts, and after a religious awakening at age 18, prepared for the ministry at Amherst College (1829) and at Andover Theological Seminary. He was ordained, married Charlotte Bass, and sailed under the American Board of Commissioners for Foreign Missions (ABCFM) for the Near East in 1833. Establishing his center at Urumia (Rezaiyeh), Persia, he received at first a warm welcome from the Nestorian people and clergy. When the patriarch later turned against the mission, the Muslim government issued an edict of toleration in 1851. Perkins was an evangelist and physician but his immense literary labors accounted for much of his influence. He prepared a writing system for modern Syriac (the Nestorian vernacular), and the printing press at Urumia produced some eighty of his works, including schoolbooks, hymnals, and translations of religious classics. Perkins's periodical *Rays of Light* was devoted to "religion, education, science, missions, juvenile matters, miscellany, and poetry." His translations of the New Testament (1846) and the Old Testament (1852) were printed in both ancient and modern Syriac. He contributed to journals of the American Oriental Society and the Deutsche Morgenländische Gesellschaft and wrote *A Residence of Eight Years in Persia among the Nestorian Christians* (1843), *Missionary Life in Persia* (1861), *Historical Sketch of the Mission to the Nestorians* (1861), and a *Memoir* (1853) of his daughter Judith, one of his several children who died in childhood. Failing health caused him to return to the United States in 1869. He died in Chicopee, Massachusetts.

BIBLIOGRAPHY H. M. Perkins, *Life of Rev. Justin Perkins, D.D.* (1887). *Missionary Herald* 66 (1870): 422–446; also numerous other articles indexed in the *Missionary Herald* from 1835 to 1860. Rufus Anderson, *History of the Missions of the ABCFM to the Oriental Churches,* 2 vols. (1872), chapters on the Nestorian Mission.

David M. Stowe

Perroton, (Marie) Françoise (Marie du Mont Carmel) (1796–1873), pioneer Catholic missionary in the Pacific. Born in Lyons, France, and well educated, Perroton became a governess. Wanting to be a missionary from 1820, she helped Pauline *Jaricot's Society for the Propagation of the Faith for many years. At age 49 she determined to go to the Pacific, bypassed churchmen who would have opposed the idea, and worked her passage unassisted, reaching Uvea Island, Wallis Islands, in October 1846. Overcoming Bishop Pierre-Marie *Bataillon's cool welcome, she survived intense loneliness, and her work proved the need for women missionaries. Bataillon told her story in Europe in 1856, inspiring many to volunteer to join her. Marist authorities accepted three, who left in 1857. Perroton received them joyfully, making profession in 1858 in the Marist Sisters as Marie du Mont Carmel. By 1861 other arrivals brought their number to eleven in the Vicariate of Central Oceania and New Caledonia. Much-needed religious training was begun in Lyons under Marie du Coeur de Jesus (Barbier). Barbier, however, gave her trainees a new direction, founding the Sisters of Our Lady of the Missions. The Pacific pioneers, including Perroton, joined the new congregation but lost enthusiasm because of problems with Barbier. A painful split was taking place when Perroton died on Futuna. The pioneers withdrew, most again organizing as Marist sisters, which in 1931 became the Missionary Sisters of the Society of Mary. Perroton's courage and example inspired many who followed her to the Pacific.

BIBLIOGRAPHY Marie Cécile de Mijolla, *Origins in Oceania: Missionary Sisters of the Society of Mary, 1845–1931* (1984). Perroton's letters are in the archives of the Missionary Sisters of the Society of Mary, Rome, and archives of Religious of Our Lady of the Missions, Rome. All are included in the privately published five-volume series *Our Pioneer Sisters* (1972–1977).

John Hosie, SM

Peter of Ghent (c. 1480–1572), Franciscan lay missionary in Mexico. Born in the Flemish part of Belgium, Peter joined the Franciscan order in 1519 as lay member. He was one of three Flemish Franciscans who arrived in Mexico in 1523, where he worked until his death. For nearly 50 years he identified himself with the Indians of Mexico, considering himself to be no more than a servant of the defeated and marginalized. He mastered the Nahuatl language and wrote two catechisms in pictographic Nahuatl form (1528 and 1553). He founded a hospital for the Indians and constructed a large chapel of St. Joseph of the Indians next to the church of St. Francis in Mexico City. Near that chapel he erected the school of St. Joseph for the children of Aztec nobility. Faithfully visiting the numerous catechetical centers he had organized, he also taught various trades and professions to Aztec youth so that they were able to contribute to a revival of their culture, notwithstanding the Spanish assault on it.

BIBLIOGRAPHY Juan Guillermo Durán, *Monumenta catechetica hispanoamericana (siglos XVI–XVIII),* vol. 1 (1984), pp. 113–124; Mariano Erasti, *América Franciscana,* vol. 1, *Evangelizadores e Indigenistas Franciscanos del Siglo XVI* (1986), pp. 119–133.

Arnulf Camps, OFM

Peters, George W(ilhelm) (1907–1988), American Mennonite missiologist. Peters spent the first 19 years of his life in Chortitza (present-day Zaporozhye), Ukraine. He witnessed the execution of his father in the Machno massacre of 1919 and immigrated to Canada with his mother in 1928. In 1932 he began teaching at the Bethany Bible Institute in Hepburn, Saskatchewan. While there, he married Susan Lepp of Dalmeny and together they founded Western Children's Mission. In 1947 he earned a Ph.D. from the Kennedy School of Missions, Hartford Seminary, Connecticut. Also in 1947, he was appointed chief administrator of Pacific Bible Institute (now Fresno Pacific College), and in 1955 he became academic dean of the Mennonite Brethren Biblical Seminary in Fresno, California. He developed strong mission curricula for both schools and motivated many graduates to choose missionary service as their life's calling. From 1962 to 1976 he headed the department of missions at Dallas (Texas) Theological Seminary. Upon retirement he accepted a call from the Liebenzeller Mission to teach missions in Germany, where he became instrumental in establishing the Freie Hochschule für Mission in Korntal, near Stuttgart, a vital center for evangelical missiology and missionary training on the Continent. His major contributions include 25 years of service on the Board of Foreign Missions of the Mennonite Brethren Church, a consistent focus on the biblical view of the church in mission, and extensive publications, of which the following are used as textbooks in English- and German-speaking colleges and seminaries: *A Biblical Theology of Missions* (3d printing, 1975), *Saturation Evangelism* (1970), and *A Theology of Church Growth* (1981). On his 80th birthday a bilingual Festschrift was presented to him as a tribute to 55 years of teaching and preaching around the globe.

BIBLIOGRAPHY Hans Kasdorf and Klaus W. Müller, eds., *Reflection and Projection: Missiology at the Threshold of 2001, Festschrift in Honor of George W. Peters for his Eightieth Birthday* (1988; contains a biographical tribute by J. B. Toews, pp. 20–42 and a bibliography of Peters's publications, pp. 43–50). Unpublished papers and parts of Peters's personal library are in the Center for Training in Mission/Evangelism of the Mennonite Brethren Biblical Seminary in Fresno, California, and in the Research Center of the *Freie Hochschule für Mission* in Korntal, Germany.

Hans Kasdorf

Petersen, Anne Marie (1878–1951), Danish missionary in India. Born at Rosilde on the island of Fyn, Denmark, Petersen became a teacher. In 1909 she was sent to South India by the Løventhals Mission (established in 1873 by the Danish Lutheran missionary C. E. Løventhal). She was inspired by and worked in accordance with the mission ideas formulated by the influential Danish theologian N. F. S. Grundtvig: a people must first become conscious of its identity as a people, and then as a group turn to Christianity. Her objective was to foster an Indian indigenous Christianity.

In the mid-1920s, Petersen's support of Mahatma Gandhi and his politics resulted in a breach between her and part of the church that had sent her. A group of friends continued to support her work, now called "The Porto Novo Mission," after the town where Petersen's mission school was located. After India's independence in 1948, the new Indian authorities were positively disposed toward the school, and in 1949 the school was supplemented with a teachers' training college. After Petersen's death in Porto Novo, the leadership of the church came into Indian hands, but the school continued to be supported by the Danish Porto Novo Mission.

BIBLIOGRAPHY Marie Stougaard Pedersen, *Anne Marie Petersen* (1963); Knut B. Westman, *Nordisk Missionshistorie* (1950).

Flemming Markussen

Peterson, Paul Bernhard (1895–1978), missionary and cofounder of the Russian and Eastern European Mission (REEM), later the Eastern European Mission. Born in Chicago, Illinois, Peterson had a vision for ministry that began in 1918 at the Moody Tabernacle in Chicago during a service convened to promote the evangelization of Eastern Europe and what soon became the Soviet Union. He and his wife, Signe, served as missionaries of the Russian Missionary Society to Poland and Latvia (1924–1926).

Returning to the United States, he cofounded the Russian and Eastern European Mission in 1927 with G. Herbert Schmidt and C. W. Swanson. With Peterson as the general secretary at the home office in Chicago, Schmidt directed the field office in Gdansk, Poland. An independent agency, it supported the ministries of Ivan Efimovich *Voronaev and other missionaries in the region, as well as Nikolai *Poysti's efforts in Manchuria and eastern Siberia. REEM and the Assemblies of God cooperated by sharing personnel and providing mutual support until 1940.

Elected president of REEM in 1931, Peterson directed and promoted the mission enterprise until his death. During his long tenure, the organization expanded its ministries into other parts of Europe and to Eastern Europeans and Russians living in South American countries. The mission was renamed Eurovision in 1985; it merged with the Slavic Gospel Association in 1989.

BIBLIOGRAPHY Paul B. Peterson, *History of the First Fifty Years (1927–1977) of the Eastern European Mission* (n.d.). "He Served His Generation by the Will of God," *Gospel Call*, Jan.–Feb. 1979, pp. 2–4; Gary B. McGee, "Working Together: The Assemblies of God—Russian and Eastern European Mission Cooperation, 1927–40," *Assemblies of God Heritage* 8 (Winter 1988–1989): 12; Tom Salzer, "The Danzig (Gdanska) Institute of the Bible," published in two parts: *Assemblies of God Heritage* 8 (Fall 1988): 8–11, 18–19 and 8 (Winter 1988–1989): 10–12, 17–18.

Gary B. McGee

Peter the Venerable de Montboissier (Pierre Maurice) (1094–1156), advocate of peaceful mission to Islam. Peter the Venerable, the Abbot of Cluny (Burgundy) from 1122, was one of the commanding figures of twelfth-century Latin Christianity at the time of the Crusades against Islam. He criticized the practice of Christian "holy war" and called for the conversion, rather than extermination, of Muslims. For the gospel to be preached peacefully, he argued that Christians must first understand the religious beliefs of Islam. To this end he initiated the Latin church's first missionary study program. Locating his project in the Spanish city of Toledo, where Christian scholars were already engaged in translating Arabic secular works, he recruited scholars to translate Islamic religious texts into Latin: the Qur'an (rendered for the first time into a Western language), a selection of traditions (*hadith*) from the prophet Muhammad, an account of the prophet's origins, a summary of Islamic doctrines, and an early Christian-Muslim dialogue. His friend Bernard of Clairvaux, a Crusader theologian, refused to write a Christian apologia on the basis of the translated documents, so Peter undertook the task himself. His *Summa Totius Haersis Saracenorum* and *Liber Contra Sectam Sive Haeresim Saracenorum* mark the first attempts at a Latin account of Islam and Christian evangelization of Muslims "not by arms but by words, not by force but by reason, not in hatred but in love."

BIBLIOGRAPHY Marie-Thérèse d'Alverny, "Deux traductions latines du *Coran* au Moyen Age," *Archives d'Histoire Doctrinale et Litteraire du Moyen Age* 16 (1948): 69–131; Norman Daniel, *Islam and the West: The Making of an Image* (1960); James Kritzeck, *Peter the Venerable and Islam* (1964); James Sweetman, *Christian Theology and Islam,* part 2, vol. 1 (1945).

David A. Kerr

Pethrus, Lewi (1884–1974), Swedish pastor, promoter of missions, and international Pentecostal leader. Reared a Baptist, Pethrus became a factory worker, was later an evangelist, and studied at Bethel Seminary in Stockholm (1905–1906). After ministering at the Baptist Church in Lidköping for several years, he pastored the Filadelphia Church in Stockholm from 1911 until his retirement in 1958. In 1907, influenced by reports of the outpouring of the Holy Spirit in North America, England, and Norway, he entered the Pentecostal movement, and coming under the influence of Thomas Ball *Barratt of Oslo, Pethrus adopted Pentecostal teaching.

When he returned to Stockholm, Pethrus's congregation accepted the new teaching, but the congregation was expelled from the Swedish Baptist Convention in 1913. Pethrus retained his preference for Baptist church polity, and this became the paradigm for the Swedish Pentecostal churches. His many projects included the Filadelphia Church Rescue Mission (1911); Filadelphia Publishing House (1912); the church periodical *Evangelii Härold* (1916–); publication of *Dagen,* a national Christian daily newspaper (1945–); IBRA, an international radio network (1955); and the Lewi Pethrus Foundation of Philanthropy (1959). An international Pentecostal leader and the undisputed spokesperson for the Swedish Pentecostal churches, Pethrus hosted the 1939 World Pentecostal Conference and served as an elder statesman until his death.

While Pethrus strongly supported missions for world evangelism, through his guidance Swedish Pentencostal missions took a more holistic view of mission and a more positive attitude toward culture than did North American Pentecostals; this became an enduring characteristic of Swedish Pentecostal missiology. In recognition of his many contributions, he received an honorary D.D. from Wheaton College, Ill., in 1949 and conferral of the Vasa Order by the king of Sweden in 1973.

BIBLIOGRAPHY A prolific writer, Pethrus wrote many books, including *Memoarer,* 5 vols. (1953–1956), *Samlade Skrifter,* 10 vols. (1958–1959), and *Lewi Pethrus: A Spiritual Memoir* (1973). For further information, see ("Av Missionärer") *Apostolisk Väckelse i Brasilien* (1934); Thomas Ball Barratt, *When the Fire Fell and an Outline of My Life* (1927); Nils Bloch-Hoell, *The Pentecostal Movement* (1964); Bertil Carlsson, *Organizations and Decision Procedures Within the Swedish Pentecostal Movements* (1978); Walter J. Hollenweger, *The Pentecostals* (1972); A. Sundsted, *Pingstväckelsen,* 5 vols. (1969–1973); *Vara Missionärer och Missionsfält* (1939); an entire issue of *World Pentecost* (no. 1, vol. 5, 1975) is devoted to Pethrus's memory. His personal library and memorabilia are held at the MissionsInstitutet—PMS, Kaggeholm, 178 54, Ekerö, Sweden.

Gary B. McGee

Petitjean, Bernard-Thaddée (1829–1884), Catholic missionary in Japan. Petitjean was born in Blanzy-sur-Bourbince, Saône-et-Loire, France, and ordained a priest in 1853. He became a member of the Paris Foreign Mission Society in 1859. In 1860 he went to Japan, first to the Ryukyu Islands, then to Yokohama and Nagasaki. There on March 17, 1865, he met descendants of Japanese Christians of the former missionary era who were still secretly practicing the faith. They spoke with Petitjean about God, Jesus Christ, Mary and Joseph, Christmas, and Lent, and saw that his teaching corresponded to their tradition. Many of these people accepted him as their Christian leader. Hearing this joyful news, Pope Pius IX nominated Petitjean as vicar apostolic of Japan and titular bishop of Myriophitus (1866). Shortly afterwards an anti-Christian persecution broke out that lasted till 1873, and about 3,400 Christians were deported. After the persecution, about 14,000 Christians retained the connection they had resumed with the missionary priests, but others decided to resume their allegiance to Christianity as *Harare* (separated). Because of the differences between the north of Japan and the south, where the seventeenth-century terminology of the Jesuit mission had survived, the mission territory was divided in 1876. Petitjean took over the south (with headquarters in Osaka), Pierre-Marie Osouf the north (with headquarters in Yokohama, later in Tokyo).

Petitjean had two special ambitions: the establishment of religious communities of women and the development of an indigenous clergy. In 1872 the first missionary sisters, called Dames de Saint-Maur, came from France to Yokohama; five years later the Soeurs du Saint-Enfant-Jésus de Chauffailles also arrived. As early as 1867 Petitjean began to recruit young men from among the "Old Christians" to train for the priesthood, and in March 1873, after the persecution had abated, there were thirty candidates. Toward the end of 1873 he conferred the tonsure on the first group, in 1880 the diaconate, and on December 31, 1883, he ordained the first Japanese priests. Less than a year later Petitjean died in Nagasaki.

Through numerous letters and reports, Petitjean exercised influence beyond his own mission. These were published, for example, in the *Annales de la Propagation de la Foi, Missions Catholiques, Compte-Rendu M.E.P., Semaine Religieuse, Die Katholischen Missionen,* and *Missioni Cattoliche.* In 1868 he published a catechism, a prayer book, and a church calendar, and in 1870 an amended and enlarged edition of the *Lexicon Latino-Japonicum* (1870), originally produced by the Jesuits in 1595.

BIBLIOGRAPHY J. B. Chaillet, *Mgr. Petitjean 1829–1884 et la résurrection catholique du Japon au XIXe siècle* (1919); "Das kirchliche Sprachproblem in der neuerstandenen Japanmission," in *Monumenta Nipponica* 3 (1940): 630–636; J. Laures, *Geschichte der katholischen Kirche in Japan* (1956), pp. 167–187.

Karl Müller, SVD

Petitot, Émile (1838–1917), French Catholic missionary in the Canadian Northwest Territories. Petitot was born at Grancy-le-Château, Côte-d'Or, France. He joined the Oblates of Mary Immaculate in 1860 and was sent to the Mackenzie Valley in the Northwest Territories, where he served in several missions, including Fort Providence (1862–1864) and Fort Good Hope (1864–1873). He undertook several journeys in which he combined exploration and evangelization, going as far as the Yukon in 1870. Exhausted, he spent a year at Lac-la-Biche, Alberta, and then went to France, where he published a number of important works in various Déné Indian languages. He returned to Fort Good Hope in 1876, but three years later, his health ruined, he left the north once again. He returned permanently to France in 1883. He joined the diocesan clergy in 1886 and spent the rest of his life as pastor in Mareuil-les-Meaux. He is the author of many reputable geographical, ethnological, and linguistic studies, including *Chez les Grands Esquimaux* (1887) and *Quinze ans sous la cercle polaire* (1889). Several places in Canada's far north bear his name. The Déné Indians whom he served called him *Yaltri nezun,* the Good Father.

BIBLIOGRAPHY Pietro Cerruti, *Il Padre Emilio Petitot e le sue relazioni sul Nord-Ovest canadese* (M.A. thesis, Univ. of Genoa, 1973); Adrien-Gabriel Morice, *L'abbé Émile Petitot et les découvertes géographiques du Canada* (1923); "Émile Petitot," *Bulletin de la Société d'histoire et d'art du diocèse de Meaux* (1974); Donat Savoie, *The Amerindians of the Canadian Northwest in the 19th Century, As Seen by Émile Petitot,* 2 vols. (1970) and "Bibliographie d'Émile Petitot, missionnaire dans le Nord-ouest canadien," *Anthropologica,* n.s., 12 (1971): 159–168. Extensive materials are in the Mackenzie diocesan archives in Yellowknife, Northwest Territories.

Achiel Peelman, OMI

Petri, Ludwig Adolf (1803–1873), Lutheran pastor and champion of church-centered mission. Petri, a pastor in Hanover, belonged to the nineteenth-century missionary movement that emerged from the evangelical awakening in Germany and that aimed at a church-centered view of mission in contrast to church union at the cost of confessional compromise. His essay "Die Mission und die Kirche" (1841), though not strictly a pioneering effort, supplied the ecclesiological foundation for a missiological stance which dominated a large sector of German Lutheranism. Like his contemporary Wilhelm *Löhe in Bavaria, Petri defined mission as the church itself engaged in missionary activity. This implied for Petri that mission could not possibly maintain its integrity except by operating from a historical confessional base. Petri did not maintain that missionary societies and associations were to be ruled out altogether. In fact, he himself founded several regional organizations devoted to the promotion of home and foreign missions. But Petri's opponents did not hesitate to question his approach: Would not the resulting churchism militate against the primacy of the coming kingdom and substitute propaganda for mission? Were the sending churches to determine the spiritual integrity of the growing churches abroad? How was the conflict between catholicity and confessional loyalty to be resolved? The time was yet to come when the special connection between the mission and the unity of the church would be more widely recognized.

BIBLIOGRAPHY H. Meyer-Roscher, "Ludwig Adolf Petri und die Mission," *Lutherisches Missionsjahrbuch* 75 (1962): 21–29; James A. Scherer, *Mission and Unity in Lutheranism* (1969).

Hans-Werner Gensichen

Petrie, Irene Eleanora Verita (1864–1897), English missionary in northern India. Born and raised in London, Petrie was the daughter of an army officer. She was educated mainly at home, and was active in Christian holiness circles and in charitable organizations. In 1892 she accepted the invitation of the bishop of Lahore to work with European and Eurasian women in India. After spending five months in Lahore, she felt drawn to work with poorer Indian women. In 1895 she was accepted by the Church Missionary Society as an honorary missionary for Kashmir. In Srinagar she worked happily in zenana visitation and in medical work. In 1897 she contracted typhoid, died, and was buried in Srinagar.

BIBLIOGRAPHY Mrs. Ashley Carus-Wilson [Mary Carus-Wilson], *Irene Petrie: Missionary in Kashmir* (1900).

Jocelyn Murray

Petter, Rodolphe (1865–1947), Mennonite missionary to the Cheyenne Indians in Oklahoma and Montana. Petter was born in Vevey, Switzerland. While studying at the Basel Mission School (1883–1889), where he received a thorough preparation in linguistics and anthropology, he accepted an invitation to join the General Conference Mennonite Mission in Oklahoma. He married Marie Gerber in 1890 (d. 1910). Arriving in Oklahoma in 1891, he insisted on studying the Cheyenne culture and language, something earlier missionaries had neglected. He became an expert in Cheyenne, creating a dictionary and grammar and a songbook, and translating Bunyan's *Pilgrim's Progress,* portions of the Old Testament, and all the New Testament. The New Testament was published by the

American Bible Society. He gained a reputation as an ethnologist through his authoritative writings on Cheyenne culture and language. His second marriage (1911) was to Bertha Kinsinger, a fellow missionary to the Cheyennes. He died at Lame Deer, Montana.

BIBLIOGRAPHY Lois Barrett, *The Vision and the Reality: The Story of Home Missions in the General Conference Mennonite Church* (1983); *Mennonite Encyclopedia,* vol. 4 (1959), pp. 155–156.

Wilbert R. Shenk

Pettitt, George (1803–1873), Church Missionary Society (CMS) missionary in India. After training in the CMS college at Islington, near London, Pettitt received Church of England ordination and was sent to India, arriving in Madras in 1833. He soon was sent to Tirunelveli, South India, by John *Tucker, secretary of the Madras CMS committee. His charge was to fill the void left by the summary dismissal of Carl Theophilus Ewald *Rhenius, who had pioneered CMS work among the Tamil-speaking Shanars. Sympathizers of Rhenius in India, Europe, and America rallied to support Rhenius, and seventy-seven pastors, teachers, and catechists in Shanar congregations begged Rhenius to continue. Pettitt faced alienation, bitterness, and controversy. A flurry of polemical pamphlets appeared, including Pettitt's *Narrative of Affairs of the Tinnevelly Mission...* (1836) and *An Account of the Palamcottah Mission Church* (1844). His massive *The Tinnevelly Mission of the Church Missionary Society* (1851) reflects the trauma of these events. Only after Rhenius's death in 1838 and after the CMS had become conciliatory in its policies toward the secessionists was Pettitt able to heal wounds and partially end the schism. In 1850, after three years in England, he went to Ceylon (Sri Lanka) as secretary of the Finance Committee for the CMS in Jaffna. Resigning from the CMS in 1855, he spent his remaining years as a chaplain and vicar in Birmingham, England.

BIBLIOGRAPHY Paul Appaswamy, *The Centennary History of the C.M.S. in Tinnevelly* (1923); Robert Caldwell, *Lectures on the Tinnevelly Missions* (1857) and *Records of the Early History of the Tinnevelly Mission* (1881); Robert E. Frykenberg, "The Impact of Radical Conversion and Social Reform upon Society in South India during the Late Company Period: Questions Concerning Hindu-Christian Encounters," in C. H. Philips and M. D. Wainwright, eds., *Indian Society and the Beginnings of Modernization, c. 1830–50* (1976), pp. 187–243; Stephen Neill, *A History of Christianity in India: 1707–1858* (1985), pp. 212–235.

Robert Eric Frykenberg

Pfander, Karl Gottlieb (1803–1865), missionary polemicist in Muslim India. Born in Württemberg, Germany, Pfander served with the Basel Mission (BM) for 12 years (1825–1837) in central Asia, where he became fluent in Persian, Turkish, and Arabic. Frustrated by the lack of evangelical literature for Muslims, he wrote his own apologetic, *Mizan al-Haqq* (The balance of truth). This work defended the integrity of the Bible (against the Islamic views of its textual corruption) and the truth of Christian revelation, and impugned the veracity of the Qur'an and Muhammad's prophethood. Translated from German (*Wage der Wahrheit*) into six languages, including English, between 1829 and 1867, the book remains a classic in the literature of Christian missionary apologetic. It typified Pfander's role in shaping missionary controversy with Islam in the nineteenth century.

When Russia closed the BM's central Asian work in 1837, Pfander joined the Church Missionary Society (CMS). He was sent to India, where he engaged Muslim religious leaders in public disputations in Agra and Peshawar. His most famous debate was with Sheikh Rahmat Allah Kairanawi, also known as al-Hindi, whose counterpolemics, published in Arabic under the title *Izhar al-Haqq* (The demonstration of truth), undermined Christian confidence in the efficacy of Pfander's approach.

The three further works which Pfander authored during his 16 years in India exhibit a softening of his polemical tone. *Remarks on the Nature of Muhammedanism* (1840) dealt with popular Muslim faith, emphasizing the importance of Islamic traditions (*hadith*) in the ways Muslims interpret the Qur'an and practice their faith. *Miftah al-Asrar* (The key of mysteries, 1844) presents an account of Jesus and the Trinity. *Tariq al-Hayat* (The way of life) presents the Christian understanding of salvation as against the Islamic understanding of sin.

In 1858, following the Indian uprising against British rule, Pfander was transferred to Constantinople, where Ottoman opposition to his controversialist approach led to the suspension of CMS activity in the city. Pfander retired to Britain.

BIBLIOGRAPHY Clinton Bennett, *Victorian Images of Islam* (1992), "The Legacy of Karl Gottlieb Pfander," *IBMR* 20 (1996): 76–81; Avril Powell, "Maulana Rahmat Allah Kairanawi and Muslim-Christian Controversy in India in the Mid-nineteenth Century," *Journal of the Royal Asiatic Society* (1975–1976): 42–63, "Muslim-Christian Confrontation: Dr. Wazir Khan in Nineteenth-Century Agra," in K. Jones, ed., *Religious Controversy in British India* (1992), pp. 77–92, and *Muslim and Missionaries in Pre-Mutiny India* (1993); Lyle Vander Werff, *Christian Mission to Muslims: The Record—Anglican and Reformed Approaches in India and the Near East, 1800–1938* (1977).

David A. Kerr

Pfanner, Franz (1825–1909), Roman Catholic missionary in South Africa. Prior of the Maria-Stern Trappist Monastery in Bosnia, Pfanner was called to evangelize the indigenous people of southern Africa at the Trappist General Chapter in 1879. Accompanied by thirty-one other Trappists, he journeyed to South Africa in 1880, founding the mission station Mariannhill, near Durban. As the monks increasingly began to influence the life of the African community around them by cultivating the land, celebrating the liturgy, and teaching the people on request, it became difficult to reconcile the Trappist rule (enforced silence, complete seclusion, etc.) with their daily existence. In 1908 Pfanner therefore requested permission to set aside the Trappist rule, and in 1909 Mariannhill became a full-fledged missionary society, the

Congregation of Mariannhill Missionaries (CMM). Through their education and social involvement, the CMM exerted a lasting influence, especially on the people of Natal. Already in 1884 Pfanner decided that they would make no distinction of color or religion in their school. In the oppressive racist atmosphere of colonial society, the policy was vigorously opposed by the white colonists. With respect to culture, Pfanner's approach was typical of nineteenth-century missionaries in that he more or less equated Christianization and Western civilization. His maxim for new converts was therefore first a pair of pants and a shirt, then the primer, then the catechism, but never without regular manual work. He died at Emaus, one of the smaller CMM mission stations.

BIBLIOGRAPHY The history of Pfanner and the CMM is recounted in M. Adelgisa, *One Hundred Years Mariannhill Province* (1984); *Mariannhill and Its Apostolate* (n.a.) (1964). See also William Saayman, "The Congregation of Mariannhill Missionaries: A Pioneering Roman Catholic Contribution to Christian Mission in South Africa," *Missionalia* 22, no. 1 (1994): 36–41.

Willem Saayman

Pfeiffer, Edward (1857–1926), pioneer American theorist of missions. Pfeiffer was a graduate of Capital University and Seminary, Columbus, Ohio, and served as a Lutheran pastor before joining the faculty there in 1899. From 1902 he taught in the seminary and was known as a strong advocate of missions. In 1908 he published *Mission Studies,* which went through several editions. It was the first systematic treatment of the theory and practice of missions in English. He showed awareness of the history of American missions and drew on the thought of Rufus *Anderson, especially as reflected in the American Board of Commissioners for Foreign Missions *Outline of Missionary Policy* (1856). But the structure of his work depended directly on the German missiologist Gustav *Warneck. Although not a student of Warneck, he accepted Warneck's theoretical framework. Pfeiffer divided his work into two parts: the history of missions, and the theory or principles of missions. He recognized that mission studies were as yet inadequately defined and deserved more careful development.

BIBLIOGRAPHY Edward Pfeiffer, *Mission Studies: Outlines of Missionary Principles and Practice* (1908). Donald L. Huber, *Educating Lutheran Pastors in Ohio* (1989).

Wilbert R. Shenk

Philaret (Drozdov) (1782–1867), metropolitan of Moscow and promoter of Orthodox missions. Philaret was born Vassily Mikhailovich Drozdov in a clerical family, and was given the name "Philaret" upon taking monastic vows in 1808. At that time he was teaching rhetoric in the seminary of Troitskaya Lavra near Moscow, and was already famous for his outstanding sermons. At 30 he was appointed rector of the St. Petersburg Theological Academy; at 35 he was consecrated a bishop and shortly thereafter an archbishop. He was a member of the Most Holy Synod, and in 1826 became the metropolitan of Moscow and remained in this position until his death. Philaret was a prolific author of theological works and an excellent administrator. Most of the Russian Orthodox missions were established under his administration. He was an active member of the Russian Bible Society (founded in 1814), and from 1816 he was engaged in translation of the Bible. It was due to Philaret's effort and under his supervision that the Russian translation of the Bible was published in 1858. Perhaps the single most significant contribution he made to the Christian mission was his authorship of the *Christian Catechism of the Orthodox Catholic Eastern Greco-Russian Church* (1823). It has been translated into many European and Oriental languages, and has been widely used by Orthodox missionaries.

BIBLIOGRAPHY Philaret, *Ukazatel k Slovam i Recham* (Bibliography of sermons and speeches) (1886). Among voluminous literature about Philaret, see V. I. Belinkov, *Deyatelnost Mitropolita Philareta po Raskolu* (The activity of Metropolitan Philaret in regard of old believers) (1896); I. Korsunsky, *Svyatitel Philaret. Mitropolit Moskovskii. Ego Zhizn i Deyatelnost na Moskovskoi Kafedre po Ego Propovedyam, v Svyazi s Sobytiyami i Obstoyatelstvami Togo Vremeni, 1821–1867* (Philaret, metropolitan of Moscow: His life and work) (1894).

Evgeny S. Steiner

Philip, John (1775–1851), Scottish superintendent of the London Missionary Society (LMS) in southern Africa. Philip was converted in the Haldane revival and in 1805 began a very successful ministry in Belmont Congregational Church, Aberdeen. There he married, in 1809, Jane Ross who bore four sons and three daughters.

In 1819 the LMS work in South Africa was threatened with closure by the British authorities. John *Campbell and John Philip were sent down as directors of the LMS to investigate fully and suggest reforms, and Philip was appointed to stay on as superintendent. Three of his sons became Congregationalist ministers in South Africa, one daughter returned to Great Britain and another, Elizabeth, married John Fairbairn, the radical negrophile editor of the *Cape Commercial Advertiser.* Jane also became the *de facto* administrative secretary of the LMS in South Africa, sometimes, during many of her husband's long treks, having to act on her own initiative.

In the Cape Colony, the indigenous Khoi people had become a landless laboring class. Together with the many people of mixed race, they constituted the so-called Cape Coloured people. In 1820 they had few civil rights. The LMS had gathered many of them into a number of lively congregations, and in 1823 Philip began a campaign to gain them their civil rights. In 1828 the effort was successful, though Philip had had to spend 18 months in Britain lobbying on their behalf, during which time he wrote *Researches in South Africa.*

Beyond the Cape Colony frontier the LMS had helped the Griqua people become an independent Christian ministate, and Philip hoped this would be the model for other South African indigenous peoples. While in Europe, he recruited the Paris Evangelical Mission Society and the Rhenish Missionary Society to begin work in South Africa; by correspondence he also persuaded the American Board of Commissioners for Foreign Missions to come. As with his own LMS, he advocated to these societies the necessity of "native agency," that is, that only Africans could convert Africa.

After the Xhosa war of 1834–1836, Philip went to London with a group of Coloured and Xhosa Christians to give evidence to a parliamentary commission before which he insisted that a major share of responsibility for the war lay with the British authorities and the white colonists. For this he was never forgiven by a large section of the white population. He was bitterly condemned by the Afrikaner people, who had left the colony on their Great Trek and had created the Orange Free State and the Transvaal. The Coloured people, together with the Griqua, Sotho, and Xhosa, had a very different attitude toward him, symbolized by his grave in a Coloured graveyard in a Coloured township.

BIBLIOGRAPHY W. M. Macmillan, *The Cape Colour Question* (1927 and 1968) and *Bantu, Boer and Briton* (1963); Andrew C. Ross, *John Philip: Missions, Race and Politics in South Africa* (1986) and "John Philip," in Gerald H. Anderson et al., eds., *Mission Legacies* (1994), pp. 125–131.

Andrew C. Ross

Phillippo, J(ames) M(ursell) (1798–1879), Baptist Missionary Society (BMS) missionary in Jamaica. Phillippo was born and educated in East Dereham, Norfolk, England. He arrived in Jamaica in 1823 but had to wait until 1825 for a license from the magistrates to preach. Compelled by ill health to return to England in August 1831, he had no firsthand experience of the slave rebellion of December 1831 and its repression, which proved so crucial for his colleagues, William *Knibb and Thomas Burchell. Nevertheless, in 1832 Phillippo joined Knibb and Burchell in the conviction that an immediate end to slavery was essential for the sake of gospel freedom. Phillippo was the first of the three to return to Jamaica after the passing of the Emancipation Act in 1834 and soon became a vocal critic of the apprenticeship system. In 1835 he purchased land above Spanish Town in anticipation of the end of apprenticeship in 1838. By the end of 1840 he had founded six free townships, including Sligoville, composed of more than a hundred former slave families. Although wanting to give the former slaves economic independence, Phillippo regarded the decision of the BMS in 1842 to terminate financial aid to the Jamaican churches as premature. He outlived many of his missionary colleagues and died in Spanish Town, where he had begun his ministry.

BIBLIOGRAPHY Brian Stanley, *The History of the Baptist Missionary Society, 1792–1992* (1992); E. B. Underhill, *Life of James Mursell Phillippo: Missionary in Jamaica* (1881). Phillippo wrote an autobiography, never published, which is preserved in manuscript in the BMS archives at Regent's Park College, Oxford.

Brian Stanley

Phillips, Godfrey Edward (1878–1961), British educator and missiologist. Phillips was accepted for missionary service by the London Missionary Society (LMS) in 1901 and posted to Davidson Street Chapel, Madras, India. In 1903 he went to Tripassore and then in 1912 became principal of United Theological College, Bangalore, serving until 1925. During World War I he also served as administrator of the Leipzig mission in Shiyali, Malabar, (1915–1916) under the Orphaned Missions program. As an ecumenist, Phillips played a pioneering role in laying the foundations for the future Church of South India. As a mission statesman, he was an articulate advocate of the "Indianization" of Christianity in India. He was ahead of his time as an ecumenist and with regard to devolution and the training of Indian Christian leadership. In 1925 the LMS appointed him foreign secretary for India, from which position he brought his progressive ideas to bear on program policies. In 1936 he became professor of missions at Selly Oak Colleges, Birmingham, England, serving until his retirement in 1944. His books include *The Outcastes' Hope* (1912), *The Ancient Church and Modern India* (1920), *The Untouchables' Quest* (1936), *The Gospel in the World: A Restatement of Missionary Principles* (1939; abridged ed., 1947), *The Old Testament in the World Church* (1942), *The Transmission of the Faith* (1946), and *The Religions of the World* (1955).

BIBLIOGRAPHY Norman Goodall, *A History of the London Missionary Society, 1895–1945* (1954); Bengt Sundkler, *The Church of South India: The Movement toward Union, 1900–1947* (1954).

Wilbert R. Shenk

Phillips, Jeremiah (1812–1879), Baptist missionary to the Santals in India. Phillips was among the first appointees of the Free Will Baptist Foreign Mission Society, organized in 1832 in Maine for sending missionaries to India at the invitation of General Baptist missionaries from England working in Orissa. Phillips and his wife served at Sambalpur, Cuttack, Balasore, and Jellasore, and later at Midnapore in Bengal. He laid the foundation of the Bengal-Orissa Baptist Mission among the Bengalis, Oriyas, and Santals. He devised a writing system for the Santal language using the Bengali script, and translated parts of Matthew into Santali in that script. He also produced a grammar and dictionary and began Santal schools. Santal response resulted in village transformation. After 44 years in India, Phillips returned to the United States, where he died three years later. The merger of Free Will Baptists with Northern Baptists in 1911 brought the oversight of the mission to the American Baptist Foreign Mission Society.

BIBLIOGRAPHY James Peggs, *A History of the General Baptist Mission* (1846); Robert G. Torbet, *Venture of Faith: The Story of the American Baptist Foreign Mission Society and the Woman's American Baptist Foreign Mission Society, 1814–1954* (1955). See also various reports in the *Calcutta Christian Observer* (1855 and 1865) and the *Calcutta Missionary Herald* (1840 and 1841).

Roger E. Hedlund

Photius (c. 820–891), Byzantine patriarch and a dominant figure in Byzantine life. Born in Constantinople to an aristocratic family, Photius received an education of the first rank in philosophy, law, literature, theology, and the sciences. About 850, after serving as a professor at the university in Constantinople, he was appointed chancellor of the empire. In 851 he took part in a delegation to the caliph's court near Baghdad, for dialogue with Islamic theologians. In 858, still a layman, Photius was elected patriarch and enthroned on Christmas day, replacing Ignatius, who had been forced to resign under accusation of high treason. The resignation of Ignatius and enthronement of Photius precipitated years of debate and discord with the papacy. The main theological issue concerned the desire of church leaders in the West to add to the Nicene Creed the *Filioque* clause (stating that the Holy Spirit proceeds from the Father "and the Son"), which was rejected by Photius. In addition, Photius challenged the papacy's claims of absolute authority over the church.

In 867, following Photius's refusal to serve Holy Communion to the emperor, Basil I, on account of his murder of co-emperor Michael III, Photius was deposed and Ignatius was restored to the patriarchate. Ten years later, following the death of Ignatius, Photius was returned to the patriarchal throne. Peace was finally restored between the eastern and western churches, Photius having secured freedom and independence from Latin domination.

Photius's talents and wide-ranging intellectual aptitudes are evident in his writing and in the missionary activity initiated during his tenure. Missions among the Armenians, Georgians, Bulgarians, Slavs, and Russians brought not only Orthodox Christianity but also new civilization, laws, learning, and institutions. Under the direction of Photius, Byzantine missionaries followed three basic principles: learn the language of the people to be evangelized; prepare translations of the Bible and liturgical texts; and establish worshiping communities.

In 886, Photius was forced to resign by the new emperor, Leo II, and he died in exile. He was buried at the convent of St. Jeremiah, in a suburb of Constantinople. In recognition of his remarkable life, history has bestowed on him the title "Great." The Orthodox Church celebrates his feast day on February 6.

BIBLIOGRAPHY Francis Dvornik, *The Photian Schism: History and Legend* (1948); Asterios Gerostergios, *St. Photios the Great* (1980); John Kallos, ed., *Saint Photios, Patriarch of Constantinople* (1992); Cyril Mango, *The Homilies of Photius* (1958); Despina Stratoudaki White, *Patriarch Photios of Constantinople* (1982; contains translations of 52 of Photius's letters).

Dimitrios G. Couchell

Pickett, J(arrell) Waskom (1890–1981), American Methodist missionary and bishop in India. Pickett was born in northeast Texas, the son of a Methodist minister. He spent his boyhood days in Wilmore, Kentucky, where he later graduated from Asbury College in 1907, in the same class with E. Stanley *Jones. In 1910 he was sent to India by the Methodist Board of Missions as pastor of the Lucknow English church. For the next 25 years he served variously as pastor, superintendent, evangelist, and editor of *The Indian Witness.* In 1935 he was elected to the episcopacy and served in that capacity for 21 years, until his retirement in 1956. In retirement he served as visiting professor of missions at Boston University School of Theology.

Pickett was an able administrator. He zealously promoted the work of evangelism in his area and took keen interest in the institutional life of the church, especially schools and hospitals. He was instrumental in the founding of Leonard Theological College and the United Mission to Nepal (1953). The construction of church buildings for rural congregations was one of his chief concerns. He was also an able statesman on behalf of the entire church in India, maintaining close contact with such national leaders as Prime Minister Jawaharlal Nehru, Mahatma Gandhi, and B. R. Ambedkar, champion of the untouchable castes in India. The prime minister commended him for his efforts to organize relief for the countless victims of the bloody Hindu-Muslim riots in the aftermath of independence. Perhaps Pickett's greatest contribution was the research on group movements that he directed at the request of the India National Christian Council. The results were published in a book, *Christian Mass Movements in India* (1933). Another American missionary in India, Donald *McGavran, was greatly influenced by the research, and this eventually led to the inauguration of the modern church growth movement.

BIBLIOGRAPHY J. Waskom Pickett, *My Twentieth-Century Odyssey* (1980), *The Indian Witness,* Nov. 1, 1956, pp. 10–11. "Bishop J. W. Pickett," *Indian Witness,* Sept. 15, 1981, pp. 8–9 (obit.); John T. Seamands, "J. Waskom Pickett," in Gerald H. Anderson et al., eds., *Mission Legacies* (1994), pp. 348–354. The archives of Asbury College, Wilmore, Kentucky, contain various unclassified personal correspondence and handwritten materials left by Bishop Pickett.

John T. Seamands

Pierce, Robert (Bob) Willard (1914–1978), founder of World Vision and Samaritan's Purse. Born in Fort Dodge, Iowa, and converted as a teenager in California, Pierce made his mark as a youth evangelist in Los Angeles and Seattle and in the fast-growing Youth for Christ movement. Although he was president of the student body of Pasadena Nazarene College, he failed to return for his final year and was at first denied licensure, but was later ordained by the Church of the Nazarene. He received an honorary doctorate from Northwestern Schools in Minneapolis (now Northwestern College).

Overseas preaching assignments in China and Korea introduced Pierce to needs he could not brush aside, and his conspicuous platform and film-making skills soon became fund-raising instruments to match the obligations he assumed, founding World Vision (WV) in 1950 to back his ministry. WV sponsored orphans, built hospitals, delivered relief to refugees and victims of war and disaster, and ultimately became the world's largest Protestant agency for evangelism, development, and relief, working in more than eighty countries with a yearly budget of hundreds of millions of dollars. Pierce's well-known words "Let my heart be broken with the things that break the heart of God," reflected his Christ-like compassion for orphans, widows, and impoverished peoples everywhere. The need, to him, constituted a mandate to respond. However, his pattern of responding first and later seeking endorsement (and funding) from his board eventually led to his resignation from WV in 1967; in 1969 he established Samaritan's Purse, which he headed until his death.

The intensity of Pierce's response to his vision of the world's needs gradually eroded the foundations of his marriage to Lorraine Johnson and ended in separation and tragedy for the couple and their three daughters. The family was reconciled just four days before he died of leukemia.

BIBLIOGRAPHY Marilee Pierce Dunker, *Man of Vision, Woman of Prayer* (1980); Richard Gehman, *Let My Heart Be Broken* (1960); Franklin Graham with Jeanette Lockerbie, *Bob Pierce, This One Thing I Do* (1983); Robert W. Pierce and Ken Anderson, *This Way to the Harvest* (1949); Norman B. Rohrer, *Open Arms* (1987).

W. Dayton Roberts

Pierre Maurice. *See* Peter the Venerable de Montboissier.

Pierson, Arthur Tappan (1837–1911), mission theorist and promoter. Pierson catalyzed the late nineteenth-century American evangelical missionary movement. With a growing reputation as Bible scholar and orator, he became pastor in 1869 of the prestigious Fort Street Presbyterian Church in Detroit. In 1876, after the church burned down, Pierson held services in the local opera house and a revival resulted. Feeling he had been called to a gospel-oriented rather than a socially prominent ministry, he became pastor in 1883 of Bethany (Presbyterian) Church in Philadelphia, a church which engaged in missions among the urban poor. While he was its pastor, Pierson ran a missionary training school and developed a national reputation as a promoter of missions. In 1885, at a Bible conference sponsored by revivalist Dwight L. *Moody, Pierson called on Protestant churches to launch a worldwide missionary campaign. In 1886 he authored *The Crisis of Missions*, the major missions promotional book of the era. He also spoke on missions to a group of YMCA collegians at an 1886 summer conference convened by Moody at Northfield, Massachusetts. As a result, 100 young men volunteered to be foreign missionaries, and the Student Volunteer Movement for Foreign Missions (SVM) was born.

Pierson's belief that world evangelization would usher in Christ's return was the key to his passion for mission. He authored the watchword of the SVM, "the evangelization of the world in this generation." He promoted missions through hundreds of books, articles, speeches, and the *The Missionary Review of the World* which he edited (1888–1911), the most important nondenominational mission journal of its day. After attending the London Centenary Conference in 1888, he began to spend time in England as missions advocate and interim pastor at Charles H. Spurgeon's Metropolitan Tabernacle. He acted as elder statesman to the emerging "faith mission" movement, influencing among others the Africa Inland Mission and the Oriental Missionary Society.

Pierson devoted the final period of his life to Bible teaching and to holiness spirituality. After being rebaptized in 1896, he was excommunicated by his denomination but continued to worship as a Presbyterian. He wrote fourteen books on Bible study and was an original editor of the Scofield Reference Bible. In 1910 he set out to tour missions in East Asia, but he grew ill and returned home to Brooklyn, where he died. All seven of his children did missionary work, and mission leaders like Robert E. *Speer, Samuel *Zwemer, and Stephen *Neill traced their inspiration for missions to him or to his writings.

BIBLIOGRAPHY Arthur T. Pierson, *The Divine Enterprise of Missions* (1891), *Evangelistic Work in Principle and Practice* (1887), *Forward Movements of the Last Half Century* (1905), *The Miracles of Missions*, 4 vols. (1891–1901), and *The New Acts of the Apostles; or, the Marvels of Modern Missions* (1893). Delavan L. Pierson, *Arthur T. Pierson* (1912); Dana L. Robert, "Arthur Tappan Pierson and Forward Movements of Late Nineteenth-Century Evangelicalism" (Ph.D. diss., Yale Univ., 1984) and "Arthur Tappan Pierson," in Gerald H. Anderson et al., eds., *Mission Legacies* (1994), pp. 28–36.

Dana L. Robert

Pigneau de Béhaine, Pierre-Joseph-Georges (1741–1799), Catholic missionary and French patriot. Pigneau was born in Origny-en-Thiérache, France. In 1765 he became a member of the Paris Foreign Mission Society and the same year went to the Cochin China. In 1770 he became titular bishop of Adran and in 1771 vicar apostolic of Cochin China (area of Saigon and southern region of Vietnam). During the civil war that broke out in 1770, he helped Prince Nguyen-Anh through skillful negotiating and with the help of French soldiers to regain the throne of Cochin China and eventually to ascend the imperial throne of Annam. Pigneau personally signed the treaty between France and Cochin China (1787). As a result, under Nguyen-Anh (whose imperial name was Jalong) the Christians who had been severely persecuted were left in peace for some time and had a chance to reorganize. But this did not last long. Nguyen-Anh's successor was his son, Minh-Mang, who became emperor in 1821. Although taught by Pigneau himself, who loved him like a son, he was bitterly opposed to foreigners because of the imperialistic conquests of the colonial powers of the time. So anti-Christian persecutions broke out again.

In French history Pigneau is praised as a patriot. He is also esteemed for his linguistic work, which prepared the way for the *Dictionarium Anamatico-Latinum* (1838) published by Taberd, and the *Catéchisme Cochinchinois* (1838). He was a priest of very deep faith. He died in Saigon and was buried there. On August 3, 1861, the French emperor declared his grave a national monument.

BIBLIOGRAPHY J.-B. Piolet, *La France au dehors: Les missions catholiques françaises au XIXe siècle*, vol. 2 (1902), pp. 416–419; E. M. Durand, "Evêque et patriote: Mgr. Pigneau de Béhaine, Evêque d'Adran," *Revue d'Histoire des Missions* 3 (1926): 353–369, 549–580 (includes bibliography); A. Lannay, *Histoire de la mission de Cochinchine, 1658–1823, documentes historiques*, vol. 3 (1771–1823) (1925).

Karl Müller, SVD

Pike, Kenneth Lee (1912–), linguist and Bible translator. Born in Connecticut in a Presbyterian family, Pike's career dates from 1935, when he began to translate the New Testament into Mixtec, a language of Mexico, and soon became a leader of the Summer Institute of Linguistics (SIL). His Ph.D. in linguistics (University of Michigan, 1942), his translation work, his teaching linguistics to prospective and active Bible translators at SIL training programs, and his wide-ranging research led to important discoveries about language that have strongly influenced missionary linguistics. He taught linguistics part-time at the University of Michigan from 1948 to 1977 and traveled worldwide to consult with Bible translators and others on linguistic problems, holding seminars, and lecturing, a practice he continued in retirement. Pike's earliest work was on the sound structures of languages and included books on phonetics, the linguistic analysis of sound systems, tone languages, and English intonation. He then developed "tagmemics," an extensive theory of language and its relation to culture. He also wrote scores of papers on linguistic phenomena he found in different parts of the world, as well as poetry and prose expressions of his life and faith. Later he studied philosophy, searching for ways to inject his Christian understanding and linguistic insights into that field. Much of Pike's research and theoretical work has been done to meet the needs of translators, part of its stimulus coming out of the linguistic problems he and others were finding. A second motive has been to give SIL workers credibility with scholars and government officials through producing his own theoretically insightful and descriptively sound scholarly work, and stimulating colleagues to do the same. Pike's wife, Evelyn (Griset), has been a close collaborator in much of his later work. Eunice Victoria Pike, his sister, was one of the first two women Bible translators with SIL and made useful linguistic contributions as well.

BIBLIOGRAPHY Pike's most widely used textbook is *Phonemics: A Technique for Reducing Language to Writing*; his most extensive theoretical contribution to linguistics, with important implications for anthropology, is *Language in Relation to a Unified Theory of the Structure of Human Behavior* (1954–1960; 2d ed., 1967). A few of Pike's wide-ranging shorter writings are included in Ruth M. Brend, *Kenneth L. Pike: Selected Writings* (1972). Eunice V. Pike, *Ken Pike: Scholar and Christian* (1981) is a biography. See also Ruth M. Brend, *Kenneth Lee Pike Bibliography* (1987); Ruth M. Brend and Kenneth L. Pike, eds., *The Summer Institute of Linguistics: Its Work and Contributions* (1977).

William A. Smalley

Pilhofer, Georg (1881–1973), Lutheran missionary in Papua New Guinea. Pilhofer grew up in northern Bavaria in modest circumstances and even as a boy was attracted to mission service abroad. Papua New Guinea seemed the obvious choice because it had just been entered as a new mission field in 1886 by the Neuendettelsau Mission. Its pioneer missionary Johann *Flierl was later to become Pilhofer's father-in-law. During 34 years of service, followed by 7 arduous years of internment in Australia during World War II, Pilhofer was mainly responsible for the school system of the mission and distinguished himself as a linguist and writer, chiefly in the Kâte language, in which he wrote the first grammar and textbooks for the training of teachers. After his return to Germany he taught in the Neuendettelsau Mission seminary and wrote its official history. In 1949 he received an honorary doctorate at the University of Erlangen.

BIBLIOGRAPHY George Pilhofer, *Die Geschichte der Neuendettelsauer Mission in New Guinea,* 3 vols. (1961–1963); Herwig Wagner and Hermann Reiner, eds., *The Lutheran Church in Papua New Guinea: The First Hundred Years, 1886–1986* (1986).

Hans-Werner Gensichen

Pilkington, George Lawrence (1865–1897), Church Missionary Society (CMS) lay missionary in Uganda. A graduate of the University of Cambridge and strongly influenced by the Keswick movement, Pilkington arrived in Buganda (now Uganda) with Bishop Alfred *Tucker's party in 1891. There he found a militarized society, rent by religious factionalism and the conflicts of the colonial scramble. Pilkington's remarkable linguistic ability enabled him quickly to get alongside the Baganda soldiers and to realize their spiritual hunger and desire for literacy. In 1893, troubled by the confusion of Christianity and politics, he went on retreat to Kome Island, where he had an experience of the Holy Spirit. This sparked off a religious revival that profoundly affected the life of the Ugandan church, an inspiration to the Balokole revival of the 1930s, which looked back to Pilkington as a role model. Pilkington's other great contribution was his translation of the Bible into Luganda. Ironically, despite his desire for a purely spiritual understanding of Christianity, he was a firm believer in the benefits of British colonialism. In 1897 he accompanied his beloved Baganda soldiers as they went to quell the mutiny of Sudanese troops in eastern Uganda. Pilkington's death in battle was universally mourned.

BIBLIOGRAPHY C. F. Harford Battersby, *Pilkington of Uganda* (1898). J. V. Taylor, *The Growth of the Church in Buganda* (1958) gives a memorable account of the period.

Kevin Ward

Pinkerton, Robert (1780–1859) British and Foreign Bible Society (BFBS) pioneer in Europe. Born in Foulshiels, near Selkirk, Scotland, Pinkerton was trained as a printer by the Edinburgh Missionary Society (EMS). After serving at the EMS southern Russia station from 1805 to 1808, he withdrew from the EMS and moved to Moscow, where he had Moravian in-laws. There he worked with Princess Meshcherskaia in translating and printing tracts. John *Paterson of the BFBS arrived in Saint Petersburg in 1812, which led to the founding of the Russian Bible Society the next year. In 1814 Pinkerton also received an appointment to represent the BFBS. He worked for new Scriptures and retrieval of old texts.

In London from 1823 to 1830, Pinkerton assumed Karl F. A. *Steinkopf's duties from 1827. From 1830 supervision of continental Bible projects was transferred to Frankfurt, a major printing center. Having done much to build Europe's Bible societies, Pinkerton's challenge after the BFBS instituted regulations against publication of the Apocrypha in 1826 was to foster the colportage system of Scripture distribution. He traveled tirelessly in the task, also pioneering the placing of Bibles in hotel bedrooms. He retired, ill, in 1857.

BIBLIOGRAPHY Robert Pinkerton, *Platon* (1814; on the Orthodox Church and sects), *Extracts of Letters: Russia, Poland, Germany* (1817), and *Russia; or, Miscellaneous Observations* (1833, 1970). See also James F. Clarke, "Russian Bible Society," in *Modern Encyclopedia of Soviet and Russian History*, Joseph Wieczynski, ed. (1976), 32:69–73. See also reports of BFBS, 1813–1859.

Nancy Stevenson

Pirminius (Pirmin) (d. 753?), Benedictine missionary bishop in Germany. Pirminius (date of birth unknown), a Benedictine monk and abbot, was a pioneer missionary bishop in the upper Rhine region. Probably a Visigoth from southern Europe (Aquitaine or Spain), he had no specific diocese and was thus free to open up new territory. He founded Reichenau and other monasteries (Murbach, Gegenbach, Hornbach) as centers from which evangelization might develop. Pirminius's rather typical missionary manual, *Scarapsus,* contains the oldest surviving text of the Apostle's Creed, a history of salvation, and a commentary on the Creed. *Dicta Pirmini* is probably his own. There is a ninth-century biography. Recognized by the Roman Catholic Church as a saint, his feast day is November 3.

BIBLIOGRAPHY A. Angenendt, *Monachi peregrini: Studien zu Pirmin und den monastischen Vorstellung der frühen Mittelalters* (1972).

Anthony J. Gittins, CSSp

Pitkin, Horace T(racy) (1869–1900), Yale graduate whose death during the 1900 Boxer Rebellion influenced the founding of the Yale China Mission. Pitkin was born in Philadelphia; his mother was a direct descendant of Elihu Yale, while his father came from a long line of Pitkins that settled in Manchester, Connecticut. Entering Phillips Academy in Exeter, New Hampshire, in 1884 Pitkin took a leading role in the campus Christian Endeavor movement. Entering Yale in 1888, he excelled in music, writing, and volunteer activities. He was widely admired for his sunny disposition and strong convictions. In the summer of 1889 at Dwight L. *Moody's Northfield (Massachusetts) School, he signed the Student Volunteer Movement (SVM) pledge, indicating his intention to become a missionary. Following graduation from Yale in 1892, he entered Union Theological Seminary, New York, then spent an interim year as traveling secretary for the SVM. In 1894, with his financée, Letitia Thomas, a graduate of Mount Holyoke College, Massachusetts, he offered himself for service with the American Board of Commissioners for Foreign Missions. Following graduation from Union (1896), and then marriage to Letitia, he sailed from New York for China in November 1896, traveling via the Holy Land, Egypt, and India and reaching Tientsin (Tianjin) in May 1897. At Paoting (Baoting) barely three years later (Letitia and an infant son were then in America), Pitkin was beheaded by Chinese Boxers while defending two single missionary women. In all, fourteen Presbyterian, Congregational, and China Inland Mission missionaries were martyred at Paoting.

BIBLIOGRAPHY Sherwood Eddy, *Pathfinders of the World Missionary Crusade* (1945), pp. 48–53; Robert E. Speer, *A Memorial of Horace Tracy Pitkin* (1903) and *Young Men Who Overcame* (1905).

James A. Scherer

Pitman, Charles (1796–1884), London Missionary Society (LMS) missionary in Rarotonga, Cook Islands. Pitman was born at Portsmouth, England, in 1796, and became a Congregational Church member and a clerk and superintendent in a timber yard before applying to the LMS. He was trained at the LMS seminary at Gosport and sailed to the South Seas in 1824, accompanied by his wife, Elizabeth Nelson (Corrie), of Newport, Isle of Wight. He was ordained in Tahiti in 1825 and initially learned the Tahitian language at Raiatéa and Tahaa (1826–1827). He served soon afterward in the Cook Islands on Rarotonga, where he was stationed at Ngatangiia (1827–1855) and worked with John *Williams and Aaron *Buzacott of the Avarua station. Pitman was an accomplished scholar in biblical languages, a pastor, and a mentor of aspiring Cook Islander missionaries, including *Ta'unga. He was regarded by colleagues as a loner and a man of one station. His authoritative translations for the mission press showed his mastery of the language (partly due to Ta'unga's role as informant) and included Bunyan's *Pilgrim's Progess* in addition to the Bible. He and his wife often complained of ill health and visited Tahiti (1835–1836) and England (1837–1839) for recuperation. A final restorative visit to Sydney in 1855 led to his retirement there in that year. He survived his wife who died in 1860.

BIBLIOGRAPHY John Garrett, *To Live among the Stars: Christian Origins in Oceania* (1985); Niel Gunson, *Messengers of Grace: Evangelical Missionaries in the South Seas, 1797–1860* (1978); Richard Lovett, *The History of the London Missionary Society, 1795–1895* (1899). Pitman's papers are in the Council for World Mission collections at SOAS, Univ. of London, and the Mitchell Library, Sydney, including a six-volume journal, 1827–1842.

John Garrett

Pius XI (1857–1939), the missionary pope. Pius was born Achille Ratti at Desio, near Milan. Ordained priest in 1879, he did parish and academic ministry and served in the Ambrosian Library in Milan. In 1914 he was appointed prefect of the Vatican Library. In 1918 he was named apostolic visitor and, one year later, titular archbishop, papal nuncio to Poland, as well as chief commissioner for Silesia, East and West Prussia. He found himself in diplomatic tensions both with Poland and with Germany, a situation from which he was freed when he was appointed archbishop of Milan and cardinal. He was elected pope on February 6, 1922.

During Pius's long pontificate (1922–1939), the papacy and the Roman curia acquired unprecedented moral and religious esteem. By negotiating the Lateran Pact and Concordat with Italy in 1929, Pius downplayed the church's temporal and political interests and underlined its spiritual role. His mission program to promote evangelization in theory and in practice was outstanding, as was evident in the Vatican's 1925 missionary exhibit and the 1926 key mission encyclical *Rerum ecclesiae.* This document stressed that all the faithful are responsible for evangelization and for collaboration through prayer and sacrifice. It promoted missionary vocations, formation of local clergy and catechists, preparation of indigenous leadership, and admission of local people of both sexes into existing religious institutes. It also called for founding new institutions adapted to local conditions, and furtherance of contemplative orders in mission territories. With this encyclical Pius provided for the church's future in countries that were soon to achieve their political independence.

In an apostolic letter addressed to vicars and prefects apostolic in China, Pius ruled out involvement in political activities and stressed the purely spiritual nature of the missions and warned against setting up barriers between the foreign clergy and the native clergy. In October 1926 he personally ordained in St. Peter's the first six Chinese bishops of the modern era. One year later he ordained the first Japanese bishop, and in 1933 the first Vietnamese bishop. He would have liked to ordain the first five African bishops also, but this privilege was reserved to his successor.

BIBLIOGRAPHY Francis J. Burke, *Pius XI, Pope of the Missions* (1929); C. Confalonieri, *Pio XI, visto da vicino* (1957); J. Lavarenne, *L'oeuvre missionnaire de Pie XI* (1935); Joseph Metzler, "Pius XI," in Gerald H. Anderson et al., eds., *Mission Legacies* (1994), pp. 55–61; Armand Olichon, *Pie XI et les missions* (1928); Josef Schmidlin, *Papstgeschichte der neuesten Zeit,* vol. 4, *Pius XI (1922–1939)* (1939); Giovanni Battista Tragella, *Pio XI, Papa missionario* (1930).

Josef Metzler, OMI

Pius XII (1875–1958), pope and promoter of missions. Pius XII (r. 1939–1958) was born Eugenio Maria Guiseppe Giovanni Pacelli into a family of jurists in Rome. He studied at the Gregorian University and at the Sant' Appollinare before his ordination as priest in 1899. He obtained a doctorate of laws in 1902. Entering the secretariat of state, he became a close collaborator of Pietro Gasparri in codifying canon law. In 1914 he became secretary of the Congregation for Extraordinary Ecclesiastical Affairs. *Benedict XV consecrated him titular archbishop of Sardes and made him nuncio to Bavaria in 1917 and to the German Republic in 1920. He became cardinal in 1929 and succeeded Gasparri as secretary of state. He was elected pope to succeed *Pius XI on the threshold of World War II. Pius XII managed to get Rome declared an open city, thus protecting it from possible destruction. He organized refugee assistance and soup kitchens to help people displaced by war. He also assisted Jews, especially those in Rome, but whether he did all he could have done remains controversial.

During his long pontificate, Pius XII expounded on a wide range of doctrine. The encyclical *Mystici Corporis* helped lay the groundwork for the ecclesiology of Vatican II; *Divino afflante Spiritu* permitted Roman Catholic exegetes to use the tools of biblical criticism. He urged greater lay participation in the Mass, reformed the Holy Week rites, and relaxed eucharistic fasts. He reversed the ban on participation in rites of ancestor veneration that had been in force since *Clement XI. He wrote two encyclicals on the missions—*Evangelii praecones* (1951), which helped clarify norms and principles regarding the practice of mission, and *Fidei donum* (1957), on the state of the missions in general and Africa in particular. He urged Europe and North America to send missionaries to Latin America after World War II to protect that region's Catholics against Communism and proselytism by Protestants. This influx played an important role in the subsequent revitalization of the Latin American church.

BIBLIOGRAPHY *Acta* are to be found in *Acta Apostolicae Sedis,* vols. 31–50. Pius's allocutions and radio addresses are available in Italian in a twenty-volume edition (1939–1958); Michael Carroll, *Pius XII: Greatness Dishonoured* (1980); Alden Hatch, *Crown of Glory: The Life of Pius XII* (1958).

Robert J. Schreiter, CPPS

Planque, Augustin (1826–1907), superior of the Society of African Missions (SMA). Born in Chemy, France, Planque studied in seminaries at Cambrai and was ordained in 1850. He taught philosophy at Arras, where he developed an interest in missions. In 1856 he joined Marion *Brésillac, who was then founding the SMA. In 1859 Brésillac and four companions died of yellow fever in Sierra Leone. As the most senior of the two remaining priests in the society, Planque signaled his intention to continue the work, and Propaganda Fide responded by nominating him superior of the society and of its seminary in Lyon. Planque directed the fortunes of the society single-handedly until 1901, when a vicar general was appointed to assist him. In 1867, when the survival of the society was still at stake, Planque was nominated pro-vicar of the society's mission in Dahomey. He chose to remain in Europe and delegate authority to a mission superior. This arrangement created difficulties that were resolved only when Propaganda Fide nominated a bishop to the mission in 1891. Planque's great achievement was to put the society on a solid footing; he did this by carefully overseeing the seminary, expanding the society to other European countries, paying constant attention to funding and recruitment, obtaining additional missions in Africa, securing the cooperation of the French government, and providing firm guidance and leadership. At the time of his death there were 266 priests and brothers in the SMA.

Planque was also founder of the Congregation of Our Lady of Apostles, formed at Lyon in 1876. This international missionary sisterhood, whose members work principally on the African continent but also in the Middle East and Europe, today comprises some 1,200 members from twenty countries across the northern hemisphere and from several African countries.

BIBLIOGRAPHY Patrick Gantly, *Mission to West Africa,* 2 vols. (1991); Patrick Gantly and Ellen Thorp, *For This Cause* (1992); René F. Guilcher, *Augustin Planque* (1928).

Edmund M. Hogan, SMA

Plasencia (Portocarrero), Juan de (d. 1590), Spanish Franciscan missionary in the Philippines. Born in Portocarrero, Spain, Plasencia entered the Franciscan order in Italy and took as his surname his birthplace in Spain. Arriving with the first Franciscan mission in the Philippines in 1578, he promoted the policy of *reducción,* by which scattered populations were brought together into villages for more effective evangelization. This approach proved more successful in the relatively more densely populated territory around Laguna de Bay than in less populated areas of the country. Schools were prominent features in the many towns he created. One of the first to master the Tagalog language, he presented a manuscript grammar and dictionary to the first synod of Manila in 1582, where it was well received. The synod also accepted his catechism, which became the basis for the *Doctrina Christiana,* the first book to be published in the Philippines (1593). At government request in 1589 he wrote a treatise on the customs of the Tagalogs, which was approved as the norm for legal cases among Filipinos and which was accompanied by a description of pre-Hispanic religious beliefs and practices. Finally, he distinguished himself among many of the early missionaries, in his defense of Filipino rights against Spanish oppressors.

BIBLIOGRAPHY A biography of Plasencia is included in *Crónica de la Provincia de San Gregorio Magno de religiosos descalzos de N. S. P. San Francisco en las Islas Filipinas, China, Japón, etc., escrita por el Padre Fray Francisco de Santa Inés... en 1676* (1892), 1: 513–522. Plasencia's treatises are in ibid., 2: 590–603. An English translation of the treatises appears in Emma Helen Blair and James Alexander Robertson, *The Philippine Islands, 1493–1898* (1903–1909) 7: 173–196. See also Leandro Tormo Sanz, "Método de aprendizaje de lenguas empleado por los franciscanos en Japón y Filipinas (ss. XVI–XVII)," in Victor Sánchez and Cayetano S. Fuertes, eds., *España en Extremo Oriente: Filipinas, China, Japón: Presencia Franciscana, 1578–1978* (1978), pp. 377–405; John N. Schumacher, "The Manila Synodal Tradition," *Philippine Studies* 27 (1979): 285–348.

John N. Schumacher, SJ

Plath, Karl Heinrich Christian (1829–1901), pioneer Protestant missiologist. Born and raised in eastern Germany, Plath started his career as a Lutheran minister and missiologist in August H. *Francke's institutions at Halle in 1856. From 1863 he lived and worked in Berlin, where he became a teacher in the seminary of the Berlin Mission and then director of the Gossner Mission in 1871. He made a name for himself by fighting for the idea of having missions recognized as a separate discipline in the theological curriculum. He succeeded in obtaining a part-time lectureship in the science of mission at Berlin University and held it for more than 30 years (1869–1901) though without becoming a member of the regular teaching staff. As a missiologist he shared the views of Alexander *Duff, whom he visited in Edinburgh. He published notable studies on the history, theory, and practice of foreign missions, all of which expounded his conviction that mission should hold a central place in the life of the church and, more specifically, in academic training for the ministry. Plath thus paved the way for Gustav *Warneck's concept of comprehensive scientific missiology.

BIBLIOGRAPHY Karl H. Chr. Plath, *Die Erwählung der Völker im Lichte der Missionsgeschichte* (1867), *Drei neue Missionsfragen* (1868), *The Subject of Missions Considered under Three New Aspects* (1873), *Die Missions-gedanken des Freiherrn von Leibnitz* (1869), and *Missions-Studien* (1870). W. Bork, *K. H. Chr. Plath* (1929); Georg Plath, *Karl Plath: Inspektor der Gossnerschen Mission. Ein Lebensbild* (2d ed., 1904).

Hans-Werner Gensichen

Platt, W(illiam) J(ames) (1893–1993), British Wesleyan Methodist missionary in West Africa. In 1916, following grammar school and two years' preparation for the Wesleyan ministry at Didsbury College, Platt went to Dahomey (modern Benin) under the Methodist Missionary Society (MMS). From 1920 he superintended the Porto Novo and Anecho (Togo) circuits. Welcomed in 1924 by churches that had been inspired by the mission of William Wadé *Harris, he administered from Abidjan a new MMS French West Africa district. He integrated more than 160 Harris-related indigenous churches into Wesleyan structures, established monogamy as the standard for the 32,000 members of these churches, and provided training for illiterate thousands. In 1926 his envoy, Pierre Benoît, brought a Harris-signed document naming Platt as Harris's successor and ordering hesitant believers into the Methodist Church under threat of God's wrath. This was affirmed in a 1928 visit to Harris from Ebrié John *Ahui, who later headed the Harrist Church.

Tensions with MMS over policy differences led in 1930 to Platt's return to Great Britain, where he worked with the British and Foreign Bible Society until 1960, when he retired as general secretary. Toronto University awarded him the D.D. In 1985, the Ivorian Methodist Church celebrated autonomy in his presence, and Ivory Coast decorated him as Commander in its National Order.

BIBLIOGRAPHY W(illiam) J. Platt, "Facing Our Task on the Ivory Coast," *The Foreign Field,* August 23, 1927, pp. 261–265, *An African Prophet: The Ivory Coast Movement and What Came of It* (1934), and *From Fetish to Faith: The Growth of the Church in West Africa* (1935). Contention about the 1926 document signed by Harris is discussed in David A. Shank, *Prophet Harris, The "Black Elijah" of West Africa* (1994), pp. 243 ff.

David A. Shank

Plütschau, Heinrich (1677–1752), pioneer missionary of the Tranquebar mission. Co-worker with the pietist

Lutheran mission pioneer Bartolomäus *Ziegenbalg, Plütschau was overshadowed by the latter to the extent that his year of death has wrongly been stated as 1746. A native of Wesenberg, Mecklenburg, he was educated at Berlin and Halle, was selected for the Tranquebar mission, and arrived there in 1706. Six years older than Ziegenbalg and not nearly so brilliant a student, he was "cut out to be an admirable follower but not a leader" (Stephen Neill). According to the original plan, Ziegenbalg was to concentrate on the Portuguese language, the lingua franca on the Coromandel coast, and Plütschau on Tamil. But for unknown reasons the arrangement was soon reversed, probably to the advantage of the mission, although Plütschau later started a Tamil language study group at Halle. In any case, Plütschau assumed his share of responsibility for the growing Tamil church until he was sent home in 1711 to defend the mission against critics in Europe, including some in the royal court at Copenhagen. In 1714 he was called to a pastorate at Beidenfleth, Holstein, Germany. This was done with the concurrence of August H. *Francke, who appreciated Plütschau's faith and loyalty but did not think him qualified to become director of a proposed mission seminary at Copenhagen.

BIBLIOGRAPHY For details of Plütschau's life and work, histories of the Tranquebar mission may be consulted, especially E. A. Lehmann, *It Began at Tranquebar* (1956). See also Stephen Neill, *A History of Christianity in India,* vol. 2 (1985), pp. 28-43.

Hans-Werner Gensichen

Plymire, Victor Guy (1881-1956), missionary in Tibet and China. Born in Loganville, Pennsylvania, Plymire studied at the Missionary Training Institute at Nyack, New York, and received ordination from the Christian and Missionary Alliance. He traveled in 1908 to northwest China in order to gain access for ministry in Tibet. He waited 16 years to baptize his first Tibetan convert. After returning to the United States in 1920, he identified with the Pentecostal movement and returned to Tibet as an Assemblies of God missionary in 1922. During his long ministry, Plymire faced enormous hardships in preaching the gospel on his treks across Tibet, and he endured several deaths in his immediate family. He continued as a missionary until forced to leave in 1949 when the door for mission closed.

BIBLIOGRAPHY David V. Plymire, *High Adventure in Tibet* (1959). An autobiographical account of his early ministry can be found in *Pioneering in Tibet* (c. 1931) and is available, along with his diary, letters, and papers at the Assemblies of God archives, Springfield, Mo.

Gary B. McGee

Podmaniczky, Pál (1885-1949), Hungarian missions leader. A Lutheran pastor and theological teacher, Podmaniczky became interested in missions during his studies in Pozsony, Hungary (Bratislava in present-day Slovakia). Through János *Victor he became coordinator of the Hungarian Student Volunteer Movement (SVM) in 1912. As editor of and contributor to the popular mission periodicals *Hajnal* (Dawn) and *Missziói Lapok* (Mission pages) over almost two decades, he widened the horizons of the Hungarian Protestant churches, which were for the first time regularly informed on the modern missionary movement. In 1926 he presented the first Hungarian outline on the study of missions. Two years later he was appointed professor of the history of religion on the Lutheran theological faculty in Sporon. However, his main impact came through informal meetings on mission-related topics, which influenced several generations of Lutheran pastors. He also organized a mission working group that encouraged students to give presentations on missions in local churches. Deeply influenced by the Finnish revival movement, he emphasized the close link between mission and revival within the local churches.

BIBLIOGRAPHY Pál Podmaniczky, "A misszió tudómányának vázlata" (An outline of the study of mission) (Ph.D. diss., Debrecen), *Theológiai Szemle* 2, nos. 3-6 (1926), and "Az ágostai hitvallás egyháza és a misszió" (The church of the Augsburg confession and mission), in Karoly et al., *Hitvallás és tudomány* (Confession and science) (1930). A significant number of articles by Podmaniczky were published in the mission periodicals *Hajnal* (1913-1914, 1921-1929) and *Missziói Lapok* (1929-1934, 1939). Ilona Podmaniczky, "Egy élet gazdag áldásából valami mutatóba" (Some insights in the rich blessings of a life), *Új Harangszó* 5, no. 42 (1949): 1-2; Anne-Marie Kool, *God Moves in a Mysterious Way: The Hungarian Foreign Mission Movement (1756-1951)* (1993).

Anne-Marie Kool

Polhill, Cecil H. (1860-1938), missionary in China and promoter of Pentecostal missions. Born into a family of the landed English gentry, Polhill attended Eton, where he won a place on the college cricket team, and Jesus College, Cambridge. Converted in 1884, he was encouraged by J. Hudson *Taylor to pursue his calling as a missionary. With his brother, Arthur, and five fellow Cambridge graduates (the famous *Cambridge Seven), he went to China in 1885 with the China Inland Mission (CIM). He returned to England in 1900 due to ill health, and inherited Howbury Hall near Bedford in 1903.

News of the Welsh Revival and similar awakening in other parts of the world prompted him in early 1908 to visit the Azusa Street revival in Los Angeles, California, led in part by William J. *Seymour. Receiving the baptism in the Holy Spirit himself in February 1908, Polhill returned home. Along with Alexander A. Boddy, Anglican vicar of All Saints Church, Sunderland (whose Whitsuntide Conferences spawned the Pentecostal movement in England), he founded the Pentecostal Missionary Union for Great Britain and Ireland (PMU) in 1909. It was the first organized and successful Pentecostal missions agency; Polhill served as its president and directed its operation until 1925, when it was integrated into the newly established Assemblies of God of Great Britain and Ireland. He subsequently retired.

Polhill was the formative influence on the PMU and contributed substantially to its financial needs. It was modeled somewhat after the CIM. The first group of missionaries traveled to China in 1910, and others worked in Tibet and India. The activities of the agency were promoted through Polhill's personal efforts, reports in *Confidence* (edited by Boddy), and Polhill's publication *Fragments of Flame* (later titled *Flames of Fire*).

BIBLIOGRAPHY Edith Blumhofer, "Alexander Boddy and the Rise of Pentecostalism in Great Britain," *Pneuma: The Journal of the Society for Pentecostal Studies* 8 (Spring 1986): 31–40; Donald Gee, *Wind and Flame* (1980); Peter Hocken, "Cecil H. Polhill: Pentecostal Layman," *Pneuma: The Journal of the Society for Pentecostal Studies* 10 (Fall 1988): 116–140; John Pollock, *The Cambridge Seven* (1955). Polhill's memoirs are held in the Assemblies of God archives, Springfield, Mo.

Gary B. McGee

Pollard, Samuel (1864–1915), British missionary in China. Pollard was born at Camelford, in Cornwall. Both of his parents were preachers with the Bible Christian Church. Converted at age 11, Pollard initially prepared for a career with the civil service, but he was influenced toward missions at a London conference in 1885 and sailed for China in 1887 as a missionary of his denomination. After language study, he traveled to Chaotung (Zhaotong) in Yunnan Province and was then assigned to the provincial capital, now called Kunming. During his early missionary years, Pollard engaged in evangelism and a ministry of compassion among the Chinese. In 1907 a people's movement to Christ among the Flowery Miao, a minority nationality, reached the Chaotung area from its starting point in Anshun, Kweichow (Guizhou) Province, and Pollard became its most famed missionary leader. Until his death from typhoid, he established a center for the thousands of new believers in Shihmenkan across the Kweichow provincial border, itinerated widely, planted churches, trained leaders, obtained justice for Miao Christians from officials and landlords, developed a unique script, known as the Pollard script, and used it when he translated the New Testament into the Miao language. He is remembered by Miao Christians as their spiritual ancestor.

BIBLIOGRAPHY W. A. Grist, *Samuel Pollard: Pioneer Missionary in China* (rep., 1971); R. Elliott Kendall, ed., *Eyes of the Earth: The Diary of Samuel Pollard* (1954).

Ralph R. Covell

Polman, Gerrit Roelof (1868–1932), founder of the Dutch Pentecostal movement and missions executive. With a background in the Salvation Army, Polman and his wife, Wilhelmine, visited the United States in the years 1903 to 1905 and joined John Alexander Dowie's Christian Catholic Apostolic Church in Zion City, Illinois. Returning to Amsterdam in 1906, they founded a Dowie Zionist center. Influenced by the Welsh revival and reports of the emerging Pentecostal movement, the Polmans and their followers became Pentecostals the following year. Polman established the Dutch Pentecostal Missionary Society in 1920; it sponsored mission endeavors in Venezuela, Zaire, China, and Indonesia (formerly the Dutch East Indies).

BIBLIOGRAPHY Cornelis van der Laan, *Sectarian against His Will: Gerrit Roelof Polman and the Birth of Pentecostalism in the Netherlands* (1991).

Gary B. McGee

Pomare II (1779–1821), high chief of Tahiti. Pomare befriended the first London Missionary Society missionaries, becoming literate under their tutelage and using their presence to gain prestige among the chiefs of the island. An attack by his rivals forced him to flee to the island of Moorea, taking the missionary Henry *Nott with him. There, in adversity, he began to consider conversion to Christianity. He returned to Tahiti and in 1812 announced his acceptance of the Christian God. His cause was now identified with the Christian cause. In 1815, while he was at Sunday worship, his opponents attacked him. He fought back, shooting down the spokesperson of the opposition even before the traditional signal had been given for commencement of the fighting. In his ensuing victory he refused to permit the cruelties formerly sanctioned for victors. He then proceeded around the island, convincing the traditional believers to destroy their idols, thus depriving them of spiritual power for any rebellion and assuring their future obedience and conversion to Christianity. Tahiti's state religion became Christianity, protected and dominated by Pomare, but his many self-indulgences caused the missionaries to withhold baptism from him until 1819. In that year he promulgated the first Christian law code in the Pacific islands. Alcohol and dissolute living led to his early death.

BIBLIOGRAPHY John Davies, *The History of the Tahitian Mission*, Colin Newbury, ed. (1961); Colin Newbury, *Tahiti Nui* (1980).

Charles W. Forman

Pompallier, (Jean-Baptiste) François (1801–1871), pioneer Catholic missionary bishop of Auckland, New Zealand. Born in Lyons, France, and ordained priest there in 1829, Pompallier joined Marcellin *Champagnat as an aspiring Marist. In 1835 his name was suggested to Rome's Propaganda Fide for a proposed Pacific mission. In April 1836, he became vicar apostolic of the Prefecture of Western Oceania, a district that extended south of the equator between Tahiti and Australia. As a bishop, he did not take vows with the first Marists forming the new congregation but departed in December 1836 with four Marists priests and three brothers. After opening missions under Pierre *Bataillon on Uvea, Wallis Islands, and Pierre *Chanel on Futuna, Pompallier reached New Zealand in 1838. A dedicated missionary, quick in languages, he impressed both the indigenous Maori and Europeans. Obtaining two presses and an experienced printer through Marist superior general Jean-Claude Marie *Colin,

Pompallier wrote numerous pamphlets and booklets in Maori and English about the Catholic religion. Despite his optimistic reports of baptisms, Maori conversions were not easy, some seemingly resulting from rivalry with Protestant tribes. British acquisition of New Zealand and subsequent Maori uprisings made missionary work increasingly difficult, and suspicious English officials wrongly charged complicity when French missions were spared from Maori attacks. The work also changed character when care of European Catholic settlers became the major task. Pompallier also had serious financial inadequacies. His missioners lost confidence as he won Maori converts with expensive gifts while some Marists were almost starving. He continually pressed Colin for more funds, and when effectively bankrupt, wrote to the Society for the Propagation of the Faith and to Rome blaming Colin for his predicament. Pompallier received thirty-six men from Colin in five years but invariably vetoed the latter's practical suggestions for their care—a situation complicated by traditional church difficulties between missionary bishops and religious orders that supplied personnel. Colin managed to persuade Rome in 1842 to subdivide Western Oceania into five vicariates, reducing Pompallier's jurisdiction to the Diocese of Auckland. In 1848 Pompallier met Colin in Rome, but they agreed only that Marists would withdraw from Auckland to a new Marist diocese of Wellington.

Pompallier's later achievements were mixed. Many priests whom he recruited left him, and he was canonically investigated twice over his administration, the second time including personal accusations. He survived financially somehow, until his departure for Europe in 1868, when the diocese was found to be bankrupt. Upon retirement to France he was made an archbishop.

BIBLIOGRAPHY Pompallier's book *Ako Marama o te Hahi Katorica Romana* (Plain teaching of the Roman Catholic Church) (1840) was reprinted many times. Lillian Keys, *The Life and Times of Bishop Pompallier* (1957) includes extensive lists of Pompallier's writings; Keys added further material in *Philip Viard: Bishop of Wellington* (1968); Kevin Roach, "Jean Claude Colin and the Foundation of the New Zealand Mission," *New Zealand Journal of History* 3, no. 1 (1969): 79–83; Ernest R. Simmons, *Pompallier, Prince of Bishops* (1984). Pompallier's letters and papers, including seven books or bound pamphlets in Maori, French, or English, are preserved in the archives of the Archdiocese of Auckland, New Zealand. Other letters are in the archives of the Marist Fathers, Rome, and in the Oceania files of the Propaganda Fide, Rome, where his mission and other reports are also held.

John Hosie, SM

Ponziglione, Paul Mary (1818–1900), Jesuit missionary to Native Americans. Ponziglione was born in Cherasco, Italy, and graduated from the Jesuit University at Torino in 1839. After taking his initial religious vows, he was employed as a teacher and acting vice-minister for the Jesuit College in Genoa, Italy, until 1848, when he resigned his position and in 1851 joined John *Schoenmakers in the Jesuit mission among the Osage Indians in Kansas, where he served until 1886. During these 35 years among the Osage he was official historiographer for the mission, translated portions of the Bible and Catholic catechism into Osage, compiled an Osage dictionary, and was instrumental in establishing numerous mission stations among other Native Americans and white settlers. In 1854 he founded a mission station among the Chippewa and Ottawa in what is now Franklin County, Kansas. From 1857 to 1869 he established more than twelve mission stations among the white settlers in Kansas, and in 1867 established mission stations among the Sac and Fox tribes. Besides his teaching ministry with the Osage, Chippewa, Ottawa, Sac, and Fox Indians, he also offered Catholic instruction, sacraments, and general education to several other Native American tribes in Kansas, Nebraska, Wyoming and Oklahoma. In 1886 he was assigned to lead St. Stephen's mission among the Arapaho Indians who lived in Fremont County, Wyoming. After a short stay he returned to the Osage mission in 1887. From 1889 to 1890 he was assigned to Marquette College, Milwaukee, Wisconsin. In 1890, after a brief reassignment to the Arapaho Indians at St. Stephen's mission, he was transferred to St. Ignatius College, Chicago, where he served until his death.

BIBLIOGRAPHY Gilbert J. Garraghan, *The Jesuits of the Middle United States,* 3 vols. (1938); William White Graves, *Annals of Osage Mission* (1935); John Francis Xavier O'Connor, *The Jesuit Missions in the United States* (1892). Francis Xavier Kuppens, "Journal of Osage Mission" (unpublished manuscript) and Ponziglione's letters and papers are in the Jesuit Missouri Province archives, Saint Louis, Mo.

Paul O. Myhre

Pope, George Uglow (1820–1908), Anglican missionary and scholar in South India. Born on Prince Edward Island, Canada, Pope was sent to India by the Society for the Propagation of the Gospel in Foreign Parts. He arrived in Sawyerpuram in 1842. He founded three seminaries—one in Madras, one at Vediarpuram near Tanjore, and the third in Sawyerpuram. The seminary at Sawyerpuram (1842) developed into a college and in 1880 became affiliated with the University of Madras. Pope had a special love for the Tamil language and published metrical translations of three significant pieces of Tamil religious literature, namely *The Sacred Kurral* (1886), *The Naladiyar* (1893), and *The Tiruvacagam* (1900). He also published *First Lessons in Tamil, with an Easy Catechism in Tamil* (1891). He was for some time a fellow of the University of Madras. After serving in India, Pope returned to England in 1882 to teach at Balliol College and Indian Institute, Oxford. Pope College was founded in honor of him at Sawyerpuram in 1962. The government of the State of Tamil Nadu, India, recognizing his outstanding service to the Tamil language, erected a statue of him on the marina beach in Madras.

BIBLIOGRAPHY Hugald Grafe, *History of Christianity in India,* vol. 4, part 2 (1990); T. J. T. Rajkumar, ed., *Pope Memorial Higher Secondary School, Sawyerpuram: 150th Commemoration Souvenir (1844–1994)* (1994); J. A. Sharrock, *South Indian Mission: Containing Glimpses into the Lives and Customs of the Tamil People* (1910).

M. Thomas Thangaraj

Popley, Herbert Arthur (1878–1960), English missionary in India. Popley was born at Richmond, Surrey, England, received his B.A. at Hackney College, and was ordained October 1901. He then sailed as a missionary of the London Missionary Society (LMS) to India, settling at Erode, Tamil Nadu, where he married Lizzie Milda Bragg of the LMS Bangalore mission in 1908. He was the founder and principal of the Community Training School, which was set up at Erode on Gandhi's basic education principle "learning by doing." After 1921 he did Tamil literary work in Madras. He served as the national general secretary of the Indian YMCA in 1928 and again in 1931–1932. As evangelism secretary of the YMCA in South India, he organized several successful evangelistic campaigns. After retirement he was the correspondent of the Coimbatore Diocese and remained active in the Church of South India until his death in Coonoor, India.

Popley loved India and thoroughly identified himself with everything Indian. He was one of the pioneers of indigenization, church unity, and ecumenism. He worked closely with Sherwood *Eddy, V. S. *Azariah, and K. T. *Paul. He mastered Tamil classics such as *Thirukural* (which he translated into English), and he conducted *Katha Kalkshepams* (storytelling) in Tamil. Having mastered Carnatic music, he introduced it in church services in the form of lyrics. He wrote articles for the *Guardian* and *Young Men of India*. His most important books were *The Music of India* (1921) and *K. T. Paul* (1938).

BIBLIOGRAPHY Popley also published *Handbook of Musical Evangelism* (with L. I. Stephen) (1914), *Handbook for Workers in Evangelistic Campaigns in India* (editor) (1917), *A. S. Appasamy* (1933), and *The Village Goes to School* (1943?).

Mohan D. David

Popov, John. *See* Innocent Veniaminov.

Porres (*or* Porras), Martín de (1579–1639), popular black saint of colonial Lima. Porres was canonized in 1962 by Pope *John XXIII and named the patron saint of social justice. Born out of wedlock of a mulatto mother and a Spanish father who later became governor of Panama, Porres entered the Dominican order in Lima around 1594. He served as a doorkeeper, domestic house cleaner, and manager of an infirmary. He won fame for his charitable works, penances, and curing powers. When he died, the archbishop, the viceroy, and the entire governing board attended his funeral, along with many ordinary inhabitants who revered him as a holy man. In time he became a favorite saint for black Catholics and Christians everywhere who see him as a symbol of racial justice.

BIBLIOGRAPHY José Antonio del Busto, *Saint Martín de Porras* (1992); Stanislaus Fumet, *Life of St. Martin of Porres: Patron Saint of Interracial Justice* (1964); John Chrysostom Kearns, *The Life of Blessed Martin de Porres: Saintly American Negro and Patron of Social Justice* (1937).

Jeffrey Klaiber, SJ

Porter, Lucius Chapin (1880–1958), American missionary educator in China. Born in Tientsin, China, to missionary parents Henry and Elizabeth Porter, Porter graduated from Beloit College (1901) and Yale Divinity School (1906). He also studied at Berlin, Marburg, Jerusalem, and Union Theological Seminary (New York), and received the M.A. at Columbia University in 1916. He married Lillian Lee Dudley in 1908. Under the appointment of the American Board of Commissioners for Foreign Missions (ABCFM) he taught at North China Union College, Tungxian, until 1918, also serving as general secretary of the North China Kung Li Hui from 1917 to 1919. With the establishment of Yenching University in Beijing, Porter served as dean from 1918 to 1922 and began his many years of service as professor of philosophy (until 1949). For various periods he also served as executive secretary of the Harvard-Yenching Institute and taught at the Beijing School of Chinese Studies. During the Japanese occupation he taught at the refugee university in Sichuan Province in 1935 and took charge of the ABCFM properties in Shansi from 1937 to 1939. Interned in 1943, he refused repatriation in order to be on hand when Yenching was restored. Porter was visiting lecturer at Columbia (1924), Harvard (1928–1929, 1931–1932), Claremont (1938), and Beloit (1940–1941), and held honorary degrees from Beloit (D.D.) and New York University (L.H.D.). He was active in dramatics at Yenching and author of *China's Challenge to Christianity* (1924) and *Aids to the Study of Chinese Philosophy* (1934). His grandfather, Jeremiah Porter, was the first Congregational pastor in Chicago; his maternal grandfather, Aaron Chapin, was the first president of Beloit College. His sister, Mary H. Porter, was the first missionary of the Congregational Women's Board of Missions of the Interior; she also served in China.

BIBLIOGRAPHY Fred Field Goodsell, *They Lived Their Faith* (1961), pp. 314–316, has a vivid sketch of Porter; Dwight W. Edwards, *Yenching University* (1959) describes his role in that institution. Other information can be found in *Missionary Herald* and in the files and archives of the United Church Board for World Ministries and of the United Board for Christian Higher Education in Asia.

David M. Stowe

Pott, Francis Lister Hawks (1864–1947), educator and Protestant Episcopal Church missionary in China. Born in New York City and educated at Columbia University and General Theological Seminary, Pott was ordained to the priesthood in 1888. He married Susan N. Wong, daughter of the first Chinese priest ordained by his church in China. A professor of metaphysics, he was appointed head of St. John's College, Shanghai, in 1888, and president of St. John's University in 1896, serving a total of 53 years. He was twice decorated by the Chinese government for his service to China.

While his primary responsibility was with St. John's University, Pott was active in many other mission endeavors, particularly in the development of the fledgling Sheng Kung Hui (Episcopal Church) of China. In ecumenical circles, he served as deputy chairman of the China Centenary Missionary Conference (1907), delegate to the World Missionary Conference in Edinburgh (1910), and president of the Educational Association of China (1914–1915). He also served as president of the China Christian Educational Association (1916–1925), president of the Association of Christian Colleges and Universities in China (1919–1921), chairman of the American Red Cross Society in China during World War I, and chairman of the North China Royal Asiatic Society for two terms of office. His published writings include college-level textbooks, translations of religious studies, a life of Christ, Chinese language-study texts, and several books on Chinese history. He retired to the United States.

BIBLIOGRAPHY The archives of the Episcopal Church, U. S. A., in Austin, Texas, contain the following items: Mary Lamberton, "St. John's University"; F. L. H. Pott, Pott's annual reports from the office of the president, St. John's University; *St. John's Echo*; and Pott's private papers, including his diaries from 1895 to 1947.

Donald E. MacInnis

Potter, Philip A(lford) (1921–), West Indian mission and ecumenical leader. Potter was born in Roseau, Dominica, West Indies. Becoming a Methodist minister, he served as a missionary in Haiti for five years among poor and largely illiterate Creole-speaking people. He represented the Jamaica Student Christian Movement at the world conference on Christian youth (Oslo, 1947), was spokesperson for youth at the World Council of Churches (WCC) assemblies in Amsterdam (1948) and Evanston (1954), and from 1954 to 1960 worked in the WCC youth department in Geneva. He was general secretary of the World's Student Christian Federation and a staff member of the Methodist Missionary Society of London. In 1967 he became director of the WCC Commission on World Mission and Evangelism and editor of the *International Review of Mission*. He was appointed general secretary of the WCC in 1972 and occupied that post until the end of 1984. Afterward he continued international travel and ecumenical involvement. In a resolution honoring Potter on his retirement as general secretary, the central committee of the WCC identified some of the main thrusts which the council owed to his influence: "the insistence on the fundamental unity of Christian witness and Christian service which the gospel commands and makes possible, the correlation of faith and action, the inseparable connection between the personal and spiritual life of Christian believers and their obedient action in the world."

BIBLIOGRAPHY Phillip A. Potter, *Life in All Its Fullness* (1981). Ans J. van der Bent, comp., *The Whole Oikoumene: A Bibliography of the Works of Philip A. Potter* (1980).

Ans J. van der Bent

Pottier, François (1726–1792), missionary of the Paris Foreign Mission Society in China. Pottier was born in Chapelle-Saint-Hippolyte, near Loches, France, and was ordained priest in Tours in September 1753. He evangelized Szechwan (Sichuan) Province from 1756 until his death, during a period when Christianity was officially banned from China. Although other missionaries had been in this region before him, Pottier was the first to take residence for such a long time and to lay the foundation for the local Catholic Church. During the decade following his arrival, he was the only foreign missionary in an area that covered not only Szechwan but also the provinces of Yunnan and Kweichow (Guizhou). In 1767 the Vatican made Pottier vicar apostolic of Szechwan and administrator for the two other territories. He paid special attention to the formation of a native clergy and, with a dispensation from Rome, by 1781 began to ordain Chinese priests not trained in Latin. At the same time, he emphasized a role for catechists and celibate Chinese women in spreading and nurturing the faith. Pottier also made Chinese Christian literature available and established schools for the religious instruction of children. Intermittent persecutions, however, subjected him, his clergy, and church members to long periods in jail or forced them into hiding. At least four missionaries and one Chinese priest lost their lives because of torture. Christianity, nonetheless, grew stronger. At the time of Pottier's death, the vicariate of Szechwan counted 25,000 Chinese Catholics, six French missionaries, eleven Chinese priests, a thriving seminary, a well-organized system of catechists, and an institute for Chinese celibate women.

BIBLIOGRAPHY Léonide Guiot, *La Mission du Su-Tchuen au XVIIme Siècle. Vie et Apostolat de Mgr. Pottier* (1892); Adrien Launay, *Histoire générale de la Société des Missions-Etrangères*, vol. 2 (1894); Société des Missions-Etrangères de Paris, *Mémorial de la Société des Missions-Etrangères* (1888).

Jean-Paul Wiest

Poullart-des-Places, Claude-François (1679–1709), founder of the Congregation of the Holy Ghost (Spiritans). Poullart-des-Places was born in Rennes, France, where he studied at the Jesuit Secondary College and struck up a friendship with Louis-Marie *Grignion de Montfort. His parents, who were wealthy, sent him to Nantes to study law. In 1702, however, he announced he wanted to be a missionary, and he decided to study for the priesthood at the Jesuit College of Louis-le-Grand in Paris. During his studies, when only 24 years old, he founded a small community for a dozen poor students in theology, feeding them physically and spiritually. He dedicated the group to the Holy Spirit, a flourishing focus of devotion in Brittany at that time, thanks to disciples of Louis Lallemant. This community led to the establishment of the Seminary of the Holy Ghost in 1703, which became the cradle for the foundation of the Congregation of the Holy Ghost, a missionary community of men who made themselves available for the most needy areas of France, especially rural missions, and after 1731 also for foreign missions. Ordained as a priest in 1707, Poullart-des-Places died two years later at age 30.

BIBLIOGRAPHY Claude-François Poullart-des-Places, *Spiritual Writings*, H. J. Koren, ed., (1959). H. J. Koren, *To the Ends of the Earth: A General History of the Congregation of the Holy Ghost* (1983).

Joseph Lévesque, PSS

Poysti, Nikolai (1893–1971), missionary in Liberia and Manchuria, and promoter of Finnish Pentecostal missions. Born in St. Petersburg, Russia, of Swedish and Russian parentage, Poysti was converted at age 15 and joined the Methodist Church. Although he participated in ministry, he did not fully surrender his life to Christ until he nearly died from pneumonia. In 1916, after he married Martta Finskas in Viipuri, Finland, the couple began their ministry in St. Petersburg following the Russian Revolution. From there they traveled to Siberia and established several churches. In 1923 they moved to Manchuria, and while ministering to the Russian population, came into contact with the Pentecostal movement. Returning as Pentecostals to Finland, they joined the Filadelphia Church (a Pentecostal congregation) in Helsinki, where Poysti served as pastor for a short time.

Poysti promoted a heightened awareness of the need for world missions among Pentecostal congregations in Finland. In 1927 he helped inaugurate the Finnish Free Foreign Mission and served as its first president. He and his wife returned to Manchuria in 1931, the same year as the Japanese invasion, and remained there until 1935. They later retired in the United States.

BIBLIOGRAPHY K. B. Westman et al., *Pohjoismaiden Lahetyshistoria* (1948); Lauri Ahonen, *Missions Growth: A Case Study of Finnish Free Foreign Mission* (1984).

Gary B. McGee

Prasad (*or* Prisada), Krishna (c.1785–1806), first Brahmin convert of Serampore Mission, Bengal, India. From Nadia in Bengal, Prasad converted to Christianity and was baptized at Serampore early in 1803. Despite failing health, he worked as an evangelist until his death in July 1806. Earlier that year, he had been elected a deacon of the church in Serampore. Though Prasad did not live long, his baptism was given special importance by the small Christian community in Bengal. To their knowledge he was the first Brahmin to become a Christian in that province. If even one from so high a caste as that of the Kulin Brahmins could resist the social pressures against conversion so then too could others. The small Christian community at Serampore was disappointed in this hope. Following his baptism Prasad broke strong caste taboos when he drank from the communion cup passed to him after Krishna *Pal, a low caste convert, had drunk from it. A few months after his baptism he broke another caste barrier, by marrying Anandamayi, the daughter of Krishna Pal. It was said that he was instrumental in persuading members of his Hindu family to discontinue the practice of widow burning (sati). He was encouraged by William *Carey to continue dressing in the Brahmin manner, including wearing the sacred thread. As in the case of the other early converts at Serampore, Prasad kept his given name, even though it was the name of a Hindu deity. Carey did not believe in the practice of giving converts new "Christian" names.

BIBLIOGRAPHY A number of books written about the Serampore Mission include references to the subject, e.g., S. Pearce Carey, *William Carey* (1923). Rajaiah D. Paul's *Changed Lives* (1968) contains an extract about the subject from a Serampore publication, *Brief Memoirs of Four Christian Hindus Lately Deceased* (1816).

Frederick S. Downs

Pratt, George (1817–1894), London Missionary Society (LMS) missionary to Samoa. Born at Portsea, England, Pratt was a member of the Above-Bar Congregational Church at Southampton. He was ordained in July 1838, and after marrying Mary Hobbs, sailed under appointment by the LMS to Samoa. They settled at Matautu on Savai'i, where he served as a member of the talented mid-century LMS staff in Samoa. After his wife died in 1844 he married Elizabeth Bicknell. He became expert in Samoan and the related Polynesian language of Niue. He spent periods of study on Niue and in 1862 accompanied W. G. *Lawes, when Lawes began work on that island. By 1859 Pratt had revised the Samoan Bible and had prepared materials for his authoritative grammar and dictionary. During the 1870s he served the LMS Samoa district committee by visiting outstations in Melanesia and Polynesia. After spending two years (1873–1875) on the Samoan island of Tutuila, he went back to his old station, Matautu. He retired to Sydney, Australia, with his family in 1879 but continued to translate for the mission press in Samoa. In 1887 he briefly visited the LMS in Papua, where many Samoans were serving. He died in Sydney at age 76.

BIBLIOGRAPHY George Pratt, *A Grammar and Dictionary of the Samoan Language* (1878). John Garrett, *To Live among the Stars: Christian Origins in Oceania* (1982); Niel Gunson, *Messengers of Grace: Evangelical Missionaries in the South Seas, 1797–1860* (1978); Richard Lovett, *The History of the London Missionary Society, 1795–1895*, 2 vols. (1899); George Turner, *Samoa a Hundred Years Ago and Long Before...* (1884). Pratt materials are in the LMS South Seas collection at the SOAS, Univ. of London (available on microfilm).

John Garrett

Pratt, Henry B(arrington) (1832–1912), pioneer American Presbyterian missionary in Colombia. A graduate of Princeton Theological Seminary, Pratt was sent by the Presbyterian Board of Foreign Missions to Nueva Granada (present day Colombia) in 1856. He returned to the United States in 1859 to serve as a chaplain in the Confederate army during the Civil War. Returning to Colombia in 1869, he pioneered evangelistic work that developed into established churches in Bogotá and Bucaramanga. Again, returning to the United States in 1877, he was commissioned next to work in Tlalpan, Mexico, for the American Bible Society in the revision of the sixteenth century Reina-Valera translation of the Bible. Later he worked on the *Versión Moderna* translation of the Bible into modern Spanish (first published in 1893) and became appreciated especially at the scholarly level. His plan to write a Spanish commentary for each book of the Bible was interrupted by death after he completed three volumes.

BIBLIOGRAPHY Francisco Ordóñez, *Historia del cristianismo evangélico en Colombia* (1956). Alexander M. Allan, "Before the mast and behind the pulpit," unpublished manuscript kept at the Day Missions Collection, Yale Divinity School Library.

Samuel Escobar

Pratt, Josiah (1768–1844), secretary of the Church Missionary Society (CMS). Pratt was born in Birmingham, England, into a devout Anglican home. Following graduation from Oxford, and ordination in the Church of England, he went to London in 1795 as curate to Richard Cecil. He joined the Eclectic Society, a center of evangelical innovation, in 1797. He played a primary role in the founding of the CMS (1799), the *Christian Observer* (1802), and the British and Foreign Bible Society (1804). In 1813 he launched a monthly journal, the *Missionary Register,* as a private initiative; it became a model for many subsequent missiological journals in its comprehensive statistical reporting of all missions on all continents and its attention to emerging missiological issues. Pratt was elected secretary of the CMS in 1802 and held this position until 1824. He became the main architect for CMS programs: development of support structures at home through local associations, missionary training, ecumenical relations with other missionary societies, negotiating appointment of German missionaries to fill the still vacant ranks of the CMS in its first years, and establishment of CMS missions in Africa, India, the Middle East, and New Zealand. He took a direct hand in the campaign to change the charter of the East India Company in 1813 to allow missionary work. As a dedicated evangelical, Pratt maintained a lifelong membership in the Society for the Propagation of the Gospel in Foreign Parts. He was widely trusted by other denominations because of his "largeness of heart," remarkable ability to translate ideas into action, keen discernment of the times, and a "constitutional modesty" that made him prefer to do his work behind the scenes. A prodigious worker, he held pastoral charges concurrent with his administrative duties, which eventually led to a breakdown in health. He died in London.

BIBLIOGRAPHY Josiah Pratt and John Henry Pratt, *Memoir of the Rev. Josiah Pratt, BD* (1849); Eugene Stock, *History of the Church Missionary Society,* 3 vols. (1899).

Wilbert R. Shenk

Price, Francis (Frank) Wilson (1895–1974), Presbyterian missionary in China. Born in China of Southern Presbyterian missionary parents, Price was fluent in Chinese from childhood days. In 1923, after receiving a thoroughgoing American education at Davidson College, Columbia University, and Yale Divinity School, he returned to China with his bride, Essie (McClure), to become a professor at Nanking Seminary. During the next 20 years he contributed to the leadership of many causes: educational reform, rural reconstruction, the Church of Christ in China, and the ecumenical movement. A major undertaking was the establishment of the Rural Training Center and a five-year survey of rural churches. When war broke out with Japan in 1937, he supported the national war effort, and as a personal friend and occasional critic of Chiang Kai-shek, served as China's advocate in America. In 1948 he traveled over the Burma Road to western China, where he served at the Nanking Seminary in exile.

Price attended the Organization Conference of the United Nations in San Francisco in 1945 as adviser to the Chinese delegation. In 1948 his optimism turned to disillusionment, but rather than go to Taiwan, he resolved to stay in China. After the Communist victory in 1949, he came under attack for his close association with the Nationalist government. The Prices were held in virtual house arrest for 22 months before being given permission to leave in 1952. Returning to the United States, Price became director of the Missionary Research Library, New York City, in 1956 and was elected moderator of the Presbyterian Church, U.S. (Southern) in 1957. His contributions to the missionary cause are legion: love of China, scholarship, support of rural church programs, and commitment to a Christian social witness.

BIBLIOGRAPHY Among Price's published works, the following are of special significance: *As the Lightning Flashes* (1948), *Marx Meets Christ* (1957), and *The Rural Church in China,* 2d ed. (1948). (The first edition was lost by the publisher during the Japanese occupation of Shanghai and never printed.) Also to be noted are Price's translations of Chinese hymns and of Sun Yat-sen's *Three Principles of the People* (1924, 1981). The best brief account of Price's China years and writings is H. McKennie Goodpasture, "China in an American, Frank Wilson Price: A Bibliographical Essay," *Journal of Presbyterian History* 49 (1971): 353–364. See also Samuel Chiow, "Religious Education and Reform in Chinese Missions: The Life and Work of Francis Wilson Price (1895–1974)" (Ph.D. diss., St. Louis Univ., 1988). Many of Price's papers are to be found in the Price Collection at Union Theological Seminary in Richmond, Va.

G. Thompson Brown

Price, Jonathan David (1796–1828), medical missionary in Burma (Myanmar). Born in Elizabethtown, New Jersey, Price was a graduate of Princeton (M.A., 1814) and the University of Pennsylvania (M.D., 1820). He also attended Princeton Theological Seminary (1816–1817). Commissioned by the Baptist foreign mission society to serve in Burma, he arrived in Rangoon with his wife and infant daughter in 1821. His wife died of dysentery five months later. His instructions were to utilize his medical aptitude to help missionaries and "heathen" but to regard these skills "as subordinate and subservient" to his responsibility as a preacher of the gospel. Price soon gained favor with the emperor and was provided a house near the palace in Ava, causing Adoniram *Judson to hope that an edict of religious toleration and freedom to preach throughout the country could be gained, but this did not happen. Price subsequently married a young Burmese woman of Thai descent who had been left blind after he had attempted cataract surgery on her. When the Anglo-Burmese War began, he and Judson were imprisoned as spies. Following their release, Price resigned as a missionary to become the Burmese court physician. He died of tuberculosis, only months after his second wife had died of cholera.

BIBLIOGRAPHY Courtney Anderson, *To the Golden Shore* (1956); Robert G. Torbet, *Venture of Faith* (1955); Walter N. Wyeth, *A Galaxy in the Burman Sky* (1892).

Alan Neely

Price, Roger (1834–1900), London Missionary Society (LMS) missionary in southern Africa. Price was born in Merthyr Cynog, Brecknockshire, Wales, to a Welsh-speaking farming family. He trained for the Independent (i.e., Congregational) ministry at Western College, Plymouth, and offered for service with the LMS. He and several others were accepted for the Kololo and Ndebele missions proposed by David *Livingstone following his first great journey, and in 1858 Price sailed with his bride, Isabella (Slater). It took the party nearly six months to get from Cape Town to Robert *Moffat's base at Kuruman, from where the Prices, with a more experienced missionary, Holloway Helmore and his family, and several Kuruman Africans, set off to the Kololo, then at Dinyanti in the Zambesi basin. The journey was harsh in the extreme; a child was born to Isabella Price en route; Livingstone (who had by now broken with the LMS) was not at Dinyanti; and the Kololo did not want the mission. Then, between March 7 and April 21, 1860, eight of the party, including Helmore, his wife, and the Price's child, all died—probably from malaria, though poison was suspected at the time. Hostility to the Prices continued, and they at last turned back. Isabella died in July; in September, John *Mackenzie rescued an exhausted Price and the Helmore children. Thereafter Price was always lame and subject to recurrent malarial attacks.

Price worked from 1862 to 1866 at the Ngwato capital Shoshong, where he got to know and value the young *Khama, and married Elizabeth (Bessie), a daughter of Robert Moffat. From 1865 to 1875 they were at Molepolole, the new capital of the Kwena king Sechele, who had become a Christian through Livingstone.

In 1876, while on furlough in England, Price was appointed to survey the route for a new LMS mission, funded by Robert *Arthington, to be established at Ujiji on Lake Tanganyika. East African travel then depended on human carriers, and Price wanted to introduce South African–style wagons. He got wagons to Mpapwa, but the next year when he took the first LMS missionary party (including E. C. *Hore) to Lake Tanganyika, the oxen died, presumably of tsetse.

Price returned to Molepolole in 1879, continuing there until 1885, when he became principal of the Moffat Institution, the educational complex at Kuruman, with superintendence of the church of the district. The institution was overambitious and understaffed—Price called it a white elephant. It closed in 1897, Price proposing another institution with higher standards (later realized by W. C. *Willoughby in the Tiger Kloof Institution). The Prices were still at Kuruman when the Boers occupied it during the Anglo-Boer War. Price died there soon afterward.

Price spoke Sechuana well and was much involved in Bible and other translation work. His farm background showed in his agricultural and mechanical skills. His long service spanned the extension of white rule into the interior; in political matters he was less ready than many colleagues to protest against government actions. Bessie Price, whose voluminous correspondence illuminates their work, raised their large family. She retired to the Cape Town area, adopting exceedingly liberal theological views in her later years, and lived until 1919.

BIBLIOGRAPHY J. C. Harris, *Roger Price* (1927); London Missionary Society, *Report of the Rev. R. Price of His Visit to Zanzibar and the Coast of Eastern Africa* (1876); Una Long, ed., *The Journals of Elizabeth Lees Price, Written in Bechuanaland, Southern Africa* (1956); J. Sibree, *London Missionary Society: A Register of Missionaries, Deputations, etc.* (1923), no. 541; A. Sillery, *Sechele: The Story of an African Chief* (1954); E. W. Smith, *Great Lion of Bechuanaland: The Life and Times of Roger Price, Missionary* (1957).

Andrew F. Walls

Price, Thomas Frederick (1860–1919), cofounder of the Maryknoll priests and brothers. Born in Wilmington, North Carolina, Price was the first Catholic in that state ever to reach the priesthood. Ordained in 1886, he became a pioneer in evangelizing non-Catholics in rural districts. At first, his missionary apostolate was limited to preaching wherever he could get a hearing, but in 1897 he began a magazine called *Truth* to reach more of the primarily Protestant population of North Carolina. Although Price's mission experience was in the southern United States, his vision of mission encompassed the world. In the fall of 1902 he opened Regina Apostolorum, a seminary to train and recruit priests for the mission in North Carolina, the poorest sections of the United States, and ultimately, overseas work. In 1911 he cofounded, with James Anthony *Walsh of Boston, the Catholic Foreign Mission Society of America, commonly known as Maryknoll. He traveled several months at a time each year to speak in parishes, schools, and seminaries about foreign missions and Maryknoll. He left for China in 1919 and was appointed superior of the first group of Maryknoll priests sent there, but died a few months later in Hong Kong from appendicitis. He is remembered by those who knew him for his simple and humble deportment, his practice of poverty, and his special devotion to the Virgin Mary and Bernadette Soubirous of Lourdes.

BIBLIOGRAPHY A copy of 3,000 pages of diary written by Price between 1908 and 1919 is in the Maryknoll Mission archives, Ossining, New York. Raymond A. Lane, *The Early Days of Maryknoll* (1951); John C. Murrett, *Tar Heel Apostle: Thomas Frederick Price, Cofounder of Maryknoll* (1944); Albert J. Nevins, *The Meaning of Maryknoll* (1954); George C. Powers, *The Maryknoll Movement* (1926); Robert E. Sheridan, *The Founders of Maryknoll* (1980) and ed., *Very Rev. Thomas Frederick Price, M.M., Co-Founder of Maryknoll: A Symposium (1956) with Supplement* (1981).

Jean-Paul Wiest

Price, William Salter (1826–1911), agent of the Church Missionary Society (CMS) in India and East Africa. Price, who came from Staffordshire, England, received his theological education at the Church Missionary College, Islington (London). He arrived in Bombay in 1849 and was involved in educational work there, and later at Sharanpur, near Nasik. At this time the British Navy was landing freed slaves at Bombay, and in 1860, C. W. *Isenberg, in charge of the work in Sharanpur, began to accept them. Known as the "Nasik boys," they were educated and taught crafts, and many were baptized. David *Livingstone recruited a number of them to work with him in central Africa. In 1864 several went to Mombasa to aid Johannes *Rebmann.

In November 1874 Price, who had been in England since April 1873, was transferred to Mombasa to revitalize CMS work in East Africa. He was accompanied by Jacob Wainwright, a "Nasik boy" who had been with Livingstone. Rebmann, blind and weak, was sent back to Germany; Price established Frere Town, and from 1875 Africans freed by the British Navy were settled there. He stayed only until July 1876, when he retired to Suffolk. But in 1881 and again in 1888 he returned in emergencies to Frere Town.

Men from Frere Town were with Bishop James *Hannington on his last journey; their leader, William Henry *Jones, had gone to Mombasa in 1864. The freed slaves trained by Price accompanied many other explorers and missionaries.

BIBLIOGRAPHY Donald Simpson, *Dark Companions: The African Contribution to the European Exploration of East Africa* (1975); Eugene Stock, *The History of the Church Missionary Society: Its Environment, Its Men and Its Work* (1899).

Jocelyn Murray

Priest, James M. (?–1883), African American Presbyterian missionary in Liberia. Little is known of Priest's early life. He was raised a slave and belonged to a "Mrs. Means" of Lexington, Kentucky, who emancipated her slaves in 1832 in order to send them to Africa. In 1843 Priest graduated from New Albany Theological Seminary in Chicago (now McCormick Theological Seminary). He and his wife, Ann, sailed to Liberia in the spring of the same year as missionaries of the Northern Presbyterian Church. They were first appointed to the station at Settra Kroo, and in 1844 were transferred to King Will's Town. Priest organized a church at Kentucky in 1847. After four years at King Will's Town, he was moved to Greenville. He spent the rest of his life serving the church and community there. As founder of the Presbyterian Church at Greenville, he erected a small church building and doubled the membership. He also conducted a Sabbath and day school. His ministry was largely among Americo-Liberian colonists, but he had a friendly relationship with indigenous Liberians. The Priests had at least five children. Ann Priest died in 1880. After 40 years of service in Liberia, Priest died at Greenville.

BIBLIOGRAPHY Arthur Judson Brown, *One Hundred Years: A History of the Foreign Missionary Work of the Presbyterian Church in the U.S.A.* (1936); William Rankin, *Memorials of Foreign Missionaries of the Presbyterian Church USA* (1895).

Sylvia M. Jacobs

Prip, Einar (1868–1939), Danish missionary among Muslims in Syria. Born in Egense near Svendborg, Denmark, Prip was the son of a local vicar. He graduated in 1894 with a degree in theology from the University of Copenhagen and became curate in his father's parish in Svendborg, where he served from 1895 to 1898. Supported by a group of friends, he was sent out in March 1898 to the Syrian Orphanage in Jerusalem. Later the same year this group of supporters became the "Österlandsmissionen" (the Orient Mission or the Near East Mission [NEM]). In 1905 NEM took over a mission field from the Irish Presbyterian mission. It comprised five small mission stations in the Kalamun district north of Damascus. Prip moved to this district with a doctor, Fox-Maule, and continued medical and school mission work. Over time they were joined by others, including Alfred *Nielsen, pastor and linguist.

The local churches attached to the mission stations were mostly made up of Christians who had converted from the old churches. Prip and his co-workers did not see the gospel received by many Muslims. In Denmark, Einar Prip's many influential letters were studied in many mission groups. Some of them were published in *Breve fra Einar Prip* (Letters from Einar Prip) (1946). In 1934 Prip returned to Denmark because of health problems, and he died in Copenhagen.

BIBLIOGRAPHY Johs. Nordentoft, *Einar Prip: Et Livsbillede* (Einar Prip: A Life) (1946); Chr. Siegumfeldt, *Österlandsmissionen* (The Near East Mission), vols. 1 and 2 (1923, 1927).

Flemming Markussen

Probowinoto, Basoeki (1917–1989), a founder of the Council of Churches in Indonesia (DGI), of the Christian party Parkindo, and of the East Asia Christian Conference. After studying at the Yogyakarta Seminary, Probowinoto was a pastor and minister of the Reformed Kwitang Church in Jakarta during the Japanese occupation. In that difficult and multiethnic situation he showed his missionary talents. Even then he had an ecumenical attitude, serving as the secretary of the Jakarta Christian Council. Right after the war he initiated a consultative body of churches in Indonesia, a predecessor to the Council of Churches in Indonesia. He was active in the Indonesian Bible Society, the board of the Christian University Satya Wacana, in Salatiga, Central Java, and the World Council of Churches (WCC), serving on the Central Committee.

From 1946 to 1967 he was the director of the synodal office of the Gereja Kristen Jawa, in Salatiga. He helped to shape a new relationship between that church and the mission board of the Gereformeerde Kerken in the Netherlands. He made important contributions toward clarifying the proclamation of the gospel in an independent nation, the role of missionaries and of indigenous ministers, and the task of laypersons. He was particularly stimulated by the reports from the Evanston assembly (1954) of the WCC and the writings of Hans-Ruedi Weber. He was cofounder of the important lay training institute of his church and for many years edited several Javanese church papers.

BIBLIOGRAPHY Few of Probowinoto's writings have appeared in Western languages. An extensive biography together with contributions about Probowinoto and some of his earlier writings appear in [N. L. Kana and Daldjoeni, eds.] *Ikrar dan Ikhtiar dalam hidup pendota Basoeki Probowinoto* (Commitment and freedom in the life of the Reverend Basoeki Probowinoto) (1987); see also J. Verkuyl, *Gedenken en verwachten* (1983), pp. 158–161.

Alle G. Hoekema

Prokhanov, Ivan Stepanovich (1869–1935), leader of the Russian Evangelical Christian movement. Born in the Caucasus, Prokhanov supported himself as an engineer but soon emerged as a religious leader. In addition to preaching, he wrote numerous articles for periodicals, including journals that he helped to found. He edited ten songbooks that contained more than 600 poems he composed and 400 hymns he translated from English and German into Russian. He organized a publishing association, Raduga, and wrote an autobiography and other books.

Raised in a family that had joined the Baptist movement, Prokhanov established a separate denomination, the Evangelical Christians, an organization that by 1914 numbered more than 30,000 members. Through this union he organized churches, a theological seminary, bookstores, women's circles, and other entities. He was a delegate to the 1911 Baptist World Alliance in Philadelphia, where he was elected a vice-president.

In 1905 he founded the Union of Freedom, Truth and Love of Peace, a political organization, and in 1917 organized the Christian Democratic Party Resurrection. In 1894 he had organized a Christian agricultural commune, and after the Bolshevik Revolution (1917), he organized other communes. Before immigrating to Germany in 1928, he was incarcerated under the Communists for two months in 1921 and for four months in 1923. Although often opposed by the Russian Orthodox Church prior to the Bolshevik Revolution and persecuted later by the Communists, Prokhavon subtitled his autobiography "The Life of an Optimist in the Land of Pessimism." He died in Berlin.

BIBLIOGRAPHY I. S. Prokhanoff, *In the Cauldron of Russia* (1933). Andrew Quarles Blane, "The Relations Between the Russian Protestant Sects and the State, 1900–1921" (Ph.D. diss., Duke Univ., 1964); J. A. Hebly, *Protestants in Russia* (1976); Walter Sawatsky, *Soviet Evangelicals since World War II* (1981); Paul D. Steeves, "Prokhanov, Ivan Stepanovich," *The Modern Encyclopedia of Russian and Soviet History*, vol. 30 (1982).

Peter Deyneka, Jr.

Proksch, Georg (1904–1986), Society of the Divine Word (SVD) missionary in India. Born in Czechowice, Silesia (present-day Poland), Proksch was ordained in 1932 at the Divine Word seminary in Mödling, Austria. The same year he was sent by the SVD to India, where he came to be regarded as perhaps the leading European musicologist, composer, choreographer, and playwright devoted to traditional Indian art forms. Under the tutelage of Indian masters, he became an expert in Indian musical and dramatic arts, and in Hindi, Sanskrit, and Hindu sacred scriptures. He mastered a variety of musical instruments and excelled in folk dancing and singing. A promoter of the policy of missionary accommodation, he was convinced that Christianity would not be accepted in India except through the centuries-old methods of the gurus. The Bible would have to be dramatized in ballets; preachers would have to sing the Good News in ballads (*kathas*) and in traditional hymn styles (*bhajans*). "The Christ that Indians can truly understand," he insisted, "must come in Indian garb and from Indian streets."

Inspired by Mahatma Gandhi at a seminar and with the blessing of Cardinal Valerian Gracias of Bombay, Proksch founded a Christian ashram in which he attempted to integrate Indian culture and the Christian faith. At the Gyan-Prakash Ashram (Gyan-Prakash, meaning "Wisdom's Light," is a play on his family name), located in Andheri, a suburb of Bombay, he required his disciples to be both artists and evangelizers. He built up a professional theatrical troupe and conducted numerous performances in India and overseas, at all times focusing on Indian art as an essential vehicle for communicating the Christian message. Among his works are hymns, Masses, films, and a novel. For more than 40 years he lived in India as a scholar, teacher, ascetic, evangelizer, and composer. He died in Vienna.

BIBLIOGRAPHY For autobiographical sketches, see the SVD publications *Word in the World* (1964, 1975) and *Lead Me to Light* (1975). Proksch wrote 35 books of plays, songs, ballets, and a novel, all in Hindi. He set to music the Book of Psalms and composed a "Life of Christ" in traditional Indian ballad form, as well as elaborate ballets with biblical themes. He also published a widely accepted hymnal, *Shraddhanjali*. Archival materials are in the Gyan-Prakash Ashram.

Louis J. Luzbetak, SVD

Protten, Christian Jacob (1715–1769), pioneering Moravian missionary in Ghana. Born in Christiansborg, on the coast of present-day Ghana, of a Danish father and a Ga mother, Protten was sent to Denmark to be educated in 1726. King Frederick IV took a great interest in him and served as godfather when he was baptized in Copenhagen. In 1735, at the Danish court, he met Nikolaus *Zinzendorf, leader of the Moravians, and joined the Moravian fellowship. Zinzendorf sent him back to his native country in 1737 with the assignment of founding a school for Euro-African children in Elmina. Because of a war being waged at this time between the Dutch and the Dahomey, he was not successful in this effort, was imprisoned, and fell ill with malaria. Recalled to Europe in 1740, he went briefly to the West Indies, where he married a mulatto Moravian, Rebecca Freundlich. From 1756 to 1761 and again from 1764 to his death, he taught at the mission school in Christiansborg. During those years he prepared a trilingual catechism with the text in Danish, Ga, and Twi. The appendix to this booklet, intended to assist European missionaries in learning Ga and Twi, was the first published grammar of a Ghanaian language.

BIBLIOGRAPHY Hans Debrunner, *A History of Christianity in Ghana* (1967); P. Steiner, *Ein Blatt aus der Geschichte der Brüdermission* (1888).

Otto Dreydoppel, Jr.

Q

Quaque, Philip (1741–1816), first African ordained into the ministry of the Anglican Church. Quaque was the son of Cudjo, a Fanti chief from Cape Coast Castle in the Gold Coast (Ghana). When Cudjo was asked by Thomas *Thompson, the first missionary with the Society for the Propagation of the Gospel (SPG) in West Africa, to select three boys for education in England, he included his son Philip. Quaque spent 11 years in England, forgetting his mother tongue but proceeding to baptism in 1759 and ordination in 1765. His first wife was English. In 1765 he returned under the auspices of the SPG as "missionary, catechist and schoolmaster to the negroes of the Gold Coast of Africa." Later, his son, Samuel, also educated in England, assisted him. It was from those educated at the school established in his memory (1822) that the invitation to the Methodist mission was extended from the so-called Cape Coast Bible Band. It was Quaque who had originally implanted in the members of the Bible Band a desire for Bible teaching.

BIBLIOGRAPHY F. L. Bartels, *The Roots of Ghana Methodism* (1965) and "Philip Quaque, 1741–1816," in *Transactions of the Gold Coast and Togoland Historical Society,* vol. 1, pt. 5 (1955); C. F. Pascoe, *Two Hundred Years of the SPG, 1701–1900* (1901); Margaret Priestley, *West African Trade and Coast Society* (1969); H. P. Thompson, *Into All Lands* (1951).

Timothy Yates

Quinn, Edel Mary (1907–1944), Catholic lay missionary who brought the Legion of Mary to Africa. Born in Ireland, Quinn grew up in a comfortable, middle-class family. By chance she was introduced to the Legion of Mary, a Catholic lay apostolate organization founded in 1921. She became a devoted member, later president, of a local branch (or "praesidia") which met weekly to pray and to report on the work, like visiting the sick and prostitutes and teaching catechism. In 1932, about to become a Poor Clare, Quinn became seriously ill and spent 18 months in a sanatorium. Still of delicate health, but cheerful and determined, she accepted a call from Africa in 1936. Despite immense problems, such as having to deal with the numerous tribal languages, she founded many praesidia and curia (regional committees of praesidia representatives) in Kenya, Tanganyika (Tanzania), Uganda, Nyasaland (Malawi), Mauritius, and Reunion, traveling enormous distances under extremely difficult conditions. In 1941 she collapsed and was hospitalized in South Africa. She resumed work in 1943 but died a year later.

BIBLIOGRAPHY Robert Bradshaw, *Edel Quinn—Envoy for Mary* (1986); Franck Duff, *Les débuts de la Légion de Marie* (1993); Léon-Joseph Suenens, *Edel Quinn, Heroine of the Apostolate (1907–1944): Envoy of the Legion of Mary to Africa* (1954).

Leny Lagerwerf

Quiroga, Vasco de (1470–1565), Spanish humanist and protector of the Indians in New Spain. Quiroga was one of the most important representatives of the utopian phase of the evangelization of the New World. After serving as an adviser in the court of Charles I, he was sent to Mexico in 1530 as a member of the second Audiencia (governing board). In 1532, with royal permission and his own money, he founded the Hospital (settlement) of Santa Fe, a colony for the protection of the Indians, near Mexico City. Shortly afterward he founded a second settlement, in Michoacán. In his *Reglas y ordenanzas para los hospitales de Santa Fe* (Rules and ordinances for the settlements...) Quiroga cites Thomas More's *Utopia* (1515–1516) as his model and source of inspiration. Known by the Indians as Tata Vasco, he himself acted as patron and protector of the colonies. In 1536 he was ordained a priest and consecrated the first bishop of Michoacán. The settlements fell into decline after his death and had ceased to function by the end of the colonial period.

BIBLIOGRAPHY Paul Lietz, "Vasco de Quiroga, Oidor Made Bishop," *Mid-America* 32 (1950): 13–32; Josefina Muriel, *Hospitales de la Nueva España,* vol. 1, *Fundaciones del siglo XVI* (1956); Fintan B. Warren, *Vasco de Quiroga and His Pueblo-Hospitales of Santa Fe* (1963); Silvio Zavala, *Sir Thomas More in New Spain: A Utopian Adventure of the Renaissance* (1937, 1955).

Jeffrey Klaiber, SJ

R

Raaflaub, Fritz (1909–1993), Basel Mission (BM) missionary in Cameroon and BM secretary for Africa. Raaflaub was born of farming parents in Gstaad, Canton of Bern, and trained at Unterstrass Teachers' Seminary in Zurich. After joining the BM he worked as an ordained pastor and as a teacher and inspector of schools in Cameroon (1932–1945, 1947–1950). During his home leave he received a D. Phil. from the University of Zurich with a dissertation on BM schools in Cameroon (1947). In 1950 he was called to serve on the BM home board as the first secretary for Africa who had experience on a mission field. On his several visits to the partner churches in Ghana and Cameroon he encouraged them in their initiative to become independent. He also launched the beginning of BM work in northern Nigeria in cooperation with the Church of the Brethren (U.S.). In 1964 he was elected president of the Council of Swiss Missions (Schweizerischer Evangelischer Missionsrat; 1964–1976) and after his resignation from the presidency acted as its secretary (1976–1984). He received an honorary D.Theol. degree from the University of Basel in 1976.

BIBLIOGRAPHY Fritz Raaflaub, *Gebt uns Lehrer: Geschichte und Gegenwartsaufgabe der Basler Missionsschulen in Kamerun* (D.Phil. diss., Univ. of Zurich, 1947), *Der bleibende Auftrag: 150 Jahre Basler Mission* (1956), ed., *Basel Mission Schools Become Presbyterian Schools* (1966), and *Kirche, Kakao und Kliniken: 150 Jahre Missionsarbeit in Ghana* (1978). Raaflaub authored numerous articles and reports in *Evangelisches Missions Magazin, L'Actualité Missionaire* (1965; 1966) and in various BM publications. Correspondence and reports from Cameroon are in the BM archive, Basel, Switzerland.

Waltraud Ch. Haas

Raban, John (c. 1795–1841), Church Missionary Society (CMS) missionary in Sierra Leone. Raban was one of the first English clergymen to join the earlier missionaries from Germany recruited by CMS. He served at Freetown, Sierra Leone, for short periods between 1826 and 1834, ill health requiring regular leaves in England, and was head of Fourah Bay Institution from 1831 to 1832 and 1833 to 1834. Like his respected acquaintance Hannah *Kilham, the Quaker advocate of the use of African languages in African schools, he investigated many of the languages spoken at Freetown by liberated slaves. In 1832–1833 he published three tiny volumes on the Yoruba language, representing the earliest study of that Nigerian language. Although elementary and crude, Raban's studies encouraged further linguistic work in the Sierra Leone mission. They were the link between the earlier work on local languages, such as that by Gustavius Reinhold *Nyländer, and the later, more refined work on Nigerian languages, such as that of James Frederick *Schön and Samuel Ajayi *Crowther, Raban's former pupil.

BIBLIOGRAPHY P. E. H. Hair, *The Early Study of Nigerian Languages* (2d ed., 1995), S. A. Walker, *The Church of England Mission in Sierra Leone* (1847). Raban materials are held in the CMS archives, Univ. of Birmingham.

P. E. H. Hair

Rabary (1864–1947), Malagasy teacher and writer. Rabary, a second-generation Christian, was of noble descent. His family lived in different villages of the central part of Madagascar due to the demands of his evangelist father's work. He was the youngest pupil to be admitted to the London Missionary Society normal school in 1876 and to the local medical school four years later. He experienced a spiritual crisis and thought he would find comfort in Catholicism, but kept the matter secret and lived in torment for some time. His father's recommendation on his deathbed in 1879 guided his choice: Rabary was to succeed his father as a pastor and evangelist. His studies were interrupted when he was called to join the courtiers' circle of Queen Ranavalona II, but in 1882 one of the pastors of the palace church urged him to become a teacher.

Rabary taught various subjects in different schools and circumstances while pursuing his studies with the assistance of missionaries. He became one of the first Malagasy to study in France, going to Paris in 1896, but stayed only for a few months. In 1900 he became pastor of the church of Avaratr'Andohalo but continued to teach and began to write. As a member of a patriotic movement against French colonization, he was imprisoned in 1915 and exiled from the capital from 1916 to 1918. His literary works covered many fields. Rabary is mainly remembered for his accounts of the progress of Christianity—more precisely of Protestantism—in Madagascar. His first book, *Ny Maritiora Malagasy* (Malagasy martyrs), appeared in 1910. A celebration of his achievements took place on his eightieth birthday, followed by others after his death.

BIBLIOGRAPHY Many of Rabary's works were published by the mission press in Antananarivo. L. A. Rabarison, *Le Pasteur Rabary* (1979); C. Rajoelisolo, *Andriamatoa Rabary sy ny Maritiora* (Rabary and the martyrs) (1944). The most extended biography is G. Ranaivo, *Andriamatoa Rabary* (1954).

Yvette Ranjeva Rabetafika

Rabinowitz, Joseph Ben David (1837–1899), father of the contemporary Messianic Jewish missionary movement. Rabinowitz founded the first modern Jewish Christian community without church missionary personnel, earning him the nickname "the Herzl of Jewish Christianity" (after the Zionist leader Theodor Herzl). He was born in Bessarabia, Russia, living most of his life in the town of Kishinev. His early years were spent in a Hasidic ethos, but in his teens he was attracted to post-Enlightenment liberal rationalism. At this time of open-mindedness he was given a Hebrew New Testament, which he read and kept. He became a successful legal advisor and journalist. During the Russian pogroms of 1881–1882 he advocated Jewish settlement in Palestine, but on a reconnaissance there he became disconsolate at the desolation and oppression in Jerusalem. While on the Mount of Olives, grieving for the city, he remembered Jesus doing the same, and then he recalled other New Testament passages. He returned home convinced of Jesus' messiahship.

Although exhilarated about introducing Jewish people to his discovery, he soon discerned that they would only listen if acceptance of his message did not entail losing their Jewishness. Russian law stipulated that if a Jew became a Christian, he or she was no longer Jewish. Therefore Rabinowitz never joined a church, nor sought to establish one. Instead, he obtained permission from the authorities to form a kind of synagogue. This community, which rapidly grew in size and in influence throughout Europe, maintained circumcision, Sabbath observance, and the Jewish festivals. His own baptism was conducted in 1885 in a Bohemian-Lutheran church in Berlin by a Congregational minister, before English witnesses, following his own seven-point Hebrew creed. He is the role model for the successful congregation-planting ministry of the modern Messianic Jewish movement.

BIBLIOGRAPHY The best resouce is Kai Kjaer-Hansen, *Joseph Rabinowitz and the Messianic Movement* (1995). Eric Gabe, "The Hebrew Christian Movement in Kishineff," *The Hebrew Christian* 60, no. 2–64, no. 2 (1987–1991); Adolph Saphir, *Rabinowich and His Mission to Israel* (1888).

Walter Riggans

Rada, Martín de (1533–1578), Augustinian missionary to the Philippines. Born in Pamplona, Spain, Rada, who earned a reputation as an expert mathematician and cosmographer, was assigned to the Augustinian Mexican mission in 1553. In 1564 he sailed from Mexico to the Philippines with four other Augustinian missionaries in an expedition headed by Miguel López de Legazpi. When Rada's confrere Andrés de *Urdaneta returned to Mexico, Rada stayed behind in Cebu. Elected the first provincial superior of the Augustinians in the Philippines in 1572, he opened several mission stations that consolidated the work of conversion his confreres had begun. Distressed by an oppressive system of taxation on a hapless people, he wrote a strong condemnation of colonial policy, prompting an immediate reply from the governor general and other royal officials defending their action. Rada's initiative sparked what might be called the "fight for justice" in the conquest of the Philippines. Unlike Urdaneta, Rada maintained that the Philippines were within the Spanish sphere of influence. After a trip to China made to promote better relations with the imperial government, he joined Governor Francisco de Sande (1575–1580) on a military expedition to Borneo, which he opposed. He died aboard ship returning to Manila.

BIBLIOGRAPHY Rada's letters have been edited by Isacio Rodríguez Rodríguez in *Historia de la Provincia Agustiniana del Santísimo Nombre de Jesús de Filipinas,* vol. 14 (1978). Brief biographies can be found in A. M. Castro, *Misioneros Agustinos en el Oriente (Osario Venerable),* M. Merino, ed. (1954), pp. 221–222; M. Merino, "Semblanzas misioneras. Fray Martín de Rada," *Missionalia Hispanica,* vol. 1 (1944), pp. 167–212; and P. Martínez Vélez, "El Agustino Fray Martin de Rada: Insigne Misionero Moderno," in *Archivo Histórico Hispano-Agustiniano,* vol. 38 (1932), pp. 340–363. An English version of Rada's opinion on the Philippine tribute and the answer it provoked is in Emma H. Blair and James A. Robertson, *The Philippine Islands: 1483–1803,* vol. 3 (1903), pp. 253–271.

José S. Arcilla, SJ

Rader, Paul (1879–1938), missions advocate and one of America's best-known evangelists. Born in Denver, Colorado—one of ten children of Daniel Leaper Rader, a Methodist minister, missionary evangelist, and editor—Paul Rader epitomized the rugged individualism, energy, and enterprise of the American West. He was educated at the Universities of Colorado and Denver, later serving on the staff of the University of Puget Sound and as athletic director of Hamline University in St. Paul, Minnesota. As a boy he was converted under his father's ministry and early displayed unusual preaching gifts. He was ordained to the Congregational ministry in 1904 but did not come to a settled faith until 1911, when after a successful foray into the business world, he confirmed his faith and calling in a life-changing spiritual encounter in New York City. Soon after, he began his association with the Christian and Missionary Alliance (C&MA) in Pittsburgh, Pennsylvania. He was called to the pastorate of Chicago's Moody Memorial Church in February 1915, where his preaching attracted 5,000 worshipers on Sunday evenings. He was elected vice president of the C&MA while at Moody Church, succeeding A. B. *Simpson to the presidency after the latter's death in 1919. By September 1921 Rader had left Moody, though continuing to serve as president of the C&MA until 1923. During his tenure, the number of missionaries under appointment doubled from 250 to 500.

Visiting C&MA fields after taking up the presidency, Rader met R. A. *Jaffray and traveled with him into China, commencing a lifelong friendship. Later, Rader assisted Jaffray in establishing the Chinese Foreign Missionary Union. In 1922 Rader published *'Round the Round World: Some Impressions of a World Tour,* in which he further defined his vision for world evangelization. For a time, his role as leader of C&MA included the presidency of the Nyack (New York) Missionary Training Institute, although he soon delegated the administration of the school to others.

A pioneer in the use of radio for the communication of the Gospel, he began broadcasting as early as 1922 from the Chicago Gospel Tabernacle, which he founded. During his ministry there (1922–1933), he formed Worldwide Gospel Couriers, a missionary sending agency. In 1926 he established the Maranatha Bible and Missionary Conference in Michigan. A uniquely gifted missionary motivator, he directly influenced the lives and ministries of a remarkable number of evangelical mission leaders, including Bob *Pierce, founder of World Vision, International; Clarence *Jones, founder of HCJB Radio, Quito, Ecuador; Oswald J. *Smith, People's Church, Toronto; Howard Ferrin, president of Barrington College in Rhode Island; Charles E. Fuller, radio evangelist and founder of Fuller Theological Seminary; Bishop Jens Christensen of Pakistan; Dwight H. Ferguson, founder of Men for Missions, OMS, International; Paul *Fleming, New Tribes Mission; and Peter *Deyneka, whom he assisted in organizing the Slavic Gospel Association in 1934. Rader published more than fifteen books, many of which communicated his passion for world evangelization. He was 58 when he died in Hollywood, California, after establishing further tabernacle ministries in Fort Wayne, Indiana, and Los Angeles.

BIBLIOGRAPHY Paul Rader, *God's Blessed Man* (1922), *Big Bug: A Novel* (1935), and *Life's Greatest Adventure* (1938). R. L. Niklaus, J. S. Sawin, and S. J. Stoesz, *All for Jesus: God at Work in the Christian and Missionary Alliance over One Hundred Years* (1986); W. Leon Tucker, *The Redemption of Paul Rader* (1918).

Paul A. Rader

Rafiringa, Paul (1850–1925), Malagasy layleader of the Roman Catholic community in Madagascar. Rafiringa was born at Antananarivo into a family some of whose members adhered to the traditional religion and some to the Reformed Church introduced by missionaries of the London Missionary Society (LMS). Rafiringa, however, attended one of the newly established Catholic schools and was baptized in the Catholic Church at the age of 14. As Catholicism had been brought in 1861 by French Jesuits, it became unpopular as conflict between France and Madagascar intensified. War broke out twice, from 1883 to 1885 and from 1894 to 1895, Catholic missionaries were driven out, and many new converts returned to Protestantism or to ancestor worship. People who remained faithful Catholics were gathered into a Catholic Union, which Rafiringa headed. During the first war he was a civil servant and a friend of some people at court and in government circles, but in spite of his connections and family duties he showed great zeal and dedication, traveling every weekend outside the capital to exhort Catholic communities, comfort the sick and destitute, organize religious services, and preach and lecture on the vocation of the laity. Among his co-workers, one of the most outstanding was Victoire *Rasoamanarivo. Rafiringa wrote a report on the activities of the Catholic Union to Leo XIII and a letter to their bishop, Cazet, asking for non-French priests to celebrate Mass. His activities continued when the clergy left again at the outbreak of the second war, during which he wrote a 900-page diary. This Malagasy manuscript is a valuable document on the history of the society and church when the country was about to lose its independence.

BIBLIOGRAPHY Pietro Lupo, "L'Église confiée aux laïcs, d'après l'histoire-journal de Paul Rafiringa" (Ph.D. diss., the Sorbonne, 1980). See also Bruno Hubsch, ed., *Madagascar et le Christianisme* (1993). Rafiringa's letters and reports are kept in the archives of the Malagasy Catholic Church at Andohalo, Antananarivo.

Yvette Ranjeva Rabetafika

Ragland, Thomas Gajetan (1815–1858), Anglican missionary in South India. Of English and Italian descent, Ragland was born at Gibraltar, after the death of his father, an army officer, and was brought up in England by an uncle. He entered Cambridge in 1837, performing well academically and obtaining a fellowship. Volunteering to the Church Missionary Society (CMS), he was sent in 1845 to Madras, where he served as secretary to the CMS corresponding committee. Convinced that new initiatives in evangelism were needed, he proposed that several missionaries (preferably unmarried) and Indian catechists should itinerate from village to village. As a result, in 1854 the North Tinnevelly Itinerancy was begun. Ragland, whose colloquial Tamil was poor, was much helped by David Fenn and Robert Meadows. He eventually settled at Sivagasi, where he died suddenly. Though his missionary career was short, the Itinerancy continued, and by 1877 a Tinnevelly church was well established.

BIBLIOGRAPHY Amy Carmichael, *Ragland Pioneer* (1931); M. E. Gibbs, *The Anglican Church in India, 1600–1970* (1972); Thomas Thomason Perowne, *A Memoir of the Rev. Thomas Gajetan Ragland...* (1861).

Jocelyn Murray

Rahner, Karl (1904–1984), Roman Catholic theologian. Born in Freiburg im Breisgau, Germany, the son of a secondary school professor, Rahner entered the Society of Jesus in 1922. After pursuing the usual course of studies, he was ordained a priest in 1932. He was sent to the University of Freiburg to pursue a doctoral program in philosophy. His dissertation was rejected by his adviser but was published in 1939 as *Geist in Welt* (God in the world). He had a theological dissertation accepted at Innsbruck in 1936 and began teaching there in 1937. When the Nazis closed the theological faculty, Rahner went to Vienna, worked in a pastoral institute, and served a brief time as parish pastor. He returned to Innsbruck after the war and remained there until 1964, when he succeeded Romano Guardini in the chair of theology at Munich. In 1967 he moved to Münster, where he taught until his retirement in 1971. He remained active until a few days before his death, shortly after his eightieth birthday, in Innsbruck.

Rahner, whose literary output was prodigious, is widely regarded as the most important Roman Catholic theologian of the twentieth century. His theological essays, in English translation, are collected in *Theological Investigations* in 23 volumes. He co-edited, among others, the second edition of *Lexikon für Theologie und Kirche, Sacramentum Mundi,* and the *Quaestiones Disputatae* series. He also co-founded the international journal *Concilium.* His theology during and after the Second Vatican Council helped show how human history is played out within an invitation to divine grace. For mission history he is important for his proposals of how to see Christianity vis-à-vis other religions. He tried to demonstrate that the grace of Christ is at work implicitly in other religions, giving rise to the infelicitous term "anonymous Christianity," which actually obscures the intent and subtlety of Rahner's argument. In his final years, he developed a more trinitarian proposal, speaking of the interaction of Christ and the Holy Spirit in the world's religions. His concept of the world church helped broaden the horizons of many.

BIBLIOGRAPHY There is no complete bibliography of Rahner's publications. Roman Bleistein and E. Klinger, eds., *Bibliographie Karl Rahner, 1924–1969* and Roman Bleistein, ed., *Bibliographie Karl Rahner, 1969–1974* (1974) cover much of the bibliography. A good source of biographical material is Herbert Vorgrimler, *Understanding Karl Rahner* (1986). For an assessment of his proposals on Christ and other religions, see Joseph Wong, "Anonymous Christians: Karl Rahner's Pneuma Christocentrism and an East-West Dialogue," *Theological Studies* 55 (1994): 609–637. For an overall review of his thought, see William Dych, *Rahner* (1993).

Robert J. Schreiter, CPPS

Railton, George Scott (1849-1913), major figure in early formation of the Salvation Army. Born of Wesleyan missionary parents in Arbroath, Scotland, Railton was drawn to William *Booth's Christian Mission in 1873 by its militant evangelism, and was instrumental in the mission's transition in 1878 to the Salvation Army. In 1880 he was appointed by Booth to head a mission to the United States; subsequently he provided leadership in Germany and France. From 1885 onward he traveled indefatigably on every continent as Booth's mendicant ambassador, reconnoitering new mission fields with what Bramwell *Booth called the "restless, fearless, struggling spirit of advance." A prime contributor to the constitutive doctrinal statement of the Army and its earliest *Orders and Regulations,* Railton championed a strongly Wesleyan theology, an aggressive, unconventional mode of evangelism, the equality of women in ministry, and the sacramentalization of the whole of life. He believed the Army to be a modern adaptation of St. Francis's Little Brothers of the Poor, ordained for self-denying toil at the world's margins. A leader of uncommon learning and linguistic gifts among his contemporaries, Railton transmuted popular jingoism into impassioned Christian internationalism expressed by the lyrics of his many songs. Most importantly, perhaps, he proved a faithful—and sometimes critical—friend of the founders, a stubborn custodian of "the one great aim" in the Army's burgeoning array of human services. "The life of a soul-saver," he wrote, "is the grandest, merriest, strangest life that can be lived on earth." He died at a Cologne railway station while on a preaching tour in Germany.

BIBLIOGRAPHY George Scott Railton, *Twenty-One Years' Salvation Army* (1886), *Heathen England: Being a Description of the Utterly Godless Condition of the Vast Majority of the English Nation and of the Establishment, Growth, System and Success of an Army for Its Salvation* (1891) and *The Authoritative Life of General Booth* (1912). John D. Waldron, comp., *G. S. R.: Selections from Published and Unpublished Writings of George Scott Railton* (1981); Bernard Watson, *Soldier Saint: George Scott Railton, William Booth's First Lieutenant* (1970).

Lyell M. Rader, Jr.

Raimondi, Timoleone (1827-1894), first Catholic bishop of Hong Kong. Raimondi was born in Milan, Italy. Immediately after his ordination, he entered the newly founded Milan Foreign Missions Seminary in 1850 and was a member of the first group of Catholic missionaries who went to Micronesia/Melanesia in 1852. He began his missionary activity on the island of Woodlark, an extraordinarily difficult and thankless mission field. From 1856 to 1858 he worked on Borneo and Labuan. He was then transferred to Hong Kong, where his real missionary career began. In 1861 Louis Ambrosi, the prefect apostolic, made him his assistant. When Ambrosi died in 1867, Raimondi took his place, first as pro-prefect, then as prefect, and from 1874 as first bishop of the newly established vicariate apostolic, which, after the Convention of Peking (1860), included the Kowloon peninsula. The rapid growth of the mission was due to his tireless zeal. He got along well with the British administration in Hong Kong. He summoned the Christian Brothers for the education of boys. He worked well with the Canossian Sisters and the Sisters of St. Paul of Chartres, who looked after the girls. He founded brotherhoods and associations. He rebuilt the churches and schools destroyed by a cyclone in 1874. He built Hong Kong Cathedral. To collect the necessary funds he made visits to the Philippines, the United States, and Mexico. Raimondi was truly a pioneer missionary; his death meant the "end of an epoch," in the words of mission historian T. F. Ryan.

BIBLIOGRAPHY "Die im Jahre 1894 verstorbenen Bischöfe," *Die katholischen Missionen* (1895): 148; H. auf der Heide, *Die Missionsgenossenschaft von Steyl: Ein Bild der Ersten 25 Jahre ihres Bestehens* (1900); T. F. Ryan, *The Story of a Hundred Years* (1959); G. B. Tragella, *Le missioni estere di Milano,* 3 vols. (1950–1963).

Karl Müller, SVD

Ramabai Dongre Medhavi (Pandita Ramabai Sarasvati) (1858–1922), Indian Christian social reformer, educator and Bible translator. Ramabai Dongre (Dongre was her family name, Medhavi her married name) was born into a high-caste Hindu family. Her father was a wandering professional reciter of Hindu epic and mythological texts. Though it was then unusual in the case of a woman, Ramabai was taught Sanskrit and many of these texts. After her parents' death in the 1874 famine, she and her brother continued the family tradition. Going to Calcutta in 1878, the titles "Pandita" and "Sarasvati" were bestowed on her as an acknowledgement of her learning. She joined the Brahmo Samaj (a reformist Hindu association) and in June 1880 married a man of much lower caste than hers. Her only child, Manorama, was born in April 1881. Less than a year later her husband died of cholera, leaving her in the unenviable situation of a high-caste Hindu widow. Her hearing was by this time severely impaired. Through the influence of Nehemiah *Goreh's apologetical writings she became intellectually convinced that whatever was true in the Brahmo theology was actually Christian in origin, and in 1883, during a visit to England, she was baptized in the chapel of the (Anglican) Community of St. Mary the Virgin in Wantage, England, some of whose members she had met in Poona (Pune). She was in Europe to pursue a medical degree, which in the end her deafness made impossible. From 1883 to 1886 Ramabai was in the formal sense an Anglo-Catholic, while insisting that at heart she was still a Hindu.

The years 1886 to 1888 were spent in the United States, lecturing and studying social reform and education. In 1887 she published her first English book, *The High-Caste Hindu Woman,* a merciless indictment of Hindu India's treatment of its women, which was persuasive because it was written from the inside. Two years later she returned to India, and with American support, opened a non-proselytizing institute for the education of young Hindu widows. This was the *Sharna Sadan* (Abode of wisdom) in Bombay. It soon moved to Poona. The more famous orphanage, *Mukti* (Salvation) opened at Kedgaon in 1898. In the meantime, Ramabai herself had passed through a second conversion, this time an evangelical one, and for the remainder of her life her Christianity was close to the Keswick "holiness" pattern. A Pentecostal-style revival began at Mukti in 1905. Ramabai herself gave increasing attention to Marathi Bible translation. Because her health was poor, the running of Mukti was left mainly to others. Her daughter Manorama died in 1921, and Ramabai herself died the following year.

BIBLIOGRAPHY Shamsundar Manohar Adhav, ed., *Pandita Ramabai* (1979); Nicol Macnicol, *Pandita Ramabai* (1926); A. B. Shah, ed., *The Letters and Correspondence of Pandita Ramabai, compiled by Sister Geraldine, CSMV* (1977).

Eric J. Sharpe

Ramazotti, Angelo Francesco (1800–1861), founder of the Milan foreign mission seminary. Born in Milan, Ramazotti became a member of the Oblates of Saint Ambrose and Charles in Rho in 1828. Ordained to the priesthood in 1829, he became a strong advocate of missions, and as early as 1844 he wanted to found a foreign mission seminary. He was elected superior of Rho in 1839, 1841, and 1847. In 1847 Pius IX asked Archbishop Romilli of Milan to establish an institute for foreign missions. So in 1849, when Ramazotti was appointed bishop of Pavia, he was able to realize his vision. He chose the parish priest, Giuseppe Marinoni, to direct the institute, and in 1850 Pius IX and the Austrian government (to which the Milan region then belonged) approved of it. The seminary, known as the Pontifical Institute for Foreign Missions and dedicated exclusively to foreign missions, was opened on December 1, 1850. In 1860 Ramazotti sent the first Italian sisters to the foreign missions. He died the next year in Milan. In 1926 *Pius XI combined the seminary with the Pontifical Seminary of the Apostles St. Peter and Paul (founded 1868).

BIBLIOGRAPHY Alfonso Bassan, *Da avvocato a patriarca: Cenni biografici di mons. Angelo Ramazotti (1800–1861), fondatore del Pontificio Istituto Missioni Estere, Vesovo di Pavia, Patriarca di Venezia* (1960); Alberto Morelli, *La spiritualità missionaria del Patriarca Ramazotti, fondatore del P.I.M.E.* (1961); Giovanni Roncalli, *Monsignor Angelo Ramazotti* (1960). A special issue of *Le Missioni Cattoliche* 90 (1961): 361–436 was dedicated to Ramazotti.

Willi Henkel, OMI

Ramsey, Evelyn (1923–1989), Church of the Nazarene missionary doctor. Born in 1923 in Richmond, Kentucky, Ramsey was educated at Trevecca Nazarene College, Nashville; Eastern Nazarene College, Wollaston, Massachusetts; Vanderbilt University, Nashville; and Tufts University School of Medicine, Boston. From 1956 to 1968 she served in the Raleigh Fitkin Nazarene Hospital in Manzini, Swaziland. In 1969 she accepted transfer to the Nazarene Hospital in Kudjip, Papua New Guinea. Here a lifelong interest in linguistics blossomed, and her missionary activities expanded into translation work. She had studied French, Greek, Hebrew, and German, and in Africa she had learned both Zulu and Swazi. For the previously unrecorded Middle Wahgi language of Papua New Guinea, she developed a dictionary and compiled a concordance of the New Testament and Psalms in Pidgin. Her skills in medicine and in linguistics made a lasting impact in both Swaziland and Papua New Guinea. Retiring in 1988, she returned to Indianapolis, Indiana, where she died.

BIBLIOGRAPHY L. David Duff, *The Ramsey Covenant* (1985); J. Fred Parker, *Mission to the World* (1988).

Robert H. Scott

Ramseyer, Fritz (1840–1914) *and* **Rosa (Bontemps)** (1841–1906), Swiss missionaries in Ghana. Fritz and Rosa Ramseyer were by far the longest-surviving married couple among the missionaries of the Basel Mission (BM) in Ghana in the century before 1914. They were married there in 1866. Their life was unusually turbulent and endangered by war on the colonial frontier. Between 1875 and 1896 they maintained a missionary presence on the southeastern border of Asante in the district of Kwahu, which until 1888 was formally outside the British protectorate. They were held as hostages by the kingdom of Asante from 1869 to 1874 and were thus, with two other hostages, the Europeans who lived longest in independent Asante before its colonial subjection in 1896. Invited by the British colonial authorities to start a mission in the Asante capital, Kumase, they were besieged there during the Yaa Asantewa revolt in 1900 and were forced to flee with the greater part of the garrison. They returned to Europe together in 1904, and Rosa died in Switzerland. Fritz was back in Ghana from 1906 to 1908. He returned to Switzerland in 1908, where he died.

The Ramseyers are major figures in the oral tradition in the areas where they worked. For many Ghanaians they are the honored founders of the church, with churches, schools, and a lay-training center named after them. For others they are symbols of the colonial role of missionaries; some Ghanaians even refer to them as spies of the British. From about 1888 Fritz Ramseyer operated a camera. His excellent photographs capture missionary lifestyles as well as the indigenous environment in Kwahu in the 1890s.

BIBLIOGRAPHY Fritz Ramseyer, *Achtzig Ansichten von der Goldküste nach Originalaufnahmen des Missionars Fritz Ramseyer* (1895) and *Vier Jahre in Asante: Tagebücher der Missionare Ramseyer und Kühne aus der Zeit ihrer Gefangenschaft, bearbeitet von H. Gundert* (2d ed., 1875; this edition is to be preferred to the first German edition and to the English version prepared by Mrs. Weitbrecht, *Four Years in Ashantee* [1875]). Peter Haenger, "Die Basler Mission im Spannungsbereich afrikanischer Integrationsversuche und europäische Kolonialpolitik (Kawhu/Ghana, 1875–1888)" (M.A. thesis, Univ. of Basel, 1989); Adam Jones, "'Four Years in Asante': One Source or Several?" *History of Africa* 18 (1991): 173–203; M. A. Kwamena-Poh, *The Reverend F. A. Ramseyer and the Foundation of the Presbyterian Church in Kumase* (1974). Albums of Fritz Ramseyer's photographs are deposited in the Basel Mission archive and in Yale University.

Paul Jenkins

Rankin, Melinda (1811–1888), American independent missionary in Mexico and probably the first Protestant woman missionary in Latin America. Born in New England, Rankin began her work among Catholics in the Mississippi Valley. Encouraged by reports she received from North American soldiers who were returning to the United States after the war with Mexico, she moved to the Mexican border at Brownsville, Texas, in 1852. There, supported by the Presbyterian Board of Education, she developed a school for Mexican children in 1854. In 1857, when religious liberty was secured in Mexico, she moved to Matamoros, and later made her way to Monterrey, where she established a school and began distributing Bibles. She purchased property and subsidized converts to do missionary work. During those years she was associated with the small congregations gathered around James Hickey, a Baptist clergyman from Texas, and Thomas Martin Westrup, an Englishman of Anglican background. This independent movement did considerable evangelism among the mestizo population in the vicinity of Monterrey. In January 1864 the group was established as the first Baptist Church in Monterrey (the first organized evangelical church in Mexico). Later controversy between Rankin and Westrup, the pastor of the congregation, resulted in the division of the congregation. In 1869 Rankin invited a pastor of the Presbyterian Church, U.S.A., A. J. Park from Brownsville, to take the leadership of her small work. He developed a Presbyterian church which was the foundation of Presbyterian work in Mexico, while Westrup and his followers remained Baptists. In 1872 Rankin returned to the United States because of health problems. As a result of her work in organizing and mobilizing Mexican nationals to evangelize their country, fourteen congregations had been established, which were later incorporated into the Presbyterian Church.

BIBLIOGRAPHY Melinda Rankin, *Twenty Years among the Mexicans: A Narrative of Missionary Labor* (1875). Francis E. Clark and Harriet A. Clark, *The Gospel in Latin Lands* (1909); Tomás S. Goslin, *Los evangélicos en la América Latina* (1956); William A. Ross, *Sunrise in Aztec Lands* (1922); W. Reginald Wheeler, Dwight H. Day, and James B. Rodgers, *Modern Missions in Mexico* (1925).

Pablo A. Deiros

Ranson, Charles W(esley) (1903–1988), Methodist theological education adminstrator in India. Ranson was born in Ballyclare, County Antrim, Northern Ireland, studied at Edgehill Theological College and Queens University, Belfast, and later earned the B.Litt. degree at Oxford University (Oriel College, 1937). In 1929 he was ordained a minister of the Irish Methodist Conference and became a Methodist missionary to India. He studied Tamil and served in and around Madras, becoming acquainted with leaders of that city, both Christian and Hindu. His service in India, both rural and urban, involved evangelistic, educational, and social work. During World War II he was pastor in the summer capital of the (British) Government of India at Simla, where Viceroy Lord Linlithgow was often in attendance. In 1943 he joined the staff of the National Christian Council of India, Burma and Ceylon and was editor of its *Review.* Responsible for theological education, he made a survey that resulted in an important book, *The Christian Minister in India.* He became research secretary of the International Missionary Council (IMC) in 1946 and its general secretary the next year, serving in both London and New York, guiding the organization toward integration with the World Council of Churches in 1961. As founding director of the Theological Education Fund (1958–1963), he influenced theological training throughout the younger churches. During 1961 and 1962 he was president of the Irish Methodist Conference. From

1962 to 1968 he was professor of ecumenical theology at Drew University, Madison, New Jersey, and he was dean of its seminary from 1964 to 1966. From 1968 to 1972 he was professor of theology and ecumenics at Hartford Seminary, then pastor of the Congregational Church, Salisbury, Connecticut, until his retirement in 1975. Ranson knew and interacted with all the leading ecumenical figures of his time, and his many contributions to the world church placed him among the leading ranks. His name is associated with the Whitby, Willingen, and Ghana meetings of the IMC. He received the King George V medal (1935), the D. Theol. from Kiel University (1953), and an honorary S.T.D. from Dickinson College (1965).

BIBLIOGRAPHY Charles W. Ranson, *A City in Transition: Studies in the Social Life of Madras* (1938), *The Things That Abide* (1940), *The Christian Minister in India* (1946), *Renewal and Advance* (as editor) (1948), *Three Addresses* (1952), *That the World May Know* (1953), and *A Missionary Pilgrimage* (1988; his autobiography). James K. Mathews, "Charles W. Ranson," in Gerald H. Anderson et al., eds. *Mission Legacies* (1994), pp. 608–615. Ranson's papers are at Yale Univ. Divinity School Library.

James K. Mathews

Raphael, Brother. *See* Rasoamanarivo, Victoire.

Rasa, Clorinda (c. 1750–c. 1802), founder of the church of Tinnevelly, South India. Clorinda was the baptismal name given by C. F. *Schwartz in 1778 to Rasa, a Marathi Brahmin widow saved from committing sati (or suttee) by an English officer, Lyttelton, who was stationed at the court of the rajah of Tanjore. He took her in and instructed her in the faith but failed to marry her. Schwartz would not baptize her until after Lyttelton died. With courage and generosity she founded in her home in Palayankottai, in 1780, the oldest church in Tinnevelly. In 1784 she undertook the dangerous journey to Tanjore to plead for a missionary, and in 1785 Schwartz came and consecrated the church, still in use today, which she had built with the Lyttelton legacy. Schwartz found a house church of fifty-one converts and a village daughter church of twenty-four additional converts. The names on the register indicate that the fellowship was completely intercaste. She sent three young men to Tanjore for training as catechists and her adopted son for education by Schwartz. Unable to maintain a European missionary there for long, Schwartz stationed *Satthianadhan, an outstanding Indian priest and evangelist in Palayankottai. The church continued growing, despite fierce persecution. In 1821 John Hough, an evangelical chaplain, persuaded the Church Missionary Society to adopt the station. Criticized by Schwartz for her alleged pride and frivolity (which suggests a very human, independent-minded woman, as other reports show), Rasa's piety and faithfulness were unquestionable. A flourishing Church of South India diocese is now based there.

BIBLIOGRAPHY Robert Caldwell, *Records of the Early History of the Tinnevelly Mission* (1881); C. B. Firth, *An Introduction to Indian Church History* (1963); Hugh Pearson, *Life of Schwartz*, vol. 2 (1839), pp. 45–46.

E. M. Jackson

Rasalama, Rafaravavy (c. 1810–1837), first Malagasy Christian martyr. Rasalama was probably one of the earliest pupils in village schools set up by the London Missionary Society in 1824. When her family moved to Manjakaray on the outskirts of the capital, she joined the first Christian community at Ambodin'Andohalo, near the royal palace. She was among the first Malagasy to be baptized (May 1831) and to take part in the Lord's Supper at Ambatonakanga, the earliest church, on June 5, 1831. In 1835 when the new queen, Ranavalona I, declared Christianity illegal, Rasalama went into hiding. The cave where she took refuge near her house was discovered, and in July 1837 she was arrested and given to a courtier as a slave. She patiently bore ill treatment until she refused to work on a Sunday and provoked her master's anger by asserting her faith. She was sentenced to death on the ground of rebellion against the queen's will. On August 14, after a night of suffering in irons, Rasalama was taken to Ambohipotsy. Her walk to the place of execution, which she filled with prayers and hymns, has become legendary. She was speared and her body was left unburied. A memorial church stands on the site today. Her martyrdom made a deep impression on her fellow countrymen and British Protestants; a memorial plaque was put in Brunswick Chapel in Bristol, England.

BIBLIOGRAPHY R. Lovett, *The History of the London Missionary Society, 1795–1896* (1896); G. Mondain, *Un siècle de mission à Madagascar* (1926). Commemorations of her martyrdom have been the occasions for the production of numerous works, such as Rabary's *Ny Maritiora Malagasy* (1957).

Yvette Ranjeva Rabetafika

Rasoamanarivo, Victoire (1848–1894), first Malagasy beatified by the Roman Catholic Church. Rasomanarivo was born into the wealthiest and most powerful family of Madagascar. Entering the first Catholic girls' school in 1861, she became so attached to the nuns that she resisted her family's attempts to transfer her to a Protestant school. Victoire was the name given to her on her christening in 1863. She continued her schooling even after her marriage in 1864 to a cousin in compliance with family tradition. The union was unhappy because of the divergent interests of the couple. Victoire was absorbed in religion, going out at dawn to attend daily Mass, heading a Catholic women's association, and practicing charity. She consented, however, to remain within the court circle, whose frivolous tastes were more suited to her husband. Her courage was remarkable during the Franco-Malagasy War of 1883–1885, when Malagasy Catholics had to fend for themselves because of the departure of the French missionary priests. The latter entrusted her with the protection of the church, knowing her piety and privileged position as the niece and daughter-in-law of the prime minister, who was a Protestant. Thanks to her support, the Catholic Union headed by Paul *Rafiringa succeeded in safeguarding the church, and she was heralded as its guardian by the Catholic missionaries on their return. Despite illness, she devoted the rest of her life to active charity. Her body now rests in a chapel in front of the Catholic cathedral in Antananarivo. Her beatification was announced by *John Paul II in Madagascar on April 30, 1989.

BIBLIOGRAPHY Articles on Rasoamanarivo appear in biographical and historical dictionaries, such as *Hommes et destins,* vol. 3, *Madagascar* (1978) and *Dictionnaire historique et géographique de Madagascar* (1966). A. Boudou, *Madagascar, la mission de Tananarive* (1940); E. Colin and P. Suau, *Madagascar et la mission catholique* (1895); E. Fourcadier, *La vie héroïque de Victoire Rasoamanarivo* (1937); J. L. C. Ramahery, *L'ange visible de l'église naissante a Madagascar* (1970).

Yvette Ranjeva Rabetafika

Ratisbonne, Marie-Théodore (1802–1884) *and* **Marie-Alphonse** (1814–1884), founders of Catholic missions to Jews. Marie-Théodore Ratisbonne was the second eldest son of the most important Jewish family in Alsace. In 1827, partly through the influence of Simon Liebermann and Louis Bautin, and partly because of his own study of the Bible and church history, he was converted to Christianity. Ordained a Catholic priest in 1830, he taught in the minor seminary of the diocese of Strasbourg until 1840, when he moved to Paris. To promote understanding between Christians and Jews, and to work for the conversion of Jews, he founded the Congregation of Notre Dame de Sion (Sisters of Sion) in 1843 and the Fathers of Sion in 1852.

Marie-Alphonse Ratisbonne was the ninth child of the family and became a lawyer and a banker. At first he was very bitter about his brother having become a Christian, but on a trip to Rome in 1842 he was converted after claiming to have had a vision of Mary. He subsequently joined the Jesuits and was ordained a priest, but he left the Jesuits to help his brother in his work. In 1855 he went to Palestine, where he spent the rest of his life working to convert Jews and Muslims. He was a strong promoter of the devotion to the Miraculous Medal, a devotion that was begun by St. Catherine Labouré in 1830. He claimed that the Madonna of the medal was the one that had appeared to him and had effected his conversion to Christianity.

BIBLIOGRAPHY Marie-Théodore Ratisbonne, *Histoire de St. Bernard et de son siècle* (1840), *Manuel de la mère chrétienne* (1859), *Nouvelle manuel des mères chrétienne* (1870), and *La question juive* (1868). M. J. Eagan, *Christ's Conquest: The Coming of Grace to Theodore Ratisbonne* (1945) and *Our Lady's Jew: Father M.A. Ratisbonne* (1953); M. D. Gros, "Ratisbonne, Marie-Théodore," *Dizionario degli Istituti di Perfezione,* vol. 7 (1983), pp. 1214–1215; B. Raas, *Popular Devotions* (1992), pp. 105–106.

Stephen B. Bevans, SVD

Rauch, Christian Henry (1718–1763), first Moravian missionary among the American Indians. Rauch was born at Bernburg, Anhalt-Bernburg (now in Germany), and united with the Moravian Church at Marienborn in 1739. He became an assistant to Count *Zinzendorf in mission work and arrived in New York in 1740, under commission of the Marienborn synod, to begin work among the Native Americans in New York. He married Ann Elizabeth Robins at Philadelphia in 1742, after he had already established work at Shekomeko, New York. His success among the Indians was due largely to the strategy he used in his initial visit among them. Upon arriving at their camp, he spoke to them of the person and work of Jesus rather than trying to convince them of the existence of God, and upon finishing his message, he lay down in their midst and slept peacefully. This degree of trust and faith in God's providence moved the Indians beyond any prior mission strategies and gained for him an open door. He was ordained in 1740 and continued work among the Mohegans in Dutchess County, New York, where he baptized the first three converts, naming them Abraham, Isaac, and Jacob. He served as pastor of the German congregations at Warwick, Pennsylvania, and at Bethabara, North Carolina.

In 1756 Rauch went to Jamaica as superintendent of the mission. The methods he had used with the Indians did not work well among the Jamaican slaves, but Rauch imposed his approach on his fellow missionaries, and the work declined as a result. He died and is buried at Old Carmel, Jamaica.

BIBLIOGRAPHY *Bethlehem Diary* 26; J. T. Hamilton and K. G. Hamilton, *History of the Moravian Church* (1967); S. U. Hastings and B. L. MacLeavy, *Seedtime and Harvest* (1979); Karl-Wilhelm Westmeier, *The Evacuation of Shekomeko and the Early Moravian Missions to Native North Americans* (1994).

Albert H. Frank

Ravoux, Augustin (1815–1906), French Catholic missionary in the American Northwest Territory. Ravoux was born at Langeac, Auvergne, France. While studying theology, he transferred to the diocese of Dubuque, Iowa, arriving in the United States in 1837. After ordination in 1840, he was sent to minister to the frontiersmen of Prairie du Chien, Wisconsin. In 1841 he began his missionary work among the Sioux Indians of the Minnesota River Valley, the first priest to serve the area in almost one hundred years. He mastered three dialects and in 1843 published a catechism and hymnal called *Wakantanka Ti Ki Chanku* (The path to the house of God). Because he was the only priest in Minnesota from 1844 to 1851, Catholic settlers in the Saint Paul area came to require most of his attention. Still, he continued to visit the Sioux villages. When thirty-eight Indians were condemned to be hanged for leading an uprising in 1862, all but five of them asked for Ravoux to prepare them for death. In 1850, largely through his efforts, the diocese of Saint Paul was created. He eventually retired to its cathedral rectory, where he wrote *Reminiscences, Memoirs and Lectures* (1890), *Labors of Mgr. A. Ravoux at Mendota, St. Paul and Other Localities* (1897), *Catholic Life in St. Paul* (1899), and *Tempus tacendi et tempus loquendi* (1901).

BIBLIOGRAPHY Mary Aquinas Norton, *Catholic Missionary Activities in the Northwest, 1818–1864* (1980); J. M. Reardon, *The Catholic Church in the Diocese of St. Paul* (1952).

Achiel Peelman, OMI

Rawlinson, Frank Joseph (1871–1937), longtime editor of the *Chinese Recorder.* Born in England and raised in a conservative Plymouth Brethren home, Rawlinson went to China in 1902 as a Southern Baptist missionary but in 1921 was separated from that mission for his liberal views and became a missionary of the American Board of Commissioners for Foreign Missions. Living his entire career in Shanghai, he was at the center of ferment, both in church and mission, and in the national scene, as China struggled to find national unity while the Protestant churches sought ways for interchurch unity. He was the liberal, outspoken editor of the *Chinese Recorder* from 1914 until his death in Shanghai in 1937, which occurred as a result of Japanese bombing.

In later years Rawlinson constantly questioned his own missiology and role, his personal struggles reflecting those in church and nation. As he contemplated the enormity of social problems in China, he looked for solutions in ecumenical cooperation, such as the National Christian Conference (1922) and the National Christian Council of China. He was a principal organizer of the Moral Welfare League of Shanghai and, beginning in 1922, was editor of the *China Christian Yearbook,* published by the China Christian Council. Always sympathetic to Chinese nationalism, he hoped that China might some day have a universal religion, based on Christianity and supported by the weight of Chinese tradition. His writing constantly probed the questions of the day, asking "Whither China?" or "Whither church and mission?" An early issue of *Life* magazine called him "one of the most influential white men in China." He was a prototype for the progressive, socially concerned missionary of his time. The best source of his thinking can be found in the many articles he wrote for the *Chinese Recorder.*

BIBLIOGRAPHY Katherine Lodwick, ed., *The Chinese Recorder Index: A Guide to Christian Missions in Asia, 1867–1941* (1991); Wallace Merwin, *Adventure in Unity: The Church of Christ in China* (1974); John Lang Rawlinson, *Rawlinson, the Recorder, and China's Revolution: A Topical Biography of Frank Joseph Rawlinson, 1871–1937* (1990).

Donald E. MacInnis

Read, James (1777–1852), London Missionary Society (LMS) missionary pastor among the Cape Coloured of South Africa. Born in Essen, England, Read, like so many other LMS volunteers, was a skilled artisan, a carpenter. In 1798 he was sent to the South Seas by the LMS, but his ship was captured by the French. Eventually Read got back to Britain. In 1800 he went to the Cape Colony to help J. Van der *Kemp. He aided in the setting up of Bethelsdorp, a large settlement of Khoi and people of mixed race. These were soon to be deemed, along with freed slaves, one people, the Cape Coloureds. At Bethelsdorp and the other settlements of the LMS the Coloureds enjoyed more freedom than anywhere else in the colony.

Read married Sara, a Khoi. Of their children, James, Jr., became a leading evangelist and minister; their daughters were teachers; and Joseph was a hero of the frontier as an officer of the Cape Regiment. Read helped many people bring charges of ill treatment against their masters to the new British courts set up in 1811, for which many whites never forgave him. He then went north of the Orange River outside the colony, contacting a number of groups among the Tswana people, which prepared the way for Robert *Moffat.

Serving as John *Philip's right-hand man, Read played an important role in the campaign that achieved equality for all before the law in 1828. In 1829, the newly created Kat River settlements of the Coloured people called Read to be their minister and he stayed there for most of the rest of his life. Under Read's leadership, the church at Kat River became an active evangelistic community; it also created good relations with the Xhosa across the frontier. All of this was destroyed in the frontier war of 1850–1851 when the old man had to leave Kat River. He removed to nearby Elandi Port, where he died.

BIBLIOGRAPHY Christopher Saunders, "James Read: Towards a Reassessment," in Collected Seminar Papers, Institute of Commonwealth Studies, London (1977). See also Andrew C. Ross, *John Philip* (1986).

Andrew C. Ross

Rebmann, Johannes (1820–1876), missionary, explorer, and linguist in East Africa. A German Lutheran trained at Basel Mission seminary in Switzerland, Rebmann was accepted by the Church Missionary Society (CMS) for work in East Africa and received Anglican orders in 1845. He joined Johann Ludwig *Krapf in Mombasa in 1846 and remained in East Africa continuously, apart from two short visits to Egypt, until 1875. During his first visit to Egypt he married a widowed teacher, Mrs. Tyler, who died in 1866. He made several journeys into the hinterland and in 1848 became the first European to sight Mount Kilimanjaro and report that it was snow-covered. He visited Chaga country around Kilimanjaro three times. In 1855, together with Johann Erhardt (another CMS missionary), he published a map based on local information that placed Mounts Kenya and Kilimanjaro approximately correctly and indicated the existence of a huge inland sea. This provided the stimulus for the journeys of the British explorers Speke and Burton, the discovery by Europeans of Lakes Victoria and Tanganyika, and of the kingdom of Buganda, where Christian missions had their first major success in East Africa.

After Krapf was invalided to Europe in 1855, Rebmann remained at Rabai just inland from the coastal plain with a tiny handful of converts. In 1864 he was joined by Ismael Semler (later ordained). Semler originally came from Mozambique, was freed from slavery by the British, and was raised in a CMS settlement in India, where Karl Wilhelm *Isenberg worked for a time. In 1875 the CMS established a freed slave settlement near Mombasa, new missionaries arrived, and Rebmann, now blind and ill, returned to Germany where he joined Krapf at Korntal. The following year, just before he died, he married Mrs. Finkh (a widow), who survived him.

Rebmann's contributions to East African history were his geographical discoveries and his linguistic achievements: he compiled vocabularies in several languages and translated the Gospels of Luke and John into Swahili.

BIBLIOGRAPHY The main sources for Rebmann's life are Eugene Stock, *The History of the Church Missionary Society,* vol. 2 (1899), pp. 124–138, and J. L. Krapf, *Travels, Researches and Missionary Labours* (1860). The *Church Missionary Intelligencer* also contains useful material.

M. Louise Pirouet

Reed, George C. (1872–1966), American missionary to Morocco and Mali. Born to Christian parents in Weeping Water, Nebraska, Reed was educated at Oberlin College. He joined Gospel Missionary Union (GMU) in 1896 and arrived in Morocco in 1897. He learned Arabic and the difficult Berber dialect of Shilha. With Clinton Reed, a cousin, he translated Matthew, John, Acts, and Romans into colloquial Arabic. He lived among the Berbers, witnessing and preaching. In 1913 he accompanied George S. *Fisher, GMU founder, on the first-ever survey of the French Sudan by Protestant missionaries. They spent six weeks at Timbuktu, preaching and teaching. The Treaty of St. Germain opened up the French Sudan to missions, and Reed and two companions took up work there in 1919. They crisscrossed the country (present-day Mali) with walking trips of over 300 miles. Reed preached in the open air whenever possible and set up a systematic visitation program that reached a thousand people per month. His translation of the Bible into Bambara, an important trade language of West Africa, was published by the British and Foreign Bible Society—the New Testament in 1937 and the entire Bible in 1963. He was honored with the Cross of the Legion of Honor by the French minister of colonies in 1950 at the public square in Bamako. He retired from the field in 1951 having served 54 years in Morocco and Mali.

BIBLIOGRAPHY Reed's letters and reports were published in the *Gospel Message* (1897–1952), a magazine of the GMU. GMU holds "George C. Reed and the French Sudan," a manuscript by Dick L. Darr based on articles in the *Gospel Message,* oral history interviews with Reed's earliest co-workers, and personal conversations with Reed in his retirement years. See also Don P. Shidler, *Exploits of Faith* (1982), pp. 114–121.

Dick L. Darr

Reed, Mary (1854–1943), American missionary to lepers at Chandag, India. At age 16, Reed became an active Methodist. For a decade she taught school; then feeling called to zenana work (evangelism among secluded women in India), she applied to the Woman's Foreign Missionary Society (WFMS) of the Methodist Episcopal Church. In 1884 she arrived in India and undertook teaching and zenana visitation. In 1890 she returned to America for her health, but her symptoms were not alleviated by surgery. She realized in a vision that she had leprosy and that God planned for her to work among India's lepers. Receiving medical confirmation of leprosy, she returned to India without bidding farewell to her family.

In 1891 Bishop James *Thoburn approached the Mission to Lepers in India and the East on her behalf. While continuing as WFMS district missionary, she became supervisor of the leper asylum at Chandag. She upgraded the housing, food, education, and medical care of the lepers. By 1897, of the 85 lepers in the colony, 67 had become Christians. In 1898 Reed severed her ties with the WFMS to work full-time with the lepers. Believing in divine healing, Reed refused medical treatment and by 1899 her health seemed restored. She supervised the leper asylum until 1938. She died in India of an accident due to her failing eyesight.

BIBLIOGRAPHY John Jackson, *Mary Reed: Missionary to the Lepers* (c. 1900). Short accounts include a profile in Annie Ryder Gracey, *Eminent Missionary Women* (1898); Lee S. Huizenga, *Mary Reed of Chandag* (1939); and Julia Lake Kellersberger, *Mary Reed, My Jewel* (n.d.).

Dana L. Robert

Reekie, Archibald Brownlee (1867–1942), pioneer Canadian Baptist missionary in Bolivia. Reekie was born of Scottish lineage in Kincardine, Ontario, Canada, converted at 16 and baptized at 20 in the Tiverton Baptist Church. He was possessed from early youth by an attraction to South America, and his sense of a divine call to Bolivia came while he was pursuing studies at McMaster University in Toronto, Ontario. After ordination, some pastoral experience, and an investigatory visit to Bolivia in 1896, he was commissioned by the Canadian Baptist Board of Foreign Mission to begin in 1898 the first permanent Protestant work in Bolivia. This was the last country in Latin America for such permanent work to begin. The persecution that Reekie and his co-workers had to endure was intensified by a constitutional prohibition until 1905 of all public exercise of non-Roman Catholic religion. From 1899 the control by the liberal party for 20 years progressively reduced the opposition. Church growth, however, was discouragingly slow. Day schools for both Spanish and Indian populations, an agricultural project that became a model for later land reform, and supportive mutual relations with the Methodists and the Bolivian Indian Mission contributed greatly to the development of Bolivian Protestantism. In 1990 there were 15,000 members in the church he founded. Largely because of his wife's extended illness, Reekie retired to Canada after 23 years of service.

BIBLIOGRAPHY *Annual Report,* 1897–1911 and 1912–1966, Board of Foreign Mission, Baptist Convention of Ontario and Quebec; William H. Brackney, ed., *Bridging Cultures and Hemispheres: The Legacy of Archibald Reekie and Canadian Baptists in Bolivia* (1997); Norman H. Dabbs, *Dawn over the Bolivian Hills* (1952); H. E. Stillwell, *Pioneering in Bolivia* (1923). See also Wilson T. Boots, "Protestant Christianity in Bolivia: Mission Theory and Practice in Three Mission Churches" (Ph.D. diss., American Univ., 1971).

Sidney H. Rooy

Reeve, William (1794–1850), pioneer London Missionary Society (LMS) worker in southern India. Reeve came from northern England. Like all nonconformists at that time, he was barred from studying at a university, but was trained at Gosport by the notable David *Bogue. Reeve was only 22 when he arrived in India in 1816 with several other LMS recruits, at a time when British policy in India made mission expansion possible. He was located at Bellary, northwest of Madras, a Kanarese-speaking area, and remained there until 1824. After leave in England he returned to Bangalore, where he spent another seven years, working on a Kanarese-English dictionary. He had previously cooperated in the Kanarese translation of the New Testament (1821), and later the Old Testament (1827). In 1834, he left India for health reasons and in 1836 he took up a pastorate at Oswestry, England, where he served until his death. In helping to make the Bible available, he contributed to the building up of the local church in Travancore and Mysore.

BIBLIOGRAPHY R. Lovett, *The History of the London Missionary Society, 1795–1895,* 2 vols. (1899).

Jocelyn Murray

Reginhar (*or* Renharius; Regenharius) (d. 838), bishop of Passau in Bavaria. Reginhar sent Frankish missionary priests to work in Moravia, but later lore that credits him with the conversion of the entire region is not entirely trustworthy. He evidently did visit Moravia and organized synods to strengthen the missionaries there. One of the unusual aspects of his mission was to appoint archpriests for each diocese as representatives of the bishop. Missionaries worked under them. Mojmír, leader of the Moravian tribes, was baptized during Reginhar's missionary leadership.

BIBLIOGRAPHY Francis Dvornik, *Byzantine Missions among the Slavs: Sts. Constantine-Cyril and Methodius* (1970), pp. 79–80.

Frederick W. Norris

Régis, Jean-Baptiste (1663–1738), Jesuit missionary and cartographer in China. Born in Istres près d'Aix, Bouches-du-Rhône, France, Régis entered the Society of Jesus at Avignon in 1679. He left La Rochelle in March 1698, reaching Canton (Guangzhou) in November, and was called to Peking (Beijing) because of his knowledge of astronomy and mathematics. To fulfill the 1708 imperial rescript ordering the Jesuits to make an atlas of the empire, Régis and several confreres first completed a map of the area from the Great Wall to Peking. After this initial success, he was occupied until 1715 with mapping Manchuria, seven provinces of China, and the island of Taiwan. During such travel he and his confreres were able to establish several new mission stations. Returning to Peking in early 1717, Régis and his colleagues assembled fifty maps into an atlas presented to the emperor in 1718. They were later engraved and published in Paris. Régis was the first missionary to translate the *I-ching* (Book of changes), then considered the oldest of the Chinese classics and one of the most difficult to comprehend. Some of his essays on that work and on Chinese chronology were published after his death in Peking.

BIBLIOGRAPHY *Huang-ch'ao yü-ti tsung-t'u* (General atlas of the empire, compiled by Régis et al.) (1718). M. d'Anville, *Atlas Général de la Chine* (1730–1734); Jean-Baptiste du Halde, *Description géographique, historique, chronologique, politique et physique de l'Empire de la Chine et de la Tartarie chinoise,* 4 vols. (1735; 1736), 4:1–32, 423–451, 459–472, and the 25 maps; Walter Fuchs, *Der Jesuiten Atlas der K'ang-hsi Zeit* (1943). See also *I-king, antiquissimus Sinarum liber,* 2 vols. (1834–1839); "Agreement of the Chronology of the Chinese Annals with the Epochs of Ancient History," *North China Herald,* no. 64 (October 18, 1851); *Shanghai Miscellany for 1852* and *Shanghai Miscellany for 1853.*

John W. Witek, SJ

Reichelt, Karl Ludvig (1877–1952), Norwegian Lutheran missionary to China and scholar of Chinese religion. Reichelt was born in the south of Norway and while still a young man became a noted revivalist preacher. After missionary training for the Norwegian Missionary Society (NMS) in Stavanger, he arrived in China in October 1903. For some years he carried out unspectacular work, first in local churches, and after 1913 in theological education. But already he had a dream of a specialist mission directed toward China's Buddhist monks. In 1919 he met and baptized a young monk, Kuantu, and in 1920 he inaugurated what eventually became the Christian Mission to Buddhists, at first under NMS auspices (1922–1926), but later independent. Its first center in Nanking was destroyed in the civil war of 1927. After some uncertainty, a new site was found at Shatin in the New Territories of Hong Kong, and Tao Fong Shan (The hill from which the wind of the spirit blows) was dedicated in 1931. It is now known as Tao Fong Shan Christian Centre. Reichelt had a pietist background, but intellectually he was moderately liberal, a believer in the Johannine *logos* doctrine and the fulfillment relationship between Mahayana Buddhism and Christianity. At the Tambaram International Missionary Council conference in 1938 he emerged as a critic of, and was criticized by, Hendrik *Kraemer on these grounds. Mostly he wrote in Norwegian and Chinese, relatively little being translated. *Religion in Chinese Garment,* the best known of his books, appeared in English in 1951 (originally published in 1913). He also wrote *Truth and Tradition in Chinese Buddhism* (1930).

During the Japanese occupation of Hong Kong, Reichelt was held under house arrest at Tao Fong Shan. After the liberation he returned to Norway, but in 1951 he was back again in Hong Kong, where he died early the following year. He is buried in the Tao Fong Shan cemetery.

BIBLIOGRAPHY Håkan Eilert, *Boundlessness: Studies in Karl Ludvig Reichelt's Missionary Thinking* (1974); Filip Riisager, *Forventning og Opfyldelse* (Expectation and fulfillment) (1973, in Danish); Eric J. Sharpe, *Karl Ludvig Reichelt: Missionary, Scholar and Pilgrim* (1984); Notto Reidar Thelle, "Karl Ludvig Reichelt," in Gerald H. Anderson et al., eds., *Mission Legacies* (1994), pp. 216–224.

Eric J. Sharpe

Reid, Gilbert (1857–1927), missionary reformer in China. A graduate of Hamilton College and Union Theological Seminary, New York, and self-educated in Chinese classics and culture, Reid began his 45-year career in China in 1882 as a Presbyterian missionary. Frustrated by unsuccessful efforts to help the Ching (Qing) government manage the yearly flooding of the Yellow River and by the violent opposition of local officials as he sought to buy mission property in Tsinan (Jinan), Shantung (Shandong) Province, he proposed a new focus for missionary work. He saw clearly that the principal opposition to Christianity in China came from the "higher classes"—ministers of state in the capital, local officials, and the local elite. This led him in 1894 to propose founding the Mission among the Higher Classes in China (MHCC). This vision was too radical for his Presbyterian board to accept, and Reid was forced to resign. His approach was to make friends with officials rather than to evangelize, and to help them to see how the Christian faith and other religions would give moral stamina and spiritual vision to the country. The MHCC, later called the International Institute of China, was officially sanctioned by the government in 1897 and influenced significantly the Chinese reformers of 1898. Failure of the reform movement and the Boxer uprising caused Reid to move the MHCC to newly erected facilities in Shanghai, where it was approved both by the Manchu government in 1909 and the new republic in 1914. In this new setting the MHCC promoted the values of Western civilization and better understanding between Westerners and Chinese.

BIBLIOGRAPHY Gilbert Reid, *Glances at China* (1892), *China, Captive or Free? A Study of China's Entanglements* (1921), and *A Christian Appreciation of Other Faiths* (1921). The best account of Reid's life is "Gilbert Reid's Biographical Record," Presbyterian Historical Society, Philadelphia. See also Mingteh Tsou, "Christian Missionary as Confucian Intellectual: Gilbert Reid in China, 1882–1927" (Ph.D. diss., Michigan State Univ., in preparation).

Ralph R. Covell

Reindorf, Carl Christian (1834–1917), pioneer Ghanaian pastor and historian. Reindorf was born into a Ghanaian trading family in Accra that had known some intermarriage with Danish officials and merchants. Trained by the Basel Mission (BM), he became a teacher, and later pastor, in the BM church in Ghana. He was the first African to publish a full-length Western-style history of a region of Africa. The background to this work is obscure, but Reindorf was partly inspired by the linguistic and publishing work of his BM colleague J. G. *Christaller, who worked on oral tradition during his time in Ghana in the third quarter of the nineteenth century. Reindorf interviewed more than 200 people of both sexes in assembling his history. Unfortunately, both Reindorf and his Church Missionary Society pastor colleague in Yorubaland, Samuel *Johnson, who published the pioneering history of the Yoruba, have been ignored in the second half of the twentieth century. Reindorf's career with the BM is little known, but family records indicate that he was well respected for his healing powers, and the BM archive suggests that he was well able to articulate an independent line over against the missionaries when he felt this was necessary.

BIBLIOGRAPHY Carl Christian Reindorf, *The History of the Gold Coast and Asante* (1895, 1966). Raymond Jenkins, "Gold Coast Historians and Their Pursuit of the Gold Coast Pasts, 1882–1918" (Ph.D. diss., Univ. of Birmingham, 1985). C. D. Reindorf, *Remembering Rev. Carl Reindorf* (1984).

Paul Jenkins

Rein-Wuhrmann, Anna (1881–1971), missionary teacher for the Basel Mission (BM) in Cameroon and gifted photographer. Rein-Wuhrmann was born as Anna Wuhrmann in Marseille, France, of Swiss parents. She was educated in Switzerland and trained as a teacher. In 1910 she was accepted by the BM and was sent to Cameroon in 1911, at that time under German colonial rule. She became principal of a girls' school in Foumban, the seat of the influential Bamum king, Njoya. Her special relationship with Njoya enabled her to create a unique pictorial record of his kingdom before its conversion to Islam. In 1915 all Basel missionaries were interned by the British, and Anna Wuhrmann was forced to return to Switzerland. She went back to Foumban in 1920 in the service of the Paris Evangelical Missionary Society, as this part of Cameroon was now under French mandate. She returned to Switzerland in 1922; the next year she married R. Rein, a German teacher, and went to live in Germany, where she also took up teaching. Her husband died in 1943, and Anna Rein-Wuhrmann returned to Switzerland in 1945. She wrote a number of books, tracts, and articles on Cameroon and the people she had worked with.

BIBLIOGRAPHY Anna Rein-Wuhrmann, *Mein Bamumvolk im Grasland von Kamerun* (1925), *Fumban, die Stadt auf dem Schutte: Arbeit und Ernte im Missionsdienst in Kamerun* (1948) and *Niemals zurueck, Erzaehlung aus dem Grasland von Kamerun* (1948). Rein-Wuhrmann's photographs are reproduced and commented on in Henri Nicod and A. Rein-Wuhrmann, *La danseuse du roi* (1950) and in Christraud M. Geary, *Images from Bamum: German Colonial Photography at the Court of King Njoya* (1988). Her tracts and articles as well as correspondence and photographic collection are in the BM archive.

Waltraud Ch. Haas

Reischauer, August Karl (1879–1971), Presbyterian missionary in Japan. Born in Jonesboro, Illinois, Reischauer graduated from Hanover (Indiana) College and McCormick Seminary and was ordained to the Presbyterian ministry. In 1905 he married Helen S. Oldfather. They had two sons and one daughter; their son Edwin became a Harvard professor of Japanese studies and U.S. ambassador to Japan (1961–1966). The Reischauers were appointed by the Presbyterian Board in 1905 as missionaries to Japan, where Reischauer's principal assignment was to teach ethics and philosophy at Meiji Gakuin College in Tokyo. In 1913 he worked with David B. *Schneder of Tohoku Gakuin and Arthur Berry of Aoyama Gakuin on plans for a union Christian university, but these hopes did not achieve fruition until after World War II. The Reischauers were instrumental in founding Tokyo Woman's Christian College (1918) and the Japan Deaf Oral School (1920), the latter begun from concerns about their daughter, Felicia, who was deaf. Reischauer taught at the Japan Theological Seminary and helped in its eventual merger with other theological schools to form what later became Tokyo Union Theological Seminary. He was also involved in founding the National Christian Council of Japan (1922). An astute scholar, his book on Japanese Buddhism was used as a text in Japanese Buddhist schools. Reischauer retired to Duarte, California, where he died.

BIBLIOGRAPHY August Karl Reischauer, *Buddhist Gold Nuggets* (1912), *Studies in Japanese Buddhism* (1917; his most influential work), *The Task in Japan: A Study in Modern Missionary Imperatives* (1926), and *The Nature and Truth of the Great Religions: Toward a Philosophy of Religion* (1966).

James M. Phillips

Remigius of Reims (c. 436–c. 533), Apostle of the Franks and bishop of Reims. Born in Château-Porcien, north of Reims, of noble parents belonging to the senatorial class, Remigius manifested gifts of scholarship and holiness that led to his election as bishop of Reims at the age of 22 (c. 458). He witnessed the collapse of Roman rule in Gaul and the emergence of new kingdoms. He established bishoprics in surrounding cities like Tournai, Cambrai, Arras, and Laon. He wrote a letter to King Clovis on his accession to the throne (c. 481), setting up the ideal of the Christian ruler who listens to his advisers (including the bishops), protects widows and orphans, and fights for justice and against corruption. The moral authority emanating from this and other messages, the influence of Clovis's wife, Clotilde, and the eagerness of the Franks to "follow the immortal God preached by Remigius," led to the conversion of Clovis to Latin Christianity. Remigius baptized and anointed Clovis on December 25, 499, urging him to renounce idolatry: "Bow your head softly, Sigamber [the name of the tribe]; adore what you have burnt, burn what you have adored."

BIBLIOGRAPHY Kurt Schäferdiek, "Remigius von Reims," *Zeitschrift für Kirchengeschichte* 94 (1983): 256–278 (bibliography). See also Eugen Ewig and Kurt Schäferdiek, "Christliche Expansion im Merowingerreich," *Kirchengeschichte als Missionsgeschichte* 1 (1978): 116–145; Laurent Theis, *Histoire du Moyen Age français* (1992).

Marc R. Spindler

Renner, Melchior (c. 1770–1821), pioneer German missionary in Sierra Leone. Renner was one of two German Lutherans who became the earliest missionaries of the Church Missionary Society (CMS) in West Africa. Recruited in 1801 by the Berlin Mission seminary, accepted by CMS, and given Lutheran orders in 1803, he was sent to Freetown, Sierra Leone, in 1804. At the society's urging, in 1808 he founded a station on the mission frontier to the north, located on the Rio Pongas among the Susu people. He attempted to study the Susu language and ran schools with his wife, who was of African extraction. But the mission was judged to be unsuccessful, and in 1815 he returned to Freetown where he served churches in the Sierra Leone peninsula. He lived in Africa until his death.

BIBLIOGRAPHY *CMS Register* (1905); Charles Hole, *The Early History of the CMS. . . to 1814* (1896); S. A. Walker, *Missions in Western Africa* (1845). Renner materials are held in the CMS archives, Univ. of Birmingham.

P. E. H. Hair

Reynolds, Hiram Farnham (1854–1938), general superintendent of the Church of the Nazarene and influential missions leader. Converted in a Methodist church in 1876, Reynolds briefly studied at Burr and Burton Congregationalist Seminary and Montpelier Methodist Seminary, both in Vermont. He began his ministry in 1879, the same year in which he married Stella Byerd. Identifying with the Wesleyan holiness movement, Reynolds left the Methodist church in 1895 and joined the Association of Pentecostal Churches of America (APCA). Because of his strong support for missions, he became its home and foreign missions secretary two years later.

When the APCA merged with Phineas F. Bresee's Church of the Nazarene to form the Pentecostal Church of the Nazarene in 1907 (after 1919, the Church of the Nazarene), Reynolds became a general superintendent along with Bresee, serving at that post for 25 years. He became missionary secretary (1907–1919) and president of the missionary board (1907–1923). In 1913–1914 he toured Nazarene missions overseas to assess and encourage the work; his reflections are found in *Worldwide Missions* (1915). With his wife and others, he helped initiate the church-related Woman's Foreign Missionary Society (the present-day Nazarene World Mission Society for women and men). Reynolds played a formative role in the development of the Church of the Nazarene and vigorously supported its mission enterprise until his death.

BIBLIOGRAPHY Amy N. Hinshaw, *In Labors Abundant* (1938); Mervel Lunn, *Hiram F. Reynolds: Mr. World Missionary* (1968); J. Fred Parker, *Mission to the World: A History of Missions in the Church of the Nazarene through 1985* (1988); Timothy L. Smith, *Called unto Holiness. The Story of the Nazarenes: The Formative Years* (1962); Mendell Taylor, *Fifty Years of Nazarene Missions,* 3 vols. (1952–1958). The papers of Hiram F. Reynolds are housed at the Nazarene archives, Kansas City, Mo.

Gary B. McGee

Rhenius, Carl Theophilus Ewald (1790–1838), linguist and missionary among the Tamil population of

South India. According to Stephen *Neill, Rhenius was "one of the greatest among the missionaries in India." He was born in West Prussia, trained in Johann *Jänicke's mission seminary at Berlin, and in 1814 was sent out by the Church Missionary Society (CMS) to Madras where he studied Tamil and became a linguist of remarkable ability. But only after transfer by the CMS to Palayankottai, Tirunelveli, in 1820 was he able to display his talents to the full, in cooperation with a group of like-minded German and Swiss missionaries. The CMS mission in that remote part of South India had begun as a branch of Tanjore in the time of C. F. *Schwartz, and followed the Lutheran Tranquebar tradition. Rhenius and his colleagues were evangelists of unusual zeal. In 1825 they reported more than 3,000 converts in ninety villages. But a crisis arose when Rhenius proposed that some evangelists should be ordained according to Lutheran custom, without participation of a bishop. However, by that time an Anglican bishop had arrived at Calcutta, and the CMS committee at Madras disagreed with Rhenius. After extended debate, the CMS declared in 1835 that Rhenius's connection with it had come to an end. His fellow continental missionaries resigned with him. But when his catechists pleaded with him to return, Rhenius yielded to their urging and began to work independently with his German and Swiss colleagues as the German Evangelical Mission, consisting of 67 out of the 293 Tirunelveli congregations. Only after Rhenius's death did the remaining German missionaries and their congregations return to the CMS. Today Rhenius is remembered not only as one of the ablest writers and translators in Tamil, but also as one of the fathers of the Tirunelveli church.

BIBLIOGRAPHY J. Rhenius, ed., *Memoir of the Rev. C. T. E. Rhenius* (1841); Hans Jacob Cnattingius, *Bishops and Societies: A Study of Anglican Colonial and Missionary Expansion* (1952).

Hans-Werner Gensichen

Rhodes, Alexandre de (1591–1660), pioneer Jesuit missionary to Vietnam. Rhodes was born in the papal enclave of Avignon, now part of France. He entered the Society of Jesus in 1612 and in 1623 was sent to Macao, the center for missions in eastern Asia. He entered Vietnam in 1624, was forced to leave in 1626, returned in 1627, and was again forced to leave in 1630. At that time, Vietnamese was written in Chinese characters, but he devised a system for writing it in Roman letters; this became the official writing system for the language. He also wrote the first books in that alphabet—a catechism, a dictionary of French-Vietnamese, and a Vietnamese grammar. A phenomenal linguist, Rhodes spoke twelve languages fluently. With his brother Jesuits, his missionary efforts in Vietnam were successful, despite intermittent opposition. By 1640 they had won 100,000 Vietnamese to the church. He returned again to Vietnam in 1642 and was forced to leave for the last time in 1645.

Because he advocated the formation of a Vietnamese clergy, a measure contrary to the *padroado* (the patronage agreement the Portuguese had established with Rome), Rhodes was blacklisted by the local Portuguese authorities and was denied access to the sea route via the Cape of Good Hope. Consequently in 1650 he had to make the journey back to Europe overland. In 1655, after a stay in Rome and then in Paris, where he advocated policies of inculturation of the church in Asia, he went to Persia, where he learned the language well enough to converse with the shah. His funeral in 1660 in Ispahan was a state occasion attended by the shah.

BIBLIOGRAPHY Alexandre de Rhodes, *Phep Giang Tamngay: Catechismus in octo dies divisus* (1651[?], 1993). See also William V. Bangert, *A History of the Society of Jesus* (1972); J. Lacouture, *Jesuites: Une multibiographie,* 2 vols. (1991).

Bartholomew Lahiff, SJ

Ricci, Matteo (1552–1610), founder of Roman Catholic missions in China during modern times. Ricci was born in Macerata, Italy, went to Rome in 1568 to study law, and entered the Society of Jesus in 1571. A volunteer to the missions in Asia, he arrived in Goa, India, in 1578 and two years later was ordained a priest. Alessandro *Valignano, the Jesuit superior in Asia, instituted a policy of inculturating Christianity in Asia and assigned Ricci to Macao to study Chinese. In 1583 Ricci and his Jesuit confrere Michele *Ruggieri received permission from Chinese officials to settle at Chao-ch'ing (Zhaoqing), west of Canton (Guangzhou). The interest of Chinese visitors in the world map displayed in the Jesuit residence led Ricci to translate the names into Chinese. Although a new governor general ordered him expelled in 1589, Ricci persuaded officials to allow him to move to Shao-chou (Shaozhou). By translating into Latin the Four Books (the basic works for all Chinese scholars of that day) and developing the first system of romanizing Chinese, Ricci became the founder of Western sinology. In 1596 the first edition of his catechism in Chinese appeared. Two years later he was in Peking (Beijing), but then because of the Japanese invasion of Korea and Chinese suspicion that all foreigners were spies, he returned to Nanking (Nanjing). He amazed scholars by his prodigious memory of Chinese texts and discussions on philosophy and mathematics.

In 1601 Ricci returned to Peking to get imperial permission to preach Christianity. He became acquainted with several leading scholars and statesmen, among them *Hsü Kuang-ch'i. Ricci considered the honors to Confucius that the scholars were required to offer to be academic rather than religious acts and that ancestor veneration was perhaps not superstitious. These aspects of his policy led to the Rites Controversy that was not finally settled by the papacy until 1742. Because of Ricci's publications, which ranged from Christian ethics to translations of the first six chapters of Euclid's *Elements,* scholars from every province going to Peking to take the metropolitan examinations wanted to meet him. Ricci presented foreign clocks and other items to the Wan-li emperor but not a copy of his world map, since it represented China as only one part of the world, not its center as the Chinese claimed. The emperor's interest in the map led Ricci to present a special edition for use in the palace. Not long before his death in Peking, Ricci completed a historical account of the introduction of Christianity into China. The emperor, whom Ricci had never met, granted him a burial place at Ch'a-la (Zhala), just outside the old western city gate. This recently restored site is known today as the *Li Madou mu* (Matteo Ricci cemetery), with more than sixty tombstones of Jesuits and other missionaries.

BIBLIOGRAPHY H. Bernard, *Matteo Ricci's Scientific Contribution to China* (1935); Chou K'ang-hsieh (Zhou Kangxie), ed., *Li Matou yen-chiu lun-chi* (Research essays on Matteo Ricci) (1971); V. Cronin, *The Wise Man from the West* (1955); P. d'Elia, ed. *Fonti Ricciane,* 3 vols. (1942–1949); L. Gallagher, *China in the Sixteenth Century: The Journals of Matthew Ricci* (1953); Lo Kuang, ed., *International Symposium of Chinese-Western Cultural Interchange in Commemoration of the 400th Anniversary of the Arrival of Matteo Ricci, S.J. in China* (1983); E. Malatesta, ed., *The True Meaning of the Lord of Heaven (T'ien-chu shih-i)* (1985); L. Polgar, *Bibliographie de l'histoire de la Compagnie de Jésus, 1901–1980,* 3 vols. (1990), vol. 1, pt. 3, pp. 65–78; Jonathan Spence, *The Memory Palace of Matteo Ricci* (1983); P. Tacchi-Venturi, *Opere storiche del P. Matteo Ricci, S.J.,* 2 vols. (1911–1913); C. Zeuli, ed., *Lettere del manoscritto Maceratese* (1985).

John W. Witek, SJ

Rice, Benjamin (1814–1887), London Missionary Society (LMS) missionary to India. After conversion, Rice's classical studies and Sunday school teaching led to his appointment by the LMS and to training at Homerton. Rice and his wife, Jane Peach (Singer), reached Bangalore in December 1836. Facility with languages—primarily Kannada but also Tamil and Telugu—led to preaching tours and production of textbooks and tracts. His revision of the Kannada Bible, a major work done in collaboration with Methodist and Basel Mission personnel in Bangalore and Mangalore, was accompanied by the building of a school system. Schools for girls were expanded by his second wife (daughter of C. T. E. *Rhenius and widow of J. J. Muller). After a home-furlough tour (1853–1856), he established a high school and college for training pastors and teachers. For 50 years he contributed to culture, education, and public life within the princely state of Mysore (now Karnataka). Rice's son Benjamin Lewis Rice (1837–1927) became a renowned scholar, teacher, and public official of Mysore.

BIBLIOGRAPHY Edward Peter Rice, *Benjamin Rice; or, Fifty Years in the Master's Service* (1890).

Robert Eric Frykenberg

Rice, Luther (1783–1836), initiator and organizer of Baptists for foreign missions in the United States. Born in Northborough, Massachusetts, Rice united with the Congregational Church in 1802. While a student at Williams College, he became a member of the secret Society of Brethren led by Samuel J. *Mills, Jr., for promoting foreign missions. In 1810 Adoniram *Judson and three of the Brethren appealed to the Congregational General Association to appoint them as foreign missionaries, a move that resulted in the formation of the American Board of Commissioners for Foreign Missions. En route to India in 1812 with Adoniram Judson, Samuel *Newell, Samuel *Nott, and their wives, together with Gordon *Hall, Rice pondered and debated the subject of infant baptism with a British Baptist missionary traveling on the same ship, and soon after arriving in Calcutta, he declared himself a Baptist and was immersed by William *Ward. Two months earlier the Judsons had taken this step, which necessitated separation from the Congregational board. This, together with immigration problems in India and pressing financial needs, led them to decide that Rice should return to the United States to rally support for the new mission.

Though it was expected that he would return and join the Judsons, who went on to Burma, Rice spent the remainder of his life motivating Baptists in the United States to cooperate for the support of missions. Traveling continually, Rice led in the convening and organization of the first Baptist national convention in Philadelphia in 1814. Later known as the Triennial Convention, it was a federation of local missionary societies and Rice became its principal agent. As a result of his urging, the Convention founded Columbian College (now George Washington University) in Washington, D.C., in 1821, began publishing a weekly newspaper, and organized a tract society that eventually became the American Baptist Publication Society. Overworked and unable to manage his manifold responsibilities, Rice resigned most of his positions, but he continued to travel and raise funds for the college and for the expanding missionary work. At the time of his death, the Convention had under appointment more than a hundred foreign missionaries. If he had a single conspicuous fault, one of his successors wrote, it was his "excessive hopefulness."

BIBLIOGRAPHY Luther Rice, *Dispensations of Providence: Journal and Letters of Luther Rice,* W. H. Brackney, ed. (1984). William A. Carleton, *The Dreamer Cometh* (1960); "Luther Rice: Man of Vision and Toil," in John Allen Moore, *Baptist Mission Portraits* (1994), pp. 109–131; Edward B. Pollard, *Luther Rice: Pioneer in Missions and Education* (1928); Evelyn W. Thompson, *Luther Rice: Believer in Tomorrow* (1967).

Alan Neely

Richard, Timothy (1845–1919), Baptist Missionary Society (BMS) missionary in China. Richard was born in south Wales and was converted during the revival of 1858 to 1860. While a student at Haverfordwest Baptist College, he offered himself for service with the China Inland Mission but was advised to apply instead to the BMS. This he did, and in 1869 he was accepted for the small BMS mission in Shantung (Shandong) Province. From 1870 to January 1875 he worked in Chefoo (Yantai), a coastal town served by three different missions. Richard, at this stage an admirer of James Hudson *Taylor and his indigenous principles, felt that Chefoo was not a strategic location, and in 1875 he moved inland to Ch'ing-Chou-Fu, an important administrative capital and religious center. Here he adopted Chinese dress and distributed tracts and rudimentary medical aid.

At Ch'ing-Chou-Fu, Richard's missionary principles took shape. He became convinced that the church in China must be self-supporting, and he argued that itinerant evangelism should be left largely to Chinese Christians. Missionaries should, rather, focus their attention on the key leaders of society, who in this context were the religious teachers and leaders of the reforming religious sects and the scholar-gentry who staffed the imperial civil service. Richard was deeply affected by the devastating famine that struck Shantung and much of north China from 1876 to 1879. He was prominent in relief work, first in Chingzhou, and then, from 1877, in Taiyuan, capital of Shansi Province. The catastrophe of the famine convinced Richard that only Western scientific expertise could avert similar disasters and that the right approach in China was to target the educated and religious elite with a message that yoked Christianity to the attractions of Western civilization.

Many of Richard's BMS colleagues and superiors now regarded his theology as too liberal and his strategic convictions as unfounded. He left Shansi in 1887 and for a time worked on a virtually freelance basis, in Peking (Beijing), Tsinan (Jinan), and from 1890, in Tientsin (Tianjin), where he edited a reforming newspaper. In 1891 the BMS seconded him to the Society for the Diffusion of Christian and General Knowledge among the Chinese, later the Christian Literature Society, of which he became secretary. At last free to pursue his distinctive vision of literary and educational work aimed at the intelligentsia, Richard influenced the Chinese national reform movement of 1897–1898, which promised much for Christianity until the reaction of the Boxer uprising of 1899–1900. The Republican Revolution of 1911–1912 appeared for a time to vindicate his ideas. Ill, he retired in 1915 and died in London.

BIBLIOGRAPHY Richard's publications include an autobiography, *Forty-Five Years in China* (1916) and *Conversion by the Million in China: Being Biographies and Articles*, 2 vols. (1907). Paul R. Bohr, *Famine in China and the Missionary: Timothy Richard as Relief Administrator and Advocate of National Reform, 1876–1884* (1972); W. E. Soothill, *Timothy Richard of China* (1924); Brian Stanley, *The History of the Baptist Missionary Society, 1792–1992* (1992); H. R. Williamson, *British Baptists in China, 1845–1952* (1957). Richard's papers are preserved in the BMS archives at Regent's Park College, Oxford.

Brian Stanley

Richards, Henry (1851–1928), British and American Baptist missionary in the Congo. Born in Somersetshire, England, the son of farmers, Richards was raised in an Anglican home and worked for his father. He joined the Congregationalists and then the Baptists, among whom he preached for a time. Alfred Tilley, a Baptist pastor and secretary to the Livingstone Interior Mission, invited Richards to become a missionary with that society. After studies in medicine and at Harley College, London, Henry and his spouse Mary (d.1881), sailed for Africa in 1879. In 1884, when the work was transferred to the American Baptist Missionary Union, Richards remained under American appointment. Two years later he began a study of the missionary methods of the Apostles, and this led to a remarkable conversion experience for more than one thousand Bantus at Banza Manteke, in the Upper Congo, in August 1886. A. J. *Gordon at Clarendon Street Baptist Church in Boston was so impressed with what came to be known as the Pentecost on the Congo that he persuaded his church to build a chapel and transport it to the Congo, where it was carried 60 miles up river under Richards's supervision. In addition to organizing the mission, Richards studied carefully the languages of the Congo river basin and, in a major linguistic breakthrough, categorized them into four distinct groups. Henry and his second wife, known only by the initial "E" (d.1884) spent much time engaged in translation work. He retired with his third wife, Mary Elizabeth, in 1919.

BIBLIOGRAPHY The Richardses both wrote extensively, as illustrated in his *The Pentecost on the Congo* (1906) and her *Itinerating on the Congo* (n.d.). Details on Richards's early life are lacking. The best biographical material is in Charles H. Stuart, *The Lower Congo and the American Baptist Mission to 1910* (1969) and Martin S. Engwall, "The Pentecost on the Congo: An Appreciation of Rev. Henry Richards," *The Baptist*, July 13, 1929, pp. 917–918. A brief typescript autobiography exists at the American Baptist Historical Society, Rochester, New York.

William H. Brackney

Richards, William (1793–1847), American missionary and Hawaiian official. Richards was born in Plainfield, Massachusetts, and graduated from Williams College (1819). In 1822 he graduated from Andover Theological Seminary, was ordained, married Clarissa Lyman, and joined the Sandwich Islands Mission of the American Board of Commissioners for Foreign Missions (ABCFM). For 13 years he worked at Lahaina, Maui, as preacher, teacher, physician, artisan, and Bible translator. In 1837 he visited the United States to promote the cause of missions and to press the Hawaiian chiefs' request that the ABCFM send someone to teach them "the practice of enlightened countries." He reluctantly left the ABCFM in 1838 to become chaplain, counselor, teacher, and translator for the king. The influence of his lectures on political economy and the science of government is seen in the bill of rights of 1839, the constitution of 1840, and the legislation of 1838 to 1842. In 1842, as ambassador to Great Britain, he secured explicit recognition of the independence of Hawaii by that country, the United States, and France. In 1846 he was appointed to head the commission charged with reorganizing the entire system of landholding and was also appointed Hawaii's first minister of public instruction. Richards translated thirteen books of the Bible and prepared schoolbooks in Hawaiian on geography, geometry, and zoology. He wrote a memoir of Queen Keopuolani (1825) and translated and edited the *Constitution and Laws of the Hawaiian Islands* (1842).

BIBLIOGRAPHY Samuel Williston, *William Richards* (1938); *Missionary Album* (1969), pp. 162–163; *Missionary Herald*, 1823–1837.

Richards's papers and journals are with the ABCFM papers at Harvard Univ., and histories of Hawaii describe his public activity.

David M. Stowe

Richier, Pierre. *See* Léry, Jean de.

Richter, Enrique (1652–1695), German Jesuit missionary in the Peruvian Amazon. Born in Bohemia, Richter studied at the University of Prague, entered the Society of Jesus in 1670, and was sent in 1684 to work in the Peruvian mission territory assigned to the Jesuits and known as Mainas. Richter arrived with Samuel *Fritz, a fellow German Bohemian Jesuit, and the two together became the most outstanding mission builders in the Peruvian Amazon basin in the seventeenth century. In 1641 the Jesuits in Quito assumed responsibility for the entire jungle of eastern Ecuador and northern Peru. Richter was sent to work along the Ucayali River, which is a major north-south tributary of the Marañón and Amazon Rivers. Based in Laguna, he worked especially among the Conibos, but he also had contact with the Piros and the Campas. In twelve years he founded nine reductions, or mission towns, along the Ucayali River.

Richter's encounter with Franciscan missionaries at the southern end of the Ucayali prompted the necessity for demarcating mission territories: northern Peru for the Jesuits, and central and southern Peru for the Franciscans. In 1691 Richter set out with a large expedition of Conibos and Spanish soldiers in an attempt to evangelize the warlike Jívaro Indians in present-day Ecuador. The attempt failed and many groups of Jívaros remained untouched until the twentieth century. Richter was killed by Piro Indians, who were incited by a Conibo whose wife had been stolen by a Spanish soldier. Richter, who is considered the Apostle of the Ucayali, wrote catechisms and vocabularies in the languages of the Conibo, Piro, Campa, and Cocama Indians.

BIBLIOGRAPHY José Chantre y Herrera, *Historia de las misiones de la Compañía de Jesús en el Marañón español* (1901); José Jouanen, *Historia de la Compañía de Jesús en la antigua provincia de Quito, 1570–1774,* vol. 1 (1943); Rubén Vargas Ugarte, *Historia de la Iglesia en el Perú,* vol. 3 (1960).

Jeffrey Klaiber, SJ

Richter, Julius (1862–1940), German Protestant missiologist. Born and raised in a parsonage in central Germany and educated at Halle, Leipzig, and Berlin, Richter served as a pastor for 25 years. After an arduous period of preparation, he qualified as a lecturer in missions and in 1920 was called to the first full professorship in that discipline at the University of Berlin. Even after his retirement in 1930 he continued to write, lecture, and edit. He wrote some thirty books and countless essays on virtually all missiological subjects, and is considered the most prolific writer of his generation in missiology. While his mentor and model Gustav *Warneck laid the foundation of a modern theory of missions, Richter was the first German missiologist to concentrate on the overseas mission fields and their churches in the encounter with non-Christian religions. In contrast to most of his predecessors, Richter took great pains to keep in touch with the international missionary and ecumenical movement by means of extensive travel and correspondence. He was able to build up a worldwide network of communication, which, though badly disrupted during World War II, proved to be advantageous to German missions in the difficult years of postwar recovery.

BIBLIOGRAPHY M. Schlunk, "Julius Richter zum Gedächtnis," *EMZ* 1 (1940): 164–169; Richard V. Pierard, "Julius Richter and the Scientific Study of Christian Missions in Germany," *Missiology* 6 (1978): 485–506.

Hans-Werner Gensichen

Ricke, Jodoco (1498–1578), Flemish Franciscan, founder of the first Franciscan mission in Quito, Ecuador. Born of a noble family in Ghent, Ricke was among the first Franciscans in Peru. In 1534 he accompanied the Spanish conqueror Pedro de Alvarado to Quito. He founded the monastery of San Pablo and built the first church of his order in Quito and in all of South America. He used the mission as a base for educating the Indians in all types of crafts and trades. He taught them music, reading, and writing, as well as new agricultural techniques. For a brief moment Ricke became involved in politics when he supported the Pizarro brothers in the civil war against Diego de Almagro (1537–1541). He served as custodian of the Franciscan monastery in Quito between 1538 and 1552, and until 1551 he also acted as superior of all Franciscans in Peru and Ecuador. His educational efforts among the Indians inspired the founding in Quito of the College of San Andrés, modeled on Santiago of Tlatelolco in Mexico, the first school for Indians in the New World. San Andrés (1555–1650) taught crafts and trades to the Indians. In 1569 Ricke left Quito for Popayán in New Grenada (Colombia), where he founded the convent of San Bernardino, and where he died.

BIBLIOGRAPHY Antonine Tibesar, *Franciscan Beginnings in Colonial Peru* (1953); José María Vargas, *Historia de la Iglesia en el Ecuador durante el Patronato Español* (1957).

Jeffrey Klaiber, SJ

Ricoldo da Monte Cruce. *See* Pennini, Ricoldo.

Ridley, William (1819–1878), linguist and missionary to Australian Aborigines. An English Presbyterian scholar of classical languages, in 1849 Ridley accepted an appointment to the Australian College in Sydney, viewing it as a missionary calling. He was ordained in 1850 by the Presbyterian Synod of New South Wales and taught at the college, but failed to obtain permanent appointment to a church. In 1853 he began an itinerant ministry to colonists and Aborigines. He rapidly acquired the Kamilaroi language of northern New South Wales and published reading materials in Kamilaroi and other languages. His booklet *Gurre Kamilaroi* (1856) contained the first Christian materials published in any Aboriginal language. Ridley proposed a mission on remarkably progressive principles, using Aboriginal languages, incorporating Aboriginal activities, and recognizing Aboriginal cultural differences. But indifferent fellow-colonists declined to provide sufficient funds.

From 1860, Ridley supported himself as a journalist to fund his own continuing itinerant ministry, returning whenever able to the Kamilaroi people. He published extensively on Aboriginal languages and is recognized among the founders of Australian anthropology. Ridley's enduring significance lies in the acute observations and deep insights he left behind.

BIBLIOGRAPHY William Ridley, *Gurre Kamilaroi* (1856) and *Kamilaroi and Other Australian Languages* (1875). B. J. Bridges, *Ministers, Licentiates and Catechists of the Presbyterian Churches in New South Wales, 1823–1865* (1989); John Harris, *One Blood* (1990).

John W. Harris

Riedel, Johann (Gerard) Friedrich (1798–1860), German missionary of the Netherlands Mission Society in Indonesia. Riedel received his missionary training at the Mission School of Johann *Jänicke in Berlin (1822–1827) and at the Mission House in Rotterdam (1827–1829). He served in the northeastern region of Celebes, Indonesia, from 1831 to 1859, based in Tondano, Minahasa. His name is associated with that of Johann Gottlob *Schwarz (1800–1859), also German by birth, who served as missionary of the same mission society in Langoan, Minahasa (1831–1859).

Riedel was a missionary pioneer. By his preaching, teaching, and pastoral care in the Malay and Tondano languages, he vigorously propagated Christianity and diminished the influence of tribal religion. He built churches and schools, trained schoolteachers, and also did some medical work. His simple life-style and his welcoming of Minahasa youth to stay in his house impressed people. He helped to stop the wars between the Tomohon and Tondano. By 1851, some 2,000 people attended his Sunday church services. He baptized more than 9,000 people, including a former tribal priest. Today's large Minahasa Evangelical Christian Church has its roots in the pietistic missionary work of Riedel and Schwarz.

BIBLIOGRAPHY H. Dijkstra, *Johann Friedrich Riedel* (1896); R. Grundemann, *Johann Friedrich Riedel: ein Lebensbild aus der Minahasa auf Celebes* (1873); E. F. Kruyf, *Geschiedenis van het Nederlandsche Zendelinggenootschap en zijne zendingsposten* (1894); *Het begon met Riedel: Perspectieven van gemeenschappelijke Hoop: Brochure bij de gelijknamige Tentoonstelling*; M. Schouten, *Minahasa and Bolaangmongondow: An Annotated Bibliography (1800–1942)* (1981); P. Steiner, *Joh. Friedrich Riedel: ein Deutscher Missionar auf der Insel Celebes* (1920).

Jan A. B. Jongeneel

Riedemann, Peter (1506–1556), Anabaptist missionary in Moravia, Austria, and central Germany. Riedemann was born in Silesia, Germany, and became an early Anabaptist leader. A shoemaker by trade, he had many natural opportunities for witness. During imprisonment in Gmunden, Upper Austria (1529–1532), he prepared the first draft of his *Confession.* On arriving in Moravia late in 1532, he was commissioned as a minister and married to Katharina. Sent to Franconia on a missionary journey, he was again arrested, spending over four years (1533–1537) in prison in Nürnberg (Nüremberg). On his return to Moravia, he helped restore order among divided groups within the Anabaptist settlement and stressed the importance of community ownership of goods. Early in 1540, on his third missionary journey, he was arrested again and jailed in Marburg, Hesse. Here he wrote the second *Confession,* as well as many hymns. Fortunately, his imprisonments were mild. When in 1542 the Moravian community wrote begging for his help in a leadership crisis, he managed to escape. Unassuming in manner, gentle and helpful, he made the love and grace of God central to his *Confession,* with the Apostles' Creed as the core. While he may have been influenced somewhat by the writings of Hubmaier, Denck, and Hut, his theology seems to be quite original. He died in Slovakia.

BIBLIOGRAPHY Peter Rideman [Riedemann], *Confession of Faith* (1950, 1970, 1993). Robert Friedmann, "Peter Riedemann: Early Anabaptist Leader," *Mennonite Quaterly Review* 44 (1970): 5–44; John J. Friesen, trans. and ed., *The Confession of Peter Riedemann* (1997); Leonard Gross, *The Golden Years of the Hutterites* (1980); George H. Williams, *The Radical Reformation,* 3d rev. and enlarged ed. (1992).

Cornelius J. Dyck

Riggs, Elias (1810–1901), American linguist and missionary in the Near East. Educated at Amherst Academy and College (1829, LL.D., 1871), in 1832 Riggs graduated from Andover Theological Seminary, published *A Manual of the Chaldee Language…,* married Martha Jane Dalzel, and sailed for Greece under the American Board of Commissioners for Foreign Missions (ABCFM). Having begun the study of Greek at age 9 and Hebrew at 13, he could use seven ancient and fourteen modern languages. He served in Athens, Argos, and Smyrna until 1844, then turned his attention to translating for the Armenians. Under his leadership the Bible in modern Armenian appeared in 1853. In Constantinople, where he was now located, he produced books, tracts, and hymns. Beginning in 1859 he took up translation of the Bible into modern Bulgarian, taught in mission schools, edited vernacular magazines, and preached frequently. After the publication of the Bulgarian Bible in 1871, he joined a committee working on a standard Turkish Bible, published in 1878. Other publications in Bulgarian included a Bible dictionary (1884) and a three-volume commentary (1898). He wrote or translated 478 Bulgarian hymns and also translated Bulgarian folklore. Of Riggs's eight children, three became ministers and three missionaries; with more than a dozen later descendants and their spouses, the family accounted for more than a thousand years of missionary service through five generations.

BIBLIOGRAPHY Riggs wrote a number of books in English: *Brief Grammar of the Modern Armenian Language* (1847), *Outline of a Grammar of the Turkish Language as Written in the Armenian Character* (1856), and numerous biblical studies. J. K. Green, *Leavening the Levant* (1916); F. F. Goodsell, *They Lived Their Faith* (1961), pp. 147–148, 402, 410–411; *Missionary Herald* 97 (1901): 98–103.

David M. Stowe

Riggs, Stephen Return (1812–1883), missionary to the Dakota Indians. Educated at Jefferson College, Pennsylvania (1834; LL.D., 1873), and Western Theological Seminary, he was ordained in 1837 to the Presbyterian ministry, married Mary A. C. Longley, and joined the Dakota Mission (to the Sioux Indians) of the American Board of Commissioners for Foreign Missions in Minnesota, serving at Lac qui Parle and Traverse des Sioux until 1854. Riggs then moved to New Hope, where several families of Christian Indians organized the "Hazelwood Republic" with a democratic constitution. Narrowly escaping death in the Sioux outbreak of 1862, Riggs ministered among the hundreds of captive Indians. After Mary Riggs died in 1869, he married Annie B. Ackley. Riggs prepared a writing system for the Dakota language and produced more than fifty volumes in that tongue, literary and religious, translated and original, including textbooks, catechisms, hymns, *Pilgrim's Progress,* and *The Constitution of Minnesota.* He translated nearly the entire Bible (published in 1880). He also wrote in English a grammar and a 16,000-word dictionary of the Dakota language, published for the Smithsonian Institution in 1852, and many articles. Four of his nine children became missionaries, and at least a dozen other descendants through four generations.

BIBLIOGRAPHY Riggs wrote *The Gospel among the Dakotas* (1869), *Mary and I: Forty Years with the Sioux* (1880), and articles in *Minnesota Historical Society Collections,* vols. 1 and 3, and in *Contributions to American Ethnology,* vols. 7 and 9. Charles A. Maxfield, "The Presbyterian and Congregational Churches among the Dakotas" (M.Th. diss., Union Theological Seminary, Richmond, 1891); *Missionary Herald* 79: 378–379; J. H. Wallace, *Genealogy of the Riggs Family* (1901). Riggs's papers are at the Minnesota Historical Society and in the ABCFM collection in the Houghton Library, Harvard Univ.

David M. Stowe

Riis, Andreas (1804–1854), Danish pioneer missionary in Ghana. By 1839 Riis and his wife, Margarethe (sometimes Anna) Wolters, were the only survivors of three parties of Basel Mission (BM) missionaries who had landed since 1828. Their survival is often credited to taking native remedies rather than the deadly cures for tropical diseases prescribed at the time by European doctors. In 1835 Riis transferred the center of BM operations from the coast to Akropong, an inland town on an escarpment in the traditional kingdom of Akwapim. On furlough in 1840, he urged continued investment in the Ghana mission and won approval for a plan to recruit Christian ex-slaves from the West Indies to found a black Christian community in Ghana; he began to implement this plan during a journey to Ghana via the West Indies in 1842–1843. (See also Johannes *Zimmermann.) Earlier BM accounts tended to mythologize Riis for his persistence and bravery. Recent literature, however, has adopted a more nuanced view, acknowledging that in the 1840s his stubbornness was the center of much conflict between the missionaries and between them and the West Indian settlers. In 1845 he was recalled and asked to leave the BM. He went to Stavanger, Norway, where it is said he played a key role in cultivating Norwegian support for mission.

BIBLIOGRAPHY M. A. Kwamena-Poh, *Government and Politics in the Akwapim State, 1730–1850* (1973); John Middleton, "150 Years of Christianity in a Ghanaian Town," *Africa* 53 (1983): 2–17 (on Akropong); Jon Miller, *The Social Control of Religious Zeal: A Study of Organizational Contradictions* (1994); Wilhelm Schlatter, *Geschichte der Basler Mission,* vol. 3 (1915).

Paul Jenkins

Rijnhart, Susanna (Carson) (1868–1908), pioneer doctor, explorer, and founder of the Disciples of Christ mission to Tibet. Born in Chatham, Ontario, Canada, Susanna Carson was dedicated to missions at age 11, when her father, a Methodist school inspector, registered her for medical school. She graduated from Toronto Women's Medical College in 1888, in its second class. In 1894 she married Petrus Rijnhart, who had joined the China Inland Mission (CIM) in 1890. Stationed in Lanchow (Lanzhou), Kansu (Gansu) Province, the last Chinese city on the Silk Road before central Asia, Susanna and her husband were influenced by Annie Royale Taylor, the "lone wolf of Tibet," and Cecil *Polhill-Turner of the *Cambridge Seven. In 1893 the CIM summarily dismissed Petrus Rijnhart, claiming that he was an imposter.

Supported by the Disciples of Christ in Toronto, the Rijnharts traveled six months to Tsinghai (Qinghai) Province, or Outer Tibet. At a Buddhist monastery they became friends with a Living Buddha and witnessed a battle between Tibetans and Muslims. After four years on the border of Tibet, they set out with their infant son and enough food for a year to walk to Lhasa, the Tibetan capital. During the nightmarish journey, the baby died and Petrus, seeking help from some nomads, disappeared. Two months later Susanna stumbled into Tatsienlu (Kangding), Szechwan (Sichuan).

Recuperating in Toronto, she wrote *With the Tibetans in Tent and Temple,* a testament to her husband's "burning ambition to be of service in evangelizing Tibet—whether by his life or his death, he said, did not matter." In 1902 she returned to Tatsienlu with a few Disciples of Christ missionaries, where she married James Moyes of the CIM. When her health failed, they returned to Chatham in 1907. She died there a year later, perhaps of complications from childbirth.

BIBLIOGRAPHY Accounts of Rijnhart's life are ultimately based on her autobiography, *With the Tibetans in Tent and Temple: Narrative of Four Years Residence on the Tibetan Border, and of a Journey into the Far Interior* (1901, reprinted 1911). Other sources include biographical files in United Church Archives, 11 Soho Street, Toronto, and Univ. of Western Ontario Library, London, Ont. Petrus Rijnhart's relations with the CIM are discussed in A. J. Broomhall, *Hudson Taylor and China's Open Century,* vol. 7, *It Is Not Death to Die!* (1989). Susanna Rijnhart appears in accounts of exploration in Tibet, e.g., Peter Hopkirk, *Trespassers on the Roof of the World: The Race for Lhasa* (1982).

Alvyn Austin

Ringeltaube, Wilhelm Tobias (1770–1816?), pioneer missionary in South India. One of several German missionaries working in India for English mission societies in the early nineteenth century, Ringeltaube was born into a Lutheran pastor's family in Silesia and studied at Halle. As the Danish-Halle mission was unable to accept him due to its decline in the late eighteenth century, Ringeltaube applied to the Society for Promoting Christian Knowledge, which sent him to Calcutta in 1797. After a short and unsatisfactory experience he resigned and returned to England, offered his services to the London Missionary Society (LMS), and arrived in Tranquebar, South India, in 1804. J. C. Kohlhoff, the successor of C. F. *Schwartz in the Danish-Halle mission, and his Indian convert, Vedamanickam, arranged for Ringeltaube to settle in Tirunelveli, and, after 1809, in Mayiladi, a village in the princely state of Travancore, where Vedamanickam had gathered a group of Christians. This was to be the last station in Ringeltaube's missionary career. His total disregard of comfort and prestige attracted people to faith in Christ. He convinced them "to waive all views of temporal advantage . . . and not to imagine that they would be exempt from the Cross." In 1813 he reported a community of 600 with seven small churches, each congregation served by a teacher-catechist. Soon thereafter Ringeltaube felt his health beginning to fail, and he entrusted the mission to Vedamanickam, who had become his chief catechist, until a successor could be found. In 1815 he was unable to continue the work. The last act of his ministry was to ordain Vedamanickam on January 23, 1816, with the laying on of hands, clothing him in his own surplice. After a visit in Madras, Ringeltaube sailed to Malacca, after which nothing is known about his fate. He probably died at sea on his way to Batavia without knowing that the LMS had dispatched a successor, Charles Mead, who arrived in 1817 and continued the work in the spirit of Ringeltaube.

BIBLIOGRAPHY W. Robinson, *Ringeltaube the Rishi* (1902); Stephen C. Neill, *A History of Christianity in India,* vol. 2 (1985), pp. 223–226.

Hans-Werner Gensichen

Ritchie, John (*or* Juan) (1878–1952), Scottish missionary to Peru. Born in Kilmarnock, Scotland, Ritchie left school at the age of 11 and served an apprenticeship as a printer. Converted in 1894 through the ministry of revivalist D. J. Findlay, he became a baptized member of Glasgow's Findlay Tabernacle. Its ecclesiology and emphasis on missions made a lasting impact on him. He studied at Harley House Bible Institute, situated to serve the poor of London's East End, and was accepted for missionary service in 1905 by the South American and Indian Council of the Regions Beyond Missionary Union (RBMU) associated with Harley House. A member of RBMU in Peru from 1906 to 1911, he then entered the recently formed Evangelical Union of South America until missiological tensions over evangelism and social action caused him to resign in 1927. During that period his most salient contribution was his writing, editing, and printing of two widely circulated periodicals: *El Heraldo* (1911–1918) and *El Cristiano* (1916–1921), renamed *Renacimiento* in 1921.

Between 1913 and 1915 Ritchie played an active part in the political constitutional struggle for religious liberty in Peru. He was also a prominent contributor to the Panama Congress on Christian Work in Latin America of 1916. In 1932 he was appointed secretary of the Upper Andes Agency of the American Bible Society. He continued teaching, writing, and distributing pamphlets for the Iglesia Evangélica Peruana, the denomination that he helped establish in 1921. He was also the instigator of the Peruvian National Evangelical Council of Churches, founded in 1940, more than two decades after he had first advocated the concept. It was the first association of its kind in Latin America.

Ritchie's view of the indigenous church resulting from his practical experience of church planting and governance is perhaps his main contribution to the English-speaking world. For the Hispanic world, his ability to address all levels of society, his emphasis on holistic mission in an era of dichotomy, and his vision of transforming individuals and society through the gospel are his greatest contributions. He died in Lima.

BIBLIOGRAPHY John Ritchie, *Indigenous Church Principles in Theory and in Practice* (1946). Saúl Barrera C., "Juan Ritchie: Fundador, organizador y conductor de la Iglesia Evangélica Peruana," in *Orígenes y desarrollo de la Iglesia Evangélica Peruana* (1993); G. Stewart McIntosh, *The Life and Times of John Ritchie, Scotland and Peru, 1878–1952* (1988) and "The Legacy of John Ritchie," *IBMR* 19, no. 1 (1995): 26–30.

G. Stewart McIntosh

Roberts, Issachar Jacox (1802–1871), Baptist missionary in China. Born in Sumner County, Tennessee, Roberts was ordained after a term at South Carolina's Furman Academy. In 1837 he financed his own passage to Macao, where he preached in a colony for persons with leprosy. Joining the Foreign Mission Board of the Baptist Triennial Convention in 1841, he became the first permanent resident Protestant missionary in Hong Kong in 1842, and in June of that year he baptized the first Chinese convert in Hong Kong. He affiliated with the Southern Baptist Convention's Foreign Mission Board following the Baptist schism in 1845 but became an independent missionary in 1852. In 1844, inspired by Karl *Gützlaff's millennialist hope for the "blitzconversion" of China, he became the first Protestant missionary to move outside the foreign trade area of Canton (Guangzhou) to conduct evangelistic ministries. Between March and May 1847, he gave daily catechism to *Hung Hsiu-ch'üan (Hong Xiuquan), founder and "Heavenly King" of the Taiping Rebellion (1850–1864). Roberts's evangelical zeal, moral rectitude, condemnation of "idolatry," liturgy, and church constitution were linked by Hung with Chinese elements to form Taiping doctrine, worship, and organization. This religious synthesis inspired and guided the Taiping millenarian campaign to supplant the Manchu dynasty and Confucianism with a theocratic "Heavenly Kingdom of Great Peace" along biblical lines in China.

For 15 months between 1860 and 1862, Roberts served as the Taiping's "director of foreign affairs" at their "Heavenly Capital" in Nanking (Nanjing). Initially, he worked hard to rally Western support for the Taiping's cause but later turned against the rebels after Hung refused to abandon his claim to being Jesus Christ's younger brother. In 1866 Roberts retired to Upper Alton, Illinois, where he eventually succumbed to complications from the leprosy he had contracted earlier in Macao.

BIBLIOGRAPHY P. Richard Bohr, "The Politics of Eschatology: Hung Hsiu-ch'üan and the Rise of the Taipings, 1837–1853" (Ph.D. diss., Univ. of California, Davis, 1978); Margaret Morgan Coughlin, "Strangers in the House: J. Lewis Shuck and Issachar Roberts, First American Baptist Missionaries to China" (Ph.D. diss., Univ. of Virginia, 1972); William R. Doezema, "Western Seeds of Eastern Heterodoxy: The Impact of Protestant Revivalism on the Christianity of Taiping Rebel Leader Hung Hsiu-ch'üan, 1836–1864," *Fides et Historia* 25 (1993): 73–98; George B. Pruden, Jr., "Issachar Jacox Roberts and American Diplomacy in China during the Taiping Rebellion" (Ph.D. diss., American Univ., 1977); Jonathan D. Spence, *God's Chinese Son: The Taiping Heavenly Kingdom of Hong Xiuquan* (1996); Yuan Chung Teng, "Reverend Issachar Jacox Roberts and the Taiping Rebellion," *Journal of Asian Studies* 23, no. 1 (1963): 55–67.

P. Richard Bohr

Robinson, John Alfred (1859–1891), Anglican mission administrator in West Africa. Born at Keynsham, near Bristol, Robinson was the son of an Anglican priest. He went to Liverpool College and the University of Cambridge (Christ College), where he took a first in his theological tripos. After a curacy and a period of teaching in Germany, he became the Church Missionary Society (CMS) secretary for the Niger in 1887. This was a difficult assignment, as dissatisfaction with the African administration of Samuel A. *Crowther had been brewing for some time. Nonetheless, Robinson managed the task moderately successfully until he came under the influence of G. W. *Brooke in 1889. Apparently accepting Brooke's ideas almost immediately, he began to argue for European missionaries, a European episcopal replacement for Crowther, and a simpler missionary life-style. He played a leading part in a confrontation with Crowther and the leading African clergy at Onitsha in 1890. The memorandum he wrote for the CMS on the state of the Niger mission was devastatingly critical and distinctly unbalanced. When the CMS failed to support their Niger missionaries in the way Robinson felt was merited, he reacted in extreme anger, threatening to write to the church press. In the midst of the ensuing crisis, he died at Lokoja of meningitis, "partly arising," judges Eugene *Stock, "from the mental strain caused by his dissatisfaction with the Committee's decision." He was an able man, driven to extremism by the spiritual intensity of the period. Five of his seven brothers were ordained; one of his brothers was Joseph Armitage Robinson, a noted New Testament scholar and an eccentric dean of Westminster and later dean of Wells; another, Arthur, was the father of J. A. T. Robinson, later bishop of Woolwich and author of *Honest to God.*

BIBLIOGRAPHY Frieder Ludwig, "The Making of a Late Victorian Missionary," *NZM* 47 (1991): 269–290; Eugene Stock, *The History of the Church Missionary Society: Its Environment, Its Men, and Its Work,* 4 vols. (1899–1916).

Peter Williams

Robinson, William (1784–1853), Baptist Missionary Society (BMS) missionary in Bengal, Java, and Sumatra. A member of John Sutcliff's Baptist church at Olney, Buckinghamshire, England, Robinson was accepted by the BMS in 1804 and sailed for Bengal (area of the province of West Bengal, India, and of modern Bangladesh) in 1806. He was married five times, losing his first four wives on the mission field. Soon after arriving in Bengal, he was ordered to leave by the British authorities, who were afraid of evangelical missions following the Vellore mutiny of June 1806. Robinson was accordingly sent to Bhutan, in the Himalayan foothills, but this mission was not a success. In 1813 the Serampore missionaries sent him to open a new mission in Batavia, Java. There he translated the Gospel of Matthew into Malay, opened a school, and preached to the British troops. Following the return of Java to Dutch rule in 1816, Robinson moved to Bencoolen, Sumatra, where he continued translating the Bible into Malay. In 1825 he returned to Bengal to be pastor of the Lal Bazaar Baptist church in Calcutta. During his ministry there he encouraged William *Carey during the distressing years of controversy between the Serampore missionaries and their younger brethren in Calcutta; he also baptized over 250 converts. From 1839 until his death, Robinson was pastor of the Baptist church in Dhaka, where he is buried.

BIBLIOGRAPHY Ernest A. Payne, *The First Generation: Early Leaders of the Baptist Missionary Society in England and India* (1936) and *Southeast from Serampore: More Chapters in the Story of the Baptist Missionary Society* (1945).

Brian Stanley

Roboredo, Manuel. *See* Bonaventura da Sardegna.

Rocha, João da (1565–1623), Jesuit missionary in China. Da Rocha was born in Santiago de Priscos, Braga, Portugal. In 1583 he entered the Society of Jesus in Coimbra, and shortly after his novitiate he left for Goa, India, where he completed three years of philosophical studies. He then went to Macao for his theological training and ordination. In 1598 he was in Shao-chou (Shaoguan) and later in Nanking (Nanjing) with his confrere, Lazzaro *Cattaneo. While in Nanking, da Rocha had extensive discussions about Christianity with *Hsü Kuang-ch'i that led to the baptism of Hsü. During the persecution of 1616 da Rocha was in Chien-ch'ang (Jianchang; today part of Nancheng), Kiangsi (Jiangxi) Province, where several Christians kept him in hiding. Afterward, he was able to expand that mission station because of the conversion of several scholars who assisted him in translating a Portuguese catechism into Chinese. He built the first church in Chia-ting (Jiading; today part of metropolitan Shanghai). When another persecution arose shortly thereafter, he took refuge in Hangchow (Hangzhou). There with Hsü, he wrote a memorial defending the missionaries. By the time it was to be presented to the emperor in Peking (Beijing), the officials responsible for the persecution had been relieved of office. Named vice-provincial of the mission in 1622, da Rocha died the following year in Hangchow and was buried in the Jesuit cemetery outside that city.

BIBLIOGRAPHY Pasquale M. d'Elia, ed., *Fonti Ricciane,* 3 vols. (1942–1949), 1:383–384; Williard J. Peterson, "Why Did They Become Christians? Yang T'ing-yün, Li Chih-tsao, and Hsü Kuang-ch'i," in C. Ronan and B. Oh, eds., *East Meets West: The Jesuits in China, 1582–1773* (1988), pp. 129–152.

John W. Witek, SJ

Rodgers, James B(urton) (1865–1944), first permanent Protestant missionary in the Philippines. Rodgers was born in Albany, New York, and graduated from Hamilton College and Auburn Theological Seminary. Following ordination and marriage to Anna Van Vechten Bigelow, Rodgers was appointed in 1889 to service in the Brazil mission of the Presbyterian Church. After returning to Brazil for a second term in June 1898, he was transferred to the Philippines. He arrived in Manila on April 21, 1899, and pioneered for 36 years in evangelistic, educational, and ecumenical work. He was instrumental in the founding of the Evangelical Union and reaching of the comity agreement in 1901; the Union Theological Seminary in Manila in 1907 (where he taught theology from 1908 to 1932); and the United Evangelical Church in 1929.

Rodgers also served as a member of the Presbyterian deputation to Mexico in 1922, the China Evaluation Conference in 1926, and the deputation to Korea in 1936. He received an honorary D.D. degree in 1905 from Union University in Jackson, Tennessee. He retired in the Philippines in 1935, and in 1940 he published his memoirs, *Forty Years in the Philippines.* He died in Baguio City in April 1944, during the Japanese occupation.

BIBLIOGRAPHY Gerald H. Anderson, "Providence and Politics behind Protestant Missionary Beginnings in the Philippines," *Studies in Philippine Church History* (1969); Kenton J. Clymer, *Protestant Missionaries in the Philippines, 1898–1916* (1986); Anne C. Kwantes, *Presbyterian Missionaries in the Philippines, 1899–1910* (1989).

Gerald H. Anderson

Roehl, Karl (1870–1951), linguist and Bible translator in East Africa. Born and educated in Germany, Roehl combined his training for the ministry with linguistic studies, including Arabic and Swahili, with a view to mission service abroad. In 1896 the newly founded Protestant Mission Society for German East Africa (later the Bethel Mission) sent him as one of their pioneer missionaries to Usambara, in present-day Tanzania, where he took a leading part in translating the New Testament into Kishambala. He was transferred to Rwanda in 1906 and there translated the four Gospels into Kinyarwanda. Later, after his retirement from mission service in 1935, he concentrated on his main assignment, a new Bible translation in Swahili (1938; 2d ed., 1950). Roehl and his African helpers succeeded more than others in rendering the biblical message in African thought forms. He also tried to avoid terms and phrases which carried specific Islamic connotations. While his Bible translation has met with criticism and is unlikely to be generally accepted for modern usage in East Africa, it continues to stimulate improvements in the indigenization of the biblical message among Swahili speaking people. Roehl will also be remembered for his contributions to the development of Swahili grammar and literature.

BIBLIOGRAPHY E. Dammann, "In memoriam Dr. K. Roehl," *EMZ* 8 (1951): 92.

Hans-Werner Gensichen

Rogers, Mary Josephine (Mother Mary Joseph) (1882–1955), founder of the first Catholic missionary institute for women in the United States. Born in Boston, Massachusetts, "Mollie" Rogers, while a student at Smith College (1901–1905), was strongly influenced by the Student Volunteer Movement of the Protestants. From 1906 to 1908, while teaching biology at Smith, she formed a mission study club for Catholic students. Searching for mission study resources, she met James A. *Walsh at the Boston office of the Society for the Propagation of the Faith (SPF). Rogers's enthusiasm for mission, awakened during her student and faculty years at Smith, found in Walsh an extraordinary vision and a keen focus for her own missionary call. Within two years she became his coworker at the SPF office in Boston, assisting in the publication of the *Field Afar* magazine and other materials. In 1911 Pope Pius X authorized the establishment of the Catholic Foreign Mission Society of America, a project proposed by Walsh and Thomas F. *Price and approved by the U. S. bishops. Rogers made her decision to join in the initiation of this new mission movement at Maryknoll in Ossining, New York, and is recognized as one of the three Maryknoll founders.

As leader of the small group of women gathered at Maryknoll in 1912 to serve as auxiliary workers, she gracefully combined two essential roles: translator/author for the magazine, and spiritual formator/director of the women's community that became the Maryknoll Sisters. Because of her wisdom, creativity, and mission spirit, no task was too small or too big for Rogers, who was given the title "Mother Mary Joseph" once canonical approval was obtained (1920). In 1921 her dream of sending Catholic women to the foreign mission fields was realized; six Maryknoll Sisters were sent to China. Thus began a constant stream of mission-sending; in the 1920s, sisters went to Hong Kong, China, Korea, Manchuria, Philippines, and the Hawaiian Islands. In her lifetime the Maryknoll Sisters numbered over a thousand. At the time of her death missions had also been established in Japan, Bolivia, Panama, Nicaragua, the western Caroline Islands, Tanzania, Ceylon, Mexico, the Marshall Islands, Chile, Peru, Mauritius, Taiwan, and Guatemala.

Rogers served as Superior General of the Maryknoll Sisters until her retirement in 1946 and continued to be their major inspiration through her retreats, talks, articles, and letters until her death.

BIBLIOGRAPHY Camilla Kennedy, *To the Uttermost Parts of the Earth* (1987); Penny Lernoux, *Hearts on Fire: The Story of the Maryknoll Sisters* (1993); Jeanne Marie Lyons, *Maryknoll's First Lady: The Life of Mother Mary Joseph, Foundress of the Maryknoll Sisters* (1964). Mother Mary Joseph Rogers' Collection containing personal documents, correspondence, conferences, articles, diaries, notebooks, and memorabilia is held in the Maryknoll Mission archives, Maryknoll, New York.

Barbara Hendricks, MM

Rolland, Samuel (1801–1873), pioneer French Protestant missionary in South Africa. Rolland was trained at the Institut d'evangélistes of Glay, Doubs, France, in a Lutheran environment. Appointed by the Paris Evangelical Missionary Society (PEMS), in 1829 he sailed for southern Africa with Isaac *Bisseux and Prosper *Lemue. In 1835, on the right bank of the Caledon River, he established the multi-ethnic settlement, which was named Beerseba. This community acknowledged the suzerainty of *Moshoeshoe of Lesotho, in whose country three other PEMS missionaries (*Casalis, *Arbousset, and Gosselin) were already working. Aided by his wife, Elizabeth (Lyndall), an LMS teacher, Rolland founded a model Christian village, where evangelization, education, agriculture, homecrafts, and language teaching were combined to "civilize" the population. He helped translate parts of the New Testament, which was printed at Beerseba beginning in 1845. The settlement was twice destroyed by Afrikaner Voortrekkers, who finally annexed the region into the Orange Free State. Rolland and several Sotho families then moved to Hermon, inside the Lesotho kingdom, where he lived until the end of his life.

BIBLIOGRAPHY Frantz Balfet, *Un pionnier de la Mission du Lessouto, Samuel Rolland, 1801–1873* (1914), *Samuel Rolland (1801–1873): Pionier van die sending in die Vrystaat* (1984); Jeanne-Marie Léonard, "Beerseba et Thaba-Bossiou, stations de la Société des Missions Evangéliques de Paris au Lesotho, 1833–1848," *Les réveils missionnaires en France du Moyen-Age à nos jours (XIIe–XXe siècles)* (1984), pp. 311–320, and "Samuel Rolland (1801–1873)," *Hommes et Destins,* vol. 5 (1984), pp. 475–476.

Jean-François Zorn

Romero y Galdamez, Oscar Arnulfo (1917–1980), martyred Catholic archbishop of San Salvador. Romero was born in Ciudad Barrios, San Miguel, El Salvador. He served as a priest in San Francisco and San Miguel, became the bishop of Santiago de María in 1970, and reluctantly accepted the post of archbishop of San Salvador in 1977. Known as a studious, spiritually oriented, morally severe and retiring priest, he was chosen by the political and church authorities to lead the church in repressive and violent times. The torture and murder of hundreds of the poor, including close clerical friends such as Rutilio Grande, Octavio Cruz, Rafael Palacios, and Alirio Napoleón Macías, brought about Romero's conversion to enhanced support of the poor. He came to believe that the promotion of justice is a fundamental part of the church's mission of evangelization. He summoned the nation and the church to a radical and sweeping conversion, to incarnational ministry in the world of the poor and oppressed. The gospel, he said, addresses the full range of historical reality. For this integral missionary message he was shot and killed on March 24, 1980, while celebrating Holy Communion. His prophetic witness against the powers, economic and military, challenged the Christian conscience in Latin America and abroad to make concern for present suffering a test for authentic discipleship of Jesus Christ.

BIBLIOGRAPHY Oscar Arnulfo Romero, *A Martyr's Message of Hope: Six Homilies by Archbishop Oscar Romero* (1981). James Brockman, ed., *The Word Remains: A Life of Oscar Romero* (1982), and *The Church Is All of You: Thoughts of Archbishop Oscar Romero* (1984); Placido Erdozain, *Archbishop Romero: Martyr of Salvador* (1981); I. Martín-Bozó and Jon Sobrino, eds., *La Voz de los Sin Voz* (1980; Eng. tr., *Archbishop Oscar Romero: Voice of the Voiceless,* 1985).

Sidney H. Rooy

Rommerskirchen, Johannes (1899–1978), missiologist, bibliographer, and librarian. Born in Germany at Neuenhoven, Aachen, Rommerskirchen entered the Missionary Oblates of Mary Immaculate in 1916. He studied missiology at the University of Münster under Joseph *Schmidlin and obtained his doctoral degree in 1930 with a dissertation on the Oblate missions in Ceylon (Sri Lanka). After Robert *Streit died in 1930, Rommerskirchen was assigned to Rome to assist Johannes *Dindinger in editing *Bibliotheca Missionum* and in strengthening the Pontifical Missionary Library, where he helped Dindinger develop the library catalogue. After some bibliographical contributions in *Zeitschrift für Missionswissenschaft,* he founded *Bibliografia Missionaria,* a bibliography of current scholarly literature on mission studies that counted forty issues by the time of his death. He was also professor of mission history at the Missiological Institute of the Propaganda Fide Athenaeum from 1933 to 1955.

BIBLIOGRAPHY A Festschrift for Rommerskirchen is *De Archivis et Bibliothecis Missionibus atque Scientiae Missionum inservientibus* (1968) (*Euntes Docete* 21 [1968]), with his bibliography on pp. 23–32. Willi Henkel, "In memoriam P. Johannes Rommerskirchen," *Etudes Oblates* 37 (1978): 185–189, "Johannes Rommerskirchen," in Gerald H. Anderson et al., eds., *Mission Legacies* (1994), pp. 395–401, and "P. Johannes Rommerskirchen O.M.I. zum Gedächtnis," *NZM* 34 (1978): 309–310.

Willi Henkel, OMI

Rønne, Bone Falch (1764–1832), Danish Lutheran minister, educator, missionary organizer, and a founder of the Danish Missionary Society. Rønne was born in Fredericia. After university studies, ordination, and a period as tutor to King Christian VIII and his sister, he became vicar (*sognepraest*) of the parish of Kongens Lyngby, in which post he remained until his death. A great and indeed nervous activist, Rønne in his young days concerned himself with matters as diverse as education, philanthropy, farming, and beekeeping. Later his energies became channeled through the evangelical revival spreading outward from England in the wake of the *Wesleys. For the last 20 years of his life his work took on an almost Methodist character, with emphasis on the distribution of Bibles and edifying tracts. In 1820 he founded the Lyngby Evangelical Tract Society, the missionary cause having a prominent place. When the Danish Missionary Society was created in the following year, Rønne became its president, a post he held until his death. His initiatives did not go unopposed; Rønne was an "enthusiast" in both negative and positive senses, and he was sometimes tactless. His work as an evangelical pioneer in Denmark, however, was of lasting importance.

BIBLIOGRAPHY N. Bundgaard, *Det danske Missionsselskabs historie*, vol. 1 (1935); *Kirke-Leksikon for Norden*, vol. 3 (1911), p. 859.

Eric J. Sharpe

Rønning, Halvor (1862–1950), pioneer Norwegian-American Lutheran missionary in China. Born to poor tenant farmers in Telemark, Norway, Rønning as a youth excelled in skiing, tended mountain sheep, and taught school. The local church was strongly influenced by Haugean revivalism. When a new minister remarked that even sons of tenant farmers might receive pastoral training in America (unheard of in Norway) and urged the young man of 21 to go, Rønning packed his bags and entered the Hauge Synod seminary at Redwing, Minnesota. After four years of theological study (1883–1887), during which he tutored classmates in Norwegian and taught in a parochial school, Rønning was called to serve as pastor of a three-point parish near Faribault, Minnesota. A revival broke out in each congregation, accompanied by intense interest in and prayer for missions. The appearance of two Norwegian China missionaries precipitated the formation of a China Mission Society at the 1890 Hauge Synod convention and caused Rønning himself to hear a "Macedonian call." He and his sister Thea, later joined by Hannah Rorem (who became Rønning's wife), responded to the call, sailed from San Francisco, and arrived in Shanghai in December 1891. A field of service was located in Fancheng, in northwest Hupei (Hubei) Province, with the help of the legendary Griffith *John of the London Missionary Society. Here Rønning labored for 15 years (1893–1899, 1901–1908). When his wife died in 1907, he returned to America with his children. At age 46 he embarked on a second pioneering ministry as a frontier missionary in Alberta, Canada.

BIBLIOGRAPHY H. N. Ronning and N. N. Ronning, *The Gospel at Work* (1943).

James A. Scherer

Roothaan, Johann Philipp (1785–1853), superior general of the Jesuits. Roothaan was born in Amsterdam, where he did classical studies under Jakob van Lennep. Influenced by the former Jesuit Adam Beckers, he entered the Society of Jesus in Russia in 1804. After a period of teaching classics in Russia (1806–1809), he did his philosophical and theological studies at Polotsk and was ordained in 1812. From 1812 to 1820 he was professor of rhetoric and preaching missions at Dünaburg College (in eastern Latvia). When the Jesuits were banned from Russia in 1820, he fled to Brig, Switzerland, where he taught, assisted the Jesuit vice-provincial Nicolas Godinot, and became acquainted with the situation in central Europe. He was founder and became rector of a college at Turin in 1823. He was elected superior general of the Jesuits in 1829, after which he wrote eleven letters to all members of the society about reorganizing the society and regaining its prestige and efficiency. He renewed Jesuit missions in all the continents. In 1851 the society counted 975 missionaries out of a total number of 5,000 members. Asking for volunteers for the United States, Roothaan made Maryland a Jesuit province with 89 members; later, St. Louis was also made a province. In 1848, exiled European Jesuits founded Marquette University in Milwaukee, Wisconsin.

BIBLIOGRAPHY J. P. Roothaan, *Epistolae*, 5 vols. (1935–1940). The most recent bibliography is Lázló Polgár, *Bibliographie sur l'histoire de la Compagnie de Jésus, 1901–1980*, vol. 3 (1990), pp. 99–103. See also A. Neu, *P. Johann Philipp Roothaan, der bedeutendste Jesuitengeneral* (1928); R. North, *The General Who Rebuilt the Jesuits* (1944); Joseph Albert Otto, *Gründung der neuen Jesuitenmission durch General Pater Johann Philipp Roothaan* (1939); C. Sommervogel, *Bibliothèque de la Compagnie de Jésus*, vol. 7 (1890–1900), pp. 117–127.

Willi Henkel, OMI

Roots, Logan H(erbert) (1870–1945), American Episcopal Bishop of Hankow (Hankou), China, from 1904 to 1937. Roots was born in Illinois, graduated from Harvard in 1891 and Episcopal Theological School in 1896, served several years as traveling secretary for the International Committee of the YMCA, and went to China in 1896. He spent his entire career (1896–1938) in the cities of Hankow and Wuchang on the Yangtze River in central China. In the 1910s and 1920s he was a leader in the ecumenical movement in China and held leading posts in several interdenominational bodies, including the National Christian Council.

In the 1930s, Roots maintained personal contact with several foreign and Chinese leftist journalists and political leaders, such as Edgar Snow, Agnes Smedley, and Chou En-lai (Zhou Enlai). Some called him the Red Bishop, but he was not himself a political activist; he was also on very good terms with Chiang Kai-Shek and his government. His home was a forum for gatherings of officials and journalists of several nationalities, especially while Hankow was the temporary capital of China (late 1937 to late 1938). After 1938, Roots lived in New York City, where he was a leader of the Moral Rearmament movement.

BIBLIOGRAPHY *New York Times*, September 25, 1945 (obit.); John McCook Roots, *Warrior's Testament* (n.d., c. 1945). Roots's voluminous official papers are in the Protestant Episcopal Church historical archives at the Episcopal Seminary, Austin, Texas.

Daniel H. Bays

Rosenkranz, Gerhard (1896–1983), German Protestant missiologist. Rosenkranz was born and raised in a teacher's family in Brunswick, Germany. He took up theological studies in Marburg in 1919, after his return from service in World War I, in which he was severely wounded. He was deeply influenced by Marburg's great religious scholar, Rudolf Otto. In 1931, after pastoral service in several parishes, Rosenkranz was appointed inspector for the East Asia Mission at Heidelberg, where he also obtained his doctorate in 1935. Having received a lectureship in missiology and comparative religion in 1939, he qualified for a full professorship in 1941 in spite of constant harassment by the Nazi secret police. In 1948 he was called to the chair of missions at Tübingen University, a position he held until his retirement in 1964. He served on most representative agencies of Protestant missions in Germany and managed in his teaching, research, and writing to cover a wider field than most of his colleagues. In 1937 he published an outline (expanded in 1951) of what he called Christian "Religionskunde," an effort to accommodate both a scientific approach to religions and a theological interpretation of God's own mission (missio Dei), while avoiding a total synthesis and disintegration of both concerns. Halfway through his postwar career Rosenkranz published the first amplification of his program, a comprehensive survey of the Christian encounter with world religions (1967), and toward the end of his life the counterpart, a massive encyclopedic analysis of the missionary task of the church (1977).

BIBLIOGRAPHY Gerhard Rosenkranz, *Evangelische Religionskunde* (1951), *Religionswissenschaft und Theologie* (1964), *Der christliche Glaube angesichts der Weltreligionen* (1967), and *Die christliche Mission—Geschichte und Theologie* (1977). O. Schumann, "Gedanken zur Aktualität einer 'Evangelischen Religionskunde,'" *ZMiss* 13 (1987): 91–98.

Hans-Werner Gensichen

Ross, John (1842–1915), Scottish Presbyterian missionary in Manchuria. Born in northern Scotland, Ross served several Gaelic-speaking churches before leaving for China under the United Presbyterian Church in 1872. His ministry deeply touched two areas, Manchuria and Korea. By 1873 he had preached his first sermon in Chinese and had pioneered Manchurian work through wide itineration from his post in Shenyang (Mukden). Known for his generous spirit toward Confucianism and Chinese ancestral rites, he supported the idea of a Chinese church that would not be a Western replica. In 1873, living on the northern border of a Korea still closed to outsiders, he met traders from the "hermit kingdom." His growing interests produced the first Korean primer (1877) and grammar (1882) in English, the first history of Korea in any Western language (1879), and, under his direction, the first Korean translation of the New Testament (1887). Its unheralded distribution in Korea produced an authentic church there before Protestant missionary itineration began widely within the country. He retired to Scotland because of ill health in 1910 but continued to write and lecture.

BIBLIOGRAPHY John Ross, *Chinese Foreign Policy* (1877), *The Manchus* (1880), *The Boxers of Manchuria* (1901), *The Original Religion of China* (1909), and the posthumous *Origin of the Chinese People* (1916). Ross's most widely acclaimed work was *Mission Methods in Manchuria* (1903). Sung-il Choi, "John Ross (1842–1915) and the Korean Protestant Church" (Ph.D. diss., Edinburgh Univ., 1992); James H. Grayson, *John Ross: First Missionary to Korea* (in Korean; 1982). A limited number of Ross's letters are available in the records of the United Presbyterian Church housed in the National Library of Scotland; some materials are also available in the National Bible Society of Scotland, Edinburgh.

Harvie M. Conn

Ross, William (1895–1973), explorer and pioneer Catholic missionary in New Guinea. Originally from Orange, New Jersey, Ross received his theological training at the Society of the Divine Word (SVD) seminary at Techny, Illinois, was ordained in 1922, and was sent by the SVD to New Guinea in 1926. Imbued with an unusual pioneering spirit, he was convinced that the potential for church growth was not on the coast but in the still unexplored interior—the Ramu River area and the Bismarck Range. Along with Alfons *Schäfer and others, and with the blessing of the bishop and government officers, he made deeper and deeper forays into the dangerous and unexplored interior, seeking possibilities for new mission stations. The interior beyond the Bismarck Range was commonly assumed to be inhospitable and uninhabited, but in 1933 Australian gold prospectors and government patrols discovered a fertile upland plateau (the Simbu-Wahgi-Mount Hagen region) with a robust and relatively dense population, equaling the population of the rest of New Guinea. Ross, Schäfer and their companions were close behind, deepening and extending the first contacts, teaching, serving, and baptizing. In 1971 Ross was honored by Queen Elizabeth II as Honorary Officer of the British Empire. In 1976 a commemorative stamp was issued by Papua New Guinea honoring "Father Ross, Pioneer Missionary."

BIBLIOGRAPHY Among Ross's publications are his ethnographical and historical works: "Ethnological Notes on Mount Hagen Tribes," *Anthropos* 31 (1936): 341–363 and his "The Catholic Mission in the Western Highlands," in *The History of Melanesia* (1968). Mary R. Mennis, *Hagen Saga* (1982), is a full-length biography of Ross. Autobiographical material can be found in his fifteen articles in the SVD *Christian Family* magazine (1927–1946). Archival materials are kept by the Catholic Mission in Papua New Guinea.

Louis J. Luzbetak, SVD

Rossano, Pietro (1923–1991), Catholic scholar of interreligious dialogue and theology of religions. Rossano was born in Italy at Vezza, Alba, and was ordained a priest in 1946. He studied at the Pontifical Biblical Institute and obtained a doctorate in theology at the Pontifical Gregorian University, and a second doctorate in classical languages at the University of Turin. Both degrees reflect Rossano's interest in non-Christian religions and cultures. He was one of the founders of the Italian Biblical Association and published several books in biblical studies. In 1966 Paul VI appointed him undersecretary and in 1973 secretary of the papal secretariat for non-Christian religions. He held this position until 1982, when John Paul II appointed him auxiliary bishop of the diocese of Rome and rector of the Lateran University. Rossano made a considerable contribution to the development of the secretariat in its early stages.

BIBLIOGRAPHY Rossano's publications include *L'uomo e la religione* (1968), *Il problema teologico delle religioni* (1975), "Christ's Lordship and Religious Pluralism in Roman Catholic Perspective," in Gerald H. Anderson and Thomas F. Stransky, eds., *Christ's Lordship and Religious Pluralism* (1981), pp. 96–110, and *Vangelo e cultura* (1985). From 1967 to 1990 Rossano wrote some thirty-five articles in English and French on the theology of religions and dialogue in *Bulletin Pontificium pro Dialogo inter Religiones*. Anna Civran, "Mons. Pietro Rossano, insigne ed umile maestro promotore del dialogo interreligioso," *Unitas* 46 (1991): 95–101; Willi Henkel, "Mgr. Pietro Rossano (1923–1991), Wegbereiter des Dialogs mit den nichtchristlichen Religionen" *ZMR* 76 (1992): 159–161; Aloysius Pieris, "Pietro Rossano, 1923–1991," *Dialogue* 18 (1991): 86–89; "To the memory of Mgr. Pietro Rossano," *Bulletin Pontificium Consilium pro Dialogo inter Religiones* 26 (1991): 305–370, with an editorial by Francis Arinze as well as contributions by Marcello Zago, Michael L. Fitzgerald, Thomas Michel, and Mariasusai Dhavamoney (pp. 331–338, 360–370).

Willi Henkel, OMI

Rossel, Jacques (1915–), Swiss missionary in India and mission administrator. Rossel was born in Tramelan, Canton of Bern, Switzerland. While still a student, he attended the 1938 World Mission Conference of the International Missionary Council at Tambaram, India. After graduating (1939) he served in the Swiss army (1939–1941) and worked as a pastor in Bulle and Romont (1941–1946). He joined the Basel Mission (BM) in 1946 and with his wife Anne-Marie (Courvoisier) went to India, where he was a lecturer at Mangalore Theological Seminary. He was an important mediator in the struggle for church union within the Church of South India until he returned to Switzerland in 1959. Under his presidency (1959–1979), the BM constitution was changed to fit the requirements in a time of partnership with independent churches overseas. He was also cofounder of the Swiss Association of Churches and Missions and the Association of Missions in Southwest Germany. As a member of the World Council of Churches (WCC) executive committee (1968–1980), he worked in various commissions, including the Commission for Special Assistance to Social Projects, and was an ardent defender of the Program to Combat Racism. After his resignation from the BM he became a pastor at Pully, Canton of Vaud, until his retirement in 1980. Throughout his career he was an outstanding integrative ecumenical leader who made a lasting contribution to the understanding of partnership in church and mission and to the question of dialogue with other religions. He received an honorary D.Th. degree from the University of Bern in 1965.

BIBLIOGRAPHY Jacques Rossel, *Découverte de la mission* (1945), *Dynamik der Hoffnung* (1967), *Sharing in the Ecumenical Fellowship* (1984), "The Basel Mission in India: Perspective and Challenge, the Legacy of the Basel Mission in India," in Godwin Shiri, ed., *Wholeness in Christ* (1985), and "A Movement in the Making," in Franz Baumann, ed., *No Bird Flies with Just One Wing! 175 Years of Basel Mission. Reflections on the History and Identity of the Basel Mission* (1990). Rossel was also coeditor of *ZMiss* from 1964 to 1974. He wrote numerous reports and articles in BM and WCC publications. His letters and reports from India are in the BM India archive, Basel, Switzerland.

Waltraud Ch. Haas

Rossum, Willem van (1854–1932), cardinal prefect of Propaganda Fide. Born in Zwolle, Netherlands, Rossum entered the Redemptorist congregation in 1874. He taught theology and was rector of the Theological School of Wittem until 1911, when Pius X made him a cardinal. In 1918 *Benedict XV appointed him prefect of Propaganda Fide, in which position he contributed greatly to realizing Benedict's encyclical *Maximum Illud,* with its program of renewal in mission, especially for overcoming colonialism and establishing indigenous clergy. Rossum proposed six Chinese bishops, who were ordained by *Pius XI in 1926. Under Rossum, membership of the Redemptorists was increasingly internationalized. He established apostolic delegations, arranged for apostolic visitations, promoted missionary synods, forbade political activity by missionaries, and asked the missionary societies to give special attention to local clergy. He created a new and larger campus for the Urban College in Rome, where he provided a chair for missiology, and in 1932 the college became a missiological institute. He was involved in the Vatican mission exhibition of 1925, which formed the nucleus of what became the Pontifical Missionary Library and Missionary Museum. In 1920, under his administration, the statutes of the Pontifical Society of St. Peter for the Indigenous Clergy were approved, and it was placed under Propaganda Fide. In 1922 he moved the Pontifical

Mission Aid Societies from France to Rome. In 1927 he founded the International Fides Agency with editions of its publications in four languages. In 1927 he asked Pius XI to introduce the yearly mission Sunday and to declare St. Francis *Xavier and *Theresa of Lisieux patrons of the missions. His biographer calls him a "second founder of the [Propaganda Fide] Congregation."

BIBLIOGRAPHY Jos. Maria Drehmanns, "Kardinaal Van Rossum, Prefect der Propaganda," *Het Missiewerk* 4 (1932–1933): 140–164, and *Kardinaal Van Rossum, korte levensshets* (1935); Josef Metzler, "Präfekten der Kongregation in der neuesten Missionsära (1918–1972)," *Sacrae Congregationis de Propaganda Fide Memoria Rerum, 1672–1972,* vol. 3, pt. 2 (1976), pp. 303–312.

Willi Henkel, OMI

Roth, Heinrich (1620–1668), pioneer Jesuit authority on Sanskrit. Roth was born at Dillingen, Germany, and joined the Society of Jesus in 1639. Ordained a priest in 1649, he arrived in India in 1652. From Goa he was transferred to the empire of the Great Mogul, and from 1654 onward he stayed at the Jesuit College at Agra. He was fluent in Hindustani and Persian, and for six years he studied the sacred Sanskrit language. Between 1660 and 1662 he wrote a Sanskrit grammar and transcribed and annotated two Sanskrit texts, the first scholar from the West to do so. In 1662 two Jesuits from China, Johann *Grüber and Albert *d'Orville, arrived at Agra by way of an overland route intending to continue their journey to Rome. Instead, they were ordered by the Jesuit general to discover an alternate route from China to Europe in order not to be dependent on Portuguese ships. D'Orville died in Agra and Roth took his place. With his manuscripts in Sanskrit, he accompanied Grüber from September 4, 1662, to February 20, 1664, when they arrived at Rome. Roth was unsuccessful in getting the manuscripts printed either in Italy or in Austria, so he took them back on his return journey overland to India in 1664. But he lost them at Scutari, Turkey, as they were misplaced in the luggage of Grüber, who got ill and was left behind. Roth arrived in India in 1666 and died at Agra. His Sanskrit grammar and manuscripts were lost until 1967, when Arnulf Camps discovered them in the National Library at Rome. Roth's interest in Sanskrit and Hinduism shows that he had understood that the majority of the people in the Mogul Empire were Hindus and not Muslims and that he was trying to change the policy of the Jesuit Mogul Mission.

BIBLIOGRAPHY Arnulf Camps and Jean-Claude Muller, *The Sanskrit Grammar and Manuscripts of Father Heinrich Roth S.J. (1620–1668), Facsimile Edition of Biblioteca Nazionale, Rome, MSS. OR. 171 and 172, with an Introduction* (1988).

Arnulf Camps, OFM

Rottler, John Peter (1749–1836), German missionary in South India. Born at Strasbourg and educated there and in Copenhagen, Rottler was ordained in 1775 and left for Tranquebar to serve in the Danish East India Mission. He not only engaged in the usual religious activities there but also carried out botanical studies, for which the Imperial Academy in Vienna awarded him an honorary doctorate in 1795. When C. W. *Gericke died in 1803, the British governor in Madras invited Rottler to come and take charge of the Society for the Propagation of Christian Knowledge (SPCK) mission at Vepery and serve as secretary and chaplain of the Female Asylum (a girls' orphanage). He then left the Lutheran work at Tranquebar and became an Anglican. When serious differences arose between him and C. W. Paezold, the other SPCK worker at Vepery, Rottler gave up that position and began conducting services at Black Town Chapel and ministered at the nearby Dutch enclave of Pulicat as well. When Paezold died in 1817, the SPCK's Madras District Committee asked him to resume the work among Europeans and Indians at the Vepery Mission. In 1819 he published the first translation of the Book of Common Prayer into Tamil. He also revised the Tamil-English dictionary of J. F. *Fabricius. He worked and died in India without ever returning to Germany.

BIBLIOGRAPHY J. Ferdinand Fenger, *History of the Tranquebar Mission* (1863); James Hough, *The History of Christianity in India* (1845); Arno Lehmann, *Es Begann in Tranquebar* (1955); Frank Penny, *The Church in Madras* (1904); W. Taylor, *A Memoir of the First Centenary of the Earliest Protestant Mission at Madras* (1847).

Richard V. Pierard

Rougemont, François de (1624–1676), Jesuit missionary in China. Born in Maastricht, Belgium, de Rougemont entered the Society of Jesus at Malines in 1641. Several months after his priestly ordination in November 1654, he applied to go to the missions. After arriving in Macao in July 1658, and spending a year in Hangchow (Hangzhou), Chekiang (Zhejiang) Province, he labored in the military garrison at Soochow (Suzhou), Kiangsu (Jiangsu) Province, where he made a number of converts. To develop the Christian community in Ch'ang-shu (Changshu), some 20 miles to the north, he established fourteen congregations headed by scholarly leaders. During the persecution of 1665 to 1671, de Rougemont was exiled to Canton (Guangzhou), where he participated in a conference dealing with missionary methods. Later he became pastor for fourteen churches and twenty-one chapels, which he administered with the assistance of lay brothers. *Wu Li, the famous Ch'ing (Qing) dynasty painter and later a Jesuit, accompanied de Rougemont on one of his mission tours. Besides several catechisms in Chinese, de Rougemont wrote an important essay on the need for an indigenous clergy and an account of his exile in Canton. Preparing to go to the island of Ch'ung-ming (Chongming), he died at T'ai-ts'ang (Taicang), near Shanghai, and was buried in Ch'ang-chou (Changzhou), Kiangsu.

BIBLIOGRAPHY François de Rougemont, *Historia Tartaro-Sinica nova* (1673). A biography and de Rougemont's Chinese works are in Louis Pfister, *Notices biographiques et bibliographiques sur les Jésuites de l'ancienne mission de Chine* (1932–1934), pp. 333–337. F. Bontinck, *La Lutte autour de la liturgie chinoise aux XVIIe et XVIIIe siècles*

(1962), pp. 113–120; H. Bosmans, "Documents relatifs à la liturgie chinoise. Le mémoire de François de Rougemont à Jean-Paul Oliva," *Analecta Bollandiana* 32 (1914): 274–293, and "Lettres inédites de François de Rougemont," *Analectes pour servir à l'histoire ecclésiastiques de la Belgique* 39 (1913): 21–54; Laurence C. S. Tam, *Six Masters of Early Qing and Wu Li* (1986), pp. 69–72.

John W. Witek, SJ

Rouse, C(lara) Ruth (1872–1956), missionary, student evangelist, and ecumenical pioneer. Born in Clapham in south London, Rouse came from a devout evangelical family in the Church of England. She early developed a capacity to understand other Christian traditions and, while never forgetting her spiritual aim, she became a convinced advocate of Christian reconciliation and unity. Rouse graduated from Girton College, Cambridge, when women were not yet granted degrees. Joining the Student Volunteer Movement during her college years, she started her vocational career as editor of the British *Student Volunteer* and pioneered in British, Scandinavian, and North American universities as traveling secretary among women students. In 1899 she went to India as a missionary but after two years returned to England because of ill health. While on convalescent leave she was asked by John R. *Mott to visit various European countries in order to promote Christian work among women students. She was appointed a World's Student Christian Federation (WSCF) secretary in 1905 and served in this position until 1924. While proving to be an effective organizer, speaker, leader, fund-raiser, and traveler, she remained first and foremost a missionary and evangelist. Through her worldwide service, she vitalized the missionary interest among students over three decades. After World War I she worked to restore international friendship and to relieve suffering and was instrumental in launching the European Student Relief.

From 1925 to 1939 Rouse served the missionary cause as educational secretary of the Missionary Council of the National Assembly of the Church of England. A post with responsibility for top-level cooperation with bishops and other church leaders, this was one of the most prestigious and difficult positions offered to a woman in the Church of England. For decades she was one of the most influential women in the international Christian community. She was a member of the World's YWCA Executive Committee (1906–1946) and YWCA president from 1938 to 1946. She was an active writer, producing a number of pamphlets, articles, and reviews over a span of more than 50 years. After retirement she won a reputation as a historian.

BIBLIOGRAPHY Works by Rouse include *The World's Student Christian Federation: A History of the First Thirty Years* (1948) and, together with Stephen Neill, edited *A History of the Ecumenical Movement, 1517–1948* (1954). Ruth Franzén, "Ruth Rouse," in Gerald H. Anderson et al., eds., *Mission Legacies* (1994), pp. 93–101. The most extensive international sources of Rouse's reports, correspondence, and other documents are in the WSCF collections in the Yale Divinity School library, New Haven, Conn.; in the World Council of Churches Library, Geneva; and in the YWCA collections in the World's YWCA Library, Geneva.

Ruth Franzén

Rouse, George Henry (1838–1909), English Baptist missionary scholar and Bible translator in India. Rouse was born in Suffolk, England. Although his grandfather and a brother were Anglican priests, he became a Baptist at age 16. Educated at Stepney (now Regent's Park) College, he gained the LL.B. and M.A. from London University, winning the Gold Medal. In 1861 he proceeded as a Baptist Missionary Society missionary to Calcutta, where he "found himself in touch with those who had known Dr. Carey, a fact which he . . . recalled with keen pleasure." After three years, ill health forced him back to England. From 1867 until 1872 he taught at Haverfordwest Baptist College, where he tutored and befriended Timothy *Richards. Improved health allowed him to return to India as secretary of the Baptist India Mission and head of the Baptist Mission Press. His linguistic abilities resulted in his revision of the Bengali Bible (1893–1907); interest in Islam resulted in his *Tracts for Muhammadans* (1893), which, although banned in Egypt, reveals considerable sympathy toward Islam and was widely acclaimed. He encouraged William *Goldsack to devote himself to Muslim apologetics. Twice married, Rouse was survived by several children. Throughout his career, he supported himself by his modest private income. In 1899 he received the honorary D.D. from Hillsdale College, Michigan.

BIBLIOGRAPHY George Henry Rouse, *The Extent of Atonement* (1875), *Who Wrote the Epistle to the Hebrews?* (1882), and *Old Testament Criticism in New Testament Light* (1903). C. E. Wilson, "A Notable Missionary: G. H. Rouse, M.A., LL.B., D.D. (1838–1909)," *MH,* May 1909, pp. 145–148 (obit.). Rouse's personal papers are in the BMS archives, Regent's Park College, Oxford.

Clinton Bennett

Rovenius, Philippus (1574–1651), Dutch Catholic missions advocate. Born in Deventer, Netherlands, Rovenius studied theology at the University of Louvain, Belgium, and was ordained a priest in 1599. In Cologne, Germany, he taught theology at the Dutch College from 1602 until 1606, when he started his pastoral work in Oldenzaal, Netherlands. Pope Paul V appointed him apostolic vicar of the mission to the Netherlands in 1614; his episcopal consecration took place in 1620. He was exiled for the rest of his life, and his possessions were confiscated by the Calvinist state authorities in 1640, but he often stayed in a safe house at Utrecht, where he died.

Rovenius was a great organizer of the mission of the Propaganda Fide in the Netherlands, establishing an effective administration and a unified liturgy and catechetics. He wrote *Treatise on Missions* in 1624 (2d ed. 1625), which was disapproved by the papal nuncio at the instigation of the regular clergy. The third edition of 1626 is a revised one. In Rovenius's view, mission in all parts of the world is an urgent task to be fulfilled under the leadership of the vicar of Christ and by well-prepared missionaries. He gave special attention to the missionary way of life.

BIBLIOGRAPHY Philippus Rovenius, *Tractatus de Missionibus ad propagandam fidem et conversionem infidelium et haereticorum instituendis* (1626). P. W. F. M. Hamans, *Geschiedenis van de Katholieke*

Kerk in Nederland, vol. 1 (1992), pp. 252-253; Alphons Mulders, *Missiologisch Bestek* (1962), pp. 88-89.

Arnulf Camps, OFM

Rowe, Phoebe (1855-1898), first indigenous Christian to receive full missionary appointment from the Woman's Foreign Missionary Society (WFMS), Methodist Episcopal Church. Born of a Scottish father and a Eurasian mother in Allahabad, India, Rowe by age 14 was teaching Sunday school and evangelizing railroad workers. At age 16 she became a teacher in Lucknow for Isabella *Thoburn, founder of a girls' school that later became Asia's first women's college. Deeply pious, especially after experiencing sanctification, Rowe was an outstanding spiritual presence among Indian and Eurasian girls.

Because of her remarkable ability to reach poor people for Christ, she was appointed a missionary of the WFMS. She sang the gospel to the people and superintended the work of Bible women. In 1882 the India Methodist Conference made her a full missionary and deployed her for urban and village evangelism. In 1887 she visited the United States and spoke in missionary meetings to wide acclaim. After returning to India, she was appointed India's first deaconess by Bishop James *Thoburn. Until her death from diphtheria, she conducted itinerant village evangelism throughout the most difficult Methodist mission fields in India.

BIBLIOGRAPHY The most complete account of Phoebe Rowe's life is her biography, including copious journal extracts, *Phoebe Rowe* by Isabella Thoburn (1899). Short sketches are included in Frances Baker, *The Story of the Woman's Foreign Missionary Society of the Methodist Episcopal Church, 1869-1895* (1896, 1987); and Louise Manning Hodgkins, *The Roll Call* (1896).

Dana L. Robert

Rowlands, John Francis (1909-1980), Pentecostal missionary in Natal, South Africa. Rowlands was born in Bristol, England, of Quaker parents. In 1921 his family immigrated to South Africa, where they became Pentecostals. In 1931 Rowlands formed Bethesda Temple in Durban, "a house of prayer for all nations," though the work was to be primarily among Indians. The church joined the Full Gospel Church of God and Rowlands was ordained as one of its ministers. The work grew rapidly, and Indian pastors and evangelists were trained and appointed. Some seventy branch churches were formed in Natal, as well as additional churches in India, Ceylon (Sri Lanka), Nepal, Malaysia, and Mauritius. The impact of this work upon the local community was such that in 1938 some Hindus threatened to burn down the Bethesda churches and kill Rowlands, which led to police protection. His strategy was not to condemn other religions but to foster pride in national culture by showing slides of his visits to India; to oppose all racist laws of the government, particularly the Group Areas Act, which uprooted thousands of Indians; and to organize large campaigns, giving pictorial presentations of the gospel. When Rowlands died there were 30,000 members in various branches of the work.

BIBLIOGRAPHY G. C. Oosthuizen, *Moving to the Waters—50 Years of Pentecostal Revival in Bethesda* (1975).

Norman H. Cliff

Roy Ladurie, Marie Le. *See* Marie de l'Assomption.

Ruatoka (1846-1906), Cook Islands missionary to Papua. Ruatoka was a member of the first band of missionaries from the Cook Islands to Papua in 1873. He labored for 32 years in Papua and became the most famous of the Pacific islander missionaries there. He and his companions started work at Manumanu, but soon Ruoatoka led them to Port Moresby, which had just been discovered by the outside world. There he became the chief associate of W. G. *Lawes, who arrived in 1874 as the first white man to settle in Papua. Ruatoka explored inland regions never before seen by outsiders, making journeys of as much as 500 miles. At Port Moresby he established both school and church. He had difficulty teaching since the children were not accustomed to discipline, but he was an impressive preacher and built up a large congregation. White missionaries came and went, but it was he who provided stability and kept the church going. When gold prospectors arrived, he became their protector, saving their lives by going unarmed into villages which had planned to kill them. He never returned to his homeland, and after his first wife's death he married a Papuan. A Christian training college was named for him and he is still widely honored by the people of Papua.

BIBLIOGRAPHY Marjorie Tuainakore Crocombe, "Ruatoka, a Cook Islander in Papuan History," in *Polynesian Missionaries in Melanesia,* Marjorie Tuainakore Crocombe et al., eds. (1982), pp. 55-78; John Garrett, *To Live among the Stars: Christian Origins in Oceania* (1982).

Charles W. Forman

Ruggieri, Michele (1543-1607), Jesuit pioneer missionary in China. Born in Spinazzola in Puglia, Italy, Ruggieri was a civil lawyer in the government of Philip II, king of Naples. Upon entering the Society of Jesus in 1572, he changed his given name, Pompilio, to Michele. He volunteered for the missions in Asia, was ordained a priest in Lisbon in 1578, and a few weeks later left for Goa, India. Alessandro *Valignano, the superior of all the Jesuit missions in Asia, set down a new policy of inculturation of Christianity in Asia and assigned Ruggieri to Macao to study the Chinese language and customs. Arriving in 1579, Ruggieri impressed Chinese merchants during short trips to Canton with his ability to speak Chinese, and succeeded in making contacts with Chinese officials. Matteo *Ricci joined him in Macao, and with the permission of the governor general, they built a residence and a church at Chao-ch'ing (Zhaoqing), Kwangtung (Guangdong) Province, in 1583. This was the first Catholic mission site in China since the medieval period. Two years later Ruggieri founded a mission in Chekiang (Zhejiang) Province, and in 1587 he did the same in Hukwang (Huguang) Province (area today embraced by the four provinces of Hubei, Hunan,

Guangdong, and Guangxi). He composed the first Catholic catechism in Chinese and worked with Ricci in compiling a Portuguese-Chinese dictionary. The recently published Chinese poetry he composed reflects a mature grasp of the language.

In 1588 Valignano sent Ruggieri to Rome to propose that a papal embassy be sent to the emperor to obtain his permission to preach Christianity in China. The death of four popes in quick succession prevented Ruggieri from accomplishing that goal. In poor health even when in China, Ruggieri remained in Italy and died at Salerno.

BIBLIOGRAPHY Michele Ruggieri, *T'ien-chu shih-lu* (True Record of the Lord of Heaven) (1584). Henri Bernard, *Aux portes de la Chine* (1933) and *Le Père Mathieu Ricci et la societé chinoise de son temps,* 2 vols. (1937), 1:33, 47, 59, 78, 88, 95, 127; Albert Chan, "Michele Ruggieri (1543–1607) and His Chinese Poems," *Monumenta Serica* 41 (1993): 129–167; Pasquale M. d'Elia, ed. *Fonti Ricciane,* 3 vols. (1942–1949), 1:147, 174–177, 264; George H. Dunne, *Generation of Giants* (1962), pp. 18, 28, 48; Eugenio Lo Sardo, ed., *Atlante della Cina di Michele Ruggieri, S.J.* (1993).

John W. Witek, SJ

Ruiz, Manuel (1803–1860), Spanish Franciscan martyr. After volunteering in 1831 for service in the Near East missions, Ruiz was assigned to his order's language school in Damascus. When illness forced his return to Europe in 1836, he resided at the Franciscan missionary college in Rome and probably taught Arabic. Returning to Damascus in 1841, he served as pastor of the parish attached to the language school. In 1844 he held the same position at Acre. He returned to Spain in 1847, taught Hebrew one year at the Burgos seminary, and served as pastor of a small parish near his hometown until 1857, when he returned to Damascus as president of the language school.

In 1856 the sultan of Turkey granted full civil liberties to Christians within his empire. In protest, the Druses began an anti-Christian terrorist campaign. The Franciscans at Damascus believed their enclave's thick wall and stout gates afforded them safety, but during the night of July 9–10, 1860, a mob entered through an unsecured rear door and killed the eight members of the Franciscan community and three Maronite brothers (siblings) who were lay teachers at the school. *Pius XI beatified all eleven martyrs on October 10, 1926.

BIBLIOGRAPHY Agustín Arce, "El beato Manuel Ruiz (1804–1860), arabista y profesor de hebreo," *Miscelánea de Tierra Santa* 3 (1974): 301–324, and *Franciscan Martyrs of Damascus (1860)* (1926 pamphlet); Ignacio Omaechevarria, *Los once de Damasco* (1960); Pellegrino Paoli, *I beati Emmanuele Ruiz e i suoi sette compagni dell'ordine frati minori, martiri a Damasco, 10 Luglio 1860* (1926).

Cyprian J. Lynch, OFM

Ruiz de Montoya, Antonio (1585–1652), Peruvian Jesuit missionary to the Guaraní Indians. After a disorderly youth in Lima, the city of his birth, Ruiz experienced a conversion and entered the Society of Jesus in 1606. As a novice he volunteered for the Paraguay missions and finished his studies for the priesthood in Córdoba, Argentina. He began working in 1613 in the region known as Guairá, in Brazil, where he established eleven mission settlements for the Guaraní Indians. Between 1620 and 1637 he served as superior of the Guaraní missions. Faced with the problem of raiders from São Paulo who carried Indians off into slavery, he organized a major migration of 12,000 Indians who left the Brazilian missions for a site a thousand miles to the south, by the Paraná River in Argentina. In 1537 he went to Spain to seek favors for the mission from Philip IV. At Ruiz de Montoya's urging, the king, and later the viceroy in Lima, granted the Jesuits permission to arm the Indians. With muskets and cannons, and aided by the martial discipline provided by Spanish officers and some of the Jesuits who had been soldiers, the Indians decisively defeated the Paulista slave raiders in 1641 and in subsequent battles. While in Spain, Ruiz de Montoya wrote *The Spiritual Conquest of Paraguay,* a chronicle of the Paraguay missions from their origins until 1637. He also composed the first grammar (1639) and the first dictionary of the Guaraní language (1640), both published in Madrid. He returned to Peru in 1643, where he pressed the viceroy to reapprove the special permissions he obtained in Madrid. While in Lima he struck up a friendship with Francisco del Castillo, a fellow Peruvian Jesuit who preached to the Indians. This friendship led him to write a treatise on mysticism and the spiritual life, *Silex of Divine Love.* He died while on a return visit to Lima. A delegation of Guaraní Indians crossed the continent in order to carry his body back to the mission of Loreto, which he had founded.

BIBLIOGRAPHY Ruiz de Montoya's chronicle was translated into English by Clement McNaspy, and others, under the title *The Spiritual Conquest* (1993). His treatise on the spiritual life, *Sílex del Divino Amor,* was published with a commentary by José Luis Rouillón (1991). On Ruiz de Montoya and the Paraguayan missions, see Philip Caraman's *The Lost Paradise* (1975, 1990), and Silvio Palacios and Ena Zoffoli, *Gloria y tragedia de las misiones guaraníes* (1991).

Jeffrey Klaiber, SJ

Rundle, Robert Terrill (1811–1866), Methodist pioneer missionary in Saskatchewan. Rundle departed from his native Cornwall (England) to become the first Methodist missionary to the Saskatchewan country of the Hudson's Bay Company, arriving at Fort Edmonton in October 1840. He adapted heartily to the rough life of the frontier, traveling extensively from his Edmonton base to Lesser Slave Lake Fort, Fort Assinaboine, Rocky Mountain House, and Gull Lake, twice traveling south, deep into Blackfoot country, and preparing the way for his successor, Benjamin Sinclair. A mountain bearing his name commemorates his journey in 1844 past the first ranges of the Rocky Mountains. He quickly mastered the Cree language, and his journals record the significant adjustments he made to the Cree syllabary originally devised by James *Evans. During the eight-year span of his missionary career, Rundle was not successful in establishing a permanent mission before he returned to Cornwall in 1848. He did, however, earn the respect of both the men of Hudson's Bay Company and the indigenous peoples, thus laying the groundwork for substantial Methodist achievement in western Canada.

BIBLIOGRAPHY Alfred Carter, "The Life and Labors of the Reverend Robert Terrill Rundle, Pioneer Missionary to the Saskatchewan, Canada" (Ph.D. diss., Boston Univ., 1952); Hugh A. Dempsey, ed., *The Rundle Journals, 1840–1848* (1977); Keith Wilson, *Robert Terrill Rundle* (1986).

Jonathan J. Bonk

Russell, William Armstrong (1821–1879), Church Missionary Society (CMS) missionary and bishop in China. Russell, from Tipperary, Ireland, was educated at Trinity College, Dublin, and was ordained in 1847 after attending the Church Missionary College at Islington (London), England. He left for China in the same year with two other missionaries, the first to be sent out by CMS following exploratory visits. He was located in Ningpo, one of the treaty ports, which remained his base for his whole service, although he spent much time in itinerations. In 1852 he married Mary Ann Leisk (1828–1887), born in Batavia to Scottish parents, who from about 1840 had been the ward and protégée of Mary Ann *Aldersey, independent pioneer missionary teacher. From 1862 to 1868, the Russells went on leave in England, where they were engaged in Bible translation, but also awaited the outcome of a dispute over whether a new diocese should be set up for mainland China, separate from the colonial diocese of Victoria, Hong King. Finally, in December 1872, Russell was consecrated first bishop of North China. He returned to Ningpo in 1873 and was active in organizing the church, ordaining four Chinese clergy in 1875 and 1876. He died at Ningpo. Mary Ann Russell was accepted as a missionary in her own right and served until her death in 1887.

BIBLIOGRAPHY CMS, *Register of Missionaries and Native Clergy* (1904); Eugene Stock, *The History of the Church Missionary Society: Its Environment, Its Men, and Its Work,* 3 vols. (1899); E. Aldersey White, *A Woman Pioneer in China: The Life of Mary Ann Aldersey* (1932).

Jocelyn Murray

Ruysbroeck, Wilhelm de. *See* William of Rubroek.

Rycroft, W(illiam) Stanley (1899–1993), Presbyterian lay missionary, educator and administrator in Latin America. The son of a Wesleyan lay preacher, Rycroft was born in Lancaster, England. As a pilot for the Royal Air Force during World War I, he was shot down three times and wounded in action. In 1922, after he graduated from Liverpool University, the Free Church of Scotland sent him to the Anglo Peruvian College in Lima, Perú, where he served for 18 years as professor of English, and from 1926 as vice-principal. For 15 years he was a professor in San Marcos University, where he received his degree of doctor of philosophy in 1938. The same year the Evangelical Alliance of Perú, of which he was then president, delegated him to attend the meeting of the International Missionary Council in Madras, India. He was secretary of the Committee on Cooperation in Latin America (CCLA) from 1940 until 1950. In 1946 he was instrumental in organizing the United Andean Indian Mission in Ecuador. As secretary for Latin America of the American Presbyterian Board of Foreign Missions (1950–1969) and as secretary for research (1960–1966), he played a vital role in raising the consciousness of his church and the public in the United States as to the importance of an integral mission approach in Latin America. A lifelong friend of John *Mackay and a frequent traveling companion of John R. *Mott, Rycroft became one of the most noted Protestant lay missionaries of the twentieth century. He died in Princeton, New Jersey, eight days after the death of his wife of fifty-eight years, Margaret (Robb).

BIBLIOGRAPHY William Stanley Rycroft, *On This Foundation: The Evangelical Witness in Latin America* (1942); Rycroft also edited or coedited *Indians in the High Andes* (1946), *Religion and Faith in Latin America* (1953), and *Memoirs of Life in Three Worlds* (1976). Rycroft was coauthor with Myrtle M. Clemmer of a series of factual studies on Africa, the Middle East, Asia, and Latin America, and also *A Study of Urbanization in Latin America* (1962, rev. 1963). "W. Stanley Rycroft, Latin America Missiologist," interview by John H. Sinclair, *American Presbyterians: The Journal of Presbyterian History* 65 (Summer 1987): 117–133.

Sidney H. Rooy

Ryland, John (1753–1825), founding member and second secretary of the Baptist Missionary Society (BMS). Ryland was son of John Collett Ryland, a Particular Baptist minister, and joined and eventually succeeded his father in the pastorate of College Lane Baptist Church, Northampton, England. About 1775 he was moved from his father's hyper-Calvinist principles by reading Jonathan *Edwards's *Treatise on the Freedom of the Will,* and shortly afterward he became a close friend of Andrew *Fuller. He baptized William *Carey at Northampton in 1783. In October 1792 he joined Fuller, Carey, and twelve others in founding the BMS. A year later he moved to Bristol to become pastor of Broadmead Baptist Church and principal of Bristol Baptist Academy, where he trained many of the early missionaries of the BMS. He was largely responsible for the commencement of the BMS Jamaica mission in 1814. In the difficult circumstances occasioned by Fuller's death in 1815, Ryland took over as secretary of the society, an office he shared first with James Hinton and then with John *Dyer. It fell to Ryland to bridge the widening gap between the Serampore missionaries in India and the London regime that had seized control of the Society after Fuller's death. Subsequently, Ryland's role was more nominal, with Dyer acting as the effective secretary. Ryland published a biography of Fuller in 1816.

BIBLIOGRAPHY J. E. Ryland, *Pastoral Memorials: Selected from the Manuscripts of the Late Revd. John Ryland, D.D., of Bristol: With a Memoir of the Author,* 2 vols. (1826); Brian Stanley, *The History of the Baptist Missionary Society, 1792–1992* (1992).

Brian Stanley

S

Sabatier, Ernst (1886–1965), French missionary in the Gilberts (present-day Kiribati) and authority on the island culture. Born in Auvergne, France, Sabatier traveled widely for his education. After elementary schooling in France, he studied in Italy, England, Spain, and Switzerland. He joined the Missionaries of the Sacred Heart and was ordained a priest in 1912. In the same year he left for the Gilberts, where he would spend the rest of his life on the island of Abemama. Sabatier assiduously studied Gilbertese language and lore from local elders. He compiled a Gilbertese-French dictionary, later translated into English. In addition to his epic history of Abemama, *Le poème de l'île,* he wrote a compendium of Gilbertese customs and *Sous l'équateur du Pacifique,* a chronicle of Catholic mission work in the islands. This latter work became a classic and in 1977 was translated into English as *Astride the Equator.* Sabatier's long residence in the Gilberts (53 years in all) and his limitless intellectual curiosity made him the foreigner most knowledgeable about the Gilbertese people and their traditions.

BIBLIOGRAPHY The introductions to the French and English editions of *Astride the Equator* furnish biographical sketches of Sabatier. The English edition, edited by Harry Maude (1977), contains a bibliography of Sabatier's publications.

Francis X. Hezel, SJ

Sadrach Surapranata (1835–1924), Javanese evangelist and leader of an indigenous Christian movement in Central Java. Born in northern Central Java, Sadrach became a *santri* (Muslim student) and found his way to the gospel through missionary J. E. *Jellesma in East Java. For several years he was a student of *Tunggul Wulung in Bondo, whose methods he followed in discussions with other *ngelmu* (wisdom) teachers. Like Tunggul Wulung, Sadrach had certain eschatological expectations about the coming of the *Ratu Adil* (Righteous King). Unlike Tunggul Wulung, however, he had a thorough knowledge of the Bible. After leaving Bondo, Sadrach served with Mrs. C. P. Philips-Stevens in Purworejo as an evangelist before establishing his own movement in Karangjoso.

Sadrach became an authoritative *guru,* as his adopted name Surapranata (he who makes the regulations) shows. He provided his congregations with a good structure and drafted regulations for baptism, marriage, and commemorative days. His Javanese Christianity adopted religious forms of Islam and *ngelmu* (Javanese wisdom). That and other differences caused a deep conflict between Sadrach and the Dutch Gereformeerde mission, so that relations with that mission were finally terminated in 1893. Following F. L. *Anthing, Sadrach then became an apostle of the Apostolic Church. After his death the movement was reunited with the mission congregations.

BIBLIOGRAPHY L. Adriaanse, *Sadrach's King* (1899); C. Guillot, *L'Affaire Sadrach: Un essai de Christianism à Java au XIXe siècle* (1981); P. Quarles van Ufford, "Why Don't You Sit Down?" in R. Schefold, ed., *Man, Meaning and History* (1980). An interpretation by Javanese theologian Sutarman S. Partonadi is *Sadrach's Community and Its Textual Roots: A Nineteenth Century Javanese Expression of Christianity* (1988).

Alle G. Hoekema

Safdar, Ali (c. 1830–1899), lay theologian of the church in India. Born of an orthodox Muslim family in Agra, Safdar received an Islamic education before graduating from a British government college. He became inspector of schools in Rawalpindi and Jabalpur. A respected Muslim *maulvi,* in 1854 he attended the debates between Karl *Pfander and Muslim religious leaders in Agra. Criticism of Christianity was part of a personal religious quest that brought him to Sufism. Friendship with the Hindu convert Nehemiah *Goreh led him to study the Psalms and New

Testament. Adopting Goreh as his spiritual guide, he was baptized on Christmas Day 1864 by E. Champion, the CMS missioner in Jabalpur. Though he was the first Indian Muslim religious scholar to receive baptism, two other Muslim teachers converted with him, and this news may have influenced *Imad ud-Din, who converted in 1866. Unlike Imad, Safdar was never ordained, and his writings, though fewer, were less polemical. His preference for poetry is exemplified in his best-known work, *Ghaza e Ruh,* in which he recounted his conversion. In his major systematic work, *Niygaz Nama,* he defended the integrity of the Christian Scriptures without rehearsing old themes of Muslim-Christian polemics. He constantly urged overseas missionaries to live and articulate the gospel in spiritually appropriate ways among Muslims.

BIBLIOGRAPHY C. F. Andrews, *North India* (1908); E. Champion, "The Two Converts," *Church Missionary Intelligencer,* n.s. 2 (February 1866): 46–50; C. E. Gardner, *The Life of Father Goreh* (1900); R. Paul, *Lights in the World: Life Sketches of Maulvi Safdar Ali and the Rev. Janni Alli* (1969); E. M. Wherry, *The Muslim Controversy* (1905).

David A. Kerr

Safford, Anna Cunningham (1837–1890), missionary educator in China. A native of Athens, Georgia, and principal of a women's college, Safford applied to the (Southern) Presbyterian Church, U.S. (PCUS) for missionary service in 1873. She was appointed for women's work in Soochow (Suzhou) and sailed shortly thereafter. As a seasoned educator, she developed a systematic, holistic approach to the cause of women that included village itineration, home visitation, and special classes and worship services just for women. Because of poor health, she was often in pain; during such times when she was unable to itinerate, she turned to the preparation of literature, her most lasting achievement. She wrote or translated a dozen or more books and pamphlets in a style that simple women could understand. As editor of the interdenominational magazine *Woman's Work in the Far East,* she was invited to address the historic 1890 missionary conference in Shanghai, but illness prevented her attending, and her paper was read to the assembly by a colleague. She died soon afterward and was buried in Shanghai.

BIBLIOGRAPHY Letters from Safford describing her work among women appear in the *Missionary* (Southern Presbyterian missionary journal), 1873–1883. Her Chinese books and pamphlets include *Anatomy, Physiology and Hygiene, Child's Catechism, Child's Universal History, A Form of Prayer, God in Nature; or, Reasons for Familiar Things, Important Doctrines of Jesus, Line upon Line,* and *Peep of Day.* Biographical data appear in P. Frank Price, *Our China Investment* (1927) and James E. Bear, "The China Mission of the Presbyterian Church in the United States" (1965), vol. 3 (manuscript in the library of Union Theological Seminary, Richmond, Va.).

G. Thompson Brown

Sahagún, Bernardino de (1499–1590), Franciscan missionary in Mexico. Born in the village of Sahagún in the province of León, Spain, Sahagún studied at the University of Salamanca and, while a student, joined the order of the Franciscans of the Observantia Strictissima. In 1529 he went to Mexico in the company of nineteen other friars. For more than 60 years—up to his death—he labored in central Mexico. He spent most of those years at the College of Santa Cruz, Tlatelolco, as a teacher and researcher. He thoroughly mastered Nahuatl and trained many informants, becoming an excellent ethnologist. His most famous work is *Historia general de las cosas de Nueva España,* in twelve volumes, in which he described the various religious, cultural, and secular aspects of the life of the Aztecs. He also translated the Gospels, wrote catechisms and prayerbooks, and published sermons and a manual for missionaries. His account of the culture of the Indians was meant to serve as an instrument for detecting idolatry, but it also served the Indians in their striving after a *religión yuxtapuesta,* or synthesis of old and new faiths.

BIBLIOGRAPHY Bernardino de Sahagún, *Florentine Codex, General History of the Things of New Spain,* tr. from the Aztec into English by A. J. O. Anderson and Charles E. Dibble (1950–1974). Ellen T. Baird, *The Drawings of Sahagún's Primeros Memoriales: Structure and Style* (1993); Claude Blankaert, *Naissance de l'ethnologie? Anthropologie et missions en Amérique, XVIe–XVIIIe siècle* (1985); Miguel León-Portilla, *Bernardino de Sahagún* (1987).

Arnulf Camps, OFM

Sahak (d. 439), catholicos of Armenia. In troubled times from 387 to 439, Sahak commissioned the former royal secretary, *Mesrob, whom he ordained to the priesthood, to combat residual paganism and menacing heresy throughout the country. Sahak endorsed Mesrob's plan and obtained royal support for establishing a thirty-six-letter alphabet for the Armenian language, paving the way for the translation of the Bible and liturgies out of Greek and Syriac into the vernacular. An added benefit for the nation was that it unified the eastern, Persian-controlled portion with the western, Greek-dependent portion. Sahak is remembered in Armenia as "the Great."

BIBLIOGRAPHY Aziz S. Atiya, *History of Eastern Christianity* (1968), pp. 324–325.

Paul D. Garrett

Saint, Nathanael (Nate) (1923–1956), pioneer of missionary aviation, martyred in Ecuador. Raised in the Philadelphia area in a family built on strict biblical principles, Saint accepted Christ at age 13. From childhood he demonstrated unusual inventive aptitudes and an insatiable interest in flying. During World War II he served three years in the U. S. Army Air Corps. Following the war he spent a year at Wheaton College, Illinois, then married Marjorie Farris. In 1948 they went with Missionary Aviation Fellowship (MAF) to Ecuador where he opened a base in Shell Mera, on the edge of the eastern jungles. MAF served as a vital supply link for missionaries and Indians in remote jungle and mountain areas. A stickler for air safety, Saint invented a number of techniques that today are standard procedures in missionary aviation.

In 1955, he located from the air a village of Auca (now known as Waorani) Indians, a remote tribe notorious for killing outsiders. For twelve weeks, Saint, Jim *Elliot, and Ed McCully flew weekly over the village, dropping gifts with an ingenious bucket drop system Saint had developed. In January 1956 two colleagues, Roger Youderian and Peter *Fleming, joined them, and the five men established a base on a beach of the Curaray River, near Auca territory. They had an initial friendly contact with three Aucas, but on January 8, 1956, a larger group of Aucas killed all five with wooden spears. The missionaries were buried at that spot by a rescue team composed of several missionaries, Quichua Indians, and U.S. military personnel from Panama.

BIBLIOGRAPHY Elisabeth Elliot, *Through Gates of Splendor* (1957); Russell T. Hitt, *Jungle Pilot: The Life and Witness of Nate Saint* (1959).

David M. Howard

Saint, Rachel Bradford (1914–1994), Wycliffe Bible Translators (WBT) missionary to the Waoranis (formerly the Aucas) in Ecuador. Born in Jenkintown, Pennsylvania, Saint attended the Philadelphia School of the Bible before working for 12 years with recovering alcoholics at the Keswick Colony of Mercy in New Jersey. In 1949 she went with the WBT to Peru, where she first heard of the Aucas, a jungle tribe that for decades had violently resisted contact with the outside world. In 1955 she began linguistic work with Dayuma, a young Waorani woman working at a hacienda near Waorani territory. After the tragic death of her brother, Nate *Saint, and four other missionaries killed by hostile members of the tribe, Rachel Saint and Dayuma came to national attention in 1957 with their appearance on the American television program *This Is Your Life*. In 1958 Dayuma returned to her Waorani family, and subsequently, Rachel Saint and Elisabeth Elliot, wife of James *Elliot, one of the slain missionaries, became the first outsiders to live with the tribe. Saint stayed at Tiwaeno until 1976, translating portions of the New Testament and overseeing the growth of the young church, which became a center for ministry by Waorani missionaries to their scattered family groups. After Saint retired from Wycliffe, she returned to Ecuador, where she spent her remaining years living near her Waorani friends.

BIBLIOGRAPHY Elisabeth Elliot, *The Savage My Kinsman* (1961, 1981); Ethel Emily Wallis, *The Dayuma Story* (1960) and *Aucas Downriver* (1973). Critical viewpoints of the Wycliffe mission to the Waoranis can be found in Rosemary Kingsland, *A Saint among Savages* (1980) and in David Stoll, *Fishers of Men or Founders of Empire? The Wycliffe Bible Translators in Latin America* (1982). James A. Yost, "Twenty Years of Contact: The Mechanisms of Change in Wao ('Auca') Culture," in Norman E. Whitten, Jr., ed., *Cultural Transformations and Ethnicity in Modern Ecuador* (1981), pp. 677–704, provides the assessment of an anthropologist hired by Wycliffe to study the Waoranis.

William L. Svelmoe

Saint Andrews Seven. Six Scottish students and their mentor Thomas *Chalmers at St. Andrews University, Scotland. The six were members of the St. Andrews University Missionary Association while Chalmers taught at St. Andrews from 1823 to 1828. Among them they gave 141 years of missionary service to India. The students were Alexander *Duff, John Urquhart, John Adam, Robert *Nesbit, William Sinclair Mackay, and John Ewart.

BIBLIOGRAPHY Stuart Piggin and John Roxborogh, *The St. Andrews Seven* (1985).

John Roxborogh

Saker, Alfred (1814–1880), Baptist Missionary Society (BMS) missionary in the Cameroons. Saker was born in Kent, England, and married Helen Jessup in 1840. While employed in the Devonport naval dockyard in 1842, he heard John *Clarke and G. K. Prince speak about the new BMS mission being established at Fernando Póo, an island off the coast of West Africa. Saker and his wife volunteered to the BMS and in 1843 sailed with Clarke for Jamaica and West Africa. Saker and his colleagues found the freed slave community at Clarence, Fernando Póo, responsive to Christianity, but their chief concern was with the Cameroonian mainland. When Saker and his first convert from Clarence, T. H. Johnston, took up residence at Cameroons Town (modern Douala) in 1845, they found the task much harder. They had to wait until 1849 for the baptism of the first convert.

After 1858, difficulties multiplied. In that year, the Spanish authorities prohibited all Protestant worship on Fernando Póo. An admirer of David *Livingstone, Saker established a new settlement for the freed slaves on the mainland in hopes that it would become a base for the advance of Christianity, commerce, and civilization into the interior. From 1859 he had to endure a sustained campaign of criticism from a missionary colleague, Alexander Innes, who accused him of exercising dictatorial powers over the community at Cameroons Town. Saker also found other colleagues increasingly critical of his emphasis on civilizing the Douala by industry and commerce. He was twice recalled to London for consultations with the BMS committee, and in 1869 the BMS sent out their senior secretary, E. B. *Underhill, to investigate the charges. Although Saker was substantially exonerated, there is no doubt that he was an authoritarian figure. In 1872 he completed a translation of the Bible into the Douala language, building on foundations laid by Joseph Merrick, one of the pioneering settlers from Jamaica. In 1876 he retired to England in failing health.

BIBLIOGRAPHY E. M. Saker, *Alfred Saker: Pioneer of the Cameroons* (1929); J. van Slageren, *Les Origines de L'Église Évangélique du Cameroun* (1972); Brian Stanley, *The History of the Baptist Missionary Society, 1792–1992* (1992); E. B. Underhill, *Alfred Saker: Missionary to Africa* (1884). Innes published a vitriolic "biography" of Saker, *More Light . . . The Only True Biography of Alfred Saker and his Cruelties* (1895). Some relevant primary sources are preserved in the BMS archives at Regent's Park College, Oxford.

Brian Stanley

Salazar, Domingo de (1512–1594), first bishop of the Philippines. Salazar was born in La Rioja, Spain, and joined the Dominican order in 1545 in the convent of San Esteban, Salamanca, a seedbed of missionaries and scholars. He was a disciple of Francisco de *Vitoria and Bartolomé de *Las Casas. He sailed for America with Gregorio de Beteta in 1554. Working in Mexico for 23 years (1554–1576), he dedicated himself to the conversion of the Indians of the Mixtec and Zapotec regions of Oaxaca. He joined Tristan de Luna's ill-fated expedition to Florida (1559–1561). His last years were spent in Mexico City, teaching in the university and defending the Amerindians. To represent the Dominicans and to serve as a defender of the Indians, he sailed for Spain in 1576. On February 6, 1579, Philip II presented him to Pope Gregory XIII as first bishop of the Philippines. He sailed from Seville in June 1580 and by September 17, 1581, he was in Manila. Salazar worked in the Philippines for a decade (1581–1591).

With Salazar's arrival the struggle for justice intensified. He defended the Filipinos, denouncing the *encomenderos* (estate owners) and the local *datus* (headmen) in a crusade for human liberation. He fought against slavery and for the peaceful preaching of the gospel. Salazar was the catalyst for the rapid growth of Christianity in the Philippines in its pioneering age. Yet he also looked forward to the opening of China to the gospel.

Salazar left Manila for Madrid in June, 1591. There he addressed Philip II and the Council of Indies, disputed with the royalists (arguing that Spain's title to the Philippines was purely spiritual), and wrote well-reasoned memorials. Through his effort, legislation favorable to the people of the Philippines was enacted. He died in Madrid.

BIBLIOGRAPHY Helen E. Blair and James A. Robertson, *The Philippine Islands: 1493–1898,* vols. 5–8 (1905–1909); Lucio Gutiérrez, *Domingo de Salazar, O.P., Primer Obispo de Filipinas (1512–1594)* (1979). See also articles by Gutiérrez in *Philippiniana Sacra,* as indexed in vol. 26 (1991): 124–125. Salazar's literary production is mainly found in the Archivo General de Indias in Seville, Spain, Audiencia de Filipinas, Legajos 74, 84.

Lucio Gutiérrez, OP

Sale, Elizabeth (Geale) (1818–1898), Baptist Missionary Society (BMS) missionary and pioneer of zenana work in India. Elizabeth Geale was born in the south of France to Anglican parents but grew up in Devonshire and London, where she became a Baptist. She married John Sale in 1848 and shortly afterward the couple sailed for Bengal with the BMS. They worked first in Barisal, then in Jessore, and from 1858 in Calcutta. In Jessore in 1854 Elizabeth Sale first gained entry to a Hindu zenana (the secluded women's section of a high-caste Hindu home). Similar opportunities followed in which she taught reading and needlework as a means of reaching high caste Hindu women. Sale continued this work in the Entally district of Calcutta. Here she became a close associate of Marianne *Lewis, who was inspired by Sale's zenana visiting to write the pamphlet that led in 1867 to the formation of the Baptist Zenana Mission. John Sale's ill health confined the couple to England for four years, but they returned to India in 1864. Elizabeth ran a girls' school, the Sale Institution, from 1864 to 1874, when her husband's health compelled her permanent return to Britain.

BIBLIOGRAPHY Ernest A. Payne, *The Great Succession: Leaders of the Baptist Missionary Society during the Nineteenth Century* (1938).

Brian Stanley

Salvado, Rosendo (1814–1900), Spanish Benedictine missionary in Australia. Born in Tuy, Spain, Salvado entered St. Martin's Benedictine monastery at Compostela in 1829, distinguishing himself as a musician. When religious houses in Spain were suppressed in 1838, he left for Cava, near Naples, completed his studies, and was ordained. Considered unsuitable for mission, in 1846 he joined several Irish priests going to Perth, Western Australia, as pastors. Bent upon mission, he seized an opportunity and trekked inland with a confrere. Joining some Aboriginal nomads for a while, but deciding that a settled life was necessary, he founded a mission and school for both whites and Aborigines. Salvado's memoirs regarding his missionary work, Aboriginal life and languages, colonization, and Australian natural history were published in Rome in 1851. In 1867 the mission and school, now named New Norcia, became a monastery and base from which further missions were sent to the far north. Salvado was its first abbot and continued in that office until his death. Taking part in the First Vatican Council (1869–1871), Salvado wrote but was unable to present a paper on missionary needs. He died on his last visit to Rome (1899–1900), and his body was returned to New Norcia and buried behind the high altar.

BIBLIOGRAPHY Salvado originally wrote his diary and memoirs in Italian, published in Rome as *Memorie Storiche dell'Australia* (1851). They were translated into Spanish (*Memorias historicas sobre la Australia,* 1853, 1946), French (*Memoires historique de L'Australie,* 1854), and English (*Salvado Memoirs,* E. J. Stormon, ed. and tr., 1977). On later developments at New Norcia, including further missions springing therefrom, see Eugene Perez, *The Diary of Bishop Torres* (1987).

Kenelm Burridge

Samartha, S(tanley) J(edidiah) (1920–), Indian theologian in the Church of South India. Samartha has played a leading role in Christian reflection on interreligious dialogue and theology of religions. Born and raised in present-day Karnataka State, India, he studied at Madras University; United Theological College (UTC), Bangalore; Union Theological Seminary, New York; and Hartford Seminary, with a Ph.D. dissertation, "The Modern Hindu View of History according to Representative Thinkers" (1958). He also did postgraduate studies at the University of Basel, Switzerland. As lecturer and principal of the Basel Mission Theological Seminary in Mangalore (1947–1960), as professor of history of religions and philosophy at UTC (1960–1966), and as principal at Serampore College (1966–1968), he was deeply involved in the life of the

Christian churches in multireligious India. As associate secretary of the Department on Studies in Mission and Evangelism of the World Council of Churches (WCC) (1968–1971), and as the first director of the subunit Dialogue with People of Living Faiths and Ideologies of WCC (1971–1980), he became a major architect of interreligious dialogue. In 1986 he received an honorary doctorate from the University of Utrecht, Netherlands. Back in India in retirement, he continues to give account of the Christian concern in religious pluralism. In *One Christ—Many Religions: Toward a Revised Christology* (1991) he developed a pluralist theology of religions.

BIBLIOGRAPHY Stanley J. Samartha, *The Hindu Response to the Unbound Christ* (1974), *Courage for Dialogue: Ecumenical Issues in Inter-Religious Relationships* (1981), *The Search for New Hermeneutics in Asian Christian Theology* (1987), *Between Two Cultures: Ecumenical Ministry in a Pluralist World* (1996; autobiography), and ed., *Living Faiths and the Ecumenical Movement* (1971). Constantine D. Jathanna, ed., *Dialogue in Community: Essays in Honour of Stanley J. Samartha* (1982); Eeuwout Klootwijk, *Commitment and Openness: The Interreligious Dialogue and Theology of Religions in the Work of Stanley J. Samartha* (1992; includes biography and extensive bibliography).

Eeuwout van der Linden

Sambeek, Jan van (1886–1966), Dutch missionary bishop in Tanzania. Born in Veldhoven, North Brabant, Netherlands, Sambeek entered the Society of Missionaries of Africa (also known as White Fathers) in 1910. After some years of further study and teaching, he arrived in Chilubula, Bangweolo, Zambia, in 1919, became educational secretary in the vicariate, and was invited to the meetings of the British Advisory Board on Education in Livingstone, Rhodesia, from 1925 to 1927. He composed several African language grammars and dictionaries (in Kinyakusa, Kisafwa, Kiha, and Kibemba). His Kibemba grammar and dictionary remain the standard works. In 1936 he was appointed vicar apostolic of Tanganyika (Tanzania), then the largest vicariate in East Africa. In 1946 the vicariate was divided and he opted for the northern, poorer part in the Buha region and became the bishop of Kigoma. He insisted that missionaries should have a sound knowledge of the language and local customs of the people they worked with. Even in the years of retirement in Kabanga, Tanzania, he continued producing books for the use of Christians and young missionaries.

BIBLIOGRAPHY "Mgr. Jan van Sambeek," *Petie Echo*, Missionaries of Africa, Rome, no. 579 (June 1967): 273–291.

J. G. Donders, M Afr

Saminathapillai Gnanapragasar (1875–1947), Sri Lankan Catholic priest and scholar. Known among Tamils as Swami Gnanapragasar, Saminathapillai was born of Hindu parents at Manipay, Ceylon (Sri Lanka). His original given name, Vaithilingam, was changed to Gnanapragasar (Aloysius) after his widowed mother embraced Catholicism in 1878. In 1895 he joined the Missionary Congregation of the Oblates of Mary Immaculate and was ordained priest in 1901. A man of remarkable apostolic zeal, intellectual acumen, and spiritual depth, he stood for justice and equality for the Tamil Hindu low-caste communities and was a pioneer missionary among such people in the outskirts of Jaffna. By preaching and catechizing, he converted over 5,000 low-caste Hindus to Catholicism, despite opposition from high-caste Hindus. Known for his eloquent preaching and exemplary missionary life, he established several primary schools for children of the poor and depressed classes, founded over thirty mission substations, and built chapels in remote Hindu villages. His method of conversion provoked Hindu-Christian rivalries, and doubts prevailed that some conversions were motivated by material gain. Recognized as a convincing Catholic apologist, author, itinerant preacher, missionary historian, etymologist, philologist, and polyglot, he also published several tracts in Tamil on Christianity, combining theology and catechism. He spearheaded a vernacular liturgical reform by translating the Massbook into Tamil and by publishing commentaries on the Gospels, besides launching a massive Tamil lexicon, of which he published six parts.

BIBLIOGRAPHY Gnanapragasar Saminathapillai, *Historical Aspects of Christianity and Buddhism* (1921), *A History of the Catholic Church in Ceylon: Period of Beginnings, 1505–1602* (1924), *Tamils: Their Early History and Religion* (1932), and *Etymological and Comparative Lexicon of the Tamil Language*, pts. 1–6 (1938–1946). Adaikalamuthu Savarimuthu, *Nenje Ninai: A Biography of Swami Gnanapragasar* (in Tamil) (1975); S. M. Selvaratnam, ed., *Swami Gnanapragasar Centenary Souvenir* (1975).

A. J. V. Chandrakanthan

Samkange, Thompson Douglas (1893–1956), Zimbabwean Methodist minister. Samkange was born as Mushore, son of Mawodzewa of the Gushungo royal clan of the Zwimbi chieftaincy in the Lomagundi district of Southern Rhodesia (present-day Zimbabwe). A first-generation Christian under the tutelage of John *White, he rose to Methodist leadership successively as teacher, evangelist, and ordained minister. With White he organized in 1928 the Southern Rhodesia Native Missionary Conference. For 20 years as its secretary, Samkange was the voice of African Christian unity in church and state in that country. In 1938 he attended the International Missionary Conference at Tambaram, India, as the sole African delegate from his country. Inspired by the zeal for unity and self-reliance of Asian Christians, meetings with Gandhi and Nehru, and friendship with Albert *Luthuli, Samkange returned to Southern Rhodesia with renewed commitment to African leadership in church and state. At Pakame he sought to build a self-reliant African rural church and educational center at a time of missionary dominance in the church and white settler control in government. Passionately committed to a unity that supersedes divisions of tribe, region, social status, or religious affiliation, Samkange helped to found the Southern Rhodesia Bantu Congress in 1938, uniting existing associations in a national political movement. He served as its president from 1943 to 1948. Under his leadership the congress aspired for mass membership and demanded full democratic rights, which became the hallmarks of later nationalist movements.

BIBLIOGRAPHY Terence Ranger, *Are We Not Also Men? The Samkange Family and African Politics in Zimbabwe, 1920–1964* (1995; a collective biography of Thompson Samkange and of two of his sons, Sketchley and Stanlake).

Norman E. Thomas

Sandegren, Johannes (1883–1962), Swedish missionary with the Leipzig Mission in South India. Born in Madurai, South India, into a virtual dynasty of Swedish and German missionaries, Sandegren was brought up in Germany and Sweden. As a student of theology at Uppsala he was strongly influenced by professor Nathan *Söderblom. After ordination in 1906, he opted for service in India, where he arrived in 1907, joining his father as a missionary at a time when the Swedish staff of the mission was increasing rapidly. During and after the critical years of World War I he helped to reorganize the Tamil Lutheran church on a more democratic and autonomous basis. In 1927 he became the first principal of the newly founded divinity school of the church at Madras. He also served as president of the newly formed Federation of Lutheran Churches in India, and for 22 years (1934–1956), as the third bishop of Tranquebar. He was able to hand the office over to the first Indian bishop, Dr. R. B. *Manikam. During and after World War II, Sandegren rendered outstanding service by forging links of fellowhip with Christians and with churches in Pakistan, Indonesia, and Malaya.

BIBLIOGRAPHY J. D. Asirvadam, *Johannes Sandegren* (1962).

Hans-Werner Gensichen

Sanders, J(ohn) Oswald (1902–1980), general director of the Overseas Missionary Fellowship (formerly the China Inland Mission [CIM]). Sanders was born in Invercargill, New Zealand, and was converted in his youth. At age 16 he became a law clerk and studied for law part-time, gaining his degree in 1922. He dedicated himself to missionary service at age nineteen and attended the new Bible Training Institute in Auckland. In 1926 he joined its staff, becoming superintendent in 1931; also in 1931 he married Edith Mary Dobson.

His forthright preaching and writing led to invitations to preach in Australia and then his acceptance of the position of Australian representative of the CIM in March 1946. Over the next few years, the CIM was thrown into turmoil as its missionaries were expelled from China and had no other fields to go to. At a conference in 1952 in Bournemouth, England, the various directors of the CIM, including Sanders, forced the general director, Bishop A. T. Houghton, to resign on account of the high-handed way in which he had handled the crisis. Two years later they appointed Sanders to the position, with somewhat curtailed powers. While Sanders had no experience as a missionary, he ably led the reoganization of the CIM into the Overseas Missionary Fellowship (OMF). An incisive and clear-headed activist, he reestablished a sense of direction, promoted the mission to the public, particularly its expanding American support-base, inspired disappointed missionaries, and sought opportunities for the mission in new fields. He was a pioneer in accepting Asians as missionaries. He could be blunt in his opinions, but he was also pastorally sensitive and was able to keep the mission steady in the face of evangelical controversies over such issues as the charismatic movement. His work restored to the OMF its premier position among interdenominational missions and gave it a strategic role in the development of East Asian churches.

Sanders retired in 1969, but his worldwide preaching and prolific writing ministry continued until his death in New Zealand at the age of 78. In retirement, he served for two years (1973–1974) as principal of the Christian Leaders Training College in Banz, New Guinea.

BIBLIOGRAPHY J. Oswald Sanders, *This I Remember* (1982). Leslie T. Lyall, *A Passion for the Impossible: The China Inland Mission, 1865–1965* (1965); Ron and Gwen Roberts, *To Fight Better: A Biography of J. Oswald Sanders* (1989).

Peter Lineham

Sandoval, Alonso de (1576–1652), Jesuit author of a treatise on black slaves in colonial Colombia. Born in Seville, Spain, Sandoval went as a youth to Peru, where his father served in the viceregal government. In Lima he entered the Society of Jesus, and in 1605 he was sent to Cartagena, in Nueva Granada, present-day Colombia. He chose as his mission in life the evangelization of the black slaves from Africa who arrived in Cartagena each year by the thousands. He catechized the slaves, baptized them, and attended to their physical needs. He introduced to this work another Jesuit, Peter *Claver, who in time would become more famous. Sandoval's unique contribution was his *De Instauranda Aethiopum Salute,* a lengthy treatise on the black slaves, their places of origin in Africa, their customs and rites, and the techniques he used to evangelize them. Published in Seville in 1627, it remains to this day one of the few works on the black population written by missionaries in Latin America. Although Sandoval deplored the sufferings to which the slaves were submitted, he refrained from condemning slavery itself. Besides attending to the slaves, he also served as general procurator of the Jesuit province of Colombia, and in 1642 as rector of the college of Cartagena. He fell prey to a contagious disease that led to his death a few years later.

BIBLIOGRAPHY Alonso de Sandoval, *Un Tratado sobre la Esclavitud,* introduction by Enriqueta Vila Vilar, ed. (1987); Vincent Franklin, "Bibliographical Essay: Alonso de Sandoval and the Jesuit Conception of the Negro," *Journal of Negro History* 158 (1973): 349–360; Norman Meiklejohn, "The Observance of Negro Slave Legislation in Colonial Nueva Granada" (Ph.D. diss., Columbia Univ., 1968).

Jeffrey Klaiber, SJ

Santori, Giulio Antonio (1532–1602), cardinal who pioneered in establishing a supervisory interest in missions outside Europe. Born in Caserta, Italy, Santori was guided by his father into a legal career in Rome, but influenced by his mother, he was ordained a priest in 1557 and returned to Caserta as vicar general. In 1563 he was transferred to Naples, where he worked with the young Cardinal Alfonso Carafa. Accused with Carafa of plotting to poison Pius IV, he was brought to Rome but he convinced the pope and his nephew, Carlo Borromeo, of his innocence. In 1566 Pius V appointed Santori a consultant at the Holy Office and in 1570 elevated him to be a cardinal. At Santori's suggestion, in 1573 Gregory XIII established a curial congregation for the reform of priests and monks of the Greek rite in Italy, and Santori was recognized as Protector of the Orient, assisting and advising missions to Syria, Egypt, Persia, and the Balkans. With Jesuit helpers, he sought to extend papal influence among the Christian communities under Muslim rule. Anxious to strengthen the indigenous Catholic clergy in the Levant, he founded the Collegio Greco in Rome, proposed one for the Armenians, and assisted the Ethiopian community, which was centered on their church of St. Stephen in the Vatican.

Santori entered the conclave of 1592 as the strongest candidate for the papacy. Although blocked by one faction among the cardinals, *Clement VIII greatly respected him, and on May 6, 1599, agreed with him on the creation of a curial congregation known as the Propaganda Fide, with responsibility not only for the Levant but also for Protestant Europe and the Indies. The congregation, which met regularly in Santori's palace, included two papal nephews and the prominent reforming cardinals Baronio, Gederico Borromeo, and Bellarmine. Although reported to have been still functioning in 1605, the congregation achieved little after Santori's death, but its organization and method of working clearly provided a precedent for its successor established in 1622.

BIBLIOGRAPHY A. Castelucci, "Il risveglio dell'attività missionaria e le prime origini della S. C. de Propaganda Fide," in *Le Conferenze al Laterano, Marzo-Aprile 1923* (1924), pp. 117–222; the appendix (pp. 223–254) contains the minutes of the congregation.

Richard Gray

Santo Tomás, Domingo de (1499?–1570), pioneer Dominican missionary and bishop in Latin America. Born in Seville, Santo Tomás entered the Dominican order in 1520. In 1540 he went to Peru to undertake missionary work. His early work on the coast and in the mountains enabled him to gain first-hand knowledge of the culture and language. He prepared the first grammar and vocabulary of the Quechua language, both published in 1560. In the debates over language policy he was an effective advocate of the use of the vernacular. He developed parish schools and helped set up San Marcos University in Lima in 1551. By 1553 he was provincial of the order and played a key role in the initial organization of the church in the viceroyalty, making significant contributions in the first and second Lima Councils (1551, 1567). He actively defended the indigenous population from injustice and campaigned against the *encomienda* system. During a visit to Europe in the late 1550s, he joined forces with fellow Dominican Bartolomé de *Las Casas in the struggle for justice for the indigenous peoples of the New World. He was consecrated bishop of La Plata in 1563. The Spanish population there fiercely opposed his activities on behalf of his Andean parishioners. The latter mourned his death by the thousands.

BIBLIOGRAPHY Domingo de Santo Tomás, *La primera gramática quichua* [1560], with introduction by José Maria Vargas (1947).

William Mitchell

San Vitores, Diego Luis de (1627–1672), Spanish Jesuit missionary, founder of the first lasting mission in Oceania. Born of a noble family in Burgos, Spain, San Vitores entered the Society of Jesus in 1640. After studies in Spain and ordination to the priesthood in 1651, he carried on a successful ministry in preaching and retreat work for some years. In 1659 his repeated request for missionary work was granted and he was assigned to the Philippines. En route to his new assignment, his ship called at Guam, Mariana Islands, where San Vitores was moved by the plight of the people. From his arrival in the Philippines, he petitioned the Spanish crown to establish a mission in the Mariana Islands. The words of Scripture—"I have sent you to proclaim the gospel to the poor"—were addressed to him, he wrote. When the queen mother, Mariana of Austria, finally acceded to his requests, he and five other Jesuits were sent to Guam in June 1668 to begin mission work in Oceania. After early successes, San Vitores and his companions encountered hostility from the Islanders. Even after one of the Jesuits and several lay helpers were killed, San Vitores forbade the Spanish troops accompanying him to use their weapons except in extreme necessity. San Vitores visited the northern islands of the group, making peace between warring factions, teaching, and baptizing. In April 1672, while making pastoral visits, San Vitores was accosted by two men, stabbed, and hacked to death, and his body was thrown into the sea. Known as the Apostle of the Marianas, San Vitores was honored by beatification in the Catholic Church in 1985.

BIBLIOGRAPHY Ward Barrett, *Mission in the Marianas* (1975); Paul Carano and Pedro Sanchez, *A Complete History of Guam* (1968); Francisco Garcia, *Vida y Martirio de el Ven. Padre Diego Luis de San Vitores* (1683); Juan Ledesma, *The Apostle of the Marianas* (1970).

Francis X. Hezel, SJ

Sarasin, Dorothee (1894–1968), first woman member of the governing committee of the Basel Mission (BM) home board. Sarasin was born in Basel into one of the oldest and most influential of the city's families. A grandfather and an uncle served on the BM home board. She was one of the founders and also the full-time secretary of the Swiss Girls' Bible Groups (Mädchen-Bibel-Kreise). In 1928 she was appointed by the BM home board as the first woman secretary of the BM Women's Mission Committee, and the first woman member of the Conference of Mission Inspectors (Inspektorenkonferenz), though without the title "Inspektor." In spite of her appointment, the Women's Mission Committee continued to be headed by the mission's director, Karl *Hartenstein, until his resignation and return to Germany in 1939, when Sarasin succeeded him as chairperson. Only then was she also accepted as the first woman member of the home board. She remained in this post until her retirement in 1962. Under her leadership the Women's Committee was much strengthened and was finally allowed a degree of independence in the selection and preparation of women candidates for overseas service. She was also editor of the newsletter for the women's mission and of a book on women in mission.

BIBLIOGRAPHY Dorothee Sarasin, ed., *Mitteilungen aus der Basler Frauenmission* (1927–1930), *Unser Dienst in der Frauenmission* (1931–1956; a monthly newsletter for women in mission), and *Was Er euch sagt, das tut, Bilder aus der Frauenmission* (1936; a collection of articles on women in mission). Reports, circular letters, and correspondence are in the BM archives; also numerous articles on women in mission in various mission publications.

Waltraud Ch. Haas

Sarasin, Karl (1815–1886), banker, politician, and Basel Mission (BM) leader. Sarasin was born into a family belonging to the Protestant business and political elite of Basel. He had a major career in cantonal politics in Basel-Stadt and left an impressive record of initiatives for the social well-being of the city. As a long-standing member of the cantonal government with responsibility for building and town planning, Sarasin played a key role in removing the city walls and in public health improvements, especially in response to the cholera and typhus epidemics in Basel in 1855 and 1865. However, due to his paternalistic tendencies, many of his pioneering ideas for government intervention in the fields of factory conditions and insurance reform were not well received. Sarasin was closely linked to the BM, serving as a member of its directing committee (1852–1862 and 1879–1884) and chairman of its industrial commission. He is credited with founding the Halbbatzen Kollekt (Halfpenny Fund), an organization of voluntary collectors in the towns and villages of southwestern Germany and Switzerland who regularly visited their neighbors to encourage giving—even of very small amounts—to the BM.

BIBLIOGRAPHY Paul Burckhardt, *Geschichte der Stadt Basel, von der Zeit der Reformation bis zur Gegenwart* (1942); Jon Miller, *The Social Control of Religious Zeal: A Study of Organizational Contradictions* (1994).

Paul Jenkins

Sarasvati, Pandita Ramabai. *See* Ramabai Dongre Medhavi.

Saravia, Adrianus (*or* Adriaan de; Adriaan van) (1532–1613), early Protestant advocate of missions. Saravia was born in Vieil-Hesdin, Belgium, of Protestant parents, and was educated at Paris. In the early years of his career he served as headmaster of schools at Guernsey and Southampton, England, and as minister at Gent and Antwerp. He established a Walloon church at Brussels, and assisted in drafting the Belgic Confession of the Reformed faith (1561). From 1584 to 1587 he was professor of divinity at Leiden. Because of his involvement in political turmoil during his professorship at Leiden, he left for Britain, where he became an Anglican and was a canon of Canterbury and also of Westminster Abbey in London until his death. He became vicar of Lewisham (London) in 1595 and rector of Great Chart in 1609. He was one of the translators of the Authorized (King James) Version of the Bible; the renown of that version testifies to his erudition and command of languages.

In 1590 Saravia published *De diversis ministrorum evangelii gradibus,* in which he argued for episcopacy, which he regarded as a divine right. Presbyterian government, he argued, causes divisions of opinion; the church needs bishops to maintain unity. Basing the mandate for missions on Matthew 28, he deemed that bishops were the successors of the apostles. (The reformer Theodore Beza opposed this view, arguing that the mandate was limited to the apostles.) Hence the church has a missionary task because of the presence of the Lord Jesus Christ, who sends his church into all the world to reevangelize the Middle East and to evangelize all heathen people. Saravia intertwined ecumenics and missions; church divisions, he claimed, hamper missions.

BIBLIOGRAPHY The English translation of Saravia's major work is *A Treatise on the Different Degrees of Christian Priesthood,* A. W. Street, tr. (1840). G. Kawerau, "Adrian Saravia und seine Gedanken über Mission," *AMZ* 26 (1899): 333–343; W. Nijenhuis, *Adrianus Saravia (c. 1532–1613)* (1980); Luke B. Smith, "The Contribution of Hadrian A. Saravia (1531–1613) to the Doctrine of the Nature of the Church and Its Mission: An Examination of His Doctrine as Related to That of His Anglican Contemporaries" (Ph.D. diss., Univ. of Edinburgh, 1965).

Leendert J. Joosse

Sargent, Douglas Noel (1907–1979), Church Missionary Society (CMS) missionary in China and trainer of missionaries. Born near London, Sargent earned a degree in mathematics at Cambridge and then went to the London College of Divinity in 1930. After ordination he was for three years a curate in St. Alban's Diocese before proceeding in 1934 to Chengtu (Chengdu), Szechwan (Sichuan) in western China, under the CMS. He studied Chinese and then lectured at the West China Union University. He was later chaplain to Bishop Song of Western China and assistant secretary for CMS, West China. In 1942 he married Imogene Ward, born in Foochow (Fuzhou), the daughter of American Methodist missionaries. In 1947 and 1948 he studied at Union Theological Seminary, New York (S.T.M.). On their return to China in 1949, the Sargents realized that their presence endangered their Chinese colleagues, and they moved to Hong Kong in 1951. They were then asked by CMS to head the men's missionary training at Chislehurst, Kent, England, where the women's training was already located. Sargent's personality and experience made a deep impression on the trainees. He continued at Chislehurst until 1962, when he was consecrated bishop of Selby (suffragan to the archbishop of York), an office he held until 1972, when he resigned after a heart attack. He died in York.

BIBLIOGRAPHY Douglas Sargent, *The Making of a Missionary* (1960).

Jocelyn Murray

Sargent, Edward (1815 or 1816–1889), missionary bishop in South India. Sargent claimed he was born in Paris, son of a soldier victorious at Waterloo, but others assert he was born in Madras, son of a soldier escort of convicts bound for Australia. He was adopted by an evangelical chaplain, William Sawyer, who sent him to the Church Missionary Society (CMS) college at Islington, London, in 1838, after two years of work as a lay evangelist in Tinnevelly. He was ordained, returned to India, and worked as a district missionary until he took charge of the Preparandi Institute, Palayankottai, spearheading the drive for an Indian ordained ministry. He purchased much land and property for the mission and twice extended Holy Trinity Church (now cathedral). Having written a number of religious books in Tamil, he was awarded a Canterbury honorary D.D. when on furlough in 1876. In 1877 he was consecrated assistant bishop of Tinnevelly together with Robert *Caldwell of the Society for the Propagation of the Gospel, an arrangement that worked only because of their great friendship and mutual admiration. They collaborated on prayer book translation and other projects. In 1875 they organized a magnificent welcome for the Prince of Wales at Tuticorin with 53 Indian clergy and 5,000 converts, a fraction of the masses they shepherded in the waves of the "mass movements." Sargent organized effective relief following the 1877 famine. In 1883 he lost his wife, Mary (b. 1809), who had given 28 years of missionary service, running what is now the Mary Sargent Girls Higher Secondary School and conducting services for women. After the 1888 Lambeth Conference, Sargent insisted on returning to India, where he died.

BIBLIOGRAPHY Paul Appasamy, *The Centenary History of the CMS in Tinnevelly* (1923); George Muller, *The Birth of the Bishopric: The History of the Tirunelveli Church from Early Beginnings to 1896* (1992); Eugene Stock, *History of the Church Missionary Society*, vol. 1 (1899).

E. M. Jackson

Satthianadhan, William Thomas (Tiruvengadam) (c. 1830–1892) *and*
Annal Arokium (1832–1890), South Indian church leaders. Born in Sinthupathurai, Tinnevelly, with the name Tiruvengadam, W. T. Satthianadhan came from a very conservative Vaishnavaite family who nevertheless sent him to the Church Missionary Society school in Palamcottah to learn English. Under the influence of William Cruikshank, he became a Christian. In 1847, after a vision in a dream, he applied for baptism on the eve of an arranged marriage he rejected. Standing firm when his outraged family hauled him before the magistrate, he went ahead with his baptism and changed his name. In 1849 he joined Thomas *Ragland and the North Tamil Itineracy until Ragland died in 1858. Satthianadhan began writing a stream of books and articles in Tamil and English, which marked him as a creative thinker and competent theologian. He edited (and published at a loss) a Tamil journal, *Desabimani*. He argued for self-support, putting his ideas into practice as minister of Zion Church, Chintadripet, Madras (1861–1892), and chairman of the North Madras Church Council. His outstanding work as an evangelist suggested that the CMS should nominate him assistant bishop of Tinnevelly, but the dominant group in the church, the Nadars, would not accept as their spiritual leader one who came from the Vaishya (merchant) caste.

Bishop Gell of Madras also objected that he could not afford to lose the contribution of Satthianadhan's wife, Annal Arokium (anglicized as Anna John). The daughter of John *Devasahayam, Annal Satthianadhan pioneered zenana education for secluded Hindu women and organized the Napier Girls' High School. She made a deep impact on public opinion when she toured England with her husband in 1878. A beautiful, serene character, she kept the ideal Christian home in Madras, a haven of peace for all races, and wrote highly popular books. *The Good Mother* was a best seller, translated into many Indian languages. She died at age 58, leaving her husband so grief stricken he did not long survive her. In 1972, their great grandson Sundar Clarke became the first Indian Bishop of Madras.

BIBLIOGRAPHY Mildred E. Gibbs, *The Anglican Church in India 1600–1970* (1972); P. A. Krishnasamy, *W. T. Satthianadhan* (1930); Rajaiah Paul, *Chosen Vessels* (1961); S. Satthianadhan, *W. T. Satthianadhan* (1893) and *Sketches of Indian Christians: Collected from Different Sources* (1896).

E. M. Jackson

Sava (c. 1169–1235), first archbishop and patron saint of the Serbian church. Sava was the third son of the Serbian prince Symeon Nemanja. Born Rastko, he assumed the name Sava after seeking monastic life at Mount Athos (in northeastern Greece). He was joined there by his father in 1197, and together they established the monastery of Hilandari in 1199. A year later, Sava's father died, provoking a rivalry for the kingship between Savas's brothers Stephen and Vukan, both of whom sought support from the see of Rome, with Stephen ultimately successful. Returning to Serbia, Sava worked to reconcile his brothers and became a force for religious and national unity focused on the Serbian Orthodox church. When Stephen persisted in relating the country to Rome, Sava returned to Athos, and went from there to the kingdom of Nicea. In 1219 the ecumenical patriarchate declared Serbia independent and Sava, archbishop. With the support of Stephen, Sava established the center of the Serbian church at the monastery of Zitsa and formed eight dioceses. Upon Stephen's death (1227), Sava crowned Stephen's son, Radislav, as king. Voluntarily resigning his office in 1233,

Sava died in Veliko Turnovo, Bulgaria. Remembered as the primary figure in the indigenization of Christianity among the Serbs, he is commemorated by the Serbian and other Orthodox churches on January 14.

BIBLIOGRAPHY Veselin Kesich, "The Spiritual Heritage of the Serbian Church," *Greek Orthodox Theological Review* 21 (1976): 1–18; John Meyendorff, "St. Sava, Ohrid and the Serbian Church," *St. Vladimir's Theological Quarterly* 35 (1991): 209–221; Daniel M. Rogich, "St. Sava on Athos: His Monastic Rule," *Sobornost* 11 (1989): 69–81; Nikolai Velimirovic, *The Life of Saint Sava* (1988).

Stanley Samuel Harakas

Sawabe, Paul (Takuma) (1835–1913), first Japanese convert and Orthodox priest ordained as a result of the missionary work of *Nikolai Kasatkin. Sawabe lived in Hakodate, Japan, when Nikolai was chaplain at the Russian consulate. A samurai and member of an ultranationalist party, Sawabe perceived Nikolai to be an enemy of the Japanese people and a teacher of a foreign religion. He sought a meeting to best Nikolai in argument or, failing that, to kill him. Nikolai's calm response surprised him, ultimately convincing Sawabe to listen to the Christian teaching. Sawabe eventually not only was converted to Orthodox Christianity but also began to speak of it to others in his circle. His first contacts, a physician named Sakai and another Japanese named Urano, were sent to Nikolai for instruction. During a time of persecution against Christianity, the three men were baptized in April 1886, receiving the Christian names Paul Sawabe, John Sakai, and Jacob Urano. When the persecution ceased, a missionizing catechetical system was established, which Sawabe supervised during the absence of Nikolai, who had gone to Russia seeking financial and ecclesial support for the mission. With an emphasis on inculturation and indigenization, Sawabe's work was fruitful in encouraging conversions. When Nikolai returned in February 1871, the mission was officially launched. About a year later, Sawabe advised Nikolai to move the center of the work to Tokyo, where a school and church were eventually built. A new persecution arose, and Sawabe and Sakai were imprisoned for a brief time. The persecution ended in February 1873. Two years later, in 1875, a visiting Russian Orthodox bishop ordained Sawabe to the Orthodox priesthood. During the Russo-Japanese War, Nikolai retired from public activity and worship, while Sawabe and others continued the missionary effort.

BIBLIOGRAPHY John Bartholomew, "The Missionary Activity of St. Nicholas of Japan" (M.A. thesis, St. Vladimir's Orthodox Theological Seminary, 1987); James J. Stamoolis, *Eastern Orthodox Mission Theology Today* (1986); Proclus Yasuo Ushimaru, "Japanese Orthodoxy and the Culture of the Meiji Period," *St. Vladimir's Theological Quarterly* 24 (1980): 115–127; Luke Alexander Veronis, *Missionaries, Monks and Martyrs: Making Disciples of All Nations* (1994).

Stanley Samuel Harakas

Sawyerr, Harry Alphonso Ebun (1909–1986), West African theologian. Sawyerr was born and grew up in Bona Sakrim in deeper Mende, home of a tribal people of Sierra Leone. Ordained a priest of the Anglican Diocese of Freetown, Sierra Leone, in 1943, he served there for over 40 years, becoming a canon of St. George's Cathedral and serving on numerous church committees.

Sawyerr saw the discipline of theology (and a university department of theology) to be central in the total ministry of the church in the world, equipping clergy and the people of God to address the hopes and fears of society. Consequently, scholarship and churchmanship were inextricably bound up together. His early exposure to native life led him to a profound respect for African language, religion, and culture. He published *Creative Evangelism* (1968), in which he argued for the necessity of adopting a positive stance toward African traditions and for Christianity to transcend cultural forms. After surveying African interpretations of existence and the problem of evil, he argued that the Old Testament was a stage in the transition from natural religion (e.g., African religions) to Christianity and the uniqueness of Christ. He also stressed sacrifices as the link between African religious experience and biblical revelation. Conscious of the largely nonliterate and iconic African society, Sawyerr identified liturgy as a critical aspect of Christian life, thought, and evangelism. He also fostered liturgical innovation. For instance, in "Tradition in Transit" (*Religion in a Pluralistic Society,* John Pobee, ed., 1976), he identified principles underlying adolescent initiation rites including the "will" of the cult, new birth from death, and rebirth-resurrection, all of which demanded personal strength, implicit obedience, and the establishment of a new bond among the initiated.

Sawyerr's whole life was linked with the Church Missionary Society (CMS). He was educated at the CMS school, Fourah Bay College, and at Durham University in England, which had connections with CMS. He was on the staff of Fourah Bay College (1948–1962), becoming its principal (1962–1974), and vice-chancellor of the University of Sierra Leone (1970–1972), which grew out of Fourah Bay College.

Sawyerr endeavored to carry on a dialogue between his African consciousness and the worldwide church. He brought African perspectives to committees of the Anglican communion and to discussions of the Faith and Order Commission of the World Council of Churches.

BIBLIOGRAPHY H. A. E. Sawyerr, *Springs of Mende Belief and Conduct* (1968), *Creative Evangelism* (1968), *God, Ancestor or Creator?* (1970), and *The Practice of Presence: Shorter Writings of Harry Sawyerr,* John Parrat, ed. (1995). Mark E. Glaswell and Edward Fasholé-Luke, *New Testament Christianity for Africa and the World: Essays in Honour of Harry Sawyerr* (1974; includes a bibliography of Sawyerr's writings).

John S. Pobee

Schäfer, Alfons (1904–1958), pioneer Catholic missionary and explorer in New Guinea. Born in Langenholthausen, Germany, Schäfer received his theological education at St. Gabriel Mission Seminary in Mödling, Austria. He was ordained for service with the Society of the

Divine Word (SVD) and was sent to New Guinea in 1929. He is perhaps the most prominent New Guinea highland missionary, noted for his enterprising spirit, leadership, organizational skills, and mission methods. A champion of missionary accommodation, he placed primary importance on the knowledge of the local culture and language. With a group of SVD missionaries, particularly William *Ross, he explored the unknown areas of the Ramu River and the Bismarck Range (1931–1933) and planned and initiated new missions. As soon as the government permitted (1934), he ventured into the newly discovered, heavily populated Simbu-Wahgi-Mount Hagen area. While Ross secured mission sites for future Catholic missions along the Wahgi River westward toward Mount Hagen, making certain that the chosen sites were among friendly people and large enough for future airstrips, Schäfer chose as his base the most densely populated area, Mount Hagen itself. He did much the same in the Simbu area, and made his home base Mingende, which became the largest mountain station. He died in Germany while on home leave.

BIBLIOGRAPHY For an autobiography, see Alphonse Schaefer, *Cassowary of the Mountains* (1991), and *Pionier auf Neuguinea* (1961). Archival material is at Divine Word Institute, Madang, Papua New Guinea.

Louis J. Luzbetak, SVD

Schall von Bell, Johann Adam (1592–1666), Jesuit missionary and astronomer in China. Schall was born in Cologne, Germany. After his early studies, he went to Rome to study for the priesthood at the Roman College (the Jesuit college in Rome) and entered the Society of Jesus in 1611. He volunteered for the missions, was ordained a priest in 1618, and entered Macao the next year. Schall remained there for over two years and participated in the defense of the city against Dutch invaders. In 1623 he was in Peking (Beijing), where he assisted *Hsü Kuang-ch'i in reforming the Chinese calendar. From 1627 to 1630 he was assigned to Sian (Xi'an) in Shensi (Shaanxi) Province, where he studied Chinese intensively and built a new church. Recalled to the capital to replace a confrere who was then on his deathbed, Schall compiled essays on astronomy and mathematics, which were presented to the emperor. Muslim and Chinese astronomers opposed the imperial sanction of the new methods. However, Schall set up a congregation of Christians in the palace and published several religious books. When Peking fell in 1644, first to a Chinese rebel and then to the Manchus, Schall was the only Westerner in the city to protect the Christian community. He proved his skills in astronomy to Manchu officials, who entrusted him with the calendar of the new dynasty and appointed him director of the astronomical bureau. With additional honorary titles, his position at court made him the protector of the Christian missions throughout China. In 1650 he received imperial permission to build a new mission compound in the capital, later called the Nan-t'ang (Nantang), South Church.

As the Shun-chih emperor, who in his youth called Schall *Ma-fa* (Grandpa), turned more toward Buddhism, Muslim astronomers attacked Schall's astronomical competence and his Christian teachings. On April 20, 1664, Schall suffered partial paralysis, such that his speech and movements were left impaired. Charged with treason and teaching false astronomy and a heterodox religion, Schall was imprisoned with three confreres, endured a state trial, and was condemned to death. An earthquake in Peking followed by a fire less than two weeks later frightened the judges, with the result that Schall and his confreres were set free. After Schall's death, Ferdinand *Verbiest, his successor at the bureau, asked for a new investigation, which led to the rehabilitation of Schall's name and restoration of all his titles and ranks.

BIBLIOGRAPHY Johann Adam Schall von Bell, *Historica narratio de initio et progressu missionis Societatis Jesu apud Sinenses* (1665; repr., *Historica relatio de ortu et progressu fidei orthodoxae in regno Chinansi permissionarios Societatis Jesu ab anno 1581 usque ad annum 1669,* 1672). Rachel Attwater, *Adam Schall: A Jesuit at the Court of China* (1962); H. Bernard and P. Bornet, *Lettres et mémoires d'Adam Schall, S.J., relation historique* (1942); R. Malek, ed., *Johann Adam Schall 400th Anniversary Volume* (1997); Louis Pfister, *Notices biographiques et bibliographiques sur les Jésuites de l'ancienne mission de Chine* (1932–1934; repr., 1975), pp. 162–170 (contains a list of Schall's Chinese works); A. Väth, *Johann Adam Schall von Bell: Missionar in China, Kaiserlicher Astronom und Ratgeber am Hofe von Peking, 1592–1666* (1933; repr., 1991).

John W. Witek, SJ

Schärer, Hans (1904–1947), Swiss missionary with the Basel Mission in Kalimantan (Borneo) and the Dutch East Indies. Born in Wädenswil, Switzerland, Schärer joined the Basel Mission in 1932 and served among the Ngaju Dayak of central Kalimantan until 1939. From 1939 until 1944 he studied at the University of Leiden, returning to his work in Borneo after World War II. He became well known for his anthropological studies of the religion of the Ngaju Dayak based on the ethnological methods of Josselin de Jong and other Dutch scholars. He died in Bandjermasin, Borneo, the site of his work.

BIBLIOGRAPHY Hans Schärer, *Die Gottesidee der Ngadju-Dajak in Süd-Borneo* (1946; English, *Ngaju Religion,* 1963) and *Der Totenkult der Ngadju-Dajak in Süd-Borneo* (1966).

Robert A. Hunt

Schauffler, William Gottlieb (1798–1883), American missionary in the Near East. Born in Stuttgart, Germany, Schauffler grew up in Odessa, Russia. He embarked for missionary service in Turkey in 1826, where he met Jonas *King, who persuaded him to go to America and study at Andover Theological Seminary. He graduated in 1831, was ordained, was appointed a missionary to the Jews by the American Board of Commissioners for Foreign Missions (ABCFM), and arrived in Constantinople in 1832. In 1834 he married Mary Reynolds, a missionary teacher at Smyrna. Capable of understanding twenty-six languages and of using ten with facility, he concentrated on Bible translation. He also undertook missionary trips in Germany and South Russia as well as in Turkey. His first convert was won in 1835 and his first major translation was a Hebrew-Spanish Old Testament (Spanish with some Hebrew words written with Hebrew characters). From 1839 to 1842 he supervised its publication by the American Bible Society in Vienna, where the Jewish community viewed it favorably. After Jewish missions in Turkey were transferred to the Free Church of Scotland in 1856, Schauffler turned his attention to the Turks and Armenians. He translated virtually the whole Bible into Turkish. Leaving Turkey in 1874, the Schaufflers lived and worked with their son Henry Albert Schauffler, ABCFM missionary in Moravia, until 1877 when they returned to America. Schauffler held several honorary degrees and was decorated by the king of Prussia.

BIBLIOGRAPHY William G. Schauffler, *Meditations on the Last Days of Christ* (1837). *Autobiography of William G. Schauffler,* ed. by his sons (1882); *Missionary Herald* 79 (1883): 95–98.

David M. Stowe

Schebesta, Paul (1887–1967), Catholic ethnographer, linguist, anthropologist, and missionary. Born in Gross-Peterwitz, Moravia, Schebesta was educated at St. Gabriel Mission Seminary in Mödling, Austria, and at the University of Vienna. He was ordained for service with the Society of the Divine Word (SVD) in 1911 and sent to Mozambique. During World War I, he was interned by the Portuguese colonial administration as an enemy alien (1916–1920). After his release, he joined the editorial staff of Wilhelm *Schmidt's ethnological and linguistic journal *Anthropos* in Mödling, Austria. In 1924, at Schmidt's suggestion, he went to British Malaya to study the Semang Negritos. This proved to be the beginning of his life's work—the study of the cultures, languages, and racial traits of pygmy peoples throughout the world. He made three field trips to the Ituri pygmies of the Belgian Congo (1934–1955) and two return trips to the Southeast Asian Negritos, as well as shorter visits to the Aeta Negritos of the Philippines and elsewhere. This fieldwork, especially among the African Bambuti and Southeast Asian Semang, made him a leading authority on the world's pygmies and became milestones in the history of anthropology. After World War II he devoted most of his time to training SVD missionaries in the field and at the mission seminary in Austria.

BIBLIOGRAPHY Schebesta's main works from an estimated 130 publications are *Die Bambuti-Pygmäen vom Ituri,* vol. 1 (1938) and vol. 2 (1941–1950), and *Die Negrito Asiens,* vol. 1 (1952) and vol. 2 (1954/1957). Anton Vorbichler, "Professor Dr. Paul Schebesta SVD," *Anthropos* 62 (1967): 665–685. A Festschrift containing a listing of his publications appears as no. 18 of *Studia Instituti Anthropos* (1963).

Louis J. Luzbetak, SVD

Schellenberg, Katharina L(ohrenz) (1870–1945), first woman missionary doctor of the Mennonite Brethren Church. Born in the Molotschna, Ukraine, Schellenberg immigrated to the United States with her family and settled in Kansas in 1879. Sure of her missionary calling, she spent 12 years in preparation before sailing for India in 1906, following her graduation from the Medical Institute of Homeopathic Medicine at Kansas City, Kansas. She learned Telugu and began medical practice within the first year, covering an area from Hughestown and Hyderabad City in the north to the Tungabadra River in the south. She pioneered under primitive conditions, treating patients in missionary homes or village tents. After her mission built its first hospital at Nagarkurnool in 1912 and a new one in Shamshabad in 1928, she and her helpers treated some 8,000 outpatients and inpatients annually. With medical expertise and Christian compassion, she cared for people, always conscious that "the Great Physician is able to heal the soul as well as the body." During nearly four decades (1906–1945), Shellenberg took only two furloughs. She is buried in Hyderabad.

BIBLIOGRAPHY Katie Funk Wiebe, "The Life and Work of Dr. K. L. Schellenberg," *Youth Worker* 8 (December 1959): 20–27; Esther Jost, "Free to Serve: Katharina Schellenberg (1870–1945)," in Katie Funk Wiebe, ed., *Women among the Brethren* (1979), pp. 82–94. Schellenberg's papers and her published articles in the periodicals *Zionsbote, Licht und Hoffnung,* and *Harvest Field* are preserved in the archives of the Center for Mennonite Brethren Studies in Fresno, California.

Hans Kasdorf

Scherer, Heinrich (1628–1704), Jesuit mathematician and cartographer of missions. Born in Dillingen, Germany, Scherer entered the Jesuits in 1645 and taught mathematics, humanities, rhetoric, and Hebrew at the court of the dukes of Mantua, Italy, and then in Munich for Max Emmanuel of Bavaria. His seven-volume *Atlas Novus* was completed in 1710, after his death, but a number of volumes had been published in 1702 and 1703. His major contribution to the history of Christian missions is contained in the second volume, *Geographia Hierarchica* (1702). This pioneering work in mission geography contains maps and short historical and geographic descriptions of Roman Catholic dioceses, prelatures, and vicariates all over the world. Other volumes include natural geography (vol. 1) and a Marian atlas (vol. 3), in which the shrines and locations of Marian apparitions were detailed. The cartography of the *Atlas Novus* was the first German attempt to present maps based on astronomical data, and the seven volumes contained the essentials of the geographic knowledge of the time.

BIBLIOGRAPHY B. Duhr, *Geschichte der Jesuiten in den Ländern deutscher Zunge* (1907, 1928), vol. 3, pp. 575–576; C. Sommervogel, *Bibliothèque de la Compagnie de Jésus,* vol. 7 (1896, 1960), pp. 765–767.

Stephen B. Bevans, SVD

Scherer, James A(ugustin) B(rown) (1870–1944), pioneer American Lutheran missionary in Japan and cofounder of the Japan Evangelical Lutheran Church. Scherer was born in Salisbury, North Carolina. His grandfather, father, three older brothers, and numerous uncles preceded him in ministerial roles. At Roanoke (North Carolina) College Scherer gained highest honors, excelling in English composition and oratory. After theological self-study and brief parish experience, he was recommended by the Board for Missions of the Lutheran United Synod of the South for ordination to begin mission work in Japan. Ordained in November 1891, he arrived in Yokohama on February 4, 1892, and while studying Japanese in Tokyo, he was invited to teach English in a middle school in Saga, Kyushu, where Lutheran mission work had its beginning. With co-workers R. B. *Peery and Ryohei Yamauchi, he presided over the first Japanese Lutheran worship service on Easter Day 1893 and witnessed the first baptism. Health reasons compelled him and his wife to return to the United States in January 1897, ending their missionary connection.

Scherer took a doctorate, held a joint pastorate, taught church history at the Lutheran seminary in Charleston, South Carolina, published several books on Japan, and became president of Newberry College, South Carolina (1904–1908). He was then invited to head Throop College of Technology in Pasadena, California, an institution that he helped transform into the prestigious California Institute of Technology (1908–1920). He advocated the rights of Japanese immigrants and wrote books about Japan and California history. During the period of rising Japanese militarism, he spent five more years in Japan (1931–1936) as a close observer of Japan's expansion into Korea, Manchuria, and China. He wrote several historical books characterized by their friendly view of Japan. Yet in 1937, following Japan's invasion of China, Scherer reversed his position, attacking the Japanese military-industrial conspiracy for betraying the Japanese people and blaming America for its complicity.

BIBLIOGRAPHY An extensive biographical sketch with bibliography of over 20 books written by Scherer appears in James A. Scherer, "A Pioneer Lutheran Missionary in Japan," *Currents in Theology and Mission,* October 1992, pp. 326–338. See also Judith R. Goodstein, *Millikan's School: A History of the California Institute of Technology* (1992).

James A. Scherer

Schereschewsky, Samuel Isaac Joseph (1831–1906), Episcopal missionary and bishop. Born of Orthodox Jewish parents in a Lithuanian village, Schereschewsky early showed gifts for religious leadership and was trained for the rabbinate, with graduate studies in Germany. During these years he was drawn to a serious consideration of the Christian faith through contact with missionaries of the London Society for Promoting Christianity amongst the Jews. In 1854 he immigrated to America, and through contact with Jewish Christians, felt called to become a Christian in fulfillment of his Hebrew heritage. His gifts for leadership were immediately recognized and he was sent to Western Theological Seminary in Pittsburgh, Pennsylvania. The issue of catholicity intrigued him and eventually led him to transfer to General Theological Seminary in New York City as preparation for ordination in the Episcopal Church.

Hearing the call for missionaries for China, he left for Shanghai in 1859 and began his study of Chinese during the voyage. A gifted linguist, he translated the Bible and the Church of England Prayer Book into Mandarin. His scholarship was matched by his love for people. He was elected bishop of Shanghai in 1877, and he was consecrated in Grace Church, New York City. He helped establish St. John's College (later University) in Shanghai. He resigned his see in 1883 when he became stricken with paralysis. After treatment in the West, he returned to Shanghai in 1895 to continue his translation work. He typed some 2,000 pages with the middle finger of his partially crippled hand. While the paralysis seemed a terrible affliction, he came to believe that God guided his life so that he could do the work for which he was best fitted. His wife was his constant companion and source of help until he died in Tokyo. He is remembered in the Episcopal book *Lesser Feasts and Fasts* on October 15.

BIBLIOGRAPHY James Arthur Muller, *Apostle of China: Samuel Isaac Joseph Schereschewsky* (1937).

Paul Clasper

Schiller, Karl Emil (1865–1945), German missionary in Japan. Schiller was born at Husum, Germany, and studied at the Universities of Bonn and Berlin. In 1895 he joined the Japan mission of the Allgemeiner Evangelisch-Protestantischer Missionsverein (after 1922 Deutsche Ostasien Mission). His entire missionary career (1895–1931) was spent in Japan. After five years in Tokyo, in 1900 Schiller moved to Kyoto, where he established his mission's Kyoto church and conducted evangelistic work in Osaka and Otsu. In 1902 he founded the Kyoto German Language School, and also lectured in philosophy and German language at Kyoto Imperial University. In 1912 he became supervisor of the German mission in Japan; as such, he had to deal with the financial crisis caused by World War I. During the war, he worked to console German prisoners interned in the prisoner-of-war camp in Shikoku. In 1921 he received an honorary doctorate of theology from the University of Berlin. He was the author of *Morgenröte in Japan* (1913) and also published on Shinto and Japanese folk religions. He helped to introduce into Japan the liberal theological thought and trends in European theology. He and his German missionary colleagues greatly contributed to the development of Japanese studies in Germany and German studies in Japan.

BIBLIOGRAPHY J. Richter, *Das Buch der deutschen Weltmission* (1935).

A. Hamish Ion

Schleiermacher, Friedrich Daniel Ernst (1768–1834), German theologian. One of the most influential German theologians of his age, Schleiermacher also deserves a place among theologians of mission. Inasmuch as he was raised and educated in Silesia, and steeped in the tradition of the Herrnhut Brethren, Christian mission was always close to Schleiermacher's heart and mind, though his later emphasis on intuition and feeling in religion left little room for the Moravian priority of "winning souls for the lamb." Three of his theological ideas proved to be of missiological relevance. First, Schleiermacher maintained that there is a kind of spontaneous expansion of religious faith that requires no special effort, no sense of finality or urgency, although it may result in the conversion of others. Second, the Christian church as a whole is duty-bound to follow the leading of the Spirit to witness to its faith in obedience to Christ's example in word and deed, and thus to prove its superior religious quality as compared with other religions. Third, mission in this somewhat muted interpretation should nonetheless have a place in training for the Christian ministry, preferably in the study of ethics or practical theology—a suggestion that was taken up in a variety of ways by Schleiermacher's followers.

BIBLIOGRAPHY Olav Guttorm Myklebust, *The Study of Missions in Theological Education*, vol. 1 (1955), pp. 84–89.

Hans-Werner Gensichen

Schlunk, Martin (1874–1958), German Protestant missiologist. Schlunk was born to missionary parents in Calicut, South India. As a theological student at Halle, he was attracted to the study of missions by Gustav *Warneck. While serving as a young pastor in north Germany, he published a monograph on the French Protestant missionary François *Coillard. Appointed director of the North German Mission at Bremen in 1908, he spent a brief time at Hamburg before becoming professor of missiology at Tübingen University (1928 until his retirement in 1941). In addition to his academic activities he displayed remarkable gifts of leadership in a variety of influential positions in German Protestant missions, especially during critical situations in and between the two world wars. Schlunk was also responsible for an uncompromising witness by German missions under the Nazi regime. A member of the German delegation to the World Missionary Conference at Edinburgh in 1910, at Jerusalem in 1928, and at Tambaram in 1938, he fostered a deeper understanding of the world missionary and ecumenical movement in Germany. His competence in the scientific study of missions was amply documented in many publications on a vast range of relevant topics, in membership in scholarly associations, and in his editorship of various mission journals. Many of his writings gained the attention of the educated German public.

BIBLIOGRAPHY Martin Schlunk, *F. Coillard und die Mission am oberen Sambesi* (1904), *Die Norddeutsche Mission in Togo* (1912), *Die Weltreligionen und das Christentum* (1923), and *Die Weltmission der Kirche Christi* (1951). Walter Freytag, "Martin Schlunk," *EMZ* 15 (1958): 48–50; Gerhard Rosenkranz, "Martin Schlunk," *EMM* 103 (1959): 17–32.

Hans-Werner Gensichen

Schmelen, Johann Heinrich (1776–1848), pioneer German missionary in South-West Africa (Namibia). Schmelen was born in Cassebruch near Bremen, northern Germany. After obtaining a good education, he left Germany to escape military service. In London he was converted under Karl Friedrich Adolf, the pastor of the German congregation there. After being trained in the *Jänicke Mission Seminary in Berlin, Schmelen joined the London Missionary Society, and in 1811 was sent to southern Africa. With a group of Orlam who had migrated into Namaland (territory of the Nama Hottentot people, in southern South-West Africa), he founded the Bethany mission station, north of the Orange River. He spent seven years exploring South-West Africa, investigating potential sites for mission stations, and persuaded the Rhenish Mission to take up mission work there. With the help of his wife, a Nama, he translated the Gospels into Nama under most difficult conditions. After the printing had been done in Cape Town, his missionary society sent him to Komaggas, where he labored until he died. He transmitted to new missionaries his spirit of total unselfishness and devotion to the service of the native population. He especially influenced those who stayed with him on their way to South-West Africa and whom he introduced to missionary work. It was said that he "became a Nama to the Namas."

BIBLIOGRAPHY H. Driessler, *Die Rheinische Mission in Südwestafrika* (1932); H. Vedder, *Das alte Südwestafrika* (1934).

Theo Sundermeier

Schmelzenbach, Harmon Faldean (1882–1929) *and* **Lula (Glatzel)** (1886–1960), Church of the Nazarene pioneer missionaries in Swaziland, Africa. Born in Ohio, orphaned at age 12, and raised by a farmer, Harmon Schmelzenbach had minimal education. After his conversion, he enrolled in 1906 at the Holiness Peniel Bible College in Texas, where he decided to become a missionary. After raising his own support, he sailed for South Africa in May 1907 with nine other independent Holiness missionaries. In the group was Lula Glatzel, who was born in Baltimore, received a call to missions at a camp meeting, and studied at God's Bible School in Cincinnati. The two were married in Port Elizabeth a year later. The Schmelzenbachs first worked in Pondoland, but local officials ousted them because they were not from a recognized church body. They relocated in Natal, where Harmon mastered Zulu, and went to Swaziland in 1910 to begin a new work in the Piggs Peak District. In 1909 they affiliated with the newly formed Church of the Nazarene General Missionary Board. Etta Innis (1876–1966), an Indiana native who had been part of the 1907 group and was conducting a mission among Europeans in Cape Colony, joined the Schmelzenbachs in Swaziland. Working under extreme conditions in an area unserved by missionaries, they recorded the first convert in 1913. The three lived frugally, with minimal support from abroad, and functioned as a team. They preached, formed schools, and counseled people at their Peniel and Grace stations. Harmon Schmelzenbach learned the rudiments of medicine and carried on medical work until a doctor arrived in 1922. Widower H. A. Shirley (1879–1945), who went to Africa in 1911 as an independent missionary, joined the Nazarene mission and in 1919 married Innis. The Schmelzenbachs took only one furlough after 21 years in Africa. In 1920, the Swazi queen approved an expansion of the work, and when Harmon Schmelzenbach died in 1929 (of malaria), the Nazarene mission numbered 24 expatriate and 143 African workers and 3,000 Christians. Lula Schmelzenbach continued to labor in Swaziland until 1953, and Etta Innis Shirley until 1946. Several Schmelzenbach descendants also became missionaries.

BIBLIOGRAPHY Lula Schmelzenbach, *The Missionary Prospector: A Life Story of Harmon Schmelzenbach* (1937). Harmon Schmelzenbach III, *Schmelzenbach of Africa* (1971); Mendell Taylor, *Fifty Years of Nazarene Missions* (1952).

Richard V. Pierard

Schmemann, Alexander (1921–1983), Orthodox theologian and promoter of church and mission renewal. Born in Estonia of Russian parents and raised in France, Schmemann was educated in French schools and at the Orthodox Theological Institute of St. Sergius in Paris. He was ordained a priest in the Russian Orthodox Church in France in 1946. He went in 1951 to St. Vladimir's Orthodox Theological Seminary in New York, where he taught and served as dean from 1962 until his death. Theologian, scholar, and ecumenist, Schmemann is remembered and revered as pastor, teacher, spiritual guide, church activist, and ecclesiastical, literary, and cultural critic. His charismatic presence and eloquence spearheaded a spiritual, liturgical, and missionary renewal of Orthodox church life in North America. His weekly radio programs, in Russian, were broadcast into Eastern Europe and the former Soviet Union. Posthumously, he is a key figure in the renewal of Christian life in former Communist lands, especially in Russia, where most of his books and sermons have been published. In his liturgical theology Schmemann criticized secularization and the compartmentalizing of Christianity as a religion, viewing sacramental worship as the experience of the world created, redeemed, and sanctified by God in Christ and the Holy Spirit. He called for theological and spiritual renewal in a missionary movement grounded in eucharistic experience.

BIBLIOGRAPHY Alexander Schmemann, *For the Life of the World* (1963; expanded ed., 1973), *Of Water and the Spirit* (1974), *Great Lent* (1974), *Church, World, Mission* (1979), and *The Eucharist* (1987). Thomas Fisch, ed., *Liturgy and Tradition: Theological Reflections of Alexander Schmemann* (1990) and "Father Alexander Schmemann, Dean, 1962–1983," *St. Vladimir's Theological Quarterly* 28, no. 1 (1984).

Thomas Hopko

Schmid, Hans (?–1558), pioneer Anabaptist missionary. Born in Upper Austria, Schmid was confirmed a Hutterite Anabaptist minister in Moravia in 1548. He was an effective and fearless missioner, particularly to disaffected Anabaptists, whom he urged to go to Moravia as the haven of refuge provided by God against the dragon of the endtime (Rev. 12:6). Many Anabaptists of Swiss descent were persuaded in part through his treatise *Brotherly Union* (1556). His extant writings include thirty-five letters and fifteen hymns written in prison, as well as a treatise on original sin and the incarnation of Christ. His central emphasis was the love of God and its work in the life of believers, obedience to the dominical injunctions, and the primacy of community—including possessions—and *Gelassenheit,* a medieval mystical term calling for surrender of the will. He was executed along with four other Anabaptists on orders of the city council of Aachen, in keeping with the decree of Emperor Ferdinand I of Austria.

BIBLIOGRAPHY *Chronicle of the Hutterian Brethren* 1 (1987); Josef Hansen, "Wiedertäufer in Aachen," *Zeitschrift des Aachener Geschichtsvereins* 6 (1884); George H. Williams, *The Radical Reformation,* 3d rev. and enlarged ed. (1992).

Cornelius J. Dyck

Schmidlin, Joseph (1876–1944), pioneer Catholic missiologist. Schmidlin was born in Kleinlandau, Alsace (when it was part of Germany). He earned his doctorate in philosophy and theology (Strassburg, 1906) and qualified as a professor in church history. While professor of dogmatic theology and patrology in Münster, he was given a lectureship in missiology in 1910; in 1914 this position was raised to a chair of missiology, the first such university chair in any Catholic faculty. Henceforth Schmidlin was mainly concerned with missiology, especially mission history. For good reasons he is recognized as the Father of Catholic missiology.

Schmidlin's missiological lecturing led to the publication of substantial works in missiology, many of which became standards in the field and are still significant. These include *Einführung in die Missionswissenschaft* (2d ed., 1925), *Katholische Missionslehre im Grundriss* (2d ed., 1923) (English tr., *Catholic Mission Theory* [1931]), and *Katholische Missionsgeschichte* (1925) (English tr., *Catholic Mission History* [1933]). He published in many journals, in particular *Zeitschrift für Missionswissenschaft* (*ZM*), which he founded in 1911; during its first 25 years of publication, *ZM* included 165 of his own major articles.

In his missiology he borrowed heavily from Gustav *Warneck, but not without examining this Protestant missiologist's ideas critically, even polemically, and asserting his own personal ideas and convictions. He was the inspiration behind the so-called Münster school of missiology, which emphasized proclamation and salvation; the Louvain school, which developed during World War II, regarded planting the church to be the main goal of mission. Only after Schmidlin's death was the controversial question tackled and finally settled at the Second Vatican Council. Missiology was fostered by his initiatives in founding the Internationales Institut für missionswissenschaftliche Forschungen, *ZM,* Missionswissenschaftliche Abhandlungen und Texte, and Missionswissenschaftliche Studien. He fostered interest in the missionary cause among students by founding university mission groups. He organized mission conferences for the diocesan clergy, which led to the founding of mission associations for priests. He organized mission study weeks for teachers, missionaries on leave, and religious communities, and promoted the idea of a German missionary society for the diocesan clergy.

Schmidlin had a rather pugnacious side to his personality. Among those with whom he crossed swords in academic, political, and personal feuds were his own professor, A. Ehrhard of Strassburg, colleagues and strangers, bishops and other members of the hierarchy, Protestant missionaries and missiologists, and the German Conference of Religious Superiors. It is no wonder that he soon clashed also with the National Socialist regime. In 1934 he was forcibly retired from the university because he refused to give the Hitler salute, and settled down in Neu-Breisach. For some time he continued to edit his journal but was forced to give this up also in 1937. He was jailed for eight months. Never giving up his struggle against the Nazi regime, Schmidlin ended his days in the concentration camp of Struthof near Schirmeck in Alsace.

BIBLIOGRAPHY An autobiography is found in E. Stange, ed., *Die Religionswissenschaft der Gegenwart in Selbstdarstellungen* (1927); Karl Müller, *Joseph Schmidlin (1876–1944): Papsthistoriker und Begründer der katholischen Missionswissenschaft* (1989; with extensive bibliography), "Joseph Schmidlin: Leben und Werk," in *50 Jahre katholische Missionswissenschaft in Münster*, Josef Glazik, ed. (1961), and "Joseph Schmidlin," in Gerald H. Anderson et al., eds., *Mission Legacies* (1994), pp. 402–409.

Karl Müller, SVD

Schmidt, Georg (1709–1785), pioneer Moravian missionary in South Africa. Schmidt was born at Kunewald, Moravia, and immigrated to Herrnhut in 1725 with Christian *David. By trade a butcher, he was active in the life of the community. As a traveling evangelist for the Moravian Brethren, he was imprisoned for two years in Bohemia and served three years of penal servitude in Prague. Commissioned for overseas mission, in 1737 he arrived at Table Bay, South Africa, and began to search for a place to evangelize. Encountering opposition from the established church, he went to work among the Khoikhoi at Bavians Kloof and began teaching them in Dutch in October 1737. In April 1738 he founded Gnadendal, and by the end of the year twenty-eight Khoikhoi were living at the station. Opposition grew to the establishment of Moravian work, and in 1744 he returned to the Netherlands. Denied permission to return to the Cape, he eventually retired to the Moravian settlement of Niesky, Germany, where he died. When Schmidt's successors resumed contact in 1792, they were greeted by a small band of converts who told of his labors and displayed a Dutch New Testament he had given them.

BIBLIOGRAPHY B. Krüger, *The Pear Tree Blooms* (1966); *Missions in South Africa* (1835); A. Schultze, *Seliger Heimgang von siebenzig Kindern Gottes aus der Brüderkirche* (1876); A. C. Thompson, *Moravian Missions* (1882).

Albert H. Frank

Schmidt, Wilhelm (1868–1954), Roman Catholic anthropologist and linguist. Born in Hörde (present-day Dortmund-Hörde), Germany, Schmidt was ordained a priest of the Society of the Divine Word (SVD) in 1892. An unusually gifted, largely self-taught scholar with only a short time of study at the University of Berlin (1893–1895), he wrote more than 650 publications. As mission seminary professor at Mödling, near Vienna (1896–1938), and as professor of ethnology at the University of Vienna (1921–1938) and Fribourg, Switzerland (1942–1951), he was a stimulating teacher and a good organizer of students and colleagues. He worked at research and writing almost to his dying day in Fribourg.

Early in his career Schmidt achieved wide recognition as a linguist. For disentangling the relationships of the Southeast Asian and Oceanic languages, he received a prestigious award from the French Académie des Inscriptions et Belles Lettres and membership in the Austrian Imperial Academy of Sciences. Among his 125 linguistic works, the most important are *Die Mon-Khmer Völker* (1906), *Gliederung der australischen Sprachen* (1919), and *Sprachfamilien und Sprachkreisen der Erde* (1926).

Impressed by the potential of the so-called *Kulturkreislehre* (culture circle theory), he turned his interest more and more to anthropology, a field directly linked to his primary concerns—the history of religions and human institutions, the false claims of deterministic evolutionism, and the missionary role in the study of culture. He soon became the chief proponent and leading figure behind the theory. He sought to concretize the culture circle theory in space-time sequence and ethnographic detail in an encyclopedic cultural history of the world, *Völker und Kulturen* (1926), which he coauthored with his close SVD associate Wilhelm Koppers. A decade later he expanded and refined the theory in a step-by-step manual on the method. He is best known, however, for his monumental 12-volume study of the origin and development of religion, *Der Ursprung der Gottesidee* (1926–1955).

Schmidt influenced leading European academic, church, and political thinkers and authorities. Although the *Kulturkreislehre* became outdated, Schmidt continues to be highly regarded, particularly by students of religion, for his ability to sift, analyze, and order vast amounts of ethnographic and mythological data. His deep grasp and appreciation of tribal religions, his promotion of serious cultural study and research by missionaries, his founding in 1906 of *Anthropos,* a leading international journal of ethnology and linguistics with strong ties to missionary research, his founding of the Anthropos Institute, and the founding of the papal ethnological mission museum in Rome: these contributions and more helped to pave the way for the recognition of mission science as a discipline worthy of the respect of scholars. He also influenced Roman Catholic theological thought and practice, especially in apologetics and in the area of faith and culture.

BIBLIOGRAPHY For comprehensive biographical information, see Fritz Bornemann, *P. Wilhelm Schmidt S.V.D., 1868–1954* (1982) and Ernest Brandewie, *When Giants Walked the Earth* (1990). For an assessment of Schmidt see the Festschrift edited by Wilhelm Koppers (1928). See also Franco Demarchi, ed., *Wilhelm Schmidt un ethnologo sempre attuale* (1989); Louis J. Luzbetak, "Wilhelm Schmidt, S.V.D.," in Gerald H. Anderson et al., eds., *Mission*

Legacies (1994), pp. 475–485. Archival materials are kept at the Anthropos Institute (now located at Sankt Augustin, Germany) and at the SVD Generalate in Rome.

Louis J. Luzbetak, SVD

Schnarre, Johannes Christian (c. 1791–1820), missionary pioneer in South India. Born in Germany, and accepted as a missionary by the Church Missionary Society (CMS) committee in August 1811 on the condition that he obtain Lutheran orders, Schnarre appeared before the committee in October 1812 together with his fellow Berlin Mission school student, C. T. E. *Rhenius. After further study under Thomas Smith, in 1813 Schnarre was dispatched to Tranquebar, a Danish colony in southern India, to assist Christoph *John and await the renewal of the East India Company Charter in 1814 when it was anticipated that restrictions on missionaries working in British India would be lifted. But after working with Rhenius in founding the CMS mission in Madras, he transferred to the Society for Promoting Christian Knowledge and worked with J. C. Kolhoff and A. F. Cammaerer superintending schools in Tranquebar until his death.

BIBLIOGRAPHY Mildred E. Gibbs, *The Anglican Church in India, 1600–1970* (1972); Eugene Stock, *History of the Church Missionary Society*, vol. 1 (1899).

E. M. Jackson

Schneder, David Bowman (1887–1938), Reformed Church missionary in Japan and second president of Tohoku Gakuin in Sendai. Born in Lancaster County, Pennsylvania, Schneder graduated from Franklin and Marshall College and Seminary and was ordained a minister of the German Reformed Church in the United States. He married Anna Schoenberger, and they were appointed in 1887 by their church's mission board to serve in Japan. Assigned to Sendai, the Schneders both taught in the Sendai Theological Training School (founded 1886), which came to be known as Tohoku Gakuin (North Japan College). Upon the resignation of its first president, Schneder served as the college's second president (1902–1936) and proved to be a tireless promoter, fund-raiser, and eventually elder statesman for the college and other Christian causes in Sendai and throughout Japan. He also tried to bridge growing U.S.-Japan antagonisms by sharing Christian viewpoints on reconciliation with his many contacts, from students and church members to prime ministers and presidents. After retirement, the Schneders remained in Sendai, where he died.

BIBLIOGRAPHY Schneder wrote many articles on Japan mission topics for *The Christian World, The Outlook of Mission, The Reformed Church Messenger, The Reformed Church Review,* and *The Japan Evangelist.* He also wrote two pamphlets about his school, *Tohoku Gakuin* (1902) and *North Japan College* (c. 1910). C. William Mensendiek, *A Man for His Times: The Life and Thought of David Bowman Schneder* (1972).

James M. Phillips

Schneller, Johann Ludwig (1820–1896), German missionary in Palestine and founder of the Syrian Orphanage in Jerusalem. Born in Erpfingen in Württemberg, Schneller was the son of a weaver. He received little formal education but passed the teachers' examination with distinction. His faith was firmly rooted in the heritage of Swabian pietism. In 1847, because of his strong performance as a student in the Pilgrims Mission Seminary for artisans in St. Chrischona, Basel, Switzerland, the founder-director, C. F. *Spittler, appointed him as the first warden of the seminary. In 1850 he was sent to Jerusalem to open a training center for Chrischona graduates, who were to work with the Falashas in Ethiopia. The Muslim massacre of Christians in Lebanon and Syria in 1860 moved him to help widows and orphans of the victims in the area of Tyre and Sidon. The experience of their misery presented him with a lifetime challenge. In 1860 he founded the Syrian Orphanage in Jerusalem. It developed into a Christian center for the training of pastors, evangelists, and teachers for the Arabic churches, as well as for his own institutions. It also provided high school facilities and training for artisans. His initiative and dedication resulted in significant contributions of Christian service to the Arabic people in Palestine. In 1896 his son Theodor followed him as director of the Schneller center, which by that time had grown to include nine boarding schools and 600 students, which made it the largest and most important mission institution in the Near East. In 1939 the British Mandatory government expropriated the property, closing the center; in 1948 it was expropriated by the Israeli government. New branches were opened in Lebanon (1952) and in Jordan (1959).

BIBLIOGRAPHY The leading biography of Schneller is by his son Ludwig, *Vater Schneller: Ein Patriarch der evangelischen Mission im heiligen Lande* (1898, 1925; Dutch tr., 1908, also Arabic tr.); Hermann Schneller, *100 Jahre Syrisches Waisenhaus in Jerusalem, 1860–1960* (n.d.), offers a useful retrospect. An important contextual study is Karl Hammer, "Die christliche Jerusalem-Sehnsucht im 19. Jahrhundert: Der geistige und geschichtliche Hintergrund der Gründung J. L. Schnellers," *Theologische Zeitschrift der Universität Basel* 42 (1986): 255–266. Johann Ludwig Schneller's correspondence with Christian Friedrich Spittler is in the Staatsarchiv in Basel; papers and other letters are in the Archiv der Pilgermission St. Chrischona, Bettingen, near Basel, Switzerland.

Lothar Schreiner

Schoenmakers, John (1807–1883), Jesuit missionary to Native Americans. Schoenmakers was born in Waspick, Netherlands, and was educated in the De Nef school in Tournout, Belgium. There he was strongly influenced by Pierre-Jean De Nef, a Catholic layman who served as its director. De Nef encouraged him and many other students, including Pierre *DeSmet and Christian *Hoecken, to consider missionary work among Native Americans. Schoenmakers was ordained a secular priest in Belgium in 1833. During this same year the political struggles in the Netherlands and Belgium intensified, so he left Belgium in 1833 and went to Georgetown, Maryland, where he entered the Society of Jesus in 1834. Assigned to Florissant,

Missouri, from 1834 until 1846 he was responsible for administrative tasks for the Society of Jesus in Missouri. In 1846 he began to serve the Osage Indians and was selected to act as superintendent for the Osage mission station in Kansas, which he established the following year. The mission included schools for boys and girls; the curriculum reflected Schoenmakers's ideas on the education of youth through teaching both the Catholic faith tradition and Western civilization. He, along with the other Jesuit missionaries, also taught Western agricultural practices to the Osage. During the Civil War, Schoenmakers established temporary mission stations for Federal troops stationed at forts and military camps near the Osage mission. In 1866 he also established mission stations for white settlers in Carthage, Kansas, and Newtonia, Missouri. He died at the Osage station.

BIBLIOGRAPHY Gilbert J. Garraghan, *The Jesuits of the Middle United States,* 3 vols. (1938); William White Graves, *Annals of Osage Mission* (1935) and *Rev. Father John Schoenmakers: Apostle to the Osage* (1928); Paul Mary Ponziglione, "Record of Missionary Stations and Churches Established by the Fathers of the Mission of St. Francis of Jerome amongst the Osage Indians in the State of Kansas from the Year 1847 to 1870," unpublished manuscript in the Jesuit Missouri Province archives, Saint Louis, Mo. Schoenmakers's letters and papers are also held in the Jesuit Missouri Province archives.

Paul O. Myhre

Scholtz, Ödön (1869–1948), Hungarian Lutheran mission advocate. Scholtz was born in Szentjakab, Province Abauj, in Slovakia, and studied theology in Sopron, Hungary, and Halle, Germany. From 1893 to 1938 he served as Lutheran pastor of Ágfalva (Agensdorf). In 1896 he founded the first Hungarian Lutheran foreign mission periodical, *Külmisszió* (Foreign mission), known since 1906 as *Missziói Lapok* (Mission pages), which he edited until 1915. This journal did much to lay the foundation of the Hungarian Lutheran Foreign Mission Society, established in 1909, and the Hungarian branch of the Leipzig Mission, which he served as president until 1928. Stressing the mission task of Hungarians among the Muslims in the Balkans, and the church's responsibility to preach the gospel in faraway fields "according to the Augsburg Confession, purely and genuinely," Scholtz challenged the widespread rationalism then influencing the Lutheran Church. He aimed first to win the ecclesiastical structures for the mission cause, and through them, to reach the common people. Although his work created interest in mission among the Hungarian German-speaking Lutheran churches in upper Hungary (Slovakia) and West Hungary (present-day Austria), his strong emphasis on the unity of church, mission, and the Lutheran confession had limited impact on Hungary as a whole.

BIBLIOGRAPHY Ödön Scholtz, *Gróf Zinzendorf Miklós Lajos, a herrnhuti testvérgyülekezet és misszió alapitója* (Count Nicholas L. Zinzendorf, founder of the Brethren community of Herrnhut) (1900), "Mohamedán misszió" (Mission among Muslims), *Külmisszió* 5, no. 4 (1900): 87–92, "Egyházi misszió" (Church-based mission) *Külmisszió* 6, no. 4 (1901): 65–68, and *Az evangélikus misszió ügy fejlődése Magyarországon kezdettől fogva az Országos Misszióegyesület megalapitásáig* (The development of the Lutheran mission cause in Hungary from its beginning to the establishment of the National Mission Association) (1940). Anne-Marie Kool, *God Moves in a Mysterious Way: The Hungarian Protestant Foreign Mission Movement (1756–1951)* (1993).

Anne-Marie Kool

Schomerus, Hilko Wiarda (1879–1945), Indologist and missionary in South India. Son of a country doctor in East Friesland, Germany, and educated by his father, Schomerus enrolled at the seminary of the Leipzig Mission in 1897 after fewer than three years of high school. In 1902 he was ordained for mission service in South India, where his elder brother, Rudolf, had served since 1891. In preparation he had studied Paul Deussen's newly published Indological works, but they proved to be of little help in a setting where Tamil and village religion prevailed over Sanskrit and Vedanta. While Rudolf concentrated on problems of the outcastes, Schomerus II, as he was called, devoted his talents to the encounter of Christianity and popular Hinduism. Working in the town of Erode, he made steady progress in gaining a more profound understanding of Hindu religion and ethics in general, and of South Indian Saiva-Siddhanta philosophy in particular, which became the subject of his first major book. In 1912 the mission board granted him a sabbatical in Germany. When the outbreak of World War I prevented Schomerus from returning to India, Rudolf Otto and archbishop Nathan *Söderblom helped him embark on an academic career, culminating in a call to Gustav *Warneck's former chair of missions at Halle University in 1925. In the next two decades he published a series of major Indological works, all of them testifying both to his scholarly competence and his devotion to the missionary task. Although he did not live to see it, Schomerus paved the way for the reopening of Halle University, which had been closed by the Nazi regime.

BIBLIOGRAPHY H. W. Schomerus, *Missionswissenschaft* (1935), and *Indien und das Christentum,* 3 vols. (1931–1933). H.-W. Gensichen, "H. W. Schomerus, Missionar und Indologe," in H. W. Schomerus, *Arunantis Sivajnanasiddiyar,* vol. 1 (1981), pp. 11–16.

Hans-Werner Gensichen

Schön, Jakob Friedrich (James Frederick in his books) (1803–1889), German-born missionary linguist and pioneer in West African language studies. Schön was trained at the Basel Mission seminary and the Church Missionary Society college at Islington, London. After he was ordained in the Church of England, he was sent to Freetown, Sierra Leone, in 1832 and worked in the peninsula until 1847. When ill-health obliged him to leave West Africa, he settled at Chatham, England, where chaplaincies at the naval base gave him time for linguistic research. In 1854 he became a naturalized British subject.

While in Sierra Leone Schön first studied the local Bullom language (his first wife was the daughter of Gustavus

*Nyländer, the pioneer of Bullom studies). In 1841 he served as principal CMS representative on the Niger Expedition inspired by Thomas Fowell *Buxton, on which he and Samuel *Crowther carried out a reconnaissance of the languages of the lower Niger. In Freetown he had begun to study the Ibo and Hausa languages, and on his return he concentrated on the latter as his life's work. His first publication in Hausa was published in 1843, his last in 1888. Schön was "the great discoverer of the Hausa language," declared the French West African scholar Maurice Delafosse. His Hausa writings earned him a gold medal from the Institut de France in 1877, and in 1884 he was awarded an honorary Oxford D.D. At Chatham, for 40 years he also acted as unpaid advisor and editor with respect to most of the linguistic work of the CMS missionaries in West Africa. His scholarship was sound, if limited by lack of linguistic training. His formal connection with the CMS ceased in 1853, but he remained devoted to the mission cause.

BIBLIOGRAPHY *Allgemeine Deutsche Biographie* (1967-1971); *Church Missionary Intelligencer,* May 1889, pp. 305-306; *CMS Register* (1905); P. E. H. Hair, *The Early Study of Nigerian Languages* (2d ed., 1995); E. Stock, *History of the Church Missionary Society* (1899). Schön materials are held in the CMS archives, Univ. of Birmingham.

P. E. H. Hair

Schreiber, August Wilhelm (1867-1945), German administrator and promoter of missions. Born into a missionary family in Sumatra, Indonesia, Schreiber studied theology and served as a parish pastor in north Germany. In 1900 he was appointed director of the North German Mission at Bremen, succeeding Franz Michael *Zahn. He continued Zahn's campaign against the liquor trade in Africa, although he was not quite so outspoken in criticizing colonial ambitions in mission. Schreiber took part in the World Missionary Conference at Edinburgh in 1910 and in the Stockholm conference on Life and Work of the Church in 1925. From 1914 to 1925 he held an influential position as first director of Deutsche Evangelische Missionshilfe, the central German agency for the promotion of missions among the educated German public. In that position Schreiber was also responsible for publishing a popular mission magazine and a yearbook. In addition he made numerous contributions of his own to missiological literature, and also promoted linguistic and ethnological research. His ecumenical outlook enabled him to accept a leading position in the administration of the central Protestant church agency in Berlin (1925-1933). Characteristically, even after retirement he accepted a call back to Bremen for a second term in the directorate of the North German Mission (1934-1937).

BIBLIOGRAPHY August Wilhelm Schreiber, *Die Edinburgher Weltmissionskonferenz* (1910), *Bausteine zur Geschichte der Norddeutschen Mission* (1911), and *Internationale Kirchliche Einheitsbestrebungen* (1921). Erich Ramsauer, "D. A. W. Schreiber—Ein Leben im Dienste der Mission," in *Gehet hin. 125 Jahre Norddeutsche Mission* (1961).

Hans-Werner Gensichen

Schrenk, Elias (1831-1913), German missionary in Ghana and evangelist in Germany and Switzerland. Schrenk worked for the Basel Mission (BM) in Ghana from 1859 to 1873. His formal role was that of administrator-treasurer, but his character and intelligence made him a force to be reckoned with in the whole range of BM work in Ghana. In 1865-1866, during a furlough in Europe, he distinguished himself by effective lobbying in the House of Commons against British plans to give up the Gold Coast Colony. After his permanent return to Europe he was an evangelist, serving from 1879 with the Evangelical Society of Canton Bern (in Switzerland), and then based in Marburg, Barmen, and Bethel. He was widely respected as an inspiring speaker and an experienced pastor with great personal authority. Records in the BM archives show that, in this latter phase of his life he maintained pastoral contact with a large number of people and practiced faith healing by the laying on of hands.

BIBLIOGRAPHY Elias Schrenk, *What Shall Become of the Gold Coast* (1865) and *Pilgerleben und Pilgerarbeit* (1905).

Paul Jenkins

Schreuder, Hans Paludan Smith (1817-1882), Norwegian missionary and bishop. Schreuder was born in Sogndal in an old clergy family and graduated from the University of Oslo (Christiania) in 1841. In 1842 he published an appeal to the Church of Norway on the Christian duty with regard "to the salvation of non-Christians." He was ordained the same year and sent by the Norwegian Missionary Society (NMS) to South Africa, where he was a missionary in Zululand in northeast Natal from 1843 to 1882 and a bishop from 1866. Schreuder used the medical knowledge he had acquired at the university to treat the Zulu king Mpande, and after many difficulties, he obtained permission from the king to start mission work among the Zulus. Schreuder was intellectually and physically well equipped. He mastered the Zulu language and wrote the first complete Zulu grammar book and a textbook for the study of the langauge. He also pioneered in translating the Bible into Zulu. In cooperation with other missionaries he was the founder of the Lutheran Zulu Church. He also contributed to the establishment of the Lutheran Church in Madagascar. He had such an impressive personality that King Mpande called him *indoda* ("man") and *mankankana* ("the powerful"). A conflict between Schreuder and the NMS about administration and ecclesiology led to his withdrawal from NMS in 1872, but he continued his work independently. For more than a century the "Schreuder Mission" worked in South Africa, supported by Norwegians and by the American Lutheran Church, until it merged with the NMS in 1977. Schreuder died in South Africa.

BIBLIOGRAPHY Olav Guttom Myklebust, *H. P. S. Schreuder: Kirke og misjon* (1980); O. G. Myklebust, *En var den Første: Studier og tekster til forstaaelse av H. P. S. Schreuder* (1986), "H. P. S. Schreuder," in Gerald H. Anderson et al., eds., *Mission Legacies* (1994), pp. 148-154.

Nils E. Bloch-Hoell

Schultz, Stephan (1714–1776), German pietist pastor and missionary to Jews. After receiving training at Johann Heinrich *Callenberg's Institutum Judaicum at Halle, Schultz spent the years 1740 to 1756 traveling across Europe and to Egypt and Palestine, evangelizing Jews and recruiting others for the Jewish mission. His method was to visit Jewish ghettos and synagogues, to demonstrate understanding and respect for the Jewish culture and religion, and to emphasize the experience of the love of God manifest in Jesus Christ rather than apologetics. He did not baptize converts but rather entrusted them to the care of state church pastors for catechesis and baptism in local congregations. In 1760 he succeeded Callenberg as director of the Halle Institute. His program there was to publish Christian literature for Jews; to teach his students Jewish languages, literature, and religious thought in preparation for their mission; and to raise support for the Jewish mission in pietist circles and state church congregations. As successful as he had been as an evangelist, he lacked Callenberg's organizational abilities, and the institute declined under his leadership, finally closing in 1792.

Bibliography Göte Hedenquist, *The Church and the Jews* (1961); J. F. A. de le Roi, *Die Evangelische Christenheit und die Juden,* 3 vols. (1884–1892) and *Stephan Schultz* (1871).

Otto Dreydoppel, Jr.

Schultze, Benjamin (1689–1760), missionary of the Danish-Halle Mission in South India. Born at Sonnenburg (in what was then Brandenburg), Germany, Schultze studied theology at Halle and arrived with two colleagues in Tranquebar in September 1719, seven months after *Ziegenbalg's death. Soon he was ordained and assumed a leading position in the mission, where he encountered tensions among co-workers and with the local Danish authorities that he was unable to relieve. In 1726 he moved to Madras in order to begin a new mission supported by the English Society for Promoting Christian Knowledge. Repeated conflicts with colleagues caused him to return in 1744 to Halle, where he continued his literary activities. He completed Ziegenbalg's translation of the Bible into Tamil (first printed in 1728), and continued with a New Testament in Telugu. He was responsible for translating part of Genesis into a southern form of Hindustani, called Dakkhini, printed at Halle in Arabic characters in 1745, followed by Psalms, Gospels, and Epistles. He also compiled a grammar of the Telugu language (1728; not printed until 1984, at Halle) as well as a grammar of Hindustani (first printed at Halle in 1745, and reprinted in 1986). A treatise on the Marathi and Gujarati languages was published at Leipzig in 1748. Regrettably, most of Schultze's literary work was done in such haste that it was susceptible to criticism.

Bibliography Heike Pelikan-Liebau, *Die "Grammatica Hindostanica" des Benjamin Schultze* (1983); Johannes Mehlig, "Benjamin Schultze's Activities in India," *GDR Review* 20, no.9 (1975): 33–35; Anders Nørgaard, "Missionar Benjamin Schultze als Leiter der Tranquebarmission," *NZM* 33 (1977): 181–201.

Hans-Werner Gensichen

Schurhammer, Georg (1882–1971), historian of sixteenth-century Jesuit missions in Asia. Born in Glottertal, Germany, Schurhammer entered the Society of Jesus in 1903 and volunteered for the Asian missions. He studied Marathi and Sanskrit before leaving to teach in a secondary school in Bombay, where excessive work and the humid climate led to nervous exhaustion. On a pilgrimage to Goa in honor of Francis *Xavier, he promised that if cured, he would write a comprehensive scholarly biography of Xavier. He returned to Europe, was ordained in August 1914 and then was assigned to the staff of the journal *Katholische Missionen* in Bonn. His *Vida de San Francisco Javier en imagines* (1921) was translated into twenty-two languages. The 1925 Jesuit mission congress in Rome called by Wladimir *Ledochowski adopted as worldwide Jesuit policy Schurhammer's proposal that all newly arrived missionaries first study the native language for two years in specially established schools. In 1932 Schurhammer became a professor of Asian history at the Gregorian University in Rome. By the time the first volume of his biography of Xavier appeared in 1955, he had published an inventory of sources and numerous articles on all historical aspects of Xavier's career. Just days before he died, he finished the final volume with the help of Joseph *Wicki.

Bibliography Georg Schurhammer, *Die zeitgenössischen Quellen zur Geschichte Portugiesisch-Asians und seiner Nachbarländer zur Zeit des Hl. Franz Xaver (1538–1552)* (1932), *Franz Xaver: Sein Leben und seine Zeit,* 4 vols. (1955–1973); also in English, *Francis Xavier: His Life, His Times* (1973–1982), and Spanish, *Francisco Javier, su vida y su tiempo* (1992). The Spanish edition includes a life of Schurhammer by Francisco Zurbano, vol. 1, pp. xxxi–xliv. Schurhammer also published *Gesammelte Studien,* 5 vols. (1962–1965).

John W. Witek, SJ

Schurmann (*or* Shurman), Johannes Adam (1810–1852), pioneer missionary in Varanasi (Benares) and Bible translator. Born in Westphalia, Germany, Schurmann studied in Berlin before being accepted by the London Missionary Society (LMS). He was ordained in Southwark, June 1833, and sent to Bengal. Tragedy and disaster dogged his ministry. He got into serious debt; his first-born child died; his Indian-born wife, Julia (Cammaerer) of Tranquebar, suffered an emotional breakdown, never recovering her sanity after the birth of her fourth child. Schurmann soldiered on, however, taking furlough from 1843 to 1846 but still managing to complete a new translation of the whole Bible into Urdu. He caused outrage by using the latest German methods of textual criticism, but precisely for this reason, as well as because of the beauty and integrity of the translation, his work endured as the standard version.

Bibliography LMS Bengal Mission, CWM archives, SOAS, London.

E. M. Jackson

Schütte, Johannes (1913–1971), Catholic missiologist and administrator. Born in Essen-Oldenburg, Germany,

Schütte took his first vows in the Society of the Divine Word (SVD) in 1934. After his ordination in 1939 and a short period of military service, he went to China in 1940, where he worked in the prefecture apostolic of North Honan (Henan). In 1947 he became acting prefect apostolic of Sinsiang (Xinxiang), and the following year the regional superior of the order. In 1949 the territory was taken over by the Communists. Schütte had to undergo interrogations, trials, threats, and house arrest. Finally, after seven months of rigorous imprisonment and a show trial broadcast over the whole province, he was expelled "forever" from China.

Back in Germany he earned a doctorate in missiology at the University of Münster with an honors thesis "Die katholische Chinamission im Spiegel der rotchinesischen Presse" (1957). He then lectured in missiology in St. Augustine's Major Seminary near Bonn and in 1955 became mission secretary in the generalate of the SVD in Rome. In 1958 he was elected superior general of the order. In this position (1958–1967) his natural talent for leadership, his missionary experience and formation, as well as his energy and tenacity stood him in good stead. Under his administration the society took over new missionary activities in Formosa, Angola, Colombia, Ecuador, and Mexico. Among his constant concerns were the maintenance of missionaries; the fostering of vocations throughout the world; the establishment and extension of universities, institutes, and seminaries; the advanced training of personnel for different positions in the Society; and the intensification of mission promotion. As a superior general, he was a participant ex officio with voting rights at the Second Vatican Council. In 1964 he became president of the subcommission for the revision of the schema *De Missionibus;* in this capacity he made a substantial contribution to the compilation of the mission decree *Ad Gentes.* In 1967 the commentary *Mission nach dem Konzil* (1967) appeared under his name. After the council he was elected to the Council of 24 in the Congregation for the Evangelization of Peoples. He was a member of the first Roman Synod of Bishops. In 1968 he became vice-secretary of the Pontifical Commission Justitia et Pax. He was only 58 when he died in Rome as a result of a car accident.

BIBLIOGRAPHY *In Memoriam: P. Johannes Schütte. Sechster Generalsuperior SVD* (1972); "In Memoriam P. Dr. Johannes Schütte SVD," *ZMR* 56 (1972): 52; J. Schmitz, "P. Johannes Schütte, 6. Generalsuperior SVD," *Steyler Missionschronik* (1973): 167–168.

Karl Müller, SVD

Schütz, Paul (1891–1985), German theologian and critic of mission. Schütz began his career as a theologian with a brief assignment as a mission leader. In 1926 he was unexpectedly called from his country parish in Hesse to direct the mission founded by Johannes *Lepsius, a comparatively small enterprise directed to the Islamic Near East, combined with relief work for persecuted Armenian Christians. Schütz found himself confronted with the difficulties of having to coordinate evangelistic and humanitarian objectives, and after two years he gave up. He used his report about his tour of the countries of the Near East, "Zwischen Nil und Kaukasus" (1930), to mount a frontal attack against churches and missions of the West which, he claimed, were themselves totally secularized and unconverted yet presumed to convert others. Western missions ought to withdraw, he said, the sooner the better, and leave the so-called pagans alone. Walter *Freytag, Karl *Hartenstein, and others replied that in spite of legitimate criticisms, Christ's eschatological mandate to his church called for mission, not for flight. After World War II Schütz took pains to explain that he had never meant to call for the discontinuance of missions.

BIBLIOGRAPHY H.-W. Gensichen, "Zur Orient—und Missionserfahrung von Paul Schütz," *ZMR* 77 (1993): 152–159.

Hans-Werner Gensichen

Schuurman, Barend Martinus (1889–1945), Dutch Reformed missionary in Java, Indonesia. Born in Enschedé, Netherlands, Schuurman studied at the Free University of Amsterdam and wrote his dissertation in 1933 under the supervision of Emil Brunner at Zürich. He served in Java at Kediri (1922–1926) and at Malang (1927–1945), where he taught at Bale Wijata, a theological institute established in 1927 to prepare candidates for the ministry in the East Java Christian Church. He was interned by the Japanese during World War II and died in a Japanese camp.

Schuurman was one of the few missionaries in the colonial era who attempted to contextualize Christianity. His main work was a textbook on Christian dogmatics in the Javanese language: *Pembijaké Kekeraning Ngaurip* (Disclosure of the secrets of life), 2 vols. (1939, 1951). It explains the Christian faith in Javanese mystical terms: God is the secret or mystery of life; Jesus reveals God's secret, and at the same time, the secrets of human life.

BIBLIOGRAPHY Barend Martinus Schuurman, *Mystik und Glaube im Zusammenhang mit der Mission auf Java* (1933) and *Over Alle Bergen: Geschriften van Dr. B. M. Schuurman, Zendeling-Leraar op Java* (1952, a collection of his articles, edited by Hendrik Kraemer). See also G. Hoekstra, "Dr. Barend M. Schuurman: zijn Persoon en Werk als Zendingstheoloog op Java" (M.Th. thesis, Evangelische Theologische Faculteit Heverlee, 1989).

Jan A. B. Jongeneel

Schwager, Friedrich (1876–1929), Catholic pioneer of mission education. Born in Altenhagen, Germany, Schwager studied at the motherhouse of the Society of the Divine Word (SVD), Steyl, Netherlands, and at St. Gabriel's Major Seminary, Mödling, Vienna, where he made his final religious profession and was ordained in 1899. He wanted to go to China but instead was appointed to Steyl, where among other things he taught mission history. In 1900 he also became editor of the SVD publication *Kleiner Herz-Jesu-Bote,* which he soon developed into a solid missionary magazine with the new name *Steyler Missionsbote.* A fruit of his editorial activity was the four-volume *Die katholische Heidenmission der Gegenwart im Zusammenhang mit ihrer grossen Vergangenheit* (1907–1909). He spent much time and effort to found a Catholic scholarly mission journal modeled on Gustav *Warneck's *Allgemeine Missionszeitschrift.* He finally persuaded Joseph *Schmidlin, a church historian, to carry out the plan. In 1911 the first issue of *Zeitschrift für Missionswissenschaft* (today *Zeitschrift für Missions- und Religionswissenschaft*) appeared. Schwager made a considerable contribution to the journal with regular reports from the mission fields, numerous reviews, and basic articles.

Schwager took part actively and zealously in all organizations of the Catholic missionary movement of the time. In 1912 his *Die katholische Heidenmission im Schulunterricht* (a textbook for catechists and teachers) appeared. In 1914 he published a "clarion call to Catholic women": *Frauennot und Frauenhilfe in den Missionsländern.* He followed with interest and even admiration the progress of the Protestant mission movement and its literature. After World War I he worked hard for a return to overseas fields of the German and Austrian missionaries expelled by the war. In 1923 he had to abandon his numerous responsibilities because of failing health.

Schwager went to the United States to promote the idea of a missiological journal there but did not succeed. To everyone's surprise, in 1925 he decided to leave the Catholic Church and join the German Congregationalists in the United States. He married and got a job as librarian in Redfield College, South Dakota, where he also attended lectures in Protestant theology. He died four years later.

BIBLIOGRAPHY Karl Müller, "Friedrich Schwager," in Gerald H. Anderson et al., eds., *Mission Legacies* (1994), pp. 102–109, and *Friedrich Schwager: Pionier katholischer Missionswissenschaft* (1984).

Karl Müller, SVD

Schwartz, Carl August Ferdinand (1817–1870), Jewish convert to Christianity and leader of missions to Jews. Born in Meseritz in eastern Prussia (now Poland), Schwartz wanted to become a rabbi but was converted and baptized in Berlin in 1837. After studying theology in Halle and in Berlin, he was assigned in 1842 to Constantinople by the London Society for Promoting Christianity amongst the Jews. In 1843 he transferred to the Free Church of Scotland and worked in Berlin until 1848. Thereafter he served in Amsterdam (1849–1864) and in London (1864–1870). In Amsterdam he and Isaac *da Costa established the Scottish Seminary for Mission at Home and Abroad (1852–1860) and supported the founding of the Netherlands Society for Israël (1861). In London he became minister of the Palace Garden Church, founded the Hebrew Christian Alliance (1865), and became editor of *The Scattered Nation* (1866).

Schwartz baptized a number of Jews, including Rabbi Theodor J. *Meyer, who became his successor. Because of his aggressive missionary strategy, the Jewish community of Amsterdam accused him of proselytism. In 1858, on his way into the pulpit, he was stabbed by Samuël Abraham Hirsch (later a teacher at Jew's College in London), but Schwartz recovered. He was the first president of the Netherlands Reformed Missions Association (1859). He criticized the liberalism of the Netherlands Mission Society and advocated the abolition of slavery in Surinam.

BIBLIOGRAPHY Carl August Ferdinand Schwartz, *Seek the Lord While You Are Young!* (1865), *Praying to Christ: A Reply to Bishop Colenso* (1866), and *What Is the Talmud?* (n.d.). W. de Greef, *Carl A. F. Schwartz, 1817–1870* (1990); P. Hoekstra, "C. A. F. Schwartz, A. M. J. Rottenberg, S. P. Tabaksblatt: Exempels van Messias-belijdend Joods Denken in de Nederlandse Hervormde Kerk voor, tijdens en na de Shoa" (M.Th. thesis, Utrecht Univ., 1990).

Jan A. B. Jongeneel

Schwartz, Christian Friedrich (1726–1798), Lutheran missionary evangelist in South India. Born at Sonnenburg, Prussia, Schwartz was trained in Halle like his predecessor Benjamin *Schultze, was ordained in Copenhagen in 1749, and arrived in India in 1750. He served for 11 years at Tranquebar, where he mastered Tamil, Portuguese, and English. In 1762 he followed some Indian converts to Tiruchirapalli, an important fort-town ruled by the *nawab* (prince) of Arcot, where he ministered not only to Indian Christians of the Tranquebar mission but also to Hindus and soldiers of the English garrison. He learned Urdu in order to converse with Muslims, in particular, the representatives of the ruling prince. Visitors reported that he did the work of several missionaries.

Along with his untiring zeal as an evangelist and his deep understanding of Indian character, Schwartz displayed a saintly disposition and integrity that go far to account for his extraordinary influence. It has been rightly said that "he retrieved the character of Europeans from imputations of general depravity." His ecumenical spirit, which led him to accept an appointment as chaplain to the British community in Tiruchirapalli, was another important factor. But he never neglected his duties as a missionary to non-Christians or abandoned his loyalty as a Lutheran.

Another remarkable aspect of Schwartz's ministry was his involvement in politics. After he had moved to the town of Tanjore, he quickly gained the confidence of the Hindu rajah, who on his deathbed appointed Schwartz guardian and trustee of his young heir. Although Schwartz declined, he later assisted the young prince. He also tried to be of use to the British, who on one occasion sent him as a special envoy of peace to Haider Ali, the despot of Mysore. Schwartz returned with respect for the Muslim ruler but complained of the insincerity and avarice of the British.

Finally, Schwartz contributed significantly to the strengthening of an indigenous church in India. He made every effort to find and train young Indians for the ministry, often supporting them from his own pocket. He also encouraged the spontaneous expansion of small groups of Christians, such as those discovered during a visit to Palamcottah in 1778, the nucleus of what later became the large and vigorous Tinnevelly church. He was also responsible for the education of Vedanayagam, son of a catechist who trained under Schwartz; Vedanayagam was to become one of the greatest Tamil poets and hymn composers. Schwartz died in Tanjore.

BIBLIOGRAPHY H. Pearson, *Memoirs of the Life and Correspondence of the Rev. Christian Frederick Swartz,* 3d ed., 2 vols. (1835); W. Germann, *Missionar Christian Friedrich Schwartz* (1870); G. H. Lamb, *C. F. Schwartz* (1948).

Hans-Werner Gensichen

Schwarz, Johann Gottlob (1800–1859), German missionary of the Netherlands Mission Society (NMS) in Indonesia. Schwarz was born in Köningsberg, Prussia (later Kaliningrad, Russia) and was converted at age 18. He received his missionary education at the mission school of Johan *Jänicke in Berlin (1822–1827) and at the NMS mission house in Rotterdam (1828–1829). He served in Indonesia from 1831 to 1859, based in Kakas, and thereafter in Langoan, Minahasa (the northeastern-most region of the Celebes). His name is associated with that of Johann Friedrich *Riedel. Schwarz traveled more than Riedel and had a wider impact in the Minahasa area. After a difficult start, he built many schools and churches. Between 1834 and 1852 he baptized 9,652 persons. He introduced the Reformed Church order in the newly established congregations, starting with Kakas and Remboken (1850). After his death in Manado, an anonymous biography was published based mainly on his diary and letters. It includes not only a survey of the Christianization process in Kakas, Langoan, and their neighborhood, but also a description of Minahasa ceremonies and customs. A son, Johannes Albert Traugott Schwarz, also served as missionary in the Minahasa region, based in Sonder.

BIBLIOGRAPHY J. G. Schwarz and F. H. Linemann, "Verslag aangaande de Bijbel verspreiding in de Menahasse van Menado," *Med.* 3 (1859): 251–261. E. F. Kruyf, *Geschiedenis van het Nederlandsche Zendelinggenootschap en zijne zendingsposten* (1894) and "Leven en werkzaamheden van J. G. Schwarz, den zendeling van Langowan," *Med.* 4 (1860): 253–302, 5 (1861): 3–38, 6 (1862): 357–406, 7 (1863): 1–71; M. Schouten, *Minahasa and Bolaangmongondow: An Annotated Bibliography (1800–1942)* (1981).

Jan A. B. Jongeneel

Schweitzer, Albert (1875–1965), medical doctor in Gabon. Schweitzer was born in Kayserberg, German Alsace (a region later ceded to France), son of a Lutheran pastor. He attended the universities of Strasbourg, Paris, and Berlin. Before age 30 he had earned doctorates in philosophy, theology, and music and was an ordained minister, a professor at Strasbourg, and a renowned organist.

Schweitzer began studying medicine in 1906, vowing to devote the rest of his life to serving others. After marrying Helene Bresslau in 1912, in 1913 he completed an M.D. degree and the couple embarked for Lambarene on the Ogowe River in Gabon, West Africa. There he founded a hospital in association with the Paris Evangelical Missionary Society but with funds raised privately. By mutual consent he was never a regularly appointed missionary of that agency or any other.

In 1917 the Schweitzers were interned in France as German civilian prisoners of war. They remained in Europe until 1924, mainly because of Mrs. Schweitzer's precarious health. Schweitzer returned alone to Lambarene in 1924. From 1927 to 1929 he was again in Europe raising support for his hospital. Thereafter, until his death at age 90, he spent most of the time at Lambarene, returning to Europe only for brief periods of fund-raising. He received numerous awards, including the Nobel Peace Prize in 1953. Reverence for all life became the major focus of his philosophy.

Schweitzer was a product of the colonial mentality, believing that nothing could be safely left to Africans to do by themselves. Focusing as he did on the work of his hospital, he did not give attention to the preparation of indigenous people for leadership. Nevertheless, George Seaver, one of his biographers, called Schweitzer "probably the most gifted genius of our age."

BIBLIOGRAPHY Schweitzer's many books include *On the Edge of the Primeval Forest* (1929), *The Forest Hospital at Lambarene* (1931), *Out of My Life and Thought* (1933), *Memoirs of Childhood and Youth* (1949), all translated by C. T. Compton, and *The Quest of the Historical Jesus* (1964), translated by W. Montgomery. James Brabazon, *Albert Schweitzer: A Biography* (1975) is the most complete assessment of Schweitzer's life.

Norman A. Horner

Scofield, C(yrus) I(ngerson) (1843–1921), missions advocate and promoter of dispensational premillennialism. Scofield was born in Michigan but grew up in Tennessee. He fought for the Confederacy during the Civil War, studied law in Saint Louis, Missouri, and then moved to Kansas in 1869. He served there as a state legislator and U.S. district attorney but experienced drinking and marital problems. He was converted, however, and in 1879 began work with the YMCA in Saint Louis. There he learned dispensational theology under James H. Brookes, a prominent early advocate. Scofield pastored Congregational churches in Dallas, Texas (1882–1895), Northfield, Massachusetts (1895–1903), and Dallas again (1903–1905); thereafter he devoted all his time to speaking and writing. His publications, notably *Rightly Dividing the Word of Truth* (1882), a Bible correspondence course (1890–1915), and the *Scofield Reference Bible* (1909), became the most powerful propagators of dispensational premillennialism in America.

Scofield was a regional superintendent of Congregational home missions in the 1880s, but his vision for foreign missions grew after he met James Hudson *Taylor, founder of the China Inland Mission, in 1888. In 1890 Scofield organized the Central American Mission, which placed thirty-nine missionaries in five countries by 1920. In 1914 Scofield cofounded the Philadelphia School of the Bible, which produced nearly a hundred missionaries in its first 20 years.

BIBLIOGRAPHY J. M. Canfield, *The Incredible Scofield and His Book* (1988); Mildred W. Spain, *And in Samaria* (1954; recounts the history of the Central American Mission); Charles G. Trumbull, *The Life Story of C. I. Scofield* (1920).

Joel Carpenter

Scott, David Clement Rufelle (1853–1907), Scottish missionary in Malawi and Kenya. An outstanding student in arts and divinity at University of Edinburgh, Scott was ordained in 1881 and sent immediately to Blantyre, Malawi, as head of the Church of Scotland Mission (CSM). Scott had, in effect, to restart the mission, as all the staff had either resigned or been dismissed. A brilliant linguist, he established a rarely paralleled closeness with African people. His profound grasp of African culture can be seen in the columns of his seminal *Cyclopedic Dictionary of the Cimang'anja Language.* Scott resigned in 1898, saddened by the death of his brother, his first wife, and her brother (all in 1895 of blackwater fever), and then of the infant daughter of his second wife. He was also dismayed by the decision of the church authorities in Scotland to side with his white settler critics. However, he left behind the beautiful church of St. Michael and a large band of devoted African converts who became the leaders of the future Blantyre Synod of the Church of Central Africa Presbyterian.

In 1901 Scott went to Kikuyu, Kenya, to head the CSM there, which also needed a fresh start. Scott was unable to repeat his Blantyre miracle and most of his efforts came to nothing. However, his ability to relate to African people did enable him to attract to the mission a number of outstanding Kikuyu people, including Mzee Jomo Kenyatta, later first president of independent Kenya.

BIBLIOGRAPHY The bulk of the material in the periodical *Life and Work in British Central Africa* was written by Scott in the years 1886 to 1898. See also Andrew C. Ross, "The Origins and Development of the Church of Scotland Mission, Blantyre, Nyasaland" (Ph.D. diss., Edinburgh Univ., 1968); Kenneth Ross, "Vernacular Translation in Christian Mission: The Case of David Clement Scott and the Blantyre Mission," *Missionalia* 21 (1993): 5–18.

Andrew C. Ross

Scott, George (1804–1874), pioneer Wesleyan Methodist missionary and renewer of Swedish church life. Born in Edinburgh, the son of a tailor, Scott had little formal education. Initially a member of the Church of Scotland, he became a Methodist in 1827. In July 1830 he was ordained to serve as a Wesleyan Methodist missionary to Stockholm, Sweden. His duties at first did not extend beyond the tiny group of Wesleyans already active there, which was all that Swedish conventicle law permitted. Soon, however, his connections with the British community widened his influence. In 1839 he formed a Wesleyan society, which was not a success, his impact on the national Church of Sweden being far greater. Many of his associates, among them the Baptist pioneer F. O. Nilsson, the evangelist Carl Olof Rosenius, and the Saami (Lapp) missionary Carl Ludwig *Tellström, were also leaders in the evangelical revival in Scandinavia. Scott, moreover, was an active promoter of overseas missions, a temperance worker, and a Sunday-school educator. The Swedish Missionary Society (Svenska Missionssällskapet) was founded in 1835 largely because of his enthusiasm.

There was a populist, political dimension to Scott's activities, however, and he was unable to avoid its intrigues. On Palm Sunday 1842 an anti-Scott demonstration in Stockholm forced him to leave Sweden. He spent the remainder of his life as a Wesleyan minister in various parts of England and his native Scotland. His role in promoting the cause of missions in Sweden is little known in the English-speaking world.

BIBLIOGRAPHY G. G. Findlay and W. W. Holdsworth, *The History of the Wesleyan Methodist Missionary Society,* vol. 4 (1924); Bengt Sundkler, *Svenska Missionssällskapet, 1835–1876* (1937); Gunnar Westin, *George Scott och hans verksamhet i Sverige* (George Scott and his work in Sweden), 2 vols. (1928–1929).

Eric J. Sharpe

Scott, Michael (1907–1983), Anglican priest and campaigner for justice issues. Scott, the son of a priest, was ordained in England in 1930. After some years of home ministry in which he became closely linked with the Communist Party, he went to India in 1937, where he combined work as chaplain to the bishop of Bombay with undercover work for Communism. Only slowly did he decide that while he shared many of its aims, the party's methods were unacceptable. From 1943 to 1950 he worked in the Johannesburg diocese of South Africa and was involved in numerous anti-racist campaigns. He was then declared a prohibited immigrant. By this time his principal concern had switched to Namibia and he represented the chiefs of the Heroro for many years at the United Nations in a campaign against incorporation of this U.N. Trust Territory into the Republic of South Africa. In 1952 he helped found the Africa Bureau in London to disseminate accurate information about the continent and its needs. Later, from 1964 to 1966, he devoted himself to a Nagaland Peace Mission.

Scott was a gentle, peace-loving person with a restless soul, a horror of injustice, and a determination to fight against it, cost him what it might. Though he was unmarried, poor, and unsupported by his church, his considerable achievements depended upon his passionate sincerity, perseverance, and the capacity to make friends across racial barriers.

BIBLIOGRAPHY Michael Scott, *Attitude to Africa* (1951), *A Time to Speak* (1958; autobiography), and *The Nagas in Search of Peace* (1966). Freda Troup, *In Face of Fear: Michael Scott's Challenge to South Africa* (1950).

Adrian Hastings

Scott, Peter Cameron (1867–1896), founder of the Africa Inland Mission (AIM). Scott's family emigrated from Glasgow, Scotland, to Philadelphia in 1879, where Scott took voice training and aspired to a career on the stage. Turning from a path his parents and his conscience disapproved, he enrolled in A. B. *Simpson's training college in Nyack, New York, and in 1890 sailed for West Africa under Simpson's International Missionary Alliance. Within months, his brother, John, who had joined him, succumbed to fever, and Scott rededicated himself over the grave. Suffering from parasites, he recuperated in England. Praying in Westminster Abbey at the tomb of David *Livingstone, he envisioned a new thrust into the interior from the eastern side of the continent, with stations in the highlands, where the gospel was not yet represented and Europeans and Americans might escape the deadly maladies.

In 1895 Scott, A. T. *Pierson, C. E. *Hurlburt, and others met in Philadelphia and founded AIM as a nondenominational "faith mission," along with the Central American Industrial Mission and the Philadelphia Bible Institute. Hurlburt became head of the Bible institute and of AIM's home office. With six others (including his sister Margaret) and a seventh who joined the team en route, Scott sailed in August 1895 for Zanzibar and Mombasa. The men of the party lost no time in setting out for the interior of what is now Kenya, establishing the first station at Nzawi, 250 miles from the coast. A second group of recruits, including Scott's parents and his sister Ina, soon joined the pioneers, and Scott's first annual report claimed four stations established and various ministries well under way. However, in the course of traveling 2,600 miles on foot, fevers and dysentery weakened the pioneers, and Scott succumbed to blackwater fever. Without his leadership, disillusionment and resignations quickly decimated the mission. It fell to Hurlburt, who arrived in East Africa with his family in 1901, to turn Scott's dream into reality.

BIBLIOGRAPHY Dick Anderson, *We Felt Like Grasshoppers* (1994); C. S. Miller, *Peter Cameron Scott: The Unlocked Door* (1955); Kenneth Richardson, *A Garden of Miracles* (1968)

Robert T. Coote

Scranton, Mary F. (1832–1909), founder of Ewha Haktang (Institute) in 1886, now Ewha Woman's University in Seoul. Scranton was a pioneer American Methodist missionary, a widow who went to Korea in 1885. Starting Ewha Haktang with one female student, she emphasized evangelistic and educational work for women. She started the Sang Dong Church in Seoul in 1894. She was the first chair of the Korean Woman's Conference for Methodist women. Receiving royal support from the queen, Min, she expanded her evangelistic and educational work to many regions such as Soowon and Iechon. She had a vision for modern education and for cross-cultural mission for Korean women, who led secluded lives based on Korean traditional religions. Her life was in harmony with her missionary work, and thus her witness to the gospel bore fruit. Her first student and convert, Lee Kyung-Sook, described her as a compassionate woman who worked with endless zeal. She died in Korea, and her funeral in the Sang Dong Church was attended by many students and members of the church whom she had led to Christ.

BIBLIOGRAPHY Mary Scranton wrote about her early work in *Korea Repository* (1885–1909). Mary Hillman, *Korea Mission Field* 6, no. 1 (1910); *Fifty Years of Light: Woman's Foreign Missionary Society of the Methodist Episcopal Church* (1938); Charles A. Sawer, *Within the Gate* (1934), pp. 23–29.

Chun Chae Ok

Scranton, William Benton (1856–1922), American Methodist medical missionary in Korea. Born in New Haven, Connecticut, Scranton graduated from Yale University in 1878 and the New York College of Physicians and Surgeons in 1882. After two years as a doctor in Cleveland, Ohio, he volunteered for Korea as a Methodist missionary. He was ordained (apparently without seminary training) and with his wife and mother was part of the first group of Methodist missionaries sent to Korea. The Scrantons arrived in Japan in March 1885. Because of the uncertain political situation, in May Scranton went alone to Korea, at the invitation of Horace *Allen, a Presbyterian doctor, who had been granted permission by the king of Korea to open a hospital. Scranton's wife and mother, and his Methodist colleagues the *Appenzellers, were able to join him in June. By the end of the first year, property had been purchased for a hospital.

Scranton was active in evangelism and church planting in addition to his medical practice. He was a member of the Bible translation committee and translated into Korean Romans and parts of James, Genesis, Exodus, and Psalms. He resigned from the Methodist mission in 1907 in order to engage in medical education under the Korean government.

BIBLIOGRAPHY Daniel M. Davies, *The Life and Thought of Henry Gerhard Appenzeller, 1858–1902* (1988); Everett N. Hunt, Jr., *Protestant Pioneers in Korea* (1980); Martha Huntley, *To Start a Work: The Foundations of Protestant Mission in Korea, 1884–1919* (1987); L. George Paik, *The History of Protestant Missions in Korea, 1832–1910* (1929, 1970); Charles D. Stokes, "History of Methodist Missions in Korea, 1885–1930" (Ph.D. diss., Yale Univ., 1947).

Everett N. Hunt, Jr.

Scudder, Ida Sophia (1870–1960), medical missionary in India. Born in India, Scudder was a granddaughter of the first American medical missionary and daughter of Dr. John *Scudder, who with his seven sons all became missionaries. Graduating from Northfield Seminary in Massachusetts, she returned to visit her parents in India, determined never to become one of "those missionary Scudders." Here in 1894 she received her call, that famous "three knocks in the night," when three young women died in childbirth because there had been no woman doctor to treat them. Graduating from Cornell University Medical School in the first class open to women, for two years she treated woman patients in her father's bungalow in Vellore, South India; then in 1902 she moved into Schell Hospital, built with money she herself had raised in America. She performed her first operation with no helper but the butler's wife, yet in time she became noted as a surgeon. By 1906 the number of patients she treated annually had risen to 40,000.

Scudder began training nurses, an almost unheard-of procedure in Asia. Her nursing school grew to become the first graduate school of nursing in India, affiliated with Madras University. In 1909 she started her famous roadside dispensaries, a ministry to patients in surrounding villages that expanded through the years to treat thousands each week, developing finally into Vellore's Rural Unit for Health and Social Affairs, administering public health service to a vast area.

Never satisfied, in 1918, with the help of women of many denominations, she founded a college to train women doctors. Beginning with seventeen girls, all taught by herself, it grew into a great complex of buildings in a beautiful valley, graduating thousands of skilled, dedicated doctors. In 1923, again with the support of many denominations, she built a larger hospital in the center of Vellore. Faced with new regulations by the Indian government that threatened to end her work, in 1941 she traveled the length and breadth of the United States raising money, enlisting new leadership with advanced degrees, securing the necessary upgrading of both college and hospital. Both were now open to men as well as women.

During her lifetime she saw her medical center become one of the largest in all Asia, the departments multiply to include radiation-oncology under her niece and namesake, Dr. Ida B. Scudder, thoracic surgery, nephrology, leprosy surgery and rehabilitation under Dr. Paul *Brand, microbiology, rural work, mental health, ophthalmology, and many others—a list of "firsts" in India commensurate with her abounding energy, indomitable will, and consecrated purpose. She died in Vellore.

BIBLIOGRAPHY Carol E. Jameson, *Be Thou My Vision* (1983); M. Pauline Jeffrey, *Ida S. Scudder of Vellore, India* (1951); Dorothy Jealous Scudder, *A Thousand Years in Thy Sight: The Story of the Scudder Missionaries in India* (1984); Dorothy Clarke Wilson, *Dr. Ida* (1959; German tr., *Doktor Ida,* 1962; French tr., *Docteur Ida,* 1971), *Dr. Ida, Passing on the Torch of Life* (1976), and "Ida S. Scudder," in Gerald H. Anderson et al., eds., *Mission Legacies* (1994), pp. 307-315.

Dorothy Clarke Wilson

Scudder, John (1793-1855), pioneer American physician and evangelist in Ceylon (Sri Lanka) and India. Scudder was born in Freehold, New Jersey, and was educated at the College of New Jersey (1811) and the College of Physicians and Surgeons, New York (1813). He established a successful medical practice in New York, and in 1816 married Harriet Waterbury. He sailed for Ceylon in 1819 as the first medical missionary of the American Board of Commissioners for Foreign Missions (ABCFM). Stationed among the Tamils of the Jaffna peninsula, he was ordained by fellow missionaries in 1821 and launched a ministry of intensive evangelism together with a hospital, day and boarding schools, and training of medical students. In 1836 Scudder was transferred to Madras, from where he did extensive touring. He spent 1842 to 1846 on health furlough in the United States, where he promoted missions with great success. Returning to India, he worked three years at Madura, then at Madras until 1854, when he went to South Africa on health leave, where he died.

Scudder published many tracts in Tamil and English. Immensely dedicated and energetic, he would stand for 11 hours at a time in the Indian sun, preaching and distributing literature. Scudder's heritage includes seven missionary sons and two daughters. The great Medical College and Hospital at Vellore, India, was founded by his granddaughter Ida S. *Scudder.

BIBLIOGRAPHY Rufus Anderson, *Missions of the ABCFM in India* (1875), chaps. 11 and 12; Fred F. Goodsell, *They Lived Their Faith* (1961), pp. 189-191; Dorothy J. Scudder, *A Thousand Years in Thy Sight: The Story of the Scudder Missionaries of India* (1934); J. B. Waterbury, *Memoir of the Rev. John Scudder, M.D.* (1870).

David M. Stowe

Seagrave, Gordon S(tifler) (1897-1965), missionary surgeon in Burma. Son of American Baptist missionaries in Burma, Seagrave was born in Rangoon. He graduated from Denison University, Granville, Ohio, in 1917 and completed his M.D. degree from the medical school of Johns Hopkins University in 1921. He married Marion Grace Morse in 1920, and the couple sailed for Burma with their infant daughter in 1922 under appointment by the American Baptist Foreign Mission Board. He established a hospital among the Karens at Namkahn in the Shan States bordering on China. With limited funds and discarded medical supplies, but with remarkable energy and imagination, he performed what he termed "waste-basket surgery" and trained a competent staff of Karen nurses.

In 1942 Seagrave joined the U.S. Army Medical Corps to serve the Chinese Fifth Army through the Burma Campaign. From 1945 to 1946 he was chief medical officer for the Shan States of Burma with the British government. In 1950 he was arrested by the government of Burma on political charges, tried by a special tribunal, and sentenced to six years' imprisonment. The Burmese high court ordered his release, however, and he returned to work at the Namkahn hospital. Beginning in 1953 Seagrave served as president of the American Medical Center for Burma Frontier Areas, Inc., with headquarters at Namkahn, Burma. He died in Redlands, California, his home in retirement.

BIBLIOGRAPHY Gordon S. Seagrave, *Waste-Basket Surgery* (1930), *Tales of a Waste-Basket Surgeon* (1938), *Burma Surgeon* (1943), *Burma Surgeon Returns* (1946), and *My Hospital in the Hills* (1955).

Norman A. Horner

Sedat, William (1909-1971) *and*
Elizabeth (Ruslin) (1914-), Church of the Nazarene missionaries in Guatemala. Born in Nurnischken, Germany, of devout Lutheran parents, William Sedat came to the United States in 1929 and graduated from National Bible Institute (later Shelton College, New York City). He subsequently received training with the Summer Institute of Linguistics for translation work and moved to Guatemala to associate with Wycliffe Bible Translators. In 1936 he began to live among the Kekchi Indians of Guatemala, for whom he developed both alphabet and dictionary.

Elizabeth Rusling was adopted into a missionary-minded home in San Diego and received a B.A. degree from California's Scripps College in 1936, after which she became a missionary for the Church of the Nazarene assigned to Guatemala, where she met William Sedat. They were married in 1940 and served as missionary teachers and Bible translators for the Church of the Nazarene. A Kekchi dictionary and grammar written by the Sedats were published by the Guatemala government in 1961; the Kekchi New Testament translation was published in 1967. At his death in San Francisco in 1971, William Sedat was working on a grammar of the Pokomchi language and had begun translation of the Pokomchi New Testament. Elizabeth Sedat continued this work and completed the Pokomchi New Testament (published in 1983). She served as a missionary in Guatemala for 13 years following her husband's death.

BIBLIOGRAPHY J. Fred Parker, *Mission to the World* (1988); Lorraine Schultz, *Bringing God's Word to Guatemala: The Life and Work of William and Betty Sedat* (1995). Various personal papers and documents are held in the Nazarene archives, Kansas City, Mo.

Robert H. Scott

Segovia, John of. *See* John of Segovia.

Segura, Juan Baptista (1529–1571), leader of a group of Catholic missionaries in Virginia. Segura was born in Toledo, Spain, and received his master of arts at the University of Alcalá, where he entered the Jesuits in 1556. Ordained a priest in 1557, he was rector of the colleges at Villímar, near Burgos, Monterrey, and Valladolid. In September 1567 he was named vice-provincial of a new Jesuit mission in Florida and arrived in St. Augustine in June 1568. Unsuccessful in establishing missions away from Spanish settlements, he sought a new mission field on Chesapeake Bay in Virginia, to which Don Luis, an Indian who was captured as a boy and educated in Spain, offered to lead him. In August 1570 Segura, with Don Luis, another priest, six brothers, and the young son of a Florida settler, set out from St. Elena, Florida. In September the missionaries landed at a site, probably on the James River near the future Jamestown, but then established their settlement across the peninsula on the York River. Don Luis, however, abandoned the mission to assume leadership of his people. In January 1571 he killed three Jesuit emissaries from Segura. On February 9 he led a raiding party to the mission, where Segura and the remaining missionaries were slain. (The young settler's son was spared and later rescued.) With Segura's death, the Jesuits abandoned Florida to concentrate their efforts in Mexico.

BIBLIOGRAPHY Clifford M. Lewis and Albert J. Loomie, *The Spanish Jesuit Mission in Virginia, 1570–1572* (1953).

Gerald P. Fogarty, SJ

Sell, Edward (1839–1932), Church Missionary Society (CMS) missionary in India. Educated at the CMS Islington college, London, Sell was later awarded the Lambeth B.D. (1881) and the Edinburgh D.D. (1907). In 1874 he became a fellow of Madras University. Between 1865 and 1881 he served as principal of Harris High School for Muslims, Madras, where he developed particular interest in Islam. Among other responsibilities, he was examining chaplain for the bishop of Madras, a canon at the Madras Cathedral (from 1889), and CMS secretary for Madras and Travancore. A prolific writer, Sell clearly made his primary vocation a literary one. He established the Society for the Propagation of Christian Knowledge press at Madras and edited the Islam series for the Christian Literature Society. His *Faith of Islam* (1880) established as axiomatic among missionary scholars that "to know [Islam] aright, one should know its literature and live among its people." Sell befriended and encouraged missionaries to Muslims from many different churches and societies. He was elected a member of the Royal Asiastic Society, and it is said that a letter addressed simply "Canon Edward Sell, Orientalist, London" once reached him safely in Madras. In 1906 he received the prestigious Kaiser-i-Hind gold medal, awarded on recommendation of the British government of India. When he died, Sell had served with CMS in India for 67 years.

BIBLIOGRAPHY Edward Sell, *Islam: Its Rise and Progress* (1906), *The Historical Development of the Quran* (1909), and *The Life of Muhammad* (1913).

Clinton Bennett

Selwyn, G(eorge) A(ugustus) (1809–1878), first Anglican bishop of New Zealand. Selwyn was born at Hampstead, London, educated at Eton and Cambridge, and ordained a priest in the Church of England in 1834. While not a Tractarian, he sympathized with some of their "high church" principles. Consecrated bishop of New Zealand in 1841, he helped revive synodical government and encouraged lay participation. Selwyn contributed to the growing sense of pan-Anglicanism, participating in the first Lambeth Conference in 1867 and serving as corresponding secretary for the Anglican Communion until his death.

Selwyn began the Melanesian mission in 1849 using a novel missionary strategy. Young men and later young women were brought from Melanesia to New Zealand for a period of education. They were returned to their home islands, where, it was hoped, they would become evangelists—although little success was achieved in the early years. Selwyn was caught between trying to serve the missionary-founded Maori church and the colonial settlements. Theological differences between the evangelical Church Missionary Society missionaries and Selwyn were exacerbated by tensions over his authority and the independence of the missionaries. Selwyn's bold plans for a multilevel, multiracial educational institution at St. John's College were never fully realized, in part because of missionary opposition. He was criticized for his slowness in ordaining Maori clergy. At the same time his support for Maori rights made him enemies among the colonial population. During the New Zealand wars of the 1860s, he acted as a chaplain to the British troops, thereby losing respect and influence among many Maori who rejected "missionary Christianity" in favor of their own religious movements.

Selwyn returned to England in 1868 as bishop of Lichfield. Throughout his ministry he was supported by his wife, Sarah Harriet Selwyn. Their second son, John Richardson Selwyn, was the second missionary bishop of Melanesia.

BIBLIOGRAPHY Allan K. Davidson, *Selwyn's Legacy: The College of St. John the Evangelist, Te Waimate and Auckland, 1843–1992, A History* (1993); John H. Evans, *Churchman Militant: George Augustus Selwyn, Bishop of New Zealand and Lichfield* (1964); David Hilliard, *God's Gentlemen: A History of the Melanesian Mission, 1849–1942* (1978); Warren E. Limbrick, ed., *Bishop Selwyn in New Zealand, 1841–1868* (1983); H. W. Tucker, *Memoir of the Life and Episcopate of George Augustus Selwyn, D.D., Bishop of New Zealand, 1841–1869; Bishop of Lichfield, 1867–1878*, 2 vols. (1879). The largest collection of Selwyn's papers are at Selwyn College, Cambridge, and are available on microfilm through the Australian Joint Copying Project.

Allan K. Davidson

Serampore Trio. The popular shorthand term used by mission promoters and historians to refer to the close partnership of William *Carey, Joshua *Marshman, and William *Ward, who codirected the Serampore Mission in Bengal between 1800 and 1823.

A. Christopher Smith

Seravia, Adrian. *See* Saravia, Adrianus.

Sergeant, John (1710–1749), pioneer American Congregational missionary to Native Americans. Born in Norwalk, New Jersey, Sergeant graduated from Yale in 1729 and served as a tutor at Yale from 1731 to 1735. In 1735 he was commissioned by the Boston branch of the Society in London for Propagating the Gospel in New England to serve as a missionary among Native Americans in Massachusetts and New York. The two major centers of his work were Sheffield, New York, and Stockbridge, Massachusetts. He worked mainly among the Housatonics, or River Indians, in Stockbridge, where the mission house is still preserved as a museum. At various times, Mohawks and Kaunaumeeks also came under his influence there. During his tenure among the Housatonics, Sergeant translated parts of the Bible into their language. It is reported that he baptized more than a hundred Indians into the Christian faith. Although he enjoyed some success in the work, his primary significance is seen in the people he influenced. He trained David *Brainerd in the language of the Indians during the year 1742. Later, from 1743 to 1747, he employed Jonathan *Edwards in the ministry among Indians at Stockbridge.

BIBLIOGRAPHY Jonathan Edwards, ed., *An Account of the Life of Rev. David Brainerd* (1749) and Iain H. Murray, *Jonathan Edwards: A New Biography* (1987) both contain material on Sergeant.

Wayne A. Detzler

Sergii of Valaam (*or* Valamo) (14th cent.?), missionary evangelist in northwestern Russia. Sergii, in all probability, was a Greek monk who in 1329 cofounded, with St. German, the Preobrazhenskii (Transfiguration) monastery on Valaam Island, in Ladoga Lake. He is credited with the conversion of many Finns and Korels, including pagan priests. On the place of their shrine he built a church, laboring as a mason, an architect, and an artist. A legend found in the ancient *Opoved* manuscript in the monastery's library places Sergii in the company of the apostle Andrew. Another tradition features him as a contemporary of Princess Olga (10th cent.), who baptized a local chieftain, Mung. Fanciful as these accounts may be, they reflect the high regard in which Sergii was held. He was canonized in 1819, and his commemoration days are June 28 and September 11 in the Julian calendar.

BIBLIOGRAPHY Ignatii, *Valaamskii Monastyr* (Valaam Monastery) (1856); Taisia (Solopova), *Zhitiya Svyatykh* (The lives of Russian saints) (1983, 1991).

Evgeny S. Steiner

Serra, Junípero (Miguel Jose) (1713–1784), Franciscan missionary to Mexico and California. Born on the island of Majorca, Serra was received into the Franciscan Order in 1730 and later, probably in 1738, was ordained to the priesthood. He soon began lecturing in philosophy and in 1744, after obtaining a doctorate in theology, was appointed to the chair of theology at the Lullian University in Palma. In 1749 he left Majorca to join the Franciscan missions in Mexico. Soon after his arrival in Mexico City, he volunteered to work in the Sierra Gorda missions. There he learned the language of the indigenous people, became an effective preacher, and promoted the Franciscan approach to mission, which saw each mission as both a religious and an economic reality. He returned to Mexico City in 1758 to assume various positions of authority and service at the Franciscan college of San Fernando.

In 1769 Serra enthusiastically volunteered to join the Spanish expedition to Upper California. In July he arrived at San Diego, where he founded his first mission. Under his leadership eight other missions were established. The spiritual care of four presidios and two civilian pueblos also came under the care of the Franciscans during his presidency. With the Mission of St. Charles Borromeo in Carmel serving as his headquarters, he traveled constantly, visiting the mission establishments under his care. In California he continued the style of mission to which he was accustomed in Mexico. Missions were to be centers of evangelization as well as agriculture and trade. Serra impressed his contemporaries with his purposefulness, energy, and ability to endure hardship. He was beatified by Pope *John Paul II on September 25, 1988. His feast is celebrated on July 1. His statue stands in the Statuary Hall of the U.S. Capitol. He was buried in the mission church at Carmel.

BIBLIOGRAPHY Maynard Geiger, *The Life and Times of Fray Junípero Serra, OFM*, 2 vols. (1959); Francisco Pálou, *Pálou's Life of Fray Junípero Serra*, Maynard Geiger, ed. and tr. (1955); Antonine Tibesar, *Writings of Junípero Serra*, 4 vols. (1955–1966).

William E. McConville, OFM

Seumois, André (1917–), Catholic missiologist. Born in Belgium at Flémalle-Grande, Liège, Seumois entered the Missionary Oblates of Mary Immaculate in 1935. He studied missiology at the Institute of the Propaganda Fide

Athenaeum, in Rome, obtaining a doctorate in 1948; in 1951 he received the master of arts from the University of Ottawa, Canada. He was appointed professor of missiology at the newly established Institute of Missionary Sciences at the University of Ottawa, where he taught from 1948 to 1951. In 1952 he was appointed visiting professor for the course on introduction to missiology at the Scientific Missionary Institute of the Propaganda Fide Athenaeum, and the following year, he was put in charge of the program. In 1959 Pope *John XXIII appointed him consultant to the Congregation for the Evangelization of Peoples, in 1960 a member of the committee for missions for the preparation of Vatican II, and in 1962 peritus (consultant) for the council. In 1969 he became professor of missiology at the Urban University, Rome, where he taught until he retired in 1987. From 1974 to 1977 he was dean of the faculty of missiology and a member of the senate of the university. He took part in the 1981 Plenary Session of the Congregation for the Evangelization of Peoples.

BIBLIOGRAPHY André Seumois, *Vers une définition de l'activité missionnaire* (1948; also in German, 1948), *L'introduction à la missiologie* (1952; Spanish, 1960), *La Papauté et les missions au cours des six premier sièles: Méthologie antique et orientations modernes* (1953), *L'Anima dell'apostolato missionario* (1958), *Apostolat: Structure Théologique* (1961; Spanish, 1968), *Oecuménisme missionnaire* (1970), *Théologie Missionnaire,* 5 vols. (1973–1981), and *Teologia missionaria* (1993). A Festschrift for Seumois is *Chiesa e inculturazione nella missione* (1987).

Willi Henkel, OMI

Severinus (d. 482), Apostle of Austria. From a German noble family, Severinus first became a monk somewhere in the East. He arrived in Noricum Riponse (modern Austria) after Attila's death but at a period when the Huns were still in the region. In 453 or 454 he led a Catholic community in Favianis, one distinguished from the Arians. He gave himself to relief work that led to the conversion of King Odocer and brought respite from persecution to Catholic Christians. Although he was never a bishop, he encouraged the churches in the area and founded monasteries at Göttweig and Bojotro.

BIBLIOGRAPHY Rajko Bratož, *Severinus von Noricum und seine Zeit* (1983); *Eugippius: The Life of Saint Severin,* Ludwig Bieler with Ludmilla Kerstan, trs., *The Fathers of the Church* 55 (1965); Klemens Kramert and Ernest K. Winter, *St. Severinus: Der Heilige zwischen Ost und West,* 2 vols. (1958–1959); Friedrich Lotter, *Severinus von Noricum, Legende und historische Wirklichkeit* (1976).

Frederick W. Norris

Seward, Sarah Cornelia (1833–1891), physician and Presbyterian missionary in India. Seward, born in Florida, New York, was the daughter of George W. and Tempe Wicke (Leddel) Seward, and the sister of George F. Seward (later, United States Consul General in Beijing, China). She attended the Woman's Medical College of Pennsylvania, in Philadelphia (now Allegheny University of the Health Sciences). In 1871 she was sent to Allahabad, India, as a medical missionary with the Woman's Union Missionary Society (WUMS). Under WUMS, Seward's practice with women flourished. She opened the first medical dispensary in Allahabad in 1872. The following year she transferred her connection to the Board of Foreign Missions of the Presbyterian Church, U.S.A., but she remained in Allahabad to continue her work. Under the Presbyterian board, Seward expanded her practice and was soon operating two mud-floor dispensaries. In 1890 a new building was erected in the center of the city. During the first year of operation, medical staff at the new facility treated 3,738 patients. Following a brief furlough to New York in 1889, Seward contracted cholera and died in Allahabad. Her medical work led to construction of the Sarah Seward Hospital in 1893 in Allahabad and a network of forty-four well-equipped dispensaries by 1904.

BIBLIOGRAPHY "Sarah C. Seward," *Woman's Medical College of Pennsylvania, Alumnae Transactions* 17 (1892): 26–27; "The Woman's Medical Mission at Allahabad," *Medical Missionary Record* 6 (July 1891): 181–182.

Robert Benedetto

Seymour, William Joseph (1870–1922), African American Pentecostal pastor and leader of the Apostolic Faith Mission. Born in Centerville, Louisiana, to former slaves, and raised as a Baptist, Seymour later joined the holiness movement, adopting its belief in entire sanctification and an outpouring of the Holy Spirit before the imminent return of Christ. In 1905 he came into contact with Charles F. *Parham, leader of a Midwestern Pentecostal movement. After embracing Parham's teaching that God would bestow the gift of tongues (i.e. known human languages) on Spirit-baptized believers to expedite world evangelism, he moved to Los Angeles, California. Beginning in April 1906 his band of followers met in a former African Methodist Episcopal church on Azusa Street for prayer and renewal, which led to the launching (also in April 1906) of the Apostolic Faith Mission. News of the Azusa Street revival and restoration of the gifts of the Spirit quickly spread around the world through the pages of *The Apostolic Faith* (Los Angeles 1906–1908), edited by Seymour (with Clara Lum), and also through the ministries of persons who traveled from there across America and overseas.

The uniqueness of this revival, the most influential of the century in terms of global impact, includes its eschatological orientation, spirituality, and interracial and intercultural makeup. Though distancing himself from Parham's insistence on speaking in tongues as evidence of Spirit baptism, Seymour affected the worldwide course of the Pentecostal movement and became revered, especially among African American Pentecostals, for his emphasis on love and reconciliation as a witness of the Holy Spirit.

BIBLIOGRAPHY William J. Seymour, *The Doctrines and Discipline of the Azusa Street Apostolic Faith Mission* (1915). Donald W. Dayton, *Theological Roots of Pentecostalism* (1987); Gary B. McGee, "The Azusa Street Revival and Twentieth-Century Mission," *IBMR* 12 (1988): 58–61; Iain MacRobert, *The Black Roots and White Racism of Early Pentecostalism in the USA* (1988); David J. Nelson, "For Such a Time as This: The Story of Bishop William J. Seymour and the Azusa Street Revival" (Ph.D. diss., Univ. of Birmingham, 1981); Cecil M. Robeck, Jr., "William J. Seymour and 'the Bible Evidence,'" in *Initial Evidence,* Gary B. McGee, ed. (1991).

Gary B. McGee

Shanahan, Joseph (1871–1943), Catholic missionary bishop in eastern Nigeria. Shanahan was born in Glankeen, County Tipperary, Ireland, to Daniel Shanahan, a devout Catholic herdsman, and Margaret Walsh Shanahan. He studied at the Templederry National School, and was trained by the Holy Ghost Fathers in France and Ireland. As a priest he served as a schoolmaster for some years with an eye to missionary work in Africa. The opportunity came in 1902 in the Catholic mission in eastern Nigeria. When he assumed leadership in 1906, he transformed the enterprise by using schools as means for rural evangelization. As bishop in 1920, Shanahan invited the St. Patrick's Order (formerly the Maynooth Brothers) to join the mission, and founded the Holy Rosary Congregation for educational apostolate. A consummate administrator, Shanahan was adventurous, generous, and charismatic. He retired with broken health in 1931, died in Nairobi, but was reburied in Onitsha (1955). Nigerians loved this man and named numerous institutions after him. He had revolutionized education and turned Roman Catholicism into a powerful force for good in the nation, and they called him the Apostle of Light.

BIBLIOGRAPHY Desmond Forristal, *The Second Burial of Bishop Shanahan* (1990); John P. Jordan, *Bishop Shanahan of Southern Nigeria* (1949). Shanahan's papers are in the Holy Ghost archives, Chevilly, Paris, and in the Holy Rosary archives, Dublin.

Ogbu U. Kalu

Sharkey, John Edmund (1821–1867) *and* **Ann Amelia (Nailer)** (1813–1878), Church Missionary Society (CMS) missionaries in South India. John Sharkey was an Anglo-Indian, born in Masulipatan, Andhra Pradesh. He was educated at Daniel *Corrie's School and the Church Missionary Institution in Madras. Like many others of his background, he was employed as a catechist after leaving school and had the good fortune to teach under Robert *Noble. In 1847 he married Ann Amelia Nailer, daughter of a prosperous merchant in Madras. He was also ordained an Anglican deacon, and moved from teaching to pastoral work. Ann Sharkey immediately started a school for girls in Masulipatan. From a small beginning it prospered, and for over 16 years the couple continued as faithful workers in the CMS Telugu mission. In November 1864 a great cyclone and tidal wave devastated the school, and thirty-three of the boarders (out of sixty-six), as well as other members of the mission, were drowned. John Sharkey himself then died three years later, but Ann was enrolled by CMS as a full member and continued her work rebuilding the girls' school until her own death. In 1879 the revived school was named the Sharkey Memorial School in tribute to her.

BIBLIOGRAPHY CMS, *Register of Missionaries and Native Clergy* (1904); M. E. Gibbs, *The Anglican Church in India, 1600–1970* (1972).

Jocelyn Murray

Shattuck, Corinna (1848–1910), American missionary in Turkey. Born in Louisville, Kentucky, Shattuck was orphaned at an early age and brought up by her mother's parents in Massachusetts, where she attended Framingham Normal School and taught school for three years. At age 25 she sailed for Turkey under the American Board of Commissioners for Foreign Missions (ABCFM) and taught at the Girls' Seminary at Aintab (Gaziantep) until 1883, then at the Girls' College at Marash until 1891. From 1892 until her retirement in 1910 she worked at Oorfa (ancient Edessa), 75 miles east of the Euphrates River and three days' journey from the nearest mission station. Alone or with a woman associate, she supervised a network of schools and orphanages and a number of Bible women, while helping and advising in the work of the evangelical churches. In 1895, during mob attacks on Armenians, her presence protected hundreds of men, women, and children in her neighbohood. After the massacre she developed an extensive handicraft industry which trained and supported thousands of widows and orphans; the enterprise imported Irish linen and sold hemstitched handkerchiefs in England and America. She also opened a school for the blind and gave special attention to Bible teaching. Invalided home in 1910, she was taken off the steamer on a stretcher and died two weeks later. Armenians in the Oorfa area raised funds for a monument in the Newton, Massachusetts, cemetery which commemorates her "heroic courage at the Oorfa massacre."

BIBLIOGRAPHY *Missionary Herald* 106 (1910): 312–313 has an extensive obituary, and several issues in vol. 92 (1896) describe the Oorfa massacre and its aftermath. Elizabeth Boyd-Bayly wrote *A Brief Memoir of Ida Mellinger* (Shattuck's missionary colleague) (1899), which includes much material on Shattuck, especially pp. 85–91. Fred Field Goodsell, *They Lived Their Faith* (1961), pp. 171–172, 405–406, has a brief sketch.

David M. Stowe

Shaull, M. Richard (1919–), American Presbyterian missiologist. Born in Felton, Pennsylvania, Shaull received a B.A. from Elizabethtown College (1938), and a B.Th. (1941), a Th.M. (1946), and a Th.D. (1959) from Princeton Theological Seminary. He was ordained to the Presbyterian ministry in 1941 and served for a year as pastor in Wink, Texas. From 1942 until 1950 he and his wife were Presbyterian missionaries in Colombia. They were transferred to Brazil in 1952, where Shaull became professor of church history in the Presbyterian Seminary in Campinas. An ecumenical leader in South America, especially among students, he was elected vice-president of the Mackenzie Institute in São Paulo in 1960, and two years later, returning to the United States, he became professor of ecumenics and mission at Princeton Theological Seminary, a position he occupied until his retirement in 1980.

Few, if any, Protestant missionaries in Latin America have had as profound and widespread an impact theologically and ecumenically. A leader in the World's Student Christian Federation and the North American Congress on Latin America, Shaull was the principal Protestant forerunner of Latin America liberation theology. Beginning in the 1950s, he published a steady stream of books and articles in English, Spanish, and Portuguese, and gave numerous seminars and lectures. His most recent books are *Heralds of a New Reformation* (1984), *Naming the Idols* (1988), and *The Reformation and Liberation Theology* (1991).

BIBLIOGRAPHY Eduardo Galasso Faria, "Richard Shaull, Renovador de Pensamento Teológico Evangélico no Brasil" (Master's thesis, Instituto Metodista de Ensenio Superior, São Bernado do Campo, São Paulo, 1993); Gerd-Dieter Fischer, *Richard Shaulls "Theologie der Revolution": Ihre Theologische und Etische Argumentation auf dem Hintergrund der Situation in Latein America* (1984); Alan Preston Neely, "Protestant Antecedents of the Latin American Theology of Liberation" (Ph.D. diss., American Univ., 1977), pp. 253–268.

Alan Neely

Shaw, Archibald (1879–1956), Church Missionary Society (CMS) missionary in Sudan. Born at Edgbaston, Birmingham, England, Shaw studied at Emmanuel College, Cambridge, and in 1905 was one of a party of five young men sent out under the CMS's Gordon Memorial Sudan Mission to establish the first CMS mission on the Upper Nile. Inadequately prepared for so challenging a land and people, all except Shaw withdrew within 18 months. His dogged perseverance during succeeding decades laid the foundation for the Episcopal Church in southern Sudan. He served as secretary of the mission from 1907 until 1936, and as archdeacon of southern Sudan from 1922 until 1940. Though often understaffed and underfunded, the evangelistic and educational work of the CMS under Shaw's leadership penetrated the vast territories of the Dinka, Zande, Moru, and Bari peoples. His tenacity and courage became legendary not only among Europeans, but also among the Dinka, who remember him affectionately by his Dinka name Macour' (Machuor), taken from the color of the ox he owned. His translations of the Scriptures and worship forms, and his respect for indigenous musical idioms continue to provide inspiration for the Dinka church, which has flourished during the 1980s and 1990s under indigenous leadership. Shaw is buried in Nairobi.

BIBLIOGRAPHY Shaw served as translator and guide for anthropologist C. G. Seligman and with his encouragement published several ethnographic articles, including "Dinka Songs," *Man* 20 (1915): 35–36, "Dinka Animal Stories (Bor Dialect)," *Sudan Notes & Records* 4 (1919): 255–275, and "A Note on Some Nilotic Languages," *Man* 16 (1924): 22–25. See also Marc R. Nikkel, "The Origins and Development of Christianity among the Dinka of Sudan, with Special Reference to the Songs of Dinka Christians" (Ph.D diss., Edinburgh Univ., 1993). Shaw's records and personal correspondence are at the CMS archive, Birmingham Univ. Library (Acc. 111), England.

Marc R. Nikkel

Shaw, Barnabas (1788–1857), founder of Methodism in southern Africa. A devout Methodist Yorkshireman, Shaw was ordained in 1814. He married Jane Butler, and the two left for service in South Africa in 1815. Against the governor's orders, he ministered to the British troops in Cape Town, though he was effectively prevented from ministering to the slaves and other Africans. He therefore sought a field for mission beyond the authority of the governor and founded the first Methodist mission in southern Africa among the Nama of the Kamiesberg Mountains (present-day Langsberg Mountains, on the border with Namibia). There he helped raise the morale of a people already profoundly demoralized and bereft of most of their cattle as a result of contact with whites. Working in Dutch rather than the local language, he developed a growing Christian community. His protégé, Jacob Links, was the first southern African to become an ordained minister of a Christian church. Shaw also aided the Nama in becoming a farming as well as a sheepherding people.

Beginning in 1826, when he again made Cape Town his base of operations, Shaw was the driving force behind the development of Methodism throughout the west of the Cape Colony. In 1837 he was called to England, where he spent his time preaching and lecturing on mission. In 1843 he returned to South Africa as a simple circuit minister, still, however, capable of innovation; he purchased two farms to found model communities for freed slaves. He spent his last years ministering especially to the Cape Coloureds in one of the Cape Town suburbs.

BIBLIOGRAPHY Barnabas Shaw, *Memorials of South Africa* (1840). L. A. Hewson, "Barnabas Shaw: Founder of Methodism in South Africa," *Journal of the Methodist Historical Society of South Africa,* April 1956 (this article contains the fullest listing of sources). The unpublished diary of Shaw is in the Public Records Office, London, File C.O.417, and a collection of letters and journals are in the Methodist Library, Cape Town.

Andrew C. Ross

Shaw, William (1798–1872), the dominant figure in early South African Methodism. Born in Scotland of English parents, Shaw was ordained as a Methodist chaplain to the Sephton party, one of the many organized groups that made up the 1820 English settler movement in the eastern Cape Colony of what is now South Africa. He was appointed to the white settlers but also to further mission among the indigenous peoples. He spent his first three years building up a strong Methodist church in the new settler community, which by 1824 counted twelve congregations. A strong settler church, he insisted, was the essential base for a mission to the African peoples. It was not until 1824 that work began among the neighboring Xhosa-speaking peoples beyond the colonial frontier. By 1830 he had established six stations covering the Xhosa-speaking population, though Methodist success was not primarily among the Xhosa but among the Mfengu refugees driven from their lands by the Zulu. This linking of the settler and mission churches set a course that resulted in twentieth-century Methodism in South Africa being one church. However, in Shaw's lifetime it produced great tension, since too often funds from England were swallowed up in keeping the settler base strong. Also, in the terrible period of bloody conflict with the Xhosa between 1834 and 1852, Shaw appeared as a spokesman of the settlers. However, it was also true that he fought for African education against settler opinion and always criticized gross injustice. Having retired to England in 1856, he was still concerned for South Africa and in 1860 proposed that an autonomous South African Methodist Conference be established, but the Methodist authorities in Britain refused approval. He retired from the active ministry in 1869.

BIBLIOGRAPHY William Shaw, *My Mission in South Eastern Africa* (1860). W. B. Boyce, *Memoir of the Rev. W. Shaw* (1874); L. A. Hewson, *An Introduction to South African Methodists* (1951).

Andrew C. Ross

Shchetkovsky, Khrisanf. *See* Khrisanf (Shchetkovsky).

Shedd, William Ambrose (1865–1918). Presbyterian missionary in Persia (Iran). Shedd was born in Urumia, northwestern Persia, of American Presbyterian parents. He interrupted his education at Marietta College, Ohio, and Princeton Theological Seminary twice by spending a total of five years in Urumia, helping his father and studying the local languages. He finished seminary and was appointed a missionary by the Presbyterian Church (USA) in 1892. Upon arrival in Urumia, he engaged in all phases of the work of the mission, was president of the college, preached, and toured the mountains on evangelistic trips.

Shedd had an increasing influence because of his intellect, knowledge of the people, and devotion to the truth. His leadership was demonstrated in the first Turkish invasion of Urumia in 1915. Thousands of Christians took refuge in mission compounds and were saved from death by the American flag and Shedd's wise diplomacy. Shedd was appointed American vice-consul. As the political situation turned to anarchy, with widespread violence, Shedd held the warring factions at bay. But at the end of July 1918, the entire Syrian Christian community—more than 70,000 people—in order to escape genocide, set forth as refugees in a flight south to British-protected Hamadan and Iraq.

Shedd, although in uncertain health, felt that he could not desert the Christian population, and he and his wife Mary acted as a rear guard of protection to the fleeing refugees. He fell victim to cholera and died beside the road. He was buried in a shallow grave on a rocky mountainside. The Christian refugees finally reached safety at Hamadan. They looked back on Shedd as the savior of their community, and he is remembered as the Moses of the Assyrians.

BIBLIOGRAPHY William Ambrose Shedd, *Islam and the Oriental Churches* (1904). Mary Lewis Shedd, his wife, wrote his biography, *The Measure of a Man* (1922).

R. Park Johnson

Sheen, Fulton J(ohn) (1895–1979) American Catholic bishop and promoter of missions. Born in El Paso, Illinois, Sheen was ordained for the diocese of Peoria, Illinois, in 1919. Though he had an impressive academic background (his dissertation won the prestigious Cardinal Mercier Award) and taught philosophy and theology at the Catholic University of America (1926–1950), he was better known as a popular preacher and "convert maker." In 1930 he began the regular "Catholic Hour" on Sunday evenings on the NBC radio network. In 1950 Sheen was appointed the national director of the Society for the Propagation of the Faith (SPF), where he also edited *World Mission,* the SPF magazine. The following year, he became auxiliary bishop of New York and embarked upon his *Life Is Worth Living* television programs, which were viewed by millions of people of all faiths. Monetary contributions received from this audience provided the majority of American Catholic financial support for the SPF missions while he was national director. He was bishop of Rochester, New York, from 1966 to 1969, when he was appointed titular archbishop of Newport (Wales).

Combining wit, personal charisma, and logic, Sheen emphasized a neo-Thomistic methodology to draw attention to mission needs and to combat communism. He urged the establishment of courses in missiology at Catholic universities. The street in front of St. Agnes Rectory, New York City, which he often visited while he was the SPF national director, bears his name.

BIBLIOGRAPHY *Treasure in Clay* (1980) is Sheen's autobiography. One of his seventy books, *Missions and the World Crisis* (1963), is a collection of his editorials in the SPF *World Mission.* See also John Tracy Ellis, *Catholic Bishops: A Memoir* (1984); and Kathleen Riley Fields, "Bishop Fulton J. Sheen: An American Catholic Response to the Twentieth Century" (Ph.D. diss., Notre Dame University, 1988).

Angelyn Dries, OSF

Shelikhov, Grigorii Ivanovich (1747–1796), manager of the Russian-American Company in Alaska. Born to a merchant family in Rylsk, Russia, Shelikhov went to Siberia to seek his fortune. In 1776 he was part of the first Russian trading expedition to Alaska, and he crossed the Pacific several times before he was put in charge of a permanent settlement on Kodiak. An honorable and dedicated layman, he differed from most of the fur traders who plied those waters by seeking to incorporate the local people peacefully into Russian Orthodox society. On Kodiak, he exhorted the Koniags and Aleuts to accept Christianity and live in the faith they embraced. Returning to Russia in 1787, he implanted in civil and church officials the idea of a religious mission to Alaska and continued his advocacy until eight monks were dispatched by the Holy Synod in 1793. From Irkutsk he sent to Kodiak the agricultural colony needed to support the monks.

BIBLIOGRAPHY G. I. (Grigorii Ivanovich) Shelikhov, *A Voyage to America, 1783–1786* (1981). J. Glazik, *Die russ.-orth. Heidemmission* (1954), pp. 104–108; Richard A. Pierce, ed., *The Russian Orthodox Religious Mission in America, 1794–1837* (1978).

Paul D. Garrett

Shellabear, William Girdlestone (1862–1947), Methodist missionary in Singapore and Malaya. Born and educated in England, Shellabear joined the Methodist Mission in Singapore in 1891 after having served there as an officer in the Royal Engineers. He founded the American Mission Press, which became Methodist Publishing House (MPH) and later Malaya Publishing House. He published numerous works of classical Malay literature in an effort to promote vernacular education and literacy. Especially noteworthy was his critical edition of *The Malay Annals* (1896). In addition to his literary work, he was active in evangelism among Malays and Malay-speaking Chinese and was presiding elder in the Methodist Malaysia Annual Conference from 1896 to 1902. From 1902 until 1909 he worked under appointment to the British and Foreign Bible Society (BFBS), translating the Bible into Malay. From 1911 until 1916 he served as district superintendent of the Methodist Mission while translating evangelistic tracts and textbooks into Malay. He also served as Malay and English book editor for the MPH.

Aware of the failure of missionaries to understand Islam, he began to direct his studies toward Islam and Arabic while in the United States from 1916 to 1920. After his retirement in 1921 due to ill health, he taught Islam, Arabic, and Malay, first at Drew University, then at the Kennedy School of Missions in Hartford, Connecticut. For many years he was an associate editor of *Moslem World* and also helped to edit a revision of the Malay Bible undertaken by the BFBS and the Netherlands Bible Society. In the 1930s and 1940s he published two book-length epic poems in classical Malay style, telling the story of the Bible, and commentaries on each of the Gospels in Malay.

BIBLIOGRAPHY William G. Shellabear, *Practical Malay Grammar* (1899, 3d ed., 1912), *Malay-English Vocabulary* (1902; 3d ed., 1925), "Baba Malay," *Journal of the Straits Branch of the Royal Asiatic Society* 65 (1913): 49–63, "Christian Literature for Malaysia," *Moslem World* 9, no. 4 (1919): 379–384, and "The Gospel for the Malays," *Moslem World* 36, no. 3 (1946): 236–239. Robert A. Hunt, *William Shellabear: A Biography* (1996). Letters and papers of William G. Shellabear are found in the Hartford Seminary archives.

Robert A. Hunt

Shembe, Isaiah Mdliwamafa (1869–1935), Zulu religious leader and founder of the Nazareth Baptist Church. Shembe was born at Ntabamhlophe near Estcourt, Natal, South Africa, of Zulu parentage. After involvement with Wesleyans, he associated with Baptists and was baptized in July 1906. He seems to have acted as an itinerant evangelist prior to coming into contact with Nkabinde, a former Lutheran who was regarded as a prophet. Nkabinde led him to develop a healing ministry in 1910. A year later, he founded the iBandla lamaNazaretha (Nazareth Baptist Church), a controversial religious movement rooted in Zulu tradition. Shortly afterward he acquired a farm that became his holy city of Ekuphakameni and established an annual pilgrimage to the sacred mountain of Nhlangakazi. Shembe was noted for his vivid parables, dramatic healings, and uncanny insights into people's thoughts. He wrote many moving hymns, composed music, and provided his followers with a rich liturgical tradition based on modified forms of traditional Zulu dancing. Critics of the movement claimed that his followers regarded Shembe as the incarnation of God. Others, led by Lutheran scholar Bengt *Sundkler, argued that Shembe's theology was an Africanized form of Christianity.

After Shembe's death a succession conflict occurred before leadership passed to his third wife's son Johannes Galilee Shembe. More serious trouble erupted following J. G. Shembe's death in 1975, when the movement split between his brother, Amos Shembe, and son Londa Shembe. Amos Shembe took the title "bishop" and seems to have led his followers toward orthodox Christianity. Londa Shembe openly admitted that he was unsure whether his movement was Christian, a form of Judaism, or perhaps more closely related to some other religious tradition such as Hinduism. Today there are about one million amaNazaretha in southern Africa.

BIBLIOGRAPHY Irving Hexham, ed., *The Scriptures of the amaNazaretha of Ekuphakameni* (1994); Irving Hexham and G. C. Oosthuizen, eds., *The Oral History and Sacred Traditions of the Nazareth Baptist Church*, 3 vols. (1996–1997); G. C. Oosthuizen, *The Theology of a South African Messiah* (1967); Bengt Sunkler, *Bantu Prophets in South Africa* (1961) and *Zulu Zion and Some Swazi Zionists* (1976); Absalom Vilakazi et al., *Shembe: The Revitalization of African Society* (1986).

Irving Hexham

Shepherd, Robert Henry Wishart (1888–1971), Scottish pastor and educational missionary in South Africa. Shepherd was a missionary of the United Free Church (UFC) (after 1929, the Church of Scotland). He graduated from University of Edinburgh (1915) and New College (1918), was ordained, and married Mary Shearer Goodfellow. Under appointment by the UFC, the Shepherds sailed for South Africa in 1919. Until 1927 he worked as a rural pastor among the Xhosa, then he joined the staff of Lovedale, the most important center of black education in southern Africa. He was first chaplain and director of the press. In 1942 he became the school's fourth and last principal. In 1955 the new Bantu Education Act destroyed the old Lovedale. For 20 years after 1942, Shepherd edited the *South African Outlook* and wrote many pamphlets and books. The most important are *Lovedale, South Africa* (1940) and *A South African Medical Pioneer* (1958). Retiring in 1956, he returned to pastoral ministry in Scotland. He served as moderator of the general assembly of the Church of Scotland in 1959.

BIBLIOGRAPHY Horton Davies and R. H. W. Shepherd, *South African Missions, 1800–1950* (1954); G. C. Oosthuizen, *Shepherd of Lovedale* (1970).

Andrew C. Ross

Sheppard, William H. (1865–1926) *and*
Lucy (Gantt) (1867–c. 1940), African American Presbyterian missionaries to the Congo. Born in Waynesboro,

Virginia, William Sheppard graduated from Stillman Institute, the Southern Presbyterian school for African American ministers in Tuscaloosa, Alabama. While he was serving as a pastor in Atlanta, Georgia, his call to become a missionary to Africa was confirmed by the Presbyterian Church U.S. Committee of Foreign Missions. After a white minister, Samuel M. *Lapsley, also volunteered, in 1890 the two left for the Congo Free State (Zaire). In the remote Kasai region, 1,200 miles from the coast, they established the American Presbyterian Congo Mission. Lapsley died after two years, but their partnership established a pattern of racial collegiality which endured in the mission for three decades. Sheppard's missionary goal was the conversion of both individuals and tribes. He built churches and day schools and established homes for boys and girls rescued from slavery. His early exploration and careful study of the culture of the hitherto xenophobic Bakuba tribe resulted in his being made a fellow of the Royal Geographic Society in London in June 1893. With others he gave international publicity to the cruel exploitations of King Leopold II against the Congolese people. In this connection, he was received at the White House by three presidents. In 1909 Sheppard and his colleague William M. *Morrison were tried in the Congo for libel after publishing an article detailing the forced labor policies and brutal punishments used by the state rubber company in the Kasai. After their acquittal, conditions began to improve. Sheppard lectured widely for missionary and human rights causes and was often featured together with people like Booker T. Washington. Years after his death he came to be recognized for his accurate ethnographic description of African peoples and for his extensive collection of artifacts.

Lucy Gantt graduated from high school and college at Talladega, Alabama. At Talladega College she sang with the famous Jubilee Singers, a touring group that introduced Negro spirituals to the American public in the north. She became engaged to Sheppard in 1886 and taught in Birmingham city schools until they married in 1894, when he was home on furlough. Upon arriving in the Congo, Lucy Sheppard focused on educational work. For example, in 1897 she was principal in Luebo of a school with forty-five students. She wrote the first book ever produced in the Bakuba language, a reading primer published by the mission in 1902, and she was mainly responsible for the first hymnal published in the Bakuba language. After the Sheppards returned to the United States in 1910, they organized the Grace Presbyterian Church in Louisville, Kentucky, and Lucy Sheppard served as a social worker. The Sheppards had four children, two of whom died in the Congo.

BIBLIOGRAPHY Lucy Gantt Sheppard, *From Talladega College to Africa* (n.d.); William H. Sheppard, *Presbyterian Pioneers in Congo* (1917). Harold Cureau, "William H. Sheppard: Missionary to the Congo and Collector of African Art," *The Journal of Negro History,* Winter 1982, p. 343; Julia Kellersberger, *Lucy Gantt Sheppard* (n.d.); William E. Phipps, *The Sheppards and Lapsley: Pioneer Presbyterians in the Congo* (1991); Stanley Shaloff, *Reform in Leopold's Congo* (1970). Additional materials are located at the Department of History, Presbyterian Church (U.S.A.), Montreat, N.C., and at Hampton University archives, Hampton, Va.

John R. Hendrick and Winifred K. Vass

Shih Mei-yu (Shi Meiyu; *or* Mary Stone) (1873–1954), medical doctor in China. Shih Mei-yu's father was a Methodist pastor in Kiukiang (Jiujiang), Kiangsi (Jiangxi), and her mother was the principal of a Methodist school for girls. Having graduated from the Rulison-Fish Memorial School under the guidance of an American missionary, Gertrude *Howe, she left China in 1892 to study medicine at the University of Michigan, where she was also known as Mary Stone. In 1896 she and her friend *K'ang Ch'eng were among the first Chinese women to receive medical degrees from an American university. Upon graduation, she was sent by the Woman's Foreign Missionary Society of the Methodist Episcopal Church as a medical missionary to work in Kiukiang. In 1901, with the support of Dr. Isaac Newton Danforth, she and K'ang Ch'eng established the Elizabeth Skelton Danforth Hospital. For some 20 years, she worked there, taking care of patients, training nurses, and promoting public hygiene. Born into the first generation of girls to have grown up with unbound feet in central China, she was enthusiastic in opposing footbinding. In the 1920s she severed her ties with the Methodist mission and moved to Shanghai, where she established the Bethel Hospital and the Bethel Mission with Jennie V. Hughes.

A prominent women's leader of the Chinese church, Shih served as a member of the China Continuation Committee after the Edinburgh World Missionary Conference of 1910. In 1922 she was elected president of the Women's Christian Temperance Union in China, an organization committed to fighting alcoholism and the use of opium and cigarettes. She spoke frequently on the contribution of Christian women to the development of China. Recognizing the importance of carrying out mission work by the Chinese, she cofounded the Chinese Missionary Society in 1918. This society aimed at supporting and sending Chinese missionaries to work among the Chinese.

BIBLIOGRAPHY Shih's biography can be found in Margaret Burton, *Notable Women of China* (1912). She is the author of "What Chinese Women Have Done and Are Doing for China," *The China Mission Year Book* 5 (1914): 239–245.

Kwok Pui-lan

Shirley, H. A. *See* Schmelzenbach, Harmon Faldean and Lula (Glatzel).

Shreve, Elizabeth (Shadd) (1826–1890), black Baptist missionary advocate in Canada. Born free in Wilmington, Delaware, Shadd was one of several children of Abraham Doras Shadd and Harriet Parnell Shadd. Raised a Roman Catholic and trained by Quakers, Shadd married George Shreve. In 1851, after passage of the fugitive slave law, they joined many other blacks in following the North Star to Canada. There Elizabeth worked with her sister, Mary Shadd, copublisher of the *Provincial Freeman,* and threw herself into the work of settling the influx of black refugees in Buxton, near Chatham, Ontario. She cared for the sick, collected clothing for the needy, delivered food to the hungry, preached, and served as catalyst for nonviolent resistance when efforts were made to return slaves to their owners in the United States.

When in 1864 Mary Shadd returned to the United States, Shreve remained in Canada. In 1867 she joined the Buxton Baptist church. Giving her testimony, she was recognized as a powerful speaker. In 1882 she helped to organize the Women's Home Missionary Society of the Amherstburg Baptist Association. As its first president, she was in great demand as a preacher and evangelist. However, on her last missionary journey, her horse stumbled, and she never recovered from her injuries.

BIBLIOGRAPHY Records of the Amherstburg Association are in the Canadian Baptist archives, Hamilton, Ontario; two books by Dorothy Shadd Shreve, *The Afri-Canadian Church: A Stabilizer* (1983) and *Pathfinders of Liberty and Truth* (1940), provide photographs and accounts of Shreve's life.

Paul R. Dekar

Shuck, J(ehu) Lewis (1814–1863), *and* **Henrietta (Hall)** (1817–1844), first U.S. Baptist missionaries in China. During the 1835 meeting of the Baptist Triennial Convention, when an offering was being received for foreign missions, J. Lewis Shuck put into the offering plate a slip of paper on which he had written, "I give myself." He married Henrietta Hall the same year and they were appointed for missionary service in China by the Baptist Convention. The Shucks arrived in Macao in 1836, where they lived and worked until the end of the Opium War (1839–1842), then moved to Hong Kong and a year later organized the first Baptist church there. While her husband was involved in evangelization and publishing, Henrietta opened a school for Chinese children and began taking Chinese orphans into her home, a practice she had begun in Macao. In Hong Kong the number grew to thirty-two children whom the Shucks fed, clothed, and nurtured. Besides being the first American female missionary to China, Henrietta Hall sent supporters at home a steady stream of letters, many of which were published, and her premature death at age 27 (after she gave birth to her fifth child) gained for her a place in Baptist mission lore—especially among Southern Baptists—second only to that of Lottie *Moon.

A year after Henrietta's death in 1844, J. Lewis Shuck left on furlough, and while in the United States affiliated with the newly formed Southern Baptist Convention Foreign Mission Board (SBCFMB), married a second time, and then returned to China, accompanied by his new wife and several other newly appointed missionaries. He settled in Shanghai, the northernmost of the five new treaty ports, and with Matthew T. *Yates organized the Baptist Mission in China. Generally, they worked harmoniously together, but there arose problems compounded by the death of Shuck's wife, Eliza, in 1851, which left him with six children, three in China and three in the United States. In November 1852, still grieving, Shuck left China for the last time. He had begun three churches, built four chapels and a school, baptized at least forty Chinese converts, and written and published thirteen works in Chinese languages. After arriving in the United States in 1853, he resigned from the SBCFMB to accept appointment by the Southern Baptist Convention Domestic Board as a missionary to the Chinese in California, where, in 1855, he organized in San Francisco a Chinese-speaking Baptist church, the first in the United States. He retired to Barnwell, South Carolina, in 1861 and died shortly thereafter at the age of 49.

BIBLIOGRAPHY Inabelle Graves Coleman, *The Conquering Christ* (1935); Margaret M. Coughlin, "Strangers in the House" (Ph.D. diss., Univ. of Virginia, 1972); Thomas S. Dunaway, *Pioneering for Jesus: The Story of Henrietta Hall Shuck* (1930); Thelma Wolfe Hall, *I Give Myself: The Story of J. Lewis Shuck and His Mission to the Chinese* (1983); Jeremiah B. Jeter, *A Memoir of Mrs. H. H. Shuck* (1846).

Alan Neely

Sibbes, Richard (1577–1635), Puritan minister, theologian, and missions advocate. Sibbes, born in Suffolk County, England, from whence many Puritans emigrated to New England because of persecution, was educated (and later lectured) at Cambridge University. He was ordained a priest in the Church of England, and was curate at Holy Trinity, Cambridge, and preacher at Gray's Inn, London. He never married. He manifested the prevailing concept of *missio Dei* that pulsed through Puritan veins. The preaching of the Reformers, he maintained, brought about the conversion of many nations, which Sibbes called "the second spring of the gospel" (the "first spring" manifested in apostolic times). Sibbes believed and preached that the gospel must continue its journey far abroad to many "'til it have gone over the whole world" ("The Fountain Opened," 1638). Turks, Jews, pagans, Indians, and Roman Catholics must know that God loves humankind, and must be won by his love. The first responsibility to communicate the gospel, he taught, belongs to preachers and to ordinary believers, while merchants and navigators have a special vocation for faraway places and new peoples. His writings were widely read in New England.

BIBLIOGRAPHY Richard Sibbes, *The Complete Works of Richard Sibbes*, A. B. Grosert, ed., 8 vols. (1862). Sidney H. Rooy, *Theology of Missions in the Puritan Tradition* (1965), pp. 15–65.

Sidney H. Rooy

Sibree, James (1836–1929), English missionary in Madagascar. Born in Hull, England, Sibree began missionary work in 1863 as an architect appointed by the London Missionary Society (LMS) to superintend erecting four large, stone churches in Antananarivo, each a memorial to a particular martyr of recent persecutions. He then returned to England, studied for the ministry at Spring Hill College, married Deborah Richardson, and went again to Madagascar in 1870. He led in extending mission work outside the capital and began teaching in the theological college. Difficulties with the government forced him to withdraw for a time (1877–1883), during part of which he worked for the LMS in South India. Back in Madagascar, he became principal of the theological college, in which position he continued till retirement in 1915. In the years leading up to the French conquest, he was an outspoken champion of Malagasy independence and urged the LMS in England to be so also. He exhibited amazing industry, continually turning out plans for new mission buildings and writing numerous works in Malagasy and sixteen books in English. His books, which were accurate and popular although not scholarly, dealt with Malagasy fauna and flora, general history, and mission history in his adopted land. He was elected fellow of the Royal Geographic Society.

BIBLIOGRAPHY Sibree's major works include, *Fifty Years in Madagascar* (1923; his autobiography), *Madagascar and Its People* (1870), *The Great African Island* (1880), *The Madagascar Mission: Its History and Present Position Briefly Sketched* (1907), and *Our English Cathedrals,* 2 vols. (1911). See also Norman Goodall, *A History of the London Missionary Society, 1894–1945* (1954).

Charles W. Forman

Sigfrid (*or* Sigurd) (11th century), pioneer missionary to Sweden. According to tradition, Sigfrid was an English missionary bishop who in 1008 baptized King Olov "Skötkonung" ("The Tax King"), ministered in Växjö, and built there what later became a cathedral. At some point in the twelfth or thirteenth century he began to be venerated as a saint; he is commemorated on February 15. Although most scholars give little value to the legends that accumulated around his name, there remains the impression of a powerful personality. What is believed to have been his grave was excavated many years ago in Växjö Cathedral.

BIBLIOGRAPHY Yngve Brilioth, *Handbok i Svensk Kyrkohistoria,* vol. 1 (2d ed., Stockholm, 1959), pp. 24–26; C. J. A. Oppermann, *The English Missionaries in Sweden and Finland* (1937), pp. 61–94.

Eric J. Sharpe

Sihombing, Justin (1890–1979), Indonesian church leader and moderator of the Toba-Batak Church. Sihombing was born in Pangaribuan, Tarutung, northern Sumatra, the son of a Batak medicine man. After serving as head of a village school, he trained for the ministry and was ordained in 1925. Commissioned to evangelize his people, his fervent preaching and compelling insights produced an outstanding spiritual impact. His pastorate in the city of Medan during World War II led to his election as moderator of the Batak church, the second indigenous leader to hold this office. He was reelected for five successive terms, for a total of 20 years. He led the church to join the World Council of Churches in 1947 and to join the Lutheran World Federation in 1952. During the period of the Japanese occupation and the national independence movement, Sihombing gave fearless and faithful leadership, based on biblical convictions. In 1951 the University of Bonn conferred on him an honorary doctor of theology degree in recognition of his leadership in maintaining the unity of the church in a time of great adversity and change. Tribute was paid to him as a church father of outstanding wisdom, patience, and dedication to his office and to his people. His published writings were largely directed to the church and its coworkers. With his book *Tohonan sidjaga tondi* (Ministry of the Spirit), he undergirded Christian discipleship; in *Poda pardjamitaon,* a homiletics manual, he published his homiletics lectures at the theological seminary in Pematang Siantar. For the centenary celebration of the church in 1961 he wrote *Seratus taon Huria Kristen Batak Protestant* (A hundred years: Batak Protestant Christian Church).

BIBLIOGRAPHY Alfred Rutkowsky, "...zu treiben das Evangelium des Friedens," *Berichte d. Rhein. Mission* 113 (1963): 293–295; Edward O. V. Nyhus, *An Indonesian Church in the Midst of Social Change: The Batak Protestant Christian Church, 1942–1957* (1987); see also *In die Welt für die Welt* 15 (1979): 174 (obit.)

Lothar Schreiner

Silva, Lynn A. de (1919–1982), Sri Lankan ecumenical leader and promoter of interreligious dialogue. De Silva, an ordained minister of the Methodist Church in Sri Lanka, studied theology at the United Theological College, Bangalore, India. Well known as a preacher and theologian, he contributed primarily in three areas: comparative studies in Christianity and Buddhism, theological debate in interreligious relationships, and promoting Christian-Buddhist dialogue. These were his emphases at the Study Centre for Religion and Society, Colombo, where he was the director for many years, and where his wife, Lakshmi, was also an able partner. De Silva was the founder-editor of the journal *Dialogue,* published by the center in Colombo. For many years he was a member of the World Council of Churches (WCC) working group of the subunit Dialogue with People of Living Faiths and Ideologies. He made significant theological contributions as Sinclair Thompson Memorial Lecturer at the Thailand Theological Seminary, Chiang Mai (1964), and as William Paton Lecturer at Selly Oak Colleges, Birmingham, England (1970). During the Nairobi assembly of the WCC (1975), where dialogue was a controversial subject, he made a notable intervention urging that dialogue is not a *temptation to* syncretism but a *security against* syncretism.

BIBLIOGRAPHY De Silva wrote numerous articles both in English and Sinhala, his native language. His books include *Creation, Redemption, and Consummation in Christianity and Buddhism* (1964), *Buddhism: Beliefs and Practices in Sri Lanka* (1974), and *The Problem of the Self in Buddhism and Christianity* (1975).

Stanley J. Samartha

Silveira, Gonçalo da (1526–1561), Jesuit protomartyr of southern Africa. Born in Almeirim, Portugal, Silveira became a Jesuit in 1543 and gained a reputation as a preacher. In 1556 he was sent as provincial to Goa, India, where he collaborated closely with the viceroy. When the Jesuits received the news that Mozambique seemed ready for evangelization, Silveira and two of his confreres were sent to Mozambique, where they arrived in February 1560. The motives of this mission were not purely religious; the viceroy was interested in the riches of the "goldland," and Silveira was also in favor of making the land's resources accessible to Portugal. The Jesuits first evangelized in Inhambane. At Tongue, Silveira baptized the king, Gamba. In December he arrived at the court of Monomotapa, who received him personally and accepted baptism on January 20, 1561. Silveira was highly regarded by the nobles and the people and by March he had baptized about 300. Then Muslim traders and representatives of the traditional religion accused Silveira of being a spy and sorcerer. The young king changed his mind, and on his command Silveira was strangled to death by soldiers during the night of March 15.

BIBLIOGRAPHY Bertha Leite, *D. Gonçalo da Silveira* (1946); Joseph Wicki, ed., *Documenta Indica,* vols. 3–7 (1954–1962).

Fritz Kollbrunner, SMB

Simatupang, Tahi Bonar (1920–1990), Indonesian Christian leader in the ecumenical movement. Born to a Batak family in Sidikalang, Sumatra, Simatupang became an Indonesian army staff officer and was trained at the royal Dutch military academy in Bandung. During the war of independence he was chief of staff of the armed forces in defense of the Republic of Indonesia. After early retirement he served with the National Council of Churches in Indonesia, then was president of the Christian Conference of Asia (1973–1977) and a president of the World Council of Churches (1975–1983). He was noted as a speaker and writer on social ethics and ecumenical concerns in Indonesia and in other Asian countries and in the West. Because of his prominent role in the national movement for independence in Indonesia (1949–1954), he was able to promote the cause of the Protestant churches in relation to the government as well as in society generally. He was the author of numerous articles and books in Indonesian, some of which were translated into other languages.

BIBLIOGRAPHY T. B. Simatupang, "The Situation and Challenge of the Christian Mission in Indonesia Today," *South East Asia Journal of Theology* 10, no. 4 (1969):10–27, "Kurzer Rückblick auf die Geschichte der christlichen Kirche in Indonesien," in Rolf Italiaander, ed., *Indonesiens verantwortliche Gesellschaft* (1976), pp. 37–85, "Dynamics for Creative Maturity," in Gerald H. Anderson, ed., *Asian Voices in Christian Theology* (1976), pp. 87–116, "Doing Theology in Indonesia Today," *CTC Bulletin* 3, no. 2 (1982): 20–29, and *Gelebte Theologie in Indonesien, zur gesellschaftlichen Verantwortung der Christen* (1992).

Lothar Schreiner

Simeon, Charles (1759–1836), Anglican leader of the evangelical revival and especially of its missionary movement. Simeon was born in Reading, England, and was educated at Eton and Cambridge (King's College). His evangelical conversion as a university student in 1779 set the course of his life. In 1782 he took his degree, was made a fellow of his college, and became the minister of Holy Trinity Church in Cambridge, where he served until his death. Despite intense opposition during his first decade of ministry, Simeon became an evangelical fixture in Cambridge and the university for the next half century.

Simeon's influence on the Church of England and the British missionary movement was exercised by regular churchmanship, voluntary efforts, and patronage. His commitment to church order, imparted to his university students through innovative sermon classes and "conversation parties," helped to retain third-generation evangelical Anglicans in the established church. In 1799 he was instrumental in founding the Society for Missions to Africa and the East, later renamed the Church Missionary Society (CMS), and played major roles in the advancement of the British and Foreign Bible Society and the London Society for Promoting Christianity amongst the Jews. Significant numbers of university students were channeled toward parish ministry through his patronage, especially through a trust that still bears his name. Surprisingly few of his students pursued missionary service through the CMS, but a large number worked in India as chaplains of the British East India Company. Most notable of the latter were David *Brown, Claudius *Buchanan, Henry *Martyn, Daniel *Corrie, and Thomas Thomason. Simeon's sermons received wide circulation in Britain and abroad. His major published work, *Horae homileticae: or, Discourses . . . Forming a Commentary upon Every Book of the Old and New Testament* (7th ed., 1845), is a collection of 2,536 sermon outlines. Thomas Babington Macaulay, in an 1844 letter that became an epitaph on the Cambridge minister, reflected common opinion when he noted that Simeon's "real sway in the Church was far greater than that of any prelate."

BIBLIOGRAPHY The primary biography, which includes a large autobiographical section, is William Carus's *Memoirs of the Life of the Rev. Charles Simeon, M.A., Late Senior Fellow of King's College and Minister of Trinity Church* (3rd ed., 1848). J. C. Bennett, "Charles Simeon and the Evangelical Anglican Missionary Movement: A Study of Voluntaryism and Church-Mission Tensions" (Ph.D. diss., Univ. of Edinburgh, 1992), and "Charles Simeon," in Gerald H. Anderson et al., eds., *Mission Legacies* (1994), pp. 3–10; H. E. Hopkins, *Charles Simeon of Cambridge* (1977); A. Pollard, *Let Wisdom Judge: University Addresses and Sermon Outlines by Charles Simeon* (1959); C. H. E. Smyth, *Simeon and Church Order: A Study of the Origins of the Evangelical Revival in Cambridge in the Eighteenth Century* (1940; the Birkbeck Lectures for 1937–1938). The two primary collections of Simeon's papers are held in Ridley Hall, Cambridge, and Cambridge University Library.

John C. Bennett

Simonton, Ashbel Green (1831–1867), American Presbyterian pioneer missionary in Brazil. Simonton was born in West Hanover, Pennsylvania, and studied in the College of New Jersey (later Princeton University) but left his law studies to enter Princeton Seminary. Inspired by a sermon by Professor Charles Hodge, he committed his life to missions. He was sent to Brazil by the Presbyterian Board of Foreign Missions, arriving in Rio de Janeiro in August 1859, and was soon joined by other missionaries, among them his sister and her husband. In 1860 Simonton organized the first Sunday school, with five children, and began evangelistic work in Portuguese. With the help of a former Roman Catholic priest, José Manoel da Conceicão, whom he converted, baptized, and ordained as the first Brazilian Presbyterian minister, Simonton opened a preaching hall and began regular work in São Paulo in May 1861. The first Presbyterian church was organized in Rio de Janeiro in January 1862. He was also the founder of the first evangelical newspaper. Simonton returned to the United States in 1862 and married Helen Murdoch. She died in Rio de Janeiro in 1864 after giving birth to a daughter. In December 1865 he and other missionaries organized the first presbytery and gave special attention to theological formation by opening a seminary in Rio de Janeiro (1867). He died of yellow fever at age 36.

BIBLIOGRAPHY Julio Andrade Ferreira, *História da Igreja Presbiteriana do Brasil,* 2 vols. (1959); Klaus van der Grijp, "Protestantismo brasileiro á procura de identidade," *Estudos teológicos* 14 (1974): 14–26; Philip S. Landes, *Ashbel Green Simonton* (1956); R. L. McIntire, "Portrait of Half a Century: Fifty Years of Presbyterianism in Brazil" (Ph.D. diss., Princeton Seminary, 1959).

Pablo A. Deiros

Simpson, A(lbert) B(enjamin) (1843–1919), founder of the Christian and Missionary Alliance (C&MA). Raised as a strict Scottish Presbyterian on Prince Edward Island, Canada, Simpson was attracted as a teenager to Puritan devotional writings. In 1865 he was ordained and then served prestigious churches in Hamilton, Ontario, and Louisville, Kentucky. In 1874 he incorporated holiness ideas into his Reformed faith and was filled with the Holy Spirit, a turning point in his ministry. In 1881 he was rebaptized by immersion and experienced faith-healing of heart trouble. Resigning from the Thirteenth Street Presbyterian Church in New York City, he founded the Gospel Tabernacle, from which he launched various mission and healing activities, including rescue missions, an orphanage, healing homes, and outreach to immigrants.

Simpson believed that Jesus' return was dependent on the gospel being preached to all the world. Fulfilling the Great Commission thus became the focus of his vocation and he felt a missionary call to China. Unable to go because of family opposition, he threw himself into "home base" activities for world mission. In 1880 he published the first illustrated mission magazine in North America, *The Gospel in All Lands.* He opened the New York Missionary Training College (later Nyack College), which sought to give lay people a foundation in the Scriptures and to get them quickly onto the mission field.

At his first annual summer convention in Old Orchard, Maine, in 1887, Simpson founded the Christian Alliance and the Evangelical Missionary Alliance. The Christian Alliance spread missionary fervor at the home base, while the Evangelical Missionary Alliance acted as a foreign mission board. An interdenominational mission movement, the alliances merged a decade later and became the Christian and Missionary Alliance. By 1895, the C&MA had sent out nearly 300 missionaries. Simpson led the organization until his death. His wife, Margaret, served as financial secretary and as secretary of missionary appointment and equipment. Simpson wrote hundreds of books and articles and edited *The Word, the Work, and the World,* a weekly publication. He recruited people into the movement by holding summer mission conventions, by preaching on missions, and by educating people at his Missionary Training Institute. After Pentecostalism emerged in the early twentieth century, the C&MA lost many supporters and missionaries because Simpson refused to say that speaking in tongues was necessary for salvation. Under his leadership, the C&MA was nevertheless the most important of the early American premillennial "faith missions."

BIBLIOGRAPHY David F. Hartzfeld and Charles Nienkirchen, eds., *The Birth of a Vision: Essays on the Ministry and Thought of Albert B. Simpson* (1986); Gerald E. McGraw, "A. B. Simpson," in Gerald H. Anderson et al., eds., *Mission Legacies* (1994), pp. 37–47; Robert L. Niklaus, John S. Sawin, and Samuel J. Stoesz, *All for Jesus: God at Work in the Christian and Missionary Alliance over One Hundred Years* (1986); George P. Pardington, *Twenty-Five Wonderful Years, 1889–1914: A Popular Sketch of the Christian and Missionary Alliance* (1914, 1984); George W. Reitz, "A. B. Simpson, Urban Evangelist," *Urban Mission* 8 (1991): 19–26; A. E. Thompson, *The Life of A. B. Simpson* (1920).

Dana L. Robert

Simpson, William Wallace (1869–1961), missionary in China. Born in Tennessee and later trained at A. B. *Simpson's Missionary Training Institute, Simpson (no relation to A. B. Simpson) and several other Christian and Missionary Alliance (C&MA) missionaries traveled to China in 1892, hoping to evangelize in Tibet. Identifying with the Pentecostal movement, Simpson left the C&MA in 1916. After two years in the United States, he and his family returned to China in 1918 as Assemblies of God (AG) missionaries. Over the years, Simpson evangelized widely and focused his efforts on the training of Chinese clergy; he remained in China until 1949. In retirement in the United States he continued to promote missions. His son, William Ekvall Simpson, also an AG missionary, died at the hands of bandits on the Tibetan-Chinese border in 1932.

BIBLIOGRAPHY W. W. Simpson, *Evangelizing West China* (c. 1934). Nora Blan, *Over Rugged Mountains: W. E. Simpson,* Heroes of the Conquest Series no. 8 (n.d.). See also Paul L. King, "Early Alliance Missions in China," in *The Birth of a Vision,* David F. Hartzfeld and Charles Nienkirchen, eds. (1986); Gary B. McGee, *This Gospel Shall Be Preached: A History and Theology of Assemblies of God Foreign Missions to 1959,* vol. 1 (1986); Charles Nienkirchen, *A. B. Simpson and the Pentecostal Movement* (1992). Simpson's correspondence and published articles are located at the AG archives, Springfield, Missouri.

Gary B. McGee

Singh, Bakht (1903–), Apostle of the Indian subcontinent. Singh was born Bakht Singh Chabra in Joya, in the Punjab, near Lahore, to Hindu parents, Jawahar Mal Chabra and Lakshmi Bai, who reared him as a Sikh. Following graduation from the government college in Lahore, he enrolled in King's College, London, in 1926, later attending the Universities of Manitoba and Saskatchewan,

Canada, where he earned degrees in mechanical and agricultural engineering. Reading a New Testament resulted in his conversion to Christianity in 1929 and changed the course of his life. He returned to India in 1933, working as an itinerant unordained Anglican evangelist among the sweepers and lepers of Karachi and throughout the Punjab and Sind.

Singh's role in the 1937 revival that swept the Martinbur United Presbyterian Church inaugurated one of the most notable movements in the history of the church in the Indian subcontinent. During the summer of 1941 in Madras, he established Jehovah Shammah, a local church modeled strictly on New Testament principles, as distinct from denominational ones, thereby initiating an immensely successful indigenous movement that now numbers over 500 congregations in India, some 200 congregations in Pakistan, and a number in Europe and in North America. Frequently charged with being antidenominational and antiforeign, Singh was in fact neither, emphasizing rather the establishment of thoroughly contextualized self-supporting, self-governing, and self-propagating congregations, and refusing to accept financial assistance from the West. While the Holy Convocations held annually in Hyderabad are perhaps the most striking aspect of the movement associated with Bakht Singh, he was in great demand as a conference speaker throughout India and the West and was a plenary speaker at the first North American InterVarsity Christian Fellowship missions conference held in Toronto, Canada, in 1946.

BIBLIOGRAPHY At the time of this writing, T. E. Koshy had not yet completed Bakht Singh's official biography. Bakht Singh's publications, widely distributed in India, consist largely of compiled sermons and include *Bethany, David Recovered All, God's Dwelling Place, Joy of the Lord, Overcomer's Secret, My Chosen, Voice of the Lord, Walk before Me, Forty Mountain Peaks, The Return of God's Glory, Holy Spirit, Sharing of God's Secrets, The Skill of His Loving Hands,* and *The True Salt,* all undated. Such scattered and fragmentary biographical information as exists may be found (in declining order of significance) in Daniel Smith, *Bakht Singh of India, a Prophet of God* (1957); T. E. Koshy, "Bakht Singh's Movement Still Full of Grassroots Vitality," *Christianity Today,* February 22, 1980, p. 51; Eleanore Llewellyn, "Bakht Singh of India," in Presbyterian Church in the U.S.A., *Unforgettable Disciples* (1942); R. R. Rajamani, *Monsoon Daybreak* (1971); Norman Grubb, *Once Caught, No Escape* (1969).

Jonathan J. Bonk

Singh, Sundar. *See* Sundar Singh.

Skrefsrud, Lars O(lsen) (1840–1910), Norwegian Lutheran missionary and linguist. Born into a poor family in Faaberg, Skrefsrud spent time in prison for theft from 1858 to 1861. While there he had a conversion experience and felt a vocational call to mission service. He had an extraordinary gift for learning languages, and while still in detention he studied English and German. After a six-month course at the Gossner School of Mission in Berlin he arrived in India late in 1863. He served with the Gossner Mission from 1863 to 1865, then was an independent missionary together with the Danish missionary H. P. Boerresen, and for a short time he worked for the British Baptist Missionary Society. Then, for more than 40 years, he was in the service of the Nordic (Norwegian) Santal Mission. He was ordained in 1882. Skrefsrud was an eloquent speaker and toured Europe and the United States, raising funds for the Santal Mission.

He was a social reformer who through negotiations with the British authorities secured the social rights of the Santals and saved them from being oppressed by the Hindu landowners. He wanted to build a genuine Santal church and he used Santal tunes for his hymns. He said, "It is the heathenism we want to get rid of, not the national character. We will distinguish between Christianity and European forms of civilization; the first we will give them in their own vessels, and the second we will leave in Europe." His most important writings are *A Grammar of the Santal Language* (1873), *A Santal Hymn Book* (1876), and *The Traditions and Institutions of the Santals* (1887). He also wrote an unpublished 1400-page manuscript for a Santal-English dictionary. Skrefsrud was a member of the Norwegian Academy for Science and Letters, was made a Knight of the Order of Saint Olav, and received the Kaiser-i-Hind gold medal.

BIBLIOGRAPHY Olav Hodne, *Lars O. Skrefsrud: Missionary and Social Reformer among the Santals of the Santal Parganas* (1966).

Nils E. Bloch-Hoell

Slater, Thomas Ebenezer (1840–1912), English missionary and scholar of Hinduism. After theological studies in Birmingham, Slater served with the London Missionary Society (LMS) from 1866 in Calcutta, Madras, and Bangalore. As a result of the first Madras Missionary Conference in 1874, he was seconded by the LMS to work among "young men who had passed through English medium colleges." This remained his chief work until his retirement from the mission field in 1904. He wrote numerous notable and pioneering works, including *The Philosophy of Missions: A Present-Day Plea* (1882) and *Missions and Sociology* (1908). He is most significant for his development of the fulfillment theory of the relationship of Christianity to other forms of faith. His ideas in *The Higher Hinduism in Relation to Christianity* (1902) influenced J. N. *Farquhar and Commission Four at the Edinburgh World Missionary Conference in 1910. He also produced apologetic works for educated Hindus, such as *God Revealed: An Outline of Christian Truth* (1876), and scholarly studies of Hinduism, such as *Studies in the Upanishads* (1897) and *Transmigration and Karma* (1898).

BIBLIOGRAPHY Kenneth R. Cracknell, *Justice, Courtesy, and Love: Missionaries and Theologians Encountering the World Religious Traditions, 1846–1914* (1995); Eric J. Sharpe, *Not to Destroy but to Fulfil: The Contribution of J. N. Farquhar to Protestant Missionary Thought in India before 1914* (1965), pp. 94–108.

Kenneth R. Cracknell

Slessor, Mary Mitchell (1848–1915), pioneer Scottish missionary in eastern Nigeria. The alcoholism of Mary

Slessor's father forced the family to move from Aberdeen, where Mary was born, to Dundee where her father hoped for a new start. He did not succeed, and Mary helped the family as best she could, beginning work in the linen mills at the age of 11. As a streetwise teenager she came under the influence of a local minister and became leader of a Christian youth club of street toughs only a little younger than herself. She became convinced of a call to serve in Calabar, Nigeria, and in 1876 the United Presbyterian Church Mission Committee eventually agreed to send her to Calabar as a mission teacher. Her first mentors soon realized that she had great potential but would not fit the Calabar teamwork approach. Thus, she went alone in 1888 to work among the Okoyong. She lived in a traditional-type house with outcast women and the twins she had rescued from death. Going barefoot, clothed in a cotton shift, she exhibited to the Okoyong and to missionaries an alternative way of engaging in mission. When the British colonial authority drove further inland she felt that the mission had to help the people affected, and she spent 1903 pioneering instead of going on furlough. This led to new stations being created and wider Christian outreach. In the new area she continued to live as head of a household of African women and children until she died at Use. Her life was an example of Christian inculturation, but regrettably it was trivialized by a romantic "white queen of Okoyong" attitude toward her in Britain.

BIBLIOGRAPHY There is no satisfactory biography of Mary Slessor. The two best vary significantly: W. P. Livingstone, *Mary Slessor of Calabar* (1915) and James Buchan, *The Expendable Mary Slessor* (1980).

Andrew C. Ross

Small, Ann Hunter (1857–1945), Scottish missionary, author, and trainer of missionaries. Small was born in Falkirk, Scotland, the oldest child in a devout Presbyterian family. In 1863 her father, John, became a missionary in western India under the United Free Church of Scotland, and Ann lived in Poona until she was ten. She was sent to boarding school in England (1870–1874), and in 1876, at almost 19, she returned to India, spending 16 years in the eastern part; during home leave in 1890 and 1891 she published her first book. But in 1892 further work in India was made impossible by illness. At the age of 37, she was asked to take charge of a new missionary training college for women in Scotland, and this work became her life's vocation. She led the college, finally named St. Colm's (Edinburgh), until 1913. She was a vivid, creative, and innovative teacher; the chapel with its music and prayer was the center of college life. She provided an emphasis on home and hospitality, and on the importance of personal relations, but also kept her students' eyes on the wider world. Her sympathies were broad, but at the same time she remained a loyal Presbyterian, stressing her denomination's contributions to the world church. In her long retirement her influence increased; she settled in Edinburgh, where she died, greatly loved, in her eighty-eighth year.

BIBLIOGRAPHY Ann Hunter Small, *Light and Shade in Zenana Missionary Life* (1891), *Yeshu-das* (Lord Jesus) (1899; 4th ed., 1938), *Our First Twenty Years* (1914), and *Missionary College Hymns* (1914). Olive Wyon, *The Three Windows: The Story of Ann Hunter Small* (1953).

Jocelyn Murray

Smet, Pierre-Jean de. *See* De Smet, Pierre Jean.

Smirnov, Evgeny (*or* Eugene) Konstantinovich (*or* Eugene Smirnoff) (1845–1922), Russian Orthodox archpriest, author, and from 1880 dean of the Russian Church in London. Smirnov graduated from St. Petersburg Theological Academy and was ordained and appointed to the Russian mission in America, arriving in 1870. He wrote many articles in Russian periodicals on religious life in North America, with an emphasis on canonical and ecclesiastical problems. Immersed in a non-Orthodox environment, Smirnov laboriously investigated the canonicity of intercommunion with representatives of other Christian churches and compiled an order of reception into Orthodoxy. In 1896 his *Offices for the Reception into the Orthodox Eastern Church of Non-Orthodox Christians,* was published in London. He was also a historian of Russian missions abroad, and for many years he wrote a section on the church abroad in *Strannik* (Pilgrim), the Orthodox journal published in Saint Petersburg. In 1903 he published *A Short Account of the Historical Development and Present Position of Russian Orthodox Missions,* a brief but valuable source in English on the missionary activity of the Russian Orthodox Church.

BIBLIOGRAPHY Eugene Smirnoff, *A Short Account of the Historical Development and Present Position of Russian Orthodox Missions* (1903; Russian ed., 1904).

Evgeny S. Steiner

Smith, A(lgernon) C(harles) Stanley (1890–1978), Church Missionary Society (CMS) missionary doctor and Bible translator in Rwanda. Born in Tientsin (Tianjin), China, the son of Stanley *Smith of the *Cambridge Seven, Smith was educated at Winchester and at Cambridge. He studied medicine at St. George's Hospital, London. During World War I he served in the Royal Army Medical Corps in France and at the CMS Mengo Hospital in Kampala, Uganda. He and fellow officer Leonard Sharp felt called to the twin kingdoms of Rwanda and Burundi, soon to become Belgian trust territories. In 1921 Smith, his wife, Zoe (sister of Sharp), and Sharp began a CMS work at Kabale in the far south of Uganda. Within a few years they entered Rwanda and began medical and evangelistic work. This was the beginning of the CMS Ruanda Mission. Smith was field secretary for a number of years. He also took over from Harold Guillebaud as the mission's leading translator, completing the Bible in Kinyarwanda (1955), then the Ankole/Kigezi Bible (1964), as well as hymns, Anglican prayer book, and *Pilgrim's Progress.* Retiring from the mission in 1977, Smith died in England; his wife died in 1980. Their four children served in Africa: Nora's husband, Dick Lyth, was Anglican bishop of Kigezi, Uganda; Eve and her husband, Tony Wilmot, worked in both West and East Africa; Geoff Stanley Smith worked in Burundi as a medical doctor; and Jim Stanley Smith worked in Kenya as a teacher.

BIBLIOGRAPHY Algernon C. Stanley Smith, *Road to Revival* (1946; supplement, 1951). Jocelyn Murray, *Proclaim the Good News* (1985); Bert Osborn, *Fire in the Hills* (1991); Patricia St. John, *Breath of Life: The Story of the Ruanda Mission* (1971).

Jocelyn Murray

Smith, Amanda (Berry) (1837–1915), African American holiness evangelist and missionary. Amanda Berry was born into slavery at Long Green, Maryland. She was married in 1854 to Calvin M. Devine and her conversion followed two years later. After her husband died in the Civil War, she moved to Philadelphia and married James Smith, an ordained deacon at Mother Bethel African Methodist Episcopal (AME) Church. After visiting Green Street Church in Philadelphia, where she heard John S. Inskip, a prominent Wesleyan holiness leader, preach, she testified that she had received her sanctification there. Following the death of her second husband in 1869, she traveled as a holiness evangelist, becoming a popular speaker in many churches and camp meetings. Smith's friendships included prominent holiness and prohibition movement leaders such as Hannah Whitall Smith and Frances Willard.

Her overseas ministry began with a visit to England in 1878. From there, Smith went to India as a missionary; Methodist bishop James M. *Thoburn thought so highly of her that he wrote the introduction to her *Autobiography* (1893). In Africa, she worked with Methodist missionaries, including Bishop William *Taylor. She was honored by African Americans and whites alike. Smith spent her last years caring for needy African American children at her orphanage in Harvey, Illinois; she was also connected to the founding of the National Association for the Advancement of Colored People. Her spiritual fervor and calls for justice in society, and her work in missions inspired an expanded role for women in ministry, particularly within the AME and Methodist churches.

BIBLIOGRAPHY Amanda Berry Smith, *An Autobiography: The Story of the Lord's Dealing with Mrs. Amanda Smith, the Colored Evangelist* (1893, reprinted 1969); M. H. Cadbury, *The Life of Amanda Smith* (1916); Jualynne Dodson, "Nineteenth-Century A. M. E. Preaching Women: The Cutting Edge of Women's Inclusion in Church Polity," in *Women in New Worlds,* Hilah F. Thomas and Rosemary Skinner Keller, eds. (1981); Clara McLeister, *Men and Women of Deep Piety* (1920); Marshall William Taylor, *The Life, Travels, Labors, and Helpers of Mrs. Amanda Smith, the Famous Negro Missionary Evangelist* (1886).

Gary B. McGee

Smith, Arthur Henderson (1845–1932), American author and missionary to China. Born in Vernon, Connecticut, Henderson graduated from Beloit College (1867) and Union Theological Seminary (1870). He married Emma Jane Dickinson in 1871, was ordained to the Congregational ministry in 1872, and sailed for China under the American Board of Commissioners for Foreign Missions (ABCFM). He did evangelistic work at Tientsin among the poor, believing that "Christianity always and everywhere begins with the lowest stratum of society and works upward," as he wrote in one of many articles in the *Chinese Recorder.* He contributed frequently to the *Celestial Empire* (Shanghai), *China Mail* (Hong Kong), *International Review of Missions, Missionary Herald, Outlook* (New York), and the *North China Daily News and Herald,* China's principal English language newspaper. In 1890 Smith went to Pangzhuang, Shantung, where he did evangelistic work and began a series of books on Chinese life which helped make him a widely known interpreter of China. In 1900 he was caught at Peking in the Boxer Rebellion, described in his two-volume *China in Convulsion* (1901). While in the United States to assist an ABCFM fund-raising effort in 1906, he secured an interview with President Theodore Roosevelt and persuaded him that a substantial portion of Boxer indemnity funds should be used to create an American-style college in China; Ts'ing-hua (Qinghua) University was the result. On his return Smith was made missionary-at-large, residing at Tongzhou. He was American chairman of the China Centenary Conference in 1907, a member of the China Continuation Committee, which coordinated most Protestant efforts, and a member of the editorial board of the *Chinese Recorder.* He also attended the World Missionary Conference at Edinburgh in 1910. In 1926 he retired at Claremont, California.

BIBLIOGRAPHY Smith's best-known books were *Chinese Characteristics* (1890) and *Village Life in China* (1899); others include *Proverbs and Common Sayings from the Chinese* (1888), *Rex Christus: An Outline Study of China* (1903), *The Uplift of China* (1907), *China and America Today* (1907), and *A Manual for Young Missionaries to China* (1918). Charles W. Hayford, "Chinese and American Characteristics: Arthur H. Smith and His China Book," in Suzanne Wilson Barnet and John King Fairbank, eds., *Christianity in China: Early Protestant Missionary Writings* (1985), pp. 153–174; *Missionary Herald* 120 (1924): 414; 121 (1925): 4–5; 129 (1933): 99; Theodore D. Pappas, "Arthur Henderson Smith and the American Mission in China," *Wisconsin Magazine of History* 70 (1987): 163–186.

David M. Stowe

Smith, Edwin Williams (1876–1957), missionary anthropologist and linguist. Smith was born of missionary parents of the Primitive Methodist Mission in South Africa. After study in England, he served as a Primitive Methodist missionary for a short time in Basutoland (modern Lesotho), and then from 1902 to 1915 in Northern Rhodesia (modern Zambia) among the Baila-Batonga. In 1915 he returned to England, eventually putting his linguistic abilities to work at the British and Foreign Bible Society, first as an agent in Italy, and later by giving editorial supervision to Scripture translations in many languages. He published several scholarly works on the Ila language, most notably his *Handbook of the Ila Language* (1907), which for

50 years was considered the standard, and *The Ila-speaking Peoples of Northern Rhodesia* (1920). He also played a principal role in the translation of the New Testament.

Smith was an outstanding anthropologist, and his publications and lectures led to his becoming president of the Royal Anthropological Institute of Great Britain and Ireland in 1934 and to serving from 1940 to 1948 as editor of *Africa,* the journal of the International Institute of African Languages and Cultures (now the International African Institute). Indigenous African religious beliefs were little understood until Smith demonstrated through *The Secret of the African* (1929) and *African Belief and Christian Faith* (1936) that the whole life of the African people was permeated by religion. *The Golden Stool* (1927), a plea for sympathetic understanding of Africans by administrative authorities, and *Aggrey of Africa* (1929), which attempted to interpret whites and blacks to each other, had a beneficial impact on race relations in Africa. Missionary biography and historical research was another of his areas of interest. *The Mabilles of Basutoland* (1939) contains much valuable information on the work of the Paris Evangelical Missionary Society in Basutoland. After retirement in 1939, Smith was a visiting lecturer on African anthropology and history at the Kennedy School of Missions of Hartford Seminary. In 1942 he received an honorary D.D. from the University of Toronto.

BIBLIOGRAPHY Edwin Williams Smith, *African Ideas of God* (1950), *Robert Moffat, One of God's Gardeners* (1925), *The Life and Times of Daniel Lindley* (1947), and a biography of Roger Price, *Great Lion of Bechuanaland* (1957). See also C. M. Doke, "Obituary, Edwin Williams Smith," *African Studies* 7 (1958): 53–61. Wilma Meier, ed., *Bibliographie afrikanischer Sprachen* (1984; contains a language-related bibliography).

Philip C. Stine

Smith, Eli (1801–1857), American missionary and Orientalist. Smith was born in Northford, Connecticut, and graduated from Yale with a B.A. in 1821. In 1826 he graduated from Andover Theological Seminary, was ordained, and was sent by the American Board of Commissioners for Foreign Missions (ABCFM) to superintend the ABCFM printing press at Malta. Already competent in Greek, Latin, and Hebrew, and having some knowledge of French, German, and Italian, he later learned Turkish and Armenian. Determined to master Arabic, he went to Beirut for language study, returning to Malta in 1827. In 1829 he accompanied Rufus *Anderson in exploring mission possibilities in Greece, and in 1830, accompanied by H. G. O. *Dwight, he began a 16-month journey of exploration reported in *Researches of the Rev. E. Smith and Rev. H. G. O. Dwight in Armenia: Including a Journey through Asia Minor and into Georgia and Persia, with a Visit to the Nestorian and Chaldean Christians of Oormiah and Salmas,* 2 vols. (1833). While in the United States (1832–1833) he married Sarah L. Huntington, returning with her to Beirut in 1834. Equipped with a new press, Smith quickly began to produce materials in Arabic, including schoolbooks, Scripture portions, a hymnbook, catechisms, translations of religious classics, and his own and other missionaries' writings. He also published classics of Arabic literature, thereby contributing significantly to the renaissance of Arab culture. Intent on producing works of the highest quality, Smith designed a new typeface which became known as American Arabic. He shared actively in all the business of the mission, preached daily, and made a journey of exploration to Hauran in 1834 and undertook other journeys in 1838 and 1852 with Edward Robinson, who published *Biblical Researches in Palestine...,* 3 vols. (1841). Smith devoted his last ten years to the translation of the Bible into Arabic, a project completed after his death by C. V. A. *Van Dyke. Smith lost his first wife in 1836; in 1841 he married Maria Chapin, who died within a year. He then married Henrietta Butler in 1846 and with her had three daughters and two sons. He died in Beirut.

BIBLIOGRAPHY Smith published *Missionary Sermons and Addresses* in 1833. Margaret R. Leavy, *Eli Smith and the Arabic Bible* (1993), and "Looking for the Armenians: Eli Smith's Missionary Adventure, 1830–1831," *Transactions of the Connecticut Academy of Arts and Sciences* 50 (1992): 189–275 (contains a useful bibliography). See also *Missionary Herald* 53 (1857): 123–125, 224–229.

David M. Stowe

Smith, George (1815–1871), Church Missionary Society (CMS) missionary in China and first English bishop of Hong Kong. Smith was born in Wellington, Somerset, England, was educated at Oxford, and in 1841 was appointed vicar of Goole in Yorkshire. In 1844 he and Thomas McClatchie sailed for China as the first two CMS missionaries in that country. (Smith is not to be confused with his namesake, a pioneer CMS missionary of the Foochow [Fuzhou] mission in the 1850s.) In 1847 he published the results of a tour of Hong Kong and the treaty ports undertaken for the CMS. He and Bishop W. J. *Boone of the Protestant Episcopal Church in the U.S.A., who had preceded him in 1844, reached agreement over their respective jurisdictions. In 1849 Smith became bishop of Hong Kong. After the 1858 Treaty of Tientsin opened inland China to missionary work, he appealed for help, and the Society for the Propagation of the Gospel responded with four missionaries in 1859. After the Taiping rebels were defeated by the imperial troops under General Charles Gordon, Smith wrote public protests about the massacres perpetrated by the victors. He visited Australia, where he appealed for Christian ministry to the many Chinese immigrants there. He resigned his see in 1864 but attended the Lambeth Conference in 1867.

BIBLIOGRAPHY George Smith, *A Narrative of an Exploratory Visit...* (1847) and *Our National Relations with China* (1857). Kenneth Scott Latourette, *A History of Christian Missions in China* (1929); Jocelyn Murray, *Proclaim the Good News* (1985); Eugene Stock, *History of the Church Missionary Society* (1899); Timothy E. Yates, *Venn and Victorian Bishops Abroad* (1978).

Timothy Yates

Smith, George (1833–1919), Scottish mission administrator and biographer. Smith (the father of the noted educator and scholar George Adam Smith) went to India as a young man to be principal of Doveton College, Calcutta, a school for Eurasian pupils. After five years he became editor of the *Calcutta Review* and the *Friend of India.* Though not a missionary himself, throughout his time in India he had a deep interest in mission and missionaries, and he and his wife, Janet, were ever-welcoming hosts for traveling missionaries. His interest in Indian society and Anglo-Indian relations led to his later being appointed as a Companion of the Order of the Indian Empire by Queen Victoria. Returning to Scotland in 1875, he became secretary of the foreign mission committee of the Free Church of Scotland in 1879, a post he held for more than 30 years. He became a senior statesman in the Scottish churches and was influential in encouraging a wider interest in and support for mission. He also wrote widely on historical and geographic topics, and his books of missionary biography (e.g., Carey, Duff, Martyn, and Van der Kemp) were popular in the late nineteenth century. In many ways he is typical of the heyday of Scottish missions, stressing the importance of education as an essential part of the missionary task.

BIBLIOGRAPHY George Smith, *Fifty Years of Foreign Missions* (1879), *The Life of Alexander Duff* (1879), *The Life of William Carey* (1885), *A Short History of Christian Missions* (1886), *The Conversion of India* (1893).

T. Jack Thompson

Smith, Henry Light (1888–1924), Brethren in Christ (BC) missionary in India. Smith was born in Harrisburg, Pennsylvania, the son of Samuel R. Smith, who founded Messiah College, Grantham, Pennsylvania. He graduated from Elizabethtown College in Pennsylvania and taught at Messiah College and at Beulah (later Upland) College in California. Ordained to the ministry in 1913, he and his wife, Katie, were sent in the same year to begin BC missions in India, in the province of Bihar. Under his superintendency, the denomination organized missions at Madhipura, Saharsa, and Supaul. He also established orphanages, medical dispensaries, and relief work. On a furlough to North America in 1921, he wrote *Bible Doctrine,* the first systematic theology compiled by the BC Church. He died in India of smallpox.

BIBLIOGRAPHY Anna Engle et al., *There Is No Difference* (1950); *Evangelical Visitor,* May 12, 1924, p. 3.

E. Morris Sider

Smith, John (1790–1824), missionary in Guyana with the London Missionary Society (LMS). Smith was born in Northamptonshire, England, and apprenticed in London at age 14. While there he underwent a conversion experience and subsequently applied to the LMS. He arrived in Demerara, Guyana, in 1817, and settled at a plantation called Resouvenir. In August 1823 a slave revolt broke out, and Smith, whose sympathies with the slaves were well known, was accused of aiding and assisting the rebellion. He was tried, convicted, and sentenced to death. His sentence was remitted, but he died in prison before word reached the colony. Smith was the only missionary who could be said to have been martyred by the West Indian plantocracy.

BIBLIOGRAPHY V. Roth, ed., *The Demerara Martyr: Memoirs of the Rev. John Smith, Missionary to Demerara,* by the Rev. Edwin Angel Wallbridge, 1848, with prefatory notes containing hitherto unpublished historical matter by J. Graham Cruickshank (1943); London Missionary Society, *Report of the Proceedings against the Late Rev. J. Smith of Demerara* (1824).

Geoffrey Johnston

Smith, John Coventry (1903–1984), Presbyterian missionary statesman. Born in Stamford, Ontario, Canada, Smith graduated from Muskingum College in Ohio (B.A., 1925), Pittsburgh Theological Seminary (B.D., 1928), and Hartford Seminary Foundation (M.A., 1936). He married Floy Bauder in 1928. After a brief pastorate in Pennsylvania, Smith and his wife were appointed missionaries to Japan under the Presbyterian Church, U.S.A. They served from 1929 to 1942 in Tokyo, Sapporo, and Wakayama. Becoming a prisoner of war in December 1942, Smith was repatriated in June 1943.

From 1943 to 1948 he spoke widely throughout the United States, served a pastorate in Pittsburgh, and helped relocate Japanese-American interns. From 1948 to 1958 he was Far East Secretary of the Presbyterian Board of Foreign Missions. In 1958 he was named associate general secretary of his church's Commission on Ecumenical Mission and Relations (COEMAR). He then served as COEMAR's general secretary from 1959 until his retirement in 1970.

Smith's interdenominational leadership included service as chairman of the executive committee of Japan's International Christian University (1951–1970), chairman of the Theological Education Fund (1958–1964), member of the World Council of Churches Central Committee (1961–1972), president of the World Council of Churches (1968–1972), chairman of the Division of Overseas Ministries, National Council of Churches in the United States (1963–1966), and organizer of regular dialogue among executives of conciliar and independent mission agencies (1961–1970).

BIBLIOGRAPHY John Coventry Smith, *From Colonialism to World Community: The Church's Pilgrimage* (1982).

Norman A. Horner

Smith, Matilda (1749–1821), South African independent teacher, mission advocate, and evangelist. Born and raised in a Dutch family in the Cape Colony, Smith (Machtilt Schmidt, in Dutch; Magtildt Schmidt in Africaans) was an extraordinary woman. Twice widowed, she saw all but one of her children die young. She was a regular churchgoer, but it was H. van Lier who guided her through an evangelical conversion. At that time no missionary society was active in the Cape, and the local church was anything but missionary. Almost single-handedly she began to preach to and teach the slaves, as well as to stimulate more Christian concern on their behalf among her fellow whites. She was delighted when J. *Van der Kemp arrived in the Cape with the pioneer party of the London Missionary Society (LMS). From then on her home in the city became a home away from home for all missionaries arriving in South Africa. She helped Van der Kemp found the South African Missionary Society, and in 1806, when Van der Kemp was confined to Cape Town by the colonial authorities, she took over as superintendent of the LMS station with its attendant villages at Bethelsdorp and remained in charge for two years. She founded a number of benevolent associations, the most important of which was the Cape Ladies Society for the Relief of the Poor.

BIBLIOGRAPHY John Philip, *A Memorial of Mrs. Matilda Smith* (1824).

Andrew C. Ross

Smith, Oswald J(effrey) (1889–1986), Canadian minister and mission advocate. Smith was the founder (1928) and longtime pastor of the People's Church in Toronto, Canada, an independent congregation and one of the most dynamic and mission-minded churches in North America. He believed that "the supreme task of the church is the evangelization of the world," and everything he did revolved around that belief. In a lifetime career of itinerant evangelism and exhortation, he preached in over seventy countries, using every means available to multiply his evangelistic efforts. He wrote scores of tracts, sermons, and pamphlets, and thirty-five books, with sales of six million in 128 languages. People's Church was also a pioneer among the churches of Canada in the use of radio, television, films, and cassette tapes. Smith is perhaps best known, however, for his pioneering promotion of the Faith Promise Method of missionary giving, which has greatly multiplied giving to missions in hundreds of churches around the globe.

BIBLIOGRAPHY Lois Neely, *Fire in His Bones* (1982); Doug Hall, *Not Made for Defeat* (1969).

Gary R. Corwin

Smith, Stanley P. (1861–?), English missionary and evangelist in China. Born in London, Smith became a Christian in 1874. During his days at Trinity College, when he was a prominent member of the Cambridge rowing team, he engaged in street evangelism and participated in D. L. *Moody's 1884 London campaign. He went to China with the China Inland Mission (CIM) in 1885, as one of the famed *Cambridge Seven. Most of his missionary service was in the province of Shansi (Shanxi) in the cities of Linfen, Hongtong, Lungan (Changzhi), and Tsechou (Jincheng). Often working with the noted Chinese leader *Hsi Shengmo, he engaged in rural evangelism, ministry to opium addicts, and training of evangelists. A forceful and fluent speaker in both English and Chinese, he was widely effective in revival and evangelistic rallies. A man of strong opinions, he had difficulty in relating well to missionary and Chinese colleagues. He once shocked Hudson *Taylor by joining with other missionaries and local Christians in a Salvation Army–type parade through the streets of Lungan. In the late 1890s he espoused the universal salvation of non-Christians rather than the CIM statement asserting "eternal punishment of the lost" and as a result was asked to resign from the mission. In 1900 he published *China from Within.* After this date his name is not found in extant records.

BIBLIOGRAPHY Material on the life and ministry of Stanley Smith can be found in A. J. Broomhall, *Hudson Taylor and China's Open Century,* vols. 6 and 7 (1988, 1989).

Ralph R. Covell

Smith, Wilfred Cantwell (1916–), historian of religion. Born and educated in Toronto, Canada, Smith studied theology under H. H. Farmer and Islamics under Hamilton A. R. Gibb in England. In 1941 he went to India under the auspices of the Canadian Overseas Missions Council and taught at Forman Christian College, Lahore. Smith founded and directed McGill University's Graduate Institute of Islamic Studies (1951–1963) and directed Harvard University's Center for the Study of World Religions (1964–1973), retiring to Toronto in 1984. His experience of Christian denominationalism in Canada and of communal conflict in India sensitized him to the harm done by religious dogmatism and by the demands of group loyalty. He argued that faith, whether Christian, Muslim, or other, is the essential and saving element in human experience. He saw the tendency to ascribe absoluteness to theological propositions or moral codes as destructive. Yet he never conceded that religious truth is unrelated to reality; experience of the transcendent is neither objective nor subjective but personal.

Smith's comparative study of religious traditions led him to conclude that God is at work in our day, not to bring the nations to Christ, but rather to enlarge the partial awarenesses of God enjoyed by Christians and others, through exposure to each other. In 1967 he suggested that Western Christian bodies should reorgnize their boards for foreign mission into two boards—one for intrachurch relations, and another for dialogue with non-Christians. In 1988, troubled by the persistence of interreligious animosities around the world, Smith continued to proclaim that God's grace and bounty are available to many non-Christians through their own traditions.

BIBLIOGRAPHY Smith's major works include *Islam in Modern History* (1957), *The Faith of Other Men* (1962), *The Meaning and End of Religion* (1962), *Questions of Religious Truth* (1967), *Toward a World Theology* (1981), and *What Is Scripture?* (1994). Smith's influence on Christian theology is assessed in John Berthrong, "Wilfred Cantwell Smith: The Theological Necessity of Pluralism," *Toronto Journal of Theology* 5 (1989): 188–205, and in Richard J. Jones, "Wilfred Cantwell Smith and Kenneth Cragg on Islam as a Way of Salvation," *IBMR* 16 (1992): 105–110. His practical views are expressed in "The Mission of the Church and the Future of Missions," in George Johnston and Wolfgang Roth, eds., *The Church in the Modern World* (1967), and in "Mission, Dialogue, and God's Will for Us," *IRM* 77 (1988): 360–374. See also Smith's chapters in Donald G. Dawe and John Carman, eds., *Christian Faith in a Religiously Plural World* (1978), and Gerald H. Anderson and Thomas F. Stransky, eds. *Christ's Lordship and Religious Pluralism* (1981).

Richard J. Jones

Smith, William (1806–1875), Church Missionary Society (CMS) missionary in India. Smith, the son of a manufacturer, came from Keighley, Yorkshire, England, and was educated at the CMS college at Islington, London. He was a gifted language learner, a good translator, and an effective bazaar preacher in the vernacular. First stationed at Gorakhpur in 1832, he settled in Benares (Varanasi) where, beginning in 1832 with his close associate C. P. *Leupolt, he strengthened the CMS mission. Together with Leupolt, he expanded chapel services, orphanages, and schools for both boys and girls; he also taught at Raja Jay Narain's Christian school in Benares. He established a teacher's training school to provide Christian teachers for his twenty-one village schools, with about 1,400 students. During the Mutiny of 1857, Henry C. *Tucker, commissioner at Benares, appointed him chaplain of a refugee station at Chunar. His most notable convert in Benares was the Maharashtrian Brahman Nilakantha (Nehemiah) *Goreh (1825–1893). Goreh's father was ostracized because he did not break relations with his son and allowed Smith to conduct Bible study in his home. Goreh accompanied Smith on his furlough to England (1848–1850). (Goreh's own notable convert was the widely influential Pandita *Ramabai.) When Smith retired in 1872, his mission numbered about 450 Christians, 16 catechists, and 2 national ministers.

BIBLIOGRAPHY Smith's only known publication was a prospectus for a school to "train evangelists for work among Hindus and Muslims" (1866) in CMS, *Papers on Education in India.* Robin H. S. Boyd, *India and the Latin Captivity of the Church: The Cultural Context of the Gospel* (1974); Roger Hooker, *Journey into Varanasi* (1978); C. P. Leupolt, *Recollections of an Indian Missionary* (4 eds., 1844 to 1884); Stephen Neill, *A History of Christianity in India, 1707–1858* (1985); *Proceedings of the CMS,* vol. 21 (1851); S. Satthianadhan, *Sketches of Indian Christians* (1896); M. A. Sherring, *The Missionary Life and Labours of the Rev. William Smith* (1879); Eugene Stock, *The History of the CMS: Its Environment, Its Men, and Its Work* (1899).

Peter Penner

Snow, Benjamin Galen (1817–1880), pioneer American missionary to Micronesia. Snow graduated from Bowdoin College (1846) and Bangor Seminary (1849) and then was sent to the island of Kusaie (now Kosrae) in Micronesia by the American Board of Commissioners for Foreign Missions (ABCFM) in 1852. Soon after his arrival, he had a flourishing church and school in operation. On the foundations laid by him and his wife, the Kusaien people have kept the church at the center of the common life up to the present time.

In 1860 the new ABCFM mission in the Marshall Islands collapsed because of the illness of the workers, and Snow was asked to rescue that work. He left Kusaie reluctantly, returning on occasional visits to encourage the people there. In the Marshalls he made his center on Ebon and recruited Hawaiians to staff the other islands. Again he encouraged the church to grow in an indigenous way as part of the social fabric. He also inspired Marshallese missionaries to go to the Mortlock Islands and himself introduced the first missionary to Truk (now Chuuk). In 1876 his health failed and the next year he and his wife were taken to Hawaii and then to the United States. He returned to his birthplace, Brewer, Maine, where he died.

BIBLIOGRAPHY James Peoples, *Island in Trust: Culture Change and Dependence in a Micronesian Economy* (1985), pp. 44–51; *Missionary Herald,* June 1880, p. 105.

Charles W. Forman

Söderblom, Nathan (Lars Olof Jonathan) (1866–1931), theologian, historian of religions, ecumenical pioneer, and archbishop of Uppsala. Söderblom was born in a Swedish country vicarage and educated at the University of Uppsala (1883–1894). Involved early in student missionary and YMCA activities, in 1890 he attended D. L. *Moody's Northfield student conference and was gripped by a vision of the unity of the church. From 1894 to 1901 he was pastor to the Swedish Legation in Paris, studying at the same time for his Sorbonne doctorate, completed in 1901 with a dissertation on comparative eschatology. In 1901 he returned to Uppsala as professor, with responsibilities in comparative religion and apologetics, dividing his time from 1912 to 1914 between Uppsala and Leipzig. Most of his major scholarly work was done in these years. Theologically he was orthodox but intellectually he was liberal and not greatly appreciated by church people. His unexpected election as archbishop was therefore unwelcome in some quarters. During and after World War I, Söderblom battled to keep Christians in the warring nations in touch with one another, but it was not until 1925 that the Stockholm Life and Work conference set the seal on his efforts. He also played a part in the 1927 Lausanne Faith and Order conference. (Ill health prevented him from attending the 1928 International Missionary Council conference in Jerusalem.) In 1930 he was awarded the Nobel Peace Prize (alone of all prizewinners, he had actually known Nobel), and after a final lecture series in Scotland, he died in Uppsala and was buried in Uppsala Cathedral. Söderblom was never a missionary, but he had a lifelong commitment to mission, and as scholar, administrator, and international leader he left a profound mark on the world church, of which mission is so integral a part.

BIBLIOGRAPHY In Swedish there is a vast Söderblom literature, though there is still no definitive biography. Particularly valuable are Tor Andræ, *Nathan Söderblom* (1931); Nils Karlström, ed., *Nathan Söderblom in Memoriam* (1931); and Bengt Sundkler, *Nathan Söderblom och hans möten* (1975). In English, see Bengt Sundkler, *Nathan Söderblom: His Life and Work* (1968); Eric J. Sharpe, *Nathan Söderblom and the Study of Religion* (1990) and "The Legacy of Nathan Söderblom," *IBMR* 12 (1988): 65–70.

Eric J. Sharpe

Soga, Mina Tembeka (1893–1981?), South African missions advocate. Soga was born in the Queenstown district of the Eastern Cape. After a Scottish Presbyterian mission education, she became a schoolteacher, fully involved (though unmarried) in the social life of the community. She attended the 1938 Tambaram meeting of the International Missionary Council as an official delegate, the first African woman to represent the continent at a world missionary conference. She made a notable contribution to the conference on the theme of the Africanization of the inner life of the church, which to her was a clear priority. From Tambaram she journeyed via the Red Sea and Egypt to the United States, where she brought a forceful message about the deprivation of black South Africans. After her return to Africa from the United States, she continued to work in the Eastern Cape as teacher and social worker, concerning herself especially with the plight of blind Africans.

BIBLIOGRAPHY Soga's mission thinking is reflected in her article "The Need for the Missionary Today: His Place and Function," *IRM* 28 (1939): 217–220. Her biography was written by Ruth I. Seabury, *Daughter of Africa* (1954). Her missiological contribution is discussed by E. Utuk, *From New York to Ibadan: The Impact of African Questions on the Making of Ecumenical Mission Mandates, 1900–1958* (1991).

Willem Saayman

Soga, Tiyo (1829–1871), South African minister. Born in eastern Cape Colony, Soga went to a mission school and later received more advanced education at Lovedale. He also spent two periods studying in Scotland under the auspices of Scottish Presbyterian missionaries, qualifying first as a teacher and later as a minister at the University of Glasgow. In 1856 he was ordained in Scotland in the Presbyterian Church—the first black South African to be ordained to the Christian ministry. Back in the eastern Cape, he served as minister at Mgwali (1857–1868) and at Tutura from 1868 until his untimely death. His missionary approach was typical of the time, concentrating especially on preaching and rudimentary teaching. He had, however, a stronger interest than most in the healing dimension of Christian mission.

BIBLIOGRAPHY John A. Chalmers, *Tiyo Soga: A Page of South African Mission Work,* 2d ed. (1878); H. T. Cousins, *From Kafir Kraal to Pulpit: The Story of Tiyo Soga* (1899); W. Saayman, "Tiyo Soga and Nehemiah Tile: Black Pioneers in Mission and Church," *Missionalia* 17, no. 2, (1989): 95–102; D. Williams, *Umfundisi: A Biography of Tiyo Soga, 1829–1871* (1978) and ed., *The Journal and Selected Writings of the Rev. Tiyo Soga* (1983).

Willem Saayman

Solages, (Gabriel) Henri (Jerome) de (1786–1832), Catholic promoter of missions to the Pacific. Born at Rabastens near Albi, France, de Solages became vicar-general of the Diocese of Palmiers. Obsessed with the Pacific Islands, then largely neglected by the Catholic Church, in 1829 he accepted a post as prefect apostolic to the island of Bourbon (Reunion) east of Madagascar. He developed his Pacific plans with an experienced Irish sea captain, Peter Dillon, also anxious to promote Catholic Pacific missions, and sought funding from Pauline *Jaricot's organization, the Society for the Propagation of the Faith. In 1830 Rome's Propaganda Fide created a gigantic South Pacific prefecture and named de Solages to be in charge. (Later the Pacific was divided into several, more manageable dioceses.) Solages' 1831 arrival in Bourbon created major dissension among the missionaries. In mid-1832 he made a poorly planned visit to Madagascar, where he was arrested, confined, and later died of fever. Despite his failures, de Solages focused church attention upon the needs of the Pacific. His plans eventually led Rome to invite the Marists to undertake the South Pacific mission.

BIBLIOGRAPHY Georges Goyau, *Les grands desseins missionaires d'Henri de Solages, 1786–1832* (1933); Ralph M. Wiltgen, *The Founding of the Roman Catholic Church in Oceania, 1825 to 1850* (1979).

John Hosie, SM

Solano, Francisco (1549–1610), Franciscan missionary and preacher in Argentina and Peru. Born of a wealthy family in Andalusia, Spain, Solano studied under the Jesuits, entered the Franciscan order, and was ordained a priest in 1576. After more than 20 years of work as a novice master, preacher, and teacher in Spain, he set out for the New World in 1589 in response to the call of Philip II for more friars of the strict observance. He passed through Lima and reached Santiago de Estero, Argentina, in 1590. In 1595 he was elected custos, or superior, of the Franciscans in Tucumán and Paraguay. Besides winning fame as a preacher, he played the violin, which he used in evangelizing the Indians. Upon finishing his term as superior in 1598, he returned to Lima, where he served as guardian of the order's monastery. Esteemed in his own lifetime as a "reincarnation" of Saint *Francis, he was canonized in 1726. One of the two Franciscan provinces in Peru is named after him.

BIBLIOGRAPHY Antolín Abad Pérez, *Los Franciscanos en América* (1992); L. J. Plandolit, *El Apóstol de América: San Francisco Solano* (1963); F. Royer, *St. Francis Solanus, Apostle to America* (1955).

Jeffrey Klaiber, SJ

Song, John. *See* Sung, John Shang-chieh.

Soper, Annie (1883–1976), pioneer of evangelical missions in the jungles of Peru. Born in England and trained as a nurse, Soper volunteered for missionary service but was rejected because of poor health. She moved to Canada to work as a nurse, and there she learned of the need for a tutor at the oldest hospital in Lima. She traveled to Lima in 1916 and engaged in an innovative instruction program. In 1922 she crossed the Andes on horseback to open medical work in Moyobamba, a remote city in the northeastern Peruvian jungle. In 1929, with missionary nurse Rhoda Gould, she went further on to Lamas and opened the first hospital in that region, linked afterward to a network of clinics staffed by women missionaries. Her medical work was accompanied by evangelistic activities, and evangelical churches spread through the region. She founded a Bible institute and sent its best graduates for advanced study in San José, Costa Rica. Eventually her work became related to the Regions Beyond Missionary Union. In recognition of her achievements, the president of Peru gave Soper that country's highest award. In 1953 she returned to England where she died in her tenth decade.

BIBLIOGRAPHY Phyllis Thompson, *Dawn beyond the Andes* (1955).

Samuel Escobar

Soper, Edmund Davison (1876–1961), Methodist mission educator. Soper was born in Tokyo, Japan, of American Methodist missionary parents. Following graduation from Dickinson College, Carlisle, Pennsylvania, and Drew Theological Seminary, Madison, New Jersey, he first expressed his lifelong interest in fundamental problems of the Christian world mission as field secretary of the Missionary Education Movement (1906–1910). Beginning in 1910 as professor of missions and comparative religion at Ohio Wesleyan University, he was known as an engaging teacher. This continued in later years, at Drew Theological Seminary, Northwestern University, Duke University, and Garrett Biblical Institute; he also served visiting professorships in India, Singapore, and Manila. As the seventh president of Ohio Wesleyan University (1929–1937), he helped that Methodist institution emerge from the Great Depression with strength.

Soper's greatest contribution to missiology was through his writings, honed by years of interpreting the Christian mission to undergraduate and theological students. He thoroughly revised *The Religions of Mankind* (1921) in 1938 and 1951 in light of contemporary scholarship. In his textbook *The Philosophy of the Christian World Mission* (1943), he defended the uniqueness of Christianity and its continuity with other religions as a middle ground between William Ernest *Hocking and Hendrik *Kraemer. In two works—*Lausanne: The Will to Understand* (1928) and *Racism: A World Issue* (1947)—he introduced to a wider audience the cutting edges of ecumenical thought.

BIBLIOGRAPHY Other works by Soper include *The Faiths of Mankind* (1918), *What May I Believe?* (1927), and *Inevitable Choice: Vedanta Philosophy or Christian Gospel* (1957).

Norman E. Thomas

Soto Fontánez, Santiago (1904–1985), Baptist church planter and intellectual leader of Hispanics in the United States. Born in Puerto Rico, Soto Fontánez graduated from the normal school of Rio Piedras and worked as a rural teacher. His Baptist church sent him as a missionary teacher to El Salvador, where he served from 1925 to 1932, after which he returned to Puerto Rico as a minister in Baptist churches at Yauco and Barrio Obrero. He completed studies at the Evangelical Seminary and the University of Puerto Rico. In 1944 he moved to New York for doctoral studies at Columbia University and became a teacher at Brooklyn College, but he kept his evangelistic and pastoral activity as a bivocational pastor of the Hispanic Central Baptist Church in New York. In 1959 he was asked to give leadership to the growing Hispanic ministry of the American Baptist Churches, and in 1972 he became the first director of the Hispanic department at the denominational headquarters in Valley Forge, Pennsylvania. As a specialist in themes related to Hispanic identity, he lectured extensively about the Spanish mystics of the sixteenth century. In 1985 the Hispanic library of Eastern Baptist Theological Seminary in Philadelphia was named after him.

BIBLIOGRAPHY Soto Fontánez wrote a bilingual autobiography that offers valuable data about Baptist ministry among Hispanics in the United States, *Misión a la puerta. Mission at the Door* (1982).

Samuel Escobar

Spae, Joseph J. (1913–1989), Catholic mission specialist on modern China and interreligious dialogue. Spae was born in Lochristi, Belgium. As a member of the Scheut missionaries, he was ordained a priest in 1936 and sent to China the following year. In 1938 he went to Japan, where he studied Buddhism and worked as a missionary, pastor, and scholar. In 1947 he received a doctorate in sinology and japanology at Columbia University, New York City. He founded the journal *Japan Missionary Bulletin* (now *Japan Mission Journal*) and the Oriens Institute for Religious Research (Tokyo). From 1972 to 1975 he was secretary general of SODEPAX (Society, Development and Peace joint committee in Geneva cosponsored by the Vatican and the World Council of Churches) and worked also for the Pontifical Institute for Non-Christians (now the Pontifical Council for Interreligious Dialogue). In 1982 he founded the magazine *China Update* and remained its publisher until his death. He was a dedicated worker and often controversial. Some of his more important publications are *Christianity Encounters Japan* (1968), *De Japanese uitdaging: Oosters denken en Westers Christendom* (1977), *East Challenges West: Towards a Convergence of Spiritualities* (1979), *Church and China: Towards Reconciliation?* (1980), *World Religions: East Meets West* (1982), and *China Revisited* (1984). He died in Ghent, Belgium.

BIBLIOGRAPHY R(oman) M(alek), "Joseph J. Spae, C.I.C.M. (1913–1989)," *China heute* 9 (1990): 34–35; John Raymaker, "In Memoriam: Joseph J. Spae (1913–1989)," *Mission Studies* 7 (1990): 243–244; Bernward H. Willeke, "P. Joseph J. Spae CICM (1913–1989)," *ZMR* 74 (1990): 303.

Karl Müller, SVD

Spalding, Henry Harmon (1804–1874), American pioneer missionary to Nez Percé Indians. Spalding was born in Bath, New York, graduated from Western Reserve College, Cleveland, studied at Lane Seminary, Cincinnati, Ohio, and was ordained in August 1835. In March 1836, under appointment by the American Board of Commissioners for Foreign Missions (ABCFM), Spalding, his wife,

Eliza, Dr. and Mrs. Marcus *Whitman, and William H. Gray began a journey of more than 2,200 miles on what became known as the Oregon Trail; the mission itself became known as the Oregon Mission. The two women were the first white women to cross the Rocky Mountains. The Spaldings established a station among the Nez Percés at Lapwai (present-day Spalding, Idaho), 100 miles north of the Whitmans' station. The first six years of the Oregon Mission were marked by dissension among the missionaries. Criticism of Spalding's methods, particularly by fellow missionary Asa Bowen Smith, led to Spalding's dismissal by the ABCFM in 1842; Marcus Whitman went east to intercede with the board, and the dismissal was rescinded. The years 1843 to 1847 saw increasing Native American hostility toward the missionaries. In November 1847 the Oregon Mission was brought to an end when hostile Nez Percés attacked the Whitmans' station, leaving fourteen dead. The Spaldings moved to Kalapoolya (present-day Brownsville, Oregon), where he taught among white settlers. Spalding eventually returned to Lapwai to teach, first in a government school (1862–1865) and later under the Presbyterian Church auspices (1871–1872).

BIBLIOGRAPHY Clifford M. Drury, *Henry Harmon Spalding, Pioneer of Old Oregon* (1936) and *The Diaries and Letters of Henry H. Spalding and Asa Bowen Smith Relating to the Nez Perce Mission, 1838–1842* (1958). Drury's publication of Spalding's diary is from the original held at Whitman College, Walla Walla, Wash. See also ABCFM, "Vinton" book (1869–1910).

Martha Lund Smalley

Spangenberg, August Gottlieb (1704–1792), Moravian bishop, theologian, and administrator. Spangenberg was born in Clettenberg, Germany, and entered the University of Jena in 1722. When he received his M.A. in 1729, he was already acquainted with the Moravians. After an unhappy teaching experience in Halle, in 1733 he moved to Herrnhut as adjunct to the Moravian leader Nikolaus Ludwig von *Zinzendorf. In this role he traveled widely and provided leadership for the establishment of Moravian settlements and missions to Native Americans in Georgia, Pennsylvania, and North Carolina. He was consecrated a bishop in 1744. Following Zinzendorf's death in 1760, Spangenberg helped develop a conferential system of governance for the Moravian Church. His major literary works provide significant information regarding the formative years of Moravian theology and missions. His three-volume biography *Leben des Herrn Nikolaus Ludwig Grafen und Herrn von Zinzendorf und Pottendorf* was published from 1772 to 1775. An abridged English translation by Samuel Jackson, *The Life of Nikolaus Lewis Count Zinzendorf*, appeared in 1838. In 1779 Spangenberg issued his systematic theology, *Idea Fidei Fratrum* (translated into English by Benjamin *La Trobe as *An Exposition of Christian Doctrine* in 1796). In 1782 he produced the first summary of Moravian mission work, *Von der Arbeit Evangelischen Brüder unter den Heiden,* which appeared in an anonymous English translation in 1788 as *An Account of the Manner in Which the Protestant Church of the Unitas Fratrum, or United Brethren, Preach the Gospel, and Carry on Their Missions among the Heathen.*

In his writing Spangenberg shows himself to be a competent but rather traditional theologian. His apologetic motive is clear as he sought to address what some of his contemporaries regarded as the extremes of Zinzendorf's thought. His missiological views and practical leadership defined Moravian mission work until the mid-nineteenth century.

BIBLIOGRAPHY Spangenberg's autobiographical statement, "Dankbare Erinnerung an Eineige der Evangelischen Brüder-Unität von dem Herrn seit etlichen und fünfzig Jahren erzeigte besondere Gnadenbeweise" (1784–1785), translated by Albert F. Jordan as, "Recollections of Fifty Years," is in the Moravian archives, Bethlehem, Pennsylvania. His contributions are discussed by J. E. Hutton, *A History of Moravian Missions* (1923). Two biographies are Charles T. Ledderhose, *The Life of Augustus Gottlieb Spangenberg* (1855) and Gerhard Reichel, *August Gottlieb Spangenberg, Bischof der Brüderkirche* (1906).

David A. Schattschneider

Spartas, Christopher Reuben (c. 1900–1982), pioneer of Orthodox Christianity in East Africa. Born Reuben Sebbania Ssedima Mukasa in Uganda, Spartas, a Muganda, was baptized in the Anglican Church and educated in mission schools. He took the name "Spartas" in his teens, having been told he exemplified the spirit of the ancient Greek city Sparta. Completing his education in 1920 at King's College, Budo, he joined the King's African Rifles (KAR), where he met Obadiah Basajjakitalo, also a Muganda. In 1925 they left KAR to found Anonya Private School, near Degeya.

In 1925 Spartas learned of the founding of the African Orthodox Church (AOC) in America, which grew out of Marcus Garvey's movement in 1921. Spartas was attracted by the goal of AOC, which, as he read in *Negro World* (magazine of the AOC), was to become a universal black church in affiliation with an ancient Christian Church not known for racism or colonialism. He then wrote to George McGuire of Antigua, patriarch of the AOC of the World. In 1928 McGuire referred Spartas to Daniel Alexander, archbishop of the AOC in South Africa; and in January 1929 Spartas broke with the Anglican Church and established the AOC in Uganda. When Alexander visited Uganda in 1931–1932, he ordained Spartas and Basajjakitalo to the priesthood.

During Alexander's visit, a Greek expatriate named Vlahos invited Alexander to baptize his children. Noting that the service as conducted by Alexander did not follow proper Orthodox form, Vlahos advised Spartas to contact Nicodemos Sarikas, an Orthodox clergyman serving the Greek expatriate community in Tanganyika (now Tanzania). Spartas did so, and after Sarikas visited Uganda, Spartas severed relations with Alexander and sought recognition by the Greek Orthodox patriarchate of Alexandria. In 1943, after Spartas had been approached by Arthur Gatung'u wa Gathuna of the AOC in Kenya, a constitution was negotiated uniting the Orthodox Church in Kenya and Uganda. In 1946 Spartas visited Alexandria and was officially recognized and named vicar general for Uganda. In September 1953 the African Greek Orthodox

Church was registered in Uganda, and in 1959 the Patriarchate of Alexandria established the archdiocese of East Africa, encompassing Kenya, Uganda, and Tanzania.

BIBLIOGRAPHY Erasto Muga, *African Responses to Western Christian Religion* (1975), pp. 153 ff.; *Musalaba* (bimonthly newsletter of the Orthodox Church in Uganda) 4, no. 2 (March/April 1990): 3–7; Theodoros Nankyama, *Introduction to Orthodoxy in Uganda* (1989); Theodore Natsoulas, "Patriarch McGuire and the Spread of the African Orthodox Church to Africa," *Journal of Religion in Africa* 12:2 (1981): 83–104; F. B. Welbourn, *East African Rebels: A Study of Some Independent Churches* (1961), pp. 77–102.

Dimitrios G. Couchell

Spaulding, Levi (1791–1873), American missionary to Ceylon (Sri Lanka). Spaulding was born in Jaffrey, New Hampshire, and graduated from Dartmouth College (1815) and Andover Theological Seminary (1818). He was ordained and was married in 1818 to Mary Christie. They sailed for India in 1819 under the American Board of Commissioners for Foreign Missions (ABCFM) and reached Jaffna, Ceylon, in 1820. They served at Manepay from 1821 to 1828 and at Tellippallai from 1828 to 1833, but for most of their long career they served at Uduville, where for many years Levi was in charge of the church, schools, and evangelistic work in the villages. In 1834 he led a party exploring possible locations for a new ABCFM mission to the Tamils of South India and chose Madura as the site. From 1838 on he devoted much energy to translation, including *Pilgrim's Progress*, to the writing of tracts and hymns, and to the work of revisions for the mission press. He published a Tamil dictionary and an English-Tamil dictionary (1852). Spaulding served for many years on the commission of the Bible Society in Madras for revision of the Scriptures. Mary Spaulding, who was in charge of the girls' boarding school in Uduville for nearly 40 years, was affectionately known as Mother Spaulding. She died in 1875.

BIBLIOGRAPHY *Missionary Herald* 45 (1849): 309, 69 (1873): 307–308, and many other issues during Spaulding's years of service. C. W. Spaulding, *The Spaulding Memorial: A Genealogical History...* (1897).

David M. Stowe

Speer, Robert E(lliott) (1867–1947), Presbyterian mission administrator. Speer was born in Huntingdon, Pennsylvania, graduated from Princeton University, and itinerated as a recruiter for the Student Volunteer Movement (SVM), from 1889 to 1890. He left Princeton Theological Seminary in his middler year (1891) to accept a call as secretary of the Presbyterian Board of Foreign Missions and served in that capacity until his retirement in 1937. As a key administrator and strategist for one of the largest denominational mission agencies in America, Speer established himself as a visible and respected leader of the Protestant missionary advance in the early twentieth century. He was active in several missions and ecumenical organizations, including the SVM, the Foreign Missions Conference of North America, the Federal Council of Churches, the International Missionary Council, and the Committee on Cooperation in Latin America. In 1927 he was elected moderator of the General Assembly of the Presbyterian Church. Through his wide-ranging endeavors, he contributed significantly to a Protestant consensus, which prevailed through World War I, about the nature and purposes of the missionary enterprise. He then defended it in the 1920s and 1930s by resisting both the liberal tilt of the Laymen's Foreign Missions Inquiry and fundamentalist attempts, led by J. Gresham Machen, to purge the Presbyterian Board of allegedly unorthodox missionaries.

Speer's missiology reflected many of the principles of Rufus *Anderson. He emphasized the primary evangelistic aim of foreign missions, the necessity of developing indigenous local churches with native pastors, and the basic distinction between the proclamation of the gospel and the spread of civilization. In later years he reiterated his convictions about the uniqueness of Christ and the superiority of Christianity to other religions. Although not a theologian, he consistently set forth an evangelical and Christocentric conception of the missionary task.

Speer's compelling oratory is manifested in many of his published addresses and sermons. He also wrote numerous articles, pamphlets, and books. His major works of missiological significance include *Missionary Principles and Practice* (1902), *The Gospel and the New World* (1919), *The Church and Missions* (1926), *The Unfinished Task of Foreign Missions* (1926), *The Finality of Jesus Christ* (1933), and *"Re-Thinking Missions" Examined* (1933). His willingness to tackle controversial social problems is evident in *Of One Blood* (1924) and *Some Living Issues* (1930). He also authored several missionary biographies, Bible studies, and books on practical dimensions of Christian living.

BIBLIOGRAPHY H. M. Goodpasture, "Robert Speer," in Gerald H. Anderson et al., eds., *Mission Legacies* (1994), pp. 563–569; Bradley J. Longfield, *The Presbyterian Controversy: Fundamentalists, Modernists, and Moderates* (1991), chap. "Robert E. Speer and the Board of Foreign Missions"; James A. Patterson, "Robert E. Speer and the Crisis of the American Protestant Missionary Movement, 1920–1937" (Ph.D. diss., Princeton Theological Seminary, 1980); John F. Piper, Jr., "Robert E. Speer: His Call and the Missionary Impulse, 1890–1900," *American Presbyterians* 65 (1987): 97–108; W. Reginald Wheeler, *A Man Sent from God: A Biography of Robert E. Speer* (1956). Papers of Robert E. Speer are held at Speer Library, Princeton Theological Seminary, Princeton, N.J., and in the library at Bryn Mawr College, Bryn Mawr, Penn.

James A. Patterson

Spener, Philipp Jakob (1635–1705), founding father of German Pietism. Spener was never involved in operational missions. The year of his death was also the year in which the Danish-Halle Mission in South India was initiated, and there is no indication that Spener had an active part in the project. However, Bartholomäus *Ziegenbalg, the pioneer missionary, was familiar with some of Spener's writings, had heard him preach in Berlin, and had met him there. At Tranquebar, Spener's catechism was translated into Portuguese and Tamil and occasionally used as a textbook for students. Spener's main concern had been the reform of the church in Germany. But elements of a theology of mission were scattered over the whole vast collection of sermons, letters, reports, and other texts, most of them published, which Spener left behind. To him mission was, in the first place, a matter of obedience to the call of God, who wants all to be saved. It is not to be left to professional messengers, although they are indispensable, but rather to all believers, as implied in what Luther called the universal priesthood of believers. Thus it is Christ himself who works through his people.

While Spener never had an opportunity to participate in missions to non-Christians outside Europe, he did test his convictions in the practice of evangelism among Jews whom he met both in Frankfurt (1666–1686) and in Berlin (1691–1705). The later editions of his outline of church reform, entitled *Pia Desideria,* contained an appendix of forty pages on the "forthcoming glorious conversion of the Jewish people" (1680).

BIBLIOGRAPHY Hans-Ludwig Althaus, "Speners Bedeutung für Heiden—und Judenmission," *Lutherisches Missionsjahrbuch* 74 (1961): 22–44. No comparable account in English is available.

Hans-Werner Gensichen

Spicer, William A(mbrose) (1865–1952), church administrator and missionary leader in the Seventh-day Adventist (SDA) Church. Spicer was born in Minnesota into a Seventh Day Baptist family that became Seventh-day Adventist and moved to Battle Creek, Michigan, during his early youth. After several church assignments, including a brief term as a missionary in India, he was made secretary of the SDA Foreign Mission Board in 1901. This was followed by a long career of leadership in the General Conference as secretary (1903–1922), president (1922–1930), and general field secretary (1930–1940).

With A. G. Daniells (president of the General Conference, 1901–1922, and secretary, 1922–1926), Spicer developed a missions strategy coupling churches in colonial homelands with mission fields in their areas of influence. They also established a network of mission stations and medical and educational institutions (many of which were grant-aided) as instrumentalities of mission. Spicer was constantly involved in guiding this expansion, and in selecting, providing education for, and maintaining contact with missionaries. He traveled constantly, supervising missionary activity and generating missionary support and enthusiasm during an era of dramatic expansion of the SDA Church. He led an SDA delegation to the World Missionary Conference at Edinburgh in 1910. A prolific author, he produced more than 20 books and wrote some 2,500 articles for the *Review and Herald* and other church papers.

BIBLIOGRAPHY William A. Spicer, *The Hand of God in History* (1913), *Youthful Witness* (1921), *Our Story of Missions* (1921), *The Gospel in All the World* (1926), *Miracles of Modern Mission* (1926), *Certainties of the Advent Movement* (1929), *Pioneer Days of the Advent Movement* (1941), and *After One Hundred Years, 1844–1944* (1944). Godfrey T. Anderson, *Spicer: Leader with the Common Touch* (1983); "General Conference" and "Spicer, William Ambrose," in *Seventh-day Adventist Encyclopedia,* 2d rev. ed. (1996); Daniel A. Ochs and Grace Lillian Ochs, *The Past and the Presidents* (1974); R. W. Schwarz, *Lightbearers to the Remnant* (1979); A. W. Spalding, *Origin and History of Seventh-day Adventists,* vols. 3 and 4 (1962).

Russell L. Staples

Spieth, (Andreas) Jakob (1856–1914), German Protestant missionary in Togo, West Africa. Born to pietist parents in Hegensberg, near Esslingen, Würtemberg, Spieth entered the Basel Mission seminary in Switzerland in 1874. The Norddeutsche Missions-Gesellschaft, based in Bremen, asked the Basel Mission for help in Togo, and Spieth agreed to the unexpected assignment. In 1880 he arrived at Ho (now in Ghana), his mission base. In 1882 he married the daughter of a missionary; three of their four children were born in Africa. Interrupted only by a two-year stay in Germany to recover his health (1883–1885), Spieth spent 21 years in Togo (from 1887 as superintendent), acquiring an excellent knowledge of the language and culture of the Ewe-speaking peoples, translating the New Testament, and continuously making notes on all his travels. Plagued repeatedly by fever, he was forced to return to Germany in 1901. Living in Tübingen and aided by the Africanists Carl *Meinhof and Diedrich *Westermann, he prepared the voluminous *Die Ewestämme: Material zur Kunde des Ewevolkes in Deutsch-Togo* (1906). It was mainly for this highly praised collection of Ewe texts and their translation into German that he was awarded the honorary D.D. by the University of Tübingen in 1911. In 1904, aided by Ludwig Adzaklo, he started translating the Old Testament into Ewe (the New Testament having been published in 1898). In 1909 he went again to Africa to conclude this task with the help of a translation committee working in Lome. He spent his last years directing the mission house in Hamburg and preparing the publication of the Bible. Two hundred printed copies reached the Ewe in 1916. Spieth had died in Hamburg two years earlier and was buried in his hometown.

BIBLIOGRAPHY Spieth's *Die Religion der Eweer in Süd-Togo* (1911) was a follow-up study of the collection of Ewe texts mentioned above and remains a lasting contribution to the ethnography and history of the Ewe-speaking peoples. Many articles by Spieth in the *AMZ* from 1883 to 1913 cover traditional Ewe culture and applications to missionary work. Emil Ohly, *Andeas Jakob Spieth, der Bibelübersetzer des Ewevolkes, ein Lebensbild* (1920).

Otto Bischofberger, SMB

Spinner, Wilfri(e)d (Heinrich) (1854–1918), Swiss missionary in Japan. Spinner was born in Bonstetten in the Canton of Zurich, and was a Reformed pastor in Dinhard near Winterthur from 1878 to 1885. In 1885 the Ostasien-Mission (OAM; founded in 1884 as Allgemeiner Evangelisch-protestantischer Missionsverein), which had come out of German theological liberalism, sent him to Japan as their first missionary. Although he worked there only a few years and did not speak Japanese, he had a diverse and successful ministry. In Tokyo (1885) and Yokohama (1886) he founded German-speaking churches, and in 1888 he took over the pastoral care of Germans in the Kobe/Osaka region. In 1887 the first indigenous church of the OAM was founded (Fukyu Fukuin Kyokwai-General Evangelical Church), with about thirty members. In the same year he started a theological seminary (which existed until 1908). He taught at a school of higher education in Tokyo, gave lectures in theology and history of religions, and also founded a theological magazine in Japanese, *Shinri* (Truth).

In 1891 he returned to Germany and became church superintendent in Ilmenau/Thuringia before being promoted in 1896 to court chaplain and privy councillor of the church in Weimar. In 1891 he received an honorary doctorate of theology from the University of Zürich.

BIBLIOGRAPHY Wilfrid Spinner, *Japan-Tagebuch 1885–1891* (Japan Diary), including introduction and commentary, in German and Japanese, Heyo E. Hamer, ed. (1997), and *Dem Andenken des Herrn Geheimen Kirchenrats Dr. theol. Wilfrid Spinner in Weimar* (1918). Heyo E. Hamer, "Zur Begegnung von E. Faber und W. Spinner in Shanghai," *Monatschefte für Evang. Kirchengeschichte des Rheinlandes* 39 (1990): 291–334; Otto Hering, "Erinnerungen an D. Spinner," *ZMkR* 33 (1918): 183–191; 34 (1919): 5–12, 19–25.

Werner Raupp

Spinola, Carlo (1564–1622), Catholic missionary in Japan and martyr. Born in Genoa, son of Octavius Spinola of Tassarola, Spinola entered the novitiate of the Society of Jesus in 1584 and was ordained priest in 1594. He eventually reached Japan in 1602. In Arima he learned Japanese and helped in the seminary. The following year he was appointed to direct missionary work, located first in Arie, then in Miyako (Kyoto), and in 1612 in Nagasaki. In Miyako he founded a kind of mathematical academy through which he attracted members of the intelligentsia. In Nagasaki he was both parish priest and treasurer of the whole Jesuit mission in Japan. Spinola was one of 23 Jesuits who did not obey the expulsion decree of the emperor in 1614, but he secretly continued his work as parish priest, treasurer, and vicar general for South Japan. On December 14, 1618, he was discovered and placed under arrest. After four years in prison he was burned at the stake in Nagasaki on September 10, 1622. With him died 25 other confessors of the faith, three of whom had apostatized shortly before. Thirty others were beheaded. The solemn beatification of 205 Japanese martyrs, including Carlo Spinola, took place on July 7, 1867.

BIBLIOGRAPHY Spinola's letters from prison are published in *Analecta Bollandiana* 6 (1887): 52–57. He was the author of "Carta del beato Carlos Spinola sobre su visita a San Germán en 1597," in *El cuatricentenario de San Germán* (1971), pp. 167–173. B. B. Bitter, *Mort de héros: Le Bx. Charles Spinola SJ* (1929); R. Cornely, *Leben des seligen Märtyrers Karl Spinola* (1868); D. Donnelly, *A Prisoner in Japan: Carlos Spinola SJ* (1928); D. Pacheco, "El proceso del beato Pedro de Zúñiga en Hirado (1621), según una relación del beato Carlos Spinola," in *Boletín de la Asociación Española de Orientalistas* 3 (1967): 23–43; G. M. Pastorino, *Una gloria di Genova e del Giappone (Il B. Carlo Spinola Mart. SJ)* (1938); F. Weiser, *Der Held von Nagasaki* (1928).

Karl Müller, SVD

Spittler, Christian Friedrich (1782–1867), cofounder of the Basel Mission. Spittler was a leading layman in the south German revival and missionary movement of the early nineteenth century. Born in a country parson's family in Württemberg, he was trained as a municipal administrator. But in 1801 he was called to Basel in order to succeed his friend Karl F. A. *Steinkopf as secretary of the Deutsche Christentumsgesellschaft (German Christian Association). Employing his talents as an organizer and promoter, he helped to found the Basel Bible Society (1804) and a number of other charitable institutions. His main concern, however, was devoted to establishing the Basel Mission (1815), together with his friends Christian G. *Blumhardt and Steinkopf. Blumhardt became the first inspector of the mission.

Later, Spittler pursued his second major project, a training institute for young men of different professions who, though unable to study for the ministry, would work for the spread of the gospel in other capacities. On the outskirts of Basel, near a chapel dedicated to Chrischona, a medieval pilgrim, Spittler established the St. Chrischona Mission (1840), where members were trained and sent out as lay missionaries to the Orient and elsewhere.

BIBLIOGRAPHY E. Schick, *Christian Friedrich Spittler* (1956); F. Veiel, *Die Pilgermission zu St. Chrischona* (1940).

Hans-Werner Gensichen

Springer, Helen Emily (Chapman) Rasmussen (1868–1946), missionary explorer and founder of American Methodist education for girls in Southern Rhodesia (Zimbabwe). After hearing Bishop William *Taylor, Helen Chapman volunteered to go to Africa as a self-supporting missionary. In 1891 she sailed for the Congo (Zaire). She married a Danish missionary, William Rasmussen, whom she met during the voyage. After six months, their health broken by malaria, the Rasmussens had to leave Africa; but they returned with their son in 1894. In 1895 William died and Helen again left the field. After her son died, she sailed for Southern Rhodesia in 1901 as the first missionary there of the Methodist Episcopal Woman's Foreign Missionary Society. Living in the villages to study Shona, she translated the Scriptures and hymns and in 1905 published *A Handbook of Chikaranga*. Over several years, she laid the foundation for Methodist girls' education.

In 1905 she married John *Springer. Together they walked across Northern Rhodesia (Zambia) and founded Methodist missions in the Congo (Zaire). The Springers opened Protestant work among the Lunda and in Katanga Province. Helen did women's work, conducted ministerial training, and translated the Scriptures. On furlough in 1919, she was a powerful speaker in recruiting for the Student Volunteer Movement, and she wrote on Africa for young people. After two more years in Southern Rhodesia, the Springers returned to the Congo, where she worked until she died.

BIBLIOGRAPHY Helen Springer, *Snap Shots from Sunny Africa* (1909) and *Campfires in the Congo* (1928). John M. Springer, *Pioneering in the Congo* (1916), *Christian Conquests in the Congo* (1927), and *I Love the Trail: A Sketch of the Life of Helen Emily Springer* (1952). See also J. Tremayne Copplestone, *History of Methodist Missions,* vol. 4, *Twentieth-Century Perspectives* (1973). Helen Springer's papers, including journals and correspondence, are held in the archives of the United Methodist Church, Madison, N.J.

Dana L. Robert

Springer, John McKendree (1873–1963), founder of American Methodist Congo Mission, missionary explorer, and bishop. Springer sailed to Southern Rhodesia (Zimbabwe) in 1901 as superintendent of the Old Umtali Industrial Mission. After marrying in 1905, he and his wife Helen Emily *Springer began forays into uncharted territory. Feeling called by God to fulfill the dreams of David *Livingstone and William *Taylor to found a chain of mission stations across central Africa, the Springers set off on foot from Northern Rhodesia (Zambia) to Angola despite mission board disapproval. Reaching the coast, they returned to the United States and Springer pressed for the establishment of a Congo Mission. After raising money, the Springers undertook an arduous two-year journey to found Methodist mission stations in the Congo (Zaire), including the Fox Bible Training School.

In 1915 the Congo Mission was formally approved, and Springer was its superintendent until 1936, except from 1921 to 1923, when he supervised Methodist work in Southern Rhodesia. Under him Protestant work was opened in Lunda country, in Katanga Province, and in other locations. In 1936 Springer was elected Methodist bishop for Africa. His belief in leadership training for the indigenous church caused him to work to establish higher education. After his retirement in 1944 he devoted himself to the Congo Institute he had founded in Mulungwishi, renamed the Springer Institute in his honor. He married another Congo missionary, Helen Everett, after the death of his first wife. They returned to the United States in 1963.

BIBLIOGRAPHY John M. Springer, *The Heart of Central Africa: Mineral Wealth and Missionary Opportunity* (1909), *Pioneering in the Congo* (1916), *Christian Conquest in the Congo* (1927), and *I Love the Trail: A Sketch of the Life of Helen Emily Springer* (1952). J. Tremayne Copplestone, *History of Methodist Missions,* vol. 4, *Twentieth-Century Perspectives* (1973). Springer's papers are held in the archives of the United Methodist Church, Madison, N.J.

Dana L. Robert

Stach, Matthew (1711–1787), pioneer Moravian missionary in Greenland. Stach was born at Markendorf, Moravia (in the modern Czech Republic), and immigrated to Herrnhut, Germany, in 1728, where he worked as a servant and later a wool spinner. He joined the Moravian Brethren in 1730 and in 1731 laid out the burial ground at Herrnhut with Frederick *Böhnisch. In 1733 he went to Greenland as one of the first Moravian missionaries and in 1740 baptized the first convert, Kajarnack. He married Rosina Stach (her maiden name) in 1741 and was consecrated a presbyter in December of that year. He spent time traveling between Greenland, the Netherlands, and North America between 1742 and 1755. In 1757 Stach's wife left both him and the church, but returned to them in 1771. In 1758 he returned to Greenland and served the stations at Fischer-Fiorde, New Herrnhut, and Lichtenfels. He produced a grammar and dictionary of the Greenland Eskimo dialect that served until the revision by J. C. *Kleinschmidt in 1823. He retired from mission service in 1771 and lived at Barby, Germany, until August 1772, when he moved to Bethabara, North Carolina. There he took charge of the small Moravian congregation, which was the oldest work in the Southern Province of the Moravian Church in America. He also served as master of the boys' school at Bethabara and a member of the Aufseher Collegium at nearby Salem. A fall in 1785 left him confined to bed, and he died two years later at age 76.

BIBLIOGRAPHY J. T. Hamilton and K. G. Hamilton, *History of the Moravian Church* (1967); J. E. Hutton, *History of the Moravian Church* (1909); *Kurze Lebenschreibungen merkwürdiger Männer aus der Brüdergemeine* (1842).

Albert H. Frank

Stahl, Ferdinand A(nthony) (1874–1950), Seventh-day Adventist missionary among the Aymara Indians of Bolivia and Peru. After training in nursing at the Battle Creek (Michigan) Sanitarium, Ferdinand Stahl and his wife, Ana (Carlson), paid their own way to La Paz, Bolivia, in 1909. Later they moved their base to Platería, Peru. Their work specifically focused on the Aymara Indians and became a model of incarnational and holistic mission, well known for its effects on the social transformation of one of the most marginalized sectors of Peruvian society. The Stahls traveled extensively throughout the region, usually by muleback. Several of the mission stations and schools that they founded prospered, and by 1932 they numbered 5,000 converts. The indigenous education system they established became a model for rural education in Peru. For health reasons the Stahls moved in 1921 to the lowlands in the Amazonian region of Peru where they worked among people in the jungle. They traveled up and down the rivers in a wood-burning steam launch called *Auxiliadora,* providing extensive medical services in a vast area. The Stahls retired to the United States in 1939.

BIBLIOGRAPHY A popular book about the Stahls is Barbara Westphal, *Ana Stahl of the Andes and the Amazon* (1960). The most complete biographical account is in Floyd Greenleaf, *The Seventh-day Adventist Church in Latin America and the Caribbean,* 2 vols. (1992). Extensive research about the Stahls has been carried on by Charles Teel at Loma Linda Univ., California.

Samuel Escobar

Stallybrass, Edward (1793–1884), English missionary in Siberia and translator of the Old Testament into Mongolian. After offering himself to the London Missionary Society (LMS), Stallybrass reached Moscow in 1817 and was joined there by Cornelius Rahm from Göteborg. In 1818 they were granted an audience by Alexander I, czar of Russia, who showed warm support for their work. They reached Irkutsk in March 1818. Stallybrass and his wife settled among the Buriat people at Selenginsk in July 1819, 200 miles northeast of Lake Baikal. His first wife died in 1833, but Stallybrass returned to Selenginsk with his second wife in 1839. In 1841 the work of the LMS was closed in Russia by decree of the Orthodox synod, but Stallybrass had completed and published the Mongolian Old Testament while in Siberia in 1840 and on his return to England began a revision of the Mongolian version of the New Testament produced in 1824 by the Russian Bible Society. He and William *Swan, another LMS missionary at Selenginsk, completed this work in London, and the result was published in 1846.

BIBLIOGRAPHY R. Lovett, *The History of the London Missionary Society, 1795–1895* (1899).

Timothy Yates

Stam, John C. (1907–1934) *and*
Elizabeth ("Betty") Alden (Scott) (1906–1934), American missionary martyrs in China. John Stam, son of a devout Christian family in New Jersey, and Betty Scott, born to missionary parents and raised in China, first met at Moody Bible Institute, Chicago. Scott went to China with the China Inland Mission in 1931, and Stam followed one year later. After they had completed language study, they were married in 1933 and assigned to work in the city of Tsingteh (Jingde), in the south of Anhwei (Anhui) Province. A daughter, Helen Priscilla, was born to them in Wuhu in September 1934. Following her birth, the young couple determined to return to Anhui, despite news of impending danger. When Communist troops captured Tsingteh on December 6, 1934, the Stams were taken to the nearby village of Miaosheo and beheaded the next day on a small hill. Their baby was spared by the intervention of a Chinese Christian who was killed as a substitute for her life. A Chinese Christian doctor who pleaded for them to their Communist captors was also executed. A Chinese evangelist from the village found Helen Priscilla Stam in an abandoned house and took her to mission friends in Wuhu. The tragic death of the Stams motivated many young people to missionary service.

BIBLIOGRAPHY Mrs. Howard (Mary Geraldine) Taylor, *The Triumph of John and Betty Stam* (1935).

Ralph R. Covell

Stanley, Henry Morton (1841–1904), journalist and Africa explorer. Stanley was born John Rowland in Denbigh, north Wales. Brought up in a workhouse, he immigrated to the United States in 1858. Arriving in New Orleans, he was adopted by a merchant who gave him his own name. Stanley became a journalist and in 1869 was commissioned by the *New York Herald* to search for David *Livingstone in central Africa. His success in finding Livingstone at Ujiji in November 1871—immortalized by his greeting "Dr. Livingstone, I presume?"—made Stanley a household name on both sides of the Atlantic. After Livingstone's death, Stanley continued his exploration of central Africa. He visited the court of Kabaka Mutesa I of Buganda in 1875 and then published an appeal for missionaries to be sent to Buganda. As a result, the Church Missionary Society commenced its Uganda mission in 1877. In the same year his journey from Nyangwe to Boma at the mouth of the Congo proved that the Lualaba River was not, as Livingstone had believed, a headwater of the Nile, but the upper reaches of the Congo. Through this journey, and his work from 1879 to 1884 as an employee of Leopold II of Belgium, Stanley was instrumental in opening the Congo to Protestant missions.

BIBLIOGRAPHY Stanley's numerous books include *How I Found Livingstone* (1872) and *In Darkest Africa* (1890). I. Anstruther, *I Presume: H. M. Stanley's Triumph and Disaster* (1956); R. Hall, *Stanley: An Adventurer Explored* (1974); Frank Hird, *H. M. Stanley: The Authorized Life* (1935). D. Stanley, ed., *The Autobiography of Sir Henry M. Stanley* (1909).

Brian Stanley

Stanway, Alfred (1908–1989), Anglican missionary and bishop in Africa. Stanway was born in Wimmera District, Victoria, Australia. Trained as an accountant, he was converted in 1928, whereupon he enrolled at Ridley College to become a missionary. After graduating in 1934 he was ordained, earned a diploma at Melbourne Teachers College, and went to Kenya in 1937 under the Australian Church Missionary Society, where he served as principal of a secondary school at Kaloleni. In 1939 he married Marjory Harrison, a talented teacher and artist. In 1944 he became the rural dean of Nyanza, where he oversaw 300 village churches and an extensive school system. In 1948 he was appointed Archdeacon of Kenya, and as secretary of the African Church Council he was responsible for all educational work in the Mombasa diocese. In 1951 he was consecrated bishop of Central Tanganyika (Tanzania), where he emphasized building a strong indigenous church and engaged in extensive fund-raising for hospitals and schools. In 1955 he consecrated as his assistant Yohana Madinda, who would later be the region's first African bishop. In the years 1963 to 1966 Stanway divided the huge diocese into four separate ones, and in 1970 created the Province of Tanganyika with his African associate as archbishop. Stanway retired in 1971 but then became deputy principal of Ridley College and helped found the Australian Christian Literature Society. He spent the years 1975 to 1978 in the United States, establishing Trinity Episcopal School for Ministry in Sewickley, Pennsylvania. After this he returned to Melbourne, where he died.

BIBLIOGRAPHY Alfred Stanway, *Prayer: A Personal Testimony* (1991). Keith Cole, *A History of the Church Missionary Society of Australia* (1971); Marcus L. Loane, *Men to Remember* (1987); Marjory Stanway, *Alfred Stanway: The Recollections of a "Little M"* (1991).

Richard V. Pierard

Stauffacher, John William (1878–1944) *and*
Florence (Minch) (1881–1959), American missionaries in Kenya and Belgian Congo. Born near Monroe, Wis-

consin, John Stauffacher graduated from North Western College (now North Central College, Naperville, Illinois). Recruited by the Student Volunteer Movement, he sailed for Kenya in 1903 under the auspices of the Africa Inland Mission (AIM). Florence Minch, born in Hooppole, Illinois, arrived in Kenya in 1906, where she and John were married that year. Both possessed pioneering spirits. In 1908 John Stauffacher was appointed extension director for AIM and began the process of opening up German East Africa (now Tanzania). In 1912 the Stauffachers entered the Belgian Congo (Zaire), where they finished their long missionary career. While based there, they also spent many interim years among the Maasai in Kenya.

In many ways the Stauffachers were ahead of their time. From the beginning they practiced a contextualized evangelism. They early developed a strong educational program. On their first furlough in 1909 they took with them their language informant, a Maasai, who became the first Kenyan African to obtain higher education in the United States. John Stauffacher's passion for justice led him to denounce fellow Westerners who exploited the Maasai. He identified with Maasai resistance to government efforts to move them from their ancestral land. Some of the expatriate community therefore saw him as a major factor in the politicization of the Maasai. His concern for gradualism in the transformation of the custom of female circumcision stood in marked contrast with the position of his own and other missions. Rather than excommunicate new converts who participated in this rite, he called for patience and prayer until African believers themselves rejected the custom. Though at times the Stauffachers seemingly marched to the beat of a different drum, more than once history proved that in reality they were hearing a drumbeat that would sound decades later. They both died in Africa.

BIBLIOGRAPHY Oliver Burbridge, *Tagi* (n.d.); Gladys Stauffacher, *Faster Beats the Drum* (1977); Josephine H. Westervelt, *On Safari for God* (n.d.). The Stauffachers' personal letters and diaries are in the archives of the Billy Graham Center library, Wheaton College, Ill.

John A. Gration

Staunton, John Armitage, Jr. (1864–1944), American Episcopal missionary priest and engineer in the Philippines. Staunton was born in Adrian, Michigan, where his father served as rector of Christ (Episcopal) Church. He was educated at the Columbia School of Mines, New York, earning a bachelor's degree in engineering in 1887. Staunton also studied at Harvard (B.A., 1890) and prepared for ordained ministry at the General Theological Seminary in New York City. In 1892 he was ordained a deacon and a priest and married Eliza M. Wilkie. Staunton served for six years as assistant at the Church of St. Mary the Virgin in New York City, and later as rector of St. Peter's Church in Springfield, Massachusetts.

In 1901 Staunton volunteered for service in the Domestic and Foreign Missionary Society of the Episcopal Church (PECUSA). Stationed in the Mountain Province of the Philippines, he opened the Church of the Resurrection, the first Episcopal Church in the province, at Baguio. In 1905 Staunton and his wife, a trained nurse, moved to Sagada, in the western Bontoc sub-province, to undertake pioneering evangelistic work among the Igorot people. Staunton's dream was to build Sagada into a modern center of industry and Western civilization. Drawing on his training as an engineer, Staunton built an extensive industrial network that included a sawmill and planing mill, four stone quarries, machine and carpenter shops, and extensive farms. A staunch Anglo-Catholic, Staunton emphasized the Daily Office and high sacramental worship in Sagada's great stone church, St. Mary the Virgin. At its height, Sagada was considered the premier example of American efforts at evangelization and "civilization." Disagreements with episcopal leadership and changing priorities in the missionary society led Staunton to resign his position in Sagada. In 1925, he returned to the United States to serve St. Michael's Church, Seattle. At the age of 70, after the death of his wife, he left the Episcopal Church and was ordained a Roman Catholic priest. He died in Hammond, Indiana, leaving no children.

BIBLIOGRAPHY John Armitage Staunton, Jr., *Mission of St. Mary the Virgin, Sagada, Philippine Islands* (1908; reprint of Staunton's 1907 annual report to the Board of Missions of the Protestant Episcopal Church). William Henry Scott, "'An Engineer's Dream': John Staunton and the Mission of St. Mary the Virgin, Sagada," in Gerald H. Anderson, ed., *Studies in Philippine Church History* (1969), pp. 337–349.

Ian T. Douglas

Steere, Edward (1828–1882), Anglican missionary and bishop in Africa. Born in London and trained originally as a lawyer at University College, London, Steere studied theology privately before being ordained in 1858. He was a friend of Bishop George Tozer and accompanied him to Malawi in 1863; when the Universities' Mission to Central Africa (UMCA) withdrew from Malawi the following year, he accompanied Tozer to Zanzibar. Though Steere had intended to stay only a couple of years, Tozer's illness and return to England left him in charge at Zanzibar. He oversaw the return of the mission to the mainland before returning to England. He then returned to Africa with the Livingstone search expedition in 1872. Consecrated bishop of Central Africa in 1874, he spoke and worked against the slave trade and helped to build Zanzibar Cathedral on the site of the old slave market. He was an excellent linguist, producing dictionaries, grammars, and hymnbooks in several African languages, including Swahili and Yao, as well as translating most of the Bible into Swahili. Like several other high Anglican missionaries to Africa, he followed a very spartan life-style and clearly distinguished between Christianity and European culture. On one occasion he said, "No man will ever be a good missionary who cannot be happy among the natives." He died in Zanzibar.

BIBLIOGRAPHY Edward Steere, *An Account of Zanzibar* (1870), *Central African Mission* (1873), *Walks in Nyassa Country* (1876), and *Walks in Zaramo Country* (1880). Anne E. M. Anderson-Morshead,

The History of the Universities' Mission to Central Africa, 1859–1896 (1897); R. M. Heanley, *A Memoir of Bishop Steere* (1888); G. H. Wilson, *The History of the Universities' Mission to Central Africa* (1936).

T. Jack Thompson

Steidel, Florence (1897-1962), missionary in Liberia. Born in Greenfield, Illinois, Steidel reported that in 1924, while she was praying, the Holy Spirit showed her in a vision a country with helpless people crying out in their suffering. Having previously studied at a Bible institute in Chicago and at Benton College of Law in St. Louis, she now prepared for medical service through nurse's training at Missouri Baptist Hospital, graduating in 1928. For instruction in theology and missions, she attended the (Southern Baptist) Woman's Missionary Union Training School in Louisville, Kentucky, graduating in 1931. She later left her Baptist affiliation, joined the Pentecostal movement, and went to Liberia in 1935 as an appointed Assemblies of God missionary.

Steidel is best known for founding New Hope Town, a leper colony. Beginning in 1947 with only a hundred dollars and the labor of lepers, she supervised medical and spiritual programs, construction of over seventy buildings, planting of rubber trees to help the community become self-sufficient, and the building of an eighteen-mile road to connect the community to the nearest government road. She also established a ministerial training school. In honor of her humanitarian contributions to Liberia, President William V. S. Tubman conferred on her the decoration of Knight Official of the Humane Order of African Redemption in 1957. She was the first woman missionary to receive this honor.

BIBLIOGRAPHY (Christine Carmichael), *New Hope Town* (c. 1960); Inez Spence, *These Are My People: Florence Steidel,* Heroes of the Conquest Series, no. 4 (n.d.). The correspondence and papers of Florence Steidel are held in the editorial office files of the Division of Foreign Missions, Assemblies of God, Springfield, Mo.

Gary B. McGee

Steinkopf, Karl Friedrich Adolf (1773-1859), German pastor and missions promoter. Born into a family of devout Christians in south Germany, Steinkopf was trained for the ministry at Tübingen University and became secretary of the Deutsche Christentumsgesellschaft (German Christian Association) at Basel in 1798, where he found colleagues like Christian F. *Spittler and Christian G. *Blumhardt. Later, in 1815, Steinkopf joined his two friends in founding the Basel Mission. Steinkopf's special contribution to the missionary awakening of the early nineteenth century was to evolve during his career as minister of the German Savoy church in London, a post he had assumed in 1801. He was a cofounder of the British and Foreign Bible Society (1804) and a committee member of the London Missionary Society. He also played a leading part in communicating impulses of the continental religious awakening to Britain, as well as English incentives for effective evangelism back to the continent. In 1820 he visited some forty Bible and tract societies founded or supported by him in Switzerland, Germany, and France. He also was instrumental in making trainees of the Basel Mission available for mission service with English mission societies, introducing to English churches the Basel Mission work in the Gold Coast, organizing small-change collections for missions on a large scale, and founding a German hospital in London.

BIBLIOGRAPHY Due to irresponsible destruction of Steinkopf's diaries after his death no adequate biography has ever been produced. The only account of his life and work is Erich Schick, *Vorboten und Bahnbrecher: Grundzüge der evangelisch Missionsgeschichte bis zu den Anfängen der Basler Mission* (1943).

Hans-Werner Gensichen

Stephen (c. 975-1038), Christian king of Hungary. Stephen, along with his father, was converted in 985. In 997, upon rising to the throne, he worked to Christianize his realm by all possible means. With the support of Rome, he set up two archbishoprics at Esztergom and Kalocsa and eight bishoprics at Csanád, Eger, Bihar, Pécs, Raab, Alba Julia, Veszprém, and Waizen; he also established or endowed numerous monasteries. Although force was often used as a means of conversion, Stephen's example also played a role. He liberated his own slaves and asked for missionaries from other lands. The Slavic peoples responded well. Stephen enacted laws to enforce Christianity and included in those laws special privileges for the church and its clergy. Upon his death, paganism, which had been driven underground, revived, but the growing Hungarian Christian community remembered him as a saintly founder.

BIBLIOGRAPHY Robert Harkay, *St. Stephan from Hungary* (1979); Bálint Hóman, *König Stephan I der Heilige* (1941); Denis Sinor, *History of Hungary* (1959).

Frederick W. Norris

Stephen of Perm (1340-1396), Russian Orthodox missionary in the Mongol period. Born in Veliki Ustyug, Russia, to a clerical family, Stephen entered St. Gregory's Monastery in Rostov at an early age. There he studied Greek and patristics. Influenced by St. Sergius of Radonezh to enter the mission field, in 1379 he journeyed north toward the White Sea and settled among the Finno-Ugric Zyryan tribes living between the Pechora and Vychegda Rivers at Ust-Vim. Learning their language and devising a writing system for them, he began preaching but met strong opposition from the pagan priests. However, within five years his work had become so fruitful that he asked the Holy Synod to appoint a bishop to oversee the mission. Stephen was selected and consecrated bishop of Perm in 1383. Returning to his see, he labored another 14 years, continuing to translate the Scriptures and liturgy into Komi, organizing parishes and monasteries, and teaching children in their native tongue. He ordained the most promising students to the priesthood. Following his death in Moscow, he was canonized a saint by the Russian Orthodox Church, but his flock suffered Russification by his successors, inspired by political considerations.

BIBLIOGRAPHY Serge Bolshakoff, *The Foreign Missions of the Russian Orthodox Church* (1943), pp. 29–30; James J. Stamoolis, *Eastern Orthodox Mission Theology Today* (1986), pp. 26–27.

Paul D. Garrett

Stephens, Thomas (c. 1549–1619), pioneer Jesuit missionary and first Englishman to reside in India. Stephens was born in Bulstan (modern Bushton), Wiltshire, to a prosperous merchant. He studied in London and Oxford, and, inspired by the life of Francis *Xavier and desiring to become a missionary in India, in 1575 he joined the Jesuits in Rome. He reached Goa in 1579 and was ordained a priest in 1583. He ministered to the Brahmin converts of Salcette in southern Goa for over 35 years, besides serving as minister of the Professed House (residence for permanent members in final vows) in Goa, rector of the College at Margoa, and socius (companion-secretary) to Alexander *Valignano, who was visitor to the Jesuits working in the East.

Stephens mastered Sanskrit, Konkani, and Marathi. He wrote the first Konkani grammar, *Arte de Lingua Canarim,* and a catechism, *Doutrina Cristam en lingua Brahmana Canarim.* His major work was *Krista Purana,* a biblical epic in Marathi. First printed in 1616, it recounts the history of salvation in 95 cantos with 10,962 stanzas. It has been hailed as a Marathi classic. Stephens died in Goa.

BIBLIOGRAPHY Thomas Stephens, *The Christian Purana,* Joseph L. Saldhana, ed. (1907; contains a biographical note and introduction). Joseph Rosario, "Thomas Stephens—Pioneering Poet," *Ignis* 16 (1987): 181–183; G. Schurhammer, "Thomas Stephens, 1549–1619," *Month,* n.s. 13 (1955): 197–210.

Michael Amaladoss, SJ

Stern, Henry Aaron (1820–1885), missionary-explorer of the Middle East. Stern was born into a strict Orthodox Jewish family in Unterreichenbach, Germany. Coming across a mission station of the London Jews' Society in Hamburg, he was so impressed by the prophecies related to Jesus highlighted in the Bibles displayed there, that when visiting London, and invited to a meeting of that society, he went along. Alexander *McCaul, the speaker, so inspired him that he frequented the center and in 1840 was baptized. His potential as a missionary to Jewish people soon became apparent, and he was sent by the society to Baghdad, from where he organized extraordinary missionary journeys into Persia (Iran), Arabia, Constantinople, Abyssinia (Ethiopia), and the Crimea, where he worked among the Karaites. He galvanized rather isolated missionaries and set things on a firm foundation. In 1863 he was commissioned to establish a mission among the Falashas, but because of diplomatic intrigues he was imprisoned for about four years by the king of Abyssinia. Upon his release, he returned to England and became a successful missionary there. In 1881 the archbishop of Canterbury conferred on him the degree of D.D.

BIBLIOGRAPHY Stern wrote three invaluable missionary travelogues: *Dawning of Light in the East* (1854), *Wanderings among the Falashas in Abyssinia* (1862), and *The Captive Missionary* (1869). A. A. Isaacs, *Biography of Henry Aaron Stern, DD* (1886). See also *Church and Synagogue* 6 (1904): 103–117.

Walter Riggans

Stevens, Edwin (1802–1837), pioneer American Protestant missionary in China. Born in New Canaan, Connecticut, Stevens graduated from Yale College in 1828. After a year's teaching in New York, he entered Yale Divinity School and was ordained in 1832, leaving at once for China as chaplain to the Seamen's Friend Society. He reached Canton in October 1832 and began his ministry among the international seafaring community of Canton and Whampoa, whom he found to be tough, hard-drinking, and often inattentive, but whose respect he ultimately won. In 1835, in defiance of Ch'ing Dynasty prohibitions, he made two adventurous journeys by boat up the China coast (one with Charles *Gutzlaff and one with Walter *Medhurst) to distribute Christian tracts in Chinese translation. Appointed a missionary of the American Board of Commissioners for Foreign Missions in 1836, he continued to distribute tracts, and it was almost certainly Stevens who handed the tract called "Ch'uan-shih liang-yen" ("Good words to admonish the age," by Liang Ah-fa) to a young scholar called *Hung Hsiu-ch'uan. The tract was instrumental in Hung's conversion to Christianity, and Hung subsequently led the Taiping Rebellion (1850–1864), one of the most destructive in Chinese history, as he sought to establish a Heavenly Kingdom on earth. Stevens himself worked hard to learn Chinese (with only moderate success) and also wrote several lengthy essays on China missionaries and his own coastal journeys, published in *Chinese Repository.* He died suddenly of fever in Singapore, en route to explore the mission possibilities in Borneo.

BIBLIOGRAPHY Edwin Stevens, various essays in *Chinese Repository,* vols. 1–5 (1832–1837). See also E. C. B. [Elijah Bridgman], "Obituary of the [sic] Edwin Stevens," *Chinese Repository* 5:513–518 (March 1837); Jen Yu-wen, *Taiping Revolutionary Movement* (1973) (where "Stevens" is misspelled "Stephens"); Samuel Wells Williams, Papers, Yale Univ., Manuscripts and Archives, MS 547, Williams letters of 1835–1837; Alexander Wylie, comp., *Memorials of Protestant Missionaries to the Chinese* (1867); Yale College, *Biographical Sketches of the Class of 1828* (1898).

Jonathan Spence

Stevens, Jedediah Dwight (1798–1877), early Presbyterian evangelist in the American Midwest. Stevens, probably born in Hamilton, New York, and educated at home, first appears in September of 1829, when he and a colleague, Alvan Coe, made a preliminary visit to Fort Snelling on the upper reaches of the Mississippi River. He is thus the first Presbyterian minister known to have entered the Minnesota Territory. That was only exploratory, however, and for the next six years, Stevens resumed his duties as teacher of the Stockbridge Indians at Green Bay, Wisconsin. But in 1835 he was appointed by the Presbyterian Mission Board to return to Fort Snelling and to expand the work begun there. One of his colleagues,

Thomas S. *Williamson, ministered at Lac qui Parle and Lake Harriet while Stevens frequented Oak Grove and Prairieville. Activities at all these sites concentrated on the evangelization of local tribes known as the Dakota among themselves and as the Sioux among outsiders. Stevens is represented in letters and diaries as an overbearing authoritarian figure who created abrasive relations among his clerical colleagues. His domineering personality contributed to both physical and psychological isolation. This state of affairs reduced his effectiveness with the Dakotas who visited his missions, and it vitiated cooperation with other missionaries in the region.

BIBLIOGRAPHY Bruce D. Forbes, "Evangelization and Acculturation and the Santee Dakota Indians, 1834–1864" (Ph.D. diss., Princeton Theological Seminary, 1977).

Henry Warner Bowden

Stevenson, Marion Scott (1871–1930), Scottish missionary, teacher, and translator in Kenya. Having grown up in the manse of a Church of Scotland minister, and with two paternal missionary uncles in India, Stevenson was socialized into a missionary career. Beginning her missionary service at age 36, she served first at the Thogoto mission in Kenya (1907–1912) and then until 1929 at the Tumutumu station. As a teacher, she had a major role in shaping the whole education system of the Church of Scotland Mission (CSM) in Kenya. As head teacher of Tumutumu station, she also supervised its forty-three outstations. With other missionaries she prepared syllabi for instruction of catechumens, evangelists, elders, and ministers, together with their wives. After language study in Germany, she together with Arthur R. *Barlow and an inter-mission team of translators published the first Gikuyu New Testament (1926) as well as *Gikuyu Prayers for Public Worship* and *Gikuyu Church Laws*. She was such a campaigner for women's causes that the Gikuyu people called her "our mother, sister, teacher and friend of the girls and women." With others, she modeled Gikuyu Christian womanhood. She was among those who campaigned tirelessly against female circumcision, and she addressed a memorandum on the subject to people of influence in England just before her death.

BIBLIOGRAPHY Thomas J. Jones, *Education in East Africa: A Study of East, Central, and South Africa by the Second African Education Commission under the Auspices of the Phelps-Stokes Fund, in Cooperation with the International Education Board* (1925); Nyambura J. Njoroge, "The Woman's Guild: The Institutional Locus for an African Women's Christian Social Ethic" (Ph.D. diss., Princeton Theological Seminary, 1992); H. E. Scott, *A Saint in Kenya: The Life of Marion Scott Stevenson* (1932).

Nyambura J. Njoroge

Stewart, James (1831–1905), Scottish missionary and educator in South Africa. Born in Edinburgh, Stewart graduated in arts at the University of Edinburgh and in 1855 began the theological course at New College, Edinburgh. He also began the medical course at Edinburgh in 1859, but he interrupted his medical training to join *Livingstone's Zambezi expedition. The expedition, initiated on behalf of a Scottish committee planning a mission to support Livingstone's ideas, was to investigate the possibilities for mission in the area. Not only did this come to nothing, but Stewart became temporarily a bitter critic of Livingstone.

In 1867, having completed his medical course and having been ordained, Stewart was appointed to the Free Church of Scotland Mission at Lovedale, South Africa. He insisted almost from the beginning that the way ahead in education was general and technical education rather than higher education for the brightest. When the authorities in Scotland backed Stewart over this issue against William *Govan, the principal of Lovedale, Govan resigned, and Stewart in 1870 became principal of what was then the leading educational institution in Africa. Under Stewart, Lovedale rapidly increased in size but continued to provide education to the highest level for both its white and its black students. Indeed, Lovedale produced many of the leaders who were to found the African National Congress in 1912. During periods of leave from Lovedale, Stewart played a part in the pioneer period of both the Livingstonia Mission in Malawi and the Scottish Kikuyu mission in Kenya.

Despite a strong paternalist side, Stewart always supported the legal equality of the races in the Cape Colony and in 1870 founded a magazine, the *Kaffir Express,* which later became the *South African Outlook,* a consistent proponent of Cape liberalism. As a reply to the increasing attacks on "liberal" education for Africans, he wrote in 1887 *Lovedale, Past and Present.*

The Free Church of Scotland made him moderator of the general assembly of 1899. He died while still serving as principal of Lovedale.

BIBLIOGRAPHY James Stewart, *Dawn in the Dark Continent* (1902). S. M. Brock, "James Stewart and Lovedale" (Ph.D. diss., Univ. of Edinburgh, 1974); J. P. R. Wallis, *The Zambesi Journals of James Stewart* (1952); J. Wells, *Stewart of Lovedale* (1908).

Andrew C. Ross

Stewart, John (1786–1823), founder of the first permanent Methodist Episcopal mission among the American Indians. Born in Virginia of free parentage, Stewart was a Baptist of mixed European and African descent. After he was robbed on his way to Ohio, he attempted to drink himself to death. Suffering agony of soul, he was delivered from depression by joining the Methodists during a camp meeting. He became ill from resisting a call to preach. Recovery commenced after he agreed to obey God. He heard the voice of a woman and a man calling him to preach to the Native Americans, and he set off in a northwesterly direction. He sang and preached to the Delawares on the way to the Wyandott Indians. Reaching the Wyandotts, he was befriended by a government agent who directed him to Jonathan Pointer, an African American who had been captured by the Indians and was fluent in Wyandott. With Pointer as interpreter, Stewart began to sing and to preach to them in 1816. Despite opposition, he warned the Wyandotts to "flee the wrath to come." His singing and preaching resulted in the conversion of the chiefs, leading women, and others. Rival missionaries appeared and accused him of exercising ministerial functions without a license. Supported by native converts, Stewart requested recognition by the Methodist Episcopal Church and was accordingly licensed in 1819. The church supported his mission work financially and by appointing missionaries to continue it. Stewart's example helped to inspire the formation of the Methodist Missionary Society in 1820.

BIBLIOGRAPHY James B. Finley, *Life among the Indians; or, Personal Reminiscences and Historical Incidents Illustrative of Indian Life and Character* (n.d.); N. B. C. Love, *John Stewart, Missionary to the Wyandots* (n.d.); Joseph Mitchell, *The Missionary Pioneer, or a Brief Memoir of the Life, Labours, and Death of John Stewart (Man of Colour), Founder, under God, of the Mission among the Wyandotts at Upper Sandusky, Ohio* (1827).

Dana L. Robert

Stirling, Waite Hockin (1829–1923), missionary in Patagonia and Anglican bishop of South America. Stirling, the son of a captain in the English Navy, was educated in Exeter and at Oxford, where he graduated in 1851. He was ordained to a curacy at St. Mary's, Nottingham, in 1852 and became secretary of the Patagonia Mission in 1857. Offering to serve as superintendent of the mission in the Falkland Islands, he sailed with his wife and daughters in 1863 and settled on Pebble Island. After the death of his wife in 1864, he moved to Ushuaia, the capital of Tierra del Fuego, and lived for a time as the only European among the indigenous people. He was consecrated bishop in 1869, with jurisdiction over Anglicans everywhere in South America with the exception of British Guiana (present-day Guiana). He was responsible for the early work of Wilfred B. *Grubb, whom he sent to the Paraguayan Chaco in 1889. He resigned in 1900 and was appointed a canon of Wells Cathedral and assistant bishop in 1901. By the Lambeth Conference of 1920, the fifth such conference of Anglican bishops he had attended, he was the senior bishop by consecration.

BIBLIOGRAPHY J. McCleod Campbell, *Christian History in the Making* (1946); F. C. Macdonald, *Bishop Stirling of the Falklands* (1929).

Timothy Yates

Stock, Eugene (1836–1928), missionary editor, administrator, and historian. Stock gave a lifetime of service as a layman to the Church Missionary Society (CMS). He became one of the most influential figures in the evolution of CMS policies in the 20 years leading up to his retirement in 1906. Born in Westminster, London, he was a self-made man without the university or clerical background that secretaries of his eminence generally had. He joined the CMS as an editor in 1873 and soon became its editorial secretary with responsibility for its publications, in particular for the prestigious and influential journal *The Intelligencer.* Throughout the 1880s his influence grew, partly because his vast and unrivaled knowledge of missionary history gave him power in respect of issues where a historical perspective was often crucial. He also had a capacity to write quickly, clearly, and in a way that lent weight to his own views as a policy framer. He had a certain irreverence for traditions and became an advocate of the "new," whether it was Keswick spirituality, the need to have women missionaries, or the ever more liberal stance of the Student Christian Movement. He also had an instant appeal with "young Turks" and was particularly on the wavelength of the rising (often radical) missionary interest in the university world.

Stock's outstanding achievement was his four-volume *History of the Church Missionary Society* (1899–1916). It is without doubt the best piece of missionary history writing of the nineteenth century, and also provides some of the most incisive insights into nineteenth-century Anglican evangelicalism. Nonetheless it is a flawed work, as Stock allowed his own immediate strategic objectives to skew his presentation of the past. By the 1890s he had become convinced that the society needed to move away from its *Venn-inspired commitment to indigenous ministry and leadership to a much more pan-Anglican and consequently white-dominated vision. Thus the society's clear commitment in 1877 to overlapping, independent episcopates for different racial groups is glossed over; the resurgence of a very powerful backlash in favor of Venn's views in the relevant 1899 Centenary Review Committee is largely ignored, and little prominence is given to the non-European contribution to missionary work. He was the major architect in the society's move in 1901 to a "one church," territorial episcopate model with the inevitable likelihood, which Stock accepted, of European dominance for the foreseeable future. He was also much involved in the wider missionary scene with the Society for the Propagation of the Gospel and the Anglican Board of Missions both at a provincial and at a national level. He remained in close contact with the day-to-day affairs of the CMS during most of his long retirement (1906–1928).

BIBLIOGRAPHY Eugene Stock, *My Recollections* (1909). Georgina Gollock, *Eugene Stock: A Biographical Study, 1836–1928* (1929); Peter Williams, *The Ideal of the Self Governing Church: A Study in Victorian Missionary Strategy* (1990).

Peter Williams

Stockfleth, Nils Joachim Vibe (1787–1866), Norwegian Lutheran missionary to the Lapps. Born in Fredrikstad, Stockfleth served for a time as an army officer. Feeling a vocational calling to evangelize the Lapps, he enrolled in the University of Oslo (Christiania) and graduated in 1824. He was appointed vicar in Lappish districts in northern Norway until he resigned in 1839 to be a full-time missionary. He worked for 27 years to evangelize the Lapps and to provide them an elementary education in the vernacular. He persuaded the authorities to build small schools and to distribute Lappish textbooks. From the late 1840s the vicars in Finnmark, northern Norway, had to learn Lappish. Stockfelth taught Lappish at the University of Oslo. He had studied Lappish with Danish and Finnish experts and had practiced his knowledge with the Lapps. In 1840 Stockfleth published a new edition of the New Testament in Lappish; in 1849, Luther's small catechism; in the 1850s, two collections of sermons by Luther; and in 1860, his own diary of missionary activity. Stockfleth was a member of the Royal Society of Sciences in Trondheim and of the Finnish Society of Literature in Helsinki and was a Knight of the Danish Order of Dannebrøg.

BIBLIOGRAPHY Adolf Steen, *Samenes kristning og Kinnemisjonen til 1888* (1954).

Nils E. Bloch-Hoell

Stockton, Betsey (1798–1865), Presbyterian missionary to Hawaii. Born into slavery in Princeton, New Jersey, Stockton was given as a young child by her owner, Robert Stockton, to his daughter, Elizabeth, and her husband, Ashbel Green, Presbyterian minister and president of the College of New Jersey (later Princeton University). She was raised and tutored in the Green family. Appointed as a single woman missionary under the American Board of Commissioners for Foreign Missions, she sailed with the first group of reinforcements to the Sandwich Islands mission in 1822 as an attached member of the Charles Stewart family. As a pioneer missionary at Lahaina, on the island of Maui, she opened the first school in the islands for the lower classes. Returning to America with the Stewarts in 1826, she taught briefly in an "infant school" in Philadelphia. Later, she went for a few months to Canada to help some missionaries in a program of education for Indian children. Returning to the town of her birth, she served with distinction for many years as principal of a school for black children. Always humble in spirit, "Aunt Betsey" became a beloved figure. Her funeral was conducted by the president and senior professor of Princeton College and by Charles Hodge of Princeton Theological Seminary.

BIBLIOGRAPHY Carol Santoki Dodd, "Betsey Stockton: A History Student's Perspective," *Educational Perspectives* (University of Hawaii) 16, no. 1 (March 1977): 10–15; Constance K. Escher, "She Calls Herself Betsey Stockton," *Princeton History,* no. 10 (1991): 87; Eileen F. Moffett, "Betsey Stockton: Pioneer American Missionary," *IBMR* 19 (1995): 71–76. Several of Stockton's letters and diary entries appear in *The Christian Advocate,* vols. 1–4 (1823–1826). Ashbel Green's diary transcripts (1792–1848) are held in the Princeton Univ. Library, Princeton, N.J.

Eileen F. Moffett

Stockwell, B(owman) Foster (1899–1961), American Methodist missionary and theological educator in Argentina. Born in a Methodist parsonage in Shawnee, Oklahoma, Stockwell became a highly prominent Protestant missionary in Latin America. His theological acumen and determined spirit were recognized early during his preparatory studies at Ohio Wesleyan University and his theology and doctor of philosophy studies at Boston University. In the 1920s he served as personal secretary to John R. *Mott. He pursued advanced studies in Strasbourg, Berlin, and Tübingen. In 1948 he received the doctor of divinity degree *honoris causa* from Ohio Wesleyan University. He served as a Methodist missionary to Argentina from 1926 until his death, during most of that period as rector of the ecumenical seminary in Buenos Aires, which he helped to establish, today known as Instituto Superior Evangélico de Estudios Teológicos (ISEDET). Just over a year before his death he became bishop of the Methodist Central Conference of Costa Rica, Panama, Peru, and Chile. He contributed enormously to the Latin American church by writing theological literature in the Spanish language, stimulating and participating in ecumenical church relations, training important Latin American church leaders and pastors, editing and translating religious literature for seminaries and churches, and serving as delegate to world conferences of the International Missionary Council (1938) and the World Council of Churches (1948 and 1954). His son, Eugene L. *Stockwell, also served as a Methodist missionary in Latin America and as a mission executive in the National Council of Churches in the United States and in the World Council of Churches.

BIBLIOGRAPHY B(owman) Foster Stockwell, *Pattern of Things to Come* (1955). Stockwell's best-known writings in Spanish are *Que es el Protestantismo?* (What Is Protestantism?) (1954), *Nuestro Mundo y la Cruz* (Our world and the Cross) (1937), and *Que Podemos Creer?* (What can we believe?) (1936). An excellent biography is Tomas S. Goslin, *B. Foster Stockwell: La Historia de una Misión* (1993). Stockwell founded the magazines *El Predicador Evangélico* and *Cuadernos de Teología* and edited two important theological collections, *Obras Clásicas de la Reforma* and *Biblioteca de Cultura Evangélica.*

Sidney H. Rooy

Stockwell, Eugene L(ouden) (1923–1996), Methodist missionary in Latin America and ecumenical mission leader. Born in Boston, Massachusetts, Stockwell grew up in Buenos Aires, Argentina, where his father, B. Foster *Stockwell, founded Union Theological Seminary (known in Spanish by its acronym ISEDET). After graduating from Oberlin College (1943) and Columbia University Law School (1948), he was a lawyer in New York City until he met John R. *Mott, who persuaded him to enter the ministry. Graduating from Union Theological Seminary, New York, in 1952, he and his wife, Margaret (Smyres), went as Methodist missionaries to Uruguay from 1953 to 1962. He then served as Latin America area secretary and later as assistant general secretary of the Methodist Board of Global Ministries in New York City. From 1972 to 1984 he was associate general secretary of the National Council of the Churches of Christ in the U.S.A., leading its division of overseas ministries. From 1984 to 1989 he directed the Commission on World Mission and Evangelism of the World Council of Churches in Geneva, and was also editor of the *International Review of Mission.* When he retired from the council, he first served as a senior scholar in residence at the Overseas Ministries Study Center in New Haven, Connecticut. Then in 1990 he returned to Buenos Aires to head Union Theological Seminary. He died in Atlanta, Georgia.

BIBLIOGRAPHY Stockwell wrote *Claimed by God for Mission* (1965), "My Pilgrimage in Mission," *IBMR* 14 (1990): 64–68, and articles and editorials in *IRM* during his years as editor. "Mission as Seen from Geneva: A Conversation with Eugene L. Stockwell," *IBMR* 11 (1987): 112–117, reported an interview during his time at the WCC.

Gerald H. Anderson

Stone, Mary. *See* Shih Mei-yu.

Stosch, Johannes Richard Andreas (1878–1973), leader of the Gossner Evangelical Lutheran Church in Chota Nagpur (Bihar), India. Born into a missionary family, Stosch joined the Gossner Mission in 1907 after training for the ministry at Erlangen and Halle. He became president of the Gossner church in India shortly before World War I and was repatriated to Germany by order of the British colonial authorities in 1916. In his absence, the church declared itself autonomous in 1919 but called him back to India in 1925 because it required his assistance in reconciling tribal groups. In 1935 Stosch was called to India once more, this time with the approval of the Federation of Lutheran Churches in India, in order to settle differences between the autonomous church and the mission. In 1938 Stosch was recalled for a third term as president. During World War II, he and two women missionaries were permitted to stay on. But Stosch decided to resign in 1942 and was, together with other missionaries, interned in a British camp until his repatriation in 1947, concluding a career of 40 years of service to the Gossner church and mission in India.

BIBLIOGRAPHY There is no biography of Stosch. Most documents about his career were destroyed when the Gossner Mission archives were destroyed during the last days of World War II. J. Stosch, "Die Kolsmission im 20. Jahrhundert," in the Festschrift *Zum 100 jährigen Bestchen der Gossnerschen Mission* (1936). A number of smaller contributions by Stosch were published in periodicals of the Gossner Mission.

Hans-Werner Gensichen

Stott, John R(obert) W(almsley) (1921–), English statesman and theologian of the evangelical movement. Educated at Cambridge University, Stott is one of the most influential clergymen in the Church of England in the twentieth century. In 1950 he became rector of All Souls Church in London (the parish where he was born), and in 1975 rector emeritus. From 1952 to 1977 he led missions to university students on five continents. In 1982 he founded the London Institute for Contemporary Christianity (now part of Christian Impact), serving as director up to 1986 and president from 1986. Chaplain to the queen from 1959 to 1991, he was appointed extra chaplain from 1991 onward and was awarded a Lambeth D.D. in 1983.

Stott has contributed to the development of missiology through his international speaking and preaching (often to students); his books on mission theology, particularly *Christian Mission in the Modern World* (1975); and his deft, concise drafting of key mission statements in the *Lausanne Covenant* (1974), *Willowbank Report on Gospel and Culture* (1978), *Evangelism and Social Responsibility: An Evangelical Commitment* (1982), *Evangelical-Roman Catholic Dialogue on Mission* (1987), and the Lausanne II *Manila Manifesto* (1989). His strategic initiatives include the Evangelical Fellowship in the Anglican Communion, the Langham Trust scholarship program (which supports Third World graduate students), and the Evangelical Literature Trust. He is the New Testament editor and contributor to the expository commentary series The Bible Speaks Today.

BIBLIOGRAPHY Timothy Dudley-Smith, *John Stott: A Comprehensive Bibliography* (1995) and ed., *Authentic Christianity: From the Writings of John Stott* (1995). A biographical sketch is in Christopher Catherwood, *Five Evangelical Leaders* (1984). David Edwards, with a response by Stott, has written a critical review of his writings, with a brief biographical introduction, *Essentials: A Liberal-Evangelical Dialogue* (1988). Other significant books by Stott include *Basic Christianity* (1958; rev., 1971); *The Lausanne Covenant: An Exposition and Commentary* (1975); *The Cross of Christ* (1986), his major theological work; and *The Contemporary Christian* (1992), which has a large selection on mission concerns.

Graham Kings

Stover, Wilbur B(renner) (1866–1930), Church of the Brethren missionary in India. Born in Franklin County, Pennsylvania, Stover grew up in Illinois, where he graduated from Mount Morris College. Through Presbyterian contacts, he was converted to the cause of foreign missions; he preached widely on missions among eastern Brethren from his base as pastor of a Philadelphia congregation. In 1894 he, his wife, Mary (Emmert) (1871–1960), and Bertha Ryan (1871–1953) were sent to northern India as the first Brethren foreign missionaries. On comity principles they chose the Bulsar (Gujarat) area as their first mission station; in the years 1907 to 1920 the Stovers worked at the Anklesvar station. Converts were few until the famines and plagues of 1896 to 1904, which missionaries worked tirelessly to combat. Orphanages created to care for child survivors became the basis for Brethren congregations. Schools, hospitals, and agricultural work followed. The Stovers returned to the United States in 1920 for health reasons, pursuing pastoral ministry in Ohio and the state of Washington. Stover wrote many articles, initiated the magazine *Little Brother,* and published five books. The title of one, *The Great First-Work of the Church: Missions* (1922) was his rallying cry, influential in leading Church of the Brethren to adopt foreign missions as its leading cause in the early twentieth century.

BIBLIOGRAPHY The standard biography is John E. Miller, *Wilbur B. Stover, Pioneer Missionary* (1931); other details are found in Elgin S. Moyer, *Missions in the Church of the Brethren* (1931), Galen B. Royer, *Thirty-three Years of Missions in the Church of the Brethren* (1913), and Anet D. Satvedi, "History of the Church of the Brethren in India, 1894–1993" (D. Min. thesis, Bethany Theological Seminary, 1993). See also the memorial issue of the *Little Brother,* December 1930, and Galen Stover Beery, "Wilbur B.

Stover: India Pioneer," Church of the Brethren, *Messenger* (October 1994): 10–14.

Donald F. Durnbaugh

Strachan, Harry (1872–1946), cofounder of Latin America Mission. Strachan was born of Scottish parents temporarily resident in Fergus, Ontario, Canada. At age seven, he returned with them to Aberdeen, where he was raised until he left to seek work in Sunderland, England. There he was converted and called to missionary service in Africa after training in London at Harley College. A routine physical examination unexpectedly closed the door on African service, however, and, in 1902 he was sent instead to Argentina, where he renewed his courtship of fellow student Susan Beamish (see below). They married in 1903.

During more than 15 years of pastoral missionary work, principally in Tandil, 190 miles south of Buenos Aires, he experimented successfully with the use of tents, colportage, and horse-drawn Bible coaches in the work of evangelism. Eventually he felt called to expand this ministry throughout the continent. He therefore resigned from the Evangelical Union of South America (of which his original sponsoring mission, the Regions Beyond Missionary Union, had now become a part) to cofound with his wife the Latin America Evangelization Campaign (later known as the Latin America Mission [LAM]), with headquarters in San José, Costa Rica.

In a day of Protestant repression and timidity, Strachan pioneered with high-profile, cooperative, interdenominational evangelistic crusades in the major cities of Latin America, launching a tradition that has figured prominently in the growth of the evangelical church up and down the continent. This tradition of evangelistic priority has been projected—consciously or unconsciously—across successive generations in LAM ministries such as Evangelism-in-Depth, Christ for the City, and others. Strachan died in San José.

BIBLIOGRAPHY W. Dayton Roberts, *One Step Ahead: The Innovative Strachans and the Birth of the Latin America Mission* (1996). See also the 1921–1946 issues of *Evangelist,* the monthly publication of LAM.

W. Dayton Roberts

Strachan, R(obert) Kenneth (1910–1965), general director of the Latin America Mission (LAM). The son of missionaries Harry and Susan (Beamish) *Strachan, Strachan was born in Tandil, Argentina, and raised in Costa Rica. Educated at Wheaton College and Dallas Theological Seminary in the United States, in 1936 he joined the LAM, founded by his parents, and served in several capacities in Costa Rica before being named codirector with his mother, Susan, in 1947 and general director in 1951, after her death. He led the LAM into "Latin-Americanizing" its structures and personnel and reviving its evangelistic priorities, while broadening its base and enlarging its ministries in radio, camping, publications, and cooperative ventures with other mission agencies.

Based periodically in the U.S. home office of the mission, Strachan also participated in structural and strategic reforms within the Evangelical Foreign Missions Association and Interdenominational Foreign Mission Association. While a guest professor at Fuller Theological Seminary in Pasadena, California, he was involved in planning for the seminary's School of World Mission.

Strachan is best remembered as the architect of Evangelism-in-Depth, an evangelistic strategy based on mobilizing all Christian believers in active communication of their faith. A correlation between total mobilization and maximum growth was the fundamental theorem of his strategy. The program derived from this approach spread rapidly through Latin America in more than ten national movements and to other parts of the world, where its concepts were incorporated into Africa's "New Life for All" and "Christ for All," as well as in the Philippines, Japan, and elsewhere. The contemporary strategy of mass evangelism has been permanently altered by shifting the focus from pulpit to pew and involving the whole body of Christ in outreach and in articulating the gospel.

Strachan married Elizabeth Walker, of Columbia, South Carolina, in 1940, and fathered six children. In 1943 he received a Th.M. from Princeton Theological Seminary. He died in Pasadena, California, at age 55, from Hodgkin's disease. His major literary legacy, in addition to editorials in the *Evangelist* magazine, is *The Inescapable Calling* (1967), consisting of lectures given during his final months at Fuller Theological Seminary.

BIBLIOGRAPHY Willys Braun, *Roots and Possible Fruits of AD2000* (1992); Elisabeth Elliot, *Who Shall Ascend* (1968); *Evangelist* magazine, monthly publication of LAM; W. Dayton Roberts, "The Legacy of R. Kenneth Strachan," *OBMR* 3 (1979): 2–6, *Revolution in Evangelism* (1967), and *Strachan of Costa Rica* (1971).

W. Dayton Roberts

Strachan, Susan (Beamish) (1874–1950), cofounder of the Latin America Mission (LAM). Born of Protestant parents in predominantly Catholic County Cork, Ireland, Susan Beamish experienced personal conversion as a teenager in a small Methodist chapel, felt called to missionary work in Africa, and prepared at Harley College in London. There she met Harry *Strachan, her Africa-bound future husband. Rejected for service in Africa for health reasons, she proceeded instead to Argentina under the sponsorship of the Regions Beyond Missionary Union in 1901. Strachan subsequently experienced a similar unexpected rejection for African missionary service and in 1902 was also sent to Argentina where the couple renewed their courtship and were married, serving together in Buenos Aires and Tandil. While in Argentina, Susan's three children were born, and she became the principal founder of the still-active Evangelical League of Argentine Women.

When the Strachans felt called in 1918 to carry out continent-wide evangelism and moved to Costa Rica, Susan cofounded and became codirector (with her husband) of the Latin America Evangelization Campaign, later known as the Latin America Mission (LAM). While Harry traveled extensively to coordinate evangelistic crusades throughout the Spanish-speaking world, she organized and directed supportive ministries, such as a seminary, hospital, orphanage, and Spanish- and English-language periodicals, laying the foundation for the LAM's holistic outreach today. She died in the Clinico Biblico, the hospital she cofounded in San José, Costa Rica.

BIBLIOGRAPHY W. Dayton Roberts, *One Step Ahead: The Innovative Strachans and the Birth of the Latin America Mission* (1996). See also the 1921–1951 issues of *Evangelist* magazine, the monthly publication of LAM.

W. Dayton Roberts

Strauss, Hermann (1910–1978), German missionary in New Guinea. Strauss was a tailor by trade when he applied at the Neuendettelsau Mission seminary in Bavaria for training. One of the most gifted people ever to serve in the mission, after graduation he obtained some linguistic training at Hamburg University and arrived in the Australian trust territory of New Guinea the same year. At that time Lutheran coastal congregations had commissioned a considerable number of indigenous missionaries to the highlands. In 1936 Strauss was assigned to what was then one of the last unpenetrated areas on the globe. He was married to Elfriede Stürzenhofecker in 1939. During World War II he was interned in Australia, but he returned to New Guinea in 1949. As in prewar times, he continued to focus his disciplined and analytical mind on the study of the Melpa language and culture and on the training of local Christian leaders. He excelled at both. For this work he was awarded an honorary doctorate from the University of Erlangen-Nürnberg in 1968. His massive anthropological study of the Melpa people portrays a Melanesian society almost untouched by Westernization and modernization; it stands alongside the best in-depth studies on Melanesian cultures. He retired in 1971.

BIBLIOGRAPHY Hermann Strauss, *Die Mi-Kultur der Hagenbergstämme im östlichen Zentralneuguinea: Eine religionssoziologische Studie* (1962; Eng. tr., *The Mi-Culture of the Mt. Hagen People,* Brian Shields, tr., G. Stürzenhofecker and Andrew Strathern, eds. [1989]), *The New Testament in Melpa* (1965), and, with W. Flierl, *Kate Dictionary* (1977). Strauss's unpublished manuscripts are in the Neuendettelsau Mission archives.

Theodor Ahrens

Strehlow, Carl Friedrich Theodor (1870–1922), German missionary in central Australia. Strehlow was born to a teacher in a small village in Prussia and trained at the Neuendettelsau Mission in Bavaria. Sent to Australia at only 22 years of age, he worked for two years at the Bethesda station. Together with J. G. Reuther, he was then assigned responsibility for the station at Hermannsburg (founded in 1877), on the Finke River in the center of the Australian continent. As a member of the Hermannsburg mission, he worked among the Aboriginal Dieri and Aranda peoples. Learning the Dieri language in a comparatively short time, he assisted Reuther in the translation of the Dieri New Testament, which was printed in 1897. It was the first New Testament in an Aboriginal language in Australia. He also compiled an Aranda dictionary of about 7,500 words, wrote five volumes of *Die Aranda- und Loritja-Stämme in Zentral-Australien* (1907–1920), and published the monumental *Arenda Service Book* (1904; 2nd ed., 1924). An Aranda school primer which he prepared was printed in 1928. His translation of the *Gospel According to St. Luke* was published by the British and Foreign Bible Society in 1925, and the four Gospels in 1929. The entire New Testament, after a thorough revision of the original manuscript by his son, T. H. G. Strehlow, was published in 1956. In addition, Strehlow translated many hymns into the Aranda language.

BIBLIOGRAPHY Wilhelm Fugmann, "Das Risiko der Verwendbarkeit. Über Leben und Werk von Carl Theodor Strehlow," *Concordia* 1 (1993): 21–31; Everard Leske, ed., *Hermannsburg: A Vision and a Mission* (1977).

Ulrich van der Heyden

Streicher, Henri (1863–1952), missionary bishop of Uganda. Born at Wasselonne, Alsace, France, Streicher joined the Missionaries of Africa (also known as White Fathers) in 1884 and was ordained a priest in 1885. He volunteered for Uganda and arrived there in 1891 in the middle of civil and religious unrest. Appointed apostolic vicar of Northern Nyanza (1896), he was ordained bishop in 1897. By 1913 he had opened forty new mission posts. The growing work created three new vicariates: Lac Albert (1913), Ruwenzori (1933), and Masaka (1934). The last was the first to be entrusted to Baganda diocesan priests. Believing that Africans should be their own missionaries, he began a school for catechists (Rubaga, 1902), ordained the first two Bagandan priests (1913), and founded a congregation for Baganda sisters, the Daughters of Mary (Banabikira, 1910), and one for brothers, the Brothers of Charles Lwanga (Bannakaroli, 1927). He began the beatification process of the martyrs of Uganda and attended the consecration of the first African bishop for Masaka, Joseph *Kiwanuka in 1939. Retired at his request in 1933, he celebrated his episcopal golden jubilee in 1947.

BIBLIOGRAPHY "Monseigneur Henri Streicher," *Notices Nécrologiques, 1950–1952,* Société des Missionaires d'Afrique, Pères Blancs (1957), pp. 3–47; G. D. Kittler, *The White Fathers* (1957); Y. Tourigny *So Abundant a Harvest: The Catholic Church in Uganda, 1897–1979* (1979); J. M. Waliggo, "The Catholic Church in the Buddu Province of Buganda, 1897–1925" (Ph.D. diss., Cambridge Univ., 1976).

J. G. Donders, M Afr

Streit, Karl (1874–1935), Catholic mission cartographer. Born in Slovakia at Dittersbächel, Leitmeritz, Streit entered the Society of the Divine Word in 1895. At Mödling, near Vienna, he was a close collaborator of Wilhelm *Schmidt in promoting the periodical *Anthropos.* In 1906 he published *Katholische Missionatlas,* which included the sending missionary societies; the number of missionaries, priests, religious sisters and brothers, catechists, mission stations, and schools; the total population of region and country; and the baptized Catholics in each place. In 1913 he published the *Atlas Hierarchicus,* indexing some 20,000 cities and mission stations and containing German, French, Italian, Spanish, and English texts. A second edition appeared in 1929, and in 1930 an English edition appeared under the title *Catholic World Atlas,* with the most complete and comprehensive statistics on the Catholic Church to that time as well as useful historical and ethnological information. Streit drew the maps for the Vatican Missionary Exhibition in 1925. In 1926 he published *Sprachfamilien und Sprachenkreise der Erde* (Families of languages and linguistic groups of the world). In 1930 he founded the Cartographical Institute of the Society of the Divine Word at St. Gabriel, Mödling, to study geographic and statistical aspects of the Catholic Church.

BIBLIOGRAPHY Karl Streit, "Mission und Kartographie," *ZM* 20 (1930): 276–280. Johannes Dindinger, "Streit, Karl," *Lexikon für Theologie und Kirche,* vol. 9 (2d ed., 1937), pp. 862–863; *Steyler Chronik* 5 (1935): 76 (obit.).

Willi Henkel, OMI

Streit, Robert (1875–1930), Catholic mission librarian and bibliographer. Born in Germany at Fraustadt, Posen, Streit entered the Missionary Oblates of Mary Immaculate in 1895. In 1902 he collaborated in producing the magazine of the German Province of Oblates and served as its editor-in-chief from 1905 to 1912. During these years he collected rich materials from the missions and wrote several books. Noticing that many Roman Catholic historians dealt with missions in a very limited and superficial way, in a series of articles he dealt with exegetical, patristic, and historical issues in mission studies. He contributed to the discussions on missions and the necessity of introducing missiology into seminaries and universities. In 1911 the first Catholic chair of missiology was established at the University of Münster, Germany. Streit's greatest contribution to missiology is the *Bibliotheca Missionum,* a bibliography of Roman Catholic missions in America, Asia, and Africa, in chronological order. From the first volume onward, scholars expressed their great appreciation for such a monumental reference tool. Streit died at an early age after completing only five volumes, leaving the task of continuing the work to his successors, Johannes *Dindinger and Johannes *Rommerskirchen.

In 1922 Streit received an honorary doctorate from the University of Münster. In 1925 Cardinal Van *Rossum, prefect of Propagada Fide, called Streit to Rome to be responsible for the missionary literature at the Vatican Missionary Exposition. Pope *Pius XI encouraged Propaganda Fide to continue the collection, which formed the nucleus of what became the Pontifical Missionary Library, and Streit was appointed the library's first director.

BIBLIOGRAPHY Robert Streit, *Bibliotheca Missionum,* vols. 1–5 (1916–1929), *Die katholische deutsche Missionsliteratur* (1925), *Die Weltmission der katholischen Kirche: Zahlen und Zeichen auf Grund der Vatikanischen Missionsausstellung 1925* (1928; also in English, Italian, French, and Spanish); a short biography and bibliography appears in *Bibliografia Missionaria* 2 (1936): 5–17. Johannes Pietsch, *P. Robert Streit, O.M.I.: Ein Pionier der katholischen Missionswissenschaft* (1952); Willi Henkel, "Robert Streit," in Gerald H. Anderson et al., eds., *Mission Legacies* (1994), pp. 391–401.

Willi Henkel, OMI

Stronach, Alexander (1800–1879), London Missionary Society (LMS) missionary to the Chinese. Born in Edinburgh, Stronach worked in Penang and Singapore from 1838. He visited Hong Kong in August 1843 to attend the LMS Conference of Missionaries and the Convention of Missionaries on Bible translation. He returned to Penang and then Singapore, where he closed down the LMS mission as part of the move of the "Ultra-Ganges Mission" from the Straits Settlement to China. In 1846 he reestablished the old Malacca printing press in Hong Kong and then, with his wife, Eliza, joined his brother John *Stronach in Amoy (Xiamen). An appreciated member of the Protestant missionary community, Stronach was chiefly involved in education, evangelism, and printing. He wrote a number of hymns and published a hymnbook in Amoy in 1857. He retired in 1870 and died in London.

BIBLIOGRAPHY [Alexander Wylie], *Memorials of Protestant Missionaries to the Chinese* (1867).

John Roxborogh

Stronach, John (1810–1888), missionary in China and Bible translator of the London Missionary Society (LMS). Born in Edinburgh and trained at the Glasgow Theological Academy, Stronach with his brother Alexander *Stronach and their wives arrived in Singapore in March 1838. He was a secretary of the Singapore Tract and Book Society, assisted in English services, worked on a Malay New Testament, and encouraged a Malay girls' school run by his wife, Margaret. With Alexander he attended the August 1843 Hong Kong LMS Conference of Missionaries and the Convention of Missionaries on Bible translation. From 1844 he and Margaret pioneered LMS work in Amoy (Xiamen), but she died en route to England in 1846. From 1847 to 1850, based in Shanghai, he was involved with the Delegates' Translation of the New Testament in classical Chinese; then, following disputes over the word to be used for God and other issues, he worked with other LMS missionaries on their own version. In 1853 he returned to Amoy, where he was based until 1876. He retired in 1878 and died in Philadelphia, Pennsylvania.

BIBLIOGRAPHY [Alexander Wylie], *Memorials of Protestant Missionaries to the Chinese* (1867).

John Roxborogh

Strong, Josiah (1847–1916), American advocate of missions and of the Social Gospel. Strong was born in Naperville, Illinois, graduated from Western Reserve College, Cleveland, and studied at Lane Theological Seminary, Cincinnati, Ohio. His professional ministry included Congregational pastorates in Cheyenne, Wyoming (1871–1873), Sandusky, Ohio (1876–1881), and Cincinnati, Ohio (1884–1886). In addition, he served as chaplain and instructor at Western Reserve College (1873–1876), regional secretary for the Congregational Home Missionary Society (1881–1884), general secretary for the American Evangelical Alliance (1886–1898), and president of the American Institute for Social Service (1898–1916). In all of these roles, Strong vigorously championed urban evangelism, social Christianity, and interdenominational cooperation.

Strong defined home missions largely in terms of social reform and the gradual Christianization of American society. His most important book, *Our Country: Its Possible Future and Its Present Crisis* (1885), sounded these themes at the same time that it delineated the major dangers facing the United States. He also projected his agenda beyond America's shores with bold talk of an Anglo-Saxon cultural conquest of the world. This volume established Strong as one of the major advocates of the Social Gospel in America.

Several aspects of Strong's career suggest relevance for foreign missions. His book *The New Era* (1893) included a chapter entitled "The Mission of the Church," in which he called on Christians to extend the kingdom of God on all fronts. Toward the end of his tenure with the Evangelical Alliance, he worked closely with the American Board of Commissioners for Foreign Missions and its foreign secretary, James *Barton. In his later writings such as *Expansion under New World Conditions* (1900), *Our World: The New World Life* (1913), and *Our World: The New World Religion* (1915), he set forth a Christian internationalism that did not entirely eclipse his earlier triumphalistic nationalism. Finally, he traveled to England (1904) and South America (1909–1910) in overseas efforts to institutionalize the Social Gospel.

BIBLIOGRAPHY Wendy Jane Deichmann, "Josiah Strong: Practical Theologian and Social Crusader for a Global Kingdom" (Ph.D. diss., Drew Univ., 1991); Paul R. Meyer, "The Fear of Cultural Decline: Josiah Strong's Thought about Reform and Expansion," *ChH* 42 (1973): 396–405; Dorothea R. Muller, "Josiah Strong and American Nationalism: A Reevaluation," *Journal of American History* 53 (1966): 487–503; James Eldin Reed, "American Foreign Policy, the Politics of Missions, and Josiah Strong, 1890–1900," *ChH* 41 (1972): 230–245.

James A. Patterson

Struve, Nikita Alexelevich (1931–), member of the diaspora Russian intelligentsia and spokesperson for religious freedom. Born in Paris, Struve graduated from the Sorbonne and served on the faculty of the University of Paris where he lectured on Russian literature at the Paris Institute of Slavic Studies. He became editor of the periodical *Vesnik,* organ of the Russian Student Christian Movement, a ministry to youth in the diaspora. He also served as editor of the official church journal *Messenger Orthodoxe.* A strong opponent of Soviet antireligious measures, he wrote *Les Chrétiens en U.R.S.S.,* published in 1963 in Paris; it was translated into English (1967) and Greek (1968). He has also concerned himself with missionary themes, including an important article on the early nineteenth-century paradigmatic Russian Orthodox missionary Makarii *Glukharev, who did missionary work among the Altaics. Struve emphasized Glukarev's method of identifying himself with the people, replacing mass conversions with individual instruction and personal commitment, offering worship services in the vernacular, and translating Scripture into the language of the people. Struve lives in Paris, where he continues as editor of *Vesnik.*

BIBLIOGRAPHY Nikita Struve, "Macaire Gloukharev, A Prophet of Orthodox Mission," *IRM* 54 (1965): 308–314, and "Orthodox Missions: Past and Present," *St. Vladimir's Theological Quarterly* 27, no. 2 (1962): 44–57. Nicholas Zernov, *The Russian Religious Renaissance of the Twentieth Century* (1963).

Stanley Samuel Harakas

Stuart, Edward Craig (1827–1911), Scottish Church Missionary Society (CMS) missionary and Anglican bishop. Born in Edinburgh, Stuart was educated at Trinity College, Dublin. In 1850, after a distinguished university career, he sailed for India under appointment by the CMS. With Thomas *French, he was one of the founding staff of St. John's College, Agra, where he taught for ten years. In 1851 he married Anne Alicia de Courcy, who was invalided to England in 1857 with mental illness. (She died in 1915 in an asylum in Ireland.) After 22 years in India he went in 1876 to the New Zealand mission as a teacher at St. Stephen's Maori College. The following year he was chosen and consecrated as second bishop of Waiapu, remaining in that post until 1894. He then offered to serve in the Persia mission and was authorized to perform episcopal functions. He worked in Persia (Iran) from 1894 to 1910, accompanied by his daughter Anne. Two nieces, Emmeline Stuart, a doctor, and Gertrude Stuart, a nurse, also worked in Persia, where medical work among men and women was found by CMS to be a useful form of service and contact. Educational institutions were also established, and after his death, the CMS Boys' High School in Isfahan was renamed Bishop Stuart Memorial College. His total length of overseas service was fifty-six years, in three widely different countries.

BIBLIOGRAPHY Gordon Hewitt, *The Problems of Success: A History of the Church Missionary Society, 1910–1942,* vol. 1 (1971); Isobel M. Nicoll, M. M. Stuart, and Joseph G. S. Cameron, *A Stuart Story, 1770–1980* (1980); Eugene Stock, *History of the Church Missionary Society,* vol. 3 (1899).

Jocelyn Murray

Stuart, John Leighton (1876–1962), Presbyterian missionary and educator in China. Born in Hangchow (Hangzhou), China, the son of Presbyterian missionaries, Stuart attended schools in America from age 11, was ordained in the Presbyterian ministry, and in 1904 traveled with his wife to China, where he taught New Testament studies at Nanking Theological Seminary from 1908 to 1919. He wrote *Essentials of New Testament Greek* in Chinese and compiled the *Greek-Chinese Dictionary of the New Testament.* In 1919 he became the first president of Yenching

University, created by the merger of Peking University, North China Union College, and the North China Union Women's College. During his 27 years as president, Yenching became the preeminent private university in China, setting the standard for the other twelve Christian colleges and universities. With ties to Harvard and Princeton, it received generous support from American benefactors for its splendid new campus outside Peking.

During the student anti-Christian movement of the mid-1920s, Stuart refused to move the university into Peking, where it could be protected. Yet, while he supported student patriotism and the need for social change in China, he remained a staunch opponent of revolutionary politics. His first commitment was to Christian higher education. In the 1920s he cultivated friendships with all sides in China's civil strife. As late as 1948, hoping the university would carry on, he urged accommodation to the Communist government.

Stuart remained with the university in Peking after its capture by the Japanese in 1937 and was interned after Pearl Harbor, refusing an offer of repatriation because others were denied it. He was freed in August 1945 and resumed the university presidency. He capped a long and distinguished career by serving as American ambassador to the Republic of China from 1946 to 1952, recommended for the post by General George C. Marshall, whom he had assisted in his China peace-keeping mission. He returned to the United Sates in 1949 while continuing to hold the post of ambassador.

BIBLIOGRAPHY John L. Stuart, *Fifty Years in China: The Memoirs of John Leighton Stuart, Missionary and Ambassador* (1954). Dwight Edwards, *Yenching University* (1959); Jessie G. Lutz, *China and the Christian Colleges, 1850–1950* (1971); Yu-ming Shaw, *An American Missionary in China: John Leighton Stuart and Chinese-American Relations* (1992); Philip West, *Yenching University and Sino-Western Relations, 1916–1952* (1976).

Donald E. MacInnis

Studd, C(harles) T(homas) (1860–1931), founder of Worldwide Evangelization Crusade (WEC). Studd was the youngest of three sons born to Edward Studd, a wealthy retired jute and indigo planter in Wiltshire, England. Considered England's most outstanding cricket player, Studd, together with six other remarkable Cambridge students (the *Cambridge Seven), dedicated his life to foreign missionary service. His decision caused a sensation in the public press and lit the flame for the Student Volunteer Movement (SVM). He gave away his substantial inheritance and sailed to China under the China Inland Mission (CIM) in 1885, endorsing wholeheartedly the CIM's radical incarnational principles in the context of extreme adversity. In China he married Priscilla Steward, a young Irish missionary, and together they had four daughters.

Forced home in 1894 by poor health, Studd itinerated throughout the United States and Britain on behalf of the SVM for six years before moving to India in 1900 to serve as minister of the English-speaking church at Ootacamund. Again in poor health, he returned to England in 1906 to resume his speaking ministry. In 1910, still sickly, and against the wishes of his ailing wife, he embarked for Africa, returning a year later to establish the Heart of Africa Mission, later to become WEC. In 1913, accompanied by his future son-in-law, Alfred *Buxton, Studd began his 18-year missionary endeavor in the Belgian Congo (Zaire). Inspiring as an exemplar, he proved to be an obstinate and unreasonable leader and colleague, provoking bitter conflict with family, fellow missionaries, and Africans until his death. His wife, who remained in England throughout his tenure in Africa except for a lone visit in 1928, died in 1929. After Studd's death at Ibambi, the struggling organization that he founded began to flourish under the capable leadership of another son-in-law, Norman *Grubb. Today, WEC, evincing the radical spirit of its founder, is an international community of some 1,500 missionaries serving in fifty-one different countries.

BIBLIOGRAPHY The incorrigibility of Studd is evident in such publications as his *Fool and Fanatic? Quotations from the Letters of C. T. Studd*, Jean Walker, comp. (1980) and *Quaint Rhymes for the Battlefield* (1914). Reliable and easily accessible sources of information on Studd include Edith Buxton, *Reluctant Missionary* (1968); John Erskine, *Millionaire of God: The Story of C. T. Studd* (1968); Norman Percy Grubb, *C. T. Studd: Cricketer and Pioneer* (1933); and Eileen Vincent, *C. T. Studd and Priscilla: United to Fight for Jesus* (1988). Virtally all of Studd's personal correspondence is located at the WEC International offices at Gerrards Cross, Bucks, England, and at Fort Washington, Pa.

Jonathan J. Bonk

Studd, J(ohn) E(dward) K(ynaston) (1858–1944), English missions promoter. Studd was the eldest of three brothers (including C. T. *Studd) born in Wiltshire, England, to Edward Studd, a wealthy retired jute and indigo planter. Converted through the witness of a friend of his father, Studd became an effective promoter of evangelism, masterminding the 1882 Cambridge University crusade, which contributed significantly to the revitalization of the British missionary enterprise. With Quintin Hogg, Studd established the Regent Street Polytechnic, becoming honorary secretary from 1885, vice-president in 1901, and president from 1903 until his death. He was appointed Officer (of the Order) of the British Empire in 1919, knighted in 1923, and declared Lord Mayor of London for 1928–1929. If his earlier dream of medical missionary work in China was never fulfilled, his impact for world missions was nevertheless considerable. His 13-week tour of twenty American college campuses in 1885 (at Dwight L. *Moody's invitation), provided impetus for the Christian awakening of such notables as Wilfred *Grenfell and John R. *Mott, thus linking him to the Student Volunteer Movement, whose impact upon the twentieth-century missionary movement is inestimable.

BIBLIOGRAPHY Arthur T. Polhill-Turner, *A Story Retold: "The Cambridge Seven"* (1901); J. C. Pollock, *A Cambridge Movement* (1953). See also references in A. J. Broomhall, *Hudson Taylor and China's Open Century*, vol. 6 (1988); C. Howard Hopkins, *John R. Mott, 1865–1955: A Biography* (1979); Basil Joseph Matthews, *John*

R. Mott: World Citizen (1934); J. Edwin Orr, *Evangelical Awakenings in Southern Asia* (1975).

Jonathan J. Bonk

Sturges, Albert A. (1819–1887), American pioneer missionary to Micronesia. Sturges was born at Granville, Ohio, and trained at Yale Divinity School. He married Susan Thompson in 1851, was ordained in 1852, and went to Micronesia sponsored by the American Board of Commissioners for Foreign Missions (ABCFM) and the Hawaiian Board of Missions. He served at Ohwa, on the east coast of Pohnpei, near the ancient center of the island's Saudeleur chiefly dynasty. He controlled a smallpox epidemic in 1854, learned the language, and translated hymns and parts of Scripture. By 1864, 154 people had been baptized. The Ohwa school educated an elite, led by the young Henry *Nanpei, who became the outstanding Protestant Pohnpeian leader. Nanpei, of mixed English-Micronesian descent, received chiefly status in his home area of Kiti on the west coast. As a landowner and trader, he absorbed and applied Sturges's brisk work ethic, optimistic theology, and motivation toward self-betterment. In 1874 Sturges initiated the Interior Micronesia Mission in the Mortlock Islands, under the leadership of Micronesian students from Ohwa. He left Pohnpei for the last time in 1885 to return to the United States. He died at Oakland, California.

Bibliography Theodora Crosby Bliss, *Micronesia: Fifty Years in the Island World...* (1906); David and Leona Crawford, *Missionary Adventures in the South Pacific* (1967); John Garrett, *To Live among the Stars: Christian Origins in Oceania* (1982); David Hanlon, *Upon a Stone Altar: A History of the Island of Pohnpei to 1890* (1988); Albertine Loomis, *To All People: A History of the Hawaii Conference of the United Church of Christ* (1970). Reports and letters are in *The Missionary Herald*, manuscripts in ABCFM papers at Houghton Library, Harvard Univ., and also on microfilm, Pacific Manuscripts Bureau, Canberra.

John Garrett

Sturmius (Sturmi) (d. 779), Benedictine missionary and first abbot of Fulda. Born in Bavaria, Sturmius was *Boniface's most trusted disciple. Educated in Fritzlar, he became a priest in 740. He undertook missionary work among the Hessians there, founding the monastery of Fulda in Hesse Nassau. He visited the Benedictine abbeys in Subiaco, Monte Cassino, and Saint Andrews. When he brought the bones of Boniface to Fulda, he angered Archbishop Lullus of Mainz, who sent him away to Normandy. Pépin brought him back in 765. Charlemagne gave Sturmius the task of converting part of the newly defeated Saxon peoples around Eresburg, Hamel, and Minden, but he died before he could have much effect in the new field.

Bibliography Wilhelm Arndt, *Leben des h. Bonifazius von Wilibald, der h. Leoba von Rudoft von Fuld, des Abtes Sturmi von Eigil, des h. Lebiun von Hucbald* (1888); P. Englebert, *Die Vita Sturmi des Eigil* (1968); Charles H. Talbot, *The Anglo-Saxon Missions in Germany* (1954); J. Wehner, *Abt Sturmius von Fulda: Sein Leben in 14 Bildern* (1967).

Frederick W. Norris

Stursberg, (Engelbert) Julius (1857–1909), German mission administrator. The son of a textile factory manager and elder in the Reformed congregation in Wuppertal-Barmen, Stursberg began theological studies in 1876 at Leipzig, where, as a result of a crisis experience, he decided to devote his life fully to God. After further study at Strasbourg, Tübingen, and Bonn, he passed his exams and became a teacher. In 1880 he joined the staff of Ludwig *Doll, the parish pastor at Neukirchen in the Rhineland, and after Doll's death in 1883 assumed the direction of his Orphan and Mission Institute and married his widow. Under Stursberg's leadership the institute became an interconfessional faith mission with a Reformed orientation and close ties to the Evangelical Alliance; flourishing works were established in Java and British East Africa (Kenya). He taught the students at the society's seminary, produced a bimonthly magazine, and traveled incessantly throughout Germany and abroad to represent the Neukirchener Mission (at such places as the New York Ecumenical Missionary Conference in 1900 and the fields in East Africa and the Dutch East Indies). The society opened a third field in German East Africa (present-day Tanzania) soon after his untimely death in 1909 while he was on a visit to Java.

Bibliography Ulrich Affeld, *Er mache uns im Glauben kühn: 100 Jahre Neukirchener Mission* (1978); *Blätter der Erinnerung an den heimgegangenen Missionsinspektor Stursberg* (1910); E. Doll, *Missionsinspektor Julius Stursberg: Ein Lebensbild* (1921); Wilhelm Nitsch, *Unter dem offenen Himmel: Aus der Geschichte der Waisen- und Missionsanstalt Neukirchen, 1878–1928* (1928); Karl Rahn, *Dennoch getrost: 75 Jahre Waisen und Missionsanstalt Neukirchen* (1953); Ferdinand Würtz, *Missionar und Missionspionier im Pokomoland in Brit.-Ostafrika* (1910).

Richard V. Pierard

Subhan, John (1897–1977), Methodist bishop in India and Islamic scholar. Subhan grew up in a Sufi Muslim family in Calcutta. After hearing Samuel *Zwemer lecture at the YMCA, he converted to Christianity. Expelled from his Islamic school, he gained entry to a Church Missionary Society school. From there he proceeded to St. John's College, Agra, graduating with a B.A. in 1925. Briefly a Catholic, he became a Methodist when the Bareilly Seminary appointed him lecturer in Islamics. Between 1930 and 1944 he lectured at the Henry Martyn School of Islamic Studies as its first Indian staff member. While there, he gained the Serampore B.D. and produced several significant publications. Between 1945 and 1965 he served as a bishop of the Methodist church in South Asia. Throughout his life, he encouraged sensitive evangelism of Muslim peoples. He was especially concerned with the reception and nurture of converts. Before retiring, he received the Serampore D.D. His name is honored by the Subhan Library at the Henry Martyn Institute's Hyderabad headquarters.

Bibliography John Subhan, *Sufism: Its Saints and Shrines* (1938), *Islam: Its Beliefs and Practices* (1938), *How a Sufi Found His Lord* (1950), and *The Virgin Mary in Catholic Belief and Protestant Thought* (1970).

Clinton Bennett

Suh Sang-Yun (*or* So Sang Yoon) (1848–1926), Korean Protestant pioneer evangelist and Bible translator. Converted in 1878 in Manchuria and baptized the following year, Suh became principal assistant to the Scottish missionary John *Ross in producing the first published translation of the New Testament into Korean (1887). Earlier, in 1883, he had carried the first printed copies of the Gospels of Luke and John across the Manchurian border into Korea, and by early 1884 he was evangelizing his home village, Sorai, five months before the first foreign Protestant missionary, Horace *Allen, reached Korea. The Sorai congregation, unbaptized and with no clergyman, was already gathering for worship, making it the "cradle" of Korean Protestantism. In 1887 Suh sent his people south to Seoul for baptism by the first resident Presbyterian clergyman in Korea, Horace G. *Underwood. In 1891 Suh guided Samuel A. *Moffett and James *Gale for three months of exploration through parts of northern Korea to plan for mission expansion. In Seoul he became assistant to Underwood in the first organized Korean Protestant church. His brother, Suh Kyung-Jo, later became its first Korean pastor.

BIBLIOGRAPHY *Kidokkyo Tae Paekhwa Sajon* (The Christian encyclopedia), vol. 8 (1983); E. Wagner, "Through the Hermit's Gate with Suh Sang Yun," *Korea Mission Field* (May 1938). See also references in R. H. Baird, *William M. Baird: A Profile* (1968), L. G. Paik, *History of Protestant Missions in Korea, 1832–1910* (1929), and H. G. Underwood, *The Call of Korea* (1908).

Samuel Hugh Moffett

Suidbert (*or* Suitbert; Swibert) (d. 713), Anglo-Saxon missionary and bishop. Suidbert came from Northumbria, England, and lived as a Benedictine monk-priest in the monastery of Rathmelsigi, Ireland. From 690 he accompanied *Willibrord on his mission to Frisia (now the Netherlands and part of Belgium), where his companions elected him *chore-episcopus* (district bishop). His consecration by Wilfred of York was not recognized by Pépin of Heristal, mayor of the palace of the Frankish kingdom. The first phase of Suidbert's activity was centered in the region of the present city of Utrecht. Later he evangelized among the Germanic tribe of the Bructeri in the territory between the Upper Ems, Wupper, Ruhr, and Sieg Rivers, where his mission was a success. Because of the rise and expansion of the Saxons, however, his mission was discontinued, and he retreated to an island on the Rhine River near the present city of Düsseldorf, the island having been given to him by Pépin. He founded a monastery there, later known as Kaiserswerth, where he died. He is remembered as the patron of many churches in the areas where he worked. A saint, his feast day is March 1.

BIBLIOGRAPHY F. Flaskamp, *Suidbert* (1930); W. Levison, *England and the Continent in the Eighth Century* (1946), pp. 57–62; C. Plummer, ed., *Bedae opera historica,* vol. 11 (1896), pp. 301 ff.

Lothar Schreiner

Sundar Singh (1889–1929?), independent Christian evangelist in India. Sundar Singh (always in the literature titled "Sadhu") was born in a Punjab village and came of mixed Sikh and Hindu stock. After an erratic education, his early dislike of Christianity came to a head with a symbolical burning of at least part of the Bible. This was followed very soon by a vision of Jesus Christ, and he was baptized on his sixteenth birthday. He was determined to become a Christian *sadhu* (holy man), and though he was associated briefly with a semi-Franciscan brotherhood, and for a few months attended an Anglican theological college, he never had any formal church affiliations. Between about 1910 and 1916 Sundar Singh traveled and preached in the mountain regions from his center at Kotgarh toward the frontiers of Tibet. He told of many dangers, hardships, and adventures, and wrote about them in the Urdu Christian press. His reports formed the basis of the first two books about him, written by Alfred Zahir (1916) and Rebecca Parker (1918). In 1918 he began to travel abroad, first to Burma, Malaysia, Singapore, Japan, and China; in 1920 to Europe, North America, and Australia; and in 1922, again to Europe. After the appearance in 1921 of *The Sadhu,* an analytical book by B. H. Streeter and A. J. Appasamy, Sundar Singh was identified as a living "mystic" and a flood of books appeared about him. But while many accepted his testimony about his early adventures, some did not, and his last years were made unhappy by controversy and by increasing ill health. On April 18, 1929, he set off once more for what he called Tibet (not the country known by that name). He was never seen or heard from again, and no one knows when, where, or how he died.

BIBLIOGRAPHY A. J. Appasamy, *Sundar Singh: A Biography* (1958); Rebecca Parker, *Sadhu Sundar Singh: Called of God* (6th ed., 1927); Eric J. Sharpe, "The Legacy of Sadhu Sundar Singh," *IBMR* 14 (1990): 161–167; B. H. Streeter and A. J. Appasamy, *The Sadhu* (1921).

Eric J. Sharpe

Sundkler, Bengt (Gustav Malcolm) (1909–1995), missionary to South and East Africa, historian, ecumenist, and missiologist. Sundkler was born in the north of Sweden and educated at the University of Uppsala, where as an undergraduate he came under the influence of Nathan *Söderblom. He was ordained in 1936 and completed his doctorate in 1937 with a dissertation on the missionary movement in nineteenth-century Sweden. He served as a Lutheran missionary in South Africa from 1937 to 1942, and in Tanzania from 1942 to 1945, acquiring meticulous knowledge of Zulu and Swahili and a vast body of information having especially to do with South African Independent Churches. He returned to Uppsala in 1945, and after a year as study secretary of the International Missionary Council, succeeded K. B. *Westman in 1949 as professor of church history (with the history of mission) in the University of Uppsala, which post he occupied until his retirement in 1974. From 1961 to 1964 he served simultaneously as Lutheran bishop in Bukoba, Tanzania (delighting in signing himself Bengt Bukoba), and as a member of the Central Committee of the World Council of Churches (1961–1965). Of his many books, special importance attaches to *Bantu Prophets in South Africa* (1948), *Church of South India 1940–1947* (1954), *The Christian Ministry in Africa* (1960), and *Nathan Söderblom, His Life and Work* (1968). His magnum opus, a history of Christianity in Africa, largely completed at the time of his death, is yet to be published. Bengt Sundkler's contribution to world mission as missionary, Africanist, scholar, and writer, and as an academic missiologist and supervisor of graduate research, is practically without parallel in postwar history.

BIBLIOGRAPHY There are two Sundkler Festschriften: Peter Beyerhaus and Carl F. Hallencreutz, eds., *The Church Crossing Frontiers* (1969) and Carl F. Hallencreutz, ed., *"Daring in Order to Know": Studies in Bengt Sundkler's Contribution as Africanist and Missionary Scholar* (1984). Both contain bibliographies, though the second is the more informative on the personal level.

Eric J. Sharpe

Sung, John Shang-chieh (1901–1944), Chinese evangelist. Born in a Methodist pastor's family in Fukien (Fujian) Province, Sung received his Ph.D. in chemistry from Ohio State University and studied theology at Union Theological Seminary, New York. His reaction to the liberal theology at Union was so intense that he was confined to a mental hospital for six months. After his return to China in 1927, he engaged in widespread evangelism, teaching, and training throughout all of China and in most of the countries of the southeast Pacific. He did much of this work as a part of the Bethel Band, an indigenous revivalist organization. Wherever he went, his work resulted in widespread conversions and in renewal of the church. From 1940 to 1944 he was ill with cancer and tuberculosis, from which he died.

BIBLIOGRAPHY Leslie T. Lyall, *John Sung* (1954).

Ralph R. Covell

Sutton, Amos (1802–1854), British missionary with the General Baptist Missionary Society in Orissa, India. Sutton trained for the ministry of the General Baptist New Connexion in Derby under J. G. Pike, the founder of the Connexion's missionary society. After a period in home ministry, Sutton departed for India in 1824, two years after the first Baptist missionaries, William Bampton and James Peggs, had entered Orissa. The first Oriya conversion was recorded in 1828. Sutton devoted himself to grammatical work on the Oriya language and Bible translation. In 1841 he began training the first three Oriya evangelists at Cuttack. By 1846 there were eight students, and the class was formalized as the Cuttack Mission Academy. In addition to a number of Oriya tracts, Sutton published *A Narrative of the Mission to Orissa* (1844), *Orissa and Its Evangelization* (1850), and an autobiography, *The Happy Transformation* (1844). He died in Cuttack.

BIBLIOGRAPHY Pradip Das, "British Baptist Missionary Activity in Orissa from 1822 to 1914: A Study in Missionary Attitudes, Relationships, and Impact" (M. Litt. thesis, Univ. of Bristol, 1994); James Peggs, *A History of the General Baptist Mission* (1846).

Brian Stanley

Swain, Clara (1834–1910), world's first woman missionary doctor and founder of the first hospital for women in Asia. Born in Elmira, New York, and imbued with an urge to serve, Swain entered the Woman's Medical College of Pennsylvania, in Philadelphia. Graduating in 1869, she was sent to India by the newly organized Methodist Woman's Foreign Missionary Society. Assigned to Bareilly, birthplace of Indian Methodism, she found the needs overwhelming. By the end of six weeks she had treated 108 patients. She began training young Indian women in medicine. Deciding that she needed a hospital and coveting land adjoining the mission owned by an Indian potentate, she approached him with trepidation. Would he sell her just an acre? No, the land was not for sale—her hopes plummeted—but he was glad to *give* the whole tract, containing a palatial building, for "such a noble purpose." In this "palace" the institution later known as Clara Swain Hospital became reality. In 1873 a new dispensary was also dedicated. The work grew to include a nursing school, a large hospital complex, rural outreach, and many departments. In 1885 she became physician to women in the domain of the rajah of Khetri, a huge area in Rajputana untouched by Christian missions. In 1885 she helped Lady Dufferin, the viceroy's wife, outline the plan initiating the formation of the National Medical Association for Supplying Female Aid to the Women of India, an important milestone in Indian progress. In 1895 she retired to Castile, New York.

BIBLIOGRAPHY Clara N. Swain, *A Glimpse of India* (1909). Dorothy Clarke Wilson, *Palace of Healing* (1968).

Dorothy Clarke Wilson

Swan, William (1791–1866), Scottish missionary in Siberia. Swan was born near Kirkcaldy, Scotland, and died in Edinburgh. He studied at Glasgow Theological Academy and was appointed by the London Missionary Society for service in Siberia. Following ordination in 1818, Swan went to Russia and then made his way to Siberia, arriving in early 1819. There he began work among the Buriat people, itinerating extensively while also translating the Bible into Mongolian. In 1831 he left Siberia to arrange publication of the Mongolian Bible and to visit Great Britain. He married Hannah Cullen in 1831 and together they went to Russia in 1832. Upon their arrival in Saint Petersburg, Swan was placed under government detention until the end of 1833. In 1840 the government suppressed the Siberian mission and the Swans were forced to leave Siberia. Swan wrote *Letters on Missions* (1830), perhaps the first Protestant attempt at a comprehensive treatment of the theory and practice of missions. In his book he used the device of replying to questions posed by an interlocutor concerning missionary work.

BIBLIOGRAPHY James Sibree, ed., *A Register of Missionaries, Deputations, Etc., London Missionary Society* (1923).

Wilbert R. Shenk

Swatson, John (c. 1855–c. 1925), African missionary evangelist. Born in the Gold Coast (Ghana), Swatson worked as a clerk in Nigeria, retired to his hometown of Beyin, and then in about 1911 became the Methodist "agent" at Aboisso, Côte d'Ivoire. Consecrated by William Wadé *Harris in 1913, "Bishop Swatson" carried his work to Sanwi in the interior, then to Sefwi in the Gold Coast. He made many converts despite opposition from chiefs and colonial officials who accused him of causing social and political unrest. During 1915–1916, with help from Anglican missionaries E. D. Martinson and Archdeacon G. W. Morrison, his converts were accepted as Anglicans by Bishop O'Rourke of Accra. They became the foundation of the strong Anglican presence there today.

BIBLIOGRAPHY G. M. Haliburton, "The Anglican Church in Ghana and the Harris Movement in 1914," *Bulletin: Society for African Church History* 1, nos. 3–4 (1964): 101–106, and *The Prophet Harris: A Study of an African Prophet and His Mass-Movement in the Ivory Coast and the Gold Coast, 1913–1915* (1971); Paul Jenkins, "The Anglican Church in Ghana, 1905–1924," *Transactions of the Historical Society of Ghana* 15, nos. 1–2 (1974): 23–39, 177–200.

Gordon M. Haliburton

Sweetman, James Windrow (1891–1966), English missionary scholar of Islam and Christianity. Sweetman divided his career between India and Britain. In the service of the British Methodist Missionary Society in India, he educated himself in the languages, culture, and doctrines of Islam, acquiring excellent command of Arabic and Persian as well as Urdu. His academic work began at Forman College, Lahore, and came to maturity at the Henry Martyn Institute of Islamic Studies, Aligarh, where he held the post of librarian from 1934 to 1946. He was an honorary doctor of Serampore.

His impact on Christian thinking about Islam extended beyond his many students through the pages of the institute's publication *News and Notes,* which in 1941 became the *Bulletin of the Henry Martyn Institute.* His many articles reiterate in advice to missionaries the commitment of his own life: the imperative of understanding Islam in depth, so as to make Christianity intelligible in the idiom of the Muslim mind. He argued for missionary specialization, and at the risk of seeming "ivory-towered," devoted himself to a massive task of research from which he produced four volumes entitled *Islam and Christian Theology.* They are written as a theological inquiry more than as a history of religion, with the purpose of illustrating similarities and differences in the comparative doctrines of Islam and Christianity. The first volume was completed in Aligarh, the others in the Selly Oak Colleges, Birmingham, where Sweetman continued his missionary teaching and research from 1947 to 1962. A fifth volume of "constructive criticism" was planned but never written.

BIBLIOGRAPHY James Sweetman, *Islam and Christian Theology,* part 1, vol. 1 (1945), part 1, vol. 2 (1947), part 2, vol. 1 (1955), part 2, vol. 2 (1967), and *The Bible in Islam* (1953). John Subhan, "James Windrow Sweetman as I Knew Him," *Bulletin of the Henry Martyn Institute of Islamic Studies* 55 (1966): 2–3.

David A. Kerr

Szabó, Aladár (1862–1944), Hungarian missions advocate. Born in Tác, Hungary, Szabó began his theological studies in 1880 in Budapest. There he met Andrew Moody of the Scottish Mission, who expanded his horizons. Deeply affected by Calvinism, Szabó studied for a time in Edinburgh; he received his Ph.D. in 1891 from the Péter Pázmány University of Budapest. He established a number of home mission societies, all linked with the Hold Street revival meetings held in Budapest. János *Victor, Gyula *Forgács, and other future leaders of the Hungarian Evangelical Mission Society were deeply influenced by these meetings; the so-called Hold Street Fellowship formed the home base for Hungarian foreign mission activity in the first decade of the twentieth century.

For Szabó, in close contact with John R. *Mott since Mott's visit to Hungary in 1895, foreign mission was important in the revival of the home churches. He challenged the Hungarian nationalism and Reformed confessionalism of his day by emphasizing the need for interdenominational fellowship and by presenting the challenge of world mission. He was the herald of the twentieth-century world mission revival through his leadership and publications.

BIBLIOGRAPHY Aladár Szabó, "A protestantismus és a külmisszió" (Protestantism and foreign mission), *Protestáns Szemle* 2 (1890): 800–810, *Új Óramutató* (New clock hand) (1896), *Külmissziói Kalauz* (Foreign mission guide) (1911), "A pogánymisszió népszerűsitése" (Popularizing heathen missions), *Élet és Munka* 5, no. 4 (1913): 37–38, and *Kegyelem Altal* (By grace) (1941).

Anne-Marie Kool

T

Takayama Justus Ukon (1552–1615), early Japanese convert and Christian feudal lord. Takayama was born in Settsu Takayama, Japan. Taking the Christian name of Justus, he was baptized in 1564 by Irmão Lourenço (1526–1592), the first Japanese Christian and lay missionary. On becoming a lord of Takatsuki Castle, Takayama built a church and a seminary in the center of his territory, and completed a new and larger church in Kyoto (1576), at that time the seat of Shintoism and Buddhism. In 1580 he erected a seminary in Azuchi, the political capital. By fostering the Confraternity of Mercy, he sought to alleviate the suffering of the poor and educate people in the practical love of God and their neighbor. In the feudal society of those days to disregard class barriers and care for everyone without distinction was quite remarkable.

Takayama converted many of his subjects, and through him other feudal lords also became Christians, among them such figures as Gamo Ujisato, Kuroda Kanbe Yoshitaka, Nakagawa Hidemasa, and Makimura Masaharu. When Toyotomi Hideyoshi banished missionaries in 1587, he urged Takayama to abandon the faith. Takayama, declaring that his first allegiance was to Christ, forfeited his status and his fief and accepted a life of hardship. In 1614, one year after Tokugawa Ieyasu published a ban on the Christian faith, Takayama and 350 other Christians were banished to the Philippines, where they arrived the following year. Takayama contracted a fever and died in Manila only forty days after landing.

BIBLIOGRAPHY Luís Fróis, *Segunda parte da historia de Japan* (1938); Yakichi Kataoka, "Takayama Ukon," in *Monumenta Nipponica,* vol. 1 (1938), pp. 451–464; Johannes Laures, "Takayama Ukon: A Critical Essay," in *Monumenta Nipponica,* vol. 5 (1942), pp. 86–112, and *Takayama Ukon und die Anfänge der Kirche in Japan* (1954).

Takehiko Oda

Takla-Haymanot (c. 1215–c. 1313), Orthodox leader of renewal and mission. Takla-Haymanot was born in Silalish, Zorare (today the Bulga district of southern Ethiopia), into an ancient Orthodox clerical family whose roots in the town of Shawa extended back for ten generations. He is thought to have received his first religious instruction from his father, who was a priest. While still a young boy, and at a time when the Christian community in Shawa was a beleaguered, demoralized, and dwindling minority, he was ordained as a deacon by Egyptian Bishop Qerilos. As a young priest, Takla-Haymanot does not appear to have evinced any peculiar genius that might explain his profound influence in later years. His nine-year association with the Dabra Hayq monastery of Iyasus-Mo'a (begun when he was already well over 30 years of age) seems to have created little sensation, but it did lay the foundation for his subsequent monastic and evangelistic influence. As a middle-aged monk, he relocated to his mentor's old monastic school at Dabra Damo in Tigre Province. Here he began to attract a substantial following of young men—including Ar'ayana-Saggahu, Madhanina-Egzi, and Bartalomewos—whose personal accomplishments would ensure their mentor enduring distinction in Ethiopian church history.

After playing a sustained and key role in the revival of monasticism in Tigre, the now venerable Takla-Haymanot returned to his place of origin in Shawa as emissary of a revitalized church. His success in transmitting the spirit of revival to Shawan Christian communities marks the apogee of his influence. While it is likely that he itinerated as a preacher, his enduring legacy was the establishment of a permanent center of Christian learning and monasticism at Dabra Asbo (today known as Dabra Libanos, Ethiopia's most important monastery), which became an agent for the conversion of large segments of the pagan populations of Shawa, Damot, and Gojjam, reversing several centuries of relentless Muslim expansion in the region. It was here that Takla-Haymanot spent the three final and most fruitful decades of his life. Virtually all the church leaders and communities that emerged during this period of Christian resurgence in the districts of Katata and Grarya, as well as throughout the Shawan plateau, traced their origins either directly or indirectly to Takla-Haymanot's Dabra Asbo community, thus ensuring the success of the subsequent efforts of King Amda-Siyon (1314–1344) to consolidate and expand Ethiopia as a Christian empire.

BIBLIOGRAPHY English sources are rather sketchy, at times unreliable, and somewhat difficult to access. Among the most useful are E. A. Wallis Budge, tr., *The Life of Takla Haymanot in the Version of Dabra Libanos, and the Book of the Riches of Kings* (1906) and *The Book of the Saints of the Ethiopian Church: A Translation of the Ethiopic Synaxarium, Made from the Manuscripts Oriental 660 and 661 in the British Museum* (1928). More critical sources of information include G. W. B. Huntingford, "The Lives of Saint Takla Haymanot," in *Journal of Ethiopian Studies* 4 (July 1966): 35–40, and Taddesse Tamrat, *Church and State in Ethiopia, 1270–1527* (1972).

Jonathan J. Bonk

Takle, John (1870–1939), Baptist missionary in Bengal and founder of the League of Missionaries to Muslims. Born in England, Takle immigrated with his parents to New Zealand when he was 14 years old. Although his parents belonged to the Exclusive Brethren, he joined the Wellington Baptist Church. He was accepted by the New Zealand Baptist Missionary Society (NZBMS) for missionary service and, after two years of training in Dunedin, in November 1896 went to East Bengal, where he spent all his missionary career, mainly at Brahmanbaria. At the second World Conference of Missionaries to Muslims, held in 1911 at Lucknow, India, he proposed the formation of a league of those involved in work among Muslims. The league was founded in 1912, and Takle edited its monthly *News and Notes* until Lewis Bevan *Jones succeeded him as editor in 1920. Takle was influential as a writer on Islam and on the Christian approach to Muslims. He wrote *The Koran and the Bible; or, The Crescent versus the Sun* (1905), *The Faith of the Crescent* (1913), and articles in *Moslem World.* In ill health, he left India in December 1922 for an early furlough in New Zealand. But his health did not improve, and he resigned from the NZBMS in 1924. He died in Wellington.

BIBLIOGRAPHY L. Bevan Jones, "The Rev. John Takle," *New Zealand Baptist,* June 1940 (obit.).

Graeme A. Murray

Talmage, John Van Nest (1819–1892), American missionary to Amoy, China. An American minister with the Dutch Reformed Church, Talmage went to Amoy (Xiamen), Fukien (Fujian), China, in 1847. There he was instrumental in solidifying and expanding the new American Board of Commissioners for Foreign Missions/Dutch Reformed Church mission. Hoping to make the Bible more accessible to the general population, he and his colleague, Elihu Doty, developed a romanized script of the local Amoy language. Talmage then used this new script to produce literacy materials and to translate Christian literature and many books of the New Testament. He completed the *Amoy Colloquial Dictionary* shortly after his return to the United States in 1889.

BIBLIOGRAPHY *Report of the ABCFM* 42 (1851): 126, and 47 (1856): 167; P. W. Pitcher, *Fifty Years in Amoy, or a History of the Amoy Mission, China* (1893).

Cindy Swanson Choo

Tambunan, Albert Mangara (1911–1970), Indonesian lay leader in church and state. Born at Tarutung, North Sumatra, Tambunan was a member of the Lutheran Batak church. He studied law in Jakarta, assisted the Dutch mission consuls, and became active in the ecumenical movement. After 1945 he was a prominent member of Parliament besides playing a role in Parkindo, the Christian political party, and in the Council of Churches in Indonesia. From 1967 to 1970 he served as cabinet minister of social affairs in the national government. He received honorary doctorates in the United States from St. Olaf College, Northfield, Minnesota, and from Temple College, Chattanooga, Tennessee. He wrote several articles on religion and politics in which he emphasized the social responsibility of churches within their society and urged his fellow Christians not to be aloof, but to participate in a responsible way in the political life of the young republic. Yet he kept a critical attitude toward the government. Hence he did not really come to prominence until after 1965, the end of the period of President Sukarno. He was a sterling example of those laypersons who gave guidance to the Indonesian churches during the last decade of colonialism and the first decades of independence.

BIBLIOGRAPHY A. M. Tambunan, "Die Stellung des Laien in der H. K. B. P.," in Hans de Kleine, ed., *"...gemacht zu seinem Volk," 100 Jahre Batakkirche* (1961), pp. 99–105. Four volumes of speeches by Tambunan while he was minister of social affairs were published in Indonesian (1969–1970).

Alle G. Hoekema

Tarkkanen, Matti (1862–1938), Lutheran minister and mission leader in Finland. Tarkkanen gained international experience as a seamen's pastor in San Francisco, California (1890–1893), and successfully worked as secretary of the Finnish Seamen's Mission (1899–1906). As director of the Finnish Missionary Society (1914–1934), he found his abilities taxed to the utmost by World War I. Still, Finnish mission work made real progress, and in 1924, on an inspection tour, he ordained the first African ministers for the young Ovambo church in South-West Africa (Namibia), the first fruits of his own missionary policy. He furthered international cooperation as a member of both the Nordic Missionary Council and the International Missionary Council. At the Jerusalem 1928 missionary conference he was a spokesperson for those concerned about syncretistic tendencies. Theologically conservative and stressing the reliability of the Bible, he was a man of faith, cooperative, big-hearted, and highly trusted.

BIBLIOGRAPHY U. Paunu, "Matti Tarkkanen (1862–1938)," in Jaakko Haavio, ed., *Mikael Agricolasta E. W. Pakkalaan* (1947), pp. 623–637.

Ruth Franzén

Tatlow, Tissington (1876–1957), British ecumenical pioneer. Born in Crossdoney, County Cavan, Ireland, Tatlow was raised in a devout family active in the evangelical wing of the Anglican Church of Ireland. He was educated at St. Columba's College, Rathfarnham, and Trinity College, Dublin. In 1896 he signed the declaration of the Student Volunteer Missionary Union, "It is my purpose, if God permit, to become a foreign missionary." Though he was not to be a "missionary" in the literal sense, his whole life's work was to be based on that declaration. Ordained deacon in 1902 and priest in 1904, he soon became the general secretary of the Student Christian Movement (SCM) in Great Britain and remained in its service for more than 30 years. His services to the World's Student Christian Federation (WSCF) were many-sided—missionary, social, apologetic, educational, ecumenical, and editorial—so that he has been described as "the apostle of the student world." He maintained close relations with the Orthodox members and movements within the WSCF. He was a firm friend of the Russian SCM in exile and of the Theological Institute of St. Sergius in Paris. In 1925 he received an honorary D. D. from Edinburgh University; in 1926 he was appointed honorary canon of Canterbury. He was one of the chief architects of the British Council of Churches as well as a good many other church bodies. From the World Missionary Conference of 1910 until the WCC came into being at Amsterdam in 1948, he was a leader in the Faith and Order movement. Characteristically, he was for many years its treasurer, realizing that theological discussion without funds and without structure would not bring the churches together. He encouraged the Free churches of Great Britain to participate in the ecumenical movement. It was his life task to see that an awakening zeal would receive effective, permanent, and developing expression for the sake of Christ's church throughout the world. He died in London.

BIBLIOGRAPHY Tissington Tatlow, *The Story of the Student Christian Movement of Great Britain and Ireland* (1933). Robert Mackie, *Tissington Tatlow* (1958).

Ans J. van der Bent

Ta'unga (c. 1818–1898), Cook Islander missionary to New Caledonia, Loyalty Islands, and Samoa. Born in Rarotonga in the Cook Islands, Ta'unga went in 1842 as a pioneer missionary under the London Missionary Society (LMS) to New Caledonia. He was one of twenty-five Polynesian missionaries who served in New Caledonia before any European missionaries arrived. He was stationed at Tuauru with two Samoans whom he regarded as slothful and fearful and as failing to present adequately the love of Christ. He learned the local language and studied the customs and received an eager response from the people. A high chief on the Isle of Pines, connecting Ta'unga's success with the death and disease brought by white traders, came with twenty canoe-loads of warriors to kill him. But Ta'unga went out alone to welcome them and gave them gifts. The chief was so impressed with his bravery that he called off the attack.

However, the LMS was fearful of further dangers and moved Ta'unga, against his will, along with his companions to Mare in the Loyalty Islands in 1845. During a year of service there, Ta'unga held discussions with high chiefs of all three Loyalty Islands and converted the son of the chief of Mare. He was then returned to Rarotonga, but after a few months he went to Samoa in the hope of continuing to New Caledonia. The Samoan church asked him instead to superintend the churches of Manu'a, the easternmost part of Samoa. He did this for 30 years, receiving praise for his labors from many quarters.

Because of advancing age he asked then to be sent home, where he continued to assist the work of the churches until his death.

BIBLIOGRAPHY Marjorie Crocombe, *If I Live: The Life of Ta'unga* (c. 1970); R. G. Crocombe and Marjorie Crocombe, eds., *The Works of Ta'unga: Records of a Polynesian Traveler in the South Seas, 1833–1896* (1968).

Charles W. Forman

Taylor, Clyde W. (1904–1988), evangelical missionary statesman. Born in Fort Smith, Arkansas, Taylor attended Nyack Missionary Institute, New York, in 1924, then served in Peru (1925–1927) with the Christian and Missionary Alliance (C&MA). After receiving a Th.B. from Gordon College, Boston, Massachusetts, in 1931, he served two terms as a missionary in Colombia. In 1944, after a brief pastorate in New England, he pioneered as secretary of the Office of Public Affairs of the National Association of Evangelicals (NAE) in Washington, D.C. In the same year he helped to found the National Religious Broadcasters and the World Relief Corporation. Then in 1945, he helped found the Evangelical Foreign Missions Association, which he headed for 30 years. From his Washington office Taylor established access to government agencies and played a strategic role in aiding the cause of overseas missions. He served as general director of the NAE (1963–1974) and general secretary of the World Evangelical Fellowship (1970–1974). Visiting more than 100 countries in 40 years on behalf of evangelical missions, Taylor was reckoned by religious journalist Louis Cassels in 1968 to be among the ten most influential Protestants in the United States.

BIBLIOGRAPHY Louis Cassels, "America's 10 Most Powerful Protestants," *Christian Herald* (April 1968); "Clyde Taylor: Mr. NAE," *Christianity Today*, July 15, 1988; Carolyn Curtis, "Mr. Evangelical," *Worldwide Challenge*, January/February 1995; Arthur H. Matthews, *Standing Up, Standing Together* (1992); James D. Murch, *Cooperation Without Compromise* (1956); Bruce L. Shelley, *Evangelicalism in America* (1967).

Robert T. Coote

Taylor, James Hudson (1832–1905), founder and director of the China Inland Mission (CIM). Born at Barnsley, Yorkshire, England, Hudson Taylor sensed by the time he was 17 that God was calling him to China. He prepared himself by reading books on China, analyzing the Chinese Gospel of Luke, and studying medicine. Four years of his first term of service (1853–1860) in southeast China was under a Chinese evangelization society, founded under the inspiration of Karl *Gützlaff. In 1858 in Ningpo (Ningbo) he married Maria Dyer, who was a faithful helpmate until her death in 1870.

Although forced to return to England in 1860 because of poor health, Taylor had a continuing concern for the millions of Chinese living in provinces where no missionary had ever gone. In 1865 he summed up his growing vision in *China's Spiritual Need and Claims*. The same year, with great faith but limited financial resources, he founded the China Inland Mission. Its goal was to present the gospel to all the provinces of China. Beginning in 1866 with a group of twenty-two missionaries, including the Taylors, the mission grew rapidly in numbers and outreach. By the time of Taylor's death in 1905, the CIM was an international body with 825 missionaries living in all eighteen provinces of China, more than 300 stations of work, more than 500 local Chinese helpers, and 25,000 Christian converts. Taylor stamped his own philosophy of life and work on the CIM: sole dependence on God financially, with no guaranteed salary; close identification with the Chinese in their way of life; administration based in China itself rather than in Great Britain; an evangelical, nondenominational faith; and an emphasis upon diffusing the gospel as widely as possible throughout all of China. The last led him to encourage single women to live in the interior of China, a step widely criticized by other mission societies.

With heavy administrative responsibilities, Taylor spent as much time out of China as in, traveling to many countries to make China's needs known and to recruit new missionaries. Although often absent from China, Taylor kept in close touch with his many missionaries, and where possible, continued to engage in missionary activity. He played a prominent part at the General Missionary Conferences in Shanghai in 1877 and 1890. He retired from administration in 1901, died in Changsha, Hunan, in 1905, and was buried in Chen-chiang (Zhenjiang), Kiangsu (Jiangsu).

BIBLIOGRAPHY A standard work on Hudson Taylor is the two-volume work by his son and daughter-in-law, Howard and Mary Geraldine Taylor: *Hudson Taylor in Early Years* (1912) and *Hudson Taylor and the China Inland Mission: The Growth of a Work of God* (1919). A one-volume work is Marshall Broomhall, *Hudson Taylor: The Man Who Believed God* (1929); John Pollock, *Hudson Taylor and Maria* (1962), focuses on the early phase of Taylor's work in China. The most definitive work is James Broomhall, *Hudson Taylor and China's Open Century* (7 vols., 1981–1989).

Ralph R. Covell

Taylor, Jenny (Faulding) (1843–1904), pioneer missionary in interior China. Born in London, Jennie Faulding was one of the China Inland Mission (CIM) party which sailed for China on the *Lammermuir* in 1866. She soon proved an adaptable and resourceful missionary. In 1871 she married James Hudson *Taylor, head of the CIM, Taylor's first wife having died the year before. She bore him three more children and wholly supported her husband in his work. In 1878, when Hudson Taylor was obliged for administrative reasons to stay on in England, she returned alone to China to lead other women in relief work in the severe Shanxi famine of 1877–1878. She was the first woman to travel deep into the interior, and her success strengthened Taylor's case for appointing women in pioneering roles. During part of their married life she stayed alone in England to make a home for their teenaged children, including an adopted daughter. She helped with the administration of the CIM home office and was an assistant editor of *China's Millions*. Later she was free to travel with her husband and share in his ministry, supporting him particularly in his old age. She died in Switzerland a year before Hudson Taylor's death in Hunan, China.

BIBLIOGRAPHY A. J. Broomhall, *Hudson Taylor and China's Open Century*, 7 vols. (1981–1989); J. C. Pollock, *Hudson Taylor and Maria: Pioneers in China* (1962); Dr. and Mrs. Howard Taylor, *Biography of James Hudson Taylor* (abridged ed., 1965).

Jocelyn Murray

Taylor, John Christopher (c. 1815–1880), the Apostle of Igboland. Taylor was born in Freetown, Sierra Leone, of Igbo ex-slaves, an Isuama father and an Arochukwu mother. He studied at the Charlotte Primary School and at Fourah Bay Institution, Freetown. He served first as an Anglican catechist in the Temne mission. He was ordained a priest by the bishop of London in 1859. Thereafter, he pastored Barthust Church, Freetown, and was a schoolmaster for 16 years. He pioneered in the Niger mission (1857–1860) at Akassa (present-day Ijaw). As an enduring legacy, he translated the Scriptures and the catechism into Igbo. A man of fiery temperament and missionary zeal, his career collapsed in the Samuel *Crowther crisis in 1869. Thereafter, he trained missionaries at Fourah Bay Institution before retreating into obscurity.

BIBLIOGRAPHY John Taylor and Samuel Crowther, *The Gospel on the Banks of the Niger* (1859); see also CMS manuscripts, especially CA 3/37, Univ. of Birmingham, England.

Ogbu U. Kalu

Taylor, John V(ernon) (1914–), Anglican missionary in Uganda and general secretary of the Church Missionary Society (CMS). Taylor studied English literature and history at Cambridge and theology at Oxford. After two curacies in England he became a CMS missionary in Uganda, serving as warden of Bishop Tucker Memorial College (theological seminary) from 1944 to 1954. During his time there he encouraged his students in the creative arts, including the writing and performance of African passion plays. From 1955 to 1959 he was research assistant to the International Missionary Council, coordinating and pioneering a series of church growth studies.

In 1959 he became Africa secretary of CMS and then succeeded Max *Warren as general secretary from 1963 to 1974, also serving for a time as vice-chairman of the Theological Education Fund of the World Council of Churches. From 1975 to 1985 he was bishop of Winchester and chaired the influential doctrine commission of the Church of England (which published *Believing in the Church: The Corporate Nature of Faith,* 1981). In retirement in Oxford, Taylor continues to write, preach, and travel. He was elected honorary fellow of Trinity College, Cambridge, in 1987.

Taylor's missiology is grounded in his experience of profound cross-cultural friendships. He was persistently ahead of his time on many issues that later became conventional, particularly in his sensitivity to politics, African traditional religion, and Pentecostalism. His *Christianity and Politics in Africa* (1957) was prophetic; *The Growth of the Church in Buganda: An Attempt at Understanding* (1958) was the fruit of grassroots field research; and *The Primal Vision: Christian Presence amid African Religion* (1963) was a pioneering study on the immanence of God in Africa.

His beautifully written classic of twentieth-century mission theology, *The Go-Between God: The Holy Spirit and the Christian Mission* (1982), focused and developed many ideas already published in his monthly *CMS News-letters* (1963–1974). His major theological work in retirement is *The Christlike God* (1993).

Bibliography Other important works by Taylor include *Christians in the Copperbelt* (1961; coauthored with Dorothea Lehmann), *Enough Is Enough* (1975; an early plea for ecological living), "The Theological Basis of Interfaith Dialogue," *IRM* 68 (1979): 373–384, and *Kingdom Come* (1989); see also his autobiographical article "My Pilgrimage in Mission," *IBMR* 17 (1993): 59–61. Timothy Yates, "Newsletter Theology: CMS News-letters since Max Warren, 1963–1985," *IBMR* 12 (1988): 11–15.

Graham Kings

Taylor, Maria (Dyer) (1837–1870), pioneer missionary of the China Inland Mission (CIM). Born in Penang, Malaya, Maria Dyer was the youngest child of Samuel *Dyer, who with his wife, Maria, was a missionary with the London Missionary Society. Both parents had died by 1847, and their three children were raised in England by their mother's brother. In 1855, aged 18, Dyer went with her elder sister, Burella Dyer, to teach at the girls' school in Ningpo conducted by Mary Ann *Aldersey, an old friend of her mother. Here she met and, in 1858, married the young James Hudson *Taylor, despite Aldersey's opposition. Maria Taylor, better educated than her husband and from a different background, was from the beginning the companion and assistant he needed. Having spoken the vernacular fluently since childhood, she immediately started a small primary school. When young women CIM missionary recruits arrived, she was able to train them in language, adaptation to Chinese culture, and missionary work. She died at Chinkiang (Zhenjiang), shortly after the birth of her last child. Of her eight children, two died at birth and two in childhood. The four who survived her all later became CIM missionaries.

Bibliography A. J. Broomhall, *Hudson Taylor and China's Open Century,* 7 vols. (1981-1989); J. C. Pollock, *Hudson Taylor and Maria: Pioneers in China* (1962); Dr. and Mrs. Howard Taylor (Howard and Geraldine Taylor), *Hudson Taylor and the China Inland Mission* (1918).

Jocelyn Murray

Taylor, Richard (1804–1873), Church Missionary Society missionary in New Zealand. Taylor was born at Letwell, Yorkshire, England. He graduated from Cambridge (B.A., 1828; M.A., 1835) and was ordained a priest in the Church of England in 1829. He sailed to Australia in 1836 and in 1839 went to New Zealand, where he taught at the mission school at Te Waimate; he was transferred to Wanganui in 1843. Christianity was spreading rapidly and Taylor baptized many Maori in the 1840s and 1850s. He traveled widely, encouraging the Maori teachers and promoting peace between traditional enemies. The growth of European settlement brought conflict over land in the 1850s and 1860s. Taylor encouraged the Maori to accept European progress but was also critical of European injustices and immorality. He won the respect of many Maori, trying more than most of his colleagues to understand their society and enter into it while remaining committed to his evangelical theology. This was reflected in his writings, *Te Ika a Maui: New Zealand and its Inhabitants* (1855) and *The Past and Present of New Zealand* (1868). He also showed a great interest in the country's geology, climate, and natural history and was a fellow of the Royal Geological Society and a founding member of the New Zealand Institute. He married Mary Caroline Fox in 1829; they had two sons and two daughters. Their son, Basil, took over as head of the mission in 1860.

Bibliography A. D. Mead, *Richard Taylor: Missionary Tramper* (1966); Jenny Murray, "A Missionary in Action," in Peter Munz, ed., *The Feel of Truth* (1969) and "Moving South with the CMS," in Robert Glen, ed., *Mission and Moko: The Church Missionary Society in New Zealand, 1814–1882* (1992); Rachel Springer, *The Missionary's Daughter: Early Days at the Putiki Mission and Wanganui, from the Diaries of Laura Taylor* (1993). Taylor's journals (1825–1826, 1833–1873) are held at the Turnbull Library, Wellington, New Zealand.

Allan K. Davidson

Taylor, Richard W. (1924–1988), Methodist missionary in India. Born in Hollywood, California, Taylor did his doctoral studies in ethics and society at the University of Chicago. A minister of the Methodist Church, he served as a missionary in India from 1954. He worked as lecturer in sociology, Nagpur University (1955–1958), director of the Christian Retreat and Study Centre, Rajpur, Dehra Dun (1958–1960), and professor of ethics at Serampore College, West Bengal (1961–1969). For many years he was associated with the Christian Institute for the Study of Religion and Society (CISRS), at Bangalore and Delhi. The interpretation of Jesus in Indian paintings by both Hindu and Christian artists was one of his special concerns. He also wrote on Christian ashrams "as a style of mission in

India." His main work was on the social and ethical thought and contribution of the church to society in India. Convinced that "Christ is active outside the confines of the Christian church," he drew attention to the implications of this for the church. He wrote, "We do in some crucially important sense find Christ, meet Christ, when we go in witness and service to those who are not yet believers." He died in Srinagar, India.

BIBLIOGRAPHY Richard W. Taylor, *Jesus in Indian Paintings* (1975); many of his articles were published in the journal *Religion and Society*. A memorial volume, *Acknowledging the Lordship of Christ*, with selections from his writings, an introduction by Saral K. Chatterji, and a bibliography, was published in 1992.

Stanley J. Samartha

Taylor, William (1821-1902), Methodist Episcopal missionary bishop, mission theorist, and holiness advocate. Born to Stuart and Martha (Hickman) Taylor in Rockbridge County, Virginia, Taylor was converted in 1841 at a Methodist Episcopal camp meeting. Appointed a Methodist missionary to California (1849), he ministered without salary to Native Americans and Chinese immigrants, and to the sick and the poor. His seaman's Bethel mission complex in San Francisco burned down in 1856, forcing him to preach and write to repay loans. The first of seventeen books, *Seven Years' Street Preaching in San Francisco* (1856), sold over 20,000 copies during its first year. Taylor's experiences as an entrepreneurial missionary on the frontier became paradigmatic for the concepts he later called "Pauline missions."

Seeking to raise funds, Taylor visited Australia and New Zealand (1863–1866) and then South Africa (March to October 1866) where his evangelistic campaigns among the black population were revolutionary. In South India from 1870 to 1875, he ignored mission comity agreements, establishing self-supporting, self-propagating, and self-governing Methodist Episcopal churches, and arguing that these be recognized as the ecclesiastical equals of churches in North America. This, as well as the recruitment and appointment of self-supporting missionaries as described in his *Pauline Methods of Missionary Work* (1879), led to conflict with the Methodist mission board in New York, which attempted to define his churches as missions, thereby placing them in the control of the mission board. Taylor maintained an adversarial relationship with the board for the rest of his life.

Elected in 1884 as Methodist Episcopal missionary bishop for Africa, he established self-supporting churches in southern Liberia, Sierre Leone, Angola, Mozambique, and Zaire. He described Africa and narrated his experiences in *Story of My Life* (1895; published also as *William Taylor of California,* 1897). A folk hero for his refusal to capitulate to the demands of the Methodist mission board, Taylor became the primary mission theorist for radical Methodist and Holiness missionaries as well as Pentecostal mission efforts in Europe, Latin American, Africa, and Asia. Taylor University (Upland, Indiana) was named for him.

BIBLIOGRAPHY D. M. Balia, "Bridge over Troubled Waters: Charles Pamla and the Taylor Revival in South Africa," *Methodist History* 30 (1992): 78–90, and "Reaping Where Others Have Sown: William Taylor's Impact on Methodism," in D. M. Balia, ed., *Perspectives in Theology and Mission from South Africa* (1993), pp. 119–127; David Bundy, "Bishop William Taylor and Methodist Mission: A Study in Nineteenth Century Social History," *Methodist History* 27 (1989): 197–210, 28 (1989): 3–21, and "William Taylor," in Gerald H. Anderson et al., eds., *Mission Legacies* (1994), pp. 461–468; Eric G. Clancy, "William 'California' Taylor: First Overseas Evangelist to Australia," *Church Heritage* 6 (1990): 41–62; J. A. B. Kessler, *A Study of the Older Protestant Missions and Churches in Peru and Chile, with Special Reference to the Problems of Division, Nationalism, and Native Ministry* (1967); W. G. Mills, "The Taylor Revival of 1866 and the Roots of African Nationalism in the Cape Colony," *JRA* 8 (1976): 105–122; J. Paul, *The Soul Digger; or, The Life and Times of William Taylor* (1928).

David Bundy

Teague, Colin (*or* Collin Teage) (c. 1780–1839), pioneer African American Baptist missionary to Africa. Born a slave in Virginia, Teague was a saddler and harness maker who saved enough ($1,300) to purchase his freedom and that of his wife and two children. He had virtually no formal education but was regarded as a man of sound judgment and exemplary piety. Both he and Lott *Carey, who consistently overshadowed him, began preaching well before the two of them led in the founding of the Richmond African Missionary Society in 1815. Four years later, in 1819, Teague and Carey were appointed by the Baptist Triennial Convention in cooperation with the American Colonization Society as missionary colonists to West Africa. Before leaving the United States in 1821, Teague and Carey were ordained, and together with their wives, Teague's 16-year-old son Hilary, and a third couple, they organized themselves into a Baptist church, naming Carey as pastor. Reaching Africa 44 days later, the colonists were forced by circumstances to wait and do manual labor for a time in Sierra Leone, but they finally established themselves in Liberia in February 1822. Shortly thereafter Teague and his family returned to Sierra Leone, where they remained until after Carey's accidental death in 1828. Returning to Monrovia, Liberia, Teague became co-pastor of the Providence Baptist Church. His son Hilary later became a renowned Liberian pastor and preacher, political leader, and newspaper editor. Like Carey, Teague regarded the colonization efforts as God's design to carry the gospel to Africa, a means to establish Christian communities in a heathen wilderness and convert the indigenous inhabitants to the Christian faith. Teague died on ship enroute to the United States.

BIBLIOGRAPHY Miles Mark Fisher, "Lott Carey: The Colonizing Missionary," *Journal of Negro History* 7 (1922): 380–418; Sylvia M. Jacobs, ed., *Black Americans and the Missionary Movement in Africa* (1982); Sandy D. Martin, *Black Baptists and African Missions* (1989); Bell I. Wiley, ed., *Slaves No More* (1980).

Alan Neely

Teava (c. 1807–1876), pioneer Pacific Islander missionary to Samoa. Teava was born on Rarotonga, Cook Islands. As a youth he "fought with and captured men and cooked and helped to eat them." Converted within the missionary community of the London Missionary Society (LMS), and after training under Aaron *Buzacott at the Takamoa Training Institution at Avarua, he was ordained as an LMS missionary and in 1832 was stationed by John *Williams on the strategically chosen Samoan island of Manono. He served from 1836 onward on the larger islands of Upolu and Tutuila, sailing untiringly in an open canoe along Upolu's southern shore. He greeted and briefed Archibald W. *Murray of the LMS soon after Murray arrived at Leone on Tutuila. He helped Murray and other incoming missionaries acquire the language and remained in Samoa for 20 years with Leone as his main station. He returned to Rarotonga in 1852, where he became a copastor with Buzacott and was honored as a veteran counselor and preacher. His sermons, prayers, and wisdom moved and inspired James *Chalmers, later a pioneer of the LMS in Papua, during Chalmers's early career on Rarotonga. Later in life, when he suffered from debilitating filariasis, Teava was still widely admired for his experience and pastoral ability.

BIBLIOGRAPHY Aaron Buzacott, *Mission Life in the Islands of the Pacific* (1866); John Garrett, *To Live among the Stars: Christian Origins in Oceania* (1982); W. W. Gill, *Life in the Southern Isles* (1876); Richard Lovett, *James Chalmers: His Autobiography and Letters* (1899).

John Garrett

Tellström, Carl Ludwig (1811–1862), pioneer Swedish lay missionary to the Saami (Lapp) people of the far north of Sweden. Tellström was early apprenticed to a painter and lacked formal education. In 1833 he approached the Wesleyan missionary George *Scott in Stockholm for pastoral counseling, and was converted. His first active evangelistic work was as colporteur under the auspices of the British and Foreign Bible Society. In 1834 he began to interest himself in the spiritual welfare of Lappland and the Saami people and to study their language. In spite of his few qualifications, Scott was able to persuade the newly founded Swedish Missionary Society to accept him, and on June 13, 1836, he became the society's first missionary. He was licensed by the bishop of Härnösand as a catechist and for many years worked faithfully and successfully in the Lycksele area, though not exclusively among Lapps. His style was more Methodist than Lutheran, and he is acknowledged to have been a powerful influence on the northern Swedish style of revivalism and as a missionary motivator. A layman in a ministers' world, as an evangelist, educator, and pastor Tellström's contribution was unique.

BIBLIOGRAPHY George Scott, *Tellström and Lapland* (from a Swedish original first published in 1842); Bengt Sundkler, *Svenska Missionssällskapet, 1835–1876* (1937); Gunnar Westin, *George Scott*, 2 vols. (1928–1929).

Eric J. Sharpe

Tempels, Placide (1906–1977), Franciscan missionary and charismatic founder of the Jamaa movement in Africa. A native of Belgium, Tempels entered the Franciscan order in 1924, was ordained in 1930, and was assigned in 1933 to the Belgian Congo (Zaire). After ten years as a "bush father" in Katanga (Shaba) Province and feeling his missionary endeavors to have failed, he abandoned manuals, catechisms, and traditional methods, and devised a system of evangelization adapted to the thoughts, feelings, and inner aspirations of the Congolese. Through dialogue and encounter, he discovered the central and basic desires of the Bantu people: life, fecundity, and vital union. These values, fused with Franciscan theology and Flemish religiosity, became the basis of the creative adaptation of Catholicism to Black African culture known as the Jamaa.

In 1944–1945 Tempels published a series of articles in Flemish detailing the basic concepts of the Jamaa. Later published in book form in French, and then in English under the title *Bantu Philosophy*, this work quickly became the center of lively debate. Some insisted it deserved to be condemned for contaminating Catholic doctrine with African beliefs. Others held that, with careful guidance, the Jamaa could facilitate Catholic missionary endeavor. But when the movement emerged as a subculture within Congolese Catholicism and began to spawn a variety of what were considered to be problems, deviations, and aberrations, the enthusiasm of many of its supporters waned.

Tempels's superiors prolonged his scheduled one-year leave in Belgium from 1946 to 1949, and when he returned to the Congo, he learned that the Propaganda Fide had forbidden him to resume missionary work. Although restricted to routine pastoral and teaching tasks and frequently transferred, he maintained contact with his Jamaa lieutenants, who urged him to publish *Notre Rencontre*, a collection of *mafundisho* (lessons) in Jamaa doctrine.

Beginning in 1960, several Congolese dioceses imposed restrictions on the Jamaa, and over the next ten years all the founder-leaders of the movement left the country. Tempels returned to Belgium to undergo surgery in 1962, never to return to Africa. He was assigned to the Franciscan friary in his hometown and forbidden to publish or speak publicly. In 1964 he was summoned to Rome to face charges of heterodoxy and improper conduct, but the Holy Office never issued any condemnation of him or the Jamaa. It did, however, urge the hierarchy of Zaire to exercise prudent vigilance over Jamaa ideology and practice. Failing health plagued Tempels in his last years.

BIBLIOGRAPHY Placide Tempels, *Catéchèse bantoue* (1948), *Bantu Philosophy*, Colin King, tr. (1953), and *Notre Rencontre* (1962). Willy De Craemer, *The Jamaa and the Church: A Bantu Catholic Movement in Zaïre* (1977); Johannes Fabian, *Jamaa: A Charismatic Movement in Katanga* (1971).

Cyprian J. Lynch, OFM

Temple, William (1881–1944), archbishop of Canterbury, ecumenical statesman, missions advocate. Temple was born in Exeter, United Kingdom, son of the bishop of London who later became archbishop of Canterbury.

Temple graduated from Oxford, then taught at Queen's College, Oxford, and was ordained. He married Frances Anson in 1916. He was rector of St. James, Piccadilly, London, and canon of Westminster. He became bishop of Manchester in 1921, archbishop of York in 1929, and archbishop of Canterbury in 1942.

A leader in the Student Christian Movement, Temple served in 1910, at age 28, as a steward at the Edinburgh World Missionary Conference, where he ushered mission leaders to their seats. He grew to prominence in the world missionary movement, however, at the Jerusalem meeting of the International Missionary Council in 1928. The Jerusalem meeting, a very contentious gathering, is remembered more for its message than anything else, and the message was drafted by Temple and Robert E. *Speer. Temple later told how he wrote the final summary one night while lying on his "tummy" on the floorboards of his tent so as to avoid the breeze at table level, which would have extinguished his candle. When their work was finished, Temple read the message to the conference. The key phrase was a ringing Christological affirmation: "Our message is Jesus Christ." It repeated the statement from the 1927 Faith and Order Conference at Lausanne (in which Temple also participated): "The message of the Church to the world is and must always remain the Gospel of Jesus Christ." The very nature of the Gospel, the Jerusalem Message continued, "forbids us to say that it may be the right belief for some but not for others. Either it is true for all, or it is not true at all." When Temple finished reading the message, W. R. Hogg reports, "the assembly was hushed." The next morning, the message was unanimously approved. In 1938 Temple was elected chairman of the provisional committee of the World Council of Churches, then in the process of formation. Temple's visions and commitment to the world Christian movement was memorably stated in his enthronement sermon at Canterbury in 1942, when he spoke of the "worldwide fellowship of Christians," resulting from the missionary enterprise, as "the great new fact of our era." When he died two years later, in his prime, the world church lost one of its greatest twentieth-century advocates of mission and unity.

BIBLIOGRAPHY Temple's many publications include *Mens Creatrix* (1917), *Christus Veritas* (1925), *Nature, Man, and God* (1934), and *Christianity and Social Order* (1942), but none was more widely appreciated than his devotional study *Reading in St. John's Gospel* (1939). He wrote one of the preliminary study papers for the Jerusalem conference, "A Statement of the Case for Evangelization," which is included in the report of the meeting, *The Christian Life and Message in Relation to Non-Christian Systems* (1928). On Temple at Edinburgh in 1910 and at Jerusalem in 1928, see F. A. Iremonger, *William Temple, Archbishop of Canterbury: His Life and Letters* (1948), p. 396, and W. R. Hogg, *Ecumenical Foundations* (1952), pp. 137, 244–248.

Gerald H. Anderson

Teresa, Mother (Agnes Gonxha Bojaxhiu) (1910–1997), founder of the Missionaries of Charity. Agnes Bojaxhiu was born at Skoplje, Serbia (former Yugoslavia), in a family belonging to the Albanian minority. She was educated in Croatian at the state high school, and at the age of 18 went to Ireland to enter the Institute of the Blessed Virgin Mary (Loretta Sisters) in order to follow her desire to work in India. She sailed for India in November 1928 and arrived in Calcutta in January 1929. After nearly 20 years of work and teaching, she felt called to start a new institute of religious women for work among the poorest of the poor. This new congregation, realized in 1951, was the Missionaries of Charity. The spirit of these missionaries is one of total surrender, loving trust, and cheerfulness, as lived by Jesus and his mother. Mother Teresa, as Bojaxhiu came to be known, also founded a male branch of the congregation, the Brothers of Charity, in March 1963. This was carried out with the collaboration of an Australian Jesuit, Andrew Travers-Ball, later known as Brother Andrew. On June 25, 1976, Mother Teresa inaugurated the Sisters of the Word, a contemplative congregation, in the Bronx, New York, which eventually became part of the Missionaries of Charity. She also founded a group of contemplative brothers, which has been approved by the Vatican as a pious union rather than as a religious congregation. Mother Teresa is known throughout the world for her service to the poor and dying. She received numerous awards for her work, among them the Nobel Peace Prize in 1979. She was often asked to represent the Roman Catholic Church at large gatherings, and she also spoke to groups of affluent people in various countries, trying to awaken them to an attitude of service to poorer people. The influence of Mother Teresa is widespread, and the service of the Missionaries of Charity under her direction is recognized on all six continents.

BIBLIOGRAPHY J. G. Clucas, *Mother Teresa* (1988); Desmond Doig, *Madre Teresa: La sua Gente, Il suo Lavoro* (1980); L. C. Johnson, *Mother Teresa* (1990); B. Lee, *Mother Teresa: Caring for All God's Children* (1981); Venora Leigh, *Mother Teresa* (1986); Edward Le Joly, *Mother Teresa of Calcutta: A Biography* (1983); Catherine Podojil, *Mother Teresa* (1982); David Porter, *Mother Teresa: The Early Years* (1986).

Mary Motte, FMM

Testera (*or* Tastera), Jacobo de (d. 1543), Franciscan missionary in Mexico. Born between 1460 and 1470 at Bayonne, France, Testera became a member of the Franciscan Province of Aquitaine in southern France. In 1510 he was transferred to Spain as chaplain to Emperor Charles V. In 1529 he joined his confreres in Mexico, where he worked in central Mexico, Michoacán, and Yucatán; in 1533 he was appointed superior of all the Franciscans in Mexico. In 1540 he was sent to Spain as a delegate to the general chapter of the Franciscan order. After his nomination as commissary general of the order for the whole of Latin America in 1541, he returned to Mexico in 1543 but died the same year.

Testera was an ardent defender of the dignity and the human rights of the Indians. For them he developed two writing techniques. One system expressed Christian prayers and doctrinal texts in picture writing (e.g., three human faces with three crowns represented God). The second technique used a kind of phonetic system. Each Latin word was expressed by a figure representing a native word that sounded roughly similar to the Latin word. For example, because the Latin "pater" sounds like the Aztec "pantli" (flag), it was represented in writing by a flag. Testera's missionary methods consisted in discovering the riches the Creator had worked in the souls of the Aztecs, who were called to be Christians, without denying that they were Aztecs.

BIBLIOGRAPHY Fidel de Jesús Chauvet, "Fray Jacob de Tastera, misionero y civilizador del siglo XVI," *Estudios de Historia Novo-hispana,* vol. 3 (1970), pp. 7–33; Mariano Erasti, *América Franciscana,* vol. 1 (1986), pp. 207–215; Richard Nebel, "Missionskatechismen," in *Conquista und Evangelisation,* M. Sievernich, A. Camps, A. Müller, and W. Senner, eds. (1992), pp. 243–245; Birgit Scharlau and Mark Münzel, *Quellqay, Mündliche Kultur und Schrifttradition bei Indianern Lateinamerikas* (1986), pp. 107–111.

Arnulf Camps, OFM

Tewksbury, Elwood Gardner (1865–1945), American Congregational missionary to China. Tewksbury was born in West Newbury, Massachusetts, the son of James Gardner Tewksbury and Sarah Jane Whittier. He graduated cum laude from Harvard College (1887) and from Hartford Theological Seminary (1890) and was ordained at the East Somerville, Massachusetts, Congregational Church in 1890. That same year he and his wife, Grace (Holbrook), were appointed by the American Board of Commissioners for Foreign Missions to the North China mission. Arriving at Tungchou, Tewksbury and his wife served two terms, 1890–1898 and 1899–1906. From 1907 to 1910 he was executive secretary of the Laymen's and Young People's Missionary Movement in New York City.

In 1910 the Tewksburys returned to China where Elwood served with the World's Sunday School Association as the first secretary for the China Sunday School Union, based in Shanghai. In this role he pioneered several educational strategies. He taught religious pedagogy and Sunday school management in seminaries and institutes throughout the country, introduced mass meetings for training purposes, and advocated athletics in the curriculum of Sunday schools. He developed a graded lesson plan on the model used in the United States, and superintended translation into Chinese of a library of Sunday school books. His wife died in Shanghai in 1938. He died in Philadelphia, Pennsylvania.

BIBLIOGRAPHY Beginning in 1910 Tewksbury edited the *China Sunday School Journal.* Basic information on him is included in the "Vinton" book of biographical data produced by the ABCFM. Narratives of his work appear in Kenneth Scott Latourette, *A History of Christian Missions in China* (1929), and Frank L. Brown, *A Sunday School Tour of the Orient, by a Commission Authorized by the World's Sunday School Association* (1914).

William H. Brackney

Tha Byu. *See* Ko Tha Byu.

Thakombau. *See* Cakobau, Ratu Seru.

Thauren, Johannes (1892–1954), Catholic missiologist. Born in Bielefeld, Germany, Thauren entered the Society of the Divine Word (SVD) and was ordained in 1922. He studied missiology under Joseph *Schmidlin in Münster, where he was awarded a doctorate in theology in 1926, with a dissertation entitled "Die Akkommodation im katholischen Heidenapostolat." In the same year he was appointed professor of missiology in St. Gabriel's Major Seminary, Vienna-Mödling.

In 1933 he became lecturer for missiology at the Faculty of Catholic Theology at the University of Vienna. In 1935 he published *Die Religiöse Unterweisung in den Heidenländern* and also began publishing *Blätter für die Missionskatechese und katechetische Zusammenarbeit der Länder* (1935–1938). After the German occupation of Austria in 1938, he was arrested and lost his position at the university, although he was able to continue his teaching at the Missiological Institute of the Archdiocese of Vienna. In 1945 he returned to the university, and was appointed as associate professor in 1946. In 1952 he became a member of the scientific commission of the Institut für missionswissenschaftliche Forschungen and joined the editorial board of *Zeitschrift für Missionswissenschaft* (Münster).

By this time, however, Thauren was quite ill. He died of a heart attack at the age of 62, having been in poor health all his life as a result of old war injuries. His many articles are mostly concerned with mission reports and missionary catechesis. He was a popular speaker at academic congresses and missionary conferences and always aimed at making missiological insights useful for missionary praxis.

BIBLIOGRAPHY J. Bettray, "P. Dr. Johannes Thauren zum Gedenken," *Theologisch-praktische Quartalschrift* 103 (1955): 62–64; Josef Glazik, "In memoriam. Univ. Prof. Dr. P. Johannes Thauren SVD," *ZMR* 38 (1954): 269; Karl Müller, "Prof. Dr. Johannes Thauren 60 Jahre alt," *ZMR* 37 (1953): 65–66. C. Tauchner, "Das Verständnis von Mission bei Johannes Thauren" (Diplomarbeit St. Gabriel's Major Seminary, Vienna-Mödling, 1982) gives a more detailed biography and a comprehensive list of Thauren's publications.

Karl Müller, SVD

Theile, Friedrich Otto (1880–1945), Australian director of the Lutheran Mission New Guinea in Papua New Guinea. Born at Summerfield, Australia, Theile received his seminary training in Neuendettelsau, Germany, and became interested in mission in New Guinea. During World War I, he organized support for the isolated German missionary families in New Guinea with the help of the Church of England. In the postwar period he negotiated the future of Lutheran mission activities in New Guinea. With the support of the Anglican Church and the Lutheran Iowa Synod in the United States, Theile convinced the Australian government that the Lutheran mission fields in New Guinea should be placed under the direction of the United Evangelical Lutheran Church in Australia. As director of the Lutheran Mission New Guinea after 1923, he secured the continued presence of German missionaries and mediated the transfer of the Rhenish mission field to the Iowa Synod (1933). In 1939 he was honored with a D.D. from Wartburg Seminary, Iowa. In World War II Theile came to the aid of the evacuated and interned German missionary families. He was a longtime member of the National Missionary Council in Australia.

BIBLIOGRAPHY Friedrich Otto Theile, *One Hundred Years of the Lutheran Church in Queensland* (1936).

Gernot Fugmann

Thérèse of Lisieux (1873–1897), Carmelite nun, saint, patroness of missions. Born Marie Françoise Thérèse Martin in Alençon, France, the youngest of nine children, Thérèse grew up a sickly child, but was warm, affectionate, and deeply religious. In 1877 her mother, Azélie, died, and in 1881 her father, Louis, sold his business and moved the family to Lisieux, the town in which his wife's sister lived.

Thérèse was drawn to the contemplative life at an early age and applied for entrance at the convent of the Discalced Carmelites in Lisieux when only 14. Although her father was in favor of the decision, the ecclesiastical superior of the convent, Abbé Delatroette, advised her to postpone entrance until she was 21. Thérèse and her father, however, applied to Bishop Hugonin of Bayeux, and she was eventually permitted to enter on April 9, 1888, at the age of 15. Taking the name Thérèse of the Child Jesus, she made her first profession on September 8, 1890. In 1894, while considering going to the Carmelite convent in Hanoi, Indochina (now Vietnam), she was diagnosed as having tuberculosis, and died three years later.

At the request of her superiors, Thérèse had written an autobiography during her last years. Instead of the ordinary obituary, copies of the book were sent to other Carmelite convents. Soon requests were made for a commercial printing and the work became a phenomenon in the religious literature of its time. Even though it was written in the pious language of French religious romanticism, Thérèse's simplicity and candor nevertheless shone through. Hers was a spirituality of the ordinary, a "little way" where sanctity was achieved by paying attention to God's presence in everyday life.

The number of miracles attributed to Thérèse became so great that Rome waived the 50-year waiting period and allowed the cause for her beatification to be inaugurated. Thérèse was beatified in 1923 and canonized in 1925. Because she had prayed unceasingly for the missions and missionaries, in 1929 *Pius XI named her patroness of the missions at the time St. Francis Xavier was named patron. In 1944, because of the devotion of the French people and because France had itself become a mission country, she was named a patroness of France, along with Joan of Arc and the Blessed Virgin Mary.

BIBLIOGRAPHY Thérèse's autobiography has appeared over the years in a number of English editions and translations; two volumes of correspondence have appeared in a critical edition: J. Clarke, tr., *General Correspondence,* vol. 1, 1877–1890 (1982) and vol. 2, 1890–1897 (1988); see also J. Clarke, tr., *St. Thérèse of Lisieux: Her Last Conversations* (1977). A partial bibliography of biographies appears in E. C. Hansen, *Nineteenth-Century European Catholicism: An Annotated Bibliography of Secondary Works in English* (1989), pp. 149–152; another bibliography on Thérèse can be found in *Bibliographia Internationalis Spiritualitatis* (1966–present) under "Teresia a Sancti Infantis." C. Mahoney, *St. Thérèse of Lisieux By Those Who Knew Her: Her Testimonies from the Process of Beatification* (1975); P. O'Connor, *In Search of Thérèse* (1987); Society for the Propagation of the Faith, *Shower of Roses upon the Missions: Spiritual and Temporal Favors Obtained through the Intercession of Blessed Teresa, the Little Sister of Missionaries, 1909–1923* (1924); J. Sullivan, ed., *Experiencing St. Thérèse Today* (1990).

Stephen B. Bevans, SVD

Thévenoud, Joanny (1878–1949), missionary of the Society of Missionaries of Africa (also known as White Fathers [WF]) in West Africa. Born in Serrière-en-Chautagne, Savoie, France, Thévenoud joined the WF and in 1903 left for Mossi, part of the enormous vicariate of the Sahara and Sudan. Disturbed by the lot of women, who were not allowed to come for instruction, he opened a workplace for them in Ouagadougou as a step to their emancipation (1917). In 1921 he was appointed vicar apostolic of the newly founded Mossi Vicariate, serving the Mossi, Gourounsi, and Boussanse peoples, and opened several missions (1923–1946). Hoping for a speedy indigenization of the church, he opened a school for catechists (1923) and a junior seminary (1923) (both still functioning today at Pabré) and a major seminary at Koumi (1933). He founded the local congregations of the Sisters of the Immaculate Conception (1922) and the Brothers of the Holy Family (1946). In 1942 he ordained the first three Mossi priests, saying, "Now I can leave." Thousands attended his funeral at Ouagadougou.

BIBLIOGRAPHY "Monseigneur Joanny Thévenoud," *Notices Necrologiques, 1954–1956, Société des Missionaires d'Afrique, Pères Blancs* (1957), pp. 9–44; G. D. Kittler, *The White Fathers* (1957).

J. G. Donders, M Afr

Thoburn, Isabella (1840–1901), American Methodist missionary and educator in India. Born in St. Clairsville, Ohio, of immigrant parents from Ireland, Thoburn became a teacher. In 1866 her brother James *Thoburn, a Methodist missionary in India, wrote to her, "How would you like to come and take charge of a school [for girls] if we decide to make the attempt?" She replied that she would come just as soon as a way was opened for her to do so, but the Missionary Society of the church was unwilling to send unmarried women. When the Woman's Foreign Missionary Society of the Methodist Episcopal Church was founded in 1869 in Boston, Mass., the first missionary they appointed was Isabella Thoburn to India; then Clara A. *Swain, M.D. was appointed to join her as a medical missionary. The two single women sailed from Boston on Nov. 3, 1869, and arrived in Bombay on January 7, 1870.

Assigned to the city of Lucknow where her brother was also based, Thoburn began a program of education for Indian women that would lead eventually to the creation of the first Christian college for women in Asia. She began with six girls in one room in the bazaar in April 1870. This developed into a boarding school, then a high school, and in 1886 the college began which she named Lucknow Woman's College.

She was in the United States on furlough from 1880 to 1881, and again, in ill health, from 1886 to 1891. During this latter period she became one of the first deaconesses in the Methodist Episcopal Church, and worked with Lucy Rider *Meyer in the Chicago Training School for a year. Then in Cincinnati, Ohio, she helped to found the Deaconess Home and Training School and also Christ Hospital. In 1891 she returned to her educational work in India until 1899 when she came back to the United States to raise funds for the college. After giving three addresses at the Ecumenical Missionary Conference in New York in 1900 she returned to India. The following year she died of cholera and was buried in Lucknow. After her death the college she founded was renamed Isabella Thoburn College, which is now the women's college of Lucknow University.

BIBLIOGRAPHY In addition to many articles written for the *Indian Witness, Heathen Woman's Friend,* and *Woman's Missionary Friend,* Isabella Thoburn wrote a biography of Phoebe Rowe (1899), her "Indian Sister," who died in 1898. Thoburn's own biography was written by her brother James M. Thoburn, *Life of Isabella Thoburn* (1903); also William F. Oldham, *Isabella Thoburn* (1902).

Gerald H. Anderson

Thoburn, James Mills (1836–1922), first Methodist missionary bishop of India and Malaysia. Born in St. Clairsville, Ohio, the son of immigrants from Ireland, Thoburn graduated from Allegheny College in 1857, entered the ministry of the Methodist Episcopal Church in 1858, and was sent to India by the Missionary Society of his church in 1859. He married Sarah Minerva (Rockwell) Downey, widow of a fellow missionary in 1861; she died in 1862 after giving birth to a son.

Initially Thoburn worked with William *Butler, the first American Methodist missionary to India who had arrived in 1856, doing village evangelism and church planting in North India. Dissatisfied with the pace of expansion and the restrictions of comity agreements, Thoburn invited the American Methodist maverick evangelist, William *Taylor, to come to India to lead a revival and the expansion of Methodist work. Taylor arrived in 1870 and for nearly five years, with the support of Thoburn, established congregations in seven leading cities across India. In 1874 Thoburn began a thirteen-year pastorate of the flourishing church founded by Taylor in Calcutta. In 1880, while speaking in the United States, Thoburn met and married Anna Jones, a medical missionary candidate, in Philadelphia. He returned to India two days after the wedding; she followed two years later after completing medical school.

Thoburn initiated Methodist work in Rangoon in 1879, and in Singapore in 1885. In 1888 he was elected bishop, with episcopal responsibility for all of India, and Methodist work in Burma and Malaysia. In February 1899 he went to Manila to initiate Methodist work in the Philippines, which was then added to his area of episcopal supervision. In 1900 Thoburn addressed the Ecumenical Missionary Conference in New York City.

Thoburn presided over an era of rapid growth of the Methodist Church in India, with mass movements of converts into membership, and expansion into Southeast Asia. He was one of the founders and editors of the Methodist periodical *Lucknow Witness* (later renamed *The Indian Witness*). He persuaded his sister Isabella *Thoburn to join the work in India where she founded a college for women in Lucknow. With his wife and sister, Thoburn was instrumental in having the office of deaconess established in the Methodist Episcopal Church in 1888. His wife died in 1902, and, after a missionary career of forty-nine years, Thoburn retired in failing health to Meadville, Pennsylvania, in 1908, where he resided until his death. At the invitation of John R. *Mott, Thoburn attended the Edinburgh World Missionary Conference in 1910. He received honorary doctorates from Allegheny College and Ohio Wesleyan University.

BIBLIOGRAPHY Thoburn's journals and sermons are in the library of Allegheny College, Meadville, Pennsylvania. Thoburn's books include *My Missionary Apprenticeship* (1884), *Light in the East* (1894), *The Christian Nations* (1895), *India and Malaysia* (1892; 2nd ed. 1896), *The Church of Pentecost* (1899), *The Christian Conquest of India* (1906), and *India and Southern Asia* (1907). During 1911 he published a series of autobiographical reflections entitled "Wayside Notes" in the *Western Christian Advocate.* See also William H. Crawford, ed., *Thoburn and India* (1909) and William F. Oldham, *Thoburn—Called of God* (1918). The most thorough study of Thoburn's career is by Guy D. Garrett, "The Missionary Career of James Mills Thoburn" (Ph.D. diss., Boston Univ., 1968).

Gerald H. Anderson

Thomas, John (1796–1881), leading early representative of the Wesleyan Methodist Missionary Society (WMMS) in Tonga. Thomas was a blacksmith at Hagley, Worcestershire, England, before going to the Pacific. For two years (1826–1828) he preached with small success at Hihifo, Tongatapu. In the meantime, a Tongan chief, Pita Vi, preceded Thomas as preacher to the high chief, Taufa'ahau *Tupou, on the more northerly island of Ha'apai. Thomas followed, and baptized Tupou in 1831, naming him Siaosi (George) after King George III of England. Thomas thus provided Christian sacral sanction for his protégé's steady advance in the following years to royal status. A Tonga-wide revival movement broke out in 1835. Tupou, as champion of the Wesleyan cause, was victorious in wars on Tongatapu against pagan and Catholic-leaning chiefs. Thomas enthroned him in 1845, with English Prayer Book rites, as first king of all Tonga. He supported the king's policy of sending Tongan Wesleyan missionaries to Fiji and Samoa. However, in 1839 the WMMS in London withdrew from Samoa by gentlemen's agreement with the LMS. Thomas vigorously sought reentry, and persuaded the Australasian Wesleyan conferences, which had taken over in the Pacific from the British in 1855, to reverse the decision. However, his personal influence with the king waned after his first English furlough (1855–1856). He went into wistful retirement in England in 1859.

BIBLIOGRAPHY Sarah S. Farmer, *Tonga and the Friendly Islands* (1855); G. G. Findlay and W. W. Holdsworth, *The History of the Wesleyan Methodist Missionary Society*, vol. 3 (1921); John Garrett, *To Live among the Stars: Christian Origins in Oceania* (1982); Niel Gunson, *Messengers of Grace: Evangelical Missionaries in the South Seas, 1797–1860* (1978); Sione Latukefu, *Church and State in Tonga...* (1974); G. S. Rowe, *A Pioneer: A Memoir of the Rev. John Thomas, Missionary to the Friendly Islands* (1885; repr. 1976). Manuscript sources are found in Wesleyan Methodist Missionary Society papers (London) and Methodist Overseas Missions Papers (Mitchell Library, Sydney).

John Garrett

Thomas, John (1808–1870), pioneer missionary in South India. Born in Mydrian, Carmarthenshire, Wales, Thomas was admitted to the Church Missionary Society (CMS) college in Islington, London, in 1833. He was ordained deacon in 1835 and priest in 1836, shortly before setting off to South India as a CMS missionary. Within a year he learned Tamil well enough to preach a simple sermon and then went to one of Carl *Rhenius's stations, Megnanapuram, where he labored for 33 years until his death. In the midst of a sandy desert he dug wells and created an oasis. He then built a large church that was consecrated in 1847 and named St. Paul's. By 1857 he could report 5,500 Christians in the district, but a mass movement increased the number to over 10,000 two years later. He developed a network of schools, and reported the presence of Christians in 125 villages in 1868, shepherded by fifty-four evangelists, twelve of whom were ordained in 1869. His wife, Mary (Davies), whom he married in 1838, continued his work after his death, together with his daughter Frances, both in 1896 still superintending the Elliot Tuxford Girls' High School he had founded. Thomas is buried in Megnanapuram, where a large festive communal meal is held in his memory every year. His son, John Davies Thomas, succeeded him but moved to Colombo, where he died in 1896, also after 33 years service.

BIBLIOGRAPHY Paul Appasamy, *Centenary History of the CMS in Tinnevelly* (1923); A. H. Grey-Edwards, *Memoir of the Rev. John Thomas* (1954); Eugene Stock, *History of the Church Missionary Society*, vols. 3 and 4 (1898).

E. M. Jackson

Thomas, Mary (Davies) (1815–1899), Church Missionary Society (CMS) missionary in India. Welsh-born like her husband, John *Thomas, whom she married in South India in 1838, Mary Thomas spent her entire adult life in India. While her husband built up the Tamil church in and around Mengnanapuram, Tamilnadu, she involved herself with women and girls. Later, with her daughter Frances, she ran the Elliot Tuxford School in Mengnanapuram, which trained women teachers. Following the death of her husband in 1870, she and her daughter were recognized as full members of the CMS mission in Tamilnadu.

Thomas represented the first of three generations of Thomases working with CMS in South India. In addition to her daughter Frances, her married daughter, Mary Jane (Thomas) Dibb, and her son, John Davies Thomas, also worked among Tamils. Initially the son worked in his father's area of Mengnanapuram, and later among Tamil-speakers in Ceylon. After he died in 1896, his widow (also named Mary Jane), continued the work in Ceylon. She was assisted in this by her daughter Annie; a second daughter, Edith worked in Tirunelveli. Thus there were six closely related women from three generations working under CMS in South India. Mary (Davies) Thomas was still at her post at the time of the CMS Jubilee in 1898, having served 60 years in Tamilnadu.

BIBLIOGRAPHY CMS, *Register of Missionaries and Native Clergy* (1904); M. E. Gibbs, *History of the Anglican Church in India, 1600–1970* (1972); Eugene Stock, *The History of the Church Missionary Society: Its Environment, Its Men and Its Work*, 3 vols. (1899).

Jocelyn Murray

Thomas, M(adathilparampil) M(ammen) (1916–1996), Indian church leader and world ecumenical leader. Born in the Travancore region of Kerala, Thomas was raised in the Mar Thoma Syrian Church, whose combination of ancient sacramental liturgy with modern evangelical spirituality undergirded his life and ministry. His early Christian youth work and social action in India projected him onto the world scene after World War II. From 1947 to 1953 he was on the staff of the World's Student Christian Federation in Geneva. *The Christian in the World Struggle*, written by Thomas in 1952 with colleague David McCaughey, was an influential guide to Christian student groups in its time.

Thomas served the World Council of Churches (WCC) as moderator of its Central Committee from 1968 to 1975. Earlier, he was Asian staff member of the WCC church and society department, then chair of the departmental working committee and co-chair of the World Conference on Church and Society in Geneva, 1966. He was also secretary of the East Asia Christian Conference for church and society concerns. He was a tireless speaker and writer, stimulating ecumenical debate and forging consensus, expressed in countless conference and meeting reports he helped write. *Towards a Theology of Contemporary Ecumenism* (1978) presents some of this work.

In India, Thomas served as associate, then director, of the Christian Institute for the Study of Religion and Society from 1958 until his retirement in 1975. His work produced a library of studies and conference reports on the religious and social dimensions of Indian life in Christian perspective. He also wrote extensively in his own name, interpreting Christian faith in light of the Asian revolution, in Indian society, and in encounter with Hinduism and secular ideologies. In retirement, he continued to write biblical studies and theology in Malayalam, his mother tongue. He served as governor of Nagaland, by appointment of the government of India, from 1990 to 1992.

BIBLIOGRAPHY M. M. Thomas, "My Pilgrimage in Mission," *IBMR* 13 (1989): 28–31, *My Ecumencial Journey: An Autobiographical Memoir* (1991), ed. with P. D. Devanandan, *Christian Participation in Nation-Building* (1960), *The Christian Response to the Asian Revolution* (1966), *The Acknowledged Christ of the Indian Renaissance* (1970), *The Secular Ideologies of India and the Secular Meaning of Christ* (1976), and *Risking Christ for Christ's Sake* (1986). Several studies of Thomas's thought and work have recently appeared, among them T. M. Philip, *The Encounter between Theology and Ideology: An Exploration into the Communicative Theology of M. M. Thomas* (1986). A complete collection of Thomas's published and unpublished writings is in the archives of the United Theological College, Bangalore.

Charles C. West

Thomas, Robert Jermain (1839–1866), Welsh missionary to China with the London Missionary Society (LMS). Thomas began preaching at age 15. He graduated from New College, London University, in 1863 and was ordained, was married, and sailed to China the same year. Within three months, his wife, Caroline (Godfrey), died. A year later he resigned from the LMS, feeling that unreached fields should be given priority over already occupied Shanghai, but he soon asked to return and to be sent to Mongolia. While he was waiting for reinstatement, a chance meeting with two Korean traders, secret Catholics, led him to negotiate a trip to that forbidden country to distribute Bibles for the National Bible Society of Scotland. He spent two and a half months there in 1865 and learned some of the language. Against advice he returned to Korea in 1866 as interpreter on an armed American trading ship, arriving at a time when uninvited foreign trade was still forbidden and a raging persecution of secret Catholic believers was resulting in the execution of thousands. The ship was attacked near Pyongyang and no one survived. Thomas was reportedly beheaded giving a Bible to his executioner. He was the first Protestant martyr in Korea.

BIBLIOGRAPHY Samuel H. Moffett, "The General Sherman Affair: Thomas, First Protestant Martyr" and "Thomas' Second Trip to Korea," *The Korea Herald* (Seoul), April 22 and May 6, 1973; Lak-Geoon George Paik, *The History of Protestant Missions in Korea, 1832–1910* (2d ed., 1970), pp. 47–51. A doctoral dissertation, "Robert J. Thomas, Pioneer Missionary to Korea," by M. S. Goh, is nearing completion at the Univ. of Birmingham, England. Thomas's letters and documents are in the library of the LMS, now transferred to the School of Oriental and African Studies in the Univ. of London; the library of the National Bible Society of Scotland holds other letters.

Samuel Hugh Moffett

Thomas Aquinas (c. 1225–1274), Catholic theologian and philosopher. Aquinas was born at Roccasecca, Italy. When he was five years old, his parents sent him to Monte Cassino in hopes that he would eventually become abbot there. But while he was studying in Naples in 1240, he was attracted to the newly founded Order of Preachers (Dominicans), whom he determined to join in spite of his family's vigorous opposition. He joined the friars in 1244, and soon came under the influence of Albert the Great, the leading Dominican philosopher of the day. Albert's teaching led Aquinas to see in the newly available philosophical works of Aristotle an important aid to Christian theological affirmation. After qualifying as a lecturer in sacred Scripture, he became a master of theology at Paris in 1256. He returned there in 1269 after teaching assignments at Orvieto, Rome, and Viterbo. He spent the last two years of his life lecturing to Dominican students in Naples, and died on his way to the Council of Lyons in 1274. He was canonized in 1323.

Among Aquinas's authentic works are important commentaries on Job, the Psalms, Isaiah, the Gospels of Matthew and John, the Letters of Paul, and most of the works of Aristotle. A profound grasp of the Scriptures infuses the two monumental theological works for which he is famous and through which he has exerted his greatest influence, *Summa theologiae* and *Summa contra gentiles.* Both works exhibit a highly refined sense of the unity of divine activity in creation and redemption and incorporate interlaced philosophical, biblical, and theological patterns of argumentation. Whether or not it was composed with this aim in mind, *Summa contra gentiles* also served for generations of Dominican friars as a kind of missionary manual.

BIBLIOGRAPHY The still incomplete definitive edition of Aquinas's works is known as the Leonine Edition (1882–). Among the English translations of his chief works, the following stand out: *Summa Contra Gentiles,* Anton Pegis, tr. (1955) and *Summa theologiae,* Thomas Gilby, ed. (1964–1980). The best single biography is James A. Weisheipl, *Friar Thomas D'Aquino* (1974). See also M. D. Chenu, *Toward Understanding St. Thomas,* Brian Davies, *The Thought of Thomas Aquinas* (1992), and J. P. Torrell, *Introduction to St. Thomas Aquinas* (1995).

Joseph DiNoia, OP

Thomas of Jesus (1564–1627), Catholic mission theorist. Thomas was born at Baëza, Spain, and changed his name from Diego Sánchez Dávila when he joined the Carmelite order. He was called to Rome in 1607 where he met with a group of Italian Carmelites who were interested in missionary work. Thomas was reluctant to accept the call to come to Rome, as he preferred a more contemplative life. In Rome he became aware of missionary problems in Persia and elsewhere and came to understand the importance of well-trained missionaries. In 1610 he went to France and Belgium to found Carmelite monasteries of the Theresian Reform. At Antwerp in 1613 he published his great work, *De procuranda salute omnium gentium* (On securing the salvation of all nations), the greatest theology of missions of the seventeenth century. This work also dealt with the necessity of establishing a new Roman congregation for the propagation of the faith. Thomas was an important precursor of that congregation (Propaganda Fide), which came into being in 1622. His book also impressed some theologians of the Reformation, such as J. *Hoornbeeck. Thomas acted as provincial of the Carmelites in northern Europe from 1617 to 1623. He died in Rome.

BIBLIOGRAPHY Thomas a Jesu, *De procuranda salute omnium gentium* (1613; new ed., 1940). G. M. J. M. Koolen, *Een seer bequaem middel, onderwijs en kerk onder de 17e eeuwse VOC* (1993), pp. 82–83; Josef Metzler, "Wegbereiter und Vorläufer der Kongregation," in *Sacrae Congregationis de Propaganda Fide Memoria Rerum, 1622–1972,* vol. 1:1 (1971), pp. 70–74; Alphons Mulders, *Missiologisch bestek* (1962), pp. 80–84.

Arnulf Camps, OFM

Thompson, Ralph Wardlaw (1842–1916), foreign secretary of the London Missionary Society (LMS). Thompson was born into an LMS missionary family in India and later moved to South Africa when his father became the LMS agent there. He returned to England for college in 1861 and hoped to become a missionary, but doctors said he was not strong enough. He took pastorates in Glasgow and Liverpool and was elected, in 1874, to the board of directors of the LMS. There he made such an impression that in 1880 he was chosen as foreign secretary, the position of chief responsibility in the LMS.

As foreign secretary Thompson tried to expand mission work, though he was often beset by deficits. He urged the directors and the churches to greater effort and support. He was especially interested in educational and medical work, in women's work, and in training local church leaders. He worked for more freedom for the widespread mission networks but also tried to keep headquarters in close touch with them through visits. He made long trips to Asia, Africa, the South Pacific, and also North America. He was much beloved and appreciated because of his deep personal concern for those with whom he worked. His statesmanship also impressed political leaders. When he visited the governor of Madagascar shortly after the French conquest, he dispelled suspicions of the LMS, leading the governor to restore to the LMS nearly a hundred churches that the Jesuits had recently seized.

Thompson moved gradually into the new ecumenical outlook that emerged in his later years. He was a leader at the Edinburgh World Missionary Conference of 1910 and was elected to its Continuation Committee. When the Conference of British Missionary Societies was formed, he was elected its first chairman. He retired from active life in 1914.

BIBLIOGRAPHY Ralph Wardlaw Thompson, *My Trip on the "John Williams"* (1900); and with Arthur N. Johnson, *British Foreign Missions 1837–1897* (1899). Basil Mathews, *Dr. Ralph Wardlaw Thompson* (1917).

Charles W. Forman

Thompson, Thomas (c. 1708–1773), first Anglican missionary to Africa. Thompson was born in Gilling, Yorkshire, England, and was educated at Christ's College, Cambridge, where he later became fellow and dean. He offered himself to the Society for the Propagation of the Gospel (SPG) in 1745 and was sent to Monmouth, New Jersey. His meetings with black slaves prompted him in 1751 to approach the SPG with an offer to serve as a missionary to the Guinea coast. He settled at Cape Coast Castle, in the Gold Coast (Ghana), in 1752 and, with the help of a leading local African, Cudjo, selected three African boys for education in England. One of these, Philip *Quaque, became the first non-European to be ordained in the Church of England (1765). Thompson was forced by ill health to return to England in 1756, but Quaque returned to Africa and ministered at Cape Coast Castle as an Anglican priest for 50 years. Thompson became vicar of Reculven (1757–1761) and of Elham in Kent (1761–1773), where he died. In 1758 he wrote *Two Missionary Voyages,* an account of pagan practices and beliefs; in 1772 he wrote a pamphlet defending the slave trade.

BIBLIOGRAPHY Margaret Dewey, *The Messengers* (1975); C. F. Pascoe, *Two Hundred Years of the SPG, 1701–1900* (1901); H. P. Thompson, *Into All Lands* (1951); F. Wolfson, *Pageant of Ghana* (1958).

Timothy Yates

Thomson, James (*or* Diego) (1788–1854), Scottish missionary, Bible promoter, and educator. Thomson was born in Creetown, Kirkcudbright, Scotland. After theological studies in Glasgow and a co-pastorate with James Haldane in Edinburgh, he went to Argentina in 1818 to distribute Scriptures and establish schools on the Lancasterian system. He pioneered public education in Argentina (1818–1821), Chile (1821–1822), and Peru (1822–1824). From 1827 to 1830 he was an agent of the British and Foreign Bible Society (BFBS) in Mexico. There he found opportunities for Scripture distribution seriously curtailed by the BFBS decision not to publish the Apocrypha (a decision he had opposed) and by papal edicts against the Bible societies. He later represented the BFBS in the Caribbean (1831–1838) and in Canada (1838–1842). He was the prime mover in founding the French-Canadian Missionary Society. He returned to Central America in 1842, but a serious illness in Yucatán brought his ministry in the Americas to a close in 1843. In 1845 he represented the BFBS in Scotland and two years later went to Spain for BFBS. He also visited Portugal and North Africa. The difficulty he had in finding a place to bury his wife, who died in Madrid in 1848, led to his involvement in the quest for religious liberty in Spain. He was forced to leave the country in 1849.

Thomson helped initiate Bible translation into Quechua (in 1822–1824, during his service in Peru), Aymará (1826, London), and Nahuatl (1828, Mexico); he attempted to begin translation into Haitian Creole (1835, Haiti), Otomí (1842, Mexico), and Maya (1843, Yucatán), and he encouraged translators working in Chippewa and Cree (1830, Canada), and Catalán, Basque, and Spanish (1847–1849, Spain).

Thomson's tie with the BFBS ended in 1849, and he devoted himself to help small Protestant groups in the Iberian peninsula. He himself had earlier begun small congregations in Buenos Aires, Lima, and Mexico City. He was instrumental in founding the Spanish Evangelization Society, which came into being in 1855, the year after his death. A man of irenic disposition, catholic spirit, and warm evangelical piety, Thomson based his strategy on the "tripod" of the school society, the Bible society, and the missionary society.

BIBLIOGRAPHY James Thomson, *Epítome de Gramática Inglesa* (1823), *Letters on the Moral and Religious State of South America* (1827), *Union Liturgy* (1837), *Incense for the Private Altar* (1838), *Incense for the Family Altar* (1838), and *Spain, Its Position and Evangelization* (1853). Arnoldo Canclini, *Diego Thomson: Apostól de la enseñanza y distribución de la Biblia en América Latina y España* (1987); Donald R. Mitchell, "The Evangelical Contribution of James Thomson to South American Life" (Ph.D. diss., Princeton Theological Seminary, 1972). Thomson's correspondence with the BFBS is held in the Bible Society Library, Cambridge, England.

William Mitchell

Thomson, John Francis (1843–1933), missionary in Argentina and Uruguay. Born in Scotland to a Methodist father and a Presbyterian mother, Thomson immigrated with his family to Buenos Aires in 1851. He was converted at the age of 14 under the preaching of William Goodfellow, a Methodist missionary and church superintendent. Educated at Ohio Wesleyan University, he married Elena Goodfellow, niece of William Goodfellow and brilliant student of the sciences. Upon their return to Argentina in 1867, Thomson began preaching in the Methodist Church in Buenos Aires, the first continuing Protestant ministry of the Word in Spanish in the Argentine republic. Two years later he began Protestant work in Montevideo, Uruguay. He vigorously attacked the "obscurantism" and "paganism" which he saw in the Roman Catholicism of his time. Leading citizens heard him gladly: lawyers, politicians, judges, doctors, and educators—but also laborers, young people, uneducated citizens, and the general public. He was evangelist to the interior of Argentina and Uruguay, missionary preacher to other Latin American countries, founder of the Society for the Prevention of Cruelty to Animals (SPCA), cofounder of the first Protestant magazine, *El Estandarte,* and promoter of the extension of new church groups. He was closely associated with distinguished Bible colporteurs of his day, Andrew Murray *Milne and Thomas B. *Wood (founder of *El Evangelista*), and with two of his spiritual sons, Francisco G. *Penzotti and Juan C. Varetto.

BIBLIOGRAPHY Daniel Monti, *Presencia del Protestantismo en el Rio de la Plata durante el siglo XIX* (1969), pp. 118–120; Juan C. Varetto, *El Apóstol del Plata: Juan F. Thomson* (1943). See also the issues of *El Estandarte* and *El Evangelista* during the years of his life and ministry.

Sidney H. Rooy

Thomson, William Ritchie (1794–1891), Scottish Presbyterian missionary in Cape Colony, South Africa. Thomson was born in Tarbolton, Ayrshire. His father, Hugh Ritchie, had been closely associated with the formation of the Glasgow Missionary Society (GMS). After ordination in London in 1821, Thomson and his wife, Frances, sailed to Cape Town as missionaries of the GMS. There he was appointed both a missionary and an agent of the British colonial government in Cape Town, which was to pay his salary. He ministered to Gqona, Koikoi, and detribalized Xhosa at Chumie. In 1828, having found his two tasks incompatible, he became a minister of a Dutch Reformed Church (DRC) congregation of mostly Koikoi in Stockenstrom. He remained an honorary member of the GMS presbytery and played a significant part in the formation of the Lovedale Seminary, opened in 1841.

In 1855, forty-five Boers, newly arrived in Stockenstrom, requested that they form a separate session and observe the Lord's supper as a white group. The synod initially declined this proposal, but in 1857 separate worship was allowed on practical grounds as a concession to weakness. Although Thomson was against the change, he accepted the synod's decision, which constituted the beginning of racially separate worship in the DRC. As missionary and pastor, Thomson spoke up for the rights of the indigenous people. He did try to remain loyal to the state in its political decisions but tempered this with humanity. His first wife having died in 1836, in 1846 he married Isabella Smith (1823–1905), a teacher of missionaries' children. He died and was buried at Hertzog.

BIBLIOGRAPHY H. Davies and R. H. W. Shepherd, *South African Missions, 1800–1950* (1954); R. H. W. Shepherd, *Lovedale, South Africa: The Story of a Century, 1841–1941* (1940); D. Williams, *When Races Meet: The Life and Times of William Ritchie Thomson* (1967).

Norman H. Cliff

Thornton, Douglas M(ontagu) (1873–1907), Anglican missionary in Cairo. Thornton was born into a distinguished family in English evangelicalism. He grew in vital Christian conviction and enthusiasm, which was channeled via Marlborough College and Trinity College, Cambridge, into missionary vocation. Like Temple *Gairdner, his Church Missionary Society (CMS) colleague in Cairo, he gained experience through the Student Christian Movement and its Volunteer Missionary Union, pioneered by John R. *Mott and R. E. *Speer.

Thornton went to Egypt in 1898. His fiancée, Elaine Anderson, followed in 1899. They were married in Cairo and a son, Cecil, was born in 1901. Thornton's thoughts were directed to Islam. Gaining competence in Arabic, he combined a disciplined vision with intense energy and dedicated himself to the task of evangelism. The magazine *Orient and Occident,* which was his brainchild, circulated widely among Muslims and afforded contacts he pursued in his preaching travels in Upper Egypt. Here he had surprising occasions of positive interaction with Coptic clergy and their congregations, which he saw as crucial to his Muslim hopes. Dreaming of an ecumenical role for the CMS in the Coptic scene, he used his only two furloughs to plead for recruits. They were all too few. Supervising an edition of the Book of Common Prayer in Arabic, he wrestled with the toils of translation. In a Cairo rooftop meditation, gazing across the domes of the vast city, he "saw" the fertile Nile Delta reaching fanlike and appealingly toward Europe, with the vast desert telling of the aridity his Christ would satisfy. After only nine years of work he died of typhoid fever, his dreams and projects bequeathed to those who might follow. Within a year Gairdner wrote his biography, drawn largely from Thornton's papers and memoranda, and assumed Thornton's mantle.

BIBLIOGRAPHY W. H. Temple Gairdner, *D. M. Thornton: A Study in Missionary Ideals and Methods* (1908).

Kenneth Cragg

Threlkeld, Lancelot Edward (1788–1859), London Missionary Society (LMS) Calvinistic Methodist missionary to Tahiti and Australian Aborigines. Threlkeld was born at Exeter, Devon. He married Martha Goss in 1808 and was a druggist's apprentice and actor before being accepted for training in London under learned ministers appointed by the LMS. Ordained in 1815, he reached the Leeward Island station at Raiatea in September 1818. He and other newcomers clashed with older missionaries, who had less specialized training and were loyal to the morally backsliding King *Pomare II, whom they baptized in 1819.

Threlkeld, with John *Williams, oversaw the growth of the church on Raiatea. With its high chief, Tamatoa, they framed laws and trained Islander missionaries to go to Polynesia and Melanesia. Threlkeld, exuberant and combative, sought to establish auxiliary plantations and industries, but LMS directors in London disapproved. His wife died in 1824 and he accompanied a LMS deputation consisting of Daniel Tyerman and George Bennet to Sydney, where he married Sarah Arndell. The deputation appointed him to begin a mission to Australian Aborigines at Lake Macquarie, New South Wales. He acquired the language and defended the rights of the people but met difficulties over methods and money. The LMS severed its link with the mission in 1828 and it was later closed. Threlkeld then participated as a Congregational minister in the controversially agitated political and religious life of New South Wales until his death in Sydney at the age of 70.

BIBLIOGRAPHY John Garrett, *To Live among the Stars: Christian Origins in Oceania* (1982); Niel Gunson, *Messengers of Grace: Evangelical Missionaries in the South Seas, 1797–1860* (1978) and ed. *Australian Reminiscences and Papers of L. E. Threlkeld...*, 2 vols. (1974); Richard Lovett, *The History of the London Missionary Society, 1795–1895*, 2 vols. (1899). Threlkeld materials are in the LMS South Sea collection at SOAS, Univ. of London.

John Garrett

Thurston, Asa (1787–1868) *and*
Lucy (Goodale) (1795–1876), American pioneer missionaries to Hawaii. Asa was born in Fitchburg, Massachusetts, and graduated from Yale (1816) and Andover Theological Seminary (1819). He married Lucy Goodale on October 12, 1819, and 11 days later sailed with the pioneer company of American Board of Commissioners for Foreign Missions (ABCFM) missionaries to the Sandwich Islands. Arriving at Kailua, Hawaii, after 164 days, they established a station there at the request of King Kamehameha. In 1821 they moved to Honolulu, the king's new capital, but in 1823 they returned to Kailua, where Asa was pastor for 40 more years. After visiting California briefly in 1863, the Thurstons spent their last years in Honolulu. Asa was notable for his command of the Hawaiian language; in addition to effective preaching, he was involved in the translation of two Gospels, four Epistles, and ten major books of the Old Testament; he also translated *Sacred Geography* and *First Lesson of Arithmetic.*

The missionaries were convinced by the disastrous experience of the London Missionary Society in Tahiti that Polynesian culture would contaminate their children, especially with regard to sex. Most sent their children home to the United States at an early age or left the mission, but Lucy kept her five with her, making extraordinary efforts to isolate them. Living arrangements prevented any contact with Hawaiians until they had made profession of Christian faith and she felt their character had been formed. These arrangements and the demands of home education reduced her ability to work with Hawaiians, but she did at various times teach Sabbath school, Bible class, and "arithmetical school," and led a Friday "female meeting" which at one time had 2,600 members. A woman of commanding presence, Lucy bore with notable courage such trials as childbirth in the hold of a native ship stinking of bilge water, and cancer surgery without anesthetic.

BIBLIOGRAPHY In her old age Lucy assembled from her journals and letters *Life and Times of Mrs. Lucy G. Thurston* (1882, 1934). *Missionary Album* (1969), pp. 190–191 and *Missionary Herald* 64 (1868): 217–218 (on Asa), and 72 (1876): 413 (on Lucy) provide informative sketches. Insights into Asa's character and contribution are found in William R. Hutchison, *Errand to the World* (1987) and in John Garrett, *To Live among the Stars* (1982). Lucy is discussed in Patricia Grimshaw, *Paths of Duty: American Missionary Wives in Nineteenth-Century Hawaii* (1989) and in Mary Zweip, *Pilgrim Path: The First Company of Women Missionaries to Hawaii* (1991).

David M. Stowe

Thurston, Matilda S. (Calder) (1875–1958), missionary, teacher, and founder of Ginling College, China. Born in Hartford, Connecticut, Matilda Calder received a B.S. degree in 1896 and a Litt.D. in 1925, both from Mount Holyoke (Massachusetts) College. After beginning her teaching career in 1897 at a private school in Middletown, Connecticut, she traveled to Marash, in central Turkey, to teach at the American Board School for Girls from 1900 to 1902. In 1902 she married John Lawrence Thurston, of the Yale Mission to North China, and they moved to Changsha, Hunan Province, China, where they founded a branch of the Yale Mission. They returned to the United States the following year because of John Thurston's ill health. After his death in 1903 she served as a traveling secretary for the Student Volunteer Movement from 1904 to 1906. She returned to Changsha, China, in 1906 to teach at the boys' school of the Yale Mission and to help at the hospital there. In 1913 the Presbyterian Board of Foreign Missions in the U.S.A. appointed her to Nanking, where she helped to found Ginling College and served as its first president until 1928. Following her resignation as president, she continued at Ginling as an adviser, teacher, and supervisor of building construction from 1920 to 1936; she was treasurer of women's activities from 1939 to 1942. She was repatriated on the *Gripsholm* in 1943 and lived in Auburndale, Massachusetts, until her death.

BIBLIOGRAPHY Matilda Thurston, *Ginling College,* pt. 1 (1955). Thurston's personal papers are available at the Mount Holyoke College library/archives, South Hadley, Mass., and in the Ginling College files in the archives of the United Board for Christian Higher Education in Asia at the Yale Divinity School library/special collections.

Joan R. Duffy

Tikhomirov, Sergii (1871–1945), Russian Orthodox Metropolitan of Japan. Born as Georgii Tikhomirov, the son of protopriest Alexei Tikhomirov, in the village of Guza (near Novgorod), Tikhomirov graduated from the Novgorod Theological Seminary and Saint Petersburg Theological Academy (1896). In 1905 after serving as rector of the Academy, he took monastic vows (and the name Sergii) and became bishop of Yamburg. He joined the Japan mission of the Russian Orthodox Church in 1908 and served as bishop of Kyoto under *Nikolai Kasatkin. Within a year he had mastered Japanese sufficiently to travel around and preach without interpretation. During this time he produced numerous diaries and articles on the church in Japan and the life of the Japanese people, which were published in the Russian Christian press to encourage interest in the church of Japan. He invested much in the education and training of Japanese Christians.

He worked, as did Nikolai, toward a fully Japanese church. On the death of Nikolai in 1912, he was made head of the Japan mission. He continued the work of the mission in the difficult years when it lost its support from Russia following the Revolution. In 1923 he became archbishop and from 1930 he was also head of the Korean mission, and metropolitan and head of the East Asian Exarchate under the Moscow Patriarchate. However, he denied any persecution of the church in the USSR and thus provoked a schism among Russian emigres in Japan. In 1940 he was forced by Japanese authorities to resign. During World War II he lived in Tokyo, most of the time under house arrest. He died a few days before the end of the war and is buried near Archbishop Nikolai in Tokyo.

BIBLIOGRAPHY Sergii Tikhomirov, *Twelve Apostles* (1935, in Russian). L. Anisimov, "The Orthodox Mission in Korea," *Journal of the Moscow Patriarchate* 3 (1991): 55–60.

Karen L. Gordon

Tikhon (1865–1923), Russian Orthodox missionary bishop in Alaska and the United States. Born Vasily Ivanovich Belavin in Toropetz (Tver Province), Tikhon studied in the Pskov seminary and St. Petersburg Theological Academy. For nine years (1898–1907) he was a member of the Russian mission in America as bishop (archbishop, from 1905) of Alaska and the Aleutian Islands. Each year he traveled through his diocese from village to village in a boat and on foot. He also administered the Russian Orthodox Church in America with a see in San Francisco (in New York after 1905). He opened several schools and founded a monastery named in memory of St. Tikhon of Zadonsk (1724–1783) at South Canaan, Pennsylvania. In April 1917 he became the metropolitan of Moscow, where he had a reputation as a liberal. At the council of the Russian church in November 1917, against the backdrop of Bolshevist bombing of the Kremlin, Tikhon was elected patriarch of Moscow and all Russia, the first to occupy this position since 1700. In 1919 he issued an anathema upon the Soviet rulers. Tikhon played an active role in the Committee of Help to Starving People. He was imprisoned by the Bolsheviks and in April 1923, on the eve of his death, signed a declaration in which he called upon the clergy and the faithful to give their loyal support to the Soviet state.

BIBLIOGRAPHY M. Vostryshev, *Bozhii Izbrannik* (Chosen by God) (1990). See also M. Spinka, *The Church in Soviet Russia* (1956).

Evgeny S. Steiner

Tilak, Narayan Vaman (1862?–1919), Indian Christian Marathi poet and hymnwriter. Tilak was born into a high-caste (Chitpavan Brahman) Hindu family south of Bombay in 1862. As a young man he was already something of a literary celebrity. In his early thirties, in search of a universal religion, he began to read the Bible. He became an "intellectual convert" and was baptized in February 1895. He insisted that the ceremony be performed by an Indian pastor rather than a European or American. Eventually his wife also became a Christian, though not without a bitter family struggle. Tilak wrote constantly, chiefly poems and hymns. In the 1950s the Marathi hymnal contained 254 of his hymns, out of a total of almost 700. In his forties he underwent a conversion of the heart rather than the mind, and for the last years of his life he was an exemplary Christian *bhakta* (devotee), giving up money and possessions, though not renouncing home and family. This alarmed some missionaries, fearful of disorder, especially since in 1917 Tilak had published an open letter stating that he no longer wished to be associated with any human religious institution. He had long intended to write a life of Christ in Marathi verse, to be called *Christavan,* but on his death in 1919 it remained incomplete.

BIBLIOGRAPHY H. L. Richard, *Christ-Bhakti: Narayan Vaman Tilak and Christian Work among Hindus* (1991); Lakshmibai Tilak, *I Follow After* (1951, abridged as *From Brahma to Christ,* 1956); J. C. Winslow, *Narayan Vaman Tilak: The Christian Poet of Maharashtra* (1923). Also see Robin H. S. Boyd, *An Introduction to Indian Christian Theology* (1969), pp. 114–118.

Eric J. Sharpe

Tile, Nehemiah (d. 1891), South African indigenous evangelist and church founder. Little is known of Tile's early life before he started working as an evangelist with the Wesleyan Mission in the eastern Cape in the 1870s. After some years, he was sent to Healdtown College for theological training. Beginning in 1879 he served as a probationer in Thembuland, where he clashed with his superintendent, mainly as a result of dissatisfaction with the degree of white control in the mission. As a result, he left the Wesleyan Church in 1883 to start the Thembu National Church, forerunner of the thousands of African Initiated Churches that came into being during the twentieth century. The Thembu king was elected head of this church, a new expression of Africa consciousness in South African Christianity. Tile especially wished to cooperate with the traditional African power structures in order to fortify them against white encroachment. He led this church until his death.

BIBLIOGRAPHY D. Balia, "A Study of the Factors That Influenced the Rise and Development of Ethiopianism within the Methodist Church in Southern Africa" (M.Th. thesis, Univ. of Durban-Westville, 1985); W. Saayman: "Tiyo Soga and Nehemiah Tile: Black Pioneers in Mission and Church," *Missionalia* 17, no. 2, (1989): 95–102; C. C. Saunders, "Tile and the Thembu Church: Politics and Independency on the Cape Eastern Frontier in the Late Nineteenth Century," *Journal of African History* 11, no. 4 (1970).

Willem Saayman

Timpany, Americus Vespucius (1840–1885), Canadian Baptist missionary to India. Timpany was born in Vienna, Ontario, the son of farmers. He was educated at Canadian Literary Institute (later Woodstock College). In 1867 he married Jane Bates, a relative of John *McLaurin (later his missionary colleague in India). Under the appointment of the American Baptist Missionary Union, Timpany began work in India among the Telugus in 1868. He began several congregations and saw the number of converts increase to more than six hundred in eight years. He started the Ramapatam Theological Seminary in 1872 to train indigenous pastors and was the founder of the American Baptist Telugu Conference. For two years (1876–1878) the Timpanys toured the Canadian churches, raising support for the newly established Canadian Baptist Missionary Society; they also began publication of a periodical, *The Missionary Link.* In 1878 they returned to India, settling at Kakinada. There he conducted preaching tours, translated Scripture and practiced medicine. For a time he was a member of the Telugu Bible Revision Committee, and he served as municipal commissioner for the town of Kakinada. In one month alone he reported over 300 baptisms. In 1885 Timpany contracted cholera from a gift of raw milk and died; his death was a major event among Canadian Baptists, who held him in high regard as their first overseas missionary.

BIBLIOGRAPHY The only extant material published by the Timpanys is their editorial work in *The Missionary Link.* "A. V. Timpany," *The Canadian Missionary Link* (1885): 75–82; "Americus V. Timpany," *McMaster University Monthly,* December 1892; H. E. Stillwell, "A. V. Timpany: Missionary Pioneer from Canada," *The Baptist Missionary Review,* August 1933.

William H. Brackney

Ting, K. H. (Ding Guangxun) (1915–), preeminent Protestant leader in China in the latter half of the twentieth century. Ting was the son of a Shanghai banker who worked as an Anglican layman to make Chinese churches self-supporting. His maternal grandfather was an Anglican priest, and his mother prayed that he would enter the priesthood. As an undergraduate, he studied engineering at St. John's University in Shanghai (B.A., 1937), then went into theological studies. He completed his B.D. degree in Shanghai in 1942 and was ordained deacon and priest in the Sheng Kung Hui (Anglican) church that year. Also that year he married Kuo Siu May (Guo Siumei), a fellow graduate of St. John's University.

After World War II the Tings began five years of service and study outside China, beginning with a year on the staff of the Canadian Student Christian Movement. The next academic year was spent in New York City, where Ting completed a master's degree at Union Theological Seminary and Columbia University. This was followed by three years of service with the World's Student Christian Federation, based in Geneva, Switzerland. The Korean War interrupted plans to return to China in 1950, but in August 1951 the Tings returned to their home in Shanghai, where he became executive secretary of the Christian Literature Society.

Ting was one of the leaders who organized and led the Chinese Protestant churches beyond dependency into the current period of "three-self" autonomy and expansion. He became principal of the Nanjing Theological Seminary in 1952. In 1956 he was consecrated Anglican bishop of Chekiang (Zhejiang) Province. He attended international conferences in Europe in 1956, 1957, and 1961 and made many trips abroad since 1979. He and his wife received honorary doctorates from Victoria University, Toronto, in 1989. In 1978 he was named a vice-president of the University of Nanjing. In 1981 he was elected chairperson of the Chinese Christian Three-Self Patriotic Movement and president of the China Christian Council. He served as a representative from religious circles in the National People's Congress and was elected vice-chairperson of the Chinese People's Political Consultative Conference in 1989. (Ting's wife died in 1995.)

BIBLIOGRAPHY K. H. Ting, *No Longer Strangers: Selected Writings of K. H. Ting,* Raymond L. Whitehead, ed. (1989). Published as a special issue, *Chinese Theological Review* 10 (1995): 1–190 carries a tribute to Ting on his eightieth birthday, and includes a biographical sketch, selections from his early writings, and reflections on his life and work by colleagues and friends.

Donald E. MacInnis

Ting Li-Mei (Ding Limei) (1871–1936), Chinese Presbyterian pastor and renowned evangelist. Ting grew up in a well-known Shantung (Shandong) Christian family and was a distinguished graduate of Calvin *Mateer's Wen-hui-kuan academy. Nearly killed in the Boxer uprising of 1900, Ting served several Shantung churches after 1900. He became a compelling speaker, and after he conducted meetings at Shantung Union College in 1909, in which over a hundred students dedicated themselves to the ministry, he rocketed to national attention and received many invitations. His younger brother, Li-chieh, was also a pastor and evangelist.

In 1910 the Chinese Student Volunteer Movement (SVM) for the Ministry was established; it was affiliated with the YMCA and patterned after its SVM counterparts in the West. Ting was its first and longtime traveling secretary. By 1922 the Chinese SVM, under Ting's leadership, had received over 1,500 pledges of young people to enter the ministry. Ting was especially effective among educated young people. His meetings were not emotional; he asked for those "willing to study," not instant converts. His national prominence faded after the early 1920s.

BIBLIOGRAPHY Daniel H. Bays, "Christian Revival in China, 1900–1937," in *Modern Christian Revivals*, Edith L. Blumhofer and Randall Balmer, eds. (1993); Charles E. Scott, "Ding, the Apostle of Shantung," *MRW* 34 (1911): 125–127. Chinese language sources are numerous.

Daniel H. Bays

Tippett, Alan R. (1911–1988), Australian Methodist missiologist, anthropologist, and missionary in Fiji. Tippett earned an L.Th. (Melbourne College of Divinity), an M.A. in history (American University, Washington, D.C.), and a Ph.D. in anthropology (University of Oregon). He was a Methodist pastor in Australia before serving from 1941 to 1961 as a missionary in the Fiji Islands. He had unrivaled knowledge of the history of the Fiji mission, much of it gained through research into local affairs. He wrote valuable reviews of early Fijian missionaries and their work. While editor of the monthly *Ai Tukutuku Vakalotu*, he produced a stream of books and tracts for the Fijian church. His last four years in Fiji were as principal of the Methodist Theological Seminary, where he raised the educational standard. Under his direction, the first Fijian students earned their L.Th. diplomas from Melbourne College of Divinity.

Tippett's missiological research for various mission agencies and boards took him to Mexico, the Solomon Islands, Polynesia, Ethiopia, and Navajo Indian reservations in North America. From his extensive studies in the South Pacific came his classic *Solomon Islands Christianity* (1967). He was an authority on animism and, in 1974, addressed the Lausanne International Congress of World Evangelization on the subject.

From 1965 to 1977 he was professor of anthropology and oceanic studies at Fuller Theological Seminary's School of World Mission, Pasadena, California. He became a colleague and friend of Donald *McGavran, leader of the church growth movement. In response to what he felt were subbiblical attacks on the movement, he wrote *Church Growth and the Word of God* (1970). In 1977 he retired to his native Australia to prepare a number of manuscripts for publication. They eventually appeared in *Introduction to Missiology* (1987).

BIBLIOGRAPHY Alan R. Tippett, *People Movements in Southern Polynesia* (1971), *Verdict Theology in Missionary Theory* (1973), *Aspects of Pacific Ethnohistory* (1973), and *The Deep Sea Canoe: The Story of Third World Missionaries in the South Pacific* (1977); Darrell Whiteman, "Alan R. Tippett," in Gerald H. Anderson et al., eds., *Mission Legacies* (1994), pp. 532–538; A. Harold Wood, *Overseas Missions of the Australian Methodist Church,* 3 vols. (1975–1980).

Darrell Whiteman

Tisdall, William St. Clair (1859–1928), Church Missionary Society (CMS) missionary to Muslims. Tisdall was born in Wales and moved to New Zealand as a youth where he received an M.A. from the University of New Zealand. He taught at Bishopsdale Theological College before joining the CMS and going to India. He worked with Thomas Valpy *French at Lahore, specializing in Islam and in evangelism among Muslims, and, in 1887, became head of the Mohammedan Mission, Bombay. In 1892 he transferred to Persia (Iran). A gifted linguist, he produced grammars in Punjabi (1889), Gujerati (1892), Persian (1902), and Hindustani (1910). During the period 1900 to 1905 he delivered the James Long Lectures in the United Kingdom on comparative religion, Islam, Buddhism, and Hinduism, most of which appeared in published versions. He received the Edinburgh D.D. in 1903. He attended the Cairo Conference of Missionaries to Muslims in 1906, presenting the paper on literature work, and spoke in plenary at the Edinburgh World Missionary Conference in 1910. He also lectured at the Islington CMS college and was vicar of Deal, Kent (1913–1926). Tisdall is perhaps best remembered for his revisions of Karl *Pfander's books, including *The Balance of Truth* (1910). Despite his negative appraisal of other religions, his commitment to serious scholarship led many missionaries to recognize the need for sober, accurate, and sensitive study of non-Christian religions.

BIBLIOGRAPHY William St. Clair Tisdall, *The Religion of the Crescent* (1895, 1906, 1910, 1916), *Sources of Islam* (1900), *India: Its History, Darkness, and Dawn* (1901), and *Comparative Religion* (1912).

Clinton Bennett

Titus, Murray T(hurston) (1885–1964), American Methodist missionary in India and Islamic scholar. Titus was born in Batavia, Ohio, and graduated from Ohio Wesleyan University (B.A., 1908). He worked in India from 1910 to 1951, mostly in the United Provinces (now Uttar Pradesh) at Lucknow College, in evangelistic work in villages, and as treasurer of the Methodist Church in India. Inspired by Samuel Marinus *Zwemer, Titus made a special contribution in his outreach to Muslims. He served as secretary for work among Muslims of the National Christian Council of India, Burma, and Ceylon; was cofounder (with William *Paton and Lewis Bevan *Jones) of the Henry Martyn School of Islamic Studies in 1930 at Aligarh (now an institute at Hyderabad); in 1926 became an associate editor of *Moslem World;* published *Indian Islam* (1930), based on his 1927 doctoral dissertation at Kennedy School of Missions in Hartford; and promoted literature and conferences for understanding of Islam among Christians. In 1926 he received an honorary D.D. from his alma mater, Ohio Wesleyan University. After returning to the

United States because of his wife's failing health in 1951, he was professor of missions and world religions at Westminster (Methodist) Theological Seminary, Westminster, Maryland, until his retirement in 1955.

BIBLIOGRAPHY Titus also wrote *Islam for Beginners* (1930) and *The Young Moslem Looks at Life* (1937) and revised and expanded his major work, *Indian Islam,* as *Islam in India and Pakistan* (1959). On his life and work, see Dwight M. Donaldson, "Advisory Editor Murray T. Titus," *MW* 53(1963): 324–331; Carol Pickering, "Murray T. Titus: Missionary and Islamic Scholar," *IBMR* 19(1995): 118–20.

Gerald H. Anderson

Todd, Reginald Stephen Garfield (1908–), missionary statesman in Zimbabwe. Todd was born at Invercargill, New Zealand, of Scottish descent and was educated at Otaga University and at Glenleith Theological College. After two years as pastor of the Oamuru Church of Christ in New Zealand (1932–1934), he immigrated to Southern Rhodesia (present-day Zimbabwe), becoming superintendent of the Associated Churches of Christ in New Zealand's Dadaya Mission near Shabani (1934–1953). Under his leadership, Dadaya became a center in African education, serving 4,000 pupils, including high school students, with quality training in agriculture and construction. Acquiring his own 50,000 acre ranch above the Ngezi River, as well as a year's medical training at Witwatersrand University in South Africa, Todd was a pastor, educator, farmer, and healer.

In 1946 he entered politics as a United Party representative in the Southern Rhodesia parliament. In 1953, upon the formation of the Federation of Rhodesia and Nyasaland, he was elected leader of the governing United Rhodesia Party and prime minister of Southern Rhodesia, serving also as minister of labor (1953–1958), minister of native education (1953–1957), and minister of labor and social welfare (1958). Desiring a raceless community with equal opportunities for all, Todd succeeded in implementing the Land Husbandry Act and in rapidly advancing African education. But he was forced to resign as prime minister when his own party opposed his plan to extend the vote to more Africans. Defeated in 1958 as leader of a new United Rhodesia Party, and in 1960 as leader of the Central Africa Party, he retired from active politics.

Respectfully called the lover of the African people, Todd emerged as a more militant liberal as white politics shifted to the right. His outspokenness led not only to his political restriction by the Ian Smith regime for 12 months in 1965 and 1966, and his arrest in 1972, but also to increased respect among Zimbabwe nationalists. As an executive member of the Christian Council of Rhodesia, Todd helped that body to become an African voice in the 1960s and 1970s.

BIBLIOGRAPHY Rolf Italiaander, *The New Leaders of Africa* (1961) and Ronald Segal, *Political Africa: A Who's Who of Personalities and Parties* (1961) contain short biographical notes.

Norman E. Thomas

Tollefsen, Gunnerius Olai (1888–1966), Norwegian missionary, evangelist, and church leader. Tollefsen was born in Bergen, Norway, and was converted at a Salvation Army meeting under the preaching of Samuel L. Brengle in 1905. Two years later, he joined the Pentecostal movement and became a close friend and coworker of Thomas Ball *Barratt. He received his theological training at the Universities of Glasgow and Edinburgh.

In 1915, Tollefsen traveled to the Belgian Congo and initially worked with Southern Baptist missionaries. Later, at the invitation of Lewi *Pethrus, he surveyed potential mission fields for the Norwegian and Swedish Pentecostal churches. He returned from the Congo in 1930 and later (1945–1964) became the first mission secretary of the Norwegian Pentecostal movement, serving in that capacity until his retirement. With his adopted son, Emanuel Tollefsen-Minos, he continued in evangelistic work. In Tollefsen's later years, and because of his linguistic research in tribal languages and humanitarian contributions, he received knighthood from Belgian King Baudouin and medals from King Haakon VII and King Olaf V of Norway. Author of many books, he was also a fellow of the Royal Geographical Society.

BIBLIOGRAPHY Tollefsen's books include *Ved Milepelen, Jesu gjenkomst, Blant ville og primitive folkeslag,* and *Men Gud gav Vekst.* "Death of G. F. Tollefsen, Norway," *Pentecost,* no. 76 (June–August 1966): 9; K. B. Westman et al., *Nordisk Missionshistoria* (1949).

Gary B. McGee

Tomás de Jesús. *See* Thomas of Jesus.

Tomlin, Jacob (1793–1880), pioneer Protestant missionary in Malacca and Thailand. Born in Lancashire, England, and a fellow of St. John's College, Cambridge, in 1826 Tomlin was appointed by the London Missionary Society (LMS) to Malacca. He arrived in 1827 but moved frequently around the region, visiting Singapore, Batavia, Bali, Rhiow, and Bangkok, where he was located from August 1828 to May 1829 with Karl *Gützlaff. Tomlin then made a visit to Bali with Walter *Medhurst and from July 1831 to January 1832 was back in Thailand with David *Abeel. In Thailand the political situation provided a fair degree of freedom, and the novelty of their message and literature, including a rudimentary translation of the Gospels and Romans, attracted interest. While random tract distribution, preaching, and elementary medical work had little prospect of building a church, at the time their witness among Chinese in Thailand was seen as strategic.

Tomlin returned to Malacca as principal at the Anglo-Chinese College. In 1834 he began his own vernacular school before returning to England in 1836. He was ordained in the Church of England in 1848 and served irregularly in various parishes until becoming vicar of Wollaston in 1868. He retired in 1876. He published his missionary journals and works on the debate over the Chinese name for God.

BIBLIOGRAPHY Tomlin's publications include *Missionary Journals and Letters: Written during Eleven Years' Residence and Travels amongst the Chinese, Siamese, Javanese, Khassias, and other Eastern Nations* (1844). See also Alex G. Smith, *Siamese Gold: A History of Church Growth in Thailand* (1982), pp. 14–18; [Alexander Wylie], *Memorials of Protestant Missionaries to the Chinese* (1867), pp. 50–51.

John Roxborogh

Toribio Alfonso de Mogrovejo, Alfonso. *See* Mogrovejo, Toribio Alfonso de.

Torrance, David Watt (1862–1923), Scottish medical missionary in Palestine. Born in Airdrie, Scotland, Torrance graduated from Glasgow University in 1883. In 1884 he was sent by the Jewish Mission of the Free Church of Scotland as a medical missionary in Palestine. On his arrival he spent some time in Nazareth, where he was welcomed by the James Hubers of the Church Missionary Society; their daughter Lydia was to become his wife. At Tiberias, where Jews were three times as numerous as Arabs, Torrance established the Sea of Galilee Medical Mission, with a summer adjunct at Safed. Tiberias was rife with malaria, cholera, and dysentery so that unending calls were made upon his medical services. The hospital at Tiberias was built in 1894. In the years that followed, many thousands of Jews and Arabs passed through its wards, and not a few of them became Christians. The hospital was barely in working order when Lydia Torrance died giving birth to a daughter in 1894, and Torrance was left with a young son, Herbert, and the infant Lydia (both were later to serve as doctors in Tiberias). When on leave in Scotland in 1895, Torrance was ordained by the Presbytery of Glasgow so that he could function when needed as a minister as well as a doctor, which reinforced the distinctively Christian outlook and missionary purpose of his activity. In 1895 he married Eleanor Durie, who had been appointed head nurse of the hospital by the Jewish Mission Committee. She succumbed in a fearful cholera epidemic in 1902. In January 1908, Torrance married E. W. Curtiss, from Connecticut, who proved to be a great asset to the hospital and to his family life.

With the entry of Turkey into World War I, the Torrances were forced to leave Palestine for Scotland. Torrance soon found service during the war as a doctor in the Royal Army Medical Corps. During his absence from Tiberias, the premises of the Medical Mission were looted and damaged. However, when he returned, at the end of the war, they were rebuilt. To his great joy, he was joined by his doctor son, Herbert Watt Torrance, in 1921. After 29 years of patient, compassionate, and brave missionary service, the Galilee Doctor's health began to fail, and he died at Safed. Torrance had become legendary, as the hakim (doctor) of Tiberias, an admired physician and surgeon of intense human sympathy. He was buried in the hospital garden where other members of his family had already been laid to rest.

BIBLIOGRAPHY W. P. Livingstone, *A Galilee Doctor; Being a Sketch of the Career of Dr. D. W. Torrance of Tiberias* (1923); David McDougall, *In Search of Israel* (1941).

Thomas F. Torrance

Torrance, Thomas (1871–1959), Scottish missionary to China. Born at Shotts, Scotland, Torrance trained at Cliff and Livingstone Colleges for missionary service. In 1895 he was sent by the China Inland Mission (CIM) to Chengtu (Chengdu), Szechwan (Sichuan), and put in charge of several outstations. He survived the Boxer Uprising of 1900. At the Edinburgh Missionary Conference in 1910, he was asked by the American Bible Society (ABS) to take over their agency in Chengtu. Bible production and distribution saw immense development, and new ABS premises were established that proved an invaluable center for widespread evangelism and the training of converts. In 1911 Torrance married Annie Elizabeth Sharp of the CIM.

During the summers Torrance engaged in evangelizing visitations to the aboriginal peoples who inhabited the upper Min Valley and established churches in Wenchuan County, at the confluence of the Min and To Rivers. There he found the Chi'ang (now Qiang) tribes, who were evidently the remnants of an ancient emigration from the Middle East.

In 1927, when several missionaries were killed by Communists, the Torrances returned to Scotland. The next year, Torrance returned alone to Chengtu, where he engaged in extensive evangelistic and teaching missions in western Sichuan, not least, among the Chi'ang, large groups of whom he took to Chengtu for biblical instruction. In 1935 missionaries were once more forced to leave. All but one of the churches established in the Upper Min and To Valleys were destroyed by Mao Tse-tung's Communist army in its "long march" in an attempt to wipe out the Christian enclave.

Over the years Torrance gained a considerable reputation as a scholar through research in unpublished Chinese archives and archaeological operations and was primarily responsible for the establishing of the museum in the West China Union University.

BIBLIOGRAPHY Thomas Torrance, *The History, Customs, and Religion of the Ch'iang, An Aboriginal People of West China* (1920), *The Beatitudes and the Decalogue* (1921), *Expository Studies in St. John's Miracles* (1938), and *China's First Missionaries* (1937, 1988). The latter (T. F. Torrance, ed.) contains a selection of articles and research papers about the Ch'iang.

Thomas F. Torrance

Torrend, Jules (1861–1936), Jesuit missionary in Africa. Born in Saint Privat d'Allier, France, Torrend entered the Society of Jesus in 1878 and was ordained in 1892. He served in South Africa (1882–1888), in the Zambesi mission in Portuguese Mozambique (1894–1905), and in Rhodesia (1905–1936). A missionary with a pioneering spirit, he became famous for his ethnological and linguistic works. He published grammars of various languages in southern Africa, dictionaries, textbooks, articles in specialized journals (such as *Études, Anthropos, Studi glottologici italiani, Journal of the African Society*) and numerous missionary reports in French, Italian, German, and English missionary magazines. His *Comparative Grammar of the South African Bantu Languages* (1891) compared and analyzed more than 30 (sometimes up to 48) languages. His *Nouvelles études bantoues, comprenant surtout des recherches sur les principes de la classification des substantifs dans les langues de l'Afrique australe* was widely read. It was published in an abridged version by De Gregorio and in full by P. van Ginneken (see J. v. Ginneken, "Les classes nominales des langues bantoues," *Anthropos* 8 [1913]: 151–164; 9 [1914]: 781–800).

BIBLIOGRAPHY P. Schebesta, *Portugals Konquistamission in Südostafrika* (1966), pp. 334–337; M. Schulien, "Necrologia: P. Giulio Torrend SJ," *Annali Lateranensi* 1 (1937): 275–280.

Karl Müller, SVD

Tosari, Paulus (1813–1882), prominent East Javanese church leader. Educated to become a *santri* (Muslim student), Tosari turned to C. L. *Coolen to receive Christianized Javanese wisdom (*ngelmu*). In 1844 he was baptized in Surabaya. Then he became a leader in the new Christian settlement at Mojowarno. From 1851 to 1858 he worked closely with the missionary J. E. *Jellesma. Tosari was the organizer, pastor, and catechist of this congregation till his death. He was an excellent preacher with a deep knowledge of the Bible. He became famous, most of all, for his *tembang* (Javanese wisdom in poetic form, recited rather than published). Through these compositions he passed on catechetic and moral lessons, which were recited in the villages in the evenings. One was a poetical version of the Old Testament story of Joseph, a Christian parallel to Muslim stories of Joseph. His largest and most important work was *Rasa Sedjati* (True teaching, or Deepest feelings). In it Christ is called the perfect man who shows others the road to heavenly perfection. Tosari's terminology resembles that used in mystical forms of Javanese Islam. In these writings he shows his independence from the missionaries. *Rasa Sedjati* was published in 1925 by the Christian literature committee headed by Hendrik *Kraemer, who praised it highly.

BIBLIOGRAPHY There are no translations of Tosari's writings. Philip van Akkeren, *Sri and Christ: A Study of the Indigenous Church in East Java* (1970): pp. 66–67, 97–102, 172–180; A. G. Hoekema, *Denken in dynamisch evenwicht. De wordingsgeschiedenis van de nationale protestantse theologie in Indonesië* (1994), pp. 47–54; C. W. Nortier, *Paulus Tosari, predikant te Modjowarno, 1848–1882* (1942–1946); C. Poensen, "Paulus Tôsari," *Med.* 27 (1883): 283–316, 333–360.

Alle G. Hoekema

Toth, Alexis (1854–1909), immigrant pastor and instigator of the expansion of the Russian Orthodox Church in the United States. Born near the western border of the Russian Empire, Toth belonged by birth to the Ukrainian Greek-Catholic Uniate Church (which acknowledged the pope as head of the church while retaining traditional patterns of worship and the use of the local languages for services). Having immigrated to the United States, Toth was serving as vicar of Uniate parishes in Minneapolis, Minnesota, when, in 1891, he disobeyed orders of the Roman Catholic archbishop of Saint Paul, John Ireland. Toth made a trip to the see of the Russian Orthodox Church in America in San Francisco, where he requested admission into the Orthodox Church. Within a short time, he led all his flock (more than 10,000 people) to Orthodoxy. He founded a seminary for preparing priests for new Orthodox parishes in America and was known as an outstanding preacher.

BIBLIOGRAPHY Alexis Toth, *Selected Letters*, G. Soldatow, trans. (1978).

Evgeny S. Steiner

Tournon, Charles Thomas Maillard de (1668–1710), first papal legate to the court of China in the modern period. Tournon was born in Turin, Italy. In 1701 he was appointed patriarch of Antioch and apostolic visitor by Pope *Clement XI, who wanted to settle the controversies about the Malabar Rites and the Chinese Rites. Tournon reached Pondicherry, India, in November 1703 and in 1704 issued instructions condemning the Malabar Rites. He proceeded to Manila to settle some ecclesiastical affairs. In April 1705 he entered Macao and then Canton (Guangzhou), where he held discussions about the rites issue with missionaries of various religious orders before proceeding to Peking (Beijing). In two audiences, December 1705 and June 1706, Tournon replied evasively to the K'ang-hsi emperor's request to issue a decree settling the rites, since he did not want the emperor involved in such religious matters. In poor health and unsuccessful in the negotiations, Tournon left Peking and stopped in Nanking (Nanjing), where in January 1707 he issued an edict against the Jesuit accommodation policy. This nullified the emperor's 1706 decree allowing missionaries to stay in China with a residence permit provided they followed the interpretations of Matteo *Ricci on the rites. Subsequently the emperor banished Tournon to Macao, where under house arrest he received papal appointment as cardinal shortly before his death.

BIBLIOGRAPHY Antonio Sisto Rosso, *Apostolic Legations to China of the Eighteenth Century* (1948); Francis A. Rouleau, "Maillard de Tournon, Papal Legate at the Court of Peking," *Archivum Historicum Societatis Iesu* 31 (1962): 264–323; D. F. St. Sure, *100 Roman Documents Concerning the Chinese Rites Controversy (1645–1941)* (1992), pp. 27–30; Joseph S. Sebes, "China's Jesuit Century," *Wilson Quarterly* 2 (1978): 170–183.

John W. Witek, SJ

Townsend, Henry (1815–1886), English missionary in Yorubaland (now in Nigeria). Townsend was born in Exeter and at age 20 volunteered to the (Anglican) Church Missionary Society. He was accepted at the inferior grade of catechist and in 1836, after an abbreviated course at the society's London college, was posted to Sierra Leone. He worked in several Yoruba African villages until invalided home in 1840 to Exeter, where he married Sarah Pearse. On his return to Sierra Leone late that year, CMS chose him to investigate the missionary implications of the return of many former slaves to their Yoruba homelands. He traveled with a Sierra Leonean party to Badagry, arriving late in 1842, and thence overland to Abeokuta, in Egba land, the focus of the Yoruba returnees. En route he met T. B. *Freeman returning from similar reconnaissance for the Methodists. Impressed by Shodeke, the Egba leader, Townsend advocated the establishment of a mission at Abeokuta. After receiving ordination in 1844, he was sent first to Sierra Leone to work with the Yoruba there and soon after with a substation mission to Yorubaland that included S. A. *Crowther and C. A. *Gollmer. But Shodeke had died, leaving a power vacuum in Abeokuta, and war had cut the road to it. The party therefore opened their work in Badagry until Townsend and Crowther were able to proceed to Abeokuta in 1846.

Over three decades Townsend was the outstanding European missionary in Yorubaland. He identified with the Egba in their resistance to Dahomean aggression and also in their war against Ibadan (to the dismay of David *Hinderer, his missionary colleague there). Townsend influenced British public and official opinion about Africa. He helped to establish Yoruba orthography, worked on Bible translation, and built up a Yoruba newspaper, *Iwe Irohin.* Traveling intensively from his base in Ake township, he did much to build the Egba church and advance the Egba state; peremptory and combative, however, he also impeded the plan of Henry *Venn for an educated African Christian leadership and for Crowther's appointment as bishop. In 1867 the movement called *Ifole* led to the expulsion of all white missionaries from Abeokuta. Thereafter Townsend worked mainly from Lagos, returning to Abeokuta only in 1875. But his health was broken, and he soon retired to Exeter, the longest serving missionary in West Africa. His views on African leadership softened in his last years in Africa, and he recommended James *Johnson's appointment as a bishop.

BIBLIOGRAPHY George Townsend, *Memoir of the Rev. Henry Townsend, Late CMS Missionary, Abeokuta, West Africa* (1887). J. F. A. Ajayi, *Christian Missions in Nigeria, 1841–1891* (1965); S. O. Biobaku, *The Egba and Their Neighbours, 1842–1872* (1957); *CMS Register of Missionaries,* no. 231; P. E. H. Hair, *The Early Study of Nigerian Languages: Essays and Bibliographies* (1967).

Andrew F. Walls

Townsend, William Cameron (1896–1982), cofounder of Wycliffe Bible Translators (WBT) Summer Institute of Linguistics (SIL). Born in Eastvale, California, in a Presbyterian family, from 1917 to 1932 Townsend sold Spanish Bibles to Native Americans in rural Guatemala, organized a school for them, translated the New Testament into Cakchiquel (a Mayan language), taught literacy, and evangelized. While learning Cakchiquel he came to realize that he should analyze the language in its own terms and not presuppose the structure of Western languages. He therefore developed an alphabet and wrote a grammar using these principles. In 1933, under strong urging from Leonard L. Legters, Townsend began to explore the possibilities for Bible translation into Native American languages of Mexico. To this end, in 1934 he organized a summer camp for training prospective translators in linguistics and in understanding cultures, starting with only five students. Initially Townsend himself did some of the teaching, based on his analysis of Cakchiquel, but among his early students were Kenneth L. *Pike and Eugene A. *Nida, who began to teach in 1935 and 1937, respectively. From that small beginning, the sister organizations WBT and SIL grew to 3,700 members by the year of Townsend's death, with training programs in several countries and workers in many more. Townsend's gifts lay in his far-ranging vision, his confidence in God's leading, his charismatic personality, and his ability to make friendships with people on all levels of society, including high-level officials. His strategy for SIL expansion was to persuade officials to invite translators into their countries for linguistic analysis of minority languages and for the cultural and spiritual uplift of minority peoples, including translation of the Bible.

BIBLIOGRAPHY Ruth M. Brend and Kenneth L. Pike, eds., *The Summer Institute of Linguistics: Its Work and Contributions* (1977); Anna Marie Dahlquist, *Trailblazers for Translators: The Chichicastenango Twelve* (1995); James Hefley and Marti Hefley, *Uncle Cam* (1975); Hugh Stevens, *Wycliffe in the Making: The Memoirs of W. Cameron Townsend, 1920–33* (1995). A Festschrift, including a brief biography, is *A William Cameron Townsend en el vigésimoquinto aniversario del Instituto Lingüístico de Verano* (1961).

William A. Smalley

Tragella, Giovanni Battista (1885–1968), Catholic missiologist. Born in Milan, Tragella became a priest in 1911 and a member of the Missionary Institute of Milan. He left for Hong Kong in 1912 but remained only two and a half years in China. He returned to Rome and taught missiology at the Pontifical University Urbaniana from 1919 to 1924. He wrote an introduction to missiology (1930) and a book on missionary spirituality (1948). His great concerns were missionary formation in the seminaries and the pastoral dimension of missionary work. He was editor of the magazine *Missioni Catolliche* (1921–1954). His greatest work was a three-volume history of his Milan missionary society, published in 1950, 1959, and 1963.

BIBLIOGRAPHY A summary of Tragella's life is in J. Beckmann, "Drei verdiente Pioniere der Missionswissenschaft: Theodor Grentrup, SVD, G. B. Tragella, PIME, Anton Freitag, SVD," in *NZM,* 24 (1968): 202–206.

Jesús López-Gay, SJ

Trasher, Lillian Hunt (1887–1961), missionary in Egypt. Trasher was born in Jacksonville, Florida. Her mother, originally a Quaker, converted to the Roman Catholic Church and reared Lillian in that tradition. After conversion to the evangelical faith, Trasher enrolled at God's Bible School in Cincinnati, Ohio, in 1905 but left after one term to work in a North Carolina orphanage. Following a short time there, she went to Greenville, South Carolina, to study at Altamont Bible and Missionary Institute. She later attended a Church of God (Cleveland, Tennessee) congregation in Dahlonega, Georgia, where she became a Pentecostal.

Breaking her engagement to an evangelist who did not share her call to missions and without the approval of her parents, she left for Egypt in 1910 as an independent missionary. With the aid of her sister, Jennie, she began to care for abandoned babies and children and in 1911 established a home for them in Assiut, Egypt, now known as the Lillian Trasher Memorial Orphanage. After 1919, she affiliated with the Assemblies of God. Many of those who grew up and received schooling in the orphanage contributed to the growth of the Pentecostal movement in Egypt. Trasher's care of thousands of orphans and her heroic faith won the respect of the Egyptian government and gained her international fame. A grateful Muslim village official once said of her: "I believe that when she dies, in spite of the fact that she is a woman and a Christian, God will take her directly to paradise." She is buried at the orphanage.

BIBLIOGRAPHY Jerome Beatty, "Nile Mother," *American Magazine,* June 1939, pp. 55–56, 180, and abridged in *Reader's Digest,* July 1939, pp. 33–36; Philip Crouch, "They Called Her the Greatest Woman in Egypt," *Assemblies of God Heritage* 4 (Winter 1984–1985), pp. 7–8; Beverly Graham, ed., *Letters from Lillian* (1983); Beth Prim Howell, *Lady on a Donkey* (1960); Lester F. Sumrall, *Lillian Trasher, The Nile Mother* (1951); Lillian Trasher, *A Work of Faith and Labor of Love* (1937). Lillian Trasher's letters and papers are kept in the editorial office files of the Assemblies of God Division of Foreign Missions, Springfield, Mo.

Gary B. McGee

Trenchard, E(rnest) H(arold) (1902–1972), Plymouth Brethren missionary in Spain. Born at Woodley, Buckinghamshire, England, and educated at the University of Bristol, Trenchard first worked in the villages of central Spain (1924–1936), then made Barcelona (1949) his base and finally Madrid (1964) until his death. A gifted Bible teacher and commentator, he saw the need to train leaders for the growing number of Brethren churches (the largest group of Protestant churches in Spain until overtaken by the Gypsy churches). No narrow denominationalist, he was a founder of the Spanish Evangelical Alliance. Many of his published works originated as correspondence courses and were widely used by evangelicals in Spanish-speaking countries. His work was marked by judicious use of biblical scholarship, careful biblical exegesis, and keen theological insight. His English commentary on Acts in *A New Testament Commentary for Today* (1969) reveals the quality of his work. As well as an *Introduction to the Four Gospels,* he published commentaries in Spanish on Mark, Acts, Romans, 1 Corinthians, Galatians, and Hebrews. Of his extensive Old Testament work, only *Introduction to the Wisdom Literature* and an exposition of Job were published (posthumously). He also published studies of basic Christian doctrines; a major theological work (with J. M. Martinez), *Chosen in Christ; The Christian Family;* and *The Church, the Churches and Missionary Work.* He displayed deep pastoral concern, wise counsel, and strategic grasp of a complex situation involving virtual persecution of Protestants in Spain.

BIBLIOGRAPHY Ernest H. Trenchard, *Sketches from Missionary Life in Spain* (1932; a popular account of his early work). *Edificación Christiana,* January, 1973, is entirely devoted to "Don Ernesto Trenchard: Su vida y su obra."

Harold H. Rowdon

Trigault, Nicolas (1577–1628), Jesuit missionary in China. Trigault was born in Douai, Belgium, where he entered the Society of Jesus in 1594. He prepared himself for the missions by studying mathematics, astronomy, and geography. In 1607 he left Lisbon for Goa, India, and reached Macao by 1610. After some time in Nanking (Nanjing) for language training, he went to Peking (Beijing) to assess the state of the mission there. Appointed mission procurator to go to Rome to explain the needs to the pope and Jesuit superiors, he left Nanking in 1612 and embarked from Macao early the next year. Reaching Cochin, India, he made his way overland to Goa. He entered Rome at the end of 1614. He received papal approval for priests to recite the breviary and with covered heads to offer the sacrifice of the Mass in Chinese. He published a Latin translation of a history of Christianity in China written in Italian by Matteo *Ricci.

After traveling extensively in Europe to get support for the China mission, Trigault returned to Macao in July 1619. He established a mission in K'ai-feng (Kaifeng) and in 1624 a mission in Shensi (Shaanxi) Province, where he was the first European to see the Nestorian monument of 781. Four years later he died in Hangchow (Hangzhou).

BIBLIOGRAPHY Nicolas Trigault, *De Christiana expeditione apud Sinas suscepta a Soc. Jesu ex P. M. Riccii commentariis libri V* (1605), *Vita Gasparis Barzei Belgae e Societate Iesu B. Xaverii in India Socii* (1610), *China in the Sixteenth Century: The Journals of Matteo Ricci, 1583–1610,* Louis J. Gallagher, tr. (1953), *De Christianis apud Japonios triumphis* (1623), and *Xiru ermu zi* (Vocabulary by tones for Europeans), 3 vols. (1626). See also J. Dehergne, *Répertoire des Jésuites de Chine de 1552 à 1800* (1973), pp. 274–275; G. Dunne, *Generation of Giants* (1962), pp. 162–182; L. Polgar, *Bibliographie sur l'histoire de la Compagnie de Jésus, 1901–1980* (1990), vol. 3, pt. 3, p. 572.

John W. Witek, SJ

Trobe, Christian Ignatius la (1758–1836), English Moravian mission administrator, editor, and musician. La Trobe received his education at Moravian schools in England and Niesky, Germany. He began his career as a teacher in Niesky and in 1787, following his return to England and ordination, became secretary to the Brethren's Society for the Furtherance of the Gospel. He later held a variety of administrative posts in the English Moravian Church. In 1790 he became the first editor of *Periodical Accounts Relating to the Missions of the Church of the United Brethren Established among the Heathen,* published by the society. It was the first missionary magazine in the English language. As an administrator, he visited Moravian mission sites, including South Africa (1815–1816), which resulted in expansion of the work. A friend of William *Wilberforce, he supplied the abolitionist leader with information regarding the condition of slaves in the West Indies, though he maintained a public silence on the subject until after 1815 for fear of endangering Moravian work in the area. He was an accomplished pianist and composer of sacred music. Several of his compositions have been reissued in contemporary editions.

BIBLIOGRAPHY Autobiographical material is contained in *Journal of a Visit to South Africa, in 1815 and 1816, with Some Account of the Missionary Settlements of the United Brethren, near the Cape of Good Hope* (1818) and in *Letters to My Children* (1851). Also see J. E. Hutton, *A History of Moravian Missions* (1923).

David A. Schattschneider

Trobisch, Walter (1923–1979) *and*
Ingrid (Hult) (1926–), missionaries to Cameroon and family life counselors. Born in Leipzig, Germany, Walter Trobisch was drafted into the army at age 18. Wounded on the Russian front, he was evacuated to Vienna, where he began studies for the ministry. After the war he continued his study at Leipzig and Heidelberg and spent a year at Augustana College in Illinois. There he met Ingrid Hult, who was born of missionary parents in Tanganyika (Tanzania) and planned to serve in Africa with the Augustana Lutheran church's Sudan Mission. While in language school in Paris, she renewed her acquaintance with Walter, who now was a pastor in Germany. In 1950 she went to Cameroon, but their love grew and two years later they were married. He joined her in the mission and in 1953 they began a pioneer work at Tchollire, in northern Cameroon. In 1957 they were reassigned to Cameroun Christian College in Libamba, where Walter Trobisch taught German and Bible and served as the campus pastor. He also offered classes on sex and marriage for older students, which led to the publication in 1962 of *I Loved a Girl,* the correspondence between him and two young African Christians who were deeply in love. This became a bestseller, and further books followed. The requests for advice on family life grew so heavy that the Trobisches left Cameroon in 1963, relocated in Austria, and formed the Family Life Mission, which conducted seminars all over the world and carried on a large counseling ministry by mail. After Walter's untimely death, Ingrid Trobisch returned to the family home in Springfield, Missouri, and engaged in writing and speaking.

BIBLIOGRAPHY Walter Trobisch, *The Complete Works of Walter Trobisch* (1987); Ingrid Hult Trobisch, *On Our Way Rejoicing* (1964).

Richard V. Pierard

Troeltsch, Ernst (1865–1923), leading German theologian of the history-of-religions school. One of the greatest philosophers of history after Hegel, Troeltsch was professor of theology at Heidelberg and of philosophy at Berlin. He regarded Christian mission as an indicator of one of the most crucial problems of the Christian faith. He was convinced that the absoluteness of Christianity could never be understood within the realm of historical thought or proved by historical means. Instead, Christianity might at best be considered as a point of convergence—not culmination—of the evolution of religion in an age of pluralism. Compared with other world religions that deserve serious consideration, omitting "primitive" religions, Christianity can claim to be "the strongest and most concentrated revelation of personalistic religion." But it remains to be seen what shape it will take in the process of an ever fuller realization of the essence of religion. Meanwhile, the rule applies that "what you say to be true is true for you," and no more may be claimed. Hence Christian mission cannot offer a salvation that is absolutely superior to other offers or aim at the Christianization of all mankind. It may, instead, try to contribute to cultural and ethical harmony—proposing not a uniform system of dogma but a common striving for reliable values like those which, for the time being, were incorporated in the prevailing Western heritage of humanism and personalism. Troeltsch did not live to observe the tragic shaking of the very foundations on which that heritage seemed to rest. But his influence on modern attempts to advocate relativism and pluralism cannot be ignored.

BIBLIOGRAPHY Ernst Troeltsch, *Die Absolutheit des Christentums und die Religionsgeschichte,* 3d ed. (1929) and "Missionsmotiv, Missionsaufgabe...," *ZMR* (1907): 129–139, 161–166. Walter Köhler, *Ernst Troeltsch* (1941).

Hans-Werner Gensichen

Trollope, Mark Napier (1862–1930), English missionary and scholar in Korea. Born in London and educated at Lancing College and New College, Oxford, Trollope first went to Korea in 1890. In 1897 after six years in Seoul studying Korean language and culture and helping with the revision of the Korean New Testament, he began evangelistic work on Kangwha Island, where the Church of England's first Korean converts were made. In 1901 he returned to England, where his missionary efforts were recognized by an honorary D.D. from Oxford University. In 1911 he was recalled from parish work in London to be Anglican bishop in Korea. As bishop, he emphasized the development of a spiritually strong church, even at the expense of numerical expansion. He also eschewed public political activism but in doing so went against prevailing conditions in Korea, which identified Christianity with Korean nationalism and political activism. The mission faced serious difficulties during and after World War I because of limited financial resources and shortages of both medical and clerical staff. In 1925 Trollope built the Byzantine-style Cathedral of St. Mary and St. Nicholas in Seoul. He was an enthusiastic supporter and sometime president of the Korean branch of the Royal Asiatic Society.

BIBLIOGRAPHY Mark Napier Trollope, *The Church in Korea* (1915) and *The English Church Mission in Corea: Its Faith and Practice* (1917). Constance Trollope, *Mark Napier Trollope: Bishop in*

Corea, 1911–1930 (1936); "Obituary: The Right Reverend Mark Napier Trollope D.D., Bishop in Korea," *Transactions of the Korean Branch of the Royal Asiatic Society* 20 (1931).

A. Hamish Ion

Trotman, Dawson Earle (1906–1956), founder of The Navigators. Trotman's father, Charles Earle Trotman, immigrated to America from England in 1892. Born in Bisbee, Arizona, Trotman moved to Lomita, California, where he was converted in 1926 through Bible verses he had memorized. He did evangelism at work, on the streets, and in churches. Within three years he had memorized a thousand verses. In 1933 he introduced Bible memorization to a sailor in Los Angeles. The following year, he organized The Navigators as a ministry to sailors, with the motto "To know Christ and to make Him known." By the end of World War II, in 1945, there were Bible-memorizing Navigators on 800 or more Navy ships, stations, and Army bases.

Twice a college drop-out and never ordained to the ministry, Trotman built his work on strict personal discipline and Scripture, as well as a passion for people. His evangelical theology grew out of his devotional life. His was essentially a lay movement. He called it a self-reproducing ministry (based on 2 Tim. 2:2), emphasizing Bible memorization, small-group Bible study, evangelism, and discipleship. Known as the apostle of follow-up, he started many "Nav homes" where leaders cultivated their disciples. In 1949 his materials and methods got a major boost when evangelist Billy *Graham, then holding a crusade in Los Angeles, enlisted his assistance in counseling new converts. Many evangelical mission agencies and churches subsequently adopted Trotman's pattern of evangelism and discipleship, and the ministry spread across the United States and then overseas. By 1994 The Navigators had some 3,300 workers in 90 countries.

Trotman drowned in upstate New York while saving the life of a girl pitched overboard from a powerboat. Two of his sermons have been published: "Born to Reproduce" and "The Need of the Hour."

BIBLIOGRAPHY Bob Foster, *The Navigator* (1984); Betty Lee Skinner, *Daws* (1974); Laverne E. Tift, *Valiant in Fight* (1990); E. Wallis, *Lengthened Cords* (1958).

James W. Reapsome

Trotter, Isabelle Lilias (1853–1928), missionary and artist. Born into a comfortable home in London, England, Lilias Trotter showed considerable talent as a watercolor artist whom Ruskin admired. She was influenced by the Keswick holiness conferences and worked in parishes in London and Oxford and for the YWCA. When she felt called to work overseas, she prepared herself at the Mildmay Institute before traveling to Algiers in 1888 with three friends—all well-educated single women. Other friends also joined Trotter in what became the Algiers Mission Band, a nondenominational society. They built up personal and individual relations with women and girls, also teaching the Bible in small groups. Trotter also translated and wrote tracts that were published by the Nile Mission Press of Cairo, and spent 1915 working at the press. Her devotional writings in English, some illustrated with her paintings, made her work well known. She continued working almost until the end of her life. The Algiers Mission Band eventually became part of the North Africa Mission, which continues to the present day, now as Arab World Ministries.

BIBLIOGRAPHY I. Lilias Trotter, *Between the Desert and the Sea* (with 16 paintings), *Parables of the Cross: Parables of the Christ Life,* and *Focussed: A Story and a Song* (all published in the 1920s). Constance E. Padwick, *The Master of the Impossible Sayings, for the most part in parable, from the Letters and Journals of Lilias Trotter of Algiers* (1938); Blanche A. F. Piggott, *I. Lilias Trotter, Founder of the Algiers Mission Band* (1930); Patricia St. John, *Until the Day Breaks* (1990).

Jocelyn Murray

Trudpert (6th century), missionary in Breisgau and martyr of the Black Forest. A German hermit, Trudpert is said to have built a cell in the Breisgau Münstertal (forest), where he worked as a missionary. The surviving legends about his life are problematic. Some say he was an Irishman, or a brother of Rupert of Salzburg, or even a relative of the Hapsburg family. He was apparently murdered by a serf. His memory had an effect on the Benedictines, who built a monastery on the site of his death.

BIBLIOGRAPHY T. Jurrus, *Sankt Trudpert Münstertal: Pfarrkirche St. Peter und Paul und St. Trudpert, Märtyrer* (1976); T. Mayer, ed., *Beiträge zur Geschichte von Sankt Trudpert* (1937). See also Joseph Schmidlin, *Catholic Mission History* (1933), p. 160.

Frederick W. Norris

Trumbull, David (1819–1889), pioneer Protestant missionary to Chile. In response to appeals from English and North American residents in the port city of Valparaiso, Chile, the Foreign Evangelical Society and the Seaman's Friend Society sent Trumbull, a Yale College and Princeton Seminary graduate and son of the governor of Connecticut, to work with the expatriate community and sailors in Valparaiso. Trumbull arrived there in late 1845 and worked in Chile for the rest of his life. Meeting first in private homes as the "Free Chapel," Trumbull and his followers organized themselves as the (interdenominational) Union Church in 1847. Following his marriage, he began Protestant services in Coquimbo and Santiago, opened a school for girls and a home for abandoned children, started a publishing house, opened a bookstore, and helped initiate the Chilean temperance movement, the YMCA, and the Bible Society. He welcomed and helped other Protestant missionaries and in 1873 recommended the transfer of his work to the Presbyterian Mission Board. Though he retained his Congregational ties, Trumbull worked under the Presbyterian board. Thoroughly ecumenical, he cooperated with Roman Catholics (who had strenuously opposed him) in times of regional or national disaster, but he campaigned vigorously for religious tolerance, civil cemeteries, and civil marriage. He became a Chilean citizen in 1886, three years before his death.

BIBLIOGRAPHY Margarette Daniels, *Makers of South America* (1916); J. B. A. Kessler, Jr., *A Study of Older Protestant Missions and Churches in Peru and Chile* (1967); James H. McLean, *Historia de la Iglesia Presbyteriana en Chile* (1932); R. E. Speer, *Studies of Missionary Leadership* (1914); W. R. Wheeler et al., *Modern Missions in Chile and Brazil* (1926).

Alan Neely

Trumpp, Ernst (1828–1885), German missionary academic and philologist. Trumpp, from Würtemberg, was ordained as a Lutheran. In 1854, having earned a doctorate from Tübingen University, he sailed for Sindh, in western India (now Pakistan) under the Church Missionary Society, going to comparatively new work in Karachi. He received Anglican ordination in India. His time there was short, due to ill health, but he contributed to the study of Sindhi, Afghan, and Pushtu. He resigned at the end of 1859 and later became professor of Semitic languages at the University of Munich. He maintained his interest in Indian languages and in 1869 was asked by the British India Office to translate the *Adi Granth,* the Sikh holy scriptures. He made important philological contributions through his *Sindhi and English Dictionary, Dictionary of Afghan Terms,* and *Pushtu Grammar.*

BIBLIOGRAPHY Ernst Trumpp, *The Adi Granth, or The Holy Scriptures of the Sikhs* (1877). Church Missionary Society, *Register of Missionaries... from 1804 to 1904* (1904); Eugene Stock, *The History of the Church Missionary Society. Its Environment, Its Men, and Its Work,* 3 vols. (1899).

Jocelyn Murray

Tryphon of Pechenga (d. 1583), Russian Orthodox missionary to the Lapps and Samoyeds. Born into a clerical family in Novgorod, Russia, and trained as a military engineer, Tryphon was directed in a vision to evangelize the Lapps, and as a layman he proceeded into the Arctic region between the Pechenga and Pazrek Rivers and on the Kola Peninsula. His preaching was vigorously opposed by the pagan priesthood, yet he succeeded in converting thousands of people. Because Orthodox laypeople may baptize only in emergency situations, he had to wait patiently for a priest to perform the sacrament. After accepting monastic tonsure, he founded the Monastery of the Holy and Undivided Trinity near Petsamo, on the Pechenga. It endured as both a center of missionary activity across the north and a major trading post. After his death, Tryphon was canonized by the Russian Orthodox Church.

BIBLIOGRAPHY Serge Bolshakoff, *The Foreign Missions of the Russian Orthodox Church* (1943), pp. 54–55; James J. Stamoolis, *Eastern Orthodox Mission Theology Today* (1986), p. 27.

Paul D. Garrett

Tseng Pao Swen (Zeng Baosun) (1893–1978), Chinese Christian educator. Tseng Pao Swen was born in Hsiang Hsiang (Xiang Xiang), in Hunan Province to a prominent family; her great grandfather, Tseng Kuo-Fan, was a Confucian scholar and government official. While studying at Mary Vaughan High School for girls, she was deeply impressed by her principal, Louise Barnes, of the Church Missionary Society, and she converted to Christianity. In 1912, accompanied by Barnes, she went to London to study at Blackheath High School. She became the first Chinese woman to receive the Bachelor of Science degree with honors from Westfield College of the University of London. After receiving a year of teacher's training, she returned to China in 1917.

Determined to open a Christian school run by the Chinese, Tseng established I Fang Girls' Collegiate School in Changsha, the capital of Hunan Province. Staff and students organized the Scholars' Union, which decided the business of the school. During the May Fourth Movement of 1919, students boycotted Japanese goods. Although the school was occupied by the Communists in 1927 and later ruined by the Japanese army, Tseng reorganized it several times. She was a committee member of the National Christian Council of China, formed in 1922. In 1936, as a member of the Youth and Religion Movement team of the national YMCA, she went on a lecture tour to twelve cities in China. Concerned about women's status in China, she was involved in promoting women's education and welfare.

Tseng attended the International Missionary Conference (IMC) held in Jerusalem in 1928 and the Madras IMC meeting in 1938. She was also a delegate to the Institute of Pacific Relations Conference at Kyoto in 1929. In 1948 she was elected to the National Assembly. Moving to Taiwan in 1950, she became a member of the government's women's commission and represented the Republic of China on the women's committee of the United Nations in 1952. She published an autobiography and several essays on women's issues.

BIBLIOGRAPHY Tseng's works include *Zeng Baosun huiyilu* (The memoir of Zeng Baosun) (1970), "China's Women and Their Position in the Church," *Church Missionary Review* 48 (1917): 372–376, "Christianity and Women as Seen at the Jerusalem Meeting," *Chinese Recorder* 59 (1928): 443, and "The Chinese Woman, Past and Present," in *Symposium on Chinese Culture,* Sophia H. Chen Zen, ed. (1931). For a missionary's report on her school, see Winifred Galbraith, "An Experiment in Christian Education," *Chinese Recorder* 58 (1927): 425–430.

Kwok Pui-lan

Tsizehena, John (1840–1912), Malagasy Christian leader. Tsizehena came from the vicinity of Vohémar, on the east coast of Madagascar, where there was an Anglican mission. When he was 25, he had a severe illness and was thought to be dead. In that condition he received a vision in which he was told to go back to earth, for there was much work for him to do. He revived and was baptized in 1865. In 1884 French troops went to Vohémar, but then withdrew to Diego Suarez, in the far north of the island. Tsizehena and most of the other Christians of Vohémar went with them because of the good treatment the French had given. They settled in a village near Diego Suarez, in the wildest part of the island. They were far removed from the Anglican Church and so Tsizehena, an untrained layman, agreed to be their bishop. He began to spread the gospel through the district and established numbers of new churches, ordaining priests where needed. Thus evolved a strong church known as the Mission Lord Church, or the Diocese of the North, or the Northern Church of Madagascar. It followed the Anglican liturgy and hoped for Anglican help. A year before his death, Tsizehena received a visit from an Anglican bishop and put his church under Anglican control. In 1967 the Diego Suarez church had 4,000 members.

BIBLIOGRAPHY G. L. King, *A Self-Made Bishop: The Story of John Tsizehena, "Bishop of the North, D.D."* (1933).

Charles W. Forman

Tucker, Alfred Robert (1849–1914), first bishop of Uganda. Born in Woolwich, England, Tucker graduated from Oxford, was ordained in 1883, and went to East Africa as bishop in 1890. In 1891 Tucker arrived in Buganda (now Uganda) on the verge of civil war, with competing Muslim, Catholic, and Anglican factions. The whole region was in crisis as competing forms of colonialism threatened. Tucker vigorously promoted British support for the Protestant group in Buganda, and Captain Lugard of the Imperial British East Africa Company intervened decisively on their behalf with his Maxim machine gun. In 1893 the impending bankruptcy and withdrawal of the company provoked Tucker's return to England to garner support for the British government to retain Uganda. Having achieved this goal, Tucker was equally critical of the abuses of British colonialism. Impressed by the dynamic local leadership, Tucker ordained the first Ugandan clergy in 1893, and in 1897 proposed a radical constitution that would have integrated missionaries and Ugandans in a single church structure. He saw this as a fulfillment of Henry *Venn's ideal of a self-governing church. The missionaries were not so sanguine, being anxious to preserve their status and control; they appealed to Venn's clear separation of church and mission and to the mission's "euthanasia," rather than absorption into the church. After ten years of debate, a constitution was achieved for the "Native Anglican Church" of Uganda, giving it a measure of African responsibility and confidence that, despite the compromises, contrasted sharply with the more overtly paternalistic structures in neighboring Anglican churches. Tucker was tireless and enthusiastic in traveling, usually by foot, to oversee the newly established work in his vast diocese, which extended beyond the boundaries of Uganda. He was a man of boundless energy and optimism, a talented artist with the brush. He achieved so much despite the absence through ill-health of his wife, Josephine, who remained in England throughout his 18 years in Africa.

BIBLIOGRAPHY Tucker's own memoirs, in two volumes, are a vivid account: *Eighteen Years in Uganda and East Africa* (1908). Holger Hansen, *Mission, Church, and State in a Colonial Setting: Uganda, 1890–1925* (1984; a detailed analysis of church-state relations); A. P. Shepherd, *Tucker of Uganda: Artist and Apostle* (1929).

Kevin Ward

Tucker, Charlotte Maria (1821–1893), honorary Anglican missionary in North India. Born in England, the daughter of a family with extensive Indian connections, Tucker wrote books for children under the nom-de-plume A.L.O.E. (A Lady of England). She also edited the *Christian Juvenile Instructor.* Her brother Robert was killed in the Indian mutiny of 1857, and living with her mother, she cared for Robert's children for 18 years. In 1875, free of this responsibility but already 54, she went to India as an honorary missionary with the Indian Female Normal School Society, which in 1880 divided to become the Church of England Zenana Missionary Society (CEZMS) and the Zenana Bible and Medical Mission (interdenominational). Tucker, joining CEZMS, worked in Amritsar, Punjab, and Batala for ten years and used her literary gifts to write books which when translated were suitable for Indian women. In retirement she continued to live in India, where she died; she is buried in Amritsar. Her nephew, Frederick Tucker (see Frederick *Booth-Tucker), who married Emma Booth, was a pioneer Salvation Army missionary to India.

BIBLIOGRAPHY Agnes Gibane, *A Lady of England: The Life and Letters of Charlotte Maria Tucker* (1985); M. E. Gibbs, *The Anglican Church in India, 1600–1970* (1972); Jocelyn Murray, *Proclaim the Good News: A Short History of the Church Missionary Society* (1985); J. C. Pollock, *Shadows Fall Apart: The Story of the Zenana Bible and Medical Mission* (1958).

Jocelyn Murray

Tucker, Frederick St. George de Lautour. *See* Booth-Tucker, Frederick St. George de Lautour.

Tucker, Henry Carre (1812–1875), British civil servant in India. One of five sons of Henry St. George Tucker (a director of the East India Company) and educated at the company's Addiscombe and Haileybury colleges, Tucker displayed an evangelical zeal that far exceeded that of most of his associates and superiors, which put him out of step with the company's position of official neutrality in religion. He believed that India had been given to England as a "sacred trust," so early on he appealed at the highest level for official support to establish Christian vernacular schools at the provincial and district levels. His policy advocated "regeneration through European knowledge." In regard to the Indian Mutiny in 1857, he admitted as commissioner at Benares that, while "our Mission of light against darkness . . . , justice against tyranny and misrule," had seriously unsettled many Indian people prior to the mutinous outbreak, yet the "red line must advance on the moral and religious, as well as the political map." His brother Robert Tudor died in the rebellion. He gave generous financial support to Jay Narain's College at Benares and various mission projects. His sister Charlotte Maria (who published as A.L.O.E., "A Lady of England"), worked under the Church Missionary Society as a zenana missionary. In retirement (1860) Tucker devoted himself to promoting missions abroad and the cause of the poor at home. He died in England.

BIBLIOGRAPHY Tucker's principal mission writings were *Notes on Education* (1839), *A Letter to Lord Stanley* (1858), ed., *Conference on Missions, Held in 1860 at Liverpool* (1860), and *Thoughts on Poverty and Pauperism* (1871). J. P. Menge paid tribute to Tucker's work at Gorakhpur in *Church Missionary Register* (1849). Also see *Proceedings of the CMS,* vol. 23 (1854–1855); Edward Lake, "In Memoriam: Henry Carre Tucker," *Church Missionary Intelligencer* (1876): 15–21, 68–74; Peter Penner, *The Patronage Bureaucracy in North India: The Robert M. Merttins and James Thomason School, 1820–1870* (1986).

Peter Penner

Tucker, John Taylor (1883–1958), Congregational missionary to Angola. Tucker was born in Fremington, Devon, England. Educated at the Congregational College in Montreal, Canada, in 1912 he began more than 35 years of missionary service in Angola, serving under the Congregational Foreign Missionary Society of Canada (now a part of the United Church of Canada) in conjunction with the American Board of Commissioners for Foreign Missions (ABCFM). Gaining early fluency in Umbundu, he taught, wrote and assisted in Bible translation. Appointed first principal of the Currie Institute at Dôndi—the forerunner of Emmanuel Seminary (1947) and Emmanuel United Seminary (1957)—Tucker began to train Angolan pastors.

A member of the Phelps-Stokes Commission investigating educational needs in West and South Africa in 1922, Tucker became the most prominent Protestant missionary in church-state relations in colonial Angola. A member of the ABCFM's special commission to negotiate with the Portuguese on missionary matters, and since 1922 part-time secretary of the Missionary Conference of Angola, he worked to end forced labor and to promote the use of vernacular languages. Committed to united Christian witness, he led in the formation of the Aliança Evangélica de Angola, becoming its first full-time secretary in 1946. In 1949 he became the representative of all Angolan Protestant missions to the Portuguese government in Lisbon as director of the Liga Evangélica de Accão Missionária e Educational, and he became general secretary of the Aliança Evangélica Portuguesa in 1950.

BIBLIOGRAPHY *A Tucker Treasury: Reminiscences and Stories of Angola, 1883–1958* (1984) is a compilation by Catherine Tucker Ward of her father's writings. Other works by Tucker include *Drums in the Darkness* (1927), *Old Ways and New Days in Angola* [193?], *Angola: The Land of the Blacksmith Prince* (1933), *Currie of Chissamba* (1945), and *Compêndio de História de Missoñes* (1954). Lawrence W. Henderson, *The Church in Angola: A River of Many Currents* (1992) contains assessments of Tucker's ecumenical leadership.

Norman E. Thomas

Tucker, John Thomas (1818–1866), Church Missionary Society missionary evangelist and church builder in India. Tucker, from Dorset, England, was a qualified doctor, but does not seem to have followed his first profession while in India. Ordained in the Church of England while at the Church Missionary College, Islington, London (1841 and 1842), in mid-1842 he was sent to Paneivilei, south Tinnevelly, where he was to serve for almost 24 years. He is said to have baptized over 2,000 converts, in addition to the children of Christians. In 1866, when he died suddenly while on leave in England, almost 50 village churches had been established besides the large central church at Paneivilei. His work and that of T. G. *Ragland's North Tinnevelly Itinerant Mission together produced a strong Tamil-speaking Anglican Church, now a part of the Church of South India. Tucker's wife, Harriett, whom he married in 1842, and who survived him, organized and ran a large school for girls in Paneivilei.

BIBLIOGRAPHY CMS, *Register of Missionaries and Native Clergy* (1896); G. Pettitt, *Sowing and Reaping (A Memoir)* (1872).

Jocelyn Murray

Tucker, J. W. (1915–1964), missionary in Africa. Tucker was born in Lamar, Arkansas, and graduated from Southwestern Bible School in Enid, Oklahoma, in 1938. Tucker and his wife, Evangeline, received appointment as Assemblies of God missionaries and served in the Belgian Congo for over 25 years. The couple chose to remain there despite the dangers from the uprising after the granting of independence (1960), and Tucker was taken hostage in the city of Paulis. Fearful of an attack by American and Belgian paratroopers, Simba rebels hardened their attitudes toward the hostages. Tucker was clubbed to death and his body was later thrown into the crocodile-infested Bomokandi River. His wife and children, along with other missionaries, were later rescued by paratroopers.

BIBLIOGRAPHY Angeline Tucker, *He Is in Heaven* (1965); Derrill Sturgeon, "The Rest of the Story Must Be Told," *Mountain Movers,* May 1986, p. 11.

Gary B. McGee

Tule, Mary (Branton) (1860–1923), black Baptist missionary in Canada, South Africa, and Liberia. Born in Chatham, Canada West (now Ontario), Mary Branton joined the First Baptist Church, Amherstburg, as a teenager. In 1890 she became president of the Women's Home Mission Society of the Amherstburg Association. She went on to study at Spelman College in Atlanta, Georgia. As a National Baptist Convention missionary, Mary Branton taught in southern Africa from 1897 until 1911, when she married a South African, John Tule. She founded the Mary Branton Tule School in Cape Town in 1911.

During this period, the South African government implemented legislation that denied blacks the franchise and stripped them of their land. With her husband, Mary Tule vigorously condemned these racial policies. In 1922 the South African government barred Mary and John Tule from returning to the country after a speaking tour in Europe and North America. They went on to minister in Liberia instead, where Mary Tule established a school in Monrovia. She died in Liberia.

BIBLIOGRAPHY Dorothy Shadd Shreve, *Pathfinders of Liberty and Truth* (1940) and *The Afri-Canadian Church: A Stabilizer* (1983). See also Walter L. Williams, *Black Americans and the Evangelization of Africa, 1877-1900* (1982).

Paul R. Dekar

Tunggul Wulung, Kjai Ibrahim (c. 1800-1885), Javanese evangelist and mystic. Tunggul Wulung came to know the gospel from missionary J. E. *Jellesma in Mojowarno, East Java, in 1853 and became a fervent and independent itinerant evangelist. His name of honor, *Tunggul Wulung*, probably relates to East Javanese mythology, which continued to play a role in his religious thinking. He used Javanese poetry (*tembang*) and public debate with other teachers of Javanese wisdom in his evangelistic efforts.

Tunggul Wulung's origins were in the the Muria area of Central Java. The Mennonite missionary there, Pieter *Jansz, refused to baptize him. His baptism by Jellesma in 1854 was considered by Jansz and others premature because of Tunggul Wulung's alleged syncretism and his lack of biblical knowledge. Tunggul Wulung became well known when he established a Christian village by clearing woods at Bondo, near Jepara. His movement was joined by hundreds of people, who followed this charismatic leader partly because of certain eschatological expectations.

During his lifetime Tunggul Wulung traveled all over Java. He was influenced and respected by F. L. *Anthing, whom he visited several times. He was the guru and predecessor to *Sadrach Surapranata. After he died his movement merged with the congregations of the Mennonite missionaries in that area.

BIBLIOGRAPHY Philip van Akkeren, *Sri and Christ: A Study of the Indigenous Church in East Java* (1970), pp. 154-157; C. Guillot, *L'Affaire Sadrach: Un essai de christianisation à Java au XIXe siècle* (1981), pp. 88-95; A. G. Hoekema, "Kyai Ibrahim Tunggul Wulung (c. 1800-1885). 'Een Javaanse Apollos,'" *Nederlands Theologische Tijdschrift* 33 (1979): 89-110; Sutarman S. Partonadi, *Sadrach's Community and Its Contextual Roots: A Nineteenth Century Javanese Expression of Christianity* (1988), pp. 46-47, 60-62.

Alle G. Hoekema

Tupou, Taufa'ahau (*or* George) (1797-1893), king of Tonga. As the young chief of the Haapai Islands in Tonga, Tupou heard of the new religion, Christianity, and engaged as a teacher the recent Tongan chiefly convert Peter Vi. He then turned the old shrines into places for Christian worship. He was joined by the English Wesleyan missionary, John *Thomas, who baptized him as George in 1831. His faith was deepened by the emotional revival of the 1830s. In 1837 he conquered the main island of Tongatapu and in 1845 he inherited the highest title and was crowned king of Tonga by Thomas. The Wesleyan Church became the state church with the king as its head. He sent his own missionaries to Samoa to start the Wesleyan Methodist Church there. In Fiji he intervened with troops when the Fijian chief's forces were in serious jeopardy from non-Christian Fijian tribes, saving the day for the Christian community. At home he gave rights for the first time to commoners and provided land to every man.

He became fond of one of the missionaries, Shirley Baker, whom he made prime minister in 1880. But Baker had just been put out of the mission, and in retaliation Baker persuaded the king to start a new established church, the Free Church of Tonga, into which most of the people flocked. The kingdom remained religiously divided until long after Taufa'ahau's death.

BIBLIOGRAPHY Sione Latukefu, "King George Tupou I of Tonga," in *Pacific Islands Portraits*, J. W. Davidson and Deryck Scarr, eds. (1970); Noel Rutherford, *Shirley Baker and the King of Tonga* (1971).

Charles W. Forman

Turner, George (1818-1891), London Missionary Society (LMS) missionary to Samoa. Turner was born at Irvine, Ayrshire, Scotland, and attended the University of Glasgow and Presbyterian Relief Divinity Hall. Marrying Mary Anne Dunn in 1842, he briefly accompanied Henry *Nisbet in an unsuccessful mission to Tana, New Hebrides (Vanuatu). In 1844 he became the founding director of the Malua theological seminary, where pastor-teachers were prepared for Samoa and for Polynesian and Melanesian LMS outstations. He sailed in the mission's ships *Camden* and *John Williams* to settle and visit missionaries he had prepared. A linguist and scholar, Turner visited London in 1860 to prepare an annotated and revised second edition of the Samoan Bible for the press, and was honored by the University of Glasgow with its LL.D. His wife died in 1870, when he again visited England for the printing of a third revision. In 1872, he married Mary McNair, the widow of a missionary. He retired in 1882 because of declining health, but continued to produce Scripture commentaries in Samoan, published by the Religious Tract Society. Acknowledged as a formative participant in the growth of the LMS in Samoa, he died in London.

BIBLIOGRAPHY George Turner, *Nineteen Years in Polynesia* (1861) and *Samoa a Hundred Years Ago and Long Before* (1884). Richard Lovett, *The History of the London Missionary Society, 1795-1895* (1899). Turner materials are in the LMS South Sea collection at the SOAS, Univ. of London.

John Garrett

Turner, Harold W. (1911-), pioneer in the study of new religious movements (NRMs). Turner was born in Napier, New Zealand. After pastoral and university-related work in New Zealand and Great Britain, he encountered NRMs while teaching theology from 1955 at Fourah Bay College, Sierra Leone, and later at the University of Nigeria. Drawing on the work of phenomenologists, he defined

NRMs as a field of study and developed a theoretical framework. His comprehensive two-volume study of one of these movements, *African Independent Church* (1967), set a new standard. After 1970 he began documenting the phenomenon worldwide, producing a singular collection (now located at Selly Oak Colleges, Birmingham, England) of source materials on NRMs, resulting in the publication of a six-volume bibliography. His work demonstrated the importance of NRMs for the study of religion generally and for missiology. In 1989 Turner retired in Mt. Wellington, Auckland, New Zealand.

BIBLIOGRAPHY Turner's other major publications include "Tribal Religious Movements—New," *Encyclopædia Britannica,* vol. 18 (1974), pp. 697–705, *Bibliography of New Religious Movements in Primal Societies,* 6 vols. (1977–1992), *Religious Innovation in Africa: Collected Essays on New Religious Movements* (1978), *From Temple to Meeting House: The Phenomenology and Theology of Places of Worship* (1979), and "My Pilgrimage in Mission," *IBMR* 13 (1989): 71–74. See also A. F. Walls and W. R. Shenk, eds., *Exploring New Religious Movements: Essays in Honour of Harold W. Turner* (1990).

Wilbert R. Shenk

Turner, Henry McNeal (1834–1915), bishop in the African Methodist Episcopal Church, author, editor, human rights advocate, and fervent proponent of the "back to Africa" movement. Freeborn in South Carolina, Turner was a gifted speaker, largely self-educated. In 1848 he joined the Methodist Episcopal Church South and five years later was licensed as a lay exhorter to travel throughout the South preaching and evangelizing. In 1858 he joined the African Methodist Episcopal (AME) Church and the following year was assigned to the AME mission in Baltimore, which enabled him to enroll in Trinity College for divinity study, his first formal education. He was ordained a deacon in 1860 and an elder two years later. During the Civil War he helped recruit blacks as Union troops and was commissioned the first black army chaplain. Following the war he was sent to Georgia as a member of the reconstruction forces, but he resigned to recruit members for the AME Church in that state. He held a series of political offices in Georgia and in 1876 became director of the AME publishing house in Philadelphia. Four years later he was elected bishop of Georgia.

Turner regarded slavery as a part of the divine plan to bring Africans to America in order for them, in his words, to "come in contact with Christian civilization, and by intercourse with the powerful white race . . . fit themselves to go back to their own land and make of that land what the white man had made of Europe and of America." He contributed to African missions by founding the *Voice of Missions* (1892), promoting immigration of American blacks to Africa, and traveling there on four occasions in the 1890s to initiate and strengthen AME work. He founded AME annual conferences in Sierra Leone, Liberia, and South Africa. Disillusioned by the racism in the United States, he later moved to Windsor, Ontario, where he died.

BIBLIOGRAPHY Mongo M. Ponton, *Life and Times of Henry M. Turner* (1917); Edwin S. Redkey, *Black Exodus: Black Nationalists and Back-to-Africa Movements, 1890–1910* (1969); Edwin S. Redkey, ed., *Respect Black: The Writings and Speeches of Henry McNeal Turner* (1971); Walter L. Williams, *Black Americans and the Evangelization of Africa, 1877–1900* (1982).

Alan Neely

Turquetil, Arsène (1876–1955), French Catholic missionary and bishop in the Canadian arctic. Turquetil was born at Reviers, Calvados, France, and joined the Oblates of Mary Immaculate in 1896. In 1899, immediately after his ordination, he was sent to the Canadian Northwest. He served among the Déné Indians, at Caribou Lake, Saskatchewan, from 1900 to 1912. He first made contact with the Inuit in 1901 and briefly lived among them in 1907. In 1911 Ovide Charlebois, vicar-apostolic of Keewatin, sent him to explore around Hudson Bay. One year later, he founded the Inuit mission of Chesterfield Inlet, where he celebrated the first baptisms in 1917. He was named vicar-apostolic of Hudson Bay in 1931 and ordained bishop the next year. He continued to reside at Chesterfield Inlet until 1930, when he moved his residence to Churchill, in northern Manitoba. In 1943 he retired to the Oblate Scholasticate in Washington, D.C. He is author of *Grammaire en Esquimaux* and several articles on his missionary experience.

BIBLIOGRAPHY Michael Devaney, *Arctic Apostle: Life of Bishop Arsène Turquetil* (1959); Adrien-Gabriel Morice, *Thawing out the Eskimo* (1943). Reports by Turquetil of his work can be found in *Missions OMI,* vols. 50, 52, 54, 65, 66, and 71, *Missions Catholiques,* vols. 44, 48, and 49 and *Anthropos,* vol. 21. Archival material is in the Oblate Deschâtelets Archives, Ottawa.

Achiel Peelman, OMI

Turton, William (c. 1760–1817), Methodist missionary to the Bahamas. The son of a Barbados planter, Turton was the first Methodist to preach in Tobago, beginning as a lay volunteer. When French occupation of the island forced his departure in 1796, he went to Saint Bartholomew. He received ordination and was appointed to the Bahamas in 1799. His work in Nassau on the island of New Providence was successful among both blacks and whites. He used his small private fortune to build a chapel, but later needed to start a school as a source of income. Granted an assistant for the New Providence circuit in 1805, Turton extended his work to Harbour Island and Eleuthera. In 1807 his wife died; he himself was ill and went to the United States to recuperate. He returned to the Bahamas with his second wife after some months. The Bahamas were made a separate Methodist District in 1811, with Turton as chairman. The 1818 Methodist conference obituary calls Turton a "man of colour," and he was thus described in the first edition of G. G. Findlay's *Wesley's World Parish.* Turton's widow protested the description to Findlay, who finding no other reference to Turton as a man of mixed race, concluded that the Conference record was in error.

BIBLIOGRAPHY George G. Findlay, *Wesley's World Parish: A Sketch of the Hundred Years' Work of the Wesleyan Methodist Mission-*

ary Society (1913?); George G. Findlay and W. W. Holdsworth, *The History of the Wesleyan Methodist Missionary Society,* vol. 2 (1921–1924).

Martha Lund Smalley

Tyler, Josiah (1823–1895), American missionary to South Africa. Son of the president of Dartmouth College, Tyler was born in Hanover, New Hampshire. A graduate of Amherst College (1845) and East Windsor Theological Seminary (1848), he married Susan W. Clark on February 27, 1849, was ordained the next day, and sailed for South Africa a few weeks later under the American Board of Commissioners for Foreign Missions (ABCFM). The Tylers were just two of a larger number of notable recruits who sailed together for the Zulu mission in Natal and who helped bring about a period of rapid growth. Tyler was stationed for much of the time at Esidumbini, and his experiences are described in his book *Forty Years among the Zulus* (1891). During his last years in Africa his health was poor, but his zeal for the work was great. He was a notably effective missionary speaker, and a week before his death he delivered an address at the Congress on Africa held in Atlanta, Georgia.

BIBLIOGRAPHY *Missionary Herald* 92 (1896): 53–54 (obit.). Earlier indexed volumes contain many excerpts from his letters.

David M. Stowe

Tyndale-Biscoe, Cecil Earle (1863–1949), Church Missionary Society (CMS) missionary headmaster in Kashmir. Tyndale-Biscoe was one of several outstanding sportsmen converted during D. L. *Moody's 1883 mission to Cambridge. After ordination and a curacy, he volunteered to CMS, arriving in 1891 in Srinagar, Kashmir, where a school for boys had recently been started. He immediately set about reorganizing the school on English public school lines, with a strong emphasis on games, swimming, and public service. A western uniform replaced Kashmiri dress. In Srinagar itself he became a well-known force for reform and morality. He served as headmaster in Srinagar until India's independence, and at the end of 1946 retired in Southern Rhodesia (Zimbabwe).

BIBLIOGRAPHY C. E. Tyndale-Biscoe, *Tyndale-Biscoe of Kashmir: An Autobiography* (1951) and *Character-Building in Kashmir* (1920). See also E. D. Tyndale-Biscoe, *Fifty Years against the Stream: The Story of a School in Kashmir* (1930).

Jocelyn Murray

U

Uchimura, Kanzo (1861–1930), foremost leader of the Non-Church (Mukyokai) movement in early Japanese Protestantism. Uchimura did not reject the Christian church as such but developed a nonsacramental, largely nonliturgical mode of church life in implied criticism of historic Western Christianity. Independence rather than rejection was his positive contribution, and his influence upon the whole Christian church in Japan was second to none, as was his influence upon many intellectual leaders of modern Japan.

Like other leaders of nascent Protestantism, Uchimura was born in a samurai family that had supported the Tokugawa regime, and he turned to Western studies as the best avenue to employment. This orientation did not alter Uchimura's independent but passionately intense kind of patriotism directed to the welfare of the whole nation. His Christian faith led him to put Jesus first, but Japan followed a close second.

Born in Edo (Tokyo) in the compound of the daimyo (feudal lord) of Takasaki, Uchimura was sent to the capital of his clan to begin his education at the age of six. Showing unusual ability to learn languages, he returned to Tokyo at the age of 11 to begin English language studies in earnest. At 13 he entered the Gaikoku Gogaku (Foreign language school) with intent to enter government service, all with the warm support of his parents. With their permission, Uchimura gained admission in 1877 to the newly opened Sapporo Agriculture College (now Hokkaido University), where most lectures were in English. This was the year following the eight-month pioneering presence of William S. *Clark. Under his influence and that of Merriman C. *Harris, the whole first-year class was baptized by the latter the night before Uchimura arrived. Uchimura could not but be influenced by this highly charged atmosphere, but with his customary independence he delayed request for baptism until June 1878.

Uchimura was graduated in 1881 but not without some altercations with Harris, who served as the leader of a church formed by the new students and a few adults. As a result, he and "seven brothers" formed an independent church that became the pattern for his later Non-Church assemblies. After several years of study in the United States, Uchimura returned to Japan in 1888 to teach in a number of schools, from each of which he resigned over disagreement on principles. The most famous incident was when, in 1891, as a teacher at the First Higher School in Tokyo, he refused to bow before the signature of the emperor affixed to a copy of the new Imperial Rescript on Education. He later changed his mind and from a sickbed sent a colleague to bow for him, but the affair effectually ended his educational career.

Uchimura turned to writing and found that as an essayist he could gain readers. By 1897 he had become senior editor of the *Yorozu Choho* (Myriad reports) with outstanding success. In 1900 he began his own magazine *Seisho no Kenkyu* (Bible study), of which 357 issues were published before his death. At the same time Uchimura started teaching the Bible on Sundays at the request of his friend from Hokkaido days, Nitobe Inazo, then president of the First Higher School. From these two activities emerged both the still thriving Non-Church movement and Uchimura's abiding influence upon the whole of Japanese Christianity.

BIBLIOGRAPHY Richard H. Drummond, *A History of Christianity in Japan* (1972); John F. Howes, "Uchimura Kanzo," *Encyclopedia of Japan* (1983); Raymond P. Jennings, *Jesus, Japan, and Kanzo Uchimura* (1958); Hiroshi Miura, *The Life and Thought of Kanzo Uchimura, 1861–1930* (1997).

Richard H. Drummond

Uemura, Masahisa (1858–1925), foremost representative of the Presbyterian-Reformed tradition in the early history of Protestant Christianity in Japan. Like many others in the leadership of the first generation, Uemura was born in a family of samurai class that had supported the Tokugawa regime. As part of the losing side vis-à-vis the new Meiji government, the family moved to Yokohama, where Uemura helped to support his family and earn school expenses by raising pigs and tutoring. He turned toward Western studies and at age 15 entered the *juku* (private school) conducted by the American missionary J. H. Ballagh and later studied under Samuel R. *Brown.

Uemura was never graduated from any school, but in this period he laid the foundation for a remarkable breadth of knowledge that he nourished throughout his life by extensive reading in English, Chinese, and Japanese. The subsequent life and career of Uemura were affected even more by the faith and personal character of the missionaries under whom he studied. A religious atmosphere surrounded the entire program of instruction, and supported as it was by the life commitment and noble conduct of the teachers, it deeply moved the mind and heart of Uemura, as it did many other Japanese youths in these schools.

Uemura was baptized in 1873 at age 16 and almost at once committed himself to the life of a Christian evangelist. In 1877 he entered the new theological seminary that had been opened in the foreign settlement of Tsukiji in Tokyo. In the same year he started a preaching place in the city, the first instance of formal Protestant evangelism conducted primarily under Japanese responsibility. Characteristic of Uemura's spiritual independence was his concern, while holding firmly to classical expressions of Protestantism, to find something of the history of salvation in his own pre-Christian religious experience, as in that of his own people. Thus he came to regard Neo-Confucian *bushido* (the way of the warrior) as a gift of God to Japan and a veritable Old Testament.

Uemura remained in Tokyo after leaving the seminary, and later, as pastor of what became the citadel of Presbyterian-Reformed faith in Japan, Fujimicho Church, he found the base for his increasingly extensive and influential Christian service. He began to write for periodicals and in 1890 founded the bi-monthly magazine *Nihon Hyoron* (Japan review), which did much to introduce Christian concepts of humanity, society, literature, and art to the educated public. His first important theological work, *Shinri Ippan,* was published in 1884. He also became a member of the Old Testament translation committee and cooperated in the preparation of the first joint Protestant hymnal. He taught in the theological department of Meiji Gakuin, even as he continued in his growing pastoral work and participation in the organizational development of the Nihon Kirisuto Kyokai (Church of Christ in Japan).

In 1901, Uemura and Ebina Danjo entered into a theological debate that was carried on for several months in the pages of the journals of which the men were respectively editors. The main points of difference concerned the doctrines of the incarnation and redemption. Ebina emphasized the role of Jesus as teacher and example rather than as divine redeemer. While recognizing the human elements in the historical development of Christianity, Uemura preferred to see its origin in divine revelation and stressed the work of God in the entire Christ event. Over against Ebina's leaning toward an adoptionist view of Jesus as the Christ, Uemura believed in his deity, in a literal incarnation of the pre-existent Christ. He saw Jesus Christ as a proper object of worship, the risen, ever-living Savior to whom believers may properly pray. Uemura's clear and forceful expression of what was classical Protestant orthodoxy in his time helped to fashion and strengthen what came to be the main stream of Japanese Protestant theology for most of the twentieth century.

BIBLIOGRAPHY Richard H. Drummond, *A History of Christianity in Japan* (1972); Charles H. Germany, *Protestant Theologies in Modern Japan* (1965); Charles W. Iglehart, *A Century of Protestant Christianity in Japan* (1959); Irvin Scheiner, *Christian Converts and Social Protest in Meiji Japan* (1970); Winburn T. Thomas, *Protestant Beginnings in Japan* (1959).

Richard H. Drummond

Ulfila (*or* Ulphilas; Wulfila) (c. 311–383), apostle of the Goths. Ulfila's Cappadocian maternal grandparents were taken as captives into Gothic Dacia (now Romania); he was probably the son of a Cappadocian mother and a Gothic father. Educated at Constantinople, he was consecrated a bishop about 341 by the Arian bishop of the capital, Eusebius of Nicomedia. Ulfila went west as a missionary to the Goths, first to those around the Danube, outside the empire. Driven out after seven years, he settled with his followers among the Goths in Moesia (now Bulgaria). He devised a writing system for Gothic, drawing on Greek and Latin letters and Gothic runes. He and his circle translated much of the Scripture; apparently he excluded the book of Kings from the Old Testament to avoid encouraging Gothic warlike culture. His influence led to the conversion of many Gothic and Germanic tribes. Ulfila's work left the Roman Catholic Church in the fifth and sixth centuries with the problem of Arian communities spread throughout various regions, particularly Spain, France, Germany, northern Italy, and parts of eastern Europe.

BIBLIOGRAPHY George Friedrichsen, *The Gothic Version of the Gospels* (1926) and *The Gothic Version of the Epistles* (1939); Peter Heather and John Matthews, eds., *The Goths in the Fourth Century* (1991); Bruce Metzger, *The Early Versions of the New Testament* (1977); Philostorgius, *Ecclesiastical History* 2.5; E. A. Thompson, *The Visigoths in the Time of Ulfila* (1966).

Frederick W. Norris

Underhill, Edward Bean (1813–1901), British Baptist missionary statesman. Underhill became joint secretary of the Baptist Missionary Society (BMS) in 1849. He assumed responsibility for the foreign affairs of the society at a time when support for the BMS in the churches was at a low ebb. His first five years were accordingly devoted to reestablishing the confidence of Baptists in the society and placing its finances on a firmer footing. In 1854 he left for India, where he spent two and a half years seeking to revitalize the first and most important field of the BMS and promote greater self-sufficiency in the churches. A second missionary tour, to the West Indies in 1859 and 1860, had even more far-reaching consequences. He published his conclusions in *The West Indies: Their Social and Religious Condition* (1862). In 1865 he wrote a public letter urging government action to remedy the economic distress of the former slave population in Jamaica which contributed to unrest that culminated in the Morant Bay uprising. Much controversy in Britain followed over the brutal suppression administered by Governor Eyre, who had unjustly blamed Underhill for the disturbances. Underhill also visited the Cameroons in 1869–1870.

Underhill retired from his position in the BMS in 1876 but remained as honorary secretary until his death. His publications include biographies of the BMS missionaries James *Phillippo and Alfred *Saker.

BIBLIOGRAPHY *Missionary Herald* (1901): 347–353 (obit.); E. A. Payne, *The Great Succession: Leaders of the Baptist Missionary Society During the Nineteenth Century* (1938), pp. 29–39; Brian Stanley, *The History of the Baptist Missionary Society, 1792–1992* (1992). Underhill's papers are preserved in the BMS archives at Regent's Park College, Oxford.

Brian Stanley

Underwood, Horace Grant (1859-1916), pioneer Presbyterian missionary in Korea. Born in London, Underwood immigrated with his family to the United States in 1872. He graduated from New York University and New Brunswick Theological Seminary and was ordained to the Dutch Reformed ministry (1884). Appointed by the Presbyterian Board of Missions to Korea, he arrived there on Easter Sunday, 1885, with his friends the Rev. and Mrs. Henry G. *Appenzeller of the Methodist Episcopal Mission. He opened a Christian orphanage in Seoul, which was to become the John D. Wells Academy for Boys (1886), founded the Saemunan Presbyterian Church (1887), established the Korean Tract Society (1888), published the first Korean hymnal (1896), and chaired the board of translators of the Scriptures into Korean until his death. In Seoul in 1889 he married Lillias Stirling Horton (1851–1921), then a physician to the Korean queen, and they had one son, Horace Horton Underwood (1890–1951), who followed his parents into Korean mission work; three of his grandsons and one great-grandson also became missionaries to Korea. In 1891 Underwood helped persuade his mission to adopt John L. *Nevius's plan for self-government, self-support, and self-propagation of newly established churches. Underwood helped organize the Seoul branch of the YMCA, founded the Pierson Bible Institute (now Pierson University), and in 1916 founded the Chosen Union Christian College, which is now Yonsei University in Seoul. He died in Atlantic City, New Jersey.

BIBLIOGRAPHY Horace G. Underwood, *A Concise Dictionary of the Korean Language* (1890), *An Introduction to the Korean Spoken Language* (1890), *The Call of Korea* (1908), and *The Religions of Eastern Asia* (1910). Lillias H. Underwood, *Fifteen Years among the Top-Knots* (1904), *With Tommy Tompkins in Korea* (1905), and *Underwood of Korea* (1918).

James M. Phillips

Upadhyaya, Brahmabandhav (1861-1907), leading indigenizer of Christianity in India. Named at birth Bhawani Charan Banerjea Upadhyaya, and growing up in a high caste Bengali Brahmin family, Upadhyaya only gradually approached Christianity, attracted by the sinless life of Jesus. In 1891 he was baptized, first as an Anglican, and then six months later as a Roman Catholic. At baptism he took the name Brahmabandhav, by which he has always been known. Soon he cast aside his European clothes, took the saffron robe of a sannyasin and began to travel over India, teaching and preaching, receiving his livelihood by begging.

His lifelong concern was to rethink Christianity in such a way as to make it acceptable to India. His first move was to emphasize the theistic passages in the Vedas, claiming that ancient India was monotheistic. This, he believed, was India's natural foundation for the revealed religion of Christianity. He attacked polytheism, pantheism, reincarnation, and idolatry as aberrations that had crept into Hinduism. He insisted that Christianity was not the destroyer but the perfecter and purifier of Hinduism.

About 1898 he settled in Calcutta and became active in the nationalist movement centered there. He also moved closer to Hinduism, calling himself a Hindu, stating that he was by birth a Hindu but by his sacramental rebirth a Catholic Christian. He returned to the observance of caste and social distinctions in eating. He attempted to blend Christian theology with Vedantist philosophy, maintaining that the usual interpretation of the Vedantist belief about this world being an illusion was a mistaken interpretation. The real meaning of this belief was that this world has only conditional existence, while God alone has necessary existence. The Hindu avatars, he thought, could be accepted because they were not incarnations but only temporary manifestations of divine power.

In his last years Brahmabandhav even incorporated into his Christianity the worship of some of the Hindu gods and goddesses as attributes of God. He also began to attack bitterly the Western missionaries. As a result of these moves, the apostolic delegate attacked him and told the Catholics of India that they could not subscribe to his journal, *Sophia.* His political writings also stirred opposition, in this case from the British rulers. He was arrested and would have been sent to jail had he not died suddenly during an operation.

BIBLIOGRAPHY B. Animananda, *Swami Upadyay Brahmabandhav* (1908); Kaj Baago, *Pioneers of Indigenous Christianity* (1969), pp. 26–49, 118–150; *The Blade: Life and Work of Brahmabandhav Upadyay* (1945).

Charles W. Forman

Urban VIII (1568-1644), pope and promoter of missions. Urban VIII (r. 1623–1644) was born Maffeo Barberini into a wealthy commercial family in Florence. He studied first at the Roman College and then at the University of Pisa, where he obtained a doctor of laws degree in 1589. He entered the papal diplomatic service and in 1604 was consecrated titular archbishop of Nazareth and became nuncio to France. In 1606 he became bishop of

Spoleto and in 1617 prefect of the Segnatura. In 1621 he promoted as a papal candidate Alessandro Ludovisi (who became *Gregory XV), and he was elected as his successor in 1623.

Although remembered for his nepotism (his brother and two nephews were created cardinals) and for enriching his family with papal revenues, his personal moral life was beyond reproach. He both furthered the reform of the church and promoted missions enthusiastically. He reformed the Roman Breviary and reformulated the procedures for canonization, for the first time reserving the right of beatification to the Holy See. He enforced the decree of Trent requiring all diocesan bishops to reside in their sees. He approved a number of new religious orders, including the Congregation of the Mission (Vincentians). Urban had served in the first Propaganda Fide and he consolidated and secured its foundation early on in his papacy. In 1627 he founded the Collegium Romanum, completely renovating the palazzo in which it was housed and seeing to the endowment of scholarships for students from outside Europe. He created many new dioceses and vicariates apostolic and was solicitous for Catholic and Uniat minorities in the Turkish Empire and Persia. Many important events in missionary history occurred during his pontificate, including the entry of the Jesuits into Paraguay, the arrival of the Jesuits in Peking (Beijing), and the martyrdom of Christians in Japan.

BIBLIOGRAPHY Urban's *acta* may be found in the *Magnum Bullarium Romanum,* vols. 13–15. The English translation of Ludwig von Pastor, *History of the Popes* (1938), devotes two volumes to him (vols. 28–29). Biographies include A. Nicoletti, *Vita di Papa Urbano VIII: Storia del suo pontificato* (the MS is held in the Vatican library) and W. N. Weech, *Urban VIII* (1905).

Robert J. Schreiter, CPPS

Urdaneta, Andres de (1508–1568), navigator, cosmographer, friar and missionary. Urdaneta was born in Guipúzcoa, Spain. As a soldier he joined Garcia de Loaysa's expedition to the Moluccas in 1525, remaining there until 1535 and returning to Spain, via India and Portugal, in 1537, with a wealth of knowledge of peoples and lands. From 1538 to 1552 he held important administrative positions in Mexico, where he became an Augustinian friar in 1553. Philip II requested him to join Miguel López de Legazpi's expedition that set sail from the port of Navidad, Mexico, for the Philippines in 1564. Urdaneta was the unofficial pilot and navigator. He was also the superior of four Augustinians traveling with him. The expedition's purpose was to conquer and evangelize the Philippines and discover the return route across the Pacific. By April of 1565 they were in Cebu, Philippines. Urdaneta sailed for Mexico in the summer of the same year and arrived in Acapulco in October, finding in the process the return route from Manila to Acapulco. He continued on to Spain in 1566 to inform Philip II of what he had found. He then returned to Mexico and died in Mexico City.

BIBLIOGRAPHY Mariano Cuevas, *Monje y marino: La vida y los tiempos de Fr. Andrés de Urdaneta* (1943); Mairin Mitchell, *Friar Andres de Urdaneta, O.S.A. (1508–1568): Pioneer of Pacific Navigation from West to East* (1964); Isacio Rodríguez, *Historia de la Provincia Agustiniana del Smo. Nombre de Jesús de Filipinas: I bibliografía* (1965); Fermin Uncilla, *Urdaneta y la conquista de Filipinas* (1907).

Lucio Gutiérrez, OP

Urios, Saturnino (1843–1916), Jesuit missionary to the Philippines. Born in Játiva, Spain, Urios was sent to the Philippine Jesuit missions in 1874. Assigned to Agusan, Mindanao, he consolidated the initial efforts of his fellow Jesuits to Christianize the indigenous Manubu tribes, founding within the year fourteen settlements on both banks of the Agusan River (now the municipalities of Southern and Northern Agusan), earning the title Apostle of Agusan. In 1891 he was assigned to the Tagoloan mission in north central Mindanao, where he followed the same method of resettling the unbaptized Bukidnon tribes in permanent communities. The next year, he was assigned to Davao, in southeastern Mindanao, where he had to change his methods because the people had undergone some training in Islam. But he held to his principle that charity and patience were the only tools of the true Christian missionary. Time and love, he believed, would prepare the people to accept Christianity and the principles of authority essential in any well-ordered society. In 1900, when the Americans arrived, local hostility turned to friendly welcome after Urios assured the people that the Americans had come in good will.

BIBLIOGRAPHY Urios's letters are in various collections of Jesuit missionary reports: *Cartas de los PP. de la Compañía de Jesús de la Misión de Filipinas* (1876–1895); *Cartas de la Asistencia de España* (1904–); *Cartas y noticias edificantes de la Provincia de Aragón* (1909–), especially vol. 16, pp. 39–42. Ventura Pasual y Beltran, *Un Apostol de Civilización: El R. P. Saturnino Urios, S. J.* (1921); José S. Arcilla, "Urios and the Bagani of Agusan, 1875–1900," in *Kinaadman,* vol. 6 (1984), pp. 235–247 and *Kabar Seberang Maphilindo,* vols. 10–11 (1982), pp. 48–58. See also Pablo Pastells, *Mision de la Compañía de Jesús en Filipinas en el Siglo XIX,* (3 vols., 1916–1917); Horacio de la Costa, *Light Cavalry* (1942), pp. 162–172, 333–345.

José S. Arcilla, SJ

Urlsperger, Johann August (1728–1806), a founder of the Deutsche Christentumsgesellschaft. Urlsperger was the son of Samuel Urlsperger, Lutheran minister at Augsburg, Bavaria, and one of the early supporters of the Danish-Halle mission in South India. After studying theology at Tübingen and Halle, Urlsperger joined his father in his ministry at Augsburg. During extended journeys through Germany, Switzerland, and England, he established contacts with other friends who also attempted to extend the authentic pietist concern for a renewal of Christianity into the new age of deism and rationalism. A pietist "association of good friends" was founded at Basel in 1756, and similar groups of clerics and laypeople expressed sympathy. In August 1780 a new German Christian Association (Deutsche Christentumsgesellschaft, later known simply as Christentumsgesellschaft) was established, with headquarters at Basel, with members all over German-speaking Europe, and correspondents elsewhere. Branch associations came into being in several towns in Germany and Switzerland. But Urlsperger's ambitious program of "combatting unbelief on a theological and philosophical basis" tended to be supplanted by involvement in a variety of Christian enterprises in an ecumenical spirit, resulting in his gradual withdrawal from the association. It was left to Karl F. A. *Steinkopf, the first full-time secretary, and Christian F. *Spittler to bring the missionary potential of the association to full fruition by founding the Basel Mission in 1815.

BIBLIOGRAPHY Erich Schick, *Vorboten und Bahnbrecher* (1943), pp. 188–202; Horst Weigelt, "J. A. Urlsperger" (unpublished diss., Erlangen, 1961).

Hans-Werner Gensichen

Vahl, Jens (1828–1898), Danish missionary leader and statistician. Vahl was born in Aalborg, Denmark, and served throughout his career as a parish minister. In 1858 he helped found a tract society, and he served on the boards of the Lutheran deaconess organization and the Evangelical Alliance. He was also a warm supporter of missions to seamen. From 1870 he was on the board of the Danish Missionary Society, serving as its chair from 1889 to his death. From 1860 Vahl published a journal (in which prominence was given to missionary information), an atlas of missions, and an annual survey, *Missions to the Heathen.* On his death, his great mission library was purchased by the state and placed in the Aarhus city library.

BIBLIOGRAPHY *Kirke-Leksikon for Norden,* vol. 4 (1929), pp. 730–731.

Eric J. Sharpe

Valadés, Diego (1533–c. 1582), Mexican-born chronicler of culture and mission in New Spain. Son of a Spanish conquistador and a Tlaxacaltec woman, Valadés was one of the first American mestizos received into the Franciscan order. Besides Spanish and Latin, he spoke several indigenous languages—Nahuatl, Tarasco, and Otomí. His *Retórica Christiana* (1579), with more than two dozen drawings of Indian temples, ceremonies, dress, and adornment, was one of the first books published in Spain by a Mexican, and though some of the drawings were misleading, they contributed to shaping early concepts in Europe about Native American culture. Included in the *Retórica* is a historical chapter of events and observations by Valadés of the early missionary work done by the friars in Mexico.

BIBLIOGRAPHY E. J. Palomera, *Fray Diego Valadés: El hombre y su época* (1963) and *Fray Diego Valadés, OFM: Evangelizador humanista de la Nueva España* (1988).

Alan Neely

Valdivia, Luis de (1561–1642), Spanish Jesuit missionary in colonial Chile. Born in Granada, Valdivia entered the Society of Jesus in 1581 and was sent to Peru in 1589. He taught in Lima, served as master of novices, and then was sent to Chile in 1593. He helped organize the Jesuit missions among the Araucanian Indians and soon became their defender. He fought to put an end to personal service and expounded the thesis that the Spanish should be restricted to defensive war and not be allowed to cross the Bío Bío River, which separated the Indians from the Europeans. He pleaded his cause in Spain in 1609 and returned to Chile with religious jurisdiction over the Araucanians. In 1612 he was also named visitor general of Chile, but in 1620 he returned to Spain under pressure. He also wrote a grammar, a dictionary, and a catechism in the Araucanian language.

BIBLIOGRAPHY Beatrice Blum, "Luis de Valdivia, Defender of the Araucanians," *Mid-America* 24 (1942): 109–137; Walter Hanisch, *Historia de la Compañía de Jesús en Chile* (1974); Eugene Korth, *Spanish Policy in Colonial Chile: The Struggle for Social Justice, 1535–1700* (1968).

Jeffrey Klaiber, SJ

Valdivieso, Antonio de (d. 1550), Spanish Dominican missionary and third bishop of Nicaragua and Costa Rica. The first two Catholic bishops of Nicaragua and Costa Rica were short lived, and their deaths left the diocese without leadership for almost eight years. Valdivieso governed the diocese from 1544 in a turbulent situation that strongly affected the life of the church and the defense of the rights of the Indians. Much of the territory of the Province of Nicaragua was controlled by the clan of Rodrigo de Contreras. Valdivieso attempted to reform the situation gradually but found himself pressed into defending the poor and oppressed Indians. A year after entering his diocese, he joined with Bartolomé de *Las Casas, bishop of Chiapas, in making clear to civil-religious authorities in Spain that he was committed to justice for the oppressed. The focal point of the conflict lay in implementation of Leyes Nuevas (new laws) (1542), measures of the Crown intended to reduce the slavery of the Indians. Contreras attempted to argue the case of the *encomienda* landowners against Valdivieso in Spain before the Council of the Indies. When he lost his appeal, the encomenderos in Nicaragua rebelled against Spanish authority, looted the city of León, and murdered Valdivieso. He became the first bishop-martyr for justice to the oppressed in the Americas.

BIBLIOGRAPHY Manzar Foroohar, *The Catholic Church and Social Change in Nicaragua* (1989); Edgar Zúñiga, *Historia eclesiástica de Nicaragua, pt. 1* (1983).

Edward L. Cleary, OP

Valencia, Martín de (1473–1534), Spanish Franciscan pioneer missionary in Mexico. An intensive participant in the Franciscan mystical-spiritual reform movement in southern Spain at the beginning of the sixteenth century, Valencia was named by the general of his order, Francisco de Quiñones, to choose twelve missionaries to evangelize New Spain (Mexico). Preceded only by two priests close to the family of the conqueror Hernán Cortés and three Franciscans from Flanders, Valencia elected like-minded colleagues, mostly from his convent, San Gabriel of Extremadura. They were known as the twelve apostles to Mexico for their extraordinary dedication and self-sacrificing labors. In his first discourse to the Indians after his arrival (1524), Valencia declared, "God sent us from faraway lands not for gold or silver, nor earthly possessions, but to seek your salvation." The Indians, after some years, testified of the Franciscans, "Because they are poor and barefoot, as we are, they eat what we eat, they sit on the ground as we do, they converse in humility with us, they love us as their children, we love and seek them as fathers." Yet the friars were rigorous with the Indians: corporal punishment was sometimes prescribed for sins, temples and idols were destroyed, and ascetic practices were required. Each convent was simple, serving as a center for mission expansion and featuring a school for children, who were then used to reach the adults. The priests learned the languages, published grammars and religious tracts, preached, and baptized. In 1531, Valencia wrote to his general, "It is no exaggeration to say that we have now baptized over a million Indians." Shortly after his death, his fellow apostle Toribio *Motolinia testified that by 1535 it was five million.

BIBLIOGRAPHY There exists a brief biography of Martín de Valencia written in Spanish by his colleague Francisco de Jiménez. References in English histories of Mexico are brief. See William H. Prescott, *History of the Conquest of Mexico,* vol. 3 (1875). An excellent study is Mariano Cuevas, *Historia de la Iglesia en Mexico,* vol. 1 (1946), particularly for its extensive quotations from primary sources.

Sidney H. Rooy

Valentinus (d. 475), apostle of Noricum. Valentinus is remembered as a missionary bishop in Passau and Rätien, in the Roman province of Noricum (area, more or less, of modern Austria). Little is known of his life; medieval legends grew up around him. Venantius Fortunatus (d. c. 610), bishop of Poitiers, France, founded a number of churches in Tirol that were dedicated to Valentinus. He is buried in the church at Zenoburg near Meran, Italy.

BIBLIOGRAPHY *Eugippius: The Life of Saint Severin,* Ludwig Bieler with Ludmilla Kerstan, trs., *The Fathers of the Church* 55 (1965).

Frederick W. Norris

Valignano, Alessandro (1539–1606), organizer of the Jesuit mission in Japan and China, patron of Matteo *Ricci. Valignano was a brilliant Italian aristocratic and worldly student of canon law. After a profound religious conversion he entered the Society of Jesus in 1566. At an extraordinary early age, in 1573, he was made Visitor to the East, the Jesuit official who, when in the field, directed all Jesuit missions from Ethiopia to Japan.

Valignano from the beginning insisted on the autonomy of the society over against the Portuguese authorities, royal and ecclesiastical, in Lisbon and in Asia. For nine years he traveled his vast region, attempting to understand the problems and opportunities facing the Jesuits in widely differing situations. From 1579 to 1582 he was in Japan, where he articulated his fundamental ideas on the nature of mission. They are laid out in a form appropriate to Japan in his *Il Ceremoniale per i Missionari del Giappone* (1581), which was written with assistance from leading Japanese Christians. Its philosophic basis was that Japanese society and culture provided a base upon which Christianity could build, so that the church would be Japanese, not Portuguese or Spanish. He later made the same judgment about China.

After several years in India, Valignano went to Macao in 1588, after which he was responsible for the Jesuits in China and Japan only. During two further visits to Japan (1590–1592 and 1598–1603), his diplomatic skills sorted out difficulties with successive dictators, first Oda Nobunaga, and then Toyotomi Hideyoshi.

It was Valignano who instructed *Ruggieri and *Ricci, the first missionaries to be allowed to stay in Ming China, to translate the key texts of Confucian philosophy and to study them so as to be able to enter the world of the Confucian literati who had administered China for centuries. Ricci performed this task so well that he was accepted by the literati as one of themselves. Valignano approved of Ricci and the other Jesuits dressing as literati, the outward form of their attempt to create a Chinese Christianity that would adopt Confucian thought much as *Thomas Aquinas had adopted the thought of Aristotle. Valignano died at Macao while preparing to visit Ricci, who had gained the emperor's tacit approval for the mission and was allowed to stay in the imperial capital, Beijing.

BIBLIOGRAPHY J. F. Moran, *The Japanese and the Jesuits: Alessandro Valignano in Sixteenth-Century Japan* (1993); A. C. Ross, *A Vision Betrayed: The Jesuits in Japan and China, 1542–1742* (1994); J. F. Schutte, *Valignano's Mission Principles for Japan* (1980; includes exhaustive bibliography).

Andrew C. Ross

Valle, Juan del (?–1561), Spanish missionary bishop. Professor in the University of Salamanca, Valle gave up his post to become bishop of Popayán (in modern Colombia). Arriving there in 1548, Valle was soon in anguish because of the abuse, exploitation, and genocide the Spanish colonists were inflicting on the Indians. He wrote scathing pastoral letters and traveled from village to village risking his life in defense of the indigenous peoples. Moreover, in 1555 he convened the only diocesan synod in Spanish American history for discussing the rights, lands, and treatment of the Indians. Enraged, the colonists lodged an official protest, and the Council of the Indies responded by prohibiting such synods thereafter.

In 1560, Valle, weary from the struggle, left Popayán with a mule laden with ample documentation of the crimes being committed by the colonists against the indigenous peoples. Arriving in Bogotá, he attempted to present the evidence to the colonial court but was rebuffed. Determined to alert the Spanish court to what was transpiring, he continued on foot to Cartagena, where he boarded a ship bound for Spain. He arrived there in 1561 and laid his case before the Supreme Council, but his accusations against the colonists were dismissed. He decided therefore to appeal to the Council of Trent, scheduled to reconvene in January of 1562. Shortly after crossing the border into France, he suddenly died.

Valle's valor has hardly been equaled, but even had he been able to get to Trent, it is doubtful the Council would have heard him. Rome and the prelates were preoccupied with the spread of Protestantism in Europe, not with events in Latin America.

BIBLIOGRAPHY Enrique Dussel, *A History of the Church in Latin America* (1981), pp. 50–54; Juan Friede, *Vida y luchas de Don Juan del Valle, primer obispo de Popayán y protector de indios* (1961); Gustavo Gutiérrez, *Las Casas: In Search of the Poor of Jesus Christ* (1993), pp. 435, 547, n. 60.

Alan Neely

Van. *For most names beginning with Van or Van der, see under the following part of the name.*

Van Dyck, Cornelius Van Alan (1818–1895), medical missionary and translator of the Arabic Bible. Born in Kinderhook, New York, Van Dyck studied medicine at Jefferson College in Philadephia, was appointed a lay medical missionary by the American Board of Commissioners for Foreign Missions in 1839, and went to Syria in 1840. At once he began his study of the Arabic language, a study he kept up all his life and at which he excelled. In 1841 he met Butros Bustani, an Arabic scholar and a recent convert to the Protestant faith, and they worked together all their lives. Bustani and other prominent teachers of Arabic had helped Eli *Smith in the translation of the Bible into Arabic and they did the same for Van Dyck.

In 1842 Van Dyck married Julia Abbott. Following the death of Eli Smith in 1857, Van Dyck finished Smith's incomplete translation of the Bible. He also published, in Arabic, textbooks on mathematics, astronomy, and other sciences, and helped in the medical work of the Syrian Protestant College and the Greek Hospital of St. George. He lived in Abeih, Sidon, and Beirut and took part in founding the first Arabic Literary Society, which was influential in the Arabic Renaissance.

George Antonius, in his book *The Arab Awakening,* pays tribute to the early American Protestant missionaries for their contribution to the movement of Arab nationalism through their emphasis on the use of the Arabic language. Antonius wrote of Van Dyck, "Of all the foreigners who came to work in Syria in the 19th century, he entered more intimately into the life of the people than any other. So far as the power of example went, his was probably the most valuable and effective single influence ever exerted by a foreigner in the cultural development of the country."

BIBLIOGRAPHY George Antonius, *The Arab Awakening* (1938), pp. 47–52; Henry H. Jessup, *Fifty-Three Years in Syria* (1910), pp. 104–111.

R. Park Johnson

Vasconcelos, Simão de (c. 1596–1671), Portuguese Jesuit administrator and historian of the Jesuits in Brazil. Vasconcelos was born in Porto, Portugal, and moved with his family to Brazil as a youth. He entered the Society of Jesus in 1615 in Bahia. When news of Portuguese independence from Spain reached Brazil in 1641, he and fellow Jesuit Antonio *Vieira were selected by the viceroy to travel to Lisbon to express the support of the colony for King John IV.

Vasconcelos returned to Brazil the following year with the new governor, Antônio Teles da Silva, whom he served as confessor. He taught humanities and theology and served as rector of the Jesuit college in Rio de Janeiro and as provincial in Bahia. His *Chronica da Companhia de Jesu do Estado do Brasil* (1663), though apologetic in style, remains an indispensable account of the Jesuit missions in Brazil from their establishment in 1549 until the death of Manuel da *Nóbrega in 1570. The book contains the first edition of José de *Anchieta's poem "De Beata Virgine Dei Matre Maria." Vasconcelos's other major work is his biography of Anchieta, *Vida do Veneravel Padre Ioseph de Anchieta (1672).*

BIBLIOGRAPHY Serafim Leite, "Simão de Vasconcelos: A vida e a obra," in Simão de Vasconcelos, *Crônica da Companhia de Jesus,* 2 vols. (1977) and *História da Companhia de Jésus no Brasil,* 10 vols. (1938–1950); Francisco Rodrigues, *História da Companhia de Jesus na Assistencia de Portugal* (1931–1950); Innocencio Francisco da Silva, "Advertencia Preliminar," in Simão de Vasconcelos, *Chrônica da Companhia de Jesu do Estado do Brasil* (1865).

Thomas M. Cohen

Väth, Alfons (1874–1937), Jesuit historian of Roman Catholic missions. Väth was born in Werbachhausen, Baden, Germany. He entered the Society of Jesus in 1893 and early expressed his desire to go to the missions in Asia. From 1899 to 1903, he taught geography and history at St. Xavier's College in Bombay. He returned to Europe for his theological studies and ordination. By 1910 he was again in India, this time as professor of history at St. Xavier's College. He returned to Germany in 1916 because of World War I. Two years later he became editor in chief of *Die Katholischen Missionen,* a leading missionary journal with headquarters in Bonn. He relinquished that position in 1925 but remained on the editorial staff until his death. During this latter period he published several important books on the peoples of India and Christianity and also a biography of Johann Adam *Schall von Bell.

BIBLIOGRAPHY Alfons Väth, *Die deutschen Jesuiten in Indien: Geschichte der Mission von Bombay-Puna, 1854–1920* (1920), *La Misión de Bombay: Historie de la mision desde el año 1854 al 1920* (1924), *Im Kämpfe mit der Zauberwelt des Hinduismus: Upadhyaya Brahmabandhav und das problem der überwindung des höheren Hinduismus durch das Christentum* (1928), *Johann Adam Schall von Bell, S.J., Missionar in China* (1933, 1991), *Die Inder* (1934), and *Histoire dell' Inde et de sa culture* (1937).

John W. Witek, SJ

Vaughan, Herbert (1832–1903), founder of the Mill Hill Missionaries and cardinal archbishop of Westminster. Vaughan was the eldest son in a large landed family of English Roman Catholic recusant stock. His five sisters all became nuns and five of his brothers became priests (two also became bishops). Ordained when only 22, he decided a few years later to devote himself to the missions by establishing a new missionary training college, opened in Mill Hill, just north of London, in March 1866. Out of it developed St. Joseph's Society of Foreign Missions. In 1872 Vaughan was appointed bishop of Salford and in 1892 archbishop of Westminster but he continued to be superior general of Mill Hill. He successfully sought recruits for his society not only in England but also in the Tyrol and Holland. The mission's first work was with American blacks in Baltimore, out of which developed in 1892 a separate society, the Josephite Fathers. Further missions were accepted in the archdiocese of Madras and in Borneo and Uganda. Vaughan was a man of huge pastoral concern and intense, if romantic, spirituality. A complete ultramontane, he showed no originality in his missionary strategy; nevertheless, he represented and stimulated the rising tide of missionary concern among Catholics in the later nineteenth century.

BIBLIOGRAPHY A. McCormack, *Cardinal Vaughan* (1966); R. O'Neil, *Cardinal Herbert Vaughan* (1995); J. G. Snead-Cox, *The Life of Cardinal Vaughan* (1910).

Adrian Hastings

Vautrin, Wilhelmina (Minnie) (1886–1941), American missionary in China. Born in Secor, Illinois, Vautrin graduated from the University of Illinois in 1912. She was sent to China by the United Christian Missionary Society (Disciples of Christ) in 1912, where she first served as a high school principal in Luchowfu and then became head of the education department of Ginling College when it was founded in 1916 in Nanking (Nanjing). She served as acting president of Ginling College from 1919 to 1922, when President Matilda *Thurston returned to the United States for fund-raising. With the Japanese army advancing on Nanking in 1937, Vautrin was called upon to take charge of the college campus, as most of the faculty fled Nanking and established a refugee campus in western China. Her diary and reports provide a detailed account of the situation in Nanking under Japanese occupation, especially the atrocities known as the Nanking Massacre, which continued into the late spring of 1938. In the last entry of her diary, April 14, 1940, Vautrin wrote, "I'm about at the end of my energy. Can no longer forge ahead and make plans for the work, for on every hand there seem to be obstacles of some kind. I wish I could go on furlough at least once." Two weeks later she suffered a nervous breakdown and returned to the United States. A year to the day after she left Nanking, she ended her own life.

BIBLIOGRAPHY Mary B. Treudley, *This Stinging Exultation* (1972). Vautrin's 526-page diary, covering the period 1937 to 1941, is in the Special Collections of Yale Divinity School Library.

Martha Lund Smalley

Vaz, Joseph (1651–1711), Goan Catholic missionary to Ceylon (Sri Lanka). Born in a Christian Brahmin family in South Goa, Vaz attended the Jesuit and Dominican colleges in the old city of Goa for his preparatory and priestly training and was ordained in 1676. Religious orders dominated by foreign white clergy still controlled the ecclesiastical scene in the Portuguese colonies, did not admit Indians to their ranks, and were unwilling to support the vicars apostolic appointed by Propaganda Fide to meet the needs of native Christians in territories beyond Portuguese administrative jurisdiction. The Dutch occupation of Ceylon had led to a critical situation for the Catholic Church there. They considered the Catholic Church a tool of Portuguese influence, and sought to suppress it in order to ensure their political and commercial hold over the island. This challenge was met by Vaz, who first worked as vicar forane (vicar general) of *padroado* in Kanara, south of Goa, where he conceived a plan to go to the assistance of Ceylon. On his return to Goa after three years in Kanara he joined a newly formed community of native priests and gradually converted it into a source of missionaries to Ceylon. Despite opposition and restrictions from the Dutch, Vaz moved to Ceylon in 1687 and worked there in difficult and demeaning circumstances for 24 years until his death. He relied heavily on native missionary colleagues and catechists, and unlike foreign missionaries in the past, he used the native Tamil and Sinhalese languages for his apostolate. During his lifetime he attained a reputation for holiness among the people of the island, and by the time he died the Catholic Church of Ceylon was once again firmly established and provided with a network of churches and chapels maintained by his Oratorian brethren. The process of his beatification was delayed and only in 1989 did Pope John Paul II declared him "venerable." The decree of his beatification was issued on July 6, 1993. Vaz is acknowledged as the Apostle of Ceylon and is seen as a model missionary for the Third World, free from the trappings of colonial authority.

BIBLIOGRAPHY M. da Costa Nunes, *Documentação para a História da Congregação do Oratório de Santa Cruz dos Milagres do Clero Natural de Goa* (1966); S. G. Perera, *Life of the Venerable Father Joseph Vaz, Apostle of Ceylon* (1953); Sebatião do Rego, *Vida do Veneravel Padre Joseph Vaz* (1745; 2d ed., annotated by J. C. Barreto Miranda, 1867; 3d ed., annotated by J. A. Ismael Gracias, 1962); Teotonio R. de Souza, "To the Nations and Nation: The Apostle of the Indies and the Apostle of Ceylon," *Renovação* 15, no. 4 (1985) and "Fr. Joseph Vaz and Fr. Agnelo de Sousa: The Struggle for Sainthood," *Goa Today*, June 1989.

Teotonio R. de Souza

Vedder, Hermann Heinrich (1876–1972), German missionary in South-West Africa (Namibia). Born in Westerenger, northwestern Germany, Vedder was imbued by the spirit of the Ravensberg revival movement, which shaped the faith of the rural community where he grew up. In 1895 he joined the Rhenish Mission, which provided for his education. Having a gift for languages, he initially offered to go to China, but due to a "lack of musicality" he was appointed to South-West Africa in 1903. There, ironically, he became an expert in the language of the Ku bushmen which is rich in pitch variation. He rewrote a Nama grammar and investigated the cultural heritage of the Dama people. His scholarly activity also embraced the history of the peoples of early southwest Africa. His main missionary work was education. Under his leadership a school for evangelists was opened in Gaub in 1911. This later grew into a teachers college in Okahandja, and he became its director in 1922. Generations of teachers were trained there and imbued with Vedder's spirit. However, he neglected to train local pastors, even after he was appointed superintendent of the mission in 1937. Having grown up in German conservatism and being strongly influenced by Gustav *Warneck's mission theology, he felt the time was not yet ripe for indigenous clergy. Neither did he promote independence for the local church. After World War II, at the invitation of Prime Minister Malan, he agreed to take a seat in the South African senate (1950). For this he was criticized by the native population, especially the Herero. In recognition of his ethnological, linguistic, and historical work, he received honorary doctorates from the Universities of Tübingen and Stellenbosch. He died in Okahandja.

BIBLIOGRAPHY H. Vedder, *Die Bergdama*, 2 vols. (1923) and *Das alte Südwestafrika* (1943). J. Baumann, *Mission und Ökumene in Süd-West-Afrika, Dargestellt am Lebensweg von Hermann Heinrich Vedder* (1969); Theo Sundermeier, "Hermann Heinrich Vedder, 1876–1972," *In die Welt für die Welt* 12 (1976): 156–169.

Theo Sundermeier

Veenstra, Johanna (1894–1933), pioneer American missionary to Nigeria with the Sudan United Mission (SUM). Veenstra was born in Paterson, New Jersey. Deeply moved by hearing Karl *Kumm, founder of the SUM, she completed her missionary training at Union Missionary Training Institute in Brooklyn, then pursued midwifery classes and worked at a nearby Hebrew mission. Arriving in Nigeria in 1920, she faced many hazards merely to reach her remote mission area in the south-central part. Her many-faceted ministry to the Kuteb people became an inspiration to her fellow missionaries, but perhaps even more to her home constituency, the Christian Reformed churches. Her impressive presence and compelling messages galvanized supporters and ultimately the denomination's mission board. Though a strong disciplinarian, in time she won the respect and affection of the Kuteb. The boarding school and clinic she founded offered many opportunities for culturally contextualized evangelism. She was a person of great stamina, exemplified in far-flung trekking; her extensive writings demonstrated also a profoundly caring and tender spirit. Her sudden death at age 39 was followed by a flowering of missionary awareness in her home churches and remarkable growth of the church among the Kuteb, Jukun, and surrounding peoples in Nigeria.

BIBLIOGRAPHY Johanna Veenstra, *Pioneering for Christ in the Sudan* (1921) and *Black Diamonds* (1929). Henry Beets, *Johanna of Nigeria* (1937); Eva Stuart Watt, *Aflame for God* (1937); Gerald L. Zandstra, *Daughters Who Dared* (1992).

Eugene Rubingh

Vénard, Jean Théophane (1829–1861), Catholic missionary martyred in Vietnam. Born in Saint-Loup-sur-Thouet, France, Vénard joined the major seminary in Poitiers and later entered the seminary of the foreign missions at Paris. In 1852 he was sent to China, arriving in Hong Kong in March 1853. His wish to be a missionary in Tonkin (Vietnam) was realized in 1854.

In 1847, shortly after he came to power, the Vietnamese emperor, Tu-Doc, ended a brief period of peace by starting violent persecution of Christians, as he was afraid that the French missionaries intended to prepare the country for colonization by France. In 1858–1859 French forces—later assisted by the Spanish army—occupied Saigon and some regions in the south. Missionaries and local Christians fled to the mountains. The occupation was meant to halt the persecution, but it only raised greater suspicion of the French missionaries. Vénard took refuge in the province of Hanoi but was captured on November 30, 1860, and brought to the city. The emperor judged his case personally and condemned him to death by decapitation. The execution took place in Hanoi.

In 1988 Pope John Paul II canonized 117 martyrs of Vietnam, of whom 96 were Vietnamese. Vénard was one of the foreign martyrs.

BIBLIOGRAPHY S. Delacroix, *Histoire universelle des missions catholiques*, vol. 3 (1958), pp. 229–244; Guy-Marie Oury, *Le Vietnam des martyrs et des saints* (1988); Christian Simonnet, *Les dix saints martyrs français du Vietnam* (1989).

Arnulf Camps, OFM

Veniaminov, Innokenti (Father John Popov). *See* Innocent Veniaminov.

Venn, Henry (1796–1873), Anglican missions administrator and theorist. Venn was born at Clapham, London, into a leading evangelical Anglican family. His grandfather, Henry Venn (1725–1797), was an outstanding pastor-evangelist identified with the Evangelical Revival. His father, John *Venn (1759–1813), pastor to William *Wilberforce and the Clapham Sect, presided over formation of the Church Missionary Society (CMS) in 1799 and helped found the *Christian Observer* (1802). Educated at Queens' College, Cambridge (B.A., 1818; M.A., 1821; B.D., 1828), Venn was ordained a deacon (1819) and a priest (1821). While serving Drypool Parish, Hull, he married Martha Sykes in 1829. He became vicar of St. John's, Holloway, in 1834. In 1846 he was made a prebendary of St. Paul's Cathedral. His return to London allowed him to resume regular attendance at meetings of the CMS, of which he became a member in 1820. His administrative gifts were soon evident, and despite precarious health, he accepted appointment as CMS clerical secretary in 1841.

Venn was one of the most influential mission statesmen of the nineteenth century. An efficient and effective administrator with a prodigious capacity for work, he led in forging a new character for the Anglican communion by the establishment of eight bishoprics overseas. In 1841 CMS had 107 European and 9 African and Asian missionaries in service. By 1873 there were 230 European and 148 African and Asian missionaries. During Venn's 32 years as clerical secretary, 498 clergy were sent out as missionaries. He stood in the front ranks of evangelicals for a generation and was twice appointed to royal commissions to represent this tradition. He both defined the evangelical position vis-à-vis Anglo-Catholics and Latitudinarians and sought to moderate the extremes of partisanship and eschatological theories that cropped up among evangelicals in the latter half of the nineteenth century, exerting his influence especially through the *Christian Observer,* which he edited during the last years of his life.

Venn is best remembered, however, as a mission theorist. Largely independent of one another, Venn and his American contemporary Rufus *Anderson (1797–1880) sought to clarify the main goal of mission and the most effective means of realizing it. The concept of the indigenous church emerged as the central construct of mission theory. A church was judged to be indigenous when it was self-propagating, self-financing, and self-governing. Venn developed his theory of mission in a series of pamphlets and policy statements written in the years 1846 to 1865. He also wrote a book on the life of Francis Xavier and numerous pamphlets and policy statements.

BIBLIOGRAPHY Henry Venn, *The missionary life and labours of Francis Xavier taken from his own correspondence: with a sketch of the general results of Roman Catholic missions among the heathen* (1862). William Knight, *Memoir of the Rev. H. Venn: The Missionary Secretariat of Henry Venn, B.D., Prebendary of St. Paul's and Honorary Secretary of the Church Missionary Society* (1880; 2d ed., 1882). Wilbert R. Shenk, *Henry Venn, Missionary Statesman* (1983; includes a bibliography of Venn's writings), "Henry Venn," in Gerald H. Anderson et al., eds., *Mission Legacies* (1994), pp. 541–547, and "Rufus Anderson and Henry Venn: A Special Relationship?" *International Bulletin of Missionary Research* 5, no. 4 (Oct. 1981): 168–172; Max Warren, ed., *To Apply the Gospel: Selections from the Writings of Henry Venn* (1971); C. Peter Williams, *The Ideal of the Self-Governing Church: A Study in Victorian Missionary Strategy* (1990); T. E. Yates, *Venn and Victorian Bishops Abroad: The Missionary Policies of Henry Venn and Their Repercussions upon the Anglican Episcopate of the Colonial Period, 1841–1872* (1978).

Wilbert R. Shenk

Venn, John (1759–1813), a founder of the Church Missionary Society (CMS). Venn was rector of Clapham parish in London (1793–1813) and confidant to the Clapham Sect, a group of evangelical leaders who were influential in organizing the CMS and other philanthropic societies. He formulated the enduring principles that guided the work of the CMS, and took the first steps to gain from the Church of England hierarchy recognition of CMS as a voluntary society; he was its administrative officer during the first three years. Venn deftly defined the CMS's ecclesiastical position, saying it should be "founded upon the Church principle, not the High Church principle." He thereby distinguished the CMS from the (High Church) Society for the Propagation of the Gospel and the nondenominational London Missionary Society. His elder son, Henry *Venn (1796–1873), served as clerical secretary of the CMS from 1841 to 1873.

BIBLIOGRAPHY John Venn, *Sermons,* 3 vols. (1814–1817) and *Annals of a Clerical Family: Being Some Account of the Family of William Venn, Vicar of Otterton, Devon, 1600–1621* (1904). Michael Hennel, *John Venn and the Clapham Sect* (1958); Eugene Stock, *History of the Church Missionary Society,* vol. 1 (1899).

Wilbert R. Shenk

Vennard, Iva May Durham (1871–1945), Methodist deaconess and founder of the Chicago Evangelistic Institute. Born in Prairie City, Illinois, she was converted in 1883 and became a lifelong member of the Methodist Church. Later, she graduated from Illinois State University and attended Wellesley College. As the Methodist Church did not ordain women to preach, she joined the church-related deaconess movement, receiving appointment in 1898 as deaconess-at-large by the Woman's Home Missionary Society. In 1904, she married Thomas Vennard, an architect and masonry contractor.

As the movement shifted away from evangelism, Mrs. Vennard, with approval of Methodist bishops, opened Epworth Evangelistic Institute in Saint Louis in 1903 to focus on preparing women for evangelism. Fierce opposition, however, forced her resignation in 1909 because of her de facto training of women preachers for home and foreign missions. Moving to Chicago, she established the (independent) Chicago Evangelistic Institute (CEI) in 1910 for women and men to continue the vision of Epworth. Identifying with the National Association for the Promotion of Holiness, Vennard played a leading role in the founding of its missions agency in 1910, now known as the World Gospel Mission. In 1923, Taylor University conferred on her an honorary D.D., an unusual honor for a woman at that time. CEI was renamed Vennard College in 1951 and moved to University Park, Iowa.

BIBLIOGRAPHY Vennard published a collection of her sermons in *Upper Room Messages* (1916). Mary Ella Bowie, *Alabaster and Spikenard, The Life of Iva Durham Vennard, D.D.* (1947). Her papers are housed at Vennard College, University Park, Iowa.

Gary B. McGee

Vera Cruz, Alonso de la (1504–1584), Spanish missionary in Mexico. Born in Caspueñas, Toledo, Vera Cruz received an M.A. as a disciple of Francisco de *Vitoria in Salamanca. In 1535 he went to Mexico, where he joined the Hermits of St. Augustin, and became novice master for three years. In 1540 he was appointed professor of theology in the college of Tiripitío, in the state of Michoacán. In 1548 he was elected provincial. In 1553 he accepted the chair of Sacred Scripture of the new University of Mexico, and in 1557 was elected again as provincial. Three times he declined the offer of bishoprics, as well as the office of commissioner general of the order; he chose to dedicate himself instead to writing and to missionary work. Vera Cruz is considered to be the father of Mexican philosophy. He also defended the rights and privileges of the Indians. As provincial, he traveled to Spain to defend the privileges of the religious orders. In response to his intervention, Pius V in *Exponi nobis* granted the rights of parish priests to members of religious orders in America. Vera Cruz returned to Mexico in 1573, assuming again the office of provincial.

BIBLIOGRAPHY *The Writings of Alonso de la Vera Cruz,* original texts with Eng. tr., Ernest Burrus, ed., 5 vols. (1968–1972). John F. Blethen, "The Educational Activities of Fray Alonso de la Vera Cruz in Sixteenth Century Mexico," *The Americas* 5 (1943): 31–47; A. Bolaño e Isla, *Contribución al estudio bibliográfico de Fray Alonso de la Vera Cruz* (1947); E. J. McCarthy, *The Augustinians in Primitive Mexico, 1533–1572* (1938).

Willi Henkel, OMI

Verbeck, Guido Herman Fridolin (1830–1898), pioneer Protestant missionary to Japan. Verbeck was the youngest of six Protestant missionaries who arrived in Japan with their families in 1859. Born and educated in Holland, equally conversant in German and Dutch, and with considerable knowledge of French, he received ministerial training in the Congregational-Presbyterian Auburn Seminary, New York, and became thoroughly at home in English. Verbeck married an American girl but was not resident long enough in the United States to obtain American citizenship. Having lost his Dutch citizenship, he remained stateless the remainder of his life, except that from 1891 he received from the Japanese Minister of Foreign Affairs a passport indicating he was under the protection of the empire of Japan. This unusual situation is at least partly responsible for Verbeck's receiving from the Japanese government a degree of confidence beyond that of any other Christian missionary of his time.

Verbeck was sent first by the Reformed Church in America to Nagasaki, where he attracted to himself a small but extraordinarily able group of samurai students who later became key leaders in the Meiji government that was to come into power in 1868. He regularly included the Bible and the American Constitution in his curriculum of English, social sciences, and Western technology. Among his students were Itō Hirobumi (later prime minister, 1885–1888, 1892–1896, 1898, 1900–1901). Ōkubo Toshimichi, Ōkuma Shigenobu, Soejima Taneomi, and others of prominence. Verbeck went to Tokyo in 1869, by recommendation of Ōkuma and with the approval of his mission board, to become the virtual head of the new Imperial government school that was to become Tokyo University.

From this post Verbeck gave advice to numerous officials and civilians, all in a spirit of urbane and gracious courtesy. Probably more than any other foreigner, he could be called one of the makers of modern Japan. His advice was key to the establishment of the prefectural system of local government (1871) and the sending of the Iwakura Mission to the West (1871); the latter led to the removal of the anti-Christian edict signs throughout the empire. Verbeck's role was critical also in the framing of the Education Order (1872) and the military Conscription Ordinance (1873). He subsequently served as a legal consultant and official translator until he left government service in 1877 to devote the remainder of his life exclusively to missionary work. Verbeck himself always considered his educational work and government service as Christian mission in the context providentially given him.

BIBLIOGRAPHY Richard H. Drummond, *A History of Christianity in Japan* (1972); William Elliot Griffis, *Verbeck of Japan: A Citizen of No Country* (1900); Hideo Satō, "Verbeck, Guido Herman Fridolin," *Encyclopedia of Japan* (1983).

Richard H. Drummond

Verbiest, Ferdinand (1623–1688), Jesuit missionary, astronomer, and diplomat at the court of China. Verbiest was born in Pitthem, near Courtrai, Belgium. In 1647 and again in 1655 he was ready to embark for the missions of South America. Spanish authorities, however, did not want Belgians in their territories, so he turned his interests toward China. He arrived in Macao in 1658 and worked in Sian (Xi'an), Shensi (Shaanxi) Province. Called to Peking (Beijing) in 1660 to assist Johann Adam *Schall von Bell in astronomical calculations, he arrived in June. Persecution of Christianity and opposition by Chinese astronomers against Western methods led to his imprisonment. Freed in 1669, he sought and obtained the rehabilitation of Schall, who had died in disgrace. Later that year an imperial inscription was placed on Schall's tomb, and Verbiest himself was appointed head of the tribunal of mathematics. He corrected the calendar calculations and became a trusted official of the emperor. On trips to Mongolia and Manchuria, he had lengthy discussions with the emperor and his officials about scientific and religious matters. To assure continuity of friendly relations with local officials who came to the capital for audiences with the emperor, Verbiest visited them to recommend the missionaries and the Chinese Christians in the provinces. Named vice-provincial of the Jesuit mission, Verbiest wrote an important letter to his confreres in Europe in which he outlined the need for personnel. Supportive of an indigenous clergy, he made many efforts to have the emperor remove Christianity as a prohibited sect in China. Verbiest was trusted to carry out the court's relations with Russia and its delegations at Peking. Author of more than two dozen books in Chinese, Verbiest worked assiduously to promote the mission throughout all of China. The refurbishing of his tombstone as well as those of Matteo *Ricci, Johann Adam *Schall von Bell, and others was part of a major restoration project of the Shala (Zhalan) cemetery in 1986.

BIBLIOGRAPHY Louis Pfister, *Notices biographiques et bibliographiques sur les Jésuites de l'ancienne mission de Chine* (1932–1934; repr., 1975), pp. 338–362 (with a list of Verbiest's Chinese works); J. Witek, ed., *Ferdinand Verbiest (1623–1688): Jesuit Missionary, Scientist, Engineer, and Diplomat* (1994; with thirty-one essays, including recent biographical and bibliographic data).

John W. Witek, SJ

Verbist, Théophile (1823–1868), founder of the Congregation of the Immaculate Heart of Mary (CICM). Born into a middle-class Flemish family, Verbist became a priest of the Archdiocese of Mechelen (Malines), Belgium, in 1847. He first worked in the minor seminary, then as chaplain of the école Militaire in Brussels; in 1860 he became national director of the Holy Childhood Association in Belgium. During that time he requested permission to establish a Belgian mission in some port city of China, and was urged by Propaganda Fide in Rome to establish a congregation of foreign missionaries. Accordingly, he founded the CICM and was elected superior general in 1862. In 1864 he pronounced perpetual vows in the chapel of Our Lady of Grace in Scheut, a suburb of Brussels, whence the congregation received its popular name in Belgium. (In the United States it is known as Missionhurst.) Appointed pro-vicar apostolic of the Apostolic Vicariate of Mongolia, he and a companion, Alois van Segvelt, arrived in Hsi-wan-tzu in 1865, and Verbist undertook direction of the major seminary there.

During his time in the very difficult mission of Mongolia, Verbist stressed establishing orphanages, further instructing Catholics, and developing the native clergy, but he did very little evangelizing because he never fully mastered the language. During an inspection tour of his vicariate in 1868, Verbist became fatally ill, probably with typhus. In 1931 his remains were taken back to Scheut.

BIBLIOGRAPHY V. Rondelez, *Scheut, Congregation Missionaire* (1962; includes bibliography of works by and about Verbist); D. Verheest, *La Congrégation du Coeur Immaculé de Maire (Scheut). Édition critique des sources. 1. Une naissance laborieuse, 1861–65* (1986).

Stephen B. Bevans, SVD

Verjus (or Verius), Henri (1860–1892), pioneer Catholic missionary, explorer, and founder of the Papuan mission of the Missionaries of the Sacred Heart (MSC). Verjus was born in southwest Italy of an Italian mother and a French father. Even as a child he spoke of becoming a missionary and suffering martyrdom. He was ordained for the MSC and sent to found a mission on Yule Island, off the coast of Papua New Guinea. As missionary and superior he emphasized holiness, self-discipline, sacrifice, knowledge of the language and culture of the people ministered to, and respect for local customs and authority structures. His vision was to make the Yule Island mission a springboard to greater possibilities on the Papuan mainland, which required expeditions into extremely difficult, unknown, and dangerous areas—expeditions welcomed by Verjus and his companions. In 1889 he became coadjutor bishop to his ailing friend and superior, Archbishop Navarre. Only three years later, Verjus's own bad health ended his life at the age of 33. The young mission then had 25 churches and chapels, 29 day schools, 11 stations for mission sisters, a boarding school, an orphanage, a catechist training school, and over 3,000 converts.

BIBLIOGRAPHY George Delbos, *The Mustard Seed: From a French Mission to a Papuan Church, 1885–1985* (1985); Philip Seveau, *A Life for a Mission: Bishop Henri Verius, 1860–1892* (1985).

Louis Luzbetak, SVD

Verkuyl, Johannes (1908–), Dutch missionary statesman. Verkuyl was born in Nieuw Vennep, the Netherlands. Upon completion of his theological training in 1932, he was ordained pastor of a small Reformed (*Gereformeerde*) congregation in the town of Laren, and in 1937 was appointed chaplain to Asian students in the Netherlands. Two years later he was sent as a missionary to Central Java, Indonesia, where for the next 24 years he served in a variety of capacities. From 1942 to 1945 he and his wife and children spent three and a half years in separate Japanese prison camps. Wholly supportive of the drive to national self-expression among the people of Indonesia, Verkuyl became directly involved in the anticolonial struggle for Indonesian independence. On home leave in 1948 he completed work on his Th.D. at the Free University in Amsterdam. From 1954 to 1962 he taught at the interdenominational theological seminary in Djakarta.

In 1963 Verkuyl became general secretary of the Netherlands Missionary Council, a post he held until 1968. In 1965 he was appointed part-time and in 1968 full-time professor of missiology at the Free University, where he remained until his retirement in 1978. He helped found the International Association for Mission Studies, the Interuniversity Institute for Missiology and Ecumenics in Leiden and Utrecht, and the Dutch ecumenical missiological journal *Wereld en Zending,* which he also edited for several years. Active in ecumenical circles, he played a prominent role in the anti-apartheid and world justice and peace movements. A prolific writer, Verkuyl authored 66 books and some 400 articles in the areas of social ethics, apologetics, interreligious dialogue, evangelism, and missiology. His best known work is *Contemporary Missiology: An Intro-*

duction (1978). Upon his retirement he was honored with a Festschrift entitled *Zending op Weg naar de Toekomst* (*Mission enroute to the future*), edited by J. D. Gort and H. J. Westmaas (1978).

BIBLIOGRAPHY Johannes Verkuyl, *Break Down the Walls: A Christian Cry for Racial Justice* (1973), *Inleiding in de Evangelistiek* (Introduction to evangelism, 1978), *De "New Age" Beweging* (The New Age movement, 1989), *De Kern van het Christelijk Geloof* (The heart of the Christian faith, 1992), and *Met Moslims in Gesprek over het Evangelie* (Speaking with Muslims about the Gospel, 1994, 2d rev. and enlarged ed.). The Festschrift referred to above, with essays in English and Dutch, contains a biographical portrait of Verkuyl in Dutch and a bibliography of his publications in six languages up to 1978. Further accounts of Verkuyl's life are to be found in his autobiography, *Memoires: Gedenken en Verwachten* (Remembrance and expectation, 1983), and "My Pilgrimage in Mission," *IBMR* 10 (1986): 150–154. Verkuyl's personal collection of letters, papers, and documents are to be donated to the Historical Documentation Center for Post-Eighteenth Century Dutch Protestantism at the Free Univ. (Amsterdam).

Jerald D. Gort

Vernier, Frédéric (1841–1915), missionary of the Paris Evangelical Mission (PEMS) in French Polynesia. Vernier was born at Faures de Barcelonne, Drôme, into a staunch French Reformed family. Trained at Geneva, he went in 1867 to serve the Tahitian church pioneered by the London Missionary Society. He became an expert in the Tahitian language, a constant traveler in small schooners to tend to and encourage the dispersed Protestants, a respected intermediary with French officials, and a chaplain and confidant of the Tahitian queen Pomare IV. The French subsidized and supervised the church; Vernier acted with Tahitian leaders in setting up and presiding over its governing council, which guarded Tahitian styles of life. With Charles Viénot he required instruction in Tahitian alongside French in the church's schools, ensuring survival of the vernacular. In 1896 he mediated unofficially, and unsuccessfully, between French authorities and the rebel chief Teraupoo of Raiatea. In 1907, after 40 years in Tahiti, he retired to Crest, Drôme, where he died in 1915. His sons, Charles and Paul, and his grandson, Henri, followed him as missionaries in Tahiti.

BIBLIOGRAPHY John Garrett, *To Live among the Stars: Christian Origins in Oceania* (1982) and *Footsteps in the Sea: Christianity in Oceania to World War II* (1992); Henri Vernier, *Au vent des cyclones: Missions protestantes et Église Évangélique à Tahiti et en Polynésie Française* (1985). *Journal des Missions Évangéliques* carries reports of Vernier's work; the Paris Evangelical Mission manuscript sources are at 102, Bd. Arago, Paris.

John Garrett

Veronis, Alexander J. (1932–), developer of Eastern Orthodox missionary programs in North America. Veronis studied at Lafayette College, Easton, Pennsylvania (B.A., 1954), Holy Cross Greek Orthodox School of Theology, Brookline, Massachusetts (B.D., 1958), Boston University (S.T.M., 1960), and the University of Athens (licentiate in theology, 1961). Early interest in missions cultivated at Holy Cross was further stimulated through contacts with African Orthodox students in Athens. Upon assuming the pastorate at Annunciation Church in Lancaster, Pennsylvania, in 1961, he instituted nationwide missionary support programs. Beginning in 1966, he presided over the Standing Committee on Missions of the Greek Archdiocese; in 1958 it became a department of the archdiocese and relocated to St. Augustine, Florida. In 1994 the department was expanded to include several other Orthodox jurisdictions. Veronis was designated as president emeritus of the mission board and elected a lifetime member; the headquarters building of the St. Augustine Mission Center was named in his honor in 1988. He has served as a short-term foreign missionary and raised $1 million for a chair in missiology at Holy Cross. In 1994 he was awarded the D.D. by Lebanon Valley College, Annville, Pennsylvania.

BIBLIOGRAPHY Alexander Veronis, "Orthodox Concepts of Evangelism and Mission," *Greek Orthodox Theological Review* 27, no. 2 (1982): 44–57, and "World Mission and Evangelism: WCC/CWME Conference (San Antonio, Texas-May, 1989)," *Greek Orthodox Theological Review* 35, no. 3 (1990): 261–270.

Stanley Samuel Harakas

Veuster, Joseph Damien de. *See* Damien of Molokai.

Vialar, Émilie de (1797–1856), French aristocrat, mystic and founder of the Sisters of St. Joseph of the Apparition. Vialar forsook wealth to live in poverty and founded a missionary congregation to teach poor children and to care for the hungry and ill. From her base in Caillac, France, she started mission posts in the new French colony of Algeria (1835), Tunisia, the Levant, Burma, and Australia. However, she had to withdraw her sisters from Algeria after refusing to subject them to the jurisdiction of the newly installed bishop. She was canonized in 1951.

BIBLIOGRAPHY Agnès Cavasino, *Émilie de Vialar, fondatrice: Les soeurs de Saint Joseph de l'Apparition, une congrégation missionnaire* (1987); P. E. Collier, *The story of Sisters of St. Joseph of the Apparition and Their Foundress, Blessed Émilie de Vialar* (1947); Chanione Esprit Darbon, *Émilie de Vialar, fondatrice des soeurs de St. Joseph de l'Apparition: Souvenirs et documents* (1901; Eng. tr., 1987).

Leny Lagerwerf

Vicedom, Georg Friedrich (1903–1974), German Protestant missiologist. Vicedom was born into a farmer's family in northern Bavaria and was trained in the seminary of Neuendettelsau, with additional ethnological preparation at Hamburg University. In 1929 he took up pioneer mission service in the highlands of central New Guinea, following the example of Christian *Keysser. The outbreak of war in 1939 forced his return to Germany where he confronted the challenge of combining a leading post at the mission headquarters with teaching assignments in the mission seminary, at the church faculty of Neuendettelsau, and later, on a part-time basis, at Erlangen University. His wide-ranging publications are an indication of Vicedom's significance as teacher and researcher. While a massive ethnological survey of the Mbowamb tribe in New Guinea (*Die Mbowamb*, 3 vols., 1943) established his reputation in the field of anthropology, there followed a whole range of missiological studies, centered around the biblical foundation of missions, the importance of mission for the church, and the dialogue of religions. Vicedom's bibliography contains more than 400 titles, a dozen of them major books. He also exercised a profound influence on world Lutheranism as a whole and in the ecumenical movement. On behalf of the Presbyterian Church of Canada, Vicedom undertook a survey of Christianity among the hill tribes of Taiwan, published under the title *Faith That Moves Mountains* (1967). His missiological heritage will be widely remembered in connection with the term *missio dei*, which, though not coined by him, he interpreted with a theocentric emphasis for the theology of mission.

BIBLIOGRAPHY There is as yet no adequate biography of Vicedom. Vicedom's influential book on the theology of mission was *Missio Dei* (1958), published in English as *The Mission of God* (1965). Klaus Wilhelm Müller, "Peacemaker. Missionary Practice of Georg Friedrich Vicedom in New Guinea, 1929–1939" (Ph.D. diss., Univ. of Aberdeen, Scotland, 1993).

Hans-Werner Gensichen

Vicelin (c. 1090–1154), apostle of Holstein, Germany. Born in Hameln, Saxony, educated in Paderborn, by 1123 Vicelin was a cathedral scholar at Bremen. Later he studied in France, and in 1126 was ordained a priest. *Adalbert, bishop of Bremen, sent him that year to evangelize the Wagrians. By 1127 he was working in Holstein among the Wends, where he founded monasteries at Neumünster and Faldera, as well as many churches. The crusades of the Wends in 1147 destroyed much of his work.

BIBLIOGRAPHY F. Hertermann, *St. Vicelin* (1926); George F. Maclear, *Apostles of Mediaeval Europe* (1869, 1986); Peter Meinhold et al., eds., *Schleswig-Holsteinische Kirchengeschichte: Anfänge und Ausbau I* (1977).

Frederick W. Norris

Victor, Janós (1888–1954), Hungarian Reformed pastor, theological teacher, and mission leader. Victor was born in Budapest, Hungary, where he grew up in a family deeply influenced by the British and Foreign Bible Society and the Scottish Mission in Hungary. While in high school he was among the pioneers of the Hungarian Student Christian Movement (MEKDSz) in 1904. Profoundly influenced by John R. *Mott, he, along with Lutheran pastor Pál *Podmaniczky, prepared to establish the small but influential Hungarian mission branch of the World's Student Christian Federation in 1912. Victor was also the translator of Mott's book *The Decisive Hour of Christian Missions*. Throughout his life he played a leading role in the Hungarian Christian (later Reformed) Mission Society, which sprang up from MEKDSz in 1913. His overall objective was to awaken the whole Reformed Church to its foreign mission responsibility. Thus he was characterized as a missionary theologian. He believed that Hungary had a special responsibility for mission among the Muslims in the Balkans and further eastward. He also initiated a fundamental theological discussion challenging Sándor *Makkai's limited Hungarian understanding of mission.

BIBLIOGRAPHY János Victor, tr., John R. Mott, *A keresztyén missziók döntö órája* (The decisive hour of Christian missions) (1913), "Keresztyénség külmisszió nélkül" (Christianity without foreign mission), *Hajnal* 19, no. 4 (1933): 1, "Mi a 'missziói munka'?" (What is mission work?) *Református Világ Szemle* 10, no. 1 (1941): 12–24, and "A 'missziói munka' theológiájához" (A theology of mission work), *Theológiai Szemle* 17 (1941): 84–89. Barna Nagy, "Dr. Victor János, a teológus. Emlékbeszéd a Budapesti Református Teológiai Akadémia 1954 október 10-i ünnepélyén" (Dr. János Victor, the theologian: Memorial speech at the Reformed Theological Academy on October 10, 1954), *Református Egyház* 6, no. 14 (1954): 3–12; Anne-Marie Kool, *God Moves in a Mysterious Way: The Hungarian Foreign Mission Movement (1756–1951)* (1993).

Anne-Marie Kool

Vidal, Owen Emeric (1819–1854), first Anglican bishop of Sierra Leone. After serving a pastorate in Sussex, England, Vidal was appointed bishop of the Anglican work in West Africa. He had already studied several Asian and African languages and had advised on the revision of some of the translations into Yoruba prepared by Samuel *Crowther. During his short episcopate (he died within two years of his appointment) he visited the Yoruba mission in the part of his diocese later termed Nigeria, proposed a reorganization of the local church and of the Church Missionary Society (CMS) mission at Sierra Leone on the lines laid down by Henry *Venn, consecrated a cathedral at Freetown, and carried out the first Church of England ordinations within Africa of both Europeans and Africans. Besides encouraging African workers such as Crowther and John *Taylor, Vidal published a pioneering analysis and classification of Yoruba and suggested, correctly, an affinity between Temne and the Bantu languages, drawing on correspondence with J. L. *Krapf in East Africa.

Vidal's daughter later served with the CMS in India.

BIBLIOGRAPHY Christopher Fyfe, *A History of Sierra Leone* (1962, 1994), pp. 272–273; P. E. H. Hair, *The Early Study of Nigerian Languages* (1967, 1994), "Temne and African Language Classification before 1864," *Journal of African Languages* 4 (1965): 46–56; E. Stock, *History of the CMS* (1899), with a photograph of Vidal.

P. E. H. Hair

Vieira, Antônio (1608–1697), Portuguese-Brazilian Jesuit preacher, statesman, and missionary. Vieira was born in Lisbon but was taken at the age of six to Salvador, Bahia, Brazil, when his father was posted there. Educated by the

Jesuits, he joined the order and was assigned to missionary work in the Bahia region. His oratorical gifts and keen intellect led to his being sent to the Jesuit college in Recife (formerly Pernambuco) as teacher of rhetoric, although he preferred to continue his missionary work. When the Spaniards were expelled from Portugal and a Portuguese king, John IV of Braganza, acceded to the throne in 1640, Vieira took part in a delegation to Lisbon to declare the loyalty of the governor of Bahia to the new king. The latter was so impressed with Vieira's oratory that he appointed him court preacher. In this position he became a close adviser to the monarch, who sent him on various missions in Europe on matters of state. Vieira insisted that the Inquisition refrain from persecuting Jews and so-called New Christians (converts), which earned him the lifelong enmity of the Inquisition, dominated in Portugal by the Dominicans.

As the king's health waned, Vieira lost his influence in court, and in 1652 the Jesuits took advantage of this and sent him as a missionary to Maranhão Province in Brazil. There he immediately sided with the Indians to protect them from enslavement by the colonists. In his capacity as chief of the mission, he made numerous trips into the Amazon region, converting, protecting, and learning several local languages. Some of his most eloquent and cogent sermons were delivered at this time as he inveighed against the outrages perpetrated by the colonists. When King John died and his unbalanced son, Afonso VI, succeeded him, Vieira lost whatever protection he had. In 1661 a mob of colonists almost lynched him and his missionaries but instead returned them to Portugal. The Inquisition authorities finally imprisoned him and brought him to trial for heresy in 1663. The charges were based on Vieira's belief in the prophecies of the sixteenth-century shoemaker Bandarra. Based on Bandarra's verses, Vieira predicted the imminent coming of the Fifth Empire with a resurrected John IV as Christ's temporal ruler in the final battle against the Turks. Vieira would not recant and was condemned to perpetual silence.

In 1668 Pedro overthrew his brother and ruled as regent, releasing Vieira from prison. The next year Vieira traveled to Rome, where he obtained a papal decree absolving him of all accusations by the Inquisition, past, present, and future. When he returned to Lisbon he was disappointed by his lack of influence in the court of Pedro II. In 1681 he was back in Bahia, where he edited his sermons and his prophetic books (*History of the Future* and *Clavis Prophetarum*) and meddled in local and Jesuitical politics, for which he was reprimanded. He died in Salvador.

BIBLIOGRAPHY Antônio Sérgio and Hernâni Cidade, eds., *Antônio Vieira: Obras Escolhidas,* 11 vols. (1954); João Lúcio de Azevedo, *História de Antônio Vieira,* 2 vols. (1920).

Gregory Rabassa

Vieter, Heinrich (1853–1914), Catholic missionary and bishop in Cameroon. Born in Kappenberg, Germany, Vieter became a Pallotine father, was ordained in 1887, and went to Brazil in 1889. In 1890 he was nominated prefect apostolic of a mission in Cameroon, then a German colony. When the missionaries arrived in 1891 they found only five Catholics. The first mission station, established in Edea, was named Marienberg. In 1891 a new, climatically more suitable mission station was opened in Kribi in the hinterland. That same year two missionaries died; a year later, a third also succumbed. In the first decade death claimed 14 of the first 60 missionaries; 37 others left the mission due to health reasons, and Vieter himself was often close to death. Despite these setbacks, the mission progressed. From 1891 to 1904, when Vieter became bishop, 4,300 Cameroonians were baptized. As World War I broke out, there were 15 main stations with 34 priests, 36 brothers, 29 sisters, and 223 local teachers. There were 19,576 children in the Catholic schools. In 1913 alone 37,592 children and adults were baptized. In 1914, while on a confirmation tour, Vieter heard about the destruction of Duala mission station and the arrest of the missionaries because of the war. He did not live to see the expulsion of all the missionaries, as he died some weeks later. He was praised as a pioneer, untiring worker, beloved superior, and wise mission organizer, and as a modest, pious, and extremely humble man. His episcopal coat of arms bore the motto "Ego servus tuus."

BIBLIOGRAPHY "Die im Jahre 1914 verstorbenen Missionsbischöfe," *Die katholischen Missionen* 43 (1914/1915): 266–267; H. Skolaster, *Die Pallottiner in Kamerun: 25 Jahre Missionsarbeit* (1924).

Karl Müller, SVD

Vietor, Johann Karl (1861–1934), Bremen merchant and leading supporter of missions in Germany. Vietor began working in West Africa for his family firm in 1884 and soon expanded its operations along the coast. When his uncle died in 1906, he combined the holdings into one company under his own name. He was a Lutheran church deacon in Bremen, supported various religious charities, and sat on the North German Mission board from 1900 to 1932. Because of his business interests in Togo and the Gold Coast, he was appointed to the Imperial Colonial Council in 1901. In keeping with the times, his fervent advocacy of missions tended to be paternalistic. Wanting Africans to become freehold farmers who could be integrated into the export economy, he created the German Congo League in 1910 and the German Aborigines Protection Society in 1913 to promote free trade and combat the introduction of plantation culture and forced labor. He was also against the alcohol trade. In 1909 he founded the magazine *Koloniale Rundschau* to be the voice of "liberal" colonialism. Diedrich *Westermann, its editor, was a North German Society missionary in Togo (1900–1907). Vietor's firm never recovered from its World War I losses and failed in 1931.

BIBLIOGRAPHY J. K. Vietor, *Geschichtliche und kulturelle Entwickelung unserer Schutzgebiete* (1913). Otto Diehn, "Kaufmannschaft und deutsche Eingeborenenpolitik in Togo und Kamerun von der Jahrhundertwende bis zum Ausbruch des Weltkrieges" (Ph.D. diss., Hamburg, 1956); Stefan Weissflog, "J. K. Vietor und sein Konzept des leistungsfähigen Afrikaners," in Werner Ustorf, ed.,

Mission im Kontext: Beiträge zur Sozialgeschichte der Norddeutschen Missionsgesellschaft im 19. Jahrhundert (1986).

Richard V. Pierard

Villaverde, Juan (1841–1897), Dominican missionary and road builder in the Philippines. Villaverde was born in Navarra, Spain, and joined the Dominican order in the convent of Ocaña, Toledo, in 1861. After his ordination he sailed for the Philippines in 1867. From 1868 to 1897 he worked in the Dominican missions of northern Luzon as a frontier missionary, spending some 30 fruitful and creative years among the hill-people of Ifugao and Nueva Vizcaya. He worked in the *reduccion* of the Igorots, creating villages and towns and opening lands for cultivation and irrigation. Many roads today connecting the towns and provinces of Isabela, Ifugao, Nueva Vizcaya, and Pangasinan were designed by Villaverde. His dream was to ameliorate the difficult living conditions of the people. Road building was for him a work of mercy, a form of apostolate and mission building. Villaverde believed that the missionary should address the social and economic welfare of the people to promote human and Christian liberation. Physically exhausted yet spiritually vibrant, Villaverde left for Spain, dying on board ship just before reaching Barcelona. He was buried at sea.

BIBLIOGRAPHY Juan Villaverde, *El Correo Sino-Anamita* (1870–1897). Guillermo Tejón, *Juan Villaverde, O.P., Missionary and Road-Builder* (1982); Dean C. Worcester, ed., "The Ifugaos of Quiangan and Vicinity by Fr. Juan Villaverde," *Philippine Journal of Science* (July 1909); Villaverde's papers are in the Archivo de la Provincia del Santísimo Rosario in Avila, Spain, Sección Cagayan.

Lucio Gutiérrez, OP

Villegagnon. *See* Léry, Jean de.

Villota y Urroz, Gerardo (1839–1906), founder of the Seminario Español de Misiones Extranjeras de Burgos. Villota was born in Santoña, Santandar, Spain, ordained a priest in December 1864, and at first engaged in pastoral ministry. From 1866 to 1870 he was professor of theology at the seminary of Monte Corbán. In 1875 he began working for the bishop of León and in 1883 for the archbishop of Burgos. The following year he became a canon of the cathedral there. By means of the *Anales de la Propagación de la Fe* he kept in touch with events in the missionary world. In connection with the preparation for the First Vatican Council he delivered expert reports on the missionary activity of the church. As a priest he always supported the missionary concerns of the church through prayer, sacrifices, and financial contributions. He assisted the refugees of the Latin American wars of secession. In the archdiocese of Burgos he was active in support of Propaganda Fide and of missionary training of priests and women religious. He conceived the idea of establishing in Spain a missionary seminary for diocesan priests along the lines of similar institutions in Paris, Lyons, and Milan. He began the process in 1897 by financially helping young clerics who were prepared to go to Latin America as missionaries. In 1899 he was able to found an institute, Colegio Eclesiástico de Ultamar y Propaganda Fide, that had the goal of serving the Latin American bishops and especially the Indian missions. After his death the college had difficulties and was entrusted by Pope *Benedict XV to Bishop Juan *Benlloch y Vivo, who revitalized it and reorganized it into the Spanish Institute for Foreign Missions. It received papal approval in 1919. Its first missionaries went to Latin America in 1923 and from 1949 onward also to other parts of the world.

BIBLIOGRAPHY Villota's principal work is *Colegio eclesiástico para la propagación de la fe* (1905); his many articles in missionary magazines are listed in *Boletín de la unión misional de clero de España* 1 (1923): 80–93. *España misionera* 4 (1947): 634–635; *Diccionario de historia eclesiástica de España,* vol. 4 (1975), p. 292; L. P. Platero, "El fundador Villota, apóstol de las vocaciones misioneras," *Semana misionera 1955–56* (1957), pp. 515–519; C. Ruiz Izquierdo, *Temple de apóstol y fundador* (1947).

Karl Müller, SVD

Vincent de Paul (1581–1660), founder of the Congregation of the Mission (known as Vincentians and Lazarists) and of the Daughters of Charity. Vincent de Paul was born in Pouy (present-day Saint-Vincent de Paul), near Dax, France. After his studies in theology in Toulouse University, he was ordained priest in 1600. Around 1613, Philippe-Emmanuel de Gondi, general of galleys in the French fleet, chose him as private tutor for his eldest son. However, wanting to dedicate his life to the poor, especially the peasants in the countryside, he took up the pastorate of Châtillon-les-Dombes in 1617. There he founded the Confraternity of Charity, an association of laywomen who helped the poor and the sick. Coming back to Paris in 1624, he was appointed chaplain for the Collège des Bons Enfants, which became the cradle of the Congregation of the Mission. This congregation was established and endowed in 1625 by Mrs. de Gondi, and Vincent de Paul became the founding father superior. In the beginning it had only two or three missionaries. Very soon, however, it spread through France, Italy, the British Isles, Poland, and even to Madagascar. In 1633 Vincent de Paul established the Daughters of Charity in collaboration with Louise de Marillac. He was canonized in 1737.

BIBLIOGRAPHY Vincent de Paul, *Correspondence, entretiens, documents,* Pierre Coste, ed., 14 vols. (1920–1925); a 15th volume consists of unpublished writings and a bibliography of 397 titles, in André Dodin, ed., *Mission et Charité* (1970). Pierre Coste, *The Life and Works of Saint Vincent de Paul,* 3 vols. (1934, 1952); André Dodin, *Initiation à Saint Vincent de Paul* (1933) and "Vincent de Paul," in *Dictionnaire de Spiritualité* (1992), cols. 841–863.

Joseph Lévesque, PSS

Vinco, Angelo (1819–1853), Catholic missionary pioneer in the southern Sudan. Vinco was born at Cerro Veronese, Italy, received theological training at the Mazza Institute in Verona, and in 1847 joined the first expedition of the institute's mission to central Africa. On a fund-raising venture in Italy after his 1849 voyage up the White Nile, he showed an enthusiasm that inspired the young Daniel *Comboni, later vicar apostolic of Central Africa, to enter the African apostolate. Needing to arrange a second voyage, Don Angelo, as he was universally known, agreed to collect ivory for a Savoyard merchant, establishing his base among the Bari at Lado. There he gained facility in the Bari language, explored the surrounding territories, and succeeded in winning respect to the extent that he served as arbitrator in local disputes. After 14 vigorous months on the White Nile, he succumbed to fever. His memory was hallowed by Europeans such as Guglielmo Lorenzo *Massaja, who likened him to Francis *Xavier, and by the Bari, who sang his praises long after his death.

BIBLIOGRAPHY E. Crestani, *Don Angelo Vinco* (1941); "Angelo Vinco, First Christian to Live among the Bari: His Journeys, 1851–1852," in Elias Toniolo and Richard Hill, eds., *Opening of the Nile Basin: Writings by Members of the Catholic Mission to Central Africa on the Geography and Ethnography of the Sudan, 1842–1881* (1974).

Marc R. Nikkel

Vingren, Adolf Gunnar (1879–1933), Swedish Pentecostal missionary and a founder of the Assemblies of God in Brazil. Vingren arrived in Belém in 1910 with Daniel *Berg, both of whom were of Swedish origin and Baptist affiliation. They had attended the Pentecostal congregation of W. H. Durham in Chicago, where they had been caught up in the Chicago stirrings that followed the 1905 awakening and the 1906 Pentecostal revival. According to Vingren's own account, he was baptized in the Holy Spirit in 1909. Through a dream, he was told in a word of prophecy to serve God together with Berg as missionaries in Pará. To discover the location of Pará, they consulted an atlas in the State Library in Chicago. They were dedicated by Durham as missionaries to Brazil. On arriving at Belém, in Pará State, they became members of a recently organized Baptist church, founded by a Southern Baptist missionary, William B. *Bagby. Vingren was without support, hence he worked hard to sustain himself. After learning Portuguese, he began to preach "redemption and the baptism in the Holy Spirit." Vingren and Berg organized prayer meetings in the basement of the Baptist chapel and looked for a revival. In 1911, after five days of prayer, Celina de Alburquerque was baptized in the Holy Spirit. Some other members of the small group began to speak in tongues and manifested evidence also of having been baptized in the Spirit. This led to controversy between Vingren and the Baptist missionaries, so he and Berg were asked to leave the congregation, and eighteen members went with them. They moved to Alburquerque's home, where, according to Berg, "the first Pentecostal religious service was officially performed in Brazil"—the beginning of the Assemblies of God in Brazil. From Belém they moved to the Amazon region. During 1930 and 1931 they went to the south of the country, where they founded large congregations in Rio de Janeiro, São Paulo, Porto Alegre, and other cities. In 1913 they began to send missionaries to Portugal, then to Madagascar and France. Vingren was diagnosed with cancer in 1930. In 1932 he returned to Sweden, where he died.

BIBLIOGRAPHY Daniel Berg, *Enviado por Deus: Memórias de Daniel Berg* (1959); Emilio G. Conde, *História das Assembléias de Deus no Brasil* (1960); Walter Hollenweger, *The Pentecostals* (1972); A. N. de Mesquita, *História dos batistas no Brasil* (1940); Ivar Vingren, *Pfonjärens dagbok: Brasilienmissionären Gunnar Vingren* (1968).

Pablo A. Deiros

Vining, Leslie Gordon (1885–1955), first Anglican archbishop and metropolitan of West Africa. Vining was educated at Emmanuel College, Cambridge, and trained for the ministry at Ridley Hall. After ordination, he served at St. Gabriel, Bishopwearmouth, at County Durham (1911–1914), a training ground for a number of missionary clergy. He became domestic chaplain to the bishop of Bristol in 1914 and served as chaplain to the British forces (1915–1918), his bravery recognized twice in dispatches. For 20 years he was an incumbent in Bristol at St. Alban's, Westbury Park, Clifton (1918–1938), and a commissary for the diocese of the Niger (1922–1938). Assigned to West Africa in 1938, he was consecrated as an assistant bishop on the Niger; in 1940 he was tranferred to the diocese of Lagos. He made vigorous attempts to deepen the spiritual life of his people and began "bishop's camps" in 1941, at the first of which 130 teachers attended. In 1951 he became archbishop of West Africa and metropolitan when a new province of West Africa was inaugurated. He was widely esteemed as a religious leader by both Christians and Muslims in Nigeria. He never married. After a period of ill health, he died at sea on his way to England.

BIBLIOGRAPHY G. H. G. Hewitt, *Problems of Success: A History of the Church Missionary Society, 1910–1942* (1971). Obituary, *Times*, March 7, 1955.

Timothy Yates

Vinton, Justus Hatch (1806–1858) *and* **Calista (Holman)** (1807–1864), American Baptist missionaries to the Karens of Burma (Myanmar). While attending the Baptist Seminary in Hamilton, New York, Justus Vinton through prayer and fasting decided to become a missionary. Calista Holman had decided to become a missionary after receiving baptism, which stimulated her recovery from two years of invalidism. Lacking seminary training, she prepared herself by mastering Greek, Latin, and Hebrew, thereby shaming her future husband into studying the languages. After a year spent studying Sgau Karen, they married in 1834 and sailed to Burma. The Vintons immediately began to itinerate among Karen villages in the jungle. Finding that they were equally adept in using the language, they soon divided the work and itinerated separately with native assistants. Calista traveled by boat and visited villages along the rivers, preaching, ministering to the sick, founding prayer meetings for women, and beginning schools. Justus hiked through the mountains, evangelizing the Karens and attracting them by his fine singing. For 24 years during the annual dry season, the Vintons continued their pattern of itineration. In the rainy season, they settled in Moulmein, where she taught school and he worked with the Burmese and did Bible translation into Sgau Karen. Calista translated hundreds of hymns into Karen.

War between the Burmese and the British in the 1850s caused the Burmese to increase the torture and murder of the Karens, who were a subject people. Thousands of Karens became disease-ridden refugees, and Justus Vinton bought rice and distributed it among them, moving the mission to Rangoon to help the people. The Baptist Missionary Union censured him for unauthorized activity, so the Vintons and other missionaries resigned in 1856 to affiliate with the American Baptist Free Mission Society. After Justus's death, Calista took on his work at the request of the native pastors. Both the Vintons' children became missionaries in Burma.

BIBLIOGRAPHY Aileen Sutherland Collins, "Calista Holman Vinton: Not Just a Missionary's Wife," *American Baptist Quarterly* 11 (September 1993): 210–222; Calista V. Luther, *The Vintons and the Karens: Memorials of Reverend Justus H. Vinton and Calista H. Vinton* (1880); Robert G. Torbet, *Venture of Faith: The Story of the American Baptist Foreign Mission Society and the Woman's American Baptist Foreign Mission Society, 1814–1954* (1955).

Dana L. Robert

Virgil of Salzburg (c. 700–784), apostle of Carinthia (southern Austria). An Irishman, Virgil, or Fergal (the Celtic form of his name), was on a pilgrimage in Europe when Pepin recommended him to Odio of Bavaria. A noted mathematician, Virgil oversaw the diocese of Salzburg, Austria, and built its cathedral without being consecrated its bishop. *Boniface, who disliked Virgil's science and his irregular leadership, accused him of heresy. The charge was never proved, but it did lead to Virgil's consecration as bishop of Salzburg, in either 755 or 767. When the Carinthians sought help from invading Avars in 772, Virgil met their needs on the condition that these Alpine Slavs convert to Christianity. (Virgil should probably not be identified with the monk, and later abbot, of that name at Aghaboe.)

BIBLIOGRAPHY Francis Betten, *St. Boniface and St. Virgil* (1927); Heinz Dopsch and Roswitha Juffinger, eds., *Virgil von Salzburg, Missionar und Gelehrter* (1985); John Ryan, ed., *Irish Monks in the Golden Age* (1963).

Frederick W. Norris

Visdelou, Claude (1656–1737), Jesuit missionary in China. Visdelou was born in Trébry, Côtes-du-Nord, France. One of the royal mathematicians sent by Louis XIV to the court of China, he arrived in Peking (Beijing) in 1688. Not chosen to stay at court, Visdelou was allowed to preach anywhere in China. Quickly gaining fluency in Chinese, he worked in several mission stations and at times served as the imperial official to welcome incoming missionaries to China.

At the 1705 Canton discussions on the Chinese Rites issue with Charles Maillard de *Tournon, the papal legate, Visdelou openly rejected the Jesuit accommodation position. Three years later the emperor banished Visdelou to Macao, where the next year Tournon secretly consecrated him a bishop. He left immediately for Pondicherry, India, where until his death he continued to send to Rome extensive translations from Chinese historical sources.

BIBLIOGRAPHY H. Gourdon, "Description du royaume de Laos et des pays voisins, présentées au roi du Siam en 1687 par des ambassadeurs du roi de Laos," *Revue Indochinoise* 18 (1912): 203–206; K. F. Neumann, "Claude Visdelou und das Verzeichnis seiner Werke," *Zeitschrift der Deutschen Morgenländischen Gesellschaft*, vol. 4 (1850), pp. 225–242; J. Witek, *Controversial Ideas in China and in Europe: A Biography of Jean-François Foucquet, 1665–1741* (1982), pp. 37–40, 110–115.

John W. Witek, SJ

Visser 't Hooft, Willem A(dolf) (1900–1985), first general secretary of the World Council of Churches (WCC). Visser 't Hooft was born in Haarlem, Netherlands, and graduated from the University of Leiden. During his student days he was drawn into the Student Christian Movement (SCM), where he learned for the first time that Christian faith could be a dynamic reality. A meeting with John R. *Mott kindled his vision of the worldwide mission of Christ, which shaped all his subsequent work. Reading Karl *Barth's *Epistle to the Romans* in 1922 gave him the assurance that the word of God had an authority that could challenge all the ideologies of modernity. There was a message to match the mission.

In 1924 Visser 't Hooft moved to Geneva to head the international work of the YMCA among boys, an assignment that nurtured his wide knowledge of and sensitivity to international issues. From 1932 he was general secretary of the World's Student Christian Federation (WSCF), and from 1938 he was the first general secretary of the WCC "in process of formation." He retired from the WCC in 1966.

The focus of Visser 't Hooft's passion can be seen in the titles of some of his books: *None Other Gods* (1937), *The Kingship of Christ* (1948), and *No Other Name* (1963). The churches of Europe were hindered from their world mission by unlawful alliances with nationalism and with liberal ideologies. In this syncretistic entanglement, he believed, they could not meet the onslaught of the new paganisms. The absolute authority of Christ as God's living word required both unity and mission, for how could the Good Shepherd gather all the nations if his own flock was scattered? The world mission of the church must be at the heart of ecclesial life, not relegated to peripheral bodies.

Visser 't Hooft was not a major theological writer, but his work in the WSCF and in the WCC, his ceaseless traveling, speaking, and writing, and during World War II his often dangerous work of keeping Christians on opposing sides in contact with one another were of decisive importance in shaping the ecumenical movement of the twentieth century.

BIBLIOGRAPHY Willem Adolph Visser 't Hooft, *Memoirs* (1973, 1987). Lesslie Newbigin, "W. A. Visser 't Hooft," in Gerald H. Anderson et al., eds., *Mission Legacies* (1994), pp. 117-122. Visser 't Hooft's papers are in the WCC archives in Geneva and include a list of over 1,760 items—books, articles, and unpublished papers.

Lesslie Newbigin

Vitoria, Francisco de (1483?-1546), Dominican scholar, and lecturer, and advocate for Indian rights in the New World. Born in the Basque country, Vitoria entered the Dominican order, studied and taught at the University of Paris, and from 1526 until his death, held the prime chair of theology at the University of Salamanca. Among his most famous *relecciones* (class lectures) are his treatises *De Potestate Civili* (1528), *De Indis,* and *De Jure Belli* (both in 1539), all published after his death. Vitoria applied Thomas *Aquinas's concept of natural law to the state of the world of his time, and in so doing he influenced a generation of missionaries and became one of the fathers of contemporary international law. He upheld the principle that all natural communities of human beings, or nations, have rights that cannot be denied by others, even in the name of the pope or Christianity. He applied that norm specifically to the Indians of the New World and thus lent intellectual support to the struggle of his fellow Dominicans, especially Bartolomé de *Las Casas. He also defended the just war theory, which radically invalidated earlier notions of the rights of Christians to conquer infidels and limited the grounds upon which war could be legitimately declared.

BIBLIOGRAPHY Francisco de Vitoria, *Relecciones teológicos del Maestro Fray Francisco de Vitoria,* 3 vols., L. G. Alonso Getino, ed. (1933-1936). Anthony Pagden and Jeremy Lawrence, eds., *Political Writings, Francisco de Vitoria* (1991); James B. Scott, *The Spanish Origins of International Law* (1934); David Traboulay, "16th Century Scholasticism and the Colonization of America: Francisco de Vitoria and His Influence," *ZMR* 70 (1986): 15-37.

Jeffrey Klaiber, SJ

Vives y Marjá, Juan Bautista (1545-1632), founder of the college of Propaganda Fide. Vives was born in Valencia, Spain, in a family of humanists. He was ordained in 1591 and served as a Roman agent for the Spanish Inquisition and ambassador in Rome for the Kingdom of Congo. In 1622, when *Gregory XV founded the Congregation of Propaganda Fide, he appointed Vives a prelate of the congregation. Sometime between 1624 and 1626, Vives offered to Pope *Urban VIII the Ferratini palace in Rome (which he had bought in 1613), along with scholarship funds for missionary training, for a college where secular priests of any nation could study and prepare for the missions. The Congregation of Propaganda Fide asked Vives to prepare the rules and statutes for the college. With the papal bull *Immortalis Dei Filius* of August 1, 1627, Urban VIII accepted the donation and the conditions proposed by Vives. He opened the college under the patronage of St. Peter and Paul, calling it Collegium Pontificium Urbanum. In 1628 Vives also proposed a tax of 10 percent on all contributions to the church, to go to Propaganda Fide in order to support the missions.

BIBLIOGRAPHY Benito de V. Arana, "Cuarto centenario de monseñor Juan Bautista Vives, fundador del Colegio Urbano de Propaganda Fide," *Illuminare* 21 (1943): 10-12; Andrés del Niño Jesús, "Recordando un centenario Mons. Juan Bautista Vives y Marjá, 1545-1945," in *La Obra Máxima,* vol. 25 (1945), pp. 163-165, 191-193, 214-216; C. de Rosa, "I Teatini e le origini del Collegio Urbano di Propaganda Fide," *Regnum Dei* 4 (1948): 277-304; Juan de Unzalu, "Monseñor Juan Bautista Vives y Marjá, fundador del Colegio Urbano de Propaganda Fide," *El Siglo de las Misiones* 30 (1943): 150-153, and "Mons. Juan Bautista Vives y Marjá: Pregón de un centenario," *Illuminare* 22 (1944): 9-13.

Willi Henkel, OMI

Vladimir of Kiev (c. 956-1015), prince who made Christianity the official religion in Russia. Born into the royal Norman-Russian line of Rurik, Vladimir defeated his half-brother, Yaropolk, to consolidate by 980 modern European Russia and Ukraine (the duchies of Novgorod and Kiev). Despite the presence of a fervent witness to Christianity within the palace (his grandmother, Olga, and his mother, Malusha, having been baptized in Constantinople in 957), Vladimir remained a pagan, continued his polygamy, and practiced indigenous rites including human sacrifice. A mutual need for military alliance against the Bulgars and the Germans led to his contact with Christian Byzantium, cemented in 987 by his marriage to Princess Anna Porphyrogeneta, sister of the Greek emperor Basil II, and acceptance of baptism on January 3, 988, following a three-month preparation. According to the popular story in the eleventh-century *Russian Primary Chronicle,* Vladimir sent embassies to examine the rites of the Latin Germans, the Khazarian Jews, and Bulgarian Muslims, as well as those of Byzantium. They found the first three religions incompatible with various traits of the Russian people, while in Constantinople's Hagia Sophia they knew not whether they were in heaven or on earth. The result, according to uncritical contemporary hagiographies, was Vladimir's sudden and complete conversion and the rapid transformation of his realm into a Christian nation. More reliable sources indicate that the convert prince (renamed Basil in baptism) did indeed immediately order that the Dnieper River mark the place both of the baptismal rebirth of his subjects and the symbolic drowning of the god Perun. This change was brought about by Greek clergy, whom he welcomed into the duchy. He made clear that those who rejected the new faith were enemies of the state, and he recruited a large contingent of priests, monks, iconographers, architects, and other artisans needed to re-create Byzantine culture in Kievan Rus' and truly transform society. The Slavic translations of the Scriptures and liturgy pioneered by *Cyril and *Methodius were imported from Bulgaria. The reality of his personal conversion is seen in his introduction of educational, philanthropic, and judicial reforms inspired by the gospel. He also supported the missionary work of the German bishop *Bruno of Querfurt among the northern Pechenegs (to the extent of offering his son as hostage). Centuries after his death, Vladimir was canonized by the Russian Orthodox Church as "Equal to the Apostles."

BIBLIOGRAPHY L. Muller, ed., *Der Metropoliten Ilarions Lobrede auf Vladimir den Heiligen und Glaubensbekenntnis* (1962); Andrzej Poppe, "St. Vladimir as a Christian," in J. Breck, et al., eds., *The Legacy of St. Vladimir* (1990), pp. 41–46; S. A. Zenkovsky, ed., *Medieval Russian Epics, Chronicles, and Tales* (1974).

Paul D. Garrett

Voetius, Gisbertus (*or* Gijsbert Voet) (1589–1676), Dutch Reformed theologian and first Protestant to write a compehensive theology of mission. Voetius was born in Heusden, North Brabant, Netherlands. He studied theology at Leiden, served as a Reformed minister in Vlijmen and in Heusden (1610–1634), and was the founder of Utrecht University, where he served as professor of Semitic languages and theology (1634–1676). His first engagement with mission issues occurred at the national synod of Dordrecht (1618–1619), where he dealt with the question of whether baptism could be administered to children from non-Christian backgrounds living with Dutch families in the East Indies. In 1643 he wrote a treatise on religious freedom. His theology of mission is found in *Selectae Disputationes Theologicae* (5 vols., 1648–1669) and in *Politica Ecclesiastica* (3 vols., 1663–1676).

Voetius emphasized that missions are grounded in both the hidden and the revealed will of God. Only apostles and assemblies such as synods have the right to establish missions; it is not the right of the pope, nor princes and magistrates, nor companies to do so. The goals of mission are the conversion of non-believers, heretics, and schismatics; the planting, gathering, and establishing of churches; and the glorification and manifestation of divine grace. Mission churches, he maintained, should not be subordinated to the sending churches in Europe.

The period after 1800 saw the growth of interest in Voetius's missionary thinking. Abraham Kuyper (1837–1920) borrowed heavily from him, especially in the field of apologetics. The synod of the Reformed Churches at Middelburg (1896) decided in favor of "ecclesiastical mission" (in contrast to the William *Carey model of mission by means of para-church agencies). Both Johannes H. *Bavinck and Johannes *Verkuyl made Voetius's missiology known outside the Netherlands. Johannes C. *Hoekendijk at Utrecht University, a fervent opponent of Voetius's views, considered his emphasis on church planting too akin to Roman Catholic missiology.

BIBLIOGRAPHY H. A. van Andel, *De Zendingsleer van Gisbertus Voetius* (1912); J. A. B. Jongeneel, "The Missiology of Gisbertus Voetius, the First Comprehensive Protestant Theology of Missions," in *Calvin Theological Journal* 26 (1991): 47–79.

Jan A. B. Jongeneel

Von. *For names beginning with Von or Von der, see under the following part of the name.*

Vories, William Merrell (*or* William Merrell Vories Hitotsuyanagi) (1880–1964), missionary in Japan and founder of the Omi Brotherhood. Born in Leavenworth, Kansas, Vories graduated from Colorado College. After volunteering for mission service with the Student Volunteer Movement (SVM), he accepted an invitation relayed through the SVM headquarters to teach English at a school in Omi-Hachiman, Japan. Arriving there in 1905, he was soon dismissed from the school because of his Christian evangelistic activities. With the help of Japanese Christians, he founded the Omi Brotherhood as a demonstration of practical Christianity. The Brotherhood came to include not only a YMCA and a church but also Christian schools, a tuberculosis sanatorium, and various industrial and commercial enterprises. He supported such programs primarily through his work as an architect, eventually designing over two thousand buildings throughout Japan. In 1919 he married Maki Hitotsuyanagi, from an aristocratic daimyo's family, who was a great support to him especially as antagonism between the United States and Japan mounted. Just before the Pearl Harbor attack, he became a Japanese citizen and took his wife's maiden name as his own. Staying on in Japan during the war, his hopes for Japanese-American reconciliation were vindicated in the postwar era, and he was the recipient of many honors from the Japanese government and civic groups. He is the author of the missionary hymn "Let There Be Light." He died at Omi-Hachiman.

BIBLIOGRAPHY Merrell Vories Hitotsuyanagi (as he is listed in libraries) wrote *A Mustard-Seed in Japan* (1913), *The Evangelization of Rural Japan* (1915), *From Buddhist Priest to Christian Evangelist* (1917?), *The Omi Brotherhood in Nippon* (1934), and *Poems of the East and West* (1960). Grace Fletcher wrote a biography of the Hitotsuyanagis in the *The Bridge of Love* (1967).

James M. Phillips

Voronaeff, Ivan Efimovich (1886–1940s), early Russian Pentecostal leader. Born in central Russia and later member of a Cossack regiment, Voronaeff (or Voronaev) was converted in 1908. He served as a pastor before migrating to the United States. While pastoring a Russian Baptist church in New York City in 1919, he visited Glad Tidings Tabernacle, an Assemblies of God (AG) congregation, and subsequently became a Pentecostal.

With appointment as an AG missionary and the financial backing of Glad Tidings Tabernacle and the Russian and Eastern European Mission, Voronaeff returned to his homeland in 1920 via Bulgaria; his brief ministry there inaugurated the Bulgarian Pentecostal movement. With Odessa as his residence, he traveled widely in the Ukraine and in Russia, evangelizing and promoting the founding of hundreds of local churches with thousands of converts. When the first Pentecostal congress met at Odessa in 1926, Voronaeff received appointment as the first president of the Council of the All-Ukrainian Union of the Christian Evangelical Faith. He also edited the Union's *Evangelist* magazine and attempted to establish a ministerial training school.

When persecution of Christians intensified, Voronaeff and his wife, Katherine, were imprisoned in Siberia (1930), along with hundreds of others. After release and further imprisonment, Voronaeff died in Siberia sometime after 1940; Katherine was released in 1953.

BIBLIOGRAPHY Steve Durasoff, *Bright Wind of the Spirit* (1972); Walter J. Hollenweger, *The Pentecostals* (1972); Katherine Voronaeff, "20 Years a Soviet Slave," interview by Norman Rohrer, *Eternity*, July 1961, pp. 8–10, 39; J. [Ivan] E. Voronaeff, "Report of Assemblies in Russia," *Pentecostal Evangel*, September 1, 1928, pp. 10, 12; Paul Voronaeff, *My Life in Soviet Russia* (1969). Reports and other information on his ministry can be found in issues of *Gospel Call* and *Pentecostal Evangel*.

Gary B. McGee

Vos, Michiel C(hristiaan) (1759–1825), pioneer South African missions advocate. Born in Cape Town, Vos went to Utrecht, Netherlands, in 1780 to study theology and ministered in the Netherlands for nine years before returning to the Cape in 1794. There he was concerned especially about the spiritual condition of the slaves in the Cape Colony. In his Dutch Reformed congregation at Roodezand (now Tulbagh), his first sermon was on Mark 16:15, "Go ye into all the world and preach the gospel to every creature." He told his congregation that he would therefore preach to the slaves and Khoi-Khoi (Hottentots)—something that was not generally done at the time. He also used his personal influence to improve the position of the Moravian missionaries in the Cape. In 1802 he went to England, and from there to Tranquebar, India, in 1804, where he ministered until his return to the Cape in 1809. He made a lasting impression through his catechesis, pastoral care, and mission enthusiasm in all the congregations he served.

BIBLIOGRAPHY Vos's autobiography was published in Amsterdam in 1824 as *Merkwaardig verhaal* (Remarkable story). An analysis of Vos's contribution, as well as a full bibliography, appears in R. Murray, "Michiel Christiaan Vos (1759–1825): Tussem reformasie en piëtisme" (M.Th. thesis, Univ. of South Africa, 1983).

Willem Saayman

Voskamp, Carl Johannes (1859–1937), German missionary in China. Born in Antwerp, Belgium, and raised in Duisburg, Germany, Voskamp studied in a local gymnasium (high school) and then transferred to the seminary of the Berlin Mission in 1879. Completing his studies in 1884, he left at once for service in the South China field. He was ordained in Canton (Guangzhou) in 1887 and ministered in various communities in the area, where he learned to relate to both simple folk and Confucian intellectuals. He married Maria Lutze in 1887 (she died in 1902) and Emmy Palm in 1907. While home on furlough in 1897 and 1898, Voskamp was named superintendent of the new mission station at the German Kiaochow (Chiao Hsien) Bay naval base in Shantung (Shandong) Province. By 1899 he and his Berlin co-workers had built a church and mission house in Tsingtao and soon were operating schools, preaching stations, and even a hospital in the enclave.

He was a prolific writer; his major works include *Unter dem Banner des Drachen und im Zeichen des Kreuzes* (c. 1892), *Zerstörende und aufbauende Mächte in China* (1898), *Gestalten und Gewalten aus dem Reiche der Mitte* (1906), and *Das Alte und das neue China* (1914). His son was killed during the Japanese siege of Kiaochow in fall 1914, but he was allowed to stay in Tsingtao under house arrest and continue a limited work. After the war the work suffered from financial exigency, and in 1925 Berlin turned over much of it to the American Lutherans. In 1931 Voskamp retired in the field. He died in Tsingtao.

BIBLIOGRAPHY C. J. Voskamp, *Aus der belagerten Tsingtau* (1915). Julius Richter, *Geschichte der Berliner Missionsgesellschaft* (1924) and *Berliner Missionsbericht* 114 (1937): 157–158 (obit.).

Richard V. Pierard

Voth, Henry R. (1855–1931), Mennonite missionary anthropologist. Voth was born in the Ukraine and immigrated to the United States in 1874. After studying at Wadsworth Mennonite Institute, Ohio, and Evangelical Seminary, Missouri, in 1882 he began working among the Cheyenne Indians at Darlington, Oklahoma (then known as Indian Territory). In 1892 he transferred to Arizona to assist with a mission among the Hopis. During the next nine years Voth conducted extensive ethnographic studies of Hopi life and religion and developed an outstanding collection of artifacts that were subsequently placed with the Field Museum, Chicago. His work as an ethnographer won him praise for insightfulness and accuracy but blame for having removed artifacts the Hopis valued. A number of Voth's monographs on Hopi culture were published in the Anthropological Series of the Field Columbian Museum, including *The Oraibi Powamu Ceremony* (1901), *The Oraibi Oaquoel Ceremony* (1903), *Oraibi Natal Customs and Ceremonies* (1905), *Brief Miscellaneous Hopi Papers* (1912), *Hopi Proper Names* (1912), and *The Oraibi Marau Ceremony* (1912). Voth and George A. Dorsey coauthored several other works on Hopi religion.

BIBLIOGRAPHY Marlin W. Adrian, *Mennonites, Missionaries, and Native Americans: Religious Paradigms and Cultural Encounters* (1989); Lois Barrett, *The Vision and the Reality: The Story of Home Missions in the General Conference Mennonite Church* (1983); E. G. Kaufman, *The Development of the Missionary and Philanthropic Interest among the Mennonites of North America* (1931).

Wilbert R. Shenk

Waddell, Hope Masterton (1804–1895), Presbyterian missionary in Jamaica and Nigeria. Waddell was born in Dublin, Ireland, and at age 16 was apprenticed to Andrew Pollock and Co., druggists and general merchants in the city. In 1822 he felt called to missionary service and in 1825 was accepted by the Scottish Missionary Society. He married Jessie Simpson and, after some years of study, was ordained by the Edinburgh Presbytery of the United Secession Church of Scotland. He and his wife left for Jamaica in 1829 and settled at Cornwall and Cinnamon Hill, two sugar estates on the north coast between Falmouth and Montego Bay. He was an active observer both of the slave revolt of 1832 and of emancipation in 1838. Following emancipation, Waddell founded Mt. Horeb, a settlement in the mountains south of Montego Bay, as part of the movement of freed slaves away from the plantations.

In 1844 the Jamaica Missionary Presbytery, of which he was a member, appointed Waddell to lead their mission to Calabar, in what is now southeastern Nigeria. He arrived in 1846, accompanied by three others from the church in Jamaica. His first location was in Duke Town, the largest of the Calabar communities. The following year, on the death of his colleague William *Jameson, he moved across the Cross River to another part of Calabar called Creek Town. He was "head of station" in Creek Town until he retired to Ireland in 1858 for medical reasons. In 1863 he published his autobiography, a comprehensive and level-headed narrative which remains a major source of information for both Jamaican and Nigerian history. He died in Dublin.

BIBLIOGRAPHY Hope Masterton Waddell, *Twenty-Nine Years in the West Indies and Central Africa: A Review of Missionary Work and Endeavour, 1829–1858* (1863; reprinted with an introduction by G. I. Jones, 1970); Geoffrey Johnston, *Of God and Maxim Guns: Presbyterianism in Nigeria, 1846–1966* (1988). Waddell's diaries for the years 1849–1856 are in the National Library, Edinburgh.

Geoffrey Johnston

Wade, Jonathan (1798–1872) *and*
Deborah (Lapham) (1801–1868), American Baptist missionaries in Burma (Myanmar). Jonathan Wade was baptized at age 18 and enrolled as one of the first students at the Baptist Seminary, Hamilton, New York. He met his wife at the local church, which had an active missionary society. After graduating in 1822, he began to study Burmese. The Wades were the first missionaries to go from Hamilton, and they sailed to Burma with Ann *Judson when she returned from furlough in 1823. In 1824 war with England broke out. Wade was arrested with other missionaries but released after one day. The Wades stayed in Calcutta for the duration of the war, working on a Burmese dictionary. In 1826 they returned to Burma and took in the daughter of Ann Judson (who had died not long after her husband's release from prison). Moving to Moulmein, Deborah Wade freed girl slaves, opened day schools, and undertook evangelistic work while Jonathan worked on translations.

As religious interest emerged among the Karens, a tribal people, the Wades began itinerant evangelism in the jungles. Jonathan Wade devised a writing system for the Sgau Karen language and engaged in Bible translation. After a furlough in which they taught Burmese and Karen for a year to prospective missionaries, they returned in 1834 with a group of new missionaries. During the dry season, they conducted village evangelism, itinerating separately with junior missionaries. Deborah gave Bible instruction and did medical work, and Jonathan examined and baptized the candidates she trained. During the rainy season, she taught school and he did translation work. After the death of Adoniram *Judson, they took over the Moulmein mission, returning to settled work among the Burmese. Jonathan directed ministerial education for a decade and continued his translations. The crown of his work was a five-volume Sgau Karen dictionary. The Wades died in Burma.

BIBLIOGRAPHY Jonathan Wade, *A Vocabulary of the Sgau Karen Language* (1849), *Thesaurus of Karen Knowledge* (compiled from 1847 to 1850), *A Dictionary of the Sgau Karen Language* (1896), *Karen Vernacular Grammar* (3d ed., 1897); Deborah B. L. Wade, *The Burman Slave Girl; Also, Narrative of the First Burman Inquirer, and of the First Converted Burman . . .* (n.d.). Walter N. Wyeth, *The Wades* (1891). Deborah Wade's correspondence with her family from 1850 to 1863 is held by the American Baptist Historical Society in Rochester, N.Y.

Dana L. Robert

Wagenseil, Johann Christoph (1633–1705), German Protestant pioneer scholar and advocate of missions to Jews. Born in Nürnberg, Wagenseil is widely considered to be one of the fathers of European Hebrew studies and is cited in the *Encyclopedia Judaica* as a noted Christian Hebraist. He was a professor at the University of Altdorf, first of history (1667), then Oriental languages (1674), and finally ecclesiastical law (1697). His academic focus was always related to his desire to see Jewish people acknowledge Jesus as their Messiah, and he devoted much of his time to enabling students to train for ministry among Jewish people, focusing especially on the need to learn Yiddish language and culture. Significantly for his generation, he was a firm opponent of anti-Semitism and of any attempts to use pressure to influence Jewish people in their consideration of the Christian message. His major missiological work, published in 1681, was entitled *Tela Ignea Satanae* (The flaming arrows of Satan), an anthology of, and commentary upon, Jewish works used to refute Christian proofs of the Messiahship of Jesus. It became one of the standard apologetic works in Jewish evangelism for several generations.

BIBLIOGRAPHY *Encyclopedia Judaica,* vol. 16 (1972), pp. 239–240; A. Lukyn Williams, *Missions to the Jews: An Historical Retrospect* (1897).

Walter Riggans

Wakefield, Thomas (1836–1901), United Methodist Free Church (UMFC) missionary in East Africa. Wakefield was born in Derby, England, left school at ten, and was later apprenticed as a printer. At age 22 he became a full-time preacher of the UMFC and from 1858 to 1861 served circuits in Cornwall. In 1861 he was accepted for a new mission undertaken by the UMFC in response to the writings of Johann *Krapf, who stressed the missionary significance of the Galla, or Oromo, people. Krapf himself led a party including Wakefield and James Woolner of the UMFC and two St. Chrischona Swiss missionaries, which reached Zanzibar in January 1862 and chose Ribe (in what is now Kenya) as the Methodist station. The Swiss soon withdrew, and first Woolner and then Krapf were forced to leave through illness. The still-raw Wakefield was left alone until joined by Charles *New in April 1863. For 27 years Wakefield was the backbone of the mission, and often its sole representative. Other missionaries died or left broken in health (W. H. During, a Sierra Leonean, was an exception); Wakefield, though often ill, persisted. Ribe, and later Jomvu, became church centers with notable African workers.

Migrant Oromo were a major element in these churches, but Ribe was essentially a Nyika town, and the Nyika were not a dominant people. Never forgetting that the mission was first intended for the Galla, Wakefield constantly sought contact with Oromo and campaigned, with eventual success, for new mission resources to reach them. He built up a detailed knowledge of coast-to-interior trading routes, drawing on Arab, Swahili, and African sources. Major explorers (James Grant, Joseph Thomson) respected him, and the Royal Geographical Society recognized his work with a grant in 1882 and a fellowship in 1889 and also wanted him to lead one of their African expeditions (a proposal vetoed by the mission). He was also known as an ethnographer and a naturalist. Despite the limitations of his education he became an enthusiastic translator into Swahili, Nyika, and Oromo. Genial and buoyant in temperament ("a very prince of African good fellows," said Joseph Thomson), Wakefield had excellent relations with other missions in East Africa, including the (high church) Universities' Mission. Bishops Tozer and *Hannington were his friends. He was widely known in his denomination, and in 1888, his first year after retiring from Africa, was elected its president. He served various English circuits, attended the Ecumenical Missionary Conference in New York in 1900, and died the next year in Southport.

During his first furlough in 1869 he married Rebecca Brewin, who died in childbirth in Ribe in 1874. In 1881 he married Elizabeth Sommers, who became his biographer.

BIBLIOGRAPHY O. A. Beckerlegge, ed., *United Methodist Ministers and Their Circuits, 1792–1932* (n.d.); Robert Brewin, *Memoirs of Mrs. Rebecca Wakefield* (1879); A. J. Hopkins, *Trail Blazers and Road Makers: A Brief History of the East African Mission of the United Methodist Church* (n.d.); E. S. Wakefield, *Thomas Wakefield: Missionary and Geographical Pioneer in East Equatorial Africa* (1904); Barbara Wolstenholme, *Not Clear to Themselves: The Story of Thomas and Rebecca Wakefield and the Establishment of the Methodist Church in East Africa* (1994; includes transcribed journals); *United Methodist Free Churches Conference Minutes,* 1902, p. 30, and *Missionary Echo,* 1902, p. 19, obits.

Andrew F. Walls

Walaeus, Antonius (*or* Anton de Wale) (1573–1639), founder of the first Protestant institute for training missionaries. Born in Gent, Belgium, Walaeus was the son of influential parents who settled as refugees in Middelburg, Netherlands. He studied at Leiden, traveled throughout Europe, and became pastor at Middelburg in 1605. There he trained Matthias van den Broecke and Zacharias Heyningus, the first two ministers sent by the local classis to the East Indies in 1609. Along with his colleague Herman Faukelius, Walaeus was appointed professor in Leiden in 1618, where the two emphasized that academic training was needed for missionaries sent to the Indies. In 1616 they proposed establishing a seminary for advanced academic study and for training in the

Malay language and Indies culture. This proposal was contrary to the early intention of the Amsterdam church authorities, who wished to send out non-academically educated pastors or young students.

Walaeus's vision was finally established at Leiden in April 1622; the Seminarium Indicum was founded as a private institution at the expense of the East India Company, with Walaeus as its director. There he educated about twenty missionary candidates for the East and West Indies in line with his book *Het ampt der kerckendienaeren* (The Office of Ministers, 1615) which was translated into French and Latin. He advocated that church and secular authorities should become mutually dependent with ministers deciding on the doctrine and discipline of the church and secular authorities serving the public well-being of the church. According to Walaeus, as successors of the apostles and as shepherds of local churches, ministers bear responsibility for spreading the gospel among all nations. He proposed that missionaries must be able to read the Qur'an in order to persuade Muslims to convert to Christianity.

In 1633 the seminary was closed because the company felt there were enough ministers overseas. Later on it was continued by Robertus *Junius. Until his death Walaeus stayed in touch with the missionaries in the East and West Indies.

BIBLIOGRAPHY L. J. van Gelder, *La missionologie théorique carmelitaine: Ses sources et son influence,* vol. 1 (1940); L. J. Joosse, *Scoone dingen sijn swaere dingen: Een onderzoek naar de motieven en de activiteiten in De Nederlanden tot verbreiding van de gereformeerde religie* (1992); G. J. M. J. Koolen, *Een seer bequaem middel: Onderwijs en Kerk onder de 17e eeuwse VOC* (1993). See also O. G. Myklebust, *The Study of Missions in Theological Education,* vol. 1 (1955).

Leendert J. Joosse

Waldo (*or* Valdez), Peter (c. 1140–1217), French leader of church reform and renewal. As a wealthy merchant in the city of Lyons, Waldo gave away all his property, which he had acquired by lending money at high rates of interest, and assumed a life of poverty. A deep religious experience had turned his thoughts to a "simple gospel," and he translated portions of the Bible into the local dialect in an effort to preach more effectively. As he preached in the streets to both rich and poor, many men and women began to follow him. The "Poor of Lyons," as his followers were called, espoused traditional orthodoxy but insisted that all believers had a right to proclaim the gospel, which drew vehement opposition from local clergy. The archbishop of Lyons ordered Waldo and his followers to stop preaching; when they persisted, they were banned from the city. In 1184 Pope Lucius III (r. 1181–1185) included them among the sects that were excommunicated from the Roman Catholic Church, making them subject to persecution, torture, and death. Crushed by the great political and religious powers, the Waldensian societies were scattered from the Languedoc and Provence in France to Lombardy in Italy. They joined the Calvinistic Reformation and survived in a small area of the western Alps, later expanding to other Italian regions.

BIBLIOGRAPHY Magda Martini, *Pierre Valdo: Le pauvre de Lyon* (1961); Giorgio Tourn, *The Waldensians: The First 800 Years* (1980).

Ans J. van der Bent

Walker, Thomas (1859–1912), evangelist and missionary in India. Born in Matlock Spa, Derbyshire, Walker graduated from St. John's College, Cambridge, in 1882. Ordained deacon in the Church of England the same year, he served first at St. John's Church, Stratford, and then at St. James' Church, Holloway. He arrived in Tinnevelly, South India, in 1885 at the request of the Church Missionary Society (CMS) Madras corresponding committee and was assigned to assist the ailing Edward *Sargent, with particular responsibility for the North Tinnevelly Itineracy. (See under Thomas *Ragland.) Following Sargent's death in 1889, Walker became district chairman of Tinnevelly with oversight of fifty clergy, and conducted a purge against indiscipline and immorality. In 1890 he married Mary Elizabeth Hodge of the Church of England Zenana Missionary Society, and from 1892 to 1893 went on furlough because of his wife's poor health. On his return he was stationed in Palayankottah. In 1897 he resigned as district chairman to concentrate on evangelism and on preparing Tamil candidates for ordination. He wrote a number of New Testament commentaries in Tamil but later became more and more involved in conducting retreats and revival meetings.

Walker's abiding legacy is the self-sufficiency of the Church of South India diocese of Tirunelveli, his support for the ministry of Amy *Carmichael (who wrote his biography) and the Dohnavur Fellowship, the establishment of the Keswick tradition in South India, and the great annual Maramon convention of the Syrian churches in Kerala, which he cofounded in 1896. Severing his connection with the CMS in 1899, he retired to Dohnavur and died on his way to a convention in Masulipatam in 1912 after 27 years of service.

BIBLIOGRAPHY Amy Carmichael, *Thomas Walker of Tinnevelly, 1859–1912* (1916) and *Walker of Tinevelly* (1932); Eugene Stock, *History of the Church Missionary Society,* vol. 4, (1899).

E. M. Jackson

Walker, William (1800–1855), first missionary to Australian Aborigines. Following training and ordination in England, Walker was appointed by the Wesleyan Missionary Society to the Aborigines of New South Wales. Arriving in Sydney in 1821, he befriended the dispossessed Sydney Aborigines and baptized the first Aboriginal convert, Thomas Coke Walker Bennelong. Although considered to be the best educated man in the colony and a preacher of extraordinary power, Walker was never able to find an appropriate role for himself, a problem exacerbated by tensions between clergy and secular authorities, clergy of different denominations, and Wesleyan clergy themselves. His educational plans for the Aborigines received little support, yet when he associated himself with Governor Macquarie's Native Institution and the Female Orphan School, he was severely criticized by his fellow clergy. He was dismissed as a missionary, quite unjustly, in 1826. Taking up farming, he remained popular with Wesleyan families who attended his unofficial services. According to Joseph Orton, later chairman of the Wesleyan's New South Wales district, Walker was "a clever man. . . . injudiciously managed by those who were placed over him." Unfortunately, on Walker's death, his request that his many manuscripts be burned was carried out.

BIBLIOGRAPHY James Colwell, *The Illustrated History of Methodism: Australia* (1904); John Harris, *One Blood* (1990). Material related to Walker may be obtained from Bonwick Transcripts, Box 53, Mitchell Library, Sydney, and in *Historical Records of Australia* 1, no. 1 (1893): 10–15.

John W. Harris

Waller, Edward Henry Mansfield (1874–1943), missionary bishop in South India. Having obtained a classics degree in 1893 at Corpus Christi College, Oxford, Waller was a tutor at the London School of Divinity (1893–1897) during which time he was ordained deacon (1894) and priest (1895) in the Church of England. He then joined the staff of the Church Missionary Society (CMS) theological college in Allahabad, India, serving as vice-principal (1897–1903) and principal (1903–1905) before becoming a district missionary in Benares (Varanasi) (1907–1909) and then area secretary (1910–1914). After two years in London as CMS secretary for India and Persia, he was elected bishop of Tinnevelly in Tamil Nadu, South India. A shy and sensitive soul with an exceptionally lucid and quick mind, Waller, who understood Tamil, could not speak fluently or preach in it. Nevertheless, he negotiated the first stage of the disestablishment of the Anglican Church in India and the replacement of the Book of Common Prayer and the Thirty-Nine Articles with a more "Indian" constitution, which enabled the southern dioceses to move forward into union in the Church of South India. He was responsible also for creating ecumenical relationships in place of hostility between CMS (evangelical) and Society for the Propagation of the Gospel (Anglo-Catholic) missions and between them and the religious communities they established. He worked hard to integrate mission administration and finance into the diocesan church structure and pressured the CMS headquarters to achieve this (1924). In the process he provoked the Alvaneri schism, resulting in the formation of the separate Tinnevelly CMS Evangelical Church.

BIBLIOGRAPHY Edward H. M. Walker, *Priest and Parish in India* (1928) and *The Story of the Negotiations for Church Union in South India* (1930). Mildred E. Gibbs, *The Anglican Church in India 1600–1970* (1972).

E. M. Jackson

Walls, Andrew F(inlay) (1928–), pioneer and academic statesman in the study of missions and world Christianity. With insight and clarity, Walls has expounded the salient features of his subject and placed it in the forefront of serious academic inquiry. Born in Scotland, he was educated at Oxford and subsequently became librarian at Tyndale House, Cambridge, before going to Sierra Leone, West Africa, in 1957 to teach theology at the University College of Sierra Leone. In 1962 he moved to Nigeria, which had gained its independence two years earlier, to head the new Department of Religious Studies at the University of Nigeria at Nsukka. While in Africa, he promoted the study of Christianity in its non-Western forms, an initiative that he later developed into the Centre for the Study of Christianity in the Non-Western World (CSCNWW), first at Aberdeen in 1982 and then at Edinburgh since 1987. He returned in 1966 to Britain to teach at the University of Aberdeen, where in 1970 he founded and headed the Department of Religious Studies. He retired in 1985 and moved to the University of Edinburgh as honorary professor.

Walls founded and edited several periodicals: *Sierra Leone Bulletin of Religion, Bulletin of the Society for African Church History, West African Religion,* and *Journal of Religion in Africa.* He edited the *Annual Survey of Literature on Christianity in the Non-Western World* and for many years compiled the quarterly bibliography in the *International Review of Mission.* He was secretary of the Scottish Institute of Missionary Studies and of the Society for African Church History, a president of the British Association for the Study of Religions, and general secretary of the International Association for Mission Studies. He is a Fellow of the Royal Society of Arts (Scotland) and is an active lay preacher of the Methodist Church in Scotland. In recognition of his public service in Scottish municipal government, museums, and art galleries, he was awarded the Order of the British Empire by the queen in 1987. He received an honorary Doctor of Divinity degree from the University of Aberdeen in 1993. The CSCNWW at Edinburgh represents Walls's legacy of scholarly activity, ecumenical partnership, and global collaboration.

BIBLIOGRAPHY Andrew F. Walls, *The Missionary Movement in Christian History: Studies in the Transmission of Faith* (1996), biographical studies of Thomas Fowell Buxton, Samuel A. Crowther, and David Livingstone in Gerald H. Anderson et al. eds., *Mission Legacies* (1994), "Structural Problems in Mission Studies," *IBMR* 15 (1991): 146–155, and a magisterial survey of Scottish missions in *Dictionary of Scottish Church History and Theology* (1993), pp. 567–594.

Lamin Sanneh

Walpot, Peter (c. 1518–1578), Hutterite Anabaptist minister in Moravia. Born in Upper Austria and a cloth cutter by trade, Walpot evinced such administrative and theological skills that historians speak of the mid-1500s as the "Walpot Era." Among Hutterites it was a time of relative peace, prosperity, and intense missionary activity, with missioners going to almost every area of Europe as far north as Denmark; Walpot himself worked his way north to Danzig (Gdansk). To promote unity among Hutterites in 1545, Walpot wrote *The Five Articles of the Greatest Strife between Us and the World*—baptism, the Lord's Supper, community of goods, *Gelassenheit* (surrender of the will), government, and divorce—which he later enlarged as the *Great Article Book.* He prepared manuals of discipline for the various trades. Far in advance of his time was his *School Discipline* (1578). Medical supplies were produced for use both within and beyond Hutterite settlements by Hutterite physicians, who were in great demand across Europe. So also were wagons, cutlery, furniture, pottery, wine, and innumerable other items produced by them. With Walpot's help, Caspar Braitmichel began the *Chronicle,* perhaps the first Anabaptist church history, bringing it to 1542; it was continued by others through the centuries. The Moravian Hutterite communities may have numbered over 20,000 baptized persons by the time of Walpot's death.

BIBLIOGRAPHY *Chronicle of the Hutterite Brethren,* vol. 1 (1987); Robert Friedmann, *Glaubenszeugnisse oberdeutscher Taufgesinnter, II* (1967) and *Hutterite Studies* (1961); Leonard Gross, *The Golden Years of the Hutterites* (1980); George H. Williams, *The Radical Reformation,* 3d rev. and enlarged ed. (1992).

Cornelius J. Dyck

Walsh, James A(nthony) (1867–1936), cofounder of the Maryknoll priests and brothers. Born in Cambridge, Massachusetts, Walsh's interest in missions was awakened and cultivated by Sulpician priests on the faculty of St. John's Seminary in Brighton, Massachusetts, where he studied until his ordination in 1892. In 1903 he became the archdiocesan director of the Society of the Propagation of the Faith in Boston. He was a tireless speaker for missions and founded the Catholic Foreign Mission Bureau to stimulate vocations as well as spiritual and financial backing. While working to persuade American Catholics to shoulder their mission responsibilities, he encountered Mary Josephine *Rogers, a young woman who shared his vision. In 1906 she helped him launch *Field Afar,* an illustrated missionary magazine that became the official organ of Maryknoll and still appears under the name *Maryknoll.* Their partnership and friendship led in 1920 to the official founding of the Foreign Mission Sisters of St. Dominic, known as the Maryknoll Sisters.

Meanwhile, in September 1910, Walsh met with Thomas Frederick *Price of North Carolina at the Eucharistic Congress in Montreal, where they worked out a plan for an American foreign mission seminary. The plan was approved at a meeting of the American hierarchy in April 1911, and the two priests then sailed for Rome where on June 29 they received formal approval from Propaganda Fide to start the Catholic Foreign Mission Society of America and to open a seminary. Maryknoll, as the society is commonly known, became a reality in August 1912, when Walsh purchased a property on Sunset Hill near Ossining, New York. Walsh, who had been elected society superior, became director of the seminary. In 1917, as the first seminarians approached ordination, he traveled through the Far East in search of a mission field, until Jean-Baptiste de *Guébriant of Canton entrusted the territories of Yangchiang (Yangjiang) and Loting (Luoding), Kwantung (Guangzhou) Province, to Maryknoll. The fall of the following year, the first group of Maryknoll priests set out for that part of south China. In 1929 Walsh relinquished direction of the seminary. He was, however, reelected superior general of Maryknoll and remained in that function until his death. Under his leadership, the society expanded very quickly, new training institutes were started in the United States, and new mission fields were opened in the Far East. Convinced that Maryknoll needed widespread support from mission-minded U.S. Catholics if it was to survive, he wrote prolifically and was a strong advocate of mission education. In 1933 the Holy See named him titular bishop of Siene. He died at Maryknoll, New York.

BIBLIOGRAPHY The 1907–1939 issues of *Field Afar* contain many of Walsh's writings. *Observations in the Orient by a Maryknoller* (1919) is the diary of his first trip to the Far East. Robert E. Sheridan compiled Walsh's various addresses, talks, and circular letters in *Discourses of James Anthony Walsh, M.M.* (1980). Biographical accounts include Raymond A. Lane, *The Early Days of Maryknoll* (1951); Albert J. Nevins, *The Meaning of Maryknoll* (1954); George C. Powers, *The Maryknoll Movement* (1926); Daniel Sargent, *All the Day Long: James Anthony Walsh, Cofounder of Maryknoll* (1941); Robert E. Sheridan, *The Founders of Maryknoll* (1980).

Jean-Paul Wiest

Walsh, James E(dward) (1891–1981), Maryknoll missionary in China. Born in Cumberland, Maryland, Walsh received his missionary calling in 1912, when he came across a copy of the Maryknoll magazine, *Field Afar.* He became one of the first six students to enroll in the seminary at Maryknoll, New York, founded by the Catholic Foreign Mission Society of America, which itself was founded for the express purpose of being the overseas missionary wing of the U.S. Roman Catholic Church. In 1918 he was among the first four Maryknollers to leave for the missions. He had been in south China barely one year when he was chosen to become the leader of this pioneering effort, and was soon responsible for a mission territory one and one-half times the size of his native Maryland. His early years in China were filled with tense events as he was captured by bandits and caught in bloody local wars. In 1927, at the age of 36, he became Maryknoll's first bishop, and in 1936 was called back to the United States to become the first superior general to succeed James A. *Walsh (not related), the founder of Maryknoll, who had just died. During his ten-year term he supervised Maryknoll's first mission efforts to Latin America and Africa. He then returned to China, to accept the post of executive secretary of the Catholic Central Bureau, an agency newly founded to coordinate all missionary, cultural, welfare, and educational efforts of the Catholic Church throughout China. After the fall of Shanghai in 1949, the Communist authorities put the bureau under increasing surveillance and finally ordered it closed. Even though he knew his arrest was inevitable, he chose to stay and not desert his flock. In 1958 he was apprehended for alleged crimes of espionage and conspiracy and, two years later, sentenced to 20 years in prison. In July 1970 he was released before the expiration of his sentence. At the age of 79 he became the last missioner expelled from China.

To Walsh the successful missionary was one who "has ceased to be an American and has become Chinese." His years of imprisonment were a long, purifying test of his adjustment and total dedication to the Chinese people as reflected in his writings on the necessity of adaptation, the power of prayer, and the place of suffering in a missioner's life. He died at Maryknoll, New York.

BIBLIOGRAPHY Walsh's major published works include *Mission Manual of the Vicariate of Kongmoon* (1937), *Maryknoll Spiritual Directory* (1947), *The Church's World Wide Mission* (1948), *Blueprints of the Missionary Vocation* (1956), and *Zeal for Your House* (1976). Biographical accounts include Robert E. Sheridan, *Bishop James E. Walsh As I Knew Him* (1981); Frank Paul Le Veness, "Bishop Walsh's China: The Life and Thought of an American Missionary in China," *Chinese Culture* 14 (June 1973): 21-36; and Jean-Paul Wiest, "The Spiritual Legacy of Bishop James E. Walsh of Maryknoll," *Tripod* 51 (June 1989): 21-28, 56-67.

Jean-Paul Wiest

Walther, Christoph Theodosius (1699-1741), Danish-Halle missionary in India. Walther was born in Schildberg near Soldin in Brandenburg, Prussia, studied at Halle, and in 1725 was ordained and posted to the Danish mission at Tranquebar, where he was appointed its leader. He served during the mission's most flourishing period, a time when the congregation grew from 280 to 1,321 communicants (3,766 if those in the surrounding villages are included) and the first Tamil pastor was ordained (1733). However, he is most remembered for his literary and translation work. Because he knew Hebrew, he contributed to the revision of the Tamil Old Testament and is credited with introducing the word *Parabaran* (The Most High) as the name for God in the Tamil church language. He also continued the work of his predecessors on developing a Tamil lexicon, published a church history in 1735, contributed to apologetic literature by authoring a conversation between a Christian and a Muslim, and compiled a Sanskrit grammar (which was never published). In 1728 he married a Danish woman, but she and their five children all died in India. Walther's health broke in 1735, but fearing that the mission might suffer in his absence, he stayed on for another four years. Finally in 1739 he was forced to return to Germany, where he continued to promote missions and the idea of the universal church. Although as enthusiastic as ever for the cause, he was now quite frail and died at the age of 41 while visiting church leaders in Dresden.

BIBLIOGRAPHY J. Ferdinand Fenger, *History of the Tranquebar Mission* (1863); Wilhelm Germann, *Lifsbilder urden evangelisk-lutherske missionen bland Tamulfoket i Ostindien, 1705-1804* (1897-1898); E. Arno Lehmann, *It Began at Tranquebar* (1956); Clarence H. Swavely, ed., *The Lutheran Enterprise in India* (1952).

Richard V. Pierard

Wang, Ming-tao (Wang Mingdao) (1900-1991), popular independent pastor in Peking (Beijing). In the 1930s Wang founded the Christian Tabernacle, an independent church. He was widely known as an evangelist, as editor of the *Spiritual Food Quarterly*, and, in the 1950s, for his adamant refusal to join the Protestant Three-Self Movement. His reasons were not political but theological, for he was an inflexible opponent of biblical modernism. In September 1954 an accusation meeting was called by the authorities, with attendance required from all churches of the city. Despite speech after speech of denunciation, popular feeling was on his side, and he was freed. His attacks on the Three-Self Movement continued, until he was arrested again in August 1955. After a year in prison he was released, and his purported confession was published, but this he later repudiated. He was arrested again, and after 22 years in prison, was released in 1979.

BIBLIOGRAPHY David Adeney, "Wang Mingdao," *Pray for China Fellowship*, October and November 1991; Francis P. Jones, *The Church in Communist China* (1962); National Council of Churches of Christ in the USA, *Documents of the Three-Self Movement* (1963); *Tian Feng* (Shanghai), various issues, especially 1955-1956; Bob Whyte, *Unfinished Encounter: China and Christianity* (1988).

Donald E. MacInnis

Wangemann, Hermann Theodor (1818-1894), leader of the Berlin Mission. Born and brought up in Brandenburg, Wangemann joined the Berlin Mission after several years as a schoolteacher of religion. With spiritual and theological roots in the Prussian revival, he was able to win active support for the cause of mission among the awakened church members in the eastern provinces. As a missionary strategist he drew up new guiding principles for mission (1882) and helped achieve the entrance of Berlin missionaries in Transvaal, German East Africa, and Kwangtung (Guangdong) in southern China. A prolific writer, Wangemann produced a comprehensive church history of Prussia (1859-1860) and a major investigation into the Prussian church union (3 vols., 1883-1884) that have retained their value to the present. His monumental history of the Berlin Mission in South Africa (4 vols., 1872-1877) became no less popular. His biography of Gustav Knak, spiritual leader and hymn composer of the awakening in Pomerania (1879), once again pursued the connection between revival and mission which was the foundation of Wangemann's own life and thought.

BIBLIOGRAPHY H. Petrich, *H. Th. Wangemann* (1895).

Hans-Werner Gensichen

Wangerin, Theodora S(charffenberg) (1888-1978), Seventh-day Adventist (SDA) missionary in Korea. One of three notable missionaries from the same Milwaukee, Wisconsin, German-American family, Wangerin went to Korea with her missionary husband, Rufus, in 1909. He contracted tuberculosis and the family returned to the United States in 1916. Impelled by a strong sense of divine guidance and missionary responsibility, she returned to Korea with her two daughters in 1917, a few months after her husband's death. At the outset she was employed in conducting training classes, cottage meetings, and small group activities in the churches. In spite of the fact that she had little formal education beyond the eighth grade, her facility with the language and ability as a writer led to her appointment as general editor of the SDA press in

Seoul in 1931. She occupied this post for some 20 years, and in this capacity she made her greatest missionary contribution. Under her editorship, *Signs of the Times* (English title), a religious monthly, achieved a circulation of 40,000 by the late 1930s—said to be the largest circulation of any Korean monthly at the time. She was also instrumental in producing literature for church members through her own writing and translating and by encouraging Korean authors whose work supported a corps of young colporteurs. After the Korean War broke out in 1950, she continued editing in Japan for more than a year but returned to the United States permanently when it was not possible to export materials from Japan to Korea. Under her supervision, the central core of Ellen *White's writing was published in Korean.

BIBLIOGRAPHY In addition to her Korean publications, Wangerin wrote half a dozen books for the English press, including *High Adventure in Korea* (1960), *God Sent Me to Korea* (1968), and many shorter pieces. Gil G. Fernandez, ed., *Light Dawns Over Asia* (1990); S. Peterson, *It Came in Handy* (1969); R. S. Schwarz, *Light Bearers to the Remnant* (1979); "Wangerin, Rufus Conrad" and "Korea," in *Seventh-day Adventist Encyclopedia*, 2d rev. ed. (1996).

Russell L. Staples

Wanless, William J(ames) (1865–1933), Canadian-born medical missionary in India. Wanless, who was supported and sent to India by the Presbyterian Church in the U.S.A., worked for nearly 40 years at Miraj, Maharashtra. While a student at University Medical College, New York City, he joined the Student Volunteer Movement (SVM) as one of its early members and published for the SVM the pamphlet *Facts on Foreign Missions* (n.d.) and later *The Medical Mission—Its Place, Power, and Appeal* (1898). The latter contained his talks to students at universities throughout the United States during his first furlough. His medical (especially surgical) work at Miraj and the successful treatment of leading nobles and politicians (including Gandhi) made him famous and secured the substantial financial support needed to develop the Presbyterian hospital under his charge into the most extensive and effective medical missionary center in India of those days. At Miraj he also founded the Miraj Medical School (1897), the first important medical school in India, and a leprosy asylum (1900). He received the Kaiser-i-Hind Medal for public service in India, and in 1928, the same year that failing health forced him to return to the United States, he was knighted for his outstanding service. He died in Glendale, California.

BIBLIOGRAPHY William Wanless, *An American Doctor at Work in India* (1932). L. E. Wanless, *Wanless of India—Lancet of the Lord* (1944).

Christoffer H. Grundmann

Wanyoike wa Kamawe (c. 1888–1978), Kenyan church pioneer and educator. Wanyoike was born at Kimathi in central Kenya. As a shepherd boy he came into contact with John E. Henderson, a Baptist missionary doctor at the nearby Kambui mission of the Gospel Missionary Society (GMS), based in Connecticut. In 1906 he became one of the first six Kikuyu Christian converts to be baptized. After schooling at the mission, he became a teacher and missionary to his people as well as a Kikuyu language teacher of missionaries in the Kambui area. After training under Henderson between 1926 and 1929, Wanyoike was ordained in June 1930 at Kambui Church by Henderson and by W. P. Knapp. In the late 1930s, GMS churches in Connecticut were unable to continue their support of the work in Kenya. Wanyoike then helped negotiate an agreement turning GMS work over to the Church of Scotland Mission, incorporating it into the Presbyterian Church of East Africa (PCEA) in 1945. Wanyoike continued to work within the PCEA until he retired in 1959. He died in Komothai near Kambui.

BIBLIOGRAPHY R. Macpherson, *The Presbyterian Church in Kenya* (1970); E. N. Wanyoike, *An African Pastor* (1974).

Gerishon M. Kirika

Ward, William (1769–1823), key leader of the British Baptist mission in Bengal. Born in Derbyshire, England, Ward was apprenticed to a printer who published *The Derby Mercury*, a regional weekly newspaper. A collector and disseminator of European news, Ward functioned as a social and political commentator in the English Midlands during Europe's revolutionary years (1789–1797). After some early setbacks, he decided in 1797 to train for full-time Christian ministry among England's Particular Baptists. While studying in Yorkshire, he was discovered by his denomination's mission board. William *Carey needed a missionary printer, but Ward's republican record caused Baptist Missionary Society officials great concern. Two years passed before they dared to send him as a missionary to Bengal, where the British East India Company had no time for people with republican tendencies. Few could then foresee the irenic ministry he would carry out among Serampore's missionaries and their Bengali contacts. He married Mary Fountain, a widow, in India.

Ward became indispensable to the Serampore Mission between 1800 and 1823 as a practical administrator, printing press manager, cross-cultural pastoral counselor, and peacemaker. One of Carey's closest colleagues, he produced Serampore's strategic "Form of Agreement" (1805); he also authored various missiological documents and a classic on Hindu mythology. After a two-year furlough in Britain and the United States, he died suddenly from cholera near Calcutta, in the prime of his life. Ward's missiological legacy has been overlooked by mission promoters and biographers who focused on the story of Carey without properly assessing the role of his brethren in the *Serampore Trio.

BIBLIOGRAPHY William Ward, *A View of the History, Literature, and Mythology of the Hindoos: Including a Minute Description of Their Manners and Customs, and Translations from Their Principal Works* (various eds. and reprints between 1806 and 1863). Samuel Stennet, *Memoirs of the Life of the Rev. William Ward* (2d ed., 1825; a simple introductory biography); A. Christopher Smith, "William

Ward, Radical Reform, and Missions in the 1790s," *American Baptist Quarterly* 10 (1991): 218–244. Some of Ward's letters and papers are in the archives of the Baptist Missionary Society, housed in Regent's Park College, Oxford.

A. Christopher Smith

Wardlaw, John Smith (1813–1872), missionary in India with London Missionary Society (LMS). Wardlaw was born in Glasgow and trained at the University of Glasgow. In 1842 he arrived at the Bellary mission of the LMS, northwest of Madras, India. In addition to building up the English congregation there, in 1846 he founded the Wardlaw Institute, an English and vernacular school that strove for the intellectual and moral uplift of boys. His wife, Anna Bella, meanwhile superintended an orphanage and boarding school for Indian girls. In 1855 he moved to Vizagapatam to do important work with a colleague, John Hay, on revising and improving the translation of the Scriptures into Telugu. A revised New Testament came out in 1856. Wardlaw had to leave for England in 1858 for health reasons, but in 1863 became president of Farquhar House Highgate, an LMS institute for training missionaries for a year after their college course. This was an early pioneer attempt at direct missionary training. In 1870 he received a doctorate of divinity from the University of Glasgow.

BIBLIOGRAPHY Richard Lovett, *The History of the London Missionary Society, 1795–1895,* 2 vols. (1899); John Owen Whitehouse, comp., *A Register of Missionaries and Deputations of the London Missionary Society from 1796 to 1877* (1877).

Frank Whaling

Warneck, Gustav (1834–1910), pioneer of missiology as an academic discipline. Warneck was born and raised in a humble German craftsman's family near Halle. After serving several years as a pastor, he went on to become an internationally renowned professor of mission at Halle (1897–1908), in the first chair of its kind in Germany. He is rightly regarded as the founder of the science of mission studies. With a significant portion of his vast missiological productivity devoted to an encounter with Roman Catholic missions, he is recognized as the first to stimulate the creation of Roman Catholic missiology as well. Warneck was also the first to initiate an objective and responsible treatment of missiological topics in his monthly journal *Allgemeine Missions-Zeitschrift* (1874), the first to produce a comprehensive compendium on the science of missions (1892–1903), and the first to promote effective cooperation in missions by means of conferences on local, regional, and national levels that were later to lead to the creation of a representative central agency of German Protestant missions. Warneck achieved all this after only three years in a kind of apprenticeship in the Rhenish Mission but without ever having done actual mission work or having set foot in an overseas mission field. He did travel to Brighton, England, once (1876) in order to meet Robert Pearsall Smith, whose emphasis on renewal and sanctification attracted him.

After retirement in 1908 Warneck remained active as a writer. Much of his influence must be attributed to the continuing impact, even after his death, not only of his authoritative *Evangelische Missionslehre* (3 vols. in 5, 1892–1903) but also his survey of the history of Protestant missions (1882), which was reprinted ten times (English tr., *Outline of a History of Protestant Missions from the Reformation to the Present Time,* 1884). A large number of smaller books and essays produced by Warneck cover virtually the whole range of the theory and practice of mission.

Critics of Warneck appeared rather late on the scene, at a time when a radical reassessment of the *missio dei* in a changing world was called for. However, his work has stood the test of time remarkably well. Warneck himself would have been the last to maintain that his missiology could be passed on to later generations without modification. His work was bound to be marked by the period to which it belonged. Nevertheless, it was based on Scripture and experience in a contextual link-up which allowed both for obedience to the gospel and freedom of the Spirit, for the extension of the eternal kingdom of God and the founding of indigenous churches as the special harvest of missionary labor. It is in this sense that missiology as the science of mission owes more to Warneck than to anyone else.

BIBLIOGRAPHY There is yet no definitive biography of Warneck; most of his unpublished papers were lost shortly after his death. For a comprehensive study of the man and his work, his environment, and his critics see Hans Kasdorf, *Gustav Warnecks missiologisches Erbe* (1990). For a summary in English, see Kasdorf's essay in Gerald H. Anderson et al., eds., *Mission Legacies* (1994), pp. 373–382. See also J. Dürr, *Sendende und werdende Kirche in der Missionstheologie Gustav Warnecks* (1947). A Festschrift was presented to Warneck on his seventieth birthday (*Missionswissenschaftliche Studien,* 1904).

Hans-Werner Gensichen

Warneck, Johannes (1867–1944), German missionary in Indonesia. The son of Gustav *Warneck, Warneck was born in Dommitzsch, Saxony, and studied theology at Halle, where Martin *Kähler influenced him to become a missionary. In 1892 he was ordained and sent by the Rhenish Mission (RM) to work among the Batak people in Sumatra. He served first as a pioneer missionary and then as a teacher at the seminary in Sipoholon, where he developed a program for training an indigenous ministry. In 1908 he joined the board's home staff at Barmen, Wuppertal, where he supervised its Indonesian mission and, from 1912, taught missions at the theological school in nearby Bethel. During this time Warneck produced scholarly works on the language, literature, and belief system of the Bataks, wrote a history of the Indonesian mission, and served as co-editor of the *Allgemeine Missions-Zeitschrift.* In 1920 he returned to Sumatra to be overseer of the burgeoning Batak church and designed the constitution that made it autonomous in 1930. From 1932 to 1937 he served as the director of the RM, and thereafter he lived in retirement. Through his many literary works Warneck fostered a deeper understanding of missions among the general public in Europe and America.

BIBLIOGRAPHY Johannes Warneck, *The Living Force of the Gospel* (1954; first published in German in 1908 as *Die Lebenskräfte des Evangelismus: Missionserfahrungen innerhalb des animistischen Heidentums;* the 1909 English translation was titled *The Living Christ and Dying Heathenism*), *50 Jahre Batakmission in Sumatra* (1912), and *Werfet eure Netze aus: Lebenserinnerungen* (1938). Paul B. Pedersen, *Batak Blood and Protestant Soul* (1970).

Richard V. Pierard

Warnshuis, Abbe Livingston (1877–1958), Reformed Church in America missionary in China. Born in Clymer, New York, Warnshuis was educated at Hope College, Michigan, and New Brunswick (New Jersey) Theological Seminary. He served in the Amoy mission from 1900 to 1920. He constantly advocated strengthening the indigenous church in China and was instrumental in writing the first book of church order for the South Fukien Church. After five years as national evangelistic secretary of the China Continuation Committee, he served as cosecretary with J. H. *Oldham for the International Missionary Council (IMC) from 1925 until his retirement in 1942. With William *Paton, Warnshuis carried chief responsibility in the arrangements for the IMC World Missionary Conferences held in Jerusalem (1928) and Tambaram, India (1938). In 1944 he represented American churches in planning interchurch aid and relief in Europe, and became the first executive vice-chairman of Church World Service. He brought to each area of mission service the superb skill of an administrator, the vision of a statesman, and the insight of one whose life is centered on God's revelation for redemption, peace, justice, and service to the victims of war and poverty.

BIBLIOGRAPHY Abbe Livingston Warnshuis, *Heidelberg Catechism in Chinese* (1907), *Lessons in Amoy Vernacular* (coauthor, 1911), *The Church's Battle for Europe's Soul* (1945), and *Church Growth and Group Conversion* (coauthor, 1956). Norman Goodall, *Christian Ambassador: A Life of A. Livingston Warnshuis* (1963).

Eugene Heideman

Warren, Max (Alexander Cunningham) (1904–1977), general secretary of the Church Missionary Society (CMS) and major British missionary statesman. Born in Dun Laoghaire, Ireland, of Irish missionary parents, Warren spent his early years in India. After schooling in England, he studied at Cambridge—history at Jesus College and theology at Ridley Hall. As a student, he was a member of the Hausa Band, whose members committed themselves to evangelizing Muslims in northern Nigeria. However, less than a year after arriving at Zaria with CMS in 1927, he contracted tubercular iritis and had to be invalided home. After physical and mental recuperation, ordination, and youth ministry in Winchester Diocese, he served as vicar of Holy Trinity, Cambridge (Charles *Simeon's church) from 1936 to 1942.

As general secretary of CMS from 1942 to 1963, Warren foresaw and interpreted the decolonization period, played a major role in mission conferences, acted as international adviser to Archbishop Geoffrey Fisher, and educated the Christian public through the monthly *CMS News-letter.* From 1963 to 1973 Warren was canon and subdean of Westminster Abbey, London. A strategic organizer behind ecclesiastical and political scenes, an external examiner for Cambridge University, a valued counselor to key people in public life as well as to young mission scholars, he received a constant stream of visitors from all over the world. He was elected an honorary fellow of Jesus College, Cambridge in 1967.

A trained and perceptive historian, Warren stressed God's involvement in the whole of history and God's action among peoples outside the covenant. His *CMS Newsletter* had a worldwide circulation of about 14,000. In it he interpreted current missiological books and reflected vividly and theologically on key issues of the day, drawing on his regular personal correspondence with missionaries. Avidly read by diplomats and politicians as well as by missionaries and bishops, he saw himself as on a watchtower like his favorite prophet, Habakkuk. Averse to bureaucracy and centralizing control and delighting in flexible initiatives, his writings stressed personal friendship as the heart of mission and the importance of the voluntary missionary societies.

Warren edited the Christian Presence series and gave two stimulating series of lectures in the Faculty of Divinity, Cambridge University, which were published as *The Missionary Movement from Britain in Modern History* (1965) and *Social History and Christian Mission* (1967). Other major missiological works include *The Christian Mission* (1951), which was an early exposition of holistic mission; *Interpreting the Cross* (1966), which contains addresses given to South African clergy; and the final affirmation that summed up his life, *I Believe in the Great Commission* (1976).

BIBLIOGRAPHY Warren's autobiography is *Crowded Canvas: Some Experiences of a Lifetime* (1974). A crucial article that focuses his later concerns is "The Uniqueness of Christ," *Modern Churchman* 18 (1974): 55–66, in which he critiques John Hicks's theology of religions. F. W. Dillistone, *Into All the World: A Biography of Max Warren* (1980); Dillistone also wrote about Warren in Gerald H. Anderson et al., eds. *Mission Legacies* (1994), pp. 616–623. For Warren's influence, major books, and articles, see Timothy Yates, "Evangelicalism without Hyphens: Max Warren, the Tradition and Theology of Mission," *Anvil* 2 (1985): 231–245 and "Anglican Evangelical Missiology, 1922–1984," *Missiology* 14 (1986): 147–157; and Graham Kings, "Max Warren: Candid Comments on Mission from His Personal Letters," *IBMR* 17 (1993): 54–58. Three theses have been written on his missiological thought: P. G. C. Meiring (Pretoria, 1968), F. E. Furey, (Louvain, 1974), and O. Haaramäki (Helsinki; published as *Max A. C. Warrenin Missionaarinen Ekklesiologia,* 1982, includes a full bibliography and a short summary in English).

Graham Kings

Watchman Nee. *See* Nee, (Henry) Watchman.

Watson, Minnie (Cumming) (1865–1949), Church of Scotland (CSM) missionary teacher in Kenya. A schoolteacher from Dundee, Scotland, Minnie Cumming arrived in Kenya in 1899, and at Freetown near Mombasa soon married her fiancé of eight years, the Church of Scotland missionary Thomas Watson. However, Thomas Watson died in December of the following year. Minnie Watson continued in Kenya at Thogoto, teaching and administering the CSM school for refugee children and supervising stone quarrying, which produced material for building school and church. In 1907 she and Arthur Ruffelle *Barlow started a boys' boarding school, and two years later one for girls. The curriculum for girls included English, sewing, hygiene, child-rearing, and laundry. The program she designed has been generally followed by other mission schools. She was also a tireless campaigner against Kikuyu female circumcision. Her missionary work under the CSM covered 32 years.

BIBLIOGRAPHY R. Macpherson, *The Presbyterian Church in Kenya* (1970); E. N. Wanyoike, *An African Pastor* (1974).

Gerishon M. Kirika

Watson, William (1798–1866), missionary among Australian Aborigines. Born in Yorkshire, England, and raised a Methodist, Watson married Ann Oliver in 1819. A grocer turned school teacher, he offered his services to the Church Missionary Society (CMS). After brief training, the bishop of London ordained him to work among the Australian Aborigines. The Watsons arrived in Wellington, New South Wales, in 1832. The compassionate ministry that he and his wife provided the sick gave him wide acceptance among the local Wiradjuri people. He learned their language and translated parts of Genesis, Matthew, and the Anglican liturgy. He conducted church services and a day school for the Aboriginal children, whom he believed would "equal if not outvie . . . the now civilised and polished nations of Europe."

As head of the Wellington mission, Watson clashed with the other missionaries, and in 1840 the CMS dismissed him. Taking the Aboriginal children with them, the Watsons set up Apsley mission, an independent ministry, on donated land near Wellington. In 1849 the bishop confirmed one of the mission's grown children, Jane Christian Marshall, the first Aboriginal admitted into full membership of any church. After 1855 the Watsons supported themselves by farming, providing an itinerant ministry in New South Wales.

BIBLIOGRAPHY Barry Bridges, "The Church of England and the Aborigines of New South Wales" (Ph.D. diss., Univ. of New South Wales, 1978); John Harris, *One Blood* (1990). The Watson Papers are held in Mitchell Library, Sydney.

John W. Harris

Way, Lewis (1773–1840), missionary statesman in the development of nineteenth-century missions to Jews. A wealthy Englishman, Way heard a story about one family's devotion to the cause of the Jews which so inspired him that he re-directed his life and fortune to such ministry. He became an early pioneer with the London Jews' Society (LJS), working with it in London. He became a role model for Christians wishing to combine a vision for the restoration of the Jews to Palestine with a conviction of the need for evangelism among them. He was devastated by the Christian persecution of Jews in Europe and believed that only after receiving full civil rights could Jews be attracted to the gospel. He therefore believed that complete political emancipation of the Jews was a necessary precondition for successful mission. He boldly submitted memorandums to this effect to the European congress of monarchs at Aix-la-Chapelle in 1818, and the good reception he received ensured that Jewish emancipation in Europe and Jewish restoration to the Holy Land became key issues for subsequent Jewish missions.

BIBLIOGRAPHY Way's most significant book was *Thoughts on the Scriptural Expectations of the Christian Church* (1828). His memorandums were published as *Memoire sur l'état des Israelites dédies à leurs majestés imperiales et royales réunies au congrès D'Aix-la-Chapelle* (1819). W. T. Gidney, *The History of the London Society for Promoting Christianity amongst the Jews* (1908).

Walter Riggans

Webb, Mary (1779–1861), pioneer in organizing American women for the support of missions. Born in Boston, Massachusetts, Webb contracted a disease at the age of five that confined her to a wheelchair for the rest of her life. In 1800, at age 21, she successfully challenged the prevailing view of the role of women in society by organizing a group of thirteen women who founded the Boston Female Society for Missionary Purposes. Webb served as the society's secretary and treasurer for 56 years. Although a Baptist, she was ecumenical in her approach to world evangelism. She furthered the cause of mission for more than 50 years, inspiring the founding of numerous mission and benevolent organizations and promoting cooperation among more than 200 women's missionary societies. Webb encouraged women to contribute a sum of two dollars annually to support the efforts of various missionary societies at home and abroad and to provide for the translation and publication of the Scriptures. Despite her accomplishments, she chose to remain in obscurity from the public eye.

BIBLIOGRAPHY R. Pierce Beaver, *American Protestant Women in World Mission: A History of the First Feminist Movement in North America* (1980); Helen Barrett Montgomery, *Western Women in Eastern Lands* (1987); Ruth A. Tucker, *Guardians of the Great Commission: The Story of Women in Modern Missions* (1988); Albert L. Vail, *Mary Webb and the Mother Society* (1914).

Joan R. Duffy

Webster-Smith, Irene (1888–1971), missionary with the Japan Evangelistic Band (JEB) and founder of the Sunrise Home for girls. Born to an Irish Protestant family in Connah's Quay, Wales, Webster-Smith became a Quaker after undergoing a conversion experience at age 16. In

1916 she went to Japan with JEB to work in a rescue home for prostitutes. Discouraged at the home's lack of long-term effectiveness, she recognized the need to rescue unwanted girls at a much younger age, or, as she put it, to "erect a fence at the top of the precipice rather than driving an ambulance at the bottom." In Kyoto in 1922 she founded her first Sunrise Home, a ministry marked by the kind of day-to-day "miracles" that characterized the orphanages of George *Müller. The work flourished until 1940, when she was forced to leave Japan. After the war, General Douglas MacArthur personally requested her return. In 1950, in conjunction with InterVarsity Christian Fellowship, she founded the Ochanomizu Christian Student Center at Tokyo University. Her remarkable personality and influence are perhaps best illustrated by the visitors who came to see her during a hospital stay late in her life. Members of the Imperial family (she once spent a summer caring for their children), Sunrise girls, missionaries, college students, GIs, generals, and businessmen came to pay their respect to the woman they called "Sensei" (teacher).

BIBLIOGRAPHY Russell T. Hitt, *Sensei: The Life Story of Irene Webster-Smith* (1965); I. R. Govan Stewart, *A Heart on Fire: Irene Webster-Smith of Japan* (1972).

William L. Svelmoe

Weerasooriya, Arnolis (1857–1888), first non-Westerner to attain the rank of colonel in the Salvation Army and a leading figure in revivals that established the Army's work in India and Ceylon (Sri Lanka). Born at Dodanduwa, Ceylon, of a prominent family, Weerasooriya underwent an evangelical conversion while an instructor at Trinity College, Kandy, and immediately became active in evangelistic ventures. The simplicity and force of preaching by William Gladwin, Salvation Army pioneer in Ceylon, led Weerasooriya to offer himself to this ministry in 1883. While a Salvation Army cadet, he was the chief catalyst in a revival among the villages of Gujarat (western India) that began a mass movement to Christian faith. Similar revivals occurred under his influence in the Tamil, Malayalam, and Telugu areas of India as well as in the southern coastal and heartland areas of Ceylon. As an associate of Frederick Tucker (later *Booth-Tucker), Weerasooriya came to prominence at the defining moment when Salvation Army missionaries in India renounced European dress and lifestyle and adopted the apparel and privations of the rural poor—sleeping under trees to avoid caste constraints, marching barefooted, and begging for food—while they preached the gospel in the national idiom and built a vast infrastructure of relief and development operations. Taking what he called a "desperate stand" against Europeanization of Indian mission, Weerasooriya trained some one hundred of the first generation of Army missionaries with uncompromising candor in the meaning and means of servanthood. In a revolutionary move, Weerasooriya was appointed chief secretary, or second-in-command, of the Army in the sub-continent, with the Western missionary force among his subordinates. He died of cholera, which he contracted while nursing fellow officers.

BIBLIOGRAPHY Bramwell Booth, ed., *Colonel Weerasooriya* (1905); F[rederick] Booth-Tucker, *Muktifauj or Forty Years with The Salvation Army in India and Ceylon* (1922); Mrs. Colonel [Minnie] Carpenter, *Some Notable Officers of The Salvation Army* (n.d.); Solveig Smith, *By Love Compelled: The Story of 100 Years of the Salvation Army in India and Adjacent Countries* (1981); Arch R. Wiggins, *The History of the Salvation Army*, vol. 4 (1886–1904) (1964).

Lyell M. Rader, Jr.

Wei, Francis C(ho) M(in) (1888–1976), Chinese Christian scholar and educator. Born in Kwangtung (Guandong) Province, Wei graduated from Boone University (1911), which was founded and supported by the American Episcopal mission in Wuchang (part of modern Wuhan), Hupei (Hubei) Province, and became a member of its faculty. In the same year he converted to Christianity, taking the name Francis, and joined the Protestant Episcopal Church, U.S.A. in the District of Hankow (Hankou; also part of modern Wuhan). With the help of the church he went to study at Harvard (M.A., 1919) and at the University of London (Ph.D., 1929). In 1929 he became president of Huachung (Central China) University, which was set up cooperatively in Wuchang by five missionary societies from North America and Great Britain; he served there for 22 years. In 1922 he was a delegate to the National Christian Conference held in Shanghai. He taught at Yale University Divinity School in 1937 and 1938. In 1945 he was the first Henry W. Luce visiting professor at Union Theological Seminary, New York, and he went to Britain on invitation to preach at Westminster Abbey and Saint Paul's Cathedral. He enjoyed great prestige in China's Christian community because of his research in philosophy, theology, and Eastern culture. He was a prolific writer in Chinese and English, including *The Political Principles of Mencius* (1916), *The Spirit of Chinese Culture* (1947), *Ten Talks on the Apostle's Creed* (1955, in Chinese), and *Basic Elements of the Christian Faith* (1965, in Chinese). After 1949 he taught at Central China Normal College and remained one of the leading figures in China's Christian community for the rest of his life. He died in Wuhan.

BIBLIOGRAPHY Howard L. Boorman, ed., *Biographical Dictionary of Republican China,* vol. 3 (1970); John L. Coe, *Huachung University* (1962). Other material is held in the archive of Huachung (College) University, record group 11, nos. 163–171, at Yale Divinity School Library.

Min Ma

Weinland, William (1861–1930), pioneer Moravian missionary in Alaska and among the Indians of southern California. Weinland was born in Bethlehem, Pennsylvania, and educated at Moravian College and Theological Seminary there. In 1884, while still a seminarian, he was sent to the Kuskokwim region of Alaska to seek a place to begin mission work among the Yup'ik Eskimos. The next year he and his wife, Caroline (Yost), returned to establish that mission, along with John and Edith *Kilbuck and an older lay missionary, Hans Torgerson, who drowned on the journey. The two young couples spent their first winter in Alaska on the edge of subsistence. The mission was just barely begun when ill health required the Weinlands to leave the field in 1887. After two years of parish ministry in Iowa, where several members of his congregation volunteered for service in Alaska, Weinland was called to begin a mission on the Potrero and Morongo Indian reservations near Banning, California. He remained in active service there until his death, enduring resistance from the Indians, opposition from Catholic missionaries, and hostility from U.S. government officials. A turning point in the work came with the conversion of John Morongo, one of the most influential members among the Indians, who became Weinland's interpreter, adviser, and friend.

BIBLIOGRAPHY Edmund deSchweinitz Brunner, *The History of the Moravian Mission to the Indians of Southern California* (1914); Carol F. Eastman, *Morongo Echoes: Through 75 Years* (1964); James W. Henkelman and Kurt Vitt, *Harmonious to Dwell: The History of the Alaska Moravian Church, 1885–1985* (1985); Anna B. Schwalbe, Gertrude Trodahl, and Harry Trodahl, *Dayspring on the Kuskokwim: The Story of Moravian Missions in Alaska* (1985). Weinland's diary for the 1884 survey expedition to the Kuskokwim is in the Moravian archives, Bethlehem, Pennsylvania; his other papers on Alaska and on the Morongo mission are in the Huntington Library, San Marino, California.

Otto Dreydoppel, Jr.

Weir, Andrew (1873–1933), Presbyterian missionary in Manchuria. Born near Cookstown, Northern Ireland, and educated at the Queen's College, Belfast, Weir was influenced by the Student Volunteer Movement and pledged himself to missionary service in 1898. He arrived in Manchuria in 1899 and served at various centers, including Chaoyang, Kuyushu, and especially Changchun. After his first wife Eva (Simms) died in 1915, he married fellow missionary Margaret Grills in 1917. Personally humble and self-effacing, Weir was one of the outstanding missionaries of his time. He was interested in evangelism and at the same time opposed to rigid dogma in communicating the gospel. Far more aware than most of his colleagues of the need for a genuinely Chinese church, he worked both for the training of Chinese leadership and for the growth of indigenous church structures. Beside being responsible for two large districts for much of his missionary career, he had important administrative duties as clerk of the Chinese synod for 27 years and treasurer of the Irish Presyterian mission. He helped in forming the Church of Christ in China in 1926 and was an influential member of the National Christian Council of China. He died at Changchun in Manchuria.

BIBLIOGRAPHY R. H. Boyd, *Waymakers in Manchuria* (1940); Austin Fulton, *Through Earthquake, Wind, and Fire: Church and Mission in Manchuria, 1867–1950* (1967); A. J. Weir, "China," in Jack Thompson, ed., *Into All the World: A History of the Overseas Work of the Presbyterian Church in Ireland, 1840–1990* (1990); Margaret Weir, *Andrew Weir of Manchuria* (1936).

T. Jack Thompson

Welch, James Ely (1789–1876), American Baptist home missionary. Little is known of Welch's early life, except that he was born near Lexington, Kentucky, and was a frontiersman. In 1810 he was converted by the fiery western evangelist Jeremiah Vardeman. Following studies at William Staughton's theological school in Philadelphia, Welch was appointed in 1817 by the Baptist Board of Foreign Missions to the western territories, with particular emphasis upon the Indians of Missouri. Welch and his wife arrived on the field in early 1818, after a trip through the Ohio valley, where they organized numerous auxiliary missionary societies for the Baptist Board. From his base in Saint Louis, Welch covered an expansive territory encompassing the Fox, Osage, and Delaware tribes. He started the First Baptist Church in Saint Louis and a school, which he administered for a time with John Mason *Peck. The interest of the Baptist Board in the St. Louis Mission waned after two years and Welch became an agent for the American Sunday School Union, starting schools throughout the Mississippi valley. Largely on Welch's experience, the Baptist Board shifted its Indian mission work to the vicinity of tribal lands, rather than in urban environments.

BIBLIOGRAPHY Welch left no publications; a few of his letters survive in *American Baptist Magazine* and in *Latter Day Luminary*. Biographical data is found in *Minutes of the Missouri Baptist General Association* (1876) and in *Proceedings of the New Jersey Baptist State Convention* (1876).

William H. Brackney

Welz, Justinian von (1621–c.1668), Lutheran mystic and visionary of missions. Welz was born into the family of an Austrian nobleman forced to leave his country on account of his Lutheran faith. When the family found refuge at Ulm, Germany, Welz was able to study law at Leiden, the Netherlands, and there published a booklet on tyranny. There is no record of activity again until 1663, when his largest work appeared, a tract on the merits of a solitary existence. Thereafter intensive study of the Bible, of the writings of Luther, and of ascetic-mystical literature initiated a radical change in him, documented in four tracts, all devoted to a passionate appeal for Protestant Christianity to engage in world mission (1663–1664). Welz offered nothing less than a detailed blueprint for a mission society, somewhat similar to the cultural and scientific societies of the baroque age but unique in its focus on foreign missions. The Roman Catholic example certainly played a part in this vision, although Welz remained a loyal Lutheran. Unable to win the approval of most church authorities, he associated himself with spiritualist enthusiasts. He is said to have lost his life as a freelance missionary in the Dutch colony of Suriname. It was only after the pietist missionary revival that his vision was at least in part realized.

BIBLIOGRAPHY Fritz Laubach, *Justinian von Welz* (1989) provides an authoritative biography and reprint of all of Welz's writings; James A. Scherer, *Justinian Welz* (1969).

Hans-Werner Gensichen

Wenger, John (1811–1880), translator of the Bible into Bengali and Sanskrit. Born in Bruchenbühl, Switzerland, Wenger had an unsettled upbringing as an orphan in Canton Berne. He trained for ministry in the Swiss Reformed Church but declined ordination in 1833 for doctrinal reasons. During the next six years, he tutored the children of Henry Leeves, an English agent of the British and Foreign Bible Society in Greece, and traveled with the family around Europe. During leave in 1838, he met John *Dyer and other Baptist Missionary Society (BMS) personnel in London. He was baptized, became a BMS missionary, and sailed for Calcutta with W. H. Pearce in 1839. Because of his linguistic talent, he succeeded William *Yates and concentrated on the long-term Bible translation and revision project that William *Carey had started. He undertook many other responsibilities as a mission leader in Bengal and in 41 years returned to Europe only twice on furlough. Rhode Island University awarded him the D.D. in absentia.

Bibliography E. A. Payne, *The Great Succession: Leaders of the Baptist Missionary Society During the Nineteenth Century* (1936), pp. 87–98; E. B. Underhill, *The Life of the Rev. John Wenger, D.D.* (1886).

A. Christopher Smith

Wenjaminow, Innokentij. *See* Innocent Veniaminov.

Wesley, Charles (1707–1788), pioneer Methodist hymn writer. Wesley was born in Epworth, England. After early education from his mother, he attended Westminster School in London and Christ Church college, University of Oxford. Ordained an Anglican priest in 1735, he accompanied his younger brother, John *Wesley, to the new American colony of Georgia, where he served as private secretary to Governor James Oglethorpe until his return to England in 1736. Experiencing conversion in 1738, he joined his younger brother in field preaching and itineration throughout England until his marriage in 1749. For the next 40 years he ministered to Methodists in London, opening many new chapels, while retaining Anglican orders and concern for the renewal of the Church of England. Unsurpassed as a hymn writer, he revolutionized congregational worship through his hymns. His poetry expressed Methodist piety and beliefs, while the singable tunes conveyed fervor and enthusiasm. "O for a thousand tongues to sing my great Redeemer's praise," he wrote; and many thousands responded by going out to spread "scriptural holiness" throughout England and to other lands, as they sang:

> My gracious Master and my God,
> Assist me to proclaim,
> To spread through all the earth abroad,
> The honors of thy name.

Bibliography Thomas Jackson, *The Life of the Rev. Charles Wesley*, 3 vols. (1841), John Telford, *The Life of the Rev. Charles Wesley* (1886, 1900), Charles Wesley Flint, *Charles Wesley and His Colleagues* (1957), Frederick C. Gill, *Charles Wesley: The First Methodist* (1964) are standard but not critical biographies. Richard P. Heitzenrater, "Charles Wesley and the Methodist Tradition," in *Charles Wesley: Poet and Theologian*, S. T. Kimbrough, Jr., ed, (1992), contains an assessment of Charles Wesley's importance in Methodism's missionary vision. John Lawson, *A Thousand Tongues* (1987), also published as *The Wesley Hymns* (1988), and S. T. Kimbrough, Jr., *Lost in Wonder* (1987) include the texts of Wesley hymns with analyses. See also Betty M. Jarboe, *John and Charles Wesley: A Bibliography* (1987).

Norman E. Thomas

Wesley, John (1703–1791), founder of the Methodist movement. Wesley was born in Epworth, England. Early on he developed a keen interest in missions from his father, Samuel Wesley, an Anglican rector who wrote a comprehensive scheme of missions for India, China, and Abyssinia, and from his mother, Susanna Wesley, who included accounts of the India missionaries Bartholomew *Ziegenbalg and Heinrich *Plütschau in his tutoring. Following education for the Anglican priesthood at Christ Church, Oxford, ordination, and election as a fellow of Lincoln College, Wesley sailed for Georgia in 1735 with his brother, Charles *Wesley, both as missionaries of the Society for the Propagation of the Gospel. While his primary responsibility was as chaplain to English settlers, Wesley reached out to Native Americans (Choctaws and Chickasaws), to African Americans, and to Jews. Finding his motive of missionary benevolence insufficient, Wesley was troubled in heart and spirit. Helped by the witness of Moravian missionaries, Wesley returned to London in 1737 and on May 24, 1738, experienced a spiritual rebirth and a sense of vocation that remained the mainstay of his life and work for more than half a century.

Wesley's motivations for mission are his major legacy. They include a personal inner conviction of a call to proclaim the gospel, to glorify God, and to be in ministry and mission with the whole people of God. With his conviction that every Christian community should be in mission, he would not be constrained in his witness by traditional parish boundaries, declaring, "I look upon the world as my parish." He emphasized that the church exists for service and for mission—locally, nationally, and globally. His 50 years of home missionary labors in Great Britain were unrivaled in intensity and far-reaching results. He never used the term "missionary" to refer to himself or his movement, preferring to have all Christian workers "devoted to God" and "breathing the whole spirit of missionaries."

Mission for Wesley embraced both evangelism and social action. With passion he opposed the major social problems of his day: alcoholism, slavery, illiteracy, poverty, and a degrading penal system. His faith in the capacity of the poor to produce their own leaders was actualized in Methodist societies and bands, and later, in trade unions. Wesley's "scriptural holiness" provided a balanced concern for personal and social salvation that remains a missionary ideal today. He encouraged pioneer ventures by the laity. Nathaniel Gilbert, a distinguished lawyer and Speaker of the House of Assembly in Antigua, visited England to hear Wesley in 1758 and returned to encourage slaves to embrace Christianity through Methodist societies.

Laymen also introduced Methodism in the American colonies, with Wesley appointing Richard Broadman and Joseph Pilmoor as preachers in 1769, and Francis *Asbury and Thomas *Coke as superintendents in 1784, following the war of independence from Great Britain. Later appointments included missionaries to Newfoundland and the West Indies in 1788, and a management committee for Methodist missions in 1790 shortly before his death in London.

BIBLIOGRAPHY Of the many Wesley biographies, Henry D. Rack, *Reasonable Enthusiast: John Wesley and the Rise of Methodism* (1989) contains the best coverage of Wesley's contribution to early Methodist missions. See volume 1 of Wade Crawford Barclay, *History of Methodist Missions* (1949) for Wesley's guidance of Methodist expansion to North America, and Barclay and Theodore R. Doraisamy, *What Hath God Wrought* for Wesley's missionary motives. Martin Schmidt analyzes Wesley's Georgia mission experience in *The Young Wesley: Missionary and Theologian of Missions* (1958) and his theology of mission in *John Wesley: A Theological Biography,* 2 vols. (1962).

Norman E. Thomas

Westcott, Brooke Foss (1825–1901), English churchman, theologian, and New Testament scholar. Although never himself a missionary, Westcott was the motive power behind the Cambridge Mission to Delhi. Born and educated in Birmingham, he entered Trinity College, Cambridge, in 1844, and was elected a fellow in 1849. For some years he taught at Harrow, but he was too diffident to be a good schoolmaster. He found his place only in 1870, when he returned to Cambridge as Regius Professor of Divinity. Already he had been led to compare India with early Christian Alexandria and believed that universities were "providentially fitted to train men who shall interpret the faith of the West to the East, and bring back to us new illustrations of the one infinite and eternal Gospel." The scheme for a Cambridge Mission to Delhi took shape and became firm late in 1876. Among its members the most celebrated was no doubt C. F. *Andrews.

In 1883 Westcott became canon of Westminster, and in 1890 bishop of Durham, in a coal-mining district of northeast England, where, like his mentor, F. D. Maurice, he was deeply respected, if not always understood. Westcott was a "social Christian" and at the same time a warm supporter of the church's mission. Four of his seven sons became missionaries to India, two of them Anglican bishops, while during his time at Durham, no fewer than thirty-six "men in orders" took up overseas work. Westcott's chief claim to fame is as a New Testament scholar and socioethical theologian. However, his place in Anglican mission history was no less important. He was buried in the chapel of Auckland Castle, County Durham.

BIBLIOGRAPHY H. Scott Holland, *B. F. Westcott* (1910); Arthur Westcott, *Life and Letters of Brooke Foss Westcott* (2 vols., 1903). Also see Martin Maw, *Visions of India* (1990), ch. 3; Stephen Neill, *The Interpretation of the New Testament 1861–1961* (1966), pp. 91ff.

Eric J. Sharpe

Westcott, Foss (1863–1949), Anglican missionary and bishop in India. Foss Westcott, son of Brooke Foss *Westcott, was educated at Cheltenham and Peterhouse, Cambridge. Ordained deacon in 1886 and priest in 1887, he served his curacy in the industrial northeast of England before joining the Cawnpore Mission of the Society for the Propagation of the Gospel, together with his brother George. Beginning in 1889 he took charge of the mission's evangelistic work, and later he initiated and developed an industrial program while also providing pastoral care for European residents in the area. In 1905 he succeeded his uncle, J. C. Whitley, as Anglican bishop of Chhota Nagpur, in which post he remained until 1919, earning much respect for his skill and tact in dealing with the German Lutheran Mission and its missionaries during World War I. In 1919 he succeeded G. A. *Lefroy as bishop of Calcutta and metropolitan of India, and his time there was later characterized as showing "statesmanship, sympathy, and sincerity." In the late 1930s he was recognized as the unofficial leader of Frank Buchman's Oxford Group Movement (subsequently known as Moral Rearmament) in India. He retired in 1945 but remained in India until his death.

BIBLIOGRAPHY E. Chatterton, *History of the Church of England in India* (1924); C. H. Robinson, *The Story of the Cawnpore Mission* (1909).

Eric J. Sharpe

Westen, Thomas von (1682–1727), Norwegian Lutheran missionary known as the Apostle to the Lapps. Von Westen was born in Trondheim and graduated from the University of Copenhagen in 1699, when he was only 17. He married a wealthy widow in Copenhagen and was appointed vicar of Veöy, Romsdal, where he served from 1709 to 1716. In 1716 he was appointed the leader of a new mission to the Lapps in northern Norway in the service of the Committee for the Propagation of the Gospel, founded in 1714 in Copenhagen. In 1717 he established in Trondheim the Seminarium Lapponicum for the training of missionaries to the Lapps. He was energetic and zealous but also autocratic as a leader, and he rejected any kind of accommodation to pre-Christian customs and thinking. The mission work he started led eventually to the incorporation of the Norwegian Lapps into the Lutheran Church of Norway. He used his private resources for the benefit of the mission and died a poor man. His ecclesiastical description of northern Norway, *Ex Topographia Ecclesiastica Findmarkiae* (reprinted in 1934), was published after his death.

BIBLIOGRAPHY Adolf Steen, *Samenes kristning og Finnemisjonen til 1888* (1954).

Nils E. Bloch-Hoell

Westermann, Diedrich Hermann (1875–1956), pioneer of African linguistics. Born in Baden, Germany, Westermann studied at Basel and Tübingen prior to being sent to Togoland (modern Togo) by the North German Mission as a teacher. There he developed an interest in the Ewe language that was to shape the direction of the rest of his life. Two major publications from this period were *Wörterbuch der Ewe-Sprache* (vols. 1 and 2, 1905, 1906) and *Grammatik der Ewe-Sprache* (1907). In 1908 he left missionary service to begin lecturing on Ewe, Ful, and Hausa at the Orientalisches Seminar in Berlin. In 1910 he replaced the Bantuist Carl *Meinhof as professor, later taking up the chair of African Languages and Cultures at Berlin University, where he remained until retiring in 1950. The studies he had begun in Togoland led to an interest in the Sudanic languages, early results of which were published as *Die Sudansprachen* (1911), but his classification of the languages was continually modified over the years, most notably in "Charakter und Einteilung der Sudansprachen" (*Africa,* 1935) and, with M. A. Bryan, *The Languages of West-Africa* (1952). ("Sudan" in that period included most of West Africa as well as areas to the east.) His main interest was in the languages at the western end of the family, such as Mande or Kpelle and Gola of Liberia, but his bibliography shows extensive publications on languages across West Africa. From 1928 to 1939, along with D. G. Brackett (1929–1939), he served as editor of *Africa,* the journal of the International Institute of African Languages and Cultures (now the International African Institute).

Westermann particularly enjoyed working on phonetics and tonetics. *Practical Phonetics for Students of African Languages* (1933, 1973), written with Ida C. Ward, benefited students for many years. Cultural change and African development also had his attention, and *Geschichte Afrikas* (1952) was an attempt at a comprehensive survey of the history of the African people. The cumulative effect of his work was to help Africanists see the continent as an indivisible whole.

BIBLIOGRAPHY Westermann's writings on language groupings also include *Die westliche Sudansprachen und ihre Beziehungen zum Bantu* (1927). Wilma Meier, ed., *Bibliographie afrikanischer Sprachen* (1984) contains a language-related bibliography. Cecil Douglas Trotter, *A Grammatical Guide and Numerous Idioms and Phrases in Ewe* (1921) is an English translation of Westermann's *Grammatik der Ewe-Sprache.* Obituary, *African Studies* 15, no. 4 (1956).

Philip C. Stine

Westman, Knut Bernhard (1881–1967), Swedish Lutheran historian, educational missionary, missiologist, and ecumenical leader. Westman was born in Härnösand, in the north of Sweden. He was educated at the University of Uppsala, coming under the influence of professor (later archbishop) Nathan *Söderblom and in 1915 gaining his doctorate with a dissertation on St. Birgitta. He was much involved in the work of the Student Volunteer Movement and the World's Student Christian Federation. In 1914 he became Söderblom's international secretary. Although professionally a medievalist, in 1923 he went to China to become principal of an embryo Swedish "university" (in reality no more than a high school) at Tao Hwa Lun, Hunan Province. The experiment was short-lived, mainly due to the chaotic politics of the time, and in 1930 Westman returned to Sweden as professor of mission history in Uppsala. Although immensely learned, Westman wrote relatively little, and then mainly in Swedish, which somewhat inhibited the recognition he deserved. In his career, personality, and style, he has been compared to the legendary Kenneth Scott *Latourette of Yale. He retired in 1949.

BIBLIOGRAPHY Bengt Sundkler, "Knut B. Westman, 1881–1967," *Svensk Missionstidskrift* 58 (1970): 45–76.

Eric J. Sharpe

Weston, Frank (1871–1924), Anglican missionary and bishop of Zanzibar. The son of a London tea broker, Weston was educated at Dulwich College and Trinity College, Oxford, where he graduated with honors in theology. After ordination in 1894 he served two curacies in London (1894–1898) before offering himself to the Universities' Mission to Central Africa. He was sent to Zanzibar and became principal of St. Andrew's Training College, Kiungani (1901–1908). While there he wrote *The One Christ,* a widely respected essay in kenotic Christology. He became bishop of Zanzibar in 1908.

Weston's chief claim to respect lay in his work as a vigorous missionary bishop with great understanding of Africans, one who gave an example of Christian character that was both ascetic and attractive. He is also remembered, however, for his part in certain debates. In 1913 he denounced the bishops of Uganda (J. J. *Willis) and Mombasa (W. G. Peel) to the archbishop of Canterbury, Randall Davidson, as having compromised Anglican ecclesiology by entering into agreements with nonepiscopal bodies, including intercommunion. In the debates about ecumenism at the Lambeth Conference of 1920, however, he was a leading influence behind the "Appeal to all Christian People," a milestone in Anglican ecumenism. During World War I Weston led the Zanzibar Carrier Corps, a body of over 2,000 men, for which he was awarded the Order of the British Empire. After the war he entered into another vigorous controversy over forced labor with Alfred Milner, British secretary of state for the colonies. His *Serfs of Great Britain* contributed to the withdrawal of an earlier memorandum by Milner's successor, Winston Churchill. Weston was admired as a fine orator and spokesman for Anglo-Catholicism in England, an upholder of Africans' rights, an able theologian and polemical writer, and an outstanding Christian leader and ecumenist.

BIBLIOGRAPHY Frank Weston, *The One Christ* (1907), *Ecclesia Anglicana—For What Does It Stand?* (1913), *The Fulness of Christ* (1916), *Christ and His Critics* (1919), and *Serfs of Great Britain* (1920). A. E. M. Anderson-Morshead and A. G. Blood, *The History of the Universities' Mission to Central Africa* (1909, 1937); G. K. A. Bell, *Randall Davidson, Archbishop of Canterbury* (1935); B. Cross, "The Christology of Frank Weston," *Journal of Theological Studies,* n.s. 21 (1970): 73–90; M. Dewey, *The Messengers* (1975); G. Hewitt, *The Problems of Success* (1971); R. Lloyd, *The Church of England, 1900–1965* (1966); H. Maynard Smith, *Frank Weston, Bishop of Zanzibar* (1926); S. C. Neill, *Anglicanism* (1958); G. H. Wilson, *History of the Universities' Mission to Central Africa* (1936); *Times,* November 4, 1924 (obit.).

Timothy Yates

Westropp, Clara E. (1886–1965), promoter of support for Catholic missions. Born in Cleveland, Ohio, Westropp and her sister, municipal judge Lillian Mary Westropp, cofounded the Women's Federal Savings Bank, the first institution of its kind to be directed and managed solely by women. Her financial expertise carried over to the formation of the Francis Xavier Mission Circles (1946), each composed of twelve women who through "prayer, sacrifice, and funds" maintained personal contact with Catholic missionaries from the Cleveland diocese. By 1960 Cleveland had over 250 mission circles. While this plan was not unique, Westropp influenced the spread of this method in Los Angeles, Detroit, and Chicago. Further fund-raising partially underwrote some of the support of her friend Bishop Fulton J. *Sheen's television programs in the 1950s. By 1961 she was the diocesan chairperson of missions, and she aided the inauguration of the Cleveland Latin America Association in the 1960s. This group sponsored Jean Donovan and Sister Dorothy Kazel, who were martyred in El Salvador in 1980. Clara was a prominent Cleveland citizen and a member of the National Catholic Welfare Council. In 1954 she received the papal medal, "Pro Ecclesiae et Pontifice," for her mission and philanthropic efforts. Her death was noted in the U.S. Congressional Record for the House of Representatives.

BIBLIOGRAPHY "Westropp, Clara E.," in David D. Van Tassel and John J. Grabowski, eds., *The Encyclopedia of Cleveland History* (1987). The Clara Westropp Papers are at the Schlesinger Library, Radcliffe College, Cambridge, Massachusetts.

Angelyn Dries, OSF

Wheelock, Eleazar (1711–1779), pioneer in Indian missions and education, leader in the Great Awakening, and founder of Dartmouth College (1769). Wheelock was born in Windham, Connecticut, and graduated from Yale College (1733). Ordained a Congregational minister in 1734, he pastored the Second Congregational Church in Lebanon, Connecticut, for 35 years. A fervent itinerant preacher, he collaborated with Jonathan *Edwards to lead the Great Awakening in Connecticut. He is especially remembered for his initiatives in Native American missions. In 1743 he began to instruct Samson *Occom, the Connecticut-born Mohegan Indian, who later returned as a missionary to his tribe. In 1754 Wheelock established Moor's Indian Charity School in Lebanon to prepare Native Americans for tribal missions. He included in his strategy Native American females who would live nearby, receive instruction, and accompany male graduates back to their people. With the English victory in the French and Indian War, the school attracted members of different tribes from New England and New York, including the Six Nations. Between 1764 and 1766 Samson Occom and others raised £12,000 in England that enabled Wheelock to found a college, named for the Earl of Dartmouth, in Hanover, New Hampshire, for "the education and instruction of Indian Youth...and Christianizing Children of Pagans." Although tangible successes of Wheelock's Native American educational and missionary efforts were limited, Wheelock's college kept local tribes from joining the British in the Revolutionary War, and for years it classically and theologically educated a coterie of Indian youths while preparing a larger number of whites for mission service.

BIBLIOGRAPHY *A Plain and Faithful Narrative of the Original Design, Rise, Progress, and Present State of the Indian Charity-School at Lebanon, in Connecticut* (1763) and the eight continuing narratives (1765–1775) by Eleazar Wheelock are key primary sources. *Memoirs of the Rev. Eleazar Wheelock* (1811), David McClure and Elijah Parish, eds., remains a helpful collection of Wheelock's writings. See also *The Letters of Eleazar Wheelock's Indians,* James D. McCallum, ed. (1932). James D. McCallum, *Eleazar Wheelock* (1969) is the most comprehensive biography available. The founding of Dartmouth College is detailed in Wilder D. Quint, *The Story of Dartmouth* (1914) and in Leon B. Richardson, *History of Dartmouth College,* 2 vols. (1932). Wheelock's correspondence is in the Dartmouth College archives.

Thomas A. Askew

Wherry, Elwood Morris (1843–1927), American Presbyterian missionary in North India. Born in South Bend, Pennsylvania, Wherry graduated from Jefferson (now Washington and Jefferson) College (A.B., 1862) and Princeton Theological Seminary (1867). In 1867 he was ordained, married Clara Maria Buchanan, and the following year they went to India as missionaries of the Presbyterian Church. Wherry's years (1883–1888) as a professor at the Ludhiana Mission seminary in Saharanpur, North India, corresponded with a period of transition in the mission's orientation. Initially supportive of public disputation with Muslim religious leaders, Wherry turned toward a more irenic approach. He wrote a summary of Urdu-language Christian literature which includes notes on nineteenth-century Punjabi Christian evangelists. Responding to the need for better educational resources on Islam, he published a four-volume annotated translation of the Qur'an, with a 40-page English concordance. His work marks the first attempt to make the Muslim scripture more intelligible to Christian missionaries. The preface urged a tactful approach in contrast to his earlier controversial assault on Islam. His editorship of the Ludhiana periodical, *Nur Afshan,* also evidenced a shift from religious dispute to growing sympathy with the nationalist aspirations in the Indian independence movement. He helped organize international missionary conferences on Islam in Cairo (1906) and Lucknow (1911). On his return to America in 1922 he wrote the history of the Ludhiana Mission and served as associate editor of the *Moslem World* until 1926. He was buried in Cincinnati, Ohio.

BIBLIOGRAPHY Works by Wherry include *A Comprehensive Commentary on the Quran,* 4 vols. (1896), *The Muslim Controversy* (1905), *The Mohammedan World of Today: First Missionary Conference on Behalf of the Mohammedan World, Cairo* (1906), *Islam and Christianity in India and the Far East* (1907), *Islam and Missions: Second Missionary Conference on Behalf of the Mohammedan World, Lucknow* (1911), and *Our Missions in India 1834–1924* (1926). Stanley Brush, "Presbyterians and Islam in India," *Journal of Presbyterian History* 62, no. 3 (1984): 215–222 (repr. in *Indian Church History*

Review 19, no. 2 [1985]: 128–136); Lyle Vander Werff, *Mission to Muslims: The Record* (1977).

David A. Kerr

White, Andrew (1579–1656), Jesuit missionary in Maryland. White was born in London, England. At 16 he entered an English Catholic seminary in Spain, returning to England after his ordination. In 1605, as a consequence of an abortive effort by some Catholics to blow up the English Parliament, he was expelled from the country. Less than a year later, White joined the Society of Jesus in Flanders, and for the next two decades he divided his time serving both as a missionary in England and a professor in the English Jesuit colleges on the continent. In London he assisted George Calvert (Lord Baltimore) in planning his second colony in British America and in 1633 headed the Jesuit mission that accompanied the first settlers of Maryland. Having gone to Maryland primarily to work among the indigenous peoples, White evangelized the local tribes from Point Lookout to the site of present-day Washington, D.C., including the Patuxents, Piscataways, and Anacostians, with particular success among the latter two. To aid this effort he composed a catechism in Piscataway as well as a grammar and dictionary and was responsible for installing the first printing press in the colony to make these works widely available. Despite two near fatal attacks of yellow fever and problems generated by failing hearing, White survived in Maryland until 1645, when insurgents overthrew the Calvert government and sent him and a Jesuit companion back to England in chains. There he was once more exiled to Europe. Nearly seventy, he unsuccessfully volunteered to return to Maryland, but he eventually reentered England, where he died.

BIBLIOGRAPHY White's *Relatio Itineris in Marylandiam* and *Declaratio Coloniae Domini Baronis de Baltimore* were published in translation by the Maryland Historical Society in 1874. See also R. Emmett Curran, *American Jesuit Spirituality: The Maryland Tradition, 1634–1900* (1988).

R. Emmett Curran, SJ

White, Charlotte Hazen Atlee (fl. 1815), Baptist missionary in India. Born in Pennsylvania, White was baptized in 1807 at First Baptist Church in Haverhill, Massachusetts. Shortly after the organization of the Baptist Board of Foreign Missions in 1814, White, a widow, offered herself as a missionary to work with the children and women of Burma, along with a gift of her property, about fifteen hundred dollars. The proposal prompted a debate over the definition of missionary. While a minority of the administrative committee held that only preachers should be appointed as missionaries and that women were not to be employed, White became the first woman missionary appointed by the American Baptists (sustained by her own funds). When she arrived in India in 1816, she met and married a widower, Joshua Rowe, under appointment of the English Baptist Missionary Society, and she transferred from the American Baptist Board to the English society. At Digah, near Serampore, she became the valued director of a large school. When her husband died in 1823, she returned to the United States. In the 1830s she was listed as teaching English, music, and drawing in an academy at Loundesboro, Alabama.

BIBLIOGRAPHY Little is known of Charlotte White. The American Baptist Board records contain a brief notation of her appointment, and board minutes detail the controversy over her appointment. Robert G. Torbet, *Venture of Faith: The Story of the American Baptist Foreign Mission Society and the Women's American Baptist Foreign Mission Society, 1814–1954* (1955) contains the most informative narrative on her career.

William H. Brackney

White, Ellen G(ould) (Harmon) (1827–1915), cofounder of the Seventh-day Adventist (SDA) Church. Ellen Harmon was born and reared in Gorham, Maine, in a devout Christian home. Her father was an exhorter in the Methodist Church, and her Christian experience was nurtured in Methodist class meetings. Having accepted the teaching of William Miller regarding the imminent return of the Lord, the family was forced out of the Methodist Church. In 1846 Ellen married James White, a fellow Millerite, and together they consolidated the group of Millerites that became the Seventh-day Adventist Church in Michigan in 1861. Although she was never ordained and did not hold formal administrative office, she was accepted as a messenger of the Lord and exerted powerful influence in the young church. Largely under her influence the church developed a worldwide view of its mission and particular ideals regarding education and health, using them and Christian literature to propagate the message. In due course these views gave a particular shape to the Adventist mission endeavor. Her residence and work in Europe (1885–1887) and Australia (1892–1901) did much to inspire Adventist missionary consciousness, and this, together with the reorganization of the church's administrative structure in 1901–1903 in effect turned the General Conference into a church-wide missionary society. During the ensuing 30-year administrative tenure of A. G. Daniels and W. A. *Spicer, the Adventist Church was planted virtually around the globe in fulfillment of the vision she had helped to generate. She wrote about missions as a generalist, providing vision, inspiring and encouraging faithfulness, and suggesting broad outlines, rather than as a specialist analyzing particular problems or giving specific directions. She wrote voluminously. At the time of her death, 24 of her books were in circulation and she had contributed some 4,600 articles to denominational periodicals.

BIBLIOGRAPHY Ellen G. White, *Education* (1903), *Gospel Workers* (1915), *Medical Ministry* (1932), and *Evangelism* (1946). M. Ellsworth Olson, *A History of the Origin and Progress of Seventh-day Adventists* (1925); Arthur W. Spalding, *Origin and History of Seventh-day Adventists,* vols. 1–4 (1961–1962); William A. Spicer, *Our Story of Mission for Colleges and Academies* (1921); Arthur L. White, *Ellen G. White,* vols. 1–6 (1981–1986); "White, Ellen Gould (Harmon), Writings of," and "White, James Springer," in *Seventh-day Adventist Encyclopedia,* 2d rev. ed. (1996).

Russell L. Staples

White, Hugh Vernon (1889–1984), American theologian of mission. After undergraduate studies at the University of California, White graduated from the Pacific School of Religion (1917), Harvard (S.T.M., 1919), and Stanford University (Ph.D., 1931). He served Disciples of Christ and Congregational churches in Hawaii and California. In 1931 he became educational secretary of the American Board of Commissioners for Foreign Missions, with "specific responsibility for the interpretation of Christian missions in terms of modern thought for church leaders." He visited missions around the world, traveled extensively in the United States, and wrote numerous articles and reviews on philosophy, religion, and missions. From 1944 to 1959 he was professor of theology at the Pacific School of Religion, where he expounded a form of personalism. He participated prominently in the 1930s' debate over *Rethinking Missions,* the report of the Laymen's Inquiry, through articles and the booklet "Rethinking Foreign Missions with the American Board." Although the report recommended cooperation with other religions and emphasized humanitarian work, White insisted that the religious dimensions of mission are fundamental and that Christianity is significantly truer and better than other religions; its essential truth and values must be disseminated throughout the world. Christian mission should avoid proselytizing and instead emphasize Christian service and nurture.

BIBLIOGRAPHY White's books are *A Theology for Christian Missions* (1937), *A Working Faith for the World* (1938), and *Truth and the Person in Christian Theology* (1963); his major articles include "Religion and Mission," *Missionary Herald* 128 (1932): 88 ff., "The Christian Message in a Non-Christian World," *Missionary Herald* 134 (1938): 464 ff., "New Missionary Dimensions," *Christendom* 1 (1935): 612 ff., and "Task and Opportunity at Madras," *Christendom* 3 (1938): 497–506. Biographical notes are found in Fred Field Goodsell, *They Lived Their Faith* (1961), pp. 77–81, 219–220, 393.

David M. Stowe

White, John (1866–1933), Wesleyan Methodist missionary in Rhodesia. White was born at Dearham, in England's Lake District. Following education for missionary service at Didsbury Theological College, Manchester, he was ordained and in 1892 began service at Klerksdorf in the Transvaal, South Africa. Transferred to the Mashonaland Mission (Zimbabwe) in 1894, he served from 1901 to 1926 as chairman and general superintendent of the Rhodesia District where he was known as a wise and farseeing administrator and as a promoter of African leadership and church extension. He first reached Northern Rhodesia (Zambia) in 1907 and led in opening Methodist missions there in 1912. In 1898 he founded the Nenguwo Training Institution (later renamed Waddilove), which provided the first Methodist training in Rhodesia for teachers, evangelists, and pastors. His was the first translation of the New Testament (1907) into the Shona language. He was a champion of African interests, and it was said of him "that no act affecting African life ever became law in Southern Rhodesia without John White having something to say on it." As president of the Southern Rhodesia Missionary Conference (1924–1928), which he had cofounded in 1903, White attempted to move the conference from accommodation to prophetic criticism of government policies in African education, land, and labor—a church-state relationship not seen again in that country until the 1960s.

BIBLIOGRAPHY C. F. Andrews, *John White of Mashonaland* (1935; repr., 1969).

Norman E. Thomas

White, John Campbell (1870–1962), Presbyterian minister, educator, and leader of the Laymen's Missionary Movement. Born in Wooster, Ohio, White graduated from the College of Wooster with a B.A. (1890) and an M.A. (1893). "Cam" White became John R. *Mott's assistant, and Mott married White's sister, Leila, in 1891. White served as secretary for the YMCA (1890–1891), traveling secretary for the Student Volunteer Movement in the United States and Canada (1891–1892), and general secretary of the YMCA in Calcutta (1893–1903). In 1906 he assisted Stephen B. Capen in founding the Laymen's Missionary Movement, which White served as general secretary from 1907 to 1915. The primary purpose of this movement was to promote missionary interest among laypeople. In 1915 he was granted an honorary LL.D. from Ursinus College in Pennsylvania. The same year he returned to the College of Wooster as president, a position he held until 1919. From 1920 to 1927 he was vice-president of Biblical Seminary in New York, and he served as acting president in 1938 and 1939. He was general secretary of the Church League of New York (1927–1930) and pastor of the West 49th Street Presbyterian Church in New York City from 1930 to 1942. Thereafter he returned to Ohio as pastor of the First United Presbyterian Church of Mansfield (1942–1947). In 1947, he became executive chairman of the Christ for the World Movement.

BIBLIOGRAPHY John Campbell White wrote numerous pamphlets, including "The Genesis and Significance of the Laymen's Missionary Movement" (1909). Further information is found in G. S. Eddy, *Pathfinders of the World Missionary Crusade* (1969) and John R. Mott, *The Decisive Hour of Christian Missions* (1910).

Wayne A. Detzler

White, Moses Clark (1819–1900), American Methodist pioneer missionary in China. Born in Paris, New York, White studied both theology and medicine at Yale University after graduating from Wesleyan University. He and his wife, Jane (Atwater), together with Judson D. *Collins, arrived in Foochow (Fuzhou) in September 1847, and opened the first Methodist work in China. In 1851, three years after the death of his wife, White married Mary Seely shortly after her arrival in China.

Like the American Board and Anglican missionaries who preceded them, the American Methodists met opposition and hostility. White was beaten by a mob in 1848. In the "White-Colder" case, they encountered bitter and protracted opposition to the construction of mission residences on property they had purchased. They opened a chapel where White preached to the curious who came in from the street. They printed a hymnal, with colloquial translations of Western hymns, and printed a colloquial version of Matthew's gospel, all translated by White. Although their primary goal was to make converts to Christianity, White and his colleagues practiced medicine and opened small day schools.

Because of Mary's poor health, the Whites were forced to return to the United States in 1852, never to return to China; the first Methodist convert was not baptized until five years later. White undertook further medical studies and for many years was a well-known professor of medicine at Yale while continuing as a superannuated clergy member of the Methodist Church.

BIBLIOGRAPHY Wade Crawford Barclay, *History of Methodist Missions,* pt. 2, *The Methodist Episcopal Church, 1845–1939,* vol. 3, *Widening Horizons, 1845–1895* (1957); Ellsworth C. Carlson, *The Foochow Missionaries: 1847–1880* (1974); Walter N. Lacy, *A Hundred Years of China Methodism* (1948); J. M. Reid and J. T. Gracey, *Missions and Missionary Society of the Methodist Episcopal Church,* vol. 1 (1895). White MSS relating to the founding of Methodist Missions in Foochow, China, are in the Methodist archives, Madison, N.J.

Donald E. MacInnis

White, Paul Hamilton Hume (1910–1992), the Australian "Jungle Doctor." Born in Sydney and converted at age 16, White became a medical student at the University of Sydney, where the newly founded Evangelical Union became his Christian training ground. He married Mary Bellingham, and they sailed for Tanganyika (Tanzania) as Church Missionary Society missionaries in 1938. At his makeshift hospital at Mvumi, west of Dodoma in central Tanzania, without running water, electricity, or operating theater, White learned Swahili and Chigogo just to be understood by the endless queues of patients. Mary's illness forced their repatriation in 1941. Back in Australia, White began writing and launched his "Jungle Doctor" radio program, which lasted for 25 years. His *Jungle Doctor* books, full of African life and folklore and missionary adventure, were acclaimed worldwide and translated into more than eighty languages.

Supporting himself by part-time medical practice, White devoted his life to student evangelism and Christian media. He was instrumental in the postwar revitalizing of evangelical Christian student groups, in developing Christian television, and in promoting Australian Christian publishing. His appeal to young and old owed much to his superb storytelling skill, always with humor and a spiritual punchline. He is estimated to have spiritually influenced thousands of persons.

BIBLIOGRAPHY Paul White, *Alias Jungle Doctor: An Autobiography* (1977; contains full list of *Jungle Doctor* books).

John W. Harris

Whitefield, George (1714–1770), British itinerant evangelist. Born in Gloucester, England, Whitefield won admission to Oxford, where he was converted to the new "methodist" piety of classmates John and Charles *Wesley. While parting company with these eventual founders of the Methodist denomination on the issue of free will and predestination (he remained a Calvinist), Whitefield retained much of the Wesley's teaching on piety and disciplined living and applied it to his preaching.

Perhaps no eighteenth-century religious figure was better known to his Anglo-American audiences than Whitefield. As evangelical preacher on two continents (chiefly England, Scotland, and North America), he was without peer. He combined itinerant ministry, outdoor preaching, weekday sermons, and extemporaneous speech to produce mass, popular audiences that numbered in the millions. He was Anglo-America's first itinerant missionary; he was an evangelist who had no settled parish (except the Bethesda Orphan House in Georgia) and who depended on the free-will offerings of his hearers on both sides of the Atlantic. His international missions to English-speaking audiences virtually redefined evangelicalism. His revivals were themselves a new religious form, neither "church" nor "sect." In effect, they were the first "parachurch" in Anglo-America, the first in a long line of extra-institutional religious associations designed to function outside of normal confessional and denominational lines and forge new religious associations premised on revival and the New Birth.

Whitefield's missionary activities taught the valuable lesson that traditional, state-supported churches were a thing of the past. Churches in Anglo-America, no less than distant foreign lands, were essentially mission fields. In Whitefield's revivals, existing churches were not supplanted so much as they were sidestepped in the interest of creating larger, translocal associations. His mode of revivalism—emotional, nondenominational, international, experience-centered, and self-consciously promoted through print media and word-of-mouth—would outlive his Calvinism and prove as receptive to Arminian as to Calvinist prophets. In time, his methods would transcend print and embrace radio and television. In this sense Whitefield stands as the greatest prophet of modern evangelicalism.

BIBLIOGRAPHY Stuart Clark Henry, *George Whitefield, Wayfaring Witness* (1957); Frank Lambert, *"Pedlar in Divinity": George Whitefield and the Transatlantic Revivals* 1737–1770 (1994); Harry S. Stout, *The Divine Dramatist: George Whitefield and the Rise of Modern Evangelicalism* (1991).

Harry S. Stout

Whitehead, Henry (1853–1947), Anglican missionary in India and bishop of Madras. Whitehead was educated at Sherborne School and Trinity College, Oxford, where he was elected fellow in 1878. In 1884 he went to India as principal of Bishop's College, Calcutta, an Anglican college for the training of an Indian ministry, a post he occupied for 15 years. For the last nine of these years he was also superior of the (Anglo-Catholic) Oxford Mission to Calcutta, which had been founded in 1890. He was consecrated bishop of Madras in 1899. He was always deeply concerned to help bring about an indigenization in the Indian church, and during his Madras years his early Tractarian leanings gave place to a large-hearted ecumenicity. Perhaps his most impressive move, though controversial at the time, was his choice of an Indian, V. S. *Azariah, as his assistant bishop; and of an obscure railway junction, Dornakal, as a center of Telugu evangelistic work. Bishop Whitehead traveled widely in the fulfillment of his duties, and on a basis of his firsthand observations of Indian village life was able to write his first book, *The Village Gods of South India* (1916), a very remarkable study for its time. After his retirement in 1922 he wrote three more books, *Indian Problems in Religion, Education, Politics* (1924), *Christ in the Indian Villages* (1930), and *Christian Education in India* (1932).

BIBLIOGRAPHY Eyre Chatterton, *A History of the Church of England in India* (1924), pp. 198 ff.; Carol Graham, *Azariah of Dornakal* (1946), pp. 33 ff.; George Longridge et al., *A History of the Oxford Mission to Calcutta* (1910); Bengt Sundkler, *Church of South India: The Movement toward Union, 1900–1947* (1954), esp. chap. 3.

Eric J. Sharpe

Whiting, John Bradford (c. 1829–1914), Anglican mission strategist. Whiting graduated from Cambridge University in 1850 and was ordained in the Anglican Church. After a curacy he became an association secretary for the Church Missionary Society (CMS) from 1856 to 1861, before returning to parish work first at Thanet and then at St. Luke's Ramsgate from 1875 to 1905. He is best known for his work as an active committee member, strategist, and occasional stand-in secretary for the CMS. He stood in the tradition of Henry *Venn and was an enthusiastic Afrophile, acting as "commissary" (nominated delegate) in England for Samuel *Crowther (1889–1891) and later for James *Johnson (1901–1914). He served as a representative of the CMS on a number of important occasions, traveling to Madeira in 1881 for a crucial conference about the future of Bishop Samuel A. *Crowther's diocese. He was the society's choice for the vacant episcopal see of Sierra Leone in the same year but was rejected on medical grounds. In the 1890s he became increasingly disenchanted by the Europeanization of the CMS and its effective discarding of Venn's principles, and he fought strongly but unsuccessfully against the new orthodoxy. A mark of his alienation was his refusal to contribute an obituary for his great friend Crowther in the CMS journal *The Intelligencer.*

BIBLIOGRAPHY *Church Missionary Review,* September 1914, p. 522 (obit.); Eugene Stock, *A History of the Church Missionary Society: Its Environment, Its Men, and Its Work,* 4 vols. (1899–1916).

Peter Williams

Whitman, Marcus (1802–1847) *and*
Narcissa (Prentiss) (1808–1847), Presbyterian missionaries to Native Americans of the Oregon Territory. Whitman and Prentiss came from New York state; both underwent spiritual renewal as youths during revivals of the early nineteenth century, and as a result both became interested in missionary outreach to Native Americans in the Far West. Prentiss was a preschool teacher, Whitman a medical specialist who had received his training by "riding with a doctor." Their common interest brought them together in marriage, and under the auspices of the American Board of Commissioners for Foreign Missions (ABCFM), they traveled overland to the Oregon Territory as newlyweds in the spring of 1836. Accompanied by other ABCFM missionaries, they established a mission in the lush valley at Waiilatpu, near present-day Walla Walla, Washington.

The Whitmans' initial enthusiasm for mission work diminished as problems arose with other missionaries and as new immigrants arrived, and their efforts to convert Native Americans to Christianity proved slow and unrewarding. Two years after they arrived, their only child, Alice, drowned in a stream. The Cayuse Indians distrusted their motives as they watched with alarm the influx of white settlers. Further distrust developed after disease struck the local tribe and efforts to vaccinate only exacerbated the problem. Some of the Cayuse believed that Whitman was trying to poison them. The disastrous end of the mission work at Waiilatpu came suddenly in November 1847. Without warning, several Cayuse men attacked the compound, and within hours fourteen people were dead, including both Whitmans. News of the "Whitman Massacre" spread quickly, and missionaries and white settlers were ordered out of the area while federal troops moved in to apprehend the suspects. The mission compound, later restored as a historic site, is a reminder of the deep distrust between Native Americans fearful of losing their land and well-meaning missionaries.

BIBLIOGRAPHY Opal S. Allen, *Narcissa Whitman: An Historical Biography* (1959); Clifford M. Drury, *Marcus and Narcissa Whitman and the Opening of Old Oregon* (1973); Nard Jones, *The Great Command: The Story of Marcus and Narcissa Whitman and the Oregon Country Pioneers* (1959).

Ruth A. Tucker

Whittemore, Emma (Mott) (1850–1931), founder of Door of Hope missions for street women. Emma Mott grew up in a wealthy home in New York and married wealthy Marcus Whittemore. Her life was filled with social activities until a back injury left her an invalid. Through the encouragement of A. B. *Simpson, founder of the Christian and Missionary Alliance, Whittemore sought prayer for healing, which was answered. Soon after, she joined in inner-city mission work with Simpson, who provided her a building in New York City for her first Door of Hope. In the decades that followed she established nearly 100 more Doors of Hope in large cities of China, Japan, western Europe, Africa, and elsewhere. Most of the young women who were brought into the mission houses were prostitutes who had no other means of support, many of whom had been sold or hired out by their relatives when they were young children. She was believed to be "instrumental in saving more fallen women than any other person." She also worked with other city mission leaders, and served as the president of the International Union of Gospel Missions from 1914 to 1918.

BIBLIOGRAPHY Regina G. Kunzel, *Fallen Women, Problem Girls* (1993); Norris Magnuson, *Salvation in the Slums: Evangelical Social Work, 1865–1920* (1977); F. A. Robinson, ed., *Mother Wittemore's Records of Modern Miracles* (1947); Ruth A. Tucker, *Guardians of the Great Commission: The Story of Women in Modern Missions* (1988).

Ruth A. Tucker

Wicki, Josef (1904–1993), historian of the Jesuit missions of Asia, especially of India. A native of Zurich, Switzerland, in 1922 Wicki entered the Society of Jesus at Feldkirch, Austria. After his ordination to the priesthood at Innsbruck in 1933, he completed his theological studies and began courses in history at the University of Innsbruck. Assigned to the Jesuit Historical Institute in Rome in 1935, he embarked on a career of publishing the documents of the early Jesuit mission in India. He completed his doctorate at the Gregorian University in 1942 with a dissertation on the early years of Alessandro *Valignano in the East Indies; it was published two years later. He collaborated with Georg *Schurhammer in editing a two-volume collection of the letters of St. Francis *Xavier. In 1948 he published the first volume of *Documenta Indica,* which reached a total of eighteen volumes by 1988. Also from 1948 until 1984 he was a professor of church history at the Gregorian University in Rome. He presented his research to major international conferences, especially in India and Sri Lanka. A member of professional historical associations, Wicki was a "scholar of merit" in the Lisbon Academy of Portuguese History. He died at Feldkirch, Austria.

BIBLIOGRAPHY Josef Wicki, ed., *Epistolae S. Franciscii Xaverii,* 2 vols. (1944–1945), *Documenta Indica,* 18 vols. (1948–1988), and author, *Missionskirche im Orient. Ausgewählte Beiträge über Portugiesisch-Asien* (1976; includes bibliography of Wicki's work). For a biography see "Fr. Josef Wicki, S.J.," *Archivum Historicum Societatis Iesu* 54 (1985): 473–496 (with a bibliography of 286 items).

John W. Witek, SJ

Widmann, Rosina (Binder) (1826–1908), German missionary in West Africa. Rosina Binder was born of farmer parents at Korntal, a pietist settlement in Württemberg. In 1846 she became engaged to Georg Widmann, a missionary of the Basel Mission (BM) who had been serving in Akropong, Ghana, since 1843. She sailed for West Africa from London in November 1847, and the wedding took place at the Akropong mission station on January 21, 1848, six days after her arrival in Ghana. She founded a girls' school within days of her wedding. She gave birth to twelve children, one of them stillborn. Three children died in Akropong, one in Korntal, and another in the BM boarding school in Basel. She wrote a unique personal diary covering the time from the day of her consecration as a mission bride (September 17, 1847) to the birth and baptism of her first son in December 1849. Having to send her own children for schooling in Europe, she became a mother to numerous African so-called "six-finger children" (children born with six fingers), who were rejected by their own communities. She became a beloved sister to the African women to whom she ministered as midwife, nurse, and adviser. The Widmanns lived and worked at Akropong for almost 30 years. In 1877 after the death of her husband, Rosina Widmann returned to Korntal.

BIBLIOGRAPHY Waltraud Ch. Haas, *Mission History from the Woman's Point of View* (1990; a short biography), pp. 28–37, and *Erstritten und erlitten: Der Befreiungsweg von Frauen in der Basler Mission 1816–1966* (1994), pp. 81–94. Widmann's diary, as well as her letters from Ghana, are in the BM Ghana archive, Basel, Switzerland.

Waltraud Ch. Haas

Wieger, Georges Frédéric Léon (1856–1933), physician, sinologue, and Jesuit missionary in China. Born in Strasbourg, France, where he completed six years of classical studies and six years of medical school, Wieger practiced medicine for two years in civilian life and then two years in the army. He entered the Society of Jesus in 1881 in Belgium because the order was outlawed in France at that time. Several months after his ordination in July 1887, he arrived in the mission of southeastern Chihli (roughly present-day Hubei) Province. With his medical skills, Wieger developed a regimen of hygiene for missionaries and for the Chinese.

His study of the language convinced him of the need to publish systematic works on Chinese culture. In addition to a considerable number of homiletic and catechetical books for missionaries to preach in Chinese languages (including the Hejianfu dialect), he wrote a ten-volume history of modern China and works on Chinese language and customs. Many appeared in several editions; some were also translated from French into English and are still in use today. For his outstanding contributions to sinology the Académie des Inscriptions et Belles-Lettres in Paris three times awarded him the Stanislas Julien Prize.

BIBLIOGRAPHY [Georges Frédéric] Léon Wieger, *Chine moderne,* 10 vols. (1920–1932), *Histoire des croyances religieuses et des opinions philosophiques en Chine* (2d ed., 1922), *Caractères chinois* (4th ed., 1924), *La Chine à travers les ages* (2d ed., 1924), *A History of the Religious and Philosophical Opinions in China* (1927; repr., 1969), *China throughout the Ages* (1928), *Les pères du système taoiste* (2d ed., 1950), and *Chinese characters* (2d ed., 1965). H. Bernard, "Au service des missions et des missionnaires de Chine. Bibliographie méthodique des oeuveres du P. L. Wieger," *Collectanea Commissionis Synodalis* 5 (1932): 975–984, and "Missions, médecine et sinologie: Le P. Wieger et ses études sur la Chine," ibid. 7 (1934): 710–733; Pierre Delattre, "Le Père Léon Wieger," *Revue d'histoire des missions* 10 (1933): 243–258.

John W. Witek, SJ

Wilberforce, Samuel (1805–1873), third son of the slave trade abolitionist William *Wilberforce. Wilberforce, though raised in an evangelical family, was influenced by the Tractarian movement and became a high churchman; unlike his friend J. H. Newman or his own brother Henry, however, he never considered conversion to Roman Catholicism. As rector of Brightstone in the Isle of

Wight (1830–1840) and in later appointments, he was a leading advocate and eloquent spokesperson of the Society for the Propagation of the Gospel. His high view of the episcopate led him also to embrace the ideal of the "missionary bishop" as pioneer evangelist and leader of the mission. This was in direct conflict with the view of his contemporary Henry *Venn of the Church Missionary Society, who saw the bishop as the "crown" of the indigenous church rather than its initiator. Wilberforce supported the launching of the Universities' Mission to Central Africa (originally the Oxford and Cambridge Mission to Central Africa of 1858). Its leader, C. F. *Mackenzie, was appointed as bishop to the Zambezi and epitomized Wilberforce's views. Wilberforce became bishop of Oxford in 1845, where he founded Cuddesdon Theological College in 1854; he became bishop of Winchester in 1869. His eloquence and energy made him possibly the most influential Anglican churchman of his time.

BIBLIOGRAPHY Samuel Wilberforce, *Speeches on Missions* (1874). O. C. Chadwick, *Mackenzie's Grave* (1959) and *The Victorian Church* (1966, 1970); M. Dewey, *The Messengers* (1975); D. L. Edwards, *Leaders of the Church of England* (1971); S. Meacham, *Lord Bishop* (1970); D. Newsome, *The Parting of Friends* (1966); T. E. Yates, *Venn and Victorian Bishops Abroad* (1978).

Timothy Yates

Wilberforce, William (1759–1833), leader of the campaign to abolish the slave trade in the British empire. Wilberforce grew up in the Yorkshire town of Hull, for which he became Member of Parliament in later life. As a student at St. John's College, Cambridge, he became a friend of William Pitt the younger (later prime minister). He was one of a group of Anglican evangelicals known as the Clapham Sect, who sought to apply their Christian insights to social and missionary causes. Abolition occupied him intensively for 20 years (1787–1807). A further campaign followed for emancipation of all slaves, in which he took a leading part. He heard of its success only on his deathbed. By then he had been a founding member of the Church Missionary Society, a supporter of the colony for freed slaves in Sierra Leone, and the provider of a chaplain (Richard Johnson) for the first convicts dispatched to Australia in 1787. He was also responsible for the inclusion of clauses in the renewed East India Company charter of 1813 that provided for an ecclesiastical establishment and permission for missionary work. He possessed great personal charm and was one of the leading speakers of his time.

BIBLIOGRAPHY William Wilberforce, *A Practical View of the Prevailing Religious System of Professed Christians...* (1797). R. Anstey, *The Atlantic Slave Trade and British Abolition, 1760–1810* (1975); R. Coupland, *Wilberforce—a Narrative* (1923); R. Furneaux, *William Wilberforce* (1974); C. Fyfe, *A History of Sierra Leone* (1962); M. Hennell, *John Venn and the Clapham Sect* (1958); C. Hole, *The Early History of the Church Missionary Society* (1896); J. C. Pollock, *Wilberforce* (1977); J. Stephen, *Essays in Ecclesiastical Biography* (1849); R. I. and S. Wilberforce, *The Life of William Wilberforce* (1838).

Timothy Yates

Wilder, Grace E(veline) (1861–1911), promoter of the Student Volunteer Movement (SVM) and missionary in India. Born in Saratoga Springs, New York, Wilder spent most of her childhood in Kolhapur, India, where her parents were New School Presbyterian missionaries. She returned to the United States with her family in 1875 and graduated from Mount Holyoke College in 1883. As a student, she was a leader of the Mount Holyoke Missionary Association, which developed a pledge for missions very similar to the one used later by the Princeton Foreign Missionary Society and the SVM. Following graduation, she lived with her parents in Princeton and prayed extensively with her brother, Robert *Wilder, for a missionary revival among collegians in America. By encouraging her brother and other Princeton students, she provided considerable moral and spiritual support for the Mount Hermon student conference in 1886. In 1887, following the death of her father, Royal *Wilder, Grace and her mother, Eliza, returned to India under the Presbyterian Board of Foreign Missions. Originally stationed at Kolhapur, she later opened a center for village settlement work at Islampur, where she died suddenly only a year after her mother.

John R. *Mott attributed to her "the spirituality and higher success" of the early SVM. She also wrote *Shall I Go? Thoughts for Girls* (1887) and *An Appeal from India* (1890) for the initial SVM pamphlet series.

BIBLIOGRAPHY Biographical data appear in Ruth E. Braisted, *In This Generation: The Story of Robert P. Wilder* (1941). See also Thomas Russell, "Can the Story Be Told without Them? The Role of Women in the Student Volunteer Movement," *Missiology* 17 (1989): 159–175. Documents on Grace Wilder are kept in the Robert Parmelee Wilder Papers, Yale Divinity School Library.

James A. Patterson

Wilder, Robert P(armelee) (1863–1938), pioneer of the Student Volunteer Movement (SVM). Wilder was born in Kolhapur, India, of New School Presbyterian missionaries. In 1875 he and his family moved to Princeton, New Jersey, because of the poor health of his father, Royal G. *Wilder. As an undergraduate at Princeton University, he helped to organize the Princeton Foreign Missionary Society. After graduation in 1886, he participated in Dwight L. *Moody's summer conference for collegians at Mount Hermon, Massachusetts, and played a key role in enlisting 100 students to sign a pledge for foreign missionary service. This precipitated the launching of the SVM, and Wilder served for the next five years as its chief organizer and recruiter. He also completed his studies at Union Theological Seminary in New York.

In 1891 the Presbyterian Board of Foreign Missions appointed Wilder to student work in India. He arrived there in 1892 after assisting in the formation of the Student Volunteer Missionary Union of Great Britain and Ireland. Wilder's ministry in India lasted almost a decade, interrupted by an SVM stint in the United States (1897–1899) and resumed under the auspices of the Indian YMCA in 1899. Health problems forced him to leave India in 1902, and eventually he served in Europe with the Student Christian Movement and the World's Student Christian

Federation. In 1916 he accepted a YMCA post in the United States. Then in 1919 he returned to the SVM as general secretary. He ended his active missionary career in Egypt after six years as executive secretary for the Near East Christian Council (1927–1933). He retired with his wife in her native Norway, where he died. He is buried in Oslo.

Wilder exemplified as well as anyone the spirit and vision of the early SVM, and his labors contributed significantly to the SVM's spiritual and institutional viability. In addition, he provided personal reminiscences of the student mission enterprise in *The Student Volunteer Movement for Foreign Missions* (1935) and *The Great Commission* (1936).

Bibliography Ruth E. Braisted, *In This Generation: The Story of Robert P. Wilder* (1941); G. Sherwood Eddy, *Pathfinders of the World Missionary Crusade* (1945), chap. "Robert Wilder and the Student Volunteer Movement"; Matthew Hugh Kelleher, "Robert Wilder and the American Foreign Missionary Movement" (Ph.D. diss., St. Louis Univ., 1974); James A. Patterson, "Robert P. Wilder," in Gerald H. Anderson et al., eds., *Mission Legacies* (1994), pp. 71–78. The Robert Parmelee Wilder Papers are in the library at Yale Divinity School.

James A. Patterson

Wilder, Royal G(ould) (1816–1887), American missionary in India, author and editor. Born in Bridport, Vermont, Wilder graduated from Middlebury College and Andover Theological Seminary, where his commitment to foreign missions grew through participation in the Society of the Brethren and the Society of Inquiry. He sailed to India in 1846 as a New School Presbyterian missionary serving under the American Board of Commissioners for Foreign Missions (ABCFM). For six years he supervised a boarding school in Ahmednagar and also helped to develop elementary schools in the city and surrounding villages. In 1852 his dissatisfaction with some ABCFM policies brought a transfer to Kolhapur, where his desire to pursue educational work provoked a heated controversy with ABCFM secretary Rufus *Anderson. In 1857 Wilder returned to the United States for health reasons, and continuing disagreements with administrators led to his dismissal from ABCFM in 1860. He resumed his ministry in Kolhapur in 1861 as an independent missionary, and then in 1870 he affiliated with the Presbyterian Board of Foreign Missions. In 1875 poor health and his children's educational needs prompted a move to Princeton, New Jersey, where he challenged college students to consider the call of missions and founded (1878) the *Missionary Review,* which he edited until his death.

A dissenter from a missiology that viewed auxiliary enterprises with suspicion, Wilder left a legacy as a staunch defender of educational missions. He promoted this cause in *Mission Schools in India of the American Board of Commissioners for Foreign Missions* (1861) and through articles in the Bombay *Times and Gazette* (1861–1869). A manuscript history of Kolhapur and a diary of his career in India were lost at sea. After his death, his wife, Eliza, and his daughter, Grace *Wilder, returned to the Presbyterian mission in Kolhapur; his son, Robert *Wilder, also served as a missionary in India, among other places.

Bibliography "In Memoriam: Rev. Royal Gould Wilder," *MRW* 11 (1888): 7–16; Robert A. Schneider, "Royal G. Wilder: New School Missionary in the ABCFM, 1846–1871," *American Presbyterians* 64 (1986): 73–82. Documents on Royal Wilder may be found in the Robert Parmelee Wilder Papers, Yale Divinity School Library.

James A. Patterson

Wilfrid (634–709), English missionary and bishop of York. A Northumbrian noble's son educated at Lindisfarne, Canterbury, and Rome, Wilfrid (Wilfrith) spent three years at Lyons and was consecrated a bishop there. When he became abbot of Ripon in 660, he introduced *Benedict's rule. His bishopric at York, begun in 666, was disputed. Wilfrid preferred large sees like those he had known in Gaul, but his opponent, Theodore, divided York into three sees, and then five, on the basis of population centers as well as tribal and political units more on the pattern of *Gregory the Great. While exiled, Wilfrid built new churches in Hexham and Ripon and improved the liturgy of the region. He also evangelized Sussex and established a monastery at Selsey.

Bibliography Bede, *Ecclesiastical History,* 5:19; Betram Colgrave, ed. and tr., *St. Eddius: The Life of Bishop Wilfrid* (1927, 1985); William Foley, *St. Wilfrid of York* (1986); Henry Mayr-Harting, *The Coming of Christianity to Anglo-Saxon England* (1972, 1977, 1991).

Frederick W. Norris

Wilkes, Paget (1871–1934), Anglican missionary to Japan and founder of the Japan Evangelistic Band. Wilkes was born in Titchwell, Suffolk, England. His father was an evangelical Anglican clergyman, and his mother a Welsh woman of musical and artistic talent. He experienced conversion during F. B. Meyer's visit to Ipswich in 1892. He was educated in Bedford and at Lincoln College, Oxford, where he was a leading member of the Oxford Intercollegiate Christian Union and a contemporary of W. H. Temple *Gairdner and J. H. *Oldham, who remembered him as an "outstanding figure." Wilkes married Gertrude Barthorp in 1897 and offered himself the same year to the Church Missionary Society to work with Barclay *Buxton in Japan, where for over 30 years he lived the life of a traveling evangelist, basing his work at Kobe. In 1903 he founded the Japan Evangelistic Band as an evangelistic auxiliary to the churches' work. Like Wilkes himself, who advocated "entire santification," the band owed much to the spirituality fostered by the Keswick Convention. In addition to evangelism and the work of holiness conventions, Wilkes wrote a number of widely read works, including *The Dynamic of Service,* which was translated into Japanese and other languages. He also composed devotional verse and hymns, some of which reflect his mother's artistic gifts. His life was marked by an emphasis on prayer, focus on the work of the Holy Spirit, and evangelistic zeal.

Bibliography Paget Wilkes, *Missionary Joys in Japan* (1913), *Missionary Journeys in Japan* (1913), *The Dynamic of Faith* (3d ed., 1925), *The Dynamic of Redemption* (1928), *The Dynamic of Life*

(1931), *The Dynamic of Service* (1939), and *Santification* (12th ed., 1949). M. W. Dunn Pattison, *Ablaze for God: The Life Story of Paget Wilkes* (1937); I. R. G. Stewart, *Dynamic: Paget Wilkes of Japan* (1957).

Timothy Yates

Wilkins, Ann (Green) (1806–1857), Methodist Episcopal missionary in Liberia. Born in the Hudson Valley, New York, the eldest of five children born to Mary (Kronkhyte) and James Green, Ann Green was married at age 17 to Henry F. Wilkins. He later deserted her, and she supported herself as a teacher. In 1836 at a camp meeting at Sing Sing, New York, she heard an address by John Seys, a missionary recently returned from Liberia. When the collection for missions was taken, she offered herself as a teacher. She sailed for Liberia in June 1837 and taught at the White Plains Manual Labor School and at the Liberia Conference Seminary in Monrovia. She organized a school at Caldwell and a Female Boarding School at Millsburg. The latter, founded in 1839, was her most significant achievement.

In an era when missionaries succumbed to illness at an alarming rate, Wilkins's relative longevity was remarkable. She briefly returned to the United States in 1841 for her health and in 1853 was so ill that she left Liberia, presumably for the last time. However, the following year she sailed again, accompanying three women teachers. She retired in 1856 and arrived in New York on April 23, 1857. Seven months later she died.

BIBLIOGRAPHY There is no published biography of Wilkins, but Wade Crawford Barclay, *History of Methodist Missions,* vol. 1 (1949), contains helpful information, as does Louise McCoy North, *The Story of the New York Branch of the Woman's Foreign Missionary Society of the Methodist Episcopal Church* (1926).

Susan E. Warrick

Willehad (c. 745–789), Anglo-Saxon missionary and bishop. Willehad came from Northumbria, England, was educated in York, reached Frisia in 765, and evangelized with varying results in the region of Dokkum, on the northeast coast of the Netherlands. Several times his life was in danger. Commissioned by Charlemagne, he went to evangelize the Saxons on the lower Weser River (region of Wigmodi) in 780 but had to give up this work because of the rebellion of the Saxons in 782. After a pilgrimage to Rome, he lived in the monastery of Echternach, Luxembourg, where he made a copy of the letters of the Apostle Paul. After Widukind, the leader of the Saxons, was baptized in 785, Willehad was recalled to the Saxon mission, which he expanded to include the region between the Weser and Ems Rivers. In 787 he was consecrated missionary bishop of Bremen. In 789, one week before he died in Blexen, near Nordenham, he consecrated the cathedral of Bremen. His relics were kept in St. Peter's, Bremen, until the Reformation. A saint, his feast day is November 8.

BIBLIOGRAPHY K. D. Schmidt, "Willehad und die Christianisierung von Bremen-Verden," *Zeitschrift der Gesellschaft für niedersächsische Kirchengeschichte* 41 (1936): 5–23.

Lothar Schreiner

Willeke, Bernward H. (1913–1997), Franciscan missiologist. Born at Münster, Germany, Willeke joined the Franciscan order in 1932 and was ordained a priest in 1939. Expecting to go to China, he studied sinology at Columbia University, New York, where he received his doctorate in 1945. His dissertation was on imperial government and Catholic missions in China during the years 1784–1785. From 1948 to 1950 he did research in Roman archives and collected a wealth of information on the China missions. In Japan, where he worked from 1950 to 1956, Willeke founded the Franciscan Language School. In 1956 he was appointed professor of missiology at the School of Philosophy and Theology of the Franciscans at Paderborn, Germany, and at the same time taught missiology at the University of Münster (1959–1962). In 1962 he became a professor of missiology at the University of Würzburg, continuing until he retired in 1984. Willeke was an authority on Franciscan mission history, with specialization in China and Japan.

BIBLIOGRAPHY Josef Glazik, ed., *50 Jahre Katholische Missionswissenschaft in Münster, 1911–1961* (1961), pp. 58–59; Hans Waldenfels, *Denn Ich bin bei Euch (Mt 28,20): Perspektiven im christlichen Missionsbewusstsein heute. Festgabe für Josef Glazik und Bernward Willeke zum 65. Geburtstag* (1978; includes biography and bibliography).

Arnulf Camps, OFM

William of Rubroek (*or* Rubruck) (13th century), Franciscan missionary pioneer in Asia. William was born in the early thirteenth century in Rubroek, a Flemish-speaking village in northern France. He joined the Franciscan order and around 1248 went to join the Franciscans in the Holy Land. In 1252 he started from Acre for a journey to the court of the Great Khan, Möngke, at Karakorum. He passed through Constantinople, southern Russia and central Asia, finally reaching the court at the south of Lake Baikal. Taking a little more southerly route, he returned to Acre in 1255. There he wrote his report for King Louis IX, "The Itinerary of Friar William." He briefly visited Paris, where he exchanged geographic information with Roger Bacon in 1257. Nothing is known of his whereabouts after that year.

William contributed much to knowledge of the geography, languages, customs, and religions of the countries and peoples he visited. In Karakorum he had discussions with representatives of Buddhism, Lamaism, Islam, and Nestorian Christianity. He held the traditional theological position of his day, which viewed other religions as idolatrous. In politics he was a realist as he advised King Louis not to be optimistic about an alliance with the Mongols against the Muslims.

BIBLIOGRAPHY Guillaume de Rubrouck, *Voyage dans l'Empire Mongol, 1253–1255,* Claude et René Kappler, tr. (1985) and *The Mission of Friar William of Rubruck, His Journey to the Court of the Great Khan Möngke, 1253–1255,* Peter Jackson, ed. and tr., with David Morgan (1990); *Sinica Franciscana,* vol. 1, Anastasius van den Wyngaert, ed. (1929), pp. 145–332.

Arnulf Camps, OFM

William of Tripoli (c. 1220–1273), Dominican missionary theorist and practitioner. William of Tripoli rejected holy war in favor of irenic evangelism in the last century of the Crusades. Born of European parents who had settled in the Latin Crusader County of Tripoli in northwest Syria, he was contemporary with King Louis IX (1226–1270) and Pope Gregory X (r. 1272–1276). While the pope dreamed of defeating Islam militarily and the king of using the Crusades as a means of converting Muslims, William called for pacifistic evangelism by preaching the gospel "without philosophical arguments and without military arms."

Fluent in Arabic and Latin and familiar with Muslim and eastern Christian sources, William wrote his *Tractatus de Statu Saracenorum et de Mahumeti Pseudopropheta* (1273), partly in response to Pope Gregory's request for information on heretics and infidels. In contrast to contemporary Latin polemic, he attempted a fair account of Muslim beliefs and history, with substantial reference to the Qur'an. Seeing the common ground between Christian and Muslim beliefs as the bridge to Muslim evangelism, he read the political events of his day as auspicious for the conversion of Islam: the Mongol destruction of the Abbasid Caliphate (1258) seemed to threaten the survival of Islam.

His claim to have won a thousand converts, though probably exaggerated, reflects missionary optimism on the basis of Muslim conversions during the Crusades. Yet within 20 years of William's death, the Ayyubid sultan Salah ah-Din (Saladin, 1138–1193) expelled the last Crusaders from Acre. If William was of unsound political judgment, the irenicism of his missionary thought influenced later generations of Dominican scholars of Islam.

BIBLIOGRAPHY William of Tripoli, *Kulturgeschichte der Kreuzzuge: Tractate de Statu Saracenorum et de Mahumeti Pseudopropheta*, H. Prutz, ed. (1883). Willem Bijlefeld, "European Christians and the World of the Mamluks: Some Impressions and Reactions," *Muslim World* 73 (1983): 208–233; Norman Daniel, *Western Views of Islam: The Making of an Image* (1966); Richard Southern, *Western Views of Islam in the Middle Ages* (1962); James W. Sweetman, *Islam and Christian Theology*, part 2, vol. 1 (1955); Palmer Throop, *Criticism of the Crusades: A Study of Public Opinion and Crusade Propaganda* (1975).

David A. Kerr

Williams, Channing Moore (1829–1910), pioneer Anglican missionary in Japan. Williams was born in Richmond, Virginia, and graduated with John *Liggins from the Virginia Theological Seminary in 1855. Both men volunteered as missionaries and were sent by the Episcopal Church to Shanghai, China. When Japan was opened to foreign missionaries in 1859, he and Liggins were assigned to begin work in Nagasaki. Later he moved to Osaka and then to Tokyo. He was consecrated Episcopal bishop of China and Japan in 1866, serving as such until 1874, when he was named first missionary bishop of Yedo (Tokyo). His personal piety and administrative ability made a deep impression on the Japanese, and he, in turn, responded to their eagerness for Western education. He founded both a theological college and a school for boys in Tokyo that later grew to become St. Paul's University (Rikkyo).

In 1887 Williams and Edward *Bickersteth drew up the Constitution and Canons for the Holy Catholic Church of Japan (Nippon Sei Ko Kai), the first autonomous province of the Anglican Communion to result from missionary work outside the Anglo-Saxon world. These efforts were intended to provide the minimum forms necessary for the development of a Japanese church in the Anglican tradition but looking toward the eventual union of all Christians in that land. In 1889 Williams resigned as bishop, but he continued work as a missionary until his return to the United States in 1908.

BIBLIOGRAPHY The only full biography of Williams is in Japanese, by Joseph Sakunoshin Motoda (The Life of Bishop C. M. Williams) (1970). A collection of Williams's correspondence and photographs is in the library of the General Theological Seminary, New York. Helen Boyle, *The Anglican Church in Japan* (1938); Otis Cary, *History of Christianity in Japan* (1909); Hisakazu Kaneko, *A Story of Channing Moore Williams: the Bishop of Yedo* (1965); Maria Minor, *Channing Moore Williams: Pioneer in Japan* (1959) ("Pioneer Builders for Christ" pamphlet series published by the Episcopal Church).

Charles Henry Long

Williams, Henry (1792–1867), leading British missionary in New Zealand. Williams was baptized at Gosport, Hampshire, England. After serving for ten years in the Royal Navy during the Napoleonic wars, he was accepted as a Church Missionary Society (CMS) missionary and ordained a priest in 1822. Sent to head the New Zealand mission in 1823, he exercised firm leadership by ending missionary involvement in musket trade and by breaking dependence of the mission on the Maori for such things as food and transport. Convinced of the correctness of evangelical Christianity, he emphasized evangelization, education, and literacy. He stood firm in the face of intertribal conflict and Maori hostility, gaining great respect for his fearless stand as a peacemaker. The mission achieved considerable success in the 1830s as it expanded out from the Bay of Islands.

The growing European contact with New Zealand caused Williams and the mission concern. He initially opposed colonization and was critical of the New Zealand Company's beginnings in the Wellington area. In 1840 he cooperated with Captain William Hobson, the British representative, playing a controversial role in translating the Treaty of Waitangi and gaining Maori adherence to it. He later felt betrayed by the way in which Maori land was appropriated by the government. He attempted to mediate between the Maori and Pakeha peoples during the Northern War, 1844–1845. He and other missionaries were charged by Governor Grey, supported by Bishop G. A. *Selwyn, with having excessive land holdings and causing the war, so that the CMS dismissed him in 1850. His brother William *Williams, while in London in 1851, unsuccessfully defended Henry's actions. Although he was reinstated in 1854, Williams's extensive influence in New Zealand had been undermined except among northern Maori.

His wife, Marianne, was a missionary in her own right through her teaching and contact with Maori women. They had eleven children, including Samuel, who was ordained a priest and was a great benefactor and pioneer of Maori secondary education.

BIBLIOGRAPHY H. F. Carleton, *The Life of Henry Williams,* 2 vols. (1874, 1877); Lawrence M. Rogers, ed., *The Early Journals of Henry Williams: Senior Missionary in New Zealand of the Church Missionary Society, 1826–1840* (1961) and *Te Wiremu: A Biography of Henry Williams* (1973). Williams's papers are held by the CMS and are available on microfilm, and in the Auckland Institute and Museum Library, Auckland, New Zealand.

Allan K. Davidson

Williams, John (1796–1839), London Missionary Society (LMS) missionary in the South Pacific. Williams was born at Tottenham High Cross, London. He acquired skills as an apprentice in the metal work trade. Converted at the City Road Tabernacle, he volunteered for missionary service with the LMS, was ordained, and married Mary Chauner in 1816. They reached Tahiti in 1818. Unhappy with the policies and ways of older LMS missionaries, he and Lancelot E. *Threlkeld went together to build a model station on the Windward island of Raiatea. They formed a church in cooperation with the island's high chief, Tamatoa, who also sponsored Williams's purchase of his first ship, the schooner *Endeavour.* Not content "within the narrow limits of a single reef," Williams set out to reach more of Polynesia and then of Melanesia. He took *Endeavour* to and from Rarotonga in the southern Cook Islands, where he often worked between 1823 and 1833, although the LMS directors were critical of these initiatives. On Rarotonga he built the *Messenger of Peace,* also called *Olive Branch.* In 1830 and 1832, he also pioneered in Samoa for the LMS, leaving Islanders as evangelists and church planters on both occasions. He cultivated the leading chiefs, Makea of Rarotonga and Malietoa of Samoa. Williams's image and fame spread rapidly among Polynesian Islanders. His solid physique and his reputation as a godly mariner who possessed the *mana* (sacral power) associated with high chiefs, was acknowledged by the Islanders in their use of his surname in local form as *Viriamu.*

Williams visited England between 1834 and 1838 to see the revision of the Rarotongan New Testament through publication. He toured the country, speaking and raising funds from noble patrons and the public, to buy and equip his own ship, *Camden.* In 1837 he published *Missionary Enterprises,* which sold briskly. Back in Rarotonga, he set out toward Melanesia leaving Mary and his eldest son, John Chauner Williams, in Samoa. The latter set himself up in trade there, using goods unloaded from the *Camden.*

In 1839 Williams was attacked and murdered on a beach at Eromanga, New Hebrides (Vanuatu), while fleeing from distrustful Islanders. Portrayed as a martyr, he became a legend and inspiration for Islander missionaries and the LMS "at home and abroad." Seven of the society's ships subsequently bore his name.

Mary Williams retired to England in 1842 and died in 1852. She had often voyaged loyally with her husband, though she was a poor sailor. She was pregnant eight times; three children survived.

BIBLIOGRAPHY John Williams, *A Narrative of Missionary Enterprises in the South Sea Islands...* (1837). Gavan Daws, *A Dream of Islands: Voyages of Self-discovery in the South Seas* (1980); Niel Gunson, "John Williams and His Ship: The Bourgeois Aspirations of a Missionary Family," in D. P. Crook, ed., *Questioning the Past...* (1972); Basil Mathews, *Williams the Shipbuilder* (1915); Cecil Northcott, *John Williams Sails On* (1939); Ebenezer Prout, *Memoirs of the Life of the Rev. John Williams, Missionary to Polynesia* (1843).

John Garrett

Williams, John Elias (1871–1927), Presbyterian educator in China. Born and raised in Ohio, Williams was a coal miner in his teenage years but later graduated from Marietta College, Ohio, and Auburn Seminary, New York. He applied to the Presbyterian Board of Missions and was assigned to China. He married Cora Lilian Caldwell, daughter of missionaries, on August 8, 1899, and sailed with her to China that same month. They raised four children.

After language study, Williams served for several years as principal of the Presbyterian Academy in Nanking, a boys' school. Later, after a year of teaching at Waseda University, Tokyo, he felt called to a career in higher education. He returned in 1907 to Nanking, where he helped to open Union College, formed by the union of several mission schools. Through his and others' efforts, funds were raised in the United States, the campus expanded, and Union College became Nanking University, a top-ranked institution with colleges of arts and science, agriculture, and forestry. Williams served as acting dean of the college of arts and science and as vice president. He was a staunch advocate of interchurch cooperation.

On March 24, 1927, Williams was shot and killed by a marauding Chinese soldier on the campus of Nanking University. He had served the Presbyterian Church, USA, in China for 28 years. According to a resolution of the Board of Managers of the university, Williams was remembered for "his unfailing insistence on the positive emphasis in higher education work of the life and teachings of Jesus Christ."

BIBLIOGRAPHY Arthur Judson Brown, *One Hundred Years: A History of the Foreign Missionary Work of the Presbyterian Church in the U.S.A.* (1950); "In Remembrance: John E. Willimas," *Chinese Recorder* (1927); William R. Wheeler, *John E. Williams of Nanking* (1937).

Donald E. MacInnis

Williams, Ralph Darby (1902–1982), pioneer Assemblies of God (AG) missionary in Central America. A native of Monmouthshire, England, Williams was influenced by Alice *Luce, an Anglican who had embraced Pentecostalism as a missionary in India and who was a proponent of Roland *Allen's theories of indigenization. In 1922 Williams and his brother Richard, who later died as an AG missionary in Peru, followed Luce to the Glad Tidings Bible Institute in San Francisco and then in 1924 worked at her Berean Bible Institute in San Diego. Williams was teaching in Mexico City in 1928 when he met Francisco Arbizú, a young Salvadoran Pentecostal and accepted his invitation to work in El Salvador, arriving there in December 1930. The council they convened was boycotted by about half of the two dozen churches that had been associated with Frederick *Mebius, while the remaining delegates drafted the Reglamento Local, a standard of doctrine and church practice that has influenced AG churches throughout much of Latin America. Despite Williams's absence after 1934 for six of the next nine years, the Salvadoran churches developed rapidly with little foreign assistance or oversight. After 1940 Williams served in leadership positions as a missionary-at-large in most of the Central American and Caribbean countries, always encouraging national administrative autonomy and the training of national pastors.

BIBLIOGRAPHY Melvin Hodges, *The Indigenous Church* (1953); Luisa Jeter de Walker, *Siembra y cosecha,* vol. 1 (1990); Everett A. Wilson, "Identity, Community, and Status: The Legacy of the Central American Pentecostal Pioneers," in Joel A. Carpenter and Wilbert R. Shenk, eds., *Earthen Vessels: American Evangelicals and Foreign Missions, 1880–1980* (1988) and "Sanguine Saints: Pentecostalism in El Salvador," *ChH* 52 (June 1983): 186–198.

Everett A. Wilson

Williams, Roger (1603?–1683), Puritan pioneer of religious liberty and missionary to Native Americans. Born in London, a Cambridge graduate in 1627 (B.A.), and a Puritan minister, Williams immigrated with his wife Mary (Barnard) to the Massachusetts Bay Colony, arriving there in 1631. Ensuing conflict with the authorities over his religious views, however, resulted in his banishment in 1635. To escape being sent back to England, Williams fled with his family and a few companions into the wilderness of what is now Rhode Island, but not before initiating what proved to be a lifelong relationship of trust and understanding with Native Americans. He learned their language, cultivated their goodwill, defended their rights, interceded on their behalf, and promoted their general well being. He openly challenged the royal charters, which ostensibly legalized English seizures of Indian lands, and he became the one individual who could act as a mediator and promoter of peace between the colonists and the Indians. During the winter of his exile, 1635–1636, Williams likely would have perished had his Indians friends not come to his aid.

In the late spring of 1636, Williams and his small group settled on a site he had purchased from the Narragansett. He called the new settlement Providence and established the first colony in America where freedom of religion was guaranteed for everyone. With Ezekiel Holliman, Williams organized the first Baptist church in America. Though Williams is often referred to as one of the earliest English missionaries to Native Americans, his mission was hardly typical and can best be understood by reading his *A Key into the Language of America* (1643) and his pamphlet *Christenings Make Not Christians* (1645). In all his relations with the Indians, including his preaching to them, Williams respected the integrity of their culture and was a consistent Christian presence among them. He was critical of accepted evangelization methods and strenuously opposed all forced or enticed conversions. In contrast, Williams engaged the Indians in dialogue, honored their religious notions, and sought to move them gently toward Christ. He was, however, reluctant to call them Christians, or to gather them into churches. That he presented the gospel to them and lived among them as an apostle cannot be denied, but he left their eternal destiny to the determination of God.

BIBLIOGRAPHY *The Complete Writings of Roger Williams,* 7 vols. (1963). See also John Garrett, *Roger Williams: Witness beyond Christendom* (1970); Edwin S. Gaustad, *Liberty of Conscience: Roger Williams in America* (1991); Perry Miller, *Roger Williams: His Contribution to the American Tradition* (1966); Ola Elizabeth Winslow, *Master Roger Williams* (1973).

Alan Neely

Williams, S(amuel) Wells (1812–1884), American missionary in China, scholar, and diplomat. Williams, born in Utica, New York, went to China with the American Board of Commissioners for Foreign Missions (ABCFM) in 1833 as a printer for the Canton mission press. There he worked closely with Elijah Coleman *Bridgman on *The Chinese Repository* and produced several monographs on the Chinese language. From 1845 to 1848 he was in the United States, where he married Sarah Walworth and gave the lectures that developed into *The Middle Kingdom* (2 vols., 1848). This remained for decades the standard English-language work on China.

Williams had learned some Japanese in the late 1830s in an attempt to return some shipwrecked Japanese sailors to Japan, and in 1853 and 1854 he acccompanied the Perry expedition to Japan as interpreter. His *Journal of the Perry Expedition to Japan, 1853–1854,* was published much later (1910). In 1856 he became secretary-interpreter of the U.S. legation to China. In 1858, having resigned from the ABCFM in 1857, he accompanied the legation to Tientsin (Tianjin), where he helped to fashion the Treaty of Tientsin. From 1860 to 1862 he was in the United States but returned in 1862 to the U.S. legation in Peking, where he remained until 1876, several times acting as head of legation. During this time he also wrote his most important language reference work, *A Syllabic Dictionary of the Chinese Language* (1874).

In 1877 Williams retired to New Haven, Connecticut, where he was appointed professor of Chinese language and literature at Yale University. With the help of his son, Frederick Wells Williams, he substantially revised *The Middle Kingdom* (2 vols., 1883), modifying many disparaging judgments of his early missionary days. He also spoke against restrictions on Chinese immigration.

BIBLIOGRAPHY Martin R. Ring, "Anson Burlingame, S. Wells Williams, and China, 1861–1870: A Great Era in Chinese-American Relations" (Ph.D. diss., Tulane Univ., 1972); Frederick Wells Williams, *The Life and Letters of Samuel Wells Williams* (1889). The Williams family papers are in Sterling Memorial Library, Yale Univ.

Daniel H. Bays

Williams, William (1800–1878), Anglican missionary bishop in New Zealand. Williams was born at Nottingham, England. He graduated from University of Oxford in 1824, was ordained a priest in 1825, studied at the Church Missionary College at Islington, near London, and went to New Zealand in 1826 under the Church Missionary Society (CMS). He took a leading part in translating the New Testament and the Book of Common Prayer into Maori and producing a Maori dictionary. While teaching at the mission's English boys' school (1827–1839), he undertook several important missionary journeys. In 1840 he set up a new missionary station at Turanga and gave significant leadership to the emerging Maori church, serving as archdeacon of the East Cape from 1842. As the first bishop of Waiapu (1857–1876), Williams encouraged the training and ordination of Maori clergy. He withdrew to Paihia in 1865 during the conflict with Maori that saw the destruction of his mission station. His *Christianity among the New Zealanders* (1867) was a defense of CMS work. In 1867 he moved to Napier as his diocese now incorporated Hawke's Bay and a growing European population.

Williams supported the Treaty of Waitangi in 1840, and was critical of government actions that undermined Maori land rights. He and his wife, Jane, had nine children, including Leonard Williams, who became the third bishop of Waiapu.

BIBLIOGRAPHY Frances Porter, ed., *The Turanga Journals, 1840–1850: Letters and Journals of William and Jane Williams, Missionaries to Poverty Bay* (1974). Many of Williams's papers are held by the CMS and are available on microfilm. Other major collections are in the Alexander Turnbull Library, Wellington, and the Auckland Institute and Museum Library, Auckland, New Zealand.

Allan K. Davidson

Williams, William Frederic (1818–1871), American missionary in the Near East. Born at Utica, New York, Williams studied at Yale in 1837 but left after two terms due to illness. He worked as a civil engineer and in 1844 entered Auburn Theological Seminary. He offered his service to the American Board of Commissioners for Foreign Missions (ABCFM) in 1846 "as a matter of duty"; in 1848 he was ordained and married Sarah Pond. They sailed in January 1849 and after two years in Beirut were assigned to Mosul. In 1859 Williams founded the station at Mardin in the mountains at the head of the Mesopotamian plain. He did extensive evangelistic touring on horseback and concentrated much effort on a school for boys. Somewhat inclined to distrust his own judgment and to look on the darker side of things, he was nevertheless admired and held in affection by colleagues and by the Turkish people. He was a strong advocate of self-support in missions, and worked indefatigably. He suffered deeply in his personal life through the loss of three wives: Sarah Pond died in 1854; Harriet B. Harding, whom he married in 1857, died only eight months later; Carolyn P. Barbour, a teacher of missionaries' children when he married her in 1861, died in 1865. He married his fourth wife, Clarissa C. Pond, a mission teacher at Harpoot, in 1866. Williams himself died at Mardin. Williams was a younger brother of Samuel Wells *Williams, ABCFM missionary noted for his writings on China and his role in developing American diplomatic relationships with that country.

BIBLIOGRAPHY *Missionary Herald* 67 (1871): 162–167, has an extensive obituary and tribute, and indexed volumes of the magazine have many excerpts from his letters and reports in the years of his service.

David M. Stowe

Williamson, Alexander (1829–1890), Scottish missionary in China. Williamson was appointed a missionary to China with the London Missionary Society and arrived in Shanghai with his wife in 1855. He returned in ill health to Scotland after two years and remained there in ministry for six years. In 1863 he was appointed the first overseas agent of the National Bible Society of Scotland. In this position he traveled extensively in Bible distribution and preaching in north China, Mongolia, and Manchuria. At the General Missionary Conference in Shanghai in 1877, of which he was one of the conveners, he was appointed secretary of the School and Textbook Series Committee. During a second period of recuperation in Scotland, he formed a Chinese Book and Tract Society. The funds raised through this organization were used to found a publishing house in Shanghai and helped establish the Society for the Diffusion of Christian and General Knowledge among the Chinese. Williamson's vision was for this society to influence the higher classes in China through literature on the Christian faith designed to show the fruits of Christianity in Western countries. (In 1906 this organization became the Christian Literature Society for China.) He contributed many articles on natural theology during 1857 and 1858 for the *Shanghai Serial,* edited by Alexander *Wylie, and also wrote *Journeys in North China* (2 vols., 1870).

BIBLIOGRAPHY Kenneth S. Latourette, *A History of Christian Missions in China* (1929); A. J. Broomhall, *Hudson Taylor and China's Open Century,* vol. 6 (1988).

Ralph R. Covell

Williamson, H(enry) R(aymond) (1883–1966), British missionary in China and Baptist Missionary Society (BMS) foreign secretary. Williamson was born in Rochdale, Lancashire, England. Sensing a call to China, he entered Bristol Baptist College and in 1908 was accepted by the BMS for service in Shansi province. There he remained until 1926, engaged primarily in educational and famine relief work. Williamson was an accomplished Chinese scholar. At one point, wanting to remain a missionary, he declined to allow his name to be nominated as professor of Chinese studies at the University of London. From 1926 to 1938 he was director of the Whitewright Institute and Museum in Tsinan (Jinan), Shantung (Shandong). He was appointed China field secretary of the BMS in 1932 and in 1938 was recalled to London to succeed C. E. *Wilson as foreign secretary. In that role Williamson directed BMS policy during the turbulent decade of the 1940s. A born optimist, he believed that contemporary political changes would lead to new missionary opportunities. To preside in his closing years of office over the evacuation of BMS missionaries from China was thus a saddening experience. After his retirement in 1951, he wrote a valuable history of the BMS China mission, *British Baptists in China, 1845–1952* (1957). From 1947 to 1953 he was chairman of the China Christian Universities Association.

BIBLIOGRAPHY J. B. Middlebrook, *Memoir of H. R. Williamson: In Journeyings Oft* (1969); Brian Stanley, *The History of the Baptist Missionary Society, 1792–1992* (1992).

Brian Stanley

Williamson, Thomas Smith (1800–1879), American missionary to the Dakota Indians. Williamson was born in South Carolina, graduated from Jefferson College, Pennsylvania, and received an M.D. from Yale College in 1824. After several years of medical practice in Ripley, Ohio, he studied theology at Lane Seminary in Cincinnati and was appointed a missionary by the American Board of Commissioners for Foreign Missions in 1834. Following a tour up the Mississippi river to explore possibilities for establishing a mission among the Dakota Indians, Williamson and his wife, Margaret (Ponge), left Ripley in 1835, organized a church at Fort Snelling (in present-day Minnesota), and went on to Lacqui Parle, the location selected for a station. In 1846 Williamson moved to a new station in Kaposia, where a church was organized in 1849. He established a station in Yellow Medicine beginning in 1852, working under very difficult circumstances. An attack by Native Americans in 1862 led to the death of 600 white settlers, though an additional 100 lives were saved by Christian Dakotas loyal to the whites. When the attacking Native Americans were defeated by government forces, many were placed in prison. Williamson and others worked among the prisoners, leading to more than 300 baptisms before his visits were forbidden by the officer in charge. Williamson continued his work among the Dakotas, serving under the Presbyterian mission board after 1872.

BIBLIOGRAPHY Writings of Williamson include *The Sioux or Dakotas: A Sketch of our Intercourse with the Dakotas on the Missouri River, and Southwest of That Stream* (1880) and various translations of portions of the Bible into the Dakota language. Memorial tribute, *Missionary Herald,* August 1879; Stephen Return Riggs, *In Memory of Rev. Thos. S. Williamson, M.D.* (1880); "Vinton" book of ABCFM biographical material.

Martha Lund Smalley

Willibald (c. 700–786), missionary in Thuringia and bishop of Eichstätt. A relative of *Boniface, Willibald was educated in a monastery at Waltham in Hants, England. After a pilgrimage in 720 to Rome, where he spent more than two years becoming familiar with the Latin world, he traveled east for more than seven years, visiting Sicily, Cyprus, Palestine, Tyre, and Constantinople, where he learned to appreciate the worlds of the Bible and Byzantium. During these travels he was imprisoned by some Muslims but rescued by other Muslims. He spent nearly a decade in Monte Cassino (730–739), after which he was sent back to Germany by Gregory III as a missionary in Thuringia, founded a monastery, and worked in Franconia to build up the church there.

BIBLIOGRAPHY Brun Appel, Emanuel Braun, and Siegfried Hofmann, eds., *Heilige Willibald 787–1987* (1987); Harald Dickerhof, Ernst Reiter, and Stefan Weinfurter, eds., *Der Heilige Willibald: Klosterbischof oder Bistumsgründer* (1990); Charles H. Talbot, *The Anglo-Saxon Missions in Germany* (1954).

Frederick W. Norris

Willibrord (*or* Willibrordus), Clemens (c. 657–739), English Benedictine missionary in the Netherlands and apostle of the Frisians. Born in Northumbria, England, Willibrord was trained by *Wilfrid in the monastery of Ripon, near York, and by Ecgberct in the monastery of Rathmelsigni, Ireland, where he was ordained a priest. In 690 he embarked for Europe with eleven companions and settled in Utrecht, an area under Frankish control. The ruler of the Franks, Pépin II, supported his desire to do missionary work, regarding Willibrord as an ally against the Frisian king Radbod. Willibrord was sent by Pépin to obtain papal blessing for the work among the Frisians. In 695, again at the request of Pépin, Willibrord went to Rome to be consecrated by Pope Sergius I as bishop (later archbishop) of the Frisians.

Willibrord labored through decades of vicissitudes. Radbod rebelled after Pépin's death in 714; he destroyed Christian shrines, restored paganism, and forced Willibrord to leave Utrecht. When Charles Martel, Pépin's son, restored Frankish order, Willibrord returned; Radbod, however, remained a pagan until his death in 719. One source indicates that Willibrord was so discouraged by the resistance of the Frisians to the gospel that he went to Denmark in order to win converts there; but the conversion of Denmark seemed to be just as difficult as that of Friesland. Willibrord had more success in the southern part of the Netherlands and in Luxembourg. He built churches and set up monasteries in Utrecht, Antwerp, Echternach, and Susteren. For a time, *Boniface worked under Willibrord. Alcuin of York wrote his biography, *Vita Willibrordi.*

BIBLIOGRAPHY A. Grieve, *Willibrord, Missionary in the Netherlands (691–739), Including a Translation of the Vita Willibrordi by Alcuin of York* (1923); H. Löwe, "Pirmin, Willibrord, und Bonifatius," in *Kirchengeschichte als Missionsgeschichte,* vol.2, part 1, H. Frohnes et al., eds. (1978), pp. 192–226; C. Wampach, *Sankt Willibrord: Sein Leben und Lebenswerk* (1953); H. A. Wilson, ed., *The Calendar of St. Willibrord, from ms. Paris. Lat. 10837: A Facsimile with Transcription, Introduction, and Notes* (1918).

Jan A. B. Jongeneel

Willis, John Jamieson (1872–1954), Church Missionary Society (CMS) missionary in Uganda and Kenya. Born in England and educated at Haileybury School, Pembroke College (Cambridge) and Ridley Hall (Cambridge), Willis was ordained priest in 1896. Arriving in East Africa in 1900, he pioneered missions first in Ankole in western Uganda, and then in the Kavirondo region of western Kenya, where he founded the Maseno School in 1906. He was Anglican bishop of Uganda from 1912 to 1934, the first to have had extensive prior missionary experience. His experience of intense missionary competition among Protestants in Kenya led him to cooperate closely with Charles *Hurlburt of the Africa Inland Mission and John Arthur of the Church of Scotland Mission. Their endorsement of a plan for a united African church at the 1913 Kikuyu Conference provoked the charge of heresy by *Frank Weston, bishop of Zanzibar. In Uganda, Willis's concern for the institutional structures of church life led him to stress missionary leadership at the expense of African responsibility, which had been a feature of the Ugandan church in its early years. His hopes for an ecclesiastical province in East Africa were not shared by Ugandans, who feared the wider political implications of domination by Kenyan European settlers.

BIBLIOGRAPHY Willis wrote about the ecumenical stirrings in Kenya in his *Towards a United Church* (1947). His papers are in Lambeth Palace Library, London. For his impact on the institutional life of the church in Uganda, see J. V. Taylor, *The Growth of the Church in Buganda* (1958).

Kevin Ward

Willoughby, W(illiam) C(harles) (1857–1938), missionary in Bechuanaland (now Botswana). Born in Cornwall, England, Willoughby studied at Spring Hill Theological College, Birmingham. Ordained as a Congregational minister in 1882, he was appointed by the London Missionary Society (LMS) to central Africa but returned home the following year with malaria. He then served Congregational churches in Perth and Brighton. In 1885 he married Charlotte Elizabeth Pountney; they had three sons and two daughters. In 1892 LMS appointed him to the Bechuanaland Protectorate, and he went to Palapye in 1893 to work among the BaNgwato of *Khama III. In 1895 he accompanied Khama, Bathoen, and Sebele to England and helped them preserve their country from South African capitalist Cecil Rhodes.

In about 1903, when the LMS built a much-needed central school for its community, Willoughby was appointed the first principal. He chose to establish the Tiger Kloof Native Institution on a farm near Vryburg in the Cape Colony, and led it until 1915. The school developed a fine reputation that attracted African pupils from all over southern Africa.

From 1919 until retirement in 1931, Willoughby was professor of African missions in the Kennedy School of Missions of Hartford Seminary in Connecticut. Upon his retirement, the Hartford Seminary conferred upon him an honorary doctor of sacred theology degree.

During his missionary years Willoughby published several small books, including *Native Life on the Transvaal Border* (1900) and *Tiger Kloof* (1912). His interest in African traditions led to *The Soul of the Bantu: A Sympathetic Study of the Magico-Religious Practises and Beliefs of the Bantu Tribes of Africa* (1928). Other works were *Race Problems in the New Africa* (1923) and *Nature Worship and Taboo* (1932). He died in Birmingham, England.

BIBLIOGRAPHY J. Mutero Chirenje, *A History of Northern Botswana, 1850–1910* (1977); Norman Goodall, *A History of the London Missionary Society, 1895–1945* (1954). Obituary in the London *Times*, June 23, 1938. Letters of Willoughby from 1915 to 1938 are in the Hartford Seminary Library.

Gordon M. Haliburton

Wilson, C(harles) E(dward) (1871–1956), Baptist Missionary Society (BMS) foreign secretary. Born in Southwark (London), Wilson trained for the Baptist ministry at Regent's Park College and in 1894 was accepted by the BMS for service in Bengal. After a year in Jessore, he taught at Serampore College until 1905, when he was recalled to London to succeed A. H. *Baynes as general secretary of the BMS. When the society appointed W. Y. Fullerton home secretary in 1912, Wilson modestly accepted a reduction of his position to foreign secretary. Wilson was the first BMS secretary to have field experience, and in the course of his 34 years in office, made six visits to BMS fields in India, Ceylon (Sri Lanka), China, the Congo (Zaire), and the West Indies. His visit to India and Ceylon in 1931 and 1932, undertaken at a time of great financial difficulty in the society, proved crucial in accelerating the process of devolution from mission to church in Bengal and Ceylon. Wilson attended the World Missionary Conference at Edinburgh in 1910 and the Jerusalem meeting of the International Missionary Council in 1928. He played a leading role in the Conference of British Missionary Societies from its formation in 1912. He retired in 1939.

BIBLIOGRAPHY Brian Stanley, *The History of the Baptist Missionary Society, 1792–1992* (1992).

Brian Stanley

Wilson, Daniel (1778–1858), fifth Anglican bishop of Calcutta. The son of a silk manufacturer in Spitalfields, London, Wilson experienced conversion at the age of 18 and received nurture from John Newton. He studied for ordination at St. Edmund Hall, Oxford, and became vice-principal of this evangelical college. He was vicar of Islington (1824–1832) and a strong supporter of the Church Missionary Society (CMS) against its critics in the Church of England. On arrival in India in 1832, he was invited to become president of the CMS corresponding committee. He fostered Bishop's College, Calcutta, which had been founded by Thomas *Middleton, as a place for training Christian leaders, and was responsible for building the Anglican cathedral of St. Paul's in Calcutta. Wilson was active in India for 26 years and made a considerable impression on church life. His opposition to caste in the church was particularly significant.

BIBLIOGRAPHY J. Bateman, *Life of Bishop Daniel Wilson* (1860); M. E. Gibbs, *The Anglican Church in India 1600–1970* (1972); S. C. Neill, *A History of Christianity in India, 1707–1858* (1985);

E. Stock, *The History of the Church Missionary Society* (1899); H. P. Thompson, *Into All Lands* (1951); T. E. Yates, *Venn and Victorian Bishops Abroad* (1978).

Timothy Yates

Wilson, Edward Francis (1844–1915), Anglican missionary educator in Canada and linguist. Born in England to a family prominent in the evangelical wing of the Church of England, Wilson set out for Canada in 1865. After experiencing a call to work among Indians there, he studied at Huron College, London, Ontario, and then returned to England. Ordained a deacon in 1867, he married Frances Spooner the next year. Returning to Canada as a Church Missionary Society (CMS) agent, Wilson served five years in Sarnia, Ontario. In 1873, he severed his CMS ties and established the Shingwauk boys' school and Wawanosh girls' school in Sault Sainte Marie, Ontario. In 1893, he retired to Salt Spring Island, a gulf island between Vancouver and Vancouver Island, where he devoted himself to church planting and farming.

The Shingwauk and Wawanosh schools pioneered a residential school system that aimed to implement government cultural replacement policy. Influenced by Henry *Venn, by a growing group of Canadian anthropologists, and by his travels among Indians in the United States, Wilson became disillusioned with this policy and instead advocated cultural synthesis. His writings established his reputation as a leading missionary ethnographer and linguist.

BIBLIOGRAPHY Edward Francis Wilson, *Missionary Work among the Ojebway Indians* (1886), *The Ojebway Language* (1874; repr. 1975), and articles in *The Canadian Indian* and *Our Forest Children.* John Webster Grant, *Moon of Wintertime* (1984); Bea Hamilton, *Salt Spring Island* (1969); Paulette Jiles, "Reverend Wilson and the Ojibway Grammar," *This Magazine* 10 (February–March 1976): 15–17; David A. Nock, *A Victorian Missionary and Canadian Indian Policy* (1988); J. Donald Wilson, "A Note on the Shingwauk Industrial Home for Indians," *Journal of the Canadian Church Historical Society* 16 (1974): 66–71. CMS, Algoma, and Huron diocesan archives house Wilson's papers and documents.

Paul R. Dekar

Wilson, Eleanor (1891–1972), teacher, ordained minister, and captain of the mission vessels *Morning Star VI* and *VII.* Wilson was born at Norwalk, Connecticut, and educated at the Cambridge (Massachusetts) Latin School, Simmons College, and New York Biblical Seminary. In 1925, after serving the YWCA in Kalamazoo, Michigan, she went overseas under the American Board of Commissioners for Foreign Missions (ABCFM) and became a high school teacher in Japan, where she later directed the Kobe Theological Seminary for women. She returned to the United States in 1933 to work at the mission's Boston headquarters. Her knowledge of Japan's Micronesian mission led her to volunteer in 1936 to work alongside the experienced sisters Elizabeth and Jane *Baldwin at the mission's training school at Mwot, on Kosrae. Following Elizabeth Baldwin's death, she accompanied Jane Baldwin, by way of Japan, to retirement in the United States shortly before the Pacific war broke out. After the war she was ordained and commissioned in Honolulu and returned to the Marshall Islands, where she was summoned at short notice—and without specialized training—to become captain of *Morning Star VI,* a mission vessel operated by the ABCFM. Never seasick, she discharged this appointment with typical adaptability. Later she raised $50,000 to buy and commission *Morning Star VII.* Retiring as missionary emeritus in 1961, she ministered to a new church on Kauai, Hawaii, for three years before finally moving to Claremont, California, where she died. She was privately interred in the Cambridge (Massachusetts) City Cemetery by the minister of Boston's Park Street Church.

BIBLIOGRAPHY Eleanor Wilson, *"Too Old?" A Saga of the South Pacific* (1972). Maribelle Cormack, *The Lady Was a Skipper* (1956, with autobiographical introduction by Eleanor Wilson); Clarence W. Hall, "She Is Skipper of the *Morning Star,*" *Reader's Digest,* November 1957, pp. 127–132; C. D. Ketchum, *The Great Waters* (1956). Wilson materials are contained in the archives of the ABCFM and ABCFM Women's Board and in the files of *Missionary Herald.*

John Garrett

Wilson, James (1760–1814), English captain of the mission ship *Duff.* Wilson was born the nineteenth child of a sea captain at Newcastle-upon-Tyne. He fought in the British army at Bunker Hill and Lexington, Massachusetts, during the American Revolution and spent nine years with the British East India Company as master of a merchantman. He was imprisoned by the South Indian ruler Hyder Ali and survived the notorious black hole of Seringapatam. Having made his fortune, and retiring early to Portsea, he was converted from aloof deism to heartfelt Calvinism. Responding to an appeal in the *Evangelical Magazine,* he bought and outfitted the *Duff* and engaged a crew of hymn-singing believers. Described as "a floating church," the ship carried the first contingent of London Missionary Society (LMS) missionaries to the South Pacific (1796–1797). Wilson sailed round the Cape of Good Hope to Tahiti, the Marquesas Islands, and Tonga, returning via Hong Kong, where he loaded a cargo of tea to defray the expenses of the voyage. Moving to Denmark Hill, London, he married the only daughter of a rich local church member by the name of Holbert. They had one son and four daughters. He lost his investments in a declining wartime market and died in failing health.

BIBLIOGRAPHY [James Wilson], *A Missionary Voyage to the Southern Pacific... in the Ship* Duff (1799); William Smith, *Journal of a Voyage in the Missionary Ship Duff...* (1813, with an appendix on Wilson's life); Herbert Stead, *Captain James Wilson* (n.d.).

John Garrett

Wilson, J. Christy, Sr. (1891–1973), Presbyterian missionary in Iran. Wilson was born in Nebraska and spent his early years in Idaho. He graduated from the University of Kansas in 1914 and from Princeton Theological

Seminary in 1919. In 1917 he married Fern Wilson (not related). He was ordained a year before graduation and served as an army chaplain in World War I. Appointed as a Presbyterian evangelistic missionary to Iran in 1919, he was stationed in Tabriz, where he preached in Persian and Turkish, took part in the medical and educational work, and wrote several books in Persian about the Bible and evangelism. At the request of the Persian government, he also wrote a textbook on the history of Iranian art. He was the author of several books in English, including a popular paperback, *Introducing Islam* (1950) and an official biography of Samuel M. *Zwemer, *Apostle to Islam* (1952).

Wilson's broad learning, strong evangelical faith, and outgoing personal influence brought him into positions of leadership in such organizations as Near East Relief and Near East Council of Churches. Because of Russia's occupation of northern Iran in World War II, it was not possible for the Wilsons to return from furlough to Tabriz. Instead, Wilson served on the faculty of Princeton Theological Seminary as associate professor of ecumenics from 1940 to 1962.

BIBLIOGRAPHY Princeton Theological Seminary, "Faculty Memorial Minute," May 9, 1973. An information sheet on J. Christy Wilson, Sr., was distributed in 1949 by the Board of Foreign Missions, Presbyterian Church, U.S.A. Elmer G. Homrighausen, address at memorial service, April 23, 1973, Princeton Theological Seminary (audio tape).

R. Park Johnson

Wilson, John (1804–1875) *and*
Margaret (Bayne) (1795–1835), Scottish missionaries and pioneer educators in Bombay. Born in Lauder, Scotland, John Wilson graduated from University of Edinburgh and married Margaret Bayne in 1828. They went to India as missionaries of the Church of Scotland, arriving in Bombay in early 1829. Initially they studied Marathi in Harnai, a village on the west coast, then returned to Bombay, where in 1831 John organized the Ambroli Church (now on Wilson Street). In 1832 he established an English school and in 1836 added a college section. Margaret, a pioneer in women's education, established several girls' schools in 1829, and in 1832 opened the first girls' boarding school in western India. Today it is called St. Columba High School. She died in 1835, and in 1837 two of her sisters went to India to carry on her work.

John served as principal of Wilson High School and College until he died in Bombay. He introduced Western education, prepared textbooks, and conducted examinations. In 1857 he helped to establish Bombay University and became its vice-chancellor in 1869. He was a pioneer of education for the low castes and served as an adviser to the government on educational policy. He mastered Sanskrit, Gujarati, Hebrew, Greek, Latin, Urdu, Hindustani, Persian, Arabic, and Zend (the language of the Zoroastrian scriptures). He became a leading orientalist and was president of the Asiatic Society of Bombay (1835–1842). A prolific author, he wrote *Parsi Religion* (1843), *History of the Suppression of Female Infanticide in Western India* (1855), *Aboriginal Tribes of the Bombay Presidency* (1876), and *Indian Caste* (1877). As an archaeologist, he wrote *The Caves of Karla* (1861) and *Religious Excavations of Western India, Buddhist, Brahamanical, and Jaina* (1875). He helped decipher Brahmi script by reproducing Asokan Girnar inscriptions and was the first to write about the origin of Bene-Israelis in western India. One of his early initiatives was the publication of the *Oriental Christian Spectator* (1830–1862), the first scholarly research journal in western India that dealt with religion, society, culture, and Western influence. Wilson entered into dialogue with the leaders of other religions, and organized public lectures, "speaking the truth in love." He attracted a few high-caste Hindus and the first Parsi converts to Christianity. He also influenced many social reformers of western India. For nearly half a century, Wilson was indeed a towering figure in Bombay.

BIBLIOGRAPHY John Wilson, *A Memoir of Mrs. Margaret Wilson* (1838), *India Three Thousand Years Ago* (1838), *Evangelisation of India* (1849), and *Memoir of the Cave Temples and Monasteries and Ancient Remains in Western India* (1850). George Smith's *Life of John Wilson* (1878) is a detailed biography; M. D. David, *John Wilson and His Institution* (1975) is an assessment of John and Margaret Wilson's work. Some of John Wilson's correspondence is in the National Library, Edinburgh, Scotland.

Mohan D. David

Wilson, John Leighton (1809–1886), missionary in Africa and Presbyterian missions administrator. Wilson was born near Salem, South Carolina, and graduated from Union College, Schenectady, New York, and Columbia (South Carolina) Theological Seminary (now in Decatur, Georgia). In 1833 he studied Arabic at Andover Theological Seminary, Massachusetts, and later that year sailed on an exploratory trip along the coast of West Africa. He returned to Africa in 1834 as a missionary with the American Board of Commissioners for Foreign Missions in Cape Palmas, Liberia. There he planted a church, started a boarding school, developed a writing system for the Glebo language, and translated portions of Scripture. Although he initially supported the American Colonization Society and resettled his wife's slaves in Liberia, he eventually opposed the colonization movement. In 1842 he launched missionary work among the Mpongwe in Gabon, with a continuing emphasis on educational, linguistic, and translation projects. He openly attacked the Atlantic slave trade and slavery in America, although he experienced difficulties trying to emancipate two slaves that he had inherited. Wilson returned to America in 1852 because of poor health and became a secretary for the Presbyterian Board of Foreign Missions in 1853. During that tenure he wrote *Western Africa: Its History, Condition, and Prospects* (1856). In 1861 he helped to organize the Executive Committee of Foreign Missions for the (Southern) Presbyterian Church and served as its executive secretary until his retirement in 1885.

BIBLIOGRAPHY Henry H. Bucher, Jr., "John Leighton Wilson and the Mpongwe: The 'Spirit of 1776' in Mid-Nineteenth Century Western Africa," *Journal of Presbyterian History* 54 (1976):

291–315; Hampden C. DuBose, *Memoirs of Rev. John Leighton Wilson* (1895).

James A. Patterson

Wilson, Mary Ann (Cooke) (1784–1868), British missionary educator in India. Born in England, Mary Ann Cooke was a governess in the family of the Earl of Mulgrave and accompanied him in 1820 when he was recruited by the British and Foreign Schools Society to assist the Calcutta Schools Society in India. When funds failed in 1822, she was enrolled as a member of the Church Missionary Society (CMS), and in 1823 she married CMS missionary Isaac Wilson. Starting a school in Calcutta with just one pupil, she went on to found a school for girls, assisted by the Ladies' Female Education Society (also organized by her). In 1834 these initiatives led, in England, to the founding of the Society for Promoting Female Education in the East (SPFEE). Her husband died in 1828, but she continued her work for girls. She later started a female orphanage at Agarpura, north of Calcutta. In 1842, having failed to command the support she felt she deserved, and having come under the influence of Anthony Norris *Groves, the Plymouth Brethren evangelist, she left the Church of England. Her orphanage was continued by the CMS, eventually becoming a boarding school for girls. Wilson appears to have left India, after 22 years' service, and is said to have taught in Syria and Italy. She encouraged other women to come and set up schools in India through the pages of the SPFEE magazine *The Female Missionary Intelligencer.* She was the fourth woman to appear in the CMS list of female missionaries.

BIBLIOGRAPHY Eugene Stock, *History of the Church Missionary Society: Its Environment, Its Men, and Its Work,* vol. 1 (1899); Mrs. [Mary] Weitbrecht, *The Women of India and Christian Work in the Zenana* (1875).

Jocelyn Murray

Wilson, Robert Orr (1906–1967), medical missionary in China. Born in Nanking (Nanjing), China, the son of Methodist missionaries William F. and Mary (Rowley) Wilson, Wilson graduated from Princeton University (B.A., 1927) and Harvard Medical School (M.D., 1933). He was appointed to the staff of the University of Nanking Hospital in 1935, arriving in 1936. He contined working in the hospital throughout the Japanese occupation, although most Chinese doctors had left Nanking well before the city was captured. He carried an incredibly heavy load of medical work with the help of a few nurses during the occupation. In April 1938 two doctors and two nurses arrived from St. Andrew's Hospital in Wu-hsi (Wuxi) to give Wilson and his staff some relief. In June 1938 he was able to leave Nanking for a furlough in Shanghai, and in 1940 he and his family left China for a furlough in the United States. When they sought to return to China the following year, his wife was unable to obtain a passport because of war conditions, so they stayed in the United States. Wilson served as a surgeon in Panama during World War II (1943–1944). After the war he practiced medicine in Arcadia, California.

BIBLIOGRAPHY Wilson's diaries and letters are held in the Special Collections of Yale Divinity School Library; excerpts published in Martha Lund Smalley, ed., *American Missionary Eyewitnesses to the Nanking Massacre, 1937–1938* (1997), provide a valuable eye-witness account of the atrocities committed by the Japanese army in the Nanking Massacre.

Martha Lund Smalley

Wilson, Samuel Graham (1858–1916), American Presbyterian missionary in Persia. Born in Indiana, Pennsylvania, Wilson graduated from Princeton University (1876) and Western Theological Seminary in Pittsburgh (1879). He was ordained in July 1880 and left for Persia (Iran) soon after. Although intending to specialize in translation work, he was soon preaching and making evangelistic tours on horseback over wide areas. In 1882 he was appointed principal of a small school for boys in Tabriz, which ten years later became the Memorial Training and Theological School. While on furlough in 1886, he married Annie Dwight Rhea, the daughter of Samuel Audley Rhea, who was himself a pioneer missionary in Persia. They eventually had four children. He translated a catechism into Armenian and a church history textbook and an arithmetic primer into Azeri Turkish. Biographical works and other works by him describing Armenian customs and the work of the mission were very popular and were translated into German and Russian. In November 1912 he was seriously injured in a railroad accident while on furlough in the United States, and he was further delayed in returning to Persia by the outbreak of World War I. He eventually returned in November 1915, after having been appointed chairman of a commission sent by the American Committee for Armenian and Syrian Relief. He traveled by way of Norway, Archangel, and Petrograd (St. Petersburg) and spent several months in Russia administering relief among Armenian refugees fleeing from Turkey. Fatigue, overwork, and exposure to extremes of cold left him so weak that he fell a victim to typhoid soon after reaching Tabriz, where he died. He was respected by Muslims and revered by Armenians as a martyr to their cause.

BIBLIOGRAPHY The main sources for Wilson's life are the manuscript records of Princeton Univ. and obituaries in the *New York Herald* and *Princeton Alumni Weekly* (1916).

Ronald E. Davies

Wimmer, Gottlieb August (1791–1863), Hungarian coordinator for the British and Foreign Bible Society (BFBS). Born in upper Hungary, Wimmer was a Lutheran pastor in Oberschützen (West Hungary) from 1818 to 1849. He established institutes of learning and an orphanage. From 1835 he coordinated the work of the BFBS in Hungary. To arouse an interest in mission among common people, he organized the first mission festival in his church in 1845. From this missionary-minded congregation, Samuel Böhm was sent as the first Hungarian missionary to Africa with the Bremen Mission in 1859.

In his comprehensive Christocentric approach, Wimmer combined deep personal piety with a concern for the social needs of his congregation and a fervent interest in the worldwide mission cause. In the following decades his pioneering work had an impact on German-speaking Lutherans throughout Hungary. For political reasons, however, he was expelled from the country in 1849. He died in Vienna.

BIBLIOGRAPHY John V. Eibner, "British Evangelicals and Hungary, 1800–1852," *Journal of the United Reformed Church History Society* 3, no. 2 (1983): 44 ff.; Anne-Marie Kool, *God Moves in a Mysterious Way: The Hungarian Protestant Foreign Mission Movement (1756–1951)* (1993), pp. 82–97; Bernhard H. Zimmermann, "G. A. Wimmer, der Erwecker des Missionssinnes in Ungarn," *NAMZ* 16, no. 8 (1939): 235–242, "Reformtätigkeit in der Pfarre Oberschützen," in *Jahrbuch der Gesellschaft für die Geschichte des Protestantismus in ehemaliger und neuer österreich,* vol. 61 (1940), pp. 159–179, and *Gottlieb August Wimmer, 1791–1863* (1965).

Anne-Marie Kool

Winans, Roger (1886–1975) *and*
Ester (Carson) (1891–1928), Church of the Nazarene pioneer missionaries to the Aguaruna Indians of Peru. Born to a poor family in Osawkie, Kansas, Roger Winans felt an early call to work with the Indians of Peru. After two years of Bible college and brief work among Mexican peoples in Texas and New Mexico, he secured passage in 1914 on a ship, arriving in Pacasmayo, Peru, without money for a night's lodging. Obtaining work as a colporteur, he familiarized himself as much as possible with the Peruvian Indians and became a missionary with the Church of the Nazarene. His first wife, Mary (Hunt), died during this period.

Ester Carson was born in California where her parents dedicated her to missionary work before her birth. She demonstrated extraordinary intensity and sense of calling to missions from her earliest years. In 1918 she went to Peru under appointment as a missionary for the Church of the Nazarene, and there she met the recently widowed Roger Winans. They were married in 1919 and with pack animals set out for Peru's upper interior country to open work on the Maranon River among the Aguaruna Indians. They met life-threatening resistance but persisted with work that developed an alphabet and recorded a word list for subsequent translation of the Gospel of Luke. They established churches, schools, and medical care up and down the Maranon River. Ester died in Peru, and Roger continued the work until 1944. He retired at Casa Robles Missionary home in California.

BIBLIOGRAPHY Roger Winans, *Gospel over the Andes* (1955). J. Fred Parker, *Mission to the World* (1988); Mendell Taylor, *Fifty Years of Nazarene Missions* (1956). Various personal papers and documents are held in the Nazarene archives, Kansas City, Mo.

Robert H. Scott

Winfried. *See* Boniface.

Winslow, Harriet Wadsworth (Lathrop) (1796–1833), American missionary to Ceylon (Sri Lanka). Born in Norwich, Connecticut, Harriet Lathrop married Miron *Winslow in January 1819 and in June embarked with him for Ceylon under the American Board of Commissioners for Foreign Missions (ABCFM). They were stationed at Uduvil, where they worked among the Jaffna Tamils. Harriet gave particular attention to the education of girls, first taking them into her own family. When a central boarding school for girls was established in January 1824, the Winslows took charge of what became the well-known Uduvil School. Harriet wrote out the lessons in arithmetic and geography and supervised instruction in sewing and the household arts. Deeply concerned for the spiritual life of the school, she remembered one girl each day in her prayers, just as she did her own children. Every girl who graduated in the first 50 years became a Christian. Winslow also served as her husband's secretary. In January 1833 she died suddenly in childbirth. Her sister, Elizabeth Coit Lathrop Hutchings, sailed to join the Ceylon mission in July before word of the death had reached the United States. Harriet was buried beside two other sisters, both missionaries, Charlotte H. Cherry and Harriet Joanna Perry. Miron Winslow was widowed three more times before his last marriage in 1856.

BIBLIOGRAPHY Miron Winslow wrote *A Memoir of Mrs. Harriet Wadsworth Winslow, Combining a Sketch of the Ceylon Mission* (1835). There is an obituary in *Missionary Herald* 28 (1833): 300–301, and her efforts in the education of girls are described in Minnie Hastings Harrison's *Uduvil, 1824–1924...* (1925).

David M. Stowe

Winslow, John ("Jack") C(opley) (1882–1974), pioneer of the Christian ashram movement in India. Born and educated in England, Winslow was a missionary in India with the Society for the Propagation of the Gospel (SPG) from 1914 to 1934. A friend of C. F. *Andrews, he opposed the racial divide between missionaries and Indian people as well as a Westernized church. He and seven Maratha men and women formed the Christa Seva Sangha Ashram at Miri in 1921, moving in 1922 to Poona (modern Pune), where it soon grew to twenty members, including Verrier *Elwin. Winslow's *Christa Seva Sangha* (1930) illustrates his creative liturgical inculturations, reflected also in his *Eucharist in India* (1920) and his "Liturgy for India" included in the Indian Anglican *Book of Common Prayer* (1960). Winslow's Indian work also includes a fine study of his friend Narayan Vaman *Tilak, translation of Tilak's poetry, support for Gandhi and the national movement, and writing on inculturation in spirituality.

Winslow left the Sangha ashram in 1934, unhappy at a Westernizing phase (subsequently reversed). Returning to England, he worked for some years with the Oxford Group Movement (Moral Re-armament). Later he was instrumental in founding a retreat center, Lee Abbey, with its attendant Fellowship, in Devon. Two months after a brief, joyful return to Pune, he died in England.

BIBLIOGRAPHY Winslow's autobiography is *Eyelids of the Dawn* (1954). He also wrote *Christian Yoga* (1923), *The Indian Mystic* (1926), and with V. Elwin, *The Dawn of Indian Freedom* (1931). Barbara Noreen, *Crossroads of the Spirit* (1994) is an account of

Winslow and the Sangha under his leadership. The Sangha journal, initially *Servant of Christ,* then the *C. S. S. Review,* is an important source. Winslow's reports are in the SPG papers at Rhodes House Library, Oxford, and other unpublished papers on the Sangha are at Bishop's College, Calcutta, and the Franciscan Friary at Hilfield, Dorset, U.K.

Daniel O'Connor

Winslow, Miron (1789–1864), American missionary to Sri Lanka and India. Born in Williston, Vermont, Winslow felt a call to mission after some years in business. He entered Middlebury College in 1813 and graduated in 1815. After graduation from Andover Theological Seminary (1818) he was ordained; in 1819 he married Harriet Wadsworth Lathrop (see article above) and sailed for Ceylon under the American Board of Commissioners for Foreign Missions (ABCFM), along with the *Scudders, *Spauldings, and Woodwards. Stationed at Uduvil, he worked among the Jaffna Tamils until 1833, doing evangelistic and translation work and giving leadership in pastoral training, and, with his wife, to a pioneering school for girls. At the death of Harriet in 1833 he returned to America with three of his own children and eight others; while there, he married Catherine Waterbury Carman in 1835. He returned to Ceylon briefly and in 1836 opened a new station at Madras especially for Tamil printing and publication. In 1837 Catherine died; he was then married to Anne Spiers (1838–1843) and Mary Billings Dwight (1845–1852).

Winslow served for many years as secretary of the Madras Bible Society committee, revising the Tamil Bible, and worked to complete a Tamil-English dictionary. He visited the United States in 1856–1857; at that time he married Ellen Augusta Reed, his fifth wife, who survived him. He received the D.D. from Harvard in 1858. In 1864 he withdrew from the mission because of ill health. He died at Cape Town, where he was buried near John *Scudder, his longtime missionary colleague in India.

BIBLIOGRAPHY *Missionary Herald* 61 (1865): 65–69, has a full obituary. Before sailing to Asia, Winslow wrote *A Sketch of Missions, or History of the Principal Attempts to Propagate Christianity Among the Heathen* (1819). He also wrote *A Memoir of Mrs. Harriet Wadsworth Winslow, Combining a Sketch of the Ceylon Mission* (1835) and published *Comprehensive Tamil and English Dictionary of High and Low Tamil* (1862). See also Rufus Anderson, *History of the Missions of the ABCFM in India* (1875), pp. 146–171, and chap. 11, on the Madras Mission, pp. 220–234; Helen I. Root, comp., *A Century in Ceylon* (1916).

David M. Stowe

Winter, Ralph D(ana) (1924–), Presbyterian missionary and founder of the U.S. Center for World Mission. Born in Los Angeles, California, Winter was raised in a godly Presbyterian home. After naval service in World War II, he earned a degree in engineering from California Institute of Technology. He then attended several other institutions, including Columbia University (M.A. in teaching English as a second language), Cornell (Ph.D. in structural linguistics), and Princeton Theological Seminary (ordination degree, 1956). Under the Presbyterian Church, U.S.A., he and his wife, Roberta (Helm), served ten years among Mayan Indians in Guatemala, where he pioneered in Theological Education by Extension (TEE). He edited *Theological Education by Extension* (1969), which popularized TEE to the world church thanks to widespread distribution of the book by the Theological Education Fund. In 1966 he joined the faculty of Fuller Theological Seminary's fledgling School of World Mission. During this period he established the William Carey Library, which specializes in the publication of mission books, including dissertations produced by graduate students at the School of World Mission. In 1972 he and Gerald H. Anderson were instrumental in founding the American Society of Missiology and launching its journal *Missiology,* with Alan *Tippett as editor. Winter is particularly remembered for his presentation at the 1974 International Congress on World Evangelization, held in Lausanne, Switzerland, which set a new agenda for world mission to "unreached peoples" (in contrast to the 1910 Edinburgh World Missionary Conference's unreached territories). In 1976 he left Fuller Seminary to establish the U.S. Center for World Mission, Pasadena, California, which includes on-site cooperative efforts of about 50 U.S. mission agencies and strategy institutes, all focused on the unfinished task of world mission—"unreached peoples." Winter's vision also led to the founding of the Association of Church Mission Committees (now Advancing Churches in Missions Commitment) and William Carey International University, Pasadena. The Frontier Mission Fellowship, another of Winter's initiatives, has helped carry the unreached peoples vision throughout the United States and beyond. A college-level course on missions called Perspectives on the World Christian Movement, also launched by Winter, is offered annually at numerous sites across the United States and overseas, helping to give the laity a deeper grasp of the world Christian movement.

BIBLIOGRAPHY Ralph D. Winter, "The 25 Unbelievable Years" in Kenneth Scott Latourette, *A History of the Expansion of Christianity* vol. 7 (1970 edition), *The Evangelical Response to Bangkok* (1973), "The Highest Priority: Cross-cultural Evangelism," in J. D. Douglas, ed., *Let the Earth Hear His Voice* (1978), pp. 213–241, ed. with Steven Hawthorne, *Perspectives on the World Christian Movement* (1981; rev. 1992) and "My Pilgrimage in Mission," *IBMR* 19 (April 1995): 56–60. Tim Stafford, "Ralph Winter: An Unlikely Revolutionary," *CT,* Sept. 7, 1984.

Robert T. Coote

Winthuis, Josef (1876–1956), German Catholic missionary in Papua New Guinea. Born in Kleve, Winthuis completed his studies in Salzburg and Hiltrup, where he was ordained in 1900. As a member of the Missionaries of the Sacred Heart (MSC), he arrived in Melanesia in 1902 and worked among the Gunantuna on the Gazelle Peninsula of New Britain. His first scientific article was published in *Anthropos* in 1909, and he was co-author of *A Katekismo katolik* (1914). In 1914 he was unable to return from leave in Germany because of World War I so he started to write about his experience in a book on missionary work and local customs, *Zur Psychologie und Methode der religiös-sittlichen Heidenunterweisung* (1929). He earned his doctorate from the University of Innsbruck and published a study of sexuality, *Das Zweigeschlechterwesen bei den Zentralaustraliern und anderen Völkern* (1928). He believed he had discovered the fundamental sexual perspective of the myths and rituals of the Melanesian peoples. In the Melanesian worldview, as Winthuis perceived it, a bisexual god is the source of life, and humans must ritually imitate the god's eternal embrace in order to secure life on earth. This triggered heated debate, his most famous adversary being Wilhelm *Schmidt. The disagreement continued for years and involved many people. Winthuis eventually left the MSC and published no more books or articles after 1936. A few years before his death he rejoined the MSC.

Bibliography Winthuis's *Zwoelf Jahre unter Suedseekannibalen* (n.d.) is autobiographical and covers his 12 years in Melanesia. His publications, which mainly defend his theory, include: *Die Wahrheit über das Zweigeschlechterwesen, durch meine Gegner bestätigt* (1930), *Einführung in die Vorstellungswelt primitiver Völker* (1931), *Mythos und Kult der Steinzeit* (1935), and *Mythos und Religionswissenschaft* (1936). A biography with bibliography was published by Carl Laufer in *Anthropos* 51 (1956): 1080–1082.

Otto Bischofberger, SMB

Wiser, William H(endricks) (1890–1961) *and* **Charlotte (Viall)** (1892–1981), Presbyterian missionaries in India. William Wiser and Charlotte Viall went to India in 1915 and 1916, respectively, as rural missionaries of the Presbyterian Church in the U.S.A. They married in Allahabad in December 1916. Their first term was devoted to teaching in Allahabad and to social work in Kanpur. During their second term in Mainpuri, Uttar Pradesh, (1925–1930), they lived in the village of Karimpur in order to get to know village people and village life. From this experience came their pioneer work in Indian anthropology, *Behind Mud Walls* (1930), which is still a standard text; and also William's seminal *Hindu Jajmani System* (1936) and Charlotte's *Foods of a Hindu Village of North India* (1937). From 1933, when William completed his doctorate at Cornell University, until 1941, they taught at North India Theological College in Saharanpur. He was a co-opted member of the Tambaram meeting of the International Missionary Council in 1938, and his research is quoted extensively in *The Economic Basis of the Church.* In 1945 they established the India Village Service, which became a model for agencies involved in rural community development. William died soon after retirement in 1959, but Charlotte maintained her contacts with India and Karimpur, updating *Behind Mud Walls* (1963, 1971) and doing further writing.

Bibliography William H. Wiser and Charlotte Viall Wiser, *For All of Life* (1943); Charlotte V. Wiser, *Four Families of Karimpur* (1978). John Bathgate, "Presbyterians and Rural Development in India," *Journal of Presbyterian History* 62 (Fall 1984): 237–245.

John C. B. Webster

Witte, Johannes (1877–1945), mission administrator, academic, and publisher. Born and brought up in Pomerania, Germany, Witte served as a pastor until his appointment as director of the German East Asia Mission in 1914. His academic career began in 1921, when he became lecturer in missiology and comparative religion at Berlin University. In 1930 he succeeded Julius *Richter as professor, until his retirement in 1939. Before 1930 Witte attempted with little success to change the traditional liberal stance of his mission by infusing it with Barthian theology. For a brief time he changed direction and joined the ultranationalist movement of the German Christians. His return to Barth's position is documented in Witte's major work on the Christian message and the world religions *Die Christus botschaft und die Religionen* (1936), which, however, soon fell into oblivion, just as did most of his numerous earlier works on East Asia in general and on Eastern religions in particular. From 1909 until 1932 Witte edited the renowned liberal publication *Zeitschrift für Missionskunde und Religionswissenschaft.*

Bibliography No biography of Witte is available. For an excellent synopsis, see Heinrich Balz, "Berliner Missionstheologie und Karl Barth," in G. Besier and C. Gestrich, eds., *450 Jahre Evangelische Theologie in Berlin* (1989), pp. 426–430.

Hans-Werner Gensichen

Wolff, Joseph (1795–1862), missionary to Jews. Wolff was born in Weilersbach, Bavaria, Germany, into a Levitical Jewish family. He proved to be such a brilliant student that he was sent to a prestigious Roman Catholic college where he was inspired by the life of Francis *Xavier and resolved to become a Christian and a missionary. After studying Roman Catholic and Lutheran theology and mastering several Oriental languages, he was expelled from the Propaganda Fide institute in Rome because of his increased attraction to Anglican theology. He therefore went to England and was baptized in the Anglican Church in 1819 and began to train with the London Jews' Society. In 1821 he was commissioned as a missionary to the Jews "in the East." The following decades saw him initiate missions in Egypt, Palestine, Syria, Persia (Iran), Asiatic Turkey, the Greek Islands, Bukhara (part of modern Uzbekistan), India, Abyssinia (Ethiopia), and Yemen. All of this involved constant danger and hardship. He was a traveler and adventurer (frequently compared to David *Livingstone), and he lived out Xavier's words, "Who would not travel over land and sea to be instrumental in the salvation of one soul?" In 1845 he returned to England, where he had pastoral oversight of people who were training for service in western Asia.

Bibliography Wolff wrote three missionary travelogues: *Researches and Missionary Labours among the Jews, Mohammedans, and Other Sects* (1835), *Narrative of a Mission to Bokhara, in the Years 1843–1845* (1846), *Travels and Adventures of the Rev. Joseph Wolff, DD, LLD* (1861). Hugh Evan Hopkins, *Sublime Vagabond: The Life of Joseph Wolff* (1984); H. P. Palmer, *Joseph Wolff, His Romantic Life and Travels* (1935).

Walter Riggans

Wolfgang (c. 924–994), missionary in Hungary and bishop of Regensburg (Ratisbon). Evidently born in Pflullingen, Schwabia, and educated at the Reichenau monastery on an island in Lake Constance, Wolfgang became dean and head of the cathedral school at Trier. While there he taught Giesela, who became *Stephen of Hungary's wife. Probably at her behest, Wolfgang for a time joined the work of Christianizing Hungary. As a teacher he was noted not only for his learning but also for his ability to lead his students into lives of disciplined virtue. He entered the Benedictine Order at Einsiedeln in 964; in 972 he was consecrated a bishop. He worked for reform not only by emphasizing the spiritual life but also by separating the office of bishop from that of abbot so that both positions might be more effective.

BIBLIOGRAPHY Kuno Bugmann, "Der Mönch Wolfgang," *Studien und Mitteilungen zur Geschichte des Benediktiner-Ordens* 78 (1968): 9–27; Paul Mai, ed., *Auf den Spuren des heiligen Wolfgang* (1973); Georg Schwaiger and Josef Staber, eds., *Regensburg und Böhmen: Festschrift zum Tausendjahrfeier des Regierungsantrittes Wolfgangs von Regensburg und der Errichtung des Bistums Prag* (1972).

Frederick W. Norris

Wood, A(lfred) Harold (1896–1989), Australian Methodist missionary, minister, and administrator. Wood served in Tonga as principal of Tupou College from 1924 to 1937, transforming it into a school with an excellent academic record and spiritual reputation. He continued to keep in touch with Tonga for the rest of his life but went on to become the principal of the Methodist Ladies' College in Melbourne from 1939 to 1966. Under his leadership it became the largest girls' school in Australia.

He served as president of the Methodist Conference of Victoria and Tasmania and president-general of the Methodist Church of Australasia. His best-known writing is the four-volume history *Overseas Missions of the Australian Methodist Church* (1978–1980), with separate volumes entitled *Tonga and Samoa, Fiji, Fiji-Indian and Rotuma,* and *North India (Lucknow-Banares District).* His other books include *History and Geography of Tonga* (1932) and *Church Unity without Uniformity: A Study of Seventeenth-Century Church Movements and of Richard Baxter's Proposals for a Comprehensive Church* (1963). He was also a keen hymnologist and wrote a few small books on hymns as well as a popular column for the local Methodist and Uniting Church newspapers. In his ministry he combined a strong emphasis on evangelism with deep commitment to social responsibility. He was known as a champion for peace and campaigned for temperance and Christian unity.

BIBLIOGRAPHY Cecil Gribble, "Alfred Harold Wood," *Church Heritage* 6 (March 1990): 63–67.

Darrell Whiteman

Wood, Thomas B(ond) (1844–1922), American Methodist missionary and strategist for religious freedom in South America. Born in Lafayette, Indiana, Wood graduated from Indiana Asbury (later DePauw) University in 1863. From 1870 to 1877 he worked in Rosario, Argentina, where he became well known as a church planter, educator, and member of the city council. From 1879 to 1889 he lived in Montevideo, Uruguay, and became superintendent of missions of the Methodist Episcopal Church in South America. He developed a cooperative strategy with Andrew *Milne of the American Bible Society, and trained colporteurs for Bible distribution and church planting in Brazil, Paraguay, Bolivia, Peru, and Ecuador. In 1891 he volunteered to move with his family to Callao, Peru, where Francisco *Penzotti had pioneered Protestant work. Wood became involved in a long political struggle for religious freedom in alliance with Free Masons, of which he was a high-ranking member in the York and Scottish rites. His wife, Ellen, and daughters Elsie, Amy, and Angie cooperated actively in the vast educational work he developed in Peru. In 1912 he returned to the United States after 42 years of missionary service in South America.

BIBLIOGRAPHY The most complete account of Wood's missionary work is Paul E. Kuhl, "Protestant Missionary Activity and Freedom of Religion in Ecuador, Perú, and Bolivia" (Ph.D. diss., Southern Illinois Univ. at Carbondale, 1982).

Samuel Escobar

Woods, C(harles) (Wilfred) Stacey (1909–1983), evangelical leader in ministry to students. Australian by birth, C. Stacey Woods was a world Christian with a vision for reaching university and high school students. Following undergraduate studies at the University of Sydney, Australia, in 1930 he came to America, where he received degrees from Dallas Theological Seminary, Texas, and Wheaton College, Illinois, graduating in 1934. The newly formed InterVarsity Christian Fellowship (IVCF) of Canada called him to be their first full-time general secretary that same year. Observing that student Christian witness in the universities of the United States was almost nonexistent, in 1937 Woods began survey trips which resulted in the establishment of IVCF-U.S.A. in 1940. He served as general secretary in both Canada and the United States until 1952, when the Canadian Board released him to give full time to the United States.

In the 1940s the Student Foreign Missions Fellowship and Christian Nurses Fellowship (now Nurses Christian Fellowship) joined IVCF-U.S.A. Woods initiated the first IVCF student missionary conference, held in 1946 in Toronto. In 1948 the conference shifted to the University of Illinois at Urbana to establish the continuing triennial Urbana Missions Conventions.

Seeing the needs beyond North America, in 1944 Woods began a survey trip of student work in Latin America. In 1947 he helped form the International Fellowship of Evangelical Students (IFES) and continued pioneering student work around the world. He left leadership of the U.S. movement in 1960 to become the first full-time general secretary of IFES, moving its headquarters to Switzerland in 1962. He continued to be active in Christian ministry long after passing on IFES leadership to Chua Wee Hian in 1972.

BIBLIOGRAPHY C. S. Woods, *Some Ways of God* and *The Growth of a Work of God* (1978). David M. Howard, *Student Power in World Missions* (1979); Keith and Gladys Hunt, *For Christ and the University: The Story of InterVarsity Christian Fellowship of the U.S.A., 1940–1990* (1991); Douglas Johnson, *A Brief History of the IFES* (1964).

Keith Hunt

Woolston, Beulah (1828–1886) *and*
Sarah H. (?–1910), founders of the first American Methodist girls' school in Asia. The Woolston sisters graduated from Wesleyan Female College in Wilmington, Delaware, and became teachers. Answering an appeal from the mission board of the Methodist Episcopal Church to begin "woman's work" in China, they sailed for Foochow (Fuzhou) in 1858. They were supported by the Ladies' China Missionary Society of Baltimore, founded in 1848 as one of the earliest women's missionary societies in America. The Woolstons in 1859 founded a girls' boarding school in Foochow to train teachers. Known as Uk Ing, the school continued through the Nationalist period, graduating many physicians, teachers, and pastors' wives. In 1871 the Ladies' China Society merged into the Methodist Episcopal Woman's Foreign Missionary Society and the Woolstons became its first missionaries. After their furlough, they led other single women missionaries to China. They itinerated and supervised day schools in the country and edited the *Child's Illustrated Paper* in Chinese. In 1877 the Woolstons attended the Shanghai Missionary Conference, where Sarah's paper "Feet Binding" was read and the women missionaries resolved that missionaries should discourage the practice. They resigned from the mission in 1883 because they opposed the introduction of English and the Chinese classics into the curriculum of the boarding school. The Woolstons believed that learning English would render the pupils unfit for return to village life as mothers and day-school teachers. The Woolston sisters returned to the United States for their final years.

BIBLIOGRAPHY The Woolstons contributed articles to *Heathen Woman's Friend.* A sketch of Beulah Woolston appears in *Eminent Missionary Women* by Annie Ryder Gracey (1898). See also Frances Baker, *The Story of the Woman's Foreign Missionary Society of the Methodist Episcopal Church, 1869–1895* (1896, 1987).

Dana L. Robert

Worcester, Samuel Austin (1798–1859), missionary to the Cherokee Indians. Born in Massachusetts, Worcester graduated from the University of Vermont (1819) and Andover Theological Seminary (1823). He was ordained a Congregationalist minister in 1825 and was appointed the same year to a mission station in eastern Tennessee. Since the Cherokee leader Sequoya, a native genius, had already created a syllabary, Worcester used it to translate tracts and large portions of the Bible into Cherokee. He also set up a print shop at New Echota, a principal native settlement in Georgia, and in 1827 he inaugurated the *Cherokee Phoenix,* the first native-language newspaper in the country. His advocacy of Christian salvation mixed with white cultural standards prompted many conversions, especially among families of mixed blood who were not averse to adopting selected aspects of Western ideas and technology. An 1830 Georgia statute prohibited whites from living among native tribes without a license, but Worcester and missionaries from several other denominations defied the law. They were arrested, mistreated, convicted, and sentenced to prison terms of several years each. Worcester alone refused to accept a pardon and took his case to the U.S. Supreme Court, which in 1832 ruled in his favor. After his release he moved to Indian Territory (later Oklahoma) in 1835 and at Park Hill Mission built houses, a church, a school, a printing office, and a book bindery. He supervised the Cherokee Bible Society and through it distributed thousands of testaments, hymnbooks, and primers. As head of the Cherokee Temperance Society, he continued to advocate habits of sober industry that had benefited the people for so long. The Indians in turn, for generations after his death, repaid his loyalty to them by retaining the faith that he embodied.

BIBLIOGRAPHY R. S. Walker, *Torchlights to the Cherokees: The Brainerd Mission* (1931).

Henry Warner Bowden

Wright, Frank Hall (1860–1922), Choctaw minister to Native Americans. Born at Old Boggy Depot, Indian Territory (today part of Oklahoma), Wright was the son of a full-blooded Choctaw Indian minister and a New England mother. He attended Union College, New York, and Union Theological Seminary, and was ordained by the Presbyterian Church in 1885. He contracted tuberculosis working among his own people and went to New York City to recuperate. In 1895 he accepted the commission of the Reformed Church of America (RCA) Women's Board to begin work among Native Americans in Oklahoma. There he regained his strength and became known as the Singing Indian Evangelist. For two decades he walked and rode long distances on the plains, organizing churches among the Cheyennes, the Comanches, and the Fort Sill Apaches. The famous Apache, Geronimo, became a Christian and was baptized at Fort Sill in 1903 during Wright's ministry there. Today many of Geronimo's descendants are members of the Apache Reformed Church of Apache, Oklahoma.

BIBLIOGRAPHY Arie R. Brower, *Reformed Church Roots* (1977); Eugene Heideman, *A People in Mission: The Surprising Harvest* (1980) and *A People in Mission: Their Expanding Dream* (1984); Dennis E. Shoemaker, *A People of Hope* (1978). See also material in RCA archives, New Brunswick Theological Seminary, New Brunswick, N.J.

Charles E. Van Engen

Wright, Isaac. *See* Coker, Daniel.

Wu, Y. T. (Wu Yao-tsung) (c. 1895–1979), Chinese Christian reformer and founder of the Protestant Three-Self Movement. Born into a non-Christian family, Wu made first contact with Christianity in a YMCA camp in 1911. He later attended evangelistic services led by Sherwood *Eddy and Frank Buchman and in 1918 joined the Congregational Church in Beijing. The turning point of his life was reading the Sermon on the Mount: Jesus "captured me and I was unable to escape." Leaving a remunerative customs service job, Wu joined the YMCA staff in 1920. He studied at Union Theological Seminary, New York, from 1924 to 1927, where Harry Ward was a prominent advocate of radical social reform. Wu received an M.A. from Columbia University in 1927 and returned to work in the schools department of the China National YMCA. After another half year at Union in 1936–1937, Wu headed the YMCA publishing house, and in 1945 founded *Tien Feng,* which became the quasi-official magazine of Chinese Protestantism. Having found in Jesus' teachings a guide to action, Wu's concern for the improvement of Chinese life moved from spiritual reform to social reform to social revolution. In the spring of 1950 he arranged meetings with the new Communist government and was principal author of a "Christian manifesto" denouncing missionary imperialism and calling for a self-governing, self-supporting, and self-propagating church. Within a year the Three-Self Patriotic Movement became the exclusive organ of Protestantism in China, to be guided by Wu in its intimate relations with the Chinese government until his death.

BIBLIOGRAPHY Xu Rulei, "True Israelite," *Chinese Theological Review* 6 (1990): 92–102, is a tribute to Wu. Ng Lee-ming, "A Study of Y. T. Wu," *Ching Feng* 15 (1972): 5–54, analyzes Wu's developing thought. Articles by Wu in English may be located through Ng's citations. *Documents of the Three-Self Movement* (1963) contains a number of definitive articles by Wu, together with other documents defining and describing the early Three-Self Movement. Wu is dealt with critically in Richard Bush, *Religion in Communist China* (1970), and sympathetically in Philip L. Wickeri, *Seeking the Common Ground* (1988).

David M. Stowe

Wu Li (Wu Yü-Shan; *or* Simon à Cunha) (1632–1718), Jesuit priest and a premier Chinese artist of the Ch'ing period. A native of Ch'ang-shu (Changshu), Kiangsu (Jiangsu) Province, Wu Li was the youngest of three sons who, after his father's death, was guided by his mother to teachers of poetry, painting, and music. By 1660 his poetry and painting were winning the praise of leading scholars. In 1665 he visited a Buddhist monastery where he produced an album of ten paintings. Wu Li was deeply affected by the death of the abbot, which was followed shortly by the death of his wife and later of his Confucian master. He began conversations with the Jesuit François de *Rougemont at the Catholic church located near his ancestral home. After he too died, Wu Li continued his discussions with another Jesuit, Philippe *Couplet, who probably baptized him in late 1679 or early 1680. Two years later he entered the Society of Jesus in Macao. Together with two Jesuit confreres, Wu Li was ordained in Nanking (Nanjing) in 1688 by a Chinese Dominican bishop, an important step in the development of an indigenous Chinese clergy. For the rest of his life he was an active pastor in Shanghai.

BIBLIOGRAPHY Jonathan Chaves, *Singing of the Source: Nature and God in the Poetry of the Chinese Painter Wu Li* (1993); Chen Yuan, "Wu Yu-shan. In Commemoration of the 250th Anniversary of His Ordination to the Priesthood in the Society of Jesus," *Monumenta Serica* 3 (1938): 130–170; Chou K'ang-hsieh, ed., *Wu Yü-shan (Li) yen-chiu lun-chi* (1971; a reprint of eleven articles on Wu Li with three new ones); A. Lippe, "A Christian Chinese Painter: Wu Li (1632–1718)," *Metropolitan Museum of Art Bulletin* 11 (1952): 123–128; M. Tchang and P. de Prunelé, *Le Père Simon à Cunha, S.J. (Ou Li Yu-chan), L'homme et l'oeuvre artistique* (1914).

John W. Witek, SJ

Würz, Friedrich (1865–1926), theologian, pastor, and mission administrator. Würz was born in Calw, Württenberg, Germany. Beginning in 1888 he taught theology at the Basel Mission (BM) Seminary in Basel. He was assistant to the mission inspector Theodor *Oehler with the title of theological secretary from 1891, then home secretary from 1895. He was also a cofounder of the "Verein und Institut für Ärztliche Mission" (Institute for Medical Mission) at Tübingen and editor of *Evangelisches Missions Magazin* from 1911 to 1926. A promoter of women's mission, he worked for fundamental change in outlook on women's work and in 1901 revived the Women's Mission Committee of the BM, founded in 1841 but never allowed to become an effective instrument. He served as its president until 1915. He was a personal friend of J. H. *Oldham and James Hudson *Taylor, had many connections with other missionary societies, and was a member of the BM delegation to the World Missionary Conference in Edinburgh (1910).

BIBLIOGRAPHY Friedrich Würz, *Die Basler Mission in Kamerun und ihre gegenwaertigen Aufgaben* (1902), *Die mohammedanische Gefahr in West-Afrika* (1904), and *Une heure décisive dans la Mission de Bâle* (1918). In addition to editing *EMM,* he wrote articles in various other mission magazines. Extensive correspondence is held in the BM archive.

Waltraud Ch. Haas

Wylie, Alexander (1815–1887), English missionary publisher in China. Born in London, Wylie was sent to China in 1847 by the London Missionary Society to be superintendent of its printing press in Shanghai. While engaged in this task, he served as editor for the *Shanghai Serial,* published from 1857 to 1858. During his time in Shanghai he collected the material needed to publish his noted work *Memorials of Protestant Missionaries to the Chinese* (1867), which gives bibliographic details on all Protestant missionaries in China from 1807 to the early 1860s. Lists and descriptions of their writings are given in both Chinese and English. After 1863 Wylie was an agent of the British and Foreign Bible Society (BFBS). He and his colporteurs distributed one million New Testaments in fifteen of China's eighteen provinces and surveyed new areas to be occupied for mission work. When failing eyesight caused him to leave China in 1877, he continued to work with the BFBS in London.

BIBLIOGRAPHY The best source for material on Wylie is his *Memorials of Protestant Missionaries to the Chinese* (1867), and in the LMS archives on China. See also Henri Cordier, "The Life and Labours of Alexander Wylie... A Memoir," *Journal of the Royal Asiatic Society of Great Britain and Ireland,* n.s. 19 (1887): 351-368.

Ralph R. Covell

Xavier, Francis (Francisco de Jassu y Xavier) (1506–1552), pioneer Spanish Jesuit missionary to Asia. Born in the Castle of Xavier, Navarre, Xavier lost his father in 1515. He entered the University of Paris in 1525 and became *magister artium* in 1530. He lived in the same college as *Ignatius of Loyola, which led to Xavier's conversion in 1533. With Ignatius and five others (the original Society of Jesus), he made his vows at Montmartre in 1534; they were ordained priests in Venice in 1537. At the request of Pope Paul III and the Portuguese king, John III, Xavier was assigned to the missions of the East Indies and in 1541 he left Lisbon for India.

After a brief stay in Mozambique, Xavier arrived in Goa in May 1542. He brought with him four papal briefs, in which he was asked to visit all regions and islands of the Orient and to inform the pope of the moral and spiritual situation in this part of the world. He began by traveling along the southern coast of India—Pescheria, Travancor, and Cochin (October 1542–December 1544). At one point he baptized 10,000 in one month. He visited Ceylon in 1544–1545, then worked for two years in the Molucca Islands (present-day eastern Indonesia). He returned to Goa and then to Malacca to prepare for his mission to Japan. Somewhat aware of the sociocultural structure of Japan, where he arrived in August 1549, he changed his methodology and began to work with the feudal lords and local religious leaders. Realizing that in order for the Orient to be converted Christianity had to be established in China, in 1552 he returned to Goa, and later in the same year sailed with a few companions for China. But worn out by his labors, he fell ill and died off the coast of China on the island of Shang-ch'uan (Saint John Island).

In India, Xavier gave special attention to children, young people, servants, and the Paravas (Bharathas), or poor fisherfolk. He was above all a catechist. He wrote three catechisms. The first, *La Dottrina Cristiana* (1542), was written in Portuguese but was immediately translated into Tamil and Malay, and he worked to get it translated into Japanese. The contents are descriptive; after some prayers, the creed and the commandments are explained. The second catechism was his *Dichiarazione del Simbolo della Fede* (1546), originally in Portuguese, but translated into Tamil and Japanese, which Xavier also worked to translate into Chinese. The rhythmic text seems to have been written to be sung. His third catechism, *Instructio pro catechistis Societatis Iesu,* was published in Latin in Malacca (c. 1545), with practical directives on teaching the faith. Xavier also founded an organization of lay catechists, with funds from the Portuguese monarchy, who dedicated themselves full-time to teaching doctrine. Xavier's letters, read throughout Europe, aroused widespread interest in the missions. For his pioneering work and his role in awakening the Christian world to the missionary task, he was canonized in 1622, then proclaimed the Patron of Missions by Pope *Pius XI on December 14, 1927.

BIBLIOGRAPHY *Epistolae s. F. Xaverii,* vols. 1 and 2, Monumenta Historica Societatis Iesu (1944–1945); *The Letters and Instructions of Francis Xavier,* tr. and introduced by M. Joseph Costelloe (1992). J. Brodrick, *St. Francis Xavier* (1952); G. Schurhammer, *Francis Xavier: His Life, His Time,* M. Joseph Costelloe, tr., 4 vols. (1973–1982; original in German). On the fourth centenary of his death, many journals dedicated special numbers to Xavier: *Studia Missionalia* 7 (1952); *Missionalia Hispanica* 27 (1952); *Archivium historicum Societatis Iesu,* 53 (1953).

Jésus López-Gay, SJ

Xavier, Jerome (1549–1617), founder of the third Mogul Mission in India. A grandnephew of Francis *Xavier, Xavier was born in Beire in the Spanish province of Navarre. He entered the Society of Jesus at the age of 19 and was ordained a priest in 1575. In 1581 he arrived at Goa, India. He was a missionary in Goa, Bassein, Cochin, and again in Goa, from where he was sent in 1594 to the court of the emperor Akbar of the Mogul Empire, arriving in Lahore in May 1595. Xavier was on good terms with Emperor Akbar, whom he accompanied on various expeditions. From 1601 to 1605 Akbar resided at Agra, where he died in October. He was succeeded by Emperor Jahangir (1605–1627), who resided at Lahore and Agra. In 1613 war broke out between the Moguls and the Portuguese, and Xavier was sent by the emperor to Goa to use his influence for peace. In 1614 Xavier signed a treaty of peace for the Mogul party at Surat. From 1615 onward he lived at Goa, where he was found burned to death in his room on June 27, 1617, not knowing that he had been elected coadjutor-archbishop of Cranganore.

Xavier established the missionary methods of the Mogul Mission: good relations with the emperors; creation of Christian literature written in Persian; the development of an original method of disputation with Muslims and Hindus; conducting oral debates with Muslims in public places; and a full display of Christian religious life through liturgy, ceremonies, and exhibitions of Western art. The Mogul Mission continued until 1803.

BIBLIOGRAPHY Arnulf Camps, *Jerome Xavier S.J. and the Muslims of the Mogul Empire: Controversial Works and Missionary Activity* (1957) and "Persian Works of Jerome Xavier, a Jesuit at the Mogul Court," *Islamic Culture* 35 (1961): 166–176; Roberto Gulbenkian, *Os quatro Evangelhos em Persa da Biblioteca Nacional de Lisboa* (1979) and *The Translation of the Four Gospels into Persian* (1981).

Arnulf Camps, OFM

Xenos, Ioannes (c. 970–after 1027), monk, saint, and itinerant missionary preacher on Crete. Born to a wealthy family in the village of Siba in Crete, Xenos rejected wealth and imitated the great missionary *Nikon, whose work was well known on the island. He conducted his mission in the island's western part, traveling from mountain to mountain, preaching and establishing several monasteries. It is not known whether he preached among apostates and converts to Islam. He attributed his mission to "visions" and "voices." He wrote several homilies on the Gospel of Matthew and a number of church hymns. He is honored on October 7.

BIBLIOGRAPHY H. Delehaye, *Deux typica byzantius de l'époque des Paléologues* (1921), pp. 191–196; N. Tomadakis, "Ho hagios Ioannes ho Xenos kai hé diatheke autou," *Kretika Chronika,* vol. 2 (1948), pp. 47–72, and "Hymnographika kai hagiologika tou Xenou," *Epeteris Etaireias Byzantiuo Spoudon,* vol. 20 (1950), pp. 314–330.

Demetrios J. Constantelos

Xu, Candida (1607–1680), foremost Chinese Christian laywoman of her time. Xu, a granddaughter of the eminent convert *Hsu Kuang-ch'i (1562–1633), was deeply religious from childhood. After she was widowed at the age of 46, she dedicated herself to serving the church. With zeal and ingenuity, undeterred by the restrictions the secluded life of an upper-class woman in traditional Chinese society placed on her, she worked to spread Christianity in China. Through the influence of her father and son, she secured for the Jesuit missionaries the good will of many provincial and local officials. She promoted the work of lay spiritual associations among Chinese Christians and was the leader of Christian women in the Shanghai area. Having by diligence and thrift raised a private income, she donated generously to the living expenses of the missionaries, financed the building of nearly forty churches and chapels, and funded publication of many Christian doctrinal and devotional works in Chinese. Called by the Jesuit missionaries the Apostle of China, Xu and her story of faith, devotion, and good works became known in Europe in the late seventeenth century through the biography written by her Jesuit confessor, Philippe *Couplet.

BIBLIOGRAPHY Philippe Couplet, *Histoire d'une dame chrétienne de la Chine* (1688). Biographies of Xu are also included in Jean Charbonnier, *Histoire des Chrétiens de Chine* (1992), and in Fang Hao, *Zhongguo tianzhujiaoshi renwuzhuan* (Biographies of people in the history of the Catholic Church in China), vol. 2 (1970).

Gail King

Xu Guangqi. *See* Hsu Kuang-ch'i.

Y

Yamamuro, Gumpei (1872–1940), pioneer Japanese leader of the Salvation Army in Japan. Born in rural Okayama Prefecture in a family of limited means, Yamamuro first became acquainted with Christian faith through street preaching and was baptized at age 17 (1888). Sensing a call to serve the common people, he studied briefly at the American-operated evangelical seminary in Tokyo and then gained his foundational higher education from five years at the Congregational Church-related Doshisha school in Kyoto (1889–1894). He served some years as a worker in the pioneer Christian orphanage founded by Ishii Juji in Okayama, doing evangelistic work on the side.

The first group of Salvation Army workers arrived in Japan from England in 1895, fourteen in number, and soon established corps (church centers for worship and social service) in Tokyo and in various other parts of the empire. Yamamuro returned to Tokyo in 1899. His background and particular sense of mission attracted him to the kind of work carried on by the Salvation Army, and he became a member of a local corps in the same year.

In his first year with the Salvation Army, Yamamuro published his famous *Heimin no Fukuin* (The gospel of the common people), which had over 500 printings and became a publishing phenomenon in twentieth-century Japan. Yamamuro was married in 1899, and with his wife, Kieko, became active in rehabilitating prostitutes. His ability, understanding, and zeal soon brought him recognition, and he was promoted to the rank of major. In 1909 the practice of street solicitation of funds began, and the range of the Salvation Army's institutional work expanded. Its first hospital opened in 1912, and a sanatorium in 1916.

The Salvation Army distinguished itself by its zeal in relief work following the great earthquake in the Tokyo-Yokohama area in 1923. For this work Yamamuro was decorated by the emperor in 1924. In 1926 he was promoted to brigadier general and appointed commander of the entire Japanese division and later made major general. He performed his social service without neglecting to use every opportunity to proclaim the gospel by word of mouth and print.

BIBLIOGRAPHY Richard H. Drummond, *A History of Christianity in Japan* (1972); Akira Tanaka, "Yamamuro Gumpei," *Encyclopedia of Japan* (1983).

Richard H. Drummond

Yang T'ing-yün (1562–1627), one of the so-called Three Pillars of Christianity in China during the Ming dynasty. Yang was a native of the Jen-hu district in Hangchow (Hangzhou), Chekiang (Zhejiang) Province. He passed the difficult palace examinations in 1592 and became a district magistrate in Anfu, Kiangsi (Jiangxi) Province, for seven years. Committed to loyalty and morality, he was several times appointed a censor, but his reports of corruption were not welcomed by those involved. During his first extended retirement from public life (1609–1622), he learned about the death of the father of *Li Chih-tsao (Zhizao), his fellow townsman and another of the Three Pillars. At Li's residence he met three Jesuits and invited them to live in a building on his property. After many discussions about Christianity and a long interior struggle, Yang was baptized. Several family members subsequently became converts. He founded a benevolent society to take care of the destitute, participated in discussion sessions concerning Scripture, built four chapels, purchased land for a Catholic cemetery, and published eight books explaining Christianity. On the occasion of his funeral, his son, John, rejecting requests by non-Christian friends and family members for a Buddhist funeral, insisted on Chinese Christian ceremonies as a symbol for all those attending.

BIBLIOGRAPHY Willard J. Peterson, "Why Did They Become Christians? Yang T'ing-yün, Li Chih-tsao, and Hsü Kuang-ch'i," in C. Ronan and B. Oh, eds., *East Meets West: The Jesuits in China,*

1582–1773 (1988), pp. 129–152; Nicolas Standaert, *Yang Tingyun: Confucian and Christian in Late Ming China* (1988; includes a complete bibliography of Yang's works).

John W. Witek, SJ

Yannoulatos, Anastasios (1929–), Greek Orthodox missiologist. Born in Piraeus, Greece, and a graduate of the University of Athens in 1952, Yannoulatos served in the Greek army (1952–1954) and in 1955 entered the Zoe Brotherhood, an organization committed to the spiritual renewal of the church in Greece. In 1960 he was ordained deacon and founded Porefthendes Inter-Orthodox Mission Center in Athens to revive the mission conscience of the church. He participated in the 1963 Mexico City conference of the Commission on World Mission and Evangelism (CWME). He served as vice-president of Syndesmos, an international Orthodox youth movement, from 1964 to 1977.

Ordained a priest in 1964, Yannoulatos studied at the universities of Marburg and Hamburg, Germany (1965–1969), and received a Th.D. summa cum laude in 1970 from the University of Athens. He was secretary for the World Council of Churches office for Relations with the Orthodox Churches (1969–1970) and from 1971 to 1975 he directed the Inter-Orthodox Center of the Church of Greece and the Center of Missionary Studies at the university in Athens, where he became associate professor of world religions in 1972. That same year he was elected bishop of Androussa and was named general director of Apostoliki Diakonia, the publishing, research, and mission organ of the Church of Greece. A chair of missiology was established at the university in 1976, and Yannoulatos was appointed full professor. In 1981 he began the quarterly mission magazine of the Church of Greece, *Panta Ta Ethni* (All the nations), remaining editor through 1991.

From 1981 to 1991 he was acting archbishop of the Archbishopric of Irinoupolis (Kenya, Uganda, and Tanzania). He opened the Archbishop Makarios III Seminary in Nairobi and promoted translations of liturgical services and the construction of new churches, clinics, and schools. From 1984 to 1991 he was moderator of CWME, and in 1987 he received the Silver Medal from the Academy of Athens for pioneer work in Orthodox missions. In 1991 he was called to the Orthodox Church of Albania, following the collapse of communism. The following year, delegates from Orthodox parishes in Albania elected him primate of the Autocephalous Orthodox Church of Albania. He established a seminary, increased the number of clergy, erected new churches, and fostered significant church growth.

BIBLIOGRAPHY Anastasios Yannoulatos, *The Spirits Mbandwa and the Framework of Their Cult* (1970), *The Dawn of Orthodoxy in Japan* (1971), *Various Christian Approaches to the Other Religions* (1971), *Ruhanga: The Creator* (1975), and *Islam: A General Survey* (1979). Luke Veronis, *Missionaries, Monks and Martyrs* (1994), *Panta Ta Ethni* (Greek mission quarterly), no. 43, 3d quarter, 1992, "Anastasios Yannoulatos: Modern-day Apostle," *IBMR* 18, no. 3 (1995): 122–128.

Dimitrios G. Couchell

Yate, William (1802–1877), British missionary to New Zealand. Yate was born at Bridgnorth, Shropshire, England. He trained at the Church Missionary Society (CMS) college at Islington, near London. Ordained a deacon in the Church of England in 1825 and a priest in 1826, he arrived in New Zealand in 1828. He was a gifted teacher and preacher. Twice he went to Sydney to have printed the first translations into Maori of biblical excerpts, hymns, and catechisms. He returned to England in 1834 and wrote the first published book about the CMS in New Zealand. When he returned to Sydney in 1836, he was accused of sexual immorality and dismissed by the CMS. Failing to gain a proper hearing for his case, he returned to England, but could only secure temporary clerical appointments until 1846, when he began chaplaincy work among sailors in Devon, which he continued until his death.

BIBLIOGRAPHY J. Binney, ed., *An Account of New Zealand and of the Church Missionary Society's Mission in the Northern Island* (1835, 1970); J. Binney, "Whatever Happened to Poor Mr. Yate? An Exercise in Voyeurism," *New Zealand Journal of History* 9 (1975): 111–125. Yate's journal and diary (1833–1845) are held at the Turnbull Library, Wellington, New Zealand.

Allan K. Davidson

Yates, Matthew Tyson (1819–1888), pioneer Southern Baptist missionary to China. Born in Wake County, North Carolina, Yates and his wife, Eliza (Moring) (1821–1894), were the first missionaries appointed from their state and among the earliest Southern Baptist missionaries to China. Although he grew up in a very poor home, he was blessed with parents who were devout Christians and who shaped their son's life accordingly. Converted at the age of 17, Yates soon sensed a call to ministry. In order to secure an education he worked his way through Wake Forest Academy and College from which he received a B.A. in 1846. Appointed as a missionary to China by the Southern Baptist Convention Foreign Mission Board (SBCFMB) in August of that year, Yates married in September and was ordained in October. One year later the couple arrived in Shanghai, the most northern of the recently opened treaty ports, and they labored there for 42 years. Working under extremely adverse conditions, Yates learned the language, endured the Chinese xenophobia, survived the Taiping Rebellion, overcame loneliness and severe illness, adapted to the culture, and enjoyed a productive ministry. He organized churches, built houses of worship, established schools, and laid the foundation for what came to be known as the Central China Mission of the Southern Baptist Convention Foreign Mission Board.

Intermittently, he was required to support himself and his family by working as an interpreter, a teacher of Chinese to English businessmen, a municipal employee, and U.S. vice-consul in Shanghai. He was offered several diplomatic posts, including that of consul-general, and was also invited to become president of Wake Forest College, but declined all these opportunities in favor of his missionary work. His publications included *First Lessons in Chinese*, for learning the language, and a colloquial Chinese translation of the New Testament. By his work and his shrewd investments, Yates bequeathed a number of legacies to Christian causes. Both Yates and his wife died in China and are buried in Shanghai.

BIBLIOGRAPHY F. Catharine Bryan, *At the Gates: The Life Story of Matthew Tyson and Eliza Moring Yates* (1949); Robert E. Speer, *Servants of the King* (1909), pp. 115–136; Charles E. Taylor, *The Story of Yates the Missionary* (1898).

Alan Neely

Yates, William (1792–1845), Baptist Missionary Society (BMS) missionary in India. After studies at Bristol Baptist Academy, Yates was sent to Bengal in 1815. The first BMS missionary to receive a license from the East India Company, he was taught Bengali and Sanskrit at Serampore by William *Carey. Disagreements with the Serampore missionaries led Yates to move to Calcutta. There Yates devoted himself primarily to linguistic and translation work. He published a Sanskrit grammar and New Testament, and in 1833, the first of several editions of a Bengali New Testament more idiomatic in nature than Carey's earlier version. With John *Wenger he completed a Bengali Old Testament in 1844.

BIBLIOGRAPHY James Hoby, *Memoir of William Yates, D.D., of Calcutta* (1847); E. D. Potts, *British Baptist Missionaries in India, 1793–1837* (1967).

Brian Stanley

Yen, Y. C. James (1893–1990), founder of mass education movement in China. Born in western China, Yen became a Christian while studying at a mission school. With degrees from Yale and Princeton, he founded a mass literacy movement while working as a YMCA leader with 20,000 Chinese laborers in France in 1918. He served as director of the Mass Education Movement in China from 1924 to 1951, founded and directed the Tinghsien Rural Reconstruction Experiment in Hopei (Hebei) Province from 1929 to 1936, and was president of the College of Rural Reconstruction in Tinghsien (Dingzhou) from 1940 to 1951. After the political changeover in China, he moved his base of operations to the Philippines, becoming president of the International Mass Education Movement (1951–1965), adviser to the Philippine Rural Reconstruction Movement, (1952–1975), and founder and president of the International Institute of Rural Reconstruction in the Philippines (1960–1975).

BIBLIOGRAPHY Pearl S. Buck, *Tell the People: Talks with James Yen about the Mass Education Movement in China* (1945); Sherwood Eddy, *Pathfinders of the Missionary Crusade* (1940), pp. 227–238; Sidney D. Gamble, *Ting Hsien: A North China Rural Community* (1954).

Donald E. MacInnis

Yergan, Max (1892–1975), African American YMCA secretary in Africa. Yergan was born in Raleigh, North Carolina, the grandson of a slave. He graduated from Shaw University with honors and joined the YMCA in 1915. During World War I the YMCA sent him to India and after a short time transferred him to East Africa, where he served African regiments of the British Army for two years. After suffering numerous cases of fever he returned to the United States, but not before helping six other African American YMCA secretaries continue the work he started. After serving in the U.S. Army as a chaplain, he sought to return to Kenya to continue his YMCA work. This thrust him into a controversy about African American missionaries that reached the highest levels of the British Colonial Office, the international office of the YMCA, and the International Missionary Council. He was eventually color-barred from Kenya, which effectively ended African American involvement in missions in Kenya for three decades. He and his family eventually went to South Africa, where he served most of his 25 years of association with the YMCA, helping to establish thirty-six YMCA organizations. In 1933 the National Association for the Advancement of Colored People awarded him the Spingarn Medal for interracial achievements.

BIBLIOGRAPHY Max Yergan, *God and Poverty in South Africa* (1938), *The Negro and Justice: A Plea for Earl Browder* (1941), and *Africa in the War* (1942). Yergan's papers and correspondence are in the YMCA archives at the Univ. of Minnesota, Minneapolis; in the International YMCA archives at Geneva, Switzerland; and in the Moorland Collection at Howard Univ., Washington, D.C.

Rodney H. Orr

Yi, Ki-Poong (*or* Lee Ki-Poong) (1865–1942), first Korean Protestant missionary. After a reckless youth in which he stoned Samuel A. *Moffett, the first foreign missionary he ever saw, Yi was converted by a Korean evangelist and baptized in 1894 by Presbyterian missionary W. L. Swallen. In 1907 Yi was a member of the first graduating class of the Presbyterian Theological Seminary in Pyengyang, whose seven members were ordained at the founding meeting of the first presbytery of the Presbyterian Church of Korea that same year. Volunteering immediately for missionary service under the newly formed Korean church, he was sent to a remote, resistant island off the south coast where he himself was stoned but did not die. In 1921 he was elected moderator of the general assembly of the Korean Presbyterian Church. In the Shinto Rites controversies before World War II, he was imprisoned by the Japanese and tortured, and he died from his mistreatment.

BIBLIOGRAPHY *Kidokkyo Tae Paekhwa Sajon* (The Christian encyclopedia), vol. 12 (1985). See also references in H. Rhodes, *History of the Korea Mission, Presbyterian Church USA, 1884–1934* (1934), and Allen D. Clark, *A History of the Church in Korea* (1971); Neil Verwey and Peggy Verwey, *Even Unto Death: A Thrilling Story from Korea* (1980, a popular, journalistic biography).

Samuel Hugh Moffett

Ying, Lien-Chih (*or* Lianzhi) (1867–1926), Chinese Catholic editor and educator. Ying was born in a Manchu family that had no religious affiliation. Interest in philosophy led him to search the literature of Confucianism, Buddhism, Islam, and Taoism and to become familiar with both Protestant and Catholic writings. His association with the Sisters of Charity in Peking (Beijing) resulted in his conversion to the Catholic faith in 1895. He never made any secret of his faith, as it served to stimulate further his already strong sense of social responsibility. In 1902 he founded and became editor-in-chief of the Tientsin (Tianjin) *Da gong bao,* a daily newspaper noted for its firm commitment to democratic ideals, the service of public interests, and language reform. After the Chinese revolution of 1911, he sold the newspaper and turned his full attention to higher education. In 1912 he and another distinguished Catholic thinker, Ma Hsiang-po, successfully petitioned Pope Pius X for a Chinese Catholic university in Peking. In October 1925, in preparation for the eventual university, Ying founded the Fu Jen She, also known as the MacManus Academy of Chinese Studies. Three months later, he succumbed to cancer of the liver, but the academy kept expanding. Within four years, it grew into a full-fledged university. Forced to close in 1952, Fu Jen Catholic University reopened in Taiwan, where it has continued to develop.

BIBLIOGRAPHY Howard L. Boorman, ed., *A Biographical Dictionary of Republican China* (1968), vol. 3, pp. 56–58; Fang Hao, comp., *Ying Lien-chih hsien-sheng jih-chi yi-kao,* 3 vols., (1974); Ruth Hayhoe, "A Chinese Catholic Philosophy of Higher Education in Republican China," *Tripod* 48 (December 1988): 16–21, 49–60.

Jean-Paul Wiest

Yoder, Charles Frances (1873–1955), Brethren missionary, editor, and teacher. Yoder was born in Wayne County, Ohio. After studying at Taylor University and Manchester College in Indiana, he graduated with honors from the University of Chicago (B.A., 1899; B.D., 1902). Declining a teaching fellowship in church history at the University of Chicago, he became editor of the *Brethren Evangelist* (1903) and taught Bible and theology courses at Ashland (Ohio) College. In 1904 he married Pearl Lutz (1876–1943), a schoolteacher. In Ashland, Yoder served as general secretary of the Brethren Church Foreign Missionary Society (1903–1906) and compiled material for *God's Means of Grace* (1908), an extensive exposition of Brethren ordinances and doctrine. Ashland College awarded him an honorary Ph.D. in recognition of this work. He investigated the potential for mission work by the Brethren Church in Persia (Iran) but advised against entering that field. In 1909 he was asked to become the first Brethren missionary in Argentina, eventually settling at Rio Cuarto, where he taught biology at the National College (1912–1923). This position gave the Brethren mission great respectability. In 1923 he discontinued teaching to devote his time to evangelism.

As theological tension increased among the Brethren in the late 1930s, Yoder returned to the United States, where he helped reestablish the *Brethren Evangelist* after the church divided in 1939. He returned to Argentina in 1940 to reorganize work under the auspices of the Missionary Board of the Brethren Church. He retired as superintendent in 1945 but remained in Argentina until his death.

BIBLIOGRAPHY Henry R. Holsinger, *History of the Tunkers and the Brethren Church* (1901), p. 758; Homer A. Kent, *Conquering Frontiers, A History of the Brethren Church* (1972), pp. 175–177; Albert T. Ronk, *History of the Brethren Church* (1968); Dale R. Stoffer, *Background and Development of Brethren Doctrine 1650–1987* (1987), pp. 173–176, 186–187.

Robert G. Clouse

Youderian, Roger. *See* Elliot, Philip James.

Young, George Armstrong (1898–1991), Baptist Missionary Society (BMS) missionary and educator in China. Young was born in Leicester, England, into a working-class family of Scottish background. He joined the English civil service at 16 and fought with the British army in World War I. He traced his conversion to a crisis experience in the battle of Ypres (1917) and his call to missionary service to his Baptist pastor in Bloomsbury. After four years of study at Rawdon Baptist College, he went to China in 1924 with the BMS. During his 23 years in China, largely in Shensi (Shaanxi) Province, he dealt with a variety of problems—mediating between government and rebel armies, encouraging Christians undergoing persecution, and helping people in famine relief. He engaged in both rural and urban evangelism and taught Bible classes in churches and in the Sian Bible Training Institute. He vigorously promoted cooperative church endeavors and helped to lead the Shensi Baptist Church into the (united) Church of Christ in China. From 1952 to 1968 he was minister of Adelaide Place Baptist Church in Glasgow.

BIBLIOGRAPHY Young's *The Living Christ in Modern China* (1947) describes his life and ministry. He also wrote *The Fish or the Dragon* (1985).

Ralph R. Covell

Young, Samuel Hall (1847–1927), Presbyterian missionary in Alaska. Born in Butler, Pennsylvania, Young graduated from the College of Wooster (Ohio) in 1874 and Western Theological Seminary, Pittsburgh, Pennsylvania, in 1878. Recruited by Sheldon *Jackson, Young was one of the first Protestant missionaries in Alaska. He spent nearly 50 years ministering among the native population and with the Klondikers who in the years 1897 to 1904 came in search of gold. He also accompanied the great American naturalist John Muir on several expeditions. Young participated in efforts to have Alaska designated a U.S. territory and served as the first secretary of the Alaska legislature and as chaplain of the Alaska senate in 1924.

BIBLIOGRAPHY S. Hall Young, *Alaska Days with John Muir* (1915), *The Klondike Clan: A Tale of the Great Stampede* (1916), and *Hall Young of Alaska, "The Mushing Parson": The Autobiography of S. Hall Young* (1927).

Robert Benedetto

Young, T(homas) Cullen (1880–1955), missionary and anthropologist. Born in Edinburgh, Young trained as an accountant, but contact with the Student Volunteer Movement convinced him of a call to be a missionary. After training at Trinity College, Glasgow, and New College, Edinburgh, he joined the Livingstonia mission in Malawi in 1904. He was ordained in 1914 while on furlough in Edinburgh.

Young quickly became fluent in Tumbuka and so immersed himself in the life of the peoples of northern Malawi that he gained a profound knowledge and appreciation of their culture. He came to believe that indigenous culture provided a foundation upon which Christianity could be built. He also believed that education to the highest level should be open to Africans, and he was one of the missionaries who encouraged the organization of the native associations which later became the basis of the Nyasaland African National Congress.

In 1931 his wife's health forced Young's retirement from missionary service. In Britain he devoted himself to preparing literature for Africa and played a major role in the formation of the United Society for Christian Literature. Back in Scotland in retirement, he played an important part in the production of the Tumbuka Old Testament. Edinburgh University granted him an honorary M.A. in recognition of his pioneering anthropological work.

BIBLIOGRAPHY T. Cullen Young, *Notes on the Speech and History of the Tumbuka-Henga Peoples* (1923), *Notes on the Customs and Folklore of the Tumbuka-Henga Peoples* (1931), *African Ways and Wisdom* (1944), and with H. Kamuzu Banda, *Our African Way of Life* (1946). See also P. G. Forster, *T. Cullen Young: Missionary and Anthropologist* (1989).

Andrew C. Ross

Yui, David Z. T. (*or* Yu Jih-Chang; Yu Rizhang) (1882–1936), longtime leader of the Chinese YMCA and of the National Christian Council. A Hupeh (Hubei) pastor's son, Yui studied at the Episcopal schools of Boone (Wuchang) and St. John's University (Shanghai) before receiving a Harvard M.S. in education in 1910. From 1911 to 1916 he held a variety of increasingly visible posts in education, journalism, and government. His affiliation with the YMCA began in 1913, and in 1916 he became secretary-general, a post he held until 1932.

Under Yui's energetic direction, the YMCA grew rapidly until the mid-1920s, when, despite its record of Chinese leadership, it was hard hit by nationalistic critics. Yui led the organization through these stresses, but at great cost to his own health. Meanwhile his talents carried him into issues far beyond the YMCA. He was one of two private Chinese observers at the Washington Conference on disarmament (1921–1922), and in 1922 he led a successful movement to raise funds to redeem Chinese railroads from Japanese control. When the ecumenical National Christian Council was formed in 1922, Yui became its first chairperson; the balancing of competing interests in this Sino-foreign body took all his tact and flair for mediation. Yui also helped to found, and was first chair of, the Institute of Pacific Relations, an important scholarly forum; and he played a prominent role at the 1928 Jerusalem meeting of the International Missionary Council.

In the United States to rally American opinion after the Japanese invasion of Manchuria, Yui suffered a cerebral hemorrhage in early 1933 and was incapacitated until his death. Yui always believed in nation building through individual Christian character, and he saw the YMCA as an instrument of China's national, as well as individual, development.

BIBLIOGRAPHY David Z. T. Yui et al., *China Today Through Chinese Eyes* (1927); several articles by Yui are in the *Chinese Recorder* and *China Mission* (later, *Christian Year Book*). Howard L. Boorman and Richard Howard, eds., *Biographical Dictionary of Republican China,* vol. 4 (1971), pp. 64–66; Shirley Garrett, *Social Reformers in Urban China: The Chinese YMCA, 1895–1926* (1970). Much of the Yui correspondence and official papers is in the YMCA archives in St. Paul, Minn.; documentation from his years in the U.S. is in the Yale Divinity Library archive, manuscript group 13, records of the Chinese Students' Christian Association in North America.

Daniel H. Bays

Yu Kuo-chen (*or* Yu Guozhen) (1852–1932), Chinese independent church leader. Yu, who was born and raised in Chekiang (Zhejiang) Province, is sometimes known by his alternate name, Yu Tsung-chou (Yu Zongzhou); in some English sources he is called Yu Koh-tsung. In 1894 he became pastor of Hongkou Presbyterian Church in Shanghai. As Shanghai's Christian community became more educated and wealthy, a movement for independence from foreign missions developed, and Yu was one of its first leaders. This began informally about 1903, with the formation of the Chinese Christian Union. In 1906 Yu changed the name of his own church to the Chapei Independent Presbyterian Church. In 1910–1911 he formed the Chinese Independent Protestant Church (CIPC), with several congregations in the Shanghai area and with himself as its head. The Chinese Christian Union remained as a moderate group, with a newspaper, *Chi-tu-t'u pao;* but Yu established a more militant independence from missions, leaving the Union in 1911 and founding a new paper, *Sheng-pao,* to give voice to his independent church.

Yu remained pastor of the Chapei congregation until 1924. Until his death he remained head of the CIPC, which eventually had hundreds of congregations and tens of thousands of members nationwide.

BIBLIOGRAPHY There are almost no English-language sources on Yu. A few scattered references to him are in the *Chinese Recorder.* See also "Chinese Independent and Self-Supporting Churches," *China Mission Year Book* 3 (1912).

Daniel H. Bays

Yun, Tchi-Ho (*or* Ch'i-ho) (1865–1945), Korean nobleman, Methodist educator, and pioneer of Korea's modernization. At age 14 Yun was sent with a select group of aristocratic youths to Japan for foreign language study.

There his ability in five languages (Korean, Chinese, Japanese, English, and French) so impressed the first American minister to Korea, General Lucius C. Foote, that he was brought back to Korea as interpreter at the American legation. But when his participation in the failed reform movement of 1884 alarmed the court, he left Korea for safety in Shanghai. Enrolling in the Methodist's mission Anglo-Chinese college, he became a Christian in 1887, then went to America for further study at Emory College and Vanderbilt University (1887–1893), becoming a vigorous supporter of the new Student Volunteer Movement for Foreign Missions.

In 1895 the Korean government invited him to return to a political career as vice-minister of education, and then briefly as vice-minister of the Foreign Office. But when once more he joined young reformers like Philip Jaisohn and Syngman Rhee in founding the Independence Club and in editing two early Korean newspapers, his advocacy of free speech and public assembly brought him banishment to the provinces. From 1904 to 1906 he was recalled to government posts, but resentment of rising Japanese intervention turned him from politics to the cause of Christian education. In 1907 he founded an Anglo-Korean school in Songdo (Kaesong), patterned after his Chinese alma mater. He was a delegate to the 1910 World Missionary Conference in Edinburgh. Imprisoned by the Japanese in the "Conspiracy Case" (1911–1913), and hoping, upon release, to help the cause of Korea, he accepted an offer of a Japanese baronetcy, which in some Korean eyes tarnished his reputation as a patriot. But he served effectively as general secretary of the Korean Young Men's Christian Association (1915–1920) and from 1930 to 1941 was the first Korean president of the present Yonsei University in Seoul.

BIBLIOGRAPHY Donald N. Clark, "Yun Ch'i-Ho", in J. B. Palais and M. D. Lang, eds., *Occasional Papers on Korea,* no. 4 (1975); *Diary of Yun Tchi Ho,* 5 vols., in Chinese, Korean and English segments (1973–1975); J. Earnest Fisher, "Pioneers of Modernization, Yun: Statesman, Scholar," in *The Korea Times,* August 27, 1972; J. S. Ryang, ed., *Southern Methodism in Korea* (1927).

Samuel Hugh Moffett

Z

Zahn, Franz Michael (1833–1900), director of the Bremen Mission. Born in Moers, Germany, Zahn combined Lower Rhine Pietist roots with a politically liberal and upper-class background. Theologically, he followed the Lutheran Bible-centered Erlangen School; his brother Theodor later became a well-known New Testament scholar of that school. His father, an important representative of Pestalozzi pedagogy, focused on the question of how Christian truth in a pluralist context could become again the "mother" of all education. Zahn applied both the Erlangen tradition on the centrality of Christian truth in education to the African context during his four decades as director (1862–1900) of the Bremen Mission, which worked entirely in what is now Ghana and Togo.

Zahn was cofounder of the Continental Mission Conference (1866) and a close friend of Gustav *Warneck. He supported and later coedited Warneck's *Allgemeine Missions-Zeitschrift,* the leading missiological journal on the Continent. He contributed important articles on indigenous churches, mission and colonialism, mission and the vernacular, and missionary methods. Rejecting not only the increasing "ethnic pathos" of his German colleagues but also the three-self-formula of the *Venn-*Anderson tradition, he wished to bring about a truly African Christianity; mission he felt should not aim so much at establishing a church as at the personal "formation of the heart" and the "future, complete reign of God."

In 1885 Zahn became the first secretary of the German Missionary Council. However, he resigned in 1890 because he was not willing to support the pro-colonial line of his colleagues. He wanted to defend what he called "the freedom of mission." He warned that to accept government money would mean the "bondage of the church" and to "sell out freedom for some peanuts."

BIBLIOGRAPHY In *AMZ* Zahn published "Die evangelische Heidenpredigt" (1895), "Die Muttersprache in der Mission" (1895), "Giebt das Neue Testament für alle Zeiten bindende Vorschriften über die Methode der christlichen Mission?" (1898). R. Schäfer presented a theological tribute to Zahn in E. Schöck-Quinteros and D. Lenz, *150 Jahre Norddeutsche Mission 1836–1986,* (1986). A comprehensive study of Zahn's missionary methods is Werner Ustorf, *Die Missionsmethode Franz Michael Zahns und der Aufbau kirchlicher Strukturen in Westafrika* (1989); see also Ustorf's "The Legacy of Franz Michael Zahn," *IBMR* 21 (1997): 124–127. Zahn's missionary correspondence and papers are in the Staatsarchiv Bremen, Depositum 7, 1025.

Werner Ustorf

Zäkaryas (c. 1845–1920), Ethiopian prophet. Zäkaryas was born to Muslim parents in Bägémder Province, Ethiopia, around 1845, and emerged as an influential teacher within the Muslim community. Beginning in 1892, he had visions which eventuated in the greatest movement of Muslims to Christianity in modern Ethiopian church history. Zäkaryas initially attempted to bring Islam into closer harmony with its Jewish and Christian antecedents. A frequent object of Muslim-initiated litigation, he displayed a grasp of the Qur'an and a dialectical aptitude that not only earned him vindication before the courts but also resulted in the conversion of numerous Muslim dignitaries. Following one such case in 1907, Emperor Menilek issued an official proclamation giving Zäkaryas freedom to teach anything he wished in any Muslim area of the country, and making it illegal for anyone to bring charges against either him, his followers, or those helped by his teaching.

Zäkaryas was baptized at Däbrä Tabor during Easter of 1910, assuming the Christian name Newayä Krestos (possession of Christ). While his nascent evangelicalism, stressing the scriptural basis of religious truth, ensured that his relationship to the Ethiopian Orthodox Church was at times an uneasy one, between 1907 and 1920 thousands of Muslims converted to Christianity. By 1935, however, the movement had virtually disappeared as a distinctive entity within Ethiopian Orthodox Christianity.

BIBLIOGRAPHY Donald Crummey, "Shaikh Zäkaryas: An Ethiopian Prophet," *Journal of Ethiopian Studies,* 10, no. 1 (January 1992): 55–66; J. Iwarsson, "A Moslem Mass Movement toward Christianity in Abyssinia," *Moslem World* 14 (1924): 286–289. Zäkaryas's 95-page "The Fixed and Permanent Collection" (quranic and biblical proof texts compiled around 1906) is the most reliable source on the actual content of his teaching. A photocopy is located in the Institute of Ethiopian Studies, Addis Ababa, Ethiopia.

Jonathan J. Bonk

Zaleski, Vladislaw Michal (1852–1925), apostolic delegate for India. Zaleski was born in Vilnius (then under Russian rule). Since there were then no Polish schools in Vilnius, he did his primary and secondary schooling privately and went to Warsaw for his theological studies. Soon afterward he transferred to the Academia dei Nobili Ecclesiastici in Rome and then to the Gregorian University, also in Rome. After his ordination in 1882 he entered the Vatican diplomatic service. In 1885 he accompanied Archbishop A. Agliardi to India and described his experiences in the book *Voyage à Ceylon et aux Indes* (1888). Thus began his extraordinary literary activity, which he himself estimated as 14,650 pages (of which 7,761 were printed).

While at the nunciature in Paris (1889–1890), Zaleski was commissioned by Pope Leo XIII to study the question of native clergy in India. After two more visits to India he was nominated titular archbishop of Thebes and apostolic delegate of "the East Indies" in 1892. He worked in this capacity until 1916, when Pope *Benedict XV nominated him titular patriarch of Antioch and recalled him to Rome. Zaleski is remembered especially for his commitment to a native clergy and the restructuring of the Indian church. In 1893 he opened the general seminary in Kandy, Ceylon (Sri Lanka). From December 1893 to May 1894 he presided at the provincial synods of Bombay, Agra, Calcutta, Madras, Ootacamund, and Verapoly. He announced the founding of four diocesan seminaries for 1895 (Agra, Lahore, Nagpur, and Ranchi). Much of his time and energy was taken up with the question of the Portuguese protectorate over the dioceses of the Malabar Coast.

In 1887 special vicariates were created for the Uniate Thomas Christians; since 1896 they have had their own native bishops. During his term of office 8 archdioceses and 27 dioceses were established. He was overjoyed when, in 1923, he received the news that three Indians had been made bishops, the first among the forty Indian bishops of India. He promoted and organized the lay apostolate. He was particularly fond of children and youth. As he left India after 25 years, he wrote: "I will remain with you in heart and will do everything within my means to help you in your work." He died in Rome.

BIBLIOGRAPHY Witold Malej, *Ks. W. M. Zaleski, Delegat Apostolski Indii Wschodniej Arcybiskup Teb, Patriarcha Antiochii* (1965; an abridged English version, *Patriarch Ladislas Zaleski: Apostolic Delegate of the East Indies*). Joseph Schmidlin, "Die geganwärtigen Missionshandbücher als missionsmethodische Quellen," *ZM* 13 (1923): 185–198.

Karl Müller, SVD

Zameza, José (1886–1957), Catholic missiologist and founder of the Spanish school of missiology. Zameza became a Jesuit in 1903. After his studies he taught at the Oña Faculty of Patrology (1919–1920) and Church History (1920–1921). He edited the missiological magazine *El siglo de las misiones* from 1924 to 1930. He was elected the first dean of the Faculty of Missiology of the Pontifical Gregorian University in Rome (1932–1957) and began to publish the journal *Studia Missionalia* in 1942. The Spanish school of missiology he started is based on the theology of Saint *Augustine in *Totus Christus,* in which everyone is called to Christ, and on the encyclical *Mystici corporis* of *Pius XII of 1943, in which the church, as the Mystical Body of Christ, has an impetus for growth *ad extra* (universal expansion) and assimilation *ad intra* (catholicity). His ideas are present in the decree *Ad gentes* of the Second Vatican Council.

BIBLIOGRAPHY José Zameza, *Amemos a la Iglesia: Instrucciones patristico-misionales para sacerdotes,* 2d ed. (1944), *La conversión del mundo infiel en la concepción del "Totus Christus" de San Agustín* (1942), and "St. Agustin and the Infidel World," *Worldmission* (1955): 70–79. A complete list of Zameza's publications is in A. Santos, *Una misionología española* (1958), pp. 119–162. On Zameza and the Spanish school of missiology, see A. Santos, "Escuela Española (José Zameza)," in *Teología sistemática de la misión* (1991), pp. 84–154.

Jesús López-Gay, SJ

Zapłata, Feliks (1914–1982), Polish Catholic missiologist. Zapłata studied in Mödling, Austria, and at Steyl, Netherlands, then joined the Steyler Missionaries of the Divine Word (SVD) and was ordained a priest. After World War II he returned to Poland, working as a parish priest and schoolteacher. In 1955 he became the SVD provincial and began lecturing in the local seminary. In 1968 he began editing *Missiological and Religions Bulletin,* and in 1969 he founded and occupied the first chair of missiology at the Academy of Catholic Theology (ATK) in Warsaw, the first and only Catholic chair of its kind in a Communist country. In 1965 the first Polish Catholic missionaries left to work overseas, marking the rebirth of missionary sending by the church in a country under Communist rule. In 1975–1976 and again in 1980 his missiological research took him to Africa.

Zapłata published widely and organized a series of missiological symposia, published in *Zeszyty misjologiczne ATK.* His academic work, as well as his efforts in preparing persons for mission work and in renewing interest in missions, especially its ecumenical dimension in the pastoral activity of the church, are his legacy. He was a pioneer of Catholic missiology in Poland and Eastern Europe.

BIBLIOGRAPHY Jan Górski, "Twenty Years Missiology in Warsaw (ATK)," *Mission Studies* 13 (1990): 93–94; Władysław Kowalak, "Symposium de missiologie a l'ATC de Varsovie, 1976," *NZM* 33 (1977): 67; Roman Malek, "In Memoriam P. Feliks Zapłata SVD (1914–1982)," *NZM* 39 (1983): 223–227.

Jan Górski

Zaremba, Felician von (1794–1874), Polish nobleman and Basel missionary in the Caucasus. Zaremba experienced conversion as a young man and was accepted for training in one of the very first classes of the Basel Mission (BM) seminary in Basel. In 1822 BM sent him to its new mission in the Caucasus, where he was stationed in Shusha and worked not only with Armenian Christians but also with Tatars. The openness to pietism characteristic of ruling circles in Russia at the end of the Napoleonic Wars declined in the 1820s and 1830s. Like the rest of his Basel colleagues conducting missionary work, Zaremba was forced to leave Russia at the end of the 1830s. He spent the rest of his life based in Basel, helping maintain the BM's contacts with its constituency in central Europe and the German-speaking Protestant diaspora in eastern Europe and European Russia.

BIBLIOGRAPHY Wilhelm Schlatter, *Geschichte der Basler Mission,* vol. 1 (1915); Andreas Waldburger, *Missionare und Moslems: Die Basler Mission in Persien, 1833–1837* (1984).

Paul Jenkins

Zeisberger, David (1721–1808), Moravian Apostle to the Indians. Born in Moravia (present-day Czech Republic), Zeisberger spent his childhood in Herrnhut, Germany, center of the Moravian missionary movement, where his parents had emigrated in search of religious freedom. As a youth, he accompanied Moravian missionaries to Georgia in 1738. He came into his life's vocation when he began mission work among Native Americans in New York State in 1745. His goal was to establish converts in villages that would provide protection from European settlers and non-Christian Native Americans. His work took him west through Pennsylvania. Despite many setbacks, he successfully established several Moravian Indian villages in eastern Ohio (present-day Tuscarawas County) beginning in 1772. However, this area soon became embroiled in hostilities marking the end of the American Revolution. While Zeisberger was defending his neutrality before British officials in Detroit in 1782, some ninety-six of his converts were massacred in Gnadenhutten, Ohio, by American militia. He eventually reestablished his mission in Fairfield, Ontario, and then led a few families back to Ohio in 1798. Efforts were made to establish new villages, but it was no longer possible to maintain exclusive communities, and the work eventually ceased. After 62 years in missionary service, Zeisberger died and was buried in Goshen, Ohio, the site of his last residence.

Zeisberger spoke several Native American languages fluently and produced a number of literary works that aided him in his efforts. These include biblical translations, hymns, catechetical materials, and general educational materials. He also produced grammatical studies and dictionaries that presented Native American languages with both English and German equivalents. Portions of his diaries have been published, and his manuscript "The History of the North American Indians" written in 1779–1780, has been translated and published by Archer B. Hulbert and William Schwarze in *Ohio Archaeological and Historical Society Publications* 19 (1910): 1–173.

BIBLIOGRAPHY Hartmut Beck, *Brüder in vielen Völkern: 250 Jahre Mission der Brüdergemeine* (1981); Edmund DeSchweinitz, *The Life and Times of David Zeisberger* (1870); Elma Gray and Leslie Robb, *Wilderness Christians: The Moravian Mission to the Delaware Indians* (1956). Zeisberger's manuscript materials are in the Moravian archives, Bethlehem, Pennsylvania. Autobiographical material appears in Eugene F. Bliss, tr., *Diary of David Zeisberger, a Moravian Missionary among the Indians of Ohio* (1885), and Paul E. Mueller, tr., *David Zeisberger's Official Diary, Fairfield, 1791–1795* (1981).

David A. Schattschneider

Zeng Baosun. *See* Tseng Pao Swen.

Ziegenbalg, Bartholomäus (1682–1719), pioneer German missionary in South India. Ziegenbalg, the prototype of German pietist Lutheran missionaries, was born in Pulsnitz, Saxony. He had a conversion experience while in high-school, after the early loss of his parents. Repeated illness and inner conflicts interrupted his studies at Berlin and Halle. But under the guidance of the pietist leaders Joachim Lange and A. H. *Francke, he underwent a demanding program of studies, including Greek and Hebrew, which was to stand him in good stead in India. When King Frederick IV of Denmark found little Danish interest in taking up mission work among non-Christian subjects overseas, he instructed his German court chaplain Franz J. *Lütkens to find suitable candidates in Germany. After consultation with Lange, Lütkens was soon able to present Ziegenbalg and his fellow student Heinrich *Plütschau, who were ordained at Copenhagen and arrived at the Danish trade establishment of Tranquebar, South India, on July 9, 1706.

The mission depended in its formative years primarily on Ziegenbalg's creative vision and ability. There was no end of difficulties, and Ziegenbalg's own impetuosity was at least partly responsible. Yet often he seemed to grow under pressure, not least on account of his practice of dealing with unforeseen challenges by intensive prayer and by accounting for his actions in incredibly extensive reporting and correspondence.

There was, first, the challenge of the local languages—Portuguese and, more urgently, Tamil. With the assistance of indigenous helpers, Ziegenbalg quickly acquired command of both the spoken and the written forms of Tamil, prepared dictionaries, published a grammar (1716), and collected Tamil manuscripts. He thus became a pioneer in the Western study of South Indian culture, society, and religion, although three of his translations and his two major works on Hindu religion remained unpublished for a long time as they did not meet with approval at Halle. His translation of the Bible, on the other hand—the whole New Testament, for the first time in any Indian language, and the Old Testament up to the book of Ruth—was printed at Tranquebar on a Tamil press sent out from Halle. Tamil hymnbooks, catechisms, and other Christian literature followed. Schools for boys and girls were established, and a seminary for the preparation of Indian assistants was opened. All this underscored Ziegenbalg's conviction that the indigenous church would be Lutheran in faith and worship but Indian in character.

However, a dispute over policy with the Danish mission secretary, Christian Wendt, undoubtedly contributed to his sudden death in 1719, before he had completed his thirty-sixth year. Much later it would be recognized that with him "a new epoch in the history of the Christian mission had begun" (Stephen Neill).

BIBLIOGRAPHY There is a large body of literature on the history of the Tranquebar mission; see especially Daniel Jeyaraj, *Der Beitrag der Dänisch-Halleschen Mission zum Werden einer indisch-einheimischen Kirche, 1706–1730* (1996), and E. A. Lehmann, *It Began at Tranquebar* (1956). The only adequate biography of Ziegenbalg translated into English is Erich Beyreuther, *Bartholomäus Ziegenbalg* (1955).

Hans-Werner Gensichen

Zimmermann, Johannes (1825–1876), German missionary and linguist in Ghana. Zimmermann was a baker who joined the Basel Mission (BM) after reading the mission's literature in the house of his German pietist parents in a Württemberg village. Sent to Ghana in 1850, he was stationed in Accra, Abokobi, and Odumase-Krobo in the Ga-Adangme language area, where he became the pioneer BM authority on the languages of the area. In the 1850s he promoted a scheme for the settlement of pietist farmers and craftsmen from Württemberg at Abokobi, an open site in Ghana unattached to any traditional settlement; he also bought land personally. The death rate of Europeans in Ghana caused this plan to be abandoned, but Zimmermann remained true to the ideal of propagating Christian village life in West Africa. He took a sympathetic approach to African culture. In the 1860s, when the mission debated the morality of various traditional slave statuses in Ghanaian society, he adopted a positive outlook, viewing them as reflecting the patriarchal order of society in the Old Testament. Odonkor Azu of Manya-Krobo, in whose capital Zimmermann worked for many years, had a traditional stool made for Zimmermann to use when he sat with his circle of councilors. Zimmermann is also said to be named in drum histories of this royal family as the foster father of two of Odonkor Azu's sons.

In 1851, Zimmermann married without obtaining the prescribed permission from Basel. His wife, Catherine (c. 1825–1891), who had probably been born in Angola, was enslaved as a child and transported across the Atlantic to Jamaica. There her colonial family gave her the name Mulgrave, freed her, and trained her as a teacher. Subsequently she volunteered to return to Africa as part of a group of Christian ex-slaves to found Christian colonies in connection with the BM in southern Ghana. (See also Andreas *Riis.) En route to Ghana, she married a Liberian by the name of George Thompson. She separated from him a few years later, and Zimmerman married her. She is said to have assisted him in his pastoral and ethnographic work.

BIBLIOGRAPHY Johannes Zimmermann, "Letztes Wort eines alten afrikanischen Missionars an sein deutsches Vaterland," *EMM* 21 (1877): 225–245 and *Vocabulary of the Akra- or Ga-Languages, with an Adangme Appendix* (1858). Jon Miller, *The Social Control of Religious Zeal: A Study of Organizational Contradictions* (1994); Karl Rennstich, *Handwerkertheologen und Industriebruder als Botschafter des Friedens: Entwicklungshilfe der Basler Mission im 19. Jahrhundert* (1985); Cornelia Vogelsanger, *Pietismus und afrikanische Kultur an der Goldküste: Die Einstellung der Basler Mission zur Haussklaverei* (1977).

Paul Jenkins

Zinzendorf, Nikolaus Ludwig von (1700–1760), German nobleman, Pietist leader, and theologian of Moravian missions. Zinzendorf was born in Dresden. At the age of ten, following tutoring at home, he attended a boarding school in Halle conducted by August Hermann *Francke. From 1716 to 1721 he traveled and studied law at the University of Wittenberg. He became a legal councilor at the Dresden court of the Saxon elector August the Strong in 1721. Following his marriage in 1722 to Countess Erdmuthe Dorothea von Reuss, he established his manorial home at Berthelsdorf in eastern Germany. Zinzendorf was released from state service in 1727 and devoted his life to leadership of the Moravians.

Refugees from Bohemia and Moravia (present-day Czech Republic) had arrived on his land beginning in 1722, bringing with them the heritage of the suppressed Hussite Unity of the Brethren (*Unitas Fratrum*). Together with German Pietists, these people formed the nucleus of the new town of Herrnhut and were the first members of the Moravian Church, which emerged as a separate denomination by the 1740s. As leader of the Moravians, Zinzendorf traveled to oversee activity in Europe, England, the West Indies, and the eastern United States. His activities often aroused controversy, as he sought to guide the development of unique forms of Moravian witness. Self-sufficient settlement congregations were established to enhance the spirituality of the inhabitants and to serve as homes for those who traveled to conduct renewal activities within established state churches or as missionaries among those who had never heard the gospel. He was consecrated a bishop in 1737. His greatest contribution to missiology was his awakening within Protestantism of an awareness of cross-cultural mission as a fundamental task of the church. Though not a systematic writer, he revealed in his published materials a consistent desire to seek contemporary expression of Christian theology.

BIBLIOGRAPHY *Nikolaus Ludwig von Zinzendorf: Nine Public Lectures on Important Subjects in Religion,* George W. Forell, tr. (1973). See also Erich Beyreuther and Gerhard Meyer, eds., *Nikolaus Ludwig von Zinzendorf: Hauptschriften* (1962–1963) and *Ergänzungsbände zu Den Hauptschriften* (1964–1985). Anthony J. Lewis, *Zinzendorf: The Ecumenical Pioneer* (1962); John R. Weinlick, *Count Zinzendorf* (1956, 1984).

David A. Schattschneider

Ziorov, Nikolai. *See* Nikolai.

Zumárraga, Juan de (c. 1468–1548), first bishop and archbishop of Mexico. Born at Tavira de Durango, near Bilboa, Spain, Zumárraga entered the Franciscan order and became provincial superior. In 1527 he was appointed first bishop of Mexico. Without episcopal consecration he went to Mexico, where he undertook the difficult task of organizing the new diocese. The Spanish court appointed him "protector of the Indians," and when some members of the Mexican government opposed him, he excommunicated them and placed Mexico under ecclesiastical censure. King Charles V called him back to Spain to justify his actions, and he was able to defend himself against the accusations to the full satisfaction of the king, who invited him to receive episcopal consecration in Valladolid in 1533. In 1534 he returned to Mexico with a group of artisans plus some women to educate Indian girls. He built churches, convents, hospitals, schools, and colleges for Indian boys and girls. In 1536 he founded the college of Tlatelolco to train young men for the priesthood. He planned for a university, which was opened after his death. In 1539 he opened the first printing office in Mexico. At his own expense he published catechisms and ascetic and liturgical books. In 1546 he became the first archbishop of Mexico and developed the ecclesiastical organization of the country, creating the dioceses of Chiapas, Oaxaca, Guatemala, and Miochoacán; he also proposed *Las Casas and Vasco de *Quiroga as bishops. He convened councils of the bishops in Mexico that were forerunners to the Mexican provincial councils. The council of 1536 settled controversies concerning the administration of baptism and marriage of converts. Some of its decisions were confirmed by Paul III in the bull *Altitudo divini consilii* (1537). The council of 1539 dealt with administration of the sacraments. From 1535 to 1543 Zumárraga held the office of inquisitor. He tried to protect the faith of the converted Indians, but despite his good intentions, the Spanish court removed him from office. During his time many temples, idols, and ancient writings were destroyed. Nevertheless, Zumárraga remains a dominant figure of the early church in Mexico, a bishop of great moral rectitude and zeal, which partially explains some of his excesses. He died in Mexico.

BIBLIOGRAPHY Joaquin Garcia Icazbalceta, *Don Fray Juan de Zumárraga, primer obispo y arzobispo de México,* de Rafael Aguayo Spencer and Antonio Castro Leal, eds., 4 vols. (1947; 1st ed., 1881); Fidel de J.Chauvet, *Fray Juan de Zumárraga* (1948); Alberto Maria Carreño, *Don fray Juan de Zumárraga: Téologo y editor, humanista y inquisidor* (1950); R. E. Greenleaf, *Zumárraga and the Mexican Inquisition, 1536–1543* (1962); "Don Fray Juan de Zumárraga, First Bishop and Archbishop of Mexico: In Commemoration of the Fourth Centenary of His Death," *The Americas* 5 (1948–1949): 261–341.

Willi Henkel, OMI

Zwemer, Samuel Marinus (1867–1952), Apostle to Islam. One of the most celebrated Protestant missionaries of the twentieth century, Zwemer made his home in Arabia and Egypt for most of 38 years (1890–1929). Initially an evangelist, he became a writer, publisher, and peripatetic conference speaker who, as much as anyone, introduced twentieth-century Christians to Islam. The son of Dutch immigrant parents, he was born in Vriesland, Michigan, where his father was a Reformed pastor. He graduated from Hope Academy and College (B.A. 1887; M.A., 1890) and New Brunswick Seminary (B.D., 1890) and became an early recruit of the Student Volunteer Movement (SVM). In 1889, when Zwemer and his classmate James Cantine could find no agency to send them as missionaries to Muslims, they established the American Arabian Mission, which five years later the Reformed Church agreed to sponsor. Zwemer lived for a time in the United States (1905–1910) serving primarily as a promoter, recruiter, and publicist for the Arabian Mission, field secretary for the Reformed Board, and traveling secretary for the SVM. Besides writing twenty-nine books and coauthoring another nineteen, Zwemer founded, and edited for 37 years, the journal *The Moslem World.* He organized two major missionary conferences on Islam, one in Cairo (1905) and one in Lucknow (1911). In 1929 Zwemer accepted the professorship of the history of religion and Christian missions at Princeton Theological Seminary, continuing in that post until 1937. After formal retirement, he moved to New York City and taught at the Biblical Seminary of New York and the Nyack Missionary Training Institute. A lifelong student of Islam, Zwemer never ceased to contend for the finality of Christ. Though unusually prolific as a writer and effective in recruiting missionaries and inspiring interest in missions, particularly in the Muslim world, Zwemer saw only a few Muslims openly profess the Christian faith.

BIBLIOGRAPHY Samuel M. Zwemer and James Cantine, *The Golden Milestone* (1938). Sherwood Eddy, *Pathfinders of the World Missionary Crusade* (1945), pp. 240–247; Alfred DeWitt Mason and Frederick J. Barney, *The History of the Arabian Mission* (1926); William M. Miller, *A Man Sent from God* (1966); J. Christy Wilson, Sr., *Apostle to Islam: A Biography of Samuel M. Zwemer* (1952) and *Flaming Prophet* (1970); J. Christy Wilson, Jr., "The Legacy of Samuel M. Zwemer," *IBMR* 10 (July 1986): 117–121.

Alan Neely

Zwingli, Huldrych (*or* Ulrich) (1484–1531), reformer in German Switzerland. Zwingli was born in Wildhaus, Switzerland, studied in Vienna and Basel, and was ordained as priest in 1506. He worked as pastor in Glarus (1506–1516), Einsiedeln (1516–1519), and Zürich, until his death on the battlefield at Kappel. He was strongly influenced by Renaissance humanism, especially by *Erasmus. In 1522 he initiated the Reformation in Zürich. His ministry had a strong social character, for he taught that the glorified Christ is Lord over all areas of life. Soon the Reformation spread to Berne and other cantons of Switzerland.

Zwingli's theology differs from *Luther's, especially regarding the Eucharist. He looked upon it as a community meal of thanksgiving, without any magical aspects: not the bread but the community changes. A colloquy in 1529 between Luther and Zwingli in Marburg, Germany, failed to reconcile their differences. Thereafter, Lutheranism and Reformed Protestantism developed separately.

Zwingli argued in *Expositio fidei* (1531) that pagans such as Socrates and Aristides were among the saved. This opinion was vehemently disputed by other Protestant reformers. For Zwingli, the working of the Holy Spirit reaches beyond the frontiers of Palestine and the church. God *may* also draw pagans to Christ; the number of the elect remains God's secret. The post-apostolic church, he believed, does not have a missionary task. In Zwingli's view paganism is mainly present in the Roman Catholic Church. In the context of the advances of the Turks against Europe, Zwingli suggested that mission among the Muslims would be better than the horrors of war.

BIBLIOGRAPHY G. W. Locher, *Zwingli's Thought* (1981); G. R. Potter, *Zwingli* (1976). On Zwingli and missions, see Paul Drews, "Die Anschauungen reformatorischer Theologen über die Heidenmission," *Zeitschrift für praktische Theologie* 19 (1897): 217–223; W. Holsten, "Reformation und Mission," *Archiv für Reformationsgeschichte* 44 (1953): 19–22; Rudolf Pfister, *Die Seligkeit erwählter Heiden bei Zwingli* (1952).

K. M. Witteveen

Appendix

The following lists will help readers find biographies according to particular categories of interest. Every biography in the dictionary can be found in the list by time period. Some biographies, however, do not fall easily within other categories the editors believe will suit most readers' interests. Please refer to the body of the work for biographies that cannot be found in the following lists.

- Baptists
- Basel Mission (Lutheran and Reformed)
- Church Missionary Society (predominantly Anglican)
- Dominicans (Roman Catholic)
- Franciscans (Roman Catholic)
- Jesuits (Roman Catholic)
- London Missionary Society (predominantly Congregational)
- Lutherans
- Methodists
- Orthodox Churches
- Presbyterians/Reformed
- Roman Catholics Born after 1500
- Society of the Divine Word (Roman Catholic)

Biographies of Non-Western Persons

- Africa
- Asia and the Middle East
- Caribbean Region and Latin America (including Mexico, Central America, and South America)
- Pacific Islands (including Hawaii)

Biographies by Type of Work

- Bible Translation
- Medical Services
- Study of Culture and Language
- Work with Women and Children

BIOGRAPHIES BY TIME PERIOD

Born up through 800

Adalbert
Addai
Aidan
Alopen
Amandus of Elnon
Ambrose
Augustine of Canterbury
Augustine of Hippo
Baradaeus, Jacob (or Bar'adai; Barada'i)
Barsauma (or Barsumas)
Bede
Benedict
Birinus
Boniface (or Bonifatius)
Chrysostom, John
Columba (or Colum Cille)
Columban (or Columbanus)
Constantine the Great
Corbinian
Cuthbert
Denis (or Denys; Dionysius) of Paris
Eligius
Eusebius of Caesarea
Ezana
Fridolin (or Fridold)
Frumentius
Gall (Gallus)
Gregory I (the Great)
Gregory Thaumaturgus
Gregory the Illuminator
Gudwal (or Gurwal; Gurvalus)
Honoratus
Irenaeus of Lyons
Jing Jing
Julian
Justin Martyr
Kentigern (St. Mungo)
Kilian (Kyllena)
Leander of Seville
Lebuin
Lioba
Longinus
Ludger (or Luidger; Liudger)
Martin of Tours
Mesrob (or Mashtots)
Ninian (or Nynias; Niniavus)
Nino
Origen
Palladius
Pantaenus
Patrick
Paulinus of York
Pirminius (Pirmin)
Remigius of Reims
Sahak
Severinus
Sturmius
Suidbert (or Suitbert; Swibert)
Trudpert
Ulfila (or Ulphilas; Wulfila)
Valentinus
Virgil of Salzburg
Wilfrid
Willehad
Willibald
Willibrord (or Willibrordus), Clemens

Born from 801 to 1500

Adalbert of Bremen
Adalbert of Prague
Affonso (Alphonse)
Alexander VI
Anastasius
Andrew of Perugia
Anselm
Ansgar (or Anskar)
Arseny of Konev
Betanzos, Domingo de
Boris
Brun(o) of Querfurt
Bucer, Martin
Buyl (or Boyl; Boil), Bernal
Catalani, Jordan
Clement of Ochrid
Córdoba, Pedro de
Cyril-Constantine
Dominic
Erasmus, Desiderius
Eulogius
Formosus
Francis of Assisi
Garcés, Julián
Gregory VII (Hildebrand)
Haraldsson, Olav
Henry (or Henrik) of Uppsala
Hut, Hans
Ignatius of Loyola (or Ióigo López de Loyola)
Innocent IV
Isaiah of Rostov
John of Montecorvino
John of Pian di Carpine (or Plano de Carpine)
John of Segovia
Kuksha
Las Casas, Bartolomé de
Loayza, Gerónimo de
Lull, Raymund (or Ramón)
Luther, Martin
Manso, Alonso
Methodius
Montesinos, Antonio de (or Antón Montesino)
Motolinía (Toribio de Benavente)
Nicholas
Nicholas IV (Girolamo Masci)
Nicholas of Cusa
Nikon the Metanoeite
Odorico of Pordenone
Otto (or Otho) of Bamberg
Padilla, Juan de
Paracelsus
Pennini, Ricoldo (da Monte Cruce)
Peter of Ghent
Peter the Venerable de Montboissier (Pierre Maurice)
Photius
Quiroga, Vasco de
Reginhar (or Renharius; Regenharius)
Ricke, Jodoco
Sahagún, Bernardino de
Santo Tomás, Domingo de
Sava
Sergii of Valaam (or Valamo)
Sigfrid
Stephen
Stephen of Perm
Takla-Haymanot
Testera (or Tastera), Jacobo de
Thomas Aquinas
Valencia, Martín de
Vicelin
Vitoria, Francisco de
Vladimir of Kiev
Waldo (or Valdez), Peter
William of Rubroek (or Rubruck)
William of Tripoli
Wolfgang
Xenos, Ioannes
Zumárraga, Juan de
Zwingli, Huldrych (or Ulrich)

Born from 1501 to 1800

Abdul Masih, Salih
Abraham Malpan
Acosta, José de
Acquaviva, Rudolf
Adam, William
Aldersey, Mary Ann
Aleni, Giulio
Alexander, Michael Solomon
Allen, David Oliver
Allouez, Claude Jean
Altham, John
Amiot, Jean Joseph Marie
Anchieta, José de
Anderson, Christopher
Anderson, Rufus
Anderson, William
Andrade, Antonio de
André, Louis
Andrews, Lorrin
Archbell, James
Arriaga, Pablo José de
Asbury, Francis
Auna
Azevedo, Ignacio de
Bacon, Sumner
Baldaeus, Philippus
Ball, Dyer
Baraga, (Irenaeus) Frederic
Barreira, Balthazar (or Baltesar)
Barth, Christian Gottlob
Barzaeus (or Barzäus; Berze), Gaspar
Barzana, Alonso de
Baxter, Richard
Benavides, Miguel de
Benedict XIV
Bernardino, Ignazio da Asti
Beschi, Constanzo Giuseppe
Bettendorf, Johann Philipp
Biard, Pierre
Bibliander, Theodor
Bickersteth, Edward
Bicknell, Henry
Billiart, (Marie Rose) Julie
Bingham, Hiram and Sybil (Moseley)
Bishop, Artemas
Black, William
Blanchet, Francis Norbert
Blumhardt, Christian Gottlieb
Bogue, David
Böhler, Peter
Böhnisch, Frederick
Bolaños, Luis
Bolotov, Ioasaf
Bonaventura da Sardegna
Bonnand, Clément
Bourgeoys, Marguerite
Bouvet, Joachim
Bowley, William
Brainerd, David
Brainerd, John
Brancati de Laurea, Lorenzo (Giovanni Francesco)
Braun, Peter
Bray, Thomas
Brébeuf, Jean de
Breton, Raymond (Guillaume)
Britto, João de
Broughton, William Grant
Brown, David
Brownlee, John
Brückner, Gottlob
Bruillard, Philippe de
Brunton, Henry
Buchanan, Claudius
Buglio, Lodovico
Butler, Elizur
Buxton, Thomas Fowell
Buzacott, Aaron
Byington, Cyrus
Cabral, Francisco
Callenberg, Johann Heinrich
Calvin, John
Campbell, John
Cáncer de Barbastro, Luis
Candidius, Georgius
Capadose, Abraham
Capillas, Francisco de
Capitein, Jacobus Elisa Joannes
Cardoso, Mattheus
Carey, Charlotte Emilia (von Rumohr)
Carey, Felix
Carey, Lott
Carey, William
Carneiro Leitão, Melchior Miguel
Carroll, John
Case, Isaac
Case, William
Castiglione, Giuseppe
Castro, Matheus de
Cattaneo, Lazzaro
Cavazzi da Montecuccolo
Céspedes, Gregorio
Chabanel, Noël
Chalmers, Thomas
Chamberlain, John
Chaminade, Guillaume Joseph
Champagnat, Marcellin (Joseph Benôit)
Chaumont, Denis
Chavoin, Jeanne-Marie (Mother Saint Joseph)
Chong Yak-Jong, Augustine
Chou Wen-Mo (Zhou Wenmo)
Clark, Ephraim W.
Claver, Peter
Clement VIII
Clement XI
Coates, Dandeson
Cobo, Bernabé
Cocceius, Johannes
Coke, Thomas
Coker, Daniel
Colin, Jean-Claude Marie
Comenius (or Komensky), Jan Amos
Coolen, C(oenraad) L(aurens)
Corrie, Daniel
Costa, Isaac da
Coudrin, Pierre Marie Joseph
Coughlan, Laurence
Couplet, Philippe
Cox, Melville Beveridge
Criminali, Antonio
Crook, William Pascoe
Crosby, Aaron
Cross, William
Dablon, Claude
Daniel, Antoine
Darling, David
David, Christian
Davies, John
Day, John
Desideri, Hippolytus
Devasahayam, John
Dober, Johann Leonhard
Dobrizhoffer, Martin
Dorville, Albert
Druillettes, Gabriel
Dubois, Jean Antoine
Duchesne, Rose Philippine
Dufresse, Jean-Gabriel-Taurin
Duncan, John
Dyer, John
Edwards, Jonathan
Egede, Hans (Povelsen)
Eliot, John
Ellis, William and Mary Mercy (Moor)
Emde, J(ohannes)
Enbaqom (Abu l-Fath)
England, John
Errico, Gaetano Cosma Damiano
Evarts, Jeremiah
Ewing, Greville
Fabricius, Johann Philipp
Falkner, Thomas
Feller, Henriette Odin
Filofei (Leshchinsky)
Fisk, Pliny
Focher, Juan
Forbin-Janson, Charles de
Foucquet, Jean-François
Francke, August Hermann
Freeman, John Joseph
Frey, Joseph Samuel C(ristian) F(rederick)
Fridelli, Xaver-Ehrenbert (or Ernbert)
Fritz, Samuel
Fróis, Luis
Fuller, Andrew
Gardiner, Allen Francis
Garnier, Charles
Gebhre Michael
George, David
Gerbillon, Jean-François
Gericke, Christian Wilhelm
Gilbert, Nathaniel
Gilmour, John
Glen, William
Glukharev, Makarii (Mikhail Yakovlevich)
Gnecci-Soldi, Organtino
Gobat, Samuel
Goes, Bento de

Gogerly, Daniel John
González de Santa Cruz, Roque
Goodell, William
Gossner, Johannes Evangelista
Goupil, René
Grant, Charles
Grassman, Andrew
Gregory XV
Gregory XVI
Griffiths, David
Grignion de Montfort, Louis Marie
Grotius, Hugo (or Huigh de Groot)
Groves, A(nthony) N(orris)
Grüber, Johannes
Gründler, Johann Ernst
Gubernatis, Dominicus de
Gulick, Peter Johnson and Fanny Hinckley (Thomas)
Hahn, Heinrich
Hale, Sarah Josepha (Buell)
Hall, Gordon
Hallbeck, Hans Peter
Hambroeck (Hambroek), Antonius
Hanxleden, Johann Ernst
Hartmann, Maria
Haven, Jens
Haweis, Thomas
Hawley, Gideon
Heber, Reginald
Heckewelder, John Gottlieb Ernestus
Henderson, Ebenezer
Henriques, Henrique
Herman of Alaska
Hermosilla, Jeronimo
Herrero, Andrés
Heurnius, Justus
Heyer, John Christian Frederick
Heyling, Peter
Hill, John Henry
Hill, Mary (Beardsmore)
Hodgson, Thomas Laidman
Holmes, Elkanah
Hoornbeeck (or Hoornbeek), Johannes
Hopkins, Samuel
Horne, Melville
Horton, Azariah
Hough, George H.
Hsu Kuang-ch'i (Xu Guangqi)
Iakinf (Bichurin)
Ingoli, Francesco
Innocent Veniaminov (Ivan Popov-Veniaminov)
Intorcetta, Prospero
Ioasaf (Hotuntsevsky)
Isakovich, Nikolai Fedorovich
I Sung-Hun, Peter
Iuvenalii (Iakov Fedorovich Govorukhin)
Jaca, Francisco José de
Jacobis, Justin de
Jänicke, Johann
Jaricot, Pauline-Marie
Jartoux, Pierre
Javouhey, Anne-Marie
Jefferson, John Clark
Jeune, Paul le
Jogues, Isaac
John, Christoph Samuel
Johns, David
Johnson, William Augustine Bernard
Jones, David
Jones, Evan and John Buttrick
Jones, John
Jowett, William
Judson, Adoniram
Judson, Ann ("Nancy") (Hasseltine)
Junius (de Jonghe), Robertus
Kaahumanu
Kähler, Christiane (Mues)
Kals, Jan Willem
Kam, Joseph
Kemp, Johannes Theodorus van der
Kendall, Thomas
Kersten, Christoph
Kiernander, John Zacharias
Kilham, Hannah (Spurr)
Kincaid, Eugenio
King, Jonas
Kingsbury, Cyrus
Kino, Eusebio Francisco
Kircher, Athanasius
Kircherer, Johannes Jacobus
Kirkland, Samuel
Kleinschmidt, Johann Conrad
Kosmas Aitolos (or Cosmas of Aitolia)
Ko Tha Byu
Lacroix, Alphonse François
Lafitau, Joseph-François
La Lande, Jean de
Lalemant, Gabriel
Lalemant, Jérôme
Lambert de la Motte, Pierre
La Salle, Jean-Baptiste de
Le Comte, Louis
Leibniz, Gottfried Wilhelm von
Lenkeevich, Nikolai (Nikodim)
Leontiev, Maxim
Léry, Jean de
Leydecker, Melchior
Liang Fa
Li Chih-tsao (Li Zhizao)
Lieberkühn, Samuel
Liele, George
Llinás, Jesús Maria Antonio
Lopez, Gregorio (Lo Wen-Tsao)
López de Mendoza Grajales, Francisco
Lourenço da Silva de Mendonça
Love, John
Loveless, Sarah (Farquhar)
Lütkens, Franz Julius
Lyon, Mary
Macgowan, Edward
Mack, John
Mack, (Johann) Martin
Maigrot, Charles
Mailla, Joseph Marie Anne de Moyriac de
Makemie, Francis
Maldonado de Buendía, Alonso
Margil, Antonio
Marie de l'Incarnation (Marie Guyart)
Marquette, Jacques
Marsden, Samuel
Marshman, Hannah (Shepherd)
Marshman, John C(larke)
Marshman, Joshua
Martin, Frederick
Martines, Francesco
Martínez, Pedro
Martínez Compañón y Bujanda, Baltasar Jaime
Martini, Martino
Martyn, Henry
Mason, Francis
Massanet, Damian
Mather, Cotton
Mayhew, Experience
Mayhew, Thomas, Jr.
Mazenod, Charles-Joseph-Eugène de
McCaul, Alexander
McCoy, Isaac
McDowell, Robert James
Medhurst, Walter Henry
Megapolensis, Johannes
Mel, Conrad
Ménard, René
Mendez, Alphonsus
Mendieta, Jerónimo
Meneses, Aleixo de
Mezzabarba, Carlo Ambrogio
Middleton, Thomas Fanshaw
Millar, Robert
Mills, Samuel John, Jr.
Milne, Rachel (Cowie)
Milne, William
Mingo de la Concepción, Manuel
Moffat, Robert
Mogrovejo, Toribio Alfonso de
Moirans, Epifanio de
Morales, Juan Bautista de
Moreau, Basile Antoine
Morris, John Webster
Morrison, Mary (Morton)
Morrison, Robert
Morse, Jedediah
Moshoeshoe (also Moshesh, and various other spellings)
Moulton, Ebenezer
Moya de Contreras, Pedro
Moye (or Moÿe; Moyë), Jean-Martin
Murillo Velarde, Pedro
Murray, Andrew, Sr.
Nacquart, Charles
Navarrete, Domingo Fernandez de
Nerinckx, Charles
Nettleton, Asahel
Newell, Maria
Newell, Samuel and Harriett (Atwood)
Nicolai, Philipp
Nitschmann, David
Nobili, Robert de
Nóbrega, Manoel da
Nott, Henry
Nott, Samuel, Jr.
Ntsikana
Nunes Barreto, João
Nyländer, Gustavus Reinhold
Obookiah (or Opukahaia), Henry
Occom, Samson
O'Donel, James Louis
Oldendorp, Christian Georg Andreas
Oviedo, André de
Paez, (Xaramillo) Pedro (or Pero Paez)

Pal, Krishna
Palafox y Mendoza, Juan de
Pallotti, Vincent
Pallu, François
Papeiha
Parsons, Levi
Paterson, John
Paucke, Florian
Paul of the Cross (Paolo Francesco Danei)
Payeras, Mariano
Peck, John Mason
Pedraza, Cristóbal de
Pedro de la Madre de Dios
Peet, Joseph
Peña Montenegro, Alonso de
Perroton, (Marie) Françoise (Marie du Mont Carmel)
Philaret (Drozdov)
Philip, John
Phillippo, J(ames) M(ursell)
Pigneau de Béhaine, Pierre-Joseph-Georges
Pinkerton, Robert
Pitman, Charles
Plasencia (Portocarrero), Juan de
Plütschau, Heinrich
Pomare II
Porres (or Porras), Martín de
Pottier, François
Poullart-des-Places, Claude-François
Prasad (or Prisada), Krishna
Pratt, Josiah
Price, Jonathan David
Protten, Christian Jacob
Quaque, Philip
Raban, John
Rada, Martín de
Ramazotti, Angelo Francesco
Rasa, Clorinda
Rasalama, Rafaravavy
Rauch, Christian Henry
Read, James
Reeve, William
Régis, Jean-Baptiste
Renner, Melchior
Rhenius, Carl Theophilus Ewald
Rhodes, Alexandre de
Ricci, Matteo
Rice, Luther
Richards, William
Richter, Enrique
Riedel, Johann (Gerard) Friedrich
Riedemann, Peter
Ringeltaube, Wilhelm Tobias
Robinson, William
Rocha, João da
Rønne, Bone Falch
Roothaan, Johann Philipp
Roth, Heinrich
Rottler, John Peter
Rougemont, François de
Rovenius, Philippus
Ruggieri, Michele
Ruiz de Montoya, Antonio
Ryland, John
Salazar, Domingo de
Sandoval, Alonso de
Santori, Giulio Antonio
San Vitores, Diego Luis de
Saravia, Adrianus (or Adriaan de; Adriaan van)
Schall von Bell, Johann Adam
Schauffler, William Gottlieb
Scherer, Heinrich
Schleiermacher, Friedrich Daniel Ernst
Schmelen, Johann Heinrich
Schmid, Hans
Schmidt, Georg
Schnarre, Johannes Christian
Schultz, Stephan
Schultze, Benjamin
Schwartz, Christian Friedrich
Schwarz, Johann Gottlob
Scudder, John
Segura, Juan Baptista
Sergeant, John
Serra, Junípero (Miguel Jose)
Shaw, Barnabas
Shaw, William
Shelikhov, Grigorii Ivanovich
Sibbes, Richard
Silveira, Gonçalo da
Simeon, Charles
Smith, John
Smith, Matilda
Solages, (Gabriel) Henri (Jerome) de
Solano, Francisco
Spangenberg, August Gottlieb
Spaulding, Levi
Spener, Philipp Jakob
Spinola, Carlo
Spittler, Christian Friedrich
Stach, Matthew
Stallybrass, Edward
Steinkopf, Karl Friedrich Adolf
Stephens, Thomas
Stevens, Jedediah Dwight
Stewart, John
Stockfleth, Nils Joachim Vibe
Stockton, Betsey
Stronach, Alexander
Swan, William
Takayama Iustus Ukon
Teague, Colin (or Collin Teage)
Thomas, John
Thomas of Jesus
Thompson, Thomas
Thomson, James (or Diego)
Thomson, William Ritchie
Threlkeld, Lancelot Edward
Thurston, Asa and Lucy (Goodale)
Tomlin, Jacob
Tournon, Charles Thomas Maillard de
Trigault, Nicolas
Trobe, Christian Ignatius la
Tryphon of Pechenga
Tupou, Taufa'ahau (or George)
Turton, William
Urban VIII
Urdaneta, Andres de
Urlsperger, Johann August
Valadés, Diego
Valdivia, Luis de
Valdivieso, Antonio de
Valignano, Alessandro
Valle, Juan del
Vasconcelos, Simão de
Vaz, Joseph
Venn, Henry
Venn, John
Vera Cruz, Alonso de la
Verbiest, Ferdinand
Vialar, Émilie de
Vieira, Antônio
Vincent de Paul
Visdelou, Claude
Vives y Marjá, Juan Bautista
Voetius, Gisbertus (or Gijsbert Voet)
Vos, Michiel C(hristiaan)
Wade, Jonathan and Deborah (Lapham)
Wagenseil, Johann Christoph
Walaeus, Antonius (or Anton de Wale)
Walker, William
Walpot, Peter
Walther, Christoph Theodosius
Ward, William
Watson, William
Way, Lewis
Webb, Mary
Welch, James Ely
Welz, Justinian von
Wesley, Charles
Wesley, John
Westen, Thomas von
Wheelock, Eleazar
White, Andrew
White, Charlotte Hazen Atlee
Whitefield, George
Wilberforce, William
Williams, Henry
Williams, John
Williams, Roger
Williamson, Thomas Smith
Wilson, Daniel
Wilson, James
Wilson, Mary Ann (Cooke)
Wimmer, Gottlieb August
Winslow, Harriet Wadsworth (Lathrop)
Winslow, Miron
Wolff, Joseph
Worcester, Samuel Austin
Wu Li (Wu Yü-Shan; or Simon à Cunha)
Xavier, Francis (or Francisco de Jassu y Xavier)
Xavier, Jerome
Xu, Candida
Yang T'ing-yün
Yates, William
Zaremba, Felician von
Zeisberger, David
Ziegenbalg, Bartholomäus
Zinzendorf, Nikolaus Ludwig von

Born from 1801 to 1850

Abeel, David
Aea, Hezekiah and Debora
Agnew, Eliza
Alcina (or Alzina), Francisco Ignacio
Alexander, William Patterson
Ali, Wallayat
Allen, Young John
Alli, Janni
Amadeus, Mary
Anderson, David
Anderson, John
Anderson, Louisa (Peterswald)
Anderson, William
Andrianaivoravelona, Josefa
Anthing, F(rederik) L(odewijk)
Arbousset, (Jean) Thomas
Armstrong, Annie Walker
Armstrong, Hannah Maria (Norris)
Armstrong, Richard
Armstrong, William Frederick
Arthington, Robert
Ashmore, William
Auer, John Gottlieb
Baedeker, Friederich Wilhelm
Bailey, Wellesley C(osby)
Baker, Amelia Dorothea (Kohlhoff)
Ballantine, Henry
Banerjea, Krishna Mohan
Barclay, Thomas
Barton, John
Bashford, James Whitford
Bataillon, Pierre Marie
Bax, Jacques
Baynes, Alfred Henry
Belcourt, Georges Antoine
Bennett, Cephas
Berthoud, Paul
Bessieux, Jean Rémi
Besson, Pablo Enrique
Bettelheim, Bernard Jean
Beyzym, Jan
Bickersteth, Edward
Bigandet, Paul Ambroise
Bigard, Stephanie and Jeanne
Bingham, Hiram, Jr.
Bird, Mark Baker
Bishop, Isabella Lucy (Bird)
Bisseux, Isaac
Blackstone, William Eugene
Bliss, Daniel
Bliss, Edwin Munsell
Bliss, Isaac Grout
Blyden, Edward Wilmot
Boardman, George Dana
Boaz, Thomas
Bodelschwingh, Friedrich von
Bohner, Heinrich
Bompas, William Carpenter
Bonjean, Ernest Christophe
Boone, William Jones, Sr.
Booth, Catherine (Mumford)
Booth, William
Borghero, Francesco Saverio
Borrow, George
Bosco, Giovanni (John)
Boudinot, Elias (Galagina)
Bowen, George
Bowen, Thomas Jefferson
Boyce, William Binnington
Bradley, Dan Beach
Breck, James Lloyd
Brett, William Henry
Bridgman, Elijah Coleman
Bridgman, Eliza Jane (Gillette)
Bronson, Miles
Broomhall, Benjamin
Brown, Alfred (Nesbit)
Brown, George
Brown, Nathan
Brown, Samuel Robbins
Buchan, Jane
Buchner, Charles
Bulmer, John
Bulu, Joeli
Burns, William Chalmers
Buss, Ernst
Butler, Fanny Jane
Butler, William and Clementina (Rowe)
Cabrini, Frances Xavier
Cakobau, Ratu Seru
Caldwell, Robert
Calhoun, Simeon Howard
Callaway, Henry
Calvert, James
Canut, Juan Bautista
Cargill, David
Carpenter, Chapin Howard
Casalis, Eugène
Caspari, Carl Paul
Chalmers, John
Chamberlain, Jacob
Chanel, Pierre Louis
Chapdelaine, Auguste
Chappotin de Neuville, Hélène de (Marie de la Passion)
Chatterjee, Kali Charan
Chavara, Kuriackos Elias
Chevalier, Jules
Child, Abbie B.
Christaller, Johannes Gottlieb
Christlieb, Theodor
Claret, Anthony Mary
Clark, Robert
Clark, William Smith
Clarke, John
Clough, John Everett and Emma (Rauschenbusch)
Coan, Titus
Cochran, George
Cochran, Joseph Gallup
Codrington, Robert Henry
Coillard, François
Colenso, Elizabeth (Fairburn) and William
Colenso, John William
Colley, William W.
Collins, Judson Dwight
Comboni, (Anthony) Daniel
Condit, Azubah Caroline
Cooke, Sophia
Coombs, Lucinda L.
Cope, Marianne
Copleston, Reginald Stephen
Coppin, Fanny Marion (Jackson)
Corbett, Hunter
Corrado, Alejandro María
Cotton, George Edward Lynch
Cousins, William E(dward)
Couvreur, Séraphin
Crawford, T(arleton) P(erry) and Martha (Foster)
Creux, Ernest
Crosby, Thomas
Crowe, Frederick
Crowther, Dandeson Coates
Crowther, Samuel Adjai (or Ajayi)
Crummell, Alexander
Cushing, Ellen Winsor (Howard) Fairfield
Cust, Robert Needham
Dahle, Lars Nilsen
Damien of Molokai
Darling, Thomas Young
Daüble, Carl Gustav
Davidson, Andrew
Day, George Edward
Day, Lal Behari
Day, Samuel Stearns
Dean, William
Delitzsch, Franz Julius
Dennis, James Shepard
Depelchin, Henri
De Smet, Pierre-Jean
Dirks, Heinrich
Doane, Edward T(oppin)
Dole, Charlotte (Close) Knapp
Doll, Ludwig
Donders, Peter
Doremus, Sarah Platt (Haines)
Douglas, Carstairs
Droese, Ernest
Dubose, Hampden Coit
Duff, Alexander
Duncan, William
Duparquet, Charles
Dutton, Ira Barnes
Dwane, James Matta
Dwight, Harrison Gray Otis
Dyer, Samuel
Edersheim, Alfred
Edkins, Joseph
Edwards, Mary (Kelley)
Ehrenfeuchter, Friedrich
Ellinwood, Frank F(ield)
Elliott, Walter
Elmslie, William J. and Margaret (Duncan)
Ely, Charlotte Elizabeth and Mary Ann Caroline
Epalle, Jean-Baptiste
Evans, James
Evans, R(obert) M(ilton)

Fabri, Friedrich
Farrington, Sophronia
Favier, Pierre-Marie Alphonse
Feild, Edward
Fenn, Christopher Cyprian
Ferguson, Abbie Park and Bliss, Anna Elvira
Ferguson, Samuel David
Fielde, Adele M.
Figurovskii, Innokentii
Fiske, Fidelia
Fison, Lorimer
Fjellstedt, Peter
Flad, Johann Martin
Fleming, John
Fliedner, Federico
Forman, Charles William
Forsyth, Christina Moir
Fox, Henry Watson
Freeman, Thomas Birch
French, Thomas Valpy
Gabet, Joseph
Geddie, John
Gérard, Joseph
Giannecchini, Doroteo
Giannelli, José
Gibson, John Campbell
Gill, William Wyatt
Gilmour, James
Goble, Jonathan
Goddard, Josiah
Goldie, Hugh
Gollmer, Charles Andrew (Carl Anders)
Gomer, Joseph
Gomer, Mary (Green)
Gordon, A(doniram) J(udson)
Gordon, Andrew
Goreh, Nilakantha (Nehemiah)
Gorham, Sarah E.
Govan, William
Grandin, Vital Justin
Grant, Anthony
Grant, Asahel
Grant, Judith (Campbell)
Graul, Karl
Gray, Robert
Graybill, Anthony Thomas
Green, Samuel Fiske
Grenfell, George
Gribble, John Brown
Grimké, Charlotte (Forten)
Grundemann, Peter Reinhold
Gual, Pedro
Guerrant, Edward Owings
Guinness, Henry Grattan
Gulick, Alice (Gordon)
Gulick, Luther Halsey and Louisa Mitchell (Lewis)
Gulick, Orramel Hinckley and Ann Eliza (Clark)
Gundert, Hermann
Gützlaff, Karl Friedrich August
Hadfield, Octavius
Hagenauer, Friedrich August
Hahn, Carl Hugo
Hale, Mathew Blagden
Hamlin, Cyrus
Hamlin, James
Hannington, James
Happer, A(ndrew) P.
Hardy, Robert Spence
Harms, Ludwig
Harris, Merriman Colbert
Hartmann, (Joseph Alois) Anastasius
Hastings, Eurotas Parmelee
Hawkins, Ernest
Hebich, Samuel
Hecker, Isaac Thomas
Hepburn, James Davidson
Herschell, Ridley Haim
Hill, David
Hinderer, David and Anna (Martin)
Hislop, Stephen
Hobson, Benjamin
Hoecken, Christian
Hoëvell, Wolter Robert van
Hoffman, C(adwallader) Colden
Hoffmann, L(udwig) F(riedrich) Wilhelm
Hofmeyr, Stefanus
Hogg, John
Holly, James Theodore
Honda Yoichi
Hore, Edward Coode
Howe, Gertrude
Hsi Shengmo (Pastor Hsi)
Huc, Évariste-Régis
Hughes, Thomas Patrick
Hume, Robert Allen
Hume, Robert Wilson
Hung Hsiu-ch'uan (Hong Xiuquan)
Hunt, John
Hunt, Phineas Rice
Ilminskii, Nikolai Ivanovich
Imad ud-Din
Ingalls, Marilla Baker
Inglis, John
Isenberg, Karl Wilhelm
Jackson, Sheldon
Jaeschke, Heinrich August
Jameson, William
Janes, Leroy Lansing
Janssen, Arnold
Jansz, Pieter
Jellesma, J(elle) E(eltjes)
Jensen, Christian
Jessup, Henry Harris
John, Griffith
Johnson, Amelia Dorothea (Baker)
Johnson, James
Johnson, Mammie
Johnson, Samuel
Jones, Charles Colcock, Sr.
Jones, Edward
Jones, John Peter
Jones, John Taylor
Jones, William Henry
Jordan, Johann Baptist (Francis Mary of the Cross)
Josenhans, F(riedrich) Joseph
Juanmartí y Espot, Jacinto
Judd, Gerrit Parmele
Judson, Emily Chubbock
Judson, Sarah (Hall) Boardman
Kafarov, Petr Ivanovich
Kähler, Martin
Kalkar, Christian
Kalley, Robert Reid
Kasatkin, Nikolai (Ivan Dmitriyevich)
Kaundinya, Hermann Anandaraja
Keasberry, Benjamin Peach
Kekela, James
Kerr, John Glasgow
Khama III
Kidder, Daniel Parish
Kidder, Mary Eddy
Kim, Andrew Tae-kon
King, Johannes
Kittel, Ferdinand
Kitto, John
Klein, Frederick Augustus
Klinkert, Hillebrandus Cornelius
Knibb, William
Knoblecher, Ignaz
Kobès, Aloÿs
Koelle, Sigismund Wilhelm
Koyi, William Mtusane
Krapf, Johann Ludwig
Krishna Pillai (Henry Alfred)
Lacombe, Albert
Laurie, Thomas
Laval, Jacques Désiré
Lavigerie, Charles
Lawes, W(illiam) G(eorge)
Lawrence, Edward A(lexander)
Lechler, Paul
Lechler, Rudolf
Lee, Daniel
Lee, Jason
Legge, James
Legge, Mary Isabella (Morison)
Lemue, Prosper
Leupolt, Charles Benjamin
Lewis, Marianne (Gould)
Libermann, François Marie Paul
Lichtenstein, Isaac
Liggins, John
Lindley, Daniel
Livingstone, David
Livingstone, Mary (Moffat)
Livinhac, Auguste Simon Léon
Lockhart, William
Löhe, Johann Konrad Wilhelm
Lohr, Oscar T.
Long, James
Lowe, John
Lowrie, John C(ameron)
Luquet, Jean Félix Onésime
Lyman, David Belden
Lyons, Lorenzo
Mabille, Adolphe
MacDonald, Duff
Machray, Robert
Mackay, Alexander M(urdoch)
Mackay, George Leslie
Mackenzie, Charles Frederick
Mackenzie, John
Mackenzie, John Kenneth
Maclay, Robert Samuel
Makarii Altaiskii (Mikhail Andreevich Nevskii)
Maretu

Marion Brésillac, Melchior Joseph de
Marks, John Ebenezer
Marmoiton, Blaise
Marston, Sarah Hall
Martin, William Alexander Parsons
Marty, Martin
Massaja, Guglielmo
Mateer, Calvin Wilson
Mather, Robert Cotton
Matthews, Daniel and Janet (Johnson)
Matthews, Thomas Trotter
Matthopoulos, Eusebius
Maunsell, Robert
Ma Xiangbo
Mazzuchelli, Samuel
McBeth, Sue L.
McCartee, Divie Bethune
McDonald, Alexander
McDonald, Robert
McDougall, Francis Thomas
McFarland, Samuel Gamble
McFarlane, Samuel
McGilvary, Daniel
McKechnie, Elizabeth
McLaurin, John
Merensky, Alexander
Merrick, James Lyman
Meyer, Lucy Jane (Rider)
Meyer, Theodore J(onas)
Miller, William
Milman, Robert
Milne, Andrew Murray
Mitchell, John Murray
Moegling, Herrmann Friedrich
Moffat, John Smith
Mongiardino (or Monguiardino; Monnggiardino), José
Montgomery, Henry Hutchinson
Moody, D(wight) L(yman)
Moon, Charlotte ("Lottie") Diggs
Moore, Joanna Patterson
Moule, Arthur Evans
Moule, George Evans
Mouly, Joseph Martial
Muir, William
Mullens, Joseph and Hannah (Lacroix)
Müller, George
Murdoch, John
Murray, Andrew, Jr.
Murray, Archibald Wright
Murray, William H.
Nassau, Robert Hamill
Nesbit, Robert
Netsvetov, Iakov Egor
Nevius, John Livingston
New, Charles
Newcomb, Harvey
Newton, John
Nicolayson, John (or Hans Nicolajsen)
Niijima, Jo (or Joseph Hardy Neesima; Neeshima)
Nisbet, Henry
Noble, Robert Turlington
Nommensen, Ingwer Ludwig
North, Frank Mason
Noyes, Harriet Newell
Oehler, Theodor Friedrich
Officer, Morris
Pamla, Charles
Pandosy, Charles
Pao'o
Parker, Peter
Paton, John G(ibson)
Patteson, John Coleridge
Pearse, Joseph
Peck, Edmund James
Perboyre, Jean-Gabriel
Percival, Peter
Perkins, Justin
Petitjean, Bernard-Thaddée
Petitot, Émile
Petri, Ludwig Adolf
Pettitt, George
Pfander, Karl Gottlieb
Pfanner, Franz
Phillips, Jeremiah
Pierson, Arthur Tappan
Planque, Augustin
Plath, Karl Heinrich Christian
Pompallier, (Jean-Baptiste) François
Ponziglione, Paul Mary
Pope, George Uglow
Pratt, George
Pratt, Henry B(arrington)
Price, Roger
Price, William Salter
Priest, James M.
Rabinowitz, Joseph Ben David
Ragland, Thomas Gajetan
Railton, George Scott
Raimondi, Timoleone
Ramseyer, Fritz and Rosa (Bontemps)
Rankin, Melinda
Rasoamanarivo, Victoire
Ratisbonne, Marie-Théodore and Marie-Alphonse
Ravoux, Augustin
Rebmann, Johannes
Reindorf, Carl Christian
Rice, Benjamin
Richard, Timothy
Ridley, William
Riggs, Elias
Riggs, Stephen Return
Riis, Andreas
Roberts, Issachar Jacox
Rolland, Samuel
Ross, John
Rouse, George Henry
Ruatoka
Ruiz, Manuel
Rundle, Robert Terrill
Russell, William Armstrong
Sadrach Surapranata
Safdar, Ali
Safford, Anna Cunningham
Saker, Alfred
Sale, Elizabeth (Geale)
Salvado, Rosendo
Sarasin, Karl
Sargent, Edward
Satthianadhan, William Thomas (Tiruvengadam) and Annal Arokium
Sawabe, Paul (Takuma)
Schereschewsky, Samuel Isaac Joseph
Schneller, Johann Ludwig
Schoenmakers, John
Schön, Jakob Friedrich (James Frederick)
Schrenk, Elias
Schreuder, Hans Paludan Smith
Schurmann (or Shurman), Johannes Adam
Schwartz, Carl August Ferdinand
Scofield, C(yrus) I(ngerson)
Scott, George
Scranton, Mary F.
Sell, Edward
Selwyn, G(eorge) A(ugustus)
Seward, Sarah Cornelia
Sharkey, John Edmund and Ann Amelia (Nailer)
Shattuck, Corinna
Shreve, Elizabeth (Shadd)
Shuck, J(ehu) Lewis and Henrietta (Hall)
Sibree, James
Simonton, Ashbel Green
Simpson, A(lbert) B(enjamin)
Skrefsrud, Lars O(lsen)
Slater, Thomas Ebenezer
Slessor, Mary Mitchell
Smirnov, Evgeny (or Eugene) Konstantinovich (or Eugene Smirnoff)
Smith, Amanda Berry
Smith, Arthur Henderson
Smith, Eli
Smith, George
Smith, William
Snow, Benjamin Galen
Soga, Tiyo
Spalding, Henry Harmon
Stanley, Henry Morton
Steere, Edward
Stern, Henry Aaron
Stevens, Edwin
Stewart, James
Stirling, Waite Hockin
Stock, Eugene
Stronach, John
Strong, Josiah
Stuart, Edward Craig
Sturges, Albert A.
Suh Sang-Yun
Sutton, Amos
Swain, Clara
Talmage, John Van Nest
Ta'unga
Taylor, James Hudson
Taylor, Jenny (Faulding)
Taylor, John Christopher
Taylor, Maria (Dyer)
Taylor, Richard
Taylor, William
Teava
Tellström, Carl Ludwig
Thoburn, Isabella
Thoburn, James Mills
Thomas, John
Thomas, Mary (Davies)
Thomas, Robert Jermain
Thompson, Ralph Wardlaw
Thomson, John Francis

Tile, Nehemiah
Timpany, Americus Vespucius
Tosari, Paulus
Townsend, Henry
Trumbull, David
Trumpp, Ernst
Tsizehena, John
Tucker, Alfred Robert
Tucker, Charlotte Maria
Tucker, Henry Carre
Tucker, John Thomas
Tunggul Wulung, Kjai Ibrahim
Turner, George
Turner, Henry McNeal
Tyler, Josiah
Underhill, Edward Bean
Urios, Saturnino
Vahl, Jens
Van Dyck, Cornelius Van Alan
Vaughan, Herbert
Vénard, Jean Théophane
Verbeck, Guido Herman Fridolin
Verbist, Théophile
Vernier, Frédéric
Vidal, Owen Emeric
Villaverde, Juan
Villota y Urroz, Gerardo
Vinco, Angelo
Vinton, Justus Hatch and Calista (Holman)
Waddell, Hope Masterton
Wakefield, Thomas
Wangemann, Hermann Theodor
Wardlaw, John Smith
Warneck, Gustav
Wenger, John
Westcott, Brooke Foss
Wherry, Elwood Morris
White, Ellen G(ould) (Harmon)
White, Moses Clark
Whiting, John Bradford
Whitman, Marcus and Narcissa (Prentiss)
Whittemore, Emma (Mott)
Widmann, Rosina (Binder)
Wilberforce, Samuel
Wilder, Royal G(ould)
Wilkins, Ann (Green)
Williams, Channing Moore
Williams, S(amuel) Wells
Williams, William
Williams, William Frederic
Williamson, Alexander
Wilson, Edward Francis
Wilson, John and Margaret (Bayne)
Wilson, John Leighton
Wood, Thomas B(ond)
Woolston, Beulah and Sarah H.
Wylie, Alexander
Yate, William
Yates, Matthew Tyson
Young, Samuel Hall
Zahn, Franz Michael
Zakaryas
Zimmermann, Johannes

Born from 1851 to 1900

Abel, Charles William
Abraham, Samuel
Abraham Mar Thoma
Abrams, Minnie F.
Adriani, Nicolaus
Agbebi, Mojola (David Brown Vincent)
Aggrey, James Emman Kwegyir
Ahui, John (or Jonas)
Akinyele, Isaac Babalola
Allamano, Joseph
Allan, George and Mary (Sterling)
Allen, Horace Newton
Allen, Roland
Allier, Raoul
Allshorn, Florence
Ambrazis, Nicholas
Amu, Ephraim Kwaku
Andel, H(uibert) A(ntonie) van
Anderson, William H(arrison)
Andrews, Charles Freer
Anzer, Johann Baptist (von)
Appasamy, Aiyadurai Jesudasen
Appenzeller, Henry Gerhard
Arnot, Frederick Stanley
Arthur, John William
Atiman, Adrian
Atkinson, Maria W. (Rivera)
Aufhauser, Johannes Baptist
Augouard, Prosper Philippe
Avison, Oliver R.
Axenfeld, Karl
Axling, William
Azariah, Vedanayagam Samuel
Bach, T(homas) J(ohn)
Bachmann, (Johann) Traugott
Báez-Camargo, Gonzalo
Bagby, William Buck
Baird, William M.
Bakker, D(irk)
Baldwin, Elizabeth and Jane
Ball, Henry Cleophas
Baller, Frederick William
Barber, Margaret
Barlow, Arthur Ruffelle
Barratt, Thomas Ball
Bartel, Henry Cornelius
Barth, Karl
Barton, James Levi
Bates, M(iner) Searle
Bavinck, Johan Herman
Beach, Harlan Page
Becker, Carl
Becker, Christoph Edmund
Belksma, J(ohannes)
Bell, L(emuel) Nelson
Bender, Carl Jacob
Benedict XV
Benlloch y Vivó, Juan
Bennett, Belle Harris
Bentley, William Holman
Berg, Daniel
Bergmann, Wilhelm (H. F.)
Berkeley, Xavier
Bermyn (or Bermijn), Alphonse
Bernard-Maitre, Henri
Berron, Paul (Émile)
Bickel, Luke Washington
Bill, Samuel Alexander
Bingham, Rowland Victor
Bird, Mary Rebecca Stewart
Birkeli, (Otto) Emil
Birraux, Joseph Marie
Bishop, William Howard
Blackmore, Sophia
Boberg, Folke Anders Adrian
Bodding, Paul Olaf
Boismenu, Alain de
Bondolfi, Pietro
Booth, Ballington and Maud (Charlesworth) Ballington Booth
Booth, Evangeline Cory
Booth, Joseph
Booth-Tucker, Frederick St. George de Lautour and Emma Moss (Booth)
Borden, William Whiting
Bosshardt, R(udolf) Alfred
Bouey, Elizabeth Coles
Braden, Charles Samuel
Braide, Garrick Sokari
Brand, Evelyn (Harris)
Brent, Charles Henry
Brockman, Fletcher Sims
Bromilow, William E.
Brønnum, Niels Høegh
Brooke, Graham Wilmot
Broomhall, Marshall
Brown, Arthur Judson
Brown, Edith Mary
Browne, Laurence Edward
Brubaker, Henry Heisey
Buck, Pearl S(ydenstricker)
Builes, Miguel Angel
Buker, Raymond Bates, Sr.
Burgess, Paul
Burton, John Wear
Burton, William Frederick Padwick
Buxton, Alfred
Buxton, Barclay Fowell
Buxton, B(arclay) Godfrey
Cable, (Alice) Mildred
Caffray, D(aisy) Willia
Cairns, David Smith
Calder, Helen
Calverley, Edwin Elliot
Camphor, Alexander Priestly
Carmichael, Amy Beatrice
Carver, William Owen
Cary, Maude
Cash, William Wilson
Cassels, William Wharton
Chakkarai, V(engal)
Chang, Barnabas
Chao T(zu) C(h'en) (Zhao Zichen)

Charles, Pierre
Chatterton, Percy
Cheek, Landon N(apoleon)
Cheese, John Ethelstan
Chen, Wen-Yuan
Chenchiah, Pandipeddi
Ch'eng Ching-Yi (Cheng Jingyi)
Chesterman, Clement C(lapton)
Chestnut, Eleanor
Chilembwe, John
Ching T'ien-Yin (Jing Dianying)
Chi-Oang
Chitambar, Jashwant Rao
Christie, Dugald
Christoffel, Ernst Jakob
Church, John E. ("Joe")
Clark, Charles Allen
Clark, Henry Martyn
Classe, Léon
Clifford, James
Cochran, Joseph Plumb
Cochrane, Thomas
Coerper, Heinrich Wilhelm
Comber, Thomas James
Conforti, Guido Maria
Considine, John Joseph
Cook, Albert Ruskin
Cook, J. A. B.
Costantini, Celso
Cotta, Anthony
Cowman, Charles Elmer and Lettie (Burd)
Crawford, Daniel
Crawford, Isabelle (Belle)
Cripps, Arthur Shearly
Cushing, Richard James
Dake, Vivian Adelbert
Dalman, Gustav Hermann
Dandoy, Georges
Datta, S(urendra) K(umar)
Daubanton, François Elbertus
Davidson, Benjamin
Davidson, H. Frances
Davis, J(ohn) Merle
Day, David A(lexander)
Deck, (John) Northcote
Delany, Emma Bertha
Dengel, Anna
Dennis, Thomas John
Deyneka, Peter
Dick, Amos Daniel Maurice
Dickson, James and Lillian (Glazier)
Dindinger, Johannes
Dobinson, Henry Hughes
Dodge, Grace Hoadley
Doke, Clement Martyn
Doke, Joseph John
Donaldson, Dwight Martin
Draper, Minnie Tingley
Drebert, Ferdinand
Drexel, Katherine
Drummond, Henry
Du Plessis, Johannes
Dyer, Alf(red) John
Eastman, Elaine (Goodale)
Eastman, George Herbert
Eddy, G(eorge) Sherwood
Eddy, Mary Pierson
Edmiston, Althea (Brown)
Edwins, August W(illiam)
Elia, Pasquale d'
Elliott, Benjamin Franklin
Elmslie, Walter Angus
Evald, Emmy C(hristina) (Carlsson)
Ewing, James C(aruthers) R(hea)
Farquhar, John Nicol
Fernbaugh, Hettie Luzena
Fisch, Rudolf
Fisher, George S.
Fisher, Welthy (Honsinger)
Fitch, George A(shmore)
Fleming, Archibald Lang
Fleming, Daniel Johnson
Fleming, Louise ("Lulu") Cecilia
Flierl, Johann
Florovsky, Georges V(asilievich)
Flynn, John
Ford, Francis X(avier)
Forgács, Gyula
Foucauld, Charles Eugène de
Fox, Charles Elliot
Frame, Alice Seymour (Browne)
Francescon, Luigi
Francis, Mabel
Francke, August Hermann
Franson, Fredrik
Fraser, Alexander Garden
Fraser, Donald
Fraser, James Outram
Fraser, John (Andrew) Mary
Fraser, Kenneth
Freinademetz, Joseph
Freitag, Anton
French, Evangeline ("Eva") and Francesca
Freytag, Walter
Fries, Karl
Friesen, Abraham J.
Frost, Henry W(eston)
Fuller, Jennie (Frow)
Fulton, Thomas Crosby
Fumasoni-Biondi, Pietro
Furman, Charles Truman
Gaebelein, A(rno) C(lemens)
Gairdner, W(illiam) H(enry) Temple
Gale, James Scarth
Galland, Emmanuel Arnold
Galvin, Edward J.
Gamewell, Frank (Francis) Dunlap
Garr, A(lfred) G(oodrich), Sr.
Gaspais, Auguste Ernest
Gebauer, Paul
George, Eliza (Davis)
Geyer, Francis Xavier
Giffen, J(ohn) Kelly
Gilman, Frank Patrick
Glass, Frederick C.
Glover, Archibald Edward
Glover, Robert Hall
Gockel, Mary
Goforth, Jonathan and Rosalind (Bell-Smith)
Goh, Hood Keng
Goldie, John Francis
Goldsack, William
Good, Adolphus Clemens
Goodall, Norman
Gowans, Walter
Goward, William E(dward)
Goyau, Georges
Graham, James Robert III
Graham, John Anderson
Grenfell, Wilfred Thomason
Grentrup, Theodor
Gribble, Ernest Richard
Griswold, Hervey DeWitt
Grossman, Guido
Groves, Charles Pelham
Grubb, Kenneth George
Grubb, Norman P(ercy)
Grubb, W(ilfrid) Barbrooke
Gsell, Francis Xavier
Guébriant, Jean-Baptiste Budes de
Gulliford, Henry
Gunning, Jan Willem
Gurney, Samuel
Gusinde, Martin
Gutmann, Bruno
Gwynne, Llewellyn Henry
Hall, Elizabeth Garland
Hall, Marian (Bottomley)
Hall, R(onald) O(wen)
Hall, Sherwood
Halliwell, Leo B(lair) and Jessie (Rowley)
Hanlon, Henry
Harada Tasuku
Haringke Bai
Harnack, Adolf von
Harris, George Kaufelt
Harris, William Wadé
Harrison, Paul Wilberforce
Hartenstein, Karl
Hastings, Harry
Hawaweeny, Raphael
Haymaker, Edward M.
Heath, George Reinke
Heim, Karl
Heine, Carl
Hemans, James Henry Emmanuel
Henderson, James
Heras, Enrique (or Henry)
Hetherwick, Alexander
Hiebert, N(ikolas) N(ikolai)
Higginbottom, Sam
Hinsley, Arthur
Hitchcock, John William
Hocking, William Ernest
Hodgkin, Henry Theodore
Hoffmann, Johannes Baptist
Hogg, Alfred George
Holland, Henry Tristram
Höltker, Georg
Hooper, Handley Douglas
Hoover, James Matthews
Hoover, Willis Collins
Hoste, Dixon Edward
Howard, Leonora
Howells, George
Hoy, William Edwin
Huegel, Frederick J(ulio)
Hueting, André
Hulbert, Homer Bezaleel
Hulstaert, Gustaf

Hume, Edward H(icks)
Hunnicutt, Benjamin Harris
Hunter, George W.
Hunter, Leslie Stannard
Hurlburt, Charles E.
Hyde, John
Hynd, David
Ibuka Kajinosuke
Iglehart, Charles W(heeler)
Ihmels, Carl
Ingram, James Henry
Inman, Samuel Guy
Isherwood, Annie Cecile
Ivanovskii, Nikolai Ivanovich
Jabavu, Davidson Don T(engo)
Jabavu, John Tengo
Jaffray, Robert Alexander
Janzen, Aaron A.
Jarlin, Stanislas François
Johanns, Pierre
Johanssen, Ernst
John XXIII
Johnson, Thomas Sylvester (Claudius)
Johnson, William Percival
Jones, Clarence W(esley)
Jones, David Picton
Jones, E(li) Stanley
Jones, George Heber
Jones, Lewis Bevan
Jones, Mabel Lossing
Jones, Nancy
Jones, Thomas Jesse
Jordan, Lewis G(arnett)
Judd, Walter H(enry)
Junod, Henri Alexandre
Kafiar, Petrus
Kagawa, Toyohiko
Kalbermatter, Pedro
Kamwana, Elliot Kenan
Kanamori, Tsurin ("Paul")
K'ang Ch'eng (Kang Cheng; or Ida Kahn)
Karrer, Otto
Keith-Falconer, Ion G(rant) N(eville)
Keller, Otto C.
Kellersberger, Eugene R(oland) and Julia Lake (Skinner)
Kelley, Francis Clement
Kempers, John R. and Mabel (van Dyke)
Keough, George D(orkin)
Kepler, Asher Raymond
Kerr, George McGlashan and Isabel (Gunn)
Kevin, Mother (Kearney, Teresa)
Keysser, Christian (J. E.)
Khrisanf (Shchetkovsky)
Kigozi, Blasio
Kijne, I(zaak) (Samuel)
Kilbourne, Ernest Albert
Kilbuck, John Henry
Kilger, Laurenz
Kim, Helen
Kimbangu, Simon
King, Clifford J.
King, Copland
Kinsolving, Lucien Lee
Kitagana, Yohana
Kivebulaya, (Waswa) Apolo
Kiwanuka, Joseph
Knak, Siegfried
Knight-Bruce, George Wyndham Hamilton
Koechlin, Alphons
Koo, T. Z. (Koo Ts-Zung; [Ku Zi-Zong])
Kraemer, Hendrik
Kraus, Johannes
Krawielitzki, Theophil
Kruyt, Albertus Christiaan
Kugler, Anna Sarah
Kulp, H(arold) Stover
Kumm, (Hermann) Karl Wilhelm and Lucy Evangeline (Guinness)
Laiser, (Loirera) Lazarus
Lake, John Graham
Lambie, Thomas A.
Lambuth, Walter Russell
Lanneau, Sophie Stephens
Lapsley, Samuel Norvell
Larsen, Lars Peter
Larson, Reuben E(mmanuel)
Latourette, Kenneth Scott
Laubach, Frank Charles
Launay, Adrien
Laws, Robert
Le Roy, Alexander
Lebbe, Frédéric-Vincent
Leber, Charles Tudor
Ledóchowska, Maria Teresa
Ledochowski, Wladimir
Leenhardt, Maurice
Lefroy, George Alfred
Leite, Serafim
Lemmens, Leonard
Lepsius, Johannes
Le Roux, Pieter Louis
Lewis, Thomas
Lievens, Constant
Lijadu, Emmanuel Moses
Limbrock, Eberhard Michael
Lith, Franciscus van
Liu, Timothy Ting-Fang (Lew, T. T.)
Lloyd, Arthur
Lock, Annie
Lohmann, Ernst
Lohrenz, Henry W.
Lombard, Eva
Long, Retta Jane (Dixon)
Loosdrecht, A(ntoine) A(ris) van de
Lorrain, James Herbert
Lourdel, Siméon
Louw, Andries Adriaan
Lubac, Henri de
Lucas, Bernard
Lucas, William Vincent
Luce, Alice Eveline
Luce, Henry Winters
Lugo, Juan Leon
Luthuli, Albert John Mbumbi
Lyon, D(avid) Willard
Maas, Otto
Mabie, Catherine Louise Roe
MacCallum, (Frank) Lyman
Macdonald, A(nnie) Caroline
Macdonald, Andrew Buchanan
Macdonald, Duncan Black
MacGillivray, Donald
Mackay, John A(lexander)
Mackenzie, Jean Kenyon
Mackichan, Dugald
Mackie, Robert Cuthbert
Maclaren, Albert Alexander
MacNicol, Nicol
MacVicar, Neil
Magee, John G(illespie)
Main, D(avid) Duncan
Makkai, Sándor
Malinki, James M(orrison)
Manikam, Rajah B(ushanam)
Manna, Paolo
Marie de l'Assomption (Marie Le Roy Ladurie)
Massignon, Louis
Mather, Percy Cunningham
Maturana, Margarita Maria
McCandliss, Henry M.
McDowell, Henry Curtis
McGavran, Donald A(nderson)
McLaurin, John Bates
McNairn, A. Stuart
McPherson, Aimee (Kennedy) Semple
Mebius, Frederick
Meeuwsen, Johanna
Meinhof, Carl (Friedrich Michael)
Melrose, Margaret (Rae)
Meyer, Louis
Miller, Harry W(illis)
Miller, Walter Richard Samuel
Miller, William McElwee
Mills, W(ilson) Plumer
Miner, Luella
Mirbt, Carl
Misley, Róza (Puchlin)
Mizeki, Bernard
Moe, Malla
Moffett, Samuel Austin
Mokone, Mangena Maake
Molnár, Mária
Monchanin, Jules (Parama-Arubi-Ananda)
Mondreganes, Pio M. de
Money, Herbert
Moninger, (Mary) Margaret
Monnier, Henri
Monsen, Marie
Montalbán, Francisco Javier
Montgomery, Helen Barrett
Moody, Campbell Naismith
Moomaw, Ira W.
Moorshead, Robert Fletcher
Morris, William Case
Morrison, William McCutchan
Mott, John R(aleigh)
Mulders, Alfonsus Joannes Maria
Mulia, Todung Gelar Sutan Gunung
Murray, William Hoppe
Mutendi, Samuel
Muthiah, Narayana
Myers, Estella Catherine
Nakada Juji
Nanpei, Henry
Nau, Semisi
Neill, Stephen Charles
Nelson, Daniel
Neumann, J(ohan) H(einrich)

Newell, James Edward
Ngizaki, Gapenuo
Nielsen, Alfred Julius
Nikolai (Ziorov)
Nino, Bernardino de
Nsibambi, Simeon
Ohm, Thomas
Oldham, J(oseph) H(ouldsworth)
Oldham, William F(itzjames)
O'Neill, Frederick W. S.
Oppong, (Kwame) Sam(p)son
Orimolade, Moses
Owen, Walter Edwin
Padwick, Constance Evelyn
Parham, Charles Fox
Parrish, Sarah Rebecca
Paton, Francis Hume Lyall
Paton, William
Paul VI
Paul, K(anakarayan) T(iruselvam)
Payne, William Smith
Peabody, Lucy Whitehead (McGill) Waterbury
Peery, R(ufus) B(enton)
Pennell, Theodor Leighton
Penzotti, Francisco G.
Perbal, Albert
Pereira, Eduardo Carlos
Perkin, Noel
Petersen, Anne Marie
Peterson, Paul Bernhard
Pethrus, Lewi
Petrie, Irene Eleanora Verita
Petter, Rodolphe
Pfeiffer, Edward
Phillips, Godfrey Edward
Pickett, J(arrell) Waskom
Pilhofer, Georg
Pilkington, George Lawrence
Pitkin, Horace T(racy)
Pius XI
Pius XII
Platt, W(illiam) J(ames)
Plymire, Victor Guy
Podmaniczky, Pál
Polhill, Cecil H.
Pollard, Samuel
Polman, Gerrit Roelof
Popley, Herbert Arthur
Porter, Lucius Chapin
Pott, Francis Lister Hawks
Poysti, Nikolai
Price, Francis (Frank) Wilson
Price, Thomas Frederick
Prip, Einar
Prokhanov, Ivan Stepanovich
Rabary
Rader, Paul
Rafiringa, Paul
Ramabai Dongre Medhavi
Rawlinson, Frank Joseph
Reed, George C.
Reed, Mary
Reekie, Archibald Brownlee
Reichelt, Karl Ludvig
Reid, Gilbert
Rein-Wuhrmann, Anna
Reischauer, August Karl
Reynolds, Hiram Farnham
Richards, Henry
Richter, Julius
Rijnhart, Susanna (Carson)
Ritchie, John (or Juan)
Robinson, John Alfred
Rodgers, James B(urton)
Roehl, Karl
Rogers, Mary Josephine (Mother Mary Joseph)
Rommerskirchen, Johannes
Rønning, Halvor
Roots, Logan H(erbert)
Rosenkranz, Gerhard
Ross, William
Rossum, Willem van
Rouse, C(lara) Ruth
Rowe, Phoebe
Rycroft, W(illiam) Stanley
Sabatier, Ernst
Sambeek, Jan van
Saminathapillai Gnanapragasar
Samkange, Thompson Douglas
Sandegren, Johannes
Sarasin, Dorothee
Schebesta, Paul
Schellenberg, Katharina L(ohrenz)
Scherer, James A(ugustin) B(rown)
Schiller, Karl Emil
Schlunk, Martin
Schmelzenbach, Harmon Faldean and Lula (Glatzel)
Schmidlin, Joseph
Schmidt, Wilhelm
Schneder, David Bowman
Scholtz, Ödön
Schomerus, Hilko Wiarda
Schreiber, August Wilhelm
Schurhammer, Georg
Schütz, Paul
Schuurman, Barend Martinus
Schwager, Friedrich
Schweitzer, Albert
Scott, David Clement Rufelle
Scott, Peter Cameron
Scranton, William Benton
Scudder, Ida Sophia
Seagrave, Gordon S(tifler)
Seymour, William Joseph
Shanahan, Joseph
Shaw, Archibald
Shedd, William Ambrose
Sheen, Fulton J(ohn)
Shellabear, William Girdlestone
Shembe, Isaiah Mdliwamafa
Shepherd, Robert Henry Wishart
Sheppard, William H. and Lucy (Gantt)
Shih Mei-yu (Shi Meiyu; or Mary Stone)
Sihombing, Justin
Simpson, William Wallace
Small, Ann Hunter
Smith, A(lgernon) C(harles) Stanley
Smith, Edwin Williams
Smith, Henry Light
Smith, Oswald J(effrey)
Smith, Stanley P.
Söderblom, Nathan (Lars Olof Jonathan)
Soga, Mina
Soper, Annie
Soper, Edmund Davison
Spartas, Christopher Reuben
Speer, Robert E(lliott)
Spicer, William A(mbrose)
Spieth, (Andreas) Jakob
Spinner, Wilfri(e)d (Heinrich)
Springer, Helen Emily (Chapman) Rasmussen
Springer, John McKendree
Stahl, Ferdinand A(nthony)
Stauffacher, John William and Florence (Minch)
Staunton, John Armitage, Jr.
Steidel, Florence
Stevenson, Marion Scott
Stockwell, B(owman) Foster
Stosch, Johannes Richard Andreas
Stover, Wilbur B(renner)
Strachan, Harry
Strachan, Susan (Beamish)
Strehlow, Carl Friedrich Theodor
Streicher, Henri
Streit, Karl
Streit, Robert
Stuart, John Leighton
Studd, C(harles) T(homas)
Studd, J(ohn) E(dward) K(ynaston)
Stursberg, (Engelbert) Julius
Subhan, John
Sundar Singh
Swatson, John
Sweetman, James Windrow
Szabó, Aladár
Takle, John
Tarkkanen, Matti
Tatlow, Tissington
Temple, William
Tewksbury, Elwood Gardner
Thauren, Johannes
Theile, Friedrich Otto
Thérèse of Lisieux
Thévenoud, Joanny
Thornton, Douglas M(ontagu)
Thurston, Matilda S. (Calder)
Tikhomirov, Sergii
Tikhon
Tilak, Narayan Vaman
Ting Li-Mei (Ding Limei)
Tisdall, William St. Clair
Titus, Murray T(hurston)
Tollefsen, Gunnerius Olai
Torrance, David Watt
Torrance, Thomas
Torrend, Jules
Toth, Alexis
Townsend, William Cameron
Tragella, Giovanni Battista
Trasher, Lillian Hunt
Troeltsch, Ernst
Trollope, Mark Napier
Trotter, Isabelle Lilias
Tseng Pao Swen (Zeng Baosun)
Tucker, John Taylor
Tule, Mary (Branton)

Turquetil, Arsène
Tyndale-Biscoe, Cecil Earle
Uchimura, Kanzo
Uemura, Masahisa
Underwood, Horace Grant
Upadhyaya, Brahmabandhav
Väth, Alfons
Vautrin, Wilhelmina (Minnie)
Vedder, Hermann Heinrich
Veenstra, Johanna
Vennard, Iva May Durham
Verjus (or Verius), Henri
Victor, Janós
Vieter, Heinrich
Vietor, Johann Karl
Vingren, Adolf Gunnar
Vining, Leslie Gordon
Visser 't Hooft, Willem A(dolf)
Vories, William Merrell (or William Merrell Vories Hitotsuyanagi)
Voronaeff, Ivan Efimovich
Voskamp, Carl Johannes
Voth, Henry R.
Walker, Thomas
Waller, Edward Henry Mansfield
Walsh, James A(nthony)
Walsh, James E(dward)
Wang, Ming-tao (Wang Mingdao)
Wangerin, Theodora S(charffenberg)
Wanless, William J(ames)
Wanyoike wa Kamawe
Warneck, Johannes
Warnshuis, Abbe Livingston
Watson, Minnie (Cumming)
Webster-Smith, Irene
Weerasooriya, Arnolis
Wei, Francis C(ho) M(in)
Weinland, William
Weir, Andrew
Westcott, Foss
Westermann, Diedrich Hermann
Westman, Knut Bernhard
Weston, Frank
Westropp, Clara E.
White, Hugh Vernon
White, John
White, John Campbell
Whitehead, Henry
Wieger, Georges Frédéric Léon
Wilder, Grace E(veline)
Wilder, Robert P(armelee)
Wilkes, Paget
Williams, John Elias
Williamson, H(enry) R(aymond)
Willis, John Jamieson
Willoughby, W(illiam) C(harles)
Wilson, C(harles) E(dward)
Wilson, Eleanor
Wilson, J. Christy, Sr.
Wilson, Samuel Graham
Winans, Roger and Ester (Carson)
Winslow, John ("Jack") C(opley)
Winthuis, Josef
Wiser, William H(endricks) and Charlotte (Viall)
Witte, Johannes
Wood, A(lfred) Harold
Wright, Frank Hall
Wu, Y. T.
Würz, Friedrich
Yamamuro, Gumpei
Yen, Y. C. James
Yergan, Max
Yi Ki-Poong
Ying Lien-chih (Lianzhi)
Yoder, Charles Frances
Young, George Armstrong
Young, T(homas) Cullen
Yui, David Z. T. (Yu Jih-Chang; Yu Rizhang)
Yu Kuo-chen (Yu Guozhen)
Yun, Tchi-Ho
Zaleski, Vladislaw Michal
Zameza, José
Zwemer, Samuel Marinus

Born after 1900

Adejobi, Emmanuel Owoade Adelek
Adeney, David H(oward)
Aina, J. Ade
Akrofi, Clement Anderson
Amalorpavadass, Duraiswami Simon
Anawati, Georges Chehata
Anderson, James Norman Dalrymple
Ao, Longri (Longritangchetba)
Arias, Mortimer
Armstrong, Philip E.
Arrupe, Pedro
Aylward, Gladys
Babalola, Joseph Ayo
Baëta, Christian G(oncalves) K(wami)
Bang Ji Il
Baughman, Burr
Beaver, R(obert) Pierce
Beckmann, Johannes
Benignus, Pierre
Bieder, Werner
Birkeli, Fridtjov (Søiland)
Bliss, Kathleen Mary Amelia (Moore)
Bloch-Hoell, Nils Egede
Bolshakoff, Serge N. (or Sergey Nikolaevich Bolshakov)
Bosch, David J(acobus)
Bowman, Robert H.
Brand, Paul Wilson
Brechter, Heinrich Suso
Breda, Gregorius van
Brennecke, Gerhard
Bright, William ("Bill") Rohl
Broger, John C(hristian)
Broomhall, Anthony James
Browne, Stanley G(eorge)
Bühlmann, Walbert
Bulck, Gaaston (or Vaast) van
Buntain, D(aniel) Mark
Camara, (Dom) Helder Pessoa
Camps, Arnulf
Carlson, Paul
Castro, Emilio
Chakko, Sarah
Chandran, J(oshua) Russell
Chawner, C(harles) Austin
Choi Chan Young
Coe, Shoki (C. H. Hwang)
Congar, Yves
Cook González, Eulalia
Costas, Orlando E(nrique)
Cragg, Albert Kenneth
Dahl, Otto Christian
Dalle Périer, Luis
Dammann, Ernst
Danbolt, Erling Gauslaa
Daniélou, Jean
Dehergne, Joseph
Dehqani-Tafti, H(assan) B(arnaba)
Devanandan, Paul David
Dodge, Ralph E(dward)
Doig, Andrew Beveridge
Dooley, Thomas Anthony
Draskóczy, László
Dunger, George Albert
Du Plessis, David Johannes
Dürr, Johannes
Elliot, Philip James ("Jim")
Elwin, H(arry) Verrier H(olman)
Emmerich, Heinrich
Eto, Silas
Evans, Robert Philip
Fleming, Paul William
Fleming, Peter Sillence
Forman, Charles W(illiam)
Freed, Paul E.
Gensichen, Hans-Werner
Gih, Andrew (Ji Zhiwen)
Glasser, Arthur Frederick
Glazik, Josef
González Carrasco, Justo
Graham, William ("Billy") Franklin
Grant, G(eorge) C(opeland) ("Jack") and Ida Madeline (Russell)
Greene, Elizabeth ("Betty") Everts
Griffiths, Bede (Alan Richard)
Haines, Byron Lee
Han Kyung Jik
Hayward, Victor E. W.
Heinrichs, Maurus
Henry, Antonin-Marcel
Hernández, Venancio
Herron, Walter
Hodges, Melvin Lyle
Hoekendijk, J(ohannes) C(hristiaan) ("Hans")
Hofinger, Johannes
Hogan, J(ames) Philip
Holsten, Walter
Huddleston, Trevor Ernest Urban
Hunt, Bruce Finley
Ibiam, (Francis) Akanu
Itzem, Julio

Jocz, Jakób
John Paul II
Kagame, Alexis
Kamma, F(reerk) (Christiaan)
Kane, J(ames) Herbert
Kats, Wilma
Kivengere, Festo
Kowalsky, Nicolas
Kuder, John
Kuhn, Isobel Miller
Lamburn, Roger George Patrick
Laufer, Carl
Ledyard, Gleason H.
Leeuwen, Arend Th. van
Lehmann, E. Arno
Leimena, Johannes
Lenshina Mulenga, Alice
Le Saux, Henri (Swami Abhishiktananda)
Liddell, Eric Henry
Liggett, Thomas J.
Lindell, Jonathan Luther
Lindsay, Gordon
Little, Paul Eagleson
Litwiller, John T(imothy) N(elson)
Lozada, Jorgelina
Luzbetak, Louis J.
Lyall, Leslie Theodore
Mackenzie, Helen Pearl
Mamora (or Sinamora), Lucius
Maranke, John
Margull, Hans Jochen
Martin, Marie-Louise
Masson, Joseph Armand
Matthews, Z(achariah) K(eodirelang)
McClure, W(illiam) Don(ald)
Men (or Menn), Aleksandr Vladimirovich
Menasce, Pierre Jean de
Merwe, Willem J(acobus) van der
Meyendorff, John
Moffett, Samuel Hugh
Moses, David G.
Motta, Waldomiro
Mukhia, David
Müller, Karl
Myklebust, Olav Guttorm
Nagenda, William
Nankyama, Theodoros
Naudé, C(hristiaan) F(rederick) Beyers
Nee, (Henry) Watchman (Ni To-sheng; Ni Tuosheng)
Neuner, Joseph
Newbigin, J(ames) E(dward) Lesslie
Nida, Eugene Albert
Niles, D(aniel) T(hambyrajah)
Norton, H(ugo) Wilbert
Ofori-Atta, William Eugene Amoako-Atta
Orchard, Ronald Kenneth
Orr, J(ames) Edwin
Oshitelu, Josiah Olunowo
Otto, Josef Albert
Panikkar, Raimundo
Papasarantopoulos, Chrysostom
Parrinder, (Edward) Geoffrey (Simons)
Parrott, J(ohn) Grady
Paton, David Macdonald
Payne, Ernest A(lexander)
Péan, Charles
Peters, George W(ilhelm)
Pierce, Robert (Bob) Willard
Pike, Kenneth Lee
Potter, Philip A(lford)
Probowinoto, Basoeki
Proksch, Georg
Quinn, Edel Mary
Raaflaub, Fritz
Rahner, Karl
Ramsey, Evelyn
Ranson, Charles W(esley)
Romero y Galdamez, Oscar Arnulfo
Rossano, Pietro
Rossel, Jacques
Rowlands, John Francis
Saint, Nathanael (Nate)
Saint, Rachel Bradford
Samartha, S(tanley) J(edidiah)
Sanders, J(ohn) Oswald
Sargent, Douglas Noel
Sawyerr, Harry Alphonso Ebun
Schäfer, Alfons
Schärer, Hans
Schmemann, Alexander
Schütte, Johannes
Scott, Michael
Sedat, William and Elizabeth (Ruslin)
Seumois, André
Shaull, M. Richard
Silva, Lynn A. de
Simatupang, Tahi Bonar
Singh, Bakht
Smith, John Coventry
Smith, Wilfred Cantwell
Soto Fontánez, Santiago
Spae, Joseph J.
Stam, John C. and Elizabeth ("Betty") Alden (Scott)
Stanway, Alfred
Stockwell, Eugene L(ouden)
Stott, John R(obert) W(almsley)
Strachan, R(obert) Kenneth
Strauss, Hermann
Struve, Nikita Alexelevich
Sundkler, Bengt (Gustav Malcolm)
Sung, John Shang-chieh
Tambunan, Albert Mangara
Taylor, Clyde W.
Taylor, John V(ernon)
Taylor, Richard W.
Tempels, Placide
Teresa, Mother (Agnes Gonxha Bojaxhiu)
Thomas, M(adathilparampil) M(ammen)
Ting, K. H. (Ding Guangxun)
Tippett, Alan R.
Todd, Reginald Stephen Garfield
Trenchard, E(rnest) H(arold)
Trobisch, Walter and Ingrid (Hult)
Trotman, Dawson Earle
Tucker, J. W.
Turner, Harold W.
Verkuyl, Johannes
Veronis, Alexander J.
Vicedom, Georg Friedrich
Walls, Andrew F(inlay)
Warren, Max (Alexander Cunningham)
White, Paul Hamilton Hume
Wicki, Josef
Willeke, Bernward H.
Williams, Ralph Darby
Wilson, Robert Orr
Winter, Ralph D(ana)
Woods, C(harles) (Wilfred) Stacey
Yannoulatos, Anastasios
Zapłata, Feliks

BIOGRAPHIES OF WOMEN

Abrams, Minnie F.
Aea, Debora. *See under* Aea, Hezekiah.
Agnew, Eliza
Aldersey, Mary Ann
Allan, Mary (Sterling). *See under* Allan, George.
Allshorn, Florence
Amadeus, Mary
Anderson, Louisa (Peterswald)
Armstrong, Annie Walker
Armstrong, Hannah Maria (Norris)
Atkinson, Maria W. (Rivera)
Aylward, Gladys
Baker, Amelia Dorothea (Kohlhoff)
Baldwin, Elizabeth and Jane
Barber, Margaret
Bennett, Belle Harris
Bigard, Stephanie and Jeanne
Billiart, (Marie Rose) Julie
Bingham, Sybil (Moseley). *See under* Bingham, Hiram.
Bird, Mary Rebecca Stewart
Bishop, Isabella Lucy (Bird)
Blackmore, Sophia
Bliss, Anna Elvira. *See under* Ferguson, Abbie Park.
Bliss, Kathleen Mary Amelia (Moore)
Booth, Maud (Charlesworth) Ballington. *See under* Booth, Ballington.
Booth, Catherine (Mumford)
Booth, Evangeline Cory
Booth-Tucker, Emma Moss (Booth). *See under* Booth-Tucker, Frederick St. George de Lautour.
Bouey, Elizabeth Coles
Bourgeoys, Marguerite
Bridgman, Eliza Jane (Gillette)
Brown, Edith Mary
Buchan, Jane
Buck, Pearl S(ydenstricker)
Butler, Fanny Jane

Butler, Clementina (Rowe). *See under* Butler, William.
Cable, (Alice) Mildred
Cabrini, Frances Xavier
Caffray, D(aisy) Willia
Calder, Helen
Carey, Charlotte Emilia (von Rumohr)
Carmichael, Amy Beatrice
Cary, Maude
Chakko, Sarah
Chappotin de Neuville, Hélène de (Marie de la Passion)
Chavoin, Jeanne-Marie (Mother Saint Joseph)
Chestnut, Eleanor
Child, Abbie B.
Chi-Oang
Clough, Emma (Rauschenbusch). *See under* Clough, John Everett
Colenso, Elizabeth (Fairburn)
Condit, Azubah Caroline
Cooke, Sophia
Cook González, Eulalia
Coombs, Lucinda L.
Cope, Marianne
Coppin, Fanny Marion (Jackson)
Cowman, Lettie (Burd). *See under* Cowman, Charles Elmer.
Crawford, Isabelle (Belle)
Crawford, Martha (Foster). *See under* Crawford, T(arleton) P(erry).
Cushing, Ellen Winsor (Howard) Fairfield
Davidson, H. Frances
Delany, Emma Bertha
Dengel, Anna
Dickson, Lillian. *See under* Dickson, James.
Dodge, Grace Hoadley
Dole, Charlotte (Close) Knapp
Doremus, Sarah Platt (Haines)
Draper, Minnie Tingley
Drexel, Katherine
Duchesne, Rose Philippine
Eastman, Elaine (Goodale)
Eddy, Mary Pierson
Edmiston, Althea (Brown)
Edwards, Mary (Kelley)
Ellis, Mary Mercy (Moor). *See under* Ellis, William.
Elmslie, Margaret (Duncan). *See under* Elmslie, William J.
Ely, Charlotte Elizabeth and Mary Ann Caroline
Evald, Emmy C(hristina) (Carlsson)
Farrington, Sophronia
Feller, Henriette Odin
Ferguson, Abbie Park
Fernbaugh, Hettie Luzena
Fielde, Adele M.
Fisher, Welthy (Honsinger)
Fiske, Fidelia
Fleming, Louise ("Lulu") Cecilia
Forsyth, Christina Moir
Frame, Alice Seymour (Browne)
Francis, Mabel
French, Evangeline ("Eva")
French, Francesca. *See under* French, Evangeline.
Fuller, Jennie (Frow)
George, Eliza (Davis)
Gockel, Mary
Goforth, Rosalind (Bell-Smith). *See under* Goforth, Jonathan.
Gomer, Mary (Green)
Gorham, Sarah E.
Grant, Ida Madeline (Russell). *See under* Grant, G(eorge) C(opeland) ("Jack").
Grant, Judith (Campbell)
Greene, Elizabeth ("Betty") Everts
Grimké, Charlotte (Forten)
Gulick, Alice (Gordon)
Gulick, Louisa Mitchell (Lewis). *See under* Gulick, Luther Halsey.
Gulick, Ann Eliza (Clark). *See under* Gulick, Orramel Hinckley.
Gulick, Fanny Hinckley (Thomas). *See under* Gulick, Peter Johnson.
Hale, Sarah Josepha (Buell)
Hall, Elizabeth Garland
Hall, Marian (Bottomley)
Halliwell, Jessie (Rowley). *See under* Halliwell, Leo B(lair).
Hartmann, Maria
Hill, Mary (Beardsmore)
Hinderer, Anna (Martin). *See under* Hinderer, David.
Howard, Leonora
Howe, Gertrude
Ingalls, Marilla Baker
Isherwood, Annie Cecile
Jaricot, Pauline-Marie
Javouhey, Anne-Marie
Johnson, Amelia Dorothea (Baker)
Johnson, Mammie
Jones, Mabel Lossing
Jones, Nancy
Judson, Ann ("Nancy") (Hasseltine)
Judson, Emily Chubbock
Judson, Sarah (Hall) Boardman
Kaahumanu
Kähler, Christiane (Mues)
K'ang Ch'eng (Kang Cheng; or Ida Kahn)
Kats, Wilma
Keller, Marian (Weller). *See under* Keller, Otto C.
Kellersberger, Julia Lake (Skinner). *See under* Kellersberger, Eugene R(oland).
Kempers, Mabel (van Dyke). *See under* Kempers, John R.
Kerr, Isabel (Gunn). *See under* Kerr, George McGlashan.
Kevin, Mother (Kearney, Teresa)
Kidder, Mary Eddy
Kilham, Hannah (Spurr)
Kim, Helen
Kugler, Anna Sarah
Kuhn, Isobel Miller
Kumm, Lucy Evangeline (Guinness). *See under* Kumm, (Hermann) Karl Wilhelm.
Lanneau, Sophie Stephens
Ledóchowska, Maria Teresa
Legge, Mary Isabella (Morison)
Lenshina Mulenga, Alice
Lewis, Marianne (Gould)
Lindsay, Freda Theresa (Schimpf). *See under* Lindsay, Gordon.
Lioba
Livingstone, Mary (Moffat)
Lock, Annie
Lombard, Eva
Long, Retta Jane (Dixon)
Loveless, Sarah (Farquhar)
Lozada, Jorgelina
Luce, Alice Eveline
Lyon, Mary
Mabie, Catherine Louise Roe
Macdonald, A(nnie) Caroline
Mackenzie, Helen Pearl
Mackenzie, Jean Kenyon
Marie de l'Assomption (Marie Le Roy Ladurie)
Marie de l'Incarnation (Marie Guyart)
Marshman, Hannah (Shepherd)
Marston, Sarah Hall
Martin, Marie-Louise
Matthews, Janet (Johnson). *See under* Matthews, Daniel.
Maturana, Margarita Maria
McBeth, Sue L.
McKechnie, Elizabeth
McPherson, Aimee (Kennedy) Semple
Meeuwsen, Johanna
Melrose, Margaret (Rae)
Meyer, Lucy Jane (Rider)
Milne, Rachel (Cowie)
Miner, Luella
Misley, Róza (Puchlin)
Moe, Malla
Molnár, Mária
Moninger, (Mary) Margaret
Monsen, Marie
Montgomery, Helen Barrett
Moon, Charlotte ("Lottie") Diggs
Moore, Joanna Patterson
Morrison, Mary (Morton)
Mullens, Hannah (Lacroix). *See under* Mullens, Joseph.
Myers, Estella Catherine
Newell, Maria
Newell, Harriett (Atwood). *See under* Newell, Samuel.
Nino
Noyes, Harriet Newell
Padwick, Constance Evelyn
Parrish, Sarah Rebecca
Peabody, Lucy Whitehead (McGill) Waterbury
Perroton, (Marie) Françoise (Marie du Mont Carmel)
Petersen, Anne Marie
Petrie, Irene Eleanora Verita
Quinn, Edel Mary
Ramabai Dongre Medhavi (Pandita Ramabai)
Ramsey, Evelyn
Ramseyer, Rosa (Bontemps). *See under* Ramseyer, Fritz.
Rankin, Melinda
Rasa, Clorinda
Rasalama, Rafaravavy
Rasoamanarivo, Victoire

Reed, Mary
Rein-Wuhrmann, Anna
Rijnhart, Susanna (Carson)
Rogers, Mary Josephine (Mother Mary Joseph)
Rouse, C(lara) Ruth
Rowe, Phoebe
Safford, Anna Cunningham
Saint, Rachel Bradford
Sale, Elizabeth (Geale)
Sarasin, Dorothee
Satthianadhan, Annal Arokium. *See under* Satthianadhan, William Thomas (Tiruvengadam).
Schellenberg, Katharina L(ohrenz)
Schmelzenbach, Lula (Glatzel). *See under* Schmelzenbach, Harmon Faldean.
Scranton, Mary F.
Scudder, Ida Sophia
Sedat, Elizabeth (Ruslin). *See under* Sedat, William.
Seward, Sarah Cornelia
Sharkey, Ann Amelia (Nailer). *See under* Sharkey, John Edmund.
Shattuck, Corinna
Sheppard, Lucy (Gantt). *See under* Sheppard, William H.
Shih Mei-yu (Shi Meiyu; or Mary Stone)
Shreve, Elizabeth (Shadd)
Shuck, Henrietta (Hall). *See under* Shuck, J(ehu) Lewis.
Slessor, Mary Mitchell
Small, Ann Hunter
Smith, Amanda Berry
Smith, Matilda
Soga, Mina
Soper, Annie
Springer, Helen Emily (Chapman) Rasmussen
Stam, Elizabeth ("Betty") Alden (Scott). *See under* Stam, John C.
Stauffacher, Florence (Minch). *See under* Stauffacher, John William.
Steidel, Florence
Stevenson, Marion Scott
Stockton, Betsey
Strachan, Susan (Beamish)
Swain, Clara
Taylor, Jenny (Faulding)
Taylor, Maria (Dyer)
Teresa, Mother (Agnes Gonxha Bojaxhiu)
Thérèse of Lisieux
Thoburn, Isabella
Thomas, Mary (Davies)
Thurston, Lucy (Goodale). *See under* Thurston, Asa.
Thurston, Matilda S. (Calder)
Trasher, Lillian Hunt
Trobisch, Ingrid (Hult). *See under* Trobisch, Walter.
Trotter, Isabelle Lilias
Tseng Pao Swen (Zeng Baosun)
Tucker, Charlotte Maria
Tule, Mary (Branton)
Vautrin, Wilhelmina (Minnie)
Veenstra, Johanna
Vennard, Iva May Durham
Vialar, Émilie de
Vinton, Calista (Holman). *See under* Vinton, Justus Hatch.
Wade, Deborah (Lapham). *See under* Wade, Jonathan.
Watson, Minnie (Cumming)
Webb, Mary
Webster-Smith, Irene
Westropp, Clara E.
White, Charlotte Hazen Atlee
White, Ellen G(ould) (Harmon)
Whitman, Narcissa (Prentiss). *See under* Whitman, Marcus.
Whittemore, Emma (Mott)
Widmann, Rosina (Binder)
Wilder, Grace E(veline)
Wilkins, Ann (Green)
Wilson, Eleanor
Wilson, Margaret (Bayne). *See under* Wilson, John.
Wilson, Mary Ann (Cooke)
Winans, Ester (Carson). *See under* Winans, Roger.
Winslow, Harriet Wadsworth (Lathrop)
Wiser, Charlotte (Viall). *See under* Wiser, William H(endricks).
Woolston, Beulah and Sarah H.
Xu, Candida

BIOGRAPHIES OF MARTYRS

This list includes those who were killed as a consequence of their Christian witness and service.

Acquaviva, Rudolf
Adalbert of Prague
Ali, Wallayat
Auca Five (Ecuador Martyrs)
Azevedo, Ignacio de
Boniface (or Bonifatius)
Brébeuf, Jean de
Britto, João de
Brun(o) of Querfurt
Cáncer de Barbastro, Luis
Capillas, Francisco de
Carlson, Paul
Catalani, Jordan
Chabanel, Noël
Chanel, Pierre Louis
Chapdelaine, Auguste
Chestnut, Eleanor
Chong Yak-Jong, Augustine
Chou Wen-Mo (Zhou Wenmo)
Criminali, Antonio
Daniel, Antoine
Denis (or Denys; Dionysius) of Paris
Dufresse, Jean-Gabriel-Taurin
Elliot, Philip James ("Jim")
Eulogius
Fleming, Peter Sillence
Ford, Francis X(avier)
Garnier, Charles
Gebhre Michael
González de Santa Cruz, Roque
Goupil, René
Hambroeck (Hambroek), Antonius
Hannington, James
Heine, Carl
Henry (or Henrik) of Uppsala
Hermosilla, Jeronimo
Heyling, Peter
Iuvenalii (Iakov Fedorovich Govorukhin)
Jogues, Isaac
Justin Martyr
Kim, Andrew Tae-kon
Kosmas Aitolos (or Cosmas of Aitolia)
Kuksha
La Lande, Jean de
Lalemant, Gabriel
Loosdrecht, A(ntoine) A(ris) van de
Lull, Raymund (or Ramón)
Marmoiton, Blaise
Martines, Francesco
Martínez, Pedro
McClure, W(illiam) Don(ald)
Men (or Menn), Aleksandr Vladimirovich
Mizeki, Bernard
Molnár, Mária
Mongiardino (or Monguiardino; Monnggiardino), José
Montesinos, Antonio de (or Antón Montesino)
Nelson, Daniel
Padilla, Juan de
Patteson, John Coleridge
Perboyre, Jean-Gabriel
Pitkin, Horace T(racy)
Rasalama, Rafaravavy
Richter, Enrique
Romero y Galdamez, Oscar Arnulfo
Ruiz, Manuel
Saint, Nathanael (Nate)
San Vitores, Diego Luis de
Segura, Juan Baptista
Silveira, Gonçalo da
Smith, John
Spinola, Carlo
Stam, John C. and Elizabeth ("Betty") Alden (Scott)
Thomas, Robert Jermain
Trudpert
Tucker, J. W.
Valdivieso, Antonio de
Vénard, Jean Théophane
Whitman, Marcus and Narcissa (Prentiss)
Williams, John
Williams, John Elias
Yi Ki-Poong

BIOGRAPHIES BY REGION OF SERVICE

Africa

North Africa (including Egypt)

Anawati, Georges Chehata
Augustine of Hippo
Borden, William Whiting
Cary, Maude
Cash, William Wilson
Foucauld, Charles Eugène de
Freed, Paul E.
Gairdner, W(illiam) H(enry) Temple
Giffen, J(ohn) Kelly
Heyling, Peter
Hogg, John
Julian
Keough, George D(orkin)
Klein, Frederick Augustus
Knoblecher, Ignaz
Lavigerie, Charles
Longinus
Lull, Raymund (or Ramón)
Massignon, Louis
Nunes Barreto, João
Origen
Padwick, Constance Evelyn
Reed, George C.
Thornton, Douglas M(ontagu)
Trasher, Lillian Hunt
Trotter, Isabelle Lilias
Zwemer, Samuel Marinus

Sub-Saharan Africa and Madagascar

Adejobi, Emmanuel Owoade Adeleke
Affonso (Alphonse)
Agbebi, Mojola (David Brown Vincent)
Aggrey, James Emman Kwegyir
Ahui, John (or Jonas)
Aina, J. Ade
Akinyele, Isaac Babalola
Akrofi, Clement Anderson
Allamano, Joseph
Allshorn, Florence
Amu, Ephraim Kwaku
Anderson, Louisa (Peterswald)
Anderson, William
Anderson, William H(arrison)
Andrianaivoravelona, Josefa
Arbousset, (Jean) Thomas
Archbell, James
Arnot, Frederick Stanley
Arthur, John William
Atiman, Adrian
Auer, John Gottlieb
Augouard, Prosper Philippe
Babalola, Joseph Ayo
Bachmann, (Johann) Traugott
Baëta, Christian G(oncalves) K(wami)
Barlow, Arthur Ruffelle
Barreira, Balthazar (or Baltesar)
Becker, Carl
Bender, Carl Jacob
Benignus, Pierre
Bentley, William Holman
Bernardino, Ignazio da Asti
Berthoud, Paul
Bessieux, Jean Rémi
Beyzym, Jan
Bill, Samuel Alexander
Bingham, Rowland Victor
Birkeli, (Otto) Emil
Birkeli, Fridtjov (Søiland)
Birraux, Joseph Marie
Bisseux, Isaac
Blyden, Edward Wilmot
Bohner, Heinrich
Bonaventura da Sardegna
Booth, Joseph
Borghero, Francesco Saverio
Bosch, David J(acobus)
Bouey, Elizabeth Coles
Bowen, Thomas Jefferson
Boyce, William Binnington
Braide, Garrick Sokari
Brønnum, Niels Høegh
Brooke, Graham Wilmot
Browne, Stanley G(eorge)
Brownlee, John
Brubaker, Henry Heisey
Bühlmann, Walbert
Bulck, Gaaston (or Vaast) van
Buxton, Alfred
Callaway, Henry
Calvert, James
Campbell, John
Camphor, Alexander Priestly
Capitein, Jacobus Elisa Joannes
Cardoso, Mattheus
Carey, Lott
Carlson, Paul
Casalis, Eugène
Cavazzi da Montecuccolo
Chawner, C(harles) Austin
Cheek, Landon N(apoleon)
Cheese, John Ethelstan
Chesterman, Clement C(lapton)
Chilembwe, John
Christaller, Johannes Gottlieb
Church, John E. ("Joe")
Clarke, John
Classe, Léon
Coillard, François
Coker, Daniel
Colenso, John William
Colley, William W.
Comber, Thomas James
Comboni, (Anthony) Daniel
Cook, Albert Ruskin
Coppin, Fanny Marion (Jackson)
Cousins, William E(dward)
Cox, Melville Beveridge
Crawford, Daniel
Creux, Ernest
Cripps, Arthur Shearly
Crowther, Dandeson Coates
Crowther, Samuel Adjai (or Ajayi)
Crummell, Alexander
Dahl, Otto Christian
Dahle, Lars Nilsen
Dammann, Ernst
Danbolt, Erling Gauslaa
Davidson, Andrew
Davidson, H. Frances
Day, David A(lexander)
Day, John
Delany, Emma Bertha
Dennis, Thomas John
Depelchin, Henri
Dobinson, Henry Hughes
Dodge, Ralph E(dward)
Doig, Andrew Beveridge
Doke, Clement Martyn
Doke, Joseph John
Dunger, George Albert
Duparquet, Charles
Du Plessis, Johannes
Dwane, James Matta
Edmiston, Althea (Brown)
Edwards, Mary (Kelley)
Elmslie, Walter Angus
Enbaqom (Abu l-Fath)
Ezana
Farrington, Sophronia
Ferguson, Abbie Park and Bliss, Anna Elvira
Ferguson, Samuel David
Fisch, Rudolf
Flad, Johann Martin
Fleming, Louise ("Lulu") Cecilia
Forsyth, Christina Moir
Fraser, Alexander Garden
Fraser, Donald
Fraser, Kenneth
Freeman, John Joseph
Freeman, Thomas Birch
Frumentius
Gardiner, Allen Francis
Gebauer, Paul
Gebhre Michael
George, David
George, Eliza (Davis)

Gérard, Joseph
Geyer, Francis Xavier
Giffen, J(ohn) Kelly
Gobat, Samuel
Goldie, Hugh
Gollmer, Charles Andrew (Carl Anders)
Gomer, Joseph
Gomer, Mary (Green)
Good, Adolphus Clemens
Gorham, Sarah E.
Govan, William
Gowans, Walter
Grant, G(eorge) C(opeland) ("Jack") and Ida Madeline (Russell)
Gray, Robert
Grenfell, George
Griffiths, David
Groves, Charles Pelham
Grubb, Norman P(ercy)
Gurney, Samuel
Gutmann, Bruno
Gwynne, Llewellyn Henry
Hahn, Carl Hugo
Hall, Elizabeth Garland
Hallbeck, Hans Peter
Hanlon, Henry
Hannington, James
Harris, William Wadé
Hastings, Harry
Hemans, James Henry Emmanuel
Henderson, James
Hepburn, James Davidson
Hetherwick, Alexander
Heyling, Peter
Hinderer, David and Anna (Martin)
Hitchcock, John William
Hodgson, Thomas Laidman
Hoffman, C(adwallader) Colden
Hofmeyr, Stefanus
Hooper, Handley Douglas
Hore, Edward Coode
Horne, Melville
Huddleston, Trevor Ernest Urban
Hulstaert, Gustaf
Hurlburt, Charles E.
Hynd, David
Ibiam, (Francis) Akanu
Isenberg, Karl Wilhelm
Isherwood, Annie Cecile
Jabavu, Davidson Don T(engo)
Jabavu, John Tengo
Jacobis, Justin de
Jameson, William
Janzen, Aaron A.
Johanssen, Ernst
Johns, David
Johnson, James
Johnson, Mammie
Johnson, Samuel
Johnson, Thomas Sylvester (Claudius)
Johnson, William Augustine Bernard
Johnson, William Percival
Jones, David
Jones, David Picton
Jones, Edward
Jones, Nancy
Jones, William Henry
Julian
Junod, Henri Alexandre
Kagame, Alexis
Kähler, Christiane (Mues)
Kamwana, Elliot Kenan
Kats, Wilma
Keller, Otto C.
Kellersberger, Eugene R(oland) and Julia Lake (Skinner)
Kemp, Johannes Theodorus van der
Kevin, Mother (Kearney, Teresa)
Khama III
Kigozi, Blasio
Kilham, Hannah (Spurr)
Kimbangu, Simon
Kircherer, Johannes Jacobus
Kitagana, Yohana
Kivebulaya, (Waswa) Apolo
Kivengere, Festo
Kiwanuka, Joseph
Knight-Bruce, George Wyndham Hamilton
Kobès, Aloÿs
Koelle, Sigismund Wilhelm
Koyi, William Mtusane
Krapf, Johann Ludwig
Kulp, H(arold) Stover
Kumm, (Hermann) Karl Wilhelm and Lucy Evangeline (Guinness)
Laiser, (Loirera) Lazarus
Lake, John Graham
Lambie, Thomas A.
Lamburn, Roger George Patrick
Lapsley, Samuel Norvell
Laval, Jacques Désiré
Laws, Robert
Le Roy, Alexander
Lemue, Prosper
Lenshina Mulenga, Alice
Le Roux, Pieter Louis
Lewis, Thomas
Lijadu, Emmanuel Moses
Lindley, Daniel
Livingstone, David
Livingstone, Mary (Moffat)
Livinhac, Auguste Simon Léon
Longinus
Lourdel, Siméon
Louw, Andries Adriaan
Lucas, William Vincent
Luthuli, Albert John Mbumbi
Mabie, Catherine Louise Roe
Mabille, Adolphe
Macdonald, Andrew Buchanan
MacDonald, Duff
Mackay, Alexander M(urdoch)
Mackenzie, Charles Frederick
Mackenzie, Jean Kenyon
Mackenzie, John
MacVicar, Neil
Malinki, James M(orrison)
Maranke, John
Marion Brésillac, Melchior Joseph de
Martin, Marie-Louise
Massaja, Guglielmo
Matthews, Thomas Trotter
Matthews, Z(achariah) K(eodirelang)
McClure, W(illiam) Don(ald)
McDowell, Henry Curtis
Meeuwsen, Johanna
Mendez, Alphonsus
Merensky, Alexander
Merwe, Willem J(acobus) van der
Miller, Walter Richard Samuel
Mizeki, Bernard
Moe, Malla
Moffat, John Smith
Moffat, Robert
Mokone, Mangena Maake
Monnier, Henri
Morrison, William McCutchan
Moshoeshoe (also Moshesh, and various other spellings)
Murray, Andrew, Jr.
Murray, Andrew, Sr.
Murray, William Hoppe
Mutendi, Samuel
Myers, Estella Catherine
Myklebust, Olav Guttorm
Nacquart, Charles
Nagenda, William
Nankyama, Theodoros
Nassau, Robert Hamill
Naudé, C(hristiaan) F(rederick) Beyers
New, Charles
Norton, H(ugo) Wilbert
Nsibambi, Simeon
Ntsikana
Nyländer, Gustavus Reinhold
Officer, Morris
Ofori-Atta, William Eugene Amoako-Atta
Oppong, (Kwame) Sam(p)son
Orimolade, Moses
Oshitelu, Josiah Olunowo
Oviedo, André de
Owen, Walter Edwin
Paez, (Xaramillo) Pedro (or Pero Paez)
Pamla, Charles
Papasarantopoulos, Chrysostom
Parrinder, (Edward) Geoffrey (Simons)
Péan, Charles
Pearse, Joseph
Perbal, Albert
Pfanner, Franz
Philip, John
Pilkington, George Lawrence
Planque, Augustin
Platt, W(illiam) J(ames)
Price, Roger
Price, William Salter
Priest, James M.
Protten, Christian Jacob
Quaque, Philip
Quinn, Edel Mary
Raaflaub, Fritz
Raban, John
Rabary
Rafiringa, Paul
Ramsey, Evelyn
Ramseyer, Fritz and Rosa (Bontemps)
Rasalama, Rafaravavy
Rasoamanarivo, Victoire
Read, James
Rebmann, Johannes
Reindorf, Carl Christian

Rein-Wuhrmann, Anna
Renner, Melchior
Richards, Henry
Riis, Andreas
Robinson, John Alfred
Roehl, Karl
Rolland, Samuel
Rowlands, John Francis
Saker, Alfred
Sambeek, Jan van
Samkange, Thompson Douglas
Sawyerr, Harry Alphonso Ebun
Schebesta, Paul
Schmelen, Johann Heinrich
Schmelzenbach, Harmon Faldean and Lula (Glatzel)
Schmidt, Georg
Schön, Jakob Friedrich (James Frederick)
Schrenk, Elias
Schreuder, Hans Paludan Smith
Schweitzer, Albert
Scott, David Clement Rufelle
Scott, Michael
Scott, Peter Cameron
Shanahan, Joseph
Shaw, Archibald
Shaw, Barnabas
Shaw, William
Shembe, Isaiah Mdliwamafa
Shepherd, Robert Henry Wishart
Sheppard, William H. and Lucy (Gantt)
Sibree, James
Silveira, Gonçalo da
Slessor, Mary Mitchell
Smith, A(lgernon) C(harles) Stanley
Smith, Edwin Williams
Smith, Matilda
Soga, Mina
Soga, Tiyo
Spartas, Christopher Reuben
Spieth, (Andreas) Jakob
Springer, Helen Emily (Chapman) Rasmussen
Springer, John McKendree
Stanley, Henry Morton
Stanway, Alfred
Stauffacher, John William and Florence (Minch)
Steere, Edward
Steidel, Florence
Stevenson, Marion Scott
Stewart, James
Streicher, Henri
Studd, C(harles) T(homas)
Sundkler, Bengt (Gustav Malcolm)
Swatson, John
Takla-Haymanot
Taylor, John Christopher
Taylor, John V(ernon)
Taylor, William
Tempels, Placide
Thévenoud, Joanny
Thompson, Thomas
Thomson, William Ritchie
Tile, Nehemiah
Todd, Reginald Stephen Garfield
Tollefsen, Gunnerius Olai
Torrend, Jules
Townsend, Henry
Trobisch, Walter and Ingrid (Hult)
Tsizehena, John
Tucker, Alfred Robert
Tucker, John Taylor
Tucker, J. W.
Tule, Mary (Branton)
Turner, Harold W.
Tyler, Josiah
Vedder, Hermann Heinrich
Veenstra, Johanna
Vidal, Owen Emeric
Vieter, Heinrich
Vietor, Johann Karl
Vinco, Angelo
Vining, Leslie Gordon
Vos, Michiel C(hristiaan)
Waddell, Hope Masterton
Wakefield, Thomas
Walls, Andrew F(inlay)
Wanyoike wa Kamawe
Warren, Max (Alexander Cunningham)
Watson, Minnie (Cumming)
Weerasooriya, Arnolis
Westermann, Diedrich Hermann
Weston, Frank
White, John
White, Paul Hamilton Hume
Widmann, Rosina (Binder)
Wilkins, Ann (Green)
Willis, John Jamieson
Willoughby, W(illiam) C(harles)
Wilson, John Leighton
Yergan, Max
Young, T(homas) Cullen
Zakaryas
Zimmermann, Johannes

Asia

Central and Northern Asia (including China, Mongolia, Tibet, Nepal, Afghanistan, Siberia)

Abeel, David
Adeney, David H(oward)
Aldersey, Mary Ann
Aleni, Giulio
Allen, Roland
Allen, Young John
Alopen
Amiot, Jean Joseph Marie
Andrade, Antonio de
Andrew of Perugia
Anzer, Johann Baptist (von)
Ashmore, William
Aylward, Gladys
Baedeker, Friederich Wilhelm
Ball, Dyer
Baller, Frederick William
Bang Ji Il
Barber, Margaret
Barclay, Thomas
Bartel, Henry Cornelius
Bashford, James Whitford
Bates, M(iner) Searle
Bax, Jacques
Beach, Harlan Page
Beaver, R(obert) Pierce
Bell, L(emuel) Nelson
Berkeley, Xavier
Bermyn (or Bermijn), Alphonse
Bernard-Maitre, Henri
Boberg, Folke Anders Adrian
Boone, William Jones, Sr.
Bosshardt, R(udolf) Alfred
Bouvet, Joachim
Bridgman, Elijah Coleman
Bridgman, Eliza Jane (Gillette)
Brockman, Fletcher Sims
Broomhall, Anthony James
Broomhall, Marshall
Buck, Pearl S(ydenstricker)
Buglio, Lodovico
Burns, William Chalmers
Cable, (Alice) Mildred
Cabral, Francisco
Candidius, Georgius
Capillas, Francisco de
Carneiro Leitão, Melchior Miguel
Cassels, William Wharton
Castiglione, Giuseppe
Cattaneo, Lazzaro
Chalmers, John
Chang, Barnabas
Chao T(zu) C(h'en) (Zhao Zichen)
Chapdelaine, Auguste
Chen, Wen-Yuan
Ch'eng Ching-Yi (Cheng Jingyi)
Chestnut, Eleanor
Ching T'ien-Yin (Jing Dianying)
Chi-Oang
Choi Chan Young
Christie, Dugald
Cochrane, Thomas
Coe, Shoki (C. H. Hwang)
Collins, Judson Dwight
Coombs, Lucinda L.
Corbett, Hunter
Costantini, Celso
Cotta, Anthony
Couplet, Philippe
Couvreur, Séraphin
Crawford, T(arleton) P(erry) and Martha (Foster)
Dehergne, Joseph

Desideri, Hippolytus
Dickson, James and Lillian (Glazier)
Dorville, Albert
Douglas, Carstairs
Dubose, Hampden Coit
Dufresse, Jean-Gabriel-Taurin
Edkins, Joseph
Edwins, August W(illiam)
Elia, Pasquale d'
Favier, Pierre-Marie Alphonse
Fernbaugh, Hettie Luzena
Fielde, Adele M.
Figurovskii, Innokentii
Fisher, Welthy (Honsinger)
Fitch, George A(shmore)
Ford, Francis X(avier)
Foucquet, Jean-François
Frame, Alice Seymour (Browne)
Francke, August Hermann
Fraser, James Outram
Fraser, John (Andrew) Mary
Freinademetz, Joseph
French, Evangeline ("Eva") and Francesca
Fridelli, Xaver-Ehrenbert (or Ernbert)
Fulton, Thomas Crosby
Gabet, Joseph
Galvin, Edward J.
Gamewell, Frank (Francis) Dunlap
Gaspais, Auguste Ernest
Gerbillon, Jean-François
Gibson, John Campbell
Gih, Andrew (Ji Zhiwen)
Gilman, Frank Patrick
Gilmour, James
Glasser, Arthur Frederick
Glover, Archibald Edward
Glover, Robert Hall
Glukharev, Makarii (Mikhail Yakovlevich)
Goddard, Josiah
Goes, Bento de
Goforth, Jonathan and Rosalind (Bell-Smith)
Graham, James Robert III
Grüber, Johannes
Guébriant, Jean-Baptiste Budes de
Gulick, Luther Halsey and Louisa Mitchell (Lewis)
Gützlaff, Karl Friedrich August
Hall, R(onald) O(wen)
Hambroeck (Hambroek), Antonius
Happer, A(ndrew) P.
Harris, George Kaufelt
Hayward, Victor E. W.
Heinrichs, Maurus
Hill, David
Hobson, Benjamin
Hodgkin, Henry Theodore
Hofinger, Johannes
Hoste, Dixon Edward
Howard, Leonora
Howe, Gertrude
Hoy, William Edwin
Hsi Shengmo (Pastor Hsi)
Hsu Kuang-ch'i (Xu Guangqi)
Huc, Évariste-Régis
Hume, Edward H(icks)
Hung Hsiu-ch'uan (Hong Xiuquan)
Hunter, George W.
Iakinf (Bichurin)
Iglehart, Charles W(heeler)
Intorcetta, Prospero
Ioasaf (Hotuntsevsky)
Jaffray, Robert Alexander
Jarlin, Stanislas François
Jartoux, Pierre
Jing Jing
John, Griffith
John of Montecorvino
John of Pian di Carpine (or Plano de Carpine)
Judd, Walter H(enry)
Junius (de Jonghe), Robertus
Kafarov, Petr Ivanovich
Kane, J(ames) Herbert
K'ang Ch'eng (Kang Cheng; or Ida Kahn)
Kepler, Asher Raymond
Kerr, John Glasgow
Kilbourne, Ernest Albert
Kim, Andrew Tae-kon
King, Clifford J.
Koo, T. Z. (Koo Ts-Zung; [Ku Zi-Zong])
Kuhn, Isobel Miller
Lambuth, Walter Russell
Lanneau, Sophie Stephens
Latourette, Kenneth Scott
Launay, Adrien
Lebbe, Frédéric-Vincent
Lechler, Rudolf
Le Comte, Louis
Legge, James
Legge, Mary Isabella (Morison)
Leontiev, Maxim
Liang Fa
Li Chih-tsao (Li Zhizao)
Liddell, Eric Henry
Limbrock, Eberhard Michael
Lindell, Jonathan Luther
Liu, Timothy Ting-Fang (Lew, T. T.)
Lockhart, William
Lopez, Gregorio (Lo Wen-Tsao)
Luce, Henry Winters
Lyall, Leslie Theodore
Lyon, D(avid) Willard
MacGillivray, Donald
Mackay, George Leslie
Mackenzie, John Kenneth
Maclay, Robert Samuel
Magee, John G(illespie)
Maigrot, Charles
Mailla, Joseph Marie Anne de Moyriac de
Main, D(avid) Duncan
Makarii Altaiskii (Mikhail Andreevich Nevskii)
Martin, William Alexander Parsons
Martines, Francesco
Martini, Martino
Mateer, Calvin Wilson
Mather, Percy Cunningham
Ma Xiangbo
McCandliss, Henry M.
McCartee, Divie Bethune
McKechnie, Elizabeth
Medhurst, Walter Henry
Melrose, Margaret (Rae)
Mezzabarba, Carlo Ambrogio
Miller, Harry W(illis)
Mills, W(ilson) Plumer
Milne, Rachel (Cowie)
Milne, William
Miner, Luella
Moffett, Samuel Hugh
Moninger, (Mary) Margaret
Monsen, Marie
Montalbán, Francisco Javier
Moody, Campbell Naismith
Moon, Charlotte ("Lottie") Diggs
Morales, Juan Bautista de
Morrison, Mary (Morton)
Morrison, Robert
Moule, Arthur Evans
Moule, George Evans
Mouly, Joseph Martial
Moye (or Moÿe; Moyë), Jean-Martin
Mukhia, David
Murray, William H.
Navarrete, Domingo Fernandez de
Nee, (Henry) Watchman (Ni To-sheng; Ni Tuosheng)
Nelson, Daniel
Nevius, John Livingston
Noyes, Harriet Newell
O'Neill, Frederick W. S.
Pallu, François
Parker, Peter
Paton, David Macdonald
Perboyre, Jean-Gabriel
Pitkin, Horace T(racy)
Plymire, Victor Guy
Polhill, Cecil H.
Pollard, Samuel
Porter, Lucius Chapin
Pott, Francis Lister Hawks
Pottier, François
Poysti, Nikolai
Price, Francis (Frank) Wilson
Raimondi, Timoleone
Rawlinson, Frank Joseph
Régis, Jean-Baptiste
Reichelt, Karl Ludvig
Reid, Gilbert
Ricci, Matteo
Richard, Timothy
Rijnhart, Susanna (Carson)
Roberts, Issachar Jacox
Rocha, João da
Rønning, Halvor
Roots, Logan H(erbert)
Ross, John
Rougemont, François de
Ruggieri, Michele
Russell, William Armstrong
Safford, Anna Cunningham
Sargent, Douglas Noel
Schall von Bell, Johann Adam
Schereschewsky, Samuel Isaac Joseph
Schütte, Johannes
Shih Mei-yu (Shi Meiyu; or Mary Stone)
Shuck, J(ehu) Lewis and Henrietta (Hall)
Simpson, William Wallace
Smith, Arthur Henderson
Smith, George

Smith, Stanley P.
Spae, Joseph J.
Stallybrass, Edward
Stam, John C. and Elizabeth ("Betty") Alden (Scott)
Stevens, Edwin
Stronach, Alexander
Stronach, John
Stuart, John Leighton
Sung, John Shang-chieh
Swan, William
Talmage, John Van Nest
Taylor, James Hudson
Taylor, Jenny (Faulding)
Taylor, Maria (Dyer)
Tewksbury, Elwood Gardner
Thomas, Robert Jermain
Thurston, Matilda S. (Calder)
Ting, K. H. (Ding Guangxun)
Ting Li-Mei (Ding Limei)
Torrance, Thomas
Tournon, Charles Thomas Maillard de
Trigault, Nicolas
Tseng Pao Swen (Zeng Baosun)
Valignano, Alessandro
Vautrin, Wilhelmina (Minnie)
Verbiest, Ferdinand
Verbist, Théophile
Visdelou, Claude
Voskamp, Carl Johannes
Walsh, James E(dward)
Wang, Ming-tao (Wang Mingdao)
Warnshuis, Abbe Livingston
Wei, Francis C(ho) M(in)
Weir, Andrew
Westman, Knut Bernhard
White, Moses Clark
Wieger, Georges Frédéric Léon
William of Rubroek (or Rubruck)
Williams, John Elias
Williams, S(amuel) Wells
Williamson, Alexander
Williamson, H(enry) R(aymond)
Wilson, Robert Orr
Woolston, Beulah and Sarah H.
Wu, Y. T.
Wu Li (Wu Yü-Shan; or Simon à Cunha)
Wylie, Alexander
Xavier, Francis (or Francisco de Jassu y Xavier)
Xu, Candida
Yang T'ing-yün
Yates, Matthew Tyson
Yen, Y. C. James
Ying Lien-chih (Lianzhi)
Young, George Armstrong
Yui, David Z. T. (Yu Jih-Chang; Yu Rizhang)
Yu Kuo-chen (Yu Guozhen)

India, Pakistan, Bangladesh, Sri Lanka

Abdul Masih, Salih
Abraham Malpan
Abraham Mar Thoma
Abrams, Minnie F.
Acquaviva, Rudolf
Adam, William
Agnew, Eliza
Ali, Wallayat
Allen, David Oliver
Amalorpavadass, Duraiswami Simon
Anderson, John
Andrade, Antonio de
Andrews, Charles Freer
Ao, Longri (Longritangchetba)
Appasamy, Aiyadurai Jesudasen
Armstrong, Hannah Maria (Norris)
Armstrong, William Frederick
Azariah, Vedanayagam Samuel
Bailey, Wellesley C(osby)
Baker, Amelia Dorothea (Kohlhoff)
Baldaeus, Philippus
Ballantine, Henry
Banerjea, Krishna Mohan
Barton, John
Barzaeus (or Barzäus; Berze), Gaspar
Becker, Christoph Edmund
Beschi, Constanzo Giuseppe
Bickersteth, Edward
Bliss, Kathleen Mary Amelia (Moore)
Boaz, Thomas
Bodding, Paul Olaf
Bonjean, Ernest Christophe
Bonnand, Clément
Booth-Tucker, Frederick St. George de Lautour and Emma Moss (Booth)
Bowen, George
Bowley, William
Brand, Evelyn (Harris)
Brand, Paul Wilson
Britto, João de
Bronson, Miles
Brown, David
Brown, Edith Mary
Brown, Nathan
Browne, Laurence Edward
Buchanan, Claudius
Buntain, D(aniel) Mark
Butler, Fanny Jane
Butler, William and Clementina (Rowe)
Cabral, Francisco
Caffray, D(aisy) Willia
Caldwell, Robert
Camps, Arnulf
Carey, Charlotte Emilia (von Rumohr)
Carey, Felix
Carey, William
Carmichael, Amy Beatrice
Carneiro Leitão, Melchior Miguel
Castro, Matheus de
Catalani, Jordan
Chakkarai, V(engal)
Chakko, Sarah
Chamberlain, Jacob
Chamberlain, John
Chandran, J(oshua) Russell
Chappotin de Neuville, Hélène de (Marie de la Passion)
Chatterjee, Kali Charan
Chavara, Kuriackos Elias
Chenchiah, Pandipeddi
Chitambar, Jashwant Rao
Clark, Henry Martyn
Clark, Robert
Clough, John Everett and Emma (Rauschenbusch)
Copleston, Reginald Stephen
Corrie, Daniel
Cotton, George Edward Lynch
Criminali, Antonio
Cust, Robert Needham
Dandoy, Georges
Darling, Thomas Young
Datta, S(urendra) K(umar)
Daüble, Carl Gustav
Davidson, Benjamin
Day, Lal Behari
Day, Samuel Stearns
Dengel, Anna
Devanandan, Paul David
Devasahayam, John
Dick, Amos Daniel Maurice
Donaldson, Dwight Martin
Droese, Ernest
Dubois, Jean Antoine
Duff, Alexander
Eddy, G(eorge) Sherwood
Elmslie, William J. and Margaret (Duncan)
Elwin, H(arry) Verrier H(olman)
Ewing, James C(aruthers) R(hea)
Fabricius, Johann Philipp
Farquhar, John Nicol
Fenn, Christopher Cyprian
Forman, Charles W(illiam)
Forman, Charles William
Fox, Henry Watson
Francke, August Hermann
French, Thomas Valpy
Friesen, Abraham J.
Fuller, Jennie (Frow)
Garr, A(lfred) G(oodrich), Sr.
Gensichen, Hans-Werner
Gericke, Christian Wilhelm
Gogerly, Daniel John
Goldsack, William
Gordon, Andrew
Goreh, Nilakantha (Nehemiah)
Graham, John Anderson
Grant, Charles
Graul, Karl
Green, Samuel Fiske
Griffiths, Bede (Alan Richard)
Griswold, Hervey DeWitt
Groves, A(nthony) N(orris)
Gründler, Johann Ernst
Gulliford, Henry
Gundert, Hermann

Haines, Byron Lee
Hall, Gordon
Hall, Marian (Bottomley)
Hanlon, Henry
Hanxleden, Johann Ernst
Hardy, Robert Spence
Hartmann, (Joseph Alois) Anastasius
Hastings, Eurotas Parmelee
Heber, Reginald
Hebich, Samuel
Henriques, Henrique
Heras, Enrique (or Henry)
Heyer, John Christian Frederick
Hiebert, N(ikolas) N(ikolai)
Higginbottom, Sam
Hill, Mary (Beardsmore)
Hislop, Stephen
Hoffmann, Johannes Baptist
Hogg, Alfred George
Holland, Henry Tristram
Howells, George
Hughes, Thomas Patrick
Hume, Robert Allen
Hume, Robert Wilson
Hunt, Phineas Rice
Hyde, John
Imad ud-Din
Isenberg, Karl Wilhelm
Jaeschke, Heinrich August
Johanns, Pierre
John, Christoph Samuel
Johnson, Amelia Dorothea (Baker)
Jones, E(li) Stanley
Jones, John Peter
Jones, Lewis Bevan
Jones, Mabel Lossing
Kaundinya, Hermann Anandaraja
Kerr, George McGlashan and Isabel (Gunn)
Kiernander, John Zacharias
Kittel, Ferdinand
Krishna Pillai (Henry Alfred)
Kugler, Anna Sarah
Lacroix, Alphonse François
Larsen, Lars Peter
Lefroy, George Alfred
Lehmann, E. Arno
Le Saux, Henri (Swami Abhishiktananda)
Leupolt, Charles Benjamin
Lewis, Marianne (Gould)
Lievens, Constant
Lohr, Oscar T.
Lombard, Eva
Long, James
Lorrain, James Herbert
Loveless, Sarah (Farquhar)
Lowe, John
Lowrie, John C(ameron)
Lucas, Bernard
Luce, Alice Eveline
Luquet, Jean Félix Onésime
Mack, John
Mackichan, Dugald
MacNicol, Nicol
Manikam, Rajah B(ushanam)
Marion Brésillac, Melchior Joseph de
Marshman, Hannah (Shepherd)
Marshman, John C(larke)
Marshman, Joshua
Martyn, Henry
Mather, Robert Cotton
McGavran, Donald A(nderson)
McLaurin, John
McLaurin, John Bates
Meneses, Aleixo de
Middleton, Thomas Fanshaw
Miller, William
Milman, Robert
Mitchell, John Murray
Moegling, Herrmann Friedrich
Monchanin, Jules (Parama-Arubi-Ananda)
Moomaw, Ira W.
Moses, David G.
Muir, William
Mullens, Joseph and Hannah (Lacroix)
Murdoch, John
Muthiah, Narayana
Neill, Stephen Charles
Nesbit, Robert
Neuner, Joseph
Newbigin, J(ames) E(dward) Lesslie
Newell, Samuel and Harriett (Atwood)
Newton, John
Niles, D(aniel) T(hambyrajah)
Nobili, Robert de
Noble, Robert Turlington
Nott, Samuel, Jr.
Nunes Barreto, João
Odorico of Pordenone
Pal, Krishna
Pantaenus
Paton, William
Paul, K(anakarayan) T(iruselvam)
Peabody, Lucy Whitehead (McGill) Waterbury
Peet, Joseph
Pennell, Theodor Leighton
Percival, Peter
Petersen, Anne Marie
Petrie, Irene Eleanora Verita
Pettitt, George
Pfander, Karl Gottlieb
Phillips, Godfrey Edward
Phillips, Jeremiah
Pickett, J(arrell) Waskom
Plütschau, Heinrich
Pope, George Uglow
Popley, Herbert Arthur
Prasad (or Prisada), Krishna
Price, William Salter
Proksch, Georg
Ragland, Thomas Gajetan
Ramabai Dongre Medhavi
Ranson, Charles W(esley)
Rasa, Clorinda
Reed, Mary
Reeve, William
Rhenius, Carl Theophilus Ewald
Rice, Benjamin
Rice, Luther
Ringeltaube, Wilhelm Tobias
Robinson, William
Rossel, Jacques
Roth, Heinrich
Rottler, John Peter
Rouse, C(lara) Ruth
Rouse, George Henry
Rowe, Phoebe
Safdar, Ali
Sale, Elizabeth (Geale)
Samartha, S(tanley) J(edidiah)
Saminathapillai Gnanapragasar
Sandegren, Johannes
Sargent, Edward
Satthianadhan, William Thomas (Tiruvengadam) and Annal Arokium
Schellenberg, Katharina L(ohrenz)
Schlunk, Martin
Schnarre, Johannes Christian
Schomerus, Hilko Wiarda
Schultze, Benjamin
Schurhammer, Georg
Schurmann (or Shurman), Johannes Adam
Schwartz, Christian Friedrich
Scudder, Ida Sophia
Scudder, John
Sell, Edward
Seward, Sarah Cornelia
Sharkey, John Edmund and Ann Amelia (Nailer)
Silva, Lynn A. de
Singh, Bakht
Skrefsrud, Lars O(lsen)
Slater, Thomas Ebenezer
Small, Ann Hunter
Smith, Amanda Berry
Smith, George
Smith, Henry Light
Smith, Wilfred Cantwell
Smith, William
Spaulding, Levi
Spicer, William A(mbrose)
Stephens, Thomas
Stosch, Johannes Richard Andreas
Stover, Wilbur B(renner)
Stuart, Edward Craig
Studd, C(harles) T(homas)
Subhan, John
Sundar Singh
Sutton, Amos
Swain, Clara
Sweetman, James Windrow
Takle, John
Taylor, Richard W.
Taylor, William
Teresa, Mother (Agnes Gonxha Bojaxhiu)
Thoburn, Isabella
Thoburn, James Mills
Thomas, John
Thomas, Mary (Davies)
Thomas, M(adathilparampil) M(ammen)
Tilak, Narayan Vaman
Timpany, Americus Vespucius
Tisdall, William St. Clair
Titus, Murray T(hurston)
Trumpp, Ernst
Tucker, Charlotte Maria
Tucker, Henry Carre
Tucker, John Thomas
Tyndale-Biscoe, Cecil Earle

Upadhyaya, Brahmabandhav
Väth, Alfons
Vaz, Joseph
Walker, Thomas
Waller, Edward Henry Mansfield
Walther, Christoph Theodosius
Wanless, William J(ames)
Ward, William
Wardlaw, John Smith
Wenger, John
Westcott, Foss
Wherry, Elwood Morris
Whitehead, Henry
Wilder, Grace E(veline)
Wilder, Robert P(armelee)
Wilder, Royal G(ould)
Wilson, Daniel
Wilson, John and Margaret (Bayne)
Wilson, Mary Ann (Cooke)
Winslow, Harriet Wadsworth (Lathrop)
Winslow, John ("Jack") C(opley)
Winslow, Miron
Wiser, William H(endricks) and Charlotte (Viall)
Wolff, Joseph
Xavier, Francis (or Francisco de Jassu y Xavier)
Xavier, Jerome
Yates, William
Zaleski, Vladislaw Michal
Ziegenbalg, Bartholomäus

Japan and Korea

Allen, Horace Newton
Appenzeller, Henry Gerhard
Arrupe, Pedro
Avison, Oliver R.
Axling, William
Baird, William M.
Bettelheim, Bernard Jean
Bickel, Luke Washington
Bickersteth, Edward
Brown, Nathan
Brown, Samuel Robbins
Buxton, Barclay Fowell
Cabral, Francisco
Carneiro Leitão, Melchior Miguel
Carpenter, Chapin Howard
Céspedes, Gregorio
Chong Yak-Jong, Augustine
Chou Wen-Mo (Zhou Wenmo)
Clark, Charles Allen
Clark, William Smith
Cochran, George
Cowman, Charles Elmer and Lettie (Burd)
Davis, J(ohn) Merle
Francis, Mabel
Fraser, John (Andrew) Mary
Fróis, Luis
Gale, James Scarth
Gnecci-Soldi, Organtino
Goble, Jonathan
Gulick, Luther Halsey and Louisa Mitchell (Lewis)
Hall, Marian (Bottomley)
Hall, Sherwood
Han Kyung Jik
Harada Tasuku
Harris, Merriman Colbert
Heinrichs, Maurus
Honda Yoichi
Hoy, William Edwin
Hulbert, Homer Bezaleel
Hunt, Bruce Finley
Ibuka Kajinosuke
Iglehart, Charles W(heeler)
I Sung-Hun, Peter
Ivanovskii, Nikolai Ivanovich
Janes, Leroy Lansing
Jones, George Heber
Kagawa, Toyohiko
Kanamori, Tsurin ("Paul")
Kasatkin, Nikolai (Ivan Dmitriyevich)
Khrisanf (Shchetkovsky)
Kidder, Mary Eddy
Kilbourne, Ernest Albert
Kim, Helen
Lambuth, Walter Russell
Liggins, John
Lloyd, Arthur
Macdonald, A(nnie) Caroline
Mackenzie, Helen Pearl
Maclay, Robert Samuel
Moffett, Samuel Austin
Moffett, Samuel Hugh
Nakada Juji
Nevius, John Livingston
Niijima, Jo (or Joseph Hardy Neesima; Neeshima)
Peery, R(ufus) B(enton)
Petitjean, Bernard-Thaddée
Pierce, Robert (Bob) Willard
Reischauer, August Karl
Ross, John
Sawabe, Paul (Takuma)
Scherer, James A(ugustin) B(rown)
Schiller, Karl Emil
Schneder, David Bowman
Scranton, Mary F.
Scranton, William Benton
Smith, John Coventry
Spae, Joseph J.
Spinner, Wilfri(e)d (Heinrich)
Spinola, Carlo
Suh Sang-Yun
Takayama Iustus Ukon
Thomas, Robert Jermain
Tikhomirov, Sergii
Trollope, Mark Napier
Uchimura, Kanzo
Uemura, Masahisa
Underwood, Horace Grant
Valignano, Alessandro
Verbeck, Guido Herman Fridolin
Vories, William Merrell (or William Merrell Vories Hitotsuyanagi)
Wangerin, Theodora S(charffenberg)
Webster-Smith, Irene
Wilkes, Paget
Willeke, Bernward H.
Williams, Channing Moore
Wilson, Eleanor
Xavier, Francis (or Francisco de Jassu y Xavier)
Yamamuro Gumpei
Yi Ki-Poong
Yun Tchi-Ho

Southeast Asia

Abel, Charles William
Abraham, Samuel
Adriani, Nicolaus
Alcina (or Alzina), Francisco Ignacio
Aldersey, Mary Ann
Andel, H(uibert) A(ntonie) van
Anthing, F(rederik) L(odewijk)
Armstrong, Hannah Maria (Norris)
Armstrong, Philip E.
Armstrong, William Frederick
Bakker, D(irk)
Baughman, Burr
Bavinck, Johan Herman
Belksma, J(ohannes)
Benavides, Miguel de
Bennett, Cephas
Bergmann, Wilhelm (H. F.)
Bigandet, Paul Ambroise
Blackmore, Sophia
Boardman, George Dana
Boismenu, Alain de
Bowman, Robert H.
Bradley, Dan Beach
Brent, Charles Henry
Bromilow, William E.
Brown, George
Brown, Nathan
Brückner, Gottlob
Buker, Raymond Bates, Sr.
Capillas, Francisco de
Carey, Felix
Carpenter, Chapin Howard
Chatterton, Percy
Chitambar, Jashwant Rao
Choi Chan Young
Condit, Azubah Caroline

Cook, J. A. B.
Cooke, Sophia
Coolen, C(oenraad) L(aurens)
Cushing, Ellen Winsor (Howard) Fairfield
Dean, William
Dirks, Heinrich
Dooley, Thomas Anthony
Dürr, Johannes
Dyer, Samuel
Emde, J(ohannes)
Fielde, Adele M.
Fleming, Paul William
Flierl, Johann
Goddard, Josiah
Goh, Hood Keng
Gsell, Francis Xavier
Haringke Bai
Hermosilla, Jeronimo
Heurnius, Justus
Hoekendijk, J(ohannes) C(hristiaan) ("Hans")
Hoëvell, Wolter Robert van
Hofinger, Johannes
Höltker, Georg
Hoover, James Matthews
Hough, George H.
Hueting, André
Ingalls, Marilla Baker
Jaffray, Robert Alexander
Jansz, Pieter
Jellesma, J(elle) E(eltjes)
Jones, John Taylor
Juanmartí y Espot, Jacinto
Judson, Adoniram
Judson, Ann ("Nancy") (Hasseltine)
Judson, Emily Chubbock
Judson, Sarah (Hall) Boardman
Kafiar, Petrus
Kam, Joseph
Kamma, F(reerk) (Christiaan)
Keasberry, Benjamin Peach
Keysser, Christian (J. E.)
Kijne, I(zaak) (Samuel)
Kincaid, Eugenio
King, Copland
Klinkert, Hillebrandus Cornelius
Ko Tha Byu
Kraemer, Hendrik
Kruyt, Albertus Christiaan
Kuder, John
Lambert de la Motte, Pierre
Laubach, Frank Charles
Laufer, Carl
Lawes, W(illiam) G(eorge)
Leeuwen, Arend Th. van
Leimena, Johannes
Leydecker, Melchior
Limbrock, Eberhard Michael
Lith, Franciscus van
Loosdrecht, A(ntoine) A(ris) van de
Maclaren, Albert Alexander
Mamora (or Sinamora), Lucius
Manna, Paolo
Marks, John Ebenezer
Marston, Sarah Hall
Mason, Francis
McDougall, Francis Thomas
McFarland, Samuel Gamble
McFarlane, Samuel
McGilvary, Daniel
Medhurst, Walter Henry
Molnár, Mária
Mulia, Todung Gelar Sutan Gunung
Murillo Velarde, Pedro
Neumann, J(ohan) H(einrich)
Newell, Maria
Nommensen, Ingwer Ludwig
Ngizaki, Gapenuo
Oldham, William F(itzjames)
Pallu, François
Parrish, Sarah Rebecca
Pigneau de Béhaine, Pierre-Joseph-Georges
Pilhofer, Georg
Plasencia (Portocarrero), Juan de
Price, Jonathan David
Probowinoto, Basoeki
Rada, Martín de
Ramsey, Evelyn
Rhodes, Alexandre de
Riedel, Johann (Gerard) Friedrich
Robinson, William
Rodgers, James B(urton)
Ross, William
Ruatoka
Sadrach Surapranata
Salazar, Domingo de
San Vitores, Diego Luis de
Schäfer, Alfons
Schärer, Hans
Schebesta, Paul
Schuurman, Barend Martinus
Schwarz, Johann Gottlob
Seagrave, Gordon S(tifler)
Shellabear, William Girdlestone
Sihombing, Justin
Simatupang, Tahi Bonar
Staunton, John Armitage, Jr.
Strauss, Hermann
Stronach, John
Tambunan, Albert Mangara
Theile, Friedrich Otto
Tomlin, Jacob
Tosari, Paulus
Tunggul Wulung, Kjai Ibrahim
Urdaneta, Andres de
Urios, Saturnino
Vénard, Jean Théophane
Verjus (or Verius), Henri
Verkuyl, Johannes
Villaverde, Juan
Vinton, Justus Hatch and Calista (Holman)
Wade, Jonathan and Deborah (Lapham)
Warneck, Johannes
White, Charlotte Hazen Atlee
Winthuis, Josef
Yen, Y. C. James

Australia and New Zealand

Boyce, William Binnington
Broughton, William Grant
Brown, Alfred (Nesbit)
Bulmer, John
Colenso, Elizabeth (Fairburn) and William
Doke, Joseph John
Dyer, Alf(red) John
Flynn, John
Gribble, Ernest Richard
Gribble, John Brown
Gsell, Francis Xavier
Hadfield, Octavius
Hagenauer, Friedrich August
Hale, Mathew Blagden
Hamlin, James
Kendall, Thomas
Lock, Annie
Long, Retta Jane (Dixon)
Marsden, Samuel
Matthews, Daniel and Janet (Johnson)
Maunsell, Robert
Montgomery, Henry Hutchinson
Pompallier, (Jean-Baptiste) François
Ridley, William
Salvado, Rosendo
Sanders, J(ohn) Oswald
Selwyn, G(eorge) A(ugustus)
Strehlow, Carl Friedrich Theodor
Stuart, Edward Craig
Taylor, Richard
Threlkeld, Lancelot Edward
Walker, William
Watson, William
Williams, Henry
Williams, William
Yate, William

Europe (including western Europe, the British Isles, Russia, Ukraine, and other countries of eastern Europe)

Adalbert
Adalbert of Bremen
Adalbert of Prague
Aidan
Alexander VI
Allier, Raoul
Amandus of Elnon
Ambrazis, Nicholas
Ambrose
Anastasius
Anderson, Christopher
Anderson, James Norman Dalrymple
Anselm
Ansgar (or Anskar)
Arseny of Konev
Arthington, Robert
Aufhauser, Johannes Baptist
Augustine of Canterbury
Axenfeld, Karl
Barratt, Thomas Ball
Barth, Christian Gottlob
Barth, Karl
Baxter, Richard
Baynes, Alfred Henry
Beckmann, Johannes
Bede
Benedict
Benedict XIV
Benedict XV
Benlloch y Vivó, Juan
Bibliander, Theodor
Bickersteth, Edward
Bieder, Werner
Bigard, Stephanie and Jeanne
Billiart, (Marie Rose) Julie
Birinus
Bliss, Kathleen Mary Amelia (Moore)
Bloch-Hoell, Nils Egede
Blumhardt, Christian Gottlieb
Bodelschwingh, Friedrich von
Bogue, David
Böhnisch, Frederick
Bolshakoff, Serge N. (or Sergey Nikolaevich Bolshakov)
Bondolfi, Pietro
Boniface (or Bonifatius)
Booth, Catherine (Mumford)
Booth, William
Boris
Borrow, George
Bosco, Giovanni (John)
Brancati de Laurea, Lorenzo (Giovanni Francesco)
Bray, Thomas
Brechter, Heinrich Suso
Breda, Gregorius van
Brennecke, Gerhard
Broomhall, Benjamin
Bruillard, Philippe de
Brun(o) of Querfurt
Brunton, Henry
Bucer, Martin
Buchner, Charles
Bühlmann, Walbert
Bulck, Gaaston (or Vaast) van
Buss, Ernst
Buxton, B(arclay) Godfrey
Buxton, Thomas Fowell
Cairns, David Smith
Calhoun, Simeon Howard
Callenberg, Johann Heinrich
Calvin, John
Camps, Arnulf
Capadose, Abraham
Caspari, Carl Paul
Castro, Emilio
Chalmers, Thomas
Chaminade, Guillaume Joseph
Champagnat, Marcellin (Joseph Benôit)
Charles, Pierre
Chaumont, Denis
Chavoin, Jeanne-Marie (Mother Saint Joseph)
Chevalier, Jules
Christlieb, Theodor
Clement VIII
Clement XI
Clement of Ochrid
Coates, Dandeson
Cocceius, Johannes
Coerper, Heinrich Wilhelm
Colin, Jean-Claude Marie
Columba (or Colum Cille)
Columban (or Columbanus)
Comenius (or Komensky), Jan Amos
Conforti, Guido Maria
Congar, Yves
Corbinian
Costa, Isaac da
Coudrin, Pierre Marie Joseph
Cuthbert
Cyril-Constantine
Dalman, Gustav Hermann
Danbolt, Erling Gauslaa
Daniélou, Jean
Daubanton, François Elbertus
David, Christian
Delitzsch, Franz Julius
Denis (or Denys; Dionysius) of Paris
Deyneka, Peter
Dindinger, Johannes
Doll, Ludwig
Dominic
Draskóczy, László
Drummond, Henry
Duncan, John
Dyer, John
Edersheim, Alfred
Egede, Hans (Povelsen)
Ehrenfeuchter, Friedrich
Eligius
Emmerich, Heinrich
Erasmus, Desiderius
Errico, Gaetano Cosma Damiano
Eulogius
Evans, Robert Philip
Ewing, Greville
Fabri, Friedrich
Filofei (Leshchinsky)
Fjellstedt, Peter
Fliedner, Federico
Forbin-Janson, Charles de
Forgács, Gyula
Formosus
Francis of Assisi
Franson, Fredrik
Freitag, Anton
Frey, Joseph Samuel C(ristian) F(rederick)
Freytag, Walter
Fridolin (or Fridold)
Fries, Karl
Fuller, Andrew
Fumasoni-Biondi, Pietro
Gabet, Joseph
Gall (Gallus)
Gensichen, Hans-Werner
Glazik, Josef
Goodall, Norman
Gossner, Johannes Evangelista
Goyau, Georges
Grant, Anthony
Grassman, Andrew
Gregory I (the Great)
Gregory VII (Hildebrand)
Gregory XV
Gregory XVI
Gregory the Illuminator
Grentrup, Theodor
Grignion de Montfort, Louis Marie
Grotius, Hugo (or Huigh de Groot)
Grubb, Kenneth George
Grubb, Norman P(ercy)
Grundemann, Peter Reinhold
Gubernatis, Dominicus de
Gudwal (or Gurwal; Gurvalus)
Guinness, Henry Grattan
Gulick, Alice (Gordon)
Gundert, Hermann
Gunning, Jan Willem
Hahn, Heinrich
Haraldsson, Olav
Harms, Ludwig
Harnack, Adolf von
Hartenstein, Karl
Haven, Jens
Haweis, Thomas
Hawkins, Ernest
Heim, Karl
Henderson, Ebenezer
Henry, Antonin-Marcel
Henry (or Henrik) of Uppsala
Herschell, Ridley Haim
Hill, John Henry
Hinsley, Arthur
Hoffmann, L(udwig) F(riedrich) Wilhelm
Holsten, Walter

Honoratus
Hoornbeeck (or Hoornbeek), Johannes
Hunter, Leslie Stannard
Hut, Hans
Ignatius of Loyola (or Iñigo López de Loyola)
Ihmels, Carl
Ilminskii, Nikolai Ivanovich
Ingoli, Francesco
Innocent IV
Irenaeus of Lyons
Isaiah of Rostov
Isakovich, Nikolai Fedorovich
Jänicke, Johann
Janssen, Arnold
Jaricot, Pauline-Marie
Javouhey, Anne-Marie
Jensen, Christian
Jocz, Jakób
John XXIII
John of Segovia
John Paul II
Jordan, Johann Baptist (Francis Mary of the Cross)
Josenhans, F(riedrich) Joseph
Jowett, William
Justin Martyr
Kähler, Martin
Kalkar, Christian
Kalley, Robert Reid
Karrer, Otto
Kentigern (St. Mungo)
Kilger, Laurenz
Kilian (Kyllena)
King, Jonas
Kircher, Athanasius
Kleinschmidt, Johann Conrad
Knak, Siegfried
Koechlin, Alphons
Kosmas Aitolos (or Cosmas of Aitolia)
Kowalsky, Nicolas
Kraus, Johannes
Krawielitzki, Theophil
Kuksha
La Salle, Jean-Baptiste de
Lavigerie, Charles
Leander of Seville
Lebuin
Lechler, Paul
Ledóchowska, Maria Teresa
Ledochowski, Wladimir
Leibniz, Gottfried Wilhelm von
Lemmens, Leonard
Lenkeevich, Nikolai (Nikodim)
Libermann, François Marie Paul
Lichtenstein, Isaac
Lieberkühn, Samuel
Lioba
Löhe, Johann Konrad Wilhelm
Lohmann, Ernst
Lourenço da Silva de Mendonça
Love, John
Lubac, Henri de
Ludger (or Luidger; Liudger)
Luther, Martin
Lütkens, Franz Julius
Maas, Otto
Mackie, Robert Cuthbert
Makkai, Sándor
Margull, Hans Jochen
Marie de l'Assomption (Marie Le Roy Ladurie)
Martin of Tours
Masson, Joseph Armand
Matthopoulos, Eusebius
Maturana, Margarita Maria
Mazenod, Charles-Joseph-Eugène de
McCaul, Alexander
Meinhof, Carl (Friedrich Michael)
Mel, Conrad
Men (or Menn), Aleksandr Vladimirovich
Menasce, Pierre Jean de
Mesrob (or Mashtots)
Methodius
Meyer, Theodore J(onas)
Millar, Robert
Mirbt, Carl
Misley, Róza (Puchlin)
Mondreganes, Pio M. de
Moorshead, Robert Fletcher
Moreau, Basile Antoine
Morris, John Webster
Mulders, Alfonsus Joannes Maria
Müller, George
Müller, Karl
Nicholas
Nicholas IV
Nicholas of Cusa
Nicolai, Philipp
Nikon the Metanoeite
Ninian (or Nynias; Niniavus)
Nino
Nitschmann, David
Oehler, Theodor Friedrich
Ohm, Thomas
Oldham, J(oseph) H(ouldsworth)
Orchard, Ronald Kenneth
Otto, Josef Albert
Otto (or Otho) of Bamberg
Palladius
Pallotti, Vincent
Paracelsus
Parrinder, (Edward) Geoffrey (Simons)
Paterson, John
Patrick
Paul VI
Paulinus of York
Paul of the Cross (Paolo Francesco Danei)
Payne, Ernest A(lexander)
Pedro de la Madre de Dios
Peters, George W(ilhelm)
Peterson, Paul Bernhard
Peter the Venerable de Montboissier (Pierre Maurice)
Pethrus, Lewi
Petri, Ludwig Adolf
Philaret (Drozdov)
Pinkerton, Robert
Pirminius (Pirmin)
Pius XI
Pius XII
Plath, Karl Heinrich Christian
Podmaniczky, Pál
Potter, Philip A(lford)
Poullart-des-Places, Claude-François
Poysti, Nikolai
Pratt, Josiah
Prokhanov, Ivan Stepanovich
Rabinowitz, Joseph Ben David
Rahner, Karl
Railton, George Scott
Ramazotti, Angelo Francesco
Reginhar (or Renharius; Regenharius)
Remigius of Reims
Richter, Julius
Riedemann, Peter
Rommerskirchen, Johannes
Rønne, Bone Falch
Roothaan, Johann Philipp
Rosenkranz, Gerhard
Rossano, Pietro
Rossum, Willem van
Rouse, C(lara) Ruth
Rovenius, Philippus
Ryland, John
Sahak
Santori, Giulio Antonio
Sarasin, Dorothee
Sarasin, Karl
Saravia, Adrianus (or Adriaan de; Adriaan van)
Sava
Scherer, Heinrich
Schleiermacher, Friedrich Daniel Ernst
Schmid, Hans
Schmidlin, Joseph
Schmidt, Wilhelm
Scholtz, Ödön
Schreiber, August Wilhelm
Schrenk, Elias
Schultz, Stephan
Schütz, Paul
Schwager, Friedrich
Schwartz, Carl August Ferdinand
Scott, George
Sergii of Valaam (or Valamo)
Seumois, André
Severinus
Sibbes, Richard
Sigfrid
Simeon, Charles
Söderblom, Nathan (Lars Olof Jonathan)
Spener, Philipp Jakob
Spittler, Christian Friedrich
Stach, Matthew
Steinkopf, Karl Friedrich Adolf
Stephen
Stephen of Perm
Stern, Henry Aaron
Stock, Eugene
Stockfleth, Nils Joachim Vibe
Stott, John R(obert) W(almsley)
Streit, Karl
Streit, Robert
Struve, Nikita Alexelevich
Studd, J(ohn) E(dward) K(ynaston)
Sturmius
Stursberg, (Engelbert) Julius
Suidbert (or Suitbert; Swibert)
Swan, William
Szabó, Aladár

Tarkkanen, Matti
Tatlow, Tissington
Tellström, Carl Ludwig
Temple, William
Thauren, Johannes
Thérèse of Lisieux
Thomas Aquinas
Thomas of Jesus
Thompson, Ralph Wardlaw
Tragella, Giovanni Battista
Trenchard, E(rnest) H(arold)
Trobe, Christian Ignatius la
Troeltsch, Ernst
Trudpert
Tryphon of Pechenga
Ulfila (or Ulphilas; Wulfila)
Underhill, Edward Bean
Urban VIII
Urlsperger, Johann August
Vahl, Jens
Valentinus
Vaughan, Herbert
Venn, Henry
Venn, John
Vialar, Émilie de
Vicedom, Georg Friedrich
Vicelin
Victor, Janós
Villota y Urroz, Gerardo
Vincent de Paul
Virgil of Salzburg
Visser 't Hooft, Willem A(dolf)
Vitoria, Francisco de
Vives y Marjá, Juan Bautista
Vladimir of Kiev
Voetius, Gisbertus (or Gijsbert Voet)
Voronaeff, Ivan Efimovich
Wagenseil, Johann Christoph
Walaeus, Antonius (or Anton de Wale)
Waldo (or Valdez), Peter
Walls, Andrew F(inlay)
Walpot, Peter
Wangemann, Hermann Theodor
Warneck, Gustav
Warren, Max (Alexander Cunningham)
Way, Lewis
Welz, Justinian von
Wesley, Charles
Wesley, John
Westcott, Brooke Foss
Westen, Thomas von
White, Andrew
Whitefield, George
Whiting, John Bradford
Wicki, Josef
Wilberforce, Samuel
Wilberforce, William
Wilfrid
Willehad
Willeke, Bernward H.
Willibald
Willibrord (or Willibrordus), Clemens
Wilson, C(harles) E(dward)
Wimmer, Gottlieb August
Witte, Johannes
Wolfgang
Würz, Friedrich
Xenos, Ioannes
Yannoulatos, Anastasios
Zahn, Franz Michael
Zameza, José
Zapłata, Feliks
Zaremba, Felician von
Zinzendorf, Nikolaus Ludwig von
Zwingli, Huldrych (or Ulrich)

Middle East (including western Asia)

Addai
Alexander, Michael Solomon
Baradaeus, Jacob (or Bar'adai; Barada'i)
Barsauma (or Barsumas)
Barton, James Levi
Berron, Paul (Émile)
Bird, Mary Rebecca Stewart
Bliss, Daniel
Bliss, Edwin Munsell
Bliss, Isaac Grout
Calhoun, Simeon Howard
Calverley, Edwin Elliot
Cheese, John Ethelstan
Christoffel, Ernst Jakob
Chrysostom, John
Cochran, Joseph Gallup
Cochran, Joseph Plumb
Constantine the Great
Cragg, Albert Kenneth
Dehqani-Tafti, H(assan) B(arnaba)
Dennis, James Shepard
Donaldson, Dwight Martin
Dwight, Harrison Gray Otis
Eddy, Mary Pierson
Ely, Charlotte Elizabeth and Mary Ann Caroline
Eusebius of Caesarea
Fisk, Pliny
Fiske, Fidelia
Foucauld, Charles Eugène de
Glen, William
Gobat, Samuel
Goodell, William
Grant, Asahel
Grant, Judith (Campbell)
Gregory Thaumaturgus
Groves, A(nthony) N(orris)
Hamlin, Cyrus
Harrison, Paul Wilberforce
Jessup, Henry Harris
John of Montecorvino
Keith-Falconer, Ion G(rant) N(eville)
Kitto, John
Klein, Frederick Augustus
Lambie, Thomas A.
Laurie, Thomas
Lepsius, Johannes
MacCallum, (Frank) Lyman
Macgowan, Edward
Merrick, James Lyman
Miller, William McElwee
Nicolayson, John (or Hans Nicolajsen)
Nielsen, Alfred Julius
Odorico of Pordenone
Parsons, Levi
Pennini, Ricoldo (da Monte Cruce)
Perkins, Justin
Photius
Prip, Einar
Ratisbonne, Marie-Théodore and Marie-Alphonse
Riggs, Elias
Ruiz, Manuel
Sahak
Schauffler, William Gottlieb
Schneller, Johann Ludwig
Shattuck, Corinna
Shedd, William Ambrose
Smith, Eli
Stuart, Edward Craig
Torrance, David Watt
Van Dyck, Cornelius Van Alan
William of Tripoli
Williams, William Frederic
Wilson, J. Christy, Sr.
Wilson, Samuel Graham
Wolff, Joseph
Zwemer, Samuel Marinus

North America

Caribbean Region

Anderson, Louisa (Peterswald)
Anderson, William
Betanzos, Domingo de
Bird, Mark Baker
Braun, Peter
Breton, Raymond (Guillaume)
Buyl (or Boyl; Boil), Bernal
Claret, Anthony Mary
Clarke, John
Coke, Thomas
Cook González, Eulalia
Córdoba, Pedro de
Evans, R(obert) M(ilton)
Gilbert, Nathaniel
Goldie, Hugh
Hall, Elizabeth Garland
Holly, James Theodore
Jaca, Francisco José de
Knibb, William
Liele, George
Lugo, Juan Leon
Makemie, Francis
Manso, Alonso
Martin, Frederick
Moirans, Epifanio de
Navarrete, Domingo Fernandez de
Phillippo, J(ames) M(ursell)
Potter, Philip A(lford)
Turton, William
Waddell, Hope Masterton

Central America

Betanzos, Domingo de
Burgess, Paul
Cáncer de Barbastro, Luis
Cook González, Eulalia
Costas, Orlando E(nrique)
Crowe, Frederick
Furman, Charles Truman
González Carrasco, Justo
Grossman, Guido
Haymaker, Edward M.
Heath, George Reinke
Hodges, Melvin Lyle
Ingram, James Henry
Itzem, Julio
Las Casas, Bartolomé de
Margil, Antonio
Mebius, Frederick
Motolinía (Toribio de Benavente)
Pedraza, Cristóbal de
Romero y Galdamez, Oscar Arnulfo
Sedat, William and Elizabeth (Ruslin)
Strachan, Harry
Strachan, R(obert) Kenneth
Strachan, Susan (Beamish)
Townsend, William Cameron
Valdivieso, Antonio de
Williams, Ralph Darby
Winter, Ralph D(ana)

Mexico

Atkinson, Maria W. (Rivera)
Báez-Camargo, Gonzalo
Betanzos, Domingo de
Butler, William and Clementina (Rowe)
Cobo, Bernabé
Elliott, Benjamin Franklin
Focher, Juan
Garcés, Julián
Graybill, Anthony Thomas
Greene, Elizabeth ("Betty") Everts
Hernández, Venancio
Huegel, Frederick J(ulio)
Ingram, James Henry
Inman, Samuel Guy
Kempers, John R. and Mabel (van Dyke)
Kino, Eusebio Francisco
Las Casas, Bartolomé de
Llinás, Jesús Maria Antonio
Mackay, John A(lexander)
Maldonado de Buendía, Alonso
Margil, Antonio
Mendieta, Jerónimo
Montesinos, Antonio de (or Antón Montesino)
Motolinía (Toribio de Benavente)
Moya de Contreras, Pedro
Padilla, Juan de
Palafox y Mendoza, Juan de
Payeras, Mariano
Peter of Ghent
Pike, Kenneth Lee
Pratt, Henry B(arrington)
Quiroga, Vasco de
Rankin, Melinda
Sahagún, Bernardino de
Salazar, Domingo de
Serra, Junípero (Miguel Jose)
Testera (or Tastera), Jacobo de
Thomson, James (or Diego)
Townsend, William Cameron
Urdaneta, Andres de
Valadés, Diego
Valencia, Martín de
Vera Cruz, Alonso de la
Zumárraga, Juan de

United States and Canada

Allouez, Claude Jean
Altham, John
Amadeus, Mary
Anderson, David
Anderson, Rufus
André, Louis
Arias, Mortimer
Armstrong, Annie Walker
Asbury, Francis
Bacon, Sumner
Ball, Henry Cleophas
Baraga, (Irenaeus) Frederic
Beach, Harlan Page
Belcourt, Georges Antoine
Bennett, Belle Harris
Biard, Pierre
Bishop, William Howard
Black, William
Blackstone, William Eugene
Blanchet, Francis Norbert
Bliss, Edwin Munsell
Böhler, Peter
Bolotov, Ioasaf
Bompas, William Carpenter
Booth, Ballington and Maud (Charlesworth) Ballington Booth
Booth, Catherine (Mumford)
Booth, Evangeline Cory
Booth-Tucker, Frederick St. George de Lautour and Emma Moss (Booth)
Boudinot, Elias (Galagina)
Bourgeoys, Marguerite
Brainerd, David
Brainerd, John
Brébeuf, Jean de
Breck, James Lloyd

Bright, William ("Bill") Rohl
Broger, John C(hristian)
Brown, Arthur Judson
Buchan, Jane
Butler, Elizur
Byington, Cyrus
Cabrini, Frances Xavier
Caffray, D(aisy) Willia
Calder, Helen
Cáncer de Barbastro, Luis
Carroll, John
Carver, William Owen
Case, Isaac
Case, William
Chabanel, Noël
Child, Abbie B.
Coke, Thomas
Considine, John Joseph
Coughlan, Laurence
Crawford, Isabelle (Belle)
Crosby, Aaron
Crosby, Thomas
Cushing, Ellen Winsor (Howard) Fairfield
Cushing, Richard James
Dablon, Claude
Dake, Vivian Adelbert
Daniel, Antoine
Day, George Edward
De Smet, Pierre-Jean
Dober, Johann Leonhard
Dodge, Grace Hoadley
Doremus, Sarah Platt (Haines)
Draper, Minnie Tingley
Drebert, Ferdinand
Drexel, Katherine
Druillettes, Gabriel
Duchesne, Rose Philippine
Duncan, William
Du Plessis, David Johannes
Eastman, Elaine (Goodale)
Edwards, Jonathan
Eliot, John
Ellinwood, Frank F(ield)
Elliott, Walter
England, John
Evald, Emmy C(hristina) (Carlsson)
Evans, James
Evarts, Jeremiah
Feild, Edward
Feller, Henriette Odin
Fisher, George S.
Fleming, Archibald Lang
Fleming, Daniel Johnson
Fleming, John
Fleming, Paul William
Florovsky, Georges V(asilievich)
Forbin-Janson, Charles de
Franson, Fredrik
Frost, Henry W(eston)
Gaebelein, A(rno) C(lemens)
Garnier, Charles
Geddie, John
Gilmour, John
Gockel, Mary
Gordon, A(doniram) J(udson)
Goupil, René
Graham, William ("Billy") Franklin
Grandin, Vital Justin
Grenfell, Wilfred Thomason
Grimké, Charlotte (Forten)
Guerrant, Edward Owings
Hale, Sarah Josepha (Buell)
Haven, Jens
Hawaweeny, Raphael
Hawley, Gideon
Hecker, Isaac Thomas
Heckewelder, John Gottlieb Ernestus
Herman of Alaska
Hiebert, N(ikolas) N(ikolai)
Hocking, William Ernest
Hoecken, Christian
Hogan, J(ames) Philip
Holmes, Elkanah
Hopkins, Samuel
Horton, Azariah
Innocent Veniaminov (Ivan Popov-Veniaminov)
Iuvenalii (Iakov Fedorovich Govorukhin)
Jackson, Sheldon
Jeune, Paul le
Jocz, Jakób
Jogues, Isaac
Jones, Charles Colcock, Sr.
Jones, Evan and John Buttrick
Jones, John
Jones, Thomas Jesse
Jordan, Lewis G(arnett)
Kelley, Francis Clement
Kilbuck, John Henry
King, Clifford J.
Kingsbury, Cyrus
Kino, Eusebio Francisco
Kirkland, Samuel
Lacombe, Albert
Lafitau, Joseph-François
La Lande, Jean de
Lalemant, Gabriel
Lalemant, Jérôme
Latourette, Kenneth Scott
Lawrence, Edward A(lexander)
Leber, Charles Tudor
Ledyard, Gleason H.
Lee, Daniel
Lee, Jason
Liggett, Thomas J.
Lindsay, Gordon
Little, Paul Eagleson
Lohrenz, Henry W.
López de Mendoza Grajales, Francisco
Luce, Alice Eveline
Luzbetak, Louis
Lyon, Mary
Macdonald, Duncan Black
Machray, Robert
Mack, (Johann) Martin
Mackay, John A(lexander)
Makemie, Francis
Margil, Antonio
Marie de l'Incarnation (Marie Guyart)
Marquette, Jacques
Martínez, Pedro
Marty, Martin
Massanet, Damian
Mather, Cotton
Mayhew, Experience
Mayhew, Thomas, Jr.
Mazzuchelli, Samuel
McBeth, Sue L.
McCoy, Isaac
McDonald, Alexander
McDonald, Robert
McDowell, Robert James
McGavran, Donald A(nderson)
McPherson, Aimee (Kennedy) Semple
Megapolensis, Johannes
Ménard, René
Meyendorff, John
Meyer, Louis
Meyer, Lucy Jane (Rider)
Mills, Samuel John, Jr.
Montgomery, Helen Barrett
Moody, D(wight) L(yman)
Moore, Joanna Patterson
Morse, Jedediah
Mott, John R(aleigh)
Moulton, Ebenezer
Nerinckx, Charles
Netsvetov, Iakov Egor
Nettleton, Asahel
Newcomb, Harvey
Nida, Eugene Albert
Nikolai (Ziorov)
Nitschmann, David
North, Frank Mason
Occom, Samson
O'Donel, James Louis
Oldendorp, Christian Georg Andreas
Orr, J(ames) Edwin
Padilla, Juan de
Pandosy, Charles
Panikkar, Raimundo
Parham, Charles Fox
Parrott, J(ohn) Grady
Payeras, Mariano
Peabody, Lucy Whitehead (McGill) Waterbury
Peck, Edmund James
Peck, John Mason
Peters, George W(ilhelm)
Petitot, Émile
Petter, Rodolphe
Pfeiffer, Edward
Pierson, Arthur Tappan
Polman, Gerrit Roelof
Ponziglione, Paul Mary
Price, Thomas Frederick
Rader, Paul
Railton, George Scott
Rankin, Melinda

Ranson, Charles W(esley)
Rauch, Christian Henry
Ravoux, Augustin
Reynolds, Hiram Farnham
Riggs, Stephen Return
Rogers, Mary Josephine (Mother Mary Joseph)
Rønning, Halvor
Rundle, Robert Terrill
Salazar, Domingo de
Schmemann, Alexander
Schoenmakers, John
Scofield, C(yrus) I(ngerson)
Segura, Juan Baptista
Sergeant, John
Serra, Junípero (Miguel Jose)
Seymour, William Joseph
Sheen, Fulton J(ohn)
Shelikhov, Grigorii Ivanovich
Shreve, Elizabeth (Shadd)
Simpson, A(lbert) B(enjamin)
Smirnov, Evgeny (or Eugene) Konstantinovich (or Eugene Smirnoff)
Smith, Amanda Berry
Smith, Oswald J(effrey)
Soper, Edmund Davison
Soto Fontánez, Santiago
Spalding, Henry Harmon
Spangenberg, August Gottlieb
Speer, Robert E(lliott)
Stach, Matthew
Stevens, Jedediah Dwight
Stewart, John
Stockton, Betsey
Stockwell, Eugene L(ouden)
Strong, Josiah
Taylor, Clyde W.
Taylor, William
Teague, Colin (or Collin Teage)
Thompson, Thomas
Thomson, James (or Diego)
Tikhon
Toth, Alexis
Trotman, Dawson Earle
Turner, Henry McNeal
Turquetil, Arsène
Vennard, Iva May Durham
Veronis, Alexander J.
Voth, Henry R.
Walsh, James A(nthony)
Webb, Mary
Weinland, William
Welch, James Ely
Westropp, Clara E.
Wheelock, Eleazar
White, Andrew
White, Ellen G(ould) (Harmon)
White, Hugh Vernon
White, John Campbell
Whitefield, George
Whitman, Marcus and Narcissa (Prentiss)
Whittemore, Emma (Mott)
Williams, Roger
Williamson, Thomas Smith
Wilson, Edward Francis
Winter, Ralph D(ana)
Woods, C(harles) (Wilfred) Stacey
Worcester, Samuel Austin
Wright, Frank Hall
Young, Samuel Hall
Zeisberger, David

Pacific Islands (including Hawaii)

Aea, Hezekiah and Debora
Alexander, William Patterson
Andrews, Lorrin
Armstrong, Richard
Auna
Baldwin, Elizabeth and Jane
Bataillon, Pierre Marie
Bicknell, Henry
Bingham, Hiram and Sybil (Moseley)
Bingham, Hiram, Jr.
Bishop, Artemas
Bromilow, William E.
Brown, George
Bulu, Joeli
Burton, John Wear
Buzacott, Aaron
Cakobau, Ratu Seru
Calvert, James
Cargill, David
Chanel, Pierre Louis
Clark, Ephraim W.
Coan, Titus
Codrington, Robert Henry
Cope, Marianne
Crook, William Pascoe
Cross, William
Damien of Molokai
Darling, David
Davies, John
Deck, (John) Northcote
Doane, Edward T(oppin)
Dole, Charlotte (Close) Knapp
Dutton, Ira Barnes
Eastman, George Herbert
Ellis, William and Mary Mercy (Moor)
Epalle, Jean-Baptiste
Eto, Silas
Fison, Lorimer
Fox, Charles Elliot
Geddie, John
Gill, William Wyatt
Goldie, John Francis
Goward, William E(dward)
Gulick, Luther Halsey and Louisa Mitchell (Lewis)
Gulick, Orramel Hinckley and Ann Eliza (Clark)
Gulick, Peter Johnson and Fanny Hinckley (Thomas)
Heine, Carl
Hunt, John
Inglis, John
Jefferson, John Clark
Judd, Gerrit Parmele
Kaahumanu
Kekela, James
Leenhardt, Maurice
Lyman, David Belden
Lyons, Lorenzo
Maretu
Marmoiton, Blaise
Murray, Archibald Wright
Nanpei, Henry
Nau, Semisi
Newell, James Edward
Nisbet, Henry
Nott, Henry
Obookiah (or Opukahaia), Henry
Pao'o
Papeiha
Paton, Francis Hume Lyall
Paton, John G(ibson)
Patteson, John Coleridge
Perroton, (Marie) Françoise (Marie du Mont Carmel)
Pitman, Charles
Pomare II
Pratt, George
Raimondi, Timoleone
Richards, William
Sabatier, Ernst
San Vitores, Diego Luis de
Snow, Benjamin Galen
Solages, (Gabriel) Henri (Jerome) de
Stockton, Betsey
Sturges, Albert A.
Ta'unga
Teava
Thomas, John
Threlkeld, Lancelot Edward
Thurston, Asa and Lucy (Goodale)
Tippett, Alan R.
Tupou, Taufa'ahau (or George)
Turner, George
Vernier, Frédéric
Williams, John
Wilson, Eleanor
Wood, A(lfred) Harold

South America

Acosta, José de
Allan, George and Mary (Sterling)
Anchieta, José de
Arias, Mortimer
Arriaga, Pablo José de
Auca Five (Ecuador Martyrs)
Azevedo, Ignacio de
Bach, T(homas) J(ohn)
Bagby, William Buck
Barzana, Alonso de
Berg, Daniel
Besson, Pablo Enrique
Bettendorf, Johann Philipp
Bolaños, Luis
Braden, Charles Samuel
Brett, William Henry
Builes, Miguel Angel
Camara, (Dom) Helder Pessoa
Canut, Juan Bautista
Castro, Emilio
Claver, Peter
Clifford, James
Cobo, Bernabé
Córdoba, Pedro de
Corrado, Alejandro María
Dalle Périer, Luis
Dobrizhoffer, Martin
Donders, Peter
Elliot, Philip James ("Jim")
Falkner, Thomas
Fleming, Peter Sillence
Francescon, Luigi
Fritz, Samuel
Galland, Emmanuel Arnold
Gardiner, Allen Francis
Giannecchini, Doroteo
Giannelli, José
Glass, Frederick C.
González de Santa Cruz, Roque
Grubb, W(ilfrid) Barbrooke
Gual, Pedro
Gusinde, Martin
Halliwell, Leo B(lair) and Jessie (Rowley)
Hartmann, Maria
Herrero, Andrés
Herron, Walter
Hoover, Willis Collins
Hunnicutt, Benjamin Harris
Jones, Clarence W(esley)
Kalbermatter, Pedro
Kalley, Robert Reid
Kals, Jan Willem
Kersten, Christoph
Kidder, Daniel Parish
King, Johannes
Kinsolving, Lucien Lee
Larson, Reuben E(mmanuel)
Las Casas, Bartolomé de
Leite, Serafim
Léry, Jean de
Liggett, Thomas J.
Litwiller, John T(imothy) N(elson)
Loayza, Gerónimo de
Lozada, Jorgelina
Mackay, John A(lexander)
Martínez Compañón y Bujanda, Baltasar Jaime
McNairn, A. Stuart
Milne, Andrew Murray
Mingo de la Concepción, Manuel
Mogrovejo, Toribio Alfonso de
Moirans, Epifanio de
Money, Herbert
Mongiardino (or Monguiardino; Monnggiardino), José
Montesinos, Antonio de (or Antón Montesino)
Morris, William Case
Motta, Waldomiro
Nino, Bernardino de
Nóbrega, Manoel da
Paucke, Florian
Payne, William Smith
Peña Montenegro, Alonso de
Penzotti, Francisco G.
Pereira, Eduardo Carlos
Perkin, Noel
Porres (or Porras), Martín de
Pratt, Henry B(arrington)
Reekie, Archibald Brownlee
Richter, Enrique
Ricke, Jodoco
Ritchie, John (or Juan)
Ruiz de Montoya, Antonio
Rycroft, W(illiam) Stanley
Saint, Nathanael (Nate)
Saint, Rachel Bradford
Sandoval, Alonso de
Santo Tomás, Domingo de
Shaull, M. Richard
Simonton, Ashbel Green
Smith, John
Solano, Francisco
Soper, Annie
Stahl, Ferdinand A(nthony)
Stirling, Waite Hockin
Stockwell, B(owman) Foster
Stockwell, Eugene L(ouden)
Strachan, Harry
Strachan, Susan (Beamish)
Taylor, Clyde W.
Thomson, James (or Diego)
Thomson, John Francis
Trumbull, David
Valdivia, Luis de
Valle, Juan del
Vasconcelos, Simão de
Vieira, Antônio
Vingren, Adolf Gunnar
Winans, Roger and Ester (Carson)
Wood, Thomas B(ond)
Yoder, Charles Frances

BIOGRAPHIES BY SELECTED MAJOR AGENCIES, ORDERS, AND RELIGIOUS TRADITIONS

This list highlights missionaries and mission leaders from selected agencies, religious orders, and major faith communities, along with a number of other significant persons who influenced the course of Christian missions.

American Board of Commissioners for Foreign Missions (predominantly Congregational)

Abeel, David
Aea, Hezekiah and Debora
Agnew, Eliza
Alexander, William Patterson
Allen, David Oliver
Anderson, Rufus
Andrews, Lorrin
Armstrong, Richard
Baldwin, Elizabeth and Jane
Ball, Dyer
Ballantine, Henry
Barton, James Levi
Beach, Harlan Page
Bingham, Hiram and Sybil (Moseley)
Bingham, Hiram, Jr.
Bishop, Artemas
Bliss, Daniel
Bliss, Edwin Munsell
Bliss, Isaac Grout
Boudinot, Elias (Galagina)
Bradley, Dan Beach
Bridgman, Elijah Coleman
Bridgman, Eliza Jane (Gillette)
Butler, Elizur
Byington, Cyrus
Calder, Helen
Calhoun, Simeon Howard
Clark, Ephraim W.
Coan, Titus
Cochran, Joseph Gallup
Doane, Edward T(oppin)
Dole, Charlotte (Close) Knapp
Dwight, Harrison Gray Otis
Edwards, Mary (Kelley)
Ely, Charlotte Elizabeth and Mary Ann Caroline
Evarts, Jeremiah
Fisk, Pliny
Fiske, Fidelia
Fleming, John
Frame, Alice Seymour (Browne)
Friesen, Abraham J.
Goodell, William
Grant, Asahel
Grant, Judith (Campbell)
Green, Samuel Fiske
Gulick, Alice (Gordon)
Gulick, Luther Halsey and Louisa Mitchell (Lewis)
Gulick, Orramel Hinckley and Ann Eliza (Clark)
Gulick, Peter Johnson and Fanny Hinckley (Thomas)
Hall, Gordon
Hamlin, Cyrus
Hastings, Eurotas Parmelee
Heine, Carl
Hume, Robert Allen
Hume, Robert Wilson
Hunt, Phineas Rice
Jones, Nancy
Judd, Gerrit Parmele
Judd, Walter H(enry)
Kanamori, Tsurin ("Paul")
Keasberry, Benjamin Peach
King, Jonas
Kingsbury, Cyrus
Laubach, Frank Charles
Laurie, Thomas
Lindley, Daniel
Lyman, David Belden
Lyons, Lorenzo
McDowell, Henry Curtis
Merrick, James Lyman
Mills, Samuel John, Jr.
Miner, Luella
Morse, Jedediah
Newell, Samuel and Harriett (Atwood)
Niijima, Jo (or Joseph Hardy Neesima; Neeshima)
Nott, Samuel, Jr.
Obookiah (or Opukahaia), Henry
Parker, Peter
Parsons, Levi
Perkins, Justin
Pitkin, Horace T(racy)
Porter, Lucius Chapin
Rawlinson, Frank Joseph
Richards, William
Riggs, Elias
Riggs, Stephen Return
Schauffler, William Gottlieb
Scudder, John
Shattuck, Corinna
Smith, Arthur Henderson
Smith, Eli
Snow, Benjamin Galen
Spalding, Henry Harmon
Spaulding, Levi
Stevens, Edwin
Sturges, Albert A.
Thurston, Asa and Lucy (Goodale)
Tyler, Josiah
Van Dyck, Cornelius Van Alan
Williams, S(amuel) Wells
Williams, William Frederic
Williamson, Thomas Smith
Wilson, Eleanor
Wilson, John Leighton
Winslow, Harriet Wadsworth (Lathrop)
Winslow, Miron

Anglicans

Personnel from agencies whose workers were predominantly Anglicans, including Church of England Zenana Missionary Society, Episcopal Church (U.S.), Society for the Propagation of Christian Knowledge (U.K.), Society for the Propagation of the Gospel (U.K.), South American Missionary Society (U.K.), Universities' Mission to Central Africa (U.K.), and others. See also *Church Missionary Society.*

Alexander, Michael Solomon
Allen, Roland
Anderson, David
Anderson, James Norman Dalrymple
Andrews, Charles Freer
Appasamy, Aiyadurai Jesudasen
Azariah, Vedanayagam Samuel
Baedeker, Friederich Wilhelm
Banerjea, Krishna Mohan
Barber, Margaret
Bettelheim, Bernard Jean
Bishop, Isabella Lucy (Bird)
Boone, William Jones, Sr.
Bray, Thomas
Breck, James Lloyd
Brent, Charles Henry
Brett, William Henry
Bridgman, Elijah Coleman

Bridgman, Eliza Jane (Gillette)
Brown, David
Browne, Laurence Edward
Buchanan, Claudius
Bulmer, John
Butler, Fanny Jane
Buxton, B(arclay) Godfrey
Buxton, Thomas Fowell
Caffray, D(aisy) Willia
Caldwell, Robert
Callaway, Henry
Cassels, William Wharton
Cheese, John Ethelstan
Codrington, Robert Henry
Colenso, John William
Copleston, Reginald Stephen
Corrie, Daniel
Cotton, George Edward Lynch
Coughlan, Laurence
Cousins, William E(dward)
Cragg, Albert Kenneth
Cripps, Arthur Shearly
Crummell, Alexander
Dehqani-Tafti, H(assan) B(arnaba)
Dwane, James Matta
Elwin, H(arry) Verrier H(olman)
Feild, Edward
Ferguson, Samuel David
Fox, Charles Elliot
Gardiner, Allen Francis
Glover, Archibald Edward
Goreh, Nilakantha (Nehemiah)
Grant, Anthony
Grant, Charles
Gray, Robert
Grenfell, Wilfred Thomason
Gribble, Ernest Richard
Griffiths, David
Grubb, W(ilfrid) Barbrooke
Hale, Mathew Blagden
Hall, R(onald) O(wen)
Haweis, Thomas
Hawkins, Ernest
Heber, Reginald
Hemans, James Henry Emmanuel
Hill, John Henry
Hill, Mary (Beardsmore)
Hobson, Benjamin
Hoffman, C(adwallader) Colden
Holly, James Theodore
Hore, Edward Coode
Huddleston, Trevor Ernest Urban
Hunter, Leslie Stannard
Isherwood, Annie Cecile
Jocz, Jakób
John, Griffith
Johns, David
Johnson, Samuel
Johnson, William Percival
Jones, David
Jones, David Picton
Jones, William Henry
Kiernander, John Zacharias
Kigozi, Blasio
King, Copland
Kinsolving, Lucien Lee
Kivebulaya, (Waswa) Apolo
Kivengere, Festo
Knight-Bruce, George Wyndham Hamilton
Krishna Pillai (Henry Alfred)
Lamburn, Roger George Patrick
Lefroy, George Alfred
Legge, James
Legge, Mary Isabella (Morison)
Liggins, John
Lijadu, Emmanuel Moses
Lloyd, Arthur
Lucas, William Vincent
Macgowan, Edward
Machray, Robert
Mackenzie, Charles Frederick
Maclaren, Albert Alexander
Magee, John G(illespie)
Marks, John Ebenezer
Marsden, Samuel
Martyn, Henry
McCaul, Alexander
McDonald, Robert
McDougall, Francis Thomas
Middleton, Thomas Fanshaw
Millar, Robert
Milman, Robert
Milne, Rachel (Cowie)
Mizeki, Bernard
Montgomery, Henry Hutchinson
Morris, William Case
Mullens, Joseph and Hannah (Lacroix)
Nagenda, William
Nicolayson, John (or Hans Nicolajsen)
Nsibambi, Simeon
Oldham, J(oseph) H(ouldsworth)
Pearse, Joseph
Pope, George Uglow
Pott, Francis Lister Hawks
Quaque, Philip
Rasa, Clorinda
Reeve, William
Roots, Logan H(erbert)
Rottler, John Peter
Rouse, C(lara) Ruth
Schereschewsky, Samuel Isaac Joseph
Schurmann (or Shurman), Johannes Adam
Scott, Michael
Selwyn, G(eorge) A(ugustus)
Sibbes, Richard
Sibree, James
Simeon, Charles
Singh, Bakht
Staunton, John Armitage, Jr.
Steere, Edward
Stern, Henry Aaron
Stirling, Waite Hockin
Stott, John R(obert) W(almsley)
Stronach, Alexander
Stronach, John
Swan, William
Swatson, John
Tatlow, Tissington
Taylor, John Christopher
Temple, William
Thompson, Thomas
Threlkeld, Lancelot Edward
Ting, K. H. (Ding Guangxun)
Trollope, Mark Napier
Tsizehena, John
Tucker, Alfred Robert
Tucker, Charlotte Maria
Vidal, Owen Emeric
Wardlaw, John Smith
Way, Lewis
Wei, Francis C(ho) M(in)
Wesley, Charles
Wesley, John
Westcott, Brooke Foss
Westcott, Foss
Weston, Frank
Whitehead, Henry
Wilberforce, Samuel
Wilberforce, William
Williams, Channing Moore
Willoughby, W(illiam) C(harles)
Winslow, John ("Jack") C(opley)
Wolff, Joseph

Baptists

Personnel from agencies whose workers were predominantly Baptists, including American Baptist Foreign Mission Society, Baptist Missionary Society (U.K.), Southern Baptist Convention Foreign Mission Board (U.S.), Woman's Baptist Foreign Mission Society (U.S.), Woman's Missionary Union of the Southern Baptist Convention (U.S.), and others.

Adam, William
Agbebi, Majola (David Brown Vincent)
Ali, Wallayat
Anderson, Christopher
Ao, Longri (Longritangchetba)
Armstrong, Annie Walker
Armstrong, Hannah Maria (Norris)
Armstrong, Philip E.
Armstrong, William Frederick
Arthington, Robert
Ashmore, William
Axling, William
Bagby, William Buck
Baynes, Alfred Henry
Bender, Carl Jacob
Bennett, Cephas
Bentley, William Holman
Besson, Pablo Enrique

Bickel, Luke Washington
Boardman, George Dana
Booth, Joseph
Bouey, Elizabeth Coles
Bowen, Thomas Jefferson
Brand, Evelyn (Harris)
Bronson, Miles
Brown, Edith Mary
Brown, Nathan
Browne, Stanley G(eorge)
Brückner, Gottlob
Buchan, Jane
Buker, Raymond Bates, Sr.
Carey, Charlotte Emilia (von Rumohr)
Carey, Felix
Carey, Lott
Carey, William
Carpenter, Chapin Howard
Carver, William Owen
Case, Isaac
Chamberlain, John
Cheek, Landon N(apoleon)
Chesterman, Clement C(lapton)
Clarke, John
Clough, John Everett and Emma (Rauschenbusch)
Colley, William W.
Comber, Thomas James
Crawford, Isabelle (Belle)
Crawford, T(arleton) P(erry) and Martha (Foster)
Crowe, Frederick
Cushing, Ellen Winsor (Howard) Fairfield
Day, John
Day, Samuel Stearns
Dean, William
Delany, Emma Bertha
Doke, Clement Martyn
Doke, Joseph John
Dunger, George Albert
Dyer, John
Fielde, Adele M.
Fleming, Louise ("Lulu") Cecilia
Fuller, Andrew
Gebauer, Paul
George, David
George, Eliza (Davis)
Gilmour, John
Goble, Jonathan
Goddard, Josiah
Goldsack, William
Gordon, A(doniram) J(udson)
Grenfell, George
Hall, Elizabeth Garland
Hayward, Victor E. W.
Holmes, Elkanah
Hough, George H.
Howells, George
Ingalls, Marilla Baker
Johnson, Mammie
Jones, Evan and John Buttrick
Jones, John Taylor
Jones, Lewis Bevan
Jordan, Lewis G(arnett)
Judson, Adoniram
Judson, Ann ("Nancy") (Hasseltine)
Judson, Emily Chubbock
Judson, Sarah (Hall) Boardman
Kincaid, Eugenio
Knibb, William
Ko Tha Byu
Lanneau, Sophie Stephens
Latourette, Kenneth Scott
Lewis, Marianne (Gould)
Lewis, Thomas
Liele, George
Lorrain, James Herbert
Mabie, Catherine Louise Roe
Mack, John
Marshman, Hannah (Shepherd)
Marshman, John C(larke)
Marshman, Joshua
Marston, Sarah Hall
Mason, Francis
McCoy, Isaac
McDonald, Alexander
McLaurin, John
McLaurin, John Bates
Montgomery, Helen Barrett
Moon, Charlotte ("Lottie") Diggs
Moore, Joanna Patterson
Moorshead, Robert Fletcher
Morris, John Webster
Motta, Waldomiro
Moulton, Ebenezer
Pal, Krishna
Payne, Ernest A(lexander)
Peabody, Lucy Whitehead (McGill) Waterbury
Peck, John Mason
Phillippo, J(ames) M(ursell)
Phillips, Jeremiah
Prasad (or Prisada), Krishna
Price, Jonathan David
Reekie, Archibald Brownlee
Rice, Luther
Richard, Timothy
Richards, Henry
Roberts, Issachar Jacox
Robinson, William
Rouse, George Henry
Ryland, John
Saker, Alfred
Sale, Elizabeth (Geale)
Seagrave, Gordon S(tifler)
Shreve, Elizabeth (Shadd)
Shuck, J(ehu) Lewis and Henrietta (Hall)
Soto Fontánez, Santiago
Sutton, Amos
Takle, John
Teague, Colin (or Collin Teage)
Tewksbury, Elwood Gardner
Timpany, Americus Vespucius
Tule, Mary (Branton)
Underhill, Edward Bean
Vinton, Justus Hatch and Calista (Holman)
Wanyoike wa Kamawe
Ward, William
Webb, Mary
Welch, James Ely
Wenger, John
White, Charlotte Hazen Atlee
Williams, Roger
Williamson, H(enry) R(aymond)
Wilson, C(harles) E(dward)
Yates, Matthew Tyson
Yates, William
Young, George Armstrong

Basel Mission (Lutheran and Reformed)

Akrofi, Clement Anderson
Auer, John Gottlieb
Barth, Christian Gottlob
Bieder, Werner
Blumhardt, Christian Gottlieb
Bohner, Heinrich
Christaller, Johannes Gottlieb
Dürr, Johannes
Fisch, Rudolf
Gundert, Hermann
Hartenstein, Karl
Hebich, Samuel
Hoffmann, L(udwig) F(riedrich) Wilhelm
Josenhans, F(riedrich) Joseph
Kaundinya, Hermann Anandaraja
Kittel, Ferdinand
Koechlin, Alphons
Lechler, Rudolf
Lombard, Eva
Moegling, Herrmann Friedrich
Oehler, Theodor Friedrich
Raaflaub, Fritz
Ramseyer, Fritz and Rosa (Bontemps)
Reindorf, Carl Christian
Rein-Wuhrmann, Anna
Riis, Andreas
Rossel, Jacques
Samartha, S(tanley) J(edidiah)
Sarasin, Dorothee
Sarasin, Karl
Schärer, Hans
Schrenk, Elias
Spieth, (Andreas) Jakob
Spittler, Christian Friedrich
Steinkopf, Karl Friedrich Adolf
Wangemann, Hermann Theodor
Widmann, Rosina (Binder)
Würz, Friedrich
Zaremba, Felician von

Church Missionary Society (predominantly Anglican)

Abdul Masih, Salih
Alli, Janni
Baker, Amelia Dorothea (Kohlhoff)
Barton, John
Bickersteth, Edward
Bird, Mary Rebecca Stewart
Bompas, William Carpenter
Bowley, William
Brooke, Graham Wilmot
Broughton, William Grant
Brown, Alfred (Nesbit)
Brunton, Henry
Buxton, Barclay Fowell
Carmichael, Amy Beatrice
Cash, William Wilson
Church, John E. ("Joe")
Clark, Henry Martyn
Clark, Robert
Coates, Dandeson
Colenso, Elizabeth (Fairburn) and William
Cook, Albert Ruskin
Cooke, Sophia
Crowther, Dandeson Coates
Crowther, Samuel Adjai (or Ajayi)
Cust, Robert Needham
Darling, Thomas Young
Daüble, Carl Gustav
Dennis, Thomas John
Devasahayam, John
Dobinson, Henry Hughes
Droese, Ernest
Duncan, William
Dyer, Alf(red) John
Edwins, August W(illiam)
Elmslie, William J. and Margaret (Duncan)
Fenn, Christopher Cyprian
Fleming, Archibald Lang
Fox, Henry Watson
Fraser, Alexander Garden
Fraser, Kenneth
French, Thomas Valpy
Gairdner, W(illiam) H(enry) Temple
Gobat, Samuel
Gollmer, Charles Andrew (Carl Anders)
Grubb, Kenneth George
Gwynne, Llewellyn Henry
Hadfield, Octavius
Hamlin, James
Hannington, James
Hinderer, David and Anna (Martin)
Holland, Henry Tristram
Hooper, Handley Douglas
Horne, Melville
Hughes, Thomas Patrick
Imad ud-Din
Isenberg, Karl Wilhelm
Johnson, Amelia Dorothea (Baker)
Johnson, James
Johnson, Thomas Sylvester (Claudius)
Johnson, William Augustine Bernard
Jones, Edward
Jowett, William
Kendall, Thomas
Kitto, John
Klein, Frederick Augustus
Koelle, Sigismund Wilhelm
Krapf, Johann Ludwig
Leupolt, Charles Benjamin
Long, James
Mackay, Alexander M(urdoch)
Main, D(avid) Duncan
Marsden, Samuel
Maunsell, Robert
Miller, Walter Richard Samuel
Moule, Arthur Evans
Moule, George Evans
Neill, Stephen Charles
Noble, Robert Turlington
Nyländer, Gustavus Reinhold
Owen, Walter Edwin
Padwick, Constance Evelyn
Paton, David Macdonald
Patteson, John Coleridge
Peck, Edmund James
Peet, Joseph
Pennell, Theodor Leighton
Petrie, Irene Eleanora Verita
Pettitt, George
Pfander, Karl Gottlieb
Pilkington, George Lawrence
Pratt, Josiah
Price, William Salter
Raban, John
Ragland, Thomas Gajetan
Rebmann, Johannes
Renner, Melchior
Rhenius, Carl Theophilus Ewald
Robinson, John Alfred
Russell, William Armstrong
Sargent, Douglas Noel
Sargent, Edward
Satthianadhan, William Thomas (Tiruvengadam) and Annal Arokium
Sawyerr, Harry Alphonso Ebun
Schnarre, Johannes Christian
Schön, Jakob Friedrich (James Frederick)
Sell, Edward
Sharkey, John Edmund and Ann Amelia (Nailer)
Shaw, Archibald
Simeon, Charles
Smith, A(lgernon) C(harles) Stanley
Smith, George
Smith, William
Stanway, Alfred
Stock, Eugene
Stuart, Edward Craig
Taylor, John V(ernon)
Taylor, Richard
Thomas, John
Thomas, Mary (Davies)
Thornton, Douglas M(ontagu)
Tisdall, William St. Clair
Townsend, Henry
Trumpp, Ernst
Tucker, John Thomas
Tyndale-Biscoe, Cecil Earle
Venn, Henry
Venn, John
Vining, Leslie Gordon
Walker, Thomas
Waller, Edward Henry Mansfield
Warren, Max (Alexander Cunningham)
Watson, William
White, Paul Hamilton Hume
Whiting, John Bradford
Wilkes, Paget
Williams, Henry
Williams, William
Willis, John Jamieson
Wilson, Daniel
Wilson, Edward Francis
Wilson, Mary Ann (Cooke)
Yate, William

Dominicans (Roman Catholic)

Anawati, Georges Chehata
Benavides, Miguel de
Betanzos, Domingo de
Breton, Raymond (Guillaume)
Cáncer de Barbastro, Luis
Capillas, Francisco de
Catalani, Jordan
Congar, Yves
Córdoba, Pedro de
Dominic
Garcés, Julián
Henry, Antonin-Marcel
Hermosilla, Jerónimo
Las Casas, Bartolomé de
Loayza, Gerónimo de
Lopez, Gregorio (Lo Wen-Tsao)
Mazzuchelli, Samuel
Menasce, Pierre Jean de
Montesinos, Antonio de (or Antón Montesino)
Morales, Juan Bautista de
Navarrete, Domingo Fernandez de
Pennini, Ricoldo (da Monte Cruce)
Porres (or Porras), Martín de
Salazar, Domingo de
Santo Tomás, Domingo de
Thomas Aquinas
Valdivieso, Antonio de
Villaverde, Juan
Vitoria, Francisco de
William of Tripoli

Franciscans (Roman Catholic)

Andrew of Perugia
Bernardino, Ignazio da Asti
Bolaños, Luis
Bonaventura da Sardegna
Brancati de Laurea, Lorenzo (Giovanni Francesco)
Breda, Gregorius van
Bühlmann, Walbert
Camps, Arnulf
Cavazzi da Montecuccolo
Chappotin de Neuville, Hélène de (Marie de la Passion)
Cope, Marianne
Corrado, Alejandro María
Focher, Juan
Francis of Assisi
Giannecchini, Doroteo
Giannelli, José
Gual, Pedro
Gubernatis, Dominicus de
Hartmann, (Joseph Alois) Anastasius
Heinrichs, Maurus
Herrero, Andrés
Jaca, Francisco José de
John of Montecorvino
John of Pian di Carpine (or Plano de Carpine)
Kevin, Mother (Kearney, Teresa)
Lemmens, Leonard
Llinás, Jesús Maria Antonio
Lopez, Gregorio (Lo Wen-Tsao)
Maas, Otto
Maldonado de Buendía, Alonso
Margil, Antonio
Massaja, Guglielmo
Massanet, Damian
Mendieta, Jerónimo
Mingo de la Concepción, Manuel
Moirans, Epifanio de
Mondreganes, Pio M. de
Motolinía (Toribio de Benavente)
Nicholas IV (Girolamo Masci)
Nino, Bernardino de
O'Donel, James Louis
Odorico of Pordenone
Padilla, Juan de
Payeras, Mariano
Peter of Ghent
Plasencia (Portocarrero), Juan de
Ricke, Jodoco
Ruiz, Manuel
Sahagún, Bernardino de
Serra, Junípero (Miguel Jose)
Solano, Francisco
Tempels, Placide
Testera (or Tastera), Jacobo de
Valadés, Diego
Valencia, Martín de
Willeke, Bernward H.
William of Rubroek (or Rubruck)
Zumárraga, Juan de

Jesuits (Roman Catholic)

Acosta, José de
Acquaviva, Rudolf
Alcina (or Alzina), Francisco Ignacio
Aleni, Giulio
Allouez, Claude Jean
Altham, John
Amiot, Jean Joseph Marie
Anchieta, José de
Andrade, Antonio de
André, Louis
Arriaga, Pablo José de
Arrupe, Pedro
Azevedo, Ignacio de
Barreira, Balthazar (or Baltesar)
Barzaeus (or Barzäus; Berze), Gaspar
Barzana, Alonso de
Bernard-Maitre, Henri
Bettendorf, Johann Philipp
Beyzym, Jan
Biard, Pierre
Bouvet, Joachim
Brébeuf, Jean de
Britto, João de
Buglio, Lodovico
Bulck, Gaaston (or Vaast) van
Cabral, Francisco
Cardoso, Mattheus
Carneiro Leitão, Melchior Miguel
Castiglione, Giuseppe
Cattaneo, Lazzaro
Céspedes, Gregorio
Chabanel, Noël
Charles, Pierre
Claver, Peter
Cobo, Bernabé
Couplet, Philippe
Couvreur, Séraphin
Criminali, Antonio
Dablon, Claude
Dandoy, Georges
Daniel, Antoine
Daniélou, Jean
Dehergne, Joseph
Depelchin, Henri
Desideri, Hippolytus
De Smet, Pierre-Jean
Dobrizhoffer, Martin
Dorville, Albert
Druillettes, Gabriel
Elia, Pasquale d'
Falkner, Thomas
Foucquet, Jean-François
Fridelli, Xaver-Ehrenbert (or Ernbert)
Fritz, Samuel
Fróis, Luis
Garnier, Charles
Gerbillon, Jean-François
Gnecci-Soldi, Organtino
Goes, Bento de
González de Santa Cruz, Roque
Goupil, René
Gregory XV
Grüber, Johannes
Hanxleden, Johann Ernst
Henriques, Henrique
Heras, Enrique (or Henry)
Hoecken, Christian
Hoffmann, Johannes Baptist
Hofinger, Johannes
Ignatius of Loyola (or Iñigo López de Loyola)
Intorcetta, Prospero
Jartoux, Pierre
Jeune, Paul le
Jogues, Isaac
Johanns, Pierre
Juanmartí y Espot, Jacinto
Kino, Eusebio Francisco
Kircher, Athanasius
Lafitau, Joseph-François
La Lande, Jean de
Lalemant, Gabriel
Lalemant, Jérôme
Le Comte, Louis
Ledochowski, Wladimir
Leite, Serafim
Lievens, Constant
Lith, Franciscus van
Lubac, Henri de
Mailla, Joseph Marie Anne de Moyriac de
Marquette, Jacques
Martines, Francesco
Martínez, Pedro
Martini, Martino
Masson, Joseph Armand
Ménard, René
Mendez, Alphonsus
Montalbán, Francisco Javier
Murillo Velarde, Pedro
Neuner, Joseph
Nobili, Robert de
Nóbrega, Manoel da
Nunes Barreto, João
Otto, Josef Albert
Oviedo, André de
Paez, (Xaramillo) Pedro (or Pero Paez)
Paucke, Florian
Ponziglione, Paul Mary
Rahner, Karl
Régis, Jean-Baptiste
Rhodes, Alexandre de

Ricci, Matteo
Richter, Enrique
Rocha, João da
Roothaan, Johann Philipp
Roth, Heinrich
Rougemont, François de
Ruggieri, Michele
Ruiz de Montoya, Antonio
Sandoval, Alonso de
San Vitores, Diego Luis de
Schall von Bell, Johann Adam
Scherer, Heinrich
Schoenmakers, John
Schurhammer, Georg
Segura, Juan Baptista
Silveira, Gonçalo da
Spinola, Carlo
Stephens, Thomas
Torrend, Jules
Trigault, Nicolas
Urios, Saturnino
Valdivia, Luis de
Valignano, Alessandro
Vasconcelos, Simão de
Väth, Alfons
Verbiest, Ferdinand
Vieira, Antônio
Visdelou, Claude
White, Andrew
Wicki, Josef
Wieger, Georges Frédéric Léon
Wu Li (Wu Yü-Shan; or Simon à Cunha)
Xavier, Francis (or Francisco de Jassu y Xavier)
Xavier, Jerome
Zameza, José

London Missionary Society (predominantly Congregational)

Abel, Charles William
Anderson, William
Auna
Bicknell, Henry
Bliss, Kathleen Mary Amelia (Moore)
Boaz, Thomas
Bogue, David
Brownlee, John
Buzacott, Aaron
Campbell, John
Chalmers, John
Chatterton, Percy
Cochrane, Thomas
Cousins, William E(dward)
Darling, David
Davidson, Andrew
Davies, John
Dyer, Samuel
Eastman, George Herbert
Edkins, Joseph
Ellis, William and Mary Mercy (Moor)
Farquhar, John Nicol
Freeman, John Joseph
Frey, Joseph Samuel C(ristian) F(rederick)
Gill, William Wyatt
Gilmour, James
Goodall, Norman
Goward, William E(dward)
Griffiths, David
Haweis, Thomas
Hemans, James Henry Emmanuel
Hepburn, James Davidson
Hill, Mary (Beardsmore)
Hobson, Benjamin
Hore, Edward Coode
Jefferson, John Clark
John, Griffith
Johns, David
Jones, David
Jones, David Picton
Kam, Joseph
Kemp, Johannes Theodorus van der
Khama III
Kircherer, Johannes Jacobus
Lacroix, Alphonse François
Lawes, W(illiam) G(eorge)
Legge, James
Legge, Mary Isabella (Morison)
Liang Fa
Liddell, Eric Henry
Livingstone, David
Livingstone, Mary (Moffat)
Lockhart, William
Love, John
Loveless, Sarah (Farquhar)
Lowe, John
Lucas, Bernard
Mackenzie, John
Mackenzie, John Kenneth
Marsden, Samuel
Mather, Robert Cotton
Matthews, Thomas Trotter
McFarlane, Samuel
Medhurst, Walter Henry
Milne, Rachel (Cowie)
Milne, William
Moffat, John Smith
Moffat, Robert
Morrison, Mary (Morton)
Morrison, Robert
Mullens, Joseph and Hannah (Lacroix)
Murray, Archibald Wright
Newell, James Edward
Newell, Maria
Nott, Henry
Orchard, Ronald Kenneth
Pearse, Joseph
Philip, John
Phillips, Godfrey Edward
Pitman, Charles
Popley, Herbert Arthur
Pratt, George
Price, Roger
Read, James
Reeve, William
Rice, Benjamin
Ringeltaube, Wilhelm Tobias
Schmelen, Johann Heinrich
Schurmann (or Shurman), Johannes Adam
Sibree, James
Slater, Thomas Ebenezer
Smith, John
Stallybrass, Edward
Stronach, Alexander
Stronach, John
Swan, William
Ta'unga
Teava
Thomas, Robert Jermain
Thompson, Ralph Wardlaw
Threlkeld, Lancelot Edward
Tomlin, Jacob
Wardlaw, John Smith
Williams, John
Williamson, Alexander
Willoughby, W(illiam) C(harles)
Wylie, Alexander

LUTHERANS

Personnel from agencies whose workers were predominantly Lutherans, including American Lutheran Church, Augustana Lutheran Church (U.S.), Australian Lutheran Mission, Berlin Mission Society, Bethel Mission (Ger.), Danish-Halle Mission, Danish Lutheran Mission, Danish Missionary Society, Evangelical Lutheran Church of America, Gossner Mission (Ger.), Hermannsburg Mission (Ger.), Leipzig Mission (Ger.), Lutheran General Synod Mission Board (U.S.), Lutheran United Synod of the South (U.S.), Neuendettelsau Mission (Ger.), North German (Bremen) Mission, Nordic Santal Mission (Nor.), Norwegian Lutheran Mission, Norwegian Missionary Society, Swedish Missionary Society, and others. See also *Basel Mission.*

Axenfeld, Karl
Bergmann, Wilhelm (H. F.)
Berron, Paul (Émile)
Birkeli, (Otto) Emil
Birkeli, Fridtjov (Søiland)
Bloch-Hoell, Nils Egede
Bodding, Paul Olaf
Bodelschwingh, Friedrich von
Brennecke, Gerhard
Bucer, Martin
Callenberg, Johann Heinrich
Chakkarai, V(engal)
Dahl, Otto Christian
Dahle, Lars Nilsen
Dalman, Gustav Hermann
Dammann, Ernst
Danbolt, Erling Gauslaa
Day, David A(lexander)
Delitzsch, Franz Julius
Egede, Hans (Povelsen)
Ehrenfeuchter, Friedrich
Evald, Emmy C(hristina) (Carlsson)
Fabricius, Johann Philipp
Fjellstedt, Peter
Flierl, Johann
Francke, August Hermann
Freytag, Walter
Gensichen, Hans-Werner
Gericke, Christian Wilhelm
Gossner, Johannes Evangelista
Graul, Karl
Grundemann, Peter Reinhold
Gründler, Johann Ernst
Gutmann, Bruno
Gützlaff, Karl Friedrich August
Hahn, Carl Hugo
Haringke Bai
Harms, Ludwig
Harnack, Adolf von
Heim, Karl
Heyer, John Christian Frederick
Holsten, Walter
Ihmels, Carl
Jänicke, Johann
Jensen, Christian
Johanssen, Ernst
Kähler, Martin
Kalkar, Christian
Keysser, Christian (J. E.)
Knak, Siegfried
Kuder, John
Kugler, Anna Sarah
Laiser, (Loirera) Lazarus
Larsen, Lars Peter
Lehmann, E. Arno
Leibniz, Gottfried Wilhelm von
Lepsius, Johannes
Löhe, Johann Konrad Wilhelm
Luther, Martin
Lütkens, Franz Julius
Manikam, Rajah B(ushanam)
Merensky, Alexander
Monsen, Marie
Myklebust, Olav Guttorm
Nelson, Daniel
Ngizaki, Gapenuo
Nicolai, Philipp
Officer, Morris
Peery, R(ufus) B(enton)
Petri, Ludwig Adolf
Pfeiffer, Edward
Pilhofer, Georg
Plath, Karl Heinrich Christian
Plütschau, Heinrich
Podmaniczky, Pál
Reichelt, Karl Ludvig
Roehl, Karl
Rønne, Bone Falch
Rønning, Halvor
Sandegren, Johannes
Scherer, James A(ugustin) B(rown)
Schlunk, Martin
Scholtz, Ödön
Schomerus, Hilko Wiarda
Schreiber, August Wilhelm
Schreuder, Hans Paludan Smith
Schultze, Benjamin
Schwartz, Christian Friedrich
Sihombing, Justin
Skrefsrud, Lars O(lsen)
Söderblom, Nathan (Lars Olof Jonathan)
Spener, Philipp Jakob
Stockfleth, Nils Joachim Vibe
Stosch, Johannes Richard Andreas
Strauss, Hermann
Strehlow, Carl Friedrich Theodor
Sundkler, Bengt (Gustav Malcolm)
Tambunan, Albert Mangara
Tarkkanen, Matti
Tellström, Carl Ludwig
Theile, Friedrich Otto
Trobisch, Walter and Ingrid (Hult)
Urlsperger, Johann August
Vahl, Jen
Vicedom, Georg Friedrich
Vietor, Johann Karl
Voskamp, Carl Johannes
Walther, Christoph Theodosius
Warneck, Gustav
Warneck, Johannes
Welz, Justinian von
Westen, Thomas von
Westermann, Diedrich Hermann
Westman, Knut Bernhard
Zahn, Franz Michael
Ziegenbalg, Bartholomäus

METHODISTS

Personnel from agencies whose workers were predominantly Methodists, including African Methodist Episcopal (U.S.), African Methodist Episcopal Zion (U.S.), Methodist Board of Missions (U.S.), Methodist Missionary Society (U.K.), Wesleyan Methodist Missionary Society (U.S.), and others.

Abraham, Samuel
Abrams, Minnie F.
Allen, Young John
Appenzeller, Henry Gerhard
Archbell, James
Arias, Mortimer
Asbury, Francis
Báez-Camargo, Gonzalo
Ball, Henry Cleophas
Bashford, James Whitford
Baughman, Burr
Bennett, Belle Harris
Bird, Mark Baker
Black, William
Blackmore, Sophia
Blackstone, William Eugene
Bowen, George
Boyce, William Binnington
Braden, Charles Samuel
Bromilow, William E.
Brown, George

Bulu, Joeli
Burton, John Wear
Butler, William and Clementina (Rowe)
Calvert, James
Camphor, Alexander Priestly
Canut, Juan Bautista
Cargill, David
Case, William
Castro, Emilio
Chen, Wen-Yuan
Chitambar, Jashwant Rao
Cochran, George
Coke, Thomas
Coker, Daniel
Collins, Judson Dwight
Cook Gonzalez, Eulalia
Coombs, Lucinda L.
Coppin, Fanny Marion (Jackson)
Cox, Melville Beveridge
Crook, William Pascoe
Crosby, Thomas
Cross, William
Dodge, Ralph E(dward)
Evans, James
Farrington, Sophronia
Fisher, Welthy (Honsinger)
Fison, Lorimer
Freeman, Thomas Birch
Gaebelein, A(rno) C(lemens)
Gamewell, Frank (Francis) Dunlap
Gilbert, Nathaniel
Gogerly, Daniel John
Goh, Hood Keng
Goldie, John Francis
Gorham, Sarah E.
Gribble, John Brown
Groves, Charles Pelham
Gulliford, Henry
Gurney, Samuel
Hall, Marian (Bottomley)
Hall, Sherwood
Hardy, Robert Spence
Harris, Merriman Colbert
Hill, David
Hocking, William Ernest
Hodgson, Thomas Laidman
Honda Yoichi
Hoover, James Matthews
Hoover, Willis Collins
Howard, Leonora
Howe, Gertrude
Hunt, John
Iglehart, Charles W(heeler)
Jabavu, Davidson Don T(engo)
Jabavu, John Tengo
Jones, E(li) Stanley
Jones, George Heber
Jones, Mabel Lossing
K'ang Ch'eng (Kang Cheng; or Ida Kahn)
Kerr, George McGlashan and Isabel (Gunn)
Kidder, Daniel Parish
Kim, Helen
Koyi, William Mtusane
Lambuth, Walter Russell
Lee, Daniel
Lee, Jason
Maclay, Robert Samuel
Mamora (or Sinamora), Lucius
Meyer, Lucy Jane (Rider)
Mokone, Mangena Maake
Mott, John R(aleigh)
Nau, Semisi
New, Charles
Niles, D(aniel) T(hambyrajah)
North, Frank Mason
Oldham, William F(itzjames)
Oppong, (Kwame) Sam(p)son
Pamla, Charles
Parrinder, (Edward) Geoffrey (Simons)
Parrish, Sarah Rebecca
Percival, Peter
Pickett, J(arrell) Waskom
Platt, W(illiam) J(ames)
Potter, Philip A(lford)
Ranson, Charles W(esley)
Reed, Mary
Rowe, Phoebe
Rundle, Robert Terrill
Samkange, Thompson Douglas
Scott, George
Scranton, Mary F.
Scranton, William Benton
Shaw, Barnabas
Shaw, William
Shellabear, William Girdlestone
Shih Mei-yu (Shi Meiyu; or Mary Stone)
Silva, Lynn A. de
Soper, Edmund Davison
Springer, Helen Emily (Chapman) Rasmussen
Springer, John McKendree
Stewart, John
Stockwell, B(owman) Foster
Stockwell, Eugene L(ouden)
Strachan, Susan Beamish
Subhan, John
Swain, Clara
Sweetman, James Windrow
Taylor, Richard W.
Taylor, William
Thoburn, Isabella
Thoburn, James Mills
Thomas, John
Tippett, Alan R.
Titus, Murray T(hurston)
Tupou, Taufa'ahau (or George)
Turner, Henry McNeal
Turton, William
Vennard, Iva May Durham
Wakefield, Thomas
Walker, William
Walls, Andrew F(inlay)
Wesley, Charles
Wesley, John
White, John
White, Moses Clark
Whitefield, George
Wilkins, Ann (Green)
Wood, A(lfred) Harold
Wood, Thomas B(ond)
Woolston, Beulah and Sarah H.
Yun, Tchi-Ho

Orthodox Churches

Personnel from Orthodox churches, including Armenian, Coptic, Ethiopian, Greek, Russian, Syrian.

Abraham Malpan
Ambrazis, Nicholas
Arseny of Konev
Bolotov, Ioasaf
Bolshakoff, Serge N. (or Sergey Nikolaevich Bolshakov)
Boris I
Chakko, Sarah
Chrysostom, John
Clement of Ochrid
Constantine the Great
Cyril-Constantine
Enbaqom (Abu l-Fath)
Figurovskii, Innokentii
Filofei (Leshchinsky)
Florovsky, Georges V(asilievich)
Frumentius
Glukharev, Makarii (Mikhail Yakovlevich)
Gregory Thaumaturgus
Gregory the Illuminator
Hawaweeny, Raphael
Herman of Alaska
Iakinf (Bichurin)
Ilminskii, Nikolai Ivanovich
Innocent Veniaminov (Ivan Popov-Veniaminov)
Ioasaf (Hotuntsevsky)
Isaiah of Rostov
Isakovich, Nikolai Fedorovich
Iuvenalii (Iakov Fedorovich Govorukhin)
Ivanovskii, Nikolai Ivanovich
Julian
Kafarov, Petr Ivanovich
Kasatkin, Nikolai (Ivan Dmitriyevich)
Khrisanf (Shchetkovsky)
Kosmas Aitolos (or Cosmas of Aitolia)
Kuksha
Lenkeevich, Nikolai (Nikodim)
Leontiev, Maxim
Makarii Altaiskii (Mikhail Andreevich Nevskii)
Matthopoulos, Eusebius
Men (or Menn), Aleksandr Vladimirovich
Mesrob (or Mashtots)
Methodius
Meyendorff, John
Nankyama, Theodoros
Netsvetov, Iakov Egor
Nikolai (Ziorov)
Nikon the Metanoeite
Nino

Origen
Papasarantopoulos, Chrysostom
Philaret (Drozdov)
Photius
Sahak
Sava
Sawabe, Paul (Takuma)
Schmemann, Alexander
Sergii of Valaam (or Valamo)
Shelikhov, Grigorii Ivanovich
Smirnov, Evgeny (or Eugene) Konstantinovich (or Eugene Smirnoff)
Spartas, Christopher Reuben
Stephen
Stephen of Perm
Struve, Nikita Alexelevich
Takla-Haymanot
Tikhomirov, Sergii
Tikhon
Toth, Alexis
Tryphon of Pechenga
Veronis, Alexander J.
Vladimir of Kiev
Xenos, Ioannes
Yannoulatos, Anastasios
Zakaryas

Presbyterians/Reformed

Personnel from agencies whose workers were predominantly from the Reformed tradition, including Church of Scotland Mission, Dutch Reformed Church, Reformed Mission League (Neth.), Netherlands Mission Society (NZG), Neukirchen Mission (Ger.), Paris Evangelical Mission Society, Presbyterians (Can., U.S., U.K., et al.), Reformed Church in Africa (NGK), Reformed Church in America, and others. See also *Basel Mission.*

Allen, Horace Newton
Allier, Raoul
Amu, Ephraim Kwaku
Andel, H(uibert) A(ntonie) van
Anderson, John
Anderson, Louisa (Peterswald)
Anderson, William
Anthing, F(rederik) L(odewijk)
Arbousset, (Jean) Thomas
Arthur, John William
Avison, Oliver R.
Bacon, Sumner
Baëta, Christian G(oncalves) K(wami)
Baird, William M.
Bakker, D(irk)
Baldaeus, Philippus
Bang Ji Il
Barclay, Thomas
Barlow, Arthur Ruffelle
Bavinck, Johan Herman
Beaver, R. Pierce
Belksma, J(ohannes)
Bell, L(emuel) Nelson
Benignus, Pierre
Berthoud, Paul
Bibliander, Theodor
Bill, Samuel Alexander
Bisseux, Isaac
Blyden, Edward Wilmot
Bosch, David J(acobus)
Brainerd, David
Brainerd, John
Brown, Arthur Judson
Brown, Samuel Robbins
Buck, Pearl S(ydenstricker)
Burgess, Paul
Burns, William Chalmers
Buss, Ernst
Cairns, David Smith
Calverley, Edwin Elliot
Calvin, John
Candidius, Georgius
Capitein, Jacobus Elisa Joannes
Casalis, Eugène
Chalmers, Thomas
Chamberlain, Jacob
Chatterjee, Kali Charan
Chestnut, Eleanor
Choi Chan Young
Christie, Dugald
Clark, Charles Allen
Cocceius, Johannes
Cochran, Joseph Plumb
Coe, Shoki (C. H. Hwang)
Coillard, François
Condit, Azubah Caroline
Cook, J. A. B.
Corbett, Hunter
Creux, Ernest
Daubanton, François Elbertus
Day, Lal Behari
Dennis, James Shepard
Dickson, James and Lillian (Glazier)
Doig, Andrew Beveridge
Doll, Ludwig
Donaldson, Dwight Martin
Douglas, Carstairs
Draskóczy, László
Drummond, Henry
Dubose, Hampden Coit
Duff, Alexander
Duncan, John
Du Plessis, Johannes
Eddy, Mary Pierson
Edersheim, Alfred
Edmiston, Althea (Brown)
Edwards, Jonathan
Ellinwood, Frank F(ield)
Eliot, John
Elmslie, Walter Angus
Ewing, James C(aruthers) R(hea)
Ferguson, Abbie Park and Bliss, Anna Elvira
Fleming, Daniel Johnson
Flynn, John
Forgács, Gyula
Forman, Charles W(illiam)
Forman, Charles William
Forsyth, Christina Moir
Fraser, Donald
Fulton, Thomas Crosby
Gale, James Scarth
Geddie, John
Gibson, John Campbell
Giffen, J(ohn) Kelly
Gilman, Frank Patrick
Goforth, Jonathan and Rosalind (Bell-Smith)
Goldie, Hugh
Good, Adolphus Clemens
Gordon, Andrew
Govan, William
Graham, James Robert III
Graham, John Anderson
Graybill, Anthony Thomas
Grimké, Charlotte (Forten)
Griswold, Hervey DeWitt
Guerrant, Edward Owings
Gunning, Jan Willem
Haines, Byron Lee
Hambroeck (Hambroek), Antonius
Han Kyung Jik
Happer, A(ndrew) P.
Harrison, Paul Wilberforce
Hastings, Harry
Haymaker, Edward M.
Henderson, James
Hetherwick, Alexander
Heurnius, Justus
Higginbottom, Sam
Hislop, Stephen
Hitchcock, John William
Hoekendijk, J(ohannes) C(hristian) "Hans"
Hovell, Wolter Robert van
Hofmeyr, Stefanus
Hogg, Alred
Hogg, John
Hoornbeeck (or Hoornbeek), Johannes
Hopkins, Samuel
Horton, Azariah
Hoy, William Edwin
Hueting, André
Hunnicutt, Benjamin Harris
Hunt, Bruce Finley
Hyde, John
Ibiam, (Francis) Akanu
Ibuka Kajinosuke
Inglis, John
Itzem, Julio
Jackson, Sheldon
Jameson, William
Janes, Leroy Lansing
Jellesma, J(elle) E(eltjes)

Jessup, Henry Harris
Jones, Charles Colcock, Sr.
Junius (de Jonghe), Robertus
Kals, Jan Willem
Kamma, F(reerk) (Christiaan)
Kats, Wilma
Kellersberger, Eugene R(oland) and Julia Lake (Skinner)
Kempers, John R. and Mabel (van Dyke)
Kepler, Asher Raymond
Kerr, John Glasgow
Kidder, Mary Eddy
Kijne, I(zaak) (Samuel)
Kraemer, Hendrik
Kruyt, Albertus Christiaan
Lambie, Thomas A.
Lapsley, Samuel Norvell
Laws, Robert
Leber, Charles Tudor
Leenhardt, Maurice
Leeuwen, Arend Th. van
Lemue, Prosper
Le Roux, Pieter Louis
Léry, Jean de
Leydecker, Melchior
Litwiller, John T(imothy) N(elson)
Loosdrecht, A(ntoine) A(ris) van de
Louw, Andries Adriaan
Lowrie, John C(ameron)
Luce, Henry Winters
Mabille, Adolphe
Macdonald, Andrew Buchanan
MacDonald, Duff
MacGillivray, Donald
Mackay, George Leslie
Mackay, John A(lexander)
Mackenzie, Helen Pearl
Mackenzie, Jean Kenyon
Mackichan, Dugald
MacNicol, Nicol
MacVicar, Neil
Makemie, Francis
Makkai, Sándor
Martin, Marie-Louise
Martin, William Alexander Parsons
Mateer, Calvin Wilson
Mather, Cotton
McBeth, Sue L.
McCandliss, Henry M.
McCartee, Divie Bethune
McClure, W(illiam) D(onald)
McDowell, Robert James
McFarland, Samuel Gamble
McGilvary, Daniel
Meeuwsen, Johanna
Megapolensis, Johannes
Mel, Conrad
Melrose, Margaret (Rae)
Merwe, Willem J(acobus) van der
Meyer, Theodore J(onas)
Millar, Robert
Miller, William
Miller, William McElwee
Mills, W(ilson) Plumer
Misley, Róza (Puchlin)
Mitchell, John Murray
Moffett, Samuel Austin
Moffett, Samuel Hugh
Molnár, Mária
Moninger, (Mary) Margaret
Moody, Campbell Naismith
Morrison, William McCutchan
Mukhia, David
Murray, Andrew, Jr.
Murray, Andrew, Sr.
Murray, William Hoppe
Nassau, Robert Hamill
Naudé, C(hristiaan) F(rederick) Beyers
Nesbit, Robert
Neumann, J(ohan) H(einrich)
Nevius, John Livingston
Newbigin, J(ames) E(dward) Lesslie
Newton, John
Nisbet, Henry
Noyes, Harriet Newell
O'Neill, Frederick W. S.
Paton, Francis Hume Lyall
Paton, John G(ibson)
Pereira, Eduardo Carlos
Pierson, Arthur Tappan
Pratt, Henry B(arrington)
Price, Francis (Frank) Wilson
Priest, James M.
Rankin, Melinda
Reid, Gilbert
Reischauer, August Karl
Ridley, William
Riedel, Johann (Gerard) Friedrich
Rodgers, James B(urton)
Rolland, Samuel
Ross, John
Rycroft, W(illiam) Stanley
Safford, Anna Cunningham
Saravia, Adrianus (or Adriaan de; Adriaan van)
Schneder, David Bowman
Schuurman, Barend Martinus
Schwartz, Carl August Ferdinand
Schwarz, Johann Gottlob
Scott, David Clement Rufelle
Sergeant, John
Seward, Sarah Cornelia
Shaull, M. Richard
Shedd, William Ambrose
Shepherd, Robert Henry Wishart
Sheppard, William H. and Lucy (Gantt)
Simonton, Ashbel Green
Slessor, Mary Mitchell
Small, Ann Hunter
Smith, George
Smith, John Coventry
Soga, Tiyo
Speer, Robert E(lliott)
Stevens, Jedediah Dwight
Stevenson, Marion Scott
Stewart, James
Stockton, Betsey
Stuart, John Leighton
Stursberg, (Engelbert) Julius
Suh Sang-Yun
Szabó, Aladár
Talmage, John Van Nest
Thomson, John Francis
Thomson, William Ritchie
Thurston, Matilda S. (Calder)
Ting Li-Mei (Ding Limei)
Torrance, David Watt
Turner, George
Uemura, Masahisa
Underwood, Horace Grant
Verbeck, Guido Herman Fridolin
Verkuyl, Johannes
Vernier, Frédéric
Victor, Janós
Visser 't Hooft, Willem A(dolf)
Voetius, Gisbertus (or Gijsbert Voet)
Vos, Michiel C(hristiaan)
Waddell, Hope Masterton
Walaeus, Antonius (or Anton de Wale)
Wanless, William J(ames)
Warnshuis, Abbe Livingston
Watson, Minnie (Cumming)
Weir, Andrew
Wherry, Elwood Morris
White, John Campbell
Whitefield, George
Whitman, Marcus and Narcissa (Prentiss)
Wilder, Grace E(veline)
Wilder, Robert P(armelee)
Wilder, Royal G(ould)
Williams, John Elias
Wilson, J. Christy, Sr.
Wilson, John and Margaret (Bayne)
Wilson, Samuel Graham
Winter, Ralph D(ana)
Wiser, William H(endricks) and Charlotte (Viall)
Wright, Frank Hall
Yi Ki-Poong
Young, Samuel Hall
Zwemer, Samuel Marinus
Zwingli, Huldrych (or Ulrich)

Roman Catholics Born after 1500

Roman Catholic religious orders, including Augustinians, Benedictines, Carmelites, Congregation of the Sacred Hearts of Jesus and Mary, Holy Cross, Lazarists, Marists, Maryknoll, Marianists, Mercedarians, Mill Hill, Missionaries of the Sacred Heart, Oblates of Mary Immaculate, Pallotines, Paris Foreign Mission Society, Paulists, Spiritans, Redemptorists, White Fathers, secular clergy, and others. See also *Dominicans; Franciscans; Jesuits; Society of the Divine Word.* For other Christian figures born prior to 1500, see the appendix lists under *Biographies by Time Period.*

Affonso (Alphonse)
Aidan
Alexander VI
Allamano, Joseph
Amadeus, Mary
Amalorpavadass, Duraiswami Simon
Atiman, Adrian
Aufhauser, Johannes Baptist
Augouard, Prosper Philippe
Bailey, Wellesley C(osby)
Baraga, (Irenaeus) Frederic
Bataillon, Pierre Marie
Bax, Jacques
Becker, Christoph Edmund
Beckmann, Johannes
Belcourt, Georges Antoine
Benedict XIV
Benedict XV
Benlloch y Vivó, Juan
Berkeley, Xavier
Bermyn (or Bermijn), Alphonse
Beschi, Constanzo Giuseppe
Bessieux, Jean Rémi
Bigandet, Paul Ambroise
Bigard, Stephanie and Jeanne
Billiart, (Marie Rose) Julie
Birraux, Joseph Marie
Bishop, William Howard
Blanchet, Francis Norbert
Boismenu, Alain de
Bondolfi, Pietro
Bonjean, Ernest Christophe
Bonnand, Clément
Borghero, Francesco Saverio
Bosco, Giovanni (John)
Bourgeoys, Marguerite
Brechter, Heinrich Suso
Bruillard, Philippe de
Builes, Miguel Angel
Cabrini, Frances Xavier
Camara, (Dom) Helder Pessoa
Carroll, John
Castro, Matheus de
Chaminade, Guillaume Joseph
Champagnat, Marcellin (Joseph Benôit)
Chanel, Pierre Louis
Chapdelaine, Auguste
Chappotin de Neuville, Hélène de (Marie de la Passion)
Chaumont, Denis
Chavara, Kuriackos Elias
Chavoin, Jeanne-Marie (Mother Saint Joseph)
Chevalier, Jules
Chong Yak-Jong, Augustine
Chou Wen-Mo (Zhou Wenmo)
Claret, Anthony Mary
Classe, Léon
Clement VIII
Clement XI
Colin, Jean-Claude Marie
Comboni, (Anthony) Daniel
Conforti, Guido Maria
Considine, John Joseph
Costantini, Celso
Cotta, Anthony
Coudrin, Pierre Marie Joseph
Cushing, Richard James
Cuthbert
Dalle Périer, Luis
Damien of Molokai
Dengel, Anna
Dindinger, Johannes
Donders, Peter
Dooley, Thomas Anthony
Drexel, Katherine
Dubois, Jean Antoine
Duchesne, Rose Philippine
Dufresse, Jean-Gabriel-Taurin
Duparquet, Charles
Dutton, Ira Barnes
Elliott, Walter
England, John
Epalle, Jean-Baptiste
Favier, Pierre-Marie Alphonse
Forbin-Janson, Charles de
Ford, Francis X(avier)
Foucauld, Charles Eugène de
Fraser, John (Andrew) Mary
Fumasoni-Biondi, Pietro
Gabet, Joseph
Galvin, Edward J.
Gaspais, Auguste Ernest
Gebhre Michael
Gérard, Joseph
Geyer, Francis Xavier
Glazik, Josef
Gockel, Mary
Goyau, Georges
Grandin, Vital Justin
Gregory XVI
Griffiths, Bede (Alan Richard)
Grignion de Montfort, Louis Marie
Gsell, Francis Xavier
Guébriant, Jean-Baptiste Budes de
Hahn, Heinrich
Hanlon, Henry
Hecker, Isaac Thomas
Hinsley, Arthur
Hsu Kuang-ch'i (Xu Guangqi)
Huc, Évariste-Régis
Hulstaert, Gustaf
Ingoli, Francesco
I Sung-Hun, Peter
Jacobis, Justin de
Jaricot, Pauline-Marie
Jarlin, Stanislas François
Javouhey, Anne-Marie
John XXIII
John Paul II
Jordan, Johann Baptist (Francis Mary of the Cross)
Kagame, Alexis
Karrer, Otto
Kelley, Francis Clement
Kilger, Laurenz
Kim, Andrew Tae-kon
Kitagana, Yohana
Kiwanuka, Joseph
Knoblecher, Ignaz
Kobès, Aloÿs
Kowalsky, Nicolas
Lacombe, Albert
Lambert de la Motte, Pierre
La Salle, Jean-Baptiste de
Laufer, Carl
Launay, Adrien
Laval, Jacques Désiré
Lavigerie, Charles
Le Roy, Alexander
Lebbe, Frédéric-Vincent
Ledóchowska, Maria Teresa
Le Saux, Henri (Swami Abhishiktananda)
Libermann, François Marie Paul
Li Chih-tsao (Li Zhizao)
Livinhac, Auguste Simon Léon
López de Mendoza Grajales, Francisco
Lourenço da Silva de Mendonça
Lourdel, Siméon
Luquet, Jean Félix Onésime
Maigrot, Charles
Manna, Paolo
Marie de l'Assomption (Marie Le Roy Ladurie)
Marie de l'Incarnation (Marie Guyart)
Marion Brésillac, Melchior Joseph de
Marmoiton, Blaise
Martínez Compañón y Bujanda, Baltasar Jaime
Marty, Martin
Massignon, Louis
Maturana, Margarita Maria
Ma Xiangbo
Mazenod, Charles-Joseph-Eugène de
Meneses, Aleixo de
Mezzabarba, Carlo Ambrogio
Mogrovejo, Toribio Alfonso de
Monchanin, Jules (Parama-Arubi-Ananda)

Moreau, Basile Antoine
Mouly, Joseph Martial
Moya de Contreras, Pedro
Moye (or Moÿe; Moyë), Jean-Martin
Mulders, Alfonsus Joannes Maria
Nacquart, Charles
Nerinckx, Charles
Ohm, Thomas
Palafox y Mendoza, Juan de
Pallotti, Vincent
Pallu, François
Pandosy, Charles
Panikkar, Raimundo
Paul VI
Paul of the Cross (Paolo Francesco Danei)
Pedraza, Cristóbal de
Pedro de la Madre de Dios
Peña Montenegro, Alonso de
Perbal, Albert
Perboyre, Jean-Gabriel
Perroton, (Marie) Françoise (Marie du Mont Carmel)
Petitjean, Bernard-Thaddée
Petitot, Émile
Pfanner, Franz
Pigneau de Béhaine, Pierre-Joseph-Georges
Pius XI
Pius XII
Planque, Augustin
Pompallier, (Jean-Baptiste) François
Pottier, François
Poullart-des-Places, Claude-François
Price, Thomas Frederick
Quinn, Edel Mary
Rada, Martín de
Rafiringa, Paul
Raimondi, Timoleone
Ramazotti, Angelo Francesco
Rasoamanarivo, Victoire
Ratisbonne, Marie-Théodore and Marie-Alphonse
Ravoux, Augustin
Rogers, Mary Josephine (Mother Mary Joseph)
Romero y Galdamez, Oscar Arnulfo
Rommerskirchen, Johannes
Rossano, Pietro
Rossum, Willem van
Rovenius, Philippus
Sabatier, Ernst
Salvado, Rosendo
Sambeek, Jan van
Saminathapillai Gnanapragasar
Santori, Giulio Antonio
Schmidlin, Joseph
Seumois, André
Shanahan, Joseph
Sheen, Fulton J(ohn)
Solages, (Gabriel) Henri (Jerome) de
Spae, Joseph J.
Streicher, Henri
Streit, Robert
Takayama Justus Ukon
Teresa, Mother (Agnes Gonxha Bojaxhiu)
Thérèse of Lisieux
Thévenoud, Joanny
Thomas of Jesus
Tournon, Charles Thomas Maillard de
Tragella, Giovanni Battista
Turquetil, Arsène
Upadhyaya, Brahmabandhav
Urban VIII
Urdaneta, Andres de
Valle, Juan del
Vaughan, Herbert
Vaz, Joseph
Vénard, Jean Théophane
Vera Cruz, Alonso de la
Verbist, Théophile
Verjus (or Verius), Henri
Vialar, Émilie de
Vieter, Heinrich
Villota y Urroz, Gerardo
Vincent de Paul
Vinco, Angelo
Vives y Marjá, Juan Bautista
Walsh, James A(nthony)
Walsh, James E(dward)
Westropp, Clara E.
Winthuis, Josef
Xu, Candida
Yang T'ing-yün
Ying Lien-chih (Lianzhi)
Zaleski, Vladislaw Michal

Society of the Divine Word (Roman Catholic)

Anzer, Johann Baptist (von)
Emmerich, Heinrich
Freinademetz, Joseph
Freitag, Anton
Grentrup, Theodor
Gusinde, Martin
Höltker, Georg
Janssen, Arnold
King, Clifford J.
Kraus, Johannes
Limbrock, Eberhard Michael
Luzbetak, Louis J.
Müller, Karl
Proksch, Georg
Ross, William
Schäfer, Alfons
Schebesta, Paul
Schmidt, Wilhelm
Schütte, Johannes
Schwager, Friedrich
Streit, Karl
Thauren, Johannes
Zapłata, Feliks

BIOGRAPHIES OF NON-WESTERN PERSONS

This list emphasizes the role of persons born outside Europe, Canada, and the United States. In an effort to highlight the involvement of non-Western persons, the following lists exclude persons who were born in the non-Western world to parents from the West. Otherwise it includes all others regardless of race or place of education.

Africa

Adejobi, Emmanuel Owoade Adeleke
Affonso (Alphonse)
Agbebi, Mojola (David Brown Vincent)
Aggrey, James Emman Kwegyir
Ahui, John (or Jonas)
Aina, J. Ade
Akinyele, Isaac Babalola
Akrofi, Clement Anderson
Amu, Ephraim Kwaku
Anawati, Georges Chehata
Andrianaivoravelona, Josefa
Augustine of Hippo
Babalola, Joseph Ayo
Baëta, Christian G(oncalves) K(wami)
Bosch, David J(acobus)
Braide, Garrick Sokari
Capitein, Jacobus Elisa Joannes
Chilembwe, John
Crowther, Dandeson Coates
Crowther, Samuel Adjai (or Ajayi)
Du Plessis, David Johannes
Du Plessis, Johannes
Dwane, James Matta
Enbaqom (Abu l-Fath)
Ezana
Gebhre Michael
Harris, William Wadé
Hofmeyr, Stefanus
Ibiam, (Francis) Akanu
Jabavu, Davidson Don T(engo)

Jabavu, John Tengo
Johnson, James
Johnson, Samuel
Johnson, Thomas Sylvester (Claudius)
Jones, William Henry
Kagame, Alexis
Kamwana, Elliot Kenan
Khama III
Kigozi, Blasio
Kimbangu, Simon
Kitagana, Yohana
Kivebulaya, (Waswa) Apolo
Kivengere, Festo
Kiwanuka, Joseph
Koyi, William Mtusane
Laiser, (Loirera) Lazarus
Lenshina Mulenga, Alice
Le Roux, Pieter Louis
Lijadu, Emmanuel Moses
Louw, Andries Adriaan
Luthuli, Albert John Mbumbi
Malinki, James M(orrison)
Maranke, John
Matthews, Z(achariah) K(eodirelang)
Meeuwsen, Johanna
Menasce, Pierre Jean de
Merwe, Willem J(acobus) van der
Mizeki, Bernard
Mokone, Mangena Maake
Moshoeshoe (also Moshesh, and various other spellings)
Mutendi, Samuel
Nagenda, William
Nankyama, Theodoros
Naudé, C(hristiaan) F(rederick) Beyers
Nsibambi, Simeon
Ntsikana
Ofori-Atta, William Eugene Amoako-Atta
Oppong, (Kwame) Sam(p)son
Origen
Orimolade, Moses
Oshitelu, Josiah Olunowo
Pamla, Charles
Protten, Christian Jacob
Quaque, Philip
Rabary
Rafiringa, Paul
Rasalama, Rafaravavy
Rasoamanarivo, Victoire
Reindorf, Carl Christian
Samkange, Thompson Douglas
Sawyerr, Harry Alphonso Ebun
Shembe, Isaiah Mdliwamafa
Smith, Matilda
Soga, Mina
Soga, Tiyo
Spartas, Christopher Reuben
Swatson, John
Takla-Haymanot
Taylor, John Christopher
Tile, Nehemiah
Tsizehena, John
Vos, Michiel C(hristiaan)
Wanyoike wa Kamawe
Weerasooriya, Arnolis
Zakaryas

Asia and the Middle East

Abdul Masih, Salih
Abraham, Samuel
Abraham Malpan
Abraham Mar Thoma
Ali, Wallayat
Alli, Janni
Alopen
Amalorpavadass, Duraiswami Simon
Ao, Longri (Longritangchetba)
Appasamy, Aiyadurai Jesudasen
Azariah, Vedanayagam Samuel
Banerjea, Krishna Mohan
Bang Ji Il
Baradaeus, Jacob (or Bar'adai; Barada'i)
Barsauma (or Barsumas)
Boris I
Bowley, William
Castro, Matheus de
Chakkarai, V(engal)
Chakko, Sarah
Chandran, J(oshua) Russell
Chang, Barnabas
Chao T(zu) C(h'en) (Zhao Zichen)
Chatterjee, Kali Charan
Chavara, Kuriackos Elias
Chen, Wen-Yuan
Chenchiah, Pandipeddi
Ch'eng Ching-Yi (Cheng Jingyi)
Ching T'ien-Yin (Jing Dianying)
Chi-Oang
Chitambar, Jashwant Rao
Choi Chan Young
Chong Yak-Jong, Augustine
Chou Wen-Mo (Zhou Wenmo)
Chrysostom, John
Coe, Shoki (C. H. Hwang)
Coolen, C(oenraad) L(aurens)
Darling, Thomas Young
Datta, S(urendra) K(umar)
Day, Lal Behari
Dehqani-Tafti, H(assan) B(arnaba)
Devanandan, Paul David
Devasahayam, John
Enbaqom (Abu l-Fath)
Eusebius of Caesarea
Gih, Andrew (Ji Zhiwen)
Goh, Hood Keng
Goreh, Nilakantha (Nehemiah)
Gregory Thaumaturgus
Han Kyung Jik
Harada Tasuku
Haringke Bai
Hawaweeny, Raphael
Honda Yoichi
Hsi Shengmo (Pastor Hsi)
Hsu Kuang-ch'i (Xu Guangqi)
Hung Hsiu-ch'uan (Hong Xiuquan)
Ibuka Kajinosuke
Imad ud-Din
Irenaeus of Lyons
I Sung-Hun, Peter
Jing Jing
Julian
Justin Martyr
Kafiar, Petrus
Kagawa, Toyohiko
Kanamori, Tsurin ("Paul")
K'ang Ch'eng (Kang Cheng; or Ida Kahn)
Kaundinya, Hermann Anandaraja
Kim, Andrew Tae-kon
Kim, Helen
Koo, T. Z. (Koo Ts-Zung; [Ku Zi-Zong])
Ko Tha Byu
Krishna Pillai (Henry Alfred)
Leimena, Johannes
Liang Fa
Li Chih-tsao (Li Zhizao)
Liu, Timothy Ting-Fang (Lew, T. T.)
Longinus
Lopez, Gregorio (Lo Wen-Tsao)
Mamora (or Sinamora), Lucius
Manikam, Rajah B(ushanam)
Martines, Francesco
Ma Xiangbo
Moses, David G.
Mukhia, David
Mulia, Todung Gelar Sutan Gunung
Muthiah, Narayana
Nakada Juji
Nee, (Henry) Watchman (Ni To-sheng; Ni Tuosheng)
Ngizaki, Gapenuo
Niijima, Jo (or Joseph Hardy Neesima; Neeshima)
Niles, D(aniel) T(hambyrajah)
Pal, Krishna
Paul, K(anakarayan) T(iruselvam)
Photius
Prasad (or Prisada), Krishna
Probowinoto, Basoeki
Ramabai Dongre Medhavi
Rasa, Clorinda
Rowe, Phoebe
Sadrach Surapranata
Safdar, Ali
Samartha, S(tanley) J(edidiah)
Saminathapillai Gnanapragasar
Satthianadhan, William Thomas (Tiruvengadam) and Annal Arokium
Sawabe, Paul (Takuma)
Sharkey, John Edmund and Ann Amelia (Nailer)
Shih Mei-yu (Shi Meiyu; or Mary Stone)
Sihombing, Justin
Silva, Lynn A. de
Simatupang, Tahi Bonar
Singh, Bakht
Subhan, John
Suh Sang-Yun
Sundar Singh
Sung, John Shang-chieh
Takayama Iustus Ukon
Tambunan, Albert Mangara

Thomas, M(adathilparampil) M(ammen)
Tilak, Narayan Vaman
Ting, K. H. (Ding Guangxun)
Ting Li-Mei (Ding Limei)
Tosari, Paulus
Tseng Pao Swen (Zeng Baosun)
Tunggul Wulung, Kjai Ibrahim
Uchimura, Kanzo
Uemura, Masahisa
Upadhyaya, Brahmabandhav
Vaz, Joseph
Wang, Ming-tao (Wang Mingdao)
Wei, Francis C(ho) M(in)
William of Tripoli
Wu, Y. T.
Wu Li (Wu Yü-Shan; or Simon à Cunha)
Xu, Candida
Yamamuro, Gumpei
Yang T'ing-yün
Yen, Y. C. James
Yi Ki-Poong
Ying Lien-chih (Lianzhi)
Yui, David Z. T. (Yu Jih-Chang; Yu Rizhang)
Yu Kuo-chen (Yu Guozhen)
Yun, Tchi-Ho

Caribbean Region and Latin America (including Mexico, Central America, and South America)

Anderson, Louisa (Peterswald)
Arias, Mortimer
Báez-Camargo, Gonzalo
Builes, Miguel Angel
Camara, (Dom) Helder Pessoa
Castro, Emilio
Costas, Orlando E(nrique)
Gilbert, Nathaniel
González Carrasco, Justo
González de Santa Cruz, Roque
Hemans, James Henry Emmanuel
Hernández, Venancio
Itzem, Julio
Johnson, Mammie
Kalbermatter, Pedro
King, Johannes
Lourenço da Silva de Mendonça
Lozada, Jorgelina
Lugo, Juan Leon
Motta, Waldomiro
Pereira, Eduardo Carlos
Potter, Philip A(lford)
Romero y Galdamez, Oscar Arnulfo
Ruiz de Montoya, Antonio
Turton, William
Valadés, Diego

Pacific Islands (including Hawaii)

Aea, Hezekiah and Debora
Auna
Bulu, Joeli
Cakobau, Ratu Seru
Eto, Silas
Kaahumanu
Kekela, James
Maretu
Nanpei, Henry
Nau, Semisi
Obookiah (or Opukahaia), Henry
Pao'o
Papeiha
Pomare II
Ruatoka
Ta'unga
Teava
Tupou, Taufa'ahau (or George)

BIOGRAPHIES BY TYPE OF WORK

This list includes four categories of work. Evangelism, church planting, and education are not listed here because so many people would be included.

Bible Translation

Adriani, Nicolaus
Akrofi, Clement Anderson
Allan, George and Mary (Sterling)
Allen, David Oliver
Allen, Young John
Anderson, Christopher
Andrews, Lorrin
Appenzeller, Henry Gerhard
Auer, John Gottlieb
Bachmann, (Johann) Traugott
Baëta, Christian G(oncalves) K(wami)
Báez-Camargo, Gonzalo
Baird, William M.
Bakker, D(irk)
Baldaeus, Philippus
Baldwin, Elizabeth and Jane
Ballantine, Henry
Baller, Frederick William
Barclay, Thomas
Barlow, Arthur Ruffelle
Baughman, Burr
Bentley, William Holman
Bergmann, Wilhelm (H. F.)
Berthoud, Paul
Bettelheim, Bernard Jean
Bingham, Hiram and Sybil (Moseley)
Bingham, Hiram, Jr.
Bishop, Artemas
Bliss, Isaac Grout
Bodding, Paul Olaf
Bompas, William Carpenter
Boone, William Jones, Sr.
Borrow, George
Boyce, William Binnington
Brett, William Henry
Bridgman, Elijah Coleman
Bromilow, William E.
Brønnum, Niels Høegh
Brown, Nathan
Brown, Samuel Robbins
Brückner, Gottlob
Burgess, Paul
Byington, Cyrus
Callaway, Henry
Carey, Felix
Carey, William
Casalis, Eugène
Chalmers, John
Chamberlain, Jacob
Chatterton, Percy
Ch'eng Ching-Yi (Cheng Jingyi)
Christaller, Johannes Gottlieb
Clark, Ephraim W.
Colenso, Elizabeth (Fairburn) and William
Colenso, John William
Cousins, William E(dward)
Crawford, Daniel
Crowther, Samuel Adjai (or Ajayi)
Cushing, Ellen Winsor (Howard) Fairfield
Cyril-Constantine
Dahle, Lars Nilsen
Daniel, Antoine
Darling, David

Darling, Thomas Young
Davies, John
Day, Samuel Stearns
Dean, William
Delitzsch, Franz Julius
Dennis, Thomas John
Dobinson, Henry Hughes
Doke, Clement Martyn
Drebert, Ferdinand
Droese, Ernest
Dyer, Samuel
Eastman, George Herbert
Edkins, Joseph
Eliot, John
Ellis, William and Mary Mercy (Moor)
Fabricius, Johann Philipp
Fleming, John
Fox, Charles Elliot
Francke, August Hermann
Fraser, James Outram
Gale, James Scarth
Geddie, John
Gibson, John Campbell
Glen, William
Glukharev, Makarii (Mikhail Yakovlevich)
Gobat, Samuel
Goble, Jonathan
Goddard, Josiah
Goldie, Hugh
Gollmer, Charles Andrew (Carl Anders)
Good, Adolphus Clemens
Goodell, William
Gossner, Johannes Evangelista
Griffiths, David
Gulick, Orramel Hinckley and Ann Eliza (Clark)
Gützlaff, Karl Friedrich August
Hall, Gordon
Hambroeck (Hambroek), Antonius
Hamlin, James
Happer, A(ndrew) P.
Haringke Bai
Hartmann, (Joseph Alois) Anastasius
Heath, George Reinke
Henderson, Ebenezer
Hetherwick, Alexander
Heurnius, Justus
Heyling, Peter
Hinderer, David and Anna (Martin)
Hulstaert, Gustaf
Hunt, John
Hunter, George W.
Ilminskii, Nikolai Ivanovich
Inglis, John
Jaeschke, Heinrich August
Jansz, Pieter
John, Griffith
John of Montecorvino
Jones, David Picton
Jones, Evan and John Buttrick
Jones, George Heber
Jones, John Taylor
Judson, Adoniram
Judson, Ann ("Nancy") (Hasseltine)
Kafarov, Petr Ivanovich
Kagame, Alexis
Kamma, F(reerk) (Christiaan)
Kasatkin, Nikolai (Ivan Dmitriyevich)
Keasberry, Benjamin Peach
Keysser, Christian (J. E.)
Kleinschmidt, Johann Conrad
Klinkert, Hillebrandus Cornelius
Kuhn, Isobel Miller
Kulp, H(arold) Stover
Lapsley, Samuel Norvell
Larsen, Lars Peter
Lawes, W(illiam) G(eorge)
Ledyard, Gleason H.
Leenhardt, Maurice
Leydecker, Melchior
Lijadu, Emmanuel Moses
Lorrain, James Herbert
Louw, Andries Adriaan
Mabille, Adolphe
MacCallum, (Frank) Lyman
Maclay, Robert Samuel
Makarii Altaiskii (Mikhail Andreevich Nevskii)
Mamora (or Sinamora), Lucius
Marshman, Joshua
Martin, William Alexander Parsons
Martyn, Henry
Mason, Francis
Mateer, Calvin Wilson
Mather, Robert Cotton
Matthews, Thomas Trotter
Maunsell, Robert
Mayhew, Experience
McDonald, Robert
McLaurin, John
Medhurst, Walter Henry
Mesrob (or Mashtots)
Miller, Walter Richard Samuel
Milne, William
Mizeki, Bernard
Moffat, John Smith
Moffat, Robert
Monnier, Henri
Morrison, Robert
Morrison, William McCutchan
Mulia, Todung Gelar Sutan Gunung
Murray, Archibald Wright
Murray, William Hoppe
Myers, Estella Catherine
Nesbit, Robert
Netsvetov, Iakov Egor
Neumann, J(ohan) H(einrich)
Nida, Eugene Albert
Nisbet, Henry
Nott, Henry
Paton, Francis Hume Lyall
Peck, Edmund James
Percival, Peter
Perkins, Justin
Petter, Rodolphe
Philaret (Drozdov)
Phillips, Jeremiah
Pike, Kenneth Lee
Pilhofer, Georg
Pilkington, George Lawrence
Pitman, Charles
Pollard, Samuel
Ponziglione, Paul Mary
Pratt, George
Pratt, Henry B(arrington)
Price, Roger
Ramabai Dongre Medhavi
Rebmann, Johannes
Reed, George C.
Reeve, William
Rice, Benjamin
Richards, William
Riggs, Elias
Riggs, Stephen Return
Robinson, William
Roehl, Karl
Rolland, Samuel
Ross, John
Rouse, George Henry
Russell, William Armstrong
Sahagún, Bernardino de
Saint, Rachel Bradford
Saker, Alfred
Saravia, Adrianus (or Adriaan de; Adriaan van)
Schauffler, William Gottlieb
Schereschewsky, Samuel Isaac Joseph
Schmelen, Johann Heinrich
Schreuder, Hans Paludan Smith
Schultze, Benjamin
Schurmann (or Shurman), Johannes Adam
Scott, William and Elizabeth (Ruslin)
Scranton, William Benton
Sedat, William and Elizabeth (Ruslin)
Sergeant, John
Shaw, Archibald
Shellabear, William Girdlestone
Smith, A(lgernon) C(harles) Stanley
Smith, Edwin Williams
Smith, Eli
Spaulding, Levi
Spieth, (Andreas) Jakob
Springer, Helen Emily (Chapman) Rasmussen
Stallybrass, Edward
Steere, Edward
Stephen of Perm
Stevenson, Marion Scott
Stockfleth, Nils Joachim Vibe
Strauss, Hermann
Strehlow, Carl Friedrich Theodor
Stronach, John
Sturges, Albert A.
Suh Sang-Yun
Sutton, Amos
Swan, William
Talmage, John Van Nest
Taylor, John Christopher
Thomson, James (or Diego)
Thurston, Asa and Lucy (Goodale)
Timpany, Americus Vespucius
Townsend, Henry
Townsend, William Cameron
Tucker, John Taylor
Turner, George
Uemura, Masahisa
Ulfila (or Ulphilas; Wulfila)
Underwood, Horace Grant
Van Dyck, Cornelius Van Alan
Vinton, Justus Hatch and Calista (Holman)

Wade, Jonathan and Deborah (Lapham)
Waldo (or Valdez), Peter
Walther, Christoph Theodosius
Wardlaw, John Smith
Wenger, John
White, John
White, Moses Clark
Williams, William
Williamson, Thomas Smith
Wilson, John Leighton
Winslow, Miron
Worcester, Samuel Austin
Yates, William
Young, T(homas) Cullen
Zeisberger, David
Ziegenbalg, Bartholomäus

Medical Services

Allen, Horace Newton
Arthur, John William
Atiman, Adrian
Avison, Oliver R.
Ball, Dyer
Becker, Carl
Becker, Christoph Edmund
Bell, L(emuel) Nelson
Bettelheim, Bernard Jean
Beyzym, Jan
Bird, Mary Rebecca Stewart
Bishop, Isabella Lucy (Bird)
Bradley, Dan Beach
Brand, Paul Wilson
Brønnum, Niels Høegh
Broomhall, Anthony James
Brown, Edith Mary
Browne, Stanley G(eorge)
Butler, Elizur
Butler, Fanny Jane
Carey, Lott
Carlson, Paul
Chamberlain, Jacob
Chesterman, Clement C(lapton)
Chestnut, Eleanor
Christie, Dugald
Church, John E. ("Joe")
Clark, Henry Martyn
Cochran, Joseph Plumb
Cochrane, Thomas
Cook, Albert Ruskin
Coombs, Lucinda L.
Davidson, Andrew
Deck, (John) Northcote
Dengel, Anna
Dickson, James and Lillian (Glazier)
Dobinson, Henry Hughes
Dooley, Thomas Anthony
Dubose, Hampden Coit
Dutton, Ira Barnes
Eddy, Mary Pierson
Elmslie, Walter Angus
Elmslie, William J. and Margaret (Duncan)
Falkner, Thomas
Feller, Henriette Odin
Fisch, Rudolf
Fleming, Louise ("Lulu") Cecilia
Fraser, Kenneth
Glover, Robert Hall
Goupil, René
Grant, Asahel
Grant, Judith (Campbell)
Green, Samuel Fiske
Grenfell, Wilfred Thomason
Guerrant, Edward Owings
Gulick, Luther Halsey and Louisa Mitchell (Lewis)
Gurney, Samuel
Hall, Elizabeth Garland
Hall, Gordon
Hall, Marian (Bottomley)
Hall, Sherwood
Halliwell, Leo B(lair) and Jessie (Rowley)
Happer, A(ndrew) P.
Harrison, Paul Wilberforce
Hastings, Harry
Heyer, John Christian Frederick
Hitchcock, John William
Hobson, Benjamin
Holland, Henry Tristram
Howard, Leonora
Hume, Edward H(icks)
Hynd, David
Ibiam, (Francis) Akanu
Johnson, Mammie
Judd, Gerrit Parmele
Judd, Walter H(enry)
Kalbermatter, Pedro
Kalley, Robert Reid
K'ang Ch'eng (Kang Cheng; or Ida Kahn)
Kellersberger, Eugene R(oland) and Julia Lake (Skinner)
Kerr, George McGlashan and Isabel (Gunn)
Kerr, John Glasgow
Kevin, Mother (Kearney, Teresa)
Kugler, Anna Sarah
Lambie, Thomas A.
Lamburn, Roger George Patrick
Lambuth, Walter Russell
Laws, Robert
Leimena, Johannes
Lockhart, William
Lohr, Oscar T.
Lombard, Eva
Lowe, John
Mabie, Catherine Louise Roe
Macdonald, Andrew Buchanan
Macgowan, Edward
Mackenzie, Helen Pearl
Mackenzie, John Kenneth
MacVicar, Neil
Main, D(avid) Duncan
Mather, Percy Cunningham
McBeth, Sue L.
McCandliss, Henry M.
McCartee, Divie Bethune
McDougall, Francis Thomas
McKechnie, Elizabeth
Miller, Harry W(illis)
Miller, Walter Richard Samuel
Molnár, Mária
Monnier, Henri
Moorshead, Robert Fletcher
Myers, Estella Catherine
Nassau, Robert Hamill
Parker, Peter
Parrish, Sarah Rebecca
Pearse, Joseph
Pennell, Theodor Leighton
Perkins, Justin
Price, Jonathan David
Ramsey, Evelyn
Reed, Mary
Richards, William
Schellenberg, Katharina L(ohrenz)
Schweitzer, Albert
Scranton, William Benton
Scudder, Ida Sophia
Scudder, John
Seagrave, Gordon S(tifler)
Seward, Sarah Cornelia
Shih Mei-yu (Shi Meiyu; or Mary Stone)
Smith, A(lgernon) C(harles) Stanley
Soper, Annie
Stahl, Ferdinand A(nthony)
Steidel, Florence
Swain, Clara
Timpany, Americus Vespucius
Torrance, David Watt
Van Dyck, Cornelius Van Alan
Veenstra, Johanna
Wanless, William J(ames)
White, Moses Clark
White, Paul Hamilton Hume
Whitman, Marcus and Narcissa (Prentiss)
Wieger, Georges Frédéric Léon
Wilson, Robert Orr

Study of Culture and Language

Adriani, Nicolaus
Akrofi, Clement Anderson
Alcina (or Alzina), Francisco Ignacio
Amiot, Jean Joseph Marie
Amu, Ephraim Kwaku
Anawati, Georges Chehata
Anchieta, José de
Anderson, James Norman Dalrymple
André, Louis
Archbell, James
Baller, Frederick William
Baraga, (Irenaeus) Frederic
Barlow, Arthur Ruffelle
Belcourt, Georges Antoine
Bender, Carl Jacob
Bentley, William Holman
Bergmann, Wilhelm (H. F.)
Bernard-Maitre, Henri
Berthoud, Paul
Beschi, Constanzo Giuseppe
Bessieux, Jean Rémi
Bigandet, Paul Ambroise
Bodding, Paul Olaf
Bouvet, Joachim
Bowen, Thomas Jefferson
Boyce, William Binnington
Brett, William Henry
Brown, George
Browne, Laurence Edward
Brunton, Henry
Bulck, Gaaston (or Vaast) van
Burgess, Paul
Byington, Cyrus
Caldwell, Robert
Callaway, Henry
Calverley, Edwin Elliot
Cardoso, Mattheus
Carey, William
Cargill, David
Casalis, Eugène
Cattaneo, Lazzaro
Chalmers, John
Christaller, Johannes Gottlieb
Cobo, Bernabé
Codrington, Robert Henry
Colenso, Elizabeth (Fairburn) and William
Colenso, John William
Copleston, Reginald Stephen
Couplet, Philippe
Couvreur, Séraphin
Crawford, Daniel
Cust, Robert Needham
Dahl, Otto Christian
Desideri, Hippolytus
Dick, Amos Daniel Maurice
Dobinson, Henry Hughes
Dobrizhoffer, Martin
Doke, Clement Martyn
Donaldson, Dwight Martin
Douglas, Carstairs
Drebert, Ferdinand
Droese, Ernest
Egede, Hans (Povelsen)
Elmslie, Walter Angus
Elwin, H(arry) Verrier H(olman)
Evans, James
Farquhar, John Nicol
Fison, Lorimer
Fleming, John
Foucquet, Jean-François
Fox, Charles Elliot
Francke, August Hermann
Fraser, Alexander Garden
French, Thomas Valpy
Fróis, Luis
Gairdner, W(illiam) H(enry) Temple
Gale, James Scarth
Gebauer, Paul
Gogerly, Daniel John
Goldie, Hugh
Good, Adolphus Clemens
Griswold, Hervey DeWitt
Grubb, W(ilfrid) Barbrooke
Gsell, Francis Xavier
Gundert, Hermann
Gusinde, Martin
Gutmann, Bruno
Haines, Byron Lee
Hall, Gordon
Hanxleden, Johann Ernst
Hardy, Robert Spence
Hartmann, (Joseph Alois) Anastasius
Heras, Enrique (or Henry)
Hoecken, Christian
Hoffmann, Johannes Baptist
Höltker, Georg
Huc, Évariste-Régis
Hughes, Thomas Patrick
Hulstaert, Gustaf
Iakinf (Bichurin)
Ilminskii, Nikolai Ivanovich
Intorcetta, Prospero
Isakovich, Nikolai Fedorovich
Isenberg, Karl Wilhelm
Jansz, Pieter
Johanns, Pierre
Johanssen, Ernst
Johnson, Samuel
Juanmartí y Espot, Jacinto
Junod, Henri Alexandre
Kafarov, Petr Ivanovich
Kagame, Alexis
Kamma, F(reerk) (Christiaan)
Kendall, Thomas
Keysser, Christian (J. E.)
Kilham, Hannah (Spurr)
King, Copland
Kircher, Athanasius
Kittel, Ferdinand
Klein, Frederick Augustus
Kleinschmidt, Johann Conrad
Klinkert, Hillebrandus Cornelius
Koelle, Sigismund Wilhelm
Kraemer, Hendrik
Krapf, Johann Ludwig
Kulp, H(arold) Stover
Lafitau, Joseph-François
Laufer, Carl
Le Roy, Alexander
Leenhardt, Maurice
Legge, James
Lijadu, Emmanuel Moses
Lorrain, James Herbert
Luzbetak, Louis J.
Macdonald, Duncan Black
MacGillivray, Donald
MacNicol, Nicol
Marquette, Jacques
Martyn, Henry
Mather, Percy Cunningham
McDonald, Robert
Medhurst, Walter Henry
Meinhof, Carl (Friedrich Michael)
Menasce, Pierre Jean de
Merensky, Alexander
Milne, William
Mitchell, John Murray
Moegling, Herrmann Friedrich
Morrison, Robert
Motolinía (Toribio de Benavente)
Muir, William
Neumann, J(ohan) H(einrich)
Newell, James Edward
Newton, John
Nida, Eugene Albert
Nino, Bernardino de
Nobili, Robert de
Nyländer, Gustavus Reinhold
Oldendorp, Christian Georg Andreas
Parrinder, (Edward) Geoffrey (Simons)
Patteson, John Coleridge
Paucke, Florian
Pennini, Ricoldo (da Monte Cruce)
Percival, Peter
Perkins, Justin
Peter the Venerable de Montboissier (Pierre Maurice)
Petitot, Émile
Petter, Rodolphe
Pigneau de Béhaine, Pierre-Joseph-Georges
Pilhofer, Georg
Plasencia (Portocarrero), Juan de
Pope, George Uglow
Popley, Herbert Arthur
Pratt, George
Proksch, Georg
Raban, John
Ramsey, Evelyn
Rebmann, Johannes
Reindorf, Carl Christian
Rhenius, Carl Theophilus Ewald
Rhodes, Alexandre de
Rice, Benjamin
Richards, Henry
Ridley, William
Riggs, Stephen Return
Roehl, Karl
Roth, Heinrich

Sabatier, Ernst
Sahagún, Bernardino de
Sambeek, Jan van
Saminathapillai Gnanapragasar
Santo Tomás, Domingo de
Schäfer, Alfons
Schärer, Hans
Schebesta, Paul
Schmidt, Wilhelm
Schön, Jakob Friedrich (James Frederick)
Schreuder, Hans Paludan Smith
Schultze, Benjamin
Schuurman, Barend Martinus
Scott, David Clement Rufelle
Sedat, William and Elizabeth (Ruslin)
Shellabear, William Girdlestone
Sheppard, William H. and Lucy (Gantt)
Skrefsrud, Lars O(lsen)
Slater, Thomas Ebenezer
Smith, Arthur Henderson
Smith, Edwin Williams
Smith, Eli
Spaulding, Levi
Spieth, (Andreas) Jakob
Stach, Matthew
Steere, Edward
Stephens, Thomas
Stockfleth, Nils Joachim Vibe
Strauss, Hermann
Strehlow, Carl Friedrich Theodor
Sundkler, Bengt (Gustav Malcolm)
Sutton, Amos
Sweetman, James Windrow
Taylor, John V(ernon)
Tippett, Alan R.
Tisdall, William St. Clair
Torrance, Thomas
Torrend, Jules
Townsend, William Cameron
Trumpp, Ernst
Turner, Harold W.
Underwood, Horace Grant
Vedder, Hermann Heinrich
Vernier, Frédéric
Vicedom, Georg Friedrich
Vidal, Owen Emeric
Visdelou, Claude
Voth, Henry R.
Wade, Jonathan and Deborah (Lapham)
Wakefield, Thomas
Ward, William
Warneck, Johannes
Westermann, Diedrich Hermann
White, Andrew
Whitehead, Henry
Wieger, Georges Frédéric Léon
William of Rubroek (or Rubruck)
Williams, S(amuel) Wells
Williams, William
Wilson, Edward Francis
Wilson, John and Margaret (Bayne)
Winslow, Miron
Winthuis, Josef
Wiser, William H(endricks) and Charlotte (Viall)
Wood, A(lfred) Harold
Yates, William
Young, T(homas) Cullen
Zimmermann, Johannes

Work with Women and Children

Agnew, Eliza
Anderson, Louisa (Peterswald)
Armstrong, Hannah Maria (Norris)
Aylward, Gladys
Berkeley, Xavier
Butler, William and Clementina (Rowe)
Carmichael, Amy Beatrice
Chappotin de Neuville, Hélène de (Marie de la Passion)
Cooke, Sophia
Daüble, Carl Gustav
Dodge, Grace Hoadley
Doremus, Sarah Platt (Haines)
Elmslie, William J. and Margaret (Duncan)
Evald, Emmy C(hristina) (Carlsson)
Ferguson, Abbie Park and Bliss, Anna Elvira
Fielde, Adele M.
Fuller, Jennie (Frow)
Gomer, Mary (Green)
Gorham, Sarah E.
Gulick, Alice (Gordon)
Hall, Elizabeth Garland
Hill, Mary (Beardsmore)
Howe, Gertrude
Johnson, Mammie
Jones, Nancy
Judson, Ann ("Nancy") (Hasseltine)
Kähler, Christiane (Mues)
K'ang Ch'eng (Kang Cheng; or Ida Kahn)
Kugler, Anna Sarah
Lewis, Marianne (Gould)
Macdonald, A(nnie) Caroline
Marie de l'Incarnation (Marie Guyart)
Marshman, Hannah (Shepherd)
Medhurst, Walter Henry
Meeuwsen, Johanna
Montgomery, Helen Barrett
Mullens, Joseph and Hannah (Lacroix)
Ramabai Dongre Medhavi
Safford, Anna Cunningham
Sale, Elizabeth (Geale)
Schneller, Johann Ludwig
Scranton, Mary F.
Shattuck, Corinna
Shuck, J(ehu) Lewis and Henrietta (Hall)
Slessor, Mary Mitchell
Stevenson, Marion Scott
Stover, Wilbur B(renner)
Trotter, Isabelle Lilias
Trumbull, David
Tucker, Charlotte Maria
Watson, Minnie (Cumming)
Webster-Smith, Irene
Whittemore, Emma (Mott)
Widmann, Rosina (Binder)
Wilson, Mary Ann (Cooke)
Winslow, Harriet Wadsworth (Lathrop)

INDEX

This index of geographical, institutional, and personal names does not employ the methodology of the appendix, which is organized around region of service, major sponsoring agencies of mission work, and similar broad categories. Instead it is organized along the following lines:

Geographical names. Country and city names important in the careers of the subjects of this dictionary are indexed. Name forms contemporary with the subjects' lives are preferred, but common alternative forms and spellings will also be found.

Institutional names (i.e., churches and other organizations). Local institutions, not the larger global organizations of which they may be part, are indexed. The names of schools, seminaries, colleges, and universities where the subjects studied are not included in the Index.

Personal names. Only names mentioned within the body of an article are indexed. A personal name that is mentioned in an article and is, in addition, the subject of an entry is set in **boldface** type, although the page number for the main entry is not included.

Note that the index does not list each of the nearly 2,400 biographical entries included in this dictionary. It does, however, list the names of all contributors, followed by the page numbers of their articles.

A

B

F

G

H

I

J

K

M

N

O

P

Q

R

S

T

U

X

Y

Z

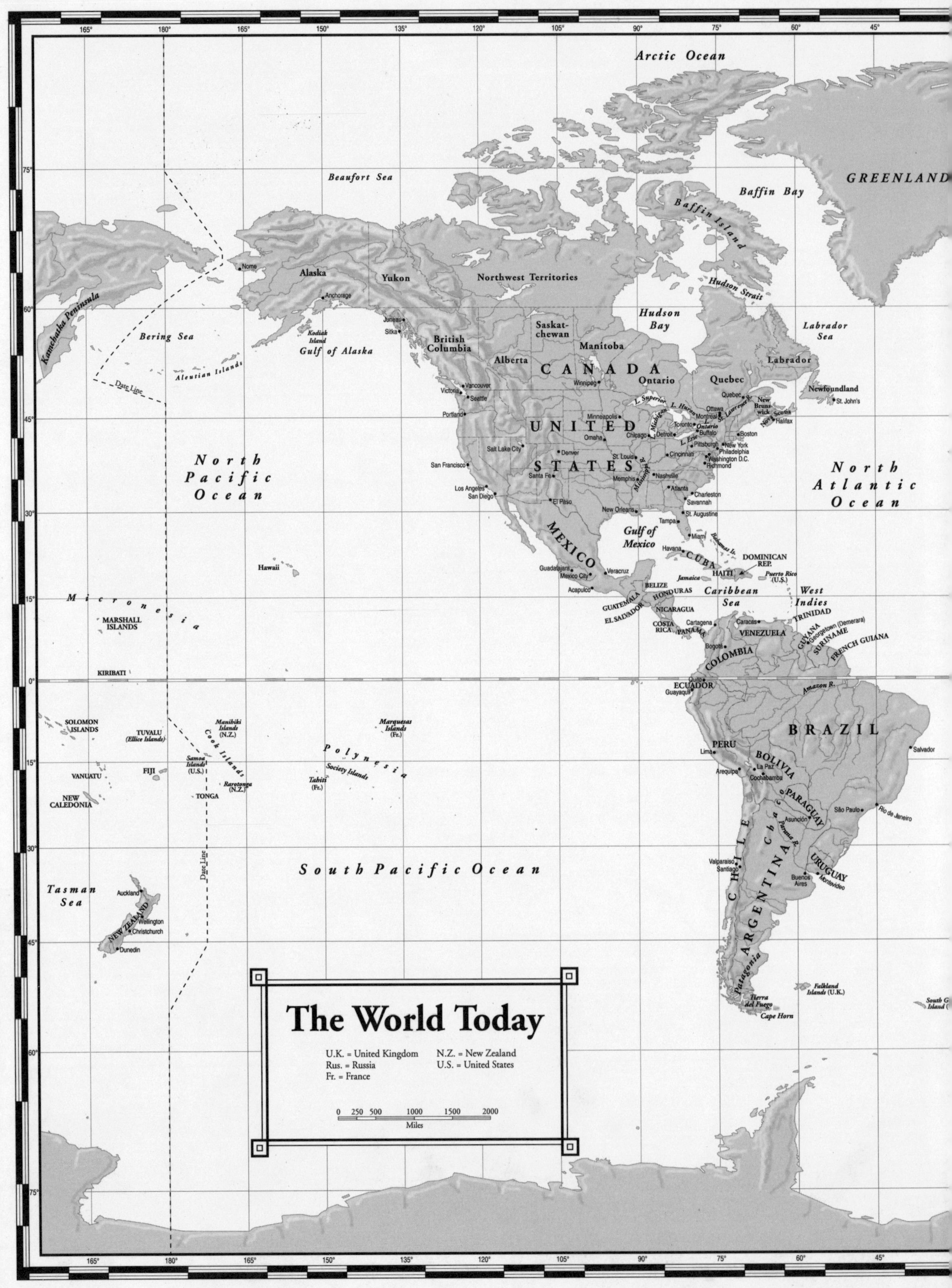
The World Today
U.K. = United Kingdom
Rus. = Russia
Fr. = France
N.Z. = New Zealand
U.S. = United States
0 250 500 1000 1500 2000
Miles
Arctic Ocean
GREENLAND
Baffin Bay
Baffin Island
Beaufort Sea
Hudson Strait
Hudson Bay
Labrador Sea
Labrador
Newfoundland
St. John's
Kamchatka Peninsula
Bering Sea
Aleutian Islands
Date Line
Nome
Alaska
Anchorage
Kodiak Island
Gulf of Alaska
Juneau
Sitka
Yukon
Northwest Territories
British Columbia
Alberta
Saskat-chewan
Manitoba
CANADA
Ontario
Quebec
Winnipeg
Vancouver
Victoria
Seattle
Portland
L. Superior
L. Huron
L. Michigan
L. Ontario
L. Erie
St. Lawrence R.
Ottawa
Montreal
Quebec
New Brunswick
Nova Scotia
Halifax
Toronto
Buffalo
Boston
Minneapolis
UNITED STATES
Omaha
Chicago
Detroit
Pittsburgh
New York
Philadelphia
Washington D.C.
Richmond
Salt Lake City
Denver
St. Louis
Cincinnati
San Francisco
Santa Fe
Memphis
Mississippi R.
Nashville
Los Angeles
San Diego
El Paso
Atlanta
Charleston
Savannah
St. Augustine
New Orleans
Tampa
Miami
North Pacific Ocean
North Atlantic Ocean
Gulf of Mexico
MEXICO
Bahamas Is.
Havana
CUBA
DOMINICAN REP.
HAITI
Puerto Rico (U.S.)
Jamaica
Guadalajara
Mexico City
Veracruz
Acapulco
BELIZE
HONDURAS
GUATEMALA
EL SALVADOR
NICARAGUA
COSTA RICA
PANAMA
Caribbean Sea
West Indies
TRINIDAD
Hawaii
Micronesia
MARSHALL ISLANDS
KIRIBATI
Cartagena
Caracas
VENEZUELA
GUYANA
Georgetown (Demerara)
SURINAME
FRENCH GUIANA
Bogotá
COLOMBIA
Quito
ECUADOR
Guayaquil
Amazon R.
BRAZIL
Salvador
PERU
Lima
BOLIVIA
La Paz
Arequipa
Cochabamba
Chaco
PARAGUAY
Asunción
Paraná R.
São Paulo
Rio de Janeiro
SOLOMON ISLANDS
TUVALU (Ellice Islands)
Cook Islands
Manihiki Islands (N.Z.)
Marquesas Islands (Fr.)
Polynesia
Society Islands
Samoa Islands (U.S.)
VANUATU
FIJI
Rarotonga (N.Z.)
TONGA
Tahiti (Fr.)
NEW CALEDONIA
South Pacific Ocean
CHILE
ARGENTINA
Valparaiso
Santiago
URUGUAY
Buenos Aires
Montevideo
Tasman Sea
Auckland
NEW ZEALAND
Wellington
Christchurch
Dunedin
Patagonia
Tierra del Fuego
Cape Horn
Falkland Islands (U.K.)